Women Writers of Great Britain and Europe

Garland Reference Library of the Humanities, vol. 1980

Women Writers of Great Britain and Europe
An Encyclopedia

Editors
Katharina M. Wilson
Paul Schlueter
June Schlueter

Garland Publishing, Inc.
New York & London
1997

Library of Congress Cataloging-in-Publication Data

Women writers of Great Britain and Europe : an encyclopedia / editors, Katharina M. Wilson,
    Paul Schlueter, June Schlueter.
            p.   cm. — (Garland reference library of the humanities ; vol. 1980)
        Includes indexes.
        ISBN 0-8153-2343-3 (alk. paper)
        1. Women authors, European—Biography—Encyclopedias.   2. Authors, European—
Biography—Encyclopedias.   3. Women authors, English—Biography—Encyclopedias.
4. Authors, English—Biography—Encyclopedias.   5. European literature—Women
authors—Encyclopedias.   6. European literature—Bio-bibliography—Encyclopedias.
I. Wilson, Katharina M.   II. Schlueter, Paul, 1933–   .   III. Schlueter, June.   IV. Series.
PN471.W565   1997
809'.89287'094—dc21
[B]   97-1409
                                                                                              CIP

Cover photograph: Sidonie-Gabrielle Colette, reprinted courtesy of CORBIS-BETTMANN
Cover design by Robert Vankeirsbilck
Book design by Karin Badger

Printed on acid-free, 250-year-life paper
Manufactured in the United States of America

Contents

Introduction

Women Writers of Great Britain and Europe bears testimony to the manifold and varied contributions women have made throughout the centuries (from antiquity to the present) to cultural, literary, social, political, and religious history. Indeed, there are no epochs and no regions, not even the most notoriously patriarchal and/or misogynistic ones, that entirely lack works composed by women. It is this continuous flow (even if it is only a trickle, at times) of female voices that we would like to present in this encyclopedia. It is the diversity of these voices which we would like to underscore in the three lists following the text: One list categorizes each author by the country she identified with throughout her career. There is also a list of pseudonyms (or in some cases lesser-known names), and a list of authors by century, which indicates the time period in which each author flourished.

In order to arouse interest as well as to facilitate further research, we opted for a format in the individual essays which will, it is hoped, accomplish both. Each entry provides a discussion of the author's life and works, her accomplishments and contributions, as well as her significance in regards to the larger literary scene. Each essay is followed by a listing of the writer's works both in the original language and in English translation.

As all editors of reference works, we, too, had to make some difficult choices, often sacrificing completeness for relative brevity, all-inclusiveness in favor of conciseness and balance. Thus, while *Women Writers of Great Britain and Europe* is not a comprehensive encyclopedia of all British and European women writers, it is a representative sampling of the variety of female voices throughout the centuries and a tribute to the rich legacy they left for us.

Katharina M. Wilson
Paul Schlueter
June Schlueter

Contributors

Kristiaan P. Aercke
J.T. Alexander
Lynn M. Alexander
Kristine Anderson
Kathy Saranpa Anstine
Brigitte Edith Zapp Archibald
C.M. Arroyo
Leonard R.N. Ashley
Francis Assaf
Marina Astman
Jane Augustine
Dean R. Baldwin
Charlene Ball
Angelika Bammer
Carol L. Barash
Peter I. Barta
Enikő Molnár Basa
Fiora A. Bassanese
Michael F. Bassman
Susan Bassnett
Kate Begnal
Edith J. Benkov
Joseph Berrigan
Maya Bijvoet
Randi Birn
Michael Bishop
Pål Bjørby
Beth Bjorklund
Merritt R. Blakeslee
Alda Blanco
Ronald Bogue
Jan Calloway
Balance Chow
Birutė Ciplijauskaitė
Susan L. Clark
Albrecht Classen
Gunnel Cleve
Lina L. Cofresi
Carol Colatrella
Mary S. Comfort
Paula Connolly
Barbara L. Cooper
Nancy Cotton
Robert D. Cottrell

Joanne V. Creighton
Mary R. Davidson
Ruth P. Dawson
Terence Dawson
Christy Desmet
Josephine Donovan
Aliki P. Dragona
V. Kim Duckett
Margaret Eifler
Dyan Elliott
Eileen Finan
Valeria Finucci
Gabriela Fiori
Rhoda L. Flaxman
Kathleen Fowler
Lee Arthur Gallo
Aristoula Georgiadou
Daniel Gerould
Tony Giffone
Mary E. Giles
Jerry Glenn
Sanda Golopentia
Cristina González
Marjanne E. Goozé
Helena Goscilo
Joseph A. Grau
Catherine S. Green
Diane Greene
Sayre N. Greenfield
Jutta Hagedorn
Peggy Hager
Stephen Hale
Margaret P. Hannay
Elaine Tuttle Hansen
Katherine Hanson
Laura Hapke
Robert Harrison
Susan Hastings
Thomas Head
Marie-France Hilgar
Dianne Van Hoof
Robert E. Hosmer, Jr.
Bruce Hozeski
Liisi Huhtala

Charles A. Huttar
Paula T. Irvin
Lanae Hjortsvang Isaacson
Rosemary Jann
Neda Jeni
Jorun B. Johns
Sheila Johnson
Judith L. Johnston
James W. Jones
Jean E. Jost
JoAnne C. Juett
Clara Juncker
Carey Kaplan
Päivi Karttunen
Catriona Kelly
Christine Kiebuzinska
Blossom S. Kirschenbaum
Helen Dendrinou Kolias
Jürgen Koppensteiner
Jadwiga Kosicka
Gail Kraidman
Ruth L. Kreuzer
Kai Laitinen
David H.J. Larmour
Anne Larsen
Valerie Lastinger
Ellen Laun
Oscar Lee
Gertrud Jaron Lewis
Stanley Longman
Ruth Lundelius
Clinton Machann
Loralee MacPike
Michèle M. Magill
Coro Malaxecheverría
Laura Jo Turner McCullough
Glenda McLeod
Cynthia Merrill
Kate Beaird Meyers
Colette Michael
Elsie B. Michie
Catherine Milsum
Stephen A. Mitchell
Cornelia Niekus Moore

Maureen E. Mulvihill
Marie Murphy
Paul D. Nelsen
Patricia W. O'Connor
Karen Offen
Patricia A. O'Hara
Jeanne A. Ojala
William T. Ojala
Stephanie B. Pafenberg
Lydia A. Panaro
Louis J. Parascandola
Paul Pascal
Zoja Pavlovskis
Jean Pearson
Maya Peretz
Janet Perez
Mary Ferguson Pharr
Richard J. Pioli
Richard Poss
Zelda Provenzano
Carol Pulham
Rosetta Radtke
Lila F. Ralston
Ann Marie Rasmussen
Alan Rauch
Anne-Marie Ray

Earl Jeffrey Richards
Helene M. Kastinger Riley
Warwick J. Rodden
J.R. Rothschild
Norma L. Rudinsky
Rinaldina Russell
Ute Marie Saine
Paul Schlueter
Harold B. Segel
Carole Shaffer-Koros
Philip Shashko
Robin Sheets
Gale Sigal
Rimvydas Šilbajoris
Michael Skakun
Marilyn B. Skinner
Marilynn J. Smith
Paula Sommers
Sarah Spence
Robert Spoo
Sandra Ballif Straubhaar
Judith Tarr
Frances Teague
Senni Timonen
John Timpane
Christine Tomei

Betty Travitsky
Richard Unger
Noël M. Valis
Ria Vanderauwera
Eleni Varikas
Henk Vynckier
Cory L. Wade
Glenda Wall
Robyn R. Warhol
Frank Warnke
Elissa B. Weaver
Hanna Kalter Weiss
Rebecca West
Duey White
Charity C. Willard
Audrone B. Willeke
Charles G.S. Williams
Katharina M. Wilson
Carolyn Woodward
Reiko Yonogi
Karl A. Zaenker
Phyllis Zatlin
Ingeborg Zeiträg
Mary F. Zirin

Portrait Credits

The following photographs are reprinted courtesy of the New York Public Library:

Bettine von Arnim
Jane Austen
Clare of Assisi
Frances Burney
Caterina da Siena
Catherine II (the Great)
Anne Frank
Mme Guyon (Jeanne-Marie Bouvier de la Motte)
Heloise
Lady Caroline Lamb
Marquise de Maintenon
Hannah More
Ann Ward Radcliffe
Christina Rossetti
Sappho
Mary Stuart, Queen of Scots

Reprinted courtesy of the Grolier Club:

Charlotte Brontë
George Eliot
Queen Elizabeth I
Elizabeth Simpson Inchbald
Frances Anne Kemble
Sophia Lee
Margaret of Austria
Marguerite de Navarre
Mary Russell Mitford
Elizabeth Montagu
Katherine Philips
Hester Piozzi
Christine de Pizan
Jane Porter

Reprinted courtesy of the German Consulate:

Ilse Aichinger
Hannah Arendt
Rosa Luxemburg
Nelly Sachs
Christa Wolf

Reprinted courtesy Gyldendal:

Suzanne Brøgger
Inger Christensen
Isak Dinesen (Karen Blixen)

Reprinted courtesy the Letterkundig Museum:

Catharina Irma Dessaur
Virginie Loveling
Elizabeth Wolff-Bekker

Reprinted courtesy CORBIS-BETTMANN:

Saint Teresa of Jesus
Sidonie-Gabrielle Colette

Reprinted by permission of SOVFOTO:

Sofia Kovalevskaia
Marina Tsvetaeva

Reprinted courtesy ITAR-TASS/SOVFOTO:

Bélla Akhátovna Akhmadúlina

Reprinted courtesy RIA-NOVOSTI/SOVFOTO:

Anna Akhmatova

Reprinted courtesy the Instituto Cervantes:

Carmen Martín Gaite

Reprinted courtesy the Norwegian Consulate:

Sigrid Undset

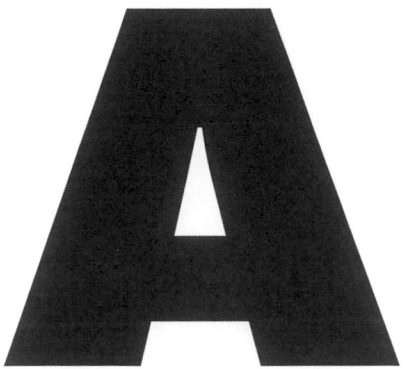

Ilse Aichinger
1921–

Born November 1, 1921, Vienna, Austria
Genre(s): novel, short story, radio play
Language(s): German

This Austrian novelist, poet, short story writer, and radio playwright was born in Vienna, spent her childhood in Linz, and completed gymnasium in Vienna in 1939. Aichinger was of partly Jewish descent, and after the *Anschluss* with Germany, she and her family were persecuted and forced to do compulsory service during World War II. She began medical studies after 1945, discontinuing them in the fifth semester to complete her first novel, *Die grössere Hoffnung* (1948; translated in English as *Herod's Children*, 1963). From 1949 to 1950, in Vienna and later in Frankfurt, she was employed as a reader with S. Filcher Verlag, which later became her publisher. In 1953 she married the German poet Günter Eich (1907–1972), whom she had met as a fellow member of the post–World War II writers' association "Gruppe 47," which had its first meeting in 1947. At each meeting a prize was offered for the best work, and Aichinger received this prize in 1952 for "Rede unter dem Galgen" ("Speech under the Gallows"), published in Germany in the collection *Der Gefesselte* (1953; translated in English as *The Bound Man and Other Stories*, 1955).

Ilse Aichinger is a master of the "unpretended language." Her works are marked by their unobtrusiveness and clarity. Her only novel, *Die grössere Hoffnung*, introduced many of the themes that have preoccupied Aichinger and established what may be called her style. Set against the background of World War II in a country dominated by the Nazis, the novel tells the story of a group of children who try through emigration to escape their threatened fate. The cen-

Ilse Aichinger

tral figure, Ellen, is a half-Jewish girl who is precocious and perceptive. Although Ellen is killed in the end, the novel ultimately offers a "greater hope" suggested by its title, even in the midst of suffering: "all things work together for good in them that love God." When the novel was published in English as *Herod's Children*, its resemblance to the works of Kafka was immediately noted. Like Kafka, she uses the convergence of dream and reality; similarly, the simplicity of her style heightens its overall effect. She uses the language and vocabulary of everyday experience, but captivating metaphors and unusual characters produce a feeling of alienation from the world.

In the title story of *Der Gefesselte*, her debt to Kafka is evident. In this story, a man wakes up one morning and finds that he has been bound with ropes that allow him very limited freedom of movement; he learns to live with his fetters. Sartre's idea of man constantly bound to the human condition finds expression in this story. The topic of the acceptance of human bondage recurs in several other stories.

In 1953 Aichinger presented her first radio play, "Knöpfe" ("Buttons"), the story of a group of workers in a button factory who spend their working lives in monotonous, repetitive routines. In doing so, these workers begin to lose their individuality, and they gradually turn into buttons.

Speaking about the nature of Aichinger's work, the critic J.C. Alldridge says that the reading public is startled by the unobtrusiveness of her work: "One has often had the impression, when reading one of her works for the first time, of a silent figure, by whom one has been observed and of whose existence one has been unaware."

Works

Die grössere Hoffnung, novel (1948). *Rede unter dem Galgen*, short stories (1952; published in Germany as *Der Gefesselte*, 1953). "Knöpfe," radio play (1953). *Zu keiner Stunde*, dialogues (1957). *Besuch im Pfarrhause*, radio play (1961). *Wo ich wohne*, stories, dialogues, poems (1963). *Eliza, Eliza*, stories (1965). *Nachmittag in Ostende* (1968). *Ausland*, radio plays (1969). *Nachricht von Tag*, stories (1970). *Dialoge, Erzählungen, Gedichte*, dialogues, stories, poems (1971). *Schlechte Wörter*, stories and radio plays (1976). *Meine Sprache und ich. Erzählungen*, all prose pieces written by the late 1970s (1978). *Verschenkter Rat. Gedichte*, thematically arranged poems written between 1955 and 1978 (1978). *Zu keiner Stunde. Szenen und Dialoge*, extended edition of *Zu keiner Stunde*, 1957 (1980).

Translations: *The Bound Man and Other Stories* [*Rede unter dem Galgen*], tr. Eric Mosbacher (1955; American ed. 1956). *Herod's Children* [*Die grössere Hoffnung*], tr. Cornelia Schaeffer (1963). *Selected Short Stories and Dialogues*, tr. James C. Alldridge (1968). *Selected Poetry and Prose of Ilse Aichinger*, tr. Allen H. Chappel (1983).

Reiko Yonogi

Bélla Akhátovna Akhmadúlina
1937–

Born 1937, Moscow, the Soviet Union
Genre(s): poetry, translation, prose
Language(s): Russian

Bélla Akhátovna Akhmadúlina

One of modern Russia's most powerful voices, Akhmadúlina writes poems centered on the chills caused by non-conformity and the fever wrought by an acute awareness of the difficulty of being different in a highly structured society. Although she shares much with other contemporary poets such as Voznesenskii, her accent on almost brazen individuality and the inability to fit in is strongly reminiscent of the early Mayakovsky.

Born in 1937, in Moscow, Akhmadúlina began to publish quite early, at the age of eighteen. She then began to attend the Gorki Institute for writers, but was expelled in 1960. Her first book, a collection of poems called *Struna* (1962; The String) was published during the period of expanded freedom of expression called the "thaw" and was a resounding success. Her next collection of poems, *Oznob* (1968; The Chill) was published abroad in Frankfurt. One more collection would see publication during the sixties, *Uroki muzyki* (1969; Music Lessons).

Then in 1977, as though long pent-up, three volumes appeared: *Svecha* (The Candle), *Metel'* (The Snowstorm), and *Sny o Gruzii* (Dreams of Georgia), the last including translations and prose writings. Since then, three more volumes have appeared, *Taina* (1983; The Secret), *Sad* (1987; The Garden), and *Bella Akhmadúlina* (1988) that includes poems from many earlier collections.

Though criticized in the official circles for being overly personal and not sufficiently socially instructive, Akhmadúlina actually is quite critical herself—of her surroundings and the people who conform rigidly and unthinkingly to the established behavior. She often describes herself as ill and in need of a sedative to calm the force inside her, as in "The Chill": "Explained the doctor: /—Your illness is simple. / It would be completely harmless, / except that the frequency of your oscillations / interferes with the examination—you're invisible." Her substance and condition elude traditional scrutiny so the doctor administers a shock to her system. Then he pronounces her normal at which she is saddened: "I alone knew / my access to a higher normalcy." Often she is childishly boisterous and disorderly as in "The Boat": "And somewhere, whistling on a pipe /not observing the flowers or their beds / a strange child runs wild / and devastates their order."

Akhmadúlina's power resides in her almost unnerving ability to weave between the intensely personal and the clearly drawn constraints of social life. Vivid images erupt from the subliminal threshhold only to smash flatly against the staircases, walls and various edifices of the society which surrounds her. The joy of the force of life is what she most highly prizes and is precisely the cause of suspicion and discomfort in those who find themselves near her. She herself is like a flower without a garden to surround her. Akhmadúlina reads her poetry to large, closely packed audiences filled with admirers.

Works

Struna, poetry (1962). *Oznob*, poetry (1968). *Uroki muzyki* (1969). *Strikhi* (1975). *Metel'* (1977). *Sny o Gruzii*, poetry, translations, prose (1977). *Svecha* (1977). "*Mnogo sobak i sobaka*," *Metropol* (1879). *Taina* (1983). *Sad* (1987). *Bella Akhmadúlina*, poetry (1988). *Poberezh'e,* poetry (1991).

Translations: *Sloneczna dolina*, ed. I. Piotrowska, et al. (1964). *Struna*, tr. V. Daněk (1966). *Fever and Other New Poems*, tr. G. Dutton and I. Mezhakoff-Koriakin (1968). *The New Russian Poets* (bilingual), ed. and tr. G. Reavey (1968). *Russian Poetry: The Modern Period*, ed. J. Glad and D. Weissbort (1978). *Three Russian Poets*, ed. and tr. E. Feinstein (1979).

The Garden, ed. G.S. Smith (1993). *Contemporary Russian Poetry,* ed. G. S. Smith (1993).

Christine Tomei

Anna Akhmatova
1889–1966

a.k.a. Anna Gorenko
Born June 11, 1889, Odessa, Russia
Died March 5, 1966, Domedovo (near Moscow)
Genre(s): poetry
Language(s): Russian

Anna Akhmatova

Anna Akhmatova, along with Boris Pasternak, Osip Mandel'shtam, and Marina Tsvetaeva, is widely regarded as one of the leading Russian poets of the twentieth century. Akhmatova, her first husband Nikolai Gumilev, and Mandel'shtam were the major proponents of Acmeism, a reaction in the 1910s and 1920s against the vague mysticism and ethereality of the Symbolist movement. The Acmeists preferred to use simple, classical diction and concrete imagery and to emphasize the immediateness of human situations. Although Akhmatova's later poetry moves away from the emotional restraint of her earlier poems, her writing is always characterized by its economy and control. In addition to poetry, Akhmatova wrote a number of biographical and critical essays on writers and artists, including Modigliani, Blok, Mandel'shtam, and Pushkin.

Akhmatova grew up in a well-to-do family in Tsarskoe Selo, near St. Petersburg. There she met the young poet Nikolai Gumilev, whom she was later to marry. She attended the university at Kiev to study law, but a year later she left to study literature in St. Petersburg. Her marriage to Gumilev in 1910 was a difficult one in spite of their intellectual kinship; in 1914 Gumilev enlisted in the cavalry, and in 1918 they were divorced. Akhmatova's love poetry from this period often reflects the turbulence of their relationship. Her association with Gumilev (executed as a counterrevolutionary in 1921) and the relatively apolitical nature of her poetry drew the suspicion of the government in the 1920s. Her son Lev Gumilev was arrested several times in the 1930s and 1940s, mainly as a means of censoring Akhmatova; her hardships and suffering during this experience are recounted in the poem *Requiem*. Akhmatova wrote and published patriotic poetry in the 1940s, but her two major late works, *Requiem* (finished in 1940) and *Poem Without a Hero* (begun in the 1940s and finished in 1962), were not published in the Soviet Union. In 1964 she traveled to Italy to accept the Taormina Prize for Poetry and the following year to Oxford for an honorary D. Litt. The Soviet government had slowly begun to rehabilitate her work during the thaw of the post-Stalin era. The first significant collection of her work without major censorship, *Beg vremini* (The Course of Time), was published in 1964, and in the following year A.I. Pavlovsky's book-length study appeared. Akhmatova was given the funeral obsequies of the Orthodox church at Komarovo near Leningrad.

Akhmatova's early poems—particularly those in the collections *Evening*, *Rosary*, and *White Flock*—are brief lyrics dealing mainly with the theme of love, usually unrequited or tragic, and use clear, precise images and a restrained tone. Often a personal object, an architectural detail, or a natural phenomenon will connote the emotional state of the speaker, as in "The Song of the Last Meeting," in which the distraught persona puts her left glove on her right hand. In the longer poem *By the Sea Shore*, published in the magazine *Apollon* in 1915, Akhmatova develops the concept of the double, a theme to which she would return often, most notably in *Poem Without a Hero*. With *Plantain* and *Anno Domini*, Akhmatova begins to deal with broader, more political issues in reaction to the worsening political climate. The persona often laments a lost order and an indefinite future: "All has been plundered, betrayed, sold out, / The wing of black death has flashed by, / All has been gnawed away by hungry anxiety." The poet's concern with the public sphere and with her responsibility as poet is further marked by the greater use of allusion. The speaker of "Lot's Wife," for example, describes how the wife turns back to look once more at the familiar sights of home; this desire reflects not only the post-revolutionary nostalgia for the past society but also the artist's fear of having to relinquish the poetry of her beloved concrete images in favor of a more dogmatic, politically "correct" way of writing, and the speaker vows that she will remember and grieve for this tragic act of looking backward. Akhmatova's two masterpieces, *Requiem* and *Poem Without a Hero*, seek to resolve the dilemma of choosing between the public and the private. *Requiem*, first published in Munich in 1963, describes the poet's own grief at the imprisonment of her son. The speaker, in a series of increasingly emotional sections, confronts despair, death, and finally madness, but in the tenth section, "Crucifixion," the subjective perspective gives way to calm, objective description of the solitary grief of the Virgin Mary, who is forbidden to weep. The epilogue returns to the perspective of the grieving mother, but this persona now feels the suffering of all the other women beside her; she vows to commemorate their suffering, asking that, if she should be remembered, it should be with a statue outside the unopened prison doors, so that the snow might melt on her bronze eyelids, as the pigeons coo and the ships sail down the Neva. *Poem Without a Hero*, first published in New York in 1960, is a cryptically allusive retrospective of the poet's life and career. Friends and acquaintances from the pre-revolutionary past appear to the speaker/poet, disguised as literary figures. Roles and identities blur, and the experiences of characters in the poem double with those of the poet. Though rich with cultural allusions, the poem nevertheless depicts the inability of the past alone—exemplified in the tragic, self-destructive romanticism of 1913 Petersburg—to redeem the present. The poem ends without a definite conclusion, and its final images depict the devastated city of Leningrad in 1943—the embodiment of a Russia which continues to survive, just as the poet survives, by maintaining her sense of suffering and loss.

With the growing numbers of translations and studies of her works, Akhmatova's importance as a modern writer is becoming increasingly apparent. The disciplined refinement of her earlier lyrics, combined with a probing analysis of the self, place Akhmatova among the best of traditional modern poets; the bolder formal experiments of the middle and late poems, with their synthesis of personal and cultural history, clearly establish her as one of the most original and innovative of all twentieth-century writers.

Works

Vecher [Evening] (1912). *Chyotki* [Rosary] (1914). *Belaya staya* [White Flock] (1917). *Podorozhnik* [Plantain] (1921). *Anno Domini MCMXXI* (1921, 1923). *Iz shesti knig* [From Six Books] (1940). *Izbrannoe* [Selected Poems] (1943). *Stikhotvoreniya 1909–1945* [Poems 1909–1945] (1945). *Izbrannye stikhi* [Selected Poems] (1946). *Stikhotvoreniya* [Poems] (1958). *Stikhotvoreniya 1909–1960* [Poems 1909–1960] (1961). *Requiem* (1963). *Beg vremini* [The Flight of Time] (1965). *Sochineniya* [Works], 2 vols. (1967, 1968). *Tale Without a Hero and Twenty-two Poems by Anna Akhmatova* (1973). *Izbrannoe* [Selected Works] (1974). *Stikhi i Proza* [Poems and Prose] (1976). *Stikhotvoreniia i poemy* [Selected Works] (1976). *Zapiski ob Anne Akhmatovoi* [Letters of Anna Akhmatova], vol. I, 1930–1941 (1976); vol. II, 1952–1962 (1980). *Anna Akhmatova: Stikhi/Perepiska/Vospominaniia/Ikonografiia* [Anna Akhmatova: Poems/Correspondence/Reminiscences/Iconography] (1977). *Anna Akhmatova o Pushkine* [Anna Akhmatova on Pushkin] (1977). *Izbrannie Sochinenie* [Selected Works] (1977).

Selected translations: *Selected Poems of Anna Akhmatova*, tr. Richard McKane (1969). *Poems of Akhmatova*, tr. Stanley Kunitz with Max Hayward (1974). *Selected Poems*, tr. Walter Arndt, with *Requiem*, tr. Robin Kemball, and *Poem Without a Hero*, tr. Carl R. Proffer (1976). *White Flock*, tr. Geoffrey Thurley (1978). *You Will Hear Thunder*, tr. D.M. Thomas (1985).

Stephen Hale

Sibilla Aleramo
1876–1960

a.k.a. Rina Faccio
Born 1876, Alessandria, Italy
Died 1960, Rome
Genre(s): poetry, novel, diary
Language(s): Italian

Sibilla Aleramo's life and works are inextricably related. Her prose and poetry are autobiographical and confessional attempts at self-affirmation that reflect her always tempestuous existence. Born into a middle-class family, she adored her liberal-minded businessman father for whom she worked as a young girl in the glassworks he managed, first in the progressive atmosphere of Milanese culture, then in the more primitive and backward world of the Italian Marches where he had moved the family for work-related reasons in 1887. In 1892, young Rina was raped by one of her father's employees and the following year was constrained to marry him. The horror of that loveless marriage and her subsequent escape from it into a life in letters are vividly described in her first, and most successful, novel entitled *Una donna* (A Woman), published in 1906 and greeted with resounding praise in Italy, France, and Germany. Even before the publication of this book, she had begun what was to prove to be a long and complex involvement with the literary and political worlds of male-dominated Italian culture. She wrote for several early feminist journals, including *L'Italia Femminile*, and became involved in socialism. In 1902 she left her husband and young son and moved to Rome where she lived with Giovanni Cena, a well-known poet who encouraged her to write *Una donna* and gave her the pen name she used throughout her career. She would remain with him until 1910; during their eight-year relationship she came to know many important cultural, political, and literary figures including Pirandello, Maria Montessori, and Gorky. Cena was the first of a great number of famous men with whom Aleramo had affairs and to whom she looked for personal and professional fulfillment. From 1910 until 1920, Aleramo was intensely involved in the Florentine literary scene and had passionate affairs with the poet Vincenzo Cardarelli, the Futurist painter Umberto Boccioni, the writers Giovanni Papini and Giovanni Boine, and, most notably, the poet Dino Campana. Their letters were published by Vallecchi in 1958 and reveal the fevered and highly literary nature of Aleramo's attachments.

Aleramo's second novel, *Il passaggio* (The Passage), was published in 1919; although it was a lyrical autobiography, it met with a generally negative critical response. Her poetry, much of which had already appeared in diverse journals, was collected under the title *Momenti* (Moments) and published in 1921. Having traveled extensively throughout Italy and Europe, Aleramo settled in Rome in 1925. By then, she had come under the powerful sway of D'Annunzianism and her future works would reflect her unfortunate desire to become the female D'Annunzio. Aleramo did not possess the authentic lyrical talent of her model, and her confessional expressions of thwarted passions and troubled affairs did not reach the level of true art. Several such works were published in the mid- and late twenties, but none attained the success of her first novel. Among them are the failed play *Endimione* (1924); the epistolary novel *Amo, dunque sono* (I Love, Therefore I Am), published in 1927 and recounting her recent affair with Giulio Parise; and *Il frustino* (The Riding Whip), published in 1932 and telling the story of yet another affair with Giovanni Boine. By the advent of Fascism, Aleramo had abandoned her political and social conscience almost entirely in favor of the intimistic art she was practicing. Although she signed Benedetto Croce's antifascist manifesto, for example, she accepted state support from Mussolini's government for many years before his fall in 1943, a decision she would later openly regret. In 1936 she met and became involved with the very young poet Franco Matacotta (1916–1978); he was to be her last great love. Under his influence she became a member of the Communist Party in 1946, and wrote a great deal of ideological verse for various Party publications. She won the Versilia Prize for poetry in 1948 for her collection of verse, *Selva d'amore* (Forest of Love), in which she brought together her poetry written between 1922 and 1942. In the last decade of her life, many of her early works were republished; she traveled twice to Russia and enjoyed the friendship of other Party members. She died in relative poverty in 1960.

Una donna remains Aleramo's masterpiece. Hailed at its appearance as equal in feminist power to Ibsen's *A Doll's House*, it is still a book that speaks eloquently in moving and yet controlled prose to the problem of women's self-definition and fulfillment. Next to it, Aleramo's most important work is her diary, kept over a period of twenty years from 1940 to 1960. It is not great literature, but it is an invaluable source of information on the cultural, political, and literary scenes of modern Italy, and it reveals Aleramo's intelligence and passion. She was a vital presence within Italian letters for most of her long life; her overall worth as a writer is more difficult to assess. By her own admission, she never fully recovered from the traumatic rape and subsequent abandonment of her son, events that shaped her sensibility much more than literary or political influences. Aleramo cannot simply be called an early feminist, nor can she be dismissed as a minor imitator of decadent models such as D'Annunzio. Her work is, instead, an excellent example of the "life as art" and "art as life" mode, an aesthetic attitude that determined much of twentieth-century art and whose intricacies are still open to exploration.

Works

Una donna [A Woman], prose (1906). *Il passaggio* [The Passage] (1919). *Andando e stando*, prose (1921). *Momenti* [Moments], poetry (1921).

Transfigurazione, prose (1922). *Endimione*, drama (1924). *Amo, dunque sono* [I Love, Therefore I Am], prose (1927). *Poesie*, poetry (1929). *Gioie d'occasione*, prose (1930). *Il frustino* [The Riding Whip], prose (1932). *Sì alla terra*, poetry (1934). *Orsa minore*, prose (1938). *Dal mio diario*, prose (1945). *Selva d'amore* [Forest of Love], poetry (1947). *Aiutatemi a dire*, poetry (1951). *Gioie d'occasione e altre ancora*, prose (1954). *Luci della mia sera*, poetry (1956). *Lettere: Sibilla Aleramo-Dino Campana*, letters (1958). *Diario di una donna: Inediti 1945/1960*, prose (1978). *Un amore insolito: Diario 1940–1944*, prose (1979).

Translations: *A Woman*, tr. Rosalind Delmar, introd. Richard Drake (1980).

Rebecca West

Leonor de Almeida de Portugal
1750–1839

a.k.a. Alcipe, Marquesa de Alorna
Born 1750, Lisbon, Portugal
Died 1839, Lisbon
Genre(s): poetry, translation, paraphrase, letters
Language(s): Portuguese

Following the political execution of her grandmother, the Marquesa de Távora, in 1758, Alcipe, her sister Maria, and her mother, D. Leonor de Almeida, were detained in the convent of Chelas by the Marquês de Pombal. Alcipe spent her youth there, amusing herself with poetry, music, and reading. She was tutored by Filinto, P. Francisco Manuel do Nascimento (b. 1734), until King Jose's death in 1777. It was Filinto who gave her the Arcadian name of "Alcipe." In 1779 she married a German officer and Portuguese citizen, the Count of Oeynhausen, who became Portuguese Ambassador to Vienna in 1780. Alcipe was widowed in 1793, with six children to educate. In response to the Napoleonic invasion, she founded the Society of the Rose and was exiled, near destitute, to London in 1804. Returning to Portugal in 1814, she inherited the Marquisate of Alorna and spent her last twenty-five years near Lisbon, where she founded a literary salon that became the focus for new aesthetic ideas.

Alcipe influenced Portuguese literature to the extent that the contemporary poet Herculano called her "Staël portuquesa." Her reading of Locke, Voltaire, and the Encyclopedia formed the basis for her attack on tyranny and fanaticism as well as her enthusiasm for progress and scientific reason. A pervasive sense of high ideals and love of liberty were constants in her work. With Macedo, Alcipe formed a link between poets of the *Arcadia* and the nineteenth century.

Often inspired by political events, her works contain over 2,000 pages of verse. Her style is an excellent example of the new sensibility, the pre-Romantic mode. Romantic fatalism, exclamation, and violent adjectives tint her vision; she likes solitude and melancholy and has a tendency toward the nocturnal, the funereal, and the pathetic fallacy. However, she still retains and celebrates neo-classical forms, such as epithets and odes, and uses a good deal of mythological references and classical allusion. A prime example is her use of Cocytus in a sonnet on the death of her infant son.

Alcipe's range of works is most comprehensive. She wrote sonnets, eclogues, elegies, epithets, and odes, as well as translations or paraphrases of Homer, Horace, Claudian (*De raptu Proserpinae*), Pope (*Essay on Criticism*), Wieland, Thomson (*Seasons*), Goldsmith, Lamartine, and the Psalms. Her letters are expressive and graceful, showing acute social and political understanding; at the same time they convey the spontaneity of life. No subject was not fit or interesting material for Alcipe. A long poem of hers on botany described over 100 kinds of scented geraniums. Fireflies, the climate of England, Leibniz, and Robertson's flight in a balloon all fascinated her. Her six-volume master work, *Obras Poéticas*, touched on all themes, genres, and structures of literature.

Works

Obras Poéticas (Lisbon, 1844).

Rosetta Radtke

Concha Alós
1922–

Born May 24, 1922, Valencia, Spain
Genre(s): novel, short story
Language(s): Spanish

Concha Alós's father was a waiter. Her grandfather was a shepherd. This working-class background, which is not usually found in writers from Spain, provided Concha Alós with a great deal of thematic and descriptive material, particularly for her early novels. Her mother hoped she would become a dressmaker, but the future novelist's interests and talents took another turning. In 1936 the Spanish Civil War erupted, forc-

ing the family, then located in Castellón, to flee from Franco's troops to a small town in the province of Murcia. Meanwhile, her father had been called to serve in the Republican forces. After the war, he was imprisoned and her mother died. The family, like many others in Spain, suffered humiliating and wrenching hardships during this period. Alós would eventually marry and move to Palma de Mallorca, where she taught school for two years and started writing. All this experience would be incorporated into her fiction. In 1957 she won a prize from the Mallorcan magazine *Lealtad* for her short story, "El cerro del telégrafo" (Telegraph Hill). In 1959, her marriage over, she left for Barcelona, where she resides today.

Alós's work needs to be situated within the dual context of women's writing and post–Civil War literature in Spain. The appearance of *Nada* (Nothing) by Carmen Laforet in 1944 seemed to signal a resurgence of fiction by women, among them Ana María Matute, Carmen Martín Gaite, Dolores Medio, and Elena Quiroga. At the same time the dominant aesthetic during much of the Franco period was social realism. Alós's early novels are good examples, rooted as they are in the miseries and deprivations of the lower classes and of women in particular. Her first novel, *Los enanos* (1962; The Dwarfs), is set in a modest boarding house, filled with desperate characters living on the margins of life and surrounded by hostile, impersonal forces over which they have no control. The "Ship of Fools" framework highlights the importance of circumstance and destiny, while the setting itself, redolent of Balzac's Pension Vauquer and Cela's *colmena* or beehive, suggests a gritty and despairing microcosm of the human condition. Alós's second novel, *Los cien pájaros* (1963; The Hundred Birds), continues in the same vein of social realism, this time focusing on the coming of age of a young, working-class girl. The theme of female liberation from male domination and an oppressive family structure is stated quietly and simply through first-person narration.

The Civil War and its aftermath provided the story line for *El caballo rojo* (1966; The Red Horse) and *La madama* (1969; The Madam). The fear of Franquist reprisals after the war, which is hinted at in the first-named novel, is fully realized in the second. *La madama* is structured around the implicit notion of two interconnecting circles of hell: the literal prison of Clemente, a former Republican soldier, and the dismal domestic struggle for survival of his family. Clemente's hopeless situation and his family's ultimate prostitution point, once again in Alós's fiction, to a bitterly deterministic, even defeatist, perspective of human existence.

In *Las hogueras* (1964; Bonfires), the absence of love provides a dense smoke screen for characters suffocating in their personally created vacuum of boredom, loneliness, and isolation. In this, the novel, though no less representative of social realism than Alós's earlier efforts, does anticipate a new line of development in her work: the exploration of the individual psyche as a bizarre dream world secretly inhabiting ordinary reality. Her first significant step away from the limitations of social realism came in *Rey de gatos* (1972; King of the Cats), a series of nine "narraciones antropófagas," or "cannibal stories," narrated mostly in first person. Here, she deals with such themes as the war between the sexes (also found in *Las hogueras*), jealousy, alienation, and crises of identity but places them within a surreal and hallucinatory cannibalistic universe in which the loss of the human is paramount.

Readers were jolted, however, by the radical departure from conventional linear narration and character construction which her 1975 novel, *Os habla Electra* (Electra Speaks to You), represented. Concentrating on the thematic dichotomy between fertility and the threat of universal destruction, Alós outlined a story of mythic and archetypal proportions, in particular, the struggle between patriarchal and matriarchal modes of being, in which the female—Electra, all Electras—strove to regain a sense of wholeness and personal identity. Weaving deftly between the real and the imaginary, with a series of oneiric images and a fragmented, often deliberately confusing narrative structure, Alós moved fully into experimental fiction with this novel. Unfortunately, she has not been able to sustain the effort. Her next two novels, *Argeo ha muerto, supongo* (1982; Argeo's Died, I Guess), and *El asesino de los sueños* (1986; The Dream Murderer), are an uneasy and sometimes awkward blend of reality and dream, in which she continues to deal with the themes of identity confusion, self-alienation, and the loss of illusion and first love, this time in a more conventional format. The use of a more straightforward casting of fictional events may also reflect a general trend in recent Spanish fiction of the 1980s: the return of storytelling itself. Where this will take Concha Alós is difficult to say. While her work from the 1960s represents a worthy contribution to Spanish neorealism, it is the innovative "deconstructed reality" of *Os habla Electra* that signals a more radical breakthrough in Concha Alós's development as a novelist.

Works

Cuando la luna cambia de color, unpublished ms. (1958). *Los enanos* (1962). *Los cien pájaros* (1963). *Las hogueras* (1964). *El caballo rojo* (1966). *La madama* (1969). *Rey de gatos (Narraciones antropófagas)* (1972). *Os habla Electra* (1975). *Argeo ha muerto, supongo* (1982). *El asesino de los sueños* (1986).

Noël M. Valis

Loula Anagnostaki
ca. 1937–

a.k.a. Loula Anagnostakē
Born ca. 1935–1940, Thessalonikē, Greece
Genre(s): drama
Language(s): Greek

Loula Anagnostaki belongs to the new generation of modern Greek playwrights who made a break with the past, writing about characters and situations that are not particularly Greek. In fact, her characters have no country, for they dwell in an *absurd* world in which they are not at home. Anagnostaki is not concerned about theatrical conventions of the past, such as logical development of the plot with a beginning, middle, and end, defined setting, interaction between the characters on stage, or clearly stated relationships. Her plays move in unexpected ways toward unexpected finishes, and the audience is put in the position of having to make sense of what is presented. In Anagnostaki's post-modern world, nothing is logical, and time is irrelevant; characters take on "European" dimensions (the influences of Beckett, Sartre, Pinter, and Brecht are obvious); and the play, rather than moving toward a resolution, is a depiction of irresolution, for nothing is resolved, and individuals are not closer to any type of recognition at the end than they were at the beginning. But all is not for nought, for Anagnostaki puts on stage our individual alienation, confusion, and lack of control over our lives, as well as our selfishness and outright meanness, expressed in petty ways that are nevertheless universal. The characters on stage may not relate with each other, but they depict the need to relate, to encounter "the other" in order to reduce the oppressive isolation that envelops them. Thus they are Anagnostaki's version of today's Everyman and Everywoman.

Her first play, *Dianyktereusē* (Overnight Stop), deals with the different fears of two people of different generations (and thus their lack of understanding of each other). In *Ē Polē* (The City), Elizabeth and Kimon entice an older man, a photographer, to break out of his isolation, but he is left more lonely at the end than he was at the beginning, for they were only playing with his emotions. In *Parelasē* (Parade), two children, Aris and Zoë, act as reflections of what is happening outside their drab room where "leaders" are savagely manipulating gullible crowds.

All of the above are one-act plays, first performed in 1965 and published in 1974 under the general title *Ē Polē* (The City). The *polē* is a modern version of the classical word *polis*, but in Anagnostaki's plays this is what her characters lack, a place they can call their own, a home. This theme is elaborated further in her subsequent works. In *Ē Synanastrophē* (Social Encounter—first performed in 1967), the setting is a place where people gather to make each other miserable. In *Antonio ē to mēnyma* (Antonio or the Message—first performed in 1972), the setting is misty, like the characters, a house that does not appear to belong to anyone in particular, an undefined place where people encounter each other in ways that bespeak lack of communication, despite the long speeches, and lack of relationships, despite the attempts to establish connections. In fact, in this play that takes place in a house, and during which we see a total of twenty-four people come on stage, there are no blood relationships. The place is just a temporary abode or meeting room for people on their way to another temporary abode or meeting room, people forever on the go, not knowing where they belong or where they want to be.

In Anagnostaki's *Ē Nikē* (Victory—first performed in 1978), one place is replaced by another as members of a family, having left their village in northern Greece and later their home in Piraeus, attempt to improve their situation in a city somewhere in Germany. The mother does not feel at home in her new surroundings and wants to go back. Her daughter, however, tries to relate to the world around her and encourages her brother to marry a German girl, but, before the play is over, he is killed by a "friend." The search for a new home makes people aware of their lack of home and of the fact that they are aliens in more ways than one.

Anagnostaki's works have been performed by Karolos Koun's Art Theater and by the National Theater of Greece. They have also been performed in France, England, Italy, Poland, and Cyprus and have been presented on the BBC, RAI, and Cypriot television.

Works

Dianyktereusē [Overnight Stop], *Ē Polē* [The City], and *Parelasē* [Parade], published under the general title *Ē Polē* (1974; *Parelasē* [Parade] also published in *Theatro* [1965], pp. 225–232). *Ē Synanastrophē* [Social Encounter]. *Antonio ē to menyma* [Antonio or the Message] (1971, 1980). *Ē Nikē* [The Victory]. *Ē Kassetta* [The Cassette]. *O echos tou oplou* [The Echo of the Gun] (1986). *Diamantia kai Mplouz* [Diamonds and Blues] (1991).

Translations: "The Town," tr. Aliki Halls. *The Chicago Review* 21, 2 (1969).

Helen Dendrinou Kolias

Anyte
ca. 300 B.C.

Born Tegea, Arcadia (Greece); exact birth and death dates unknown; flourished approximately 300 B.C.
Genre(s): epigrams
Language(s): Greek

We know nothing of the personal life of Anyte, but an anecdote told by Pausanias connects her with a miracle performed by the healing god Asclepius and the subsequent construction of his shrine at Naupactus. Her interest in the woodland god Pan is appropriate for a native of Arcadia.

The most important and influential of the Hellenistic women epigrammatists, Anyte is usually credited with twenty-one extant poems, all but one preserved in the *Greek Anthology*. Three other pieces once ascribed to her are not now considered her genuine work. Ancient sources inform us that she also wrote lyric poetry and perhaps epic (Antipater of Thessalonica terms her "the female Homer"), but only her epigrams have survived.

Thematically, Anyte's epigrams may be grouped into four categories: commemorations of objects dedicated to divinities, epitaphs for human beings, epitaphs on animals, and landscape poems. The first two are standard types of epigram found in the earliest verse inscriptions, but the latter two are apparently Anyte's own invention, and her introduction of bucolic motifs into Greek epigram is crucial for the later development of the European pastoral.

Even in her highly conventional dedicatory and sepulchral quatrains, Anyte displays elegance, exceptional learning, and marked originality. Poem 2, for example, is a bold artistic experiment in which the dedication formula is reduced to its starkest elements (object, dedicator, divine recipient, maker of object) and the reader is forced to infer the rationale for the gift from slight textual hints. The funerary epigrams for human beings are devoted exclusively to the pathetic fate of the young—soldiers fallen in war, girls perishing before their nuptial day. The attitudes expressed are orthodox, even androcentric: marriage is viewed as the natural and desirable lot of women without any trace of that anxiety over sexual initiation pervading Erinna's *Distaff* (q.v.). In contrast to most male epigrammatists, however, Anyte does stress the emotional impact of death upon the survivors. In poem 4 she apparently compares young soldiers who have lost their captain to children mourning a mother—a gender reversal so unusual that most editors obelize the text.

By anthropomorphizing their subjects and, thereby, blurring the distinction between the human and animal realms, Anyte's five epitaphs for beasts and insects affirm the essential importance of such "lesser" lives. Thus poem 9 recounts the fate of a slain war horse in epic language and invests him with the grandeur of a fallen Homeric hero. In her longest piece, poem 12, a dolphin cast ashore laments his end, recalling his former pride in seeing his own image serving as the figurehead of a ship. A quatrain consoling a young girl, Myro, on the loss of her two insect pets displays remarkable tact in its ability to dignify a child's simple grief without becoming precious or falsely sentimental. Anyte's interest in children and capacity to participate imaginatively in their world are also evident in the dedicatory poem 13, in which a description of a picture of boys riding a goat carries witty undertones of equestrian events at the great Pan-Hellenic athletic contests and so conveys the children's conception of themselves as potential Olympic contenders.

While Anyte's animal poems were much imitated in antiquity, her bucolic landscape pieces had a far greater impact upon subsequent literature. In each of these works, she creates the sensuous picture of an idyllic resting place, the domain of Hermes or his son Pan, offering the tired wayfarer shade, a fresh breeze, and a drink of cold spring water in the parching heat. This vision of the sweet and welcoming but finally temporary "green haven" is taken up by her imitator Nicias and, after him, by Theocritus, the recognized founder of the European pastoral tradition. Noting that Vergil's *Eclogues* are set in an artificial "Arcadia" bearing no resemblance to geographical reality, Reitzenstein suggested that the Roman artist's mythic pastoral homeland is a literary tribute to Anyte and her role in shaping the bucolic genre.

Highly popular in antiquity, Anyte was imitated not only by later generations of Greek epigrammatists but by Roman authors such as Catullus and Ovid. In her hands the epigram, though remaining a minimalist poetic form, becomes capable of evocative and emotionally convincing representation of children, animals, and wild nature.

Works

English tr. in *The Greek Anthology*, tr. W.R. Paton. Loeb

Classical Library, 5 vols. (Cambridge, Mass., 1916) and in D. Rayor, *Sappho's Lyre: Archaic Lyric and Women Poets of Ancient Greece* (Berkeley and Los Angeles, 1991). Commentary in *The Greek Anthology: Hellenistic Epigrams*, eds. A.S.F. Gow and D.L. Page, 2 vols. (Cambridge, 1965). Greek texts and German tr. in Homeyer, H., *Dichterinnen des Altertums und des frühen Mittelalters* (Paderborn, 1979).

Marilyn B. Skinner

Tullia d'Aragona
ca. 1510–ca. 1570

Born ca. 1510, Rome, Italy
Died ca. 1570, Rome
Genre(s): poetry and prose dialogues
Language(s): Italian

Tullia d'Aragona was born in Rome probably in 1510, illegitimate daughter of Giulia Campana, a celebrated beauty from Ferrara, and Archbishop Pietro Tagliavia d'Aragona, grandson of the king of Naples. She was highly educated and as a child was reputed to have been able to carry on disputations in excellent Latin.

Biographical accounts vary, and the more romantic versions claim that Tullia was forced to become a courtesan on the death of her father. This appears to be total fiction since his death is not recorded until 1558. What is known for certain is that by 1531 she was involved in a relationship with Filippo Strozzi, the Florentine banker who conspired against Cosimo de Medici, ruler of the city, who had him killed in 1538. Letters written by Strozzi confirm his relationship with Tullia, though she seems to have continued to live in Rome until at least 1541. In that year some sonnets written by her were received and included in the collected papers of the Roman Academia degli Umidi. One of these sonnets, "Almo pastor," is addressed to Cosimo. She eventually moved to Florence under the patronage of Duchess Elenora of Toledo.

Tullia d'Aragona's biography is full of contradictions and problems. Some biographers have mentioned a husband, but she appears to have been known by the same name throughout her life. Her degree of education is unquestionable, and she ran a literary salon first in Rome and later in Florence after 1555, though the years between 1541 and 1555 are poorly documented. She may have lived for a time in Venice and in Ferrara, her mother's native city. There is also an anecdote that appears in various forms, relating how Tullia d'Aragona transgressed laws concerning the proper dress to be worn by a courtesan. One version of the story has Tullia in Florence, wearing clothes to which, as a courtesan, she was not entitled, and other versions set the story in Venice or Florence, with Tullia refusing to wear the yellow cloak that would mark her out as a courtesan. All versions of the story attest to Tullia's strong-mindedness on this issue and the general belief that she was indeed a courtesan first and a writer second.

Her two best known works were *Guerrino Il Meschino*, a poem of approximately 30,000 lines in 36 cantos of ottava rima and her *Dialogue on the Infinity of Love* published in Venice in 1547. In her preface to *Guerrino*, she defends the rights of women to education and attacks those writers who include indecent material in their books, even including Ariosto in her criticisms. Her *Dialogue on the Infinity of Love* is an account of the conversations between herself and Benedetto Varchi, the Florentine philosopher and historian. Tullia d'Aragona appears to have returned to Rome and to have died in 1569–1570. A portrait supposedly of her, by Alessandro Bonvicino, known as Il Moretto, is in the Martinengo Gallery at Brescia.

The absence of concrete information about Tullia d'Aragona means that romanticized accounts of her life have flourished unhindered. What all have in common is a constant denigration of her abilities as writer and intellectual. She has been criticized for her immoral behavior, for her lovers and reputation as a great beauty, and for the fact that she wrote poetry to the ruler who had her lover Filippo Strozzi murdered. Later she was accused of hypocrisy when she criticized the immorality of other writers. It appears to have been impossible for Victorian critics especially to reconcile the fact that a courtesan might also have been an intellectual and a writer. This, however, is the only sensible conclusion that a contemporary reader can reach. Tullia d'Aragona was her own woman, taking wealthy and powerful lovers as a means of financial support, a practice that was by no means uncommon for a single woman at the time. She seems to have consistently moved in high social circles and to have been well thought of by some of the leading Humanist intellectuals of her time, and she has left a very large body of work as evidence of her talent as a writer.

Works

Dialogo Della Signora Tullia D'Aragona sull'infinita di amore (Venice, 1547).

Susan Bassnett

Hannah Arendt
1906–1986

Born October 14, 1906, Hanover, Germany
Died December 1986, New York
Genre(s): scholarly works
Language(s): German, English

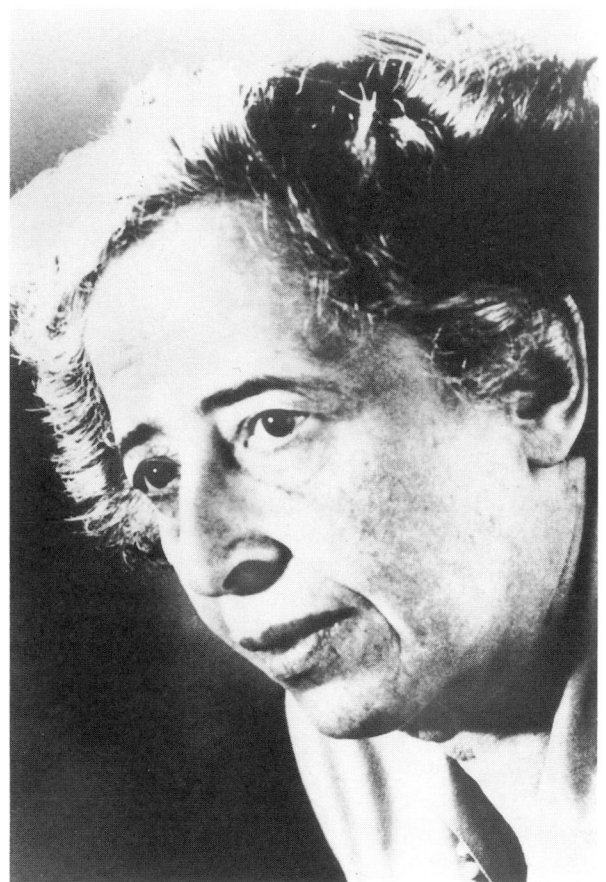

Hannah Arendt

Hannah Arendt spent her youth in Königsberg, East Prussia, where her grandfather was a city official. She studied with the important German philosophers of the period, Heidegger and Bultmann (Marburg), Jaspers (Heidelberg), and Husserl (Freiburg). In 1929, her first book on the concept of love in St. Augustine was published, presumably based on a dissertation. After having been arrested by the Gestapo in 1933, she fled to Paris, where she married the philosophy professor Heinrich Blücher. In 1940, she emigrated to the United States, where she immediately began to contribute to journals such as *Partisan Review*, *Commentary*, and *Review of Politics*. From 1944 to 1946, she held a leading research position with the *Congress for Jewish Relations*. From 1945 to 1952, she was the secretary of the Jewish Cultural Reconstruction, which attempted to find Jewish manuscripts that had been lost during the Nazi regime. Subsequently, she lived as an independent author, occasionally accepting guest professorships at American universities. From 1963 to 1967 and 1967 to her death, she was professor at the University of Chicago and the Graduate Faculty of the New School for Social Research in New York, respectively.

A philosopher by training and temperament, Hannah Arendt was thrust by the times into becoming one of the foremost thinkers analyzing European fascism. She became internationally known in that capacity through her *magnum opus, The Origins of Totalitarianism*, in which she presents a brilliant analysis of late nineteenth-century European economic and social conditions as having produced a certain type of personality with an affinity for totalitarianism. First published in English in 1951, it appeared in German in 1955, revised and enlarged as well as translated by Hannah Arendt, a pattern that was to repeat itself with her other main books. In 1958, her biography of the romantic Rahel Varnhagen was published in German, a work that she had nearly finished by 1933. Her observations of the 1958 Hungarian revolution *Die ungarische Revolution und der totalitäre Imperialismus* were amplified in her second most important book *On Revolution*, published in English and German simultaneously in 1963. Sent by the magazine *The New Yorker*, Hannah Arendt covered the Eichmann trial in Jerusalem, publishing her report in 1963 with a now famous subtitle: *On the Banality of Evil*. Her philosophical legacy is *On Violence* (1970), also published in German in the same year.

Works

Der Liebesbegriff bei Augustin (1929). *The Origins of Totalitarianism* (1951). *Elemente und Ursprünge totalitärer Herrschaft* (1955). *Fragwürdige Traditionsbestände im politischen Denken der Gegenwart* (1957). *Die ungarische Revolution und der totalitäre Imperialismus* (1958). *Rahel Varnhagen. Lebensgeschichte einer deutschen Jüdin aus der Romantik* (1959). *Von der Menschlichkeit in finsteren Zeiten. Gedanken zu Lessing* (1960). *Vita activa oder Vom tätigen Leben* (1960). *Between Past and Future. Six Exercises in Political Thought* (1961). *On Revolution* (1963). *Über die Revolution* (1963). *Eichmann in Jerusalem. A Report on the Banality of Evil* (1963). *Eichmann in Jerusalem. Ein Bericht von der Banalität des Bösen* (1964). *On Violence* (1970). *Macht und Gewalt* (1970). *Crisis of the Republic. Lying in Politics. Civil Disobedience. Thoughts on Politics and Revolution* (1972).

Ingeborg Zeiträg

Bettine von Arnim
1785–1859

Born April 4, 1785, Frankfurt-am-Main, Germany
Died January 29, 1859, Berlin
Genre(s): letters, political and social-critical essays
Language(s): German

Bettine von Arnim

Bettine (or Bettina) von Arnim was perhaps the most important woman writer of the German Romantic era; she also had considerable influence on the generation of German writers known as "Jung Deutschland" ("Young Germany"). She was born Elisabeth Catharina Ludovica Magdalena Brentano in 1785, the daughter of Peter Anton Brentano, a merchant of Italian origin who lived in Frankfurt, and Maximiliane Laroche (or La Roche), who had earlier been a friend of the young Goethe. Bettine's grandmother, Sophie von Laroche, had achieved prominence as a novelist, and Bettine's brother Clemens was to become one of the principal lyric poets of the German Romantic movement. In 1801 Bettine became acquainted with the young poetess Karoline von Günderode and was deeply upset when her friend committed suicide in 1806. In 1807 she had her first meeting with Goethe in Weimar and soon began writing enthusiastic and often explicitly amorous letters to the aging poet, whose epistolary replies to her were considerably more reserved. In 1835, after Goethe's death, she published a fictionalized adaptation of this correspondence, entitled *Goethes Briefwechsel mit einem Kinde* (Goethe's Correspondence with a Child). In 1811 Bettine married the German Romantic poet and novelist Achim von Arnim, a friend of her brother Clemens, with whom he had published the collection of folk songs known as *Des Knaben Wunderhorn* (The Boy's Magic Horn). The Arnims eventually settled at Achim's family estate at Wiepersdorf, Brandenburg, where they raised a large family. After Achim's death in 1831, Bettine resided frequently in Berlin, where she gradually devoted herself to the cause of political reform and to the plight of the poor and the oppressed in her country. She died in Berlin in 1859 after several years of illness following a stroke.

Her first significant publication was the above-mentioned adaptation of her correspondence with Goethe. This was followed in 1840 by *Die Günderode* (Miss Günderode), an epistolary account of the brief life of the young poetess. In 1843 she published *Dies Buch gehört dem König* (This Book Belongs to the King), which describes and deplores the human suffering brought about by industrialization in Prussian territories. The book appeals directly to the King of Prussia, Friedrich Wilhelm IV, as the one man able to remedy or at least to alleviate some of these problems. In 1844, Bettine published a tribute to her brother's lyric genius, *Clemens Brentanos Frühlingskranz* (Clemens Brentano's Spring Wreath). Her last major publication, *Gespräche mit Dämonen* (1852; Conversations with Demons) is, like the earlier book addressed to the king, devoted to issues of political and social reform.

Critics have noted that Bettine von Arnim's earlier work, especially the highly popular and influential *Goethes Briefwechsel mit einem Kinde*, expresses what might be regarded as the epitome of a "romantisches Lebensgefühl" ("romantic feeling of life"): an extreme intensity and vivacity of emotion combined with a rare generosity of enthusiasm. It is this same generosity, applied to social and political issues and expressed in some of her later works as well as in her personal, active devotion to the welfare of the poor and the oppressed, that earned her the great respect of the younger generation of German writers and intellectuals in the 1840s and 1850s.

Works
Goethes Briefwechsel mit einem Kinde [Goethe's Correspondence with a Child] (1835). *Die Günderode* [Miss Günderode] (1840). *Dies Buch gehört dem König* [This Book Belongs to the King] (1843). *Clemens Brentanos Frühlingskranz* [Clemens Brentano's Spring Wreath] (1844). *Gespräche mit Dämonen* [Conversations with Demons] (1852). *Sämtliche Werke*, ed. W. Oehlke, 7 vols. (1920–1922). *Werke und Briefe*, vol. 1–4, ed. G. Konrad (1959); vol. 5, *Briefe*, ed. J. Müller (1961).

Richard Unger

Aspāzija
1865–1943
Born March 16, 1865, Zemgale, Latvia
Died November 5, 1943, Dubulti, Latvia
Genre(s): drama, lyric poetry, memoirs, journalism
Language(s): Latvian

Aspāzija, whose real name was Elza Rozenberga, can be numbered among the four or five most distinguished lyric poets in Latvian literature and is one of the most outstanding playwrights in its exceptionally rich tradition of national drama. She was born into a well-to-do farmer's family; her early education was good for her time, but mainly because of parental resistance, she was unable to complete secondary school. After a disastrous early marriage that ended in divorce and after the financial ruin of her parents, she went to Riga to support herself, mainly as a writer. This she was able to do with brilliant success; by the turn of the century she was famous and greatly admired as a dramatist. Her play *Sidraba šķidrauts* (1905; The Silver Veil) created a furor, for it was understood to symbolize a call for revolution and Latvian national independence from Russia. A mark of her extraordinary popularity was the appearance in 1904 of her collected works in a 700-page volume.

In 1897 she married Jānis Pliekšāns, who soon became famous under his pseudonym of Rainis and is considered Latvia's greatest writer. Aspāzija shared her husband's political exile in Switzerland (1906–1920). Their interdependence and mutual influence is very complex and has not been sufficiently studied. It is certain that she greatly furthered his development as a poet, she was his main critic and (to an unverifiable degree) his collaborator. From 1906 on, her reputation was to some extent eclipsed by that of her husband, but she continued producing high-caliber work until her death.

After Latvia gained independence, Aspāzija and Rainis returned from exile. An ardent feminist, she was politically active in the women's rights movement for several years. Since her political views changed throughout her life, she managed to antagonize in turn almost all Latvian political parties and factions, which to some extent harmed her popularity. Her reputation rests assured, however, on the basis of the colorful, bold, and passionate language of her poetry, both lyric and dramatic, with its virtuosic rhythms and extraordinary gift for metaphor. She is also celebrated for the rich mythical and folkloric content of her plays, such as *Zalša līgava* (1928; The Sea Serpent's Bride). Although the folklore on which she most immediately draws is Latvian, the mythical themes and archetypes are universal. Her plays are complex, revealing multiple levels of meaning. Her work succeeds in synthesizing Christian and pagan, romantic, and classical assumptions.

Works

In the following list an attempt is made to indicate the date of first publication of each work; since first performance sometimes predates publication, and since Russian censorship delayed the printing of some of the early works, the dates are not always clear. *Atriebēja* (1888). *Prologs* (1894). *Vaidelote* (1894). *Zaudētas tiesības* (1894). *Ragana* (1894). *Saules Meita* (1894). *Naizsniegtais mērķis* (1895). *Sarkanās puķes* (1897). *Zeltīte* (1900). *Dvēseles krēsla* (1904). *Sidraba šķidrauts* (1905). *Saulainais stūrītis* (1910). *Ziedu klēpis* (1912). *Laime* (1913). *Izplesti spārni* (1918). *Raganu nakts* (1923). *Aspāzija* (1923). *Zila debess* (1924). *Boass un Rute* (1925). *Trejkrāsaina saule* (1926). *Torņa cēlējs* (1927). *Asteru laikā* (1928). *Zalša līgava* (1928). *Zelta mākoņi* (1938). *Pūcesspiegelis* (1932). *Velna nauda* (1933). *Dvēseles ceļojums* (1933). *Rudens lakstīgala* (1933). *Kaisītas rozes* (1936). *Zem vakara zvaigznes* (1942).

Translations: *The Silver Veil* and *The Sea Serpent's Bride*, tr. A.B. Stahnke. [Selected poems], *A Century of Latvian Poetry*, ed. and tr. W.K. Matthews (1957).

Zoja Pavlovskis

Marie-Catherine le Jumel de Barneville, Baronne d'Aulnoy ca. 1650–1705

Born 1650 or 1651, Barneville-la-Bertrand, France
Died January 13, 1705, Paris
Genre(s): novel, fairy tale, travel literature, memoirs, short story, devotional literature, correspondence
Language(s): French

Possibly one of the most enigmatic figures of her age, Marie-Catherine le Jumel de Barneville, Madame d'Aulnoy, was born at Barneville-la-Bertrand in 1650 or 1651, the daughter of Nicholas-Claude le Jumel and Judith-Angelique Coustelier. Little or nothing is known about the circumstances of her childhood, but she must have received the usual training given daughters of a minor aristocratic family—lessons in painting, music, and several foreign languages, including Spanish and English. She was also considered a witty, elegant, and easy conversationalist, and in her own works she uses her French to remarkably good effect. Additionally, references to other literary works in her texts reflect a wide acquaintance with popular literature, including Ovid, parodic Renaissance poetry, Spanish drama, and the French medieval *fabliaux*.

In 1666, when not yet seventeen, she was married to a man three times her own age, François de la Motte, baron d'Aulnoy and one of the household officers of César de Vendôme. It is more than likely that the marriage was arranged and less than welcome to the young bride. The baron, who had purchased his title, possibly with money given by Vendôme for sexual favors, was a handsome, wealthy, but also irritable and high-tempered man. Shrewd, ambitious, avaricious, he drank to excess, chased women, and was a noted supporter of the Parisian brothels. Three years after it began, the marriage ended in scandal and execution, with Marie-Catherine fading from public view for nearly twenty years to come.

Although our understanding of those events is less than complete, it appears likely that Marie-Catherine's mother, possibly with her daughter's consent, persuaded two Norman friends to accuse the baron of lèse-majesté. Although immediately arrested and taken to the Bastille at Colbert's order, he convinced the authorities of his innocence. His denouncers were then arrested and sent to join d'Aulnoy in prison where, after numerous trials, they confessed under torture that the affair had been carefully planned by d'Aulnoy's mother-in-law. Her objective was to obtain the baron's money while disencumbering both herself and her daughter of his person. The two Normans were beheaded at the Place de Grève, the baron was released after paying the crown a rather hefty fine, and Madame d'Aulnoy and her mother disappeared.

The degree of Madame d'Aulnoy's complicity in the crime, as well as her whereabouts after the executions, is unknown. A forced sojourn in a Parisian convent is likely. Certainly she was in Paris in October of 1676 for the birth of her fifth child. In the years to come, she may have traveled extensively—

to Flanders, to England, and to Spain, where her mother had fled and where she served as a double agent for both the French and Spanish governments. At any rate, when Marie-Catherine next appears in public records, it is 1685, and she is installed in a convent outside Paris.

By now middle-aged, the baronne turned her hand to writing, most probably as a means of financial support. In 1690, she made her literary debut with her first, and arguably her best, novel, *Histoire d'Hypolite, Comte de Douglas* (The Story of Hypolite, the Count of Douglas). This was a rousing tale of love, adventure, and narrowly averted incest that also included France's first published fairy tale, the "Ile de la Félicité" (The Isle of Happiness) which predates Perrault's more famous collection by a good seven years. The book was an immense success, and within a year had been reprinted by one of France's most prestigious booksellers and publishers, Claude Barbin.

Success brought prosperity and respectability. Madame d'Aulnoy moved to the quartier Saint-Sulpice soon afterward, delaying little in establishing a salon frequented by such luminaries as the Princess de Conti, the Comtesse de Murat, and Madame and Mademoiselle Desholières. She set to work at a feverish rate, trying her hand at a number of genres. Her *Mémoires de la cour d'Espagne* (1690; The Memoirs of the Spanish Court), also a huge success, was followed in 1691–1692 by another travelogue, *Relation du voyage d'Espagne* (The Story of a Voyage to Spain), another historical novel, *Jean de Bourbon, prince de Carency* (Jean of Bourbon, Prince of Carency), an interesting experiment with the *novella* form, *Nouvelles espagnols* (1692; Spanish Short Stories), and her only two devotional works—*Sentiments d'une âme penitente* (1691; Sentiments of a Penitent Soul) and *Le retour d'une âme à dieu* (1691; The Return of a Soul to God). In 1693, she turned to historiography for her seventh book, *Nouvelles ou mémoires historiques* (Stories or Historical Memoirs), a history of Louis XIV's war against Holland. Her last two novels, *Mémoires de la cour d'Angleterre* (1695; Memoirs of the English Court) and *Le Comte de Warwick* (1703; The Count of Warwick), returned to an English locale for their exotic setting, and continued to explore her favorite theme, the connections between love and power. Though little read today, these, too, were best-sellers of their day. Her most lasting successes, however, were her two collections of fairy tales—*Les contes de fées* (Fairy Tales), published in 1697 and *Les contes nouveaux ou les fées à la mode* (New Fairy Tales, or Fairies in Fashion), which appeared the following year. Countless re-editions of both works have been printed, fourteen in the eighteenth century alone, and they are still being read and enjoyed today.

By the close of the 1600s, Madame d'Aulnoy stood at the height of her literary fame. A respectable and best-selling author, she was one of nine French women holding membership in the venerable Accademia del Ricovvati of Padua. In just thirteen years, she had produced twenty-eight volumes, including novels, novellas, fairy tales, a history, edifying verse, travel books, memoirs, and letters. It was at this moment, when she seemed at her most secure from social reprobation, that scandal once again erupted in a curious replay from the events of her youth. Her close friend Madame Ticquet was accused of attempting to have her husband, a counselor at the Parlement de Paris, murdered at his own front door. Madame Ticquet, who was reported to have been at Madame d'Aulnoy's on the day of the crime, was arrested, brought to trial, put to torture, and executed at the Place de Grève. D'Aulnoy, tainted by the haunting similarity to the trial of her youth, shared in the reprobation and once more retired from public life. Six years later, on January 13, 1705, she died. She was survived by four of her six children.

While Madame d'Aulnoy was not the leading literary figure of her day, neither is she interesting solely for her unusual life. Her works display linguistic talent, an unsettling sense of humor, a gift for rapid narration and parody, an ability to analyze emotions with finesse and delicacy, and a quick ear for coining arresting new words. In her novels, her thematic emphasis upon constancy, faithful love, and "la delicatess des sentiments" leads her to adopt a critical attitude toward a code of morality that often denied freedom of action to women. This stream of social critique, hidden at times, more open at others, is the underground stream feeding much of Madame d'Aulnoy's literary production. Unlike so many of their predecessors, her heroines are not martyrs for love. They are victims of society—of unfeeling parents, of cruel husbands, of constricted opportunity, of isolation, of malevolent circumstances, but most of all of role definitions that force women to live for, in, and through their marriages. Marriage is rarely a happy state in Madame d'Aulnoy's work, and though the ceremony itself often provides the traditional comic ending of her tales, she usually mitigates its appeal with curiously disturbing overtones, most often the death or the bereavement of a woman protagonist. Interestingly, while the heroines of her novels are distinguished principally by their passive suffering, the heroines of the fairy tales are capable of action and function as figures of power. Soldiers, lovers, courtiers, and rulers, they change the worlds of Madame d'Aulnoy's imagination, reminding us that the original audience was not children but adults, the elegant women of salon society during the reign of Louis XIV.

Madame d'Aulnoy has often been undervalued, particularly in reference to her fairy tales, but the complexity of her seemingly conventional stories and the ambiguous moral stances they imply are now attracting the attention that they deserve. In addition to her considerable skills as a story teller, she has claims on our interest as a covert, but pointed moralist. New editions of many of her works are now needed to enable us to reassess her achievement and her position in French literature.

Works

Histoire d'Hypolite, Comte de Douglas [The Story of Hypolite, the Count of Douglas] (1690). *Mémoires de la cour d'Espagne* [Memoirs of the Spanish Court] (1690). *Relation du voyage d'Espagne* [The Story of a Visit to Spain] (1691). *Jean de Bourbon, prince de Carency* [Jean of Bourbon, Prince of Carency] (1692). *Sentiments d'une âme penitente* [Sentiments of a Penitent Soul] (1691). *Le retour d'une âme à dieu* [The Return of a Soul to God] (1691). *Nouvelles espagnols* [Spanish Novellas] (1692). *Nouvelles ou mémoires historiques* [Stories or Historical Memoirs] (1693). *Mémoires de la cour d'Angleterre* [Memoirs of the English Court] (1695). *Les contes de fées* [Fairy Tales] (1697). *Les contes nouveaux ou les fées à la mode* [New Tales, or Fairies in Fashion] (1698). *Le Comte de Warwick* [The Count of Warwick] (1703).

Translations: *The Earl of Douglas, An English Story, from the French* [Histoire d'Hypolite] (1774). *The History of John of Bourbon, Prince of Carency. Containing a Variety of Entertaining Novels, . . . Written in French, . . . translated into English* [Jean de Bourbon] (1723). *The Diverting Works of the Countess d'Anois . . . Containing: I. Memoirs of Her Own Life. II. All Her Spanish Novels and Histories. III. Her Letters. IV. Tales of the Fairies . . . Newly done into English* [Nouvelles espagnols, among others] (1707). *Memoirs of the Court of England in 1675* [Mémoires de la cour d'Angleterre, Mrs. William Henry Arthur, tr.] (1913). *The History of the Earl of Warwick* [Le Comte de Warwick] (1708).

Glenda Wall

Jane Austen
1775–1817

Born December 16, 1775, Steventon, Hampshire; England
Died July 18, 1817, Winchester, Hampshire
Genre(s): novel
Language(s): English

A "small square two inches of ivory" is the way Austen once described her own work. Yet this same work, apparently being lightly dismissed, is among the most enduring and most popular literature of the nineteenth century. Categorized as novels of manners, the careful detail given to both setting and character in Austen's works has captivated readers for over a century.

Born in 1775, Austen was the seventh of eight children born to the rector of Steventon, Hampshire. She began writing at about age eleven. Her notebooks containing "novels," chiefly parodies of eighteenth-century sentimental novels, were passed around her family for their entertainment. Austen and her family were, as she said, "great Novel readers and not ashamed of being so."

Austen's writing and publishing history is somewhat confusing. Her writing falls into two groups of three novels with a "silent" decade between, yet her publishing history does not reflect this division. The following chronology shows the dates of composition, revision, and publication of her novels:

c. 1790–1793: *Love and Freindship* [sic] *Volume the First;* juvenilia.

Before 1796: *Elinor and Marianne* (not extant); recast, 1797–1799, as *Sense and Sensibility;* further revision, 1809–1810; published, 1811.

1792–1796(?): *Lady Susan;* survives in a fair copy of c. 1805 or later; first published in *Memoir* (Austen–Leigh), 2nd ed., 1871.

1796–1797: *First Impressions* (not extant); rewritten, c. 1812, as *Pride and Prejudice;* published, 1813.

1797–1798: *Susan* (not extant); recast and much expanded as *Northanger Abbey,* 1805; posthumously published, 1818.

1803: *The Watsons* (a fragment); first published in *Memoir* (Austen–Leigh), 1871.

1811–1813: *Mansfield Park;* published, 1814.

1814–1815: *Emma;* published, late 1815 or, more probably, early 1816.

1815–1816: *Persuasion;* published posthumously, 1818.

1817: *Sanditon* (a fragment, given title by Austen family); first published from manuscript, 1925.

Many scholars believe that Austen's silent period was caused by discouragement after *First Impressions* was rejected unread and *Northanger Abbey* was picked up by a publisher in 1803 for a pittance but never issued (after which Austen bought back the manuscript in 1816). Although she probably made some minor revisions, *Northanger Abbey* appears to be the earliest example of her work. It is, however, a mistake to differentiate too sharply between the novels of the two periods. For the first group of three were being revised while Austen was writing the second group. The most obvious influence occurs in the change of genre in *Sense and Sensibility* and *Pride and Prejudice;* in their original forms, *Elinor and Marianne* and *First Impressions* were both epistolary novels, a technique Austen dropped in revision and never again employed.

According to Austen, "three or four Families in a Country Village is the very thing to work upon." She concentrated on a limited part of English society, provincial gentry and the aligning of the rural upper-middle class with the aristocracy. Austen wrote about that with which she was familiar; and when her niece sought her advice about a novel, Austen advised her to "stick to Bath" where she was "quite at home."

Austen resisted the temptation to stray from familiar ground, even when nudged by royalty. When the domestic chaplain to the Prince of Wales suggested that in her next novel she might delineate the character of a clergyman, Austen realized that the hints he supplied were based on his own experiences. She replied, somewhat mischievously, that she might be able to do "the comic parts of the characters" but "not the good, the enthusiastic, the literary."

Such an answer, with its somewhat stinging implications, was typical. Her satirical treatment of social standards and literary expectations in her novels and her acidic comments in her letters have earned her a reputation for a sharp tongue. After her death in 1817, her sister, Cassandra, burned many of Austen's letters, implying to some critics that the worst, the sharpest, of the letters were destroyed. But it is more likely that the more personal letters, the ones most likely to show the gentler side, were destroyed to protect her privacy even after death. It is important to realize how fiercely Austen and her family guarded her privacy. All her novels were published anonymously and their authorship was a well-kept secret.

Nevertheless, much of her personality, tastes, and interests can be discerned through her novels. In *Northanger Abbey,* for example, she satirizes gothic romantic mysteries (Radcliffe's *Mysteries of Udolpho* in particular) and presents what was to become a re-

Jane Austen

current theme: feminine self-delusion. The latter theme is picked up again in *Sense and Sensibility* and *Pride and Prejudice* but demonstrates its pitfalls by contrasting the actions and reactions of two sisters. In *Sense and Sensibility,* the two sisters, Elinor and Marianne Dashwood, represent "sense" and "sensibility," respectively. Each is deserted by the young man from whom she has been led to expect a matrimonial offer. Reacting with sense, Elinor eventually untangles the complications surrounding her lover and they become engaged; Marianne, on the other hand, reacts with sensibility and impetuosity. She gradually comes to realize the foolishness of her love and to see her real affection for another, a quieter and more serious lover. In *Pride and Prejudice* the contrast between sisters is more subtle and further complicated by a parallel male pairing, Bingley and Darcy. One of the most popular of Austen's novels, *Pride and Prejudice* introduces many of the stylistic devices commonly associated with her work: witty, cutting dialogue between couples; strong-willed heroines without a strong role model (her mother is either weak and ineffectual, or dead); settings that reveal the underlying character of the male protagonist (in this instance, Pemberley); and an ironic undertone, often established in the opening lines of the novel ("It is a truth universally acknowledged that a single man in possession of a good fortune must be in want of a wife").

Mansfield Park marks a slight diversion from the pattern established in Austen's earlier novels, for here the heroine is an orphan adopted into her rich uncle's family. Despite being condescendingly treated as a poor relation, Fanny's honesty and modest disposition gradually make her an indispensable part of the household, particularly when her uncle is away on business for an extended period and the family's sense of discipline is relaxed. In this novel, it is the male characters, particularly Edmund Bertram and Henry Crawford, who represent contrasting personalities, and it is Edmund who is self-deluded and eventually comes to see Fanny's virtues. To many critics, *Mansfield Park* is one of Austen's lesser novels, perhaps because of her reversal of her usual male and female portrayals, a reversal she did not repeat.

In contrast, the novels that followed—*Emma* and *Persuasion*—are considered by many to be her best works. The heroine in *Emma* is again virtually alone in the world: her mother is dead, her father is absent-minded and ineffectual, and her governess-companion has left to be married. But unlike Fanny in *Mansfield Park,* Emma is not especially wise. In this novel Austen again deals with the theme of feminine self-delusion, but the focus on a single, strong-willed character makes the impact stronger than in previous works. In *Persuasion* Austen returns to the contrasting of sisters but focuses primarily on the second of three (Anne Elliot). Anne is pretty, intelligent, amiable, but also malleable. She is persuaded by a trusted friend, Lady Russell, to break off a long-standing engagement despite her feelings for her lover. During the resulting confusion both lovers become entangled in other relationships but eventually realize that their affection for each other still exists. In this, Austen's last complete work, the satire and ridicule take a milder form, the tone is graver and tenderer, the interest lies in a more subtle interplay of characters. Austen herself apparently recognized the difference in tone, for she wrote of Anne: "She is almost too good for me."

Although well received, Austen was not immediately successful; few of her works reached a second edition during her lifetime. In fact, the collected edition of 1853 supplied the market until 1882. Attention began to increase during the 1890s as indicated by the appearance of biographies and critical pieces. Today, almost 175 years later, all of her books are in print and Austen is one of the top-selling authors. No doubt much of her popularity is due to a desire to escape to a better place and time. Yet because much of her work depends on character analysis, many readers still identify with much of her work. Others are captivated by her style, her careful construction and use of the dramatic method where characters are introduced through dialogue before putting in an appearance. To some she is one of the greatest ironists who ever lived. And to most she is a challenge. As Austen herself put it, "I do not write for dull elves who cannot think for themselves."

Works

Sense and Sensibility (1811). *Pride and Prejudice* (1813). *Mansfield Park* (1814). *Emma* (1815). *Northanger Abbey* (1818). *Persuasion* (1818). *Lady Susan* (1871). *The Watsons* (1871). W. Austen-Leigh, and R.A. Austen-Leigh, *Jane Austen: Her Life and Letters, a Family Record* (1913). *The Novels of Jane Austen,* ed. R.W. Chapman (1923). *Sanditon* (1925). *The Letters of Jane Austen,* ed. R.W. Chapman (1923). *Minor* Works, ed. R.W. Chapman (1954). *Letters 1796–1817,* ed. R.W. Chapman (1955). *Love and Freindship* [sic], *and Other Early* Works (1978). *Letters,* 3rd ed., ed. D. Le Faye (1995).

Lynn M. Alexander

Sophie Louise Charlotte (von Klenow) Baden
1740–1824

Born November 21, 1740, Copenhagen, Denmark
Died June 6, 1824, Copenhagen
Genre(s): novel, essay, journalism
Language(s): Danish

Sophie Louise Charlotte Baden attained a prominent place in Danish letters as a novelist, correspondent, and a frequent contributor to *Bibliotek for det smukke Kiøn* (Library for the Fair Sex), a journal especially for aristocratic literary and literate women in Copenhagen. Baden's work as a novelist first took the form of a story in letters, *Den fortsatte Grandison* (1784; The Grandison Continuation); together with a series of letters and another shorter story, *Den fortsatte Grandison* was first published as a complete novel in 1792, upon the recommendation of enthusiastic readers and the editors of the *Bibliotek*. Charlotte Baden became a prominent spokeswoman for such cardinal personal virtues as true sensitivity, authenticity, and rural simplicity. Baden also contributed anonymous sketches and letters to *Morgenposten* (The Morning Post) and *Birchs Billedgallerie* (Birch's Picture Gallery); one of her sketches in the latter journal, "Billeder af en Københavnsk Dukke" (Pictures of a Copenhagen Doll), depicts (through letters) the shallowness, superficiality, and *coquetterie* of the Copenhagen writer, Dorette, in contrast to the wholesomeness of the unaffected rural girl, Lovise (Dalager, pp. 117–118). Charlotte Baden built her major work, *Den fortsatte Grandison*, upon the precursor novel of Samuel Richardson, the very popular English novelist; Richardson's novel, *The History of Sir Charles Grandison* (1753–1754) served as the form and contextual precedent for Baden's own sequel in letter form. Baden also adapted Richardson's view of women as the true ennobling moral force that holds socially destructive tendencies (and male passions) at bay.

Sophie Louise von Klenow was the daughter of First Lieutenant, later Major, Gustav Ludvig von Klenow (1703–1772) and Bolette Catharine From (1696–1788). She was born in Copenhagen on November 21, 1740, and died on June 6, 1824; she was buried at Our Lady Church in Copenhagen. Charlotte became the wife of the preeminent university professor, lecturer, and scholarly critic, Jacob Baden, who fulfilled an illustrious academic career at the University of Copenhagen.

In 1784, Charlotte Baden began writing a continuation in letter form of the life of Clementine, one of the secondary characters of Richardson's novel of manners and mores, *Sir Charles Grandison*. The conflict in Richardson's novel had centered on the opposition between love and religion; in *Den fortsatte Grandison*, Charlotte Baden changed the conflict to one of love and duty, focusing on Clementine's love for the married Grandison and her duty toward her "proper" suitor, the nobleman Belvedere. Of her own choosing, and to avoid her duty, Clementine retreats to a cloister; instead of serving as a place of respite, escape, and solace, Clementine's cloister becomes a symbol of the family's and society's (united) efforts to discipline and prepare Clementine for marriage. Clementine marries her intended Belvedere; the wedding, depicted symbolically as Clementine's deathday, represents Clementine's martyrdom and ultimate acquiescence to her family.

Not only did Charlotte Baden continue Richardson's highly popular novel in letter form; she also adopted Richardson's worldview: women were the primary force for morals, integrity, sincerity, and ethical values; while the character of the man was determined to be passionate (erotic), the woman was depicted as the virtuous being (*par excellence*). Richardson, aristocratic Danish women literatæ, and Charlotte Baden considered women the essence of honor and virtue against more primitive male passions and instincts; as such, women were expected to improve family morals, to hone their natural virtues, and to serve as positive social (and socializing) influences over and against more base, always threatening, male passions. The exemplary, didactic novels of Richardson led the way to a reevaluation of women's roles; Richardson's works gained enthusiastic, eager response among the female reading public in Denmark, leading to letters and correspondence among literate women, to discussion and debate in the reform aristocratic circles, and to a totally new self-awareness of significance for women's (growing) literary engagement. The new engagement and interest in Richardson's intentionally didactic novels gave initial impetus to the extensive prose works of Charlotte Dorothea Biehl and to the direct dramatization of Richardson's novels by Frederikke (Münster) Brun; both of Baden's immediate Danish predecessors considered Richardson's works a model for life. Baden followed on Biehl's and Brun's heels, publishing *Den fortsatte Grandison*, a great many letters defending women's keen sensitivity in reading and reading choices, and sketches such as "Billeder af en Københavnsk Dukke" for prominent literary journals. Charlotte Baden added new psychological dimension (and insights) to Richardson's earlier novel while building the essential conflict between love, the heart's domain, and duty to family, to peers, and to society.

With Charlotte Baden, a voice speaks out for a new reform: an aristocratic moral based on sincerity, sensitivity, integrity, and duty. Following Richardson's lead, Charlotte Baden didactically depicts women as the essential force for virtue, ethics, and engagement in the immediate family and the Danish aristocratic society.

Works
Den fortsatte Grandison, novel (1784). "En Fortælling i et Brev" [A Story in a Letter]. [Articles, letters], in *Morgenposten* and *Birchs Billedgallerie*, "Billeder af en Københavnsk Dukke," *Birchs Billedgallerie*. [Letters, articles, sketches], in *Bibliotek for det smukke Kiøn* (*Den fortsatte Grandison*).

Lanae Hjortsvang Isaacson

Teresa Landucci Bandettini
1763–1836
a.k.a. Amarelli Etrusca
Born 1763, Lucca, Italy
Died 1836, Lucca
Genre(s): poetry
Language(s): Italian

Teresa Bandettini was born in Lucca of Benedetto and Maria Alba Micheli. At age seven she was orphaned, and with her family in difficult financial condition, she was not able to follow a regular course of study. Instead, she studied the classics, and at age fifteen she became a professional dancer. Between 1779 and 1789 she traveled across Northern Italy, earning fame as a literary ballerina. While in the theater, she would read Dante during the intervals. One day in Verona she demonstrated her great talent for poetic improvisation by chance. Attending a session given by an improviser, she answered him in rhyme; he was so pleased with her skill that he gave her lessons, which were enough to allow her to tour the principal towns of Italy, achieving great success wherever she went.

She traveled to Imola in 1789, where she contracted a marriage with Peter Landucci, by whom she had three sons and a daughter. He recognized her marvelous inspiration, freshness, and elevated poetic sentiments and helped her gain public recognition. Shortly thereafter, she met the Count L. Savioli, who introduced her to the literary society of Bologna and helped in the composition of the poem "La morte di Adone," in octaves, which she published in Parma in 1790. She soon abandoned dance to dedicate herself to poetry. She held first place in numerous academies of improvisation, elaborating in rhyme whatever arguments were presented on the spot. Her great successes in Ferrara, Padua, and Verona brought her in contact with the famous improvisor G. Mollo, also traveling at the time. When in Mantua, she and her husband entertained G. Murari dalla Corte, who introduced her to A. Bozzoli and S. Bettinelli, with whom she was friends until the latter's death. In 1793, Bandettini performed for the public in Parma and Pavia. After that time she was introduced to A. Mazza, F. Arrivabene, and Bodoni. She was a great success, and on this occasion L. Mascheroni dedicated the sonnet "Deh, come dietro al buon cantor di Enea" to her.

In March 1794, she was honored with the name "Amarelli Etrusca," and her work was preserved in the appendix along with that of A. Kauffman. When she returned to Lucca, she was admitted to a women's literary circle held by Marchese E. Bernardini; she also joined the Academia deglio Osruri and other prestigious groups.

Despite her noteworthy success, Bandettini was constantly preoccupied with financial problems. The situation worsened with the fall of the government. Although she remained apolitical, she left Lucca because of Jacobinism. In 1800, she went first to Venice, meeting several dignitaries, and then to Parma and Vienna, where she was disappointed in being denied a stipend by the Austrian Court, despite her popularity. In 1805, she was awarded an annual pension from the Duke of Modena following the publication of the poem *La•Teseide* in twenty cantos, and the translation of Q. Smirneo Calabro's *Paralipomeni* (1815, 1818). Desiring to return to the town of her birth, Bandettini sought a pension from the Court of Modena with permission to continue receiving compensation from Lucca. In 1819 she returned to that city with her husband, who was gravely ill and who died soon after.

Despite illness, Bandettini continued to write throughout her life, publishing *Discorso sulla poesia* in 1831. Her poetry affected many, and she was honored as the greatest poet of her time, recalling the great masters such as Pareni, Mascheroni, Monti, and Alfieri, among whom Bandettini will be remembered.

Works

La Teseide (1805). *Discorso sulla poesia* (1831). A collection of Bandettini's improvised poems can be found in B. Croce, "Gli Improvvisatori," in *La Letteratura italiana del Settecento* (Bari, 1949), pp. 299–311.

Jean E. Jost

Natalie Clifford Barney
1876–1972
Born October 31, 1876, Dayton, Ohio
Died February 2, 1972, Paris, France
Genre(s): autobiography, epigram, essay, dialogue
Language(s): French

Natalie Clifford Barney was born into a wealthy family in Dayton, Ohio, in 1876. From her mother, a portrait painter who studied with Whistler, she inherited her interest in the arts; from her father, she inherited two million dollars. When at the age of 21 she became independently wealthy, she settled in Paris, where she became a central figure in artistic and literary circles, and where her salon at 20 Rue Jacob became a gathering place for artists and intellectuals for over fifty years.

Although Barney's works include epigrams, sketches, plays, essays, and a novel, she is better known for her life than for her works. She lived openly as a lesbian in a time when such a life was completely unacceptable to conventional society although both psychoanalysis and homosexual rights movements in Germany and England were drawing attention to homosexuals and lesbians and were helping to create a climate in which such "deviance" could be acknowledged.

Barney had many love affairs and many more lasting friendships. The most famous of her lovers were the poet Renée Vivien (Pauline Tarn) and the painter Romaine Brooks (the latter relationship lasted over fifty years). Her literary and artistic friends included the writer Remy de Gourmont, Gertrude Stein, Colette, and Ezra Pound.

Her influence on the artistic and intellectual life of Paris was greatest during the 1920s and 1930s. Her salon at 20 Rue Jacob was a gathering place for artists and writers, who congregated there at 4:00 P.M. each Friday to consume tea and cucumber sandwiches and to read and perform their works. Gertrude Stein, Colette, Mata Hari, Virgil Thomson, Georges Antheil, Ezra Pound, Ernest Hemingway—all were guests at Natalie Barney's salon.

Barney appears as a character in several fictional works. Remy de Gourmont first made her famous as the "Amazone" in his *Lettres à l'Amazone* (Letters to the Amazon), and Barney then took the name of "The Amazon" in two of her own works, *Pensées d'une amazone* (Reflections of an Amazon) and *Nouvelles Pensées de l'Amazone* (New Reflections of the Amazon). She appears as a character in an autobiographical novel by Liane de Pougy, which tells the story of Pougy's affair with Barney. Renée Vivien portrays her as "Vally" in her novel *Une femme m'apparut* (A Woman Appeared to Me); a figure resembling Barney also appears in much of Vivien's melancholy love poetry. Djuna Barnes satirized her and her circle in *The Ladies' Almanack*. And Radclyffe Hall, in *The Well of Loneliness*, gives the most memorable portrait of Barney in her character of "Valerie Seymour," a symbolically named tower of strength who looks out over the turbulent world and serves as a beacon that guides and inspires less courageous souls.

Prior to the 1970s, Barney's unconventional life had seemed more interesting to biographers than her literary work. Her accomplishments are now being re-evaluated, and she is now seen as a precursor of the "second wave" of the women's movement. Along with Renée Vivien, she sought to create poetry in which women and women's experience were central. Barney and Vivien were influenced by French Symbolist poetry, the courtly love tradition, and the poetry of the Greek poet Sappho, as Karla Jay has shown in *The Disciples of the Tenth Muse: Natalie Clifford Barney and Renée Vivien.*

Barney's works include epigrams, biographical studies, and meditations on love and friendship. Like the epigrams of La Rochefoucauld and Oscar Wilde, hers are trenchant critiques on manners and society. Her essays reveal a vision of a future world without sex roles or guilt over sexual relations, yet they never lose their elegant lightness of tone nor their irony. Radclyffe Hall's "pale yet ardent light of the fanatic" (Hall, *The Well of Loneliness*) may show through in such essays as "L'Amour défendu" ("Love Defended"), "Des amours à l'Amour" ("From Loves to Love"), and "Aspects d'un ange" ("Aspects of an Angel"); but it is always veiled in humor, charm, and a manner that manages to be both self-deprecating and egotistical.

Barney indeed remains a paradox: an eighteenth-century wit, sedate and old-fashioned in appearance and manner, she lived in quiet defiance of her age. She hated its egalitarianism, its introspection and self-absorption, its preoccupation with psychoanalysis and with the self. She was anti-fascist yet elitist, pacifist yet apolitical; mystical yet anti-religious; self-absorbed yet generous. She sought total freedom to control her own life. Thanks to her great wealth, she achieved that freedom. Natalie Clifford Barney belongs to those nineteenth- and twentieth-century pioneers who sought to define and justify homosexuality not only as a sexual choice but as a way of life. She also stands among women's rights advocates—though she never spoke for rights nor engaged in political action. Her whole life, however, was a political act, for she openly chose her own sex as lovers and companions with pride and without repentance. As an original if minor voice in French literature, as a patron (matron?) of the arts, and as an outspoken and fearless model of women's independence as well as for freedom for gays and lesbians, Natalie Barney remains one of the most original and provocative literary figures of the early twentieth century.

Works

Quelques portraits-sonnets de femmes (1900). *Cinq petits dialogues grecs* (Antithèses et parallèles) (1902). *Actes et entr'actes* (1910). *Je me souviens* (1910). *Pensées d'une amazone* (1920). *Poems et poèmes: autres alliances* (1920). *Aventures de l'Esprit* (1975).

The One Who Is Legion, or A.D.'s After-Life (1930). *Nouvelles Pensées de l'Amazone* (1939). *Souvenirs indiscrets* (1960). *Traits et portraits* (1975). "The Woman Who Lives with Me" (n.d.)

Translations: *Selected Writings of Natalie Clifford Barney*, ed. and introd. Miron Grindea (London, 1963).

Charlene Ball

Emilia Pardo Bazán
1851–1921

Born 1851, La Coruña, Spain
Died 1921, Madrid, Spain
Genre(s): novel, short story, literary criticism, history
Language(s): Spanish

Emilia Pardo Bazán stands out in the history of Spanish literature as one of Spain's few recognized women writers before the twentieth century. She was famous in her own time not only as a novelist, short story writer, literary critic, and historian of the first order but also as a woman of amazing versatility and independence. In an age when women were advised to remain in the roles assigned by convention—wife, mother, nun—Pardo Bazán audaciously wrote feminist essays and introduced into Spain the shocking theories of French naturalism propounded by Émile Zola. Although she never subscribed to the determinist theories of Zola's naturalism, she did employ its techniques and themes. Pardo Bazán's literary interests, however, exceeded any one literary school or method, and during her long career she wrote in the traditional style of Spanish realism and the spiritual-mystical mode in fashion during the turn of the century. She also incorporated the dictates of naturalism, modifying them to suit the temper of her talent and times. Eclectic is the word that best applies to Pardo Bazán.

Emilia Pardo Bazán's intellectual curiosity and determination were manifested early; she virtually educated herself, reading avidly and widely in classical and modern literature, learning English so that she could read that literature, reading French and Italian literature in the original languages, and delving into philosophical and aesthetic problems. She wrote essays and books on subjects as varied as St. Francis and Christian mysticism, modern French and Russian literature, and the Russian revolution. No subject seemed inappropriate to this energetic woman who even founded a literary magazine for which she herself wrote all the material for several years.

Although married and the mother of three children, she spent most of her time apart from her husband, maintaining a home in Madrid where she reigned over a literary salon. In recognition of her intellectual abilities and acute knowledge of modern literature, she was honored as the first woman to occupy a professorship at the University in Madrid.

Pardo Bazán was a controversial figure, inspiring both acclaim and disdain, but she was nonetheless accepted, even by those less than enthusiastic about her insistence on proving herself as a writer and intellectual, and becoming one of the most significant writers of her time. Her reputation has grown in the years since her death. Today Pardo Bazán is seen as a major writer and critic and as a pioneer in women's issues. She wrote twenty novels, several volumes of literary criticism and history, hundreds of short stories, and hundreds of essays.

Works

Obras completas, 44 vols. (1886–1926). *Obras completas*, ed. Federico Carlos Sainz de Robles, 2 vols. (1947).

Translations: *Short Stories by Emilia Pardo Bazán*, ed. Albert Shapiro and F.J. Hurley (1933). *The Son of the Bondwoman*, tr. Ethel Harriet Hearn (1976).

Mary E. Giles

Salomėja Bčinskaitė-Bučienė 1904–1945

a.k.a. Salomėja Nėris
Born 1904, Kiršai, Lithuania
Died 1945, Moscow
Genre(s): poetry
Language(s): Lithuanian

Salomėja Nėris was designated Lithuanian SSR People's Poet in 1954. She studied Lithuanian literature, German, and pedagogics at the University of Kaunas, Lithuania and taught high school from 1928 to 1941. She published her first collection of poems, *Anksti rytą* (Early in the Morning) in 1927. Youthful romantic and religious leanings led Nėris to a conservative Roman Catholic worldview. Later, extensive travels in Western Europe brought Nėris closer to a leftist political stance, leaning toward a certain romantic idealism reminiscent of Louis Aragon, Bertholt Brecht or,

even more, Federico Garcia Lorca. In 1931 Nėris publicly joined the left-wing Lithuanian artists' group "The Third Front," declaring that henceforth her poetry was to become political and serve the working class. In 1937, while in Paris, Nėris joined the sculptor Bernardas Bučas in a common-law marriage and returned to live in Kaunas. In 1938 Nėris received the Lithuanian republic State Prize for Literature for her collection *Diemed'iu 'ydėsiu* (I'll Bloom Like Wormwood). In 1940, as Soviet tanks were rolling across Lithuania, Nėris wrote an adulatory "Poem to Stalin" and read it at a Plenary Session of the USSR Supreme Soviet to welcome Lithuania's inclusion into the Soviet Union. In 1941 Nėris became a deputy to the Lithuanian SSR Supreme Soviet. In the same year she withdrew to Russia under the German attack and lived in Moscow, Penza, and Ufa, writing strident antifascist poetry in praise of the Soviet country and regime. She returned to Lithuania in 1944, became seriously ill, and was taken to Moscow for special care, where she soon died.

Nėris was well-read in several languages. Tolstoy, Dostoevsky, Romain Roland, and Stefan Zweig were among her favorites in prose, and Friedrich Schiller, Johann Wolfgang von Goethe, Heinrich Heine, and Alexander Pushkin, as well as Anna Akhmatova, Alexander Blok, Paul Verlaine, Rainer Maria Rilke, and Charles Baudelaire among her favorite poets. Nėris has also translated a number of works from these authors.

Her poetry might best be characterized by its melodious passion. There is a vibrant intensity in the experience of life that reaches, and swells, at the point of pain as it transforms itself into deceptively simple, yet extremely subtle, poetic language. In it, sound recurrences combine with grammatical, intonational, and emotional points of stress to produce a haunting, persistent feeling of rhythm, simultaneously enchanting and relentless, driving readers to draw their breath in pain to hear her story.

In her early period, until about 1940, that story is predominantly personal. The poet tells us with poignant openness how wonderful and how painful it is to experience the process of living as a continuous becoming. There is defiance in her verse, particularly toward the bourgeois values that, she felt, made her an outcast at home because of her unconventional marriage; her work takes a challenging stance against the norms and mores of her society and time. There is also contemplation, where the poet's word reaches out gently, precariously, to touch the highly sensitive, indeed, agonizing, issue of one's own mortality that confronts the surging passion to live, to drink deeply of beauty, freedom, and love. In this thematic frame, a number of poems subtly utilize associations with the imagery and diction of Lithuanian folk songs without, however, any direct imitation of their style or prevalent themes.

While it is quite likely that Nėris turned to the left at least partially out of contempt for what she thought was the Philistine, mindless life of the bourgeoisie, it could also be that the horrors of Stalin's regime did reach her attention to some extent, but it was too late; she had allowed herself to be trapped in an ideological dead-end, with capitalist greed, fascist insanity, and Russia's monumental inhumanity blocking every exit. All she had left was the Soviet war machine—she was now part of it, was functioning as one of its cogs, in effect independently, of her own will. Only the searing yearning for her homeland, boundless love, and desperate burden of dispossession shines through her later, politically committed poetry to sustain in her readers that strange enchantment they had always felt toward her verse. Even stylistically, the harsh and often wooden verbal structures of Bolshevik rhetoric seems mixed in a peculiar, elusive way with passages of the previous graceful, luminous beauty, so full of love for the native land.

Placed in a historical framework, Nėris fills a transitional stage between the rhetorical patriotic romanticism of such poets as the "bard of national awakening" Jonas Mačiulis-Maironis (1862–1932) and the intimate, experimental, modernistic, or expressionistic verse of such major Lithuanian poets of the twenties, thirties, and forties as Bernardas Brazd'ionis (b. 1907), a poet of great lyrical pathos whose passion for the ideal has similarities with the works of Nėris or Jonas Aistis (1904–1973), a soulful lover of the spare and sometimes harsh Lithuanian landscape who nevertheless liked to experiment with modernistic turns of style and vocabulary, and perhaps especially Antanas Miškinis (1905–1983) whose bucolic, folkloric, passionate verse was enchanted, enthralled, with song. At the other end of the spectrum, her poetry has given a personal tinge and some human feeling to the Socialist Realist doggerel pursued by an entire host of Soviet Lithuanian poets that did not end their song until approximately the sixties. A number of women poets, Judita Vaičiūnaitė (b. 1937), Janina Degutytė (b. 1928), Violeta Palčinskaitė (b. 1943) and others, have acknowledged their thematic and emotional, if not necessarily stylistic, indebtedness to Nėris, by all means one of the major leading Lithuanian poets of any time.

Works

Anksti ryţa, poems (1927). *Pėdos smėly*, poems (1931). *Diemed'iu 'ydėsiu*, poems (1938). *Eglė 'alčiu karalienė*, poem/tale (1940). *Poema apie Stalina* (1940). *Dainuok, širdie, gyvenimą*, poems and tales in verse (1943). *Lakštingala negali nečiulbėti*, poems (1945). *Bolševiko kelias*, narrative poem (1960). *Marija Melninkaitė*, narrative poem (1963). *širdis mana–audrų daina*, collected poems (1974). *Kaip 'ydėjimas vyšnios*, collected poems (1978). *Salomėja Nėris. Poezija*, collected poems (1979).

Rimvydas Šilbajoris

Madame Jeanne-Marie Le Prince de Beaumont
1711–1780
Born April 26, 1711, Rouen, France
Died 1780, Chavanod, Haute-Savoie, France
Genre(s): novel, didactic work
Language(s): French

Madame Le Prince de Beaumont was a popular novelist and a prolific writer of educational works for women and children, Christian apologetics, and moral tales which were widely read throughout Europe and America between 1750 and ca. 1830.

Coming from a large artistic family—the painter Jean-Baptiste Le Prince was her younger brother—Jeanne Marie Le Prince taught at a convent school for teachers in Rouen. When her unhappy marriage was annulled in 1745, she turned to writing to supplement a meager income. Her first novel, *Le Triomphe de la Vérité*, was published in 1748, the same year as two works in which she argues that women's natural qualities are superior to those of men. Shortly after, she settled in London, where she quickly established a reputation as a governess and started a monthly magazine, *Le Nouveau Magasin Français*, aimed primarily at women. She also wrote full-length didactic works such as *Éducation complète* (1753), which was used by the Princess of Wales, *Civan, roi de Bungo* (1754), which was set in Japan, and the *Anecdotes du XIVe siècle* (1759), as well as the highly popular epistolary novels, *Lettres de Madame Du Montier* (1756) and *La nouvelle Clarisse* (1767). Many of her books ran to several editions and were translated into every major European language. In 1758 she bought a house near Annecy, France, to which she retired with her second husband and where she continued writing until her death.

The most important of her works, the *Magasin des Enfants* (1756), is divided into journées in which a governess called Mme Bonne converses with seven pupils (Ladies Sensée, Spirituelle, Tempête, etc.) who are aged between five and thirteen. Each day, the lessons on history, geography, and science are alternated with Bible stories and fairy tales, including the classic version of "La Belle et la Bête" (adapted from a rambling 362-page story by Mme de Villeneuve, q.v.). Though always present, the morality is never saccharine, and many of the tales (e.g. "Le Prince au long nez") reveal considerable humor. It is the first work written not for a specific child, but for children in general; the first to address children as children and not as mini-adults, and to do so without being condescending. She continued her success with the *Magasin des Adolescentes* (1760), which introduces the same girls and others in their teens (Miss Frivole, Lady Sincère, etc.) to philosophy, and with *Instructions pour les jeunes Dames* (1764), which outlines the duties of a wife. One of her themes throughout is that women should rely not on men but on their own inner resources and to do this they must understand religion. In *Les Américaines* (1770), Mme Bonne asks the same young women, now her friends, to imagine how they would react in a European city if they had been transported there suddenly from the forests of America. The ensuing dialogue introduces the women to theology. In spite of her generally conservative views, Mme Bonne is constantly respectful of her pupils' individuality: "Each Lady is made to speak according to her particular Genius, Temper and Inclination." The question-and-answer technique is designed to stimulate their independent thought, greater self-awareness, and ability to conduct a reasoned debate. At a time when women received virtually no formal education, this intention was revolutionary.

Mme Le Prince de Beaumont's achievement can be measured by the success which her works enjoyed and the rapid improvement in women's education between 1760 and 1785. The *Magasin des Enfants* was frequently reprinted; in the nineteenth century, its format was much copied but never equalled. When her books fell out of fashion, except for two or three of her fairy tales—notably "La Belle et la Bête" (Beauty and the Beast)—none was ever republished. They were the first victims of a movement that she did much to create. She was the first editor of a woman's monthly magazine, the founder of children's literature in France, and an indefatigable promoter of women's equal right to learning.

Works

Le Triomphe de la Vérité, ou, Mémoires de M. de la Villette (1748; tr. *The Triumph of Truth, or, Memoirs of Mr. de la Villette*, 1755). *Lettre en réponse à "L'Année merveilleuse"* (1748). *Arrêt solennel de la nature* (1748). *Lettres diverses et critiques* (1750). *Le Nouveau Magasin français, ou, Bibliothèque instructive* (1750–1752, 1755). *Éducation complète, ou, Abrégé de l'histoire universelle, mêlée de géographie, de chronologie . . . à l'usage de la famille royale de la princesse de Galles* (1753). *Civan, roi de Bungo, histoire japonnoise, ou, Tableau de l'éducation d'un prince* (1754; tr. *Civan, King of Bungo*, 1800). *Lettres de Mme. Du Montier à la marquise de ***, sa fille, avec les réponses* (1756; tr. *The History of a Young Lady of Distinction. In a Series of Letters Which Passed between Madame Du Montier, and the Marchioness De ***, Her Daughter*, 1758). *Magasin des Enfants, ou, Dialogues entre une sage gouvernante et plusieurs de ses élèves* (1756; tr. *The Young Misses Magazine, or, Dialogues between a Discreet Governess and Several Young Ladies of the First Rank under Her Education*, 1757?). *Anecdotes du XIVe siècle, pour servir à l'histoire des femmes illustres de ce temps* (1758). *Lettres curieuses, instructives et amusanntes, ou, Correspondance historique, galante, etc. entre une dame de Paris et une dame de province* (1759). *Magasin des Adolescentes . . . Pour servir de suite au "Magasin des Enfants"* (1760; tr. *The Young Ladies Magazine . . .* , 1760). *Principes de l'Histoire-Sainte* (1761). *Instructions pour les jeunes Dames qui entrent dans le monde et qui se marient . . . Pour faire suite au "Magasin des Adolescentes"* (1764; tr. *Instructions for Young Ladies on Their Entering into Life, Their Duties in the Married State, and Towards Their Children*, 1764). *Lettres d'Émérance à Lucie* (1765; tr. *Letters from Émérance to Lucy*, 1766). *Mémoires de Madame la Baronne de Batteville, ou, La Veuve parfaite* (1766; tr. *The Virtuous Widow: or, Memoirs of the Baroness de Batteville*, 1768). *La nouvelle Clarisse, histoire véritable* (1767; tr. *The New Clarissa: a True History*, 1768). *Magasin des Pauvres, des Artisans, des Domestiques et des Gens de la campagne* (1768; tr. *Dialogues for Sunday Evenings; Translated from a Work of Madame Le Prince de Beaumont Called "Magasin des Pauvres,"* 1797?). *Les Américaines, ou, La Preuve de la Religion Chrétienne, par les lumières naturelles* (1770). *La Double Alliance, ou, Les heureux naturels, histoire du marquis D**** (1772/73). *Le Mentor moderne, ou, Instructions pour les garçons et pour ceux qui les élèvent* (1772). *Manuel de la Jeunesse, ou, Instructions familières, en dialogues* (ca. 1773). *Contes moraux* (1774; tr. *Moral Tales,*

1775). *Oeuvres mêlées de Mme. Le Prince de Beaumont: Extraites des Journaux & Feuilles périodiques qui ont paru en Angleterre pendant le séjour qu'elle y a fait* (1775: reprint of *Le Nouveau Magasin français*). *Nouveaux Contes moraux* (1776). *La Dévotion éclairée, ou, Magasin des Dévotes* (1779).

Terence Dawson

Simone de Beauvoir
1908–1986

Born January 9, 1908, Paris, France
Died April 14, 1986, Paris
Genre(s): novel, essay, travel books, short story, drama, autobiography
Language(s): French

Simone de Beauvoir was one of the most important literary figures in France after the Second World War. Her name is permanently linked to Existentialism and Jean-Paul Sartre, her companion for 51 years.

Born into an upper middle-class family, she enjoyed a secure and happy childhood, accepting her privileged position in society and the Catholic beliefs and bourgeois values of her parents without question. Educated in a strict girls' school in Paris, Simone soon rebelled against her bourgeois world which she found shallow and insincere. By age fourteen, she had lost faith in God and was determined to become a writer and teacher, rejecting marriage and children. Her growing alienation from family and friends of her class brought her to an early awareness of solitude and death which were later common themes in her writing. Realizing that men held a favored position in society, she began to consider her own role as a woman, the importance of love, and an ideal relationship with a man.

Simone wanted to pursue higher education, but her parents objected to her studying philosophy, which she preferred, so she studied literature and the classics. Her first attempts at writing (a novel and short stories) were disappointing and her education was unsatisfying. She completed her undergraduate work in 1928 and planned a higher degree thesis on Liebniz. While preparing for the *agrégation*, she met Sartre. She placed second on the national list for the exam; Sartre was first. Simone had finally met someone she considered intellectually superior to her, and she no longer felt alone. "It was the major event of my life," she said. Sartre's ideas conflicted with her staid, puritan, bourgeois world, but in Sartre she had found her

ideal man. "I trusted him so completely that he guaranteed me the sort of absolute security formerly provided by my parents and by God."

The first phase of her life had ended. She began teaching part-time and tried to write, at times only because Sartre insisted that she persevere. Her dependence on him was obvious, a situation that often concerned her. They had agreed not to marry, not to lie to one another, and to be free to have love affairs without recrimination. For several years they taught in different towns, but their relationship was never interrupted. Simone had no success in writing, abandoning one project after another because she was not able to incorporate her experiences into her works. She and Sartre were not yet involved in politics though they associated with many leftist intellectuals who sympathized with the working classes. They traveled extensively, first in Europe, and eventually all over the world. They had failed to recognize the Nazi threat to peace in the 1930s until they were shocked into action with the German occupation of France in 1940. Only then did they discard their self-centered, self-satisfied existence and become involved in the world around them.

When the war began de Beauvoir and Sartre were both teaching in Paris. His literary career was launched in 1936, but she could not get any of her stories or novels published. Sartre was mobilized in 1939, and taken prisoner in June 1940. Simone fled Paris when the Germans entered the city but returned shortly and led a constrained, austere, though not uncomfortable lifestyle during the war years. After Sartre returned to Paris (1941), they finally became involved in affairs outside of themselves. They collected and distributed information for the French Resistance, which was their way of dealing with a situation beyond their control. De Beauvoir was dismissed from her teaching post for vague "moral" reasons in 1943. There was great literary activity in Paris during the Occupation, and she finally had two works published, *L'Invitée* (She Came to Stay) and *Pyrrhus et Cinéas*. Along with Albert Camus, she and Sartre began devising a new philosophy for the post-war world. Her only play, *Les Bouches inutiles* (1945), was not well-received and closed after fifty performances. But her novel, *Le Sang des autres* (1945; The Blood of Others) won great acclaim. It is one of the few good novels about the Occupation and has been underrated by many critics.

In 1945 Sartre and de Beauvoir started a new literary and political journal, *Les Temps modernes*, a vehicle for the dissemination of existentialism, which was now in favor among French intellectuals. In her writing de Beauvoir concerned herself with moral and ethical issues, including feminism. She toured America in 1947 and began a love affair with Nelson Algren. *L'Amérique au jour le jour* (1948; America Day by Day) reveals her anti-American attitude; she and Sartre were pro-Soviet at this time, and strongly anti-Gaullist which cost them popularity in France. When her controversial two-volume *Le Deuxième Sexe* (1949; The Second Sex) was published, de Beauvoir was harshly attacked for her frank discussion of sex, motherhood, and women's inferior status. As in much of her work, the influence of Sartre's ideas, even his terminology, is obvious. Woman as "other," as an appendage of man, is not complete in herself. Undoubtedly, this reflected her own situation, her dependence on Sartre and Algren. She admitted that she was depressed when she and Algren broke up after four and a half years; it signaled sexual decline and advancing age. These dreaded feelings diminished when, in 1952, she began living with Claude Lanzmann, a twenty-seven-year-old writer; the affair lasted six years. Her spirit was rejuvenated, but her relations with Sartre did not change. Sartre and Lanzmann had embraced Marxism and de Beauvoir followed, as usual.

In 1954 de Beauvoir won the prestigious Prix Goncourt for her novel, *Les Mandarins* (The Mandarins), about a small circle of leftist intellectuals whose hopes for a better society were shattered after the Liberation. Following a trip to China and Russia the next year, she wrote *La longue Marche* (The Long March), a rather tedious, pedantic study of China, which she felt embodied the hope for the future. But political activism could not eradicate her fear of growing old. She had begun writing the autobiography in four volumes that was to be a tremendous success: *Mémoires d'une jeune fille rangée* (1958; Memoirs of a Dutiful Daughter); *La Force de l'âge* (1960; The Prime of Life); *La Force des choses* (1963; Force of Circumstances); *Tout compte fait* (1972; All Said and Done). Writing kept her fears at bay: "Creation is adventure; it is youth and freedom." Her book on old age, *La Vieillesse* (1970; The Coming of Age), examines the biological aspects of aging and the situation of the elderly from antiquity to the present. Like women, the elderly are passive, inert; they are also defined as "Other."

By 1970 de Beauvoir was active in the *Mouvement de libération des femmes*; she later became president of the feminist group, *Choisir*, and the *Ligue du droit des femmes*. Refusing to be labeled a feminist, she advocated women's rights, contraception, and abortion. She signed the "Manifesto" along with several hundred women who said they had had illegal abortions.

Sartre lost the sight of his one good eye in 1973, and until his death in 1980, de Beauvoir devoted herself to helping him with his work. She published an account of his last ten years, based on interviews, in 1981, *La Cérémonie des Adieux* (Adieux: A Farewell to Sartre); it was her last published work. Much of her literary work was based on Sartre's philosophical ideas: man is "essential," the subject; woman is "inessential," the object. Men must have "projects" which define and give meaning to life; lacking "projects," women do not achieve a full identity but remain passive, not active. All de Beauvoir's works revolve around her own feelings and experiences; at times her views are too personal to be completely valid, but she also spoke forcefully for the disinherited, the oppressed, the "other."

Works

L'Invitée (1943). *Pyrrhus et Cinéas* (1944). *Le Sang des autres* (1945). *Les Bouches inutiles; pièce en deux actes et huit tableaux* (1945). *Tous les hommes sont mortels* (1946). *Pour une morale de l'ambiguité* (1947). *L'Amérique au jour le jour* (1948). *L'Existentialisme et la sagesse des nations* (1948). *Le Deuxième Sexe*, 2 vols. (1949). *Les Mandarins* (1954). *Privilèges* (1955; includes "Faut-il brûler Sade?" "La Pensée de droit, aujourd'hui." "Merleau-Ponty et le pseudo-Sartrisme."). *Mémoires d'une jeune fille rangée* (1958). *Brigitte Bardot et le mythe de Lolita* (1960). *La Force de l'âge* (1960). *Djamila Boupacha*, with Gisèle Halimi, (1962) [1962; Djamila Boupacha; The Story of the Torture of a Young Algerian Girl Which Shocked Liberal French Opinion]. *The Marquis de Sade; An Essay*, ed. Paul Dinnage (1962). *La Force des choses* (1963). *Une Mort très douce* (1964). *Les Belles Images* (1966). *La Femme rompue* (1967). *La Vieillesse* (1970). *Tout compte fait* (1972). *Quand prime le spirituel* (1979). *La Cérémonie des Adieux, suivi de Entretiens avec Jean-Paul Sartre* (1981).

Translations: *The Blood of Others* [*Le Sang des autres*] (1948). *The Ethics of Ambiguity* [*Pour une morale de l'ambiguité*] (1949). *She Came to Stay* [*L'Invitée*] (1949). *America Day by Day* [*L'Amérique au jour le jour*] (1952). *The Second Sex* [*Le Deuxième Sexe*] (1952). *All Men Are Mortal* [*Tous les hommes sont mortels*] (1955). *The Mandarins* [*Les Mandarins*] (1956). *Brigitte Bardot and the Lolita Syndrome* [*Brigitte Bardot et le mythe de Lolita*] (1960). *The Prime of Life* [*La Force de l'âge*] (1962). *Force of Circumstances* [*La Force des choses*] (1964). *A Very Easy Death* [*Une Mort très douce*] (1966). *Les Belles Images* (1968). *The Woman Destroyed* [*La Femme rompue*] (1969). *The Coming of Age* [*La Vieillesse*] (1972). *All Said and Done* [*Tout compte fait*] (1974). *Memoirs of a Dutiful Daughter* [*Mémoires d'une jeune fille rangée*] (1974). *Old Age* [*La Vieillesse*] (1977). *Adieux: a Farewell to Sartre* [*La Cérémonie des Adieux, suivi de Entretiens avec Jean-Paul Sartre*] (1981). *When Things of the Spirit Come First: Five Early Tales* [Quand prime le spirituel] (1982).

Jeanne A. Ojala
William T. Ojala

Aphra Behn
1640–1689
a.k.a. Astrea
Born 1640, Harbledown, Kent (?) England
Died April 16, 1689, London
Genre(s): drama, poetry, novel, translation
Language(s): English

Behn's origins are uncertain, but recent evidence suggests that she was the Aphra Johnson christened in 1640 in Harbledown, Kent, although the yeoman status of her supposed father does not accord with her education, which is that of a gentlewoman. According to her novel *Oronooko* (1688), she traveled to Surinam in 1663–1664 when she was a young woman. Tradition has it that upon her return to London she married a merchant named Behn, of Dutch extraction, who perhaps died of the plague in 1665; however, she never once refers to such a person. The earliest indisputable external evidence about her life is a series of letters documenting her employment in 1666 as a secret agent for the English government. She was sent to Antwerp to get information about exiled Cromwellians and to relay Dutch military plans. She used Astrea as her code name as a spy and later as her literary name. In the Netherlands she ran into debt, and in 1667 when she returned home, went briefly to debtor's prison. She was noted among a wide circle of friends and fellow writers for her beauty, wit, and generosity; Sir Peter Lely and Mary Beale painted portraits of her. Her strong Tory sentiments and personal loyalty to the royal family led to a political outspokenness that earned her enemies among some powerful Whigs. She satirized the Earl of Shaftesbury, the Whig leader, in *The City Heiress* (1682) but offended the king in the same year when she attacked the Duke of Monmouth in an epilogue, for which she was arrested. During her life she was forced to fend off not only political and personal attacks but also attacks on her as a woman who wrote with the same freedoms as a man. In her last years she suffered from poverty and a painful crippling disease, and her political hopes were crushed by the Revolution of 1688.

Behn first achieved literary celebrity as a playwright, entering the theater in 1670 and producing seventeen extant plays; two more plays have been lost—*Like Father, Like Son* (1682) and *The Wavering Nymph* (1684). Four anonymous plays have been attributed to her—*The Woman Turned Bully* (1676), *The Debauchee* (1677), *The Counterfeit Bridegroom* (1677), and *The Revenge* (1680); these, however, may have been written by Thomas Betterton. Behn's dramatic specialty was the "Spanish" comedy of intrigue written in brisk, colloquial prose. Typically she manipulates several sources into a complex and witty play of expert stage craftsmanship. A number of couples—eluding the unwanted marriages arranged for them—meet, bed, and/or wed after innumerable intrigues, mistaken identities, duels, disguises, and practical jokes. Her plays abound in bedroom farce and scenes of comic lowlife with delightful portrayals of landladies, bawds, buffoons, and prostitutes. She provides spectacle in masquing, costuming, and dance and uses stage machinery and other technical resources ro create special effects.

The best of Behn's intrigue comedies is *The Rover; or, The Banished Cavaliers* (1677), set at carnival time in Naples, where impoverished English cavaliers-in-exile become entangled with Spanish ladies and win their persons and fortunes. Behn's rover, Willmore, is her distinctive version of a favorite Restoration character, the wild gallant. *The Rover* stayed in the repertory until the middle of the eighteenth century, the role of the witty heroine being taken by such famous actresses as Elizabeth Barry, Anne Bracegirdle, Anne Oldfield, and Peg Woffington. Also among Behn's best plays is *Sir Patient Fancy* (1678), an amusing tangle of the amours of two neighboring London families. Her *Emperor of the Moon* was an instant success in 1687. A gay and extravagant combination of *commedia dell'arte,* operatic spectacle, sumptuous costuming, dance, song, satire, intrigue, and a bit of manners comedy, the play was performed for nearly a hundred years.

A number of her plays deal centrally with her most distinctive theme, her attack on forced marriage. She titled her first play *The Forced Marriage* (1670) and went on to write *The Town Fop* (1676) and *The Lucky Chance* (1686), respectively a sentimental and a harder treatment of the same subject. While New Comedy in general depicts the witty stratagems of young lovers who outwit their elders in order to marry according to their own choice, Behn goes beyond this to attack the arranged marriage as an institution. In doing so, she uses in distinctive ways two stock characters, the courtesan and the amazon. In *The Rover,* Parts I and II (1677, 1681), and *The Feigned Courtesans* (1679), Behn uses the courtesan to suggest that marriage for money is a form of prostitution. In *The Young King* (1679) and *The Widow Ranter* (1689), the woman warrior in both romantic and comic versions provides a visual metaphor for the battle of the sexes and suggests the compatibility of lovers who are equals in wit and war.

Behn was a versatile and sometimes distinguished poet. She wrote topical and witty prologues and epilogues for the theater. Her elegies and panegyrics in baroque pindarics for members of the royal family and the nobility were usually published in folio or quarto to celebrate a state occasion. Her elegies for the Earl of Rochester and the Duke of Buckingham display her personal affection and admiration for these two fellow wits. Behn had a fine lyric gift; her elegant and sophisticated songs appeared both in her plays and in contemporary collections. Her best-known song, "Love in Fantastic Triumph Sat," appeared in her one tragedy, *Abdelazer* (1676), and has often been reprinted.

In the latter part of her career, Behn made a number of miscellaneous translations from Latin and French, apparently for the money. She had no Latin and worked from a prose paraphrase of Ovid and Cowley; her French, however, was fluent, and she produced able, sometimes improved, versions of Tallement, La Rochefoucauld, Bonnecorse, Aesop, and de Fontenelle.

In the last years of her life she also wrote fiction, producing more than a dozen novels, some of which were published posthumously. Her novels achieved great popularity: two were dramatized, and collections of her novels appeared throughout the eighteenth century; some continue to be reprinted. In her fiction Behn pioneered in the transition from romance to novel by providing extensive circumstantial detail. Her two best tales—*The Fair Jilt* (1688) and *Oronooko* (1688)—are based on events she herself witnessed. *Oronooko,* the story of an African prince enslaved in Surinam, displays great originality in theme and structure and is perhaps her best-known work.

Behn wrote ably in a number of genres. She is significant not only as an artist but also as the first professional woman writer and the first woman whose writing won her burial in Westminster Abbey. On her tombstone are these verses: "Here lies a proof that wit can never be / Defence enough against mortality."

Works

The Forced Marriage (1670). *The Amorous Prince* (1671). *The Dutch Lover* (1673). *Abdelazer* (1676). *The Town Fop* (1676). *The Rover* (1677; edited by F. Link, 1967). *Sir Patient Fancy* (1678). *The Feigned Courtesans* (1679). *The Young King* (1679). *The Sec-* *ond Part of the Rover* (1681). *The False Count* (1681). *The Roundheads* (1681). *Like Father, Like Son* (1682). *The City Heiress* (1682). *Poems upon Several Occasions* (1684). *Love Letters between a Nobleman and His Sister* (1684). *The Wavering Nymph* (1684). *A Pindaric on the Death of Our Late Sovereign* (1685). *A Poem to Catherine Queen Dowager* (1685). *A Pindaric Poem on the Happy Coronation* (1685). *The Lucky Chance* (1686). *The Emperor of the Moon* (1687; edited by L. Hughes, *Ten English Farces,* 1948). *To Christopher, Duke of Albemarle* (1687). *To the Memory of George, Duke of Buckingham* (1687). *The Amours of Philander and Sylvia* (1687). *A Congratulatory Poem to Her Most Sacred Majesty* (1688). *The Fair Jilt* (1688). *A Congratulatory Poem on the Happy Birth of the Prince of Wales* (1688). *Oronooko* (1688). *Agnes de Castro* (1688). *A Poem to Sir Roger L'Estrange* (1688). *To Poet Bavius* (1688). *A Congratulatory Poem to Queen Mary* (1689). *The History of the Nun* (1689). *The Lucky Mistake* (1689). *A Pindaric Poem to the Reverend Dr. Burnet* (1689). *The Widow Ranter* (1689). *The Younger Brother* (1696). *The Adventures of the Black Lady* (1698). *The Court of the King of Bantam* (1698). *The Nun* (1698). *The Unfortunate Happy Lady* (1698). *The Wandering Beauty* (1698). *The Dumb Virgin* (1700). *The Unhappy Mistake* (1700). *Works,* 4 vols., ed. J. Todd (1992). *Love Letters Between a Nobleman and His Sister* (1684–1687; modern ed. 1987).

Nancy Cotton

Maria Elisa Belpaire
1853–1948

Born January 31, 1853, Antwerp, Belgium
Died June 9, 1948, Antwerp
Genre(s): essay, memoirs, biography
Language(s): Dutch

Called "The Wise Woman of Flanders" and "the Mother of the Flemish Movement," Maria Elisa Belpaire played a central role in the artistic and social emancipation of a region that, having lost its medieval splendor, had become a cultural backwater from the seventeenth century onward. French had gradually become the only language for administration and education, and the native tongue Flemish (a term denoting the variety of Dutch spoken in Flanders) had been more or less actively suppressed, especially since the foundation of the Belgian state in 1830.

Born into the French-speaking upper class in Flanders, Maria Elisa Belpaire nevertheless decided to use Flemish in her writings. She first tried her hand at poetry and, true to her ideal of edifying the Flemish people, collected and translated a large number of fairy tales in collaboration with two other women writers. She soon settled for the genre that suited her best: the essay.

Brought up in a highly cultured milieu and personally acquainted with many artists and intellectuals, it seemed natural that she would write about art, music, and literature. Throughout her many essays, among them studies on Beethoven and Dickens and the varied collection *Kunst-en levensbeelden* (1906, 1913, 1919; Images of Art and Life), her style and tone remained those of a nineteenth-century Romantic: impassioned and lyrical. So did her value judgments: the literature and art she appreciated had to deal with love, genius, spiritual passion, ecstasy, and the religious drive for infinity. She joined the Christian thinkers of her time in defending a Christian-humanistic ideal of art: art is not value free but the expression of "moral grandeur," "higher life," or an "ideal image," and a union of "truth" and "beauty." In her programmatic essay *Christen ideaal* (1899; Christian Ideal), she argued that the Christian ideal of art, like that of holiness, could be found in the eight beatitudes of the Sermon on the Mount.

Though she lived well into the twentieth century, Belpaire never warmed to the new artistic and literary movements emerging at the turn of the century. She denounced the moderns for showing the seamy side of life, and she deplored the secularization of art and literature, for there could be no artistic inspiration without a sense of God.

While in many ways a woman belonging to the "old" order, Belpaire was in the vanguard of nascent Christian democratic movements, shifting emphasis from traditional Christian charity (many of her relatives were involved in philanthropy) to organized social action. She set up women's organizations, and was very active at the Yser Front in World War I where she took up the cause of Flemish soldiers commanded by French-speaking officers they could not understand. She co-founded *De Belgische Standaard*, a newspaper for the front, in which she promoted Catholic ethics and wrote many contributions on the rights of Flemings. Her work at the front—when she was already in her sixties—earned her the epithet "mamieke," little mother. *De vier wondere jaren* (1920, 1938; The Four Wondrous Years) is an interesting account of her experiences at the front.

An advocate of women's education, Belpaire founded and financially supported a number of Catholic schools for girls, which she wanted to be run by lay personnel, not nuns, and open to non-Catholics who subscribed to broad humanistic ideals, and also a prestigious women's college. Her reasons were typical of her bourgeois background, and of the many nineteenth-century feminists who paved the way for more radical changes later. In "Vrouweninvloed" (Woman's Influence), published in *Kunst-en levensbeelden*, Belpaire advanced the thesis that, though men are intellectually superior to women, women outdo their partners in the moral field and are generally "wiser." Furthermore, because woman's realm is the intimacy of the home, her influence is not always visible, yet it is much more effective than man's, whose realm is the outside world. Obviously a good education could only enhance the quality of woman's impact. It seems a curious reasoning for a woman who herself never nurtured a family and whose impact on public life was, without any doubt, direct and immense.

Yet Belpaire only commented at rare moments on her "peculiar" position as a woman in a male-dominated cultural and social environment. On co-signing a letter of protest addressed to the Belgian Archbishop, Cardinal Mercier, who had proclaimed that Flemish was not a language fit for science and scholarship in the context of a heated debate on reforming education in Flanders and ending French supremacy, she wrote: "He [the cardinal] will always keep looking for the priest who put me up to this, since it has not entered his mind that a woman can have a conviction of her own, and act according to it."

Throughout her life Belpaire remained a patron of the arts and a promoter and initiator of many cultural initiatives. She brought about and financed the fusion of two Catholic journals into *Dietsche Warande en Belfort*, which became the authoritative voice of broad-minded Catholic Flemish intellectuals.

She also translated, from Danish, works by Björn Björnson and Johannes Jörgensen, a young Catholic convert. She received the Literary Prize of the Province of Antwerp in 1933 and became Doctor Honoris Causa of the University of Louvain in 1937. Her most valuable writings are probably the vast volumes on the life and history of her relatives, *De families Teichmann en Belpaire* (1925–1934), and her own memoirs, *Gestalten in 't verleden* (1947; Figures in the Past), which all offer a fascinating insight into the life of the socially committed bourgeoisie and the cultural history of a period that witnessed many crucial changes.

Though Maria Elisa Belpaire was duly honored during her long life, a full study on the work and significance of this extraordinary and perseverant woman who firmly believed in the edification of a suppressed people and, to a lesser extent, of a suppressed sex, has yet to be written.

Works

Uit het leven (1887). [With H. Ram and L. Duykers], *Wonderland* (7 vols., 1894–1924). *Herfstrozen* (1897). *Christen ideaal* (1899, 1921). *Het landleven in de letterkunde der XIXde eeuw* (1902, 1923). *Kunst-en levensbeelden* (1906, 1913; Vol. 2, 1919). *Constance Teichmann* (1908, 1926). *Beethoven* (1911, 1947). *Na veertig jaar* (1912). *Antwerpen vóór honderd jaar, 1814* (1919). *De vier wondere jaren* (1920, 1938). *Alphonse Belpaire* (1922). *Na vijftig jaar* (2 vols., 1924). *August Cuppens* (1925). *De families Teichmann en Belpaire* (3 vols., 1925–1934). *Charles Dickens* (1929). *Reukwerk* (1932). *Gestalten in 't verleden* (1947).

Ria Vanderauwera

Illuminata Bembo
ca. 1410–1496

Born ca. 1410, Venice, Italy
Died May 18, 1496, Bologna, Italy
Genre(s): hagiography
Language(s): Italian

Illuminata, the daughter of a prominent Venetian noble family, was a nun of the Franciscan order (Poor Clares) and author of the *Mirror of Illumination*, a life of the noted visionary and spiritual writer, St. Catherine of Bologna.

Illuminata entered the monastery of Corpus Domini in Ferrara in 1430. Catherine of Bologna, who entered the same monastery the following year, soon gained renown for her piety and visions. In 1456, she became the abbess of a new monastery in her native Bologna and died there in 1463. Some of the nuns of Corpus Domini, including Illuminata, followed her to Bologna. By 1172, Illuminata had become abbess of the community. She composed the *Mirror of Illumination* in Italian at some unknown time after Catherine's death. This very personal portrait of Catherine differs significantly in tone from her "official" life, written in Latin by Catherine's confessor for use in the canonization procedures. Although Illuminata does recount such events as the beginnings of the new community in Bologna, the *Mirror* is less a biography than a meditation on the spiritual life of

the saint intended for the continuing instruction of the community's members. It tells not only of Catherine's visions and devotional practices but describes how she acted as a spiritual director for the nuns of her community. Illuminata includes reminiscences about conversations between the saint and Illuminata herself, who had lived in an adjoining cell. The manuscript of the work was kept and used at the monastery, where it remains today, but the work was not printed until over three centuries later. A shorter version of Catherine's life, edited by van Ortroy, is also probably the work of Illuminata.

The *Mirror of Illumination* reflects the memory of a great teacher composed by a student trying to continue her work. It provides a remarkable portrait of life in a vigorously reformed convent of the fifteenth century.

Works

Specchio d'illuminazione sulla vita di s. Caterina da Bologna (1787; reprinted in G. Melloni, *Atti o memorie degle uomini illustri in santita nati o morti in Bologna*, vol. IV ([ed. A. Benati and M. Fanti; 1971], pp. 289–300). Nuñez, L.M., *La santa nella storia, nelle lettere, e nell'arte* (1912), pp. 158–160.

Thomas Head

Catherine Bernard
1662–1712

Born 1662, Rouen, France
Died September 16, 1712, Paris
Genre(s): lyric poetry, narrative fiction, tragedy
Language(s): French

When at twenty-three Catherine Bernard abjured the reformed religion of her family, she was known well enough to be given a special notice in the *Mercure galant* praising her "ouvrages galants." She had begun precociously to write verse and had received compliments from her cousin Fontenelle while still very young. She was also complimented by the attribution of a romance, *Frédéric de Sicile* (by Pradon?), as well as her cousin's *Relation de l'île de Bornéo*. At eighteen she had left her native Rouen to make her fortune as an author in Paris. She remained poor but in the fullest sense became a professional woman of letters.

Her first novel, *Eléonore d'Yvrée* (1687), inaugurated a series exemplifying "Les malheurs de l'amour." Published with a dedication to the Dauphin and a moralizing preface, the novel in its use of history, narrative structure, and theme of the dutiful sacrifice of passion followed self-consciously in the tradition of Mme de Lafayette's *La Princesse de Clèves*. Praising its economy of plot and dialogue, concision of style, and portrayal of psychological nuance in the *Mercure* (September 1687), Fontenelle underscores this renewal of the novel whose innovations he himself had lauded. *Le Comte d'Amboise* (1689) at greater length continues to explore the noble refusal of passion and reaffirms the heritage of the novelist's first model. Seeking variation as Mme de Lafayette herself had in *Zaïde*, Bernard complicates her plot in the more adventure-laden *Inès de Cordoue* (1696). The drama of its heroine's sacrifice has brought less attention to this last novel than has one of its two preliminary *contes de fées*, "Riquet à la Houppe." Probably with her blessing, Charles Perrault retold the tale in his *Contes* (1697). Bernard's novels were republished in the widely circulated "Bibliothèque de campagne" (1739, 1785).

Bernard was the most successful woman tragedian in seventeenth-century France. *Laodamie* (1689), the last new tragedy staged at the Guénégaud theatre, had a long, profitable first run of twenty-three performances (with three more in 1690–1691). *Brutus*, dedicated to the Duchesse d'Orléans, ran for twenty-seven and was restaged eight times before 1700. It was revived with the collaboration of the Comédie-Française in 1973. Effectively unified, both plays show the mixture of Cornelian and Racinian models common in tragedies of the 1690s. *Laodamie*, a reversal of Racine's *Bérénice*, dramatizes (as does *Eléonore d'Yvrée*) the rivalry of two women whose characters remain noble despite differing responses to love. An already considerable dramatic interest given to "the people" is amplified in the more Cornelian *Brutus*, a dramatization of the problematics of love versus patriotism that pits Brutus's sons against their father. Bernard humanizes Brutus but by shifting heroic focus to Titus creates a political study of tyranny. Ample and unacknowledged borrowing by Voltaire for his *Brutus* (1730) was denounced in the *Mercure* (March 1731).

Having reached the summit of a poet's career that successful tragedy represented, Bernard renounced the theatre and the more showy and fashionable early verse, with the support of the patronage of the Chancelière de Pontchartrain, whose austerity seconded her own tendency to moral severity. Some dozen poems continued, however, to appear in worthy collections (notably *Bouhours*, 1693, 1701), including an epigram playing on Pontchartrain's capitation tax reform and a bantering petition to the king for payment of a pension of 200 francs that had rewarded her encomiastic verse, for which she three times won the coveted poetry prize of the Académie française (1691, 1693, 1697). Decorated also in the *Jeux floraux*, Bernard was given her place in the Parnassus of women writers by the Paduan Ricovrati. These honors and patronage were continuously sought by dedications and verse, but they only just rescued Bernard during the last decades of her life from an abject poverty that she never sought to relieve by lesser means than those she conceived to be part of the noble profession of letters.

Works

Les Malheurs de l'amour. Première nouvelle: Eléonore d'Yvrée (1687). *Le Comte d'Amboise, nouvelle galante* (1689). *Laodamie, reine d'Epire, tragédie* (1689). *Brutus, tragédie* (1690). *Inès de Cordoue, suivi de l'histoire d'Abenamar et de Fatime* (1696). *Recueil des plus beaux vers . . . Bouhours* (1701). *Pièces de poésies qui ont remporté le prix de l'Académie française* (1763; for 1691, 1693, 1697).

Charles G.S. Williams

Sister Bertken
1427–1514

a.k.a. Berta Jacobs
Born 1427, Utrecht, The Netherlands
Died 1514, Utrecht
Genre(s): poetry, religious prose
Language(s): Dutch

At the age of twenty-four, Sister Bertken (Dutch: Suster Bertken), in all likelihood a daughter of a well-to-do Utrecht middle-class family, became a canoness in the monastery of Jerusalem near Utrecht, a monastery of Augustinian regulars where she remained for six years. In 1457, at the symbolically significant age of thirty, Bertken was granted permission by Bishop David of Burgundy to be enclosed as a recluse in a cell built into the wall of the "Buurkerk" in Utrecht. There she lived for the next 57 years. Only on June 25, 1514, after this long period of steadfast endurance, did she die. She was buried, in accordance with her own wishes and in the presence of Utrecht's church and city authorities as well as many citizens, in her cell in the Buurkerk. A Latin *vita* of this local *mulier sancta* was enclosed in a bottle and placed in Bertken's coffin by the authorities, and the prior of the monastery of regular Augustinian canons in Utrecht, who supervised the Jerusalem-monastery and guarded the keys of Bertken's cell during her life, inscribed a Dutch translation of the *vita* on the title page of the *Legenda Aurea* of his monastery.

Two small volumes of prose and poetry are all that remain of Bertken's *oeuvre*: *Een boecxken gemaket ende bescreven van Suster Bertken die lvii jaren besloten heeft gheseten tot Utrecht in dye buerkercke* (A Little Book Composed and Written by Sister Bertken Who Was a Recluse at the Buurkerk in Utrecht for 57 Years) and *Suster Bertken's boeck dat sy selver gemaect ende becreven heeft* (The Book of Sister Bertken Which She Composed and Wrote Herself)—both published post-humously in 1516 by the Utrecht printer Jan Berntsz. The first is a series of meditations on the passion of Christ and the second a miscellaneous collection of prayers, "A Pious Colloquy between the Loving Soul and Her Beloved Bridegroom Jesus," "A Vision of the Birth of Christ," and eight poems.

Bertken's *oeuvre* or, rather, whatever Jan Berntsz decided to publish from the manuscripts found in Bertken's cell following her death, has received little scholarly attention and less true understanding in Dutch literary scholarship as its study has suffered from the imprudent application of the stereotype of the charming, simple, and pious Middle Ages. Reinder P. Meijer's assertions, in his *The Literature of the Low Countries* that "Her religious world was simple and so was her representation of it" and that "the cliché of 'charming medieval simplicity' might have been coined to describe her work" (1971, p. 69) are typical of this approach. Yet, increasingly, Bertken has been shown to be a significant medieval woman writer who drew from a long literary, didactic, theological, and mystical tradition—a tradition going back to *Canticles* and the Church Fathers and continuing into her own age and culture, especially in the remarkable works of Hadewych of Antwerp, Jan Ruusbroec, Beatrice of Nazareth, and the spirituality associated with the beguine movement and the *devotio moderna*. Viewed in the light of this tradition and the special thematic concerns which her 57-year-long existence as *reclusa* imposed on Bertken, her writings reveal a consistent and original literary and mystical program—a program that revolves around the expression, in an often oblique and demanding language and rhetoric, of a number of related voices inside Bertken, those of the woman, the *mystica*, and the recluse.

Works

Johanna Snellen, ed., *Een boecxken gemaket ende bescreven van suster Bertken die lvii jaren besloten heeft gheseten tot Utrecht in dye buerkercke. Naar den Leidschen druk van Jan Seversen* (1924). van de Graft,

C. Catharina, ed., *Een boecxken . . .* (1955). The Snellen-text is based on the edition of Bertken by the Leiden printer Jan Seversen, whereas de Graft reproduces the text of the earliest published version by the Utrecht printer Jan Berntsz. See also Henk Vynckier, "Poetry from Behind Bars: Some Translations from the Dutch Recluse Sister Bertken (1430–1517)." *Mystics Quarterly* (Fall 1988).

Henk Vynckier

Kata Bethlen
1700–1759

a.k.a. "Árva" [Orphan]
Born November 25, 1700, Bonyha, Hungary
Died July 29, 1759, Fogaras, Hungary (now Romania)
Genre(s): memoirs
Language(s): Hungarian

Bethlen is one of the earliest writers of memoirs in Hungary. She was led to writing by her unhappy first marriage and subsequent religious conflicts with the children of that first marriage. She was throughout her life active in the cultural and intellectual life of her country as a member of the important Bethlen family, the niece of the Chancellor of Transylvania Miklos Bethlen, as well as, in her second marriage, the wife of the son of a later Chancellor, Mihály Teleki. Her first marriage was politically motivated, and the antagonism between her strong Protestant views and the Catholicism of her husband's family wounded her deeply. The Heller family denied her access to her children, and her daughter's malicious teasing seems to have touched her most deeply, for it is mentioned in her writings. After the death of her first husband, she remarried and, as the mistress of her husband's large estates, was active in fostering education in Transylvania. This marriage was happier, but her husband and the children of this marriage died early, therefore the epithet "orphan."

Her diary was written primarily as a personal response to the pressures her first husband's family put on her to convert. She published her writings under the titles: *Védelmező erős pajs* (1759; Protecting, Strong Shield) and *Bujdosásának emlékezetkönyve* (1733, 1735; The Memoirs of Her Exile) and the collected work which includes her letters: *Életének maga által való rövid leírása Széki gróf Teleki József özvegye, Bethleni Bethlen Kata grófnő írásai és levelezése* (1759; Her Life, Written by Herself, the Writings and Correspondence of . . .). Her writings, however, mirror more than her personal troubles, for they also reflect the political struggles of the day and the duties and tasks of the leading families in this conflict.

Her correspondence shows a clever, skillful woman who encouraged industrial development on her estates. She established gardens and nurseries to propagate better stock, had a papermill and glass works, and employed numerous artisans, including embroiderers, a major cottage industry of the time. She studied natural science to counteract the effects of natural disasters and sought to aid her tenants in adopting progressive farming practices. She learned medicine and pharmacology to better minister to the needs of her community and contributed generously to the advance of learning by establishing schools and scholarships. She also contributed to the education of girls, which she felt was sadly neglected. As a patron of Péter Bód, the Protestant scholar and publisher, she fostered printing and scholastic reform. The library he assembled for her was one of the most important of the age. While he was her chaplain (1743–1749), he collected over 500 manuscripts in addition to numerous books. Unfortunately, an 1847 fire destroyed the library.

It was her memoirs, however, that assured Bethlen a place in Hungarian literature. Her life's story (*Életének maga által . . .*) is a personal history shot through with the concerns of the day. She is not merely a religious writer, though her pietistic leanings would suggest that: she sees the religious struggle in national terms, within the context of the forcible re-conversion efforts of the Hapsburg family in the eighteenth century; her pietistic comments are eclipsed by her determined political views. In this, she is a good representative of the Hungarian Baroque and unites the literature of her day with that of the Reform period of the nineteenth century.

Her memoirs, in succinct, almost colloquial, language, are surprisingly open in spite of their melancholic nature. They give details and personal reactions that are lacking in the works of her male contemporaries such as Francis Rákoczi II. Perhaps her goal of justifying God's ways to man, rather than of accounting for her own actions, accounts for this openness.

Also important are her letters, which are remarkable even when compared with the correspondence of predecessors such as Zsuzsanna Lorántffy, Anna Bornemissza, or Ilona Zrinyi. Especially after the death of her second husband, she wrote extensively and brought a new, intimate style to this genre. Although not free of Baroque ornament and formality, they nevertheless exhibit a simplicity and elegance of language that make them akin to the letters of Mme de Sevigné and others at the Court of Louis XIV.

Between 1742 and 1751 she wrote a collection of poetic prayers, which she published under the title *Védelmező erős pajs*. These show an interesting blend of traditional meditative lyrics, the popular genres of the day, and her strongly Puritanical views. The style of the letters is also reflected in her major work, the memoirs, on which she worked from 1740 on. We do not have a complete manuscript, and the printed version stops in mid-sentence at June 20, 1751. She followed, in style, the memoirs of János Kemény and Miklos Bethlen, which she knew, but her work is also closely related to the *Confessions* of Francis Rákoczi. In the preface she endeavors to give a moral and didactic framework to her autobiography; in reality, it is her personal life and her commentary that provide interest. The compactness and economy of earlier parts is diluted later, but here the details of everyday life are more numerous. The interspersed prayers give it both a more personal and a more lyrical flavor.

Works
Védelmező erős pajs (1759). *Bujdosásának emlékezetkönyve* (1733; 7 editions in her lifetime). *Életének maga által való rövid leírása*, ed. Miklós K. Pap (1881). *Széki gróf Teleki József özvegye Bethleni Bethlen Kata grófnő írásai és levelezése, 1700–1759*, ed. Lajos Szadeczky-Kardoss (1922–1923). *B.K. Önéletleírasa*, intro. Mihaly Sűkösd (1963).

Enikő Molnár Basa

Charlotte Dorothea Biehl
1731–1788
Born June 2, 1731, Copenhagen, Denmark
Died May 15, 1788, Copenhagen
Genre(s): drama, short story, novel, autobiography, translation, historical letter
Language(s): Danish

The literary production of Charlotte Dorothea Biehl positions itself in the struggle between the feudal aristocracy and the emerging bourgeoisie that characterized Danish society and its theater in the mid-eighteenth century. Inspired by French and English moral-sentimental drama, Biehl was the major Danish dramatist in the 1764–1772 period. With a series of sentimental comedies and *singspiels*, as well as later fiction and prose, she represents a new bourgeois morality, which internalized aristocratic hierarchies and ceremonies as "inner nobility."

Born into a family of Castellans, Biehl spent her childhood years at Copenhagen Castle and her mature life at Charlottenborg Castle. She was consistently subjected to the whims of an authoritarian father, who prevented his intelligent daughter from reading and, ultimately, from marrying. As a member of the bourgeoisie, yet living among the aristocracy and as a victim of the patriarchal family yet seemingly supporting the institution, Biehl expressed in her writings the contradictions of her life.

Biehl's first and most successful play, *Den Kierlige Mand* (1764; The Loving Husband), sets the high moral tone that characterized her theatrical productions. By appealing to her maternal feelings, a husband rescues his normally dutiful wife from the temptations of festivity and flirtation. *Den Forelskede Ven* (1765; The Friend in Love) and *Den Ædelmodige* (1767; The Noble One) establish a morality of love, while the subtly subversive *Den Listige Optraekkerske* (1765; The Shrewd Fraud) depicts a fraudulent, seductive exploiter of men, duly punished in the end. Seven of Biehl's plays were collected in *Comedier* (1773; Comedies), published at the end of her most productive years in the theater. Her successful translation of Cervantes's *Don Quixote* appeared in 1776 or 1777.

Moralske Fortaellinger I–IV (1781–1782; Moral Tales) opened the second phase of Biehl's career with a series of tales advocating control, self-repression, and rationality in response to the German sentimental-rebellious novel epitomized by Goethe's *Leiden des Jungen Werthers* (1774).

The third phase of Biehl's production began with her monumental epistolary novel, *Brevvexling Imellem Fortroelige Venner* I–III (1783; Correspondence between Intimate Friends), with Richardson's *Pamela* (1740) as her model. In 1784, she furthermore recorded in letter form her memories of Danish royalty. In 1787, she offered her autobiography, entitled *Mit Ubetydelige Levnetsløb* (My Insignificant Life) as a birthday present to a friend.

While often heavy-handedly moralistic, Biehl's literary works, written under absolute monarchy and patriarchy, represent a new bourgeois consciousness as well as a new feminine voice.

Works

Comedier (1773). *Betragtning over Jesu Lidelse og Død* (1773). *Silphen* (1773). *Kierligheds-Brevene* (1774). *Den Prøvede Troskab* (1774). *Euphemia* (1775). *Den Sindrige Herremands Don Quixote af Mancha Levnet og Bedrifter* (1776). "Søster B.: En Tale Holden i Kiede-Forsamlingen d. 13de Martii 1778" (1778). *Et Oratorium af Gio. Batta Pergolesi. Poesien af C.D. Biehl* (1780). *Moralske Fortaellinger I–IV* (1781–1782). *Brevvexling Imellem Fortroelige Venner I–III* (1783). *Den Tavse Pige eller De Ved Tavshed Avlede Mistanker* (1783). "C.D. Biehls Anekdoter om Christian VI i 2 Breve til Joh. v. Bulow" (1784). "Upartiske Anmaerkninger til en Falsk og Ondskabsfuld Historie" (1784). *Interiører fra Kong Frederik den Femtes Hof: C.D. Biehls Breve og Selvbiografi* (1784). *Interiører fra Kong Christian den Syvendes Hof: Efter Charlotte Dorothea Biehls Breve* (1784). *Orpheus og Eurydice* (1786). "Hovmesterinden" (1786). *Den Uforsigtige Forsigtighed* (1787). "Til Hs. Kgl. H. Cronprindsen d. 4. April 1784" (1794). "Regeringsforandringen den 14de April 1784" (n.d.).

Clara Juncker

Anna Bijns
1493–1575

Born 1493, Antwerp, Belgium
Died 1575, Antwerp
Genre(s): poetry
Language(s): Dutch

Born in the almost superstitiously pious Catholic lower middle class of Antwerp, Anna Bijns became a private school teacher in that city upon the death of her father in 1516. Franciscan Minorites had tutored her and had probably stimulated her early talent for verse-making in the flourishing style of the Chambers of Rhetoric, though it is not certain whether she actually ever belonged to such a Chamber. Bijns remained closely connected with Minorites throughout her sad and rather isolated life as a poor schoolmistress and spinster. The Franciscans were the most militant and the most intellectual among the local clergymen to resist the swiftly rising fortunes of, first, the Lutherans (from 1515 until 1526), the Anabaptists (1534–1539), and the Calvinists (after 1526) in Antwerp. Despite ever harsher countermeasures imposed by the Spanish government of the Low Countries, these three reformational movements (and Calvinism foremost) succeeded in weaning ever larger segments of the cosmopolitan and well-to-do Antwerp bourgeoisie and aristocrats away from Catholicism.

Bijns had been writing light "foolish" and "amorous" refrains in the rhetorical style of *nugae difficiles* in the early decades of the sixteenth century, but the adverse fortunes of orthodox Catholicism changed her inclination. Bijns blamed the progress of "heresy" (all the phenomena of which she conveniently but rather inaccurately designated as "Lutherie") partly on the ineffective preaching of the well-intending but hopelessly unprepared parish clergy. The Reformation was effected in the Southern Netherlands to a great extent by means of polemical pamphlets. It was in this often vile and vulgar logomachy that Bijns engaged as *miles christi*—though not without fear that her "frail womanhood" might make her fail in this self-ordained task as "the "avenging angel of the insulted faith." It is not unlikely that Bijns undertook this task after some prodding by Minorite acquaintances who knew her talent and temperament.

Whether Bijns really understood all the delicate nuances of the reformational arguments or the intricacies of Catholic orthodoxy at that very complex time hardly matters. Hers was the only strong Catholic voice in print against a whole army of anonymous Protestant poets. She saw the poet's—any poet's—mission as dual but indivisible: as a artist (s)he must draw beauty from pure devotion and as *miles christi* (s)he must make use of this talent in defense of the beleaguered Church.

As a sensitive woman from the ranks of the people, Bijns recognized that the excesses of both Reformation and Counter-Reformation were entangling ever more ordinary people, and she felt that the parish clergy were failing in their task as shepherds of the common flock. This attitude would explain the tone and lay-out of the polemic counter-reformational refrains that make up her first collection in print.

A thicker, more aggressive volume was published in 1548, this time openly under Franciscan aegis and perhaps not entirely under the author's control. Generally, Bijn's counter-reformational poems are specifically anti-Lutheran. She presents Luther as her personal enemy, his life as odious, and his doctrines as the devil's own. There is obviously no sophistication in her argument that murder, theft, sacrilege, countless orphans, and runaway monks are all evils directly traceable to Luther's greed and pride. Bijns's metaphorical arsenal and vituperative tone clearly suggest that it was her purpose to protect the ordinary, simple flock of well-meaning souls against Luther's temptations by means of a presentation of "Lutherie" as an utterly nauseating and blinded life-style. Images of light versus dark, health versus corruption, underlie her black-and-white ideas. She extracted hyperbolic images from execution scenes, daily life, and official revocations of former heretics, and her inductive and apostrophic arguments were designed to appeal to her audiences' emotions.

A third volume (over 250 pages) was published in 1567 as a fund-raiser for the restoration of the Franciscan monastery, which had fallen victim to a reformed arsonist's anger. This collection contains a variety of themes, and some refrains were already decades old. The general tone of the volume matched the rather defeatist *mea culpa* attitude of the Catholic camp, following the apparent success of the Reformation in Antwerp. The selection includes refrains very different from those previously published, such as tender expressions of self-accusation, contemplative meditation, Bonaventuran praises of Nature, *ars moriendi* poems, and refrains expressing pity for the damned.

At least until 1533, Bijns had been accumulating a body of "amorous" and "foolish" refrains twice the size of that of her counter-reformational and spiritual work. Published only in the late nineteenth century, these sometimes scatological, sometimes folksy, witty refrains reveal quite another Anna Bijns. Eros is treated whimsically. There are some sensitive anatomy refrains, for instance those with the "Bonaventura" acrostic—probably a reference to the Franciscan Bonaventura, a staunch advocate of celibacy and asceticism—but mostly the poems are bellicose and suggest amorous frustration. Bijns attacks male hypocrisy in many misandric refrains, and (typically) associates the unfaithful lover with Luther. "Man" is, like Luther, a faithless hypocrite. "Woman" is an innocent, trusting, easily ensnared believer. Some refrains express a rather grotesque view of marriage.

It is obvious that, for Bijns as a woman, independence comes first and that she sees Man, that wolf in sheep's clothing, as rather an inferior creature. Yet she is a poet full of surprises and contradictions, and so there are some genuinely tender love lyrics in the *oeuvre* of this versatile writer. Though her contra-reformational collections were published several times and earned her during her lifetime the epithet "Brabantian Sappho," and in spite of a highly unusual early translation into Latin of some of her work, Anna Bijns was buried with a pauper's service in the Cathedral of Antwerp. Her burial confirmed her life's motto: "Sour rather than sweet." By the time of her death in 1575, "Lutherie" was on the wane again, crushed under ever heavier Spanish pressure.

Katharina Boudewijns is generally considered the foremost of Bijns's successors, but this Brussels aristocrat had little, indeed, of the raciness of her Antwerp predecessor. Anna Bijns achieved mastery of the difficult rhetorical refrains to a greater degree than any other poet using that poetic form in the Dutch language. Bijns was also the first in her literature to deny the all importance of the rhyme scheme. No rigid syllable count clogs her refrains; rather, a rhythmical qualitative verse not earlier achieved in the language proved the perfect vehicle for her warm-blooded concerns.

Works

Konstighe Refereyne vol schoone Schrifturen ende Leeringhen (1646). *Den Gheestelijcken Nachtegael* (1623). *Anna Bijns, Refreinen* (1949). *Anna Bijns. Meer zuurs dan zoets* (1975).

Translations: "Anna Bijns, Lesbia Teutonica," in *Renaissance Women Writers* (1986), tr. Kristiaan Aercke with critical introduction. "Antwerp's Sharpest Tongue Against Luther," tr. Kristiaan Aercke, in *Vox Benedictina* II, 3 (1985): 224–238.

Kristiaan P. Aercke

Louise Cathrine Elisabeth Bjørnsen
1824–1899

a.k.a. Elisabeth Martens
Born April 9, 1824, Roholte, Denmark
Died December 27, 1899, Copenhagen
Genre(s): novel
Language(s): Danish

With her novels depicting the promise, hopes, and resignation of talented, intelligent women, Louise Cathrine Elisabeth Bjørnsen earned contemporary recognition and a faithful following of readers. Bjørnsen chose to depict the intellectual woman who often lives on the fringe of society, working for others economically better situated in life and resigning herself to a cordial "understanding," a less-than-passionate married life. Bjørnsen's works deal with idealistic, hopeful young women who ultimately (and necessarily) settle for less than they envision and deserve and then pay an additional price in bitterness, lost illusions, and regret.

Louise Cathrine Elisabeth Bjørnsen, born in Roholte, Denmark, on April 9, 1824, was the daughter of the parish priest in Kongsted, Frederik Cornelius Eberhard Bjørnsen (1781–1831), and Rebekka Adolphine Rabeholm (1786–1858). Bjørnsen's father died when she was still very young, and her education, in housekeeping and literature, fell completely to her mother, Rebekka Rabeholm.

Bjørnsen lived as a novelist until her death in Copenhagen on December 27, 1899; she never married. In 1855, Louise Bjørnsen made her literary debut with *Hvad er Livet?* (What Is Life?). Written under the pseudonym Elisabeth Martens, *Hvad er Livet* depicted "the position of the governess in society, familiar and intimate, but based on deprivation and insufficient employment opportunity for unmarried women" (Stig Dalager and Anne-Marie Mai, *Danske kvindelige forfattere* 1, 1983, p. 173). *Hvad er Livet* was an immediate success, followed by a second printing in 1857 and a third in 1881. *Hvad er Livet* traces the lives of Anna, "clever and industrious, the very best student in school," and Mathilde who "lacks ability and industry but (uses) her social status (to avoid) the teacher's reprimands." Bjørnsen employs her characters Anna and Mathilde in order to sketch two types of education for young women: the social education of Mathilde and Anna's practical knowledge and experience with the demands of living. Anna lives as a governess in the house of an affluent, influential family; she serves partially as society dame, partially as servant, (always) condescendingly treated by the household. Anna falls head over heels in love with a young painter, only to lose him to the favored, fortunate daughter of her "family"; Anna eventually marries into the civil service class, resigning the grand (romantic) love to a secure marriage. *Hvad er Livet* is a poignant account of a fate all too common for the daughters of the middle and poor classes. Reality for many such young women meant a large measure of resignation, bitterness, and disappointment.

Louise Bjørnsen's second novel, *En Qvinde* (1860; A Woman), also struck a responsive chord with the reading public; the work deals with the same theme as *Hvad er Livet*: resignation of hopes, dreams, and expectations. In *En Qvinde*, the protagonist, Thora, possesses both the material and intellectual gifts for emancipation; she writes, performs, composes, reads scholarly journals. Yet Thora's dreams and expectations come to naught; the narrator reveals and corrects Thora's faulty vision of the future, and the central character ends in complete resignation, with religious and social engagement as a replacement for the illusions of her youth. Both *Hvad er Livet* and *En Qvinde* reflect the moral tone, the bitterness, and the resignation of the first novels of Danish women writers. Bjørnsen continued her literary career with *Fortællinger* (1866; Stories); *Hvad behøvedes der for at leve?* (1869; What Was Necessary to Live?); *Fra Fortid og Nutid* (1878; From the Past and Present); and, *Til Høstaftenerne* (1893; For Autumn Evenings).

Such works did not win as much acclaim as her two earlier novels, but they did attract the attention of a firmly loyal circle of Bjørnsen readers. Two additional novels, *Sangerinder* (1876; Songstresses) and *To Søstre* (1890; Two Sisters), are important because of Bjørnsen's stylistic *rapprochement* to the social drama of the 1870s (*Sangerinder*) and because of the author's skillful, accurate portrayal of a young woman in love (*To Søstre*).

Louise Bjørnsen's novels won both contemporary audience and, later on, many steady, loyal readers. Her works, *Hvad er Livet* and *En Qvinde* among them, describe the hopes, dreams, and disappointments of many talented women bravely but idealistically facing life, work, and love on their own.

Works

Hvad er Livet (1855; 1857; 1881). *En Qvinde* (1860). *Fortællinger* (1866). *Hvad behøvedes der for at leve?* (1869). *Sangerinder* (1876). *Fra Fortid og Nutid* (1878). *To Søstre* (1890). *Til Høstaftenerne* (1893).

Lanae Hjortsvang Isaacson

Ana Blandiana
1942–

Born 1942, Timiş Dara, Romania
Genre(s): poetry, short story, essay, journalism, children's literature, translation
Language(s): Romanian

Ana Blandiana is the most important representative of a generation referred to in Romanian literary criticism as "the generation of the struggle against inertia."

She studied in Oradea and Cluj graduating in Philology in 1967, worked as an editor with *Viaţa studenţească* and *Amfiteatru* and, since 1975, as a librarian at the Institute of Fine Arts in Bucharest. She has been for a long time a regular columnist in the Writers' Union weekly magazine *România literară* and made her poetic debut in 1964 with the jubilant, intensely vital volume *Persoana întîi plural* (First Person Plural). This was followed by, at a regular pace, the volumes *Călcîiul vulnerabil* (1966; The Vulnerable Heel), and *A treia taină* (1969; The Third Sacrament), in which the voice of the poet is energetic and severe, proclaiming the Midas-like destiny of the writer ("All that I touch transforms into words") and acknowledging with lucid fervor and pain the "great law of maculation," which informs life, love, and reflec-

tion as well. In 1970 Blandiana was awarded the Poetry prize of the Writers' Union for *A treia taină* and published the first retrospective selection of poems—*Cincizeci de poeme* (Fifty Poems) which brought her the Mihai Eminescu Academy prize for poetry. The themes of sensual love, mature poetic consciousness, sin and purification, sarcasm and suffering combine in the strong volumes *Octombrie, noiembrie, decembrie* (1972; October, November, December), *Poezii* (1974; Poems), *Somnul din somn* (1977; The Sleep in Sleep), *Poeme* (1978; Poems, a retrospective selection published in the prestigious collection "Cele mai frumoase poezii" [The most beautiful poems] and prefaced by A. Philippide), and *Ora de nisip* (1983; Hour of Sand).

Blandiana is a unique singer of the couple, with its agonizing affective and cognitive complementations, blind spots, and atrophies ("You see only the moon, / I see only the sun, / You yearn for the sun, / I yearn for the moon, / But we stay back to back, / Bones united long ago, / Our blood carries rumours / From one heart to the other / . . . / How equal are we? / Are we to die together or will one of us carry, / For a time / The corpse of the other stuck to our side / Infecting with death, slowly, too slowly, / Or perhaps never to die completely / But carry for an eternity / The sweet burden of the other, / Atrophied forever, / The size of a hunch, / The size of a wart . . . / Oh, only we know the longing / To look into each other's eyes / And so at last understand, / But we stay back to back, / Grown like two branches / . . .")

At the same time, the poet put into words Romania's unnoticed "transhumance" (or "emigration") to sleep, dream, and *încănemoarte* (stillnotdeath), its gradual exit from human communication, its systematic destruction by "venomous winters," under moons "as precise as the handcuff(s)," its "almost happy despair." Blandiana's verse is, by now, one of the best introductions to a contemporary perception of existence in Romania ("It's snowing with malice, / The snow falls with hate / Above waters icy with loathing, / Above orchards blossomed by evil, / Above embittered birds who suffer, / . . . / Only I know / That once a flurry of snow / Was love at the beginning. — / It's so late / And hideously it's snowing, / And my mind's stopped working / So I wait / To be of use / To this wolf that's starving.").

In December 1984, Blandiana published in the student magazine *Amfiteatru* a group of poems that were widely circulated and intensely commented on throughout Romania. The authorities reacted by retrograding the poetry editor of the magazine and depriving the freelance author of the right to publish for several months. The best known among the incriminated poems came to be the poignant "Children's Crusade" in which the poet rose her voice against the official natalist policy forced upon Romanian women at times of economic and political disaster ("An entire people not yet born, but doomed for birth, / already in columns before being born, fetus next to fetus . . . / An entire nation which cannot see, cannot hear, / cannot understand, but which advances through / the cramps of woman's body by the blood and / womb of mothers which have not been asked"). Less explicit in its exasperated invocation of the commonplaces of daily misery, the companion poem "Totul" (Everything) remains an expression of the Eastern European ghetto in which the political connotations of each of the members of the enumeration are hard to understand for the Western readers who will perceive the hiatus between two different worlds rather than the blunt Romanian context to which Blandiana refers (". . . leaves, words, tears, / cans, cats, / streetcars from time to time, queueing for flour / [with] ladybugs, empty bottles, speeches, / eternal T.V. images, / Colorado bugs, gas, / little flags, the European championship [soccer] cup, / buses running with propane cylinders, / same old portraits, / apples not accepted abroad, / newspapers, rolls, / fake oil, carnations, / airport welcomes, cico lemonade, [chocolate] sticks, / Bucharest salami, diet yogurt, / Gypsy women selling Kent cigarettes, Crevedia eggs, / rumours, / the Saturday T.V. serial, / surrogate coffee, / the peoples' struggle for peace, the choirs, / the yield crop, Gerovital; the cops on Calea Victoriei, / the "Singing of Romania," adidas, / the Bulgarian compote, political jokes, Ocean fish, / everything").

A recent poem continues this political pamphlet trend in Blandiana's poetry. It speaks about President Ceausescu in the frame of the ancient (and itself problematic) Romanian myth of "Master builder Manole." Like Manole, who walled his wife and child in the church he was erecting to make sure the construction endures through time, Ceausescu the church-destroyer is paradoxically viewed as a ". . . builder of our private inferno . . . / Grand master surpassing all the others / Not through his knowledge, / but through the exasperation to build" who has managed to wall in a whole nation.

A volume regrouping the articles Blandiana had published under the rubric "Antijurnal" (Anti-journal) in the literary magazine *Contemporanul* appeared in 1970 under the title *Calitatea de martor* (The Quality of Witness). It marked the beginning of a sustained writing of essay and short stories, and was followed by the volumes *Eu scriu, tu scrii, el, ea scrie* (1976; I

Write, You Write, He, She Writes), *Cele patru aotimpuri* (1977; The Four Seasons), *Cea mai frumoasă dintre lumile posibile* (1982; The Most Beautiful of All Possible Worlds), and *Coridoare de oglinzi* (1984; Corridors of Mirrors); for this volume Blandiana was granted the 1984 Journalism prize of the Writers Union.

Blandiana's prose, centered upon moral meditation and the quest for superior transparence raises many of the acute ethical questions facing Romanian intellectuals today. It speaks in terms which deserve future analyses about the strength to persist in not winning (*Calitatea de martor*) and exposes the reader to contrasting perceptions of Europe, Romania, and the United States by a traveler whose soul stays poetic (*Cea mai frumoasă dintre lumile posibile*) or to the eternal dilemmas of choosing between speech and silence, acting and bearing, winning and losing which ground not only Blandiana's art but also her generation's basic encounter with life.

Works

Persoana întîi plural [First Person Plural] (1964). *Călcîiul vulnerabil* [The Vulnerable Heel] (1966). *A treia taină* [The Third Sacrament] (1969). *Cincizeci de poeme* [Fifty Poems] (1970). *Calitatea de martor* [The Quality of Witness] (1970; 2nd ed., 1972). *Octombrie, noiembrie, decembrie* [October, November, December] (1972). *Poezii* [Poems] (1974). *Convorbiri subiective* [Subjective Conversations] 1975). *Eu scriu, tu scrii, el, ea scrie* [I Write, You Write, He, She Writes] (1976). *Somnul din somn* [The Sleep in Sleep] (1977). *Cele patru anotimpuri* [The Four Seasons] (1977). *Poeme* [Poems], preface by A. Philippide (1978). *Cea mai frumoasă dintre lumile posible* [The Most Beautiful of All Possible Worlds] (1982). *Ora de nisip* [Hour of Sand] (1983). [With Romulus Rusan], *Coridoare de oglinzi* [Corridors of Mirrors] (1984).

Translations: Bosquet, Alain, ed., *Anthologie de la poésie roumaine.* (1968; "Elegie de dimineață"/"Pastel de matin"; "Fii înțelept"/"Sois sage"; and "Din clipa . . ."/"C'est à partir . . ." tr. Claude Sernet; "Ar trebui"/"il faudrait" tr. Alain Bosquet). De Micheli, Mario, ed. and tr., *Poeti romeni del dopoguerra* (1967; "Triptic"/"Trittico"). *Literatura rumana contemporánea*, in *Union,* special issue dedicated to contemporary Romanian literature (1968; "Ochii statuilor"/"Los ojos de las estatuas," "Calmă"/"Cálma" tr. Belkis Cuza Malé). Mesker, Stefan, ed., *Werk uit Roemenie. Poëzie* (1966; "Elegie de dimineață"/ "Ochtendpastel"). *Poesía rumana actual,* special issue, *Cuadernos Hispanoamericanos* 221 (1968) ("Ochii statuilor"/"Los ojos de las estatuas"; "Iarba"/"La hierba"). *Poètes et prosateurs roumains d'aujourd'hui*, special issue, *Marginales. Revue bimestrielle des Idées, des Arts et des Lettres* 23 (1968): 119–120 ("Elegie de dimineață"/"Pastel du matin"; "Din clipa . . ."/ "Dès l'instant . . ."). Sarov, Taško, ed. and tr., *Antologija na romanskata poezija* (1972; "Pieta"; "Goană"/ "Gonenje"). *Signos* 1, issue dedicated to Romania (1970) ("Iarba"/"La hierba"; "Ora spitalelor"/"Hora de los hospitales"). Špoljanskaja, D., ed., *Šal'noe leto—Molodye pisateli Rumynii. Stihi i proza.* (1968; "Restul pe masă"/"Sdača na stole"; "Fii înțelept"/"Bud' mudrym"; "În liniștea mare"/"Spokojstvie"; "Știu, puritatea . . ."/"Kto zaet . . ."; "Ora spitalelor"/"Čas bol'nic"; "Pînă la stele"/"Do zvezd" tr. V. Kornilova). *30 poeți români/ 30 poètes roumains* (1978; "Genealogie"/"Généalogie" and "Din auster și din naivitate"/"L'austère et la naïveté" tr. Irina Radu).

English Translations: Deletant, Andrea, and Brenda Walker, tr., *Silent Voices. An Anthology of Contemporary Romanian Women Poets* (1986), pp. 21–36 (poems from *Octombrie, noiembrie, decembrie*, 1972; *Somnul din somn*, 1977, and *Ora de nisip*, 1983). Duțescu, Dan, ed. and tr., *Romanian Poems* (1982), pp. 231–233 ("Fall," "Herder of Snowflakes," and "Which One of Us"). Emery, George, ed., *Contemporary East European Poetry* (1983), pp. 344–347 ("From a Village," "Song," and "Dance in the Rain" tr. Irina Livezeanu; "Links" tr. Michael Impey). Impey, Michael H., tr., "Three Romanian Poems—Ana Blandiana; Constanța Buzea; Gabriela Melinescu. Translated from the Romanian by M.H.I.," *Books Abroad* 50, 1 (1976): 34–35. MacGregor-Hastie, Roy, ed. and tr., *Anthology of Contemporary Romanian Poetry* (1969) ("Din clipa . . ."/"From That Moment . . .").

Sanda Golopentia

Ilse Blumenthal-Weiss
1899–1987

Born October 14, 1899, Berlin-Schöneberg, Germany
Died August 10, 1987, Greenwich, Connecticut
Genre(s): poetry
Language(s): German

Ilse Blumenthal-Weiss has only very recently begun to receive recognition as a poet, although her first postwar collection appeared in 1954. Since she failed to leave Europe and spent the war years in a concentration camp, she did not fit the standard definition of an "exile poet" and, accordingly, was not included in the numerous scholarly studies of exile literature. Now, however, her poetry is coming to be acknowledged as one of the most poignant memorials to the victims of the Holocaust.

Blumenthal-Weiss, the daughter of Gottlieb Weiss, the owner of a large clothing store, and Hedwig Weiss-Brock, led an active and eventful life in pre-Hitler Germany. She earned a diploma as a physical education teacher, traveled extensively, corresponded with Rilke, and published a volume of poetry, *Gesicht und Maske* (1929; Face and Mask). She married the dentist Herbert Blumenthal in 1920. In 1937 she fled to Holland, where she remained until being deported to Theresienstadt in 1944. Her husband and son Peter died in concentration camps. After the war Blumenthal-Weiss and her daughter Miriam emigrated to the United States. For many years she lived in New York, where she worked as a librarian at the Leo Baeck Institute.

In the verse of *Das Schlüsselwunder* (1954; The Key Miracle) and *Mahnmal* (1957; Memorial), traditional forms predominate and the content is with few exceptions based on the Holocaust. In spite of the general similarities, there is a wide variety of form (blank verse and numerous stanzaic and rhyme patterns), tone (from satiric to elegiac), and perspective (personal and universal, religious, humanistic, and, in a broad sense, political). *Ohnesarg* (1984; Coffinless) is also dominated by the memory of the Holocaust, but the form and style of the poems are less traditional: most are written in a laconic free verse. This book also contains an interesting factual account of the author's experiences during the war.

Blumenthal-Weiss will be remembered as one of the few survivors of a concentration camp to memorialize the victims of the Holocaust in German verse. Although not a prolific poet, her wide range of thematic variations and poetic forms is reflective of the variety of responses to the Holocaust.

Works

Gesicht und Maske (1929). *Das Schlüsselwunder: Gedichte* (1954). *Mahnmal: Gedichte aus dem KZ* (1957). *Begegnungen mit Else Lasker-Schueler, Nelly Sachs, Leo Baeck, Martin Buber* (1977). *Ohnesarg: Gedichte und ein dokumentarischer Bericht* (1984).

Jerry Glenn

Anne-Marie Fiquet du Bocage
1710–1802

Born October 22, 1710, Rouen, France
Died August 8, 1802, Paris
Genre(s): poetry, drama, letters, travel writing
Language(s): French

The life and professional literary career of the celebrated Mme Bocage records one of the most privileged examples of female achievement and notoriety in the eighteenth century.

Unlike so many literary women of the early-modern era, Bocage enjoyed the distinct advantages of a comfortable and enlightened family background, formal education in the liberal arts, a supportive and literary spouse, and opportunities to benefit from the work of her contemporaries through extensive travel and the cultural exposure of the salon world. She reportedly was also a great beauty and gifted conversationalist. The motto of her admirers was "*Forma Venus, arte Minerva*" ("A Venus in form, a Minerva in art"). Voltaire, an ally, called her "La Sappho de Normandie." Fontenelle and Clairaut were also enthusiastic promoters of her work.

Bocage was born into a well-established, bourgeois family of Rouen, the La Pages. Her father, a successful official with the Department of Commerce, encouraged the precocious Bocage from an early age to develop her obvious aptitude for writing, especially poetry. After formal training at an exclusive Parisian convent, Bocage married, at the age of seventeen, Pierre-Joseph Fiquet du Bocage, an established poet-translator with special interests in English literature (see his *Melanges*, 3 vols., 1751; and his *Lettres*, 2 vols., 1752). These two devotees of the contemporary cultural scene became well known throughout the Rouen arts community. Around 1734, they began to spend about eight months of each year in Paris, where their custom was to open up their house one night each week to the literati of the city. The Bocage salon in Paris attracted French, British, American, Italian, and German writers and intellectuals. Jean-François Marmontel, a chronicler of eighteenth-century salon life, complained, however, that the Bocage salon lacked the color and verve of other contemporary salons.

In addition to their salon activities, the Bocages traveled throughout England, Holland, and Italy. Mme Bocage, in her diverting letters to her sister, provides a good account of their travels, and she also documents the international recognition given her and her husband. This particular body of literature shows Mme Bocage to be a skilled and entertaining epistolarist and valuable travel writer, whose eye for foreign manners and morals compares most favorably with that of her celebrated English contemporaries in the genre—Mrs. Thrale, Lady Mary Wortley Montagu, and Celia Fiennes.

Mme Bocage did not rush into the public light of professional authorship, but rather launched her career in her mid-thirties, after first having benefited from the guidance of parents, educators, spouse, and distinguished friends, and from extensive travel and cultural exposure. It was not until 1746, at the age of thirty-six, that Mme Bocage distinguished herself as a literary professional. In that year, she won the First Prize for Poetry from The Academy of Rouen for her verse "De influence mutuel des beaux-arts et des sciences" ("On the Mutual Influence of the Fine Arts & the Sciences"). Bocage's maiden success was followed by her *Le Paradis terrestre* (1748), a poem inspired by John Milton's great epic *Paradise Lost*. Her *Paradis*, cast as an epilogue to Milton's poem, was harshly criticized by the German writer Friedrich Melchior Grimm as a cold, servile imitation of its English master. Johann Christoph Gottsched was more supportive. In his *Anmuthige Celehrsamketi* (1754), he instances Bocage's poem as an example of the equality of the female mind. Other contemporary supporters of Bocage's work, outside of France, included the Spanish writer Ignacio de Luzan (*Memorias literarias de Paris*, 1750) and Josefa Amar y Borbon ("Discuso," *Mem. Lit.*, 32, 1786). Bocage's Miltonic imitation was followed by another work, also inspired by a great English poet, Alexander Pope, whose *Temple of Fame* (1715) Bocage adapted in her *Temple de la Renommee* (1749).

One of Bocage's principal longer works, and the one best known today, especially by feminists, is her play *Les Amazones* (1749), performed by the Comediens Ordinaire du Roi eleven times in July and August of 1749. Although it was widely translated (into Italian, 1756; into German, 1762), Bocage's *Amazones* was only a middling success. Precedents for the play's theme, gynecocracy (the rule of women), existed in the writings of the late medieval French feminist Christine de Pizan, as well as in the plays of several seventeenth-century English male playwrights—Fletcher (*Sea Voyage*, 1622), Howard (*Woman's Conquest*, 1670 and *Six Days Adventure*, 1671), D'Urfey (*Commonwealth of Women*, 1685), et al. Assuming the existence of an Amazon state as historical fact, Bocage represents her heroines as feminist paradigms of capable governance and high civic principles, even if their ideology is tested by Queen Orinthe's fatal love for Theseus, King of Athens. Although a tragedy, Bocage's play does not conclude with the dissolution of the matriarchal community. The dialogues in the play between the Amazon Menalippe and Theseus lay out the principles of the Amazon "counterculture" (quite literally) and reflect to some degree the more extreme features of radical seventeenth- and eighteenth-century feminist thought, which surely attracted the conservative but intellectually alert Bocage and her sororal circle. Regrettably, she was embarrassed during the run of *Les Amazones* by charges of plagiarism. It was thought that the play's authentic author was either her friend Abbe de Resnel or Monsieur Linaut. Perhaps because of this episode, which slightly blemished her early reputation, Bocage never again wrote for the stage. (French women, it might be noted, would not begin to make significant advances in the theater until the work of Mme de Graffigny, in the 1750s.)

Bocage's *Amazones* was followed in 1756 with an original epic poem that suggested an apparent change in her literary repertoire, *La Columbiadne* (1756). This long poem of ten cantos celebrated the discovery of America and the heroism of Columbus. It also revealed Bocage's continuing interest in historical models of individuality and accomplishment. Bocage's feminist attraction to the Amazon prototype is still apparent, several years later, in *Columbiadne*, when Columbus falls in love with a powerful Indian queen, described by Bocage as a "mighty Amazon," more ferocious than Penthesilea.

During the 1760s, Bocage returned to her fondness for imitation and produced *La Mort d'Abel*, a paraphrase in verse of *Tod Abels* (1758), a species of idyllic heroic prose-poems by Salomon Gessner, a Swiss pastoral poet. Bocage's choice of subject matter again demonstrates her preoccupation with heroic figures of the past. With the death of her devoted husband in August 1767, she was left a relatively wealthy widow, free to pursue her literary interests with minimal domestic and social obligations.

Overall, Bocage's *oeuvre* shows a broad range of genres: verse-drama, light social verse, epic verse, pastoral verse, travel literature, and letter writing. She was most successful as a writer of society verse, then much in vogue. But Bocage also distinguished herself as a student of feminism, even if her writings are not stridently polemical (cf. Marie du Gournay, Jacquette Guillaume). Bocage was a delightful, fresh presence on the eighteenth-century literary scene, and she attracted wide attention on the Continent and in England. Several recent scholars of eighteenth-century women writers have begun to give fresh attention to Bocage, resulting in new editions of her work; useful investigations into her life, supportive networks, and career; valuable contextualizations of her broad literary achievement, addressing its visionary features; and original analyses of the sensitive intersection of gender and publicity in the print culture of eighteenth-century France.

Works

De influence mutuel des beaux-arts et des sciences (1746). *Lettre de Madam * * * . . . sur l'Opera comique* (1746). *Le Paradis terrestre, poem imite de Milton* (1746; sometimes recorded "1748"). *Temple de la Renommee*, translation of Pope's *Temple of Fame*, 1715 (1749). *Les Amazones, tragedie en cinq actes* (1749). *Lettres de Madame du Bocage* (1750, 1757, 1758). *La Columbiadne, ou la Foi portee au Nouveau Monde* (1756). *La Mort d'Abel* (1760). *Le Recueil des Oeuvres de Mme du Bocage*. 3 vols. (1762, 1764, 1770). *Lettres Concerning England, Holland, and Italy, By the celebrated Madame du Bocage . . . written during her Travels. Translated from the French*, 2 vols. (1770). *Oeuvres poetiques editees de Madame du Bocage*, 2 vols. (1788).

Maureen E. Mulvihill

Cecilia Böhl de Faber y Larrea
1796–1877

a.k.a. Fernán Caballero
Born December 25 or 27, 1796, Morges, Switzerland
Died April 7, 1877, Sevilla, Spain
Genre(s): novel, short story
Language(s): Spanish

Fernán Caballero was the unusual product of an unlikely alliance between a German Hispanicist and an early Spanish feminist who also espoused Catholic traditionalist views. This rich and divergent cultural background would play a key role in her intellectual and literary development. Another influence came later in the lively friendship she struck up with Washington Irving in 1828–1829. Undoubtedly, the experience of her three marriages would also sift indirectly into her fiction, most notably in *Clemencia* (1852). Her first husband, Captain Planels, was, by all accounts, a brute, but mercifully for Cecilia died in 1817. She then married the Marqués of Arco-Hermoso in 1822, who unfortunately left her afterward in much strained economic circumstances. Sometime after his death in 1835, she met an English aristocrat whom we know from correspondence only as "Federico Cuthbert." It was a short, unhappy love affair. This 1836 episode was followed by one last attempt at matrimony in 1837, when Cecilia, then almost forty-one, married twenty-three-year-old Antonio Arrom de Ayala. In 1859 Arrom de Ayala committed suicide after a series of financial and business debacles. Fernán Caballero's last years were lonely ones, marked by gradual impoverishment and emotional depression over her own life and the fall of her patroness, Queen Isabel II, in 1868. By the time she died in 1877, her literary fortunes and popularity were on the wane, and a rising young writer, Benito Pérez Galdós, would soon surpass the tentative and contradictory strides she had made toward the modern realist novel.

Fernán Caballero's best-known novel, *La Gaviota* (The Sea Gull), originally appeared in 1849 as a magazine serial (several of her novels and stories would first see the light in this form). She was immediately hailed as the "Spanish Sir Walter Scott." Given the rather barren literary period—1850–1870—it is not surprising that the idealized setting, lachrymose romanticism and melodramatic touches of *La Gaviota* would be equally appealing for its fresh realistic sketches of the Andalusian character and customs. Fernán Caballero's enthusiasm and love for local folkways and traditional beliefs spilled over into several volumes of *costumbrista* sketches and tales (sometimes also awkwardly inserted in her longer fiction).

Cecilia's ideological outlook is essentially one of romantic conservatism, that is, an idealized embellishment of Spain's Catholic and monarchical institutions, emphasizing submission to authority and the natural adherence to customs and a living tradition. Her hostility to modern-day liberalism and foreign influence surfaced in such ideologically polarized fictions as *Elia, o la España treinta años ha* (1857; Elia, or Spain Thirty Years Ago) and *Un servilón y un liberalito, o tres almas de Dios* (1859; A Loyalist and a Liberal, or Three Souls of God). On an individual level, conservatism, when disclosed in personal and especially marital relationships, meant a strong and sometimes quite inflexible belief in the application of reason to sentiment. Such is the case for *Clemencia*: here, the beneficent and civilized use of reason as opposed to the savagely destructive force of passion (and more explicitly, raw sexuality) is the principal dichotomy exploited imagistically as the tension between civilization-garden and barbarism (i.e., passion)-tree.

Despite her ideological distortions, overtly moralizing stance, and failure to move beyond *costumbrismo*, Fernán Caballero cannot be lightly dismissed in Spanish literary history. As the initiator of both the regional novel and the thesis novel of ideological conflict, she remains a significant figure in the renaissance of nineteenth-century Spanish narrative.

There are six Madrid editions of her *Complete Works*, none reliable (the first in 1855–1858, and the latest in 1917–1928). Several of her novels—*La Gaviota* (1972), *Clemencia* (1975), *Elia* (1968), *La familia de Alvareda* (1979)—have been reedited in more accessible, modern editions.

Works
Clemencia (1852). *Cuadros de costumbres populares andaluzas* (1852). *Lágrimas* (1853). *La estrella de Vandalia* (1855). *Obras completas*, 19 vols. (1855–1858). *Con mal o con bien a los tuyos te ten* (1856). *La familia de Alvareda* (1856). *La Gaviota* (1856). *Una en otra* (1856). *Cuadros de costumbres* (1857). *Elia, o la España treinta años ha* (1857). *Lady Virginia* (1857). *Relaciones* (1857). *Un verano en Bornos* (1858). *Cuentos y poesías populares andaluces* (1859). *Un servilón y un liberalito, o tres almas de Dios* (1859). *Deudas pagadas* (1860). *Vulgaridad y nobleza* (1860). *San Telmo, recuerdos del l de enero de 1861* (1861). *El Alcázar de Sevilla* (1862–1863). *Colección de artículos religiosos y morales* (1862). *La farisea* (1863). *Las dos gracias o la expiación* (1865). *La mitología* (1867). *Cuentos, oraciones, adivinas y refranes populares e infantiles* (1877). *Epistolario* (1912). *El refranero del campo y poesías populares* (1912–1914). *Obras de Fernán Caballero*, 5 vols. (1961).

Translations: *Alvareda Family* [La familia de Alvareda] (1872). *Elia, or Spain Fifty Years Ago* [Elia] (1868). *The Old and the New* [Un servilón y un liberalito] (1882). *The Sea Gull* [La Gaviota] (1965). See also R.S. Rudder, *The Literature of Spain in English Translation* (1975).

Noël M. Valis

Elisabeth Borchers
1926–
Born February 27, 1926, Homberg/Niederrhein, Germany
Genre(s): poetry, short story, radio drama, children's literature, essay, translation
Language(s): German

Elisabeth Borchers grew up in Alsace and worked, after studies in France and the United States, at the University for Designing in Ulm. She lived in Neuwied and Berlin from 1960 to 1971. Since 1971 she has been working as a reader for a publishing house. Her poems excel in mystic metaphors and a different kind of reality. In her short stories she reveals the ordinary life of the common man in modern society. *Eine glückliche Familie* (A Happy Family) talks about the triviality of the German and American affluent society. Borchers's radio plays became very popular in Germany and abroad. She also demonstrated her skills in numerous translations. She received the Radio Prize and the Writer's Prize of the South German Radio Station in 1967 for her radio play *Rue des Pompiers* from her collection *Nacht aus Eis* (Night Full of Ice). In 1967 she received the Cultural Prize of the German Industry and in 1976 the Roswitha-Medal from the City of Gandersheim.

Works

Poems: *Gedichte* [Poems] (1961). *Der Tisch, an dem wir sitzen* [The Table, at Which We Are Sitting] (1967). *Gedichte* [Poems] (1976). *Wer lebt* [He Who Is Living] (1986).

Radio plays: *Nacht aus Eis. Szenen und Spiele* [Night Full of Ice. Scenes and Games] (1965). *Feierabend* [After Work] (1965). *Rue des Pompiers* (1965). *Anton S. oder die Möglichkeiten* [Anton S. or the Possibilities] (1967). *Ist die Stadt denn verschlossen* [Is the City Locked?] (1967).

Children books and short stories: with D. Blech, *Erzählungen: Bi, Be, Bo, Ba, Bu—die Igelkinder* [Short Stories: Bi, Be, Bo, Ba, Bu—The Hedge Hog Children] (1962). [With D. Blech], *Und oben schwimmt die Sonne davon* [And Above Us the Sun Is Swimming Away] (1965). *Das alte Auto* [The Old Car] (1965). *Das rote Haus in einer kleinen Stadt* [The Red House in a Small Town] (1970). *Eine glückliche Familie* [A Happy Family, short stories] (1970). *Das große Lalula* [The Big Lalula] (1971). *Papperlapapp sagt Herr Franz der Rennfahrer* [Papperlapapp says Mr. Franz the Car Racer] (1971). *Schöner Schnee* [Beautiful Snow] (1972). *Das sehr nützliche Merk-Buch für Geburtstage* [The Very Useful Memory Book for Birthdays] (1975). *Briefe an Sarah* [Letters to Sarah] (1977). *Die Zeichenstunde* [The Drawing Hour] (1977). *Das Insel-Buch für Kinder* [The Insel Book for Children] (1979). *Das Adventbuch* [The Advent Book] (1979). with W. Schlote, *Paul und Sarah oder wenn zwei sich was wünschen* [Paul and Sarah, or When Two Are Wishing Something] (1979). with W. Schlote, *Heut wünsch ich mir ein Nilpferd* [Today I Am Wishing a Hippopotamus] (1981). with L. Brierly, *Der König der Tiere und seine Freunde* [The King of the Animals and His Friends].

Essays: *Lektori salutem* (1978).

Translations: *Poems*, tr. Ruth and Matthew Mead (1969).

Albrecht Classen

Anna Louisa Geertruida Bosboom-Toussaint
1812–1886

Born September 16, 1812, Alkmaar, The Netherlands
Died April 13, 1886, 's-Gravenhage
Genre(s): novella, historical novel
Language(s): Dutch

A descendant of Huguenot refugees, Geertruida (Truitje) Bosboom-Toussaint became Holland's most prolific and popular nineteenth-century historical novelist.

After her broken engagement to the critic and historian R.C. Bakhuizen van den Brink, she moved into lodgings, unmarried, at age thirty-six—a thing unheard of among the respectable Dutch bourgeoisie of the period. (It is no coincidence that independent and headstrong women occasionally occur in her work.) In 1851, she married the painter Jan Bosboom, five years her junior. By that time, she had already established herself as a major writer.

Her debut novella, *Almagro* (1937), was based on an episode of Schiller's *Die Räuber. De graaf van Devonshire* (1838; The Count of Devonshire), Bosboom-Toussaint's first historical novel, was inevitably inspired by Sir Walter Scott and the French Romantics, but it also announced her own specific use of the genre. The historical facts, though meticulously documented and researched, serve mainly as a background for the psychological conflicts of the protagonists.

Bosboom-Toussaint chose the seventeenth century—Holland's most glorious period—as the setting of her next major novel, *Het huis Lauernesse* (1840; The House of Lauernesse). This was in line with the leading critical journal *De Gids*, which wanted Holland to produce a proud nationalistic literature of its own. The treatment of the material, however, clearly bore the author's own stamp. Using a complex plot involving the story of a young noblewoman who angers and alienates her Roman Catholic fiancé by adopting the reformed religion, Bosboom-Toussaint depicted the sometimes drastic effect of the Reformation on social and domestic life. It became her most popular work.

Her most ambitious piece of work is certainly the Leicester series (1846–1855), which some critics regard as her masterpiece. In an attempt to "interpret" history, Bosboom-Toussaint pictured Leicester very favorably. He may have failed as a statesman (e.g., his abortive mission in Holland), but he was saved as a Christian because he preserved his spiritual integrity. Other important historical novels are *Graaf Pepoli*

(1860; Count Pepoli) and the three-volume *De Delftsche wonderdokter* (1870–1871; The Delft Quack).

Though Bosboom-Toussaint also wrote some minor novels—an apparent effort to alleviate her family's constant money problems—she undoubtedly stood out among contemporary historical novelists, such as Oltmans and Van Lennep, not in the least because she was able to combine romantic sentimentality and imagination (adventures, escapes, disguises . . .) with skillful characterization and a "modern" psychological approach. She was a master at writing dialogues and devising complex, dramatic plots. Her style occasionally suffered from ornamentality and digressions slowing down the plot line. Curious is the deliberate use of archaic language (on the instigation of *De Gids*), which sometimes led to unwanted anachronistic effects.

Her religious views, present throughout her work, are akin to those of the Réveil, a conservative evangelical movement of the period. In *Het Huis Lauernesse*, which was basically meant as a tribute to Holland's reformist fervor, Bosboom-Toussaint did not refrain from referring to the pain and destruction caused by the religious schism. Her sympathy clearly lies with figures who embody Christian humanistic ideals rather than fanatic militancy, such as the kind-hearted preacher in *Het Huis Lauernesse* or Gideon Florenzs, Leicester's religious counselor in the book of the same name.

Two works are of special interest to modern feminist criticism: *Mejonkvrouwe de Mauléon* (1848; Mademoiselle de Mauléon), a historical novel about Bossuet's alleged mistress, and *Majoor Frans* (1874; Major Francis), a contemporary novel of manners made up of letters and journal fragments. In Bosboom-Toussaint's interpretation, Mademoiselle de Mauléon sacrificed her love for Bossuet to the higher ideals of the Church and, as the author suggests with characteristic insight, to his career as a prominent churchman. Yolande de Mauléon, like the woman hiding behind the nickname Major Francis, is the victim of malicious gossipers for whom young unattached women are naturally suspect. The clearly emancipationist note in *Majoor Frans*—the protagonist wants to be financially independent and has but little respect for received values—is toned down at the end when she fulfills her greatest wish, subjecting herself to the man she loves (a rich heir into the bargain) and serving him.

Truitje Bosboom-Toussaint was not only immensely popular with the general public, she was also on equal footing with the major men of letters of the period. She seemed to have emancipated herself successfully, though not without difficulty, from the condescending tone with which women writers were usually approached. When, at the peak of her career, she was criticized by the religious authorities for the lack of an edifying message in *Majoor Frans*, Bosboom-Toussaint, a devout Christian herself, typically replied that she did not consider it necessary to "constantly psalmodize in order to fight for the true religion."

Works

Almagro (1837). *De graaf van Devonshire* (1838). *Het Huis Lauernesse* (1840). *Eene kroon voor Karel den Stouten* (1842). *De graaf van Leycester in Nederland. De vrouwen uit het Leycestersche tijdvak. Gideon Florensz* (1846–1855). *Mejonkvrouwe de Mauléon* (1848). *Het huis Honselaarsdijk in 1638* (1849). *Media-Noche* (1852). *Graaf Pepoli* (1860). *De Delftsche wonderdokter* (1870–1871). *Majoor Frans* (1874; film version, 1915). *Langs een omweg* (1878). *Raymond de schrijnwerker* (1880). *Het kasteel Westhoven op Walcheren in Zeeland* (1882). *Volledige romantische werken* (25 vols., 1885–1888; rpt. 1898–1901). Tazelaar, C. *Onuitgegeven brieven van mevrouw Bosboom-Toussaint* (1934).

Translations: *Major Francis* [*Majoor Frans*], tr. J. Ackroyd (1885).

Ria Vanderauwera

Katharina Boudewijns
ca. 1520–1603

Born ca. 1520, Brussels, Belgium
Died after 1603, Brussels
Genre(s): contrareformational and dramatic poetry, translation
Language(s): Dutch

The daughter of the Clerk to the mighty Council of Brabant, Katharina married another aristocrat, Nicholas de Zoette, lawyer and secretary to the same Council. When Nicholas died, his well-educated wife was left with five children. She then acquired the protection of the Countess d'Arenberg, as appears from the dedication of Boudewijns' collection of spiritual poetry, *Het Prieelken der Gheestelijker Wellusten* (1587, 1603; The Bower of Spiritual Voluptuousness).

In this volume Boudewijns used rhetoricians' poetical forms to express her disappointment with the Calvinist domination of Brussels (1581–1586). Calvinist rule resulted, for example, in the temporary closing of churches. Genuine fear arose among Catholics concerning the future of their creed in Brussels and the Southern Netherlands. Boudewijns' sensitive poems do not seem to have been intended as a bulwark for Catholic orthodoxy to check Calvinist (and democratic) progress. Very much unlike the polemical rhetoric and the virulent scorn heaped upon the followers of the Reformation some decades earlier by the Antwerp teacher Anna Bijns, Boudewijns's resigned and rather nostalgic lyric poetry expresses consolatory concerns in a quite impersonal style. Her longing for mystical (re)union with the Lost Husband is almost purely medieval. More refined than Anna Bijns, more medieval in inspiration, Boudewijns is also a far more discreet poet. Invectives are scarce in her poetry, and the conventional catalogue of the opponents' vices and sins in contrareformational poetry is reduced to the charge of rebellion, of tyranny. The lack of humility and obedience of the Calvinists must surely lead to spiritual and economic decline, according to Boudewijns. A despairing tone of *fin du siècle* awareness can thus be detected in her poetry, which emphasizes the return to God and Christ as the only alternative to the evil of the times.

In the 1580s, Boudewijns also wrote a brief morality play. Very likely this *Schoon Spel van Sinnen van Twee Personen, te weten Liefde ende Eendrachtigheyt* (A Beautiful Morality for Two Persons, to Wit Love and Concord), was never performed. The allegorical voices of Love and Concord debate the issues of contemporary vice; Concord has to concede that embracing a pure and blessed poverty is the only way toward a better life for "radix malorum est cupiditas."

Boudewijns also responded to the contemporary interest in systems of meditation and the improvement of one's personal spiritual life. In 1567, she translated into Dutch a Spanish tract on discretion, "very necessary and profitable for all those aspiring to Christian perfection," by Seraphin de Fermo (Brussels, 1568).

Works

Het Prieelken der Gheestelijker Wellusten (1927). "Het Prieelken der Gheestelijker Wellusten," "Een Schoon Spel van Sinnen van Twee Personen . . . ," and various other poems, in *Het Prieelken der Gheestijker Wellusten* (1872). *Een schoon tractaet, sprekende van der excellenter Deucht des Discretiens* (1568).

Kristiaan P. Aercke

Elizabeth (Dorothea Cole) Bowen
1899–1973

Born June 7, 1899, Dublin
Died February 22, 1973, London
Genre(s): novel, short story
Languages(s): English

Like two scissors blades working against one another, Bowen's identification with the Anglo-Irish gentry and her sense of being an outsider to English culture sharpen her perception of social change during the twentieth century. Her characters fascinate and engage readers' imaginations, but her plots are sometimes improbable. Her elegant prose encompasses both the distortions of her characters' observations and the cold-eyed judgment of an authorial intelligence. Influenced by Marcel Proust, Henry James, and Jane Austen, Bowen utilized their technical narrative devices, but her fiction, rarely solemn, succeeds by exploiting the witty, satirical insights of moral comedy.

At the age of seven, Bowen was moved from Dublin to Folkestone, on the coast of Kent, and she credits that split between her Irish heredity and her English childhood with making her a novelist. She was raised by her mother alone after her father certified himself insane. At the age of thirteen, Bowen lost her mother to cancer (Bowen herself later died of lung cancer), and her aunt assumed responsibility for her niece's education and social training. Bowen transformed some of her schoolgirl experiences in *The Little Girls* (1964), and she set down her impressions of the Kentish resort town "Seale-on-Sea" in several of her novels. In 1917, she left school to live with her recovered father in Ireland, which had been occupied by the British army since 1916. The Bowens, as members of the Anglo-Irish gentry, entertained the British officers, and Bowen was briefly engaged to a British lieutenant. Without a clear sense of vocation, Bowen attended a London school of art for two terms, quit, and began her literary career by showing some short stories to the established novelist Rose Macaulay, who offered both encouragement and introductions to the London literary circles. Bowen's first collection of stories, *Encounters,* was published in 1923, the same year Bowen married a British World War I veteran, Alan Cameron, with whom she lived until his death in 1952. The couple resided where his work as educational administrator took them, first to Northamptonshire, then to Oxford in 1925, to London in 1935. After spending World War II in London, they chose to retire in County Cork at Bowen's Court.

As the only child of an Anglo-lrish landowner, Bowen inherited Bowen's Court in 1930 and, as long as she was financially able, spent part of each year writing and entertaining at her Irish country estate. During 1921, she had feared Bowen's Court would be burned down by Irish rebels; her nightmares prompted by that fear are recorded in her novel, *The Last September* (1929). Bowen often retreated to Bowen's Court to write in solitude. Her love for the great house and her sense of being rooted there may be seen in the family history she wrote, *Bowen's Court* (1942).

Bowen's first novel, *The Hotel* (1927) succeeds as a satirical comedy of a young woman, Sydney, attracted too suddenly to the sexuality of an older man. In the character of Mrs. Kerr, Bowen creates the first of many overly protective aunts and mothers who break off the young heroines' precipitous love affairs.

The Last September (1929), set during the Irish civil war, depicts the conflicting loyalties and hostilities felt by the Anglo-Irish gentry for their Irish tenants and their English guests. Lois, the heroine, loves the Irish great house which closely resembles Bowen's Court, but she also loves an English soldier stationed in Ireland. In a lightly comic style, Bowen depicts the nineteen-year-old Lois's inexperience: "She could not remember, though she had read so many books, who spoke first after a kiss had been, not exchanged but— administered." Her aunt, Lady Naylor, discourages Lois's lover by suggesting, first, that Lois is too young, and, then, that the young man is too far below her class. Suddenly shifting to tragedy, Bowen has the English soldier killed and has Lady Naylor's great house burned by the Irish rebels.

Bowen's third novel, *Friends and Relations* (1931), is a competent light comedy. Her sharply focused comic vision produced Elfrida's entrance: "Down the long shop, narrow and cumbered like the past, with its dull mirrors, she came very tall, *distraite,* balancing nervously in her speed like a ship just launched." *To the North* (1932) is a better novel, because Bowen makes her readers believe the naive, humorless character of Emmeline, slow to make connections. When Markie almost apologizes for not wanting to marry her, saying, "Sorry. . . . But you knew I was always out for what I could get," Emmeline does begin to see, but, nevertheless, she compliantly continues their relationship. In an unconvincing and melodramatic conclusion, Emmeline drives with reckless speed, as if trying to escape the past, though Markie is her passenger in the car; as they crash, her final word to him is "Sorry."

In her next novel, *The House in Paris* (1935), Bowen explores the divided personality of Karen, who becomes a deceiver in order to carry on an illicit affair with Max. Less impressively, Bowen characterizes Max as a French Jew, treating his rootlessness unsympathetically, and she ridicules his nervous fiancee, Naomi, because her eyes "start out of her head." In this history, "fate . . . creeps like a rat."

Bowen's two finest novels, *The Death of the Heart* (1938) and *The Heat of the Day* (1949), depict characters who respond to contemporary moral problems. *The Death of the Heart* explores the cultural and psychological aftermath of World War I through the overly sensitive perceptions of an adolescent orphan, Portia, who has come to live in London with her brother, Thomas, and her sister-in-law, Anna. *The Heat of the Day* explores the psychological and moral problems of loyalty in the context of the trying years of World War II.

Her lyrical, allusive descriptions of Regent's Park are an unmatched achievement in British fiction. While walking in Regent's Park, Anna, in *The Death of the Heart,* gradually thaws her frozen feelings and begins, painfully, to allow compassion a role in her life. In *The Heat of the Day,* the Londoners in wartime Regent's Park take refuge from and, paradoxically, wrestle with their moral choices. Bowen's visual and psychological images make the locale emblematic of changes suffered by individuals caught in a particular historical moment.

Written as if history did not matter, *A World of Love* (1955) juxtaposes the passionate dreams of the adolescent Jane with the unsatisfied dreams of the adults around her in a shabby Irish great house. *The Little Girls* (1964) depicts three old women excavating their own childhood secrets. *Eva Trout* (1968) is a broad social comedy dominated by the wealthy, clumsy, troublemaking Eva, who is killed by her adopted child. These last three novels won public acclaim, but they are not as finely written as *The Death of the Heart* and *The Heat of the Day.*

Bowen's development as a fiction writer is reflected in her short stories. *Encounters* (1923) and *Ann Lee's* (1926) offer mannered observations that are, as Bowen herself acknowledged, "a blend of precocity and naivete." In her stories of wartime London, collected in *The Demon Lover* (1945), she skillfully captures the eeriness, the trauma, and the intensity she experienced during the blitz. The melodramatic turns of plot that sometimes mar her novels succeed in the tighter shape of her short stories.

In her novels, Bowen sometimes failed to create credible plots, which proceed inevitably from actions taken by her characters. It does not seem possible that Stella, the sensible, self-controlled heroine of *The Heat of the Day,* would carry on an affair for months without knowing much about her lover, without suspecting that he feels no patriotic loyalty, and without having any information to verify or deny a charge that he is a traitor selling secrets to the Nazis. Nor is Bowen's explanation for the lover's behavior very credible: Robert betrays his country as part of his rebellion against a grasping, middle-class family who lacks a gentrified attachment to the land. Max, whom Karen loves in *The House in Paris,* hardly seems capable of fathering Karen's child or of committing suicide. Markie, in *To the North,* is such a complete cad that his desire for Emmeline cannot be comprehended. Bowen succeeds brilliantly, however, in her portrait of Portia's adolescent sensibility in *The Death of the Heart,* so that her disturbing behavior precipitates action.

Bowen's reputation as a fiction writer rests on her creation of memorable characters, on her imaginative evocation of the atmosphere of a particular locale at a precise moment, and on her brilliant, mannered English prose.

Works

Encounters (1923). *Ann Lee's and Other Stories* (1926). *The Hotel* (1927). *The Last September* (1929). *Joining Charles* (1929). *Friends and Relations* (1931). *To the North* (1932). *The Cat Jumps* (1934). *The House in Paris* (1935). *The Death of the Heart* (1938). *Look at All Those Roses* (1941). *Seven Winters* (1942). *Bowen's Court* (1942) *English Novelists* (1942). *The Demon Lover* (1945; American ed., *Ivy Gripped the Steps and Other Stories,* 1946). *The Heat of the Day* (1949). *Collected Impressions* (1950). *The Shelbourne* (1951). *The Early Stories* (1951). *A World of Love* (1955). *Stories by Elizabeth Bowen* (1959). *A Time in Rome* (1960). *Afterthought* (1962; American ed., *Seven Winters and Afterthoughts,* 1962). *The Little Girls* (1964). *The Good Tiger* (1965). *A Day in the Dark and Other Stories* (1965). *Eva Trout* (1968). *Pictures and Conversations* (1975). *Collected Stories* (1981). *A World of Love* (1981). *The Mulberry Tree: Writings of Elizabeth Bowen,* ed. H. Lee (1987). *A Time in Rome* (1990).

Judith L. Johnston

Karin Boye
1900–1941

Born 1900, Gothenburg, Sweden
Died 1941, Alingsås, Sweden
Genre(s): lyric poetry, essay, prose fiction
Language(s): Swedish

Karin Boye has always been recognized as one of the major modern writers of Swedish literature. Born into the upper middle class, she completed high school in 1920 and went on to a teacher's seminary where she took her exam as public school teacher in 1921. She continued her studies at Uppsala University from 1921–1926 and two more years at Stockholm's "högskola," from where she received her master's degree in 1928. After graduation she taught at various schools at different times in her short life. But already during her high school years Boye was profoundly interested in political issues, and soon she became a member of the left radical *Clarté.* Another major interest was Freud's psychoanalytical theories, which just then were becoming more generally known. Together with Erik Mesterton and Josef Riwkin she co-founded the journal *Spektrum* in 1931. During the same year she was elected into the distinguished Swedish literary society *Samfundet de Nio.* In 1929 Boye married her *Clarté* colleague Leif Björk, but this marriage soon ended with a divorce in 1931. More openly yielding to her homosexual leanings after that, she lived with her German girlfriend in her home in Stockholm. Boye's split between the social bourgeois mores of her upbringing and her strong innate desire to be free of them early became the major theme in Boye's literary work. Her erotic split showed itself in periodically severe depressions for which she sought psychoanalytical help, especially during the years 1932–1933 while she was in Berlin. The treatment did not alleviate her deep inner anguish, later compounded by the fact that her girlfriend was dying of cancer. In April 1941 she walked out into her beloved Swedish woods outside of Alingsås and committed suicide.

Even in her earliest poetry Boye gave expression to her inner battle between moral commitment and spontaneous abandonment to life's vital forces. Her first poetry collection, *Moln* (Clouds), came out in 1922 and became an immediate success. Its lyric quality deepened in *Gömda land* (Hidden Countries), and with her third collection *Härdarna* (The Hearths), in which a courageous trust in providence fights victoriously the forces of social estrangement, she completes the poetry of her youth. Eight years later she published the deeply psychological *För trädets skull* (1935; For the Sake of the Tree), a collection that is unique not only in Swedish, but world literature. The symbolic language in these poems both conceals and concedes her tragic personal problem. Thematically intertwined with the political developments on the European scene, which just then began to threaten the personal freedom of each individual, the "tree," whose roots are threatened below the earth's surface, stands as the symbol of the individual. *De sju dödssynderna* (1941; The Seven Deadly Sins) came out posthumously, edited by her friends Victor Svanberg and Hjalmar Gullberg, who also wrote an introduction to the selection. Pitting love and death against each other, Boye had tried for a last time to solve her problem—without success.

Boye began her prose publications with her novel *Astarte* (1931), which won her the prize in the Nordic Novel Competition. Here, too, she discusses the confrontation between the will to live free versus the demands of cultural traditions. In her next novel *Merit vaknar* (1933; Merit Awakens), she takes a stand for reality against an exaggerated idealism. The same theme is variously repeated in her short stories *Uppgörelser* (1934; Settlements), and the novel *Kris* (1934; Crisis). Though she takes a stand for life and gratification in *Kris*, the conflict between free abandonment to life's forces and duty ends in a sad defeat in her next novel *För lite* (1936; Too Little). The next collection of short stories *Ur funktion* (1940; Out of Function) is again concerned with moral problems. Boye's last, completed, and possibly greatest work was the novel *Kallokain* (1941). Again inspired by the political developments on the European continent, Boye shows the psychological danger to the individual in a futuristic "police state" of the twenty-first century. *Bebådelse* (Annunciation), a novel fragment, short stories, and sketches, came out posthumously in 1941. Boye even tried her hand at playwriting. Her play *Hon som bär templet* appeared in *Bonniers Litterära Magasin* in 1941, and was put on stage by an ensemble in Stockholm that same year. Four of her essays, "Dagdrömmeriet som livsåskådning," "Om litteraturkritiken," "Språket bortom logiken," and above all "Rädslan och livet," (Daydreaming as Philosophy of Life, About Critic of Literature, The Language Beyond Logic, Fear and Life), which she published in *Spektrum* during the years 1931–1932, are important for any study of Karin Boye and her work.

Karin Boye's work, especially her novel *Kallokain*, has been translated into numerous languages, such as English, German, Danish, Norwegian, Hungarian, and Portuguese.

Over the years, Boye's poetry and prose have been republished in editions and selections too numerous to list here, and interest in her work is increasing as time goes by.

Works

Boye's opus is collected in *Samlade Skrifter*, 1–11 (Stockholm, 1947–1949), with introductions by her friend and biographer Margit Abenius. Her poetry is brought together in *Dikter* (Stockholm: 1942). S. Linder edited a reprint of selected poems under the title *Till dig* (Stockholm: 1963).

Individual works are discussed in the article.

Translations: *Kallokain*, tr. Gustaf Lannestock, intro. Richard B. Vowles (Madison, Wis., 1966; New York, 1985).

Hanna Kalter Weiss

Sophia Elisabet (Weber) Brenner
1659–1730

Born 1659, Stockholm, Sweden
Died 1730, Stockholm
Genre(s): poetry
Language(s): Swedish, German, Latin, Italian, French

Sophia Brenner is considered Sweden's first Swedish-language female poet of significance, but modern readers and scholars seem to give her little attention. Most of her efforts were occasional poetry (to a great extent poems for weddings and funerals), where her sure sense of rhyme, meter, and rhetorical flourishes made her extremely popular during her own lifetime.

Brenner's childhood and married life provided fortuitous circumstances for the development of her poetic gifts. Her father, a merchant of German extraction, believed in the education of women, and she received instruction in Latin and other unusual subjects for girls at the time. She married Elias Brenner, a Finnish-Swedish numismatist and miniaturist, in 1680. He, too, encouraged his wife's writing, and they often played host to the outstanding cultural figures of the time, including Urban Hjärne, Haquin Spegel, and Jacob Frese. These two factors were of great importance in establishing her literary "career" and fame. Their marriage was a long and happy one, although thirteen of their fifteen children died during Sophia Brenner's lifetime, and their financial situation never allowed them to feel secure.

Brenner utilized alexandrines for most of her verse, which showed Carolingian piety, common sense, and occasional irony, expressing the values and outlook of the Swedish bourgeoisie. At their best, her lyrics are charming and gracious, often revealing her (for that time) "feminist" views. She believed in the equality of the sexes and in women's right to an education. However, she expressed contentment with her role as wife and mother. In addition to occasional poems, she composed religious verse which displays Pietistic influences.

Although Sophia Brenner is all but forgotten today, her position as the "Honored Lady" of Swedish verse was firmly and unanimously proclaimed by her contemporaries.

Works

Minne öfwer den förundrans-wärde stora americanska aloen [Regarding the Wonderful Large American Aloe Plant . . .] (1708). *Poetiska dikter* [Lyric Poems] (1713). *Vårs Herres och Frälsares Jesu Christi alldra heligaste pijnos historia rijmvijs betrachtad* [The Story of the Most Holy Passion of Our Lord and Savior Jesus Christ in Verse Form] (1727). *Poetiska dikter II* [Lyric Poems II] (1732; published posthumously).

Kathy Saranpa Anstine

Bridget of Sweden
ca. 1303–1373

Born ca. 1303, Uppland, Sweden
Died July 23, 1373, Rome, Italy
Genre(s): divine revelations
Language(s): writings in Latin (dictated in Swedish)

Bridget is representative of a number of women (such as Hildegard von Bingen or Caterina da Siena) who achieved prominence in the high and late Middle Ages through the reception of visions or revelations that were believed to be of divine origin. This inspiration provided Bridget with an authority and assured her of an audience which would otherwise have been denied a woman of her times. Like other female visionaries, she assumed an active role in public life and used her position to criticize corruption in both Church and State. Bridget's writings also reflect an acute awareness of the problems which were peculiar to the fourteenth century—the devastation of the One Hundred Years War, the bubonic plague, the "Babylon Captivity" of the popes in Avignon, and civil unrest in Rome.

Bridget was the seventh child born to a powerful family of Swedish nobles. Her father, Birger Persson, was lawman (governor) for Uppland. In 1316 at the age of thirteen or fourteen, Bridget was married to Ulf Gudmarsson (later made lawman for Närike in East Gothland). Bridget's married life was a model of conventional piety, but she was nevertheless absorbed by the responsibilities and the distractions of her station: she bore eight children and was required to attend the young king and his wife at court for several years. In 1341, Bridget and Ulf made a pilgrimage to Santiago de Compostella in Spain. On the return trip, Ulf sick-

ened and voluntarily withdrew into the Cistercian monastery of Alvastra.

Ulf's death in 1344 was the turning point in Bridget's life and the first of her visions date from this time. A celestial voice concealed in a bright cloud greeted Bridget as Christ's spouse and God's mouthpiece, who was especially appointed to convey His will to humanity. In 1345, she was directed to found a religious order, for which Christ dictated the rule (*Regula Sancti Salvatoris*). The order of the Holy Saviour, which became familiarly known as the Brigittines, received papal approval in 1371.

After living in retreat at the monastery of Alvastra for several years (1345–1349), Bridget was commanded to go to Rome for the Jubilee year of 1350, where she was told to remain until the Pope and the Emperor met in that city. (This was an unlikely event in that the papacy had resided at Avignon since 1309 and was estranged from the German Emperors.) Except for the various pilgrimages she undertook (including one to the Holy Land in 1371), Bridget remained in Rome until her death in 1373, constantly urging the return of the pope from Avignon. She was attended by her daughter, Catherine (later canonized) and her two confessors—Peter Olaf, canon of Skenninge, and Peter Olaf, prior of Alvastra. Bridget also acquired a large popular following due to her reputation for piety, her almsgiving, and her prophecies. Her prophecies likewise earned her a considerable number of enemies in that she was an unabashed supporter of papal politics, her visions served to buttress the corrupt system of indulgences for the remission of sins, and she occasionally made prophetic forays into secular politics. This divided reaction to Bridget is reflected by the events surrounding her canonization. After many delays, she was canonized in 1391. Even so, her cult remained a bone of contention, and her canonization required confirmation first at the Council of Constance (1414–1418), later at the request of the Swedish king (1419), while the orthodoxy of the *Revelaciones* had to be defended at the Council of Basle (1431–1443). The validity of her revelations and her claims to sanctity were questioned by churchmen as eminent as Jean Gerson in his work *De probatione spirituum* (1415).

Although Bridget remained awake for her visions she experienced the rapture and ecstasy often associated with mystical transcendence. She received the visions in Swedish but was instructed that they should be translated into Latin. The task of translation fell primarily to her confessors, the two Peters, although it was initially undertaken in Sweden by Master Mathias, canon of Linköping cathedral and an eminent theologian. On her deathbed she appointed Alphonse of Pecha, the retired bishop of Jaen, who had acted as her spiritual director, occasional confessor, and translator, as her literary executor. It was he who edited and divided the *Revelaciones* into seven books in time for the opening of the canonization process (1377). Book Eight and a final book of additional revelations (*Extravagentes*) were added to the original seven (these latter books also being augmented) around 1380. Unfortunately, Alphonse of Pecha showed little skill as an editor. The work follows no logical or chronological sequence and tends to be repetitious. Considering Bridget's dependence on others in the translation and presentation of her work, it is difficult to ascertain how much control she had over the final product. Bridget herself tells us that she permitted her translators to make minor additions to heighten the effect of her revelations, while she gave her assistants a free hand in changing anything that was not entirely orthodox. Nevertheless, Bridget, following a divine prompting, did begin to learn Latin, which Peter of Skenninge later testified was sufficient for her to oversee the production of her works.

The *Revelaciones* themselves are a series of short, didactic passages which sometimes take the form of a dialogue. The identity of the celestial speaker alternates between Christ, the Virgin Mary, or another saint, while Bridget is invariably referred to as the Bride of Christ. Very often, the vision is presented as a warning to a particular individual who is in need of reform. There are a number of themes that recur throughout the *Revelaciones*: unregenerate society is continuously warned of God's wrath, urged to repent and do penance, bullied by graphic descriptions of souls in Hell or purgatory, and periodically reassured of God's mercy. Church corruption is contrasted with projections of a purified Church, which can only be realized with the pope's return to the Holy See. On the devotional side, Bridget is particularly concerned with Christ's passion and the veneration of His Virgin Mother. Unlike the writings of many medieval visionaries, the *Revelaciones* tend to be pragmatic and didactic rather than speculative, devotional rather than mystical. Moreover, while many prophets of this period were revolutionaries who were hostile to the Church Militant, and predicted its overthrow, Bridget differed in that her enemies were those who opposed the organized Church. While denouncing outright corruption, not even sparing the pope himself, she aggressively defended the *status quo*.

The Latin of the *Revelaciones* is poor, the style plain, and the organization scanty; nevertheless, Bridget's stern message of repentance had consider-

able impact on her age and her prophecies (and some spurious ones attributed to her) were still influential after her death, especially in the fifteenth century. The religious order that she founded is still in existence. Bridget was and still remains a controversial figure in so far as many were repelled by the aggressive and outspoken nature of her revelations and challenged the source of her inspiration. Even so, Bridget's visions were the vehicle by which she transcended the usual barriers of education and gender and played an active role in religion and politics.

Works
Revelaciones and minor works, ed. B. Ghotan (1492); ed. C. Durante (1606). A modern critical edition is in progress in *Samlingar utgivna av Svenska Fornskrift–sällskapet*, Latinska Skrifter, Ser. 2 (1956–).

Translations: Fourteenth-century Swedish tr. in *Heliga Birgittas Uppenbarelser*, ed. G.E. Klemming. 5 vols. (1857–1884). Fifteenth-century English extracts in *Revelations*, ed. R. Cummings, EETS, O.S. 178 (1929). *Revelations and Prayers of St. Bridget of Sweden: Being the "Sermo Angelicus" or Angelic Discourse concerning the Excellence of the Virgin Mary* (1928), tr. E. Graf. See extracts in Obrist, ("The Swedish Visionary Saint Bridget of Sweden," in *Medieval Women Writers*, ed. K.M. Wilson, Athens, Ga., 1984, pp. 227–251) and in *Revelations* (1972), tr. Anthony Butkovich.

Dyan Elliott

Marguerite Briet
ca. 1510–ca. 1552
Born ca. 1510, Abbeville, France
Died ? (after August 1552)
Genre(s): novel, letters, allegorical treatise, translation
Language(s): French

One of the first novelists in French literature, Hélisenne de Crenne was born into a Picardian family of minor nobility sometime around 1510. Her real name, recorded in the Latin chronicle *De Abbavilla*, was Marguerite Briet. What little we know about her life comes primarily from her long, semi-autobiographical novel, *Les Angoysses douloureuses qui procedent d'amours* (The Sad Agonies Which Come from Love). Such a source is naturally suspect since it is impossible to determine which of its incidents are fictional and which are not. If we trust Part I (generally considered the most autobiographical), Marguerite was very young when she wed Philippe Fournel, seigneur de Crasnes. We know from various legal documents that the couple had a son (Pierre Fournel), that their stormy marriage ended in separation before 1552, that a love affair precipitated the divorce and furnished material for Marguerite's novel; that this novel was a great popular success; that it was followed by three other volumes—a collection of letters, an allegorical treatise, and a translation of the first four books of the *Aeneid*. Further details, however, are unavailable. We do not know why Marguerite chose her *nom de plume*, which two years later was also given to a character in *Amadis de Gaul* by another Picardian writer. Nor do we know how Marguerite de Briet met Denis Janot, who published not only her novel but also *Amadis*.

It seems likely that some incidents in the novel—the tragic love, Hélisenne's cruel imprisonment by her husband, her torture at the hands of other in-laws—had a factual basis. In writing *Les Angoysses* (The Sad Agonies), which appeared in three parts from 1538 to 1560, she avowed two motives: (1) to encourage women to evade the "embrasements" ("hugging and kissing") of love and (2) to relieve her sufferings and anxieties by telling of them. Both aims were traditional to sixteenth-century literature. Both, however, come to perfect fruition in the plot, which records a fascinating exploration of feminine sexuality within Renaissance society.

Since the novel was probably published in installments, its plan is rather confused. Part I is told by Hélisenne herself, who also figures as narrator and heroine. It tells of her early life, the beginning of her tragic affair, and her imprisonment by an angry husband. The narrative voice in Part II is her lover's, Guénélic, who tells of the adventures he and his friend Quezinstra encounter as they seek the missing lady all over Europe. They find her in Part III, which is also narrated by Guénélic but concentrates on Hélisenne's sufferings. While the two young men rescue the heroine, she immediately succumbs to a fatal disease. Her death bed/repentance scene is followed by Guénélic's death and by the couple's descent to the Elyssian Fields, guided by Mercury. After the lovers' death, Venus and Athene briefly squabble over who has the rights to Hélisenne's book, but Jupiter has it carried to Paris where it is published to perpetuate the couple's memory.

At least the last event is verifiable. Published in eight editions from 1538 to 1560, this sprawling and operatic story was an immediate success. Kitty Delle Robbins-Herring credits its popularity to the novel's continuation of themes treated in poems, prose romances, and love complaints of the period. Indeed, Hélisenne's plot and characterizations are deeply indebted to Boccaccio's *Fiammetta* and Antoine de la Sale's *Petit Jehan de Saintré*; her style is heavily influenced by Lemaire de Belges. A.M. Schmidt, however, traces the novel's success to Marguerite's bold manipulation of her own story. Readers were enthralled by these confessions of a fallen woman and abused wife. The novel's mixture of fact and fiction is still one of its most attractive features. Marguerite herself seems to have been taken with it. She continued to publish under Hélisenne's name despite Hélisenne's death at the end of the book.

Despite the use of her romantic heroine's name, Marguerite wrote her other works in a heavily didactic strain, continuing the novel's avowed intention of dissuading women from the pursuit of love. A collection of public epistles or essays, *Les epistres familières et invectives* (Informal and Invective Letters), and an allegorical treatise, *Le songe de Madame Hélisenne . . . la considération duquel est apte à instiguer toutes personnes de s'aliéner de vice et s'approcher de vertu* (The Dream of Madame Hélisenne . . . the consideration of which is apt to instigate all people to avoid vice and approach virtue) appeared in 1532. In 1541, she published a translation of the first four books of Vergil's *Aeneid*.

Even though Hélisenne's themes were familiar ones for her time, neither the book nor its author was bereft of originality. She invested her story with a novel intensity; her analysis of her own fall and her subsequent equations between "lovelessness and liberty" were evidence of a distinct voice. Her exploration of feminine sensuality was explicitly, even daringly, specific, not only in the details of Hélisenne's violent passion but also in the author's emphasis upon clothing, hair, facial expressions, and body movements. Most critics have noted the novel's voyeuristic appeal. Not only must we consider Hélisenne's scrutiny by her husband (named after the many-eyed Greek giant Argus) but also our own delight as readers in spying upon their affairs. The book offers a complex study of the heroine's impossible situation and of passion's destructive role in our own lives. Its moral—that women should flee love—was amply supported by the details of its narrative.

A word should also be said about Briet's language, which has been the subject of much critical debate. The novel is nothing short of extravagant, often excessive in its style. Although representative of her period in general, the frequency with which she embellishes can be disconcerting to modern readers. Her language abounds in Latinisms, convoluted syntax, repetitions, obsolete French words, and neologisms, either original with the author or borrowed from other writers. It has often been criticized as overextravagant, verbose, pretentious, and Latinate. The humanist Étienne Pasquier believed that Rabelais had her in mind when he mocked the Latin jargon of the Limousin school. Claude Colet's editing of her collected works in 1550 implicitly asserted that her language needed correcting, as did his preface, which notes that the work was undertaken at the urging of two women who found the book unreadable as written. Such criticism, however, often says more about the critic's assumptions than Briet's writing. Her style is difficult—she never uses a common word if she can find a learned and obscure one—but so is the language of Rabelais and Maurice Scève. Moreover, the prose model that she followed—middle French—sanctioned her extravagance. Middle French prose relished complicated syntax and vocabulary, repetitions, long sentences, and scholastic terminology. When compared with the other writers of her day, she did as well as most and better than some. Her books were read before Colet's editions; some readers who deplored her Latinisms praised them as stylistic features in texts by men. It seems at least probable that the learned style and overtly sensuous subject were disconcerting—both in her day and our own—because they issued from the pen of a woman. It's at least possible such criticism explains Briet's relatively short career and her turn to edifying or scholarly genres in her work after *Les Angoysses* (The Agonies).

Many twentieth-century critics, sensing that she has been misjudged, have reassessed her work. Some (Gustave Reynier and Henriette Charasson) credited her novel with breaking new ground for the pastoral (*L'Astrée*), psychological (*La Princesse de Clèves*), and sentimental novel. Others (L.M. Richardson) have taken note that in *Familiar and Invective Letters* Hélisenne defends her sex with a vigor unequaled by any other French Renaissance woman. Indeed, a translation of the letters along with two new critical editions of *Les Angoyssesses douloureuses*, Part I, have recently been published. This work indicates that we have only begun to evaluate her position.

Marguerite/Hélisenne left readers a fascinating legacy. Her novel is both frank confession and elaborate artifice, moral tract and sensuous narrative, self-assertion and self-doubt. *Les Angoysses* (The Agonies) gives us a powerful experience of the Renaissance woman.

Works

Les Angoyssesses douloureuses qui procedent d'amours: Contenantz troys parties, Composees par Dame Hélisenne: Laquelle exhorte toutes personnes a ne suyvre folle Amour [The Sad Agonies which come from love: contents in three parts written by Lady Hélisenne, which book exhorts all people not to follow foolish love] (1538). (Part I has been published in a new edition by Paule Demats, *les Angoyssesses douloureuses qui procedent d'amours (1538), Première partie* [Paris, 1968] and by Jérôme Vercruysse, same title [Paris, 1968]). *Familieres et invectives de ma dame Hélisenne, composes par icelle dame, De Crenne* [Intimate and Invective letters of My Lady Hélisenne, composed by this lady of Crennes] (1539). *Les quatre premiers livres des Eneydes du treselegant poete Virgile, traduictz de latin en prose Françoyse par ma dame Hélisenne, à l'elucidtation et decoration desdictz libres, diriqez à tresillustre et tresauguste Prince Françoys, premier de ce nom invictissime Roy de France* [The first four books of the *Aeneid* of the most polished poet Virgil, translated from Latin into French prose by my lady Hélisenne, in the translating of which there are many thoughts which by means of phrasing are added here: which serves greatly to the elucidation and decoration of these books, dedicated to the most famous and august Prince Francis, the first of that name, invincible King of France] (1541). *Le Songe de madame Hélisenne, composé par ladicte Dame, la considération duquel est apte à instiguer toutes personnes de s'aliéner de vice et s'approcher de vertu* [The Dream of Madame Hélisenne, composed by this lady, the consideration of which is apt to instigate all people to avoid vice and approach virtue] (1532). *Les oeuvres de ma dame Hélisenne q'elle a puis naqueres recogneues et mises en leur entier. Cest ascavoir les angoisses douloureuses qui procedent d'amours, Les Epistres familieres et invectives. Le songe de ladicte dame, let tout mieulx que pr cy devant redigees au vray, et imprimees nouvellemet par le commandement de ladicte Dame de Crenne* [The Complete and recognized works of my lady Hélisenne. That is, The Sad Agonies which come from love. Intimate and Invective letters. The Dream of this Lady, all better than before, composed according to the truth and printed anew by the said Lady De Crennes' command] (1543).

Translations: *A Renaissance Woman: Hélisenne's Personal and Invective Letters* [*Les Epistres familieres et invectives*] (1986).

Glenda Wall

Anna Brigadere
1861–1933

Born October 1, 1861, Zemgale, Latvia
Died June 25, 1933, Zemgale
Genre(s): drama, novel, short story, lyric poetry
Language(s): Latvian

Of the numerous Latvian women writers, Anna Brigadere and Aspāzija are the most distinguished, their contribution to the rich national theater unsurpassed (although equaled) by other Latvian dramatists. Brigadere's novels are also outstanding.

Daughter of a farm laborer, Brigadere was able to complete only three years of primary school and subsequently became an autodidact. Her childhood in the country was permeated with the influence of Latvian folklore, which is strongly felt in her work. When her mother died in 1874, the family moved to the town of Jelgava and later to Ventspils. During a succession of jobs as seamstress and shopgirl, and later as teacher, she garnered a store of observations of all walks of life, which she later used in her writing. Between 1882 and 1884 Brigadere found employment as a governess in Russia, largely because of her self-acquired familiarity with German language and literature. In 1885 she succeeded in finishing a teachers' course and continued working as tutor and governess. Influenced by a prolonged stay at a hospital, she wrote her first story, "Slimnīcā" (1896; In the Hospital), which was published in 1896.

Beginning in 1897 she was able to devote herself fully to literature, both as writer and as editor of several magazines. Her popularity was very great: her later years were spent at a country home of her own, Sprīdīši, given to her by the nation in recognition of her achievement. After Brigadere's death Sprīdīši was turned into a museum in her memory.

Along with her contemporaries Jānis Poruks (1871–1911) and Kārlis Skalbe (1879–1945), Brigadere is a quintessentially Latvian writer, occupying a position midway between Western emphasis on reason and Eastern European emphasis on feeling yet with a share in both. Although firmly ensconced in the middle class, she exposes its shallowness in her realistic stories and novels. At the same time she is an idealist, and her writing is frequently symbolic. Her masterpiece, the autobiographic trilogy of novels, *Dievs, daba, darbs* (1927; God, Nature, Work), *Skarbos vējos* (1931; Harsh Wind), and *Akmeņu sprostā* (1933; In a Stone Cage) has always been one of the most widely admired works in Latvian literature, especially the first novel. The whole forms a *bildungsroman* full of well-drawn characters, particularly women, notable for its profound love of nature, deep religious feeling, and belief in the ennobling power of work—attitudes that are basic to the Latvian national character. Latvian folklore shaped Brigadere's literary style, its often laconic concentration, its precision and clarity, as well as her ethical outlook, which is marked by optimism, insistence on inner clarity, and emphasis upon human dignity and worth. Her folkloric plays, such as *Sprīdītis* (1903; Thumbling) and *Maija un Paija* (1921; Maija and Paija), rival the trilogy in effectiveness and popularity. In these she combines a variety of fairytale motifs and situations to express her views in highly poetic form and language. Of her other plays, the comedies are realistic and distinguished by lively satire. Her psychological plays are less successful, since the resolution of the plots often fail to emerge convincingly from the nature of the characters. Her lyric poetry is limpid and perfect in form. Brigadere's highest achievement, however, is in the autobiographic trilogy and the folkloric plays.

Works

Aiz lidzrietības (1897). *Atkalredzēšanās* (1901). *Izredzētais* (1901). *Sprīdītis* (1903). *Ceļa jūtīs* (1904). *Ausmā* (1907). *Čaukstenes* (1907). *Pie latviešu miljonāra* (1909). *Zvanīgs zvārgulītis* (1909). *Kopoti raksti* [Complete Works], 20 vols. (1912–1939). *Princese Gundega un karalis Brusubārda* (1912). *Dzejas* (1913). *Raudupiete* (1914). *Spēka dēls* (1916). *Mazā majā* (1918). *Ilga* (1920). *Maija un Paija* (1921). *Paisums* (1921). *Hetēras mantojums* (1924). *Sniegputenī* (1924). *Lielais loms* (1925). *Sievu kari ar Belcebulu* (1925). *Lolitas brīnumputns* (1926). *Dievišķā seja* (1926). *Dievs, daba, darbs* (1927). *Kvēlošā lokā* (1928). *Kad sievas spēkojas* (1929). *Šuvējas sapnis* (1930). *Skarbos vējos* (1931). *Pastari* (1931). *Karaliene Jāna* (1932). *Akmeņu sprostā* (1933). *Kalngali* (1934).

Translations: *Maija and Paija*, tr. Ilze Raudsepa, in *The Golden Steed*, ed. Alfreds Straumanis (1979). [Selected poetry], in *A Century of Latvian Poetry*, ed. and tr. W.K. Matthews (1957).

Zoja Pavlovskis

Vera Brittain
1893–1970

Born December 29, 1893, Newcastle-under-Lyme,
Staffordshire, England
Died March 29, 1970, London
Genre(s): autobiography, poetry, history, essays,
speeches, novels
Language(s): English

An ardent pacifist and feminist, Brittain wrote over twenty-five books, which range from poetry to history and which discuss women's contribution to politics around the world. Brittain said that she wrote both of her famous autobiographies—*Testament of Youth* (1933) and *Testament of Experience* (1957)—to work through personal pain and to interpret history in terms of personal events. Her haunting and relentless spiritual self-evaluation has been compared to one of her major influences, the nonconformist John Bunyan, especially his *Grace Abounding to the Chief of Sinners* (1666).

The only daughter of a leisured provincial family, Brittain claimed that her life was molded by feminism and her experience of World War I. While attending St. Monica's boarding school, she read Olive Schreiner's *Woman and Labour* (1911), which made her a feminist, and convinced her reluctant parents to let her go up to Somerville College, Oxford, in 1914. After a year at Oxford, she became a Voluntary Aid Detachment nurse and went abroad to help the British effort in World War I. In *Testament of Youth,* she describes the personal and sexual liberation involved in caring for wounded soldiers and prisoners of war. She says that she became a pacifist when she realized the absurdity of struggling to save the same soldiers her brother and his friends were trying to kill farther north. Through the deaths of her brother, her fiancé, and her closest friends, Brittain came to realize the way an entire society, particularly women, bears the emotional shock of war.

Returning from abroad, Brittain and other women who had served the war effort fought to gain degree status for female students at Oxford. She also helped to edit a volume of *Oxford Poetry* (1920) that launched the careers of many students who would become prominent writers, including Robert Graves and Winifred Holtby. Brittain met Holtby in 1920 and they remained close friends, encouraging one another's political and creative writings, until Holtby's death in 1935. Using Elizabeth Gaskell's biography of Charlotte Brontë as its model, *Testament of Friendship* (1940) discusses the relationship between Holtby's family background and her writings, particularly the constant struggle faced by a woman who believes in

numerous causes but who also requires time alone to write well. This struggle was Brittain's as well.

After graduating from Oxford, she settled in London with Holtby and committed her career to social and political change. She became a lecturer for the League of Nations Union in 1922, giving as many as four speeches a week, while contributing regularly to the *Manchester Guardian, The Nation,* and the feminist journal *Time and Tide* and completing her first published novel, *The Dark Tide* (1923).

While Brittain's novels are more traditional in structure and tone than those of "modern" writers like Virginia Woolf and May Sinclair, the smooth nap of her prose consistently explores feminist themes. From the frank discussion of women students and teachers at Oxford in *The Dark Tide* to the attempted rape in *Born 1925* (1948), Brittain builds her novels around the vastly different constraints and expectations that shape men's and women's lives. As with her friend Radclyffe Hall's *Well of Loneliness* (1928), Brittain's *Honourable Estate* (1936) shows both the power of male and female homoerotic relationships and the ways in which those relationships are crippled by socially imposed distance and silence. *Honourable Estate's* exposure of the need for more open attitudes toward homosexuality and abortion, as well as its portrayal of both old and new-style marriages, are part of Brittain's lifelong plea for the removal of double standards of sexual morality.

Between the wars, her political energies were focused on feminist concerns. In the 1920s she was closely aligned with Lady Margaret Rhondda and the women writers who centered around *Time and Tide* and the Six Point Group. The group's goals—vast changes in human attitudes, a new concept of marriage, women's advancement to political and economic equality, improved social services for women, radical changes in sexual morality, and a new understanding of women's potential—formed the basis of her theoretical writing in *Women's Work in Modern England* (1928), *Halcyon* (1929), and *Lady into Woman* (1953). *Women's Work* encourages women to pursue their own careers as it exposes the legal obstacles that have prevented them from doing so in the past. Brittain was perhaps most original in *Halcyon's* ideal of "semi-detached" marriage, a call for women's freedom to travel and to development of both emotional equality and independent careers. *Lady into Woman* brings feminist achievements from around the world to bear on the specific political situation of contemporary English women. During World War II, she became vice-president of the Women's International League for Peace and Freedom and campaigned for improved Anglo-Indian relations.

Testament of Experience (1957) traces Brittain's

commitment to pacifism through the Peace Pledge Union and World War II. On behalf of world peace, she wrote numerous pamphlets and contributed to hundreds of periodicals internationally. *Seed of Chaos, or What Mass Bombing Really Means* (1944) was the most widely known and scathing of these critiques. Brittain's unpopular advocacy of peace made her an enemy of both the Home Office and the Gestapo during the war, and it obliterated the sale of her books in the United States. In the novel *Born 1925* (1948), her experience of two wars is spread out among the three major characters.

Brittain's marriage to political philosopher George Catlin was much like the ideal she described in *Halcyon* and *Lady into Woman*. She traveled internationally on behalf of peace and feminism and remained devoted to her women friends, particularly Winifred Holtby, who lived with Brittain most of her married life. Brittain had two children, John Edward and Shirley (Williams), who was a Member of Parliament when her mother died in 1970. True to her diverse sympathies, Brittain was still participating in demonstrations and sit-ins and working on several books, including the final *Testament of Time,* when she died.

Works

Verses of a V.A.D. (1918). *The Dark Tide* (1923). *Good Citizenship and the League* (1924). *Not Without Honour* (1924). *Women's Work in Modern England* (1928). *Halcyon, or the Future of Monogamy* (1929). *Testament of Youth* (1933). *Poems of the War and After* (1934). *Honourable Estate* (1936). *Thrice a Stranger* (1938). *Testament of Friendship, the Story of Winifred Holtby* (1940). *War-Time Letters to Peace Lovers* (1940). *England's Hour* (1941). *Humiliation with Honour* (1942). *Law Versus War* (1944). *Seed of Chaos or What Mass Bombing Really Means* (1944, U.S. title *Massacre by Bombing*). *Account Rendered* (1945). *Conscription or Cooperation?* (1946). *On Becoming a Writer* (1947, U.S. title *On Being an Author,* 1948). *Born 1925: A Novel of Youth* (1948). *Vera Brittain Writes on How Shall the Christian Church Prepare for the New World Order?* (194?). *In the Steps of John Banyan* (1950, U.S. title *Valiant Pilgrim*). *The Story of St. Martin's: An Epic of London* (1951). *Search After Sunrise: A Traveller's Story* (1951). *Lady into Woman: A History of Women from Victoria to Elizabeth II* (1953). *Testament of Experience* (1957). *Long Shadows* (with G.E.W. Sizer, 1958). *The Women at Oxford: A Fragment of History* (1960). *The Pictorial History of St. Martins-in-the-Fields* (1962). *Pethwick-Lawrence: A Portrait* (1963). *The Rebel Parson: A Short History of Some Pioneer Peace-*
Makers (1964). *Envoy Extraordinary: A Study of Vijaya Lakshmi Pandit and Her Contribution to Modern India* (1965). *Radclyffe Hall: A Case of Obscenity?* (1968). *Chronicle of Youth* (1981).

Carol L. Barash

Ivana Brlić-Ma'uranić 1874–1938

a.k.a. I.B.M.
Born 1874, Ogulin, Yugoslavia
Died 1938, Zagreb
Genre(s): children's literature
Language(s): Croatian

One of Yugoslavia's outstanding writers of children's literature, Ivana Brlić-Ma'uranić excelled in creating original stories and fables, the characters and motifs of which were drawn extensively from Slavic folklore. In some respects, then, her creative contribution shares the neoromantic orientation of some of her contemporaries, notably Nazor and Vidrić. This establishes her connection with the Croatian Moderna, although she was never a part of the symbolism or impressionism most often associated with that movement. Brlić-Ma'uranić was lovingly called the "Croatian Andersen," a tribute both to her great artistic success and her popularity that still prevails.

Brlić-Ma'uranić was never a stranger to creative literature. Her father was Vladimir Ma'uranić, a writer and historian as well as a member of three Academies of Science, the Yugoslavian, Czech, and Polish. Vladimir was the eldest son of the great poet Ivan Ma'uranić who wrote *Smrt Smail-age Čengić* (The Death of Smail-Aga Čengić).

Her first collection of poems and stories appeared in 1902 in a limited edition (for her friends) under the title, *Valjani i nevaljani, zbirka pripovijedaka i pjesmica za dječaka* (The Worthwhile and the Worthless, a Collection of Tales and Poems for Children). Both this book and the following one, *Škole i praznici* (1905; Schools and Holidays), attracted some favorable attention. Her third work, *Slike* (1912; Pictures) augured the tremendous acclaim her next two works were to have. The most influential literary figure of the time, Antun Gustav Matoš, responded very positively to both *Pictures, I* and her next production, *Čudnovate zgode šegrta Hlapića* (1913; The Strange Fortunes of the Novice Hlapić). In *Priče iz dauvnine* (1916; Stories from Long Ago), though, he discerned "a classic book."

Stories from Long Ago is considered to be Brlić-Ma'uranić's greatest work. One modern critic calls the stories "our most beautiful fables." Another points out that *Stories from Long Ago* is not just valuable as a literary work and a part of the cultural heritage, "but is considered our own story of the past, the story that we always happily remember." *Stories from Long Ago* has gone through twelve editions so far, testifying to the accuracy of the critics' estimation. It has been translated into ten languages, adapted as a play, radio show, television production, and puppet theater performance, to mention some of its popularizations.

Although she wrote two more collections of tales, *Knjiga omladini* (1923; A Book to Young People), *Dječja čitanka o zdravlju* (1927; Children's Reader about Health) and her novel, *Jaša Dalmatin, Potkralj Gud'erata* (1937; Jasa Dalmatin, Viceroy of Gud'erat), which were published by some of the most prestigious publishing houses in Yugoslavia, it was for *Stories from Long Ago* that Brlić-Ma'uranić was thrice nominated for the Nobel Prize in Literature. In 1937, a year before her death, Brlić-Ma'uranić became the first female member of the Yugoslavian Academy of Sciences and Arts.

As a writer, Brlić-Ma'uranić is best known for her clarity of images and rhythmic and sonorous prose. She described her style as the process of representing "the heart in pictures" (*srce u sliku*). The musicality of her prose enhances the wealth of magical and mythological beings that people her creations and creates a picturesque impression not unlike certain types of oral literature. The following line from *Stories from Long Ago* illustrates her control over both the euphonic flow of words and the evoked imagery: *Jutro bijelo, kano krilo golubovo, a mekane magle nad ponikvom prohode, rekao bi: bijelorune ovce.* ("The morning is white like a pigeon's wing and the fogs pass by over the hollow as, one might say: white-fleeced sheep.") The first five words sound like a traditional line from the *deseterac*, the decasyllabic folk-line that regularly displays caesura after the fourth syllable. The sentence is saturated with alliteration and assonance producing a musical effect. The image, also, is poetic, the white morning like a pigeon's wing suggesting both the dove-like color and the emotional association of peaceful protection. This single example may illustrate the power of her creative production. Brlić-Ma'uranić's art transcends its generic design of children's literature and has become a part of the national culture. *Stories from Long Ago* still retains great popularity in Yugoslavia, ensuring Brlić-Ma'uranić a lasting position in Yugoslavian literature.

Works

Valjani i nevaljani (1902). *Škole i praznici* (1905). *Slike* (1912). *Čudnovate zgode šegrta Hlapiča* (1913). *Priče iz dauvnine* (1916). *Knjiga omladini* (1923). *Dječja čitanka o zdravlju* (stihovi) (1927). *Mir u duši, Posebni otisak iz Hrvatske revije* (1930). *Zgode i nezgode šegrta Hlapiča* (no date). *Jaša Dalmatin, Potkralj Gud'erata* (1937). *Srce od licitara* (1938).

Translations: *Croatian Tales of Long Ago*, tr. F.S. Copeland (1924). *La Paix de L'Âme*, tr. Cécile Baron d'Ottenfels (1929). *Leggende Croate, favole antiche*, tr. Umberto Urbani (1957). *Die Verschwundenen Stiefel. Die Wunderbaren Erlebnisse des Schuster-jungen Gottschalk*, tr. Else Byhan (1959). *Das Schlangenmädchen aus dem Zauberwald* (1966). *Lavendel og Rosmarin*, tr. Thorkil Barfod (1929).

Christine Tomei

Suzanne Brøgger
1944–

Born November 18, 1944, Copenhagen, Denmark
Genre(s): essay, autobiography, novel, poetry, translation, journalism
Language(s): Danish

The perspective of an exile who regards all social verities with a fresh, skeptical eye seems to suit Suzanne Brøgger, who grew used to moving between cultures at an early age. Some of her literary heroes—Karen Blixen, Henry Miller, Anais Nin, and Emmanuelle Arsan—also belonged to an international society and experienced similar uprootings. Her insights, like theirs, confront human sexuality and thus have the power to shock.

Suzanne Brøgger has been a world-traveler since childhood, when her stepfather, Svend Brøgger, was assigned to Ceylon and then Thailand. She therefore received part of her schooling in Denmark (Bernadotte-skolen in Hellerup, Th. Langs pigekostskole in Silkeborg, and Copenhagan University) and part in the Middle East. Her consequent facility with Eastern languages gained her freelance employment as a journalist reporting from the Soviet Union and the Middle East. The collection *Brøg* (1980; Brew) includes articles she wrote from abroad between 1965 and 1980. A strikingly beautiful woman who has also had experience as an actress, notably in the role of Helena in the Danish Royal Theater's production of *Troilus and Cressida*, she knows how to present herself in the media with flair and to dramatize her role as author.

Suzanne Brøgger

She has been the recipient of several Danish literary prizes, including the "Golden Laurel" in 1982 and a Danish State's Art Foundation lifelong grant from 1985.

Brøgger stepped into the international limelight with her work *Fri os fra kærligheden* (1973; Deliver Us from Love), a highly polemical and controversial critique of western mores which was translated into more than seven languages. Mingling essays, short stories, and slice-of-life accounts of personal experiences, Brøgger called into question a number of assumptions about western values such as the nuclear family, privacy, and the incest taboo. Although *Fri os fra kærligheden* was subtitled "A radical feminist speaks out" in one of its English editions, Brøgger denies this connection. Indeed, she often takes feminists to task for accepting and working within patriarchal structures instead of trying to break free of them and forge new ways of living. She is particularly contemptuous of the monogamous couple unit that is considered the ideal social arrangement in western society, finding it too stifling. "What there will be a need for in future is not specialization, but generalization: to be able to love more than one person, more than one race, more than one sex—and not merely a single representative of the opposite sex," she has asserted. She continued to write in the same vein in her next published book, *Kærlighedens veje og*

vildveje (1975; The Right and Wrong Ways of Love).

In her autobiographical works, *Crème fraiche* (1978; Fresh Cream) and *Ja* (1979; Yes), Brøgger writes frankly about her own sexual relationships, continuing to protest against exclusive forms of love to promote her own somewhat utopian ideal of universal love. Despite reservations about Brøgger's brand of utopianism, Danish critics consider these two works her best; Jens Kistrup goes so far as to call *Crème fraiche* one of the major works of contemporary Danish literature.

With *En gris som har været oppe at slås kan man ikke stege* (1979; A Pig That's Been Fighting Can't Be Roasted) Brøgger breaks with the cosmopolitan world of her international travels to concentrate on a lyrical description of life in a rural Danish community and her relationship with her neighbors there. In this work, she eschews linear form for repetition of mythic themes to reflect her beliefs about cyclical nature and a holistic universe.

Tone, an epic commemorative prose poem about Tone Bonnen, a milliner, appeared in 1981. Here, Brøgger draws on Nordic and Greek mythology to recount and celebrate the life of an obscure and now-forgotten woman who nevertheless passionately loved life, suffered and eventually died of bone cancer. Although some critics have thought the form of *Tone* gets in the way of readers' ability to relate to the character, nevertheless, the work as a whole reveals Brøgger's ongoing development as an initially popular writer who continues to take her craft more and more seriously.

Brøgger has steadfastly remained loyal to her original point of view and continued to write about her own characteristic themes. Her style, however, has steadily changed in a more literary direction and increasingly involves much experimental play among genres.

Works

Fri os fra kærligheden [Deliver Us from Love] (1973). *Kærlighedens veje og vildveje* [The Right and Wrong Ways of Love] (1975). *Crème fraiche* [Fresh Cream] (1978). *Ja* [Yes] (1979). *En gris som har været oppe at slås kan man ikke stege* [A Pig That's Been Fighting Can't Be Roasted] (1979). *Brøg* [Brew] (1980). *Tone. Epos* (1981). *Den pebrede susen. Flydende fragmenter og fixeringer* [The Pepper Whistle. Floating Fragments and Fixations] (1986). *Edvard og Elvira. En ballade* (1988).

Translations: *Deliver Us from Love*, tr. Thomas Teal (1976). "No Man's Land" (excerpt from *Kærlighedens veje og vildveje*), tr. Christine Badcock, in *No Man's Land: An Anthology of Modern Danish Women's Literature* (1987). "A Visit with Henry Miller," tr. Gregory Stephenson, *Seahorse*, 2, 4 (1983): 1–6.

Kristine Anderson

Anne Brontë
1820–1849

a.k.a. Acton Bell
Born January 17, 1820, Thornton, England
Died May 28, 1849, Scarborough
Genre(s): novel, poetry
Language(s): English

The youngest of the famous Brontë sisters, Anne Brontë is often regarded as the least talented and therefore overlooked. Whether she deserves this reputation has become the subject of much debate. Her novels, *Agnes Grey: An Autobiography* (1847) and *The Tenant of Wildfell Hall* (1848), for which she is best known, demonstrate her eye for detail and talent for storytelling, in addition to an unmistakably Brontëan taste for the unconventional. Although she wrote a great deal of poetry, it has, for the most part, been neglected.

She escaped attending the Clergy Daughters' School at Cowan Bridge with her sisters because of her age. After the deaths of the two elder girls, Maria and Elizabeth, Charlotte and Emily returned home. During much of their childhood the four remaining Brontë children were allowed to roam and play freely in the Yorkshire moors. Such play encouraged extensive development of their imaginations.

The children created the Glass Town Confederacy—stories of twelve toy soldiers involving conquest, civil war, personal jealousies, loyalties, and loves. In 1831 Charlotte left for Miss Wooler's School at Roe Head, and at this point Emily and Anne began chronicling the happenings of their own imaginary kingdom of Gondal. Gondal is the setting for a series of poems characterized by romantic characters and language. Though Emily continued to be absorbed by this fantasy world, Anne apparently lost interest during her late teens and early twenties, contributing Gondal poetry only under Emily's influence.

Anne Brontë was initially educated at home by Charlotte and then spent two years as a student at Roe Head. In the spring of 1841 she was forced by economic need to find employment as a governess, as was Charlotte. Her experience at Blake Hall was brief and unhappy, and she soon returned home. She then assumed a position at Thorpe Green, securing a job for her brother as well, but becoming shocked by Branwell's growing obsession with the mistress of the house. Ashamed of Branwell's behavior and unable to endure the separation from her sisters, Anne quit her position and returned home. Branwell's subsequent decline into madness is reflected in the writings of all his sisters but particularly in Anne's *The Tenant of Wildfell Hall*. In 1844 the Brontë sisters attempted to start their own school. The endeavor was not successful; they did not receive a single application.

Poems by Currer, Ellis and Acton Bell, a slim volume containing sixty-one poems was published in May 1846. The Brontës selected male pseudonyms partly to protect themselves from prejudice against women writers and partly to meet Emily's demands for anonymity. Even before all the publication details had been completed, the sisters began working on novels, perhaps inspired by the ease with which their initial dreams of publication had become a reality. But publication did not mean success; by mid-July only two copies of their poems had been sold, despite several complimentary reviews.

By the end of June 1846, the Brontë sisters had each finished a novel—Charlotte, *The Professor*; Emily, *Wuthering Heights*; and Anne, *Agnes Grey*—and were trying to locate a publisher who would offer the three novels as a triple decker. In July 1847 Thomas Cautley Newby accepted *Wuthering Heights* and *Agnes Grey* but refused *The Professor*. *Agnes Grey* appeared with *Wuthering Heights* in December 1847.

Newby promised early sheets of *The Tenant of Wildfell Hall* to an American publisher with the statement that it was his belief that it was by the author of *Jane Eyre*. The resulting publicity caused problems with Charlotte's publishers who had promised her next novel to another American publisher. To straighten out the confusion and prove that the novels were the work of two authors, Charlotte and Anne traveled to London to visit Messrs. Smith and Elder, Charlotte's publisher. Upon arriving in London the sisters were caught in a severe storm and Anne developed a respiratory infection. When they returned home Charlotte and Anne were faced with a series of domestic trials. Branwell died of consumption in September. Emily's health then showed symptoms of collapse, and not until shortly before her death in December 1848 would she agree to see a doctor. After Emily's death Anne, who had never completely recovered from the illness caused by her soaking in London, quickly sickened. Consumption was soon obvious. On May 24, 1849 she left Haworth for Scarborough, dying there four days later. The poem "I hoped that with the brave and strong" was her last composition.

Most critics find Anne's work more conventional and therefore less interesting than that of her sisters. Still, more than her sisters, Anne sought a realistic approach to fiction without sentimentalizing or romanticizing her characters. Charlotte's Jane Eyre marries far above her station, whereas Anne's *Agnes Grey* is allotted a thoroughly respectable though unglamorous clergyman. Anne believed that her duty as a writer was to teach rather than entertain or fantasize.

As the last surviving Brontë, Charlotte greatly influenced the literary reputations of her sisters. Unfortunately, her condescending and apologetic attitude toward Anne's literary talent has set a precedent for much subsequent criticism. Some critics, however, have objected to Charlotte's picture of "gentle Anne." Indeed, the vigor with which Anne approached her subjects does not substantiate Charlotte's opinion. Many critics find merit in the presentation of the evils and fallacies of the double standard exercised in child-rearing in *Agnes Grey*. Her approach is similarly forthright in *The Tenant of Wildfell Hall* where the heroine leaves her husband. These novels, with their feminist overtones, were considered immoral and sensational when originally published.

Still, Anne's work does have weaknesses. Critics note that her attempt to portray the tedium of a governess's life in *Agnes Grey* results in many tedious passages. *The Tenant of Wildfell Hall* is often criticized for its weak structure, since the main body of the story is told through the protagonist's diary rather than by the character herself. In spite of her flaws, many critics feel that Anne was a talented writer who deserves separate and careful consideration.

Works

Poems by Currer, Ellis and Acton Bell (as Acton Bell) (1846). *Agnes Grey: An Autobiography* (as Acton Bell) (1847). *The Tenant of Wildfell Hall* (as Acton Bell) (1848). *The Brontës' Life and Letters* (1908). The Complete Poems of Anne Brontë (1920). *Poems,* ed. E. Chitham (1979).

Lynn M. Alexander

Charlotte Brontë
1816–1855

a.k.a. Currer Bell
Born April 21, 1816, Thornton, England
Died March 31, 1855, Haworth
Genre(s): novel, poetry
Language(s): English

Charlotte Brontë is recognized by literary historians for her contributions to the development of the novel. Her fame and influence rests on four novels and con-

tributions to a single volume of poetry. Although much of her reputation is based upon the immediate success of *Jane Eyre* (1847) and the romantic appeal of her personal history, especially as presented by Elizabeth Gaskell (whose biography of Charlotte Brontë is preeminent in its genre), her real contribution was in the fictional exploration of emotional repression and of the female psyche. Brontë's work introduced new depth and intensity to character development and the portrayal of emotion in fiction.

In 1824 her father, a Church of England clergyman, sent his two eldest daughters, Maria and Elizabeth, to the Clergy Daughters' School at Cowan Bridge, and in August of the following year he sent Charlotte to join them. According to Brontë, "typhus fever decimated the school periodically, and con-

Charlotte Brontë

sumption and scrofula in every variety of form, [which] bad air and water, and bad insufficient diet can generate, preyed on the ill-fated pupils." Both Maria and Elizabeth fell victim to consumption and returned home to die. Charlotte was particularly close to Maria and later eulogized her in the portrait of Helen Burns in *Jane Eyre*.

After the deaths of his two eldest daughters, Mr. Brontë decided to educate his children at home. The children read Shakespeare, Milton, Bunyan, Dryden,

Scott, Wordsworth, Byron, the *Arabian Nights,* and journals such as *Blackwood's Edinburgh Magazine.* Thrown upon their own resources, the children invented two kingdoms inhabited by twelve soldiers given to their brother Branwell by Mr. Brontë: Charlotte and Branwell created the kingdom of Angria, Emily and Anne the kingdom of Gondal, and the children wrote the histories and adventures of the characters inhabiting their kingdoms. In 1845 Emily and Anne were still devising plots for Gondal, but in 1839 Charlotte consciously rejected Angria in order to free herself from what she felt to be an unhealthy obsession.

In January 1831 she attended Roe Head, a small private school near Mirfield, where she stayed for a year and a half and returned in 1835 as an assistant teacher. Here Charlotte made two lifelong friendships: Ellen Nussey and Mary Taylor. The three women corresponded for over twenty years, and Charlotte's periodic visits provided her with scenes and impressions upon which to draw when writing. In December 1837 she returned to Haworth; however, financial circumstances soon forced her to seek employment once again, and in May 1839 she became a governess for three months and again in March 1841 for nine months, after which she traveled to Brussels with Emily. The three Brontë sisters wished to open their own school, and in order to strengthen their credentials Emily and Charlotte wished to spend a half-year in school on the Continent improving their foreign languages. They arrived at the Pensionnat Héger on February 15, 1842, but returned at the end of October when their aunt died.

Charlotte returned to Brussels toward the end of January 1843 and formed a passionate, but unrequited, attachment to Constantin Héger, her married instructor. Portraits of her relationship and feelings for Héger can be seen in *The Professor* (1857) and *Villette* (1853), and many scholars believe that Héger inspired the character of Fairfax Rochester in *Jane Eyre.* But by the end of the year, her loneliness and homesickness became too much for her and she left Brussels on January 1, 1844. The sisters' plan to open a school proved to be fruitless; not one prospective pupil applied and by the close of the year the plan was abandoned.

Upon her return from Belgium, Charlotte discovered that Emily and Anne, like herself, had been writing poetry. The three published at their own expense *Poems by Currer, Ellis, and Acton Bell,* assuming male pseudonyms to preserve secrecy and to avoid the patronizing treatment they believed critics accorded women. The book received few reviews and sold only two copies.

Their lack of success, however, did not deter the sisters; even before the appearance of the *Poems* they began working on fiction. Each wrote a short novel— *Wuthering Heights* by Emily, *Agnes Grey* by Anne, and *The Professor* by Charlotte—intended to be one volume of a triple decker. Publication, however, proved to be elusive. The novels were rejected by half a dozen publishers before Thomas Cautley Newby agreed, in July 1847, to publish *Wuthering Heights* and *Agnes Grey* if the authors contributed fifty pounds toward production costs. But Newby refused to include *The Professor.* The sisters agreed and Charlotte continued, unsuccessfully, her search for a publisher for *The Professor.* When one publishing house agreed instead to consider a lengthier, more exciting novel, she immediately completed and submitted *Jane Eyre,* which she had begun several months earlier. The work, which appeared before that of her sisters, was an immediate success.

Charlotte's publisher, George Smith, was eager to follow up the success of *Jane Eyre* with another work, and in early 1848 she began working on what was to become *Shirley.* The composition of the novel was arrested half way through by a series of tragedies: her brother and two sisters fell ill with tuberculosis, and all died within the space of nine months. At thirty-three, Charlotte was the sole survivor of the six Brontë children. Although grief-stricken, she found solace in writing and pressed on with *Shirley,* completing it in August 1848. Although many scholars cite the subdued tone of the ending as a major weakness, *Shirley* nevertheless provides readers with one of Charlotte's most charming heroines: Caroline Helstone. Even though a somewhat passive victim, Caroline did make a plea for opportunities for women that was both novel and rousing: "I believe single women could have more to do—better chances of interesting and profitable occupations than they do now possess. . . . The brothers of these girls are every one in business or in professions; they have something to do; their sisters have no earthly employment, but household work or sewing; no earthly pleasure but an unprofitable visiting; and no hope, in all their life to come, of anything better. This stagnant state of things makes them decline in health. . . . The great wish—the sole aim of everyone of them—is to be married, but the majority will never marry; they will die as they now live." The protagonist of the novel, Shirley Keeldar, is an idealized portrait of Emily Brontë, but, Charlotte's desire to eulogize her sister resulted in a character so saintly that she lacks substance. The plot of *Shirley* deals with the hardships of the Yorkshire unemployed and the bitter confrontations of masters and men. And it is by interweaving the stories of Caroline and Shirley with the theme of industrial conflict that Charlotte Brontë can explore the failure of Victorian society to give women the opportunity to develop their abilities, realize their potential, and control their lives.

The publication of *Shirley* brought Charlotte the friendship of Elizabeth Gaskell, Harriet Martineau, Thackeray, and other writers. And it was mainly at Gaskell's home that she wrote *Villette,* a novel which some critics feel is her richest and most completely integrated work, in the three years following *Shirley.* With *Villette,* she returned to the autobiographical mode that had given *Jane Eyre* much of its coherence and conviction. But this time, unlike *The Professor,* she avoided an uncritical identification with her protagonist. Although Lucy Snowe embodies much of Brontë's own experience and is in many respects a projection of her inner self, she is not simply an enactment of her secret dreams and fantasies or a fictionalized expression of personal feelings. With *Villette* she comes full circle, returning to the fictionalized presentation of her experiences in Brussels first discussed in *The Professor.* But unlike the earlier portrayal, in *Villette,* Brontë is able to distance herself from the character and present a stronger, more mature exploration of the experience.

In the year following the publication of *Villette,* Charlotte married her father's curate. She found married life congenial and satisfying, and her husband daily revealed qualities that won her respect and increased her attachment to him. But her happiness was short-lived. In January 1855 she discovered she was pregnant. She suffered from extreme nausea and vomiting, conditions that her constitution, already weakened by incipient tuberculosis, was unable to bear. She died on March 31, 1855, ten months after her marriage, one month before her fortieth birthday.

Works

Poems by Currer, Ellis and Acton Bell (1846) ("Edited by Currer Bell"). (as Currer Bell) *Jane Eyre: An Autobiography* (1847). (as Currer Bell) *Shirley: A Tale* (1849). (as Currer Bell) *Villette* (1853). *The Professor: A Tale* (1857). *The Twelve Adventurers and Other Stories,* ed. C.K. Shorter and C.W. Hatfield (1925). *Legends of Angria: Compiled from the Early Writings of Charlotte Brontë,* ed. F.E. Ratchford and W.C. de Vane (1933). *Five Novelettes,* ed. W. Gerin (1971). *Complete Edition of the Early Writings of Charlotte Brontë, 1826–1832.* Vol. 1: *The Glass Town Saga,* ed. C. Alexander (1987). *Letters,* vol. 1, ed. M. Smith (1995).

Lynn M. Alexander

Emily Brontë
1818–1848

Born July 30, 1818, Thornton, England
Died December 19, 1848, Haworth
Genre(s): novel, poetry
Language(s): English

Emily Brontë's actual development as a writer began in 1831 when her sister Charlotte left for school at Roe Head. At this time Emily and her sister Anne began to record the saga of Gondal. Previously they had helped with the Glass Town Confederacy but Charlotte and their brother Branwell were the leaders in those creations.

Another factor in Emily's creative development was the freedom she and her siblings were allowed. Free to roam and play upon the Yorkshire moors as they wished, the girls expanded their imaginations beyond the usual boundaries. Also contributing to their mental stimulation was the free access they had to their father's library, where they found histories, biographies, and poetry—including the complete works of Byron. Emily's writing shows the influence of the moors and the romanticism of writers such as Byron and Scott: the poetry of Gondal depends on landscape for its major effects and is filled with the reckless actions of outlaws and rebels fleeing from justice or from pursuing armies and sheltering in the hollows of rocks or down in the glens where their secret haunts were located.

On the eve of Emily's seventeenth birthday, she and Charlotte left for Roe Head School, Charlotte was to teach and Emily's acceptance as a pupil was partial payment of Charlotte's salary. Her stay lasted only three months, as she sickened physically and mentally, pining for the moors. Many years later, when preparing a memoir for Emily's publisher, Charlotte tried to explain her sister's strong reaction to the strictures of boarding school: "Liberty was the breath of Emily's nostrils; without it, she perished. The change from her own home to a school, and from her own very noiseless, very secluded, but unrestricted and inartificial mode of life, to one of disciplined routine (though under the kindliest auspices) was what she failed in enduring. Her nature proved here too strong for her fortitude. Every morning when she woke, the vision of home and the moors rushed on her and darkened and saddened the day that lay before her. Nobody knew what ailed her but me—I knew only too well. In this struggle her health was quickly broken; her white face, attenuated form, and failing strength threatened rapid decline. I felt in my heart she would die, if she did not go home, and with this conviction obtained her recall."

Anne was sent to Roe Head in her place, leaving Emily without the companionship at home that she craved. At this same time Branwell returned home from his unsuccessful attempt to establish himself in London. Because both felt their attempts to confront the outside world to be steeped in failure, a new bond developed between them. This period of close association lasted for two years, and it was during this time that her preoccupation with the themes of guilt and failure began to take root.

Abruptly, in the autumn of 1837, Emily took a position as a teacher in a large school near Halifax. Exact details as to how and why are not known, but it is generally assumed that, while the position was secured by Charlotte, a desire to be near Branwell, who went as an usher at a boys' school that autumn, was behind the decision. Although Emily did not particularly enjoy her stay at Law Hill School—she once told a classroom of unruly girls that the only individual she liked in the whole establishment was the house dog—it was to have a lasting effect on her, for much of the salient features of the history of Law Hill found their way into *Wuthering Heights*. The evidence as to the length of her stay at Law Hill is conflicting, but the recent discovery that a letter from Charlotte, complaining of the harsh conditions under which Emily worked, dated by most biographers October 2, 1837, is clearly postmarked October 9, 1838, would seem to fix Emily's stay in the winter of 1838 to 1839.

Scholars regard Emily's stay at Law House as important because a nearby house, High Southerland Hall, is believed to be the model for the house known as Wuthering Heights, and it has been suggested that the kernel of the Heathcliff story was found in the recollections of a local Halifax man, Jack Sharp. However, the parallels are not exact, and there is another credible possibility for a model—Top Withens, near Haworth.

Emily returned to Haworth in 1839 and remained there until February 1842 when she and Charlotte left for Brussels to study foreign languages and equip themselves to open their own school. Forced to return home by the death of their aunt in October 1842, Emily decided to remain at Haworth when Charlotte returned to Brussels. It was at this time that she wrote much of her poetry. By 1844 the three sisters' plan to start a school had floundered through lack of response, and the sisters found themselves in low spirits, trying to conceive of earning their livings in a congenial manner.

It was at this point that Charlotte discovered a notebook of Emily's poetry, which she thought to be quite good. Anne soon admitted that she too, had been writing poetry, as had Charlotte. Together the sisters published *Poems by Currer, Ellis and Acton Bell.* The male pseudonyms were used at the insistence of Emily to maintain anonymity and protect their privacy. Not even the publishers knew the actual identities of the authors.

The three sisters, perhaps inspired by the ease with which they were able to publish their poems, quickly decided to try their hand at writing fiction. By July 1846 each had written a novel—Charlotte, *The Professor*; Anne, *Agnes Grey*; and Emily, *Wuthering Heights*. The sisters wished to publish the three works as a triple decker and after some searching a publisher, Thomas Newby, was found who would publish *Agnes Grey* and *Wuthering Heights*, but not *The Professor*. Charlotte wrote *Jane Eyre* in the interval and quickly found a publisher of her own. *Wuthering Heights* was published in two volumes and *Agnes Grey* in one volume in December 1847. Reviewers were baffled and shocked by *Wuthering Heights,* though some expressed admiration for its strange power. Even modern critics have difficulty dealing with the novel, tending either toward a stress on its eccentricity or concentration on very small sections.

Setting the tone with the Yorkshire word, "wuthering," an adjective referring to turbulent weather, Emily created a novel of such intensity that it is the standard by which subsequent gothic novels are measured. Heathcliff's violent obsession for Catherine and the almost incestuous nature of their relationship has fascinated critics and scholars since the novel's publication. The narrative itself is a stylistic challenge with its multiple narrators and the two Catherines, mother and daughter. The passionate tone of the novel was so shocking to Victorian readers that when it was revealed that the author was a woman, there was immediate speculation that Emily's brother, Branwell Brontë had written it. However, comparisons with extant juvenilia and poetry leave no doubt that Emily wrote *Wuthering Heights*.

It is not known what Emily did after finishing *Wuthering Heights*. A letter from Newby, fitting an envelope addressed to Ellis Bell and referring to another novel, has been found, but Newby tended to confuse the sisters and the novel mentioned could be Anne's *The Tenant of Wildfell Hall* (published June 1848). It has also been suggested that Emily's time was taken up with expanding *Wuthering Heights* from one to two volumes. Whatever work she might have done in the two years between the finishing of *Wuthering Heights* and her death, however, remains conjecture.

Branwell, who had been declining mentally and physically ever since he returned home in disgrace, died of consumption on September 24, 1848. His physical and spiritual welfare caused anxiety for all three sisters; and there are stories of Emily, the largest of the three, bearing the brunt of looking after him and carrying him about. Soon after his death Emily was reported to have a cough and a cold, which quickly developed into consumption. She struggled to continue her everyday tasks until almost the day of her death, refusing, according to most biographers, all medical assistance. She died suddenly on December 19, 1848.

Emily Brontë remains enigmatic because so little is known about her, and what is known is often contradictory. Her life seems one of self-isolation and conformity; her writings seem designed to shock and outrage. Her defiance of rigid categories and refusal to divide characters into obvious categories—good and bad, saints and sinners, aristocracy and servants—is very un-Victorian, but does not seem out of keeping with her temperament.

Works

Poems by Currer, Ellis and Acton Bell (1848). (as Ellis Bell) *Wuthering Heights* (1848). *The Life and* Works *of Charlotte Brontë and Her Sisters* (1899–1900). *Poems of Emily Brontë* (1906). *The Complete* Works *of Emily Jane Brontë* (1906). *The Complete Poems of Emily Jane Brontë* (1924). "An Unpublished Verse by Emily Jane Bronte" (1931). *Two Poems. Love's Rebuke, Remembrance* (1934). *The Gondal Saga* (1934). *Gondal Poems, Now First Published from the Manuscript in the British Museum* (1938). *The Complete Poems* (1941). *Five Essays Written in French by Emily Jane Brontë* (1948). *The Complete Poems* (1951). *A Diary Paper* (1951). *Gondal's Queen: a Novel in Verse* (1955). *Complete Poems*, ed. J. Gezari (1992). *Poems*, ed. B. Lloyd-Evans (1992).

Lynn M. Alexander

Anita Brookner
1938–

Born July 16, 1938, London
Genre(s): art history, novel
Language(s): English

Anita Brookner was educated at James Allen's Girls' School, King's College, University of London, the Courtauld Institute, and in Paris. A visiting lecturer at the University of Reading from 1959 to 1964, she

was Slade Professor of Fine Arts at Cambridge, the first woman to hold the position. A Fellow of New Hall, Cambridge, she currently teaches at the Courtauld Institute. An internationally respected authority on eighteenth- and nineteenth-century French art, she is the author of eight specialized studies in the field, including *Watteau* (1968); *The Genius of the Future* (1971); *Greuze* (1972); and *Jacques-Louis David* (1974). In addition, she is the author of more than fifteen novels.

Brookner's work in art history has earned her the respect of colleagues, critics, and students. Her scholarly articles and texts are characterized by meticulous research, fluent expression, and extraordinary erudition. Her lectures give evidence of the same careful attention to logic, detail, and style; she is known as one of the Courtauld's finest tutors.

Brookner has also demonstrated skill as a novelist. *The Debut* (1981) published as *A Start in Life* in the U.K. tells the story of Dr. Ruth Weiss, a quiet scholar devoted to the study of Balzac. At the age of forty, Dr. Weiss decides that literature has ruined her life: Balzac was right—the virtuous are passive victims doomed to unsatisfying lives. Temporarily freeing herself from clinging parents who are little more than spoiled, overgrown adolescents, she goes to Paris in search of a great romantic affair. Inevitably disappointed, she returns to London and ends up caring for her invalid, widowed father and is consumed anew by her study of virtue and vice in the fiction of Balzac.

Providence (1982) is the story of Kitty Maule, daughter of a long-deceased British army colonel and his French wife. A university lecturer who specializes in the Romantic tradition, Kitty delivers a series of presentations on Benjamin Constant's *Adolphe*, a short novel about failure. She lives in two worlds, one of her doting but demanding French grandparents, the other of British academe. Her perceptions clouded by fantasies, Kitty misreads the meaning of an affair with a colleague and retreats to a life of disappointment, unable to change, an intelligent heroine defeated.

Her third novel, *Look at Me*, (1983) is a work of metafiction. Frances Hinton, cataloguer in an art library devoted to pictorial representations of medical illness, seems to crave companionship; living with an ancient housekeeper in a tomb-like flat, she catalogues and observes rather than experiences the people she meets. As an outsider with sensibilities too fine to allow her to develop the attributes she needs to survive in a social world, she returns, disappointed, to the bed in which her mother died in order to write the novel we read. Initially described as a "beggar at the feast," Frances ends up taking revenge, consuming her enemies while making literature a substitute for life.

Edith Hope, the protagonist of *Hotel du Lac* (1984), is a writer of romantic fiction sent into temporary exile after an "unfortunate lapse"; her scandalous behavior has caused her friends to banish her to Switzerland. At the elegant Hotel du Lac, she spends her time in genteel fashion, joining in the rituals of hotel residence with a number of interesting, eccentric characters, writing undelivered letters to her lover, and working on sections of a new novel. Edith achieves some insight into her own predicament but chooses to reject a life of practical, pragmatic arrangements in favor of returning to London and a life of romantic fictions.

In these four novels Brookner presents several consistent concerns while demonstrating considerable technical advance. From *The Debut* through *Hotel du Lac,* she portrays a woman of early middle age, often an exile or orphan, bound to, if not oppressed by, traditions, whether intellectual or social, and alienated. Lonely and inhibited, she nonetheless ventures, albeit timidly, into a love affair that will follow a preordained course: infatuation, disappointment, and failure, followed by accentuated isolation, with the whole experience transmuted to artistic creation of one sort or another.

Typically, the Brookner heroine has yearnings for the romantic and the impossible, a desire for courtly love in Chelsea, as it were. Though she is perceptive and intelligent, she appears incapable of recognizing the impossibility of translating romantic fantasy into quotidian existence; when she does achieve some insight, as in the case of Edith Hope, she ignores it and returns to her customary life, incapable, or perhaps just unwilling, to change.

Brookner's mastery of technical elements has increased. The earlier novels showed a rather tentative hand outlining a plot perhaps more suited to a short story, a voice neither fully modulated nor smoothly inflected. In *Providence* and, to a greater extent, in *Hotel du Lac,* Brookner creates a developed plot of substance and breadth with well-paced events; sure wit and irony enrich a repertory of voices. Particularly in the case of the latter, the prose is controlled, graceful, and richly evocative. Her style, accurately described as "hyperliterate" and distinguished by references to Dickens, Balzac, Colette, and Henry James, holds a decided appeal for an audience both literate and literary. In a world rather carefully circumscribed, Brookner succeeds, particularly in *Providence* and *Hotel du Lac,* in depicting the plight of a twentieth-century woman with a comic richness deeply suggestive of more serious concerns.

Yet little in any of these novels prepared readers for Brookner's 1985 novel, *Family and Friends,* a striking departure and an answer to those critics who have claimed that her fiction is essentially autobiographical. *Family and Friends* chronicles the affairs of a wealthy Jewish family, the Dorns, during the late 1930s and 1940s. The story of a powerful matriarch, Sophia (Sofka), and her four children, Frederick, Alfred, Mimi, and Betty, this novel embraces not only a larger cast of characters but also a wider geography than the previous four. Transplanted to London in the hectic days preceding the outbreak of World War II, the family continues to prosper without their recently deceased patriarch. Sofka assumes his place and dominates the life of the clan, openly favoring Frederick and Betty. Brookner traces the Dorn family story from London to Paris and the Riviera to Hollywood, integrating new relations and acquaintances as she creates a rather densely populated narrative. *Family and Friends is* rich and robust, full-bodied and sparkling. The greater narrative breadth of this novel has enabled Brookner to portray characters of far greater complexity and range than in her previous novels; they are so finely modeled, with such carefully limned sensibilities (and hungers), that these wonderful black-and-white family photographs described a half-dozen times in the novel actually come to life as full-color cinema. With *Family and Friends,* Brookner has given a significant demonstration of extended range and power as a writer of fiction; she has created a vital, engaging tale of absorbing interest, characteristically fluent articulation, and emotional resonance.

Works

An Iconography of Cecil Rhodes (1956). *Utrillo* (translator, 1960). *The Fauves* (translator, 1962). *Gauguin* (translator, 1963). *Watteau* (1968). *The Genius of the Future: Studies in French Art Criticism: Diderot, Stendahl, Baudelaire, Zola, the Brothers Goncourt, Huysmans* (1971; 1988). *Greuze: The Rise and Fall of an Eighteenth-Century Phenomenon* (1972). *Jacques-Louis David* (1974). *A Start in Life* [*The Debut*] (1981). *Providence* (1982). *Look at Me* (1983). *Hotel du Lac* (1984). *Family and Friends* (1985). *A Misalliance* (1986). *A Friend from England* (1987). *Latecomers* (1988). *Lewis Percy* (1989). *Brief Lives* (1990). *A Closed Eye* (1991). *Fraud* (1992). *A Family Romance* [*Dolly*] (1993). *A Private View* (1994). *Incidents in the Rue Laugier* (1995).

Robert E. Hosmer, Jr.

Elizabeth Barrett Browning
1806–1861

Born March 6, 1806, Durhall, England
Died June 30, 1861, Florence, Italy
Genre(s): poetry, letters
Language(s): English

A celebrated nineteenth-century poet whose work has recently enjoyed an important feminist critical revaluation, Browning was the oldest of twelve children. Educated at home by tutors, she was endowed with a profound desire for knowledge and engaged in a remarkable curriculum of languages, classics, literature, and philosophy. Late in 1820 her father suffered financial losses, and shortly thereafter she was stricken with her first serious illness for which opium, which became a lifetime habit, was prescribed. Elizabeth's mother died in 1828, and in 1832 the Barretts left their beloved Hope End estate, settling first in Sidmouth, then London.

By 1838 Browning had published three volumes of poetry but had not yet earned any real critical attention. She moved that year with her favorite brother, Samuel, to the gentler climate of Torquay for her health, but returned to London two years later when he drowned, for Elizabeth a terrible and traumatic loss. Although *Poems* (1844) gained her a wide and admiring reading public, she lived a circumscribed life until her elopement with Robert Browning in 1846.

The courtship of Elizabeth Barrett and Robert Browning, which resulted in volumes of letters and the famous *Sonnets from the Portuguese,* began with Browning's 1845 letter to the famous poetess in which he declared: "I do . . . love these books with all my heart—and I love you too." She concealed the romance from her father, who opposed the marriage of any of his children. In September 1846 the couple was secretly married and shortly after left for the Continent, settling ultimately in Florence. The change of climate and mode of living vastly improved her health, and in 1849 she gave birth to a son, Robert Wiedman Barrett-Browning (Pen). During the years 1850–1859 the Brownings traveled a great deal, passing summers in England but always returning to Florence as their home. She never again communicated with her father, who had disowned her upon her marriage, and in 1857 Mr. Barrett died, never reconciled to his favorite daughter. In 1861 Elizabeth died and was buried in Florence. Her life, particularly her marriage to Robert Browning, has been the subject of many critical and romantic biographies. The last few years have

witnessed several important studies that explore the influence of Elizabeth and Robert Browning on each other's work.

Today her early poetry is neither widely read nor highly regarded; nonetheless, these volumes reveal her erudition and her passionate commitment to poetry. *The Battle of Marathon* (1820) and *An Essay on Mind* (1826) are long, didactic, neoclassical poems in heroic couplets. *The Battle of Marathon* narrates the 490 B.C. battle between the Greeks and the Persians. *An Essay on Mind* is a metaphysical and epistemological enquiry that asserts the primary value of the imagination and poetry. Her earlier works also include a translation of Aeschylus's *Prometheus Bound* (1833) and *The Seraphim and Other Poems* (1838), a diverse collection of poems marked by a religious preoccupation and a certain morbidity.

Poems (1844) was Barrett Browning's first volume to draw wide attention. Although "Lady Geraldine's Courtship" was a favorite, she considered "A Drama of Exile" the best poem in the volume. "The Cry of the Children" is noteworthy, for it marks her commitment to political and social issues, in this case the child labor system. She became increasingly convinced that women writers must devote themselves and their work to pressing contemporary issues and injustices, a conviction that shapes her later poetry. Only in the last twenty years have critics addressed her political commitment.

Browning's next major work was *Sonnets from the Portuguese,* published with *Poems* in 1850 but written several years earlier for Robert Browning during their courtship. Because of their highly personal nature, she titled them to suggest a translation. *Sonnets* which enjoyed enormous popularity, is a sequence of forty-four poems that traces the call of love, the attendant fears, doubts, and insecurities, and the final triumph of love. Several of these poems are considered masterful executions in the genre of amatory verse. Greater critical attention has recently been paid to *Sonnets,* a result of feminist revaluation of Browning's work and its place in the tradition of women's writing.

It is mainly her later poetry, largely concerned with political and social issues, that has been the subject of feminist reconsideration. In 1851 she published *Casa Guidi Windows,* a well-crafted poem, which moves from optimism and hopefulness for the cause of Italian liberty to disillusionment. Her passionate commitment to Italian politics, which is just beginning to receive critical consideration, is also reflected in many of the poems in *Poems Before Congress* (1860). However, one poem in this volume, "A Curse for a Nation," is a condemnation of slavery in America. The poem embodies Browning's convictions about the power and responsibility of women to raise their voices in protest against injustice, claiming that "A curse from the depths of womanhood / Is very salt, and bitter and good."

Aurora Leigh (1857), a long epic poem, remains the most widely discussed poem of her later years. In the narration of the trials, travels, and career of an independent woman poet, she explores feminist, political, and aesthetic issues. *Aurora Leigh,* which Browning prefaced as the work "into which my highest convictions of work and art have entered," was admired by Swinburne, Ruskin, and the Rossetti brothers, but received mixed, often highly critical reviews and was largely forgotten until Virginia Woolf urged reconsideration of the "stimulating and boring, ungainly and eloquent, monstrous and exquisite" poem that "commands our interest and inspires our respect" (*Second Common Reader*). The critical interest in the poem initiated by feminist criticism continues to produce fascinating and important psychoanalytic and feminist work on the poem. Recent criticism emphasizes the subversions, anger, and gender conflicts in her poetry and relocates Browning in a women's literary tradition. As a result, a greater degree of seriousness has become attached to her work, and a fuller portrait of this Victorian woman poet of deeply held convictions has emerged.

Works

The Battle of Marathon: a Poem (1820). *An Essay on Mind, with Other Poems* (1826). *Prometheus Bound, Translated from the Greek of Aeschylus,* and *Miscellaneous Poems* (1833). *The Seraphim and Other Poems* (1838). *Queen Annelida and Falce Arcite,* in *The Poems of Chaucer Modernized* (1841). (with R. H. Horne) *A New Spirit of the Age* (1844). *Poems* (1844). *Poems: New Edition* (1850). *Sonnets* [or] *Sonnets from the Portuguese,* in *Poems* (1850). *Casa Guidi Windows: A Poem* (1851). *The Cry of the Children,* in *Two Poems* (1854). *Aurora Leigh* (1857). *Poems Before Congress* (1860). *Last Poems* (1862). *Poetical Works* (1866). *Letters Addressed to R. Hengist Horn,* ed. S.R. Townshend Mayer (1877). *Poetical* Works *from 1826 to 1844,* ed. J.H. Ingram (1887). Kenyon, F.G., ed. *Letters of Elizabeth Barrett Browning* (1897). *Letters of Robert Browning and Elizabeth Barrett Browning 1845–1846* (1899). *Complete Works,* ed. C. Porter and H. Clarke (1900). *Poetical Works* (1904). Meynell, A. ed., *The Art of Scansion: Letters of E.B. Browning to Uvedale Price* (1916). Wise, T.J., ed. *Letters of Eliza-*beth Barrett Browning to Robert Browning and Other Correspondents (1916). Huxley, L., ed. *Letters to Her Sister 1846–59* (1929). *Twenty-two Unpublished Letters of Elizabeth Barrett Browning and Robert Browning (to Her Sisters)* (1935). Benet, W.R., ed. *From Robert and Elizabeth Browning: A Further Selection* (1936). Miller, B., ed. Elizabeth Barrett to Miss Mitford: Unpublished (1954). McCarthy, B.P., ed. *Elizabeth Barrett to Mr. Boyd: Unpublished Letters* (1955). Landis, P., and R.E. Freeman, eds. *Letters of the Brownings to George Barrett* (1958). Shackford, M.H., ed. *Letters to B.R. Haydon* (1959). Kelley, P., and R. Hudson, eds. *Diary of E.B.B.: The Unpublished Diary of Elizabeth Barrett Browning, 1831–1832* (1969). Heydon, P., and P. Kelley, eds. *Elizabeth Barrett Browning's Letters to Mrs. David Ogilvy, 1849–1861* (1974). Kelley, P., and R. Hudson, eds. *The Brownings' Correspondence,* vols. I and II (1984); vol. III (1985). Kelley, P. and B. Coley, eds. *The Browning Collections: A Reconstruction with Other Memorabilia* (1984).

Patricia A. O'Hara

Friederike (Frederikke) Brun
1765–1835

Born June 3, 1765, Gräfentonna-Gotha, Sachsen (Saxony) Germany
Died March 25, 1835, Copenhagen, Denmark
Genre(s): poetry, letters, travelogue
Language(s): German

At her beloved, elegant Sophienholm on Bagsværd Lake, a salon of international and, to a certain degree, aristocratic character, and in Merchant Constantin Brun's (refined) salons in the Palace on Bredgade, Friederike Brun was a catalyst for the refined, cosmopolitan, literary circles of her day. Like her more provincial contemporary, Karen Margrethe (Kamma) Rahbek of Bakkehuset, Brun offered a cultural home for intellectuals, artists, and writers. With her great talent as a storyteller and her knowledge and experience in European literary salons, such as that of Madame de Staël in Geneva, Friederike Brun drew Danish and European literati to a meeting point, to a center of entertainment, sensitive conversation, and social refinement.

Sophie Christiane Friederike (Frederikke) Münter (Brun) was born in Gräfentonna-Gotha, Sachsen (Saxony), on June 3, 1765. She was the daughter of the presiding church superintendent in Gräfentonna, Balthasar Münter (1735–1793), and Magdalena Sophia Ernestine Friederike von Wangenheim (1742–1808), and she was the sister of the writer, Friederich Münter. When Friederike Münter was barely a few weeks old, Balthasar Münter accepted an appointment as parish priest of Skt. Petri Church in Copenhagen; in the Danish capital, the Münters quickly joined the influential and culturally prominent German society circles (of) A.P. Bernstorff and Ernst Schimmelmann. Friederike Münter was a very precocious child, fond of reading and dramatizing Samuel Richardson's novels and capable of reading Ossian in English at thirteen and Tasso in Italian at fourteen. She also made her first attempt at poetry in 1782, with a collection of German poems privately printed by her father. Friederike's first trip abroad, to Germany with her parents, acquainted her with such prominent literary figures as Herder, Klopstock, Bürger, and Wieland and led to her first travel journal, *Tagebuch meiner ersten Reise* (1782; Diary of my First Journey). With her lively wit, spirit, and intelligence, Friederike Münter attracted many suitors; her father's mild insistence and concern for her economic security led Münter to accept the hand of the Copenhagen merchant, Constantin Brun; he and Münter were married shortly after her eighteenth birthday. There were five children from the marriage, among them Ida, the later Comtesse de Bombelles. After the birth of Ida, Friederike Brun developed a severe case of influenza; when the attack subsided, Brun was left deaf. Her severe deafness never impeded Brun's later social prominence or the liveliness of conversation, sociability, and entertainment at Sophienholm. Brun embarked on a series of travels for treatments and recreation, with Constantin Brun or alone. From 1790 to 1791, the Bruns traveled through France and Switzerland, meeting the German poet, Friedrich Matthisson, and the Swiss writer, Charles Victor de Bonstetten. Friederike Brun shared the companionship of both men, first primarily Matthisson's in Lugano and Rome (1795–1796), but Bonstetten eventually stepped definitively into the foreground becoming the completely dominating (passion) of Brun's life. Even managing to win over Constantin Brun with his charm, Bonstetten and his son moved into the Brun home in Copenhagen; the Bonstettens shared the residence with Friederike and Constantin Brun from 1798 to 1801. Brun accompanied Bonstetten on his return to Switzerland, remaining with him there until 1803, when she returned alone—and inconsolable—to Copenhagen.

In 1805, Brun made her final trip south, first to Geneva, where she resided with Madame de Staël and Bonstetten, then to Rome, where she lived in the same congenial company from 1807 to 1810. In 1810, Constantin Brun issued an ultimatum to his wife; she was either to forsake her daughter Ida and remain with Bonstetten on a fixed pension or to return to Denmark immediately. Brun chose the latter course, never to see Bonstetten again but to continue writing to him until his death (1832). The relationship between the Bruns, never passionate, was not restored to harmony: Brun gave up her travels and friend, while (Constantin) had to reconcile himself to foreigners (and) a salon of European format where the most prominent intellectuals and artists met with the aristocrats, foreign diplomats and travelers. Sophienholm and the Palace on Bredgade became the centers of cultural life and *belles lettres*, with Friederike Brun at the helm of it all, until her death on March 25, 1835.

Friederike Brun's extensive collections (in 15 volumes) of poetry, letters, artistic and literary articles, personal sketches, and travel descriptions are nearly exclusively written in the German of her literary circle and cultural heritage. In addition to the early editions of her poems (1782) and the poems published by Friedrich Matthisson (*Gedichte*, 1795, Poems), Brun wrote two additional volumes of poetry, *Neue Gedichte* (1812; New Poems) and *Neueste Gedichte* (1820; Newest Poems); her poetry belongs stylistically to the *Empfindsamkeit* category, but with a certain classical quality. More remarkable and noteworthy are Brun's many travel descriptions, characterizations of noted individuals, and depictions of life in Europe: "In many instances genres cross each other in (her) individual works, which often combine travel, personal sketches, and art and cultural descriptions from (Brun's) many European trips" (Dalager, Stig, and Anne-Marie Mai, *Danske kvindelige forfattere* 1, p. 139). Such works as *Prosaische Schriften I–IV* (1799–1801; Prose Writings), which included *Tagebuch über Rom* (1795–1796; Diary of Rome) and *Episoden aus Reisen I–II* (1806–1809; III, 1816; IV, 1818; Episodes from Travels); *Briefe aus Rom* (1808–1810; Letters from Rome); and, her last book, *Römisches Leben I–II* (1833; Life in Rome), reveal Brun's perceptive, precise, artistic sense, her sympathetic feelings for Italian nature, art, and culture, and her ability to sketch the significant personalities she had met in Rome and elsewhere. Friederike Brun's most important work is certainly her fine autobiography of the first fifteen years of her life in the cultured Danish-German Münter milieu in

Copenhagen, *Wahrheit aus Morgenträume* (began 1810, published 1824; Truth from Morning Dreams; in Danish, *Ungdomserindringer*, Memories of Youth). The work includes an addition, *Idas ästhetische Entwicklung* (1824; Ida's Aesthetic Development), in which Brun, as representative of German-Danish ennobling cultural humanism, provided an educational program for the development of the feminine *forte*, the exemplary aesthetic and artistic talents inherent in women.

Idas ästhetische Entwicklung is dedicated to Madame de Staël, the most complete incarnation of Brun's aesthetic humanistic ideal. Brun also carried on an extensive correspondence with her contemporaries, among them the mild governess of Bakkehuset, Karen Margrethe (Kamma) Rahbek, of course Madame de Staël of Geneva and Italy and Bonstetten, and especially, over twenty years, Caroline von Humboldt, with whom Brun shared her deepest bitterness and boredom with life and her constant comparison between "the man God gave me and the man my heart chose."

The cultural background, education, and experience, and the various travels of Friederike Brun were those of a European cosmopolitan, of a representative of the refined, artistic-literary salon tradition of European savants and connoisseurs. Yet Brun enjoyed her acquaintance with many Danish artists, poets, and writers, B. Thorvaldsen, Johannes Edwald, Jens Baggesen, Adam Øhlenschläger, J.H. Heiberg, and B.S. Ingemann. Brun's personality was a unique meld of sentimentality and practicality, of clarity, romance, vision, and a deep understanding of the famous and less notable people she came to know. Friederike Brun's writings and her salons at Sophienholm and Bredgade reflect her internationally oriented intellect as well as her sensitivity and knowledge of Danish cultural life *and* her personal *ennui* after a life of extensive travel and one great passion.

Works

Gedichte (1782). *Tagebuch meiner ersten Reise* (1782). *Gedichte* (1795). *Tagebuch über Rom* (1795–1796). *Prosaische Schriften*, I–IV (1799–1801). *Episoden aus Reisen* I–IV (1806–1809; 1816; 1818). *Briefe aus Rom* (1808–1810). *Wahrheit aus Morgenträume* (1810–1824). *Neue Gedichte* (1812). *Neueste Gedichte* (1820). *Idas ästhetische Entwicklung* (1824). Briefe, Artiklen, Beiträge. *Hören*; *Musenalmanach*; *Iris*; *Nytaarsgave for Damer*; *Minerva*; *Tilskueren*. *Römisches Leben*, I–II (1833).

Lanae Hjortsvang Isaacson

Janina Brzostowska
1907–1986
Born July 7, 1907, Wadowice, Poland
Died 1986
Genre(s): poetry, novel
Language(s): Polish

Brzostowska was born in Wadowice in the mountain area of Beskidy, in a middle-class family of intelligentsia. Her father, Jan Dorozinski, was a high school principal and teacher, author of poetry published under the penname of Julian Mrok, and the author of "Zarys psychologii elementarnej" (An Outline of Basic Psychology); her mother, Julia née Berner, was a pianist. Brzostowska started writing poetry at eleven, and several years later her poems "Matka" (Mother) and "Sen w ogrodzie" (A Dream in the Garden) appeared in a school newspaper *Nasz lan* (Our Field). Brzostowska studied Polish and French at Jagiellonian University in Cracow, where her family moved, and continued her poetic activity.

In the summer of 1924 she joined the group of poets of the Beskidy region called "Czartak," founded by such well-known men of letters as Emil Zegadlowicz, Edward Kozikowski, and Jan Nepomucen Miller, who organized in order to "pour the light onto the world from the top of this Hilly Republic according to the age-old truth that all joy comes from the mountains," and "prove with a new form of art that Poland has the right to occupy her newly acquired place among the free nations. . . ." Brzostowska's ties with the poets of the "Czartak" were ones of friendship rather than of program; because of a lung disease she developed in her youth, she lived and worked alone.

Her formal debut was made in 1925 with a volume of poems connected with urban rather than country life, and it was very favorably received due to its original language, "organically isolated," as one of the critics put it. The source of her poetry was perceived in a "desire to define that which cannot be expressed and her fear of what is transitory but unfamiliar." The eighteen-year-old was praised for her wisdom concerning the vanity of things and her calm meditation on death. The title of the volume of poems called *O ziemi i mojej milosci* [1925; On Land and My Love] was viewed as a definition of her poetic program: to write about the land, not only that of her region and its people, but to involve herself with human life in a broader sense. Her poetry describing love, nature, and the life of common people met with general recognition. The last book she published with the "Czartak" was the volume of subtle and meditative lyrical poems entitled *Erotyki* [1926; Erotic Poems]. She formally left the group in 1929, yet she remained close to the friends of her youth and remembered them warmly. In the same year she moved permanently to Warsaw but never joined another literary group and was always perceived as an isolated phenomenon in Polish literature. Though relatively little known, she was included among the important women poets next to Kazimiera Illakowiczowna and Maria Pawlikowska-Jasnorzewska by prominent historian of literature and critic Aleksander Brueckner.

Having moved to the capital city, Brzostowska attempted prose and in 1933 published her first novel *Bezrobotni Warszawy* [1933; The Jobless of Warsaw] in the vein of a series of journalistic reports, dubbed by the critics as "a cry of protest" of the unemployed from the depth of their physical and moral misery. That first novel was soon withdrawn from publication by censorship. Brzostowska's second novel describes a woman's coming of age and, according to the critics, reveals the author's subtle psychological insight on social questions. From 1938 to 1939 Brzostowska was an editor of the bimonthly *Skawa*, devoted to the problems of her native region of Beskidy. One of its collaborators was the famous artist, philosopher, and man of letters Stanislaw Ignacy Witkiewicz, known as Witkacy. After almost a decade, Brzostowska returned to poetry with her two volumes of verse published in 1939, which remained basically unknown for their circulation was interrupted by the outbreak of war. The main subjects of her lyrical poetry are love and the passage of time.

Brzostowska spent the years of the German occupation in Warsaw and engaged in the conspiratorial activity of patriotic resistance; deported from Warsaw with the rest of the inhabitants after the 1944 uprising, she was one of the first who returned to settle among the ruins of the totally razed city. She wrote poetry but published little during the times of relative lack of political oppression of art; translating poetry became her main occupation, her greatest achievement being the 1961 translation into Polish of the complete "Songs" of Sappho. In 1969 in Vienna, those poems were sung in Polish by the Japanese singer Emiko Iiama with music by the Polish composer Andrzej Hundziak.

Works

Poetry: *Szczescie w cudzym miescie* [Happiness in a Strange City] (1925). *O ziemi i mojej milosci* [On Land and My Love] (1925). *Erotyki* [Erotic Poems] (1926). *Najpiekniejsza z przygod* [The Most Beautiful of Adventures] (1929). *Naszyjnik wiecznosci* [A Necklace of Eternity] (1939). *Zywiol i spiew* [The El-

ements and the Song] (1939). *Plomien w cierniach* [Flame among Thorns] (1947). *Giordano Bruno*, historical poem (1953). *Wiersze* [Poems] (1957). *Zanim noc . . .* [Until the Night] (1961). *Czas nienazwany* [Time without Name] (1964). *Obrona swiatla* [In Defense of Light] (1968). *Pozdrowienie* [Greetings] (1969). *Szczescia szukamy* [In Search of Happiness] (1974). *Poezje wybrane* [Selected Poetry] (1974). *Eros* (1977). *Spiew przedwieczorny* [A Song at Nighttime] (1979). *Poezje zebrane* [Collected Poems] (1981).

Novels: *Bezrobotni Warszawy* (1933; rpt. 1947, 1950). *Kobieta zdobywa swiat* [A Woman Conquers the World] (1937).

Maya Peretz

Lukrecija Bogašinović Budmani
1710–1784

Born October 26, 1710, Dubrovnik, Yugoslavia
Died June 8, 1784, Dubrovnik
Genre(s): poetry
Language(s): Croatian

Although today Lukrecija Bogašinović Budmani is forgotten (none of her works having ever been printed), she was one of the most popular poets of Baroque Dubrovnik. Other than the fact that she was the only child of her parents, and the granddaughter of the poet Petar Toma Bogašinović, who in 1684 published what proved to be a popular epic concerning the recent defeat of the Turks by the King of Poland at Vienna, nothing is known about her childhood and youth. However, they could hardly have been happy because of her father's misfortune. Employed as a clerk by the government of Dubrovnik, he was apparently unjustly accused in 1710 of being chiefly responsible for the great shortage in the state granary and was sentenced to five years of galley labor and banishment from Dubrovnik, with the additional obligation of paying a huge fine to the government in yearly installments, which he did until his death. So Lukrecija did not even live with her father from her birth up to her thirty-third year, when his banishment was revoked and he returned to Dubrovnik. When she first started writing is unknown. On the evidence of her works it is clear that she knew Italian and had a considerable knowledge of the poetry of her time.

Very late, in her forty-third year, Lukrecija married Šimun Budmani, a merchant by profession. Ten years later she was a childless widow. Although her husband left her no property, she was supported in her widowhood by the real estate that she had inherited from her father's brother and her mother's sister. When she died in 1784, she was accorded a solemn funeral in the Dominican church of Dubrovnik and was laid beside her parents, not her husband, who had been buried in another church.

Only four works of Lukrecija have been preserved in manuscript, even though it is likely that she wrote more. All four treat a Biblical theme, and all four were written after her fiftieth year, so that it is reasonable to suppose that they were not her first attempts at poetry. The first three are epics: *Posluh Abrama Patrijarke* (1763; The Obedience of Patriarch Abraham) in 760 verses, *Život Tobije i njegova sina* (1763; Life of Tobith and His Son) in 1684 verses, and *Život Josefa Patrijarke* (1770; Life of Patriarch Joseph) in 1996 verses. The fourth work is a pastoral eclogue, *Razgovor pastirski vrhu porodenja Gospodinova* (1764; The Shepherds' Conversation on the Lord's Nativity) in 1504 verses. All those works are written in stanzas of four verses, each verse consisting of four trochees, with the rhyme scheme *abab*, the usual stanza of the Baroque poetry of Dubrovnik.

The adaptation of Biblical tales into vernacular epics, primarily for moralistic and didactic purposes, is almost unknown today, but it was very popular in the Baroque, and Lukrecija had many Italian and Croatian predecessors for her epics. Although she did not have her works printed, so many manuscripts—now in various libraries and archives of Dubrovnik and Zagreb—have been preserved (many of these contain, naturally, faulty and abridged versions), that they must have been popular and admired during her life and well into the nineteenth century. Perhaps the chief merit of Lukrecija's epics is in the psychological truth and realism of her Biblical adaptations. Where the Bible gives little more than the facts of the story, she tries to account for the characters' psychology and motivation, in order to make them more familiar to the readers. She was not a great poet, but her epics deserve our interest by their strong dramatic element, shown in the many dialogues in the crucial moments, and in the skill with which the author had given her own contemporary setting to the Biblical stories, so that they read as if they took place in eighteenth-century Croatia. The author, with an obvious moralistic purpose, often addressing her young female readers in particular, stresses the importance of the family and analyzes the relations between its various members. Her heroes—Abraham, the heavily tested father and husband, the saintly Tobith, Joseph, the ideal man in his just and magnanimous treatment of his brothers—are presented as moral examples to the readers by their nobility, generosity, and, above all, unshakable piety.

Works

Posluh Abrama Patrijarke (1763). *Život Tobije i njegova sina* (1763). *Život Josefa Patrijarke* (1770). *Razgovor pastirski vrhu porodenja Gospodinova* (1764).

Neda Jeni

Frances (Fanny) Burney
1752–1840
Born June 13, 1752, King's Lynn, Norfolk, England
Died January 6, 1840, London
Genre(s): novel, memoir
Language(s): English

Frances Burney was the daughter of a music-master and organist later to gain renown as a historian of music and member of Samuel Johnson's circle. She was a shy and seemingly backward child but displayed an early talent for mimicry and a remarkably reten-

Frances (Fanny) Burney

tive memory. Her mother died in 1762, and five years later her father married Elizabeth Allen, a widow with a keen interest in literature. Frances became a voracious reader and began an extensive experimentation with writing. In 1767 her stepmother concluded that Frances and her sister Susan were taking their writing too seriously, and the girls dutifully consigned their "scribblings"—including the draft of a novel by Frances, "Carolyn Evelyn"—to a bonfire. In 1768 Burney began keeping a detailed diary, and in 1778 her first novel, *Evelina, or a Young Lady's Entrance into the World,* was published. The novel was published anonymously, but the secret of its authorship quickly leaked out and Burney found herself the center of a whirlwind of adulation. Samuel Johnson, Hester Thrale Piozzi, Sir Joshua Reynolds, Richard Brinsley Sheridan, and other well-known people were effusive in their praise. Burney quickly became the darling of the Streatham set and the special pet of Johnson.

She next tried writing a comedy for the stage, but the project was dropped at the urging of her father and Samuel "Daddy" Crisp, an old family friend. They apparently feared the play's sharp satire on female "wits" would offend the influential "bluestockings." Another novel, *Cecilia,* appeared in 1782. In 1784 Burney lost three close and important friends. "Daddy" Crisp died that April. Then, that summer, the widowed Mrs. Thrale announced she would marry an Italian singing master. Her family and friends reacted with shocked disapproval, and she turned to Frances for support. The very conservative and socially punctilious Burney responded coldly, and the friendship ended. In December, Johnson died.

In 1785 Burney was presented to King George III and Queen Charlotte and was soon offered the post of second keeper of the robes for Queen Charlotte, entering the royal service in July. She soon found the restrictive nature of her post disagreeable, and she resented the petty tyrannies of her immediate superior. In 1790 she voiced her discontent to her father, but he was reluctant to allow her to resign. The next year, though, her health began to fail, and she left the post in July 1791 with a pension of £100 a year. In January 1793 Burney visited a friend at Norbury Park in Surrey and was introduced to a colony of French refugees who had rented nearby Juniper Hall. Among them was a former army officer, Alexandre d'Arblay, who had been adjutant general to the Marquis de Lafayette and accompanied Lafayette when he fled to Austria. A romance blossomed, and Burney and d'Arblay were married on July 28, 1793. Their only child, Alexandre, was born December 18, 1794.

Shortly after her marriage, Burney wrote *Brief Reflections Relative to the Emigrant French Clergy,* a pamphlet encouraging charity toward Catholic priests who had fled revolutionary France. March 1795 saw a performance at Drury Lane of *Edwy and Elgiva,* a tragedy written during her years at court. It was a dismal failure, withdrawn after one performance. *Camilla,* Burney's third novel, was published in 1796. A successful subscription sale made the novel a strong moneymaker, but critical reaction was mixed. In 1801 General d'Arblay returned to France to try to reclaim the property he had lost during the revolution, and Burney joined him in 1802, intending to stay only a few months. But war broke out again, trapping her in France until 1812. Her last novel, *The Wanderer, or Female Difficulties,* appeared in 1814. It sold well but it was a pitiful example of the deterioration of a once-skilled writer's abilities. Burney was surprised and hurt by the harsh criticism it received.

She returned to France after the fall of Napoleon and was present there during the "Hundred Days." The d'Arblays returned to England in 1815 and settled in Bath, where the general died in 1818. Burney moved to London and spent a quiet and retired old age. In 1832 she published the *Memoirs of Doctor Burney,* based on manuscript notes left by her father and fleshed out with her own anecdotes and recollections. The public found the work entertaining, but the critics condemned it roundly. Burney became a recluse and died quietly at the age of eighty-seven.

Her fame as a novelist depends almost entirely on her first published work, *Evelina.* It is an epistolary novel, written in an easy and still readable style, and the first important example of the domestic novel of manners. It combined a good-humored but sometimes biting social satire with a sentimentality much more appreciated in her age than in our own. Its sentimentality and occasionally heavy-handed moralizing discomfit the modern reader, but these were important plusses in Burney's day. In fact, the completely moral tone of her works has been cited as an important influence in the establishment of the novel as a respectable literary genre.

In her second novel, *Cecila,* discerning readers noted a disturbing change in Burney's style: a movement toward use of "elevated," more elegant language. This was so marked that there was widespread but unfounded speculation that Samuel Johnson had a hand in the novel's composition. Burney had begun to lose her touch, and her style continued to decline into a stilted, pompous verbosity that makes *Camilla* tedious and *The Wanderer* almost unreadable.

Many factors have been advanced as the cause of

this decline: a desire to imitate Johnson's style, a striving to enhance the respectability of her novels by elevating their tone, a loss of familiarity with the rhythms of English prose during her absence in France, loss of spirit occasioned by the need to write for money rather than as purely creative expression, and a simple drying up of the creative juices. Most probably, each of these elements had its effect.

Although *Evelina* is the only one of her novels to claim lasting readership, Burney was not a "one-shot novelist." *Cecilia* and *Camilla*, too, were widely read and admired in their day. She did much to make the novel a respectable literary form and novel-writing an acceptable occupation for women. The influence of her works on Jane Austen has long been acknowledged, and traces of Burney's influence have been discerned in the works of Maria Edgeworth, Charlotte Smith, and others.

However, Burney was no pioneer. Other women had written novels before her. She simply happened to write quite a good novel on her first attempt, and circumstances (particularly her involvement with Johnson and the Streatham set) caused it to get perhaps more attention than it deserved. Nor was she an innovator in matters of style and technique. In *Evelina* she used proven novelistic techniques, and her later works show no real stylistic inventiveness. What was fresh and engaging about *Evelina* was Burney's choice of her young heroine as the *persona* from whose viewpoint we observe the events of the plot—and her exceptional talent for depicting manners, social behavior, and conversation.

Several modern scholars have suggested the presence of a nascent feminism in Burney's novels. These suggestions should be taken with extreme caution. Burney was an almost unswervingly conservative and conventional lady, and it would certainly be surprising to find any progressive social notions in her works. Her heroines struggled to improve their lot, but they strove only to regain their proper place in the social order. In Burney's novels, the appropriate reward for a woman's perseverance through adversity is a comfortable marriage to a socially acceptable gentleman.

With the first publication of her journals and correspondence two years after her death, her position of importance in literary history was assured. When she produced her *Memoirs of Doctor Burney*, the volumes provided fascinating glimpses of famous figures of the previous century—unfortunately smothered in turgid and tortuous prose. In her diaries and letters, though, the characters of her life stand out clearly and vividly. Burney rivals James Boswell as a recorder of conversation, and her descriptions of people are con-

siderably more lifelike. Keenly attuned to the externals of character and behavior, she provides portraits that are often superficial but also detailed and animated. She is an excellent storyteller, and she had plenty of good stories to tell—especially about Johnson and the members of his circle, her days at Court, and her time in France during the Napoleonic Wars.

Works

Evelina (1778). *Cecilia* (1782). *Brief Reflections Relative to the Emigrant French Clergy* (1793). *Edwy and Elgiva* (staged 1795; ed. M.J. Benkovitz, 1957). *Camilla* (1796). *The Wanderer* (1814). *Memoirs of Doctor Burney* (1832). *Diary and Letters of Madame d'Arblay*, ed. C. Barrett (1842–1846). *Selected Letters and Journals*, ed. J. Hemlow (1987). *Early Journals and Letters*, ed. L. Troide et al. (1988–). *Complete Plays*, ed. P. Sabot et al. (1995).

Joseph A. Grau

Constanţa Buzea
1941–

Born 1941, Bucharest, Romania
Genre(s): poetry, children's literature
Language(s): Romanian

Constanţa Buzea graduated in philology at the Bucharest University in 1967, having made her debut in 1957 in the literary journal *Tînărul scriitor* and published her first volume of verse in 1963. Since 1973 she has functioned as an editor for the journal *Amfiteatru*. Buzea, who is the author of 15 volumes of poetry, is unanimously recognized as one of the greatest contemporary Romanian poets.

Her voice rang deep and true almost from the beginning. The poet abandoned from her second volume the militant accents of *De pe pămînt* (1963; From the Earth). *La ritmul naturii* (1966; In the Rhythm of Nature) and *Norii* (1968; Clouds) are already volumes of fluent abstract meditation upon poetry, love, and spiritual change. In 1970 Constanţa Buzea produced a volume on death, sickness, and satiation—*Agonice* (Agonizing [Poems])—and one on maternity and its drive—*Coline* (Hills). Since 1971 she has published, for a while on a yearly basis, mature volumes of essential lyricism such as *Sala nervilor* (1971; Hall of Nerves), *Leac pentru îngeri* (1972; Remedy for Angels), *Răsad de spini* (1973; Thorn Transplant), *Pasteluri* (1974; Pastels), *Ape cu plute* (1975; Rivers with Rafts), *Limanul orei* (1976; Haven of the Hour), *Ploi de piatră* (1979; Stony Rains), *Umbra pentru cer* (1981; Shadow for the Sky), and *Planta memoriei* (1985; Memory Plant).

Buzea's reflexive poetry dwells in "the poor valleys of the mind." The poet practices a kind of superior oblivion, she "thoroughly forgets" whatever might bring her back to the surface and the concrete. In the *camera obscura* of the soul, like Hölderlin, Rilke, or Trakl, the "mild savage" "saddled with words hanging round [her] neck" celebrates the austere genesis of the poem, the privileged moment of inspiration which sets forth the coagulation of poetic feeling into verse and image. Unflinching in this poetic vigil—or, if one looks at it from the outside world, in this poetic somnolence ("Poetry is itself a sleep/ From which you don't wake up")—the "imprudent" poet produces a superlative confession, one might say a meta-confession, in which external biography is rejected in favor of a quintessential exposure of her most hidden lyrical pulsations.

In proclaiming the autonomy of one's poetic destiny, Buzea grants her poems a survival dimension which is far beyond any political or ideological connotations. In her poetic universe, the mind "in which [the poet] still reside[s] as in a kingdom" has as its nearest equivalent the "shell of laughter" which protects the child. Even when speaking of "gifts [changed] into farce" or of "raw bread under a burnt crust," of "death-mill[s]" and "the process of becoming gentle invalids" the poet stays detached, imperative and serene, for degradation, devaluation, and disintegration are always counterbalanced in the long run by the inalterable regenerative power of living poetry.

Buzea's verse is ceremonial, majestic, severely disciplined in its amplitude, one is tempted to say apodictic. The poet masters like few others the choice of "hurtful words/ beautiful and cold"; she knows that, in the end, lyricism is coldness rather than warmth ("Accumulating a coldness which is all mine/ Would have been generous"), that one encounters one's soul especially when it snows, that dying is "a beautiful illness," and that the poet true to self never hesitates. At times, the last strophe of a poem would indicate to the reader, in a glimpse, its lyrical etymology. In her lucid invocation of the lyrical forces of the soul Buzea has managed to transform her poems into deeply energizing though still melancholic texts. In this, as well as in the organic musicality of her verse, she reminds the Romanian reader of Mihai Eminescu.

Buzea wrote a number of books for children such as *Cărticică de doi ani* (1970; Booklet for the Two-year-old), *Aventurile extraordinare ale lui Hap Pap* (1970; The Extraordinary Adventures of Hap Pap) in collaboration with poet-husband Adrian Păunescu), *Cărticică de trei ani* (1972; Booklet for the Three-year-old), *Cărticică de patru ani* (1974; Booklet for the Four-year-old), *Cărticică pentru fetițe veverițe și băieți vevereți* (1979; Booklet for Squirrel-girls and Squirrel-boys).

In 1972 Buzea was awarded the Poetry prize of the Writers Union for her retrospective volume (1963–1971) *Leac pentru îngeri* (Remedy for Angels). In 1974 she received the Academy prize "Mihai Eminescu" for her volume *Pasteluri* (Pastels).

Works

De pe pămînt [From the Earth] (1963). *La ritmul naturii* [In the Rhythm of Nature] (1966). *Norii* [Clouds] (1968). *Agonice* [Agonizing (Poems)] (1970). *Coline* [Hills] (1970). *Cărticică de doi ani* [Booklet for the Two-year-old] (1970). *Sala nervilor* [Hall of Nerves] (1971). *Leac pentru îngeri* [Remedy for Angels] (1972). *Cărticică de trei ani* [Booklet for the Three-year-old] (1972). *Răsad de spini* [Thorn Transplant] (1973). *Pasteluri* [Pastels (Still-Life Poems)] (1974). *Cărticică de patru ani* [Booklet for the Four-year-old] (1974). *Ape cu plute* [Rivers with Rafts] (1975). *Limanul orei* [Haven of the Hour] (1976). *Poeme* [Poems] (1977). *Ploi de piatră* [Stony Rains] (1979). *Cărticică pentru fetițe veverițe și băieți vevereți* [Booklet for Squirrel-girls and Squirrel-boys] (1979). *Umbra pentru cer* [Shadow for the Sky] (1981). *Planta memoriei* [Memory Plant] (1985). [with Adrian Păunescu], *Aventurile extraordinare ale lui Hap Pap* [The Extraordinary Adventures of Hap Pap] (1970).

Translations: *Poeti romeni del dopoguerra* ["Ľetà"/ "Vîrstă"], ed. and tr. Mario De Micheli (1967). *Antologija na romanskata poezija* ["Sonot na bojata"/ "Cîntec pentru luptător"], ed. and tr. Taško Sarov (1972). *30 poeți români/30 poètes roumains* ["Septembre"/"Septembrie" and "Golgotha"/"Golgota" tr. Ileana Vulpescu] (1978), pp. 215–223.

English Translations: *Silent Voices. An Anthology of Contemporary Romanian Women Poets*, tr. Andrea Deletant and Brenda Walker (1986), pp. 37–47 (poems from *Poeme*, 1977; *Ploi de piatră*, 1979; *Umbră pentru cer*, 1981 and *Planta memoriei*, 1985). *Romanian Poems*, ed. and tr. Dan Dutescu (1982), pp. 226–228 ("The Dreams of Colour"; "The Wing"; "About the Fall of Leaves"). Impey, Michael, "Three Romanian Poets—Ana Blandiana; Constanța Buzea; Gabriela Melinescu," *Books Abroad* 50, I (Winter 1976): 34–35.

Sanda Golopentia

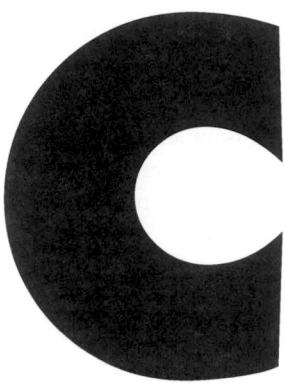

Wilhelmina "Minna" Ulrika (Johnson) Canth
1844–1897

a.k.a. Wilja, M.C., Teppo, -nn-, Airut, X
Born March 19, 1844, Tampere, Finland
Died May 12, 1897, Kuopio, Finland
Genres: drama, journalism, short story, aphorism, translation
Language(s): Finnish (one play in Swedish)

Minna Canth ranks among Finland's best dramatists, working above all with social issues: the plight of the worker, of women, of the poor. Her gift for dialogue and plot have made her plays among Finland's most frequently produced. She remains one of the harshest and most outspoken critics of social injustice in Finland and retains a respected place in the Finnish literary Parnassus.

Canth was the first-born daughter of a working-class family in the industrial town of Tampere. The family's move to Kuopio in 1853 marked an improvement in economic and social status; her father opened a shop there and became a successful merchant. He encouraged the gifted child in her reading and musical pursuits, and she received an education of the quality usually reserved for the (primarily Swedish-speaking) upper class. Throughout her career, Canth was thus able to understand and portray the entire spectrum of Finnish society.

In 1863, Minna left home to attend the newly established teachers' seminary in Jyväskylä, the first of its kind to offer instruction in Finnish and to accept both male and female students. The atmosphere of burgeoning Finnish nationalism there sealed Minna's fate: she vowed to dedicate herself to the education of the Finnish people. In Jyväskylä she met her future husband, the science teacher Johan Ferdinand Canth. They married in 1865, a

union which produced six children. She assisted her husband in editing two newspapers, *Keski-Suomi* and *Päijänne* and contributed articles and short stories that dealt for the most part with social issues, including women's emancipation. She lost her husband in 1879 and, to support her family, took over her father's shop in Kuopio in 1880. By this time she had written her first play, *Murtovarkaus* (published in 1883 but completed in 1879); her second, *Roinilan talossa*, appeared in 1885 (but had been finished in 1883). These "innocent" comedies did little to prepare audiences for her next play, *Työmiehen vaimo* (1885), which attacked working conditions, women's subservient role in the household (even when she clearly could manage better than her husband), and alcoholism. The play *Kovan onnen lapsia* (1888) was even more acerbic in its social criticism, so much so that it nearly put an end to her dramatic career, for even the more "radical" Finnish writers found it too strong, not to mention the conservative owners of the Finnish theater. She then turned to somewhat less controversial matters in *Papin perhe* (1891), a play about the "generation gap," with a runaway daughter who becomes a successful actress; the curtain closes on a proud and reconciled family. With *Sylvi* (1893), Canth turns to more psychological portrayals. This play deals with adultery and the destructive force of erotic feelings. It was written in Swedish for the theater in Stockholm; she had become frustrated with the Finnish theater direction and looked for more appreciation in Sweden. *Anna Liisa* (1895), her last and possibly best play, signals her reconciliation with the Finnish theater. This tragedy presents the fate of a woman who murders her own (illegitimate) baby, a not uncommon crime among young peasant girls at the time. Some critics have seen the influence of Tolstoy in this drama.

Though Canth's plays are of greatest importance, her short stories deserve attention as well; they treat for the most part the same issues discussed in the dramas of the mid-1880s and often satirize the (usually Swedish-speaking) middle class. Canth also created and edited the short-lived journal *Vapaita aatteita* (Free Ideas) from 1889–1890. She continued to contribute articles on social issues to Finnish periodicals throughout her lifetime (most of her short stories were also first published in this format). Canth died of a heart attack, the last of a series which had plagued her for a year and a half, in 1897.

Minna Canth has become a legend in Finland. She was the first Finnish-speaking feminist in her country and is considered a seminal figure not only in the women's rights movement but for social reform in other areas as well. She considered herself a socialist but believed in a religion-based socialism although she attacked the church itself. The contribution she made to the then-embryonic Finnish-language literature can hardly be overestimated. Her work is uneven, sometimes more political polemics than inspired literary achievement, but her artistic genius can be witnessed in some of her finer works, in *Anna Liisa* or *Papin perhe*. A champion of women and of the proletariat, she has been honored with a statue in downtown Kuopio, the nurturing mother, tireless reformer, and literary artisan in one woman.

Works

Plays: *Murtovarkaus* (1883). *Roinilan talossa* (1885). *Työmiehen vaimo* (1885). ("From the Drama *The Worker's Wife*." Excerpt translated by Elli Tompuri in *Voices from Finland*, 1947). *Kovan onnen lapsia* (1888). *Papin perhe* (1891). *Sylvi* (1893). *Anna Liisa* (1895).

Short stories: *Novelleja ja kertomuksia* (1878). *Hanna* (1886). *Koyhää kansaa* (1886). *Kansan ääniä* (1889). *Novelleja* (1892).

Other prose: *Hän on Sysmästä* (1893). *Spiritistinen istunto* (1894). *Kotoa pois* (1895). *Arvostelu neiti Ellen Keyn viime lausunnoista naisasiassa* (1896). *Suolavakka*. [Collected aphorisms] (1954).

Kathy Saranpa Anstine

Jane Welsh Carlyle
1801–1866
Born July 14, 1801, Haddington, Scotland
Died April 21, 1866, Chelsea, London
Genre(s): letters
Language(s): English

The only child of a respected country doctor, Jane Welsh displayed a powerful intellect at an early age and distinguished herself at local schools. By the age of thirteen she had written a novel, a five-act tragedy, and had convinced her parents that "like a boy" she ought to learn Latin. Edward Irving, a young clergyman was appointed her tutor. Jane's father, to whom she was extremely devoted, died when she was eighteen, leaving her the estate of Craiggenputtock and a substantial income. Shortly later, she was introduced to Thomas Carlyle, who became not only her friend but her mentor, and later her husband.

Jane's intelligence and wit were complemented by a distinctive appearance; according to one description, she was "bright and beautiful with a certain starlike radiance and grace." She did not lack for suitors, many of whom are satirized in her letters, but only Irving, Carlyle, and the sculptor George Rennie appear to have been viewed seriously by her. Jane's meeting with Carlyle in 1821 was the beginning of a deep intellectual relationship with very little romance. In spite of the affectionate tone that develops in their correspondence until their marriage in 1826, there is very little passion. Later, the biographer J.A. Froude was to characterize their union as a "partnership not marriage," reflecting, among other things, the asexual element of their married life.

After spending two years in Edinburgh, the Carlyles moved to the remote estate of Craiggenputtock where Thomas labored over *Sartor Resartus*. The six years spent there were among the worst of Jane's life; without society, she had no outlet for her conversation and wit, and what is worse, she had to contend with her husband's very changeable moods. In 1834 the Carlyles set up permanent residence at No. 5 Cheyne Row in Chelsea, London. Thomas Carlyle had emerged as an important literary figure and their home became something of a cultural center. Regular visitors at the Carlyles' evenings at home included Macaulay, Dickens, Ruskin, and Tennyson. Geraldine Jewsbury, who originally visited Cheyne Row to meet Thomas, and eventually became Jane's closest friend and regular correspondent.

Jane was extremely attentive to the domestic concerns of Cheyne Row and supervised frequent renovations and redecorations, including the construction of the "quiet place," a room where Thomas could work without having his fragile disposition disturbed. Insulating him from the daily activities of the world occupied much of Jane's time, and these efforts form the subject of many of her letters. Carlyle, she tells one correspondent, "dislikes nothing in the world so much as going into a shop to buy anything, even his own trowsers and coats; so that, to the consternation of cockney tailors, I am obliged to go about them." Elsewhere, in the journal she kept in 1855, Jane Carlyle provides a witty and biting description of the Tax Commissioners whom she sees on Thomas's behalf (November 21, 1855). As much as her writing sparkles when she writes of her domestic tasks, it is clear that they wore her down, particularly as she began to feel neglected by her husband.

Jane was encouraged both by Thomas and by friends to write a novel, and although she may have started one, nothing of it remains. What emerges in her letters is a clear and simple style that draws strength from her canny sense of detail and her cynical wit. Occasionally her writing is much more subdued, and a tone of sadness and fatigue emerges. She complained of a weak constitution and severe headaches throughout her life and was often depressed about Thomas's inattention to her. Only after her death, which though sudden appeared to be of natural causes, did Thomas (after reading her letters) fully appreciate the stress she bore for his sake. Exactly how great a drain he had been on Jane's spirit is not clear; by her own admission, she had recognized genius in Thomas, had "married for ambition," and was prepared "to take the consequences."

Works

The Collected Letters of Thomas and Jane Welsh Carlyle (1970).

Alan Rauch

Ana Caro Mallen de Soto
ca. 1600–ca. 1650

Born ca. 1600, probably in Seville, Spain
Died ca. 1645–1650
Genre(s): drama, poetry
Language(s): Spanish

Ana Caro enjoyed considerable fame during her lifetime and was praised by numerous contemporary authors, including the dramatist Matos Fragoso as well as Vélez de Buevara, who referred to her as the "tenth muse" of Seville and member of a fictitious literary academy in his picaresque novel *El diablo cojuelo* (The Lame Devil). She was also eulogized by the sixteenth-century antiquarian Rodrigo Caro as "a famous poetess who has written many plays and other works of poetry."

However, very little is now known of her life, and some of her literary manuscripts may have perished. She was born into a distinguished Andalusian family and must have received a far more meticulous education than the average girl of her time, for she demonstrates familiarity with the humanistic learning of that age. That she was able to indulge her literary inclinations bespeaks a life of financial ease and social prestige. Most of her life was spent in Seville, and numerous references of civic pride are found in her writings. Many of her works are long poetic narratives of local events, written in the highly embellished, metaphoric style typical of the baroque, and are of interest today only to scholars. These include the following: "Narration of the Grand Celebrations in the Convent of San Francisco of Sevilla for the Holy Martyrs of Japan" (1628), "The Grand Victory that Jorge de Mendoza y Piçaña, Governor-general of Ceuta, Won over the Moors of Tetuán" (1633), and "The Narration of the Grand Celebration in the Church of San Miguel in Sevilla on the Occasion of the Events in Flanders" (1635).

In January 1637, Ana Caro went to Madrid, where she was evidently received into the innermost literary and social circles. Here she met and befriended the short story writer and outspoken feminist, María de Zayas. During her short stay in the capital she wrote the *Account of the Royal Celebrations in the Palace of the Buen Retiro for the Coronation of the King of the Romans and Entry into Madrid of the Princess of Cariñán* (1637). This lengthy poetic narrative in three parts describes the lavish festivities of the Court during February 1637, in honor of the naming of Ferdinand III as Holy Roman Emperor and the arrival of the Princess of Cariñán, who had some importance for Spanish politics. The work is typical of courtly poetry with its abundance of hyperbole, mythological allusions, inverted syntax, and the extravagant praise of Philip IV as the Sun King and of his minister, the Duke of Olivares.

Early in 1637 she was back in Seville. Her works from this period include a short piece in verse, the "Sacramental Loa . . . in four languages" for the Corpus Christi celebrations of 1639. She also wrote several *autos sacramentales* or short verse dramas performed in the streets on movable stages. Her last known work—a prefatory sonnet—appeared in 1645, and she must have died soon afterward. Most of her poetry was closely connected to her native city of Seville. She is little known today, principally for two extant plays: *El Conde de Partinuplés* (The Count of Partinuples) and *Valor, agravio y mujer* (Valor, Dishonor, and Woman). Both depict popular female stock characters: the woman averse to love and marriage and the woman disguised as a man.

El Conde de Partinuplés, first published in the *Laurel de comedias de diferentes autores. Quarta Parte* (1653), is based on a popular romance of chivalry. The plot always hinges on a beautiful lady—in this play, the Princess Rosaura—who remains invisible to her suitor. However, Rosaura is not actually disdainful of men but rather fearful of an ominous prophecy. The plot develops in an atmosphere of magic and romance and, through the supernatural powers of Aldora, the lovers are brought together in a happy conclusion. *Valor, agravio y mujer* is a delightful comedy of errors that incorporates most of the stock situations of Golden Age drama: disguise and mistaken identity, intrigue, misdirected love, misspoken conversations, *double entendre*, and so on, until the heroine, Leonor, ingeniously resolves the complications and gets her man. In this play the author shows a considerable talent for comic dialogue and skillful craftsmanship.

Many of Ana Caro's works were described or published by Serrano y Sanz in the *Apuntes para una biblioteca de escritoras españolas*, and several of the poetic narratives have recently been edited.

Works

El Conde de Partinuplés. In *Biblioteca de autores españoles*. Vol. 49: *Dramáticos posteriores a Lope de Vega* (1924). *Contexto de las reales fiestas que se hizieron en el Palacio del Buen Retiro a la coronación del Rey de Romanos, y entrada en Madrid de la Señora Princesa de Cariñán*. Facs. ed. Antonio Pérez y Gómez (1951). "Grandiosa vitoria que alcançó de los Moros de Tetuán Iorge de Mendoça y Piçaña, General de Ceuta, quitándoles gran suma de ganados cerca de las mesmas puertas de Tetuán." ed. Francisco López Estrada. In *Homenaje a Blecua* (1983). "Loa sacramental, que se representó en el carro de Antonio de Prado, en las fiestas del Corpus de Sevilla, este año de 1639." ed. F. López Estrada. In *Revista de Dialectología y Tradiciones Populares* (*Homenaje a Vicente García de Diego*), 32 (1976): 263–274. "Relación de la grandiosa fiesta, y octava, sobre los sucesos en Flandes, que en la iglesia parroquial del glorioso San Miguel de la Ciudad de Sevilla, hizo don García Sarmiento

de Sotomayor. . . ." (1635). "Relación, en que se da cuenta de las grandiosas fiestas, que en el convento de N.P.S. Francisco de la Ciudad de Sevilla se an hecho a los Santos Mártires del Iapón." ed. F. López Estrada. In *Homenaje a Antonio Pérez y Gómez*. 2 vols. (1978). *Valor, agravio y mujer*. ed. Manuel Serrano y Sanz. In *Apuntes para una biblioteca de escritoras españolas*. 2 vols. (1898; rpt. in *Biblioteca de Autores Españoles*, vol. 268, 1975).

Ruth Lundelius

Barbara Cartland
1901–

a.k.a. Barbara McCorquodale
Born July 9, 1901
Genre(s): romance novel, drama, journalism
Language(s): English

The most prolific romance novelist, according to the *Guiness Book of World Records,* and one of the top five best-selling authors of all time (long past the 100,000,000 copy mark set in 1979), Cartland has also been a playwright, biographer, journalist, pageant designer, decorator, glider pilot, county councillor, philanthropist, businesswoman, and world traveler.

Cartland runs her estate at Canfield and has raised three children, a daughter born during her six-year marriage to Alexander McCorquodale, and two sons, born during her twenty-seven year union with Alexander's cousin, Hugh. Each son manages either the financial affairs or the extensive corrections for each book.

Barbara Cartland began her career as a writer after World War I, when she was invited by publisher Lord Beaverbrook to contribute paragraphs of gossip to the *Daily News.* Insisting on anonymity for much of this material, as she "preferred to work behind the scenes," she expanded the market for her columns to other newspapers: *Daily Mail, Daily Mirror,* and *Tatler.*

Her first novel, *Jigsaw* (1925), described as "Mayfair with the lid off," drew, in part, from Cartland's own experiences and echoed the styles of favorite authors: Ethel M. Dell (especially *The Sheik*) and Elinor Glyn. *Jigsaw* has a freshness and charm rarely found in her later novels. It concerns the adventures of Mona Vivien, a "strikingly beautiful" young woman who has graduated from convent school and is ready to enter London society. Despite a brief fling with the mysterious, worldly half-brother of her "true love," a Marquis, Mona recognizes that her source of future happiness depends on making the right decision and eventually accepts the Marquis' proposal. Some criticisms of the novel were favorable as in the statement that the book was "a dramatic conflict of emotions, written with zest," but not all concurred. Others bitingly commented that the writing was "amateurish" and one stated "If this is Mayfair, then let me live in Whitechapel." Critics notwithstanding, Cartland's first work was published in six editions and five other languages, setting a precedent that has not ceased.

Cartland's fictional formula rarely changes. A chaste heroine, whose name must end with the letter "a," meets the handsome, wealthy hero in an exotic nineteenth-century setting. Love blooms; obstacles are overcome; the couple marries and only then give in to the passion that has beset them throughout the novel. Variations only involve the scene for each romance, her vast travels have inspired many of her stories. The conclusion of each work is relatively similar; lines or passages from one have even been found in other Cartland works.

Her lack of pornographic filigree has earned her over 400,000,000 readers. "I am their escape from the depression and boredom and lack of romance in modern life," she once explained to an interviewer. Each thin volume, usually no more than 60,000 words, is dictated to a series of secretaries. Scorning long paragraphs and complicated subplots, she avoids lengthy explanations or needless descriptions.

Cartland's literary strength is thorough research. Attention to factual or epistolary evidence is most visible in several of her historical biographies, as is the added attraction of a "romantic angle." One such example is *Metternich: The Passionate Diplomat* (1964), which required thirty sources, including material from the Viennese Court and State Archives as well as numerous histories and biographies in addition to Cartland's own work on Josephine, Empress of France. The text centers on Metternich's political importance: his influence on the development of the Congress of Vienna and his ability to engage Austria in European affairs during the period of 1815–1848. But the ambivalent nature of the man is also pursued with an exposé of his relationships with three wives and four mistresses: "The loves of . . . Metternich, within the marital state or beyond it, softened the character of someone whose icy intellect produced a figure of superhuman coldness, objectivity, and brilliance," Cartland concludes in the text.

Cartland has one film scenario to her credit (*The Flame Is Love*), which had twenty-four million viewers when shown in America on NBC.

Because of a serious illness Cartland became interested in nutrition, especially proper diet and vitamins, and eventually created a series of books on the importance of good health on individual appearance (among them *Be Vivid, Be Vital*, 1956; *Look Lovely, Be Lovely*, 1958; and *Vitamins for Vitality*, 1959).

Cartland is known as "The Queen of Romance," an accolade that captures the writer's sincere desire to keep alive the fantasy her readers crave: the Cinderella story that ends "happily ever after." She "keeps the faith" with her Regency novels, and her audience happily and constantly responds by demanding more Cartland.

Works (a partial list)

Jigsaw (1925). *Blood Money* (1925). *Sawdust* (1926). *If The Tree Is Saved* (1929). *For What?* (1930). *Sweet Punishment* (1931). *A Virgin in Mayfair* (1932). *Just off Piccadilly* (1933). *Not Love Alone* (1933). *A Beggar Wished* (1934). *Touch the Stars* (1935). *Dangerous Experiment* (1936). *But Never Free* (1937). *Broken Barriers* (1938). *The Gods Forget* (1939). *Stolen Halo* (1940). *Now Rough, Now Smooth* (1941). *Ronald Cartland* (1942). *The Isthmus Years 1919–1939* (1943). *Yet She Follows* (1944). *The Years of Opportunity, 1939–1945* (1948). *A Duel of Hearts* (1949). *The Knave of Hearts* (1950; repub. as *The Innocent Heiress*, 1975). *Love Is an Eagle* (1951). *Love Is the Enemy* (1952). *The Passionate Pilgrim* (1952). *Elizabethan Lover* (1953). *Desire of the Heart* (1954). *The Fascinating Forties: A Book for the Over-Forties* (1954, 1973). *Love Me for Ever* (1954). *Wings on My Heart* (1954). *The Kiss of the Devil* (1955). *Bewitching Women* (1955). *Marriage for Moderns* (1955). *Be Vivid, Be Vital* (1956). *The Coin of Love* (1956). *The Outrageous Queen* (1956). *Polly, My Wonderful Mother* (1956). *The Caged Bird* (1957). *Love, Life and Sex* (1957). *The Scandalous Life of King Carol* (1957). *The Thief of Love* (1957). *Look Lovely, Be Lovely* (1958). *The Private Life of Charles II* (1958). *The Kiss of Silk* (1959). *The Private Life of Elizabeth, Empress of Austria* (1959). *Vitamins for Vitality* (1959). *Love under Fire* (1960). *The Price of Love* (1960). *Josephine, Empress of France* (1961). *The Messenger of Love* (1961). *Diane de Poitiers* (1962). *The Many Facets of Love* (1963). *Etiquette for Love and Romance* (1964). *The Fire of Love* (1964). *Living Together* (1964). *Metternich: The Passionate Diplomat* (1964). *Sex and the Teenager* (1964). *A Ghost in Monte Carlo* (1965). *Love Holds the Cards* (1965). *Love on the Run* (1965). *Woman—the Enigma* (1965). *A Virgin in Paris* (1966). *Danger by the Nile* (1967). *I Search for the Rainbow: 1946–1966* (1967;

repub. as *I Search for Rainbows*, 1973). *The Enchanting Land* (1968). *Love Is Contraband* (1968). *The Youth Secret* (1968). *A Hazard of Hearts* (1969). *Love in Hiding* (1969). *Love Is Dangerous* (1969). *The Unknown Heart* (1969). *The Unpredictable Bride* (1969). *Cupid Rides Pillion* (1970). *The Hidden Evil* (1970). *The Hidden Heart* (1970). *The Magic of Honey* (1970). *The Reluctant Bride* (1970). *Street Adventure* (1970). *We Danced All Night, 1919–1929* (1970). *After the Night* (1971). *Armour against Love* (1971). *The Enchanted Waltz* (1971). *The Golden Gondola* (1971). *Health Food Cookery Book* (1971). *Husbands and Wives* (1971). *If We Will* (1971). *The Kiss of Paris* (1971). *The Little Pretender* (1971). *Out of Reach* (1971). *Stars in My Heart* (1971). *The Black Panther* (1972). *Book of Beauty and Health* (1972). *The Dream Within* (1972). *The Enchanted Moment* (1972). *Halo for the Devil* (1972). *The Irresistible Buck* (1972). *Lines on Life and Love* (1972). *Lost Enchantment* (1972). *Love is Mine* (1972). *No Heart Is Free* (1972). *Audacious Adventurer* (1973). *Blue Heather* (1973). *The Coin of Love* (1973). *The Daring Deception* (1973). *The Leaping Flame* (1973). *A Light to the Heart* (1973). *Lights of Love* (1973). *Love Forbidden* (1973). *The Little Adventure* (1973). *Men Are Wonderful* (1973). *The Pretty Horse-Breakers* (1973). *Where Is Love?* (1973). *The Wicked Marquis* (1973). *Against the Stream* (1974). *The Bored Bridegroom* (1974). *The Castle of Fear* (1974). *The Cruel Count* (1974). *The Dangerous Dandy* (1974). *The Glittering Light* (1974). *Journey to Paradise* (1974). *No Darkness for Love* (1974). *No Time for Love* (1974). *The Penniless Peer* (1974). *The Ruthless Rake* (1974). *An Arrow of Love* (1975). *As Eagles Fly* (1975). *Bewitched* (1975). *Call of the Heart* (1975). *Desperate Defiance* (1975). *The Devil in Love* (1975). *Fire on the Snow* (1975). *The Flame Is Love* (1975). *Food for Love* (1975). *A Frame of Dreams* (1975). *The Frightened Bride* (1975). *A Gamble with Hearts* (1975). *The Impetuous Duchess* (1975). *The Karma of Love* (1975). *A Kiss for the King* (1975). *Love Is Innocent* (1975). *The Mask of Love* (1975). *Say Yes, Samantha* (1975). *The Shadow of Sin* (1975). *A Sword to the Heart* (1975). *The Tears of Love* (1975). *Towards the Stars* (1975). *A Very Naughty Angel* (1975). *Where Is Love* (1975). *An Angel in Hell* (1976). *The Blue-Eyed Witch* (1976). *Conquered by Love* (1976). *The Disgraceful Duke* (1976). *The Dream and the Glory* (1976). *The Elusive Earl* (1976). *Escape from Passion* (1976). *The Golden Illusion* (1976). *The Heart Triumphant* (1976). *The Husband Hunters* (1976). *The Magic of Honey Cookbook* (1976). *Moon over Eden* (1976). *Passions in the Sand* (1976). *The Slaves of Love* (1976). *Vote for Love* (1976). *The Wild Cry of Love* (1976). *A Duel with Destiny* (1977). *Kiss the Moonlight* (1977). *Look, Listen and Love* (1977). *Love and the Loathsome Leopard* (1977). *Love Locked In* (1977). *The Love Pirate* (1977). *The Marquis Who Hated Women* (1977). *No Escape from Love* (1977). *Recipe for Lovers* (1977). *A Rhapsody of Love* (1977). *The Saint and the Sinner* (1977). *A Sign of Love* (1977). *The Temptation of Torilla* (1977). *A Touch of Love* (1977). *The Wild Unwilling Wife* (1977). *Alone in Paris* (1978). *The Chieftain without a Heart* (1978). *Flowers for the God of Love* (1978). *The Ghost Who Fell in Love* (1978). *The Irresistible Force* (1978). *I Seek the Miraculous* (1978). *The Judgement of Love* (1978). *Lessons in Love* (1978). *The Light of Love: Lines to Live by Day by Day* (1978). *Love and Lovers* (1978). *Love, Lords and Ladybirds* (1978). *Magic or Mirage* (1978). *The Mysterious Maid-Servant* (1978). *The Passion and the Flower* (1978). *A Princess in Distress* (1978). *The Problems of Love* (1978). *The Race for Love* (1978). *The Twists and Turns of Love* (1978). *The Captive Heart* (1979). *The Drums of Love* (1979). *The Duke and the Preacher's Daughter* (1979). *The Prince and the Pekingese* (1979). *Ashes of Desire* (1980). *Barbara Cartland* (1980). *Barbara Cartland's Scrapbook* (1980). *Bride to the King* (1980). *The Bridge of Kisses* (1980). *The Broad Highway* (1980). *Charles Rex* (1980). *The Dawn of Love* (1980). *Free from Fear* (1980). *A Gentleman in Love* (1980). *The Goddess and the Gaiety Girl* (1980). *The Great Moment* (1980). *Greatheart* (1980). *A Heart Is Stolen* (1980). *The Horizons of Love* (1980). *Imperial Splendour* (1980). *A Kiss of Silk* (1980). *Little White Doves of Love* (1980). *Lost Laughter* (1980). *Love at the Helm* (1980). *Love for Sale* (1980). *Love Has His Way* (1980). *Love in the Moon* (1980). *Lucifer and the Angel* (1980). *Money, Magic and Marriage* (1980). *My Brother, Ronald* (1980). *The Obstacle Race* (1980). *Ola and the Sea Wolf* (1980). *The Perfection of Love* (1980). *The Power and the Prince* (1980). *The Price of Love* (1980). *The Price of Things* (1980). *Pride and the Poor Princess* (1980). *The Prude and the Prodigal* (1980). *Punished with Love* (1980). *Rainbow in the Spray* (1980). *The Runaway Heart* (1980). *The Sequence* (1980). *Signpost to Love* (1980). *Six Days* (1980). *A Song of Love* (1980). *Son of the Turk* (1980). *The Sons of the Sheik* (1980). *The Sweet Enchantress* (1980). *The Waltz of Hearts* (1980). *Who Can Deny Love?* (1980). *Women Have Hearts* (1980). *Afraid* (1980). *The Amateur Gentleman* (1981). *The Complacent Wife* (1981). *Count the Stars* (1981). *Dollars for the Duke* (1981). *Dreams Do Come True* (1981). *Enchanted* (1981). *The Explosion of Love*

(1981). *For All Eternity* (1981). *From Hell to Heaven* (1981). *A Gamble with Hearts* (1981). *Gift of the Gods* (1981). *The Heart of the Clan* (1981). *His Official Fiancée* (1981). *In the Arms of Love* (1981). *An Innocent in Russia* (1981). *The Kiss of Life* (1981). *The Lion Tamer* (1981). *The Lioness and the Lily* (1981). *Love at the Helm* (1981). *Love in the Dark* (1981). *Love Wins* (1981). *Lucky in Love* (1981). *A Night of Gaiety* (1981). *A Portrait of Love* (1981). *Pure and Untouched* (1981). *The River of Love* (1981). *Romantic Royal Marriages* (1981). *A Shaft of Sidelight* (1981). *Tetherstones* (1981). *Touch a Star* (1981). *Towards the Stars* (1981). *The Wild, Unwilling Wife* (1981). *Winged Magic* (1981). *The Wings of Ecstasy* (1981). *Wings on My Heart* (1981). *Written with Love: Passionate Love Letters* (1981). *Again This Rapture* (1982). *The Audacious Adventures* (1982). *Barbara Cartland Picture Romances* (1982). *Barbara Cartland's Book of Celebrities* (1982). *The Call of the Highlands* (1982). *Camfield Romances* (1982). *Caught by Love* (1982). *For All Eternity* (1982). *The Frightened Bride* (1982). *From Hate to Love* (1982). *The Incredible Honeymoon* (1982). *Keep Young and Beautiful* (1982). *A King in Love* (1982). *Kneel for Mercy* (1982). *Lies for Love* (1982). *Light of the Gods* (1982). *Looking for Love* (1982). *Love and the Marquis* (1982). *Love at the Helm* (1982). *Love Leaves at Midnight* (1982). *Love on the Wind* (1982). *Love Rules* (1982). *Love to the Rescue* (1982). *Love Wears a Veil* (1982). *A Marriage Made in Heaven* (1982). *A Miracle in Music* (1982). *Mission to Monte Carlo* (1982). *Moments of Love* (1982). *Music from the Heart* (1982). *The Naked Battle* (1982). *The Odious Duke* (1982). *Open Wings* (1982). *The Poor Governess* (1982). *The Power and the Prince* (1982). *The Secret Fear* (1982). *Secret Harbour* (1982). *The Smuggled Heart* (1982). *Touch a Star* (1982). *The Unknown Heart* (1982). *The Vibrations of Love* (1982). *Winged Victory* (1982). *Diona and a Dalmatian* (1983) *The Dragon and the Pearl* (1983). *The Duke Comes Home* (1983). *A Duke in Danger* (1983). *Free from Fear* (1983). *From Hate to Love* (1983). *Gypsy Magic* (1983). *A Heart Is Broken* (1983). *Help from the Heart* (1983). *In the Arms of Love* (1983). *Journey to a Star* (1983). *A King in Love* (1983). *The Kiss of Life* (1983). *Lies for Love* (1983). *Lights, Laughter and a Lady* (1983). *Love and Lucia* (1983). *Love in the Dark* (1983). *Love in the Wind* (1983). *Love to the Rescue* (1983). *The Magic of Honey* (1983). *The Magic of Love* (1983). *A Miracle in Music* (1983). *The Poor Governess* (1983). *Riding to the Moon* (1983). *Tempted to Love* (1983). *The Unbreakable Spell* (1983). *Wish for Love* (1983). *Bride to a Brigand* (1984). *The Call of the Highlands* (1984). *A*

Dream from the Night (1984). *The Duke Comes Home* (1984). *Etiquette for Love and Romance* (1984). *Fire in the Blood* (1984). *Getting Older, Growing Younger* (1984). *Help from the Heart* (1984). *Hungry for Love* (1984). *The Island of Love* (1984). *Journey to a Star* (1984). *Light of the Gods* (1984). *Little White Doves of Love* (1984). *Looking for Love* (1984). *Lord Ravenscar's Revenge* (1984). *Love Comes West* (1984). *Miracle for a Madonna* (1984). *Moonlight on the Sphinx* (1984). *The Peril and the Prince* (1984). *Princess to the Rescue* (1984). *A Rebel Princess* (1984). *Revenge of the Heart* (1984). *The Romance of Food* (1984). *The Unbreakable Spell* (1984). *Royal Punishment* (1984). *The Scots Never Forget* (1984). *Secrets* (1984). *The Storms of Love* (1984). *The Taming of Lady Lorinda* (1984). *Theresa and a Tiger* (1984). *The Unbreakable Spell* (1984). *The Unwanted Wedding* (1984). *White Lilac* (1984). *Winged Victory* (1984). *A Witch's Spell* (1984). *Alone and Afraid* (1985). *Barbara Cartland's Book of Health* (1985). *The Castle Made for Love* (1985). *The Devilish Deception* (1985). *Escape* (1985). *The Etiquette of Romance* (1985). *A Fugitive from Love* (1985). *Hungry for Love* (1985). *Look with Love* (1985). *Love Is a Gamble* (1985). *Love Is Heaven* (1985). *Love on the Wind* (1985). *Miracle for a Madonna* (1985). *The Outrageous Lady* (1985). *Paradise Found* (1985). *Polly: My Wonderful Mother* (1985). *The Proud Princess* (1985). *Safe at Last* (1985). *Temptation of a Teacher* (1985). *A Very Unusual Wife* (1985). *A Victory for Love* (1985). *An Angel Runs Away* (1986). *Count the Stars* (1986). *Crowned with Love* (1986). *The Devil Defeated* (1986). *A Dreams in Spain* (1986). *A Gentleman in Love* (1986). *The Golden Cage* (1986). *Haunted* (1986). *Helga in Hiding* (1986). *The Hell-Cat and the King* (1986). *Listen to Love* (1986). *Love Casts Out Fear* (1986). *Love Climbs In* (1986). *Love Joins the Clan* (1986). *The Love Trap* (1986). *Never Forget Love* (1986). *The Peril and the Prince* (1986). *The Secret of the Mosque* (1986). *A Serpent of Satan* (1986). *Terror and the Sun* (1986). *Bewildered in Berlin* (1987). *The Curse of the Clan* (1987). *Dancing on a Rainbow* (1987). *The Devilish Deception* (1987). *The Earl Escapes* (1987). *Escape* (1987). *For All Eternity* (1987). *Forced to Marry* (1987). *A Heart Is Stolen* (1987). *Journey to a Star* (1987). *Lies for Love* (1987). *Love and Kisses* (1987). *Love Casts out Fear* (1987). *Love on the Wind* (1987). *The Love Puzzle* (1987). *Lovers in Paradise* (1987). *Never Laugh at Love* (1987). *The Perfume of the Gods* (1987). *Punishment of a Vixen* (1987). *A Runaway Star* (1987). *The Secret of the Glen* (1987). *Starlight over Tunis* (1987). *Wanted: A Wedding Ring* (1987). *A World of Love* (1987).

Zelda Provenzano

Castelloza
ca. 1150–1200

Flourished late twelfth or early thirteenth centuries, Mayonne (Haute-Loire), Southern France
Genre(s): canso
Language(s): Occitan

Castelloza is the author of three cansos (or love songs) that carry her name and a fourth that can confidently be attributed to her on the basis of its juxtaposition with her other songs in manuscript N and its thematic similarities to them [Paden et al., "The Poems of the *Trobairitz* Na Castelloza," *Romance Philology* 35 (1981–1982) 163–165]. Her songs are preserved in five manuscripts, in four of which she is the subject of a short biography or *vida*, while her conventionalized portrait miniature illustrates her songs in three. According to her biography, she was the wife of Turc de Mairony and loved Arman de Breon, who was the subject of her love songs. Turc de Mairony, whose existence is independently confirmed by a reference to him in 1212, was presumably the lord of the castle of Mayonne, situated in the commune of Venteuges (arr. Le Puy, Haute Loire). A family of Brion held a castle of that name in the commune of Compains (arr. Issoire, Puy de Dôme), but there is no record of an Arman. Castelloza addresses one poem to the *trobairitz* (or woman troubadour) Almois de Castelnou, mentioned in a document dated 1219, while one song (Song IV) shows marked similarities to a piece by the troubadour Peirol, who flourished between 1185 and 1221. Hence, Castelloza's poetic activity may be situated sometime in the last two decades of the twelfth and the first two decades of the thirteenth centuries.

It has been persuasively argued that the four texts of the reconstituted Castelloza canon compose "a brief lyrical cycle, where an inner progression can be perceived, and where reverberations from one piece to the next heighten poetic meaning, so that the group as a whole is imaginatively richer than the four pieces considered separately" [Dronke, Peter, "The Provençal *Trobairitz* Castelloza," in *Medieval Women Writers*, ed. K. Wilson (1984), p. 132]. Song I, "Amics, s'ie.us trobes avinen," propounds a series of antitheses that the next three poems attempt to resolve. The disdainful lover is envisaged as both "charming, humble, open, and compassionate" (I: 1–2) and "wicked, despicable, and haughty" (I: 4). The poetic voice admits that it might be said that she is in error in pleading her own cause with a knight (I: 19), but she prizes less highly the demands of convention and social mores than those of her heart. In the final three stanzas of the song, the antitheses enunciated in the first three stanzas—the hostile versus the acquiescent lover, her (feigned) rejection of him versus her fidelity toward him, her vigorous prosecution of her suit versus her resigned silence, and her death from unhappy love versus her healing accomplished through perseverance in her one-sided affection—are resolved in favor of fidelity, perseverance, and joy through or beyond the indignities of her unfaithful knight. He who would reprove her choice is, she avers, much of a fool who "doesn't know how it is with me, nor has seen you with the eyes I saw you with, when you told me not to worry, for at any time it could happen that I would again have joy" (I: 26–31). This hope appears to buoy her up, leading her to choose to praise her beloved publicly and privately to remain faithful to him, although it does not prevent her from addressing to him her pleas and reproaches, which she declines to entrust to a messenger. Her course of action is determined: she will espouse loyalty and will find her joy in the very act of proclaiming her love. Yet, in a swift reversal, she concludes that she must die "if you choose not to permit me any joy" (1: 45–46).

Songs II, III, and IV reiterate the elements of Song I: hope and despair, acceptance and indifference, salvation and death; but the depiction of the lady's plight darkens with each successive text. Song I suggests the first recognition by the lady of the beloved's indifference, shortly after she has declared her own passion to him. In Song II ("Ja de chantar non degr'aver talan"), the poetic voice admits to knowing that the knight loves another and recounts an episode in which she purloined a glove belonging to the knight only to return it for fear of causing him harm through the suspicions of his mistress. In Song III ("Mout avetz faich long estatge,"), speaking as though her liaison is at an end and with it all hope of reciprocation and joy in love (III: 8–12), she alludes repeatedly and graphically to her own death (III: 6, 15–16, 39–40). However, she concludes with the promise of forgiveness and welcome should her beloved chose to return after hearing her song. In Song IV ("Per joi que d'amor m'avenga,"), which begins "henceforth" (IV: 2), the note of resignation has deepened, for the lady laments that another reigns in her place (IV: 9–10). Conspicuously lacking in the songs of Castelloza is the presence in the abstraction *joi*, so frequently invoked by the poetic voice, of a transcendental power that would permit the elevation of that joy to the status of an ideal. The object, the knight, fails utterly to embody a system of values having the power automatically to ennoble the striving of the subject towards an absolute. The pretense of the poetic voice to find wholeness, identity, and fulfillment—*joi*, in a word—in her posture of noble fidelity rings hollow; for in this poetic universe *joi* exists only as its obverse, a shadowy reflection of itself.

Merritt R. Blakeslee

Caterina da Siena
ca. 1347–1380

Born 1347 (?), Siena, Italy
Died April 29, 1380, Rome
Genre(s): letters, mysticism, autobiography
Language(s): Italian

A Doctor of the Church and patroness of Italy, Caterina da Siena is one of the most influential authors of late medieval Europe. The daughter of Jacopo Benincasa and Lapa Piagenti, Caterina was the youngest of more than twenty children. She refused to marry and became a Dominican tertiary. Soon enough a group of disciples gathered around her and she became a powerful force in Italy during the second half of the four-

Caterina da Siena

teenth century. Although she never learned to write, she has left a large number of letters dictated to secretaries and a Dialogue of Divine Love. Gifted with a very strong personality, she tended to identify her views with both the Church and God. Her most important role came at the very end of her life when she went to Rome to rally support for Urban VI at the inception of the Great Schism. Her devotion to the papacy guaranteed that she would remain influential even after her death.

Works
Libro della divina dottrina [The Book of Divine Teaching], ed. Matilde Fiorilli (Bari, 1912). *Le lettere di S. Caterina da Siena* [The Letters of St. Catherine], ed. Piero Misciatelli, 6 vols. (Florence, 1970). Bell, *Holy Anorexia*, 22–53. *DBI* 22, 361–379.

Joseph Berrigan

Catherine II (the Great), Empress of Russia
1729–1796

Born April 21/May 2, 1729, Stettin, Pomerania
Died November 6/17, 1796, St. Petersburg, Russia
Genre(s): treatise, law, letters, translation, memoirs, history, criticism, comparative word list, comedy, comic operas, drama, fable, collection of proverbs, satire
Language(s): Russian, French

Varied literary activity and patronage of literature were only two of the many interests pursued by Empress Catherine II, born Sophie Auguste Friedrike, princess of Anhalt-Zerbst. Brought to Russia in 1744 to marry Grand Duke Peter Fedorovich, the Holstein-born crown prince of Russia, her cousin, and the future Peter III, Sophie converted to Russian Orthodoxy with the new name of Ekaterina Alekseevna, Catherine in English. Her marriage in 1745 proved to be unhappy and politically perilous, for the young couple had trouble producing the desired heir for the childless Empress Elizabeth (Grand Duke Peter may well have been sterile and impotent). When after several miscarriages Catherine finally gave birth to Paul in 1754 (probable father: Sergei Saltykov), the baby was taken away to be raised by Empress Elizabeth. Catherine involved herself in other romantic and political intrigues in the next several years as Empress Elizabeth's health deteriorated and her husband's defects became

Catherine II (the Great), Empress of Russia

blatant. Her romance with Stanislas Poniatowski produced a daughter who died early, and her romance with Grigory Orlov produced a son, Aleksei Bobrinskoi, born two months before the coup d'etat of June 28–July 8, 1762 that displaced Peter III, who was killed a week later. Proclaimed Catherine II and officially crowned in Moscow in September 1762, she began an extraordinary reign of more than thirty-four years that left its mark on Russian, European, and world history. The hallmarks of her reign were policies of "enlightened absolutism" that aimed at order and stability, economic growth and cultural development, military power, territorial expansion, and international repute.

Literature interested Catherine even before she came to Russia. She learned French well and had at least heard of the works of Voltaire and of Molière, Racine, and Corneille. In the difficult years before she won the throne she read avidly and widely, learned Russian quite well, and began to write informally including an early draft of memoirs for her mentor, British envoy Sir Charles Hanbury-Williams, with whom she corresponded frequently in 1756–1757 on mainly political subjects. By then she already sensed a great destiny. Upon gaining the throne she soon established contact with the French philosophers Diderot, D'Alembert, and Voltaire, whom she sought to enroll in her efforts to enlighten Russia. Some of her letters to them were published at the time and served fur-

ther to advertise her enlightened program. She also encouraged other Russian writers and the translation of foreign works into Russian. The average number of titles published annually in Russian rose from 161 in the early 1760s to 373 in the 1790s.

Her first widely known full-scale treatise was the famous *Nakaz* (Instructions) of 1767–1768 to the newly convened Legislative Commission, a compendium of some 655 articles borrowed largely from Montesquieu, Beccaria, and the German cameralists that provided guidelines for the work of the commissioners. It came out in many Russian editions and the Academy of Sciences issued a quadrilingual version in Russian, German, French, and Latin. It was quickly translated into all the main European languages and published abroad in English, Dutch, Italian, Swedish, Polish, and modern Greek. Subsequent Russian legislation often cited this work, which announced that Russia was a European state, argued that absolute monarchy was the best government for such a large and diverse empire, and advocated a general program of benevolent-sounding reforms to promote progress in economic, social, and cultural development under firm central guidance. The *Nakaz* was composed in French, then rendered into Russian by assistants, and edited by the empress in consultation with various advisers. Catherine's authorship in this and many other instances involved other people. Especially obscure was her participation in the first Russian satirical journals in 1769. Apparently she supplied some items for the periodical *Vsiakaia vsiachina* (All Sorts and Sundries), but exactly which ones is uncertain. The same is true of her part in *Antidote*, a work that aimed to counteract some negative views about Russia popularized in France by Jean Chappe d'Auteroche.

Catherine's five comedies of the early 1770s all satirized such common foibles as gossiping, hypocrisy, hypochondria, parental tyranny, and religious superstition. All were issued without her name but were performed first at court. At least one, *O Vremia!*, drew upon a foreign model, Gellert's *Betschwester*. She undoubtedly received considerable assistance in writing these plays, especially from her secretary and long-time friend Ivan Elagin. Later Catherine dismissed such writings as "trifles" that she indulged in merely for diversion. Their quality in literary terms was certainly quite low, but they may still be important as facts of Russian intellectual and cultural history, and as examples to others.

In the 1780s Catherine's literary activity revived and broadened to include several works for her grandsons, Alexander and Konstantin. These were the fables about Khlor and Fevee, a Russian ABC, a conversation and stories, and selected Russian proverbs. In 1780 she published her first antimasonic work, which was deliberately misdated 1759. In 1785–1786 her trilogy of antimasonic comedies appeared: *The Deceiver*, *The Deluded*, and *The Siberian Shaman*, all three of which attacked freemasonry as an international conspiracy and ridiculed its devotion to ritual. All three were quickly translated into German and published by C.F. Nicolai. She also indulged in two adaptations of Shakespeare's *The Merry Wives of Windsor* and *Timon of Athens* as *Vot kakvo* (This 'Tis to Have Linen and Buck-Baskets) and *Rastochitel'* (The Spendthrift), both in 1786. Later she offered two "imitations" of Shakespeare. Her comic operas, written with Aleksandr Khrapovitskii, were quite popular mainly because they employed the best composers, musicians, set designers, and elaborate stage machinery and costumes. She professed to see in them a form of therapy (for depression in particular).

In the 1780s Catherine also took an interest in Russian history and supervised the compilation of excerpts from the medieval chronicles, a chronology from 862 to 1462, and a genealogy of the princes of the house of Riurik. The first three parts of these materials had been serialized in the new journal *Sobesednik liubitelei rossiiskogo slova* in 1783–1784. She also sponsored the compilation of a comparative word list of selected terms in all known languages, including those of American Indian tribes.

Catherine wrote some seven different drafts of an autobiography beginning in the mid-1750s and concluding in the 1790s. None was finished, and none was published until long after her death. Indeed, the first printed version appeared outside Russia under the sponsorship of the revolutionary emigré Aleksandr Herzen as an attack on the legitimacy of the Romanov dynasty. Fairly full Russian editions were printed in the early twentieth century. The different versions contradict each other in many details, and none gives much treatment of her life beyond her accession to the throne. They were written mostly in French, with some Russian passages and fragments. She dedicated them to different friends, but she seems to have had no intention of publication. It is slightly ironic, therefore, that her literary reputation abroad should be mainly based upon these memoirs of her life before she became empress. Some editions include a number of her letters, the genre in which she wrote the most words; her known letters number more than 10,000, and the Russian state archives undoubtedly hold even more.

In fiction Catherine certainly displayed little literary talent, yet she did show some audacity and fore-

sight in setting an example of toying with various genres, especially in adapting foreign works to Russian tastes and customs. Certainly she received considerable direct assistance in the composition and editing of her works, some of which may be considered to have been written "by committee," as it were. The same is true of much of her nonfiction, especially of her *Nakaz*, and her authorship of important state documents such as the Charter to the Nobility of 1785. She may have demonstrated greater originality in some of her letters to friends, particularly those to her Parisian agent and confidant Melchior Grimm.

Works

Nakaz o sochinenii proekta novogo ulozheniia (1767). Anonymous contributions to *Vsiakaia vsiachina* (1769). *Antidote, ou examen du mauvais livre intitulé: Voyage en Sibérie en 1761* (1770). *O Vremia!* (c. 1772). *Peredniaia znatnogo boiarina* (1772). *Vlositel'* (1772). *Gospozha Vestnikova s sem'eiu* (1774). *Imianiny gospozha Varchalkinoi* (1774). *Taina protivonelepnogo obshchestva (Anti-absurde) otkrytaia ne prichastnym onomu* (1780). *Skazka o tsareviche Khlore* (1781). *Rossiiskaia azbuka dlia obucheniia iunoshestva chteniiu* (1781). *Razgovor i razskazy* (1782). *Vybornyia rossiiskiia poslovitsy* (1783). *Skazka o tsareviche Fevee* (1783). *Komediia "Obmanshchik"* (1785). *Vol'noe, no slaboe perelozhenie iz Shakespira, Komediia "Vot kakovo imet' korzinu i bel'e"* (1786). *Komediia "Obol'shchennyi"* (1786). *Komediia "Shaman Sibirskoi"* (1786). *Rastochitel'* (1786). *Novgorodskii boratyr' Boeslaevich'* (1786). *Opera komicheskaia "Fevei"* (1786). *Podrazhanie Shakespiru. Istoricheskoe predstavlenie bez sokhraneniia featral'nykh obyknovennykh pravil, iz zhizni Riurika* (1786). *Zapiski kasatel'no rossiiskoi istorii*, pt. I–VI (1787–1794). *Nachal'noe upravlenie Olega* (1787). *Opera komicheskaia "Khrabroi i smeloi vitias' Akhrideich'"* (1787). *Komediia "Razstroennaia sem'ia ostorozhkami i podozreniiami"* (1788). *Skazka o Gore-bogatyre Kosometoviche i opera komicheskaia iz slov skazki sostavlennaia* (1789). *Fedul s det'mi* (1790).

Editions of collection works: *Sochineniia*, 3 vols., ed. A. Smirdin (1849–1850). *Sochineniia*, 3 vols., ed. V.F. Solntsev (1893). *Sochineniia*, ed. A.I. Vvedenskii (1893). *Sochineniia, na osnovanii podlinnykh rukopisei*, vols. I–V, VII–XII, ed. A.N. Pypin (1901–1907).

Translations into English: *Memoirs of the Empress Catherine II, Written by Herself* (1859). *Memoirs of Catherine the Great*, tr. Katharine Anthony (1927). *The Memoirs of Catherine the Great*, ed. Dominique Maroger (1955). *Voltaire and Catherine the Great:*

Selected Correspondence, ed. A. Lentin (1974). "Catherine the Great's Instructions (NAKAZ) to the Legislative Commission, 1767," in Paul Dukes, ed., *Russia under Catherine the Great,* vol. II (1977).

J.T. Alexander

Margaret Cavendish, Duchess of Newcastle
1623–1673

Born 1623, St. John's Abbey, Colchester, Essex, England
Died December 15, 1673, Welbeck Abbey, Nottinghamshire
Genre(s): poetry, fiction, drama, oration, letters, philosophical treatise, biography, autobiography
Language(s): English

Margaret Cavendish was among the most conspicuous and prolific female writers of the seventeenth century and the first to experiment with a broad variety of genres. During her lifetime she wrote and published a dozen books of poetry, fiction, plays, orations, letters, philosophical treatises, biography, and autobiography, earning a reputation for genius and eccentricity that has endured for more than three hundred years.

The youngest child of Thomas Lucas, a wealthy landowner who died soon after her birth, and Elizabeth Leighton, she was raised to be "virtuous . . . modest . . . civil . . . [and] honorable." She passed an idyllic childhood in rural Essex learning little more than the traditional accomplishments and otherwise devoting her time to the cultivation of her imagination. Upon the outbreak of civil war, she fled with her family to Oxford, where in 1643 she became a maid of honor to Queen Henrietta Maria. Despite her painful shyness, she braved the loss of her protective family and the ridicule of the court to follow the Queen into exile in Paris. There she met William Cavendish, Marquis of Newcastle, her brother Charles's commander and a Royalist hero of the siege of York. They were married in 1645 and until the Restoration lived in Paris, Rotterdam, and Antwerp.

Although William was a widower and thirty years older than she, Cavendish never tired of rehearsing her husband's virtues: sometime military hero, sometime poet and playwright, an amateur in philosophy and the natural sciences, William was the definitive romantic cavalier, his most serious work was a study of the gentlemanly art of horsemanship. In the face of enormous debt, William maintained luxurious households on the Continent where he entertained the famous philosophers of the time, interpreting for his young wife the matter of their discussions. The father of five children from his first marriage, he apparently submitted to her contempt for "breeding women" and encouraged only the growth of her intellect and imagination; in pride and gratitude for such an "Extraordinary Husband," Cavendish wrote, "I cannot for my Life be so good a Huswife as to quit Writing . . . you are pleased to Peruse my Works and Approve of them so well, as to give me Leave to Publish them, which is a Favour few Husbands would grant their Wives. . . ."

Six years after their marriage, Margaret Cavendish returned to England in an unsuccessful attempt to obtain money due on William's sequestered estates. During her eighteen-month stay she composed her first book, *Poems and Fancies,* which was published in London in 1653. Her theory that, for her, poetry must be grounded in the rational "distinguishment" she had learned from the philosophers and the imaginative "similizing" retained from her childhood play was already apparent, but so too was her habitual dislike of revision: "there was more pleasure in making than mending," she later wrote, and more than once made the preponderance of thoughts in her head her excuse: "I did many times not peruse the copies that were transcribed, lest they should disturb my following conceptions." *Poems and Fancies* was followed within two months by *Philosophical Fancies,* like the first book an enchanting blend of fantasy and the popularization of current scientific inquiry, but because of its uncontrolled leaps from the rational steps of evidence, division, and order into the realm of the imagination, an object of frequent derision. Aware of her shortcomings, she had tried to apologize to her critics: "The Reason I write in Verse is Because I thought that Errors might better pass there, than in Prose, since poets write most Fiction and Fiction is not given for Truth but for pastime"; failing to convince them of the value of her work, but still encouraged by her husband and confident of her own "native wit," she turned to prose. During her remaining years in exile she published three books, which united her desire for personal fame with a growing feminist awareness.

The World's Olio, a collection of essays compiled upon her return to Antwerp, concludes with a defense against charges of plagiarism, ironic because of the censure she suffered, but a theme already common in women's writing. In the dedication of her next book, *The Philosophical and Physical Opinions* (1655), to the universities of Oxford and Cambridge, Cavendish straightforwardly attacked the customs that shut women out of education and power, using a familiar female image to "similize" her argument: ". . . we are kept like Birds in Cages, to Hop up and down in our Houses, not Suffer'd to fly abroad, to see the several Changes of Fortune and the Various Humors, Ordained and Created by Nature, and wanting the Experience of Nature, we must needs want the Understanding and Knowledge." *Natures Pictures Drawn by Fancies Pencil to the Life* (1656), a collection of tales of romantic heroines facing fantastic adversity, presented Cavendish's ideal woman in fiction, formless by modern standards and obviously the product of her vision of herself. The short autobiography attached to *Natures Pictures,* "A True Relation of my Birth, Breeding, and Life," is, however, charming in its "plain natural style," and like the *Life* of her husband she published twelve years later is as direct a portrait of personal experience as ever came out of that dramatic period of English history.

When, after the Restoration, Charles II made William Duke of Newcastle and restored some of his property, they retired to Welbeck Abbey. There, isolated from the distractions and criticisms of society, Cavendish continued writing, producing within the next eight years a remarkable quantity and variety of works. The fourteen closet dramas included in her *Playes* were obviously modeled upon William's amateur attempts, but within their chaotic dramatic structures they present extraordinary women, skilled in the art of systematic public debate. "Female Orations," a section of *Orations of Divers Sorts* (1662), her next book, laid bare the customs and prejudices that had brought women to their current state of powerlessness. Even in its forthright feminist polemic, however, it could not escape the hallmarks of her "similizing" imagination: "The truth is, we live like bats or owls, labour like beasts, and die like worms." *CCXI. Sociable Letters* (1664) and *Philosophical Letters* (1664) marked Cavendish's return to her most successful style, witty, enthusiastic, personal, and supremely confident that whatever she had to say was, for the moment, reasonable and right. *Observations upon Experimental Philosophy* (1666) was a return to her interest in science, but almost predictably rescinded her earlier opinions about experimentation; the science-fiction story attached to it, *The Description of a New Blazing World,* combined her passion for scientific speculation with her romanticized vision of the new woman. *The Life of the Thrice Noble, High and Puissant Prince William*

Cavendishe and a new book of *Playes* were the last of her original productions, yet her interest in writing seems never to have flagged. In the last years of her life she probably regretted the haste of her earlier composition; always proud of her work, she must have overseen its new editions and made the revisions she thought necessary to insure her fame.

In 1667 Cavendish was an invited guest at the Royal Academy, honored for her scientific achievements, which were not, after all, very much more implausible than those circulating during the period. Still, with her eccentric dress and her embarrassing habit of publishing her own writing, she was a curiosity for the Londoners who flocked to stare at her carriage. She returned to Welbeck Abbey after her triumphant visit, died in 1673, and was buried in Westminster Abbey. In 1676 William collected and published *Letters and Poems in Honour of the Incomparable Princess Margaret Duchess of Newcastle,* a volume containing praise from Hobbes but also the sound criticism of Walter Charleton: "Your fancy is too generous to be strained, your invention too nimble to be fettered. . . . Hence it is that you do not always confine your sense to your verse, nor your verses to rhythm! nor your rhythm to the quantity and sounds of syllables." Cavendish was hampered in her writing, surely, by her lack of disciplined intellectual training and in her philosophy by her necessary dependence upon the observations of others. Yet in her work there is an inescapable exuberance that makes Virginia Woolf's judgment, "She has the irresponsibility of a child and the arrogance of a Duchess," seem more tribute than blame.

Works

Poems and Fancies: Written by the Right Honourable, the Lady Margaret Countesse of Newcastle (1653, 1664, 1668). *Philosophical Fancies Written by the Right Honourable, the Lady Newcastle* (1653). *The World's Olio. Written by the Most Excellent Lady the Lady M. of Newcastle* (1655, 1671). *The Philosophical and Physical Opinions, Written by her Excellency, The Lady Marchionesse of Newcastle* (1655, 1663, 1668). *Natures Pictures Drawn by Fancies Pencil to the Life. Written by the Thrice Noble, Illustrious, and Excellent Princess, the Lady Marchioness of Newcastle. . . .* (1656, 1671). *Playes Written by the Thrice Noble, Illustrious and Excellent Princess, the Lady Marchionesse of Newcastle* (1662). *Orations of Divers Sorts, Accommodated to Divers Places. Written by the Thrice Noble . . .* (1662, 1668). *CCXI. Sociable Letters, Written by The Thrice Noble . . .* (1664). *Philosophical Letters: or, Modest*

Reflections upon some Opinions in Natural Philosophy, Maintained by Several Famous and Learned Authors of this Age, Expressed by Way of Letters: By the Thrice Noble . . . (1664). *Observations upon Experimental Philosophy. To Which is Added, the Description of a New Blazing World. Written by the Thrice Noble . . .* (1666, 1668). *The Life of the Thrice Noble, High and Puissant Prince William Cavendishe, Duke, Marquess, and Earl of Newcastle . . .* (1667, 1675). *Playes, Never before Printed. Written by the Thrice Noble . . .* (1668).

Susan Hastings

Laura Cereta
1469–1499

Born 1469, Brescia, Italy
Died 1499
Genre(s): letters, oration, invective
Language(s): Latin

Cereta was born to noble parents, Veronica di Leno and Silvestro Cereta, a jurisprudent and humanist, who was often employed in the bureaucracy of Brescia. She was tutored first in a convent, then at home in the humanities by her father. From her writings we learn that she also studied mathematics and astrology and read extensively on religious subjects. At fifteen, she married the merchant Pietro Serina but was widowed after only 18 months. It seems certain that Cereta discussed philosophical questions at meetings of learned people in convents and in private homes. She died suddenly at thirty and was buried in the church of San Domenico in Brescia.

Most of Cereta's literary output is in the form of Latin epistles, one of the genres more assiduously cultivated by fifteenth-century humanists. Written when she was between sixteen and eighteen years of age, her letters are addressed to members of her family, to prelates, and to professional people of her community. In many of them she expresses her grief for the death of her husband, who shared her interest in learning. What is apparent in all of them are the values current among humanists of her time: a love of truth, a great respect for learning as the only activity that distinguishes humanity, a driving wish to immortalize her name. Cereta does not make much of the often-debated conflict between learning and religious belief; she upholds them equally and quotes instances of people who were religious as well as erudite. In-

dicative of her mental attitudes is the motivation that she gives for her love of astrology as her desire to read the rational language that God has used in the workings of the spheres. Cereta had a strong sense of her own intellectual value, which she vehemently defended against detractors in a letter conceived as a traditional "invective."

Thirteen of her letters were titled and written as formal orations on a series of topical subjects: avarice, death, fate and chance, war and its causes, the Turkish menace, the advisability of marriage for men and women, the advantages of an active life, self-control, and ensuing happiness. One letter gives geographical details upon a request. There is also an amusing funeral oration on the death of an ass, which is to be read as a parody of a much-practiced genre.

For the modern reader what is most striking is Cereta's defense of women and of their right to receive an education on an equal footing with men. She touches on the relation between the sexes in several letters and at considerable length in the notes she addressed to Bibulus Sempronius. Very revealing are her complaints about the isolation she faced as a female scholar, about the difficulty in finding time to study, and about the envy driving men and women of her town to detract from her achievements. In the last years of her life, she was subject to considerable pressure to abandon her studies and embrace the religious life.

Works

Laurae Ceretae Brixiensis Feminae Clarissimae Epistolae jam primum e MS in lucem productae a Jacopo Philippo Thomasino, qui eius vitam et notas addidit (1640). Albert Rabil, Jr., ed., *Laura Cereta: Quattrocento Humanist* (1981), pp. 109–175. "Letter to Augustinus Aemilius, Curse against the Ornamentation of Women." "Letter to Bibulus Sempronius, Defense of the Liberal Instruction of Women." "Letter to Lucilia Vernacula, against Women Who Disparage Learned Women." *Her Immaculate Hand: Selected Works by and about the Women Humanists of Quattrocento Italy*, eds. Margaret L. King and Albert Rabil, Jr. (1983), pp. 77–86.

Rinaldina Russell

Ernestina de Champourcín (y Morán de Loredo)
1905–

Born 1905, Vitoria, Alava, Spain
Genre(s): poetry, novel, essay
Language(s): Spanish

Chronologically, Champourcín belongs to the "Generation of 1927," which included Lorca, Aleixandre, Alberti and many other famous poets (her late husband, the poet Juan José Domenchina, may be classed a lesser member of the same group). Champourcín shares with other members of the generation a formation under the aegis of the "Generation of 1898," and especially the poetic hegemony of Juan Ramón Jiménez, with whom she was personally acquainted (publishing her memoirs of him in 1981). In a general way, the group exhibits initial traits of European modernism, subsequently evolving through a modified surrealism, and still later in the direction of neorealism, social engagement, and existentialist concerns. These broad outlines can also be discerned in the evolution of Champourcín's work, although she herself has divided the development of her poetry into three stages: human love, divine love, and retrospection. The first stage lasted from 1926 when her first collection, *En silencio* (In Silence), appeared, until 1936, when the Spanish Civil War (1936–1939) erupted. This was also the year of Champourcín's marriage, and she was soon to accompany her husband into exile in Mexico where he died in 1959 (she remained, working as a translator, until the mid-1970s). Exile produced a rupture in Champourcín's poetic production, as well as in her vital circumstances, resulting in a sixteen-year period in which no poems appeared. When she returned to the publication of poetry, the thematic character of her poems had changed radically, becoming religious and biblical, and her form is more prosaic. The divine love period spanned from 1952 to 1974, as the poet sought inspiration in the Scriptures and characterizes herself as a seeker of light and truth in search of mystical or cosmic union with the deity. In 1974, she published her first collection after return from exile, following some six years of silence, seemingly ending her period of metaphysically inspired poetry. The works composed after return from exile exhibit certain traces of earlier periods, but are on the one hand much more immediate in their concern with such worldly problems as war and human alienation and on the other hand are more personal and biographical as the poet looks backward at life in exile, old friends, travels, loneliness, and longing.

During her first decade of publishing, Champourcín produced four poetry collections and a novel, *La casa de enfrente* (1936; The House Across the Street), which adopts the format of a diary to reconstruct the childhood and adolescence of a girl up to and including her first love affair. Significant poetry collections during this period are *Ahora* (1928; Now), reminiscent of poetic greats of the previous generation such as Antonio Machado and Juan Ramón Jiménez, and exhibiting the cult of metaphor typical of the Generation of 1927; *La voz en el viento* (1931; Voice in the Wind), in which the "human love" themes are especially noteworthy; and *Cántico inútil* (1936; Useless Canticle), her longest and most surrealist collection, although it is varied both metrically and thematically to an extent that makes it difficult to characterize. While displaying the fully developed "human love" themes, it also anticipates the early traits of the "divine love" stage to follow much later.

Presencia a oscuras (1952; Presence in Shadows) is illumined by the poet's belief that "God is in all poetry," initiating a poetry of praise and religious aspiration more fully developed in *El nombre que me diste* (1960; The Name You Gave to Me), *Cárcel de los sentidos* (1964; Prison of the Senses), *Hai-kais espirituales* (1967; Spiritual Hai-kus), *Cartas cerradas* (1968; Closed Letters), and *Poemas del Ser y del Estar* (1974; Poems of Being and Becoming—actually an untranslatable play on the two Spanish verbs "to be"). Religious themes are minimized in the poet's final works, although cosmic gropings are not entirely absent. *Primer exilio* (1978; First Exile) and *La pared transparente* (1984; The Transparent Wall) coincide in being inspired more in memory than in emotions and mystic meditations giving rise to the first and second periods, respectively. Now past eighty, Champourcín is unlikely to modify her poetic trajectory again (indeed, retrospective verse is a frequent characteristic of aged poets). However, she has begun to receive some of the recognition she was denied for decades in Spain because of her exile and may eventually be acclaimed as the most important woman poet of the Generation of 1927.

Works

En Silencio (1926). *Ahora* (1928). *La voz en el viento* (1931). *Cántico inútil* (1936). *La casa de enfrente* (1936). *Presencia a oscuras* (1952). *El nombre que me diste* (1960). *Cárcel de los sentidos* (1964). *Hai-kais espirituales* (1967). *Cartas cerradas* (1968). *Poemas del Ser y del Estar* (1974). *Primer exilio* (1978). *La pared transparente* (1984).

Janet Perez

Gabrielle-Emilie le Tonnilier de Breteuil Châtelet-Lomont 1706–1749

Born 1706, Paris, France
Died 1749, Luneville
Genre(s): letters, poetry, philosophical and scientific treatises
Language(s): French

This extraordinarily gifted intellectual spanned the disciplines, performing experiments in physics, chemistry, and math; writing poetry; and translating Vergil, Ovid, and Horace into fluid French. In 1735, she wrote an essay on Newton's discoveries on optics and later translated and analyzed his *Principia Mathematica*, thus furthering the revival of French science. Her works reflect the influence of Gottfried Leibniz's epistemology. Regarded as one of the great beauties of the early eighteenth century, she possessed remarkable determination, energy, and influence in the aristocratic and intellectual circles of France.

Madame du Châtelet, the youngest of four children, was her father's indulged favorite, and thus developed exorbitantly expensive tastes. The five-foot-nine-inch beauty towered over most of her lovers, including Richelieu and Voltaire. As an ungainly youth, she desperately sought affection, finding it with hard study from her tutors. Her excellence in gymnastics, fencing, and riding derived from talent and diligence. Luck, a head for mathematics, and an instinct for cards brought her money, which she rapidly spent. But it was the works of Descartes, Newton, Locke, Pope, and Leibniz that excited her fertile intellect.

In 1725, she wed the Marquis Florent-Claude du Châtelet-Lomont, a heavyset man with florid face, loud voice, and a love of food and drink. Ten years her senior, he allowed her freedom from interference in her life and demanded the same. Edwards notes that "the story to the effect that the bride halted the ceremony in order to correct the clergyman's pronunciation of a Latin phrase may be apocryphal." She spent three months completely and lavishly refurbishing her groom's townhouse behind the Louvre. During this period she became pregnant with Gabrielle-Pauline, who inherited both her mother's good looks and her intellect. The following year, son and heir Florent-Louis-Marie was born; the son took after his military father. Seven years later, Victor-Esprit was born but did not survive infancy.

Madame du Châtelet lived the typical aristocratic life, awakening at mid-morning to breakfast in bed, spending several hours preparing for afternoon guests and philosophical conversation (when she was pregnant, she received guests from her bed) but also reading far into the night. Requiring only two to four hours sleep, she absorbed volumes—in the original Greek and Latin, modern French, German, English, and Spanish—during the wee hours. Also, like other aristocrats, she accepted her husband's open affairs and engaged in her own. Du Guebriant and the Comte de Vincennes, the one physically dashing and the other intellectually stimulating, and Duke de Richelieu, a lifelong friend, preceded the love of her life, François Arouet, or Voltaire. This genius was in intellectual matters her equal and her spur. The intensity of their minds matched that of their passion. Together they flouted custom, appearing together at inns and operas and even before King Louis.

The Marquis de Châtelet's chateau at Cirey was a high, rambling structure in the deep woodlands at the eastern edge of Champagne not far from Holland. The building was badly in need of repair. Madame du Châtelet, providing the direction, and Voltaire, providing the funds, lavishly refurnished it as their hideaway. This proved a safe retreat for the provocative Voltaire, whose political writings kept him in permanent danger. Working with the intense fury of the compulsive, Voltaire accomplished miracles in three months. Here the two cultivated all the arts and wrote prodigiously, organizing meals and meetings around their writing schedules. Occasionally Madame du Châtelet's husband Florent-Claude would visit, with or without his current mistress, and all remained extremely civil, if interested in dissimilar matters. Life at Cirey seemed ideal and solved many problems—it offered work space, co-habitation, and safety. Additionally, she was able to keep Voltaire cut off from Paris life and the charms of other attractive women.

Social life continued apace as well, although Madame du Châtelet was not comfortable when Voltaire was invited to the homosexual court of Crown Prince Frederick of Prussia. This storm she weathered, and for a while, that of Voltaire's niece, Madame Denis, who wheedled great sums of money from her devoted uncle. Others attended the couple at Cirey for long or short visits, always keeping the occupants' lives stimulated. Meanwhile, Madame du Châtelet's growing reputation spread across the continent as her brilliant books were reviewed with awe. Voltaire's controversial dramas continued to get him in trouble, sometimes leading to seclusion.

Sometime between 1745 and 1747 Voltaire began an affair with his niece, the widowed Madame Denis, unbeknownst to Madame du Châtelet. The stress of his double life lead to irascibility and dyspepsia, and to Madame du Châtelet's further neglect. Voltaire's waning interest brought her sorrow, despite her calm acceptance of the situation. Finally she turned to the handsome and vigorous thirty-two-year-old Saint-Lambert, a passionate man who helped her forget her humiliation. By him, the forty-three-year-old Madame du Châtelet became pregnant, and in 1749, soon after childbirth, she died, presumably of a heart ailment. Voltaire mourned greatly, writing "I have not lost merely a mistress, I have lost the half of myself—a soul for which mine was made, a friend whom I saw born. The most tender father does not love his only daughter more truly."

The contributions left by Madame du Châtelet are so extensive and diverse that they mark her as a greatly influential intellectual, known and respected by the scholars of her day. Her great energy, zeal, and devotion to knowledge are unsurpassed, and her legacy is one to be emulated.

Works

Aeneid, tr. in *Les Lettres de la Marquise du Châtelet*. Theodore Bestermann, ed. (Geneva, 1958). *Dissertation sur la nature et la propagation du feu* (1744). *Doutes sur les religions reculées adresses a Voltaire* (1792). *Institutions de Physique* (1740). *Traduction des principles mathematiques de la philosophie naturelle de Newton* (1759). *Traité Sur le Bonheur* (1744).

Jean E. Jost

Inger Christensen
1935–

Born January 6, 1935, Vejle, Denmark
Genre(s): poetry, novel, drama, translation
Language(s): Danish

Christensen is considered by some to be the most important writer of the "sixties generation" in Denmark. She has been called a modernist although her treatment of such topics as self, language, writing, and the word, plus her use of strictly structured systems to expose the artificiality of all systems, are characteristics of postmodernism.

Christensen was trained as a teacher at the Århus Seminarium, where she took her teacher's examination in 1958. While still a student, she began to publish her first poems in the magazine *Hvedekorn*, and under the influence of Poul Borum, to whom she was married

from 1959 to 1976, became interested in modernist philosophies and methods, which she found congenial to her own talent. Her first book was *Lys* (Light), a collection of poems published in 1962, shortly followed by *Græs* (Grass) the following year. A three-year Arts Foundation grant gave her the opportunity to finish *Det* (It), her masterwork, in 1969. She has received numerous other Danish prizes, including the Kjeld Abell prize in 1978 and the Søren Gyldendal prize in 1983.

Inger Christensen

In 1978 she became a member of the Danish Academy. She resides in Copenhagen.

Christensen's major theme is the relationship between the self and the world, encompassing nature, other people, and language. A rigorously intellectual writer strongly influenced by contemporary European currents, especially structuralism, she once said in an interview, "The structure of a work of art is not generally seen as a kind of philosophy. But I think about it as such, and have done so since my first poetry collection." This was *Lys*, which is structured around the progression of the seasons as the I-narrator, who is, in the first poem, located in a desolate, snow-driven landscape, and goes from winter to summer and comes out of the darkness into the light. If the title of this collection reflects its visionary, abstract character, the title of the next one, *Græs*, reflects a concern with more earthly things. The most important section of this book is "Møde" (meeting), a series of short poems in which the French poet Rimbaud is featured as a main character. "Møde" ends the book on a note stressing the individual's need for a meeting with the rest of the world, especially other people.

These two poetry collections were followed by two novels, *Evighedsmaskinen* (1964; The Perpetual Motion Machine) and *Azorno* (1967). *Evighedsmaskinen* takes place in a small town dominated by a fundamentalist religious sect that believes a new savior will be born to them on Christmas night. The community will ensure that his life imitates Christ's in all its main events. When such a child is born, however, his parents try to protect him from his assigned fate. Despite their best efforts, the inevitable happens: on his thirtieth birthday, he is seized and buried alive. He manages to dig his way out of his burial chamber and goes wandering into the night.

Her next novel, *Azorno*, begins as letters written by several woman characters who are competing with each other to be the one who gets to meet Azorno, the protagonist of a romantic novel the writer Sampel is working on. The epistolary form eventually becomes a diary. *Azorno* expresses the idea that we are all characters in each other's novels.

As impressive as all her work up to this point may be, it was only an apprenticeship for her masterwork, *Det* (1969; It), which one critic has called a "word-cathedral." It is a book-length poem constructed on a mathematical number system based on linguistic theory. Its three main sections are "Prologos," a long prose poem about the creation of the world; "Logos," further divided into three parts: "The Scene," "The Action," and "The Text"; and "Epilogos." Each of the three chapters of the "Logos" section consists of eight series of eight poems each; each series is named after categories in the Danish linguist Viggo Brøndal's book on prepositions. The source for Christensen's development and variations on sentence structure in *Det* is Noam Chomsky's theory of transformational grammar. As for subject matter, *Det* encompasses many of the philosophical and ideological debates taking place during the sixties, such as the influence of the Chinese Cultural Revolution in Denmark, French structuralism, and the anti-psychiatry of R.D. Laing. In spite of its formidable intertextuality and structure, *Det* is a very readable book and was a bestseller as well as a critical success in Denmark.

Christensen's next major work was *Det malede værelse* (1976; The Painted Room), a historical novella about the Renaissance painter Andrea Mantegna, who is best known for his frescoes in the *camera degli sposi* in the royal castle in Mantua. A person entering this room has the illusion of being in the middle of the activity portrayed on the walls and the ceiling. This effect inspired the structure of Christensen's work, which is written in three parts, from three different viewpoints. Her interest in painting also plays a role in some of her dramatic works, for example the television play *Ækteskabet mellem lyst og nød* (1978; The Marriage between Lust and Need), in which there is a discussion of decorating a young girl's room with Renaissance and Surrealist paintings.

In 1979 Christensen published another book of poetry, *Brev i April* (Letter in April), an autobiographical narration in short poems of a trip taken by a woman poet with her small son. She ironically contrasts her own intellectualizations with the child's ingenuous response to nature. *Alfabet* (Alphabet) followed in 1981. Like *Det*, this poetry collection is also constructed on a mathematical principle: each section, beginning with a new letter of the alphabet, contains the number of lines equal to the sum of the number of lines in the preceding two sections. The series does not finish the alphabet, however, but breaks off at the letter "n."

Christensen's other writings include essays, a number of translations, mostly of German works into Danish, and original dramatic works. Her drama is influenced by absurdists like Ionesco and Beckett. It includes her radio trilogy composed of *Speljltigeren* (1966; The Mirror-Tiger), *Klædt på til at overleve* (1967; Dressed to Survive), and *Et uhørt Spil* (1969; An Unheard Play), a stage play, *Intriganterne* (1972; The Intriguers), the libretto for Ib Nørholm's opera *Den unge park* (1972; The Young Park), and two television plays.

Christensen's election to the Danish Academy and the respectful discussion she receives in histories of contemporary Danish and Scandinavian literature attests to her importance to contemporary Danish letters. Poul Borum has said that *Det* belongs to world literature; yet, the translations of it into French and English have not yet been published. In general, she has been translated less than some of her contemporaries with lesser reputations and has thus not yet received the international reputation she seems to deserve.

Works

Lys [Light] (1962). *Græs* [Grass] (1963). *Evighedsmaskinen* [The Perpetual Motion Machine] (1964). *Speljltigeren* [The Mirror-tiger], radio play (1966). *Azorno* (1967). *Klædt på at overleve* [Dressed to Survive], radio play (1967). *Det* [It] (1969). *Et uhørt spil* [An Unheard Play], radio play (1969). *Den unge park* [The Young Park], libretto for an opera by Ib Nørholm; television broadcast (1972). *Intriganterne* [The Intriguers] (1972). *En aften på Kgs. Nytorv* [An Evening in Kongens Nytorv], radio play (1975). *Ørkenens luftsyn* [The Desert's Air-Scene] television play (1975). *Det malede værelse: en fortælling fra Mantua* [The Painted Room: A Tale from Mantua] (1976). *Ægteskabet mellem lyst og nød* [The Marriage between Lust and Need], television play (1978). *Brev i April* [Letter in April] (1979). *Masser af sne til de trængede får* [Masses of Snow for the Needy Sheep], radio play (1979). *Alfabet* [Alphabet] (1981). *Del af labyrinten* [Part of the Labyrinth] (1982). *Den lange ukendte rejse* [The Long, Unknown Journey] (1982). *En vinteraften: Ufa og andre spil* [A Winter's Evening in Ufa and Other Plays] (1987). *Æter* [Ether] (1987). Christensen has also contributed numerous short pieces to Danish periodicals and anthologies.

Translations: *Azorno* (German), tr. Hanns Grössel (Frankfurt: S. Fischer, 1972). *Lettre en avril*, tr. Janine and Karl Poulsen. *Arcane* 17 (1985). For English translations of individual poems in periodicals and anthologies, see Carol L. Schroeder, *A Bibliography of Danish Literature in English Translation, 1950–1980*. Susanna Nied writes about her translation of *Det* in the *Danish Literary Journal* in 1982, and excerpts appeared in *No Man's Land: An Anthology of Modern Danish Women's Literature* (Copenhagen, 1987), but this translation has not yet been published in its entirety.

Kristine Anderson

Agatha Christie
1890–1976

Born September 15, 1890, Torquay, Devon, England
Died January 12, 1976, Wallingford
Genre(s): mystery novel
Languages(s): English

Agatha Christie's career, from *The Mysterious Affair at Styles* (1920), written in response to her sister's demand for a detective story not as easily solved by the reader as the popular fiction then in vogue, to *Curtain* (in which she finally disposed of her famous sleuth Hercule Poirot in 1975) and *Sleeping Murder* (serialized in a popular magazine in the year of her death, 1976), was phenomenal. She wrote some 130 or 140 short stories, more than half that many novels, a score of radio and stage plays, a couple of volumes of poetry, a travel book, and an autobiography. The film *Murder on the Orient Express* (one of more than a dozen which brought her work to the screen), based

on one of her novels (*Murder on the Calais Coach*), made more money than any other British film up to that date. A play (*The Mouse Trap*), originating in her story "Three Blind Mice," opened in 1952 and is still running, having long since become the most successful play in the history of the English theatre. Her books have sold hundreds of millions of copies and have been translated into more languages (over 100) than has Shakespeare. "A Christie for Christmas" was for generations a British publishing tradition. Quite simply, she was the most famous British woman writer of her half a century or so of fame and the most commercially successful woman writer of all time.

All this production (she called herself "a perfect sausage machine") and practice did not make her an artistic writer. Her first novel was refused by a number of publishers before John Lane bought it for The Bodley Head. Some of the stories in *Poirot Investigates* (1924) and her very controversial novel *The Murder of Roger Ackroyd* (1926) are among her best work; she did not improve over fifty years, perhaps because she was quite good enough for her readers from the start and also perhaps because she was proud of the fact that "though I have given in to people on every [other] subject under the sun, I *have never given in to anyone over what I write.*"

Her skill was said to lie in ingenious plotting, but real invention was not really needed. She simply rang the inevitable changes on the conventions of the genre. She could not have "nobody did it" (suicide being a solution rejected by readers), but she could and did have "everybody did it," one of the "corpses" did it, the narrator did it—just about everything but Stephen Leacock's crazy suggestion in his spoof on the red herrings and tortuous twists of mystery writing: he has the murder committed by two people who are just barely mentioned in the book—they are, in fact, the publishers, noted only at the bottom of the title page.

Julian Symons in his history of the crime novel, *Bloody Murder,* adds to the fact that "her skill was not in the tight construction of plot," that she did not often "make assumptions about the scientific and medical knowledge of readers," though her war work in pharmacies gave her a certain pride in the way she brought in poisons, playing (as she said) with "the phial" in her little "domestic murders." Nor were her characters or scenes especially well drawn. She created, actually, a "never-never" world of fiction (as critic Edmund Crispin and others have noted) and seems to have had little interest in the world in which she lived. With characters that are "flat" and a rural English setting that had largely disappeared before she could write much about it, she moved from her early sensational claptrap (*The Seven Dials Mystery,* 1929, has been called "almost embarrassing" in its "bright young things, beautiful Balkan spies, and sinister anarchists") to her very own brand of upper-class twits gathered in the library of some country house to hear the detective unravel the mystery. This plot is exactly the sort that is spoofed at the start of the 1980 film version of her *The Mirror Crack'd,* which begins with the showing of *Murder at Midnight* in the village hall of St. Mary Mead, which all the world knows is the home of her eccentric but lovable Miss Marple. Her world, like that of her contemporary P.G. Wodehouse, remained firmly that of times long past, before Labour lords with low-class accents, when garden fêtes and jumble sales, not socialism and common markets, were topics of discussion. In her novels the action is in the library, not in the bedroom.

"What I'm writing is meant to be entertainment," she told Francis Wyndham in 1966. As the creator of Tommy and Tuppence Beresford (*Partners in Crime,* etc.), Parker Pyne (*Parker Pyne Investigates,* etc.), Harley Quin (*The Mysterious Mr. Quin,* etc.), Superintendent Battle (*The Secret of Chimneys,* etc.), Col. John Race (*The Man in the Brown Suit,* etc.), Mark Easterbrook (*The Pale Horse*), Arthur Calgary (*Ordeal by Innocence*), Inspector Narracott (*The Sittaford Mystery*), the bases of films such as *Witness for the Prosecution, And Then There Were None,* and *Death on the Nile* (among others), and—most of all—the great Belgian detective Hercule Poirot, with his dapper little moustache, irritating little mannerisms (Christie's substitute for characterization) and "little grey cells," Agatha Christie was indubitably a genius at popular entertainment.

In a genre with magnificent milestones ever since Wilkie Collins's *The Moonstone* (1868), with Poe and Conan Doyle and many more (including women such as Dorothy Sayers, Josephine Tey, P.D. James, and others whose work is not nearly as "abominably careless" as the London *Times* found, but truly literary), Christie by sheer popularity and persistence carved out a lasting place for herself that can be enjoyed as well as respected by everyone except curmudgeons such as Edmund Wilson, who damned the whole detective fiction genre with the nasty question: "Who Cares Who Killed Roger Ackroyd?"

Works

The Mysterious Affair at Styles: A Detective Story (1920). *The Secret Adversary* (1922). *The Murder on the Links (1923). The Man in the Brown Suit* (1924). *Poirot Investigates* (1924; in U.S., 1925). *The Secret of Chimneys* (1925). *The Murder of Roger Ackroyd* (1926). *The Big Four* (1927). *The Mystery of the Blue Train* (1928). *The Seven Dials Mystery* (1929). *Partners in Crime* (1929). *The Underdog* (1929). *The Mysterious Mr. Quin* (1930; also as *The Passing of Mr. Quin*). *The Murder at the Vicarage* (1930). (as Mary Westmacott) *Giants' Bread* (1930). *The Sittaford Mystery* (1931; in U.S. as *The Murder at Hazelmoor*). *Black Coffee* (produced 1931, published 1934). *Peril at End House* (1932). *The Thirteen Problems* (1932; in U.S. as *The Tuesday Club Murders,* 1933; also as *Miss Marple and the Thirteen Problems*). *The Hound of Death and Other Stories* (1933); *Witness for the Prosecution,* produced 1953, published 1956. *Lord Edgware Dies* (1933; in U.S. as *Thirteen at Dinner*). *Why Didn't They Ask Evans?* (1934; in U.S. as *Boomerang Clue,* 1935). *Parker Pyne Investigates* (1934; in U.S. as *Mr. Parker Pyne, Detective*). *The Listerdale Mystery and Other Stories* (1934). *Murder on the Orient Express* (1934; in U.S. as *Murder on the Calais Coach*). *Murder in Three Acts* (1934; in U.S. as *Three Act Tragedy,* 1935). (as Mary Westmacott) *Unfinished Portrait* (1934). *Death in the Clouds* (1935; in U.S. as *Death in the Air*). *The ABC Murders: A New Poirot Mystery* (1936). (with F. Vosper) *Love from a Stranger* (1936; based on the story, "Philomel Cottage"). *Cards on the Table* (1936). *Murder in Mesopotamia* (1936). *Death on the Nile* (1937; in U.S., 1938; produced as *Murder on the Nile,* 1946). *Murder in the Mews and Other Stories* (1937; in U.S. as *Dead Man's Mirror and Other Stories*). *Dumb Witness* (1937; in U.S. as *Poirot Loses a Client;* also as *Murder at Littlegreen House* and *Mystery at Littlegreen House*). *Appointment with Death: A Poirot Mystery* (1938; and published as play, 1945). *Hercule Poirot's Christmas* (1938; in U.S. as *Murder for Christmas: A Poirot Story,* 1939; also as *A Holiday for Murder*). *The Regatta Mystery and Other Stories* (1939; also as *Poirot and the Regatta Mystery*). *Murder Is Easy* (1939; in U.S. as *Easy to Kill*). *Ten Little Niggers* (1939; in U.S. as *And Then There Were None,* 1940, produced 1943, published 1944; produced in U.S. as *Ten Little Indians,* 1944, published 1946). *One, Two, Buckle My Shoe* (1940; in U.S. as *The Patriotic Murders,* 1941). *Sad Cypress* (1940). *Evil under the Sun* (1941). *N or M? The New Mystery* (1941). *The Body In the Library* (1942). *The Moving Finger* (1942; in U.S. 1943). *Five Little Pigs* (1942; in U.S. as *Murder in Retrospect;* produced and published as *Go Back for Murder,* 1960). *Death Comes as the End* (1942; in U.S., 1945). *Towards Zero* (1944; with G. Verner, produced 1956; also as *Come and Be Hanged*). (as Mary Westmacott) *Absent in the Spring* (1944). *Sparkling Cyanide* (1945; in U.S. as *Remembered Death*). *The*

Hollow: A Hercule Poirot Mystery (also as *Murder After Hours*). (1946; produced as *The Hollow*, 1951, published 1952). *Come Tell Me How You Live* (1946). *The Labours of Hercules: Short Stories* (1947; in U.S. as *Labors of Hercules: New Adventures in Crime by Hercule Poirot*). *Witness for the Prosecution and Other Stories* (1948). *Taken at the Flood* (1948; in U.S. as *There Is a Tide*). (as Mary Westmacott) *The Rose and the Yew Tree* (1948). *Crooked House* (1949). *The Mousetrap and Other Stories* (1949; in U.S. as *Three Blind Mice and Other Stories*, 1950; title story produced as *The Mousetrap*, 1952, published 1956; as radio play, 1952). *A Murder Is Announced* (1950). *They Came to Baghdad* (1951). *The Under Dog and Other Stories* (1951). *They Do It with Mirrors* (1952; in U.S. as *Murder with Mirrors*). *Blood Will Tell* (1951; in U.S. as *Mrs. McGinty's Dead*, 1952). (as Mary Westmacott) *A Daughter's a Daughter* (1952). *After the Funeral* (1953; in U.S. as *Funerals Are Fatal*; also as *Murder at the Gallop*). *A Pocket Full of Rye* (1953; in U.S., 1954). *The Spider's Web* (produced 1954, published 1957). *Destination Unknown* (1954; in U.S. as *So Many Steps to Death*, 1955). *Hickory, Dickory, Dock* (1955; in U.S. as *Hickory, Dickory, Death*). *Dead Man's Folly* (1956). (as Mary Westmacott) *The Burden* (1956). (with G. Verner) *4:50 from Paddington* (1957; in U.S. as *What Mrs. McGillicuddy Saw!*, 1961). *Ordeal by Innocence* (1958). *Verdict* (produced and published 1958). *The Unexpected Guest* (produced and published 1958). *Cat Among the Pigeons* (1959). *The Adventures of the Christmas Pudding, and Selection of Entrées* (1960). *Personal Call* (radio play, 1960). *Double Sin and Other Stories* (1961). *13 for Luck: A Selection of Mystery Stories for Young Readers* (1961; in U.S. as *13 for Luck: A Selection of Mystery Stories*, 1966). *The Pale Horse* (1961; in U.S., 1962). *The Mirror Crack'd from Side to Side* (1962; in U.S. as *The Mirror Cracked*, 1963). *Rule of Three: Afternoon at the Seaside, The Patient, The Rats* (produced 1962, published 1963). *The Clocks* (1963; in U.S., 1964). *A Caribbean Mystery* (1964; in U.S. 1965). (as A.C. Mallowan) *Star over Bethlehem and Other Stories* (1965). *At Bertram's Hotel* (1965). *Surprize! Surprize! [sic] A Collection of Mystery Stories* (1965). *13 Clues for Miss Marple: A Collection of Mystery Stories* (1965). *Third Girl* (1966; in U.S., 1967). *Endless Night* (1967; in U.S., 1968). *By the Pricking of My Thumbs* (1968). *Halloween Party* (1969). *Passenger to Frankfurt* (1970). *Nemesis* (1971). *The Golden Ball and Other Stories* (1971). *Fiddlers Three* (produced 1971). *Elephants Can Remember* (1972). *Akhnaton* (1973). *Postern of Fate* (1973). *Hercule Poirot's Early Cases* (1974).

Curtain: Hercule Poirot's Last Case (1975). *Sleeping Murder* (1976).

Leonard R.N. Ashley

Christine de Pizan
ca. 1365–ca. 1430

Born ca. 1365, Venice, Italy
Died ca. 1430, Poissy, France
Genre(s): poetry, history, literary criticism, autobiography, essay, letters, narrative
Language(s): French

Christine de Pizan

Although born in Italy into a family that originated in Pizzano, near Bologna, from whose celebrated university both her father and grandfather held degrees, she moved at an early age to Paris, where her father was appointed medical advisor and astrologer to the French king, Charles V (1365–1380). Nevertheless, her origin undoubtedly influenced her ideas so that she combined her Italian heritage with her observations on French life and thought.

From her early years she apparently showed signs of unusual intellectual curiosity that were encouraged by her father, although her opportunities for formal education were limited because of contemporary attitudes toward the education of women and because at fifteen she was married to Etienne du Castel, a young Picard notary who, the year of the marriage (1380) was given a promising appointment as secretary in the royal chancellory.

The marriage was a happy one, producing two sons and a daughter, but after ten years Etienne died suddenly and unexpectedly, the victim of an epidemic. Thus Christine, aged twenty-five, was left a widow with young children and an elderly mother in her care. Her sorrow was profound and her lack of preparation to cope with her new responsibilities almost complete, but out of these misfortunes her career as a writer developed.

At the beginning she wrote poetry to express her grief and to find comfort for it in the popular forms of her day: balades, rondeaux, and virelais. It is also possible that she served a sort of apprenticeship copying manuscripts for the blossoming Parisian book-trade. At the same time, she started on a program of self-education through reading, beginning with a translation of Boethius's *Consolation of Philosophy* and the medieval *Ovide Moralisé* (Ovid Moralized). This led to her first long allegorical, mythological work, *L'Epîstre d'Othéa* (The Letter of Othea), which took the form of a letter from the goddess of wisdom (Othéa) to a young man who had reached the age of knighthood concerning the proper moral and spiritual education for a young knight. The education of the young would be a favorite concern throughout her career, and her ideas on the subject were well in advance of her times.

Her writing gained increased attention through her part in a literary debate concerning the merits of Jean de Meun's continuation of the *Romance of the Rose*. This pitted her wits against those of several members of the royal chancellery, her husband's former colleagues, but she was supported in her protestations against the misogyny and exaggerated popularity of the poem by the Chancellor of the University of Paris, Jean Gerson. The discussion inspired her to write two further works in defense of women: *La Livre de la Cité des Dames* (The Book of the City of Ladies), intended to correct Boccaccio's ironical view of women in the *De Claris Mulieribus* (Of Famous Women), and *Le Livre des Trois Vertus* (The Book of the Three Virtues), a guide to enable women to enjoy a more respected place in society.

These works and a biography of Charles V, the *Le Livre des Fais et Bonnes Meurs du Sage Roi Charles V* (The Book of the Deeds and Good Character of the Wise King Charles V), commissioned by the late king's younger brother, the Duke of Burgundy, turned Christine from writing poetry to prose, usually didactic in inspiration. Before this, however, she had composed a long allegorical and historical poem entitled *La Mutacion de Fortune* (The Changes of Fortune). Her subsequent writing included a semiautobiographical *L'Avision-Christine* (Christine's Vision) and more educational treatises, notably *Le Livre du Corps de Policie* (The Book of the Body Politic), *Le Livre des Faits d'Armes et de Chevalerie* (The Book of the Deeds of Arms and of Chivalry) on preparation for warfare and knighthood, and *Le Livre de la Paix* (The Book of Peace), addressed to the French dauphin Louis de Guyenne concerning his duties to his country. She demonstrated increasing concern for the state of France, threatened by both internal conflict and a renewal of war with England. She appealed in turn to those she thought had a responsibility to try to save the country, to Isabeau de Bavière in her "Epîstre à la Reine" ("Letter to the Queen") and to the elderly Duke de Berry, the king's uncle, in her "Lamentacions sur le Maux de la Guerre Civile" ("Lamentations on the Evil of Civil War") as well as to Louis de Guyenne. But no amount of good will could stem the misfortunes that soon overtook France, the Cabochian revolt in 1413, a veritable reign of terror, and the French defeat by the English at Agincourt two years later. This was soon followed by the death of Louis de Guyenne, the prince on whom Christine had pinned so many hopes. Soon after writing a letter to console the widows and other relatives of the victims of Agincourt, the "Epîstre sur la Prison de Vie Humaine" ("Letter on the Prisonhouse of Human Life"), Christine retired to the Dominican Abbey in Poissy, where her daughter had been a nun for many years. Her voice was heard only one more time when she hailed the victory of Joan of Arc at Orleans and the coronation of Charles VII at Reims. Her "Dittié sur Jeanne d'Arc" ("Song on Joan of Arc"), dated July 31, 1429, was the first poem to celebrate these events which were bringing about a change in France's fortunes. This was the last that was heard from her, but her works were copied, printed, and read well into the sixteenth century.

Works
First poetry (1392–1402). *Epître au Dieu d'Amour* [Letter of the God of Love] (1399). *Le Débat de Deux Amants* [The Debate of the Two Lovers] (c. 1400). *Le Livre des Trois Jugements* [The Book of the Three Judgments]. *Le Dit de Poissy* [The Tale of Poissy]. *L'Epistre d'Othéa* [The Letter of Othéa]. *Les Epistres sur le Roman de la Rose* [The Letters on the Romance

of the Rose] (1401–1402). *Le Dit de la Rose* [The Tale of the Rose] (1402). *Le Chemin de Long Estude* [The Long Road of Learning] (1403). *La Mutacion de Fortune* [The Changes of Fortune] (1404). *Le Livre des Faits et Bonnes Meurs du Sage Roy Charles V* [The Book of the Deeds and Good Character of Wise King Charles V] (1404). *Le Livre de la Cité des Dames* [The Book of the City of Ladies] (1405). *Le Livre des Trois Vertus ou le Trésor de la Cité des Dames* [The Book of the Three Virtues or the Treasure of the City of Ladies] (1405). *L'Epistre à la Reine de France* [The Letter to the Queen of France] (1405). *L'Avision-Christine* [Christine's Vision] (1404). *Le Livre de la Prod'homie de l'Homme* [The Book of Man's Prudence. Also called *Le Livre de Prudence*] (1406). *Le Livre du Corps de Policie* [The Book of the Body Politic] (1407). *Sept Psaumes Allegorisés* [Seven Psalms Allegorized] (1409). *Le Livre des Faits d'Armes et de Chevalerie* [The Book of the Deeds of Arms and of Chivalry] (1410). *La Lamentacion sur les Maux de la Guerre Civile* [Lamentation on the Ills of Civil War] (1410). *Le Livre de la Paix* [The Book of Peace] (1412–1413). *L'Epistre de la Prison de Vie Humaine* [The Letter of the Prisonhouse of Human Life] (1418). *Les Heures de Contemplacion sur la Passion de Nostre Seigneur* [The Hours of Contemplation on the Passion of Our Lord] (1422–1424). *Dittié de Jeanne d'Arc* [The Song of Joan of Arc] (1429).

Translations: *The Book of the City of Ladies* [*Le Livre de la Cité des Dames*], tr. Earl Richards (1981). *La Cité des Dames* [*Le Livre de la Cité des Dames*], tr. Thérèse Moreau and Eric Hicks (1986 in modern French). *The Book of Faytes of Armes and of Chyvalerie* [*Le Livre des Faits d'Armes de le Chevalerie*], tr. William Caxton, ed. A.T.P. Byles (1931). *A Medieval Woman's Mirror of Honor* [*Le Livre des Trois Vertus*], tr. Charity Cannon Willard (1989).

Charity C. Willard

Caryl Churchill
1938–

Born September 3, 1938, London
Genre(s): drama
Language(s): English

Caryl Churchill is a playwright, among the best now writing, who addresses social and political questions with audacity and wit. The talents of her political cartoonist father and her model-actress-secretary mother

are extended in the style and substance of her plays. Born in London, she moved with her family to Canada in 1948 where she attended the Trafalgar School, Montreal. Returning to England in 1956 as a young adult gave her a shocked outsider's view of the class system despite her distant relationship to one of that system's staunchest defenders, Sir Winston Churchill. At Lady Margaret Hall, Oxford, she began to write plays. *Downstairs* and *Having a Wonderful Time* were produced there before she received her B.A. in English in 1960 and the Richard Hillary Memorial Prize in 1961.

After her marriage in 1961, she stayed at home raising three sons and writing more than a dozen plays for radio and television. Feeling isolated at home politicized her so that, although she dislikes labels, she now counts herself as a socialist and a feminist. In theme, her plays connect personal and political oppression, often expressed in conflicts about sexuality, mothering, and violence. In form, they are often Brechtian, using popular devices like song in a dance of ideas that emphasizes social rather than psychological conflicts.

In 1972, Michael Codron commissioned Churchill to write a play for the Royal Court, the theatre that nurtured John Osborne, David Storey, and David Hare. Her play was *Owners,* about property values, mates, rowhouses, butcher's meat, infants, and senile mums. Edith Oliver found its American production promising, but, seconding Churchill's own estimate of the influence of her father's cartoons, said that the characters talk like the captions in *Punch* cartoons or horror comics. The style reflects Joe Orton's savage mockery of cozy family life as a patriarchal butcher plans to murder his ambitious wife.

As resident dramatist at the Royal Court (1974–1975), Churchill wrote a science-fiction play, now called *Moving Clocks Go Slow,* and *Objections to Sex and Violence. Objections,* staged in 1975, puts a middle-class divorcee into a caretaker's job and involves her with terrorists, flashers, and pornography. In *Traps,* the next play she wrote, Churchill began to experiment with time and illusion. Four men, two women, and an infant explore the possibilities of change in a commune which is like a Möbius strip or an impossible Escher drawing. Their changing relationships form flexible traps like the traps that prevent the audience from knowing whether the commune is in the city or the country, whether Syl has a child she doesn't want or wants a child she doesn't have. With one small hope for Utopia, the play ends as the characters bathe serially in an old wash tub, the most violent one bathing last, and smiling, in the deepest, dirtiest water of all. Written early in 1976, *Traps* was first produced at the Royal Court Theatre Upstairs in January 1977.

Through *Traps,* Churchill had worked alone on plays about contemporary life. She then began to work with fringe theatre workshops, a method that she found exhilarating, exhausting, and fruitful. With Monstrous Regiment, a feminist touring company, she wrote *Vinegar Tom* (1976), a play about witches with no witches in it. The play shows that the witch hunts of the seventeenth century used nonconforming women (old, poor, single, or skilled as healers) as scapegoats in a time of social unrest. Having finished a rough draft of *Vinegar Tom,* Churchill began work with the Joint Stock Theatre Group and its director, Max Stafford-Clark, on *Light Shining in Buckinghamshire* (1976). Ideas derived from improvisations enriched a play about the attempt of Diggers, Levellers, and Ranters to build a New Jerusalem in England's green and pleasant land in the 1640s. Both plays use a historical perspective to show that change can occur, both set groups of people in a political context, both are ensemble pieces without star roles, and both use short, self-contained scenes, interrupted by songs, to raise questions.

Floorshow (1977) was also worked out with Monstrous Regiment and with co-authors David Bradford, Bryony Lavery, and Michelene Wandor as sketches and lyrics for a cabaret about women and work. As Churchill's career took off, some of her earlier radio plays were done as lunchtime plays in the fringe theatre. She wrote a television play called the *Legion Hall Bombing* (1978) about the trial without jury of Willie Gallagher in Northern Ireland but withdrew her name when the BBC censored it.

In a workshop on sexual politics with Joint Stock, Churchill developed *Cloud Nine* (1979), a satirical farce set in an African colony in 1880 and in a London park about 1980. Through music hall devices and cross-sex casting, she connects colonial, sexual, and class oppression. In the first act, Clive, the Victorian patriarch, insists that his family and his Africans must live out his ideas. A male actor plays his wife, Betty, in an exaggerated stereotype of feminine compliance. Because he has assumed white values, a white actor plays African Joshua, for whom the walls of Empire finally come tumbling down. In exuberant farcical action, a white hunter tempts wife, son, and servant, but when he tempts Clive himself, he is forced to marry the lesbian governess. In the second act of Churchill's best-known play, the members of Clive's family are twenty-five years older and they are no longer his. With new working-class characters, they meet in the public space of a London park and try out new arrangements in a quieter, tenderer questioning of class, gender, and homophobic oppression. *Cloud Nine* opened at the Royal Court in 1979, and the 1981 New York production, which ran for two years, won three Obie awards.

Three More Sleepless Nights (1980), about two couples trying to change by changing partners, followed *Cloud Nine* but did not achieve its critical acclaim. Then *Top Girls* (1982) led Benedict Nightingale to rank Churchill as one of the half-dozen best contemporary dramatists. Its brilliant opening brings achieving women from the past millennium to a dinner celebrating Marlene's latest promotion. Of the top girls, only Dull Gret, from a Brueghel painting, has challenged the patriarchal hierarchy. Pope Joan, Lady Nijo, and the others, like Marlene, have sacrificed sexuality, maternity, and self-assertion in order to succeed in a man's world. In more naturalistic scenes in Marlene's employment agency and in her sister's working-class home, we see that nothing has changed at the bottom, although there are some places for women at the top.

Remembering *Top Girls,* several critics referred to Churchill's next play as "Bottom Girls." *Fen* (1983) peoples a bleak East Anglia landscape with figures, five women and one man, in twenty-two roles on the potato farms. Designer Annie Smart filled the stage with furrowed earth and built the walls of a room around it so that one set serves for each brief scene. Fog steams from the fen to obscure distinctions between past and present, illusion and reality. If there is a heroine, it is Val, torn between lover and children, unable, like the others, to give up and live. Churchill won the Susan Smith Blackburn prize for *Fen* in 1984.

In 1984, Churchill wrote a cabaret on crime and punishment called *Softcops.* A man of reason in nineteenth-century France tries to control crime with educational placards that explain how each punishment fits its crime. Vidocq, a robber who became a chief of police, plays against Lacenaire, a glamorous criminal whose publicity distracts attention from genuine threats to authority. Its provocative structure and the music of a string quartet pleased some critics but most found the play too highbrow, too dependent on its inspiration in *Discipline and Punish* by French philosopher Michel Foucault.

Churchill is an intellectual playwright, putting new ideas into new theatrical forms based on popular entertainment. In *Midday Sun* (1984), a script for a dance group at the Institute of Contemporary Arts, four British tourists fantasize, experience, and then remember a holiday on a Moroccan beach and an encounter with an Arab beggar. In plays marked by beauty, anger, and generous humor, she continues to seek change and to challenge authority and centralized control.

Works

Downstairs (1958). *Having a Wonderful Time* (1960). *Easy Death* (1961). *Schreber's Nervous Illness* (1972). *Owners* (1972). *Moving Clocks Go Slow* (1975). *Objections to Sex and Violence* (1975). *Light Shining in Buckinghamshire* (1976). *Vinegar Tom* (1976). *Floorshow* (with others, 1977). *Traps* (1977). *Cloud Nine* (1979). *Three More Sleepless Nights* (1980). *Top Girls* (1982). *Fen* (1983). *Softcops* (1983). *Midday Sun* (1984). *Serious Money* (1987). *Lives of Great Poisoners* (1993). *The Skiker* (1994).

Mary R. Davidson

Hélène Cixous
1937–

Born 1937, Oran, Algeria
Genre(s): fiction, essay, critical-theoretical text
Language(s): French

Hélène Cixous is one of the most well known and important French women writers at work today. A professor of literature at the University of Paris VIII—Vincennes at St. Denis, she co-founded the school and initiated its Women's Studies program. Her first published text, *Le Prénom de Dieu*, appeared in 1967; her doctoral thesis in 1968 was entitled *L'Exil de James Joyce ou l'art du remplacement*. Also that year she founded the review *Poetique* with Gérard Genette and Tzvetan Todorov. In 1969 *Dedans* was awarded the Prix Médicis and in 1973 she began to write on questions of sexual difference and on female experience and writing. In the mid-seventies she published exclusively with Editions des femmes in a gesture of political commitment to, and in solidarity with, the women's movement. By 1982 she stopped publishing with des Femmes so that she could continue to experiment with a variety of other creative forms.

Cixous denies that she is a theorist, preferring her writing to be seen as a process of working to recast the mythic past with a newer, more subversive feminism. This project makes it difficult to label her a novelist as well. Rather her texts are combinations of majestic energies that find their sources in poetry, fable, and the wonder of "tableaux." The wide array of myth employed in her work undergoes a significant re-writing with the aim of surpassing the traditional phallocentric authority of the present (and past) social order. This reading *otherwise* of myths directs its power to the reinstallation of the female voice that has been silenced by masculine discourse. Such a transformation becomes a new ground upon which Cixous's "methodology" of female self-discovery, recovery and rewriting rests. In reassembling patriarchal myths Cixous employs a more useful and appropriate female mythopoetic creativity to reach a great liberation. Because of this activity, it is perhaps better to understand Cixous as a poet-theoretician of women's approaches to writing with myth or through myth.

This re-employment of myth, past and present, underscores Cixous's belief in the central concern of language as a co-opted entity, co-opted by the idealized version of man. Thus, with the critique of this status of language offered by Lacan and Derrida, both of which have greatly influenced her, Cixous exposes and dismantles the logic of phallocentrism. The book becomes the property of *écriture feminine* or feminine writing, the property of a kingdom of libidinal and maternal affirmation.

In her 1975 manifesto, "The Laugh of the Medusa," Cixous entreats women to write, without defining the feminine practice of writing in theoretical language. Instead, she shares a vision of writing that would be free of any limitation or boundary, a writing that constantly reinvents new representations of formerly impossible realities. In this manner she opposes the demonstrations and justifications of philosophy for the openness of the poetic, thereby privileging the vocal and musical elements of language as well. In the same year, Cixous and Catherine Clément published *La jeune née*, one of the most popular works in feminist studies. Clément and Cixous analyze the nature and operations of representations of women in Western culture. The second half of the book is a dialogue between these two disagreeing writers.

Works

Le Prénom de Dieu (1967). *Dedans* (1969). *L'Exil de James Joyce ou l'art du remplacement* (1969; The Exile of James Joyce). *Le Troisième Corps* (1970). *Les Commencements* (1970). *La Pupille* (1971). *Un Vrai Jardin* (1971). *Neutre* (1972). *Tombe* (1973). *Prénoms de personne* (1974). *Portrait du soleil* (1974). *Révolutions pour plus d'un Faust* (1975). *La Jeune Née* [The Newly Born Woman] (1975). *Un K. incompréhensible: Pierre*

Goldman (1975). *Souffles* (1975). *Portrait de Dora* (1976). *La* (1976). *Partie* (1976). *La Venue à l'écriture* (1977). *Angst* (1977). *Préparatifs de noces au delà de l'abîme* (1978). *Chant du corps interdit/Le Nom d'Oedipe* (1978). *Vivre l'orange* (1979). *Anankè* (1979). *Illa* (1980). *Ou l'art de l'innocence* (1981). *Limonade tout était si infini* (1982). *Le Livre de Promethea* (1983). *La Prise de l'école de Madubaï* (1984). *L'Histoire terrible mais inachevée de Norodom Sihanouk roi du Cambodge* (1985). *La Bataille d'Arcachon* (1986). *Entre l'écriture* (1986). *L'Indiade ou l'Inde de leurs rêves* (1988).

Translations: *Reading with Clarice Lispector* (1990). *The Book of Promethea* (1991). *Coming to Writing and Other Essays* (1991). *Three Steps on the Ladder of Writing* (1993). *The Terrible but Unfinished Story of Norodom Sihanouck* (1994). *Manna: For the Mandelstams for the Mandelas* (1994).

Richard J. Pioli

Clare of Assisi

Clare of Assisi
1193–1253
Born 1193, Assisi, Italy
Died 1253, Assisi
Genre(s): works of monastic spirituality
Language(s): Latin

As a young woman of noble standing in Assisi (the daughter of Favarone and Ortolana), Clare was attracted to the ideal of poverty espoused by her contemporary, Francis of Assisi. Following Francis's example, Clare founded an order of religious women known as the Poor Ladies of Assisi (like Francis's Poor Men), and later as the Clarissas or Poor Clares in her honor.

Like Francis, Clare focused her life on the practice of the ideal of poverty and looked suspiciously on the composition of theology. The few writings that survive contain a strong, pragmatic statement of the ideals which inspired her and governed the order: four letters of spiritual advice addressed to Agnes of Prague between 1234 and 1253; the *Rule* for her new order composed in 1254; and an autobiographical reflection, known as the *Testament*, probably written shortly before her death. While the authenticity of these works has been frequently discussed, they are all generally accepted as genuine although the Latinity of both the *Rule* and *Testament* was improved by scribes at the papal chancery. A letter to Ermentrude of Bruges is probably a summary of two authentic letters made in the seventeenth century, and there is no guarantee of the authenticity of a blessing included in the *Legend of St. Clare.*

While Clare's spiritual ideals and life were predicated on the faithful imitation of the genius of Francis, she demonstrated her own genius in translating those ideals into a feminine version.

Works
"Epistolae ad b. Agnetem," in W. Seton, ed., *Archivum franciscanum historicum* 17 (1924): 513–519. "Regula." *Seraphicae Legislationis Textus Originales* (1897), pp. 49–75. "Testamentum." *Ibid.,* pp. 273–280. *Escritos de santa Clara y documentos contemporaneos,* I. Omaechevariia, ed. (1970).

Translation: Vaughn, J., and I. Brady, eds., *Francis and Clare. The Complete* Works (1982).

Concordance: Godet, J-F., and G. Mailleux, eds., *Opuscula Sancti Francisce, Scripta Sanctae Clarae.* Corpus des sources franciscaines, vol. 5 (1976).

Thomas Head

Lady Anne Clifford
1590–1676

Born January 30, 1590, Skipton Castle, Yorkshire
Died March 22, 1676, Brougham Castle,
Westmorland
Genre(s): diary, letters
Language(s): English

Only three diaries survive that were kept by women who lived during the reign of Queen Elizabeth I. Of these, Clifford's diary is the most interesting historically. Those by Margaret Hoby and Grace Mildmay concentrate on the routine of daily life and on religious faith, whereas Clifford includes accounts of events such as Queen Elizabeth's death and funeral and talks with Queen Anne and John Donne as well as information about the history of her family. Her diary continues to hold our interest both because she led a remarkable life and because she wrote well, recording telling details. When she writes of her first presentation to King James I, for example, she comments that the fashion at court had certainly changed from Queen Elizabeth's time, for everyone in her party came away bitten by lice.

Her life had three stages. As a child, she was dutiful; as a wife, she was unhappy; as a widow, she came into her own. Her parents' marriage was troubled, and Clifford's sympathies were with her mother, whom she adored. From her mother, she inherited a love of literature. Her reading ranged from works on religion to Ovid, Chaucer, and Jonson. Lady Margaret Russell was one of Spenser's patrons and employed Samuel Daniel as her daughter's tutor; Clifford, in turn, erected monuments to both of these poets and befriended Donne and George Herbert. From her father, she inherited troublesome lawsuits, for he willed the family lands to his brother rather than his child, and Clifford spent years suing to regain her estates.

When she married, Clifford probably hoped that her husband would help her in these suits, but instead Dorset tried to force her to stop the case because he thought settling it would provide him with ready money and please the king. After Dorset's death, Clifford remarried. Like Dorset, Pembroke was unfaithful and a spendthrift; unlike him, he sympathized with his wife's claims. Finally in 1643, she received the property, and six years later she left her husband in London to go to her estates. Soon after she arrived, word came that Pembroke was dead.

The long lawsuit, with its frustration and unhappiness, probably led Clifford to begin writing. From 1605 until 1643, her time and energy had been en-

gaged in lawsuits, and she wished to leave a careful account of what had happened for her two daughters. This desire, her interest in her family's history, and her pleasure in recording her daily activities led to a number of manuscripts: one in third-person and another in first-person that tell of her life, and others that summarize her family history. (The first-person autobiographical manuscript is referred to as her diary.)

After the death of her second husband, Clifford spent the rest of her life as the industrious chatelaine of her property. She not only ran her large estates but also built or restored six castles, two almshouses, and seven churches and a chapel. As the *DNB* remarks, "Her passion for bricks and mortar was immense." For nearly thirty years she built, administered, wrote, and pleased herself. Mildly eccentric (she pinned scraps of paper with *sententiae* all around her rooms) and extraordinarily generous, Clifford was a remarkable woman. Her diary offers a lively account of the life that the well-to-do led in the seventeenth century.

Works

Lives of Lady Anne Clifford and Her Parents, ed. J.P. Gilson (1916). *The Diary of Lady Clifford*, ed. V. Sackville-West (1923). *Clifford Letters of the Seventeenth Century*, ed. A.G. Dickens (1962). *The Diaries of Lady Anne Clifford*, ed. D.J.H. Clifford (1990). *The Diary of Anne Clifford 1616–1619*, ed. K. Acheson (1995).

Frances Teague

Sidonie-Gabrielle Colette
1873–1954

Born January 28, 1873, Saint-Sauveur-en-Puisaye,
France
Died August 3, 1954, Paris
Genre(s): novel, essay
Language(s): French

Colette spent her first twenty years in her native Burgundy. In 1893 she married Henry Gauthier-Villars (known as Willy), a Parisian publisher and habitué of the demimonde. Fifteen years her senior and always in need of money, Willy urged his young wife to write her girlhood memoirs. "And that" Colette explained later, "is how I became a writer."

Her first novel, *Claudine á l'école* (1900; Claudine at School, published under Willy's name) was an immense commercial success. Three more "Claudine" novels followed, taking the heroine from her country

Sidonie-Gabrielle Colette

school to Paris and marriage. Separated from Willy in 1906 (the divorce became final in 1910), Colette supported herself by working as a mime and dancer in various music-halls. She continued to write, however, and in 1910 published *La Vagabonde* (The Vagabond), a novel about a music-hall dancer who yearns for the comforting presence of a man but who ultimately chooses the lonely life of independence. In 1912, Colette married Henry de Jouvenel. They were divorced in 1925. During World War I, she turned to journalism, but returned to fiction in 1920 with the publication of *Chéri*, the novel that firmly established her reputation in France. In 1925, she began a liaison with Maurice Goudeket, who was seventeen years her junior. They were married in 1935, the year Colette was elected to the Belgian Royal Academy. Other honors followed. In 1945 she was elected to the Goncourt Academy, and in 1953 she was named Grand Officer of the Legion of Honor.

Beginning in the late 1930s, Colette began to suffer from arthritis. During her last years, she was confined to her bed, which she liked to call her "raft." At her death, the French government accorded her a state funeral.

Colette's work can be divided into two broad categories: on the one hand, fiction; on the other hand, chronicles, journals, and reminiscences. The fiction deals with the pangs of love and the ravages of desire. In most of the novels, the protagonist is a woman who longs to "submit" to love even while rebelling against the loss of freedom that inevitably accompanies love. In *Chéri*, Colette depicts an aging demimondaine, Léa, who, when confronted with the shocking fact that she is growing old, renounces love and, accepting her status as "an old woman," gives her young lover in marriage to a woman half her age.

Acceptance of the inevitable is a fundamental principle in the moral code of Colette's heroines, many of whom live on the fringe of society as music-hall dancers or courtesans. Another is the imperative to be happy, which for Colette means controlling the appetites, reducing as much as possible the gap between desire and fulfillment, and finding beauty and joy in ordinary things. These, in fact, are the themes of her books of reminiscences. In *La Maison de Claudine* (1929; My Mother's House) and *Sido* (1953), she idealized her mother, Sido, whose love of nature and lucid, unsentimental view of human affairs Colette describes in prose that is a model of elegance.

Colette may be accused of focusing on a narrow range of human experience. She had no interest in philosophy, religion, or politics. She was concerned, rather, with love (maternal and passionate, heterosexual and homosexual) and with what she called the female's "mission to endure." A first-rate stylist, Colette has now attained the status of a classic French author.

Works

Claudine á l'école [Claudine at School] (1900). *Claudine à Paris* [Claudine in Paris] (1901). *Claudine en ménage* [The Indulgent Husband] (1902). *Claudine s'en va* [The Innocent Wife] (1903). *Minne* [Minnie] (1904). *Dialogue de bêtes* [Creatures Great and Small] (1904). *Les égarements de Minne* [Minnie's Misconduct] (1905). *Sept dialogues de bêtes* [Creatures Great and Small] (1905). *La retraite sentimentale* [The Retreat from Love] (1907). *Les vrilles de la vigne* [The Vine's Tendrils] (1908). *L'ingénue libertine* [The Innocent Libertine] (1909). *La vagabonde* [The Vagabond] (1911). *L'envers du music-hall* [Music-Hall Sidelights] (1913). *L'entrave* [The Shackle] (1913). *Mitsou ou comment l'esprit vient aux filles* [Mitsou] (1919). *Chéri* [Chéri and The Last of Chéri] (1920). *Le blé en herbe* [Ripening Seed] (1923). *La femme cachée* [The Hidden Woman] (1924). *L'enfant et les sortilèges. Musique de Maurice Ravel* [The Boy and the Magic] (1925). *La fin de Chéri* [Chéri and The Last of Chéri] (1926). *La naissance du jour* [Break of Day] (1928). *La seconde* [The Other One] (1929). *La Maison de Claudine* [My Mother's House] (1929). *Ces plaisirs* (1932. Reedited in 1941 as *Le pur et l'impur* [The Pure and the Impure]. *La Chatte* [The Cat] (1933). *Duo* [Duo] (1934). *Mes apprentissages* [My Apprenticeship] (1936). *Bella-Vista* [Bella-Vista] (1937). *Le Toutounier* (1939). *Chambre d'hôtel* [Chance Acquaintances] (1940). *Journal à rebours* [Looking Backwards] (1941). *Julie de Carneilhan* (1941). *De ma fenêtre* (1942). *Gigi et autres nouvelles* (1944). *Trois . . . six . . . neuf* [Three . . . Six . . . Nine] (1944). *L'étoile vesper* [The Evening Star] (1946). *Le fanal bleu* [The Blue Lantern] (1949). *Sido* (1953). Other works include: books on animals; books of reminiscences; collections of short stories; several volumes of correspondence; hundreds of newspaper articles; film scripts; stage adaptations of some of her novels.

Robert D. Cottrell

Camilla Collett
1813–1895
Born 1813, Kristiansand, Norway
Died 1895, Kristiania (Oslo)
Genre(s): novel, essay
Language(s): Norwegian

Camilla Collett stands out as a true pioneer in the literary and cultural history of her country. She was born just at the time that 400 years of Danish rule over Norway was ending, and during her lifetime she witnessed tremendous changes in Norwegian society, politics, and culture and the flowering of a national literature. Camilla Collett participated in this process by writing Norway's first novel, *Amtmandens Döttre* (The Governor's Daughters), published in 1854–1855. With its realistic and critical depiction of contemporary society, *The Governor's Daughters* anticipated the social realism that characterizes Norwegian novels of the 1870s and 1880s. And in its portrayal of marriage as an often loveless and spiritually void institution, which stifles women in particular, Collett's book represents Norway's first feminist novel. Camilla Collett did not produce much fiction after *The Governor's Daughters*, but she continued to engage herself in improving the situation of women, and she has been credited with laying the foundation for the women's emancipation movement in Norway.

Camilla Collett was born into a prominent Norwegian family. Her father, Nicolai Wergeland, was one of the signers of the Norwegian constitution in 1814,

and her brother, Henrik Wergeland, has been hailed as Norway's greatest romantic poet. A child of the Enlightenment, Nicolai Wergeland brought his children up in keeping with the writings of Rousseau. For Henrik this meant an opportunity for almost limitless exploration and development, but for Camilla, Rousseau did not prescribe the same education—a woman's duty was to serve the needs of her husband and this should be instilled in her as a child. Accordingly, Camilla was sent to finishing schools, first a year in Kristiania (present-day Oslo), and then two years in Germany.

Camilla Wergeland is said to have possessed a delicate, even ethereal beauty and, with her charm and many talents, could have attracted any suitor she chose. But when she was seventeen, it was her ill fortune to fall hopelessly in love with J.S. Welhaven, a man who was the bitter opponent of both her father and her brother in a conflict that split the country's authors and cultural leaders into two hostile camps. For a period of several years, Camilla and Welhaven met each other at social events and carried on a correspondence, but social conventions prevented Camilla from expressing her emotions and Welhaven carefully guarded his. Finally, all hope was lost when Welhaven declared that no affair of the heart could take precedence over commitment to his cause. This unhappy love affair had a profound and lasting affect on Camilla. It was obviously an impetus for her novel *The Governor's Daughters*, and she wrote openly about it in her journals and letters (compiled and published between 1926–1934) and in her memoirs *I de lange Nætter* (1862; During the Long Nights).

In 1841, at twenty-seven years of age, Camilla married Peter Jonas Collett. He respected her talent and ambition and gave her the necessary support and encouragement to pursue her writing. His untimely death in 1851 was a great personal loss, and it also left her in the difficult position of being a widow with four sons. With stubborn determination, she completed her novel and for the next thirty years there was a steady stream of stories, articles, and essays from her pen.

Camilla Collett was in many ways a citizen of Europe. She lived abroad—in Copenhagen, Rome, Dresden, Paris—for extended periods of time, and through her travels and her reading came in contact with current ideas and trends. She admired the writings of George Sand in particular, but at the time she wrote *The Governor's Daughters*, Collett felt that many of Sand's ideas were too radical. Though she does lament in her novel the fact that young girls were deprived of the education and training that would enable them to develop their talents, Collett does not argue that women should have the opportunity to pursue a life and a career independent of marriage. There is no question but that marriage promised the happiest and most fulfilling future for the Governor's four daughters. But it should be a marriage based on mutual love and respect, not a union forced upon young women by parents whose primary interest was social and financial status. *The Governor's Daughters* is sharply critical of the superficiality and injustice of social conventions, but its underlying message is a plea for love. And woman, Collett contends, with her greater emotional capacity, is better able to recognize love and should therefore be free to declare her love.

On the issues of love in marriage and the importance of women's personal emancipation (a woman's right to assert her personality and to develop her abilities), Collett stood firm throughout her life. But as the years went by, she understood more clearly the need for social and political change as well. Her views became increasingly radical, and her writing took on a polemic tone. Her many articles and essays first appeared in newspapers and magazines, and she periodically compiled and published them in book form.

When these articles were first printed in the press, they were anonymous (*The Governor's Daughters* was also published anonymously, though the author's identity was not kept secret for long). The stigma attached to a woman who made her writing public was keenly felt by Collett, who nonetheless did not hesitate to attack this prejudice in her own writing. She wrote book reviews and essays on literature, some of which were the first examples of feminist literary criticism in Norway. She called for a new image of woman, denouncing the typical role in which women were cast as self-effacing, self-sacrificing saints. There can be little doubt that Collett was heard and heeded by her male contemporaries, most notably Henrik Ibsen.

For most of her life Camilla Collett was a solitary figure with no female colleagues to join her in her struggle. However, she lived to see arise a generation of women writers and activists who, inspired by her example, carried on the work to which she had dedicated her life.

Works

Novels: *Amtmandens Döttre* (1854–1855).

Stories and memoirs: *Fortællinger* (1860). *I de lange Nætter* (1862).

Articles and essays: *Sidste Blade I–V* (1868–1873). *Fra de Stummes Leir* (1877). *Mod Strömmen I–II* (1879–1885).

Letters and journals: *Dagböker og breve I–V*, ed. Leiv Amundsen (1926–1934).

Translations: *An Everyday Story. Norwegian Women's Fiction*, ed. Katherine Hanson (1984).

Katherine Hanson

Ivy Compton-Burnett
1884–1969
Born June 5, 1884, Pinner, Middlesex, England
Died August 27, 1969, London
Genre(s): novel
Language(s): English

The eldest child of Dr. Compton Burnett's second wife, Katharine, Ivy Compton-Burnett was brought up with five older step-brothers and sisters and six younger brothers and sisters in suburban Hove. Her father was a homeopathic doctor who wrote many books and pamphlets defending his kind of medicine. She received a classical education from the family tutor and took a degree in classics at Royal Holloway College, London, in 1902.

A series of family disasters occurred when she became a young adult. First, her father died in 1901, and her mother went into formal mourning. Her younger brother Guy, to whom she had a strong attachment, died of pneumonia in 1905. In 1911 her mother died after a painful, lingering illness. She then took over as overbearing head of the house until her sisters rebelled and the family home was broken up in 1915. In 1916 her brother Noel was killed on the Somme. At the end of the next year, her two youngest sisters, believed to be suicides, died of overdoses of veronal. Compton-Burnett herself nearly died in the influenza epidemic of 1918.

The outward turmoil seemed to have ceased when in 1919 she began to share living quarters with Margaret Jourdain, a writer and historian of furniture and other antiques. The two lived together until Jourdain died in 1951. During this time, she wrote the bulk of the novels for which she is famous.

Her first novel, *Dolores* (1911), with its self-sacrificing heroine, is thought to be immature, written in a crude style. She later deprecated the book, saying that her brother Noel had had too great a hand in it. Her next, *Pastors and Masters* (1925), is the first novel in which she achieved her mature style and the distinctive universe she presents in her fiction.

Critics usually note first the idiosyncrasies of Compton-Burnett's technique. Her novels are set in the English countryside, seemingly sometime between

1880 and 1910. The feeling is late Victorian or Edwardian with the family that is depicted an almost self-enclosed set. She explained her typical time frame by saying that she knew the stable society at the beginning of the century, but that it is very difficult to see the present completely and organically when one is living in the midst of it. Critics also speak of the claustrophobic atmosphere of the novels: no character gets to escape very far for very long, and the reader does not get to follow the fugitive on his journey. Her writing remains closeted with the family, the relatives, the children, the servants, and sometimes a few friends; she said that, universally, family relationships and personal experiences are central to everyone, remarking on the amount of destruction and affection in families. Intelligent and unsentimental, Compton-Burnett is said to have crossed Victorian domestic fiction with Greek tragedy.

Another notable technique of her fiction is that her novels are predominantly expressed in dialogue with very sketchy descriptions of the characters, with almost no authorial comment, and with no exploration of the characters' thoughts as such. She suggests that her sketchy descriptions allow readers to picture the characters in their own imaginations. Abstaining from authorial comment is a modernist technique, reflecting James Joyce's ideal of the author as God, off paring his fingernails while his world seems to exist in its own right. Her reliance on dialogue functions as a deliberately formal technique, abstracting and elevating the characters and their conflicts. The characters' use of language reveals their moral and intellectual natures. Unlike the villains, her good characters do not use clichés or slang, and they tell the truth, sometimes disconcertingly. Nathalie Sarraute has described the dialogue as reflecting the fluctuating border between conversation and subconversation, between what is said and what is almost said, what is on the tip of the tongue. Of course, in families much of the subconversation is understood by the members, whether or not it is ever articulated.

Part of the tension of Compton-Burnett's novels derives from the contrast of the polished manners and speech with ruthless clashing of wills and egos. Her typical theme concerns power or domination or egotism. She often uses melodramatic devices—like wills destroyed, significant conversations overheard, or illegitimate children newly claimed—to reveal the secret lives of her characters. Frederick Karl complains that these recognition scenes do not lead to reformation or salvation as in Greek tragedy or Christian comedy; instead, the characters try to hush up the scandal and carry on (in the broadest sense of the term).

Other critics bemoan the lack of poetic justice. Some call Compton-Burnett amoral because her wicked flourish and her good continue to suffer. However, she is a realist, not an allegorist, and she is depicting family life, where love and hate meet most intensely. After a shocking revelation, families have to ignore or forget it, at least on the surface. The alternative would be to break apart. The family is home, the ground. To lose it would be an unthinkable, primal disaster.

The comedy of Compton-Burnett's writing is another contradiction. Critics find her dialogue witty, brilliant, and epigrammatic. Some name her a creator of great comic characters like the parasites and busybodies, and all find her ironic. But part of the force of her comedy is her black comedy, the laughter in the face of outrageous statements and actions, laughter as an expression of shock like the audience's reaction to the plays of Harold Pinter. As in Freud's theory of the joke, we laugh at the emperor with no clothes, at authority denuded.

Manservant and Maidservant (1947), published in America as *Bullivant and the Lambs,* is thought by many to be her best novel. Critics praise the juxtaposition of the servants' world with that of the upstairs family. They appreciate the character of the butler Bullivant and that of the serving boy George, a character who seems too modern to settle down in the world of masters and servants. The conflict between parents and children is particularly pointed and poignant here, with the children skeptical of their father's reforming because the memory of their past suffering remains so painfully real.

In America periods of neglect of Compton-Burnett's fiction alternate with periods of qualified critical interest. In England, her reputation as one of the most original and significant novelists of the twentieth century is stable. Her books were never bestsellers, but fellow writers acknowledge her importance. A number of contemporary British writers seem to have been influenced by her fictional practices. The modernity of her work caused her to be compared to Cubist painters, to writers of the *nouveau roman,* and to Harold Pinter with his absurdist dramas. Compton-Burnett is both an innovator and a classicist.

Works

Dolores (1911). *Pastors and Masters* (1925). *Brothers and Sisters* (1929). *Men and Wives* (1931). *More Women and Men* (1933). *A House and Its Head* (1935). *Daughters and Sons* (1937). *A Family and a Fortune* (1939). *Parents and Children* (1941). *Elders and Betters* (1944). *Manservant and Maidservant* (1947, published in America as *Bullivant and the*

Lambs). Two Worlds and Their Ways (1949). *Darkness and Day* (1951). *The Present and the Past* (1953). *Mother and Son* (1955, James Tait Black Memorial prize). *A Father and His Fate* (1957). *A Heritage and Its History* (1959, dramatized by Julian Mitchell, 1965). *The Mighty and Their Fall* (1961). *A God and His Gifts* (1963). *The Last and the First* (1971).

Kate Begnal
Janet Perez

Corinna
ca. 200 or 400 B.C.

Born third or fifth century B.C., Tanagra, Boeotia (Greece), but the date is strongly disputed; the earliest references to her occur in first century B.C. authors
Death date unknown
Genre(s): poetry
Language(s): Greek

Corinna, next to Pindar the most renowned Boeotian poet in antiquity, is firmly associated with him in the ancient biographical tradition: various anecdotes represent her as his teacher (Plutarch, *Glor. Athen.* 4.347F) or, alternatively, his poetic rival, victorious over him in singing contests once or several times (Pausanias 9.22.3; Aelian, *VH* 13.25; Suda s.v. "Korinna"). Literary citations preserve only a few lines of her work; when, at the beginning of this century, substantial passages on papyrus were first brought to light, scholars unhesitatingly deemed Corinna's style and subject matter "primitive." Her interest in retelling obscure local legends in a simple, straightforward manner and in a literary dialect colored by Boeotian vocabulary, pronunciation, and spelling was considered evidence of a limited, parochial talent. Consequently, she was relegated to the category of "minor [and not particularly interesting] voices."

In 1930 Edgar Lobel presented a strong stylistic argument for jettisoning the ancient biographical evidence and moving Corinna's date down to the third century B.C. The subsequent learned controversy, not yet resolved, forced scholars into an attentive rereading of her fragments and ultimately led to a new appreciation of her art. Corinna is now thought to be a subtle, engaging, and occasionally quite witty storyteller. The recent discovery of a new fragment (*PMG* 655), apparently from the prologue to a published verse collection, reveals her as a self-conscious artist:

there she titles her poems *Weroia* (the word may mean "narratives"), assigns them to the lyric genre of *partheneia* or compositions to be sung and danced by choruses of young girls, and boasts of the esteem her "clear-teasing voice" has brought her native city. The fragment breaks off as she is summarizing the contents of these choral lyrics, which apparently dealt with the exploits of such mythic figures as Cephisus and Orion.

The "Berlin Papyrus" (*PMG* 654), the longest extant sample of her poetry, contains passages from two tales: first, the account of a musical competition between the eponymous heroes of two Boeotian mountains, Helicon and Cithaeron; second, the prophecy of Acraephen, denizen of Apollo's oracle on Mount Ptoios, regarding the fate of the nine daughters of the river Asopus. The "Contest of Helicon and Cithaeron" is much admired for its economy, verve, and humor. In only twenty-three lines (all that is legible of the preserved text), Corinna recapitulates the finale of one competitor's prize song and then briskly informs us that the gods, under the supervision of the Muses, decided the winner by dropping secret ballots into golden urns. When Cithaeron is proclaimed victor and garlanded, Helicon throws a violent tantrum, hurling a boulder on high and smashing it into a thousand pebbles. This personification of a peak with unruly human impulses is a lively and delightful touch. Since tradition from Hesiod onward makes Mount Helicon the principal haunt of the Muses, the poet may have finally described how the goddesses mollified the sore loser by promising to honor him with their abiding presence. In the "Daughters of Asopus," a much lengthier fragment, Acraephen advises Asopus, who is searching for his nine missing daughters, that they were secretly abducted by Zeus, Poseidon, Apollo and Hermes and will eventually become the mothers of a race of demigods. To lend authority to his prediction, the prophet summarizes the history of his oracular seat. At his urging, Asopus apparently submitted to the will of the gods and accepted the loss of his daughters. As these female figures bear the names of nine major Greek settlements, Corinna is clearly providing an etiological account of how each came to be associated with its particular patron divinity. Her poem, furthermore, had patriotic overtones, for the single bride she bestowed upon Hermes was her own native city Tanagra (Pausanias 9.20.2).

It should be noted that Corinna, though she writes compositions for young girls to sing, is by no means a woman-oriented poet. Her narratives seem to have dealt principally with the feats of male gods and heroes—Hermes and Ares, Orion, Orestes, the "Seven against Thebes." She views her mythic heroines from a traditional, fully patriarchal perspective. Raped by Zeus and his companions, the Asopids may count themselves blessed in their semi-divine offspring; late references mention tales of the daughters of Minyas, who refused to worship Dionysus and were punished with madness, and of Metioche and Menippe, who sacrificed themselves to save their city. Finally, in the most enigmatic of her fragments (*PMG* 664a), she reproaches Myrtis, another Boeotian poet (q.v.), because "being a woman, she entered into contention (*eba . . . pot erin*) with Pindar." The Greek phrase can mean either participation in an actual contest or literary emulation. In either case, it suggests that Myrtis's rivalry with a male poet is unseemly, as she must necessarily fall short of Pindar's greatness due to her sex. Corinna's delicate *Weroia* therefore serve as an illustration of what the proper woman poet can and should compose.

Works

Greek texts and German translations in Homeyer, H. *Dichterinnen des Altertums und des frühen Mittelalters* (Paderborn, 1979). Greek texts in *Poetae Melici Graeci*, ed. D.L. Page (Oxford, 1962). English translations in *Greek Lyric IV*, tr. D.A. Campbell, Loeb Classical Library (Cambridge, Mass., and London, 1982) and in Rayor, D., *Sappho's Lyre: Archaic Lyric and Women Poets of Ancient Greece* (Berkeley and Los Angeles, 1991).

Marilyn B. Skinner

Natalia de Oliveira Correia
1923–

Born September 13, 1923, Isle of S. Miguel, Azores
Genre(s): essay, journalism, literary criticism, novel, poetry, short story, drama
Language(s): Portuguese

Natalia Correia is an institution in Portuguese letters of the twentieth century. Born in the Azores, she was educated in mainland Portugal and started early a long and distinguished career that would touch virtually every field of literature, from works of children's literature, theater, novel, essay, literary criticism, and travel books to poetry, the medium in which she has received the most critical attention. Correia's intellectual life bears witness to the political and sociological changes of contemporary Portugal. Correia was di-

rector and editor of several journals and worked as a consultant to the Department of Culture. She was elected to the National Congress and was an important part of the movement of resistance against the fascist dictatorships of Salazar and Caetano. Her *Antologia de poesia erotica e satirica* (1966) was censured by the government of Antonio Salazar, and she was condemned to two years of house arrest for "abusing the freedom of the press."

Correia's trajectory as a poet started in 1947 with the publication of *Rios de nuvens*, and from that book through fourteen more volumes she has developed the themes of love, nature, and the telluric forces of women. Her collection of poems, *O armisticio* (1985), has as its main theme the need for the current patriarchal system to give way to a government based on female wisdom as the only hope for world survival.

In the theater and novel, Correia is equally important and versatile. Her first novel, *Anoiteceu no barrio* (1946), deals with the impact of a changing society on the everyday life of common people, while her most famous play, *Erros meus, ma fortuna, amor ardente*, commissioned in 1981 by the National Theater in commemoration of the four-hundredth anniversary of the death of the poet Luis de Camoes, deals with the life and works of this distinguished member of Portuguese letters. As a literary critic and essayist, Correia is also important. Her anthologies and critical essays range from the work of the medieval troubadours to the surrealist poets and each one has expanded the realm of Portuguese literary history. A perceptive observer, her travel diaries range from a chronicle of a visit to the United States in *Descobri que era europeia* (1951) to a reflection on contemporary life in *Nao percas a Rosa* (1978). She has also worked in children's literature and is an excellent painter. Natalia Correia is truly one of the most talented members of twentieth-century Portuguese intellectual life.

Works

Poetry: *Rios de nuvens* [Rivers of Clouds] (1947). *Poemas* [Poems] (1955). *Dimensao encontrada* [Found Dimension] (1957). *Passaporte* [Passport] (1958). *Comunicacao* [Communication] (1959). *Cantico do pais emerso* [Canticle of the Emersed Country] (1961). *O vinho e a lira* [Wine and Lyre] (1966). *Matria* (1968). *As macas de Oreste* [Orestes' Apples] (1970). *A mosca iluminada* [The Illuminated Fly] (1972). *O anjo de ocidente a entrada do ferro* [The Angel of the West at the Iron Door] (1972). *Poemas a rebate* [Poems to Alarm] (1975). *Epistola* aos Iamitas [Epistle to the Iamitas] (1976). *O diluvio e a pompa* [Deluge and Pomp] (1979). *O armisticio* [The Armistice] (1985).

Novels: *Anoiteceu no barrio* [Dusk in the Neighborhood] (1946). *A madona* [The Madonna] (1968).

Plays: *O progresso de Edipo* [Oedipus' Progress] (1957). *O homunculo* [The Dwarf] (1965). *O Encoberto* [The Concealed] (1969). *Erros meus, ma fortuna, amor ardente* [My Mistakes, My Fortune, Impassioned Love] (1981).

Essays: *Poesia de arte e realismo poetico* [Art, Poetry and Poetic Realism] (1958). *Uma estatua para Herodes* [A Statue for Herodes] (1974). *A lingua portuguesa en perigo* [The Portuguese Language in Peril] (1979).

Anthologies and Literary Criticism: *A questao academica de 1907* [The Academic Question of 1907]

(1962). *Antologia da poesia erotica e satirica* [Anthology of Erotic and Satirical Poetry] (1966). *Cantares galego-portugueses* [Galician-Portuguese Ballads] (1970). *Trovas de D. Dinis* [The Songs of D. Dinis] (1970). *A mulher* [Women] (1973). *O surrealismo na poesia portuguesa* [Surrealism in Portuguese Poetry] (1973). *Antologia de poesia portuguesa no periodo barroco* [Anthology of Baroque Portuguese Poetry] (1983). *A ilha de Sam Nunca* [Sam Nunca's Island] (1982).

Diaries and Travel Books: *Descobri que era europeia* [I Discovered That I Was a European] (1951). *Nao percas a Rosa* [Do Not Miss the Rose] (1978).

Children's Literature: *Grandes aventuras dum Pequeno Heroi* [The Grand Adventures of Little Hero] (1947).

Lina L. Cofresí

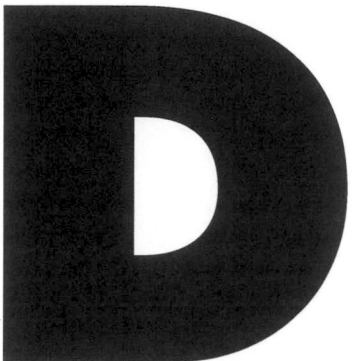

Maria Dąbrowska
1889–1965

Born 1889, Kalisz, Poland
Died 1965
Genre(s): short story, novel, drama, translation
Language(s): Polish

Several times proposed as a candidate for a Nobel Prize for Literature—an honor she never received—Maria Dąbrowska enjoys a secure place in the history of Polish literature as the outstanding woman prose writer of the twentieth century. Born Maria Szumska near the city of Kalisz, she was educated mostly in private schools in Kalisz and Warsaw and pursued university studies in the natural sciences in Lausanne, Switzerland (1908–1909) and in Brussels, Belgium (1909–1912). While in Brussels she also began studying economics, philosophy, and sociology at the Université Nouvelle. In the years that she was out of Poland, Dąbrowska was actively involved in Polish émigré circles, especially in the Belgian capital. Her keen interest in social and economic issues, particularly the cooperative movement, was strengthened by her marriage in 1911 to Marian Dąbrowski (who died in 1925), a Socialist activist who was forced to emigrate from Russian Poland after the revolution of 1905–1907. Following her return to Poland in 1914, Dąbrowska began a career as a journalist writing mainly about economics and politics. From 1918 to 1924 she was also employed in the Ministry of Agriculture in Warsaw.

Dąbrowska's strong sense of social justice and her liberal political views set her on an inevitable collision course with the regime of Marshal Józef Piłsudski in the interwar period. She took up the cause of the political opposition, vigorously opposed the intensifying anti-Semitism of the 1930s, especially in the period from Piłsudski's death in 1935 to the outbreak of war in September 1939, and became a passionate advocate of land reform to improve the lot of the peasants. During the

German occupation of Poland from 1939 to 1945, Dąbrowska lived in Warsaw where she played an active role in the underground cultural life of the city. Inactive publicly as a writer during the postwar Stalinist decade, Dąbrowska resumed her prolific literary career in 1955. Her later years brought her well-deserved national acclaim. In 1957 she received an honorary doctorate from the University of Warsaw and in 1962, on the occasion of the fiftieth anniversary of her literary career, the Polish Academy of Sciences organized an international symposium in her honor in Kalisz and Warsaw. The proceedings of the symposium were published in 1963, two years before her death at the age of seventy-five.

Although her earliest work of fiction, the novella *We Francji . . . ziemi cudzej* (In France . . . a Foreign Land) was written in 1912, Dąbrowska's first literary success was the collection of stories about poor rural people entitled *Ludzie stamtąd* (Folk from over Yonder), which appeared in 1926. This was followed in 1932 by the first two volumes of the four-volume novel *Noce i dnie* (Nights and Days) which was her greatest literary accomplishment and the basis of her fame as a writer. The remaining two volumes of the immense work were published in 1933 and 1934. The great bulk of Dąbrowska's subsequent literary work consists of collections of stories, among them *Znaki życia* (1938; Signs of Life) and *Gwiazda zaranna* (1955; *The Morning Star*, translated into English under the title *A Village Wedding and Other Stories*). A second attempt at a large "family saga"—*Przygody człowieka myślącego* (The Adventures of a Thinking Man)—remained unfinished and was published in book form posthumously in 1970. Long interested in the career of Joseph Conrad, Dąbrowska began writing a series of essays about him in the early 1930s; the entire collection was published in book form in 1959 under the title *Szkice o Conradzie* (Essays on Conrad). Dąbrowska's oeuvre also includes two weak historical plays—*Geniusz sierocy* (1939; The Orphan Genius) and *Stanisław i Bogumił* (1948; Stanislaus and Bogumił)—and a translation of the *Diary* of Samuel Pepys which she undertook during the wartime occupation and which was published in 1952.

Nights and Days, the work of fiction for which Dąbrowska is most admired and for which she will be most remembered, is a family chronicle. In it, the author's principal interest—the impact on a remote provincial farm of the transformations of Polish society from the January insurrection of 1863 down to 1914 and World War I—is traced through the family histories of its two main characters, Bogumil Niechcic and Barbara Ostrzeńska. A sweeping panorama of fifty years of turbulent Polish history, *Nights and Days* compensates for its great length with a number of finely etched character portraits, faithfully and often arrestingly recreated historical episodes, and an unerring sense of social dynamics. Although intended originally as a psychological novel, the immense work grew into a novel of vast social proportions far exceeding the boundaries of its original village setting. Of the many interesting feminine portraits in the novel by far the most commanding is that of the central character, Barbara, a superb study of a highly complex woman set in the frame of great change in Polish society, the Polish family, and the role of women.

Works
Uśmiech dzieciństwa. Wspomnienia (1923). *Ludzie stamtąd* (1926). *Noce i dnie* (4 vols., 1932–1934). *Znaki życia* (1938). *Geniusz sierocy* (1939). *Stanisław i Bogumił* (1948). *Gwiazda zaranna* (1955). *Myśli o sprawach i ludziach* (1956). *Szkice z podróży* (1956). *Szkice o Conradzie* (1959). *Przygody człowieka myślącego* (1970).

Harold B. Segel

Madame du Deffand
1697–1780
Born September 25, 1696, Château de Chamrond, France
Died September 23, 1780, Paris
Genre(s): letters
Language(s): French

Daughter of Gaspard and Anne Brulard de Vichy de Chamrond, Marie Anne married Jean-Baptiste de La Lande, Marquis du Deffand, in 1719. Marie Anne de Vichy de Chamrond, whom history knows as Mme

du Deffand, was born in her family's chateau in Burgundy in 1696, a daughter of an ancient, though not rich, family. Her mother died when she was a child, and she had two elder brothers and a younger sister. Her father, although a nobleman, was concerned solely with tending his land. At the age of five Marie was sent to a convent in Paris, a well-known establishment for girls of noble families, where she was to spend twelve years. Since the only goal of a girl's education was acquiring the social graces necessary to courtly society, Mlle de Vichy was taught barely more than how to read and write, a situation that troubled her greatly in her later years. Her teachers in their turn were astonished by her total indifference to religion and her rebellious, independent spirit.

When Marie was twenty-one, her father arranged her marriage to the Marquis du Deffand. Even the first weeks of marriage disappointed the young wife, who found her husband hopelessly dull. Remarkable for her beauty and wit, she tried to find amusement in parties, gambling, and love affairs at the court of the Regent, the Duc d'Orléans. Her behavior was scandalous even for her dissolute society, so that in 1724 she and her husband separated for good. However, the multitude of her love affairs was not the result of a passionate but, on the contrary, of a cold, cynical nature, desperately trying to escape the boredom that was to plague her all her life.

After the death of the Regent in 1723 Mme du Deffand attached herself to the court of the Duchesse du Maine, a royal princess exiled from Paris because of her political intrigues. The Duchesse gathered round herself a court of various people not welcome to the royal court, including such intellectuals as Voltaire. There the unparalleled wit and intelligence of Mme du Deffand could find full scope.

Her income was not great for a woman of her class, for her dowry was under the control of her husband. She had only enough to keep a small apartment with a few servants in Paris. Yet it was enough for her to open a salon. Soon her fame was rivaled only by that of Mme Geoffrin, another great salonnière who was not, however, of noble birth. Mme du Deffand was visited on equal terms by the aristocracy and by the foremost intellectuals of that era—Voltaire, Montesquieu, d'Alembert, Diderot. Even foreigners traveling through Paris would beg to be introduced to her.

In 1750 the Marquis du Deffand died. His death left his widow in comfortable financial circumstances, so that she moved into a larger, better set of rooms in the convent of Saint Joseph, henceforth one of the most famous apartments in Europe. Yet, despite her social success, the rest of her life held many misfortunes. In 1752 she became blind. She spent a few months in her native place in Burgundy, now owned by her brother. There she met Julie de Lespinasse, her brother's illegitimate daughter by his own mother-in-law, an exceptionally intelligent girl of twenty. Mme du Deffand took a great liking for her young niece. Since the blind marquise needed a companion, two years later she installed Mlle de Lespinasse in Paris in an apartment below her own.

Mlle de Lespinasse was, unfortunately, too talented a companion. Certain guests of Mme du Deffand, mostly the Encyclopedists led by d'Alembert, liked her conversation so well that little by little they started spending some time in her apartment before visiting her mistress. In 1764, when the egoistic Mme du Deffand found it out, she considered it an act of betrayal and threw her young relative out of her house. Many friends of Mme du Deffand considered her unjust, dissociated themselves from her, and started visiting the salon that Julie now opened, which was to become perhaps the most brilliant of all. One of them was d'Alembert, despite his long friendship with Mme du Deffand, because he was then and ever after in love with Mlle de Lespinasse.

This was a shattering blow for Mme du Deffand's pride. However, she could not really grieve that the Encyclopedists had left her. Although her spirit was intensely skeptical, her outlook was conservative, and she had always received the progressive thinkers only because of d'Alembert, whom she greatly liked and admired. She continued to keep her salon, but from then on not the intellectuals but the worldly, aristocratic representatives of the old, reactionary views visited her. In consequence Mme du Deffand complained that the conversation had become dull. Even worse was to follow. In her sixty-eighth year the blind old woman fell passionately in love for the first time and with a man twenty years younger than herself, the English writer Horace Walpole, who visited Paris periodically. Naturally, although he liked her and cultivated her friendship, he did not reciprocate her passion.

The old age of Mme du Deffand was extremely unhappy. The carefree society of her youth had given place to the new, serious, and progressive spirit, which she did not like, her old friends were dead or not living in Paris, the man she loved did not love her, she suffered from boredom, insomnia, and melancholy. Finally, in 1780 she departed the life she found so intolerable.

After her death the publication of Mme du Deffand's letters to various people—mostly to Voltaire, her intimate friend the Duchesse de Choiseul, and Horace Walpole—established her as one of the greatest writers of the eighteenth century by virtue of the incomparable elegance and precision of her style. But even without her letters she would live in history as the mistress of one of the greatest salons of her age, and a most interesting human being—a supremely intelligent and unhappy woman, who, in spite of the many advantages she possessed, was tormented all her life by pessimism, cynicism, and, most of all, boredom.

Works

Letters of the Marquise du Deffand to Horace Walpole, ed. Mary Berry, 4 vols. (1810). *Correspondance complète de la marquise du Deffand avec ses amis, le Président Hénault, Montesquieu, d'Alembert, Voltaire, Horace Walpole*, ed. M. de Lescure, 2 vols. (1865). *Correspondance de Mme du Deffand avec la duchesse de Choiseul, l'Abbé Barthélémy et M. Craufurt, publiée avec un introduction par M. le Marquis de Sainte-Aulaire*, 3 vols. (1866). *Lettres de la Marquise du Deffand à Horace Walpole*, ed. Mrs. Paget Toynbee, 3 vols. (1912). *Madame du Deffand: Lettres à Voltaire*, ed. Joseph Trabucco (1922). *Letters to and from Madame du Deffand and Julie de Lespinasse*, ed. Warren Hunting Smith (1938). *Horace Walpole's correspondence with Madame du Deffand and Wiart*, ed. W. S. Lewis and Warren Hunting Smith, 6 vols. (1939).

Neda Jeni

Shelagh Delaney
1939–
Born November 25, 1939, Salford, Lancashire
Genre(s): drama, screenplay, short story
Language(s): English

"To talk as we do about popular theatre, about new working class audiences, about plays that will interpret the common experiences of today—all this is one thing, and a good thing, too. But how much better even, how much more exciting, to find such theatre suddenly here, suddenly sprung up under our feet! This was the first joyful thing about Theatre Workshop's performance of *A Taste of Honey*." So Lindsay Anderson wrote during the summer of 1958 of the first play of a nineteen-year-old girl from a working-class family from the north of England. With the critical and popular success of *A Taste of Honey,* Delaney was catapulted into prominence as an extraordinarily promising and precocious writer of the new drama. Although in 1960 she produced a second play, *The Lion in Love,* the hopes of many exuberant early supporters for a bountiful body of writing from her has not been rewarded.

Delaney was raised in Salford, an industrial suburb of Manchester that serves as background setting for both of her plays. She left school at age seventeen and found employment variously as a salesgirl, a milk depot clerk, and as an usherette at a local cinema. She had an ambition to write, however, and had begun work on a novel at the time she was working as an usherette. The novel was transformed to playscript when, upon going to the theatre one evening and seeing a touring production of Terence Rattigan's bourgeois entertainment, *Variations on a Theme,* she was so disgusted by the febrile character of Rattigan's tea-tinkling conventions that she became convinced she could do better herself. When she completed the script, she sent a copy to Joan Littlewood, director of the Theatre Workshop at the Theatre Royal Stratford-East, expecting only, perhaps, some helpful criticism. Within two weeks, *A Taste of Honey* was in rehearsal with Miss Littlewood directing.

Set in a "comfortless flat," *A Taste of Honey* examines the misfortunes of Jo, a sensitive and awkward teenager who defends herself with a sometimes caustic tongue and hardened outer shell of indifference to the general squalor of life that surrounds her. The play, written in two acts, progresses by examining Jo's relationships, within the context of a sordid environment she can never fully overcome, with her sluttish mother, a lover, and a new-found friend. In turn, Jo is abandoned by each of them. Her mother agrees to marry a current lover and leaves Jo to fend for herself. Her lover, a black seaman, ships out leaving her with an engagement ring from Woolworth's and a child in her womb. Her friend Geof, a spirited homosexual lad, helps Jo during her pregnancy and, by drawing her away from being overwhelmed by hate and self-pity, introduces her to the joy of simple affection (the taste of honey). Geof proposes marriage to Jo and is refused. He also departs when the prodigal mother returns, her own fling at marriage in ruin, to reclaim rudely the territory.

Audiences and critics alike were impressed by the unaffected honesty of character and relationships. What may have been the material of cliché melodrama came off with such vitality and directness that the pathos of situation was illuminated all the more

clearly by the brightness of the ironic humor found in Joan Littlewood's glowing production performed in a style blending elements of modern naturalism with the presentational openness of the traditional music hall. Indeed, some suggested that director Littlewood (widely known for her success at shaping theatrically effective productions out of unlikely sources) had substantially rewritten the script during the course of rehearsal. However, John Russell Taylor's examination of the original typescript (provided by Littlewood) determined that "The dialogue throughout has been pruned and tightened—rather more, evidently, than is usual in rehearsal—but most of the celebrated lines are already there . . . and the character of Jo, the play's *raison d'être, is* already completely created and unmistakably the same. . . . The play is obviously much superior in the final version, but it is not so different, and the only modifications which one might find out of keeping are very minor. . . ."

The *eclat* that accompanied *A Taste of Honey*'s 1958 premiere brought its then nineteen-year-old author international attention. The play was produced in New York in 1960 and received enthusiastic critical acclaim as well as The New York Drama Critics Award for "Best Foreign Play." Delaney's screenplay for the 1962 cinema adaptation, written with the film's director Tony Richardson, brought her a British Film Academy Award and the Robert Flaherty Award for "Best Screenplay."

Some observers of the theatre scene, inclined to categorize Delaney as the "angry young woman" of the new drama, were cautioned in a program note for the original production that because Delaney "knows what she is angry about," she may well be the antithesis of the so-called angry young men. Unlike Jimmy Porter, in Osborne's *Look Back in Anger,* Jo does not account for her situation in terms of bitter denunciations directed against the government of socioeconomic injustice. In dramatic situations where she might be moved to anger, Jo's commentary is colored by statements like, "I hate love!" Lindsay Anderson, in his 1958 review of *A Taste of Honey,* compares Jo to Holden Caulfield of J.D. Salinger's *A Catcher in the Rye.* "Like Holden, Josephine is a sophisticated innocent," notes Anderson. "Precious little surprises her; but her reactions are pure and direct, her intuitions are acute, and her eye is very sharp. . . . But Josephine is luckier than Holden in some ways: she is tougher, with common-sense Lancashire working-class resilience that will always pull her through. And this makes her different too from the middle-class angry young man, the egocentric rebel. Josephine is not a rebel; she is a revolutionary." Rather than being a social philosopher who deliberately tries to move an audience with didactic messages, Delaney is a careful and compassionate observer of life; her audiences are moved to ponder the implications of what they see.

Her second (and, to date, only other) play, *The Lion in Love,* was originally presented in September 1960 at the Belgrade Theatre, Coventry, for a run outside London before moving to the Royal Court in late December. The script draws its title from an Aesop fable which moralizes, "Nothing can be more fatal to peace than the ill assorted marriages into which rash love may lead." Naturalistic in style, the play examines a strained marriage, problems and difficulties of each generation in search of what it wants, and the "waywardness of life itself." Unlike *A Taste of Honey,* the play has a large cast, a complex interweaving of story-lines, and direct statements of social-consciousness by a number of the characters. It was not a popular success and received mixed critical reactions. Although most reviewers considered it verbose, poorly constructed, and thematically unfocused, Kenneth Tynan found the realistic qualities of the piece to have "authenticity, honesty, restraint and . . . a prevailing sense of humor." John Russell Taylor found some merit in the characterization, particularly the mature perspicuity of one of the play's young females, but hoped *The Lion in Love* would eventually prove only a transitional work.

In 1963, Delaney published a collection of autobiographical short stories entitled *Sweetly Sings the Donkey.* Reviewers thought the writing uneven, but, at its best, composed "in that same arresting voice," in Marion Magid's words, "without literary pretension, honest to the point of brutality, that made Miss Delaney's first work so striking." Since 1963, she has written screenplays for two films—*The White Bus* (1966) and *Charlie Bubbles* (1968)—and several scripts for television including "The House That Jack Built" (1977), which was performed without accolade in 1979 as a stage production Off-Broadway.

Works

A Taste of Honey (1958; screenplay 1961) *The Lion in Love* (1960). *Sweetly Sings the Donkey* (1963). *The White Bus* (1966). *Charlie Bubbles* (1968). *Did Your Nanny Come from Bergen?* (1970). *St. Martin's Summer* (1974). *The House That Jack Built* (1977). *Find Me First* (1981). *So Does the Nightingale* (1981). *Don't Worry about Matilda* (1983). *Dance with a Stranger* (1985). *Railway Station Man* (1992).

Paul D. Nelsen

Grazia Deledda
1871–1936

a.k.a. Ilia di Sant'Ismael
Born September 27, 1871, Nuoro, Sardinia
Died August 15, 1936, Rome
Genre(s): novel, drama, poetry, short story
Language(s): Italian

One of Italy's most important modern novelists, Grazia Deledda is often seen as a transitional figure, combining the form of the nineteenth-century novel with the existential outlook of twentieth-century fiction. Critics have linked her with several nineteenth-century movements—romanticism, *verismo* (the late nineteenth-century naturalistic movement that dealt realistically with common problems faced by the lower classes), and decadence (with its emphasis on the complex psychological portrayal of unusual states of mind)—but her work is much too varied (over forty novels and short story collections published between 1890 and 1937) and too complex to be categorized so easily.

Deledda was born into a middle-class family in Nuoro, Sardinia. Educated only through elementary school, Deledda read passionately a variety of popular and serious nineteenth-century writers. These two influences—her birthplace and her reading—were to shape practically all of her work. Except for her last novels, all of Deledda's work centers on the people of Sardinia and their ancient customs and beliefs and describes in detail the harsh, desolate landscape that surrounds them. Deledda once stated that she wished to do for Sardinia what Tolstoy had done for Russia, and her emphasis on individuals caught up in tragic circumstances often beyond their control is reminiscent of the Russian novelists. Deledda married in 1900 and moved to Rome with her husband, Palmiro Madesani; although she remained in Rome for the rest of her life, she continued to write about her native island, recalling and distilling people, places, and customs. In 1926 Deledda won the Nobel Prize for literature. She died in Rome in 1936, and her last novel, the autobiographical *Cosima,* was published the following year.

Deledda's earliest works, such as *Nell'azzurro* (1890) and *Stella d'oriente* (1891), show most clearly the influence of the romantic novel, with its emphasis on adventure and exaggerated plot devices. But in the 1890s her novels and stories begin to concentrate more on the Sardinian land and people, particularly such works as *Anime oneste* (1895) and *La via del male* (1896), and in 1895 Deledda published a study of

Sardinian culture, *Tradizioni popolari di Nuoro in Sardegna*. The Sardinian setting was to furnish her with characters and themes for almost all of her novels even after she moved to Rome. Often the poetic descriptions of the wild countryside and fierce climate serve to characterize the harshness of the characters' lives or the inner conflict of the protagonist. The customs of her Sardinian characters reflect the survival of an ancient, even pre-Christian way of life; these old beliefs inevitably come into conflict with the demands of the modern world, a conflict which dominates Deledda's work. In *Dopo il divorzio* (1902, revised as *Naufraghi in porto* in 1920), the protagonist Constantino Ledda is sent to prison for 27 years for killing his uncle; a new divorce law allows his wife Giovanna, who is living in poverty, to remarry a landowner, but her new life proves worse than her poverty and she is scorned by the villagers. After the real murderer of Constantino's uncle confesses, the innocent man, shattered by what he considers to be his wife's betrayal, returns to his village and eventually begins a passionate but loveless affair with Giovanna. Unable to find happiness, he eventually kills Giovanna's cruel mother-in-law and is sentenced to hard labor in prison; Giovanna's life deteriorates still further. Deledda shows how on the one hand the traditional prohibition of divorce, which had provided security and stability, also proved inflexible and repressive, while on the other hand the new order fails to support those whom it purports to liberate.

In many novels the decay of the old order is typified by the dissolution of the patriarchal family unit; often the patriarch is harsh and unyielding, or he is absent and the remaining male protagonists are weak or isolated from the real world. The almost certain failure of the protagonist to resolve the conflict between the old and the new gives Deledda's novels a sense of fatalism and even futility; but the public failure does not eliminate the obligation to act ethically, and this defeat often leads a character to seek a private expiation, often through self-renunciation. In *Elias Portolu* (1903), a young man (Elias) falls in love and has an affair with his brother's fiancee; Elias plans to become a priest, but then his brother dies. Elias' own son by the affair dies, and he decides not to marry his brother's widow, as custom demands, but to become a priest. The title character of *La Madre* (1920; The Mother) threatens to expose her son, a priest, for his love for a parishioner. He gives up his lover, but his mother plans to denounce him in church. Unable to do so, she dies at Mass in front of her son. After 1921, Deledda began to concentrate on the psychological states of her characters, as in *Il*

segreto dell'uomo solitario (1921; The Secret of the Solitary Man) and less on Sardinia as a setting. Her last novels have thinner, more allegorical plots and are often situated in undefined, atemporal settings, for example *Il paese del vento* (1931; The Country of the Wind).

While Deledda is certainly significant as a historical figure, linking nineteenth-century forms and techniques with a modern skepticism, her work is also important as a document of a particular place and time and as a treatment of the universal problems of guilt and moral responsibility in a world of contradictory values.

Works

Nell'azzurro [In the Blue] (1890). *Stella d'oriente* [Star of the East] (1891) pseud. Ilia di Saint'Ismail. *Amore regale* [Royal Love] (1892). *Fior di Sardegna* [Flower of Sardinia] (1892). *Racconti sardi* [Sardinian Tales] (1894). *Anime oneste* [Honest Souls] (1895). *Tradizioni popolari di Nuoro in Sardegna* [Popular Traditions of Nuoro in Sardinia] (1895). *La via del male* [The Way of Evil] (1896). *Il tesoro* [The Treasure] (1897). *L'ospite* [The Guest] (1897). *Giffah, Nostra Signora del Buon Consiglio, Le disgrazie che puo causare il denaro, I tre talismani* [Giffa, Our Lady of Good Counsel, The Disgraces That May Produce Money, The Three Talismans] (1899), four fables published as separate volumes. *Le tentazioni* [The Temptations] (1899). *La giustizia* [Justice] (1899). *Il vecchio della montagna* [The Old Man of the Mountain] (1900). *La regina delle tenebre* [The Queen of the Shadows] (1901). *Dopo il divorzio* [After the Divorce] (1902); revised as *Naufraghi in porto* [Shipwreck in Port] (1920). *Elias Portolu* (1903). *Cenere* [Ashes] (1904). *Nostalgie* [Nostalgias] (1905). *I giuochi della vita* [The Games of Life] (1905). *Amori moderni* [Modern Loves] (1907). *L'ombra del passato* [The Shadow of the Past] (1907). *Il nonno* [The Grandfather] (1908). *Il nostro padrone* [Our Master] (1910). *Sino al confine* [To the Boundary] (1910). *Nel deserto* [In the Desert] (1911). *Chiaroscuro* (1912). *Colombi e sparvieri* [Doves and Hawks] (1912). *Canne al vento* [Reeds in the Wind] (1913). *Le colpe altrui* [The Guilt of Others] (1914). *Marianna Sirca* (1915). *Il fanciullo nascosto* [The Hidden Boy] (1915). *L'incendio nell'oliveto* [The Fire in the Olive Grove] (1918). *Il ritorno del figlio* [The Return of the Son]. *La bambina rubata* [The Stolen Baby] (1919). *La madre* [The Mother] (1919). *Cattive compagnie* [Bad Company] (1921). *Il segreto dell'uomo solitario* [The Secret of the Solitary Man] (1921). *Il Dio dei viventi* [The God of the Living] (1922). *Il flauto nel bosco* [The Flute in the Forest] (1923). *La danza della collana* (The Dance of the Necklace). *A sinistra* [On the Left] (1924). *La fuga in Egitto* [The Flight to Egypt] (1925). *Il sigillo d'amore* [The Seal of Love] (1926). *Annalena Bilsini* (1927). *Il vecchio e i fanciulli* [The Old Man and the Children] (1928). *Il dono di Natale* [The Christmas Gift] (1930). *La casa del poeta* [The House of the Poet] (1930). *Il paese del vento* [The Country of the Wind] (1931). *La vigna sul mare* [The Vineyard on the Sea] (1932). *Sole d'estate* [Summer Sunlight] (1933). *L'argine* [The Embankment] (1934). *La chiesa della solitudine* [The Church of Solitude] (1936). *Cosima* (1937). *Il cedro del Libano* [The Cedar of Lebanon] (1939).

Selections of works: *Versi e prosi giovanili* [Early Prose and Poetry] (1938), ed. A. Scano. *Romanzi e novelle* [Romances and Novels] (1941–1955), ed. E. Cecchi, 4 vols.

Theater: with C. Antona Traversi, *L'edera* [Ivy] (1912). (with C. Guastalla and V. Michetti) *La grazia* [Grace] (1921).

Poetry: *Paesaggi sardi* [Sardinian Landscape] (1896). "Lauda di Sant'Antonio" [Laud of Saint Anthony] (1893).

Translations: *After the Divorce*, tr. Maria Lansdale (1905). *Eugenia Grandet* by Balzac (1930). *After the Divorce*, tr. Susan Ashe (1985). *Ashes*, tr. Helen Colvill (1908). *The Mother*, tr. Mary Steegman (1923) (preface by D.H. Lawrence).

Stephen Hale

Marie Dentière
ca. 1500–1561

a.k.a. "Un marchand de Genève," "Un femme chrestienne de Tornay," Marie d'Enntière
Born ca. 1500, Tournai, Belgium
Died 1561, Geneva, Switzerland
Genre(s): history, polemic
Language(s): French

A Protestant pamphlet writer and preacher, Dentière was involved in the reform movement in Geneva and was one of the few published female authors of early Protestantism.

Born to a noble family of Tournai, Dentière entered a local Augustinian convent. Joining the reform movement alongside other members of her family, she left her abbey in the 1520s and married Simon Robert, a former priest of that diocese who had become an evangelical pastor. After Robert's death, she married another evangelical preacher, Antoine Fromment, with whom she went to Geneva during the violent controversies of the early 1530s. Dentière became personally active in the reform movement, preaching to female audiences and publishing two works during the turbulent course of that decade.

The War for and Deliverance of the City of Geneva, Faithfully Prepared and Written Down by a Merchant Living in That City provided a lively and partisan interpretation of the long struggle between the Catholic duke of Savoy and the Protestant citizens of Geneva in the years 1524–1536. It was a hard-hitting document intended to influence public opinion during the reorganization of the secular and religious governance of the city immediately after the defeat of the Savoyard regime.

By 1539 a number of Dentière's friends, including the recently arrived John Calvin, had been exiled from Geneva. In that year she wrote *A Most Beneficial Letter, Prepared and Written Down by a Christian Woman of Tournai, and Sent to the Queen of Navarre, Sister of the King of France, Against the Turks, the Jews, the Infidels, the False Christians, the Anabaptists and the Lutherans*. This work was intended to win support for those exiles, by bringing their plight before Marguerite de Navarre, the sister of the French king, Francis I, and a woman sympathetic to the evangelical cause. The religious rulers of her city were described as schemers and "cockroaches" who spread dissension and looked out for their own economic interests. Dentière defended evangelical theology through attacks on Catholic and even Lutheran opinion, buttressed by a series of sophisticated citations of canon law and other traditional theological sources. She also included an opening "Defense of Women," a consideration of the role of women in theological discourse. For Dentière the priesthood of all believers included women: "For we ought not, any more than men, hide and bury within the earth that which God has . . . revealed to us women. Although we are not permitted to preach in assemblies and public churches, nevertheless we are not prohibited from writing and giving advice in all charity one to the other."

The work was impounded by the city council. Dentière and Fromment fought an ongoing legal battle to gain its release but were unsuccessful even after the return of Calvin. Her radical stance on theological issues was unacceptable to her former allies. The couple became the objects of ridicule among the Genevan pastorate, and Dentière died in 1561 shortly after her husband, who had long since resigned his parish, had been charged with adultery. No printed copies of the *War and Deliverance* and only one of the *Beneficial Letter* survive today. She was a fine rhetorician, who offered one of the earliest feminist critiques of the role of women in the life of the Christian community.

Works

La guerre et deslivrance de la ville de Genesve, fidèlement faicte et composèe par ung Marchant demourant en icelle (1536). *Epistre très utile, faicte et composèe par une femme chrestienne de Tornay, envoyèe à la Royne de Navarre, seur du Roy de France, contre les Turcz, Juifz, Infideles, Faulx chrestiens, Anabaptistes et Lutheriens* (1539). The entire text of *La guerre et deslivrance* and extracts from the *Epitre très utile* are printed in Albert Rilliet, "Restitution de l'écrit intitulé: *La guerre de deslivrance de la ville de Genesve* (1536)," *Mémoires et documents publiées par la société d'histoire et d'archéologie de Genève* 20 (1881): 309–384. Other extracts from the *Epistre très utile* are printed in Aimé-Louis Herminjard, ed. *Correspondance des réformateurs dans les pays de langue française*, 9 vols. (Geneva: 1866–1897), V, pp. 295–304. The only surviving copy of this work is in Geneva, Bibliothèque municipale, D. Den. 1.

Thomas Head

Catharina Irma Dessaur
1931–

a.k.a. Andreas Burnier
Born July 3, 1931, Gravenhage, The Netherlands
Genre(s): poetry, novel, essay, short story
Language(s): Dutch

Andreas Burnier recalls that, growing up in hiding during the war years, she became aware of the fact that women enjoyed only limited freedom in a masculine society and, much more dramatically, that she felt like a boy trapped in a girl's body. It was almost inevitable that Burnier's first attempts at functioning in an adult masculine world failed: her studies in philosophy were thwarted by a male professor who refused to supervise her and her marriage ended in a divorce after ten painful years. She went back to school and made a career in academe. She has been professor of criminology at the University of Nijmegen since 1973.

Her first novel, *Een tevreden lach* (1965; A Contented Laugh), was an instant success with the critics, to a great extent because of its experimental and clever structure. Burnier shifts from first to third person narrative, mixes various text types and genres, and alternates narrative with lyrical prose, the purpose of which is to convey the main character's search for identity, individual freedom, and full development. Though her main character, Simone, is a lesbian, and lesbianism is a recurring motif in Burnier's work, she insists that it is not the main theme. Homosexuality mainly serves to emphasize woman's angst and basic loneliness in a man's world. Similar

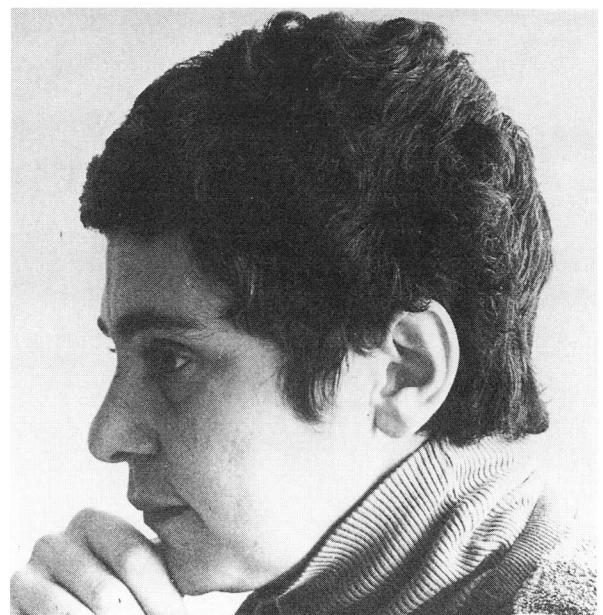

Catharina Irma Dessaur

themes are elaborated in *Het jongensuur* (1969; The Boys' Hour), a novel, and in *De verschrikkingen van het noorden* (1967; The Horrors of the North), a collection of short stories.

From 1970 onward, Burnier's work has become more militant and essayistic. In *De huilende libertijn* (1970; The Crying Libertine), she showed the absurdness of both superfluous feminism and male "sex fascism" by depicting a society that is the grotesque (feminist) reverse of our present male-dominated world. Disappointed, the main character, Jean, begins to write a scientific essay entitled "Beyond Reductionism." The exposure of the reductionist course (Western) civilization is taking and the possible remedies are the main themes in Burnier's further work—fiction or nonfiction.

Darwin, Marx, and Freud, the "anti-trinity," are at the root of this reductionist tendency, according to Burnier. They stripped both men and women of their spiritual values and reduced them to animal dullness, materialist greed, and sex drive. This theme underlies *De reis naar Kíthira* (1976; The Journey to Kíthira), a novel (though Burnier later said that the form of the essay would have better suited the ideas expressed in it), *De zwembadmentaliteit* (1979; The Swimming Pool Mentality), a collection of essays, and, again, the novels *De litteraire salon* (1983; The Literary Salon) and *De trein naar Tarascon* (1986; The Train to Tarascon) (the latter is Burnier's most traditionally structured work of fiction). Women, suggests the author, can save this sadly dehumanized world.

Feminism is for Burnier more than a fight for concrete women's rights and interests; it involves a total metamorphosis of civilization as we know it. Humanity can be saved and reborn, thanks to the full integration of feminine creativity (spiritual values) with abstract masculine thinking (rationalism, empiricism). Burnier argues her point referring to concepts and symbols from antiquity, eastern philosophy, and lost utopian civilizations. A desire to be assimilated in a big cosmic plan of divine love and the conviction that reincarnation is a step toward the projected better world increasingly prevail. *De droom der rede* (1984; The Dream of Reason), written under her real name, C.I. Dessaur, which she uses for her academic publications, is a philosophical treatment of these ambitious themes.

Andreas Burnier is also the writer of poetry, many lectures, book reviews and articles. She has spoken out for homosexual causes and against abortion and euthanasia, which she persistently associates with Nazist practices. More a "woman of ideas" than a novelist or even an essayist, Andreas Burnier has a special place in the present-day Dutch world of letters.

Works

Een tevreden lach (1965). *De verschrikkingen van het noorden* (1967). *Het jongensuur* (1969). *De huilende libertijn* (1970). *Poëzie, jongens en het gezelschap van geleerde vrouwen* (1974). *De reis naar Kíthira* (1976). *De zwembadmentaliteit* (1979). *Na de laatste keer* (1981). *De litteraire salon* (1983). *Belletrie 1965–1981* (1985). *Essays 1968–1985* (1985). *De trein naar Tarascon* (1986).
[C.I. Dessaur, pseud.], *Foundations of theory-formation in criminology; a methodological analysis* (1971). *De droom der rede* (1984).

Ria Vanderauwera

The Countess of Dia
ca. 1100–ca. 1200
Flourished late twelfth century, Dia (Drôme), Southern France
Genre(s): canso
Language(s): Occitan

The four *cansos* (or love songs) attributed to the Countess of Dia by the manuscripts in which they figure make her the *trobairitz* (or woman troubadour) with the largest extant corpus, both in terms of securely ascribed works and of the number of copies of those songs. "A chantar m'er" figures in no fewer than fifteen manuscripts, one of which also gives its melody. A short *vida* (or biography) of the Countess survives in four manuscripts, and conventionalized portrait miniatures illustrate nine of her songs. Although she has traditionally been referred to as "Beatritz de Dia," there is no textual authority for this usage, and it is more accurate to refer to her as the "Contessa de Dia," the only denomination used in the manuscripts that contain her poems.

Her *vida* says that she was the wife of William of Poitiers and later fell in love with Raimbaut d'Aurenga, about whom she composed many good songs. She has been identified with Philippa, wife of Aimar II of Poitiers, Count of Valentinois and Dia, with Beatrix, wife of William II of Poitiers, and with Isoarde, daughter of the Count of Dia. On the evidence of her *vida* and of the geographical proximity of Dia and Orange (*Aurenga* in Occitan), it has traditionally been asserted that she was the co-author, with the celebrated troubadour Raimbaut d'Aurenga, of the *tenso* (or dialogue poem) "Amics, en gran consirier." However, the historical accuracy of the *vida* is suspect, and there is no firm evidence to confirm this conjecture. To the contrary, the three manuscripts that contain the *tenso* ascribe it only to Raimbaut. The Raimbaut referred to in the *tenso* is not necessarily the troubadour of that name (d. 1173) but perhaps his grand-nephew Raimbaut IV (d. 1214). Alternatively, it is not impossible that author of the *vida*, noting thematic and linguistic similarities between the *tenso* and the Countess' songs, especially "Estat ai en greu consirier," simply invented the liaison between the two. Finally, it has been suggested that the *vida* is to be read metaphorically. The names of Raimbaut and William of Poitiers (which would refer to the first troubadour, who flourished in the late eleventh and early twelfth centuries) would represent the two styles of poetry practiced by the Countess.

In only one song, "Ab joi et ab joven m'apais," is

the joy of love evoked in terms of unalloyed happiness. In this song, which demonstrates considerable technical virtuosity in joining morphological pairs at the rhyme, the Countess celebrates the qualities of her beloved, whom she addresses under the pseudonym Floris, the protagonist of the romance *Flore et Blancheflor*. "Fin joi me don' alegranssa" begins as a celebration of the joy of love but degenerates into a denunciation of the slanderers and the envious who place obstacles in the way of love. "A chantar m'er," is a lament of unhappy love by a lady. The poetic voice protests against the indifference and arrogance of her beloved, complaining that her exceptional qualities are of no avail in preserving his affections. "Estat ai" is an erotic reverie. The latter two songs, both separation laments, conform to the paradigm of the Occitan *canso* with a feminine poetic voice as practiced by all of the other *trobairitz* (or woman troubadours) who composed in this genre. On the other hand, the Countess' other two songs ("Ab joi et ab joven" and "Fin joi me don' alegranssa") are unique among the *cansos* of the *trobairitz* in being simple transpositions of the troubadour *canso* with a masculine poetic voice.

Merritt R. Blakeslee

Isak Dinesen
1885–1962

a.k.a. Karen [Tanne] Christence Dinesen Blixen-Finecke
Born April 17, 1885, Rungsted, Denmark
Died September 7, 1962, Rungstedlund,
buried in the garden at Rungstedlund
Genre(s): novel, poetry, essay, drama
Language(s): Danish, English

With her fantastic tales and her fantastic life of adventure, heartache, suffering, and challenge, the Danish writer Karen Blixen has enjoyed international *renommé*. Writing in English and in Danish, Blixen won recognition in the United States, in Great Britain, in her native Denmark, indeed, internationally, for her extraordinary tales. Set in the past, in the aristocratic old order of *noblesse oblige*, Blixen's stories and her accounts of life in Africa attain a timeless quality. Her life as a member of an upper-class Danish family; as an aristocratic adventurer, the Baroness; and, as the storyteller *par excellence*, Isak Dinesen-Karen Blixen, is itself a legendary account of passion, pride

and pain, of glory and suffering, of fate, rise and fall for an idea—and an ideal.

Karen Christence Dinesen was born at Rungstedlund in Rungsted, Sjælland, Denmark, on April 17, 1885. The building in which she was born, the former

Isak Dinesen

Rungsted Inn, had had an interesting history prior to her birth: The king of Sweden, Karl II, had lodged there in 1700; the poet Johannes Ewald had made the Inn his home (1773 to 1776), indeed Karen Blixen's later study had been *Ewalds Stue*, Ewald's quarters; and Wilhelm Dinesen, Karen's father, had purchased and resided at Rungstedlund from 1879 to 1895, writing *Boganis Jagtbreve* (Boganis's Letters from the Hunt) during the decade 1880–1890. At the time of Dinesen's birth, Rungstedlund was still spartan in structure but close to the shore and the charming fishing villages. Dinesen's parents were the author and aristocratic landowner Wilhelm Dinesen (1845–1895) and Ingeborg Westenholz (1856–1939), the daughter of Regnar Westenholz, a member of the mercantile, financially prominent, and governing classes. Her upbringing, family, and orientation were all patrician, in complete harmony with the upper classes and removed from radical social and feminist movements. Together with her two sisters and her younger brothers, Dinesen was educated at home, under the supervision of her mother Ingeborg and her maternal aunt, Moster Bess, and a series of select house tutors. Dinesen's typically upper-class education concentrated on the role of woman as wife, mother, and participant in cultured leisure pursuits. From her father, Dinesen inherited an inclination for adventure, self-fulfillment, and freedom. Her mother's ideas of respectability, duty, and responsibility contrasted markedly to the free aristocratic ideals and adventurous spirit of her father, who had lived among the North American Indians (hence the name, Boganis), served in the 1864 Danish war with Prussia; participated in the Franco–Prussian War (1970–1971), the Commune Movement in Paris (*Paris under Communen*, 1889), *and* the Russian–Turkish War of 1877; and had also been a member of the Danish Parliament until his suicide in Copenhagen, on March 28, 1895.

With the unexpected death of Wilhelm Dinesen, Karen Dinesen, her brothers, and her sisters fell under the even more stringent discipline of Ingeborg Westenholz Dinesen and Moster Bess; as her mother before her, Ingeborg Dinesen was left a widow with five young children to bring up and with the attendant responsibilities at Rungstedlund and her own childhood home, Folehave. Many years later, Karen Dinesen (Blixen) recalled her mother's harsh directive to behave better than other children, as well as her own deep sorrow at her father's death when she was but an impressionable ten-year-old.

As a very young girl, Karen Dinesen found expression for her considerable fantasy in her own plays, poems, and stories for the families at Rungstedlund and Folehave. Her first play, "Hovmod staar for Fald" (Pride Goeth before a Fall), was performed by the eleven-year-old Karen, her family, and friends in May, 1896. The only revised, published comedy from her childhood was entitled "Sandhedens Hævn" (The Revenge of Truth). Between the ages of fifteen and twenty, Dinesen also published several poems, among them, "Medvind" (Breeze) and "Roersang" (The Rower's Song). Danish folktales, the Icelandic family sagas, and the Norwegian sagas were all important to Karen Dinesen's writing, even influencing her saga, "Grojotgard Alveson of Aud." In this early work, Karen Dinesen first expressed an ideal central to her entire oeuvre: "A man achieves the destiny he alone can claim, the fate he alone can bear." Dinesen's extensive study of Danish classical literature and English prose and poetry encouraged youthful dreams and fantasies.

As a young girl of the upper classes, Karen Dinesen frequented the family estates, Katholm in Jutland (the home of her paternal uncle, Wentzel Laurentzius

Dinesen) and, during the continual round of summer parties and balls, Frijsenborg, the home of her half-cousins, Daisy and Inger Frijs. Dinesen also visited her Swedish relatives in Skåne, members of the Blixen–Finecke family, including the brothers, Hans and Bror. The young Karen Dinesen fell head-over-heels in love with her cousin Hans, and she was later to marry (unhappily, as it turned out), Hans' twin, Bror. In 1898–1899, Karen Dinesen studied in Switzerland with a close friend, Else Bardenfleth; Dinesen's early love of Shakespeare was also encouraged and enriched by a stay in Oxford in 1904. From an early age, Karen Dinesen had demonstrated considerable talent for drawing, and she enrolled in Charlotte Sode's Drawing School in Copenhagen. In 1903, Dinesen was accepted as an art student at the Royal Academy, with Professor Viggo Johansen as her principal teacher. In addition to studying art, Karen Dinesen wrote short stories; three of these were accepted for publication under the pseudonym Osceola. On reading the first story, the literary historian and critic of the day, Valdemar Vedel, acknowledged the talent of its author. A literary career was a distinct possibility for Dinesen. However, she feared being trapped in a literary career. In a sense, Dinesen was already trapped by the female role; she yearned to pursue her dreams (and she did so, briefly, by excursions to Paris "to study art" in 1910 and to Rome in 1912), but she and her clever sisters were perhaps too unusual for many young men and not bohemian enough for the artistic life in poetry, song, and music.

On the twenty-third of December, 1912, Karen Dinesen announced her formal engagement to Bror Blixen-Finecke of Näsbyholm; the couple had no definite plans, only a determination to leave both Denmark and southern Sweden. A relative had recently returned from British East Africa (Kenya) and spoke glowingly of the prospects there. Bror Blixen left early in 1913 for Africa to find a suitable property in Kenya for a coffee plantation. With financial help from the Dinesen and Westenholz families, the couple acquired M'Bagathe and M'Bogani Estates with the intention of growing coffee as the Karen Coffee Co., Ltd. The elevation of the property proved far too high for coffee. Karen Dinesen left Denmark in December 1913 to join her fiancé, and the couple was married in a civil ceremony in Mombasa, on January 14, 1914.

For the first time in her life, Karen Blixen felt completely happy at the farm near Nairobi, under the Ngong Hills; she later poignantly expressed her feelings of belonging, of home and the rightness of her life in her work, *Den afrikanske Farm* (1937; Out of Africa). Karen Blixen quickly became involved in the lives of the European, principally English, settlers and in the affairs of the natives, the Kikuyu and the Masai. The farm proved a financial disaster from the very beginning, and Karen Blixen's life in Africa proved one of great economic trials and personal suffering, of great passion, love, *and* the adventure she had longed for. The marriage to Bror Blixen quickly collapsed; Bror Blixen had no real interest in the farm when the prospect of adventure and ready, more easily won, capital loomed on the horizon in the form of safaris into Kenya's wilderness. In addition, Bror Blixen infected his young wife with syphilis, and in 1915 she had to return to Denmark to undergo secret and belated treatment. Bror and Karen Blixen separated in 1921, finally divorcing in 1925; from 1921 on, Karen Blixen tried single-handedly during her long absences in Denmark, with help from her brother Thomas and her servant Farah Aden, to keep the coffee plantation from failing. At this point, Karen Blixen began to write stories, preparing for an inevitable return to Denmark and a possible literary career. In 1925, Blixen visited the prominent critic Georg Brandes in Copenhagen; with his assistance, her very early marionette comedy, "Sandhedens Hævn" (The Revenge of Truth), was published in *Tilskueren* in May 1926 under the name of Karen Blixen-Finecke.

Despite her fears and doubts, the failure of her health, her farm, her finances, and her marriage, Karen Blixen retained a belief in her own talent; her brother, Thomas Dinesen, was her loyal companion and support during her early literary comeback years in Kenya, even before she left Africa for good. Not only did she receive encouragement from Thomas; she also received literary and artistic critique from her one love, the English aristocrat and emigré, Denys Finch Hatton (1887–1931). Finch Hatton listened to her stories, commenting freely and competently on her efforts; he read the Bible and fine literature with her. Denys Finch Hatton was, quite simply, the decisive catalyst for Karen Blixen. Denys Finch Hatton died in an airplane crash on May 4, 1931, toward the end of Karen Blixen's stay in Kenya. By 1931, even before Finch Hatton's death, it was only too apparent that the farm would fail despite all Karen Blixen's efforts, loans, and struggles, and in August of 1931, accompanied by the ever-faithful Farah, Karen Blixen retraced her route of 18 years before, returning via Mombasa to Europe and an uncertain future.

Karen Blixen returned to Rungstedlund, her mother, and home with a determination to continue writing in English but with no literary contacts. With the financial help of Thomas Dinesen and a warm welcome from her mother Ingeborg Dinesen, Karen Blixen worked continually, alone, in two separate rooms of the family home. All her efforts to create a literary life in place of all she had lost in love, health, finances, and hopes for Africa resulted in her first successful collection of stories in English, *Seven Gothic Tales*, published initially by the American publishers Harrison Smith and Robert Haas, in April 1935. For this collection, Karen Blixen chose the pseudonym Isak Dinesen as part of a literary stratagem and mask to free herself from literary tastes for realism. The name Isak, which means laughter in Hebrew, was also particularly appropriate for the ironic wit of an author who had already experienced much joy—and sorrow—in life. *Seven Gothic Tales* was an immediate success in the United States, England, and Sweden. Karen Blixen's own translation *Syv fantastiske fortællinger*, was published in September 1935. *Seven Gothic Tales* depicted individuals invariably driven toward the fulfillment of their destiny. Blixen's use of an archaic narrative style and her inclusion of the irrational link the author to trends in modern European literature.

Karen Blixen's next work, the beautiful and poignant account of her African adventure and life, *Den afrikanske Farm* (Out of Africa), was written in Skagen in Jutland (in both Danish and English) and was published in 1937. The work begins on a note of tragedy, with mention of a farm once owned and now lost for good: "I had a farm in Africa at the foot of the Ngong Hills" (*Den afrikanske Farm*, p. 9). In *Den afrikanske Farm*, Karen Blixen combines autobiography and myth and deeper personal insights. In Africa, in a time of joy and tragedy, Karen Blixen's horizons widened far beyond youthful conflicts between bourgeois Christian responsibility and a free life of danger, love, and nature. Blixen came to view the free aristocrat as an ideal, one who fully comprehends destiny, joy, and tragedy. In *Den afrikanske Farm*, Blixen no longer writes of responsibility, of "doing the right thing," but of the duty to live as God planned, to fulfill one's special destiny, however tragic, in a universal design or an even greater mosaic. The writer Karen Blixen gained in stature and nobility by understanding God's intention and living according to her own destiny. As she eloquently expressed it, "Yes, certainly, I thought, that was the intention, and now I understand it all" (*Den afrikanske Farm*, p. 205). In her work on the African experience, Karen Blixen's defeat is transformed to victory, her own fate becomes a blessing, for she has lived her part in God's plan; Blixen has realized final triumph in the sheer telling of her tale—and myth— of Kenya before the land was changed by commerce and a new world.

Karen Blixen's ideals of duty, honor, and destiny, of aristocratic *noblesse oblige*, and of the elemental grandeur of tragedy are also important in *Vintereventyr* (1947; Winter's Tales). In *Vintereventyr*, characters either fulfill or betray God's plan, and their destiny. The tale "Sorg-Agre" (Sorrow Acre), for example, is a deceptively simple story built on a 1634 legend from southern Jutland. In the legend, a young man has been accused of setting fires on the estate of a country lord. The Blixen story from *Vintereventyr* takes place around 1775 and includes reference to the Danish author, Johannes Ewald, and his "new work" *Balders Død* (Balder's Death). The youth's mother strikes a bargain with the old lord, agreeing to reap, harvest, and bind an entire field of corn, "sorrow acre," a superhuman feat, in exchange for her son's life. Anne-Marie, a simple farmer's wife, wins her son's freedom by offering her own life. But Blixen's reworking of the legend into her tale is not as simple as it would appear. The old feudal order, represented by the aristocratic lord, apparently triumphs, for the lord stands by his word and by the terrible tragic bargain, come what may, and Anne-Marie pays the supreme price for her son's life. However, a new voice speaking for the individual enters the tale in the person of Adam. The young, aspiring nephew of the old lord, Adam, will inherit the landed estates, the old lord's young wife, and a new era. The old system of feudal lord and subject will end—or has already ended—but, in spite of its demise, the aristocratic order of honor, law, and tragedy still holds a fascination. Despite his enthusiasm for the new time, Adam recognizes a pattern of order and harmony beyond the fate, tragic or fortuitous, of a single individual ("Sorg-Agre," *Fra det gamle Danmark*: 2, 233).

Vintereventyr appeared during World War II (1947), a difficult, trying time in Denmark as elsewhere, when Blixen's readers needed fantasy and heroic tales of tragedy. For Karen Blixen, World War II brought another round of financial duress, as she was unable to secure the American and English honoraria for her works, *Seven Gothic Tales*, *Out of Africa*, and *Winter's Tales*. As financially threatened as ever, Karen Blixen was on the point of selling Rungstedlund. In 1944, Blixen published another book, what the Danes call "en gyser" (a thriller), *Gengældelsens Veje* (1946; The Angelic Avengers), under the fantastic pseudonym Pierre Andrézel. The book caused quite a stir, and Blixen later disclaimed, then acknowledged, authorship. Between 1942 and 1956, Blixen worked on a monumental novel of one hundred chapters, *Albondocani*, a religious work or work with a religious theme. She was unable to realize her plan for

Albondocani, but her finances, as precarious as her health, pressed her onward, and she did complete a single chapter of the work, *Kardinalens tredje Historie* (The Cardinal's Third Story) in 1952.

In the late 1940s, Blixen's Rungstedlund—and the mythical Baroness herself—became a drawing card for a group of younger Copenhagen intellectuals. The editors of the new literary periodical *Heretica*, Thorkild Bjørnvig and Bjørn Paulsen; the authors Frank Jæger, Aage Henriksen, and Jørgen Gustava Brandt; the publisher-actor Ole Wivel; and the actor, Erling Schroeder, were all drawn to the aristocratic aura, to the "baroness-myth," which Blixen revelled in and was only too eager to foster, and to Rungstedlund, which had become a literary salon.

Karen Blixen also began a series of radio conversations, commentaries, stories, and readings: *Daguerrotypier* (1951; Daguerrotypes). Blixen's own English stories, "Uncle Seneca" (1951; Onkel Seneca), "Babette's Feast" (1950; Babettes Gæstebud), and "The Ghost Horses" (1950; Spøgelseshestene), were also translated into Danish and read on the radio. Blixen also used the radio to speak out on a variety of causes: humane treatment of animals, the dispossessed, and, finally, efforts to preserve and designate Rungstedlund as a national monument. After her near-fatal illnesses of 1955–1956, Blixen's literary career was necessarily curtailed. *Sidste Fortællinger* (Last Tales) appeared in 1957 and *Skæbne-Anekdoter* (Anecdotes of Destiny) in 1958, but both books were reduced in terms of formal plan. "Ringen" (The Ring), the last story of the last collection, is true to Blixen's oeuvre in dealing with the mystery that fatefully changes life—for good or ill.

Karen Blixen had first won acclaim in the United States and, at the very end of her life, in early 1959, she accepted an invitation from the Fund for the Advancement of Education, Ford Foundation, to appear in New York, Washington, and Boston. The four-month stay and her reading/lecture tour proved very taxing, and Blixen returned home greatly weakened. She continued writing, producing the Danish version of *Shadows on the Grass* (1960; Skygger paa Græsset) at Dragør, the home of her friend and secretary, Clara Svendsen. At Dragør and Rungstedlund, Blixen continued to receive visitors, writers, family, and friends until her death at seventy-seven on September 7, 1962. She died in the home where her fantastic, eventful, and (as she described it) wholly, entirely happy life had begun.

Karen Blixen has been called both an author of timeless works, of works pitting individuals of any age against fate, universal plan, and destiny, and "a foreign bird in Danish literature," a writer removed from her land and time and from contemporary modernism and realism. The self-created (and sustained) baroness-of-Rungsted-myth; the aristocratic ideal of *Out of Africa*; the fascination with the archaic, feudal aristocracy, all seem to distance her from our century, from our time and culture. However, in creating symbolic characters, Blixen explores inner powers warring within an individual. Shared archetypal myths, symbols, and beliefs live on universally as part of a greater pattern and plane, as Blixen explores the mind of the individual, the self, and the I, as well as the force, direction, and influence of life's pattern on the symbolic characters of her story-myths. Karen Blixen's oeuvre shares much with modernism in its presentation through reflections, reversals, and breaks with tradition; her authorship is also distinguished from modernism by its reworking of the historical-social bases for interpretation. With her fantastic stories of the past, of other enchanting, fanciful, and often tragic times, and with her mythically poignant and grand story of Africa, her life and symbolic dream of life in *Den afrikanske Farm*, Karen Blixen has created a symbolic world filled with wonder and a sense of individual destiny within a far greater, more impressive universal scheme.

Works

"Grjotgard Alveson of Aud" (1905). "Eneboerne" [The Hermits] (1907). "Pløjeren" [The Plowman] (1907). "Familien deCats" [The deCats Family] (1909). "Sandhedens Hævn" [The Revenge of Truth] (1926). *Seven Gothic Tales* [*Syv fantastiske fortællinger*] (1935). *Den afrikanske Farm* [Out of Africa] (1937). "Sorte og hvide i Afrika," Foredrag afholdt i Lund (1938); *Blixeniana* (1979). *Vintereventyr* [Winter's Tales] (1947). *Gengældelsens Veje* [The Angelic Avengers] (1944, 1946). *Breve fra et Land i Krig* [Letters from a Land at War] (1940, 1948). "The Ghost Horses." *Ladies' Home Journal* (October 1951). *Daguerrotypier* (1951). *Kardinalens tredje Historie* [The Cardinal's Third Story] (1952). *Sidste Fortællinger* [Last Tales] (1957). *Skæbne-Anekdoter* [Anecdotes of Destiny] (1958). "Babettes Gæstebud" [Gabriel Axel, Babettes Gæstebud] (1958; film, 1987). "Rungstedlund: En radio-tale" (1958). "On Mottoes of My Life" (1960). "Introduction," Truman Capote, *Holly* (1960). *Shadows on the Grass* [Skygger paa Græsset] (1960). "Sandhedens Hævn" [The Revenge of Truth: A Marionette Comedy] (1960). "Introduktion," Basil Davidson, *Det genfundne Afrika* (1962). *Osceola: 1962* ("Grojtgard Alvesøn og Aud," "Pløjeren," "Eneboerne," "Familien deCats"; Poems: "Vinger," "Maaneskin," "Medvind," "Vuggesang,"

"En Stjerne," "Balladen om mit Liv," "Ex Africa.") *Ehrengard* (1963). *Fra det gamle Danmark I-II*, From old Denmark I–II (1963). *Kongesønnerne og andre efterladte fortællinger* [The Princes and Other Posthumous Tales]. "Karen Blixen fortæller," Louisiana Grammofonplader (1964).

Essays: Essays, 1965: "Mit Livs Mottoer" [My Life's Mottos] (1960). "Daguerrotypier" [Daguerrotypes] (1951). "En Baaltale med 14 Aars forsinkelse" (1953). "Fra Lægmand til Lægmand" [From Layman to Layman] (1954). "Breve fra et Land i Krig" [Reunion with England] (1944). "Om Retskrivning" (1938). "H.D. Branner: Rytteren" (1952). *Samlede Essays* [Collected Essays] (1969, 1977). *Moderne Ægteskab og andre Betragtninger* [Modern Marriage and Other Considerations] (1924; first published 1977). *Breve fra Afrika: 1914–1931* [Letters from Africa: 1914–1931 (1978–1979, 1984, 1986, 1991). *Kongesønnerne og andre efterladte Fortællinger* [The Princess and Other Posthumous Tales] (1985, 1992). *Samlede Essays* [Collected Essays] (1985, 1992). *Karyatiderne. En ufuldendt Historie* (1993); *The Caryatid. An Unfinished Tale.* (1993).

Lanae Hjortsvang Isaacson

Margaret Drabble
1939–

Born June 5, 1939, Sheffield, Yorkshire, England
Genre(s): novel, short story, screenplay, biography, journalism
Language(s): English

Widely read and well received by both critics and the general audience, Margaret Drabble plays a lively role in British culture. In addition to her novels, she has written several stories, screenplays, and a biography of Arnold Bennett. She has written or edited several books on literary subjects and scores of reviews and other pieces for journals, newspapers, and magazines. She writes on popular and literary topics for school children and adults, for scholars and laymen. Frequently interviewed and photographed, the subject of several feature articles as well as much critical commentary, she also appears on televized literary programs, participates on governmental councils and Arts Council tours, and teaches adult education one day a week at Morley College.

Drabble went from The Mount, a Quaker boarding school in York, to Newham College, Cambridge

University, on scholarship, receiving a brilliant starred-First in English literature. While her fiction is located within, enriched by, and played off against the literary language, traditions, and characters she knows so well, she deliberately chooses not to be a high-culture artist disengaged from day-to-day realities. Eminently accessible and readable, she is attuned to herself and to ordinary experience, vividly rendering the ordinary with intelligence, learning, insight, and humor. Her informal, intimate, personal voice seems to speak directly for a whole generation of readers, particularly women, in Great Britain, the United States, and other countries.

The protagonists of Drabble's novels have followed the course and concerns of her own life: young women leaving university, getting married and separated, birthing children, having affairs, raising progressively older children, reaching midlife, and wondering what next. The surface lucidity of her early novels and the seeming candor of her first-person narrators have misled some readers into assuming that little critical distance separates the author from her narrators. In fact, the tension between surface and meaning gives to Drabble's work an unresolved, exploratory quality quite different from the popular women's fiction it deceptively resembles. Her fiction at its best is a virtual "double-voiced discourse" exemplifying the tension that many women experience who are struggling to define themselves within a patriarchal frame of reference. She examines with subtlety and moral acuity the very tissue and structure of women's lives. From her first comparatively slight novel, *A Summer Bird-Cage* (1963), her first-person characterizations have grown in depth and subtlety, reaching their culmination in the portrait of Jane Gray in her most technically experimental narrative, *The Waterfall* (1969). Whereas each of these narrators lives in a solipsistic world and uses her body as a decorative front and self-protective retreat from external realities, *The Waterfall* records Jane Gray's orgasmic breaking out of the constrictions of female identity. The significance of this experience is equivocally examined by Jane as are the lives and experiences of the narrators who precede her.

The third-person novels of Drabble's middle period move further out of the solipsistic spaces of the early novels. They record a more graphic exodus from the constricting world of childhood: its geography, classbound values, and moral outlook. Northern landscapes are rejected in each novel for the cosmopolitan environment of London, duplicating the journey Drabble herself made from Sheffield to London. Although born into a liberal, professional, middle-class family, Drabble draws from her family's rural, working-class roots in her fiction, dramatizing particularly the "need to escape" from oppressive provincial limitations. "By will and by strain" her characters create new selves and new worlds out of preconceived "golden" fantasies: a golden Jerusalem, a Bunyanesque holy city, realms of gold. Literary influence continues to be important: *Jerusalem the Golden* (1967) was, Drabble admits, "profoundly affected" by Bennett and by his character Hilda Lessways. *The Needle's Eye* (1972) is characterized by its skillful adaptation of Jamesian central intelligence and its probing psychological and moral complexities. The interconnected network of characters, images, literary allusions, and levels of reference of *The Realms of Gold* (1975) initiates her more expansive later style.

While these novels link up to the sociomoral tradition of the English novel—which Drabble outspokenly values over modernist experiments—they, like her earlier work, continue to be in many ways double-voiced and equivocal, mediating between traditional realistic humanism and modern perspectives. "Omniscience has its limits," the narrator of *The Realms of Gold* candidly admits, calling attention to the fictionality of this carefully constructed world. Similarly, character is not at all stable, and perhaps not knowable. Because the characters' lives are such a composite of psychological determinism and willful self-creation, the boundaries between the real and the imagined are equivocal for characters and readers alike. Furthermore, her use of houses and landscapes as objective correlatives of mental states lends considerable subtlety and depth to these works, dramatizing her intense preoccupation with the "effect of landscape upon the soul." Drabble is resolutely traditional in her liberal belief that the individual must link up to something larger than the self—a place, a community, shared values, the past. All of her work is about the conflict between free will and determinism, between the search for free feeling and the desire for some measure of control and judgment. The search for a suitable moral and human habitation is the compelling genesis of her art. The tension within these middle novels resides in the apparent freedom of the individual to create a new self coupled with his or her necessary circumspection within geographical, communal, and historical contexts.

In *The Ice Age* (1977) and *The Middle Ground* (1980), Drabble focuses on the commonly shared contexts and experiences of urban middle-class life, detailing the texture, the trends, and the trappings of mass culture. The most vividly memorable passages of both books depict the dehumanized, noisy, dirty, ugly, and graffiti-ridden world that is modern urban Britain. The environment in which characters live is largely shaped from without. The individual may be, like Anthony Keating in *The Ice Age,* no more than a "weed upon the tide of history" doomed to enact a drama that differs only in particulars from other members of his or her generation.

Like their author, the characters, successful in their professional lives, are now experiencing a midlife reappraisal of self. The characters are less obsessed with the past than they are with the quality and significance of the lives they are now leading, lives which strikingly resemble those of their associates. Drabble's characters crave connection, and in midlife the connection they seek is increasingly social and metaphysical. What is happening to individuals reflects, in turn, what is happening to the British nation as a whole, which is getting older, tired, staid, facing crises, going through some strange and disorienting metamorphosis. *The Ice Age* is highly controlled, a visibly plotted work, and so too are the lives of the characters it chronicles, whereas *The Middle Ground* is plotless and shapeless; the novel's structure is open to contingency just as the lives of its characters are.

Because she refuses to stay in the same spot, her fiction is constantly nourished by her own personal development. As a result, Drabble, perhaps more than any other contemporary British woman novelist, has the opportunity to produce a distinctively female work that surpasses gender limitations. Her mediating position between "male" and "female" concerns and traditions, literary and popular issues and perspectives, the literary and the real, the traditional and the modern gives equivocal resonance and strength to her fiction. Her attempt to "only connect" these diverse strains is the generating energy of her work.

Works

A Summer Bird-Cage (1963). *The Garrick Year* (1964) *The Millstone* (1965). *Wordsworth* (1966). *Jerusalem the Golden* (1967). *The Waterfall* (1969). *The Needle's Eye* (1972). *Virginia Woolf: A Personal Debt* (1973). *Arnold Bennett: A Biography* (1974). *The Realms of Gold* (1975). *The Ice Age* (1977). *For Queen and Country: Britain in the Victorian Age* (1978). *A Writer's Britain: Landscape in Literature* (1979). *The Middle Ground* (1980). *The Tradition of Women's Fiction: Lectures in Japan* (1982). *The Radiant Way* (1987). *Natural Curiosity* (1990). *Concise Oxford Companion to English Literature,* ed. (1990), *The Gates of Ivory* (1993).

Joanne V. Creighton

Stéphanie Ducrest, Countess of Genlis
1746–1830

Born January 25, 1746, Champercy, near Autun, France
Died December 31, 1830, Paris
Genre(s): poetry, novel, tract, children's literature, drama, memoirs
Language(s): French

Mistress to the Duke of Orleans (later Philippe-Egalité), tutor to the future Louis Philippe I and his royal siblings, friend of Talleyrand, and correspondent to Napoleon, Stéphanie de Genlis was involved in political events from before the French Revolution through the Revolution of 1830. She was a prolific and popular writer of novels, educational tracts, children's literature, and personal memoirs. Her works total approximately 140 volumes.

Caroline-Stéphanie-Félicité Ducrest de Saint Aubin, Countess of Genlis and later Marquise of Sillery, lived a life lifted from romance. After her father's financial disaster, Genlis went to Paris, where at the age of ten she began to develop a lifelong taste for high society, theater, and learning; she also studied music avidly, devoting as many as ten hours a day to practice. Genlis was always a formidable presence; in Paris, her beautiful face and voice, plus her skill at playing the harp, became her ticket to aristocratic society. Genlis's marriage also belongs to the world of romance. Charles-Alexis Bruslart, who had seen a miniature of Genlis when he met her father in an English prison, went to Paris upon his release and fell in love with her; their marriage was secret, and met with strong opposition from his family. Genlis was seventeen.

Genlis became the mother of three children and a social phenomenon; she met the Duke of Chartres (later the Duke of Orleans, and finally Philippe-Egalité) and probably became his mistress. At thirty-one Genlis retired to Bellechasse with the Duke of Chartres's young princesses, her own children, and an "adopted daughter" who may have been Genlis's illegitimate daughter with the Duke; later, Genlis became tutor or "gouvernante" to the young princesses, an unprecedented move that raised scandal.

During the tumult of the French Revolution, Genlis took the Princess Adelaide, her most devoted student, to safety in England, then brought her back to France at the Duke's insistence. Labeled as émigrés, Genlis and Adelaide were ordered to leave France and finally took refuge in a Swiss convent; Genlis's husband and the Duke of Orleans were both executed.

From 1793 until 1800 she lived as an exile, often unwelcome, sometimes in danger, and always poor. Genlis received help from her son-in-law, from her protector General Dumouriez, and from her friend Talleyrand; she eked out her meager funds by painting, giving harp lessons, and by writing. She produced a great deal of work from 1794 on that sold readily. Finally Genlis was permitted to return to Paris, but had great difficulty adjusting to the now unfamiliar city.

In 1804 she received a pension from the emperor Napoleon and corresponded with him. In 1812 new editions of her works came out; Napoleon gave her the honorary title of Inspector of the schools in her Parisian borough. She lived through the Revolution of 1830; having seen her former student come to the throne as Louis-Philippe I and having expressed the opinion that he lacked the strength necessary to be king. Shortly afterword she died.

A large number of Genlis's early writings concern education. Her *Theatre of Education* (1779–1780), the *Theatre of Society* (1781), *The Annals of Virtue* (1782), *Adelaide and Theodore, or Letters on Education* (1782), and *Tales of the Castle* (1784) all reflected her experience at Bellechasse; some characters in *Tales of the Castle* even bear the names of those children who listened to the stories. *Adelaide and Theodore* is a response to Rousseau's *Émile*. Rousseau's Sophie was a secondary character existing primarily as a future wife for Émile, but Genlis focuses on Adelaide's rather than on the boy's education. Genlis believed that since girls were born to a "monotonous and dependent life," they should receive their education at home from their mothers, preparing themselves for future life as wives who counsel their husbands wisely while remaining submissive to them, and as mothers who mold their own children's characters. Genlis believed, in opposition to Rousseau, that "man, if left to himself, would be necessarily vengeful and would consequently be lacking in spiritual nobility and generosity." The *Theatre of Education* offers plentiful examples of young boys and girls who, exiled to convents, permitted to travel around Europe following fashion, or left to the care of a lazy governess, risk becoming incorrigible fools, liars, and gossips.

Genlis's *Theatre of Education* puts her principles into practice. Although the moral message of her little plays can be heavy-handed and although the good characters espouse only the most virtuous sentiments, the pleasure of histrionic performance is manifest. The plays are primarily for girls, although there are some parts for brothers and fathers.

While Genlis indulges a taste for melodrama, the importance of social responsibility is also hammered home. Even in "Beauty and the Monster," a reworking of the fairy tale, the heroine can overcome her aversion to the monster (who of course becomes a prince) not only because he loves her but because he charitably provides a haven for the "unhappy." From these plays, one also glimpses the wisdom Genlis must have gained from her hard experience with court intrigue; "The Generous Enemies," for instance, shows how two devoted friends can be turned against one another by a scheming sister-in-law and a profligate husband. Most poignant, perhaps, is "The Good Mother" who is willing to separate from her best-loved daughter in order to make her a good match. Considering Genlis's closeness to her charges and their devotion to her, the plays' insistence on the primacy of a mother or governess who acts as mother is both touching and coercive.

Although Genlis's works for children stress the individual's power to save himself from bad habits and influences, her novels, written primarily during her exile and the years of poverty after her return to France, recognize more clearly the pernicious effects of illicit love and intrigue in the adult world. *The Knights of the Swan*, the first novel published during her exile, is different in form and intent from most of Genlis's novels. A highly artificial "troubadour novel" celebrating the old regime symbolically through the court of Charlemagne, the novel contrasts the constitutional monarchy of Charlemagne with the anarchic rebellion of the Saxons, who represent the Jacobins during the Reign of Terror. Genlis apparently hoped to ingratiate herself with the French émigrés as well as to earn badly needed money. Her best known historical novels, *La Duchesse de la Vallière* (1804) and *Mademoiselle de Clermont* (1802) (often considered her best novel) are more melodramatic.

In *The Influence of Women on French Literature*, Genlis argues that women are not suited to epic or tragedy, but to "real actions." Genlis takes her own advice in three novels dealing with unmarried mothers: *The Rival Mothers* (1806), *Alphonsine* (1806), and *Alphonse* (1809). Her choice of this topic is especially interesting because Pamela, Genlis's adopted daughter, was rumored to be her illegitimate child, fathered by the Duke of Orléans. The mothers in these novels, having become entangled in illicit affairs, resist attempts to deprive them of their children; eventually they give the children to the care of another family but supervise their education, either at close quarters or from afar.

Genlis's *Memoirs* came out in 1825; and although they contain inaccuracies caused by failure of memory or Genlis's need to justify herself, they contain valuable information about people and events of the eighteenth century. In her last years, Genlis hoped to rewrite Diderot's *Encyclopedia* to make it reflect orthodox religious and moral principles. Her reverence for religion and morality remained unshaken.

Genlis's educational works were popular in England during the 1780s and went through multiple editions but were less popular in the nineteenth century. Her novels sold well, but she was treated with contempt by later Victorian critics. The contradiction between Genlis's devotion to religion, morality, and feminine submission and her social and literary career, plus the close relationship between her life and art, make her a fascinating subject for study.

Works

Théâtre à l'usage des jeunes personnes (1779–1780). *Théâtre de Société* (1781). *Les Annales de la Vertu ou cours d'histoire à l'usage des jeunes personnes* (1782). *Adèle et Théodore ou Lettres sur l'éducation* (1782). *Les Veillées du Château ou cours de morale à l'usage des enfants par l'auteur d'Adèle et Théodore* (1784). *Discours sur l'éducation de M. le Dauphin et sur l'adoption* (1790). *Discours sur la suppression des Couvens de religieuses et l'éducation publique des femmes* (1791). *Lecons d'une Gouvernante à ses Elèves* (1791). *Les Chevaliers du Cygne ou la cour de Charlemagne* (1795). *Précis de la conduite de Madame de Genlis depuis la Révolution* (1796). *Les Petits Émigrés ou Correspondence de quelques enfants* (1798). *Les Voeux téméraires ou L'enthousiasme* (1799). *La Petit La Bruyère ou Caractères et moeurs de ce siècle à l'usage des enfants* (1799). *Les Mères Rivales ou la Calomnie* (1800). *Nouvelle heures à l'usage des enfants* (1801). *Nouvelle méthode d'Ensignement pour la première enfance* (1801). *Projet d'une Ecole rurale pour l'éducation des filles* (1801). *Mademoiselle de Clermont, Nouvelle Historique* (1802). *L'Epouse impertinente par air, suivet de Mari corrupteur et de la femme philosophe* (1804). *Souvenirs de Félicie L.* (1804). *La Duchesse de la Vallière* (1804). *Le Comte de Corke ou la séduction sans artifice* (1805). *Madame de Maintenon* (1806). *Alphonsine ou la Tendresse maternelle* (1806). *Suite des Souvenirs de Félicie* (1807). *La Siège de La Rochelle ou le Malheur de la conscience* (1807). *Bélisaire* (1808). *Sainclair ou la victime des Sciences et des Arts* (1808). *Alphonse ou le Fils naturel* (1809). *La maison rustique* (1810). *De l'Influence des femmes sur la littérature française comme protectrices des Lettres ou comme auteurs* (1811). *Les Bergères de Madian ou la Jeunesse de Moise* (1812). *Mademoiselle de La Fayette, ou le Siècle de Louis XIII* (1813). *Les Hermites des Marais Pontins* (1814). *Histoire de Henri le Grand* (1815). *Jeanne de France, Nouvelle Historique* (1816). *Le Journal de la Jeunesse* (1816). *Les Battuécas* (1816). *Dictionnaire critique et raisonné des étiquettes de la Cour, usages du monde, etc.* (1818). *Les Voyages poétiques d'Eugène et d'Antonine* (1818). *Almanach de la Jeunesse en vers et en prose* (1819). *Les Parvenus ou les Aventures de Julien Delmours* (1819). *Pétrarque et Laure* (1819). *L'Intrépide* (1820). *Le Siècle de Louis XIV* (1820). *Palmyre et Flaminie* (1821). *Six Nouvelles morales et Religieuses* (1821). *Les Jeux champêtres des Enfants* (1821). *Six Nouvelles morales et religieuses* (1821). *Les Dîners du baron d'Holbach* (1822). *Les Veillées de la chaumière* (1823). *Les Prisonniers* (1824). *Mémoires inédits sur le 18ᵉ siècle et la Revolution Française* (1825). *Oeuvres Complètes* (1825). *Thérésina ou l'Enfant de la Providence* (1826). *Inès de Castro, nouvelle suivie de la mort de Pline* (1826). *Les Soupers de la Maréchale de Luxembourg* (1828). *Le Dernier Voyage de Nelgis ou Mémoires d'un vieillard* (1828). *Manuel de la jeune feMme Guide Complet de la maîtresse de maison* (1829). *Athénaïs ou le Château de Coppet en 1807* (posthumous) (1831). *Lettres inédits de Mme de Genlis à son fils adoptif Casimir Baecker* (1902). *Dernieres lettres d'amour. Correspondence inedites de la comtesse de Genlis avec le comte Anatole de Montesquiou* (1954).

Translations: *Theatre of Education* (1781). *Adelaide and Theodore: or Letters on Education* (1783). *The Beauty and the Monster* (1785). *Hagar in the Desert* (1785). *Sacred Dramas*, tr. Thomas Holcroft, in *Three Centuries of Drama: England, 1751–1800* (1785). *Tales of the Castle*, tr. Thomas Holcroft (1785). *Adventures of Alphonso after the Destruction of Lisbon* (1787). *The Beauties of Genlis* (1787). *Lessons of a Governess to her Pupils* (1792). *The Knights of the Swan; or, the Court of Charlemagne* (1796). *Short Account of the Conduct of Mme de Genlis, since the Revolution* (1796). *The History of the Duchess of C—* (1798). *Alphonso and Dalinda: or, The Magic of Art and Nature*, tr. Thomas Holcroft (1799). *Rash Vows: or The Effects of Enthusiasm* (1799). *The Young Exiles; or, Correspondence of Some Juvenile Emigrants* (1799). *La Bruyere the Less: or, Characters and Manners of the Children of the Present Age* (1800). *A New Method of Instruction for Children* (1800). *The Rival Mothers* (1800). *The Depraved Husband and the Philosophic Wife* (1803). *Panrose; or The Palace and the Cottage* (1803). *The Castle of Kolmeras, to Which Is Added Ida Molten* (1804). *The Duchess of la Valliere* (1804). *Alphonsine: or, Maternal Affection* (1806). *Madame de Maintenon* (1806). *The Juvenile Theater* (1807). *The Duke of*

Lazun; an Historical Romance (1808). *The Earl of Cork: or, Seduction without Artifice* (1808). *Recollections of Felicia L.* (1808). *The Siege of Rochelle; or, The Christian Heroine* (1808). *The Traveller's Companion* (1809). *Belisarius; a Historical Romance* (1810). *Sainclair, or The Victim to the Arts and Sciences* (1813). *Mademoiselle de La Fayette, an Historical Novel* (1814). *Jane of France, an Historical Novel* (1816). *A Manual Containing the Expressions Most Used in Travelling* (1817). *Placide, A Spanish Tale* (1817). *The New Era: or, Adventures of Julien Delmours: Related by Himself* (1817). *The Solitary Family: or, The Norman Hut*, in Garret, William, *A Right Pleasant and Famous Book of Histories* (1818). *Petrarch and Laura* (1820). *Six Tales, Moral and Religious* (1822). *Child of Nature*, tr. Elizabeth Inchbald, in *Three Centuries of Drama: English, 1751–1800* (1825). *Memoirs of the Countess de Genlis* (1825). *New Moral Tales* (1825). *Eugene and Iolotte; a Tale for Children* (1828). *Joseph and his Brothers; Fruits of a Good Education*, in *Three Centuries of Drama: American* (1843).

Christy Desmet

Amandine-Aurore-Lucie Dupin, Baronne Dudevant
1804–1876

a.k.a. George Sand, Jules Sand
Born July 1, 1804, Paris, France
Died June 8, 1876, Nohant
Genre(s): novel, essay, tale, drama, political articles, letters, autobiography
Language(s): French

Born into the provincial aristocracy, Aurore was raised by her paternal grandmother, an admirer of Rousseau, at the family château de Nohant in Berry and educated at the Couvent des Anglaises in Paris. She returned to Nohant where she was allowed the freedom to develop intellectually and to become acquainted with provincial life. She resumed reading Rousseau, Shakespeare, Byron, Chateaubriand, and other Romantics whose influence on her literary style and romantic point of view was apparent from the beginning of her writing career. In 1822 she married the baron Dudevant, a coarse, narrow-minded retired army officer. After eight years of loveless marriage and two children, she fled to Paris where she took up the bohemian life and tried to earn her living by writing.

Dressed like a man ("in order to be free," she said), smoking cigarettes, and engaging in a series of amorous liaisons (usually with younger men), Aurore soon made her reputation as a "free spirit" and a writer. It took courage for her to live an independent life, earning her own living, and openly defying public morality. In 1831 she wrote, "I am embarking on the stormy sea of literature. I need to live. . . . [Social] conventions are rules for people without soul and without virtue. [Public] opinion is a prostitute who gives herself to those who pay her most dearly." Thus, Aurore launched her long and productive career which falls into roughly three phases: the Romantic period when she attacked society and decried the restricted lives of women; her support of the various "isms" that would lead to a better (utopian) society; the idyllic pastoral novels which were set in her native Berry, and also the more prosaic novels of manners.

In 1831 she collaborated with her lover, Jules Sandeau, on a novel, *Rose et blanche, ou la Comédienne et la religieuse* (1831; Rose and White, or the Comedienne and the Nun), using the pseudonym "Jules Sand." Writing alone for the first time under the name George Sand, she published a romantic novel, *Indiana* (1832; in English, 1935), which was the first of her successful works. This novel was based on personal experience, though she denied it was a self-portrait. However, one can find the author in all her works—the independent individual, sensitive, misunderstood, and suffering from societal restrictions. Themes of romantic passion dominated the first phase of her literary career which included her novels *Indiana* and *Valentine* (1832; in English, 1902), *Lélia* (1833) *Jacques* (1834; in English, 1847), and *Mauprat* (1837; in English, 1847). Trapped in an unhappy marriage and personally affected by the legal and social inequalities that limited women's choice of lifestyle, she proclaimed their right to pursue free and unshackled lives. Her early novels were considered immoral in the 1830s; she advocated the emancipation of women, justified and even idealized adultery, and described the Romantic idea of passion as the motive force in life. Her own turbulent liaison with Alfred de Musset was described in *Lettres d'une voyageur* (1834–1836; in English Letters of a Traveller, 1847); their disastrous trip to Italy, during which they both engaged in outside sexual ventures, terminated their affair and provided the material for her novel, *Elle et lui* (1859; in English, She and He, 1902). While suing for a legal separation from Dudevant (c. 1840), Sand was involved in a lengthy, stormy affair with Frederick Chopin; their exasperating visit to the island of Majorca became the subject of her novel,

Un Hiver à Majorque (1841; in English, Winter in Majorca 1956). During this first period her writing always reflected the men and ideas that were most prominent in her life. Her characters struggled against conventional mores imposed on the individual and flaunted their romantic passions in the face of public censure, just as Sand herself did. That she preferred the company of men to women is evident in her love affairs and documented in her novels.

Sand's association with Félicité-Robert de Lamennais, Pierre Leroux, Michel de Bourges, Charles-Augustin Saint-Beuve, and others convinced her that the artist should take an active role in social reform. During the second phase of her literary career, Sand produced a number of novels denouncing the evils of class distinctions, marriage, and property. She also despised revealed religion and social customs that restricted people's lives and interfered with relations between the sexes. Socialism, humanitarianism, and republicanism were enthusiastically embraced; her works such as *Spiridon* (1838), *Le Sept Cordes de la lyre* (1839), *Le compagnon du tour de France* (1843; The Journeyman Joiner or The Companion of the Tour de France, 1847), *Consuelo* (1842–1843; in English, 1846), *La comtesse de Rudolstadt* (1843–1845; in English, The Countess of Rudolstadt, 1847), and *Le Meunier d'Angibault* (1845; in English, The Miller of Angibault, 1863), included portraits of her friends and distillations of their theories on the regeneration of society. Her advocacy of democracy and glorification of plebeian virtues dismayed the entrenched bourgeoisie as had Sand's espousal of complete sexual freedom. In her novel, *Spiridon*, Leroux's vague humanitarianism appears as a deistic religion that would supplant Christianity. This theme is treated in a more philosophical vein in *Sept Cordes de la lyre*, the lyre symbolizing the harmony to which humanity ought to aspire. Harmony through socialism was one of the themes of *Consuelo* and its inferior sequel, *La comtesse de Rudolstadt*; a melange of discussions on the occult and free-masonry, the transmigration of souls, the brotherhood of man, and of course, the suffering endured by lovers are skillfully blended into a unique pseudo-philosophical utopia. In *Meunier d'Angibault*, Sand attacks inequality of birth and wealth. The working-class hero and the upper-class woman he loves rid themselves of the burden of her fortune and find fulfillment in spreading the gospel of brotherhood. Here socialism is treated in less mystical, more concrete terms.

After 1839 Sand lived a rather bourgeois, though not sedate, existence at her home in Berry. She continued to write, tended to her household, played host-

ess to her friends, and spent time with her grandchildren. However, the Revolution of 1848 lured her back to Paris. She welcomed the revolution, and she edited and wrote articles for the *Bulletin de la République* under the direction of Ledru-Rollin. A group of republican feminists nominated Sand for the National Assembly in 1848 without her consent; she refused this "honor" for she did not believe women's place was in politics. She felt she served the people by her writing on social problems and editing the *Bulletin*, but she was not prepared to expose herself to the rigors of the masculine political arena. Her idealism was soon dashed by the insurrections of June 1848 and the bloody civil war; the coup d'état of Louis Napoleon Bonaparte finished any hope for a more equitable, free society, and Sand returned to Nohant. Her interest now turned to the pastoral novel, the genre in which Sand made a major contribution to literature.

La Mare au diable (1846) [1890; The Haunted Pool] is the first and perhaps best of her rustic novels that are considered masterpieces of regionalist literature. Sand was no longer bent on reforming the world. In clear, graceful, and quiet language the author depicted the natural beauty of her province, peopled with slightly idealized and sanitized countryfolk. In *La petite Fadette* (1849; Little Fadette; A Domestic Story), *François le Champi* (1850) [1889; Francis the Waif], and *Les Maîtres sonneurs* (1852) [1890; The Bagpipers] Sand set the standard for French provincial literature. She changed her attitude toward literature during this period: "In the arts the most simple is the noblest thing to try, but the most difficult to attain." There is a poetic perfection in these works, a successful combination of narrative skill and the characterization of "real" people with human problems. Sand had fashioned the regional novel and given the peasant a prominent place in literature unequalled by earlier writers. After 1860 she turned to the more mannered and less individualistic novel; *Jean de la Roche* (1859), *le Marquis de Villemer* (1861) [1871; The Marquis de Villemer], and *Les Beaux messieurs de Bois-Doré* (1858) [1890; The Gallant Lords of Bois-Doré] are Romantic in style but also more predictable in plot and character development.

Another important literary contribution made by this prolific and creative artist was her correspondence (edited by Georges Lubin, 1964–1985) which comprises 20 volumes. Her *Histoire de ma vie* [Story of My Life] in 4 volumes (1854–1855) is also interesting for her frank assessments of her contemporaries; she admired Dumas and Flaubert, hated Mérimée, and disliked Balzac. For over 40 years Sand produced a torrent of novels, tales, essays, and plays. The latter were enthusiastically received by her contemporaries but are of scant interest today. Her writing style was effortless and lyrically descriptive; she wrote with conviction and an idealism and sensuality that distinguished all of her works. Sand embodied the many facets of the Romantic spirit of the nineteenth century; visionary, passionate, caring, free-spirited, and contemptuous of rigid bourgeois morality, she was called "la harpe éolienne de notre temps," by her contemporary, Ernest Renan. Sand's popularity has waned, but her contributions to the genre of regional literature has secured her reputation in the French literary world.

Works

Adriani (1853). *Les ailes de courage* (1916) [1931; Wings of Courage]. *Les amours de l'age d'or* (1871). *André* (1835) [1947; André]. *Antonia* (1863) [1870; Antonia]. *Autour de la table* (1875). *Le beau Laurence* (1870) [1880; Handsome Lawrence]. *Les beaux messieurs de Bois-Doré* (1862) [1890; The Gallant Lords of Bois-Doré]. *Césarine Dietrich* (1871) [1871; Césarine Dietrich]. *Les Charmettes*, n.p., n.d. *Le château des désertes* (1851) [1856; The Castle in the Wilderness]. *Le compagnon du tour de France* (1843) [1847; The Journeyman Joiner or The Companion of the Tour de France]. *La comtesse de Rudolstadt* (1844) [1847; The Countess of Rudolstadt]. *La confession d'une jeune fille* (1865) [1865; Young Girl's Confession]. *Constance Verrier* (1869). *Consuelo* (1842–1843) [1846; Consuelo]. *Contes d'une grand'mère* (1873) [1930; Tales of a Grandmother]. *Les dames vertes* (1863). *La Danielle* (1857). *Le dernier amour* (1867). *La dernière Aldini* (1857) [1871; The Last Aldini: A Love Story]. *Dernières pages* (1877). *Les deux frères* (1875). *Le diable aux champs* (1857). *Elle et lui* (1859) [1902; She and He]. *La famille de Germandre* (1861). *La filleule* (1853). *First and True Love: A Thrilling Novel* (1853) [in English only]. *Flamarande* (1877). *Flavie: les maioliques florentines* (1872). *Francia: une bienfait n'est jamais perdu* (1872). *François le champi* (1850) [1889; Francis the Waif]. *Gabriel* (1840). *Garibaldi* (1860). *Gamiani, ou, Deux nuits d'excès Paris* (1870). *Germaine's Marriage: A Tale of Peasant Life in France* (1892) [in English only]. *Un hiver à Majorque* (1841) [1956; Winter in Majorca; with José Quadrado's Refutation of George Sand also 1902; George Sand and Chopin; a Glimpse of Bohemia]. *Un hiver au midi de l'Europe* (1841). *L'homme de neige* (1856) [1898; The Snowman]. *Horace* (1842). *Impressions et souvenirs* (1873) [1877; Impressions and Reminiscences]. *Indiana* (1832) [1835; Indiana]. *Isidora* (1847). *Jacques*

(1834) [1847; Jacques]. *Jean de la Roche* (1860). *Jeanne* (1844). *Journal d'un voyageur pendant la guerre* (1871). *Journal intime* (posthumous) (1926) [1975; The Intimate Journal of George Sand]. *Laura: voyages et impressions* (1865). *Lavinia* (1844). *Légendes rustiques* (1858). *Lélia* (1833). *Leone Leonie* (1837). *Lettres au peuple* (1848). *Lettres d'un voyageur* (1837) [1847; Letters of a Traveller]. *Lucrezia Floriani* (1846). *La mare au diable* (1846) [1847; The Devil's Pool; also 1890; The Haunted Pool]. *Ma soeur Jeanne* (1874) [1874; My Sister Jeanne]. *Mademoiselle La Quintinie* (1860). *Mademoiselle Merquem* (1868) [1868; Mlle Merquem, a Novel]. *Les maîtres mosaïstes* (1838) [1895; The Master Mosaic-Workers]. *Les maîtres sonneurs* (1852) [1890; The Bagpipers]. *Les Majorcains* (1843). *Malgrétout* (1870). *Marianne* (1876). *Le marquis de Villemer* (1861) [1871; The Marquis de Villemer]. *La marquise* (1888). *Mauprat* (1837) [1847; Mauprat]. *Mélanges* (1843). *Melchior* (1842). *Le meunier d'Angibault* (1845) [1863; The Miller of Angibault]. *Les mississipiens, proverbe* (1840). *Monsieur Sylvestre* (1866) [1871; Monsieur Sylvestre; a Novel]. *Mont-Revêche* (1853). *Mouny-Robin* (1842). *The Naiad; A Ghost Story* (1892) [in English only?]. *Nanon* (1872) [1890; Nanon]. *Narcisse* (1859). *Nouvelles lettres d'un voyageur* (1877). *Nouvelles* (1869). *Le nuage rose* (n.d.) [1902; The Rosy Cloud]. *Oeuvres de George Sand* (1860–1892). *Oeuvres choisies* (1851). *Pauline* (1841). *Le péché de Monsieur Antoine* (1846; The Sin of Monsieur Antoine). *La petite Fadette* (1849; Little Fadette; A Domestic Story). *Le Piccinino* (1847) [1900; Piccinino: The Last of the Aldinis, 2 vols.]. *Pierre qui roule* (1870) [1871; A Rolling Stone]. *La politique et le socialisme* (1845). *Pourquoi les femmes à l'Académie?* (1863). *Princess Nourmahal* (1888) [in English only?]. *Procope le Grand* (1844). *Promenades autour d'un village* (1866). *Quelques refléxions sur J.-J. Rousseau* (1854). *Questions d'art et de littérature* (1878). *Questions politiques et sociales* (1879). *Recollections by George Sand in Mérimée, Letters to an Incognita* (1874). *Réponse à diverses objections* (1846). *Le secrétaire intime* (1834) [1843; The Private Secretary]. *Les sept cordes de la lyre* (1839). *Simon* (1836) [18__?; Simon; A Love Story]. *Sketch of Talleyrand*, n.p., n.d. [in English only?]. *Souvenirs de 1848 . . .* (1880). *Souvenirs et impressions littéraires* (1862). *Spiridon* (1848). *Tamaris* (1862). *Teverino* (1845) [1855; Teverino: a Romance; also 1870; Jealousy or Teverino]. *Théâtre de Nohant* (1861). *La tour de Percemont. Marianne* (1876) [1881; The Tower of Percemont and Marianne]. *L'Uscoque* (1838) [18__?; The Uscoque, or, the Corsair]. *Valen-*

tine (1832) [1902; Valentine]. *Valvèdre* (1861). *Une vieille histoire in Heures du soir* (1833). *La ville noire* (1861). *Voyage à Majorque* (18__?). *Voyage d'un moineau de Paris à la recherche du meilleur gouvernement*, in *Vie privée et publique des animaux* (1868).

Plays: *La baronne de Muhldorf* (1853). *Cadio* (1868). *Claudies* (1841). *Cosima: ou, la haine dans l'amour* (1840). *Le démon du foyer* (1852). *Le drac* (1865). *La petite Fadette* (1864). *Flaminio* (1854). *Françoise* (1856). *Le lis du Japon* (1866). *Lucie* (1856). *Maître Favilla* (1855). *Marguerite de Saint-Gemme* (1859). *Le mariage de Victorine* (1851). *Mauprat* (1837?). *Molière* (1851). *Le pavé* (1862). *Le pressoir* (1853). *Les vacances de Pandolphe* (1852).

William T. Ojala
Jeanne A. Ojala

Marguerite Duras
1914–1996

Born 1914, Cochin China
Died March 3, 1996
Genre(s): novel, drama, movie director
Language(s): French

Marguerite Duras was born in Cochin China (which was later called South Vietnam), where she spent most of her youth. In 1932, she moved to Paris where she studied law and mathematics (her father was a mathematics teacher, her mother an elementary school teacher), and enrolled in the Faculty of Political Sciences. In 1939 she married Robert Antelme, author of *L'Espèce Humaine* (The Human Species); three years later she met Dyonis Mascolo, author of *Le Communisme* (Communism), with whom she had a son. She became a militant Communist but later left the party. She was a prominent figure for feminist readers and critics, her texts focusing on the relation between desire and language, sexuality and gender. She is also considered one of the leading French writers of her time.

Over the past forty years, she wrote novels, plays, and numerous essays. She contributed to many films, starting with the script she wrote for *Hiroshima mon amour* (Hiroshima, My Love), which was directed by Alain Resnais, and created quite a stir at the 1960 Cannes Festival. She collaborated on movies adapted from her novels (*Un barrage contre le Pacifique* [The Sea Wall], *La Musica*, *Dix heures et demie du soir en* été [Ten-Thirty PM in the Summertime], *Le Marin de Gibraltar* [The Sailor from Gibraltar], *Moderato Cantabile*), and later directed them (*Détruire, dit-elle* [Destroy, She Said], *Jaune le Soleil* [Yellow the Sun], *Nathalie Granger*).

Because the same themes and scenes often reappear in her novels, plays, and films, her work resisted generic classification and covered several fields at the same time: many of her published scripts can be read as novels (*Hiroshima mon amour*, *India Song*, *Aurélia Steiner*), some of her novels are made of visual figures (*Le Ravissement de Lol V. Stein* [The Ravishing of Lol V. Stein], *L'Homme Atlantique* [The Atlantic Man]; in some of her theater and films the actors actually read their parts, instead of acting them (*Le Camion* [The Truck], *La Maladie de la mort* [The Malady of Death]).

The versatility of her narrative defies any classification and is reiterated by the elusiveness of her texts, always repeated but never quite the same, which creates both familiarity and defamiliarization. One can define three stages in her work, stages that show a continuation of her themes (childhood, solitude, encounter, love, sexuality, incommunicability, boredom, death, and time), and an evolution in her style.

Her earliest novels (1943–1960) have a simple, coherent plot, a linear and chronological development, and a great thematic unity. Often set during vacations in a hot Mediterranean summer, they tell the story of a crisis in the life of a couple, of love encounters. Many of her characters are passive and drink heavily, but their passivity is often composed of wisdom and silence. They are fascinated by passion and death. Often a peculiar event takes place in their surroundings (fatal accident, crime of passion, suicide). Though these elements are quite ordinary and their repetition rather monotonous, Duras has renewed the art of the novel by her rejection of traditional psychology, her peculiar use of dialogue, her preference for what is suggested rather than explicit and above all by the overwhelming role given to time and duration. The encounter between man and woman leads to a slow, progressive, cautious discovery of love, a love that ignores social barriers and boundaries, and reveals the failure of communication. Time is perceived as both necessary and threatening and creates in Duras's novels an unusual, if sometimes irritating, slow rhythm.

In her later works, the obsession with memory and desire uses repetition even more. The narrative movement is reduced to a minimum; each text is related to the previous ones and can be seen as fragments of a longer narrative. These intertextual repetitions require from the reader a willingness to reread rather than to consume the text.

Finally, in her more recent novels, Duras reshapes not only her work but her own image in the eyes of the public. With *L'Amant* (The Lover: Prix Goncourt 1984), she became a popular writer. Part of its success might be due to its advertisement as an "exotic, erotic autobiographical confession," which hides its deep ambivalence: by her narrative use of "I" and "she," Duras pretends to confess but is not committed to truthfulness and plays a seductive game of veiling and unveiling her life.

Works

Les Impudents (1943). *La Vie tranquille* (1944). *Un barrage contre le Pacifique* (1950). *Le Marin de Gibraltar* (1952). *Les petits chevaux de Tarquinia* (1953). *Des journées entières dans les arbres* (1954). *Le Square* (1955). *Moderato Cantabile* (1958). *Les Viaducs de la Seine-et-Oise* (1960). *La Musica, Dix heures et demie du soir en été* (1960). *Hiroshima mon amour* (1960). *L'Après-midi de Monsieur Andesmas* (1962). *Le Ravissement de Lol V. Stein* (1964). *Théâtre I, II* (1965). *Le Vice-Consul* (1966). *L'Amante anglaise* (1967). *Détruire, dit-elle* (1969). *Abahn, Sabana, David* (1970). *L'Amour* (1972). *India song texte-théâtre-film* (1973). *Nathalie Granger, suivi de La Femme du Gange* (1973). With Xavière Gauthier. *Les Parleuses* (1974). *Le Camion, suivi d'Entretien avec Michelle Porte* (1977). *L'Eden cinéma* (1977). With Michelle Porte, *Les Lieux de Marguerite Duras* (1977). With Joël Farges and François Barat, *Marguerite Duras* (1979). *Le Navire Night* (suivi de *Césarée, Les Mains négatives, Aurélia Steiner, Aurélia Steiner, Aurélia Steiner*) (1979). *L'Eté 80* (1980). *L'Homme assis dans le couloir* (1980). *Les Yeux verts* (1980). *Agatha* (1981). *Outside: papiers d'un jour* (1981). *L'Homme Atlantique* (1982). *La Maladie de la mort* (1982). *Savannah Bay* (1982). *L'Amant* (1984). *La Douleur* (1985). *La Pute de la côte normande* (1986). *Les Yeux bleus, cheveux noirs* (1986). *La Vie matérielle: Marguerite Duras parle* (1987). *Eden Cinéma* (1988). *La Pluie d'été* (1990). *L'Amant de la Chine du Nord* (1991). *Yann Andrea Steiner* (1992). *Ecrine* (1993). *C'est tout* (1995).

Translations: Duras's works have been translated in many languages. The following translations in English: *Hiroshima mon amour* (1961). *Four Novels*, tr. Richard Seaver (1965). *The Ravishing of Lol V. Stein*, tr. Richard Seaver (1966). *The Square*. Three Plays, tr. Barbara Bray and Sonia Orwell (1967). *The Vice-Consul*, tr. Eileen Ellenbogen (1968). *L'Amante anglaise*, tr. Barbara Bray (1968). *Destroy, She Said*, tr. Barbara Bray (1970). *India Song*, tr. Barbara Bray (1976). *The Little Horses of Tarquinia*, tr. Peter Du Berg (1980). *The Sailor from Gibraltar*, tr. Barbara Bray (1980). *Whole Days in the Trees and Other Stories*, tr. Anita Barrows (1984). *The Lover*, tr. Barbara Bray (1985). *The Malady of Death*. Five Novels (1985). *The Sea Wall*, tr. Herrma Briffault (1985). *The War*, tr. Barbara Bray (1986). *Emily L.* (1990). Green Eyes (1990). *Summer Rain* (1992).

Michèle M. Magill

Emily Eden
1797–1869

Born March 3, 1797, London, England
Died August 5, 1869, Richmond, Surrey
Genre(s): memoir, novel
Languages(s): English

Emily Eden lived her life in the aristocratic surroundings she depicts in her two novels. She was the twelfth child and seventh daughter of the First Baron Auckland, a commissioner in America after the Revolutionary War, Chief Secretary in Ireland, Minister-Plenipotentiary to Versailles, and Ambassador to both Spain and Holland. Her uncle, Robert Eden, was the last colonial governor of Maryland. Her family's descendants were equally illustrious: novelist Eleanor (Lena) Eden was her niece; Violet Dickinson, friend of Virginia Woolf and Vita Sackville-West, was her great-niece; and Prime Minister Anthony Eden was her greatgreat nephew.

Eden was well educated by governesses and then by the same tutor who taught her brother Robert. She was conversationally at ease amid topics of Whig politics and foreign affairs. She never married, a personal choice rather than an effect of the growing surplus of women over men as the nineteenth century advanced. She and her sister Frances (Fanny) lived with her brother George (later Lord Auckland), first in London, where he was First Lord of the Admiralty, and then, from 1835 to 1842, in India, where George was Governor-General and Emily and Fanny served as his "first ladies." Two of her books describe this experience. *"Up the Country": Letters Written to her Sister from the Upper Provinces of India* (1866), is an account of Eden's two-and-one-half year tour of India. Although she was largely unconscious of her brother's role in initiating the nadir of British rule in India through his mismanagement of the First Afghan War,

she does give an accurate contemporary glimpse into the life of the British in India, including a sympathetic comprehension of the Indian dislike of British arrogance and self-righteousness. *"Up the Country"* was Eden's most popular work and has continued to be of interest to contemporary travelers to India, with modern reprintings in 1930, 1978, and 1983.

Portraits of the Princes and People of India (1843) is a beautifully printed volume of Eden's sketches and watercolors, which elicited praise for her as "one of the most accomplished amateur artists in India in the early nineteenth century." Her drawings were highly enough regarded that they received a showing by the Viceroy of India in 1916, and some 200 of them are still on display in the Victoria Memorial in Calcutta. Her portrait of Ranjit Singh has influenced subsequent portraitists.

It is for her novels, however, that Eden is most enduringly remembered. *The Semi-Detached House* (1859) and *The Semi-Attached Couple* (1861) have both been readily available since their initial publication, most recently in Virago Press editions. In them Eden shows an Austenesque love-and-marriage market among the very rich. In *House* young Lady Blanche Chester awaits the birth of her son, establishes herself as a force in country society, and comes to know the Hopkinsons and to help promote the marriages of Janet and Rose, thwarting meanwhile the snobbery of Baroness Sampson. The semi-detachment of the house reflects Eden's democratic belief in human worth and relatedness despite class differences. *Couple* details the difficulties that a young married couple face in learning to know one another; romance takes a back seat to very real differences of upbringing, sensitivity, and activity, as Lord Teviot's hearty loving frightens young Helen. In addition, the houseguests, hunting, and ambassadorial duties incumbent upon their lifestyle make it impossible for the couple to become intimate. In the midst of a borough election, Helen learns both how to yield and how to stand up for herself, and Teviot sees the roughness of his prideful ways. In both books the dry drollery of Eden's presentation remains as fresh and captivating as it was over a century ago. She is aptly characterized as a minor Jane Austen.

Works

Portraits of the Princes and People of India (1843). *The Semi-Detached House* (1859). *The Semi-Attached Couple* (1861). *The Journals and Correspondence of William Lord Auckland,* ed. G. Hugge (1861–1862). *"Up the Country": Letters Written to Her Sister from the Upper Provinces of India* (1866; reprinted as *Letters From India* 1872). *Catalogue of Exhibition of Paintings by the Hon. Miss Eden* (at Victoria Memorial Exhibition, Belvedere, Calcutta, 1916). *Miss Eden's Letters,* ed. V. Dickinson (1919).

Loralee MacPike

Maria Edgeworth
1768–1849

Born January 1, 1768, Black Bourtont Oxfordshire, England
Died May 22, 1849, Edgeworthstown, Ireland
Genre(s): novel, short story, drama, essay
Languages(s): English

In the preface to his *Waverley Novels* Sir Walter Scott wrote: "Without being so presumptuous as to hope to emulate the rich humor, pathetic tenderness, and admirable tact which pervade the work of my accomplished friend, I felt that something might be attempted for my own country, of the same kind with that which Miss Edgeworth so fortunately achieved for Ireland." Maria Edgeworth—an Anglo-Irish novelist, short story writer, dramatist, and educational essayist—is known chiefly for her work in the tradition of the novel of manners although she is also remembered for her contributions to educational theory. Her reputation as a novelist has suffered from inevitable comparisons to Jane Austen; however, literary historians have long acknowledged her many innovations to English fiction.

Much of Edgeworth's work was inspired and motivated by her father, a politician, inventor, and educator. Married four times, he fathered twenty-two children. Besides her responsibilities as agent and secretary of the family estate (Edgeworthstown, Ireland, where she lived from age fifteen until her death), she had control of her father's ever-increasing family. To entertain them she composed stories, first on a slate and then, if they approved, in ink. In this manner she perfected her skills as a storyteller.

Formal collaboration between Edgeworth and her father occurred on only two books, most notably *Practical Education,* which espouses many ideas on education taken from Rousseau, but her father's hand is noticeable in almost all her work. Not only did he urge her to write moralistic and didactic stories, but he edited her manuscripts, deleting and inserting, rearranging and rewriting to his own taste. Most critics agree that his presence within Edgeworth's work is more of a hindrance than a help. Yet some maintain that the dichotomy of highly imaginative fiction with extreme pragmatism creates an interesting puzzle.

Castle Rackrent: An Hibernian Tale (1800) is considered by most to be her best work. Written while her father was traveling, the novel is free from the overt didacticism of much of Edgeworth's other works. Although surpassed in many of her efforts by later writers, Edgeworth implemented several new narrative techniques in *Castle Rackrent.* Of major importance is her narrator, Thady Quirk. Not only is he active rather than passive but the narrative is presented from his perspective (a narrative device later adopted by Austen). The first regional novel, *Castle Rackrent* depicts speech, mannerisms, and activities of a specific group—a technique which greatly influenced Scott as well as others such as William Thackeray and James Fenimore Cooper. Ivan Turgenev said that his *Sportsman's Sketches* were also influenced by *Castle Rackrent* in their full development of lower-class characters.

Edgeworth's other Irish tales are also considered to be worthy of note. *Belinda is* a picture of society at the close of the eighteenth century and is commented on by Austen in *Northanger Abbey.* Also included in this group is *The Absentee* and *Ormond.* Concerned with social and economic problems and showing great understanding for Irish culture, these are generally grouped among Edgeworth's best work.

Thus, because of her innovations to narrative technique in the English novel, her sensitivity to local atmosphere, and her sympathetic portrayal of national character, Edgeworth influenced some of England's best-known authors (most notably Austen and Scott) and is an important figure in the history of the English novel.

Works

Adalaide and Theodore (1784). *Letters for Literary Ladies* (1795). *The Parent's Assistant* (1796). *Practical Education,* with R.L. Edgeworth (1798). *Castle*

Rackrent (1800). *Early Lessons* (1801). *Moral Tales* (1801). *Belinda* (1801). *The Mental Thermometer* (1801). *Essay on Irish Bulls* (1802). *Popular Tales* (1804). *The Modern Griselda* (1805). *Leonora* (1806). *Essays on Professional Education*, with R.L. Edgeworth (1809). *Tales of Fashionable Life* (1812). *Patronage* (1814). *Continuation of Early Lessons* (1814). *Comic Dramas* (1817). *Harrington, a Tale;* and *Ormond, a Tale* (1817). *Rosamond: A Sequel to Early Lessons* (1821). *Frank: A Sequel to Frank in Early Lessons* (1822). *Harry and Lucy Concluded: Being the Last Part of Early Lessons* (1825). *Thoughts on Bores, Janus* (1826). *Little Plays for Children* (1827). *Garry-Owen* (1829). *Helen, a Tale* (1834). *Orlandino* (1848). *The Most Unfortunate Day of My Life* (1931).

Lynn M. Alexander

Egeria
ca. 350–A.D. 430
Flourished ca. A.D. 400
Genre(s): pilgrimage memoir
Language(s): Latin

In the late fourth or early fifth century, a Latin-speaking woman from the western part of the Roman Empire made the arduous pilgrimage to the Holy Land, where she traveled extensively and resided for three years in Jerusalem itself. She composed a memoir of her travels that provides one of the most precious records of late antique Christian pilgrimage and worship.

Since the discovery of the sole manuscript of the work, by Gamurrini in 1884, both the identity of the author and the date of her journey have occasioned much discussion. That manuscript is fragmentary and the extant portions are not continuous, so it is unclear how much of Egeria's record has been lost. The clipped and precise descriptions of the work contain few biographical details. Scholarly consensus has attributed the work to "the blessed nun Egeria," a pilgrim mentioned by the seventh-century Spanish monk Valerius. Egeria's work is generally called the *Itinerarium*, or *Travels*, on the basis of a now-lost manuscript which bore that title under Egeria's authorship in the catalogue of a medieval monastic library. Internal evidence suggests that Egeria came from a region on the Atlantic coast, but she could equally have been a Gallo-Roman from the Aquitaine or a Spaniard from Galicia. She was clearly a member of a monastic community and apparently recorded her description largely for the benefit of her sisters. The economic resources required for her journey and the welcome which she was accorded in the Holy Land by such figures as the Bishop of Edessa suggest that she was of high social standing. Although Egeria did not have as firm a command of Latin literary style as such late antique Christian women as Proba, she was well educated and possessed a firm grounding in both Scripture and the Christian literary tradition. She rejoiced when the bishop of Edessa gave her a copy of *The Letter of King Abgar* that she deemed superior to that found in her library at home.

The most vexing question concerning the work is the date of Egeria's journey. This is a matter of some scholarly importance because her description of the liturgy practiced in Jerusalem, a liturgy which served as the basis of various later Eastern rites, is important to the history of the development of those Christian liturgies. The text must have been composed between 363 and 540, but most theories have focused on the years ca. 400. Devos, refining arguments first made by Baumstark, has placed Egeria's stay in Jerusalem as lasting from 381 to 384. A persistent set of counter-arguments, begun by Lambert and continued by Gingras, have suggested the years 414–416. Other dates have been put forth by various single commentators. The recent consensus of scholarly opinion has been in agreement with Devos.

The surviving narrative is almost evenly divided between Egeria's journey around the Holy Land and the passages on Jerusalem itself and its liturgy. Egeria desired to bring home specific information to her community about such topics as biblical geography, Christian historical traditions, and liturgical rites. She frequently addressed its members directly, as in her description of the Jerusalem liturgy, "Loving sisters, I am sure it will interest you to know about the daily services they have in the holy places. . . ." Earlier, she had introduced the precious copy of the *Letter of Abgar*, "You yourselves must read it when I come home, dearest ladies, if such is the will of Jesus our God." Like most travelers, she was eager to share her novel experiences with her friends. Like most pilgrims, she was eager for them to share in the spiritual benefits which she had gained. While Egeria's Latin is of a rather plain style, the very descriptive gifts and attention to detail which she placed at the service of her community serve the modern historian extremely well.

Works
The most recent critical editions are O. Prinz, *Itinerarium Egeriae* (1960), and E. Francheschini and R. Weber, *Itinerarium Egeriae*, in *Itineraria et alia*

geographica (Corpus Christianorum, Series Latina, vol. 175; 1965). English translations and commentary can be found in G.E. Gingras, *Egeria, Diary of a Pilgrimage* (Ancient Christian Writers, vol. 38; 1970); P. Wilson-Kastner et al., *A Lost Tradition. Women Writers of the Early Church* (1981); and John Wilkinson, *Egeria's Travels to the Holy Land* (1971, revised 1981). Valuable notes and a French translation can be found in P. Maravel, ed., *Ethérie. Journal de voyage (Itinéraire)* (Sources Chrétiennes, vol. 296; 1982).

Thomas Head

Marianne Ehrmann
1755–1795

a.k.a. Beobachterin [Observing Woman], Verfasserin der Amalia, Verfasserin der Philosophie eines Weibes, Maria Anna Antonia Sternheim
Born November 25, 1755, Rapperswyl, Switzerland
Died August 14, 1795, Stuttgart, Germany
Genre(s): periodical, novel, short essay, short story
Language(s): German

Marianne Ehrmann was important for her journalism and for a novel and several stories that describe milieus seldom represented in eighteenth-century literature, especially that written by and for women. Remarkable pre-feminist ideas characterize much of her later work.

Nothing is known about Ehrmann's early childhood; neither her parents nor her place of birth, beyond the family name Brentano, can be confirmed. She is said to have been raised by an uncle in Frankfurt. Her first marriage, to a man who is routinely identified only as a good-for-nothing, ended in divorce. Thereafter, Ehrmann apparently earned her own living, perhaps with a respectable stint as a governess, definitely for a while as an actress, calling herself Sternheim, after the virtuous heroine of Sophie von La Roche's first novel.

In about 1781 the young woman met and married T.F. Ehrmann, seven years her junior, and soon began writing. After publishing an anti-feminist essay in the tradition of Rousseau, three novels, and one play, and after assisting her husband with several periodicals that he put out, she established a monthly of her own: *Amalia's Leisure Hours, Dedicated to Germany's Daughters*. It survived for three years (fairly typical for periodicals of the time) before a dispute with her publisher forced Ehrmann to give it up. She promptly started another: *The Hermit from the Alps*,

which was brought to an end two years later by Ehrmann's ill health. On August 14, 1795, at age thirty-nine, she died. Her husband continued to publish more of her works until 1798, including her most important novel, originally published in 1787 as *Amalie, A True Story in Letters*, and republished in 1796 and 1798 as *Antonie von Warnstein, A Story of Our Times*.

Ehrmann is important for producing *Amalia's Leisure Hours*, one of the best magazines for women in eighteenth-century Germany. It contains articles on an impressive variety of subjects, poetry by some of the best writers of the day (including Schiller and Hölderlin), and stories and essays by the editor that are frequently remarkable for their freshness and candor. The monthly magazine was a good vehicle in which Ehrmann could develop both her style and her thoughts, which came increasingly into conflict with the dominant confining and complacent view of women. Ehrmann is now recognized as an important representative of pre-feminism. Her novel *Amalie* boldly depicts and justifies the life of an actress and more cautiously discusses the dangerous topic of divorce.

Works

Philosophie eines Weibs [A Woman's Philosophy. Tr. into French] (1784). *Leichtsinn und gutes Herz oder die Folgen der Erziehung. Ein Original-Schauspiel in 5 Aufzügen* [Frivolity and a Good Heart, or the Consequences of Education. An original play in 5 acts] (1786). *Amalie, eine wahre Geschichte in Briefen* [Amalie, a True Story in Letters] (1787); republished as *Antonie von Warnstein. Eine Geschichte aus unserm Zeitalter* [Antonie von Warnstein. A Story of Our Times. 2 vols.] (1796–1798). *Ninas Briefe an ihren Geliebten* [Nina's Letters to Her Beloved] (1788). *Graf Bilding, eine Geschichte aus dem mittlern Zeitalter, dialogisirt* [Count Bilding, a Story of the Middle Ages in Dialogue] (1788). *Kleine Fragmente für Denkerinnen* [Small Fragments for Thinking Women] (1788). *Amaliens Erholsstunden. Teutschlands Töchtern geweiht* [Amalia's Leisure Hours, Dedicated to Germany's Daughters. 3 vols.] (1790–1792). *Die Einsiedlerinn aus den Alpen. Eine Monatsschrift zur Unterhaltung und Belehrung für Deutschlands und Helvetiens Töchter* [The Hermit from the Alps. A Monthly for the Entertainment and Instruction of Germany's and Helvetia's Daughters. 2 vols.] (1793–1794). *Erzählungen* [Tales] (1795). *Amaliens Feierstunden. Auswahl der hinterlassenen Schriften* [Amalia's Free Hours. A Selection from the Posthumous Writings. 3 vols.].

Ruth P. Dawson

George Eliot
1819–1880

a.k.a. Mary Ann Evans
Born November 22, 1819, South Farm, Arbury,
Warwickshire, England
Died December 22, 1880, London
Genre(s): translation, novel, short story
Languages(s): English

In his recollection of Eliot, F.W.H. Myers wrote: "She . . . taking as her text the three words . . . *God, Immortality, Duty,*—pronounced, with terrible earnestness, how inconceivable was the *first,* how unbelievable the *second,* and yet how peremptory and absolute the *third.*" Eliot herself recognized something of the kind in her work as the following comments reflect:

The idea of God so far as it has been a high spiritual influence, is the ideal of a goodness entirely human (i.e., an exaltation of the human).

I am just and honest, not because I expect to live in another world, but because having felt the pain of injustice and dishonesty towards myself, I have a fellow-feeling with other men who would suffer the same pain if I were unjust or dishonest towards them.

If art does not enlarge men's sympathies, it does nothing morally; I have had heart-cutting experience that opinions are a poor cement between human souls: and the only effect I ardently long to produce by my writings is, that those who read them should be better able to imagine and to feel the pains and the joys of those who differ from themselves in everything but the broad fact of being struggling, erring, human creatures.

Born Mary Ann Evans, Eliot was the daughter of a Warwickshire land agent, a man of strong Evangelical Protestant feeling. She and her father became very close after her mother's death in 1836, but in 1842 an emotional conflict developed that severed communication between them: Eliot refused to attend church with her father. In the early 1840s Eliot became familiar with Higher Criticism, the new biblical and theological scholarship from Germany that applied science and history to the Bible. In 1844 Eliot began to translate Strauss's *Das Leben Jesu,* published in 1846 as *The Life of Jesus, Critically Examined.* Three years later she began translating Spinoza's *Tractatus Theologico-Politicus.* In May 1849 her father died, and she decided to accompany the Charles Bray family to the Continent.

George Eliot

When Eliot returned to England in 1850, she met John Chapman and lived for much of 1851 to 1853 (under difficult emotional circumstances) as a resident of his London house. She became assistant editor of the *Westminister Review* when Chapman bought it in 1851, a post she held until 1854. It was at this time that she became a close friend of Herbert Spencer, with whom she believed herself in love, and through him met George Henry Lewes. In 1853 she began translating Feuerbach's *Das Wesen des Christenthums* (published as *The Essence of Christianity* in 1854).

The year 1853 also marked the beginning of one of the most famous liaisons in nineteenth-century Victorian England, that of Eliot and Lewes. Although Lewes was separated from his wife, the laws of the time made divorce impossible. However, Eliot's union with him lasted until his death in 1878. They called themselves man and wife and were accepted as such by their friends.

Eliot was in her mid-thirties when she finally gave in to the urging of Lewes and tried her hand at writing fiction. It was in 1857 that the pseudonym of George Eliot was adopted, chiefly to avoid notoriety following the publication of her first three short stories in *Blackwood's Edinburgh Magazine*—"Amos Barton," "Mr. Gilfil's Love Story," and "Janet's Repentance," published together in 1858 as *Scenes of Cleri-*

cal Life. This same year she also began working on her first novel, *Adam Bede* (1859).

The plot of *Adam Bede* is based on a story about a confession of child murder made to Eliot's aunt, Elizabeth Evans, by a girl in prison. Elizabeth Evans was a Methodist preacher and the original of the Dinah Morris character. With its pairings of contrasting characters—the two brothers, Adam and Seth, and Dinah and Hetty—the novel provides an early example of Eliot's skill at characterization. Likewise, the garrulous Mrs. Poyser is a memorable supporting character.

The Mill on the Floss, published in 1860, is viewed by many scholars as her most autobiographical work. The heroine, Maggie Tulliver, is highly strung and intelligent, of intense sensibility, and possessing artistic and poetic tastes. From conflicting temperaments within her family and the incongruity of Maggie's character with her surroundings spring unhappiness and ultimate tragedy. Her love for her brother, Tom, is thwarted by his lack of understanding, and the intellectual and emotional sides of her nature are starved. Eventually Maggie is turned out of her brother's house and ostracized by the community after being innocently but irremediably compromised by her cousin's fiancé. The situation appears irreconcilable; but a flood descends upon the town, and Maggie courageously rescues Tom from the Mill. There is a moment of revelation for Tom before the boat is overwhelmed and both brother and sister are drowned.

With the publication of *Silas Marner* in 1861, Eliot again focuses on the innocent individual wrongly driven out of a seemingly virtuous community. Gradually Marner finds happiness through his love for an orphan, Eppie. A solemn and somewhat bleak story, Eliot intended *Silas Marner* "to set in a strong light the remedial influences of pure, natural, human relations."

Romola (1863), Eliot's only historical novel, is set during the Italian Renaissance. According to Lewes, contemporary reviewers met it "with a universal howl of discontent." Eliot, however, thought it her best work. "There is no book of mine," she wrote, "about which I more thoroughly feel I could swear by every sentence as having been written with my best blood."

With her next book, *Felix Holt, the Radical* (1866), Eliot again departed from her usual rendering of rural communities and townsfolk, this time capturing the urban environment in her only overtly political novel. In the novel she provides a political model for reforms: Felix is noble-minded and self-sacrificing, deliberately choosing the life of a humble artisan in order to show his fellow workers that the hope of improving their condition lies in education and learning to think for themselves, not in legislative programs.

Eliot returned to the rural with her next, and finest, novel, *Middlemarch* (1871–1872). Originally conceived as two separate works, "Miss Brooke" and "Middlemarch," the novel presents a broad canvas of community life with parallel plots concerning unhappy marriages with one partner outgrowing the other, and false hopes of scientific discoveries prevented or marred because of the arbitrariness of time, medical and social reforms blocked because of ignorance, and the cancerous effect of money on human relationships. Despite the broad scope and complications of intertwining stories, *Middlemarch* presents some of her strongest characterizations and plotting. Subtitled "A Study of Provincial Life," it is a complex panoramic work focusing on the social, religious, economic, political, and personal interrelationships among a number of characters. Eliot states her basic premise in the work's "Prelude": a natural conflict occurs between personal growth and ambition when an individual is faced with social or other adversaries. Hence her provincial characters are concerned more with materialism and conformity than with personal substance, and her two protagonists, Dorothea Brooke and Tertius Lydgate, must overcome apathy and intolerance to exercise their idealism. Her handling of plot, as a carefully worked-out organic whole with every character and incident forming a "contributory and integral part," as David Cecil called it, is excellent, as are her many carefully delineated, psychologically complex characters, her sensitivity to setting, and her complete awareness of the cultural and intellectual currents of her day. The concern above all for a rational approach to life enables her to see the shallow hypocrisies and narrow prejudices of the majority of the people in the world she describes. Compared to the overwhelming novels of her day, as F.R. Leavis noted, *Middlemarch* can be best compared with the work of Tolstoy.

Between *Felix Holt* and *Middlemarch*, Eliot tried her hand at writing a closet drama, *The Spanish Gypsy* (1868). Although contemporary reviews were positive, Henry James's evaluation of the work reflects the attitude of most modern critics: "*The Spanish Gypsy* is not a genuine poem," he declared. "It lacks the hurrying quickness, the palpitating warmth, the bursting melody through a glass smoked by the flame of meditative vigils."

Eliot's last novel, *Daniel Deronda* (1876), is considered by many critics to be one of the finest, most sensitive portrayals of Jewish life ever created by a non-Jewish writer. Two years after its publication, Lewes died, and on May 6, 1880, Eliot married John Cross, a clergyman. She became ill in October the same year and died on December 22.

Eliot's fiction centered around moral problems and the moral growth and development of her characters. This preoccupation with moral dilemmas gives her work an overt didacticism that many twentieth-century readers find heavy-handed. Yet few fail to admire her ability to construct on a vast scale while maintaining a close attention to detail. Her works are carefully crafted and capture much of the rugged beauty and hardships of rural nineteenth-century England.

Works

Translations: *The Life of Jesus Critically Examined, by D.F. Strauss* (1846). As Marian Evans *The Essence of Christianity, by L. Feuerbach* (1854). *Ethics*, by B. Spinoza, ed. T. Deegen (1981). *Tractatus Theologico-Politicus*, by B. Spinoza (unpub.).

Short Stories: *Scenes of Clerical Life* (1858).

Novels: *Adam Bede* (1859). *The Mill on the Floss* (1860). *Silas Marner* (1861). *Romola* (1863) *Felix Holt, the Radical* (1866). *The Spanish Gypsy* (1868). *Middlemarch* (1871–1872). *Daniel Deronda* (1876).

Other: *Letters*, ed. G. Haight (1955). *A Writer's Notebook, 1819–1880, and Uncollected Writings*, ed. J. Wiesenfarth (1981).

Lynn M. Alexander

Elisabeth Charlotte Pfalzgräfin, Herzogin von Orléans
1652–1722

a.k.a. Lisalotte von der Pfalz
Born May 27, 1652, Heidelberg, Germany
Died August 12, 1722, Saint-Cloud, France
Genre(s): letters, correspondence, memoir
Language(s): German, French

Elisabeth Charlotte, Countess and Duchess of Orléans, was the daughter of the Elector Karl Ludwig of the Palatine and of Charlotte, Princess of Hessen. Her parents' marriage was not a very happy one and they were divorced; her father remarried a chambermaid by whom he had many children and to whom Elisabeth Charlotte became very attached.

In the year 1671 she was married to Philipp, the Duke of Orléans, who was recently widowed by the death of his first wife, Henrietta of England. A condition of her marriage to this wealthy and influential personage was her conversion to Catholicism. It was a political marriage, by which the Elector of the Palatine hoped to gain friendship and peace with France. However, it was not a very happy marriage; Elisabeth Charlotte never really felt at home in the French court. However, she did love the theatre and often read and attended the plays of Molière; she met, was acquainted with, and highly respected the works of Corneille and Racine. Elisabeth Charlotte had three children. The first died in early childhood, and her eldest son was betrothed to the bastard daughter of the King of France, Louis XIV. Her relationship to the French court and its courtesans became so unbearable that she eventually withdrew from them altogether and retreated to her own garden, devoting herself to the study of gems and precious stones, art and engraving, and, above all else, cultivating an extensive correspondence with her stepsisters, with her aunt in Hannover, and with friends and relatives. Her correspondence was a source of joy to her friends in Germany; Leibnitz, the famous philosopher, who apparently read some of her letters, is said to have marveled at her rich language and her unique expressions and considered her epistles more than mere letters; he called them works of art. She wrote over four thousand letters.

The letters provide us with a rich source of the cultural life of that time, especially of German and French cultural expressions. Life at court, bourgeois traditions, religious practices, work habits and entertainment, music, theatre, medicine, and health care are discussed in detail. Elisabeth Charlotte never recovered from her homesickness for Germany. In the year 1701 her husband, Philipp of Orléans, died, and Elisabeth Charlotte experienced feelings of reconciliation for her husband and for his country.

Works

Anekdoten vom Französichen Hofe vorzuglich den Zeiten Ludwigs XIV und des Duc Regent aus Briefen der Madame d'Orléans . . . Herzog Philipp I von Orléans Witwe, herausgegeben von A.F. Veltheim [Anecdotes from the French Court Particularly of the Time of Louis XIV and of the Duke Regent Taken from the Letters of Madame of Orléans, the Widow of Duke Philipp I] (1789). *Bekenntnisse der Prinzessin Elisabeth Charlotte von Orléans. Aus ihren Originalbriefen* [Confessions of the Princess Elisabeth Charlotte of Orléans from the Original Letters] (1791). *Memoires sur la court de Louis XIV et de la Regence*

[Memoirs of the Court of Louis XIV and of the Regency] (1823). *Memoires, fragments, historiques et correspondance* [Memoirs, Fragments, Histories and Correspondence] (1832). *Briefe an die Raugräfin Louise 1676–1722* [Letters to the Countess Louise 1676–1722; letters to her stepmother] (1843). *Die Briefe der Herzogin Elisabeth Charlotte von Orléans aus den Jahren 1676–1722* [Letters of the Duchess Elisabeth Charlotte of Orléans from the years 1676–1722] (1867–1881). *Briefe an Leibnitz herausgegeben von Zeitschrift des historischen Vereins fur Niedersachsen* [Letters to Leibnitz edited by the Journal of the Historical Society of Neidersachsen] (1884). *Aus den Briefen der Herzogin Elisabeth Charlotte von Orléans an Kurfürstin Sophie von Hannover herausgegeben von E. Bodemann, 2 Bande* [Letters from the Duchess Elisabeth Charlotte of Orléans to the Princess Sophie of Hannover, edited by E. Bodemann, 2 volumes] (1891). *Briefe über die Zustände am französischen Hofe unter Ludwig XIV. Ausgewählt aus den Jahren 1672–1720, herausgegeben von R. Friedmann* [Letters about the Conditions of the French Court under Louis XIV. Selections from the years 1672–1720, edited by R. Friedmann] (1903).

Brigitte Edith Zapp Archibald

Elisabeth of Nassau-Saarbrücken
ca. 1397–1456

Born after 1393 (1397?), Vézélise, France
Died 1456, Saarbrücken
Genre(s): prose romance
Language(s): German

Elisabeth of Nassau-Saarbrücken, with whose name the beginnings of a prose fiction tradition in Germany are connected, came from a French-speaking court in Lorraine and was raised by a mother steeped in the tradition of the late medieval *Chansons de geste*. Married to a German count at an early age, Elisabeth combined the tasks of raising her sons and administering her lands (she was widowed in 1429, her oldest son succeeded to the throne in 1438), as well as translating and introducing French chivalric literature to a German courtly audience. Her family relations extended to the leading cultural centers in Lorraine and Burgundy on the one side and Heidelberg on the other, the home of the younger Countess Palatine Mechthild,

the foremost patroness of German literature in southern Germany of the later fifteenth century. Elisabeth's tomb lies in the Collegiate Church of St. Arnual in Saarbrücken.

The French sources of the four romances attributed to Elisabeth are rhymed *Chansons de geste* connected loosely with the romanticized figures of Charlemagne, his successors, and his enemies. In an ambiguous phrase at the end of *Loher und Maller*, Elisabeth's mother Margarethe of Vaudémont is credited with having written the French version; it is more likely to assume, however, that Margarethe had copies of the *Chansons de geste* produced for herself or her daughter, compilations and adaptations of romances of the thirteenth and fourteenth centuries. Elisabeth must have completed her translations into German prose by 1437, the date found in the *subscriptio* of the second last work, *Loher und Maller*.

The first of Elisabeth's romances is commonly referred to as *Herpin*. Its lengthier title in Simrock's uncritical edition *Der weiße Ritter oder Geschichte von* Herzog Herpin von Bourges *und seinem Sohne* Löw indicates the three major strands of the narrative that relates the trials of Charlemagne's maligned and exiled retainer Herpin and his son Löw. Various fairy-tale motifs play a major role in the plot; for example, young Löw (Lion de Bourges) is nurtured by a lioness, four fairies cast their spells over the infant, a grateful ghost (the white knight) comes to his aid in his later heroic fights, and a magic horn can only be blown by him. The work was repeatedly printed between 1514 and 1659.

The second romance, *Sibille*, on the other hand, did not achieve this degree of popularity and exists only in the sumptuous set of folio manuscripts of Elisabeth's oeuvre produced after her death by her son Johann. It is the story of the unjustly maligned consort of Charlemagne, Sibille, who while in exile gives birth to Ludwig and is finally reinstated in her honor and reunited with the emperor.

The third romance, *Loher und Maller*, takes the reader a generation further to the struggle for the imperial title between Ludwig and his brother Loher (a fictional conglomerate of the Merovingian Clotaire I of the sixth century and the Carolingian Lothair of the ninth). Loher is banned from the French court and while in exile wins the hand of the East Roman Emperor's daughter. With the aid of his devoted friend Maller he fights the heathens, the Greeks, and the Franks, is crowned Roman Emperor by the Pope but loses his beloved wife in childbirth, accidentally kills his friend Maller, and ends in despair as a hermit. This work exists in various manuscript copies of the fifteenth and early prints of the sixteenth centuries and was rediscovered and reprinted in an abridged and modernized form by an outstanding *femme de lettres* of the Romantic movement, Dorothea Schlegel, in 1806, under her husband Friedrich Schlegel's name.

The last and most interesting of Elisabeth's romances is that of *Huge Scheppel* based on the *chanson de geste Hugues Capet*. In an entirely fictional manner, it relates the dynastic change from the Carolingians to the Capetians, the ascent of Hugh, the butcher's grandson, to the French throne by winning the deceased Ludwig's daughter through a series of ruthless feats of arms. *Der schneed Gebuwer* ("the loathsome proletarian"), as he is called by his aristocratic enemies, succeeds in blotting out the blemish of his low birth by beating the established caste at their own game: that of warfare, dueling, or murdering (the butcher's grandson excels in that, as the author slyly remarks), and at that of courting and seducing noble ladies. His ten bastard sons who appear at court at an inopportune moment increase his fame rather than his disgrace: "ist wol in Buelschaft groß Thorheit; so ist ouch große Freud und Wollust darin," he justifies his amorous exploits ("while there is great folly in the pursuit of love, there is also great joy and pleasure in it").

Modern critics have pointed out that Elisabeth merely produced a close translation of the French originals without adapting them to the new medium and without shaping the contents herself. The crudity of the source texts whether in the description of brutalities or in the seemingly emotionless erotic encounters is only slightly mitigated. Indeed, the purpose of Elisabeth's literary activity seems to have been to transmit into Germany subject matters popular among the contemporary French aristocracy. In doing so she uses the medium of prose familiar to late medieval French fiction but in Germany hitherto used only for religious or factual texts. Elisabeth thereby stands at the beginnings of a trend in German literature that lasted for over two centuries and produced numerous offshoots (e.g., *Pontus und Sidonia* attributed to Eleonore Von Österreich). In its many printed versions, this type of literature (the so-called *Volksbücher*) reached the well-to-do bourgeois readers well into the eighteenth century who would marvel at the glorious feats and tribulations of these romantic heroes and heroines but would also be reassured by the message that everybody is bound to the Wheel of Fortune and that submission to God's will is quintessential in everybody's life.

Works

Herpin in K. Simrock. *Die deutschen Volksbücher* 11 (1892; rpt. 1974), pp. 213–445. *Der Roman von der Königin Sibille in drei Prosafassungen d. 14. u. 15. Jahrhunderts*, ed. H. Tiemann (1977), pp. 117–186. *Loher und Maller* (abridged) in Friedrich Schlegel, *Sammlung von Memoiren und Romantischen Dichtungen des Mittelalters aus Altfranzösischen und Deutschen Quellen*, ed. L. Dieckmann (1980), pp. 377–456. *Huge Scheppel*, in H. Kindermann, *Volksbücher vom sterbenden Rittertum* (1928), pp. 23–114.

Karl A. Zaenker

Elisabeth von Schönau
1129–1164
Born 1129
Died June 18, 1164, Schönau, Germany
Genre(s): visions
Language(s): Latin

Elisabeth entered the Benedictine monastery of Schönau at twelve years of age and was professed in 1147. Schönau near St. Goarshausen on the Rhine was founded c. 1130 as a double Benedictine monastery run by an abbot. From 1157 to her death, Elisabeth was the magistra of the women's monastery. Her literary work was written as guidance for her fellow nuns.

In poor health during all her life, Elisabeth went through a severe crisis in 1152 that led to visionary experiences (a vision of the Trinity among them) that recurred during the remainder of her life. In 1155, Elisabeth urged her brother (Ekbert) (Eckbert, Egbert) to enter the Schönau monastery. Ekbert of Schönau (d. 1184) became Elisabeth's spiritual advisor, often urging her to find in her visions answers for crucial questions prevalent in the church and state of their time. Upon Elisabeth's dictations in both Latin and German, Ekbert also composed her visionary works in Latin.

Typical of Elisabeth's visions is the presence of St. John or of an "angel" who interprets to her what she has seen but may not have understood and whose theological concepts at times differ from those of Ekbert (cf. especially Elisabeth's vision of Christ as a woman).

Elisabeth of Schönau is a younger contemporary of Hildegard von Bingen (see entry) whom she met and admired and with whom she corresponded. Although a visionary like Hildegard, Elisabeth is unequal to her in scope or originality. Yet, like Hildegard, she exhorts monks and bishops to an inner reform of the church; in fact, at times, she attacks the abuses within the church and the offensive behavior of its representatives.

While some of Elisabeth's visions were ridiculed even by her contemporaries, other parts of her work experienced great popularity during the Middle Ages. Over 150 manuscripts are still extant, several among them from the twelfth century, and some spread as far as England and Iceland as early as the twelfth century. There has never been a critical edition nor a complete translation into any vernacular language of Elisabeth's works.

Elisabeth's three most important "visionary cycles" (Köster) are: *Liber viarum Dei* (1156–1157), influenced by Hildegard von Bingen's *Scivias; Revelationes de sacro exercitu virginum Coloniensium* (1156–1157), a visionary account of the phantastic legend of St. Ursula and her 11,000 companions (the number presumably a misreading of the name Ximilla). This account was the most widely circulated of Elisabeth's works and exerted an enormous influence on her contemporaries, no doubt accounting for Elisabeth's popularity in her time; and *Visio de resurrectione beatae Mariae virginis* (1156–1159), a response to the great contemporary interest in the details of Mary's life.

Elisabeth's visions were collected, edited, and prefaced by Ekbert von Schönau in three books, *Liber I-III visionum* (1152–1164). About twenty of Elisabeth's letters are also extant.

Elisabeth von Schönau's books have never been acknowledged by the church, nor has she ever been canonized; she is venerated as a local saint only in the Limburg diocese where Schönau is located. Her works were popular throughout the Middle Ages and during the baroque and pietistic periods. A critical edition of *Visiones* is needed for a proper evaluation of her work.

Works

Die visionen der hl. Elisabeth und die Schriften der Aebte Ekbert und Emecho von Schönau, ed. F.W.E. Roth (Brünn, 1884) (Latin text). *Acta SS.* 1st ed. (June 3, 1701), pp. 604–643 and 3rd ed. (June 4, 1867), pp. 400-532. *Liber I–III visionum* edited by Ekbert von Schönau.

Gertrud Jaron Lewis

Queen Elizabeth I
1533–1603
Born September 7, 1533, Greenwich, England
Died March 24, 1603, Richmond
Genre(s): poetry, translation, letters, oration
Language(s): English

After a youth that saw her mother's execution in 1536, her brother's accession to the throne in 1547, and her own imprisonment under her Catholic sister's reign, Elizabeth I began her rule of England in 1558, bringing a long period of relative peace, military success, and enhanced political importance to the nation. Her popularity at home was matched with a sometimes grudging respect from allies and enemies abroad, not only for her political astuteness but for her learning.

Roger Ascham and his pupil William Grindal, both leading Protestant humanist scholars, educated her and praised her aptitude. While queen, Elizabeth continued to study history and classical literature, but it was her capabilities as a linguist that produced the largest portion of her writings. She was expert enough in Greek, Latin, French, and Italian to write *A Book of Devotions* in English and these tongues. Probably compiled in the 1570s, even these private prayers show her as conscious of her political image.

Elizabeth's linguistic ability also produced translations from all four of these foreign languages ar various times in her life. She rendered the 13th Psalm into English tetrameter verse and Marguerite de Navarre's *Le Miroir de l'ame pécheresse* (Mirror of the Sinful Soul) into prose when only about eleven years old. When sixty-five, she tackled Horace's "Ars Poetica." Her most polished piece, an early one done in verse, is of 90 lines from Petrarch's "Trionfo Dell'Eternita," and her longest is of Boethius's *De Consolatione Philosophiae* (1593). In many of these works, the alliteration may alienate the modern ear, but certain passages have considerable vigor. The great speed at which she translated may account for some mistranslations and a rhythmically awkward Latinate word order, but the devotion of effort to such a task amid state duties is remarkable.

She also wrote original poems, though not all those subsequently ascribed to her. Of the six definitely genuine pieces, three are only two-to-four-line epigrams, and the others under twenty lines. This small body of work, nonetheless, has distinct characteristics: the poems touch her particular situations, political and personal. They do not so much complain against fortune as assert her determination to overcome it. One, perhaps the latest, relies on the

Queen Elizabeth I

Elizabeth I's political position and talents have made her literary fame more as a subject of masterpieces like Spenser's *Faerie Queene* than as an author in her own right. Her contemporaries recognized, however, that she was immensely learned and a skillful writer in a wide variety of forms.

Works

Mirror of the Sinful Soul, ed. P. Ames (1897). *Queen Elizabeth's Englishings of Boethius . . . Plutarch . . . Horace*, ed. C. Pemberton (1899, rpt. 1973). *The Letters of Queen Elizabeth*, ed. G. Harrison (1935, rpt. 1968). *The Public Speaking of Queen Elizabeth*, ed. G. Rice (1951). *The Poems of Queen Elizabeth I*, ed. L. Bradner (1964). "Ah silly pugge" in L. Black, *TLS* (May 23, 1968). *A Book of Devotions Composed by Her Majesty Elizabeth R*, trans. A. Fox and intro. J. Hodges (1970). *Proceedings in the Parliaments of Elizabeth I*, ed. T. Hartley (1981). *Elizabethan England and Europe: Forty Unprinted Letters*, ed. E. Kouri (1982). *Elizabeth's Glass with "The Glass of the Sinful Soul" (1544) by Elizabeth I*, ed. M. Shell (1993). "The French Verse," ed. and trans. S. May and A. Prescott, *ELR* (1994).

Sayre N. Greenfield

paradoxes of Petrarchan love poetry, whereas the two other main pieces have the occasional alliteration and rougher meter characteristic of mid-century lyrics.

Elizabeth's numerous letters penned in her roles as princess and queen exhibit a variety of styles suited to the particular situations and correspondents. She could be remarkably direct, even with other monarchs, but could, when her own feelings were ambivalent or when her purposes required that she not commit herself, write in a cloudy language of high diction, extended metaphors, and philosophical aphorisms.

Over a dozen of her speeches survive, and, though their occasions vary, they typically express trust in her people's good-will and a desire for their security. Although some rhetorical features, like a dependence on deductive reasoning and a penchant for comparisons and metaphors, remain fairly constant, her style changes. Early speeches rely on an obfuscating adorned prose. When her political confidence increases, later performances grow more bold, if only in stating her evasiveness. In one case, she herself calls her response to a request an "answer answerless." The two most famous speeches, that at Tillbury to her troops as the Spanish Armada approached and her final "Golden" oration to Parliament, are unusually direct and dramatic.

Dorothe Engelbretsdatter
1643–1716

Born January 16, 1643, Bergen, Norway
Died February 19, 1716, Bergen
Genre(s): religious poetry (hymn), occasional poetry, rhymed letters
Language(s): Danish (the written language in Norway at this time)

Dorothe Engelbretsdatter is recognized as Norway's first woman writer. Although women wrote before her, she is without doubt the first Norwegian woman to be taken seriously and to gain recognition for her writing.

Born in 1643 in Bergen, Norway's largest and most influential city in the seventeenth century, little is known of her early life. At age eighteen she married Ambrosious Hardenbeck, a pastor, who later took over her father's position as pastor of the cathedral in Bergen. As the daughter and wife of religious leaders, she lived in a very pious milieu. Her social position also afforded her the opportunity to write; it was acceptable for women of her background to read and write.

Dorothe Engelbretsdatter bore nine children and she outlived all of them. Seven of them died in childhood; one disappeared; and one fell in battle. Her husband died in 1683, leaving her to live alone the last thirty years of her life. It is understandable why many critics have emphasized the role sorrow has played in her work and readily point to it as a source of inspiration for her writing.

Her first book, *Siælens sangoffer* (Song Offerings of the Soul), published in 1678, was a collection of religious poetry. Many of the poems were set to popular music and became favorite hymns. The book was published after she had buried seven of her children, and in the introduction she comments that "new sorrows have produced new songs."

Two important factors should be mentioned in connection with this book. First, it was written and published in the vernacular. This was significant because much was still being written in Latin. Second, the book was published in Christiania (present-day Oslo). Most books at this time were still being published in Copenhagen. (Copenhagen began printing books in 1482; Norway did not receive its first printing press until 1643). These two factors contributed to making the book accessible to a larger audience.

The book was extremely successful; in fact, it was a bestseller. Twenty-five editions appeared; the last in 1868. There were six editions alone in the period from its publication in 1643 to 1700. Stories are told of people rushing to the bookstore to obtain a copy, only to be turned away. The book was as popular in Denmark as it was in Norway.

Shortly after her husband's death, she published her second book, *Taareoffer* (Tear Offerings), in 1685. This, however, was not an original work. Rather, it was a paraphrase of a manuscript by the Norwegian pastor Peder Møller, which in turn was a translation of a work by a German writer, Heinrich Müller, published in Germany in 1675.

Following her husband's death, Dorothe Engelbretsdatter was concerned about how she would be able to provide for herself. In 1684 the king granted her life exemption from government taxes. This is regarded as the first artist's stipend in Norway.

It is impossible to view Dorothe Engelbretsdatter's work separate from the religious and political climate of the 1600s. The modern secular mind finds it difficult to grasp this setting. The church (dominated by a strict Lutheran orthodoxy) was the ultimate authority, and there existed a very rigid political order (in the form of an absolute monarchy). Literature had a powerful religious and political function. Poets wrote to entertain and glorify the monarchy as well as to serve the church; the hymn was an integral part of the church service. The genres that Dorothe Engelbretsdatter chose (religious and occasional poetry) fulfilled these two important functions. She also followed very closely the conventions of these two genres.

Her poetry is in some ways very typical of the baroque poetry of the day. Her form was strictly controlled. She was very deft at rhyme, and she employed many of the rhetorical devices of the baroque poet. However, there were some important differences. Her poetry had a very personal, direct tone. It was not intellectualized, but came, as she said "from the heart." One must ask why she was so popular in her time. Her poetry was sincere; she presented a very personal and approachable God. Her imagery was connected to the events of everyday life; people found it very easy to relate to. Filled with emotion, it was different from much of the heavy scholarly literature of the day.

Literary histories have traditionally either overlooked Dorothe Engelbretsdatter or, referring to her as a "tearjerker," dismissed her as a popular, but unimportant writer. However, there has been a renewed interest in her work. In the 1950s her collected works were published in a revised and annotated edition. This made her work more accessible to the Norwegian audience.

Recently, critics have maintained that her image as a "tearjerker" is unfair. It seems to be a judgment based on her second book, a much more sentimental piece of writing and one that is not her original work. These critics maintain that emphasis must be placed on her first work, which is her original writing. In addition, one must keep in mind that she was working within the limits of a specific genre. Stronger emphasis has also begun to be placed on her occasional poetry and letters, of which about fifty remain. In doing so, a different picture of her emerges; it is a lighter picture, where humor is also present.

Ludvig Holberg, the famous Danish/Norwegian writer of the eighteenth century lauded Dorothe as "the best poetess the North has known." Although one cannot say that she has maintained her popularity through time, there is still interest in her. In 1986, a contemporary Norwegian writer published a novel with Dorothe as a main character. This book (*I Dorotheas hus* by Torill Thorstad Hauger, Oslo: Gyldendal, 1986), attempts to bring the world of Dorothe Engelbretsdatter closer to the modern reader.

Works

Siælens Sangoffer [Song Offerings of the Soul] (1678). *Taareoffer* [Tear Offerings] (1685). *Leilighetsbrev/brev* [Occasional Poetry and Letters]. *Samlede skrifter I–II* [Collected Works] (1955–1956).

Peggy Hager

Erinna
ca. 370 b.c.

Born approximately 370 b.c.(?), possibly on Telos, a small island in the southeast Aegean, near Rhodes (according to the consensus of some modern scholars)
Genre(s): poetry, epigram
Language(s): Greek

Ancient critics deemed Erinna a woman poet second only to Sappho, as supreme in hexameter verse as Sappho was in her lyrics; her fame rested upon a three-hundred-line poem entitled the *Distaff*, whose metrical craftsmanship was rated "equal to Homer's." References to this work in subsequent literature indicate that it enjoyed a remarkable vogue among poets writing in the first half of the third century b.c. and continued to be cherished, at least by the erudite, down through the Hellenistic period and the early centuries of the Roman empire. Learned interest in Erinna was stimulated by a sentimental legend that she was an unmarried girl who had written the *Distaff* at the age of nineteen and died, still a virgin, shortly thereafter. In actuality, no biographical data had been handed down, as is evident from the fact that even her birthplace and date are variously given.

Until 1928, Erinna's work was known to us solely through three epigrams preserved in the *Greek Anthology* and a few brief citations in later authors. In that year, however, Italian archaeologists discovered some badly mutilated papyrus fragments of the *Distaff* that have now been pieced together, restored and supplemented to provide about twenty lines of continuous text. These restorations are highly conjectural, and several commentators have expressed grave doubt that much real sense may be made of the whole. It is agreed, though, that Erinna's greatly praised poem was a lament for the speaker's dead friend Baucis, once her girlhood playmate and more recently a bride. This observation in itself signals a clear departure from earlier Greek poetic tradition and a direct influence upon succeeding authors: prior to Erinna, hexameters had not been associated with funerary poetry, but later Hellenistic writers, including Theocritus, readily employ them for that purpose.

If the scholarly conjectures are accurate, the preserved text apparently begins in the middle of the speaker's reminiscences of her childhood life with Baucis. She may have alluded to a girls' tag game in which the "It" player assumed the role of a tortoise who weaves a shroud for her dead son, to playing with dolls, to the household activities of someone's mother, and lastly to the shape-changing nursery monster Mormo; she also apparently spoke of Baucis's forgetfulness of things heard from her mother, this in the context of marriage and Aphrodite. Finally she seems to have turned back to her immediate sorrow, lamenting that she could not leave the house, look upon Baucis dead, or mourn with uncovered head, for which she felt *aidos*, "shame." Further remains of the left-hand side of a column contain possible references to the speaker's present age, nineteen (or, alternatively, to Baucis's age at death); to grey hairs; and to shouts in praise of Hymen, god of marriage, punctuated with cries of grief over Baucis.

The problem of providing a coherent explanation of this fascinating fragment has proven extremely difficult for scholars, not only because the lines themselves are so mutilated but also because ancient and modern critics alike tend to interpret the *Distaff* according to their own preconceptions of its creator. When the work was rediscovered, its use of a first-person speaker prompted autobiographical surface readings that treated it as a young girl's naive and spontaneous expression of sorrow over a friend's death. After the techniques of close literary analysis had disclosed the poem's consummate artistry, one scholar cynically branded it an elaborate literary forgery perpetrated by an unknown male writer, designed to appeal to Alexandrian tastes by passing itself off as the pathetic outcry of a damsel in distress. In contrast, feminist classical scholars have recently argued cases for approaching the *Distaff* as a genuine masterpiece of women's art incorporating a female-ordered perspective upon experience. The focus of that experience is a matter of debate: for Arthur, the poem is a symbolic meditation upon selfhood and personal identity; Pomeroy thinks it concerned itself chiefly with literary creativity; Skinner contends that it examined the fragility of women's bonding and their enforced isolation within a patriarchal society. Because of its important aesthetic and cultural value, it should continue to attract the interest of all students of the female tradition in world literature.

The new concern for the *Distaff*, has diverted attention from Erinna's three surviving epigrams. These, however, provide the opportunity to observe how the poet exercises her artistic talents within a smaller compass and may therefore throw light upon the themes of her longer hexameter poem. Two of these pieces are funereal epigrams for Baucis in which the dead girl herself speaks. In the first, the more conventional of the pair, she addresses her own gravestone, bidding it tell passers-by first, that she had been a bride; second, her name and birthplace; third, that her friend Erinna had had this epitaph inscribed upon it. The markedly original companion piece makes her accuse the king of the underworld of personal malice, in a phrase that became famous: *baskanos ess', Aida*, "you are jealous, Hades." Elaborately varying the commonplace "bride of death" motif, the last four lines depict Baucis's father-in-law lighting her pyre with the torches kindled for her wedding while the hymeneal song modulates into a threnody. These innovative poetic ideas—which were quickly absorbed into the tradition and soon became clichés—all eroticize the experience of death, or at least forge a subliminal connection between a woman's heterosexual initiation and her death. Remains of verse beginnings and endings suggest that the same emotional association between marriage and death was exploited in the *Distaff*. A third, very different piece celebrates the verisimilitude of a girl's portrait; its self-conscious preoccupation with the *sophia* of the artist lends weight to Pomeroy's belief that the *Distaff* dealt with the situation of the woman poet. This quatrain, the first known ekphrastic (vividly descriptive) epigram in Greek literature, seems to have directly inspired the work of Nossis and, to a lesser extent, of Anyte. Anyte also appears to borrow from Erinna for her own funerary epitaphs on maidens, especially by appropriating and conventionalizing the link between marriage and death as related polarities of female experience. In this way Erinna probably served as the model for an entire later generation of women epigrammatists.

Works

Greek text of the *Distaff* fragments in *Supplementum Hellenisticum*, eds. H. Lloyd-Jones and P. Parsons (Berlin, 1983). Text and English tr. in *Select Papyri III*, ed. D.L. Page, Loeb Classical Library (Cambridge, Mass., 1950). Greek texts and German translations of the epigrams in Homeyer, H., *Dichterinnen des Altertums und des frühen Mittelalters* (Paderborn, 1979). Commentary in *The Greek Anthology: Hellenistic Epigrams*, eds. A.S.F. Gow and D.L. Page, 2 vols. (Cambridge, Mass. 1965). English tr. in *The Greek Anthology*, tr. W.R. Paton. Loeb Classical Library, 5 vols. (Cambridge, Mass., 1916). English tr. of all fragments and epigrams in Rayor, D., *Sappho's Lyre: Archaic Lyric and Women Poets of Ancient Greece* (Berkeley and Los Angeles, 1991).

Marilyn B. Skinner

Florbela de Alma da Conceição Espanca
1894–1930

Born 1894, Vila Vicosa, Alentejo, Portugal
Died 1930, Matosinhos
Genre(s): poetry, short story
Language(s): Portuguese

Espanca, cited as "her country's foremost woman poet" in the *Columbia Dictionary of Modern European Literature*, was born illegitimately in the Alto Alentejo province of Portugal. Married at the age of sixteen, she rebelled against the second-class status of Portuguese women. By the time of her divorce at eighteen, she had begun to write lyric poems and short stories in the manner of the symbolist-decadent style then popular. These early works were not published until 1931. Espanca began studying law in Lisbon in her early twenties and soon married for a second time. Her first collection of poems, *Livro das mágoas* (Book of Woes), was published in 1919. This early phase of her work reveals the influence of her mentor, Antonio Nobre. Following her second divorce in 1923, she published the *Livro de Sóror Saudade* (Book of Sister Saudade), the title of which refers to the name given her by Américo Durão, a friend and fellow poet. This collection represents a second phase of her career, and her uninhibited self-disclosure of amorous encounters invites comparison with *The Portuguese Letters* of Sóror Mariana Alcoforado. Espanca's quest for love here reaches cosmic proportions. These two early works went unnoticed by critics of the day, probably due to their unorthodoxy and "impropriety."

Espanca married for a third time and was preparing two collections of poetry when she died, possibly a suicide, on her birthday in 1930. This third phase of her production included the works *Charneca em Flor* (Flowering Heath) and *Reliquiae* (Relics), both published in 1931. The poet here reaches her artistic height, abandoning her barren pursuit of love and experiencing moments of inner peace, which find expression in her sonnets of "sculptural perfection" (*Literatura Portuguesa Moderna*). Her short stories, according to the *Columbia Dictionary of Modern European Literature*, are "... dated examples of erotic art nouveau."

Works

Poetry: *Livro das mágoas* (1919; Book of Woes). *Livro de Sóror Saudade* (1923; Book of Sister Saudade). *Charneca em Flor* (1931; Flowering Heath). *Reliquiae* (1931; Relics). *Juvenilia* (1931).

Short Stories: *As Mascaras do Destino* (1931; The Masks of Destiny). *Domino Negro* (1931; Black Domino).

Paula T. Irvin

Concha Espina
1869–1955

a.k.a. Concepción Espina [de la Maza]
Born 1869, Santander, Spain
Died 1955, Madrid
Genre(s): novel, short story, drama, poetry
Language(s): Spanish

Espina has been termed the first Spanish woman writer to earn her living exclusively from her writings, a possibly inaccurate statement but one that reflects her wide popularity. Twice nominated for the Nobel Prize (once lost by a single vote), she won several prizes, including the Royal Academy's prestigious Fastenrath for *La esfinge maragata* (1914; English translation, Mariflor, 1924); the National Prize for Literature for *Altar mayor* (1954; High Altar), and a major theatrical prize for *El jayón* (1918; The Foundling). Espina's prestige sufficed to have her named a cultural representative of King Alfonso XIII to the Antilles (1928), and she later served as a visiting professor at Middlebury College. Although generally conservative and rarely considered a feminist, Espina was among the most successful women writers in the first quarter of the twentieth century.

Raised in a religious home and educated in a convent, Espina hastily married in 1892 following her mother's death and her father's bankruptcy, accompanying her husband to Chile where two of their five children were born. Financial difficulty prompted her to begin writing as a newspaper correspondent, but her journalism compounded incipient marital problems, which ultimately led to separation in 1916.

Espina is associated with the regional variant of realism, with early novels usually set in rural Santander and featuring detailed descriptions of nature and conservative ideology. The author of some fifty books, including novels, plays, and poetry, she is best known for her fiction. While influenced by post-romantic sentimentalism as well as realistic currents, she remained essentially apart from major literary movements. Her importance for feminists is her focus on female protagonists. As a sentimentalist, she often wrote of unrequited or impossible love yet had suffi-

cient vision to portray some women as victims of their own sentimentality, trapped in an intellectual vacuum by the conflict between romantic illusion and the harsher realities of daily life with the then-typical male-female relationships. In later works, Espina moves beyond her native region and one-to-one relationships to study the impact of varied social realities on her characters. Her plays were few, concentrating on internal moral dilemmas of women in their roles as mother, daughter, fiancée, and wife. Two collections of Espina's brief fiction explore critical issues in Spanish history during the early twentieth century: the need for national reform, the conflict between traditional values and progress, materialism versus idealism, and the hostilities of the civil war.

The popular *folletín* (serialized novel of the nineteenth century), with its melodrama, suspense, and dependence on coincidence, provided a model for Espina's first foray into long fiction, *La niña de Luzmela* (1909; The Girl from Luzmela), which also includes the sentimental novel and moralistic fiction among its forebears. Plot takes primacy over characterization, and style is superior to both the one-dimensional characters and soap-opera plot. The writer's concept of suffering as a fundamental part of human existence and her depiction of virtue in conflict with evil appear here and in *Despertar para morir* (1910; To Awake to Die), although more sophistication is evident in the latter, which analyzes moral decadence in Madrid's turn-of-the-century aristocracy and develops the tragic consequences of marriage as an economic transaction. In *Agua de nieve* (1911; English translation, *The Woman and the Sea*, 1934), suffering continues as a major avenue for plumbing life's deeper meaning, but simplistic conflicts between good and evil are replaced by analysis of the Spanish woman and the heroine's internal struggles in her quest for happiness.

Among Espina's best and most successful novels is *La esfinge maragata* (1914; English translation, *Mariflor*, 1924), which refines the best of her regionalistic vision of northern Spain while incorporating some of the fervor for national regeneration of the "Generation of 1898." *La esfinge maragata* is set in the isolated, backward, impoverished, semi-desert Maragatería district of León's border with Galicia. Following classic realistic/naturalistic procedure, Espina spent months there observing details of village life, geography, and social environment, and documenting local dialect and folklore. While provincial and localistic, the novel is also a vigorous denunciation of social and familial situations of women. Florinda, the heroine, raised in Galicia (humid and green), returns to live with her grandmother, Dolores, in a desolate, sterile land, her once wealthy family now impoverished. Modern, independent, frank, cultured, and optimistic, with an urban mentality, Florinda contrasts with her traditional grandmother's feudal outlook; coarse, uneducated ways; lack of independence; and rural mentality. Another contrast is established between the strong, silent, long-suffering women, and the men who are brutal, domineering, and dehumanized, or else weak. Life in Maragatería is an endless cycle of emigration and living at the subsistence level. Harsh economic realities eventually triumph and Mariflor ends by accepting the same economic basis for matrimony as generations of Maragatan women before her.

Unlike its predecessors, *El metal de los muertos* (1920; The Metal of the Dead) is most emphatically social protest fiction. Following World War I, Spain was experiencing unrest prior to the Civil War, and Espina moved closer to the left, although remaining moderate. This social epic, her most ambitious work, has been ranked by most critics among her best achievements, and for it also the diligent author personally researched the area and way of life described (in the Río Tinto copper mines in the Andalusian province of Huelva). Espina depicts a miners' strike between 1910 and 1920, a struggle supported by a group of bourgeois intellectuals inspired by humanitarian socialism (a term avoided by the novelist, whose chief organizer speaks instead of return to early Christian values). Contemporary concern with pollution, industrial wastes, and poisonous by-products lends an up-to-date air to this novel of nearly seven decades ago. Espina introduces a large cast, ranging from brutalized prostitutes to oldtime miners, administrators and labor officials, achieving something approaching the collective protagonist. The main plot is complicated by involved amorous subplots, but the primary conflict remains the struggle between capitalism and the workers' welfare.

Espina's most nearly feminist novel is *La virgen prudente* (1929; The Wise Virgin), examining societal pressures and cultural prejudices that condition women's attitudes and produce internal contradictions. The symbolically named protagonist, Aurora de España (Dawn of Spain), an idealistic young lawyer, struggles with family, friends, and suitors, intent on independence despite their resistance. The contrast between this work and her novels from the mid-1930s onward is enormous, as wartime experiences rendered Espina extremely pro-Franco, producing highly politicized post-war texts of national exaltation, tending again to the melodrama of her apprenticeship years, with their Manichean duality of good and evil. *Altar*

mayor, awarded the highest recognition of any of Espina's works, the National Prize for Literature (for more than six decades the most prestigious literary prize won by any woman writer in Spain), is aesthetically inferior to *La esfinge maragata* and lacks the dramatic impact and social significance of *El metal de los muertos*. Conceived as an exaltation of traditional Spanish values and national history, it is set in Covadonga (Asturias) where the Reconquest began in 711.

Blind from 1937 on, Espina continued to write, and two novels of her final years are of interest for the feminist scholar. *El más fuerte* (1947; The Strongest) presents a male protagonist who, after eighteen years of successful marriage, faces (with his wife) the test of parenting three children through adolescence. In the process, he acquires self-knowledge and becomes better acquainted with the younger generation, but his wife founders in a futile effort to recover the past. *Un valle en el mar* (1950; A Valley in the Sea) focuses on the theme of rape and its consequences in a stratified rural Cantabrian village. The delineation of social values is informative and reasonably objective, and the two central characters transcend the unidimensional flatness and melodramatic traits of the minor personages to rank among Espina's more memorable creations.

An independent figure who resists facile categorization, Espina changes repeatedly during her half-century career, with neither her ideology nor her themes remaining constant. Although her aesthetics are not innovative, her frequent changes in setting and subject matter evince a desire for novelistic progress. Espina was especially interested in feminine psychology, although her analyses were less of individuals than of a type: the woman who was forebearing, long-suffering, self-abnegating, chaste, born "to love and suffer." Her poetics are eclectic and results are uneven. From today's perspective, some works seem outmoded because she often drew upon the past's more dated literary manifestations (postromanticism, melodrama, sentimentalism). Her move to the right after the Civil War also hurt her fame and created an "ideology gap" for many readers. Her wartime *Esclavitud y libertad: diario de una prisionera* (1938; Slavery and Liberty: Diary of a Prisoner) recounts her incarceration by radical leftists and helps to explain her changed attitude. Nevertheless, her writing as a whole is representative of a broad social spectrum and interests sociologically because of her middle-class origins and identification. The enhanced respect she won for women writers in official circles through her own popular success continues to benefit her successors.

Works

La niña de Luzmela (1909). *Despertar para morir* (1910). *Agua de nieve* (1911). *La esfinge maragata* (1914). *La rosa de los vientos* (1916). *El jayón* (1918). *El metal de los muertos* (1920). *El caliz rojo* (1923). *Dulce nombre* (1921). *Llama de cera* (1925). *La virgen prudente* (1929). *Flor de ayer* (1934). *Retaguardia* (1937). *Alas invencibles* (1938). *Esclavitud y libertad: diario de una prisionera* (1938).

La tiniebla encendida (1940). *El fraile menor* (1942). *Moneda blanca* (1942). *La Otra* (1942). *Victoria en América* (1944). *El más fuerte* (1947). *Un valle en el mar* (1950). *Una novela de amor* (1953). *Altar mayor* (1954).

Translations: *Mariflor*, tr. Frances Douglas (1924). *The Red Beacon*, tr. Frances Douglas (1924). *The Woman and the Sea*, tr. Terrell Tatum (1934).

Janet Perez

Camilla Faa' Gonzaga
1599–1662

Born, 1599, Casale, Italy
Died 1662, Ferrara
Genre(s): memoirs
Language(s): Italian

Camilla Faa's life can be read as an example of how unprotected women are in a system in which people in positions of authority can dictate all rules and change all laws. Born into an influential family in the Monferrato region (her father Ardizzino was ambassador to the Gonzagas and her mother Margherita Fassati was a wealthy local heiress), Camilla was educated in a convent before becoming lady-in-waiting at the Gonzaga Court in Mantua. She was fifteen when Duke Ferdinando Gonzaga started to woo her while also trying to convince her father of the seriousness of his intentions. Before long Camilla and Ferdinando were secretly married. Happiness was short lived. Their son was not yet born when the Duke had to bow to political pressures and to petition the Pope to annul his first nuptials in order to marry into a more powerful family. Having become a pawn in a game too difficult for her to understand, Camilla hoped she would be left alone with her child. Instead, he was taken away soon after his birth while she was purposely kept in the dark about events at Court and then repeatedly asked to remarry or to take religious vows. Camilla tried to resist the pressure for five years in the hope that her situation would improve and a way out of her predicament could be found. Finally, she accepted her unwanted destiny of reclusion and became a Clarissa nun. Camilla wrote her memoir in 1622 with the understanding that her Mother Superior would keep it within the convent's walls to avoid possible retaliation.

The title "Storia di donna Camilla Faa di Bruno Gonzaga" was most probably not Camilla's own but given to the short memoir by its editor. The manuscript copy is in the Archives of the Convent of the Corpus Domini in Ferrara. The first published edition is that of 1895, prepared by Giuseppe Giorcelli for *Rivista di Storia, Arte, Archeologia della provincia di Alessandria*. Camilla's "Storia" is a short, terse rendering of the events which first led her to marry Ferdinando and then determined her exclusion from the Court, her seclusion from friends, and her reclusion in a faraway convent. The writing is not a plea of innocence nor is its purport to chastise Ferdinando and his counsellors. Camilla seems somehow able to maintain her objectivity and to keep political obligations in mind. This constitutes in many ways the strength of her memoir. She chooses to be proud rather than pathetic; instead of insisting upon her victimization, she decides to write of her survival; in place of vituperative sarcasm, she offers articulate questioning. Her dismissal from the Court, the denial of her status, the pressure put on her to become a nonentity as a woman should have doomed and mastered Camilla in the long run. It did not happen. She chose to write in fact exactly when everything seemed lost and when speaking for herself of her self would have made no difference in her status. Camilla spent the rest of her remaining forty years isolated in Ferrara. Today we can read her "Storia" as one of the earliest examples in Italian literature, or possibly the earliest altogether, of female autobiography, and an assertive one at that.

Works

"Storia di donna Camilla Faa di Bruno Gonzaga." *Rivista di Storia, Arte, Archeologia della provincia di Alessandria* 10.4 (1895): 90–99. Rpt. with slight changes as "Historia della Sig.ra Donna Camilla Faa Gonzaga," in F. Sorbelli Bonfa, *Camilla Faa Gonzaga: Storia Documentata* (1918).

Valeria Finucci

Oriana Fallaci
1930–

Born June 29, 1930, Florence, Italy
Genre(s): journalism, narrative prose
Language(s): Italian

Oriana Fallaci is one of the most familiar names in contemporary international journalism, renowned for her brilliant and pointed interviewing techniques. Her individual portraits and social studies are celebrated and criticized for their honesty, accuracy, and acute insights if not for their impartiality. Fallaci claims that her journalism is personal, even autobiographical; she is also a subject as interviewer and investigator. As a novelist, the writer blends realistic description with emotional subjectivity. Naturalist scenes unite with meditations, memory, allegorical dreams, musings, and lush imagery in a blend of tones, hues, and narrative techniques joined through the omnipresent psyche of the narrator.

Born of a poor working-class family, Fallaci was drawn to her political and ideological issues at an early age thanks to her father's involvement in the Socialist Party as well as her own experiences in the war. In fact, the adolescent Fallaci acted as a courier for the partisans and Allies, helping save downed fliers and escaped prisoners. During her studies in medicine at the University of Florence, Fallaci began working part time for an uncle, the founder of the magazine *Epoca*. She soon abandoned her medical books for a career in journalism.

After covering the night police beat for a Florentine daily, Fallaci began a long working rapport with another Italian magazine, *Europeo*, as a special correspondent. Working with a tape recorder and notebook, the journalist traveled worldwide covering such disparate events as wars and weddings. Her books record her interpretation of these experiences: distasteful celebrity interviews became *Gli antipatici* (1963; The Egotist); a world tour on the status of women resulted in *Il sesso inutile* (1961; The Useless Sex); her interest in space produced *Se il sole muore* (1965; If the Sun Dies), an investigation of scientists, NASA, astronauts, and science fiction; her three tours of duty in Viet Nam translated into *Niente e così sia* (1969; Nothing and So Be It), a documentary of the horrors, propaganda, and madness of war.

By the late 1960s, Fallaci was an international celebrity herself and a popular subject for other interviewers. In demand for her inquisitive and somewhat inquisitorial questioning, the journalist began contributing to several American periodicals, including *Look*, *Ms.*, *New Republic*, *The New York Times Magazine*,
and the *Washington Post*. Multilingual, she conducts interviews in several languages, which often afford revealing glimpses into the nature and thoughts of her subjects.

Concerned with power and its misuse, injustice, and oppression, her pieces confront these issues by employing journalistic methods to disconcert figures of power, such as statesmen and politicians, and ideologues into unexpected revelations. Her most famous conversations are published in *Intervista con la Storia* (1974; Interview with History). With its fourteen interviews of individuals ranging from the Shah of Iran to Golda Meir, this book is an exemplar of Fallaci's contention that the journalist is a direct witness to the flow of history.

Never married, Fallaci became the companion of Greek freedom fighter Alexandros Panagoulis after an interview, and they remained attached until his suspicious death in 1976. The story of his life and beliefs and their love, blended with political and philosophical meditations on the struggle for human freedom and dignity, are the basis for Fallaci's most famous novel *Un uomo* (1979; A Man).

Another popular and controversial novel is *Lettera a un bambino mai nato* (1975; Letter to a Child Never Born), the tale of a woman's reactions to an unexpected and inconvenient pregnancy as she battles with her own desire for autonomy, the demands and rights of the child, and her conscience and guilt at his loss. Told as a monologue, or confession to the child, this book has been viewed as a strong feminist statement on maternity and social responsibility.

Passionate, involved, and politically engaged, Oriana Fallaci is a model of subjective journalism at its best and most controversial. Rejecting professional remoteness, the writer sees the journalist as a creative artist, a witness to history in process, and a participant in the investigative act. Fallaci's verve, raw energy, and blunt honesty have won her both detractors and admirers. Nevertheless, she has twice won the Saint-Vincent prize for journalism, Italy's equivalent of the Pulitzer, as well as the Viareggio Literary Award for her fiction (1979).

Works

Essay collections: *I sette peccati di Hollywood* (1958). *Il sesso inutile: Viaggio intorno alla donna* (1961). *Gli antipatici* (1963). *Se il sole muore* (1965). *Niente e così sia* (1969). *Quel giorno sulla luna* (1970). *Intervista con la Storia* (1974).

Novels: *Penelope alla guerra* (1962). *Lettera a un bambino mai nato* (1975). *Un uomo: romanzo* (1979). *Insciallah* (1990).

Translations: *The Useless Sex*, tr. Pamela Swinglehurst (1964). *Penelope at War*, tr. Pamela Swinglehurst (1966). *The Egotists: Sixteen Surprising Interviews*, tr. Pamela Swinglehurst (1968). Also published in England as *Limelighters. If the Sun Dies*, tr. Pamela Swinglehurst (1966). *Nothing, and So Be It*, tr. Isabel Quigly (1972). Also published in England as *Nothing and Amen. Interview with History*, tr. John Shepley (1976). *Letter to a Child Never Born*, tr. John Shepley (1976). *A Man*, tr. William Weaver (1980). *Inshallah*, tr. James Marcus (1992).

Fiora A. Bassanese

Cassandra Fedele
1465–1558

Born 1465, Venice, Italy
Died 1558
Genre(s): letters, poetry, oration, treatise
Language(s): Latin

Cassandra was born to Angelo Fedele and to Barbara Leoni, both descendants of noble families exiled from Milan at the fall of the house of Visconti. She was first tutored by her father. At the age of twelve, she began to study theology and the sciences with Gasparino Borro but continued to cultivate the classical languages until she was twenty-two. After marrying a doctor from Vicenza, Giovan Maria Mapelli, she traveled to Crete and lived in Retino (Rethimnon) from 1495 to 1520. On the return journey, the ship was caught in a severe storm, and the Mapellis lost most of their property. After her husband's death in 1520, Cassandra dedicated herself to learning. As her fame grew, she received invitations from Louis XII of France, from Leo X, and from the Queen of Spain to move to their courts, but the Doge forbade her to leave and, in his words, "deprive Venice of its best adornment." Cassandra, however, soon found herself in reduced circumstances. Only when, at the age of eighty, in 1547, she appealed for help to Pope Paul III, was she made prioress of the girls' orphanage attached to the church of S. Domenico di Castello in Venice. She held that position until her death, eleven years later.

Only three orations and some letters of Cassandra's much larger body of writing have come down to us. She was also known as a poet and, as such, celebrated by Politian, Sansovino, and Panfilo Sasso. A few verses are included in her letter to Pope Paul III. We read of a treatise, *De scientiarum ordine* (On the Order of Sciences), in her letters and in those of her friends, who wrote about it as of a work well known to them. Two more writings are mentioned: *Digressioni morali* (Moral Digressions) and *Elogi degli uomini illustri* (Praises of Illustrious Men).

Cassandra's orations, all of encomiastic nature, were delivered by her at official occasions. When young, she was favored by the Doge of Venice, Agostino Barbarigo, and she was invited to state banquets and private gatherings. The speech on the birth of Christ which she addressed to the town dignitaries in San Marco, during the Christmas celebrations, has not come down to us. One of her extant speeches is a praise of literature and was given in the presence of the ambassadors from Brescia. What won Cassandra her fame in Italy and abroad was the oration she delivered at the University of Padua in 1557 on the occasion of the degree conferred on a relative. The speech was given before the president of the university, many professors, and students and was published the same year with the title of "Oration for Bertuccio Lamberti, Receiving the Honors of the Liberal Arts." According to Cavazzana, in the State Library of Munich, there is a letter dated 1558 addressed to Cassandra by a humanist from Nurenberg, Peter Danhauser, who later became professor of Roman Law in Vienna. After hearing of Cassandra from his friend, Hartman Schadel, who had been present at her speech in Bologna, Danhauser wrote to compliment her most enthusiastically and to ask for some of her poetry. The third extant oration was the official speech of welcome that Cassandra was asked to deliver upon the arrival in Venice of Bona Sforza, Queen of Poland. Cassandra was then ninety-one years old.

Fedele's correspondence included letters to many dignitaries and men of letters who were prominent in northern Italy, such as Giorgio Sommariva, Lodovico Cendrata, Matteo Bosso, Adriano Cappelli, as well as to Popes Leo X and Paul III, and to Ludovico Sforza, Duke of Milan. From a letter to Girolamo Monopolitano, dated 1514 and not published by Tomasini, we gather that she had been studying philosophy and classical history. Some historians of the University of Padua state, contrary to Tomasini's denial, that Cassandra taught philosophy there in substitution for her relative, Alberto Leonardi.

Among the women who in fifteenth-century Italy achieved a high degree of erudition and literary skill and won fame among their contemporaries, Cassandra is an exception in so far as she was allowed to display her capacities publicly and was appointed as speaker by state authorities. A portrait of her, now lost, was painted by Gentile Bellini. It depicted a young girl in elegant dress with her hair piled high on her head, according to the contemporary Venetian fashion, later severely forbidden by the State. The print shown in Tomasini's edition and a medal in the collection of Papazzo dei Dogi, were drawn from that portrait.

Works

Cassandrae virginis venetae, oratio pro Bertuccio Lamberti canonico concordiensi, liberalium artium insignia suscipiente. Habita in Gymnasio patavino (1487). *Clarissinae feminae Cassandrae Fidelis venetae, epistolae et orationes posthumae,* ed. J.F. Tomasini (1636). Petrettini, M., *Vita di Cassandra Fedele* (1814). Simsonsfeld, H., "Zur Geschichte der Cassandra Fedele." *Studien zur Literaturgeschichte, Michael Bernays gewidmet* (1893), pp. 101–108. Cavazzana, C., "Cassandra Fedele erudita veneziana del Rinascimento." *Ateneo veneto* 29 (1906): App. 9, 386–387. "Oration to the Ruler of Venice, Francesco Venerio, on the Arrival of the Queen of Poland," "Oration for Bertuccio Lamberti, Receiving the Honors of the Liberal Arts," "Oration in Praise of Letters," "Letter to Alessandra Scala: Whether Marriage Is to Be Preferred to Studies by a Learned Woman, 1492." In M.L. King and A. Rabil, Jr., eds., *Her Immaculate Hand. Selected* Works *by and about the Women Humanists of Quattrocento Italy* (1983), pp. 48–50, 69–73, 74–77, 87–88.

Rinaldina Russell

Susan Edmonstone Ferrier
1782–1854

Born September 7, 1782, Edinburgh, Scotland
Died November 5, 1854, Edinburgh
Genre(s): novel, letters
Language(s): English

Susan was the tenth and last child of James Ferrier and Helen Coutts Ferrier, who died when Susan was fourteen. As a child and a young woman, she knew and visited many people (in Edinburgh society and elsewhere in Scotland) a number of whom turn up later as thinly disguised characters in her novels. Among the homes she visited was that of the Duke of Argyle, where she established a friendship with Charlotte Wavering that was to develop into a very pro-

ductive literary relationship. Wavering and Ferrier initially considered joint authorship, but differing tastes and writing styles precluded this. Wavering did contribute a chapter to Ferrier's first novel, *Marriage* (1818), but her main value to Ferrier the writer was as a keen and thoughtful critic.

Ferrier has been grouped with the Scottish didactic novelists (Brunton, Hamilton, etc.) and with the Scottish regionalists (Gait, Porter, Scott), and has even been termed the Scottish Austen. However, in the end, it is the considerable merits of her own novels that have maintained Ferrier's vitality as a writer. Her novels are pointedly witty studies of Scottish society, animated by the sprightly dialogue of wonderfully comic characters, although occasionally the energy is checked and the sparkle dimmed by long tendentious moral commentary. She wrote three novels: *Marriage, The Inheritance* (1824), and *Destiny* (1831). Critics generally agree that the novels successively diminish in spontaneity, freshness, and originality while they increase in technical control, artistic shaping, and overall stylistic mastery. It should not be surprising, then, that the middle novel, *The Inheritance,* is generally regarded as Ferrier's best.

Marriage opens with an encounter between the very elegant and very squeamish Englishwoman, Lady Juliana, and her husband's Highland relatives, including his three eccentric aunts and his five "great purple" sisters. This group of deliciously odd creatures is reinforced by their still odder neighbor, Lady MacLaughlan. The result is a mighty clash of culture, sentiments, and values. Juliana is horrified and disgusted by this Highland family and its homeland, but the family itself remains cheerfully oblivious to her attitude. Juliana flees from stingy Scotland to extravagant London, where she raises one of her twins to be even more spoiled and self-centered than she herself and leaves the other twin, Mary, to be raised in the Highlands by her gentle and sensible sister-in-law, with predictably different results. The second part of the book brings Mary to her mother's house, where she is highly unwelcome and out of place. Mary is eventually rewarded for her patient endurance and her charity. She marries the MacLaughlans' heir and returns to her beloved Highlands.

The next novel, *The Inheritance,* is less a study of manners in conflict than a history of a young woman, Gertrude St. Clair, who nearly forfeits her inheritance by choosing a lover of whom the lord disapproves. Gertrude, while of good instincts and generous heart, is too easily led by her selfish lover. Consequently, she lives extravagantly for several years until she learns that she is really the child of Mrs. St. Clair's nurse and an heiress only by fraud. Instantly repudiating her wealth and title, she loses her false lover, who can now inherit in his own right. After a period of despair, she is helped to mature by her cantankerous but kindly Uncle Adam and by her true lover who at once restores her to position and wealth. The book offers acute insights about a heroine who struggles vainly against the skilled and ruthless manipulation of her "mother" and the more overt tyranny of her guardian. The only hope for a woman to be happy and worthy alone, Ferrier suggests, is to devote herself to a higher master and to a life of faith and good works, as do Mrs. St. Clair's unmarried sisters.

Ferrier owes obvious debts to Austen, and the opening line of *The Inheritance*, "It is a truth universally acknowledged, that there is no passion so deeply rooted in human nature as that of pride," has often been cited. But the differences between the two writers are more marked than their similarities. This very quotation is symptomatic: This line is pedantic and moralistic; she seems completely to have missed the light irony in the original line. Nor does Ferrier's wit resemble Austen's; it is consistently broader, more acerbic, and more dependent on caricature and farce in the Smollettian tradition.

The final novel, *Destiny*, was written after her life had become increasingly narrowed by the loss of many of her siblings and by her own long confinement with her ill father. Critics generally maintain that her gallery of originals was exhausted and her material wearing thin. The novel is precisely articulated and symmetrical almost to a fault. Providence, in keeping with the title, is the justification for the remarkable coincidences of the book, but it remains difficult fully to admire the strong authorial hand. For all this, the book remains quite readable, and the great comic clergyman, Mr. McDow, makes amends for pages of overly sentimental prose. What critics find the most original aspect of the book, setting Ferrier apart from other Scottish regionalists, is her portrait of the petty, selfish, irascible Glenroy who is fiercely proud of his family name and unforgivably blind to his daughter's virtues, her love for him, and even her basic needs for survival. Here, for once, is an unromantic portrayal of a Highland chieftain. Here, too, is the charming Mrs. Macauley, who is generally agreed to be one of the few completely realized and fully successful sentimental figures in literature. And here, finally, is the aging society belle, Lady Elizabeth Waldegrave, Glenroy's English wife, who provides her own contribution to the humor,

although she also elicits more pity than did her predecessor, Lady Juliana.

Walter Scott, an old friend, assisted Ferrier in negotiating terms for the publication of *Destiny*. She visited Abbotsford late in life, but besides this visit and trips to London about her failing vision, Ferrier's later life was almost entirely homebound. She declined requests that she write another work, although she did make revisions for the 1849 reappearance of her books in Bentley's Standard Novels.

Works

Marriage (1818). *The Inheritance* (1824). *Destiny, or the Chief's Daughter* (1831).

Kathleen Fowler

Margita Figuli
1909–1995

a.k.a. Morena, Ol'ga Morena
Born October 2, 1909, Vyšný Kubín, then in Austria-Hungary, later Czechoslovakia
Died March 27, 1995
Genre(s): novel, short story
Language(s): Slovak

Margita Figuli's work has passed through impressionist short stories and expressionist historical prose based on New and Old Testament themes to unfinished efforts at socialist realism with a complete but disjointed socialist novel in 1974. In the same year she received the title "National Artist."

Born in northern Slovakia, Figuli finished business school and worked in a Bratislava bank. After a few insignificant poems, her first published stories in the 1930s brought critical approval, but her antiwar story *Olovený vták* (The Leaden Bird) in 1940 caused her dismissal from her job. Her next novella was very popular as was her long historical novel; both are basically Christian works. After World War II she published various fragments indicating an effort to change her ideological position, which was apparent in her last novel as well as her various books for children.

Figuli's first impressionist stories were collected as *Pokušenie* (Temptation) in 1937. Contemporary critics related them to the "lyrical prose" that had developed as a form of expressionism, and this relation became explicit with the "naturism" of her next and most important book, *Tri gaštanové koně* (Three

Chestnut Horses) in 1940. Immediately a popular success, it was reprinted seven times in the next seven years. Though little more than a hundred pages long, this is an epic treatment of the love of a village tramp and a rich farmer's daughter. Their spiritual growth through tragedy to a happy ending is mythologized by three horses symbolizing the goodness, beauty, and strength of nature as well as the same three qualities gained by obedience to the Christian moral code. With the rich rhythms and imagery of biblical prose, the work masterfully sustains the atmosphere and tone of fated drama without obscuring the detailed description of Tatra mountain forests or the naive optimism of both villagers. In the same period Figuli published two anti-war stories, *Olovený vták* and *Tri noci a tri sny* (Three Nights and Three Dreams) in 1942. Her longest work was *Babylon* in 1946, a four-volume historical novel about the Babylonian kingdom in sixth century B.C., its capture of the Jews, battles with Persia, and so on. Although there were obvious pacifist analogies to the past war, Stalinist critics condemned *Babylon* as escapist and "merely aesthetic." It was republished in 1956 in a changed version as was also *Tri gaštanové koně* in 1958. Figuli's last novel, *Víchor v nás* (The Whirlwind within Us) in 1974, begins expressionistically with a magical blacksmith and a troubled girl whose hallucinations are realistically explained through her origin in the rape of her mother by a bestial Nazi soldier. This confusion of mythic and documentary elements persists although midway in the novel the conflict turns into a banal factory problem to illustrate the "building of socialism."

Despite her later failures, Figuli's *Tri gaštanové koně* and *Babylon* remain classics of Slovak literature.

Works

Uzlík tepla [A Tiny Bit of Warmth] (1936). *Pokušenie* [Temptation] (1937). *Olovený vták* [The Leaden Bird] (1940). *Tri gaštanové koně* [Three Chestnut Horses] (1940). *Tri noci a tri sny* [Three Nights and Three Dreams] (1942). *Babylon* (1946). *Víchor v nás* [The Whirlwind within Us] (1974).

Translations: *Tri gaštanové koně*: Czech: *Tři gaštanové koně* (1942, 1971). Magyar: *Három pejló* (1960). *Három gesztenyepej* (1980). Polish: *Trzy kastanki* (1962). English: "Three Chestnut Horses" (1962) (excerpt). Russian: *Trojka gnedych* (1965). Slovenian: *Trije rjavci* (1973). Bulgarian: *Tri doresti konja* (1979). *Babylon*: Russian: *Vavilon* (1968); German: *Babylon* (1968); Czech: *Babylon* (1971).

Norma L. Rudinsky

Emilie Flygare-Carlén
1807–1892

Born August 8, 1807, Strömstad, Sweden
Died February 5, 1892, Stockholm
Genre(s): novel, tale, memoir
Language(s): Swedish

Emilie Flygare-Carlén was Sweden's first regional novelist, writing about the Bohuslän skerries, the rugged coastal life, and the seafaring people she knew intimately from her childhood. Her novels were so popular among middle-class readers in the nineteenth century that she accumulated a small fortune by writing to meet public demand. Because she was able to earn a good living from her literary production, she has been called Sweden's first professional author.

She was born Emilie Smith in Strömstad, a little town on Sweden's west coast. Her father, Rutger Smith, was a successful shopkeeper and shipowner of Scottish descent. The youngest of fourteen children, Emilie received little formal education but gained much practical knowledge of life and people from the freedom of activity she was allowed. As a teenager she accompanied her father on his travels through the skerries, eagerly absorbing impressions from the lives of sailors and fishing folk. She also schooled herself by reading popular novels. Independent and imaginative, Emilie had a strong element of superstition in her nature. But it was her own dramatic and tragic experience of life that turned her into an author.

In 1827 Emilie married the physician Axel Flygare and moved with him to Småland. Their brief life together was a struggle with poverty and illness. Four children were born of whom two died. In 1833 her husband died of tuberculosis. Emilie then returned to Strömstad with her surviving son and daughter only to experience the rapid decline of her family's fortune after the death of her father. In 1834 she became engaged to Reinhold Dalin, a gifted lawyer. She was pregnant when Dalin suddenly died during a cholera epidemic. Curiously, Emilie had refused his request for a death-bed marriage, even though the stigma of illegitimacy would mean social ostracism for both mother and child.

To conceal her pregnancy, Emilie moved to Dalsland where she gave birth to a daughter at the home of a relative of Dalin's. This daughter grew up to become Rosa Carlén (1836–1883), author of numerous novels including *Agnes Tell* (1861) and *Tattarens son, ur svenska folklivet* (1866; The Vagabond's Son; from Swedish Folklife). During the stay in Dalsland, Emilie's daughter by her first marriage died. Regarding this as a punishment from God, Emilie gave up her newborn daughter to be adopted by Dalin's relatives. The later relationship between Emilie and Rosa Carlén was fraught with the psychological complications of abandonment. Each author eventually wrote a novel that features an abandoned child.

In 1837 Emilie returned to Strömstad with her son Edvard. The following year she published her first novel, *Waldemar Klein* (1838), a salon novel modeled after Sophie von Knorring's *Cousinerna* (The Cousins). Although this work was a popular success, it marked the beginning of a lifelong rivalry between the young middle-class author and her aristocratic colleague von Knorring. In 1839 Emilie and her son moved to Stockholm, where she brought out several more salon novels in quick succession. In order to gain acceptance in higher social circles, she concealed that period of her life surrounding Rosa's birth. In 1841 she married the lawyer and writer Johan Carlén and shortly thereafter began to write the novels that established her fame as an author.

In her five "west coast" novels, set in her native region of Bohuslän, Emilie Flygare-Carlén wrote about the people and landscape she knew best. The first of these was the tragic story of murder and retribution *Rosen på Tistelön* (1842; The Rose of Thistle Island. A Tale of the Swedish Coast). Held by some critics to be one of the masterpieces of Swedish literature, this novel displays naturalistic tendencies. Its exciting, skillfully developed plot was based on an actual criminal case. *Pål Värning* (1844; Paul Värning), one of her shortest and most well-constructed novels, is a humorous tale of travel and adventure. The author's conscious use of the local dialect of the west coast skerries helps to achieve a humorous, familiar tone, in spite of the dramatic episode in which Nora, Pål's fiancée, tries to conceal the unwanted child she conceived in a brief affair with another man. Her other "west coast" novels from the 1840s include *Enslingen på Johannis-skäret* (1846; The Hermit of St. John's Islet) and *En Natt vid Bullersjön* (1847; One Night at Bullar Lake).

In 1852 Emilie's son Edvard died. Grief-stricken, Emilie now insisted that her only remaining child, Rosa, come to live with her. Against her own wishes, Rosa moved to Stockholm in 1853. Three years later Rosa married Rickard Carlén, the brother of her mother's husband. Thus the unique situation arose in which mother and daughter became sisters-in-law by marriage. Their relationship remained strained, however. Rosa refused to read her mother's novels, and Emilie never encouraged her daughter's writing.

For six years after the death of her son, Emilie Flygare-Carlén published nothing. When she again began to write, she published *Ett köpmanshus i skärgården* (1860–1861; A Merchant House in the Archipelago), the "west coast" novel that is generally considered to be her best work. Set in the short-lived boom period of the herring-fishing industry, this work has been called by Victor Svanberg the first novel to sympathize with free enterprise. It contains strong realistic characterizations and many autobiographical elements.

In 1862 Emilie Flygare-Carlén received the gold medal of the Swedish Academy. Her long, often tragic, but fascinating life is recounted in her three autobiographical writings: *Skuggspel* (1865; Shadow Play), which tells of her youth, *Tidsmålningar och ungdomsbilder* (1865; Pictures of the Age and Memories from Youth), and *Minnen av svenskt författarliv* (1878; Reminiscences of the Lives of Swedish Authors), in which she writes of her encounters with Sophie von Knorring, C.J.L. Almqvist, and other famous contemporaries.

Together with Fredrika Bremer and Sophie von Knorring, Emilie Flygare-Carlén was one of the three major female novelists of prose realism in mid-nineteenth-century Sweden. Of the three she enjoyed the widest popularity among Swedish readers, and nearly twenty of her novels appeared in English translation during her lifetime. Her real literary achievement was her five "west coast" novels. Unlike Fredrika Bremer, Flygare-Carlén was much more interested in telling a story than in advocating reform of social ills. Though she did not take an open stand on the question of women's emancipation, she often portrayed female characters who are or become independent. Especially in her novels of the 1840s one can find women who are rational, practical, and capable of earning their own living. Her novels sometimes suffer from stylistic flaws. Yet Flygare-Carlén drew her characters deeply and vividly, and their passions and actions are psychologically convincing. Next to Fredrika Bremer she was the most widely translated Swedish author before Strindberg.

Works

Waldemar Klein (1838). *Representanten* [The Representative] (1830). *Gustaf Lindorm* [Gustavus Lindorm] (1839). *Professorn och hans skyddslingar* [The Professor and His Favorites] (1840). *Fosterbröderne* [The Foster Brothers] (1840). *Kyrkoinvigningen i Hammarby* [The Consecration of the Church of Hammarby] (1840–1841). *Skjutsgossen* [The Carriage Boy] (1841). *Kamrer Lassman* [Head Clerk Lassman] (1842). *Rosen på Tistelön* [The Rose of Thistle Island] (1842). *"Ända in i döden"* [Even unto Death] (1843). *Pål Värning* [Paul Värning] (1844). *Fideikommisset* [The Birthright]

(1844). *Vindskuporna* [The Attics] (1845). *Bruden på Omberg* [The Bride of Omberg] (1845). *Ett år* [One Year] (1846). *Enslingen på Johannisskäret* [The Hermit of St. John's Islet] (1846). *En Natt vid Bullarsjön* [One Night at Bullar Lake] (1847). *Jungfrutornet* [The Maiden's Tower] (1848). *En nyckfull qvinna* [A Whimsical Woman] (1848–1849). *Romanhjältinnan* [The Heroine of a Novel] (1849). *Familjen i dalen* [The Family in the Valley] (1849). *Ett rykte* [A Rumor] (1850). *Ett lyckligt parti* [A Fortunate Match] (1851). *Förmyndaren* [The Guardian] (1851). *Inom sex veckor* [Within Six Weeks] (1853). *Ett köpmanshus i skärgården* [A Merchant House in the Archipelago] (1860–1861). *Stockholmsscener bakom kulisserna* [Scenes from Stockholm Behind the Stage-Scenes] (1864). *Berättelser från landsorten* [Tales from the Provinces] (1864–1865). *Skuggspel* [Shadow Play] (1865). *Tidsmålningar och ungdomsbilder* [Pictures of the Age and Memories from Youth] (1865). *En hemlighet för världen* [A Secret from the World] (1876). *Minnen av svenskt författarliv 1840–1860* [Reminiscences of the Lives of Swedish Authors from 1840 to 1860] (1878). *Efterskörd från en 80–årings författarebana* [Gleanings from the Literary Career of an Octogenarian] (1888). *Brev* [Letters, ed. Jan Smith] (1960).

Translations: *The Birthright* (1851). *The Bride of Omberg* (1853). *A Brilliant Marriage* (1852, 1856, 1865). *The Brother's Bet or Within Six Weeks* (1867, 1868). *The Events of a Year* (1855). *The Guardian* (1865). *Gustavus Lindorm or "Lead Us Not into Temptation"* (1853, 1854). *The Hermit* (1853). *The Home in the Valley* (1854). *Ivar or The Skjuts-boy* (1852, 1864). *John; or, Is a Cousin in the Hand, Worth Two Counts in the Bush?* (1853, 1854, 1857). *Julie or Love and Duty* (1854). *A Lover's Strategem or The Two Suitors* (1852, 1865). *The Magic Goblet or The Consecration of the Church of Hammarby* (1845). *The Maiden's Tower. A Tale of the Sea* (1853). *Marie-Louise or The Opposite Neighbors* (1853, 1854). *One Year or Julia and Lavinia. A Tale of Wedlock* (1853). *The Professor and His Favorites* (1843, 1854). *The Rose of Tistelön. A Tale of the Swedish Coast* (1844, 1850). *The Smugglers of the Swedish Coast or The Rose of Thistle Island. A Romance* (1844, 1845). *The Temptation of Wealth or The Heir by Primogeniture* (1846, 1847). *Twelve Months of Matrimony* (1853, 1854, 1862, 1882). *The Whimsical Woman* (1852, many editions). *Woman's Life or The Trials of Caprice* (1852, 1856, 1858).

Jean Pearson

Marie Louise von Françoise
1817–1893

Born June 27, 1817, Herzberg, Saxony
Died September 25, 1893, Weissenfels, Saxony
Genre(s): novel
Language(s): German

Von Françoise belonged to the school of realism and corresponded with Marie von Ebner-Eschenbach and C.F. Meyer and was herself the author of vigorously realistic novels.

Marie Louise von Françoise was the daughter of a wealthy aristocratic officer, whose family derived from an old noble French family. Her mother was of the Saxon nobility. Although wealthy, Marie Louise was not granted an education suitable to her station. She therefore educated herself by reading the works of Adolph Müllner and Fanny Tarnow.

Her father's untimely death, her mother's remarriages, and Marie Louise's removal to her uncle's custody in Potsdam started her on her writing career. After her guardian squandered her inheritance, Marie Louise's fiancé, Count Alfred of Görtz, broke their engagement, leaving Françoise alone. She moved back to live with her aging mother and ill stepfather to care for them in Weissenfels, where she stayed till the end of her life. She established a friendship with Marie von Ebner-Eschenbach and C.F. Meyer during this time. At the age of fifty-four she was successful in publishing a great novel: *Die letzte Reckenburgerin* (The Last Lady of Reckenburg). Critics agree that this great book is Marie Louise von Françoise's contribution to the permanent fund of literature. In it the poet presents with surprising realism a picture of patriarchal existence at the end of the eighteenth century and the beginning of the nineteenth. Her three great novels, *Die letzte Reckenburgerin*, *Frau Erdmuthens Zwillingssöhne* (1872; Mrs. Ermuthen's Twin Sons), and *Stufenjahre eines Glücklichen* (1877; The Pinnacle Years of a Fortunate One), belong to the historical novels of, respectively, the Napoleonic Era, the War of Prussian Independence, and the War of 1848. Some critics consider the moral tendencies evident in her works to be a weakness, but these tendencies really show her dependency on eighteenth-century literature. Her novels show a strong acerbity, a certain reserve, an earnestness, and a goodness of character. Her conservatism remains free of the decadence of the epigones.

Marie Louise von Françoise holds a high place among German writers. Her works are the products of a penetrating, energetic, yet gentle and forgiving mind.

Works

Ausgewählte Novelle [Selected Short Stories] (1867). *Die letzte Reckenburgerin* [The Last Lady of Reckenburg] (1871). *Erzählungen* [Stories] (1871). *Frau Erdmuthens Zwillingssöhne* [Mrs. Erdmuthen's Twin Sons] (1872). *Geschichte der Preussischen Befreiungskriege 1813–1815. Ein Lesebuch für Schule und Haus* [History of the Prussian War of Independence 1813–1815. A Reader for School and Home] (1873). *Hellstadt und andere Erzählungen* [Hellstadt and Other Stories] (1874). *Natur und Gnade nebst anderen Erzählungen* [Nature and Grace and Other Stories] (1876). *Stufenjahre eines Glücklichen* [The Pinnacle Years of a Fortunate One] (1877). *Der Katzenjunker* [The Squire of Cats] (1879). *Phosphorus Hollunder* (1881). *Zu Füssen des Monarchen* [At the Feet of the Monarchy] (1881). *Der Posten der Frau. Lustspiel* [The Situation of the Woman. A Comedy] (1882). *Judith, die Kluswirthen* [Judith, the Inn keeper's Wife] (1883). *Das Jubliäum und andere Erzählungen* [The Anniversary and Other Stories] (1886). *Briefwechsel mit C.F. Meyer, hrsg. A. Bettelheim* [Correspondence with C.F. Meyer, edited by A. Bettelheim] (1905). *Gesammelte Werke* [Collected Works] (1918).

Brigitte Edith Zapp Archibald

Anneliese ("Anne") Frank
1929–1945

Born June 12, 1929, Frankfurt am Main, Germany
Died March 1945, Bergen-Belsen Concentration Camp
Genre(s): diary, essay, fable, short story
Language(s): Dutch

Anne, born in Frankfurt-am-Main on June 12, 1929, was the second daughter of Otto and Edith Frank. As Jews, the family fled Nazi Germany in 1933 and settled in Amsterdam. Anne, a gifted student, hoped to become a writer or a journalist. With the Nazi occupation of Holland in 1940, Jews were soon forbidden to attend public schools. As a result, Anne was enrolled in a Jewish school. Life became increasingly more difficult for Dutch Jews, with deportation to the East beginning in 1942. The Frank family decided to go into hiding on July 9 of that same year. They, along with four others, spent two years in small rooms (the "Secret Annex") behind the offices where Otto Frank had worked. Several non-Jewish friends brought them provisions and news from the outside. Then, on August 4, 1944, the hiding place was discovered and the occupants were arrested. They were first taken to Westerbork and then to Auschwitz; later, Anne and Margot, her sister, were sent to Bergen-Belsen where Anne died in March of 1945 (two months before the liberation of Holland).

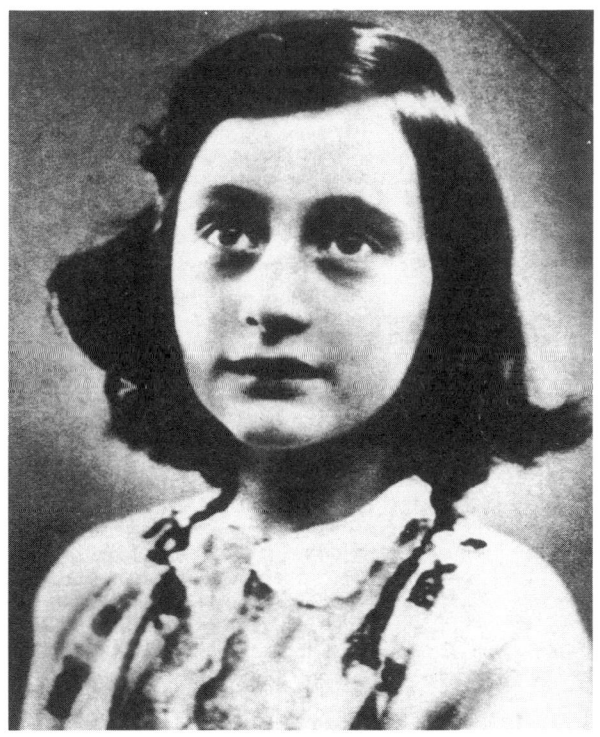

Anneliese ("Anne") Frank

Of the original eight inhabitants of the Secret Annex, only Otto Frank survived. Miep, a friend of the family who had brought them food during the two years, gave him Anne's diary and other writings when he learned that Anne had perished. The writings, which the Nazis had overlooked, were discovered by Miep on the floor of the Secret Annex. The diary, first appearing in published form in 1947 under the title *Het Achterhuis* ("The House Behind"), was soon translated into other languages and became an immediate success. The English edition, *Anne Frank: The Diary of a Young Girl* came out in 1953 and was followed by dramatic and film versions. Anne's short stories, essays, and fables were published after her father's death in 1980 with the English translation, *Anne Frank's Tales from the Secret Annex*, appearing in 1984. The Anne Frank House, containing the Secret Annex, is now a museum as well as the headquarters for a youth organization dedicated to world peace.

The diary, which Anne addresses as "Dear Kitty," begins on June 12, 1942, and has August 1, 1944, as a final entry. As a preface, Anne wrote: "I hope I shall be able to confide in you completely, as I have never been able to do in anyone before, and I hope that you will be a great support and comfort to me." The diary reveals the thoughts of an inquisitive, observant, and sensitive adolescent over a two-year period. Anne raises questions on a variety of issues, ranging from the personal to those relating to mankind in general. She speculates on such topics as the problems of becoming a woman, attitudes about sex, the war, being a Jew. Anne comments: "Sometime this terrible war will be over. Surely the time will come when we are people again, and not just Jews." A growing self-awareness as well as an optimistic outlook, in spite of the adverse conditions, are evident in the diary. As Anne states: "In spite of everything, I still believe that people are really good at heart."

Works

Anne Frank: The Diary of a Young Girl (1953). *The Diary of Anne Frank*, play (1955). *The Diary of Anne Frank*, film (1959). *Anne Frank's Tales from the Secret Annex* (1984).

Michael F. Bassman

Dora Petrova Gabe
1886–1983

a.k.a. Bogdan Haritov, Ranina
Born August 28, 1886, Dŭbovik, Bulgaria
Died February 18, 1983, Sofia
Genre(s): poetry, short story, children's literature, criticism, memoirs
Language(s): Bulgarian

Gabe is one of Bulgaria's foremost women poets. Her literary creative work is addressed equally to children, youth, and adults. She was the daughter of a Bulgarian journalist whose family returned from Russia and settled in Dobrud'a. She grew up in Dobrud'a, and its plains and fields, its seashore and sunsets had a great influence on her creative work. Gabe attended elementary school in her village and the resort city of Balčik and completed her secondary education in Šumen and Varna. In 1904 she enrolled at the University of Sofia and then in the fall of 1905 traveled to Geneva and in 1907 graduated from the University of Grenoble with a specialization in French language and literature.

Her first poem was published in 1900 and soon after she became a contributor to the journal *Misŭl*. Her first collection of poems *Temenugi* (1908; Violets) was imbued with an ardent yearning for an ideal love. Significantly, the last poem was entitled "Now I Stand Lonely, Hopeless on the Crossroad." The same year she married Bojan Penev, one of Bulgaria's great literary critics and professor of literature at the University of Sofia.

After World War I she actively collaborated in the journal *Zlatorog* and her new collections of poetry appeared as *Zemem pŭt* (1928; Earthly Way) and *Lunatička* (1932; The Sleepwalker). The heroine of *Lunatička* wanders in a strange city, sympathizing with the unhappiness of the working people but unable to offer any comfort and aid. At the end the heroine exclaimed: "My own helplessness is a burden to me like a guilt." Gabe wrote many poems, short stories, and novels for children and published about thirty volumes in her seventy-five years as a writer. In addition, she edited *Biblioteka za malkite* (Library for the Young) and the journal *Prozorče* (Little Window). According to Gabe a children's writer should always preserve in him/her "the child he/she once was," and be able to see the world from the child's perspective. A few of the titles of her books are characteristic of her writings for children: *Malki pesni* (1923; Little Songs), *Kalinka-malinka* (1924; The Ladybug), *Velikden* (1930; Easter), *Malka Bogorodica* (1937; Little Mother of God), *Naiobicam zalugalki* (1955; I Like Toys the Best) and *Maika Paraškeva* (1971; Mother Paraškeva).

After 1944 there were some changes in her thematic orientation, especially in her writings for children. *Maika Paraškeva* is not only the mother of Georgi Dimitrov, the hero of the Reichstag Fire Trial and leader of Bulgaria, but a hero-mother herself and the embodiment of the primal characteristics of Bulgarian mothers.

In the poem *Vela* (1946), Gabe presents the heroic struggle of a partisan woman. Vela, unlike the Sleepwalker, has a clearly defined goal in life and a determination to fight for a better world. Gabe wrote some of her best poetry during the later years of her life. Many new collections of her writings appeared: *Novi stihove* (1958; New Poetry), *Počakai slŭnce* (1967; Wait a Little, Sun!), *Nevidimi oči* (1970; Invisible Eyes), *Glŭbini: Razgovori s moreto* (1976; Depths: Conversations with the Sea) and *Svetŭt e taina* (1982; The World Is a Mystery). Her poetry is intimate and optimistic, and the writer shows concern for real people. She treats even the simplest event or idea within a dialectical framework and asks penetrating philosophical questions on life and death. If Gabe had some power over nature she would never permit people to become old. She loved life and beauty and made them the primary subject in her poetry.

Gabe was actively involved in the cultural life of her country. She translated the writings of many Polish, Czech, Russian, and Greek poets into Bulgarian. She was one of the founders and for many years the president of the Bulgarian PEN club. A number of her works have been translated into Czech, Greek, English, French, Polish, Russian, Spanish and other languages. Gabe was awarded many honorary titles and prizes for her writings and public activity.

Works

Temenugi (1908). *Malki pesni* (1923). *Kalinka-malinka* (1924). *Njakoga* (1924, 1971). *Zvŭnčeta* (1925, 1929). "Das Tor de Welt." In *Europaische Lyrik der Gegenwart* (1927), p. 217. *Malkijat dobru'anec* (1927, 1936, 1970). *Zemem pŭt* (1928). *Velikden* (1930). *Mulgalivi geroi* (1931–1940, 1945, 1968, 1980) in 2 vols. *Lunatička* (1932). *Bjala liulčica* (1933). *Gorskata kuštička* (1934, 1954). *Malka Bogorodica* (1937). *Červenoto cvete: Razkazi* (1946). *Naiobicam zalugalki* (1955). *Nespokoino vreme* (1957). *Izbrani tvorbi* (1958). *Novi stihove* (1958). *Lirika: Izbrani stihotvorenija* (1966). *Počakai slŭnce* (1967). *Za nas malkite* (1967). *Nevidimi oči* (1970). *Maika Paraškeva* (1971). *Sgŭstena tisina: stihove* (1973). *Stihotvorenija* (1975). *Glŭbini: Razgovori s moreto* (1976). *Izbrani stihove* (1978) in 2 vols. *Izbrani stihotvorenija* (1982). *Poemi* (1982). *Svetŭt e taina* (1982).

Translations: *Depths. Conversation with the Sea*, tr. John Robert Colombo and Nikola Roussanoff (1978).

Philip Shashko

Madame Gacon-Dufour
ca. 1762–?

Born ca. 1762, France
Death date unknown
Genre(s): polemical essay, novel
Language(s): French

This very erudite woman, known only as Madame Gacon-Dufour, had many publications to her credit and is among the first women of her time to have taken a frankly feminist stand in her *Mémoire Pour le Sexe Féminin Contre le Sexe Masculin* (1787). In this daring pamphlet, an attack on the chevalier de Feucher who had severely criticized women, Madame Gacon-Dufour asks if the latent and blatant corruption found in eighteenth-century society is not due more to men

than to women. In a forceful diatribe, she describes the life of an aristocratic woman, with all the submissiveness involved: "This worthy knight, who has spurred so much furor against us, who has had the gall to soil us with all possible crimes and by taking as examples five or six contemptible women scorned by both sexes, has tried in vain to justify his culpable assertions. He never had the decency to cite even one of our virtues, nor did he enumerate any of them. This worthy knight might think perhaps that he covered himself with great glory and that he has thus achieved some dignity among men. . . . [but] all the male gender cannot be as unfair and ridiculous as he is."

Madame Gacon-Dufour was a champion of education for women, publishing in 1807 (Year XIII of the Revolutionary calendar) a volume entitled *De la Nécessité de L'Instruction Pour les Femmes*, on the need of a proper education for women. Also an agronomist, the most famous among her works is her treatise on rural economy. She also wrote several handbooks on the fabrication of assorted soaps and a manual for people living in the country, detailing the chores that had to be handled during the year. These manuals can truly be considered among the first do-it-yourself books, as well as an "encyclopedia" of sciences and arts. Her novel *L'Héroine Moldave* (1818), almost forgotten today, was a lengthy work in three volumes; she also translated from the English a morality novel, entitled *Georgeana*. In collaboration with other women (Mmes de Lavallière, de Montespan, de Fontanges, de Maintenon and other illustrious personalities), she published the *Mémoires, Anecdotes Secrets Galantes, Historiques et Inédites* (1807).

Works

Mémoire Pour le Sexe Féminin Contre le Sexe Masculin (1787, in-12, 50p.). *Recueil Pratique D'Economie Rurale et Domestique* (1804, in-12, 243p.). *De la Nécessité de L'Instruction Pour les Femmes* (1807, in-12, xii-307p.). *Rapport Fait à L'Athénée des Arts Sur les Farines de Pommes de Terre* (s.l., Imp. de C.-F. Patris, s.d., in-8, 8p.). *Manuel de la Mènagére, à la Ville et à la Campagne, et de la Femme de Basse-Cour* (1805, 2 vol. in-12, with portraits). *Manuel complet de la Maitresse de Maison et de la Parfaite Ménagère ou Guide Pratique Pour la Gestion D'Une Maison à la Ville et à la Campagne* (1826, in-12, 262p.). *Manuel du Patissier et de la Patissière, à l'Usage de la Ville et de la Campagne* (1825, in-18, x-288p.). *Manuel Théorique et Pratique du Savonnier, ou l'Art de Faire Toute Sortes de Savons, par une Réunion de Fabricants* (1827, in-18, viii, 272p.).

Colette Michael

Veronica Gambara
1485–1550

Born November 30, 1485, Pratalboino, Italy
Died June 1550, Correggio, Italy
Genre(s): lyric poetry, letters
Language(s): Italian, Latin

Daughter of Count Gianfrancesco da Gambara and Alda Pia, Gambara was a poet and patron of the early sixteenth century. She ruled the small territory of Correggio and presided over a flourishing court where poets, courtiers, and dignitaries gathered. She wrote poetry in the Petrarchist manner of her friend Pietro Bembo, as well as numerous letters. Her friends were prominent political and literary figures of the day.

Gambara was born on November 30, 1485, on her family's estates in Pratalboino, near Brescia. Born into a noble and well-connected family, she received a thorough humanistic education that included studies in Greek and Latin, philosophy, scripture, and theology. In 1502 she began correspondence with Pietro Bembo, who was the reigning literary figure of the century and the leader of a resurgence of Petrarchism. He became her poetic mentor, and they remained friends until his death in 1547. In 1509 Gambara was married to Count Giberto X, lord of Correggio. Their small court became a fashionable salon for the cultured nobility. Among her guests were Pietro Arentino and Isabella d'Este. As a patron she encouraged the development of the painter Antonio Allegri, known as Corregio. On August 26, 1518, Giberto died, and Gambara was plunged into bitter mourning. She continued to rule Correggio herself and to write poetry. Gambara numbered among her friends the Emperor Charles V, King Frances I of France, Pope Leo X, and numerous cardinals and princes. In 1530, Gambara attended the coronation of the Emperor in Bologna. Both the Emperor and the king of France visited her in Correggio. She died in June 1550 in Correggio.

Gambara's writings consist of some 50 poems and over 130 letters. The poems are mostly sonnets, but she employs other forms including the madrigal, the ballad, and stanze in ottava rima. Her poetry includes several love poems to her husband in the Petrarchan manner, poems on political issues, devotional poems, and Vergilian poems in praise of the countryside of Brescia and Correggio. Many of her poems are addressed to political figures she knew (Emperor Charles V, Francis I, Pope Paul III), exhorting them to stop fighting wars and to make peace. She also addressed poems to other literary figures, such as Pietro Bembo and Vittoria Colonna. Her love poems are generally more interesting. Written to her husband Giberto, they are full of Vergilian and Petrarchan echoes. She employs the Petrarchan terminology formalized by Bembo, and because her poetry adheres closely to Bembo's doctrine of imitation, it often seems overly refined and artificial. Her letters are addressed to her friends, among them Pietro Bembo, the Marchese del Vasto, and Isabella d'Este. Some are familiar and affectionate; others are formal and conventional. Gambara's poetry was circulated privately, and some poems appeared in sixteenth-century anthologies. The first collected edition of her writings (Rizzardi's) appeared in 1759.

Gambara is a good example of the Italian Renaissance woman. She acted as governor, patron, writer, wife, and mother. She approached writing casually and probably did not think of herself as a writer by vocation. Her court at Correggio was famous and influential. She is considered to be one of the three foremost women poets of sixteenth-century Italy, along with Vittoria Colonna and Gaspara Stampa.

Works

Amadduzzi, Luigi, ed., *Undici Lettere inedite di Veronica Gambara e un'ode latina tradotta in volgare* (Guastalla, 1889). Chiappetti, Pia Mestica, ed., *Rime e lettere* (Florence, 1879). Costa, E., ed., *Sonetti amorosi inediti e rari* (Parma, 1890). Rampini, A.L., ed., *Sonetti inediti* (Padua, 1845). Rizzardi, Felice, ed., *Rime e lettere* (Brescia, 1759). Salza, A., ed., *Rime inedite e rare di Veronica Gambara* (Cirié, 1915).

Richard Poss

Elizabeth Gaskell
1810–1865

a.k.a. Mrs. Gaskell, Cotton Mather Mills, Esq.
Born September 29, 1810, London, England
Died November 12, 1865, Holybourne, Hampshire
Genre(s) novel, biography
Language(s): English

In November 1865, when reporting her death, *The Athenaeum* rated Gaskell as "if not the most popular, with small question, the most powerful and finished female novelist of an epoch singularly rich in female novelists." Today she is generally considered a lesser figure in English letters, remembered chiefly for her minor classics *Cranford* and *Wives and Daughters: An Every-Day Story*. Her early fame as a social novelist began with the 1848 publication of *Mary Barton: A Tale of Manchester Life,* in which she pricked the conscience of industrial England through her depiction and analysis of the working classes. Many critics were hostile to the novel because of its open sympathy for the workers in their relations with the masters, but the high quality of writing and characterization were undeniable, and critics have compared *Mary Barton* to the work of Friedrich Engels and other contemporaries in terms of its accuracy in social observation. The later publication of *North and South* (1855), also dealing with the relationship of workers and masters, strengthened Gaskell's status as a leader in social fiction. Her fiction was deeply influenced by her upbringing and her marriage. The daughter of a Unitarian clergyman who was a civil servant and journalist, Gaskell was brought up after her mother's death by her aunt in Knutsford, a small village that served as the prototype not only for Cranford but also for Hollingford in *Wives and Daughters* and the settings of numerous short stories and novellas. In 1832 she married William Gaskell, a Unitarian clergyman in Manchester in whose ministry she actively participated and with whom she collaborated to write the poem "Sketches among the Poor" in 1837.

"Our Society at Cranford" now the first two chapters of *Cranford,* appeared in Dickens's *Household Words* on December 13, 1851, and was itself a fictionalized version of an earlier essay, "The Last Generation in England." Dickens so liked the original episode that he pressed Gaskell for more; at irregular intervals between January 1852 and May 1853 eight more episodes appeared.

Two controversies marred Gaskell's literary career. In 1853 she shocked and offended many of her readers with *Ruth,* an exploration of seduction and illegitimacy prompted by anger at moral conventions that condemned a "fallen woman" to ostracism and almost inevitable prostitution—a topic already touched on in the character of Esther in *Mary Barton.* The strength of the novel lies in its presentation of social conduct within a small dissenting community when tolerance and rigid morality clash. Although some element of the "novel with a purpose" is evident, her sensitive portrayal of character and, even more, her feel for relationships within small communities and families show a developing sense of direction as a novelist. Although critics praised the soundness of the novel's moral lessons, several members of her husband's congregation burned the book and it was banned in many libraries. Even Gaskell admitted that she prohibited the book to her own daughters, but she nevertheless stood by the work.

The second controversy arose following the 1857 publication of *The Life of Charlotte Brontë.* The biography's initial wave of praise was quickly followed by angry protests from some of the people dealt with in the book. In a few instances legal action was threatened; however, with the help of her husband and George Smith the problems were resolved without recourse to law. The most significant complaint resulted from Gaskell's acceptance of Branwell Brontë's version of his dismissal from his tutoring position (he blamed it on his refusal to be seduced by his employer's wife) and necessitated a public retraction in *The Times,* withdrawal of the second edition, and a revised third edition, the standard text. Despite the initial complications and restrictions necessitated by conventions of the period (the book did not, for example, deal with Brontë's feelings for Constantin Héger), *The Life of Charlotte Brontë* has established itself as one of the great biographies; later biographies have modified but not replaced it.

During 1858 and 1859 Gaskell wrote several items, mainly for Dickens, of which two are of particular interest. *My Lady Ludlow,* a short novel cut in two by a long digressive tale, is reminiscent of *Cranford,* yet the setting and social breadth anticipates *Wives and Daughters.* The second work, *Lois the Witch,* is a somber novella concerning the Salem witch trials that prefigures her next work, *Sylvia's Lovers,* by its interest in morbid psychology. *Sylvia's Lovers is* a powerful, if somewhat melodramatic, novel. The first two volumes are full of energy; they sparkle and have humor. The ending, however, shows forced invention rather than true tragedy. Regarded by Gaskell as "the saddest story I ever wrote," *Sylvia's Lovers* is set during the French Revolution in a remote whaling port with particularly effective insights into character relationships.

Most critics agree that *Cousin Phillis* is Gaskell's crowning achievement in the short novel. The story is uncomplicated; its virtues are in the manner of its development and telling. *Cousin Phillis is* also recognized as a fitting prelude for her final and most widely acclaimed novel, *Wives and Daughters: An Every-Day Story,* which ran in *Cornhill* from August 1864 to January 1866. The final installment was never written, yet the ending was known and the novel as it exists is virtually complete. The plot of the novel is complex, relying far more on a series of relationships between family groups in Hollingford than on dramatic structure. Throughout *Wives and Daughters* the humorous, ironical, and sometimes satirical view of the characters is developed with a heightened sense of artistic self-confidence and maturity.

Gaskell was hostile to a biography of her being

written in her lifetime. Only months before her death, she wrote to an applicant for data: "I disapprove so entirely of the plan of writing 'notices' or 'memoirs' of living people, that I must send you on the answer I have already sent to many others; namely an entire refusal to sanction what is to me so objectionable and indelicate a practice, by furnishing a single fact with regard to myself. I do not see why the public have any more to do with me than buy or reject the ware I supply to them" (June 4, 1865). After her death the family sustained her objection, refusing to make family letters or biographical data available.

Critical awareness of Gaskell as a social historian is now more than balanced by awareness of her innovativeness and artistic development as a novelist. While scholars continue to debate the precise nature of her talent, they also reaffirm the singular attractiveness of her best works.

Works

Mary Barton: A Tale of Manchester Life (1848). *Lizzie Leigh: A Domestic Tale* (1850). *The Moorland Cottage* (1850). *Cranford* (1853). *Ruth* (1853). *Lizzie Leigh and Other Tales* (1855). *North and South* (1855). *The Life of Charlotte Brontë* (1857). *My Lady Ludlow* (1858). *Right at Last and Other Tales* (1860). *Lois the Witch and Other Tales* (1860). *Sylvia's Lovers* (1863). *A Dark Nights Work* (1863). *Cousin Phillis: A Tale* (1864; republished as *Cousin Phillis and Other Tales*). *The Grey Woman and Other Tales* (1865). *Wives and Daughters: An Every-Day Story* (1866). *The Letters of Mrs. Gaskell,* ed. J.B.V. Chapple and A. Pollard (1966).

Lynn M. Alexander

Gertrud of Helfta
1256–ca. 1301

Born January 6, 1256
Died November 17, 1301/1302, Helfta, Germany
Genre(s): mysticism
Language(s): Latin

Gertrud of Helfta, also called Gertrud the Great, is of unknown ancestry. She spent her entire life in the convent of Helfta (near Eisleben in today's German Democratic Republic). Her thorough schooling included the seven *artes liberales* as well as comprehensive studies in theology.

Helfta, a Benedictine, Cistercian-oriented convent, was founded in 1229. Under its famous abbess, Gertrud of Hackeborn (in office: 1251–1291), the convent developed into a renowned center of culture and mysticism.

The three Helfta representatives in the literature of medieval mysticism are the abbess' sister, Mechthild of Hackeborn (see entry), the beguine Mechthild of Magdeburg, and Gertrud the Great; the latter remained the least known. Contemporary reception of Gertrud's work, judging by the few manuscripts extant, remained at most lukewarm. A Middle High German translation, *Ein botte der götlichen miltekeit,* of her major Latin work *Legatus divinæ pietatis* appeared about 100 years after her death; it is a shortened version (mainly of Books III to V of the *Legatus*) with moralizing intent.

The Cologne Carthusian Johann Gerecht of Landsberg (Lanspergius) made this mystic known with his first edition of Gertrud's Latin work in 1536. The 1875 first critical edition of Gertrud's work by the Benedictines of Solesmes is now superseded by the Sources Chrétiennes edition.

Gertrud wrote both secular poetry and theological exegetical treatises in Middle High German as well as Latin, but all of this is lost; only an occasional German term or, at most, short passages written in German can be found in her Latin prose. Her Latin work consists of the *Legatus divinæ pietatis* (The Messenger of Loving Kindness) and the *Exercitia spiritualia,* a book of mystical meditations and prayers. Gertrud of Helfta is also one of the writers responsible for Mechthild of Hackeborn's work, *Liber specialis gratiæ.*

Gertrud's *Legatus* is extant in five manuscripts: the best one is clm. 15.332 (1412), Bayerische Staatsbibliothek, Munich; cod. 4224 (1487) österreichische Nationalbibliothek, Vienna; cod. 77/1061 (fifteenth century), partial ms., Stadtbibliothek Trier; cod.13 (fifteenth century) Stadtbibliothek, Mainz; cod.84 (1473), partial ms., Hessische Landesbibliothek, Darmstadt. The *Legatus divinæ pietatis* consists of five books, but only Book II was written by Gertrud herself. Book I represents a *vita* of Gertrud; Books III to V contain an account of Gertrud's spiritual experiences based on Gertrud's dictation, notes, and conversations. There are no manuscripts of the *Exercitia spiritualia* extant. Its authenticity was established through a comparison with Book II of the *Legatus.*

Gertrud of Helfta's writing is influenced by Bernard of Clairvaux's style and diction and, in general, by texts of the daily liturgy and scriptures, especially the *Song of Songs* and the psalms. A predominant characteristic of Gertrud's work is the intertwining of liturgy with mystical meditations in which bridal imagery (*Brautmystik*) is a major theme. At times Gertrud's use of terms of sweetness—which is quite common for medieval spiritual works in general—may divert today's reader from the fact that her prose is also highly poetic and characterized by startling oxymora and a wealth of almost harsh imagery.

The *raison d'être* for Gertrud's work is Gertrud's mystical experience on January 27, 1281. But she started to compose her memorial, now Book II of the *Legatus*, only in 1289 when she felt a divine call to communicate her inner transformation and mystical experiences. This work is now considered one of the classics of Christian mystical writings. It is characteristic of Gertrud that the experience of *unio mystica* liberates her in such a way that she feels unrestrained by petty rules and regulations. Nonconformist in many ways, she often suggests areas in the church that are in need of reform. She sees herself with authoritative priestly power in the spiritual guidance of fellow nuns and lay people seeking her advice. It is perhaps because of these passages that her work experienced some censorship.

Within the theological context of the thirteenth century, the themes that capture Gertrud's interest most are the eucharist and the veneration of the heart of Jesus. The heart as the intellectual, spiritual, and affective center of the human being in medieval thinking becomes the focus of Gertrud's mystical love of Christ. Her understanding is based on John 7:37f. and 13: 23–25 and is best symbolized in the famous Christ–John-sculpture. The veneration of Jesus' heart is also closely intertwined with and inseparable from the theme of the motherhood of God, as shown in beautiful imagery throughout the *Legatus* and *Exercitia*.

Due to the markedly Benedictine spirituality in her writings, Gertrud has been venerated as a saint within the Benedictine order since the seventeenth century. In 1738 her cult was extended to the entire church. Gertrud is the only German woman ever to receive the title of "the Great."

While in many ways comparable to other mystical works, Gertrud of Helfta's writings are unique in their emphasis on joy, praise, and thanksgiving. Her inner detachment (*libertas cordis*) leads Gertrud not to dwell on the human condition as sinful and suffering, but to burst out at every possible occasion into songs of jubilation. Her beautiful jubilus (*Exercitia*, VI) is a masterpiece of mystical poetry.

Works

Oeuvres spirituelles (Sources Chrétiennes) [Latin-French ed.], 1967 ff. with introductions. *Ein botte der götlichen miltekeit*, ed. Otmar Wieland (1973); *Revelationes Gertrudianae ac Mechtildianae*, ed. Louis Paquelin (1875), *Insinvationvm divinæ pietatis*, ed. Johannes Lansperger (1536).

Translations: *Legatus* (1865), tr. M. Frances Clare Cusak. *Exercitia* (1823), tr. Thomas Alder Pope (1956), tr. Columba Hart; (1989), tr. Gertrud Jaron Lewis and Jack Lewis; excerpts in *The Soul Afire*, ed. H.A. Reinhold (1944).

Gertrud Jaron Lewis

Natalia Ginzburg
1916–

a.k.a. Alessandra Tornimparte
Born July 14, 1916, Palermo, Sicily
Genre(s): novel, short story, drama, essay, biography, translation
Language(s): Italian

In her own country, Natalia Ginzburg is recognized as one of Italy's major twentieth-century writers. Best known for her fiction and drama, she is also an essayist, biographer, and translator. She first won the notice of critics after World War II. Since then, she has received numerous literary awards. Ginzburg has also gained an international audience through translations into English, French, Spanish, German, Danish, and Hungarian.

The youngest of five children, Natalia Ginzburg was born in Sicily to Giuseppe and Lydia Levi. Her father's family was Jewish and from Trieste; her mother's family was Catholic and from Milan. After three years, the family moved to Turin, where Natalia grew up. Family interests included science (her father was Professor of Anatomy at Turin University), politics (her father and brothers were involved in socialist and antifascist activities), and literature (the children read extensively, recited poems, and told stories). At the age of seven she wrote her first poem; at seventeen she completed her first story. In 1933 she met Leone Ginzburg, a Russian expatriate writer and political activist. She soon began working at Einaudi, the Turin publishing house, which was to be her publisher for many years. In 1938 she married Leone Ginzburg; he died in 1944 while a political prisoner in Rome. They had three children. In 1950 Natalia Ginzburg married Gabriele Baldini, Director of the Italian Institute in London and later Professor of English Literature at Rome University. The marriage ended with his death in 1969. Since her first childhood poems, through years of personal tragedy and political upheaval, Natalia Ginzburg has continued to write. She is now living in Rome.

Works

La strada che va in citta e altri raconnti (1945; under pseudonym Alessandra Tornimparte, 1942). *Estato cosi* (1947). *Tutti i nostri ieri* (1952). *Valentino* (1957). *Romanzi del 900* (with Giansiro Ferrato; 1958). *Le voci della sera* (1961). *Le piccole virtu* (1962). *Lessico famigliare* (1963). *Cinque romanzi brevi* (1964). *Ti ho sposato per allegria e altre commedie* (1968). *Mai devi domandarmi* (1970). *Caro Michele* (1973; videorecording, 1970). *Paese di mare e altri commedie* (1973). *Vita imaginaria* (1974). *Sagittario* (1975; part of *Valentino*, publ. in 1957). *Famiglia* (1977). *La carta del cielo* (1980; racconti di Mario Soldati; edited by Ginzburg). *Diari, 1927–1961* (1982; di Antonio Delfini edited by Ginzburg and Giovanna Delfino). *La famiglia Manzoni* (1983). *La citta e la casa* (1984).

Translations: *Dear Michael* (1975). *No Way* (1974; 1976). *La route qui m'ene a la ville: quatre romans courts* (1983). *The Advertisement* (1969). *The City and the House* (1986). *The Road to the City/The Dry Heart: Two Novelettes* (1949; rpt. 1990). *Las pequenas virtudes* (1966). *The Little Virtues* (1985, 1986). *Familiealbum* (1968). *Family Sayings* (1967, 1984, 1986). *Voices in the Evening* (1963). *Die Stimmen des Abends* (1970). *Never Must You Ask Me* (1973). *Dead Yesterdays* (1956). *A Light for Fools* (1957). *All Our Yesterdays* (1985, 1986). *Todos nuestros ayeres* (1958). *Alle unsere Jahra* (1967). *Valamennyi tegnapunk* (1979).

Lydia A. Panaro

Zinaida Gippius
1869–1945

a.k.a. Hippius
Born November 20, 1869, Belev, Tula District, Russia
Died September 9, 1945, Paris
Genre(s): poetry, short story, drama, literary journalism
Language(s): Russian, French

One of this century's most remarkable lyric poets writing in Russian, a prolific writer of prose, drama, and criticism, and a voluminous correspondent, Gippius was an initiator of Russian symbolism, one of the largest and most influential literary movements in Russia this century. Gippius was not only a leading and well-regarded writer but also wielded considerable institutional power in the avant garde literary establishment of St. Petersburg from the 1890s until her emigration in 1915. With her husband, the writer Dmitrii Sergeevich Merezhkovskii, she was closely involved with the planning and editorial selection of such journals as *New Path*, *World of Art*, and *The Scales*; she was also a contributor to the French symbolist journal *Mercure de France*. The famous literary-philosophical gatherings which she organized were attended by most of the leading lights of intellectual Petersburg. She was a central figure in the Religious–Philosophical Society, which sought to reconcile the disaffected Russian intelligentsia with the Orthodox Church; other members included Nicholas Berdyaev and Vasilii Rozanov. After emigration, when she and her husband settled in Paris, she continued organizing philosophical and literary activities, most notably in the form of a discussion society called *The Green Lamp*.

Gippius's institutional prominence, combined with a certain calculated *épatage* of dress and behavior which emerges in the well-known portrait of her by Leon Bakst, made the shocked conventional public regard her as the epitome of decadence. It is doubtful whether any of her contemporaries attracted such violent hostility. Some of this came from writers who were offended by her highhanded treatment or wittily acerbic attacks, some from observers who found Gippius and her husband's mystical religious beliefs antipathetic or absurd—the poet Innokentii Annenskii, for example, wrote of the Merezhkovskiis: "They have no capacity for abstraction, only instincts and damnable self-love, they haven't a single idea, only a gold ring they wear on their ties." But some of the hatred must undoubtedly be attributed to resentment, in a male-dominated society, that any woman should be so powerful and so flamboyant. The many sexist appellations which she attracted confirm this impression: she was known as "Messalina" and "the white she-devil," and Trotsky wrote of her, "I do not believe in witches in general, not counting the above-mentioned Zinaida Gippius, in whose reality I believe absolutely, though about the length of her tail I can say nothing definite" (*Literature and Revolution*, chapter 1).

Gippius's unorthodox sexuality also led to adverse comment. She rejected stereotyped notions of women's roles, writing in 1928 to the young poet Nina Berberova, "Frankly, I feel no maternal feelings for you; in fact, in general I don't seem to be capable of such feelings." Her marriage to Merezhkovskii was based on affectionate companionship, not on sexual interest—Gippius herself encouraged rumors that it had not been consummated. In relationships with other men she herself acted as initiator and hunter, particularly in the case of her long infatuation with Dimitrii Filosofov, whom she treated as a kind of male Muse. Sexual ambivalence was another aspect of Gippius's hostility to convention; this theme emerges especially strongly in her diaries and in some of her short stories, for example "The Mother-of-Pearl Cane."

On the other hand, the complications of Gippius's personality were great, and it is unwise to claim that her ideas can easily be appropriated by modern feminism. She was capable of writing very dismissively of "female psychology," describing it as unstable and unreliable. She reacted to other women with suspicion; she was, for example, violently jealous of Marina Tsvetaeva, and seemed happiest in a dominating, patronizing role with a younger woman, such as Berberova. Her attitude to lesbianism was likewise contradictory: her views on sexual freedom had been initiated by an erotic interest in male homosexuality. She regarded actual sexual contact as secondary to spiritual communication, writing to Filosofov "It was all in God, from God, through Him. A moment of religious feeling (not only for you but for God and for nature) touched my spirit and my soul and *my flesh*." Her relations with women seem also to have been emotional or sentimental rather than sexual. All in all, she was an advanced case of the so-called Queen Bee complex; that is, a woman who regards freedom as uniquely her prerogative.

Gippius's lyrics present problems for the modern reader. The emotional pain and confusion brought about by the physical state of being a woman, delineated by other women writers such as Shkapskaya and Tsvetaeva, are absent; and the domestic realities of women's lives she ignored as completely as any male writer. Her concern is with the supernatural, the otherworldly; the external world exists only as a collection of deliberately patterned and formulaic attributes, or as props for a metaphysical conflict. The only tradition of women's writing in which she can perhaps be placed is that of the Gothic occult tale or ghost story; her early volume *Mirrors* has some similarity to the writing of Isak Dinesen, for example.

Though hot-house eroticism, often with demonic overtones, is certainly characteristic of Gippius's lyrics, genuine sexual ambivalence is harder to find. She does use masculine pseudonyms and masculine narrators in her lyrics, and female narrators are distanced

from the poet's own person (see for example "Annunciation," 1904). But, like all the symbolists, Gippius had a dualistic philosophy, and the contrast between "femininity" and "masculinity" is only one of many polarities in her poetry; at least as important are the contrasts between fear and resolution, and between the moral extremes of God and the Devil. Besides, in keeping with the abstraction of her poetry, it is more satisfactory to read the male and female poems as representations of psychological types, centering round a conventional binary opposition between the female—emotional and fearful—and the male—intellectual and courageous. The term "androgynous" used by some critics is probably the most fitting for her poetry.

Arguably, Gippius's finest achievements as a poet are those to which gender is irrelevant. She has been described as one of Russia's finest religious poets. Her claim to this rests less on those poems where she expresses pious resignation, in the female voice, or encounters such resignation at second hand, in the male voice; there is usually a note of affectation here. More impressive are the poems in which she starkly, and without hint of gender, portrays metaphysical evil; she writes, for example, with chilling strength in the opening lines of her long poem *The Last Circle*:

The waves of otherworldly nausea foam up,
Break into spray and scatter in black mist,
And into darkness, into outermost darkness,
As they return to subterranean ocean.
We call it pain here, sorrowful and heartfelt,
But it's not pain, for pain is something else.
For subterranean and endless nausea
There are no earthly words, for words are not
    enough.

               Translated by S. Karlinsky

Gippius's political poetry, which was highly praised by D.S. Mirsky, a critic of outstanding discernment, is equally resolute. The mode is vatic and commanding, as in this attack on the October Revolution:

Will those pure heroes forgive us?
For we have not kept their commandment.
We have lost all that is sacred;
The shame of our souls, the honour of the earth.
[. . .]
The nocturnal flock whistles and croaks,
The Neva's ice is bloody and drunken. . . .
O, Nicholas' noose was cleaner
Than these grey monkeys' fingers!

While the above is in the nineteenth-century publicistic tradition of Pushkin and Tyutchev, it is doubtful whether either could have equaled Gippius's magnificent snub to Blok:

I shall not forgive. Your soul is innocent.
I shall not forgive it. Ever.

The cerebral, rather than emotional, quality of Gippius's verse is suggested also by its construction. She was a poet of considerable technical facility, a pioneer of metrical innovations among the symbolists, such as tonic verse and half-rhyme. Her lyrics are metrically constrained, with formalized word-repetition which in some cases has the quality of a melodious refrain, but in others underlines an ironic *pointe*. The intellectual character of the verse is underlined by perpetual internal debate. Sometimes a single poem expresses conflict or paradox, sometimes alternative versions of one poem complement or contradict each other; or the same title is used for poems of radically different orientation.

Given Gippius's great prolificity, it is not surprising that her output should be uneven and sometimes repetitive. Sometimes she relied too greatly on her very considerable purely lyric talent, turning out poems which are trifling and monotonously musical. But there is no doubt that the intrinsic merits of the best of her work have survived the passage of time; and that, from a literary-historical point of view, her activities laid the foundation for the outstanding tradition of poetry by women in Russia this century.

Works

Stikhotvoreniya, 2 vols. (1972). The various volumes of her *Stories* are most accessible in the facsimile editions, ed. T. Pachmuss, published Munich, beginning 1973.

Correspondence: *Pis'ma Berberovoi i Khodasevichu*, ed. E.F. Sheikholoslami (1978).

Translations: *Selected* Works, tr. and ed. T. Pachmuss (1972). *Women Writers in Russian Modernism, An Anthology*, tr. and ed. T. Pachmuss (1978).

Catriona Kelly

Leah Goldberg
1911–1970

Born 1911, Kovno, Lithuania
Died 1970, Jerusalem
Genre(s): poetry, drama, children's literature
Language(s): Hebrew

Leah Goldberg was born in Kovno, Lithuania, in 1911, and was educated there at the Hebrew Gymnasium. She continued her education in philosophy and Semitic languages at the Universities of Bonn and Berlin, and in 1933 was awarded a Ph.D. from the University of Bonn. During this time she adopted Hebrew as her mother tongue. Early in her career, in 1935, Goldberg settled in Palestine and joined the experimental literary group Yachdev, along with Natan Alterman and Avraham Shlonsky. She worked closely with Shlonsky as a translator and editor.

Goldberg's career began as a lecturer on the history of the theater for the Habima dramatic school and advisor for its theater. She also joined the newspaper staff of the *Davar* (Word) as a drama and literary critic. She later moved to join the staff of the *Ha-Mishmar* (The Observer). In 1954 she joined the faculty of Hebrew University, Jerusalem, as a lecturer in comparative literature. Subsequently, she became Chairman of the Comparative Literature Department and remained in this position until her death in 1970.

Because of her inclusion in the Yachdev group, Goldberg is usually associated with the modernist movement of the thirties, and its Freudian and French symbolist influences. Yet, her works seem to elude any categories or traditionalism.

Part of Leah Goldberg's prolific writing was intended for the delight of children. Her partnership with photographer Anna Rivkin-Brick produced the lively works *Mal Kat Sheva ha-Ketanah* (1956; The Little Queen of Sheba) and *Harpatkah ba-Midbar* (1966; Adventure in the Desert). She also wrote poetry for children, as in *Gan ha-Hayyot* (The Zoo), where she used rhyming verses to describe animals and their matching attitudes.

There are few areas into which Goldberg has not ventured. She was extremely active in the arena of criticism, not only on various newspaper staffs, but also as the author of articles (e.g., "Aspects of Israeli Theatre") and a book on the art of the short story (*Omanut ha-Sippur,* or The Art of Narrative). Other publications include a novel, *Ve-Hur ha-Or* (1946; And He Is the Light), and a collection of essays about her native Russia, *Ha-Sifrut ha-Rusit ba-Meah ha-Tesha' Esreh* (1968; Russian Literature of the Nineteenth Century). She also did many translations, and even wrote a dramatic play, *Ba'alat ha-Armon* (1955; Lady of the Castle).

As a poet, Goldberg is daring in her imagery. In her collection *Shibboleth Yerokat ha-'Ayin* (1939–1940; Green-Eyed Ear of Corn), she creates a unique evening with such descriptive phrases as "a rug of roofs is spread before my window light," "the antenna clutches like a mast the hem of heaven heaving on the sea," and she wishfully writes, "a star will fall into my cup perchance." There is an edge of intellectual hardness in this use of artistic, sometimes shocking imagery, which serves to bring the reader to a poetic awareness. However, Goldberg felt this philosophical trend lacked a freshness she was seeking, and it was not a path she continued to pursue.

Goldberg later published a volume of poems dealing with nature, *Al ha-Pericha* (Of Bloom), which seems to fulfill her need of giving the reader beautiful imagery while conveying a depth of feeling and love of beauty. This act of moving over that edge of intellectual hardness to a world of feeling and beauty has made Goldberg one of the most beloved of Hebrew poets. Her voice penetrates the internal being of all nature, as she has trees, blades of grass, and even the moon sing to the stream, and finally offers the "stream's psalm the world extols." There is a freshness in her imagery as she compares the stone, "the constant, mystery of creation," to the stream, "I am change, its revelation." The freshness of Goldberg's poetry does not fade as she reflects on the past. She remembers not significant events, but the fleeting images of "a wheat stalk in the greenness of her youth," and "the tree in the middle of her spring." She emphasizes the constant of change in nature and the beauty that one experiences through nature's constant renewal. This is the essence of Leah Goldberg's poetry: each day is a renewal, "every day shall not be like yesterday, and the day before it, and life shall not become trite and habitual." This is the prayer Goldberg offers for not only herself, but her readers as well.

The pinnacle of honors and fame came to Leah Goldberg one year before her death, when, in 1969, the Institute of Hebrew Studies of New York University awarded her the Irving and Bertha Neuman Literary Prize. Although she died in 1970, her spirit of freshness and boldness is constantly renewed as there is a wealth of wisdom and depth of feeling yet to be discovered in her prolific works.

Works

Jabaot Ashan [Smoke Rings] (1935). *Mihtavim Minsiah Medumah* [Letters from an Imaginary Jour- ney] (1937). *Shibboleth Yerokat ha-'Ayin* [Green-Eyed Ear of Corn] (1939–1940). *Gan ha-Hayyot* [The Zoo] (1941, 1970). *Mibeti Hayashan* [From My Old House] (1942). *We-Hur ha-or* [And He Is the Light] (1946). *Luah ha-ohavim* [The Tablet of Lovers] (1950). *Sifrut yafah olamit be-tirgumaha le-lvrit* [World Literature in Hebrew Translation] (1951). *Ahavat Shimson* [The Love of Samson] (1951–1952). *Pegishah 'Im Meshorer* [Meeting with a Poet] (1952). *Nisim ve-nifla'ot* [Deeds and Wonders] (1954). *Ba'alat ha-Armon* [Lady of the Castle] (1955). *Barak BaBoker* [Morning Glory] (1955). *Malkat Sheva ha-Ketanah* [The Little Queen of Sheba] (1956). *Ayeh Pluto* [Where Is Pluto?] (1957). *The Chatelaine* (1957). *Ahdut ha-adam vehayekum bi-yetsirato Shel Tolstoi* [The Unity of Man and Survival in the Works of Tolstoy] (1959). *Mukdam ve-Menhar* [Early and Late] (1959). *Tserif Katan* [A Little Cabin] (1959). *Omanut ha-Sippur* [The Art of Narrative] (1963). *Im Halayla Hazeh* [With This Night] (1964). *Ma'aseh be-tsayar* [Work by a Painter] (1965). *Harpatkah ba-Midbar* [Adventure in the Desert] (1966). *Yedidai me-Rehov Arnon* [My Friends from Arnon Street] (1966). *Ha-Mefuzar mi-Kefar Azar* [The Scatter-Brain from Kefar Azar] (1967). *Mah osot ha-ayalot* [What Does She Do] (1967). *Ha-Sifrut ha-Rusit ba-Meah ha-Tesha' Esreh* [Russian Literature of the Nineteenth Century] (1968). *Sheloshah Sippurim* [Three Stories] (1970). *Yalkut Shirim* [The Back-Pack of Poems] (1970). *Sheerit ha-Hayyim* [Remnants of Life] (1971).

JoAnne C. Juett

Claire Goll
1891–1977

Born October 29, 1891, Nurnberg, Germany
Died March 30, 1977, Paris
Genre(s): poetry, prose, letters, autobiography
Language(s): German, French

Claire Goll is mainly known for her expressionistic-surrealistic poetry influenced to a large extent by Rainer Maria Rilke. Conveying enthusiasm and at times pathos, she never distanced herself from the issues described.

Her life was restless and often not very pleasant, but in her letters she created the image of a strong character who could even laugh in and about pain. Her pacifistic background, her own ill health, and general attitude toward humanity permitted her to feel sympathy for the outcasts, the helpless, the suppressed. In general, her poetry expresses this sympathy for and analysis of man in the twentieth century.

Born in Nurnberg, Goll spent her childhood and youth in Munich, where she visited the reform school of the pedagogue Georg Gerschensteiner. In 1911 Claire Goll married the Swiss publisher Dr. Heinrich Studer, in 1912 their daughter Dorothea was born, and in 1917 Goll divorced her husband and moved to Switzerland. Living and studying in Geneva, she was actively engaged in the anti-war movement during the First World War. In Switzerland she made the acquaintance of many of the leading literary figures of expressionism, for example Kurt Wolff, the publisher who had left his native Germany, and Franz Werfel. While living in Zurich, she had contacts with Hans Arp, James Joyce, and Stefan Zweig. Her future husband Ivan Goll had published the poem "Requiem für die Gefallenen Europas" (Requiem for the Fallen Soldiers of Europe) in the pacifist paper *Demain.* Through Henri Guilbeaux, the publisher of *Demain* and Romain Rolland, a leading pacifist, she met Ivan Goll after she had congratulated him on his poem. He visited her in Geneva and in 1917 they "married" symbolically. In 1921 a legal ceremony was performed because Ivan pressed her. In 1918 and again in 1921, Claire had spent some time with Rilke, and this very close and intimate relationship probably was the reason for Ivan to take the initiative. The liaison had been celebrated by Rilke in the enthusiastic poem "Liliane," which was Claire's second name. In 1919, Claire had followed Ivan to Paris, where he had joined the surrealist movement. There, Claire made further acquaintances and formed friendships with surrealist painters and poets such as Chaga, Delaunay, Gleizes, and Leger. Claire, who had been ill all her life, spent much time away from her husband, and a collection of their letters shows a very deep, emotional and concerned relationship. It is interesting to note that during the years between 1930 and 1939, Hitler and his regime are never directly referred to. The correspondence is full of personal and emotional issues, of detailed descriptions of her illness, of important and very trivial matters. The letters give the idea of how precisely Claire watched the world around her, how concerned she was with the "everyday." In 1937, Ivan had planned a flight to New York; his literary engagement, however, kept him from pursuing the plan. Claire left for London in 1938, and both arrived in New York in 1939, where they stayed until 1947. In New York, Ivan published the literary magazine *Hemisphere* (1943–1947). In 1950, Ivan died of leukemia in Paris. Claire traveled on a lecture tour through the United States between 1952 and 1954. In 1973, the City of Marbach, West Germany, opened the "Ivan and Claire Goll Room" in the German Archive for literature.

The title of the collection of lyrics, *Lyrische Films* (1922; Lyrical Films), already showed her extravagance. The first part of the collection are lyrical poems, the second section is called "sentimentalities," and the last part is the *Tagebuch eines Pferdes* (Diary of a Horse). This third part is a prose poem dedicated to "Ivan and all the horses." The first poem of the collection, for example, is a hymn on the twentieth century, the reference, as in all expressionistic works, is to the age of the machine. Nature became automatized: Orpheus does not sing any more, but the "gramophone" becomes the "metallic phoenix." It is a sarcastic, at times perverted, glorification of the machine's domination over man. The style of all these poems is expressionistic-surrealistic, with run-off lines, lack of rhyme, and distorted sentence structure. The first poem in "Sentimentalitäten" is dedicated *To *** (*An ***), and a comparison of body and facial features with nonhuman objects. The second poem, "Woman," is a critical analysis of woman in her relationship with man. Many poems of this part deal with mankind or especially the woman in modern society, and always, an atmosphere of coldness, criticism, of letting loose is conveyed. The third section of the collection is another sarcastic statement about man and society. The speaker is a horse and describes life in terms of "horse." The poem depicts the life of an active committee member, pulling carts, suffering, enduring, struggling, and Claire develops a picture of the working people in the early twentieth century as she saw it.

The autobiography *Ich verzeihe keinem* (1976; La poursuite du vent) depicts the literary scene of almost fifty years and is also an attempt to order her own past, especially her numerous liaisons with literary celebrities. Despite its historical and poetical importance, the autobiography, therefore, caused considerable scandal.

Works

Prose: *Der Neger Jupiter raubt Europa* (1928). *Eine Deutsche in Paris* (1928). *Ein Mensch ertrinkt* (1931). *Arsenik* (1933). *Der Gestohlene Himmel* (1962). *Memoiren eines Spatzen des Jahrhunderts* (1969). *Traumtänzerin* (1971). *Zirkus des Lebens* (1973).

Lyrics: *Mitwelt* (1918). *Lyrische Films* (1922). *Roter Mond, weißes Wild* (1955). *Das tätowierte Herz* (1957). *Klage um Yvan* (1960). *Les larmes petrifies* (1951). *Le coeur tatoue* (1958). *L'Ignifere* (1969). Collection of poems together with Yvan.

Letters, Autobiography: *Briefe mit Yvan Goll* (1966). *La poursuite du vent* (1976).

Translations: *Ich verzeihe keinem* [*La poursuite du vent*] (1976). *Arsenic* [*Arsenik*].

Jutta Hagedorn

Catherine Grace Frances Moody Gore
1800–1861

a.k.a. Mrs. Gore, Albany Poyntz, Anonymous
Born 1800, London, England
Died: January 29, 1861, Linwood, Lynhurst, Hampshire
Genre(s): novel, drama, poetry, short story
Language(s): English

When Gore died in 1861, the *London Times* praised her as "the best novel writer of her class and the wittiest woman of her age." She was known throughout novel-reading Britain, particularly among women, as the author of more than sixty "fashionable novels," works that portray the manners, romances, and scandals of high society. Yet she also published plays, poems, short stories, literary sketches, songs, and even a gardener's manual on roses. Among those who knew her personally, including Mary Russell Mitford, Thackeray, and Dickens, she was renowned for her learned and clever conversation.

Raised in East Retford, Nottinghamshire, and in London, she began writing at an early age and published her first novel, *Theresa Marchmont, or The Maid of Honour*, in 1824, a year after her marriage. The year 1829 saw the appearance of her *Hungarian Tales*, narratives blending fact and fiction. But it was in 1830, with the publication of *Women as They Are, or The Manners of the Day* that Gore joined the ranks of the "Silver-Fork School" of novelists; she ultimately became its most prolific, and possibly most popular, writer. In *Women as They Are* and dozens of subsequent novels of fashion, she depicts the gay leisure class of Regency England, complete with strutting dandies, arrogant parvenus, scheming mamas, and hopeful girls decked out in the family jewels. Her novels appealed both to the fashionables about whom she wrote and to middle-class readers as well. The romances portrayed in her works often play out the middle-class female daydream of marrying into aristocracy, and her pages are crowded with the minute details about shops, dress, and etiquette craved by those struggling themselves to rise in society. However, Gore also brought to her novels a sharp wit and keen insight into the pretensions and absurdities of the fashionable world; in fact, one reviewer cautioned her not to be too reckless in her exposure of hypocrisy.

Following the appearance of *Women as They Are*, she turned out work at an astonishing rate, producing six books and several plays in 1831 and 1832 alone. Toward the end of this period, she published *The Fair of May Fair* (1832), a collection of short stories. It was not well received, and her correspondence indicates that she was stung by the bad reviews, particularly by suggestions that she was wasting her talents. Gore had privately referred to herself as a writer of "rubbish," but in the face of public criticism, she fiercely defended the fashionable novel, contending that "every picture of passing manners, if accurate, is valuable from the drawing room to the alehouse." However, when she published *A Sketchbook of Fashion* anonymously, in 1833, Gore requested that the book be given no notice at all and confessed to her publisher that she had grown rather ashamed of her novels of fashion. Hoping to redeem her name and remind readers of her earlier success at a more serious form of literature, she also produced a collection of historical stories in 1833 and announced them as "*Polish Tales,* by the authoress of *Hungarian Tales.*"

In 1832, the Gores had moved to Paris, where she presided over a Sunday salon frequented by literary and political personalities. She published little more until 1836, when a flurry of novels appeared, occasioned, most likely, by a financial crisis. Years later, she expressed her belief that "even from an iron intellect the sparks are only elicited by collision with the flints of this world. " But in Gore's case, necessity tended to result in the frivolous novels for which she was famous rather than the serious work to which she sporadically returned.

By 1841, the Gores had returned to England, and she published her best-known novel: *Cecil, or The Adventures of a Coxcomb*. At her insistence, the novel was published anonymously to encourage readers in the belief that an exciting new talent had appeared: it created just the sensation she had hoped for. Purporting to be the autobiography of a dandy, a friend and companion of Lord Byron (*Cecil* displays an intimate acquaintance with London clubs as well as a greater knowledge of Greek and Latin than would ordinarily be attributed to a woman. Hence, no one imagined it had been written by Gore, who probably got her information about the clubs from her friend William Beckford. Throughout the novel, she mercilessly satirizes dandyism, although she also uses Cecil's travels to show off her own acquaintance with Parisian manners, cuisine, and politics.

In the same year that *Cecil* appeared, she began a series of articles in *Bentley's Miscellany* under the pseudonym "Albany Poyntz." In one of the earliest of these articles, "The Children of the Mobility versus the Children of the Nobility," she bitterly contrasts the "freedom" of poor children with the "deprivations" and discomforts supposedly suffered by the gaudily dressed children featured in the currently popular "Portraits of the Nobility." The Albany Poyntz articles also include a series of satirical sketches of members of the upper-class entourage—"The Standard Footman," "The Lady's Maid," etc.—but even in some of these, Gore reveals an understanding of and compassion for the hardships of the poor.

Her efforts at playwriting met with considerably less success than her novels and sketches. Although *The School for Coquettes* was a hit in 1831, Gore's most highly publicized play, *Quid Pro Quo, or The Day of the Dupes*, was a theatrical disaster. The play won a lucrative prize in 1844 as the best comedy of British life and manners, but when it was produced the play was hooted off the stage and assailed by the press.

In 1846, Gore's husband died, and four years later she received an inheritance from another family member that allowed her to relax her demanding pace. She had regularly turned out novels over the previous decade, but none had met with the same success as *Cecil*—not even its sequel *Cecil, A Peer* (1841), or *Adventures in Borneo* (1849), another fictional autobiography, this time in the style of *Robinson Crusoe*. Interest in the fashionable novel was waning, but when Gore fell victim to a bank scandal in 1855, she cunningly reissued her 1843 novel about a corrupt banker, *The Banker's Wife, or Court and City*—omitting, of course, the appreciative dedication she had made, ironically enough, to her own trusted banker, who later involved her funds in the scandal; 1855 also saw the appearance, fittingly, of Gore's *Mammon, or The Hardships of an Heiress*. She published her last novel in 1858. Her eyesight began to fail and she died in 1861.

The comparison of Gore's life and her work produces some odd contradictions: she courted high society even as she satirized it, and despite her own financial hardships and hard-headed business sense, her novels celebrate the virtue of womanly submission and chronicle the disastrous consequences of women's attempts at independence. Gore herself alternately disparaged and defended her fashionable writing. Had she not been driven by financial necessity, she might have produced works of more lasting stature; still, her *oeuvre* provides a revealing portrait of the follies of her era.

Works

Theresa Marchmont, or The Maid of Honour A Tale (1824). *The Bond: A Dramatic Poem* (1824). *Richelieu, or the Broken Heart* (1826). *The Lettre de Cachet: A Tale*, with *The Reign of Terror: A Tale* (1827). *Hungarian Tales* (1829). *Romances of Real Life* (1829). *Women as They Are, or The Manners of the Day* (1830). *The Historical Traveller* (1831). *The School for Coquettes* (1831). *Pin Money: A Novel* (1831). *The Tuileries A Tale* (1831). *Mothers and Daughters: A Tale of the Year 1830* (1831). *The Opera: A Novel* (1832). *The Fair of May Fair* (1832). *A Sketchbook of Fashion* (1833). *Polish Tales* (1833). *The Hamiltons, or the New Era* (1834). *The Maid of Croissey, King O'Neil,* and *The Queens Champion* (in *Webster's Acting National Drama,* 1835). *The Diary of a Désennuyée* (1836). *Mrs Armytage, or Female Domination* (1836). *Picciola, or Captive Creative* (by X.B. Saintine, ed. and trans. by Gore, 1837). *Memoirs of a Peeress, or the Days of Fox* (ed. C. Bury, 1837). *Stokeshill Place, or The Man of Business* (1837). *The Rose Fancier's Manual* (1838). *Mary Raymond and Other Tales* (1838). *The Woman of the World: A Novel* (1838). *The Cabinet Minister* (1839). *The Courtier of the Days of Charles II, with Other Tales* (1839). *A Good Nights Rest! or Two O'Clock in the Morning* (in *Duncombe's British Theatre,* 1839). *Dacre of the South, or The Olden Time: A Drama* (1840). *The Dowager, or The New School for Scandal* (1840). *Preferment, or My Uncle the Earl* (1840). *The Abbey and Other Tales* (1840). *Greville, or a Season in Paris* (1841). *Cecil, or The Adventures of a Coxcomb: A Novel* (1841), *Cecil, A Peer* (1841). *Paris in 1841* (1842). *The Man of Fortune and Other Tales* (1842). *The Ambassador's Wife* (1842). *The Money Lender* (1843). *Modern Chivalry, or A New Orlando Furioso* (1843). *The Banker's Wife, or Court and City: A Novel* (1843). *Agathonia: A Romance* (1844). *Marrying for Money* (in *Omnibus of Modern Romance,* 1844). *The Birthright and Other Tales* (1844). *Quid Pro Quo, or The Day of the Dupes: A Comedy* (1844). *The Popular Member: The Wheel of Fortune* (1844). *Self* (1845). *The Story of a Royal Favorite* (1845). *The Snowstorm: A Christmas Story* (1845). *Peers and Parvenus: A Novel* (1846). *New Year's Day: A Winter's Tale* (1846). *Men of Capital* (1846). *The Debutante, or The London Season* (1846). *Sketches of English Character* (1846). *Castles in the Air: A Novel* (1847). *Temptation and Atonement and Other Tales* (1847).

The Inundation, or Pardon and Peace: A Christmas Story (1847). *The Diamond and the Pearl: A Novel* (1849). *Adventures in Borneo* (1849). *The Dean's Daughter, or The Days We Live In* (1853). *The Lost Son: A Winter's Tale* (1854). *Transmutation, or The Lord and the Lout* (1854). *Progress and Prejudice* (1854). *Mammon, or The Hardships of an Heiress* (1855). *A Life's Lessons: A Novel* (1856). *The Two Aristocracies: A Novel* (1857). *Heckington: A Novel* (1858).

Cynthia Merrill

Luise Adelgunde Victoria Gottsched
1713–1762

a.k.a. XYZ der Jüngere, L.A.V.G., Gottschedin
Born April 11, 1713, Danzig, Germany
Died June 26, 1762, Leipzig
Genre(s): drama, journalism, polemic, translation
Language(s): German

Luise Gottsched is the most important woman writer of the early Enlightenment in Germany. Her large body of work, frequently with a satirical element, includes plays (originals and translations), polemics, reviews, and magazine articles. She was the first German woman journalist of note.

As a young woman, Luise Kulmus received an excellent education with the help of both her mother and her father, studying subjects that ranged from the usual girl's French and music to the very unusual mathematics and philosophy. Along with her education, she absorbed profound conflicts about her female role, for despite having all the tools for independent thought and for creativity, she felt that as a woman she should use them only in subordination to her husband. Under these conditions, her literary development was both enhanced and hurt by her marriage to the domineering Professor Gottsched in 1735. On the one hand, the marriage to the most influential literary man of the period gave her the opportunity to be at the center of German literary life in the only way available to a woman at the time. On the other hand, because of the ideology of a wife's subjection to her husband's will, she was unable to object when her husband directed her to stop writing plays, at which she was developing considerable skill, and instead to devote herself completely to translations for him that gave her no chance for further literary creativity. In the face of these contradictions, the gifted woman's self-confidence was crippled and her personal literary achievement restricted in ways that left her embittered and dissatisfied.

She had begun publishing anonymously in 1731 at age eighteen, four years before her marriage but two years after becoming acquainted with Gottsched. After marriage, her life is marked by no clearly identifiable major nonliterary events; she remained childless. For her husband, who was himself a phenomenally productive writer, she did a prodigious amount of translating along with article writing and book reviewing for his periodicals. This activity has earned her the label of being Germany's first important woman journalist. Her plays and translations of plays were very successful, performed frequently for years after her death. Her polemics reveal her fervent participation in the literary quarrels that marked and then marred her husband's domination of the German literature of his day.

The works that receive the most praise today, three plays, *Pietisterey*, *Das Testament*, and *Herr Witzling* (Pietism in a Whale-bone Skirt, The Will, and Mr. Witty) are comedies that show Luise Gottsched's satirical gift but also reveal undercurrents of ambivalence toward learning and toward women.

Works

Der Frau von Lambert Betrachtungen über das Frauenzimmer, tr. of Anne Thérèse de Marguenat de Courcelles de Lambert, Reflexions sur les femmes (1721); also, poems by Gottsched (1731). *Ode: Das glückliche Russland am Geburtstage Ihro Kaiserl. Majestät Anna Iwanowna* [Happy Russia on the Birthday of her Royal Highness Anna Iwanowna] (1733). *Der Sieg der Beredsamkeit*, tr. of Madeleine Angélique Poisson de Gomez, *La Triomphe de l'eloquence*, 1730 (1735). *Kato*, tr. of Joseph Addison, *Cato*, 1713 (1735). *Die Pietisterey im Fischbein-Rocke; Oder Die Doctormäßige Frau*, Version of Luise Bougeant, *La femme docteur ou la théologie janséniste tombée en quenouille* (1736). *Triumph der Weltweisheit, nach Art des Französischen Sieges der Beredsamkeit der Frau Gomez, nebst einem Anhange dreier Reden* [Triumph of World Wisdom. In the manner of the French *Triumph of Eloquence* by Madam Gomez, with an appendix of Three Speeches] (1739). *Der Zuschauer. Neun Theile*, tr. of The Spectator, 1711–1714 (1739–1943). *Horatii, als eines wohlerfahrnen Schiffers treumeynender Zuruff an alle Wolfianer* [Horatii, the Sincere Call of a Well-Meaning Sailor to All Followers of Wolfe] (1740). *Zwo Schriften, welche von der Frau Marquise von Chatelet und dem Herrn von Mairan,* das Maaß der lebendigen Kräfte in den Körpern betreffend, sind gewechselt worden, tr. of *Lettre de M. de Mairan . . . a Madame *** [la marquise du Chatelet] sur la question des forces vives, an reponse aux objections qu'elle lui fait sur ce sujet dans ses Institutions de physique*, 1741 (1741). *Cornelia, Mutter der Grachen*, tr. of Marie Anne Barbier, *Cornélie, mère des Gracques*, 1703. In *Die Deutsche Schaubühne nach den Regeln und Mustern der Alten*, vol. 2, 1741 (1741). *Das Gespenst mit der Trommel*, tr. of Destouches, *Le Tambour nocturne*, 1736. In *Deutsche Schaubühne*, vol. 2, 1741 (1741). *Alzire, oder die Amerikaner*, tr. of Voltaire, *Alzire, ou les Américains*, 1734. In *Deutsche Schaubühne*, vol. 3, 1741 (1741). *Der Verschwender*, tr. of Destouches, *Le Dissipateur*. In *Deutsche Schaubühne*, vol. 3, 1741 (1741). *Der Poetische Dorfjunker*, tr. of Destouches, *La Fausse Agnes*. In *Deutsche Schaubühne*, vol. 3, 1741 (1741). Tr. of 330 of the 635 articles in *Herrn Peter Gaylens historisches und kritisches Worterbuch.* 4 vols. (1741–1744). *Der Menschenfeind*, tr. of Moliere, *Le Misanthrope*, 1666. In *Deutsche Schaubühne*, vol. 1, 1742 (1742). *Die Widerwillige*, tr. of Charles Dufresny, *L'Esprit de contradiction*, 1700. In *Deutsche Schaubühne*, vol. 1, 1742 (1742). *Lockenraub, ein scherzhaftes Heldengedicht*, tr. of Alexander Pope, *The Rape of the Lock*, 1714; also tr. of two poems by Antoinette Deshoulières (1744). *Die ungleiche Heirath* [The Unequal Marriage; comedy]. In *Deutsche Schaubühne*, vol. 4, 1744 (1744). *Die Hausfranzösinn, oder Die Mamsell*. In *Deutsche Schaubühne*, vol. 5, 1744 [The French Governess, or Mam'selle; comedy] (1744). *Panthea* [Panthea], tragedy. In *Deutsche Schaubühne*, vol. 5, 1745 (1744). *Das Testament* [The Will], comedy. In *Deutsche Schaubühne*, vol. 6, 1745 (1745). *Herr Witzling* [Mr. Witty], one-act comedy. In *Deutsche Schaubühne*, vol. 6, 1745 (1745). *Der Aufseher oder Vormund*, tr. of Addison, *The Guardian*, 1713 (1745). *Die gestürzten Freymäurer*, tr. of G.-L. Perau, *Les Franc-maçons écrasés* and *L'Ordre des francs-maçons*, 1747 (1747). *Paisan parvenu, oder der glücklich gewordene Bauer*, tr. of Marivaus, *Paysan parvenu*, 1735 (1748). *Neue Sammlung auserlesener Stücke aus Popens, Newtons, Eachards und anderer Schriften* [New Collection of Selected Pieces from the Writings of Pope, Newton, Eachard, and others] (1749). *Geschichte der königlichen Akademie der Aufschriften und schönen Wissenschaften zu Paris, darin zugleich unzählige Abhandlungen aus allen freien Künsten, gelehrten Sprachen und Alterthümern enthalten sind* [History of the Royal Academy of Letters and Belles Lettres at Paris, Wherein Innumerable Treatises from All the Free Arts, Scholarly Languages,

and Antiquities Are Contained] (1749–1757). *Vollständige Sammlung aller Streitschriften über das vorgebliche Gesetz der Natur von der kleinsten Kraft in den Wirkungen der Körper* [Complete Collection of All Pamphlets About the Alleged Law of Nature of the Smallest Effect in the Activities of Bodies] (1752). *Cénie, oder die Großmuth im Unglücke, ein moralisches Stück*, tr. of Mme. de Graffigny, *Cénie*, 1750 (1753). *Der kleine Prophet von Bömischbroda, oder Weissagung des Gabriel Johannes Nepomucenus Franciscus de Paula Waldstörchel* [The Little Prophet from Bömischbroda, or Prediction of Gabriel Johannes Nepomuceus Franciscus de Paul Waldstörchel]. In part a tr. of Friedrich Melchior Grimm, *Le petit Prophète de Boehmischbroda*, 1753 (1753). *Der königlichen Akademie der Aufschriften und schönen Wissenschaften zu Paris ausführliche Schriften, darin unzählige Abhandlungen aus allen freien Künsten, gelehrten Sprachen und Alterthümern enthalten sind* [The Extensive Documents of the Royal Academy of Letters and Belles Lettres at Paris, Wherein Innumerable Treatises from All the Free Arts, Scholarly Languages, and Antiquities Are Contained], 2 vols. (1753–1754). *Der beste Fürst, ein Vorspiel auf das Geburtsfest der verw. Fürstin Johanna Elisabeth von Anhalt-Zerbst* [The Best Prince, a Prologue for the Birthday Celebration of the Widowed Princess Johanna Elisabeth von Anhalt-Zerbst] (1755). *Des Abts Terrason Philosophie nach ihrem allgemeinen Einflusse auf alle Gegenstände des Geistes und der Sitten*, tr. of Jean Terrasson, *La Philosophie applicable a tous les objets de l'esprit et de la raison*, 1754 (1756). *Nachrichten, die zum Leben der Frau von Maintenon und des vorigen Jahrhunderts gehörig sind*, tr. of Laurent Angliviel de La Beaumelle, *Memoires pour servir à l'histoire de Madame de Maintenon et à celle du siècle passé*, 1755–1756 (1757). *Gedanken über die Glückseligkeit, oder philosophische Betrachtungen über das Gute und Böse des menschlichen Lebens*, tr. of Louis de Beausobre, *Essai sur le bonheur*, 1758 (1758). *Briefe, die Einführung des Englischen Geschmacks in Schauspielen betreffend, wo zugleich auf den Siebzehnten der Briefe, die neue Litteratur betreffend, geantwortet wird* [Letters Concerning the Introduction of the English Taste in Plays, Where the Seventeenth Letter About the New Literature Is Answered] (1760). *Des Freyherrn von Bielefeld Lehrbegriff von der Staatskunst*, tr. of Jacob Friedrich von Bielfeld. *Institutions politiques*, 1760 (1761). *Der Frau Luise Adelgunde Victorie Gottschedinn, geb. Kulmus, sämmtliche Kleinere Gedichte* [Collected Shorter Poems, ed. by her Husband] (1763). *Briefe der Frau Louise Adelgunde Victorie Gottsched* [Letters of Madame Gottsched], ed. Dorothea Henriette von Runckel (1771).

Translation: One poem in *Bitter Healing: Anthology of German Women Authors from Pietism to Romanticism*, ed. Jeannine Blackwell and Susanne Zantop (Lincoln, 1989).

Ruth P. Dawson

Marie-Olympe de Gouges
1745–1793

Born May 7, 1745, Montauban, France
Died November 4, 1793, Paris
Genre(s): pamphlet, brochure, drama, novel
Language(s): French

Olympe de Gouges was an ardent feminist and an advocate of women's rights during the early years of the French Revolution, 1789–1793. Marie Gouge (or Gouze) was born in Montauban in 1745 (she said 1755) of lower class parents; she married a wealthy, older man, M. Aubry (but never took his name), and had a son. Not much is known of her life before age eighteen, but she had sufficient funds to support herself in Paris where she pursued a writing career, using her mother's name, Olympe, and assuming the aristocratic "de." In 1785 her first play (a comedy) was performed in the Théâtre Français; none of her verbose, loosely constructed plays was successful. She was poorly educated and never mastered spelling or grammar, a fact of which she was acutely aware.

The Revolution plunged her into the turbulent, male political world and into feminist activities that brought her notoriety, persecution, and finally death. Olympe was the first feminist during this period to call for equal rights for men and women, among the first to try to organize women's groups, and the first to draw up a feminist manifesto (1789). Her program of radical reform did not appeal to many women of any class, and men simply ridiculed and derided her efforts. The Manifesto called for (1) legal equality for men and women, (2) careers open to talent, (3) abolishing the dowry system, (4) equal education for men and women, (5) and a national theatre devoted to producing plays by women. This "high priestess of Feminism" found few supporters for her original and bold ideas. Speaking to a meeting of the Society of Revolutionary Republican Women, she called for an army of 30,000 women to go into battle, to allow women to hold positions in the government, and to put women in charge of educating the young. Her proposals were greeted with laughter and hisses from her female audience who voted to postpone discussion of them. However, nothing deterred her from speaking her mind and pursuing her goals, by violent means if necessary.

Olympe's feminism was constant and consistent, but her political allegiance vacillated between monarchist and republican. In 1789 she welcomed the Revolution, became a royalist when Louis XVI was forced to leave Versailles for Paris (October 1789), turned against the King when he attempted to flee the country (1791), and then offered to defend Louis at his trial (1792); finally, convinced that Louis was a traitor, she supported a republic. Her open opposition to Robespierre and the Terror, and her association with the terrifying female rabble, the *Tricoteuses* [Knitters], led to her downfall. The Committee of Public Safety saw her as a dangerous and divisive radical, but their attempts to silence her failed. She continued to write political and feminist tracts and to make public speeches that were considered a threat to the aims of the Revolution. Her famous *Les Droits de la Femme: à la Reine* (1791; Declarations of the Rights of Women) boldly set forth her feminist demands: women had the right to participate in politics and to choose a profession, new marriage laws should guarantee equality between partners who would hold all property in common, and the condemnation of unwed mothers must be abolished. She prophetically insisted that if "Woman has the right to mount the scaffold; she must equally have the right to mount the rostrum" (Article X). De Gouges believed women were capable of leadership: "They are the force behind everything," the force that animated man to act. Her political views, rather than her feminism, finally brought about her arrest. In a pamphlet, *Les Trois Urnes* (1793; The Three Urns), she called for a federalist system of government which was a violation of the law.

At her trial she insisted that she had always been a good citizen, a republican, as one could see in her work entitled, *L'Esclavage des noirs* (1792; The Slavery of Blacks). The Revolutionary Tribunal was unconvinced and found her guilty of several crimes against the government. She was condemned to die. Claiming to be pregnant in order to postpone her execution, de Gouges failed. At 4:00 P.M. on November 4, 1793, she was guillotined. In her will she "left her heart to her country, her honesty to men (if they needed it), and her soul to women." De Gouges and other feminists did not achieve their program of reform, but they made women aware of their inferior status in society and gave them a set of goals to work toward.

Works

Le Mariage inattendu de Chérubin (1785). Lucinde et Cardenio [not published]. *Les Comédiens démasqués, ou Madame de Gouges ruinée par la Comédie-Française pour se faire jouer (n.d.). L'Homme généreux (1786). Molière chez Ninon, ou le siècle des grands hommes (1788). Le Philosophe corrigé, ou le cocu supposé (n.d.). Adresses au Roi et à la Reine, au prince de Condé, et Observations à M. Duveyrier sur sa fameuse ambassade (n.d.). Zamore et Mirza, ou l'heureux naufrage (1788). Lettre au Peuple, ou projet d'une caisse patriotique, par une citoyenne (1788). Remarques patriotiques (1788). Oeuvres de Mme de Gouges, 3 vols. (1788). Mes Voeux sont remplis, ou le don patriotique, dédié aux états généraux (1789). Le Bonheur primitif, ou les réveries patriotiques (1789). Discours de l'aveugle aux Français (1789). Dialogue Allégorique entre la France et la Verité dediée aux Etats Généraux (1789). L'Ordre national, ou le comte d'Artois inspiré par Mentor (1789). Séance royale, motion de monseigneur le duc d'Orléans, ou les songes patriotiques (1789). Lettre à Mgr. le duc d'Orléans Prince du Sang, par l'amie de amie de tous les citoyens et du repos public (1789?). Lettre aux représentants de la nation (1789). Départ de M. Necker et de madame de Gouges, ou les Adieux de madame de Gouges à M. Necker et aux Français (1790). Action heroïque d'une Française ou La France sauvée par les femmes (1790). Le Marché des Noirs (n.d.). Le Danger du Préjugé ou l'Ecole des Hommes (n.d.). Lettre aux littérateurs français (1790?). Réponse au champion américain, ou colon très-aisé à connaître (1790). Les Droits de la Femme: à la Reine* [Declaration of the Rights of Woman] *(1791). Mirabeau aux Champs-Elysées (1791). L'Esclavage des Noirs, ou l'heureux naufrage (1792). Réponse à la justification de Max. Robespierre (1792). L'Esprit français ou Problème à résoudre sur le labyrinthe des divers complots (1792). Lettres à la reine, aux généraux, etc., avec la description de la fête du 3 juin (1792). Adresse au Don Quichotte du Nord (1792). Grande eclipse du soleil jacobiniste et de la lune feuillantine (1792?). Arrêt de Mort que présente Olympe de Gouges contre Louis Capet (1792?). Le Bon Sens Français ou l'Apologie de Vrais Nobles, dediée aux Jacobins (1792?). La France sauvée, ou le Tyran détrôné (1792?). Le Couvent, ou les Voeux forces (1792). Le Prince philosophe, 2 vols. (1792). Olympe de Gouges, défenseur officieux de Louis Capet, au président de la Convention nationale (1792). L'Entrée du Dumouriez à Bruxelles, ou les Vivandières (1793). Testament politique d'Olympe de Gouges (1793). Complots dévoilés des sociétaires du prétendu théâtre de la République (1793). Avis pressant à la Convention par une vraie républicaine (1793?). Les trois Urnes, ou le salut de la patrie (1793). Correspondence de la Cour—Compte Moral rendu et dernier mot à mes chers amis, par Olympe de Gouges à la Convention Nationale et au Peuple . . . (n.d.). Le Cri du Sage par une Femme (n.d.). Avis pressant ou Réponse à mes calomniateurs (n.d.). Pour sauver la patrie il faut respecter les trois ordres (n.d.). Observations sur les étrangers (n.d.). Dernier Mot à mes chers amis (1793?). Mémoires de madame de Valmont (n.d.).*

Jeanne A. Ojala

Marie le Jars de Gournay
1565–1645

a.k.a. La Damoiselle de Gournay, Mademoiselle
de Gournay, La Fille d'Alliance de Monsieur
de Montaigne
Born 1565, Paris
Died 1645, Paris
Genre(s): criticism, novel, translation, poetry,
polemic
Language(s): French

The editor of Montaigne's *Essays* and a scholar of international reputation, Marie de Gournay was a professional writer and woman of letters who worked to advance the cause of women and who was in France the most scholarly female critic before Mme de Staël.

The daughter of a nobleman with important functions at court, Marie spent most of her childhood at the family estate Gournay-sur-Aronde in Picardie, where she read avidly and taught herself Latin. The discovery, at the age of eighteen or nineteen, of Montaigne's *Essays* marked the beginning of her life-long enthusiasm for the book and its author. A deep friendship—or perhaps even passion—developed between the older man and his "adopted daughter." His death, in 1592, provoked her emotional breakdown and later caused her to start working on her first edition of the *Essays* (1595). After the death of her mother in 1591 she provided generously for her siblings and then moved to Paris to live by herself as a woman of letters, a decision for which her contemporaries criticized her severely. She associated with all the important authors and intellectuals of her day and frequently voiced her opinions, which gave rise to controversy and slander. She published steadily throughout her lifetime and in her last years gained

Cardinal Richelieu's favor as well as assistance from the royal exchequer. She died in Paris at the age of eighty.

Marie de Gournay did not only publish eleven different editions of the *Essays*, she also produced one short novel, translations from Virgil, Ovid, Cicero, Tacitus, and Sallust, numerous poems, many essays on the French language, poetry, theory of translation, education, morality and religion, two feminist tracts, and supervised several reprints of her collected works (1624, 1634, 1641).

For many years, Marie de Gournay was accused of opportunism and her editorial integrity questioned. A certain laudatory passage about her in the *Essays* 17:11 was said to have been written by herself. Recent scholarship has established, however, that she edited Montaigne's text with as much care and competence as any good scholar of her day would have done.

Although her work was inspired and influenced by Montaigne's, she did possess originality and creative talent. Her *Proumenoir de Monsieur Montaigne* (1594; Walking with Mr. Montaigne) is considered one of the earliest psychological novels in French literature. The plot, borrowed from Claude de Taillemont, centers on an unmarried girl who risks her reputation and accepts hardships to escape a marriage of convenience and follow the man of her choice. The novel is full of digressions in the manner of Montaigne which Marie the moralist uses to show that for women, as for men, the basis of virtue is and must be knowledge.

She was far from a radical feminist but produced very intelligent, highly readable and entertaining contributions to the debate about women's rights and roles. In *L'Egalité des hommes et des femmes* (1622; The Equality of Men and Women), and *Grief des dames* (1626; The Ladies' Grievance), she focuses on theological questions and searches philosophers and churchfathers for "evidence" in favor of Eve's equality. Moreover, to counter the low regard in which women's intelligence was generally held, she insists on the importance of education, arguing that most differences between men and women would disappear if women were given the same education as men. The author's erudition and knowledge of the classics are evident in both essays.

Whereas the effect of *L'Egalité des hommes et des femmes* is muted somewhat by its inner contradictions, the vehement *Grief* is effective moral satire. A supplement to Montaigne's "The Art of Conversation" (3: VIII), it deals with the one aspect of conversation that he ignores, namely the ladies' share in it. With fine psychological insight, Marie de Gournay shows that the responses of the male participants in this imaginary debate, which appear as so many gestures of politeness, mercy, and tolerance, are in fact evasions motivated by unconscious insecurities and fear.

Though she composed numerous poems on public and private subjects, Marie de Gournay was not much of a poet. She is remembered above all for her critical essays. Her predilection for the poetry of the Pleiade and Ronsard was old-fashioned in the eyes of her contemporaries but must be seen as a vindication of complete poetic liberty, something Malherbe's school and the neoclassicists could not appreciate.

Works

Le Proumenoir de Monsieur Montaigne (1594). *Bien-Venue de Monseigneur le Duc d'Anjou* (1608). *Adieu de l'Ame du Roy de France et de Navarre, Henry le Grand à la Royne* with *La Défense des Pères Iésuites* (1610). *Versions de quelques pièces de Virgile, Tacite et Saluste* with *L'Institution de Monseigneur, frère du Roy* (1619). *Eschantillons de Virgile* (n.d.). *L'Egalité des hommes et des femmes* (1622). *Remerciements au Roy* (1624). *Préface* to the *Essays* of Montaigne (1595, 1599, 1617, 1625, 1635; shortened versions in 1598, 1600, 1604, 1611, 1617). "La Fille d'Alliance de Monsieur de Montaigne," in *Le Tombeau du feu sieur de Sponde* (1595). *Grief des dames* (1626). *L'Ombre de la Damoiselle de Gournay* (1626). *Les Advis ou les Présens de la Demoiselle de Gournay* (1634). *Les Advis ou les Présens de la Demoiselle de Gournay* (expanded, 1641). Letters to Justius Lipsius in *Bulletin du Bibliophile*. (1862): 1296–1311. Letters to Henri Dupuy, *Nouveaux documents sur Montaigne*, ed. Payen (1850). Letter to Cardinal Richelieu, cited by P. Bonnefon in *Montaigne et ses amis*. Letter to M. Bignon, British Museum, Egerton 21, fol. 63. Letter to Anna Marie van Schuurman, Koninklijke Bibliotheek, The Hague.

Maya Bijvoet

Marie Eugenie delle Grazie
1864–1931

Born August 14, 1864, Ungarisch-Weisskirchen, Hungary
Died February 18, 1931, Vienna
Genre(s): novel, epic, poetry, drama, essay
Language(s): German

Marie Eugenie delle Grazie's career spanned approximately fifty years, during which she produced works in a variety of genres. Her epics and her novels are considered her best work, although she also wrote poetry, plays, prose tales, and essays. Her literary career was at its height during the first decade of this century, when she was regarded as one of the foremost women writers and thinkers in Germany. But even before her death, her reputation had waned considerably, due in part to her shift from free-thinker to religious writer. In her later years the liberal press lost interest in her, while Catholic publishers held back cautiously and her works did not receive the same exposure as earlier. Yet the contents of her works are typical for turn-of-the-century Austria, and she ranks second only to Ebner-Eschenbach among the important woman authors of that period.

Delle Grazie was born on August 14, 1864, in Weisskirchen, Hungary (now Bela Crkva). Her happy and secure childhood came to an end when her beloved father, a director of a coal mine company, suddenly died in 1872. The family moved to Vienna, where delle Grazie attended a girl's school and for one year a teacher's college. She had to interrupt her studies because of a nervous illness, aggravated by her mother's opposition to her attempts at writing poetry. In 1875 she met the chaplain of St. Leopold in Vienna, Laurenz Müllner (1848–1911), who later became Professor of Christian Philosophy at the University of Vienna. He recognized her talent and furthered her education beyond that of the average woman of the time. He became her mentor and encouraged and criticized her literary productions.

Müllner's death in 1911 left delle Grazie with an enormous sense of loss. During the following summer a mystical experience caused her to convert back to the Catholic faith of her youth, a change prepared by her intellectual disappointment with a number of scientific theories. All of her subsequent works, to her death in 1931, are written from the spirit of her regained faith.

Delle Grazie began composing poetry at an early age, and some of the verses included in her first collection, *Gedichte* (1882; Poems), were written when she was only ten to twelve. These poems already demonstrate her characteristic clarity of language, formal ability, and an atmosphere of pessimism and resignation. The subject matter is often the conflict between spirit and nature, the most prominent theme of all writers at the turn of the century. Her poems often concern love, some describing quiet happiness, but more often renunciation and suffering from unrequited love. Later expanded editions of the poems include discussions of philosophical, scientific, and sociological ideas. Some of the poems in the collection *Italienische Vignetten* (1892; Italian Vignettes) mirror her feelings of hopelessness and disappointment as she compares her youth to the ruins of the historical past. But she finds solace in the sight of the sea, which she perceives as a reflection of her notion of life as a monistic unity of all living things. This pantheism runs through her entire *oeuvre*, although it takes on the guise of mysticism in her later works.

Nature, as the force from which everything comes and to which everything returns, is evident in the descriptions of the Hungarian landscape in her story *Die Zigeunerin* (1885; The Gypsy), a romantic tale of a gypsy girl, Dora, who, betrayed in love, takes bloody revenge. It also plays a role in her epic *Hermann* (1883), a heroic poem about the Germanic past in which the mystique of the German forest is evoked.

Her blend of talents found its best expression in her next major work, often considered her masterwork, the epic in iambic pentameter, *Robespierre. Ein modernes Epos* (1894; Robespierre. A Modern Epic), on which she worked for ten years. It is in the classical form of twenty-four cantos but is modern in the sense that it is based on the ideas of the nineteenth-century French philosopher Hyppolyte Taine, who regards the beginning of the revolution as a social rather than a political movement, as a struggle for justice which then developed into a political struggle for basic rights. Rousseau's influence is apparent in delle Grazie's contention that in separating nature from spirit and human existence from nature, man became isolated. Modern culture and civilization are no longer in harmony with nature, and the result is nihilism. Despite some reservations about the drastic descriptions of misery, the work was considered epoch-making for modern realism, and Hans Benzmann in *Das literarische Echo* (1900/1901, vol. 3, pp. 888–893) described it as "one of the most profound and most beautiful works of art of contemporary literature."

After the success of *Robespierre*, delle Grazie turned to drama, and the première of *Schlagende Wetter* (Firedamp), a naturalistic play, was held at the Deutsches Volkstheater in Vienna on October 27, 1900. It depicts the exploitation of mine workers by the owner and shows the abyss between the two classes. This social drama in the manner of early Hauptmann was followed by *Der Schatten* (The Shadow), a symbolic play (completed in 1897) dealing with the relationship of art and life, a popular theme at the turn of the century. A poet is suddenly filled with regret for his unfulfilled life, and his envy of his friend drives him to commit crimes. When his conscience helps him overcome the dark shadow that had possessed him, the entire incident turns out to have been a product of his poetic fantasy. Through the shadow the poet was able to free himself from the demonic powers that beset the artist more powerfully and dangerously than other people. The play also shows delle Grazie's interest in the subconscious, including dreams, which she considered an emblematic representation of the unconscious, capable of giving information about art and life. Of herself she says that some of her works were conceived in dreams so vivid that she only had to write them down, like an artist who is able to paint a scene from recollection.

Der Schatten received the Bauernfeldpreis and was performed at the Vienna Burgtheater (Première; September 28, 1901)—evidence of delle Grazie's high esteem at the time. The following four one-act plays, collected under the title *Zu Spät* (1903; Too Late), were also performed at the Burgtheater. They include "Die Sphinx" (The Sphynx), a comedy that was also performed successfully in Berlin, but delle Grazie's next attempt at a comedy, *Narren der Liebe* (1905; Fools of Love), found so little critical approval that she returned to more serious subject matter that was truer to her inclinations in her next play *Ver Sacrum* (1906), which deals with the sexual awakening of a young married woman who experiences true love after having been joined to an older man in an arranged marriage. Although it remained on the stage for only two performances, the drama was awarded the Prize of the Wiener Volkstheater.

Despite the award, delle Grazie recognized that her talent was more in the genre of narrative prose. In 1907 she completed her first novel, *Heilige und Menschen* (Saints and Humans), which was serialized in the *Neue Freie Presse* in 1908 and appeared in book form in 1909. The plot, set in a girls' convent school in Rome, juxtaposes royal and papal Rome in the political and social spheres, exposes the affected piety and sanctimoniousness professed in the convent, and contrasts dogmatic religion with ethical-liberal attitudes. Delle Grazie shows how a modern scientist who rejects the religion preached in the convent can still believe in a living God in nature and how the feeling of being connected with all living things can create a more genuine ethical feeling of compassion than the pious comedy of altruism.

Ethical feelings motivated delle Grazie's reaction in 1910 to a book denouncing women's emancipation and occasioned two articles in the leading Viennese newspaper, the *Neue Freie Presse* (August 28, and December 11, 1910). Here she expressed her sympathy with the liberation movement although her profession as well as her inclination have kept her removed from the activities of public life. She feels that women who have been repressed for so long under men's laws, who have disguised themselves and humiliated and degraded themselves under the obligation of selling themselves on the marriage market, now have found the courage to tell the truth about themselves, the marriage market, and men. In addition to her support for the women's cause, she also spoke out against the unjust conditions between subjects and landowners in the novel *Vor dem Sturm* (1910; Before the Storm).

The foreshadowing and beginning of World War I form the background to the novel *O Jugend!* (1917; Oh Youth), dealing with four friends who serve as representatives of their generation, whereas the next two novels, *Donaukind* (1918; Child of the Danube) and *Eines Lebens Sterne* (1919; The Stars of a Life), both heavily autobiographical, look back to the childhood and young adulthood of a precocious, imaginative, and proud girl, Nelly. In contrast, modern life—in the trenches, on the road with refugees from Poland, and in the cities—forms the background of *Homo. Der Roman einer Zeit* (1919; Homo. The Novel of an Era), named after an orphaned boy from the war-torn city of Homonna, who becomes the symbol of true Christian love.

After World War I delle Grazie wanted to express her hope for the revival of her lost homeland, and in *Der Liebe and des Ruhmes Kränze* (1920; Wreaths of Love and Glory), set at the time of the Congress of Vienna (1815–1818), she attempts to re-create that unique period of light, brilliance, grace, and playful elegance.

Typical for delle Grazie's last works, and often considered the best work of her later period, the novella *Die weissen Schmetterlinge von Clairvaux* (1925; The White Butterflies of Clairvaux), is the tale of a religious conversion. It depicts the inner struggle between Bernard de Clairvaux and a convicted murderer and rapist, the "terror of the woods," who in the end shows true repentance and dies in a state of grace.

In the last major novel, *Unsichtbare Strasse* (1927; The Invisible Road), a convent is desecrated by murder, but this action converts the protagonist from class hatred into an advocate of brotherly love, from denying God into believing in Him. He is thus able to overcome his base drives and enter the priesthood out of conviction.

When delle Grazie died on February 18, 1931, she was in the process of putting together a collection of novellas, including "Titanic" and "Matelda." She also left a completed novel, *Die Liebe des Peter Abälard* (1921; The Love of Peter Abelard). Although she considered it one of her best works, she had not submitted it for publication, probably for fear that it could be interpreted as reflecting on her own life.

After her return to the fold of the Catholic church in 1912, the press fell rather silent about delle Grazie. Once hailed as one of the leading personalities on the literary scene, she was almost forgotten by the time of her death. Given the current interest in turn-of-the-century Vienna, this important writer, who anticipated and shared all of the major themes and techniques of the leading Viennese writers, would seem to deserve restoration to a more prominent position in the literary history of her generation.

Works

Gedichte; poems (1882; new edition, 1885, 1902). *Hermann. Deutsches Heldengedicht in 12 Gesängen*, heroic poem (1883, 1885). *Die Zigeunerin. Eine Erzählung aus dem ungarischen Heidelande*, prose tale (1885). *Saul. Tragödie in 5 Acten*, drama (1885). *Italienische Vignetten*, poems (1892). *Der Rebell. Bozi. Zwei Erzählungen*, prose tales (1893). *Robespierre. Ein modernes Epos. 2 Teile*, epic poem (1894). *Moralische Walpurgisnacht. Ein Satyrspiel vor der Tragödie*, play (1896). *Schlagende Wetter. Drama in 4 Akten*, drama (1900). *Liebe*, prose tale (1902). *Der Schatten. Drama in 3 Akten und einem Vorspiel*, drama (1902). *Sämtliche Werke*, 9 vols. (1903). *Zu Spät. Einakterzyklus.*, plays (1903). *Narren der Liebe*, comedy (1905). *Ver Sacrum*, drama (1906). *Schwäne am Land*, drama (1907). *Vom Wege. Geschichten und Märchen*, tales (1907). *Traumwelt*, prose tale (1907). *Heilige und Menschen*, novel (1909). *Vor dem Sturm*, novel (1910, 1924). *Gottesgericht und andere Erzählungen*, prose tales (1912). *Wunder der Seele*, prose tale (1913). *Zwei Witwen*, novella (1914). *Das Buch des Lebens. Erzählungen und Humoresken*, prose tales (1914). *Die blonde Frau Fina und andere Erzählungen*, prose tales (1915). *Das Buch der Liebe*, novel (1916, 1927). *O Jugend!*, novel (1917). *Donaukind*, novel (1918). *Eines Lebens Sterne*, novel (1919). *Die Seele und der Schmetterling*, novella (1919). *Der frühe Lenz*, prose tale (1919). *Homo Der Roman einer Zeit*, novel (1919). *Die Blumen der Acazia* (1920, 1932). *Der Liebe und des Ruhmes Kränze. Roman auf der Viola d'Amour*, novel (1920). *Die weissen Schmetterlinge von Clairvaux*, novella (1925). "Matelda," novella in *Heimlich bluten Herzen. Österreichische Frauennovellen* (1926). *Unsichtbare Strasse*, novel (1927). *Titanic. Eine Ozeanphantasie*, novella (1928). *Sommerheide*, novella (1928). *Das Buch der Heimat*, prose tale (1930). *Die Empörung der Seele*, novel (1930). *Die kleine weisse Stadt und andere Kurzgeschichten aus der Banater Heimat*, tales (1977).

Jorun B. Johns

Kate Greenaway
1846–1901

Born March 17, 1846, Hoxton, London
Died November 6, 1901, Hampstead, London
Genre(s): children's stories, poetry
Language(s): English

Primarily known for her illustrations of children's books, Greenaway wrote verse and other texts as well. Her children's rhymes and drawings of children and English gardens were very popular both in Europe and in America. Her parents recognized her budding talent at twelve and provided art lessons, but her formal education alternated between visiting tutors and girls' schools. Her first published works, in 1868, were designs for Christmas and Valentine cards. She soon began illustrating little books and continued this work throughout her life.

But Greenaway's writings alone would not have gained entry into the publishing world. Her writings fall into five categories: illustrated verses, datebooks, nonfiction, correspondence, and miscellaneous poetry. Her popular illustrated verses still have a special innocent charm, the almanacs and datebooks brought her some notoriety, and she also illustrated texts for art lessons and game rules.

The only two children's rhyme books that Greenaway both wrote and illustrated were *Under the Window* (1878) and *Marigold Garden* (1886). Her *An Apple Pie* (1885) has been considered original, but the text is very close to standard nursery alphabet rhymes. *Under the Window* is a series of outside scenes spotlighting Victorian emerging ladies and gentlemen, reflecting in words and images the whimsy and innocent fantasy of childhood. The rhyme is singsongy, and the theme is a combination of fantasy and etiquette. *Marigold Garden*, also manners-conscious, was more successful in capturing the fancy of a child's perspective. The illustrations and text form a complementary whole, so that the picture of the stuffy woman with her constrained, dutiful grandchildren matches the tone of the verse.

These works' popularity was a reflection of the Victorian Age of which Greenaway was certainly a part. In many ways, the innocence and beauty of her children, who in no way resemble the chimneysweeps and other poor waifs then on the streets, are directly influenced by the Pre-Raphaelite movement. She not only admired the paintings of John Everett Millais, Rossetti, and Hunt, but was a disciple of John Ruskin. The Ruskin–Greenaway correspondence began in 1880, when he wrote about the *Under the*

Window exhibition, and ended in 1900, when he died; he wrote about 500 letters, and she wrote 1,000 or more. Ruskin, the authoritarian art critic, offered advice and friendship and devoted a lecture to Greenaway called "Fairyland" on May 30, 1883. Feeling that she was wasting much effort on her illustrations and datebook art, he encouraged Greenaway to paint larger works, which she did. Greenaway subsequently illustrated over twenty books written by others. In addition to a collection of cat poems edited by Ruskin, *Dame Wiggins of Lee and Her Seven Wonderful Cats* (1885), Greenaway's best known collaborators were Bret Harte (*The Queen of the Pirate Isle,* 1886) and Robert Browning (*The Pied Piper of Hamelin,* 1888).

Her unpublished poems fill up four volumes of manuscripts, though several were subsequently published in a biography about her. Most of her poems are unpolished and amateurish, and she was never satisfied with them. They are not, however, nursery rhymes. They are lyrics, some in sonnet form, on a number of different themes, many serious and sad, many verses about love.

The artist described by her biographers was "sincere, modest, patient, intelligent, bighearted, sensitive, forgiving, and humorous," and Ruskin said that Greenaway was able to "re-establish throughout gentle Europe the manners and customs of fairyland."

Works

Self-illustrated: *Under the Window Pictures and Rhymes for Children* (1878). *Art Hours: After K. Greenaway* (1882). *Steps to Art: After Kate Greenaway* (1882). *Kate Greenaway's Almanac for 1883–95, 1897* (14 vols., 1882–1896). *Language of Flowers* (1884). *Kate Greenaway's Alphabet* (1885). *Marigold Garden: Pictures and Rhymes* (1885). *An Apple Pie* (1886). *Kate Greenaway's Book of Games* (1889). *Kate Greenaway's Pictures from Originals Presented by Her to John Ruskin and Other Personal Friends* (1921). *The Kate Greenaway Treasury: An Anthology of the Illustrations and Writings of Kate Greenaway.* ed. E. Ernest and P. Lowe (1967). *The Kate Greenaway Book,* ed. B. Holme (1976). *Kate Greenaway's Mother Goose* (1984, 1987, 1988). *Polly Put the Kettle on and Other Rhymes* (1987). *Book of Games* (1989). *Kate Greenaway's Nursery Rhyme Classics* (1990). *An Apple Pie* (1993).

Marilynn J. Smith

Lady Augusta Gregory
1852–1932

Born March 15, 1852, Roxborough, Ireland
Died May 22, 1932, Coole
Genre(s): plays, biography, essay, folklore, memoir, translation
Language(s): English

A playwright, director, folklorist, historian, translator, biographer, and co-founder of the Irish National Theatre, Lady Gregory was an important figure in the Irish Literary Renaissance of the early twentieth century. Although born into and married within the Protestant land-owning ascendancy, she developed early in life an imaginative empathy with Irish Catholic peasantry, an empathy that, along with her goal of literary nationalism, exerted the formative influence on her large and varied oeuvre.

Gregory's literary use of Irish peasants and peasant dialect formally began with her study of Gaelic in 1894. Excited by the growing interest in folklore, she began visiting the peasants around her estate, listening to and recording their oral poems and stories. W.B. Yeats, whom she met in 1896 and who became a close friend, encouraged her work, and, in 1902, she published her translations of some of the native Irish epics in *Cuchulain of Muirthemne.* She went on to translate other works from the Gaelic some of which influenced important Irish writers of the time. In 1920 she published her serious folklore study, *Visions and Beliefs in the West of Ireland,* which earned her the epithet "mother of folklore" from Thomas Wall of the Irish Folklore Commission.

Gregory later used her folklore stories and her studies of dialect to full advantage in her plays. A co-founder of the Abbey Theater (its name and location were her suggestions), she was one of the theater's most important playwrights, contributing more plays than any other author in the group and serving, with Synge and Yeats, as one of the three major directors in the theatre. Writing primarily one- and two-act plays, she worked with tragedies, comedies, and farces. She wrote peasant plays, folk history plays, a passion play, and adaptations (as well as translations) from Molière and Goldoni. Like Synge, she generally wrote in the distinctive English of the peasants of Western Ireland, a dialect rich in concrete images and metaphors and odd grammatical constructions.

Gregory's plays are characterized by her rich gift for dialogue, her ear for the saying that reveals character, and her skill in creating taut dramatic plots from simple anecdotes. She often created comic effects by writing dialogue as two monologues and was talented at raising an anecdote from the particular to the universal. In plays like *Kincora, Dervorgilla, and Grania,* she also gives intriguing studies of frustrated women, in the last presenting the Irish counterpart to the Deirdre figure used by both Synge and Yeats in their plays.

An advocate of home rule and a defendant of free speech (she defended Synge's *Playboy of the Western World* on opening night although she did not care for the play), Gregory also evidenced political and national concerns in plays such as *Caravans, The Wren Boys,* and *The Deliverer.* After her son's death in World War I, she turned her talents to children's plays, fairy plays, and a biography of her nephew, Hugh Lane. Her passion play, *The Story Brought by Briget* (1924), was written following the Irish Civil War and shows the futility of hatred as a motivating force. Her memoirs of the Abbey's history, *Our Irish Theatre* (1913), still serve as an important historical source. Gregory's last act at the Abbey was her direction of Sean O'Casey's *The Plough and the Stars.* In her last years, she lived on at her estate at Coole Park, and died there in 1932.

Long recognized for the help she offered other writers, Gregory is now being appreciated for her own creative works. In her plays, folklore collections, biographies, memoirs, essays, and translations and in her efforts to establish the Abbey as a successful theatre she was, she said, "a beggar at many doors." But her work left some of the finest one-act plays in English, provided materials other writers drew upon for their works, and introduced many English readers to the Irish sagas and native literature. Her "series of enthusiasms," only begun when she was forty-four, has left the Irish nation and all of us with a rich and varied literary heritage.

Works

Arabi and His Household (1882). *Over the River* (1888). *A Phantom's Pilgrimage or Home Ruin* (1893). (ed.) *The Autobiography of Sir William Gregory* (1894). "Ireland, real and idea" *Nineteenth Century* (Nov. 1898). (ed.) *Mr. Gregory's Letter Box 1813–1830* (1898). *Ideals in Ireland* (1901). *Cuchulain of Muirthemne* (1902). *Poets and Dreamers* (1903). *Gods and Fighting Men* (1904). *Kincora* (1905). *A Book of Saints and Wonders* (1906). *The Kiltartan History Book* (1909). *Seven Short Plays* (1909). *The Kiltartan Wonder Book* (1910). *The Kiltartan Molière* (1910). *Irish Folk History Plays,* first and second series (1912). *Our Irish Theatre* (1913). *Comedies* (1913). *The Full Moon* (1913).

The Golden Apple (1916). *The Kiltartan Poetry Book* (1919). *Visions and Beliefs in the West of Ireland* (1920). *The Dragon* (1920). *Hugh Lane's Life and Achievements* (1921). *The Image and Other Plays* (1922). *Three Wonder Plays* (1923). *Mirandolina* (1924). *The Story Brought by Briget* (1924). *A Case for the Return of Hugh Lane's Picture to Dublin* (1926). *On the Race Course* (1926). *Three Last Plays* (1928). *My First Play: Colman and Guaire* (1930). *Coole* (1931). *Spreading the News* (1932). *Collected Plays I: The Comedies* (1970) *Collected Plays II: The Tragedies and the Tragic-Comedies* (1970) *Collected Plays III: The Wonder and Supernatural Plays* (1970). Collected *Plays IV: The Translations and Adaptations* (1970). *Seventy Years: Being the Autobiography of Lady Gregory* (1976). *Journals,* ed. D.J. Murphy (Vol. I, 1978; Vol. II, 1987). *Theatre Business: The Correspondence of the First Abbey Theatre Directors: W.B. Yeats, Lady Gregory, and J.M. Synge,* ed. A. Saddlemeyer (1982).

Glenda McLeod

Maria de Groot
1937–

Born 1937, Amsterdam, The Netherlands
Genre(s): poetry
Language(s): Dutch

Maria de Groot is a major modern poet working outside the mainstream of post-war Dutch poetry in which religious themes play a negligible role.

As a child in Amsterdam, during the Second World War, Maria de Groot witnessed the deportations of the Jews, which left an indelible impression. She studied Dutch literature and theology at the university and in 1961 saw her first poem "Beatrijs" receive the first prize in a poetry contest organized by the University of Amsterdam.

The titles of her collections point to the religious nature of her work in which the old link between religion and poetry is constantly reaffirmed. The poet experiences earthly reality as being perpetually in contact with the sacred and the divine and feels that she herself stands in the tension of that contact. Refusing the rigid mold of institutionalized religion or a particular faith, she uses Jewish, Catholic, and Protestant themes and symbols.

Her point of departure is the need to write poetry, to master language, and to infuse it with spirit through rhythm and rhyme in order to make the text the meeting place of the real and the sacred. Since her experience of the contact between the two gives meaning to her life and can be expressed only through poetry, writing poetry is for Maria de Groot an existential necessity.

The poet's relation with Christ, a major theme, is presented as a relationship between a man and a woman. In this respect there is an affinity with the great Dutch mystic Hadewijch, although Maria de Groot is not a mystic herself. Earthly objects and relations stand for themselves and are not symbolic of spiritual ones.

In *Amsterdams getijdenboekje* (1966; Amsterdam Breviary, completely reprinted in her collection *Gedichten;* 1971; Poems) the poet gives expression to her awareness of death, her search for meaning, and her experience of the divine. In *Brevier van een Romaanse reis* (1975; Breviary of a Journey to Rome), she attempts to establish a connection between her own emotions and the old Roman statues of human figures seen in the South of France. The cycle deals with a journey and emphasizes the poet's bond with the earth. *Het Florentijnse circus* (1967; The Florentine Circus), a lyrical epic of 752 lines, is one of her best poems, although it went almost unnoticed by the critics when it came out. The narrator, a woman, tries to choose between Christ and Dionysus, but her dilemma remains unresolved, for both have their risks as well as their rights and to make a choice is impossible. The divine must touch human existence through the earthly and physical.

Maria de Groot has a good sense of rhythm, language, and style. Accused of being too academic and intellectual and of assuming too much knowledge on the part of her reader, she writes the kind of poetry that becomes more accessible with each reading. It is intelligent, carefully written, serious, yet alive with concrete details and decors.

Though she is not well known, Maria de Groot is one of the most important poetic talents of the post-war period in The Netherlands.

Works

Amsterdams getijdenboekje (1966). *Rabboeni* (1966). *Het Florentijnse circus* (1967). *Liedboek van Kevin* (1968). *Gedichten* (1971). *Brevier van een Romaanse reis. Het huis van de danser* (1975). *Carmel* (1977). *Album van licht* (1979). *De bronnen van Jaweh* (1981). *Vlierbessen* (1982).

Maya Bijvoet

Jeanne-Marie Bouvier de la Motte, Mme Guyon
1648–1717

Born April 13, 1648, Montargis, France
Died June 9, 1717, Blois
Genre(s): essay, poetry, pamphlet, letters, memoir
Language(s): French

Born into a prominent noble family in Montargis, Mlle de la Motte was a delicate child. At an early age she exhibited symptoms of hysteria; visions, hallucinations, morbid fears of damnation, and tendencies toward self-sacrifice caused her constant mental anguish. Educated at convents in Montargis, she returned home at age twelve, determined to enter religious life. She found spiritual comfort in the writings of St Francis de Sales and Jeanne de Chantal (foundress of the Order of the Visitation) who had a profound impact on the rejuvenation of religion in France at this time.

The young girl's desire to enter a convent was opposed by her parents who arranged her marriage, at age sixteen, to Jacques Guyon, a solid, wealthy, thirty-eight-year-old counsellor of the Parlement of Paris. Five children were born (three survived) during their twelve-year marriage. After she was widowed, Mme Guyon left her children in the hands of a guardian, abandoned her wealth, and immersed herself in the mystical teachings of the Spanish priest, Miguel de Molinos (c. 1640–1697). In 1680 she arrived at the pinnacle of mystical Quietism, called the "Peace of God" and traveled to Paris where she met d'Aranthon, Bishop of Geneva, who convinced her that she had a sincere religious calling. Through her brother, Père La Motte, she became acquainted with Père Lacombe, also a Barnabite priest, who confirmed that she was destined for an extraordinary religious mission. Lacombe became her spiritual director and in 1681 they began preaching, first at the Ursuline convent in Thonon, and then at Turin, Grenoble, and Verceil. For five years they traveled and spread their mystical beliefs; the Bishop of Geneva grew alarmed at their success and withdrew his support.

Mme Guyon's Quietism was a form of religious mysticism based on the writings of Père Molinos; he was imprisoned by the Inquisition in 1685 and his writings condemned in 1687. These beliefs centered on passive contemplation, renunciation of self, complete submission to the will of God, spiritual quietude, and total indifference to life, death, and salvation. Only the mind had value; one's soul communed directly with God, eliminating the need for the Sacraments. As long as the communion with God remained unbroken, the body could indulge in sinful acts without affecting the spiritual purity of the soul. Mme Guyon's increasingly bizarre behavior led to condemnation and persecution. She called herself the "pregnant woman of the Apocalypse," the "foundress of a New Church," prophesied that "all hell would band together against her," and claimed that she was a saint and a bride of Jesus. In her raptures Mme Guyon said that "woman would be pregnant from an internal spirit" and in fact her own body which was at times abnormally swollen seemed to give credibility to her claim.

In July 1686 Guyon returned to Paris; in 1688 she was living at the Visitation convent on the rue Saint-Antoine and frequenting the Court at Versailles and the girls' school of St-Cyr. Lacombe and Guyon were arrested in 1687 on suspicion of heresy and immorality, but Mme de Maintenon had her released. Maintenon, morganatic wife of Louis XIV and foundress of St-Cyr, supported Guyon's Quietist doctrines and had introduced her to high-placed ladies who enthusiastically embraced her beliefs. Guyon's eloquence and warmth and her genuine piety convinced many that she was a saint; she served as spiritual director to some of these devout women, replacing their priestly confessors. The King disapproved of ostentatious religious display but chose not to interfere because Mme de Maintenon encouraged and protected Guyon's activities both at Court and among the noble girls at St-Cyr. Her two early works, *Moyen court et très facile pour faire d'oraison* (The Short and Easy Method of Prayer) and *Les torrents spirituels* (1704; Spiritual Torrents), won for Guyon the devotion and friendship of François de Salignac de la Motte-Fénelon, tutor of the royal children, later Archbishop of Cambrai and member of the French Academy.

But critics of Guyon's mystical doctrines were extremely vocal; to defend her beliefs and her virtue she asked that a commission be appointed to examine charges against her. Her morals were not an issue, only the orthodoxy of her writings were in question. Mme de Maintenon never doubted that her friend's writings would be exonerated. The Conference of Issy that lasted for several months found 34 "errors" in her works, *Moyen court* and *Le Cantique des Cantiques* (Explanation of the Song of Songs), which were eventually condemned by the French church hierarchy. Guyon reluctantly accepted its judgment, and was allowed to retire wherever she chose; she returned to Paris and the controversy surrounding her soon led to her arrest and imprisonment at Vincennes and then the Bastille.

Fénelon, who had been a member of the Issy Commission, had agreed to the suppression of her

Jeanne-Marie Bouvier de la Motte, Mme Guyon

erroneous beliefs but would not condemn her personally. He and the conservative Bishop Bossuet disagreed on Guyon's methods of prayer. Due to Fénelon's support, Guyon was allowed to move to a convent in Paris. However, the King was determined to end this religious controversy and ordered Guyon back to the Bastille and Fénelon to return to his diocese. The Holy See in 1699 condemned Fénelon's work, *L'Explication des Maximes des Saints sur la vie intérieure* (Explanation of the Maxims of the Saints on the Inner Life), a defense of Quietism.

The influence of Quietism quickly subsided as its adherents bowed to the Pope's decision. Guyon was released from the Bastille in 1702 and went into exile in Blois where she engaged in charitable works for the last fifteen years of her life. In her final testament she deplored the false accusations made against her writings, especially blaming the enmity of her brother and his influence on the Archbishop of Paris for her troubles. Her works continued to be published in many languages through the eighteenth century. *Opuscules spirituels* (1704; Spiritual Pamphlets) was her first major work in which she described men's souls as naturally longing to return to and merge with God. The soul must die before it can live again. The book culminated in a description of "spiritual purity" which most mystics never attained. In *Les livres de l'Ancien et du Nouveau Testament . . .* (1713–1715; The Books of the Old and New Testament . . .), Guyon attempted to explain the Apocalypse; she played the prophet, claiming to be a vehicle for transmitting thoughts received directly from the Lord, and recounting visions. She left a manuscript (*Justifications*) and some mystical verses that were published after her death. *La vie de Mme Guyon* [The Life of Mme Guyon], published in Cologne in 1720, was probably not a single work but a collection of memoirs she had furnished to officials for the Conference of Issy. This account of her life is incomplete and inaccurate at times. Its importance lay in her claims to be able to fathom the depths of the soul and "that God had chosen her to destroy human reason and re-establish divine reason."

Mme Guyon was the greatest French mystic of the seventeenth century. Her beliefs were condemned, but her morals were never impugned. Seemingly identifying herself with an apostolic mission she stated "That which I bind will be bound; that which I unbind will be unbound." Believing that she had attained perfection, she could no longer pray to the saints or the Virgin Mary. To the end of her life she adhered to her religious mysticism, which had had a tremendous influence in France.

Works

Cantiques spirituels, ou emblèmes sur l'amour divin, 5 vols. (n.d.). *Le Cantique des cantiques de Salomon, interprété selon le sens mystique & vraie représentation des états intérieurs . . .* (1688) [*The Song of Songs of Solomon with Explanations and Reflections Having Reference to the Interior Life*], tr. James W. Metcalf (1865). *Le Moyen court et très facile pour faire d'oraison* (1688). *Recueil de Poésies spirituelles,* 5 vols. (1689). *Advice by Madame Guyon to a Young Ecclesiastik, Who Was about to Commence Preach[ing]* (170?). *Opuscules spirituels,* 2 vols. (1704). *Les torrents spirituels* (1704) [*Spiritual Torrents*], tr. A.E. Ford (1853)]. *La Vie de Mme Guyon, écrite par elle-même,* 3 vols. (1720). *Les livres de l'Ancien et du Nouveau Testament, traduits en français avec des explications et des réflexions qui regardent la vie intérieure,* 20 vols. (1713–1715) [*The Mystical Sense of the Sacred Scriptures. or, The Books of the Old and New Testaments (Including the Apocrypha), with Explications and Reflections Regarding the Interior Life*], 2 vols., tr. Thomas W. Duncan (1872). *L'Ame amante de son Dieu représentée dans les emblemes de Hermanus Hugo sur ses pieux désirs, et dans ceux d'Othon Vaenius sur l'amour divin* (1716). *Discours chrétiennes et spirituels [sic] sur divers sujets qui regardent la vie intérieure,* 2 vols. (1716). *Lettres chrétiennes et spirituelles sur divers sujets qui regardent la vie intérieure ou l'esprit du Christianisme,* 4 vols. (1717–1718). *Poésies et cantiques spirituels sur diverse sujets qui regardent la vie intérieure, ou l'esprit du vrai Christianisme,* 4 vols. (1722). *Regel der Kindheit Jesu-Genossen* (1752). *A Short and Easy Method of Prayer,* tr. Thomas Digby Brooke (1775). *The worship of God in spirit and in truth. or, a short and easy method of prayer . . . to which is added, Two letters concerning a life truly Christian . . .* (1775). *La Sainte-Bible* (1790). *Spiritual Progress, or, Instructions in the Divine Life of the Soul* [with Fénelon] (1853).

Jeanne A. Ojala
William T. Ojala

Thomasine Gyllembourg
1773–1856

Born November 9, 1773, Copenhagen, Denmark
Died July 1, 1856, Copenhagen
Genre(s): tale, novel, drama, letters
Language(s): Danish

Mother of the famous dramatist and critic Johan Ludvig Heiberg, Thomasine Gyllembourg pioneered realistic prose fiction in Denmark in the 1820s. Her highly popular "Everyday Tales" and the salon she led helped to create the "Heiberg school," whose influence dominated literary taste in Denmark for several decades.

Thomasine Christine Buntzen Heiberg Gyllembourg, more commonly known as Fru Gyllembourg, was the eldest daughter of city assessor Johan Buntzen and his second wife, Anna Bolette Sandgaard. Her mother died when she was eight. Her father encouraged his favorite daughter's literary inclinations, providing her with excellent tutors. One of these was the dramatist P.A. Heiberg, whom Thomasine married at age seventeen. The match was ill-suited temperamentally. Heiberg was a brilliant but quarrelsome rationalist, whereas Thomasine adhered to the cult of the heart à la Rousseau. The couple's only child, Johan Ludvig Heiberg, was born in 1791. Shortly before her husband was exiled from Denmark for his political views, Thomasine had fallen in love with a gallant Swedish nobleman, Baron Carl Frederik Gyllembourg. Gyllembourg was himself living in exile because of his involvement in the assassination of the Swedish King Gustav III.

The dissolution of Thomasine's first marriage, by royal decree, in 1801, and her immediate remarriage to Baron Gyllembourg was one of the most celebrated scandals in the history of Scandinavian literature. This stormy and traumatic period of her life provided Thomasine Gyllembourg with the subject matter for much of her later writing. Her love letters to Gyllembourg before their marriage are worthy rivals to those in Rousseau's novel *La nouvelle Héloïse*, while her "lettre remarquable" to Heiberg, asking for the divorce, became a standard text in Danish high-school readers.

From her anonymous literary debut in 1827 to her collected works in 1851, Thomasine Gyllembourg's writings were edited and published by her son, J.L. Heiberg. He even brought out a few of her more controversial works under his own name. In 1828 Fru Gyllembourg's story "En Hverdagshistorie" (An Everyday Tale) appeared in Heiberg's influential journal *Den flyvende Post* (The Flying Post). This story marked a clear break in Danish literature with romanticism and earlier forms of fiction. Portraying the contemporary life and problems of the Copenhagen bourgeoisie, Fru Gyllembourg here provided the psychological realism the public was seeking. "En Hverdagshistorie" was the first of a long and immensely popular series of modern prose tales and novels, all referred to as "Everyday Tales."

Her next major work, *Slaegtskab og Djaevelskab* (1830; Genealogy and Demonology), was a family chronicle inspired by Greek tragedy. It became for a time the most famous novel in Scandinavia. Though it contains some overwritten scenes of Gothic horror, it reveals Gyllembourg's psychoanalytic skill in the portrayal of compulsive neurosis and hysteria. In her four plays, published together in 1834, she tried to establish a modern realistic drama based on the psychological probing of erotic conflicts. Her plays include *Sproglaereren* (1834; The Language Teacher), on the theme of happy marriage despite age differences, and *Fregatskibet Svanen* (1834; H.M.S. Swan), a tolerant treatment of the problem of bigamy. Among her most penetrating psychological studies are two confessional novels in the style of Rousseau: *Maria* (1839) and *Een i Alle* (1840; One in All). Here Gyllembourg perceptively analyzes childhood traumas of an erotic nature and their lasting effects on character. *Een i Alle*, the more vital work, sympathetically portrays the adventures of gallant Trolle, a Don Juan figure. Fru Gyllembourg's last work, *To Tidsaldre* (1845; Two Ages), is her literary testament in the form of a novel. Here she compares the world of her youth to the world of her old age, weighing contemporary

bourgeois values against the aristocratic and revolutionary ideals of the eighteenth century. This work inspired Kierkegaard to write *The Literary Review*, a little book devoted to her novel.

After the death of her second husband, Fru Gyllembourg lived with her son and his wife, the gifted Fru Heiberg, who became nineteenth-century Scandinavia's most celebrated actress. The three of them worked together in literary and theatrical collaboration and created an exclusive and extremely influential salon. By the 1840s the "Heiberg school" was regarded as the literary establishment in Denmark.

In her "Everyday Tales" Thomasine Gyllembourg portrayed Danish middle-class life with exact attention to detail and realistic dialogue. The didactic purpose of her fiction led her to criticize the middle classes for their lack of genuine culture and to urge higher standards of education. The refinement of the heart remained her ideal. In many ways an heir of the eighteenth century, she was an unconventional, humane, and passionately intelligent artist whose work led the way to realism in Danish literature.

Works
Familien Polonius [The Polonius Family] (1827, 1834). "Den magiske Nögle" [The Magic Key] (1828). "En Hverdagshistorie" [An Everyday Tale] (1828). "Kong Hjort" [King Stag] (1830). "Den lille Karen" [Little Karen] (1830). *Slaegtskab og Djaevelskab* [Genealogy and Demonology] (1830). *Noveller, gamle og nye af Forf. til "En Hverdagshistorie"* [Stories, Old and New by the Author of "An Everyday Tale"] (1833). *Magt og List* [Force and Cunning] (1834). *Sproglaereren* [The Language Teacher] (1834). *De Forlovede* [The Engaged] (1834). *Fregatskibet Svanen* [H.M.S. Swan] (1834). *Findelön* [The Reward] (1834). *Nye Fortaellinger af Forf. til "En Hverdagshistorie"* [New Stories by the Author of "An Everyday Tale"] (1835–1836). *To Noveller af Forf. til "En Hverdagshistorie"* [Two Novelettes by the Author of "An Everyday Tale"] (1837). *Maria* (1839). *Een i Alle* [One in All] (1840). *Naer og Fjern* [Near and Far] (1841). *En Brevveksling* [A Correspondence] (1843). *Castor og Pollux* [Castor and Pollux] (1844). *Korsveien* [The Crossroad] (1844). *To Tidsaldre* [Two Ages] (1845).

Collected Works: *Skrifter af Forf. til "En Hverdagshistorie,"* ed. J.L. Heiberg, 12 vols. (1849–1851).

Letters: *Heibergske Familiebreve*, ed. Morten Borup (1943).

Jean Pearson

Hella Haasse
1918–
a.k.a. Helene Serafia Haasse
Born February 2, 1918, Batavia, Dutch Indies
Genre(s): novel, essay, poetry, drama, translation,
short story, autobiography
Language(s): Netherlandic

Hella S. Haasse is commonly acknowledged as The Netherlands' major contemporary female author. Although she is best known for her prose work and essays, Haasse made her debut as a poet. She also delivered meritorious work as a playwright and translator.

Born as the daughter of Katharina Diehm Winzenhohlen, an esteemed concert pianist, and W.H. Haasse, a government functionary, the author spent part of her youth in the Dutch Indies. Due to her mother's illness, which demanded a stay in Switzerland, Haasse was separated from her parents for three years, during which time she attended Dutch boarding school. Afterwards, she returned to Batavia where she started high school. Here, her interest in Dutch literature was stimulated. In 1938, Haasse left for The Netherlands to study Scandinavian languages at the University of Amsterdam. The following year, she met her future husband, J. van Lelyveld, who encouraged her to contribute to *Propria Cures*, a student magazine.

In time, Haasse's interest in Scandinavian languages waned, leading to her join the drama department in 1940. Three years later, she closed a contract with a company, *Centraal Toneel*, directed by Cees Laseur.

Haasse made her literary debut with poems in the literary journal *Werk*. She only gained her reputation, however, with the publication of "Oeroeg" (1948). This short narrative describes the friendship between an Indian boy, Oeroeg, and a Dutch boy, the son of an administrator from whose point of view the story is told. Both children are raised together, but they start growing apart as they approach manhood. When the Dutch boy returns to India after finishing his studies in The Netherlands, the close friendship with Oeroeg no longer exists. Oeroeg has become a fervent nationalist who despises the Dutch, including his former friend. The narrator realizes that an unbridgeable abyss separates them; Oeroeg has become a stranger whom he has never understood and never will. The author stated that she wrote "Oeroeg" as a memory to the country where she was born and from a secret feeling of guilt with respect to the population she never really had learned to know. With "Oeroeg," Haasse cut the umbilical cord that still connected her to her country of birth.

In *Het woud der verwachting* (1949), Haasse's first novel, the author relates with historical accuracy the life of Charles d'Orléans. She depicts him as a sensitive man who, against his will, got involved in intrigues of the 100-Year War. D'Orléans was captured by Henry V of England and only twenty-five years later was he released from prison. He returned to France where he spent the rest of his life doing the only thing that gave him consolation: writing poetry. *Het woud der verwachting* is often called a historical novel, a term that should be used with some reservation. Haasse has done extensive research on the political and historical background of fifteenth-century France, but her work is more than a chronicle. She has stated that she has always felt akin to d'Orléans, a dreamer who fails because he lacks practical sense. Only when he explores his literary talents does he find the satisfaction and self-confidence a political career could never offer him. Haasse says this novel mirrors her world from 1935 to 1945—"a transitional period of self-contained reveries towards a more conscious concern for people and society." She recognizes herself in the increasing loneliness the medieval poet experienced. Haasse's historical novels are not romanticized histories. Her primary aim is to discover patterns between the realities of the past and the present. Haasse says she looks at our present reality from the perspective of the past, because it renders human reality visible.

De scharlaken stad (1952) takes us back to fifteenth-century Rome. The author wrote this novel out of fascination for the enigmatic figure of Giovanni Borgia. In opposition to the previous novel, *De scharlaken stad* has a more complicated composition.

De Ingewijden (1957) refers to the "Euleusinia" or the secret rituals in honor of the goddesses Demeter and Persephone. According to Greek mythology, he who wanted to be initiated in the mysteries of life and death and experience oneness with the primordial being had to find his way through a treacherous subterranean labyrinth. Haasse gives this ancient ritual a modern setting by introducing six protagonists who meet each other by coincidence on the island of Crete shortly after World War II. Haasse contrasts ancient Greece, which evokes the Euleusian mysteries, with the cold modern period, which is controlled by war and fascism.

Een nieuwer testament (1966) is based on an imaginary trial between the last poet of the Roman Empire, the pagan Claudius Claudianus. His antagonist, the prefect Hadrianus, who represents Christianity, the official Roman religion, banned Claudius for being involved in pagan rituals. When Claudius has the audacity to return to the city, Hadrianus has him arrested. While in prison, Claudius writes a "new-er" testament, an improved version of the New Testament that emphasizes man's independent creative personality thereby rejecting the vision that the son (man) should follow the father (Christ). When Hadrianus is finally confronted with Claudianus the day of the trial, he becomes aware that he has been defending a false religion. As a manifestation of his rebellion, he sets Claudius free and commits suicide.

In *Een gevaarlijke verhouding of Daal-en Bergse brieven* (1976), Haasse introduces Mme de Merteuil, Choderlos de Laclos's evil female of *Les Liaisons Dangereuses* (1782). Haasse picks up the thread where Laclos left off. Mme de Merteuil is dwelling in The Hague in the Daal (val-) en Bergse (Mont) Lane. The marchioness defends and justifies her past way of life, which gives her the opportunity to take up a number of topics such as love in a male-oriented society and the relationship between man and wife. Although Haasse's style remains traditional throughout her career, her fictional work seems to become more and more essayistic. Large parts of this novel approach the essay form.

Mevrouw Bentinck of Onverenigbaarheid van karakter (1978) and *De groten der aarde of Bentinck tegen Bentinck* may also be considered among Haasse's historical novels. Willem Bentinck, Sr., friend and confident of the Dutch King Willem II, was one of the most remarkable figures in The Netherlands of the eighteenth century. When Haasse got access to the Bentinck archives, she became fascinated by Willem Bentinck, Jr., and his wife Charlotte Sophie von Aldenburg. Haasse composed a book in collage form, the greater part consisting of authentic texts about the doomed-to-fail marriage between Bentinck and his wife, which has not been treated extensively by Bentinck biographers. Haasse wanted to throw a different and more truthful light on the Bentinck figure, and she intended to use Charlotte Sophie's escapades as an example of female emancipation in the Age of Enlightenment.

De groten der aarde of Bentinck tegen Bentinck (1982) deals with the period 1730–1750 after Bentinck, Jr., and his wife have broken up their marriage. More so than in the previous Bentinck novel, the author narrates more in her own voice. She still uses the collage technique—although to a lesser extent—to give the impression of presenting an epic report, as she calls it. In all of her historical novels, Haasse is concerned with the same thematics, that is, the search for one's identity and the purpose of man's existence.

Haasse wrote two autobiographical novels. *Zelfportret als legkaart* (1954) combines alternatively descriptions of the author's youth in India, the wartime in Amsterdam, her studies, and her marriage. *Persoonsbewijs* (1967) may be considered as a sequel. Except for the first chapter which is biographical, the novel is dedicated to the problem of being an author and to Haasse's own literary works. Here, Haasse argues that through the process of writing, she analyzes and renders conscious that which is usually buried deep within her. As in previous novels, Haasse expresses her conviction in the interconnectedness of even unconscious happenings.

Works

Prose: *Kleren maken de vrouw* (1947). "Oeroeg" (1948). *Het woud der verwachting* (1949). *Het leven van Charles D'Orleans* (1949). *De verborgen bron* (1950). *De scharlaken stad* (1952). *Zelfportret als legkaart* (1954). *De ingewijden* (1957). *De vijfde trede* (1957). *Cider voor arme mensen* (1960). *De meermin* (1962). *Een nieuwer testament* (1966). *Persoonsbewijs* (1967). *De tuinen van Bomarzo* (1968). *Huurders en onderhuurders* (1971). *De meester van de neerdaling, De duivel en zijn moer* (1973). *Een gevaarlijke verhouding of Daal-en Bergse brieven* (1976). *Mevrouw Bentinck of Onverenigbaarheid van* karakter (1978). *De groten der aarde of Bentinck tegen Bentinck* (1982). *De wegen der verbeelding* (1983).

Major essays: *Het versterkte huis, Kastelen in Nederland* (1951). *Klein Reismozaiek, Italiaanse Impressies* (1953). *Eem kom water, een test vuur* (1959). *Anna Blaman* (1961). *Leestekens* (1965). *De tuinen van Bomarro* (1968). *Tweemaal Vestdijk* (1970). *Krassen op een rots* (1970). *Zelfstandig bijvoeglijk* (1972). *Het licht der schitterende dagen, het leven van P, C. Hooft* (1981). *Ogenblikken in Valois* (1982).

Plays: *Een Amsterdamse jongen redt de beurs* (1951). *Het treurig spel van Jan Klaassen en Katrijn Ongeschikt voor de Houwelijcke Staat* (1951). *Hoe de Scout zichzelf aan de schandpaal bracht* (1951). *Liefdadigheid naar vermogen of Graag of niet* (1957). *De vrijheid is een assepoes* (1955). *Een draad in Block. Geen Bacchanalen* (1971).

Translations: *Oeroeg* and *De verborgen bron* are translated in Welsh, *Het woud der verwachting* and *De ingewijden* in German and *De scharlaken stad* in German, English, Swedish and Serbo-Croatian.

Dianne Van Hoof

Hadewijch
ca. 1200

Date and place of birth and death unknown; probably lived in the beginning or middle of the thirteenth century in the Brussels area
Genre(s): poetry, letters, visionary literature
Language(s): Dutch (Brabant dialect)

A thirteenth-century mystic, Hadewijch is considered one of the early representatives of the so-called *minnemystiek*. Her work contains letters, visions, stanzaic poems, and a small set of poems mostly in rhyming couplets. Her stanzaic poetry belongs to the very few extant Middle Dutch love songs in the troubadour tradition and her prose, together with that of the Cistercian mystic Beatrijs of Nazareth (c. 1200–1268), is the earliest extant prose in the vernacular.

Besides her name and work, we know very little, if anything, of Hadewijch. The erudition emerging from her writing almost certainly indicates a noble or aristocratic descent. Her letters—the only source of biographical information—suggest that, though she was not a nun, she lived for some time in one or two small communities of religious women. She may also have lived part of her life as a *reclusa*. Like many other women of her time, the so-called *mulieres religiosae*, she took part in the great spiritual revival that marked the twelfth and thirteenth centuries. She must have read or, at least, known about the great mystic writers. Most probably she knew Latin: passages in her letters have been identified as translations of William of Saint Thierry and Richard of Saint Victor, though she may have borrowed from existing translations.

The basic shift of focus in religious life and thought from *knowledge* of God to *experience* of God, which had been initiated by Saint Bernard, undoubtedly inspired Hadewijch's *minnemystiek*. The central concept in her thinking was *minne*—love. A full understanding of all the connotations of Hadewijch's *minne*, often personified, has yet to be established, but it is easiest to see *minne* not so much as God or Christ but rather as the personification of an abstract quality or, better, an experience (of God). Three basic moments can further be distinguished: the awareness of a distance between *minne* and Hadewijch—*een ghebreken*, "a lack"; the complete surrendering to *minne*—*een ghebruken*, "using and enjoying"; and, finally, balance restored. The tension between *ghebreken* and *ghebruken*, that is, the mystic's craving for *minne*, runs through most of Hadewijch's work. The motifs of courtly love—unattainable lover, the submissive service to love, the complaints, the hope and despair, the all-pervading power of love—all acquire a spiritual dimension in Hadewijch's writing. She reinterprets the unattainability of *minne*, as an ontological given, which time and again she attempts to transcend by striving for and reaching a state of union with *minne*.

Developing the theme of *minne*, Hadewijch wrote her stanzaic poems in much the same way as the troubadours had done before her, elaborating the imagery and vocabulary of courtly love and the techniques of *natureingang*, tripartition, tornada, concatenation, rhyme scheme, and rhyme. Instead of using *coblas unisonas* (the same rhyme and rhyme scheme), which are hard to achieve in a Germanic language, she used *coblas singulars* (the same rhyme scheme but not the same rhyme). But her repertory of rhymes and rhyming words remains small with respect to the actual possibilities of Middle Dutch. Rather than being Romance syllabic, Hadewijch's rhythm is the Germanic stress rhythm highlighted by profuse alliteration, assonance, and repetition. Though written with great technical skill, the stanzaic poems are not entirely free of easy verse filling. Sometimes the reader is given the impression of thoughts and emotions forced into a rigid stanzaic format.

In the letters Hadewijch emerges as an accomplished, articulate, and sensitive writer. They were probably addressed to a woman (or women) who belonged to a religious community of which Hadewijch herself had once been a member. Some of the longer letters are real treatises on religious and spiritual problems and illustrate Hadewijch's powerful and passionate thinking about *minne* as well as her superior skill as a writer of prose. Others are more intimate communications in which Hadewijch gives practical advice on living a life of charity and devotion to *minne*. She developed similar themes in her nonstanzaic poetry, the so-called *mengeldichten*. Her advisory tone suggests that she must have enjoyed the high regard of whomever she wrote to; perhaps she had been the leader of the community. There are also indications that she might have been the victim of enmity and jealousy.

Hadewijch's visions are increasingly regarded as one of the greatest achievements in Dutch artistic prose of the Middle Ages, by far excelling her stanzaic poems in literary importance and aesthetic value. They were apparently written at someone's request and served as descriptions of actual ecstatic experiences. For the modern reader, unacquainted with the conventions or the psychology of mystic experiences in Hadewijch's age, the visions might, however, be difficult to appreciate, larded as they are with the allegories, symbols, angels, and seraphim typical of the genre in that period.

Hadewijch's work was known, copied, excerpted, paraphrased, and occasionally translated (into German and Latin) up to at least the late fifteenth and, particularly, in the fourteenth century. She was especially known in Brabant where the tradition of speculative mysticism was continued by Jan van Ruusbroec (1293–1381) among others. Ruusbroec built his systematic doctrine on thoughts similar to those developed by Hadewijch. At that time she was also known in Germany by the name of Saint Adelwip from Brabant.

In the seventeenth and eighteenth centuries, however, Hadewijch's work was virtually lost. She only claimed her definitive place in the Dutch literary canon with the "discovery" of the manuscripts of her work in 1838. She then came to be regarded as one of the most gifted literary women of her period and found a place in every school anthology treating Dutch literature from its very beginnings.

Works
(Three complete manuscripts of her work contain 45 stanzaic poems, 31 letters, 14 visions, 29 poems mostly in rhyming couplets [one ms. has only 16 of

them], 13 of which were probably not by her.) *Brieven*, ed. J. van Mierlo. 2 vols. (1947; with modern Dutch tr., 1954, eds. F. van Bladel and B. Spaapen). *Mengeldichten*, ed. J. van Mierlo (1952). *Strophische gedichten* (1942; 2 vols., ed. J. van Mierlo; With modern Dutch translations, 1961; eds. E. Rombauts and N. de Paepe. With modern Dutch translations, 1982; ed. M. Ortmans). *Visioenen* (1924–1925; 2 vols., ed. J. van Mierlo. With modern Dutch translations, 1979; 2 vols., ed. P. Mommaers. With modern Dutch translations, 1980; ed. H.W.J. Vekeman).

Translations: *The Complete* Works, ed. and tr. C. Hart (1980). Selected letters, in *Mediaeval Netherlands Religious Literature*, tr. E. Colledge (1965). Selected letters and poems, tr. R. Vanderauwera, in *Medieval Women Writers*, ed. K.M. Wilson (1984). Of the stanzaic poems, *Hadewijch d'Anvers. Amour est tout: poèmes strophiques*, tr. R. van de Plas, intro. A. Simonet (1984).

Ria Vanderauwera

Maša Hal'amová
1908–1995
Born August 28, 1908, Blatnica, then in Austria-Hungary and later in Czechoslovakia
Died August 17, 1995
Genre(s): lyric poetry
Language(s): Slovak

With the title of "National Artist" given her in 1983, Maša Hal'amová was doubtless the major contemporary lyric woman poet in Slovakia. She follows in the Slovak symbolist tradition of Ivan Krasko and was thus influenced by the Czech and French symbolists.

Born in a small town in central Slovakia, she attended school there, but her mother's death sent her to live in Yugoslavia until Czechoslovakia was established in 1918. She graduated from a Bratislava business school, published her first book of verse in 1928, then spent a year studying in Paris. She married physician Dr. Ján Pullman and lived in the Tatra Mountains until his death in 1956. After 1959 she began to write children's stories and has also translated children's literature from Russian, Czech, and Lusatian-Sorbian.

Her first collection of poems, *Dar* (Gift) in 1928, expressed intensely her relation to the simple facts of her small world, but it also emphasized the polarity of hope and disappointment, of good fortune and suffering. Her second collection of poems, *Červený mak* (Scarlet Poppy) in 1932, still carried this theme but with a wider social context that enlarged the framework of her poems about love and the beauty of the mountains. In some works she used the ballad form. She published nothing more until 1955, when several new poems were added to the re-edition of her earlier poems. Hal'amová's last collection appeared in 1966, occasioned by the death of her husband in 1956. Called *Smrt' tvoju 'ijem* (I Am Living Out Your Death), it was addressed to her own loneliness and to a circle of similarly suffering people.

Hal'amová is a poet "of the heart," of intimate, private experiences generalized only through their clarity and intensity. She has achieved her status with a tiny body of less than one hundred published verses and without any political attachment in a highly politicized world.

Works

Dar [Gift] (1928). *Červený mak* [Scarlet Poppy] (1932). *Básne* [Poems] (1955). *Smrt' tvoju 'ijem* [I Am Living Out Your Death] (1966). *Vyznania* (1988). *Vzácnejšia nad zlato* (1988). *Criepky* (1993).

Translations: Czech: *Dar* (1979). English: "Legend" and "Elegia" (1947). "Legenda/Legend" (1976).

Norma L. Rudinsky

Radclyffe Hall
1886–1943

Born 1886, Bournemouth, Hampshire, England
Died October 11, 1943, London
Genre(s): poetry, novel
Language(s): English

Radclyffe Hall, christened Marguerite Hall, was the daughter of Radclyffe Radclyffe-Hall, whom she barely knew but who left her a large inheritance when she turned seventeen. She was raised by her flighty mother and a moody Italian stepfather, parents who often subjected her to emotional and even physical abuse.

She started her writing career at the age of three when she wrote her first poem. Between 1906 and 1915, she published five volumes of poems. Her work improved in the later volumes, though becoming increasingly personal, and the poems' lyrical qualities enabled several composers, including Coleridge Taylor, Liza Lehmann, Woodesforde

Finden, Mrs. George Batten, and Coningsby Clarke, to set them to music.

Her first novel, *The Forge,* was a brief social comedy published in 1924, followed by *The Unlit Lamp* later the same year. This early work hints at incest and the subject of lesbianism, which she returned to in *The Well of Loneliness,* but the treatment is so muted that the book attracted little public notice. Nevertheless, the writing is powerful in its bleakness. *A Saturday Life,* a novel, was published in 1925, and another novel, *Adam's Breed,* the next year. Although *Adam's Breed* is overly sentimental, the protagonist, Gian-Luca, a headwaiter, again demonstrates a character struggling against conforming to society's demands. The story is presented with her usual honesty and won several awards, including the American Eichelberger Humane Award.

In 1928, Hall published her famous novel of "sexual inversion," *The Well of Loneliness.* The novel became a *cause célèbre* as people either defended or condemned the book, which was banned in England because, said the Magistrate, it portrayed "unnatural and depraved relationships." Whether the story of Stephen Gordon and her lover, Mary, is a good novel is another matter. Havelock Ellis claims it shows "poignant situations . . . set forth so vividly." Yet Leonard Woolf and Rebecca West, both of whom fought for its publication, consider the work flawed. Woolf states that the characters "appear to be the creation of the intellect, and for the reader they have no emotional context." West is even harsher in her remarks, saying it is "not a very good book . . . A novel which ends a chapter with the sentence 'And that night they were not divided' cannot redeem itself by having 'they' mean not what it usually does." West's complaint underlies the fact that despite its subject matter, the novel is still encased in Victorian trappings. However, regardless of its flaws, the work is important because, as Jane Rule says, it "remains *the* lesbian novel." Hall later returned to the subject in her short story, "Miss Ogilvy Finds Herself."

Hall was a devout Christian, although maintaining a strong interest in psychic research, and this became the topic of her next novel, *The Master of the House* (1932). Christophe Bénédit is the son of a carpenter, Jousé, has a mother named Marie, and a cousin Jan. The parallel to the Holy Family is obvious, and, though some critics questioned the propriety of modernizing Christ's life, Hall considered this to be her finest work.

In 1934 she published *Miss Ogilvy Finds Herself,* a collection of five stories. Her last novel, *The Sixth Beatitude,* was published in 1936. The protagonist, Hannah Bullen, a servant, is an unwed mother of two children by different fathers, who, nevertheless, is presented, as the title implies, as being pure of heart. The novel, like much of Hall's better fiction, is grim and unrelenting.

Before dying in 1943, Hall spent her last thirty years living with her lover, Lady Una Troubridge, who called Hall by the name John.

Works

'Twixt Earth and Stars (1906). A Sheaf of Verses (1908). Poems of the Past and Present (1910). Songs of Three Counties, and Other Poems (1913). The Forgotten Island (1915). The Forge (1924). The Unlit Lamp (1924). A Saturday Life (1925). Adam's Breed (1926). The Well of Loneliness (1928). The Master of the House (1932). Miss Ogilvy Finds Herself (1934). The Sixth Beatitude (1936).

Louis J. Parascandola

Aase Hansen
1893–1981

Born March 11, 1893, Frederiksværk, Denmark
Died 1981, Copenhagen
Genre(s): novel, essay, translation, scholarship
Language(s): Danish

The many significant novels of Aase Hansen deal with intelligent, intellectual women caught at cross-purposes with society; with traditional expectations, mores, and roles; and, most importantly, with the ambivalent desires, purposes, and achievements of such women and their hopes for—and fears of—independence. For all the female protagonists in Aase Hansen's novels, the promise of freedom, the merits of meaningful work, and a new equal place in society, as subjects of the story, inevitably involve scary choices, genuine fears of freedom and of an independent life. Aase Hansen's characters are torn between a longing for all important self-realization and their own *angst* in choosing and then living a life of freedom. Hansen answered the quintessential dilemma for herself with her own authorship: By remembering and retelling, she can achieve a little of that pivotal status which neither love nor a career can really bring women. Hansen's writing gave impetus to current, constant discussions concerning the difficult choices that women must make—and the negative aspects of such choices.

Aase Hansen was born on March 11, 1893, in Frederiksværk, Denmark. She was the daughter of Frederik Carl Hansen (1853–1915), the town merchant, and of Mette Kirstine Pedersen (1852–1928). In 1913, Hansen passed her entrance examinations for the university, graduating from Frederiksborg State School. She continued her education at the University of Copenhagen, finishing her university degree in the fields of Danish, German, and English, in 1921. Hansen's first position was as a visiting teacher at Ålborg Cathedral School; she later obtained a permanent appointment as Adjunct to Vejle School, but she did not secure tenure for that position, for, as she recognized, she wasn't the born pedagogue. Hansen had long nourished a childhood dream of becoming a writer, but she postponed her literary debut by working for a year in Copenhagen's Office of the National Registry and by teaching seven additional years at Ullerslev Secondary School on Fyn (Fünen). (Hansen wrote her first two books, Ebba Berings Studentertid [1929; The Academic Career of Ebba Bering] and Et Par Huse om en Station [1930; A Few Houses by a Station], while still at Ullerslev.) In 1932 Hansen resigned her post at the secondary school, returning to Copenhagen as a full-time writer and translator. Hansen's academic career set its mark on her subdued, tranquil style, and she sketched her characters with careful human and humane insight and with her own experiences and challenges as an independent intellectual in mind. Never married, Hansen died in Copenhagen in 1981, after a literary career spanning 50 years, from her 1929 debut to her final work, I Forvitringens Aar (1977; In Years of Decline).

The major theme of Aase Hansen's novels is the personal conflict between intellectual promise and the desire for a meaningful, traditional love relationship on the other. Hansen's characters desire importance, freedom, and self-reliance, but they also fear loneliness, unfulfilled dreams, and self-deception. Hansen drew on her own life experiences and her training as a scholar to sketch portraits of women facing the inherent burdens and drawbacks of their own life decisions and of their intense longing for recognition and self-acceptance.

Hansen's debut novel, Ebba Berings Studentertid, deals with the protagonist Ebba's transition from naive provincial girl to university student; Ebba and her friends share a desire to break free of a close, confining provincial background "into new experiences in the capital and at the University" (Dalager, Stig, and Anne-Marie Mai, Danske levindelige forgattere, Vol. 2. Copenhagen, 1982, p. 70). Ebba's friends all find satisfaction in language and literature studies, whereas

Ebba remains discontented, disillusioned, and uninvolved in her own political science studies. Ebba's path through academia is a rocky one because of her own lack of commitment and her disinterest and disappointment in her studies; in addition, she lacks necessary "concrete experience in the male-dominated world [of] abstract, theoretical political-science" (Dalager, p. 71), and she regrets her own choice of study. Ebba's sexual awakening with an older, married man clearly reveals her bitterness and loneliness, her disappointment, and her own admitted failure to take her studies seriously. Ebba finishes her studies unprepared for "a share in life" and cut off from "the traditional secure marriage, the role of wife and mother of which she [very belatedly] dreams" (Dalager, p. 72). Aase Hansen reveals Ebba's conflicts and lack of commitment all too clearly; her unresolved yearnings for independence and for love and security lead Ebba to a problematic, lonely existence. In *Ebba Berings Studentertid*, Aase Hansen sketches the hard decisions that educated women still face; she also discloses the essential conflict within her protagonist, Ebba's lack of dedication to science and statescraft.

In *Et Par Huse om en Station*, Aase Hansen further demonstrated her keen insights into local milieu and her ability to use her own experiences in sketching characters and setting. Hansen's novels, *Vraggods* (1933; Wreckage) and, particularly, *Stine* (1933) deal with self-conflict and self-reflection; in the latter novel, the student Rigmor loses her lover to the more earthy, direct, uncomplicated Stine. With *Stine*, Aase Hansen's stories begin to focus on the psychology and history of self-discord as a theme. Hansen's mature work, *En Kvinde kommer hjem* (1937; A Woman Comes Home), deals with a modern mature woman's return home to her dying mother, without work or lovers. Hansen's novel reveals the modern protagonist-narrator's conflicting desire and fear of freedom. This work was followed by *Drømmen om i Gaar* (1939; The Dream of Yesterday), a portrayal of the chance reunion of two school friends during a summer trip. The two women have followed entirely different life-paths, and neither way has proven happy or carefree: one has chosen traditional marriage, a demonic lover, many suicide attempts, and perpetual turmoil, whereas the narrator has resisted involvements and passions in favor of loneliness, isolation, and a position on the sidelines. Both of Hansen's characters in *Drømmen om i Gaar* reflect self-dissension which the lonely, detached narrator *might* have weathered only a little bit better and at a very high price. Aase Hansen's later novels, *Den lyse Maj* (1948; Light May) and *Skygger i et Spejl* (1951; Shadows in a Mirror) continue to sketch the life experiences of women—the love conflicts and the modern problems of work, career, hopes, and dreams. In *Skygger i et Spejl*, two women travel home together; they present two sides of essentially the same story of passion with difficult and painful love affairs. The narrator's story develops through dream and reverie in contrast to her companion's more vivid and actual accounts.

Aase Hansen's *oeuvre* focuses on the essential transitions, conflicts, and changes confronting and challenging every woman. Hansen drew on her own experiences as an intellectual and as a provincial woman who excelled academically, and, then, she confronted self-conflicts, fears, hopes, loneliness, and several hard personal decisions and found meaning and a niche in her writing. Aase Hansen's many novels, essays, and memoirs raise still-relevant questions about goals, hopes, and purposes.

Works

Ebba Berings Studentertid (1929). *Et Par Huse om en Station* (1930). *Stine* (1933). *Vraggods* (1933). *En Kvinde kommer hjem* (1937). *Drømmen om i Gaar* (1939). *De røde Baand* [The Red Bands] (1943). *Madammen i Sundgaarden, hørespil* [The Lady of Sundgaard] radio play (1933, 1942). *Tordenluft* [Thunder Air] (1945) . *Den lyse Maj* (1948). *Skygger i et Spejl* (1951). *Fra den grønne Provins* [From the Green Province], memoirs in essay form (1952). *Alt for Kort er Duggens Tid* [Much too Short Is Blossom Time] (1954). *Ursula og hendes Mor* [Ursula and her Mother] (1956). *Den lange Sommerday* [The Long Summer Day] (1957). *Nogle Dage, Nogle Time* [Some Days; Some Hours] (1966). *Gaester i Dezember* [Guests in December] (1970). *Klip af et Billedark* [Clippings from a Picture Sheet], memoirs (1973). *I Forvitringens Aar* (1977).

Lanae Hjortsvang Isaacson

Frederikke (Rinna/Renna) Elisabeth Brun Juul Hauch
1811–1896

Born June 13, 1811, Helsingør (Elsinore), Denmark
Died March 24, 1896, Frederiksberg, Copenhagen
Genre(s): novel
Language(s): Danish

Together with her husband, the poet Carsten Hauch, Renna Elisabeth Hauch presided over the literary and artistic milieu of Sorø, site of the Sorø Academy on the island of Sjælland (Denmark). Renna Hauch was well acquainted with the leading literary and intellectual figures of her day, and she maintained a life-long friendship with the very important literary critic and scholar Georg Brandes, who admired her strong and tolerant nature. Renna Hauch was very concerned with modern principles of child-rearing, in the spirit of Rousseau. A member of *Dansk Kvindesamfund* (The Danish Society of Women) in the 1870s and an elderly but still active, engaged participant in the fledgling Social Democratic Movement, Renna Hauch managed to raise a large family, preside over Sorø intellectual society, and establish her own independent intellectual connections. The author of several smaller narratives and two novels, *Tyrolerfamilien* (1840; The Tyrol Family, with an introduction by Carsten Hauch) and *Frue Werner* (1844; Mrs. Werner), Renna Hauch caused no end of consternation in Sorø with her nude bathing, her abandonment of the corsette craze, and with the freedom she accorded her daughters in connection with young men. Although she never thought of rejecting motherhood as a part of woman's nature, as the natural course for women, Renna Hauch did argue for a free upbringing for young women, for an "educational model of freedom for the individual . . . [who grows up] undeterred by society's norms and conventions" (Dalager, Stig, and Anne-Marie Mai, *Danske kvindelige forfattere*, vol. 1. Copenhagen, 1983, p. 180), in an open, free loving home.

Frederikke Renna Elisabeth Brun Juul was born on June 13, 1811, in Helsingør (Elsinore), Denmark. Her parents, who both died while still quite young, were Svend Brun Juul, the city magistrate in Helsingør (1774–1813), and Helene Elisabeth von Munthe af Morgenstierne (1781–1820) (*Dansk biografisk Lekiskon*, "Carsten Hauch," 1979, 86). Renna Juul grew up in the cultured home of her uncle Wullf; he was a military commander and a renowned translator of all the works of William Shakespeare. At the age of seventeen, Renna Juul married the 40-year-old poet, Carsten Hauch, and thereby became firmly established in the artistic and literary world of Sorø. Renna Hauch wrote her first novel, *Tyrolerfamilien*, in 1840; her husband Carsten Hauch offered a foreword to the story of Marie who flees both her family and the patriarchal Copenhagen society to become the wife of a peasant in the Tyrol. Renna Hauch's other novel, *Frue Werner*, was published in 1844, when her own daughters were nearly grown and she was thirty-three; Hauch's second novel deals with the widow Mrs. Werner's attempts to raise her daughter Marie far from the multifaceted society of the city, in a free, natural, open milieu, and, with the dual processes of sexual matu-

ration and *løsrivelse*, letting go. Renna Hauch lived a long life engaged in the radical trends of her time; many of her ideas won a ready, receptive, tolerant audience among the poets, writers, and artists of Sorø. Hauch won the recognition of her many friends and intellectual associates for her practicality, her social commitment, and her role as the poetic muse, "sagakvinden" (saga woman), as the poets admiringly called her. Renna Hauch died in Frederiksberg, Copenhagen, on March 24, 1896, at the age of eighty-five, after a life of intellectual and social commitment.

Renna Hauch's first novel, *Tyrolerfamilien*, depicts a young, motherless protagonist, Marie; Marie has family roots in the cultured civil servant class, but she flees a vindictive stepmother, who forbids Marie's piano playing, a punitive upbringing at the hands of her uncle, and a constrictive, authoritarian urban environment, to travel to the Tyrol. Marie undertakes the trip from Copenhagen to the Tyrol completely alone and frequently employs her strength, intelligence, and pluck to save herself from dangerous situations. Marie becomes the passionate, loving wife of a peasant, Franz; as Hauch suggests, Marie's passion for Franz is a dangerous feeling which burdens their mutual relationship. In *Tyrolerfamilien*, Hauch describes a marriage based solely on love; her second novel, *Frue Werner*, proposes an alternative to all-encompassing marital passion—a marriage that provides nurturing, shelter, and protection. Frue Werner has given her young daughter Marie a careful, protective upbringing, a good home. Marie falls in love with a young man, Erhard Selmer; as an informed and free-thinking widow, Frue Werner does not oppose her daughter's love but helps with the transition, the inevitable letting go. Frue Werner even negotiates the rough waters of passion with her daughter, also instructing Erhard in the need for young men to go slowly, to win the love of their young wives before they win their bodies. Erhard becomes a protective, sheltering substitute for Frue Werner; when Marie's mother suddenly falls ill, Erhard is summoned to the dying woman's bed, to marry Marie and to step in as her protector. Sexual passion between marriage partners, between Marie and Erhard as intellectual and psychological equals, is suppressed or hidden in fleeting dream episodes, in visions or symbols, and Erhard assumes the watchful role once played by the caring and careful Frue Werner.

Renna Hauch was at the center of a lively, stimulating, intellectual circle of poets, writers, playwrights, composers, and artists at Sorø. Together with Carsten Hauch, she came in close contact with the leading literary and cultural figures of the day and won their admiration and esteem. Hauch never questioned the naturalness of her role as mother or wife, and she did not dispute the given sexual division of work; Hauch did, however, support a free, positive, liberal education that would enable young women to use their talents and give their natural curiosity free rein. Renna Hauch committed herself to the causes of educational reform and social justice, and she played an active role in the Danish literary circles and society of her day.

Works

Tyrolerfamilien (1840). *Frue Werner* (1844).

Lanae Hjortsvang Isaacson

Heloise
ca. 1098–1164
Born ca. 1098
Died May 15, 1164
Genre(s): letters
Language(s): Latin

Heloise has become one of the most celebrated women of the Middle Ages, largely because of her tragic love affair with the noted philosopher Peter Abelard. She was also well known to her contemporaries as an example of feminine learning.

Born to a wealthy Parisian family, Heloise was noted for her devotion to classical studies early in life. Her family engaged Abelard as her tutor. Their subsequent affair led to the birth of a child, named Astralabe, Abelard's castration by Heloise's enraged uncle, and Heloise's eventual entrance into the convent of Argenteuil. On the close of that convent, the community took refuge at the Paraclete, an abbey founded by Abelard, who had by then left for Britanny. Heloise became the new convent's first abbess and presided over its flourishing growth. She was buried beside her former lover in the cemetery of the Paraclete, but in 1817 both their remains were moved to Père-Lachaise cemetery in Paris.

Heloise's most famous works are three letters to Abelard that survive as collected with Abelard's lengthy replies and other of Abelard's letters, including the famous *Story of My Misfortunes*. Heloise's letters indicate an abiding love for Abelard. She stressed her service to him, which continued even in her religious vocation: "I have kept nothing back for myself, unless to become yours now even more." Heloise reproached her absent lover for his refusal

to aid her. When Abelard replied, he advised her to redirect her love from him to God. This correspondence created the famous legend of their love affair, which inspired such varied writers as Jean de Meun, Dante, and Petrarch. The authenticity of this corpus, however, is problematic. Some have suggested that Abelard himself, or perhaps some third party, wrote the entire correspondence as a comprehensive treatise on love. Others have maintained the authenticity of Heloise's authorship of the letters attributed to

Heloise

her in the manuscripts. Although the question remains unanswered, the problems surrounding the authenticity of these letters are sufficient to require the historian to use them with care. In any case, the letters are valuable evidence for the development of ideas about love and the human personality in the twelfth century.

Apart from these letters, Heloise sent a series of theological questions, chiefly concerning scriptural passages, to Abelard. They survive, together with Heloise's covering letter and Abelard's replies, in a text known as the *Problemata*. A brief letter from Heloise to Peter the Venerable, the powerful abbot of Cluny who protected Abelard in his last years, also survives. No one has seriously questioned Heloise's authorship of these works.

Works

Letters to Peter Abelard in J.T. Muckle, "The Personal Letters Between Abelard and Heloise," *Medieval Studies* 1953, 15, 47–94; in J.T. Muckle, "The Letter of Heloise on Religious Life and Abelard's First Reply," *Medieval Studies* 1955, 17, 240–281; and in Peter Abélard, *Historia Calamitatum*, ed. J. Monfrin, 1967. "Letter to Peter the Venerable," in G. Constable, ed., *The Letters of Peter the Venerable*, vol. 1, 1967, pp. 400–401. *Problemata*, ed. J.P. Migne, in *Patrologia Latina*, 178, cols. 677–730.

Thomas Head

Felicia Dorothea Browne Hemans
1793–1835

a.k.a. Felicia Browne, Felicia Hemans, Mrs. Hemans
Born September 25, 1793, Liverpool, England
Died May 16, 1835, Dublin, Ireland
Genre(s): poetry, essay, translation, drama
Language(s): English

The most popular woman poet of the nineteenth century, Hemans spent most of her life in Wales, where her family moved after her father's business failures. A beautiful, precocious child, she was educated at home under her mother's direction. She studied French, Spanish, Italian, Portuguese, German, and Latin. She read Shakespeare at six, began writing poetry at eight, and published her first volume at fourteen—dedicated to the Prince of Wales and listing over nine hundred subscribers, including her future husband. Her marriage to Captain Alfred Hemans lasted less than six years. Shortly before the birth of their fifth son, Captain Hemans went to Rome "for the sake of his health" and was never seen again. Pursuing "uninterrupted domestic privacy," she devoted herself to her sons and mother.

American writer Lydia Sigourney attributed Hemans's success to the influence of "maternal culture": "by her prolonged residence under the maternal wing, she was sheltered from the burden of those cares which sometimes press out the life of song." Her mother's death in 1827 seems to have marked the beginning of her own decline. She died of tuberculosis at forty-two, mourned by Wordsworth as "that holy Spirit, / . . . who, ere her summer faded/ Has sunk into a breathless sleep."

Hemans produced numerous volumes of poetry, songs, translations, and some periodical essays. Her five-act tragedy, *The Vespers of Palermo* (1823), failed at Covent Garden but was produced more successfully in Edinburgh with the assistance of Sir Walter Scott. Hemans read, and often quoted, Shakespeare, Petrarch, Lope de Vega, Tasso, Gibbon, Schiller, Novalis, Goethe, Byron, Shelley, and Mme. de Staël. *Corinne,* she said, "has a power over me which is quite indescribable. Some passages seem to give me back my own thoughts and feelings, my whole inner being." She corresponded with Joanna Baillie and Mary Howitt, and in 1829, she visited Sir Walter Scott at Abotsford. At the instigation of Maria Jewsbury, she also became acquainted with William Wordsworth, whom she visited in 1830 at Rydal.

Although she set most of her long poems in exotic places—Moorish palaces, Carthaginian ruins, Spanish castles—and invoked stories of political rebellion and war, her real concerns are domestic. Her chosen themes are, in Sigourney's words, "the loveliness of nature, the endearments of home, the deathless strength of the affections,the noble aims of disinterested virtue, the power of that piety that plucks the sting from death. "Maternal love is a prevailing concern, especially in *Records of Woman,* poetical tales written shortly after her mother's death.

Hemans provides insight into the critical values and popular taste of the nineteenth century. She was acclaimed by such prominent reviewers as Francis Jeffrey and recommended for study in the schools by Matthew Arnold (her poems, he said, "have real merits of expression and sentiment"). In America, where she was the most frequently anthologized English writer in the gift books and annuals, critics Andrews Norton and Andrew Peabody ranked her work above Milton's and Homer's. Essay after essay defines her as the perfect lady poet.

Assuming that the "nature of this poetess is more interesting than her genius, or than its finest productions," reviewers evaluate the poetry in terms of her personality. She is applauded for living in retirement and maintaining proper "feminine reserve." Readers note her "tremulous sensibility," "delicate organization," and "intense susceptiveness," but conclude that she keeps her feelings under control. "The calm mistress of her stormiest emotions," Hemans exudes the right amount of melancholy and reveals "no unsatisfied cravings." Moreover, she has little sense of artistic self-consciousness. As Lydia Sigourney said, "Sympathy, not fame, was the desire of her being." Hemans proclaimed that she was determined not to become "that despicable thing, a woman living upon admiration!" In "Properzia Rossi," a celebrated woman sculptor decries her fame as "worthless" because her statue has no effect on the knight she adores.

Being "a genuine woman, and, therefore, a true Christian," Hemans is commended for dispensing religious and moral sentiments. According to William Michael Rossetti, she had "that love of good and horror of evil which characterize a scrupulous female mind." Her favorite poem, *The Forest Sanctuary,* concerns a sixteenth-century Spaniard who flees to North America in search of religious freedom. *The Skeptic,* a poem arguing for the necessity of deism, infuriated Byron ("too stiltified & atmospheric—& quite wrong"), but most readers saw it as appropriate for women to act as "natural guardians of morality and faith."

Women also praised Hemans in extravagant terms. Author Maria Jewsbury idolized her as "a Muse, a grace, a variable child, a dependent woman, the Italy of human beings." George Eliot, who quoted "our sweet Mrs. Hemans" frequently during the early 1840s, called *The Forest Sanctuary* "exquisite!" Elizabeth Barrett Browning and Letitia Landon wrote elegies for Hemans, while Sigourney and other American poetesses claimed her as their precursor. Indeed, it has been suggested that Hemans "ought to be read at length before trying any of the great woman poets of the nineteenth century." Despite an awkward situation that left her living without her husband, she proved that it was possible to be a poet, a lady, a mother, *and* a great popular success. But the gushing praise for her poetry reveals a double critical standard that would limit the aspirations and diminish the achievements of women poets throughout the century.

Works (Selected)

Poems (1808). *England and Spain, or Valour and Patriotism* (1808). *The Domestic Affections and Other Poems* (1812). *The Restoration of the Works of Art to Italy* (1816). *Translations from Camoens and Other Poets* (1818). *Stanzas to the Memory of the Late King* (1820). *Dartmoor* (1821). *Welsh Melodies* (1821). *The Vespers of Palermo* (1823). *The Forest Sanctuary and Other Poems* (1825). *Records of Woman* (1828). *Songs of the Affections* (1830). *Hymns for Childhood* (1834). *National Lyrics and Songs for Music* (1834). *Scenes and Hymns of Life* (1834).

Robin Sheets

Georgette Heyer
1902–1974

a.k.a. Stella Martin
Born August 16, 1902, London, England
Died July 4, 1974, London
Genre(s): novel
Language(s): English

Georgette Heyer, the eldest of three children and the only daughter of George and Sylvia Heyer, was privately educated and did not attend university. When she was seventeen she wrote a story, as she said, "to relieve my own boredom, and my brother's." Although she had written merely to entertain her brother Boris while he was recovering from an illness, her father, who himself had written several articles for *Punch,* liked the story and encouraged her to work on it for publication. She did, and in 1921 her first novel, *The Black Moth,* was published.

Despite her early success, she cared little for publicity. Throughout her writing career of over 50 years, she made no appearances and never granted an interview, even in the interest of increasing book sales. She used the pseudonym Stella Martin for her third book but thereafter used her real name. That she was an early success would, however, prove to be especially important in 1925. When her father died she became the principal means of financial support for her mother and two younger brothers.

In 1925 she married a mining engineer; in 1927 she joined him in Africa, but he was unhappy with his job and she was unhappy with their travels, so in 1929 they returned to England. There, with his wife's encouragement, he began studying to be a barrister, something he had long wished to do; Heyer's writing was now providing the basic financial support not only for her mother's family but also for her own.

Heyer was a prolific writer. She is best known for her Regency novels, her publishers noted that she "worked quickly, . . . and made few corrections, soaking herself in the Regency Period—becoming an expert on the history and manners of that time." Indeed, she kept copious notes and sketches of Regency life and fashion. This attention to detail did not encumber her style, which is marked by a verve and wit that at times has been compared to that of Jane Austen. Instead, the details of dress and use of Regency slang lend a viable sense of scene to these novels in which the functions of social class, manners, and romance figure predominantly. A 1948 *New York Times* review captured the tone of these novels when the reviewer said of Heyer that she "writes cheerful and highly unorthodox historical novels, set in Regency England, in which people never lose their lives, their virtue, or even their tempers."

Such a novel is *The Nonesuch* (1962) in which Sir Waldo Hawkridge comes to Broom Hall, setting the countryside in a turmoil as families rush to entertain him with the most stylish and engaging parties, mothers and daughters concoct matchmaking schemes, and the young men of the town try desperately to emulate this paragon of style known as the "Nonesuch." The story contains common elements of the romance genre. The hero suddenly appears in a small town, unknown but by his reputation, and falls in love with Ancilla Trent, governess of the feisty and coquettish Miss Tiffany Wield. Tiffany, "a most accomplished flirt," determines to charm the Nonesuch and at least capture the heart of the young Lord Julian. Yet in the end it is the "very gentle" but courageous Miss Patience Chartley who takes Lord Julian's heart.

Here, as in many of her Regency romances, Heyer relieves the potential melodrama of these situations with humor, wit, and a refreshing use of common sense. Characters are well-defined, and even the most annoying Tiffany is likeable. Heyer develops the potential of the genre by mirroring characters and relationships—the Nonesuch and Ancilla Trent with the young Lord Julian and Patience Chartley, the coquette with the gentle beauty, fashion with foppery. The humorous romantic complications are enlivened by the overriding satire of the society that busies itself in frenzied, albeit clumsy, attempts to marry off the Nonesuch or to imitate his fashion and skill. Good manners, "tradition, and upbringing" are the measure of the nobility of character in these novels that exemplify the best elements of the romance genre right up to the climax when the runaway Tiffany must be rescued and finally taught a lesson by the Nonesuch.

While Heyer is best known for these Regency novels, she also published a dozen mysteries, the first being *Footsteps in the Dark* (1932). Her husband, while studying for the bar, frequently collaborated with her on these novels, helping with the plot. The wit, clear characterization, and closely defined social scene that marked her Regency novels were also important elements of her detective novels. Two of her characters—Scotland Yard detectives Superintendent Hannasyde and Inspector Hemingway—make return appearances in eight of these novels as they frequently confront eccentric characters whose humor enlivens both the investigation and the novel.

At times Heyer criticized her own work as not being "real" literature, but she summarized many readers' responses as she noted that "it's unquestionably good escapist literature . . . its period detail is good, . . . and . . . I will say that it is very good fun."

Works

The Black Moth (1921). *The Great Roxhythe* (1922). *The Transformation of Philip Jettan* (as Stella Martin, 1923). *Instead of the Thorn* (1923). *Simon the Coldheart* (1925). *These Old Shades* (1926). *Helen* (1926). *The Masqueraders* (1928). *Beauvallet* (1929). *Pastel* (1929). *The Barren Corn* (1930). *The Conqueror* (1931). *Footsteps in the Dark* (1932). *Devil's Cub* (1932). *Why Shoot a Batter?* (1933). *The Unfinished Clue* (1934). *The Convenient Marriage* (1934). *Death in the Stocks* (1935). *Regency Buck* (1935). *Behold, Here's Poison!* (1936). *The Talisman Ring* (1936). *They Found Him Dead* (1937). *An Infamous Army* (1937). *A Blunt Instrument* (1938). *Royal Escape* (1938). *No Wind of Blame* (1939). *The Spanish Bride* (1940). *The Corinthian* (1940). *Envious Casa* (1941). *Faro's Daughter* (1941). *Penhallow* (1942). *Friday's Child* (1944). *The Reluctant Widow* (1946). *The Foundling* (1948). *Arabella* (1949). *The Grand Sophy* (1950). *Duplicate Death* (1951). *The Quiet Gentleman* (1951). *Detection Unlimited* (1953). *Cotillion* (1953). *The Toll-Gate* (1954). *Bath Tangle* (1955). *Sprig Muslin* (1956). *April Lady* (1957). *Sylvester: or The Wicked Uncle* (1957). *Venetia* (1958). *The Unknown Ajax* (1959). *Pistols for Two and Other Stories* (1960). *A Civil Contract* (1961). *The Nonesuch* (1962). *False Colours* (1963). *Frederica* (1965). *Black Sheep* (1966). *Cousin Kate* (1968). *Charity Girl* (1970). *Lady of Quality* (1972). *My Lord John* (1975).

Paula Connolly

Magdalena Heymair
ca. 1535–ca. 1586

a.k.a. Magdalena Heymairin
Born between 1530 and 1540, probably in Regensburg
Died after 1586, probably in Kaschau (Kosiçe, later Czechoslovakia)
Genre(s): rhymed adaptations of the Bible
Language(s): German

"This must be the end of time, when also women are publishing books." Thus exclaims an admiring Josua Opitz in his preface to Magdalena Heymair's second work, *Jesus Sirach* (1571). Heymair's entry into this hitherto male domain was, to be sure, dictated by economic necessity. Married to the Straubing schoolteacher Wilhelm Heymair, she was forced by "lack of money and food" (foreword to the *Epistles*) to supplement the meager schoolmaster's income by teaching, first as a home tutor, then as a schoolteacher in Straubing, Cham, and Regensburg. In 1586 we find her in Kaschau (presently Kosiçe) as the Hofmeisterin (governess) in the household of the widow Judith Reuber, née von Fridensheim. After 1586, nothing further is heard of Magdalena Heymair.

Heymair's works are an outgrowth of her teaching endeavors, and, as stated in titles and forewords, they are expressly intended for youth. All were adaptations of the Bible: *The Epistles* (first printed 1568), *Jesus Sirach* (1571), the *Apostelgeschichten* (1573; *The Acts*), *Tobias* and *Ruth* (1580), selections tailormade for the traditional curriculum in the "German schools" as those institutions were called that taught German reading and sometimes writing and arithmetic. *The Epistles* (with the Gospels) were recommended as reading material in many of the school ordinances; so were *The Acts*, designed to replace the legends of the Saints in the Lutheran schools. *Tobias and Ruth* were Biblical role models of children obedient to their parents. As she explains in the foreword to *The Epistles*, Heymair chose to rewrite each epistle in the form of a song in imitation of Niklaus Herman's popular *Sontagsevangelia*. According to Heymair, Herman had gotten the idea of his gospel songs from a schoolteacher, who wanted to use them as reading and memorization material in her schools. In deviation from Herman, Heymair used not only religious melodies but also secular ones and expresses the hope that her texts will replace the ones of the popular ditties sung in the streets. A valiant attempt has been made to make the Biblical material comprehensible to a child. Difficult theological concepts are glossed over, with the emphasis instead on Christian ethics. Like Herman's, her doggerel is often forced, her rhyme not very pure, the word order strained to facilitate rhyme. The naiveté and simplicity, however, make these songs very appealing and they do lend themselves well to singing.

Measured by the standards of her time, Heymair's success as an author was immediate. Her *Epistles* saw three editions, *Jesus Sirach* no less than eight, the *Apostelgeschichten* one and *Tobias and Ruth* two. That Heymair was able to break into the publishing field at all is in itself remarkable. Although schoolbooks proved to be a consistent and lucrative income for many a printer, to take the work of a new-

comer, a woman, must have posed a risk. It is likely that Heymair's reputation as a schoolteacher was a factor. The well-to-do mother of two of her pupils, Catharina von Degenwerg, appeared to have used her influence and also introduced Heymair to other acquaintances, to whom Heymair then dedicated her works and who receive favorable mention in the forewords. These women read her works and used them with their children. The immediate success of her first work must also have made further publishing easier. This reputation as a teacher and an author also accounts for the fact that Magdalena Heymair published these school texts under her own name rather than that of her husband. She was the only woman teacher to contribute in this way before the eighteenth century.

Works

Die Sontegliche Epistel vber das gantze Jar in gesangweis gestelt durch Magdalenam Heymairin Teütsche Schul maisterin zue Chamb. Mit einer Vorrede Magistri Bilibaldi Ramsbecken Stadt predigers zu Chamb [The Epistles] (1568). *Das Büchlein Jesu Syrach in Gesange verfasset vnd der lieben Jugendt zu gutem in Truck gegeben durch Magdalena Heymairin, Teutsche Schulmeisterin zu Regenspurg. Mit einer schönen Vorred . . .* [Jesus Sirach (Ecclesiastes)] (1571; Staatsbibl. Munich, Harvard, 1573, 1574, 1578) [Wolfenbüttel Herzog August Bibliothek]. *Die Apostelgeschichten Nach der Historien Gesangs weiß gestelt Durch Magtalena Heymairin, diser Zeytt Teutsche Schuelhalterin zu Regenspurg* [The Acts] (1573). *Das Buch Tobiae samt etlichen vnd 50 geistlichen Liedern vnd Kindergesprächen, wozu noch viele Weynacht-Oster-vnd Pfingstgesänge zu rechnen . . .* [The Book of Tobias] (1580). *Das Buch Tobiae Jnn Christliche Reimen Vnnd Gesangweiße gefast und gestellet Gott dem lieben Ehestand allen frommen Christleibenden Eheleuten und Jungfrewlichen Kinderschulen zu ehren erinnerung vnd Trost Durch Frauen Magdalenen Heymairin Jetz aber durch einen gut Hertzigen Christen gebessert vnnd gemehret vnd von newem mit anderen ein verleibten Gesänglen in Truck verfertiget. Anno, 1586. . . . Volget das Büchlein Ruth auch Gesangsweiß als ein zugab Durch obgemelten Auctorem vnd correctorem. M.D. LXXVI* [The Books of Tobias and Ruth] (1580).

Cornelia Niekus Moore

Hildegard von Bingen
ca. 1098–1179

Born ca. 1098, Bermersheim in Rheinhessen, Germany

Died September 17, 1179, Rupertsberg near Bingen

Genre(s): poetry; musical lyric; drama; medical, political, and religious treatises

Language(s): Latin

Hildegard von Bingen is the first major German mystic. She wrote profusely as a prophet, a poet, a dramatist, a physician, and a political moralist, communicating often with popes and princes, influential persons and common folk. Exerting a tremendous influence on the Western Europe of her time, she was an extraordinary woman who stood out from the corruption, misery, and ruin—both temporal and spiritual—of the twelfth century.

Hildegard's father was Hildebert, a knight in the service of Meginhard, the count of Spanheim. At the age of six, the child began to have the visions that continued the rest of her life and which she later recorded. At the age of eight, she was entrusted to the care of Jutta, who was the sister of Count Meginhard of Spanheim. She continued her education under Jutta, learning to read and sing in Latin. At the age of fifteen, she was clothed in the habit of a nun in the hermitage of Jutta, following the Rule of Saint Benedict. When Jutta died in 1136, Hildegard, at the age of thirty-eight, became the abbess of the community. Between 1147 and 1150, Hildegard moved her community to a dilapidated church and unfinished buildings at Rupertsberg, near Bingen. Hildegard saw to the building of a large and convenient convent that continued to attract increasing numbers. She lived here, except during her extensive travels in Western Europe, did most of her writing here, and continued as abbess until her death. She was buried in her convent church where her relics remained until the convent was destroyed by the Swedes in 1632; her relics were then moved to Eibingen.

Hildegard was a woman of extraordinarily energetic and independent mind, who wrote voluminously. She recorded her visions in three books: *Scivias* (May You Know, or Know the Ways) written between 1141 and 1151, *Liber Vitae Meritorum* (The Book of the Life of Meritorious Works) written between 1158 and 1163, and *Liber Divinorum Operum Simplicis Hominis* (The Book of the Divine Works of a Simple Man) written between 1163 and 1173. The illuminated manuscript of Hildegard's *Scivias*, the "Riesenkodex," Hessische Landesbibliothek, Wiesbaden, cod.

2 (Rupertsberg, c. 1180–1190), is an excellent preservation and is of the highest value to scholars of mysticism, history, and medieval art. The visions of *Scivias* develop Hildegard's views on the universe, on the theory of macrocosm and microcosm, the structure of man, birth, death, and the nature of the soul. They also treat the relationship between God and humans in creation, the Redemption, and the Church. *Scivias* also discusses the importance of the virtues by explaining the idea of "viriditas." "Viriditas" literally means greenness; symbolically, growth or the principle of life. According to Hildegard and other thinkers of her time, life from God was transmitted into the plants, animals, and precious gems. People, in turn, ate the plants and animals and acquired some of the gems, thereby obtaining "viriditas." People then gave out "viriditas" through the virtues, hence their importance in the chain of being. The last vision of *Scivias* contains *Ordo Virtutum*. Written between the years 1141 and 1151, the play is extremely important, since it appears to be the earliest liturgical morality play yet discovered.

Liber Vitae Meritorum describes the vision of a very large circle in which the Virtues and Vices are grouped. Hildegard gives us a description of all these Virtues and Vices, but the book is less mystical and more moral and practical than *Scivias*. *Liber Divinorum Operum Simplicis Hominis* is found in an important illuminated manuscript in the municipal library at Lucca. This book contains many of the same dogmatic and ascetic thoughts that are found in *Scivias*, but it is arranged differently. The fundamental idea of the book is the unity of creation. Hildegard herself does not use the terms macrocosm and microcosm, but she succeeds in synthesizing into one great whole her theological beliefs along with her knowledge of the elements of the universe and the structures within the human body. This work is often considered as the epitome of the science of her time.

Besides these three books recording her visions, Hildegard also wrote a long physical treatise entitled *Physica: Subtilitatum Diversarum Naturarum Creaturarum* (Physical Things: Subtitled of Various Natural Creatures) and her book of medicine entitled *Causae et Curae* (Causes and Cures). Although her theoretical knowledge of medicine as found in these works may seem crude today, she must have been successful because large numbers of sick and suffering persons were brought to her for cures. In addition, Hildegard wrote *Vita Sancti Disibodi* (The Life of Saint Disibod) and *Vita Sancti Ruperti* (The Life of Saint Rupert). Her *Solutiones Triginta Octo Quaes-*

tionum (Answers to Thirty-eight Questions) comments on various theological and scriptural subjects. Her *Explanatio Symboli Sancti Athanasii* (Explanation of the Symbol of Saint Anthanasius) is self-explanatory, as is her *Explanatio Regulae Sancti Benedicti* (Explanation of the Rule of Saint Benedict), which she wrote at the request of the Benedictine monastery of Huy in Belgium. For the nuns of her own convent, Hildegard wrote hymns and canticles—both words and music—and between 1151 and 1158 collected them into a cycle entitled *Symphonia Armonie Celestium Revelationum* (The Harmonious Symphony of Heavenly Revelations). Approximately seventy sequences of hymns, antiphons and responsories are found in the cycle and were written for a wide range of liturgical celebrations, from important Church feasts to feasts of lesser-known saints. Finally, Hildegard wrote letters to popes, cardinals, bishops, abbots, kings and emperors, monks and nuns, men and women of various levels of society both in Germany and abroad. Her letters helped Hildegard become known throughout Europe, and they unfold important political and ecclesiastical information concerning the history of her time. Migne prints one hundred and forty-five of her letters in *Patroligiae Cursus Completus, Series Latina.*

In addition to all her writings and correspondence, Hildegard was not confined to her convent. She traveled considerably for her time and circumstances. Very little is known about her means of travel, but she visited many places along the Nahe River, the Main, the Moselle, and the Rhine—the highway of Western Germany—most likely traveling by boat. The exact dates of her various travels are difficult to ascertain, but her various letters make many references to her travels. Sometimes she founded convents, as she did at Eibingen, on the opposite side of the Rhine near Rudesheim and only a mile from her own convent. Sometimes she visited courts and palaces. In 1155, Frederick Barbarossa invited Hildegard to visit him at the old royal palace that he had restored at Ingelheim (traditionally held as the birthplace of Charlemagne). Frederick Barbarossa was king at the time, but he was hoping to receive the Imperial Crown. In a letter to Hildegard that Frederick wrote several years after the visit, he comments that some of the prophecies she made to him at Ingelheim had come true.

In a letter to the people of Cologne, Hildegard comments on her earlier visits to Treves or Cologne and also comments that she was exceedingly tired, having been traveling for the last two years and preaching to various masters, doctors, and other learned men.

Sometime in her life she also visited Trier, Metz, Wurzburg, Ulm, Werden, Bamberg, and other places as distant as Belgium and Switzerland. Near the end of her life, she visited France. In the Acts of Inquisition concerning Hildegard's life and miracles, it is stated that she made a pilgrimage to the shrine of St. Martin of Tours, and then went on to Paris. It is also stated that she took three or four of her books, including *Scivias,* with her on this journey. Finally, her correspondence indicates that she preached and prophesied during her various travels, exerting a tremendous influence.

It is no surprise that Hildegard is considered significant and is sometimes compared to writers like Dante and Blake. She is the first major German mystic; the illuminated manuscripts recording her visions and their commentary—*Scivias* in particular—are important to historians and those studying mysticism as well. Her *Ordo Virtutum* at the end of *Scivias* is the earliest known morality play, and her various other writings are significant advances in the understanding of the relationship of the individual to his or her universe and in the understanding of medieval medicine. The collection of her hymns and songs is a significant one that is only now being thoroughly studied. She corresponded actively with the religious and political leaders of her day, who were molding the future of Europe in particular and the whole world in general. In her travels, preaching and prophesying, Hildegard has influenced numerous geographical areas and their peoples.

Bruce Hozeski

Octavia Hill
1838–1912
Born December 3, 1838, Wisbeck, England
Died August 12, 1912, London
Genre(s): journalism
Language(s): English

Octavia Hill was a social reformer whose work and writing centered primarily on the reform of urban housing and the improvement of the quality of urban life. She was the eighth of eleven children. In 1851 her mother, an educator, was obliged by financial necessity to move to London with her five daughters, taking a position as manager of the Ladies' Cooperative Guild, an organization founded by the Christian Socialists. In 1852 at the age of fourteen, Octavia began attending meetings of the Christian Socialists where she met the Reverend F.D. Maurice, who offered her a post in another Christian Socialist venture, taking charge of the "ragged children" employed in a toy-furniture making operation; her first article, published in *Household Words* in 1856, was an account of the lives of the poverty-stricken toy makers. Her success with the toymakers led Rev. Maurice to employ her to teach arithmetic at the newly established classes of working women at the Working Men's College and, when the Ladies' Cooperative Guild failed, Maurice offered her a salaried post as Secretary to the Women's Classes. In 1862 the Hills started a school for girls at their new home in Nottingham Place that thrived for 24 years. Hill received her certificate from Queen's College in 1864.

Through her association with the Christian Socialists, Hill met Ruskin, who gave her artistic training and commissioned work from her for the next ten years. For Ruskin, Hill copied pictures for *Modern Painters,* the Society of Antiquaries, and the National Portrait Gallery. Her association with Ruskin proved fruitful not only because he commissioned her copying work; he also assisted her in her next and most important venture, which was to launch her future career and in which she found her true vocation. In 1865, Ruskin purchased three tenanted slum-houses in Paradise Place, a court not far from Hill's home that she was to manage and improve. She improved the properties, gradually rehabilitating both living quarters and their occupants. In 1866, Ruskin further aided Hill's schemes, purchasing a row of cottages; later that year, Hill had four more dilapidated houses placed in her management. Her first article specifically about housing appeared in the *Fortnightly Review* in November 1866 and was followed by a series of others on the same subject.

In 1865, she was involved in the founding of the London Association for the Prevention of Pauperization and Crime (which later became the Charity Organization Society) to which Ruskin contributed generously. Hill read her paper, "The Importance of Aiding the Poor Without Almsgiving," at an 1869 meeting, and thereafter the Reverend W. Freemantle invited Hill to take charge of the very poor Walmer Street District in his parish. Her successful management of all these properties led to more and more similar undertakings, and her fame began to spread beyond Marylebone where her first properties were situated and soon beyond London altogether. She was asked to manage properties in Leeds (1874), Liverpool (1879), and Manchester.

In 1875 Hill became a member of the Central Council of the Charity Organization Society, and, with the demands for her property management growing, she found it necessary to train workers to whom she could delegate her increasing responsibilities. Soon her renown spread beyond England, and women from Berlin, Munich, Sweden, Holland, Russia, and America were in her training. Her system of property management was introduced by these delegates into many towns and cities outside of England. Also in 1875, five of her articles were published as a book in America under the title *Homes of the London Poor.* This work, later translated into German by Princess Alice of Hesse, led to the founding of the "Octavia Hill Verein" in Berlin. In that year, Hill became a member of the Executive Council of the Commons Preservation Society. In 1877 she and her sister, Miranda, were among the founding members of the Kyrle Society, for which Hill functioned as treasurer and her sister as president. These societies worked toward the creation and improvement of public spaces; it was, for example, largely due to Hill's efforts that Parliament Hill was secured for public use.

She is also remembered today for her part in the founding in 1895 of the National Trust, along with Robert Hunter and Canon Rawsley, which secured many important properties, including the Cliff at Barmouth, Tintagel, portions of the Lake district, and Mariners Hill, for public use and enjoyment. In 1898, J.S. Sargent painted the portrait of Hill which hangs in the National Portrait Gallery. In 1905, Hill became a member of the Royal Commission on the Poor Laws.

Works
Further Account of the Walmer Street Industrial Experiment (1872). *Letter to my Fellow Workers Accompanying the Account of Donations Received for Work amongst the Poor Daring 1872(–1911)* (1873 [–1912]). *Homes of the London Poor* (1875). *District Visiting* (1877). *Our Common Land and Other Short Essays* (1877). *Colour, Space and Music for the People* (1884). *An Open Space for Deptford: An Appeal* (1892). "Preservations of Commons: Speech at a Meeting for Securing West Wickham Common." Kent and Surrey Committee of the Commons Preservation Society (1892). *Memorandum on the Report of the Royal Commission on the Poor Laws and Relief of Distress* (1909). *Report of an Attempt to Raise a Few of the London Poor Without Gifts* (n.d.).

Gale Sigal

Esther ("Etty") Hillesum
1914–1943

Born January 15, 1914, Middelburg, Holland
Died November 30, 1943, Auschwitz Concentration
Camp
Genre(s): diary, letters
Language(s): Dutch

Esther Hillesum, a Dutch Jew, was born on January 15, 1914, in Middelburg, Holland. Her father, a teacher and a scholar, taught at schools in various cities until he was appointed headmaster of a gymnasium in Deventer. Esther's mother had come to Holland to escape persecution in her native Russia. A student of law, Esther received her degree from the University of Amsterdam. She later returned to the university to pursue interests in Slavic languages and psychology. Her passion was reading, especially Russian literature, the Bible, and Rilke.

In the early months of 1941, Esther met Julius Spier, who was twenty-eight years her senior and the founder of psychochirology. They became involved physically, emotionally, and intellectually. The following year, 1942, was crucial to the Jews of Holland as the Nazis, who had been occupying the country for two years, began deportations to the East. It was during that year, when Anne Frank and her family went into hiding, that Esther was offered a position as a typist with the Jewish Council. She found the work very monotonous; she was even more disturbed, however, by the fact that the position protected her from deportation. Esther believed that she should be with her people in the camps to share their destiny as well as to help them: "But I don't think I would feel happy if I were exempted from what so many others have to suffer." Accordingly, Esther volunteered to go to Westerbork where she remained for a year. During that time, with the assistance of the Jewish Council, she was occasionally permitted to return to Amsterdam. In 1943, Esther and her family were sent to Auschwitz where she died on November 30. Esther had previously given her diaries and "letters from Westerbork" to a gentile friend with instructions that they be published after the war. It was not, however, until 1981 that the diaries and letters appeared in print; the English version came out two years later.

Esther's diaries and letters begin on March 9, 1941, and end on August 24, 1943. They disclose the life and thoughts of an intelligent, perceptive, and sensitive woman. It is difficult for Esther to come to terms with personal issues as she witnesses the destruction of her people and her country ("I mustn't let myself be ground down by the misery outside"). Nevertheless, she manages to resolve many of her conflicts and is truly able to grow and become her own person. In her diaries and letters, Esther elaborates on her sexuality and her relationships with men, especially with her lover Spier. She discusses at length the problems raised in trying to maintain her own identity while involved with a man. Esther goes so far as to explore the status of women: ". . . the essential emancipation of women still has to come. We are not yet full human beings; we are the 'weaker sex.' We are still tied down and enmeshed in centuries-old traditions. We still have to be born as human beings, that is the great task that lies before us." Esther also struggles with other issues, such as her relationship with God ("It is difficult to be on equally good terms with God and your body").

The diaries and letters of Esther reveal, on an intense level, the engrossing thoughts of a woman who is evolving into a self-confident and independent person. What also emerges, in spite of the circumstances of the time, is an underlying optimism and faith in mankind (similar ideas were expressed by Anne Frank). As Esther says: "If there were only one human being worthy of the name of 'man,' then we should be justified in believing in men and in humanity."

Works

The Diaries (1981). *Letters from Westerbork* (1981).
Michael F. Bassman

Agneta Horn
1629–1672

Born August 18, 1629, Riga, Latvia
Died March 18, 1672, Stockholm, Sweden
Genre(s): autobiography
Language(s): Swedish

The author of one of the most intensely personal literary documents from the Age of the Swedish Empire, Horn has frequently been the object of both historical and literary scrutiny since the manuscript of her autobiography was discovered in 1885. The intrinsic aesthetic value of the text has been heightened among scholars by Horn's impressive family connections: her maternal grandfather, Axel Oxenstierna, was the Swedish Chancellor (1612–

1654), and her father, Gustav Horn, was a Field Marshal in the Swedish Army. In contrast to the memoir and diary formats of most Swedish-life writings of the period, Horn's autobiography is a fascinating and ruminative document, partly secular, partly spiritual. Born and reared in the various arenas of conflict of the Thirty Years' War, Horn uses the tragic plagues and calamitous battles of that war as a backdrop for her personal disasters: the loss of her mother, the bitter feuds with her family, her protracted resistance against a proposed spouse promoted for the sake of political advantage, the death of her husband, and so on. Her life's drama, richly narrated with an unprecedented reliance on dialogue, unfolds largely among the aristocratic circles of the Lake Mälare region and concludes with her spouse's death in the Polish campaign of 1656.

The 550 lines of quotations from *The Psalms* and *Job* which follow the narrative in the manuscript have been widely dismissed as little more than the jottings of a devout widow. It has been pointed out in a recent edition of these citations, however, that a binding error earlier in this century led to a misreading of Horn's intentions. The careful ordering and systematic personalization of the verses leave little doubt but that Horn regarded this portion of the autobiography as the spiritual counterpart to the narrative section; in it, she sought to give expression to her theodical misgivings and to equate her suffering with that of Job, David, and the Israelites. Horn also wrote a short poem treating the major themes of her autobiography. Although neither a prolific nor well-known writer, it has nevertheless been suggested that she be regarded as the author of "the first Swedish novel." Certainly she stands out as one of the most compelling and introspective narrators of the Swedish Baroque.

Works

Agneta Horn. Beskrivning över min vandringstid, ed. Gösta Holm (1959). *Agneta Horns lefverne efter Ellen Fries efterlämnade manuskript*, ed. Sigrid Leijonhufvud (1908). Fries, Ellen, "En sjelfbiografi från sextonhundratalet." *Dagny* (February 1886), pp. 33–44; (March 1886), pp. 70–80; (May 1886), pp. 129–147.

Stephen A. Mitchell

Maria Teresa Horta
1937–

Born 1937, Lisbon, Portugal
Genre(s): essay, journalism, novel, poetry, short story
Language(s): Portuguese

Maria Teresa Horta is one of the most innovative and daring writers of her generation. Born and educated in Lisbon, Horta has been connected to literature and arts since early in her life, working as a journalist, a movie and literary critic, and a magazine editor. She directed and contributed to the literary pages and supplements of such newspapers and periodicals as *A Capital, Eva, O Expresso, Flama,* and is now chief editor of the feminist magazine *Mulheres.* Horta participated in the movement to renew and preserve Portuguese music and is an important figure in the cinematic world, codirecting in 1963 with Antonio de Macedo the production of a short film entitled *Verão Coincidente,* based on her poem by the same name.

Horta's first book of poetry, *Espelho Inicial* (1960) won critical praise, and her second, *Tatuagem* (1961), established her as an important member of the movement "Poesia 61," which tried to instill new life in contemporary Portuguese poetry. Horta's emphasis on the erotic feelings of women has made some of her books controversial and hotly debated. In 1970, her first novel, *Ambas as Mãos Sobre o Corpo,* caused a critical uproar, and in 1971, so did the collection of poetry *Minha Senhora de Mim,* which calls women to exercise their rights to sensual pleasure. This book was censored.

In 1972 Maria Teresa Horta collaborated with Maria Isabel Barreno and Maria Belho da Costa in *Novas Cartas Portuguesas.* The work, an exploration of the feelings of women about love, war, the mores of society, and the erotic nature of life, was declared "offensive to public morals" under the dictatorship of Marcello Caetano, and the three writers were arrested and tried, provoking an international reaction to the dictatorship and gathering support for the nascent feminist movement in Portugal.

In 1974 Horta published her second novel, *Ana,* and in 1975 her essay, *Aborto: Direito a nosso corpo,* written with Celia Metrass, established her as the speaker for the Portuguese feminist movement. In the same year she published the collection of poetry entitled *Educação Sentimental,* which continued to probe the links between the erotic and the psychological. The volume *Mulheres de Abril* (1977) denounces the annihilating everyday life of Portuguese women and announces hope for a new order. In 1983 the book *Os Anjos* undertakes the exploration of androgyny and sensuality. In 1985 Horta published her third novel, *Ema*. Her latest work, *Minha Mae, Minha Amor* (1986) deals with the relationships of mothers and daughters.

Works

Poetry: *Espelho Inicial* [Initial Mirror] (1960). *Tatuagem* [Tatoo] (Poesia 61) (1961). *Cidades Submersas* [Submerged Cities] (1961). *Verão Coincidente* [Coincident Summer] (1962). *Amor Habitado* [Inhabited Love] (1963). *Candelabro* [Candelabra] (1964). *Jardim de Inverno* [Winter's Garden] (1966). *Cronista não é Recado* [The Chronicler Is Not the Message] (1967). *Minha Senhora de Mim* [My Lady of Mim] (1971). *Educação Sentimental* [Sentimental Education] (1975). *Mulheres de Abril* [April's Women] (1977). *Os Anjos* [The Angels] (1983). *Poesia completa*, 1: 1960–1966 [Complete Poetry, 1: 1960–1966] (1983). *Poesia completa*, 2: 1967–1982 [Complete Poetry, 2: 1967–1982] (1983).

Essays: [With Celia Metrass], *Aborto: Direito a nosso corpo* [Abortion: The Right to Our Bodies] (1975).

Novels/Short Stories: *Ambas as Mãos Sobre o Corpo* [Both Hands on the Body] (1970). [With Maria Isabel Barreno and Maria Belho da Costa]. *Novas Cartas Portuguesas* [New Portuguese Letters] (1972). *Ana* (1974). *Ema* (1985). *Minha Mae, Minha Amor* (1986).

Lina L. Cofresí

Hrotsvit of Gandersheim
ca. 935–ca. 973

Name rendered as Hrotsvit, Hrotsvita, Hrosvita, Hroswitha, Roswitha, Rotsuith
Born ca. 935, Saxony(?)
Died after 973, Gandersheim(?), Saxony
Genre(s): drama, narrative poetry (legends of saints, historical epic, verse chronicle)
Language(s): Latin

Hrotsvit, a canoness of the abbey of Gandersheim near Hildesheim in Saxony, composed medieval Latin verse in several genres. She is best known, however, as the author of six Latin plays on Christian themes, written in rhyming prose. Her unusual name, by her own witty testimony, signifies *Clamor Validus Gandeshemensis*: the Great Shout, or Loud Noise, of Gandersheim. She

lived in Saxony in the middle of the tenth century, in the convent founded by and for the family of the Holy Roman Emperor Otto the Great; the dates of her birth and death are uncertain and must be inferred from what she herself says in her writings. She was rather older than her friend, teacher, and abbess, the Ottonian princess Gerberga, who was born in 940; she lived at least until the accession of the Emperor Otto II in 973. She was most probably of noble blood and was known personally to the royal family, under whom the culture of Germany and of western Europe in general attained sufficient sophistication to have earned from modern historians the title of "Ottonian Renaissance." Hrotsvit, with her firm grounding in classical Latin learning and literature and her strongly Christian subject matter, stands forth as an important representative of her culture and her time. In the history of drama she is more important still: the first known dramatist of modern times and the first known woman dramatist of any time.

The works of Hrotsvit are contained chiefly in a manuscript, now at Munich, found in 1493 at the monastery of St. Emmeram by the German humanist Conrad Celtes. It consists of two books of verse and prose arranged apparently in order of composition, with a short verse "coda" plus an epic poem. Book I contains seven legends of saints written in Latin hexameters and based on the Bible and the Apocrypha, on the lives of the saints, and on contemporary reports, with a preface in rhyming prose by the author and a dedication to the Abbess Gerberga. Book II begins with a brief comment on the sources of the legends, followed by a second prose preface which sets forth Hrotsvit's purpose in writing her six plays. She writes, she professes, in response to a dismaying tendency among her coreligionists to immerse themselves in the pagan seductions of the Roman playwright, Terence; she undertakes to provide an antidote to Terence's six comedies of lascivious women with six edifying tales of Christian virgins. There follows a letter of dedication to certain unnamed patrons, and then the plays themselves, which, despite their Terentian form and inspiration, are based on hagiographical sources. Both the plays and the legends seem to have been put together according to a single overriding purpose, as a cycle of works on related themes: perpetual and triumphant virginity above all, and with it Christian heroism and the mercy and justice of God. The legends deal for the most part with the exploits of holy men, the plays avowedly with those of holy women. The latter were probably not performed in Hrotsvit's own time, unless perhaps in the form of dramatic readings; there is considerable debate as to whether Hrotsvit was in fact aware of the true nature of Roman drama. Hrotsvit's own plays are, however, highly performable, and have been performed successfully on the modern stage.

At the end of the final play, *Sapientia*, stand thirty-five Latin hexameters on the subject of the Apocalypse of John, followed by a third prose preface and a pair of verse prologues to the 1,500-odd lines of the *Gesta Ottonis*, "The Deeds of Otto the Great." This epic poem is, as Hrotsvit attests, the earliest comprehensive account of the first Saxon ruler to claim the throne and the title of Charlemagne.

In addition to the works collected in the St. Emmeram manuscript, Hrotsvit is also known to have composed a verse chronicle of the early years of her own monastery: *Primordia Coenobii Gandeshemensis*, "The Origins of the Convent at Gandersheim." The manuscript of the *Primordia* is no longer extant but must be reconstructed from early printed editions. The text itself is accepted by scholars as Hrotsvit's last known work; it refers to the fire which destroyed the abbey's church in 970 and to the reign of the Emperor Otto II (973–983).

Hrotsvit's position in the history of literature is assured by the simple fact of her having written plays. These plays are not, and are not intended to be, the equal of their Terentian models in style, substance, or literary excellence. They are, however, both witty and erudite, with a genuine gift for dialogue and drama. She is less gifted as a poet. Her *Primordia* is a fairly standard representative of its kind. Her legends are remarkable chiefly for the ways in which she chooses and adapts her sources. Her *Gesta Ottonis* is notable less for the virtuosity of its verse than for the fact that it is, and professes to be, an original composition based on the reports of eyewitnesses, as she had done earlier in composing the legend of St. Pelagius. This is the essence of Hrotsvit's not inconsiderable literary talent. She effectively reinvented classical drama in Christian form and substance at a time when the genre itself had ceased to exist. In the great age of reliance upon one's *auctores*, one's august predecessors, she made use of eyewitness accounts in original compositions. She was, moreover, a woman displaying a broad and conscious erudition in a patriarchal age: a fact of which she was very well aware, and which she expressed in the prefaces to her literary works with great and wicked wit, in the conventional phrases of Christian, and feminine, humility.

Works

Legends (ca. 962): *Historia nativitatis laudabilisque conversationis intactae Dei Genitricis (Maria)* [The History of the Nativity and the Praiseworthy Life of the Virgin Mother of God]. *De ascensione Domini (Ascensio)* [The Ascension of the Lord]. *Passio sancti Gongolfi martiris (Gongolfus)* [The Martyrdom of St. Gongolf]. *Passio sancti Pelagii pretiosissimi martiris qui nostris temporibus in Corduba martirio est coronatus (Pelagius)* [The Martyrdom of the Most Precious Pelagius, Who Received the Crown of Martyrdom in Cordoba in Our Own Time]. *Lapsus et conversio Theophili Vicedomini (Theophilus)* [The Fall and Redemption of the Viceroy Theophilus]. *Basilius* [Basil]. *Passio sancti Dionisii egregii Martiris (Dionysius)* [The Martyrdom of the Remarkable Saint Dionysius]. *Passio sanctae Agnetis virginis et martiris (Agnes)* [The Passion of St. Agnes, Virgin and Martyr].

Plays (ca. 967): *Conversio Gallicani principis militiae (Gallicanus)* [The Conversion of General Gallicanus]. *Passio sanctarum virginum Agapis Chioniae et Hirenae (Dulcitius)* [The Martyrdom of the Holy Virgins Agapes, Chionia, and Irene]. *Resuscitatio Drusianae et Calimachi (Calimachus)* [The Resurrection of Drusiana and Calimachus]. *Lapsus et conversio Mariae neptis Habrahae heremicolae (Abraham)* [The Fall and Redemption of Mary, Niece of the Hermit Abraham]. *Conversio Thaidis meretricis (Pafnutius)* [The Conversion of Thais the Courtesan]. *Passio sanctarum virginum Fidei Spei et Karitatis (Sapientia)* [The Martyrdom of the Holy Virgins Faith, Hope, and Charity]. *The Apocalypse of John Gesta Ottonis* [The Deeds of Otto the Great] (after 968). *Primordia coenobii Gandeshemensis* [The Origins of the Convent at Gandersheim] (after 973).

Judith Tarr

Lucy Apsley Hutchinson
1620–1675

Born January 29, 1620, London
Died after 1675
Genre(s): biography, autobiography, treatise
Language(s): English

Along with her contemporary, Margaret Cavendish, the Duchess of Newcastle, Hutchinson is one of the first significant women prose writers in English. She was born January 29, 1620 in the Tower of London, where her husband was later imprisoned in 1663. Her father, Sir Allen Apsley, was Lieutenant of the Tower at the time of her birth, and her mother, Lucy St. John, was Apsley's third wife. They had ten children; Hutchinson was the fourth, following three boys.

Though she is best known for her biography of her husband, the *Memoirs of the Life of Colonel Hutchinson*, her most interesting extant piece is an autobiographical fragment: *The Life of Mrs. Hutchinson Written by Herself.* This work gives a rare inside glimpse into the lives of upper-class young women in the early seventeenth century. It opens with a grim prefiguration of what was to be the central historical event in the lives of her and her husband—the English Civil War: "The land was then at peace [at the time of her birth] . . . if that quietness may be called a peace, which was rather like the calm and smooth surface of the sea, whose dark tomb is already impregnated with a horrid tempest." This statement is a fairly typical example of Hutchinson's style, which, despite her Puritan inclinations, retained a Latinate sophistication, derived no doubt from the strong classical training she received as a child.

That education, very unusual for a woman at that time, she received partly because she was very precocious and partly because her mother doted on her. Having had three sons, her mother "received me with a great deal of joy" and learning that the child might not live "became fonder of me." She was taught French and English simultaneously by a French "day-nurse" and could read English by the age of four. She had an excellent memory and recited sermons verbatim, much to the delight of the adults. By the age of seven she had eight tutors in such fields as languages, music, dancing, writing, and needlework, but her bent was already toward serious reading. Her mother feared that her zeal for studies would "prejudice" her health, but even during periods of prescribed play, "I would steal into some hole or other to read." In Latin she "outstripped" her brothers who were at school, even though her tutor was a "pitiful dull fellow." "Play among other children I despised," and she neglected the traditional feminine accomplishments: "and for my needle I absolutely hated it."

Hutchinson's mother met her father when he was forty-eight and she was sixteen. After their marriage they lived in the Tower, where Mrs. Apsley became active in caring for prisoners. She funded "experiments" in "chemistry" done by Sir Walter Raleigh (then in prison) and others, "Partly to comfort and divert the poor prisoners, and partly to gain the knowledge of their experiments, and the medicines to help such poor people as were not able to seek physicians. By these means she acquired a great deal of skill." She evidently taught some of her medicinal knowledge to her daughter, who ministered to the enemy wounded during the Civil War despite criticism by one of her husband's fellow officers. Hutchinson's sympathy for the poor and disabled was clearly a factor in her support of the Puritan cause. In the *Memoirs* she notes with enthusiasm how under the Republic her husband, as a member of the Council of State (from 1649 to 1651), was able to take "such courses that there was very suddenly not a beggar left in the country, and all the poor [were] in every town so maintained and provided for, as they were never so liberally . . . before nor since."

The interest in the *Memoirs of the Life of Colonel Hutchinson* lies in the anecdotes that illuminate the social life of the time as well as the character of the actors in the drama she unfolds. For example, we learn that on the day of her engagement she came down with smallpox. Despite the fact that "all that saw her were affrighted," her fiancé stood by her, the marriage took place, and "God recompensed his justice and constancy by restoring her . . . as well as before."

Much of the *Memoirs,* however, is a rather dry exposition of the events of the Civil War in which her husband was personally involved, such as the defense of Nottingham against the royalists, a strategic battle which preserved the north–south passage for the forces of parliament. Hutchinson clearly sees herself as writing military history and rejects temptations to elaborate romantic episodes. The work was written in the third person, ostensibly to recount her husband's life to her children and not intended for publication. She proposed that "a naked, undressed narrative speaking the simple truth of him, will deck him with more substantial glory, than all the panegyrics [of] the best pens." However, the weakness in the work lies in its relentless enthusiasm for her husband's improbably impeccable character. As a follower of Cromwell, Colonel Hutchinson was out of favor during the Restoration and in 1663 was arrested; he died in prison eleven months later. Hutchinson wrote the *Memoirs* shortly thereafter, probably between 1664 and 1671. It was not published until 1806, but thereafter reprinted several times, remaining one of the most popular of the Civil War memoirs.

Its author herself lived into the late 1670s, having presented a translation of Lucretius's *De Rerum Natura* in 1675, which had been written much earlier. The dedication to that work is largely a recantation of having committed "the sin of amusing myself with such vain philosophy" as Epicureanism. She asserts, however, that she did the translation only as a diversion: "I did not employ any serious study . . . for

I turned it into English in a room where my children practised . . . with their tutors, and I numbered the syllables of my translation by the threads of the canvas I wrought in"—a further glimpse into the early milieu of the woman writer. She also completed a partial translation of the *Aeneid* and wrote two treatises on religion: *On the Principles of Christian Religion*, written for her daughter, and *On Theology*, which were published in 1817. An earlier manuscript narrative of the events of her husband's life remains in the British Museum and some additional writings on moral and religious subjects were still privately owned in the early 1900s.

Works

Memoirs of the Life of Colonel Hutchinson (1806). *The Life of Mrs. Hutchinson Written by Herself* (1806). *On the Principles of the Christian Religion; Addressed to Her Daughter;* and *On Theology* (1817).

Josephine Donovan

Fotini Ikonomidou
1856–1883
a.k.a. Fimonoï, Honolulu
Born 1856, Athens, Greece
Died 1883, Athens
Genre(s): poetry
Language(s): Greek

Fotini Ikonomidou was born in 1856, in a well-to-do family of Athenian merchants and intellectuals. She received the modest education accorded to middle-class young girls of her time—a few years in a ladies' seminar. She had the opportunity, however, to complete her education by herself, reading books from her father's imposing library and listening, behind the doors, to the everyday literary and political debates that were taking place in the salon of her uncle, a university professor. She secretly started to write poetry at the age of thirteen and stuck to it, in spite of the severe objections raised by her family. Before she was twenty years old, her parents lost their fortune and died a little later; she therefore had to live in the dependent and humiliating condition of an unmarried relative in her guardian's house, facing the scorn of a society that abhorred female celibacy as much as "blue stockings."

As we learn from her writings, poetry was her only consolation, her entire *raison d'être*. Ikonomidou grew up during a period in which romanticism dominated the Greek literature and shaped the poetic vision of her generation. She was deeply marked by its atmosphere of extreme pessimism, morbidity, and desperate desire for escape, which fitted only too well her own perception of life as a woman. Her poetry is haunted by metaphors of slavery and confinement, by images of "cages," "prisons," and "chains" in which is caught the subjectivity of what she calls the "female being." Despite the rigidity of her verse and her rhetoric style, Ikonomidou is one of the most important representatives of the first generation of Greek women poets who, writing in the first person, expressed the impossibility of making their lives and feelings conform to the dominant models of femininity. Her writings suggest a desperate quest for an autonomous female identity, through the exploration of her own "unsatisfied longings" and "impudent aspirations."

Although Ikonomidou did not have the opportunity to publish a book, she was a permanent contributor to some of the most influential literary publications of her time as *Parnassos* (Parnassus), *Attikon Imerologuion* (Attic Almanac), *Vyron* (Byron), and *Pikili Stoa* (Miscellaneous Porticum). She was respected by many of her contemporary poets and critics such as Kostis Palamas who considered her verse "original, of high artistic quality and powerful expression" and who wrote a moving obituary on her death, in 1886.

Works
"Sfallo?" [Am I to Blame?]. *Vyron* II (1876). "Is tin eftyhian" [To Happiness]. *Vyron*, II (1876). "Matin" [In Vain]. *Pikili Stoa*, third year (1883). "Thiati?" [Why?]. *Pikili Stoa*, fourth year (1884).

Eleni Varikas

Elizabeth Simpson Inchbald
1753–1821
Born October 15, 1753, Stanningfield, Suffolk, England
Died August 1, 1821, Kensington
Genre(s): drama, novel
Language(s): English

Elizabeth was the eighth child in a family of nine. She ran away from home at nineteen to seek her fortune

Elizabeth Simpson Inchbald

on the London stage. As a beautiful woman with a pronounced stammer, she faced formidable obstacles in her aspirations. The stammer she could control when delivering carefully rehearsed lines, but her beauty caused difficulties of another kind, for it marked her as prey to such unscrupulous actors as James Dodd, who attempted to molest her when she applied to him for help.

The experience of independence was so thoroughly frightening that, three months after her arrival, she accepted the proposal of Joseph Inchbald, whom she had earlier rejected. Seventeen years her senior, Joseph provided her the security of marriage with a fellow Roman Catholic as well as automatic access to the stage. Ironically, or perhaps intentionally, Elizabeth's Bristol debut as Cordelia to Joseph's Lear capitalized on their age difference, and this was a role she was to repeat many times. For the first four years of their marriage, she served an apprenticeship in the regional theaters of England and Scotland, but finally, in July 1776, Joseph having quarreled with the Edinburgh audience, they moved to Paris, where he tried to earn a living by his avocation, painting, and she tried writing comedies, only to return to Brighton in September.

It was at this low period that the Inchbalds befriended Sarah Siddons and her brother, John Philip Kemble, and Elizabeth fell in love with Kemble, but she never remarried after her husband's death in June 1779.

One of Elizabeth Inchbald's earliest known literary efforts was an outline of *A Simple Story,* which she circulated among friends in 1777. By 1779, she had completed the first version of the novel, which she offered for publication several times over the next ten years. Meanwhile, she began to succeed in her dramatic writing, earning 100 guineas from the sale of her first play, *The Mogul,* which played ten days at the Haymarket in 1784. After this first play, inspired by the French craze for ballooning, she received consistently high fees for her subsequent plays, most of which were produced and printed. Inchbald's humanitarian interests are revealed in her most successful plays. Under the guise of a light summer comedy, *I'll Tell You What* (1786) raised questions about marriage and divorce. *Such Things Are* (1788), which brought £900, probed social issues by portraying, in the character Haswell, the prison reformer John Howard. Today her best-known play may be *Lover's Vows,* a rendering of a Kotzebue play that scandalizes Fanny Price in *Mansfield Park.*

Although her first gainful writing was for the theater, Inchbald is better known for her novels, *A Simple Story* (1791) and *Nature and Art* (1796). When she failed to locate a publisher for her early version of *A Simple Story,* she began a second novel in 1779, yet it was not until she combined the stories ten years later that she succeeded in selling the book to a publisher for £200. *A Simple Story,* well-received by the public, praised for its realism and its dramatic qualities, may be read autobiographically, the Dorriforth–Miss Milner relationship reminiscent of Inchbald's infatuation with Kemble (another Catholic who studied for the priesthood).

As a Catholic, Inchbald intentionally subverted the usual vilification of her religion by depicting a sympathetic priest whose tender and virtuous relationship with his ward ripens into love. Dorriforth is torn between his "prospect of futurity" in heaven and his recognition of his ward's failings on the one hand and his earthly love for Miss Milner and his desire to reform her on the other. The struggle is resolved when he inherits an earldom and, forgiven his priestly vows, is encouraged to marry as a family duty. But in the second part of the novel (set some 16 years later) Dorriforth's first instincts are proven correct, when his wife, still bent on testing the extent of his tolerance, slips into an affair in his absence. Although she dies shortly thereafter with a deathbed repentance, Dorriforth's unyielding morality continues to prosecute the sins of the mother in their daughter until the shock of her near abduction effects a reconciliation.

Nature and Art, frankly revolutionary in tone, is less psychologically acute and thought less successful now, though Inchbald's contemporaries praised it highly. The story begins with two brothers who make their way after their father's death. Henry, a fiddler, supports William until the latter has risen to a deanship; the resentment he receives in return prompts him to leave England for Africa. Later, Henry's "naturally" educated son returns to live under his uncle's protection in England and there meets his cousin, William, whose "artificial" education has molded him in the image of his own calculating father. The opposition between the two persists as William seduces a virtuous woman and later (as judge) sentences her for the prostitution he forced on her, and Henry first delivers his father from his African exile and then marries his faithful Rebecca.

Inchbald continued writing for the London stage until 1805, her last play being the comedy *To Marry, or Not to Marry* (1805). In the fall of that year, she turned to editorial work, writing a series of 125 biographical and critical prefaces for *The British Theatre* (1806–1808), a twenty-five volume collection published by Longman. She then selected plays for a seven-volume *Collection of Farces* (1809) and a ten-volume *The Modern Theatre* (1811). She also wrote articles and reviews for the *Edinburgh Review* and the *Artist* declining other offers to write for the *Quarterly Review* and to edit *La Belle Assemblee*. She lived the last two years of her life in Kensington House, a Roman Catholic residence for ladies, dying there on August 1, 1821.

Self-tutored and remarkably successful, Inchbald achieved an unusual degree of recognition for a professional woman writer of her period. She was an active playwright for more than twenty years, earning the respect of Richard Brinsley Sheridan, who commissioned *The Wedding Day* (1794). Her first novel, *A Simple Story*, praised by her contemporaries, has continued to be reissued since its publication.

Works

Appearance Is Against Them (1785). *I'll Tell You What* (1786). *The Widow's Vow* (1786). *Such Things Are* (1788). *The Mogul Tale* (1788). *Animal Magnetism* (1788). *A Simple Story* (1791). *The Massacre* (1792). *Everyone Has His Fault* (1793). *The Wedding Day* (1794). *Nature and Art* (1796). *Wives as They Were, and Maids as They Are* (1797). *To Marry, or Not to Marry* (1805).

Catherine S. Green

Luce Irigaray
1932–

Born 1932, Blaton, Belgium
Genre(s): nonfiction, feminist theory
Language(s): French

Luce Irigaray is a psychoanalyst and philosopher and a member of the Freudian school of Paris, founded by Jacques Lacan. She taught at Vincennes, Department of Psychoanalysis, from its founding after the student riots in Paris in 1968, to 1974, when her seminar was cancelled shortly after the publication of her doctoral thesis in philosophy, *Speculum de l'autre femme* (Speculum of the Other Woman). The circumstances surrounding Irigaray's dismissal from Vincennes remain obscure.

The central concern of Irigaray's work is woman's desire and woman's language. Her first book, *Le langage des déments* (1973), discusses the relationship of demented people to language, which, according of Irigaray, is similar to that of women. Both women and the demented are most frequently passive objects of discourse, spoken about rather than speakers in their own right. In *Speculum de l'autre femme* Irigaray states that female sexuality has remained the "dark continent" of psychoanalysis. Through a rereading of texts from Plato to Freud, she concludes that patriarchal discourse has castrated women, excluded them from language and history, and turned them into victims of incredible distortion. Her chief argument is against Freud, whose statements on femininity reveal the misogynist bias of the father of psychoanalysis.

In *Ce sexe qui n'en est pas un* (This Sex Which Is Not One), Irigaray compares herself to Alice in Lewis Carroll's novel, looking at the world from the other side of the mirror. The reverse side of the mirror is analogous to female desire, which according to Irigaray, is absent from the traditional scene of representation. How do we speak about that other side? How do we invent a language to express female sexuality in a way that escapes the old phallic distortions? The title of the book has a double meaning. First of all, it is a statement that female desire does not exist within patriarchal culture; second, it expresses Irigaray's hypothesis that female desire is not centered, but multiple. Female pleasure is, according to Irigaray, spread out to various parts of the body unlike male pleasure, which is centered in the phallus. This multiple sexuality is analogous to women's language, which lacks the focusing logic of male discourse. Instead, women express themselves in a fluid, tentative manner that escapes exact definition and closure.

In *Parler n'est jamais neutre* (1985), Irigaray once again returns to the language of schizophrenics, hysterics, and other marginal persons in an attempt to determine the unconscious or preconscious schemas of an individual's discourse. She concludes that language is never neutral or universal. It is always influenced by gender, history, social situation, and so on, and meaning is created on the basis of these differences. To deny differences would annul meaning. Irigaray's feminism is utopian, based on a faith in female bonding. The brief, poetic text, *Et l'une ne bouge pas sans l'autre* (1979) evokes the relationship between mother and daughter, and at the conclusion of each of her major works (*Speculum de l'autre femme*, *Ce sexe qui n'en est pas un*, and *Parler n'est jamais neutre*), Irigaray reiterates her regret for the rupture between mother and child, which feminists frequently see as the basis for the triumph of patriarchy and the exclusion of women from culture. For the balance to be restored, women must reconnect with each other to reject the sexless roles they have been assigned by the fathers, defend their own desire, and finally claim a place for it on the stage of representation.

Works

Le langage des déments (1973). *Speculum, de l'autre femme* [Speculum of the Other Woman] (1974). *Ce sexe, qui n'en est pas un* [This Sex Which Is Not One] (1977). *Et l'une ne bouge pas sans l'autre* (1979). *Amante Marine. De Friedrich Nietzsche* (1980). *Le corps-à-corps avec la mère* (1981). *Passions élémentaires* (1982). *L'oubli de l'air. Chez Martin Heidegger* (1983). *La croyance même* (1983). *L'éthique de la différence sexuelle* (1984). *Parler n'est jamais neutre* (1985). *Sexes et parentes* (1987). *Je, Tu, Nous* (1990). *J'aime a toi* (1992). *Genres culturels et interculturels* (1993).

Translations: Speculum of the Other Woman, tr. Gillian C. Gill (1985). This Sex Which Is Not One, tr. Catherine Porter and Carolyn Burke (1985). *Marine Lover of Friedrich Nietzsche* (1991). *Elemental Passions* (1992). *Sexes and Genealogies* (1992). *An Ethics of Sexual Difference* (1993). *I Love to You: Sketch of a Possible Felicity in History* (1994). *Thinking the Difference: For a Peaceful Revolution* (1994).

Randi Birn

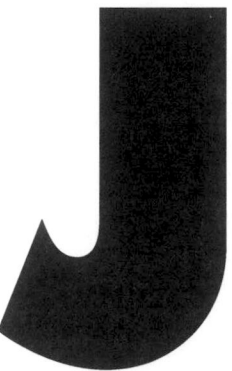

Vidmantė Jasukaitytė
1948–

Born 1948, Lithuania
Genre(s): poetry, novel
Language(s): Lithuanian

Vidmantė Jasukaitytė reaches far beyond customary socialist realism long imposed by the Soviet regime. Her first novel is a unique phenomenon in Lithuanian letters, somewhat akin to Juozas Baltušis' *Sakmé apie Juźća*; it shows affinities with Latin-American novels of magic realism but surpasses them in lyrical intensity.

She made her debut as poet but achieved fame principally with her extraordinary novel. From the very first book of verse she creates half real–half mythical worlds that later give a touch of magic to her novel. There are also allusions to the unbreakable chain of women of various generations who, like the ancient vestals, guard the eternal fire (here, the fire of femininity endowed with a sacral power). She prefers loose rhythms, abandonment, or innovative variations of rhyme, almost prosaic sequences with hardly any melody. The poetry arises from unusual imagery, superposition of temporal levels, and a deep, all-encompassing emotional note. Her poems are fragmented; there is no subject, just a series of instantaneous reactions from within combining heterogeneous elements.

Stebuklinga patvorių 'olė (1981; The Miraculous Grass along the Fences), has a tight overall structure that enhances the effects of each part. Many lyrical passages combine with a fantastic note while portraying the history of six generations of Lithuanian women. This gives the book a certain epic quality: the action of the three parts is set in periods of fight for Lithuania's independence. At the same time, it represents the emerging consciousness and independence of Lithuanian women by reaffirming their inner strength.

The novel consists of three "ballads" (this points to the musical quality and to its reliance on folklore). Each "ballad" tells the life story of a woman: the first goes back to 1863; the last reaches contemporary times. The three are united by their experience of two-fold love: one elected by the heart, the other one imposed by circumstances. It is the first one which gives almost magic power to the woman. Externally, each woman succumbs to her destiny. Internally, each develops a power of resistance that allows her to strike an affirmative note and sing a song of praise. While the details of married life are referred to in matter-of-fact prose and related to history, the secret love inspires intensely lyrical passages and leads to visions. The last part adds yet another dimension: metafiction. Thus the experience of loving in the three women becomes the experience of writing: recording the legendary message carried through a century.

In *Stebuklinga patvorių 'olė*, Jasukaitytė does not adopt a militant feminist stance. On the contrary: she shows that it is possible to retain traditional feminine qualities without feeling defenseless or submissive. Woman's task is seen here as one of taming words and endowing them with the power of incantation in order to create new myths and legends. These, in turn, affirm woman's magic gifts: she is able to communicate with the dead souls of her ancestors, see in the dead of night, hear words spoken miles away. Jasukaitytė's style shows many characteristic traits of feminine writing: cyclical time, litany-like repetitions, great fluidity, symbols of water and birds, lyrical introspective passages going back to the childhood of each protagonist, the oral aspect of discourse. With this novel Jasukaitytė has created one of the most original novels written in the last decade in Europe.

Works

Ugnis, kurią reika pereiti [Fire That Must Be Crossed] (1976). *Taip toli esu* [I Am So Far] (1979). *Stebuklinga patvorių 'olė* (1981). *Mano broli 'mogau* [Man, My Brother] (1982). "Balandė, kuri lauks." *Nemunas* 12 (1989).

Birutė Ciplijauskaitė

Ruth Prawer Jhabvala
1927–
Born May 7, 1927, Cologne, Germany
Genre(s): novel, filmscript, short story
Language(s): English

Jhabvala has lived major portions of her life in four countries. Born in Cologne, Germany, in 1927 to a Polish Jewish lawyer and his German Jewish wife, she fled from Germany to England in 1939 with her parents and brother. In 1951, after graduating from the University of London with an M.A. in English literature, she married Cyrus Jhabvala, an Indian architect, and moved with him to Delhi, India. There the Jhabvalas raised three daughhers. For both professional and personal reasons and with her husband's encouragement, Jhabvala left India in 1975 and moved to the United States.

The personal reasons that caused her to leave are presented in a powerful essay, reprinted as the introduction to *An Experience of India* (1971). Essentially India, so exhilarating at first, had become oppressive. She uses the image "living on the back of an animal" to represent her irritation at India's extreme and inescapable poverty and her inability either to affect or to overlook it.

Jhabvala chose New York because its pressures and variety somehow drew together for her the experiences of the Europe of her youth and the India of her adulthood. She also chose it because it was the home of her cinematic collaborators, James Ivory and Ismail Merchant. Ivory, an American director, and Merchant, an Indian producer, had come to India in 1961 to ask her to write the filmscript for her novel, *The Householder*. Since that time the team has produced fourteen films, including two based on Jhabvala's novels. Merchant, Ivory, and Jhabvala are personal friends as well as colleagues, all living in the same apartment house. Her recent story, "Grandmother," and novel, *In Search of Love and Beauty* (1983), explore this friendship.

To date, Jhabvala's writings on India still constitute the main body of her work. Of her novels, only the most recent, *In Search of Love and Beauty* (1983),

does not have an Indian setting. In India, she is often considered with others writing about India in English, such as Kamala Markandaya. Indian reviews are not always favorable, finding her writing able but unsympathetic.

In fact, Jhabvala's earliest novels, *Amrita* (1955) and *The Nature of Passion* (1956), while comic and satiric, present Indian life with considerable delight. However, the mood of *Esmond in India* (1958), her third novel, is darker. In it, a pretty, naive Indian heroine, much like her counterparts in the earlier novels, feels modern enough to make her own matrimonial choices. But her story, unlike theirs, does not close happily: at novel's end she is left pursuing a damaging affair with Esmond, a selfish Englishman already married to an Indian woman who had made a similar choice.

The bitterness of *Esmond* lies less in the Indian life depicted than in the effects of the intersection of Indian and Western ways. The next novel, *The Householder* (1960), returns to more purely Indian life. There Western figures appear but only as exotic yet finally irrelevant interlopers. Her last novel concerned mainly with Indian family life and told from an Indian point of view is *Get Ready for Battle* (1962). In mood it is closer to the first novels than to *Esmond*.

The next three novels, *A Backward Place* (1965), *Travelers* (1973), and *Heat and Dust* (1975), reflect Jhabvala's declaration in *An Experience of India* that she is no longer interested in India but in herself (as symbolic of the westerner) in India. The central characters in these novels are Westerners who have come to India for varied reasons. Judy, of *A Backward Place*, is an English girl married to an Indian actor. Because she has come without an agenda—neither to find herself as Lee of *Travelers* wishes to do, nor to have India give up its secrets, as the central character of *Heat and Dust* wants—Judy remains healthy and becomes more assimilated into India than any of the other Westerners. Yet Judy, Jhabvala suggests, is not a complicated girl, and other Westerners because of their natures are more likely to become trapped by India's sensuality or its mystical religions (as do Lee and the narrator of *Heat and Dust*). Or they may be unable to leave their Western background behind enough to enter into Indian life. The true meeting of East and West, Jhabvala's fiction suggests, is a rarity, and the path to that meeting is fraught with danger to travelers in either direction.

Most recently, Jhabvala has been writing more filmscripts than fiction, a kind of writing that she reports to be less taxing. Writing for films has influenced her novels. The later books tend to be written in distinct scenes with sharp cuts between people and places; a similar change has taken place in her short fiction. Her later work, then, seems more modern than her earlier work, but it is also colder and more distancing, perhaps reflecting her increasing sense of her own rootlessness.

Works

To Whom She Will (1955; published in the United States as *Amrita). The Nature of Passion* (1956). *Esmond in India* (1958). *The Householder* (1960; as filmscript, 1963). *Get Ready for Battle* (1962). *Like Birds, Like Fishes* (1964). *A Backward Place* (1965). *Shakespeare Wallah* (1965). *A Stronger Climate* (1968). *The Guru* (1969). *Bombay Talkie* (1970). *An Experience of India* (1971). *A New Dominion* (1973; published in the United States as *Travelers). Heat and Dust* (1975; as filmscript, 1983). *Autobiography of a Princess* (1975). *How I Became a Holy Mother and Other Stories* (1976). *Roseland* (1977). *Hullabaloo over Georgie and Bonnie's Pictures* (1978). *The Europeans* (1979). *Jane Austen in Manhattan* (1980). *Quartet* (1981). *In Search of Love and Beauty* (1983). *A Room with a View* (1985). *Three Continents* (1987). *Out of India: Selected Stories* (1987). *Shards of Memory* (1995).

Ellen Laun

Ragnhild Jølsen
1875–1908

Born 1875, Enebakk, Norway
Died 1908, Oslo
Genre(s): novel
Language(s): Norwegian

The period from 1890 up to 1910 represents a transition from new romanticism and symbolism to new realism in Norwegian literature. To this period Ragnhild Jølsen contributes a distinct but troubled voice. Her use of legends, tales, archaic linguistic forms combined with brilliant in-depth studies of female sexuality, in particular, stand unparalleled in Norwegian literary history.

Jølsen was born into an old, wealthy landowner family in an isolated, densely forested farm district southeast of Christiania (later Oslo). The youngest of five children she received what at the time must have been a highly unconventional female upbringing, one free of the socially expected female passivity, obedi-

ence, and demand for self-obliteration and self-sacrifice. The close proximity to nature, with its large, deep woods, its solitude and "endlessness," gave her a sense of freedom that contrasted sharply with the petit-bourgeois way of life she came to know upon the family's move to the capital. The move came as the result of financial mismanagement, which some years later led to the bankruptcy of the entire estate.

In Christiania, Jølsen entered high school. It soon became evident that she did not care for school learning, rather, she pursued other far more fascinating aspects of life in the city. Especially, the bohemian late-night life in the many city cafés attracted her. There she made acquaintances among the intellectual and artist "rebels," and in a few instances, she became sexually involved. Her behavior, which involved drugs and drinking, scandalized her family and ruined her "good name." In spite of the stir she created, Jølsen insisted on living life her way. A great beauty, she never married. At the age of thirty-three, she died from an overdose of veronal.

While in Christiania, Jølsen worked short periods as a telegraph operator and a governess. When her family returned to the estate, in a futile attempt to save what was left, she went with them. She was twenty-one.

At home, in Enebakk, Jølsen began to collect oral stories, folktales, proverbs, and songs. She had always been interested in history, especially, the Middle Ages. History subsequently became an important source of inspiration for her writing. She started to write in earnest, and with the approval of her parents she made her debut with the novel *Ve's mor* (1903). It was favorably reviewed in the daily press. Her talent was recognized and encouraged by other writers. Her description of female sexuality and female/male relationships and desire, however, surprised and shocked critics as well as readers. In her later writing Jølsen, again and again, returned to exploring female psychological development, to women's conflict-filled visions of love, and to their ill-fated experiences in "real life." These are the major themes in *Rikka Gan* (1905), and *Fernanda Mona* (1905).

Her works can perhaps be seen as thematically centered around a strong protest against the conventions that shaped and circumscribed women's lives. She wrote critically of the role religion and church exerted on women's attempts at self-development. She also wrote fiercely against the pervasive fear of sex. In Enebakk, far from her life in Christiania and the illusion of freedom she had experienced there, she had come to view the Norwegian society as an inhibitively patriarchal one.

The individual characters in her works are first and foremost seen in terms of their relationship to the family, past and present. The fate of the individual woman and man is inextricably woven together with that of the family. The attempt to separate oneself, to create a life on one's own, always fails and eventually leads to death. In her portraits of women and men, Jølsen is guided by a firm belief in nineteenth-century notions of determinism and power of sexual instincts. It is especially women who represent ancestral heritage in her writing and who are always solitary figures, hypersensitively connected to nature, never able to cross over to the larger human collective. Openly sensual, dreaming, and erotic, they fall in love with men who are capable of satisfying their sexual needs. But their love-ideal collides not only with the norms but also with itself; the men they love (physically) are not the men they can respect. Jølsen's female figures exist in the border areas between dream and reality. Their lives are marked by broken illusions. They are torn between responsible, loyal husbands, and attractive, somewhat demonic, but in the end weak, lovers.

Jølsen constructs her narratives in strong images and scenes, built around tension-filled and climactic moments, which is part of the aesthetics of the period. In Jølsen's case one may speak of a literary *Jugendstil*. Her language is apostrophic, stylized, archaic (fairy tales, ballads, legends). Motifs and milieux may resemble those of Selma Lagerlöf, as in the case of *Hollases Krønike* (1906). Imagery, in general, is characterized by an extensive use of animal and fire symbolism. In *Brugshistorier* (1907), her last work, each of the short stories are characterized by a clear, realist style, full of humor, with none of the melancholy, the grotesque, and the mysticism, which are present in her other works.

Works

Ve's mor (1903). *Rikka Gan* (1905). *Fernanda Mona* (1905). *Hollases Krønike* (1906). *Brugshistorier* (1907). *Samlede skrifter*, B. 1–3. (1909). *Efterladte arbeider*, ed. Antonie Tiberg (1980).

Translations: "Fiddlemusic in the Meadow," "Twelfth man in the Cabin," in An *Everyday Story: Norwegian Women's Fiction*, ed. Katherine Hanson (Seattle, 1984).

Pål Bjørby

Julian of Norwich
1343–ca. 1416
Born 1343, England
Died after 1416
Genre(s): mystical treatise
Language(s): English

One of the outstanding theological and mystical writers of the church, Julian of Norwich composed two versions of her book in 16 chapters (or showings), *Revelations of Divine Love*. The first version was probably written shortly after she experienced her 16 visions, and the longer text some 20 years later.

She evidences familiarity with mystical texts both from England and the Continent as well as a thorough knowledge of the Vulgate and of the writings of St. Gregory and St. Augustine. She was also recognized for her talents at spiritual counseling, as is evident from Margery Kempe's account of their meeting. Well-educated, erudite, and blessed with remarkable intellectual skills, Julian not only recorded but also interpreted her visions. Unlike the bourgeois (and uneducated) Margery Kempe, whose revelations are nonanalytic, Julian explained her mystical experiences in clear theological terms.

Like most medieval mystics, Julian strove for the perfect union through love with the Godhead.

Concerned with the spiritual welfare of her readers and intent upon sharing her message of hope, she emphasized the limitless nature of divine love and compassion by contemplating the motherhood of God. "God as Mother," or rather, Christ, the creative force of the Trinity, the *natura creatrix*, is eulogized by Julian as the ultimate (because tender and self-sacrificing in love) embodiment of true love:

The Mother may tenderly lay her child to her breast, but our Mother, Jesus, may familiarly lead us into His blessed breast by His Sweet open side. . . . This fair and lovely word, Mother, is so sweet and so kind in itself that it may not truly be said of anyone but Him and Him Who is the very life of all things. To the property of motherhood belong nature, love, wisdom, and understanding and it is God.

Julian has earned an eminent and well-deserved place in the history of Roman Catholic mysticism; in her we have a visionary of remarkable literary and imaginative powers and a compassionate, fascinatingly complex human being. Her spirituality is essentially optimistic; her message is one of hope in divine benevolence; her revelations are theologically and analytically sound, and her style is memorable.

Works

Colledge, E., and J. Walsh, eds. *A Book of Showings to the Anchoress Julian of Norwich* (1978). Glasscoe, M., ed. *Revelations of Divine Love.* (1976). Reynolds, S.A., ed. *A Shewing of God's Love: The Shorter Version of Sixteen Revelations by Julian of Norwich* (1958). Walsh, J., ed. *The Revelations of Divine Love.* (1961). Walters, C., ed. *Revelations of Divine Love* (1966).

Katharina M. Wilson

Aino Kallas
1878–1956
Born 1878, Finland
Died 1956, Estonia
Genre(s): novel, short story, diary
Language(s): Finnish

Aino Kallas was the daughter of a distinguished Finnish family. Her father, Julius Krohn, was one of the prime movers of the mid-century national movement, the man who set in motion the scholarly collection and study of Finnish oral tradition. At the age of twenty-two, she married Oskar Kallas, one of Estonia's leading folklorists.

With her marriage to Oskar Kallas she shifted from the center of the Finnish national movement to the center of the emerging Estonian national movement. Although Aino Kallas had already begun to write before her marriage, she only became fully aware of her literary calling after she had settled in Estonia. In her choice of themes and style and almost certainly in her purpose, however, she differed markedly from her own generation of Finnish writers. Her themes sprang largely from her commitment to the Estonian national movement. Although she wrote in Finnish for Finns, her writings were translated immediately into Estonian by Friedebert Tuglas, himself an outstanding author. Works such as *Meren takaa* (1904; From Beyond the Sea) and *Lähtevien laivojen kaupunki* (1913; The Town of the Departing Ships) have been characterized by one critic as "indignation realism," an attempt to evoke the centuries of suffering endured by the Estonians at the hands of the Baltic-German overlords. A selection of short stories from this period appeared in English in 1924 under the title *The White Ship* and won considerable critical acclaim.

In 1922 Oskar Kallas was entrusted with the diplomatic representation in London and the Hague. Aino Kallas described her move to London as a "leap into the ocean." Despite her close connections with literary circles in London, it is, however, difficult to detect any direct influence on her writings from this period. The seeds of inspiration continued to come from the Estonian past. During this period Aino Kallas wrote four of her most profound works, a series of novellas: *Barbara von Tisenhusen*, *Reigin pappi* (The Rector of Reigi), *Sudenmorsian* (The Wolf's Bride), and *Pyhän joen kosto* (The Revenge of the Holy River). Like her earlier stories, these are set in historical Estonia and are rich in detail; the sense of history is also heightened by the deliberate use of archaic language and often by a chronicle style. If her earlier works were historical narratives, these are historical ballads, into which the author projects her own often difficult and strained inner life, both real and imagined.

The most personal and symbolic of these stories is *The Wolf's Bride*. In this and other stories Kallas's characters wander dreamlike through life until they experience, suddenly and by accident, almost as if bewitched, a strange event. It brings the character a moment of great bliss but at the same time destroys. In the 1920s and the 1930s these works were received with enthusiastic acclaim in Finland, Estonia, and Great Britain.

Aino Kallas is one of the best-known Finnish writers outside her own country. Her books were enjoyed as masterly historical accounts of forbidden love, and they retain their attraction at this level: the very timelessness of her theme explains their continuing popularity both in Finnish and in translation. It was the appearance of the first edition of her diaries, however, that prepared the way for the appraisal of her work that is still in hand.

Works
Lauluja ja balladeja [Song and Ballads] (1897). *Kuloa ja kevättä* [Forest Fire and Spring] (1899). *Kirsti*

(1902). *Meren takaa I* [From Beyond the Sea, I] (1904). *Ants Raudjalg* (1907). *Virolaisia kansansatuja* [Estonian Folk Tales] (1910). *Merentakaisia lauluja* [Songs from Beyond the Sea] (1911). *Lähtevien laivojen kaupunki* [The Town of the Departing Ships] (1913). *Seitsemän* [Seven] (1914). *Suljettu puutarha* [The Closed Garden] (1915). *Tähdenlento* [Falling Star] (1915). *Nuori Viro* [Young Estonia] (1918). *Musta raita* [Black Stripe] (1919). *Katinka Rabe* (1920). *Vieras veri* [Strange Blood] (1921). *Barbara von Tisenhusen* (1923). *Reigin pappi* [The Rector of Reigi] (1926). *Langatonta sähkö* [Wireless Electricity] (1928). *Sudenmorsian* [The Wolf's Bride] (1928). *Novelleja* [Choice of Novellas] (1928). *Pyhän joen kosto* [The Revenge of the Holy River] (1930). *Marokon lumoissa* [Enchanted by Morocco] (1931). *Batseba Saarenmaalla* [Bath-Sheba of Saarenmaa] (1932). *Mare ja hänen poikansa* [Mare and Her Sons] (1935). *Talonpojan kunnia* [The Honor of the Peasant] (1936). *Valitut teokset I–III* [Selected Works I–III] (1938). *Kuoleman joutsen* [Swan of Death] (1942). *Kuun silta* [The Moon Bridge] (1943). *Löytöretkillä Lontoossa* [Exploring in London] (1944). *Polttoroviolla* [At the Funeral Pile] (1945). *Mallen tunnustukset* [Malle's Confession] (1945). *Kanssavaeltajia ja ohikulkijoita* [Fellow Travellers and Passers-by] (1946). *Uusia kanssavaeltajia ja ohikulkijoita* [New Fellow Travellers and Passers-by] (1946). *Kolmas saattue* [The Third Procession] (1947). *Seitsemän neitsyttä* [Seven Virgins] (1948). *Virvatulia* [Ignis Fatuus] (1949). *Rakkauden vangit* [Prisoners of Love] (1951). *Päiväkirja vuosilta 1897–1906* [Diary from the Years 1897–1906] (1952). *Päiväkirja vuosilta 1907–1915* (1953). *Päiväkirja vuosilta 1916–1921* (1954). *Päiväkirja vuosilta 1922–1926* (1955). *Päiväkirja vuosilta 1927–1931* (1956). *Vaeltava vieraskirja* [Wandering Guest Book from the Years 1946–1956] (1957). *Elämäntoveri* [Life's Companion] (1959). *Aino Kallaksen kauneimmat runot* [Aino Kallas's Most Beautiful Poems] (1959).

Translations: *Barbara von Tisenhusen. A Livland tale* (1925). *Bath-Sheba of Saarenmaa* (1924). *Eros the Slayer. Two Estonian Tales* (1927). *The White Ship. Estonian Tales* (1924). *The Wolf's Bride. A Tale from Estonia* (1930). *Three Novels* (*Barbara von Tisenhusen, Reigin pappi, Sudenmorsian*) (1975).

Kai Laitinen

Margarita Karapanou
1946–
Born 1946, Athens, Greece
Genre(s): novel
Language(s): Greek

Margarita Karapanou was born in Athens in 1946, but she spent part of her childhood in France. She studied cinema and philosophy in Paris and later worked as a nursery school and kindergarten teacher. She is the daughter of well-known Greek fiction writer Margarita Liberaki, whose works have been translated in French and English. Karapanou's first short novel, published in 1976, was *Kassandra and the Wolf*, translated into English by N.C. Germanacos. Her second novel, *O Ipnovatēs* (The Sleepwalker), was published in 1986 and Karapanou herself translated it into French. She was recently given the Goncourt Award (best foreign fiction) for *Ipnovatēs* (1988).

Her first novel discusses a young preschool-age girl's experiences of morality, love, sexuality, and class differences. As Kimon Friar says in his review of the novel's translation, "[the adult world] is seen through the eyes of a child who is neither moral nor immoral but simply amoral as a kitten."

Karapanou's second novel takes place in Hydra, a Greek island known for its intellectual and cosmopolitan non-Greek citizens. In this work, Karapanou satirizes an adult world of perverse sexuality, emotional instability, and unhappiness. Murder, death, and sexual corruption is the framework within which the characters move; Karapanou's solution to this world seems to be the appearance of an attractive yet murderous Greek policeman, who is the new God-sent Messiah, the world's second chance.

Karapanou's work ridicules contemporary upperclass Greek society and cosmopolitan "intellectuals," yet, at the same time, her writing expresses a profound concern for the state of affairs that she parodies. Even though Karapanou has published only two books, she can be considered among the most important Greek women writers.

Works
Ē Kassandra ke o Lykos (1976). *O Ipnovatēs* [The Sleepwalker] (1986). *Rien ne va plus* (1991).

Translations: *Kassandra and the Wolf.*, tr. N.C. Germanacos (1976). *Cassandre et le loup* (1976). *Kassandra och Vargen* (1979).

Critical Work: "Ē Metaphrasē: Enas Viasmos." ["Translation: A Rape."] *Ē Leksē*, 56, July–August 1986, 776–777.

Aliki P. Dragona

Zoe Karelli
1901–

a.k.a. Chryssoula Argyriadou
Born 1901, Thessaloniki, Greece
Genre(s): short story, poetry, drama, essay
Language(s): Greek

The sister of the prominent writer N.G. Pentzikis, Argyriadou studied foreign languages and music. She started her literary career with the short story "Diatheseis" (Moods) in 1935, and in 1940, she published her first poetic anthology, the *Poreia* (Course), which was followed by various other poetic collections, such as *Epochi tou Thanatou* (1948; The Season of Death), *I Fantasia tou Chronou* (1949; The Imagination of Time), *Tis Monaxias kai tis Eparsis* (1951; Of Solitude and Pride), *Chalcographies kai Eikonismata* (1952; Chalcographies and Icons), *To Ploio* (1953; The Ship), *Cassandra kai alla Poiemata* (1955; Cassandra and Other Poems), *Antitheseis* (1957; Oppositions), *O Kathreptis tou Mesonychtiou* (1958; The Mirror of Midnight) and others.

She also deployed her literary skills in writing plays and essays; her plays *O Diavolos kai i evdomi entoli* (1955; The Devil and the Seventh Commandment) and the *Suppliants* (1962), as well as her essays "About Doubt," "The Absolute in the Work of Claudel," "Waiting for Godot or the Passion of Inertness," among others gained her a very high reputation in the Greek literary elite.

Argyriadou, from the beginning of her literary career, revealed a highly personal style, that marked her entire work thereafter. Her surrealistic style, her metaphysical religious feeling, and her existentialist anxieties about death, solitude, and decay dominate her writings. Refusing to use the traditional forms of poetry, she very early began to experiment with new forms of expression. Her paratactic speech and abstract, somewhat convoluted way of expressing herself have made her writing rather inaccessible to the public.

Her collection *Oppositions* reveals a change in her attitude toward her existentialist quests and a strained search for new, inconceivable realities. Kimon Friar remarks in a review of *Kassandra and the Wolf* (in *World Literature Today*, Spring 1977, Vol. 51) that Argyriadou's "vigilant consciousness keeps watch on the ambiguous borderland between the material and the immaterial, between the time world of Heraclitean flux and the space world of eternal silence, trying to spy out a realm where space and time are coequal and codeterminate." Argyriadou strives to relate the realm of eternal silence to the material world of speech. Her themes, as Friar points out, are almost exclusively concerned with the split in the person of sensibility tormented by the attempt to find integrity and create ties of continuity in a world of spiritual disintegration.

A poem, as described in "Worker in the Workshops of Time" and in "Adolescent from Antikythera," becomes for Argyriadou "erotic shapes for whatever exists/ within time." She treats poetry not only as an aesthetic receptacle of time but also as the best spiritual medium of modern times with which to understand contemporary man's struggle to give meaning to his existence in a time of deteriorating values.

Her plays, in which the poetic element is very strong, are "poems" in dialogue form. The central idea of *The Devil and the Seventh Commandment* is the strength of voluptuousness, the negation of conventional family bonds, and the omnipotence of the demonic. Argyriadou, herself liberated from social "conventions," openly challenges her readers for further quests.

Her verse technique is a mixture of "Byzantinism" (the language of Byzantine hymnology) and free verse; she shifts the order of words, thus also producing semantic shifts, and plays with syntax. These techniques refresh her expression and incorporate rhetorical figures and abstract concepts. Her language mixes "demotic" with "archaic" (*kathareuousa*) elements. Her poetry is almost devoid of imagery and usually depends for its effects on the passionate expression of thought. Her words are bare of sentimentality and are mainly those of philosophical speculation.

In 1956, she was awarded the second State Prize of Poetry for her collection *Cassandra and other Poems*; in 1974, she obtained the first State Prize for her poems of the period 1940–1973. For her outstanding literary contribution she was awarded the "Palmes Académiques" by the French government. She is the only Greek poetess who has fully realized her role as a European poetess; her ideas, concepts, and personal anxieties reflect the anxieties of our times. Her poems have been translated into several European languages, including Polish and Hungarian.

Works

Poems: "Course" (1940). "Season of Death" (1948). "Imagination of Time" (1949). "Of Solitude and Pride" (1951). "Chalcographies and Icons" (1952). "The Ship" (1953). "Cassandra and Other Poems" (1955). "Garden Tales" (1955). "Oppositions" (1957). "The Mirror of Midnight" (1958). Two collective volumes of her poems appeared in 1973. Vol. 1 covers the period 1940–1955 and Vol. 2 the period 1955–1973, including her recent collections *The Crossroads* (1973) and the *Diary* (1955–1973).

Plays: *The Devil and the Seventh Commandment* (1955). *Suppliants* (1962). *Simonis, the Royal Child of Byzantium* (1965).

Essays: "About Doubt" (1958). "The Absolute in the Work of Claudel" (1959). "Waiting for Godot or the Passion of Alertness" (1967). "Essays on C.P. Kavafi, T.S. Eliot, J. Joyce, F. Kafka, F. Dostoyevski, L. Pirandello, N. Gogol, and A. Camus."

Translations: In Greek, T.S. Eliot's "The Family Reunion" and "The Cocktail Party."

Aristoula Georgiadou

Kassia
ca. 805–ca. 865

a.k.a. Kasia, Kassiane, Eikasia, Ikasia
Born ca. 805, probably Constantinople
Died ca. 865, in the convent she founded in Constantinople
Genre(s): Christian hymns, nonreligious gnomic poetry
Language(s): Greek

The most distinguished female poet of the Byzantine period, Kassia composed both secular and religious verse under the reigns of Theophilos (829–842) and Michael (842–867). She came from a noble family: her father was a *kandidatos* at the Imperial Court. As a young woman, she was determined to become a nun and was active in the campaign against the iconoclasts. When Theodoros Studites, the great champion of the icons, was exiled, Kassia sent him gifts and letters. The story that Kassia took part in a beauty contest at which the emperor Theophilos was to choose a wife and lost the throne with a witty riposte to one of his questions is old but apparently untrue. Later, possibly in 843, the year marking the end of the iconoclast controversy, she founded a convent bearing her name in Constantinople. There she spent the rest of her life and wrote the greater part of her poetry. The exact date of her death is unknown, but the evidence suggests she did not live beyond the reign of Michael.

After the restoration of the icons, there was an increase in the writing of hymns, and Kassia's are among the more interesting pieces. The problems concerning the authenticity of works attributed to Kassia

are highly involved, but the following are probably genuine: the kanon *On The Dead*, the tetraodion for Easter Sunday, and 21 other hymns for different days in the religious calendar. There are another 25 pieces whose authorship is disputed and 10 more falsely ascribed to Kassia. Her most famous hymn is *On Mary Magdalene* (Wednesday in Holy Week), which is still sung in the Orthodox church. Also noteworthy are *On St. Peter and St. Paul* (June 28th), *On St. Eustratios and His Fellow-Martyrs* (December 13th), and *For Christmas Day*. While there is no direct evidence, it is likely that Kassia also composed music to accompany her hymns.

In general, Kassia eschews the expression of deep spiritual thought and concentrates on the historical side of religion. Her language is ornamental and relies heavily on the use of rhetorical devices, especially antitheses, which are often, but not always, deftly employed. There are several vivid images littered throughout the corpus. The lack of any significant originality is mitigated by a trusting sincerity and a preference for expressing the more joyous aspects of the Christian faith.

Apart from the religious works, about 300 lines of Kassia's gnomic verses survive. Among these, there are a collection of epigrammatic pieces on such subjects as stupidity, woman, fortune, beauty, wealth, and the faults of Armenians, 32 verses on the theme of friendship, and a group of statements on the sublimity of the monastic life. The best of the secular verses are the 27 trimeters which all begin with "I hate" and which scrutinize human social habits with a perceptive eye. Again, there is no great originality of conception or expression, but the traditional themes are handled with a pleasing artistry.

Kassia's religious poetry stands far above that of her contemporaries. She remained a figure of influence and interest after her death and since the middle of the nineteenth century has been featured in several novels and plays by Greek and other writers.

Works

Translations: Argyropolous, J., *Kassia, Her Life and Poetry* (in Greek) (Athens, 1924). Trypanis, C.A., *Greek Poetry from Homer to Seferis* (London, 1981), pp. 435f., 445–447. Tripolitis, A., *Kassia: The Legend, the Woman, and Her Work* (New York, 1992).

David H.J. Larmour

Frances Anne Kemble
1809–1893

a.k.a. Fanny Kemble
Born November 27, 1809, London
Died January 15, 1893, London
Genre(s): journal, poetry, letters, essay, historical drama, novel, translation
Language(s): English

Born into England's first family of the theatre, Kemble exemplifies what was possible for talented, assertive nineteenth-century women. Remembered chiefly for her incomparable readings of Shakespeare in England and America, she also received attention for her inspired acting and for her literary output. Her writings, spanning the Victorian era, include journals, poetry, letters, essays, historical dramas, and one novel, as well as translations of works by Schiller and Dumas.

Kemble was the third generation of Kembles to work in the theatre, although she always preferred writing to acting. Niece of John Philip Kemble and Sarah Siddons and daughter of the actor-proprietor of Covent Garden and an actress, Kemble made her acting debut as Juliet in 1829 at Covent Garden, at the urgings of her family, to help stave off debt. Though she was an instant success, her efforts did not save her father from bankruptcy, and, in 1832, father and daughter left for a two-year American theatrical tour to recoup funds. Kemble was wildly successful in America, but she most ardently desired a literary career like that of Scott, Byron, or Keats. In April 1834, she gladly rejected a stage career in favor of marriage to Pierce Butler, an American who had avidly pursued her since seeing her act in Philadelphia two years before. As Kemble later wrote to Anna Brownell Murphy Jameson nearly five months after her wedding, "In leaving the stage, I left nothing that I regretted."

Two years after their marriage, Butler inherited a Georgia plantation that made him one of the state's largest slaveholders, and he and Kemble went to live briefly at Sea Islands. This sojourn began the inexorable destruction of their marriage and, ironically, also provided the impetus for the work her admirer Henry James was to call her best prose work, *Journal of a Residence on a Georgian Plantation in 1838–1839*. The book, based on Kemble's 100 days in Georgia, was not published until 1863, when it joined the debate over slavery at a crucial juncture in the North's will to triumph. Although Kemble wished only to bury her past, she was impelled to publish

Frances Anne Kemble

the journal to counteract the British interest in entering the Civil War. Her book undoubtedly contributed to that decision, but it came too late to play the decisive role her biographers have attributed to it. The work, though subsequently neglected, deserves to be read as an important document in American cultural history. It argues passionately against slavery and includes many brutally realistic passages describing conditions on a southern plantation before the Civil War. It is also noteworthy for its fascinating insights into the life and mind of a talented Victorian personality.

Noting in 1839 that she had been entirely ignorant of her husband's "dreadful possessions," Kemble found herself increasingly unable to overlook his values or unconventional lifestyle, though it is clear during these years that she most valued and passionately desired an intact family, especially after the birth of her two daughters. She moved away from her concern with abolition to fight to keep her family whole, but her effort failed in 1849, when Butler sued for divorce and won custody of their children until the girls came of age. Emotionally wounded by the sensational court case, Kemble returned to England, where she filled the next decade of her life by writing A *Year of Consolation* and returning to the stage. After appearing in several plays, Kemble settled into an extremely lucrative career staging readings of Shakespeare in England and America for which she won universal praise and a secure financial future.

After her antislavery journal was published in 1863, Kemble lived for thirty more years, deriving satisfaction from closeness to her daughters and their families. Her first grandchild, Owen Wister, Jr., was later to continue the literary tradition of his grandmother by writing *The Virginian*. Kemble read Shakespeare on stage, enjoyed the company of literary greats such as Robert Browning, Henry Wadsworth Longfellow, Henry James, and Edward FitzGerald, and published a play, poems, and her autobiographical *Records of a Girlhood* and *Records of Later Life*. James, her friend in old age, called these journals "one of the most animated autobiographies in the language." At eighty, she became a novelist for the first time, publishing *Far Away and Long Ago*, a curious work that correlates with her earliest expressions of desire for a life of love and adventure. Though not carried off as she had wished in girlhood—"The death I should prefer would be to break my neck off the back of a good horse at a full gallop on a fine day"—she did manage to live life to the fullest, in good Romantic fashion, ranging over England and America in stage performance and trying her hand at fiction, poetry, drama, essays, and journals. Her active life as mother, writer, actress, and political activist correctly entitles her to an early biographer's subtitle, "a passionate Victorian." Both her life and literary works await definitive scholarly study.

Works
Francis the First: An Historical Drama (1832). *Journal of F.A. Butler* (1835). *The Star of Seville, A Drama in Five Acts* (1837). *Poems* (1844). *A Year of Consolation* (1847). *Journal of a Residence on a Georgian Plantation in 1838–1839* (1863). *Plays: An English Tragedy, Mary Stuart* (tr. of Schiller), *Mademoiselle de Belle Isle* (tr. of Dugmas) (1863). *Poems* (1866). *Records of a Girlhood: An Autobiography* (1878–1879). *Notes upon Some of Shakespeare's Plays* (1882). *Records of Later Life* (1882). *Adventures of John Timothy Homespun in Switzerand: A Play Stolen from the French of Tartarin de Tareascon* (1889). *Far Away and Long Ago* (1889). *Further Records, 1848–1883* (1890). *Fanny, The American Kemble: Her Journals and Unpublished Letters*, ed. F.K. Wister (1972).

Rhoda L. Flaxman

Margery Kempe
ca. 1373–ca. 1439
Born ca. 1373, Bishop's Lynn (today King's Lynn), Norfolk, England
Died ca. 1439
Genre(s): autobiography
Language(s): English

Often labeled "fanatic" and "hysterical," Kempe is perhaps one of the most immediate, personal, and fascinating religious mystics in England. Illiterate, she dictated her autobiography, *The Book of Margery Kempe*, in old age to an amenuensis, probably a priest. *The Book of Margery Kempe* is the first vernacular autobiography in England, and it relates Kempe's life, sufferings, conversion, and subsequent conversations (dalliances) with God the Father, Christ, the Holy Spirit, the Virgin Mary, St. Catherine, St. Bridget, and other saints in great and lively detail. Throughout the book Kempe refers to herself almost invariably in the third person as "this creature" in apposition to God her Creator whose glorification is ultimately the purpose of her book. Kempe's visions are characterized by their vivid conciseness and are accompanied by sensual experiences (smells, sounds, and other sensations).

In her autobiography, Kempe reveals herself as a headstrong, determined woman. Her first vision of Christ came at the end of a long period of tribulations: an apparently very difficult birth was followed by hallucinations in which devils threatened and tortured her and Christ came to her aid, consoling, calming and healing her. This experience triggered her religious enthusiasm and initiated her path of piety, which, though frequently interrupted at the onset by worldly ambitions and self-doubts, culminated in her lively dalliances with Christ and His saints.

Having failed in several commercial ventures (brewing, milling), which she interpreted as God's punishment for her ostentation and worldly cares, she focused all her energies and determination on her religious experience. Her frequent fits of uncontrollable cryings, sighs, and lamentations not only in Church but on pilgrimages and in other public places as well earned her much scorn and criticism, occasionally even the accusation of hypocrisy. Nevertheless, firm in her faith (though not always sure of the genuineness of her revelation) and encouraged, too, by her confessors and spiritual counselors, Philip Repyngdon, bishop of Lincoln, and the Anchoress Julian of Norwich, among them, she pursued her religious career with a dogged determination and unfaltering decisiveness.

In 1413, as a result of her long insistence, she and her husband took vows of mutual continence and shortly thereafter she set out for the first of her long series of pilgrimages both abroad and in England. Her travel to the Holy Land, beset with various trials and difficulties but rich, too, in excruciatingly intense visionary experiences, is particularly informative. Accused more than once of Lollardy, because her brand of popular pietism smacked of heresy to the clerical class, she was vindicated every time as orthodox.

What makes *The Book of Margery Kempe* an invaluable literary and historic document is her uncompromising honesty even toward herself and her exuberantly vivid, clear style, devoid of theological and philosophical reflections but abounding in physical and psychological details that make Kempe and her world come alive even to today's readers.

Works

Hutler-Bowden, W., ed. *The Book of Margery Kempe: A Modern Version* (1944). Meech, S.B., and H.E. Allen, eds. *The Book of Margery Kempe* (1940).

Katharina M. Wilson

Diana Kempff
1945–

Born 1945, Thurnau, Oberfranken, Germany
Genre(s): novel, experimental prose miniature, fantastic allegory, poetry
Language(s): German

Daughter of the famous pianist Wilhelm Kempff, Diana Kempff decided she would become a writer when she was thirteen. By the age of seventeen she was writing but hesitated to publish for a long time. One of her characteristic traits, she says, is slowness. After finishing secondary education (she failed in German for "not mastering the language well enough"), she has worked as editor in several publishing houses. Presently she dedicates full time to writing. In 1983 she was awarded the Münchener Förderungspreis, and in 1983, the Heinrich-von-Kleist Preis. Some of her work has been translated into Swedish.

Kempff's turn to poetry as the first means of expression indicates her overall orientation: to move away from reality and create imaginary spaces filled with dreams and visions. Her books of poetry show preference for short units: the first consists of haiku-like miniatures pervaded by a melancholy mood, full of un-

usual images. Already in it she starts questioning the finality of life. The second presents dense vignettes whose meaning goes beyond enunciation, delving into dreams, raising uncertainties, perceiving and intuiting different truths. There is no rhyme and little rhythm: the verses surge as movements of the psyche.

Her great breakthrough came with *Fettfleck* (1979; A Blotch of Fat), her only prose work that conforms to the parameters of a novel. Construed with autobiographic elements, it can be considered as a *Bildungsroman* that relates the growing up of a solitary, very fat girl who soon finds out that life is not all roses and fairy tales. Other children shy away from her, and she is obliged to create for herself an imaginary world. The extraordinary quality of this novel rests on its artful handling of language: a mixture of dialect and child's talk, slowly evolving to a "normal" discourse. Within contemporary women's writing, such effect of immediacy is approached only in *Mandei-lhe uma boca* (1983) of Olga Gonçalves. In the choice of subject—although not in its treatment—*Fettfleck* reminds one of Marie-Louise Kaschnitz's "Das dicke Kind." The little girl's reactions transmitted in a monologue show some characteristics of feminine writing: introspective flow of thoughts, paratactic sentences; short, fragmented paragraphs, subjective perception of time. One is struck by the psychological veracity of a child's secret world, her acute perception of what is going on, her urgent need to communicate, which finally leads her to determine that she will be a writer. It is a cruel world that Kempff presents, and the closing paragraph confirms the cruelty. Yet, there is a kind of stoic acceptance on the part of the child who, through it, is able to convert some of her experiences into poetry and introduce lyric quality into the narrative.

Hinter der Grenze (1980; Beyond the Limit) oscillates between fairy tale and science fiction, between *Alice in Wonderland* and Orwell's *Animal Farm*. It presents the transformation of a little girl who goes to the zoo and suddenly steps "beyond," into "no man's land," peopled with talking and even verse-writing animals. The book is full of literary and allegorical allusions; plays on words abound: it is a literary piece. In *Der Wanderer* (1985) the fantastic note becomes even stronger, the mood more somber, although an exhortation is given to "speak of light which arises out of darkness." It shows subterranean labyrinths of the unconscious in a state of preformation rendered in long, unending paragraphs. At the very beginning, a warning is issued: "I am not I, not only I, not I alone, I, the Dreamer," pinpointing further: "there is nothing real in this game, I hide behind my 'why.'" One critic sees in it "dreamscapes of fright" filled with "postapocalyptic imagery." Others speak of nightmarish visions. Again, it is the wrestling for adequate expression that adds an affirmative note even to this nihilistic world. Between the two fantasies Kempff releases *Der vorsichtige Zusammenbruch* (1981; The Careful Breakdown), which consists of fifty short prose fragments—meditations on life and death but also on writing. It is permeated by existential *angst*, yet the experience of creating new language rings a positive note.

Kempff pays particular attention to dreams, fantasy, and experimentation with language. She is interested in inner worlds and excels in transmitting the psychological processes of a child. Often, the image of a door or a wall is used as a symbol of the necessity to go beyond reality perceived by the senses. She has a particularly fine ear for music and rhythm. Her sense of language cannot be matched easily. Working with language appears as the only solution in a depressing world, but then even its ultimate validity is put to doubt. Recurring themes in her work are solitude, selfishness, cruelty, death. Long monologues function as self-analysis. Hinted at as "a mixture of elegant sarcasm and fierce despondency," Kempff's writing stands out among her contemporaries through its mastery in combining the real with the fantastic, her ability to infuse lyricism without veering toward sentimentalism, her extraordinary gift for language, and the poetic quality born out of the struggle in her best pages, as in *Fettfleck*.

Works

Vor allem das Unnützliche [The Useless Above All] (1975). *Fettfleck* [A Blotch of Fat] (1979). *Hinter der Grenze* [Beyond the Limit] (1980). *Der vorsichtige Zusammenbruch* [The Careful Breakdown] (1981). *Herzzeit* [Time for the Heart] (1983). *Der Wanderer* (1985).

Birutė Ciplijauskaitė

Marie-Thérèse Kerschbaumer
1936–

Born August 31, 1936, Garches near Paris, France
Genre(s): prose, poetry, radio and television drama, essay, translation
Language(s): German

Marie-Thérèse Kerschbaumer has emerged in recent years as one of the leading women prose writers in German. Perhaps it was her own difficult childhood

(of which she is reluctant to speak) that subsequently led her to sympathize with the disenfranchised people of the world. Repression and exploitation of minorities and the underprivileged is her central theme in individual and highly successful artistic forms. She is also active in the European peace movement and takes a public stance on many sociopolitical issues.

Fleeing the Spanish Civil War, Kerschbaumer's Austrian mother and Spanish father went to France, where Marie-Thérèse Raymonde Angèle was born near Paris in 1936. Her childhood years were spent partly in Costa Rica but primarily with her grandparents in the Austrian province of Tyrol. To escape the unhappy family situation she went to England to work for a year when she was seventeen and subsequently to Italy. Back in Austria in 1957 she attended night school to earn her high school diploma, but her plans to study the visual arts were frustrated. In 1963 she began her studies at the University of Vienna with a concentration in Romance languages and literatures. After spending two years in Romania, where her first volume of poetry was published, she received her doctorate from the University of Vienna in 1973 with a dissertation on structural linguistics in Romanian. In 1971 she married the painter Helmut Kurz–Goldenstein; they have one son. Kerschbaumer lives today as a freelance writer in Vienna, where she manages to find time for both family and career as well as for political activities.

Kerschbaumer's best-known work to date is *Der weibliche Name des Widerstands* (1980; The Feminine Name of Resistance). It won wide recognition for the author when it was produced as a television film in 1981, and the following year it was reprinted in a prominent paperback series. Noteworthy is the fact that the book was written years before the topic of antifascism became fashionable, which is indicative of Kerschbaumer's individualistic and pioneering stance. The book consists of seven "reports" about women killed in Nazi concentration camps. Although based on historical accounts, the reports are themselves fictional, representing a unique amalgam of documentary and imaginative literature. The seven portraits present women of various types and backgrounds: writer, professor, nun, gypsy, seamstress, teacher, and working-class woman. The seven stand as representative of those who were persecuted because of their race or religion or opposition to the Hitler regime. The author describes the courageous resistance—ultimately futile—of these women to the sufferings, humiliation, and horrors of fascism. Part of the power of the work derives from the fusion of temporal categories, whereby past and present are inextricably intertwined, just as are the personal pronouns "I," "you," and "she," creating a fusion of identities. The work thus succeeds in making a general statement by focusing on particular individuals, with the language and style adapted in each case to the personality of the figure. Interspersed are reflections on the writing process itself that reveal the ethical and aesthetic commitment of the author to be one and the same.

The theme of oppressor versus victim in modern European history appeared already in Kerschbaumer's first major work, *Der Schwimmer* (1976; The Swimmer), cast against a backdrop of the Franco regime in Spain. It describes the attempt of inmates to escape from an institution and flee on a ship that is to aid the refugees. The plot line, however, remains in the background, and foregrounded are the thoughts and feelings, memories, and associations of the first-person narrator, expressed in a highly rhythmical and metaphorical language. Such experimental techniques were perfected in *Der weibliche Name des Widerstands*, which was followed by an ambitious lengthy novel, *Schwestern* (1982; Sisters). It presents the fictional account of several Austrian families against a background of twentieth-century history: collapse of the monarchy, inflation and economic crisis, political instability, and catastrophe. The red thread, consisting of the story of sisters who vie for the affection of patriarchal fathers, recurs through several generations, places, and social classes. The careers and ruinations of the fathers are reflected in the lives of the female family members, most of whom fail, although one develops into a political activist. The motif of the sisters in the novel is representative of Austrian sociopolitical structures, which are depicted as bogged down in ultraconservative entanglements. Kerschbaumer also writes radio plays, which, although not available in published form, have been highly successful on Austrian radio. One example is "Kinderkriegen" (1979; Having Kids), which deals with the deplorable situation in hospital maternity wards.

Kerschbaumer is one of the few writers successfully to unite ethical and aesthetic issues. Although the summaries may sound black and white, the author depicts the characters and situations with great subtlety and consummate skill, and her moral commitment thus requires no sacrifice of artistic quality. The protagonists in her works are women, and she is particularly interested in portraying a female perspective. She rejects, however, the concept of a specifically feminine aesthetic, and women's issues are seen rather in connection with the general struggle of oppressed individuals and classes to resist domination and repression. "Sensitivity is probably not linked with gender but rather a matter of attitude, conscience, and knowledge," stated Kerschbaumer in an interview. In contrast to autobiographical women's writing Kerschbaumer chooses historical settings, and she unites historical events and literary-philosophical reflections with sensitive character portrayals (which occasionally contain autobiographical elements). She regards literature as a means for the reflective individual to combat the misuse of power, and she sees her specific task as speaking for the underprivileged who have no audible voice of their own. As a member of the Artists for Peace organization as well as the Graz Authors' Association she works to realize the slogan "Nie Wieder Krieg" (No More Wars).

Works
Gedichte (1970). *Der Schwimmer. Roman* (1976). *Der weibliche Name des Widerstands. Sieben Berichte* (1980; rpt. 1982). *Schwestern. Roman* (1982).

Beth Bjorklund

Nadezhda Khvoshchinskaia 1824–1889
a.k.a. V. Krestovsky, V. Porechnikov, and N. Vozdvizhensky
Born May 20, 1824, Riazan' province, Russia
Died June 8, 1889, St. Petersburg
Genre(s): fiction, poetry, criticism
Language(s): Russian

Literature was primarily an avocation for the women of mid-nineteenth century Russia who were well educated enough to practice it. Nadezhda Khvoshchinskaia is the rare example of a woman who made writing her profession. For over forty years she struggled to support herself and various dependents— her mother, a sister, her brother's orphaned children and, briefly and quixotically, a much younger husband dying of tuberculosis—by writing for major journals and reprinting earlier works in separate and collected editions. Her total production comprises nearly 100 poems, mainly on civic themes, published between 1842 and 1859, including one long tale in verse "Derevenskii sluchai" (1853; A Country Case); ten novels, over forty shorter works of fiction and a few dramatic sketches; literary criticism for the magazine *Otechestvennye zapiski* (Notes of the Fatherland) from 1861–1864 and the newspaper *Russkie vedomosti* (Russian Gazette) from 1876–1881; and translations, primarily from French and Italian. It is remarkable that she managed this complex career from the provincial fastness of Riazan', 100 miles southeast of Moscow. For many years, although the fact that "V. Krestovsky" was a woman was widely publicized, the identity behind her masculine pseudonyms remained known only to her editors and colleagues. Writing came naturally to the family. Her sister Sofia was a talented author, and her youngest sister, Praskovia Khvoshchinskaia (1832–1916), published one volume of undistinguished stories under the pseudonym "S. Zimarova": *V gorode i v derevne: Ocherki i rasskazy* (1881; In the City and in the Country: Sketches and Stories).

Khvoshchinskaia perceived herself as an honest craftswoman: " . . . nobody sees better than I my blunders and ignorance—in a word, all that is justifiably ridiculed. I would have stopped writing long ago, if it were not for the necessity of working; that's why I write so much. But, once I decided on that form of day labor, I told myself that I would never utter a dishonorable word, I would not betray that truth, faith in which unites the best of people; in that faith I am the equal of those people . . . ." (Letter to N.V. Shelgunov, December 10, 1874 in *Russkaia Mysl'*, 1891). As this quotation suggests, there was a reforming impulse behind her writing from the first civic poems to her last story, "V'iuga" (1889; The Snowstorm), that depicts the fate of an exiled revolutionary. Khvoshchinskaia was an intelligent observer who portrayed the cycles of succeeding generations with a pessimism that bothered radical critics much more than her artistic lapses.

Today much of Khvoshchinskaia's prose is best read as social history, but some works stand out above the rest. Her best novel, *V ozhidanii luchshego* (1860; In Hope of Something Better) depicts a grotesque family of provincial nobles who flee abroad in fear of the impending emancipation of the serfs. "Bratets" (1858; Brother) has a bleak, satiric tone and a jaundiced view of family life that resembles the late 1870s *Gospoda Golovlevy* (The Golovlevs) by her friend and editor Mikhail Saltykov-Shchedrin. Some of her late "sketches" (*ocherki*), particularly those published in *Album: Groups and Portraits*, 1879, create effective montages of a variety of contrasting characters without confining them to a tight plot. "Ridneva" (1875) is a chilling depiction of the humiliations suffered by a feckless, poverty-stricken actress. Among Khvoshchinskaia's more striking repeated types are the careerist who is not averse even to robbing his family to further his goals ("Brother"; "Pervaia bor'ba" [1869; Early Struggles]); the aspiring girl mired in a self-sat-

isfied provincial milieu ("V doroge" [1854; On the Road]; *Bol'shaia medveditsa* [1870–1871; Ursa Major]), and the reformer or revolutionary who remains true to the ideals of his generation after his comrades and family have sold out ("Schastlivye liudi" [1874; Happy People]; *Obiazannosti* [1885; Obligations]).

In April 1883 Khovshchinskaia's literary "jubilee" was celebrated with the presentation of a watch and a commendation signed by 731 people, including some of the leading artistic and scientific figures of the day. After the death of her mother, she moved to Petersburg in 1884. When Khvoshchinskaia died in 1889, she did not leave enough money to pay for the funeral.

Works

V ozhidanii luchshego (1860). *Album: Groups and Portraits* (1879). *Polnoe sobranie sochinenii*, 6 vols. (1912–1913). *Povesti i rasskazy*, ed. and intro. M.S. Goriachkina (1963). *Poety 1840–1850kh gg* (Leningrad, 1972), pp. 259–270.

Translations: *La signora Ridneff*, tr., S. de Gubernatis-Besobrasoff (1876). *Veriaguine*, tr., Victor Derely (1888).

Mary F. Zirin

Käthe Kollwitz
1867–1945

Born 1867, Königsberg, Germany
Died 1945, Moritzburg/Dresden
Genre(s): journal, letters
Language(s): German

Käthe Kollwitz is known primarily as a graphic artist, who in her drawings, etchings, woodcuts, lithographs, and sculptures gave a deeply sympathetic portrait of the pain, rage, tenderness, and joy in the lives of working-class men, women, and children. Her insistence on a politically engaged "art for use," an operative, functional art that at the same time upholds the highest standards of artistic integrity, makes hers a political aesthetic of particular importance in twentieth-century culture. Kollwitz's view of the potential of art and the responsibility of the artist marks her literary work as well. In both her diaries and her letters she explores the relationship between art, politics, and everyday life from her position as a woman artist deeply involved in the struggles of her time.

Born in 1867 in Königsberg to a free-thinking, socially conscious, and politically active family, Käthe

Kollwitz was encouraged early on to think independently and take responsibility for her choices. Choosing to become an artist, she studied at the Women's School of Art, first in Berlin, and then in Munich. After her marriage to Karl Kollwitz, they settled in a working-class neighborhood in Berlin; his medical practice was on the first floor, their apartment on the second, and her studio on the third. Refusing to make a choice between family and career, Kollwitz structured a life in which family life, work, and political engagement were not only inseparable, but mutually sustaining and interdependent components. By the time of her death in 1945, Kollwitz had become internationally recognized as one of the primary artists of her time, the recipient of numerous prestigious awards (including the Villa Romana Prize in 1907), and the first woman elected to the Prussian Academy of the Arts. Above all, she had become known as an artist who never compromised her vision of an art that could be of service toward the construction of a more just and humane world.

Despite (or perhaps because of) her fame and broad popularity as an artist, a woman whose work is appreciated both by the art establishment and by the common people whose lives she depicted, Kollwitz's written work—her diaries and letters—has never in its totality been made available in published form. Only selections and excerpts have been published; the eleven volumes of her diary, an invaluable record of her life and times in Germany between 1909 and 1943, as yet exist only in manuscript form in the archives of the Berlin Academy of Arts. The published work includes two autobiographical sketches—"Erinnerungen" (1923; Recollections) and "Rückblick auf frühere Jahre" (1941; Looking Back at Earlier Years)—both written for and at the request of her son Hans, excerpts from her diaries, and letters to her husband, sons, friends, colleagues, and comrades.

Reluctant to focus on her self (what ultimately counts, she insisted, was not what a person *is* but what she or he *produces*), she positions herself as one of the players in the unfolding drama of history at a given moment. Like the figures depicted in her art, she emerges in her writing as an individual who is always representative of her time. Thus, the seemingly unemotional surface, the almost documentary tone of her writing, in her letters as well as in her autobiographical texts, merely reveal her passionate refusal to give in to sentimentality. Grieving the death of her youngest son Peter, killed at age eighteen in Flanders within the first months of World War I, she writes in her diary: "This morning, January 1, there is a bright, clear sky. On Peter's bed a strip of sun. Move on and get through. Take your hands, hold yourself together and look ahead" (January 1, 1919).

Whether she is writing about the death of a beloved child, difficult moments in her marriage, or times of depression in which she is unable to be productive in her work, the axiom Kollwitz lived by was always firm and clear: not to weep, but to act. Thus, her work as an artist—whether her tool is a chisel, charcoal, or a pen—is characterized by the stark simplicity of a line that focuses on the essential: "Strength: that means, taking life as it is and, without allowing it to break you—without complaining and much crying— to go about your work with energy. To not deny yourself—the person you happen to be, but to focus in on the essential (Diary entry, February 1917).

Works

Tagebuchblätter, 1909–1943 [Diaries]. Manuscript, 11 vols. *Tagebuchblätter und Briefe,* ed. Hans Kollwitz (1948, rpt. 1985) [Selection tr. Richard and Clara Winston (1955; The Diary and Letters of Käthe Kollwitz)]. *"Ich will wirken in dieser Zeit." Auswahl aus den Tagebüchern und Briefen aus Graphik, Zeichnungen und Plastik* ["I Want to Be Effective in These Times": Selections from Diaries and Letters, Graphic Art, Drawings and Sculpture], ed. Hans Kollwitz (1952, rpt. Ullstein, 1981) *Aus meinem Leben* [From My Life] (1958). *Briefe der Freundschaft und Begegnungen* [Letters of Friendship and Encounters], ed. Hans Kollwitz (1966). *Bekenntnisse* [Confessions], ed. Volker Frank (1981).

Angelika Bammer

Ljarissa Kosac
1871–1913

a.k.a. Lesja Ukrajinka
Born February 25, 1871, Zvjahel, Ukraine, Soviet Union
Died August 1, 1913, Saram
Genre(s): lyric poetry, dramatic poetry, drama
Language(s): Ukrainian

Lesja Ukrajinka was the first Ukrainian poet whose creativity transcended the process of national revival. Daughter of Olena Pcilka and niece of M. Drahomanov, Ukrajinka adopted their ideas on the necessity of cultural expansion and the elevation of the Ukrainian literary language. The cultural atmosphere in the Kosac home attracted visitors such as the playwright

Staryckyj and the composer Lysenko and stimulated Ukrajinka's creativity as well as exposed her to discussions of the function of the arts in society. In particular, she was indebted to Drahomanov for expanding her acquaintance with world literature, and this influence is reflected in her first efforts in lyric verse, a translation of Heine.

The first period of Ukrajinka's creativity as a lyric poet projects the optimism of a young girl who is gravely ill with a desperate tubercular condition and compelled to travel around the world in search of a better climate to alleviate that condition. Ultimately, despite painful operations, long sojourns in Egypt, the Caucasus, Crimea, and Georgia, Ukrajinka died in Saram and was buried in Kiev.

Lesja Ukrajinka wrote her first poems at the age of twelve. Her lyric poetry is not generally considered to be her crowning achievement although the poems display both courage and strength as well as a moving quality in the description of her intimate moods and feelings. The first anthology of her lyric poetry *Na Krylach Pisen'* (On the Wings of Song) appeared in 1892, and in 1899 was followed by the collection *Dumy i Mriji* (Thoughts and Dreams), and in 1902 by *Vidhuky* (Echoes).

It was in the writing of the second period of her creativity, particularly in such long dramatic poems as *Samson, Robert Bruce, Kassandra,* and *Davnja Kazka* (An Old Tale) that the prototypes of her future dramatic concerns emerged. The dramatic poem, then, serves as a transitory stage between the lyric and drama, and these poems provide a lyrical element and a well-developed plot as well as dramatic conflict. In these poems, Ukrajinka not only creates a mood; she provides an epic view that relates to her concerns with Ukrainian culture. The poem *Robert Bruce* gives an indication of these concerns; the hero, Bruce, the only Scottish lord who remained faithful to his people in their struggle against the invading Englishmen, leads the Scots to a victory and saves the independence of Scotland. In this poem Ukrajinka's interests in the struggle for Scottish independence reflect her commitment to the struggle of Ukrainians for their own national autonomy.

As a dramatist, Ukrajinka moved in the opposite direction from the currents in the modern theater of Ibsen, Hauptmann, or Maeterlinck to the ancient theater of Aeschylus, Sophocles, and Euripedes. Her dramas are not only classic in structure but contain elevated themes, high style, and a clearly defined structure. It is in her dramas that Lesja Ukrajinka steps beyond the confines of the current tradition of realism. Representative settings for her plays are classical antiquity, the Middle Ages, the world of Mohammed, as well as early Ukrainian history as in the play *Bojarynja* (1910; The Noblewoman) and the context of early Christianity, in such plays as *V Katakombax* (1906; In the Catacombs), *Advokat Martijan* (1913; The Advocate Martianus), and *Na rujinax* (1904; In the Ruins). The main theme of the plays is the historical process and human aspirations that are extended symbolically to Ukrainian contemporary history.

In one of her most memorable works, *Lisova Pisnja* (1911; The Forest Song), Ukrajinka uses symbolism to extend her fascination and love for nature into a conflict between the natural world and the material world. In this work, fantastic wood nymphs, fairies, and mermaids, and in particular the wood nymph Mavka, represent not only the beauty of nature but the spirit of poetry. When the poetic spirit of Mavka meets Lukash, who does not understand the spirit of the forest world, tragedy ensues. As exemplified by this work, ultimately the significance of Lesja Ukrajinka in Ukrainian literature lies in her concern for both the expansion of language and the search for new forms, thereby extending the Ukrainian realist tradition into the stream of world literature.

Works
Na Krylach Pisen' (1892). *Dumy i Mriji* (1899). *Vidhuky* (1902). *Tvory Lesi Ukrainky* (1953). *Tvory v desiaty tomakh* (1963–1965). *In the Catacombs*, tr. John Weir (1971). *Spirit of Flame. A Collection of the Works of Lesya Ukrainka*, tr. Percival Cundy. *The Babylonian Captivity. Five Russian Plays*, ed. C.E. Roberts (1946).

Christine Kiebuzinska

Sofia Kovalevskaia
1850–1891

Born January 3, 1850, Korvin-Krukovskaia, Moscow
Died January 19, 1891, Stockholm
Genre(s): mathematics, drama, poetry, journalism, memoirs
Language(s): Russian

With the abolition of serfdom in 1861, a generation of young Russian noblewomen began to hope that some of the restrictions governing their lives could be lifted also. Their hopes for higher education were dashed: after the student unrest of 1862, girls lost even the grudgingly awarded privilege of attending university lectures. By the late 1860s these frustrated Russians began streaming into Western Europe to study at institutions of higher learning. Sofia Kovalevskaia (née Korvin-Krukovskaia) is exemplary among these vital women. At her tragically early death (from pneumonia or pleurisy), she was at once a source of inspiration to talented girls throughout the world and anathema to those who feared women's aspirations outside the domestic sphere. Kovalevskaia's scientific legacy is still being explored by modern mathematicians. Her second career, as a writer whose dashing style reflects her notable gifts as conversationalist and storyteller, has given us a first-hand account of her childhood and lifelong advocacy of political reform and social justice.

Kovalevskaia's life, covered effectively in Ann Koblitz's recent biography in English (Koblitz, Ann Hibner, *A Convergence of Lives, Sofia Kovalevskaia: Scientist, Writer, Revolutionary* [Boston, 1983]), is the stuff of legend. Her great-grandfather on the maternal side was the Russianized German astronomer and mathematician Friedrich Shubert. She proved her own exceptional talent as a child by teaching herself the elements of higher mathematics from pages of a textbook used to paper the walls of her room at the family estate of Palibino, Vitebsk province (*A Russian Childhood*). Her father, a retired major-general, was persuaded somewhat reluctantly to let Sofia be tutored during the winters the family spent at the Shubert home in St. Petersburg. Since it was unlikely that he would agree to higher education abroad for his daughter, at eighteen Sofia contracted a "fictitious marriage" with the young paleontologist and publisher of scientific books, Vladimir Kovalevsky. (Such marriages were part of the romantic radical *mores* propagated in Chernyshevsky's famous novel, *What's To Be Done*, 1863.) With Kovalevsky as their "guardian," both Sofia and her elder sister, Anna, escaped to Western Europe. Sofia pursued her studies in Berlin, persuading the famous German mathematician Karl Weierstrass to tutor her and sponsor her for a doctorate *in absentia* from Gottingen University; Anna went to Paris and married a French Socialist, Victor Jaclard.

By 1874 Kovalevsky's devotion to his "wife" won her over to a real marital relationship. The young couple returned to seek academic positions in Russia, but their radical connections and Kovalevskaia's sex worked against them. They worked for a progressive new newspaper and undertook an unsuccessful project to construct rationally designed apartments in St. Petersburg. In 1878 their daughter, also Sofia, was born. Prodded by Weierstrass to return to mathematics, Sofia

Sofia Kovalevskaia

separated from her husband in 1881 and moved to Paris. The following year she took a teaching post at Stockholm University. Vladimir finally received a position at Moscow University, but it came too late; implicated in the crash of a speculative oil venture in the Russian Near East, he committed suicide in 1883.

The first woman professor in modern Europe, Kovalevskaia was internationally famous in the 1880s. Her Swedish sponsor, the mathematician Gustav Mittag-Leffler, and his sister, the writer Carlotta Leffler, became her close friends. The two women collaborated on a set of plays, one showing an unsuccessful life and the other the same life transformed by rational conditions, under the blanket title, *A Struggle for Happiness*. When Leffler married a handsome young Italian nobleman, Kovalevskaia remarked wistfully that Carlotta was "happiness," while she herself was destined to remain "struggle."

Kovalevskaia's last years continued to be marked by deep contradictions. In a vote of confidence by her colleagues in Western Europe, she was awarded the prestigious French *Prix Bordin* for her work on the revolution of a solid body about a fixed point ("Kovalevsky's top"). She never ceased hoping for a post in her native land, where she was named adjunct member of the Russian Academy of Science—and denied admission to meetings of its mathematical division. A stormy romance with the exiled Russian political scientist and historian Maxim Kovalevsky intensified the problems of combining a career and personal happiness.

All her life Kovalevskaia wrote verse. In the 1870s she produced articles on scientific and theatrical topics and in the late 1880s described visits to French hospitals and a Swedish school for leading Petersburg newspaper journalists. She began to write prose seriously during the years in Sweden and in 1890 published her charming reminiscences of childhood, in which she depicts not only the varied influences on her own life, but also her sister's search for an outlet for her literary talents. Kovalevskaia's memoir of the Polish rebellion of 1863 has only recently been printed in the Soviet Union. Six years after George Eliot's death, Kovalevskaia published a sympathetic reminiscence of two visits with the English author, one during her years with G.H. Lewes and the other during her late marriage to the much younger J.W. Cross. Kovalevskaia's unfinished novel, *Vera Barantzova* (A Nihilist Girl) the heroine of which is a self-sacrificing radical of the 1870s, was printed in Russia only in 1906.

Works

Vospominaniia i pis'ma, S. Ia. Shtraikh, ed. (2nd. rev. ed., 1961). *Vospominaniia. Povesti*, P. Ia. Polubarinova-Kochina, ed. (1974). *Izbrannye proizvedeniia* (1982).

Translations: *Vera Barantzova*, tr. Sergius Stepniak and William Westall (1895). *A Russian Childhood*, tr., ed., and intro. Beatrice Stillman, with an *Analysis of Kovalevskaya's Mathematics* by P.Y. Kochina, USSR Academy of Sciences, New York (1979).

Mary F. Zirin

Ursula Krechel
1947–

Born April 12, 1947, Trier, Germany
Genre(s): drama, novel, poetry, editions, journalism
Language(s): German

Ursula Krechel's talents are many-faceted. She is a playwright, poet, novelist, editor, and journalist. Once an activist in the student movement of the sixties, she has also been identified as a feminist.

Born in 1947, Krechel started out as a journalist while still a student. She attended university between 1966 and 1971 in Köln, studying theater, art history, and German Studies. She graduated with a disserta-tion on the film critic Herbert Ihering. In 1969–1970 and 1971–1972, she was the dramaturge at the Städtischen Bühnen Dortmund, and a theater worker for juveniles under custody. She has traveled widely and at present lives in Frankfurt.

Krechel's feminist inclinations can be found early in her career. "I write about women because of the fact that there is a contradiction between what they are and what society thinks of them. . . . I am motivated to dramatize contradictions I find in society, whatever they might be. With these words Krechel introduced her play, *Erika*, in *Theater heute* (August 1974; Theater Today). This piece for seven women characters deals with Erika's emancipatory revolt against the suppressive mechanism of marriage and work. In the play, Erika leaves her husband, but gets pregnant with a stranger. In the "happy ending," she returns ironically to her marriage and work with a baby and the realization that things could have been much more catastrophic than they are. Erika muses upon the situation: "I always thought I am dumb as a woman. . . . But a man is dumb too." The play is not merely a piece of mental propositions; drawing upon social reality, it attempts, hesitantly and painfully, to reveal contradictions in the everyday action and prattle of the petite bourgeoisie as if they were scars.

The problem of woman's identify has been a persistent theme in Krechel's writing ever since *Erika*. Her position as a feminist can be summarized in terms of an astute remark about the "New Women's Movement." "One should not," she wrote, "grasp feminism as a theory and as a mental construct (*Denkgebäude*), but rather as a ground-structure (*Grundstruktur*) for consciousness."

In her book of factual report, *Selbsterfahrung und Fremdbestimmung* (1975; Self's Experience, Other's Destiny, 2nd ed. in 1978 with the afterword "Fortsetzung des Nahkampfes mit weitsichtigeren Mitteln," or "Continuation of the Combats: The Long-Term Strategy"; new edition in 1983), Krechel further concretizes the contradictions of female existence by integrating theoretical exposition with the method of storytelling. In doing so, she attempts to force open the internal aspects of feminism itself. These "reports of the New Women's Movement" represent a collection of the positions, experiences, and struggles in the wide area of conflict in female emancipation, which she unravels and analyzes. The book is also enhanced by an aesthetic quality which some critics characterize as the production of an objective reality through an overt subjectivity. As the title of the book suggests, in the narratives one could find the authorial self's experience merging into, while still distinct from the other's destiny.

This paradoxical but apparent unity of subjective self-experience and objective observation of contemporary life accounts for Krechel's poetic style in *Nach Mainz!* (1977; To Mainz!) and *Verwundbar wie in den besten Zeiten* (1979; Vulnerable as in the Best of Times), both concerned about problems of self-identity in a world of male-gendered realities. Resisting the light-hearted sing-song jingle of the new lyrical subjectivism, poems in these volumes exhibit an angular hardness and biting harshness. *Nach Mainz!*, which opens with an eloquent story of the persona's mother, is a collection of narrative poems, condensed and distilled from embittered day-to-day activities, and from dreams and disjointed utopias. More complex but also evoking an inner world of illusions and delusions, *Verwundbar wie in den besten Zeiten* is a many-layered series of poems weaving vulnerability, sufferings, wounds, complaints, and some kind of unresigned sorrow into a thematic matrix. While mapping, through reflective thought, the causalities of these elements, Krechel experiments with complex forms of expression. In particular, the painful sense of foreignness and cold motivates her to violate the conventional use of language: "But the particulars could/ not have had any names"; "Speeches have lost their words." The result of this approach is a startling wealth of colorfully differentiated pictures and names. Her language is melodious and rhythmic but goes against syntactical and paratactical conventions.

Krechel's inclinations drew her attention not only to the flaws of society, sufferings, love, and politics, but also to the New Women's Movement and its literature. She was attracted to the writings of Irmgard Keun, whom one can now read again since Krechel's rediscovery, and to Elisabeth Langgässer's *Unauslöschliches Siegel* (Unerasable Seal), which she edited with a new afterword in 1979.

In 1981 Krechel published her first great prose, *Zweite Natur* (Second Nature). Incorporating dreams and calculated chance elements, this work adopts in part a method of organization akin to surrealism. It has a loosely structured, episodic, and serendipitous form with little if any epical integration and psychological portrayal. There is scarcely any hint at where the climactic moments are. All of these characteristics seem to suggest a rejection of bourgeois codes of narration. Despite the fact that the story is about how four young people go about trying out the "new form of life (*die neue Lebensform*) in the community (*Wohngemeinschaft*)" of Frankfurt and "fall out of the nest of biographies," this novel is no *Bildungsroman* or adolescent fiction either. It is situated at the border between reality and fiction, where the claims of both areas are constantly at odds with one another. That "heartless people deserve this state" is an experience which the young people of the novel and Krechel's writings defend against with vigor. The melancholic knowledge that it is insufficient to create these characters, and much less suitable if at another time, weighs heavily on the narrative, and determines the end of the novel, which remains rather ambivalent: three women and a pair of doves leave the community with the boys.

Rohschnitt. Gedicht in sechzig Sequenzen (Raw Cuts: Poetry In Seventy Sequences), a book-length lyric published in 1983 and composed according to the principle of film-cutting, also deals with the kind of "right dreams in the wrong reality" depicted in *Zweite Natur*. Stringed together throughout by means of narrative moments, this great cycle of poems demands understanding and double readings. As a point of departure, Krechel chooses to discourse at length on the self or "*I*," who remains astonished by and disapproving of her attributes and labels of identification: "the *I* I have been is to be/ in the grass, that have I dreamed/ that the *I* I have been is to be." The departure from the *I* means a departure from the roles, the establishments, and the realities with which we are surrounded. The *I* can be plural, as in "die Schöne die Kluge die Mutter" (The Beautiful the Intelligent the Mother)—the three travel, together with a child, into an indistinct future: "charts, folded plans, departure is invention/ is a raft made of cork, a hole from Wanting-no-more/ an idea of more." Krechel has no particular aversion to greatness of form such as that achieved in Rilke's *Duino Elegies*, but the nature of her playful narratives, which resist thematic conscription, is not conducive to it. There seems to be a number of moves associated with deconstruction, the critique of the Enlightenment, and the transvaluation of values. Perhaps the poems are just what they are: "raw cuts" which, according to film terminology, are only initial montage clippings belonging together. At any rate, the technique of ordering used already constitutes a subversion of the classical concept of the lyrical subject.

In her more recent poems, *Vom Feuer lernen* (1985; Learn from Fire), Krechel has turned to lyrical suggestiveness. As "The Common Language Sealed" ("versiegelt die geläufige Sprache," the title of the first poem in the volume) suggests, she has rejected the direct pragmatic applications of her poetry. Her language is constantly both literal and symbolic, and even intentionally oblique. In line with the shift of interest to the "New Subjectivity" in the German writing of the eighties, this latest development indicates that Krechel is also moving beyond the precepts of the student movement in which she came of age.

Krechel has worked with many genres. A recent work deserving attention is her theatrical piece *Aus der Sonne* (stage manuscript 1985; From the Sun). Introducing the play, she asks: "Why cope with the changes of life by creating out of sheer invention a world which the firm reality will outdo anyway?" In the play, Edith's first line goes: "Unplayable. I will not laugh at that. That is my life. It will be played." The idea of life as play is presented not only in terms of the blurring of the distinctive borders between life and play, but also gotten across by means of a stylish grasp of life in the forties and fifties. This idea is also the preoccupation in another novel written in 1985, *Die Papsttochter* (The Pope's Daughter), in which fiction and reality illuminate one another, and truth and fiction cross over.

Works

Creative Writings: *Erika*, play (premiered 1974, pub. 1975). *Zwei Tode* (1975). *Nach Mainz!*, poems (1977). *Verwundbar wie in den besten Zeiten*, poems (1979). *Zweite Natur*, novel (1981). *Rohschnitt. Gedicht in sechzig Sequenzen*, poems (1983). *Vom Feuer lernen*, poems (1985). *Aus der Sonne*, play (manuscript, 1985). *Die Papsttochter*, novel (manuscript, 1985).

Other Works: *Information und Wertung*, dissertation on the theater and the film criticism of Herbert Ihering (1972). *Selbsterfahrung und Fremdbestimmung* (reportage, 1975, 1978 m. Nachw. "Fortsetzung des Nahkampfes mit weitsichtigeren Mitteln," erw. neuausg. 1983). *Die Entfernung der Wünsche am belien Tag* (1977). *Women's Liberation. Frauen gemeinsam sind stark!*, texts and materials about the Women's Liberation Movement in the United States (1977). *Das Parkett ein spiegelnder See* (1979). *Lesarten*, texts about poetry (1982). *Glückselig feindselig vogelfrei* (1984). *Der Keksgigant* (1986). *Leuk und Lachen oder die Grammatick des Austausches* (1987).

Miscellaneous: Contribution to "Theater heute" (August 1974). Editor of Elisabeth Langgässer's *Unauslöschliches Siegel* (1979). "Ich bin eine erstklasige Schriftstellerin zweiter Güte." In *die Karriere der Vicki Baum*, television play by Ursula Krechel and Herbert Wiesner (1985). Afterword to Irene Brin's *Morbidezza* (1986).

Balance Chow

Louise Labé
ca. 1522–1566

Born April 1522 (?), Lyons, France
Died Lyons, April 1566
Genre(s): débat, elegy, sonnet
Language(s): French

In the sixteenth century Lyons was a major commercial and intellectual center that rivaled Paris in importance. Close to Italy, frequented by Italian traders and bankers, serving as occasional residence for the king and his court, it welcomed the intellectual contributions of the Renaissance. Labé's father, a wealthy cordier or ropemaker, allowed his daughter to profit from the more liberated trends in feminine education that prevailed among some of the French and Italian aristocracy. She learned Latin, Spanish, and Italian and became an accomplished musician. Biographers indicate that she also mastered fencing and amazed more conservative members of Lyons society by riding horseback in male costume. Her marriage to Ennemond Perrin, thirty-five years her senior, did not prevent her from pursuing her interest in literature and the arts. The *Belle Cordiére*, as she was called, entertained intellectuals and writers, among them Maurice Scève and Olivier de Magny. The latter is rumored to have been her partner in a brief but tempestuous love affair that inspired some of Labé's most celebrated poetry. In 1555 a small volume consisting of the *Débat de Folie et Amour* in prose, three elegies, and 24 sonnets appeared in Lyons as the *Euvres de Louize Labé lionnoize*. Although there are occasional references to some Latin verses by Labé, these have apparently been lost, and her literary reputation depends exclusively upon the sonnets and the *Débat*.

In the prefatory letter to her friend Clémence de Bourges, Labé argues that the time has come for women to look beyond mere domestic duties and show what they can do in the field of humanistic learning. This includes publishing their literary works so that Labé is, herself, an example of the enlightened Renaissance woman. The *Debate between Folly and Cupid* suggests a rapport with the medieval *débat*, but Labé renews the genre through her light and sophisticated manipulation of prose style and reveals the influence of Leo Ebreo and other Renaissance Neoplatonists as well as such Italian literary models as Bembo and Sannazaro. She is also indebted to Plutarch, Lucian, Erasmus, and Ovid, but the myth that provides the substance of the *Débat* is her own invention. Labé shows similar originality in the sonnets where she transforms the Petrarchan discourse of male poets into a vehicle for feminine desire and feminine emotion.

Labé's sonnets are remarkable for both technical mastery and passionate intensity, qualities that make her one of the more accessible poets of the School of Lyons and that have sustained her literary reputation from Ronsard to Rilke. In the sixteenth century the sensuous character of her love, the frank expression of longing for physical union, combined with her liberated lifestyle, place her in a difficult social position. Insulting songs and verses suggested that she was little better than a prostitute. Contemporaries like François de Billon, Antoine du Verdier, and Jean Calvin openly referred to her as a courtesan or worse. She was also accused of assisting her cousin Antonia Roccot to poison her husband Jean Yvard, but Yvard's death in Geneva prevented the case from coming to trial and spared her further scandal.

Labé apparently withdrew from Lyons society following the publication of her book and spent the remaining years of her life at her villa of Parcieu en Dombes. The *Oeuvres*, accompanied by laudatory verses from contemporaries like Scève and Pontus de Tyard, enjoyed considerable success, with a second and third edition published in Lyons by Jean de

Tournes in 1556 and a fourth edition appearing the same year in Rouen. It is not likely that Labé's departure from Lyons was occasioned by the reception accorded her poetry or even the legend of the "Belle Cordière." Lyons was in financial decline and suffered from the political and military turmoil occasioned by the outbreak of religious warfare. The city was also ravaged by plague, and a great many of the Lyons intelligentsia had died in the 1550s. The brilliant and refined Lyonese society that had surrounded and nourished the Belle Cordiére no longer existed.

Works

Euvres de Louize Labé lionnoize (1555). *Oeuvres complètes*, ed. Enzo Giudici (1981).

Translations: *Sonnets*, tr. Graham Dustin Martin (1973). *The Debate between Folly and Cupid*, tr. Edwin Marion Cox (1925).

Paula Sommers

Claire (Rose) Lacombe
1765–

Born March 4, 1765, Ariège, France
Death date unknown
Genre(s): political and feminist pamphlets, speeches
Language(s): French

Claire Lacombe, known as "Red Rosa" for her radical social and economic ideas, was one of the most active and vocal feminists of the French Revolution. Nothing is known about her early life except that she was an actress in southern France before she arrived in Paris in 1792. She was soon affiliated with the radical Enragés, including Théophile Leclerc, a journalist and deputy from Lyon, with whom she lived. Her first public appearance was before the Legislative Assembly in July 1792; she demanded that Lafayette be replaced as French Chief of Staff and that women be allowed to serve the nation in the same capacity as men: "abolish the privileges of the male sex. . . . Thirteen million slaves are shamefully dragging the chains of thirteen million despots," she declared. Women should be armed to fight in defense of *la patrie* and crush counterrevolution at home; most deputies scoffed at these would-be "grenadiers in greasy skirts." That women could fight was proven on August 10, 1792, when Lacombe, at the head of a male corps of Fédéres, stormed the Tuileries Palace in Paris; this bloody attack by enemies of monarchy overthrew the

King. Lacombe was wounded and received a civic crown from the government. To educate women about their rights and role in the new France, Lacombe and several other feminists founded the Society of Revolutionary Republican Woman (May 1793), which eventually claimed 170 members. These women were to be at least eighteen years old, virtuous, and of good moral character. It was the first club organized for lower class women with an interest in their concerns such as adequate food supplies and inflation. Lacombe was committed to bettering their lives through pressure on the government. The Society was partially responsible for the victory of the Montagnards in 1793, but a rift among members soon diminished their effectiveness. Lacombe was secretary, then president, of the Society and she favored the more radical Enragés over the Montagnards and the Jacobins.

Under her leadership the club demanded that women be allowed in the military, that national workshops be established, and that all nobles be excluded from public office. The radicalism of many feminists alienated the working-class women whom they were trying to organize and lead. Dissension over wearing the cockade and dressing in trousers and the caps of liberty caused an irreparable breach in the Society. When the Jacobins consolidated their power, Lacombe and others were targeted as enemies of the state. Lacombe especially disliked Robespierre and accused him of being a coward and an "ordinary man." Moreover, the market women of Paris sided with the Jacobins and petitioned the National Convention to abolish the Society. On October 28, 1793, members of the club were attacked by a mob of market women at their meeting hall in Saint-Eustache. This marked the end of the feminist movement in France—the Jacobins disbanded all women's clubs. The women were ordered to return to their homes and their traditional roles as wives and mothers.

Lacombe was a victim of the very women she hoped to aid and of the Jacobins' antifeminism. She was arrested on April 2, 1794, accused of being a counterrevolutionary and of immorality (for living with Leclerc), and imprisoned. By 1795 women were barred from attending meetings of the assembly and lost their right to organize clubs and petition the government. The activist revolutionary women were silenced. When she was released from prison on August 20, 1795, Lacombe became a proprietress of a tobacco shop before resuming her acting career and fading into obscurity. The efforts of Lacombe and others on behalf of women's rights failed to win the support of the leading revolutionaries, but in the nineteenth century they were lauded for their attacks on aristocratic and middle-class privilege and their efforts on behalf of the working class.

Works

Discours prononcé à la barre de l'Assemblée nationale par Madame Lacombe, le 25 juillet 1792, l'an 4, de la liberté (n.d.). *Rapport fait par la Citoyenne Lacombe à la Société des républicaines révolutionaires [sic] de qui s'est passé le 16 septembre à la Société des Jacobins concernant celle des Républicaines révolutionaires [sic] séante à S. Eustache; et les dénonciations faites contre la Citoyenne Lacombe personnellement* (n.d.).

Jeanne A. Ojala

Marie-Madeleine, Pioche de la Vergne, Comtesse de Lafayette 1634–1693

a.k.a. La Fayette
Born 1634, Paris
Died May 25, 1693, Paris
Genre(s): novels, novella, memoirs
Language(s): French

A major figure in the history of the novel, Mme de Lafayette is known primarily for *La Princesse de Clèves*, the greatest French novel of the seventeenth century and one of the acknowledged masterpieces of Western fiction.

Mme de Lafayette was born and raised in Paris and spent most of her adult life in the French capital. Christened Marie-Madeleine, Pioche de la Vergne, Mme de Lafayette was the first born of Marc Pioche, Sieur de La Vergne and Isabelle Pena, both from the lowest ranks of the nobility. Of her early years, little is known. Her father died in 1649, and a year later her mother married the Chevalier Renaud-René de Sévigné, whose elevated rank afforded both Mme de Lafayette and her mother entrée to the highest circles of the court. In 1650, Mme de Lafayette was made a lady-in-waiting to Anne of Austria, and in 1654 she made the acquaintance of Henriette-Anne Stuart (known as Henriette d'Angleterre), the future wife of Louis XIV's brother, Philippe de France, Duc d'Orléans. Mme de Lafayette was later to become the close companion of Henriette d'Angleterre and collaborate with her in the composition of her memoirs.

In 1655, Mme de Lafayette married Jean-François Motier, Comte de Lafayette, a widower twenty-eight years her senior and a member of a distinguished, albeit financially troubled, provincial family. From 1655 to 1660, the couple resided at the family chateau in the Auvergne, where Mme de Lafayette gave birth to two sons, Louis (1658) and Armand (1659). In 1660, Mme de Lafayette returned alone to Paris to tend to her husband's complicated legal suits, which she brought to a successful conclusion in 1662. Although she remained on good terms with her husband, the couple soon agreed that he would remain in Auvergne, to oversee the family estate while she resided in Paris.

Once established in Paris, Mme de Lafayette became a regular member of court and intellectual circles. She remained a life-long friend of Mme de Sévigné, later recognized as one of the century's greatest letter-writers and gradually developed a deep and fast relationship with the Duc de la Rochefoucauld, author of the masterly *Maximes*. Her own literary career began with a novella titled *La Princesse de Montpensier*, published anonymously in 1662. This tale of a young woman's arranged marriage and illegitimate, ruinous passion was quite well received, and in ensuing years it was often praised for its *vraisemblance* and its rejection of the conventions of the heroic romances, so popular in the 1640s and 1650s, of Mlle de Scudéry and la Calprenède. In 1669, she began work on a romance, titled *Zaïde*, about Moors and Christians in medieval Spain, enlisting the help of La Rochefoucauld and Jean Regnalut de Segrais in the project. Volume one of *Zaïde* appeared in 1670 under Segrais's name, the second volume in 1671. Although a collaborative effort, this popular romance was clearly more Mme de Lafayette's work that anyone else's. During the 1670s, Mme de Lafayette assiduously researched the historical background for her masterpiece, *La Princesse de Clèves*, while working indefatigably for the advancement of her sons' careers. In 1678, *La Princesse de Clèves* was published anonymously, and for more than a year the novel was the center of conversation throughout Parisian intellectual circles. The novel's controversial confession scene, in which the Princesse begs her husband to help her overcome her passion for the Duc de Nemours, led the editors of the *Mercure Galant* to solicit letters from its readers evaluating the Princesse's decision—the first such literary survey in French letters. *La Princesse de Clèves* was the last of Mme de Lafayette's writings to be published during her lifetime. After her death in 1693, one short novella and two nonfictional works were published: *La Comtesse de Tende* (1724), probably written in the 1680s, although some scholars date it much earlier; *Histoire de Madame Henriette d'Angleterre* (1720), written in 1665 and 1669–1670;

and *Mémoires de la Cour de France pour les anneés 1688 et 1689* (1731; Memoirs of the Court of France for the Years 1688 and 1689).

La Princesse de Clèves is undoubtedly Mme de Lafayette's finest work, one whose psychological analysis and dramatic intensity are perhaps only equaled in the seventeenth century by the great tragedies of her contemporary Jean Racine. The novel was not, as was once thought, especially innovative in form, nor did it directly influence novelists of the eighteenth century; nevertheless, it was immediately recognized as a great work in its day, and it has continued to enjoy an unwavering preeminence in French literature to the present. Seventeenth- and eighteenth-century readers were impressed by the verisimilitude of Mme de Lafayette's treatment of passion. Later readers have been particularly struck by the acumen with which Mme de Lafayette exposes the complex motives of her characters, their divided alliances, ambiguous self-justifications, and obliquely erotic actions. All have been intrigued by the enigmatic Princesse—above all, by her singular confession to her husband and by her striking decision, after her husband's death, to reject the Duc de Nemours.

La Princesse de Montpensier and *La Comtesse de Tende*, although lesser works than *La Princesse de Clèves*, are well-crafted novellas whose merits have not been fully recognized. *La Princesse de Montpensier* combines historical fact and fiction in an ingenious fashion and subtly parallels the devastations of love and the upheavals of the state that attend the unfortunate passion of the Princesse. *La Comtesse de Tende*, Mme de Lafayette's most bitter and cynical work, portrays with laconic rigor the self-interest, callousness, and savagery of polite society; it also shows the real and brutal dangers aristocratic women were prey to once they entered into an illicit relationship.

The romance *Zaïde* shares the limitations of its genre, but given those constraints, it is a lively and at times psychologically astute tale which stands above most of the romances of the century. Of Mme de Lafayette's works of nonfiction, her *Histoire de Madame Henriette d'Angleterre* is the most interesting. the concluding narration of the death of Madame is one of the century's great instances of neoclassical restraint and detachment in the expression of powerful feeling.

Works

Romans et nouvelles (La Princesse de Clèves, Zaïde, La Princesse de Montpensier and *La Comtesse de Tende)*, ed. Émile Magne (1970, reprint). *Histoire de Madame Henriette d'Angleterre, La Princesse de Montpensier, La Comtesse de Tende*, ed. Claudine Herrmann (1979, reprint). *Correspondance de Madame de Lafayette*, ed. André Beaunier (1942, reprint).

Translations: *The Princess of Clèves*, tr. Nancy Mitford, rev. Leonard Tancock (1978). *The Comtesse de Tende* and selections from *The History of Madame Henriette d'Angleterre*, tr. Ronald Bogue, in *Baroque Women Writers*, ed. Katharina Wilson and Frank Warnke (1987). *The Princesse de Clèves*, tr. Robin Buss. (1992). *The Princesse de Clèves; The Princesse de Montpensier; The Comtesse de Tende*, tr. Terence Cave. (1992). *The Secret History of Henrietta, Princess of England: first wife of Philippe, duc d'Orléans; together with Memoirs of the Court of France for the Years 1688–1689*, tr. J.M. Shelmerdine (1993).

Ronald Bogue

Lady Caroline Lamb
1785–1828
Born November 13, 1785, London
Died January 24, 1828, London
Genre(s): novel, poetry
Language(s): English

Lamb, an aristocratic novelist and poet of the early nineteenth century, is chiefly remembered as the flighty married woman who fell in love with Byron and who ungraciously accepted his decision to terminate their liaison. Brought up in a social class in which titled family connections and elegance ruled, Lamb was given no formal education because a doctor had advised that she "should not be taught anything or placed under any restraint." When she married William Lamb at twenty, she was described as a model of fashion and of pale, delicate complexion.

The liaison with Byron flourished under the system of literary soirées in which the evening's amusement was to complete the verses for a partner. Lamb met Byron at a ball, shortly after the success of his *Childe Harold* in 1812. They exchanged gifts and letters and appeared in public together for about nine months. The relationship slowly and tortuously died before Lamb's eyes. Byron married Anne Isabella Milbanke January 2, 1815. His marriage ended in scandal when Lady Byron signed separation papers; he subsequently left England for good. There are numerous references to Lamb in his correspondence.

Meanwhile Lamb's in-laws were plotting to separate her legally from William by having her declared insane. During this period she secretly wrote *Glenarvon*, a *roman à clef* about her affair with Byron. She published it anonymously in 1816, but the particulars were immediately discovered. As a novel, its chief interest is to Byron scholars. The complicated plots and "innumerable subsidiary characters" make the book confusing. Some scenes bring a scene or emotion to life, but writing was basically Lamb's "sole comfort" during a time when she and her husband were ostracized. The parallels between her life and her novel are easily drawn. Calantha, young, ingenious, and irresponsible, falls in love with Lord Avondale and marries him. Over time, Calantha's wild behavior and Avondale's negligence create a weak marriage. She associates with several London society ladies, all easily recognizable to Lamb's contemporaries. While Avondale is away to quiet a political disturbance, Calantha meets Glenarvon, a stranger who has appeared to lay claim to some property. They are attracted to each other and exchange gifts and letters. After numerous calamities Glenarvon marries and leaves.

Her second novel, *Graham Hamilton,* finished in 1820, is not as complicated or emotionally charged as her first. Consequently, little attention has been given to it. Her third novel, *Ada Reis,* finished in 1823, was inspired by exotic Eastern tales such as *Vathek* and was well received in its day. Jenkins says that Ugo Foscolo, the exiled Italian writer, encouraged her to write something that "would not offend." Ada Reis becomes a pirate, settles in Arabia, and meets Kabarra, a spirit of darkness, who becomes his mentor. And Lamb also wrote mostly autobiographical poems that are generally technically stilted and cliché ridden, as for example, "William Lamb's Return from Paris, Asking Me My Wish."

Always of delicate health, her final years were relatively quiet. In 1824, however, she happened to pass the cortege carrying Byron's body, and popular legend reports that Lamb's emotional stability broke as a result. Actually, she reports having been troubled at the sight, but what caused her the most pain was the biography of Byron written by Thomas Medwin shortly after the poet's death. In it, according to Jenkins, she had to "endure . . . the new anguish of seeing herself for the first time as she had been held up to the scorn of Byron's friends, and now to that of the public." Even her obituary notice in the *London Gazette* could not allow her liaison with Byron to sink into oblivion: "The world is very lenient to the mistresses of poets, and perhaps not without justice, for their attachments have something of excuse; not only in their object but in their origin, they arise from imagination, not depravity." Other writers she knew intimately were Benjamin Constant and Mme de Staël, and beginning in 1825, the young Edward Bulwer-Lytton.

Lady Caroline Lamb

Works

Glenarvon (anon., 1816; reissued as *The Fatal Passion,* 1865). *Verses from Glenarvon; To Which Is Prefixed the Original Introduction* (1816). *A New Canto* (anon., 1819). *Graham Hamilton* (anon., 1822). *Ada Reis: A Tale* (anon., 1823). *Fugitive Pieces and Reminiscences of Lord Byron with Some Original Poetry,* ed. I. Nathan (1829).

Marilynn J. Smith

Mary Ann Lamb
1764–1847

a.k.a. M.B., Sempronia
Born December 3, 1764, London
Died May 20, 1847, London
Genre(s): children's literature
Language(s): English

Mary Lamb is known chiefly as the sister of Charles Lamb, a writer of the early Romantic period. She suffered from intermittent bouts of mental illness throughout her adult years, but she was still able to work on several publishing projects to help support herself and Charles. Of the work attributed to Charles, Mary Lamb was responsible for 14 of the 20 tales in their children's Shakespeare book, all but three of the stories in *Mrs. Leicester's School,* and a third of the poems in a small volume of children's poems. In addition, she wrote an article addressing the issue of the woman's role in nineteenth-century England.

She had two brothers: Charles, born when she was eleven years old, and John, one year her senior. The family spent many years living in quarters in the Temple, property once owned by the Knights Templar, where the father was a factotum of a prominent lawyer, Samuel Salt, who had chambers in the Temple. Through Salt, John and Charles received scholarships to attend Christ's Hospital, where Charles met Samuel Coleridge. Mary's only formal schooling was briefly at William Bird's Day school.

It was necessary that the young Mary had to assist her parents taking care of Charles and doing needlework, and as her parents aged, she nursed them at home. On September 27, 1796, at the age of thirty-two, however, exhausted from the physical and emotional strain of caring for her aging parents, Mary became hysterical. In a knife-wielding charge against a young apprentice, she stabbed her mother, who was trying to stop the fracas. The wound killed Mrs. Lamb, but it wasn't for several days that Mary remembered the incident at all. Declared a lunatic, she stayed in an asylum until the following April, when she was placed under Charles's guardianship and moved to a private home, she did not return home until the death of her father in 1799. From the day of the collapse, she was never able to discuss the death of her mother, and she experienced occasional upsets, some of which necessitated hospital care.

Upon joining her brother in new lodgings, Mary and Charles received their friends at regular Wednesday evening parties and developed their writing interests. They visited regularly with Coleridge, the Wordsworths, and the Hazlitts; later they knew Leigh Hunt and Robert Southey. For Mary, one association that prepared her literary career was with the Godwins. She did not know William Godwin (1756–1836) before the death of his first wife, Mary Wollstonecraft, but she did know his second wife, Mary Jane Godwin, who began publishing and selling juvenile books. She commissioned Mary Lamb to write *Tales from Shakespear,* which appeared in 1807. Mary wrote fourteen comedies and histories, and Charles did the six tragedies, but only Charles's name appeared on the title page. The prose tales taken from some of Shakespeare's plays have been well received and are probably the best-known work of the Lambs.

Mrs. Godwin also published two other collaborations in 1809: *Mrs. Leicester's School* and *Poetry for Children.* Although unverified, approximately a third of the poems may have been Mary's and all but three of the stories were hers. This time, the title page listed no author; the stories are "autobiographical" accounts told by different school girls at the school. The book was well received, running into eight editions by 1823.

Mary's article "On Needleworking," appearing in *The British Lady's Magazine* in April 1815, addressed the issue of women's duties and how best to meet them. She proposes ways that a woman, within the framework of her feminine world, can add to the comfort and income of her household. Noting that "women have of late been rapidly advancing in intellectual improvement" and that "workwomen of every description were never in so much distress for want of employment," Lamb recommends selling the needlework so many women do to fill leisure hours. Her idea of feminine duty is to "be accounted the helpmates of *men;* who, in return for all he does for us, expects, and justly expects, us to do all in our power to soften and sweeten life." Unless parents can foresee a daughter's need for future self-sufficiency, she wrote, there is no need to "strain every nerve to bring them up to a learned profession." By doing needlework for money, "so much more nearly will woman be upon an equality with men as far as respects the mere enjoyment of life."

Works

Tales from Shakespear (1807; with Charles, Mary Lamb wrote "The Tempest," "A Midsummer Night's Dream," "The Winter's Tale," "Much Ado About Nothing," "As You Like It," "The Two Gentlemen of Verona," "The Merchant of Venice," "Cymbeline," "All's Well That Ends Well," "The Taming of the Shrew," "The Comedy of Errors," "Measure for Measure," "Twelfth Night," and "Pericles, Prince of Tyre"). *Mrs. Leicester's School; or the History of Several Young Ladies, related by Themselves* (anon., 1807, Mary Lamb wrote Elizabeth Villiers, Louisa Manners, Ann Withers, Elinor Forester, Margaret Green, Emily Barton, Charlotte Wilmot). *Poetry for Children* (by the author of *"Mrs. Leicester's School",* 1809). "On Needleworking," *The British Lady's Magazine* (by Sempronia, April, 1815; reprinted Gilchrist, 244–254). *Mary and Charles Lamb: Poems, Letters, and Remains* (ed. W. Hazlitt, 1874). *The Works of Charles and Mary Lamb,* E.V. Lucas (1903–1905). *The Works of Charles and Mary Lamb,* ed. T. Hutchinson (1924). *The Letters of Charles and Mary Lamb,* ed. E.W. Marrs, Jr. (1975–1978).

Marilynn J. Smith

Anne-Therese de Marguenat de Courcelles, Marquise de Lambert
1647–1733

Born 1647, Paris
Died July 12, 1733, Paris
Genre(s): essay, narrative fiction, letters
Language(s): French

Born to a family of old nobility, Lambert lost her father at an early age. Her stepfather, the amateur writer Bachaumont, encouraged her penchant for reading and reflection and urged her to keep journals of her readings. This the marquise continued to do after marriage to Henri de Lambert, marquis de Saint-Bris (1666). Although the son of a distinguished army commander and himself an able man, Lambert's career progressed slowly up to a final short tenure as governor of Luxembourg. Widowhood (1686) left Lambert with complicated and extended litigation to safeguard the fortunes of her two surviving children: Henri-François (b. 1677) and Marie-Thérèse (comtesse de Saint-Aulaire, 1679–1731).

Short essays like the comparison of Diogenes and Alexander published posthumously may have been written much earlier. Only three of Lambert's writings were published during her lifetime, all without her prior consent. Of these, the two *Avis d'une mère*, to her son and to her daughter, became her best-known works (the former circulated widely in English translation, going through seven printings alone with the letters of Lord Chesterfield to his son). After the unauthorized publication of the letter to her son (1726), Lambert supervised the appearance of the two (1728 and republished them in Holland in 1729 under the title *Lettres sur la véritable éducation*). Both were composed at the turn of the century. Linked by the common concern of education, this time a "continuing" one, *Réflexions nouvelles sur les femmes* (1728) was published only to counter an unauthorized printing (1727; rpt. in 1729 in part as *Métaphysique de l'amour*).

Both the letters of advice to her children and the reflections on women have given Lambert a place in the early history of feminism, the so-called theoretical, élite phase, in which education had become central. The education proposed for Mlle de Lambert, like that of her brother, is pragmatic, an education whose end is happiness in the world and whose basis is self-reliance. As for the son's letter, the title given the pirated printing, "On True Glory," gives the tone. Hero-

ism (worthy of his grandfather), however, is to be tempered by conscience and a sensitivity to humanity that adds the claims of others to those of self-worth. Although Lambert's correspondent Fénelon found ambition here to be too exalted, seemingly at the expense of religion that is nowhere literally invoked, he found nothing to criticize in the daughter. Religion in it is commended as guide to a woman's duties but also as consolation for the situation in which men's institutions have placed that duty. Education for independent judgment and broad culture goes well beyond the program Fénelon had proposed. Although attention to religion here, a stoic tone, and insistence on decorum have made Lambert seem conservative, there is no doubt of her belief in the equality of women once their self-identity is achieved through proper education. The more personal and original *Réflexions*, whose program remains individual ethical feminism, convey a message of the need for reenforcement of female identity, which will come in a felt community but must first be found in individual self-esteem, consciously cultivated in terms of the positive differences of imagination, sensibility, and love that constitute that identity.

Lambert's posthumously published treatises on friendship and on old age, like her educational reflections, show continuous meditation on modern texts, on Montaigne and Descartes especially, but also on Pascal and Nicole, Malebranche, La Rochefoucauld and Saint-Evremond. Her readings of Plato, the Stoics, Cicero, and Horace are also direct and formative. From the writings on education, several times declared as useful to herself as to her children, through those on old age, it becomes apparent that Lambert's writing reflects a conscious shaping by the humanist tradition that strives through reflection to live fittingly and that her mind was deeply affected by Cartesian rationalism. Her single narrative fiction, *La Femme hermite*, a sustained confession by a woman of quality ("qui s'est retirée du monde"), narrates the consequences of the sin of not having reflected on life and may seem an enactment of Horace's wisdom on the vanity of travel when introspection is lacking. Lambert's embodiment of this honored tradition, in an elegant *style coupé*, drew tributes at her death (notably by Fontenelle) as it had during her lifetime frequently in her own drawing room.

For more than two decades, after it began in 1710, Lambert's salon retained its preeminence in Parisian society. She realized in it long-held desires for good discussion. Society gathering simply for diversion was assigned one day, whereas afternoon discussions on specific topics—sometimes from prepared texts—was set for Tuesdays (in an "enlightened" development D'Alembert later praised, the two soon commingled to their mutual profit). Gaming and literary parlor games, like those of Mme du Maine at Sceaux, were not allowed. Nor were explicitly polemical discourses on religion and politics. Both certainly entered into discussion that was predominantly centered in moral philosophy and moved across a broad range of topics including aesthetics (with Houdar de la Motte, Du Bos), mathematics and science (Mairan, Fontenelle), and economies both political (Saint-Pierre) and hedonistic (Lassay). Playwrights like Dancourt and Marivaux, and the actress Adrienne Lecouvreur, met learned classicists like Buffier, Mongault, Louis de Sacy. And Marivaux, who left a more flattering evocation of his hostess in *La Vie de Marianne* than did the outsider Le Sage in his satirical character portrait of Marquise de Chaves, found at least one topic for a play (*La Colonie*)—and perhaps the tone for another (*La Voiture embourbée*), as did Mme de Staal (*L'Engouement, La Mode*). Staal's accounts of the court at Sceaux and communications read from the duchesse must have caught the ear of the novelists Crébillon and Duclos, as well as Mlles La Force, Murat, and Saintonge. Their worldly texts, like the *vers badins* of Chaulieu and Saint-Aulaire, refracted the Tuesdays' conversation.

In retrospect, Lambert's salon takes its place as the first of the great Enlightenment salons. Although classicists like Mme Dacier, Fraguier, and Valincour were regulars, and Lambert toyed momentarily with the rôle of mediator in the Querelle des Anciens et des Modernes, her preference was for the modern. Fontenelle remained central for her, as his broad interests did for the salon. Discussing and filtering the Moderns' positions, as it were communicating with the Club de l'Entresol, Lambert's salon seemed also an "antechamber" to a renaissant Académie française. Beyond direct and fictionalized accounts of its life, Lambert's enlivening dialogue may be rediscovered in certain readings of her writings: the treatise on old age in dialogue with Sacy, her paraphrase of Montesquieu—"Discours sur la différence qu'il ya de la réputation à la considération"—as a revealing woman's rewriting that the author himself highly valued.

Works

Avis d'une mére à son fils (1726). *Réflexions nouvelles sur les femmes, par une dame de la cour de France* (1728). *Avis d'une mére à son fils et à sa fille* (1728). *Traité de la viellesse* (posth., 1747). "Réflexions sur le goût" (posth., 1747). *La Femme hermite, nouvelle nouvelle* (posth., 1747). "Reflexions sur les richesses" (posth., 1747). "Dialogue entre Alexandre et Diogène sur l'égalité des biens" (posth., 1747). "Discours sur la différence qu'il y a de la réputation à la considération" (posth., 1747). *Lettres* (posth., 1747, 1754). *Oeuvres* (1808).

Translations: *The Works of the Marchioness de Lambert*, tr. anon. (1749; rpt. 1769, 1781). *A Mother to Her Son and Daughter: On True Education and Dialogue between Alexander and Diogenes on the Equality of Happiness*, tr. Rowell (1749). *New Reflections on the Fair Sex*, tr. J. Lockman (1729, 1737). *Essays on Friendship and Old Age*, tr. by a Lady (E.H.) (1780). *The Fair Solitary, or Female Hermit*, tr. anon. (1790).

Charles G.S. Williams

Anna Margrethe Lasson
1659–1738

a.k.a. Lassen
Born 1659, Copenhagen, Denmark
Died 1738, Odense, Denmark
Genre(s): novel, poetry, letters
Language(s): Danish

Anna Margrethe Lasson deserves a special place in Danish literature as the author of the very first Danish novel, *Den beklædte Sandhed* (1715; The Truth in Disguise, published anonymously, 1723). Lasson also wrote several honorary poems and letters of recognition and acknowledgment, most notably an honorary poem (and defense of women) for the significant Norwegian poet, Dorothe Engelbretsdatter. This poem was included in Engelbretsdatter's longer poetic work, *Taareoffer for bodfærdige Syndere* (1685; Offering of Tears for Penitent Sinners). Lasson's other verses include *Et Æreminde paa adskillige Vers over Familiens gamle Ven Oluf Borck* (1696; A Remembrance in Several Verses for an Old Friend of the Family, Oluf Borck), and the *Gratulations Vers til den Glorværdigste Danske Konge, Friderich den Fierde* (Verse in Honor of the Most Excellent Danish King, Frederik the Fourth), which Lasson wrote in her youth. Lasson has secured her position in Danish literature as an "early advocate of Danish, her mother tongue [and as a defender] of women who have dedicated themselves to scholarly matters, study and writing, which many consider uncommon, indeed improper and inadmissible concerns for women" (Friderich Schönau, *Samling af danske lærde Fruentimmer*, p. 962). Lasson advocated "true love for the mother tongue" (Fredrick Bajer, "En dansk Roman," 366), and, in the preface to her novel, she once again defended her contemporaries, literate, well-educated women. In Denmark, Anna Margrethe Lasson is remembered as the first Danish novelist, "our lovely Danish Aminda . . . who has given us the beautiful novel" (Schönau, p. 977). Modern literary critics have often taken a dimmer view of *Den beklædte Sandhed*, but the work remains important as the very first novel in Danish.

Anna Margrethe Lasson, the Aminda of *Den beklædte Sandhed*, was born in 1659 and christened on March 6, 1659, in Holmens Church, Copenhagen. She was the daughter of a gifted, avaricious, and very eccentric legal officer and country judge, Jens Lassen (1625–1706) and of Margrethe Christensdatter Lund (who died about 1690). Anna Margrethe Lasson never married. For a time, she administered the office and estate of the Dean of Our Lady Church and Parish (Vor Frue Sogn), Odense, on Fyn. She lived a humble, rather isolated life in Odense, until her death in 1738. Her writings reveal, however, an individual in close touch with the events and society of her day.

Anna Margrethe Lasson's major work is the novel, *Den beklædte Sandhed* (1715, 1723). The novel is very reminiscent of the precious, baroque *romans à clef* ("key" novels) of the seventeenth-century Madeleine de Scudery. In the novel, Lasson refers to places on Fyn, the island where she spent her life, and she exhibits intimate, detailed knowledge of "the Danish royal family and nobility . . . she had occasion to know of society's most prominent circles, if not directly, then at least through very good sources" (*Dansk biografisk Leksikon*, 1981, 8, 614). *Dansk biografisk Leksikon* further suggests that *Den beklædte Sandhed* is a very pompous, disjointed, complicated, and improbable story about knights and fair damsels; the novel is a retelling in flowery style of contemporary intrigues and scandals, possibly a fictional account of the marriage of Christian V's brother Jørgen and the English princess, Anne. In contrast to F.C. Schönau's (1753) glowing assessment of the work, modern literary historians have viewed *Den beklædte Sandhed* skeptically and critically, with little enthusiasm and interest; there have been "many assurances of the book's poor quality and insignificance in comparison with the classics." The novel seems to be a rather curious *mélange* of "high baroque, *galant*-heroic, pastorale, and late baroque, semihistorical elements" (*DbL*, 614). Even the full title of the novel immediately suggests its complexity, its flowery, flamboyant language, and its *roman à clef* precedents: *Den fordum i Ronne Bogstavs Kaabe nu i Danske Tunge-Maals Klæde iførte liden Roman kaldet "Den beklædte Sandhed," fremviist alle Liebhavere til Fornøyelse af en det danske Sprogs inderlige Elskerinde Aminda, Trykt 1723* ("The Truth in Disguise," a Little Novel, Formerly Written in the Cape of Runic Letters Now Clad in the Danish Language, Written for the Enjoyment of All Lovers by a Passionate Lover of the Danish Language, Aminda, Published 1723). However, the literary historians Stig Dalager and Anne-Marie Mai have recently taken a more positive approach to the first Danish novel. Dalager and Mai (*Danske dvindelige forgattere*, vol. 1, 1982) admit that the novel suggests "many impulses . . . [from] the pastorale's love-universe [and] the courtly novel's heroism, [to] rococo's affected descriptions of nature" (Dalager, p. 90), but they also suggest that the novel "creates an inner unity . . . [that] it points to the future . . . [and] that it contains much more than the conventional love-story: [it is] a multi-faceted love-story, sensual and spiritual, tragic and haunting, an element in a social utopia, rococo's elegant utopia" (Dalager, pp. 90–93). To Dalager and Mai, *Den beklædte Sandhed* reflects "a new opposition between rationalism and complexity of feeling, a new pensive relationship to nature, and a new interest for the emotional and passionate as something fine, intimate, and tempestuous" (Dalager, p. 93). The novel suggests a new prose wave, a turning point in Danish literature and letters; perhaps it merits more critical acclaim on that basis.

Anna Margrethe Lasson's contribution to Danish letters and literature cannot be measured in terms of wide acclaim, European recognition, and a multitude of celebrated works. We must, instead, consider Lasson a prose pioneer, one who suggested a new direction for Danish literature, enhanced the Danish language immeasurably with her "exceptionally well-composed letters" (Gustav Wad, *Fra Fyns Fortid*, 1924, p. 80), and one who asserted the worth and significant role of literate, well-educated women, both in her poems to Engelbretsdatter and Frederik IV and in her notable preface to the very first Danish novel, *Den beklædte Sandhed*.

Works

Taareoffer for bodfærdige Syndere: Vers (1685). *Et Æreminde paa adskillige Vers over Familiens gamle Ven Oluf Borck* (1696). *Gratulations Vers til den Glorværdigste Danske Konge, Friderich den Fierde* (n.d.). *Den beklædte Sandhed* (1715, 1723).

Lanae Hjortsvang Isaacson

Violette Leduc
1907–1972

Born 1907, Arras, France
Died 1972
Genre(s): novel, autobiography
Language(s): French

Violette Leduc was born in Arras in 1907 and grew up in Valenciennes, in the close atmosphere described in *La Bâtarde* (1964; The Bastardess), in which her mother and grandmother played such decisive roles, her father not recognizing his daughter. The latter book, firmly autobiographical like nearly all her books, also evokes her early life as a *pensionnaire*, her high school days in Paris and her work as editorial secretary and publicity writer with Plon, a major French publishing house, and, later, as a journalist. *La Bâtarde* and *La Folie en tête* (1970; Madness in Mind) describe in intimate detail and with her characteristic admixture of intensity and detachment her various friendships with Maurice Sachs, Jean Genet, Simone de Beauvoir, and others and the respect earned, with difficulty and yet certainty, from them and other writers such as Sartre, Jouhandeau, and Camus. Violette Leduc died in 1972 in Faucon, in the Alps of Upper Provence.

In 1946, Camus welcomed the manuscript of *L'Asphyxie* (Asphyxia) into the collection *Espoir* he was then editing. It was clearly an auspicious start for Violette Leduc although it would take many years, until the publication of *La Bâtarde* in 1964, for widespread public success. Simone de Beauvoir argued that all of Violette Leduc's books could assume the title of *L'Asphyxie*.

After *L'Affamée* (1948; Famished), which speaks, through the typical blatancy of its title, of the deep yearnings and desires that, inevitably, peopled the gaping holes of emotional and aesthetic deprivation and frustration of Violette Leduc's private and public lives, came *Ravages* (1955; Ravages). This powerful book, linked to all the others in its fundamental obsessions and aspirations (and perhaps especially to *Thérèse et Isabelle*), proceeds to narrate, with the most transparent of novelistic veils, the reciprocally ravaging effect of a double possessive passion. Jealousy, the tensions of exclusion and sharing, blindness, and lucidity, the gentleness and the (self-) destructiveness of love, the wonders and the horrors of high emotion: these are the principal elements of a book as profoundly confessional as any of the great books of self-revelation by contemporaries such as Maurois, Mauriac, de Beauvoir, Malraux, and many others.

La vieille fille et le mort (1958; The Old Woman and the Corpse), which also offers us "Les Boutons dorés," recounts the moving, pathetic gestures of a woman desperately wishing to reveal her love, incapable of finding that delicate equilibrium of giving and receiving with men, thrust up against her loneliness, her age, her inhibitions. It is a short novel of quiet tragedy and, typically, resistant, even if intransitive, hope. "Les Boutons dorés" is a short novel of youth and love, loss and "floating." Less flagrantly centered upon the self, it nevertheless partakes of the essential paradoxes and struggles at the heart of all Violette Leduc's work.

Trésors à prendre (1960; Treasures for the Taking) is, perhaps, the most splendidly resilient and, in a sense, serene of all of her works. Relating her wanderings on foot through Southern France in 1951, it demonstrates with supreme clarity Violette Leduc's passion for life. The emotional gamut is a full one: despair, solitude, fear, vulnerability, inadequacy, victimization, courage, persistence, vigor, recovery, and love. The "centers of interest" are as endless as the things of the world, and as rich, as profound, as significant. The style is characteristically telegraphic, staccato, never predictable, sharply observant.

La Bâtarde, according to Simone de Beauvoir, offers "a temperament, a style." The book depicts with intensity the strife in Violette Leduc's life, it treats her "ugliness," the stiflements and humiliations, the ambivalences and tensions of her many human interchanges. She also finds in love a crucial "instinct of self-preservation" and shows, in S. de Beauvoir's celebrated phrase, "that a life is the taking up of a destiny by a freedom." *La Folie en tête* (1970) ekes out a salvation by its intense interest in the world and deep cherishing of people. It, too, is searingly authentic, audacious, and rarely judgmental. Violette Leduc continues to be the misfit, the outsider, mistrustful yet desiring, dazzled yet lucid when faced with the literary "stars" of her epoch. This book, like all her books, bears the mark of love's burning trace upon her body and her soul.

Works

Prose: *Ma mère ne m'a jamais donné la main* (1945). *L'Asphyxie* (1946). *L'Affamée* (1948). *Ravages* (1955). *La Chasse à l'amour* (1973). *La vieille fille et le mort* (1958). *Trésors à prendre* (1960). *La Bâtarde*, préf. de Simone de Beauvoir (1964). *La Femme au petit renard* (1965). *La Folie en tête* (1970). *Thérèse et Isabelle* (1970). *Le Taxi* (1971).

Michael Bishop

Sophia Lee
1750–1824

Born 1750, London, England
Died March 13, 1824, Clifton, Bristol
Genre(s): drama, historical novel, poetry
Language(s): English

Sophia Lee

One of five daughters of the actor and theater manager John Lee, Sophia Lee lost her mother at an early age and had to be a mother to the younger family members. One of her earliest literary efforts was *The Chapter of Accidents* (1780), a five-act play based on Diderot's *Le Père de Famille*. It was first produced at the Haymarket Theatre on August 5, 1780, and later at Drury Lane and Covent Garden.

It was published in 1780, and there were subsequent editions and reprintings as well as French and German translations. From the play's profits, Lee established a school for young ladies at Belvidere House, Bath, where her sisters, including Harriet (also a novelist and playwright), came to reside. In 1803, she gave up the school, and after a residence in Monmouthshire near Tintern Abbey she settled at Clifton, Bristol.

Lee also wrote one of the first English historical romances, *The Recess, or A Tale of Other Times*, a literary landmark whose first volume appeared in 1783, with the second and third volumes following in 1785. A year later, she published *Warbeck, A Pathetic Tale*, a translation of Baculard D'Arnaud's *Varbeck* which, like *The Recess*, blended historical fact with sentimental fiction. A ballad in 156 stanzas entitled *A Hermit's Tale, Recorded by His Own Hand and Found in His Cell* followed in 1787. A second play, a tragedy in blank verse called *Almeyda; Queen of Granada*, was produced at Drury Lane in 1796. Although her sister Harriet conceived and executed the design of *The Canterbury Tales* (1797–1805), Lee contributed the introduction and two stories, "The Young Lady's Tale, The Two Emilys" and "The Clergyman's Tale, Pembroke," which together comprised one and one-half volumes of the total five volumes. Although it was not published until 1804, *The Life of a Lover*, a six-volume epistolary narrative with autobiographical overtones, constituted Lee's earliest literary effort. The comedy, *The Assignation*, Lee's final work, was produced at Drury Lane in 1807, but it was unfavorably received due to its satirical treatment of certain public figures.

Lee's literary reputation rests upon *The Recess*, one of the earliest and most influential examples of historical Gothic writing. Although this literary genre was pioneered by Thomas Leland's *Longsword, Earl of Salisbury* (1762), it was *The Recess* that inaugurated a lengthy train of successors. This work is set during the reign of Queen Elizabeth I, who figures as one of the major characters, along with Sir Philip Sidney, Sir Francis Drake, Lord Burleigh, and Lady Pembroke. The plot is as convoluted and labyrinthine as the subterranean recess that gives the novel its name. Briefly, *The Recess* tells of the extended sufferings of two fictitious daughters of Mary, Queen of Scots, by a clandestine marriage to Thomas, fourth Duke of Norfolk. The two daughters, Ellinor and Matilda, are raised in secrecy in a subterranean recess within the precincts of an abandoned abbey. Their retirement ends abruptly with the entrance of the Earl of Leicester, his secret marriage to Matilda, and the removal of both sisters from seclusion to court. There Ellinor falls in love with the Earl of Essex, but their union is thwarted. The rest of the narrative recounts the persecution both sisters undergo at the hands of a villainous Elizabeth, who discovers in their noble birth a threat to the security of her own throne.

Lee's novel clearly is indebted to the English Gothic writers Sir Horace Walpole and Clara Reeve as well as the French writers of historical romance, Abbé Prévost and Baculard D'Arnaud. Like Reeve and Walpole, Lee presents herself as the editor, rather than the author, of an authentic and antique manuscript that chronicles a by-gone era. Like Prévost and D'Arnaud, Lee interweaves fictitious and factual events with a free hand; like them, she casts over this concoction a distinctly Gothic gloom, employing such standard Gothic themes as death, incest, and madness and conventions like subterranean vaults, trapdoors, and monastic ruins. In *The Recess* history affords a basis for suggestion rather than knowledge, and dates are confused or ignored, perhaps by design, perhaps by accident. Neither Lee nor her readers seem disturbed by a rewriting of history that places the Armada invasion before the execution of Mary, Queen of Scots. The explanation behind historical events is shown to be personal and private rather than political and public. (For example, love controls Essex's behavior in Ireland and causes Sidney's death at Zutphen.) Lee deflates the grand panoramic sweep of history and brings it within the comprehension of her contemporary reading public. She reveals this intention in the novel's advertisement: "History, like painting, only perpetuates the striking features of the mind, whereas the best and worst actions of princes often proceed from partialities and prejudices, which live in their hearts and are buried with them." The narrative seeks to demonstrate not only the intensely personal motives comprising history but also the subjectivity inherent in our interpretations of history. The narrative is made up of two long letters, one by each sister, bringing to bear strikingly different viewpoints on essentially similar occurrences.

In its own time, *The Recess* was well received, with four editions by 1792, a fifth in 1804, an Irish edition in 1791, and various printings and abridgements in 1800, 1802, 1824, 1827, and 1840, as well as French and Portuguese versions. The German play *Maria Stuart und Norfolk* by actor and romanticist Christian Heinrich Speiss owed its inspiration to Lee's novel. The writing of historical romances flowered after the publication of *The Recess,* and a number of works clearly took Lee's book as their model: Mrs. Harley's St. *Bernard's Priory* (1786), Anne Fuller's *Alan Fitz-Osborne, An Historical Tale* (1787), and Rosetta Ballin's *The Statue Room* (1790). The art of Sir Walter Scott and Ann Radcliffe also bear the impress of Lee's achievement. Her use of the rationally explained supernatural reached its perfection in Radcliffe, and the strain of historical romance that Lee inaugurated culminated in Scott's novels.

Works

The Chapter of Accidents (1780). *The Recess, or A Tale of Other Times* (1783–1785). *Varbeck* by Baculard D'Arnaud (translated by Lee as *Warbeck, A Pathetic Tale,* 1786). *A Hermit's Tale, Recorded by Her Own Hand and Found in His Cell* (1787). *Almeyda; Queen of Granada* (1796). Introduction, "The Young Lady's Tale, The Two Emilys" and "The Clergyman's Tale, Pembroke," in *The Canterbury Tales* by Harriet and Sophia Lee (1797–1805). *The Life of a Lover* (1804). *The Assignation* (stage performance only, 1807).

Eileen Finan

Rosamond Lehmann
1901–1990
Born February 3, 1901, Bourne End, Buckinghamshire, England
Died March 12, 1990, London
Genre(s): novel
Language(s): English

Born into an unusually intellectual and artistically gifted family, Lehmann fit in well with her younger sister, Beatrix, who became a well-known actress, and her youngest brother, John, who became a critic, poet, founder of *New Writing,* and, for a time, manager of Leonard and Virginia Woolf's Hogarth Press. Lehmann's father, an editor of *Punch* and a regular contributor of verse and prose to that magazine, also entertained many literary figures at his home. Educated privately, Lehmann went to Girton College, Cambridge, in 1919 to study modern languages, returning home in 1922.

Partly because most of her important work was published by 1947, Lehmann's reputation did not live up to early expectations that ranked her with Elizabeth Bowen and Virginia Woolf, although she has consistently enjoyed critical esteem. Those who have objected to aspects of her writing chided her for confining herself to the world of "feminine sensibility" in which, in technically impeccable but mannered and highly charged emotional prose, women and girls are faced with disillusionment, loss of innocence, and betrayal by love and life.

Despite these problems, Lehmann's novels profoundly and lyrically investigate aspects of women's lives that are frequently ignored—lesbian relations, infidelity, suicide, hatred, and power manipulations. In her first highly acclaimed novel, *Dusty Answer* (1927), published a year before Radclyffe Hall's *Well of Loneliness,* Lehmann treated the theme of adolescent lesbianism with sensitivity and candor, using her own college experiences. *A Note in Music* (1930) and *The Weather in the Streets* (1936) both deal with the drabness and disillusionment accompanying unfulfilled middle age, an accomplishment especially in an era when there were even fewer novels than there are today depicting lives of women over thirty. *The Ballad and the Source* (1945) is her best-known and most critically acclaimed novel. Stylistically breathtaking and structurally complex, full of Jamesian experimentation with point of view, the book presents a charismatic but egomaniacal central character, the aging Mrs. Sybil Anstey Herbert Jardine, who comes to dominate the consciousness of a progressively unillusioned adolescent, Rebecca Landon, who learns variations of the story of Mrs. Jardine's life—a tale encompasing adultery, madness, suicide, and hatred—from four people who knew her. A theme introduced in this novel that remains important in Lehmann's later writing is that of the mystical and transcendent influence of the self on others. Many critics have praised Lehmann's ornate, romantic, lyrical prose. Lehmann said of herself that she wrote in a "half-trance," experiencing herself as "a kind of preserving jar in which float fragments of people and landscapes, snatches of sound, [but] there is not one of these fragile shapes and serial sounds but bears within it the explosive seed of life."

After her daughter's death of poliomyelitis in 1958, Lehmann turned increasingly to spiritualism, which she discusses in *The Swan in the Evening* (1967), a disquieting, even embarrassing but moving personal memoir.

Works

Dusty Answer (1927). *A Note in Music* (1930). *Letter to a Sister* (1932). *Invitation to the Waltz* (1932). *The Weather in the Streets* (1936). *No More Music* (1945). *The Ballad and the Source* (1945). *The Gipsy's Baby and Other Stories* (1947). *The Echoing Grove* (1953). *A Man Seen Afar* (with W. Tudor Pole) (1965). *The Swan in the Evening: Fragments of an Inner Life* (1967). (with Cynthia Hill Sandys) *Letters from Our Daughters* (1972). *A Sea-Grape Tree* (1977).

Carey Kaplan

Anna Maria (Malmstedt) Lenngren
1754–1817

Born June 18, 1754, Uppsala, Sweden
Died March 8, 1817, Stockholm
Genre(s): poetry, satire, journalism
Language(s): Swedish

"Fru Lenngren" (as she is often called in Sweden) must be included in any listing of Sweden's best poets. She ranks certainly as its best poetess. She did not care for public recognition; all of her poems and articles, save one ["Dröm" (1798; Dream)], were published anonymously. Her verse, the best of it written during Sweden's troubled 1790s, provides a bridge of sorts from the Enlightenment period to the beginnings of Romanticism, for it contains elements of both.

Anna Maria Lenngren grew up in a bourgeois household where her father, Magnus Brynolf Malmstedt, was a member of the Moravian Brethren and took the needy into his home. It has been speculated that this "turmoil" in the home gave rise to Lenngren's desire for peaceful orderliness in her own adult household. This same father, a lecturer in Latin eloquence at Uppsala University, encouraged his daughter's learning, and she received a classical education virtually unheard of for girls of her time. This schooling in the Latin classics would serve her well when she took up the pen herself; one of her greatest skills is her acute sense of stylistic propriety. Her literary debut occurred in 1772 when she published some (unoriginal) poems in a newspaper. In 1780 she married a government employee, Carl Peter Lenngren, with whom she enjoyed an ostensibly happy, if childless, marriage. Lenngren assisted her husband in editing the newborn *Stockholms–Posten* during the 1780s, where she contributed causeries and witty poems as well, it is conjectured, as articles. The 1790s saw her most mature and perfect poetic creations, and her most controversial; her most satirical poems against the nobility could not be published until the nineteenth century. She was considered for a position in the prestigious Swedish Academy, but the time was not ripe for a woman to be admitted to this literary Parnassus, no matter how gifted she might be. But Lenngren herself was always disparaging her own poetic talents and hid her pen and paper in a special cupboard when visitors came.

Lenngren's poems were collected and published for the first time after her death. Among them, some of the best are "Porträtterne" (1796; The Portraits), in which an older gout-plagued countess deigns to describe the portraits of her illustrious forebears for her servant girl, a satiric masterpiece in miniature; "Slottet och kojan" (1800; The Castle and the Cottage), which compares the simple, happy life of the poor man to the unhappy if materially comfortable one of the wealthy. "Några ord till min dotter, ifall jag hade någon" (1798; A Few Words to My Daughter, If I Had One) has been touted by some as proof that Lenngren valued the traditional wife–mother role higher than her literary efforts; others see an ironic, closet-feministic genesis for this piece. "Den glada festen" (1796; The Jolly Party) and "Grevinnans besök" (1800; The Countess' Visit) are considered her finest idylls; "Hans nåds morgonsömn" (1796; His Grace's Morning Sleep) is one of her most tart poetic commentaries, presenting the nobleman sleeping off a night of "wine, women and song" while his middle-class creditors, some in desperate need of their payment, wait for him to leave his bed.

Lenngren's poetry has aged well; she is a standard classic even today. During her lifetime and afterward, she was accorded the admiration and respect of many readers, educated and not, female and male. Her "snapshot" style does not rule out an occasional touch of sentimentality; she writes in praise of bourgeois morality and simplicity. Even so, many scholars find it difficult to encapsulate her work into a simple, all-encompassing description, and she remains one of Sweden's most enigmatic, as well as admired, poets.

Works

Skaldeförsök [Poetic Attempts] (1819).

Translations: Nelson, Philip K., Anna Maria Lenngren: 1754–1817, poems (1984). "The Portraits," "The Boy and His Playthings," and "Castle and Cottage" [respectively, "Porträtterne," 1796; "Gossen och leksakerna," 1798; and "Slottet och kojan," 1800], in Charles Wharton Stork, Anthology of Swedish Lyrics from 1750 to 1915 (New York, 1917). "Family Portraits" [Porträtterne"], in Henry Wadsworth Longfellow, Poets and Poetry of Europe (Philadelphia, 1845). (This version also appears, the translator's name unmentioned, in N. Clemmons Hunt [ed.], Poetry of Other Lands, Philadelphia, 1883.)

Kathy Saranpa Anstine

Madame Jeanne-Marie Le Prince de Beaumont 1711–1780

Born April 26, 1711, Rouen, France
Died 1780, Chavanod, Haute-Savoie, France
Genre(s): novels, didactic works
Language(s): French

Madame Le Prince de Beaumont was a popular novelist and a prolific writer of educational works for women and children, Christian apologetics, and moral tales that were widely read throughout Europe and America between 1750 and c. 1830.

Coming from a large artistic family—the painter Jean-Baptiste Le Prince was her younger brother—Marie Le Prince taught at a convent school for teachers in Rouen. When her unhappy marriage was annulled in 1745, she turned to writing to supplement a meager income. Her first novel, Le Triomphe de la Vérité, was published in 1748, the same year as two works in which she argues that women's natural qualities are superior to those of men. Shortly after, she settled in London, where she quickly established a reputation as a governess and started a monthly magazine, the Nouveau Magasin français, aimed primarily at women. She also wrote full-length didactic works such as the Éducation complète (1753), which was used by the Princess of Wale, Civan, roi de Bungo (1754), which was set in Japan, and the Anecdotes du XIVe siècle (1758), as well as the highly popular epistolary novels, Lettres de Madame Du Montier (1756) and La nouvelle Clarisse (1767). Many of her books ran to several editions and were translated into every major European language. In 1758 she bought a house near Annecy, France, to which she retired with her second husband and where she continued writing until her death.

The most important of her works, the Magasin des Enfants (1756), is divided into journées in which a governess called Mlle Bonne converses with seven pupils (Ladies Sensée, Spirituelle, Tempête, etc.) who are between five and thirteen in age. Each day, the lessons on history, geography, and science are alternated with Bible stories and fairy tales, including the classic version of "La Belle et la Bête" (adapted from a rambling 362-page story by Mme de Villeneuve, q.v.). Though always present, the morality is never saccharine, and many of the tales (e.g. "Le Prince au long nez") reveal considerable humor. It is the first work written not for a specific child, but for children in general; the first to address children as children and not as mini-adults, and to do so without being condescending. She continued her success with the *Magasin des Adolescentes* (1760), which introduces the same girls and others in their teens (Miss Frivole, Lady Sincère, etc.) to philosophy, and with *Instructions pour les jeunes Dames* (1764), which outlines the duties of a wife. One of her themes throughout is that women should rely not on men but on their own inner resources and to do this they must understand religion. In *Les Américaines* (1770), Mme Bonne asks the same young women, now her friends, to imagine how they would react in a European city if they had been transported there suddenly from the forests of America. The ensuing dialogue introduces the women to theology. In spite of her generally conservative views, Mme Bonne is constantly respectful of her pupils' individuality: "Each Lady is made to speak according to her particular Genius, Temper and Inclination." The question-and-answer technique is designed to stimulate their independent thought, great self-awareness, and ability to conduct a reasoned debate. At a time when women received virtually no formal education, this intention was revolutionary.

Mme Le Prince de Beaumont's achievement can be measured by the success her works enjoyed and the rapid improvement in women's education between 1760 and 1785. The *Magasin des Enfants* was frequently reprinted; in the nineteenth century, its format was much copied but never equalled. When her books fell out of fashion, except for two or three of her fairy tales—notably "La Belle et la Bête"—none was ever republished. They were the first victims of a movement that she did much to create. She was the first editor of a woman's monthly magazine, the founder of children's literature in France, and an indefatigable promoter of women's equal right to learning.

Works

Le Triomphe de la Vérité, ou, Mémoires de M. de la Villette (1748), tr. *The Triumph of Truth, or, Memoirs of Mr. de la Villette* (1755). *Lettre en réponse à 'L'Année merveilleuse'* (1748). *Arrêt solennel de la nature* (1748). *Lettres diverses et critiques* (1750). *Le Nouveau Magasin français, ou, Bibliothèque instructive* (1750–1752, 1755). *Éducation complète, ou, Abrégé de l'histoire universelle, mêlée de géographie, de chronologie . . . à l'usage de la famille royale de la princesse de Galles* (1753). *Civan, roi de la famille royale de la princesse de Galles* (1753). *Civan, roi de bungo, histoire japonnoise, ou, Tableau de l'éducation d'un prince* (1754), tr. *Civan, King of Bungo* (1800). *Lettres de Mme Du Montier à la marquise de ***, sa fille, avec les réponses* (1756), tr. *The History of a Young Lady of Distinction. In a Series of Letters Which Passed Between Madame Du Montier, and the Marchioness De ***, Her Daughter* (1758). *Magasin des Enfants, ou, Dialogues entre une sage gouvernante et plusieurs de ses élèves* (1756), tr. *The Young Misses Magazine, or, Dialogues Between a Discreet Governess and Several Young Ladies of the First Rank Under Her Education* (1757). *Anecdotes du XIVᵉ siècle, pour servir à l'histoire des femmes illustres de ce temps* (1758). *Lettres curieuses, instructives et amusanntes, ou, Correspondance historique, galante, etc. entre une dame de Paris et une dame de province* (1759). *Magasin des Adolescentes . . . Pour servir de suite au 'Magasin des Enfants'* (1760), tr. *The Young Ladies Magazine* (1760). *Principes de l'Histoire-Sainte* (1761). *Instructions pour les jeunes Dames qui entrent dans le monde et qui se marient . . . Pour faire suite au "Magasin des Adolescentes"* (1764), tr. *Instructions for Young Ladies on Their Entering into Life, Their Duties in the Married State, and Towards Their Children* (1764). *Lettres d'Émérance à Lucie* (1765), tr. *Letters from Émérance to Lucy* (1776). *Mémoires de Madame la Baronne de Batteville, ou, La Veuve parfaite* (1766), tr. *The Virtuous Widow: or, Memoirs of the Baroness de Batteville* (1768). *La nouvelle Clarisse, histoire véritable* (1767), tr. *The New Clarisse: a True History* (1768). *Magasin des Pauvres, des Artisans, des Domestiques et des Gens de la campagne* (1768), tr. *Dialogues for Sunday Evenings; Translated from a Work of Madame Le Prince de Beaumont Called "Magasin des Pauvres"* (1797). *Les Américaines, ou, La Preve de la Religion Chrétienne, par les lumières naturelles* (1770). *La Double Alliance, ou, Les heureux naturels, histoire du marquis D**** (1772–1773). *La Mentor moderne, ou, Instructions pour les garçons et pour ceux qui les élèvent* (1772). *Manuel de la Jeunesse, ou, Instructions familières, en dialogues* (ca. 1773). *Contes moraux* (1774), tr. *Moral Tales* (1775). *Oeuvres mêlées de Mme Le Prince de Beaumont: Extraites des Journaux & Feuilles périodiques qui ont paru en Angleterre pendant le séjour qu'elle y a fait* (1775; rpt. of *Le Nouveau Magasin français*). *Nouveaux Contes moraux* (1776). *Le Dévotion éclairées, ou, Magasin des Dévotes* (1779).

Terence Dawson

Doris Lessing
1919–

a.k.a. Jane Somers
Born October 22, 1919, Kermanshah, Persia
Genre(s); novel, short story
Language(s): English

When Doris Lessing entered the literary scene in 1950 with the conventionally realistic *The Grass Is Singing,* she began a career devoted to exploring the psychic wholeness missing in the "fragmented" modern world. In her novels, as well as in numerous stories and work in other genres, Lessing has been for many readers a kind of Cassandra or conscience of the modern age. Lessing has produced fiction of many forms, including a multivolume *Bildungsroman,* works focusing on characters seeking inner knowledge or independence, "space fiction" series, books about a young terrorist and a career woman working in the world of fashion—in short, a wide literary canvas peopled with earnest characters who have had considerable impact on intelligent readers around the world.

Lessing's first novel, *The Grass Is Singing,* published after she emigrated from Rhodesia to London, is set in, and clearly deeply concerned with the colonial world Lessing knew as a child. Mary Turner is seen in flashback as incapable of adjustment to white "superiority" on the impoverished farm she and her husband run, and her cruelty and insecurity result in her being killed by her black houseboy. Africa is also the setting for four of the five parts of Lessing's "Children of Violence" series (published from 1952 through 1969); Martha Quest is depicted from adolescence to old age and death, from colonial expectations during World War II through failed marriages and child raising, political and social involvement, emigration to England, and psychic complexities in a world hurtling rapidly toward destruction (in *The Four Gated City,* 1969) at the end of the twentieth century.

The Golden Notebook (1962) is by common consent Lessing's masterpiece. More overtly concerned with the fragmented soul than any of her other books, this novel shows how Anna Wulf divides her life into notebook narratives (black for her life in colonial Africa, red for her life as a Communist, yellow about an alter ego, and blue, a factual diary), all of which culminate in a golden one serving as therapy and reconciliation of her various "selves." In addition, several "Free Women" sections comprise a short conventional novel, also about Anna Wulf but "written" by her as counterpoint to her "real" life. Erroneously consid-

ered by some critics to be Lessing's own "confessions," the novel is instead a rich, multilayered, endlessly rewarding account of a woman's search for wholeness through Jungian therapy as well as through sex, marriage, dreams, politics, writing, and incessant analysis of news reports and of herself.

Lessing's forays into "inner space" continued with *Briefing for a Descent into Hell* (1971), a claustrophobic work somewhat indebted to Scottish psychiatrist R.D. Laing in its concern with mental imbalance and psychic phenomena. Charles Watkins, one of the few male protagonists in Lessing's novels, is a classics professor who "travels" psychically to a gathering of Greek deities (hence the book's title, with "hell" equated with earth), to World War II Yugoslavia (where he fights with partisans), and, most startling, to a raft on the ocean that lands him in a prehistoric city where strange species of animals fight and from which he escapes to "reality." After the amnesiac Watkins is found wandering in London, he is hospitalized, able to recall his various "existences" but not his "real" life; after therapy, he is restored to "sanity" but not to wholeness, freedom, and human harmony.

Restoration of psychic health is also Lessing's concern in *The Summer Before the Dark* (1973) and *Memoirs of a Survivor* (1974). The first is a realistic, somewhat clichéd account of Kate Brown's gradual awakening at age forty-five into a self-conscious "liberation"; she goes away from home and family for a series of experiences one summer that culminate in her returning, chastened and reconciled, to her routine life. The latter work, though, is an important study of a woman's solitary survival following the ultimate war; inexplicably, she must care for a preadolescent girl who rapidly matures into a sexually liberated woman and who, with her lover and a strange hybrid pet, pioneers in helping other survivors endure the end of civilization. Most impressive in the book, however, are those passages in which the narrator "walks" through a wall to "see" a series of tableaux about her own earlier life by which she rids herself of behavior and thinking invalid in her world.

Lessing's series of five "space fiction" narratives, "Canopus in Argos: Archives," the first book in the series, depict Earth's history as a battleground for opposing forces of ageless beings. The first book in the series, *Shikasta* (1979), is a prolix sequence of documents, reports, and records presenting earth's history from a cosmic perspective; as allegory, the work shows how humanity flounders helplessly from catastrophe to catastrophe, but as a novel it is unconvincing. *The Marriages Between Zones Three, Four and Five* (1980), however, is a fascinating fable that, although allegorical, also offers a convincing love story and psychological analysis of the rise and fall of civilizations. *The Sirian Experiments* (1981) contains many documents about earth's early history, but it also offers a female demi-god who slowly changes as she understands the "group mind" that runs the universe and the effects this has on and for earth. *The Making of the Representative for Planet 8* (1982) concerns the freezing death of a world whose inhabitants must prepare for their promised removal to another planet; even the "Overlords," though, are subject to inexorable cosmic forces that radically diminish earthly concerns with nationalism and historical pride. Finally, *Documents Relating to The Sentimental Agents in the Volyen Empire* (1983) again includes various documents but is also an ineffectual attempt at satire regarding the debasement of language as mere "rhetoric" in the rise and fall of societies.

In 1983 Lessing attempted a hoax by publishing *The Diary of a Good Neighbour* under the name "Jane Somers," and *If the Old Could . . .* under the same name the year after; her intent in the experiment was to see whether novels could be published on their merits instead of on an author's name and reputation. But neither realistic book, one focusing on a fashion magazine editor's relationship with a dying older woman, the other on a never-consummated love affair and relationship with her niece, is very good: characters are banal, plots are sentimental, and insights into any larger world view are limited.

The Good Terrorist (1985) is a return to a realistic approach; it concerns a young insecure middle-class woman who works with (and supports) a gang of would-be terrorists; they prefer to fight the "system" through parasitic behavior and endless discussions and demonstrations while she works as a drudge cleaning up after them, abusing her own parents, and, through misguided idealism, taking the revolution into her own hands. Topical though the book is, it lacks emotional liveliness and compelling characters.

Lessing's work has obviously changed radically over the years, especially as she has taken chances in trying new approaches and subjects. Her high prophetic seriousness (as reflective of her recent interest in Sufism) and relative lack of a sense of humor have often been noted, but at her best, when she focuses on a solitary, compulsive person (usually a woman) who has been forced to a moment of crisis, she effectively dramatizes a revaluation of personal identity.

Though her fiction is often repetitive, prolix, didactic, and trivial, her depth of character presentation and sense of character commitment have secured her place among the most powerful and compelling writers of the century.

Works

The Grass Is Singing (1950). *This Was the Old Chief's Country* (1951). *Martha Quest* ("Children of Violence" I) (1952). *Five: Short Novels* (1953). *A Proper Marriage* ("Children of Violence" II) (1954). *Retreat to Innocence* (1956). *The Habit of Loving* (1957). *Going Home* (1957). *A Ripple from the Storm* ("Children of Violence" III) (1958). *Each Her Own Wilderness*, in *New English Dramatists: Three Plays*, ed. E.M Browne (1959). *Fourteen Poems* (1959). *In Pursuit of the English: A Documentary* (1960). *Play with a Tiger* (1962). *The Golden Notebook* (1962). *A Man and Two Women* (1963). *African Stories* (1964). *Landlocked* ("Children of Violence" IV) (1965). *Particularly Cats* (1967). *The Four-Gated City* ("Children of Violence" V) (1969). *Briefing for a Descent into Hell* (1971). *The Story of a Non-Marrying Man and Other Stories* (1972; in the U.S. as *The Confessions of Jack Orkney and Other Stories*). *The Singing Door*, in *Second Playbill Two*, ed. A Durband (1973). *The Summer Before the Dark* (1973). *Memoirs of a Survivor* (1974). *A Small Personal Voice: Essays, Reviews, and Interviews*, ed. P. Schlueter (1974). *Collected Stories* (1978; in the U.S. as *Stories*). *Shikasta* ("Canopus in Argos: Archives" I) (1979). *The Marriages Between Zones Three, Four and Five* (Canopus in Argos: Archives" II) (1980). *The Sirian Experiments* ("Canopus in Argos: Archives" III) (1981). *The Making of the Representative for Planet 8* ("Canopus in Argos: Archives" IV) (1982). *Documents Relating to the Sentimental Agents in the Volyen Empire* ("Canopus in Argos: Archives" V) (1983). (as Jane Somers) *The Diary of a Good Neighbour* (1983). (as Jane Somers) *If the Old Could . . .* (1984). *The Good Terrorist* (1985). *Prisons We Choose to Live Inside* (1986). *The Wind Blows Away Our Words* (1987). *The Doris Lessing Reader* (1988; U.S. edition, with same title but different contents, 1988) *The Fifth Child* (1988). *Particularly Cats and More Cats* (1989; U.S. edition as *Particularly Cats. . . . and Rufus*, 1991). *African Laughter: Four Visits* (1992). *The Real Thing* (1992). *Under My Skin* (1994). *Love, Again* (1996).

Paul Schlueter

Astrid Lindgren
1907–

Born 1907, near Vimmerby, Småland Province, Sweden
Genre(s): children's and young adult literature
Language(s): Swedish

Astrid Lindgren was the second child of tenant farmer Samuel August Ericsson and his wife Hanna. They lived on the farm *Näs* in an old red house surrounded by apple trees where the four Ericsson children grew up much like the children she describes in her "Bullerbybooks." Already in school her classmates predicted that some day she would write stories and even went as far as calling her "Vimmerby's Selma Lagerlöf." But the very idea frightened her. Training as a secretary in Stockholm, she worked in an office, got married, and had two children. It is thanks to her children that her storytelling eventually developed.

In 1941 her daughter had pneumonia and wanted her mother to "tell a story . . . about 'Pippi Långstrump'" (Pippi Longstocking). The stories about Pippi were so successful with her daughter and her friends, that Astrid Lindgren had to repeat them time and again over the years. But it was not until 1944, when Astrid Lindgren was immobilized with a sprained ankle, that she finally wrote the Pippi Longstocking stories down and presented them to her daughter as a birthday present. Another copy she sent to a publisher. It was promptly rejected.

While waiting for the answer, Astrid Lindgren had worked on another story, *Britt-Marie lätter sitt hjärta* (Britt-Marie Eases Her Heart), and entered it in a prize competition for young adult literature in 1944. It received the second prize. When the same publisher announced another prize competition the following year, Astrid Lindgren entered the slightly edited Pippi manuscript and it won her first prize.

Other Pippi stories followed in short, steady succession: *Pippi Långstrump går ombord* (1946; Pippi Goes on Board) and *Pippi Långstrump i Söderhavet* (1948; Pippi in the South Seas). The Pippi stories became the basis and cornerstone of Astrid Lindgren's international fame despite the often stormy attacks that "no normal kid" behaves the way Pippi does. But Pippi, with her strong defiance of all adult authority and undaunted by convention, became the heroine and model for young adults all over the world who saw in Pippi their dream of freedom and power fulfilled.

In 1946 Lindgren's book about master detective Bill Bergson won her a shared first prize, but it re-mained the last book she ever entered in a competition. The same year she also published her first book about the Bullerby children whose adventures closely resemble those of her own as a youngster at Näs with its seasonal rhythm of life lived in an old Swedish farming community.

The author of about fifty books and still going strong, Astrid Lindgren has become a popular figure as a Swedish writer for children and young adults. Since 1963 she has been a member of the distinguished literary society *Samfundet De Nio*. Her books have been translated into more than 39 languages and dialects. Her inspiration does not come from either her own or other people's children and grandchildren. "There is no child that can inspire me as much as the child I myself was once upon a time," she maintains. All it takes is to remember how it was and felt at the time. She does not want to influence youngsters in any way. The only thing she dares to hope is that her books contribute to fostering some kind of basic philosophy of humanity, democracy, and love of life in those who read them. Her major satisfaction lies in brightening the lives of children. "That's enough for me," she says. And the numerous reprints of her stories attest to her success in her chosen genre.

Works

Britt-Marie lätter sitt hjärta (1944). *Kerstin och jag* (1945). *Pippi Långstrump* (1945). *Pippi Långstrump går ombord* (1946). *Mästerdetektiven Blomkvist* (1946). *Alla vi barn i Bullerbyn* (1947). *Pippi Långstrump i Söderhavet* (1948). *Mera om os barn in Bullerbyn* (1949). *Nils Karlsson-Pyssling* (1949). *Kajsa Kavat* (1950). *Kati i Amerika* (1950). *Mästerdetektiven Blomkvist lever farligt* (1951). *Bara roligt i bullerbyn* (1952). *Kati på Kaptensgatan* (1952). *Kalle Blomkvist och Rasmus* (1953). *Mio min Mio* (1954). *Kati i Paris* (1954). *Lillebror och Karlsson på taket* (1955). *Rasmus på luffen* (1956). *Rasmus, Pontus och Toker* (1957). *Barnen på Bråkmakargatan* (1958). *Sunnanäng* (1959). *Madicken* (1960). *Lotta på Bråkmakargatan* (1961). *Karlsson på Taket flyger igen* (1962). *Emil i Lönneberga* (1963). *Vi på Saltkråkan* (1964). *Nya hyss av Emil i Lönneberga* (1966). *Karlsson på Taket smyger igen* (1968). *Än lever Emil i Lönneberga* (1970). *Kati i Italien* (1971). *Bröderna Lejonhjärta* (1973). *Madicken och Junibackens Pims* (1976). *Pippi Långstrump har Julgransplundring* (1979). *Ronja Rövardotter* (1981). *När lilla Ida skulle höra hyss* (1984). *Emils hyss nr 325* (1985).

English Translations: *Pippi Longstocking*, tr. Florence Lamborn (New York, 1950, 1969, 1973). *Pippi*

Goes on Board, tr. Florence Lamborn (New York, 1957, 1973). *Pippi in the South Seas*, tr. Gerry Bothmer (New York, 1959, 1964). *The Children of Noisy Village*, selections of Bullerby children, tr. Florence Lamborn (New York, 1962). *The Six Bullerby Children*, tr. Evelyn Ramsden (London, 1963). *Happy Times in Noisy Village*, selections of Bullerby children, tr. Florence Lamborn (New York, 1963). *All About the Bullerby Children*, tr. Evelyn Ramsden and Florence Lamborn (London, 1970). *Bill Bergson, Master Detective*, tr. Herbert Antoine (New York, 1952, 1968). *Bill Bergson Lives Dangerously*, tr. Herbert Antoine (New York, 1954). *Bill Bergson and the White Rose Rescue* tr. Florence Lamborn (New York, 1965). *Kati in America*, tr. Maianne Turner (Leicester, 1964). *Kati in Italy*, tr. Daniel Dupuy (New York, 1961). *Mio, My Son*, tr. Marianne Turner (New York, 1956). *Karlsson on the Roof*, tr. Marianne Turner (New York, 1971). *Rasmus and the Vagabond*, tr. Gerry Bothmer (New York, 1968). *The Children on Troublemaker Street*, tr. Gerry Bothmer (New York, 1964). *Lotta on Troublemaker Street*, tr. Gerry Bothmer (New York, 1963). *Mischievous Meg*, tr. Gerry Bothmer (New York, 1962). *Emil in the Soup Tureen*, tr. Lilian Seaton (Chicago, 1970). *Emil's Pranks* (Chicago, 1971). *Emil and the Piggy Beast*, tr. Michael Heron (Chicago, 1973). *Seacrow Island*, tr. Evelyn Ramsden (New York, 1969). *The Brothers Lionheart*. tr. Joan Tate (New York, 1975).

Hanna Kalter Weiss

Elizabeth Lynn Linton
1822–1898

Born February 10, 1822, Cumberland, England
Died July 14, 1898, London
Genre(s); novel, journalism, essay, review, short story
Language(s): English

Linton, a prolific writer and social critic, wrote no fewer than twenty-four novels and thirteen other books in addition to scores of journal articles, essays, and reviews. Her novels were often thinly cloaked polemics centering primarily on moral conflicts, the theme of class consciousness, or the "woman question." An outspoken, energetic writer, she was an observant and accurate chronicler of the age in which she lived.

She left Cumberland for London in 1845, spending that year reading in the British Museum and writ-ing her first novel, *Azeth the Egyptian* (1846). Her second novel, *Amymone: A Romance of the Days of Pericles* (1848), received favorable reviews by Walter Savage Landor and others. On the basis of an article she submitted to the *Morning Chronicle* titled "Aborigenes," she was hired as a salaried staff writer, the first woman to hold such a position, and between August 1849 and February 1851 wrote at least 80 articles and 36 reviews. During this time she met Landor, with whom she became very close, and through him she met Charles Dickens and John Forster.

Leaving the *Morning Chronicle* in 1851, she began work on her third novel, *Realities*, which she dedicated to Landor and published that same year. During 1851 she also met Mary Ann Evans (George Eliot). After the poor reception of her third novel, she toured the Continent and in 1852 took the post of Paris correspondent for *The Leader*, also writing articles for Dickens's *Household Words*. On her return to England in 1854, she published an essay in praise of Mary Wollstonecraft in *The English Republic*, the monthly run by her future husband. Soon thereafter, however, she wrote "Rights and Wrongs of Women" in *Household Words*, which expressed strong views against "the emancipated woman."

In 1858 she married William James Linton, engraver, writer, and reformer, then a widower with seven children. In 1864 Linton collaborated with her husband on *The Lake Country*, she writing the text and he illustrating it. They lived apart from 1865 on, and her husband spent much of the rest of his life in America.

From 1865 until her death, Linton published a novel a year. In *Grasp Your Nettle* (1865) and *Lizzie Lorton* (1866), she criticized village life with *Lizzie Lorton*, set in Linton's native Cumberland receiving high praise. Among the thirty-three articles she contributed to *The Saturday Review* in 1868 is the one for which she became best known, her anonymous "Girl of the Period"; Linton vehemently attacked the idea of female emancipation arguing primarily against what she characterized as the frivolity and vulgarity of the advanced woman and arguing in favor of the ideals of feminine charm and domesticity. She also decried the overriding selfishness and immorality of the "Girl of the Period," whose concern with fashion, cosmetics, and luxury she denounced.

In addition to writing regularly for *The Saturday Review* and contributing to other journals, she also published *Ourselves: A Series of Essays on Women* (1869), which carried on her attacks against feminine emancipation. Despite her criticism of "the Girl of the

Period," Linton did argue in favor of economic and legal rights for married and divorced women. When Forster's *The Life of Landor* came out in 1869, which slighted her importance in Landor's life, Linton wrote a scathing review and published an article on Landor.

In 1872, Linton published *Joshua Davidson,* her most successful and popular novel. An adaptation of the gospel story to the condition of modern life it attacked Christian morality and the position of the Church of England. Her next novel, *The Atonement of Leam Dundas* (1876), was among her favorite works but was one of her least commercially successful and was harshly reviewed. For the next several years, Linton traveled on the Continent, turning out a stream of articles as well as writing several novels, *The World Well Lost* (1877), *Under Which Lord?* (1879), *The Rebel of the Family* (1880), a three-volume collection of long short stories titled *Within a Silken Thread* (1880), and *My Love* (1881). In 1883 her famous "Girl of the Period" essays were published under her own name in two volumes with the title, *The Girl of the Period and Other Social Essays.* Although these volumes gave her lasting fame, they did not sell well at the time. In 1883 she also published her novel, *Ione,* dedicated to Swinburne.

In 1885 she published another notable novel, the one she considered her best, *The Autobiography of Christopher Kirkland,* an autobiography in the shape of a three-volume novel in which the protagonist was male. Again focusing on the "woman question," the novel was neither a popular nor critical success. Before the end of the year she also published a short novel, *Stabbed in the Dark,* contributed an essay on George Eliot to *Temple Bar,* and produced other articles. In 1886 she published *Paston Carew, Millionaire and Miser,* which she had begun in 1884, and in 1889 *Through the Long Night.* In the next years, Linton continued writing social criticism as well as novels. Her public prominence is apparent in the fact that in 1890 she was one of the three contributors to a symposium on *Candour in English Fiction* in the *New Review;* the other two contributors were Walter Besant and Thomas Hardy.

In 1891 she published *An Octave of Friends,* and one of her best essays, "Our Illusions," was published in the April issue of the *Fortnightly Review. One Too Many,* another virulent attack upon female emancipation and higher education for women, was serialized in the *Lady's Pictorial* in 1893 and published as a book the next year. In 1893, Helen Black published a collection of interviews with "Notable Women Authors," and Linton, at the age of seventy-one, was the first woman interviewed for the series.

In 1896 Linton was elected to the Society of Authors and was honored by being the first woman to serve on its committee. She was still steadily contributing essays on the relations between the sexes, asserting in the January 1896 issue of *Woman at Home* the impossibility of platonic friendships between man and woman as well as women's inferiority and weakness. Early in 1897, she wrote an appreciation of George Eliot for a series entitled *Women Novelists of Queen Victoria's Reign* and began work on her last novel, an autobiographical work, *The Second Youth of Theodora Desanges,* which was published posthumously in 1900, as was her final work, a collection of reminiscences, *My Literary Life.*

Works

Azeth the Egyptian (1846). *Amymone: A Romance of the Days of Pericles* (1848). *Realities: A Tale* (1851). *Witch Stories* (1861). *The Lake Country* with map and illustrations by W.J. Linton (1864). *Grasp Your Nettle* (1865). *Lizzie Lorton of Greyrigg* (1866). *Sowing the Wind* (1867). "The Girl of the Period" (1868). *Ourselves: A Series of Essays on Women* (1869). *The True History of Joshua Davidson* (1872). *Patricia Kemball* (1875). *The Mad Willoughbys, and Other Tales* (1876). *The Atonement of Leam Dundas* (1876). *The World Well Lost* (1877). *A Night in the Hospital* (1879). *Under Which Lord?* (1879). *The Rebel of the Family* (1880). *Within a Silken Thread and Other Stories* (1880). *My Love* (1881). *Ione: A Novel* (1883). *The Girl of the Period and Other Social Essays* (1883). *Stabbed in the Dark: A Tale* (1885). *The Rift in the Lute: A Tale* (1885). *The Autobiography of Christopher Kirkland* (1885). *Paston Carew, Millionaire and Miser* (1886). *The Philosophy of Marriage* (1888). *Through the Long Night* (1889). *Was He Wrong?* (serialized only, 1889). *Sowing the Wind* (1890). *About Ireland* (1890). *An Octave of Friends with Other Silhouettes and Stories* (1891). *About Ulster* (1892). *Freeshooting: Extracts from the Work of Mrs. Lynn Linton,* selected and arranged by G.F.S. (Mrs. Gulie Moss) (1892). *In Haste and at Leisure: A Novel* (1895). *Twixt Cup and Lip: Tales* (1896). *Dulcie Everton* (1896). *My Literary Life* (1899). *The Second Youth of Theodora Desanges* (1900). A list of her articles is found in H. Van Thal's biography, *Eliza Lynn Linton: The Girl of the Period* (1979), pp. 229–230.

Gale Sigal

Virginie Loveling
1836–1923

a.k.a. W.G.E. Walter
Born May 17, 1836, Nevele (Ghent), Belgium
Died December 1, 1923, Ghent
Genre(s): anecdotal poetry, naturalistic novella, children's literature, novel, essay
Language(s): Dutch

Virginie Loveling

Virginie and her older sister Rosalie Loveling wrote both poetry and prose. The sisters were the daughters of a well-educated Flemish mother and a father who was a connoisseur of languages and German literature.

Virginie Loveling's literary production is astonishing both for its quantity and its diversity. Her first literary efforts were realistic poems, often with a sentimental tone; some of these were published together with poems by her sister Rosalie in 1870. The sisters also published two volumes of novellas together (1874, 1875), clearly indicating, however, who had written what. Unlike her sister, Virginie gradually expanded subsequent novellas in length and thematic diversity. From 1877 onward, she wrote some remarkable novels on controversial political-religious topics of the time with significant psychological depth in the characters (especially her women). Virginie Loveling's fictional prose was recognized as important and modern in style and themes by the foremost Belgian and Dutch literary personalities of her time (such as Potgieter, Busken Huet, Max Rooses, Karel van de Woestijne) and by commissions of both governments. Most of Virginie's novellas (which she continued to write during her entire career) were first published in prestigious literary periodicals in Holland (*De Gids, Nederland, Nederduytsch Tijdschrift, Leeskabinet*). In 1894 she was awarded the Five-Yearly (Belgian) Prize for Dutch Literature for her novel *Een dure Eed* (1891; A Costly Oath). Her series of *Kinderverhalen* (1863–1886; Children's Stories) won her the prize of the Royal Academy of Belgium.

Virginie Loveling combines the crisp observation of types with such themes as heredity, marriage, and the problems of and with children, in Flemish country and city settings. The narrative is often situated in the framework of contemporary political (including religious) discussions. Recurring themes and motives are family life, marriage (Virginie Loveling acknowledges that only marriages for love have a chance of success), the frustration of having children (or of not having children), poverty, death. Serious social drama, village amours, and the psychology of socially and physically crippled characters are rendered almost starkly, without the soothing wrapper of metaphor. Indeed, her careful avoidance of metaphor throughout her *oeuvre* is remarkable.

Virginie Loveling's first novel-length prose work was *In onze Vlaamsche Gewesten* (1877, 1882; In our Flemish Regions. Under the pseudonym W.G.E. Walter); it is subtitled "Political Sketches" and treats the then very-explosive anticlerical and liberal (in other words, conservative, in Belgium) problems of the country in her characteristic intelligent and objective manner. Loveling recognizes the absurdity and inadequacy of black-and-white characterization and typecasting—something she carefully avoids in all her novels. Hypocrisy and extremism, goodness and understanding are to be found on both sides of a political-religious controversy and in all human beings. Another "political novel" is *Sophie* (1885). The novel dates from, and is set in, the turbulent years of Belgian history known as the era of the "School War," when the Catholic and the Liberal parties fought over fundamental issues of conflict between them. *Sophie* is about a crisis of faith; it is an *étude de moeurs* as well as a critical statement against the very strong influence of Catholicism in the Flemish countryside.

Polydoor en Theodoor (1881, 1883) is interesting as a study of a half-idiotic dwarf (Polydoor) who mercilessly tyrannizes his environment and his mother in particular—another variant of the child theme that is so prominent with Virginie Loveling. A form of naturalism is announced in *Een Vonkje van Genie* (1883; A Spark of Genius). Jeroen, a child with a talent for painting, will never realize his dreams; he will die in prison. Heredity and milieu are to blame for the tragic—or rather: melodramatic—course of the lives of a potentially gifted child and his (memorably drawn) parents. This novella stands as an accusation of the world that withholds the food from the soul that craves it and thus extinguishes the spark of genius.

From now on, Loveling steers clear from happy endings! Heredity is again a major force in the novella *Onze Idealen* (1892; Our Ideals), where the melodramatic and the fantastic blend in a tale that is as gripping as any of Poe's or Maupassant's. Among Loveling's longer novellas, *Meesterschap* (1898; Mastery) deserves special mention. With this work her pessimistic, black period really begins. *Meesterschap* presents a somber view of Flemish farm life—a view that can stand as a rural equivalent of Zola's industrial city pessimism. Loveling's ugly and vicious farmers, however, become subhuman only as the result of the increasing concern with money and power in their very small economic circle, in the course of the story itself. Milieu and circumstance are thus presented as the strongest influences on personality. Money is always a negative force for Loveling. Marriage, too, it has already been noted, should exclusively be a concern of the heart. The heart, not fortune, is the condition for love.

Together with *Sophie* and *Een Dure Eed*, *Een Revolverschot* (1911; A Gunshot) is generally considered one of Loveling's masterpieces. Again a study of heredity and its effects on psyche and eros, *Een Revolverschot* presents the fatal love of two sisters for the same man. Somber horror pictures and a few touches of melodrama stand out in this gruesome tale of murder and insanity.

Throughout her literary career, Virginie Loveling was also active as essayist and translator (of English and German poetry and of essays from English, French, and Swedish into Dutch and French for various Belgian periodicals). Some of her novellas have been translated into French, German, English, Italian, Danish, and Czech, even during her lifetime. With her cousin Cyriel Buysse, another important figure in Belgian literature in Dutch, she wrote *Levensleer* (1912), a humorous novel about the francophone bourgeoisie of Ghent. Finally, Virginie Loveling was also the author of two little books for children, one on insects, the other on the solar system.

Works

Anton (1866). Detel, tr. of German novellas by Klaus Groth (1866). [With Rosalie Loveling], Gedichten (1870). Novellen (1874). Nieuwe Novellen (1875).

A selection of her major novellas and novels (dates of publication do not always correspond with date of composition): [Pseud. W.G.E. Walter]. *In onze Vlaamsche Gewesten* (1877). *Polydoor en Theodoor* (1881, 1883). *Kinderverhalen* (1883–1886). *Een Vonkje van Genie* (1883). *Sophie* (1885). *Een Dure Eed* (1891). *Onze Idealen* (1892). *Een Idylle* (1893). *De Bruid des Heeren* (1895). *Mijnheer Connehaye* (1895). *Meesterschap* (1898). *Het Land der Verbeelding* (1896). *Madeleine* (1897). *De Twistappel* (1904). *Erfelijk belast* (1906). *Jongezellenlevens* (1907). *Een Revolverschot* (1911). (with C. Buysse) *Levensleer* (1912). *Volledige Werken* [Collected Works] 10 vols., (1933–1934).

Kristiaan P. Aercke

Monica Lovinescu
1923–

a.k.a. Claude Pascal, Monique Saint-Côme
Born 1923, Bucharest
Genre(s): short story, drama, literary criticism, essay, translation
Language(s): Romanian, French

Monica Lovinescu exiled herself from Romania in 1947 and has lived since in Paris, becoming a French citizen in 1967. When she left Bucharest, at age twenty-four, she had already published a number of short stories in *Vremea* and *Revista Fundaţiilor Regale* as well as regular drama reviews in *Democraţia*. After 1947 she continued to write in Romanian for the Romanian exile periodicals *România*, *Revista scriitorilor români*, *Contrapunct*, *Limite*, *Caiete de dor*, *Micromagazin*, *Lupta*, etc. while at the same time contributing essays to the French and English publications *Preuves*, *Les Lettres nouvelles*, *East Europe*, *L'Alternative*, *Problèmes du communisme*, *La France catholique*, and *Continent*.

Between 1951 and 1974 Lovinescu worked for the Radiodiffusion Française broadcasts in Romanian. In the sixties, she became a cultural commentator for the Romanian Desk of Radio Free Europe. Since then, she airs, with utmost regularity, two weekly programs—"Actualitatea culturală românească" (Romanian Cultural News) and "Teze şi antiteze la Paris"

(Theses and Antitheses in Paris) which have the strongest impact in Romania. The Romanian public listens to far away but impeccably informed and adamantly true Monica Lovinescu more than to the local broadcasts. Lovinescu would speak the unspeakable, with poise and lucidity, denounce cultural terrorism, abuse, or institutionalized lies, rejoice at the real artistic achievements, keep Romanian audiences informed with respect to the art and literature of the Romanian and East European exiles and dissidents or with the main trends in contemporary Western thought. Many times, the dissatisfactions of the Romanian writers, systematically ignored or denied publicity by the local authorities, have been voiced first by Lovinescu and acknowledged in Romania only after this by now almost indispensable, though paradoxical step. This is to say that the Romanian authorities listen to Monica Lovinescu's broadcasts at least as much as the general public, though for different reasons and with infinitely less pleasure.

Since 1950 there have been many violent official campaigns against Lovinescu in the Romanian press. In 1977, the Romanian Secret Police backed a terrorist attack against this Iron Lady of Romanian literary criticism. According to the D.S.T. and to the French press—see the numerous articles published by *Le Monde*, *Le Matin*, *Le Quotidien de Paris*, *La Croix* as well as the important books by Wolton (1986) and Picaper (1987)—the aim was to prevent her from ever writing or broadcasting again. Luckily transported to the hospital in due time by a passer-by, Lovinescu was saved and continues to talk to Romania twice a week. In 1978 she published in a compact volume of 500 pages entitled *Unde scurte. Jurnal indirect* (Short Waves. An Indirect Journal) a small part of her essential analyses devoted to post–World War II Romanian literature. The volume has been considered potentially so dangerous by the Romanian authorities that the literary weekly *Luceafărul* initiated, under the name "Pseudo-cultura pe unde scurte" (Pseudo-culture on Short Waves) a special anti-Lovinescu column which lasted almost two years.

Lovinescu's physiognomy as a contemporary literary critic is most unusual. She airs her criticism more often than she publishes it. She addresses her refined analyses not to a sparse learned readership here and there but to a whole country which listens to them with a concern and a fervor no Occidental critic would ever dream to elicit. She is able to determine through her comments many a shift in the evolution of Romanian culture both at the individual creator's and at the institutional level. While doing so she faces risks few of her peaceful homologues would be prepared to confront for professional reasons and assumes extraliterary responsibilities toward her sources which complicate and severely challenge her expression. Finally, Lovinescu practices a double, schizoid reading, with one eye—as she put it—looking at the text from the point of view of strict truth which cannot be uttered in Romania (wherefrom the critic's permanent irritation and frustration) and the other from the point of view of the degree of boldness incorporated in its transgression of limits and interdictions (wherefrom the critic's interest and hope). While writing and speaking as a sober professional, literary criticism is for Lovinescu a means for survival, a way to continue to live in the essential space of the country she left but did not abandon.

Unde scurte (1978; Short Waves) is devoted to a critical examination of the 1961–1971 decade of "liberalization" (or de-Stalinization) in Romanian literature. It is Lovinescu's thesis that while all the other East European countries achieved their "liberalization" by means of radical contestation and as the result of a cathartic ethical quest aimed at redefining and reestablishing the abused literary contract between artists and society, Romanian writers chose to put into parentheses the Stalinist experience and outgrow it by simply refusing to express it artistically. This unusual battle of silence in which all those who had published ideological maculature between 1948–1960 were tacitly shunned from the literary memory and a whole generation reconnected itself—over the gap of more than a decade—to the interwar tradition and, among its immediate predecessors, only to those who had perished in political prison or abstained from publishing during the Stalinist years, resulted in an unprecedented aesthetic explosion of Romanian literature which might be considered as the most evolved and modern literature in the communist bloc. At the same time though, by hurriedly giving precedence to the aesthetic over the ethic, the Romanian writers missed the opportunity to break the ideological totalitarian taboos and thus, through their punitive silence, continued to serve the major interests of the regime. This basic misunderstanding on their behalf, combined with the misunderstanding of the regime which, unaware of the fact that aesthetic evasion functioned as a safety valve preventing the writers from attaining real freedom and asking essential questions, started a strong antimodernistic campaign. Thus, while most of the East European writers became part of an efficient intelligentsia renouncing, for a while, a strictly professional writers' profile, their Romanian homologues hastened to function again as real contemporary writers but missed the opportunity and the duty of transforming into a unified and active intelligentsia.

Lovinescu translated from Romanian into French Virgil Gheorghiu's *La vingt-cinquième heure* (1949; The Twenty-fifth Hour) as well as Adriana Georgescu Cosmovici's novel *Au commencement était la fin* (1952; At the Beginning Was the End).

Works

Unde scurte. Jurnal indirect [Short Waves. An Indirect Journal] (1978).

Sanda Golopentia

Rosa Luxemburg
1871–1919

Born 1871, Zamosc, Russian Poland
Died 1919, Berlin, Germany
Genre(s): letters, economic and political treatises
Language(s): Polish, German, Russian, French

Rosa Luxemburg is best known as a brilliant and original Marxist theoretician and political strategist ("the best brain after Marx," according to her first biographer, Franz Mehring). The author of major economic and political treatises [*Reform or Revolution* (1899); *The Accumulation of Capital—An Anti-Critique* (1906); *The Crisis of Social Democracy* (1916) and *Introduction to National Economy* (1925)], she became internationally known in her time as "Red Rosa," the militant fighter on the front-line of the struggle for world socialism in late nineteenth- and early twentieth-century Europe. In her letters, however, we see another, less well-known, Rosa Luxemburg: the woman, friend, and lover, who in her private writings revealed herself to be much more complex than her public persona showed.

Born in the Polish city of Zamosc in 1871 into an educated and cosmopolitan but financially struggling middle-class Jewish family, Luxemburg lived in Poland until her political activism as a high-school student in Warsaw forced her to go into exile in 1883. As an expatriate in Zurich, she engaged in a thorough study of socialist theory and organizing practice under the tutelage of Leo Jogiches, her political mentor and lover of many years, and as a student of political economy whose brilliant dissertation was immediately published as a book. Quickly rising to a position of leadership within the left wing of the international socialist movement, Luxemburg chose as her base

Berlin, the capital of European Social Democracy at that time. Although she traveled much and widely as an organizer and orator in the cause of international socialism, she also cultivated life-long, intimate friendships with a small circle of people who constituted her emotional family and home: her comrades Karl and Luise Kautsky, Clara Zetkin, Karl and Sonja Liebknecht, Mathilde Wurm, and Marta Rosenbaum; her secretary Mathilde Jacob; and her lovers Leo Jogiches and Hans Diefenbach. In 1919, shortly after founding, with Karl Liebknecht, the Spartacus League (precursor of the German Communist Party), Luxemburg was assassinated in Berlin by fanatical right-wing storm troopers.

In contrast to her public writings (treatises, analyses, newspaper articles and speeches) Luxemburg's private writings (her correspondence with comrades, friends, and lovers) were not published in their entirety until the early 1980s. Previously published selections reflect the shifts in interest in various aspects of Luxemburg as a thinker, activist, and person. They reflect changing definitions of what constitutes the political as well.

The first letters to be published, within a year of her death, were her letters from prison, written primarily to her closest woman friend Sonja Liebknecht. In these letters Luxemburg emerges as a woman in whom the intellectual acuity of her analysis is matched by the emotional depth of her compassion. Reading, thinking, watching the clouds above the prison walls and the birds outside her window, she reflects on people's inhumanity both to other people and to the creatures over whom they exercise power. She sees the fundamental interconnectedness of all things: "I am rather surprised that Karl wants you to send him a book on bird song. For me the song of birds is inseparable from their life as a whole; it is the whole that interests me, rather than any detached detail" (Letter to Sonja Liebknecht, August 2, 1917).

This sense of the connectedness of all things, which was at the heart of Luxemburg's political vision as well, is also articulated in the letters to her friends and comrades that were published next. Finally, the publication of Luxemburg's love letters, documents of her tempestuous and life-long relationship with Leo Jogiches, was a sign of the increasing public interest in Rosa Luxemburg the woman, an interest informed by a 1970s consciousness of the political nature of personal relationships. Always insisting on the legitimacy of a person's dream for personal happiness (what else, she herself asked, is political struggle for?), Luxemburg's vision of a happy and fulfilled private life is inseparable from her vision of social change on a national and international level. Her anguish was that, in practice, she found that they were in perpetual conflict.

The style of Luxemburg's letters is consonant with her political form: an activism impelled by the vision of the infinite capacity for change within ourselves and the world we live in. Ranging in tone from sharp wit and biting sarcasm through dry, factual analysis to a tenderness that is unafraid of brushing up against sentimentality, they reveal a woman of keen intellect and deep feelings. In her letters to Jogiches the quality of her style, which appears less as writing than as words spoken on paper, is particularly palpable. Writing primarily in Polish and German (the languages of her childhood), but also intermingling Russian and French and bits of Yiddish, English, and Latin, her writing is startling in its range and freedom. Considered one of the great language artists in the field of Polish literature, Luxemburg was, in her own words, "a land of boundless possibilities."

Works

Gesammelte Briefe [Collected Letters], ed. Annelies Laschitza and Günter Radczun, tr. Hildegard Bamberger and Eduard Ullman (1982–1984). *The Letters of Rosa Luxemburg*, ed. Stephen E. Bronner, tr. Stephen E. Bronner and Hedwig Pachter) (1978). *Briefe aus dem Gefängnis* [Letters from Prison], tr. Eden and Cedar Paul (1946). *Prison Letters to Sophie Liebknecht*. tr. Eden and Cedar Paul (New York: A.J. Muste Memorial Institute, 1974–1985). *Briefe an meine Freunde* [Letters to My Friends] (1985). *Briefe an Freunde* [Letters to Friends], ed. Benedikt Kautsky

Rosa Luxemburg

(1976). *Briefe an Mathilde Jacob* [Letters to Mathilde Jacob], ed. Narihiko Ito (1972). *Briefe an Karl und Luise Kautsky, 1896–1918* [*Letters to Karl and Luise Kautsky from 1896 to 1918*], ed. Luise Kautsky, tr. Louis P. Lochner (1923; rpt. 1982). *Comrade and Lover: Rosa Luxemburg's Letters to Leo Jogiches*, ed. and tr. Elzbieta Ettinger (1979).

Angelika Bammer

(Emilie) Rose Macaulay
1881–1958

Born August 1, 1881, Rugby, England
Died October 30, 1958, London
Genre(s): novel
Language(s): English

The second of seven children, Macaulay was a tomboy who believed she would grow up to be a man; in her early twenties she still hoped to join the Navy. This sense of gender ambiguity, both playful and serious, pervades her fiction. In 1887 the Macaulays left Rugby, where her father was an assistant master, and moved to Italy. In the seacoast town of Varazze, the children led an exciting and undisciplined life before the family returned to England in 1894. She attended Oxford High School and later Somerville College, Oxford, where she read modern history. After graduating in 1903, she lived with her parents, first in Aberystwyth and afterward in Cambridge. By late 1905 she had had several poems published and was at work on her first novel, *Abbots Verney* (1906).

Macaulay's early novels combine a witty, aphoristic style with themes of loss and isolation from society. *The Lee Shore* (1912) concludes by urging philosophical detachment from failure and the "lust to possess": "The last, the gayest, the most hilarious laughter begins when, destitute utterly, the wrecked pick up coloured shells upon the leeshore." After the success of this novel (which won first prize and £1,000 in a competition organized by its publisher), Macaulay moved to London where she mingled with writers and intellectuals. During "this pre-war golden age," as she once called it, she published *The Making of a Bigot*, a comic novel about the necessity of compromising the "manyfaced Truth" in order to get on in the world, and her first book of poems, *The Two Blind Countries,* which reflects the influence of Walter de la Mare

and other Georgians but succeeds in registering her own peculiar sense of the instability of institutions and social structures, which she figures as "the transient city."

Macaulay worked as a nurse for part of the First World War, and in 1916 became a civil servant in the War Office, dealing with exemptions from service and conscientious objectors. In *Non-Combatants and Others* (1916), the heroine Alix comes to realize that her pacifist mother, Daphne—one in a series of exuberant, confident, worldly women in Macaulay's fiction—is right in campaigning for a "positive" peace, "a young peace, passionate, ardent, intelligent, romantic, like poetry, like art, like religion." The novel also contains an early and sensitive study of the psychological effects of trench-fighting. Early in 1918, Macaulay was transferred to the Ministry of Information. Here she met and fell in love with Gerald O'Donovan, a married novelist with whom she had a relationship that lasted until his death in 1942. His stimulus and criticism were of much importance to her career.

During the 1920s Macaulay established her reputation for trenchant, clear-eyed social satire. Her first best-seller, *Potterism* (1920)—an attack on the popular press and the muddleheaded emotionalism it exploits—is dedicated to "the unsentimental precisians in thought, who have, on this confused, inaccurate, and emotional planet, no fit habitation." In *Crewe Train* (1926), London society and its malicious gossip are exposed through the silent, anarchic figure of Denham, who, much against her husband's will, prefers to live alone in a Cornish cottage and explore the caves beneath it. But "Life" is too strong for her; her self-sufficiency gives way to social and marital pressures. She relinquishes her cottage and the cave of her own and returns to her husband.

In the 1930s Macaulay became increasingly absorbed in the study of the seventeenth century and wrote a refreshing, informed biography of Milton.

More important is her historical novel *They Were Defeated* (1932), set in the early 1640s and featuring the poet Robert Herrick. Macaulay restricted the characters' vocabulary to words known to have existed at the period, and the dialogue is remarkably credible and fluent. The novel elegizes the Cavalier tradition and movingly portrays Herrick, whose verses celebrating simple rural joys go unheeded in a world where Donnian "conceit" is all the rage. Most poignant are the "defeats" involving women. A harmless old eccentric is hunted down as a witch; and Julian Conybeare, a brilliant and poetically gifted girl, becomes the mistress of the poet John Cleveland only to discover that he wants her to give up ideas and poetry and assume her proper role in life. Her protest, "It makes no differ, being a maid," does not avail. The story ends with her tragic, absurd death. In *Crewe Train* Macaulay had described Denham as "the Silent Woman"; Julian might be called "the silenced woman."

Macaulay visited Portugal and Spain and produced two works of great learning and wit based on her travels, *They Went to Portugal* (1946) and *Fabled Shore* (1949). In 1948 Macaulay began writing *The World My Wilderness* (1950), her first novel in almost a decade. The central symbol—the London Blitz ruins—is a variation of the cave motif used in *Crewe Train*. Barbary, a girl resembling Denham in many ways, leaves her home in a tiny French port to live in "civilized" London. But her earlier life and her participation in the French underground have made her unfit for all this, and she is at home only in the bombed-out buildings of the city. Here, the "cave" is more a symbol of widespread moral decline than an image of personal freedom.

All her life Macaulay was fascinated by religious questions, and much of her work reflects this. She had stopped receiving Communion in 1922 because of her involvement with the married O'Donovan. Yet she always considered herself an "Anglo-Agnostic," and in 1950 she began exchanging letters with an Anglican priest named Johnson. Her letters to him fill two books—*Letters to a Friend* and *Last Letters to a Friend*—and trace her return to the Anglican Communion under his spiritual guidance.

In 1956, Macaulay published *The Towers of Trebizond*, which John Betjeman considered "the best book she has written, and that is saying a lot." Partly inspired by a trip to Turkey in 1954, the novel is a masterful and picaresque compendium of her beliefs and interests, written in what she called a "rather goofy, rambling prose style." This allows her to sketch a scene swiftly or digress at length (on the history of mistresses, e.g.). The eccentric Father Chantry-Pigg, along with an insane camel and a trained ape, provide hilarity, but the work also reflects, in part, her crisis of faith. The narrator Laurie—who does not reveal herself to be a woman until the end—yearns for the Byzantine city of Trebizond, which symbolizes the Church, but her adulterous relationship prevents her from making "the pattern and the hard core" of the city her own. At the end she is still outside the city.

"Ignorance, vulgarity, cruelty" were Macaulay's "three black jungle horrors." In contrast, her work consistently offers a voice that is civilized, ironic, playful, canny, and sane. Her satire is sometimes accused of flippancy, but this is because her narrative "mimicry" and use of authorial voice are not yet properly understood. Nor are her feminism and her play on gender expectations fully appreciated. What Katherine Mansfield called "her offhand, lightly-smiling manner" thinly disguises intense commitment to difference and eccentricity and equally intense religiosity. Her pluralistic mind, like the Anglican Church as she describes it in *The Towers of Trebizond,* was "very wonderful and comprehensive."

Macaulay was made a Dame Commander of the British Empire in 1958.

Works

Abbots Verney (1906). *The Furnace* (1907). *The Secret River* (1909). *The Valley Captives* (1911). *Views and Vagabonds* (1912). *The Lee Shore* (1912). *The Two Blind Countries* (1914). *The Making of a Bigot* (1914). *Non-Combatants and Others* (1916). *What Not: A Prophetic Comedy* (1919). *Three Days* (1919). *Potterism: A Tragifarcical Tract* (1920). *Dangerous Ages* (1921). *Mystery at Geneva* (1922). *Told by an Idiot* (1923). *Orphan Island* (1924). *A Casual Commentary* (1925). *Crewe Train* (1926). *Catchwords and Claptrap* (1926). *Keeping up Appearances* (1928; in the U.S., *Daisy and Daphne).* *Staying with Relations* (1930). *Some Religious Elements in English Literature* (1931). *They Were Defeated* (1932; in the U.S., *The Shadow Flies).* *Going Abroad* (1934). *Milton* (1934). *The Minor Pleasures of Life* (1934). *Personal Pleasures* (1935). *An Open Letter to a Non-Pacifist* (1937). *I Would Be Private* (1937). *The Writings of E.M. Forster* (1938). *And No Man's Wit* (1940). *Life Among the English* (1942). *They Went to Portugal* (1946). *Fabled Shore: From the Pyrenees to Portugal* (1949). *The World My Wilderness* (1950). *Pleasure of Rains* (1953). *The Towers of Trebizond* (1956). *Letters to a Friend: 1950–1952* (1961). *Last Letters to a Friend: 1952–1958* (1962). *Letters to a Sister* (1964).

Robert Spoo

Elizabeth Mackintosh
1896–1952

a.k.a. Gordon Daviot, Josephine Tey
Born June 25, 1896, Inverness, Scotland
Died February 13, 1952, London
Genre(s): novel, drama, biography
Language(s): English

Mackintosh is best known as Josephine Tey, the author of several extraordinary novels of detection. More extensive, however, and in her own estimation more central to her career as a serious writer, was her output of fiction, plays, and biography under the pseudonym Gordon Daviot.

Born in Inverness, Scotland, she attended the Royal Academy there but declined to go on to university or art school ("I balked, too, at art—my talent is on the shady side of mediocre"). Instead she studied three years at Anstey Physical Training College, Birmingham, worked briefly as a physiotherapist, and taught physical education at schools in Scotland and England. Called home in 1923 to attend her dying mother, she remained in Inverness living with her father. She took long annual holidays in England and developed some friendships in London theatrical circles but shunned publicity and was generally reclusive. She continued her work through the year of illness that preceded her early death. Found among her papers were two novels and thirteen plays, since published.

The career of "Gordon Daviot" began about 1925 with contributions to magazines and continued in 1929 with two novels including a detective story, *The Man in the Queue*. Mackintosh then turned to drama but, on the rejection of her first effort, reworked it as a romantic novel, *The Expensive Halo* (1931). Finally in 1932 came *Richard of Bordeaux;* running in London for over a year, starring John Gielgud, as well as in New York, this remained Mackintosh's most successful play. In Gielgud's opinion "she improved on Shakespeare . . . by giving [King] Richard II] a sense of humour." *Richard* was followed by twelve other full-length plays, five of which were produced in her lifetime (Laurence Olivier played Bothwell in *Queen of Scots),* and thirteen shorter plays, including several radio broadcasts. Nearly half her plays retell stories from history or the Bible (Sarah and Hagar, Joseph, Moses, Rahab). The latter group should not be considered religious plays: it was the story that interested her, and her reading of it was typically nonsupernaturalist. Romantic themes appear occasionally in her plays; more prominent is a vein of tart satire, especially of politicians. She also wrote two

historically based prose works, a biography of the seventeenth-century Scottish royalist Viscount Dundee *(Claverhouse,* 1937), and a novel about the pirate Henry Morgan *(The Privateer,* 1952).

The pseudonym "Josephine Tey" first appeared in 1936 with A *Shilling for Candles,* and Mackintosh reserved it for detective fiction, which she deprecated as her "yearly knitting." From 1947 to 1952, indeed, one Tey novel did appear each year. These works, exhibiting her skill in dialogue (honed by writing for the stage) and attention to characterization, not only rank high in classic "golden age" detective fiction but belong to the mainstream of the novel. Exploration of character is Mackintosh's chief interest. Insight into motive and the perception of such typically "criminal" character traits as vanity are always, for her, key elements in detection, and when her detectives err, as often happens, it is by suppressing such insight and trusting more traditional, apparently objective, kinds of evidence. (One oddity in Mackintosh's presentation of character is the obsessive notion that it can be read infallibly in trivial details of facial features and expression. Her Scotland Yard inspector Alan Grant relies heavily on this method, applying it no less accurately with photographs or portraits than in the flesh. But curiously, Mackintosh hardly ever describes Grant himself.) Thematically, Mackintosh develops romance interests in some of the Tey novels and, with delightful asperity of tone, makes fun of the vanity and shallow lifestyle of the theatre and arts crowd. Another serious theme uniting these works is that of identity, ranging from initial difficulty in identifying the corpse *(Queue, Sands)* through the morally neutral effort of a prodigal to escape disgrace by resuming his old name *(Shilling)* to imposture (teenage harlot posing as innocent victim in *Franchise,* foundling cousin posing as heir in *Brat,* transvestite disguise in *Love).*

Moreover, Mackintosh feels free to depart from golden age formulas, often in ways suggesting a more skeptical postmodern sensibility. Only half the eight novels have corpses; in two no one dies, and in two long-closed cases are reopened. Especially remarkable is *The Daughter of Time,* in which a bedridden detective conducts an academic investigation into the fate of the young princes in the Tower and concludes that Henry VII, not Richard III, had them murdered. Here and twice more *(Miss Pym Disposes, The Franchise Affair)* Mackintosh ends not with order satisfyingly restored by justice but with innocence suffering and society powerless to punish the wrongdoers adequately if at all.

Among the sufferers are Mackintosh's detectives, who may be physically *(Daughter)* or emotionally *(Sands)* ill, prone to play God—hence the title *Miss*

Pym Disposes—but inept, or themselves involved in crime though fundamentally honest (*Brat*). For all Mackintosh's favorable, even sympathetic treatment of him, Grant is unusually fallible. He wastes time chasing the wrong suspect, and sometimes (*Shilling, Franchise*) it takes an amateur detective to correct his errors. Three cases (*Queue, Pym,* and *Sands*) are solved by the murderer's confession, not the detective's sleuthing, though in the last, to do Grant justice, the confession merely anticipates his independent solution; and in *The Daughter of Time* the verdict against King Henry inherently must lack the external corroboration standard for the genre.

If the police have trouble drawing the right conclusions, all the more easily is the general public hoodwinked. Mackintosh's skepticism on this score unites the Tey and the Daviot *oeuvres*. Frequently she attacks gullibility in the face of fraudulent piety, whether that of the rogue "monk" in *A Shilling for Candles* or that of the Covenanters in *Claverhouse*. Misled public opinion drives an innocent into exile in *The Franchise Affair* (a fictionalized version of an eighteenth-century case) and, in the one-act play *Leith Sands*, hangs a man for a murder that never occurred. Much of Grant's case in *The Daughter of Time* consists of questioning the reliability of accepted "evidence" and citing parallel instances of historians' naive credulity. This book is Mackintosh's best known in academic circles, being used as a textbook for raising questions on historical method. The same story appears in dramatic form in *Dickon*. She especially enjoyed rehabilitating characters vilified by history (Dundee, Morgan, Richard III) and, in fiction, portraying the character type of the honest rogue (*Kif, Brat*).

Other links between Tey and Daviot are consistent patterns in the treatment of women and a cinematic quality in Mackintosh's writing. She loved movies, habitually attending twice weekly, and several of her novels have been dramatized in film (e.g., Hitchcock's *Young and Innocent*) or television.

Works

As Gordon Daviot: *The Man in the Queue* (1929, rpt. 1953 under Josephine Tey). *Kif: An Unvarnished History* (1929). *The Expensive Halo* (1931). *Richard of Bordeaux* (produced 1932, published 1933, rpt. 1958 in *Penguin Plays*). *The Laughing Woman* (1934). *Queen of Scots* (1934). *Claverhouse* (1937). *The Stars Bow Down* (1939). *Leith Sands* [broadcast 1941] *and Other Short Plays* (1946). *The Privateer* (1952). (*Plays* 3 vols., foreword by J. Gielgud (1953–54; *The Pen of My Aunt* rpt. in *Eight Short Plays* [1968]; *Dickon* ed.

with intro., historical commentary and notes by E. Haddon [1966]).

As Josephine Tey: *A Shilling for Candles* (1936). *Miss Pym Disposes* (1947). *The Franchise Affair* (1948). *Brat Farrar* (1949). *To Love and Be Wise* (1950). *The Daughter of Time* (1951). *The Singing Sands* (1952). *Three by Tey (Miss Pym Disposes, The Franchise Affair, Brat Farrar)* intro. by J. Sandoe (1954). *Four, Five and Six by Tey (The Singing Sands, A Shilling for Candles, The Daughter of Time)* (1958).

Charles A. Huttar

Ella Maillart
1903–

Born February 20, 1903, Geneva, Switzerland
Genre(s): travel literature, journalism
Language(s): French, English

Born into a middle-class family in Geneva, the young Maillart acquired through sports the independence of mind and physical robustness that enabled her to make her now-classic treks across Asia. She played field hockey and skied competitively and from girlhood on sailed on Lake Geneva, later becoming the only woman entered in the 1924 Olympic single-handed sailing competition in Paris, in which seventeen countries participated. Self-supporting, she worked all over Europe as a language teacher, a deckhand (*Gypsy Afloat* recalls some of her voyages), and a film extra, until, succumbing to the lure of the unknown and her own indomitable sense of curiosity, she set out alone in 1930 for Russia.

Maillart's six-month stay in Moscow marked the beginning of her career as a writer and a traveler. She supported herself with journalism and wrote the volume *Parmi la jeunesse russe*, of special interest because of her contacts with the Russian film industry. But ever more distant horizons beckoned: in the early 1930s, at the time when enormous stretches of Central Asia were still only accessible by horse, donkey, or camel, Maillart made the journeys described in her finest travel books: the intrepid trek into Russian Turkestan in 1932 recorded in *Des Monts célestes aux Sables rouges* (in English as *Turkestan Solo*), and, in 1935, the transcontinental *Forbidden Journey* (*Oasis interdites*) from Peking to India, so titled because the vast northwest Chinese province of Sinkiang, racked by civil war and only nominally under the control of the Kuomintang, was strictly forbidden to foreigners.

Maillart's fascination with the dignity and strangeness of Asian ways, and her attraction to the limitless unknown, whether physical or spiritual, shaped her life. *Cruises and Caravans* (1942)—Maillart had now begun to write in English—recalls the adventuresome jaunts of the 1930s, *Ti-Puss* (1951) records the war years which Maillart spent in India, and *The Land of the Sherpas* (1955) reports briefly on her trip to Nepal. The most fascinating of her later works is *The Cruel Way* (1947), in which the central confrontation is no longer between the author and Asia, but rather between Maillart and her beautiful, sensitive, self-destructive and drug-addicted traveling companion "Christina," a pseudonym for the Swiss writer Annemarie Schwarzenbach (see separate entry). The account of their trip to Afghanistan undertaken in the spring of 1939, is an honest study of a troubled friendship and of the failure of Maillart's attempts to guide Christina out of her suffering.

During these years Maillart came to understand that her passion for traveling sprang from a search for real values: it was, in essence, a spiritual quest. She widened her horizons again by including in her search for knowledge the religious heritage of the East. Maillart now resides in French-speaking Switzerland, where she is something of a celebrity. She continues to travel widely; her last trip to Tibet was in 1986.

Maillart is a traveler first and a writer second. Her best books, such as *Forbidden Journey*, are direct, fresh, and modest. They are not political reports, for though Maillart often mentions the corruptive effect of Western materialism on Eastern culture, the mechanisms of political change do not interest her. Her works live on the spirit of adventure that thrilled to the myriad foreign sights and sounds and souls. Where Maillart is not yet fully aware of the ultimately spiritual origin of her zest for the physical universe, where her courageous journeys express more of herself than she recognizes, her writing, in all its simplicity, has the force of lived allegory. After resolving the tension between the outside world and the ultimate truths of life (which Maillart in any case sees as complementary rather than contradictory) her writing loses some of its color and force: the introspective view does not capture the reader as fully as the alert, outward gaze. Maillart's best work, however, embodies the paradox of the consummate individualist searching or reintegration with a lost completeness.

Works

"With Bonita to Greece." *The Yachting Monthly* 49,291 and 49,292 (1930). *Parmi la jeunesse russe. De Moscou au Caucase* (1932). "Tachkent et Samarcande." *La Revue de Paris* 41.6 (1934). *Des Monts célestes aux Sables rouges* (1934; 1971; 1986). *Oasis interdites. De Pékin au Cachemire.* (1937; 1971; 1982). "De la Mer Jaune à la Mer d'Oman par le Tibet." *L'Illustration* 96, 27.8 and 3.9 (1938). *Cruises and Caravans* (1942). *Gypsy Afloat* (1942). *The Cruel Way* (1947; 1986). *Ti-Puss* (1951). *The Land of the Sherpas* (1955).

Translations: *Turkestan Solo* [Des Monts célestes aux Sables rouges] (1934; 1985). *Forbidden Journey* [Oasis interdites] (1937; 1949; 1983).

Ann Marie Rasmussen

Françoise d'Aubigné, Marquise de Maintenon
1635–1719

a.k.a. Mme de Maintenon
Born November 27, 1635, Niort, France
Died April 15, 1719, Saint-Cyr
Genre(s): educational tract, letters, maxim
Language(s): French

Mme de Maintenon had one of the most remarkable careers of the Splendid Century, the Age of Louis XIV. Born in prison in Niort to a ne'er-do-well father and a placid, commoner mother, Françoise endured poverty and neglect during her youth and adolescence. In 1639 her family moved to Martinique where her father died six years later; Françoise was sent to live with an aunt in France. In this strict Calvinist household, the young girl became imbued with moral and religious beliefs that influenced her entire life. Another female relative received permission to educate the girl; at the convent of the Ursulines in Paris, Françoise was converted to Catholicism before leaving the convent at age fourteen. Living in poverty with her mother in Paris, the beautiful and spirited girl had no prospects for making a good marriage or for employment.

Fortunately she came to the attention of a neighbor, the crippled, satiric poet and playwright Paul Scarron, who offered to marry her or provide a dowry so she could enter a convent. Neither offer was accepted until her mother died, and Françoise was left with no alternative; in 1652, at age sixteen, she married Scarron. Though poor himself, Scarron's residence in the Marais was a gathering place for a brilliant and rather uninhibited society. The beautiful courtesan, Ninon de Lenclos, was a regular visitor along with free-thinking gentlemen from the *beau monde* of Paris. Mme Scarron used her charm and beauty to good advantage and

Françoise d'Aubigné, Marquise de Maintenon

earned a reputation for prudence and trying to please; ". . . everyone loved me," she wrote later in life, "I had seen everything, but [I] always acted so as not to sully my reputation. . . . I wanted to be part of society, to have my name said with admiration and respect, . . . and especially to be approved by people of quality." The illustrious company at Scarron's social gatherings admired his sensible, cautious, young wife. After his death in 1660, his widow continued to associate with this diverse, socially prominent group; at the fashionable hôtels d'Albret and Richelieu she mingled with distinguished women such as Mme de Sévigné, Mme de LaFayette, and Mme de Montespan. Once more reduced to penury, Mme Scarron retired to the Ursuline convent in Paris and lived on a small pension from the Queen Mother.

A dramatic change in her fortunes came about after the beautiful, sensuous, and passionate Mme de Montespan became the official mistress of Louis XIV. When they had children, Montespan proposed that Mme Scarron raise the children. Only after the king personally requested it did the impoverished widow agree to accept this unusual position. The arrangement was a poorly kept secret in Paris, especially when the king began visiting the residence on the rue de Vaugirard. Mme Scarron's discretion and her dedication to the children gradually developed into a kind of bond between this surrogate mother and the king. In

1673, Louis formally recognized his natural children, and they joined him at Court. Mme Scarron was given an apartment there and continued to supervise their upbringing. As a reward for her services Louis gave her the estate of Maintenon and the title of marquise (1674).

During the next six years the fortunes of Mme de Montespan waned as the king drew closer to Mme de Maintenon. By 1681 Montespan had left the Court and Mlle de Fontanges, the king's last mistress, had died. It is doubtful that Mme de Maintenon ever became Louis' mistress. In fact, she actually encouraged the king to be more attentive to his long-suffering Queen, and the latter was touchingly grateful to Maintenon. The true relationship between Louis and the Marquise has never been fully ascertained, but when the Queen died, it is certain that they were married morganatically in late 1684. The marriage was never openly acknowledged by either party nor by anyone at Court, and Maintenon was not Queen.

The Marquise never involved herself in affairs of state, but she did influence Louis on religious matters. She has been accused of encouraging the king's anti-Huguenot (Protestant) campaign that led to the revocation of the Edict of Nantes (1685), but this has not been proven. Her involvement with Quietism and sympathy for Jansenism have been cited as examples of her lack of firm religious principles. However, it was through her commitment to female education that Maintenon earned the admiration and respect of her contemporaries. In 1685 she persuaded Louis to found a secular school for poor noble girls. Neither she nor the king considered a convent education as adequate for living in the world. Saint-Cyr was completed in 1686; part secular, part religious, the school provided a better education for girls than was usual at the time. Maintenon personally oversaw the curriculum, hired and directed the instructors, and provided dowries for the pupils. Saint-Cyr was the focal point of her life. Often bored and tired of the stifling court life, she put her talents to good use at the school. Much of her writing concerned the education of young women, preparing them for life outside a convent. The great Fénelon advised her on instruction, and Racine wrote plays (*Esther* and *Athalie*) which were performed by the students. After the king died, Maintenon retired to Saint-Cyr where she died in 1719.

Most of her writings and letters were preserved in the library at Saint-Cyr. In 1756 La Beaumelle published her letters and wrote a work on Maintenon and the seventeenth century (6 vols.). This editor/author took many liberties with her style, cutting words and sentences and inserting phrases of his own. Fortunately, Lavallée used the original manuscripts, now dispersed at Versailles, the archives of Seine-et-Oise, and the Bibliothèque Nationale, for his *Oeuvres de Mme. de Maintenon . . .* (Works of Mme. de Maintenon . . .) published in the nineteenth century. Through his efforts the finesse, conciseness and restrained elegance of her writing style were aptly demonstrated. Her writings, like those of Mme de Sévigné, provide an insider's view of Paris society and the Court and are an important source for understanding the role of women in seventeenth-century France.

Works

Choix d'entretiens et de lettres (1876). *Conseils et instructions aux demoiselles pour leur conduits dans le monde*, 2 vols. (1857). *Conversations* (1828). *Correspondance générale de Madame de Maintenon*, 4 vols. (1865–1866). *Recueil des instructions que Madame de Maintenon a données aux demoiselles de St.-Cyr, d'après un manuscript original et inédit appartenant à la comtesse de Gramont d'Aster* (1908).

William T. Ojala
Jeanne A. Ojala

Nadezhda Mandelshtam
1899–1980

Born October 31, 1899, Saratov, Russia
Died December 29, 1980, Moscow
Genre(s): memoir
Language(s): Russian

Nadezhda Mandelshtam's two books, *Hope Against Hope* and *Hope Abandoned*, bear witness to her incredible tenacity in the face of relentless persecution under Stalin. The wife of Osip Mandelshtam, a poet of genius, she devoted her life to the preservation of her husband's *oeuvre* after his arrest and disappearance in the concentration camps in 1938.

She was born Nadezhda Yakovlevna Khazina in an educated Jewish family in the provincial town of Saratov. Living most of her early life in Kiev, she became an art student in the studio of A.A. Ekster. It was in 1919 in Kiev that she met her future husband, Mandelshtam, to whom she was officially married in 1922. The couple lived in Moscow, in the Herzen House, while looking for a place of their own to live. Her friendship with Anna Akhmatova, a great poet and fellow Acmeist of Mandelshtam, dates from 1925. Already in the 1920s Osip Mandelshtam was beginning to come under fire on account of his nonconformist attitude vis-à-vis the "social command" imposed upon literature by the new Soviet regime. His first arrest in 1934 was occasioned by a denunciatory poem he wrote about Stalin. After his second arrest and disappearance in 1938, Nadezhda evaded the authorities on numerous occasions by moving from one provincial town to another, teaching English to earn her daily bread. From this time until Mandelshtam's official rehabilitation, she devoted herself to preserving her husband's memory and poetry, often devising ingenious ways of hiding manuscripts from the police.

Nadezhda Yakovlevna composed her two great memoirs *Hope Against Hope* (1970) and *Hope Abandoned* (1972) in the latter half of the 1960s. These works were never published in the Soviet Union. Her first book concentrates primarily on the four years between Mandelshtam's two arrests. Although restricted to this time span, the author's style is discursive, and provides many valuable insights into the horror of Soviet life under Stalin. Indeed, to resurrect the past and to expose the moral bankruptcy of a system wherein the end justifies the means is the author's avowed purpose. This intent is even more apparent in her second book, *Hope Abandoned*, which Jane Harris has rightfully characterized as a "Book of Judgment." The author attacks the moral laxity and blindness to human suffering characteristic of those who supported Stalinism. *Hope Abandoned* in this sense is different from *Hope Against Hope*, whose focus was primarily upon Mandelshtam. In the second work greater attention is given to Nadezhda Yakovlevna's life with Mandelshtam from the beginning of their relationship up to his arrest in 1934. The author's own life, from her husband's death to the writing of the book, is also described. In this second memoir she adds "considerably to her portrait gallery of contemporaries, bringing Mandelshtam's lonely eminence into sharper relief" (Max Hayward).

In these writings Nadezhda Mandelshtam comes through to the reader as a person of great courage, whose devotion to her husband saved the works of one of the greatest poets of the twentieth century from oblivion. By virtue of her brutal honesty and powerful convictions, her moral victory over her persecutors is complete.

Works

Vospominaniya (1970). *Vtoraya kniga* (1972). *Moe zaveshchanie i drugie* esse (1982).

Translations: *Hope Against Hope*, tr. Max Hayward, introd. Clarence Brown (1970). *Hope Abandoned*, tr. with foreword by Max Hayward (1972). *Mozart and Salieri*, tr. by Robert A. McClean (1973).

Laura Jo Turner McCullough

(Mary) Delariviere Manley
ca. 1663–1724

Born April 6 or 7, 1663 (?) or 1667–1672, Jersey, England
Died July 11, 1724, London
Genre(s): memoir, drama
Language(s): English

Much is problematic about Manley's early years, including whether Mary was her first name and when and where she was born. Her own testimony, given in thinly fictionalized autobiographical narratives, is unreliable; and the little remaining documentary evidence is ambiguous. We do know that she was born in the latter part of the seventeenth century in England, possibly on the island of Jersey, or possibly at sea between Jersey and Guernsey, the daughter of Sir Roger Manley, who was Lieutenant-Governor of Jersey, a Stuart sympathizer, and an author of histories. She had three sisters and a brother. Her mother died in Manley's youth and her father c. 1688, apparently leaving her the ward of a cousin, John Manley, who later married her under false pretenses (he was already wed) and abandoned her with a son. This "bigamous marriage," which Manley recounts in *The New Atlantis* (1709) and *The Adventures of Rivella* (1714), seriously damaged her social reputation.

Shortly thereafter she became the companion of Barbara Palmer, the Duchess of Cleveland, who figures in several works. They soon quarreled, and Manley retired to Exeter, having discovered, as she put it in *The Adventures of Rivella*, that "her Love of Solitude was improved by her Disgust of the World." In Exeter she wrote the first of her works: two plays—*The Lost Lover*, a comedy, and *The Royal Mischief*, a tragedy—and an epistolary protonovel entitled *Letters Written by Mrs. Manley* (1696; retitled *A Stage Coach Journey to Exeter* in 1725). At about this time she had an affair with Sir Thomas Skipworth, who produced her plays in London in 1696. *The Lost Lover* presented at Drury Lane c. March 1696, had little success, but the tragedy, which appeared a month or so later at Lincoln's Inn Fields, helped to establish Manley's reputation and yielded her a financial profit. Both plays were preceded by important feminist prefaces. Only "prejudice against our Sex," she maintained, prevented the plays from receiving a more enthusiastic reception. Partly as a response to these statements, Drury Lane shortly thereafter exposed Manley and other women playwrights of the period to public ridicule by presenting a burlesque of the production of *The Royal Mischief* entitled *The Female Wits*. Whether this play had a chastening effect on Manley is unclear, but she gave up writing (or at least publishing) for nearly a decade. During this period she became romantically involved with John Tilly, who was married and the warden of the Fleet Street prison. Tilly was the great love of her life, but she gave him up after several years to allow him to make a financially advantageous liaison with a rich widow.

It was shortly after this (1702) that Manley began producing her most celebrated works, a series of fictionalized satires written partly to vindicate herself, partly to promote her Tory political interests, and partly to make money. The first of these, which most scholars attribute to her, is *The Secret History of Queen Zarah, and the Zarazians* (1705). It includes an important theoretical preface, which provides a critique of the then popular heroic romance. *Queen Zarah* has the distinction of being the first *roman à clef* written in English. The work is a political satire in the form of a picaresque romance, directed against Sarah Churchill, the Duchess of Marlborough, who with her husband was an influential Whig member of the court of Queen Anne. In *Queen Zarah* Sarah is portrayed as ambitious, cruel, greedy, rude, and guilty of various sexual improprieties. Perhaps because of the explicitness of the latter descriptions the book was extraordinarily popular, selling several thousand copies. In 1706 Manley produced another play, *Almyna*, considered her best tragedy.

Manley's most celebrated work, *Secret Memoirs and Manners . . . from the New Atlantis,* appeared in 1709. Like *Queen Zarah*, this satire was a kind of *roman à clef* that recounted political intrigue and sexual scandal, mainly among members of the Whig aristocracy. The work includes scenes of homosexual, as well as heterosexual, orgy, drunkenness, rape, and incest, which have given it a sensationalist reputation. The second volume, for example, opens with a piece on the New Cabal, a group of wealthy lesbians. Manley was arrested for libel on October 29, 1709, but was released under the newly enacted *habeus corpus* writ on November 5, and the case was eventually dropped in 1710. As in all Manley's works, *The New Atlantis* reveals the author's talent at realistic description, of dress, manners, and psychological motivation, as well as her wry, sarcastic wit. The last of Manley's political works, *Memoirs of Europe,* appeared in 1710, and *Court-Intrigues,* in 1711. During this period, she published *The Female Tatler,* a journal of political satire, and in 1711 succeeded Jonathan Swift, a fellow Tory, as editor of *The Examiner.*

Probably of most interest to the modern reader is Manley's *Adventures of Rivella* (1714), which remains an important early precursor to the novel. Essentially autobiographical, Rivella's story is narrated by Sir Charles Lovemore to a Chevalier d'Aumont, who is an admiring Rivella reader. Like many later novels, the central character is presented as an innocent victim of circumstances—mainly financial—and of prejudice against women. Manley is particularly exercised by the double standard: *"If she had been a Man, she had been without Fault: But the Charter of that Sex being much more confin'd than ours, what is not a Crime in Men is scandalous and unpardonable in Woman."* In addition to a feminist perspective, the work expresses a kind of cynicism reminiscent of Le Rochefoucauld (whom, indeed, Rivella reads) that contributes to the growing tradition of realism in literature. The world is portrayed as a decidedly unromantic jungle where people operate primarily according to self-interest.

Her final works included a play, *Lucius, The First Christian King of Britain*, produced at Drury Lane in 1717, *The Power of Love: in Seven Novels* (1720), and *Bath Intrigues* (1725), published posthumously; the latter may not be hers.

Her contribution lies in having forged an authentically feminist realism, in creating vigorous, true-to-life characters whose psychological behavior is finely tuned, and in having braved the negative currents that opposed women's entrance into the field of dramatic and fictional literature. She is one of the pioneers of women's literature in English, but her work has yet to receive the serious critical attention it deserves.

Works

Letters Written by Mrs. Manley (1696) (reprinted as *A Stage Coach Journey to Exeter* in 1725). *The Lost Lover; or The Jealous Husband* (1696). *The Royal Mischief* (1696). *The Secret History of Queen Zarah and the Zarazians* (1705). *Almyna; or the Arabian Vow* (1707). *Secret Memoirs and Manners of Several Persons of Quality of Both Sexes from the New Atlantis, an Island in the Mediterranean* (1709). *Memoirs of Europe, toward the Close of the Eighth Century* (1710). *Court Intrigues in a Collection of Original Letters from the Island of the New Atlantis* (1711). *The Adventures of Rivella; or the History of the Author of the Atlantis by Sir Charles Lovemore* (1714). *Lucius, the First Christian King of Britain* (1717). *The Power of Love: in Seven Novels* (1720). *Bath Intrigues* (attributed to Manley) (1725). *The Novels of Mary Delariviere Manley*, ed. and intro. by P. Köster (1971).

Josephine Donovan

Eeva-Liisa Manner
1921–

a.k.a. Anna September
Born December 5, 1921, Helsinki, Finland
Genre(s): poetry, drama, novel, translation
Language(s): Finnish

Eeva-Liisa Manner is one of the most important, innovative writers of modern Finnish poetry. The characteristic features of her work are philosophically analytical thinking, concise imagery, and a musical beauty of expression. These features are typical of her whole range—poetry, prose, and drama—the difference between the genres largely fade in her writing.

Manner was born in Helsinki in 1921. She left secondary school to work in insurance and publishing from 1940 to 1946. Since then, she has been a freelance writer and a productive translator. She spent her childhood in Viipuri (now part of the Soviet Union); later she has lived in Tampere and Churriana (Spain).

The work that marked her breakthrough and that of modernism in Finnish poetry was her collection *Tämä matka* (1956; This Journey). It was preceded by two traditional books of poetry typical of the forties and a novel describing her childhood in the early fifties. The central problems of the poet can be seen in *Tämä matka*. The themes that run through it are loneliness—her great theme, taking part in the world's suffering ("Misericordia") and opposing violence ("Strontium"). Music has been a powerful influence, especially Bach and Mozart, but equally modern jazz. A counterforce to loneliness in this and later works is the relation with nature, an experience tinged with pantheism. Much of her imagery comes from childhood experiences, dreams, and myth (the horse is an especially frequently repeated metaphor); later the relation with nature is also linked with oriental philosophy, particularly Chinese wisdom.

High points of her later work are a verse drama, *Eros ja Psykhe* (1959; Eros and Psyche), which most purely continued the themes of *Tämä matka*, and the poetry collections *Kirjoitettu kivi* (1966; Written Stone), *Fahrenheit 121* (1968), and *Kuolleet vedet* (1977; Dead Waters). *Varokaa, voittajat* (1972; Beware, Victors), a novel in limpid style, is a significant analysis of violence. It describes a southern country not precisely identified, with a political murder as a starting point. It deals with the fate of forgotten people, the oppressed, who are seen as the plague of prosperity. The novel is dominated by the theme of shared suffering that pervades her poetry.

Kirjoitettu kivi and *Fahrenheit 121* belong to the Spanish period in Manner's poetry, containing attitudes to topical events and the state of the world. They continue the voyage of discovery of *Tämä matka* into the ego world of subjective experience: "The world is the poem of my instincts / and ceases when I die." The prose passages in these works are not poetic philosophy but philosophic poetry. Often they mock the conclusions of classical philosophy, as in the poem *Kirjoitettu kivi*: "You live, you have two children, a wife, a bed, a mangy dog, you live, because it is impossible, you live, because it is impossible." Collections like *Niin vaihtuivat vuoden ajat* (1964; So Changed the Seasons) and *Paetkaa purret kevein purjein* (1971; Flee Boats with Light Sails) are noteworthy above all for their sensitive, reflective nature poetry. In *Kuolleet vedet* the thematic material has definitely deepened: it presents a view of the world in recent times as a living domain of blood and destruction. All the central imagery points the same way, to the rotting of the world, and the process is shown from the point of view of the individual, the family, and the land. The images—"sourceless light," life as a "dream," with "dead waters" around—are variations on the word of the Bible, including the beginning of St. John's Gospel, and contain points of contact with medieval mysticism: "And in the light shone darkness and / the light understood it not."

Manner's most successful play *Uuden vuoden yö* (1965; New Year's Night) describes in almost naturalistic style "cultured misery"; *Toukokuun lumi* (1967; Snow in May) stands alongside it. *Poltettu oranssi* (1968; Burnt Orange) exploits psychoanalysis and modern dramatic language: it is a picture of a family hell and the tragedy of a sick young woman.

In a different genre and under a different name, Anna September, Manner has published a cheerful detective novel *Oliko murhaaja enkeli?* (1963; Was the Murderer an Angel?). The same sort of change of tone is seen in poetry with *Kamala kissa* (1976; The Horrible Cat), a masterly book of rhymed sequences and satirical poems in the style of T.S. Eliot's cat poems.

Manner has translated into Finnish *inter alia* the prose of Willy K. Kyrklund, Yasunari Kawabata, and Herman Hesse, Shakespeare's plays, and Spanish poetry.

Works

Poetry: *Tämä matka* [This Journey] (1956). *Orfiset laulut* [Orphic Songs] (1960). *Niin vaihtuivat vuoden ajat* [So Changed the Seasons] (1964). *Kirjoitettu kivi* [Written Stone] (1966). *Fahrenheit 121* (1968). *Jos suru savuaisi* [If Sorrow Should Give Smoke] (1968).

Paetkaa purret kevein purjein [Flee Boats with Light Sails] (1971). *Kamala kissa* [The Horrible Cat] (1976). *Kuolleet vedet* [Dead Waters] (1977). *Runoja* [Poems] (1980). *1956–1977* (1980).

Plays: *Eros ja Psykhe* [Eros and Psyche, verse drama] (1959). *Uuden vuoden yö* [New Year's Night] (1965). *Toukokuun lumi* [Snow in May] (1967). *Poltettu oranssi* [Burnt Orange] (1968). *Varjoon jäänyt unien lähde* [The Source of Dreams Left in Shadow, radio play] (1969). *Vuorilla sataa aina* [In the Mountains It Always Rains, radio play] (1970).

Other: *Kävely musiikkia pienille virtahevoille and muita harjoituksia* [Walking Music for Small Hippopotami and Other Exercises, prose] (1957). [Anna September, pseud.], *Oliko murhaaja enkeli?* [Was the Murderer an Angel?] (1963). *Varokaa, voittajat* [Beware, Victors, novel] (1972).

Translations: Two poems from *Kamala kissa* [An Awful Cat], tr. Herbert Lomas. *Books from Finland* 1 (1977). Poems from *Kuolleet vedet* [Dead Waters], intro. Aarne Kinnunen, tr. Herbert Lomas. *Books from Finland* 4 (1978).

Päivi Karttunen

Olivia Manning
ca. 1911–1980

Born 1911 (?) or 1915 (?), Portsmouth, England
Died July 23, 1980, Isle of Wight
Genre(s): novel, short story, humor, history, travel, essay, review
Language(s): English

Though best known for her novels, particularly *The Balkan Trilogy* (1960–1965), Manning also wrote stories, humor, history, travel, and other works, as well as numerous essays and reviews for the (London) *Times* and such journals as *Horizon, Spectator, Punch,* and *New Statesman.* Little biographical information is available for her, and until her death even an approximate year of her birth was unknown. Her father was a commander in the Royal Navy and her husband a BBC drama producer. She served in the press office in the U.S. embassy, Cairo (1942), in the Public Information Office, Jerusalem (1943–1944), and in the British Council Office, Jerusalem (1944–1945). She was a painter; Walter Allen (*The Modern Novel in Britain and the United States*) noted her "painter's eye for the visible world" that "enabled her to render particularly well the sensual surface of landscape and places."

Manning's first novel, *The Wind Changes* (1938), dealt with the Irish uprising but differs from most other fictionalized accounts of the "troubles" in its focus on the conflicts within the central characters, a woman and two men, rather than on larger political and social issues. Her insightful handling of mental states was praised for its clarity and careful pacing, and her style, especially dialogue, was compared favorably to the work of Hemingway. The characters, however, were said to be indistinguishable in mood or act simply because of her emphasis on thought processes.

Manning's precise observation and description seemed to limit her efforts to present people and their actions adequately. Though her other early novels (*Artist Among the Missing*, 1949, *School for Love*, 1951, and *A Different Face*, 1953) were respectfully received, none made any appreciable impact. Yet all seem in retrospect to be leading, through her acknowledged gifts of humor, precision of language, sweeping sense of history, and keen appreciation of place, toward her *Balkan Trilogy*. *School for Love* is set in Jerusalem during World War II as experienced by a stranded sixteen-year-old boy. *A Different Face*, by contrast, is set on the English coast and concerns a man who discovers that his investment in a school has disappeared. In both cases, these early novels reflect Manning's skill at dramatizing essentially pessimistic, even hopeless, situations with a sharp eye for the telling detail, the vivid phrase, the ironic perspective, even though her dispassionate distance from her subjects sometimes displeased both readers and critics.

Each of these works was deservedly praised for its broad canvas, juxtaposition of individual fates against the backdrop of great European conflicts, and careful placement of characters in particular historical contexts; yet here, too, Manning's handling of her central characters came in for repeated criticism. Her acknowledged skill in penetrating the male psyche was often noted, but the individual, male or female, seemed wholly overwhelmed by the sheer magnitude of world events, so much so, in fact, that readers sometimes found the books more persuasive as historical documents than as fiction.

The Balkan Trilogy includes *The Great Fortune* (1960), *The Spoilt City* (1962), and *Friends and Heroes* (1965). *The Great Fortune* (the title presumably refers to life itself) presents a husband and wife (Guy and Harriet Pringle) in Bucharest who see how the older world is doomed but who, of course, are incapable of altering the inevitable. The cosmopolitan Guy (as seen through Harriet's eyes) is considered one of the most complex, appealing, full-bodied characters in all of modern literature; Anthony Burgess considered him a

"kind of civilization in himself." Bucharest is the "spoilt city" of the second novel; in this work, Guy tries to save the city during its occupation by the Germans, though he is scarcely able to save himself and can never wholly fathom the radical changes he is witnessing. The same emphasis on the uncertainty of events is found in *Friends and Heroes*, in which the Pringles, now in Athens, find themselves still surrounded by flux and discord; Manning seems to suggest that never again will Europe—or the world—be able to experience the previous world of stability and order.

Manning subsequently completed an additional three volumes about World War II. Also considered fine examples of the *roman fleuve* (series or sequence novel), the *Levant Trilogy* [made up of *The Danger Tree* (1977), *The Battle Lost and Won* (1978), and *The Sum of Things* (1980)] continues the story of the Pringles, now stranded in Egypt and soon to wander through Palestine and Syria. Manning's excellent sense of atmosphere continues to dominate her characters' perceptions, though critics noted her more conventional reliance on routine descriptions and incidents as they experience the sharp contrast between England and Egypt, the rich and the poor. The soberly realistic Middle East descriptions avoid the poetic or exotic temptations of, say, Lawrence Durrell's *Alexandria Quartet* as Manning dryly, wittily captures the world of military hospitals, markets, religious shrines, and cafes.

Manning's other novels include *The Rain Forest* (1974), set on an island in the Indian Ocean, again focusing on the gradual dissolution of a colonial way of life. She necessarily utilizes details of a steamy, oppressive climate as she contrasts incompetent British authority and the forbidden forest of the title. Her protagonists are a married couple who after struggling against both humans and nature are able to go on together, while others find the forest itself a primeval refuge.

Manning's talent was widely recognized, and her ambitious series novels are likely to endure as her most important works. Her concern was not with shifting political loyalties or historical topicality, despite the specific settings of her best novels, so much as with a quiet but vivid sense of the effects of setting on sensitive characters' awareness of the dissolution of empires.

Works

The Wind Changes (1938). *The Remarkable Expedition: The Story of Stanley's Rescue of Emin Pasha from Equatorial Africa* (1947; in the U.S. as *The Reluctant Rescue*). *Growing Up: A Collection of Short Stories* (1948). *Artist Among the Missing* (1949). *The Dreaming Shore* (1950). *School for Love* (1951). *A Different Face* (1953). *The Doves of Venus* (1955). *My Hus-*

band *Cartwright* (1956). *The Balkan Trilogy: The Great Fortune* (1960). *The Spoilt City* (1962). *Friends and Heroes* (1965). *A Romantic Hero and Other Stories* (1967). *Extraordinary Cats* (1967). *The Play Room* (1969; as screenplay, 1970; in the U.S. as *The Camperlea Girls*). (with others) *Penguin Modern Stories* 12 (1972). *The Rain Forest* (1974). *The Levant Trilogy: The Danger Tree* (1977); *The Battle Lost and Won* (1978); *The Sum of Things* (1980). *The Play Room* (1984). *The Weather in the Streets* (1986).

Paul Schlueter

Katherine Mansfield
1888-1923

Born October 14, 1888, Wellington, New Zealand
Died January 9, 1923, Paris
Genre(s): short story
Language(s): English

A master of the short story, Mansfield was born in New Zealand, the fourth child of wealthy parents. She received her education in London at Queen's College, where she first encountered the writings of the symbolists (an important influence on her own work) and began her writing career on the school magazine. After graduation, she returned to New Zealand with her parents, determined to become a writer and return to Europe. In 1908 she persuaded her father to let her return with a modest allowance. She never saw New Zealand again.

Some of Mansfield's first stories appeared from 1910–1912 in the Fabian-Socialist magazine *The New Age*. There she published sharp, satirical sketches, literary parodies, feminist polemics, and the "Bavarian Sketches," later collected under separate cover as *In A German Pension*. She met J.M. Murry, whom she later married, in 1911 and with him established a new periodical called *Rhythm*. It was while writing for *Rhythm* that she met such figures as D.H. Lawrence and Leonard and Virginia Woolf. The news of her brother's death in 1915, which drove her into deep despair, sparked her interest in her native New Zealand. In a burst of creativity she produced "Prelude," published in 1917 as one of the first publications of Virginia and Leonard Woolf's Hogarth Press. Other stories such as "The Man without a Temperament" and "Je ne parle pas français," written at this time, helped to enhance her growing reputation as a short story writer.

Mansfield's move away from what Woolf called the literary "underground" to the canon of accepted modern writers was accompanied by the discovery of her tuberculosis. Realizing that the diagnosis was her death sentence, she spent much of her remaining time writing. In 1920 she published *Bliss, and Other Stories,* and in 1922 *The Garden-Party and Other Stories.* From 1921–1922, as death neared, she worked with great power and intensity, completing enough short stories for two posthumous collections later published by her husband. She died in 1923 at the Gurdjieff Institute in Paris.

A many-faceted craftswoman, Mansfield wrote satirical pieces, feminist literature, and touching stories of her childhood in New Zealand, in which over half of her stories are set. Greatly influenced by the symbolist writers and often described as a writer of "lyrical" quality, she was interested not in social contexts and realities but in evoking an atmosphere or mood created through a network of concrete images and the power of the idealizing imagination. Like most Symbolists, she was also a tireless experimenter in literary form. Her stories are the quintessential modern format, with conscious epiphanies serving as focal points for the portrayal of internal crisis. Among her favorite devices are internal monologues, parallelisms, contrasts, flashbacks, and daydreams. In her later career she also experimented with the short-story cycle, in which separate stories are linked by character, setting, and repeating images and motifs.

Among Mansfield's favorite themes were the flowering of the self, sexual corruption, the terrors of childhood, the female artist, solitude, and death. From her symbolist roots, she also inherited a keen interest in expanding the poetic potentials of the prose genre, and many of the short stories are written in a lyrical prose, exploiting rhythm, image, and sound as aids to convey meaning.

Mansfield used her exquisite and delicate sensibility to create stories of solid and well-crafted structure, dealing with themes of weighty implications. Since her death, critical commentary has been unfortunately and intimately intertwined with comments on her personality. On one hand, Lawrence's picture in *Women in Love* and on the other her husband's portrait in the patiently edited and rearranged editions of her notebooks have muddied the critical waters. Today, however, critics are displaying new interest in her art and her contribution to the short story form.

Mansfield once said, "The false writer begins as an experimenter; the true artist ends as one." Her death at thirty-four cut short both her life and that experimentation, leading Elizabeth Bowen to call Mansfield "our missing contemporary."

Works

In a German Pension (1911). *Prelude* (1918). *Je ne parle pas français* (1918). *Bliss, and Other Stories* (1920). *The Garden-Party and Other Stories* (1922). *The Dove's Nest, and Other Stories* (1922). *Poems* (1923). *Something Childish, and Other Stories* (1924). *The Aloe* (1930; rev. 1984). *Novels and Novelists* (1930). *Juliet* (1970). *The Letters and Journals of Katherine Mansfield, A Selection* (1977). *The Complete Stories of Katherine Mansfield* (1978). *The Urewera Notebook* (1978). *Collected Letters,* vol. 1 (1984). *Critical Writings,* ed. C. Hanson (1987). *Collected Letters,* vol. 2 (1987).

Glenda McLeod

Gianna Manzini
1896–1974

Born 1896, Pistoia, Italy
Died 1974, Rome
Genre(s): novel, short story, memoirs, journalism
Language(s): Italian

Manzini graduated from the University of Florence with a degree in modern literature and soon began an active collaboration with the prestigious *Solaria* and *Letteratura*. These two Florentine journals were attentive to the new European fiction and to formal values; not surprisingly, Manzini showed an early preference for the stream-of-consciousness technique and a continued attention to style. In 1945–46, she directed *Prosa*, a review of international contemporary fiction. Throughout her long, productive career as a writer, Manzini enjoyed continuous critical acclaim.

Her first work, *Tempo innamorato* (1928; Time of Love), revealed a novelist with a strong lyrical vein, a figurative style, and a keen perception of unusual sensations and emotions. The story line is fractured by a free association of reminiscences and by the search of spiritual affinities among characters, of correspondences between people and the landscapes in which they live. These qualities explain her preference for the shorter narrative form. In the best stories of *Incontro col falco* (1929; Encounter with the Falcon), *Boscovivo* (1932), *Un filo di brezza* (1936; A Slight Breeze), *Rive remote* (1940; Distant Shores), *Venti racconti* (1941; Twenty Stories), *Forte come un leone* (1944; Strong as a Lion), we find autobiographical recollections of rare inner experiences, where a precious, metaphorical style turns the narrative line into a proliferation of dream-like, almost surrealistic images.

Manzini's capacity to harmonize symbolic effects and psychological states is well exemplified by *Il valzer del diavolo* (1953; The Devil's Waltz), in which the recurring presence of a cockroach becomes linked to the protagonist's new awareness of her morbid and overpowering dedication to others. In the novel, *La sparviera* (1956; The Sparrow-Hawk), a recurring cough that afflicts the main character over a period of many years, soon develops into a nightmarish awareness of something alive, hidden, and destructive. The man's bouts with the illness are intertwined with the occasional appearances in his life of a woman who exercises on him a strangely exhilarating effect. Finally he succumbs to his illness, willingly facing a death that takes on the mysterious face of his enchantress. Thanks to Manzini's controlled technique and her vivid description of threshold perceptions, the character's pathological state becomes emblematic of human existence, whereby a hazardous condition is transformed into an irresistible presence.

What makes Manzini's work unique is her capacity to sustain a prose style of continuous analogical transformations as well as to analyze feelings and moral states that imperceptibly turn into something unexpected. In *È un'altra cosa* (1961; Another Thing) the object of analysis is a writer's dilemma of compromising with his conscience and creativity or remaining faithful to himself and thus antagonizing his wife, who wishes him to adapt to the values of society and the tastes of the general public. Moral and psychological revelations are more explicitly handled in the autobiographical novel *Ritratto in piedi* (1971; Standing Portrait). This is the author's confession of her slowly coming to terms with her hidden affection for her father, whose character and principles are brought to life by her reminiscences. An anarchist who disapproved of private property and the exploitation of other human beings, Signor Manzini rejected all compromises with the bourgeois way of life and lived a lonely existence as a watch repairman. Later he faced Fascist persecution and death by the hand of a gang of Fascist youths. Manzini recollects her visits to the mountain village where her father was exiled, his participation in the Spanish civil war, his coming together with other anarchists in preparation of an international congress and, finally, her own college days, where new experiences blurred all concerns for her persecuted father. In all, a moving confession of filial appreciation for a downtrodden, peaceful man who had, in fact, renounced affections and comforts out of his own sense of love and social justice.

Although many Italian critics have praised her artistic achievements, Manzini has failed to capture the interest of the large public, and foreign publishers have generally ignored her. She stands out, however, as an innovative stylist and a masterful practitioner of psychological analysis.

Works

Tempo innamorato (1928). *Incontro col falco* (1929). *Boscovivo* (1932). *Un filo di brezza* (1936). *Rive remote* (1940). *Venti racconti* (1941). *Forte come un leone* (1944). *Carta d'identità* (1945). *Lettera all'editore* (1946). *Forte come un leone e altri racconti* (1947). *Ho visto il tuo cuore* (1950). *Cara prigione* (1951). *Animali sacri e profani* (1953). *Il valzer del diavolo* (1953). *Foglietti* (1954). *La sparviera* (1956). *Arca di Noè* (1960). *È un'altra cosa* (1961). *Il cielo addosso* (1963). *Album di ricordi* (1964). *Allegro con disperazione* (1965). *Ritratto in piedi* (1971). *Sulla soglia* (1974).

Rinaldina Russell

Margaret of Austria

Margaret of Austria
1480–1530

Born January 10, 1480, Brussels, Belgium
Died December 1, 1530, Malines
Genre(s): letters, poetry
Language(s): French

Although this daughter of an Austrian prince, Maximilian, and a Burgundian duchess, Mary, seemed destined for a brilliant future, the misfortunes of her early life would have ruined a less sturdy character. These led her to adopt the motto *Fortune Infortune Fort Une*, which may be understood to mean that the variations of Fortune can torment sorely.

Married at the age of two to the French dauphin, the future Charles VIII, she was rejected when a marriage with Anne of Brittany seemed to have more to offer France. This rejection inspired in her a life-long hatred of France. A subsequent marriage to the heir to the Spanish throne, Juan of Castille, was cut short by the prince's premature death, but in Spain she learned her first lessons in diplomacy. A third marriage, to Philibert of Savoy, was arranged for her in 1501, but this, too, was ended by the prince's unexpected death three years later. Thereafter she refused all further suggestions of marriage and turned her attention to other ways of serving her family and their

interests. In addition, she became a patroness of the arts, a musician and builder, as well as the guardian and educator of several royal children, her nieces and nephew, whose destinies were important.

The center of these activities was the court she established in Malines, midway between Brussels and Antwerp. There she assembled an art collection and a library and surrounded herself with artists and men of letters. With her courtiers she made music and wrote poetry as a respite from the political administration that dominated her life. Her public life is recorded in the letters which she exchanged, first of all with her father, by now the Holy Roman Emperor, and later with her ambassadors, her political rivals and, eventually, with her nephew Charles, King of Spain and, in his turn, Holy Roman Emperor. Many of these letters have been published, though others remain in manuscript. Their number is impressive and their contents reveal their writer's vitality, industry, adaptability, and practicality. From 1507 until her death, she governed what is now Belgium, northern France, and Holland.

Margaret's albums of poetry and many of her books still exist, along with inventories of her art collection. Two of the albums include musical scores and painted decorations as well as poetry. She was the patroness of such painters as Baren Van Orly, Jacopo de Barberi and Jean Gossaert; she admired Erasmus, lending him one of her most precious manuscripts for his translation of the New Testament. In view of such tastes, it is curious that she preferred medieval poetic forms and the sort of poetic contests that were popular in a much earlier day.

Margaret's greatest diplomatic triumph was undoubtedly the Treaty of Cambrai in 1529, also known as the Ladies' Peace, which she negotiated for Charles V with her former sister-in-law, Louise of Savoy, who was representing her son, the French King Francis I. The animosity between the two rulers had been great, sharpened by competition for the imperial crown and, even more, because of Francis I's capture by the imperial troops in Pavia in 1525 and subsequent imprisonment by the Emperor Charles in Madrid. Although released by the Treaty of Madrid in January 1526, the French King violated his part of the agreement, so it was expedient for the two ladies to try to arrange something better. Through Margaret's skill and intelligence, the new treaty, signed on August 3, 1529, was almost entirely favorable to her nephew, Charles.

The years of struggle to support his ambition had, however, taken their toll on Margaret. Although only fifty, her health declined so greatly that she died on the first day of December 1530. Her final letter to her nephew, dictated the day before, is a model of devotion and sorrowful leavetaking.

It was two more years before the memorial church she had been building for her husband at Brou was finished and she could finally be taken there to join him. In that lovely church, she lies in a tomb on two levels where she is represented in her worldly robes of state, and beneath this there is a simply clad recumbent figure prepared to meet her Maker.

Works

Correspondance de Marguerite d'Autriche et de ses ambassadeurs à la cour de France concernant l'exécution du Traité de Cambrai [The Correspondence of Margaret of Austria and Her Ambassadors to the Court of France Concerning the Execution of the Treaty of Cambrai] (1935). *Albums Poétiques de Marguerite d'Autriche* [The Poetical Albums of Margaret of Austria] (1934). *Correspondance de L'Empereur Maximilian Iᵉʳ et de Marguerite d'Autriche sa fille, gouvernante des Pays Bas* [The Correspondence of the Emperor Maximilian I and Margaret of Austria, His Daughter, the Governor of the Low Countries] (1840). *Gedichte Margarethes von Ossterreich* [Poems of Margaret of Austria] (1954). *Correspondance de Marguerite d'Autriche, gouvernante des Pays-Bas, avec ses amis sur les affaires des Pays-Bas de 1405 à 1528* [The Correspondence of Margaret of Austria, Governor of the Low Countries, with Her Friends on the Affairs of the Low Countries from 1405 to 1528] (1842–1847).

Charity C. Willard

Marguerite de Navarre
1492–1549

a.k.a. Marguerite d'Angoulême, Queen of Navarre
Born April 11, 1492, Angoulême, France
Died December 21, 1549, Château d'Odos (Tarbes)
Genre(s): poetry, novella, letters
Language(s): French

Marguerite de Navarre

Marguerite was the daughter of Louise de Savoie and Charles d'Angoulême; she married Charles d'Alençon in 1509 and Henri d'Albret, king of Navarre in 1527. Imbued with the ideals of the Italian Renaissance, Louise de Savoie provided Marguerite with an excellent education, even allowing her to share some lessons with her brother Francis. Scholars disagree on the depth of her learning, but it is clear that she had some knowledge of Latin and Italian and had at least begun to study Hebrew. She was interested in philosophical and religious questions and dazzled contemporaries with her ability to discuss subjects, ranging from Neoplatonism to contemporary Church reform. When Francis became king in 1515, Marguerite, who was more attractive and more animated than Queen Claude and who enjoyed her brother's confidence, helped set the intellectual tone of the French court. She protected gifted poets like Clément Marot and encouraged the translation of classic texts. François Rabelais, addressing her as "esprit ravy et ecstatique" dedicated to her the third volume of his adventures of Pantagruel. Although she never opposed royal policy and remained outwardly obedient to Rome, Marguerite supported reform of the Gallican Church, and Lefèvre d'Etaples, who translated the Bible into French, was one of her protégés.

When Francis I was held captive after the Battle of Pavia by Emperor Charles V, Marguerite went to visit her brother in prison and help negotiate his release. Upon Francis's safe return, she married Henri d'Albret, Charles d'Alençon having died after his return from the Battle of Pavia. The second marriage was to disturb the harmonious relationship between Marguerite and her brother. Fearing that Henri would arrange a political marriage with a Spanish prince, he took Marguerite's daughter Jeanne d'Albret out of her parents' custody and forced her into a marriage (later annulled) with the duke of Cleves. Marguerite was also distressed by the intermittent religious persecution that became a feature of her brother's reign. She remained devoted to Francis, but her influence at court gradually declined. After Francis's death in 1547 Marguerite withdrew to Navarre and devoted her final years to religious meditation and to writing.

Marguerite was a prolific poet. Her early works—allegories and meditations in *terza rima,* spiritual rondeaux, verse epistles to members of the royal family—remained in manuscript until they were rediscovered by scholars in the nineteenth and twentieth centuries. She began her public career in 1531 with the publication of *Le Miroir de l'âme pécheresse,* a controversial work that showed her adherence to the principles of *sola fides* and *sola scriptura.* The second edition of this work (1533) included the *Dialogue en forme de vision nocturne* in which Marguerite conversed with her late niece on a variety of topics including grace and free will. This edition of the *Miroir* was condemned as unorthodox by the Sorbonne, but the condemnation was retracted at the insistence of Francis I. In spite of the retraction, Marguerite was regarded by many as a Lutheran sympathizer. Perhaps because of the controversy the Queen of Navarre waited until 1547 to publish a collection of her works, *Les Marguerites de la Mar-*

guerite des Princesses. Many of the poems composed during the 1540s were omitted from the anthology, among them, *Les Prisons,* which is generally regarded as her most significant poem and *La Navire,* her final tribute to Francis. Marguerite was also interested in drama and wrote plays dealing with the birth of Christ, the visit of the three wisemen, the flight into Egypt, and the massacre of the Holy Innocents. In addition, she authored a series of symbolical "comédies profanes." The theatrical works, which may have been presented by ladies of the court, complement the poetry in conveying the principles of Marguerite's evangelical Christianity.

Critical response to Marguerite's poetry and drama has not always been enthusiastic. Her intellectual range, metrical versatility and importance as a religious poet have not been challenged, but she has been accused of lacking technical facility. While she admired Petrarch and Dante and was one of the first writers to use *terza rima,* she did not anticipate the Pléiade poets in cultivating classical genres and imitating classical authors.

Until recently, Marguerite's poetry has been overshadowed by her prose work, a collection of novellas inspired by the *Decameron.* Composed during the 1540s and incomplete at her death, the collection was first published in 1558 with the title *Histoires des amans fortunez.* A corrected and reorganized edition prepared by Claude Gruget and acknowledging Marguerite as author appears in 1559 as the *Heptaméron des nouvelles de tres illustre et tres excellente Princesse Marguerite de Valois.* Imitating Boccaccio, Marguerite presents ten French aristocrats who are isolated by spring floods in the Pyrenees and spend their time in conversation and story-telling. Deviating from her Italian model, she increases the number of women story tellers from three to five, gives much greater importance to the dialogue sequences that separate the various stories and cultivates a simpler narrative style. Because of its sympathetic yet subtle portrayal of women and severe criticism of masculine insensitivity, the *Heptaméron* can be regarded as a defense of feminine dignity. It is not, however, a feminist treatise. Marguerite's sophisticated manipulation of dialogue encourages multiple readings of the text. The *Heptaméron* reveals her interest in a variety of subjects from the *querelle des femmes* to courtly etiquette, from Neoplatonism to Scriptural exegesis and the validity of monastic life.

Works

Lettres de Marguerite de Navarre, ed. F. Génin (1841). *Nouvelles lettres de la reine de Navarre addresseés au* roi François Ier, ed. F. Génin (1842). *Les Marguerites de la Marguerite des Princesses*, ed. F. Frank, 4 vols. (1873). *Dernières poésies*, ed. A. Lefranc (1896). *Le Pater Noster*, ed. E. Parturier (1904). "Jugendgedichte Margaretes," ed. P.A. Becker, in *Archiv für das Studium der neuren Sprachen und Literaturen* (1913). *Dialogue en forme de vision nocturne*, ed. P. Jourda (1926). *Poésies inédites*, ed. P. Jourda (1930). *Théâtre profane*, ed. V.L. Saulnier (1946). *La Navire*, ed. R. Marichal (1956). *Petit oeuvre dévot et contemplatif*, ed. H. Sckommodau (1960). *L'Heptaméron (Nouvelles)*, ed. Y. Le Hir (1967). *Chansons spirituelles*, ed. G. Dottin (1971). *La Coche*, ed. R. Marichal (1971). *Le Miroir de l'âme pécheresse*, ed. J. Allaire (1972). *Les Prisons*, ed. S. Glasson (1978).

Translations: *The Heptameron*, tr. P.A. Chilton (1984). *Le Miroir de l'âme pécheresse, édition critique et commentaire suivis de la traduction faite par la princesse Elisabeth, future reine d'Angleterre*, in *The Glasse of the synneful soul*, ed. Renja Salminen (1979).

Paula Sommers

Marguerite de Valois
1553–1615

Born May 14, 1553, Saint-Germain-en-Laye, France
Died March 27, 1615, Paris
Genre(s): memoir, letters, poetry
Language(s): French

Born at Saint-Germain-en-Laye on May 14, 1553, Marguerite was the daughter of Henry II (1519–1559) and Catherine de Médicis (1519–1589). The niece of Marguerite of Savoy and the great niece of Marguerite of Angoulême, she was famous not only for her beauty but for her erudition and devotion to letters.

She was married by her brother Charles IX to Henry of Navarre, the future Henry IV (1553–1610), on August 18, 1572. The wedding occasioned the presence of many influential Protestants in Paris and was followed by a surprise attack on the Huguenots on the eve and feast day of St. Bartholomew. The Bartholomew Massacre, as it came to be known, was ordered by her brother Charles at the urging of their mother, Catherine de Médicis. The event made a strong impression on Marguerite, who later wrote an eyewitness account of it in her memoirs.

Cultivated, beautiful, and charismatic, Marguerite had had an extended liaison with the Duke of Guise before her marriage at the age of nineteen to Henry. Her sexual liberality became well known among members of the Court, as did Henry's. The couple separated not long after the marriage began, sharing little more than a penchant for self-indulgence. During their long separation Marguerite sided with her brother the Duke of Alençon in a political matter against her husband, for which she was driven from the Court and even arrested in 1583. She withdrew to Nérac before establishing residence in the chateau of Usson in Auvergne from 1587 through 1605.

There were no children from the marriage, and after Henry's accession to the throne of France the Pope dissolved the marriage. Marguerite consented to the annulment but only in December of 1599, after the death of Gabrielle d'Estrées (1573–1599), Henry's mistress for eight years and the mother of the Dukes of Vendôme. Following the annulment Henry immediately married Marie de Médicis in 1600, an arrangement that seemed not to trouble Marguerite, who retained the title of Queen. She remained friends with Henry, who consulted her regularly on matters of state. She treated Marie as an equal.

She maintained a mansion in Paris, the cost of which was an annoyance to Henry, where she held a small court of poets and scholars. Like her aunt Marguerite of Savoy, she was the patron of Pierre de Ronsard (1524–1585). François Maynard (1582–1646), poet and member of the Académie Française, was her secretary and helped her in the writing of her own poetry. Her memoirs are addressed to Pierre de Bourdeilles Brantôme, the popular court figure who was smitten with her and who featured her in his *Vies des dames illustres*, a widely circulated series of anecdotes dealing with court intrigue. Her letters reveal the same clear, exact style of her poetry and are among the best letters of the sixteenth century.

Marguerite, affectionately called La Reine Margot, died in her mansion at Paris on March 27, 1615. All her life she exhibited an almost equal attraction to piety and license, to rigor and decadence. Independent-minded from her youth, she was unaffected by popular opinion of her conduct.

Works

Les mémoires de la roine Margverite (1628). *Mémoires de la reyne Margerite*. Ed. nouv., plus correct (1665). Lauzun, Philippe, ed., *Lettres inedites de Marguerite de Valois 1579–1606* (1866).

Translations: tr. by Robert Codrington. *Memorialls of Margaret of Valoys* (London, 1649).

Cory L. Wade

Marie de France
ca. 1140–?

Supposed period of literary activity: ca. 1160–1215
Genre(s): the Breton lay (the narrative lay), fable,
saint's life
Language(s): Old French (Anglo-Norman dialect)

Marie de France has long been recognized as the first
woman writer in the French language. The details of
her life are few and not clear: she is thought to have
been born in France, yet lived in England, supposedly at the time of Henry II Plantagenet and of Aliénor
d'Aquitaine, perhaps even at their court. From her
works one learns that she knew English and Latin and
that she knew something of the geography of both
England and Normandy. She also shows her concern
to be known as a writer by those who follow her; indeed, she even mentions long evening hours spent in
poetic composition.

For about two hundred years scholars have maintained that Marie de France (so named since the first
publication of her *Fables* in 1581 by Claude Fauchet,
in Paris) is the author of at least three works, each
written in octosyllabic rimed couplets. In the order
of composition indicated by Marie herself, these
works are a group of twelve narrative poems that
editors have called *Lais*, preceded by a general Prologue; a collection of one hundred and two fables,
or an *Isopet*, translated from the English, whose author Marie mistakenly identifies as King Alfred; finally, an *Espurgatoire de Seint Patriz*, based upon a
Latin text by the monk Henry of Saltrey. Such an
ordering points to a transition from the secular to
the religious, or as one recent editor has noted, there
is "a progression from entertainment through mor-
alization to edification."

Marie de France's literary activity is generally
thought to date from ca. 1160 to 1215. It is remarkable that each one of the works, created when most
literary productions remained anonymous, is signed
by a "Marie." In the beginning lines of the *lai* of
Guigemar, the first narrative in Harley ms. 978, the
author refers to herself as "Marie, / Ki en sun tens pas
ne s'oblie"; in the Epilogue to the *Fables* she speaks of
herself as "Marie ai nun, si sui de France"; and in the
Espurgatoire, she both names herself and declares her
literary purpose: "Jo, Marie, ai mis en memoire, / Le
livre de l'Espurgatoire: / En Romanz, qu'il seit
entendables / A laie gent e covenables."

The process of attribution of the three works
mentioned took place over the course of several hundred years. Today, in spite of several recent attempts
to discredit her authorship of all the *lais* in Harley
ms. 978 (the earliest ms. and the only one to contain all twelve narratives, plus the Prologue and the
Fables), the majority of researchers believe Marie de
France to be the sole author of the three works. Furthermore, in 1974, the scholar Emanuel Mickel, Jr.,
when referring to specific similarities between the
attributed works and *la Vie Seinte Audree*, strongly
suggested that Marie is also the translator of that
particular saint's life.

Attempts to identify Marie de France with a
known historical person have led to such suggestions as the figures of Marie de Champagne; Marie
de Compiègne; Marie, daughter of Count Galeran of
Meulan and his wife, Agnès; Mary, the Abbess of
Barking; Mary, the illegitimate daughter of Geoffrey
of Anjou, and sister of Henry II, who became the
Abbess of Shaftesbury; and Mary, Abbess of Reading. The most likely identification is that of the Abbess of Shaftesbury, given the knowledge of contemporary court and legal matters shown by the poet.
Marie de France's identification with the Abbess of
Reading is not to be discounted, however, for ms. H.
was probably executed at that Abbey. As for the poet's
birthplace, it is now accepted that the phrase "de
France" refers not to the royal family of France but
to her country of origin. The exact region of her birth
is unknown. Mickel, when summing up the locali-
ties possible, mentions the wide acceptance that
Marie was "probably a native of the Ile-de-France
area or of Norman territory in close proximity" (*Marie
de France*, 17).

That the *Lais*, thought to be dedicated to either
King Henry II or to his son Henry, the Young King,
were known to and loved by Marie's courtly contemporaries is undisputable. In his work, *La Vie Seint
Edmund le Rei*, Denis Piramus offers a detailed reference to a *Dame Marie* who composed *vers de lais*.
Further attestations to Marie's popularity and to the
popularity of the genre of the narrative *lai breton*
are the translations of the *Lais*, made during the
Middle Ages, into Old Norse, Middle English, and
Middle High German. There were, moreover, adaptations, "imitations and exploitations" as well as explicit references to Marie that were written in Old
French.

The reasons for the popularity of the *Lais* are self-
evident: the theme of these narrative poems is love,
shown in multiple varieties. The stories contain penetrating psychological insights, sharply delineated
character portraits, folkloric themes and motifs (e.g.,
the man with two wives), elements of the *matière de
Bretagne* (e.g., King Arthur, his queen and court;

Tristan and Iseut), fantasy, a discriminating use of place and description, adventure, and symbolism. A *lai* is often constructed around an image or a symbol which may, in the course of the narration, accrete unto itself more and more meanings. In addition, Marie uses certain narrative themes or motifs (e.g., the wife unhappily married to a jealous husband), either primary or secondary, within an individual plot. Within the group of twelve poems, the reader will discern repetition of the themes and motifs, sometimes multiple repetitions, yet each time with a significant variation. Marie's *Lais* appeal to those who appreciate the art of a highly self-conscious story-teller. Today, many translations in a number of modern languages are available, with new translations being published almost yearly.

Although a renewed scholarly attention to Marie de France's works, begun some twenty years ago, has focused principally upon the *Lais* (five extant manuscripts), the *Fables* (twenty-three extant manuscripts) are currently beginning to receive the attention they merit. It is hoped that the studies of the late Marjorie Malvern will, in published form, reach a wider audience. The *Espurgatoire de Seint Patriz* (one manuscript only) has received the least scrutiny, in spite of its relation of a descent into Hell antedating that of Dante the poet.

Whether or not Marie de France is the creator of the novelistic genre, as is claimed by some critics, most assuredly she belongs to that group of twelfth-century tellers of tales (Thomas d'Angleterre and Chrétien de Troyes) who gave impetus to the appearance of the genre. That her influence is still felt in the twentieth century is clear from the words of John Fowles, perhaps the most significant creative writer in England today. In his collection of tales, *The Ebony Tower*, where one also finds repetitions and variations of themes, Fowles poignantly acknowledges his debt to Marie de France, saying:

One may smile condescendingly at the naïveties and primitive technique of stories such as Eliduc; but I do not think any writer of fiction can do so with decency—and for a very simple reason. He is watching his own birth.

Works

Listed in chronological order, according to Marie's own words: *Lais*; *Fables*, or *Isopet* (translation from English); *Espurgatoire de Seint Patriz* (translation from Latin text written in England).

J.R. Rothschild

Elena Maróthy-Šoltésová
1855–1939

Born January 6, 1855, Krupina, then in Austro-Hungary
Died February 11, 1939, Martin, both towns later in Czechoslovakia
Genre(s): short story, novel, autobiography
Language(s): Slovak

Elena Maróthy-Šoltésová's several short stories, one novel, and novelistic autobiography represent early realistic Slovak prose fiction conceived as part of the battle of the smaller Slavic nationalities against their political repression in the Austro-Hungarian Empire before it fell apart with its defeat in World War I.

Born in 1855 into the nationalistic family of a rural Protestant clergyman, Daniel Maróthy, who was also a minor Slovak poet, she was educated at a girls' school until age twelve. In 1875 she married an older merchant, Ľudovít Šoltés, apparently partly so that she could move to the small but nationally important town of Trenčiansky Svätý Martin. Her first story was published in 1881, and two years later she became vice-president, then president (1894–1927) of the only major women's organization, Zivena. Simultaneously (1885–1922) she edited several periodicals directed against the Germanizing and Magyarizing tendencies in the old Empire. The deaths of both her children occasioned an autobiographical work in 1923–1924, which was her only critical and international success, though her fiction was always popular with the Slovak women readers. At Šoltésová's death in 1939 she was eulogized as much for her organizational and editorial work in encouraging and supporting other writers, both men and women, as for her own prose fiction.

Šoltésová's six short stories or novellas began and ended as descriptive, simply plotted, idealized accounts of small town love affairs, misunderstandings, and deaths. However, her one novel, *Proti prúdu* (Against the Current) in 1894, pictures a Magyarized nobleman of Slovak ancestry significantly named Šavelský who like Šavel (Saul) converts into Paul and becomes a Slovak nationalist at the instigation and love of his nationalistic wife, named Laskárová (loving woman). Šavelský then works against the social current of the Magyarized or Germanized Slovak gentry. This schematic, overidealistic presentation was condemned as inartistic as well as sociologically improbable, but Šoltésová defended it by the didactic function of literature. Her autobiographical accounts of her two children's development, illnesses, and deaths, collected together as *Moje deti* (My Children) in 1923 to 1924, were detailed and tender without sentimentalism.

Šoltésová's significance is more historical than aesthetic, not only as one of the two earliest Slovak women novelists and as the leader of the women's literary movement by her editorial activity but also as the creator of a new type of heroine that sees herself as a conscious, independent part of the national struggle.

Works

Stories and novellas: *Na dedine* [In the Village] (1881). *Prípravy na svadbu* [Wedding Preparations] (1882). *V čiernickej Škole* [In the Ciernicka School] (1891). *Prvé previnenie* [First Transgression] (1896). *Popolka* [Cinderella] (1898). *Za letného večera* [One Summer Evening] (1902).

Novel: *Proti prúdu* [Against the Current] (1894).

Autobiographical works: *Umierajúce dieta* [The Dying Child] (1885). *Môj syn* [My Son] (1913). *Moje deti* [My Children] (1923–1924). *Sedemdesiat rokov 'ivota* [Seventy Years of Living] (1925).

Collected articles (edited by others): *Začatá cesta* [The Way Begun (for Women)] (1934). *Pohl'ady na literatúre* [Literary Views] (1958).

Collected works: *Zobrané spisy Eleny Maróthy-Šoltésovej* (1921–1925).

Translations: Czech: *Proti proudu* (1897). French: *Mes enfants du berceau à la tombe* (1928, 1934). Czech: *Moje deti* (1957). Magyar: *Gyermekeim* (1958, 1977). Croatian: *Moja djeca* (1925). Slovenian: *Moja otroka* (no date).

Norma L. Rudinsky

Florence Marryat
1837–1899

Born July 9, 1837, Brighton, England
Died October 27, 1899, St. John's Wood, London
Genre(s): novel
Language(s): English

Marryat, the sixth daughter of Captain Frederick Marryat, the celebrated writer of sea adventures, was a prolific popular novelist of Victorian England. Early in life she evinced an interest in writing and published her first novel, *Temper*, at age twenty-two. She scored a success five years later with *Love's Conflict*, written to distract herself while nursing her children who had come down with scarlet fever.

She married young, wedding Colonel T. Ross Church of the Madras Staff Corps when she was sixteen. Her extensive travels with him in India resulted in *"Gup": Sketches of Anglo-Indian Life and Character* (1868) ("Gup" is Hindustani for "gossip"). While emerging as a popular fiction writer of the 1870s, she also found time to publish her father's correspondence (the two-volume *Life and Letters of Captain Marryat*, 1872), to which she contributed a biographical portrait, and to edit the monthly periodical *London Society* (1872–1876).

In the 1880s and 1890s Marryat added drama and spiritualism to her growing interests, writing and starring in a comedy, *Her World* (1881), and producing among other such works *There Is No Death* (1891), a detailed account of seances and interviews with mediums. By 1890, when she married Colonel Francis Lean of the Royal Marine Light Infantry, there seemed no end to her accomplishments: she was an operatic singer, entertainer, public speaker, and manager of a school of journalism.

Marryat is remembered as a practitioner of the "sensation novel," a semi-Gothic literary form of the 1860s and 1870s featuring sinister family secrets and daring anti-heroines. Her novel *Love's Conflict* (1865) employs these elements in the story of Helen Du Broissart, a social climber and the daughter of an adulteress, who marries into the wealthy Treherne family only to be murdered by her former lover. Like her fellow sensationalists, Mary Elizabeth Braddon and Mrs. Henry Wood, Marryat both paid fascinated attention to the fallen woman and prudently punished her by the end of the story. She treated another favorite character, the cynical aristocrat who skirts immorality in *The Confessions of Gerald Estcourt* (1867), one of a string of popular works.

Many of Marryat's almost sixty novels were widely read in the United States and translated into a number of languages, including Swedish and Russian. Her fluid style (such sentences as "The affections will be their own judges" came effortlessly to her narrators), sharp eye for social pretension, and travel writer's observation of place earned her a certain success with a readership avid for details of aristocratic houses and the *mésalliances* that occurred in them.

Works

Temper (1859). *Love's Conflict* (1865). *Woman Against Woman* (1865). *Too Good for Him* (1865). *For Ever and Ever: A Drama of Life* (1866). *The Confessions of Gerald Estcourt* (1867). *"Gup": Sketches of Anglo-Indian Life and Character* (1868). *Nelly Brooke* (1868). *Veronique* (1869). *The Girls of*

Feversham (1869). *Petronel* (1870). *The Prey of the Gods* (1871). *Her Lord and Master* (1871). *Life and Letters of Captain Marryat* (1872). *Mad Dumaresq* (1873). *Sybil's Friend, and How She Found Him* (1874). *No Intentions* (1874). *Open! Sesame!* (1875). *Fighting the Air* (1875). *My Own Child* (1876). *Hidden Chains* (1876). *Her Father's Name* (1876). *A Harvest of Wild Oats* (1877). *Christmas Leaves* (1877). *Our Villas* (1877). *Written in Fire* (1878). *A Little Step-Son* (1878). *Her World Against a Life* (1879). *A Star and a Heart* (1879). *Out of His Reckoning* (1879). *The Poison of Asps* (1879). *A Scarlet Sin* (1880). *The Root of All Evil* (1880). *The Fair-Haired Alda* (1880). *Her World* (1881). *With Cupid's Eyes* (1881). *My Sister the Actress* (1881). *Phyllida, A Life Drama* (1882). *How They Loved Him* (1882). *Facing the Footlights* (with Sir C.L. Young) (1882). *A Moment of Madness, and Other Stories* (1883). *Peeress and Player* (1883). *The Heir Presumptive* (1886). *The Master Passion* (1886). *Tom Tiddler's Ground* (1886). *A Crown of Shame* (1888). *Mount Eden* (1889). *The Nobler Sex* (1890). *A Fatal Silence* (1891). *Gentleman and Courtier* (1891). *The Risen Dead* (1891). *There Is No Death* (1891). *How Like a Woman* (1892). *Parson Jones* (1893). *The Spirit World* (1894). *A Bankrupt Heart* (1894). *The Hampstead Mystery* (1894). *The Beautiful Soul* (1895). *The Heart of Jane Warner* (1895). *The Strange Transfiguration of Hannah Stubbs* (1896). *A Rational Marriage* (1899). *The Folly of Allison* (1899).

Laura Hapke

Anne Marsh-Caldwell
1791–1874

Born 1791, Linley Wood, Staffordshire, England
Died October 5, 1874, Linley Wood, Staffordshire
Genre(s): novel, short story, history, translation
Language(s): English

Anne Marsh-Caldwell, a mid-nineteenth-century domestic novelist, launched her literary career under the direction of Harriet Martineau. Daughter of a Staffordshire landholder and lawyer, wife of a failed banker, and mother of seven children, she had often written stories for her own amusement. When Martineau came to visit, Marsh-Caldwell read her "The Admiral's Daughter," a story of a young woman's adultery. After a fit of crying, Martineau expressed her amazement and admiration; after rereading the manuscript at home, she agreed to help find a publisher. The author's name was withheld from the public at the direction of her husband. "A father of many daughters," explained Martineau, "did not wish their mother to be known as the author of what the world might consider second-rate novels." Although "The Admiral's Daughter" was a sensational success, Marsh-Caldwell continued to publish anonymously. Some reviewers knew her name; others simply referred to her as "the authoress." Very little is known about the circumstances of her life. Although some attributions are still in doubt, she seems to have produced over twenty novels, two books of stories, a history of the Protestant Reformation in France, and some translations from French. When her brother died in 1858, she succeeded to her family's property at Linley Wood and resumed the surname of Caldwell. She died on the estate where she was born "lady of the manor, landholder, like her father," said the *Athenaeum* obituary.

Her best-known works were "The Admiral's Daughter" and *Emilia Wyndham*. As Margaret Oliphant observed, "Her first and most ambitious work is not addressed to her audience of young ladies." Its protagonist, a beautiful woman of Spanish descent, drifts into an illicit affair with her husband's friend. She is, therefore, a "worm," "an empty casket," a "worthless withered rose." Ridden with guilt, she can no longer feel comfortable in attending church or caring for their children. She must face a duel, her husband's fatal injury, and her lover's suicide. In contrition and love, she disguises herself as a nurse to attend her dying husband; dressed as a governess, she supervises her daughters' education. No book produced "more solemn silent showers than that heartrending story," said one paper. While Harriet Martineau believed that "the singular magnificence of that tale was not likely to be surpassed," most readers preferred the pure and patient heroines of her later novels.

In *Emilia Wyndham*, for example, "the charm of the story is the character of its heroine—her trials, her patience, her fidelity." Emilia dreams "of Una and her lion—or Clarinda and her lance," but she must follow her mother's instructions and achieve heroism in "the heavy, wearying every-day evils of every-day actual life . . . combining patience, perseverence, endurance, gentleness, and disinterestedness." "A highminded, devoted girl," she does not err; she rescues others. The novel was dedicated to William Wordsworth in recognition of "the fine influence of his poetry" and prefaced with an essay on domestic realism. The indisputable quality of the novel, she argued, is "that it should convey the sense of reality—that the people we read of should be to us as actual beings and persons—that we should believe in them." Without overstepping the bounds of easy probability, the novelist should bring "causes and their consequences into obvious connexion."

Like other domestic novelists, Marsh-Caldwell sometimes criticized the way men abused their power within the family. In *Emilia Wyndham*, she took issue with Douglas Jerrold's characterization of the nagging wife in *Mrs. Caudle's Curtain Lectures*, a series of satirical sketches in *Punch*. "Any vulgar penny-a-liner can draw Mrs. Caudle, and publish her in a popular journal; and with such success that she shall become a by-word in families, and serve as an additional reason for that rudeness and incivility, that negligent contempt, with which too many Englishmen still think it their prerogative, as men and true-born Britons, to treat their wives." Her heroine must confront a tyrannical father who torments his daughter and wife. At the end of the novel, she asks, "Is it not just possible, think you, that *some* of the discomforts of married life—a *very* small proportion, of course—might be ameliorated, if husbands now and then received a lesson in their turn, and learned to correct themselves as well as their wives?" *Punch* retaliated with a parody.

At a time when fiction was still regarded with considerable suspicion, Marsh-Caldwell seemed safe. She "writes as an English gentlewoman should write; and what is better still, she writes what English gentlewomen should read," said James Lorimer, having commended her for avoiding metaphysical precipices, moral volcanos, and "the odours of the workhouse." She was, according to Oliphant, "orthodox and proper beyond criticism." Indeed, one conservative journal saw her popularity as evidence of the nation's moral integrity. But if she helped make fiction respectable, she also made it dull: she and her heroines were "a *wee, wee* bit prosy." Moreover, she was not able to sustain her early achievements. Writing in 1855, Oliphant concluded, "She has taken to making books rather than to telling stories, and has perceptibly had the printing-press and certain editorial censors before her." A modern literary historian theorizes that Marsh-Caldwell's situation was typical of many other popular women writers of the time: working in isolation and drawing upon her own fantasies, she produced one book of considerable promise; entering the literary world and receiving suggestions from editors and readers, she lapsed into a formulaic fiction.

Works

The Old Men's Tales: "The Deformed" and "The Admiral's Daughter" (1834). *Tales of the Woods and Fields* (1836). *The Triumphs of Time* (1844). *Mount Sorel: Or, The Heiress of the de Meres* (1845). *Father Darcy* (1846). *Emilia Wyndham* (1846). *Norman's Bridge: Or, The Modern Midas* (1847). *The Protestant Reformation in France: Or, The History of the Hugonots* (1847). *Angela* (1848). *Mordaunt Hall: Or, A September Night* (1849). *Tales of the First French Revolution* (1849). *Lettice Arnold* (1850). *The Wilmingtons* (1850). *Ravenscliffe* (1851). *Time the Avenger* (1851). *Castle Avon* (1852). *The Longwoods of the Grange* (1853). *Aubrey* (1854). *The Heiress of Houghton: Or, The Mother's Secret* (1855). *Woman's Devotion* (1855). *Margaret and Her Bridesmaids* (1856). *The Rose of Ashurst* (1857). *Mr. and Mrs. Ashton* (1860). *The Ladies of Lovel-Leigh* (1862). *Chronicles of Dartmoor* (1866). *Lords and Ladies* (1866).

Robin Sheets

Harriet Martineau
1802–1876

Born June 12, 1802, Norwich, England
Died June 27, 1876, Birmingham
Genre(s): autobiography, essay, comparative sociology, journalism, novel
Language(s): English

The study of Martineau's life affords the student of nineteenth-century English and American society a view not only of an exceptional woman but of the transformations taking place during this era in politics, views of child-rearing and education, and the strain inherent in a woman's life if that woman happens to defy convention by following a calling beyond her designated sphere. Although her discerning eye and prolific ease with the written word earned her the respectful title of "the first sociologist," her accomplishments were at times threatened by debilitating disease, conflicting feelings regarding family responsibilities, and the volatile reaction of her readers on the many controversial issues she deigned to explore and popularize in her fifty-year literary career.

Martineau was described as a delicate and difficult child, the latter adjective a result perhaps of her mother's seeming indifference to her sixth child. Her childhood, however, was like that of many in the early 1800s when scrupulous attention was paid material and educational needs while emotional and nurturing components were virtually ignored. Early bouts with digestive and nervous disorders and the partial loss of hearing justify the term "delicate."

Rather than letting her past embitter or impede her personal development as an adult, Martineau used her own childhood experiences [described in detail in *Household Education* (1849) and *Autobiography with Memorials by Maria Weston Chapman* (1877)], as a catalyst for a lengthy and impassioned articulation of the deficiences of early nineteenth-century beliefs on children and childhood education; in so doing, Martineau became an early popularizer of the theories of John Locke and David Hartley. Other examples of her use of personal experience as a basis for broad social texts are *Life in the Sickroom* (1844), a description of invalidism, common of women in the nineteenth century, a book that also reads like a home-care nursing manual, and *Our Farm of Two Acres* (1865), which describes her brief venture into rural living.

Much of Martineau's writing appeared in journals and newspapers such as the *Edinburgh Review, Westminster Review, National Anti-Slavery Standard,* and, most especially, the *Monthly Repository*. In 1864 her essays published in the *Daily News* were compiled into a book, *Biographical Sketches,* many of which are formal obituaries of historical personages of her time. These miniature biographies eulogize such women as Amelia Opie, Charlotte Brontë, Mrs. Wordsworth, and Mrs. Marcet, and, as such, offer contemporary readers historical and biographical information regarding other women, known and unknown, of this era.

Her first pieces, "Female Writers on Practical Divinity" and "On Female Education," published in 1827 and 1823, reflect a constant theme of her work, that is, that any discrepancy in women and men's capabilities was due to a disparity in education, and although Martineau believes that educating women would certainly enhance women's status in their domestic sphere, she in no way believed that women should be relegated to that area.

Women were indeed an important subject in Martineau's most noted work, *Society in America* (1837). Her keen observations regarding the status of women in a nation professing freedom of opportunity for all was certainly one of the main factors in the mixed reaction of her readership in both countries. *Society in America* as well as *Retrospect of Western Travel* (1838), a more readable tract of her observations during her two-year visit to America, and *How to Observe: Morals and Manners* (1838) are considered some of the earliest instances of the science of comparative sociology, and as such won her the distinction of innovator in a field previously uncharted. Besides remaining one of the best sources of descriptive information regarding the early years of the American republic, *Society in America* is also an honest chronicle of one woman's discovery of the discrepancies between political theory and the actualities of people's lives within any social system.

Her reputation as a writer, which preceded her coming to America in 1834, was based principally on her *Illustrations of Political Economy*. In this series, written between 1832 and 1834, she defined and illustrated, in rather stilted story form, the unfolding principles of *laissez-faire* capitalism and the concepts of progress and opportunity based upon ability rather than ancestry. These popular works were originally written as separate booklets and were directed specifically at the working class in England, though they were read widely by all. Her idealistic enthusiasm regarding the mutually beneficial relationship possible between labor and capital interests was based in part on her belief that if all members of such a system understood the principles of political economy, corruption within the system was less apt to occur.

Martineau was first and foremost a natural journalist, never editing or changing her thoughts once they were committed to the page. This resulted in a prolific legacy (over fifty books and pamphlets) on a surprising range of subjects and in many styles; she is considered at her best with social descriptions and at her worst with fictional accounts. *The Hour and the Man* (1841), an example of her fiction, re-creates the life of a black Haitian revolutionary and that nation's struggle for freedom from white domination. Fiction also offered a "respite" from her usual journalistic style, said Martineau, in describing *Deerbrook* (1839), a three-volume love story.

People responded to the mature Martineau in extremes, from intense dislike, as was the case with George Eliot, to the devoted admiration of Maria Weston Chapman, her first biographer. Her passionate dual personality and frankness caused the loss of many friendships throughout the years, as did her association with such controversial issues as abolition, women's rights, and nontraditional forms of healing. Martineau remained, however, a teacher in the broadest sense of the word, an activist early called to share her observations and experiences with others through the written word. She never married but rather developed into a happily independent woman, consumed not by relationships but by her work.

Works

Devotional Exercises (1823). *Illustrations of Political Economy* (1832–1834). *Society in America* (1837). *How to Observe: Morals and Manners* (1838). *Retrospect of Western Travel* (1838). *Deerbrook* (1839). *The Hour and the Man* (1841). *Life in the Sickroom* (1844). *Household Education* (1849). *Biographical Sketches* (1864). *Our Farm of Two Acres* (1865). *Autobiography with Memorials by Maria Weston Chapman* (1877). *Harriet Martineau's Letters to Fanny Wedgewood,* ed. E. Arbuckle (1983). *Harriet Martineau on Women,* ed. G.G. Yates (1984).

V. Kim Duckett

Carmen Martín-Gaite
1925–

Born December 8, 1925, Salamanca, Spain
Genre(s): short story, novel, children's literature, essay
Language(s): Spanish

Carmen Martín-Gaite

Carmen Martín-Gaite was born in Salamanca. She received a degree in Romance Philology from the University of Salamanca and Madrid and her doctorate in history from the latter. When she moved from her native Salamanca to the capital, she associated with a group of young writers who would soon become fa-

mous as social realists, among them her future husband Rafael Sánchez Ferlosio.

Martín-Gaite's fiction reflects literary and social changes spanning a thirty-year period in Spain. The monotony of Franco's oppressive regime is depicted in her early work. A second and third novel bear witness to her progressively more subtle psychological studies as well as more imaginative and experimental fiction. She has not only employed a wide range of fictional styles, including the social novel, the fantastic, metafiction and children's fairy tales but has also written essays and historical works, and has participated in various television productions.

Martín-Gaite's fiction has received an enthusiastic response from the Spanish public and critics. She was awarded the Premio Gijón in 1955 for *El balneario*, the Premio Eugenio Nadal in 1957 for her first novel *Entre visillos*, and more recently, *El cuarto de atrás* received the coveted Premio Nacional de Literatura 1978. The latter work, translated into English, has attracted a great deal of attention from critics in the United States as evidenced by three booklength studies and frequent invitations from American universities.

Several thematic concerns appear throughout her work, unifying literary and historical interests: the restriction of women's (and men's) role in society and the contradictions that arise when women attempt to change their status; the general conformity and tedium of life under the Franco dictatorship; the difficulty of communication; and language and dialogue as an affirmation of life and love.

With the exception of the early novella *El balneario*, reminiscent of Kafka and a precursor of *El cuarto de atrás*, Martín-Gaite's first two novels and short stories have been considered social realist works. *El balneario* intermingles the protagonist's real life and her dream life, daily frustrations translating into nightmarish obsessions. The fragmentation of the two narrative levels and the surrealistic spatial configuration of this work sharply contrast with the author's straightforward first novel, *Entre visillos*. Although provincial life in all its dreary oppression is well drawn, the novel's conventionality and nearly documentary realism limit its appeal. The narrative centers upon the anguish of a few individuals struggling between rebellion and withdrawal within an overwhelmingly conformist society. As in her next novel, *Ritmo lento*, the rare characters who refuse to acquiesce to the social restrictions are condemned to loneliness.

Ritmo lento, along with Luis Martín-Santos's *Tiempo de silencio*, initiates a new social novel in Spain by eschewing the collective study of society for a focus upon a single extraordinary individual. The less "objective" and nonchronological style of *Ritmo lento* presages the author's next two novels. In *Retahílas* she finds her own voice, which can be noted in the experimental style, treatment of characters, and linguistic play. Here language becomes the very purpose of the narration, and the self defines itself and gains freedom through the word. The framing prelude and epilogue provide a literary pastiche of the nineteenth-century novel, counterpointed by the long central dialogue between two characters. The orality of this "dialogue" is undermined insofar as the simply communicative illusion of the novel is necessarily and self-consciously effaced by its written and literary quality, whereas the dialogues themselves are indeed more like monologues.

Martín-Gaite's most recent novel, *El cuarto de atrás*, continues in the self-reflexive and nostalgic vein of *Retahílas*, but its playfulness, humor and technical virtuosity make it the author's most intriguing and open work to date. The claustrophobic and apparently insoluble dilemmas of an era when women are either subservient to men or utterly alone are no longer the focus of her narratives. In this regard, it is not insignificant that Martín-Gaite began writing the novel the day Franco died. The Back Room is a world where the disparate coexists: the sublime and the corny; romantic excess and the strength to write and invent as a woman; male and female; the conscious and unconscious; history, realism, fantasy, and dreams combining into the fragmentary unity that is the unending process of living and writing. The novel is comprised of at least two stories: an encounter between the narrator and a man wearing a black hat, and the story of the novel's own generation: an emblematic pile of pages mysteriously accumulates parallel to the dialogue about writing which is the novel.

Many of Martín-Gaite's concerns in the novel are present in her nonfiction. Just as *El cuarto* exhibits an essay-like quality, so too her recent work, *El cuento de nunca acabar*, is an investigation of narrative in a style that combines both storytelling and the essay. In her historical studies of the eighteenth century, *El proceso de Macanaz* (1970) and *Usos amorosos del siglo dieciocho en España* (1972), as well as her essays in *La búsqueda del interlocutor y otras búsquedas* (1973), essential themes converge and are explored as historical investigation, philosophical musing, or linguistic play. These include the lack of communication and its opposite—the word as salvation from oblivion and from a hostile world. The issues of solitude, freedom, emotional ties, and identity are intimately connected to Martín-Gaite's formal experiments with dialogue and literature. According to her, literature is a place where the pleasure of life, love, and writing is grasped in its necessarily ephemeral and interconnected nature. Martín-Gaite's wide range of topics and modes aesthetically and intelligently manipulated in these works makes her one of the most important writers of contemporary Spain.

Works

Short Stories: *El balneario* (1955). *Las ataduras* (1960).

Novels: *Entre visillos* (1957). *Ritmo lento* (1963). *Retahílas* (1974). *Fragmentos de interior* (1976). *El cuarto de atrás* (1978).

Fairy tales: *El castillo de las tres murallas* (1981).

Essays: *La búsqueda del interlocutor y otras búsquedas* (1973).

Combination of essays and fiction: *El cuento de nunca acabar* (1983).

Historical works: *El proceso de Macanaz* (1970). *Usos amorosos del siglo dieciocho en España* (1972).

Poetry: *A rachas* (1976).

Translations into English: *The Spa. The Bonds. From Behind the Curtains. Conversational Stream. Interior Fragments. The Back Room. Never-Ending Tale.* Essays: *The Quest for an Interlocutor and Other Quests. The Trial of Macanaz. Romantic Customs of the Eighteenth Century in Spain. By Fits and Starts.*

Marie Murphy

María Martínez Sierra
1874–1974

a.k.a. María de la O Lejárraga, Gregorio Martínez Sierra
Born December 28, 1874, San Millán de la Cogolla, Spain
Died June 28, 1971, Buenos Aires, Argentina
Genre(s): drama, novel, essay, libretto, translation, autobiography
Language(s): Spanish

María Martínez Sierra, one of Spain's most popular playwrights in the early twentieth-century, did not sign her literary texts and essays with her name. Instead, she used her husband's name, Gregorio Martínez Sierra, until his death in 1947. This self-effacing gesture has set up a situation where most contemporary scholarship either erases her authorship altogether or grudgingly accepts it but only as joint authorship. Yet recent research, based on legal documents signed by Gregorio Martínez Sierra and testimonies of their contemporaries, confirms not only her contribution to their literary production but substantiates the hypothesis that María Martínez Sierra was, in many cases, the sole author of countless plays, poems, novels and essays on the "woman question."

Born in a small town in northern Spain, she moved to Madrid with her family when she was a small girl. She attended the Normal School of Madrid and became an elementary school language teacher. In 1899, she began her literary collaboration with Gregorio Martínez Sierra, seven years her junior, and married him one year later. Beyond writing, their projects were to include the creation of two literary journals: *Helios* (Sun) (a Modernist journal founded jointly with Juan Ramón Jiménez) and *Renacimiento* (Renaissance). Because their early years were economically difficult, María continued to teach and to do pedagogical research until their literary career could support them. In these years, she did a great deal of translating, wrote travel books, and collaborated with Manuel de Falla as librettist of his ballets *El sombrero de tres picos* (The Three-Cornered Hat) and *El amor brujo* (Love's Sorcery).

Until Gregorio's death in 1947, all of María's considerable work was credited to him, for such was their joint decision; it was not until after Gregorio's death that María published under her own name. *El poema del trabajo* (Labor's Poem), the first project on which the couple collaborated, are allegorical prose poems in praise of work and published in 1898, two years before their marriage. Other early works, written in the Modernistic style, included *Diálogos fantásticos* (Fantastic Dialogues), *Flores de escarcha* (Frost Flowers), and *Teatro de ensueño* (Dream Theater). These were followed by more realistic narrations, *Tú eres la paz* (You Are Peace) and *La humilde verdad* (The Humble Truth). The early works, pantheistic in tone, are set most often in rural Spain. They demonstrate strong admiration for the simple, natural life and tend to present moral lessons through parables.

In approximately 1910, María and Gregorio, realizing that their interest lay more in people than in nature, began writing for theater and eventually produced over fifty plays, most of which featured strong, practical, maternal women characters. Most of the plays, unlike the preceding narrative works, were set in Madrid. Among the best known are *Canción de*

cuna (1910; Cradle Song, 1923), *Primavera en otoño* (1911; Autumn Spring), *El reino de Dios* (1916; The Kingdom of God, 1929), *Sueño de una noche de agosto* (1918; The Romantic Young Lady, 1929), *Seamos felices* (1929; Let's Be Happy), *Triángulo* (1930; Take Two from One, 1931). The best-known play, *Canción de cuna* (Cradle Song), translated into many languages and performed all over the world, concerns a group of cloistered nuns who adopt an infant girl abandoned to them. In the first act, the women find fulfillment in maternity. The second act takes place eighteen years later and shows the wedding day of the young girl and the farewell to her mothers. Several films and television plays have also been made of this work in various countries.

In 1931, Gregorio went to Hollywood to supervise filming of some of his plays and to write movie scripts for MGM and Paramount Pictures. María remained in Spain and was elected Socialist *diputada* (representative) to the Cortes (Parliament) during the Republic. With the outbreak of the Spanish Civil war (1936), María and Gregorio separated definitively: he went to Argentina with actress Catalina Bárcena, the mother of his child. María remained in Nice (France) during and after the war. After Gregorio's death in 1946, María moved to Buenos Aires, where she remained until her death just six months short of her one hundredth birthday.

As was the case with other women writers of this period, María Martínez Sierra was interested in feminist issues and became a feminist activist in the international women's movements. In 1914, Chrystal Macmillan, the British delegate to the International Women's Suffrage Alliance (IWSA), went to Spain and named her the Spanish Secretary of this organization. Between 1916 and 1932 she also wrote five series of essays on the "woman question." Four of which were, again, published with her husband's name. In the aftermath of the debacle of the international women's movement during World War I, she continued her feminist activities. In the early 1930s, she founded the Asociación Femenina de Educación Cívica (The Women's Association for Civic Education). Yet, her concern for social issues was not restricted to the problems of women. She joined the Socialist Worker's Party of Spain (PSOE) and in the 1933 Parliamentary elections was elected to represent the city of Granada. When the Civil War broke out in 1936, the Republican government assigned her to the Spanish embassy in Switzerland as the commercial attaché. She left for Switzerland in 1936 and never again returned to Spain. Between 1938 and 1952 she lived in the south of France. In 1953, María settled in Buenos Aires where she lived until her death in 1974. In exile, she made her living by translating and writing short stories, principally for the Buenos Aires daily, *La Prensa*. She also wrote two autobiographies.

Whereas the Martínez Sierra plays were extremely popular in their time (several generations of North American high school and college students have learned Spanish reading *The Cradle Song*), they are no longer read or performed. This could possibly be attributed to their sentimental themes and style. According to Patricia W. O'Connor, the leading authority on the Martínez Sierras, the most successful aspect of their literary production was the creation of strong and independent women as the central figures for their plays and novels. In these texts the author/s advocated careers for women particularly in the areas of medicine, education, social services, and literature.

María Martínez Sierra's feminist essays contributed to the feminist polemic in Spain. She was interested not only in the role and education of women in society but was also preoccupied with the question of sexual difference. In her early essays she depicted sexual difference as stemming from a "natural essence" that made women peaceful in opposition to men who were "naturally" violent. In 1932, no longer content with this explanation, she proposed that sexual difference had been constructed socially and culturally by men through their representation of women in literature. She suggested that male writers had created an image of women and that women, in turn, had internalized and imitated this masculine construction. Her cultural analysis is possibly the first of its kind in Spain and shows both her lucidity and commitment to the "woman question."

Her autobiographies, *Una mujer por los caminos de España* (A Woman on the Roads of Spain) and *Gregorio y yo* (Gregorio and I), are splendid. In them she chronicles her life as a writer and as an activist. They capture the literary and political atmosphere of her time and reveal a unique and gifted mind.

Works

As Gregorio Martínez Sierra: *El poema del trabajo* (1989). *Diálogos fantásticos* (1899). *Flores de escarcha* (1900). *Almas ausentes* (1900). *Horas de sol* (1901). *Pascua florida* (1903). *Sol de tarde* (1904). *La humilde verdad* (1905). *La tristeza del Quixote* (1905). *Teatro de ensueño* (1905). *Motivos* (1905). *Tú eres la paz* (1906). *La feria de Neuilly* (1907). *Aldea ilusoria* (1907). *La casa de la primavera* (1907). *Aventura* (1907). *Aventura* and *Beata primavera* (1908). *El peregrino ilusionada* (1908). *Torre de marfil* (1908). *Juventud, divino tesoro* (1908). *Hechizo de amor* (1908). *La selva muda* (1909). *El agua dormida* (1909). *La sombra del padre* (1909). *El ama de casa* (1910). *El amor catedrático* (1910). *Todo es uno y lo mismo* (1910). *Primavera en otoño* (1911). *Canción de cuna* (1910). *El palacio triste* (1911). *La suerte de Isabelita* (1911). *Lirio entre espinas* (1911). *El pobrecito Juan* (1912). *Madam Pepita* (1912). *El enamorado* (1913). *Mamá* (1913). *Sólo para mujeres* (1913). *Madrigal* (1913). *Los pastores* (1913). *La vida inquieta* (1913). *La tirana* (1913). *Margot* (1913). *Las golondrinas* (1914). *La mujer del héroe* (1914). *La pasión* (1914). *El amor brujo* (1915). *Amanecer* (1915). *El reino de Dios* (1916). *El diable se rié* (1916). *Abril melancólico* (1916). *Cartas a mujeres de España* (1916). *Esperanza nuestra* (1917). *Navidad* (1916). *Feminismo, feminidad, españolismo* (1917). *La adúltera penitente* (1917). *Calendario espiritual* (1918). *Cristo niño* (1918). *Sueño de una noche de agosto* (1918). *Rosina es frágil* (1918). *Cada uno y su vida* (1919). *El corazón ciego* (1919). *Fuente serena* (1919). *La mujer moderna* (1920). *Vida y dulzura* (1920). *Granada* (1920). *Kodak Romántico* (1921). *El ideal* (1921). *Don Juan de España* (1921). *Torre de marfil* (1924). *Cada uno y su vida* (1924). *Mujer* (1925). *Rosas mustias* (1926). *Seamos felices* (1929). *Triángulo* (1930). *La hora del diablo* (1930). *Eva curiosa* (1930). *Nuevas cartas a las mujeres* (1932). *Cartas a las mujeres de América* (1941).

As María Martínez Sierra: *Cuentos breves* (1899). *La mujer española ante la república* (1931). *Una mujer por los caminos de España* (1952). *Gregorio y yo* (1953). *Viajes de una gota de agua* (1954). *Fiesta en el Olimpo* (1960).

Translations: *Ana María*, tr. Mrs. Emmon Crocker (1921). *The Cradle Song*, tr. John Garrett Underhill (1917), pp. 625–679. *The Cradle Song*, tr. John Garrett Underhill (1917). *The Cradle Song and Other Plays*, tr. John Garrett Underhill (c.1922). *Holy Night: A Miracle Play in Three Scenes*, tr. Philip Hereford (1928). *Idyll*, tr. Charlotte Marie Lorenz. *Poet Lore* 37 (1926). *The Kingdom of God: A Play in Three Acts*, tr. Helen and Harley Granville-Barker (1927). *Let Us Be Happy*, tr. T.S. Richter (n.d.). *A Lily among Thorns*, tr. Helen and Harley Granville-Barker. *Chief Contemporary Dramatists. Third Series*, ed. T.H. Dickinson (1930), pp. 457–471. *Love Magic*, tr. John Garrett Underhill. *Drama Chicago* 25 (1917): 40–61. *The Lover*, tr. John Garrett Underhill. *Stratford Journal* (1919): 33–44. *Plays of Gregorio Martínez Sierra*, tr. John Garrett Underhill. *Poor John*, tr. John Garrett Underhill. *Drama* 10 (1920): 172–180. *Reborn*, tr. Nena Belmonte (n.d.). *The Romantic Young Lady*, tr. Helen and Harley Granville-Barker (1923). *Take Two* from One, tr. Helen and Harley Granville-Barker (1925). *The Two Shepards*, tr. Helen and Harley Granville-Barker, in *Plays for the College Theatre*, ed. G.H. Leverton (1932). *The Two Shepards*, tr. Helen and Harley Granville-Barker (1935).

Alda Blanco
Patricia W. O'Connor

Chiara Matraini
1515–ca. 1604

Born June 4, 1515, Lucca, Italy
Died ca. 1604
Genre(s): poetry, letters, translation
Language(s): Italian

The Matraini family, at the time Chiara was born, belonged to the ruling class of Lucca. Their standing, however, was undermined when in 1531–1532 they played a leading role in the unsuccessful insurrection of the Straccioni. They were exiled for a brief period, and when they returned to Lucca they failed to regain their former social position. The family died out altogether in 1615, shortly after Chiara's death. Chiara, too, had an ambiguous relationship with the city of her birth. She is presented in both a negative and a positive light in local history, and she herself complains in letters and verse of unfair treatment by her husband's family, her own son, the city, and society in general, which had not permitted her the education she desired.

At the age of fifteen Chiara was married to Vincenzo Cantarini. By 1542 she had been widowed, and it seems, from documentary evidence corroborated by biographical references in her writing, that between 1547 and 1555 she was linked romantically with Bartolomeo Graziani, a married man, whose wife at least one contemporary historian depicted as the suffering victim of Chiara's villainy. Graziani was murdered in 1555, and history's recording of this event together with the love triangle, until the recent work of Giovanna Rabitti, has always had the characteristics of a sixteenth-century tragic tale. Chiara lived in Genoa in 1560–1562, during which time she was close to the circle of the Doge. She was back in Lucca by 1576, when she had her portrait made by the painter Alessandro Ardenti in the guise of the Cumaean Sibyl, part of the decoration of an altar she also commissioned for the church of Santa Maria Forisportam, where she was eventually buried. Because she was seen as a sibyl and seductress, Chiara

Matraini has been, by fanciful extension, called an enchantress and a witch; she is more often, however, deemed an important intellectual and poet, and the latter claim is borne out by her impressive verse and epistolary collections.

The biography of Chiara Matraini is inextricably linked to her most important writing. She was a Petrarchist, and her poetry collection, like those of her principal models, Petrarch, but also Vittoria Colonna and Pietro Bembo, tells an earthly love story that is at the same time the story of her poetry and her journey to God. The first edition of her *Rime*, published in 1555, follows the story of her affair with Graziani, and part one ends with references to his tragic death. The spiritual itinerary, not yet convincingly imposed on the love story in the first edition of the *Rime*, is carefully developed in the 1595 and especially in the 1597 edition after thorough revisions of many of the poems, the attenuation of biographical references not easily allegorized, a reorganization of the sequence, and the inclusion of new material. The final edition, which the author saw through publication, represents one of the highest achievements of sixteenth-century Petrarchism. While the language, imagery, and significant moments of the love story are dependent on the models, as is the division of the book into a part "in life" and another "in death" of the beloved, the particular configuration they take on in the final version of the *Rime* has an extraordinary coherence and originality of its own, rare in the annals of Petrarchist imitation. The cohesion of the book depends on the writer's technical expertise and especially on her masterful exploitation of the dominant images of the sun and moon, their respective realms of day and night, and of the many metaphorical possibilities of that semantic field. The lover is the moon to the beloved's sun, but only the hierarchy remains constant, and the relationship is explored through the use of classical mythology, the biblical tradition, and Petrarchan (and Petrarchist) conventions. Finally, the collection as a whole shows that the image of the sun, present from the first poems to the last in a myriad of forms, can and must be read spiritually and neoplatonically as the instrument of the lover's elevation and salvation, as Divine love, reflected in the world and leading beyond the world. Matraini's letters, many of which are published together with the final editions of the poetry, illuminate her life and her work; her writing during the years that intervened between the first and final editions of her poetry, largely religious in nature, contributed importantly to the final form her major collection assumed.

Virtually forgotten for centuries—there is not as yet a complete modern edition of her *Rime*, and her other writing has not been reprinted since the seventeenth century—Chiara Matraini's work has in recent times been enthusiastically reevaluated; critics compare her to Gaspara Stampa, and some name her among the most important writers of sixteenth-century Italy.

Works

Poetry and letters: *Rime e prose di Madonna Chiara Matraini Gentildonna Lucchese* (1555). *Rime di diversi signori napoletani e d'altri . . . Libro settimo*, Lodovico Dolce, ed. (1556), pp. 68–154. *Lettere della signora Chiara Matraini, Gentildonna Lucchese, con la prima e seconda parte delle sue Rime* (1595). *Lettere di Madonna Chiara Matraini Gentildonna Lucchese, con la prima e seconda parte della sue Rime [. . .]* (1597). *Inediti vaticani di Chiara Matraini*, in *Studi di filologia e critica offerti dagli allievi a Lanfranco Caretti*, I, Giovanna Rabitti, ed. (1985), pp. 225–250.

Modern anthology selections: Baldacci, Luigi, ed., *Lirici del Cinquecento* (1957), pp. 497–530. Costa-Zalessow, Natalia, ed., *Scrittrici italiane dal XIII al XX secolo. Testi e critica* (1982), pp. 93–98. Gamba, B., ed., *Lettere di donne italiane del secolo decimosesto* (1832), pp. 157–164. Ferroni, G., ed., *Poesia italiana. Il Cinquecento* (1978), pp. 244–248. Muscetta, C., and D. Ponchiroli, eds., *Poesia del Quattrocento e del Cinquecento (Parnaso italiano IV.)* (1959), pp. 1297–1300.

Other works: *Orazione d'Isocrate*, tr. from Latin (1556). *Meditazioni spirituali di Madonna Chiara Cantarini de' Matraini, Gentildonna Lucchese* (1581). *Breve discorso sopra la vita della Beata Vergine* (1590). *Considerazioni sopra i sette salmi penitenziali del Gran Profeta Davitati [. . .]* (1586). *Dialoghi spirituali di Madonna Chiara Matraini, Gentildonna Lucchese* (1602).

Elissa B. Weaver

Friederike Mayröcker
1924–

Born 1924, Vienna, Austria
Genre(s): poetry, poetic prose
Language(s): German

Friederike Mayröcker has published texts in avant-garde journals and presses since 1947, making a living teaching English language and literature at a Viennese secondary school between 1946 and 1969. Since the 1950s, she has been in contact with the writers of the Wiener Gruppe (Vienna Group), such as Artmann, Rühm, Jandl, and Bayer, whose aims she shared at the beginning and whose achievements she has by now outdone. With her companion Ernst Jandl, she has coauthored plays and prose texts. She has also provided whimsical drawings for some of her books.

Friederike Mayröcker is without doubt the most versatile and experimental of contemporary poets in the German language and also the most cosmopolitan. With her antisentimental but highly playful attitude toward language and the world—which in her compatriot Wittgenstein's seminal philosophy are all but a complex oneness—she seems as close to Brechtian estrangement and *maudit* or beat casualness as she is to the entire twentieth-century avantgarde tradition, regardless of national origin or language. While making ample use of the by-now-well-exploited iconic properties of concrete poetry, she rarely remains within their perimeter but instead combines them with other modernist techniques to achieve a powerful and supple language enriched with typographical devices. Thus she is capable of expressing simultaneously several countervailing voices in a single text without the whole appearing incoherent to the serious reader.

In 1966, her first major anthology, a retrospective, was published, through which she finally became known to a wider audience. Bold is the best description of her stance. She employs her vast and contemporary erudition not in a traditional way, like Kaschnitz, but ranges freely and purposefully in a kind of associative, illogical dream logic first analyzed by her compatriot Freud and pioneered in literature by the French surrealists. Sometimes her oneiric combinations are far-fetched and on the borderline of comprehensibility, a border that she has vowed to expand, but most of the time, her poetic exploits are nothing short of stunning. She by no means shuns reality and private life: her love poems to Jandl are among the most moving today. Moreover, there has been a perceptible development in her writing: while her early poetry shows an autobiographical strain and a separate line of the "experimental for the experimental's sake," as it were, her recent texts are a masterful, tight but nevertheless airy synthesis of both. Friederike Mayröcker's prizes are many, although she deserves still more. She has lectured widely abroad.

Works

Larifari (1956). *Metaphorisches* (1965). *Tod durch Musen* (1966). *Sägespäne fur mein Herzbluten* (1967).

Minimonsters Traumlexikon (1968). *Fantom Fan* (1971). [With Ernst Jandl], *Fünf Mann Menschen.* (1972). *Arie auf tönernen Fuszen. Je ein umwölkter gipfel* (1973). *In langsamen blitzen* (1974). *Meine träume im flugelkleid* (1974). *Das Licht in der Landschaft* (1975). *Fast ein Frühling des Markus M.* (1976). *Rot ist unten* (1977). *Heiligenanstalt* (1978). *Ausgewählte Gedichte 1944–1978* (1979). *Ein Lesebuch* (1979). *Die Abschiede* (1980).

Ute Marie Saine

Mechthild von Magdeburg
ca. 1210–ca. 1282–1294

Born ca. 1210
Died ca. 1282–1294
Genre(s): mystical revelation in prose and verse
Language(s): Low German, translated into Latin and Middle High German

Mechthild von Magdeburg was a Beguine (a member of a medieval lay religious order for women) at Magdeburg, whose loosely structured book of mystical revelations, *The Flowing Light of the Divinity,* serves as one of the rare extant examples of women's writing in medieval Germany. Originally written in Low German between 1250 and 1285, her revelations are retained in Latin and Middle High German translations and consist of seven parts, first gathered by her Magdeburg Dominican confessor, Heinrich von Halle (parts 1–6), and subsequently by the sisters at the convent of Helfte (part 7), which she entered ca. 1270. Her writings were translated first into Latin by Heinrich and then ca. 1344 into Middle High German by Heinrich von Nördlingen, a member of the Friends of God sect, and it is this manuscript (Einsiedeln Nr. 277) upon which the bulk of subsequent complete and fragmentary translations into German and English, as well as Middle High German text editions, have been based.

Not a conventionally learned woman, she apparently was literate and raised in a household that was reasonably prosperous. While her knowledge of Latin apparently did not extend beyond the liturgy, familiarity with theological issues and the courtly language of chivalry clearly are evident in her work. She often professed hesitancy and inadequacy at the God-given task of communicating her mystical experiences to others, but she was obviously a woman of strong opinions when convinced to write or to dictate her thoughts as evinced in her criticism of the clergy of her time—she found many religious people quite materialistic and misguided—and in her willingness to use the metaphoric language associated with sexual union that appears in the secular love poetry of the time as well as in the biblical prototype, *The Song of Songs.*

Mechthild's work is notable both for its variety and depth. Her revelations take the form of allegorical visions, aphorisms, prayers, poems strongly influenced by the *Minnesang* tradition, reflections on societal behavior, and numerous cryptic references to historical and biblical personages; it should be noted that Heinrich von Halle arranged these revelations somewhat arbitrarily into "chapters" that do not necessarily reflect Mechthild's spiritual development. Nevertheless, the compiler's and subsequent editors' and translators' transmission of Mechthild's revelations cannot obscure the wonderment she experiences when shown glimpses of Heaven and Hell, the puzzlement and querulousness she expresses when dealing with fellow religious women and men who do not live up to her standards, and the ecstasy she knows in mystical union with the Trinity—and the deprivation she encounters in periods of spiritual dryness and debilitating illness.

Mechthild's imagery is striking: supernatural fluidity, light, sublimated sexuality, and color mix and mingle with mundane touches, such as Christ calling for his dinner, mad dogs running in the streets, and her own loneliness in strange, new settings. The theme of the Godhead as *Trinity* occurs repeatedly in her revelations, as does the more courtly theme of love as pursuit: "And now she beholds a complete God in three persons, and professes the three persons within one God. He greets her with courtly language, not likely to be heard in the kitchen. He dresses her in clothes fit to be worn in a palace, and puts Himself at her disposal. . . . He wants to play a game with her alone, a game not known to the body, nor to the peasants behind their plows, nor the knights in their tournaments, nor even His sweet mother Mary."

Mechthild's subjects are wide-ranging. She describes, among other things, mystical union, the composition of the nine choirs of angels, the paths that lead to righteousness or damnation, and the ways holy people ought to live in the world. She powerfully sketches the landscapes of Heaven as well as Hell and draws visionary portraits of Enoch and Elias, Lucifer, the Virgin, John the Baptist, and Christ on the cross. Mechthild constantly attempts to make sense of the revelations given to her: her intent is to find verbal "likenesses" that express not only the relationship of the Divine to the human but also the Word to the world. Her words, she insists, cannot do adequate justice to what she has experienced ("One can hardly touch [it] with words"), but she must try to show, for example, how Christ is "like" a pilgrim, how man's sufferings are "like" Christ's, how the apostles are "like" bees, and how man is "like" an animal. She utilizes parables (parable equals "gelichnis" equals likeness) and dialogues to show the gap she attempts to bridge, a gap that on the earthly plane is characterized by the limits of language and the imperfect nature of man.

Mechthild's work remains as one of the few examples in the German Middle Ages of women's writings. Yet, if it were one of many examples, it would remain unique both for the breadth and depth of her visions and for their vibrant individual expression.

Works

Offenbarungen der Schwester Mechthild von Magdeburg, oder Das fliessende Licht der Gottheit, ed. P. Gall Morel (1869; rpt. 1963). New edition based on the same Einsiedeln manuscript (Nr. 277), ed. Hans Neumann, in progress. Galvani, Christiane Masch, *A Female Perspective on the Mystical Experience: Mechthild von Magdeburg's* Ein vliessendes Lieht der Gotheit *in a Complete English Translation, with Annotations and Introduction.* M.A. thesis, Rice University, 1987. Menzies, Lucy, *The Revelations of Mechthild von Magdeburg* (1953).

Susan L. Clark

Dorothea Mendelssohn-Veit-Schlegel
1763–1839

Born 1763, Berlin, Germany
Died August 1839, Frankfurt
Genre(s): novel, article, translation
Language(s): German

The daughter of Moses Mendelssohn and wife of Romantic writer and philosopher Friedrich Schlegel, Dorothea Schlegel wrote fiction, journal articles, and worked as a translator. She was at the center of the Jena Romantic movement.

The eldest daughter of the orthodox Jew and Enlightenment philosopher Moses Mendelssohn, Dorothea was educated by her father. After a long engagement she was married to Simon Veit in 1778, a banker chosen for her by her father. She bore four children, two of whom survived, Johannes and Philipp. Unhappy in her marriage, she met Friedrich Schlegel (born 1772), at the home of her friend Henriette Herz. In 1799 she separated from Veit and that autumn moved with her son Philipp to Jena to live with Friedrich and his brother August Wilhelm, and August Wilhelm's wife Caroline. The relationship between Dorothea and Caroline remained cordial for only six months. In 1800, to help support Friedrich financially, she wrote the novel, *Florentin*, which was thought to have been written by Friedrich. The novel has a male hero and reflects the influence of contemporary novels by Goethe and Tieck. Dorothea moved with Schlegel to Dresden in 1803 and then in 1804 to Paris. She was baptized a Protestant and married Friedrich on April 6, 1804. In 1805 they moved to Cologne, but in 1806 Veit got custody of the children in order to raise them as Jews. In 1808 Friedrich and Dorothea converted to Catholicism and were remarried in the faith. That year Friedrich procured an appointment as an Austrian court secretary and they settled in Vienna. Dorothea took a two-year trip to Rome in 1818 to visit her two sons, who had become ardent Catholics and painters of the Nazarene school. Simon Veit, who had continued to provide her with financial support even after the divorce, died in 1819. Friedrich Schlegel died suddenly of a stroke in 1823 and Dorothea moved to Frankfurt and lived with her son Philipp. Dorothea Schlegel died on August 3, 1839.

Dorothea belonged to the group of Jewish salonières from Berlin that included Henriette Herz and Rahel Varnhagen. She differed from these two in her literary productivity and her utter devotion to her husband. Because of Friedrich she worked hard as a writer and translator, never asking for personal recognition. In addition to her novel, *Florentin*, she contributed to Friedrich's journals. Her most important and lasting contributions are her translations, particularly of Madame de Staël's *Corinne*. She played a significant role in presenting contemporary French women writers to German readers through her translations and articles.

Although Dorothea is characterized as an independent woman in Friedrich Schlegel's novel, *Lucinde*, she was not pleased with the identification, and she should not be considered an early feminist solely on the basis of her romantic relationship. Intensely devoted to Friedrich and following him in his increasing conservatism, she contributed to the German Romantic movement only as long as financially necessary and always under her husband's name or anonymously.

Literary works and letters: *Florentin*, ed. Friedrich Schlegel (1801). *Briefe von Dorothea und Friedrich Schlegel an die Familie Paulus* (1913). *Briefe von Dorothea Schlegel an Friedrich Schleiermacher* (1918). *Der Briefwechsel Friedrich und Dorothea Schlegels 1818–1820 während Dorotheas Aufenthalt in Rom*, ed. H. Finke (1923). *Die Brüder Schlegel: Briefe aus frühen und späten Tagen der deutschen Romantik*, ed. J. Körner (1926). *Caroline und Dorothea Schlegel in Briefen*, ed. Ernst Wieneke (1914). *Dorothea von Schlegel, geb. Mendelssohn, und deren Söhne Johannes und Philipp Veit. Briefwechsel im Auftrage der Familie Veit*, ed. J.M. Raich (1881). *Florentin: Roman, Fragmente, Varianten*, ed. L. Weissberg (1986). "Dorothea Veit-Schlegel." *Frauenbriefe der Romantik*, ed. Katja Behrens (1981). "Die Mutter bei der Aussetzung Moses. Gemälde von P. Veit" (1835). *Poetisches Taschenbuch für das Jahr 1806* (1806). Two poems: "Der Stolze," "Mein Geliebter."

Contributions to journals edited by Friedrich Schlegel: In *Athenäum*: Reviews of Madame de Genlis' *Les voeux téméraires* and Ramdohr's *Moralische Erzählungen*. In *Europa*: Poems: "Zu einer Volksmelodie," "Bei der Erblickung der Handschrift eines verstorbenen Freundes" (to Novalis). Essay: "Gespräch über die neusten Romane der Französinnen," which includes critique of De Staël's *Delphine*. Also essays on Parisian life, "Pariser Neuigkeiten," including, "Ueber den Zustand der Musik in Paris," written with J. Fr. Reichardt. In *Deutsches Museum*: Review of performance of Handel's *Timotheus oder die Gewalt der Musik*.

Translations: *Corinna, oder Italien; aus dem Französischen der Madame de Staël übersetzt* (1807–1808). *Geschichte der Jungfrau von Orleans. Aus altfranzösischen Quellen, mit einem Anhange aus Hume's Geschichte von England*, ed. Friedrich Schlegel (1802). *Geschichte der Margaretha von Valois, Gemahlin Heinrich des Vierten von ihr selbst beschrieben. Nebst Zusätzen und Ergänzungen aus andern französischen Quellen*, ed. Friedrich Schlegel (1803). *Die Geschichte des Zauberers Merlin; aus dem Altfranzösischen. Sammlung romantischer Dichtungen des Mittelalters: aus gedruckten und handschriftlichen Quellen* (1804). *Lothar und Maller eine Rittergeschichte. Aus einer ungedruckten Handschrift*, ed. Friedrich Schlegel (1805). *Valerie.* By Juliane von Krüdener (1804). *Die verwegenen Gelübde, nach den Voeux téméraires der Gräfin Genlis.*

Marjanne E. Goozé

Sophie Mereau
1770–1806

Born March 28, 1770, Altenburg, Germany
Died October 31, 1806, Heidelberg
Genre(s): novel, short story, poetry, translation
Language(s): German

Sophie Mereau wrote novels, stories, and poems, translated, and published several journals. Often portrayed as a writer of German *Empfindsamkeit*, she had strong contact with Weimar Classicism and was a significant contributor to the Heidelberg Romantic movement.

Born in 1770 in Altenburg, Sophie Mereau received a traditional female education in the usual subjects but also learned Spanish, French, English, and Italian. Her mother died when she was sixteen and her father when she was twenty-one. She lived in Jena where she met Schiller, who had a major influence on her work. On April 4, 1793, Sophie married Carl Mereau; he was twenty-eight, a lawyer, librarian, and law professor, but within a year she regretted her marriage. She took a lover in 1794 and the following year traveled with another to Berlin. Sophie had two children with Carl Mereau: Gustav, born in January 1794, and Hulda, born in September 1797. After Gustav's death in 1800, Sophie Mereau decided to divorce her husband. She met Clemens Brentano in 1798; he fell in love with her immediately. Although they had a romantic relationship, Sophie severed her ties to Clemens when she left her husband and went to stay in Camburg with relatives in the summer of 1800. The time in Camburg was very productive: she edited three literary journals, published a collection of her poetry, wrote several stories, translated, and finished her novel *Amanda und Eduard* (Amanda and Edward) parts of which Schiller published in *Die Horen* (The Hours). In December 1802 she resumed her relationship with Brentano. At first she wished to live with Clemens in Marburg but would not marry him. Sophie finally consented in November 1803 when she became pregnant with their son, Achim Ariel, who was born in May 1804 and died six weeks later. Their marriage was often troubled and they spent much time apart. Her fourth child was born in May 1805 and also lived only a few weeks. Sophie then threw herself into her work. In late fall she was expecting her fifth child, but at the end of the year she suffered a miscarriage and became very ill. Her miscarriage brought about a reconciliation with Clemens, and at the end of the year they both converted to

Catholicism. The time between her conversion and her death in October 1806 was her happiest. She died at the age of thirty-six from a hemorrhage after delivering her sixth child.

Mereau's first novel, *Das Blüthenalter der Empfindung* (1794; The Blossoming Age of Sentiment), is written in the first person with a male narrator although the woman in this work is clearly more active and decisive than the man. It portrays eighteenth-century revolutionary political events and was one of the first novels of the period to depict an emigration to America for personal freedom. *Blüthenalter* deals with the conflict between society and the individual, advising individuals to be guided by their feelings. Mereau does not set feelings in opposition to reason but sees them in consort with it. Major themes in Mereau's writings are man's relationship to nature and the search for personal freedom and love. In her stories "Elise," "Julie von Arwain," and the important "Die Flucht nach der Hauptstadt" (The Flight to the Capital), Mereau advocates career choices for women and the development of one's own personality. In "Marie" (1798), Mereau is one of the first of the Romantics to support free love. Her poems reflect the same themes as her prose works. The second novel, *Amanda und Eduard* (Amanda and Eduard), was finished after the divorce and speaks against arranged marriages. Written in epistolary form, it follows the traditions of the genre in its emphasis on characters' feelings and reactions to experiences rather than plot development. Although Mereau believed that women should be allowed greater personal freedom, her female characters are motivated and guided by love since it is a woman's nature to love. Mereau points out the unjust conditions of women's lives, but she never calls for political equality.

She also worked as a translator and editor. Of greatest significance are her translations of the *Letters of Ninon de Lenclos*, Madame de Lafayette's *The Princess of Cleves*, and Boccaccio's *Fiametta*. She also translated Montesquieu's *Persian Letters* and two volumes of Spanish novellas. Between 1799 and 1801 she edited three journals: *Göttinger Roman-Calender* (Göttinger Novel-Calender), *Berlinischer Damen-Calender* (Berliner Ladies-Calender), and two volumes of *Kalathiskos*.

Works

Amanda und Eduard (1803). *Gedichte*, 2 vols. (1800, 1802). *Kalathiskos*, ed. Peter Schmidt (1968). "*Lebe der Liebe und liebe das Leben.*" *Der Briefwechsel von Clemens Brentano und Sophie Mereau*, ed. Dagmar von Gersdorff (1981). *Das Blüthenalter der Empfindung* (1982, reprint). "*Meine Seele ist bey euch geblieben.*" *Briefe Sophie Bentanos an Henriette von Arnstein*, ed. Karen Schenck zo Schweinsberg (1985).

Marjanne E. Goozé

Théroigne de Méricourt
1762–1817

Born August 13, 1762, Marcourt, Belgium
Died June 9, 1817, Paris
Genre(s): political and feminist pamphlet, speech, letters
Language(s): French

Théroigne de Méricourt (née Anne-Josèphe Terwagne) was one of the leading and most notorious feminists in the early years of the French Revolution. As a political activist she was a member of several revolutionary societies and took part in the violent and bloody clashes between rival factions. Born in Belgium, she left home at age fourteen and became a companion to a French woman living in London. Théroigne studied music and gave concerts for several years. In 1784 she went to Paris and lived under the name Mme de Campinados; she acquired a benefactor, the old marquis Ann-Nicolas de Persan, comte de Dun et de Pateau, from whom she received an annual pension of 5000 francs. However, she abandoned her "career" as courtesan and went to Italy in 1788 to pursue her musical training, hoping eventually to sing on stage in Genoa. The generous marquis de Persan continued to support her until she returned to Paris after hearing of the meeting of the Estates-General in 1789. She foresaw the possibility of major reforms to benefit mankind and immediately made contact with the early revolutionaries such as Brissot, Desmoulins, Barnave, St. Just, and Siéyès. Her passionate support of the revolution was genuine; it presaged the dawn of a new age when equality between men and women would create a true fraternity.

However, the "belle Liégeoise" was accused of being a paid agent for the political ambitions of the duc d'Orléans. This was unlikely for she hated the monarchy, especially Marie Antoinette, on whom she blamed all the ills of France. She was interested in achieving liberty for women; to this end, she advocated creating regiments of women warriors, a company of "Amazones," to fight alongside men in battle. Intelligent and committed to a cause, "l'Amazone de la Liberté" proposed using violence to achieve her goals. Dressed in bright trousers, armed with pistols and a dagger, she participated in the women's march on Versailles in early October 1789. She circulated among the marchers, urging them to stand firm in their demands for food for the capital and to remove the royal family from Versailles to Paris. Their success won her recognition among female activists and led to her founding the society of Friends of the Law (1790). This "man's woman," who did not especially like women, crusaded for women's rights and tried to inspire French women to serve their country. Her attempt to establish a club for working-class women failed; her violent nature and masculine attire alienated the very people she hoped to help realize full citizenship in an imminent utopia.

Ignored by those she tried to inspire and threatened by the revolutionary authorities, she fled to Belgium in late 1790. Arrested by the Austrians in February 1791, Théroigne was imprisoned, then sent to Vienna where she met with the Emperor Leopold III. She was subsequently freed, given 600 francs, and returned to Paris. This whole episode remains a mystery. But she was greeted as a heroine in Paris and asked to speak to the Société Fraternelle des Minimes and the Society for Revolutionary Republican Women. In her famous pamphlet, "Aux 48 sections" (1792), she called on women to enter politics to ensure full citizenship. Following her convictions, she took part in the attack on the Tuileries Palace on August 10, 1792, which resulted in the overthrow of the monarchy. During the long, bloody assault, she killed a royal defender, Suleau, and was awarded a civic crown by the National Assembly. Unfortunately, Théroigne threw her support to the moderate Girondins, whose influence was waning. In May 1793 she spoke to the National Convention; she warned them about Austrian spies working to undermine the revolution and called on members to confer political offices on women. That same month, the Montagnards set out to destroy the Girondins and intimidate their supporters. On May 15, Théroigne was assaulted, beaten, and stripped naked by a mob of radical women when she tried to enter the assembly.

Méricourt never recovered from the attack, and a year later her brother had her committed to an asylum. Théroigne was insane and died in the hospital of Salpetrière in Paris on June 9, 1817. Her efforts to encourage the development of women as equal partners in a utopian republic and to make fraternity a reality were not realized. But Théroigne de Méricourt had made women aware of female abilities and potential.

Works

"Aux 48 sections" (1792). *Discours, prononcé a la Société Fraternelle des Minimes, le 25 mars 179. . . . en presentant un drapeau aux citoyennes du Faubourg St. Antoine* (1792).

Jeanne A. Ojala

Aila Meriluoto
1924–

Born January 10, 1924, Pieksämäki, Finland
Genre(s): poetry, novel, juvenile literature, detective novel, literary biography
Language(s): Finnish, Swedish

Aila Meriluoto is one of Finland's most important poets since the Second World War. She has also written books for young people and translated Rilke's poetry. Rilke has influenced her own work, especially in its early stages.

As a poet Meriluoto gradually, in her own way, has broken away from the traditional romantic tradition. Her first collection, *Lasimaalaus* (1946; Stained Glass), marked both the last culmination of traditional poetry and the heralding of the new, modern poetry in the history of Finnish poetry. It contains both sensitive, girlish melodiousness and rhetorical strength, massiveness; it is uncompromising and passionate. In it the voice of postwar youth could be heard ("without belief or mercy"), and it was a critical and popular success. Meriluoto did not shift to free verse until the late fifties, and even later she has followed her own line in relation to the general development of Finnish poetry. In her poetry of the 1960s Lapland signified a distance, setting everything past into perspective, in *Asumattomiin* (1963; To the Uninhabited), and *Tuoddaris* (1965). She lived in Sweden from 1962 to 1974, and the language became a problem for her. She has also written in Swedish. In her poems of the 1970s there is a new, conversational, everyday tone and humor.

Central to her work is a personal, confessional approach to the roles of woman and artist and the nature of creative work. In her first collections her attitude is romantically uncompromising; later irony and humor give a sense of proportion. Her intense marriage with the writer Lauri Viita lasted from 1948 to 1956, and its traumatic quality is seen both in poems and in her biography *Lauri Viita, legenda jo eläessään* (1974; Lauri Viita, A Legend in His Lifetime).

The most revealing and distressed of her volumes of poetry is *Pahat unet* (1958; Bad Dreams), after which she becomes more objective, with imagery drawn from biology. Nature often gives an erotic coloring to Meriluoto's poems, and she has powerfully described woman's life in all its range in her poetry.

Works

Lasimaalaus [Stained Glass] (1946). *Sairas tyttö tanssii* [A Sick Girl Dances] (1952). *Pommorommo* (1956). *Pahat unet* [Bad Dreams] (1958). *Portaat* [Steps] (1961). *Asumattomiin* [To the Uninhabited] (1963). *Ateljee Katariina* [Atelier Katariina] (1965). *Tuoddaris* (1965). *Meidän linna* [Our Castle] (1968). *Silmämitta* [Eyeshot] (1969). *Peter-Peter* (1971). *Elämästä* [Of Life] (1972). *Lauri Viita, legenda jo eläessään* [Lauri Viita, A Legend in His Lifetime] (1974). *Kotimakuin mies* [Homeland Like a Man] (1977). *Varokaa putoilevia enkeleitä* [Beware of Falling Angels] (1977). *Sisar vesi, veli tuli* [Sister Water, Brother Wind] (1979). *Talvikaupunki* [Winter City] (1980). *Vihreä tukka* [Green Hair] (1982). *Lasimaalauksen läpi. Lasimaalaus ja päiväkirja vuosilta 1944–1947* [Through Stained Glass. Stained Glass and a Diary 1944–1947] (1986).

Liisi Huhtala

Charlotte Mew
1869–1928

Born November 15, 1869, London
Died March 24, 1928, London
Genre(s): poetry, short story, essay
Language(s): English

The life of Charlotte Mew lacked outward event, but her inner life possessed enormously complex vitality and intensity of feeling. Incompatible emotions warred within her, as the *personae* in her writings reveal. Whenever sexual desire arises, religious or moral renunciation blocks its expression. Obsession with death dominated everything she wrote. For none of her deepest longings could she find satisfying outlets in her life; she could only find them in her writing. Erotic love, religion, and death are the three great irreconcilable themes which create almost unbearable tensions in her poetry and prose. Although her output is quantitatively small—sixty-eight poems, eighteen stories, and thirteen essays—it is of the highest quality, utterly genuine and moving, deserving the praise it won from writers and critics in her lifetime and after. If she had written nothing but the seventeen poems of *The Farmer's Bride*, Louis Untermeyer commented, they "would have been sufficient to rank her among the most distinct and intense" of modern poets.

The bare facts of Mew's biography do little to explain her accomplishments. Her father, Frederick Mew, an architect, married his partner's daughter: of their seven children, two died in infancy, one died at the age of five, and two finished their lives in mental institutions. Mew grew close to her remaining sister, Anne, four years her junior. Believing their siblings' insanity to be hereditary, they decided not to marry lest their offspring inherit the family madness. This pledge must have been costly to Mew, for her writing shows an appreciation and enjoyment of children and also a profound intuition of the human need for sexual intimacy. Her inner religious standards, high and severe, must, however, ultimately account for her constricted life.

Mew began writing short stories in the 1890s. She published the first of these, "Passed," in *The Yellow Book* in 1894 and between 1900 and 1912 also published some poetry. In 1913 she met the novelist May Sinclair, who admired and encouraged her work, and Alida Monro, wife of Harold Monro, owner of the Poetry Bookshop and publisher of her collection, *The Farmer's Bride* (1916). The volume received discriminating critical notice and made a strong impression on such writers as Virginia Woolf, Hugh Walpole, the poet laureate Robert Bridges, and especially on Thomas Hardy, who invited Mew to visit him at Max Gate. Hardy was the one writer who, of all her contemporaries, she most admired and to whose work her own is most often compared.

Mew's mother and sister both became ill early in the 1920s and, as caring for them absorbed all her energies, she wrote very little from then on. Their financial situation was desperate until 1922 when Hardy, John Masefield, and Walter de la Mare procured for Mew a Civil List pension of £75 a year. Her mother died in 1923 and her sister in 1927. In 1928, Mew entered a nursing home for treatment of neurasthenia and there, apparently fearing that she, too, was losing her mind, committed suicide by drinking half a bottle of Lysol.

Death following renounced or thwarted love is a predominant motif in all her work. Sometimes religious principle causes the renunciation, as in the stories "An Open Door" and "In the Curé's Garden." Sometimes, as in the stories "The China Bowl," "A

Wedding Day," and "White World," parental love jealously opposes marital love; only death brings resolution. Missed opportunity is an abiding theme, as in "Passed" and "The Bridegroom's Friend." Even in the fairy tale "The Smile," the struggling heroine dies as she reaches the goddess of happiness, for the goddess happened not to be watching the struggle and so could not reward it, a paradigm of Mew's life.

Irreconcilable conflict between sexual desire and spiritual aspiration is also a principal theme of her poems, which are excellently crafted, economical in language, and usually in the form of rhymed odes. Often the poem is an interior monologue expressing the intense subjectivity of a *persona* clearly not the poet herself. These *personae* are often drawn from the fishing villages of England or France, since Mew was deeply attracted to French literature and to Catholic France, as is seen in the essay "Notes in a Brittany Convent" and the poem "The Little Portress (St. Gilda de Rhuys)." Although Christian in her thinking, she never became a Roman Catholic.

Rural settings also enabled her to express her profound love of the natural world, which she described in her essay, "A Country Book," and the long poem "Madeleine in Church," the interior monologue of a prostitute, a modern Mary Magdalen, expresses Mew's doubts concerning God's forgiveness and eternal life. The motif of "really seeing," of the intense look, recurs frequently in her work. The eyes of two beings meet in passionate contact to express boundless emotions beyond speech, as in "Ken," a poignant poem about an idiot-madman taken to an institution. The intense look also often signals falling in love, as in "The Fête," the monologue of an enamored adolescent boy who feels "half-hidden, white unrest" watching a circus performer.

Sexual love is characteristically linked to and countermanded by its inevitable contrary, religious feeling. Sexual love is by no means always the debased activity of a Madeleine or a Pécheresse. Often it is a sublime ideal of union precluded by death, as in the moving poem, "In Nunhead Cemetery." This interior monologue is spoken by a male *persona*, a husband to a dead wife, but, as Nunhead Cemetery is the actual burial place of Mew's brother Henry, the emotions in it may be seen as transmutations of her own. Here, as often in her work, grief is mixed with and heightened by sexual longing put in terms of burning. Burning suggests flames, the color red, and the red rose, all of which she uses with the traditional symbolism of sexual passion, as in "The Quiet House," a poem that she described as "perhaps the most subjective to me" of the poems in *The Farmer's*

Bride. The female *persona,* a daughter kept home to care for an ailing father, muses: "When you are burned quite through you die. / Red is the strangest pain to bear; / A rose can stab you across the street / Deeper than any knife: / And the crimson haunts you everywhere—"

Mew once said of herself: "1 have a scarlet soul." Here the *persona* continues: "I think that my soul is red / Like the soul of a sword or a scarlet flower: / But when these are dead / They have had their hour. / I shall have had mine, too, / For from head to feet, / I am burned and stabbed half through, / And the pain is deadly sweet." The oxymoron of "deadly sweet pain" sums up Mew's being. The poem's final words convey her strange premonitory self-understanding and read almost as an epitaph: ". . . No one for me—I think it is myself I go to meet; / I do not care; some day I *shall* not think; I shall not *be!*"

Works

The Farmer's Bride (1916). *Saturday Market* (1921). *The Rambling Sailor* (1929). *Collected Poems* (1953). *Collected Poems and Prose,* ed. V. Warner (1981).

Jane Augustine

Alice Meynell
1847–1922

a.k.a. A.C. Thompson
Born October 11, 1847, Barnes, England
Died November 17, 1922, London
Genre(s): poetry, essay, art history, travelogue, literary criticism, translation, journalism
Language(s): English

Though Meynell's literary output also included essays, art history, travel writing, literary criticism, translations, anthologies, and editorial work, it was primarily her poetry that brought fame in her day. A prominent late Victorian and mid-Georgian writer, her reputation, along with that of Christina Rossetti, whose aesthetic and religious interests she generally shares, suffered eclipse in the twentieth century. Critical admiration for her restrained, stylistically simple, and rhythmically disciplined verse is now returning, and her *oeuvre* is ripe for reevaluation.

In recent years feminist literary critics have become increasingly drawn to the story of Meynell's life as an example of an "early superwoman" who successfully fused a marriage of equal partners with a family (seven living children) and career while working on women's issues such as suffrage and peace. A woman of passionate attachments to male mentors—most prominently, a Father Dignam (her early spiritual guide), Francis Thompson, Coventry Patmore, and George Meredith—she managed to maintain her marriage, busy social life, and maternal obligations while turning out a large and varied body of writing.

The daughter of independently wealthy, culturally enlightened parents, Meynell was educated by daily tutorials and a life lived, in alternate seasons, in northern Italy and England. Brought up among adults and books, she wrote poems as early as seven years old and resolved to be a poet. Her famous protest, written in her diary at age eighteen, signals her seriousness of purpose: "Of all the crying evils in the depraved earth . . . the greatest, judged by all the laws of God and humanity, is the miserable selfishness of men that keeps women from work." But her diaries also reveal her struggle to balance her dedication to work with an equal interest in an active life among people.

Converting to Catholicism at the age of twenty, she caught the eye of Aubrey de Vere, and, through his interest, of Patmore, Tennyson, and Henry King, who admired her work. *Preludes* (1875), her first book of poems, earned praise from John Ruskin, Christina Rossetti, George Eliot, and others, placing her as a late-Romantic of notable stylistic economy. Her poetic themes in this first volume foreshadow her consistent poetic interests throughout her life: love, time, process, religious faith, poetic inspiration, and nature.

Her marriage to Wilfred Meynell in 1877 presages the shift in her attention from poetry to journalism, piece work against deadlines that she evidently found most compatible with raising seven children. The Meynells established and coedited the short-lived *Pen: A Journal of Literature* (1880); in 1881 her husband became owner and editor of *The Weekly Register,* a stable source of income for the next eighteen years. In addition, he founded *Merry England,* a literary magazine. Alice Meynell wrote for these journals as well as for *The Spectator, The Saturday Review, The Scots* (later, *The National), The Observer, The Tablet,* and *The Pall Mall Gazette.* Turning to prose writing in the 1880s and 1890s, she suspended poetry publishing until 1896.

When her husband sold *The Weekly Register* in 1899, she began to travel again, lecturing across the United States in 1901–1902, the date of her *Later Poems.* She remained an active writer for the rest of her life. Between 1903 and 1911 her literary output included brief essays on Wordsworth, Tennyson, Rob-

ert and Elizabeth Barrett Browning, Shelley, Keats, Herrick, Coleridge, Cowper, Arnold, Christina Rossetti, Jean Ingelow, and Blake for Blackie's Red Letter Library. *Poems* (1913) contained reissued poems as well as several new ones. In spite of her busy family life, she published four books of poetry during World War I. Though her health was failing, she wrote twenty-five new poems in the last three years of her life, dying in 1922 at the end of a long and productive literary, social, and family life.

Modern critics fault Meynell's essays for humorlessness, overprecious satirical slant, and impressionistic and underdeveloped ideas. Most of her essays, composed to fit the format of the editorial column, lack elaborately reasoned arguments. Yet it was just these qualities that earned her the praise of contemporaries as one of the first successful female literary critics and popular essayists, one who never overwrote and who left room for the reader's interpretation.

The key to both her life and art lies in the word "discipline." Among her elegant, austere lyrics, her religious poems have earned special attention for their highly controlled expression of moral, rather than mystical, religious consciousness and their lack of sentimentality. Her poetic ideas about religion emphasize a life of renunciation and understated stoicism, and she was regarded as one of England's most important Roman Catholic poets of her day.

Meynell's important ties to many of the famous writers of her period occasion her biographer's description as a woman paradoxically surrounded by friends and admirers, and yet solitary at the core. Contemporary accounts suggest that no one in her circle really felt he or she knew her. She was somewhat of an enigma to those closest to her, both welcoming relationships and protecting her privacy. In the midst of an unusually rich and interesting private life among gifted writers, she produced her highly disciplined poems and economical essays that shield as much as they reveal.

Works

As A.C. Thompson: *Preludes* (1875). *The Poor Sisters of Nazareth* (1889). (with F.W. Farrar) *William Holman Hunt, His Life and Work* (1893). *Poems* (1893, 1896). *The Rhythm of Life and Other Essays* (1893, 1896). (trans.) *Lourdes: Yesterday, To-Day and To-Morrow,* by D Barbe (1894). *The Colour of Life and Other Essays on Things Seen and Heard* (1896). *Other Poems* (1896). *The Children* (1897). *London Impressions* (1898). *The Spirit of Place and Other Essays* (1899). *John Ruskin* (1900). (trans.) *The Madonna,* by A. Venturi (1901). *Later Poems* (1902).

Children of the Old Masters: Italian School (1903). (trans.) *The Nun,* by R. Bazin (1908). *Ceres' Runaway and Other Essays* (1909). *Mary, the Mother of Jesus* (1912, 1923). *Childhood* (1913). *Poems* (1913). *Essays* (1914). *The Shepherdess and Other Verses* (1914). (trans.) *Pastoral Letter of His Eminence Cardinal Mercier, Archbishop of Malines, Primate of Belgium, Christmas* (1914). *Ten Poems* (1915). *Poems on the War* (1916). *Hearts of Controversy* (1917). *A Father of Women and Other Poems* (1917). *The Second Person Singular and Other Essays* (1921). *The Last Poems of Alice Meynell* (1923). *The Poems of Alice Meynell,* Complete Edition (1923). *Essays of To-day and Yesterday* (1926). *Wayfaring* (1929). *Selected Poems of Alice Meynell,* ed. F. Meynell (1930). *The Poems of Alice Meynell,* ed. F. Page (1940). *The Poems of Alice Meynell, 1847–1923,* Centenary Edition, ed. F. Meynell (1947, 1955). *Alice Meynell: Prose and Poetry,* Centenary Edition, ed. F. Page, V. Meynell, O. Sowerby, and F. Meynell (1947). *The Wares of Autolycus: Selected Literary Essays,* ed. P.M. Fraser (1965).

Rhoda L. Flaxman

Louise Michel
1830–1905

Born 1830, Vroncourt, France
Died 1905, Marseilles
Genre(s): poetry, novel, memoir, political text, drama
Language(s): French

Louise Michel, whose participation in the Commune earned her the nickname the "Red Virgin," is one of the premier figures of the French Socialist and Anarchist movements of the nineteenth century. Although she was neither a theoretician nor an organizer, her speeches and writings, her highly visible participation in demonstrations, and her numerous imprisonments made her a legend in her own lifetime. The details of her life come from many sources, not the least of which are her own memoirs. It is here, however, that it is sometimes difficult to sort out facts, for Michel not only eschews a chronological account but also presents a romanticized vision of the world. Michel's memoirs, when read with other sources (e.g., police surveillance records), do allow for an accurate picture of her life.

Born in 1830 at Vroncourt, the illegitimate daughter of a servant woman, her childhood was a happy one, for she was raised by both her mother and pater-nal grandparents, who treated her as if she were legitimate. She received her early education from her grandfather, a rational thinker who had fought in the French Revolution. After the deaths of her grandparents, Louise was sent to school, where she was trained as a schoolmistress, a career to which she would return at different moments in her life. Her first post was at a village not far from Vroncourt, where her mother was living. Although Louise formed many strong friendships with women and had a close companion in Théophile Ferré, her devotion to her mother was the one lasting emotional relationship she experienced.

Louise's interest in the Republican movement and her nascent revolutionary consciousness drew her to Paris, where she took a teaching job in 1856. There her activities were many. Her inherent curiosity led her to study science; to expand her political interests, she joined various Republican and women's rights groups; to ease her poverty and help support her mother, she gave music and drawing lessons and throughout she was contributing articles to journals and writing poetry and novels. This period of her life was marked by two events that shook French society and thrust Louise onto the political center stage: the Franco-Prussian War and the Commune. In 1870, France's impending defeat at the hands of the Prussians polarized political sentiments. The Republican government doubted the loyalties of the Paris revolutionaries and feared the National Guard. After the fall of Paris in 1871, the Guard declared the Paris Commune and separated itself from the Versailles government. Although the Commune barely lasted two months, the memory of its bloody battles would be long and the Communards became instant heroes or instant enemies, depending on which camp one was in. Louise, who fought on the barricades, was condemned as one of the Commune leaders. She was sentenced to perpetual banishment in New Caledonia, where she remained until a general amnesty was granted to all Communards in 1881.

The years in New Caledonia were kinder to Louise than she had expected. She set up a school for the prisoners' children and later for the Kanakas. She studied their language, collected their legends, engaged in an active correspondence concerning their rights, and was staunchly pro-Kanaka during their 1878 revolt. Louise continued to write poetry during her exile, inspired by the beauty of the islands. When amnesty returned her to Paris, it was not long before she was again arrested for her participation in a demonstration. Another arrest in 1883, this time for joining an Anarchist march and allegedly inciting looting, resulted in a six-year prison sentence.

She was granted a pardon and released from prison in 1886, but the shock of her mother's death the year before and the internal divisions in the Socialist movement seemed to sap some of Louise's spirit. When she was arrested in 1890 and threatened with a trumped-up insanity charge, she left France for a self-imposed exile in England where she would spend many of her remaining years. In England she found a greater affinity with the Anarchists than the Marxists, with whom she broke in 1895. Until her death, Louise continued her heavy schedule of speaking tours. She died in Marseilles, where the line of mourners at her burial was over a kilometer long. Yet, this was not her final resting place. Her body was disinterred and returned to Paris to be buried with all the pomp and circumstance of a national heroine, a martyr of the revolution.

Louise Michel's writings are inseparable from her life. Her output was massive and constant. Articles she composed over a period of fifty years are scattered in over a hundred journals. Much of what she wrote is still in manuscript form and much has simply been lost. And, as in the case of any writer with an enormous oeuvre, not all is of equal value. Although she wrote and published in many genres including theatre, e.g., *Le Coq rouge* (1888; The Red Rooster) and political essays, e.g., "Le Rêve" (1898; The Dream), the majority of her works take the form of novels, poetry, or memoirs. Louise felt that art had a social impact and thus should reflect political action. Her novels, often written in collaboration, were intended as a form of engaged literature that would present a realistic vision of society and inspire social change. However, her imagination and her love of drama often got the best of her, and the novels are excessively melodramatic and abound with sensationalistic murders, suicides, and the like.

The *Mémoires* (1886; Memoirs) and the *Souvenirs et aventures de ma vie* (1905–1908; Memories and Adventures of My Life) present an equally problematic side of the writer. As autobiography they are not always trustworthy since she would on occasion "tamper" with the evidence to create a more politically consistent portrait of herself. However, they contain descriptive passages that are stylistically linked to her poetry and that form a thematic bridge between her life and her art. Louise's poetry itself was marked most profoundly by Romanticism. The early poems are marked by Christian imagery as well as by her admiration of Victor Hugo, a writer who would remain a strong influence in her works. Political themes, often rendered with compelling emotion as, for example, in her pieces inspired by the Commune, and utopian visions are frequent in her poems. Yet, it is the poems of the New Caledonian exile that blossom forth with the full force of her Romantic temperament faced with the natural beauty of the islands and are by far her most successful.

Works

Lueurs dans l'ombre. Plus d'idiots, plus de fous. L'Ame intelligente. L'Idée libre. L'Esprit lucide de la terre à Dieu (1861). *Le Livre du jour de l'an, historiettes, contes et légendes pour les enfants* (1872). *La Grève dernière* (1881). (with Jean Guétre) *La Misère* (1882). (with Jean Guétre) *Les Méprisées* (1882). *Le Gars Yvon, légende bretonne* (1882). (with Jean Winter) *Le Bâtard impérial* (1883) (with Adolphe Grippa) *La Fille du peuple* (1883). *Contes et légendes* (1884). *Légendes et chants de gestes des canaques* (1885). *Les Microbes humains* (1886). *Mémoires* (1886). *L'Ere nouvelle, Pensée dernière, souvenirs de Calédonie* (1887). *Le Coq rouge* (1888). *Lectures encyclopédiques par cycles attractifs* (1888). *Le Monde nouveau* (1888). *Les Crimes de l'époque* (1888). *Le Claque-dents* (1890). *Prise de possession* (1890). *A travers la vie, poésies* (1894). "Le Rêve" in *Inquisition et Antisémitisme* (1898). *La Commune* (1898). *Oeuvres posthumes, v. I. Avant la Commune* (1905). *Souvenirs et aventures de ma vie* (published in serial form in *La Vie populaire* 1905–1908). (with Emile Gautier) *Les Paysans* (n.d.). *La Chasse aux loups* (n.d.).

In addition, Michel contributed many articles to newspapers and journals, e.g., *L'Aurore, La Bataille, L'Echo de la Haute-Marne, L'Intransigeant, Le Libertaire, La Marseillaise, La Patrie en danger, Le Pays, La Révolution sociale,* etc.

Translation: *The Red Virgin—Memoirs of Louise Michel,* eds. B. Lowry and Elizabeth E. Gunter (University, Ala.: University of Alabama Press, 1981).

Edith J. Benkov

Jóreiðr Hermundardóttir í Miðjumdal
ca. 1239–?

Born ca. 1239, Iceland
Death date unknown
Genre(s): visionary poetry
Language(s): Old Norse

Jóreiðr í Miðjumdal is credited with eight stanzas of dream verse in *Íslendinga saga*, part of *Sturlunga saga*, an account of current events written by Jóreiðr's contemporary Sturla Þórðarson. In the sort of Icelandic visionary verse of which Jóreiðr's poetry is typical, the poet attributes the origin of the poetry to a figure seen and heard in a dream or vision. In Jóreiðr's case, the dream-figure is one of the grand heroines of pagan legend, Guðrún Gjúkadóttir (from the story of Sigurd the Volsung). The verses and the frame-story that goes with them involve Jóreiðr's visions on a number of summer nights in 1255 in which she sees Guðrún dressed in dark clothing (which is often symbolic in Icelandic tradition of violent death) and mounted on a large gray horse. Jóreiðr asks the dream-woman about the fate of various of her friends and kinsmen, who are tangled up in political feuds elsewhere in Iceland. The dream-woman provides her with suitably doom-filled answers, sometimes in prose, but mostly in verse, in archaic Eddic style. Jóreiðr's poetry and the frame-story surrounding it are an evocative mirror of the apprehension and political tension characteristic of her time—the decline of the Icelandic republic. They are also noteworthy for two other reasons: (1) they represent the largest corpus attributed to any single woman *skald* in the Old Norse period; and (2) they comprise the largest body of counter-evidence to the prevailing modern belief that women composed little poetry after Iceland's conversion to Christianity.

Works

Jónsson Finnur, ed., *Den norsk-islandske skjaldedigtning* IIB (1915), p. 158. Kock, Ernst Albin, ed., *Den norsk-isländska skaldedigtningen* II (1949), pp. 84–85.

Translations: *Sturlunga saga*, tr. Julia McGrew, I, (1971), pp. 431–434.

Sandra Ballif Straubhaar

Mary Russell Mitford
1787–1855

Born December 16, 1787, Alresford, England
Died January 10, 1855, Swallowfield
Genre(s): poetry, letters, short story, essay, drama
Language(s): English

The author of *Our Village* was born into relatively favored circumstances; her mother was an heiress and her father a physician. But because of her father's profligacy, Mitford spent much of her life on the edge of poverty. Indeed, it was a desperate need for money that prompted her profuse literary production, which

began in the 1820s. Her historical dramas and "sketches" of rural life made her famous.

A precocious only child, Mitford could read by the age of three. Her mother's fortune had already been dissipated by her father by the time Mitford was six or seven, so because of their financial situation, the Mitfords moved first to London and later to Reading. While in London (in 1797), Mitford herself won a lottery prize of £20,000, which put the family back on a sound financial track for some years. The following year she matriculated at a "ladies' school" in London run by a French emigré, St. Quintin, where she won various prizes. Throughout her life she remained a voracious reader; she was conversant in French and knew some Italian and Latin. She studied at the school for over four years, after which she returned to live with her parents.

Her first publications were a collection of poems in 1810, followed by several longer poetic works. "Christina," which concerned a romance that developed in the wake of the mutiny on the "Bounty," appeared in 1811 and was very popular, especially in the United States, and went through several editions. "Blanch of Castile" followed in 1812 and "Narrative Poems on the Female Character" in 1813. These years are documented in a series of letters she wrote, some to her parents, most to Sir William Elford, a dilettante painter who became a kind of mentor. They now comprise the first volume of her collected letters, published in 1869, a mine of information on nineteenth-century manners and attitudes. The first volume reveals Mitford to be a lively, frank intelligence, given to irreverent humor, whose talent for moving descriptions of rural life is apparent early in her life. The conversational mode used in her letters became the hallmark of her fictional style, about which she once wrote: ". . . we are free and easy in these days, and talk to the public as a friend . . . we have turned over the Johnsonian periods . . . to keep company with the wigs and hoops"— an indication that Mitford saw herself as part of the democratization of art that was a central aspect of romantic literary theory.

However, Mitford remained ambivalent about the works of her romantic contemporaries, Wordsworth, Coleridge, and Byron, though she reveled in Wordsworth's and Coleridge's praise of her work. Her preference, not surprisingly (given the similarity between their work and hers), was for the prose fiction of Maria Edgeworth and Jane Austen; the other major influence on her was Washington Irving. In 1824, as the first series of *Our Village* was about to be published, she explained that the book "will consist of essays and characters and stories, chiefly of country life, in the manner of the 'Sketch Book,' but without sentimentality or pathos—two things which I abhor." Throughout her correspondence Mitford iterates her distaste for romantic sentimentalism and her preference for realism. That she herself occasionally indulged in sentimentalism reflects the romantic cast of the era but may also be due to her need to appeal to popular taste.

By 1820 the family, reduced to near destitution, had to move to humbler quarters in Three Mile Cross, a small village near Reading where Mitford was to live for more than thirty years and which she was to endow with international celebrity as the site of "our village." The first of these sketches appeared in the *Lady's Magazine* in 1819. At the same time Mitford turned her hand to a completely different literary form, tragedy. Her first attempt at drama, *Fiesco*, was not accepted, but shortly thereafter *Julian* was presented at Covent Garden on March 15, 1823, with William Charles Macready, an eminent actor, in the title role. It ran for eight performances and evidently received much sexist criticism.

Foscari, her second work, was completed in 1821 but not produced until November 4, 1826, when it ran for fifteen performances at Covent Garden with Charles Kemble in the lead. Coincidentally, Byron had put forth a tragedy on the same subject in 1821, which caused Mitford considerable consternation. Her most successful play was *Rienzi*, another romantic historical tragedy set in Renaissance Italy and concerning rival noble families who contend for power and containing a "Romeo and Juliet" subplot. Critics consider this her best play, and audiences evidently agreed, for it had thirty-four performances in London in the fall of 1828 and was very successful on the road in the United States where Charlotte Cushman played the lead female role. Mitford's other dramatic works include: *Inez de Castro* (1831), *Mary, Queen of Scots* (1831), *Charles the First* (1834), and an opera, *Sadak and Kalasrade* (1836).

Meanwhile, Mitford had begun publishing *Our Village*, the work that was to establish her as an international celebrity, in five volumes published in 1824, 1826, 1828, 1830, and 1832. She described it as "not one connected story, but a series of sketches of country manners, scenery, and character, with some story intermixed, and connected by unity of locality and of purpose." This is in fact an accurate description of the work, which did not fit into traditional notions of genre but instead created a new form, "village fiction," and provided the basis for a dominant nineteenth-century women's literary tradition, that of the local color writers. Particularly strong in the United States, it included such writers as Caroline Kirkland, Harriet

Mary Russell Mitford

Beecher Stowe, Rose Terry Cooke, and Sarah Orne Jewett—all of whom were directly influenced by Mitford. She also had an effect on American writer Catherine Sedgwick, with whom she corresponded, Irish writer S.C. Hall (*Sketches of Irish Character*), and Elizabeth Gaskell, whose *Cranford* is a direct descendant of *Our Village*.

Our Village is narrated by a persona who guides the reader through the streets of her town, describing in detail the surrounding vegetation, housing, and landscape as well as the various "characters" who inhabit the village. Their stories are sketched in, as well, which provides what little plot *Our Village* may be said to have. Writing in the heyday of romanticism, it is not surprising that Mitford saw the rural world as a kind of pastoral Utopia that nurtured authentic people who spoke truths born of their intimate experience of nature. She favors such characters and their eccentricities and resists any sign of encroaching urban homogenization. *Our Village* became a popular rage. For years, Mitford was besieged by visitors and correspondents wanting to see or learn more about the original model for such characters. Children were named after them; flowers were named after Mitford herself.

Her studies of rural life continued with *Belford Regis* (1834), *Country Stories* (1837), and *Atherton* (1854). In 1836 she met Elizabeth Barrett (later

Browning) with whom she was to form a strong friendship; numerous letters between them are extant. Despite her industrious literary production, Mitford remained impoverished in the latter years of her life, finally forced to move to a small cottage in Swallowfield, also near Reading, where she died. A charming stylist and a pioneer of an important direction in women's literature, Mitford's current obscurity is undeserved.

Works

Poems (1810). *Christina, the Maid of the South Seas; a Poem* (1811). *Blanch of Castile* (1812). *Narrative Poems on the Female Character, in Various Relations of Life* (1813). *Julian* (1823). *Our Village: Sketches of Rural Character and Scenery,* 5 vols. (1824, 1826, 1828, 1830, 1832). *Foscari* (1826). *Dramatic Scenes, Sonnets, and Other Poems* (1827). *Rienzi, A Tragedy* (1828). *Mary, Queen of Scots* (1831). *Inez de Castro* (1831). *Charles the First, An Historical Tragedy* (1834). *Belford Regis, or Sketches of a Country Town* (1835). *Sadak and Kalasrade; or The Waters of Oblivion* (1836). *Country Stories* (1837). *The Works of Mary Russell Mitford: Prose and Verse* (1841). *Recollections of a Literary Life* (1852). *Atherton and Other Tales* (1854). *The Dramatic Works of Mary Russell Mitford* (1854). *The Life of Mary Russell Mitford . . . Related in a Selection from Her Letters to Her Friends,* ed. A.G.K. L'Estrange (1869). *Letters of Mary Russell Mitford,* ed. Henry Chorley (1872). *Correspondence with Charles Boner and John Ruskin,* ed. Elizabeth Lee (1914).

Josephine Donovan

Nancy Mitford
1904–1973

Born November 28, 1904, London
Died June 30, 1973, London
Genre(s): novel, essay, biography
Language(s): English

Nancy Mitford was the oldest of the Earl of Redesdale's seven children. Though she came from a family of writers, as well as politicians and historians, her parents were convinced she needed no education, and so she (like her writer sister Jessica) got none. This contributed to her independent nature and perhaps to a certain eccentricity. She did not, however, become a fascist like two of her five sisters (one of whom married Sir Oswald Moseley, who led the British Union of Fascists). Her amusement at her family's odd behavior is reflected in her entertaining novel *The Pursuit of Love* (1945), where she treats her relatives as almost Dickensian caricatures; they were also the "hons. and rebels" Jessica wrote about.

Mitford's most familiar novels are probably *Love in a Cold Climate* (1949), *The Blessing* (1951), and *Don't Tell Alfred* (1960), but she was also the author of fiction of the Thirties: *Highland Fling* (1931), *Christmas Pudding* (1932), and *Wigs on the Green* (1935). They were appreciated in their day for a witty style and a facile, sometimes farcical, humor, and today they are read because of the fame of her later work.

In *Highland Fling* a huntress, Jane Dacre, goes after Albert Gates, despite the fact that when he invited her to see his etchings he was really thinking about art. In *Christmas Pudding* we have "one of those houses which abound in every district of rural England, and whose chief characteristic is that they cannot but give rise, on first sight, to a feeling of depression." In the house, however, is the lively young lady Philadelphia Bobbin, in search of romance. In *Wigs on the Green* Poppy St. Julien knows that Jasper Aspect has neither prospects nor scruples—which makes him irresistible to her. Reissued in the 1970s (with *Pigeon Pie* of 1940, in which a bored sophisticate, Sophia Garfield, is out to cheer up the dreariness of wartime with a skirmish in the war between the sexes), these early novels are a little dated but still have charm.

Especially dated is *Pigeon Pie,* written at the time of the "phony war" and joking about things such as espionage, sabotage, and propaganda that were soon to become serious matters. But the intrigue of the book is, in fact, like the country house and the London "smart set" backgrounds of the other books, truly incidental. Essentially the books are all satires of the Sweet Young Things, now called The Beautiful People. "Cracks in the upper crust," ran a blurb on the Penguin edition of one of Mitford's novels, were "almost Nancy Mitford's private literary domain."

Mitford knew the upper crust. As the wife of the son of a former British ambassador to Italy, she lived in Paris and reported the social life there for the *Sunday Times.* She set *Love in a Cold Climate* and some other work in Parisian diplomatic circles: Alfred in *Don't Tell Alfred* is the British ambassador to France. Most undiplomatically, Fanny, the narrator and Alfred's wife, is really Mitford herself and writes (as Norman Collins said in the *Observer*) "of the heart with a most engaging heartlessness." Fanny/Nancy satirizes the surfaces of life at least in the upper echelons (said a critic in the *Spectator*) "with more truth, more sincerity, and more laughter than a year's output of novels in the bogus significant style."

Mitford had no desire to attempt the "bogus significant" and knew she was not penetrating, that she was clever but not profound. She never gets very deeply into characters; she is at her best with eccentrics such as the couple in *The Blessing*. She is Grace Allingham, who has lived with her dashing husband only 10 days in 7 years and nonetheless adores him. He is a French marquis who loves her—and any other beautiful women he can get his hands on. Another writer might make a tragedy of this material, but Mitford plays it for laughs. She lacks the bite that makes serious satire better (if bitter); she is content to jest about aristocratic friends and foes and their horrible children and their trendies and toadies.

Horsemanship and French, she said, was all the knowledge her parents' weird ideas about education gave her to work with. The French she used to make *The Little Hut* (1951) out of André Roussin's pleasant little play and to research solid studies of *Madame de Pompadour* (1954, revised 1968), *Voltaire in Love* (1957), and *The Sun King: Louis XIV at Versailles* (1966). She also translated Mme. de Lafayette's classic *The Princess of Cleves* (1950). She educated herself widely and was able to write the essays in *The Water Beetle* (1962), a popular biography of *Frederick the Great* (1970), and *Noblesse Oblige: An Enquiry into the Identifiable Characteristics of the English Aristocracy* (1956), which made her widely known in connection with the differences between "U" and "non-U" speech. She edited the letters of Maria Josepha, Lady Stanley of Aderley, and her daughter-in-law (Henrietta Maria Stanley) as *The Ladies of Aderley* and *The Stanleys of Aderley* (both 1938), throwing interesting sidelights on Victorian women. But, like many self-educated persons, in all her work she seems attracted to curious detail rather than the large picture, to gossipy anecdotes to flash and filigree, peculiarities rather than profundities. At the same time she is nobody's fool, and she can always limn a character deftly when she wants to or conjure up the costumes and scenery of a bygone age convincingly.

Mitford lacked not so much education as malice. She would have been a better writer had she some of the nastiness of, say, Evelyn Waugh. As it is, her satire is never scathing and one wonders if there is enough salt in it to preserve it for posterity. The "hons. and rebels" are fast fading. There was a time, Mitford's mother once said, that whenever she saw "Peer's Daughter" in a sensational banner headline she knew it was "going to be something about one of you children." Today Unity (with her fascination with the Nazis) and some of the other Redesdale brood (one of whom married royalty) are far less likely to ring a bell in memory than Mitford. Whether the interest in her prewar world and her postwar eccentrics will last, or whether Mitford herself will continue to be of interest because of the autobiographical elements in *The Pursuit of Love*, remains to be seen.

One hopes Mitford's fun will not be forgotten. There was more to the Thirties than strikes and depression and, though one might not know it from reading most modern fiction, not all the world is lower class or middle class.

Works

Highland Fling (1931). *Christmas Pudding* (1932). *Wigs on the Green* (1935). *The Stanleys of Aderley* (1938). *The Ladies of Aderley* (1938). *Pigeon Pie* (1940). *The Pursuit of Love* (1945). *Love in a Cold Climate* (1949). [trans.] *The Princess of Cleves, by* Mme. de Lafayette (1950). *The Blessing* (1951). *The Little Hut* (1951). *Madame de Pompadour* (1954, 1968). *Voltaire in Love* (1957). *Don't Tell Alfred* (1960). *The Water Beetle* (1962). *The Sun King: Louis XIV at Versailles* (1966). *Frederick the Great* (1970). *A Talent to Annoy: Essays, Journalism, and Reviews,* ed. C. Mosley (1968). *Selima Hastings* (1985).

Leonard R.N. Ashley

Paula Modersohn-Becker
1876–1907

Born 1876, Dresden, Germany
Died 1907, Worpswede
Genre(s): journal, letters
Language(s): German

Paula Modersohn-Becker is today known best as one of the great women artists of this century, a radical and solitary innovator unaffiliated with any of the artistic movements or schools of her time (neo-Impressionism, Primitivism, Expressionism) whose work nevertheless both prefigured and influenced subsequent developments in twentieth-century art. Ironically, however, she first became known as a writer: when a selection of her letters and journals were published in 1919, the slim booklet became an immensely popular bestseller and was often reprinted in the German-speaking world. However, it was not until six decades later, with the publication of the complete edition of her letters and journals, that her full range as a writer could be appreciated and assessed.

Born 1876 in Dresden to a family that prized gentility and decorum, Modersohn-Becker chose to pursue a career as an artist with only minimal familial support. She studied art in London and Bremen and at the Drawing and Painting School of the Society of Women Artists in Berlin; in 1901 she married the painter Otto Modersohn and settled with him in the artists' colony of Worpswede. Several extended visits to Paris (1900, 1903, 1905, 1906) acquainted her with what she enthusiastically described as the "most most modern painters" and confirmed her passion and commitment to the life and work of an artist. Nevertheless, she returned to Worpswede and her marriage in the spring of 1907. In November of that year she gave birth to a daughter and died just a few weeks later.

Covering the events of her life from 1892 to 1907, Modersohn-Becker's diary entries and letters to family, friends, and colleagues reflect a life-long tension between dutifulness ("I am trying very hard to learn a lot so I can be a good housekeeper . . . and so that you will feel comfortable and satisfied with me"—Letter to her parents, August 19, 1892) and a passionate ambition to be a good and serious artist ("Accomplish great things in your art; there is greater satisfaction in that than in anything else life can give you"—Letter to Otto Modersohn, Paris, April 25, 1906). Like her drawings and paintings, Modersohn-Becker's literary work can be described as an art of "monumental intimacy." The directness and unaffected honesty of her writing style reflects the same powerful, almost totemic simplicity of her figures, landscapes and still lives. In the intensity of her experience, the ordinary becomes monumental, significant beyond the immediacy of the particular moment portrayed. Whether she is describing a drawing instructor's antics, the ecstasy of life in Paris, a book she is reading, or a young mother she is painting, her writing is marked not by a realism of representation (what something *is* like), but by a heightened psychological (Expressionist) "realism" (what something *feels* like). This quality of intense engagement and her fierce commitment to remain true to herself and to the path that she had chosen make her written work cohere beyond a mere collection of letters and journals. It has the grandeur and dramatic tension of a tragedy in prose.

Works

The Letters and Journals of Paula Modersohn-Becker, tr. J. Diane Radycki (1980). [Based mainly on *Die Briefe und Tagebuchblätter von Paula Modersohn-*

Becker, ed. Sophie D. Gallwitz (1920)]. *Paula Modersohn-Becker in Briefen und Tagebüchern*, ed. Günter Busch and Liselotte von Reinken (1979). *Paula Modersohn-Becker: The Letters and Journals, 1876–1907*, tr. Arthur Wensinger and Carole C. Hoey (1984).

Angelika Bammer

Karin Moe
1945–

Born 1945, West Coast, Norway
Genre(s): criticism, novel, poetry, short story
Language(s): Norwegian

Karin Moe is an experimental writer whose literary voice has left its distinct mark on the contemporary Norwegian literary scene. She has worked in advertising, as a consultant to a publishing company, and as an instructor in French at the University of Oslo. Aside from working and writing she has been one of the organizers of a "stunt-poet" group the goal of which has been to raise the awareness of the media, the government, and the general public about the dismal situation of both literature and writers in Norway. In 1986 she staged her own mock burial from a hospital bed in Oslo. Before this rather untimely "death," Moe managed to publish five exciting, experimental, and unequivocally feminist texts.

Moe's overriding concern lies with her attempt to create a female specific *écriture norvégienne*. Language is the theme of her critical writing and her fiction. The influences are several, mainly poststructuralist French. She herself points to R. Barthes, Luce Irigaray, Hélène Cixous, Annie Leclerc, and Chantal Chawaf. Their suspicion of the referentiality of language is passed on to the Norwegian reader through Moe's texts. Entrenched conventional notions of "woman," "man," "sexuality," and "gender" are deconstructed and declared useless. Next to her interest in French matters, she admits that the oral traditions of the West Coast, in particular those passed on by women, are meaningful to her writing. Her playful manipulation of Norwegian persistently breaks with literary norms. Through her spiritedly satirical critique of phallologocentrism she seeks to offer the hope of a "counter"-language, where patriarchal constructs no longer can function.

She is much amused by male critics' open dismay and misunderstanding of what they call her "obsession" with sex and genitalia. It is her way of meeting the world head-on—writing about sex is simply to describe women's reality. She cannot, of course, do without common linguistic features, but she uses these to subvert the familiar, intent on making the reader cognizant of women's silence and marginal position. Philosophy, psychoanalysis, and the natural sciences are her tools.

Her language is not ordered and linear, it is chaotic, fluid, silent, listening, of/from the body. She writes with pleasure à la Barthes, and with a keen sense of layout, space, and rhythm. Her texts are sculpted, choreographed. By contextualizing language she produces new possibilities for naming that are non-universal, pluralistic, without control. Her language is thought-in-context/contact/body-for-others, providing the reader with a point of departure for further conceptualization. Hers is a *mis-en-scène* of language as the lack it is, and her writing contains women's traces within it. Her major source of inspiration is the writings of Irigaray. Moe's linguistic maneuvers clearly have consequences for how the reader will perceive time, space, and human relations. Women writers who share her aesthetics are Christa Wolf, Alice Walker, Liv Kõltzow, Eldrid Lunden, and Chantal Chawaf.

Kyka/1984 (1984) represents an ambitious project in which not only the traditional meta-narrative is disrupted but the physical appearance of the book is part of the desire to make the reader aware of the appropriation process of "woman" into patriarchal structures, by man's lust for paradigms. *Kyka/1984* reveals the writer as a consummate literary concept-artist, an aspect of her work that is very much at play in *Mordatter* (1986) and *Sjanger* (1986). *Kyka/1984* refuses the reader the security-(ph)allacy of the macronarrative, that Moe views as representative of the social realist and postsocial realist novel writing in the 1970s and 1980s in Norway. The impossibility of hanging on to meaning, in the unfolding of the crime story (told via the "voice" of a six-year-old girl framed by a community gossip chorus, in small print in the margins of the pages, and a police report), is countered with the possibility of a new language, a different way of perceiving the "world." This (utopian) attempt is created in the writing books of the little girl, but the trust the reader puts in her story remains an illusion, as her familiar "I" vanishes. Her language however, is noncategorical and nonreflective, sharply contrastive of the Law of the Father.

Mordatter (1986) is a collection of poems in which Moe zeroes in on representations of motherhood, mother–daughter relations, and female socialization. Her veneration for the mother never becomes roman-

tic abandonment, a belief in a given, natural identity. Not wanting the young daughter to become swallowed up by the mother's body and language, Moe prevents the daughter's initiation into patriarchal paradigms. Interestingly, the grandmother has survived the fate of her own daughter, perhaps because she is too deeply rooted in women's oral traditions. She remains harmonious, a sort of ur-mother. In describing their phases of womanhood, Moe appears to say that their relationship to language mirrors the relationship to the body, however different the result. Grandmother and granddaughter share a language that is open, multilayered, and unpredictable.

In *Sjanger* (1986), a collection of reviews, articles, fiction, short essays, poems, and fictional interviews with Irigaray and J. Derrida, written between 1980 and 1986, Moe contributes her sharply critical but humor-filled perspective to the postmodernist debate in Norway. The structure of the collection is characterized by an effective contrasting of "masculine," and "feminine," as well as by a variety of genres and styles. Her discussion centers on modernist and postmodernist views of art and literature, and the connection between these and French feminist theory and fiction.

The short texts chart Moe's travels through recent feminist perspectives, and in spite of feminism's outright philosophical and political questioning of the Great Narratives, she finds that her own feminist positioning has become ambivalent. All the same, *Sjanger* does show Moe's continual curiosity with masculine codes of signification, and she still insists on the importance of women's writing, past and present, and she certainly intends her own writing to subvert reading, writing, and meaning-producing structures. She wants the difference she represents to point to new strategies of female naming and speaking. In particular, she wants postmodernists to incorporate women's analyses, what masculine discourse is weary of, namely, the body, fluids, a different mother. The pluralism she offers, she writes, should replace postmodernism with the term "transmodernism."

Works

Kjønnskrift (1980). *37 Fyk* (1983). (ed.) *Kvinne og kunstnar* (1983). *Kyka/1984* (1984). *Mordatter* (1986). *Sjanger* (1986).

Translations: "The Lady in the Coat," "Eagle Wings," from *Kjønnskrift*, in *An Everyday Story: Norwegian Women's Writing*, ed. Katherine Hanson (1984).

Pål Bjørby

Moero
ca. 320 B.C.– ?

a.k.a. Myro
Born approximately 320 B.C., Byzantium
Death date unknown
Genre(s): epigram, epic poetry, lyric poetry
Language(s): Greek

Moero or Myro (the spelling of her name is disputed) is closely linked to Anyte (see separate entry) in the prologue to the *Garland,* an anthology of epigrams compiled by Meleager of Gadara in the first century B.C. The two poets were probably contemporaries and shared the same artistic concerns; that they were personally acquainted is unlikely. In later antiquity, Moero is remembered both for her own sake and as the mother of the tragic poet Homerus (fl. 284–81 B.C.), on whose career she seems to have exercised considerable influence.

One of the most highly regarded of ancient women poets, Moero was also exceptionally versatile. In addition to her epigrams and epic poetry, samples of which survive, she is reported to have composed lyrics, a hymn to Poseidon, and a poem with the intriguing title *Arai* ("Curses"). Meleager claims to have included many of her epigrams in his anthology, but only two are preserved. The first, a striking variation upon the conventional dedicatory epigram, speaks of a cluster of ripe grapes consecrated to Aphrodite in terms of a child parted from its mother, the vine. The rich fusion of epithalamic and funerary language, together with the intense evocation of a sheltering maternal presence, suggests that the quatrain may be read as a symbolic statement about the sundering of the mother–daughter bond on the occasion of the daughter's marriage. The second, which owes much to Anyte 3, requests the Hamadryads, tree-spirits dwelling in a grove of pines beside a river, to aid the dedicant. These goddesses are pictured as nymphs treading the river-bottom with rosy feet—a vivid and fanciful image for trees whose roots extend out of the bank beneath the surface of the water. In both epigrams, Moero's capacity to visualize nature in human terms and invent daring anthropomorphic metaphors is strongly felt.

Ten lines from her epic poem *Mnemosyne* cited by Athenaeus (11.491B) expand Hesiod's account of Zeus's infancy in Crete. Doves feed the child-god on ambrosia, while an eagle brings nectar in its beak; when, fully grown, Zeus overthrows his father Cronus, he rewards his nurses with unique privileges. In typical Hellenistic fashion, Moero flaunts her erudition by neatly alluding to a long-disputed crux in Homer (*Od.* 12.62) which could refer either to doves (*peleiades*) or to the seven Pleiads, daughters of Atlas. The title meanwhile implies that the epic was primarily concerned with Zeus's encounter with Mnemosyne ("Memory") and the subsequent birth of their daughters, the nine Muses. Moero's work may therefore have been a programmatic or self-reflective pronouncement upon her own poetic craft.

Works

Greek texts and German translations in Homeyer, H., *Dichterinnen des Altertums und des frühen Mittelalters* (Paderborn, 1979). Greek texts in *Collectanea Alexandrina*, ed. J.U. Powell (Oxford, 1925). Commentary on epigrams in *The Greek Anthology: Hellenistic Epigrams*, eds. A.S.F. Gow and D.L. Page, II (Cambridge, 1965).

Translations: English translations of epigrams in *The Greek Anthology* I, tr. W.R. Paton (Cambridge, Mass.: Loeb Classical Library, 1916). Translation of the *Mnemosyne* fragment in Athenaeus, *The Deipnosophists* V, tr. C.B. Gulick (Cambridge, Mass.: Loeb Classical Library, 1955).

Marilyn B. Skinner

Dolors Monserdà de Macía
1845–1919

Born 1845, Barcelona, Spain
Died 1919, Barcelona
Genre(s): novel, poetry, journalism, drama
Language(s): Catalan, Spanish

Dolors Monserdà was born and raised in a cultured Barcelona home with an unusually well-read mother and bookbinder, bibliophile father. Her first works were written in Castilian, but by 1877, she had turned to Catalan, moving from poetry to novelettes, plays, and novels produced as part of the Catalonian *Renaixença* (Revival). Monserdà's strong interest in social issues centered around problems of the working class and working women, concerns placing her well ahead of her time. Her depiction of contemporary social conditions, her consistently realistic approach to her material, were influential in bringing women fiction writers closer to realism and eliminating much of the moralizing sentimentalism found in earlier women novelists.

Ma corona (1877; My Crown), the writer's first

collection of poetry in Catalan, was inspired by the death of her youngest daughter. *Poesies catalanes* (1888; Catalan Poems) treats patriotic, intimate, folkloric, and historic themes in addition to the maternal and religious of the first collection. *Poesies* (1911) repeats some earlier poems and adds new ones, but is not a complete compilation of all poetry published in the interim. In addition to these books of verse, Monserdà wrote lyric theater: *Sembrad y cojeréis* (1874; As You Sow, So Shall You Reap) and *Teresa o un jorn de prova* (1876; Teresa, or a Day of Trial). *Amor mana* (1930; Love Flows), Monserdà's only prose play, was written in 1913 but published posthumously.

La Montserrat (1893), Monserdà's first attempt at fiction in Catalan is a full-length novel whose female protagonist, Montserrat, is engaged to a young man whose father is obsessed with wealth and ambition. Eventually left a spinster by the would-be father-in-law's greed, Montserrat as jilted sweetheart proves much more practical than earlier stereotypes. By her example, she challenges the Spanish cultural archetype of the lonely, ridiculous, and embittered old maid, demonstrating through energetic pragmatism that a productive and reasonably happy life is still possible.

Monserdà's second novel, *La família Asparó* (1900; The Asparo Family) is experimental for its day, with an internal monologue by the male protagonist, perhaps adapted from the writer's apprenticeship in the theater. With its contemporary Barcelona setting and real characters drawn from the elegant bourgeoisie, *The Asparo Family* is a *roman à clef*, whose cast includes portraits of well-known society figures. Of a more moralizing bent than Monserdà's other fiction, this novel attempts an exposé of materialism and amorality among the fashionable upper-middle class.

La fabricanta: novela de costums barcelonines (1860–1875) (1904; The Factory Woman: Novel of Barcelona Customs) is deemed Monserdà's best and most powerful work. Notwithstanding its subtitle, concerns are more socioeconomic than *costumbrista* (a local-color genre painting regional customs). The ambient contrasts markedly with Monserdà's two earlier novels, depicting the world of cottage industries and shops of the urban lower class. The female protagonist, a weaver's daughter, sets up and operates her own loom after marrying a poor worker. Refusing to let marginalization and isolation overcome her resolve, she eventually manages to save her husband's workshop. The story line is innovative, as the "self-made woman" was rare in Barcelona at the end of the nineteenth century. The heroine's struggle is not a feminist search for autonomy, as she subordinates her interests to those of her husband and does not challenge the system. Nevertheless, with this depiction of the rise of small factories in Catalonia, Monserdà is more attuned to issues of class and gender than other women writers of her day.

In *La Quiteria* (1906), which traces the life of a foundling girl raised in a backward Catalan village, Monserdà contrasts rural and urban lifestyles. Quiteria's harsh, deprived upbringing and low self-esteem undergo modification when a city woman takes her to Barcelona as her maid. Eventually the heroine must choose between her new life with its relative self-determination and a more conventional existence as a village housewife. Perhaps predictably, Quiteria (with counseling from the local priest) chooses love and marriage.

María Gloria (1917) once again confronts problems of social class. María Gloria, the spoiled granddaughter of a formerly wealthy, newly impoverished family, indulges romantic fantasies and is pampered by her family until she is suddenly left a penniless orphan. Forced to confront stark reality, she finds her dream world replaced by working-class misery when she is taken in by her old wet-nurse. Monserdà paints in some detail the conditions under which working-class women maintained themselves by sewing and other ways of contributing to the domestic economy. Even though María Gloria marries a self-made member of the rising middle class, thereby obviating the problem of supporting herself, the novel exemplifies a heightened awareness of problems peculiar to class and gender.

In addition to these full-length fictions, Monserdà cultivated the short story, publishing a dozen tales in two slight volumes jointly entitled *Del Món* (1908; About the World). Nearly all have women as their focus, and many have first-person female narrators. The autobiographical presentation achieves optimum effects in treatment of marriage, feminine loneliness and isolation, the marginal existence of forgotten senior citizens, and the shallowness of materialism.

Monserdà focuses primarily on women, ranging from the young servant girl to the elderly middle-class widow, the self-made working woman and the amoral upper-class. She thus portrays a broad social spectrum, despite a preferential emphasis on middle- and working-class women, and re-creates the several vital stages from adolescence to old age. Although most of her works are long out of print, Monserdà is unquestionably a key figure in early Catalan feminism, and her influence in moving women's fiction in the direction of realistic depiction of contemporary social conditions was decisive. Within the bounds of Catholic liberalism, she is a major realist, comparable in significance to better-known male writers such as Alarcón, Pereda, and Valera.

Works

Sembrad y cojeréis (1874). *Teresa o un jorn de prova* (1876). *Ma corona* (1877). *Poesies catalanes* (1888). *La Montserrat* (1893). *La família Asparó* (1900). *La fabricanta; novela de costums barcelonines (1860–1875)* (1904). *La Quiteria* (1906). *Del Món*, 2 vols. (1908). *Poesies* (1911). *María Gloria* (1917). *Buscant una ánima; novela de costums barcelonines* (1919). *Amor mana; comèdia en tres actes* (1930).

Janet Perez

Elizabeth Montagu
1720–1800

Born October 2, 1720, York, England
Died August 25, 1800, London
Genre(s): essay, literary criticism, letters
Language(s): English

Elizabeth Montagu

Essayist and Shakespearean critic, Montagu was also a prolific letter writer. Her witty and vividly descriptive correspondence, spanning two-thirds of the eighteenth century, re-creates the diverse activities in which she excelled, from the London establishment of scholarly forums to the management of Berkshire farmlands and Northumberland collieries. Additionally, the letters re-veal her political interests, such as her concern for the welfare and advancement of women and her discomfort with the ethical implications of the century's newly developing capitalism. Finally, her letters tell the story of her more private life—her relationship with her husband and her several intimate and steadfast friendships.

Montagu was the fourth child and first daughter in a large, wealthy, socially prominent, and well-educated family. In her adolescence, she was energetic and gregarious, and when she was twenty-two, she married Edward Montagu, nearly 30 years her senior. Shortly after his death in 1775, Montagu adopted her young nephew Matthew Robinson (later Montagu) as her heir, who after her death became custodian of her correspondence, bringing out collections of her letters in 1809 and 1813.

Montagu's first published work consisted of three dialogues she contributed anonymously to her friend Lord Lyttelton's *Dialogues of the Dead* (1760), with the delightful "Dialogue between Mercury and a modern Fine Lady" influenced by Elizabeth Carter's "Modish Pleasures" (*Rambler,* 2 March 1751). Also during 1760, Montagu, with Carter's encouragement, began a second project, an extended essay in response to Voltaire's attack on Shakespeare in his *Dictionnaire philosophe.* In 1768, Montagu wrote to Carter, "Between attending Mr. Montague in his very infirm state, domestic Orders for the regulation of a family consisting of about thirty persons, letters of business, and my authorlike duties, I have sometimes a great hurry, and I have also some sick patients for whom I am obliged to make up Medicines, that being in some cases not to be trusted to another; poor Shakespear is last served." But she persevered, and in 1769 her *Essay on the Writings and Genius of Shakespeare* was published anonymously. Her identity was almost immediately known, and Montagu became highly esteemed as a Shakespearean critic. The *Essay* went to several editions and was translated into French and Italian.

Besides time spent in Berkshire and Northumberland, Montagu traveled in Scotland, the Rhineland, and the Low Countries, and often visited France. An enthusiastic patron of the arts, she supported many writers, architects, and painters. Among the women writers she assisted were Sarah Fielding, Hester Chapone, and Hannah More. At one point, she proposed the establishment of a women's college, and in 1767 she and her sister Sarah Scott (q.v.) were working on a plan to provide a home for unmarried gentlewomen. Among Montagu's several close female friends, Elizabeth Carter may have been the most important. The two exchanged many letters, sometimes traveled together, often visited one another, and planned to share a home in later life. But although Montagu settled a pension on Carter immediately after her husband's death, the two friends never lived together. Affectionate friendship marked the Bluestocking women, that group of London ladies with perhaps Montagu at the center, which created a forum for social, literary, artistic, and intellectual interests. The Bluestockings looked to one another for intellectual support, and in their self-sufficiency demonstrated the strengths of womanly community. Through her Bluestocking parties, Montagu brought together women and men of diverse backgrounds, interests, and beliefs to share ideas: "I have always pitied a certain set of people who some years ago called themselves the 'little world,' it is so much better to be of the general world . . . to be able to converse with ease, and hearken with intelligence to persons of every rank, degree and occupation."

Works

Lyttelton, G.L. *Dialogues of the Dead.* 3rd ed. (1760). An *Essay* on *the Writings and Genius of Shakespeare, Compared with the Greek and French Dramatic Poets.* 6th ed., corrected, to which are added *Three Dialogues of the Dead* (1810). *Letters of Mrs. Elizabeth Montagu, with Some of the Letters of Her Correspondents,* ed. M. Montagu (1809–1813). *Letters from Mrs. Elizabeth Carter to Mrs. Montagu between the Years 1755 and 1800,* ed. M. Pennington (1817). Gaussen, A.C.C. *A Later Pepys: The Correspondence of Sir W.W. Pepys 1758–1825, with . . . Mrs. Montague . . . and Others* (1904). *Elizabeth Montagu, the Queen of the Bluestockings: Her Correspondence from 1720 to 1761,* ed. E.J. Climenson (1906). Blunt, R., ed. *Mrs. Montage, "Queen of the Blues"* (1923). Anson, E. and F. Anson *Mary Hamilton at Court and at Home* (1925; contains letters from Montagu). Johnson, R.B., ed. *Bluestocking Letters* (1926).

Carolyn Woodward

Mary Wortley Montagu
1689–1762

Born 1689, London
Died August 21, 1762, London
Genre(s): essay, letters, poetry
Language(s): English

After their mother died in 1693, Mary and her three siblings were left to the care of paternal grandparents and a governess, who, says Montagu, "took so much pains from my infancy to fill my head with superstitious tales and false notions, it was none of her fault I am not at this day afraid of witches and hobgoblins, or turned Methodist." Educated in part by tutors, Montagu was largely self-taught and began writing poetry when she was twelve. In 1712 she eloped with Edward Wortley Montagu, appointed Ambassador Extraordinary to the Court of Turkey in 1716. Journeying with her husband to Constantinople, she began to write the letters that would establish her reputation as an author. The couple returned to England in 1718 and, encouraged by Pope, Montagu settled at Twickenham with their two children, Mary, who married John Stuart and became Lady Bute, and Edward, whose marriages and profligate spending constantly embarrassed his family. Resuming her travels in 1739, in part at the invitation of the Italian Count Algarotti, Montagu resided first at Avignon and then at Lovere; she returned in January 1762, after the death of her husband and at the request of her daughter, and died in August.

A vigilant observer of human nature in society and politics, Montagu's poetry, essays, and letters show her concerns as a feminist and as a moralist. As a *bel esprit,* she eschewed publication, but she circulated much of her writing in manuscript, and both the pirated printings and the unpublished works met with acclaim from contemporaries including her friend Lord Hervey, Pope, Walpole, Johnson, and Burns. Contemporary publication of Montagu's works, therefore, was sporadic and not authoritative, but her literary reputation was firmly established during her lifetime.

In her essays, some of which she published anonymously, she often started by exposing a fashionable error, an intellectual misstep. A longing for honesty and integrity in all human relationships frequently underlies her focus on specific public personalities. The voice and intention of her persona are defined in an essay from January 24, 1738: "I keep up to the character I have assum'd, of a Moralist, and shall use my endeavors to relieve the distress'd, and defeat vulgar prejudices whatever the event may be." On July 28, 1714, Montagu's essay justifying the lightheartedness of some widows appeared in the *Spectator.* In *The Nonsense of Common-Sense,* a series of nine essays published as a weekly newspaper from December 1737 to March 1738, Montagu defends Walpole against attacks in the Opposition paper, *Common Sense.* On January 3, 1738, justifying Walpole's attempts to tax wine and tobacco, she writes, "The highest Perfection of Politicks, they say, is to make the Vices of the People contribute to the Welfare of the State." In her poetry, Augustan forms and a consistently satiric tone attest to her respect for the models of her contemporaries. But her opinions and insights shape her poems, frequently occasioned by personal and public events.

Written in 1715 during a literary liaison with Pope and John Gay, three of her *Court Eclogues* were printed anonymously without her permission by Edmund Curll in 1716 as *Court Poems*. In 1718 Pope presented Montagu with his autograph copy of her manuscript of the eclogues, and Walpole printed an annotated edition of all six eclogues in 1747. The subject of the third eclogue "The Drawing Room," shows the wisdom of her decision to circulate poetry only among friends, for in it she criticizes the morality of Princess Caroline's court: "A greater miracle is daily view'd,/ A virtuous Princess with a court so lewd."

Montagu is best known for her letters. Most famous are her Embassy letters, the value of which was recognized by Mary Astell, whose preface shows her characteristic encouragement and admiration of Montagu and identifies the unique quality of her voice. "To how much better purpose the Lady's Travel than their Lords. . . . A Lady has the skill to strike out a New Path and to embellish a worn-out Subject with variety of fresh and elegant Entertainment. . . . besides that Purity of Style for which it may justly be accounted the Standard of the English tongue, the Reader will find a more true and accurate Account of the Customs and Manners of the several Nations with whom the Lady Convers'd than he can in any other Author. . . . Her Ladyship's penetration discovers the inmost follys of the heart, . . . treating with the politeness of a Court and gentleness of a Lady, what the severity of her Judgment cannot but Condemn."

In addition to the descriptive letters themselves, Montagu brought back from Turkey an enthusiastic and convincing tale of inoculation against smallpox. In a letter to Sarah Chiswell, in which she recalls her discovery, she shows her disdain for professional irresponsibility and betrays her own desire to be more assertive. "I should not fail to write to some of our doctors very particularly about it if I knew any one of 'em that I thought had virtue enough to destroy such a considerable branch of their revenue for the good of mankind, but that distemper is too beneficial to them not to expose to all their resentment the hardy wight should undertake to put an end to it. Perhaps if I live to return I may, however, have courage to war with 'em. Upon this occasion, admire the heroism in the heart of your friend."

In her letters to her sister Frances, the Countess of Mar, Montagu creates whimsical sketches of her social life. Similar subjects become polished commentary in letters to the Countess of Oxford and the Countess of Pomfret. Although they differ in their views on morality and propriety, Montagu and Lady Bute correspond openly on issues of feminism and child raising. Montagu gracefully defends having emphasized domestic training for her own daughter and then urging scholarly training for her granddaughter. "The ultimate end of your education was to make you a good wife . . . ; hers ought to make her happy in a virgin state." Montagu's individualized feminism takes its direction from the status quo: "I have heard it lamented that boys lose so many years in mere learning of words: this is no objection to a girl, whose time is not so precious: she cannot advance herself in any profession, and has therefore more hours to spare." Montagu's evaluation only lightly conceals an ironic complaint about women's limited options, but her *carpe diem* response, based on practicality and preference, precludes bitterness.

Letters to Lady Bute lament "the general want of invention which reigns amongst our writers." She wonders if England "has not sun enough to warm the imagination." Only Congreve and Fielding, Montague concludes, show originality, but, because they must publish in order to make a living they fall short of their potential genius. "The greatest virtue, justice, and the most distinguishing prerogative of mankind, writing, when daily executed do honor to human nature, but when degenerated into trades are the most contemptible ways of getting bread." And although she participates herself in a literary battle with Pope, she insists that authors should, instead of "stigmatizing a Man's name, . . . confine their censure to single Actions . . . [instead of] Satyrs and Panegyricks."

Montagu's *A Comedy/Simplicity* is a translation and adaptation of *Le Jeu de l'amour et du hasard*, a French play written by Pierre de Marivaux.

In her practical feminism she urges readers to consider that reform benefits the oppressor as well as the oppressed. She writes, "Amongst the most universal Errors I reckon that of treating the weaker sex with a contempt, which has a very bad Influence on their conduct, who, many of them, think it excuse enough to say, they are Women, to indulge any folly that comes into their Heads, and also renders them useless members of the common wealth, and only burdensome to their own Familys." It is little wonder that with a pen so merciless in exposing folly, Montagu's friends' and family's responses varied from profound affection to violent antagonism. Modern audiences discover in Montagu's writing a sensitive and sensible response to significant issues of the eighteenth century.

Works

Six Town Eclogues. With some other Poems. H. Walpole, ed. (1747). *A Collection of Poems* (printed for R. Dodsley, 1748). *Works.* J. Dallaway, ed. (1803). *Letters and Works.* Lord Wharncliffe, ed. (1837). *Letters and Works,* W. Moy Thomas, ed. (1861). *The Nonsense of Common-Sense.* R. Halsband, ed. (1947). *Complete Letters of Lady Mary Wortley Montagu,* ed. (3 vol. R. Halsband, ed. (1965–1967). *Essays and Poems and Simplicity, A Comedy.* R. Halsband and I. Grundy, ed. (1977). *The Best Letters of Lady Mary Wortley Montagu.* T. Octave, ed. (1978). *Court Eclogues, Written in the Year Seventeen Sixteen: Alexander Pope's Autograph Manuscript.* R. Halsband, ed. (1977).

Mary S. Comfort

Anne-Marie Louise d'Orléans, Duchesse de Montpensier
1627–1693

Born May 29, 1627, Paris
Died April 15, 1693, Paris
Genre(s): novel, letters, memoir
Language(s): French

Anne-Marie Louise d'Orléans, la grande mademoiselle, was the daughter of Marie de Bourbon, duchess de Montpensier, and Gaston d'Orléans, the younger brother of Louis XIII. She inherited her mother's immense fortune, which made her the richest woman in France, when Marie died a few days after giving birth. The inheritance proved a mixed blessing, however. Not only did it later present difficulties in finding an appropriate husband, but it also deprived her of her sole surviving parent during childhood. Gaston, a rebellious, discontented, fickle, and troublesome younger brother, was deeply distrusted by Cardinal Richelieu who separated father and daughter almost immediately after the mother's death. The young princess grew up alone in Paris.

She lived in apartments at Tuileries, cared for by her governess, Madame de St. George, and surrounded by a household staff numbering nearly sixty. It was not a childhood without joy. Anne-Marie was assured every physical comfort possible, and her childless aunt and uncle, the King and Queen, doted on her. As second in line to the throne of France, she grew up in more luxury than many heads of state.

When she was eleven years old several important changes took place. Queen Anne gave birth to an heir, the future Louis XIV, whose arrival placed Anne-Marie at a greater distance from the throne. Perhaps of more import personally, however, was her discovery of her father's untrustworthy nature. The executions of Cinq Mars and de Thous, whose rebellions her father had fostered and then abandoned, shocked her greatly.

In the years of her adolescence, following Louis XIII's death on May 14, 1643, more disappointments were in store. Renouncing love, she declared her interest in finding an "appropriate" establishment as the wife of a powerful European head of state. She was often proposed for several monarchs, including Frederick III, the Holy Roman Emperor; the future Charles II of England; and even Louis XIV himself. Her immense fortune, which the royal family was loath to lose, the disgraceful reputation of her father, and the political machinations of the Regent Anne and Cardinal Mazarin, blocked each and every union.

Deprived of an "establishment," she became embroiled in domestic politics and, partly from misplaced loyalty to her father, allied herself with the Prince de Condé and the Fronde in open rebellion against the King. The years of the Fronde were her years of glory. In 1652, she played a heroic role, helping to relieve the town of Orléans. Three months later she secured entry for Condé's troops into Paris, ordering the cannons of the Bastille to be turned on her cousin Louis and his royal forces.

Her decisiveness and bravery were much admired. But Louis inevitably won, and Anne-Marie's heroism, though gaining her the title of the Second Maid of Orléans, lost her the most brilliant prospect she would ever have—a place beside her cousin as queen and consort. Instead of a throne in Paris, her lot was self-exile to her estate in Saint-Fargeau. It was during this first four-and-a-half-year period of exile that she began her voluminous, fascinating, and, in Michelet's words, courageous memoirs, an undertaking inspired by her admiration for the memoirs of Marguerite de Valois, the divorced wife of Henri IV. This monumental task of authorship absorbed almost all of her energy. The rest of her exile was taken up in a series of degrading and distressing tangles with her father, who had been bleeding her estate to pay his gambling debts and to support his second wife and three daughters.

She was allowed to return to court in 1652, amid rumors of her impending wedding to Louis's younger brother, the Compte d'Anjou. She evaded such plans, however, as she also evaded the attempt in 1662 to marry her to mad King Alfonso VI of Portugal. Upon this second refusal, she was again banished from court, this time to Eu where she busied herself in establishing a school for the poor.

On her second return to Paris, she led the complex and highly codified life of a "petite fille de France." Her salon was frequented by such luminaries as the Marquis de Sévère, Madame de Lafayette, and the Marquis de la Rochefoucault. A great builder like her royal cousin, she was also one of the first patrons of Le Vau, the architect of Versailles. She dabbled in literature, writing two rather mediocre novels, *La Relation de l'île imaginaire* (The Story of an Imaginary Island) and *Histoire de la Princesse de Paphlagonie* (The Story of Princess Paphlagonie), which initially appeared under the name of her secretary, Segrais. She also patronized the arts. It was in her salon that the first complete public performance was given of Molière's *Tartuffe*.

Although in her youth she had been more interested in statecraft than in the "gallanterie" of her various marriage proposals, in middle age she fell victim to an unfortunate passion. At the age of forty, she fell in love with a Gascon captain in the King's bodyguard—Antoine Nompar du Caumont, the Compte de Lauzun. Lauzun, an adept social climber and a callous adventurer, seems to have returned her affection, at least initially, and after much subtle negotiation, they obtained permission from Louis to wed. The marriage was delayed by a few days, however, and in that small space of time political pressures brought to bear on the King compelled him to withdraw his permission. Lauzun, his former favorite, was imprisoned in the Bastille.

Although Anne-Marie worked frantically for his release, it was to take almost ten years to win his liberty. Even then, she obtained it only by giving part of her estate to Louis's illegitimate son, the Duc de Maine. It is possible that she married Lauzun shortly after he was granted a pardon in 1682, but her inability to procure additional favors at court, despite her numerous gifts of land and money, angered the Gascon lover. He turned on her, was cold, indifferent, and cruel, and they soon separated. The remainder of her life passed in charitable works, increased isolation, and the writing of her memoirs, which she began again in 1672, seventeen years after discarding them. She died of uremic poisoning at sixty-six years of age on April 15, 1693 in her apartments in Paris. A grotesquely and undeservedly comic touch marred her state funeral when a jar containing her embalmed entrails exploded, bringing the ceremonies to a temporary halt.

It is difficult to categorize the works of Mlle de Montpensier. Even her novels are a strange melange of social history and fabulous story. *La Vie de Madame Fouquerolles* (The Life of Madame de Fouquerolles), published in 1652 at Saint Fargeau, is the biography of one of her ladies-in-waiting. *La Relation de l'île imaginaire* (The Story of an Imaginary Island), written in two days in 1658 at Trévous, gives a utopian plan of government. *Histoire de la Princesse Paphlagonie* (1659; The Story of the Princess of Paphlagonie) records her support of Mlle de Vandy in that lady's quarrel with the Comtesse de Fiesque. These, and the *Divers Portraits* (Several Portraits) published in 1659, are additionally difficult to evaluate because of their almost certain rewriting at the hands of Mlle de Montpensier's various secretaries. The *Relation* (The Story) and *Histoire de la Princesse* (The Story of the Princess) were published originally under Segrais's name.

Her letters and her memoirs, on the other hand, are just as certainly her own work but also just as certainly an odd mixture of fact and fiction. Her most celebrated correspondence, with Madame de Motteville, details a fictional utopian community where marriage is outlawed. Her reasons for this structuring not only reflect events in her own life but also prefigure many feminist arguments.

Recently her *Mémoires*, a vast collection numbering 2,000 pages, have received renewed attention. In the past her lack of precision and her disregard for facts have been cited as flaws in the collection, as have failings in grammar, spelling, factual dating, and construction. However, a new interest in her work, partly fueled by the publication of a more faithful text, has revealed some intriguing and little-anticipated aspects.

Mlle de Montpensier, despite her lack of a classical education, is a vivid observer. She stuffs her pages with minute descriptions of styles, dress, gestures, courtly functions, moonlight, and architecture. Her spontaneous and consciously uncorrected style, a decided contrast to the carefully written and rewritten memoirs of Madame de Motteville, has now been stripped of the regularization and polish of former editors. It can be seen as it once was—a remarkably effective document, recording the twists and turns of Mlle's often troubled mind. Her interesting use of direct as opposed to indirect style and a number of passages of self-reflection that had previously been cut are also exciting discoveries in the work of a feminine seventeenth-century memorialist.

Mlle de Montpensier's *Mémoires*, if read in this recovered form, are the most personal and the most telling of their century. Their worth lies not so much in their illumination of great historical events as in their explorations of the pressures surrounding Anne-Marie. Written at four different intervals in her life, they are uniformly composed in places and times of exile or retreat. Their changing function makes a fascinating story in and of itself—from their first use, after the collapse of the Fronde, to affirm her individuality, to their later, Proustian utility, after her affair with Lauzun, to recapture a lost world. This changing purpose and many aspects for which they were once censured—a frequent melange of tones, a startling candidness, a lack of edifying sentiment, an occasional coexistence of contradictory codes, and an unsettling spontaneity and digressive structure—give us a unique insight not only into the court of Louis XIV but into the psyche and circumstances of a particularly difficult "fille de France." Ironically, those offenses against the classical style for which she was once censured are the very aspects that now permit us to detect wretched and fascinating states of being in this text, states that can only be inferred from the silences and lacunae of other, more polished female memoirists of the same epoch.

Works

La Vie de Madame Fouquerolles [The Life of Madame Fouquerolles] (1652). *Relation de l'île imaginaire* [The Story of an Imaginary Island] (1658). *Histoire de la Princesse Paphlagonie* [The Story of Princess Paphlagonie] (1659). *Divers Portraits* [Different Portraits] (1659). *Lettres de Mademoiselle Montpensier* [The Letters of Mademoiselle Montpensier] (1806). *Mémoires de Mlle. Montpensier* [The Memoirs of Mademoiselle Montpensier] (1858).

Glenda Wall

Giuliana Morandini
1926–

Born 1926, Udine, in the province of Friuli, Italy
Genre(s): novel, dramatic and literary criticism, journalism, children's literature
Language(s): Italian

Much has been written about Morandini's literary *oeuvre*, and virtually nothing about her life. Born in Udine, which she sometimes revisits, she used Friuli as background in her first novel, *I cristalli di Vienna* (Bloodstains), but in a stylized manner that does not reflect the contemporary reality. She has traveled extensively in Central and Northern Europe, and resides in Rome.

Long involved with theater, she has published an introduction to Samuel Beckett's *Not I* (in *Carte Segrete*, 1973, No. 22, 65–74); *Le insensate* (1975), a modern interpretation of Euripides's *The Bacchantes*; an introduction to the German edition of plays by Pasolini (1984); an introduction to Wedekind's *Lulu*; and newspaper and magazine reviews.

The crisis of psychiatric institutions during the 1960s and the evolving roles of women figure in . . . *E allora mi hanno rinchiusa* (1977, 1985; . . . And Then They Locked Me Up), introduced by an essay on the relationship between mental illness and the "woman question." The interviews with institutionalized women are prefaced by sensitive verbal portraits and bring to light the culturally distinct reality of women. Awarded the Viareggio Prize in 1977, this work has been partially translated into Finnish. The second edition contains a new essay evaluating relevant legal changes during the intervening decade.

She anthologized writings by obscure or forgotten Italian women, 1800–1900, in *La voce che è in lei* (1980; The Voice That Is in Her), which presents cultural themes and stylistic problems that generations of women have had to confront to express themselves. Used as a textbook in some schools, this work has also contributed to international feminist discourse. Morandini's collection of poetry by women is *Poesie d'amore* (1986; Love Poems). She has also published a children's book, *Ricercare Carlotta* (1979).

Each of her three novels to date lyrically explores the inner and outer worlds of its protagonist: the consciousness of a woman in crisis or quest reviewing and restructuring her past; and an environment that withholds secrets and presents threats as well as opportunities. In this sense each work is a "mystery": a spatial novel (though it has plot) that cannot be understood in linear progression but coheres through evocative language and recurrent imagery and is comprehended in its totality. Serious and psychological, the prose is not without humor—and not without awkward mannerisms. Morandini makes sensitive use of the child, or the recollected child, in these "spatial novels"—the vulnerable manipulative child who, often ignored, gains admission to situations from which adults are excluded; the child who experiences acutely, without adult comprehension but also without adult prejudice; the child whose motives, roles, and interpretations are too seldom reckoned with by others.

In her fiction Morandini has been moving eastward into Central Europe: from Friuli (1977, *I cristalli di Vienna*; Prato Prize, 1978), to Trieste (1983, *Caffè Specchi*; Viareggio Prize, 1983), to Berlin (1987, *Angelo a Berlino*; Campiello Prize, 1987). Her writing reflects a softening of either–or boundaries and a reappreciation of Central Europe. The female *bildungsroman* is recognized in its primacy and not merely as a variation on the male. Morandini's work is therefore considered not only important, but also timely.

I cristalli di Vienna is retrospective and lyrical, its plot thrusting toward new growth. It unfolds both how a girl grows up and how a soul emerges from estrangement into meaningfulness. Like novels by Curzio Malaparte (Italian) and John Horne Burns (American) set during the same period, it presents life under military occupation, showing the effect of both "enemy" and "friendly" troops on a civilian population. The orientation toward war is uncommonly maternal. (The main character sees the soldiers also as old babies.) The book implies no ultimate judgment or redemption but rather presents beleaguered people caught up in conflicts not of their own making. Recognizing a basic human attraction to both bestiality and elegance, the author seems to search out a kind of decency.

In *Caffè Specchi*, Katharina explores her inner life and the atmosphere of Trieste, finding correlations of feeling, memory, and recovered images. At stake at this point in her life is custody of her son, whom her husband, with hallucinatory rigidity, refuses to yield to her. With several languages at her command, she nevertheless remains inarticulate at critical moments. She encounters the conductor of a Berlin orchestra, a youth in a reddish-brown pullover, a Faustian old man; she walks randomly through the streets; her crisis is related to the malaise of the city and its culture, a murkiness of perception and paralysis of will. A ten-part adaptation of this novel for radio has been made by Massimo Franciosa and Luisa Montagnana.

Angelo a Berlino is set in Berlin divided by the wall, though Berlin also figures in historic dimensions and as dreamscape. The city, suspended between hostile governmental systems, threatens to overwhelm the main character with its noise, intensities, and diversity. Erika, the protagonist, is searching not only for traces of her personal aristocratic heritage (and traces of her dead sister), but also for a usable collective past. This double search, for the city's identity and her own, takes place amid American and Japanese tourists, Turkish emigrants, an African youth who smells of hibiscus. The panorama of Berlin appears more clearly as an analogue of her own inner dividedness. Just as the city must rebuild, Erika must reconstruct from a life rooted in disasters (the murdered sister, the firebombing of Dresden,

the mad mother); and she must balance memory with a sense of future possibilities for love and creativity.

Involved at an international level in cultural debates, Morandini was a member of the Italian delegation at the Cultural Forum of Budapest in 1985 and participated at a conference in Bamburg in 1986.

Works
I cristalli di Vienna (1978). *Le insensate* (1975). . . . *E allora mi hanno rinchiusa* (1977). *La voce che è in lei* (1980). *Poesie d'amore* (1986). *Ricercare Carlotta* (1979). *Caffè Specchi* (1983). *Angelo a Berlino* (1987).

Translations: *Bloodstains*, tr. Blossom S. Kirschenbaum (St. Paul, 1987).

Blossom S. Kirschenbaum

Elsa Morante
1912–1986
Born August 18, 1912, Rome
Died November 26, 1986, Rome
Genre(s): novel, fairy tale, short story, essay, poetry, translation
Language(s): Italian

Elsa Morante started to write poems and fairy tales at a very early age. A self-educated student, she studied primarily at home for five years and then in Roman high schools. She was married for a number of years to one of Italy's most prolific and well-recognized writers, Alberto Moravia, they had an intellectually competitive relationship. Morante wrote slowly and painstakingly, often resorting to quasiseclusion to better concentrate, her only company that of a cat. Her pronouncements on the literary and critical scene were rare, and as rare were her interviews. She wrote mostly novels although she also produced fairy tales, short stories, and poems.

Morante is widely recognized as a major author in the literature of this century and her production continues to draw serious critical analysis. Her most successful novel was *La storia* (1974), which came out in the Italy of the seventies, a time of political upheavals and tensions. It soon became a best-seller and was the most talked-about novel of the decade. It has since been fashionable for critics to debunk *La storia* and to read it as a pathetic tale of wartime slaughter. Morante's embrace of neo-realistic techniques was deemed anti-climatic and old-fashioned, her constructions too mystifying, her choice of down-to-earth characters to emblematize uncontrollable events too populistic. In a word, the writer was judged politically rather than artistically, a move she herself might have fostered by insisting on the publication of *La storia* at a down-to-earth price. When Marxist critics found they could not see in the novel what they thought should have been there, they put it down; critics from the right, on the other hand, did not seem satisfied with the presentation and treated it harshly.

Elsa Morante is most interesting when she relies on the power of memory to resurrect a world that no longer exists. Children are often her main characters. *Menzogna e sortilegio* (1948) is an epic of two generations doomed by impossible dreams. Elisa, the protagonist, knows that she has to remember her life with her parents if she wants to understand what attracted her to a reality that was magical in her childish eyes and yet proved destructive in her grown-up days. *L'isola di Arturo* (1957) broaches the issues of growing up and the failure of adults to satisfy children's dreams. The drama of exclusion is revisited in a mythic key, the beauty of a prelapsarian world is contrasted with the realization that the pleasure it gives is fleeting, that in order to grow the young must leave their nest. In *Aracoeli* (1982) memory brings back to life a story of defeat. Here the crisis of the family can no longer be mended, and the hope for regeneration is crushed time and again by a society that has become too violent and chaotic. As in the pessimistic *Menzogna e sortilegio*, the mother becomes the subject of conflicting allegiances, her very existence tied to a world forever lost and yet forever desired, albeit perhaps destructively. One can understand why Morante tried to commit suicide soon after its publication. She survived and spent two years confined to a hospital bed. She wrote no more.

Works

Le bellissime avventure di Cateri' dalla trecciolina [The Most Beautiful Adventures of Cateri with the Golden Braids] (1941). *Il gioco segreto* [The Secret Game] (1941). *Menzogna e sortilegio* [House of Liars] (1948). *L'isola di Arturo* [Arturo's Island] (1957). *Alibi* [Alibi] (1958). *Le straordinarie avventure di Caterina* [The Extraordinary Adventures of Caterina] (1959). *Lo scialle andaluso* [The Andalusian Shawl] (1963). *Il mondo salvato dai ragazzini* [The World Moved by Children] (1968). *La storia* [History. A Novel] (1974). *Aracoeli* [Aracoeli] (1982).

Valeria Finucci

Hannah More
1745–1833

Born February 2, 1745, Stapleton, Gloucestershire, England
Died September 7, 1833, Windsor Terrace, Clifton
Genre(s): drama, poetry
Language(s): English

Hannah More

More lived through two eras, a fact that both defined and limited her impact as a writer. Born in the century of Johnson, she died at the end of the Romantic age. Toward the close of her life she was a celebrated anachronism, refusing to accept the fundamental social and philosophical changes that accompanied Romanticism. To the last she defended what, in effect, was already gone. Yet in her own way she had helped to create change just as surely as she had tried to stop it. Too conscientious to ignore things as they were, More was too conventional to opt for radical transformation. Still, her attempts to preserve the status quo while modifying it for the better struck a chord in the hearts of an entire generation.

One of five sisters who ran a successful boarding school in Bristol, More had since childhood shown a gift beyond the others for communication in all its forms. Too, she had the peculiar distinction of having the great personal crisis of her life done with early on. Jilted three times by the rich landowner to whom she had been engaged for six years, More learned firsthand the value of compassion. Around 1773 she firmly rejected her erstwhile fiancé's pleas for another chance, but she never turned bitter. Instead, she sublimated her feelings into her religion, her family, and her ever-widening circle of friends.

While recovering from the stress of the broken engagement, More visited London in 1774 or 1775. There her intellectual and conversational gifts won over David Garrick and his wife, who introduced her to a large number of London celebrities. There More, who had begun her career as a poet and playwright in Bristol, found fame with the production of her drama *Percy* (1777), a tragedy that was the triumph of its season. Garrick edited and promoted the play for his protégée, and its success was surely due in large part to his efforts. On its own, *Percy* is neither poetic nor dramatic, merely a bland imitation of Corneille. After Garrick's sudden death in 1779, More lost interest in the stage. She produced another play, *The Fatal Falsehood* (1779), and she published *Sacred Dramas* (1782), a set of biblical stories done as closet drama; but her attention had turned elsewhere.

Wherever her attention turned, she met further success. Over her lifetime she made some £30,000 as an author, most of it predicated on her ability to communicate equally well with the great and the unknown. In London More was quickly accepted as a Bluestocking, a friend of Edmund Burke, Joshua Reynolds, and Samuel Johnson. She pleased them all with "Bas Bleu" (1782), a poem saluting London's female intellectuals, past and present. She could have continued writing such elegant trifles for the rest of her life.

Instead, in a series of didactic works, she urged the upper classes to embrace true Christianity, by which she meant an Evangelical form of the Anglican faith. As More grew older, she became convinced that human corruption and divine redemption were the key elements in Christianity and that the true Christian must not only establish a personal relationship with God but also demonstrate it in his every act. This kind of enthusiasm seemed almost Methodistic to more conservative Anglicans, and it left More open to criticism within her own Tory group; but it also gave her the strength to press that group for moderate reform. Thus, in *Thoughts on the Importance of the Manners of the Great to General Society* (1788), she urged the wealthy to respect the Sabbath as it was intended. In *An Estimate of the Religion of the Fashionable World* (1790), she held that Christianity must be embraced in its entirety rather than in part. In *Stric-*

tures on the Modern System of Female Education (1799), she suggested that women should be trained as circumstances require and as a Christian society demands.

William Cobbett once called More an "old bishop in petticoats," and she was something of the sort. She was as well, however, a parson to the poor. Following William Wilberforce, she worked for the abolition of slavery, a cause she championed in her poem "The Slave Trade" (1788). Following Robert Raikes, she and her sisters established a string of Sunday schools for the neglected rural poor. Nonetheless, even with her doctrinal leanings toward reform, she remained a staunch Tory who feared and despised the French Revolution. In 1792 she wrote "Village Politics," her first progovernment, antirevolution tract. In simple language that deliberately aped the chapbook style, she justified the English system and reviled the French. Widely praised, this bit of anti-Jacobin propaganda led to a series of *Cheap Repository Tracts* (1795–1798), distributed by the rich to the poor in an effort to quell their unrest. A prime mover in this cause, More wrote at least fifty of these tracts. How successful they were as an antidote to the "French poison" is debatable; what is certain is that they were widely circulated among a people whose concerns eventually led to reform rather than to revolution.

In 1808, More published her only novel, *Coelebs in Search of a Wife*, meant as an alternative to the romances then in fashion. The alternative was another huge success, with dozens of editions printed in England and America. Like the rest of her work, *Coelebs* is too didactic to be good reading now. Ostensibly the story of a bachelor seeking a spouse, it is in fact a general statement of More's beliefs. Characters do not so much converse as lecture on her favorite subjects: women, education, children, charity, and above all, Christianity as the center of existence.

After *Coelebs* the old "female bishop" wrote several other works on pious subjects; but though everything sold well, something was different. The Romantic age had superseded the Johnsonian era; and if Romanticism was more than revolution, its politics and metaphysics were quite distasteful to an Evangelical Tory. Romantics like Coleridge and De Quincey found More equally distasteful. Though she was still revered by many when she died quietly in 1833, England and the world had left her in another century. Yet by her work for reform she, too, had a place, not just in the past but in the continuum of those who work for the welfare of humanity.

Works

The Search After Happiness (1773). *The Inflexible Captive* (1774). *Essays for Young Ladies* (1777). *Percy* (1777). *The Fatal Falsehood* (1779). *Sacred Dramas* (1782). *Thoughts on the Importance of the Manners of the Great to General Society* (1788). *An Estimate of the Religion of the Fashionable World* (1790). *Cheap Repository Tracts* (1795–1798). *Strictures on the Modern System of Female Education* (1799). *Hints Towards Forming the Character of a Young Princess* (1805). *Coelebs in Search of a Wife* (1808). *Practical Piety* (1811). *Christian Morals* (1813). *An Essay on the Character and Practical Writings of St. Paul* (1815). *Stories for Persons of the Middle Ranks, and Tales for the Common People* (1819). *Moral Sketches of Prevailing Opinions of Manners, Foreign and Domestic, with Reflections on Prayer* (1819). *Bible Rhymes* (1821). *The Spirit of Prayer* (1825). *Works* (8 vols., 1801; 19 vols., 1818–1819; 11 vols., 1830; 6 vols., 1833–1834; 2 vols., 1848). *Poems* (1816, 1829).

Mary Ferguson Pharr

Irmtraud Morgner
1933–1990

Born August 22, 1933, Chemnitz (now Karl-Marx-Stadt), East Germany
Died May 6, 1990
Genre(s): novel
Language(s): German

The novelist Morgner's intellect and erudition, her cultural insight, historical consciousness, and philosophical woman's perspective combined with her skill as a weaver of complex narrative tapestries make her one of the outstanding writers in Germany today. Morgner's subject is contemporary reality, its historical background and its possible future; her theme is ultimately the increasingly perilous state into which the dehumanizing obsession with technical specialization, hierarchy, conquest, and war inherent in the patriarchal value system have brought humankind. Refreshingly, she filters her concerns through imaginative language and metaphor pervaded with innate humor, and she shapes them into literature with protean fantasy.

The major formative influence on Morgner is the fact that she has lived in the socialist GDR since its inception (when she was sixteen). Born into a proletarian family, she was allowed to attend the University of Leipzig (1952–1956) where she majored in *Germanistik* and *Literaturwissenschaft*, studying under Hans Mayer. After university, she moved to East Berlin and worked as an editorial assistant for the official literary magazine, *Neue deutsche Blätter*, until 1958 when she began writing full-time. Her first two books (*Das Signal steht auf Fahrt*, 1959; *Ein Haus am Rand der Stadt*, 1962) were cast basically in the prevailing mold of socialist realism. *Ein Haus am Rand der Stadt*, in particular, shows promise of an independent, questing imagination, which refuses to avoid conflicts between socialist ideal and reality; thematically, her concern about women's limited, double-burdened role is already evident. Like her contemporaries, Christa Wolf, Sarah Kirsch, and Günter de Bryn, Morgner's writing influenced GDR literature to become more subjective and less schematic while remaining socialistically engaged.

Three works belong to what might be termed Morgner's second developmental phase, *Hochzeit in Konstantinopel* (1964), *Gauklerlegende* (1970), and *Die wundersamen Reisen Gustav des Weltfahrers* (published in 1972 but written before the former two). With *Hochzeit*—a work received with considerable enthusiasm, especially in the Federal Republic (1969)—Morgner had clearly begun to find her unique voice, the ability to sustain a critical dialectic between realism and fantasy. *Hochzeit*'s ever questioning heroine Bele H., a streetcar conductor in East Berlin, makes a prenuptial "honeymoon" trip to a resort somewhere on the Yugoslav Adriatic (Bele dubs it "Constantinople"). In the course of their three weeks there, Bele tries to help Paul, her physicist fiancé, gain touch with his own feeling, human side; Scheherazade-like, she tells him twenty-one allegorical tales based on fantasized interpretations of her own experiences, with the aim of opening new perspectives about human relationships to him. Blind to her deeper purpose, he remains the one-sided theoretician. When the trip is over, she bails out of the relationship, taking her future into her own hands.

The narrative voice of her next work, *Gauklerlegende*, is again a woman's; but here, too, it is her husband, the specialist male, who clearly has the socially more significant role; the subject of the wife's tales and active figure of the book, the Pied Piper/Gaukler, is obviously male as well. In *Die wundersamen Reisen*, Gustav, again a masculine title character, is both "amazing" traveler and narrative voice. The fictive "Vorwort der Verfasserin" and "Nachwort der Herausgeberin" (Preface and Afterword) added for the 1972 publication alter the perspective to that of Bele H., Gustav's granddaughter, who claims that, in a moment of inspiration, she learned to identify her own biography with his "prevaricated" adventures born of the "creativity of the powerless." Thus, in both *Gauklerlegende* and *Die wundersamen Reisen* a further extension of Morgner's central themes emerges; the drawing together of past and present, seventeenth century *Gaukler* and modern woman, universe-traveling grandfather and granddaughter. The past, in each case, has "legendary" character and as such is used to point the way to a future in which those who are as yet powerless find the courage "to accomplish something greater" by leaps of the imagination that make it possible for them to step beyond the bounds of historical limitations.

Fantasy and humor, women's creativity, the concerns of everyday reality linked with legendary past, hope for the future; these factors come together in the third and ongoing phase of Morgner's writing, in which female figures assume the active, focal roles. With her 700-page montage/collage novel, *Leben und Abenteuer der Trobadora Beatriz nach Zeugnissen ihrer Spielfrau Laura* (1974), Morgner set a landmark of imaginative writing in German letters. Her nascent stylistic abilities based on surprising juxtapositions and funny contrasts had clearly matured and found their vehicle in conscious feminine perspectives. *Die Trobadora* combines elements as disparate as, for instance, an excerpt from an official GDR tract tabulating women's orgasms and an unpublished novel which Morgner had written in 1954 (it deals with tensions between pre- and postwar generations in the GDR, is inserted in seven *intermezzos*, and serves as background for numerous characters in *Die Trobadora*). We see the possibilities and shortcomings of the socialist state from the viewpoints of an historical twelfth-century *troubadora* from Provençe, Beatriz de Dia, and her salaried minstrel Laura Salman, a contemporary, university educated streetcar driver and single mother in East Berlin. The reawakened Beatriz (she had made a deal with a fairy that she sleep until times were better for creative women) travels to the GDR of 1968, believing it to encompass the ideal realization of women's equality; Laura is still struggling with imperfect realities. Through these women, legendary and real, Morgner takes on her own times, ranging from the May 1968 Paris uprising through Chancellor Ulbricht's Bitterfelde decree that workers write and writers work, in a critical celebration of the socialist state for whose future she still had great hopes, based especially on the gradually improving position of women that the early 1970s seemed to promise. Various chapters in this nonlinear, open-formatted work

further reflect the dynamics of the present by citing Morgner herself, Paul Wiens, editor of one of the GDR's most respected literary journals, *Sinn und Form*, and author Volker Braun, as well as other real personages. When *Die Trobadora* became available in the West in 1976, critics and the reading public made it a best-seller; feminists declared her a spokeswoman. Then almost a decade passed before Morgner published again.

Morgner's outspoken stance against capitalism notwithstanding, her open sexuality and criticism of the socialist system, particularly of its little-changed double sexual standard and commensurately unfair workplace/household load for women, made further publishing very difficult for her in the GDR. Her long-term personal relationship with Wiens and the need to raise her young son did not make writing easier. She, however, remained acutely aware of political developments in both her own country and Europe as a whole; these events, her continued reading in literature and philosophy, as well as her travels in Greece provided the basis for a continuation of the Beatriz/Laura story, *Amanda: Ein Hexenroman*, completed in 1982 and published a year later. *Amanda* is an even more complex melding of legendary past, present, and future than was *Die Trobadora*, an even more strongly contoured mosaic of the development of women's role in the world, one that stretches from pagan and Christian creation stories through the European peace movement of the late 1970s and early 1980s. Morgner's humor has darkened and tends to the grotesque, but it still pervades the structure of Amanda. Her fantasy continues to fly, not only in the guise of a mythological messenger for Beatriz but also within the world of a group of East Berlin women working for self-realization and centered around Laura. Beatriz is reincarnated as a siren, robbed of her tongue, and put in an owl's cage in the East Berlin Zoo; her role in *Amanda* is to record and interpret Laura's (i.e., ordinary women's) experience, purpose, and progress in the world. The group of women around Laura have help and positive examples from a symbolic world of activist witches, themselves captives of patriarchal powers on the Brocken, the mountain of Walpurgis Night (April 30). Amanda, head of the androgynous witches and Laura's independent-minded other half, leads the witches and a select group of creative men (from Goethe through Marx) in a victorious rebellion against the arch-patriarchs, God and the Devil, who hold them in thrall. This fantastic coup embodies the hope that Morgner still has for the victory of peaceful forces—women and men—working together in the real world. She has found her example in Goethe's re-interpretation of the Pandora myth, where Pandora is the preserver of hope and symbol of humankind's ability to love instead of hate. *Amanda* thus offers a projection into a possible future. Morgner called it "only the first half of the victory" and promised, in her closing words in the book, to supply the rest in the yet-unnamed third volume of her Beatriz/Laura trilogy.

In 1984, as part of her only trip to the United States, Morgner read at the annual Women in German Conference and various universities from her working introduction to Book III and a prepublished trial chapter. That same year, at a literary conference in Solothurn, Switzerland, she presented the chapter that appeared, along with her own introductory works, excerpts from *Amanda*, and an interview, as *Die Hexe im Landhaus: Gespräch in Solothurn* (1984). The following year (1985) Morgner was the recipient of the Hroswitha von Gandersheim Literary Prize for outstanding women authors. In November 1989, the city of Kassel honored her as the first woman to receive their "Literary Prize for Grotesque Humor." These two symbols of literary recognition from the West, along with her Heinrich Mann Prize (1975) and GDR National Prize (1977), place Morgner among the most honored women writers of this century in both Germanies.

While writer in residence at the University of Zurich (1987–1988), Morgner underwent the first of four cancer operations. She lived to see the fall of the Berlin Wall. But in February 1990, she wrote of her frustration that illness had robbed her of the chance to participate actively in her country's peaceful revolution and of her unpreparedness for the extent of the "corruption" and "moral bankruptcy" come to light in the GDR. This, nevertheless, remained her "fatherland" for whose "day after tomorrow" she had hoped and written since its inception in 1949 because, as she continued to believe, "capitalism was and is no alternative for me, or for any woman." She died just weeks after the land she would not leave and the Marxism she would not forsake were voted out of existence. As a writer, Morgner was an *agent provocateur*, whose still relevant goal was to "make not literature but a world" in which women "enter history," and whose unique humor was "a form of contending with life" that belonged to her "very being [and] therefore to [her] writing."

In his *laudatio* for Irmtraud Morgner in Kassel (1989), Walter Jens, honorary President of P.E.N. in Germany, author and professor, compares her to James Joyce and Thomas Mann in her use of allusion and appeal to the intelligence of her readers. English writing has so far brought forth no authoress comparable to Morgner. The work of the sexually explicit Erica Jong, for example, shows nothing of Morgner's insights and writer's talent. The John Barth of *Giles Goatboy* and *Sotweed Factor* or the Thomas Pynchon of *Gravity's Rainbow* approach Morgner's ability to combine outrageous fantasy, the grotesque, humor, and criticism, yet they, too, lack the scope of her vision and, more significantly, the revolutionary potential of her woman's perspective.

Works

Das Signal steht auf Fahrt. Erzählung (1959). *Ein Haus am Rand der Stadt. Roman* (1962). "Notturno. Erzählung" (1964). *Hochzeit in Konstantinopel. Roman* (1964). *Gauklerlegende. Eine Spielfraungeschichte* (1970). *Die wundersamen Reisen Gustav des Weltfahrers. Lügenhafter Roman mit Kommentaren* (1972). "Sündhafte Behauptungen [Annemarie Auer]," "Vexierbild [Günter Kunert]," "Bootskauf [Ludwig Turek]." Porträts (1972). "Das Seil. Erzählung" (1973). "Spielzeit. Erzählung" (1973). Diskussionsbeitrag zur Arbeitsgruppe II "Literatur und Geschichtsbewußtsein" (1974). "Bis man zu dem Kerne zu gelangen das Glück hat. Zufallsbegünstigte Aufzeichnungen über den Oberbauleiter vom Palast der Republik nebst Adjutanten und Ehefrau" (1974). *Leben und Abenteuer der Trobadora Beatriz nach Zeugnissen ihrer Spielfrau Laura. Roman in dreizehn Büchern und sieben Intermezzos* (1974). "Rede auf dem VII. Schriftstellerkongreß der DDR" (1978). [With Sarah Kirsch and Christa Wolf], *Geschlechtertausch* (1980). *Amanda: Ein Hexenroman* (1983). "Nekromantie im Marx-Engels-Auditorium" (1984). "Zeitgemäß unzeitgemäß: Hrotsvit. Dankrede beim Empfang des 'Literaturpreises der Stadt Gandersheim zum Gedenken an die erste deutsche Dichterin, Hroswitha von Gandersheim, die vor 1000 Jahren ihr Lebenswerk vollendete'" (1986). "Die Schöne und das Tier" (1988), and "Guten Morgen, Du Schöner" (1990): Excerpts from the not yet published "Die Cherubinischen Wandersfrauen. Ein apokrypher Salmanroman" (Book III of Morgner's trilogy).

Translation: Achberger, Karen and Fritz, "The Twelfth Book of *Die Trobadora*, 'Gospel of Velaska, Which Laura Reads as a Revelation on the Day of the Trobadora Beatriz's Burial,' by Irmtraud Morgner." *New German Critique*, 15 (Fall, 1978): 121–146.

Sheila Johnson

François Bertaut, Dame Langlois de Motteville
ca. 1615–1689

Born 1615 or 1621, France
Died December 29, 1689, Paris
Genre(s): memoir
Language(s): French

Confidante to a queen and one of the most popular of the numerous memoirists of the French seventeenth century, Françoise Bertaut was born either in 1615 or 1621. Both dates are found in her own accounts. She was the daughter of Pierre Bertaut, the secretary to Henry IV and Louis XIII and the nephew of French poet Jean Bertaut. Her mother, Louise Bessin de Mathonville, spent her youth with Spanish relatives in Spain and was appointed to the service of the young Spanish princess Anne of Austria when the latter wed Louis XIII.

Louise was a loyal confidante to the queen. She also gave her seven-year-old daughter Françoise to the service, although soon after mother and daughter were forced to retire to their family estates in Normandy. Cardinal Richelieu had exiled them to separate the Queen from Mme Bertaut, who was thought to be sending Anne's secret messages to Spain. There, from 1628–1639, Louise carefully groomed her daughter for eventual royal service, fostering her memory and love of Queen Anne and furnishing a living example of the religious piety she felt necessary for such service. In 1639, she wed Françoise to an old, childless, but rich widower of eighty, Nicholas Langlois, Seigneur de Motteville, who conveniently died two years later. His death left Françoise free to answer Anne's recall to service, a call that followed closely upon the death of Louis XIII and his cardinal-minister.

From the moment of her reunion with Anne in 1643, Madame de Motteville devoted herself body and soul to the Queen Regent. Always possessed of the Queen's confidence and favor, she avowed her intention to write her memoirs almost immediately after her return. She proceeded with the Queen's knowledge and approval, recording court events and, in fact, the history of the Queen's Regency, with a much admired balance and a quiet self-effacement.

Soon after the Queen's death on January 20, 1666, Madame de Motteville retired from court to a house in the Rue Saint-Dominique. Her visits and sojourns at the Convent de Sainte-Marie de Chaillet, where her sister was Mother Superior, became more and more frequent as she grew older. Ironically, the woman who had spent much of her life recording her memories ended her life without the ability to recall them. Gradually lapsing into complete senility, she died in Paris in 1689.

Madame de Motteville's memoirs have often been justly admired. "Ce que j'ai mis sur le papier," she wrote, "je l'ai vu et je l'ai ouï." She emerges as an intelligent, indefatigable witness, writing without passion but with great simplicity. The piety instilled in her by her mother not only accounts for her balance but also for her love of moralizing, which surfaces throughout the book. In her distinctive, always lucid style, she manages to capture the characters of those around her with great immediacy and to fill her book with vignettes of amazing power.

Never bitter, though often melancholy, the memoirs may well have achieved their balanced tone through careful rewriting. A partial copy of what appears an early draft does exist. Here less balanced judgments and a more spontaneous flow of thoughts and reflections are to be had. But whatever the circumstances of production, the memoirs as they stand are a fascinating record of their period. Their touching and faithful portrayal of the Queen Regent, a portrait that is always fair but also always sensitive to the pressures surrounding the Regency, give us a unique document—the story of a feminine regency as recorded by a feminine historian.

Works

Mémoires pour servir à l'histoire d'Anne d'Autriche [Memoirs to Serve as the History of Anne of Austria] (1878).

Glenda McLeod

(Jean) Iris Murdoch
1919–

Born July 15, 1919, Dublin, Ireland
Genre(s): novel, philosophy
Language(s): English

Born of Protestant Anglo-Irish parents in Dublin, Iris Murdoch grew up in London but has retained an active interest in Ireland, especially as setting for some of her novels. She studied classics, ancient history, and philosophy at Oxford before World War II, worked during the war for the British government, and later helped refugees for the United Nations. She continued her study of philosophy at Cambridge after the war and subsequently became a fellow at Oxford. She married John Bayley, poet, critic, novelist, and also a fellow at Oxford, in 1956.

In addition to specialized papers on linguistic analysis and existentialism, she has written a number of less technical works on ethics, aesthetics, and similar moral issues, including *Sartre: Romantic Rationalist* (1953), *The Sovereignty of Good* (1970), *The Fire and the Sun: Why Plato Banished the Artists* (1977), and *Acastos* (1986), Platonic dialogues. Though she has tried to keep her philosophic work distinct from her literary output (over twenty novels as well as stories and plays), her philosophic bent is immediately evident in her fiction.

Murdoch's fiction is characterized by a remarkable sense of humor, particularly wit and word play, farce (including wild chases), burlesque, dependence on split-second timing, and unforeseen plot twists. Her sense of parody and satire is less obvious, but her balance among various comic modes, including gentle satiric thrusts, combined as these are with serious, even polemical concerns, makes her work considerably more complex than it first appears.

She has repeatedly stated that she identifies with the tradition of George Eliot. Though she has acknowledged Henry James's influence, she has also stated that she prefers the non-Jamesian "open" novel (a spontaneous gathering of eccentric characters engaged in casual, seemingly uncontrolled activities), a claim not wholly borne out by her tightly structured books. She has used the term "transcendental realism" (in her essay "Against Dryness: A Polemical Sketch") to apply to her fiction, a term suggesting an initial acceptance of conventional concepts of plot, character, and setting with a subsequent explosion of absurd, wildly outrageous, and richly unconventional occurrences and "messy" characters. Despite the seemingly anarchic tone and nature of her novels, Murdoch is evidently pessimistic about transient humanity's chances of survival in a formless, directionless universe.

Her fiction, consequently, focuses on individuals who are required by some circumstance (possibly violent or absurd) to ponder the nature of personal freedom and commitment. They must then realize that they can know neither love nor freedom unless they accept the radical "contingency" and ultimate pointlessness of existence as prerequisite to relations with others. Murdoch's first novel, *Under the Net* (1954), for example, offers a protagonist, Jake Donaghue, who discovers the sheer joy and unknowable wonder of life through some wildly comic adventures involving continual misunderstanding of other people. *The Flight from the Enchanter* (1956), a more complex, original novel, contrasts the fascinating but amoral

Mischa Fox, who uses other people, with Rosa Keepe, who barely escapes his influence.

The Bell (1958), commonly considered (with *A Severed Head,* 1961) the best of Murdoch's earlier works, follows a variety of ordinary characters who retreat to a monastery to escape human limitations and failure, especially at love. Unable to live either in the world or out of it, they individually work out their destinies. *A Severed Head* is a remarkably effective comic account of the same efforts to understand the nature of human freedom; one of Murdoch's familiar clumsy male protagonists, Martin Lynch-Gibbon, reluctantly learns about love and sex in a series of wildly incongruous sexual couplings.

Following *A Severed Head,* Murdoch published seven novels in quick succession. *An Unofficial Rose* (1962) is a family chronicle about an elderly man's reflections on his past and his desires for his son's future; *The Unicorn* (1963) is a slight though heavily philosophical work concerned with the ambiguity of relationships, especially sexual ones; *The Italian Girl* (1964) is a short, more Gothic work set in a Scottish household; *The Red and the Green* (1965) is a historical work set in Dublin during the 1916 Easter uprising; *The Time of the Angels* (1966), Murdoch's "God is dead" novel closely related to *The Unicorn* in its concern with metaphysical concepts, is a fascinating, sensational, Gothic exploration into the nature of evil; *The Nice and the Good* (1968) is a return to her earlier concern with the conflicts inherent in spiritual and sexual love; and *Bruno's Dream* (1969) is a somewhat surrealistic account of an old man's dying thoughts as he feebly attempts to understand the world and death.

In the 1970s, Murdoch continued her rapid production, with *A Fairly Honourable Defeat* (1970) an appropriate name for the position many of her characters accept in their metaphysical quest. Though this novel breaks no new ground, she is more detailed in her evident knowledge of cuisines and cultural allusions, and this and several of her subsequent works are more expansive in scope and bulk. *An Accidental Man* (1971) focuses on the contrast between the search for love and the search for power through a kind of parallel novel-within-a-novel. *The Black Prince* (1973) is more experimental in its obsessive handling of a middle-aged man's lust for a twenty-year-old woman and with other sexual pairings reminiscent of *An Accidental Man. The Sacred and Profane Love Machine* (1974) is also about a man obsessed, in this case with his two loves, his wife (the sacred) and his mistress (the profane); this book, by far Murdoch's most violent, raises numerous moral questions but resolves few of them satisfactorily. The protagonist in *A Word Child* (1975) discovers that his adultery has been indirectly responsible for the deaths of two others and that his past is returning to haunt him; desperate to touch and love others, he eventually tries to purge his guilt by contacting the man he cuckolded.

The more thoughtful *Henry and Cato* (1976) focuses on two men who attempt individually to reconcile private impulses, especially the need for love: one, a self-exile in the United States until his brother's death, returns to England and echoes of his earlier life; the other, his boyhood friend turned Anglican priest, wrestles with forbidden love. Both men are complicated, both have muddled emotional lives, and both learn about pure evil in the forms of "fallen angels" who tempt them. *The Sea, The Sea* (1978) has been compared by Margaret Drabble to *The Tempest* and also to Homer; it deals with a theatre director who retires to the seashore but who slowly entraps his old circle of friends in his sexual obsessiveness.

The 1980s and 1990s have shown a continuation of Murdoch's prolific productivity, with no diminution of her philosophical interests but with greater abstraction in characterization. The first word of *Nuns and Soldiers* (1980) is "Wittgenstein," who has frequently been invoked in analyses of Murdoch's work; the speaker, dying on Christmas eve, hosts an entourage of friends who later intrude possessively between would-be lovers, the widow, and one of the friends. *The Philosopher's Pupil* (1983) presents an overly didactic allegorical struggle between good and evil, even to the point of identifying the narrator by an initial; similarly, *The Good Apprentice* (1985) is both allegorical and muddled, though it is much more emphatic about the protagonist's suffering through personal irresponsibility toward a friend.

Murdoch's books have steadily grown longer and more turgid, though with greater concern with her character's experiential growth and breadth. She has often written about her characters' sexuality, even promiscuity, and she has dealt with such sexual taboos as incest. As her books have grown more abstract and philosophical, they have also grown less interesting as fiction, with recent characters less memorable than those of the 1960s.

Yet she remains a fertile writer, with undiminished vigor and productivity, with meticulous detail, and above all with dense, austere, unromantic, and pessimistic perspectives on her characters' lives. These characters are not tragic, just pathetic or terrible, and comedy helps the reader to see how enslaved they are, trapped by the ideas Murdoch forces them to bear. At her best she is both entertaining and intellectually challenging; at her worst she is abstract to the point of obscurity. She deals primarily with concepts such as love, freedom, and power, and the "morality" she offers through her characters is limited in part by their own limitations, in part by the opposition of a host of authority figures, but almost always by some form of love and moral commitment.

Works

Sartre: Romantic Rationalist (1953, 1980). *Under the Net* (1954). *The Flight from the Enchanter* (1956). *The Sandcastle* (1957). *The Bell* (1958). *A Severed Head* (1961; as play, with J.B. Priestley, 1964). *An Unofficial Rose* (1962). *The Unicorn* (1963). *The Italian Girl* (1964; as play, with J. Saunders, 1968). *The Red and the Green* (1965). *The Time of the Angels* (1966). *The Nice and the Good* (1968). *Bruno's Dream* (1969). *A Fairly Honourable Defeat* (1970). *The Sovereignty of Good* (1970). *The Servants and the Snow* (1970). *An Accidental Man* (1971). *The Three Arrows* (1972). *The Black Prince* (1973). *The Sacred and Profane Love Machine* (1974). *A Word Child* (1975). *Henry and Cato* (1976). *The Sea, the Sea* (1978). *The Fire and the Sun: Why Plato Banished the Artists* (1977). *A Year of Birds* (1978). *Nuns and Soldiers* (1980). *Art and Eros* (1980). *The Philosopher's Pupil* (1983). *The Good Apprentice* (1985). *Acastos* (1986). *The Message to the Planet* (1991). *Metaphysics as a Guide to Morals* (1994). *The Green Knight* (1994). *Jackson's Dilemma* (1995).

Paul Schlueter

Vera Mutafčieva
1929–

Born March 28, 1929, Sofia, Bulgaria
Genre(s): novel, short story, criticism, film script, scholarly monograph
Language(s): Bulgarian

Mutafčieva became a novelist when she was a well-known scholar with more than fifty publications in Bulgarian and Ottoman history. The daughter of Petur Mutafčiev, one of Bulgaria's great historians, she is on her way to becoming one of Bulgaria's foremost novelists. Born, raised, and educated in Sofia, Mutafčieva graduated from the University of Sofia in 1951. She worked as a researcher at the Institute of History and the Institute of Balkan Studies of the Bulgarian Academy of Sciences and in 1978 received her doctorate in history. She has also served as director of the Center for Ancient Languages and of the Bulgarian Research Institute in Vienna. She is presently affiliated with the Institute of Literature in Sofia.

In 1960 her first popular historical works appeared, and in following years she published her first fiction with the series *Geroična letopis* (1961; Heroic Chronicle). *Letopis na smutnoto vreme* (1966–1967; Chronicle of the Time of Troubles) presents a vivid description of the Bulgarian–Ottoman time of troubles of the second half of the eighteenth century. The striking depiction of the forays, strife, and anarchy created by local freebooters is blended with the main trends of the sociopolitical struggles. Mutafčieva successfully integrates real historical events and personalities with imaginary episodes and figures to create authentic literary characters. *Slučajet D'em* (1967; The Dzem Case) is one of Mutafčieva's most successful novels. Praised by critics, it has been translated into many languages. It treats an East–West episode of the fifteenth century, the fate of an exile caught in "the great games" that states play in history. Dzem becomes a pawn in the conflict between the Ottoman Empire and the Western powers, and the Balkans are caught in the middle. In *Ricarjat* (1970; The Knight), *Alkiviad Malki* (1975; Alcibiades the Little), *Alkiviad Veliki* (1976; Alcibiades the Great), and other novels, Mutafčieva uses the past to make a point about the present. Mutafčieva evaluates each historical epoch, personality, or idea from an historical perspective.

Using her artistic skills and a psychohistorical approach, Mutafčieva analyzes each of her heroes/villains in relations to both their time and ours. Being a scholarly novelist, Mutafčieva paints objective pictures of the past and discovers in events, personalities, and ideas many common elements throughout history.

Works

Geroična letopis (1961). *Goljamata borba* (1961). *Kŭrdzaliisko verme* (1962). *Povest za dobroto i zloto* (1963). *Da se znae* (1964). *Slučajet D'em* (1967). *Eseta* (1969). *I Klio e muza* (1969). *Poslednite Šišmanovci* (1969, 1975). *Ricarjat* (1970). *Geroika. Ocerci za Kozlodui* (1972). *Procesŭt. Povest* (1972). *Belot na dve rŭce* (1973). *Bogomili. Istoriceski razkaz za deca* (1974; 1976). *Železni stupki. Istoriceski razkaz za deca* (1974). *Povest s dvoino duno* (1974). *Alkiviad Malki* (1975). *Alkiviad Veliki* (1976). *Kniga za Sofronii* (1978). *Bombite. Roman* (1985). *Sŭedinenieto pravi silata. Roman* (1985).

Philip Shashko

Christiane Benedikte Eugenie Naubert
1756–1819

a.k.a. Verfasser des Walther von Montbarry; Verfasser der Alme Verfasserin des Walther von Montbarry, Fontanges, et al.
Born September 13, 1756, Leipzig, Germany
Died January 12, 1819, Leipzig
Genre(s): novel, novella, fairy tale
Language(s): German

Christiane Benedikte Naubert was the most prolific German woman writer of her time and one of the earliest writers of historical novels and romances in German.

Naubert's father, Dr. Johann Ernst Hebenstreit, who died when his daughter was only a year old, was a distinguished medical professor at the university in Leipzig. Under the guidance of her stepbrother, also later a professor, she received an unusually good education for a woman of her day; she studied philosophy and history, learned Latin and Greek, and then taught herself Italian, English, and French. In her early twenties she wrote her first novel, the sentimental *Heerfort und Klärchen*, and published it—as she did all the rest until nearly the end of her life—anonymously. Her second book was devoted to a historical character, Emma, daughter of Charlemagne (1785). It was sufficiently successful to encourage her to publish more in this genre, for in the next year three new works appeared in six volumes. Naubert wrote rapidly, probably with no opportunity to revise. In 1788 she published five new titles in nine volumes, including three of her best known: *Geschichte der Gräfin Thekla von Thurn*, set during the Thirty Years War (2 v.), *Hermann von Unna*, about the secret tribunals of the fifteenth century (2 v., translated into French in 1801, English in 1794, and Dutch in 1802), and *Konradin von Schwaben* (2 v.), a story about the house of Hohenstaufen. In 1789 she began a five-volume series of "new fairy tales of the Germans" and came out with three new novels. This was her most prolific period; in the ten years from 1786 to 1795, starting when she was thirty, she wrote 37 books in 52 volumes, mostly historical romances. Benedikte Naubert was one of Germany's earliest professional women writers.

But her name then was still Hebenstreit. Not until 1797, when she was forty-one years old, did she marry for the first time. Her husband, Lorenz Holderieder, a merchant and estate owner in Naumburg, died after four years. She married again, another respected merchant, Johann Georg Naubert. The periods of her marriages are times of silence, with little or nothing published. As she aged, she suffered from weak eyes and deafness and thus wrote her last works by dictation.

Some of her books are among the best eighteenth-century novels by women. They demonstrate a good understanding of human nature, good use of language, and an unexpected sense of humor. Not surprisingly, they also show weaknesses that are common with rapid writing: repetition, diffuseness, overreliance on stock situations that are intended to thrill the readers. Still, Naubert attempted in her historical novels to use her sources fully; she even included footnotes to her texts. Most of the subjects are from German history, especially the Middle Ages, with occasional excursions into English history or other more exotic settings. Because all her abundant work until 1817 was published anonymously, readers were left to guess who this unusual author might be; they invariably mistook her gender.

Works

Heerfort und Klärchen; etwas für empfindsame Seelen, [Heerfort and Clara, Something for Sentimental Souls], 2 vols. (1779). *Geschichte Emmas, Tochter Karls des Grossen, und seines Geheimschreibers Eginhard* [The Story of Emma, Daughter of

Charlemagne, and His Scribe Eginhard], 2 vols. (1785). *Die Ruinen* [The Ruins], 3 vols. (1786). *Amalgunde, Königin von Italien; oder Das Märchen von der Wunderquelle. Eine Sage aus den Zeiten Theodorichs des Grossen* [Amalgunde, Queen of Italy; or the Fairytale of the Miraculous Well. A Tale from the Time of Theoderich the Great], 2 vols. (1786). *Walther von Montbarry, Grossmeister des Tempelordens* [Walter de Monbary, Grand Master of the Knights Templars], 2 vols. (1786; English tr. 1803). *Die Amtmännin von Hohenweiler: eine wirkliche Geschichte aus Familienpapieren gezogen* [The Magistrate's Wife at Hohenweiler, a True Story Drawn from Family Papers] (1787). *Geschichte der Gräfin Thekla von Thurn; oder Scenen aus dem dreyssigjährigen Kriege* [The Story of Countess Thekla von Thurn, or Scenes from the Thirty Years War] (1788). *Hermann von Unna; eine Geschichte aus den Zeiten der Vehmgerichte* [Hermann of Unna, a Series of Adventures of the Fifteenth Century, in Which the Proceedings of the Secret Tribunal . . . Are delineated . . .] (1788; English tr. 1794). *Konradin von Schwaben oder Geschichte des unglücklichen Enkels Kaiser Friedrichs des Zweiten* [Conradin of Swabia, or the Story of the Unhappy Grandson of Emperor Friedrich II] (1788). *Elfriede, oder Opfer väterlicher Vorurtheile* [Elfriede, or the Victim of a Father's Prejudices] (1788). *Pauline Frankini oder Täuschung der Leidenschaft und Freuden der Liebe* [Pauline Frankini or Delusion of Passion and Joys of Love] (1788). *Elisabeth, Erbin von Toggenburg: oder Geschichte der Frauen von Sargans in der Schweiz* [Elisabeth, Heiress of Toggenburg, or the Story of the Women of Sargans in Switzerland] (1789). *Emmy Reinolds; oder Thorheiten der Groen und Kleinen* [Emmy Reinolds, or Follies of Great and Small] (1789). *Hatto, Bischof von Mainz: Eine Legende des zehnten Jahrhunderts* [Hatto, Bishop of Mainz, a Legend of the Tenth Century] (1798). *Neue Volksmärchen der Deutschen* [New Fairy Tales of the Germans] (1789–1792). *Alfons von Dülmen; oder Geschichte Kaiser Philipps und seiner Tochter. Aus den ersten Zeiten der heimlichen Gerichte* [Alf von Duelmen, or the History of the Emperor Philip, and His Daughters] (1790; English tr., 1794). *Barbara Blomberg, Vorgebliche Maitresse Kaiser Karls des fünften. Eine Originalgeschichte in zwei Theilen* [Barbara Blomberg, Alleged Mistress of Emperor Charles IV, an Original Story in Two Parts] (1790). *Brunilde. Eine Anekdote aus dem bürgerlichen Leben des dreizehnten Jahrhunderts* [Brunilde, an Anecdote from Bourgeois Life of the 13th Century] (1790). *Geschichte des Lord Fitzherbert und seiner Freunde,*

oder die verkannte Liebe [Story of Lord Fitzherbert and His Friends, or Misunderstood Love] (1790). *Merkwürdige Begebenheiten der gräflichen Familie von Wallis* [Remarkable Events of the Family of the Count of Wallis] (1790). *Werner, Graf von Bernburg* [Werner, Count of Bernburg] (1790). *Gustav Adolf IV. aus Schauenburgischem Stamme* [Gustav Adolf IV of the Clan of Schauenburg] (1791). *Geschichte Heinrich Courtlands; oder, Selbstgeschafne Leiden* [History of Heinrich Courtland, or Selfmade Sorrows] (1791). *Edwy und Elgiva, oder die Wunder des heiligen Dunstan, eine altenglische geschichte* [Edwy and Elgiva, or the Miracle of Saint Dunstan, and Old English Story] (1791). *Gebhard Truchse von Waldburg, Churfürst von Cöln, oder die astrologischen Fürsten* [Gebhard Lord High Steward of Waldburg, Elector of Cologne, or the Astrological Princes] (1791). *Graf von Rosenberg, oder das enthüllte Verbrechen. Eine Geschichte aus der letzten Zeit des dreyssigjährigen Kriegs* [Count von Rosenberg, or the Discovered Crime, a Story from the Time of the Thirty Years War] (1791). *Lord Heinrich Holland, Herzog von Exeter; oder Irre geleitete Gromuth, eine Begebenheit aus dem Mittelalter von England* [Lord Henry Holland, Duke of Exeter, or Magnanimity Mislead, an Event from the English Middle Ages] (1791). *Marie Fürst, oder das Alpenmädchen* [Marie Fürst, or the Alps Girl] (1791). *Philippe von Geldern; oder Geschichte Selims, des Sohns Amurat* [Phillippe von Geldern, or the Story of Selim, Son of Amurat] (1792). *Konrad und Siegfried von Fehtwangen, Grossmeister des deutschen Ordens* [Conrad and Siegfried von Fehtwangen, Grand Masters of the German Knights] (1792). *Miss Luise Fox, oder Reise einer jungen Engländerin durch einige Gegenden von Deutschland* [Miss Luise Fox, or Travels of a Young Englishwoman Through Some Parts of Germany] (1792). *Ulrich Holzer, Bürgermeister in Wien* [Ulrich Holzer, Mayor of Vienna] (1792). *Lucinde; oder, Herrn Simon Godwins medicinische Leiden. Nach dem Englischen* [Lucinde, or Mr. Simon Godwin's Medical Sufferings. From the English] (1793). *Heinrich von Plauen und seine Neffen, Ritter des deutschen Ordens. Der wahren Geschichte getreu bearbeitet* [Heinrich von Plauen and His Nephews, Knights of the German Order, Faithfully Told According to the True Story] (1793). *Alma; oder Ägyptische Mährchen* [Alma, or Egyptian Fairytales] (1793–1797). *Walther von Stadion; oder Geschichte Herzog Leopolds von Öesterreich und seiner Kriegsgefährten* [Walter von Stadion, or the Story of Duke Leopold of Austria and His War Comrades] (1794). *Sitten und Launen der Grossen, Ein Cabinet* von *Familienbildern* [Manners and Moods of the Great, a Cabinet of Family Scenes] (1794). *Der Bund des armen Konrads, Getreue Schilderung einiger merkwürdiger Auftritte aus den Zeiten der Bauernkriege des 16. Jahrhunderts* [Poor Conrad's Alliance, True Description of Some Remarkable Scenes from the Time of the 16th-century Peasant Wars] (1795). *Friedrich der Siegreiche, Churfürst von der Pfalz; der Marc Aurel des Mittelalters. Frey nach der Geschichte bearbeitet* [Friedrich the Victorious, Elector from the Pfalz, the Marcus Aurelius of the Middle Ages, Freely Told According to History] (1795). *Vellada; ein Zauberroman* [Vellada, a Novel of Magic] (1795). *Joseph Mendez Pinto. Eine jüdische Geschichte* [Joseph Mendez Pinto, a Jewish Story] (1802). *Cornelie, oder die Geheimnisse des Grabes* [Cornelie or the Secrets of the Grave] (1803). *Eudoxia, Gemahlin Theodosius der Zweiten. Eine Geschichte des 5. Jahrhunderts* [Eudoxia, Wife of Theodosius the Second, a Story from the Fifth Century] (1805). *Fontanges, oder das Schicksal der Mutter und Tochter, eine Geschichte aus den Zeiten Ludwigs XIV* [Fontanges, or the Fate of a Mother and Daughter, a Story from the Times of Louis XIV] (1805). *Die Gräfin von Frondsberg, aus dem Hause Löwenstein, eine vaterländische Geschichte aus den Zeiten des Mittelalters* [The Countess of Frondsberg, from the House of Löwenstein, a National Story from the Middle Ages] (1806). *Heitere Träume in kleinen Erzählungen* [Cheerful Dreams in Little Stories] (1806). *Lioba und Zilia* (1806). *Wanderungen der Phantasie in die Gebiete des Wahren* [Fantasy's Wanderings in the Territories of the True] (1806). *Attilas Schwert oder die Azimunterinnen* [Attila's Sword, or the Azimunter Women] (1808). *Die Irrungen* [The Errors] (1808). *Elisabeth Lezkau, oder die Bürgermeisterin* [Elisabeth Lezkau or the Mayor's Wife] (1808). *Azaria. Eine Dichtung der Vorwelt* [Azaria, a Story of the Past] (1814). *Rosalba* (1817). *Alexis und Luise. Eine Badegeschichte* [Alexis and Luise, a Story at a Bath] (1819). *Der kurze Mantel, und Ottilie; zwei Volksmärchen* [The Short Cloak, and Ottilia, Two Fairytales] (1819). *Turmalin und Lazerta* (1820).

Translation: Translation of "The Short Cloak" in *Bitter Healing: Anthology of German Women Authors from Pietism to Romanticism* (Lincoln, 1989).

Ruth P. Dawson

Ada Negri
1870–1945

Born 1870, Lodi, Italy
Died 1945, Milan
Genre(s): poetry, novel, short story, translation
Language(s): Italian

Negri was born in a working-class family: her mother labored in a textile factory 12 hours a day, her grandmother, who had once been a personal maid, worked as a doorkeeper in a rich family mansion. Negri studied to become a teacher to escape what she described as the humiliating condition of the serving class. From 1888, she taught at Motta Visconti, near Pavia, and began to publish poems in *Illustrazione popolare* of Milan. Her first collection of poetry, *Fatalità* (Fate), came out in 1892 and made her suddenly famous. From then until the end of the Second World War, she published many works of poetry, novels, and short stories. The Fascist Party tried to appropriate her fame by making her a member of the Italian Academy. She officially withdrew from the party at the beginning of the Second World War.

In *Fatalità*, Negri describes the fog-bound industrial centers of northern Italy, their industrial plants, their desolate workers' districts, the humble interiors of people leading repressed, hopeless lives. The volume appeared in a period of great social unrest, characterized by strikes, by demonstrations violently suppressed, and by the women's emancipation movement. In poems, such as "Fire in the Mine," "Strike," "Unemployed," "End of the Strike," which are contained in that volume as well as in the collections *Tempeste* (1896; Storms) and *Esilio* (1914; Exile), Negri spoke to her country with the voice of the oppressed working classes and told of their everyday feelings, their aspirations, their sufferings. That was also the age of Parnassian taste in literature; by contrast, Negri's descriptions were vigorous and straightforward, and they bore that unmistakable ring of authenticity that only personal experience can give.

Equally successful are the two volumes of short stores *Le solitarie* (1917; The Lonely Ones) and *Sorelle* (1929; Sisters). Here the lonely and drab existence of disadvantaged women is described with clear vision and in unimpeachable style. Many believe her best work to be *Stella mattutina* (1921; Morning Star), in which her own painful childhood and adolescence are recollected with great delicacy and lucidity. In some works, such as *Il libro di Mara* (1919; Mara's Book), *I canti dell'isola* (1925; The Songs of the Island), *Vespertina* (1930; Evening Star), and *Il dono* (1936;

The Gift), Negri makes concessions to the literary fashions of her day, to Giovanni Pascoli's sounding of rare inner experiences and to Gabriele D'Annunzio's energetic exaltation in the sunny Mediterranean landscape. Other works, published throughout the thirties and the early war years, show a progressive adherence to conventional middle-class values. Her new interest in religion and mysticism was manifest in her last volume, *Oltre* (Beyond), published posthumously in 1946, a hagiographic life of St. Catherine of Siena.

In retrospect, Negri's value can be clearly seen in her natural narrative vein and in her literary grace. Historically, she marks the first entrance of the working class into Italian letters.

Works

Fatalità (1892; tr. A.M. Von Blomberg, 1898). *Tempeste*, from the Italian of Ada Negri (1896; tr. Isabella M. Debarbieri, 1905). *Maternità* (1904). *Dal profondo* (1910). *Esilio* (1914). *Le solitarie* (1917). *Orazioni* (1918). *Il libro di Mara* (1919). *Stella mattutina* (1921; tr. Anne Day, 1930). *Finestre alte* (1923). *I canti dell'isola* (1925). *Le strade* (1929). *Sorelle* (1929). *Vespertina* (1930). *Di giorno in giorno* (1932). *Il dono* (1936). *Erba sul sagrato* (1939). *Fons amoris (1939–1943)* (1946). *Oltre* (1946).

Rinaldina Russell

Margarita Nelken
1896–1968

Born July 5, 1896, Madrid, Spain
Died March 9, 1968, Mexico City, Mexico
Genre(s): art criticism, literary criticism, essay
Language(s): Spanish, French

In 1931, Margarita Nelken was heralded on the pages of *El Socialista* (organ of the Socialist Workers' Party of Spain) as a representative of the new type of Spanish woman because, according to her interviewer, she combined her literary and artistic talent with political activism. Art critic, journalist, and feminist, Nelken was one of a handful of Spanish women elected to the Spanish Parliament during the Republic (1931–1936). A Socialist, she was the only woman elected in the three elections held during that period. Among her books and articles, her two most significant contributions to the "woman question" in Spain are: *La condición social de la mujer en España* (1922; Women's Condition in Spain) and *Las escritoras*

españolas (1930; Spanish Women Writers).

Margarita Nelken was born in Madrid in 1896 and from a very early age trained as a painter. She studied painting in Paris with Eduardo Chicharro and Maria Blanchard. In 1914 she participated in a collective show in Vienna, and in 1916 she had an individual show in the Sala Parés in Barcelona. Her paintings were also shown in Bilbao at the Sala de Artistas Vascos (the Basque Artists Gallery). By 1911, at the age of fifteen, she was already contributing articles on painting to *The Studio*, an English journal, and to the French *Le Mercure de France*. She had to give up painting for fear of going blind. Art, though, would always be her livelihood. Before the Civil War she was an art critic and professor at the Prado Museum. After the war, in her Mexican exile, she wrote many books on art criticism and was one of the art critics of the Mexico City daily, *El Excelsior*.

Deeply affected by the German Revolution, Nelken became interested in social issues and feminism. In 1922, she published *La condición social de la mujer en España* which, from the outset, was received as a revolutionary call for the development of feminism in Spain. In it she argued that women were exploited in every aspect of their lives: the workplace, the home, their sexual relationships, the legal system, and their education. She extensively discusses comparable worth, the social ramifications of a negligible education for women, sexual hypocrisy, the Church's emotional exploitation of women, the lack of sexual education, the problem of illegitimate children, prostitution, single motherhood, and the need for divorce. This book was perceived to be groundbreaking because she did not isolate each problem and treat it as a single issue. Rather, she subsumed all of the different issues under the general category of exploitation. Her male contemporaries on the Right and the Left were shocked and upset by this book. The Right was scandalized by its tough anticlerical line. The Left was hurt because she did not exclude it from her critique. She often criticizes the Socialist Workers' Party for not paying attention to the woman question when, she argues, that women's oppression originates in the exploitation of women's labor. Her argument is that feminism can only be triumphant if the Left realizes that feminism is essential to its struggle and if the Spanish movement becomes cosmopolitan and links up with the women's movements in other countries. The importance of Margarita Nelken's position is that it proposes the unity of socialism and feminism in Spain.

Paradoxically, Margarita Nelken was against women's suffrage. Her analysis of the Spanish situation led her to conclude that women in Spain were not ready for political intervention. Already a deputy in the Parliament in 1931, she did not attend the session of the Cortes that was to vote on women's suffrage. Spanish women won the right to vote on that day.

Las escritoras españolas is a landmark book. Writing within a male-dominated literary tradition in which women writers were either considered exceptions to the rule or where copious lists of women writers were concocted in order to prove the existence of women writers, she chooses to establish the idea of a women's culture. For Nelken, there has always existed in Spain a tradition of women's writing and a strong participation of women in the world of culture. She argues that ecclesiastical censorship was always harder on women's writing than on men's, but that this censorship served as a stimulus for women writers. In fact, what she does in this book is establish a corpus and a tradition of women writers. She discovers that mysticism is the dominant theme of women's writing. In opposition to other contemporary women writers who spoke of the constraints placed on them by male writers, Nelken never mentions the difficulties of women writing within the male literary tradition. Rather, she chooses to set up an alternative and separate women's culture in opposition to the male literary tradition.

During the Civil War she was active in the defense of Madrid, participated in the International Congress of Antifascist Writers, was a reporter for several journals, and continued to lecture on art. She was first exiled in the Soviet Union, where her son Santiago died at the battle of Stalingrad, and then went on to Mexico where she died in 1968.

Works

Glosaario (Obras y artistas) (1917). *La condición social de la mujer en España* (1922). *La trampa del arenal* (1923). "La aventura de Roma" (1923). "Mi suicidio" (1924). "Una historia de adulterio" (1924). "Pitimini 'etoile'" (1924). "El viaje a Paris" (1925). *En torno a nosotras* (1927). *Tres tipos de virgenes* (1929). *Las escritoras españolas* (1930). *La mujer ante las Cortes Constituyentes* (1931). *Ramon y Cajal. La mujer: conversaciones e ideario* (1933). *Por qué hicimos la Revolución* (1935). *Las torres del Kremlin* (1943). *Historia del hombre que tuvo el mundo en la mano. J.W. von Goethe* (1943). *Los judíos en la cultura hispánica* (194?). *Primer frente* (1944). *Carlos Orozco Romero* (1951). *Escultura Mexicana contemporanea* (1951). *Historia gráfica del arte occidental* (1953). *Ignacio Asúsolo* (1962). *El expresionismo en la plástica mexicana de hoy* (1964). *Un mundo etereo: la pintura de Lucinda Urrusti* (1976).

Alda Blanco

Božena Němcová
1820–1862

Born February 4, 1820, Vienna, Austria
Died January 20, 1862, Prague
Genres: short story, novel
Language(s): Czech

Němcová was a leading figure in late Czech romanticism and the first eminent Czech woman writer. She is still considered to be one of the most significant Czech prose writers, and her novel *Babička* (1855; Grandmother) is a classic of Czech literature and one of the most frequently translated works in Czech.

Her personal life was tragic. The illegitimate daughter of household servants to the nobility in Vienna, she spent her early childhood with her grandmother in the Czech village of Ratibořice, which later became the inspiration for her most famous novel. At the age of seventeen, she married Josef Němec, a Czech customs official, who was much older than she. Although the young and beautiful Němcová became involved in the intellectual life of Prague and counted among her friends Karel Havlíček, Josef Frič, J.E. Purkyně, Václav Nebeský, and many other literary and cultural leaders, her married life became increasingly chaotic and unhappy. Her husband was periodically accused of illegal political activities by the Austrian government, and this persecution led to frequent changes of residence and a low income for the family. After a hard life, Němcová died at the age of forty two, poor, sick, and lonely. In contrast, her literary works convey a warm sympathy for humanity and faith in the goodness of Nature and God. As a disciple of Rousseau, Němcová sensed a natural harmony that transcends all social and economic distinctions.

Like her friend Karel Erben, an important Czech poet, Němcová began her literary career by collecting Czech folk tales and incorporating folk themes into her work, as in *Obrázek vesnický* (1847; Picture of the Village). Although her early stories are often sentimental and didactic, Němcová developed the narrative technique that she was to use in *Babička*.

Critics generally agree that the classic *Babička* transcends her other works. In this novel, Němcová combines autobiographical details from her childhood (the central character is obviously modeled on her own grandmother), with a sense of the universal. The figure of the grandmother is often associated with the Slavic ideal of motherhood, but in a larger sense, she represents a maternal, natural order of things, full of beauty and goodness.

Although Němcová continued to deal with similarly ethnographic materials, from *Pohorská vesnice* (1856; The Village in the Foothills) to her last tales, she was never able to repeat the artistic harmony she had achieved in *Babička*.

Němcová's literary accomplishment served as a model for future writers, and, since her time, Czech women writers have exerted a strong influence on the development of the Czech novel, an influence that is notably lacking in other Czech literary genres.

Works

Národní báchorky a pověsti (1845–1846). *Domácí nemoc* (1846). *Dlouhá noc* (1846). *Obrázek vesnický* (1847). *Baruška* (1852). *Rozárka* (1854). *Babička* (1855). *Karla* (1855). *Divá Bára* (1855). *Pohorská vesnice* (1856). *V zámku a v podzámčí* (1856). *Chudí lidé* (1856). *Dobrý člověk* (1858). *Chyže pod horami* (1858). *Slovenské pohádky a pověsti* (1857–1858).

Clinton Machann

Works

Erōsa eleğias (1924). *Sarkanā vāze* (1927). *Pie Azandas upes* (1933). *Dziesminiece* (1934). *Ciema spīgana* (1935). *Anna Dzilna* (1936). *Sieva* (1938). *Rūžu Kristīne* (1939). *Rožu pelni* (1946). *Kārdinātāja* (1949). *Katrīne Abele* (1950). *Pasaules plauksta* (1952). *Trīs Caunu sievietes* (1954). *Pilsēta pie Daugavas* (1955). *Melnā magone* (1956). *Miera ielas cepurniece* (1957). *Mūžīga Ieva* (1958). *Pērles Majores draugs* (1958). *Ugunis pār Rata kalnu* (1959). *Bulvāru čigāni* (1960). *Septītā cilpa* (1960). *Sieviete ar sarkaniem ērkšķiem* (1961). *Tas trakais kavelieru gads* (1962). *Holivudas klauns* (1963). *Līgava un sieva* (1963). *Melnas plūmes pie sarkanam lūpām*, with Andrievs Salmiņš (1964). *Indrānes oši šalc* (1965). *Trīs laimes meklētāji* (1966). *Sastapšanas pie operas kafejnīcas* (1967). *Atkal Eiropā* (1968). *Grēka ābols* (1968). *Varavīksnes pār Rīgu* (1969). *Rīga dienās, nedienās* (1970). *Adams un Ieva* (1971).

Zoja Pavlovskis

Aīda Niedra
1899–1972

a.k.a. Īda Niedra, Īda Salmiņa or Salmiņš [her married name], Aīda Nierda (a misprint)
Born March 23, 1899, in Vidzeme, Latvia
Died November 23, 1972, Santa Monica, California
Genre(s): novel, short story, lyric poetry
Language(s): Latvian

Probably the most important Latvian woman novelist after Anna Brigadere, Aīda Niedra was born and grew up in the country. Her given name was originally Īda. Early childhood experiences and impressions created close ties and love for the land, which is very evident in her work. After secondary school she worked until 1932 as secretary to a Justice of the Peace in Riga. She spent the years 1944 to 1949 as a war refugee in Germany, and then immigrated to the United States. Her novels are powerful studies of heroic, archetypal figures, especially women, whose primitive passions are purged by hard work, motherhood, and suffering, and who exemplify such national characteristics as *spīts* (stubborn defiance). To achieve the idealization necessary for her purposes, she frequently places her narratives in the nineteenth century and uses a stylized, rhetorical mode of expression.

Florence Nightingale
1820–1910

Born May 12, 1820, Florence, Italy
Died August 13, 1910, London
Genre(s): diary, letters, reports, journalism, speeches
Language(s): English

"I had so much rather live than write; writing is only a supplement for living," Nightingale told a friend. "I think one's feelings waste themselves in words; they ought all to be distilled into actions, and into actions which bring results." Florence Nightingale won her place in history through her heroic actions during the Crimean War, but her reasons for rebelling against society's expectations for women, her religious justification of her conduct, and her proposals for reforming health care and sanitation are all formulated in words: diaries, letters, government reports, journal articles, addresses to nursing students, more than two hundred books and pamphlets. For Nightingale, writing was a means to self-knowledge and an instrument for social change.

Educated at home by their wealthy, well-bred father, Nightingale and her older sister Parthenope studied history, philosophy, mathematics, and classics; they also wrote weekly compositions. At the urging of classical scholar Benjamin Jowett, Nightingale prepared an anthology of writings by medieval mystics prefaced with the statement, "This reading is good only as a preparation for work." She objected to writers who failed to understand the importance of work: poets who ignored poverty and disease in order to celebrate "the glories of this world"; "female ink-bottles" who spewed out pages of useless polemics; novelists who lured young women into fantasies of romantic love. Without action, the imagination could be dangerously self-indulgent. Dreaming, which Nightingale regarded as an all-consuming activity for many women, was a sign of despair and frustration, an alternative rather than a prelude to accomplishment.

Writing served a therapeutic function in Nightingale's private life. Early journals describe her anger and frustration with the idle life of an upper-class Englishwoman. She believed she had a call from God to undertake a life of heroic service, while her family asked her to write letters, play the piano, and entertain company, so writing enabled her to break with her family and begin her work in nursing. She told her father, "I hope now I have come into possession of myself." "Cassandra," an autobiographical fragment from this period, criticizes Victorian family structure, analyzes the ways women's time and talents are wasted, and prophesies the coming of a female Christ who will arise in the midst of suffering and complaint. Although the work remained unpublished during her lifetime, John Stuart Mill incorporated some of her criticism of domestic routine into *The Subjection of Women*. Nightingale continued to write "spiritual meditations" throughout her life: confessions of guilt, apologies for her self-obsession, communings with God.

Suggestions for Thought, the work from which "Cassandra" is derived, is, according to Elaine Showalter, "a major document of Victorian religious thought, which should be studied alongside Newman's *Apologia Pro Vita Sua.*" In 1852 Nightingale declared, "I have remodelled my whole religious belief from beginning to end. I have learnt to know God. I have recast my social belief; have them both written for use, when my hour is come." Rejecting Anglicanism, Catholicism, Protestantism, and Positivism, she argued that the laws of God could be discovered by experience, research, and analysis. God is the Universal Being who is Law, "a Being who, willing only good, leaves evil in the world solely in order to stimulate human faculties by an unremitting struggle against every form of it." Nightingale tried to impose order—digests with elaborate divisions and subdivisions, running titles, marginal glosses—but the massive manuscript is marred by rambling digressions and repetitions. Nightingale sent her jumbled "Stuff," as she called it, to Mill, who advised publication, and Jowett, who called

for extensive revision. Although she had a few copies privately printed in 1860, she lost interest in revising the book for a general audience. *Suggestions* had served its purpose: she had formulated a theological justification for her commitment to self-development and public service.

In the public sphere, Nightingale wrote her way into positions of power. Although she was a public idol when she returned from the Crimea in 1856, she had no official standing with the military or governmental agencies investigating British losses in the war. She had also become an invalid. Arrogant, manipulative, and almost demonically energetic, she used her pen to attack the administrative chaos and poor sanitary conditions in the British army. When a report was omitted from the government's publication, she paid to have five hundred copies printed in the form of a parliamentary blue book and circulated among her influential acquaintances. *Notes on Matters Affecting the Health, Efficiency, and Hospital Administration of the British Army* (1858) resulted in the establishment of a Royal Commission and passage of many of Nightingale's recommendations. Recognizing her brilliant analytic skills and knowledge of statistics, government leaders frequently sought her advice, especially on matters of public health in India. When necessary, she could organize tremendous public support through adroit use of the press.

Notes on Nursing: What It Is, and What It Is Not (1860) was Nightingale's most popular book, selling 15,000 copies in a few months and receiving scores of enthusiastic reviews; according to Harriet Martineau, it was "a work of genius." Nightingale's advice on domestic hygiene was intended for a wide audience, for she defined a nurse as anyone who has responsibility for another's health. Her belief that all disease is "more or less a reparative process" meant that the nurse must "put the patient in the best condition for nature to act upon him." The doctor's duties were diminished by her adamant opposition to the germ theory and her conviction that "nature alone cures." Nightingale's prose is clear, concrete, often epigrammatic in style, and occasionally satiric in tone; through related image patterns, she fuses moral fervor and scientific authority.

Nightingale carefully cultivated her image as the noble, self-sacrificing "lady with the lamp," but she also identified with Jesus, Joan of Arc, Correggio's Magdelen, and Queen Victoria. A skilled mythmaker, she made the nurse into a figure of epic proportions. "Una and the Lion" (1868) invokes Spenser's *Faerie Queene* to eulogize Agnes Jones, a woman who died while nursing in a workhouse, as "Una in real flesh and blood—Una and her paupers, far more untameable than lions." In actuality, Nightingale thought Jones was inept; in print, she saw an opportunity to satisfy her own ego and win converts to Christian service.

She was reluctant to align herself with women, perhaps because of unresolved conflicts with her mother and sister. She supported married women's property rights, but she resisted Mill's appeals for help in the suffrage campaign, remarking that she herself exerted more influence on government than if she "had been a borough returning two M.P.'s" Having money, position, and great personal strength, she claimed to be "brutally indifferent to the wrongs or rights of my sex." But even as she urged readers to keep clear of "both jargons"—the jargon about women's rights, "which urges women to do all that men do," and the jargon about woman's mission, "which urges women to do nothing that men do"—she set an example and gave advice that enabled many women to set out upon independent lives: "Oh, leave these jargons, and go your way straight to God's work, in simplicity and singleness of heart."

Works

Notes on Matters Affecting the Health, Efficiency, and Hospital Administration of the British Army (1858). *Notes on Hospitals* (1859). *Notes on Nursing: What It Is, and What It Is Not* (1860). *Suggestions for Thought* (1860). *Observations on the Evidence Contained in the Stational Reports Submitted to Her by the Royal Commission on the Sanitary State of the Army in India* (1863). "How People May Live and Not Die in India" (1863). "Una and the Lion" (1868). *Florence Nightingale to Her Nurses* (1914). *Selected Writings of Florence Nightingale*, ed. L.R. Seymer (1954). "Cassandra," ed. Myra Stark (1979).

Robin Sheets

Anna-Elizabeth de Noailles (de Brancovan)
1876–1933

Born November 15, 1876, Paris
Died April 30, 1933, Paris
Genre(s): poetry, novel, short story, memoir
Language(s): French

The Countess of Noailles, author of twenty works that include poems, novels, short stories, and memoirs, was known and celebrated for a very brief time dur-

ing her life before being condemned by the "intellectuals." She was much admired by Jean Cocteau, whose last work, *La Comtesse de Noailles: Oui et Non*, presents a fascinating picture of a woman both loved and despised. Her work was overtly sensual, in the tradition of Verlaine, which aroused both ire and fascination among her contemporaries; according to Cocteau, her real "fault" lay in the fact that her works did not include "un certain ennui," the sign of the serious and the privilege of a true masterpiece. Considered a "néo-romantic" by those who denigrated her work, she drew inspiration from "pagan" sources, and focused much of her attention on nature, the beautiful, and death which she referred to as "l'ombre" (shadow). Those who admired her did so with hyperbole: Joseph Reinach is reputed to have told her, "There exist three miracles in France: Joan of Arc, the Marne, and you," while Moréas nicknamed her the Hymettan Bee. She was touted by Maurice Barrés who marveled at her "obscured shivers, regal fevers," and presented her as a latter-day Sappho who—single-handedly, one surmises—revived the best of ancient Greek poetry. Colette also praised her, painting an unofficial portrait that celebrates her as poet first, beauty and aristocrat second, and includes two observations the Countess made about herself; the first, "I am wild, but without a trace of wickedness," the second, "I shall have been useless but irreplaceable." Interestingly, it was Gide and his circle of what Cocteau calls "encyclopedistes" at the *Nouvelle Revue Française* who treated Anna as a traitor to the cause.

The daughter of a Romanian father, Prince Gregory Bassaraba de Brancovan, and Greek mother, Ralouka Musurus, Anna-Elizabeth was born in Paris on November 15, 1876. Anna-Elizabeth had an older brother, Constantin, who, from 1903–1905 directed a journal called *La Renaissance Latine*, for up-and-coming writers of the era; her younger sister, Hélène, the princess Alexandre de Caraman-Chimay by marriage, died in 1929.

Anna-Elizabeth spent her youth in Paris and Amphion, on the banks of Lake Léman, and in 1897, married Mathieu, Count of Noailles. From that time on she lived almost exclusively in Paris where she gave birth to a son, Anne-Jules, in 1908. She died in Paris on April 30, 1933 and was buried in the Père-Lachaise cemetery. Her heart, however, was taken to the cemetery of Publier in Haute-Savoie where it was buried separately beneath a stele inscribed with a line from one of her poems: "C'est là que dort mon coeur, vaste témoin du monde" (Here sleeps my heart, witness to the wide world).

Anna was made a member of the Académie Royale de Langue et de Littérature Françaises in Brussels in

1922—an honor in which she was followed by Colette—and was the first French woman to be promoted to commander in the Legion of Honor.

In 1938 a monument was erected in her honor in Amphion. The majority of her manuscripts belong to the Bibliothèque Nationale, which hosted an exhibition in her honor in 1953 on the twentieth anniversary of her death. There is some indication that her star is on the rise again.

Works

Le Coeur innombrable (1901). *L'ombre des jours* (1902). *La Nouvelle espérance* (1903). *Le visage emerveille* (1904). *La Domination* (1905). *Les Eblouissements* (1907). *De la Rive d'Europe à la Rive d'Asie* (1913). *Les Vivants et les morts* (1913). *Les forces eternelles* (1920). *Poésies* (1920). *Conte Triste avec une moralité* (1921). *Les innocentes ou la sagesse des femmes* (1923). *Les Climats* (1924). *Le poeme de l'Amour* (1924). *Passions et vanités* (1926). *L'honneur de souffrir* (1927). *Poèmes d'Enfances* (1929). *Exactitudes* (1930). *Le livre de ma vie* (1932). *Derniers vers* (1934, posthumous collection).

Sarah Spence

Isotta Nogarola
ca. 1416–1466

Born ca. 1416, Verona, Italy
Died 1466, Verona
Genre(s): letters, oration, poetry, dialogue
Language(s): Latin

Together with other women humanists of fifteenth-century Italy, Nogarola was the product of a new cultural revival, whereby the arts, the humanities, and other attainments of the human mind reached unprecedented popularity, and some of the educational advantages reserved for boys were extended to girls of the privileged classes. Born to Bianca Borromeo and Leonardo Nogarola, both of noble ancestry, Isotta found in her family an environment very favorable to learning. Her aunt, Angela Nogarola, was a poet; other members of the family had distinguished themselves in literature and in the sciences. Together with her sisters, Isotta studied Greek and Latin, first under Matteo Bosso, then under Martino Rizzoni, a favorite pupil of the celebrated teacher Guarino of Verona. In 1438, she moved to Venice to avoid the plague and the war between the Venetian Republic and Milan.

After her return to Verona, in 1441, she made friends with Lodovico Foscarini, son of the Doge, who had become mayor of the city and kept a literary salon. Although she was sought after for her fame and beauty, Isotta declined marriage and pursued her studies in isolation. Sacred literature and theology became the exclusive subject of her study in the second part of her life. She was buried in the church of Santa Maria Antica in Verona.

Nogarola cultivated the genres popular with the literary elite of her times: the Latin epistle, Latin poetry, the oration, and the dialogue.

Her letters were addressed to literary men and to dignitaries of her region. In Verona, there is a letter in which Isotta congratulates the celebrated humanist, Ermolao Barbaro, on his election to prothonotary apostolic. In 1437, she worded an elegant and enthusiastic praise of Guarino of Verona, and sent it to him; hence a number of letters were exchanged between the Nogarola sisters, Guarino and his son, Girolamo. With Damiano del Borgo, she kept a lengthy correspondence, animated by reciprocal admiration and affection. To Foscarini she turned for advice and moral support. It is in disputation with Foscarini that Isotta wrote the dialogue on the relative culpability of Adam and Eve. Her letters were greatly admired in her times for their elegance and the frequent erudite citations and digressions. Their manuscripts were soon dispersed among various Italian towns and abroad. Arturo Pomello tells us that 564 of them could be found in the second half of the seventeenth century in one Parisian library alone.

One letter is written in the classical form of *consolatoria* and laments the death of J.A. Marcello's son. A second oration was written for the arrival of E. Barbaro, and a third one in praise of Saint Jerome. Isotta's best-known work, however, is the dialogue-disputation between herself and Foscarini about the relative culpability of Adam and Eve. Here Isotta finds herself in the position of defending Eve against the authority of the Bible and of Saint Augustine's commentary. Although she pleads for the weakness of the female sex, she holds Adam the guiltier of the two because of his greater knowledge and responsibility. She further argues in Eve's favor, in name of her compelling desire to acquire knowledge, a desire that is innate in humankind. The dialogue was published by the author's descendant, Count Francesco Nogarola, in 1563, in a handsome Aldine edition. The text, however, was significantly altered and the liveliness of the original exchange between Isotta and Ludovico was lost in what became an erudite treatise, more subdued from a doctrinal point of view.

Nogarola is an important figure not only in the history of feminism, but for the sociological and anthropological study of western civilization. As an early bluestocking, she soon became aware of the structural obstacles encountered by women who, for the first time in history, received an education comparable to that of men. Recurrent in her letters is the complaint of being a woman and thus being subjected to "men's denigrations in words and fact." Her dialogue clearly attests to the distressing impasse of women who could not reject the cultural and religious traditions from which society drew the justification of an order strongly upheld.

Works

Isotae Nogarolae Veroniensis dialogus quo utrum Adam vel Eva magis peccavit. Quaestio satis nota sed non adeo explicata, continetur (1563). *Isotae Nogarolae Veroniensis, opera quae supersunt omnia*, ed. E. Abel, 2 vols. (1886). Maria Ludovica Lenzi, *Donne e Madonne, L'educazione femminile nel primo Rinascimento italiano* (1982), pp. 209–216. "Of the Equal or Unequal Sin of Adam and Eve," in *Her Immaculate Hand. Selected Works by and About the Women Humanists of Quattrocento Italy*, eds. M.L. King and A. Rabil, Jr. (1983), pp. 57–69.

Rinaldina Russell

Hedvig Charlotta Nordenflycht
1718–1763

a.k.a. En Herdinna i Norden [a shepherdess in the Northland]
Born November 28, 1718, Stockholm, Sweden
Died June 29, 1763, Lugnet (near Stockholm)
Genre(s): lyric poetry, prose
Language(s): Swedish

Hedvig Charlotta Nordenflycht remains best known for the emotional intensity and candor of her poetry at a time when these elements were not yet commonly found in Swedish letters. Her lyrics combine a religious outlook with her thoughts on the philosophies of, among others, Voltaire and Rousseau. A literary figure of considerable importance during the middle of the eighteenth century, Nordenflycht, together with the poets Gustaf Creutz and Jacob Gyllenborg, established Sweden's first literary salon.

Nordenflycht was born to middle-class parents (though her father was ennobled for faithful government service in 1727) and led a life not unusual for middle-class girls of her day. She was taught to read Swedish by age five, but despite her literary bent she was given no formal education. Her brothers were allowed to tutor her in Latin and German, but this instruction was limited to their vacations from the university. She read avidly as a young girl, sometimes even while performing household chores. At age sixteen she was engaged to Johan Tideman at her dying father's request. The fiancé had inspired Nordenflycht's respect and friendship by means of his philosophical interests, but by her own reports he was physically repulsive to her. He died before they could marry, and in 1741 she married the more attractive Jacob Fabricius, a naval chaplain, with whom she enjoyed a short happy marriage. His death seven months later propelled Nordenflycht into her poetic career; her collection *Den Sörgande Turtur-Sufwan* (The Mourning Turtledove) of 1743 expresses the sorrow and despair she experienced at the death of her beloved husband. During the next six years she published four volumes of poems under the title *Qwinligit Tankespel* (Feminine Thought-Play), and in 1752 she was awarded a government pension for her literary contributions. Her poetry took on a Voltairean cast during the time of the *Tankebyggarorden* (Order of the Thought Builders), the literary salon of which she was the center. Toward the end of her life she met and fell in love with the much younger Johan Fischerström, and it is assumed that his inability to share her feelings resulted in a failed suicide attempt by drowning, during which she contracted a debilitating illness and died.

Nordenflycht's poetic production is a large one, as is the range of subject matter it encompasses. She grapples with different philosophical approaches and intense emotions, with occasional verse, women's rights, and her own private passions. The quality fluctuates, and her rhymes and meter are at times uneven. She has been accused of lacking stylistic sensitivity and of not being capable of understanding the philosophical systems she explores. But a few of her poems [one in particular, "Min lefnadslust är skuren af . . ." (My Lust for Life Is Cut Asunder)] display a true poetic gift, especially those poems inspired by Nordenflycht's intense reactions to her personal misfortune. Her particular poetic essence can be characterized by a content that is ahead of its time (the reader is reminded of the "I"-centered emotional outbursts of Romanticism) encased in a rococo package.

Nordenflycht is considered Sweden's first career poet and one of its first feminists in her belief in women's right and duty to receive an education. Although her unfortunate love experiences have been cause for ridicule, her importance for Swedish letters and her considerable talent cannot be overlooked.

Works

Den Sörgande Turtur-Sufwan [The Mourning Turtle-dove] (1743). *Qwinligit Tankespel* (1–4) [Feminine Thought-Play] (1744–1750). *Andeliga Skaldeqwäden* [Spiritual Poems] (1758). *Witterhetsarbeten* [Literary Works] (1759, 1762). *Utvalda Arbeten* [Selected Works], collected by Fischerström (1774). *Samlade Skrifter* [Collected Works] (1852). *Samlade Skrifter* [Collected Works], collected by Hilma Borelius (1925–1938).

Kathy Saranpa Anstine

Nossis
ca. 250 B.C.–?

Born in Epizephyrian Locri, southern Italy; exact birth and death dates unknown
Flourished approximately 275 B.C.
Genre(s): epigrams
Language(s): Greek

Nossis apparently belonged to one of the ranking families of Locri. In Poem 3, our single source of biographical information, she terms herself "noble" (*agaua*), names her mother Theophilis and grandmother Cleocha, and commemorates Theophilis's presentation of an elaborately worked robe to Hera Lacinia. Although we know nothing else about her private life, her epigrams indicate that she wrote exclusively for a circle of intimate women friends. At Locri, women may have enjoyed relatively high status. Archaeological evidence from an earlier period confirms the prominence of the joint cult of Persephone and Aphrodite, two fertility goddesses closely linked to the female sphere, and Persephone's supreme importance at Locri was certainly recognized in Hellenistic times. These cultural factors no doubt contributed to the intensely woman-identified nature of Nossis's poetry. It would be erroneous, however, to imagine her living in a quasimatriarchal society, which would have been impossible in the Greek world at any time or place.

Nossis owes her limited survival to the first century B.C. anthologist Meleager of Gadara, who extracted representative pieces from her published book of verses for his epigram collection, the *Garland*. In his prologue, she is praised specifically as a love poet:

Eros is said to have "melted the wax for her tablets." Furthermore, in Poem 1, which must have originally introduced her own book, the author herself proclaims: "Nothing is sweeter than *eros*. All other delights are second. . . . This is what Nossis says." Love, then, was clearly a dominant theme of her poetry, but none of the eleven epigrams now preserved in the *Greek Anthology* (the authenticity of a twelfth is suspect) is overtly erotic. However, six of her quatrains ostensibly commemorating votive dedications by women discreetly evoke the sensual attractiveness of the dedicants as reflected in their statues and portraits. Meleager's capsule account of Nossis' poetry may imply that he himself sensed erotic undertones in those descriptive pieces, for "melting wax" could refer to the process of painting on wood in encaustic—a standard ancient medium for portraiture. Finally, Nossis confirms her artistic debt to Sappho both indirectly, through regular employment of Sapphic language (*aganos*, "gentle," which Nossis applies to three different women, was the earlier poet's term for her beloved Atthis), and explicitly in Poem 11, the *envoi* to her collection. All this evidence indicates that Nossis' expressly erotic poems must have celebrated love between women. That hypothesis would also explain why her book was lost and why only a few seemingly innocuous quatrains survived the centuries.

Among the multitude of Hellenistic and later epigrammatists, Nossis is an outstanding artist, even though she appears to have exercised little direct influence upon the mainstream tradition. Challenged by the strict limitations of the epigram form, she attempts, like the acknowledged master of the genre Callimachus, to fit searching pronouncements within its restrictive framework. In particular, she is fascinated by the connection between an aesthetic representation and its subject and employs the dedicatory epigram as a vehicle for probing the relationship of artistic product to model. Since the models she deals with are women, her epigrams necessarily touch on issues of female selfhood and individuation. For example, Poem 8, which begins with the exclamation *automelinna tetuktai* ("Melinna's very being is fully wrought!") and lauds the verisimilitude of the portrait on display, goes on to observe how closely Melinna resembles her mother and concludes, "How good it is when children are like their parents." As the painter limns his model in pigments, so a mother, by analogy, replicates herself in her daughter's flesh: through her reproductive and nurturing efforts, she, too, acts as a creative artist and passes on to the next generation an image of herself. Yet the quatrain also depicts the tension between "Melinna herself," *automelinna*, and Melinna as the biological continuation of her mother: juxtaposing those two contradictory notions without reconciling them, it implicitly conveys the struggle over the daughter's autonomy inherent in the mother–daughter dyad. We may note further that this epigram appropriates the standard patriarchal sentiment that sons should resemble fathers, as evidence of their legitimacy, and transforms it into an affirmation of the exceptional biological bond between female parent and female child. In this and in several other epigrams (such as the programmatic 1 and 11, which proclaim a conscious choice of erotic themes and of Sappho as poetic model, and in 3, which examines the mother–daughter relationship autobiographically), it is clear that Nossis has assumed a firmly woman-centered stance in marked opposition to the attitudes of the dominant culture.

Nossis does try her hand at traditionally masculine themes. But even when she expresses patriotic feelings or admires the achievements of a male literary predecessor, she writes in a distinctly female voice. Thus her quatrain memorializing a Locrian victory over the indigenous Bruttians (Poem 2) voices that uncompromising hatred for a defeated enemy that women who had been confronted with the imminent possibility of rape and enslavement would understandably have felt. Similarly, her epitaph (Poem 10) for Rhinthon, author of tragic burlesques, staunchly proclaims the literary value of his supposedly slight productions and calls into question the conventional hierarchy of genres. This defense of Rhinthon is simultaneously a protest against the devaluation of women's writing, likewise confined to "lesser" poetic forms.

Living in an age when female homoeroticism was beginning to meet with strong cultural disapproval, Nossis risked much in choosing to write from a woman-identified perspective. That specimens of her poetry have survived at all is a testimony to the subtle ambiguities and delicate ironies she uses in order to convey her sensibility to an understanding reader.

Works

Greek texts and German translations in Homeyer, H., *Dichterinnen des Altertums und des frühen Mittelalters* (Paderborn, 1979). Commentary in *The Greek Anthology: Hellenistic Epigrams*, eds. A.S.F. Gow and D.L. Page, 2 vols. (Cambridge, 1965). English translations in *The Greek Anthology*, tr. W.R. Paton. 5 vols. (Cambridge, Mass., Loeb Classical Library, 1916) and in Rayor, D., *Sappho's Lyre: Archaic Lyric and Women Poets of Ancient Greece* (Berkeley and Los Angeles, 1991).

Marilyn B. Skinner

Christine Nöstlinger
1936–

Born October 13, 1936, Vienna, Austria
Genre(s): children's and youth literature, poetry
Language(s): German

Christine Nöstlinger is Austria's best-known, most productive, and most colorful author of books for children and adolescents. Following the publication of *Die feuerrote Friederike* in 1970, she has published at least one book per year and this does not take into account numerous reprints and translations into many languages. To date Nöstlinger has about seventy titles to her credit. *Wir pfeifen auf den Gurkenkönig* (1972; The Cucumber King), a humorous family novel about a twelve-year-old boy and his family who lead an uneventful life until the autocratic "Cucumber King" suddenly appears from the depths of their basement and, together with an equally autocratic father, conspires against the family, has reached an edition of well over 100,000 and has become a classic in its own right.

Nöstlinger, who grew up in a working-class district of Vienna and studied graphic arts at the Academy of Applied Arts in Vienna, started her writing career, rather inconspicuously, during a short and rather unhappy phase as a homemaker and the mother of two children in the sixties. Although she writes primarily for children, her books can be enjoyed by all age groups.

In her books, the typical Austrian setting, atmosphere, and language notwithstanding, Nöstlinger discusses topics and problems that affect children and adolescents worldwide. She writes about human shortcomings, typical family conflicts such as divorce, runaway children and restrictive grandmothers, prejudice and superstition, inhumanity, and war. Her pacifist attitude is best reflected in her popular autobiographical novel, *Maikäfer flieg!* (1973; Fly Away Home), in which she recalls what life was like for her family in Vienna toward the end of World War II. Nöstlinger's primary goal as an author, however, is to entertain her readers. To accomplish this she wraps her social message in a cloak of magic, fantasy, and grotesqueness.

Nöstlinger's status as a preeminent writer of fiction for young people was confirmed in 1984 when she received the Hans Christian Andersen medal, the first Austrian writer to receive this coveted award, which has been called the Nobel Prize of children's literature. Currently, Nöstlinger spends most of her time in the Waldviertel region north of Vienna where, in addition to her book projects, she writes columns for various newspapers and magazines.

Works

Die feuerrote Friederike (1970). *Die drei Posträuber* (1971). *Die Kinder aus dem Kinderkeller* (1971). *Mr. Bats Meisterstück* (1971). *Wir pfeifen auf den Gurkenkönig* (1972). *Pit und Anja entdecken das Jahr* (1972). *Ein Mann für Mama* (1972). *Der schwarze Mann und der groe Hund* (1973). *Sim-Sala-Bim* (1973). *Maikäfer flieg! Mein Vater, das Kriegsende, Cohn und ich* (1973). *Der kleine Herr greift ein* (1973). *Iba de gaunz oaman Kinda* (1974). *Achtung! Vranek sieht ganz harmlos aus* (1974). *Gugurells Hund* (1974). *Ilse Janda, 14* (1974). *Der Spatz in der Hand . . . ist besser als die Taube auf dem Dach* (1974). *Konrad oder das Kind aus der Konservenbüchse* (1975). *Stundenplan* (1975). *Rüb-rüb-hurra!* (1975). *Der liebe Herr Teufel* (1975). *Winterzeit. Pit und Anja entdeckendas Jahr* (1976). *Pelinka und Satlasch* (1976). *Das Leben der Tomanis* (1976). *Das will Jenny haben* (1977). *Lollipop* (1977). [With Bettina Anrich-Wölfel], *Der kleine Jo* (1977). *Luki-live* (1978). *Die Geschechte von der Geschichte vom Pinguin* (1978). *Andreas oder die unteren sieben Achtel des Eisbergs* (1978). *Rosa Riedl Schutzgespenst* (1979).

Dschi-Dsche-i Dschunior (1980). *Gestapo ruft Moskau* (1980). *Einer* (1980). *Der Denker greift ein* (1981). *Rosalinde hat Gedanken im Kopf* (1981). *Gretchen Sackmeier* (1981). *Pfui Spinne* (1981). *Zwei Wochen im Mai. Mein Vater, der Rudi, der Hansi und ich* (1981). *Das Austauschkind* (1982). *Iba de gaunz oaman Fraun* (1982). *Ein Kater ist kein Sofakissen* (1982). *Das kleine Glück. Schrebergärten* (1982). *Anatol und die Wurstelfrau* (1983). *Gretchen hat HänschenKummer* (1983). *Otto Ratz und Nanni. Leseratten* (1983). *Hugo, das Kind in den besten Jahren* (1983). *Jockel, Jula und Jericho* (1983). *Am Montag ist alles ganz anders* (1984). *Geschichten vom Franz* (1984). *Liebe Susi, lieber Paul* (1984). *Olfi Obermeier und der Ödipus* (1984). *Die grüne Warzenbraut* (1984). *Prinz Ring* (1984). *Jakob auf der Bohnenleiter* (1984). *Vogelscheuchen* (1984). *Haushalts-schnecken leben länger* (1985). *Liebe Oma, Deine Susi* (1985). *Neues vom Franz* (1985). *Der Wauga* (1985). *Der Bohnen-Jim* (1986). *Der geheime Grovater* (1986). *Geschichten für Kinder in den besten Jahren. 26 Erzählungen* (1986). *Man nennt mich Ameisenbär* (1986). *Oh, du Hölle! Julias Tagebuch* (1986). *Susis geheimes Tagebuch Pauls geheimes Tagebuch* (1986). *Iba de gaunz oaman Mauna* (1987). *Der Hund kommt* (1987). *Wetti und Babs* (1987). *Schulgeschichten vom Franz* (1987). *Der neve Pinocchio. Die Abenteuer des Pinocchio neu erzählt* (1988). *Neve Schulgeschichlen vom Franz* (1988). *Echt Susi* (1988). *Gretchen mein Mädchen* (1988).

Translations: *Brainbox Sorts It Out* [*Der Denker greift ein*], tr. Anthea Bell (1985). *But Jasper Came Instead* [*Das Austauschkind*], tr. Anthea Bell (1983). *Conrad* [*Konrad*], tr. Anthea Bell (1976). *The Cucumber King* [*Wir pfeifen auf den Gurkenkönig*], tr. Anthea Bell (1975). *Fly Away Home* [*Maikäfer flieg!*], tr. Anthea Bell (1975). *Girl Missing* [*Ilse Janda, 14*], tr. Anthea Bell (1976). *Guardian Ghost* [*Rosa Riedl Schutzgespenst*], tr. Anthea Bell (1986). *Lollipop* [*Lollipop*], tr. Anthea Bell (1982). *Luke and Angela* [*Luki-live*], tr. Anthea Bell (1981). *Marrying off Mother* [*Ein Mann für Mama*], tr. Anthea Bell (1978). *Mr. Bat's Great Invention* [*Mr. Bats Meisterstück*], tr. Anthea Bell (1978).

Jürgen Koppensteiner

Edna O'Brien
1930–

Born December 15, 1930, Tuamgraney, County Clare, Ireland
Genre(s): novel, short story, screenplay, drama, essay
Language(s): English

O'Brien, an Irish expatriate, has been sexually candid in her works. This candidness, plus being a woman, has added to her appeal to her reading public, especially in the United States, where she is criticized as much as she is celebrated. Her professional readers are, it seems, on the lookout for the least echo of Joyce, the least emotional excess, the least indication of derivative lyricism or self-indulgence. Scrutiny has been even more intense because she writes so well so often.

O'Brien writes best about what she knows, and much of her best writing draws from her personal experience. Therefore she writes better stories about Ireland than she does about London, better stories about village life than city life, and best about women facing and abandoning a Catholic, Irish heritage for a secular, passionate life in search of what O'Brien is never ashamed to call "true love." The word "girl" surfaces and resurfaces in her writing, calling up the pain involved in callow girls' traumatic education for living. For many of her women, this abandoned heritage remains in the psyche and the flesh forever; one never stops being an Irish Catholic, a daughter, a village girl.

Thus O'Brien has forged a body of work parallel to her real life. The *Country Girls* trilogy (*The Country Girls*, 1960; *The Lonely Girl*, 1962; *Girls in Their Married Bliss*, 1964), begun shortly after she had moved to London, deals with growing up, breaking ties, and learning about (and failing in) love. Her novels of the late sixties, especially *August Is a Wicked Month* (1965) and *Casualties of Peace* (1966), address the consequences of marriage's collapse (O'Brien was divorced in 1964). In 1977 she published *Johnny I Hardly Knew You,* which she has said was an exploration of the older woman's attraction for younger men, a search to reestablish the unambiguous mother–son relationship through the ambiguous medium of sex. That book may also take revenge on males in general when the heroine murders her handsome younger lover.

By the 1980s O'Brien was ensconced in a large house in Maida Vale, a largely Irish residential district in London. Her expatriation appears in two ways in her fiction: in the less successful stories about urban life collected in A *Fanatic Heart* (1984) and an exploration of things Irish in her nonfiction, including *Mother Ireland* (1976), *James and Nora* (1981), and *Returning* (1982).

O'Brien is famous for writing well (and frequently) about sex. She has taught women writers how to write lyrically and honestly about physical and emotional intimacy, but she has been most convincing when she portrays sex as part of a woman's total existence, something involving her education, her childhood, her hopes, even her career. Thus her depictions of sexual relations in stories such as "The Love Object" and "Paradise" are less convincing than those in "A Rose in the Heart of New York," "A Scandalous Woman," or in novels such as *Country Girls* or *Night* (1972).

She explores human emotions through a richly lyrical confessional prose. Perhaps the height of her lyric mode was reached in the interior monologues of Mary Hooligan in *Night.* Lyricism and confessionalism arise from the Irish narrative tradition as does her very Irish sensibility: she is looking for the very rhythms of the human soul and the rules of life. There is an intoxication with the dangers at hand for any Irish writer: sentimentality, maudlin self-absorption, facile lyricism, blather, blarney. And if she sometimes succumbs to these temptations—"That night their lovemaking had all the sweetness and all the release that earth must feel with the longawaited rain"— there are riches that more than balance the lapses.

The conviction and authenticity of superior fiction come through so often that O'Brien must be considered one of the most important writers of her time. The *Country Girls* trilogy is, as a whole, quite successful, even if there is a loss of energy and descent into pessimism in the last novel, the too obviously titled *Girls in Their Married Bliss*. Kate and Baba of the *Country Girls* books are perhaps her best-known characters. Kate, one of her most sympathetic and frustrating creations, is, quite simply, a victim of romance, as we watch her mature, we follow her through a series of amorous disappointments and disasters realizing that her unrealistic expectations of love disqualify her for happiness. Her friend and opposite, Baba, a reckless ironist, prospers in the ironic world of intimacy. True love fails for Baba, too, but she is resilient and hard enough to settle for a series of nongenuine attachments, culminating in a marriage to a rich man she does not love. One of the rewards of the *Country Girls* books is that O'Brien as author identifies ideals in which she passionately wishes to believe—and allows them to fail. By the end of the trilogy, none of these ideals are left standing. Kate fails because of her devotion to the love ideal, and Baba succeeds because of a complete absence of ideals.

Of her stories, the two best are possibly "Sister Imelda" and "A Rose in the Heart of New York." "Sister Imelda" describes a nun and her schoolgirl pupil, both obsessed with the quest for purity, who fall in love with each other and with the intensity of their quest. One of her best moments occurs when the girl realizes she must turn away from her mentor and toward a worldly future. "Rose," also about turning away, is a careful tracing of the relation of mother and daughter. If there is a single best moment in O'Brien's fiction, it may well be the moment when the daughter discovers some money her dead mother has left for her.

O'Brien has also written successfully in other genres. She has written screenplays for film versions of her novels, including *The Girl with Green Eyes* (1964), and *X, Y. and Zee* (1971). Her play *Virginia* (1981) is a very successful study of Virginia Woolf, and she is also an excellent essayist.

Her independent mind has put her at odds with other women writers who have expected her to be a spokesperson for the feminist viewpoint. "I don't feel strongly about all the things they feel strongly about," she has said. "I feel strongly about childhood, truth or lies, and the real expression of feeling." She has insisted on a real difference between the sexes. Especially unfeminist is her conviction that there is "both a conscious and an unconscious degree of submission in a woman." However, O'Brien feels that women can and must fight this submissiveness. For her future fiction, O'Brien has said that her goal is to create a truly great female character. She wishes not only to match the best of literature's women (ironically, created mostly by male authors) but also to create a truly believable heroine, a "woman who succeeds," if only to show that success is possible.

Works

The Country Girls (1960). *The Lonely Girl* (1962; rpt. as *Girl with Green Eyes,* 1964; screenplay 1964). *A Cheap Bunch of Nice Flowers,* in *Plays of the Year,* ed. J.C. Trewin (1963). *Girls in Their Married Bliss* (1964). *August Is a Wicked Month* (1965). *Casualties of Peace* (1966). *Time Lost and Time Remembered* (screenplay with D. Davis from O'Brien's story "A Woman at the Seaside,"1966). *Three into Two Won't Go* (screenplay from the novel by A. Newman, 1968). *The Love Object* (1969). *A Pagan Place* (1970). *Zee & Co.* (screenplay for the film *X, Y. and Zee,* 1971). *Night* (1972). *A Pagan Place* (1973). *The Gathering* (1974). *A Scandalous Woman and Other Stories* (1974). *Mother Ireland* (1976). *Johnny I Hardly Knew You* (1977; in the U.S. as *I Hardly Knew You,* 1978). *Arabian Days* (1978). *The Collected Edna O'Brien* (1978). *Mrs. Reinhardt and Other Stories* (1978). *A Rose in the Heart* (1979). *James and Nora* (1981). *Virginia: A Play* (1981). *Returning* (1982). *A Fanatic Heart* (1984). *The Country Girls Trilogy and Epilogue* (1986). *Banishing Ireland* (1987). *Nights* (1987). *Tales for the Telling* (1988). *The High Road* (1988). *On the Bone* (1990). *Lantern Slides* (1990). *Time and Tide* (1990). *House of Splendid Isolation* (1993). *Northern Ireland* (1993). *An Edna O'Brien Reader* (1994).

John Timpane

Annalena Odaldi
1572–1638
Born April 28, 1572, Pistoia, Italy
Died December 1, 1638, Pistoia
Genre(s): drama
Language(s): Italian

Annalena Odaldi was born Lessandra Odaldi on April 28, 1572, the daughter of Camillo di Piero Odaldi and Madonna Lucrezia Fioravanti. Her father was a merchant, part owner of a pharmacy and dry goods business. Her mother bore him fifteen children in the period of seventeen years from 1566 to 1583 (Lessandra was the sixth child, the third daughter). Camillo died in May or June of 1584, and shortly thereafter his widow saw to the marriage of her oldest daughter, Polita, and entered her second and third daughters, Laura and Lessandra, in important Pistoiese convents. In January of 1585, Lessandra entered the Franciscan convent of Santa Chiara taking the name of Sister Annalena. At least four of Annalena Odaldi's siblings, Laura, Mario, Bartolomeo, and Canida, also entered the religious life, four children died in infancy, and on the others the records are incomplete. Annalena held the convent offices of sacristan, bookkeeper (many times), and novice mistress. She died on December 1, 1638.

Annalena Odaldi was the author of five short farces. She wrote them between 1600 and 1604 when she was novice mistress for performance before an audience of nuns by the young women in her charge as part of the convent's Carnival festivities. The farces, known in a single, probably autograph manuscript in the Riccardiana Library in Florence (cod. Ricc. 2976, vol. 6), are in verse (seven-syllable lines, generally rhymed) and have no act or scene divisions, however, they amply use music and dance to suggest the passing of time and to allow for changes on stage.

The plays present traditional satires of physicians, lawyers, and old lechers, alongside those of plebeian characters. The subjects are entirely secular, but since they were intended for Carnival festivities they could be tolerated by convent authorities in the spirit of the "world upside down."

In the first of the farces, Nannuccio e quindici figliastre (1600; Nannuccio and fifteen stepdaughters), marriage is the explicit subject matter. The slim storyline is about Nannuccio di Pierone, a widower with fifteen unmarried and marriageable stepdaughters and one stepson, Beco Nero (reminiscent of Annalena's large family). Nannuccio wants to remarry himself before arranging matches and dowries for his children; but his son brings in a judge who rules against the irresponsible father. Nannuccio is Annalena's protagonist, but his lines are fewer, his part smaller that those of two women, Nencia and Pasquina, and their marriageable daughters, Fiorina and Nestasia, who argue and discuss dowries and rich prospects until the final scene of the play when Beco arrives with the judge.

Piero giuoca-asini (1600–1604; Piero Who'd Bet His Jackass) and Commedia di tre lombardi (1600–1604; The Three Lombards) stage marital squabbles, in the first case due to the husband's habit of gambling which is disastrous for the family finances. Commedia di tre lombardi opens with a husband's complaint that his wife has left him for a lover, but this is shown not to be true when the wife returns with a good excuse—motherly concern for their son. Most of the play, however, stages the humorous encounter of a lawyer from Bologna and a Tuscan physician whose dialects and predispositions prevent them from understanding one another until the subject raised by one—marriage arrangements—enormously interests the other, who happens to have a nubile daughter. Maestro Pauoloccio medico (1604; Master Pauoloccio, the Doctor) brings together a series of foolish characters. Maestro Pauoloccio is a physician who calls himself both surgeon and barber (and therefore dentist) and who kills (inadvertently, of course) rather than cures. Commedia di tre malandrini (1604; The Three Rogues) is about certain low-life characters intent on swindling some nuns; the play shows that nuns are too clever for that.

The plots of these farces are not always logical, and characters often introduce irrelevant issues, nevertheless, Annalena's writing does not fail from time to time to provide entertaining scenes, sketches, good lines, dramatic skill, and a good laugh. The unevenness is characteristic of Tuscan convent theater as a whole, since the plays were often written by a teacher, such as Annalena Odaldi, who each year at Carnival time had to have a play ready for her students' performance. The strength and appeal of Annalena's work derive from cleverly devised and written farcical actions and linguistic play which presuppose a well-developed theater tradition in Santa Chiara and at least a few able performers. The comic devices, especially the use of dialect and rustic speech, show Annalena to be familiar with popular farce and also show her to be a writer of considerable spirit and talent.

Works

Commedia di Nannuccio e quindici figliastre (1600). Commedia di maestro Pauoloccio medico (1604). Commedia di tre malandrini (1604). Commedia di tre lombardi (between 1600–1604). Commedia di Piero giuoca-asini (between 1600–1604). Early seventeenth century ms., probably autograph, Riccardiana Library, Florence, cod. Ricc. 2976, vol. 6.

Elissa B. Weaver

Margaret Oliphant
1828–1897

Born April 4, 1828, Wallyford, Midlothian, England
Died June 25, 1897, Eton
Genre(s): novel, criticism, translation, travel guide, biography, journalism, essay
Language(s): English

The last of several children born to cousins, Oliphant spent her early years in Lasswade, near Edinburgh. Her two much older brothers, the only other surviving children of the family, went to school in Edinburgh, and for much of the time Oliphant was the focus of her mother's attentions. Her mother, descended from the Oliphants of Kellie Castle in Fife, was an excellent storyteller and a dedicated reader and was one of the major influences on her literary tendencies.

When she was six years old, the family moved to a large and gloomy house in Glasgow. The lugubrious surroundings and the lack of social contacts increased her voluminous reading; Q.D. Leavis notes that at "seven or eight [Oliphant] was already a confirmed novel-reader," and what Henry James called her "immensity of reading" led naturally to an "easy flow" of writing. This "easy flow" led to an output both prodigious and varied. She published over one hundred books of fiction, criticism, translations, travel guides, and biography. In addition, the articles and essays she produced for many periodicals, chiefly Blackwood's, amount to at least another hundred volumes.

The first of her published works, *Passages in the Life of Mrs. Margaret Maitland* (1849), was written while the family was living in Liverpool, where her father had a position in the Customs House. During this period, Oliphant became engaged to a young man who was going to America for three years, after which they were to have been married, but the engagement was broken following a year of quarrelsome letters. In her *Autobiography*, Oliphant refers to this time as one of "depression and sadness." It was also a time when her mother became ill and Oliphant sat silently at her mother's bedside and began to write to amuse herself. Her brother, living in London, took the manuscript of her first book to the publishing firm of Colburn, where it was accepted for publication.

The £150 Oliphant earned for the novel financed her first trip to London, where she had gone to await its publication and to look after her eldest brother, who was perpetually in debt. Thus began the pattern of her life, ceaseless literary labors in the support of her male relatives. Ironically, it was at this time that she became acquainted with her cousin Francis

Oliphant, whom she would marry in 1852. He was an artist who had designed the stained glass windows in the Houses of Parliament, but like her father, brothers, and sons, he was never as financially successful as she was to become.

On the morning of her wedding, she received the page proofs of her novel *Katie Stewart,* published by Blackwood, an association which was to last forty-five years until her death in 1897. Her marriage to Francis Oliphant, however, lasted only seven years and ended with his death in Rome in 1859. The Oliphants had gone to Italy in search of a more healthful climate for Francis, who was suffering from consumption. The family, which by this time included a daughter and a son, settled in Florence where the weather was cold and damp, but Francis's health did not improve. The preceding years had been difficult for Oliphant; she had given birth to four children, only two of whom survived, and her mother, her greatest source of strength and support, had died shortly after the second child. Throughout this tragic time, she published dozens of articles for *Blackwood's* and at least two or three novels each year. Her third child was born six weeks after the death of her husband.

She returned to Scotland and continued with her writing, beginning what was perhaps her most famous series of novels, *The Chronicles of Carlingford.* The first two, *The Rector and the Doctor's Family* and *Salem Chapel,* were published in 1863; *The Perpetual Curate* (1864) and *Miss Marjoribanks* (1866), continued the series. The latter is considered by most critics to be her best work and the one which was most influential upon the work of other writers. Ironic, satirical, and comedic, the novel was written following the death of her twelve-year-old daughter Margaret. The success of the Carlingford series had enabled her to travel again to Italy, where the child succumbed to an attack of fever.

Oliphant returned to England and lived near Eton where she had enrolled her sons. The expenses of their education and the support of her brother Frank and his family necessitated an unending literary output, notably the concluding volume in the Carlingford series, *Phoebe Junior* (1876). The last years of her life were as unfortunate personally as the earlier ones had been. She outlived both of her sons, who had never fulfilled her hopes for them. Her nephew, whom she had educated, showed promise as an engineer but died of typhoid in India.

The tragedies of her personal life have tended to obscure her unique accomplishments as a writer. The heroines in her novels do not conform to the usual Victorian stereotypes; they are practical, clever, and articulate, and they worked (as Oliphant herself had always done). The first writer to note the "feminine cynicism" in Austen's novels, she was an original and perceptive critic.

Her last major work, the first two of the three-volume *Annals of a Publishing House* (1897), a history of Blackwood, remains as one of the most detailed, accurate, and engaging works of its kind. Her last journal article for *Blackwood's,* "'Tis Sixty Years Since," published in May 1897, honored the long reign of Queen Victoria in anticipation of the Queen's Jubilee, which was to be held in June. When she had completed the article, her doctor told her she was dying. With typical Scottish fortitude, she clung to life until two days after the celebration. She died as she had lived, pleasing others through the efforts of her pen but never totally satisfying her own desires.

Works

Passages in the Life of Mrs. Margaret Maitland (1849). *Caleb Field* (1851). *Merkland. A Story of Scottish Life* (1851). *Memoirs and Resolutions of Adam Graeme of Mossgray* (1852). *Harry Muir. A Story of Scottish Life* (1853). *Katie Stewart* (1853). *Quiet Heart. A Story* (1854). *Magdalen Hepburn. A Story of the Scottish Reformation* (1854). *Lilliesleaf. Conclusion of "Margaret Maitland"* (1855). *Zaidee, A Romance* (1856). *The Athelings, or the Three Gifts* (1857). *The Days of My Life* (1857). *Sundays* (1858). *The Laird of Nordlaw* (1858). *The House on the Moor* (1861). *The Last of the Mortimers* (1862). *The Rector and the Doctor's Family* (1863). *Salem Chapel* (1863). *The Perpetual Curate* (1864). *Miss Marjoribanks* (1866). *A Son of the Soil* (1866). *Madonna Mary* (1867). *The Brownlows* (1868). *The Minister's Wife* (1869). *John. A Love Story* (1870). *Innocent. A Tale of Modern Life* (1873). *May* (1873). *A Rose in June* (1874). *For Love and Life* (1874). *The Story of Valentine and His Brother* (1875). *Whiteladies* (1875). *The Curate in Charge* (1876). *Phoebe, Junior. A Last Chronicle of Carlingford* (1876). *Young Musgrave* (1877). *The Primrose Path. A Chapter in the Annals of the Kingdom of Fife* (1878). *Within the Precincts* (1879). *The Two Mrs. Scudamores* (1879). *The Greatest Heiress in England* (1879). *A Beleaguered City* (1880). *In Trust. A Story of a Lady and Her Lover* (1882). *Literary History of England in the End of the Eighteenth and Beginning of the Nineteenth Century* (1882). *Hester. A Story of a Contemporary Life* (1883). *It was a Lover and His Lass* (1883). *The Ladies Lindores* (1883). *Sir Tom* (1884). *Oliver's Bride. A True Story* (1886). *A Country Gentleman and His Family* (1886). *Joyce* (1888). *The Second Son* (1888). *Cousin Mary* (1888). *Lady Car: The Sequel of a Life* (1889). *Kirsteen. A Story of a Scottish Family Seventy Years Ago* (1890). *The Duke's Daughter and the Fugitives* (1890). *The Cuckoo in the Nest* (1892). *Diana Trelawny. The Story of a Great Mistake* (1892). *The Marriage of Elinor* (1892). *The Heir Presumptive and the Heir Apparent* 1892). *The Victorian Age of English Literature* (1892). *Lady William* (1893). *The Sorceress* (1893). *A Child's History of Scotland* (1895). *Two Strangers* (1895). *Sir Robert's Fortune. A Story of a Scottish Moor* (1895). *The Unjust Steward, or the Minister's Debt* (1896). *The Two Marys* (1896). *Old Mr. Tredgold* (1896). *Annals of a Publishing House* (1897). *The Lady's Walk* (1897). *The Sisters Brontë* (1897). *Autobiography and Letters of Mrs. Margaret Oliphant,* ed. A.L.W. Coghill (1899). *Selected Short Stories of the Supernatural,* ed. M.K. Gray (1986).

Gail Kraidman

Monika van Paemel
1945–

Born May 4, 1945, Poesele, Belgium
Genre(s): criticism, novel
Language(s): Flemish

The recipient of several literary prizes (for her first novel *Amazone met het blauwe voorhoofd* and the later novel *Marguerite*), Monika van Paemel is among the foremost women writers in modern Netherlandic literature.

Due to a severe illness she was bedridden from her ninth to her fifteenth year and spent most of this time reading. She decided very early on that she wanted to become a writer but first completed a course in commercial studies and entered the writing profession via journalism. She is married and has two daughters.

Her first three novels can be seen as a trilogy. In *Amazone met het blauwe voorhoofd* (1971; Amazon with the Blue Forehead), Monika van Paemel is on a search for her own identity. At the same time she brings the reader closer to his or her own identity through confrontations about country, blood relations, gender, and social prejudice. Her second book, *De confrontatite* (1974; The Confrontation), has a similar objective but proceeds in a more refined and complex manner; the central consciousness is split up into three first-person narrators with whom the reader can identify at will. *Marguerite* (1976) is again simpler and more controlled. The author places the protagonist opposite a dominant grandmother, who also appears in the earlier books, in an attempt to write the dominant woman out of her life so she can realize her autonomy and reaffirm her own identity. At the end of the novel, when the grandmother has been dead for some time and the narrator roams through a museum in Arles and sud-

denly sees an old portrait with the exact likeness of her grandmother, the narrator knows that she will carry this Marguerite with her for the rest of her life. The book is composed of flashbacks and has a circular structure. The maturing granddaughter pushes further and draws ever wider circles around her subject, until Marguerite's death closes the circle. Dominant themes in these novels are the man–woman duality, the position of the modern woman in relation to previous generations, love and lovelessness, time and timelessness. *De vermaledijde vaders* (1985; The Cursed Fathers) is again set in rural Flanders, the land of the author's childhood, and deals with similar problems.

In addition to the novels, Monika van Paemel has written many novellas and critical essays. She often uses the collage and stream-of-consciousness technique and usually fuses fiction and autobiography while emphasizing female characters and their perspectives as women. She has contributed to such prominent journals as *Nieuw Vlaams Tijdschrift*, *Dietsche Warande en Belfort*, and *De Vlaamse Gids*.

Works

Amazone met het blauwe voorhoofd (1971). *De confrontattie* (1974). *De kortste verhalen en gedichten* (1974). *Marguerite* (1976). "De stilte van de grote dagen" (1977). "Moeder waarom schrijven wij?" (1981). "Gebrek aan zolderkamers? Het Moment" (1982). "Het voorlaatste woord" (1983). "Het erotisch moment" (1983). "De westeuropese maagd," "Eerste liefde" (1983). *Zelfportret met juwelendoos. Vlaamse verhalen na 1965* (1984). *De vermaledijde vaders* (1985).

Maya Bijvoet

Vera Panova
1905–1973

a.k.a. Vera Vel'tman, V. V-an, V.V., V. Starosel'skaja, V.S.
Born March 20, 1905, Rostov-on-Don, Russia
Died March 3, 1973, Leningrad
Genre(s): novel, short story, drama, film scenario,
television adaptation, literary criticism, essay,
children's literature, memoir
Language(s): Russian

Vera Fëdorovna Panova is a highly talented and sensitive Soviet writer, whose work is noteworthy for its diversity of forms, wide choice of subject matter, and honest portrayal of ordinary people. She writes about war, work, human emotions, bringing up children, daily life, the art of writing, literature, history, and her own life. Though she has written much for the stage, screen, and television, Vera Panova is best known for her prose. Her war novel *Sputniki* (1946), which presents some of the most memorable characters of Soviet literature, and *Serëzha* (1955), a classic in the literature about children, have both been translated into many languages, including English.

Her personal life was very difficult. When she was five her father drowned in a boating accident. There was no money for formal schooling; she educated herself through reading. From age seventeen, she wrote sketches, *feuilletons*, articles, and stories for a number of Rostov newspapers and magazines, most often under the pen name Vera Vel'tman. She incorporated many of her experiences as a novice journalist during the turbulent twenties into her novel *Sentimental'nyji roman* (1958; A Sentimental Romance). Her years of practical work in journalism are reflected in her later prose style.

In 1925, Vera Panova married Arsenij Starosel'skij. The marriage ended in divorce two years later. Soon after, she married Boris Vakhtin, but this marriage did not last either. In 1937, Vakhtin was falsely denounced and arrested; he died in prison camp. Left alone to provide for her three children, she continued her journalism career and, influenced by Gorky's works, also began writing plays. Two of her dramatic works from this early period won prizes: *Il'ja Kosogor* (1939) and *V staroj Moskve* (1940; In Old Moscow). In 1941, the latter play had been staged successfully in Moscow and was already under rehearsal in Leningrad when World War II broke out. Panova, then living near Leningrad, soon was forced to flee German occupation. With her daughter she set out on foot to rejoin the rest of her family in the Poltava region. At Narva, she found shelter in a synagogue the Germans had turned into a barracks for refugees and Soviet prisoners of war. This wartime experience is the basis for her play *Metelitsa* (1942; The Snowstorm).

In 1943, Panova finally settled in Perm'. To support her family, which then included not only herself and her three children but also her mother and an orphan child, she worked long hours for the local radio and newspapers and also continued her creative writing. She began a novel, *Kruzhilikha*, about life at a large factory in the Urals. In 1944, she published her first long story, "Sem'ja Pirozhkovykh" (The Pirozhkov Family), later reworked and reprinted under the title "Evdokija" (1959). Exhausted by years of hard living and hard work, Panova accepted an unusual assignment: to write a brochure on the work aboard a military hospital train. She wrote the brochure and also the novel *Sputniki* (1946; The Traveling Companions). The immediacy of the narrative, the intimacy she achieves with her characters, and its unusual perspective on the war earned for *Sputniki* a Stalin prize and assured her a prominent place in Soviet literature.

In 1945, Panova married David Jakovlevich Ryvkin, a writer who wrote under the pseudonym of David Dar. This marriage was to last almost twenty-five years. Together with her husband and his two children, Panova resettled herself and her own family in Leningrad.

In 1947, she published *Kruzhilikha*, and it, too, won a Stalin prize although it also sparked lively controversy. Soviet critics considered Listopad, the director of the factory and the main character of the novel, a "negative hero." Though Panova defended her right to create such heroes, she took no risks with her next work, *Jasnyj bereq* (1949; Bright Shore), about postwar life on a collective farm; it followed all the accepted precepts for a Socialist Realist novel. Though *Jasnyj bereq* also received a Stalin prize, Panova openly acknowledged that it was very weak. Nonetheless, the book contains some beautifully rich pages devoted to the five-year-old Serëzha and his world. In the post-Stalin era, she returned to this young hero and made him the central figure in her short novel, *Serëzha* (1955).

Just after Stalin's death in 1953, when the icy constraints on Russian literature were beginning to thaw, Vera Panova published her most daring novel, *Vremena goda* (Seasons of the Year). In this work she boldly exposes some of the Party bureaucracy and corruption; she also disproves the myth that good Communist families produce good children. The novel was immensely popular with the reading public, but Panova was harshly censured in the press for her "naturalism" and "objectivism."

Despite her critics, she maintained her place in the top ranks of Soviet writers. At the Writers Congresses in 1954 and 1959, she was elected a member of the Presidium of the Union of Soviet Writers; she was twice awarded the Order of the Red Banner of Labor (1955, 1965). Being an established writer, Panova was allowed to travel to England, Scotland, and Italy. In 1960, she toured the United States. Her published travel notes and articles, including an epilogue to the Russian translation of *The Catcher in the Rye*, attest to her affinity for Western life and culture.

In the sixties and seventies, Panova also wrote several original film scenarios and adapted many of her own prose works for the screen, the most successful being *Serëzha* (1960; A Summer to Remember) and *Vstuplenie* (1962; Entry into Life), based on her stories "Valja" and "Volodja." Both these films won international awards.

A number of the themes and character types found in Panova's prose works also are used in the plays that she wrote in the sixties. Though many of these plays were successful, she preferred to write prose, claiming that prose forms gave her greater artistic freedom. Toward the end of her life, she experimented with a variety of prose styles: historical tales, *Liki na zare* (1966; Faces at Dawn); a novel in rough form, *Konspekt romana* (1965; Synopsis of a Novel); essays, criticism and travel sketches, *Zametki literatora* (1972; Notes of a Writer); a book of personal reminiscences, *O moej zhizni, knigi i chitateljakh* (1975; About My Life, Books, and Readers); and the fairytale novel *Kotoryj chas?* (1981; What Time Is It?).

In 1967, Vera Panova suffered a stroke that left her partially paralyzed. Though incapacitated, she continued to work, with the help of her family and numerous secretaries, until the day of her death.

The scope of Panova's writing is most impressive, but she will be remembered best for the work devoted to children and young people. Being concerned more with portraying the public and private lives of ordinary individuals than with exploring major political and social themes, Panova often did not meet the demands of Socialist Realism. Her willingness to overstep boundaries and her sincere sentiment coupled with a genuine talent for writing, assure for her a well-deserved place in world literature, as well as in Soviet literature.

Works

Prose: *Sputniki* [The Traveling Companions] (1946). *Kruzhilikha* [The Factory] (1947). *Looking Ahead* (1964). *Jasnyj bereq* [Bright Shore] (1949). *Vremena goda* [Seasons of the Year] (1953). *Serëzha* [Seryozha] (1955). *Time Walked* (1959). *A Summer to Remember* (1962). *On Faraway Street* (1968). *Sentimental'nyji roman* (1958). *Evdokija* [Jevdokia]

(1944–1959). "Valja" (1959). "Volodja" (1959). "Troe mal'chisek u vorot" (1961). "Sëstry" [Sisters] (1965). "Konspekt romana" [Synopsis of a Novel] (1965). *Liki na zare* (1966). *Kotoryj chas?* (1981).

Plays: *Il'ja Kosogor* (1939). *V staroj Moskve* (1940). *Metelitsa* (1942). *Devochki* (1945). *Provody belykh nochej* (1960). *Kak pozhivaesh' paren'?* (1962). *Skol'ko let, skol'ko zim!* [It's Been Ages!] (1966). *Nadezhda Milovanova*, also known as "Vernost'" and "Pogovorim o strannostjax ljubvi" (1967). *Eshchë ne vecher* (1968). *Tred'jakovskij i Volynskij* (1968).

Film and TV scenarios: *Serëzha* (1960). *Evdokija* (1961). *Visokosnyj god* (1962). *Vstuplenie* (1962). *Rano utrom* (1964). *Poezd miloserdija* (1964). *Rabochij posëlok* (1965). *Mal'chik i devochka* (1966). *Chetyre stranitsy odnoj molodoj zhizni* (1967). *Svad'ba kak svad'ba* (1974).

Collections: *Sobranie sochinenij v pjati tomakh* (1969–1970). *P'esy* (1985). *Selected* Works (1975).

Translations: *The Train* [Sputniki] (1949). *The Factory* [Kruzhilikha] (1949). *Looking Ahead* (1964). *Bright Shore* [Jasnyj bereq] (1950). *Seasons of the Year* [Vremena goda] (1957). *Seryozha* [Serëzha] (1956). *Time Walked* [Serëzha] (1959). *A Summer to Remember* [Serëzha] (1962). *On Faraway Street* [Serëzha] (1968). *Jevdokia* [Evdokija] (1964). "Sisters" [Sëstry] (1971). "Notes for a Novel" [Konspekt romana] (1966). "It's Been Ages!" [Skol'ko let, skol'ko zim!] (1968).

Ruth L. Kreuzer

Hortensia Papadat-Bengescu
1876–1955

Born 1876, Iveşti (Galaţi), Romania
Died 1955, Bucharest
Genre(s): novel, short story, drama, essay, poetry
Language(s): Romanian, French

Hortensia Papadat-Bengescu had an overprotected childhood with studies in a local "French pension" and a family that, out of the type of deforming love parents often dispense to daughters, barred her from going to study in Paris as she planned and did not encourage her to write although her interest in literature was quite explicit. To escape at least partially she married quite early and spent her life in many of the provincial towns of Romania (Turnu-Măgurele, Buzău, Focşani, Constanţa) before establishing herself in Bucharest. She came to public writing, first in French and then in Romanian, rather late in her life, due to the advice and action of a woman friend, Constanţa Marino-Moscu, herself a writer.

Papadat-Bengescu's first three volumes—*Ape adînci* (1919; Deep Waters), *Sfinxul* (1921; The Sphinx) and *Femeia în faţa oglinzii* (1921; The Woman in Front of the Mirror)—contained lyrical introspective short stories in which she approached the passionate "life without deeds" of urban female characters that gathered, as in Duras's "Les Dames des Roches Noires," on the terrace of a summer spa hotel and exchanged unending convergent stories evolving around essential silence, noisy gestures, violent gaze, desire, refusal, and repulsion. No one until Hortensia Papadat-Bengescu had either shown with such lucid strength the value, vitality, and dynamism of the specifically female inner experience or had the capacity to bring to consciousness and illuminate, from an unyieldingly feminine point of view, the struggle of hate between women and men in love and life. Hortensia Papadat-Bengescu was acclaimed and attacked with passion from the very beginning as a strong and daring intellectual writer, evoking Proust but at the same time radically different from him due to her unorthodox preference for the unprejudiced exploration of female intersubjectivity.

Basically at the same time, in a "document novel" entitled *Balaurul* (1923; The Dragon), Papadat-Bengescu was among the first in Europe to provide a critical account of World War I from the point of view of a female character. During the war, the writer had worked as a volunteer nurse for the Red Cross, and the novel is visibly written with an attention to the accurate reproduction of each and every detail. Pages like those devoted to the peasant soldier "whose heart was visible" as the result of a shell splinter wound were and remain powerful and paved the way for a rich series of Romanian novels dealing with World War I by Rebreanu, Sadoveanu, or Cezar Petrescu.

By combining the introspective and documentary writing hypostases Hortensia Papadat-Bengescu became the founder of the modern urban novel in Romanian literature. The most important of her novels— *Fecioarele despletite* (1926; The Dishevelled Maidens), *Concert din muzică de Bach* (1927; Concert from Bach Music), *Drumul ascuns* (1932; The Hidden Way), *Rădăcini* (1938; Roots), and the unpublished *Străina* (The Stranger Woman), which was mysteriously lost and did not resurface until recently—build up a Proustian and Freudian "comédie humaine" centered upon the different generations of a pseudoaristocratic Romanian family, the Hallipa's. Hortensia Papadat-Bengescu speaks about physical decay and moral arid-

ity, about character mutations and annihilation, about sickness and death. Hers is an ample and ironic chronicle of Romanian urban and suburban life as well as a revealing and as yet unequaled analysis of the diversity of suffering—from the medically informed unforgettable pages about men and women surveying the progression and then gradually surrendering to tuberculosis, cancer, cardiac affections, neurosis, or ulcer to the incisive pages describing the annihilation of disarmed sick wives by cold professional husbands, of erratic aristocrats by vital upstart wives, or the inexorable transformation of soft, peaceful, and devoted human beings into hateful, resentful ones because they were systematically wronged and abused by indifferent and strong life partners. There is a wide diversity of characters, from the princes, pseudo-princes, established bourgeois, and nouveaux-riches to the suburban pimp, from the submissive wives and disoriented, almost animalist daughters, who work painfully to accumulate money for their husbands, lovers, or fathers, to the feminists, from bankers, business women and men, neurologists, obstetricians, to university professors and composers, from miserable servants or poor marginal members of well-to-do families to cold and authoritative women that distractedly subdue the whole community around them, including at times a shy, loving husband.

In 1946, on the occasion of her seventieth birthday, Hortensia Papadat-Bengescu received the prestigious National Award for Prose Writing. She opened a new and important avenue for the Romanian modern novel. Nor has she been surpassed as a feminist in Romanian literature and must be considered, together with Virginia Woolf, Nathalie Sarraute, or Marguerite Duras, among the most important European women writers of our time.

Works

Ape adînci [Deep Waters] (1919). *Bătrînul* [The Old Man], play (1920–1921). *Sfinxul* [The Sphinx] (1921). *Femeia în faţa oglinzii* [The Woman in Front of the Mirror] (1921). *Balaurul* [The Dragon] (1923). *Romanţă provincială* [Provincial Romance], short stories (1925). *Fecioarele despletite* [The Dishevelled Maidens] (1926). *Concert din muzică de Bach* [Concert from Bach Music] (1927). *Desenuri tragice* [Tragic Drawings], short stories (1927). *Drumul ascuns* [The Hidden Way] (1932). *Logodnicul* [The Fiancé] (1935). *Rădăcini* [Roots], 2 vols. (1938). *Străina* [The Stranger Woman] (lost while in press at Cioflec). *Teatru* [Plays], ed. Eugenia Tudor (1965). *Opere* [Works], 3 vols., ed. Eugenia Tudor (1972, 1975, 1979).

Sanda Golopentia

Larin Paraske
1833–1904

Born 1833, Lempaala, Finland
Died 1904, Metsapirtti
Genre(s): rune songs
Language(s): Finnish

The names of thousands of rune singers are known from the Karelian cultural area on both sides of the border between Finland and Russia. At various stages of the Finnish national romantic movement, primarily during the nineteenth century, an abundance of archaic folksong, characterized by trochaic meter and alliteration, was collected from these singers. The most famous of them was Larin Paraske, an illiterate peasant woman who was Orthodox in religion.

Larin Paraske was born and raised as the daughter of a serf on the Russian side of the border. She was orphaned at a young age and, at the age of twenty, married forty-year-old Kaurila Teppananpoika from the Finnish side of the border. As his wife, she became known as Larin Paraske, named after his poverty-stricken farm. Nine children were born to them, and of these only three grew to maturity. Because her husband was sickly and the need was great, Paraske sought additional income in many ways: she pulled barges on the river, begged, and raised children from orphanages in St. Petersburg. Widowed in 1888, Paraske came upon a new source of income: the clergyman, Adolf Neovius, who was collecting folklore, noticed Paraske's talent and, paying her small sums, he began to write down the songs she had in her memory.

This was the beginning of a collaboration which lasted for many years. When he moved from Karelia to the environs of Helsinki, Neovius invited Paraske to come along as well. There he introduced the singer to numerous prominent artists of the time and continued recording her runes. It was during this time that Albert Edelfelt and Aksel Järnefelt painted their renowned portraits of Larin Paraske, and it was she who gave Jean Sibelius his most significant contact with folksong. The collection completed by Neovius contains one of the most extensive repertoires of folksongs collected from a northern European woman.

Equally represented in Larin Paraske's repertoire of 1,500 folksongs were all the primary genres of southern Karelia, including epic, lyric, wedding, and charm runes. Central to her repertoire and that of the entire poetry area, is an emphasis upon lyric verse and women's experience. It was women's song which reigned in these areas during the nineteenth century. Paraske sang an abundance of young women's songs concerned with the relationship between children and parents, particularly the mother. There are also many songs about helplessness at the death of parents. Larin Paraske's verse is rich in wedding songs concerned with the difficulties entailed in a bride's departure from her home. There are mother's songs and lullabies intuiting a child's future and sorrow at a child's death. There are some love songs, a great many songs about marriage, and, in the final phase, widow's songs. There is also an abundance of songs about care, the theme of which is a nameless, undefined sorrow. In one way or another, of course, these relate to the experience of women as do her other songs.

Although the poetic subject matter in Paraske's songs relates to general human experience, her songs are also autobiographical. Larin Paraske's tendency to improvise, to join together traditional subject matter in a new way, to continuously return to a particular subject, to rearrange certain songs, is clearly unique to her singing. In examining these dimensions of her songs, one observes, for example, that the relationship between husband and wife takes on more prominence in Paraske's songs than is usual for rune singers, making her widow's songs uniquely forceful and piercing.

Primarily, however, Paraske addresses us as one who has powerfully expressed the rich women's culture typical of her particular background. Her repertoire, which is the truest and most complete example of southern Karelian folksong, demonstrates that, even when subordinated and under difficult circumstances, women have been able to create a culture out of their own experiences and, with its aid, come to master their own lives.

Low the long-tailed duck's spirits
swimming in chilly water
   lower the orphan's
walking about the village
   cold the pigeon's heart
pecking the village haystack
chilly the sparrow's belly
   drinking chilled water:
   colder mine, poor me
   colder than any.

Translation by Keith Bosley

Senni Timonen

Emilia Pardo Bazán
1851–1921

Born 1851, La Coruña, Spain
Died 1921, Madrid
Genre(s): short story, novel, literary criticism
Language(s): Spanish

Emilia Pardo Bazán stands out in the history of Spanish literature as one of Spain's few recognized women writers before the twentieth century. She was famous in her own time not only as a novelist, short story writer, and literary critic and historian of the first order but also as a woman of amazing versatility and independence. In an age when women were advised to remain in the roles assigned by convention—wife, mother, nun—Pardo Bazán audaciously wrote feminist essays and introduced into Spain the shocking theories of French naturalism propounded by Émile Zola. Although she never subscribed to the determinist theories of Zola's naturalism, she did employ its techniques and themes. Pardo Bazán's literary interests, however, exceeded any one literary school or method, and during her long career she wrote in the traditional style of Spanish realism and the spiritual-mystical mode in fashion during the turn of the century. She also incorporated the dictates of naturalism, modifying them to suit the temper of her talent and times. Eclectic is the word that best applies to Pardo Bazán.

Emilia Pardo Bazán's intellectual curiosity and determination were manifested early; she virtually educated herself, reading avidly and widely in classical and modern literature, learning English so that she could read that literature, reading French and Italian literature in the original language, and delving into philosophical and aesthetic problems. She wrote essays and books on subjects as varied as St. Francis and Christian mysticism, modern French and Russian literature, and the Russian revolution. No subject seemed inappropriate to this energetic woman who even founded a literary magazine for which she herself wrote all the material for several years.

Although married and the mother of three children, she spent most of her time apart from her husband, maintaining a home in Madrid where she reigned over a literary salon. In recognition of her intellectual abilities and acute knowledge of modern literature, she was honored as the first woman to occupy a professorship at the University in Madrid.

Pardo Bazán was a controversial figure, inspiring both acclaim and disdain, but she was nonetheless accepted, even by those less than enthusiastic about her insistence on proving herself as a writer and intellectual, and becoming one of the most significant writers of her time. Her reputation has grown in the years since her death. Today Pardo Bazán is seen as a major writer and critic and as a pioneer in women's issues. She wrote twenty novels, several volumes of literary criticism and history, hundreds of short stories, and hundreds of essays.

Works

Obras completas. 44 vols. (1886–1926). *Obras completas*, ed. Federico Carlos Sainz de Robles. 2 vols. (1947).

Translations: *Short Stories by Emilia Pardo Bazán*, ed. Albert Shapiro and F.J. Hurley (1933). *The Son of the Bondwoman*, tr. Ethel Harriet Hearn (1976).

Mary E. Giles

Callirhoe Parren
1861–1940

a.k.a. Maïa
Born 1861, Rethymno, Crete
Died 1940, Athens, Greece
Genre(s): journalism, novel, short story, drama, essay, literary criticism
Language(s): Greek

Callirhoe Siganou was born in 1861 in a middle-class family of Crete. She studied in the best schools for girls in Athens and, in 1878, she graduated from the Arsakeion School for training teachers. After her graduation, she was invited to run the Greek community school for girls in Odessa, where she worked for two years. She also ran, for several years, the Zapeion School of the Greek community in Adrianople. In 1880 she was married to the French journalist Jean Parren, the founder of the Athens News Agency, and some years later she moved permanently to Athens.

Callirhoe Parren was the leading figure of late-nineteenth and early-twentieth-century Greek feminism. In 1887 she started publishing the *Efimeris ton Kyrion* (1887–1918; Ladies' Newspaper), the first feminist publication in Greece, exclusively edited by women. Under her editorship, the *Ladies' Newspaper* became not only the organizational center for women's emancipation but also one of the best distributed weeklies in Greece and among the Greek diaspora (5,000 copies). Its campaigns for women's rights had a big impact and resulted in the first successful protective legislation for women. Parren was closely connected to the European and American women's movement and represented the Ladies' Newspaper in several International Conferences (1888, 1889, 1896, and 1900 in Paris and 1893 in Chicago). In 1896, she founded the Union of Greek Women. She was also the founder of various welfare organizations for women (Sunday School, Asylum of Sainte Catherine, The Soup Kitchen, etc.).

Besides her unremitting activity as a pedagogue, feminist, and social reformer, Parren was also one of the main intellectual figures of the late-nineteenth-century cultural life in Athens. She was the first professional woman journalist and worked for two of the biggest daily newspapers, *Acropolis* and *Asty* (City). She published her *Women's History* in 1889. Her *salon*, known as the "literary Saturdays," attracted the most prominent representatives of the literary and artistic avant-garde of the end of the century. Her wide culture, her knowledge of foreign languages (she spoke English, French, Russian, and Italian fluently), her traveling experience but most of all her strong personality, won her a wide recognition both in Greece and abroad. Among her friends were Jules Simon and Juliette Adam as well as some of the leading figures of the literary avant-garde of the 1880s like Gavriilidis, Xenopoulos, and the national poet Kostis Palamas, who wrote a famous poem for her. A skillful tactician, she used her own exceptional admission in this male milieu to build up a policy of alliances with the women's movement. But this did not prevent her from being a fearsome polemicist who could publicly attack the most respected male intellectuals if she considered women's interests jeopardized. Her violent dispute with Roïdis, the father of Greek literary criticism, provoked the famous "*querelae* over women writers" (1893), which occupied the Athenian press for months.

For Parren writing was an invaluable arm in women's hands, a privileged means for self-assertion. As an editor of the *Ladies' Newspaper*, she did everything to promote women's literature, including the organization of literary competitions, and managed in a very short time to get contributions from nearly all the major women writers of the late nineteenth century, including those who did not consider themselves feminists. Women writers, she believed, should have a double goal: "free themselves from the implacable tyranny of public opinion which turns their writings into another evidence of their servile submission" and, at the same time, "convince the multitude that the New Woman is the moral and intellectual equal of man and deserves total liberty." This double, and to a certain extent contradictory, func-

tion she attributed to women's literature marked her own fiction, which is characterized by a permanent tension between didactic intention and genuine literary ambition. Written at a time when realism and the "urban novel" were making their first appearance in Greek literature, her novels developed a virulent critique of existing gender relations in a developing society fascinated by the most superficial expressions of the bourgeois decency in the "civilized" West, and yet largely submitted to the most obscurantist social codes of the Mediterranean traditional culture. But while showing that women bear the brunt of this transitional social order, Parren is also working out the first articulate utopian visions of gender relations, putting forward alternative social values based on gender equality, women's autonomy and self-fulfillment, female friendship, and solidarity.

Parren's novels were first published in the *Ladies' Newspaper* under the pen name *Maïa* and met with an enthusiastic response from the female readership of the journal. The first three novels were published subsequently in three volumes: *I Hirafetimeni* (1900; The Emancipated Woman), *I Mayissa* (1901; The Enchantress) and *To Neon Symvoleon* (1902; The New Contract) formed a trilogy (*Ta Vivlia tis Avyis*, The Books of Dawn) about the solitary and tormented odyssey of two generations of Greek women toward emancipation and self-accomplishment. The trilogy had a favorable reception from such critics as Grigorios Xenopoulos and Kostis Palamas who underlined the "generous contribution of Parren in the development of Greek social novel." The trilogy also served as a basis for a play called *Nea Yineka*. (The New Woman) put on in 1907 with the participation of Marika Cotopouli, the most popular dramatic actress of the 20th century, which contributed to popularize the work and ideas of its author. *The Emancipated Woman* was translated into French and published in *Journal des Débats* and *Revue Littéraire*. Her other novels, To *Maramenon Krinon* (1909; The Faded Lily) and *Horis Onoma* (n.d., Without a Name), were also published, but they have been lost. We know them, however, from their initial publication in the *Ladies' Newspaper*.

Callirhoe Parren died in 1940, in Athens. Although she was one of the most controversial and influential figures of her time, she gradually sank into oblivion until the late 1970s, when she was rediscovered by the emerging feminist scholarship. Her writings have not yet been reprinted.

Works

Istoria tis Yinekos [Women's History] (1889). *Zoi Enos Etous* [One Year of Life] (1894). *Epistole Athineas is*

Parissinin [Letters of an Athenian Woman to a Parisian] (1896–1897). *I Hirafetimeni* [The Emancipated Woman] (1900). *I Mayissa* [The Enchantress] (1901). *To Neon Symvolean* [The New Contract] (1902). *Nea Yineka* [New Woman] (1907). *To Maramenon Krinon* [The Faded Lily] (1909). *Horis Onoma* [Without a Name] (n.d.). *Ta Taxithia Mou* [My Trips] (n.d.).

Translations: "*L'Emancipée*," *Journal des Débats* (February 4 to March 18, 1907).

Eleni Varikas

Françoise Pascal
1632–ca. 1698

Born February 1632, Lyon, France
Died ca. 1698, Paris
Genre(s): drama, verse
Language(s): French

Born in the bourgeoisie, Françoise Pascal received a much better education than most girls of her social class. She had the opportunity to see dramatic performances in her native Lyons, and she soon tried to write plays. In 1655, her *Agathonphile martyr* was published in Lyons. It is taken from Camus's novel *Agathonphile*, which had already served as a source for Marthe Cosnard's *Chastes Martirs*, but Françoise Pascal probably did not know the latter's play. She did not follow the rules of classical theater; scenes are not linked, the action is not unified, it does not take place only within Rome, and it requires at least two days.

Two years later, her second play, *L'Endymion*, was published again in Lyons. It is more satisfactorily constructed; it also requires an elaborate setting, with a chariot for Diane, forest, trees, flowers, an altar, etc. That same year in her *Diverses Poésies* appeared two one-act farces, *L'Amoureuse vaine et ridicule* (The Vain and Ridiculous Amorous Woman) and *L'Amoureux extravagant* (The Extravagant Amorous Man). In the first one, the central figure, though old and ugly, is convinced that all men who see her fall in love with her. The other farce shows a ridiculous poet who is deprived of his money by a clever valet.

In 1661, Françoise Pascal went back to a five-act play with *Sésostris*. She still paid little attention to the classical unities, but the characters are moved by genuine emotion and the story is well told. This play shows considerable progress over her earlier works.

For her last play, Françoise Pascal returned to the farce. *Le vieillard amoureux* (1664; The Amorous Old Man) uses eight-syllable verse. The plot is made of tricks played by a girl and her helpers to overcome her father's opposition to her marriage. The miserly father falls in love with his daughter's lover who has disguised himself as a young woman.

Françoise Pascal also loved music and painting. In the latter part of her life she published several collections of pious verse. She was the first woman dramatist of the seventeenth century who wrote more than a single play.

Works

Agathonphile martyr (1655). *La mort du grand et véritable Cyrus* (1655). *L'Amoureuse vaine et ridicule* (1657). *L'Amoureux extravagant* (1657). *L'Endymion* (1657). *Sésostris* (1661). *Le vieillard amoureux* (1664). *Le commerce du Parnasse* (1669). *Cantiques spirituels ou noëls nouveaux* (1670). *Les réflexions de la Magdelène dans le temps de sa pénitence* (1674). *Les entretiens de la Vierge et de S. Jean l'Evangeliste* (1680).

Marie-France Hilgar

Margaret Paston
1423–1482

Born 1423, Norfolk, England
Died 1482
Genre(s): letters
Language(s): English

Prior to her marriage to John Paston, nothing is known of Margaret Paston's life except that she was the daughter of a wealthy landowner of Norfolk. From the day of her first meeting with her future husband, however, she became one of a handful of medieval women—or medieval men—whose individual experiences were recorded and preserved for future generations, in her case in a vast collection of Paston family correspondence and papers spanning almost a century. Had she married anyone else, she might or might not have ever written a letter, but in either event her experience would have been completely lost to us, and so in a very real sense the Paston we now reconstruct epitomizes the extent to which a woman's life was determined by the particular role of wife to which she was assigned. As her own words reveal, this role (for a woman of her class and times) was circumscribed and subordinate, but in no way was it marginal or powerless. Her central and formidable responsibility included and is manifest in her letter writing, but it may be misleading to think of her as a "woman writer" without an initial word of qualification. There is no evidence that Paston was in the least bit learned or interested in reading and writing in ways that we would understand; it is not even possible to be sure that she was able to write, since the 104 extant letters sent in her name were written in a number of different hands. It is most probable that she could and did write herself, but like most affluent men and women in the fifteenth century more often hired a scribe to take dictation. It is a voice rather than a hand, then, that speaks in her letters.

A single, not extraordinary circumstance (for the fifteenth century) occasioned both Paston's most remarkable activities and many of her letters: for a good deal of their married life, her husband was away from home. John Paston was a student at Cambridge when he married and left his wife with his in-laws while he finished his studies there and then went on to the Inner Temple in London. Later he spent many months of each year in London, when the courts were in session, and on a few occasions he was detained in Fleet prison as a result of the vagaries of his complex property claims and political maneuvers. The nature of the disputes in which the Pastons were involved often left Paston to defend, in a literal sense, their properties. One of the early struggles centered on a mansion in Gresham that they bought from Geoffrey Chaucer's son Thomas, to which a rival baron also laid claim. In 1449–1450, John Paston seized the property and left his wife in charge while he went to London to take further legal action. The rival claimants soon retook the house with armed forces, physically removing Paston from the premises and then looting and partially destroying the house. Similarly, when a decade later the Pastons inherited Caister Castle from John Fastolf (Shakespeare's Falstaff, and apparently a distant relative of Paston's), they were subsequently sued and attacked by various claimants. Paston was again left to fend off enemies for long periods of time, and no settlement of this private war took place until after her husband's death in 1466.

Paston also bore at least eight children, six of whom survived, and even when her husband was at home planned for and orchestrated all the daily needs of a large household of family and servants. Modern biographers often comment on what is perceived by our standards as her harshness and lack of affection for her children, and her relationship with one of her daughters is often cited. When it became known that her daughter had secretly exchanged a vow of marriage with the Pastons' bailiff, Paston attempted to block official sanction of the unapproved match. When her efforts failed, she formally refused to let her daughter back into her home, and the daughter was sheltered in a nunnery until the wedding took place.

But her function as mother and even as "housewife," in the broadest sense of the term, is not a dominant theme in Paston's writing, though occasionally she requested that her husband buy certain food or clothes for her and her family. Her letters center, however, on her part in the public spheres of property management, politics, and local warfare; Virginia Woolf described them as "the letters of an honest bailiff to his master." Her writing was never an incidental part of her life, a leisure pastime, or a vehicle of self-expression; instead, it was an integral and essential part of the job she undertook. She acted repeatedly in her husband's place to manage his large estate and the complex affairs it entailed, buying and selling goods, negotiating with his tenants and enemies, holding courts, and pleading his cases. She reported on what she had done and agreed (or in some cases refused) to perform future services for him. She passed on appeals and information from others and kept him well-advised on what was happening on the local front, since affairs of all sorts affected their family peace and prosperity. She sometimes asked for money and sometimes agreed to send him funds. In all this, she played a crucial advisory role, evaluating and proposing strategy and recommending action.

After her husband's death, most of Paston's extant letters were written to two of her sons, the eldest, Sir John Paston, and the younger John Paston. While still carrying out Sir John's occasional orders and always acting and plotting on his behalf, she advised her sons more directly and authoritatively than she did their father on increasingly troublesome financial and political matters and even resorted to threats in her efforts to force the titular head of the family to act as she thought he should. Her letters to her eldest son are filled with reproaches for spending too much, failing to work hard, forgetting to write or come home, selling off family property to pay for personal indulgence, and neglecting to buy a tombstone for his father's grave. In the later letters, she spoke more and more openly with disappointment and bitterness as well as with characteristic anxiety, as her son failed to take the charge and care to which she, for his and his namer's sake, devoted her entire life.

Works

The Paston Letters and Papers of the Fifteenth Century, ed. N. Davis (1971).

Elaine Tuttle Hansen

Heidi Pataki
1940–

Born November 2, 1940, Vienna, Austria
Genre(s): journalism, poetry, prose, essay
Language(s): German

Heidi Pataki is one of the keenest observers and sharpest critics of contemporary society. She is well known for her satirical, provocative poetry that unites language experimentation with social criticism. She is also known as an essayist and film critic, and she was one of the earliest activists in the Austrian women's movement.

Pataki was born in 1940 in Vienna, where she attended school and studied at the university with a concentration in journalism and art history. Since 1970 she has worked as editor of the journal *Neues Forum* and in the early 1980s also as editor of *Filmschrift*. She lives today as a freelance writer and journalist in Vienna, where she is a frequent contributor to newspapers and radio stations. She is a member of the Graz Authors' Association and also of various women's groups.

How does one write a poem today? Is poetry even possible any more? That is the question Pataki poses, and she answers it in the negative, as paradoxically exemplified in two outstanding volumes of poetry: *Schlagzeilen* (1968; headlines) and *Stille post* (1978; rumor). Poetry today is seen not as a moral or political problem nor even as a psychological or aesthetic one but solely as a problem of language. Is our language still usable; or has it not rather exhausted itself? Anything we say has been said a thousand times before, and this use and abuse of language has rendered it vacuous. What was once metaphor is now commonplace, profundities have become trivialities, and meaningful expression has degenerated to hackneyed phrases.

Pataki confronts the situation with clear-eyed and cold-blooded radicalism, as expressed in a theoretical statement accompanying *Schlagzeilen* entitled "Eleven Theses about Poetry": "Originality is nonsense," and "anyone who still tries to write a new poem is anachronistic." She draws the conclusions for her own poetry by picking up the "headlines"—clichés, banalities, and slogans—from ordinary discourse and arranging them in a montage-like construction. Paying more attention to the sound and rhythm than to the meaning (which is in any case absent), she establishes unexpected connections and invents unusual meanings, and the pawnshop-particles of language are powerfully evocative in their new associative context. Although she treats poetry as if it were a game, a certain sadness is also present, as exemplified in the pro-

grammatic poem, "you have taken my language away." One is driven to despair at the realization that one's language has been so co-opted by advertising, politics, and all sorts of misuse that the words no longer mean anything. Despair, however, manifests itself in irony and parody rather than sentiment or nostalgia, and the apparent debunking of language only bears witness to its vital importance for our well-being.

Stille post takes its title from the party game in which a sentence is whispered around a circle only to come out at the end in drastically mutilated form. The poetry demonstrates this crisis of language by a plundering of the literary tradition in true postmodernist fashion. Lines and fragments from the "sacred" canon of *Minnesang* and folksong, from Goethe, Eichendorff, Heine, Rilke, Trakl, and many more appear in this montage—recognizable, but radically altered by the context. "hosanna," for example, presents a collection of famous "whoever" and "whenever" lines without however any result clauses. The irony is global, but the parody is not of the tradition but of contemporary society. The philosophical and linguistic presuppositions are reflected upon in a series of poems with the illustrative titles "metaph./ysics" and "semant./ical & c.," in which unreadability itself becomes thematic.

Some of the same snippets from the tradition are taken up for further variation in "metaphor./ics & c." and intertwined with banal slogans, whereby the metaphors are phonetic and syntactic rather than semantic and thus untranslatable. In this cliché-ridden world where individuality and authenticity are mere anachronisms, the title poem ironically opens with the admonition: "mister meier, get real!" and concludes as anonymously with a "place for mister maier! / (mayer?) / meier." The crass juxtaposition of disparate elements reveals the paradox of poetry in present-day society and questions the possibility of speaking at all. The montage stands, as the author states in her "epilogue" to *Stille post*, as "a museum displaying the dried-up trophies of the indestructible tradition. To destroy the indestructible—that is the paradox of the poem."

The apparently disrespectful parody and play with language are not so much a critique of the tradition as they are a questioning of its meaning for us, given the collective, mechanized, consumer-oriented society in which we live. The aggressive act of deformation can only be understood as a result of passionate attachment. Pataki knows the literary tradition extremely well, and she demonstrates the thesis that any poem quotes its predecessors. But what happens to art that undergoes reproduction *ad nauseam*? Pataki possesses an extraordinary lyrical, rhythmic talent, and one has the feeling she could write any number of poems in the conventional manner. By taking, however, the poem itself as her topic she has created a type of metalinguistic commentary in which the poem turns back on itself to investigate the conditions of its own existence.

Pataki is obviously not the first to cry "rotten!" to "2,000 years of Western culture." A Nietzschean influence is evident in her radical critique of language and culture as well as in her vitalistic affirmation of life; Nietzschean philosophy is also the maddening disparity between social convention and utopian vision, which elicits a strong emotional reaction. With wit, humor, and irony Pataki demonstrates the "pastness" of the past, and she demands a language and art commensurate with the present. The provocative nature of the undertaking is visually represented by photographs of the author linking the spiritual striptease with a physical one. Given the excess baggage with which we are all encumbered, according to Pataki's perspective, one cannot be radical enough.

Works

Schlagzeilen. gedichte (1968). *Fluchtmodelle. zur emanzipation der frau. Politisch-soziologische satiren* (1972). *Stille post. gedichte* (1978).

Beth Bjorklund

Karolina Pavlova
1807–1893

Born July 22, 1807, Iaroslav, Russia
Died 1893, Dresden, Germany
Genre(s): poetry, translation
Language(s): Russian, French, German

Karolina Karlovna Pavlova (née Jaenisch), generally considered Russia's major nineteenth-century woman poet, was born in Iaroslav, north of Moscow, into a family that was German on her father's side and French and English on her mother's. Her father, Karl Ivanovich Jaenisch, studied medicine at Leipzig University. He then returned to Russia, married Karolina Karlovna's mother, Elisaveta, and received an appointment as professor of physics and chemistry in the Moscow Medical-Surgical Academy after Karolina Karlovna's birth.

Pavlova had an eventful and stormy life. Her earliest memory as a five-year-old, she wrote in a memoir, was fleeing Moscow with her family in 1812 at the approach of Napoleon's army. In the same memoir she recounted that in 1816, when she was nine, her seven-year-old sister died. Perhaps because

Karolina Karlovna thus became an only child, she received an unusually good education for a woman of her time through private tutors. She showed an early gift for languages and by the time she was eighteen knew French, English, German, Italian, and of course Russian, as well as some Spanish and Polish. In the course of her career Pavlova would write in and translate to and from a variety of languages. Although best known as a Russian poet, she also wrote poetry in French and German, and translated others' poetry from German, French, English, Polish, and Greek into Russian; from Russian, Polish, English, and French into German; and from Russian into French.

By 1825 when she was eighteen, Pavlova had begun to attend the literary salon of Princess Zinaida Volkonskaia, a salon that attracted leading literary and philosophical lights of the day including Aleksandr Pushkin. Here Karolina Karlovna met Adam Mickiewicz, the exiled Polish revolutionary and poet. Mickiewicz, who was impoverished, started giving her Polish lessons, and in November 1827 proposed to her. When a rich uncle who disapproved of the match threatened to disinherit Karolina Karolovna and her entire family, Mickiewicz quickly lost interest and moved to St. Petersburg. He did not, however, bother to break the engagement until 1829 when Karolina Karolovna asked him to clarify their relationship and he was about to leave Russia. Although Pavlova never saw him again, this experience appears to have affected her deeply; over the course of her life not only did she translate several of Mickiewicz's works into French, but she also wrote several poems about him, two entitled "November 10," the date of his proposal to her.

In 1833 Karolina Karlovna made her literary debut with *Das Nordlich* (Northern Lights). The book consisted of her translations into German of works by Russia's most famous poets (Aleksandr Pushkin, Vasily Zhukovksy, Nikolai Iazykov, Evgeny Baratynsky, Anton Delvig, Dmitry Venevitinov) as well as her own German poetry. *Das Nordlich*, which was published in Dresden, received excellent reviews, both in Russia and Germany, including praise from Goethe himself.

In 1836 the Jaenischs' rich uncle finally died, thus at the age of twenty-nine Karolina Karlovna suddenly found herself an heiress surrounded by eager suitors. Her choice was unfortunate. In 1837 she married Nikolai Filippovich Pavlov (1805–1864), a promising writer enjoying great success at literary salons at the time thanks to his *Tri povesti* (1835; Three Tales) which attacked the institution of serfdom. Pavlov later told his friends that he had married his wife for her money.

During the 1840s the Pavlovs ran a distinguished

literary salon where Westernizers (those who believed Russia should become part of Europe), hotly debated the Slavophiles (those who rejected Western European values), and where such writers as the Aksakovs, Evgeny Baratynsky, Afanasy Fet, Nikolai Gogol, Timofei Granovsky, and Alexander Herzen read their latest works.

In 1839 Ippolit, the Pavlovs' only child, was born, and Pavlova published two new works. *Les Preludes* consisted of Pavlova's translations, into French this time, of English, German, Polish, and Russian poetry, as well as some of her own French poetry. Pavlova's translation into French of Schiller's play, *Joan of Arc*, also appeared during this year. She had already started writing poetry in Russian, much of which began to appear in various Russian literary journals.

Meanwhile Nikolai Pavlov's literary career was not keeping pace. Reviewers expressed disappointment that his second collection of stories (1839) did not live up to the promise of the first. He stopped writing, and increasingly spent his time (and Pavlova's fortune, which he controlled) playing and losing at cards.

It was during this period that Pavlova wrote and published her best known work, *Dvoinaia Zhizn'* (1848; A Double Life). The work, which was very well received, recounts in alternating prose and poetry sections the daytime life and nighttime visions of Cecilia, an eighteen-year-old member of Moscow society. Although the prose section seems to end happily, with Cecilia marrying the man she loves, in the poetry sections Pavlova suggests that this marriage will bring Cecilia only pain, disillusionment, and the loss of her true self.

Pavlova's own marital situation grew worse. In 1849 she invited a relative, Evgeniia Aleksandrovna Tannenberg, to live with her. Pavlov fell in love with Tannenberg, moved her into a separate apartment, and had three children by her. In the meantime he continued to gamble with and lose tremendous amounts of his wife's money. In 1852 Pavlova's parents complained to the Moscow military governor about Pavlov, who had tried to mortgage his wife's estate without telling her. The governor, reportedly angry on his own account because of an epigram Pavlov had written about him, took the occasion to have Pavlov's library searched. When the search revealed forbidden books critical of the government, Pavlov was arrested and exiled to Perm for a year. Pavlov suddenly became a martyr for the liberal cause and Pavlova the object of ridicule and condemnation for causing his imprisonment.

To escape this social obloquy Pavlova and her parents moved from Moscow to St. Petersburg where misfortune quickly followed; her father died of cholera in 1853. When Pavlova did not go to the funeral, supposedly because of fear of infection, a new scandal erupted and Pavlova and her mother moved to Dorpat (Tartu), Estonia.

During this time "Razgovor v Kremle" (1854; Conversation in the Kremlin) appeared, a narrative poem perceived at the time as expressing Slavophile views. Consequently, Pavlova was once again attacked by the liberal press.

In Dorpat Pavlova became acquainted with Boris Utin, a law student twenty-five years her junior at the University of Dorpat, who between 1853 and 1855 became her last and most intense love, and the inspiration for a cycle of love poetry. Pavlova made a few short visits back to Russia in 1855 and 1857 and traveled through Europe and to the Middle East. In 1858 she settled in Dresden where, because her husband had squandered her estate, she would live in poverty until her death in 1893.

In 1859 she published *Quadrille*, a narrative poem in which four women who meet at a ball try to determine if they or society are to blame for their unhappy marriages. In 1861 the politically controversial narrative poem, *Conversation in Trianon*, was published in London. The poem, which Pavlova had written in 1848 in reaction to the French revolution of that year, expressed her idea that revolutions were both inevitable and ultimately futile since new dictators would simply replace the old. The work could not be published in Russia because the censorship forbade any reference to revolutions.

In 1863 Pavlova had her collected works published in Russia where they were not well received. The literary climate had changed in twenty years and now the most influential Russian literary critics found Pavlova's elegiac, romantic, beautifully crafted poetry old-fashioned and frivolous.

Pavlova's last important friendship was with A.K. Tolstoy, a playwright (and distant relative of Leo Tolstoy) whom she met in Dresden in 1861 and who visited her there frequently until his death in 1875. Tolstoy managed to arrange a small pension for Pavlova, perhaps in gratitude for her very popular translations of his plays into German.

Pavlova died in 1893 having outlived Mickiewicz, her husband, her son, and A.K. Tolstoy. Some of the obituaries mentioned that she left a trunk of unpublished manuscripts, others mentioned a draft for an expanded version of her complete works which she had entrusted to her grandson. Nothing further was heard of either.

Scholarship about Pavlova, as often happens with woman writers, has focused disproportionately on her relations with the various men in her life; her father, the men she loved, the men who loved her, her husband, and male critics' reactions to her work (the most famous, Vissarion Belinsky, praised her for her "muzhestvennyi energiia," her "masculine energy"). There is, however, ample evidence that women and women's experience played an important role in Pavlova's work. She wrote several works concerned with women's position in society (*A Double Life, Quadrille*, "Jeanne d'Arc") and two poems about women poets ["Three Souls" (1845) and "On Reading the Poetry of a Young Woman" (1846)]. Twentieth-century Russian women poets in their turn have honored Pavlova in their work. Sofiia Parnok (1885–1933) dedicated a poem to her and Marina Tsvetaeva (1892–1941) named one of her poetry collections *Remeslo* [Craft] after one of Pavlova's most famous poems in which she describes poetry as her "sacred craft."

Works

Polnoe sobranie stikhotvorenii. Vstupitel'naia stat'ia P.P. Gromova (Moscow, Leningrad, 1964).

Translation: *A Double Life*, tr. Barbara Heldt (1986).

Diane Greene

Caterina Percoto
1812–1887

Born 1812, Udine, Italy
Died 1887, Udine
Genre(s): short story
Language(s): Italian

Born to a noble family of Friuli, which was then under Austrian occupation, Percoto spent seven years of her adolescence in a boarding school. Her decision to live a celibate life came as a consequence of her family's opposition to her marrying the man she loved, a stand she saw as a proof of prejudice and as an act of violence. She spent her life on her farms, sharing the laborer's work, totally dedicated to her writing and to charitable works.

When her writing came to the attention of F. Dall'Ongaro, she began to publish some of her stories in the Trieste magazine, *Favilla*. Her subsequent publications—*Racconti* (1858; Short Stories), *Novelle vecchie e nuove* (1861; New and Old Tales), *Novelle scelte* (1880; Chosen Tales), *Novelle popolari edite e inedite* (1883; Popular Tales, Published and Unpublished)—are all stories and sketches of events and life

conditions of the poor people she observed around her. They give a compassionate view of the hardships and the abuses suffered by farmers and village population under the Austrian rule, by their wives and children, by curates and parish priests. Especially moving are the portraits of enduring and sacrificing women, described by her as "women of courage," whose condition she articulated in a speech as the "heavier burden befallen on that half of humanity."

Percoto's place in Italian literary history is with a group of novelists, such as Giulio Carcano, Ippolito Nievo, and Luigia Codemo, who described and denounced the condition of poverty in the forgotten countryside and thus came to represent what was called the "rustic" narrative genre. Unlike theirs, Percoto's stories are free from the easy idealism of romantic writers and from the paternalistic attitudes usually found in populist literature. Her sober and simple prose is due to her unrelenting loyalty to true stories and characters and to her refusal to change her spoken language and the Friuli dialect into Tuscanized Italian. She is seen now as the first realist writer of Italian literature, and, as such, she enjoyed a considerable revival during postwar neorealism.

Works

Racconti (1858). *Novelle vecchie e nuove* (1861). *Novelle scelte*, II (1880). *Novelle popolari edite e inedite* (1883). *Gli ultimi anni di Caterina Percoto* (*Lettere all'ab. F. Bernardi*), ed. N. Minghetti (1915). *Scritti friulani*, ed. B. Chiurlo (1929). *Sotto l'Austria nel Friuli 1847–1865*, ed. E. Levi (1918). "Lettere inedite al Dott. G. Pompili." *Bollettino della Società filologica friulana* (1938). *"L'anno della fame" e altri racconti*, ed. A. Spaini (1945). *L'album della suocera e altri racconti*, ed. A. Gatto (1945).

Rinaldina Russell

Vibia Perpetua
ca. 181–A.D. 203

Born ca. A.D. 181
Died March 7, A.D. 203, Carthage
Genre(s): autobiography, dream vision
Language(s): Latin

Early in 203 A.D., Perpetua and her companions were arrested for refusing to sacrifice to Emperor Septimius Severus on his birthday. At the time of her arrest, Perpetua was a catechumen, a candidate for baptism (she was baptized while in prison). One of her brothers was also a catechumen; her father was a pagan; and the rest of her family seem to have been Christian sympathizers though probably not Christians. Perpetua was nursing her infant son at the time of her arrest and imprisonment. Her narrative describes the discomforts of prison, her trial before the tribunal, her concern for her baby, and her father's repeated attempts to beg or bully her into recanting her faith. In addition to these events, she also describes four visions she had while in prison. These visions deal with her approaching death, the painful friction between her and her father, and her fears for the soul of her brother Dinocrates, who had died at the age of seven. In the visions, Perpetua deals forcefully and creatively with each of these problems and awakens strengthened and revitalized to continue her struggle. Her narrative ends: "This is what I have done till the day before the contest; if anyone wants to write of its outcome, let them do so." The day after she wrote this, according to the *Passio*, Perpetua was gored to death by a wild cow in the arena, and her companions were also killed by various beasts.

All that we have of Perpetua's work is contained in the (3rd century?) *Passio Sanctarum Perpetuae et Felicitatis*. The author of the *Passio* claims to have preserved Perpetua's work "as it was set down by her own hand" (*Passio* II,3), and the flavor of the passage (*Passio* III-X) seems to support his claim. Perpetua's style is immediate, colloquial, and direct. Her visions have a strikingly authentic and original quality; they do not seem to have been altered to conform to any theological or stylistic norm. Moreover, Perpetua very rarely attempts to interpret the visions or to assign allegorical meanings to them; she vividly describes what she has seen and lets it stand for itself. Her simplicity lends still more power to events and images that are striking enough in themselves. Her vision of the upcoming gladiatorial combat is riveting: she sees herself stripped naked and anointed by her supporters and transformed into a man; she defeats a huge Egyptian in hand-to-hand combat and is awarded the prize by her kind, fatherly fencing-master. She awakens realizing that she will be condemned to death and that she will win the true contest, which she will fight against the powers of evil.

Although we have only a few pages of Perpetua's work, there can be little doubt that she holds a unique place in the literary canon, both for her unaffected yet skillful literary style and for her brilliant psychological and spiritual insights. Both her life and her writing reveal a uniquely courageous and perceptive woman whom readers of any age can admire.

Works

Acta Sanctorum collecta digesta illustrata (1643), vol. VII, pp. 629–637. Van Beek, C.I.M.I., ed., *Passio Sanctarum Perpetuae et Felicitatis* (1936). Van Beek, C.I.M.I., ed. *Passio Sanctarum Perpetuae et Felicitatis, Latine et Graece* (1938).

Translations: Dronke, Peter, *Women Writers of the Middle Ages: A Critical Study of Texts from Perpetua to Marguerite Porete* (1984, rpt. 1985), pp. 2–4. Musurillo, H.R., tr., "The Passion of Ss. Perpetua and Felicitas" in Elizabeth Alvilda Petroff, ed., *Medieval Women's Visionary Literature* (1986). Ower, E.C.E. *Some Authentic Acts of the Early Martyrs* (1927).

Lila F. Ralston

Maria Petijt
1623–1677

Born January, 1623, Hazebroek, The Netherlands
Died November, 1677, Mechelen, The Netherlands
Genre(s): spiritual autobiography, confessional letters
Language(s): Dutch

Born in the wealthy, commercial Flemish middle class, Maria Petijt was educated in a boarding school before she began her novitiate with the Augustinian Canonnesses in Ghent in 1642. She had to give up her intention of becoming a regular canonness because of a lingering eye disease. Very eager nevertheless to live devoutly in sincere contemplation, Petijt submitted herself to the spiritual guidance of several Carmelite friars—at first alone, in Ghent, and from 1657 until her death, with a few other women in Mechelen (Malines). The most influential of these friars was Michael a Sancto Augustino; he became Petijt's Father Confessor and would also become directly responsible for her spiritual and literary fame. It was Michael a Sancto Augustino who initiated Petijt into the techniques of contemplative meditation. She was never a nun, but she and her companions took the vows of chastity and poverty and of obedience (i.e., to the spiritual director, Michael). It is most likely that Maria Petijt wrote her many letters to Michael, on his request; the letters show her development in the practice of meditation and her spiritual growth. Probably she began writing her spiritual autobiography for the same reason. It must be assumed that she never had purely literary or artistic intentions.

Perhaps precisely for this very reason, Petijt's prose is still eminently readable today. Her style impresses through its vivacity, its directness, and personal feeling. With a single detail she can sketch an entire situation; her self-confidence in writing reminds the reader of the powerful sparseness of her great English contemporary, John Bunyan. For instance, a practical description of what "to withdraw one's self from the world" concretely means in daily life, is contained in the following anecdote: the young woman is still living with her parents but has decided to deny herself the joys of companionship at the table, as a spiritual exercise:

As soon as I was through with my meal, I would take my plate from the table, greet those present, and then I would leave the table without saying one more word. And so I went up then to my room (my translation)

After her death, Michael a Sancto Augustino edited her manuscripts and translated a selection into Latin. The autobiography *Leven van de weerdighe moeder Maria a Sta Teresia (alias) Petijt* (The Life of the Worthy Mother . . .) appeared as Volume I of the four-volume edition. Remarkable is the analytical instead of chronological organization that Michael imposed upon the texts. It is generally assumed that he had in mind a possible beatification process of Petijt, for which the spiritual writings would have to serve as evidence—hence the Latin translation of key passages. The other three volumes of the edition contain the spiritual letters that she had directed to Michael in his role of Father Confessor.

From these letters and her autobiography, Petijt emerges as an exceptionally intelligent, sensitive mystic with a good feeling for original imagery. The development of her searching soul follows a purifying pattern from repentance, despair, and consolatory grace to exquisite mystical experiences. Merciless in her self-criticism, and preceding the intense cult of the Holy Heart (especially in France), Petijt achieved an altogether unique, Baroque symbiosis of the authentic Flemish mysticism and the Spanish type. The former emphasizes the total immersion of the soul in God (the image "as a drop of water in the sea" recurs time and time again), the latter records more ecstatic experiences. A. Deblaere writes that "because of the careful observation and the differentiated representation of the psychological effects of the mystical experiences on her spirit and her soul, her testimony is altogether unequaled in continental mystical literature" (my translation o.c., 684). Maria Petijt has been put forward as the equal in thought and expression of the great Saint Teresa of Avila.

Works

Michael a Sancto Augustino, ed., *Het leven van de weerdighe moeder Maria a Sta Teresia (alias) Petijt* (1683), 4 vols. Michael a Sancto Augustino, tr., *Vita venerabilis matris Mariae a Sta Teresia* (ms., Collegio S. Alberto, Rome, Post. III). Fragments of this text have been translated into French by L. Van Den Bossche, "De la vie 'Marie-forme' au mariage mystique," in *Et. Carmél.*, 16 (1931), pp. 236–250 and 17 (1932), pp. 279–294. In English translation: MacGinnis, T., *Union with Our Lady. Marian Writings of Ven. Maria Petyt of St. Teresa* (1954).

Kristiaan P. Aercke

Katherine Philips
1632–1664
a.k.a. Orinda
Born January 1, 1632, London
Died June 22, 1664, London
Genre(s): poem, translation
Language(s): English

Although Philips was born to a middle-class family in London and instructed nearby at Mrs. Salmon's school for girls, her life and poetic activities centered in southwest Wales. About four years after her father died in 1642, her mother married Sir Richard Phillipps of Pembroke. Philips herself, at age sixteen, married his kinsman and former son-in-law, fifty-four-year-old James Philips. They settled at Cardigan, but she traveled several times to London and once to Dublin. She began writing verse as early as 1650, and by the time of her death at thirty-two from smallpox, she had gained a considerable literary reputation, distributing poems among her acquaintances. Her two most intimate friends, often addressed in the poems by pseudoclassical names, were Mary Aubrey (Rosania) and Anne Owen (Lucasia). Other members of her circle included the Master of Ceremonies for Charles II, Sir Charles Cotterell (Poliarchus), her husband (Antenor), and, at least peripherally, such admirers as the Earl of Orrery, the theologian Jeremy Taylor, and the poets Henry Vaughan and Abraham Cowley.

Philips's extant literary works consist of approximately 120 original poems, five poems translated from French, and two translations of Corneille's dramas, *Pompey* and *Horace* (the latter incomplete). All these, except for one poem that appeared in both Tutin (1905) and Elmen (1951) and three that surfaced in 1977 (one in Mahl and Koon, two in Mambretti), were printed in her 1667 collected works. (For other uncertain attributions, see Mambretti.) An edition of 74 poems had appeared without her consent in 1664, and a very few poems saw print earlier, the first prefixed to William Cartwright's works in 1651 and two in Henry Lawes's 1655 *Second Book of Ayres*.

Katherine Philips

Of her plays, *Pompey* had been published twice in 1663, after opening successfully at Dublin's Smock Alley during the 1662–1665 season, and probably in London as well. *Horace*, completed by John Denham, was performed at court in February 1668, and nearly a year later enjoyed a London theater run. Philips's letters also attracted interest, enough for two eighteenth-century editions of those written to Cotterell and for four others to have been anthologized in 1697.

Philips's reputation rests mostly on her poetry, but she is less original in style than subject. Her verse sticks mostly to regular meters in such regular forms

as heroic couplets, tetrameter stanzas, and a few ballad stanzas. As a late Cavalier poet, she has an inclination for metaphysical conceits but usually avoids sharp incongruities and rough rhythms. Like Cartwright, who influenced her greatly, she gives most of her verse, but not necessarily her best, a smooth courtliness.

Philips's great theme is friendship, adapted from the Cavalier poets' treatment of Platonic love but, under the influence of the French *Précieuse* society, turned to Platonic friendship between women. Her poems elevate her friends, particularly Rosania and Lucasia, to the heights of beauty and goodness and exclaim her own devotion to them. Men, she sometimes felt, could not possibly deserve such a sublime being in marriage: "She is a public Deity, / And were't not very odd / She should depose herself to be / A petty household god?"

When not praising or remonstrating with her adored friends, Philips frequently lauds other acquaintances or, after the Restoration, members of the court. If these verses are insipid, two Interregnum pieces that suggest Royalist leanings, one complaining of "The dying Lion kick'd by every ass," have more power. In fact, in one poem, she angrily and wittily defends her husband, an official under Cromwell, from the taint of such verses. Though her upbringing and marriage should have put her in the Puritan camp, she had opposite political loyalties, perhaps through a youthful association with Royalist literati.

Personal relationships and situations dominate her poetry, and her own isolation from London's literary and social scene may account for a minor strain of *contemptus mundi* verse. These poems, especially her translation of Saint Amant's "Solitude," are often superior to her panegyrics. Occasionally, such subjects lead her away from personal verse to abstract philosophical poems, among the first instances of this genre in English. Though she is no master of the poetic essay, rare couplets, like, "Mean, sordid things, which by mistake we prize, / And absent covet, but enjoy'd despise," achieve a power of antithesis even the great eighteenth-century poets might not have scorned.

Works

Pompey (1663). *Poems by the Incomparable, Mrs. K.P.* (1664). *Poems by the Most Deservedly Admired Mrs. Katherine Philips The Matchless Orinda* (1667). *Letters from Orinda to Poliarchus* (1705, enlarged 1729).

Sayre N. Greenfield

Hester Lynch Salsubury Thrale Piozzi
1741–1821

Born January 16, 1741, Bodvel, Carnarvonshire,
Wales
Died May 2, 1821, Clifton
Genre(s): diary, anecdote, letters
Language(s): English

Hester Lynch Salsubury Thrale Piozzi

Informally educated in Bodvel by doting parents,
Piozzi showed early signs of intelligence and wit. She
spent the earliest years of her twenty-one-year-mar-
riage to Henry Thrale at Streatham Park near London. Of twelve pregnancies, five daughters survived
infancy, four to adulthood. Although her own children and her associates in the Bluestocking circle
objected to her second marriage to an Italian singer
and music teacher, she managed to reconcile family
and society to some extent as she pursued a career
as an author, at her best in characterizing through
dialogue.

Long an enthusiastic diarist, Piozzi kept her first
diary as a record of the progress of her daughter
Queeney. Gradually, the diary expanded to include
commentary about her growing family. Encouraged
by Samuel Johnson's suggestion and Thrale's gift of an
empty volume as repository, she began the diary she
called *Thraliana* on September 15, 1776. A rich collection of anecdotes and conversations occasionally
unified by her narrative, *Thraliana* provides insight
into English society. Piozzi selects her materials carefully, recording the words of famous persons or the
compelling comments of relatively unknown associates. A connoisseur of conversation, she supplements
overheard, spontaneous dialogue with discussions she
has herself prompted and guided, especially in her
salon among the members of the Bluestocking circle
and with Johnson, a constant companion during the
years of her marriage to Thrale. It also shows that
Piozzi was concerned less with recording daily in
strict chronological order than with aligning the
rhythm of historical event with personal circumstance. Posterity would inherit not historicity but
vivid moments captured in their entirety. While her
emphasis on the personal and individual makes her
writing more colloquial than orderly or authoritative, it recalls the rich texture and variety of a domestic life made vibrantly intellectual by the vigilant diarist's search for materials.

Much of *Thraliana* recalls Johnson's extended visits, but the *Anecdotes* and *Letters* to and from
Johnson more consistently interest Johnson schol-

ars. Piozzi's collections include Johnson's minor poetry as well as details of his daily life and sayings.
When Johnson, disapproving of her marriage to
Piozzi, terminated a long and mutually inspirational
relationship with Piozzi, he freed her to consider
more objectively his personality and thought. Thus
she tells of a different Johnson than the man portrayed by Boswell, with whom she had several battles
during the publication of numerous early reminiscences of Johnson.

An innovative author, Piozzi discovered subjects
for research and writing throughout her lifetime. With
Johnson, she began translating Boethius, and she began a discussion of art and philosophy, abandoning
the project after writing over 100 pages. Other writings chronicle travel to Wales and France. Piozzi's verse
is effective as satire, if not as poetry, a judgment she
makes of her own work when she compiles it in
Thraliana. Her ability to create compelling dialogue
has been noted in her imitation of Swift's poems on
his own death ("Three Dialogues on the Death of
Hester Lynch Thrale") and in a two-act comedy. Readers note in *British Synonymy* political commentary,
in *Observations and Reflections* a popularizing of
travel literature, and in *Retrospection* the leavening
of history with anecdote and commentary.

Works

Anecdotes of the Late Samuel Johnson, LL.D. During the Last Twenty Years of His Life (1786). *Letters to and from the Late Samuel Johnson, LL.D. to Which Are Added Some Poems Never Before Printed* (1788). *Observations and Reflections Made in the Course of a Journey Through France, Italy, and Germany* (1789). *The Three Warnings* (1792). *British Synonymy; or an Attempt at Regulating the Choice of Words in Familiar Conversation. Inscribed, with Sentiments of Gratitude and Respect, to such of her Foreign Friends as Have Made English Literature Their Peculiar Study* (1794). *Three Warnings to John Bull before He Dies. By an Old Acquaintance of the Public* (1798). *Retrospection; or, A Review of the Most Striking and Important Events, Characters, Situations, and Their Consequences, Which the Last Eighteen Hundred Years Have Presented to the View of Mankind* (1801). *Autobiography, Letters and Literary Remains*, ed. A. Hayward (1861). *Thraliana, the Diary of Mrs. Hester Lynch Thrale, Later Mrs. Piozzi* (ed. K.C. Balderson) (1942).

Mary S. Comfort

Adelheid Popp
1869–1939

Born 1869, near Vienna, Austria
Died 1939
Genre(s): autobiography
Language(s): German

Adelheid Popp's autobiography *Die Jugendgeschichte einer Arbeiterin* (1910; The Autobiography of a Working Woman) and its sequel *Erinnerungen aus meinen Kindheits- und Mädchenjahren aus der Agitation und anderes* (1915; Memoirs of my Childhood and Young Womanhood, Times of Struggle and Other Things) is important not only as one of the first proletarian autobiographies published in Europe around this time, it is also one of the most powerful and eloquently written of these texts. In addition, it is one of the relatively few books written by a woman about the particular lot of proletarian women, who were not only exploited as workers but sexually harassed, abused, and exploited as women. *Die Jugendgeschichte einer Arbeiterin* describes the social upheaval and class conflict in Austria during the years of the author's childhood and young womanhood, years of industrialization and capitalist expansion. It is a model of a socialist success story, charting a working-class child's rise out of poverty and op-

pression into the pride and dignity of a class-conscious struggle for rights and social change.

Born outside of Vienna, Adelheid Dworak was the fifteenth child of a weaver family. Her father, an alcoholic who frequently beat and abused his wife and children, died when she was six. After a mere three years of schooling, she was sent to work: domestic work in Viennese bourgeois households, piecework as a seamstress, and factory work in a variety of different establishments. Hospitalized for exhaustion as a result of overwork and inadequate physical care at age thirteen, she was able for the first time to rest, read, and think about life, work, and the options awaiting her in the future. Finding her own thoughts and experience reflected in contemporary socialist ideas, she involved herself in the Austrian socialist movement. From that time on nothing—not even marriage, two children and the need to continue wage labor—detracted her from the political path she chose: to organize and agitate for socialism and the emancipation of women and men of the working class. As an organizer, cofounder, and editor of a newspaper for women workers and the author of numerous treatises on women, politics, and work, Popp became internationally known as one of the leaders of the socialist women's movement in Austria.

Her *Jugendgeschichte*, which was first published through the support and under the auspices of the International Socialist movement (August Bebel wrote the foreword), was an immense popular success, especially among working-class women, the very audience Popp had most urgently wanted to reach. Within the first year of its publication, it had already gone through three editions; it was translated into English, French, Italian, Polish, Romanian, Swedish, Czech, and Hungarian. Beginning with her childhood and ending in the present with the death of her husband and her commitment to a life of service in the socialist cause, *Jugendgeschichte* reads as the proletarian version of the bourgeois *Bildungsroman*, detailing her ascent out of the darkness of oppression into the light of working-class consciousness. Popp describes the bleakness of a joyless childhood: the scarcity of material things, the lack of education, the fear and helpless anger that turn into familial violence. She then describes the process of reading her way up and out: beginning with the escapist fiction (romantic tales of love and adventure) produced for a poorly educated mass audience, she moves on to the classics of bourgeois high culture, until she finally discovers the literature of socialist theory and analysis. This trajectory also marks the position from which she writes. Popp's narration of the experiences of her childhood and youth is informed by her present socialist-feminist consciousness. The "philanthropy" of a factory owner at Christmas thus, in retrospect, throws into even starker relief the fundamental brutality of the relationship between the haves and have-nots in a capitalist economy. Popp tells her story in a simple and straightforward way, without embellishments or sentimentality.

Popp's narrative focus and persona stand in marked contrast to the conventional bourgeois model of autobiographical writing. Her focus is not so much on the process of self-individuation as on the relationship between individual lives and the larger structures of class and social power relations within which they are embedded. In *Erinnerungen*, a text in which the autobiographical elements are consciously backgrounded to a much more programmatic emphasis on socialist and feminist analyses, personal stories (her own and those of people she has known or heard about) serve mainly to illustrate and anchor her political theses. The personal is of interest insofar as it is exemplary and can shed light on the larger, collective, social issues. Popp makes no effort to disguise her didactic intent: "If I felt the need to write about how I became a Socialist, it was solely out of the desire to encourage those countless women workers who yearn for fulfillment with a heart full of longing, but always draw back because they have no faith in their ability to achieve anything" (*Jugendgeschichte*). For Popp, speaking as a woman worker for and to others like herself, writing is itself a politically emancipatory act.

Works

Autobiography: *Die Jugendgeschichte einer Arbeiterin* [The Autobiography of a Working Woman] (1910; tr. E.C. Harvey 1912; rpt. 1983). Note: The first, significantly edited, version of Popp's autobiography was published anonymously in 1909 as *Lebensgeschichte einer Arbeiterin von ihr selbst erzählt* [Life Story of a Working Woman as Told by Herself], in a series of working-class autobiographies published by E. Reinhardt. A late version was entitled simply *Jugend einer Arbeiterin* [Youth of a Working Woman] (1915; rpt., 1977). *Erinnerungen aus meinen Kindheits- und Mädchenjahren, aus der Agitation und anderes* [Memoirs of my Childhood and Young Womanhood, Times of Struggle and Other Things] (1915).

Political treatises: *Die Arbeiterin im Kampf ums Dasein* [The Working Woman in the Struggle for Survival] (1911). *Frauenarbeit in der kapitalistischen Gesellschaft* [Women's Work in Capitalist Society] (1922).

Angelika Bammer

Jane Porter
1776–1850

Born 1776, birthplace unknown
Died May 24, 1850, Bristol
Genre(s): biography, novel
Language(s): English

Jane Porter

Novelist and playwright, daughter of an army officer and sister of Dr. William, Anna, and Sir Robert, Porter's Edinburgh education was enhanced by an avid interest in Scottish myths and legends, many narrated to her by a poor neighbor, Luckie Forbes.

In 1797, Jane and her sister Anna assisted Thomas Frognall Dibdin in the publication of *The Quiz*, a short-lived periodical. Following its failure, the family moved to a London residence formerly owned by Sir Joshua Reynolds, where, it is believed, Jane Porter wrote her early biographical fiction. The first romance, *Thaddeus of Warsaw* (1803), was considered a product of her youthful exuberance and natural sympathy for the influx of Polish citizens seeking refuge. An equally vital source of inspiration was Robert's description of a personal meeting with the Polish hero, Thaddeus Kosciuszko, during the general's visit to England. Porter wrote that her first heroic tale was "founded on the actual scenes of Kosciuszko's suffering and moulded out of his virtues," though she masks her protagonist as a young descendant of John Sobieski. Many other characters are thinly disguised versions of various friends and family members. Acclaimed as a "work of genius" and later recognized as "the best and most enduring" of her fiction, the novel achieved wide acceptance and was published in several translations.

The ninth edition of *Thaddeus of Warsaw* and the initial printing of *The Scottish Chiefs* occurred in 1810. The latter publication, a five-volume work, is based on the life of the Scotch patriot, William Wallace. This heroic romance incorporates the childhood legends Porter loved as well as an old poem by Henry the Minstrel (Blind Harry) and bits of information on Wallace's life received from Campbell the Poet, who also supplied a list of recommended references. Wallace's career as an outlaw began when he killed an Englishman who had insulted him. As his band of brigands increased in number, they engaged the British army several times, notably at Stirling Bridge, and almost succeeded in liberating Scotland until a reinforced troop of British soldiers overpowered Wallace's men at Falkirk. Although he escaped capture at this time, he was eventually arrested, tried, and executed as a traitor, but his death provided inspiration for the country's next hero, Robert Bruce, who successfully achieved Wallace's dream of independence. Porter's interpretation of this much-loved legend found instant favor with her readers and its fame rivaled the predecessor, with numerous translations printed throughout Europe and parts of India.

The Scottish Chiefs was dubiously "honored" by Napoleon, who attempted to have its translation banned in France. It is considered one of the few historical novels printed prior to Scott's *Waverly* to have survived and has had several reprints since its initial publication.

After writing a three-volume novel dealing with the Stuart clan, *The Pastor's Fireside* (1815), Porter wrote several plays. One, *Egmont: or the Eve of St. Alyne,* sent to Edmund Kean, famed Shakesperean tragedian, was denied production by his fellow actors, and it was never published. *Switzerland* (1819) and *Owen: Prince of Powys* (1822) were eventually presented at Drury Lane but considered "lamentable failures."

George IV suggested the subject of her next novel, *Duke Christian of Lüneberg,* which she dedicated to the monarch. Her final publication, *Sir Edward Seaward's Narrative of His Shipwreck and Consequent Discovery of Certain Islands in the Caribbean Sea* (1831), harbors the mystery of its origin. Purported to have developed from an actual diary account and edited by Porter, it was described by the *Quarterly* as a well-written work of fiction. Porter insisted that the account was genuine and had been given to her by the writer's family; yet an inscription in Bristol Cathedral, supposedly placed there by Porter, cites her brother William as the actual author.

Porter received many honors and invitations, especially for her first two works. She was made a Lady of the Chapter of St. Joachim and given the gold cross of the order from Württemberg. In 1844, an organization composed of American authors, publishers, and booksellers sent a rosewood armchair "as an expression of admiration and respect," but these gifts did not alleviate the family's financial difficulties, a fact which she repeatedly noted in her unpublished diaries.

She seriously regarded her literary skill as a "religious duty" and painfully extracted each word. She often envied her sister, Anna, who had a facility for free expression and a more relaxed approach. Porter insisted that the major changes in the English novel originated with her works, rather than with the creations of Sir Walter Scott—ironically, a childhood playmate—as her reputation was in its zenith long before his first novel reached publication. She defended her ability to unite "the personages and facts of real history or biography with a combining and illustrative machinery of the imagination" although later critics deplored her manipulation of various events to secure the novel's development.

The public, however, is the final critic, and its delight in Porter's enthusiastic exaggerations cannot be denied. Scottish children, normally denied the reading of romantic stories, were encouraged to enjoy her tales, and Porter's unique blends of legend, myth, and reality remain landmark contributions to the art of fiction.

Works

A Defense of the Profession of an Actor (1800). *Thaddeus of Warsaw* (1803). *Sketch of the Campaign of Count A. Suwarrow Ryminski* (1804). *The Scottish Chiefs* (1810). *The Pastor's Fireside* (1815). *Switzerland* (1819). *Owen: Prince of Powys* (1822). *Duke Christian of Lüneberg* (1824). *Tales Round a Winter Hearth* (with A.M. Porter) (1826). *The Field of the Forty Footsteps* (1828). *Sir Edward Seaward's Narrative of His Shipwreck and Consequent Discovery of Certain Islands in the Caribbean Sea* (1831).

Zelda Provenzano

Beatrix Potter
1866–1943

Born July 28, 1866, Bolton Gardens, Kensington, England
Died December 22, 1943, Sawrey
Genre(s): children's illustrated story
Language(s): English

Born into a family whose fortune was already well established, Potter led a carefully guarded childhood. Unlike her younger brother Bertram, she was not sent to school and had virtually no friends. At an early age she showed a talent for illustration and was encouraged by her governess to practice her artwork. Potter found subject material first at local museums and later in nature when her family took extensive summer vacations in Scotland and the Lake District.

Her attachment to nature was by no means sentimental; she often dissected dead animals when she found them and had a keen eye for ecological and biological detail. Her illustrations in *Wayside and Woodland Fungi* (1967) are the work of a skilled and knowledgeable naturalist. She maintained a tie with nature even in the austere home of her parents by keeping a small menagerie. Most notable among her pets, which included mice, bats, frogs, and snails, were two of her rabbits, Peter Rabbit and Benjamin Bunny, and her hedgehog, Mrs. Tiggy-Winkle.

In 1893 the son of one of Potter's former governesses took ill. To amuse the boy during his recovery, Potter sent him illustrated letters which traced the adventures of her pets. The letters circulated among friends and Potter was encouraged to prepare the story of Peter Rabbit as a book. Failing to find a publisher, Potter had *The Tale of Peter Rabbit* printed privately in 1900. A second private printing followed in 1902 along with a private edition of *The Tailor of Gloucester*. By this time the firm of Frederick Warne & Co. offered to publish *Peter Rabbit* if Potter would do color illustrations. The success of *Peter Rabbit* established her as an important children's writer, and with each successive work, usually in the same miniature format as the first, her reputation and popularity grew.

The association between Potter and Warne & Co. was a long and happy one that lasted over the publication of 24 of her books. She was particularly close to Norman Warne, who worked in his father's firm. In 1905 Norman proposed and Potter, in spite of her parents' strenuous objections, accepted. Unfortunately, Warne died shortly after their engagement was announced. During this period Potter bought Hill Top, a farm near the village of Sawrey, using both the earnings from her books and a small legacy. Still under the rule of her parents, she leased the farm, under generous terms, to a tenant farmer and visited it only occasionally. The legal concerns of her property brought her into contact with William Heelis, a local solicitor, whom she married in 1913.

Although some books did appear after her marriage, Potter's career as a writer was essentially over. She immersed herself in the concerns of her farm and was respected enough to be elected president of the Herdwick Sheep-Breeders' Association shortly before her death. As Mrs. Heelis, Potter shunned fame, and though she referred to accolades of her work as "great rubbish," there is no question of her stature or the extent of her influence in children's literature.

Potter's stories have a simplicity that is complemented by a sense of realism and of humor. Her characters, who live in a world that can be both comforting and threatening, learn to appreciate the former by experiencing the latter. The impact of her stories is consistently emphasized by the deft accuracy and subtle playfulness of her artwork.

Works

The Tale of Peter Rabbit (1902). *The Tale of Squirrel Nutkin* (1903). *The Tailor of Gloucester* (1903). *The Tale of Benjamin Bunny* (1904). *The Tale of Two Bad Mice* (1904). *The Tale of Mrs. Tiggy-Winkle* (1905). *The Pie and the Patty-pan* (1905). *The Tale of Mr. Jeremy Fisher* (1906). *The Story of a Fierce Bad Rabbit* (1906). *The Story of Mrs. Moppet* (1906). *The Tale of Tom Kitten* (1907). *The Tale of Jemima Puddle-Duck* (1908). *The Roly-Poly Pudding* (1908; later *The Tale of Samuel Whiskers,* 1926). *The Tale of the Flopsy Bunnies* (1909). *Ginger and Pickles* (1909). *The Tale of Mrs. Tittlemouse* (1910). *Peter Rabbit's Painting Book* (1911). *The Tale of Timmy Tiptoes* (1911). *The Tale of Mr. Toad* (1912). *The Tale of Pigling Bland* (1913). *Tom Kitten's Painting Book* (1917). *Appley Dapply's Nursery Rhymes* (1917). *The Tale of Johnny Town-Mouse* (1918). *Cecily Parsley's Nursery Rhymes* (1922). *Jemima Puddle-Duck's Painting Book* (1925). *Peter Rabbit's Almanac for 1929* (1928). *The Fairy Caravan* (1929). *The Tale of Little Pig Robinson* (1930). *Sister Anne* (1932). *Wag-by-Wall* (1944). *The Tale of the Faithful Dove* (1956). *The Journal of Beatrix Potter* (1966). *Wayside and Woodland Fungi* (illustrations only, 1967). *Letters to Children* (1967). *A History of the Writings of Beatrix Potter* (1971).

Alan Rauch

Modesta Pozzo
1555–1592

a.k.a. Moderata Fonte
Born 1555, Venice, Italy
Died November 2, 1592, Venice
Genre(s): treatise, madrigal, sonnet
Language(s): Italian

Modesta Pozzo de' Zorzi, the second child of Cicilia and Hieronimo Pozzo, was born in Venice. Both her parents died in her infancy and she was raised by relatives. As customary for girls at the time, she was sent to a convent until she reached the age of nine. Back home, her relatives noticed her eagerness to learn and allowed her to start serious study of Latin, painting, music, and math. Soon Modesta came to be known as a child prodigy and was even asked by the Venetian oligarchy to recite her poems in their presence. She married Filippo de' Zorzi and had four children.

In 1581 some of Modesta Pozzo's madrigals and sonnets were published under the title *Tredici canti del Floridoro*. But Pozzo's fame rests on *Il merito della donne*, a posthumous treatise that appeared under the pseudonym Moderata Fonte. According to her daughter Cicilia, who was responsible for the publication together with Pozzo's other son, Pietro, Modesta was still working on *Il merito* the day she died.

Pozzo's treatise was one of many published during the Renaissance. Most were printed in Venice, a city famous both for the quantity and quality of its publication. Several works on women's worth are justifiably famous, such as Book 3 of B. Castiglione's *Il libro del cortegiano* (1528; The Book of the Courtier) and G.F. Capella's *Della eccellenza et degnita' delle donne* (1529; Of the Excellence and Worth of Women). But no treatise by a woman had ever been published before Pozzo's *Il merito della donne*.

Pozzo's structure is dialogic with an even number of discussants, pro and con, facing each other. In *Il merito* there are six debaters: three argue in favor of women's need for recognition, education, and independence; and three argue for maintaining the *status quo*. The conversation occurs in a garden, a place more accessible to "honest" women than either the streets or salons of earlier, male-authored treatises on women. Remarkable in Pozzo's work is the authority with which women talk about politics, medicine, and philosophy, and the familiarity they display with past and contemporary literature. Statements and verses by famous authors are occasionally quoted almost *verbatim*, but the effect is different.

What makes the difference is that women do the talking in *Il merito* and the result is startlingly original. By comparison, Castiglione had the most influential male discussants in his group take the defense of women, praise them, and talk on their behalf. But they talked as men, thus enforcing, propagandizing, and legitimizing men's opinions about women's identity and proper sphere of action. Were they interested in knowing what women think and how they value themselves, they would have asked the court ladies to join in their discussion. Instead they used women's presence to universalize their ideological assumptions; since women could not speak, let alone protest, they assumed that they approved what they heard about themselves.

In this context Pozzo's treatise is strikingly revisionary. She questions and challenges history because it excludes women. She expounds at length on herbal medicine because customarily women have known much about herbs. She praises famous antique women, but not for the conventional virtue of chastity. Her tone can be vituperative, calm, or philosophical. Whatever the scene, she is conscious of her rhetorical power and uses logic to her advantage. Today she will be remembered, together with Lucrezia Marinella and Arcangela Tarabotti, as one of the three most gifted women writers of the seventeenth century.

Works

Tredici canti del Floridoro (1581). *Le feste. Rappresentazione* (1581). *La Passione di Christo* (1582). *La Resurrettione di Giesu Christo Nostro Signore* (1592). *Il merito della donne* (1600, rpt. 1979, 1988).

Valeria Finucci

Stanisława Przybyszewska
1901–1935

a.k.a. Andrée Lynne
Born October 1, 1901, Cracow, then
in Austro-Hungary
Died August 14, 1935, Danzig (Gdańsk),
then a free city
Genre(s): historical drama, short story,
novella, letters
Language(s): Polish, German, French, English

One of the most remarkable twentieth-century Polish writers, Przybyszewska was almost totally forgotten until the late 1960s when the unpublished manuscripts of her plays were unearthed, staged, and eventually published. Her masterpiece, *The Danton Case*, probably the best drama about the French Revolution since Georg Büchner's *Danton's Death*, is now firmly established in the repertory of the Polish theatre and known throughout the world in Andrzej Wajda's 1983 film version, *Danton*, a French-Polish production starring Gerard Depardieu.

The illegitimate daughter of the then-celebrated modernist playwright and novelist Stanisław Przybyszewski and Aniela Pająk, an impressionist painter, Przybyszewska was educated in Western Europe (Austria, Switzerland, France), where she lived first with her mother, then with her maternal aunt after her mother's death. Upon her return home in 1916, Przybyszewska attended teachers college in Cracow, from which she graduated in 1919, briefly enrolled at the university in Poznań, studied piano and violin, and came into contact with the literary and artistic avant-garde. Suffering from nervous exhaustion brought on largely by her close and tragic relationship with her father, Przybyszewska moved to Warsaw in 1922, where she worked in a left-wing bookstore and was arrested and for a short time imprisoned for her alleged involvement in the socialist movement. In 1923 she married Jan Panieński, a young artist, and moved to Danzig when her husband obtained a teaching position at the Polish gymnasium. After Panieński's sudden death in 1926, Przybyszewska chose to remain in Danzig where she spent the last ten years of her life in almost total isolation and growing misery and ill health, brought on by morphine addiction—both her father and husband abused the drug—which led to her death in 1935 at the age of thirty-four.

Determined at all costs to be a writer, Przybyszewska clung stubbornly to her sense of calling and substituted literary creativity for life, convinced of her own genius and ultimate vindication at the hands of posterity. Systematic work, careful revision, and endless polishing were the foundations of her artistic method for dealing with the public issues—revolution, social justice, the role of exceptional individuals in history—that dominated her thinking. During the composition of her trilogy—*Thermidor* (1923, in German), *'93* (completed in 1928), and *Sprawa Dantona* (The Danton Case, completed in 1929)—Przybyszewska adopted the revolutionary calendar devised by Fabre d'Eglantine and began dating her correspondence according to it and talking of Danton and Robespierre as though they were her contemporaries. Living on the margin of her own age, she found herself on happier ground with the heroic figures of 1789.

Because of her deep immersion in the tumultuous world of revolutionary Paris, Przybyszewska is able to create masterful psychological portraits of the venal sentimental idealist, Danton, and the incorruptible Robespierre, genius of the revolution, who knew that by institutionalizing the Terror so that the government may survive he was bringing about his own downfall and sowing the seeds of dictatorship that would be reaped by Bonaparte. Although documentary in spirit and based on extensive research, *The Danton Case* is a contemporary reading of the past, based on the parallel that the author perceives between the events in France at the end of the eighteenth century and those taking place in Russia in the twentieth century. Przybyszewska's finest play is a brilliant study of the mechanisms of power and the inevitable drift of revolution toward totalitarianism by a writer committed to the cause of radical social change—and, in fact, by her own account, in love with Robespierre for many years.

It is in her letters that Przybyszewska most fully reveals herself and describes the discovery of her vocation as an artist, the nature of her creative struggles, and the ceaseless battle for material survival. Her correspondence (published in three volumes, 1978–1985) offers a remarkable biography of a mind confronting itself in all the anguish of loneliness and despair, while at the same time proudly asserting the cultivation of one's own consciousness to be the highest duty. Written in four languages, sometimes addressed to famous writers such as Mann, Bernanos, and Cocteau, and often unfinished and unsent, Przybyszewska's letters were her only means of communicating with those mental peers that she felt must exist somewhere and that she has finally found in future generations.

Works

Dramaty [Dramas], ed. and introd. Roman Taborski, afterword by Jerzy Krasowski (1975). *Listy* [Letters], ed. Tomasz Lewandowski, volumes 1–3 (1978–1985). *Ostatnie noce Ventôse's* [The Last Nights of Ventôse], ed. Stanisław Helsztyński (1958).

Translations: Of *Sprawa Dantona*. English—*The Danton Case* and *The Danton Affairs*, adapted by Pam Gems. *The Danton Case, Thermidor*, Two Plays, tr. Bolestaw Taborski (Evanston, Illinois, 1989). French—*L'Affaire Danton* (1982). Swedish—*Affären Danton* (1985). German—*Sache Danton* (1930).

Jadwiga Kosicka
Daniel Gerould

Barbara Pym
1913–1980

Born June 2, 1913, Oswestry, Shropshire, England
Died January 11, 1980
Genre(s): novel, journalism
Language(s): English

After receiving her B.A. with honors in English Literature from St. Hilda's College, Oxford, Pym served with the Women's Royal Naval Service in England and Italy from 1943 to 1946. She then began her long career working for the International African Institute, where she became assistant editor of its journal, *Africa,* while writing novels in her spare time.

Her first six novels, published between 1950 and 1961, achieved critical recognition and a small but loyal following. These books established Pym as the chronicler of a world small in scope but wide in relevance, the world of spinsters dedicated to the church and to more or less worthless curates; the world of small office workers, librarians, anthropologists, the Church of England clergy; and persons on the outskirts of academic life. This world of little people, especially women, leading quiet lives of compromise, resignation, and acceptance is recorded with compassion, irony, dry wit, an evocative attention to details, and an absolute absence of sentimentality.

Incredibly, Pym could not find a publisher after 1961, although she continued to write fiction, seeing it increasingly as a personal and private exercise. Despite great fortitude, though, she began to question the value of her early work. In 1974 she retired from her editorial position and went to live with her sister in an Oxfordshire village.

In February 1977, responding to an invitation from the *Times Literary Supplement* to a number of literary figures to name the most underrated writers of the century, Lord David Cecil and Philip Larkin both named Pym, suddenly catapulting her to fame and international publication after sixteen years of oblivion. Her frequently rejected novel, *Quartet in Autumn,* a small ironic masterpiece on the theme of aging, was bought by Macmillan, while Jonathan Cape reissued all her out-of-print books. *The Sweet Dove Died* followed, and *A Few Green Leaves* was published posthumously after Pym's death from cancer.

A reserved person who described her avocations as "reading, domestic life and cats," Pym was also a traditionalist in feeling that what mattered most to her in life were the Church of England and the English poetic tradition. Nonetheless, and despite a calm, conventional, though highly crafted, style, Pym's art is radical in that she insists on telling the truth about women's lives, albeit with gentle scepticism and satire. Typical is this comment in *Less Than Angels:* "It would be a reciprocal relationship—the woman giving the food and shelter and doing some typing for him and the man giving the priceless gift of himself."

Her themes are consistent throughout her books and help explain the recent upsurge in interest, especially among feminist scholars: the (often unmet) need for an appropriate and responsive recipient of one's love; the necessity for humorous acceptance of a confining existence; and the pathos of lives being lived without affection or any other aesthetic framework to dignify, amplify, and explain their significance.

Works

Some Tame Gazelle (1950). *Excellent Women* (1952). *Jane and Prudence* (1953). *Less Than Angels* (1955). *A Glass of Blessings* (1959). *No Fond Return of Love* (1961). *Quartet in Autumn* (1977). *The Sweet Dove Died* (1978). *A Few Green Leaves* (1980). *A Very Private Eye: An Autobiography in Diaries and Letters* (1985). *An Academic Question* (1986). *Civil to Strangers and Other Writings,* ed. H. Holt (1987). *A la Pym: The Barbara Pym Cookery Book,* ed. H. Pym and H. Wyatt (1995).

Carey Kaplan

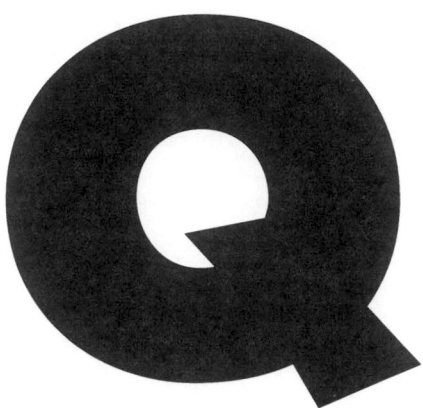

Elena Quiroga
1921–1995

Born October 26, 1921, Santander, Spain
Died October 3, 1995
Genre(s): novel
Language(s): Spanish

Upon receiving the Nadal prize of 1951 for *Viento del norte* (Northwind), Quiroga became one of several women novelists of her generation to achieve national recognition. In the years that followed, however, her work did not receive the critical attention it deserved, perhaps in part because she was writing stream of consciousness, while the dominant novelistic current in Spain was social realism. In 1983 she became the second woman elected to the Spanish Royal Academy, thereby securing her status as a major author.

Although Quiroga was born in Santander, where her mother's family lived, and attended boarding school there, she considers herself Galician. Much of her childhood and her early adult years were spent in that region, at her father's home in the province of Orense. Her mother died when Quiroga was only two years old. The absence of the mother, like the landscape of Galicia, forms an important theme in Quiroga's works. Largely self-educated, Quiroga had access to her paternal grandfather's extensive library and later to the library of La Coruña, when her father moved to that coastal city. In 1950 she married historian Dalmiro de la Válgoma and moved to Madrid. Since 1968, when her husband was named permanent secretary of the Royal Academy of History, they have lived in the building that houses the Academy.

Viento del norte, still Quiroga's most popular novel, is written in a linear structure and traditional narrative form. It presents a penetrating psychologi-

cal study of authentic Galician characters during the pre–Civil War period and is related to Quiroga's later novels by the introduction of such themes as orphanhood, loneliness, and social class distinctions. The beginning of Quiroga's mature writing, however, is marked by the publication of *Algo pasa en la calle* (Something's Happening in the Street) in 1954. Its analysis of the psychological effects of divorce was particularly daring in Franco Spain, where the model divorce law of the Second Republic had been abolished retroactively. Far removed from the traditional structure of *Viento del norte*, *Algo pasa en la calle* introduced such Faulknerian techniques as multiple perspectives and stream of consciousness.

Quiroga's second major novel of the 1950s was *La careta* (1955; The Mask). Her most developed use of stream of consciousness, it also reflects her interest in existentialist philosophy. Moisés, the alienated protagonist, has never overcome the psychological damage caused by his parents' death in the Civil War. Like *Algo pasa en la calle*, it is a daring novel for its introduction of taboo topics, including sexuality and a criticism of the Catholic Church.

Tristura (1960; Sadness) and *Escribo tu nombre* (1965; I Write Your Name) are interrelated works dealing with the childhood and adolescence of a protagonist whose life experiences are in some ways similar to the author's. Like Quiroga, Tadea is a motherless child who is sent from Galicia to live with her mother's family in Santander and attend boarding school there. *Tristura*, winner of the Critics Prize, is told from the perspective of the young child. It develops themes of absence and silence while also presenting a strong criticism of the social and religious hypocrisy of middle-class defenders of the status quo. The criticism becomes stronger in the sequel novel, where the convent school that Tadea attends is treated as a microcosm of society. The repression of freedom within the school is paralleled by the backlash against the reforms of the Second Republic that gave rise to the Civil War.

Quiroga's last published novel, *Presente profundo* (1973; Profound Present), like *Algo pasa en la calle*, presents multiple perspectives and a shifting narrative point of view. It juxtaposes the stories of two suicides, that of an older Galician woman who feels herself no longer needed by her husband and children, and that of a cosmopolitan young divorcee who, separated from the child she loves, drifts into the drug culture. The link between these narrative strands is a doctor who seeks a better understanding of himself as he reconstructs the lives of the two women.

Quiroga's use of innovative novelistic structures, her willingness to deal with topics considered taboo in Franco Spain, and her sensitive treatment of social and psychological problems, particularly those of women, have established her as a major author of postwar Spain.

Works
La soledad sonora (1949). *Viento del norte* (1951). *La sangre* (1952). *Algo pasa en la calle* (1954). *La enferma* (1955). *La careta* (1955). *Plácida, la joven y otras narraciones* (1956; includes three short novels: the title novel and two works originally published in 1953, *Trayecto uno* and *La otra ciudad*).*La última corrida* (1958). *Tristura* (1960). *Escribo tu nombre* (1965). *Presente profundo* (1973).

Phyllis Zatlin

Françoise Quoirez
1935–

a.k.a. Françoise Sagan
Born June 21, 1935, Cajare (Lot), France
Genre(s): novel, drama, short story, screenplay, song, reminiscence
Language(s): French

It sounds almost like a fairy-tale. Once upon a time a girl by the name of Françoise, having failed her exams at the Sorbonne, sat down and wrote a little book called *Bonjour tristesse* and sent it off to a big Paris publisher. No one expected very much of the little book, not even Françoise herself; her father wouldn't even let her put the family name on it, so she borrowed the name of a princess from Proust: Sagan.

Then the miracle happened. Not only was her little book published, but it won the Prix des Critiques for

1954 and within a year had sold a million copies in France alone and made its teenage author rich and famous.

In retrospect, it is easy to see why *Bonjour tristesse* was a success. It had something for everybody. For the critics there was its style: cool, analytical, lucid, understated, and yet full of unsuspected nuances. It was prose in the grand tradition of *La Princesse de Clèves* and *Adolphe* and seemed to confirm what they had always been saying about the classic style, that it could be mastered by any bright French schoolgirl. For the young there was the book's heroine, Cécile, a cool, laid-back teenager whose indifference thinly veils a naively egocentric, sentimental view of life. At her most introspective, Cécile reveals a vague sense of unease at having driven her father's fiancée to suicide. Take these ingredients, add a dash of false candor, a suggestion of incest, a hint of Raymond Radiguet, the *enfant terrible* of the 1920s, and *voila! un best-seller!*

Elizabeth Janeway comes quickly to the heart of the work: *Bonjour tristesse* was a precocious book. It stamped a pattern of impossible, though amusing events upon reality in a teen-age dream of wickedness, seduction, sophistication, and power—for Cécile controlled and manipulated the adults about her at will. Her story was pure wish-fulfillment, carried off by the intensity and immediacy with which it was told but inclined, whenever the author's concentration faltered, to turn absurd.

First novels being what they are, it was inevitable that the author should be identified with her heroine. Thanks to François Mauriac, among others, Sagan soon became in the public eye the incarnation of the Beat Generation in France. A near fatal automobile crash that led to a dependency on morphine, two unsuccessful marriages, and a chronic weakness for gambling and whisky and fast cars would seem to suggest she did her best to live up to her reputation.

In fact the image of the "charming amoral little monster" with the Jaguar and the leopard-skin coat has held up somewhat better than that of the writer. As most critics have observed over the years, Sagan's subsequent novels remain essentially what *Bonjour tristesse* was, highly stylized arrangements of idle pseudosophisticates seeking to manipulate one another's lives to find momentary relief from boredom. It is sadly ironic that when she finally did try to escape the world of *Bonjour tristesse* and wrote a novel about working-class people in a mining district of northern France (*Le chien couchant*, 1980), she was taken to court on a charge of having plagiarized it.

Little is to be gained by an itemized survey of her work, for there is little change from book to book.

Nora Rosen takes a charitable view, seeing Sagan as a sort of modern-day Gautier "who has refined her material down to its essence." The trouble is that beneath the brilliantly hard, crystalline surface there is nothing worth concealing. There are only the usual love-triangles enacted in fashionable apartments and five-star hotels and beach houses, the Ferraris and the Chanel suits and the Creed jackets, the father-figures, the generation-gap, and throughout it all, apt and epigrammatic observations about people in love.

There is throughout Sagan's work a certain exquisite quality one ordinarily associates with the craft of the miniaturist. The language of the critics is revealing here: she is "a player of boudoir chess" (Stanley Kaufmann); her stories are "fragile sand dollars—elegant, delicate designs" (*Time*); her characters "more caryatids than people" (Brigid Brophy) who "drift like those toy boats with camphor tied behind them" (Ronald Bryden) and comprise "a pricey collection of tiny figurines and minute porcelains" (Valentine Cunningham). Perhaps the best analogy is that of Anatole Broyard, who likens her characters to "exotic fish, drawn forward or sideways by whatever or whoever happens to be suspended nearest."

As one might suspect, this sort of writing comes very close to soap opera, and is saved from this fate only by Sagan's pellucid style and occasional flashes of ironic humor. It cannot approach serious literature, though, because in the final analysis the reader doesn't care what happens to her people because they don't care themselves. A novel need not be profound, nor even be about interesting people. But it has to be about things that matter, or at least about people who think they do.

The underlying mood of emptiness, far from echoing the *grito* of the Existentialist, becomes self-indulgent parody, and love is reduced to a state of being just a little less bored than usual. In *Des yeux de soie* (1976), a woman who has just been abandoned by her lover seeks solace dancing with a stranger in a night club:

He: "Life goes on, I'm still here, you're still here. We're dancing."

She: "We'll dance for the rest of our lives. We're the sort of people who dance . . . ."

Then later, in bed:

"You know," she said in a calm voice, "it's a funny thing, life, all that . . ."

"What?" he said.

"I don't know,"—and turning toward him, she fell asleep on her side.

Works

Novels: *Bonjour tristesse* (1954). *Un certain sourire* (1956). *Dans un mois, dans un an* (1957). *Aimez-vous Brahms?* (1959). *Les merveilleux nuages* (1961). *La chamade* (1965). *Le garde du coeur* (1968). *Un peu de soleil dans l'eau froide* (1969). *Des bleus à l'âme* (1972). *Un profil perdu* (1974). *Le lit défait* (1977). *Le chien couchant* (1980). *La femme fardée* (1983). *Un orage immobile* (1983). *De guerre lasse* (1985).

Shorter fiction: *Des yeux de soie* (1976). *Musiques de scènes* (1982).

Plays: *Château en Suède* (1960). *Les violons, parfois* (1962). *La robe mauve de Valentine* (1963). *Bonheur, impair et passe* (1964). *Un jardin sur la mer* (1964). *Le cheval évanoui, suivi de l'Écharde* (1966). *Un piano dans l'herbe* (1970). *Il fait beau jour et nuit* (1979).

Other: *Toxique*, autobiographical fragments (1964). *Réponses*, interviews (1974). *Avec mon meilleur souvenir*, biography (1984). *Sand et Musset: Lettres d'amour*, correspondence (1985). Also numerous screenplays, texts for collections of photographs and tableaux vivants, scenarios, and lyrics for the singer Juliette Greco.

Robert Harrison

Rachilde
1860–1953

a.k.a. Marguerite Vallette
Born February 11, 1860, Château-l'Évêque, France
Died April 4, 1953, Paris
Genre(s): novels, short story, drama, essay, criticism
Language(s): French

Born in 1860 in the Périgord as the daughter of Joseph Eymery, a colonel in the French army and Gabrielle Feytaud, the only daughter of a wealthy publisher, Marguerite Eymery cultivated her literary ambitions at an early age when, barely sixteen years of age, she published her first novels, a number of *romans-feuilleton*, in the local Périgord press. At the age of eighteen, she moved to Paris where she embarked on a prolific career as a novelist, playwright, essayist, and *grande dame* of French literature that would continue deep into the twentieth century. Together with her husband Alfred Vallette, whom she married in 1889, she participated in the founding of the *Mercure de France* in 1890—a journal that soon became the leading French literary journal and that especially championed the cause of the new symbolist and decadent authors. Rachilde was also famous for her *mardis*, a prestigious weekly salon for the Parisian writers and intellectuals associated with the *Mercure de France*. One of the most visible figures of French literature during the *fin de siècle* and the *belle époque*, Rachilde outlived the age that had brought her fame by many decades. In her later years, she fervently resisted new generations of avant gardists. Especially dadaists and surrealists found no favor in her eyes because of their contemptuous attitude toward nineteenth-century elitist doctrines concerning art and society. This inability of Rachilde to admit new developments in art and literature no doubt contributed to the sheer anonymity of her death on April 4, 1953.

Rachilde's oeuvre is vast. She published at least one volume every year throughout most of her long life, and her talents and interests led her to compose novels, short stories, plays, essays, and short criticism. Among her early novels, especially *Madame de Sans-Dieu* (1878; Madam without-God), a *roman-feuilleton* often erroneously identified as *Madame de Sangdieu*, and *Monsieur de la nouveauté* (1880; Mister Novelty), the first major novel published by Rachilde following her arrival in Paris, are memorable. Yet, it is probably *Monsieur Vénus. Roman matérialiste* (1884; Mister Venus. A Materialist Novel) that is chiefly responsible for the literary notoriety Rachilde achieved early in her career. This "materialist novel," which was published the same year as Huysmans's *A Rebours*, was banned immediately following its publication on a charge of pornography, and its female protagonist, Raoule de Vénérande, is to be ranked with Huysmans' Des Esseintes as one of the most bizarre figures in French *fin-de-siècle* fiction. Yet, Rachilde refused to be intimidated by the furor surrounding the publication of her novel and published during the next two decades no less frenetic novels such as *Nono. Roman de moeurs contemporaines* (1885; Nono. Novel of Contemporary Manners), *La Marquise de Sade* (1887; The Marquise de Sade), *Madame Adonis* (1888) and *Les Hors-nature. Moeurs contemporaines* (1897; The Unnaturals. Contemporary Manners). In fact, she continued to write this type of novel several decades into the twentieth century: e.g. *La Tour d'amour* (1914; The Tower of Love), *Au seuil de l'enfer* (1924; On the Threshold of Hell), and *Madame de Lydone, assassin* (1929; Madam of Lydone, Assassin).

Among Rachilde's plays, *La Voix du sang* (1891; The Voice of the Blood) and the psychological *Madame la Mort* (1891; Madam Death) deserve mention. She also wrote some significant literary criticism and was one of the early admirers of Alfred Jarry, whom she studied in her *Alfred Jarry ou le Surmâle des lettres*

(1928; Alfred Jarry or the Superman of Literature). Her *Portraits d'hommes* (1930; Portraits of Men) consists of a series of literary portraits.

Rachilde, who identified herself as "Rachilde homme de lettres" on her name-cards, was highly esteemed during her life by such luminaries of French literature as Maurice Barrès, Arsène Housaye, Marcel Schwob, Camille Lemoinier, Jean Moréas, Jean Lorrain, and Guillaume Apollinaire—many of whom wrote prefaces to various publications of hers. Similarly, academic scholar Mario Praz identified her in his *The Romantic Agony* of 1930 as one of the professionals of the French decadent and "sensualist" school. Rachilde's writings, indeed, typically introduce the reader to a distinctively decadent cast of characters. Dandies, sadists, androgynes, transvestites, effeminate men, Amazon women, vampires, madmen, and necrophiles proliferate—especially in her novels and short stories. Yet, it would be incorrect to completely divorce the sexual confusion, the artifice, the frenetic furor, and demented phantasmagoria that typify Rachilde's fictional universe from its deliberately pseudoscientific, antinaturalist mockery. As the subtitles of some of her studies of "contemporary manners" indicate, much of Rachilde's decadent fiction, like Huysmans', involves a frontal attack on the claim to social seriousness and mimetic accuracy of much of French nineteenth-century bourgeois literature. As such, her *oeuvre* deserves as much renewed attention as some other exponents of decadent fiction such as Huysmans, Jean Lorrain, or Villiers de l'Isle-Adam have recently enjoyed.

Works

A complete Rachilde bibliography does not exist and, in fact, is not attempted by her most recent biographer Claude Dauphiné, in his *Rachilde, femme de lettres 1900* (1985). The following is therefore a limited survey of some of Rachilde's most important writings. *Madame de Sans-Dieu* (1878). *L'étoile filante* (1879). *Monsieur de la Nouveauté* (1880). *La Mort d'une petite fille de marbre; la Petite Vierge de plâtre* (1880). *Monsieur Vénus. Roman matérialiste* (1884). *Nono. Roman de moeurs contemporaines* (1885). *La Virginité de Diane* (1886). *A Mort* (1886). *La Marquise de Sade* (1887). *Madame Adonis* (1888). *Théâtre: Madame la Mort, Le Vendeur de Soleil, La Voix du sang* (1891). *La Sanglante Ironie* (1891). *L'Animale* (1893). *Le Démon de l'absurde* (1894). *L'Heure sexuelle* (1893). *Les Hors-nature. Moeurs contemporaines* (1897). *La Jongleuse* (1900). *Le Meneur de louves* (1905). *La Tour d'amour* (1914). *Le Grand Saigneur* (1922). *La Haine amoureuse*

(1924). *Au seuil de l'enfer* (1924). *Alfred Jarry ou le Surmâle des lettres* (1928). *Refaire l'amour* (1928). *Madame de Lydone, assassin* (1929). *Portraits d'hommes* (1930). *Notre-Dame des rats* (1931). *Jeux d'artifices* (1932). *Mon étrange plaisir* (1934). *Les Accords perdus* (1937). *Face à la peur* (1942).

Henk Vynckier

Ann Ward Radcliffe
1764–1823

Born July 9, 1764, London
Died February 7, 1823, London
Genre(s): novel
Language(s): English

The mysteries and ironies of Ann Radcliffe's life are somehow appropriate for the woman who perfected the Gothic suspense tale. Arguably the most popular writer of her time, she lived a reclusive life and stopped writing for publication altogether when her mother's will made her financially comfortable. Her best novels are set in a romanticized Italian landscape, but she never traveled to Italy. Though contemporaries and writers of the next generation would tell jokes at her expense, they would also imitate her. She bequeathed more to the Romantic imagination in terms of sensibility and vocabulary than the Romantics would ever admit. By all accounts, she lived as a dutiful wife, daughter, and niece; her novels, however, are powerful explorations of female fantasy. In many of her tales apparently supernatural events arouse suspense and terror, which are alleviated when the explanation is found to be purely natural. However, her own mind tended toward melancholy and outright depression, perhaps even to madness near the end of her life.

Radcliffe's family included famous physicians and scholars. However, her father was a haberdasher, salesman, and businessman. She often visited her uncle, Thomas Bentley, who knew many eminent poets, scientists, and travelers. In her obituary her husband would write that these visits to her uncle were a major influence on her imagination. Otherwise, her education was standard. When living in Bath, Radcliffe may have been a student of Sophia Lee, who ran a woman's school there. If she did not meet Lee, she certainly read and was deeply influenced by Lee's novel *The Recess*. That book had marked a departure from the standard domestic sentimental novel. There is an interest in madness, in passion and mystery, in the psychology of the romantic sensibility. What was new about Lee's novel was its freedom from the constraints of "realism," which in most cases meant the depiction of house, home, and duty expected in women's fiction. Female characters could now be placed in wild and unpredictable circumstances, and the depiction of their perils and emotions could be freer. Thus, fantasy of a powerful kind was given a new latitude. These developments, along with an interest in the dark and the macabre (Radcliffe frequently reread *Macbeth*), left its mark on her subsequent literary work.

In 1787, she married William Radcliffe, a law student turned journalist, who encouraged her to write and critiqued her work. Her novels were almost immediately popular, and by *The Romance of the Forest* (1791), she was a well-known literary figure. Radcliffe achieved true fame with *The Mysteries of Udolpho* (1794), a book that earned her the nickname "The Great Enchantress."

Radcliffe's novels have been considered in several ways. Earlier critics, wishing to get around Radcliffe as quickly as possible, either dismissed her work as trash or praised it faintly as the precedent for much better novels, such as *Jane Eyre* and *Wuthering Heights*. Lately, critics have begun to attribute a great deal of importance to Radcliffe. Her novels can be seen as the first perfection of an enduringly popular genre (witness the recent vogue for "romance novels"). Radcliffe also wrote the first novels whose main aim was to elicit emotions of terror, horror, and suspense. Lately she has been recognized as a writer whose main theme was female fantasy—specifically, the fantasy in which the virtuous and beleaguered heroine triumphs over insurmountable difficulties to achieve her own happiness and vindicate the essential goodness of the divine order.

Clearly, Radcliffe was a writer with a formula. Keats was responding to Radcliffe's depiction of nature when he lampooned her as a writer who will "cavern you and grotto you, and waterfall you and wood you, and immense-rock you." She concocted a mixture of medieval and contemporary romance that brought ruined castles, houses with secret passageways, cryptic messages that explain everything, and dark, half-understood portents in nature into fiction; she also resurrected the apparatus of Renaissance romance, including the low-born heroine who discovers that she is nobly born, woods lushly responsive to the excesses of the heroine's emotions (as is the case with Adeline of *The Romance of the Forest*, 1791), and the reunion of deserving lovers after eventful separation. There is also a cast of characters that has become too familiar: a lonely maiden,

Ann Ward Radcliffe

an older authoritarian male figure who sooner or later becomes an out-and-out villain, a loyal servant, and a virtuous hero.

Yet Radcliffe deserves to be remembered for more than these clichés. Her writing reveals a genuine interest in the extremes of human psychology. She is acutely sensitive to the aspects of life that make us anxious and afraid. And there is a moral purpose to the excitation of terror in the reader, for terror is a test of reason, an index of the extent to which the reader trusts herself and her world. As mentioned above, the point of most of her novels is that all the terror has a natural explanation. Her heroines are heroines because they triumph over great difficulties to discover this; her villains are villains because, like La Motte of *The Romance of the Forest*, they often know the secret and try to prevent the heroine from discovering it. These villains often enjoy tormenting the unknowing heroine over their half-understood world. The extent of their evil is revealed at the end, when the heroine understands that world more clearly and has a more complete control over her life. Thus La Motte keeps the true origin of Adelie's birth from her, and Montoni of *The Mysteries of Udolpho* tries to wheedle his dead wife's money out of her daughter Emily. Emily triumphs over Montoni and over La Motte because of self reliance and inner strength.

One need not belabor the patterns that emerge so clearly from these novels—of male figures denying female figures essential information and essential power, of revelations that change the place of woman in the world. When in *Udolpho* the veil is lifted over the mysterious picture, the key to it all, Emily faints; it is as if she, allowed to see the real truth, must escape somehow from its impact. Most importantly, Radcliffe's heroines do it themselves: in the end they act to change their worlds and break free of the dark, often unconscious fetters of fear.

Part of all the fantasy is the undeniably attractive nature of some of the villains. Some readers have been quick to find Electra complexes throughout Radcliffe's fiction. More to the point, her villains are brooding, isolated, full of a mysterious inner conflict. She refined and refined this character until she perfected it in Father Schedoni of *The Italian* (1797). He has been recognized as the prototype of the aloof, preoccupied Romantic hero, a proto-Manfred: "there was something in [Schedoni's] air, something almost superhuman." Though Ellena triumphs over Schedoni in the end and marries the virtuous Vivaldi, it is his character that remains the most striking thing in a very striking novel.

The Italian was the last of Radcliffe's novels to be published during her lifetime. A year later, her father died and her husband fell ill. In March 1800, her mother died, leaving Radcliffe alone and despondent, "the last leaf on the tree." Although she wrote one more novel, *Gaston de Blondeville* (1826), she had lost the desire to publish, possibly even to be read. According to her husband's obituary, she died in a delirium.

Radcliffe is a writer who has had a remarkable and enduring impact on fiction both serious and popular. Of her works, *The Romance of the Forest* and *The Italian* hold up the best. They are still enjoyable for their suspense and attractive for their substance. Though she wrote very little about her personal life, one imagines that she would have appreciated readers who could see the moral intent of all the wildness, the twists of plot, the romance, and the fantasy. She virtually discovered a form of myth that, however it may embarrass or distress us, is still very powerful.

Works

The Castles of Athlin and Dubayne (1789). *A Sicilian Romance* (1790). *The Romance of the Forest* (1791). *The Mysteries of Udolpho* (1794). *A Journey Made in the Summer of 1794 through Holland and the Western Frontiers of Germany, with a Re-* *turn down the Rhine, to Which Are Added Observations during a Tour to the Lakes of Lancashire, Westmoreland and Cumberland* (1795; Travel Journal). *The Italian, or the Confessional of the Black Penitents* (1797). *Gaston de Blondeville, or the Court of Henry III Keeping Festival in Ardenne* (1826). *St. Alban's Abbey* (1826).

John Timpane

Radegunde
A.D. 520–587

Born A.D. 520, Thuringia
Died 587, Poitiers
Genre(s): episcopal correspondence
Language(s): Medieval Latin

Radegunde (520–587 A.D.) is the subject of three narrative sources written before 610 by contemporaries who knew Radegunde as a Merovingian queen, as the founder and a nun of the St. Croix nunnery in Poitiers, and as the patron saint for a new kind of cult worship during the period of the Catholic Christianization of barbarian Europe. The dramatic events of Radegunde's life attracted moral interpretation by the Gallo-Roman historian Bishop Gregory of Tours; the Italian poet-priest Fortunatus; and the humble Frankish nun Baudonivia.

Radegunde was born into one of the three ruling families in Thuringia, a tribal territory bordering Frankish Gaul. In early childhood, Radegunde's parents were assassinated by her uncles, and when she was ten years old, one uncle allied with the neighboring Franks to make war on the other uncle. One of the Frankish kings captured Radegunde and her younger brother in this war as his victory prizes. Catholic bishops arbitrated a judgment about Radegunde and she was taken to a Gallo-Roman villa to work and to be educated until the time of her forced marriage to Clothar I, son of Clovis I and Clothilde. At the Merovingian court in Soissons, Radegunde lived as a Catholic queen among concubines until her husband murdered her brother. Following this murder, Radegunde fled to the shrine of St. Martin in Tours. At the altar, she exchanged her jewels for the intercession of powerful churchmen against Clothar. Negotiations between several bishops and Clothar eventually enabled Radegunde to establish St. Croix, an independent nunnery for more than 200 women in Poitiers, a frontier area of Frankish conquest and

Christian conversion. The nuns lived immured under the Rule of Caesarius of Arles, communicating with the outside kingdom largely through the diplomacy of Bishop Gregory and through the pen of Fortunatus.

As both a barbarian queen and a Catholic saint, Radegunde lived on the crux of cultural assimilation for the Christianization of Merovingian Gaul. The story of Queen-Saint Radegunde is one of the earliest examples of the cultural and religious accommodation accomplished in barbarian Europe by means of a woman's example in life and in literature.

Works

Epistula ad episcopus (written before the Council of Tours, 587) in *Historia Francorum*, Bk. IX, Gregory of Tours, *Monumenta Germanica Historia Script. rer. mer.* 1–450. Internal evidence in primary sources for other correspondence, but manuscripts are not identified by scholarship to date.

Duey White

Marie Louise de la Ramée
1839–1908
a.k.a. Ouida
Born January 1, 1839, Bury St. Edmunds, England
Died January 25, 1908, Viareggio, Italy
Genre(s): novel, short story
Language(s): English

An only child, Ramée was left by the long and frequent absences of her French father to be raised almost entirely by her English mother and grandmother. The family liked to believe that the mysterious M. Ramée was involved in opposition politics in his native land and that he died during the days of the Commune. Ramée's fierce pride in her French heritage soon combined with her fantasizing temperament to inflate her surname to de la Ramée.

Her fantasies having long outgrown the narrow provinciality of Bury St. Edmunds, Ramée welcomed the move to London with her mother and grandmother in 1857. After being introduced to Harrison Ainsworth, then editor of *Bentley's Miscellany*, she began her writing career as "Ouida" (her childhood mispronunciation of "Louise"). She followed up the success of her "Dashwood's Drag; or the Derby and What Came of It," which appeared in *Bentley's* for April and May 1859, with a series of similar tales of

high society and sporting life, many collected in *Cecil Castlemaine's Gage, and Other Novelettes* (1867). *Granville de Vigne,* serialized in Ainsworth's *New Monthly Magazine* and reprinted as *Held in Bondage* (1863), typified her early fiction. Its formula of dashing military life, extravagant luxury, tortuous romantic intrigue, and a hero of almost impossible beauty, courage, and style reached its epitome in *Under Two Flags* (1867). The public attention (and financial reward) such fiction attracted allowed Ramée to live out the fantasies otherwise denied by her lack of beauty and social status. Adorned in Worth gowns and surrounded by hothouse flowers, she held court to largely male audiences in the Langham Hotel during the seventies; in later years she frequently dressed to resemble the heroines of her latest novel. Although essentially conventional in her own behavior, she flouted Victorian codes of respectability by encouraging people to smoke throughout dinner and by remaining with the men over brandy and cigars, collecting material for her novels from their conversation. *Tricotrin* (1869) and *Folle-Farine* (1871) added a new element to her fictional formulas: the peasant heroine who becomes tragically enmeshed in the snares of high society, a device she would exploit again in *Two Little Wooden Shoes* (1874).

In 1871 Ramée traveled to Europe, producing *A Dog of Flanders and Other Stories* (1872) from her observations of the Belgium peasantry and a series of novels set in Italy, among them *Pascarèl* (1873), *Signa* (1875), *In a Winter City* (1876), and *Ariadnê* (1877). She lived in the Villa Farinola outside Florence from 1871 to 1888. Of the several novels featuring fashionable members of Florentine society, the most notorious was *Friendship* (1878). Its main characters were recognized to represent Ramée, the Marchese della Stuffa (a gentleman-in-waiting to the Italian court whom she had pursued with unrequited passion), and Mrs. Janet Duff Gordon Ross, Stuffa's avowed mistress. Ramée's insistence that the novel was based on absolute truth made its idealization of her own role and its vilification of her rival all the more outrageous. Her personal disappointments helped turn her attention from the glamour to the failings of polite society. *Moths* (1880), perhaps her most successful work, shows the social fabric being eaten away by the vice and hypocrisy of society's fashionable "moths." She would increasingly lament the upper classes' failure to live up to the ideals of taste and breeding she set for them as well as their surrender to the values of the vulgar and social climbing middle classes she had all her life detested. She sentimentalized the Italian peasantry as victims abandoned by the aristocracy to the tyranny of the bourgeois bureaucracy in A *Village Commune and Other Stories* (1881). *The Massarenes* (1897) most directly condemns the *nouveaux riches* and the "smart" set that collaborated with them.

As the eighties waned, so, too, did Ramée's popularity with an audience turning from three decker romances to more realistic one-volume works. Her extravagant lifestyle continually outran her income, leaving unpaid bills and pending lawsuits behind her as she moved from place to place, her only companions after her mother's death being a faithful servant or two and the pack of spoiled dogs on which she lavished her affection. In her final years only a Civil List Pension, awarded in appreciation for her contributions to literature, stood between her and real poverty. During the nineties she turned increasingly to criticism and commentary: many of her analyses of British and European writers and her vendettas against publishers, plagiarists, cruelty to animals, female suffrage, Italian misgovernment, the Boer War, and the rising tide of vulgarity and ugliness brought on by the ascendancy of middle-class money and values were collected in *Views and Opinions* (1895) and *Critical Studies* (1900).

Ramée owed her considerable success in the 1870s and 1880s in part to her abundant imagination for sensational plotting, vivid detail, and local color, in part to the expanding market for fiction created by lending libraries and railway bookstalls. Her eccentricity, her egotism, and her flamboyance were always straining against the prosaic and sometimes sordid reality of her life; her wish-fulfilling fictions fed her own and her audience's longing for the glamour, romance, and luxury forever beyond their reach.

Works
Held in Bondage (1863). *Strathmore* (1865). *Chandos* (1866). *Cecil Castlemaine's Gage, and Other Novelettes* (1867). *Under Two Flags* (1867). *Idalia* (1867). *Tricotrin* (1869). *Puck* (1870). *Folle-Farine* (1871). *A Dog of Flanders and Other Stories* (1872). *Pascarèl* (1873). *Two Little Wooden Shoes* (1874). *Signa* (1875). *In a Winter City* (1876). *Ariadnê* (1877). *Friendship* (1878). *Moths* (1880). *Pipistrello, and Other Stories* (1880). *A Village Commune and Other Stories* (1881). *Bimbi: Stories for Children* (1882). *In Maremma* (1882). *Wanda* (1883). *Frescoes: Dramatic Sketches* (1883). *Princess Napraxine* (1884). *Othmar* (1885). *A Rainy June* (1885). *Don Guesaldo* (1886). *A House Party* (1887). *Guilderoy* (1889). *Ruffino and Other Stories* (1890). *Syrlin* (1890). *Santa Barbara, and Other Tales* (1891).

The Tower of Taddeo (1892). *The New Priesthood: A Protest against Vivisection* (1893). *Two Offenders and Other Tales* (1894). *The Silver Christ and a Lemon Tree* (1894). *Toxin* (1895). *Views and Opinions* (1895). *Le Selve, and Other Tales* (1896). *The Massarenes* (1897). *Dogs* (1897). *An Altruist* (1897). *La Strega, and Other Stories* (1899). *The Waters of Edera* (1900). *Critical Studies* (1900). *Street Dust, and Other Stories* (1901). *Helianthus* (1908).

Rosemary Jann

Lea Ráskai
ca. 1450–ca.1500
Born fifteenth century
Died sixteenth century
Genre(s): translation, copyist of ecclesiastical works
Language(s): Hungarian, Latin

Very little is known of the life of Lea Ráskai. She was a Dominican nun in the cloister on the Nyulak Szigete (Island of the Hares), known today as St. Margaret's Island, and was most likely of aristocratic birth. Her cloister had been founded by King Béla IV for his daughter, Margaret. Ráskai copied the legend of St. Margaret (*Margit legenda*), probably also translating it from the Latin. This would indicate a high degree of education, as indeed is also suggested by the reforms that were being carried out at this time: the rules call for extensive readings in liturgical works as well as the Bible, and most of this was still in Latin. The *Margit legenda* (Margaret Legend) was done in 1510. Ráskai's literary talent is demonstrated in the care she took to make each detail of her subject's life come alive by minute references to the cloister; such passages might even be embellishments of the Latin original. The Margaret legend is important as a record of the life of a princess of the House of Árpád, but Ráskai's contribution extended beyond this one work.

The *Cornides codex* is perhaps her most important work. This was copied between 1514–1519 and consists of fourteen sermons and eleven legends. The source of the sermons is a fifteenth-century collection by an unknown compiler who calls himself Paratus. These are full of parables and many similes from nature. The Easter sermon serves almost as a reply to the lament of Mary, setting forth how Jesus appears to Mary while she was still at home and how the angels, Adam and Eve and the prophets, the patriarchs, and saints glorified her. The one for All Saints Day recounts the dedication of the Pantheon in 605 to the Blessed Virgin and all the saints. For Trinity Sunday, one of the great mysteries of faith is explained in the best tradition of medieval philosophy. Most of the legends in this work are based on the *Legenda Aurea*, but the *Catalogus Sanctorum* is the source of the legend of St. Potenciana and the legend of St. Dorothy comes from the *De Sanctis* of the popular Hungarian preacher, Plébart of Temesvár. Most of the saints are virgins and martyrs from the early days of the Church, though St. Helena is included as an example of chaste widowhood. While following her sources fairly closely, Ráskai nevertheless shows some passages of rare poetic beauty, particularly in the legend of St. Dorothy. She also copied about half of the *Példák könyve* (The Book of Examples) in 1510, in 1517 the legend of life of St. Dominic, and in 1522 the *Horváth codex*. Her contribution to Hungarian literature has provided a rich source of earlier traditions.

Sister Lea belonged to the new generation of nuns to whom Hungarian literature owes a great debt for they preserved earlier legends through their copying. Though somewhat anachronistic in their dedication to the ideals of the Middle Ages on the threshold of the Renaissance, they were not untouched by the spirit of Humanism. Better educated than their predecessors, they were freer in spirit and more in touch with the world: the mother of King Matthias took an active interest in the major monasteries and had free access to the one on St. Margaret's island also. Familiar with Latin, the sisters also used Hungarian to transmit the teachings and the legends of the Church to those unschooled in the Church's language. Ráskai speaks with feeling of the peace to be found in the cells: "outside the cells there is nothing but warfare. . . . In the cells we pray, write, study, . . . read Holy Writ, or serve God." Ironically, though we do not know when Ráskai died, the disintegration of the Hungarian kingdom was sealed with the defeat at Mohács in 1526 when the young king was killed. The monasteries of Buda were no longer the refuges they had been earlier, and in 1541, when the city fell to the Turks, all of them were closed and the inhabitants were forced to flee.

Works

Margit legenda (1510). *Peldák könyve*, first part (1510). *Cornides codex* (1514–1519). *Domonkos legenda* [Legend of St. Dominic] (1517). *Horváth codex*.

Enikő Molnár Basa

Irina Ratushinskaia
1954–

Born March 4, 1954, Odessa, Soviet Union
Genre(s): poetry, short story
Language(s): Russian

A descendant of Russianized Polish nobility, a physicist and mathematician by training, Irina Ratushinskaia has been writing poetry since childhood. She realized her true vocation as a poet when at the age of twenty-five, she read Pasternak, Mandelshtam, and Tsvetaeva. She describes it in her brief autobiographical sketch "My Homeland" as a sudden encounter with the eternal light of truth, making her aware of the inhumanity of existence under the Soviet regime. The result was a profound spiritual awakening, which released an avalanche of poetic creativity.

Since that revelation she has committed herself to speak out in protest against the Soviet disrespect of basic human rights and, by that same token, become a dissident poet. Her courageous poetic attack on injustice, obviously, could not be published in the Soviet Union; instead her poetry was spread unofficially by *samizdat*, and some of it reached the West where three collections of her work were published: one in 1984, two in 1986.

Ratushinskaia's poetic activity resulted in her arrest in September 1982 and subsequent sentence to seven years' hard labor and five years' exile in March 1983. On October 10, 1986, Ratushinskaia was released before completing her term and allowed to leave the Soviet Union with her husband (she married Igor Gerashchenko in 1979) to go to England for medical treatment. For the time being she decided to stay in the West.

During the three and a half years in jail in incredible, inhuman conditions, suffering physical and mental torture, Ratushinskaia has composed more than two hundred poems writing them down with a burnt match on a piece of soap and committing them to memory until retainment. To avoid additional punishment, she washed off the lines when she knew them by heart.

Frequently, her lyric voice assumes the power of a modern Cassandra foreseeing her confinement and martyrdom. The sublimation of her own pain channels her creative impulse toward compassion for her fellow-inmates, her abandoned husband: "Lord, how is life for him? Keep a watchful eye, / Lest that bare cubbyhole apartment drive him to madness!" (April, 1983). The motif of bitter denunciation of the Soviet system's brutality is overcome by the constantly recurring theme of trust in Divine Grace and a sense of mission to bring truth to the world. Her moral anguish is fleeting and mild, she likens it to a tiny tame animal: "As a domesticated cub, my anguish / Lives in tranquillity, responds to 'shoo'! / She needs so little: Some attentive scratching." (October, 1982).

Ratushinskaia also has written short stories, one of which has appeared in the Russian emigré daily *Novoye Russkoe Slovo* [The New Russian Word] ["The Debt" (October 5, 1986)]. A collection of Ratushinskaia's short stories, *The Tale of Three Heads*, came out in Russian and English at the very end of 1986.

Ratushinskaia's lyrics range from classical meters and rhyme schemes to various modes of modern versification. Most of her poetic output, as a genuine lyrical testimony to the cruel persecution of human dignity, belongs to the, alas, well-established genre of "prison-diary."

Works

Poems: text in Russian, English, and French, tr. Meery Devergnas (French) and Philip Balla, Pamela White Hadas, Susan Layton, Ilya Nykin (English) (1984). *Vne limita* [Beyond the Limit], selected poetry (1986). *Ia dozhivu* [I'll Survive], poems (1986). *Skazka o trekh golovakh* [The Tale of Three Heads], tr. Diane Nemec Ignashev (1986).

Translations: *Grey Is the Color of Hope* (1988). *Pencil Letter* (1988). *In the Beginning* (1991).

Marina Astman

Gerlind Reinshagen
1926–

Born 1926, Königsberg, Germany
Genre(s): drama, radio play, novel
Language(s): German

Although Gerlind Reinshagen has published works of narrative prose in recent years, she is above all a playwright, one of the few women dramatists in Germany today. She began her career in the 1960s as the writer of radio plays, adapting many for stage production. Her professional success was firmly established in the early and mid-1970s when her plays *Himmel und Erde* (1974; Heaven and Earth) and *Sonntagskinder* (1976; Sunday's Children) found fre-

quent production on the major stages of West Germany. In 1974 Reinshagen received the Schiller-Förderpreis, and the Mülheimer *Dramatikerpreis* in 1977. Despite their success, these plays were not published until 1981. Since that time Reinshagen's popularity as a female dramatist and prose writer has grown, as the 1986 edition of her collected plays attests.

Reinshagen was born in Königsberg in 1926 and studied first in Braunschweig and then West Berlin, where she currently lives. Her first play to draw critical attention was the adapted radio play *Leben und Tod der Marilyn Monroe* (1971; Life and Death of Marilyn Monroe) in which she portrays the stellar rise and ultimate destruction of a female celluloid "myth." In this myth, created in the image abstracted and desired by secularized modern society, the creator seeks affirmation of its impoverished existence.

All of Reinshagen's plays are characterized by experimentation with and explosion of traditional dramatic structure. The plays are written in scenes, with only occasional act or part designations (e.g., nineteen scenes in *Leben und Tod der Marilyn Monroe*, and four stations in *Himmel und Erde*). Reinshagen frequently employs *Verfremdungseffekte* (distancing effects) such as the projection of expository titles at the start of each scene, frequent use of songs juxtaposed with eloquent dialogue, and occasional direct address of the audience by the actors. The author also suggests innovation in acting and production style. In the list of characters in *Leben und Tod der Marilyn Monroe*, Reinshagen requests that each character be played by several actors and actresses in the course of one production.

Reinshagen's plays treat a variety of themes and problems that other postwar German literary artists have also examined. The complex issue of the Third Reich, and specifically the civilian relationship to Nazism and provincial fascism, is the focus of the play *Sonntagskinder*. Here, the Nazi past is mediated through the perspective of the fourteen-year-old main character, Elsie. Reinshagen shows how through fascism and adult domination the moral and personal development of a child is slowed, arrested, and regresses. This play, with its presentation of the destruction of the child's instinctive innocence by the ruling provincial and fascist adult world, demonstrates an affinity with the works of the German playwright and novelist Marieluise Fleisser (1901–1974).

Reinshagen also employs the narrative perspective of the child in the short prose diary "Elsas

Nachtbuch" (1980; Elsa's Diary) and in the accompanying play *Das Frühlingsfest* (1980; The Springtime Celebration). Herein she addresses the economic and moral restoration of postwar Germany. Economic rehabilitation and the modern business world are introduced in Reinshagen's early play *Doppelkopf* (1971; Twohead), in which the young aspiring protagonist climbs the corporate ladder only to become sickened and repulsed by the inhumanity at the managerial pinnacle. This contemporary theme is delivered through an expressionistic play structure. The story of the ambitious but unsuccessful apprentice, who strives to enter the managerial ranks, is also told in Reinshagen's humorous first novel *Rovinato oder die Seele des Geschäfts* (1982; Rovinato or the Soul of the Company).

In her plays Reinshagen portrays predominantly female main characters without adopting a strong feminist viewpoint; however, in her latest works Reinshagen specifically addresses a feminist literary issue. In the novel *Die flüchtige Braut* (1984; The Fleeting Bride) and the play *Die Clownin* (1985; The Clown Woman) Reinshagen seeks to uncover and establish a female literary tradition through the anachronistic introduction of nineteenth-century literary figures into twentieth-century stories. In the novel Reinshagen transposes a Romantic intellectual circle in present-day West Berlin. The characters (mostly writers, scholars, and artists) adopt the characteristics of a past literary author or figure. Significantly, the main character, Dora, selects Emily Brontë as her alter ego. Both Dora and Emily reappear in *Die Clownin*.

Although hardly known outside of West Germany, Gerlind Reinshagen has become Germany's first successful contemporary female playwright. Her works offer representations of contemporary social and political issues while clearly addressing the urgent question of the importance of literary tradition for the modern writer.

Works

Plays: *Doppelkopf* (1971). *Leben und Tod der Marilyn Monroe* (1971). *Himmel und Erde* (1974). *Sonntagskinder* (1976). *Das Frühlingsfest* (1980). *Die Clownin* (1985).

Prose: *Elsas Nachtbuch* (1980). *Rovinato oder die Seele des Geschäfts* (1982). *Die flüchtige Braut* (1984).

Stephanie B. Pafenberg

Mary Renault
1905–1983

a.k.a. Eileen Mary Challans
Born September 4, 1905, London
Died December 15, 1983, Cape Town, South Africa
Genre(s): novel
Language(s): English

Mary Renault was the daughter of a medical doctor and a descendant of English Puritans. She received her early education in Bristol, graduated from St. Hugh's College, Oxford, and later completed nursing training at Radcliffe Infirmary, Oxford. She turned to nursing to observe human life first hand since she noted that her earlier writings were purely derived from other people's books. Her first novel, *The Purposes of Love* (1939), published in the United States as *Promise of Love*, was drawn from her hospital nursing experience. Her next three novels, love stories with well-drawn character portrayals, were written off duty. The last of these, *Return to Night* (1947), described by one critic as "everything Hollywood could possibly want," earned her an MGM $150,000 prize in 1947. The story is told from the male doctor's point of view, leading T. Sugrue to comment that "the objectivity of which she is so proud is a negation of feminine tenderness. . . ." This work established Renault's reputation in America.

After her nursing service during the war, she moved to Natal, South Africa, and began extensive travels through Italy, France, Greece, and the Aegean. She was most impressed with Greece, the setting for her first historical novel, *The Last of the Wine* (1956), a taut and absorbing narrative. In 1953 *The Charioteer* appeared in the United States, a book which, according to H. Saal, enters "the shadowy world of the homosexual" whose character's "untiring delicacy becomes—like a steady diet of English lady writers, tiresome—and the intrusion of some good old-fashioned heterosexual vulgarity welcome." Other critics, however, praised her sensitive delineation of love among men. She also touched upon contemporary issues by introducing conscientious objectors and the subject of pacifism into the novel.

Her 1962 novel, *The Bull from the Sea,* is a sequel, dealing with the death of Theseus. The structure is episodic, held together by the presence of the hero. At this point critics began to debate whether Renault might best be considered a writer of historical novels or historical romances. In spite of her appended "historical notes" and scholarly bibliographies, much of her writing, especially in the dialogues, is pure fiction. A unifying motif of a number of the novels is the sacrificial death of a king. Renault makes the mythological personal and humanized through her use of the first-person narrative.

The Persian Boy (1972) received mixed reviews. A panoramic view of the Asian and African conquests of Alexander the Great, the tale is told from the point of view of a castrated Persian slave whose understanding of the historical moment is unbelievable. Renault pursued her interest in the conqueror with a biography, The Nature of Alexander (1975). In The Praise Singer (1978), she returned to her earlier formula of presenting a story from the point of view of an obscure but historically representative figure, Simonides the Poet, who laments the passing of traditional Greek values in the sixth century B.C. Renault ended her Alexander trilogy with Funeral Games (1981), a complex story with a preface of forty-five "Principal Persons." An especially vivid character is the Amazonian Eurydice who fails as a "masculine" warrior. The presence of such a figure in Renault's final novel is an interesting one. While the theme of homosexuality frequently recurs in her works, the characters were usually masculine. Indeed, many critics reacted rabidly to these characters, one, H. Kenner, referred to Renault as "a male impersonator," in spite of the fact that homosexuality is always dealt with in a delicate, natural fashion throughout her work. Such attacks were perhaps directed at Renault personally because of her life-long relationship with a friend she had met during nurses' training. In spite of this kind of criticism, Renault's novels, especially The Last of the Wine and The Mask of Apollo, continue to enjoy popularity as novels of historical and entertaining value.

Works

The Purposes of Love (1939; in the U.S. as Promise of Love). Kind Are Her Answers (1940). The Friendly Young Ladies (1944; republished as The Middle Mist, 1945). Return to Night (1947). North Face (1948). The Charioteer (1953). The Last of the Wine (1956). The King Must Die (1958). The Bull from the Sea (1962). The Lion in the Gateway (1964). The Mask of Apollo (1966). Fire from Heaven (1969). The Persian Boy (1972). The Nature of Alexander (1975). The Praise Singer (1978). Funeral Games (1981).

Carole Shaffer-Koros

Franziska von Reventlow
1871–1918

Born May 18, 1871, Husum, Frisia
Died July 27, 1918, Muralto, Tessin
Genre(s): short story, essay, poetry, translation, diary, letters, novel
Language(s): German

In 1899 Fanny Liane Sophie Auguste Wilhelmine Adrienne Gräfin zu Reventlow left her parents and the world of aristocracy and changed her name to "Franziska," under which she was to become famous as a literary figure. She grew up in Lübeck (since 1889) and Hamburg, lived in Munich from 1892 to 1909, and then in Ancona, southern Switzerland. During her years in Munich she led a life free from all social conventions and tried to become a painter. Financial troubles, however, forced her to turn to writing. All her novels reflect her own life during those years. The crucial autobiographical novel Herrn Dames Aufzeichnungen (1913; Notes of Mr. Dames) caused a storm of public outcry by those who were depicted in it. Her correspondence with Emanuel Febling, a schoolmate of Heinrich and Thomas Mann, dates back to 1890, her diary to 1895. She was a fervent admirer of Friedrich Nietzsche and strongly advocated the philosophy of Life as Art and To Live Only for Art. This interest is particularly reflected in her first novel Ellen Olestjerne (1903), which mirrors many modern trends in literature and art of the turn of the century. Henrik Ibsen also deeply influenced her, which resulted in Fanny's extreme and absolute form of subjectivism and in a dominant quest for independence in her life. Thus her works include women figures of strong personality who decide on their own what to do with their life.

She concluded a brief marriage with the court assistant Walter Lübke from Hamburg on May 23, 1894, but she became pregnant by the painter Henryk Walkow and gave birth to her son Rudolf on September 1, 1897, in Munich. Her decision to raise him alone came close to a scandal in Schwabing/Munich and was another act of her self-determination. In 1912 she wrote Von Paul zu Pedro (From Paul to Pedro). In 1916 appeared Der Geldkomplex (The Money Complex) and in 1916–1918 Der Selbstmordverein (The Club of Suicidals), which was to be published only in her complete works in 1925. All these novels reveal Franziska von Reventlow to be master of a literary style influenced by French authors such as Marcel Prévost, Anatole France, and Guy de Maupassant, whose works she extensively translated for the Albert Langen publishing house. In her novels she excelled in humor, graciousness, and a very light conversational tone that often hides tragedy and suffering. Even though she had many literary contacts with R.M. Rilke, Emnil Ludwig, and Klabund, she followed her French amorous models of the nineteenth century (*Von Paul zu Pedro*). In *Der Geldkomplex* she satirized the bohemian lifestyle and talked openly about the misery and economic plight of artists.

Works

With Eugen Thosson, *Klosterjungen* [Monastery Boys], collection of humorous sketches (1897). *Ellen Olestjerne. Eine Lebensgeschichte* [Ellen Olestjerne. A Story of a Life] (1903). *Von Paul zu Pedro. Amouresken* [From Paul to Pedro. Amorous Stories] (1912). *Herrn Dames Aufzeichnungen oder Begebenheiten aus einem merkwürdigen Stadtteil* [Notes of Mr. Dames or Events in a Strange City Neighborhood] (1913). *Der Geldkomplex oder von der Kunst, Schulden mit Charme zu ertragen* [The Money Complex; or, Of the Art of Coping with Debts in a Gracious Way] (1916). *Das Logierhaus zur schwankenden Weltkugel und andere Novellen* [The Pension of the Staggering Globe and Other Short Stories] (1917). *Gesammelte Werke* [Collected Works] (1926). *Briefe* [Letters] (1929). *Tagebuch* [Diary], printed in 1971] (1895–1910).

Albrecht Classen

Jean Rhys
1890–1979

a.k.a. Ella Gwendolyn Rees Williams
Born August 24, 1890, Roseau, Dominica, British West Indies
Died May 14, 1979, Exeter
Genre(s): novel, short story, translation, autobiography
Language(s): English

The daughter of a Welsh doctor and his Scottish-Dominican wife, Rhys was educated at a convent in Roseau, Dominica, until she left the island to attend the Perse School in Cambridge, England. She studied later at the Royal Academy of Dramatic Art but left school after her father's death. Over her family's objections, she remained in England and worked as chorus girl in a musical comedy company touring the provinces. Some of her later jobs included modeling, tutoring, translating, and ghostwriting a book on furniture. She began to write after her first marriage in 1919.

Rhys wrote for many years before Ford Madox Ford encouraged her to publish her first book, *The Left Bank and Other Stories* (1927). These stories, and most of her later works as well, depict her experiences as a child growing up in Dominica and as a young woman living in London and Paris. Although there is a fine line in her work between life and art, her prose transcends autobiography by capturing the impressions of an unrepresented class in literature, those cast out by society. In his preface to *The Left Bank,* Ford characterized Rhys's innovation as "an almost lurid! [sic] passion for stating the case of the underdog." Ford also praised her sensitive ear for dialogue and her careful eye for form in fiction, stylistic qualities that reveal her conviction that one must write from life in order to portray truth in fiction. As she stated in a 1968 interview, "I am the only truth I know."

In the four novels written in the 1920s and 1930s, Rhys describes the same lonely female figure at different stages of life. In her first novel *Postures* (1928) (Rhys preferred the American title *Quartet),* she presents the *ménage à trois* of an English couple and Marya Zelli, a young married woman whose husband has been jailed. Seen by critics to be a *roman à clef* of the difficult relationship of Rhys, Ford, and Ford's common-law wife Stella Bowen, the novel details the cruel treatment of the unprotected single woman by "respectable" people, a theme that recurs often in Rhys' work. In her second novel, *After Leaving Mr. Mackenzie* (1931), Julia Martin, the former mistress of the title character, has been pensioned off by her lover and ekes out a lonely existence in a Paris hotel room. The typical Rhys heroine, like Julia, ends up alone, friendless, and broke, without the protection of a man. Rhys's own favorite of the early novels, *Voyage in the Dark* (1934), is the story of Anna Morgan, a chorus girl taken as mistress by an older man and then discarded when she asserts her independence. In Rhys's fictional world, women who abhor the hypocrisy of respectability are always at odds with those, usually men, who have law and money on their side. Women of a certain type struggle desperately for money that provides them with security, but they lose or spend money freely when they have it. Although the aging Sasha Jansen in *Good Morning, Midnight* (1939) manages, through the generosity of a friend, to live well during a trip to Paris, she cannot let down her guard to trust a gigolo who eventually reveals himself to be as vulnerable as she is. Sasha's experiences with love have scarred her and left her emotionally bankrupt.

Rhys's early novels, reissued after the success of *Wide Sargasso Sea* (1966), gained a wider audience in the 1960s and 1970s when critics pointed out that she had been a pioneer in addressing the difficulties faced by a single woman in a male-dominated society. Although in interviews Rhys revealed her opposition to a strictly feminist reading of her fiction, she raises the issue of the powerlessness of women in the nineteenth century in her last novel.

Rhys receded from the public in the 1940s and 1950s and lived in obscurity in Cornwall; she was rediscovered in 1957 when the BBC produced a radio version of *Good Morning, Midnight* and placed an advertisement in the *New Statesman* seeking its author. She had worked for years on a number of short stories and a novel based on the character of Antoinette Cosway, the mad wife of Rochester in Charlotte Brontë's *Jane Eyre*. Characteristically searching for the most appropriate words for her ideas, Rhys rewrote the novel many times with some chapters having as many as eleven versions. Her careful craftsmanship forbade her from publishing what she considered to be inferior work, and she continued to revise the manuscript of *Wide Sargasso Sea* until its publication in 1966, when it was hailed by critics as one of the greatest English novels. Rhys said she wrote the story of the Caribbean-born Antoinette to revise Brontë's nineteenth-century interpretation of the West Indian woman and to vindicate the madwoman in the attic. *Wide Sargasso Sea* is a painfully compelling story of violence and madness that questions the definition of the word "primitive" in classifying English and Caribbean culture. While her earlier novels present the alienation of the foreigner in a European setting, the portrayal of Antoinette centers on the distorted view of Caribbean culture held by the English and the ambiguous status of the white West Indian who is not at home in either culture.

In the last years of her life, Rhys published two collections of short stories and worked on her autobiography. These collections of short stories are technically superior to her first book, which Rhys felt did not merit republication although she allowed selected stories to reappear in *Tigers Are Better-Looking* (1968). The later stories in this collection are more developed and polished than the earlier sketches, but she continued to focus on the themes of an unmarried woman struggling to get along and the alienation of the West Indian living in England who is subject to British prejudices. In her last book, *Sleep It Off, Lady* (1976), Rhys ordered the stories chronologically according to the stages of her life. Stories of the Caribbean are followed by those that treat of her encounter with England, and the collection ends with the story of an old woman reviled by the inhabitants of a small English village. In her unfinished autobiography, *Smile*

Please (1979), Rhys described the real-life versions of some of these stories and revealed how closely her work is tied to her life. *The Collected Short Stories* (1987), a volume that includes some previously uncollected stories, was published posthumously. She refused to have her biography written, but the stories, novels, and her own autobiographical impressions represent articulately her courageous spirit in living.

Called by A. Alvarez in 1974 "the best living English novelist," Rhys's work has been compared to that of Françoise Sagan in their common ability to portray sadness. Although a voracious reader in her youth of Byron and Dickens, Rhys did not in later years keep up with other writers' work and thus remained outside literary movements. Her contribution to literature bridges two traditions, the British and the Caribbean, but she does not rest securely in either, as her work is at its best when it considers those who do not belong and who spit in the face of respectability.

Works
The Left Bank and Other Stories (1927). *Perversity*, by Francis Carco (1928; translated from the French by Rhys, although attributed to F.M. Ford). *Postures* (1928; in the U.S. *Quartet*, 1929). *After Leaving Mr. Mackenzie* (1931). *Barred*, by Edward de Neve (1932; translated from the French by Rhys; de Neve was a pseudonym of Jean Lenglet). *Voyage in the Dark* (1934). *Good Morning, Midnight* (1939). *Wide Sargasso Sea* (1966). *Tigers Are Better-Looking, with a Selection from the Left Bank* (1968). *Penguin Modern Stories I* (1969). *My Day* (1975). *Sleep It Off, Lady* (1976). *Smile Please: An Unfinished Autobiography* (1979). *The Letters of Jean Rhys*, ed. by F. Wyndham and D. Athill Melly (1984). *The Collected Short Stories* (1987).

Carol Colatrella

Dorothy Richardson
1873–1957
Born May 17, 1873, Abingdon, Berkshire, England
Died June 17, 1957, Beckenham, Kent
Genre(s): novel
Language(s): English

Dorothy Richardson's home life, outwardly conventional and prosperous, at least until she was twenty and her father went bankrupt, was inwardly disrupted by pretention and madness: her father urgently longed to transcend his merchant-grocer origins and be a gentleman; her mother, depressed for many years, ultimately killed herself in 1895 while on vacation with Richardson. At age five, she learned to read and spell, her only interests, at a small private school. Later she was educated, first at home by a governess whom she detested, then at Southborough House, London, an intellectually lively institution where she particularly reveled in the study of logic. Poverty forced her to become a teacher in Germany in 1891 and a governess from 1891 to 1895, experiences treated in the first volumes of *Pilgrimage*. After her mother's death, longing for independence and freedom from what she perceived as the horrors of woman's lot in a middle-class domestic setting and having learned that teaching was far too confining for her, Richardson accepted a post as a dental assistant at £1 per week and began her long romance with London. At this time she met H.G. Wells, her friend for many years, lover for a few, and husband of a school friend. Wells encouraged her to write as did others. She began with journalism and went on to nonfiction and finally to her masterwork, *Pilgrimage*. At the age of forty-four she married Alan Odle, a talented but highly eccentric and unworldly artist sixteen years younger than she, with whom she lived amicably but maternally until his death.

From the publication of *Pointed Roofs* (1915), the first chapter or volume of *Pilgrimage*, Richardson received enthusiastic and awed critical recognition, Even Virginia Woolf, who felt competitive with her, acknowledged that Richardson had "invented or . . . developed and applied to her own use, a sentence which we might call the psychological sentence of the feminine gender." In histories of the novel, she is consistently coupled with Proust, Joyce, and Woolf as a major early innovator in technique and subject and an early practitioner of the stream-of-consciousness method. Many books and studies have been written about her particularly in recent years. Remarkably, though, she remains a very nearly unread writer. Ford Madox Ford fulminated that she was "the most abominably unknown contemporary writer," and Elizabeth Bowen insisted that "until Dorothy Richardson has been given her proper place, there will be a great gap in our sense of the growth of the English novel."

Pilgrimage, the work to which she devoted most of her life, is a twelve-volume (or chapter, as she preferred) work charting and capturing the flow of consciousness through Miriam Henderson as she grows and changes from adolescence to young womanhood. At the same time, without being remotely didactic, the work gives an incomparable portrayal of the consciousness of an era. Unlike Joyce, Richardson is faithful to the waking, coherent, rational mind, despite her record of the profusion of experience. And, unlike Proust, she records without attempting to analyze. Her constant low-key awareness of the specialness of the female mind and of complex issues confronting that mind at a period of rapid and radical emancipation is highly congenial to modern feminist readers. Richardson's anti-Semitism, on the other hand, even if perceived as a reflection of the times, is unsympathetic since it is so badly presented with no irony, detachment, or distance, particularly in the last chapter-volumes.

Richardson herself knew that her work was highly original and groundbreaking but contemptuously dismissed the critical attempt to define her technique: "What do I think of the term 'Stream of Consciousness' . . . ? Just this: that amongst the company of useful labels devised to meet the exigencies of literary criticism it stands alone, isolated by its perfect imbecility."

Works

The Quakers Past and Present (1914). *Gleanings from the* Works *of George Fox* (1914). *Pointed Roofs* (1915). *Backwater* (1916). *Honeycomb* (1917). *The Tunnel* (1919). *Interim* (1919). *Deadlock* (1921). *Revolving Lights* (1923). *The Trap* (1925). *Oberland* (1927). *John Austen and the Inseparables* (1930). *Dawn's Left Hand* (1931). *Clear Horizon* (1935). *Pilgrimage* (including *Dimple Hill*), 4 vols. (1938). *Pilgrimage (including March Moonlight)*, 4 vols. (1967).

Carey Kaplan

Luise Rinser
1911–

Born March 30, 1911, Pitzling, Bavaria, Germany
Genre(s): short story, essay, autobiography, drama, novel
Language(s): German

Luise Rinser's work shows a mixture of conservativism and *Neue Sachlichkeit*, of the real and the fictitious. Her novels, short stories, and essays are attempts to deal with the past and the present; they are personal and critical and show the ability to analyze and penetrate the surface. Her work made her a dangerous enemy of the Third Reich.

Luise Rinser's life until after the war was a constant odyssey and not always a voluntary one. Each step of this odyssey was faithfully recorded and reflected in her work. She spent 1915 to 1917 in a monastery, near Weilheim; from 1916 to 1918 she attended the *Volksschule* (elementary school) in Ettlingen, and from 1918 to 1924 a school overseas, where her father was the head teacher. From 1924 to 1930, Luise attended the *Lehrerinnenbildungsanstalt* (seminary for female teachers) in Munich where, in 1928 already, with special permission, she was a guest-student for pedagogic psychology at the University of Munich. In 1932, she worked temporarily for her father as his substitute and, in 1933 she was selected to build a *Landschulheim* (summer camp for students) for the *Freiwilligen Arbeitsdienst* (voluntary work duty). In 1934 she passed the *Staatsexamen* (state exam) for female teachers and taught in a school for difficult children until 1937. Her original design to study psychology and to write on Freud and Adler had to be given up because of the political climate. Rinser continued to work as a teacher until 1939. Threatened with dismissal from school duty if she did not enter the party, she left and married Horst G. Schnell, a distinguished musician. In May of 1939, she started her literary career with a collection of twelve short stories *Die gläsernen Ringe* (1940; Rings of Glass). Both she and Schnell were vehement opponents of Hitler and his regime, with the result that in 1941 Luise was prohibited to write and expelled from the *Schriftstellerverband* (Organization of Writers). From that moment on the persecution by the regime did not stop for her or for her husband. In 1941, the family (with sons Christopher, 1940, and Stephan, 1941) moved to Rostock where Schnell became music director. In September of 1942, Schnell was drafted for "political unreliability" and sent to the Eastern Front, where he died shortly afterward. In April of 1942, Luise and her sons had left Rostock for Silesia as Rostock had been bombed, and in June she returned to Bavaria, where she lived under deplorable conditions; the last narration of *Weihnachts-Triptychon* (1963; Christmas-Triptychon) describes her experiences during that time. On October 12, 1944, a former friend and colleague denounced her, and she was arrested by the *Gestapo*, the secret police. The accusations were high treason and disruption of the military (*Wehrkraftzersetzung*). Rinser spent the rest of the war in prison, from where she was freed because her documents and the evidence against her were burnt; *Gefängnistagebuch* (1946; Prison Diary) is a documentary of that time. Through recommendations of Erich Kästner, she became a staff member of the American newspaper *Neue Zeitung*. The years until 1950 were hard, and she owed her survival mostly to friends and strangers. In 1953 she married Carl Orff but was separated from him in 1959; she moved to Rome where she bought a house.

Rinser's work is to a large extent autobiographical, and after 1950, critics no longer praise it unanimously. The change in style and atmosphere may be the result of her more harmonious life after 1950 without pressure and fear. Her first publication, *Die gläsernen Ringe*, portrays in twelve stories the life of the five- and six-year-old Luise. In *Gefängnistagebuch*, she compiled the notes she took during her prison days in 1944–1945, and in its edition of 1963, she added the facts about her liberation. In the preface to the first edition she claimed that in spite of the personal statements and experiences conveyed, she wanted to put the emphasis on the political reality of the days. In almost brutally realistic manner the inmates, the hunger, the dirt, the maltreatment of the prison camp were described. The book deserves attention for its deep psychological insight and analysis and its concern for the fate of the prisoners. The documentary closes with a letter of apology from the denouncer. *Die Stärkeren* (1948; The Stronger), which dealt with the fate of two children who grew up between 1914 and 1945, is another deep psychological study of the consequence of war and the subsequent insecurities it causes. *Jan Lobel aus Warschau* (1948; Jan Lobel from Warsaw) belongs in the same category. Completely different is *Martins Reise* (1949; Martin's Journey). A concoction of fairy-tales, history, dream, and reality, this book shows the pedagogical side of Rinser: directed toward young people, *Martins Reise* is entertaining and didactic. *Mitte des Lebens* (1950; The Middle of Life) was eventually combined with its independent continuation *Abenteuer der Tugend* (1957; Adventure of Virtue) under the title *Nina* (1961). *Mitte des Lebens* received both positive and negative criticism as did all Rinser's work from that time on. The novel is an attempt to reconstruct the desperate and fruitless love affair between Nina and Dr. Alexander Stein. Diary notes written by Stein and sent to Nina after his death reveal her life between 1922 and 1948—the indecisiveness, despair, hopes, and disillusions of both lives. The novel also presents a sister–sister relationship that is rediscovered after many years. Guilt, pain, regret, and hope are the key words of this novel; partly epistolary, partly narrative, it is written in the first person, told from the perspective of the sister Margaret. The roughness of Nina's character and the lack of emotion in the lives of the characters are reflected in the cold and abrupt style, the short sentences, and the brutal language. *Abenteuer der Tugend* is an epistolary novel describing Nina's struggle to find herself after she had fled Germany to denounce her own past. The letters reflect her attempts to understand the attitude of the Catholic church toward marriage, the sacrifices of a wife and mother, and the saving belief in God. The style of the letters is complex from the lack of dialogue partners, whose reactions and responses had to be incorporated into Nina's own letters, which slows down the pace greatly. *Der Schwerpunkt* (1960; The Emphasis) is a collection of essays on five contemporary writers. *Vom Sinn der Traurigkeit* (1962; On the Meaning of Sadness) is a treatise on the origin of melancholy. *Weihnachts-Triptychon* is comprised of three autobiographical stories about Christmas. Luise Rinser's work reflects her life, her ability to observe critically but passionately, her urge for freedom, justice, and truth. Her style is generally clear and simple as befits a representative of *Neue Sachlichkeit*.

Works

Novels: *Hochebene* (1948). *Die Stärkeren* (1948). *Mitte des Lebens* (1950). *Daniela* (1953). *Der Sündenbock* (1955). *Abenteuer der Tugend* (1957; with *Mitte des Lebens* and *Nina*, 1961). *Die vollkommene Freude* (1962). *Ich bin Tobias* (1966). *Der schwarze Esel* (1974). *Bruder Feuer* (1975). *Mirjam* (1983).

Short stories: *Die gläsernen Ringe* (1940). *Erste Liebe* (1946). *Jan Lobel aus Warschau* (1948). *Martins Reise* (1949). *Sie zogen mit dem Stern* (1952). *Eine Weihnachtsgeschichte* (1953). *Ein Bündel weier Narzissen* (1956). *Geh fort, wenn du kannst* (1959). *Weihnachts-Triptychon* (1963). *Septembertag* (1964). *Das Geheimnis des Brunnens* (1979).

Drama: *Das Ohstädter Kinder-Weihnachtsspiel* (1949).

Autobiography: *Gefängnistagebuch* (1946). *Baustelle* (1970). *Grenzübergänge* (1972). *Kriegsspielzeug* (1972–1978). *Den Wolf umarmen* (1981). *Nordkoreanisches Reisetagebuch* (1981).

Essays and other prose: *Pestalozzi und wir* (1947). *Die Wahrheit über Konnersreuth* (1954). *Fülle der Zeit. Carl Zuckmayer und sein Werk* (1956). *Der Schwerpunkt* (1960). *Vom Sinn der Traurigkeit* (1962). *Ich wei deinen Namen* (1962). *Über die Hoffnung* (1964). *Gespräche über Lebensfragen* (1966). *Hat Beten einen Sinn?* (1966). *Jugend unserer Zeit* (1967). *Gespräche von Mensch zu Mensch* (1967). *Zölibat und Frau* (1967). *Laie nicht ferngesteuert* (1967). *Fragen und Antworten* (1968). *Von der Unmöglichkeit und der Möglichkeit heute Priester zu sein* (1968). *Unterentwickeltes Land Frau* (1970). *Hochzeit der Widersprüche* (1973). *Dem Tode geweiht?* (1974). *Wie, wenn wir ärmer würden?* (1974). *Hallo Partner* (1975). *Leiden, sterben, auferstehen* (1975). *Wenn die Wale kämpfen* (1976). *Der verwundete Drache. Dialog über Leben und Werk des Komponisten I. Yun.* (1977). *Khomeini und der islamische Gottesstaat* (1979). *Mit wem reden?* (1980).

Anthology: *Mein Lesebuch* (1979).

Translation: *Nina* (1956). *Rings of Glass* [*Die gläsernen Ringe*] (1958).

Jutta Hagedorn

Lady Anne Thackeray Ritchie
1837–1919

Born June 9, 1837, Hyde Park, London, England
Died February 26, 1919, "The Porch," Freshwater
Genre(s): short story, novel, memoir
Language(s): English

The elder of the two Thackeray daughters, Anne grew up in a thoroughly literary environment. Shortly after the birth of her sister Minny (Harriet Marrion Thackeray, b. 1840), their mother began to show signs of the mental instability that would result in lifelong institutionalization. The daughters were therefore sent to live with their grandmother and step-grandfather, the Charmichael-Smyths, in Paris. Thackeray remained close to his daughters even when they were away, and in 1846 he brought them back to live with him in London. Although she had no rigorous education, Anne showed an early awareness of contemporary culture and politics; by the age of fourteen she was assisting Thackeray as his amanuensis.

During Thackeray's tours of America his daughters returned to their grandmother in Paris. Although there was an effort by Mrs. Charmichael-Smyth to provide the girls with the moral and religious education she thought they were lacking, the sisters remained open and broadminded. Reminiscences of her travels in Europe at this time, her friendship with the Dickens children (who were also in Paris), and of her acquaintances in Paris are recounted in *Chapters from Some Memoirs* (1894). Ritchie joined her father in London when he returned from America and continued to act as his secretary. Her London acquaintances included Tennyson, the Carlyles, the Brownings, and even, in her 1850 visit, Charlotte Brontë (". . . a tiny, delicate, serious, little lady, pale with fair straight hair and steady eyes").

When she was twenty-three, Ritchie's first story, "Little Scholars," was published (with the consent of publisher George Smith) in her father's new and prestigious *Cornhill Magazine*. According to Thackeray, the firm of Smith and Elder was "in raptures about Anny's style," and in 1862, her first novel, *The Story of Elizabeth*, was serialized in the *Cornhill*. The novel, a convoluted romance centered around an impetuous heroine, was an immediate success.

In 1863, on Christmas Eve, William Thackeray died leaving his daughters well off but very much alone (their grandmother died within a year). Among the ever-increasing circle of friends who watched over the Thackeray sisters was the Stephen family, and in 1867 Minny was married to Leslie Stephen. Ritchie lived with her sister and brother-in-law until 1875 when Minny died. This period was her most productive in terms of fiction. In 1867 *The Village on the Cliff*, a novel in which a woman must come to grips with unrequited love, was published. It remained one of her favorite works. Other works of fiction followed, including *Old Kensington* (1873), *Bluebeard's Keys and Other Stories* (1874), and *Miss Angel* (1875), as well as a collection of essays (*Toilers and Spinsters and Other Essays*, 1874).

Following Minny's death, Ritchie and Stephen, who called her "the most sympathetic and sociable of beings," shared a residence at Hyde Park. Here she met and was courted by her cousin Richmond Thackeray Ritchie, who though seventeen years her junior proposed and was accepted. Although he had an "uneventful" career in the India Office, his work was solid enough to merit a knighthood in 1907 and appointment as permanent Undersecretary for India in 1909, three years before he died. They had two children.

Ritchie was active until her death. She wrote introductions to the works of Mary Russell Mitford, Elizabeth Gaskell, and Maria Edgeworth. Some of her later reminiscences are recorded in *Blackstick Papers* (1908) and *From the Porch* (1913). But the most consuming project of her later years by far were the introductions she prepared for her father's collected works.

Virginia Woolf, Ritchie's "niece," describes her aunt in the character of Mrs. Hilbery in the novel *Night and Day* (1919). In the obituary she prepared for the *Times Literary Supplement*, Woolf praised Ritchie's work for its "surprisingly sharp edges." "It is Lady Ritchie," says Woolf elsewhere in the obituary, who "will be the unacknowledged source of much that remains in men's minds about the Victorian age."

Works

The Story of Elizabeth (1863). *The Village on the Cliff* (1867). *Five Old Friends* (1868). *Old Kensington* (1873). *Bluebeard's Keys and Other Stories* (1874). *Toilers and Spinsters and Other Essays* (1874). *Miss Angel* (1875). *To Esther and Other Sketches* (1876). *Madame de Sévigné* (1881). *Miss Williamson's Divagations* (1881). *A Book of Sibyls* (1883). *Mrs. Dymond* (1885). *Little Esme's Adventure* (1887). *Records of Tennyson, Ruskin, and Robert and Elizabeth Browning* (1892). *Alfred Lord Tennyson and His Friends* (1893). *Chapters from Some Memoirs* (1894). *Lord Amherst and the British Advance Eastward to Burma* (1894). *Chapters from Some Unwritten Memoirs* (1895). *Blackstick Papers* (1908). *A Discourse on Modern Sibyls* (1913). *From the Porch* (1913). *From Friend to Friend* (1919).

Alan Rauch

Mary Darby Robinson
1758–1800

a.k.a. Perdita
Born November 27, 1758, College Green, Bristol, England
Died December 26, 1800, Englefield Cottage, Surrey
Genre(s): drama, poetry, novel
Language(s): English

The daughter of a whaling ship captain of Irish descent, Robinson became an actress, a playwright, a poet, and a novelist. She was also, for a brief time, the mistress of the Prince of Wales, later George IV.

Robinson was introduced by the dancing-master at Mrs. Hervey's to David Garrick, who asked her to play Cordelia to his Lear. Although she served a period of internship at Drury Lane Theatre, her acting debut was postponed by her marriage to Thomas Robinson, a law student. After a period of high living in London, her husband, who proved to be a scoundrel, was sent to debtors' prison, where Robinson and her infant daughter, Maria, spent ten months with him.

Shortly after her marriage, she began writing poetry. With the help of her patroness, Georgianna Cavendish, the Duchess of Devonshire, Robinson published her first collection of poems, *Verses*, in 1775. Cavendish was Robinson's only female visitor in prison, a fact that led her to develop a bitter dislike for members of her own sex. In her *Memoirs*, Robinson said: "During my long seclusion from society . . . not one of my female friends even inquired what was become of me. . . . Indeed, I have almost found my own sex my most inveterate enemies; I have experienced little kindness from them; though my bosom has often ached with the pangs inflicted by their envy, slander, and malevolence."

Upon her husband's release from prison, Robinson resumed her acting career and enjoyed four highly successful seasons at Drury Lane, but her fourth season, 1779–1780, was her last. On December 3, 1779, she played the part of Perdita in *The Winter's Tale*. Her performance so captivated the Prince of Wales that he fell in love with her, and she was permanently nicknamed "Perdita." She became the Prince's mistress but was soon replaced. Humiliated by the Prince's rejection, she abandoned the stage and fled to France, where she was befriended by Marie Antoinette, in whose honor Robinson later composed "Monody to the Memory of the Late Queen of France." When she returned to England, she formed a lasting liaison with Colonel Tarleton (Sir Banastre), an officer of the British army in America.

The early 1780s marked the high point of Robinson's public fame. She regularly toured the fashionable sections of London in an "absurd chariot with a basket shaped like a coronet attached to the side," driven by her current "friend"; her husband and other hopeful admirers sat in the side-car. But her life changed drastically in 1784 when she contracted an "unknown" disease, probably rheumatoid arthritis or infantile paralysis, that left her lower body weakened and partially paralyzed. Robinson remained an invalid for the rest of her life and devoted herself completely to her writing.

Though much of Robinson's poetry now seems too affected and too sentimental, with an overabundance of eighteenth-century apostrophizing, a number of her contemporaries, most notably Samuel Taylor Coleridge, had high praise for her work and found her "a woman of undoubted genius." Coleridge not only admired her poems but imitated one of them himself: his "The Snow-Drop" was originally entitled "Lines written immediately after the perusal of Mrs. Robinson's Snow Drop." Coleridge was also very much impressed with her "Haunted Beach," a poem vaguely reminiscent of his own "Rime of the Ancient Mariner." As a final tribute, Coleridge's "The Stranger Minstrel" was subtitled: "Written [to Mrs. Robinson] a few weeks before her death." From 1788 to 1791, Robinson was part of the Della Cruscan movement led by Robert Merry. She, and other female followers of Merry (Hester Thrale Piozzi and Hannah Cowley) were viciously attacked, both personally and professionally, by literary critic William Gifford in his *Baviad*.

Robinson spent her last years in London, where she belonged to a circle of "radical" women, including Mary Wollstonecraft, Mary Hays, Charlotte Smith, and Helen Maria Williams, all of whom were accused by the Reverend Richard Polwhele, an antifeminist, anti-"Jacobin" critic, of trying to "taint" their young female readers with the "demon democracy." It was due, in part, to the influence of the Wollstonecraft circle that Robinson published two feminist tracts, "Thoughts on the Condition of Women" and "A Letter to the Women of England on the Injustice of Mental Subordination with Anecdotes by Anne Frances Randall," in 1799. She was also a close friend of William Godwin, whose influence can be seen in her most widely read novel, *Walsingham; or, The Pupil of Nature* (1797). *Walsingham*, basically a sentimental novel, though it does touch on political and ethical questions similar to those posed in Godwin's works, was especially popular in France. At the time of her death in 1800, Robinson was writing her autobiography. The work was completed by her daughter and published posthumously in 1801 as *Memoirs of the Late Mrs Robinson, Written by Herself*.

Works

Verses (1775). *Poems* (1777). *The Lucky Escape* (1779). *Poems* (1791). *Vaucenza; or the Dangers of Credulity* (1792). *Nobody* (1794). *The Widow* (1794). *Angelina* (1796). *The Sicilian Lover* (1796). *Sappho and Phaon* (1796). *Hubert de Sevrac* (1796). *Walsingham; or, The Pupil of Nature* (1797). *The False Friend* (1799). "A Letter to the Women of England on the Injustice of Mental Subordination, with Anecdotes by Anne Frances Randall" and "Thoughts on the Condition of Women" (1799). *Effusions of Love* (Robinson's correspondence with the Prince, n.d.). *Lyrical Tales* (1800). *The Mistletoe* (1800). *Memoirs of the Late Mrs. Robinson, Written by Herself* (edited by M. Robinson, 1801). *Poetical Works of the Late Mrs Mary Robinson* (edited by M. Robinson, 1806).

Kate Beaird Meyers

Dames des Roches

(pseudonym)

Madeleine Neveu
ca. 1520–1587

Born ca. 1520, Poitiers, France
Died 1587, Poitiers

Catherine Fradonnet
1542–1587

Born 1542, Poitiers
Died 1587, Poitiers

Genre(s): poetry, prose dialogue, tragicomedy,
letters, translation
Language(s): French

The Dames des Roches lived their entire lives in and
around Poitiers. Madeleine married in 1539 the lawyer
André Fradonnet who died eight years later. Catherine
was their sole surviving child. Madeleine was remarried in 1550 to Francois Eboissard, Seigneur de la Villée
et des Roches, a lawyer active in local politics. Madeleine
probably frequented humanist circles during Poitiers's
first period of literary fame (1545–1555) that included
the poets Pelletier, Tahureau, and de Baïf. Her primary
concern was Catherine's education. Madeleine and
Catherine's coauthored works and partnership over their
salon testify to a close relationship founded on esteem
and a lively exchange of ideas. Their mutual devotion
was so great that contemporary *elogia* attribute
Catherine's refusal of matrimony to her desire to remain with her mother. An unstated corollary is that
Catherine's marriage would doubtless have terminated
her venture in cooperative scholarship. Their publications first appeared in the 1570s when they were establishing a *salon*. In 1577, the court's three-month
residence in Poitiers prompted them to write poems
honoring members of the royal family. These were published the following year in a first volume of works,
followed in 1579 by an expanded second edition. By
then, their fame attracted to their *salon* Parisian lawyers present at the 1579 assizes or "grands jours" of
Poitiers. Among them was E. Pasquier who, chancing
to see a flea on Catherine's bosom, suggested a contest
of versified wit. This was the start of *La Puce de Madame des Roches*, a ninety-three folio collection containing numerous *blasons* by the habitues of the *salon*.
Madeleine and Catherine published two further volumes of works before their death of the plague in 1587.
The publications of the Dames des Roches, which include a wide variety of poetic genres, prose dialogues,
a tragicomedy, letters, and first translations of Latin
works, constitute an impressively extensive and diver-
sified body of writings. Madeleine's contribution, entirely in verse with the exception of her *missives*, dwells
on largely personal topics such as matters of health, a
thirteen-year lawsuit, her ambitions for her daughter,
the role of women, the religious wars and misfortunes
of Poitiers, marital love, and epitaphs to deceased public figures. Although her work is more limited in length
and scope than her daughter's—she published only late
in life when she became a widow—Madeleine's presence figures prominently throughout the *oeuvres*. The
valorization of the Mother is perhaps the most striking
feature of these works. Madeleine and Catherine wrote
for and of each other. Catherine frequently dedicates
individual poems to her mother whom she calls "the
life of my life." The daughter's appeal to maternal discourse is further embodied in her mythical heroines
Agnodice, Pasithee, Charite, the Amazons, Proserpina,
Pallas Athena, the "Femme forte" of Proverbs, Phyllis,
who constitute so many legitimizing "foremothers" in
her quest for poetic origins. Also integral to Catherine's
feminine economy is her praise of the distaff in her
often cited "A ma Quenoille" (1579). Catherine is the
first woman writer to challenge humanist norms that
either considered women's education as secondary to
household duties (Erasmus, More, Vives), or treated
learned women as exceptional "honorary males" unfit
for, and alienated from, the traditional occupations of
their sex.

The Dames des Roches's unique social and familial situation enabled them to combine harmoniously
the duties of a household, *salon*, and dual writing careers. They were fully integrated in a community of
humanist legists and scholars whose conservative royalist, nationalistic, and Gallican views they shared.
Their works provide a fascinating glimpse into the
vitality of humanist learning among the provincial
upper bourgeoisie and *noblesse de robe*.

Works

*Les Missives de Mes Dames des Roches de Poitiers,
mere et fille, avec le Ravissement de Proserpine prins
du Latin de Clodian. Et autres imitations et meslanges
poetiques* (1586). *Les Oeuvres de Mes Dames des
Roches de Poitiers, mere et fille* (1578). *Les
Oeuvres . . . seconde edition, corrigee et augmentee
de la Tragicomedie de Tobie et autres oeuvres
poetiques* (1579). *Les Premieres Oeuvres . . . Les
Secondes Oeuvres . . . troisieme edition* (1604). *La
Puce de Madame des Roches*, ed. D. Jouaust (1582,
1583, 1610; rpt., 1868). *Les Secondes Oeuvres de
Mes Dames des Roches de Poitiers, mere et fille* (1583).

Anne Larsen

Edith Rode
1879–1956

Born February 23, 1879, Copenhagen, Denmark
Died September 3, 1956, Frederiksberg, Denmark
Genre(s): novel, memoir, poetry, drama, journalism
Language(s): Danish

Edith Rode came of age at the turn of the century and published her first two novels in 1901 during a period in Danish literary history when writers from previously silent or overlooked social milieus, including women, began to make themselves heard. Although Rode wrote successfully in all genres, she excelled in the short story.

As the daughter of C.H.H. Nebelong, a physician to the court of King Christian IX, Rode grew up among conservative aristocrats. Nevertheless she received a fairly broad liberal education and attended Erna Juel Hansen's experimental school. After a brief early marriage that ended in divorce, she married the mystical symbolist poet, Helge Rode, who was a major figure in Danish literary circles. She traveled widely, living for periods of time in France and Italy. Her resulting exposure to different walks of life served her well; an insight into late-nineteenth-century female childhood can be gleaned from the autobiographical *De tre smaa piger* (1948); and her volumes of memoirs, *Der var engang* (1951), *Paa togt i Erindringen* (1953) and *Paa rejse i Livet* (1957), contain interesting portraits of her friendships with famous artists and poets like Edvard Munch, Sophus Claussen, and Rainer Marie Rilke. In 1913, she began writing for the Copenhagen daily newspaper, *Berlingske Tidende*. Her subsequent long career in journalism not only gave her the opportunity to develop her talent for the short story but produced two travel books, a series of cookbooks, an advice book titled *Livskunst uden filosofi* (1948), and an invaluable contribution to Danish women's history, *Den Gyldne Bog om Dansker Kvinder* (1941), which she edited. As a dramatist, she wrote two plays, *Sejren* (1913) and *Det evige Glæder* (1920), a series of radio plays, and two screenplays. Three collections of Rode's poetry were also published, in 1920, 1933, and 1952.

Rode's earliest novels, *Misse Wichmann* (1901), *Maja Engell* (1901), and *Gold* (1902) drew on her own experiences in their portrayal of young bourgeois heroines venturing among bohemian artists. One of their main themes is the incompatibility of men's expectations with women's own needs for both love and liberation. They treat a number of moral and sexual topics, such as frigidity, with a frankness that was surprising in a young woman at the time. Similar themes were also featured in her following novels, *Tilfredse Hjerter* (1905) and *Grazias Kærlighed* (1909), which both take place in Italy, thereby contrasting the mores, including sex role expectations, of the South with those of the North.

Rode had already produced two volumes of short stories, *Kvinde* (1908) and *Af Kundskabens Træ* (1912), before she began writing for the *Berlingske Tidende*, but at that point her talent for the genre really began to blossom. Her stories were reprinted in a succession of collections of which *I tidens Klo* (1949), is a distillation of the best. Many of her stories have erotic themes, treating feminine psychology with insight and irony. For example, "Den evige tilbeder" (The Eternal Adorer), her only story to have been translated into English twice, is written from the point of view of a sophisticated woman who receives a young man bearing a note from one of her female friends, advising her to kill him immediately. After several weeks of the boring young man's importunate devotion, the narrator understands her friend's note and sends him on to another friend with a note of her own. Such stories led one of her admirers to compare Rode to Guy de Maupassant.

Although at her death Tom Kristensen praised Rode's poetry for its lyrical quality and considered her a pioneer among twentieth-century Danish women poets, her insight into feminine perspectives and conflicts was most fully developed in her fiction. Susanne Fabricius considers Rode's skill with the Danish language superior to that of most writers of entertainments despite certain cloying overtones in her style. Rode perhaps deserves more attention than she has received for her understanding of sexual politics and her examination of the underlying social and psychological motives that hindered many women from participating in their own liberation.

Works

Af kundskabens Træ [From the Tree of Knowledge] (1912). *Afrodite smiler* [Aphrodite Smiles] (1920). *Det bittersøde æble* [The Bittersweet Apple] (1920). *Digte* [Poems] (1920). *Digte* [Poems] (1933). *Digte* [Poems] (1952). *Gold* [Barren] (1902). *Grazias Kærlighed* [Grazia's Love] (1909). *I tidens Klo; atten noveller, gamle og nye* [In the Claw of Time: Eighteen Short Stories, Old and New] (1949). *John Piccolo arver 60 millioner dollar* [John Piccolo Inherits 60 Million Dollars] (1932). *Idyllen, vaudeville uden sang* [Idyll: Vaudeville without Blood] (1932). *Livets Ekko, 10 noveller* [Life's Echo: Ten Short Stories]

(1932). *Livskunst uden filosofi* [The Art of Life without Philosophy] (1948). *Maja Engell* (1901). *Mennesker i mondo* [People in the World] (1935). *Misse Wichmann. Ogsaa i de andre huse* [Also in the Other Houses] (1901). *Paris i en nøddeskal* [Paris in a Nutshell] (1927). *Pige* [Girls] (1914). *Sejren; skuespil i fire akter* [Victory: A Play in Four Acts] (1913). *Smaa børn og store* [Little Children and Big] (1950). *Tilfredse Hjerter* [Contented Hearts] (1905). *De tre smaa piger* [Three Little Girls] (1948). *Den tunge dør* [The Heavy Door] (1922). *Der var engang, et kig tilbage* [Once Upon a Time: A Glance Back] (1951).

Translations: "The Eternal Adorer," tr. Evelyn Heepe, in *Modern Danish Authors* (1946, 1974). "The Eternal Adorer." *The Norseman* 8, no. 5 (Sept.–Oct. 1950): 344–346. "Illusion," trs. Ann and Peter Thornton, in *Contemporary Danish Prose. Mieze Wichmann* (n.d.). *The Three Little Girls* (extracts), tr. Evelyn Heepe, in *Modern Danish Authors* (1946, 1974). *Unfruchtbar*, tr. Helene Klepetar (1908).

Kristine Anderson

Christina Rossetti
1830–1894

a.k.a. Ellen Alleyne
Born December 5, 1830, London
Died December 29, 1894, London
Genre(s): poetry
Language(s): English

Rossetti, the foremost female poet of religious verse and orthodox Christianity in nineteenth-century England, has been ranked with John Donne, George Herbert, and Gerard Manley Hopkins as one of the great religious poets.

She was the youngest of four children born into a gifted, literary Italian–English family; the Pre-Raphaelite poet and painter Dante Gabriel Rossetti was her oldest brother, and her first book, *Verses* (1847), was printed on her grandfather's press when she was sixteen. She suffered from chronic ill health throughout her life, a condition that allowed her to escape the odious work as a governess that her sister Maria undertook to help support the family. On two occasions, Rossetti assisted her mother in conducting a day school, in 1851–1852 and again in 1853, and from 1860 to 1870 she worked at a House of Charity for "fallen" women run by Anglican nuns.

Family and religion formed the dominant centers of Rossetti's life. She was strongly attached to her mother, with whom she lived most of her life. Like her mother and sister, she was influenced by the Oxford Movement and became a fervent Anglo-Catholic. In 1850 Rossetti broke her engagement to the Pre-Raphaelite painter James Collinson because of religious differences, and again in 1866 she refused to marry a close friend, the linguist Charles Bagot Cayley, ostensibly because he did not share her religious views. Significantly, perhaps, Rossetti served as the model for Mary in several of her brother's paintings.

In 1850, seven of Rossetti's poems appeared in the Pre-Raphaelite journal *The Germ,* all under the pseudonym of Ellen Alleyn. Her brother, Dante Gabriel Rossetti, eagerly promoted his sister's poems, sending them in 1861 to the Victorian critic John Ruskin, who judged that no publisher would take them because they were too full of "quaintnesses and offenses." But in the same year Macmillan accepted her manuscript of *Goblin Market and Other Poems* (1862), the success of which established Rossetti as a leading English poet. A moral allegory of sensual temptation, fall, and redemption through sisterly love and self-sacrifice, this work is considered by some critics to be Rossetti's major claim to literary immortality. The subject of sisters, who frequently embody contrasting states of mind, occurs in a number of her poems from the 1850s and 1860s.

The title poem of Rossetti's next collection, *The Prince's Progress and Other Poems* (1866), is a richly textured Pre-Raphaelite allegorical pilgrimage of a soul and the moral crisis that results from worldly self-indulgence. A mood of world-weariness echoes through many of her poems. The themes of unhappy or unrequited love, renunciation, regret at a wasted life, and musings on death and eternal life are common. Rarely does a note of joyous exultation break through, as it does in her early and famous love poem "A Birthday" (1857). Of her more than 1,000 poems, nearly half are devotional and nearly half her poems deal with death, either as an end to suffering or as a prelude to the happier afterlife of the Christian resurrection. Rossetti renounced the fulfillment of earthly love in devotion to an ideal of spiritual love. That her love of heaven presented no easy consolation but a difficult journey is apparent in her well-known poem "Uphill" (1858).

A different side of Rossetti emerges in her poems for children, published as a collection in *Sing-Song: A Nursery Rhyme Book* (1872). These verses consist of light instructional rhymes, poems about animals, flowers, and the natural world, lullabies, Christmas carols, and a few nonsense rhymes. Rossetti's most famous poem for children, "Who Has Seen the Wind?," is still widely anthologized, as is the carol "In the Bleak Midwinter." Two collections of short stories, *Commonplace* (1870) and *Speaking Likenesses* (1874), were not popular and are of interest chiefly for their characterizations of people in the Rossetti circle. More successful is an autobiographical portrait in her youthful novella *Maude* (1897), written when she was nineteen but published posthumously. Maude, suffering from Rossetti's own character flaws of overscrupulousness and a very human and impenitent pride in her poetic accomplishments, dies when she falls out of a carriage. Rossetti presents several alternative female roles and fates in the story, though Maude's own fate is clearly the most romantic.

"Monna Innominata," a sonnet sequence on the theme of unhappy love, was originally published in *A Pageant and Other Poems* (1881). Like Elizabeth Barrett Browning before her, Rossetti intentionally reverses the male poetic tradition in these fourteen sonnets and lets the "unnamed lady" of so many love sonnets express her own love in her own voice. Another sonnet sequence published in *A Pageant and Other Poems* is "Later Life," twenty-eight poems that are essentially religious and hortatory in tone. Here, as in other poems, Rossetti uses the cycle of nature to represent the cycle of despair and of hope for rebirth in the human spirit. Her religious prose does not reveal the intensity of spiritual struggle shown in many of her poems and is often merely dutiful in tone. But works like *Annus Domini* (1874), *Called to Be Saints* (1881), and *The Face of the Deep* (1892) reflect her intimate knowledge of the Bible and the Apocrypha, and *Time Flies: A Reading Diary* (1885) is of interest for its reflections on incidents and details from her life. Although many readers have regarded Rossetti as one of the world's finest religious poets and some have called her the greatest English woman poet of the nineteenth century, her vision and power were limited by the restrictions of the Victorian world. The deep conflict between Rossetti's instinctive temperament and the demands of Victorian womanhood and authoritarian religion resulted in her withdrawal from direct experience of life into an intense and often anguished inner life. Thus much of her poetry deals, as Ralph Bellas has said, with "the self-consciousness of suffering rather than the dramatic presentation of suffering itself." Yet from within her limited angle on the world, Rossetti produced a number of memorable poems whose acute

Christina Rossetti

musicality, technical mastery, and expressive tenderness assure her of literary immortality.

Works

Verses (1847). *Goblin Market and Other Poems* (1862). *The Prince's Progress and Other Poems* (1866). *Poems* (1866). *Commonplace and Other Stories* (1870). *Sing-Song: A Nursery Rhyme Book* (1872 and 1893). *Annus Domini: A Prayer for Each Day of the Year, Founded on a Text of Holy Scripture* (1874). *Speaking Likenesses, with Pictures Thereof by Arthur Hughes* (1874). *Goblin Market, The Prince's Progress, and Other Poems* (1875). *Seek and Find: A Double Series of Short Studies on the Benedicite* (1879). *A Pageant and Other Poems* (1881). *Called to be Saints: The Minor Festivals Devotionally Studied* (1881). *Letter and Spirit: Notes on the Commandments* (1883). *Time Flies: A Reading Diary* (1885). *Poems* (1890). *The Face of the Deep: A Devotional Commentary on the Apocalypse* (1892). *Verses: Reprinted from "Called to Be Saints," "Time Flies," "The Face of the Deep"* (1893). *New Poems, Hitherto Unpublished or Uncollected* (1896). *Maude: A Story for Girls* (1897). *The Poetical Works of Christina Georgina Rossetti, with Memoir and Notes,* ed. W.M. Rossetti (1904). *The Complete Poems of Christina Rossetti,* ed. R.W. Crump (1979). *Rossetti Papers 1862–1870* ed. W.M. Rossetti (1903). *The Family Letters of Christina Georgina Rossetti,* ed. W.M. Rossetti (1908). *Three Rossettis. Unpublished Letters to and from Dante Gabriel, Christina, William,* ed. J.C. Troxell (1937).

Jean Pearson

Evdokiia Rostopchina
1811–1858

Born December 23, 1811, Moscow
Died December 3, 1858, Moscow
Genre(s): poetry, drama, short story, novel
Language(s): Russian

At the height of her renown in the 1830s, Rostopchina was one of the most copiously published, extravagantly praised, and assiduously courted Russian poets. Although her reputation subsequently plummeted, her popularity, while it lasted, was staggering.

A native Muscovite, Rostopchina came from an affluent family with literary aspirations, especially on her father's side. When Rostopchina was not yet six, her mother (Dar'ia Pashkova) died of tuberculosis. Shortly after, the government office for which her father, Petr Sushkov, worked transferred him to Petersburg. Deprived of both parents, Rostopchina and her two younger brothers remained in Moscow under the indifferent care of their maternal grandparents. Only a modicum of adult attention and guidance shaped the children's early development, however, for their grandfather secluded himself in his study, emerging only for meals, while their grandmother's waking hours revolved around social occasions, her toilette, and the hordes of guests who daily swarmed to the house.

Tutors and governesses of dubious qualifications assumed responsibility for the children's upbringing and for their irregular education. Like most young girls of the era, Rostopchina studied the Bible, Russian, French, and German, a smattering of arithmetic, and a negligible dose of history and geography in addition to the mandatory drawing, piano, and dance. Blessed with a lively intelligence, a retentive memory, and an inquiring mind, the young girl successfully filled the vast lacunae in her education on her own initiative. Later she acquired a working knowledge of both Italian and English.

In the heat of her enthusiasm for Schiller, Byron, Pushkin, and Zhukovskii, Rostopchina began scribbling verses that in 1830 caught the notice of a discriminating visitor to the Pashkov house: the poet and critic Petr A. Viazemskii. Without her knowledge he published one of her lyrics, "Talisman," in a Petersburg almanac in 1831, thereby launching her literary career. Instead of instant fame, Rostopchina's reward was a sharp rebuke from her scandalized grandparents, who deemed "versifying" an unseemly pastime for a decent unmarried young lady. That bewildering reaction effectively prevented Rostopchina from trying to publish her poetry until after she was married.

Rostopchina's marriage, paradoxically, both eased and complicated her circumstances. Her spouse, Count Andrei Rostopchin, the son of the famous governor-general of Moscow during Napoleon's invasion, was younger than Rostopchina, not of age when the couple married in 1833 and utterly incapable of fulfilling any of the customary marital obligations. Although her family and acquaintances saw the match as a brilliant coup, Rostopchina, who accepted the offer with reluctance, had profound qualms about the union, which soon proved to be justified.

However mismatched the couple was, Rostopchina nonetheless now had entree to the best society and felt free to pursue openly her literary inclinations. Published cryptically at first under the name "Countess R – – na" and then under her full name, Rostopchina's lyrics caused a near sensation. Such an exaggerated response to poems that are charming, sometimes good, very occasionally excellent, but generally unremarkable, now seems puzzling. But the author's gender—and her identity as a young woman from high society, with beauty, personal style, and grace in addition to talent—doubtless stirred the public imagination. Furthermore, Rostopchina had had solid personal ties with members of the literary circles from her childhood days at the Pashkov residence and had known the unequaled poet Pushkin from the age of eighteen. So she was no stranger to literary salons, and when she arrived in Petersburg with her husband in 1836, she had no difficulty renewing friendships or striking up new ones with the foremost representatives of Russian letters of the time. The list of cosmopolitan guests regularly gracing the soirées at the resplendent Rostopchina house included some of the most famous contemporary writers, artists, music critics, and thinkers.

Rostopchina's poetry, frequently written between social engagements and quite often recording her impressions of or emotional reactions to events transpiring during these gatherings, was published in a separate volume in 1841. It treated the conventional Romantic themes of love, disillusionment, solitude, and yearning in a manner that clearly reflected sundry West European and Russian influences. Composition came easily to her, and the rapidity and casualness with which she was able to dash off one stanza after another inevitably resulted in some rather facile images, phrases, and formulations.

Encouraged by her success in lyric poetry, Rostopchina in 1838 experimented in prose. Her two tales, "Chiny i den'gi" (Rank and Money) and "Poedinok" (The Duel), appeared above the somewhat presumptuous signature of "Iasnovidiashchaia" (Clairvoyant), and came out the following year in a book bearing the title *Ocherki bol'shogo sveta* (Sketches of Grand Society). In the preface the author expressed her views on society, which she castigated for prizing only position and wealth instead of inherent virtues. Whereas the critical reception of Rostopchina's poetry had been consistently laudatory, her prose passed practically unnoticed. Only a few spoke favorably of the tales, among them an editor who compared Rostopchina to George Sand, then the most generous of compliments. The tales, like all of Rostopchina's fiction, suffer from insignificant content, unconvincing characterization, and protracted gushes of emotional intensity couched in metaphors and similes punctuated by sighs and gasps. Drenched in the pathos for which Romanticism at its most immature had an inexplicable weakness, they have a historical and sociological value that cannot compensate for their lack of literary merit.

Between 1837 and 1839 Rostopchina had two daughters and a son, and traveled south, presumably for reasons of health. In 1840 she returned to Petersburg without her husband, and resumed the whirl of social activities that she criticizes so vehemently in her prose. In 1845 the entire Rostopchina household went abroad for two years. From Italy Rostopchina sent her ballad "Nasil'nyi brak" (The Forced Marriage), which appeared in a conservative Petersburg daily in 1846. It caused a scandal. While some read the ballad as Rostopchina's indiscreet exposé of her marital woes, many interpreted it as an allegory decrying Russia's subjugation of Poland. In any event, Rostopchina fell into disgrace at court, and the general attitude toward her cooled, steadily worsening over the next twelve years.

When Rostopchina returned to Russia in 1847 and settled down in Moscow for good, her creativity sought new and not entirely felicitous modes of expression. Instead of lyrics, she began writing prose novels and large-scale works in blank verse. In the last decade of her life, she was unusually and indiscriminately prolific, turning her hand to a wide variety of genres, including several five-act dramas in blank verse, novels [*Schastlivaia zhenshchina* (1851–1852; A Fortunate Woman), *Palazzo Forli* (1854), *U pristani* (1857; At the Pier/At a Refuge)], comedies, and a one-act verse drama called *Vozvrat Chatskogo v Moskvu* (1856; Chatsky's Return to Moscow). These were all received with repeated indifference and occasional abuse.

In 1858 Rostopchina took to her bed, fully aware that she had little time left. Her last extant written communication was in French to Alexandre Dumas, to whom she sent a letter and a note containing information about the biography of the Russian poet Mikhail Lermontov. By the end of the year Rostopchina was dead.

Rostopchina was in several significant ways a typical product of the aristocratic milieu in which she moved during her adulthood. Personally and ideologically conservative, she was cushioned from countless hardships by her social standing and her financial security. Writing for her was neither an irresistible inner impulse nor a professional necessity for the sake of earning a livelihood; it had the appeal of an agreeable hobby, a pleasurable means of whiling away the hours, even though negative reviews wounded her pride deeply. A percentage of her poems reveal a generous lyric talent, an ear for pleasing rhymes, and an instinct for poignant images and delicate effects. Some of them wonderfully capture moods of melancholy, resignation, and despair in the face of love's expectations, of disappointments, and of loss. Several evidence the poet's responsiveness to nature's beauty and her strong religious feeling. Only a handful of her poems, however, bear an individual stamp and make a lasting impression, for the rest tend to be generalized, almost anonymous. Her output as a whole smacks of the "dear diary" school of writing.

Not only the "lightness" of Rostopchina's poetry but also the privileged conditions in which she lived led the socially committed critics of the 1860s and 1870s to disparage her contribution to Russian poetry in immoderate and rather vulgar attacks on her works and her way of life. Nor was their evaluation of her prose more generous, even though they must have found much to sympathize with in her repeated diatribes against the emptiness of the *beau monde*, with its constant parties, gossip, materialism, pettiness, and insignificance. But her criticism came from within, since she was, at least for a while, one of the most prominent celebrities within that glittering set that the later generations of utilitarian critics despised. Literary criticism of the twentieth century has treated Rostopchina even more cruelly, in a sense, for its indifference has practically relegated her to the ranks of the forgotten.

Works

Collections and more significant publications: *Ocherki bol'shogo sveta: sochineniia Iasnovidiashchaia* (1839). *Stikhotvoreniia* (1841). *Neliudimka: drama v 5-i deistviiakh* (1850). *Schastlivaia zhenshchina* (1851–1852). *Palazzo Forli* (1854). *U pristani: roman v pis'makh*, 4 vols. (1857). *Stikhotvoreniia*, izd. 2 (1857–1860). *Vozvrat Chatskogo v Moskvu: prodolzhenie komedii Griboedova "Gore ot uma"* (1856). *Dnevnik devushki: roman [v stikhakh]* (1866). *Sochineniia graf. E.P. Rostopchinoi*, 2 vols.

(1890). *Sobranie sochinenii* (1910). *Dom sumasshedshidh v Moskve v 1858 godu* (1911).

Translations: "Nasil'nyi brak" [The Forced Marriage], tr. Louis Pedrotti, p. 202 and "Chiny i den'gi" [Rank and Money], tr. Helena Goscilo, in *Russian and Polish Women's Fiction* (Knoxville, 1985), pp. 50–84.

Helena Goscilo

Ulla Ryum
1937–

Born May 4, 1937, Frederiksberg, Copenhagen, Denmark

Genre(s): novel, short story, drama, poetry

Language(s): Danish

Ulla Ryum's literary oeuvre is an intriguing, intricate blend of imagery, flights of fantasy, realistic and surrealistic scenes of modern life, and keen criticism of an urban society that favors competition, mutual indifference, and hostile aggression at the expense of humanity and mutual caring. Ulla Ryum's strong Catholic upbringing is evident in her mystical view and portrayals of the city. Ulla Ryum's plays and novels challenge her readers and the audience of her plays to the full. The central theme of Ulla Ryum's plays and prose works concerns the essence of Christian love. Her protagonists are invariably women who emulate Christ by sacrificing self, by considering others first, by giving physical love and emotional affection with no qualification or reservation. For Ryum, we often fail to know ourselves, hence, we never really come to know each other. We "miss each other" in a very hostile metropolis governed solely by competition, self-concern, and total disregard for others. In her works, Ryum suggests that there may be an answer to our common search for identity in the unconditional love of women now depicted as Christ-like figures. Ulla Ryum uses surrealistic scenes, fantastic images and events, deep Catholic mysticism, and a medieval search for allegory, myth, and a faith for *Enhver* ("Everyman"), to reveal new perspectives on reality.

Ulla Ryum was born in the Frederiksberg area of Copenhagen on May 4, 1937; her parents are Sten Ryum (b. 1910), a lawyer and commission/secretariat director, and Elise Kirstine Hammer (b. 1908). Ulla Ryum began her literary career, she claims, while working in an Østerbro, Copenhagen, restaurant kitchen, as part of her training in hotel operations. Her early practical work provided the realistic ballast for a literary oeuvre of imagination, Catholic symbolism, myth, and rare fantasy. Ulla Ryum's début as a writer came in 1962, with the novel *Spejl* (Mirror); *Spejl* concerns a modern individual's efforts to realize an identity within the frightening setting of an impersonal city. The scenes of modern life in *Spejl* are terrifying, often grotesque, for individuals communicate and often act at cross-purposes. Yet, Ulla Ryum holds out a ray of hope for a solution, for a way out of the modern maze. In *Spejl*, one woman at least points the way out of the negative, counterproductive mælstrom of modern city life.

Ulla Ryum's next novel was *Natsangersken* (1963; The Night Singer). In this novel, Ulla Ryum's Christian/Catholic message of love and sacrifice comes to the fore. The alcoholic little songstress of *Natsangersken* sacrifices for others and chooses to die in reconciliation with herself and other even weaker, flawed individuals. The songstress' life has been one of diminished, reduced possibilities, of great, enclosing barriers and limits for her as *le deuxième sexe, den anden* (the second sex); her own father and all the men she has ever known have only denied and degraded her, depriving her of worth and identity.

Limits and barriers established for the songstress have also diminished the *men* who have known and used her. In denying her essential humanity, they have also clearly denied their own. In the end, the songstress dies as a Christ figure who reconciles those around her.

The novel *Latterfuglen* (The Bird of Laughter) followed *Natsangersken* in 1965. The protagonist of *Latterfuglen* is a humble dancer in a chorus line, Hortenzia, pursued and possessed by an egg merchant, Ludvig Mandelin, whose own maze of schedules and systems deprive him of love and emotion. The fearful—and fearfully insecure and immature—Mandelin simultaneously seeks to protect himself from human contact and to denigrate Hortenzia. Mandelin's efforts result in Hortenzia's suicide and, then, in a symbolic journey to find the girl, and himself, in the realm of death; Mandelin's search parodies the Orpheus Myth. In the case of *Latterfuglen*, the journey to the other world fails completely, for Mandelin is unwilling to reach Hortenzia, incapable of recognizing the needs of others and loving himself. Ulla Ryum ends her novel with a comical, fantastic, yet grotesque scene, a parody-scene "punning" the deadly serious Mandelin: Ludvig Mandelin visits a bath in a symbolic effort to cleanse, find forgiveness and a new life, but he is so scoured and rinsed by the women attendants (that) "when they are finished, there is nothing left of him."

Ulla Ryum followed *Latterfuglen* with *Jakelnatten*

(1967; The Night of Punch-and-Judy) and *Byen K* (1967; The City K), and, then, with two collections of short stories: *Tusindskove: Hændelser og Historier* (1969; Thousand Woods: Events and Stories), and *Noter om idag og igår. Nye og gamle Historier* (1971; Notes on Today and Yesterday: New and Old Stories). From 1968 on, her literary career took on dramatic—and political—dimensions, as Ryum began to write plays, screenplays, television and radio dramas. Her plays have followed in fairly rapid succession: "Den bedrøvede bugtaler" (1971; The Grief-Stricken Ventriloquist, Radioteatret); "Myterne" (1973; The Myths, Comediehuset); "Krigen" (1975; The War, Det kongelige Teater); "Cirkus" (1975; Circus, Fiolteatret); "Faster er død" (1978; Aunt has Died, TV); "Jægerens ansigter" (1978; Faces of the Hunter, Comediehuset); "Rummene" (1979; The Rooms, Århus); "Og Fuglene synger igen" (1980; And the Birds Are Singing Again, Radio). "Digt om et Døgn" is a fantastic, lively play, in which Ryum has given free rein to her considerable talents for the bizarre, the imaginary, *la farce noire*, and the humorous. In "Digt om et Døgn," the poet, Johan Herman Wessel, an historical figure from "the Spring 1783—but probably (from) today," finally awakens from alcohol-induced slumber to encounter Trude Mansdatter, the proprietress of a tavern; her son Ludvig Morten List; and the waitress, Alberte. The characters engage in continuous, fantastic discourse, approaching each other and stepping away, contacting and failing to communicate, engaging and insulting each other. After Ludvig and Alberte retreat from the scene together, in love or ready for love, Wessel pursues an implausible, curious dialogue with "the mute *Pifteren*, a tongue-less oboe and mouth-organ player," frequenting the tavern and providing music for entertainment. The dialogues of the play create an aura of absurdity and mad-cap happenstance, as Trude and Wessel, Ludvig and Alberte, speak and act past one another. The fate of the players on the scene is the fate of Everyman (or *Mansdatter*, Man's Daughter), a tragic-comic destiny which Ulla Ryum aptly describes in the subtitle to "Digt om et Døgn:" "a merry tragedy for four speakers and one player."

Ulla Ryum has also written a drama for radio, "Denne ene Dag" (1976; That One Day) as well as a long prose-poem soliloquy, *Natten* (1975; The Night), for the actress Berthe Qvistgaard. In *Natten*, Ryum has again emphasized an essential message of love, responsibility, and service. The idea of Christian love and sacrifice is a constant in Ulla Ryum's work. Ryum's most recent work is yet another novel, *Baglandstekster* (1983; Texts from Hinterland), representing a return to the genre.

Ulla Ryum has also been active politically and on behalf of Danish authors, playwrights, the theater, and film. From 1973 to 1976, Ryum served as a director of the Association of Danish Authors; she has also been a chair of the Danish Democratic Women's Association (1975) and a directing associate of the National Art Endowment's Board for Literature (1977–1980). Ryum has also taught at the National Drama School and the Film School of Denmark. She has been a member of the Commission for the National Drama School (1978) and of the Directorate for the Royal Theatre (1979) and an adviser for Bagsværd Amateur Theatre, Radio Theatre, and the Royal Theatre's *Comediehus* (Comedy Scene), which has presented her plays "Denne ene Dag," "Jægerens ansigter," and "Rejse gennem dagen." Ulla Ryum has received additional recognition in the form of a National Art Endowment Fellowship (1965–1968); an honorary award from Danish Dramatists (1975); and, in 1981, a Travel Grant from the Tagea Brandt Foundation.

Ulla Ryum's *oeuvre* is rich, diverse, and complex. Her novels introduce us to fantastic characters and events while depicting the loneliness and the lack of love and self-knowledge that seem the plight of the modern individual. Ryum's plays are strangely engaging, filled with the improbable, the absurd, the poetically beautiful, the curious, and the bizarre. Through the course of her work, Ulla Ryum has stressed essential themes: service and greater self-realization through the quintessential gift of unconditional, Christian love.

Works

Spejl (1962). *Natsangersken* (1963). *Latterfuglen* (1965). *Jakelnatten* (1967). *Byen K* (1967). *Tusindskove: Hændelser og Historier* (1969). *Noter om idag og igår. Nye og gamle Historier* (1971). "Den bedrøvede bugtaler" (1971). "Myterne" (1973). "Krigen" (1975). "Cirkus" (1975). *Natten* (1975). "Denne ene Dag" (1976). "Faster er død" (1978). "Jægerens ansigter" (1978). "Rummene" (1979). "Og Fuglene synger igen" (1980). "Digt om et Døgn" (1980). "Rejse gennem dagen" (1980). "En kærlighedshistorie" (1981). *Baglandstekster* (1983). *Kvindesprog—Udtryk og det Sete. Papirer om faglig Nr. 10.* [Women's Language—Expression and Visualization on Technical Communication Nr. 10] (1987). *Seks Skuespil.* [Six Plays] (1990). *Skjulte Beretninger: 21 Spørgsmål.* [Concealed Account Questions] (1994). "I Am the One You Think" (Jeg er den I tror) excerpt, in *New Danish Fiction: Review of Contemporary Fiction* (1995).

Lanae Hjortsvang Isaacson

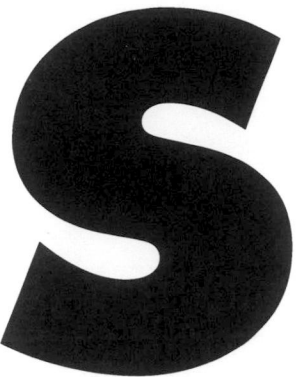

Marguerite Hessein de la Sablière
1640–1693

Born 1640, Paris
Died January 6, 1693, Paris
Genre(s): letters, maxims
Language(s): French

Marguerite Hessein de la Sablière is remembered to-day as much for her intelligence and erudition as for her brilliant salon and her long-term patronage of the French fabulist La Fontaine. She was born in 1640 into a Huguenot family most probably originating in the Low Countries. Her education was remarkably thorough for her day. She was one of the few women of her time to be able to read Greek as well as Latin, she displayed an early talent for mathematics and in later life could recall numerous verses of Vergil and Horace by heart. The influence of her uncle, Antone Menjot, a friend of Pascal, brought her to blossom in many fields.

Like all young women of her class and fortune, she was destined to marry. She wed her cousin Antoine de Rambouillet, the seigneur de la Sablière, on February 20, 1654. The couple were members of the same social milieu and class, and both were noted for their intelligence and talent. Antoine, in fact, was the author of a number of French madrigals. Initially they were happy, and the union produced three children—Anne (1655), Nicholas (1656), and a bit later Marguerite.

When Marguerite's father died, misfortune struck. Antoine discovered that the Hessein fortune had been considerably eroded by speculation. Problems developed immediately. Madame de la Sablière was obliged to move to the Convent of Charonne in 1667, and, because of continuous pressure from her husband, she sought and obtained a final, formal separation. The notice was issued on May 30, 1668. From that time on, she lived apart from both husband and children.

Her life was not totally empty, however. From 1669–1680 her apartments in the Rue Neuve de Petits-Champs were the setting for one of Paris' most interesting salons. Although not yet published, she had already acquired a degree of notoriety and was able to attract such guests as Sobiesky, Brancas, Charleval, Pellisson, Mme Scarron, les Marquises de Lamben et de Sévigné, Queen Christina of Sweden, and even Mlle de Lenclos, the former lover of Antoine. Her desire for learning was insatiable. Her library of seventy-five volumes includes works by the saints Augustine, Bernard, Cyprian, Francis Xavier, John Chrysostom, and Teresa of Avila, as well as books by Epictetus and Marcus Aurelius. Her *Traité de l'Equilibrium des liquids* (A Treatise on the Equilibrium of Liquids) and a personal telescope testify to her scientific interests. In addition, she took lessons from some of France's most illustrious savants. François Bernier taught her natural history, anatomy, and astronomy; Roberval and Sauveur, geometry and mathematics. The philosophical speculations of Gassendi and Descartes were common topics of conversation at her home.

From 1673 to 1680, she provided La Fontaine with a refuge and a home. His *Fables* may well have grown from her discussions of Descartes and his speculations about the souls of animals. Certainly "La Fable des deux rats du Renard et de l'oeuf (Discours à Madame de la Sablière)" [The Fable of the Two Rats of Renard and the Egg (Discourse to Madame de la Sablière)], and his fables of the crow, the gazelle, the tortoise, and the rat directly reflect her influence and milieu. Although his patroness did not love flattery, La Fontaine was not ungrateful and gave voice to his appreciation several times.

Indeed, most of the literary men of her day enjoyed and valued Madame de la Sablière's companionship. Although Boileau, perhaps stinging from her correction of his science in the "Fifth Epistle," attacked her learning in his "Satire sur les Femmes" (Satire on Women), Perrault answered it in his "Appreciation des Femmes" (Appreciation of Women). La Fontaine, among numerous other compliments, once wrote that she had "beaute d'homme avec grace de femme." Additionally, her studies were recognized by the king, who awarded her a pension of 2000 livres a year.

She was less happy in her private affairs, however. An unfortunate interlude with Charles de la Fare led her to embrace religion. In the 1680s she converted to Catholicism. The same year she retired to the Hôpital des Incurables. At this time, in a fervent search for solitude and with a growing distaste for worldly concerns, she penned her *Les Maximes Chrétiennes* (Christian Maxims) and her letters to Père Rancé. At the hôpital, she helped to tend the sick. She observed all the duties of cloistered life, and, in declining health, battled her way through to a fervent reconciliation with her God. She died at the hôpital on January 6, 1693.

The writings of Madame de Sablière reveal her erudition and her elegance, her talent for a precise use of the French language, and her later religious fervor. The *Maximes*, first published in 1705, are so good that they have been attributed at times to that master of the aphorism, La Rochefoucault. Her letters let her mystical temperament, her energetic and decisive character and her fervent sense of repentance unfold. The style, though tranquil, is no less passionate. In both the maxims and the letters, Madame de Sablière's learning is everywhere apparent. Although her subject matter in both is religious, one can clearly detect the personality who first brought together the French aristocracies of blood and letters.

Madame de la Sablière rests today in Saint-Sulpice in Paris.

Works

Les Maximes Chrétiennes [Christian Maxims] (1705).
Pensées Chrétiennes [Christian Thoughts] (1923).

Glenda Wall

Nelly Sachs
1891–1970

Born December 10, 1891, Berlin
Died May 12, 1970, Stockholm
Genre(s): poetry, drama, translation
Language(s): German

Nelly (Leonie) Sachs was the only child of Margarethe (nee Karger) and William Sachs, a Berlin businessman. Although she eventually became best known as "the poetess of Jewish destiny," her upbringing, like that of many cultured and wealthy assimilated German Jews, did not stress religious training, and she herself never learned either Hebrew or Yiddish. In her early youth, Sachs was interested in the dance, only turning to writing in her teenage years. This interest in theater would reemerge in later years in the form of her dramatic works. Her early writings included puppet plays (none published) and poems, many of which appeared in newspapers. Her first published book, *Legenden und Erzählungen* (1921; Legends and Tales), was a collection of short stories, many set in the Middle Ages, and dedicated to her early literary heroine and mentor, the Swedish novelist Selma Lagerlöf, with whom she was in correspondence since the age of sixteen. These early works showing the influence of nineteenth-century German Romanticism and nature poetry, did not gain much critical attention. They also did not show any traces of the influence of the avant-garde artists active in Berlin between the wars. Later in life, Sachs would distance herself from these early works, omitting them from the collections and anthologies, all published after the war.

The turning point in Sachs's life and works came with the ascent to power of the National Socialist party in 1933, with its openly antisemitic policies. No longer allowed to publish except in Jewish journals, she began her unsystematic study of Hasidic literature and the mystical tradition of the Kaballah. Hearing of the fate of deported Jews, friends of the family worked desperately to get exit visas for Nelly Sachs and her widowed mother. Through the tireless efforts of various friends, the help of Prince Eugene of Sweden and the intercession of Selma Lagerlöf, they were finally able to get permission to immigrate to the United States, which in turn enabled them to obtain the desired letters of transit through to neutral Sweden, their intended goal. They arrived in Sweden in 1940. Mother and daughter managed to escape Germany just in time, thanks to the advice of an official who recommended to the naive Sachs that she ignore the deportation notice and board the earliest flight out of Germany. A short time later, all exit visas out of Germany were cancelled. All her Jewish friends and members of her family who remained behind perished in the ensuing Holocaust. Sachs spent the rest of her life in Sweden, eventually became a Swedish citizen, and refused all suggestions and offers to return to Germany, even though she was granted honorary Berlin citizenship in 1967.

Both in her personal life and in her work, these experiences exerted an immense effect on the poet. Her new life as a fifty-year-old impoverished exile marked a complete break from the earlier comfortable bourgeois existence. This break also marked the beginning of her mature poetry, a poetry completely free of any metric conventions and stanzaic breaks, driven solely by force of themes and images, and arranged in cycles. The narrow escape from death haunts all her poetry, as she herself said in a letter: "The terrible experiences which brought me personally to the brink of death and darkness became my tutors. Had I been unable to write, I would not have survived. Death was my tutor. How could I have occupied myself with anything else? My metaphors are my wounds. Only through them is my work to be understood." Indeed, shortly after her arrival in Sweden, she tried to write a continuation of *Legenden und Erzählungen* but never finished the project. She was to publish no more creative prose the rest of her life.

Both of her early postwar collections, *In den Wohnungen des Todes* (In the Habitations of Death) and *Sternverdunkelung* (Eclipse of the Stars), as well as the play *Eli* were direct results of her attempts to come to terms with those "terrible experiences" through their disturbing images of life, death, and suffering in the concentration camps. These works, with their strong themes of pain, loss, separation, and disappointment in love, brought her international attention.

A reclusive person, Sachs seldom gave interviews, and was reluctant to reveal any details about her personal life, either past or present. She was hardly known, even in the German-speaking world, until she was awarded the Nobel Prize for Literature in 1966, which she shared with the Israeli writer S.Y. Agnon. In part, her secretiveness was due to ill health suffered after the death of her mother in 1950. Two heart attacks and a series of nervous breakdowns kept her in hospitals or sanitariums for long periods of time.

While even in the earlier mature poetry, Sachs's works evinced a trace of hermeticism, but it is the later poetry, such as the *Glühende Rätsel* (Glowing Enigmas) which has been most problematic to literary critics. Many have asserted that Sachs's works cannot be read apart from her later works. Their increasingly mystical and enigmatic language was interpreted by

Nelly Sachs

some to signify reconciliation and even forgiveness through quietism and acceptance. However, such a simplistic interpretation of the later works was one that she herself went out of the way to deny. It is obvious that these later pieces show her being increasingly influenced by her readings of cabalistic literature, especially through Gershom Scholem's (1897–1982) German translation of the Book of Sohar. But the move toward mysticism was not only through Jewish lines; other, including Eastern, mystical traditions can be evinced in these works as well. In time, the ashes of the crematoria became the dust of ages, and themes of metamorphosis and the sands of time grew more significant than the fate of the Jewish people and the sorrows of the Holocaust.

As the language of her poetry became more mystic, the poems also became more universal. Writing in German, she rejected the literary and cultural traditions associated with that language. She was a poet who managed to forge a language of her own—an ahistorical German. Exiled from her native land, she created a unique place for herself: a purely linguistic existence in response to both the Nazi dictum that "when a Jew writes in German, he lies," and the Zionist statement that the concepts of writing in German and being Jewish were mutually incompatible. She became a writer with no linguistic homeland, writing poetry which many German postwar critics had difficulty assimilating into literary history. At first, Sachs was classified, along with Paul Celan, under the rubric of "exile poet." Later on, the label of "poetess of Jewish destiny" would be used. However, neither of these characterizations adequately accounts for the movement toward mysticism in her later works, and much remains to be done before any study or assessment of her works can claim to be in any way definitive. There has, for example, been very little critical attention paid to her fourteen dramatic pieces, even though some have been performed as radio plays, and the Swedish composer Moses Pergament even set *Eli* to music.

While Sachs was awarded many prizes and awards (the city of Dortmund, which houses the Nelly Sachs archives, presented her with the first Nelly Sachs Prize in 1961), the slow recognition by some critics of her poetry could be ascribed to the publication of her early collections in East Berlin and in Amsterdam, as well as the attitude of many German critics toward German exile writers. However, the continued lack of critical attention must be ascribed to the general difficulty of her works and her refusal to include biographical details in her poetry, preferring instead to mysticize her experiences, or universalize them through such themes as exile, loneliness, or metamorphosis. To this day she remains, unfortunately, better known by reputation than by personal acquaintanceship with her works.

One important facet of Sachs's work which has been neglected is her role as translator. She was the person most responsible for introducing postwar Swedish poetry to the German-language audience, championing the works of Edfelt, Ekelof, Lindegren, and others. For this work, she was awarded a number of Swedish literary prizes.

Works

Legenden und Erzählungen [Legends and Tales] (1921). *Fahrt ins Staublose: Die Gedichte der Nelly Sachs 1* [Journey into the Dustless Realm: The Poetry of Nelly Sachs, 1] (1961). This anthology and the following one include all of her mature poetry, including posthumous works. *Suche nach Lebenden: Die Gedichte der Nelly Sachs 2* [Search for the Living: The Poetry of Nelly Sachs, 2] (1971), ed. Margarethe Holmqvist and Bengt Holmqvist. *Zeichen im Sand* [Markings in the Sand] (1962). Includes all fourteen dramatic works.

Letters: *Briefe der Nelly Sachs* [Letters of Nelly Sachs] ed. Ruth Dinesen and Helmut Müssener (1984). Includes bibliography of Sachs's translations from Swedish as well as translations of Sachs's own works into other languages.

Translations: *O the Chimneys: Selected Poems, Including the Verse Play, Eli,* tr. Michael Hamburger et al. (1967). Published in the U.K. as *Selected Poems: Including the Verse Play "Eli"* (1968). *The Seeker and Other Poems,* tr. Ruth Mead, Matthew Mead, and Michael Hamburger (1970). *Contemporary German Poetry,* selections, ed. and tr. Gertrude C. Schwebell (1964).

Oscar Lee

Vita (Victoria Mary) Sackville-West
1892–1962

Born March 8, 1892, Knole, Sevenoaks, Kent, England
Died June 2, 1962, Sissinghurst, Cranbrook, Kent
Genre(s): novel, biography, travel literature, poetry, literary criticism
Language(s): English

"I *will get* myself into English Literature." As Sackville-West herself might appreciate, her prominence therein relies upon a notoriously unconventional life as well as upon prodigious—if essentially non"modernist"—literary works. Early in life she imagined her name in histories of literature: "Sackville-West, V., poet and novelist." Excluding juvenilia (eight novels and five plays between 1906 and 1910), she produced twelve novels, five biographies, two long poems, much other poetry, and assorted travel, garden/country, and critical writing.

Anomalous among her works is the short experimental novel *Seducers in Ecuador* (1924), which Virginia Woolf praised for its "fantasticallity." It remains a delightful and disconcerting text, probably intended as a compliment to Woolf's style. In her English Georgics, *The Land* (a poem that won the 1926 Hawthornden Prize), and her superb novel, *The Edwardians* (1930)—both enormously popular—her literary conservatism triumphs: she sings the cycle of her country's year in rurally erudite verse, and recreates in brilliant, often satiric prose the overblown *vie-en-rose* of aristocrats during her childhood. Her best writing treats the extremes of gentry life, fields and salons alike. Her other work is not as well achieved artistically, betraying a lack of "central transparency" (in Woolf's phrase) and giving "the effect of having been done from the outside" (in her own)—perhaps the aesthetic price for ingrained snobbery and indirect narcissism.

That her oeuvre should continue to intrigue readers is hardly surprising, however, if only for what it reveals about Sackville-West and her relations with both *beau monde* and Bloomsbury. "I am an incredible egoist, that's the long and the short of it"; fascinated by her own personality (or personalities) and sexuality (or sexualities), she reflected creatively upon her forty-nine-year marriage to diplomat-politician Harold Nicolson and her lifelong series of love affairs with women, including Virginia Woolf. The "Author's Note" to *The Edwardians* advises, "No character in this book is wholly fictitious"; early, her novels such as *Challenge* (written in 1919) suggest psychobiographical readings of the author's fictionalized self-representation as either male or tellingly split between two characters of different gender.

Sackville-West's mixed Spanish–English heritage also divided her. Born and raised on a colossal estate held by centuries of Sackvilles (one of whom coauthored *Gorboduc* and wrote the Induction to *A Mirror for Magistrates)*, she considered it her life's tragedy as an only daughter to watch her beloved Knole pass to an uncle and a cousin. The literary compensation for this loss was extraordinary: Woolf's *Orlando* (1928), which has been called the longest love letter in history. Given an early copy (and later the manuscript, beautifully bound), Sackville-West read it on publication day, overwhelmed and flattered to be consoled for her father's death and identified with Knole for posterity.

She was more ambivalent about her maternal past. She adored and feared her mother, by turns an impulsively generous "Bonne Maman" and cruelly imperious Lady Sackville (who called Woolf "that wicked Virgin Wolf"). At midlife, Sackville-West wrote *Pepita* (1937), a biography of her grandmother, the Spanish dancer whose supposed Gypsy blood she associated with the wanderlust and passionate nature she was finally beginning to control in herself. Henceforth, "heart of darkness" themes—even latent sadomasochism, notably in *The Dark Island* (1934)— gave way to themes of leave-taking (adumbrated in 1931 by the splendid novel *All Passion Spent),* solitude (the title of a 1958 poem), and saints' lives (those of Joan and the two Teresas). Sackville-West explored "the power of being alone," specifically, in her poems of place, "the power of being alone with earth and skies."

A prolific correspondent, she wrote daily to Nicolson for most of their lives. Her letters to Woolf alone fill a volume. She kept a rich diary, and a long autobiographical memoir about her traumatic affair with Violet (Keppel) Trefusis was published posthumously in *Portrait of a Marriage,* together with ex-planatory chapters by her son Nigel amounting to a panegyric of his parents' marriage.

That relationship has been mythologized by all concerned, its ability to withstand both partners' series of homosexual lovers elevated to a principle of "caring without interference." Sackville-West and Nicolson spoke about marriage on the BBC and on tour in the United States; in transcripts (and elsewhere) one notes the slippage between feminist and aristocratic/egoistic self-assertion, between rights for all women, as women, and independence for exceptional selves who transcend gender through personal privilege. Sackville-West became conservative with age and her experience of World War II (like Woolf, she lived under the bombing path across southern England). She was surprised that one of her young female relatives wanted a career, for example. Yet in her last novel, *No Signposts in the Sea* (1961), she speaks through a narrator, lower class in background, to challenge the wealth-based assumptions of a woman who prescribes against "squalour" in marriage by recommending separate bedrooms. *Signposts* also returns to the cruise-of-life metaphor of *Seducers.*

Not generally considered a professional writer, Sackville-West in fact wrote most deliberately for money: she supported herself, and often Nicolson; sent her sons to Balliol (Oxford); paid for Long Barn and Sissinghurst Castle; and financed the creation of the celebrated Sissinghurst Garden. (She was nonetheless loyal to the Hogarth Press, ignoring mid-career other publishers' lucrative offers.) Weekly *Observer* gardening columns brought her more contemporary recognition than her poetry and novels put together, and she was awarded the Royal Horticultural Society's Gold Medal (which, in her words, "generally goes to old men over eighty, who have devoted the whole of their lives to horticulture").

Some find paradoxical her devotion to "country notes," truth-in-platitude, and formal gardens after a nonconformist youth (the "splendid arson of my reckless days" [*The Garden*]). Hugh Walpole characterizes her as a romantic hedonist. Given British social history, however, her defiant independence can be seen in a tradition of licensed aristocratic eccentricity. She took pains to avoid overt "scandal," keeping her lesbian affairs semisecret and withdrawing *Challenge*— with its portraits of Trefusis as Eve and herself as Julian—from publication. Her "open" marriage had an Edwardian aspect: members of the upper-class, including her own parents, had always tolerated discreet adultery. Her literary works reflect a personal progress toward restraint, service, and reclusivity; the result is balanced prose of great beauty brought to match her consistently decorous poetry. Sackville-West's career conjoins distinguished writing with an idiosyncratic life of struggle against sexual norms.

Works

Chatterton (1909). *Constantinople: Eight Poems* (1915). *Poems of East and West* (1917). *Heritage* (1919). *The Dragon in Shallow Waters* (1921). *Orchard and Vineyard* (1921). *The Heir* (1922). *Knole and the Sackvilles* (1922). *Challenge* (1923 in the U.S., 1974 in the U.K.). *Grey Wethers* (1923). *Seducers in Ecuador* (1924). *The Land* (1926). *Passenger to Teheran* (1926). *Aphra Behn* (1927). *Twelve Days* (1928). *King's Daughter* (1929). *The Edwardians* (1930). *Sissinghurst* (1931). *Invitation to Cast Out Care* (1931). *Rilke* (translations, 1931). *All Passion Spent* (1931). *The Death of Noble Godavary and Gottfried Kunstler* (1932). *Thirty Clocks Strike the Hour* (1932). *Family History* (1932). *Collected Poems*, vol. I. [no vol. II] (1933). *The Dark Island* (1934). *Saint Joan of Arc* (1936). *Pepita* (1937). *Some Flowers* (1937). *Solitude* (1938). *Country Notes* (1939). *Country Notes in Wartime* (1940). *English Country Houses* (1941). *Grand Canyon* (1942). *The Eagle and the Dove* (1943). *The Woman's Land Army* (1944). *Another World Than This* (with H. Nicolson, 1945). *The Garden* (1946). *Nursery Rhymes* (1947). *Devil at Westease* (1947). *In Your Garden* (1951). *In Your Garden Again* (1953). *The Easter Party* (1953). *More for Your Garden* (1955). *Even More for Your Garden* (1958). *A Joy of Gardening* (1958). *Daughter of France* (1959). *No Signposts in the Sea* (1961). *Faces: Profiles of Dogs* (1961). *V. Sackville-West's Garden Book*, ed. P. Nicolson (1968). *Dearest Andrew: Letters from Victoria Sackville-West to Andrew Rieber, 1951–62*, ed. N. MacKnight (1979). *The Letters of Victoria Sackville-West to Virginia Woolf*, ed. L. DeSalvo and M.A. Leaska (1984).

Catherine Milsum

Barbara Sadowska
1940–1986

Born February 24, 1940
Died October 1986
Genre(s): poetry
Language(s): Polish

During her funeral at the Warsaw Powazki cemetery on October 6,1986, in the presence of thousands, poet Wiktor Woroszylski spoke about Sadowska, calling her "the Polish Mater Dolorosa, a sister to all mothers of murdered sons. . . ." Sadowska's son, nineteen-year-old Grzegorz, was dragged from the street into the police station and beaten to death in May 1983. Several weeks earlier, Sadowska herself was hit on the head by "unknown thugs" who broke into St. Martin's church in Warsaw, where she was sorting out medication packages to be delivered to people arrested under the "martial law." As a consequence of that attack, the poet underwent two serious skull operations. She had been in trouble with the regime since the fifties when, as a teenager, she frequented the unofficial stage performances; she was often called for investigation, and later the police tried to link her case to the murder of a son of a well-known Catholic publications' editor committed at that time. In 1968, she supported the student revolt against the regime, and in 1976 she joined the KOR, Committee for Workers' Defense, organized by prominent intellectuals to help the jailed factory employees and their families. She joined the "Solidarity" movement at its outset, working all the time with the Archbishop's Air Committee at St. Martin's.

She made her debut as a seventeen-year-old with the poem "Mama" in issue no. 10 of the journal *Nowa Kultura*. Her first volume of poetry was warmly received by both literary critics and the wider audience. Her second volume, however, met with accusations of being "uncommunicative," "dark," and "obscure." She had to wait for almost ten years to see her next book in print. She never belonged to any literary groups and did not seek support from influential people. Her fourth volume was severely abbreviated by the censors. She published nothing through official channels for the last twelve years of her life. Her poetry was printed by underground publications.

She wrote in 1983:

> on scraps of paper
> I insult the Department of Justice
> the court of law
> and the government
> with the child
> whom you will not manage
> to kill

Works

Zerwane druty [Torn Wires] (1959). *Nad ogniem* [Over the Fire] (1963). *Nie mozesz na mnie liczyc, nie bede sie bronic* [Don't Count on Me, I Will Not Defend Myself] (1972). *Moje* [Mine] (1974). *Tumor* (1981). *Slodko byc dzieckiem Boga* [It's Sweet to Be a Child of God] (1985).

Maya Peretz

Cora Sandel
1880–1974

a.k.a. Sara Fabricius
Born 1880, Kristiania (Oslo), Norway
Died 1974, Uppsala, Sweden
Genre(s): novel, short story
Language(s): Norwegian

Cora Sandel has the distinction of having had more of her works translated into English than any other Norwegian woman writer, with the exception of Nobel Prize recipient Sigrid Undset. Sandel is best known in the English speaking world for her *Alberta* trilogy, now widely recognized as a feminist classic. Few English readers, however, realize that Sandel published five collections of short stories, and that, possibly, she achieves her greatest artistic success in this literary genre.

Cora Sandel is actually a pseudonym chosen by Sara Fabricius when, at forty-two years of age, she submitted her first story for publication in a literary magazine. She was born in 1880 in Kristiania (present-day Oslo) to middle-class parents of good standing. While their situation was not without economic difficulties, Sara's parents did manage to maintain a home based on traditional bourgeois norms and values. In 1892 the family moved to Tromsö, far above the Arctic Circle in the north of Norway, at that time a small, provincial town.

Sara Fabricius aspired to become a painter, and in 1899 she went to Kristiania to study painting with Harriet Backer. Unable to get a stipend, she had to curtail her study after one year and return to Tromsö. Finally, in 1905, she was able to leave Tromsö and resume her painting; she spent one year in Kristiania and in 1906 went to Paris. She had funds enough to keep her in Paris for only six months, but she stayed on, often living from hand to mouth, and did not return to Scandinavia until 1921. Her art studies brought her into contact with other expatriate artists, and they became her circle of friends. In 1913 she married the Swedish sculptor Anders Jönsson. The couple continued to live on the Continent throughout the war years, spending time in Florence, Paris, and Brittany. By the time they were ready to move home, Sara had abandoned painting in favor of writing; in her suitcase were notes intended for a novel based on her childhood.

They had had a child, born in Paris in 1917, and the three of them settled in Sweden, outside of Stockholm. The marriage was disintegrating, however; in 1922 she separated from her husband, and four years later they were divorced. Cora Sandel chose to make her home in Sweden and she died in Uppsala in 1974, ninety-four years old. She always wrote in Norwegian though and continued to regard herself as a Norwegian author.

Cora Sandel was very protective about her private life; she felt that an author owed no more to her public than the books she wrote, and this attitude explains much of the reason she opted to use a pseudonym. There can be no doubt that much of what she experienced went into her writing. Impulses received from living many years in France, for example, are evident in her art. Sandel's depictions of life in a northern Norwegian town, in *Alberte og Jakob* (1926; Alberta and Jacob), *Kranes konditori* (1945; Krane's Café) and several stories, are drawn from personal experience. Her own unhappy marriage ending in divorce and a custody battle over her only child is echoed in novels and stories. And finally, Sandel's struggle to become an artist, to overcome the external and internal barriers specific to her as a woman, inspired her to write the novels depicting Alberta's development as a woman and an artist.

In the first book of the trilogy, *Alberta and Jacob*, Alberta is a teenager living with her family in a middle-class home. Because of their strained economic circumstances, her parents are eager to marry their daughter off to the first eligible suitor. Unhappily, Alberta fails to meet her parents' expectations; she is plain looking and timid and not the least bit interested in learning domestic skills. She longs to continue her schooling, but since her parents can barely afford to keep her brother in school, she is forced to stay home and help her mother mend clothes and keep house. In spite of her isolation and seemingly hopeless situation, Alberta manages to keep alive her dream for a future where she will be free to learn and to realize her talents. There is a defiant spirit behind the shy and insecure exterior.

Alberta does succeed in escaping small-town existence, and when *Alberte og friheten* (1931; Alberta and Freedom) opens, she has arrived in Paris. She is now independent and can pursue her art studies, but she finds that freedom can be a hard reality for a single woman who has neither money nor saleable skills. And she discovers that neither she nor her female companions receive much support in their work from their male friends even though they, too, are struggling artists and should be sympathetic. When the relationship becomes steady, these same men seem to expect that both partners could concentrate on his career and that she should keep his house and raise his children.

In the third book, *Bare Alberte* (1939; Alberta Alone), Alberta has a husband and child. She is no longer painting—for one thing, art supplies are an expensive outlay for a poor artist couple. Instead she has started to write; notes and fragments on scraps of paper are as much as she can manage in between answering the demands made on her time and energy by child and husband. But by the end of the book, she has completed a manuscript, and she has won the self-assurance and conviction that enable her to leave her child and husband and, manuscript in hand, set out on her search for a publisher.

Thirteen years passed between the publication of the first and last books of the trilogy. Alberta underwent a long maturation process. Cora Sandel is a careful writer—her prose is perfectly shaped, and there are no superfluous or poorly chosen words. She is also a writer who is not satisfied until she has understood her characters thoroughly; consequently her portrayals demonstrate remarkable psychological depth and insight. This is not only evidenced in her *Alberta* trilogy but in her novel *Kranes Konditori* (1945; Krane's Café) and in her many and exquisitely crafted stories as well.

Works

Novels: *Alberte og Jakob* (1926). *Alberta og friheten* (1931). *Bare Alberte* (1939). *Kranes konditori* (1945). *Kjöp ikke Dondi* (1958).

Short stories: *En blå sofa* (1927). *Carmen og Maja* (1932). *Mange takk, doktor* (1935). *Dyr jeg har kjent* (1945). *Figurer på mörk bunn* (1949). *Barnet som elsket veier* (1973).

Translations: *Alberta and Jacob*, tr. Elizabeth Rokkan (1962, U.S. edition 1984). *Alberta and Freedom*, tr. Elizabeth Rokkan (1963, U.S. edition 1984). *Alberta Alone*, tr. Elizabeth Rokkan (1965, U.S. edition 1984). *Krane's Café: An Interior with Figures*, tr. Elizabeth Rokkan (1968, U.S. edition 1986). *The Leech*, tr. Elizabeth Rokkan (1960, U.S. edition 1986). *Cora Sandel: Selected Short Stories*, tr. Barbara Wilson (1985). *The Silken Thread. Stories and Sketches*, tr. Elizabeth Rokkan (1986, U.S. edition 1987). *Slaves of Love and Other Norwegian Short Stories*, ed. James McFarland (1982). *An Everyday Story. Norwegian Women's Fiction*, ed. Katherine Hanson (1984). *Scandinavian Women Writers. An Anthology from the 1880s to the 1980s*, ed. Ingrid Claréus (1989).

Katherine Hanson

Francesca Sanvitale
1928–

Born May 17, 1928, Milan, Italy
Genre(s): novel, criticism, journalism
Language(s): Italian

Born in Milan, Francesca Sanvitale lived for a while in Florence, then settled down in Rome. Beside being an accomplished novelist, Sanvitale writes for some of the most influential Italian newspapers and journals (her pronouncements on Tozzi and Neera are often quoted), and she is a skillful interviewer (her interviews of French Academician Yourcenar were made for the Italian RAI-TV).

We can reconstruct Sanvitale's youth from the lines of her quasiautobiographical novel *Madre e figlia* (1980; Mother and Daughter). The work is a reevocation, sometimes in a mythical key, often in a realistic mood, of a love–hate relationship between a mother who cannot grow and a daughter who needs assertive role models because she wants to grow. The narrative is in the third person, the point of view that of the daughter, although at times an "I" intervenes in the presentation. The tale moves between the two poles of total subjugation and sudden revolt, and between intervals of bewilderment and moments of clarity. *Madre e figlia* is the book of an impossible rebellion that is nevertheless attempted; the story of the threat that claustrophobic relationships inevitably foster and of the release that only death can bring about.

Il cuore borghese (The Bourgeois Heart) was composed early in the writer's career but published only in 1972. Like *Madre e figlia*, it is a *Bildungsroman*, but one in which the self-questioning of the intellectual leads only to failure. Salvation for the bourgeoisie is shown to be possible only when one chooses a life that is a non-life, or opts for the void that comes when indifference has thoroughly paralyzed the will. Yet this pessimistic outlook is not overriding. The action progresses by scenes rather than through an old-fashioned plot to better depict the stasis that wraps the middle class society analyzed.

L'uomo del parco (1984; The Man in the Park) is another unusually structured novel. A sequence of micronarratives tells the story of a woman's rebirth. The slow-moving action and the magical landscape function as the background for a tale of inward search. Giulia, the main character, knows that to be cured she must lucidly diagnose her disease. Only then can she—and will she—find a way out of her predicament.

Sanvitale has progressively gained recognition as one of the most promising writers of this generation, and her books have enjoyed both critical and popular success.

Works

Il cuore borghese [The Bourgeois Heart] (1972). *Madre e figlia* [Mother and Daughter] (1980). *L'uomo del parco* [The Man in the Park] (1984).

Valeria Finucci

Sappho
ca. 620 B.C.–?

Born ca. 620 B.C., Eresus on Lesbos
Death date unknown
Genre(s): poetry
Language(s): Greek

Although we possess a relatively large amount of biographical data about the supreme woman poet of antiquity, much of it may not be historically valid. Attic vase-paintings show that within a century of her lifetime Sappho had already become a figure of romantic legend; thus on a *krater* by the Brygos Painter she is shown rejecting the amorous lyric advances of her contemporary and fellow countryman Alcaeus. Fourth-century B.C. comic writers invented satiric details about her life that were incorporated into later biographies, such as the allegation that she was married to a wealthy trader from Andros called Cercylas (the name puns on *kerkis*, designating both the plectrum employed to strike the lyre strings and, on a subliterary level, the male sexual organ). They may also have manufactured the tale of her suicidal plunge from the cliff of Leucas prompted by unrequited love for the boatman Phaon—a story clearly occasioned by a lost Sapphic poem recounting Aphrodite's doomed passion for a mortal lover, either Phaon or his equally mythic counterpart Adonis (see fr. 211a–c, Campbell).

Other biographical details, however, appear to be culled directly from Sappho's poetry. We are told that her mother's name was Cleis, and that she had one daughter, named after her grandmother. In the surviving fragments the poet does mention her mother once (fr. 98a) and speaks of her daughter Cleis repeatedly (frr. 98b and 132; cf. 150 and 213A); as subject and addressee, the latter apparently played a prominent role in Sappho's compositions. A mutilated papyrus scrap (no. 14 in Campbell's collection of testimonia) informs us that Sappho wrote a poem about her brothers; their names, known from other sources, were Charaxus, Larichus, and

Sappho

Erigyius. As a youth, Larichus performed the important function of pouring wine for the assembled committee-men in the town hall, an office held only by boys of high birth, and his sister commemorated this honor in her verse (fr. 203). The sensational story that she publicly castigated Charaxus for his affair with a courtesan is borne out by frr. 5 and 15, where she welcomes her brother home, laments his past errors, and wishes ill upon his mistress Doricha. It has been suggested, however, that the "errant brother" motif is an archaic Greek literary convention employed as a point of departure for moralizing blame poetry; this would explain why the poet is not ashamed to expose a family scandal.

Sappho composes for her female companions (fr. 160); some, like Atthis, are expressly singled out as addressees. The nature and purpose of this circle of listeners and her exact relationship to its members are subjects that have generated much controversy. Later antiquity imagined her a teacher of well-born young women, but Wilamowitz's chivalrous idea of Sappho as prim mistress of a girls' finishing school is an amusing anachronism. The current popular notion of her as leader of an organized female separatist group also conflicts with all we know of the behavior of women in the archaic Greek world. In reality, nothing in the fragments implies that Sappho's poetic activities or social situation were unusual for a woman of her rank. The Greek concept of song as quintessentially feminine, incarnated in such mythic emblems as sirens, sphinxes, and the nine Muses, permitted women to express themselves in choral dance and solo lyric performance and so prepared Sappho's male contemporaries to recognize and cherish a female poetic genius. Likewise, the evidence of social history suggests that at all temporal periods Greek women, though restricted in their dealings with men not blood relatives, freely interacted with other women in broadly based same-sex networks and derived prestige and satisfaction from their position within such networks.

Sappho's lesbian thematics—her eloquent appreciations of female beauty and intense evocations of homosexual desire—can also be situated within her own social and historical context. Her verse, like all archaic lyric, must have been intended as a public rather than a personal statement. It does not automatically follow, however, that the quasiautobiographical confessions of passion in Sappho's poetry are wholly conventional, divorced from any private feeling. With its marked separation between men's and women's cultures, the society of archaic and classical Greece, while strongly patriarchal, seems to have been remarkably tolerant of deep emotional bonding and actual homoerotic relationships between women. Certainly Sappho's poetry would not have attained a widespread popularity throughout Greece or been collected and preserved by Alexandrian scholars had it expressed sentiments repugnant to Greek men. Thus, while this body of verse affords a distinctly female perspective upon reality and reflects a woman-identified consciousness, its presentation of women's experience must have conformed, at least in broad outline, to the expectations prevailing within the dominant culture.

The poems of Sappho are monodies, solo songs performed to the accompaniment of the lyre. Several characteristics set her work apart from that of male lyric poets: a preoccupation with intimate relationships and with the subjective emotional state of the speaker or her addressee; direct and familiar encounters with the divine world; personalized treatment of myth; and the subtle employment of sensual imagery, especially that of sight, sound, and touch. In particular, Sappho's concept of the erotic relationship is clearly distinguished from attitudes toward love found elsewhere in archaic Greek poetry. Male poets treat sexual activity as agonistic, fitting it to a pattern of dominance and submission in which the lover takes his keenest pleasure from the difficult pursuit and mastery of the unwilling beloved, whether boy or woman. Sappho depicts the ideal sexual encounter as egalitar-

ian and reciprocal, with the participants displaying a like measure of desire and need for each other. She is fond of appropriating the language and conventions of Homeric combat scenes to portray the psychological tensions of the erotic situation, but her erotic wars are always struggles between equally matched combatants, and for her the female sphere of love and desire is as charged with the potential for sublime heroism as is the male sphere of military conflict. Many of the surviving fragments are imbued with an atmosphere of romantic yearning for a lost companion. In fr. 94, for example, the speaker urges remembrance of past happiness as a partial anodyne for the grief of separation. The girls who leave go unwillingly and long for their friends left behind (fr. 96). The circumstance behind these shattering departures was evidently an arranged marriage, the young woman being given no choice in the matter. Implicitly, then, Sappho depicts women's homoerotic love as precarious and fragile, readily sacrificed to patriarchal and heterosexual convenience: female lives are adequately lived only in the interstices of the public social structure.

Yet her poetry is not always romantically despondent; the fragments reveal that she devoted her creative energies to a remarkable variety of themes. Many of Sappho's songs invoke Aphrodite, sometimes in company with the Muses, and her single surviving complete text the so-called "Ode to Aphrodite" (fr. 1), is a profound realization of the compelling personality of that goddess; similarly, fr. 2 summons Aphrodite to an imagined garden of sensual enchantment to join the speaker and her companions in feasting. Several citations make it clear that Sappho attacked other women in verse. While her targets are generally assumed to be sexual rivals, it appears that some polemics had political overtones (e.g., fr. 71), and the tradition of her exile in Sicily may have been prompted by outspoken denunciations of the female members of families hostile to her own. Finally, several short quotations from her *epithalamia* and the broken text of a lengthy description of the wedding procession of Hector and Andromache (fr. 44) indicate that she could represent marriage as a joyful occasion and write of heterosexual love with no less delicacy of feeling.

Works

Greek texts in *Poetarum Lesbiorum Fragments*, eds. E. Lobel and D.L. Page (Oxford, 1955). *Sappho et Alcaeus*, ed. E.-M. Voigt (Amsterdam, 1971). Texts, testimonia, and English translations in *Greek Lyric 1*, tr. D.A. Campbell, Loeb Classical Library (Cambridge, Mass., and London, 1982).

Marilyn B. Skinner

Galateia Sarantë
ca. 1920–

a.k.a. Galateia Saranti
Born 1920(?), Patras, Greece
Genre(s): novel, novella, short story, children's literature
Language(s): Greek

Galateia Sarantë studied law at the University of Athens but gave that up to devote her time to writing. She has written five novels, three novellas, three volumes of short stories, and several children's books. She has been recognized as an important figure in modern Greek literature and has received several awards for her work.

Her first book, *To vivlio tēs charas* (The Book of Joy), published in 1947, includes two short works, both of which deal with the theme of breaking up and going apart in male–female relationships. The potential union in each case is not quite achieved.

Her second published work, *To vivlio tou Giochanes kai tēs Marias* (The Book of Johannes and Maria), which was published in 1952 but first appeared in 1947 in *Nea Estia*, takes place during the Nazi occupation of Greece: A physician and his daughter take into their home a Jewish family. The young man, Johannes, falls in love with the physician's daughter, Maria, but his love remains pure and unrequited, for her heart is already given to another. In all three of these early works we find the seeds of what will mark her later writing: the delicate sensibility of the author reflected in the insightful portrayal of her characters; the lyrical flow of her prose; the nostalgia for family traditions and customs, her preoccupation with relationships. Her major characters are good people, above malice, hatred, and selfish interest, and many of her young people are idealists and dreamers with intellectual and spiritual yearnings.

In her *Paschalies* (1949; Lilacs), *Epistrophē* (1953; Return), and *To palio mas spiti* (1959; Our Old Home), Sarantë lingers in the security of familiar surroundings seen against the background of World War II. *Paschalies* contrasts conditions in Greece before the war and afterward as they affect one closely-knit family and their *patriko* home in the country where the lilacs bloom (or bloomed before they and the house were burned). It is a tale of love and war told from a female point of view. The main character is the youngest girl in the family, Lina, who has inclinations toward writing and in this most autobiographical of Sarantë's novels is probably a spokesman for the author herself.

The main character of *Epistrophē*, Anna Xerou, returns home after ten years of studying abroad and has to deal with problem of readjusting to conditions and situations in Greece after the war among physical, financial, and human ruin.

To palio mas spiti (Our Old Home) deals with two people, a brother and a sister, who try to keep their dignity and that of their family, despite the financial ruin of their father and many other misfortunes, including a broken engagement, a necessary end to the brother's studies, a broken heart, and the death of a loved one. They find strength and comfort in each other, and, although saddened, they are not completely defeated. The brother, a war veteran with a slight limp, finds peace in his books.

Her best-known novel, *Ta oria* (The Boundaries), published in 1966, deals with a woman who is rejected by a lover and, being the mother of a child and lacking the protection of a husband, becomes gradually estranged from society and eventually feels completely alienated.

In her short story "Elene," published in her 1982 collection of short stories by the same title, Sarantë depicts a situation where the break-up of a "perfect" marriage is inevitable because of the childish concepts the marriage was based on.

Sarantë's strength and emphasis lie not in plot development but in the fine shadings of feeling. Her subtle portrayal of character, especially of the women characters, gives the reader a deep insight into human relationships. The world she describes is an inner world of thought and emotion. Unfortunately, sometimes this inner world becomes too abstract, her characters too good to be true, and their thoughts too indefinite and unspecific to be convincing. But, nevertheless, her creations are memorable and sometimes disturbing, especially when she depicts the outsider within the group, the one who does not quite fit in. As the supportive family of her early period gives way to the alienating tendencies of modern society in her later work, one cannot help but notice the writer's personal development from "the way we would like things to be" to acceptance of "the way things are."

Works

Novels: *To vivlio tēs charas* [The Book of Joy] (1947). *Paschalies* [Lilacs] (1949, 1973). *To vivlio tou Giochanes kai tēs Marias* [The Book of Johannes and Maria] (1952). *Epistrophē* [Return] (1953). *To palio mas spiti* [Our Old Home](1959). *Ta oria* [The Boundaries] (1966). *Rögmes* (Cracks).

Short stories: *Chrōmata empistosynēs* [Colors of Trust] (1962). Na *Thymasai tē Vilna* [Remember Vilna] (1972). *Elenē: Diēgēmata* [Helenē: Short Stories] (1982).

Children's literature: *Sta chronia tou Pavlou Mela: To liontari kai to phidi* [In the Time of Pavlos Melas: The Lion and the Snake] (1962). *Charazei ë lephteria: Oi mparoutomyloi tës Dëmëtsanas* [Freedom Is Breaking: The Gunpowder Mills of Demetsana] (1971).

Translations: *Hilmu fataten*, Tr. Naiim Atia (1978). *Polawiacze Gabek. Antologia greckich opowiadan morskich. Wybor, przeklad, wstep i aneks biograficzny Nikos Chadzinikolaou* (1981). *Nygrekiska berättare. Sammanställningoch översättning Senta Hadjópoulos Slöör* (1964).

Helen Dendrinou Kolias

Nathalie Sarraute
1900–

Born 1900, Ivanovo-Voznessensk, Russia
Genre(s): novel, essay, drama
Language(s): French

Nathalie Sarraute was born in Ivanovo-Voznessensk, Russia, in 1900. She grew up in a milieu of Russian intellectuals: her mother published numerous novels under a masculine pseudonym, and her father, an industrialist, encouraged her interest in scholarly achievements. Her parents divorced when Nathalie was just two. She spent her early childhood with her mother in France and spent vacations with her father in Russia and Switzerland. When she was eight, she moved to Paris with her father and lived with him and her stepmother permanently.

Nathalie Sarraute was a brilliant student at the Sorbonne (B.A. in English), at Oxford (where she started a B.A. in history), and Berlin (where she studied sociology), and was fluent in Russian, French, German, and English. In 1922 she entered the University of Paris Law School, where she met Raymond Sarraute, whom she married three years later. She was a member of the Paris bar from 1925 to 1941, and had three daughters.

In 1932 she wrote a few texts, which she published in 1939 as *Tropismes* (Tropisms). Her work had a favorable welcome from Jean-Paul Sartre and Max Jacob but otherwise was unnoticed. During World War II, she hid from the Germans in a little town near Paris. She took the name of Nicole Sauvage, and posed as her own daughters' governess. During the war she met Jean-Paul Sartre, who wrote the preface for her second novel, *Portrait d'un Inconnu* (Portrait of a Man Unknown), finished in 1946, and published in 1948.

Although she refuses this label to her work (or any other label), Nathalie Sarraute is considered a pioneer of the "New Novel" school. Like the other writers of this school, she demands an active collaboration from the reader, reflects on the creative act that produces the work within the work itself, and uses new methods aimed at renewal of the genre of the novel. Her many theoretical essays present literature as a search for new ways of perceiving reality and insist that form cannot be separated from content. She sees the work of art as an entity in itself, and creating constitutes an end in itself. Thus she does not believe in any didactic use of literature, even for worthwhile causes (this disinvolvement among the New Novelists has caused the most passionate objections from their critics).

Sarraute's work is based on human sensations and relationships although she offers no moral lessons. The reader has to perceive reality through the anonymous "characters'" consciousness, rearrange a fragmented reality, and supply the missing elements of the text (missing words, unfinished sentences, mixture of "real" and imaginary scenes, repetition of the same scenes through different points of view). The suppression of plot and chronology, the disappearance of narrative discourse gives way to immediate, spontaneous, and ordinary dialogues (conversations and "subconversations") between undefined, interchangeable characters presented as "she," "he," "I" or "we."

Whereas the New Novelists have an obsession with objective description (in which the critics see an aim to the "reification of the external world), Sarraute's work is centered on what Robbe-Grillet has called a "psychology of the depth," or interior movements and changes. Her earliest novels presented the tensions and conflicts threatening family members. Her later works unmask the danger of social fear, ignorance, and intolerance for individuals. In her latest novel, *Enfance* (1983; Childhood), for the first time in eighty-three years, she explores her own "tropisms," her own contradictory feelings, by writing about her childhood and her personal relationships with her father, mother, and stepmother. As in her other works (and this has been a reproach often made to her) she talks only about herself, but more openly, and even more deeply. She unveils what hides human anxiety (certitudes, hopes, traditions, dogma), and speaks to and about every human being. According to Claude Mauriac, she, "of all living writers, is the one who has most profoundly and fundamentally renewed our knowledge of mankind." Her works have been translated into 23 languages.

Works

Tropismes (1939). *Portrait d'un Inconnu* (1948). *Mancreau* (1953). *Le Planetarium* (1959). *Les Fruits d'or* (1963). *Le silence, suivi de Le Mensonge* (1967). *Entre la vie at la mort* (1968). *Isma,* suivi de *Le Silence* et *Le Mensonge* (1970). *Vous les entendez* (1972). *C'est beau* (1973). *Disent les imbéciles* (1976). *Elle est là* (1978). *Enfance* (1983). *Nathalie Sarraute* (1987). *Tu ne t'aimes pas* (1989). *Le Silence* (1993).

Michèle M. Magill

Albertine Sarrazin
1937–1967

Born September 1937, Algiers
Died July 10, 1967, Montpellier
Genre(s): novel
Language(s): French

In September 1937, a newborn baby was abandoned at the "Bureau d'Assistance Publique" in Algiers. She was named Albertine Damien. At age two she was adopted by a middle-aged couple. As an adolescent, she was a brilliant, but undisciplined, student and her adoptive parents decided to place her at *Le.Bon Pasteur.* She escaped from this school of correction and hitchhiked to Paris, where she became a prostitute. Hoping to give up that kind of life, she attempted a hold-up that failed, and was condemned to seven years in prison. She escaped by jumping over a wall, and broke the bone called "l'astragale (astragalus), which is the title of her most famous work. A passer-by, Julien Sarrazin, helped her, hid and nursed her: two years later they got married. They both spent much of their time in prison, and though their life together was brief, their love has become legendary.

While in jail, Albertine wrote two novels, *La Cavale* (On the Run), and *L'Astragale,* which instantly became bestsellers in the fall of 1965. In 1966, she received the Prix des Quatre-Jurys in Tunis. Her works are mainly autobiographical: they evoke her life in jail and its boredom and her thirst and passion for life when she is free. The themes of love, desire, and death are dominant in all of them. Though writing was always a passion for her, it became her way of escaping beyond the bars, if only in her mind, and gave her a sense of freedom she may not have found otherwise.

Her happiness, money, and fame were short-lived: on July 10, 1967, she died during surgery in Montpellier. She was not yet thirty. Her husband sued the doctors, who were found guilty of grave negligence. With the money, he opened a publishing house for the unedited texts left by Albertine.

Since her death, her work has inspired many critical studies and dissertations, in France and abroad. Albertine the novelist, the poet, the moralist might even be surpassed by the epistolarian. Her letters to Julien and her friends, written quickly and spontaneously, reveal a style as refined as in her other texts. The abandoned child of Algiers is now considered a true classical writer, whose liveliness, originality, humor, and courage are widely admired.

Works

Journal de Prison (1959). *La Cavale* (1965). *L'Astragale* (1965). *La Traversière* (1966). *Oeuvres* (novels, letters, poems) (1967). *Poèmes* (1969). *Lettres à Julien 1958–1960* (1971). *Lettres de la Vie Littéraire* (1974). *Bibiche* (short story). *Le Passe-Peine* (diary) 1949–1967 (1976). *Biftonsde Prison* (1977).

Articles: *Les Lettres Françaises* (Jan. 1967; July 1967; July 1969; June 1972). Le Figaro Litteraire (Nov. 11, 1965; Dec. 1, 1966; July 17, 1967; May 20, 1972). *Le Magazine Litteraire* (Dec. 1972; March 1972). *Les Nouvelles Littéraires* (March 1966; July 1967). *L'Express* (Jan. 2–8, 1967; December 18–22, 1968). *Revue des Deux-Mondes* (Jan. 1966; Jan. 1969). *The Times Literary Supplement* (Feb. 3, 1966; Jan. 12, 1967). *The New York Times Book Review* (June 9, 1968, Jan. 1966). *Esprit* (Jan. 1966). *Réalités* (Nov. 1965.). *Le Monde* (Jan. 13, 1967). *Elle* (Feb. 7, 1972.)

Translations in almost twenty languages. *L'Astragale* was adapted for cinema by G. Casaril in 1968 and *La Cavale* by M. Mitroni in 1971.

Michèle M. Magill

Catherina Anna Maria de Savornin Lohman
1868–1930

Born January 1, 1868, Assen, The Netherlands
Died September 23, 1930, The Hague
Genre(s): novel, article, essay
Language(s): Dutch

Anna de Savornin Lohman was one of a few women authors who, at the turn of the century, wrote about the social and ethical position of women in contemporary society. Born into the Hague upper class, she passed a cheerless childhood and youth. She was thwarted in her desire to pursue higher education (a course of life open only to her brothers). She lost some of her close relatives too soon and suffered disappointment in love. When her father was financially ruined, she was forced to earn her living and turned to writing.

In her numerous novels, essays, pamphlets, and literary reviews, she took a firm and controversial stand not only on the "woman's question," as it was then called but also on matters of literature and religion, and she used her sharp pen to relentlessly attack the fake propriety and stern Calvinism of the top circles in The Hague.

Disillusionment with the world, often culminating in bitterness, and profound doubts about the rigorous faith of her parents run through her novels. She is very effective in portraying a slice in the life of a number of closely related characters (relatives, friends, couples), often without any climax of plot line, and in observing the way in which they cope with the growing awareness that human existence is essentially flawed. Their doubts about the discrepancy between the misery of daily life and the ideals of their faith, between positive rational thinking and mystic belief are best pictured in her most successful novel, which carries the significant title *Vragensmoede* (1896; Question-weary). Central in the book is the couple Uytweerde, young ambitious Calvinists—he, politically, she socially, active. The birth of a retarded child upsets their blind belief in a God whom the wife especially comes to see as utterly cruel and loveless. It is typical for Savornin Lohman that the character who deals best with the imperfections of human existence is the serene and humane agnostic Dr. Vrede, an old friend of the couple and, as they see it, an unfortunate unbeliever.

Savornin Lohman's opinions on the position of woman in the social fabric are best expressed in *De liefde in de vrouwenquestie* (1898; Love in the Woman's Question) and *Vrouwenliefde in de moderne literatuur* (1902; Woman's Love in Modern Literature). *De liefde in de vrouwenquestie* is a pamphlet partly written in response to the novel *Hilda van Suylenburg* (1898) in which the feminist author Cécile Geokoop pictured two women who combined a successful career with a happy marriage. Though Savornin Lohman was an advocate of the equal work–equal pay principle and a defender of women's education, the latter because that would make it possible for women to earn a living if they had to (think of her own plight), she considered the pursuit of a career to be chiefly a substitute for love. A successful combination of love and career is impossible, and women who wish to imitate men are ridiculous. Woman's highest aspiration is to find a man she can love with unconditional surrender.

But Savornin Lohman also fulminated against the marriages of convenience of which she professed to see too many in the Hague upper class. She exposed it as immoral for mothers to promote a union between their innocent daughters and men too much about town but blessed with wealth and title. On the other hand, she went as far as advocating free love (though she would not always admit it), curiously enough in the configuration one man–more women, her rationale being that too many women were leading a lonely life or were trapped in a loveless union.

The most extreme illustration of her conviction that woman's highest happiness is the love for a man is the novel *Het ééne noodige* (1897; The One and Only Need). It is the curious and somewhat morbid story of Katie de Reth who actually "falls in love" with and "devotes" her life to a man she never meets. On the news of his death she burns her poetry and commits suicide.

Savornin Lohman also wrote many book reviews, some of which were later collected in *Over boeken en schrijvers* (1903; On Books and Writers). She had no affinity at all with the avant-garde of her time and their art for art's sake principle, but she persistently admired writers who wrote openly about sensuality and sex, especially from the woman's point of view.

Her memoirs, *Herinneringen* (1909), were candid, personal and, at times, high-tempered. From 1903 till 1917 she edited *De Hollandsche Lelie*, a woman's weekly. In her very last book, *Levensraadselen* (1921; Life's Mysteries), published when she had been widowed after a short but happy union (during which she had given up writing), she held a much more cheerful view of her fellow human beings than in the rest of her work. Instead of perceiving God as cruel and loveless, she now saw him as loving and forgiving.

A restless and belligerent mind, Savorin Lohman was a widely read and self-made intellectual whose writing lacked discipline. Her style and language are often careless (partly due to the fact that she had to be prolific to earn a living) and larded with needless repetitions. Her nonchalance, unchecked emotions, and bitterness tended to undercut the effectiveness of her polemics, and she was an easy victim of the derision of male colleagues. She was, however, a fluent storyteller and a sharp observer, who had a keen understanding of the conflicts between men and women and between children and parents. Her fiction can be read as a series of novels of manners mirroring Dutch upper-class life at the turn of the century.

Though Lohman's viewpoints on the position of woman are certainly dated today, she should be appreciated in her own time when ideas about women pursuing a career or women capable of sensual love were only slowly coming to fruition. She was also immensely popular at the time and therefore deserves a space in reference works and women's studies larger than the one usually allotted to her.

Works

Miserere (1895). *Vragensmoede* (1896). *Het ééne noodige* (1897). *Levens-ernst* (1897). *De liefde in de vrouwenquestie* (1898). *Geloof* (1899). *Naschrift op de liefde in de vrouwenquestiei* (1899). *Smarten* (1900). *Na het ontwaken* (1901). *Vrouwenliefde in de moderne literatuur* (1902). *Over boeken en schrijvers* (1903). *Gelukswegen* (1903). *Jonge roeping* (1903). *Letterkundig leven* (1904). *Van het inwendige leven* (1904). *Liefde* (1905). *Kleine levensdingen* (1905). *In den opgang* (1906). *Uit de sfeer gerukt* (1908). *Herinneringen* (1909). *Uit Christelijke kringen* (1911). *Zedelijkheids-apostelen* (1912). *Levensraadselen* (1921). *Wat nooit sterft* (n.d.). *Om de eere Gods* (n.d.).

Ria Vanderauwera

Dorothy L. Sayers
1893–1957

Born June 13, 1893, Oxford, England
Died December 17, 1957, Witham, Essex
Genre(s): novel, short story, translation, drama, essay, biography
Language(s): English

Sayers is best known for her Lord Peter Wimsey detective novels, witty mysteries that portray English society between the wars. The only child of The Rev. Henry Sayers and Helen Leigh Sayers, she was born June 13, 1893, in Oxford. After an isolated childhood, largely in the Fens, she went to Somerville College in 1912; many of her contemporaries at Oxford died in the trenches of World War I. In 1915 she won first class honors in modern languages but no degree because of her sex; in 1920 she was awarded both a B.A. and an M.A. with the first group of women to be granted degrees from the University of Oxford. Blackwell's published her first work, two volumes of poetry, *Op. I* (1915) and *Catholic Tales and Christian Songs* (1918); she worked at Blackwell's as an editor, taught at a boys' school in southern France, and then in 1922 joined Benson's Advertising Agency in Lon-

don as a copywriter. In 1924 she managed to hide her pregnancy from her family and close friends; after her marriage to Captain Oswald Arthur (Mac) Fleming in 1926, she legally adopted her own son without revealing his parentage.

Whose Body?, a rather conventional detective puzzle, introduced Lord Peter Wimsey in 1923. Wimsey's flippant delight in the corpse was gradually replaced by an attitude of moral responsibility in the later books. In *Clouds of Witness* (1926) he saved his brother, the Duke of Denver, from a murder conviction by brilliant sleuthing that included a daring cross-Atlantic flight just prior to Lindbergh's. *Unnatural Death* (1927, *The Dawson Pedigree* in the U.S.) introduced Wimsey's resourceful ally, Miss Climpson. *The Unpleasantness at the Bellona Club* (1928) concerns the effects of World War I on veterans, a theme that recurred in the series as Lord Peter's own war service and subsequent breakdown were gradually revealed. (Sayers's own husband suffered psychologically from his war experience; she supported him for most of their marriage, which lasted until his death in 1950.) By 1928, Lord Peter had made her famous. In that year she published *Lord Peter Views the Body*, a collection of twelve short stories, and edited *Great Short Stories of Detection, Mystery and Horror* (1928, *The Omnibus of Crime* in the U.S.), supplying a significant essay analyzing the detective tradition.

When her father died in 1928, leaving her a small legacy, Sayers bought a home in Witham, Essex, a pleasant train journey from her London publishers. With Anthony Berkeley, G.K. Chesterton, and other mystery writers, she founded the Detection Club, complete with rituals such as swearing a sacred oath on a skull named "Eric." She also completed *Tristan in Brittany*, a translation of the twelfth-century *Romance of Tristan* (1929). The following year she collaborated on *The Documents in the Case* with "Robert Eustace" (pseudonym, probably for Eustace Fraser Rawlins; see Trevor Hall's book on Sayers) and published *Strong Poison*, the novel that introduced Harriet Vane as a mystery writer suspected of poisoning her lover. In 1931 Sayers published *The Five Red Herrings*, edited another volume of detective stories, and collaborated on *The Floating Admiral*, a detective parody written by members of the Detection Club, including G.K. Chesterton and Agatha Christie. *Have His Carcase* (1932) was a less successful Wimsey/Vane story; leaving out the "love interest" Sayers wrote two masterful mysteries, *Murder Must Advertise* (1933), set in an advertising agency rather like Benson's, and *The Nine Tailors* (1934), set in the Fen country where she had spent her childhood.

After giving a speech at the Somerville College Gaudy (reunion) in 1934, she published *Gaudy Night* (1935), a Wimsey/Vane novel set in a women's college at Oxford. Her best novel, it focuses on the theme of intellectual integrity and explores the conflict between head and heart. By telling the story from Harriet Vane's perspective, Sayers is able to present Wimsey as a fully rounded character, beset with fears about the European situation and about his own aging; the book ends with Wimsey's famous proposal in Latin on Magdalen bridge. In the following year, Sayers collaborated with her friend Muriel St. Clare Byrne to produce *Busman's Honeymoon* on stage (1937), portraying the start of Harriet's life as Lady Peter Wimsey; the subsequent novel version was appropriately subtitled "A Love Story with Detective Interruptions." That was the end of the published Wimsey saga, except for some short stories and a few wartime essays and advertisements. Later her friend Wilfred Scott-Giles published *The Wimsey Family*, telling the history of the Wimseys since 1066, a saga that Sayers and her friends had made up as a game. An unfinished Wimsey/Vane novel, *Thrones, Dominations*, begins just after the honeymoon; the manuscript is in the Marion E. Wade Collection at Wheaton College (Illinois).

In 1937 Sayers "turned from her life of crime," as one schoolboy put it, and devoted her writing to theological drama. *The Zeal of Thy House* followed her friend T.S. Eliot's *Murder in the Cathedral* at the Canterbury Festival (1937). Other dramas include *The Devil to Pay*, a reworking of the Faust legend for the Canterbury Festival (1939); *The Just Vengeance* (Litchfield Festival 1946); *The Man Born to Be King*, a series of 12 radio dramas on the life of Christ, broadcast in monthly segments in 1941 and 1942 and published 1943; and *The Emperor Constantine* (Colchester Festival Play, 1951). She also wrote several radio plays for children; *Love All*, a farce staged in London (1940); several volumes of short stories featuring Lord Peter or her other detective, Montague Egg; a book on aesthetics, *The Mind of the Maker* (1941); a series of witty essays on theology and social issues, including feminism, a translation of *The Song of Roland* (1957); and an unfinished biography of Wilkie Collins (1977).

Her final years were primarily devoted to Dante. One night on her way to the air raid shelter, she grabbed a copy of *The Divine Comedy* in the original Italian and was entranced. She subsequently translated *Hell* (1949) and *Purgatory* (1955) for Penguin classics in a lively *terza rima*, documented with erudite and witty notes. At the invitation of her friend Barbara Reynolds, Sayers gave a series of lectures at Cambridge, later published as *Introductory Papers on Dante* (1954) and *Further Papers on Dante* (1957). While at work on the *Paradiso*, she died suddenly in her home on December 17, 1957; the translation was completed by her friend Barbara Reynolds.

Although she wrote in many genres, Sayers's work is unified by a concern with craftsmanship, with the value of worthwhile work done well. Appropriately, her memorial tablet in Somerville College is inscribed, "Praise Him that He hath made man in His own image, a maker and craftsman like Himself."

Works

Op. I (1915). *Catholic Tales and Christian Songs* (1918). *Whose Body?* (1923). *Clouds of Witness* (1926). *Unnatural Death* (1927). *The Unpleasantness at the Bellona Club* (1928). *Lord Peter Views the Body* (1928). (trans.) *Tristan in Brittany* (1929). (with Robert Eustace) *The Documents in the Case* (1930). *Strong Poison* (1930). *The Five Red Herrings* (1931). (with others) *The Floating Admiral* (1931). *Have His Carcase* (1932). *Murder Must Advertise* (1933). *Hangman's Holiday* (1933). *The Nine Tailors* (1934). *Gaudy Night* (1935). (as edited by M. Wimsey) *Papers Relating to the Family of Wimsey* (1936). *Busman's Honeymoon* (1937). *The Zeal of Thy House* (1937). *The Greatest Drama Ever Staged* (1938). *Double Death* (1939). *Strong Meat* (1939). *The Devil to Pay* (1939). *In the Teeth of the Evidence* (1939). *He That Should Come* (1939). *Begin Here* (1940). *Creed or Chaos?* (1940). *Love All* (1940). *The Mysterious English* (1941). *The Mind of the Maker* (1941). *Why Work?* (1942). *The Other Six Deadly Sins* (1943). *The Man Born to Be King* (1943). *Even the Parrot* (1944). *The Just Vengeance* (1946). *Unpopular Opinions* (1946). *Making Sense of the Universe* (1946). *Creed or Chaos and Other Essays* (1947). *Four Sacred Plays* (1948). *The Lost Tools of Learning* (1948). (trans.) *The Comedy of Dante Alighieri the Florentine: Cantica I: Hell* (1949). *The Emperor Constantine* (1951). *The Days of Christ's Coming* (1953). *Introductory Papers on Dante* (1954). (trans.) *The Comedy of Dante Alighieri the Florentine: Cantica II: Purgatory* (1955). *Further Papers on Dante* (1957). (trans.) *The Song of Roland* (1957). *The Comedy of Dante Alighieri the Florentine: Cantica III: Paradise* (1962). *The Poetry of Search and the Poetry of Statement* (1963). *Christian Letters to a Post-Christian World* (1969). *Lord Peter: A Collection of All the Lord Peter Wimsey Stories* (1972). *Talboys* (1972). *A Matter of Eternity* (1973). *Striding Folly* (1973). *Wilkie Collins: A Critical and Biographical Study* (1977). *The Wimsey Family* (1977).

Margaret P. Hannay

Solveig Margareta von Schoultz
1907–

Born August 5, 1907, Borgå, Sweden
Genre(s): children's literature, poetry, short story, drama, autobiography
Language(s): Swedish

Solveig von Schoultz is a very sensitive writer, whose imagination derives from lyricism, but she transfers her keen application of associative language to her prose works as well. She is an untiring observer of human relationships, above all relationships between women and between mother and child. Her descriptions of relations between men and women are acutely seen from the woman's point of view.

Her very first book was a book for children, *Petra och silverapan* (1932; Petra and the Silver Monkey); it was followed by *December* (1937).

Her first three volumes of poetry, *Min timme* (1940; My Hour), *Den bortvända glädjen* (1943; The Froward Joy) and *Eko av ett rop* (1945; Echo of a Cry) are filled with a warm feeling for life. In these works, her poems still have rhymes; perhaps she needed them at the time to harness her fountainlike fantasy. But from *Nattlig äng* (1949; Night Meadow) on, her language is more serene and controlled, and the rhymes have disappeared.

In her first collection of short stories, her psychological approach and fine sense of shades in people's reactions already establish themselves; later they become the hallmark of her prose. *Ingenting ovanligt* (1947; Nothing Special) was followed by short stories in which the tone is more experimental, as, for example, in *Närmare någon* (1951; Closer to Someone), but in *Den blomstertid* (1958; The Time of Summer Flowers) she reverts to a style that comes naturally to her, exact and penetrating, but womanly and warm. She decidedly concentrates on what she knows best: the feelings, reactions, and moods of women, their tensions and reflections. Women are constantly in focus: she studies children, young girls and maturing women, middle-aged women, and old women. She has also written a study of her two daughters, called *De sju dagarna* (1942; The Seven Days), referring to the seven days of creation in which a human being matures. This book is one of the most intriguing and most informative books in Swedish literature on the relation between parents and child.

In the series of related short stories, *Ansa och samvetet* (1954; Ansa and Conscience), she uses material from her own childhood and from that of her girls. Ansa is finding her feet in the incomprehensible world of adults; the stories cover a child's experience of guilt and remorse, of anxiety, and of the need to be cared for.

Twenty years later Solveig von Schoultz reverted to autobiographical material in *Där står du* (1973; There You Stand), and in *Porträtt av Hanna* (1978; Portrait of Hanna); the latter covers a liberation process from her mother, Hanna.

In *Allt sker nu* (1952; All Happens Now) a new independence asserts itself; this book is more concerned with clarifying her own stands, as a woman, than the earlier ones. It uses more stringent language, a feature that becomes fully apparent in *Nätet* (1956; The Net), her lyric masterpiece. *Terrassen* (1959; The Terrace) is an experiment in dense Japanese form, and in the subsequent *De fyra flöjtspelarna* (1975; The Four Fluteplayers) and *Bortom träden hörs havet* (1980; Beyond the Trees, Hark—the Sea) all irrelevant items have vanished, and the language carries weight in every word.

Solveig von Schoultz has also written plays, especially for radio and television, but the short stories and sometimes almost novella-like stories and lyrics are her proper media.

Her more recent short stories cover *Även dina kameler* (1965; Your Camels, Too), *Rymdbruden* (1970; Space Bride), *Somliga mornar* (1976; Certain Mornings), and *Kolteckning, ofullbordad* (1983; Charcoal Drawing, Unfinished). Personal relations, a wide variety of them, remain her focal interest. The relationships are looked at from the woman's point of view: the wife's perspective, the mother's perspective.

Solveig von Schoultz wrote as she did long before the feminist movement came to the fore, and by its representatives she was at first criticized for conservatism. Now winds have changed, and she is recognized for the strength her female characters expose, admittedly a maternal kind of strength, as she looks upon women as "mothergods," encompassing everything in their strength. There seems to be a constantly ongoing debate about women and their relations to the surrounding human beings in all her works. In that sense, she is one of the first "feminist" writers in this country. She herself declares that lyricism is her mother tongue, a statement that holds good for her prose style as well.

Works

Prose: *Petra och silverapan* [Petra and the Silver Monkey] (1932). *December* (1937). *De sju dagarna* [The Seven Days] (1942). *Nalleresan* [The Bear Journey, A Children's Story] (1944). *Ingenting ovanligt*

[Nothing Special] (1947). *Närmare någon* [Closer to Someone] (1951). *Ansa och samvetet* [Ansa and Conscience] (1954). *Den blomstertid* [The Time of Summer Flowers] (1958). *Millaskolan* [The Milla School, A Children's Book] (1960). *Även dina kameler* [Your Camels, Too] (1965). *Rymdbruden* [Space Bride] (1979). *Där står du* [There You Stand] (1973). *Somliga mornar* [Certain Mornings] (1976). *Porträtt av Hanna* [Portrait of Hanna] (1978). *Kolteckning, ofullbordad* [Charcoal Drawing, Unfinished] (1983). *Ingen dag förgäves* [No Day in Vain] (1984).

Poetry: *Min timme* [My Hour] (1940). *Den bortvända glädjen* [The Froward Joy] (1943). *Eko av ett rop* [Echo of a Cry] (1945). *Nattlig äng* [Night Meadow] (1949). *Allt sker nu* [All Happens Now] (1952). *Nätet* [The Net] (1956). *Terrassen* [The Terrace] (1959). *Sänk ditt ljus* [Lower Your Light] (1963). *Klippbok* [Cuttings] (1968). *De fyra flöjtspelarna* [The Four Fluteplayers] (1975). *Bortom träden hörs havet* [Beyond the Trees, Hark—the Sea] (1980). *En enda minut* [One Single Minute] (1981). A number of short plays for radio performance.

Gunnel Cleve

Olive Emilie Albertina Schreiner
1855–1920

a.k.a. Mrs. S.C., Ralph Iron
Born March 24, 1855, Wittebergen, Basutoland
(now Lesotho), South Africa
Died December 11, 1920, Wynberg
Genre(s): novel, essay, letters
Language(s): English

Known primarily for her feminist novel *The Story of an African Farm* (1883) and for *Woman and Labour* (1911), the "Bible" of the early twentieth-century British women's suffrage movement, Schreiner was probably the first white woman to write novels about the African colonial situation.

The ninth of her missionary parents' twelve children and named for three dead brothers, she was often estranged from her religious family. She claimed that she became a mystical "free thinker" after the death of her younger sister and that this early impulse was further shaped by reading the works of Darwin, Herbert Spencer, John Stuart Mill, Shelley, Goethe, and Emerson, from whom she probably derived her pseudonym, Ralph Iron. She had a little bit of educa-

tion at home but never attended public school. When her family's home broke up because of poverty, she was shuttled between older siblings until she left to become a governess. It was at this time that she began to write seriously. In seven years of loneliness and isolation, she wrote the bulk of three novels—*Undine* (1929), *The Story of an African Farm*, and *From Man to Man* (1926)—the manuscripts of which she took with her when she left South Africa for England in 1881.

The Story of an African Farm has two major sections, childhood and adulthood, which are separated by a long, meditative passage about the birth and growth of a mystical belief shared by the novel's central characters, Lyndall and Waldo. Lyndall's understanding of Victorian culture's construction of masculinity and femininity is both passionate and profound. However, like the heroine Rebekah in *From Man to Man*, Lyndall seems unable to act on her feminist impulses, choosing instead a brief, masochistic liaison, which ends in her shame and death. While her best male characters often incorporate Victorian women's tasks into their own sense of work—they nurture the women they love and think of their creations as offspring—her ugliest, most vicious characters are usually women and many of her women characters, such as Em in *African Farm* and Bertie in *From Man to Man*, seem emotionally as well as economically tied to a system that treats them as commodities for men's aggrandizement and exchange.

Soon after it was published, *The Story of an African Farm* pushed Schreiner to the center of London's literary and intellectual circles. She was an early member of the Men and Women's Club, an elite group that met weekly to discuss sexual reform and "sex morality," and she became close friends with group members Edward Carpenter, Havelock Ellis, and Karl Pearson. Her intense and dependent relationship with Ellis in particular is traced in *The Letters of Olive Schreiner* (1924). Schreiner chose to live among prostitutes while in London, but she seems to have had few close women friends, with the notable exceptions of Eleanor Marx and the suffragist Constance Lytton.

Schreiner suffered from severe attacks of asthma, which may have been psychological in origin and which often prevented her from writing, talking, or traveling. Although she struggled to finish *From Man to Man* and an introduction to Mary Wollstonecraft's *A Vindication of the Rights of Woman* (1792), the only works she completed in England were short, allegorical pieces, collected in *Dreams* (1890), *Dream Life and Real Life* (1893), and the posthumous *Stories, Dreams and Allegories* (1923). Although her husband radically edited the original letters and destroyed what he did not publish, the *Letters* and *The Life of Olive Schreiner* (1924) remain important sources in understanding her work.

When she returned to South Africa in 1889, her writing became primarily political. *Trooper Peter Halket of Mashonaland* (1897) is a bitter parody of Cecil Rhodes in which a Dutch soldier sacrifices his own life to free a black man who has been convicted and sentenced to death because of British racism. Here, as in *An English South African's View of the Situation* (1899) and *Thoughts on South Africa* (1923), Schreiner's criticism of antinative colonial policies was radical for her time. She claimed that blacks act as a laboring class on which the South African economy depends, that race is a metaphysical as well as a physical reality, and that women understand what unites the races better than men because of their common experience of mothering. On the other hand, Schreiner tended to idealize her own culture, particularly the traditional beliefs and roles of Boer women, in her attempt to imagine an interracial South Africa. In her later years she remained in contact with the militant suffragists and with Gandhi's nonviolent *satyagraha* movement. She broke with the Cape Colony Women's Enfranchisement League when it failed to endorse native men's and women's, along with white women's, suffrage.

Although it is no longer well known, Schreiner's *Woman and Labour* was read by thousands of women in prewar England. *Woman and Labour* brought together her allegorical and political impulses; she considered it her most significant work. Stories are told of suffragettes' reading *Woman and Labour* to one another in jail and of women's "conversion" to feminism from reading this work. The work addresses women's emotional complicity in their economic oppression, making scathing attacks on what Schreiner calls "parasitic" upper-class women and prostitutes. As the title suggests, *Woman and Labour* tends to elide women's labor in the work force with their reproductive labor implying that the knowledge gained from mothering should both enable and transform other kinds of professional work. She argues that men and women will benefit equally from women's improved economic status and that equality will lead to improved sexual relations between women and men. Many of her arguments continue to inform contemporary feminist theory.

When Schreiner married Samuel Cronwright in 1894, he changed his name to Cronwright-Schreiner, but for most purposes she did not. Because of her asthma and her political involvement, she spent long periods of time away from her husband. A month after her fortieth birthday, she gave birth to a child that lived less than a day. This dead daughter remained a haunting presence in her life and later writing, and she chose to be buried next to the child overlooking the *kopje* that inspired *The Story of an African Farm*. Schreiner has been an influence on numerous white African writers, including Doris Lessing and Nadine Gordimer.

Works

The Story of an African Farm (1883). *Dreams* (1890). *Dream Life and Real Life* (1893, republished 1977). *The Political Situation* (with S.C. Cronwright-Schreiner, 1896). *Trooper Peter Halket of Mashonaland* (1897, republished 1974). *An English South African's View of the Situation. Words in Season* (1899). *A Letter on the Jew* (1906). *Closer Union* (1909). *Olive Schreiner's Thoughts about Women* (1909). *Woman and Labour* (1911, republished 1979). *Thoughts on South Africa* (1923). *Stories, Dreams and Allegories* (1923). *The Letters of Olive Schreiner*, ed. S.C. Cronwright-Schreiner (1924). *From Man to Man; or, Perhaps Only . . .* (1926, republished 1982). *Undine* (1929). *A Track to the Water's Edge: The Olive Schreiner Reader*, ed. H. Thurman (1973), *Olive Schreiner Reader*, ed. C. Barash (1987). *Letters, Vol. I: 1871–1899*, ed. R. Rive (1987).

Carol L. Barash

Anna-Maria van Schurman
1607–1678

Born 1607, Cologne, Germany
Died 1678, Wieuwerd (Dutch Frisia)
Genre(s): translation, poetry, treatise
Language(s): Dutch, Latin, French, others

Called a "marvel" and the "star of Utrecht," Anna-Maria van Schurman was considered the most learned woman of her age. She was highly accomplished both in the arts and in a great number of scientific disciplines. The living proof of women's intellectual capacities, she supported the idea of education and scholarship for women yet held a conservative view of the feminine role in society.

The daughter of staunchly Reformed parents, Anna-Maria grew up in an orthodox Calvinist milieu. Her exceptional artistic talents and intellectual abilities manifested themselves very early. She was given the same education as her brothers, and under the tutelage of her father she learned quickly and eagerly a wide variety of subjects: arithmetic, geography, astronomy, music, Latin, Greek, Hebrew, and a large number of Oriental and modern languages as well as theology, which became increasingly important for her. To avoid persecution, the family moved from Cologne to Utrecht in 1615. They moved to Franeker in 1623, so that Anna-Maria's brothers could attend the university there, but went back to Utrecht when her father died shortly thereafter. When the new university of Utrecht opened its doors, rector Voetius arranged for Anna-Maria to attend the lectures unseen by the other (male) students. Under Voetius, she studied languages and theology and began gradually to drop art and poetry as frivolous pursuits. The death of her mother in 1637 left her with the care of two blind and old aunts, who demanded her full attention. Though she was by now known all over Europe and great thinkers like Descartes made a point of looking her up when in Utrecht, she turned away from her scholarship to devote herself to her family and became increasingly involved with the saintly Pietist, Labadie, whose community she joined and followed, from Amsterdam to Herford and Altona in Germany to Wieuwerd in Friesland, where she died completely detached from Europe's intellectual scene.

Despite her glorious accomplishments as an artist and a scholar, Anna-Maria van Schurman remained modest and reluctant to display her gifts. She would not have published anything were it not for the insistence and pressure of her friends. Her *Amica Dissertatio* . . . (1638; Friendly Dissertation . . .) is written in scholastic format and debates whether the study of letters befits a Christian woman. A careful and conservative defender of the feminist cause in the early seventeenth century, van Schurman advocates education and knowledge mostly for those women whose hands are free of household tasks, and warns that learning should never become the basis for claiming one's superiority. Moreover, the desire to glorify God should always be in the student's mind. In *Eucleria* (1675), her autobiography written during her stay with the Labadist community in Altona and Wieuwerd, she explains her reasons for joining Labadie's group, a sort of commune, thus answering her contemporaries' objections to this step. *Over de Paelsteen onzes Levens* (1639; About the End of Our Life) is a theological treatise that attempts to answer the question of whether divine decisions about the end of our life are changeable. The author shows that everything depends on God's unchangeable decision and that the term of our life is fixed. In *Mysterium Magnum* (1699), she contemplates the future of the divine kingdom.

Though Anna-Maria van Schurman renounced in her old age most of what she had achieved and promoted earlier on, she made a permanent contribution to the cause of female education.

Works

Amica Dissertatio inter Annam Mariam Schurmanniam et Andr. Rivetum de capacitate ingenii muliebris ad scientias (1638; 1641). *Over de Paelsteen onzes Levens* (1639). *Opuscula Hebraea, Graeca, Latina, Gallica, Prosaica et Metrica* (1648). *Eucleria seu melioris partis electio* (1675). *Mysterium Magnum* (1699). *Uitbreiding ov er de drie eerste Capittels van Genesis and Vertoog van het Geestelijk huwelijk van Christus met de Geloovigen* (1732).

Translations: *Question Célèbre, s'il est nécessaire, ou non, que les filles soient scavantes* [*Amica Dissertatio*], tr. G. Colletet (1646). *De Vitae Termino* [*Paelsteen van den Tijt onzes Levens*] (1639). *Eucleria of Uitkiezing van het Beste Deel* [*Eucleria seu melioris partis electio*] (1684).

Maya Bijvoet

Alice Schwartzer
1942–

Born 1942, Wuppertal, West Germany
Genre(s): essay, documentary
Language(s): German

Alice Schwartzer has become known in the German-speaking countries and France in particular since the 1960s through her almost radical feminism and her provocative attitude toward everything "male."

Born in 1942 in Wuppertal, Alice Schwartzer worked as a journalist and publicist, in Paris as much as in Germany. The major aim of her work is the analysis of the female position in modern postwar Germany, especially in areas where women obviously have never enjoyed an equal opportunity, such as in their professional life. In her opinion, women are exploited by employers, husbands, children, the law, and thus, by society in general. Women, the larger part of society, have been made its slaves and outsiders. Schwartzer tries to analyze the reasons for the underprivileged situation of women and sees men not only as woman's counterpart but as woman's arch-enemy. Most of her works are based on interviews and personal statements of women on working conditions, on abortion, or on love.

Her radical attitude provoked Ester Vilar to establish a different perspective; trying to analyze man's behavior, she came to the conclusion that man is woman's victim, calling her most famous book: *Der dressierte Mann* (The Trained Man). In a famous television discussion in Paris in the 1960s Ester Vilar and Alice Schwartzer had the opportunity to present and exchange their opinions, but the discussion culminated in mutual insults, misunderstanding, and intolerance.

In *Frauen gegen den Paragraphen zweihundertachtzehn* (1973; Women Against Paragraph 218), Schwartzer collected opinions and statements of women on the abortion paragraph in the German criminal code: combining individual viewpoints with short personal comments, Alice Schwartzer tries to establish that women have a right to decide what happens to their own bodies and are unwilling to let men tell them what to do. Schwartzer sees the abortion paragraph as an unjustified intervention from the part of man. *Frauenarbeit-Frauenbefreiung* (1973; Women's Labor–Women's Liberation) analyzes the exploitation women experience on the job with documents and personal statements of working women.

The book that established her fame, *Der "kleine" Unterschied und seine großen Folgen* (The "Little" Difference and Its Big Consequences), marks the beginning of the women's liberation discussion in Germany in a more radical vein. It discusses, like almost all of her works, the "little" biological difference that supposedly justifies the tremendous exploitation of women. *Simone de Beauvoir heute-Gespräche aus zehn Jahren* (Simone de Beauvoir Today) introduced this French feminist and companion of Sartre to the German audience.

Alice Schwartzer is provocative in style, expression, and opinion. Even though her opinions are hardly ever objective, she achieves credibility by giving women the chance of expressing their own opinions and using their statements and these documentary materials to prove her own point and to establish credibility.

Works

Der "kleine" Unterschied und seine großen Folgen. Frauen über sich-Beginn einer Befreiung; Frauen gegen den Paragraphen zweihundertachtzehn; Frauenarbeit-Frauenbefreiung. Praxis Beispiele und Analysen (1973). *Simone de Beauvoir heute-Gespräche aus zehn Jahren; Durch dick und dünn. Mit Leidenschaft: Text 1968–1982* (1982). *So fing es an! Die neue Frauenbewegung* (1983). *Lohn: Liebe. Zum Wert der Frauenbefreiung* (1986).

Translations: *Simone de Beauvoir Today*.

Jutta Hagedorn

Sibylle Schwarz
1621–1638

Born February 14, 1621, Greifswald, Germany
Died July 31, 1638
Genre(s): poetry drama, novella, letters
Language(s): German

Sibylle Schwarz was born on February 14, 1621, and died seventeen years later of dysentery on July 31, 1638. A native of the northern German city of Greifswald, she was the youngest child of upper-class parents, which accounted for her formal education in reading, catechism, music, mathematics, and the memorization of psalms. Schwarz's letters, written in a time when few women read, wrote, or passed on thoughts in print, document additional independent study, tutoring, and exchange of books with her university-educated brothers and mentors, among whom were Greifswald University's mathematics and medicine professor Johann Schoner, logic and metaphysics professor Alexander Christian, and theology professor Barthold Krakewitz. Her work, which includes sonnets, numerous "occasional" poems, a Susanna-drama, a tragedy commemorating the burning of the family's country estate at Fretow, a bucolic novelette, and a number of letters, demonstrates that she could read and write German and translate from Dutch and Latin, and was familiar not only with contemporary German Baroque poetry but also with figures and myths from classical antiquity. Schwarz's father's various civil service positions also brought the family into contact with royalty and nobility, and several of Schwarz's "occasional" poems accordingly celebrate events in their lives, for example, the matriculation of the Duke Ernst von Croy at the University of Greifswald.

Just as social status offered Schwarz an education and powerful connections, so did the family's comfortable economic situation provide a buffer against extreme hardship during the Thirty Years War. When first imperial troops and then Swedish forces descended on Greifswald, Schwarz and other young children were sent to safety at Fretow, which is idealized and eulogized in several of her poems, letters, and dramas as the most beautiful place on earth, a symbol of friendship and the virtuous life. The burning of Fretow was as traumatic for Schwarz as the sudden death of her mother on January 25, 1630. Her father was posted to Stettin from 1629 to 1631, and the Schwarz children, left in Greifswald, were effectively orphans. Care of the household was first turned over to the eldest daughter, widowed Regina, and then, upon her remarriage, to Emerentia, whose nuptials occurred the day Schwarz died from a sudden illness.

Not only a prodigy in producing verse, but also a phenomenon in the sense that she was a female writer and a prolific one at that, Schwarz left as her written legacy two substantial volumes of verse and prose, which total over one hundred and fifty pages. Routinely her efforts go beyond predictable rhyme schemes and themes and exhibit metrical skill, intense communication of feelings, a variety of poetic voices, and mastery of current poetic techniques. On the one hand, Schwarz worked to join the literary establishment, often praising Opitz and consciously emulating him or at the very least drawing from his models. On the other hand, she was aware that she wrote "in a different voice" in her age, as the German Baroque was a time of ornamentation that did not take kindly to women who wanted to be more than ornaments. Schwarz's consciousness of being female in a male literary community gave her an unusual status, as well as access to a group of writers who, critics themselves, were in the position to make judgments about what constituted good and publishable material, yet the little girl dubbed "the Pommeranian Sappho" was viewed by many in somewhat the same manner as Samuel Johnson's talking dog. In short, Schwarz chronicled marker events in the lives of many females around her but did not participate in their rites of passage.

In the final analysis, Schwarz offers a unique window into female experience in the Baroque era. While her work expresses the conventional Baroque sentiments that echo in the works of her male contemporaries—life's transitoriness, pacifistic beliefs, awareness of God's destructive and restorative aspects, the pains and pleasures of love, and the pleasant existence of shepherd and shepherdesses, for example—as well as adheres to the formal elements that prescribed and described German Baroque prose and verse, the additional dimensions to Schwarz's writings came about because she grew up female and died tragically young in an age not noted for an enlightened attitude toward women and in a country devastated by war.

Works

Deutsche Poetische Gedichte, Nuhn zum ersten mahl aus ihren eignen Handschriften, herausgegeben und verleget durch M. Samuel Gerlach, aus dem Hertzogtuhm Würtemberg, und zu Danzig Gedrukt, bey seel. Georg Rheten Witwen, im M.D.C.L. Jahr. *Ander Teil Deutscher Poëtischer Gedichten,* Nuhn zum ersten mahl aus ihren eignen Handschriften herausgegeben und verleget von M. Samuel Gerlach, au dem

Hertzogtuhm Würtemberg, und zu Danzig Gedrukt, bey seel. Georg Rheten Witwen, im M.D.C.L. Jahr.

The above are accessible in Curt von Faber du Faur, *German Baroque Literature: A Catalogue of the Collection in the Yale University Library* (New Haven, 1958–1969). The Faber du Faur collection is available on microfilm at most major research libraries. Schwarz's work comprises Volumes 271 and 272 of this collection.

Susan L. Clark

Annemarie Schwarzenbach
1908–1942

a.k.a. Clarac, Clark, Clark-Schwarzenbach
Born May 23, 1908, Zurich, Switzerland
Died November 15, 1942, Sils, Switzerland
Genre(s): prose fiction, poetry, biography, travel literature, journalism, photography
Language(s): German

It is an irony of sorts that the wealthy, powerful, and privileged family of beautiful, talented Annemarie Schwarzenbach was in many ways a destiny she could not transcend. Her father's wealth derived from the textile industry; her maternal grandfather was the influential Swiss General Ulrich Wille, and her maternal grandmother was born a von Bismarck, third cousin of the chancellor Otto von Bismarck. Schwarzenbach, neither robust nor self-confident, was never able to extricate herself from the destructive love–hate bond that tied her to her strong-minded, traditionalist, and politically conservative mother.

Schwarzenbach's profound rebellion against everything her family stood for broke out in 1931, during an eighteen-month stay in Berlin. Its forms remained constants in her life: antifascist politics, intimate friendship with Erika and Klaus Mann (the eldest children of Thomas Mann), the overweening drive to write, lesbianism, and morphine addiction. After 1933 her life was one of restless, unceasing travel, punctuated by the cycle of hospitalization for drug withdrawal in Switzerland and relapses into drug abuse. Her whereabouts changed with a rapidity that suggests desperation as Schwarzenbach unsuccessfully sought to find peace within herself: 1934, Moscow and Central Asia; 1935, after a suicide attempt, Persia, where she suddenly married a French diplomat; 1936 to 1938, the United States, Danzig, Moscow, Vienna, and Prague; 1939, Afghanistan (with Ella

Maillart); 1940, a return trip to America that included a love affair with Carson McCullers and ended as a nightmare voyage through the insane asylums of New York; 1941, the Belgian Congo; 1942, the final return to Switzerland, where she died as the result of head injuries sustained in a cycling accident.

Schwarzenbach lived to suffer, and she lived to write. She completed a Ph.D. in history at the University of Zürich, and her numerous magazine and newspaper articles reveal a practiced critical eye for the political and social complexities of the many lands she visited. Her fictional work, on the other hand, can overwhelm the reader with an unrelenting, static subjectivity that is often frozen in its obsession with the extremes of fear, despair, and loneliness. Where she retains control of her text, however, Schwarzenbach convincingly depicts the torments of her hauntingly inconsolable characters and produces lyric moments of great beauty. The paradoxes of her work surely reflect her own inner contradictions. Unfortunately, some of Schwarzenbach's papers (including diaries and correspondence) seem to have disappeared after her death. Since the rediscovery of Schwarzenbach in 1987, however, collections of her photojournalism have appeared, unpublished works have appeared in print, and out-of-print works republished.

Works

Beiträge zur Geschichte des Oberengadins im Mittelalter und zu Beginn der Neuzeit [Contributions to the History of Upper Engadin in the Middle Ages and in the Early Modern Era], Diss. U. of Zürich (1931). *Freunde um Bernhard* [Friends of Bernhard], short story (1931). with Hans Rudolf Schmid, *Das Buch der Schweiz. Ost und Süd* [The Book About Switzerland. East and South], journalism (1932). with Hans Rudolf Schmid, *Das Buch der Schweiz. Nord und West*. [The Book About Switzerland, North and West], journalism (1933). *Lyrische Novelle* [Lyrical Novella], short story (1933). *Winter in Vorderasien. Tagebuch einer Reise* [Winter in the Near East. A Travel Journal], travel literature (1934). *Lorenz Saladin. Ein Leben für die Berge* [Lorenz Saladin. A Life Lived for the Mountains], biography (1938). *Das glückliche Tal* [The Fortunate Valley], novel (1940, 1987). "Die Schweiz—Das Land, das nicht zum Schuss kam." *Der Alltag* 2 (1987): 17–22 (written 1940). "Das Wunder des Baums," excerpt from unpublished novel of same title, completed 1942, *Der Alltag* 2 (1987): 23–33. *Jenseits von New York: Ausgewählte Reportagen, Feuilletons und Fotographien aus den USA 1936–1938* [journalism and photojournalism] (1992).

Ann Marie Rasmussen

Madeleine de Scudéry
1607–1701

Born 1607, Le Havre, France
Died June 2, 1701, Paris
Genre(s): novel
Language(s): French

Better educated than most of the women of the period, Madeleine de Scudéry had learned several foreign languages and read extensively when she joined her brother in Paris in 1639. She quickly became a social feature in the salon of Catherine de Vivonne, Marquise de Rambouillet. *La chambre bleue d'Arthénice* (Arthenice's Blue Bedroom) was then a renowned meeting place for intellectuals and fashionable society. It was there that the movement first developed that which was later known as *preciosité*—overly stressing refinement of language and manners. The glory of the Hotel de Rambouillet declined after the death of Vincent Voiture and of the Marquis de Rambouillet, and interest shifted to the salon, in the Marais in Paris, of Mademoiselle de Scudéry. She invited well-known *gens de lettres* (men of letters) such as Conrart, Pellison, Ménage, Godeau, Chapelain, and d'Aubignac. Each year, Mlle de Scudéry published one or more volumes of her serial novels—*roman fleuve*. The first edition of *Artamène ou le Grand Cyrus* was published between 1649 and 1653 (10 vols.) under her brother Georges de Scudéry's name. It was followed (1654–1661) by *Clélie*, also in 10 volumes.

Although Mlle de Scudéry's novels are situated in ancient times and in faraway places [*Ibrahim ou L'illustre Bassa* (1641) in Turkey, *Le Grand Cyrus*, in ancient Persia, *Clélie* in Rome], her guests are recognizable in her heroes. Mlle de Scudéry herself is Sappho; Pellison is Acante; Godeau is Mage de Sidon; la Marquise de Rambouillet, Cléomire; Voiture, Callicrate; Jullie d'Angennes, Philonide, and so on. In his study of seventeenth-century society, Victor Cousin has identified many of the author's contemporaries. The heroes act and talk in measured and polite terms; their conversations are witty and learned, setting the tone for polite conversations of polite society. In this sense, Mlle de Scudéry had a great influence on the mores of her time, but her novels no longer have much appeal. They are endless stories of adventures with no apparent plot. Yet, her novels were translated in many languages, including German, English, Italian, Spanish, and Arabic. The *carte du tendre* in *Clélie* was much admired as the map to the roads of true love. The receptions in Mlle de Scudéry's salon no doubt had a great influence on the literary personalities of the time such as La Rochefoucauld, Mme de La Fayette, and Madame de Sévigné.

Works

Almaiide ou L'esclave Reine (1660–1663). *Artamène ou le Grand Cyrus* (1649–1653). *Clélie, Histoire Romaine* (1654–1660). *Ibrahim ou L'illustre Bassa* (1641). *Conversations sur Divers Sujets* (1680). *Conversations Nouvelles sur Divers Sujets* (1684). *Conversations Morales* (1686). *Nouvelles Conversations Morales* (1688).

Colette Michael

Anna Seghers
1900–1983

Born November 19, 1900, Mainz, Germany
Died June 1, 1983
Genre(s): novel, short story
Language(s): German

Anna Seghers studied art history and sinology at Heidelberg University, finishing in 1924 with a doctoral thesis on the Jewish tradition in the work of Rembrandt. In 1925 she married the sociologist and writer Lászlo Radvanyi and decided in 1928 to join the Communist Party; both were to be life-long affiliations. In 1933 she immigrated to France; her books were banned by the National Socialist Regime. During the Spanish Civil War she was an active supporter of the Republicans and in 1941 escaped to exile in Mexico. Returning to East Germany in 1947, she became prominent as an author and participant in cultural politics, unswervingly, though at times critically, supporting the official organs of the GDR, receiving many high awards and presiding from 1952 to 1978 over the Deutsche Schriftstellerverband der DDR. Seghers's literary work has become internationally acclaimed in eastern as well as in western critical circles. The general esteem for her work rests on her concern for humanity, altruism, social justice, solidarity, and personal responsibility as well as on her progressive art consideration, which often defied conformist cultural politics. She must have appreciated Christa Wolf's reverence for her and been proud to see her leading the next generation. Anna Seghers's style of prose writing was formed by the French and Russian realists of the nineteenth century, and her topics are all narrative commentaries of epochal social experiences. Her very first short story, *Grubetsch* (for which she used

the name Seghers), was a milieu study, the next, *Aufstand der Fischer von Santa Barbara*, in 1928 (filmed by Piscator in the Soviet Union, 1934) was a piece about striking fishermen and their plight of poverty and exploitation. *Auf dem Wege zur amerikanischen Botschaft* (1930) deals with the execution of Sacco and Vanzetti. Her first novel, *Die Gefährten* (1932), describes the defeat of revolutionary movements after World War I, *Der Kopflohn* (1933) confronts the thought processes of an SA-man and an antifascist worker; and *Der Weg durch den Februar* (1935) depicts the failure of resisting Viennese workers, explaining that a revolutionary ideology without power is doomed. Her most famous novel *Das siebte Kreuz* appeared in 1942 (filmed in the United States in 1944), a moving epic about the terrors of concentration camp and exile life. It was followed by *Transit* (1944), a further exploration of emigration, the anguish of uprootedness, being reduced to the uncertainty of chance and helpless moments of waiting before passage into exile. After *Der Ausflug der toten Mädchen* (1946), which begins a process of recapitulation by fusing present, dream, and memory, Seghers produced a new novel, *Die Toten bleiben jung* (1949, filmed in 1968, for which Christa Wolf wrote the film script), in which the authoress tried to summarize her view of events from 1918 to 1945. The historical structures of continuation from 1947 to 1953, which reflect Seghers's personal conviction for a new German state with Marxist social behavior, are portrayed in the novel *Die Entscheidung* (1959), followed by the sequel *Das Vertrauen* (1968). The titles indicate that decision and trust are necessary to build this new world, signified by the literary composite of dialectical opposition, the fight of western against eastern, reactionary versus progressive, capitalist versus socialist, bourgeois versus marxist forces. Her many anthologies of short stories round out her positions on the political and social experiences of her time.

Works

Jude und Judentum im Werke Rembrandts, Diss. (1924). *Grubetsch*, short story (1927). *Aufstand der Fischer von Santa Barbara*, short story (1928). *Auf dem Wege zur amerikanischen Botschaft*, anthology (1930). *Die Gefährten*, novel (1932). *Der Kopflohn*, novel (1933). *Die Stoppuhr*, short story (1933). *Ernst Thälmann. What He Stands For* (1934). *Der Weg durch den Februar*, novel (1935). *Der letzte Weg des Koloman Wallisch*, short story (1936). *Die Rettung*, novel (1937). *Die schönsten Sagen vom Räuber Woynok, Sagen von Artemis* (1940). *Das siebte Kreuz*, novel (1942). *Transit*, novel (1944). *Der Ausflug der toten Mädchen,* anthology (1946). *Das Ende,* short story (1948). *Die Toten bleiben jung,* novel (1949). *Die Hochzeit von Haiti,* anthology (1949). *Die Linie,* anthology (1950). *Crisanta,* short story (1951). *Die Kinder,* short stories (1951). *Der Mann und sein Name,* short story (1952). *Der erste Schritt,* short story (1953). *Frieden der Welt,* collection of speeches (1947–1953). *Die groe Veränderung in unserer Literatur,* speech (1956). *Brot und Salz,* short story (1958). *Die Kraft des Friedens,* speech (1959). *Die Entscheidung,* novel (1959). *Karibische Geschichten,* anthology (1962). *Über Tolstoy. Über Dostojewski,* essays (1963). *Die Kraft der Schwachen,* anthology (1965). *Das wirkliche Blau. Eine Geschichte aus Mexiko* (1967). *Vietnam in dieser Stunde* (1968). *Das Vertrauen,* novel (1968). *Briefe an Leser* (1970). *Über Kunstwerk and Wirklichkeit,* essays (1970–1971). *Überfahrt. Eine Liebesgeschichte* (1971). *Sonderbare Begegnungen,* anthology (1973).

Translations: *The Dead Stay Young* (1950). *Revolt of the Fisherman of Santa Barbara. A Prize on His Head* (1960). *The Seventh Cross* (1968).

Margaret Eifler

Sophie de Ségur
1799–1874

a.k.a. La Comtesse de Ségur, née Rostopchine
Born July 19, 1799, St. Petersburg
Died January 31, 1874, Paris
Genre(s): children's literature
Language(s): French

The daughter of the Count Rostopchine, minister of Tzar Paul I, and of Anna Protassov, the countess lived either at Woronowo, her father's feudal domain, or at the court of Alexander I until the age of seventeen. Her education was very closely supervised by her mother, who, strongly influenced by the French philosophers of the eighteenth century, imposed on her children the most ascetic regimen. Anna Protassov, who suddenly converted to Catholicism against the will of the count, battled relentlessly to win their children over to the Catholic faith. Sophie eventually followed her mother over to the Catholic side of the family. In 1816, the count, feeling in political disfavor, decided to exile his family to Paris, where the young Sophie was very soon married, in 1819, to the Count Eugene de Ségur. The Count Rostopchine presented the young couple with a chateau in Normandy, Les Nouettes, where Sophie de Ségur was to spend the major part of her life. The marriage was not a very happy one, and she decided to live in Normandy with her eight children. Though she had always been a good story teller, it is only when her grandchildren moved away to England that she started to write, mailing them the stories they had enjoyed so much at home.

Upon the insistence of Louis Veuillot, director of the ultramontane newspaper *L'Univers,* she decided to publish her work. In 1856, Louis Hachette published *Les Nouveaux contes de Fées* (New Fairy Tales), with illustrations by Gustave Doré. The book was an instant success and during the next thirteen years the countess wrote about twenty novels for children, the best known of which are *Les Malheurs de Sophie* (1859; Sophie's Misfortunes), *Les Petites filles modèles* (1857; Exemplary Little Girls), *Les Mémoires d'un Ane* (1860; Memoirs of a Donkey). She also wrote more didactic books, such as *l'Evangile d'une grand-mère* (1866; A Grandmother's Gospel), *La Bible d'une grand-mère* (1870; A Grandmother's Bible), *Les Actes des Apôtres* (1866; The Acts of the Apostles) and *La Santé des enfants* (1857 and 1862; Children's Health), an essay on childcare. Her novels and fairy tales are still widely read and studied today despite some harsh criticism.

Her literary style contributes much to her success. She succeeds in mixing the theatrical genre, by using the direct style extensively, with the narrative, providing the very young reader with a novel that is easy to read and interesting. However, it is probably her approach to children's literature that best explains her popularity: in her works, the didactic intentions, which weighed so heavily in the books of her predecessors, become secondary. She presents the reader with heros who are on a more human scale. Good does not always prevail, instincts are always taken into account.

Some critics have made psychoanalytical readings of the countess and have strongly expressed their concern about her sadomasochistic tendencies and the dangers that she represented to society as a whole.

These characteristics of her work are still very passionately discussed in France, some critics going so far as to ask that her books be banned from young children's libraries or that they be heavily censored. The main points of controversy in her work are related to her depictions of nineteenth-century French society from an aristocratic perspective, according to which there is little hope for the members of the lower classes. However, her writings are of considerable interest to historians, who have been able to reconstitute from her descriptions the day-to-day life of a wide range of the society of the Second Empire.

The most interesting aspect of the countess' work

is her relentless effort to express her understanding of childhood and, to a lesser extent, of adulthood. Throughout her writing there emerges a genuine concern for children and the role of parenting at all levels.

Probably influenced by the teaching of her mother, who was a great admirer of Rousseau, the countess advocates a simple lifestyle: clothing is to be comfortable and practical, allowing the young child to get physical exercise through play. Food is to be natural and abundant: she severely condemns both gluttony and the starvation of children by parents as a means of punishment. Skills taught to children—even those of aristocratic families—must be of a practical nature as well as of an intellectual one. Parents must provide children with a basic healthy routine that forbids late nights, mundane amusement, and luxury, but which must fulfill the child's need for sleep, food, and physical exercise. Her conception of childhood is original for the nineteenth century in the sense that it recognizes the child as a person having legitimate needs different of those from his or her parents.

The countess also spoke about adulthood. She did it primarily in the name of women showing many a woman as head of a household successfully managing important domains without the help of a husband, a brother, or any kind of male support. Even more daringly, she depicted mothers totally in charge of the spiritual fate of their children, excluding the intervention of priests. She imprinted in her readers' mind the portrait of women as potentially the total equals of men, as self-reliant human beings. In her later works, intended for teenage readers, she tried to fight on more specific grounds, such as the right for girls to choose their husbands, the necessity of a marital relationship based on love, respect, and understanding on the part of both the husband and the wife. She even revealed to her readers how sexual power could be used by women to change a relationship, also advocating that women have a right to see their sexual desire adequately fulfilled by their husbands. Her young heroines show a very positive understanding of sexual feelings, taking the leadership role in the couple's private life.

However, the countess also showed that men were unjustly treated by society: she therefore tried to see that her male characters be treated sensibly. She demanded that men be nurturing to their children, affectionate, and even tender.

The variety of themes and problems expressed in the works therefore justifies her place of honor among nineteenth-century French writers. In the past few years, the process toward her canonization has begun, with the inclusion of some of her works in high school curricula.

Works

Les Nouveaux contes de fées (1856). *La Santé des enfants* (1857 and 1862). *Les Petites filles modèles* (1857). *Les Vacances* (1859). *Les Malheurs de Sophie* (1859). *Les Mémoires d'un ane* (1860). *Pauvre Blaise* (1860). *La Soeur de Gribouille* (1861). *Les Bons enfants* (1862). *L'Auberge de l'Ange-Gardien* (1862). *Les Deux nigauds* (1862). *François le Bossu* (1863). *Un Bon petit diable* (1865). *Jean qui grogne et Jean qui rit* (1865). *La Fortune de Gaspard* (1866). *Le Général Dourakine* (1866). *Le Mauvais Geenie* 9 (1866). *l'Evangile d'une grand-mère* (1866). *Comédies et proverbes* (1866). *Dikoy le Chemineau* (1867). *Quel amour d'enfant* (1868). *Après la pluie le beau temps* (1871). *Les Actes des Apôtres* (1866). *La Bible d'une grand-mère* (1870).

English translations: *The Misfortunes of Sophie* (1936). *The Wise Little Donkey* (1931). *The Angel Inn* (1976). *Old French Fairy Tales* (1920). *The Acts of the Apostles for Children* (1912). *A Life of Christ for Children* (1909).

Valerie Lastinger

Séverine
1855–1929

a.k.a. Caroline Remy, Mme Adrien Guebhard
Born April 27, 1855, Paris
Died April 23, 1929, Pierrefonds
Genre(s): journalism, essay, drama, autobiography, lecture
Language(s): French

Séverine ranks as a major French journalist of the late nineteenth and early twentieth centuries; certainly she was the stellar woman journalist of her era. Trained on the job by a talented mentor, Jules Vallès, for whom she worked as a copyist, Séverine assumed the editorship of *Le Cri du peuple* following Vallès' death in 1885. She and her husband, Adrien Guebhard, later sold the paper. She subsequently made a good living as a freelance journalist, publishing in a wide spectrum of Parisian newspapers. These included the all-woman daily *La Fronde* (1897–1903), edited by her old friend Marguerite Durand, for which she covered the Dreyfus Affair.

Séverine's career as a journalist was far from preordained. She was the only child of a petit-bourgeois municipal employee and his wife, who raised their daughter by very strict disciplinary standards designed to break her spirit. They did not succeed. She fled into marriage at the age of seventeen. By the time she began working for Vallès in the 1880s she had been separated for many years from her first husband, Henri Montrobert, from whom she had run away following the birth of their son. In the interim she had been living with Adrien Guebhard, whom she met while employed as a reader for his mother. She bore a son by him and married him after the 1884 divorce law allowed her to terminate her marriage to Montrobert. Meanwhile she had met Vallès in Brussels. After his return to Paris she went to work for him and soon became Vallès's spiritual daughter. Her two sons were sent out to nurse and then away to school.

Through the press and her flair for self-dramatization, Séverine became a Parisian celebrity. She pioneered first-hand investigative reportage and interviews in the French press. After 1900 she embarked on a new career as a speaker, generally for advanced political causes. Always an enemy of authoritarianism, whether on the political right or the left, and insistent on maintaining her liberty of ideas and action in the face of pressures to affiliate with parties, causes, and so on, Séverine surprised many in 1921 by joining the emergent French Communist Party. Several years later, however, she was purged for refusing to abandon her concurrent support for the League of Rights of Man. She was particularly noted for her support of anarchism, women's rights, and pacifism.

Séverine's book-length publications include five volumes of her articles, culled from the six thousand and more she published, a play, and *Line,* an autobiography covering her early years. Her correspondence with Vallès found later publication in his collected works. Séverine also composed many prefaces for books by colleagues, a number of speeches, and published longer essays in various publications such as the *Revue philanthropique.* There is no complete critical edition of her works.

Works

Ed., *Le Cri du peuple* (1885–1888). *Pages rouges* (1893). *Notes d'une Frondeuse (de la Boulange au Panama)* (1894). *Pages mystiques* (1895). *En marche* (1896). *Affaire Dreyfus—Vers la lumière—Impressions vécues* (1900). *A Sainte-Hélène, pièce en 2 actes, en prose* (1904). *Sac-à-tout* (1906). *Line (1855–1867)* (1921). *Correspondance entre Séverine et Jules Vallès,* in Vallès, *Oeuvres complètes* (1972). *Séverine: Choix de papiers, du Cri du peuple à la Fronde,* annotés par E. Le Garrec (1982).

Karen Offen

Marie de Rabutin-Chantal, Marquise de Sévigné
1626–1696

Born February 5, 1626, Paris
Died April 15, 1696, Grignan
Genre(s): letters
Language(s): French

Marie de Rabutin-Chantal was born in the fashionable Marais quarter of Paris in 1626. Her father, from an old and illustrious aristocratic Burgundian family, married the wealthy daughter of a recently ennobled Parisian tax-farmer. Orphaned at the age of seven, Marie was raised by maternal relatives, the de Coulanges, in a warm, loving atmosphere. She was well educated for a girl and was allowed a great deal of freedom; she knew Latin and Spanish and was fluent in Italian. History, literature, and writing, along with religious instruction, riding and dancing lessons produced the well-rounded, independent, self-confident woman who became the most famous *epistolière* of the seventeenth century. At age eighteen, the beautiful, wealthy heiress married Henri de Sévigné, a charming but extravagant and faithless Breton nobleman. They were members of the Parisian *beau monde,* habituées of the famous salons of the capital, where they mingled with writers and ministers, courtesans, and courtiers. In 1651 de Sévigné was killed in a duel, leaving his wife with two young children. Choosing not to remarry (to take another "master" as she put it), the twenty-five-year-old widow embarked on a full and independent life. She never regretted this decision; "the state of matrimony is a dangerous disease," she could write after 38 years of widowhood. Mme de Sévigné continued to spend most of her time in Paris, but she also lived for long periods at her château of Les Rochers in Brittany and at her uncle's Abbey of Livry outside of Paris; her lyrical descriptions of these rural retreats clearly reveal a love of nature and the countryside that was unusual among her contemporaries. Numerous estates provided the financial security Mme de Sévigné needed to live well and to ensure her children's future. Her son, Charles, had an unsatisfying military career before he took up the life of a country gentleman at his mother's favorite estate of Les Rochers. Witty, intelligent, and charming, Charles never received the passionate devotion that Mme de Sévigné lavished on her daughter, Francoise-Marguerite, "the prettiest girl in France." Two years after marrying the comte de Grignan, this beloved daughter moved to Provence where her husband was the

Lieutenant General (Governor), and the famous correspondence between mother and daughter commenced.

Over 1500 of Mme de Sévigné's letters are extant; unfortunately those of her daughter were destroyed by her granddaughter, Pauline de Simiane, who had intended to burn the entire correspondence. Mme de Sévigné's letters are unmatched in style and tone. They provide a vivid and immediate account of aristocratic life during the reign of Louis XIV. She wrote in a natural, conversational style, moving easily from subject to subject, infusing life into people and events of the time. There is a sense of immediacy in her writing that holds the reader's interest and transports him or her into her world. Mme de Sévigné was an intelligent, keen observer with a realistic view of life. Without moralizing or merely gossiping, she gave character and depth to the men and women of her acquaintance. She described life at court, lavish fêtes and gruesome executions, wars and love affairs, dreaded illnesses and horrendous medical practices, the dread of growing old, and the agonies of dying. One of the most interesting people found in this vast correspondence is Mme de Sévigné herself. Few historical figures are as well-known as she—her daily routine, her health (very robust), her diet, her friends, her frequent travels, her moods and character, her fears and joys are all revealed in her incomparable style. Her love of reading, her periodic need for solitude, and her appreciation of nature were unusual for women of her class and time. Cultured, witty, friendly, and cheerful, Mme de Sévigné displayed a *joie de vivre* that was only occasionally tinged with melancholy. Her attractive personality is one of the reasons for the appeal of her letters. Although she was not a professional writer, she was an accomplished stylist and knew the importance of writing well. She could make anything interesting, even the weather or a walk in her woods. In her letters Mme de Sévigné bequeathed an eternal vitality and vivacity to the momentous and trivial aspects of the Splendid Century.

Works

The Letters of Madame de Sévigné, 7 vols. (1927). Duchêne, Roger, ed., *Madame de Sévigné: Correspondence,* 3 vols. (1972–1978).

Jeanne A. Ojala
William T. Ojala

Anna Sewell
1820–1878

Born March 30, 1820, Yarmouth, England
Died April 25, 1878, Old Catton, near Norwich
Genre(s): novel
Language(s): English

The obscure author of only one book, the classic horse story *Black Beauty,* Sewell experienced a typical Victorian upbringing in a strict Quaker family. Except for two sojourns at spas in Germany and several extended visits with relatives, she remained at home, never married, and was nursed during her slow decline and last illness by her devoted and domineering mother, the writer Mary Sewell. From earliest childhood, Anna Sewell displayed a lively interest in horses and fierce outrage at any mistreatment of animals. At age fourteen she fell while running and seriously injured her ankles, which brought to an end her brief attendance at a local day-school; inappropriate medical treatment caused her to become a semi-invalid for the rest of her life, and she came to depend on horses for companionship as well as freedom of movement.

During Sewell's year-long medical treatment in Boppard, Germany, in 1856, her mother began to write ballads for children and working people. Sewell helped her prepare several collections of verse and prose for publication, and two of Mary Sewell's ballads (including "Mother's Last Words") became unprecedented bestsellers. In the town of Wick, near Bath, where the family lived from 1858 to 1864, Sewell and her mother founded a library, a Temperance Society, a Hall for Mothers' Meetings, and an Evening Institute for Working Men, where mother and daughter taught reading, writing, and natural history three times a week. Sewell liked to improvise little humorous stories in verse which were occasionally written down and kept by friends, but one serious poem by her survives from this period.

At age fifty-one, Sewell's health deteriorated to the point that she gave up her own horse. To repay her debt of gratitude to the many horses she had ridden throughout her adult life, she began to write a book that would show "what gentle and devoted friends horses can be." At first she dictated the book to her mother, but gradually she felt strong enough to write the story of *Black Beauty* down in pencil, which her mother then transcribed. Between November 1871 and August 1877, only three entries in Sewell's journal note her progress on her famous story. The book was published in 1877 and began to be widely and enthusiastically reviewed in January 1878. When she died three months later, 91,000 copies had already been sold and she was happily aware that her work was a success.

Sewell designated *Black Beauty* as "the autobiography of a horse" with herself as the translator "from the original equine," and wrote the book not for children but for working men who dealt daily with horses. Her aim was not to create a lasting work of literature but "to induce kindness, sympathy, and an understanding treatment of horses." The title character is a thoroughbred stallion who falls to the lowest social station, that of a hired carthorse, through no fault of his own but through human mistreatment. The book contains much technical information on the care and training of horses; so accurate were the descriptions of horse care that one expert horseman declared the book to be written by a veterinarian.

Black Beauty is an "improving" book of the kind that was popular in the Victorian era. That *Black Beauty*'s fame has survived while the vast majority of such books are now forgotten testifies to the originality and sincerity of Sewell's storytelling. She wished particularly to portray the difficult situation of London cabmen, but although she sought practical alleviation for the working class, she subscribed to an inherently feudal, hierarchical, ordering of the world, with the benevolent master at the head of both family and society. She considered it the duty of the lower classes to serve the upper, just as horses were created to serve men. It was the responsibility of the masters, in turn, to look after those beneath them and to prevent cruelty, wrong-doing, and suffering wherever they occurred. Sewell disliked the changes brought about by the Industrial Revolution and technology, and the city represents corruption and evil for Black Beauty. Of social evils, alcoholism is the worst, often the cause of cruelty to horses. The ethic of humaneness, however, is clearly heralded throughout the novel in the words and behavior of compassionate men, women, and children.

Works

Black Beauty: His Grooms and Companions. The Autobiography of a Horse (1877).

Jean Pearson

Marietta Shaginian
1888–1982

a.k.a. Jim Dollar
Born March 21, 1888, Moscow, Russia
Died March 1982
Genre(s): journalism, history, literary criticism, poetry, fiction
Language(s): Russian

Marietta Shaginian's career spanned seventy-five years, from her first poem, published in a provincial newspaper in 1903, to the final pages of *Chelovek i vremia* (Man and Time), which she signed as finished at age "ninety years and four months" in 1978. After a brief flirtation with modernism and the "decadent" ideals of the first decade of the twentieth century, Shaginian put her considerable talents, intellect, and wide-ranging interests (among others, philosophy, music, psychology, and textiles) to the service of the new revolutionary Soviet society, both propagating and exemplifying the tenets of a committed literature faithfully and ingeniously.

Shaginian was born into a family of Russified Armenians. Her father was a hard-working medical doctor, a lecturer at Moscow University, a convinced atheist, and an admirer of Goethe; his daughter inherited much of his intellect and ideals. Left unprovided for by his early death in 1902, Shaginian's mother returned to her family in Nakhichevan' near Rostov on the Don. Despite worsening otosclerosis, young Marietta returned to Moscow and began earning her living at fifteen. She tutored and published poetry, prose fiction, and literary and art criticism for provincial journals in order to complete her education at the pre-revolutionary equivalent of a women's college. For several years Shaginian's work reflected the Symbolism and apocalyptic philosophy ("revolution with the cross") of the Petersburg circle, which revolved around the historical novelist Dmitry Merezhkovsky and his wife, the writer Zinaida Gippius. She broke with the Merezhkovskys in 1912. As she pointed out, life with her younger sister in one windowless room and constant financial struggle "created a healthy antidote to any refined decadence" (*Sovietskie pisateli*, 646). Her first novel, *Svoia sud'ba* (1916; One's Own Fate, first published in full in 1923), is already programmatic, outlining an antiFreudian method of treating psychological disfunction that, rather than burrowing into the "negative" past, reinforces positive social behavior.

Shaginian spent the years of the 1917 revolution and succeeding civil war in Nakhichevan', where she founded a textile school. The reversals and chaotic situation in the Don region over that period are synthesized in her kaleidoscopic short novel *Peremena* (1923; Change). From 1920 to 1927 she lived in Petrograd-Leningrad where, under the sponsorship of Maxim Gorky, she began her "participation in the great and difficult process of creating a Soviet literature. . . . I suddenly felt a need to write for newspapers as a lyric necessity. . . . And this sensation of a lyric, vital need for the newspaper word remained with me for the rest of my life."

Responding to the call for popular, ideologically correct reading for the masses, Shaginian, under the pseudonym "Jim Dollar," produced *Mess Mend* (1923), a fantastic spy novel devoted to the adventures in New York and the Soviet Union of a band of American radical superheroes working to counter an evil capitalist plot. The work, issued as a serial in ten parts, was wildly successful, but even Shaginian herself found it difficult to develop much enthusiasm for its two sequels. "*Kik*" (the title is an acronym for the Russian words for Witch and Communist), a tale that treats the mysterious disappearance of a Soviet official, is Shaginian's idiosyncratic protest against specialization by genre in literature. The story is developed through newspaper accounts and by four witnesses who put their testimony in the form of a poem, a novella, a melodrama in verse, and the outline for a documentary film.

Shaginian's most popular prerevolutionary book of poetry, *Orientalia* (five editions between 1913 and 1922), is based on Armenian themes. Her marriage in 1917 to the philologist Ia. S. Khachatrianets sealed her return to her roots. During the 1920s she made frequent journalistic forays to study the transformation of her homeland under the Soviets, and she describes herself from 1927 as no longer a guest in the republic, but a constant dweller in Armenia." There she closely followed the construction of a hydroelectric dam and described it in a novel of industrialization, *Gidrotsentral'* (1929; Hydroelectric Plant). *Journey through Soviet Armenia* (1950) is a summary of her many studies of her homeland.

The 1930s to the mid-1950s were marked by intensive journalistic forays all over the Soviet Union and Western Europe. After spending World War II writing propagandistic literature in the Urals, Shaginian displayed her erudition in major studies of literary figures as diverse as Goethe, the twelfth-century Persian writer Nizami Ganjawi, and the nineteenth century Ukrainian poet Taras Shevchenko. The 1957 edition of a tetralogy (two "chronicle" novels and two sets of sketches) devoted to Lenin and his family, on which Shaginian worked for over thirty years, was awarded the Lenin Prize in 1972. She was admitted to the Communist Party in July 1942, and in 1950 she was named a corresponding member of the Armenian Academy of Sciences. Her philosophical memoir of Russia in the last years before the revolution, *Man and Time,* brought her long, active career to a triumphant end.

Works
Orientalia (1913–1922). *Svoia sud'ba* (1916). *Mess Mend* (1923). *Peremena* (1923). *Gidrotsentral'* (1929). *Sovietskie pisateli: Avtobiografii,* Ia. Brainina i E.F. Nikitina, comp. (Moscow, 1959), vol. 2, pp. 640–660. *Sobranie sochinensi,* 9 vols. (Moscow, 1971–1975). *Chelovek i vremia: Istoriia chelovecheskogo stanovleniia* (Moscow, 1980).

Translations: "Man and Time" [excerpt], tr. Helen Tate. *Soviet Literature,* 9 (1980): 33–107. *Mess Mend: The Yankees in Petrograd,* tr. S.D. Cioran (Ann Arbor, Mich., 1987).

Mary F. Zirin

Mary Wollstonecraft Shelley
1797–1851
Born August 30, 1797, London
Died February 1, 1851, London
Genre(s): novel
Language(s): English

Of his wife Mary, Percy Bysshe Shelley wrote in the dedication to *The Revolt of Islam,* "They say that thou wert lovely from thy birth, / Of glorious parents, thou aspiring child." William Godwin, radical philosopher, and Mary Wollstonecraft, author of *A Vindication of the Rights of Woman* (1792), were those "glorious parents." Wollstonecraft had died as a result of giving birth to Mary, and Godwin's remarriage to the widow Mary Jane Clairmont four years later created bitter feelings and resentment for Mary. These feelings and her strong attachment to her father led to her removal to Scotland in 1812 to ease tensions in the family, which included Shelley, Fanny Imlay (Wollstonecraft's "love child") Charles, Jane (later Claire), and William.

In 1812, Mary met the poet Shelley and his wife, Harriet Westbrook. Mary was nearly seventeen when she and Shelley met again in May 1814; he and his wife were estranged by this time, and almost immediately they became lovers. By July she was pregnant, and the couple eloped to the Continent. Her first book, *History of a Six Weeks' Tour,* published anonymously in 1817, describes the trip through France, Switzerland, and Germany that Mary, Shelley, and Shelley's stepsister Claire Clairmont took following the elopement. Mary's earlier writing has all been lost, but with Percy Bysshe Shelley's aid and encouragement, her best-known work would be published the following year.

Frankenstein; or, The Modern Prometheus was published anonymously in 1818. Percy, Mary, and Claire had taken residence in Geneva near Byron (Claire's somewhat reluctant lover) and John Polidari. *Frankenstein,* a novel of the scientific creation of life severed from moral concerns and social affiliation, became a literary sensation in London. It apparently grew in Mary Shelley's imagination in response to a casual competition to create a ghost story as well as to a conversation about contemporary experiments with galvanic electricity on dead tissue. *Frankenstein,* according to Ellen Moers, "is most interesting, most powerful, and most feminine: in the motif of revulsion against newborn life, and the drama of guilt, dread, and fright surrounding birth and its consequences."

For Mary, the consequence of giving birth was tragedy. Before she reached the age of twenty-two, she had given birth to three children, all of whom had died. These deaths separated her emotionally from Percy. Her only surviving child was born in 1819. In addition, her half-sister Fanny Imlay had committed suicide in 1816, as did Harriet Shelley (abandoned by Shelley earlier the same year and pregnant by an unknown lover). Harriet's death freed Percy to wed Mary two weeks later. Her greatest loss, however, was the death by drowning of Percy Bysshe Shelley himself in July 1822. Still somewhat emotionally estranged from him at this time, Mary Shelley, an impoverished widow at twenty-four, attempted through her grief and guilt to establish Shelley's literary reputation (against his father's express wishes) and to support her son through her writing.

She wrote other novels, several biographies, and many stories, most of which were published in *The Keepsake;* some have elements of science fiction while others are Gothic. Among them is the novella *Mathilda* (1819), in which Shelley is fictionalized as Woodville. This largely biographical work explores the estrangement between Mary and Percy after their daughter Clara's death at age one.

Valperga (1823) and *The Last Man* (1826) are widely considered Mary Shelley's best work after *Frankenstein. The Last Man* represents a creative landmark in her work. Though marred by overwriting and excessive length, the book commemorates her husband as she was unable to do in a biography. Her characterization of Adrian, second Earl of Windsor, is the only acknowledged portrait of Shelley: "I have endeav-

oured, but how inadequately, to give some idea of him in my last published book—the sketch has pleased some of those who best loved him." This idealized view of Shelley, a variation on the "Noble Savage" motif, is set in the future and describes the gradual destruction of the human race by plague; its narrator, Lionel Verney, begins life as a shepherd boy and after many years finds himself amid the ruined grandeur of Rome in the year 2100.

The same theme is found in *Lodore* (1835): the heroine Ethel is taken as a child by her father, Lord Lodore, to the wilds of Illinois and raised amid the grandest objects of Nature after which she returns to a life of romance and penury in a London reminiscent of Mary Shelley's early years. She also wrote *The Fortunes of Perkin Warbeck* (1830) and *Falkner* (1837) and another novella, *The Heir of Mondolfo* (published posthumously in 1877). In addition to her many stories, Shelley also wrote biographical and critical studies of continental authors and published several editions of her husband's work. She also worked on, but never completed, biographies of Percy Bysshe Shelley and of her father. In short, she spent her widowhood as a productive and successful woman of letters.

In 1844, her father-in-law died, leaving his title and estate to Shelley's son. Only then was she secure financially. The devotion of her son and his marriage to her friend Jane St. John made her last years comfortable. She died February 1, 1851, eight days after falling into a coma.

Works

History of a Six Weeks' Tour Through a Part of France, Switzerland, Germany, and Holland, with Letters Descriptive of a Sail round the Lake of Geneva and of the Glaciers of Chamouni (with P.B. Shelley) (1817). *Frankenstein* (1818). *Mathilda* (1819). *Valperga; or The Life and Adventures of Castruccio Prince of Lucca* (1823). *The Last Man* (1826). *The Fortunes of Perkin Warbeck. A Romance* (1830). *Lodore* (1835). (with others) *Lives of the Most Eminent Literary and Scientific Men of Italy, Spain, and Portugal* (1835–1837). *Falkner: A Novel* (1837). (with others) *Lives of the Most Eminent Literary and Scientific Men of France* (1838). *Rambles in Germany and Italy in 1840, 1842, and 1843* (1844). *The Swiss Peasant* (in *The Tale Book,* with others, 1859). *The Choice. A Poem on Shelley's Death* (1876). *The Heir of Mondolfo* (1877). *Tales and Stories,* ed. R. Garnett (1891). *The Romance of Mary W. Shelley, John Howard Payne, and Washington Irving* (1907; the Payne–Shelley letters, ed. F.B. Sanborn). *Letters Mostly Unpublished* (ed. H.H. Harper, 1918). *Proserpine and Midas. Two Unpub-*

lished *Mythological Dramas,* ed. A. Koszul (1922). *Letters,* ed. R.L. Jones (1944). *Mathild,* ed. E. Nitchie (1959). *Journals,* ed. L. Robinson (1947). *My Best Mary: The Selected Letters,* ed. M. Spark and D. Stanford (1953). *Collected Tales and Stories,* ed. C.E. Robinson (1976). *Letters,* ed. B.T. Bennett. vol. 1 (1980), vol. 2 (1983). *Journals 1814–44,* ed. P.R. Feldman and D. Scott-Kilvert (1987).

Anne-Marie Ray

Frances Sheridan
1724–1766

Born 1724, Dublin, Ireland
Died September 26, 1766, Blois, France
Genre(s): novel, comedy
Language(s): English

Sheridan, forbidden by her father to learn to write, was educated in Latin and botany as well as in written English by her older brothers. When she was fifteen years old, she wrote her first novel, *Eugenia and Adelaide,* on paper given to her for the household accounts. In 1743, when she was nineteen, she entered the fray of a pamphlet war, defending a man whom she had not yet met but was later to marry. Both the pamphlet, "A letter from a Young Lady to Mr. Cibber," and a poem "The Owl," published in the *Dublin News Letter* were in protest to the attacks of Theophilus Cibber on Thomas Sheridan, a popular actor and manager of the Theatre Royal, Smock Alley, Dublin.

In 1747, she married Thomas Sheridan, but she did not again write for publication until 1759. During these years she was made intimately aware of birth and death. She bore six children, two of whom died, her beloved uncle died, both her parents died, and her close friend, Miss Pennington died. Sheridan herself was plagued with illness; lame since childhood, she was stricken in her early thirties with maladies that stayed with her until her death, variously described as rheumatism in the head, violent headaches, disorders of the stomach, and fainting seizures. Yet she was noted for her vivacity and charm, and from 1759 until her death she worked steadily at the profession of writing.

To get away from Dublin theatre disturbances and from financial debts, Sheridan and her husband settled in London in 1754. She became friends with Samuel Johnson, David Garrick, and Samuel Richardson, and with several literary women, such as Hester Mulso

Chapone, Sarah Fielding, and Catherine Macauley. Samuel Richardson read *Eugenia and Adelaide,* contemplated but decided against publishing it, and encouraged Sheridan to begin writing again.

During the winter of 1759–1760, busy with household management and with the supervision of her children's education, grieving for Miss Pennington's death, and suffering from her own illnesses, Sheridan wrote her novel *Memoirs of Miss Sidney Bidulph.* It was published in March in both London and Dublin, and by July a second London edition came out. Her next effort was a comedy *The Discovery,* which in late 1763 opened at Drury Lane, where it played to packed houses for seventeen nights. The following year, she wrote another comedy, *The Dupe* which opened in December at Drury Lane. Although it closed after only three performances, sales of the printed play were so brisk that she was paid £100 above the usual copyright fee.

In September of 1764, in response to her worsening health and to continuing financial distress, the family moved to France. Over the next two years, she wrote four works. For some time her health seemed to improve, but in early September 1766 she was seized with fainting fits and a fever and died two weeks later. An autopsy revealed, as her husband wrote, that "all the noble parts were attacked, and any one of four internal maladies must have proved fatal." Two works were published posthumously in 1767: *Nourjahad,* an exotic moral tale, and a two-volume continuation of *Sidney Bidulph;* a dramatic tragedy based on this continuation was lost in manuscript. A third comedy, *A Journey to Bath* was refused by Garrick and not published until 1902, at which time a three-act fragment, credited to her, was included in W. Fraser Rae's edition of her son Richard Brinsley Sheridan's plays.

Sheridan's youthful effort, *Eugenia and Adelaide* (published 1791), depicts the Gothic adventures of two girlhood friends. *Sidney Bidulph* noted by Johnson for its power of feeling, was immensely popular during the eighteenth century, running to five London editions and at least one Dublin edition. In translation, it was avidly read on the continent: for instance, twenty years after its first publication, a French bookseller remarked that she had sold more copies of *Sidney Bidulph* than of any other novel. Here, Sheridan's interest is in exploring the passions, perhaps encouraged as much by grief for the deaths of loved ones as by the inspiration of Richardson's *Clarissa.* The plot is sentimentally tragic, but Sheridan's language is energetic and direct and comic interludes break the general air of sorrow. One such interlude, the story of a rich relation from the West Indies who disguises himself as a beggar in order to test the kindness of Sidney and her brother, was picked up by Sheridan's son Richard Brinsley in *The School for Scandal*. Themes in the novel are the powerlessness of women in patriarchy and the bonds of consolation formed among women. A destructive kindness exists between Sidney and her mother; oppression as women binds Sidney and the maidservant Patty Main, while class difference separates them; and romantic friendship offers solace but no hope for change. In the 1767 continuation, Sidney's powerlessness is destructive to her own daughters.

As early as mid-1763, *The Discovery* had been published in London, Dublin, and Edinburgh, with a second London edition printed before the year was out; the play saw repeated revivals during the eighteenth century, was anthologized and adapted well into the nineteenth century, and in 1924 Aldous Huxley offered a modern version. In *The Discovery* women assure harmony through placating and indirectly guiding villainous or foolish men. Here, as in her other comedies, Sheridan achieves effect through an awareness of language from which her son learned much. For instance, the contrasting personalities of Lord Medway and Sir Anthony are caught by the language they use: Lord Medway, "the shorter we make the wooing—women are slippery things—you understand me!" Sir Anthony, "Your Lordship's insinuation, though derogatory to the honour of the fair-sex, (which I very greatly reverence) has, I am apprehensive, a little too much veracity in it." Aptly, Sir Anthony's nephew refers to him as "uncle Parenthesis."

The Dupe might have been a stage success a half-century earlier, but in 1763, its satire offended the moral sensibilities of its bourgeois audience. The play closed to "an almost universal hiss" from the critics, who found it "low and vulgar" and who censured its author for "conduct so unbecoming, so unfemale." In the printed version, Sheridan's language was sanitized. For instance, "Spawn of a Chimney Sweeper" and "Cinder Wench" are expunged, and the description of the name of *wife* as worse "than ten thousand blistering Plaisters" dwindles to "worse than ten thousand daggers."

In *A Journey to Bath*, Mrs. Surface, a landlady whose parlor is "a Mart of Scandal," uses language hypocritically. Sheridan had her most fun, however, with Mrs. Tryfort, who later metamorphosed into Mrs. Malaprop. Among her frequent linguistic manglings are these: "to teach my Lucy, and make her illiterate," "Oh in everything ma'am he is a progeny! a perfect progeny!" and "But my Lord Stewkly is so embellished, Mrs. Surface! No body can be embellished that has not been abroad you must know. Oh if you were to hear him describe contagious countries as I have done, it would astonish you. He is a perfect map of geography."

Nourjahad, which Sheridan had planned as the first in a series of Oriental moral tales, is a whimsical fable with a complicated plot having a true surprise ending. In the story, a young man who values pleasure above all else is granted his desire for eternal youth and wealth; but the world remains mortal and he learns what loss is. Gradually he discovers new values. The tale was often reprinted in the eighteenth and nineteenth centuries and as recently as 1927.

Criticism of Sheridan's work focuses on what her son learned from her, which was significant. But her work has more to offer than evidence of her son's comedic training. *Sidney Bidulph* is fascinating for the ways in which it questions how completely woman's life is bound by patriarchy. The comedies are lively explorations of the use and misuse of language. Finally, *Nourjahad* is a delight in its inventive plot, its finely sketched characterization, and its tone of poignant simplicity.

Works

A Letter from a Young Lady to Mr. Cibber (1743; in *Cibber and Sheridan*). *The Owl: A Fable* (1743; in *Dublin News Letter*). *Memoirs of Miss Sidney Bidulph* (1761). *The Discovery* (1763). *The Dupe* (1764). *The History of Nourjahad* (1767). *Eugenia and Adelaide* (1791). *Letters and Ode to Patience* (1799; in *A Miscellany*). *A Journey to Bath* in *Sheridan's Plays . . . and His Mother's Unpublished Comedy*, ed. W.F. Rae (1902). *Verses on Thomas Sheridan* in *Sheridan*, ed. W. Sichel (1909). *The Plays of Frances Sheridan*, ed. R. Hogan and J.C. Beasley (1984).

Carolyn Woodward

Mary Sidney, Countess of Pembroke
1561–1621

Born October 27, 1561, Penshurst, Kent, England
Died September 25, 1621, Crosby Hall
Genre(s): poetry, translation
Language(s): English

Sidney was born to a family of power in Elizabeth's court. Her mother was the daughter of John Dudley, Duke of Northumberland, who had died for his attempt to put Lady Jane Grey on the English throne.

Northumberland's surviving sons—Robert Dudley, Earl of Leicester, and Ambrose Dudley, Earl of Warwick—were primary patrons for Protestant writings in England, supported Elizabeth against her Catholic rivals, and advocated military intervention on the Continent on behalf of Protestants there. Northumberland's daughters married men who strongly supported the Protestant cause: Katherine Dudley married the Earl of Huntington, Lord President of the Council in the North, Mary Dudley herself married Sir Henry Sidney, Lord President of the Marches of Wales and Lord Deputy of Ireland, who had been educated with the young King Edward. Among them, Sidney's father and uncles ruled approximately two thirds of the land under Elizabeth's rule.

After the death of her older sister, Ambrosia, Sidney went to Elizabeth's court at the Queen's express invitation. Her uncle Robert Dudley, Elizabeth's favorite and reputedly the most powerful man in England, arranged for her marriage at age fifteen as the third wife of one of the great Protestant lords, the middle-aged Henry Herbert, Earl of Pembroke, and contributed substantially to her dowry. As the Countess of Pembroke and the mistress of huge estates near Salisbury, in Wales, and in London, she used her money and influence to encourage such writers as Edmund Spenser, Abraham Fraunce, and Samuel Daniel.

Her brother, Sir Philip Sidney, was the hope of Protestants on the Continent. Endeavoring to influence Elizabeth to support the Huguenots against the Catholic Valois in the French religious wars, the Earls of the Dudley/Sidney alliance met at her London home to plan a letter dissuading Elizabeth from marrying the Duc d'Anjou. Philip served as spokesman for the alliance, infuriating the Queen, who forced him to leave the court. Philip spent his time of enforced idleness with Sidney at Wilton, her country estate. There he wrote the *Arcadia*, the most popular prose fiction in English for two centuries. After Philip died, Sidney edited the *Arcadia* for publication (1593) as well as his sonnet sequence *Astrophil and Stella* (1598).

Sidney also helped to create a hagiography, establishing Philip as a Protestant martyr. She wrote two poems mourning his death, "The Doleful Lay of Clorinda," published with other elegies for Philip in Spenser's *Colin Clouts Come Home Again*, and "To the Angell Spirit of the most excellent Sir Philip Sidney," which exists in one manuscript copy, a presentation copy of her Psalms. Her other two original poems praise Elizabeth. "A Dialogue between Two Shepheards . . . in Praise of Astrea" was written for the Queen's visit to Wilton; it is unfortunately undated. "Even Now That Care" dedicates Sidney's translation of the Psalms to Queen Elizabeth (1599).

In addition to these original poems, she translated four works in the 1590s: Robert Garnier's *Marc Antonie*, Philippe de Mornay's *A Discourse on Life and on Death*, Petrarch's *Trionfo della Morte*, and the Psalms of David. The first three works deal with the theme of death, which was particularly appropriate to her at that time; her three-year-old daughter Katherine had died the same day her son Philip was born in 1584; her father, mother, and her brother Philip all had died in 1586; by 1595, her youngest brother Thomas and all of her powerful uncles had died as well.

Sidney's major literary achievement was her translation of the Psalms. Philip had translated the first 43 psalms into sophisticated English verse patterns modeled on the French psalter of Clemont Marot and Theodore de Beze. After his death, Sidney revised some of those psalms and translated the rest. Rarely repeating a verse pattern, her work is a triumph of English prosody and consists more of meditations on the Psalms than of literal translations. John Donne praised her Psalms, saying "They tell us *why,* and teach us *how* to sing," a statement more accurate than hyperbolic, as recent studies of George Herbert and others have recognized.

The Psalms were never presented to the Queen, and Sidney's prestige waned with her husband's. Pembroke had long been plagued with ill health and in his physical weakness had lost most of his power in Wales. In January 1601 he died, leaving his widow the castle and town of Cardiff, Wales, along with some other properties. When he came of age, her son William, third Earl of Pembroke, assumed her role as patron of writers; the first folio edition of Shakespeare, for example, is dedicated to her sons William and Philip. Although both William and Philip attained great wealth and power in the court of James I, Sidney largely retired from court life after the accession festivities. She attempted to put down insurrections in Cardiff, continued her literary friendships, and spent much time taking the waters for her health in the fashionable Continental town of Spa.

Her continued, although diminished, importance as a patron is seen in Aemilia Lanyer's dedication of *Salve Deus Rex Judaeorum* to her (and other women of her circle) in 1611. She died in 1621 at the advanced age of fifty-nine and was buried "in a manner befitting her degree."

Samuel Daniel had prophesied that by her Psalms Sidney's name would live even when her great house at Wilton "lies low leveled with the ground." In 1647, Wilton burned, destroying most of the records of her life and quite possibly some additional writings alluded to in contemporary correspondence. Nevertheless, her Psalms do stand as one of the most significant poetic achievements during Elizabeth's reign.

Works

A Discourse of Life and Death; Antonius: A Tragoedie (1592; *The Countess of Pembroke's Antonie,* ed. A. Luce, 1897; *Narrative and Dramatic Sources of Shakespeare* 5, ed. G. Bullough, 1966). "A Dialogue Between Two Shepheards . . . in Praise of Astrea." *A Poetical Rhapsody,* ed. E. Davison (1602). *The Psalms of Sir Philip Sidney and the Countess of Pembroke,* ed. J.C.A. Rathmell (1963). *The Triumph of Death and Other Unpublished and Uncollected Poems by Mary Sidney, Countess of Pembroke (1561–1621),* ed. G.F. Waller (1977). *The Countess of Pembroke's Translation of Philippe de Mornay's "Discours de la Vie et de la Mort,"* ed. D. Bornstein (1983). *Collected Works,* ed. M. Hannay et al. (1997).

Margaret P. Hannay

Ieva Simonaitytė
1897–1978

Born 1897, Vanagai, Lithuania Minor, the Klaipėda (Memel) district
Died 1978, Vilnius
Genre(s): novel
Language(s): Lithuanian

Because of poor health, Simonaitytė did not attend regular schools and became a self-educated person. In early youth Simonaitytė worked as an itinerant seamstress. In 1921, she came to Klaipėda, learned typing and stenography, and worked in various offices. The first longer piece, a story called "Tu am'inai mane minėsi" (You Will Remember Me Forever) was published in 1933. In 1939 Simonaitytė published her first novel-length story, *Aukštujų Šimonių likimas* (The Fate of the Simonys of Aukštujai), which received the Lithuanian State Prize for Literature and is indeed the best work of her career. The novel deals with the decline and eventual obliteration of an ancient family of Lithuanian nobles living in the territory that was known previously (before the Russians settled there in 1944) as "Lithuania Minor"—actually, East Prussia. The territory was long occupied

and colonized by the Germans, but the Lithuanian element did nevertheless remain quite strong into the nineteenth century. We first see this family, the Simonys, in the Middle Ages, resisting the onslaughts of the German Teutonic order with great determination but ultimately without effect. The main part of the novel, however, deals with the period of established German rule in the eighteenth and nineteenth centuries. The family begins gradually to assimilate; its members lose their sterling old-time Lithuanian moral qualities and enter a decline both spiritually and in social status. Worst of all, they lose their national identity, blend in with the Germans, and ultimately become just another ordinary family of German burgers and farmers—a pitiful condition indeed, because Simonaitytė in her personal and historical anti-German indignation, paints them all, without exception, in the blackest hues of her palette. As an artistic chronicle of this long decline, the story reaches an epic quality and remains unique to this day as the only large-scale artistic commentary upon the destiny of the Lithuanian nation, or at least this particular "Prussian" part of it, from which so many of the best scholars and artists had come in those centuries when the main body of Lithuania was kept in darkness and stagnation by the Russian Tsars.

When Hitler took the Klaipeda district in 1939, Simonaitytė came to live in Lithuania itself. There she met the Soviet occupation and the Second World War, during which she remained in the country and was harassed by the German occupiers. When the Soviets came to power, Simonaitytė entered with great dedication into postwar reconstruction work, most particularly as an artist, producing a great number of large prose works, inevitably in the spirit of "Socialist realism"—a strangely convoluted esthetic predicated upon its function as a tool of the totalitarian Soviet dictatorship. The story "Pikčiurnienė" (1953) portrays the long life of a well-to-do peasant woman, a "kulak"; this designation was invented by Stalin to mark people that were to be destroyed as "class enemies." Naturally, Pikčiurnienė lives up to her name (which translates approximately as "the nasty hag") and cheats, scolds, persecutes others all her life, only to say on her deathbed that she thought she'd lived honestly and for the good of others. Aside from the political idiocies of Socialist realism, there is also an impersonal, dark spirit in the novel. There is the presence of a relentless force of evil, very much like that of the Germans in the Simonys novel, who, like Pikčiurnienė, were not only evil persons but also somehow the embodiment of a destiny of almost Shakespearean darkness. The main hero of the novel

Vilius Karalius (Vilius the King, first part published in 1939, others in later years, under the Soviet regime) is again a similar figure of decay and evil, again a representative of the exploiting classes, a "kulak." Other heroes are portrayed as positive, painfully searching and eventually finding ideals worthy of commitment, those of the Soviet society. In this novel, however, Simonaitytė does demand personal responsibility (and implicitly recognizes the personal power) of each individual for his own destiny, whatever the dark force over everybody's heads. *Vilius Karalius* is written in conventional third-person narrative, without any attempts at modernistic style, or even without any of the grand, solemnly poetic, rhetorical cadences that can be found in *Aukštujų Šimonių likimas*.

Simonaitytė has written three more novels, *Pavasarių audroj* (1938; In the Storm of Springtime), *Be tėvo* (1941; Without Father), *Pakutinė Kūneliio kelionė* (1968; The Last Journey of Kūnelis), and a number of short stories and tales, some autobiographical.

Some critics have considered Simonaitytė, not altogether without reason, to be herself a harsh, hard-bitten person, self-righteous, graceless, tyrannical, and a believer in the prevalence of evil over good. Nevertheless, there is genuine power in her prose, and a grim honesty straight into the face of any evil force, be it the Germans, the kulaks, Socialist realism, or even she herself. Hers were the habits and bearing of an imperious literary figure, which, in Lithuania, she has indeed remained, standing there as a pillar of strength and forging a link between the older and the younger generations in Lithuanian prose.

Works

Aukštujų Šimonių likimas, novel (1939). *Pavasarių audroj*, novel (1938). *Vilius Karalius*, novel (1939). *Be tėvo*, novel (1941). "Pikčiurnienė," story (1953). *Collected Works*, 6 vols. (1957–1958). *O buvo taip . . .* , *Ne ta pastogė* (1963), and *Nebaigta knyga* (1965), both autobiographical tales. "Meilutis ir Gu'iukas," story for children (1967). *Gretimos istorijėlės*, autobiographical tales. *Pakutinė Kūneliio kelionė*, novel (1968).

Rimvydas Šilbajoris

María del Pilar de Sinués de Marco
1835–1893

Born 1835, Zaragoza, Spain
Died 1893, Madrid
Genre(s): novel, conduct book, translation
Language(s): Spanish

María del Pilar de Sinués is one of a group of professional women writers who, in the second half of the nineteenth century, wrote women's fiction and conduct books advocating the cult of domesticity. She also directed a magazine for women, *El ángel del hogar* (1859; The Angel of the House). Although she published some one hundred extremely popular novels and conduct books, her name is mostly absent from literary histories. When included, her critics describe her writing as "costume jewelry prose" and belittle it for being liked by the "simple classes of Spain." Yet, Sinués is an important writer worthy of study for several reasons. From a sociological perspective, her prolific and successful literary career suggests the existence of a substantial female audience, which can begin to explain the emergence of professional women novelists during this period. Also, if one reads her domestic fiction as narratives about female subjectivity rather than as, simply, badly fictionalized conduct books for women, Sinués becomes a key figure in the creation of the discourse of Spanish womanhood.

What little is known about her life seems to be very contradictory. She married the playwright José Marco y Sanchís sight unseen and their marriage ended in a separation. Because of this she was forced to support herself by writing. In contrast to her novels where romantic love triumphs in the face of adversity and her women characters—given their domestic talents of frugality and selflessness—live happily ever after, she died alone and in poverty having squandered a great deal of money.

In her conduct books and novels, she advocated the virtuous woman, bourgeois domesticity, and Christian motherhood. But it is also common to find in her works negative portrayals of the aristocratic lady, the woman of letters, and women who favor women's education. She argued that women should be educated and write only if they were willing to give priority to their domestic duties and behave like "angels in the house." Sinués's contemporaries noted her habit of receiving visitors while immersed in her needlework, thereby proving her own domesticity. They also remembered that she never seemed to finish her pieces.

Sinués argued that women should not write novels given their tendency to write romantic fiction. She believed that the writing of this type of narrative unleashed the writer's passion, which for her was associated with a form of illicit sexual activity antithetical to the notion of "the virtuous woman." In spite of this admonition, she herself wrote passionate and romantic novels. In her two-volume conduct book, *El ángel del hogar* (The Angel of the House), this contradiction can be seen clearly. She does not limit herself to an analysis of the different types of women in society and the behavior appropriate to their position (as does Mrs. Ellis, her English equivalent). She intercalates several novellas to explain and exemplify her analysis and advice. Yet, these short narratives are not presented as fiction. Rather, they are narrated as "real life" stories seen or heard by the narrator. Clearly, though, given the symmetry of characters and plot, these narratives are fiction. This paradox underscores the ambivalence felt by Pilar de Sinués, and many other women writers of her period, about writing in a society with a very weak women's novelistic tradition and where women writers were thought to be committing, in her own words, a grave sin.

The importance of a writer such as Pilar de Sinués is not only her astounding productivity but also her articulation of the contradictions facing women writers at this historical moment in Spain. On the one hand, she exalts the woman as the angel of the house with all of its constraining implications for the woman of letters and, on the other, she cannot control her need to write. She conforms and, in her own way, rebels. María del Carmen Simón Palmer, one of the few critics to address this question, has argued that many of the women writers of this period became spokeswomen for the angel in the house because they could be then forgiven for the "offense" of writing.

Works

Mis poesías (1855). *Amor y llanto. Colección de leyendas* (1857). *La diadema de perlas* (1857). *Margarita* (1857). *Premio y castigo* (1857). *Rosa* (1857). *La ley de Dios* (1858). *El ángel del hogar. Obra recreativa dedicada a la mujer* (1859). *El ángel del hogar. Estudios morales acerca de la mujer* (1862). *Flores del alma* (1860). *A la sombra de un tilo* (1861). *Fausta Sorel* (1861). *Un nido de palomas* (1861). *A la luz de la lánoara* (1862). *El lazo de flores* (1862). *La rama del sándalo* (1862). *Memorias de una joven de la clase media* (1862). *Narraciones del hogar. Primera serie* (1862). *Celeste* (1863). *Hija, esposa y madre* (1863). *Dos venganzas* (1863). *La virgen de las lilas* (1863). *La senda de la gloria* (1863). *El sol de invierno* (1863). *El almohadón de rosas* (1864). *El centro de flores* (1865). *Sueños y Realidades. Memorias de una madre para su hija* (1865). *No hay culpa sin pena* (1864). *Galeria de mujeres célebres* (1864–1869). *El alma enferma* (1864). *El ángel de la tristeza* (1865). *Querer es poder* (1865). *A rio revuelto* (1866). *Cuentos de color de cielo* (1867). *Elcamino de la dicha. Cartas a dos hermanos sobre la educación* (1868). *Veladas del Invierno en torno de una mesa de labor* (1866). *Volver bien por mal* (1872). *Las alas de Ícaro* (1872). *Una hija del siglo* (1873). *Un libro para damas* (1875). *El becerro de oro* (1875). *La vida íntima, en la culpa va elc astigo* (1876). *Combates de la vida. Cuadros sociales* (1876). *Plácida* (1877). *Un libro para las madres* (1877). *La mujer en nuestros días* (1878). *Las mártires del amor* (1878). *Palmas y flores* (1878). *Cortesanas ilustres* (1878). *Damas elegantes* (1878). *Las esclavas del deber* (1878). *La gitana* (1878). *Reinas mártires* (1878). *Glorias de la mujer* (1878). *La abuela* (1878). *Tres genios femeninos* (1879). *Luz y sombra* (1879). *La primera falta . . .* (1879). *Un libro para jóvenes* (1879). *La Dama elegante. Manual práctico y completísimo del buen tono y del buen orden doméstico* (1880). *Armas galantes* (c. 1880). *Una herencia trágica . . .* (1882). *Verdades dulces y amargas. Páginas para la mujer* (1882). *Dramas de familia . . .* (1883–1885). *La vida real* (1884). *Leyendas morales* (1884). *Mujeres ilustres* (1884). *Una historia sencilla* (1886). *La misión de la mujer* (1886). *La expixción* (1886). *Páginas del corazón* (1887). *Isabel. Estudio del natural . . .* (1888). *Cómo aman las mujeres . . .* (c. 1889?). *Novelabs cortas* (1890). *Morir sola* (1890). *Los ángeles de b tierra* (1891). *Cuentos de niños* (1897).

Alda Blanco

Dame Edith Sitwell
1887–1964

Born September 7, 1887, Scarborough, Yorkshire, England
Died December 11, 1964, London
Genre(s): poetry, literary criticism, biography, novel
Language(s): English

Dame Edith Sitwell, a poet and public figure who provoked controversy, was associated with avant-garde styles and thought for fifty years. She became a public figure because she not only read her poems on lecture tours but wrote and performed poetry designed to be accompanied to music.

A child of an aristocratic family, she and her younger brothers Osbert and Sacheverell were brought up in legendary elegance. She was educated at home and was introduced to French symbolist poetry, especially Rimbaud's, through her governess Helen Rootham, with whom she lived in the 1920s. When Sitwell moved to London, she published at her own expense her first volume, *The Mother and Other Poems* (1915), and edited the annual volumes of *Wheels* (1916–1921).

Sitwell also became notorious by performing her poems in *Facade* (1922), set to music by William Walton, in a concert hall. Many of the titles of these poems were dance names such as "Waltz," "Polka," or "Fox Trot." She not only explored the rhythms of word order but the sounds as well. In "Waltz," for example, the sound and rhythm create the 1–2–3 beat of the dance: "Daisy and Lily, / Lazy and silly, / Walk by the shore of the wan grassy sea— / Talking once more 'neath a swan-bosomed tree." Criticism, much of it hostile, responded to the seemingly meaningless poems and the theatricality of her performance. Other poems published in the 1920s also reflect her experimentation in synesthesia and the social disillusionment of the times. Her friends of the period included T.S. Eliot, Aldous Huxley, and Virginia Woolf.

In the 1930s much of Sitwell's work was written to support herself, so there are several anthologies and general prose works: a study of Pope (1930), a book about Bath (1932), *English Eccentrics* (1933), *Aspects of Modern Poetry* (1934), a biography of Queen Victoria (1936), and a novel about Jonathan Swift's loves, *I Live Under a Black Sun* (1937). She resumed writing poetry in 1938.

Poems after World War II reflect a change in style and philosophies, as in *Green Song & Other Poems* (1944), *Song of the Cold* (1945), *Shadow of Cain* (1947). In these poems, lines are longer and her despair over the destruction of life through the bomb "rains" can be seen in her openly pacifist poems. "The Shadow of Cain," Sitwell insists in her introduction to her *Collected Poems* (1954), shows her outrage at the bombing of Hiroshima: "This poem is about the fission of the world into warring particles, destroying and self-destructive."

Later poems are more metaphysical and spiritual. In 1955 Sitwell was accepted into the Roman Catholic Church, and many poems of the late 1940s and 1950s seek to "give holiness to each common day." In her 1962 *The Outcasts,* Sitwell called poetry the "deification of reality."

In her last years honors and praise made her well known. In 1948 and 1950 Sitwell toured the United States reading her poems, which contributed to her reputation. In 1951 the University of Oxford gave her an honorary D.Litt., and in 1954 the Queen made her a Dame Commander of the Order of the British Empire. Most of her manuscripts, sold in auction at Sotheby's, were sent to the library of the University of Texas.

Works

The Mother and Other Poems (1915). *Twentieth-Century Harlequinade and Other Poems* (with Osbert Sitwell, 1916). *Clowns' Houses* (1918). *The Wooden Pegasus* (1920). *Facade* (1922). *Bucolic Comedies* (1923). *The Sleeping Beauty* (1924). *Troy Park* (1925). *Poor Young People* (with Osbert and Sacheverell Sitwell, 1925). *Poetry and Criticism* (1925). *Elegy on Dead Fashion* (1926). *Rustic Elegies* (1927). *Gold Coast Customs* (1929). *Alexander Pope* (1930). *Collected Poems* (1930). *Bath* (1932). *The English Eccentrics* (1933; revised and enlarged, 1957). *Five Variations on a Theme* (1933). *Aspects of Modern Poetry* (1934). *Victoria of England* (1936). *Selected Poems* (1936). *I Live Under a Black Sun* (1937). *Poems New and Old* (1940). *Street Songs* (1942). *English Women* (1942). *A Poet's Notebook* (1943, 1950). *Green Song & Other Poems* (1944). *The Song of the Cold* (1945). *Fanfare for Elizabeth* (1946). *The Shadow of Cain* (1947). *The Canticle of the Rose* (1949). *Poor Men's Music* (1950). *Facade and Other Poems 1920–1935* (1950). *Selected Poems* (1952). *Gardeners and Astronomers* (1953). *Collected Poems* (1954). *The Outcasts* (1962). *The Queens of the Hive* (1962). *Taken Care Of* (1965). *Selected Poems of Edith Sitwell,* ed. J. Lehmann (1965).

Marilynn J. Smith

Amalie Skram
1846–1905

Born 1846, Bergen, Norway
Died 1905, Copenhagen, Denmark
Genre(s): novel, short story, drama
Language(s): Norwegian

With the publication of *Constance Ring* in 1885, Amalie Skram broke taboos that had silenced generations of women. Like her predecessor Camilla Collett, whom she greatly admired, Skram attacked the institution of marriage. But where Collett had leveled her criticism at the way in which marriage was arranged,

Skram denounced the double standard and deplored the sexual ignorance of young women at the time they entered marriage. Never before had there been such a frank discussion of woman's sexuality in a Norwegian book—by a female author, no less—and public and critics alike were scandalized.

Amalie Alver was born in 1846 in Bergen. Her father was a merchant, though not a terribly successful one, and the family's economic situation was never secure. In 1863 her father went bankrupt, and he left for America to try his luck there. Later that same year Amalie, an extraordinarily beautiful seventeen-year-old, was engaged to marry a man nine years her senior. Her fiancé was the captain of a merchant ship and after they were married, the Müllers sailed together for a number of years, visiting distant ports all over the world.

Amalie showed herself to be a good sailor; she was never seasick and obviously enjoyed being on deck when the ship was under sail. These experiences were to inspire some of the best depictions of life at sea in Norwegian literature, in *Forraadt* (1892; Betrayed) and the second volume of her tetralogy *Hellemyrsfolket* (1887; The People of Hellemyr). But even though she took well to the sea voyages, her marriage with Müller proved to be difficult and unhappy. Initial attempts to break away from the marriage were frustrated by her family, who sought to discourage her because of the scandal associated with divorce. This plus the resistance she encountered in trying to obtain custody of her two sons created a tremendous emotional strain, and in 1877 she suffered a nervous breakdown and had to be admitted to Gaustad mental hospital in Kristiania (present-day Oslo).

She was released after three months and at that time (1878) was granted her divorce and took up residence with her brothers and her sons. Needing an income, Amalie Müller turned to writing. Her first published pieces were reviews of works by Ibsen, the Danish author J.P. Jacobsen, Camilla Collett, to mention a few. She was exposed to radical ideas and attitudes both through her reading and her social interactions, and book reviews written during this period reveal a growing receptivity to a naturalistic philosophy.

In 1884 Amalie Müller married the Danish writer Erik Skram, and she went to live with him in Copenhagen where she remained for the rest of her life. From the time of their first meeting, Erik Skram had encouraged Amalie to write fiction, and the first ten years of their marriage marked a period of intense creative productivity. But the stress of trying to fulfill three demanding roles—wife, mother, and writer—took its toll, and in 1894 Amalie Skram once again had a nervous breakdown. She was committed first to a psychiatric ward and then, much against her will, was transferred to a mental hospital. Fortunately, she succeeded in convincing a doctor that she was not mentally ill, and he arranged her release. This traumatic experience resulted in two books, *Professor Hieronimus* and *Paa St. Jörgen* (At St. Jörgen's), both published in 1895. Through a fictitious character, Skram tells of the treatment she received at mental institutions, and her descriptions gave rise to a heated debate in Copenhagen and actually resulted in improved conditions for psychiatric patients.

Skram's condition had hardly improved, however. Her health had suffered considerably as had her nerves, and in 1899 her marriage with Erik Skram ended in divorce. She continued to write, albeit sporadically because of her broken health, until she died in 1905.

Marriage and the problematic relationship between the sexes were issues that occupied Skram throughout her life, and she wrote four novels and several short stories on this subject. After *Constance Ring*, Skram went on to write *Lucia* (1888), *Fru Inés* (1891), and *Forraadt* (1892), all novels dealing with women who experience unhappy marriages. Skram was intent on exposing marriage as a hypocritical institution. Her heroine Constance Ring grows up believing that marriage is sacred, instituted by God. But when, having learned that her husband has made the servant girl pregnant, she goes to her mother and aunt and finally to her pastor for help in obtaining a divorce, she is rebuffed by all. They explain to her that men are by nature promiscuous and that this, contrary to what they had taught her earlier, is the reality of married life. Furthermore, it was her Christian duty to stay with her husband and to wield a positive influence over him. Although Constance does agree to abandon her divorce suit, she is not able to reconcile herself with a life she perceives to be built on lies and deceit. Some years after this crisis, her husband dies in a sailing accident, and Constance, initially overcome by guilt and depression, finally does open herself to new relationships with men. But the double standard is ever-present and, as Constance is unable to cope with disillusionment, each new attempt to find love founders.

Women would be much better equipped to deal with marriage, even the double standard, Skram argued, if they were given a proper education in their youth. Mothers avoided all discussion of sexuality. Teenaged brides were given in marriage to older, established men without ever being told that they would share the same bed on their wedding night. This obviously hindered women from developing a natural and healthy attitude toward their own sexuality and the sexual desires of their husbands, to the ultimate unhappiness of both partners. Ory, the young bride in *Betrayed*, responds with fear and shock to her husband's sexual overtures on their first night together. She comes to regard sex as something ugly and repulsive, and though she longs to be a good wife and to love her husband, she remains cold to all his attempts at intimacy. Her own sexuality having been thwarted, she takes a perverse interest in hearing about her husband's earlier sexual encounters. This becomes an obsession that eventually causes him to lose his mind.

Amalie Skram was driven by a need to tell the truth and depict life as she saw it in everything she wrote. That she was influenced by the French naturalists can be seen in her earliest stories, and concerning her novel *Constance Ring*, she asked that it be regarded as a *document humain*. The determining influence of heredity and environment is most fully developed in her four-volume work *The People of Hellemyr*, the story of a family through several generations. This tetralogy is considered to be the finest example of a naturalistic work in Norwegian literature. For many years Amalie Skram's place in literary history rested on her reputation as one of Norway's foremost representatives of naturalism. Recent scholarship, however, has focused on her "marriage" novels, pointing out her important contribution as an outspoken feminist author.

Works

Novels: *Constance Ring* (1885). *Hellemyrsfolket* (tetralogy): *Sjur Gabriel* (1887). *To venner* (1887). *S.G. Myre* (1890). *Axiom* (1898). *Lucia* (1888). *Fru Inés* (1891). *Forraadt* (1892). *Professor Hieronimus* (1895). *Paa St. Jörgen* (1895). *Julehelg* (1900). *Mennesker* (1902–1905).

Short stories: *Börnefortællinger* (1890). *Kjærlighed i nord og syd* (1891). *Sommer* (1899).

Drama: with Erik Skram, *Fjældmennesker* (1889). *Agnete* (1893).

Letters: *Mellom slagene*, ed. Eugenia Kielland (1955).

Criticism: *Optimistisk Læsemaade. Amalie Skrams litteraturkritikk*, ed. Irene Engelstad (1987).

Translations: *Betrayed*, tr. Aiken Hennes (1986). *Constance Ring*, tr. Judith Messick with Katherine Hanson (1988). *Norway's Best Stories*, ed. Hanna Astrup Larsen (1927). *Slaves of Love and Other Norwegian Short Stories*, ed. James McFarlane (1982). *An Everyday Story. Norwegian Women's Fiction*, ed. Katherine Hanson (1984).

Katherine Hanson

Božena Slančiková
1867–1951

a.k.a. Timrava
Born October 2, 1867, Polichno, then in Austro-Hungary
Died November 27, 1951, Lucenec, both towns now in Czechoslovakia
Genre(s): short story, novella, poetry, drama
Language(s): Slovak

Arguably the best Slovak woman writer to date, Timrava has been categorized as a "critical realist" by Marxist scholars for her condemnation of the materialistic and hypocritical small-town society she portrayed. She received the title of "National Artist" in 1947.

Born into the family of Protestant minister Pavol Slančik in southern Slovakia, Timrava was educated at home except for one year in a girls' school at age fourteen. She spent four unhappy months as companion to a rich widow in 1900 but otherwise lived all her creative life in the village where she was born and in a neighboring village. Unmarried, she lived with her family and worked as a nursery school teacher to supplement her royalties, which were meager for most of her life. The financial instability of a single woman increased Timrava's insight into current women's issues, and she portrayed many female characters whose rebellion against their position usually remained internal and only half-understood. Less nationalistic than her older sister writers Elena Maróthy-Šoltésová and Terézia Vansová, Timrava did not see the solution of the national problem as the solution to women's inequities.

Timrava's fifty or more stories and novellas are primarily autobiographical or based on close observation of the village society she lived in. Her early slightly satiric verses about her family and friends were never published, but she developed them into ironic stories of courtship leading to marriage as a financial bargain that remind one of Jane Austen's novels written over a half-century earlier. Among the best of them are *Bez hrdosti* (No Self-Respect) in 1905, *Veľké Šťastie* (Her Great Good Fortune) in 1906, and *Strašnýkoniec* (An Awful Ending) in 1912—all showing rebellious females who despise their position as pawns but who resign themselves to a loveless "prudent" marriage or to a lonely single life. During the same period Timrava was also writing a separate series of powerful, often tragic stories about the second village caste, the peasants. *Tá zem vábna* (That Alluring Land) in 1907 showed the problem of massive emigration from the point of view of those left behind. The longest and best of these peasant stories, *Ťapákovci* (The Ťapak Clan) in 1914, was immediately acclaimed by critics as an epiphany of the backward extended family so downtrodden they no longer wanted to improve their lives. The clear dramatic and philosophical contrast between a sister who loves the old ways and a young wife who demands progress is characteristically complicated by the tragic element of the sister's crippled legs that embittered her life. In a masterpiece of irony, the pacifist novella *Hrdinovia* (Great War Heroes) in 1928, Timrava showed both the rich and the poor and how differently the Great War affected them. Two stories present an interesting though incomplete autobiographical picture of a woman writer in the national movement: *Skúsenost'* (Experience) in 1902 and *Všetko za národ* (Give Your All for the Nation) in 1930.

Timrava is unique among Slovak writers (men as well as women) for the perceptive, realistic clarity of her characters and the bitter terseness of her satire. Much praised by Marxist critics for her early recognition of many of the contradictions of capitalism, she is also striking for her early perception that women were at least inwardly rebelling against their limitations, that some ordinary young girls were already incipient feminists.

Works

Skúsenost' [Experience] (1902). *Tá zem vábna* [That Alluring Land] (1907). *Márnost' vštko* [The Vanity of It All] (1908). *Ťapákovci* [The Ťapak Clan] (1914). *Dedinské povosti* [Village Tales] (1920). *Hrdinovia* [Great War Heroes] (1928). *Všetko za národ* [Give Your All for the Nation] (1930). *Dve doby* [Two Epochs] (1937). *Novohradské dedina* [A Novohrad Village] (1937). *Výber z diela* [Selected Works] (1937). *Výber z rozprávok* [Selected Tales] (1937). *Prvé kroky* [First Steps] (1938). *Zobraneé spisy* [Collected Works] (1921–1945).

Translations: Czech: *Zkusenost* (1958). Russian: *Bez radosti* (1960). Magyar: *Hözök* (1960, 1975). English: "The Ťapák Family" (excerpt) (1962). Polish: *Za kogo wyjść* (1984). English: "The Assistant Teacher," "That Alluring Land," "No Joy at All," "An Awful Ending," "The Ťapák Clan," "Great War Heroes" (1990).

Norma L. Rudinsky

Smara
1857–1944

a.k.a. Smara Gîrbea, Smaranda Garbini[u], Frusinica, Baba Vişa
Born 1857, Tîrgovişte, Romania
Died 1944, Bucharest
Genre(s): novel, short story, drama, poetry, essay, children's literature, journalism, memoir, translation
Language(s): Romanian

Smara (Smaranda Gheorghiu, née Andronescu) combined in one person and under a variety of pseudonyms a determined feminist, an enlightened and dynamic cultural entrepreneur, and a vigorous militant writer.

She traveled widely in Romania, Italy, Belgium, France, Sweden, Denmark, Greece, etc., lecturing on education and women's emancipation, was among the organizers of the Universal Union of Women's Congress for Peace, and represented Romania repeatedly at international congresses such as the Orientalists' Congress (1889) and the Latin Congress (1902). Smara founded a literary circle attended by the superlative Romanian poet Eminescu among other prestigious writers of the time. In 1890, one year after the tragic death of Veronica Micle, she published a monograph acknowledging that romantic woman poet's contribution to Romanian literature. In 1893, Smara issued a literary journal—*Altiţe şi bibiluri* (Lace and Frills). The name of the journal was meant to draw the attention of the cultivated public to women's needlework folk art and, more generally, of folk costume sewing as a legitimate constituent of Romanian culture. In books like *Feciorii şi fiicele noastre* (1896; Our Sons and Daughters) and *Inteligenţa femeii* (1896; Women's Intelligence), Smara advocated equal education for girls and boys while opposing male chauvinistic cultural policies and ideologies of the time. After years of tenacious campaigning Smara managed to introduce and popularize the idea of outdoor schools.

A regular contributor to *Convorbiri literare*, *Fîntîna Blanduziei*, *Revista literară*, *Literatorul*, *Revista poporului*, *Românul literar*, *Tribuna literară*, *Universul*, *Adevărul*, *Şsoala romănă*, etc., Smara published several novels among which *Fata tatii* (1912; Daddy's Girl), *Băiatul mamii* (Mom's Boy), and *Domnul Bădină* (Mr. Bădină) are best known. In the second, the principal character, an unhappily married woman, becomes a feminist and, subsequently, depressed by the baseness of her lover, commits suicide. In the other novels, the female characters are also weakened and humiliated by selfish, despotic, and opportunistic husbands and lovers.

Her short stories, some of which were collected in the volumes *Novele* (1890; Short Stories) and *Dumitriţe brumate* (1937; Hoarfrosted Marigolds] are either nostalgic evocations of rural life or compassionate depictions of the life of the poor, of recruits, convicts, etc.

Smara's long plays focus upon incest (*Mîrza*, 1904) or plead for legally enforcing men's paternal responsibilities (*Ispăşire*, 1905; Expiation). Smara's short plays are circumstantial celebrations of the Union of the Romanian principalities (*La 24 Ianuarie,* 1905; On January 24th), of patriotism (*Dorul de ţară*, 1905; Homesickness), or of human work (*Meseriaşii*, 1905; The Craftsmen).

Her volumes of erotic, contemplative, or patriotic poetry—such as *Ţara mea* (1905; My Country) and *Spade strămoşeşti* (n.d., Ancestors' Swords) are rather conventional.

Smara's numerous lecture trips provided the material for rich and vivid travel recollections such as *Schiţe şi amintiri din Italia* (1900; Sketches and Memories from Italy), *Schiţe şi amintiri din Cehoslovacia* (1925; Sketches and Memories from Czechoslovakia), and especially *O româncă spre Polul Nord* (1932; A Romanian Woman toward the North Pole) in which Smara recounts Denmark, Sweden, Finland, and her encounter with Ibsen.

Smara translated works by E.A. Poe and James Fenimore Cooper into Romanian.

Works

Din pana suferinţei [Suffering's Pen] (1888). *Novele* [Short Stories] (1890). *Veronica Micle. Viaţa şi operile sale* [Veronica Micle. Her Life and Works] (1892). *Feciorii şi fiicele noastre* [Our Sons and Daughters] (1896). *Inteligenţa femeii* [Women's Intelligence] (1896). *Mozaicuri* [Inlays] (1897). *Schiţe din Tîrgovişte* [Sketches from Tîrgovişte] (1898). *Schiţe şi amintiri din Italia* [Sketches and Memories from Italy] (1900). *Calvar* [Calvary] (1901). *Mîrza* [Mîrza] (1904). *Dorul de ţară. Meseriaşii. La 24 Ianuarie. Ispăşire* [Homesickness. The Craftsmen. On January 24th. Expiation] (1905). *Ţara mea* [My Country] (1905). *Conferinţe şi discursuri* [Speeches and Addresses] (1905). *Stîlpi de pază* [Watch Studs] (1906). *Fata tatii* [Daddy's Girl] (1912). *Băiatul mamii* [Mom's Boy] (n.d.). *Spade strămoşeşti* [Ancestors' Swords] (n.d.). *Schiţe şi amintiri din Cehoslovacia* [Sketches and Memories from Czechoslovakia] (1925). *Simfonii din trecut* [Symphonies from the Past] (1927). *O româncă spre Polul Nord* [A Romanian Woman Toward the North Pole] (1932). *Domnul Bădină* [Mr. Bădină] (n.d.). *Corbul cu pene de aur* [The Raven with Golden Feathers] (1925). *Dumitriţe brumate* [Hoarfrosted Marigolds] (1937). *Cîntă Dorna* [Dorna Is Singing] (1939).

Sanda Golopentia

Florence Margaret Smith
1902–1971

a.k.a. Stevie Smith
Born September 20, 1902, Hull, Yorkshire, England
Died March 7, 1971, London
Genre(s): poetry, novel, short story, radio play, book review
Language(s): English

Author of whimsical, deceptively simple verse, Smith also wrote three novels, ten short stories, a BBC radio play, and book reviews. She was given the nickname "Stevie," which she used for all her published work, for her resemblance to a small, popular jockey. Smith and her older sister were raised by their mother and their aunt and by the aunt alone after their mother's death during Stevie's sixteenth year. Throughout her adult life, she made her home with her aunt in a northern suburb of London, Palmers Green. Disguised under the names "Bottle Green" and "Syler's Green," Palmers Green became the setting for fiction and essays in which she comments wryly on the community's "fairly harmless snobbery" and describes nostalgically the woods she and her older sister explored as children. She attended Palmers Green High School and North London Collegiate School for Girls, where the subjects she studied were those studied in boys' schools—an unorthodox curriculum that she appreciated. At school, she learned to love the musical rhythms of the poems she memorized, and she often built her own poetry upon quantitative musical measures. For thirty years she worked as a secretary for two London magazine publishers, employment that gave her time to write poetry, fiction, and book reviews. Her literary reputation grew slowly from 1936 until 1957, when the publication of *Not Waving but Drowning* won her wider critical acclaim. Her lively, humorous letters to other writers, friends, and editors reveal her intelligence as witty, whimsical, serious, philosophical, and not morbid, though in many of her poems she considers death a welcome guest. When she died of a brain tumor in 1971, she had won a popular audience for her poems, which she read on BBC radio programs. The 1975 publication of her *Collected Poems* was welcomed with appreciative reviews, and a movie, *Stevie,* based on a play by Hugh Whitemore and starring Glenda Jackson, appeared in 1978.

Placing herself within a cultural tradition and also challenging its values, Smith wrote several poems in which she imaginatively recreates the voice of legendary and literary characters. "I Had a Dream I Was Helen of Troy" offers a critique of the simpering, thoughtless, and inconsistent character in Homer's *Iliad.* "The Last Turn of the Screw" retells Henry James's tale from the perspective of the not-so-innocent child Miles. Other poems revise the characters of Hamlet's mother Gertrude and her new husband Claudius, of Dido, of Persephone, of Antigone, and of Phaedra (in which she criticizes Marcel Proust's interpretation of Jean Racine's tragic heroine).

In metaphysical poems both serious and comic in tone, she questions Christian doctrine. "How Cruel Is the Story of Eve" explores the traditional interpretation of women as seducers, responsible for original sin. Her speaker notes that the legend has been employed to "give blame to women most/And most punishment." In another poem, "How Do You See," she questions the definitions given for the "Holy Spirit," adopting a style that echoes and mocks a catechism. The poem asks, quite seriously, whether Christianity may not have played out its role in human history. After an allusion to the armed nations ready to destroy each other, she concludes grimly "we shall kill everybody."

Smith's novels are set during times of war, espionage, betrayal, and social unease, but she employs a narrator who breezes through these crises with a crooked smile and an acid tongue. Commenting on England's possible response to the Italian invasion of Abyssinia, the narrator in *Over the Frontier* (1938) notes of herself: "we do not so much like the peace-at-any-price people who go about today to apologise for England and to pretend that she hasn't really got so much of the earth's surface, it only looks that way on these jingo maps. . . . For if we are not nowadays the conquerors and pioneers, we are at least the beneficiaries under empire, and at least and basest we have cheap sugar." She deflates the self-righteous polemic of imperialists and pacifists, then knocks out from under herself any pretentious stand of moral superiority. Her novels sparkle with political insights that are human and funny. Most critics focus on her nonsense verse, her poems built upon odd and charming patterns of sound. Although they share with children's nursery rhymes certain simple aural pleasures, these poems are only superficially simple in tone

and attitude. (The doodling drawings which Smith attached to her published poems also suggest a simplicity in attitude, but her cartoons work, as James Thurber's do, upon the fantasies and candid dream images of the unconscious.) Like T.S. Eliot, Smith could use chiming rhymes for whimsical satire. Her "The Dedicated Water Bull and the Water Maid," written, as her subtitle suggests, in response to a performance of Beethoven's Sonata in F, Opus 17, for Horn and Piano, wittily mocks self-important pomposity: "O I am holy, oh I am plump." Her "The Singing Cat" seems at first a transparent description of an amusing, inconsequential incident in a commuter train but develops a mild critique of those who transform others' pain into their own aesthetic pleasure. Her subtitles often suggest that her verses were prompted by a brief experience, but the poems are not lightly occasional. After reading two paragraphs in a newspaper, she wrote "Valuable," which explores the complex moral and psychological situation of young girls who bear illegitimate babies because they lack a sense of their own worth. An unsympathetic speaker begins the poem in a self-righteous and superior tone of voice, but that stance is challenged both by the image of a panther in a cage and by the voice of one of the young girls, who protests that her low self-esteem merely reflects the community's evaluation of her. Smith's poem, hardly sentimental, implies that the illegitimate babies are the mutual responsibility of society and individuals.

By creating a fiercely comic persona for her poems, fiction, and essays, Smith gave voice to her serious questions on Christian doctrine, contemporary morality, the abuse of power, and the literary tradition. In her eccentric voice, she ridiculed the perfect idiocy of much human behavior while revealing her compassion for fellow creatures caged in a prison.

Works

Novel on Yellow Paper (1936; retitled *Work It Out for Yourself,* 1969). *A Good Time Was Had by All* (1937). *Over the Frontier* (1938). *Tender Only to One* (1938). *Mother, What Is Man?* (1942). *The Holiday* (1949). *Harold's Leap* (1950). *Not Waving but Drowning* (1957). *Some Are More Human Than Others: Sketchbook by Stevie Smith* (1958). *Selected Poems* (1962). *The Frog Prince and Other Poems* (1966). *The Best Beast* (1969). *Two in One* (includes *Selected Poems* and *The Frog Prince,* 1971). *Scorpions and Other Poems* (1972). *Collected Poems* (1975). *Me Again: Uncollected Writings of Stevie Smith* (1981). *New Selected Poems* (1988).

Judith L. Johnston

Edith Irene Södergran
1892–1923

Born April 4, 1892, St. Petersburg, Russia
Died June 24, 1923, Raivola (now Rosjtjino),
Finland
Genre(s): lyric poetry
Language(s): German and Swedish

Edith Södergran occupies a unique place among Swedish writers in Finland in that she opened the gates to European and modernist influence on a type of poetry that had lived a rather secluded life of its own. Educated at the German Girls School in St. Petersburg (now Leningrad), she grew up in a cosmopolitan atmosphere and even in Raivola, the village on the Carelian isthmus, where her family lived, the mixture of Finnish and Russian culture was clearly present. The specific nature of her home village, the cosmopolitan atmosphere of St. Petersburg, and a certain eccentric preoccupation with her "self," peculiar to the only child type of writer, color her poetry, which is new in form, fresh in expression, and bears the clear signature of its author. Much of it can only be understood against these three background factors: Raivola, St. Petersburg, and the fact that she was her mother's only child and was brought up almost entirely by her mother, who always stayed with her during terms in St. Petersburg. Her father died of consumption in 1907, an illness that was to end his daughter's life as well less than twenty years after his death. In 1909 it was discovered that she had the contamination, and the rest of her life was a constant fight against the illness.

It is important to notice that her switch from German to Swedish, which was her mother tongue, coincides with this crisis in her life. From 1909 on, her poetry becomes all her own with the typical Södergran features of free form, no rhymes, "catalogue" poems that resemble some of Walt Whitman's poetry, and the intensely feminine use of language that is one of her chief characteristics. At this time her mother was still wealthy, and she tried to find a cure for her daughter in Switzerland. The years 1911–1913 were spent on the Continent, and when Edith returned home early in 1914, she was filled with dreams of a literary future. She visited several people in 1915, asking them for an evaluation of her poems. She published her first volume, *Dikter* (Poems), in 1916. She could hardly foresee the reaction. Stylistic features that she was familiar with from the Continent—rhymelessness and a dashing swiftness of associations—were so new to the Swedish reading public that people were shocked, and this harsh reaction seems to have taken Edith Södergran

entirely by surprise. All her desperate attempts to establish contacts with what she terms "literary personalities" were refuted, and she returned to Raivola in 1917 to remain there for the rest of her life. In November, the Russian Revolution deprived Edith and her mother of all their property, except the house in Raivola, and in the spring of 1918, the war spread to the village and was followed by famine in the summer. But at that time Nietzsche had become the source of inspiration for Edith, and there is a deep contrast between her creative heights and the poverty and illness she was living in. Her second book, *Septemberlyran* (1918; The September Lyre) reflects both the first beginnings and her almost ecstatic final embracement of Nietzsche's teachings. In them she finds the strength to cope with her illness and poverty, facts that are not tolerated in the sublime world of her poetry. Critical appraisal moved from chilly to cold, but one person, Hagar Olsson, herself a critic and writer, appreciated Edith's poems and entered upon a correspondence with Edith that led to a lifelong friendship. Södergran's visionary poetry is maintained in *Rosenaltaret* (1919; The Rose Altar) but there are also specimens of her early lyric poems. *Framtidens skugga* (1920; The Shadow of Future) is the summit of her lyric achievement: prophetic, visionary and Södergranian. She has now made acquaintance with Steiner's religious views and is about to give up writing all together.

By 1920 other modernists had established themselves, and they looked to Edith Södergran as their idol. But her physical strength was now broken, and though she now gained the friendship of people who appreciated her, and even occasionally resumed writing herself, she was unable to fight her illness much longer. She died on Midsummer Day, 1923.

Hagar Olsson published posthumously a collection of late poems called *Landet som icke är* (1925; The Country That Is Not). In a volume called *Edith's Letters* (1955), she published their correspondence, a fascinating portrait of two friends and two important women writers.

Edith Södergran opened a new era of poetry in Finland and reached out across the language barrier to Sweden. She has been rated as the most important Swedish lyric writer in Finland in the twentieth century.

Works

Dikter [Poems] (1916). *Septemberlyran* [The September Lyre] (1918). *Rosenaltaret* [The Rose Altar] (1919). *Brokiga iakttagelser* [Gaudy Observations] (1919). *Framtidens skugga* [The Shadow of Future] (1920). *Landet som icke är* [The Country That Is Not] (1925).

Gunnel Cleve

Nadezhda Sokhanskaia
1823–1884

a.k.a. Kokhanovskaia
Born February 17, 1823, near Korocha, Russia
Died December 3, 1884, "Makarovka" (manor)
Kharkov province
Genre(s): short story, autobiography, publicity,
ethnography-history
Language(s): Russian

If Nadezhda Sokhanskaia ("Kokhanovskaia") had been born fifteen years earlier and begun publishing as a contemporary of Nikolai Gogol, she would have had a better chance to be recognized as one of the great regionalists of Russian literature. In the postemancipation era of the 1860s and 1870s, however, she was clearly out of step: sympathetic to the Slavophiles, she published most of her works in Ivan Aksakov's newspapers and other conservative forums. Deeply religious, she supported the Cyril and Methodius societies created to protect Orthodox Ukrainians in the western borderlands. Her journalism displayed antisemitic bias, and her contentious character made the protest letter one of her most practiced genres. Prescriptive critics failed to appreciate the internal logic of Sokhanskaia's fiction. Because she described her simple protagonists' adventures from their own viewpoint in a stylized voice that drew heavily on oral tradition, she was accused of approving their mores and casting a rosy glow over the harsh realities of rural life under serfdom. The Soviets seemed content to let this reputation stand and Western scholars have yet to evaluate Sokhanskaia's original talent.

Born into near poverty, Sokhanskaia was educated as a scholarship student at the Kharkov Institute, one of the infamous "closed" boarding schools for girls. After she returned at seventeen to "Makarovka," the humble family manor in the eastern Ukraine, she made the interpretation of the history and contemporary life of the area her life work. She published several articles of collected popular songs, and her fiction is steeped in folklore. The protagonists of her stories were drawn from the impoverished gentry, Cossack, and merchant classes; she reported on peasant attitudes in brief reports to newspapers (under rubrics like "S khutora" [From the Farm]), but the peasantry plays only a subordinate role in her fiction. Her most admired work, "Starina" (1861; Olden Times), was a set of sketches of her ancestors, including a woman who turned her hand to banditry. This historical compilation was complemented by several fictional tales set in the eighteenth century: "Iz provintsial'noi gallerei

portretov" (1859; From a Provincial Portrait Gallery), "Roi Feodosii Savvich na pokoe" (1864; Swarm—the hero's nickname, because he was born in an apiary—Feodosii Savvich at Rest), and "Krokha slovesnogo khleba" (1874; A Literary Breadcrumb—so called because the story appeared in a book published for charity; Sokhanskaia usually referred to it as "Prus" after the nickname of her hero, a veteran of the Prussian wars who travels to Petersburg to seek justice in a land dispute).

Sokhanskaia's weakest story is the most realistic and autobiographical ("Gaika," 1856–1860; meaning "nut" or "screw" but in context best translated as "The Linchpin"). She was clearly fascinated by the challenge of depicting larger-than-life characters like Swarm and all three heroes—father, daughter, and suitor—of "From a Provincial Portrait Gallery." For virtually the first time, and very nearly the last, in Russian literature, Sokhanskaia depicts the entrepreneur as a positive type ("Gaika"; "Kirilla Petrov i Nastas'ia Dmitrova," 1861). Despite her affectionate tone and the exuberant language and glittering stylization in which she describes her protagonists' flamboyant ways, Sokhanskaia never loses sight of the despotism and patriarchal mores that rule their world. In this rigid society her female characters suffer most. In "Posle obeda v gost'iakh" (1858; An After-Dinner Visit), Liubov' Arkhipovna tells the narrator how she learned to cherish the clumsy, kind merchant her mother forced her to marry. It takes a single question from her listener to reveal the full extent of the girl's tragic loss of a chance for happiness with a lover whose quicksilver character and talents matched her own.

When Sokhanskaia sent her first efforts at fiction to a St. Petersburg editor in 1846, he suggested that the neophyte hone her craft by writing the history of her own life. This remarkable autobiography, written before she was twenty-five, was published posthumously in *Russkoe obozrenie* (The Russian Review, 1896, 6–9). It evokes still fresh memories of Sokhanskaia's carefree childhood, unhappy years at school, and the shock of her return to an earth-floored house in a region composed largely of women living alone on isolated farms and estates. Much of her later life is covered in correspondence with Ivan Aksakov and his wife (*Russian Review*, 1897, 2–12). A long article she wrote in answer to criticism of "From a Provincial Portrait Gallery" offers valuable information about her creative priorities [*Russkaia Beseda* (Russian Colloquy), 1859, 6, crit., pp. 123–152]. While her widowed mother and spinster aunt were still vigorous, Sokhanskaia had time to write; from the late 1860s, she had to devote most of her energies to caring for them and the farm they had struggled to build. At her death she left unpublished only a fragment of reminiscences from her aunt's life, "Sumerechnye rasskazy" (Twilight Tales), and the historical introduction to a projected novel, "Stepnaia baryshnia sorokovykh godov" (A Young Lady of the Steppes of the '40s).

Works
Povesti, 2 vols. (1863).

Translation: "Les Ames du bon Dieu," N.A. Kolbert, tr., *Barines et moujiks* (1887).

Mary F. Zirin

Mary Somerville
1780–1872

Born December 26, 1780, Jedburgh Manse, Burntisland, Scotland
Died November 29, 1872, Naples
Genre(s): science text, translation, memoir
Language(s): English

A self-taught mathematician, Somerville wrote books on physical science, mathematics, and astronomy. Her youth was spent in Scotland where she received fitful spurts of education in writing, reading, needlework, cooking, drawing, dancing, and playing the piano but was discouraged from pursuing any formal education or even home-study unrelated to domestic concerns. Her love of nature and her scientific curiosity were viewed as inappropriate, eccentric, and dangerous by her family. Her thirst for knowledge therefore prompted surreptitious reading and study; she quietly taught herself Latin and began to learn about astronomy. Upon seeing algebraic symbols in a monthly magazine, she developed a strong ambition to learn higher mathematics. She studied Euclid, other basic texts, and taught herself Greek.

At the age of twenty-four she married a distantly related cousin, Captain Samuel Grieg, who became Russian consul in London. Grieg, like most of Somerville's family, disparaged her studies and ambitions, but she persevered, teaching herself plane and spherical trigonometry, conic sections, and some astronomy. The couple had two children, one of whom died while very young, and three years after they were married Grieg died.

Having solved an algebraic problem in a mathematical journal, Somerville received a silver medal. Wallace, the editor of the journal and later professor of mathematics of Edinburgh University, encouraged Somerville and helped her select books for a small library. At the age of thirty-three, with independent means, she had accumulated the sought-after books and was openly able to pursue her interests.

In 1812, she married another cousin, Dr. William Somerville, whose attitude toward her studies was one of admiration and encouragement. A true companion, he was an excellent classicist and shared many of her scientific interests, including mineralogy and geology, and assisted her studies in many ways. They lived in Edinburgh for the first years of their marriage, Dr. Somerville becoming the head of the Army Medical Department of Scotland, then moving to Hanover Square, London, when he was appointed a member of the Army Medical Board in 1816. In London, Mary Somerville attended lectures at the Royal Institution where she met many of the leading thinkers and scientists of the day. On a visit to Paris, the Marquis de la Place, impressed with her erudition, gave her an inscribed copy of the *Système du Monde*. He later said that she was the only woman who understood his work. Back in London, she met, among others, Maria Edgeworth, who became a close friend.

In 1826, Somerville presented her paper, "The Magnetic Properties of the Violet Rays of the Solar Spectrum," to the Royal Society. Although the theory presented in this paper was subsequently refuted by Moser and Ries, the work was nonetheless considered original, speculative, and ingenious and brought her recognition.

She was then asked to write a popularized English version of la Place's *Le Mécanique Céleste*. The publication of this book, titled *The Celestial Mechanism of the Heavens* (1831), placed her among the first rank of scientific writers. It was immediately adopted as a textbook at Oxford—a university that did not then admit women. She was elected an honorary member of several British and foreign learned societies, including the Royal Astronomical Society, which elected Somerville and Caroline Herschel—their first female members— at the same time, and her bust, executed by Chantrey, was placed in the Great Hall of the Royal Society. Her next book, *On the Connexion of the Physical Sciences* (1834), a summary of research into physical phenomena, went through nine editions and several revisions and was translated into German and Italian; a pirated edition was printed in the United States. A sentence in the 1842 edition is credited by John Couch Adams (1767–1848) with sparking the calculations from which he deduced the orbit of Neptune.

Somerville was elected an honorary member of the Royal Academy of Dublin (1834), of the Sociètè de Physique et d'Histoire Naturelle (Geneva 1834), and of the British Philosophical Institution (c. 1835). Also in 1835 she wrote a lengthy essay on comets for *Quarterly Review*. In 1836, her paper "Experiments on the Transmission of Chemical Rays of the Solar Spectrum Across Different Media" appeared in *Comptess Rendus Hebdomadaires des Séances de L'Académie des Sciences*. While in London, she was asked by Lady Byron to direct the mathematical studies of her daughter, Ada Byron (later Lady Lovelace). She was further honored by being made the recipient of a lifelong pension of £200, later raised to £300.

Although the Somervilles moved to Italy in 1838 because of her husband's failing health, Somerville continued to write important scientific works and to conduct scientific experiments on the solar spectrum and the juices of plants. Her *Physical Geography*, on which she worked for many years, was published in 1848 and went through seven subsequent editions. A year later, when her husband died, she remained in Italy. In 1869, at age eighty-nine, she published *Molecular and Microscopic Science*, a summary of the most recent discoveries in chemistry and physics. In that year she was the recipient of the first gold medal awarded by the Italian Geographical Society as well as the Victoria gold medal of the Royal Geographical Society. She returned to pure mathematics late in life, working until her death on *Theory of Differences*. She died within a month of her ninety-second birthday and was buried at the English Campo Santo at Naples.

Somerville wrote on scientific and astronomical matters with simplicity and power, explaining complicated subjects with an unpretentious and energetic clarity so that even those unfamiliar with the subject could absorb difficult principles. The prefaces to her works were published separately for the general public, while the actual works were used as textbooks for university students and mathematics scholars. Her *Personal Recollections*, friendly and engaging, resonates with her enthusiasm for experimentation and the excitement of discovery. She also recounts many customs of Scotland during her girlhood as well as good-naturedly detailing her many frustrations at not being allowed to pursue learning. Interested in promoting education for women, her name headed the Women's Suffrage petition of 1868. She was commemorated after her death in the foundation of Somerville College, Oxford, and in the Mary Somerville scholarship for women in mathematics. A crayon portrait of her which James Swinton executed in 1848 hangs in the National Portrait Gallery, and a copy of the bust made by Lawrence Macdonald in 1844 at Rome was presented to the National Portrait Gallery in Scotland. Her bust adorns not only the Great Hall of the Royal Society but also graces a room in the Royal Institution.

Works

The Celestial Mechanism of the Heavens (1831). *A Preliminary Dissertation on the Mechanism of the Heavens* (1832). *On The Connexion of the Physical Sciences* (1834). *Physical Geography* (1848). *Molecular and Microscopic Science* (1869). *Personal Recollections from Early Life to Old Age of Mary Somerville with Selections from her Correspondence* by her daughter, Martha Charters Somerville (1873).

Gale Sigal

Somerville and Ross
(pseudonym)
Edith Oenone Somerville
1858–1949
a.k.a. Geilles Herring, Viva Graham
Born May 2, 1858, Corfu
Died October 8, 1949, Castle Townshend, Ireland

Violet Florence Martin
1862–1915
a.k.a. Martin Ross
Born June 11, 1862, Ross House, County Galway, Ireland
Died December 21, 1915, Cork, Ireland

Genre(s): novel, travel, literature, short story, dictionary
Language(s): English

Writing during the time of the Irish Literary Revival, Somerville and Ross depicted Ireland not mythically but realistically, evoking the era when changes in the Land Laws brought about the end of the Anglo-Irish Ascendancy.

Second cousins and members of prominent English families that had established themselves in Ireland in the twelfth and sixteenth centuries, Somerville and Ross grew up in "big houses," and Somerville was to spend much of her energy trying to find money to maintain the Somerville House and her own pack of hounds, even introducing and successfully raising Friesian cattle in Ireland. When Ross met her in 1886, Somerville had already established herself as a professional illustrator, studying art in Paris with Delecluse and Colarossi and sketching Pasteur in his clinic. The two then began a literary collaboration that was so successful that critics have found it almost impossible to separate their styles; that continued even after Ross's death, with Somerville asserting that she remained in spiritual communication with her partner and signing both their names to the works she published.

Following in the tradition of Maria Edgeworth, a close friend of their great-grandmother, the two were particularly interested in language and dialect, first working together on *The Buddh Dictionary*, a collection of phrases used by Somerville's family, and throughout their lives collecting instances of the Irish use of English. Yeats praised the accuracy of the reported Irish speech in their work. These details of Irish life were the most effective aspect of their first novels, *An Irish Cousin* (1889) and *Naboth's Vineyard* (1891), both of which are burdened with Gothic and melodramatic plot devices. *The Real Charlotte* (1894) was their most effective novel and was honored as a World Classic by Oxford University Press in 1948. Set against the background of Anglo-Irish society as portrayed through the decaying Dysart family, it focuses particularly on two women, Francie, an uneducated but beautiful lower-class girl, and Charlotte, an unattractive, driven middle-class woman who is successful in her business dealings but fails in her personal relations. The novel, like much of their work, is a study of frustrated desire and has been compared favorably with Austen's novels, George Eliot's *Middlemarch*, and Balzac's *Cousine Bette*. Their subsequent novel, *The Silver Fox* (1898), was less successful, perhaps because it deals so intensely with Irish mysticism.

To support themselves, Somerville and Ross also wrote, at the same time as their novels, a series of comic sketches of their travels through Ireland and Europe, *Through Connemara in a Governess Cart* (1893), *In the Vine Country* (1893), *Beggars on Horseback* (1895), and *Stray-Aways* (1920). Many of these were first published in periodicals, as were the Irish R.M. stories, which first appeared in the *Badminton Magazine* in October 1898. Their agent, J.B. Pinker, who also worked for Henry James and Arnold Bennett, suggested they work on a series of comic stories about hunting which led to the publication of *Some Experiences of an Irish R.M* (1899). This work, depicting the adventures of a Resident Magistrate, Major Sinclair Yeates, trying to cope with the Irish peasants and his crafty landlord, Flurry Knox, brought its authors international fame. From then until Ross's death, the pair continued to write mainly hunting stories, *All on the Irish Shore* (1903), articles in *Some Irish Yesterdays*

(1906), and a hunting novel, *Dan Russel the Fox* (1911).

After Ross's death, with the worsening situation in Ireland, Somerville wrote a series of novels that dealt more specifically, though it had always been a concern of theirs, with the social and political problems of Ireland, particularly with how sectarianism was undermining Irish life. In *Mount Music* (1919), Somerville writes about religious schisms, in *An Enthusiast* (1921) about political ones. And in *The Big House of Inver* (1925), Somerville writes a novel, thought to be as effective as *The Real Charlotte* about the decay and collapse of the "big houses" in Ireland, with the house modeled on Ross House, Ross's ancestral home.

Somerville and Ross are interesting because, as Lord Dunsany said of the Irish R.M. stories, readers can get "more of Ireland from that book than from anything I can tell them" and because of the relation between the two women. As Somerville puts it, "the outstanding fact . . . among women who live by their brains, is friendship. A profound friendship that extends through every phase and aspect of life, intellectual, social and pecuniary."

Works

S. *The Kerry Recruit* (1889). S. as Geilles Herring and R. *An Irish Cousin* (1889). S. and R. *Naboth's Vineyard* (1891). S. and R. *In the Vine Country* (1893). S. and R. *Through Connemara in a Governess Cart* (1893). S. and R. *The Real Charlotte* (1894). R. and S. *Beggars on Horseback* (1895). R. and S. *The Silver Fox* (1898). S. and R. *Some Experiences of an Irish R.M.* (1899). R. and S. *A Patrick's Day Hunt* (1902). S. and R. *All on the Irish Shore* (1903). S. *Slipper's ABC of Fox Hunting* (1903). S. and R. *Some Irish Yesterdays* (1906). S. and R. *Further Experiences of an Irish R.M.* (1908). S. and R. *Dan Russel the Fox* (1911). S. *The Story of the Discontented Little Elephant* (1912). S. and R. *In Mr. Knox's Country* (1915). S. and (nominally) R. *Irish Memories* (1917). S. and (nominally) R. *Mount Music* (1919). S. and R. *Stray-Aways* (1920). S. *An Enthusiast* (1921). S. and (nominally) R. *Wheel-Tracks* (1923). S. and (nominally) R. *The Big House of Inver* (1925). S. and (nominally) R. *French Leave* (1928). S. *The States Through Irish Eyes* (1930). S. and (nominally) R. *An Incorruptible Irishman* (1932). S. and (nominally) R. *The Smile and the Tear* (1933). S. and (nominally) R. *The Sweet Cry of Hounds* (1936). S. and (nominally) R. *Sarah's Youth* (1938). S. and Boyle Townsend Somerville. *Records of the Somerville Family of Castlehaven and Drishane from 1174 to 1940* (1940). S. and (nominally) R. *Motions in Garrison* (1941). S.

and (nominally) R. *Happy Days!* (1946). S. and (nominally) R. *Maria and Some Other Dogs* (1949).

Elsie B. Michie

Joanna Southcott
1750–1814

Born April 25, 1750, Devonshire, England
Died December 27, 1814, London
Genre(s): religious tract
Language(s): English

Prophet, priestess, and mystic, Southcott wrote and published 65 religious pamphlets from 1792 to 1814 and was the center of a large religious movement known as the Southcottians, which some have estimated as having up to 100,000 members. Born the fourth daughter of an unsuccessful farmer, Southcott sought employment as a domestic servant; she rejected numerous marriage proposals from farmers' sons, determined to remain single. During the 1790s, she wrote down her prophecies predicting famine that she felt was caused by failure to take her other prophecies seriously. In 1801, she published her first work, *The Strange Effects of Faith*, financed by her own savings. It attracted a small group of followers, mostly women and members of the working class but also including several Anglican ministers and the engraver William Sharp. Southcott believed that she heard the Lord's voice and received visions that permitted her to distribute a commonplace seal and stated the millennium was exclusively available for her followers, "the sealed people." In 1802, she visited London, and in 1803 she toured the North and West. From 1804 to 1814, Southcott lived in London in the house of the wealthy Jane Townely, who was her patron and secretary. In 1809, the movement began to decline when the witch and murderess Mary Bateman was associated with a Yorkshire congregation, but it achieved a second impetus in 1814, when Southcott, then sixty-four, promised to give birth to the son of God. Of the nine doctors who examined her, six declared that she was pregnant, and she developed all the signs of pregnancy. At the time of the expected birth, she suddenly died; an autopsy performed on her body revealed no pregnancy. After her death, the movement did not die out but persisted until the end of the nineteenth century. In the early twentieth century, Alice Seymour reissued Southcott's writings, and there is still a small body of followers today. Southcott's work attracted commentators who are either fervent defenders or detractors. Among her contemporaries, Keats referred to her as a nuisance, Southey referred to her as a freak, and Byron alludes to her failure to give birth to the son of God in attacking Wordsworth in *Don Juan*. Her writing was attacked for alleged vulgarity and indecent allusions. Recent criticism has attempted to be more objective, seeing Southcott and her radical religious fervor as part of Romanticism.

Critics have pointed out that the movement appealed strongly to women since Southcott believed that just as a woman had been responsible for the Fall, so she would be for the salvation. In *Strange Effects of Faith*, she asks, "Is it a new thing for a Woman to deliver her people? Did not Esther do it? Did not Judith do it?" The movement also appealed to the working classes' adjustments to economic, agricultural, and military upheavals. Critics have pointed out, however, that her prophecies did not provoke her followers toward political action but instead emphasized personal salvation and thus was in the Methodist tradition.

Southcott expected Methodist support but was rejected by the Exeter Methodist community and grew disillusioned. Critics see *Divine and Spiritual Communications* (1803) as one of her rare polemical works in which she accuses the Methodists of being Calvinistic. She was a devout member of the Church of England, and most of her efforts were directed at persuading individual clergymen and bishops to reexamine her prophecies. She believed that all religious sects were to be united with the Church of England. Her purpose was not to form a competing sect, but her followers eventually founded their own chapels and named them after her. Just as Southcott perceived herself as a mere vehicle of God, so she perceived her writings; they were not intended for any aesthetic purpose but to spread her message. Critics have noted that her style is a mixture of the mystical and the literal in which biblical allusions combine with autobiographical references. Her handwriting is often illegible, giving the sense of being written in a moment of mystical revelation. Later, her pamphlets had to be dictated to her secretary. The pamphlets, however, were not the only way that Southcott reached her audience; her actions were widely commented on and debated in the press so that even those who never read any of her pamphlets were aware of her beliefs and activities. Ironically, she never wanted herself to be the focus of the movement but saw herself as a mere intermediary. Although she is often associated with and admired Richard Brothers, a religious leader who declared himself King of the Hebrews and Nephew of God, Southcott felt that he succumbed to moral pride.

Today, she is rarely if ever read, but she provides an interesting footnote to the literary, religious, and social history of early nineteenth-century England.

Works

The Strange Effects of Faith (1801). *A Continuation of the Prophecies* (1802). *Dispute Between the Woman and the Powers of Darkness* (1802). *Answer of the Lord to the Powers of Darkness* (1802). *Books of Sealed Prophecies* (date unknown). *Second Book of Visions* (1803). *A Word in Season* (1805). *A Word to the Wise* (1803). *Divine and Spiritual Communication* (1803). *Sound an Alarm in My Holy Mountain* (1804). *A Warning to the World* (1804). *On the Prayers for the Fast Day* (1804). *Letters on Various Subjects* (1804). *Copies and Parts of Copies* (1804). *Letters and Communications* (1804). *The Trial of Joanna Southcott* (1804). *Answer to Garrett's Book* (1805). *Answer to the Five Charges in the Leeds Mercury* (1805). *True Explanation of the Bible* (1805). *Explanation of the Parables* (1805). *Kingdom of Christ Is at Hand* (date unknown). *Answer to Rev. Foley* (1805). *Controversy with Elias Carpenter* (1805). *An Answer to the World* (1806). *Full Assurance That the Kingdom of Heaven Is at Hand* (1806). *The Long Wished for Revolution* (1806). *Answer to Mr. Brother's Book* (1806). *Caution and Instruction to the Sealed* (1807). *An Account of the Trials on the Bills of Exchange* (1807). *Answer to a Sermon by Mr. Smith* (1808). *Answer to False Doctrines* (1808). *True Explanation of the Bible, Part VII* (1809). *A True Picture of the World* (1809). *Controversy of the Spirit* (1811). *An Answer to Thomas Paine* (1812). *The Books of Wonders* (1813–1814). *Prophecies Announcing the Birth of the Prince of Peace* (1814).

Tony Giffone

Muriel Spark
1918–

Born February 1, 1918, Edinburgh, Scotland
Genre(s): novel, short story, translation, plays, literary criticism, biography, children's fiction, poetry
Language(s): English

The wit and style of Spark's novels and short stories express vividly the many themes present in her work. The various genres in which she works range from translations of Horace, Catullus, and Guillaume Apollinaire to radio plays (*Voices at Play,* 1961), stage plays (*Doctors of Philosophy,* 1963), essays, literary criticism, children's stories, biography, poetry, short stories, and novels. Her sense of the comic is visible throughout her work although it is used most often to express serious themes. She is a genius at describing the surfaces of social situations in a way that is anything but flippant.

Spark was born to a Presbyterian mother and a Jewish father. Educated at James Gillespie's Girls School, a Protestant school in Edinburgh, she started learning classical languages at the age of seven. She completed her schooling in 1936 and left the following year for Africa, living in Rhodesia and South Africa until 1944. While in Africa she married S.O. Spark, an Englishman, but soon after the birth of their son the marriage was dissolved. Returning to wartime London, she worked in the Political Intelligence Department of the British Foreign Office until the war was over.

Her first writing job was on the staff of the *Argentor,* a jeweler's trade magazine, but she also worked as editor of *The Poetry Review* for two years as well as putting out two issues of her own journal, *Forum,* and she also worked as a part-time editor for a publisher. During this time her main literary interests developed in the direction of poetry and criticism; she had been publishing her poetry since 1951 and was on the fringe of London's literary bohemia. Her poems in *The Fanfarlo and Other Verse* (1952) are of many types, the title poem influenced heavily by the Scottish border ballad form.

From 1950 to 1957 her attention was focused mainly on nonfiction work. She edited *The Brontë Letters* (1954) and, with Derek Stanford—her literary partner until 1957 and friend of many years who wrote a study of her entitled *Muriel Spark: A Biographical and Critical Study* (1963)—edited the *Letters of John Henry Newman* (1957) and those of Mary Wollstonecraft Shelley in *My Best Mary: The Selected Letters of Mary Wollstonecraft Shelley* (1953) as well as *Tribute to Wordsworth: A Miscellany of Opinion for the Centenary of the Poet's Death* (1950). She concentrated at this time on literary criticism, producing such diverse volumes as *Emily Brontë: Her Life and Work* (1953)—she wrote the biographical first section of this work and Stanford the critical second section—*John Masefield* (1953), and *Child of Light: A Reassessment of Mary Wollstonecraft Shelley* (1951).

Spark turned seriously to fiction only after winning a short story contest sponsored by *The Observer* in 1951 with her short story "The Seraph and the Zambesi." Macmillan, interested in her work, invited her to try novel writing, and she responded (with the additional help of a stipend from Graham Greene) with

The Comforters in 1957, an experimental work, and the first of her many critically well-received novels. Her attitude toward the novel form has always been mistrustful. Commenting on her first novel, Spark explained that she wrote it to try out the form: "So I wrote a novel to work out the technique first, to sort of make it all right with myself to write a novel at all—a novel about writing a novel."

A major influence on Spark's life and her work was her conversion to Catholicism in 1954. "All my best work has come since then," reports Spark. Religion, as well as the self-conscious craft of novel writing itself, is a major theme in her work; in The Comforters for example, she heavily criticizes "professional" Catholics. Her second novel, Robinson (1958), is an adventure story and allegory, and her third, Memento Mori (1959), was adapted for the London stage in 1964.

The first collection of her short stories, The Go-Away Bird and Other Stories (1958), brought together much of the short fiction Spark had been placing in a variety of publications. More of her stories and poems were collected in separate volumes in 1967, including many that were first published in the New Yorker. Her stories reveal this talented writer's range, which moves easily from comedy and fantasy ("Miss Pinkerton's Apocalypse") to tragic experience ("Bang-Bang You're Dead"), to laying open, as delicately as a fine surgeon, the characteristic hypocrisy of human beings ("The Black Madonna").

Probably her best-known work, The Prime of Miss Jean Brodie (1961) is the story of the influence of an unusually romantic teacher on her students in a girls' school in Edinburgh. Like many of Spark's works, this novel has been adapted for the stage (1964) and screen (1967) and even television (1978). Again like most of her early works, this book focuses on a small society described in accurate detail, in a detached satiric tone that is often described by critics as that of a "dandy." Partly because of the success of this novel, Spark left London to live first in New York and then in Rome, where she now makes her home. Along with this change in place has come a change in the tone of her novels, which are increasingly harsher and more virulent than her early work, although she is still often described as a writer of comedy. The Abbess of Crewe: A Modern Morality Tale (1974) is an example of a work combining these two elements. An allegory of Watergate set in a nunnery, it points out the pervasive influence of the mass media on the modern world.

Spark's work has been burdened by the insistence of traditional scholarship on labeling and categorizing any writer considered a respectable member of the canon. Her changing styles and autobiographical bent have influenced critics who have overlooked her work on the basis of these "faults." Newer critical methods with more inclusive approaches, however, open her work to more extensive study, as shown by her inclusion in Judy Little's study Comedy and the Woman Writer: Woolf, Spark and Feminism. Also examined recently in terms of her use of cinematic technique, psychological exploration of characters, and her quasidetective fiction, Spark's innovative uses of time and form demand further attention.

Works

Child of Light: A Reassessment of Mary Wollstonecraft Shelley (1951). The Fanfarlo and Other Verse (1952). Emily Brontë: Her Life and Work (1953). John Masefield (1953). The Comforters (1957). The Go-Away Bird and Other Stories (1958). Robinson (1958). Memento Mori (1959). The Bachelors (1960). The Ballad of Peckham Rye (1960). The Prime of Miss Jean Brodie (1961). Voices at Play (1961). The Girls of Slender Means (1963). Doctors of Philosophy (1963). The Mandelbaum Gate (1965). Collected Poems I (1967). Collected Stories I (1967). The Very Fine Clock (1968). The Public Image (1968). The Driver's Seat (1970). Not to Disturb (1971). The Hothouse by the East River (1973). The Abbess of Crewe: A Modern Morality Tale (1974). The Takeover (1976). Territorial rights (1979). Loitering with Intent (1981). The Only Problem (1984). The Stories of Muriel Spark (1985). Mary Shelley: A Biography (1987). A Far Cry from Kensington (1988). Curriculum Vitae (1992). The Essence of the Brontës: A Compilation of Essays by Muriel Spark (1993).

Jan Calloway

Maria Luisa Spaziani
1924–

Born 1924, Turin, Italy
Genre(s): poetry, journalism, translation, scholarship
Language(s): Italian

Spaziani began her journalistic activities at a young age; she founded the review Il Dado as a student, and contributed to it and other reviews in the early forties. In 1948 she received her college degree with a thesis on Marcel Proust. Her first collection of poetry, Le acque del Sabato (The Sabbath's Waters) was published by Mondadori in 1954. After several years of extensive travels from England to the Soviet Union, from Belgium to Greece, and after stays in Milan and Paris, she moved to Rome where she lives today. Since 1964 Spaziani has taught French language and literature at the University of Messina. She has written many collections of poetry, several of which have won literary prizes; she has also published numerous translations from French and German as well as scholarly studies on French topics. Spaziani is currently president of the "Centro Internazionale Eugenio Montale," a center for the dissemination and study of poetry that awards the "Eugenio Montale International Prize" for translations and publications of Italian verse.

Spaziani's early poetry was greatly influenced by the hermetic tendencies of the thirties and forties and, more specifically, by certain formal and thematic aspects of Ungaretti's and Montale's verse. Highly literary and technically controlled, the poems of *Le acque del sabato*, for example, reveal her debt not only to the hermetic influence but also to the Italian high lyric tradition from Leopardi through the early twentieth century. In that first volume, Spaziani succeeded in forging a genuine voice, however, that far surpasses mere imitation or technical excellence. Memory and an acute sensitivity to the natural world inform her well-wrought poems; the voice is at once highly subjective and distanced by the elegant formal control. There is nothing confessional or easily melodic about these poems, yet they have the emotive and musical intensity of authentic song.

Her succeeding volumes (*Il gong*, 1962; *Utilità della memoria*, 1966; *L'occhio del ciclone*, 1970; *Geometria del disordine*, 1981; *La stella del libero arbitrio*, 1986) remain true to her vocation as a highly literary, essentially anti-romantic poet. Always present is a strong and immediate sense of the natural living world, but equally powerful is the debt to poetry as tradition and inherited richness. Spaziani's sense of culture, especially Italian and French, permeates even her most autobiographical verse. The poems reverberate with echoes of other poets, yet the heritage is consistently transformed by Spaziani's sensibility and intelligence.

Although indebted to many poets of many times and places, Spaziani is particularly close to Eugenio Montale both in technical excellence and in her refusal to use poetry as an instrument of self-display. She was, in fact, the source of inspiration for Montale's poetic woman, known as "Vixen" and immortalized in a series of poems called "Madrigali privati" (Private Madrigals) included in his 1956 volume *La bufera e altro*. There, she is portrayed as an intensely earthy and sensual presence by whom the poet is overwhelmed. One poem in the series, "Da un lago svizzero" (From a Swiss Lake), contains an acrostic of

Spaziani's name, the only example of such word play in all of Montale's verse.

In a series of responses to questions pertaining to feminist poetry published in the anthology *Donne in poesia* (1976; Women in Poetry), Spaziani makes clear her implicit refusal of such a label. She is sympathetic to the feminist movement but characterizes it as simply another step "in the transformation of Ptolemaic man into Copernican man." Her debt to other women writers is not greater than her debt to other writers in general, given that "the unique voice of a woman poet has worth in and of itself, for its emotive and moral singularity, the same singularity that differentiates important books written by men." Her own contribution to poetry proves, in its consistent excellence, that important books can and should be gender-free.

Works

Poetry: *Le acque del Sabato* [The Sabbath's Waters] (1954). *Primavera a Parigi. Luna lombarda* (1959). *Il gong* (1962). *Utilità della memoria* (1966). *L'occhio del ciclone* (1970). *Ultrasuoni* (1976). *Transito con catene* (1977). *Geometria del disordine* (1981). *La stella del libero arbitrio* (1986). Poems anthologized in *Donne in poesia: Antologia della poesia femminile in Italia dal dopoguerra ad oggi,* ed. Biancamaria Frabotta (1976).

Poems anthologized and translated in *The Defiant Muse: Italian Feminist Poems from the Middle Ages to the Present,* Beverly Allen, Muriel Kittel, Keala Jane Jewell, eds. (1986).

Scholarly works: *Ronsard fra gli astri della Pléiade* (1972). *Il teatro francese del Settecento* (1974). *Il teatro francese dell'Ottocento* (1975). *Il teatro francese del Novecento* (1976). *Alessandrino e altri versi fra Ottocento e Novecento* (1978).

Rebecca West

Adrienne von Speyr
1902–1967

Born September 20, 1902, La-Chaux-de-Fonds (Swiss Jura)
Died September 17, 1967, Basel
Genre(s): essay, memoir
Language(s): German

Von Speyr's life is marked by two features: the wish to become a medical doctor and supernatural signs (the first being the meeting with Ignatius de Loyola when she was six, on Christmas 1908) that led her to convert from Protestantism to Catholicism (meaning for her "unity and wholeness of faith") on All Saint's Day, 1940, under the spiritual leading of Hans Urs von Balthasar, S.J., the well-known theological writer. Their cooperation continued until von Speyr's death (Balthasar is still leading both the St. John's Community they founded together in 1945 and the publishing house Johannesverlag-Einsiedeln, which he founded in 1946 to print von Speyr's writings). From 1941 to 1954, she was a physician visiting from 60 to 80 patients a day. She offered them free treatment if necessary and was always considerate of their family, religious, and economic problems. Yet every year she also experienced a series of "Passions" (sympathy with Jesus' inner pains) and descents to "Infernos." In 1942, she received visible stigmata that she begged in her constant state of prayer to be made invisible. Besides, she was sent on "Journeys" nightly, out of her body, wherever need be of help in war concentration camps, seminaries, confessionals, Roman curia, totally neglected churches. The main features of her character were happiness—joyfulness, humor, zest for surprise amidst incomprehensions, tortures of physical diseases—and courage. She worked as a physician from 1941 to 1954 when her illness (diabetes, arthrosis, heart disease) obliged her to stop. She enjoyed reading, especially French literature and women's writings (Colette was her favorite); among her greatest friends were the essayist Albert Béguin, Henri de Lubac, Gabriel Marcel, Romano Guardini, Hugo Rahner. She mostly dictated her many writings for twenty to thirty minutes a day; Balthasar wrote them in shorthand. He decided to stop this real flood of inspired texts ca. 1950, for they had reached the sixty volumes and he thought "a limit of readableness had been attained." Her first book, *Magd des Herrn* (Handmaid of the Lord), written from the end of January to the beginning of February 1946 and published in 1948, gives the basic meaning of her mysticism. The first chapter is entitled "The light of consent." Mary's life is concentrated in her consent: it is faith, hope, and charity all in one. She becomes pure space made free for the incarnation of the Word. From Mary all can take a form: the soul opens to the dimension of the Church consent (which is Marian) and is plastic in the hands of God. Von Speyr's mysticism is "radically anti-psychologic, theologic and historic-eschatological" (Balthasar). She meant it as a service to the whole of the Church in order not to develop dogma, but to deepen and enliven the center of the universal Church. Through the mystery of the Trinity life of charity, a mystery which we enter through the Christ and His

obedience as a Son, we utter and live the original prayer, i.e., the root of our service.

Works

Das Johannesevangelium—Das Wert wird Fleisch [Meditations on the Gospel of St. John 1, 19–5, 47 (1959)], pp. 191, abridged (1949). *The Word. A Meditation on the Prologue to St. John's Gospel 1, 1– 19* (1953) pp. 159. *Magd des Herrn* (1948; The Handmaid of the Lord, 1956, pp. 174). *The Handmaid of the Lord* (1985; new translation), pp. 178. *Die Welt des Gebetes* (1951; pp. 288, The World of Prayer, 1985, pp. 311).

Gabriela Fiori

Marguerite-Jeanne Cordier de Launay, Baronne de Staal
1684–1750

Born August 30, 1684, Paris
Died July 15, 1750, Gennevilliers, France
Genre(s): memoir, comedy, lyric poetry, letters
Language(s): French

Born to an impoverished mother, who had left her émigré husband in England, Rose Delauney was given her mother's name and retained it. She had no subsequent knowledge of her father. Charmed by her precocious intelligence and good manners, the prioress of Saint Louis (Rouen) took charge of the child. She was given a solid education, which she continued on her own, and treated with a distinction that later conflicted with the subservience demanded by the "in service" positions she needed for a livelihood. From a premature attraction to the religious life, Staal passed briefly through enthusiasm for novels to a more lasting apprenticeship in philosophy. A short treatise has survived from this period. It more significantly marks both her letters and memoirs. It was through her letters, first collected for publication at the request of the duc de Choiseul, that she first began a disillusioning ascent in the world guided by Fontenelle and the scholar-poet Nicolas Malézieu. Her conversational letters like those to Mme du Deffand show both the philosophical control exerted to master that disillusion and the consolation of the friendship she enjoyed, especially in the salon of Mme de Lambert with Chaulieu and Voltaire, with Valincour and Dacier (who courted her).

For the duchesse du Maine's pleasures, in the "Divertissements de Sceaux" and its *Grandes Nuits*

(1713–1714), Staal produced verse, wrote, and sang songs (sometimes to music by Campra), planned fireworks, and composed two three-act comedies in prose: *L'Engouement* and *La Mode*. Eschewing Molière's broader farce, which was severely criticized in the Hôtel de Lambert, Staal's light-handed comedy of manners continues in both plays to treat concerns for women's education discussed there. Both are character studies of women with sole responsibility for a family but without the education to manage it properly. Both absence of education and the society that fosters frivolity in its place are satirized.

The journey from downstairs to upstairs splendors at Sceaux narrated in Staal's *Mémoires* meant more than participation in the team of retainers supplying the duchesse's pleasures and patience in serving the often imperious and capricious granddaughter of the Great Condé. At the cost of a year's imprisonment in the Bastille (from December 1718), Staal learned the dangers of political intrigue. Loyalty to her mistress, if nothing more, implicated her in the abortive Cellamare conspiracy, by which the duchesse had hoped to further the political fortunes of her husband. The unexpected boon in the Bastille was a lasting friendship with another prisoner, the chevalier de Ménil, and a rallying of old friends. But imprisonment became philosophically emblematic to the writer of the *Mémoires* and deepened her experience of writing itself, which becomes an intellectually sustained effort to balance past promises against present failures, the constraining forces of others in her life against a freedom of self-definition in writing. Account-settling with Mme du Maine is left for other occasions. The *Mémoires* end with the death of the duc du Maine and seemingly were not written after 1741 and her marriage to the obscure baron de Staal arranged by Mme du Maine. After being delivered to the altar, "bound and decorated," Staal wrote, no more was to be said. Nothing of a personal nature is known of the last years of Staal's life.

Although Staal offers her views of historical events from her privileged point of view, the history she makes is her own. By discreet and subtle turns of narrative, juxtapositions, and ellipses that betray her introspective quest for self-definition, Staal moves the historically oriented seventeenth-century genre of memoirs fully into autobiography. As Grimm wrote when they first appeared (1755), they "enriched our literature by a work unique in its genre."

Works

Abrégé de métaphysique, ed. Léa Gilon (posth., 1978). *Mémoires* (posth., 1755). *L'Engouement* (posth., 1755). *La Mode* (posth., 1755). *Lettres,* ed. abbé Barthélemy (posth., 1755). *Lettres,* ed. abbé Barthélemy (posth., 1801). "Portrait de Mme la duchesse du maine," ed. La Harpe (posth., 1801).

Translations: *Memoirs of Madame de Staal-De Launay,* tr. Cora Bell (1892).

Sanda Golopentia

Germaine Necker, Baronne de Staël-Holstein
1766–1817

Born April 22, 1766, Paris
Died July 14, 1817, Paris
Genre(s): novel, essay, literary criticism, tales, drama, letters
Language(s): French

Mme de Staël was one of the major precursors of Romanticism and modern criticism whose writings reflected the liberal Republican spirit of the late eighteenth century. An avid supporter of the revolutionary ideals of 1789, she became disenchanted with the radicals who instituted the Terror. Similarly, she admired Napoleon until he shattered her hope for a liberal republic in France.

Her father, Jacques Necker, whom she idolized, was a wealthy Swiss Protestant financier; he was appointed Controller-General of Finance in 1777 by Louis XVI. Germaine's youth was spent among the great figures of the Enlightenment (Buffon, Diderot, Grimm, Talleyrand) who frequented her mother's salon in Paris. She was a precocious child; at age twelve, she wrote a comedy, and at twenty-two, a work on Rousseau. In 1785 she made an unhappy marriage with Baron de Staël-Holstein, Swedish ambassador to France. Three children were born before the couple separated in 1798.

In 1789 Mme de Staël welcomed the Revolution, predicting that it would inaugurate a new age of liberty and justice. Disillusioned with the bloodshed and quarrelsome political factions, she left France for England in early 1793, finally settling at her family's estate of Coppet, near Geneva, during the Terror. She began a long, stormy liaison with the politician and writer Benjamin Constant and continued her writing. She returned to Paris in 1795 but was forced to leave by the Directory government. Two years later she was back in Paris and reopened her salon. Her liberal sentiments and open criticism of Napoleon forced her into exile several times during his fifteen-year rule. Undaunted by the emperor's antipathy toward her,

Mme de Staël traveled widely in Europe, where she won sympathy as a victim of Napoleon's tyranny. During her travels she met with European intellectuals and rulers and gathered materials for her writings. She was convinced that she had a mission to acquaint the parochial French with cultures beyond the Rhine. For many years she lived at Coppet, which became a lively center of cosmopolitan culture and of open resistance to Napoleon. Only after the Emperor's abdication in 1814 was she able to return to Paris.

Mme de Staël represented the cosmopolitan spirit of the eighteenth century in the best sense of the term: a product of aristocratic Parisian society, liberal, free-thinking, imbued with ideas of progress, liberty, and the natural goodness of humanity. She favored the enlightened political and moral ideas of Montesquieu and Rousseau, from which she never wavered. She had a passion for "polite society" and the good taste it embodied. The solitude of her country house at Coppet did not appeal to her; Mme de Staël was a social being and longed for the urbane, brilliant society of Paris. Her intelligence, wealth, and position were not sufficient for her. She wanted to be accepted as an intellectual equal by her male contemporaries. Consequently, she felt a deep sense of the isolation of genius, especially of a woman of genius. Her dynamic (at times strident) and domineering personality and her strong will often alienated people, which caused her suffering and increased her feelings of isolation and loneliness. She had a quick and penetrating mind and did not hesitate to make value judgments on people, events, or cultures. Her writings were extremely subjective; her verbose and colorless style was overcome only when a character or experience was close to her own.

In her writings she strove to show the linkage between political ideas, ethics, literature, and cultural differences. Her "L'Essai sur les Fictions" (Essay on Fiction) concerned the role of writers as moral guides, a popular theme among later Romantic writers. Another moral essay, "De l'influence des passions sur le bonheur des individus et des nations" (1796; The Influence of Passions on the Happiness of Individuals and Nations), is devoted to passions, such as love, that cause unhappiness and how to combat them. The object of her famous work *De la littérature considerée dans ses rapports avec les institutions sociales* (1800; Literature Considered in Relation to Social Institutions), was, in her words, "to examine the influence of religion, customs, and laws on literature, and the influence of literature on religion, customs, and laws," an ambitious project for which she lacked the depth or breadth of knowledge necessary to handle these subjects. However, she was one of the first to study literature as a reflection of national mentality, growing out of a particular society. The book lacks synthesis, but it demonstrates her analytical abilities. Another influential work, *De l'Allemagne* (1810; On Germany), attempts to acquaint the French with Germany and its culture which she admired. Actually she had little more than a superficial knowledge of her subject and did not fully understand the brand of German nationalism she so ardently admired. It is, however, a good illustration of her romantic attitudes and spiritual concepts.

The heroines of Mme de Staël's two novels, *Delphine* (1802) and *Corinne* (1807), are well-drawn self-portraits; the other characters are, however, rather one-dimensional. *Dix années d'exil* (1821; Ten Years of Exile) is a fragmentary autobiography describing her experiences as she traveled in Austria, Poland, and Russia in 1812. Finally, Mme de Staël returned to Paris in 1814, via Stockholm and England after Napoleon's downfall, but she was forced to seek refuge at Coppet again during the Hundred Days. She had ambiguous feelings about Napoleon's return; she mistrusted his liberal pronouncements, but she feared that France would be crushed and punished by the Allies if Napoleon were defeated again.

In her last three years, she secretly married Albert Rocca, a young Swiss officer, and wrote a book on the Revolution that clearly reveals her liberal idealism and her dislike of Napoleon. His major flaw (as she saw it) was his lack of respect for humankind. She died in Paris at age fifty-one. Mme de Staël's reputation rests primarily on *De la littérature* and *De l'Allemagne*, and not on her novels. Although her scholarship was often inadequate, her critical analyses of a variety of subjects were often insightful and original.

Works

Considérations sur les principaux événements de la Révolution française (1818). *Correspondance générale*, ed. B. Jasinski, 6 vols. (1960–). *Corinne* (1807). *De l'Allemagne* [On Germany] (1810). *Du charactère de M necker et de sa vie privée* (1804). "De l'influence des passions sur le bonheur des individus et des nations" [The Influence of Passions on the Happiness of Individuals and Nations] (1796). *De la littérature considerée dans ses rapports avec les institutions sociales* [Literature Considered in Relation to Social Institutions] (1800). *Delphine* (1802). *Dix années d'exil* [Ten Years of Exile] (1821). "Essai sur les fictions" [Essay on Fiction] (1795). *Lettres sur les ouvrages et le caractère de J.-J. Rousseau* (1788). *Reflexions sur le suicide* [Reflections on Suicide] (1813).

Jeanne A. Ojala
William T. Ojala

Elsbeth C. Stagel
ca. 1300–ca. 1360

Born beginning of fourteenth century
Died ca. 1360, Töß, Switzerland
Genre(s): convent chronicle
Language(s): Middle High German

Elsbeth Stagel (Stagelin, Stägelin), daughter (presumably) of Senator Rudolf Stagel, was a nun and later a prioress in the Dominican convent of Töß, in Winterthur near Zürich. Töß was founded in 1233 and placed under the spiritual direction of the Dominicans of Zürich. By 1350 the convent had ca. 100 members. The convent of Töß became famous for its scriptorium, its convent school, and a library (whose catalogue is not extant). Töß was dissolved in 1525.

Elsbeth Stagel is perhaps best known for her association with the mystic Heinrich Seuse (Suso), whom she met ca. 1336. Their twenty-five year long relationship, documented by their correspondence, is one of the famous spiritual friendships of the Middle Ages. Seuse, also known as "Amandus," is often seen as the *minnesinger* among the German mystics.

It is under Seuse's influence that Elsbeth Stagel began to study and to copy writings of the mystics. Eventually she translated a number of works in prose and even rendered some of Seuse's Latin material into German verse. Seuse calls Elsbeth Stagel his "spiritual daughter." Their friendship is responsible for Seuse's *vita* (1365) which is written for edification and based on material (sermons, letters, conversations) secretly collected by Elsbeth Stagel. The second part of this *vita* is a description of Elsbeth Stagel's own life.

Elsbeth Stagel also began to write herself. She is the author of several of the *vitae* of the *Tösser Schwesternbuch*, i.e., the convent chronicle of Töß. This chronicle of Töß contains a nucleus, namely, two lives that had been written earlier, that of Sophia von Klingnau and of Mechthilt von Stans, around which some thirty-six lives of members of the convent from its beginning until ca. 1340 are gathered.

The Töß chronicle is perhaps the most famous one of its genre. Its date is ca. 1340, its language is Middle High German. The text is extant in three fifteenth-century manuscripts, the best of which is cod. 603 (Stiftsbibliothek St. Gallen).

The *Tösser Schwesternbuch* concentrates on the ascetic striving (*ir hailig ubung*) and the signs of grace (*die usgenomnen gnaden und wunder*) apparent in the lives of mystically inclined nuns of the convent. It was written with the intent of spiritually revitalizing convent life. Among the noteworthy *vitae* are those of

Anna von Klingnau (*ain luchtendes liecht an hochem leben*), Mezzi von Klingenberg, who donated paintings and German books to the convent, Margret Finkin (of whom it is said that *die gnad hat sie usgenomenlich, das sy als luttseliklich von Got rett*); and especially that of Jûtzi Schulthasin, in whose *vita* the intellectual insights (*erkantnus*) this sister gained during seven years of visions are emphasized.

The *Tösser Schwesternbuch* is the first known attempt of biographical writing in German. While abounding in clichés and repetitions, the work contains some notable passages, and its author(s) coined a number of powerful new terms, such as the various compounds for love: *minnebewegung, minvund, minzaichen,* etc.

Works

La Vie mystique d'un monastère de Dominicaines au Moyen-Age d'après la Chronique de Töss, ed. Jeanne Ancelet-Hustache (Paris, 1928). *Deutsches Nonnenlegen: Das Leben der Schwestern zu Töß. . . .* ed. Margarete Weinhandle (München, 1921). *Das Leben der Schwestern zu Töß beschrieben von Elsbeth Stagel, samt der Vorrede von Johannes Meyer,* ed. Ferdinand Vetter (Berlin, 1906). Pez, Bernardus, *Bibliotheca ascetica antiquo-nova* (Regensburg, 1725; rpt. 1967), pp. 448–452. Murer, Henricus, ed., *Helvetia Sancta* (1643, 2nd ed. Luzern, 1648), pp. 358–369.

Gertrud Jaron Lewis

Gaspara Stampa
ca. 1524–1554

Born ca. 1524, Padua, Italy
Died 1554, Venice
Genre(s): lyric poetry
Language(s): Italian

Gaspara Stampa occupies a distinctive and distinguished place among Italian lyric poets of the sixteenth century. Born in Padua of a bourgeois family, she moved to Venice while still a girl and seems, with her siblings Cassandra and Baldassare, to have become a member of the brilliant demimonde of that city—then at the zenith of its political and cultural power. In all probability, Gaspara was a *cortigiana onesta,* or "honest courtesan," in no simple sense a prostitute but a member of a social class that enjoyed, in Renaissance Venice, not only admiration but indeed respect. The *cortigiana onesta,* who did not bestow her favors lightly or promiscuously, normally had a liaison with only one man—at least during the period of the liaison—and her "protectors" often included great nobles, princes of the Church, and famous writers, artists, and intellectuals.

Gaspara's protector was the young Count Collaltino di Collalto, and her passionate love for him, both before and after his abandonment of her, is the source of her art, virtually her sole theme. Like all sixteenth-century love poets, she is an imitator of Petrarch, but her sexual identity enforces certain adaptations of Petrarchan conventions—adaptations that the Venetian poet effects with imagination, ingenuity, and brilliance. Not distant and unattainable, like Petrarch's Laura, Collaltino has been her lover, albeit a faithless one. Despite her reiterated assertions of his superiority to her, it becomes clear in her sequence of sonnets and songs that Gaspara's fidelity and intensity of passion have made her in fact the superior one, and that the validation of that superiority is her art—an art that, despite its severely limited subject matter, continues to sound across the centuries its notes of erotic joy, hopeless desire, and pain. Dramatic vigor and inventive imagery are among the hallmarks of her poetry.

Gaspara Stampa's poems were collected and published after her death by her sister. In the course of the nineteenth century her greatness was recognized, and she is now seen to be a very important figure in Italian poetry.

Works
Rime, ed. Abdelkader Salza (1913).

Translations: *Three Women Poets; Renaissance and Baroque*, ed. Frank J. Warnke (1986). *Women Writers of the Renaissance and Reformation*, ed. Katharina M. Wilson (1987).

Frank Warnke

Lucy Hester Stanhope
1776–1839
Born March 12, 1776, Chevening, Kent, England
Died June 23, 1839, Djoun, Lebanon
Genre(s): memoir
Language(s): English

Noted traveler to the Levant, mystic, and eccentric, Stanhope drew to her mountain convent in Lebanon such visitors as the fabled literary voyagers Alexander Kinglake, Alphonse de Lamartine, and Eliot Warburton. She embodied the essence of that melancholy romanticism, aristocratic disdain, and extravagant temperament that fired the imagination of European writers of the early nineteenth century. Although her reputation today is wrapped in obscurity, in her heyday her forcefulness of character and the seductiveness of her glamor convinced the Arab tribes of Syria and Palestine among whom she lived of the essential truth of her many oracular pronouncements.

As the granddaughter of the first Lord Chatham, whom she resembled, and daughter of the third Earl Stanhope, the radical politician and famed experimental scientist, she possessed a very definite sense of her station in life. She quickly came to the attention of William Pitt the Younger, her uncle, whom she served as trusted confidante and private secretary. So closely did she identify with this role, a drawing room ornament of the first order, that she wished for nothing more than to be known as "Mr. Pitt's niece." Poorly educated by the standards of the day, having no instruction in the classics when such was the norm, her irrepressible wit and acerbic tongue nevertheless left their marks. With the ascension of William Pitt to the office of Prime Minister in 1804, Stanhope assumed enormous social importance, dispensing much patronage and arranging official banquets.

Proud, imperious, restless—a first-rate conversationalist and a fiery haranguer—she quit the Pitt household upon the Prime Minister's death. She retired to the solitude of Wales after the demise of her favorite brother, Major Stanhope, and Sir John Moore, an admirer and one of her uncle's favorite generals. Subject to fierce bouts of dejection and contempt for a society that no longer recognized her worth, she renounced Europe for the Levant in 1810. In what would later become typical for the Victorian age, she traveled in the grand manner, her entourage growing as she moved east, taxing her financial resources to the limit. After entering Jerusalem and Damascus with great style, she struck east to the famed ruins of Palmyra, the first European woman ever to do so. She finally settled in a half-ruined convent in Djoun on the slopes of Mount Lebanon, eight miles from Sidon. Such was her sway over the neighboring Druses that the most fearsome tribal chieftains and their Turkish overlords came to respect her and heed her word. Not only did she make prodigal provision for her entourage but she also provided a haven for fleeing Europeans after the battle of Navarino (1827) and compelled Ibrahim Pasha to solicit her neutrality when he sought to invade Syria. She was known to have given Pasha, the fierce lieutenant of Mehmet Ali, the Viceroy of Egypt, more trouble than all the insurgent tribes of Syria and Palestine combined.

For writers such as Kinglake, her name was almost as familiar as that of Robinson Crusoe; Kinglake, the author of *Eothen,* the most famous of English travelogues to the Near East and a minor masterpiece much beloved by Winston Churchill, wrote "both [Crusoe and Stanhope] were associated with the spirit of adventure; but whilst the imagined life of the castaway mariner never failed to seem glaringly real, the true story of the Englishwoman ruling over the Arabs always sounded to me like a fable." Combining the charm and commanding temper of her aristocratic line and the melancholy of a stubborn recluse going to partial seed in the East, she could not help but fascinate literary travelers. Although many sought interviews with her, she was loath to grant them. Disgruntled with Europe, she barricaded herself against its influence, never consulting its books or newspapers but trusting to astrology alone. As a mimic of savage repute, she could obliterate any target of her choice. Byron, with his many affected airs, was a natural favorite, and she was known to have attributed to the Romantic poet a "curiously coxcombical lisp." Among her other distinguished victims was Lamartine, whom she found overrefined, bearing himself, in her phrase, "like the humbler sort of English dandy."

In the Levant, Stanhope came to be regarded as a seer and was respected as such; even sober westerners, with a healthy dash of skepticism, could not escape the magnetism of her personality. For the voyager with literary ambitions, she was an obligatory sight on a journey east. Kinglake, her most famous English visitor, characterized her religious beliefs as a curious mélange of the different religions of the Ottoman empire although he emphasized that she never lost her practical streak and her famed abhorrence for any display of exquisiteness.

Known by such sobriquets as "The Mad Nun of Lebanon" or such self-styled ascriptions as "Queen of the Arabs," Stanhope died alone and abandoned in 1839, walled up in her half-ruined convent. Deeply in debt in her last years, she reacted with fury when Lord Palmerston approved the appropriation of her pension to settle the insistent claims of her many creditors. Ever the aristocrat, she refused to accept any visitors and declined into hopeless indigence in her proud tower of isolation.

Works

Memoirs of the Lady Hester Stanhope as Related by Herself in Conversations with Her Physician (1845). *Travels of Lady Hester Stanhope Forming the Completion of Her Memoirs Narrated by Her Physician* (1846).

Michael Skakun

Anna Stanislawska
ca. 1653–ca. 1701
Born between 1651 and 1654
Died between October 15, 1700 and June 2, 1701
Genre(s): poetry
Language(s): Polish

Called a "rhymemaker" by historians of literature, Stanislawska was the first woman poet who wrote in Polish in the seventeenth century, when the majority of Polish poets still used Latin. Born in an aristocratic family with lands in the east of Poland and the Ukraine, she was a daughter of a high provincial dignitary and administrator. Her mother died when Anna was very young, and she was raised at a monastery and in 1668 forced by father and stepmother to marry a degenerate son of a wealthy governor, J.K. Warszycki; the marriage was annulled a year later by King John III (Sobieski), her protector after her father's death. At the end of 1669, she married Cpt. Jan Z. Olesnicki who was killed in 1675 during the war with Turkey, and in the summer of 1677, Chamberlain Jan B. Zbaski, who died during the siege of Vienna in November 1683. Widowed, she managed all her property and finances and represented herself in court in her effort to regain the lands she inherited from her father, which were newly liberated from the Turks. She established several charitable foundations, which was probably the reason why she was shunned by her family and left to die alone. The exact dates of her birth and death are not known.

Works

An autobiographic poem, *Transakcja albo opisanie calego zycia jednej sieroty przez zalosne treny od tejze samej pisane roku 1685.* Publ. A. Brueckner: *Wiersze zbieranej druzyny. Pierwsza autorka polska i jej autobiografia wierszem* (Biblioteka Warszawska, 1893), vol. 4, pp. 424–429.

Maya Peretz

Enid (Mary) Starkie
1897–1970

Born August 18, 1897, Killiney, Dublin, Ireland
Died April 21, 1970, Oxford
Genre(s): literary criticism, autobiography
Language(s): English

A scholar of French literature, Starkie wrote more than fifteen books on nineteenth- and twentieth-century writers. After receiving her undergraduate education at Alexandra College in Dublin, Starkie received her training in French literature at the Sorbonne, University of Paris, where she earned her doctorate in 1928. Starkie taught French literature at Exeter University, in several American universities on visiting appointments, and, for most of her career, at Oxford University starting in 1929. She described her childhood and college years in her only autobiographical book, *A Lady's Child*, in 1941.

Starkie used such biographical sources as manuscripts and correspondence to write her critical studies of French writers and was the first outsider allowed to use Arthur Rimbaud's papers for her 1937 study of the writer's life and works. She felt that better understanding of a work comes from knowing the artist's personality. As she wrote in her *Introduction to Baudelaire* (1958), "True, the intrinsic value of a work of art depends from the artistic point of view, on itself alone, but those who enjoy it, responding to it sympathetically, will always be interested to discover all they can about the nature of the man who could produce it, and wish to come into contact deeply with his personality."

Always the scholar, Starkie's studies of Rimbaud, Baudelaire, Pétrus Borel, André Gide, and Flaubert are known for their careful documentation of sources and assimilation of biographical information into a critical analysis. Her studies provide what critics have called a "joy of continuous discovery." Her last book, published posthumously, was the second volume of her two-part study of Gustave Flaubert, a book called by Flaubert scholar and translator Francis Steegmuller "the most sympathetic, best written modern account in English, or in French, of Flaubert's complete later career. It is a worthy monument to the great novelist and to his indomitable biographer."

Honors in her life include election to the Irish Academy of Letters, being made Commander of the Order of the British Empire in 1967, and being made Chevalier of the French Legion of Honor in 1948. The Faculty of Modern Languages at the University of Oxford conferred on her the Doctorate of Letters in 1939.

Starkie was remembered for her individualistic personality, and her obituaries even included references to her touches of rebellious dress and behavior. She campaigned for her choices of candidates for Oxford's prestigious Chair of Poetry, a post decided in an election by the Masters of Arts of the university, and through her efforts W.H. Auden was elected to the post in 1956. Among the French writers she knew well and was instrumental in bringing to Oxford for honors and lectures were Jean Cocteau and André Gide; she also knew British writer Joyce Carywell.

Starkie spent several months in America teaching at Berkeley and Seattle in 1951. She was, however, so warmly received at Hollins College in Virginia during her term in 1959 that she bequeathed her fortune to the college.

Works

Les Sources du lyricisme dans la poésie d'Emile Verhaeren (1927). *Baudelaire* (1933; rewritten 1957). *Arthur Rimbaud in Abyssinia* (1937). *A Lady's Child* (1941). *Pétrus Borel en Algerie: sa carrière comme inspectateur de la colonisation* (1950). *André Gide* (1953). *Pétrugs Borel* (1954). *Introduction to Baudelaire* (1958). *From Gautier to Eliot: The Influence of France on English Literature 1851–1939* (1960). *Flaubert: The Making of the Master* (1967). *Flaubert: The Master* (1971).

Marilynn J. Smith

Christina (Ellen) Stead
1902–1983

Born July 17, 1902, Rockdale, Australia
Died March 31, 1983, Sydney
Genre(s): novel, short story, screenplay, novella, review, translation
Language(s): English

Stead trained at the Sydney Teachers College and became a public school teacher, work she later saw herself unfit for. After studying typing and shorthand for a business career, in 1928 she sailed to England, working in England and France as a grain clerk and a bank clerk. She met and formed an alliance with William Blake, whom she married in 1952. From 1937 to 1946, she lived in the United States, publishing several novels and writing scripts for MGM in Hollywood. In 1946 she traveled to Europe again with Blake, returning to England to refresh her feel for the English language. In 1974 she returned to Australia.

Although Stead is best known for her eleven novels, she began her writing career with a collection of short stories, *The Salzburg Tales* (1934), parables, allegories, and stories of the grotesque. *The Puzzleheaded Girl* (1967) is a collection of four novellas, exploring the figure of the young woman in America. In addition, she wrote reviews and translated novels from French to English, and she edited two anthologies of short stories, one with her husband. In 1974 she received the Patrick White Award, recognizing her excellence as an Australian novelist.

The Man Who Loved Children (1940) is Stead's acknowledged masterpiece. Ignored for twenty-five years, the novel was reissued in 1965 with an afterword by Randall Jarrell, naming the novel great because it does one thing better than any other fiction—makes the reader part of one family's day-to-day intimate existence. The novel depicts three characters of mythic proportions: the father Sam, the mother Hetty, and the daughter, a potential artist, Louisa (Louie). The fiction portrays basic conflicts between parents and child for power and independence, between man and woman for identity and understanding, between parents for the soul and allegiances of their child. In a virtuoso performance, Stead establishes personality through the distinctive speech of the three principal characters with their obsessions and individual blindnesses. The woman's movement solidified the reputation of the novel and procured a new generation of readers for the unsentimental depiction of a family tearing itself apart.

The Man Who Loved Children can also be seen as a portrait of the artist as a young woman with Louie forming herself out of the conflicting force fields of Sam and Hetty, declaring her resistance in a play about tyranny that she wrote in a language she made up for herself. For Louie, school means the opportunity to make a friend and to create an ego ideal, her teacher Miss Aiden, a muse to dedicate her poetry to. Louie's "I will not serve" encompasses her willingness to kill both her parents and ultimately to run away, to go on her walk around the world.

Stead's novel *House of All Nations* (1938) won critical acclaim and popular success at the time of its publication. Critics have called this exploration of the workings of banking and international finance her greatest intellectual achievement because of its scope and complexity. The huge novel displays her mature style, charting a world of avarice with people living not just on but for money and money-making.

Her third great novel is *Dark Places of the Heart* (1966), also titled *Cotter's England*. In one sense, it is a depiction of the poverty and ugliness of Britain's industrialized north. In another, it is an analysis of another family and of Nellie Cotter Cook's influence on the people around her. A central concern is the relationship between Nellie and her brother Tom. Like Michael and Catherine Baguenault, the brother–sister pair in *Seven Poor Men of Sydney* (1934), Nellie and Tom seem too close to each other, engaged in a battle for power and personal survival. The dark places of Nellie's heart manifest themselves in a fascination with death, a compulsion to manipulate other people, and a dangerous desire to be more than human, to achieve a charismatic destiny. As in all of Stead's strongest fiction, the plot of the novel is subordinant to the drama of character. Her writing here is sparer and more controlled than in her other novels.

Stead set only two novels in Australia: her first, *Seven Poor Men of Sydney,* and her fifth, *For Love Alone.* According to Michael Wilding, the first novel is organized to display the lives and interactions of seven poor men connected to each other by friendship, family, and work. The varieties and different effects of poverty give the novel its unity, imperfect because of other important characters and because of romantic and grotesque passages not directly integrated with the theme. *For Love Alone* depicts the poverty of the central character, Teresa Hawkins, and her relationship to her demanding family, but it also portrays her successful flight to England, a place of wider opportunity. The novel raises questions of women's sexuality and of the difficulty of achieving satisfying relationships between men and women. Teresa seeks her fulfillment in her relationship to a man, Quick, a wealthy American, but she retains to some extent her sexual freedom and her right to a separate consciousness.

Although recognition of her achievement has been slow in coming, Stead is now acknowledged to be a significant twentieth-century fiction writer, still mainly because of *The Man Who Loved Children.* She continues the tradition of nineteenth-century realistic novelists, especially the French and Russians. A novelist with a modern, post-Freudian sensibility, Stead depicts people's social connections with an understanding of the underlying economic forces that shape their lives. She is compared to Dickens for her density of realistic detail, for her comic eye and ear for exaggerated rhetoric, for her use of the grotesque, and for her commentary on social conditions. Stead uses her characters' language to reveal their deceptions and illusions. The characters express this individuating language in dialogues, in interior monologues, and in letters to each other. Stead identified herself as a psychological writer, expressing the drama of the person.

Works

Seven Poor Men of Sydney (1934). *The Salzburg Tales* (1934). *The Beauties and the Furies* (1936). *House of All Nations* (1938). *The Man Who Loved Children* (1940). *For Love Alone* (1944). *Letty Fox: Her Luck* (1946). *A Little Tea, A Little Chat* (1948). *The People with the Dogs* (1952). [trans.] *Colour of Asia* by F. Gigon (1955). [trans.] *The Candid Killer* by J. Giltene (1956). [trans.] *In Balloon and Bathyscape* by A. Piccard (1956; also titled *Earth Sky and Sea*). *Dark Places of the Heart* (1966). *The Puzzleheaded Girl* (1967). *The Little Hotel* (1974). *Miss Herbert: The Suburban Wife* (1976). *The Christina Stead Anthology*, ed. J.B. Read (1979). *Ocean of Story: The Uncollected Stories of Christina Stead*, ed. R.G. Geering (1986). *I'm Dying Laughing: The Humourist* (1987). *The Little Hotel* (1992).

Kate Begnal

Edith Stein
1891–1942

a.k.a. Teresia Benedicta a Cruce
Born October 12, 1891, Breslaw, now Wroclaw
Died August 9 (presumably), 1942, Auschwitz
Genre(s): autobiography, philosophy, social and theological essay
Language(s): German

Deeply rooted in a Jewish family, the last and most cherished of eleven children, Stein was brought up with love, strength, and respect for her great intelligence by her mother Augusta Courant who, a widow as early as 1893, conducted with courage and strong religious ethics both her numerous family (seven living children) and the business her husband had left in debt. She supported university studies for all her children who wanted them. Although she was fond of school since age six, out of an existential crisis at puberty, Stein quit the gymnasium to live for a time with her married sister Elsa in Hamburg. Voluntarily abandoning Jewish religious practice, she resumed studies in the Lyceum 1908–1911 and, declaring herself an atheist, became intensely involved in women's problems and a Prussian group for "votes for women" during her university years in Breslaw. Here (1911–1913) Stein studied German philology (out of her love for languages), history (as an instrument for facing the present "with a sense of social responsibility"), and psychology (to understand the "*person* problem").

After deciding she had been deceived by the positivistic psychological view of Hönigswald and Stern, Stein went to Göttingen University to attend Edmund Husserl's (1859–1938) lectures. Through the revelation of Husserl's *Logical Researches*, Stein saw phenomenology as the way to prepare "the conceptual instruments psychology needed to acquire as its basic "clear principles." In Göttingen (1913–1915) where, though an atheist, she felt a continuous "thirst for truth," which was also a form of "endless prayer," her friendship with A. Reinach, Max Scheler, and others of Husserl's disciples who valued the religious phenomenon as well as a return to her mother's faith led Stein toward Catholicism. She was convinced all of a sudden, after reading one night St. Teresa of Avila's *Autobiography* and was christened in January of 1922.

After a period of nursing work in World War I, Stein became assistant to Husserl at Freiburg University and worked on a thesis on empathy (1916). Stein's academic career was interrupted, first because of her Catholicism (Heidegger, Husserl's successor in Freiburg, rejected her in 1931 although Stein was already a well-known essayist and lecturer), and then by Nazi anti-Semitic decrees which prevented her appointment at the German Institute of Scientific Pedagogy (Münster, 1932). At last, with peaceful certainty Stein saw her way: Carmel. There were obstacles: age (42), poverty, her mother's sorrow, even greater at Stein's conversion.

After acceptance from Köln Carmel, Stein took the veil in 1934, received an order to complete a theoretical work on Aquinas's thought and afterward wrote her metaphysical text *Eternal Being and Limited Being*. As the Transcendent Being is also "He who mercifully turns down to his creature," the Eternal Being is in fact the foundation and support of the limited one. The contemplation of Christ is Stein's strength. After the notorious anti-Semitic *Kristallnacht* (November 9, 1938), Stein asked to join the Echt Community in Holland to be safer and was joined by her sister Rosa. In Echt Stein wrote *Ways to the Intuition of God* under the inspiration of Pseudo-Dionysius, *Treatises, and Letters*. The *Ways* are the signs and calls of nature, which send us back to the One who mysteriously reveals Himself so. We can experience "a person-to person encounter with God." Stein begins to write *Scientia crucis* (unfinished because of her imprisonment), a study on St. John of the Cross, and reached the conclusion that "the nuptial union of the soul with God—the aim of its creation—has been obtained through the Cross, consummated on the Cross and sealed with the Cross for all eternity. On March 26, 1939 (Passion Sunday) in a message to her prioress, Stein asked for permission to offer herself to Jesus' Heart on behalf of Jews, to hinder the coming war. On August 2, 1942, the SS came and took Stein with Rosa to Westerbork camp; on August 7 they were taken to Auschwitz.

Works

Complete Works, ed. Lucy Gerber (1950) (some vols. also in French). *Zum problem der Einfühlung,* Ph.D. thesis, 1917 (English tr. *On the Problem of Empathy,* 1970). "Jarbuch für Philosophie und Phänemenologische Forschung." *Psychische Kausalität* [Psychic Casualty] (1922). *Eine Untersuchung über den Staat* [A Research on the State] (1925). *Husserl's Phänomenologie und die Philosophie des Thomas van Aquino* [Husserl's Phenomenology and Aquinas's philosophy] (1929). Several writings on women, mostly from her Austrian, German, and Swiss lectures.

Autobiography: *Aus dem Leben einer jüdischen Familie—Kindheit und Jugend* [Life of a Jewish Family—Childhood and Youth] (1933). *Wie ich in dem Kölner Karmel Kam* [How I Came to Köln Carmel], Christmas gift to her prioress and first biographer, Mother Teresia Renata de Spiritu Sancto (1938), essays (1952; transl.). Teresia Matre a Dei, essays (1971; transl.). Elisabeth de miribel, essays (Paris, 1954 and 1984).

Gabriela Fiori

Anne Stevenson
1933–

Born January 3, 1933, Cambridge, England
Genre(s): poetry
Language(s): English

Stevenson was born in Cambridge, England, in 1933 when her father, the philosopher C.L. Stevenson *(Ethics and Language)* was studying there. Her birthplace appears to have been determinative. Like Henry James, T.S. Eliot, and H.D., she has become an American writer unable to live in America. All of her adult life she has lived in Great Britain—in England, Scotland, and Wales for a few years each; she is now settled near Durham in an ex-mining village. Her present choice of rural life, trying, as she says, "to keep away from 'fame' and 'personalities,'" manifests values evidently formed in the Vermont of her childhood—appreciation of natural locale and personal reticence. These qualities characterize her poetry from early to late.

She began writing poetry with Donald Hall when she was a student at the University of Michigan (B.A. 1954, M.A. 1962). Her first book of poems, *Living in America,* appeared in 1965. Tension between domesticity and the need for a larger scope—an analogue of the tension between America and England—is a strong and perennial motif in Stevenson's work. In her early volume, *Reversals* (1969), which includes poems from *Living in America,* marriage, pregnancy, and motherhood claustrophobically enclose the poet but also force her to get outside "the house." Yet joy often prevails over negativity, as in "The Victory," written after childbirth: "Snail! Scary knot of desires! / Hungry snarl! Small son. / Why do I have to love you? / How have you won?" In "On Not Being Able to Look at the Moon," she warns herself against pathetic fallacy, "a mania for / stealing moonlight and transforming it into my own pain." Here she is defining her poetic stance: the world is self-existent, to be observed with accuracy and delight, not to be appropriated by ego. Therefore the poem itself, she notes in "Morning," is "not made but discovered."

Stevenson's great poetic strength lies in this discovery of the poem in the place. She continually finds the natural world a rich "objective correlative" for both her emotions and intelligence. In her poems description and commentary therefore subtly blend, as in "England": "The paths are dry, the ponds dazed with reflections. / . . . A pearly contamination strokes the river / As the cranes ride or dissolve in it." Contrapuntal to "England" is "Sierra Nevada," a poem evoking that western mountain range: "Landscape without regrets whose weakest junipers / strangle and split granite, whose hard, clean light / is utterly without restraint." Stevenson's characteristic adherence to forms—to rhyme, although flexible and slant, to long lines and declarative sentences—reflects her respect for the similarly stringent forms of the world. Her poems are thus tight yet detailed, even explanatory, and honest; she works hard not to mislead or be misunderstood.

In her more recent poetry, the forms have loosened and become more experimental. An ambition to combine prose and poetry produced *Correspondences: A Family History in Letters* (1974), in effect, a novel in a book-length poem series. Tracing an evolution of attitudes through six generations, these poem-epistles reveal interrelationships between members of the Chandler family of Clearfield, Vermont, a family that resembles Stevenson's own. Their revelations paint a broad historical portrait of nineteenth-century America's influence on the twentieth century. The ancestors' greed, intolerance, sexual repression, and misplaced religion are seen as having bred broken family ties, anger, frustration, and profound uncertainty in the modern descendents. Although Stevenson echoes each character's voice with historically plausible accents, history perhaps concerns her less than paying tribute to her mother. An obituary of the fictive mother, Ruth Chandler Arbeiter, opens the narrative and frames it. She has died young, of cancer (as Stevenson's own mother did at the age of fifty-four), and her daughter, Kay Boyd, a poet living in England, sees her mother's life as unfulfilled, following a pattern of nonfulfillment in her female forebears.

Traveling Behind Glass: Selected Poems 1963– 1973 (1974) emphasizes the metaphor of "glass," which is both barrier between self and world and transmitter of light to see that world. The title poem, a version of Jack Kerouac's *On the Road*, also examines the itinerant life, whose fragmented experiences and lonely questionings create disheartened confusion: "I have forgotten what / home it was I came for. / . . . this sun is so dull and / estranged that I know / this dark glass as / the only living possession of the valley." In her final vision glass shatters "into its stars, and the stars / scatter, flashing like kingfishers, / into the emptiness." Even this much light, however, is little consolation. Fragmentation and pain prevail.

This grappling with stark landscapes—that is, with harsh experiences—extends on into *Enough of Green* (1977), set in Scotland where rocky coasts smell "of fish and of sewage" and "salt-worried faces" and "an absence of trees" abound. Loneliness and transience are expressed by indicative titles: "Temporarily in Oxford," "Hotel in the City," "Goodbye! Goodbye!" Darkness, ruins, and abandoned houses preoccupy her as objective correlatives of domestic breakdown and as if to live in greenery and comfort were a suspect luxury her New England-trained psyche must deny itself.

This conflict between "green" and "black" continues, though eased, along with motifs of glass and consciousness of time passing, in *Minute by Glass Minute* (1982), written after the poet had moved to Wales. The thematically central long poem, "Green Mountain, Black Mountain" is an elegy to her dead parents, to her father particularly, which links memories of her Vermont youth with present-day realities of Welsh life. Because her father, musician as well as philosopher, had made music central to his daughters' lives, it becomes—as does poetry, by extension—almost a kind of religion. Cantatalike in form, the poem resolves in a coda uniting memory and language—the green mountains— with the wind, soil and birdsong of the black mountains: "Swifts twist on the syllables of the wind currents. / Blackbirds are the cellos of the deep farms."

Several poems in *The Fiction-Makers* (1985) are also elegies to the dead, including the especially moving "Red Rock Fault" and "Willow Song," in memory of her poet-friend Frances Horovitz. Although informed by sadness and loss, these poems become celebrations, for wreckage and energy strangely coexist in them. The poet observes how damaged terrain around old minepits now produces a lush growth of wild flowers. The breakdown of her illusions has rejuvenated her psychic landscape. She says of this volume: "*The Fiction-Makers* is an effort to disencumber myself of the illusion of believing in my own 'story.'" Thus in "A Legacy," written on her fiftieth birthday, she gives away to friends the fixed components of her "story" in recognition of temporality and the final dissolution to come.

For Stevenson the external world provides an anchor for the mind, which cannot give birth to this world but can mirror it. To mirror truthfully has been her lasting poetic project. This uncommon integrity, like "the genuine" praised by T.S. Eliot in the work of Marianne Moore, is both formal and personal, making Stevenson's poetry one of the most solid achievements in contemporary British letters.

Works

Living in America (1965). *Elizabeth Bishop* (1966). *Reversals* (1969). *Correspondences: A Family History in Letters* (1974). *Traveling Behind Glass: Selected Poems 1963–1973* (1974). *Correspondences* (1975). *Child of Adam* (1976). *Enough of Green* (1977). *A Morden Tower Reading* 3 (1977). *Cliff Walk* (1977). *Minute by Glass Minute* (1982). *The Fiction-Makers* (1985). *Selected Poems 1956–1986* (1987). *Bitter Fame* (1989). *The Other House* (1990). *Four and a Half Dancing Men* (1993).

Jane Augustine

Veronika Strēlerte
1912–1995
Born October 10, 1912, Dobele, Latvia
Died May 1995 in Huddinge, Sweden
Genre(s): lyric poetry, short story
Language(s): Latvian

Veronika Strēlerte was the most outstanding modern Latvian woman poet of the twentieth century. Originally her first name was Rudīte. As daughter of the editor of a periodical, she was born into an intellectual family; her interest in literature led her to study Romance philology in Riga and to translate (mainly while in exile) numerous Italian and French classics into Latvian. Her poetry is highly sophisticated; her early works showed a strong influence of the Italian Renaissance. At the approach of the Soviet forces in 1945 she, like many other Latvians, especially intellectuals, went into voluntary exile in Sweden, where she had been active since then not only as poet and translator but also as editor of the literary periodical *Daugava* and of a selection of Latvian folksongs (*dainas*). She was married to the Latvian essayist and critic Andrejs Johansons; previously she was married to the Latvian historian and poet Arvēds Svābe.

Strēlerte's poetry is characterized by perfection of form and melodiousness. Its deep emotion is presented in a restrained and aloof manner. This combination of qualities pervades her work with an ambiguity that belies its surface clarity and simplicity. Her worldview often seems correspondingly dualistic.

Works

Vienkārši vārdi (1937). *Lietus lāse* (1940). *Mēness upe* (1945). *Zem augstiem kokiem* (1951). *Gaismas tuksneši* (1951). *elastības gadi* (1961). *Pusvārdiem* (1982). Numerous pieces in various collections and periodicals.

Translations: Samples of her work in *A Century of Latvian Poetry,* ed. and tr. W.K. Matthews (1957).

Zoja Pavlovskis

Lorenza Strozzi
1514–1591

Born 1514, Capalle, Italy
Died 1591, Prato
Genre(s): hymn, poetry
Language(s): Latin

Zaccaria di Battista di Giovanni Strozzi, of the famous Florentine family, had five children. His fourth-born was named Francesca. As a very young child she was sent as a boarder ("in serbanza") to the Dominican convent of San Niccolo in Prato, a common practice in Florence in the sixteenth century. By the time she was seven, we are told by her nephew and biographer, Zaccaria Monti, she was well loved by the nuns of that convent. At age thirteen she entered San Niccolo officially, changing her name to Sister

Lorenza, and by 1529 she had taken her vows. San Niccolo was a popular convent for the Strozzi women, and in 1529 a list of the professed nuns of the convent included five Strozzis, one of whom, Antonia, Lorenza's aunt, had been prioress, another, Maddalena, was then subprioress. Lorenza's older sister Elisabetta married, while her younger sister, Maria Salome, became a Franciscan nun in the convent of San Giorgio, also in Prato. Like her brother Ciriaco, who taught Greek and philosophy at the University of Bologna, and her other brother Francesco, a doctor of law, Lorenza had scholarly inclinations, which she was able to pursue in the convent while performing her normal duties. She was prioress a number of times, held other offices, and was closely associated with Catherina de' Ricci, a nun in San Niccolo who was later to be canonized.

It was clear from the time she was very young that Lorenza was exceptionally intelligent. While she was a school girl at the convent a special tutor, undoubtedly sent by her family, was brought in to give her lessons in Latin and Greek. When she was not at divine services Lorenza studied the classics, and by the time she was eighteen she was writing poetry in Latin herself. She seems to have known the famous religious reformers Bernardino Ochino and Pietro Martire Vermigli, both of whom later became Protestants and fled Italy. Like many of her contemporaries, while she was attracted by the desire for reform and the spirit of religious renewal, she remained a faithful Catholic. The strength of her faith is confirmed by the religious hymns she wrote and for which she became famous in her time.

The hymns are indebted primarily to Horace's odes and to famous liturgical songs for their meter, and there is one for each of the important feasts of the liturgical calender of the Florentine diocese. Individual compositions are preceded by references to their Horacian source. One hundred and four hymns, all in Latin, composed by 1587, were published at the Giunta Press in Florence in 1588; Lorenza dedicated them to the Bishop of Pistoia, Lattanzio de'Lattanzi, the prelate who had jurisdiction over the convents of Prato. Her hymns were later translated into French by Simeon Georges Pavillon, set to music by Jacques Maudint, and published in Paris in 1601 with a dedication written by her nephew Zaccaria Monti to the Queen of France, Lorenza's compatriot, Maria de' Medici. Lorenza Strozzi's hymns were sung in churches throughout Italy, and she is remembered and praised in the writing of many Tuscan literary historians and of Dominican scholars.

Works

Ven. Laurentiae Strozziae Monialis S. Dominici di Monasterio Divi Nicholai de Prato, in singula totius anni solemnia, Hymni . . . (1588); and again with French translation by Simeon Georges Pavillon and music by Jacques Maudint (1601).

Elissa B. Weaver

Mary Stuart, Queen of Scots
1542–1587

Born 1542, Linlithgow Palace, Scotland
Died February 8, 1587, Fotheringay Castle
Genre(s): poetry, prose
Language(s): English

A center of controversy in her lifetime, Mary Stuart has remained an enigma to later ages. Queen of Scotland from the sixth day of her life, she was, when a young child, sent by her mother, the queen regent, to the French court, where she was raised with the children of Francis I in a scintillating, somewhat corrupt Roman Catholic atmosphere. After the death of her young husband, Francis II of France, Stuart elected to return to Scotland, a relatively rude, semifeudal staunchly Protestant kingdom, foregoing the luxury—and the difficult intrigues—of the French court but entering tumultuous waters in Scotland. Her marriage to Henry Stuart, Lord Darnley, her cousin, strengthened her claim to the English throne and incurred the suspicion of Elizabeth I and her advisers, for in 1565 Elizabeth was still quite insecure on her throne and fearful of sedition by Catholic subjects for whom Stuart was a rallying point. On the other hand, Stuart was most unappealing as a ruler to the Scottish reformed church, and her position in Scotland was also undermined by Darnley, from whom she became increasingly alienated. The birth of their son, later James VI of Scotland and James I of England, on June 19, 1566, did not strengthen her position; Darnley refused to attend the child's christening.

It is probably impossible to determine the truth concerning her involvement in the most serious of the crimes attributed to her: the murder of Darnley by the Scottish nobles, led by James Hepburn, Earl of Bothwell, on February 10, 1567. It is also impossible to be certain what her feelings for Bothwell were: whether she feared him or was passionately in love with him. What is known is that she and Bothwell

Mary Stuart, Queen of Scots

were married, in a Protestant ceremony, on May 15, 1567, that the event followed a supposed kidnapping of the queen by Bothwell's forces, and that it led to open, tumultuous outcries against the queen, who was separated forcibly from Bothwell by alienated noblemen and forced to abdicate her throne in favor of her son, James, on July 24, 1567. James, also separated from her, was raised by her enemies in the Protestant faith.

Imprisoned by her nobles in Lochleven, Stuart escaped and raised an army but was defeated at Langside. She then decided to throw herself on the protection of Elizabeth, her cousin and sister-queen, a political blunder that she never overcame. She was kept in varying conditions of captivity by Elizabeth for nineteen years but finally was recognized by her cousin as a grave threat, tried for various political intrigues in which she had been embroiled, and condemned to death. She was executed in Fotheringay Castle on February 8, 1587 and interred in Petersborough. On October 11, 1612, her body was reinterred in Westminster, by order of her son.

A product of the high Renaissance in France, Stuart was educated by outstanding French writers. She composed occasional verse and prose at critical moments throughout her life. As George Ballard has noted, her verses have never been accorded serious attention as literature: "the many writers of her history," he states, "have been so full in their accounts of her misfortunes and tragical end, and so warmly engaged either in heightening or depressing her reputation in regard to her conduct in life, that they have almost all forgot to transmit to posterity an account of her education and what part she bore in the republic of letters." Nonetheless, her writings are indeed worthy of attention. Stuart did not publish them herself, but many of her pieces appeared in works by her contemporaries and others were collected after her death and printed in several collections, the most important of which are noted below.

Of her writings, the so-called "casket letters and sonnets," produced at her first English trial as evidence of her complicity in the murder of Darnley, are the most contested. While the letters do speak of the assassination and may be open, therefore, to the suspicion of having been manufactured as evidence against her, the sonnets, which are truly great poems, do not implicate her in the crime but merely attest to her feelings for Bothwell. On that account, they may be more readily recognized as her own work, and they constitute a unique group of passionate love sonnets in a woman's voice. That they can easily be related to the course of Stuart's association with Bothwell adds to their poignancy. Her other poetry ranges from a mourning dirge for Francis II to appeals to Elizabeth and a moving type of poetry of resignation and acceptance.

Works

Collection de Manuscrits, Livres Estampes et Objects d'art relatifs a Marie Stuart Reine de France et D'Ecrosse (1931). *Last Letter of Mary Queen of Scotland Addressed to her brother in law Henry III King of France on the night before her execution at Fotheringay Castle 8th February 1587* (1927). *Latin Themes of Mary Stuart*, ed. Anatole de Montaignon (n.d.). *Letters and Poems of Mary, Queen of Scots, supposed author*, ed. and trans. Clifford Bax (1947). *Poems of Mary Queen of Scots*, ed. Julian Sharman (1873). *Poems of Mary Queen of Scots, to the Earl of Bothwell* (1932). *Queen Mary's Book, A Collection of Poems and Essays by Mary Queen of Scots*, ed. Mrs. P. Stewart Mackenzie-Arbuthnot (1907). *Recueil des Letteres et Memoires de Marie Stuart*, ed. Prince Alexander Labanoff (Lobanov-Rostovski) (1844).

Betty Travitsky

Sulpicia
ca. 95 B.C.–?
Flourished late 1st c. B.C., Rome
Death date unknown
Genre(s): elegiac poetry
Language(s): Latin

Sulpicia was the niece and probably the ward of M. Valerius Messalla Corvinus, the eminent literary patron of the Augustan Age; his circle included, among others, Tibullus and Ovid. Sulpicia is the author of six short love elegies that are preserved together with the works of Tibullus as part of the *Tibullianum Corpus* (Book IV.7–12). She is thus the only example of a *docta puella* whose works survive. The *doctae puellae* were the "learned" female companions of the elegists, often mentioned by Catullus, Ovid, Propertius, and others as an important element in their social and creative lives. While Sulpicia's extant works total only forty lines, they still manage to represent a wide variety of themes, for the most part traditional ones in elegy. All her poems deal with her love for an aristocratic Roman youth whom she addresses by the pseudonym Cerinthus. In them she exults over the consummation of their love (IV.7); laments that she must go to the country with Messalla to celebrate her birthday, rather than remain in the city with Cerinthus as she would prefer (IV.8); rejoices that Messalla has changed his plan, and that she will spend her birthday with Cerinthus after all (IV.9); complains of Cerinthus's unfaithfulness to her, with a woman she describes as sordid and of low class (IV.10); reports that she is ill with a fever but that her principal concern is whether Cerinthus really cares about her recovery (IV.11); and apologizes for her apparent coolness to him on one occasion (IV.12). Attempts have been made, as with Catullus's Lesbia sequence, to place these miscellaneous poems into some reasonably coherent chronological order; all such attempts must by their nature be based largely on subjective considerations. Critics are divided on the poetic merit of Sulpicia's works; but there is general agreement on their deeply felt emotion and sincerity. Some have professed to find, not only in the quality of the emotions expressed in Sulpicia's poems, but also in their syntax, metrics, and style, specifically "feminine" characteristics. In view of the smallness of the sampling, and because there is literally nothing else in Latin literature to compare with it, it is probably prudent to reserve judgment in this regard. This Sulpicia is not to be confused with another poet of the same name who lived about a century later.

Paul Pascal

Margarete Susman
1874–1966

a.k.a. Reiner
Born October 14, 1874, Hamburg, Germany
Died January 16, 1966
Genre(s): poetry, scholarship, novel, philosophy
Language(s): German

Margarete Susman is the maiden name of Margarete von Bendemann-Susman. A German poet, writer, scholar, theorist, artist, public speaker, and socialist activist, her reputation rests mainly on her being a controversial woman philosopher of religion who spoke up for the Jews.

Susman was born to the family of a wealthy businessman in Hamburg in 1874. Her training as an artist began early. At the age of eight, she was sent to Zürich, where she attended a *höhere Töchterschule*. Her upbringing, a religious one with Protestant inclinations, was rather open-minded. In spite of her parents' liberal attitudes, however, she was not given a formal education. Instead, having undergone rigorous initial academic training under her father, she attended the Arts Academy in Düsseldorf and studied painting, where she met Eduard von Bendemann, a painter and historian who later became her husband. While studying art in Paris, Munich, and Berlin, she also became a regular auditor in philosophy lectures, which proved to have a decisive impact on her career. She was a welcome guest in the seminars of Theodor Lipps and, especially, Georg Simmel, whom she rewarded with a book in her final years, *Die geistige Gestalt Georg Simmels* (1959; Georg Simmel's Mental Gestalt). These academic activities turned Susman into a great learner and scholar on her own.

In 1901, Susman made her debut as a lyrical poet with a volume of poems, *Mein Land* (My Land), though an earlier collection had been printed privately in 1892. Academic thinking obviously had no adverse affect on her creativity, for she turned out volume after volume of poetry. However, Susman was destined to claim her laurels off the beaten track: she decided to be a philosopher of religion when an article she contributed to the *Frankfurter Zeitung* (May 16, 1907) caused a great sensation. In her article, "Judentum und Kultur" (Jewry and Culture), she went against the grain by questioning the current tendency toward the solution of the problem of Jews. As a matter of principle, she proposed, the relationship between Jews and Germans had to be taken into consideration. The article was a point of departure for her. Thereafter, she devoted herself to articles, lectures, and books on religion, sociology, and psychology. The major concern of these efforts focused on the general question of the relationship between "God's people" (the Jews) and Christians and Germans in the history of ideas. In her most significant work, *Das Buch Hiob und das Schicksal des jüdischen Volkes* (1946; The Book of Job and the Fate of the Jewish People), she arrived at the most profound answer of her own: between the synagogue and the church, no barrier should ever exist.

Since her first article, Susman remained one of the most important contributors to the *Frankfurter Zeitung*, for which she was a regular literary correspondent between 1900–1920. Her book, *Das Wesen der moderne deutschen Lyrik* (The Nature of Modern German Lyrical Poetry), was a result of this activity. She had also been a long-time contributor to the *Morgen*. In 1912, she published *Vom Sinn der Liebe* (Of the Desire of Love). After World War I and the dissolution of her marriage, reminiscences of which were given in *Ich habe viele Leben gelebt* (1964; Much Life Have I Lived), she published a series of major works including *Frauen der Romantik* (1929, rev. 1960; Women of the Romantic Age); the book on Goethe and Charlotte von Stein, entitled *Deutung einer großen Liebe* (1951; Interpretation of a Great Love Affair); and the collection of essays, *Gestalten und Kreise* (1954; Creators and Circles); *Vom Geheimnis der Freiheit* (1965; The Secret of Freedom).

In 1933, Susman immigrated to Zürich, where she was actively involved in the socialist religious circle of the theologian Leonhard Ragaz ("Neue Wege. Blätter für den Kampf der Zeit"; New Paths—Papers for the Combat of the Time). Because of this, she was suspected to be an extreme leftist, and in 1937 she was banned from speaking and writing. As a result, she had to publish in part under the pseudonym of "Reiner" in Swiss newspapers and magazines. Susman continued to live in Zürich after the war. Although she lost her eyesight in her old age, Susman was still constantly at work until she died in 1966.

Susman was one of those German writers who, after withdrawing to a simplified order of life, remained unknown to or misunderstood by the general public. Seeking to reconcile the various strains of antitheses in herself, she received, ironically, both rejection and applause from the wrong people. In France, where such ambivalence was more readily appreciated, she was the only important German representative to attend the famous talks of Pontigny (1925–1928).

Her poetry is closely akin to the melancholy and

weariness of the New Romantics; themes of an early expressionism are also present. For Susman, writing was also a part of the effort to cope with the world's problem in the interest of a new community. Owing to her determined will to action and dedication to the destiny of the time, and because of formal problems and on the grounds of the discussions with Karl Wolfskehl, at one point she withdrew copies of *Mein Land* from circulation. Susman's lyrical poetry is characterized by serious interrogations of and direct engagement with life. Mostly written in meditative blank verse, there is an original voice of her own throughout. Nevertheless, the volumes of poems including *Neue Gedichte* (1907; New Poems), *Die Liebenden* (1917; Loved Ones), *Lieder von Tod und Erlösung* (1922; Songs of Death and Redemption), and even the later collection *Aus sich wandelnder Zeit* (1955; From Changing Times) as well, can only be regarded as by-products of her entire output.

Her prose was derived from experience, with the evidence of a pure subjectivity identifying itself with the object. Whether on Kafka, Moses Mendelssohn, Franz Rosenzweig, Dostoyevsky, Nietzsche, or Goethe, her essays attend to suggestiveness rather than seek to provide mere information. The essays are in general philosophical, and one has to get used to her bold, deliberate, and occasionally irritating interpretations of facts. She is fond of conjuring a host of images to invoke a call to action; hers is a rhetorically and rhythmically structured prose with intentions that she did not even seek to hide. Revolving around herself as a center, what her writing attempted to do was the expansion of personal existence to a wider circle of influence. Like Bloch, Buber, Gurewitsch, Landauer, Lukács, Rosenzweig, and Leopold Ziegler, over the years she played a decisive part through the *Frankfurter Zeitung* in contribution to the development of the spirit of revolution. Susman was also associated, closely or briefly with well-known figures such as Simmel, Groethuysen, George, Wolfskehl, and (in her last years) Celan.

Susman's discursive writing was often intended to provoke the public. In her numerous articles and reviews, there is an acute attention to that which was new in her times. She sympathized, for instance, with the cause of Jewish women, particularly Berta Pappenheim. Writing had a special meaning to Susman, because her attempt to reconcile her role as a writer and as a wife and woman eventually failed. As her marriage broke to pieces, she underwent a state of psychological crisis. In a sense, she found a way out through literature and philosophy, for which she had a constant love. From these there issued, for her,

such a great fascination that she was more than willing to be a spokeswoman of her time through her writing.

Works

Poetry: *Gedichte* (1892, privately printed). *Mein Land* (1901). *Neue Gedichte* (1907). *Die Liebenden* (1917). *Lieder von Tod und Erlösung* (1922). *Aus sich wandelnder Zeit,* anthology (1955).

Philosophy, critical studies, prose: *Vom Sinn der Liebe* (1912). *Das Wesen der modernen deutschen Lyrik* (1912). *Die Revolution und die Frau* (1918). *Das Kruzifix,* novel (1922). *Frauen der Romantik* (1929, 1960). *Das Buch Hiob und das Schicksal des jüdischen Volkes* (1946). *Deutung einer großen Liebe* (1951). *Gestalten und Kreise* (1954). *Deutung biblischer Gestalten* (1956). *Die geistige Gestalt Georg Simmels* (1959). *Ich habe viele Leben gelebt,* autobiographical reminiscences (1964). *Vom Geheimnis der Freiheit: Gesammelte Aufsätze 1914–1964,* selected essays, ed. Manfred Schlösser (1965).

Other works: with H. Simon, *Philosophie der Romantik* by E. Kircher (1906). Introduction to *Brücke und Tür,* ed. M. Landmann (1957). Contributions to *Frankfurter Zeitung.* Contributions to *Neue Wege. Blätter für den Kampf der Zeit.* Contributions to *Morgan.*

Balance Chow

Berta von Suttner
1843–1914

a.k.a. B. Oulet
Born July 9, 1843, Prague, Czechoslovakia
Died June 21, 1914, Vienna, Austria
Genre(s): novel, short story, lyric, drama text, essay, autobiography
Language(s): German

Berta von Suttner's work brought her fame in the first place because of its themes and the engagement and the enthusiasm it conveys.

Berta von Suttner stems from an old prestigious family of the Austrian aristocracy. Her father was a high-ranking officer, her mother came from a family of poets and writers; she was born a Korner. The militaristic-aristocratic background of von Suttner and the political climate of the second half of the nineteenth century determined her career, the themes of her work, and her engagement in antiwar propaganda.

Born in 1843, von Suttner married young and against the will of her family. Her husband was Arthur von Suttner, a writer of reputation and a member of the nobility himself. Husband and wife left Austria to escape the altercations with her parents and lived in Tiflis, now in the Soviet Union, where Arthur worked as an engineer and a war correspondent and Berta became a teacher. Later they moved back to Austria, where both became literarily and politically active. Both were independent, liberal thinkers, who could not agree with the contemporary sociopolitical climate. Arthur von Suttner joined his wife in her antiwar activities, while he himself was engaged in a league in Vienna, fighting anti-Semitism. In 1883, Berta's first novel had appeared, called *Inventarium einer Seele* (Inventory of a Soul). When her greatest success was published in 1889, she thus was already an established and accredited author. *Die Waffen nieder* (Lay Down Your Arms), became the basis for her world fame. The positive and negative letters of response, collected and preserved by Berta herself, have all been published in her *Memoiren* (1905; Memoirs). Alfred Nobel congratulated her and asked her to work for him again, as she had been his personal secretary before she married Arthur, an offer that she declined. Leo Tolstoy compared the novel to Harriet Beecher Stowe's work, so that *Die Waffen nieder* received the unofficial subtitle "The 'Uncle Tom's Cabin' of the Peace Movement." Felix Dahn wrote a satire on the novel and attacked von Suttner for her antiwar propaganda. The Social Democrats on the other hand, again tried to use her and her reputation for their own work. In 1891 she founded the Austrian Peace Society and supported Alfred Nobel in his efforts to establish a society in Germany in 1892. Between 1892 and 1899 von Suttner was the chief editor and publisher of the pacifist newspaper *Die Waffen nieder*, founded an International League, and received in 1905, the first woman ever to do so, the Nobel Prize for Peace through the initiative of Alfred Nobel himself.

Her knowledge and the serious dedication to whatever she was doing are reflected in the novel *Das Maschinenzeitalter* (1899; Age of the Machine) and in the reaction to this work. Critics of the time were convinced that leading scholars and scientists had compiled the information. *Die Waffen nieder* became the most politically influential novel in Europe. The last printing appeared in 1914, shortly before World War I broke out. The book title can be regarded as a summary of her life and aspirations, and her battle cry until her death. The novel covers the time period between the childhood of the fictitious heroine and the Franco-Prussian War in 1870–1871. The fictitious

autobiography carries traits of Berta's own life and has led readers to believe that Berta and the heroine must be identical. Except for the fact that Berta's husband did not die during the war, the background, the education of the heroine, the attitudes and expectations toward life and war, the lifestyle of the family and the heroine all parallel Berta's own life too much as not to see her behind her heroine. Looking back, the heroine remembers the past forty years of her life, especially the long list of battles and wars. It is as if "normal" life and the problems of everyday situations are completely irrelevant when it comes to fighting for the glory of the fatherland. The image of a perverted society, of a perverted age, is painted. The irony, the sarcasm, the wit with which Berta/Martha described the military enthusiasm of a seventeen-year-old girl is overwhelming. Berta's language and her ability to play with it are perfect. She involves the reader and allows him or her to feel with the heroine as she presents the pros and cons of warfare objectively and rationally. The novel is not only a sentimental story but also a thorough survey of the actual political and social conditions of the time. Here, as in other works, von Suttner proved that she was not only an idealistic woman but a serious and critical observer of her age and an educated witness of Europe's past.

Works

Novels and novellas: *Inventarium einer Seele* (1883). *Ein Manuskrip* (1884). *Ein schlechter Mensch* (1885). *Daniela Dormes* (1886). *Highlife* (1886). *Verkettungen* (1887). *Erzählte Lustspiele* (1888). *Schriftsteller-Roman* (1888). *Die Waffen nieder* (1889). *An der Riviera* (1892). *Eva Siebeck* (1892). *Die Tiefinnersten* (1893). *Trente-et-quarante* (1893). *Vor dem Gewitter* (1893). *Im Berghause* (1893). *Phantasie über "Gotha"* (1893). *Es Löwos* (1893). *Das Maschinenzeitalter* (1899). *Der Krieg und seine Bekämpfung* (1904). *Marthas Kinder* (1902). *Ketten und Verkettungen* (1904). *Briefe an einen Toten* (1904). *Babies siebente Liebe* (1905). *Stimmen und Gestalten* (1907). *Gesammelte Werke* (1907). *Der Menschheit Hochgedanken* (1911). *Rüstet ab!* (1960).

Short stories: *Doktor Hellmuths Donnerstage* (1892). *Krieg und Frieden* (1895). *Der Kaiser von Europa* (1897). *Schmetterlinge* (1897). *Franzl und Mirzl* (1905).

Essays: *Randglossen zur Zeitgeschichte* (1906). *Der Kampfum die Vermeidung des Weltkrieges* (1917). *Rüstung und Überrüstung* (1909). *Die Barbarisierung der Luft* (1912). *Aus der Werkstatt des Pazifismus* (1912). *Der Kampf um die Vermeidung des Weltkrieges* (1917).

Other: *Frühlingszeit, eine Lenzes-und Lebens-gabe,* lyrics (1896). *Schach der Qual,* drama text (1898). *Die Haager Konferenz,* autobiography (1900). *Memoiren,* memoirs (1905).

Translations: *Lay Down Your Arms!* (1891). *Memoirs of Berta von Suttner* (1972).

Jutta Hagedorn

Henriette de Coligny, Comtesse de La Suze
1618–1673

Born 1618, Paris
Died March 10, 1673
Genre(s): lyric poetry, letters
Language(s): French

The third of four children of Gaspard III de Coligny, maréchal-duc de Châtillon, and Anne de Polignac, Henriette was raised by a pious mother in an austerity thought fitting for one of France's most prominent re-formed families. Related to the French royal family, and the House of Nassau, the Coligny daughters were sought as prestigious alliances: Henriette's sister Anne by George of Wunemburg and Teck, and she herself by Thomas Hamilton, 3rd Earl of Haddington. After his premature death (February 1645) ended a short resi-dence in war-torn England, where Queen Henrietta received her at Oxford, she returned to a marriage ar-ranged by her mother (1647) to Gaspard de Cham-pagne, comte de La Suze. Virtually cloistered by her husband at Belfort (Alsace), then Lumigny (Brie), the comtesse managed to establish permanent residence in their Marais *hôtel* only in 1653 after the comte's rearguard action in the Fronde failed and forced him into German exile. The marriage ended in a much-pub-licized divorce granted to the wife for cause of impo-tence by the Paris Parlement (1661). An equally publi-cized earlier conversion to Catholicism had been effected by a council of bishops assisted by her spiri-tual directors La Milletière and Père Léon, both of whom published accounts of it. Abjuration in high pomp (July 20, 1653) was ritually observed on the arms of the Queen and Gaston d'Orleans. From her scruples came the brief epigram "Oui, j'aime Charenton."

First sparked to write verse by a belated and brief period at the Hôtel de Rambouillet, whose spirit con-tinued in her own circle, Mme de La Suze sought a succession of tutors beginning with the learned Urbain Chevreau and later including Montplaisir and Subligny. She received numerous poetic tributes, early on the "Vers pour Iris" sequence by Jacques (not Hercule) de Lacger, and she became in them "la dixième muse." But it was Madeleine de Scudéry, Pellison, and their group who most encouraged her writing with friendship and supported it in published compliments. An elaborate compliment to her elegies, which had been read out in the Académie de Castres, appeared in Book VIII of Scudéry's *Clélie.* Boileau's critical praise helped to consecrate the elegies, which remained through the eighteenth century her most often praised lyric mode. Admitted to *Le Parnasse francais* by Tithon du Tillet, she retained her place there through the *Parnasse des Dames* (1773).

La Suze became queen of the *recueils collectifs.* Her single independent volume of verse (21 poems, 1666) collected the airs and madrigals, verse portraits and epigrams, *stances* and elegies that first appeared prominently (18 poems) in the collective volume pro-duced by the Parisian bookseller Charles Sercy in 1653 and several times reedited, along with a prose por-trait of the Grande Mademoiselle that originally fig-ured in the album of *Portraits divers* (1659) published under her name. La Suze's poetry was similarly used by the publisher Quinet for a new collection of "pieces galants" that, after a first appearance in 1664, contin-ued in expanded reeditions until the mid-eighteenth century to associate her name with the "new" and "le plus beau" of lyric poetry (1666, 1668, 1674, 1680, 1684; continued by Cavelier, 1691, 1698; and by Trévoux, 1725, 1741, 1748). Among the 32 new po-ems in these and other anthologies, from 1667 through 1692, airs/chansons and elegies largely predominate. Her *oeuvre* is almost completely represented in the 1725 collection.

In the directness of her confessional expression of love, as in her independence in publishing, and her flamboyant pleasures (among which writing was prominent), the highly born La Suze encouraged by her example younger women poets like Mlle Lheritier and Mme d'Esche. Although she remains the Doralise of Somaize's *Dictionaire des précieusses,* her airs and other short lyric pieces and especially her elegies con-tributed to the transformation of mid-seventeenth-century *préciosité.* Simplification of figures, conver-sational rhythms, and evident sensibility all would later seem more "natural" to Regency poets of *vers badins.*

Works

Poésies de Madame la Comtesse de La Suze (1666). *Recueil de pièces galantes, en prose et en vers, de Mme la Comtesse de La Suze* (1664–1725).

Charles G.S. Williams

Karin Sveen
1948–

Born August 17, 1948, Ringsaker, Norway
Genre(s): short story, poetry, drama, novel
Language(s): Nynorsk (New Norwegian) and
Bokmál (Dano Norwegian)

Karin Sveen has emerged as an important Norwegian writer in the 1980s. Born in a small rural town in Norway to working-class parents, she was educated as a teacher. Despite her education and present social position, she strongly identifies with the working class. This class consciousness is evident in her writing, as she often focuses on class differences in Norway. She currently lives in Hamar, Norway, and is active politically in the left wing in the Socialist Party (SV).

Sveen distanced herself from the social realists of the 1960s and early 1970s. While many of the central literary figures at this time believed they were creating a new form of literature for the working class, Sveen viewed the results as illusionary and unrealistic.

Sveen debuted with a collection of poems in 1975 (*Vinterhagen*, The Winter Garden), followed closely by two more collections, *Mjøsa gär* (1976; The Lake Mjøsa Flows) and *Den svarte hane* (1977; The Black Cock). The fact that the collections are written in New Norwegian, her regional dialect (from Hedemark), and Dano Norwegian, respectively, is witness to her linguistic versatility.

Døtre (1980; Daughters), a collection of short stories, gained widespread recognition and popularity in Norway. The thirteen stories in the collection deal with different aspects of motherhood and daughterhood: daughters' attempts to gain independence, mothers' difficulties in letting go, the barriers that mothers create for their own daughters and, at the same time, the disillusionments of motherhood for women who were themselves once daughters.

Sveen's first novel, *Utbryterdronninga* (1982; The Escape Queen), has been called a modern folk tale. It has a strong feminist message. There are elements of the fantastic, but they are firmly rooted in a realistic framework. A young girl, Marja, whose past is unknown, is found drifting in a boat by a childless couple who adopt her. She is confronted with the cruel and hostile world of adults and children and she learns to survive—not by adapting but by developing a strong identity of her own. Marja discovers her special talent as an escape artist, and when her talents become known to others she is viewed as both a hero and a witch.

Sveen's second novel, *Den reddende engel* (1984; The Saving Angel), is a sensitive and often humorous portrayal of the Norwegian society in the 1950s, seen through the eyes of a young girl. This girl (also called Marja) describes episodes from her early years growing up with her twin brother and under the care of a man whom we believe to be her father. The novel has some surprising twists and, through the naive but observant eyes of Marja, we gain insight into some of the social and psychological implications of class differences in Norway.

The language situation in Norway is complicated. Sveen is keenly aware of the connection between language and social class. In developing her characters she is able to unveil, through language, the strong class differences in Norway. Her prose is lyrical, despite the fact that she most often deals with common, everyday themes. Sveen's focus on the mother/daughter relationship and on the issue of parenthood in general has added to the debate of the 1980s surrounding these issues.

Works
Vinterhagen [The Winter Garden] (1975). *Mjøsa gär* [The Lake (Mjøsa) Flows] (1976). *Den svarte hane* [The Black Cock] (1977). *Døtre* [Daughters] (1980). *Litt av et ord* [The Word] (1981), in *Sá stor du er blitt* [You Have Gotten So Big]. *Utbryterdronninga* [The Escape Queen] (1982). *Snart 17* [Soon 17], script (1983). *Hanna* [Hanna], script (1984). *Den reddende engel* [The Saving Angel] (1984). *Kroppens sug, hjertets savn* [The Body's Urge, the Heart's Longing] (1985).

Translations: *Det gode hjertet* from *Døtre* [A Good Heart], in *An Everyday Story*, tr. and ed. Katherine Hanson (1984), pp. 203–209. *Litt av et ord* from *Sá stor du er blitt* [*The Word* from *You Have Gotten So Big*], tr. Joan Tate. *The Norseman*, 5 (September 1985): 8–9.

Peggy Hager

Magda Szabó
1917–

Born October 5, 1917, Debrecen, Hungary
Genre(s): poetry, novel, children's literature, drama, translation
Language(s): Hungarian

Szabó wás educated in Debrecen, where she earned a doctorate in Latin and Hungarian in 1940. Her dissertation, *A Romaikori szépségápolás* (The Cult of Beauty in the Roman Age), was later published. From

1940 to 1944 she was a secondary school teacher, and after 1945 she accepted a position in the ministry of culture. She returned to teaching between 1950 and 1959. After 1950, like so many other Hungarian writers, she did not or could not publish anything. This silence was broken in 1958, and the following year she left teaching to devote herself full time to writing. Szabó's first poems were published in the journals *Magyarok* (Hungarians) and *Ujhold* (New Moon). The poetry volumes, *Bárány* (1947; Lamb) and *Vissza az emberig* (1947; Back to Man), document the tragedy of war. Her poetry is meditative and intellectual with a firm commitment to form. Nineteen fifty-eight saw the publication of a third volume of poetry, *Neszek* (Sounds), and it was also the year her first novel, *Freskó* (Fresco), was published. For this she won the Jozsef Attila Prize in 1959.

Like so many of her generation, Szabó is interested in the decline of the old order and the effect of societal changes on women. In *Freskó* she presented the disintegration of a provincial clerical family. Her criticism is unusually harsh as she shows the failure of traditional moral values and blames this, as well as the conservatism of the provincial intelligentsia, for the demise of the family. *Az óz* (1959; The Fawn) is more psychologically oriented as it studies the rivalry of two women, Eszter and Angela. The former is jealous of the ease with which Angela seems to gain everything, but in the end, when Eszter might have satisfaction, she finds that only hatred can fill her heart. Later novels, such as *Disznótor* (1960; Pig Killing), *Pilátus* (1964; Pilate), *A Danaida* (1964; Danaide), and *Katalin utca* (1969; Katalin Street) also study loneliness through heroines who are generally passionate and suffering women. She uses the techniques of the modern novel, particularly the interior monologue; her sensitive and accurate understanding of psychological motivations, as well as her timely topics, make her a popular writer. As in her poetry, so in her prose style, a strong sense of form prevails.

Beginning with the sixties, her interest broadened and the themes of her novels reflect this wider view. In *Mózes egy, huszonkettö* (1967; Moses One, Twenty-two) she examines the conflicts between the older and the younger generation. The differences between Eastern and Western Europeans and particularly the Eastern European's view of himself are the central themes of *A szemlélők* (1973; The Spectators). *Ókút* (1970; The Ancient Well) evokes the world of her childhood, and *Régimodi történet* (1977; An Old-Fashioned Tale) uses family reminiscences to evoke the life of a provincial town at the turn of the century. She is able to unite an inner realism and a historical distance in the characterization of her personae. Her books for children and young people, while designed to be instructive, are popular with the readers. Many of her works, also, have been translated into German, English, and French among other languages. In addition to poetry and novels, she has written plays, film scripts, and radio plays, and has several major translations to her credit. From English, she rendered Galsworthy, Shakespeare's *Two Gentlemen of Verona*, and Kyd's *Spanish Tragedy*. Her dramas, *Kigyó marás* (1960; Snake-bite) and *Leleplezés* (1962; Unveiling), were performed in Poland and in Yugoslavia in 1964.

Works

Poetry collections: *Bárány* (1947). *Vissza az emberig* (1947). *Neszek* [Sounds] 1958. *Szilfán halat, összegyüjtött versek* [Fish on the Elm Tree, Collected Poems] (1975).

Novels: *Freskó* (1958). *Az óz* (1959; English ed., *The Fawn*, 1963). *Disznótor* (1960). *Pilátus* (1964). *A Danaida* (1964). *Katalin utca* (1969). *Mózes egy, huszonkettö* (1967). *A szemlélók* (1973). *Ókút* (1970). *Régimodi történet* (1977).

Short stories: *Alvók futása* [Race of the Sleepers] (1967).

Juvenile novels: *Mondják meg Zsófinak* (1958; English ed., 1963, *Tell Sally*). *Sziget-kék* [Island-blue] (1959). *Álarcosbál* [The Masquerade-ball] (1961). *Születésnap* [The Birthday] (1962). *Abigél* [Abigail] (1978). *Tünder Lala* [Fairy Louis] (1965).

Children's books: *Bárány Boldizsár* [Who Lives Where], a verse tale (1958). *Marikáék háza* [Mary's House] (1959).

Plays: *Kigyó marás* (1960). *Leleplezés* (1962). *Fanny hagyomanyai* [The Posthumous Papers of Fanny] (1964). *Kiálts város* [Cry, City] (1973). *Az a szép, fényes nap* [That Beautiful, Bright Day] (1976). *A mérani fiú* [The Boy of Meran] (1980). *Béla király* [King Bela] (1984), collected in *Eleven képet a világnak* [A Living Picture for the World] (1966) and *Erök szerint* [According to Forces] (1980).

Film script: *Vöröstinta* [Red Ink] (1959).

Radio play: *A hallei kirurgus* [The Chirurgeon of Halle] (1963).

Critical essays: *Kívül a körön* [Outside the Circle] (1980).

Travelogues: *Hullámok kergetése* [The Pursuit of Waves] (1965). *Zeusz küszöbén* [On Zeus's Threshold] (1968).

Enikő Molnár Basa

Wislawa Szymborska
1923–

Born July 2, 1923, Kornik, Poland
Genres: poetry
Language(s): Polish

According to Krynski and Maguire, Szymborska "is regarded as one of the three best representatives, since World War II, of the rich and ancient art of poetry in Poland" (and the only woman among them). They claim that the 10,000 copies of Szymborska's 1976 *Poezje* (Poems) were sold out within a week. Unlike the other two poets who, the critics stress, "have by and large continued to cultivate their familiar territory, Szymborska constantly opens fresh themes and elaborates new techniques. Her verse shows the high seriousness, delightful inventiveness, and prodigality of imagination that we expect of first-rate poetry; and it bears the stamp of unmistakable originality."

Szymborska moved to Cracow from Kornik at the age of eight and has lived there ever since. She studied sociology and Polish literature at the Jagiellonian University and made her debut with the poem "Szukam slowa" (I Seek the Word) in *Walka* (Struggle), the 1945, no. 3 supplement to the Cracow newspaper *Dziennik polski* (Polish Daily). Officially criticized for writing "in a manner unintelligible to the masses" and dwelling morbidly on the experiences of the war . . . at the expense of the new theme of building socialism (Krynski and Maguire), her first volume of poetry, ready in 1948, was not published for four years until, apparently convinced that the times called for art to serve an important immediate goal, she rewrote it. Even though she sincerely tried to raise an authentic poetic voice in tune with the revolutionary era, she was found wanting. Her later publications included fewer and fewer poems on political themes and dealt more and more with lyrical subjects. She has won many literary prizes, written extensively on books by both Polish and foreign writers, and translated French poetry, mostly from the sixteenth and seventeenth centuries. She is poetry editor of the weekly *Zycie literackie* (Literary Life) in Cracow. The beautiful bilingual American publication of her seventy poems contains an extremely interesting and sensitively written introduction to her work and her ideas about poetry.

In 1996 Szymborska was awarded the prestigious Nobel Literature Prize. She is the fifth Pole or Polish-born writer and the second consecutive poet to win the literature award.

Works

Dlatego zjemy [That's Why We Live] (1952, 1954). *Pytania zadawane sobie* [Questions Put to Myself] (1954). *Wolanie do Yeti* [Calling Out the Yeti] (1957). *Sol* [Salt] (1962). *Sto pociech* [A Million Laughs] (1967). *Poezje wybrane* [Selected Poems], chosen and with introduction by the author (1967). *Poezje* [Poems] (1970, 1977). *Wszelki wypadek* [There but for the Grace] (1972, 1975). *Wybor wierszy* [Selected Poems] (1973, 1979). *Tarsjusz i inne wiersze* [Tarsius and Other Poems] (1976). *Wielka liczba* [A Great Number] (1976, 1977).

Translations: *A Million Laughs. A Bright Hope* [*Sto pociech*], tr. Krynski and Maguire. *There But for the Grace* [*Wszelki wypadek*], tr. Krynski and Maguire.

Publications in periodicals abroad: *Les lettres nouvelles* (Paris, 1965). *The Literary Review* (New Jersey, 1967). *Micromegas* (Iowa City, 1968). *Wiadomosci* (London, 1968). *Monat* (Hamburg, 1970).

Poems in anthologies: *Anthologie de la poesie polonaise* (1965). *Lektion der Stille* (1959). *Neue polnische Lyrik* (1965). *Panorama moderner Lyrik* (1960). *Polish Writing Today* (1967). *Polnische Poesie des 20. Jahrhunderts* (1965). *Postwar Polish Poetry* (1965). *Vertige de bien vivre* (1962). *The New Polish Poetry. A bilingual collection*, compiled and edited by Milne Holton and Paul Vangelisti (1978). *Sounds, Feelings, and Thoughts: Seventy Poems by Wislawa Szymborska*, tr. and introd. by Magnus J. Krynski and Robert A. Maguire (1981).

Maya Peretz

Arcangela Tarabotti
1604–1652

a.k.a. Galerana Baratotti
Born 1604, Venice, Italy
Died 1652, Venice
Genre(s): tract
Language(s): Italian

Elena Cassandra Tarabotti, born in Venice in 1604, became Sister Arcangela in the Benedictine convent of St. Anna, where she took the veil in 1620 and shortly afterwards, it is not known exactly when, took her final vows. She did not have a religious vocation and all of her life protested her confinement and that of other of women through her writing, much of which was published and known to a large community, even beyond the city of Venice. Her works are critical of family and state politics, which protected wealth and nobility by relegating potentially expensive daughters to a life of imprisonment and by denying them as well a good education. She exposed the hypocrisy of the fierce contemporary criticism of female vanity, pointing out that men were just as vain and suggesting that their concern was not so much for the virtue of their wives and daughters as for their money, which they would more readily spend on themselves and on the prostitutes with which they liberally associated. She argued for the merit of women and their right to attend to their beauty and adornment, one of the few areas of their lives in their control. Tarabotti wrote forcefully and convincingly, despite her lack of adequate formal training, and she unnerved her critics to the point that they mercilessly attacked her for the least evidence of literary shortcomings, indeed criticized her for typographical errors in a published work. She always responded promptly and fearlessly and seems to have had support and sympathy from many noblewomen and not a few erudite men.

Her first work, *La tirannia paterna* (Paternal Tyranny), written in her early years in the convent, decried the injustice of her situation, laying the blame on fathers and the State whose common interests were being served. This early work, somewhat transformed, was published posthumously in 1654 under a different title, *La simplicità ingannata* (Simplicity Deceived). Her second polemical tract, *L'Inferno monacale* (Convent Hell), on the misery of the lives of vocationless nuns, was never published, but its sequel, *Il paradiso monacale* (Convent Paradise), was, for obvious reasons. This latter work has been variously interpreted as expressing Sister Arcangela's repentance and acceptance of her religious vocation and, more convincingly, as a failed attempt to reconcile herself to that vocation, a failure that is expressed in conflicting attitudes and in a continuation, although attenuated, of her lifelong feminist polemic, an unfaltering defense of the merit of women. This polemic returns to the center of her attention in the works that followed, in the *Antisatira* (Antisatire), a reply to F. Buoninsegni's *Contro il lusso donnesco* (Against the Luxuries of Women), in her published letters, and in her response, *Che le donne siano della spetie degli uomini. Difesa delle donne* (That Women Are of the Same Species as Men. A Defense of Women) to the work of Acidalius Valens, an erudite German, the *Disputatio perjucunda qua anonimus probare nititur mulieres homines non esse* (A Most Delightful Disputation in Which an Anonymous [Author] Strives to Prove That Women Are Not Men), translated into Italian by Orazio Plata and published in 1595. Some historians have believed the Latin tract to be a joke though Arcangela did not and argued, or rather inveighed, against its heresy and its misogyny. The Church, too, took it seriously and put it on the Index for its heretical ideas in 1651. The *Antisatira* and the *Lettere* take up the defense of women, affirming that the ignorance of women derives from their having been deprived by men of an education. She refutes the argument that mixing men and women together in schools would lead women to sins of impurity, objecting that women cannot be held responsible for the lust of men. She argues for the "light of reason," a natural gift that has helped her overcome her educational handicap and permitted her to read with understanding, for example, the political works of Machiavelli, with, of course, the permission of her Superiors. She answers the accusation of vanity with counter accusations, often witty as well as accurate (for example, in answer to criticism of the excessively ornate dress of women, their exaggerated make-up, she replies that in contemporary fashion the "mustaches of men, that should fall down over the mouth to inhibit the production of obscene masculine language, are forced by iron and fire to rise menacingly towards the sky").

Besides being intelligent, clever, and combative, Arcangela Tarabotti was also ambitious; she wanted to be heard and appreciated. She corresponded with important men and women, dedicated her writing to some of them, and even sent a copy of her *Antisatira* to Cardinal Mazarin. Through her pen she made herself quite important for her time and condition, and scholars are now beginning to recognize what an extraordinary feat that was. She is the subject of a biography (by Zanette, 1960), but it does not present her life and works clearly with the critical detachment she deserves. Her role as one of the early voices of Italian feminism has been firmly established and has begun to produce interesting analyses and to stimulate the scholarly interest she merits.

Works

As Galerana Baratotti: *La simplicità ingannata* (1654), written twenty years earlier and entitled *La tirannia paterna*. *L'Inferno monacale* (n.d., unpublished, one ms. known to belong to the private collection of Count Giustiniani). *Il paradiso monacale* (1663 [1643]). *Antisatira*, (n.d., publ. anonymously by DAT [donna Arcangela Tarabotti] in F. Buoninsegni, *Contro il lusso donnesco, satira menippea* (1644). *Lettere familiari e di complimento* (1650). *Che le donne siano della spetie degli uomini. Difesa delle donne di Galerana Barcitotti [pseud.] contro Horatio Plata* (1651).

Elissa B. Weaver

Sabine-Casimir-Amable Voïart Tastu
1798–1885

Born August 31, 1798, Metz, France
Died January 11, 1885, Palaiseau
Genre(s): poetry, short fiction, pedagogy, literary history and criticism, travelogue
Language(s): French

The literary production of Amable Tastu falls into two somewhat overlapping phases, one "creative" and the other "professional": her lyric poetry, composed predominantly before her husband's financial difficulties, reflects characteristic features of French Romanticism. Her prose works, written under financial pressure, show how she adapted her talents to financial exigencies. In both periods, though, it is striking how successful her publications were, invariably going through many editions.

She was born in Metz, her father a public official and her mother the sister of the Minister of War under the First Republic. Her mother died when she was seven, an event that apparently reinforced her disposition to melancholy. She devoted much of her childhood and youth to reading and, encouraged by her father's second wife, steeped herself in the poetry of Gessner, Ossian, Bernardin de Saint-Pierre, and Chateaubriand. In 1809 she composed her first poem "Le Réséda" (The Mignonette) in honor of the Empress Josephine, and the work won her an audience with the Empress. In 1816 her father published another poem of hers, "Le Narcisse" (The Daffodil), in the journal *Le Mercure* without her knowledge. The eighteen-year-old protested to her father that she was confronted by the dilemma of marriage or work: if he wanted her poetry published, then he would have to accept her remaining single. Her father showed her letter of protest to the publisher of *Le Mercure*, Joseph Tastu, who promptly married the young woman. Their marriage seems to have been happy: they had one son, Eugène, who later became a French diplomat with assignments in Larnaca (Cyprus), Bagdad, Cairo, and eastern Europe. In 1820 and 1823 she won the "Silver Lily" (Lys d'argent) from the Académie des Jeux-Floraux (Academy of Floral Games), an academy founded in 1324 at Roussillon for the encouragement of poetry; the Académie des Jeux-Floraux at this time played an influential role in encouraging Romanticism in France; the significance of this award can be appreciated if one recalls that it was the Académie des Jeux-Floraux that first recognized Victor Hugo in 1819, the year before it recognized Amable Tastu, before comparable recognition from the Académie Française. Amable Tastu's status as a poet is further attested by the fact that she was asked to compose a poem in honor of the coronation of Charles X in 1824, "Les oiseaux du sacré" (The Birds of the Coronation). In 1826 her husband published her first collection of poetry. Three works stand out here: "L'Ange gardien" (The Guardian Angel), praised by Sainte-Beuve for its serene tone and for being a model of the "domestic elegy"; "Shakespeare," which presents selections from *Julius Caesar, Romeo and Juliet, King Lear*, and A *Midsummer Night's Dream* and which merits attention as part of the discovery of Shakespeare in France in the wake of Stendhal's *Racine et Shakespeare* (1823/25); and "A Victor Hugo," which must be viewed as one of the earliest tributes to the then-twenty-four-year-old poet. The Revolution of 1830 led to the gradual financial ruin of Joseph Tastu, and perhaps the fall of Charles X also had ramifications for the literary fortunes of the poet who had sung his coronation. In any event after 1830 a new phase in Amable Tastu's career began: she embarked on a series of publication ventures that stand in marked contrast to her earlier poetic works: a new translation of Robinson Crusoe (1835; reprinted 1839, 1845); children's literature; pedagogical treatises; historical writings; short fiction; literary criticism (her *Éloge de Mme. de Sévigné* [Praise of Madame de Sévigné] from 1840 was awarded a prize by the Académie Française and reprinted in subsequent editions of letters of Madame de Sévigné); literary history (her studies of both German and Italian literature were frequently reprinted throughout the nineteenth century); and travelogues. Following her husband's death in 1849, she joined her son during his various diplomatic assignments, at one time being the only European woman in Bagdad. In the course of these wanderings she lost her sight, which could only be partially restored later. She returned to Paris in 1865, experienced both the siege of Paris and the Commune before she retired to Palaiseau where she died in 1885. Her early lyrical works bear reexamination; her literary criticism should be seen as part of more general movements.

Works

The following lists attempt to systematize the often contradictory listings found in the catalogues of the Bibliothèque Nationale, British Library, and National Union pre-1956 imprints. *Album poétique des jeunes personnes* [Poetic Album for Young People] (1861, 1869, 1876). *La Chevalerie française* [French Chivalry] (1821). *Chroniques de France* [Chronicles of France] (1820, 1829, 1831, 1837). *Cours d'histoire de France* [A Course on French History] (1836). *L'Éducation maternelle* [Maternal Education] (1835). *Éloge de Mme*

de Sévigné (1840). *Les Enfants de la vallée d'Andlau, ou Notions familières sur la religion, la morale et les merveilles de la nature* (1837; English tr. as *Education, moral and religious, or familiar illustration of the importance of industry, sobriety, economy, kindness, benevolence, knowledge and piety, for children and youth*, tr. Rev. C. Newell 1842). *Le Livre de la jeunesse et de beauté* [The Book of Youth and Beauty] (1834). *Le Livre des Femmes, choix de morceaux extraits des meilleurs écrivains français sur le caractère, les moeurs et l'esprit des femmes* [The Book of Women, Choice of Selections from the Best French Authors on the Character, Behavior and Mind of Women] (1823). *Poésies* (1826, 5th edition 1833). *Poésies nouvelles* (1835, 4th edition 1839). *Prose* (1836). *Les Récits du maître d'école* [Tales of the Schoolmaster] (1844). *Soirées littéraires de Paris* [Literary Evenings in Paris] (1832). *Tableau de la littérature italienne* [Survey of Italian Literature] (1843). *Tableau de la littérature allemande* [Survey of German Literature] (1843, 1844). *Voyage en France* [Traveling in France] (1846). Under this title, a number of subsequent expanded editions were published that collect many of Amable Tastu's scattered travelogue writings.

Earl Jeffrey Richards

Elizabeth Taylor
1912–1975

Born July 3, 1912, Reading, Berkshire, England
Died November 19, 1975, Grove's Barn, Penn, Buckinghamshire
Genre(s): novel, short story
Language(s): English

Fine ironies and a polished style, a retiring life, and a dedicated readership have caused some critics to mention in the same breath Jane Austen and the modern Englishwoman Elizabeth Taylor. She was born Elizabeth Coles in Berkshire in 1912 and worked as a governess and a librarian before her marriage in 1936. Having had two children and started to bring them up, she turned in 1945 to full-time authorship after the success of her first novel, *At Mrs. Lippincote's*. She dedicated herself to the short and not-so-simple annals of the British middle class, which she viewed with a penetrating eye and a gentle but not wholly uncontemptuous amusement.

She was especially good at catching the individuating gesture and in penetrating the often-elaborate disguises that stockbrokers and other middle-class suburbanites put on those actions that they think are beneath them and nevertheless perform for some real or imagined advantage. She was not at all surprised to discover in the group of people who "had advantages"—and were typically anxious always to "take advantage" to increase that "superiority"—startling inconsistencies; she was able to render these carefully without ever creating characters who were merely puzzling bundles of contradictions. She was able to get right to the heart of characters who were, deep down, at war with the surfaces they deliberately and ingeniously adopted or unfortunately and uncomfortably were compelled by society to adopt.

She chronicled in novels and exquisite short stories (said to be so subtle as to be an acquired taste) the incongruous situations in which perfectly ordinary middle-class people were to be observed doing the most extraordinary things. Hers was the world of human foibles and contradictions that Logan Pearsall Smith described as inhabited by "meat-eating vegetarians" and similar strange but everyday people.

Eschewing the sensational, Taylor opted for plots that permitted her sometimes improbable characters to exhibit themselves without attracting undue attention to the machinery of the fiction. At the same time she was completely aware that even a pillar of the middle-class is, on occasion, liable to appear among the respectable in an outrageously loud tie, or kick over the traces and run away with someone's wife, or do in a rich and elderly relative, or take off with the most unpredictable and "unsuitable" companion to some place impossibly distant or declassé. Her characters inhabited a world of modulated voices and clichéd emotions, a world in which only a few "advanced" or "artistic" persons were expected to be eccentric in manner or extravagant in speech and gesture. She made it perfectly credible for the momentous to interrupt the mundane.

In character, plot, and dialogue she added a seasoning of malice, a dash of censure or contempt (but never toward the reader, who was invited to be on the side of the Right). We are shown how in their genteel and fundamentally British hypocrisy the characters sometimes fool even themselves, and we are invited to sit in judgment of what fools such mortals can be.

Taylor's work is quintessentially British in its shrewd tolerance and its "superior" correction, in its admixture of snobbery with morality, in its skillful combination of the delicious secret guilt of gossip with the properly public stance of "sorting things out." Along with her feminine intuition and village-scandal-monger cattiness—admittedly frequently leavened by a sincere sympathy for characters one might have thought deserved nothing but condemnation—she has an un-

flinching dedication not only to *setting* things right but also *getting* things right. Her glance is penetrating. Her work is highly crafted, deliberate in every effect, calculated when it seems the most casual. Telling us all about her subjects, also, she wastes little or nothing, except perhaps some compassion on a few wayward people who ought to have known better. All of her people we recognize. Some of them we ought not to like as much as her kindness and art make us like them.

Taylor's wit is the kind vaguely described as "dry," which is to say that it prompts smiles, not guffaws, even at the outrageous. Margaret Willy (in the best brief estimate of Taylor's achievement) notes that Taylor's ironies have been compared with Austen's and then cleverly adds:

Another attribute shared by these tolerantly amused, intensely feminine delineators of human foible was a distaste for sensational subject-matter and personal publicity alike. This perhaps in part accounts for the comparatively limited recognition, in favour of flashier fictional attractions, accorded to one of the most quietly distinguished talents of our time.

Arguably the simplest explanation of why a dozen novels from *At Mrs. Lippincote's* to the posthumous *Blaming* (1976) have been so "quietly" received by critics is that most book reviewers over that period were men, and Taylor writes best about and for women. Men may not be able to feel to the same extent the "shock of recognition" at her economical and precise depiction of a young girl's dreams and embarrassments, at a middle-aged woman's hypocrisies and insecurities, at an old woman's disappointments and forced adjustments. Male critics have to acknowlege Taylor's art; female critics keep telling us of her heart.

Her skill is evident in novels. Her collections of short stories prove that she is also the mistress of the briefer form, but here the influence of her favorite writer (Jane Austen) is perhaps less.

Works

At Mrs. Lippincote's (1945). *Palladian* (1946). *A View of the Harbour* (1947). *A Wreath of Roses* (1949). *A Game of Hide-and-Seek* (1951). *The Sleeping Beauty* (1953). *Hester Lilly and Other Stories* (1954). *Angel* (1957). *The Blush and Other Stories* (1958). *In a Summer Season* (1961). *The Soul of Kindness* (1964). *A Dedicated Man and Other Stories* (1965). *Mossy Trotter* (1967). *The Wedding Group* (1968). *Mrs. Palfrey at the Claremont* (1971). *The Devastating Boys* (1972). *Blaming* (1976).

Leonard R.N. Ashley

Emma Tennant
1937–

a.k.a. Catherine Aydy
Born October 20, 1937, London
Genre(s): novel, journalism, literary criticism
Language(s): English

Shortly after Tennant was born, her family moved to Scotland, where she lived for nine years before moving back to London. She attended a village school in Scotland, St. Paul's Girls' School in London, and a finishing school in Oxford, where she was inspired to learn more about art. At fifteen she traveled to Paris to study art history at the École de Louvre. When she returned to England, Tennant became a debutante and was presented at Court in 1956.

In 1961 she began to contribute occasionally to the *New Statesman.* Two years later she became travel correspondent for *Queen.* Her first novel, *The Colour of Rain,* was published with a pseudonym in 1963. In 1966 she became features editor for *Vogue.* When *The Time of the Crack* (1973) was published, Tennant became a full-time novelist.

Tennant was the founding editor of *Bananas* a literary magazine of the British Arts Council, from 1975 to 1978. In 1978 she began writing book reviews for the *Guardian,* to which she still contributes. She also became general editor of *In Verse* in 1982 and *Lives of Modern Women* in 1985. Tennant became a Fellow of the Royal Society of Literature in 1982.

Novelist, critic, and editor, Tennant cannot be pigeonholed. Three of her novels—*The Time of the Crack* (1973), *The Last of the Country House Murders* (1974), and *Hotel de Dream* (1976)—are science-fiction publications. The rest of her novels contain varying amounts of realism. Tennant herself does not believe that prose literature has an obligation to be realistic. She has said, "I would like to feel that I can go off in any direction that seems right." Consequently, her novels cannot be categorized. She does, however, admit that "a lot of my books have actually been a blend of Calvinism and romanticism—having to do with murder and morals. . . ." By some critics she has been called a "woman writer" as opposed to a "writer"; that is, she does treat the feminist viewpoint, examining it and at times exhorting it, in most of her works. Nevertheless, she says about feminism, "the theory must never stand in the way of creativity."

After *The Colour of Rain* (1963), a realistic and critical view of English upper-class society, there was a ten-year hiatus in publishing, mainly because she lost confidence as a result of a disparaging remark reportedly made about her book during judging for the Prix Formentor. Tennant reentered the publishing market by way of the science-fiction genre, whose writers gave her support and confidence, with *The Time of the Crack* (1973). In this novel a huge crack opens unexpectedly in the Thames, separating the North from the South and throwing into chaos the strict separation between social classes that had existed before. The plot also involves two analysts who attempt to cure their patients by regression; the novel is an early example of Tennant's criticism of the theories of "experts" in trying to explain a world that includes myth, imagination, and unexplainable phenomena. The *Times Literary Supplement* called the novel "Lewis Carroll technique applied to H.G. Wells material."

The Last of the Country House Murders (1974) is set in an England with a "Big Brother" government some time in the near future. In this parody of an English murder mystery, the murder of a remaining decadent aristocrat is going to be staged by the government for the entertainment of tourists. His only freedom: Jules Tanner gets to choose his murderer. In *Hotel de Dream* (1976) fantasy and reality intermingle as inhabitants of a boarding-house enter each other's dreams, spending much of their time escaping reality by sleeping. These three novels, which Tennant has called "political satire-fantasy," received fairly good reviews, noting her skill at describing settings and feelings, her intelligent humor, and her satire of modern society.

In *The Bad Sister* (1978), Tennant broke away from fantasy and returned to a more realistic mode, using "documents" to make up the novel. The bulk of this murder mystery consists of "The Journal of Jane Wild," sandwiched by comments from the "editor" of this journal. Here Tennant explores the theme of doubles, coupled with a critical look at both patriarchal tradition in society as well as its confrontation by militant revolutionary movements and militant feminism. As the clergyman Stephen remarks in the novel, "'It's the modern evil, I believe, this jumble of Marxism and Tantrism and anything else thrown in, which is used to persuade people to kill each other.'" This novel is based on James Hogg's *The Private Memoirs and Confessions of a Justified Sinner* (1824).

In her next two novels, *Wild Nights* (1979) and *Alice Fell* (1980), Tennant was less interested in plot and more in perception. Both novels, she has said, were "intended to be short works of poetic prose." *Wild Nights* is a first-person, "fictional childhood memoir," set in the Tennants' family home in Scotland. She has described *Alice Fell* as a novel about "the fall of a girl, using the myth of Persephone." These two novels, along with her next, *Queen of Stones* (1982), use the theme of childhood. All three were inspired by her daughters' growing up.

Queen of Stones, a female version of *Lord of the Flies*, uses documents to reconstruct a fictional event. Besides presenting the lives of adolescent girls, the novel also satirizes society's official interpretation of adolescence, particularly Freudian analysis. The narrator pontificates: "Thus, perhaps, will the psychopathology of the developing female be more fully comprehended; as also the mythology sustaining our concept of the feminine in society." The narrator, whom Tennant has described as "pretty stupid," ends by blaming all the sinister events in the novel on the arrival of the first menstrual period of one of the main characters.

In *Woman Beware Woman* (1983), Tennant tried to evoke character more strongly than in her previous novels. Each of the three women in this story must beware of the others after the famous husband of one has been found dead. Tennant has said that the book is about "the horrors of the 'perfect' family, and what in fact goes on underneath, the entrapments and tensions." She emphasizes that the characters do not represent women in our time.

Black Marina (1985), another mystery, brings the left-wing politics and feminism of the Portobello Road area, in London, to St. James, a tiny Caribbean Island. The book is also about the search for identity—not only for Marina, a young girl searching for her "roots," but for the entire island. Tennant's evocation of place is superb. She describes the library of the last of the white colonial landowners as a place "where the peeling-off spines of the books hang like moths half out of their cocoons. . . ." This is a perfect metaphor for the entire island, which is stuck halfway between its colonial past and the modern world of resorts and condominiums—not to mention revolutions and invasions.

Tennant's later novel, *The Adventures of Robina by Herself*, "edited" by Emma Tennant (1986), is a picaresque, autobiographical novel using eighteenth-century idiom but set in the 1950s. It traces the adventures of an incredibly naive young woman from Oxford to Paris to London and is based on the premise that "the ways and manners of a certain section of the society in which we live are virtually unchanged since the early eighteenth century."

Tennant's success has been in evoking a sense of place. Although she has said, "I think, in most writers, there's some sort of pattern," her own writing exemplifies another statement of hers: "Every different thing demands its own expression."

Works

The Colour of Rain (as Catherine Aydy, 1963). *The Time of the Crack* (1973). *The Last of the Country House Murders* (1975). *Hotel de Dream* (1976). *The Bad Sister* (1978; with M. Rayner) *The Boggart* (1979). *Wild Nights* (1979). *Alice Fell* (1980). *The Search for Treasure Island* (1981). *Queen of Stones* (1982). *Woman Beware Woman* (1983; U.S. ed. *The HalfMother*). *Black Marina* (1985). *The Ghost Child* (1984). *The Adventures of Robina by Herself*, ed. Emma Tennant (1986). *The House of Hospitalities* (1987). *A Wedding of Cousins* (1988). *Two Women of London: The Strange Case of Ms. Jekyll and Mrs. Hyde* (1989). *The Magic Drum: An Excursion* (1989). *The ABC of Writing* (1992). *Faustine* (1992). *Tess* (1993). *Pemberley or Pride and Prejudice Continued* (1993). *An Unequal Marriage or Pride and Prejudice Twenty Years Later* (1994).

Carol Pulham

Teresa de Cartagena
ca. 1400–?

Born fifteenth century, Spain
Death date unknown
Genre(s): treatise
Language(s): Spanish

Teresa de Cartagena belonged to an illustrious Christian family of Jewish origin, which achieved great prominence in Castile due to the literary accomplishments of its members. Teresa was the granddaughter of Pablo de Santa María, who was first chief rabbi and later bishop of Burgos. Among other writers, Álvar García de Santa María and Alonso de Cartagena were her relatives. Given her unusual background, it is not surprising that Teresa de Cartagena studied in Salamanca, became a nun, and wrote a couple of treatises.

Having lost her hearing in her youth, Teresa composed a book entitled *Arboleda de los Enfermos* (The Grove of the Sick), mostly to console herself by studying in great detail the many positive aspects of illness, which in her opinion leads to God. To demonstrate this, she quoted not only the Bible, but also authors such as Saint Augustine and Saint Bernard. The knowledge and skill that Teresa displayed in this work, and even the fact that she had written it, caused bewilderment in Castile, where there were practically no women authors at the time. She was accused of having plagiarized the works of others and even of not having composed the work herself.

To answer these accusations, Teresa composed a book entitled *Admiraçión Operum Dey* (Wonder at the Works of God), which some critics consider the first example of feminist writing in the Iberian Peninsula. She defends the idea that women are not inferior to men in the eyes of God. In her opinion, both sexes complement each other, and if God made men stronger physically and to some extent mentally than women, it was so that they would be able to deal with the outside world. Women stay inside and therefore do not need to be as strong as men. Having made this concession, Teresa stresses that although there are important natural differences between men and women, many differences are cultural, and the attitude with respect to literature is one of them. She explains that women do not write because they are not trained or encouraged to do it. Teresa attributes the bewilderment her literary activities had caused to the fact that people believed women did not write because they were not capable of doing it. She states that the ability to write is a gift from God to the individual, man or woman, and people should wonder at this gift and not at the identity of the receiver. She concludes that to deny that both men and women can receive this gift is to deny the power of God.

As can be seen, Teresa de Cartagena was capable not only of expressing herself in writing but also of reflecting about the writing process. These were very unusual accomplishments for a woman in Medieval Castile. Some critics think she became a writer because she was marginalized by her Jewish origin and acute deafness. No doubt these circumstances had something to do with her desire to express herself in writing. However, she could do it because, having come from a literary family, she had the necessary training and encouragement. The same thing can be said of Florencia Pinar, a poet who also came from a literary family. As for the historian Leonor López de Córdoba, although she did not come from a literary family, she was familiar enough with the writing process to dictate her work to a notary. The only three significant women authors of medieval Castile wrote because, apart from the desire to do so, they had direct or indirect access to the pen. Teresa de Cartagena's analysis of the situation was indeed accurate.

Works

Arboleda de los Enfermos (mid-fifteenth century).
Admiraçión Operum Dey (second half of the fifteenth century).

Cristina González

Saint Teresa of Jesus
1515–?

Born March 28, 1515, Avila, Spain
Death date unknown
Genre(s): mystical treatise
Language(s): Spanish

Saint Teresa of Jesus

Saint Teresa of Jesus was born in Avila, as the daughter of Alonso Sánchez de Cepeda, the son of a converted Jew from Toledo. Alonso Sánchez married for the first time in 1505; his wife, Catalina del Peso, died two years later, leaving him two children. In 1509 Alonso married Beatriz de Ahumada, Teresa's mother. The couple had ten children. Beatriz had a fondness for romances of chivalry, which she had to read with her children unbeknownst to her husband. Teresa was captivated by the romances. At the age of five she persuaded one of her brothers to flee the paternal house and go with her to "the land of the Moors" to seek martyrdom.

Teresa wrote four long works: *The Book of Life* (1588), *The Way of Perfection* (1564), *Book of the Foundations* (1573), and *The Dwelling Places of the Interior Castle* (1577). All except the second one begin with an assertion of the advantages of good lineage as an omen of future accomplishments. The first chapter of *The Book of Life* is titled: "To have had virtuous and God-fearing parents along with the graces the Lord granted me should have been enough for me to have led a good life, if I had not been so wretched."

Teresa wrote the first draft of her *Book of Life* in 1562. Although the book went through several revisions and was not published until 1588, we know that it was scrutinized by theologians and inquisitors for several years since the book, which narrated extraordinary experiences, was written by an "idiot"—a person who did not know Latin—and a woman.

The first ten chapters tell of her life up to the moment of the conversion, when she began to receive the mystical experiences. Chapter eleven is devoted to a description of the degrees of prayer or mercies that she had received up to the moment of drafting the book. This chapter is emblematic of Teresa's mystic writing. She avoids abstract doctrine in favor of events; she avoids concepts and tries to be understood through images. The way of perfection is compared in this chapter to the irrigation of a garden, and the different stages along the way are four different modes of irrigation. The resort to images accounts for Teresa's literary mastery. At some points the images are so deep and sublime that the reader cannot anticipate the possibility of surpassing them. And yet, he is always surprised by Teresa's genius in finding new comparisons that convey ever greater intensity and beauty.

Four degrees of prayer are described in *The Book of Life*: recollection, quiet, sleep of the faculties, and union. Recollection can be attained through human effort. It is not a struggle with the human faculties as it was in the Franciscan school; it is simply a decision to renounce worldly values and attitudes. The other three degrees are all "supernatural," that is, unattainable by natural means; they are mercies from God.

The Way of Perfection was written for the nuns of the reformed monastery of Avila in 1564. The book consists of two parts: chapters 1 to 42 contain the basis of spiritual perfection for the nuns. Humility is posited as the foundation of the spiritual edifice. All values of the world, especially honor in the sense of lineage, must be renounced. The second part (chapters 43–73) is commentary on the *Pater noster*.

Her last and most acclaimed book, *The Dwelling Places of the Interior Castle* (1577), describes the way of perfection as a quest for the center. The soul is portrayed as a castle with different mansions. In the innermost mansion or center of the soul God dwells with his infinite majesty, love, and light. Messages and inspirations radiate from that center to the faculties,

inviting them to see from the dangerous outskirts of the castle (sin) and from the exterior chambers (dispersion), and reach to God and themselves. For Teresa, the conquest of God is the conquest of our personal identity.

The Dwelling Places of the Interior Castle is divided into seven sections of different lengths, each one devoted to a set of dwelling places or mansions. The division of the book into seven sections may have been inspired by the popular septenaries of the Catholic Church: seven virtues, seven deadly sins, or seven sacraments. But the book is not an allegory based on numerical symbolism; in it Teresa narrates her own life, the nuances of her experiences being more important than the external frame of the book.

To appreciate Teresa's cultural and literary originality, one must measure her accomplishments against the handicaps she had to overcome: she was a woman in sixteenth-century Spain, of Jewish descent, a nun in a monastery of closure, and severely ill since the age of twenty-two. Settled in God as her center, she had a clear hierarchy of values, was able to appreciate or deride social and religious institutions, had an exemplary sense of freedom, gave a new impulse to religious life and mystical literature, and through her insistence on courage, provides us with a formula that is still valid to banish the ghost of alienation.

Works

Obras completas de Santa Teresa, ed. Efrén de la Madre de Dios and Otger Steggink (1967).

Translations: *The Collected Works of St. Teresa of Avila*, tr. Kieran Kavanaugh and Otilio Rodriguez, 2 vols. (1979–1980). *The Complete Works of St. Teresa of Jesus*, tr. E. Allison Peers. (1946)

C.M. Arroyo

Laura Terracina
1519–1577

Born 1519, Naples, Italy
Died 1577
Genre(s): narrative and lyric poetry
Language(s): Italian

Laura Terracina was the most prolific woman poet of the Italian Renaissance. She was the daughter of Diana Onofra of Sorrento and of Paolo Terracina, a nobleman who held several offices at the Neapolitan court and died at the age of 110. Laura did not receive a classical education but was encouraged in her poetic endeavors by Marcantonio Passero, a retired professor of the University of Padua, who kept a private register of Neapolitan poets, and by Lodovico Domenichi, a literary factotum and entrepreneur of the publishing business. The decade 1549–1559 was the happiest in her life: ensconced in the family residence in the then-pastoral as well as aristocratic district of Chiaia, Laura, in the bloom of her youth, savored the attention of the people who frequented the court, the university, and the academies. For the Terracinas, staunch supporters of the monarchy, these were years of success. Laura's propensity for highly placed men and women was strengthened during the street riots of 1547, when her entire family was threatened with extinction because of a tax imposed by her uncle Domenico. At the age of forty, she married a relative, Polidoro Terracina. The marriage was very unhappy, mostly on account of his obsessive jealousy. In the volumes published at this time and later, Laura laments her restricted life, her isolation, and the ingratitude of the powerful. Between 1570 and 1575, she traveled to Rome, perhaps in the hope of ingratiating herself with the Papal Court. Her last piece of writing is a letter dated November 30, 1577.

Most of Terracina's output can be seen as a poetic correspondence in the current Petrarchistic mode. About 80 poems were sent to as many literati of the peninsula, at least 200 more were addressed to members of the Neapolitan nobility. Thematic and stylistic commonplaces are used to praise the recipient and to celebrate private or public occasions. The metrical schemes are those of the sonnet, the *canzone*, the madrigal, the sestet, the octave, *terza rime*, and *capitoli*.

Relatively few are love poems. In her fourth volume, she evades the sexual entreaties of Alfonso Mantegna di Maida, professor of the Studium; when he finally turns his attention elsewhere, Terracina composes a poem in praise of the lady. Some poems of unrequited love maintain the male point of view and the manner of address to the beloved is characteristic of Petrarchism. Modern scholars see them as a gauge of the degree of depersonalization present in the socialized applications of the lyric code. Most of Terracina's poetry of courtship, however, is addressed to well-known women of high rank and was very probably written in the voice of and by request of male suitors. Other poems are complaints over the lover's betrayal in the person of fictional characters and can be easily traced to the popular genre of the "woman's lament."

The prevailing tone of Laura's poetry is depreca-tory and moralistic. Contemporary society is upbraided for its greed, treachery, and ferocity. In the manner of Petrarch, she laments Italy's political upheavals and the devastations of cities and countryside brought about by invading armies. In a more personal vein, she expresses nostalgia for her past successes. Many poems written in her last years and never published belong to the genre of *rime spirituali*, much favored in the new religious climate of the Counter-Reformation. In her prayers and meditations on death, Terracina attains a level of intimate pathos.

A *Discorso sopra tutti i primi canti d'Orlando Furioso* (1549; Summary of the Content of the First Cantos of *Orlando Furioso*) summarizes Ariosto's poem in 46 swift and graceful cantos interspersed with moralistic considerations. In Canto V, Terracina upholds the intellectual equality of the sexes and attributes the limited achievements attained by her sex to the small number of women dedicated to literary work. First published by Giolito in 1549, the *Discorso* was reissued five times by him before 1561 and at least four more times by other publishers before the end of the century. In 1567, she wrote a second *Discorso*, this one about Ariosto's additional Cantos, when her reluctance was overcome by Valvassori, the publisher.

Exaggeratedly praised during her most productive years, Terracina outlived the popularity of the genres to which she had applied her facile vein. After her death, she became the butt of sexual and literary ridicule on the part of dyspeptic satirists. Most famous is the portrayal of her made by T. Boccalini in his *Ragguagli di Parnaso* (Reports from Parnassus). Her literary prolificacy and pro-Spanish sympathies are here ferociously, though wittily, chastised in what is essentially an *ad feminam* attack of political nature. Since then, Terracina has scored very low in the scale of sixteenth-century poetic achievement. It is, therefore, a surprise to discover considerable facility and rhetorical skill in many of her verses. More recently she has been called a professional of literature, who capably answered the demands of a middle-brow public. As such, in a social-historical view of Renaissance literature, she fits the description given by her contemporary admirers as that of a "marvel of the female sex."

Works

Rime (1548). *Rime seconde* (1549). *Discorso sopra tutti i primi canti di Orlando Furioso* (1549). *Quarte rime* (1550). *Quinte rime* (1552). *Seste rime* (1558). *Sovra tutte le vedove di questa citta di Napoli* (1561). *La seconda parte de' Discorsi sopra le seconde stanze de' Canti d'Orlando Furioso* (1567).

Rinaldina Russell

Maria Tesselschade
1594–1649

Born March 15, 1594, Amsterdam, The Netherlands
Died June 20, 1649, Amsterdam
Genre(s): poetry, letters
Language(s): Dutch

Maria Tesselschade Roemersdochter lived through the first half of the Dutch Golden Age, an era in which political power and economic prosperity were matched by intense cultural activity. She wrote poetry, including sonnets, and kept up a lively correspondence with some of the great writers and intellectuals of the time, such as Hooft, Huygens, and van Baerle or Barlaeus. Mostly written on the occasion of, or as a reaction to, private and public events, Tesselschade's letters and poems are not only fine examples of Dutch Renaissance literature (which was late in developing compared to Southern Europe), but they also offer valuable insights into the bustling intellectual, literary, and religious climate of the young Dutch republic.

Her father, the wealthy grain merchant and poet Roemer Pieterszoon Visscher (1547–1620), had given her the middle name Tesselschade to "memorize" the heavy losses he suffered following a storm off the Frisian island Texel three months before she was born (*Tessel* is Texel; *Scha* is *schade*, or damage). Tesselschade (like her equally talented sister Anna Roemer Visscher) received an excellent education in the liberal arts. They knew both French and Italian, read foreign authors, wrote and translated, and were hostesses at the frequent gatherings of artists and intellectuals in their father's house. Later Tesselschade became a very welcome guest of the so-called *Muiderkring* or Muiden Circle, a rather loose group of literati, scholars, merchants, and holders of public office who met irregularly at the house of the poet and historiographer P.C. Hooft for poetry, music, and discussions.

Tesselschade's charm and her many accomplishments (singing, engraving, writing) attracted poets and artists. But in 1623 she married Allard Crombalgh, a naval officer with no literary or artistic pretensions. He died in 1634. As a widow in her forties, Tesselschade was still courted, half in jest, half in earnest, by two prominent members of the Muiden Circle. In 1641 or 1642, she converted to Catholicism, a courageous act of faith at a time when Roman Catholics were an unpopular minority. Both occasions characteristically gave rise to a lively poetic and epistolary exchange among Tesselschade and her friends. Faithful to the memory of her beloved husband, she never gave in to her "suitors," sending them level-headed and, often, witty replies. She countered the sometimes vicious attacks on her return to Roman Catholicism with remarkable serenity and occasional playfulness.

A true child of the Renaissance, Tesselschade craftily explored the possibilities of the vernacular, making use of various rhyme schemes and prosodic patterns. She had a predilection for ingenious wordplay, complex imagery, and oblique allusions. An admirer of the Italian poet Marino, she did not keep her work free from frivolous punning and mannerisms.

Classical ideals prevail throughout her writing. The motto with which she occasionally signed her poems and letters, "Elck zyn Waerom"—"to each his why"—points toward her independent mind and her tolerance toward others. Her very aversion to intolerance and rigidity in religious and other matters may have turned her away from rigorous Calvinism, which, in her opinion, was seriously curtailing the freedom of the republic's citizens (including their freedom of religion). Tesselschade confronted grief—her own grief and that of others—with equanimity and stoic composure. In one of her most accomplished poems, a sonnet written on the death of the Lady of Sulekom, Huygens's wife, Tesselschade implored her friend to "confide to paper not to memory," since "paper was the weapon with which I fought the wish to die ere heaven could reclaim me."

Maria Tesselschade died in 1649, not only surviving her husband but also her two daughters and some of her closest friends. Though her beauty and talents had been extensively sung in poetry and prose during her lifetime, only a few of her poems had actually been printed. More verse was published in various anthologies later in the century, but on the whole relatively little survived. Her work on a translation of Tasso's *Gerusalemme Liberata* is entirely lost except for one stanza. Among her most appreciated poems are the sonnet already mentioned, the beautifully solemn "Mary Magdalen at the Feet of Jesus," emphasizing man's repentance and God's mercy, and "Onderscheyd tusschen een wilde, en een tamme zangster" (The Distinction Between a Wild and a Tame Singer), a crafted illustration of "the ars naturae aemula" theme.

Though Maria Tesselschade is generally not counted among the century's great, her work remains of interest today as one of the few testimonies of a highly intelligent, sensitive, and witty woman who participated, apparently with great zest, in the exciting cultural life of the Netherlands' most illustrious age.

Works

Een onwaerdeerlycke vrouw. Brieven en verzen van

en aan Maria Tesselschade, ed. J.A. Worp (1918; rpt. 1976). 't Hoge huis te Muiden. Teksten uit de Muiderkring, ed. M.C.A. Van der Heijden, 2nd ed. (1978).

Translations: Selected poems and letters, tr. R. Vanderauwera, in *Renaissance Women Writers*, ed. K.M. Wilson (1987).

Ria Vanderauwera

Anne Teyssiéras
1945–
Born 1945
Genre(s): poetry
Language(s): French

Anne Teyssiéras's first volume of poetry, aptly titled *Epervier ma solitude* (Sparrowhawk My Loneliness), was published in 1966 and followed soon by *Fragments pour une captive* (1969; Fragments for a Prisoner). The latter is an intense, compact collection centered upon an intimate though discreet elaboration of themes of disappearance and absence, waiting and possible future gesturing. A "hymn of Death," it struggles with factors of (self-)imprisonment and devastation, determination, and invention. *L'Ecaille entre les eaux* (1975; The Shell between the Waters), written under the sign of Artaud, shows just how difficult this struggle is: the bare, elegant texts swarm with unspeakableness, suffocation, pain, and impotence, and, although the final section speaks of rebirth and maintains a sense of feasibility, it, too, is threatened with failure and cloaked in uncertainty.

Anne Teyssiéras's sixth volume, *Parallèles* (Parallels), appeared in 1976 (republished in 1982 with *La Boule de cristal*, The Crystal Ball). *Parallèles* offers us poems of great emotional intensity, in which love and the poet's ceaseless interrogation of signs are repeatedly met with frustration and forced to the brink of "madness." The power of resistance is, however, great; death is not absolute, the (absent) other remains a "high keeper of my song," while the *hic et nunc* retains its vital compulsion: "I shall not wear mourning / Elsewhere summons me / Here is my obligation wherein I cleanse a swamp." *Le Pays d'où j'irai* (1977; The Land from Where I Shall Go), liminally inspired by Michaux, betrays similar tensions: marginally more positive in tone and centered upon departure and future event, the volume nevertheless displays the many sober traces of the wretchedness of things as well as

the exile wrought paradoxically by poetry itself. *Juste avant la nuit* (1979; Just Before Night) specifically articulates these paradoxes and tensions via a contrapuntal rhetoric in which the "intertwinement of speech" is delicately explored and enacted, and factors of poetic place and non-place, recognition and non-recognition, going and (non-)arrival, loss and regrowth are subtly and evocatively elaborated.

Les Clavicules de Minho (The Clavicles of Minho) was published in 1986. Taking up the interrogations Anne Teyssiéras began in part in *La Boule de cristal* (1982), "It is," she says, "the end consequence of a period of reflection on, if one wants, the result of the 'gropings' that went before." It is, at all events, both a powerfully felt and a brilliantly lucid assessment of the problematics of poetic voice and, indeed, all artistic expression. As such it stands alongside the writings of contemporaries such as Yves Bonnefoy, Michel Deguy, and Bernard Noël. It happily avoids all pretentiousness and tendentiousness. Poetry and art, for Anne Teyssiéras, offer an oddly intransitive knowledge, a kind of "laughter . . . in response to all questions." They are predicated upon "belief," desire, "promise"; they hesitate between sense and non-sense; their "focusing" is illusory, their contact is with nothingness. They are, one might say, living "deconstruction." The poet, as Anne Teyssiéras says, "seeks shelter in the eye of the cyclone, whereas you exhaust yourself at the fringes of non-sense." Poetry and art are thus "movement not achievement." Myth, she rightly argues, comes precisely from poetry's/art's "detour." Other forces, however, are infinitely greater, and, possibly, less mystifying: love, the forces of being beyond us, the "distant effusion" of which poetry and art are but an "echo." The latter are merely "the saliva of nothingness"—but "everything is in Nothingness"— and require our compassionate but lucid laughter to show both their skeletalness and their residual potential for illumination. *Les Clavicules de Minho* gives us the revealed originality of Anne Teyssiéras as poet and theoretician.

Works
Epervier ma solitude (1966). *Fragments pour une captive* (1969). *Cinq étapes pour une attente* (1971). *Dernier état* (1974). *L'Ecaille entre les eaux* (1975). *Parallèles* (1976). *Le Pays d'où j'irai* (1977). *Juste avant la nuit* (1979). *Parallèles, suivi de La Boule de cristal* (1982). *Poèmes en Kabbale* (1984). *Les Clavicules de Minho* (1986). *Le chemin sous la mer* (1992). *Instants pour la seconde vie* (1994).

Michael Bishop

Ilse Tielsch
1929–

Born March 20, 1929, Hustopeče (formerly Auspitz) near Brno (formerly Brünn), formerly Czechoslovakia
Genre(s): poetry, short story, novel, radio drama
Language(s): German

Ilse Tielsch is one of the most popular authors on the contemporary Austrian scene. She writes in a readily accessible style with conventional themes and forms and with a keen sense for what is topical in present-day society. Although her poetry is noteworthy, she is best known for her historical novels dealing with the Second World War and the immediate postwar period.

Tielsch was born in 1929 in southern Moravia, and her family was thus a part of the German minority in Czechoslovakia. She was ten years old when World War II broke out, and her teenage years were shaped by ensuing events. A few months before the end of the war, the fifteen-year-old Ilse was sent on a train to relatives in Upper Austria, and she experienced first-hand the chaos as the refugees sought food and shelter in the war-torn country. After much moving around Tielsch studied journalism at the University of Vienna and received her doctorate in 1953. In 1950 she married Rudolf Tielsch, a medical doctor, and they have two children. Tielsch began writing in the mid-1960s, and the recognition she achieved in the 1970s became fame in the 1980s. Her works prior to 1979 appear under a hyphenated name, which she then shortened to Tielsch by dropping the family name Felzmann. Tielsch lives today as a freelance writer in Vienna, where she is a member of the PEN Club and coeditor of the literary journal *Podium*.

Tielsch's historical works begin with a short narrative, *Erinnerungen mit Bäumen* (1979; Reminiscences with Trees), and culminate in two lengthy novels, *Die Ahnenpyramide* (1980; The Ancestor Pyramid) and *Heimatsuchen* (1982; Searching for Home). *Erinnerungen* presents a quasibiographical account of the events of 1945 from a present-day perspective. A trip to a writers' conference in Upper Austria serves as occasion for a trip into the past as the protagonist Anna visits the area where she had lived temporarily as a young girl more than three decades prior to the time of narration. The landscape becomes a soul-scape as Anna recalls the war and the ensuing events. In contrast to the inferno of that time, the present narrative stance is reflective and meditative, and the titular designation "with Trees" articulates the metaphorical level of memory, raising also the question of continuity of identity between then and now.

Tielsch's major novels continue the theme of personal past interwoven with modern European history. *Die Ahnenpyramide* offers a family chronicle from a present-day perspective, looking back to the earliest mention of the family in church records in 1580 and extending to departure from the area in 1945. It is at the same time a social history of German enclaves in the Czech territories of Bohemia and Moravia, and it attempts to understand the historical relations between the Sudeten Germans and the native Slavic population. Realizing that "totality" is a utopian vision, the narrator points to the discontinuity of historiography; and she presents realistic vignettes describing the everyday life and work of people in a small town, as based on documentary evidence culled from newspapers, photographs, and records of the time. The thematic center is the childhood of the protagonist, a thinly veiled autobiographical figure named Anni F., and the events of her life between the ages of nine and sixteen are narrated in conjunction with the events of World War II between 1938 and 1945. The child, like an oscillograph, registers the vibrations of a world run amok and plunging headlong toward destruction. The long expedition into the past is motivated by a search for the self, for "what we are began long before us." It is also an attempt to liberate the concept of "home" (*Heimat*) from the odium of its nationalistic and imperialistic associations. Without idealization, sentimentality, or revisionism the narrator describes an era that is recognized as past and that stands as experience to be integrated into the present.

Heimatsuchen begins where the previous work left off at the end of the war in 1945 when the twelve million Germans living in the Sudetenland and other Eastern European countries were required to leave their homes and seek a new life elsewhere. The sixteen-year-old Anni and her family stand at the center as representative of the millions of refugees that poured into Austria as well as into East and West Germany. The work narrates the chaos of the times: the hardships and dangers of flight, cold, hunger, illness, and exhaustion, separation from and death of loved ones, search for a place to stay, the black market, suspicion and rejection by the indigenous population—and also the help and comfort that was offered and the hope for a new beginning. Without pathos or self-pity and also without bitterness or resentment the author presents a realistic, well-documented account of the time. Whereas the sociopolitical issue of the refugees, the "Heimatvertriebene," is a sensitive topic that had been virtually taboo for over three decades, Tielsch offers a reconciliatory book. While refusing to provide grist for the mill of right-wing politics, it illuminates the past in the true spirit of "Vergangenheitsbewältigung." The work is in some ways comparable to Christa Wolf's *Kindheitsmuster* (1976), and although Tielsch's account is less subjective, it too constitutes an experiment in remembering. It is also an effort to understand the past and forgive its wrongdoings, and above all it is a cry against the repetition of history.

Tielsch has published several collections of short stories that demonstrate her superb stylistic ability even apart from the gripping material of recent history. *Ein Elefant in unserer Straße* (1977; An Elephant in Our Street) is a collection of satires on modern consumer society. With irony and humor the author parodies the drive for material wealth and social status, the grotesque manifestations of which, as indicated by the title, lead to absurdity and alienation. *Fremder Strand* (1984; Foreign Shore), set in the context of a trip to the North Sea, narrates the mid-life crisis of a typical modern woman. As wife, mother, and artist she had placed her family before her own professional ambitions; but with the children grown she finds herself estranged from her husband, alone and aging, and overwhelmed by the distance to her own self as well as to the ostensibly familiar outside world.

Since poetry has in general a more limited appeal than prose, Tielsch's poetry has been somewhat overshadowed by her large novels. But Tielsch would be a prominent author even if she had written only poetry, for her six lyric volumes have been well received. The breakthrough came in 1975 with *Regenzeit* (Rain Time), which was reprinted in 1981—a rare occurrence with poetry. Another volume, *Nicht beweisbar* (Not Provable), also appeared in 1981, and a further volume in 1986, *Zwischenbericht* (Interim Report). A development is noticeable over the past two decades away from the traditional certainties toward a more questioning, skeptical stance, as indicated also by the recent titles. Topics include childhood memories, landscapes, social criticism, and the hopes and fears attached to our fragile constructs. In short free-verse lines the author presents an amalgam of thought and feeling, experience and impression, often with a slight narrative line and a surprising twist at the end. The poems speak dynamically and directly, as indicated by the following self-commentary: "Metaphors don't save us when we fall" (from *Regenzeit*). Of course Tielsch also deploys metaphor very widely, but her images are readily understandable and stand in the service of life rather than art.

In contrast to the exclusiveness and elusiveness of hermetic poetry or experimental literature, Tielsch writes in a traditional realistic mode. The issues that concern her are practical and empirical rather than theoretical or abstract. If her work has not received full recognition from the literary establishment it is probably because it does not have the philosophical depth or aesthetic finesse associated with great literature. Tielsch's faith in the knowability of reality and in the adequacy of language to convey it stands in contrast to the modern tradition of language skepticism. On the other hand, Tielsch's books have reached a wider audience than many works in the intellectual tradition, and they stand as good literature for the general reading public.

Works

In meinem Orangengarten. (1964). *Herbst, mein Segel.* (1967). *Anrufung des Mondes.* (1970). *Begegnung in einer steirischen Jausenstation.* (1973). *Regenzeit.* (1975; rpt. 1981). *Ein Elefant in unserer Straße oder Geschichten mit Paul.* (1977). *Erinnerungen mit Bäumen.* (1979). *Südmährische Sagen* (1979). *Die Ahnenpyramide.* (1980). *Nicht beweisbar.* (1981). *Heimatsuchen.* (1982). *Fremder Strand.* (1984). *Zwischenbericht.* (1986). *Der Solitär.* (1987).

Translation: *Memories with Trees*, tr. David a. Scrase (1993).

Beth Bjorklund

Märta Eleonora Tikkanen
1935–
Born April 3, 1935, Helsinki, Finland
Genre(s): novel
Language(s): Swedish

Märta Tikkanen took a B.A. degree in humanities at Helsinki University in 1958, worked as a journalist and later as a secondary school teacher for several years, then became headmistress of a Citizens' Further Education Institute. Her second husband encouraged her writing. At first her writing seemed to emerge as one part of the dialogue in this marriage, the other being provided by her husband in his own novels.

Her first novel, *Nu imorron* (1970; Now Tomorrow), is an intense monologue, the ultimate purpose of which seems to be a search for the writer's self, and the autobiographical element recurs in her second novel, *Ingenmansland* (1972; No Man's Land). The first novel uses the first-person narrative throughout, describing a wife wanting a life of her own or at least a kind of total acceptance but unable to secure even enough time to read the newspaper. In the second novel the third-person narrative creates a certain distance between writer and work in debating the nature of freedom that the female protagonist seeks. In the time between these two novels, Märta Tikkanen had become acquainted with the American Women's Liberation movement and was definitely influenced by their ideas, but her female protagonist seems too naive and too isolated to be able to live up to any feminist ideals: she remains in a no-man's-land, but she is aware of the necessity of some kind of liberation for both partners. The works that earned her international fame were *Män kan inte våldtas* (1975; Men Cannot Be Raped) and *Århundradets kärlekssaga* (1978; The Love Story of This Century). The latter has been called a confessional poem and belongs in the genre of autobiographical stories that has dominated Swedish literature in Finland for some twenty years.

Her most recent work, *Rödluvan* (1986; Little Red Riding Hood), continues her constant focus on womanhood as well as her autobiographical line; it is a report obviously on her own maturing process through childhood and marriage, sorrow and liberation.

Märta Tikkanen has already offered many valid arguments in the ongoing debate on women and their new position. She is quite likely going to continue along these lines, as the issues involved seem to catch and keep her interest together with her analytical observation of her own self.

Works

Nu imorron [Now Tomorrow] (1970). *Ingenmansland* [No Man's Land] (1972). *Vem bryr sig om Doris Mihailov?* [Who Cares for Doris Mihailov?] (1974). *Män kan inte våldtas* [Men Cannot Be Raped] (1975) (translated into five languages, also English). *Århundradets kärlekssaga* [The Love Story of This Century] (1978). (with Katarina Michelsson), *Mörkret som ger glädjen djup* [Darkness That Gives Joy Its Depth] (1981). *Sofias egen bok* [Sophy's Own Book]. *Rödluvan* [Little Red Riding Hood] (1986). A few radio and television plays.

Translation: *Love Story of the Century* (1988).

Gunnel Cleve

Tat'iana Tolstaia
1951–

Born 1951, Leningrad, Russia
Genre(s): short story, drama criticism
Language(s): Russian

A granddaughter of Aleksandr Nikolaevich Tolstoi (1882–1945), famous for his *Aelita* (1922–1923) *Peter the First* (1929–1945), and *The Road to Calvary* (1922–1941), Tolstaia has earned a name for herself among the literati. She graduated in 1974 from the Department of Philology at the State University of Leningrad, a training that partially accounts for her inventive and rigorous attitude toward language. Although she whimsically claims to have dreamed since childhood of pursuing a nursing career, her attraction to literature manifested itself early in the several years she spent working at a publishing house after graduation. Her literary debut in 1983 with the excellent story "Na zolotom kryl'tse sideli" (1923; On the Golden Porch) unaccountably aroused little attention. But the publication of her longer narrative "Peter" just three years later in *New World* sparked lively enthusiasm in both Moscow and Leningrad. It established her reputation as an original and exciting young talent.

Tolstaia's stories focus on the isolation of the individual personality, the universal inability to grasp the essence of other human beings, and the indifference on the part of the overwhelming majority to the psychological complexity of others. Especially children and the elderly, situated at the two extremes of the age spectrum, suffer from the incomprehension and callousness of those around them. Many of Tolstaia's protagonists lead lives that go unnoticed or misunderstood. Victims of ridicule and condescension, they reside at the fringe of society, with scant opportunity for fulfillment or success.

Convinced that the significance of a life becomes partially revealed only after the person dies, Tolstaia treats the experience of death as a moment of epiphany in such works as "Na zolotom kryl'tse sideli," "Sonia," and "Svidanie s ptitsei" (Rendezvous with a Bird). Yet whatever insights death may vouchsafe, individual identity in Tolstaia's world eludes definition, being located somewhere in the interstices of seemingly irreconcilable contradictions. Children, whom Tolstaia frequently endows with bold imagination and unexpected insights, conceive of life as a miraculous adventure and thus appear particularly receptive to the inexplicable paradoxes inherent in human nature. Hence the girl in Tolstaia's first story sees her bookkeeping neighbor Uncle Pasha as a downtrodden husband, a happy lover, a helpless old man, a khalif, a prince, King Solomon, etc. Delight in provocative enigmas that reflect the mysterious nature of life and personality virtually disappears with adulthood, which is why Tolstaia tends to associate childhood with the Edenic state. "Na zolotom kryl'tse sideli," for example, explicitly equates childhood with the prelapsarian happiness of perceptions uncorrupted by commonplace forms and categories.

Tolstaia spotlights characters who range from the mildly unheroic to the unsettlingly pathetic. Since she entertains an unidealized, skeptical, even bleak, view of romantic love, her protagonists' amorous aspirations and involvements appear in a humorous or grotesque light. Elevated notions of love crumble under the assault of myopic delusions on the one hand and brute physicality on the other. In general Tolstaia's fictional universe is aggressively physical, populated by countless objects, bodies, and faces that she evokes vividly in striking metaphors and similes. Yet the relationship of Tolstaia's protagonists to this tangible reality is curiously unstable, and reality itself seems contingent, incessantly open to multiple interpretations.

Probably the single most distinctive aspect of Tolstaia's writing, her instantly identifiable signature (with the exception of her weakest effort, "Chistyi list" [Tabula Rasa], which by her own admission failed to come off), is her exuberant, condensed style. Above all, the prose of Tolstaia's eccentric narrators, descended from Laurence Sterne's and Nikolai Gogol's garrulous storytellers, pulses with iridescent vitality. rife with contradictions and illogicalities, ellipses, erratic shifts from pathos to humor, flaunted lapses of memory side by side with perfect recall of apparently irrelevant and minute details, this obtrusive narrative voice indulges in digressions, disclaimers, apostrophes, and exclamations as it freely mixes colloquialisms with elevated and poetic diction. Tolstaia's narrator disgorges a series of images startling in their originality and unexpectedness ("the garden waved its handkerchief," "the small change had slipped like minnows into the lining," "the calendar's viscous sleep," "the crystal of Sonia's foolishness"). Rather than serving a purely decorative function, these images tend to derive from a key concept that dominates the narrative. For instance, the opposition between material phenomena and intangibles around which the story "Sonia" revolves finds expression in a central image: "To chase after you would be like trying to catch butterflies by waving a shovel." That focal simile is sustained by the related images of dragonfly wings and dried forget-me-nots as well as by a consistent association between Sonia's spiritual qualities and the enamel dove of her brooch. The latter contrasts revealingly with the picture of "someone killing someone else" depicted on the brooch of Sonia's "snakelike" counterpart Ada, who is regularly portrayed against a backdrop of plenty, communicated through Tolstaia's list of food, furniture, etc. Many of Tolstaia's strongest effects, in fact, proceed from the interplay between the inner world of people's thoughts and emotions and the outer world of objects. And Tolstaia suggests the intricate nature of human relationship to the physical world of things through the device of animating objects and objectifying people.

Tolstaia's irrepressible humor manifests itself not only in the irony, grotesque portrayals, and comic formulations of her stories, but also in parody, as for example in a piece like "Utamonogatari," a purported attempt to re-create a Japanese poetic genre, with amusing results. Her negative review of a book devoted to her grandfather shows another facet of Tolstaia—her capacity for outspoken, acerbic criticism, grounded in close textual analysis.

Given the limited quantity of Tolstaia's output thus far, a summary assessment of her abilities as a writer seems premature. But she gives every indication of possessing abundant creative powers in the sphere of short fiction.

Works

Stories: "Na zolotom kryl'tse sideli," in *Avrora* (1983). "Svidanie s ptitsei," in *Oktiabr'* (1983). "Sonia," in *Avrora* (1984). "Chistyi list," in *Neva* (1984). "Reka Okkarvil'," "Milaia Shura" and "Okhota na mamonta," in *Oktiabr'* (1985). "Peter," in *Novyi mir* (1986). "Poet i muza," "Fakir," and "Serafim," in *Novyi mir* (1986). *Na zolotom kryl'tse sideli* (Moscow, 1987).

Translations: "Rendezvous with a Bird" [Svidanie sptitsei], tr. Mary Fleming Zirin: "Sonia," tr. Nancy Condee; "Peter," tr. Mary Fleming Zirin, in *HERitage and HEResy: Recent Fiction by Russian Women*, ed Helena Goscilo (1983). *On the Golden Porch* (1990). *Sleepwalker in a Fog* (1991).

Parody: "Utamonogatari," *Voprosy literatury* (1984).

Review article: "Kleem i nozhnitsami," *Voprosy literatury* (1983)

Helena Goscilo

Flora Célestine Thérese Henriette Tristan
1803–1844

a.k.a. Flore Tristan, Flore Tristan-Morcoso
Born April 7, 1803, Paris
Died November 14, 1844, Bordeaux
Genre(s): novel, essay, autobiography
Language(s): French

Tristan was a leading figure in the socialist and feminist movements in nineteenth-century France. She was born to a wealthy Peruvian–Spanish nobleman and a French mother. After her father died, the French government refused to recognize the marriage, confiscated Tristan-Morcoso's property, and declared Flora illegitimate. Living in poverty and shunned by family, she went to work at age eighteen in a lithography shop. She eventually married the owner and had three children (one died). Chazal was an abusive alcoholic, and in 1825 Flora left him. To support her family she took a position as a ladies' companion, traveling to England several times during this nine-year period. Harassed by her husband, barely able to eke out a living, and determined to receive her rightful share of her father's property and to be recognized by his family, she sailed to Peru unchaperoned. She failed to accomplish her goals, but her uncle did grant her a small pension which provided her a modicum of independence. Tristan's semi-autobiography, *Pérégrinations d'une paria* (1838; Peregrinations of a Pariah), described this voyage and her year spent in Peru; these experiences also provided the background for her novel, *Méphis* (1838).

Back in Paris in January 1835, she found that her husband had been awarded custody of their son and daughter; and that she had no legal recourse. When Chazal sexually assaulted his eleven-year-old daughter, Flora took him to court and won custody of the girl but not of her son. In 1838 Chazal shot Flora on a street in Paris. Finally she was able to obtain a legal separation and permission to use her own name. Still, she was not free to remarry. Forever bound to a man she despised by laws she considered discriminatory, Tristan began her campaign to crush the forces that oppressed women, workers, and the inarticulate masses. These injustices that affected her personally thrust Tristan into feminist and socialist activities to which she dedicated the rest of her life.

Tristan had already been in touch with the Fourierists and had attended regular meetings of the *Gazette des femmes* (Women's Gazette). She published several short articles on socialism and women; she also deluged the Chamber of Deputies with petitions for a revised divorce law and against capital punishment. In 1839 Tristan went to England to observe firsthand the conditions of the working class. Her observations were recorded in *Promenades des Londres* (1840; Walks in London), which was acclaimed by socialists and republicans. Her most famous work, *l'Union ouvrière* (1843; The Workers' Union), contained her program which called for the working class to free itself from oppression; she was the first socialist to do this. Tristan's major purpose was to organize "the working class by means of a compact, solid, indissoluble Union." Five years before Marx's *Communist Manifesto* she saw workers as a distinct class and that their power lay in solidarity; "Isolated you are weak. . . . Union creates strength." Workers would tax themselves to establish 'Workers' Palaces' where their children would be educated and care given to injured and aged workers. Her program stressed the rights of workers: the right to work, to an education, and to political representation. Tristan wanted to reform the social order to allow for the full development of the individual personality. All of this would be accomplished without class conflict or violence, which she vehemently rejected.

Closely linked to emancipation of the worker was the liberation of women. An entire chapter of her book dealt with "The Necessity for Women's Emancipation," which, anomalously, was addressed to male workers whom she believed would lead the struggle to free women. As long as women remained enslaved, she insisted, workers could not be free. Though she stressed women's unique domestic role, she refused to confine them to family responsibilities. The subordination of women in marriage was her *bête noir*; she advocated the right of women to work for wages equal to men's and the right to divorce. Marriage was to be freely chosen and equality between spouses was essential to happiness in the home. Women should not be forced to sell themselves, as she had done, to gain security as this puts them on the same level as prostitutes. Her radical stance on freedom for women is clearly delineated in *L'émancipation de la femme; ou, Le testament de la paria* (1846; The Emancipation of Woman, or The Testament of a Pariah). Tristan argued forcefully that the emancipation of women was in the best interest of men. Her influence on notions of a universal union of workers and on feminism were truly remarkable. More than anyone else of her time she combined these two movements into one. Women and workers were everywhere exploited and enslaved by their powerlessness, ignorance, and poverty; if they would unite they could eradicate these evils.

Tristan had an overwhelming sense of mission; as the "Woman Messiah," she would lead the oppressed masses to freedom. She also felt isolated—she was, as she said, a pariah. Serious in purpose and determined to uplift the masses, she undertook an exhausting tour of France to spread her gospel. She contracted typhoid and died at Bordeaux at age forty-one. Tristan failed to create the Utopian socialist society she dreamed of, but her ideas survived and became part of modern socialist and feminist thought.

Works

Pérégrinations d'une paria, 2 vols. (1838). *Méphis* (1838). *A messieurs les membres de la Chambre des députés* (1838?). *Promenades des Londres* (1840). *l'Union ouvrière* (1843). *L'émancipation de la femme; ou Le testament de la paria* (1846).

Jeanne A. Ojala
William T. Ojala

Frances Milton Trollope
1779–1863

Born March 10, 1779, Stapleton, near Bristol, England
Died October 6, 1863, Florence, Italy
Genre(s): novel, travelogue
Language(s): English

Although the author of thirty-four novels, Trollope has been more widely recognized as the mother of Anthony Trollope and as the author of a popular travel book, *Domestic Manners of the Americans* (1832), than for her fictional achievements. Yet her controversial social-reform novels and her recurring use of a new, strong heroine makes Trollope a significant pioneer in nineteenth-century fiction. Her use of fiction to advocate legal reform and attack social abuses and her development of complex feminine characters influenced the work of many of her contemporaries.

Trollope was a Bristol clergyman's daughter who lost her mother early and was educated by her father in languages, the classics, and the arts. When her father remarried, she went to London with her brother and sister for five years, not marrying until she was nearly thirty. Her marriage was somewhat of a surprise to those who knew her well, for her husband, by whom she had seven children in eight years, was a serious and retiring barrister. After eighteen years in London and Harrow, where the family built a stately home, the Trollopes found themselves on the brink of bankruptcy.

Faced with destitution, Trollope decided to join an experiment in utopian living in the United States. But the venture was a disappointment, and she went on to Cincinnati where she tried to find work. Here her life alternated between plans for grandiose business and cultural schemes and devastating failure. At fifty-two, destitute again, she returned to England and published her first book, *Domestic Manners of the Americans,* an instant and controversial bestseller. Exposing "the lamentable insignificance of the American woman" and attacking many of America's most prized beliefs, the book generated some of the harshest criticism of its time, yet went through many editions in America, England, and the Continent.

Domestic Manners of the Americans, which achieved an almost unheard-of success for a first work, is a chronological account of her experiences during her almost four-year stay in the United States. The book's appeal lies in Trollope's brilliant selection of detail and the way she transformed her material into representative and amusing vignettes of nineteenth-century American life. According to Mark Twain, her work was accurate enough to be called "photography." The most original part of the book is her underlying thesis that the sins and flaws of America stem mainly from the exclusion of women from the mainstream of American life, a situation resulting, she believed, from male preference, not economic necessity. Throughout the work she documents a hostility toward women lurking beneath the surface of American life.

Thus at fifty-three Trollope was launched on a writing career. But even the earnings from her subsequent travel books on Germany and Paris and several popular novels failed to keep the family afloat, and they were forced to abandon their home and flee to Belgium, where her husband could not be sued by his creditors. For several years the Trollopes lived in rented lodgings in Brussels while Trollope wrote frantically to support the family. At the same time, she nursed several of her children who were dying of tuberculosis; she often spent her time alternating between the care of the mortally ill and the grinding out of fiction.

She continued to make tours, however, hoping to repeat the success of *Domestic Manners of the Americans.* She soon realized, though, that much of what she earned was spent in transporting herself and her family to the places she needed to see. Thus for economic as well as domestic reasons, Trollope turned primarily to writing fiction.

Through her concentration on social abuses she became one of the first novelists to bring unpleasant subject matter squarely into what had been aptly called "the fairy land of fiction." Her first social-reform novel, *The Life and Adventures of Jonathan Jefferson Whitlaw* (1836), grew out of her strong revulsion against American slavery. Telling the story of a cruel overseer, Trollope's work anticipated the more famous Harriet Beecher Stowe's *Uncle Tom's Cabin* by fifteen years. Her next contribution to social-reform fiction was *The Vicar of Wrexhill* (1837), an attack upon evangelical excesses and their unfortunate effects upon women.

In the course of her literary career Trollope was twice prompted to write a novel advocating legislative reform. In 1839 she began publishing *The Life and Adventures of Michael Armstrong, the Factory Boy* to dramatize the need for passage of a Ten-Hours Bill, and in 1843 she published *Jessie Phillips: A Tale of the Present Day* to demonstrate the weaknesses of the New Poor Law, particularly the bastardy clauses. Both works met with only mediocre popular success and both were harshly criticized although for different reasons. As far as most critics were concerned, *Michael Armstrong* revealed nothing about child labor that the 1832 republication of John Brown's *A Memoir of Robert Blincoe* and the 1837–1838 publication of Charles Dickens's *Oliver Twist* had not already shown. Yet despite the charge that it all had been said before and that reform was on the way, Trollope's novel was very much of its time. She investigated factory conditions herself, finding that while some changes had been made many abuses still existed; even so the Ten Hours Bill was not passed until 1847.

Jessie Phillips was also often criticized as a second-rate novel dealing with a topic, the New Poor Law, already portrayed in more finely executed works, particularly *Oliver Twist* and Thomas Carlyle's *Past and Present*. Much of the criticism leveled at Trollope was for having "sinned grievously against good taste and decorum" by dealing with the bastardy clauses of the New Poor Law; yet precisely because it deals with the bastardy clauses *Jessie Phillips* is unique. Trollope was by no means a first-rate novelist, but her weakness is in her presentation, not her subject matter. Stereotypical and exaggerated characterization and intrusive narrators are her major weaknesses although significant improvements can be seen when later novels are compared with earlier ones.

After her daughter's death in 1848, Trollope returned to Florence where she embarked upon her last fictional innovation: a group of novels in which the heroines are triumphant, whose most obvious quality is an aggressive independence, and whose most frequent trials are confrontations with tyrannical fathers or marriages to weak or evil men. In her last novel,

Fashionable life; or, Paris and London (1856), Trollope moves from these dominant ladies to a vision of a community of females living in peace, harmony, and cooperation—happier than they had ever been with the men in their lives.

While never becoming a novelist of special distinction, Trollope did develop as a writer. Her growing understanding of how the structures of the novel—such as characterization, parallelism, and continuity—work to form a whole made her a popular novelist during her lifetime and an interesting figure for study in light of her influence both on society and on other writers.

Works

Domestic Manners of the Americans (1832). *The Refugee in America: A Novel* (1832). *The Mother's Manual; or, Illustrations of Matrimonial Economy: An Essay in Verse* (1833). *The Abbess: A Romance* (1833). *Belgium and Western Germany in 1833* (1834). *Tremordyn Cliff* (1835). *Paris and the Parisians in 1835* (1836). *The Life and Adventures of Jonathan Jefferson Whitlaw; or, Scenes on the Mississippi* (1836). *The Vicar of Wrexhill* (1837). *Vienna and the Austrians* (1838). *A Romance of Vienna* (1838). *The Widow Barnaby* (1839). *The Life and Adventures of Michael Armstrong, the Factory Boy* (1839–1840). *The Widow Married: A Sequel to The Widow Barnaby* (1840). *One Fault: A Novel* (1840). *Charles Chesterfield; or, The Adventures of a Youth of Genius* (1841). *The Ward of Thorpe Combe* (1841). *The Blue Belles of England* (1842). *A Visit to Italy* (1842). *Jessie Phillips: A Tale of the Present Day* (1842–1843). *The Barnabys in America; or, Adventures of the Widow Wedded* (1843). *Hargrave; or, The Adventures of a Man of Fashion* (1843). *The Laurringtons; or Superior People* (1844). *Young Love: A Novel* (1844). *The Attractive Man* (1846). *The Robertses on Their Travels* (1846). *Travels and Travellers: A Series of Sketches* (1846). *Father Eustace: A Tale of the Jesuits* (1847). *The Three Cousins* (1847). *Town and Country: A Novel* (1848). *The Young Countess; or Love and Jealousy* (1848). *The Lottery of Marriage: A Novel* (1849). *The Old World and the New: A Novel* (1849). *Petticoat Government: A Novel* (1850). *Mrs. Mathews; or Family Mysteries* (1851). *Second Love; or Beauty and Intellect: A Novel* (1851). *Uncle Walter: A Novel* (1852). *The Young Heiress: A Novel* (1853). *The Life and Adventures of a Clever Woman. Ilustrated with Occasional Extracts from Her Diary* (1854). *Gertrude; or, Family Pride* (1855). *Fashionable Life; or, Paris and London* (1856).

Lynn M. Alexander

Birgitta Trotzig
1929–

Born November 9, 1929, Göteborg, Sweden
Genre(s): novel, prose poetry, essay
Language(s): Swedish

Birgitta Trotzig (née Kjellén) has been called one of Sweden's "most important and original" contemporary writers because of her visionary perspective and aesthetic purity of style. She studied literature and art history at the University of Göteborg, then wrote critical essays on art and literature for some of Sweden's most important newspapers. Among them were *Sydsvenska Dagbladet, Dagens Nyheter*, and *Aftonbladet*. Her aesthetic writings also appeared in such collections as *Endeavor and Proposal* (1963), which contains her essays from 1955 to 1962. Topics discussed include Russian iconography, the painters Chagall and Soutine, and the philosopher Chardin. Literary journals such as *Bonniers Litterära Magasin* also published her essays. In 1949 she married the artist Ulf Trotzig. She moved to Paris, France, in 1955, but resides presently in Lund, Sweden.

Trotzig's work shows a strong ethical component that betrays personal involvement: "I write in order to understand life and thereby prepare myself for death," she once wrote. Part of this understanding derives from a contemplation of history. Therefore some of her novels aptly take the form of the *legend* or of the historical novel. Her first novel, *De Utsatta* (1957; The Exposed; transl. into German, *Die Ausgesetzten*, 1967), is a legendary tale set in the last decade of the sixteenth century, when the province of Skaane was captured from Denmark by the Swedes and a merciless repatriation of the population ensued. Similarly, the novel *En berättelse fraan kusten* (1961; A Report from the Coast) takes the form of a medieval chronicle of the city of Aahus. The lives, deeds, beliefs, and prejudices of its leaders, citizens, and beggars are probed, and the picture that emerges is one of suffering humanity waiting for God's redemption. The novel's motifs are taken from stark contrasts such as light/darkness, birth/death, height/depth, and a supporting symbolism of transubstantiation and transcendence. Central to the novel is the theme that while yet in darkness and despair, humanity longs for redemption through Christ but is unable to recognize the truth. The Christ-symbolism is evident chiefly in the figure of the humpback Merete in whose deformed body a child grows as the result of rape—a ray of hope in the midst of evil. The perfectly formed child dies, however, as the first of a number of such deaths in the midst of want and disease. Merete is accused of having brought this evil upon the city. She is stoned to death and buried at sea. Biblical sentences (e.g., "who was the first to take up a stone") underscore the religious symbolism of the sacrificial lamb slain for the sins of others in the "flower month" of May. The novel's last sentence is both didactic and bitter: "This happened in Aahus on the east coast of Skaane in the year 1500 after Christ's birth. . . ."

Trotzig's development as a writer has been influenced by Spanish and Russian mystics, and by Walt Whitman, Selma Lagerlöf, Pär Lagerkvist, Kafka, and others.

Works

Ur de älskandes liv (1951). *Bilder* (1954). *De utsatta* (1957); German tr. Solita Felter, *Die Ausgesetzten* (1967). *Ett landskap* (1959). *En berättelse fraan kusten* (1961). *Utkast och förslag* (1962). *Levande och döda* (1964). *Sveket* (1966). *Ordgränser* (1968). *Sjukdommen* (1972). *I kejsarens tid* (1975). *Jaget o världen* (1977). *Dirättelser* (1977). *Dykungens dotter* (1985).

Helene M. Kastinger Riley

Marina Tsvetaeva
1882–1941

Born September 26, 1882, Moscow, Russia
Died August 31, 1941, Elabuga, Soviet Union
Genre(s): poetry, prose
Language(s): Russian

Marina Tsvetaeva, one of the greatest Russian poets of the twentieth century, once wrote about herself: "I can be grasped only in terms of contrasts, i.e., of the simultaneous presence of everything. . . . I am many poets; as to how I've managed to harmonize all of them is my secret." Her thoroughly disinterested poetic stance prevented her from siding with movements and ideologies. She spent her most productive years in the midst of constant literary and political struggles which she tended to regard as nonsensical. In her lifetime, her work was regarded as undesirable both abroad and in the Soviet Union by all except the greatest writers, among them Andrei Bely, Rainer Maria Rilke, Boris Pasternak, and Anna Akhmatova.

As a child she often felt unwanted by her family. Her upbringing, however, was intellectually stimulating. Her father, a professor at the University of Moscow, founded one of Russia's best-known museums. Her mother, a highly educated, cosmopolitan woman

Marina Tsvetaeva

and a musician, had her learn the piano, which was to contribute considerably to the rhythmic novelty and musicality of her poetry. In 1912, she married Sergei Efron, a sickly and charming but rather talentless man. His inability to contribute to the family budget and his various political activities proved to be a heavy and tragic burden for Tsvetaeva. A devoted mother to her children, she had several love affairs with both men and women. After the October revolution in 1917, she was trapped in Moscow for five years. Her fragmentary documentary writings in *Omens of the Earth*, which was published only in excerpts, give a fascinating account of her experiences during this period. After one of her children starved to death, she joined her husband in the West in 1922. Following her initial success during her visit to Berlin and her three-year stay in Czechoslovakia, the family moved to Paris in 1925. Soon after her arrival, Tsvetaeva suggested in her essay *A Poet on Criticism* (1926) that only those who understand modern art can evaluate it. Her tone offended established figures in the emigré community. Her husband's pro-Soviet activities, in addition, resulted in her isolation and poverty in the years to come. Yielding to pressure from her family, she returned to Moscow in 1939, only to have all her relatives, except for her son, arrested (her husband was executed), and to find herself shunned by the Soviet literary elite. In August 1941, after Hitler attacked the Soviet Union, she was evacuated to Elabuga, where she committed suicide and where she is buried in an unmarked mass grave.

She started writing poetry at the age of six. Her first two collections of verse, *The Evening Album* (1910) and *The Magic Lantern* (1912), offer a myth-like evocation of childhood experiences. *The Evening Album* was received favorably by such established writers as Briusov and Gumilyov. Her poems in the collection *Mileposts I.* (1921) present a consecutive lyrical chronicle of the year 1916 in a diary format. Her use of more than one kind of foot in the line is a major innovation in Russian versification. Similarly novel is her simultaneous use of the archaic and colloquial dialects. A lyric chronicle of 1917, the year of two Russian revolutions, is offered in the collection *The Demesne of the Swans*, written between 1917 and 1921 and published in 1957. In her poetic diary, *Craft* (1923), personal themes merge with concerns about postrevolutionary Russia. This and another collection, *After Russia* (1928), represent the peak of Tsvetaeva's achievement. Inspired by her experiences in a provincial and philistine Czech town, she wrote perhaps her best work, the long, satirical poem, *The Pied Piper* (1925–1926), which is based on a German legend. The "Poem of the Staircase," written in 1926, is a lyrical narrative of the Paris squalor, in which the impoverished poet had to make her home. Also in Paris she wrote her two neoclassical verse tragedies, *Ariadne* (1927) and *Phaedre* (1928). Her only piece of prose fiction is the *Letter to an Amazon*, written in 1932, which examines lesbian love. In 1938–1939, before her return to the Soviet Union, she wrote her "Verses to Czechoslovakia," which voice her strong sympathies with the invaded people.

An uncommon wealth of topics, a ready receptiveness to foreign literatures, and the confident mastery of Russian culture highlight the literary activity of Marina Tsvetaeva. Her original prose, expansive correspondence, and, in particular, the sonorous versification and strophic experimentation which typify her poetry finally started to receive due attention in the late 1950s in the Soviet Union and abroad. Even today, hitherto unnoticed aspects of Tsvetaeva's work and life are being uncovered.

Works

Izbrannye proizvedeniia [Selected Works] (1965). *Pis'ma k A. Teskovoi* [Letters to A. Teskova] (1969). *Neizdannye pis'ma* [Unpublished Letters] (1972). *Izbrannaia proze v dvukh tomakh* [Selected Prose in Two Volumes] (1979). *Stikhotvoreniia i poemy v piati* tomakh [Poetry and Long Poems in Nine Volumes] (1980).

Translations: *Modern Russian Poetry*, eds. Vladimir Markov and Merill Sparks (1967), pp. 429–449. *Russian Poetry: The Modern Period* (1978), pp. 140–148. *Selected Poems*, tr. E. Feinstein (1981). *A Captive Spirit: Selected Prose*, tr. J.M. King (1980). *In the Inmost Hour of the Soul: Selected Prose* (1989). *After Russia/Posle Rossii* (1992). *Art in the Light of Conscience* (1992).

Peter I. Barta

Esther Tusquets
1936–

Born August 30, 1936, Barcelona, Spain
Genre(s): novel
Language(s): Spanish

Esther Tusquets was born on August 30, 1936, into a well-established Catalan family. She completed her secondary education in the *Colegio Alemán* in Barcelona (a Spanish version of a German High School) and later studied *Filosofía y Letras* (History) at the University of Barcelona and the University of Madrid. In 1960, she became the director of Editorial Lumen, a position that she still holds.

Born in the first year of Spain's convulsive Civil War, Tusquets's writing career was initiated much later—in the early years following Franco's death. This period in Spain is marked not only by an explosion of political parties, but also by a loosening of sexual and social taboos, and an artistic and literary boom. Tusquets's novels have attracted attention for their experimental and poetic qualities. Her erotic and heterodox feminist writing displays a penetrating engagement with various aspects of life. While her carefully circumscribed and intense psychological narrative has aptly been compared to Virginia Woolf's fiction, the latter's modernist epiphanies are rather more undermined than celebrated in Tusquets's work. Two major thematic strands, the illustrated Catalan upper class and women's lives and loves, weave a complex narrative tapestry, combining the specificity of contemporary Barcelona with a universality that has prompted acclaim in Spain as well as the translation of her works into many languages.

Tusquets did not begin her literary career until 1978, the year her first novel, *El mismo mar de todos los veranos* (The Same Sea of Every Summer), ap-

peared. This work constitutes the beginning of a trilogy, continued by *El amor es un juego solitario* (1980; Love Is a Solitary Game), and completed by *Varada tras el último naufragio* (1980; Stranded After the Last Shipwreck). In 1981, she published a collection of short stories which are very closely interrelated, and another short story was published one year later in the collection of women's stories compiled by Ymelda Navajo entitled *Doce relatos de mujeres* (Twelve Stories by Women). Her last main work appeared in 1985 under the title *Para no volver* (To Not Return). She has also published a children's book *La conejita Marcela* (1979; Marcela, The Little Rabbit) and various articles in the magazine *Destino*. She is also an active collaborator for the most important newspaper in Barcelona, *La Vanguardia*.

The action of Tusquets's trilogy—as well as most of her narrative—is set in Barcelona, and her characters are part of the middle-class society that shows its mediocrity through its overall satisfaction with life. Tusquets's protagonists are women in search of their own identity, a search that leads them to a vast variety of homosexual and heterosexual experiences. The novels in the trilogy share, in addition to the theme of searching for oneself, the same protagonist, Elia. The first part of the trilogy, *El mismo mar de todos los veranos*, is written in the first person and could be considered as the first part of that search: the narrator, a professor of history, seeks to be reborn through a lesbian relationship. Clara, Elia's lover, will be the permanent companion throughout the different stages of Elia's search. Mythological and literary allusions are frequently used by Tusquets. The second volume of the trilogy, *El amor es un juego solitario*, deals with another form of quest. This time it is the desire to escape from a bourgeois, mediocre life which pushes middle-aged Elia to involve herself in a series of experiences with two adolescent lovers. Sexual experiences are, for a time, equated with love and fulfillment. This proves to be a temporary escape and not the solution to Elia's existential dilemmas. *Varada tras el último naufragio* concludes Elia's search. In this novel, the protagonist witnesses the end of her marriage and her false ideals of happiness and of idyllic wedlock, carefully learned during childhood through fairy tales and other myths. This time the search will be directed toward finding life and happiness in reality as opposed to fantasy. In this case, the search is a confrontation rather than an escape through sexual adventures.

Set in the snobbish Catalan society of Barcelona's elite, the novel explores the protagonist's menopausal crisis marked by the onset of old age, an estranged marriage, and a reevaluation of her life. Tusquets interrogates the role of females in society, focusing upon the protagonist's dislike of her mother and daughter in sharp contrast to her love for the young Clara, an androgynous alternative to traditional women and love relationships. The anatomical differences of lesbian sexuality (total body contact rather than more exclusively genital contact and the lack of dichotomy between penetrator and penetrated), as well as the ultimate equality between the lovers, implicitly undermines phallocentric ideology—underscored by the narrative's tenderness and feminine images. Although the protagonist fails to escape a prescribed wifely role, the dreamlike erotic sequence in the novel's central section introduces a world of youthful hope—presaging different roles for other women, who, like Clara, can combine love, literature, and political activism in a more daring way than their older counterparts. The juxtaposition between the protagonist's (uneasy) acquiescence to cultural norms and her experience of otherness with Clara is paralleled by the structural counterpoint between the traditional framing story and the disruption of story expectations and literary norms in the long central portion of the novel. This strategy, along with the bold treatment of a forbidden subject matter, contributes to making this a very impressive novel.

In her next work, *Siete miradas en un mismo paisaje* (1981), Tusquets continues with the main themes presented in earlier works. Here she chooses the short story as a means to analyze female psychological growth when faced with the expectations of society and of the family. The book is formed of seven stories that represent seven critical moments in the protagonist's (Sara's) life. Tusquets again explores homosexual as well as heterosexual love relationships and gives a sharp depiction of the social background against which Sara struggles. Tusquets's latest novel, *Para no volver* (1985), does not differ enormously from previous works from the point of view of content. Now, we truly witness a psychoanalytical search. This theme,

which was omnipresent in other works, takes the form here of the relationship between the analyst and his patient, a middle-aged woman named Elena. The novel is a serious reflection on life and on the futility of success, suggesting that failure could be an almost desirable goal for human activity. Love and the suffering it entails are the only tools to understand oneself and others.

Tusquets's prose style, which has been called baroque, is indeed quite an achievement. Her writing is sumptuous, full of lyrical images and metaphors, and is both suggestive and sensual. She uses mainly the extended monologue to convey the autoanalysis her protagonists undergo. She is able to combine plasticity with cultural issues. Freud and Jung hide in almost every page. Her novels suggest the idea of a "life puzzle" that the protagonist must put together. Tusquets is a feminist writer in more ways than one: her feminism goes to remote corners of the feminine psyche. As is the case of other women writers in Spain, she deals with common themes such as love, mother–daughter relationships, and solitude. Yet, she goes a little farther; she treats feminine sexuality in a way rarely found in other novelists. Tusquets's protagonists may not like their present existence, but they do like their bodies. The female body is sometimes described through metaphor, other times less elliptically in sensuous, open, positive ways. This will possibly suggest paths to other writers' treatment of the too-often taboo subject of female sexuality.

Works
El mismo mar de todos los veranos (1978). *La conejita Marcela* (1979). *El amor es un juego solitario* (1980). *Varada tras el último naufragio* (1980). *Seite miradas en un mismo paisaje* (1981). "Las sutiles leyes de la simetría." *Doce relatos de mujeres* (1982). *Para no volver* (1985).

Coro Malaxecheverría
Marie Murphy

Julia Uceda
1925–

Born October 21, 1925, Sevilla, Spain
Genre(s): poetry
Language(s): Spanish

Julia Uceda's formative years were spent in the Andalusian city of Seville, where she received her doctorate from the University with a thesis on the poet José Luis Hidalgo. Later, she would also publish a study on Hidalgo. In 1966 she left to teach Spanish literature at Michigan State University for seven years. She has not lived in Seville since then. In an interview, she observed: "You have to understand what Sevilla was like in those years. [The Franco period] was a very difficult and destructive era, and if we survived . . . it was probably because we were too close to the situation and couldn't compare it to anything else. . . . Not only the poets of our generation left Sevilla, the university people too . . . because they realized how oppressive our situation was. They left for their own good. We were a very unlucky generation. . . ." Uceda would later move around, from the United States to Oviedo, Albacete, Ireland, and eventually back to Spain once more, where she resides and teaches in the northern province of Galicia. She has contributed steadily over the years to such journals as *Insula*, *Cal*, *Cuadernos Hispanoamericanos*, *Revista de Occidente*, and others. In addition, she now heads a small publishing house called Colección Esquío de Poesía.

Uceda has been regarded as part of the Generation of the 1950s, a group of Spanish poets noted especially for their social and political concerns and use of everyday language and imagery (Angel González, Manuel Mantero, Gloria Fuertes, Claudio Rodríguez, for example). Nevertheless, she possesses a poetic voice and spirit of her own, one which Manuel

Mantero admiringly calls "strange," and which makes her difficult to categorize. Her poetry, which is always intimate and mysterious and yet never forgets the social context, has gravitated increasingly toward the metaphysical and existential.

Her first book, *Mariposa en cenizas* (Butterfly in Ashes), was published in 1959, but her poetry had been appearing regularly in small literary magazines and anthologies before that date. As she herself notes, she arrived "late" to poetry: late, yes, but with a surprising depth and purity of her poetic persona. This first book is basic for understanding her poetry, since it already contains some of the themes and the lyrical intellectualism of her more mature work. *Mariposa en cenizas*, though primarily love poetry, also deals with death and alienation, in poems like "Mariposa en cenizas" (Butterfly in Ashes) where she sees her death as "not yet ripe" in God's fields, and "La extraña" (The Stranger) where she senses herself radically cut off from another, mysterious existence.

Extraña juventud (1962; Strange Youth), a finalist for the prestigious Adonais Poetry Prize of 1961, develops the existentialist vein more fully, with an emphasis on the feeling of being both "strange" and "foreign," as the poet questions her own sense of authenticity and identity, pressured by mortality itself. "Julia Uceda," she asks herself, "what have you done with your shadow?" Her language, intense and strong, also opens out into wider concerns in this book, which is dedicated "to men of my time." *Extraña juventud* implicitly denounces a repressive and unjust political system, the inequalities, and the collective and individual alienation of Franco Spain.

By her third volume of poetry, *Sin mucha esperanza* (1966; Without Much Hope), Uceda had reached the end of one phase—what could be called "historical existentialism"—and the beginning of another, in which she takes a much more introspective and metaphysical turning. As in her earlier books, the poet, though intensely aware of man's social and political plight, never sets the collective over and against the individual. For her, "without the salvation of the individual we are lost." Thus such themes as loss of identity, lack of freedom, alienation, lost childhood, exile, and death are treated together, merging singular and plural concerns into one. Particularly poignant are the poems "Eterno oleaje" (Eternal Wave) and "Una patria se ve desde la cumbre" (A Country Seen from Afar), in which images of inner and outer exile from "an impossible country" are juxtaposed.

Poemas de Cherry Lane (1968; Cherry Lane Poems) consists of fourteen poems, written in free verse and reflecting much of Uceda's experiences in the United States. This book, which at times approaches the hallucinatory in its imagery, has been called by one critic "fundamental" in the canon of Spanish postwar poetry. Her vision of reality is simply but profoundly expressed in this line from "Condenada al silencio" (Condemned to Silence): "Nada más natural. Nada más misterioso" (Nothing more natural. Nothing more mysterious).

Uceda's fifth book, Campanas en Sansueña (1977; Bells in Sansueña), clearly anticipates Viejas voces secretas de la noche (1981; Ancient Secret Voices of the Night), in its metaphysical and visionary search for illumination. For it is only the light, she writes, that, paradoxically, has substance. Reworking the traditional imagery of the dark side of the soul, Uceda seeks revelation in darkness, in the night which possesses its own light, its own knowledge, or as she puts it, "la noche es caminar/buscando ángulos de luz" (night is out walking/searching for the angles of light). It is this powerful union of the intimate with the metaphysical that marks Uceda's poetry and makes her one of Spain's strongest and most singular poetic voices today.

Works

Mariposa en cenizas (1959). Extraña juventud (1962). Sin mucha esperanza (1966). Poemas de Cherry Lane (1968). José Luis Hidalgo: Estudio y antología (1970). Campanas en Sansueña (1977). Viejas voces secretas de la noche (1981). Julia Uceda: Poesía. Ed. Francisco J. Peñas-Bermejo (1991). Del camino de humo (1994).

Unpublished works: Los andaluces. Antología histórica de la poesía andaluza. En elogio de la locura.

Translations: American Poetry Review (Nov.–Dec. 1986). Prairie Schooner (Winter 1985). Anthology of Magazine Verse and Yearbook of American Poetry, 1986–1988 ed. (1988). New Orleans Review (Spring 1987). Touchstone (Spring 1988). Ulula (1987). The Poetry of Julia Uceda. Trans. Noël Valis (1995).

Noël M. Valis

Liesl Ujvary
1939–

Born October 10, 1939, Bratislava (formerly Pressburg), Czechoslovakia
Genre(s): photography, poetry, prose, radio drama, essay
Language(s): German

Liesl Ujvary is one of the most radical representatives of contemporary "experimental literature," the specifically Austrian avant-garde movement that originated with the Vienna Group in the late 1950s. Readers are often baffled by her texts, which defy genre classification and resist conformity with conventional literary norms. Ujvary seems to specialize in clichés and banalities, which, however, she turns around to expose the underlying thought processes. Behind the ostensible nonsense is a sharp mind and a keen observer of contemporary life in Western society.

Ujvary was born in Czechoslovakia of Austrian parents in 1939, and she retains her Austrian citizenship. She studied Slavic and Old Hebrew literature and art at the universities of Vienna and Zurich and received her doctorate from the University of Zurich in 1968. From 1965 to 1970 she taught Russian at a language institute in Zurich, and thereafter she spent a year teaching Russian in Tokyo; the following year, 1971–1972, she pursued postdoctoral studies at the University of Moscow. Since then she has lived as a freelance writer in Vienna, where she is a member of the Graz Authors' Association. From 1960 to 1963 she was married, and she has one daughter who grew up with her grandparents in Tyrol. Ujvary also works occasionally as a translator and contributor to Austrian and German newspapers and radio stations.

Given Ujvary's advanced academic degrees and international cultural experience one may be inclined to look for erudite representations of it in the text, but in vain, for her works are not representational, and biographic experiences manifest themselves only indirectly. Sicher & Gut (1977; Safe & Good) and rosen, zugaben (1983; roses, additions) are her leading volumes of poetry, and their central theme is language itself. Language is seen less as a means of communication than as a barrier to it, and the shortcomings and absurdities of conventional speech are poetically foregrounded against an implicit background of total otherness. The short poems and prose pieces present phrases and slogans, statements and questions from everyday life arranged in a montagelike constellation to express the author's critical stance toward verbal behavior. The sentences are intentionally banal so that no traditional image arises, and the author deliberately avoids aesthetic effects. For example, "the sky is blue in Vienna / the sky is blue in Rome / the sky is blue in New Orleans / the sky is blue in Tokyo" (from "Peter Stuyvesant Takes a Trip") is obviously not a statement about particular cities but about the form of speaking itself. Whereas *Sicher & Gut* operates largely with such repetitions, *rosen, zugaben* presents short texts that look like poems but are written in a nondiscursive, highly experimental mode. Both works derive their power from the lack of convergence between superficial context and actual meaning.

Ujvary's basic philosophy is described more explicitly in her autobiographical prose work, *Schöne Stunden* (1984; Beautiful Hours). It gives an account of the author's development as a creative writer, which is equated with her development as a human being. Narration is in the form of an inner monologue in which two separate strains are nevertheless discernible. The first discusses the problem of the individual in a society that is seen as restrictive and dehumanizing; the second reflects the thoughts and feelings of the author as she writes. The "beautiful hours" of the ironic title are those in which she is entirely at one with herself, that is, almost never. With wit but also with sadness Ujvary registers the distance between her utopian vision and the verbal norms that regiment our lives. The tension between the surface appearances and the various realities behind them is also the topic of her recent prose work, *Geheimer Verkehr* (Secret Communication). Her radio plays, some of them written together with Bodo Hell, have been frequently broadcast by Austrian radio stations.

Ujvary writes in the tradition of radical language criticism stemming from Mauthner, Wittgenstein, and Kraus, and extending to the postwar Vienna Group and contemporary experimental writers. Language is weighed in the balance and found wanting. The intent is to question the epistemology behind the linguistic structures and thus to undermine the conventional certainties we all take for granted. Language, according to Ujvary, consists of verbal and graphic clichés that—particularly since the advent of modern media and advertising—intervene between the individual and his or her natural way of feeling. Language criticism is also sociopolitical criticism, for it specifically targets the normative behavior and ideological pressures foisted upon us by society. By showing the schematic, stereotypical forms of speech (and thus of thought) to which we are all enslaved, Ujvary hopes for emancipation to new and nonmanipulative modes of thought and communication. Ujvary's idealism vacillates between euphoria and disillusionment, but her lapidary reduction of formal means is in any case highly provocative.

Works

Ed., *Freiheit ist Freiheit. Inoffizielle sowjetische Dichtung* (1975). *Sicher & Gut* (1977). *Fotoroman Bisamberg* (1980). *rosen, zugaben* (1983). *Menschen & Pflanzen Porträts* (1983). *Schöne Stunden* (1984). *Geheimer Verkehr* (1992).

Beth Bjorklund

Leonora Christina Ulfeldt
1621–1698

Born July 8, 1621, Frederiksborg, Denmark
Died March 16, 1698, Maribo
Genre(s): autobiography, biography, poetry
Language(s): Danish, French, German

Born in 1621 as the daughter of King Christian IV and Kirstine Munk, Leonora Christina belonged to the educated, leisured aristocracy that dominated the cultural activities of her time. Yet Leonora Christina's autobiography, *Jammersminde* (published 1869; Memory of Woe), transcends the literature of seventeenth-century learned noblewomen not only in the suffering, the strength, and the courage of its author but also in its psychological and social realism.

Leonora Christina's marriage at fifteen to Corfits Ulfeldt, prime minister of Denmark until the death of Christian IV in 1648, catapulted her into innumerable political schemes and intrigues. The Ulfeldts' activities resulted first in exile and, in 1663, culminated in Leonora's imprisonment in Blaataarn (Blue Tower), where she remained for twenty-two years. Only after the death of her archenemy, the queen of Frederik III, was Leonora released in 1685. She spent her remaining years at Maribo Kloster.

The earliest writings of Leonora Christina include "Rejsen til Korsør" (1656; Journey to Korsør), a travelogue recounting the exiled Leonora's return to Denmark on behalf of her husband to seek reconciliation with the Danish king, and "Confrontationen i Malmø" (1659; The Confrontation in Malmø), Leonora's account of her legal defense of Ulfeldt, who was on trial for high treason against the Swedish king. The events of "Rejsen til Korsør" recur in *Den Franske Selvbiografi* (1673; The French Autobiography), intended for inclusion in Otto Sperling the Younger's never-published *De Foeminis Doctis* (About Learned Women).

Leonora's masterpiece is *Jammersminde*, which describes her long incarceration in Blaataarn. Presenting her sufferings in religious terms by identifying with Job, Leonora recounts her day-to-day prison existence in a document of strength and dignity against all odds. Her vivid descriptions of characters and incidents at Blaataarn point toward much later psychological realism and naturalism.

In a biography of (pre)historical female regents, *Haeltinners Pryd* (written 1684; The Ornaments of Heroines), Leonora celebrated the qualities with which she herself had been generously endowed. Of the three parts, on combative, faithful and virtuous, and steadfast heroines, respectively, only the first part survives.

Leonora Christina's *Jammersminde* remains unsurpassed in Danish literature as the autobiography of a woman who outshone her contemporaries, male and female, not only in riches and tragedies but also in intelligence, courage, and creativity. While her guilt or innocence is still being debated, the verdict on her literary mastery is unanimous.

Works

Den Franske Selvbiografi (1673; 1881). *Jammersminde* (1663–1685; 1869). *Haeltinners Pryd* (1684; 1977). *Jammersminde og Andre Selvbiografiske Skrifter* (1969).

Translations: *Memoirs of Leonora Christina, Daughter of Christian IV of Denmark: Written During Her Imprisonment in the Blue Tower at Copenhagen 1663–1685*, tr. F.E. Bunnett (1872).

Clara Juncker

Regina Ullmann
1884–1961

Born December 14, 1884, St. Gallen, Switzerland
Died January 1, 1961, Ebersberg, Bavaria
Genre(s): short story, poetry
Language(s): German

Regina Ullmann was born to parents of Jewish origin in St. Gallen, where her Austrian father was a well-to-do businessman. A dreamy, slow, difficult child, she suffered the loss of her father in 1887 and moved to Munich in 1902 with her mother and older sister. Here she fell in with a circle of avant-garde thinkers, poets, and literati—throughout her life she was to count eminent writers, among them Thomas Mann and Hans Carossa, among her acquaintances—and began de-

veloping the talent for storytelling that had already revealed itself in her childhood. Though she traveled frequently, Ullmann and her mother remained settled in the Munich area until 1935. In 1906 and 1908 she bore illegitimate daughters, who were raised by farmers in the vicinity of Munich, though Regina Ullmann visited them regularly and took charge of their education. Also, 1908 marks the beginning of Ullmann's friendship with the poet Rainer Maria Rilke, which had a profound influence on her writing and on her publishing career.

In 1911 Regina Ullmann converted to Catholicism. The years until 1935 were productive, though she periodically suffered from depressions and crises in her creative work and always lived in financially precarious circumstances, her various attempts at supporting herself (beekeeping and gardening among them) coming to naught. Expelled from the Deutscher Schriftsteller-Verband (German Writer's Association) because of her Jewish ancestry in 1935, she and her mother immigrated to Austria in 1936, where her mother died in the early days of 1938. Following the German occupation of Austria the same year, Regina Ullmann returned to Switzerland and found lodgings in a home run by nuns in St. Gallen, where she wrote and lived for the next twenty years. She died in Munich while visiting her daughter.

Regina Ullmann's work has never found a large following: it is in some ways as difficult and taciturn as the author herself. Although she was a born storyteller, the act of writing and the expectation that she live up to the calling of poet were constant obstacles in her path. While her early poems and prose pieces are in the neoromantic vein—exalted expressions of feeling largely detached from descriptions of reality—her mature prose strikes a course between realism, symbolism, and deep piety that demands much of today's reader. Particularly fond of portraying peasant life, she often treats moments in the lives of the defenseless and powerless. An example is "Der goldene Griffel," a story based on a childhood memory, in which a slow and disturbed child's unexpected success in completing a schoolroom task leads not to the promised reward of a "golden" slate pencil but to a scolding for laziness and naughtiness. Ullmann is not sentimental, and her style is at times rough and imperfect; it wanders and breaks like Ullmann herself, restless, troubled, and clear-sighted.

Works

Feldpredigt. Dramatische Dichtung [Sermon in the Field, A Dramatic Poem] (1907, 1915). *Von der Erde des Lebens* [On the Earth of Life], prose poems (1910).

Gedichte [Poems] (1919). *Die Landstrasse* [The Country Highway], short stories (1921). *Die Barockkirche, von einer Votivtafel herab gelesen, zugleich mit etlichen Volkserzählungen* [The Baroque Church, Interpreted from a Votive Tablet, and Including a Number of Folk Stories] (1925). *Vier Erzählungen* [Four Stories] (1930). *Vom Brot der Stillen*. 2 vols. [The Bread of the Silent], short stories (1932). *Der Apfel in der Kirche und andere Geschichten* [The Apple in the Church and Other Stories] (1934). *Der Engelskranz* [The Angelic Wreath], short stories (1942). *Madonna auf Glas und andere Geschichten* [Madonna on Glass and Other Stories] (1944). [Coeditor], *Erinnerungen an Rilke* [Remembrances of Rilke] (1945). *Der ehrliche Dieb und andere Geschichten* [The Honest Thief and Other Stories] (1946). "Sammlung der Vergesslichen. Ein Selbstporträt aus jüngsten Jahren, mit der Feder gezeichnet" [The Forgetful One's Anthology. A Recent Self-portrait Drawn with a Quill Pen]. *Gruss der Insel an Hans Carossa* (1948), pp. 221–236. *Von einem alten Wirtshausschild* [About an Old Sign at an Inn], short stories (1949). *Schwarze Kerze* [Black Candle], short stories (1954). *Gesammelte Werke*. 2 vols. [Collected Works] (1960, 1978, 1980). *Kleine Galerie. Eine Auswahl aus ihren Erzählungen* [Small Gallery. A Selection from Her Stories] (1975). *Erzählungen, Prosastücke, Gedichte*. 2 vols. [Collected Works but with bibliography, afterword, and biographical documents], stories, prose, poems (1978). *Ausgewählte Erzählungen* [Selected Stories] (1979).

Ann Marie Rasmussen

Umiltà of Faenza
1226–1310

Born 1226, Faenza, Italy
Died May 22, 1310, Florence
Genre(s): sermon, tractate, prayer, hymn
Language(s): Latin

Umiltà's given name was Rosanese; she was the only daughter of a noble family in Faenza. In her youth she underwent a religious conversion and wished to enter a convent; but her parents refused. When Rosanese's father died she was married to a nobleman named Ugolotto. For nine years she attempted to convince him to live a chaste life with her but to no avail. During this time she bore two sons, both of whom died shortly after their baptism, and she may have had other children as well. Finally Ugolotto became

seriously ill, and his physicians advised him that he would die unless he abstained from sex. Rosanese then convinced Ugolotto, much against his will, to allow her to enter the convent of St. Perpetua near Faenza. She became a choir nun and he joined the same house as an extern brother. Rosanese then took the name Umiltà (Humility); she was twenty-five at the time. Her conduct as a nun was exemplary, earning her the admiration of her sisters.

Umiltà was illiterate, but when the other sisters asked her to read at mealtime she miraculously "read" a marvelous sermon, which later could not be found in the book she had had before her. After this, the convent provided her with a teacher who taught her to read and write.

Umiltà soon found that the convent was too lax for her taste and could not offer her the solitude she craved in order to devote her life to prayer. With the help of a miracle she escaped over the wall of the monastery, crossed a river, and walked to a nearby convent of the Order of St. Clare. The Abbess there placed Umiltà under the care of one of her relatives until a cell was built for her next to the church of St. Apollinaris in Faenza. She lived in this cell for the next twelve years.

Umiltà left her cell at the request of several clerics, among them the Abbot of the Greater Vallombrosan Order, who asked her to construct a monastery in Faenza. She founded a house and became its Abbess, an office she filled with great distinction. Later, in response to a vision of St. John the Evangelist she left her convent with several nuns (among them her close companion Blessed Margarita of Faenza [1230–1330]), obtained relics of the Evangelist, and built a church in his honor in Florence. Two years later she founded another convent in Florence, where she lived until her death.

Having miraculously healed herself of a tumor of the kidneys while at the convent of St. Perpetua, Umiltà soon became renowned as a healer and counselor, famous for her ability to detect unconfessed sins in others and for her eloquent preaching.

Nine of Umiltà's sermons and fragments of several others, along with several of her prayers, have been preserved in an Italian *Life* edited by Giudiccius in 1632, and in the *Analecta*, based on this *Life* and written in the fourteenth century. Her works were for the most part dictated in Latin to one of her followers. Umiltà's writings as we have them are filled with extravagant praises of Christ and Mary, of her patron saint John the Evangelist, and of her two guardian angels. Her style is sensual, even erotic, and at times quite ornate, particularly in her descriptions of the

Virgin Mary and in her devotion to John the Evangelist, whom she calls her "sweetest Bridegroom."

Umiltà's sermons are usually meditative in tone and are often addressed to Christ, Mary, or St. John the Evangelist. She writes in the first person most of the time, occasionally using parables or extended allegories to illustrate a doctrinal point. The difficulty of her life and work and the support she receives from the divine realm are recurring themes.

Umiltà's lauds were apparently well received during her lifetime. They were still being used by the nuns of St. Salvio in the late fourteenth century and were translated into the vernacular. Her sermons also appear in the vernacular in the Italian *Life*.

Works

Sala, T., *Sermones S. Humilitatis de Faventia* (1884). Zama, Piero, *Santa Umiltà: La Vita e i "sermones"* (2nd ed., 1974).

Translations: Pioli, Richard J., tr. "St. Umiltà of Faenza, *Sermons*," in Elizabeth Alvilda Petroff, ed., *Medieval Women's Visionary Literature* (1986).

Lila F. Ralston

Marie Under
1883–1980

Born March 27, 1883, Tallinn, Estonia
Died September 25, 1980, Stockholm, Sweden
Genre(s): poetry, essay, translation
Language(s): Estonian

Born in what is now again Estonia, Marie Under enjoyed the privilege of attending a German school, where she also studied Russian and French. Both her parents had come originally from Hiiumaa Island (Dagö) off the Estonian coast. Her father was a schoolteacher. Under had acquired the ability to read as early as age four and by age thirteen had commenced her career in poetry, writing in German initially. However, she was not to publish her first collection, *Sonetid* (Sonnets), until she was thirty-four.

The Estonian public was taken by surprise by the overt eroticism of Marie Under's first publication in 1917. The subjective, sensual treatment of love is continued in her next two verse collections, *Eelõitseng* (First Flowering) and *Sinine Puri* (The Azure Sail), both of which appeared in 1918. By this time Under had become the leading voice of the Siuru group of poets, referred to as both rebellious and colorful. European travel following World War I ultimately accounted for the influence of German Expressionist poetry in Under's subsequent work. She even translated into Estonian a selection of verse by George Heym, Franz Werfl, Ernst Stadler, and Walter Hasenclever. Postwar, her poetry changed radically in its outlook and was marked by anxiety, inner conflict, and a preoccupation with hopelessness and death.

Marie Under had already received a number of literary prizes and seen her work translated into several languages by the appearance of her fourth and fifth collections of poems, *Verivalla* (1920; Bleeding Wound) and *Pärisosa* (1923; Heritage). Her most significant period of literary creativity commenced with the publication of *Hääl Varjust* (1927; Voice from the Shadows).

As a result of the second Soviet annexation of Estonia in 1944, Marie Under decided to flee to Sweden across the Baltic; in this self-imposed exile her poetic voice remained clear and powerful. Her subsequent publications are characterized by a language now more simple and direct.

Among other distinctions, Marie Under was elected to honorary membership of International PEN in 1937 and was repeatedly nominated for the Nobel Prize. As a distinguished translator she brought a total of twenty-six works into Estonian from German, English, French, and Russian, including *Doctor Zhivago* and Rilke's poetry. She also translated Goethe, Schiller, Ibsen, and Baudelaire. Her own original poetry has been translated into English, French, German, Russian, Swedish, and Finnish. Her critical essays were written largely in the 1920s.

Marie Under's total *oeuvre* amounts to around four hundred poems published in thirteen collections, spanning some six decades of literary creativity. It is justifiably argued that her voice has yet to be heard clearly in the West; when it is, she would deservedly rank among the best six women poets in twentieth-century European literature.

Under easily claims to be Estonia's real national poet, and her poignant voice remains the clearest and most audible of all her contemporaries. Her themes range from nature and pantheism to biblical legends, her tone from the erotic to the indignant. Under constantly employs metaphor, comparison and symbol, and images of wind, sea, and fire. Her neoromantic verse, at times quasi-impressionistic and philosophical, conveys a suffering both personal and universal, an aesthetic ecstasy and an essentially extroverted spirituality. Marie Under's zest for life is balanced by a sometimes somber introspection in poetry imbued with the alive, open senses of Estonia's most important poet.

Works

Sonetid [Sonnets] (1917). *Eelõitseng* [First Flowering] (1918). *Sinine Puri* [The Azure Sail] (1918). *Verivalla* [Bleeding Wound] (1920). *Pärisosa* [Heritage] (1923). *Hääl Varjust* [Voice from the Shadows] (1927). *Rõõm Uhest Ilusast Päevast* [Delight in a Beautiful Day] (1928). *Õnne Varjutus: Ballaadid ja Legendid* [Eclipse of Happiness: Ballads and Legends] (1929). *Lageda Taeva All* [Under the Open Sky] (1930). *Kivi Südamelt* [A Stone off the Heart] (1935). *Mureliku Suuga* [With Sorrowing Lips] (1942). *Sädemed Tuhas* [Sparks Under Ashes] (1954). *Ääremail* [On the Brink] (1963).

Collections: *Ja Liha Sai Sõnaks* [And Flesh Turned into Word] (1936). *Kogutud Teosed* [Collected Works I–III] (1940). *Sõnasild* [Bridge of Words] (1945). *Südamik* [The Core] (1957). *Kogutud Luuletused* [Collected Poems] (1958). *Valitud Luuletused* [Selected Poems] (1958).

Translations: *Modern Estonia Poetry*, 20 poems and ballads, tr. W.K. Matthews (1953). *The PEN in Exile I and II*, Selections (1954, 1966). *Child of Man*, tr. W.K. Matthews (1955).

Warwick J. Rodden

Sigrid Undset

Sigrid Undset
1882–1949

Born 1882, Kalundborg, Denmark
Died 1949, Lillehammer, Norway
Genre(s): novel, essay, short story, poetry, drama, children's literature, biography
Language(s): Norwegian

In the English-speaking world there are few Norwegian authors whose popularity exceeds that of Sigrid Undset. She is best known for her trilogy *Kristin Lavransdatter* (1920–1922), an epic set in medieval Norway. Soon after it was written, this masterpiece was translated into numerous foreign languages (including English), and it became an international bestseller even before Undset was awarded the Nobel Prize for Literature in 1928.

Sigrid Undset was born in 1882 in Kalundborg, Denmark, at the home of her maternal grandfather, a chancery councillor of that small town. Her father, originally from Trondheim, was an archaeologist whose scholarship had earned him an international reputation, and Ingvald Undset kindled in his daughter an interest in history and the Middle Ages that was to bring her even greater renown. Other important influences from her childhood home included a fine library and a rich tradition of storytelling—folktales and legends but also purely imaginative stories. In 1884 the family moved to Kristiania (present-day Oslo), where Ingvald Undset had a position at the University Museum. For several years her father had suffered from poor health and in 1893, when Sigrid was only eleven years old, he died. The deep attachment Sigrid Undset felt toward her father was to later find expression in her fiction; the moving relationship between Kristin and her father, Lavrans (*Kristin Lavransdatter*), comes immediately to mind, and we have a second example in *Jenny* (1911), where the protagonist idolizes the father she lost during her childhood.

Making ends meet was difficult for a widow with three children, and Sigrid, the oldest child, felt a responsibility toward her mother and two younger sisters. She therefore decided not to pursue a university education but rather to enroll in a commercial college. She finished the program in one year and then took a job in an office where she remained for ten years. These were hardly lost or wasted years for Undset; she read a great deal during this period, both history and literature, and she was also writing. The first manuscript she completed and submitted to a publishing house was a story set in medieval Norway. It was rejected, but the editor nonetheless encouraged her to try her hand at something modern. This she did and in 1907 her first novel, *Fru Marta Oulie*, was published, thereby launching her career as a writer. The following year brought two more publications, and in 1909 she received a travel stipend which allowed her to quit her office job and travel to Italy.

In Rome Sigrid Undset met her future husband, the painter Anders Svarstad. They were married in 1912 in a civil ceremony in Antwerp and spent the first year of their marriage living abroad, in London and Rome. Between 1913 and 1919 Sigrid Undset gave birth to three children; Svarstad had three children from a previous marriage and these children came periodically to live with their father and stepmother. Even while managing a busy household, Undset found time for her writing.

The novels and stories written before 1920 comprise the first phase of Undset's production. During this period Undset wrote about people and places she had observed firsthand: the setting is Kristiania; the time, the early years of this century; the people, ordinary middle-class citizens who shared Undset's workplace and neighborhood. In vivid and realistic prose Undset re-creates those sections of the capital city she had known as a child and young woman. She displays a fine ear for dialogue, even capturing the dialects within the city, and her character portrayals evidence human warmth and keen insight. The women in this early fiction are typically caught between their dreams for happiness and fulfillment and the reality of their situation with its inherent limitations. The Undset heroine believes in ideal love, and she longs to fall in love with a man in whom she can find fulfillment and to whom she can submit herself. These are ideals and expectations not easily realized; failure to do so cannot be blamed on circumstance or fate, however, for Undset insists that her characters possess a free will and that they are therefore morally responsible for their lives.

Jenny, in the novel bearing her name, is twenty-eight years old and has still not experienced love. An attractive and intelligent woman who has developed her talents as an artist, she nonetheless feels that she, as a woman, cannot find true fulfillment in her work, and so she longs for marriage and children. She chooses to match herself with a man who is not her equal, and this initial error leads to other and more serious mistakes. At the end of her life, she recog-

nizes that she should have waited until she met the man who could claim her unreserved love and respect.

The trials and errors of Jenny and other female protagonists reflect the author's own quest for a set of values and norms that would endure the stress of great social change. Jenny had yearned to submit herself wholly to love, a husband, and family, but as Undset continued to struggle and to search for some kind of authority, she looked more and more to religion and the church. The Lutheran Church, Norway's state church, did not answer her needs, and she eventually converted to Catholicism. In 1924 she was officially received into the Catholic Church. She and her husband had been separated since 1919 when she and the children moved to Lillehammer, and their marriage was now annulled.

The second phase of Undset's authorship coincides with her move to "Bjerkebæk," the name she gave her home in Lillehammer. This is the period of her great medieval epics, first *Kristin Lavransdatter* (1920–1922), followed by *Olav Audunssön i Hestviken* (1925–1927; The Master of Hestviken). Undset was a meticulous scholar and the historical authenticity of these novels has been well documented. *The Master of Hestviken* takes place at the end of the thirteenth century, and *Kristin Lavransdatter* is set in the first half of the fourteenth. Detailed descriptions of farm buildings and routine chores, of how people dressed and what they ate never seem dry or obtrusive, so artfully are they woven into the narrative. The political situation, the role of the church (Norway was Catholic until the Reformation), the family structure, customs, and celebrations—these are also part of the fabric of the books.

Kristin Lavransdatter is unquestionably the more popular of the two largely because the narrative centers around the main character, tracing her development from the time she is a child to her death as a mature woman. *Kristin Lavransdatter* stands out as one of the finest character portrayals in Norwegian literature. The novel's central conflict derives from Kristin's headstrong and sensuous nature: in following her desires, she thereby sets her own will against that of a higher authority. She challenges the authority first of her father and later her husband, and not until she is dying does she realize that in all these acts of independence and willfulness she has resisted the will of God.

Undset's Christian faith is reflected in everything she wrote after 1920. Following the medieval epics, she again wrote novels in a contemporary setting but now from a distinctly Catholic point of view. In *Gymnadenia* (1929; The Wild Orchid) and *Den brændende busk* (1930; The Burning Bush) Undset depicts her protagonist's gradual conversion to Catholicism, and one assumes there is more than a trace of autobiography in these books.

Undset's production includes an impressive number of articles and essays, ranging from scholarly articles on Norwegian medieval history and portraits of Catholic saints, to essays on religious, moral, and social issues and current political ideologies. She took a firm stand against both Communism and Nazism and, in fact, had been such an outspoken critic that when Norway was invaded by Nazi Germany in April 1940, she was advised to flee the country. She went first to Sweden and then crossed Siberia to Japan where she sailed to San Francisco. She remained in the United States until Norway was liberated in 1945 and during this time was an active diplomat for her country, writing articles and giving speeches all over America. She returned to Lillehammer in 1945 and two years later, on her birthday, King Haakon VII conferred upon her the Grand Cross of the Order of Saint Olav for service to her country.

Works

Novels: *Fru Marta Oulie* (1907). *Fortællingen om Viga-Ljot og Vigdis* (1910). *Jenny* (1911). *Vaaren* (1914). *Splinten av troldspeilet* (1917). *Kristin Lavransdatter* (trilogy): *Kransen* (1920). *Husfrue* (1921). *Korset* (1922). *Olav Audunssön i Hestviken* (1925). *Olav Audunssön og hans börn* (1927). *Gymnadenia* (1929). *Den brændene busk* (1930). *Ida Elisabeth* (1932). *Elleve aar* (1934). *Den trofaste hustru* (1936). *Madame Dorthea* (1939).

Short stories: *Den lykkelige alder* (1908). *Fattige skjæbner* (1912). *De kloge jomfruer* (1918).

Poetry: *Ungdom* (1910). *Ungdom. Dikt. Med forfatterens egne tegninger* (1986).

Books for children: *Fortællinger om Kong Artur og ridderne av det runde bord* (1915). *Sigurd og hans tapre venner*, tr. into Norwegian (1955).

Drama: *I grålysningen* (1952). *Prinsessene i berget det blå* (1973).

Biography: *Caterina av Siena* (1951).

Essays: *Et kvindesynspunkt* (1919). *Sankt Halvards liv, dod og jærtegn* (1925). *Katholsk propaganda* (1927). *Etapper* (1929). *Hellig Olav, Norges konge* (1930). *Etapper. Ny række* (1933). *Norske helgener* (1937). *Selvportretter og landskapsbilleder* (1938). *Tilbake til fremtiden* (1945). *Lykkelige dager* (1947). *Artikler og taler fra krigstiden*, ed. A.H. Winsnes (1952). *Kirke og klosterliv. Tre essays fra norsk middelalder*, intro. Hallvard Rieber-Mohn (1963). *Artikler og essays om litteratur*, ed. Jan Fr. Daniloff (1986).

Letters: *Kjære Dea*, ed. Christianne Undset Svarstad (1979). *Sigrid Undset skriver hjem: en vandring gjennom emigrantårene i Amerika*, ed. Arne Skouen (1982).

Originally published in English: *Sigurd and His Brave Companions. A Tale of Medieval Norway* (1943). *True and Untrue and Other Norse Tales* (1945).

Translations: *Jenny*, tr. W. Emmë (1921). *Kristin Lavransdatter: The Bridal Wreath*, tr. Charles Archer and J.S. Scott (1923). *The Mistress of Husaby*, tr. Charles Archer (1925). *The Cross*, tr. Charles Archer (1927). *The Master of Hestviken: The Axe*, tr. Arthur G. Chater (1928). *The Snake Pit*, tr. Arthur G. Chater (1929). *In the Wilderness*, tr. Arthur G. Chater (1929). *The Son Avenger*, tr. Arthur G. Chater (1930). (Single volume, *The Master of Hestviken*, was published in 1934.) *The Wild Orchid*, tr. Arthur G. Chater (1931). *The Burning Bush*, tr. Arthur G. Chater (1932). *Christmas and Twelfth Night. Reflections*, tr. E.C. Ramsden (1932). *Ida Elisabeth*, tr. Arthur G. Chater (1933). *Stages on the Road*, tr. Arthur G. Chater (1934). *Saga of Saints*, tr. E.C. Ramsden (1934). *The Longest Years*, tr. Arthur G. Chater (1935). *Gunnar's Daughter*, tr. Arthur G. Chater (1936). *The Faithful Wife*, tr. Arthur G. Chater (1937). *Images in a Mirror*, tr. Arthur G. Chater (1938). *Men, Women and Places*, tr. Arthur G. Chater (1939). *Madame Dorthea*, tr. Arthur G. Chater (1940). *Return to the Future*, tr. Henriette C.K. Naeseth (1942). *Happy Times in Norway*, tr. Joran Birkeland (1942). *Norway's Best Stories*, ed. Hanna Astrup Larsen (1947). *Four Stories*, tr. Naomi Walford (1959). *An Everyday Story. Norwegian Women's Fiction*, ed. Katherine Hanson (1984). "Gardens," tr. Sherrill Harbison. *Landscape* 30, no. 2 (1989).

Katherine Hanson

Johanna Charlotte Unzer
1724–1782

Born November 17, 1724, Halle an der Saale, Germany
Died January 29, 1782, Altona
Genre(s): poetry, nonfiction
Language(s): German

Johanna Charlotte Unzer(in) is the only significant German woman writer of "anacreontic" poetry, publishing two volumes of poems, each with an expanded second edition. She is also one of very few German women in the eighteenth century who wrote books of nonfiction, producing popular accounts of philosophy and natural history for female readers.

Born in Halle an der Saale, a university town and center of pietism, Johanna Charlotte Ziegler came from a respectable family. Her father, who had studied with Johann Sebastian Bach, was an organist, composer, and music teacher. Her mother came from a family of clock makers. Johanna Charlotte received a minimal education as a young girl, apparently learning some French, though not enough to read extensively in that language. When she was older, however, perhaps in her late teens, she began trying to make up for what she had missed. She was probably stimulated in this effort by her maternal uncle, Johann Gottlob Krüger, ten years her senior and a professor of medicine at the university, and by Johann August Unzer, two years her junior. This man, who was a student of her uncle in medicine and of her father in music, became her husband in 1751.

That was the most eventful year in her life. She made her literary debut, publishing three books at once. Her uncle moved away from Halle, and she, now that both parents were dead, married Unzer and moved from the provincial and deeply religious region of Thuringia to the far north of Germany, to Altona, a liberal Danish-controlled town next to Hamburg. Two years later, she was well established in her new surroundings, contributing poetry to two periodicals there, publishing an enlarged edition of her earlier poetry collection, being crowned poet laureate of the University of Helmstedt (where her uncle was now Vice-rector), and becoming an honorary member of two literary societies, the "Deutsche Gesellschaften" of Göttingen and Helmstedt. In 1754 she published a new volume of poetry. Immediately after this flurry of activity a long period of silence began. Two beloved and long-mourned infants died, and Unzer herself suffered from a sickness that lingered on for nine years. Finally, in 1766, she began publishing again. She must have been writing well before that date, however, because again three works appeared in one year, a new collection of poetry and revisions of both earlier volumes. The next year she published a revised version of her monumental book on philosophy, *The Fundamentals of Comprehensive Knowledge for Ladies*. From then on, for the fourteen years until her death at age fifty-seven, she published nothing more, although she continued to be interested in literature, as is shown by her name on a subscription list (in 1773) for a novel by one of her famous contemporaries, Christoph Martin Wieland, and by her role as an agent collecting subscribers for Wieland's later venture into journalism with a monthly called *Der Teutscher Merkur*. Her husband, whose medical practice and literary activity showed no major interruptions during these decades, died seventeen years later.

Unzer first became known because of her ambitious undertaking for women readers, the composition of a popularized account of "comprehensive knowledge": it contained mostly philosophy, leavened with poems by various authors. For this long work (over 600 pages) Unzer relied on three sources, Christian Wolff for the sections on logic, Alexander Baumgarten for those on Metaphysics, and Krüger, her uncle, for those on science. It was extraordinary in eighteenth-century Germany for a woman to undertake a project of this kind. The follow-up volume, on the basics of natural history, seems to have been less successful. Her more lasting reputation rests however on her poetry. Johanna Charlotte Unzer-Zeigler accepted the conventions of wine, women, and song that characterized the anacreontic poetry of her day and wrote drinking songs laden with pastoral allusions, songs of cheerful flirtation, rationalist odes and nature poems, and (least successfully) verse tales. Her first volume of poetry claims to be primarily joking (*Scherzhaft*), while the second, written after her marriage, contains poems she described as tender and moral. Many include illuminating autobiographical references and reflect Unzer's interest in philosophical issues and methods.

Works

Grundri einer Weltwei heit für das Frauenzimmer [Fundamentals of Comprehensive Knowledge for Ladies] (1751). *Grundri einer natürlichen Historie und eigentlichen Naturlehre für das Frauenzimmer* [Fundamentals of Natural History and of Nature Study Itself for Ladies] (1751). *Versuch in Scherzgedichten* [Experiment in Witty Poems] (1751). *Versuch in sittlichen und zärtlichen Gedichten* [Experiment in Moral and Tender Poems] (1754). *Fortgesetzte Versuche in sittlichen und zärtlichen Gedichten* [Continued Experiments in Moral and Tender Poems] (1766).

Ruth P. Dawson

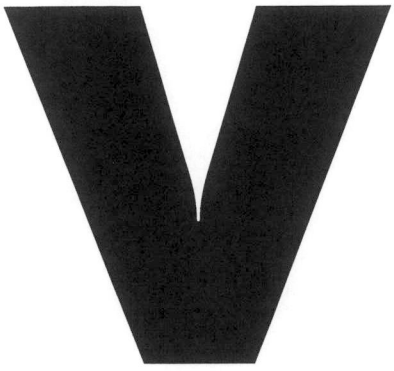

Helenē Vakalo
1921–

a.k.a. Eleni Vakalo
Born 1921, Constantinople
Genre(s): poetry, art criticism
Language(s): Greek

Helenē Vakalo studied archaeology at the University of Athens and art history at the Sorbonne in Paris. With her husband, the artist and stage designer George Vakalo, and others, she founded the School of Decorative Arts "Vakalo" in Athens in 1958, where she has been teaching art history. Since 1949 she has also been writing articles for newspapers and journals and has served as the art critic of *Ta Nea* and *Zygo* for many years.

She started writing poems in 1945 and has published thirteen poetry collections since then. She apparently has found a kindred spirit in Marianne Moore, the only poet she has translated into Greek. Translations of her own poetry have appeared in English, French, and Russian anthologies.

Vakalo's poetry is highly personal and deliberately antilyrical. Except for her *Genealogia*, it can be described as surrealistic or postsurrealistic. She is one of the so-called "Poets of Essence," a group of poets who did most of their writing after World War II, the Nazi Occupation, and the Greek Civil War and had to deal with the ruins (physical and emotional) that were the result of those historical events and with the accompanying feelings of estrangement and alienation. Distrusting the senses, they chose to write in simple and direct language, avoiding ornamentation, the complexities of syntax, and the demands of form. Vakalo's poetry appears to be formless and prosaic; it is a poetry of nouns and verbs, with few adjectives and even fewer adverbs. This type of writing seems to be in agreement with her definition of what it is to be creative: to push things beyond the given shapes and forms. She is at the forefront of those Greek poets who experimented with new ways of writing and new ways of looking at the world.

Although Vakalo's language is simple, her poetry is highly subjective and requires of the reader a "suspension of disbelief" and a commitment to the journey that is each poem. But her entire *oeuvre* is a journey also, a larger journey, for the reader and for the poet. In her early poems Vakalo practiced a type of automatic writing while exploring the world of the subconscious. Starting with *To dasos* (1954; The Forest), however, and reacting against sentimental writing, she has attempted to write a poetry "beyond lyricism," a poetry of essence. Like a blind person (*E ennoia tōn typhlōn*—The Meaning of the Blind) who has to learn "to see" differently than other people, the poet tries to make her way through the forest (*To dasos*) of experience and distinguish essence from illusion before she arrives at an understanding of things (*O tropos na kindynevoume*—The Manner of Our Endangering), comes to terms with her own "archaeology" in *Genealogia* (1971; Genealogy), and realizes that there are countless Madame Rodalinas (*Oi palavres tēs kyra-Rodalinas*—The Follies of Madame Rodalina) and that we all are both one of them and all of them.

Works

Themata kai parallages [Themes and Variations] (1945). *Anamnēseis apo mia ephialtikē politeia* [Recollections from a Nightmarish City] (1948). *Ste morphe ton theorēmaton* [In the Form of Theorems] (1951). *To dasos* [The Forest] (1954). *Toichographia* [Frescoes] (1956). *Hēmerologio tēs ēlikias* [Journal of Age] (1958). *Perigraphē tou sōmatos* [Description of the Body] (1959). *Ē ennoia tōn typhlōn* [The Meaning of the Blind] (1959). *O tropos na kindynevoume* [The Manner of Our Endangering] (1966). *Genealogia* [Genealogy] (1971). *Tou Kosmou* [Of the World]

(1978). *Prin apo tōn lyrismo* [Before Lyricism] (1981). *O Mythos tēs hellēnikotētas: E Physiognomia tēs metapolemikēs technēs stēn Hellada* [The Myth of Hellenicity: The Physiognomy of Postwar Art in Greece] (1983). *Oi palavres tēs kyra-Rodalinas* [The Follies of Madame Rodalina] (1985).

Translations: *The Charioteer: Annual Review of Modern Greek Culture* 15 (New York, 1974). *Contemporary Greek Poetry* tr., intro., biographies, and notes by Kimon Friar (Athens, 1985). *Genealogy*, tr. Paul Merchant (1971; new and revised ed. 1977). *The Greeks. A Celebration of the Greek People through Poetry and Photographs*, ed., tr., with an epilogue by Kimon Friar, commentary by Odysseus Elytis (New York, 1984). *Modern European Poetry*, ed. Willis Barnstone et al. (New York, 1966). Greek poems tr. Kimon Friar, in *Modern Poetry in Translation*, No. 4; No. 34. *Six Modern Greek Poets.*, ed. and tr. John Stathatos (London, 1975). *Resistance, Exile and Love. An Anthology of Post-War Greek Poetry*, tr. and ed. Nikos Spanias (New York, 1977).

Helen Dendrinou Kolias

Helena Valentí
1940–

Born 1940, Barcelona, Spain
Genre(s): novel, short story
Language(s): Catalan

Born to a bourgeois family in postwar Barcelona, Helena Valentí grew up under the Franco regime, experiencing the restrictions typical of the period in Spain. To escape this repression, she lived and studied in England, obtaining her doctor of literature from Cambridge University. Her marriage to an Englishman ended in divorce, and Valentí lived a bohemian existence in London for five years, during which she became active in the women's liberation movement. Returning to Catalonia in 1974, she lived for a time in Barcelona but soon moved to the coastal village of Cadaques. She then returned to Barcelona.

Valentí's first book, *L'amor adult* (1977; Adult Love), is a collection of thematically related stories with both autobiographical and feminist substrata. Motifs drawn from personal experience abound: the foreign female in England, the tolerant, enlightened British husband, posters advertising women's lib, quantities of gin, the feminist movement per se, and the "liberated" but not satisfied female. Additional themes include the unwanted pregnancy, hostility within matrimony, the lack of marital communication, frequent separations of lovers and spouses, and aggressively unconventional sexual behavior. Whatever common ground there may be among the eleven stories inheres in the use of the liberated woman as protagonist or central consciousness. A dominant note is the battle of the sexes, from which not even motherhood nor infancy provides a respite. Nearly all characters appear hypnotized by the mystique of their respective sexes and consequently suffer from inability to mature. Valentí's feminism in this collection is balanced without being unduly aggressive or defensive.

In *La solitud d'Anna* (1981; Anna's Loneliness), Valentí amplifies existential preoccupations implicit in the previous work. Anna is, as the title implies, an incarnation of existential solitude (the feminine lot). Masculine characters play strictly secondary roles and are portrayed as insensitive, indifferent, and ineffectual but necessary for procreation. Brutal, infantile, or criminal, they appear as exploiters, all but devoid of emotion, so lacking in understanding as to be unaware of their offenses against womankind. Anna decides to have an abortion, which spells the end of her relationship with her lover, Luis, after three years of living together. Luis disappears while Anna is in the clinic, leaving a handful of money. The novel holds out little hope for heterosexual love or for marriage as an institution.

La dona errant (1986; The Errant Woman) is a novel without beginning or end, a narrative whose action is directly melded to the daily adventure of people in the street. Somewhat as in a giant chess game without players, its pieces move regardless of their own wishes, as if impelled by mysterious cosmic forces. As a social commentary upon the contemporary generation of Spanish adolescents, the novel describes their search for a niche in the world and the disorientation resulting from having inherited from preceding generations various modes of conduct which they intuitively reject as erroneous. Concern with the "generation gap" in values is a major theme.

With three strong feminist statements to her credit to date, Valentí is one of the definitive voices of Catalan feminism in the 1980s. Her fiction is intelligently written and cosmopolitan in its outlook, and even when seemingly guilty of a certain dualistic conception of male and female characters, strikes a telling blow for openness, communication, and feminine self-sufficiency. Without limiting her focus to feminist issues and the war between the sexes, Valentí deals with broader philosophical questions and problems of contemporary society which transcend the matter of gender.

Works

L'amor adult (1977). *La solitud d'Anna* (1981). *La dona errant* (1986).

Janet Perez

Marja-Liisa Vartio
1924–1966

Born September 11, 1924, Sääminki, Finland
Died June 17, 1966, Savonlinna
Genre(s): poetry, short story, novel, radio scripts
Language(s): Finnish

Marja-Liisa Orvokki Vartio died at the age of forty-two. Both of her parents were teachers; her mother was also a lay preacher and reciter. Vartio's upbringing was religious. Her parents divorced a few months before she was born; as a child she spent part of her time with her mother, part with her father. In 1950 she took a degree in art history. In 1945 she married the manager of an art shop, Valter Vartio; they divorced in 1955. She then married the writer Paavo Haavikko.

Vartio is said to have been a splendid teller of stories, who easily cast a spell over her listeners. This can be observed in her poems, which are often long and narrative. The role of folk poetry and Finnish mythology in her verse is unique, particularly so at the time when she was writing. Vartio wrote both in an adapted *Kalevala* meter and in the free verse favored by the postwar modernists. Skillful use of rhythm and great gushes of imagery give an atmosphere of magic and incantation to her poetry.

Her collection of short stories, *Maan ja veden välillä* (1955; Between Earth and Water), is a bridge between poetry and prose. She has herself said that writing is by nature close to dreaming. Characteristics of her stories—timelessness, lack of comment, namelessness, metaphor, and a strongly suggestive atmosphere—justify calling them dream stories. The real and unreal levels of her writing are not opposed but appear side by side; the best example of this is her story "Vatikaani" (The Vatican).

Vartio played her part in the renewing of prose writing in the 1950s. The attempt to achieve "objectivity" by means of more external description can be seen in her work. Vartio's narrator may leave the reader to provide conclusions and explanations. Irony and humor appear when the narrator and the characters approach matters in different ways. Vartio's narrative methods are versatile and interesting, with her use of viewpoint and free indirect discourse.

In her novels Vartio describes country folk, the upper classes, and the new suburban dwellers of the fifties, particularly women. One of the principal themes in her work is the search for woman's identity, the attempt to break free from the demands set by her environment. The young girls in her novels *Mies kuin mies, tyttö kuin tyttö* (1958; Any Man, Any Girl) and *Tunteet* (1962; Feelings) strive hard to achieve a situation where they can decide things for themselves. Vartio's women do not always succeed in their endeavors. The longing for connection is great, and human contacts are difficult, often only death provides the possibility of realizing something about another person in the world of her novels.

Dreams and fancies are important in Vartio's five novels. The tragedy of a character may be the inability to realize dreams, as in *Kaikki naiset näkevät unia* (1960; All Women Have Dreams), or the central character may be a person already dead who dominates the imaginations of others, as in *Se on sitten kevät* (1957; So It's Spring). Vartio's posthumous novel, *Hänen olivat linnut* (1967; Hers Were the Birds), an undisputed classic of modern Finnish literature, contains complex symbolism. The structure of the whole novel is built around a collection of birds, which is an important departure point for both the plot and the meaning of the book. The fancies connected with the birds help the main characters to stay alive and maintain their connection to each other.

Works

Poetry: *Häät* [Wedding] (1952). *Seppele* [Wreath] (1953). *Runot ja proosarunot* [Poems and Prose Poems] (1966).

Short stories: *Maan ja veden välillä* [Between Earth and Water] (1955).

Novels: *Se on sitten kevät* [So It's Spring] (1957). *Mies kuin mies, tyttö kuin tyttö* [Any Man, Any Girl] (1958). *Kaikki naiset näkevät unia* [All Women Have Dreams] (1960). *Tunteet* [Feelings] (1962). *Hänen olivat linnut* [Hers Were the Birds] (1967).

Radio plays: *Säkki* [The Sack] (1959) in *Suomalaisia kuunelmia, 1952–1963* (Finnish Radio Plays), ed. Jyrki Mäntylä (1964). *Saara* (1964) in *Suomalaisia kuunelmia, 1964–1965*, ed. Jyrki Mäntylä (1966).

Translations: "The Vatican," a short story; three prose poems; two extracts from the novel *Hänen olivat linnut* [Hers Were the Birds], tr. Aili and Austin Flint, intro. Pirkko Alhoniemi, in *Books from Finland* (March 1986): 136–149.

Päivi Karttunen

Elizabeth Vesey
ca. 1715–1791

Born ca. 1715, Ireland
Died 1791, London
Genre(s): letters
Language(s): English

Elizabeth Vesey was born in Ireland about 1715. Sometime before 1746 she married her second husband, Agmondesham Vesey, accountant-general of Ireland, amateur architect, and womanizer. Dividing her time between the family home in Ireland and a house she maintained in London, Vesey attracted many friends and from 1770 until 1786 was a leading Bluestocking. Of her letters, Lord Lyttleton wrote to David Garrick, "You will be charmed (as I am) with the lively coloring and fine touches in the epistolary style of our sylph, joined to the most perfect ease." Vesey's letters reflect the sprightly wit and good humor by which she inspired convivial talk among the continental and British literati, philosophers, and scholars who gathered regularly in her "blue room" during the London winter season.

In 1751, Mary Delany dubbed her "the Sylph." Elizabeth Montagu praised the "musick" of her voice and the "gentle vivacity" of her wit. Horace Walpole asked, "What English heart ever excelled hers?" Her witty sallies were commonly aimed at herself, as when, denouncing second marriages, she seemed to overlook her own, finally exclaiming, "Bless me, my dear! I had quite forgotten it." Even when ill she kept up her self-mockery, once remarking that her only happy moment in fourteen days had been a fainting fit, another time fearing for the loss of "seven or eight" of her senses.

But this fascination with her own illnesses suggests a dark side. She herself said she had "a mind formed for doubt." Her friend Elizabeth Carter believed that because Vesey scarcely ever enjoyed "any one object, from the apprehension that something better may possibly be found in another," she lived in "a perpetual forecast of disappointment." Once, Vesey told Carter of the sublime thrill of reading the agnostic Abbé Raynal during violent thunderstorms. Carter, who saw in her friend "coral groves and submarine palaces," was alarmed, writing back, "'Tis a dangerous amusement to a mind like yours."

When she was forty-seven years old, Vesey captivated Laurence Sterne, who for five years sought her out and wrote her love letters. Sterne's appreciation must have been a joy, for Mr. Vesey's peccadillos were unceasing. But when her husband died in 1785, he left her hardly anything out of an income of £4000 except their London house while settling on his mistress a legacy of £1000. Although reportedly the nephew and heir "acted with great kindness and liberality," assuring Vesey of at least a "competency," this double stroke—her husband's death, and evidence of his neglect of her—blasted her already skeptical and apprehensive mind. From age seventy until her death at seventy-six, she was in a state of decline, from uncontrolled weeping to passivity, violent outbursts, and, finally, childlike vulnerability.

While Bluestocking gatherings derived from French salons, the name seems to have been inspired by Vesey's assurances, "Pho, Pho, don't mind dress! Come in your blue stockings!" Through studied informality, Vesey created a casual atmosphere for her conversations. Vesey's aim was to draw together the most exciting thinkers in various realms and to get them talking, sometimes stimulated by a reading from a new work. In this way, ideas were kept in motion. Additionally, such literary arts as letter writing and biography owe much to Bluestocking conversations in which the real social world and the world of ideas met in talk that was at once gossipy, thought-provoking, and artful.

Vesey's letters sometimes reveal the excesses of imagination that worried her friends: when ill in 1779, she writes to Montagu, "I find the lamp of the mind sinking in its socket and had I courage to face the World unknown I should wish the flame quite extinct." But this same letter also reveals the value she placed on civilized conversation between friends, for she goes on to create solace for herself through her communication of news events, gossip, and political analysis, ending abruptly and wittily with, "here is Ann come with the dressing basket how I hate to look at my own face when I can talk to you." Vesey's letters primarily show her delight in language play. They are full of sharp sensuous detail, often in surprising combinations, as in a series that closes her thanks to Lord Lyttleton for his concern while she was ill: "& since you set any value upon my life I don't regret the blisters bleedings & the Boluses they cram'd down my throat." And sometimes her bright details are used in a game of self-mockery, as when she teases Lyttleton, in 1768, about his supposed proposition that they elope.

Her language play often involves comic hyperbole, and active verbs keep her reader rushing along. For instance, she creates a picture of ridiculous extravagance in the preparations she and Mr. Vesey are making for a party to be held in Lyttleton's honor: "half a dozen oaks stript of their bark, the bed of the River dug up for rustick Stones the bogs and Heaths uncover'd of their Moss the Labourer taken from Harvest the Housekeeper robb'd of her Bread and barley to tempt the Birds to build their nests in Malvina's Bower—and there they are now—such a flight—whistling and singing the fish leaping the Farmer scolding and I almost crying to give up all hopes of seeing you there till next year which is to me for ever." The "whistling and singing" series, dashing from comedy to pure affection, is typical of Vesey's prose style. Through her letters one can appreciate the bright spirit that for fifteen years created conversation and good humor among a richly diverse group of friends.

Works

Selected letters in the following: *A Series of Letters Between Mrs. Elizabeth Carter and Miss Catherine Talbot 1741–70 . . . Letters from Mrs. Elizabeth Carter to Mrs. Vesey 1763–87*, ed. M. Pennington (1809). *Memoirs of the Life and Correspondence of Mrs. Hannah More*, ed. W. Roberts (1834). *Mary Hamilton at Court and at Home, from Letters and Diaries 1756 to 1816*, ed. E. Anson and F. Anson (1925). *Bluestocking Letters* , ed. E.B. Johnson (1926).

Carolyn Woodward

Björg Vik
1935–

Born 1935, Oslo, Norway
Genre(s): short story, drama, journalism
Language(s): Norwegian

It is as a writer of short stories that Björg Vik has risen to her status as one of Norway's foremost contemporary authors. Before becoming a full-time writer of fiction, Vik studied journalism and for five years was a journalist for a newspaper in Porsgrunn, where she currently makes her home. Her journalistic skills are evident in her fiction, in her uncomplicated and realistic style, her precise and finely tuned use of language, and her ability to detect a story in even the most undramatic and ordinary situations.

Björg Vik's stories, then, are realistic depictions of ordinary people in everyday situations. These stories are generally (though not exclusively) about women in various stages of development, from childhood to old age. Vik's characters are often undergoing a transition or are faced with a personal crisis: The protagonist may be a child responding with fear and confusion to outbursts of anger and violence between parents; an adolescent yearning for the happiness and fulfillment denied her mother; a house-

wife and mother questioning the meaning of her existence; an elderly widow struggling to cope with loneliness. There is relatively little dramatic action in Vik's stories—the author is more interested in depicting the psyches of her characters and in exploring the nuances of their relationships with others. Björg Vik possesses a remarkable ability to enter into her characters and illuminate their innermost feelings and thoughts.

An undercurrent of longing—for love, personal fulfillment, freedom—runs throughout Vik's work. Female protagonists in her first three books long to experience love and warmth. They have a tendency to seek self-realization through love relationships with men and to equate freedom with sexual liberation. As Vik indicates in the title of her second collection, *Nödrop fra en myk sofa* (1966; Cry for Help from a Soft Sofa), the characters in these early stories belong to the upper-middle class and represent a traditional lifestyle.

In *Kvinneakvariet* (1972; An Aquarium of Women), Vik's concerns are more specifically feminist. To her gallery of characters have been added women and girls from the working class, professional women, and artists. While interpersonal relationships continue to be a major focus, the protagonist in these stories is awakening to the social and political factors influencing her life. She is beginning to perceive that male domination extends beyond the confines of her home and that personal freedom is consequently far more complicated than merely loosening the bonds of marriage. The problem of freedom is further explored in Vik's next collection, *Fortellinger om frihet* (1975; Stories of Freedom), and here there are several stories in which men are also shown to be victims of an impersonal, profit-oriented society.

With *En håndful lengsel* (1979; A Handful of Longing), one notes a thematic shift. The characters are still filled with a sense of longing, but the insight gained through sharpened perception has tempered their expectations and they often choose not to change their situations but to accept and make the best of their lots. There is an aura of resignation over these stories that persists in *Snart er det höst* (1982; Soon It Will Be Autumn) and *En gjenglemt petunia* (1985; A Forgotten Petunia), Vik's most recent collections. Many of the protagonists in these latest stories feel they have freed themselves of false illusions; some of them are learning to deal with death; most of them have come to recognize their own loneliness as something inevitable.

Björg Vik has also had success as a dramatic writer of stage and radio plays. Her play *To akter for fem kvinner* (1974; Two Acts for Five Women) has been performed in all the Scandinavian countries, Germany, and Austria; in addition, there have been two Off-Broadway productions. The subjects and themes of her dramatic pieces are much the same as in her prose fiction.

The recipient of many literary prizes in Norway, Björg Vik has also been nominated for the prestigious Nordic Council Literary Prize on three occasions. She is regarded as one of the finest short story writers not only in her native Norway but throughout Scandinavia.

Works

Novels: *Gråt elskede mann* (1970). *Små nøkler store rom* (1988).

Short stories: *Söndag ettermiddag* (1963). *Nödrop fra en myk sofa* (1966). *Det grådige hjerte* (1968). *Kvinneakvariet* (1972). *Fortellinger om frihet* (1975). *En håndfull lengsel* (1979). *Snart er det höst* (1982). *En gjenglemt petunia* (1985).

Drama: *To akter for fem kvinner* (1974). *Hurra, det ble en pike!* (1974). *Sorgenfri* (1978). *Det trassige håp* (1981). *Fribillett til Soria Moria* (1984).

Translations: *Out of Season and Other Stories*, tr. David McDuff and Patrick Browne (1983). *An Aquarium of Women*, tr. Janet Garton (1987). *Slaves of Love and Other Norwegian Short Stories*, ed. James McFarlane (1982). *An Everyday Story. Norwegian Women's Fiction*, ed. Katherine Hanson (1984). *View from the Window. Norwegian Short Stories*, tr. Elizabeth Rokkan and Ingrid Weatherhead (1986). *Scandinavian Women Writers. An Anthology from the 1880s to the 1980s*, ed. Ingrid Clareus (1989). *Two Acts for Five Women*, performed in two Off-Broadway productions. *Free Pass to Soria Moria*, performed by Pan Viking company in New York, March 1987. *New Norwegian Plays*, tr. Janet Garton and Henning Sehmsdorf (1989).

Katherine Hanson

Madame de Villedieu
ca. 1640–1683

a.k.a. Marie-Catherine Desjardins
Born 1640 (?), France
Died 1683
Genre(s): poetry, letters, novel, reviews, drama
Language(s): French

Neither Marie-Catherine Desjardins's place nor year of birth is certain: she was born perhaps in Alençon; she grew up until age fifteen in or around this Normandy town. Her death certificate, in 1683, gives her age as forty-five, but in a letter dated May 15, 1667, she claims that she has "[. . .] the experience gained from twenty-seven years of life." She could have been born either in 1638 or in 1640.

In 1655, young Marie-Catherine fell in love with one of her cousins, handsome François Desjardins, a dashing cavalry lieutenant. Her father, Guillaume Desjardins, a stubborn, ill-tempered man, perpetually in debt from bad business deals and grandiose schemes to amass wealth, went to court and succeeded in having the engagement broken. Outraged by this callous action, Catherine Ferrand, his wife, obtained a legal separation and moved to Paris, taking her two daughters with her. It is around this time that Marie-Catherine, to forget her grief over losing François, began to write verse.

In 1658, she met the man who was to become her lifelong love: Antoine de Boëssert de Villedieu, a lieutenant in the *Régiment de Picardie*. Six years later (she was twenty-four or twenty-six, depending on chronology), she and Villedieu signed before a priest a solemn promise to be married, just before Antoine sailed away with his regiment. Having written in 1664 a tragicomedy, *Le Favory*, which Molière was staging, Marie-Catherine insisted that she be known henceforth as "Madame de Villedieu" publicly and privately. She demanded that her name as the play's author be so changed, a whim that created conflict with and resentment among some of the actors. Not without difficulty, Molière persuaded her to change her mind.

Her relationship with Antoine de Villedieu was both intense and stormy. Marie-Catherine was very possessive, a trait that did not sit well with her lover. In 1667, he publicly denied any attachment or obligation he might have had toward her and sought to marry someone else, a decision that, although based partially on financial considerations, failed to affect her love, or rather, her obsession.

Marie-Catherine left France around that time for the Netherlands, officially to tend to a lawsuit she had pending there. She stayed awhile in Belgium, then went on to The Hague. Back in Belgium, she learned with dismay that her former lover had turned over (or, more likely, sold) her correspondence with him to the well-known Paris bookseller Barbin, who was about to publish it. Appalled that her most intimate—and passionate—declarations to Antoine were to become fodder for public curiosity, she begged her Parisian correspondent to stop Barbin. Too late: the best that could be done was to remove her name as author from the *privilège*.

On August 22, 1667, Antoine was killed at the siege of Lille. His death coincided with the losing of her Dutch lawsuit and with her own father's demise. Marie-Catherine was brokenhearted as well as penniless. She accepted the hospitality of the Duchess de Nemours, an early benefactress and protectress, at Neufchâtel, until the end of spring 1668. There she composed her first major novel, *Cléonice*. She also adopted permanently the name Madame de Villedieu from that time on, with the consent, indeed with the blessings, of Antoine's family.

Beginning in 1669, she made the name of Villedieu illustrious in the world of letters: a very prolific author, her works sold quite well until 1672, when her production slowed down because of a certain world weariness that induced her to seek the asylum of a convent. Monastic life, however, soon proved itself unsuitable to her independent nature, nor could she long bear the frustration of having to give up writing, especially poetry, an avocation deemed too secular for a nun. She left the convent in 1675.

In 1677, thirty-seven-year-old Marie-Catherine secretly wed fifty-five-year-old Claude-Nicolas de Chaste, likely more for reasons of convenience than for love. She bore him a son, Louis. Her husband died less than two years later, leaving her in financial difficulty despite a pension of 2,500 livres granted the young child by Louis XIV. Marie-Catherine retired with her son to the Desjardins family's country estate of Clinchemore where she died in 1683, having spent her twilight years in pious retreat. There is some evidence that she harbored Jansenist sympathies in the latter part of her life.

Works

Epigramme (1663). "Jouissance" (1658). *Alcidamie* (1661). *Recueil* (1662). *Manlius Torquatus*, a *drame* performed at the Hôtel de Bourgogne (1662). *Carrousel* for the *Dauphin* (1662). *Nitétis* (1663). "Lisandre" (1663). *Le Favory* (1664). "Carmente, histoire grecque" (1667). *Anaxandre* (1667). *Cléonice* (1668). *Nouveau recueil* (1668). *Relation d'une Revue des Troupes d'Amour* (1668). *Recueil de quelques lettres en relations galantes* (1668). *Amours des grands hommes* (1670). *Exilés de la Cour d'Auguste* (1670). *Fables et histoires allégoriques* (1671). *Mémoires de la vie d'Henriette-Sylvie de Molière* (1672). *Galanteries grenadines* (1672). *Nouvelles afriquaines* (1672). *Le Portefeuille* (1674). *Les Désordres de l'amour* (1674).

Francis Assaf

Gabrielle-Suzanne Barbot Gallon, Dame de Villeneuve
ca. 1695–1755

a.k.a. Mme de Vxxx
Born 1695(?)
Died December 29, 1755, Paris
Genre(s): "nouvelle," fairy tale, novel
Language(s): French

Mme de Villeneuve wrote the original version of "La Belle et la Bête" (Beauty and the Beast), a tale which has become the French prototype of the eighteenth-century literary fairy tale. Yet for a long time Mme de Villeneuve did not receive due credit because her carefully constructed narrative of considerable length reached its wide distribution only in the severely abridged form included by Mme Le Prince de Beaumont in her *Magasin des Enfants* of 1756.

The daughter of a nobleman of La Rochelle, Gabrielle-Suzanne Barbot married Jean-Baptiste Gallon de Villeneuve, a lieutenant-colonel of the French infantry. Finding herself without financial resources after her husband's death, Mme de Villeneuve sought to improve her lot through writing. She was rewarded with considerable success as her second full-length novel, *La Jardinière de Vincennes* (1753), became a mid-century bestseller. In contrast to the more prominent female authors of the first half of the century, like Mme de Graffigny or Mme de Tencin, whose personal flamboyance was coupled with public notoriety, Mme de Villeneuve pursued her life and literary career in relative obscurity. Her latter years were spent in the company of Crébillon père, Voltaire's arch-rival, whom—as Casanova reports—she assisted in his duties as royal censor while conducting the affairs of his household in general.

A review of the publishing history of Mme de Villeneuve's works suggests that, as a writer, she was decidedly aiming at commercial success, as she conformed in her literary expression to the dominant genre and style of the time, shifting from "nouvelle," to fairy tale, to novel. The "nouvelle" *Le Phénix conjugal* of 1734 depicts the fate of a young nobleman who is persecuted by his father for marrying a working-class girl. Her first book sets both the thematic and the formal parameters for her subsequent works; love and virtue, money and social class are the central issues of her fictional universe; multiple subplots and puzzle-effects characterize the construction of her narratives.

As the raging literary fashion of the declining seventeenth century—the fairy tale—underwent a short revival in the 1740s, Mme de Villeneuve published her two collections of tales. In *La Jeune Américaine ou les contes marins* (1740–1741) we find her masterpiece "La Belle et la Bête," set in the frame of a transatlantic sea voyage. There are few better-loved fairy tales than that of the young prince cursed to bear the likeness of a repulsive beast-like creature until he is released through the devoted love of an unselfish maiden. The second tale, "Les Nayades," elaborates the motif of the rivalry between the kind and the rude stepsister, who each receive the magical gifts they deserve. The third posthumous tale, "Le Temps et la Patience" (1768), blends fairy tale with allegory as the reader follows the adventures of an errant princess and her exiled brothers.

Mme de Villeneuve's second collection of tales, *Les Belles Solitaires* (1745), is a puzzling work of uneven quality that seems to explore the nature of fictional discourse through concrete examples. A countess gives an autobiographical account improbable enough to be called fantasy and a marquise presents two fairy tales whose gratuitous invention is rendered plausible through logical explanation.

It is in her best and most successful novel, *La Jardinière de Vincennes* (1753), that Mme de Villeneuve's feminist orientation becomes most visible. The heroine, an impoverished aristocratic widow, defies the reigning social order that disallows manual labor for the aristocracy. She resorts to work in order to bring up her children in dignity and independence. The plight of women's destiny is treated less optimistically in *Mesdemoiselles de Marsange* (1757), a somber tragedy set in motion by a young woman who challenges the patriarchal order that preordained her younger sister for the convent.

In Mme de Villeneuve's two other novels, the occasionally heavy-handed complications of the plot relegate most ideologic concerns to the background. *Le Beau-frère supposé* (1752) is a novel of pure intrigue and adventure, complete with abductions, blackmail, and murder, whereas the action of *Le Juge prévenu* (1754) revolves around the familiar issue of marriage across class barriers.

Despite certain stylistic flaws in her work, Mme de Villeneuve should be remembered as a woman and a writer who succeeded in conveying subtly and skillfully her distinct awareness of the social injustice produced by the aristocratic patriarchal ideology. Her brand of feminism, however, is decidedly undogmatic because she propounds pragmatism not only as an ultimate value but also as an effective means to bring about social change. Avoiding the trap of *sensibilité* that swept the century, Mme de Villeneuve presented an ideologically cohesive and consciously constructed narrative universe that relies on the reflection of social reality and not on the dissection of love.

Works

Le Phénix conjugal (1734). *La Jeune Américaine ou les contes marins* (1740–1741). *Les Belles Solitaires* (1745). *Le Beau-frère supposé* (1752), *La Jardinière de Vincennes* (1753). *Le Juge prévenu* (1754). *Mesdemoiselles de Marsange* (1757). *Le Temps et la Patience* (1768).

Barbara L. Cooper

Renée Vivien
1877–1909

a.k.a. Pauline Mary Tarn
Born June 8, 1877, London
Died November 18, 1909, Paris
Genre(s): poetry, prose poem, translation, novel, fairy tale, short story
Language(s): French

The problematic and uncertain facts concerning the birth and childhood of Renée Vivien (née Pauline Tarn) epitomize some of the complexities that her life and work represent. According to some biographers she was born in London, according to others, in Long Island in the United States as the child of a presumably English father and an American mother whose wealth derived mainly from the dry goods business. In 1898, the young Pauline escaped to Paris where she became a spirited and often scandalous member of the *fin-de-siècle bohème*. Her stormy lesbian relationships with, among others, Natalie Clifford Barney and Baroness Hélène Van Zuylen de Nyevelt—relationships that are reflected in her work and literary preferences—soon attracted the attention of the *beau monde* of turn-of-the-century Paris. Her early death in 1909, at the age of thirty-three, of the combined effects of excessive alcohol use, nervous fatigue, and a final exhausting and mysterious lesbian affair, concludes the almost classic *fin-de-siècle* career of Renée Vivien.

In spite of her early death, Renée Vivien published extensively. Much of her poetry, especially the collections *Etudes et Préludes* (1901), *Cendres et Poussières* (1902), *Evocations* (1903), her translation of Sappho's lyrics (1903), and the two collections of prose poems *Brumes de Fjords* (1902) and

Du vert au violet (1903), deserve attention. Renée Vivien also published two volumes written in collaboration with Hélène V.Z. (Hélène Van Zuylen de Nyevelt) under the collective pseudonym of Paule Riversdale: *L'Etre double* (1904) and *Netsuké* (1904). Yet, Vivien is also the author of some intriguing prose texts, such as the short fiction and lesbian fairy tales of *La Dame à la Louve* (1904), the quasiautobiographical novel *Une femme m'apparut* (1904), and the only-recently-published *Anne Boleyn* (1982), a short narrative whose intended publication in 1909 was halted by the author's death.

The significance of the *oeuvre* of this woman writer who refused to be condemned to "the ugliness of men" resides in her ability to transform standard decadent and symbolist myths and themes in terms of her female and lesbian sensitivities and eroticism. Thus, the Baudelairian "delicate art of vice," the decadent's sense of artifice and predilection for autumnal moods, the symbolist's fascination with death, religion, and mysticism, and classical Sapphic and modern lesbian motifs combined to form Vivien's private poetic universe. The dream of a new Lesbos—which Renée Vivien and Natalie C. Barney briefly tried to realize during their stay on Lesbos (Mytilene) in 1904 in the form of an artistic enclave for lesbian poets and intellectuals—is, in this respect, the feminist and lesbian counterpart of the male ivory tower of, for example, Mallarmé's soirées or the more solitary "refined *thébaïde*" of J.-K. Huysmans's *Des Esseintes*. Although Renée Vivien has never gained widespread acceptance for either her literary talents or her militant views on the role of women, she has increasingly been the object of attention of both gay and feminist intellectuals and academic scholars of the *fin de siècle*.

Works

Poetry: For Renée Vivien's collected poems, see *Poèmes de Renée Vivien*, 2 vols. (1923–1924) or the one-volume facsimile reprint by Arno Press in 1975.

Short fiction: *La Dame à la Louve* (1904).

Novel: *Une femme m'apparut* (1904). *Anne Boleyn*, ed. Jean-Paul Goujon (1982).

Translations: *Sappho* (1903). *Les Kitharèdes* (1904). *Sapho et huit poétesses grecques* (1909).

English translations: *A Woman Appeared to Me*, tr. Jeannette H. Foster (1976). *The Muse of the Violets*, tr. Margaret Porter and Catherine Kroger (1977). *At the Sweet Hour of Hand-in-Hand*, tr. Sandia Belgrade (1979). *The Woman of the Wolf*, tr. Karla Jay and Yvonne M. Klein (1983).

Henk Vynckier

Suzanne Voilquin
1801–ca. 1877

Born December 17, 1801, Paris
Died late 1876 or early 1877, near Paris
Genre(s): journalism, autobiography
Language(s): French

Suzanne Monnier Voilquin is best known for her autobiographical writings, particularly her *Souvenirs d'une fille du peuple* (1866) and more recently for her *Mémoires d'une Saint-Simonienne en Russie*, which remained unpublished until 1979. Most of the biographical information we now possess comes from her own accounts. She sometimes signed letters as "Jeanne," "Jenny," or "Jeanne S. Voilquin."

Suzanne was the third of four children, and the first daughter, of Parisian skilled workers. Her father was a hatter and an enthusiastic participant in revolutionary politics during the Revolution. She attended a convent school for a few years, then was briefly in apprenticeship when she suffered a breakdown and returned home. Her mother turned over responsibility for her new little sister Adrienne when Suzanne was just nine years old. During her teens she lost her religious faith.

In her early twenties, Suzanne was courted, seduced, and abandoned by a young medical student who had promised marriage. She later married Eugène Voilquin, who promptly infected her with venereal disease, thus thwarting her dreams of motherhood. In 1830 she and Voilquin joined the Saint-Simonian sect, and in 1832 she affiliated with a group of young working women to edit a paper, *La Femme libre*, defending the cause of women within and beyond Saint-Simonian circles. This paper, under various names, published 40 issues in the course of two years. Suzanne and her husband separated in early 1833 (divorce was illegal in France), and he left France for Louisiana with another woman. Later that year Suzanne took up the study of homeopathic medicine.

In 1834 Suzanne cast her lot with the Saint-Simonians who were going to Egypt. She became the community's laundress in Cairo. During an outbreak of plague she apprenticed herself to several resident French doctors and declared she had discovered her true vocation. She then apprenticed medicine in an Egyptian military hospital. In May 1836 she bore a child, but it died within the month. She then left Cairo for France and returned to Paris nearly penniless.

By her own account, Suzanne earned a diploma in midwifery from the Paris Faculty of Medicine in November 1837 and returned to the study of homeopathic medicine. As a midwife she supported her aged father as well as herself and attempted to found an association to aid unwed mothers. In 1839 she went to Russia, to seek her fortune by earning enough money to become economically independent, but the Russian climate inflicted severe stress on her health. She returned to Paris in 1846, reestablished her midwifery practice, and engaged in various unsuccessful but pioneering attempts to found institutions that would expedite the hiring of wet nurses, aid midwives, and so on.

After the collapse of the Revolution in 1848, she left France for Louisiana with her father and niece to nurse her mortally ill sister Adrienne. She remained there until 1859, but no record of these years has come down to us.

In 1866 Suzanne published her *Souvenirs*. These autobiographical writings cover her life up to her 1839 departure for Russia. She then consolidated the letters she had written to her sister from Russia with the notion of keeping them safe "until women have their own archives." These letters miraculously survived and found their way to the Bibliothèque Marguerite Durand; they were published as *Mémoires* in 1979. Suzanne's later years were plagued by ill health and she reportedly died in a convalescent home outside Paris.

Suzanne Voilquin's contribution to literature and history lies in her distinctive contribution to women's journalism and in her two published volumes, the *Souvenirs* and the *Mémoires*. These published writings provide exceptional records of the adventurous life of a gifted and articulate working-class Frenchwoman, blessed with a keen sense of womanly dignity and a heightened consciousness of the injustice of women's lot in nineteenth-century French society.

Works

Ed., *La femme libre* (also published under the titles, *La Femme de l'avenir*, *La Femme nouvelle*, *Tribune des femmes*, *L'Apostolat des femmes*, 1832–1833). Préface de Suzanne à Claire Demar, *Ma Loi d'avenir* (1834; rpt. 1976). Two articles in *La Providence*, August and October 1838 [concerning Suzanne's project for an association to aid unwed mothers]. *Souvenirs d'une fille du peuple, ou la Saint-Simonienne en Egypte, 1834 à 1836* (1866; rpt. 1978, with introduction by Lydia Elhadad). *Mémoires d'une Saint-Simonienne en Russie, 1839–1846*, présenté et annoté par Maïté Albistur and Daniel Armogathe (1979).

Translations: Excerpt from *Souvenirs d'une fille du peuple* in *Victorian Women: A Documentary Account of Women's Lives in Nineteenth-Century En-*gland, France, and the United States* (1981), from an unpublished annotated translation of the *Souvenirs* by Elizabeth C. Altman.

Karen Offen

Henny de Vreede
1936–

a.k.a. Mischa de Vreede
Born September 17, 1936, Batavia (present-day Djakarta)
Genre(s): poetry, novel, children's literature
Language(s): Dutch

Born in the former Dutch East Indies of missionary parents, Mischa de Vreede came to the Netherlands in 1946 after spending four years of her childhood in Japanese internment camps. From a very young age she was determined to become a writer.

Her first collection of poetry, *Met huid en hand* (1959; With Skin and Hand), is a pun on the Dutch expression "met huid en haar" ("haar" means hair) meaning "completely" and was an instant success. One of the poems was awarded the Poetry Prize of the city of Amsterdam. The unpretentious free verse, lacking punctuation and capital letters and deriving its poetic effect from casual alliteration and repetition, was considered refreshing after the elaborate, experimental poetry of the fifties generation in the Netherlands, the so-called "Vijftigers." De Vreede's emphatic "bodily" imagery was, however, directly inspired by the Vijftigers. Her motifs were loneliness, the search for love and affection, and, most prominently, the yearning to merge with the beloved. The melodious "groot slaaplied" ("great cradlesong"), in which the author expressed her desire to return to the unborn state of union with her daughter Catelijne, figures in a great number of anthologies today.

Mischa de Vreede later turned to prose and published various novels chronicling the difficulties and tensions that occur in relationships between men and women. Her main character is invariably a woman, wife and/or mistress, often caught between a desire for security and a desire for freedom and noncommitment. The protagonist tends to identify emancipation with "being candid about sex"—a trait she shares with other heroines of feminist fiction written in the seventies. De Vreede's prose, like her poetry, is unpretentious, fluent, and simple, mimicking the reflections and broodings of the heroine, whose preoccupation with domestic routines and actions is often painstakingly reported.

Onze eeuwige honger (1973; Our Eternal Hunger), advertised on the cover as "a shameless tearjerker," pictures a lonely woman desperately longing for sex and affection. She picks the wrong friend and ends up committing suicide. *13—Een meisjesboek* (1976; 13—A Girls' Book), *Eindelijk mezelf* (1977; Finally Myself), and *Over* (1980) are meant as a trilogy portraying women at different crucial stages in their lives: Lili at thirteen, experiencing sexual awakening; Agaath, at thirty-three, enjoying divorce, men, and freedom, willfully deciding to have the child of her married lover; and the former nude model Margot, at fifty-three, winning back her philandering husband after a life of patience and acceptance. The more polished story "*Van jou hou ik*" (1982; It's You I Love) turned out to be a commercial success. It portrays an adulterous young woman whose husband, a tabloid journalist, is interested more in other people's sex lives than in his own. At the end the heroine decides to record her "confession" on tape to be sure to get through to him, only to find out later that she mistakenly erased one of his interviews instead of registering her own words.

In 1983–1984, Mischa de Vreede was writer-in-residence at Ann Arbor, Michigan. Her critical view of American society is expressed in *Persoonlijk* (1986; Personally), a collection of autobiographical sketches and poetry, and in the novel *Bevroren* (1985; Frozen) in which a middle-aged woman tries to cope with her husband's death, the rift with her daughter, and her disillusion with the United States. De Vreede is also a writer of children's books (with a slightly moralizing touch), and she has translated work by Bellow and Kosinsky.

The critical acclaim Mischa de Vreede won for her poetry was never matched later. Frequently attacked for being trendy, boring, and picturing characters that lack depth and substance, her popular feminist fiction has nevertheless earned her a steady readership. Her most compelling and intense writing to date remains, however, *Een hachelijk bestaan* (1974; A Hazardous Existence), an "autobiographic collage" of her experiences as a child in Japanese internment camps and as a twice-divorced young mother of two trying to eke out a living. While some of her novels may date easily, Mischa de Vreede should be credited for the candor with which she writes about herself. It invests her work with a unique sense of authenticity and vulnerability.

Works

Met huid en hand (1959). *Eindeloos* (1961). *Oorlog en liefde* (1963). *Binnen en buiten* (1968). *Onze eeuwige honger* (1973). *Een hachelijk bestaan* (1974). *Eindeloos en verder* (1975; revised edition of *Eindeloos* and *Oorlog en liefde*). *Oude mensen in kinderboeken: een onderzoek naar het beeld van oude mensen in de jeugdliteratuur* (1976). *13—Een meisjesboek* (1976). *Eindelijk mezelf* (1977). *Over* (1980). *Mijn reis* (1981). "*Van jou hou ik*" (1982). *Het leven een film* (1984). *Bevroren* (1985). (As Henny de Vreede) *De afspraak* (1985). *Persoonlijk* (1986).

Ria Vanderauwera

Walladah bint al-Mustakfi
994–1077

Born 994, southern Spain
Died 1077 or 1091
Genre(s): lyric poetry
Language(s): Arabic

The immortality of this poet and patron of writers in Arab-dominated southern Spain has been preserved primarily by the poems of Ibn Zaidūn, one of which (his *qaṣīda in nūn*) the distinguished Spanish authority Emilio García-Gómez has called the most beautiful work of all Hispano-Arabic love poetry. Fragments of this poem appear anonymously in the famous *A Thousand and One Nights*.

Princess Walladah (literally "fecund") was the daughter of the Calif of Cordova, Muhammad III al-Mustakfī, an abusive ruler whose seventeen-month reign ended when he was poisoned in 1025. At age thirty Walladah inherited a fortune and made her home a popular gathering place for fellow writers. She enjoyed great notoriety and was a remarkable woman for her circumstances. The works of her contemporary, the renowned philosopher Ibn Hazam, and those of Ibn Bassām in the following generation, testify to her fame. She was reputed to be exceptionally beautiful, with light skin, blue eyes, and blondish-red hair. Historians report that her character was likewise exceptional—volatile, independent, and marked by extreme passions, as demonstrated by her defying precepts of the *Koran* (such as refusing to wear a veil), by her leaving the harem, by the verses she had embroidered on her robe ("I . . . bestow my kiss on him who craves it"), and by her possibly lesbian friendship with the poetess Muhga.

Walladah's most tender and personal poems are those written in her late thirties, at the beginning of her intriguing and scandalous relationship with Ibn Zaidūn (1003–1071). These verses, using frequent images from nature, constitute a bold and exquisite confession of feminine passion: "I feel a love for you that, if felt by the stars, the sun would not shine." After only a few months, however, she became jealous of her black maid and rejected the poet to form a new alliance with the wealthy and influential vizier Abū 'mir ibn 'Abdūs. Although she never married, eventually she went to live in Ibn 'Abdūs' harem and lived to be quite old.

Walladah's poems are significant for the insights they offer into a writer of remarkable creativity, intelligence, freedom, education, and stature. She was an accomplished poet in her own right; nevertheless, her few extant poems are published almost exclusively in collections of Ibn Zaidūn's works. Likewise, critical analyses of her verses are scant and appear most often in conjunction with his writings.

Lee Arthur Gallo

Maxie Wander
1933–1977

Born 1933, Vienna, Austria
Died 1977, Kleinmachnow/Berlin, East Germany
Genre(s): documentary literature, journal, letters
Language(s): German

Maxie Wander's work played a pivotal role in the development of the new body of women's literature produced in the German Democratic Republic (GDR) in the course of the 1970s. It contributed significantly to, and is itself emblematic of, the growing and, from mid-decade on, increasingly publicly articulated consciousness among GDR women of the ways in which their lives as citizens within a socialist state are shaped by sexual politics as well.

Born 1933 in Vienna, Wander worked as a secretary, photographer, and journalist; she wrote screenplays and short stories. In 1958 she moved to the GDR, where she lived with her husband, the Austrian writer Fred Wander, and their children until her death of cancer in 1977. As a writer, Wander became known primarily for two important documentaries: *Guten Morgen, du Schöne. Protokolle nach Tonband* (1977; Good Morning, My Lovely. Tape-recorded Interviews), a documentary of GDR women's lives from the perspective of the 1970s, and *Tagebücher und Briefe* (1980; Journals and Letters), a record of her own life's journey through illness toward death.

Guten Morgen, du Schöne is a collection of minimally edited autobiographical sketches of seventeen contemporary GDR women. The women interviewed range in age from sixteen to seventy-four; they live a variety of different lifestyles; many are mothers and most work. Unlike previous "documentations" about life in the GDR, these stories are no longer measured by the standards of Socialist Realism; instead they are based on the authenticity of each individual's different and subjectively rendered experience. In its acknowledgement of difference and its insistently subjective definition of "truth," this collection of life stories by women speaking out in their own voices and unafraid to be critical of either their own or their society's shortcomings, marked a turning-point in the history of GDR women's culture. In her foreword "Berührung" (In Touch) Christa Wolf describes *Guten Morgen, du Schöne* as exemplary of the belief in a concrete utopia that is at once a socialist and a feminist ideal; a society in which women and men are striving to live fully as human beings, subjects of a history they are in the process of shaping.

Wander's *Tagebücher und Briefe*, posthumously published and edited by her husband, re-creates the texture of Wander's daily life as a woman and a writer and an Austrian expatriate in the GDR. Divided into three parts, the selections span events from 1968 to 1977. Part I describes her treatment (mastectomy and radiation therapy) for breast cancer in 1976, her fear of pain and death and her struggle to come to terms with a body that has been mutilated. Part II records her engagement, emotionally, intellectually, and politically, with the lives of people around her. The immediacy of Wander's style makes palpable the intimacy of a life shared with family and friends: her unresolved grief over the fatal accident of her young daughter, the continuing balancing act of her marriage, the sustaining quality of her friendship with her colleague Christa Wolf. Part III tells a story of a life lived richly and fully, even as the writer is in the physical process of dying. Wander's writing is marked by an extraordinary degree of self-consciousness, always balanced between her writer's perception that life, in a sense, is a book, and her knowledge that writing itself grows out of the rich and complex materiality of common lives simply lived. This doubled sense of herself as both observer and participant in her own and other's lives blurs the boundary between autobiography and documentary in Wander's texts. As her reflections on death—her own and that of her child—show, living to her means being attentive to the significance of the minutia of everyday life: "Actually every woman is interesting when one has the energy to pay attention to her."

Works

Guten Morgen, du Schöne. Protokolle nach Tonband [Good Morning, My Lovely: Tape-Recorded Interviews] (1977); West German ed.: *Guten Morgen, du Schöne. Frauen in der DDR* (1978). with Fred Wander, *Provenzalische Reise* [Visit to the Provence] (1978). *Tagebücher und Briefe* [Journals and Letters], ed. Fred Wander (1980); West German ed.: *Leben wär' eine prima Alternative: Tagebuchaufzeichnungen und Briefe* [Life Would Be a Great Alternative: Journal Notes and Letters] (1980).

Angelika Bammer

Sylvia Townsend Warner
1893–1978

Born December 6, 1893, Harrow, Middlesex, England
Died May 1, 1978, Maiden Newton, Dorset
Genre(s): novel, short story, letters, poetry
Language(s): English

Warner was the daughter of a schoolmaster at Harrow but was educated privately, first by her mother and then by a governess and tutors. Given free run of her father's library, she read widely on her own and can thus be considered largely self-educated. She originally aspired to a career in music and at one point intended to study composition with Arnold Schönberg, but the intervention of World War I turned her to musicology. As a young woman, she was the only female editor of the monumental *Tudor Church Music* (10 vols., 1925–1930); however, the encouragement of David Garnett and T.F. Powys helped her decide in favor of literature. In a career spanning more than fifty years, she produced poems, novels, short stories, biographies, and translations. For these accomplishments she was elected a fellow of the Royal Society of Literature and an honorary member of the American Academy of Arts and Letters.

From an early age, Warner showed an interest in the supernatural, which is evident in works throughout her career. Her first novel, *Lolly Willowes* (1926), the first book selected by the Book-of-the-Month Club, chronicles the life of a woman who rejects traditional roles and turns to witchcraft. Stories written over many years deal in various ways with supernatural themes, while her novel *The Corner That Held Them* (1948) shows an intimate knowledge of the occult and herbal medicinal lore in its portrayal of life in a fourteenth-century convent. *The Kingdoms of Elfin* (1977) is a collection of *New Yorker* stories, all of which treat the world of elves, fairies, werewolves and other such creatures as ordinary inhabitants of the planet that mortals think of as exclusively their own. Warner never exploits the supernatural for its own sake or for cheap effects. Her interest is primarily in extending the limits of vision or in using the extraordinary as a means of exploring human psychology.

In her novels Warner is less interested in social and political themes than in the interior struggles of her characters. Lolly Willowes chooses witchcraft after a lifetime of searching for a fulfilling alternative to the sterile and boring life that Victorian society permits her; even so, witchcraft is more a symbol of individual freedom than an indictment of social policies. *Mr. Fortune's Maggot* (1927) takes its main character, an innocent missionary, to the tropical island of Fuana where he is sorely tempted by the delights of the pagans he is sent to convert. Far more complex, and often considered Warner's masterpiece, is *The Corner That Held Them*. Its roguish and picaresque central character, Ralph Kello, enters Oby convent during the Black Death, claiming to be a priest, and spends the rest of his life wrestling with the moral consequences and complications of this sin. Others at Oby are similarly torn between worldly temptations and the demands of the church. Complex, detailed, learned, and spirited, this novel has been called a "sustained delight." Similar in theme though Victorian in setting is *The Flint Anchor* (1954), in which John Barnard is moved by experiences as a student to strive for moral perfection only to find that the everyday concerns of business and family life frustrate his lofty ideals. Moreover, idolatry toward his daughter Mary leads to neglect of other family members, each of whom is warped by his tyranny and inability to love. *Summer Will Show* (1936) resembles *The Flint An-*

chor in period, but the struggles of its heroine are for identity and purpose in a male-dominated culture that permits little scope or assertiveness for its women.

Warner is best known and most highly regarded for her short stories, which range broadly over the British cultural scene but focus mainly on the middle classes. The majority of her characters are women. Often written in the "plotless" vein pioneered by Chekhov, her stories range from brief impressionistic sketches to novella-length studies and, like the novels, focus on character and situation, frequently exploring with wit and irony the follies and foibles of ordinary people. A master of technique and storycraft, Warner never settled into a pattern or formula. "The Phoenix" can be construed as a sophisticated joke or as an allegory; "A Garland of Straw" is a disturbing excursion into madness and thwarted love; "The Museum of Cheats" requires only forty pages to satirize the greed and vanity of two and a half centuries; "Winter in the Air" is a realistic portrayal of a woman whose husband has rejected her for another; "The One and the Other" intertwines the "material world with the immaterial" in a tale at once fantastic and realistic.

In all her fiction, Warner is an acute observer of manners, morals, the minutiae of daily existence, and the secret ways of the human heart. Her concern with appearance and reality is humane and liberal; she seldom condemns, preferring to look instead for the secret beneath the surface which enlivens and even ennobles her humblest characters.

She belongs to the broad mainstream of British fiction and has often been compared with Jane Austen and Katherine Mansfield. Her style exhibits clarity, restraint, precision, and simplicity in both poetry and prose. Wit, grace, humor, subtlety, and charm are frequently noted characteristics, but her special quality resides in a precise yet original use of language. She has a genius for metaphor, drawing on art, music, and nature as the sources of her imagery. Although sometimes criticized for writing with more attention to style than substance, Warner is never boring or trite. Readers are required to look carefully, for her effects are often subtle and demand an alert and sensitive audience. These qualities will probably deny her a large following, but critical appreciation of her work is growing and a place for her in twentieth-century letters is assured.

Works

The Espalier (1925). *Lolly Willowes* (1926). *Mr. Fortune's Maggot* (1927). *Time Imported* (1928). *The True Heart* (1929). *Some World Far from Ours* and *Stay, Corydon, Thou Swain* (1929). *Elinor Bar-*

ley (1930). *A Moral Ending and Other Stories* (1931). *Opus 7: A Poem* (1931). *Rainbow* (1932). *The Salutation* (1932). with Valentine Ackland, *Whether a Dove or a Seagull* (1933). *More Joy in Heaven and Other Stories* (1935). *Summer Will Show* (1936). with Graham Greene and James Laver, *Twenty-four Stories* (1939). *Cat's Cradle Book* (1940). *A Garland of Straw: Twenty-Eight Stories* (1943). *Portrait of a Tortoise: Extracted from the Journals of Gilbert White* (1946). *The Museum of Cheats: Stories* (1947). *The Corner That Held Them* (1948). *Somerset* (1949). *Jane Austen: 1775–1817* (1951; rev. ed. 1957). *The Flint Anchor* (1954). *Winter in the Air and Other Stories* (1955). *Boxwood* (1958; rev. ed. 1960). *A Spirit Riser: Short Stories* (1962). *Sketches from Nature* (1963). *Swans on the Autumn River: Stories* (1966). *A Stranger with a Bag and Other Stories* (1966). *T.H. White: A Biography* (1967). *King Dufus and Other Poems* (1968). *The Innocent and the Guilty* (1971). *The Kingdoms of Elfin* (1977). *Scenes from Childhood and Other Stories* (1982). *Letters,* ed. William Maxwell (1983). *Collected Poems,* ed. Claire Harman (1983). *One Thing Leading to Another and Other Stories,* ed. S. Pinney (1984). *Selected Poems,* ed. S. Pinney (1984). *Selected Stories* (1988).

Dean R. Baldwin

Beatrice Potter Webb
1858–1943

Born January 22, 1858, Standish House,
Gloucestershire, England
Died April 30, 1943, Passfield Corner, Hampshire
Genre(s): essays, journalism, history
Language(s): English

Webb, reformer, researcher, and Fabian Socialist, was the seventh of eight daughters born to Richard Potter, a wealthy and cultivated merchant. Although frequent childhood illness limited her formal education, her father encouraged all his daughters to read widely and independently. She had frequent contact with such free-thinking family friends as T.H. Huxley, John Tyndall, and James Martineau and developed a close relationship with Herbert Spencer.

Intensely introspective, Webb grew up haunted by her lack of a meaningful faith and a useful purpose in life. The socialism that finally provided her with alternatives to both religion and profession opposed Spencer's laissez-faire philosophies, but his scientific investigation of social institutions exercised a lasting influence upon her. Her early involvement with the Charity Organisation Society and the Octavia Hill housing projects in London left her dissatisfied that such philanthropic efforts did nothing to reach the roots of poverty. She welcomed the opportunity to investigate working-class labor for Charles Booth's *Inquiry into the Life and Labour of the People of London,* and her essay on "Dock Life in the East End of London" first appeared in *The Nineteenth Century* in 1887. She disguised herself as a seamstress to gather data on the East End tailoring trade later that same year. The articles based on her experiences resulted in her being called to testify before a House of Lords Committee on the Sweating System in 1888. There she made clear her growing conviction that such exploitation was endemic in capitalism itself.

In an effort to develop a more systematic criticism of capitalism, she turned her attention in 1889 to cooperative societies and trade unionism. Research for *The Co-operative Movement in Great Britain* (1891) first introduced her to Sidney Webb, the Fabian Socialist she married, over the objections of friends and family, in 1892. For the next fifty years they formed an intellectual, political, and emotional partnership devoted to furthering Fabian policies of gradual reform, collectivism, and administration by an intellectual elite. Their home at 41 Grosvenor Road became the salon of Fabian thinkers and the workshop for the methodical and meticulously researched studies of social phenomena that were their trademark. Their first joint effort was *The History of Trade Unionism* (1894), followed by *Industrial Democracy* in 1897. In 1894 they used a £10,000 bequest to the Fabian Society to found an institution for the study of political economy that later became the London School of Economics.

In 1905 Webb was appointed to a Royal Commission on the Poor Law, which she induced to sponsor many investigations into the impact of government policies on the poor. Although she was unsuccessful in moving the Commission toward changes that might prevent rather than cure poverty, as outlined in her Minority Report of 1909, she had the satisfaction in later years of seeing many of her recommendations adopted. The Webbs' hopes of organizing an Independent Socialist Party in the years before World War I were disappointed by infighting among those who disagreed with their gradualist and collectivist policies and resented their domineering personalities. A project of more lasting effect was their founding of *The New Statesman* in 1913, dedicated to the furthering of Fabian Socialism and the scientific study of social problems.

During and after the war, Webb served on the McLean Committee on the reform of local government, the Reconstruction Committee, and the War Cabinet Committee on Women in Industry. Her defense of equality in *The Wages of Men and Women—Should They Be Equal?* (1919) suggests a sensitivity to sexual discrimination missing in her attitudes toward female suffrage and protective factory legislation. She was highly successful with the Seaham Harbour constituency that her husband represented in Parliament from 1919 to 1928, promoting a regular series of educational activities for its members and writing a monthly "News Letter to the Women of Seaham." The useful activities of the Half-Circle Club that she organized in London to bring together the wives of other Labour Party M.P.s were somewhat undercut by members' resentment about Webb's often unsubtle attempts to make them more socially presentable. During the twenties she and Sidney published *English Prisons* (1922), *Statutory Authorities* (1922), revised studies of trade unionism and the cooperative movement, and *English Poor Law History* (1927–1929). *The Decay of Capitalist Civilization* (1923) presented their strongest indictment of the economic and moral bankruptcy of the prevailing system, and *A Constitution for the Socialist Commonwealth of Great Britain* (1920) their impracticably utopian alternatives. In 1929 she gave a series of talks for the BBC on their research techniques, which appeared in 1932 as *Methods of Social Study.* Between 1924 and 1926 Webb composed *My Apprenticeship,* her autobiography up to her marriage. Like the diaries it is based upon, this work gives compelling testimony to her own literary gifts. Its projected two-volume sequel, *Our Partnership,* was begun in the late twenties; the only completed volume (1892–1911) appeared after her death in 1948.

In 1929 the Webbs moved from London to Passfield Corner in Hampshire. Sidney chose the title "Baron Passfield" when granted a peerage in 1929, although Webb herself steadfastly refused to share the title with him. Despite their earlier skepticism about Soviet Russia and their continued awareness of its many repressive policies, a visit in 1932 made them "fall in love" with this society that seemed to embody so many of their most cherished ideals: production for use rather than for profit, centralized planning and collective ownership, party support for "the vocation of leadership," an intense spiritual commitment to political ideals. They recorded their views in *Soviet Communism: A New Civilisation* (1935) and remained staunch defenders of Russia to the ends of their lives. Webb resigned from the Executive Committee of the Fabian Society in 1933 and published her farewell address to it in the *Fabian News* for 1941. Before her death from kidney disease in 1943, she had received honorary degrees from the Universities of Manchester, Edinburgh, and Munich and had become the first woman ever elected to the British Academy. After her husband's death in 1947, their ashes were moved to Westminster Abbey.

Webb found her vocation in social science and public service. What struck some observers as arrogance resulted from her confidence in her own vision of the social good and her urgency about making it a reality. She dedicated her life to defining and promoting a society in which economic justice would foster moral and social progress.

Works

Most of her works were written with Sidney Webb: *The Co-operative Movement in Great Britain* (1891). *The History of Trade Unionism* (1894). *Industrial Democracy* (1897). *The Webbs' Australian Diary* (1898). *The Problems of Modern Industry* (1902). *The History of Liquor Licensing in England* (1903). *London Education* (1904). *The Parish and the County* (1906). *The Manor and the Borough* (1908). *Minority Report to the Royal Commission on the Poor Law* (1909). *The State and the Doctor* (1910). *English Poor Law Policy* (1910). *The Prevention of Destitution* (1911). *Grants in Aid* (1911). *The Story of the King's Highway* (1913). *An Appeal to Women* (1917). *The Wages of Men and Women—Should They Be Equal?* (1919). *A Constitution for the Socialist Commonwealth of Great Britain* (1920). *The Consumers Co-operative Movement* (1921). *English Prisons Under Local Government* (1922). *Statutory Authorities for Special Purposes* (1922). *The Decay of Capitalist Civilisation* (1923). *My Apprenticeship* (1926). *English Poor Law History: The Old Poor Law* (1927). *English Poor Law History: The Last Hundred Years* (1929). *Methods of Social Study* (1932). *Soviet Communism: A New Civilisation* (1935). *Soviet Communism: Dictatorship or Democracy?* (1936). *The Truth About Soviet Russia* (1942). *The Constitution of the USSR* (1942). *Our Partnership* (1948). *Diaries, 1912–1924* (1952). *Diaries, 1924–1932* (1956). *American Diary, 1898* (1963). *The Diaries of Beatrice Webb, Vol. I, 1873–1892,* ed. Norman and Jeanne MacKenzie (1982). *The Diaries of Beatrice Webb, Vol. II, 1892–1905,* ed. Norman and Jeanne MacKenzie (1983).

Rosemary Jann

(Gladys) Mary Webb
1881–1927

Born March 25, 1881, Leighton, Shropshire,
England
Died October 8, 1927, St. Leonards-on-Sea, Sussex
Genre(s): novel
Language(s): English

A transitional novelist between Victorianism and Modernism, Webb lived most of her life in her native county of Shropshire, whose nature she apotheosized in her writings. Eldest of six children born to a Welsh schoolmaster and a distant relative of Sir Walter Scott, Webb was educated at home by her governess and lifelong friend, Miss E.M. Lory. Webb also attended a finishing school in Southport, Lancashire, for three years. Upon returning from school, she was expected to supervise the education of her younger siblings. At age twenty, Webb suffered a collapse from Graves' Disease, which left her with a disfiguring goiter. During her long convalescence she devoted herself to writing essays and poems.

From the beginning, nature was Webb's central subject. As her brother recalled: "Her God was Nature." Her first completed work was a collection of nature essays, written between the time of her father's illness and death in 1909 and her marriage in 1912 to Henry Webb, a Shropshire schoolmaster. First published in 1917 as *The Spring of Joy*, these essays, though rather old-fashioned in tone, contain the core of Webb's pantheistic nature mysticism and reveal her precise, minute observation of natural phenomena. They express her faith that health and divine vitality are to be found in "the spiritual ties between man and nature."

At the time of her marriage, Webb received a substantial allowance from her mother. With this, Webb and her husband were able to establish a modest home near Shrewsbury. For several years they worked as market gardeners, an activity that provided more material for her future novels than income. In the spring of 1915, in three weeks' time, Webb wrote her first novel, *The Golden Arrow* (1916). Spasmodic and rapid writing was typical of her manner of composition, and she seldom revised her work.

All six of Webb's novels are love stories; all but one end happily for the lovers. Yet it is nature that seems to be the true hero and heroine of her novels. Webb's nature mysticism acts as a vital, transforming force in her characters' lives. Deborah in *The Golden Arrow* experiences this force in her "apocalypse of love" as a presence "behind light and shadow, under

pain and joy . . . —too intangible for materialization into words, too mighty to be expressed by any name of man's." Prue Sarn in *Precious Bane* (1924) experiences the mystical union as "a most powerful sweetness that had never come to me afore. It was not religious, like the goodness of a text heard at a preaching. It was beyond that." Webb may be described as a "transcendental realist," portraying human characters and the natural world with the vision of a poet and the eye of a naturalist.

Webb's most pantheistic work is her memorable tragic novel, *Gone to Earth* (1917), which also marks an impressive technical advance over her earlier writing. Rebecca West, in her review of this work, declared it the novel of the year and pronounced its author "a genius." Here the landscape and its myriad lives are active presences, taking sides in the drama surrounding Hazel Woodus, a wild and graceful child of nature who "can never adjust herself to the strait orbit of human life." Like Catherine in Emily Brontë's *Wuthering Heights,* Hazel "did not want heaven; she wanted earth and the green ways of earth." The fate of the girl who wants only to "be her own" is determined by the conflict between her two lovers, the cruel sensualist Reddin and the tormented idealist Marston. Hazel, more truly spiritual and attuned to the spirit of nature than the conventionally religious world that condemns her, is literally hounded to death by hunters as she chooses to die with her pet fox rather than sacrifice it to the "death pack." Written in the dark days of World War I, the novel echoes "the keening—wild and universal—of life for the perishing matter that it inhabits."

In 1917 Webb and her husband moved into "Spring Cottage," a small bungalow they had built according to Webb's own design. Her next novel, *The House in Dormer Forest* (1920), takes for its theme the destructive influence of lifeless tradition on the inheritors of an entailed estate. Webb often pits her visionary characters against those whose lives and souls have been stifled by rigid codes of behavior.

The success of *Gone to Earth* had paved the way for greater recognition of Webb's gifts and she began to receive advance royalties for her novels. In 1921, she and her husband moved to London. Though ultimately disappointed in the literary life there, Webb met writers and editors, wrote reviews for the *Bookman* and the *Spectator,* and had several short stories published in the *English Review.* She made the acquaintance of Walter de la Mare, who published three of her poems in his anthology *Come Hither.* In London, she wrote *Seven for a Secret* (1922), for which Thomas Hardy's novels served as model. She asked and received permission from Hardy to dedicate the book to him.

Precious Bane (1924), her last completed work, was the novel Webb and many of her critics considered her best work. Here nature mysticism is offset by dominant Christian symbolism. Set in England at the end of the Napoleonic wars, *Precious Bane is* a first-person retrospective narrative of the life of a "hare-shotten" young woman. Prue Sarn's harelip is viewed as a sign of witchcraft, the "devil's mark," by the highly superstitious villagers. At the end of the novel, an angry mob nearly drowns Prue on a ducking stool, but she is rescued by the ideal man and her ideal lover, the weaver Kester Woodseaves. Webb's knowledge of the dark side of human nature is balanced here by her passionate faith in the healing power of love. Her portrayal of female sexual feeling is surprisingly bold rather than sentimental. As in her other novels, Webb's prose style reaches heights of lyrical intensity, especially in her descriptions of the landscape. *Precious Bane* was awarded the Prix Femina for the best English novel of 1924–1925.

Webb's last novel, *Armour Wherein He Trusted* (1928), remained a fragment and was first published posthumously in a collection of her short stories. Her essays were reissued posthumously, together with some of her poems, as *Poems and the Spring of Joy* (1928), for which Walter de la Mare wrote the introduction, and a final collection of *Fifty-One Poems* was published posthumously in 1946.

Her genius as a novelist remains obscure. Her use of dialect, local traditions, and folklore has led to her being classified as a regional or rural writer by some critics, while others have regarded her as a "hierophant" of the "cult of the primitive." Charles Sanders, who compiled an excellent annotated bibliography on Webb, finds that in spite of her rhapsodic treatment of nature, her novels are essentially modern in their probing of the fear and insecurities of twentieth-century humanity and in their analysis of the "herd instinct" of conventional society.

Works

The Golden Arrow (1916). *The Spring of Joy* (1917; reissued as *Poems and the Spring of Joy*. 1928). *Gone to Earth* (1917). *The House in Dormer Forest* (1920). *Seven for a Secret* (1922). *Precious Bane* (1924). *Armour Wherein He Trusted* (an unfinished novel, together with ten short stories, 1928). *Fifty-One Poems* (1946). *Collected Prose and Poems,* ed. G.M. Coles (1977).

Jean Pearson

Simone Weil
1909–1943

a.k.a. Émile Novis
Born February 3, 1909, Paris
Died August 24, 1943, Ashford, England
Genre(s): political article, poetry, essay, notebook
Language(s): French

Simone Weil published political articles and poems under her own name and "Émile Novis" (an anagram); her major works—essays and fragmentary writings on society and religion—appeared posthumously. A political activist and the author of wide-ranging articles on society and its injustices, Simone Weil's private notebooks also contain some of the most powerful reflections on religious experience written in the twentieth century.

The daughter of cultivated agnostic Jews, Simone Weil was deeply influenced by Alain, her philosophy teacher at the Lycée Henri IV. At the École Normale Supérieure she gained a reputation for her left-wing sympathies. On graduating in 1931, the Ministry of Education posted her as a philosophy teacher to the remote town of Le Puy, where she irritated the authorities by participating in workers' demonstrations. The following year she was moved to Auxerre; the next, to Roanne (see *Leçons de philosophie de Simone Weil,* 1959). In 1934 she took a leave of absence to gain experience as a factory worker. When the Spanish Civil War broke out, she volunteered for noncombat duties. She returned to teaching, but ill health forced her to take further leave. While visiting an Italian church in 1937, an experience of "something" stronger than herself compelled her to kneel for the first time in her life and awoke an interest in Christianity. During the war she lived with her parents in Marseille. Restless to participate in the Allied cause, she devised several plans (e.g., the formation of a group of front-line nurses), none of which was accepted. Meanwhile, she was increasingly drawn to Catholicism and became a close friend of Father Perrin. In 1941 he arranged for her to take part in the grape harvest in the Ardèche, where she met Gustave Thibon. In 1942 she traveled with her parents to New York; from there she went alone to England, where she worked for the Free French forces. Crippled by ill-health, largely owing to self-deprivation, she died in a sanatorium at age thirty-four.

Throughout her life, Simone Weil was profoundly concerned with the relation between the individual and society. Within months of taking up her first teaching post, she became involved in a demonstration for higher wages for quarry workers. Although she was frail and suffered from excruciating headaches, she insisted on going down a mine and working with miners' equipment. In December 1933 she led a demonstration of 3,000 miners through the streets of Saint-Étienne. The following year she did exhausting piece-work in various factories, including Renault, an experience, she claimed, that marked her for life. Meanwhile she was writing articles for left-wing publications on workers' conditions and movements, industrial problems, social oppression, and pacifism. She distrusted the achievements of communism. In "Perspectives" (1933), starting from the premise that a state is not a workers' state if the workers in it are at the complete disposal of a bureaucratic elite, she argues that socialism must discover a closer union between manual and intellectual labor. Non-Stalinist Marxists praised the essay; Trotsky, to whom it was largely addressed, was stirred to write an article in reply. The most important of her early essays, "Réflexions sur les causes de la liberté et de l'oppression sociale" (1934) was not published in her life. It has four parts: a critique of Marxism, an analysis of the nature of political oppression, a theoretical outline of a free society, and a lucid description of society and its ills. L'Enracinement, which she wrote in London in 1943, represents a synthesis of her later ideas. It discusses how to rebuild a just society in France after the liberation. Its axioms are that human rights are subservient to obligations incumbent on individuals and society alike, and that each individual has needs (besoins de l'âme) such as Order, Liberty, Obedience, Responsibility, Rootedness, etc. As a blueprint, these ideas are wildly impracticable; as theses, they merit consideration. Weil argues that an individual cannot realize his potential unless he actively participates in the life of a community rooted in long-standing traditions. (It was for this reason that she admired the twelfth-century Cathars.) Albert Camus, who was responsible for publishing the unfinished manuscript in 1949, was greatly impressed by it.

When Simone Weil died, her manuscripts were collected and edited by friends. Gustave Thibon, to whom she had given twelve of her private notebooks, was the first to compile a collection of pensées from them under the title La Pesanteur et la Grâce. Its publication in 1947 revealed a facet of her personality known previously only to close friends: the opinionated social philosopher was also a mystic dedicated to the annihilation of her ego in order to experience God.

"L'Iliade, ou le poème de la force" (1940–1941) bridges Weil's sociopolitical and religious thought. In her view, the "hero" of the poem is the impersonal "force" that turns a man into a thing and makes a corpse out of him. The greatness of Homer's epic lies in the fact that it does not take sides: it testifies. Her antipathy to Judaism, the Roman Empire, and the Christian Church as an institution stems from her view that each in its way has identified itself with force. In contrast, she admired the Gospels as the summum of Greek thought and as an expression of the antithesis of force: Grace. From 1938 onward, she had repeated experiences that she described as Christ taking possession of her. In her notebooks, she strove to express the meaning that religious experience had for her. In 1942 she wrote a series of letters to Father Perrin explaining her commitment to Christianity as well as her reasons for refusing to be baptized. He published these in Attente de Dieu (1950), the most accessible of her works. Other collections of her often startling reflections on religion are La Conaissance surnaturelle (1950), Intuitions pré-chrétiennes (1951), Lettre à un religieux (1951), La Source grecque (1953), and Pensées sans ordre concernant l'amour de Dieu (1962).

A tension of opposites conditions everything that Simone Weil was and wrote. A philosopher, she was drawn to physical labor. A Jew, she was drawn to Catholicism. A Catholic, she would not be baptized. Suspicious of the growth of individualism and the related loss of collective values, her writings constantly return to her own remarkable personality. The Marxist activist became one of the outstanding religious thinkers of her time, and this, in turn, deepened her sociopolitical ideas. Interest in her work has grown steadily since her death. Perhaps no other figure has written more impressively on both the individual in society and the individual and God.

Works

La Pesanteur et la Grâce (1947). L'Enracinement: Prélude à une déclaration des devoirs envers l'être humain (1949). Attente de Dieu (1950). La Conaissance surnaturelle (1950). Cahiers, 3 vols. (1951–1956; revised edition, 1970–1974). La Condition ouvrière (1951). Intuitions pré-chrétiennes (1951). Lettre à un religieux (1951). La Source grecque (1953). Oppression et Liberté (1955). Venise sauvée, tragédie en trois actes (1955). Écrits de Londres et dernières lettres (1957). Leçons de philosophie de Simone Weil: Roanne 1933–1934, ed. Anne Reynaud (1959). Écrits historiques et politiques (1960). Pensées sans ordre concernant l'amour de Dieu (1962). Sur la Science (1965). Poèmes, suivis de "Venise sauvée," Lettre de Paul Valéry (1968).

Translations: Waiting for God (1951). Gravity and Grace (1952). The Need for Roots (1952). Letter to a Priest (1953). The Notebooks of Simone Weil (1956).

Intimations of Christianity (1957). *Oppression and Liberty* (1958). *Selected Essays, 1934–1943* (1962). *Seventy Letters* (1965). *On Science, Necessity and the Love of God* (1968). *First and Last Notebooks* (1970). *Gateway to God* (1974). *The Simone Weil Reader* (1977). *Lectures on Philosophy* (1978). *Simone Weil: An Anthology* (1986).

Terence Dawson

Fay Weldon
1933–

Born September 22, 1933, Alvechurch,
Worcestershire, England
Genre(s): novel, short story, play, radio and televison drama, scholarship
Language(s): English

"It took me a long time to believe that men were actually human beings," Weldon wrote. Brought up in New Zealand and raised by her mother and sister after her parents' divorce, she attended convent school. In the 1950s she completed her M.A. in economics and psychology at St. Andrews University and was an unmarried mother—"a solitary experience," as she has written. The result of her early life was a unique perspective on the world: "I believed the world was female, whereas men have always believed the world is male. It's unusual for women to suffer from my delusion." Weldon's subject has largely been the generation of women that grew up after World War II; her theme is how these women survive being human.

To read a Weldon novel is to encounter a densely truthful depiction of the claims people make on one another. Each of her novels traces the complex interweavings of human relations and how these inevitably constrain women. *Down among the Women* (1971) follows a group of women of her own "generation" as they variously fight, deny, and fail to transcend the label of "woman." In *Praxis* (1978), the expectations forced on women figure in the fate of Praxis Duveen, in prison for infanticide. *Puffball* (1980) is part supernatural parody, part autobiography—about Liffey, going through a pregnancy separated from the father, who has a full and busy life in London while Liffey comes to term amid witches and hauntings in Somerset. *Female Friends* (1975), one of Weldon's best novels, records how the concatenation of personal failings and male exploitation defeat even the most modest dreams.

Weldon has both claimed and disclaimed the feminist viewpoint. She has written that she belongs to the last pre-feminist generation: women without power, without theory, often aware of their impotence and oppression, often angry, frustrated, and despairing but also trying to make a life of it. Thus the last words of *Down among the Women* are "We are the last of the women." One feels that the last two words might be enclosed in their own quotation marks.

Weldon's best work is less didactic than it is moral; it seeks less to draw a lesson than to depict the truth. Readers have sensed a distance between her fictional practice and the strident moralism that mars other feminist writing. Weldon has acknowledged the strong, even lopsided, moral intention in her fiction. She has admitted that she intentionally rounds out her female characters more fully than her male characters: "I just make [male characters] behave, talk, and I don't add any justification for their behaviour. Whereas my women characters are all explained." Male behavior is so well established that it hardly needs explication; male domination is such an accomplished fact that it hardly needs mention. Fiction becomes a way of "redressing a balance so far tilted as to be all but unworkable."

Though Weldon accords her women a fuller explanation, she does not idealize them. Throughout her fiction and drama there is a refusal to invest women characters with unusual courage, resources, or integrity. Lily of *Remember Me* (1976), Chloe of *Female Friends,* Ruth of *Life and Loves of a She-Devil* (1983)— all are women with failings, all dole out their share of hurt and disappointment, and all contribute to their respective fates. All we have is what happens: the ironies of relationships with men; the successes and failures of friendships between women; the demands of motherhood; the coming to terms with menstruation, pregnancy, the physical aspects of being a woman, the lack of an alternative to male-defined roles; and always, isolation. Weldon's women often end neither better nor wiser than before. In place of great expectations, they have a clearer view of themselves and of their chances for happiness. Indeed, this final clarity verging on optimism rescues Weldon's work from what some readers find is a tragic pessimism relieved only by black humor. Chloe of *Female Friends* searches for some parting wisdom to give the reader, and her conclusions are characteristically concrete: "Take family snaps, unashamed. Dress up for weddings, all weddings. Rejoice at births, all births. For days can be happy—whole futures cannot."

Weldon may be an even better writer for the stage than she is a novelist; much of her best fiction has been adapted from her dramatic works. Her best single piece of writing, "Polaris," has succeeded equally well as drama, radio play, and short story. Dramatic technique often surfaces in the experimental aspects of her fiction: staccato sentences, short paragraphs, jagged alternations between chronologies and points of view. A novel like *Female Friends* may be rendered largely in stage dialogue, exploiting the inherent irony of the dramatic situation. Her best work delivers what good drama delivers: the impression of voiceless objectivity combined with that of an unmistakable voice.

Weldon writes about a sharply delimited, not to say claustrophobic, world, which may lead some readers to the impression of sameness from work to work. In the 1980s and the 1990s, a productive period for this very productive writer, she has sought to widen her scope, with her adaptation of and reflections on Jane Austen (1980 and 1984), her book on Rebecca West (1985), and novels such as *The Hearts and Lives of Men* (1987) and *The Rules of Life* (1987). Of the novels, the former is a mock fairy tale and the latter a vicious satire on religion. *The Shrapnel Academy* (1986) explores a theme that has always been in her work: the obsolescence and brutality of war. In these, as in all of her other writings, Weldon struggles against the sermonizing impulse, the desire to bash the reader over the head with the moral import of the tale. She sometimes gives in to this impulse. On the other hand, she has produced a great number of truly good plays, dramas, and pieces of fiction; she is a much better writer than many better-known writers.

Works

Wife in a Blonde Wig (1966). *The Fat Woman's Tale* (1966). *The Fat Woman's Joke* (1967; in the U.S. as . . . *And the Wife Ran Away* [1968]). *What About Me* (1967). *Dr. De Waldon's Therapy* (1967). *Goodnight, Mrs. Dill* (1967). *The 45th Unmarried Mother* (1967). *Fall of the Goat* (1967). *Ruined Houses* (1968). *Venus Rising* (1968). *The Three Wives of Felix Hall* (1968). *Hippy Hippy Who Cares* (1968). *£ 13038* (1968). *The Loophole* (1969). *Smokescreen* (1969). *Poor Mother* (1970). *Office Party* (1970). *Permanence* (1970). *Upstairs Downstairs* (1971). *On Trial* (1971). *Down among the Women* (1971). *Old Man's Hat* (1972). *A Splinter of Ice* (1972). *Hands* (1972). *The Lament of an Unmarried Father* (1972). *A Nice Rest* (1972). *Time Hurries On*, in *Scene Scripts*, ed. M. Marland (1972). *Spider* (1973). *Comfortable Words* (1973). *Housebreaker* (1973). *Desirous of Change* (1973). *In Memoriam* (1974). *Mr. Fox and Mr. First* (1974). *Words of Advice* (1974). *The Doctor's Wife* (1975). *Poor Baby* (1975). *Friends* (1975). *Female Friends* (1975). *The Terrible Tale of*

Timothy Bagshott (1975). *Aunt Tatty* (1975; from the story by E. Bowen). *Moving House* (1976). *Remember Me* (1976). *Words of Advice* (1977; in the U.K. as *Little Sisters*, [1978]). *Act of Rape* (1977). *Married Love* (1977). *Act of Hypocrisy* (1977). *Chickabiddy* (1978). *Mr. Director* (1978). *Polaris* (radio and stage drama, 1978). *Praxis* (1978). *Weekend* (1979). *All the Bells of Paradise* (1979). with P. Anderson and M. Stott, *Simple Steps to Public Life* (1980). *Action Replay* (1980). *Puffball* (1980). *Pride and Prejudice* (1980, from the novel by J. Austen). *Honey Ann* (1980). *Life for Christine* (1980). *Watching Me, Watching You* (television drama, 1980; novel, 1981). *I Love My Love* (radio drama, 1981; stage play, 1984). *After the Prize* (1981). *Woodworm* (1981). *The President's Child* (1982). *Little Mrs. Perkim* (1982, from the story by P. Mortimer). *Redundant! or, The Wife's Revenge* (1983). *Life and Loves of a She-Devil* (novel, 1983; television serial, 1986). *Letters to Alice: On First Reading Jane Austen* (1984). *The Western Women* (1984). *Bright Smiler* (1985). *Rebecca West* (1985). *Polaris and Other Stories* (1985). *Jane Eyre* (drama, from the novel by C. Brontë, 1986). *Face at the Window* (1986). *A Dangerous Kind of Love* (1986). *The Shrapnel Academy* (1986). *The Heart of the Country* (television serial and novel, 1987). *The Hole in the Top of the World* (1987). *The Good Woman of Setzuan* (1987, adapted from Brecht). *Scaling Down* (1987). *The Hearts and Lives of Men* (1987). *The Rules of Life* (1987). *Polaris and Other Stories* (1989). *The Cloning of Joanna May* (1991). *Wives and Husbands* (1991). *So Very English* (1991). *Moon over Minneapolis* (1992). *Darcy's Utopia* (1992). *Affliction* (1995). U.S. ed. *Trouble*, 1993). *Life Force* (1993). *Bram Stoker's "Dracula"* (1994). *Angel, All Innocence and Other Stories* (1995). *Wicked Women: A Collection of Short Stories. Worst Fears* (1996).

John Timpane

Lina Wertmuller
1923–

Born August 14, 1923, Rome, Italy
Genre(s): film drama, novel
Language(s): Italian

Lina Wertmuller is known primarily as a film director, but, she has written the screenplays for her movies as well as stage plays and one novel. She was born with the remarkably full name of Arcangela Felice

Assunta Wertmuller von Elgg Spanol von Braueich, the daughter of Maria Santa Maria and Federico Wertmuller, a successful Roman attorney. Her great-great-grandfather, Baron Erich Wertmuller von Elgg, is said to have fled Zurich for Italy after killing a rival in a duel. By Lina Wertmuller's own account, her father was an autocrat who made domestic life miserable until her mother walked out on him after fifty years of marriage. Yet, he was also quietly anti-Fascist, protecting partisans and harboring a family of Jews in his own home. Lina Wertmuller herself has served on the central committee of the Italian Socialist Party. Her work reflects this socialist orientation and a certain feminism by keeping film audiences alive to the exploitation rampant in the society in which they live. Her writing nevertheless exhibits little programmatic content, and she is often ambivalent enough to outrage both socialists and feminists.

She began her career after studying stage directing in the dramatic academy of Pietro Sciaroff, who, along with Tatiana Pavlova, had introduced Stanislavsky's ideas to Italy. She spent a decade up to the early sixties in a wide variety of theatrical endeavors: acting, writing, directing, stage managing, and puppetry. She founded a short-lived theater of her own, the "Arlecchino," then joined Maria Signorelli's touring puppet theater, doing a repertory of plays adapted from such authors as Franz Kafka (upsetting parents who expected fairy tales). She also worked with director Guido Salvini, director-actor Giorgio De Lullo, and finally Federico Fellini, whom she served as assistant on the movie *8 ½*. Then, with partial backing from Fellini, she wrote and directed her first film, *I Basilischi* (The Lizards) produced in 1963. It portrays the youth of a Southern Italian town in their aimless lethargy which they occasionally punctuate with bursts of empty violence. It is nevertheless a strangely amusing film. It won the "Silver Sail" prize at the Lucarno Festival and a young director's award at Cannes.

In 1965 she wrote and directed her second feature film, *Questa volta, parliamo di uomini* (This Time, Let's Talk About Men, called simply *Let's Talk About Men* in its U.S. release), a group of four vignettes exploring abusive male–female relationships. It presents an array of styles, ranging from an almost farcical theatricality to serious realism and overt surrealism. From the middle sixties on into the seventies, she wrote and directed a number of television musicals. They included *Il Giornalino di Gian Burasco* (1965; Gian Burasco's Diary), *Rita la zanzara* (1966; Rita the Mosquito), and *Non stuzzicate la zanzara* (1967; Don't Sting the Mosquito), all of them starring Rita Pavone. She returned to the stage in 1968, when Franco

Zeffirelli directed her play *Due piu due non fan piu quattro* (Two Plus Two Don't Equal Four Any More) starring Giancarlo Giannini with sets by sculptor-designer Enrico Job, Lina Wertmuller's new husband. She has since worked often with both of these men, the one as lead actor, the other as art director.

In association with Giannini, she established her own production company, Liberty Films. The first result of this new enterprise was the 1972 film, *Mimi metallurgico ferito nell'onore* (Mimi, Metalworker, Wounded in His Honor), which appeared in the United States under the title *The Seduction of Mimi*. This film established both a pattern for Wertmuller and her reputation. Like her subsequent films, it is a story about a "little man." Mimi, played by Giannini, is a Sicilian worker caught up in maintaining his male honor and challenging the authority of the Mafia, only to find himself swallowed up in the "brotherhood." In 1973, her next film appeared: *Film d'amore e d'anarchia* (released as *Love and Anarchy*). It, too, featured Giannini in the main role of Tunin. After seeing Fascists murder his friend, he comes to Rome to have vengeance by assassinating Mussolini. An anarchist prostitute helps him in his plans and he falls in love with another girl in the same brothel. Between the two, his plans go awry, he goes berserk, and the Fascist police beat him to death.

Wertmuller's films now came in rapid succession. In 1974 appeared *Tutto a posto, niente in ordine* (Everything in its Place, Nothing in Order, released as *All Screwed Up*) about Southern Italian workers who live in a commune in Milan as they become swallowed up in a bourgeois society of conspicuous consumption. In that same year another film appeared: *Travolti da un insolito destino nell'azzuro mare d'agosto* (Swept Away by an Unusual Fate upon an Azure August Sea, released simply as *Swept Away*) dealing with a curious reversal of social and sexual roles between a female ship passenger and a male deck hand once they find themselves shipwrecked and alone. Then in 1975 came *Pasqualino settebellezze* (Pasqualino Seven-Beauties, released as *Seven Beauties*). This was a considerable success, although highly controversial. It deals with prostitution in the fullest sense of the word: Pasqualino is a macho Neopolitan who has defended his seven ugly sisters against other macho types, but then goes to war, deserts the Fascist army, lands in a Nazi war camp, and ends up corrupted by the female prison commandant. He is finally welcomed back to Naples by his seven sisters, all of them now whores.

On the strength of these films, Warner Brothers signed Wertmuller to a contract which obligated her to produce four English language films. The first and only product of this agreement was *The End of the World in Our Usual Bed in a Night Full of Rain* (1978), the story of the marriage of a macho Italian Communist journalist (Giancarlo Giannini) and an American feminist photographer (Candice Bergen). It was generally regarded as a failure, enough so at the box office that Warner cancelled its contract.

In the next year, 1979, Wertmuller directed her own stage play, *Amore e magia nella cucina di mama* (Love and Magic in Mama's Kitchen) which she had begun in 1970 at the urging of Franco Zeffirelli. The play is based on the sensational 1945 trial of Leonarda Cianciuli, who had become unbalanced after the deaths of her twelve chidden at birth, murdered her best friends, and turned them into soap and candle wax, all in the fervent belief they would reappear reincarnated, more beautiful and more perfect than before. The play opened at the festival of Two Worlds in Spoleto, with scenery by Enrico Job. It played in Rome and was scheduled to open at Cafe La Mama in New York in April 1980. It was cancelled shortly before its announced appearance. Her next film appeared the same year, featuring Giannini, Marcello Mastroianni, and Sofia Loren, a love triangle with the Mafia and Fascists on the periphery, all under the grand title, *Fatto di sangue fra due uomini a causa di una vedova. Si sospettano moventi politici* (Blood Feud Between Two Men Over a Widow. Political Motives Are Suspected, released in the United States as *Revenge* and in England as *Blood Feud*).

Wertmuller has continued to produce films. They include the 1983 *Scherzo di destino in aqquato dietro un'agolo come un brigante di strada* (A Twist of Fate Waiting in Ambush Around the Corner Like a Street Thief), about a government bureaucrat trapped in his bulletproof, overdone limousine; *Sotto sotto* (1984; Softly, Softly), a marital farce satirizing the Catholic Church, sexual hangups, macho posturing, and the institution of marriage. Then, in 1986, two films appeared: *Un complicato intrigo di donne, vicoli e delitti* (A Complicated Intrigue of Women, Alleys and Crimes, released as *Camorra*), about a group of women taking on Naples' drug dealers and gangsters, and *Notte d'estate con profilo greco, occhi a mandorla e odore di basilico* (Summer Night with Greek Profile, Almond-shaped Eyes and Scent of Basil) presenting the sexual fireworks that erupt when a wealthy, lusty woman kidnaps a political terrorist. Beyond these releases, she has also produced a novel, *La Testa di Alvise* (1981; published in English in 1982 as *The Head of Alvise*). It tells the story of Sammy Silverman's lifelong bitter hatred for Alvise Ottolenghi Portaleoni inspired by his awful sense of inferiority that began in

their boyhood when the Italian Jew saved the American Jew in a mad flight from Treblinka to Spain and on to New York. It ends now, forty years later, when the rich hack writer Sammy meets Nobel Prize author Alvise and thinks he kills him in a mad dance likened to Salome's over the head of John the Baptist.

Her work, taken generally, has addressed the difficulties people encounter trying to live together against the odds of sexual and political entanglements that undercut integrity and purpose in human life. In an angular, nervous, and staccato style, she portrays life as a grotesque comedy.

Works

Films: *I Basilischi* (1963). *Questa volta, parliamo di uomini* (1965). *Mimi metallurgico ferito nell'onore* (1972). *Film d'amore e d'anarchia* (1973). *Tutto a posto, niente in ordine* (1974). *Travolti da un insolito destino nell'azzurro mare d'agosto* (1974). *Pasqualino settebellezze* (1975). *The End of the World in Our Usual Bed in a Night Full of Rain* (1978). *Fatto di sangue fra due uomini a causa di una vedova. Si sospettano moventi politici* (1979). *Scherzo di destino in aqquato dietro un'agolo come un brigante di strada* (1983). *Sotto sotto* (1984). *Un complicato intrigo di donne, vicoli, e delitti* (1986). *Notte d'estate con profilo grecco, occhi a mandorla, e odore di basilico* (1986).

Published screenplays: *The Screenplays of Lina Wertmuller*, tr. John Simon (1977; includes *The Seduction of Mimi*, *Love and Anarchy*, *Swept Away*, and *Seven Beauties*).

Stage plays: *Due piu due non fan piu quattro* (1968). *Amore e magia nella cucina di mama* (1979).

Novel: *La testa di Alvise* (1981).

Stanley Longman

Rebecca West
1892–1983

a.k.a. Cicily Isabel Fairfield, Corinne Andrews
Born December 25, 1892, London
Died March 15, 1983, London
Genre(s): novel, journalism, biography, history, literary criticism
Language(s): English

By voicing her ideas memorably in prose that could be raucous, elegant, and precise and by remaining an active writer for more than seventy years, West earned for herself a unique position in twentieth-century British letters. Working as a novelist, literary and political journalist, biographer, historian, and commentator on the morality of her time, West repeatedly demonstrated a brilliant fusion of rational analysis and spirited engagement.

Throughout her career, she published under the pseudonym "Rebecca West," chosen for Henrik Ibsen's defiant character in *Rosmersholm,* and she proclaimed herself a radical feminist not only in her political essays but also in her fictional characters and plots, in her biography of St. Augustine, in her historical analyses, and in her literary criticism. Her imaginative grasp of abstract theories—whether Hegel's dialectic or Jung's unconscious or the Manichean myth of good and evil—enabled her to create characters and narrative structures embodying those concepts she believed essential to understanding twentieth-century history. That she could command a forceful rhetoric to connect disparate concepts and events is evident in *Black Lamb and Grey Falcon* (1941) as she wryly comments on d'Annunzio's seizure of Fiume: "All this is embittering history for a woman to contemplate. I will believe that the battle of feminism is over, and that the female has reached a position of equality with the male, when I hear that a country has allowed itself to be turned upside-down and led to the brink of war by its passion for a totally bald woman writer." Her satire of individual or cultural imbecility combined ruthlessness and wit.

As a literary critic, West praised the achievements and deplored the inadequacies of her fellow authors. Her literary judgment in *Henry James* (1916) is both irreverent and astute, for, without idolizing the master of psychological insights, she acknowledges his class-conscious aversion to vulgarity and his limited imaginative grasp of women's characters; hers is the first feminist study of James's fiction. She admired James Joyce's "Marion Bloom, the great mother who . . . lies in a bed yeasty with her warmth and her sweat," and she compared Molly's monologue to the "unified beauty" of Beethoven's Fifth Symphony, but she also noted that Joyce "pushes his pen about noisily and aimlessly as if it were a carpet-sweeper, whose technique is a tin can tied to the tail of the dog of his genius." West wrote a sensitive, appreciative sketch of D.H. Lawrence but brazenly called his genius eccentric.

As a fiction writer, she chose to adopt a different pattern with each book, but she always created characters in conflict, wrestling with ideas that symbolize real forces in history. Her most radical fiction was a short story, "Indissoluble Marriage," published in the first issue (June 1914) of *Blast* (and reprinted in 1982 in *The Young Rebecca).* In it, West draws upon Jungian symbolism to explore the sexual politics of a marriage. The dramatic tale, narrated by an unsympathetic husband, depicts his wife's powerful sensuality, evident in her body and her voice, and her self-determined spirit, evident in her advocacy of woman's suffrage. She is indestructible; he nearly drowns. West, affirming the power of female sexuality, undermines the aggressive, misogynist assumptions of Vorticist and Futurist theory.

Her two novels about World War I are unequal in literary quality. *The Return of the Soldier* (1918) imaginatively fleshes out a Freudian interpretation of neurosis, in this case shell shock induced by war. The fictional love triangle contrasts the natural, passionate, lusty, erotic drives with the repressive, materialistic and tyrannical, death-loving drives, both competing for the psyche of the soldier. The shell-shocked soldier, suffering amnesia, remembers only his prewar lover, a common woman whom his family would never have accepted into their class; he has forgotten his family obligations, his proper, cold wife, and his dutiful participation in the war. West in her exposition of the story links war's aggression with society's class consciousness, both exemplary of patriarchal tyranny over the individual. Prompted by the memory of his young son who had died, the soldier regains his memory and returns to his wife and to the war. By contrast with this brilliant fiction, her anonymous fictional memoir, *War Nurse: The True Story of a Woman Who Lived, Loved and Suffered on the Western Front* (1930), ostensibly written by "Corinne Andrews," seems an attempt to earn easy money quickly by competing with the war novels and films of the time.

The Judge (1922) explores the familial triangle of an independent, self-determined woman, her weakling husband, and his domineering, tyrannical mother. The power struggle between daughter-in-law and mother-in-law reveals aspects of West's rebellion against and respect for her own mother. *Harriet Hume: A London Fantasy* (1929) oddly combines a moral parable with a romantic comedy in an episodic plot that turns on the artistic heroine's ability to read the thoughts of her beloved, an ambitious politician. At the end, the lovers unite, as if two halves of a personality are finally reconciled.

Of the four short novels published under the title *The Harsh Voice* (1935), the most impressive creates a memorable character, Alice Pemberton, who is "the Salt of the Earth." Alice carefully controls her life, repressing her own and her husband's desires, smothering her family's love for her, and expecting incompetence, carelessness, and inconsiderateness from all around her. As she rubs salt into wounds, she believes herself to be acting sensibly and selflessly in the best interests of her victim. The husband's decision to poison Alice provides a satisfying fictional conclusion.

A partial definition of the happy marriage between female and male power occurs in *The Thinking Reed* (1936) in a dialogue where each spouse admits admiring the other as superior. Isabella, the rational heroine, widowed at the beginning of the novel, rejects an aristocratic French lover because he is a tyrant (she compares him to the Arc de Triomphe, embodying male patriotic glory), then marries a kind-hearted, intuitive Frenchman who has peasant ancestors but who now owns profitable automobile factories. He can behave like an ass, and she can behave like a maenad, but together they are morally superior to both the imbecilic ruling class and the envious, mean-spirited politicians. She saves her husband's career from disaster, but her action destroys their unborn child; Isabella and her husband heal their estrangement, but West clearly signals the loss of their wealth in the stock market crash.

During World War II, West published a short, propagandistic novel, *The Second Commandment* (1942), depicting the courage of a Danish actress during the Nazi occupation of Copenhagen, but her next major novel was not published until 1956: *The Fountain Overflows*. West's childhood is partially represented in this fictional account of a poor, intellectual family of three sisters, one brother, and a mother who manages their affairs despite periodic financial reversals caused by their impractically idealistic journalist father. Their overflowing love for each other gives them the strength not only to suffer genteel poverty but to offer shelter and support to others.

In *The Birds Fall Down* (1966), West creates a fiction about expatriate Russians before the 1917 Revolution, pairing a young woman, daughter of an English aristocrat and a Russian emigré, with a double agent for the Czar and the Revolutionaries. Each character is formed by two antithetical forces at work within: political forces for the double agent, cultural forces for the young woman. The death of the young woman's czarist grandfather provides the crisis that brings these two characters in contact. The double agent passionately explains to the Russian–English woman Hegel's "theory of the dialectic," combining thesis and contradictory antithesis into a new synthesis, so that the reader realizes, as the young woman does not, that he loves her. In her eyes, the double agent threatens her life, and she arranges for his assassination.

West's fascination with the mind divided against itself, with the formation of nationalist loyalty and the betrayal of that loyalty, may also be seen in her collected essays on the Nuremburg trials, on the trial of a British Fascist, on the Profumo affair, and on other "sordid and undignified" crimes: *The Meaning of Treason* (1947) and *The New Meaning of Treason* (1964).

The most famous of West's books is her *Black Lamb and Grey Falcon* (1941), a two-volume narrative of her travels in Yugoslavia in the spring of 1937. She mixes travelogue, history, fiction, autobiography, and political analysis in a compelling, entertaining, informative work explaining the cultural differences among the Slavic peoples, narrating a history of violent insurrection against tyranny exposing the origins of a passionate, cruel nationalism. She wrote down her evaluations of Yugoslavian, Austrian, and German motives, "convinced of the inevitability of the second Anglo-German war." Of all her works, *Black Lamb and Grey Falcon* best exemplifies her intellectual range, her ability to move and inform, her imaginative grasp of philosophical, political, and historical movements, her brilliant rhetorical style, and her self-assured judgment.

Works

Henry James (1916). *The Return of the Soldier* (1918). *The Judge* (1922). *The Strange Necessity* (1928). *Harriet Hume: A London Fantasy* (1929). *War Nurse: The True Story of a Woman Who Lived, Loved and Suffered on the Western Front* (Anon., as by "Corinne Andrews," 1930). *D.H. Lawrence: An Elegy* (1930). *A Letter to a Grandfather* (1930). *Ending in Earnest: A Literary Log* (1931). *St. Augustine* (1933). *The Harsh Voice: Four Short Novels* (1935). *The Thinking Reed* (1936). *Black Lamb and Grey Falcon: A Journey through Yugoslavia* (1941). *The Second Commandment* (1942). *The Meaning of Treason* (1947). *A Train of Powder* (1955). *The Fountain Overflows* (1956). *The Court and the Castle* (1957). *The New Meaning of Treason* (1964; English ed., *The Meaning of Treason, rev. ed.,* 1965). *The Birds Fall Down* (1966). *1900* (1981). *The Young Rebecca: Writings of Rebecca West, 1911–1917*, ed. J. Marcus (1982). *This Real Night* (1985). *Sunflower* (1986). *Family Memories,* ed. F. Evans (1987).

Judith L. Johnston

Christa Winsloe
1888–1944

Born December 23, 1888, Darmstadt, Germany
Died June 6 (or 10), 1944, Cluny, France
Genre(s): narrative prose, film script
Language(s): German

Winsloe fashioned her life against the grain of the expectations from her family and her society and created a body of fiction that portrays the difficulties felt by a woman who does not wish to conform.

The daughter of a German army officer, Christa Winsloe was educated at a strict girls' school in Potsdam and then sent to a finishing school in Switzerland. She had been educated to become an officer's wife; instead, she went to Schwabing, an area of Munich where many artists lived and pursued a career as a sculptress. Viewed as a dilettante, she achieved little success.

In 1913, she did indeed marry into the station expected of her. Her husband was the Hungarian Baron Ludwig Hatvany, who had made his fortune in sugar cane. At this time, Winsloe wrote a novel, *Das schwarze Schaf* (The Black Sheep), which she never published, perhaps because it mirrored her life too closely. It concerned a girl who is an outsider at school and in the art world where she seeks a career, but who discovers an entrance to the realm of acceptance through marriage to the right man.

Her real life took a different turn, however. Due to her husband's numerous affairs, Winsloe left him and returned to Munich where she pursued anew her artistic ambitions, this time sculpting only figures of animals. She also began to write for publication and soon contributed articles on cultural events to the Munich newspapers and to the prestigious *Querschnitt*, a journal of the arts. With her novella, *Männer kehren heim* (date unknown; Men Return Home), Winsloe began to voice the concern that would occupy the rest of her fiction, namely the question of sexual identity within a society stratified according to gender roles. During World War I, a girl is attacked by several soldiers, and, to avoid future degradations, she wears her brother's clothes for the rest of the war.

In 1930 Winsloe created the work that made her name as a writer. In that year, her drama *Ritter Nérestan* (Knight Nérestan) premiered in Leipzig. It was a success but was retitled for its Berlin premiere as *Gestern und heute* (Yesterday and Today). Most well known, however, is the film version, entitled *Mädchen in Uniform* (1931; Girls in Uniform). This work tells of the schoolgirl Manuela von Meinhardis who is forced into the strict confines of a Prussian girls' school. She finds solace and love in her relationship to one of her teachers, Fräulein von Bernburg. After performing the lead male role in the school play, Manuela has too much to drink and openly declares her love for her teacher. The headmistress views such feelings as "sinful" and "morbid" and decides Manuela must leave the school. Unable to face separation from her beloved, Manuela commits suicide. Two conclusions were filmed. In one, Manuela dies, but in the other she is saved by her classmates. This latter version was deemed unacceptable by American censors. The former was for decades the only version shown in the United States.

The success of this work brought Winsloe's career as a sculptress to an end. In 1934, already in exile, she published the novelized version of this story, *Das Mädchen Manuela* (The Child Manuela). Here, too, Manuela commits suicide. The more erotic elements of the relationship between Manuela and Bernburg are downplayed, and Winsloe brings out Manuela's need for maternal love as the source of her attraction. Ultimately, however, all three versions do treat the love between two females extremely sympathetically and with extraordinary verisimilitude.

A turning point in her life seems to have been her love relationship with the American journalist Dorothy Thompson in 1932–1933. Winsloe accompanied Thompson to the United States, where, however, the latter decided she did not want to be part of a long-term lesbian relationship. Winsloe returned to Europe, settling in the south of France. Her novel, *Life Begins* (1935), published only in English, describes a young sculptress who gains the courage to attempt to live openly with the woman she loves. Her last novel, *Passagiere* (1938; Passengers), has lost that confidence. The heroine is on board a ship where no one knows her. She loses her identity, as a woman and as an individual, and achieves her goal of becoming part of the mass of passengers.

In the 1940s, Winsloe wrote several film scripts, including one for the German director G.W. Papst, *Jeunes filles en détresse*, about girls whose parents are divorced. Another, *Aiono* (1943), depicts a Finnish refugee who dresses in male clothing, a similar theme to that in her earlier novella.

Winsloe was active in the antifascist movement in France, even hiding refugees in the home she shared with her lover, the Swiss author Simone Gentet. They were murdered under circumstances that have never been fully explained. The official account attributes their deaths to the hand of a common thief.

Christa Winsloe is best known for her vivid evocation of the cruel repression exercised upon those who could not or would not fit into the narrow bounds drawn by a culture that proscribed behavior according to a strict code of the acceptable and the normal. In her life and her work, she struggled against those rules that denied the validity of any but the voice of the acceptable majority.

Works

Plays: *Ritter Nérestan* (1930). *Gestern und heute* (1930) (English tr., 1933). *Der Schritt hinüber* (1940).

Novels: *Männer kehren heim* (date unknown). *Das Mädchen Manuela* (1934). *Life Begins* (1935; in the U.S., *Girl Alone*, 1936). *Passegiere* (1938).

Film: *Mädchen in Uniform* (1931). *Jeunes filles en détresse*. *Der Schritt hinüber* (1940). *Schicksal nach Wunsch* (1941). *Aiono* (1943).

James W. Jones

Christa Wolf
1929–

Born March 18, 1929, Landsberg/Warthe (now Gorzów, Poland)
Genre(s): novel, short story, essay, film script
Language(s): German

Christa Wolf's prose belongs to the most highly respected literature of the second half of this century. Not only has she won critical acclaim as a novelist, short story writer, and essayist in both Germanies, her work is also widely read and respected in English translation.

From Wolf's earliest years, the political events of her times have directly affected her life and form the bases of her writing. She was four when Hitler became Chancellor, ten when the war began, and sixteen when her family fled their home, the small city of Landsberg, east of the Oder River (now the Eastern border of the GDR), settling in Mecklenburg, an area that became part of the Soviet zone. As a schoolgirl, Wolf participated in Nazi organizations and did not question the only ideology to which she had been exposed. However, after she had completed her *Abitur* (diploma granted when university preparation examinations are passed) in 1949, she became an active member of the SED (the ruling party of the GDR). From 1949–1953, Wolf studied *Germanistik* at the Universities of Jena and Leipzig, where Hans Mayer, renowned scholar of literary history and philosophy,

supervised her *Diplomarbeit*, "Problems of Realism in the Work of Hans Fallada."

In 1953, Wolf moved to East Berlin, which is still her home, and began working as reader for and, then editor of the journal, *Neue Deutsche Literatur*. She was also chief editor of the publishing house Neues Leben (until 1959) and reader for the Mitteldeutschen Verlag (publisher) in Halle (1959–1962). Since 1962, she has written full time, remaining, nevertheless, active in various writers' associations (an official in the writers' union, 1955–1977; member of PEN, GDR; member of the Academy of Arts, GDR), as well as being part of the Central Committee of the SED from 1963 through 1967. Wolf has received numerous, prestigious literary prizes from both Germanies.

Her earliest published work, *Moskaver Novelle* (1961; Moscow Novella), an idyllic German/Russian love story laced with reflections on Fascism and Socialism rightly evoked little literary stir. In contrast, Wolf's first novel, *Der geteilte Himmel Erzählung* (1963; Divided Heaven), a work stimulated by the erection of the Berlin Wall (the story is set in 1961), quickly sold out several printings, was widely translated, and made into a controversial film (1964). The plot is again both a romance and an argument for the values of Socialism. Rita, a pretty and intelligent young woman from a village in the GDR, falls in love with Manfred, a doctoral candidate in chemistry from Berlin (East); she goes to the city to be with him and begin studies to become a teacher. Before the semester starts, Rita finds work in a brigade that builds railroad cars and gets personally involved with the socialist production process; this aspect of the novel reflects Wolf's positive response to the late fifties' *Bitterfelder Weg* behest of Chancellor Ulbricht to intellectuals to participate in the reconstruction efforts of the state (Wolf herself worked in a factory for a time). Such aspects of *Divided Heaven* as long passages about worker relations and Rita's choosing her work brigade over a crass materialistic life with Manfred, who "deserts" to West Germany, reflect the conventions of socialist realism—the doyenne of the genre, Anna Seghers, had considerable influence on Wolf. But the book also shows promise of Wolf's developing individual style, particularly with respect to free-flowing perspective change, passages of remembering, and intense self-reflection and questioning on the part of the heroine. Although the Wall itself is never mentioned, there were sufficient controversial topics touched on (for instance, the integration of ex-Fascists, the weaknesses of the socialist production system) to prevent Wolf from publishing for the next five years. Numerous GDR writers of the time suffered similar fates when they chose to write about the problems of East to

West migration, for instance Uwe Johnson, who had to publish his *Speculations About Jacob* (1959) in the West. Publicly, officially sanctioned sources in the East focused on Wolf's tendency to "inwardness," condemning it as decadent.

The publication of her next major work, *Nachdenken über Christa T.* (1968; The Quest for Christa T.), demonstrated that Wolf had clearly matured into a writer of considerable subtlety and merit. In her fiction, Wolf has tended to work backward through her own biography. *Christa T.*, for example, reaches back to the period in which Wolf herself was a *Gymnasium* (secondary school) student and extends through the mid-sixties. The structure of the first-person narrator's reflections is not chronological, beginning instead with the title character already dead; the perspective and time changes are more complicated than those of earlier works. Christa T., a friend of the narrator, embodies the concept of the individual striving for the right of subjective self-realization within the socialist state. Not the events of her life—study, teaching, marriage, children, death from leukemia—make her unique, but rather Christa T.'s constant refusal to stagnate and abnegate personal responsibility for the quality of her life. Christa's dynamic individualism contrasts with and yet affects the lives she touches, most profoundly that of the self-reflective narrator in her quest to comprehend Christa. In *Christa T.*, Wolf begins to define motifs suggested in *Divided Heaven* but central to this and future work: the question of what had become of the Hitler generation; the difficulty of saying "I" or the endless way to one's self; the possibility for a person (and thereby society) to change; the significance of the inner person; the lessons of history, in particular of the literary history of the nineteenth century; the necessity of remembering.

Following the initially unappreciative critical reception of *Christa T.*, Wolf published a series of conceptually experimental short stories and a collection of important literary-theoretical essays between 1969 and 1974. With these essays, *Lesen und Schreiben* [Reading and Writing], she establishes an analytical basis for her own fiction, one that is grounded in her artistic philosophy that the dimension of self is essential for the presentation of truth in literature. The links between her essays and fiction continue into her most recent writing; through her fiction, her research and theoretical concepts are imbued with life. A central principle of Wolf's writing is that of "subjective authenticity" ("Conversation with Hans Kaufmann," 1974). In a short essay, "Brecht and Others" (1966), she attests to the "determinative" influence this revolutionary author had on her writing; pivotal for her is

Christa Wolf

the concept that a literature that can capture the essence of modern social tensions has the possibility to change that society. By 1983, however, she had distanced herself from Brecht's aesthetic, suggesting that such objective definition as his tends to negate the potential of literature to express "the vital experience of countless subjects" ("Frankfurt Poetic Lectures").

Wolf's continuing concern with understanding what had made Fascism possible is reflected in the major novel, *Kindheitsmuster* (1976; A Model Childhood), which appeared during a time of relative openness in the GDR to the exploration of its Fascist background (see, for example, Hermann Kant's *Der Aufenthalt*). Convinced that individual responsibility is a cornerstone of sociohistorical developments, Wolf, in keeping with her concept of authorial subjective authenticity, chose as the core of the work characters and events closely linked with those of her own family. The actual occurrence is a trip in 1971 made by Wolf, her sixteen-year-old daughter, her husband, and her brother back to her birthplace, Landsberg, now Gorzów, in Poland. British critic, Neal Ascherson, aptly describes *A Model Childhood* as "a complex book of reminiscence and reflection." The complexity stems from the varied, free-flowing shifts in perspective and voice as well as in the chronological levels of the narrative. The events reach back to the Hitler years and involve the central character as a child, Nelly, referred to in the third person, the Wolf persona experiencing the trip and remembering her past, addressed as *du* (the familiar form of "you"), and the ongoing voice of the narrator, actually writing the story in the first person in active search for self-understanding, acutely aware of the necessity of the "candid 'I.'" In an attempt to hinder the falsification of history, the narrator assumes a further moral imperative by interlacing her text with real names and reports of contemporary events from November 1972 through May 1975, the period in which Wolf actually wrote the book. The question posed throughout: "How did we become what we are?" While paying indirect homage to Thomas Mann in certain passages (particularly to his "Mario and the Magician"), Wolf has clearly broken from traditional nineteenth-century narrative strictures; in *A Model Childhood* she adds her own voice to the innovative literary structures of the twentieth century, uniquely reflecting the complexity of contemporary reality.

Included among the theoretical concepts that Wolf has developed in her attempt to find "a new way to write" through "a new way to be in the world" are the reexamination of historical roots, especially those of the nineteenth-century romantics, where she finds the emergence of the intellectual woman in Germany, and the literary realization of the *Subjektwerden des Menschen* (presentation of human beings as subjects of literature rather than objects), while retaining artistic objectivity through epic distancing.

The 1979 novel, *Kein Ort. Nirgends* (1979; No Place on Earth) (the title in German is a play on the word *utopia*, no place), grew, for example, out of Wolf's essayistic considerations of the largely forgotten romantic author, Karoline von Günderode (1780–1806) and Heinrich von Kleist (1777–1811), a writer condemned as decadent in the GDR in line with Georg Lukác's theory of bourgeois writers. Wolf preceded her novel with considerable research reevaluating the subjectivity of the romantics, the women in particular (see her excellent essay, "Der Schatten eines Traumes" [The Shadow of a Dream], introducing her edition of Günderode's works, 1979). In *No Place on Earth*, Wolf concentrates the action into a single afternoon, a fictive encounter of Günderode and Kleist at a tea. Karoline longs to have the right to assume the active role in life reserved for men in her times; Kleist protests the limitations on men's expression of their feelings. Wolf's suggestions for the breaking down of societal role barriers to achieve human wholeness and yet preserves unique female and male voices remind one of those of Virginia Woolf although she read Woolf

only later. Wolf's own experience with the ingrained traditional sex-role prejudices in the GDR enters the narrative in the reiterated question "Who is speaking?" and in her concept of the "relationship and closeness" of writers' problems in the romantic period to those of the present. Additional research into the nineteenth century are evidenced in her republication of Bettina von Arnim's *Die Günderode* with an essay Afterword, "A Letter About Bettina" (1980).

With her recent novel, *Kassandra* (1983; *Cassandra*), Wolf found a plot basis even farther removed from the present—in the prehistorical period of classical myth, a not uncommon setting for writers in the GDR (for example, Irmtraud Morgner, Anna Seghers, Erich Arendt, Peter Hacks). Wolf concentrates on a period building up to the Trojan War that she dubs *Vorkrieg*, that time when war is still preventable. She links her own fears about modern man's moral bankruptcy, self-destructive tendencies, especially with regard to nuclear armament, and her own frustrations as a writer trying to tell the truth, with the fate of Cassandra, cursed to foresee her people's fate but to be considered insane. (Wolf had introduced both "Cassandra" and "pre-war" in *A Model Childhood*.) *Cassandra* begins in the present with the narrator at the ruins of a Mycenean palace, the legendary place of Cassandra's execution after the Greeks had defeated Troy. Without transition Cassandra enters: "With this tale, I approach my own death." Her story unfolds as recollection and reflection in the brief time span between her arrival in the executioner's cart before the palace gates and her beheading at Clytemnestra's order. The "I" is thus distanced into a realm beyond the limitations of actual time or history, yet the text remains intensely personal, the theme of the fatality of the patriarchal power mentality frighteningly current. Wolf calls the work a *roman à clef* and documents its evolution exhaustively in the accompanying *Four Essays*.

The latter 1980s saw a progressively pessimistic view of humankind's future on Wolf's part. Her concern about the destructive tendencies of nations with relation to nature and armament culminated in the short work *Störfall* (1987), an autobiographically based, analytical interpretation of the Chernobyl debacle and the questions it raised about the direction humanity has chosen and the relation and responsibility of the individual to that direction within the context of his or her everyday reality.

Her recent works of fiction, *Sommerstück* (1989; Summer Play) and *Was bleibt* (1990; What Remains), constitute reworkings of earlier manuscripts. Typically, each has as its structuring center a reflective woman.

Sommerstück, based on Wolf's own experiences between 1975 and 1983, when she wrote the original version, takes place in the Mecklenburg country home of the principal character, where close friends come, go, and interact. Wolf has called it "my most personal book," dealing with the intensely introspective theme through multi-perspective, third-person narrative and affirming personal bonds, reminiscent of Chekhov, and the bond with her *Heimat*. The state ostracism that she and other intellectuals were subjected to as a result of their protesting Wolf Biermann's expulsion (1976) from the GDR is not dealt with here. In contrast, *Was bleibt*, first written in 1979 (i.e., closer to the time Wolf was expelled from the executive committee of the Berlin Writers' Union as a result of having signed the "open letter" in support of Biermann) is a first-person narrative focusing on one day during the period when she was under surveillance by the State Security Police (Stasi). Both of these works of "association" stood in the center of media controversy surrounding Wolf in the months of transition from the Cold War to a unified Germany, *Sommerstück* because it had not been published ten years earlier.

Wolf's response to the events leading to the disappearance of the GDR as a political reality can be found in a collection of her texts written between November 1988 and March 3, 1990, and published as *Christa Wolf im Dialog: Aktuelle Texte* (1990; Current Texts). These speeches, interviews, and letters document a painful death of illusions and hope for a German socialist state. As in her other works, which question both past and present in relation to the future, Wolf continues to question, but the verb "become" ("Wie sind wir so geworden . . . ?"), which had characterized her *oeuvre*, has been replaced with a query about what of all that, which has *become*, has the possibility to *endure* ("Was wird wohl bleiben?"). The failures of the first generation of GDR idealists in dealing with their own history and their resultant failure to guide the second generation, the children of the 1950s and 1960s, to political responsibility is a dominant theme: "But the children of the parents, who were not able to establish real relationships with them, are now the young people who are leaving" (p. 154). Wolf herself left the Socialist Union Party (Communist) in the latter part of 1989. As a writer, the concepts of hope and utopia continue to occupy her and, reflecting on her own writing of the later 1980s, she sees both deriving ultimately from "everyday life" rather than "theory" (162). The constant in Wolf's thinking is the necessity to analyze the "authenticity" of her own reality and to confront the dominant powers, whatever they be (168).

The ever-growing control and complexity of Wolf's narrative voice combines with her involvement with language use and philosophical development to fix her achievements among those of the outstanding writers in our times. In her search for expression of woman's subjective perspective, she explicitly rejects the historical tradition of subjugating women, in general, and the prevailing male literary standard, in particular. Western feminists, including writers and filmmakers, have long been positively influenced by her work. Wolf herself cites Ingeborg Bachmann and Marie-Luise Fleisser as forerunners of a new art form in which the writer rejects the role of object and finds new forms and the self-confidence in which to express herself as active subject. With her extensive involvement in political life, her world travels, and strong commitment to change without regard to political party, she serves as a model for those concerned with pushing back prevailing limits toward self-realization as writers and as individuals.

Works

Moskauer Novelle (1961). *Der geteilte Himmel Erzählung* (1963). *Nachdenken über Christa T.* (1968). *Lesen und Schreiben. Aufsätze und Betrachtungen* (1972). [With Gerhard Wolf], *Till Eulenspiegel. Erzählung für den Film* (1973). *Unter den Linden. 3 unwahrscheinliche Geschichten* (1974; rev. 1977). *Kindheitsmuster* (1976). *Fortgesetzter Versuch: Aufsätze, Gesprächte, Essays* (1979). *Kein Ort. Nirgends* (1979). *Gesammelte Erzählungen:* "Blickwechsel," "Dienstag, der 27. September," "Juninachmittag," "Unter den Linden," "Neue Lebensansichten eines Katers." "Kleiner Ausflug nach H.," "Selbstversuch. Traktat zu einer Protokoll" (1980). *Lesen und Schreiben. Neue Sammlung* (1980). *Kein Ort. Nirgends/Karoline von Günderode. Der Schatten eines Traumes,* ed. and intro. Christa Wolf (1981). *Kassandra. Erzählung und Frankfurter Poetik-Vorlesungen* (1983). [With Gerhard Wolf], *Ins Ungebundene gehet eine Sehnsucht. Gesprächsraum Romantik. Prosa, Essays* (1985). *Die Dimension des Autors. Essays und Aufsätze, Reden und Gespräche. 1959–1985* (1986). *Störfall. Nachrichten eines Tages* (1987). *Ansprachen. Reden, Briefe, Reflexionen* (1988). *Sommerstück* (1989). *DDR, Journal zur Novemberrevolution: August bis Dezember 1989: vom Ausreisen bis zum Einreißen der Mauer: Chronik* (1989). *Was bleibt* (1990). *Christa Wolf im Dialog. Aktuelle Texte* (1990).

Screenplays: [With Gerhard Wolf], *Der geteilte Himmel* (1964). [With Gerhard Wolf], *Fräulein Schmetterling* (1965–66; never distributed). [With others], *Die Toten bleiben jung*, adaptation of the novel by Anna Seghers (1968). [With Gerhard Wolf], *Till Eulenspiegel. Eine historische Legende nach Motiven des Deutschen Volksbuches* (1975). [With Alfried Nehring], *Selbstversuch*, film for GDR TV (1990).

Translations: *Divided Heaven* [*Der geteilte Himmel*], tr. J. Becker (1965). *The Quest for Christa T.* [*Nachdenken über Christa T.*] (1970). *Reading and Writing: Essays, Sketches, Memories* [*Lesen und Schreiben*], tr. J. Becker (1977). *A Model Childhood* [*Kindheitsmuster*], tr. Molinaro/Rappolt (1980). *No Place on Earth* [*Kein Ort. Nirgends*], tr. J. van Heurck (1982). *Cassandra: A Novel and Four Essays* [*Kassandra und die Frankfurter Poetik-Vorlesungen*], tr. J. van Heurck (1984). *What Remains* [*Was bleibt*] (Farrar, Straus & Giroux, 1991). *A Day's News*, trs. H. Schwarzbauer and Rick Takvorian (1989). *The Author's Dimension: Selected Essays*, trs. Jan Van Heurck and ed. Alexander Stephan (1990).

Sheila Johnson

Elizabeth Wolff-Bekker
1738–1804

Born July 24, 1738, Vlissingen, The Netherlands
Died November 5, 1804, 's Gravenhage
Genre(s): poetry, novel, essay
Language(s): Dutch

Born in 1738 in Vlissingen, as the youngest child in a strict Calvinist merchant family, Elizabeth Bekker studied Latin and theology and early in life developed a talent for literature. After an unsuccessful one-night elopement with the ensign Matthijs Gargon, she had to suffer the censorship of the Calvinist bigots (Dutch: "fijnen") of Vlissingen, one of whom was her brother, whose moral and religious intolerance and hypocrisy she would combat all her life. In 1752, to escape from the unforgiving community of Vlissingen, she married Adriaan Wolff, a fifty-two-year-old widower and minister at Beemster in the province. This "philosophical marriage"—as Wolff called it—lasted 25 years until the death of Reverend Wolff in 1777. Yet, this pragmatic and generally uneventful marriage allowed Elizabeth to bring to fruition her literary potential, and within 15 years of her marriage, she achieved national recognition as one of Holland's most gifted but also most controversial authors. After the death of her husband in 1777, Wolff invited Aagje Deken, with whom she had been acquainted since 1776, to stay at her house. Even though Deken and Wolff initially pursued their literary careers individually, they soon started an intellectual collaboration that would last the rest of their lives. Together these two remarkable women wrote some of the most engaging and commercially successful literature of the Age of Enlightenment in Holland, and their novel *Historie van Mejuffrouw Sara Burgerhart* (1782; The History of Miss Sara Burgerhart) has been called the first modern Dutch novel. In 1787, following the Prussian intervention in the conflict between the Patriotic and the Orangist parties, Wolff and Deken, who sympathized with the patriotic party, went into exile in Trévoux in France and, due to dire financial problems, did not return to Holland until 1797 when they moved to The Hague. Upon their return, they found Holland and the literary tastes of its readers changed. Wolff and Deken could not repeat their former literary triumphs and supported themselves mainly with translations and contributions from admirers and friends. They stayed together until Elizabeth's death on November 5, 1804. Deken died only eight days after the death of her life-long companion.

Wolff's earliest publications, two volumes of poetry entitled *Bespiegelingen over het genoegen* (Reflections on Joy) of 1763 and *Bespiegelingen over den staat der rechtheid* (Reflections on the State of Righteousness) of 1765, betray the influence of Alexander Pope and the philosophical poem in the neo-classical tradition. In 1769 follows *Walcheren*, a mixed epic and pastoral poem, about the region of Holland with the same name. The first really remarkable work by Wolff is the utopian *Holland in het jaar 2440* (Holland in the Year 2440), which was published anonymously in 1770 and which, in epistolary form and satirical tone, deals with the state, education, and the role of women in the Holland of the future. In 1772 Wolff continues her expert satirical attack on contemporary Dutch society with her *Zedenzang aan de Menschenliefde* (Moral Song to Human Love)—a spirited *riposte* to religious fundamentalists who saw the fire of the theatre of Amsterdam, in which several people died, as a sign of divine wrath. The same year she published *De menuet en de dominee's pruik* (The Menuet and the Reverend's Wig)—an amusing mock-epic and satirical narrative about the forced resignation of an elder of a local church who had been observed dancing at the wedding of his daughter. Wolff's didactic and reformist concerns resurface in her *Proeve over de opvoeding, aan de Nederlandsche moeders* (Essay Concerning Education. To the Mothers of Holland), which was published in 1780. The essay is prefaced with an introductory poem by Deken and as such testifies to the gradual development of their unified literary expression. The first real product of Wolff and Deken's collaboration, a three-volume series of poems addressed to the poor of Holland which was entitled *Economische liedjes* (Domestic Songs), appeared in 1781. Yet the lasting fame of this literary team depends on their first novel, *Historie van Mejuffrouw Sara Burgerhart* of 1782. The novel's success was phenomenal (it achieved three editions in four years) and was soon translated into English and French. *The History* is a two-part epistolary novel and, though it betrays the influence of Samuel Richardson and Rousseau, the warning of its title page "Not Translated" (Dutch: "Niet Vertaalt") should be accepted fully. The novel is, indeed, entirely original in its detailed and perceptive portrayal of the Dutch middle class and its values, vices, triumphs, and miseries. The bigots who had caused her so much hurt in her youth and whom she had already denounced vehemently in her previous writings were once again assaulted without pity in *Sara Burgerhart*. Yet the realism of this novel should be understood in terms of its didactic ramifications. As the authors indicate, the book is intended for the instruction and edification of young ladies: "Our main purpose is to prove: That an excess of vivacity, and a resulting desire for entertaining distractions—justified by Fashion and Luxury—often put the best girls in danger of falling into lamentable tragedies which will make them despised in the eyes of such who will never be able to be their equal in probity of heart and moral perfection."

In 1784–1785, Wolff and Deken followed up with *Historie van den heer Willem Leevend* (The History of Mister Willem Leevend), a novel in eight parts, which in its first two parts is as intense and captivating as their first novel but which becomes increasingly philosophical and long winded in the latter part of the novel, as the authors' didactic and speculative bent of mind seems to have overpowered their creative instincts. *Willem Leevend* was not as successful as *Sara Burgerhart* and marked the beginning of the decline of Wolff and Deken's popularity. During the ten years of their exile in Burgundy, they published *The Letters of Abraham Blankaart* (1787), a verse account of their stay in France entitled *Wandelingen door Bourgogne* (1789; Walks in Burgundy), and another epistolary novel, *The History of Miss Cornelia Wildschut* (1793–1796). Yet, none of these works was sufficient to keep alive the popularity of the absent authors with their native audience. Following their return to The Hague in 1797, Wolff and Deken tried to remedy their financial woes, but the recently published *The History of Miss Cornelia Wildschut* did not appeal widely to the reading public, nor did the

Elizabeth Wolff-Bekker

two-volume pseudo-autobiographical *Geschrift eener bejaarde vrouw* (The Writing of an Aged Woman) of 1802 bring them much relief.

Thanks to the outstanding scholarship of P.J. Buijnsters and others in the twentieth century, Wolff and Aagje Deken have gained acceptance, after a century of neglect, as a lasting presence in the history of our literature. Their wit, humor, refinement and progressive approach to such issues as the role of women, education, and religion at a time when women who had literary ambitions in Holland were almost exclusively confined to the role of what is known in Dutch literature as *zedendichtster*, i.e., moral poetess, are a source of continued fascination to the modern reader.

Works

Dyserinck, J. ed., *Brieven van Betje Wolff en Aagje Deken* (1904). Brandt Corstius, J.C., ed., *Lotje Roulin* (1954). Minderaa, P., ed., *De menuet en de dominees pruik* (1772; 1954). de Wolf, H.C., ed., *Proeve over de opvoeding, aan de Nederlandsche moeders* (1780; 1978). Huygens, G.W., ed., *Holland in het jaar 2440* (1780; 1978). Buijnsters, P.J., ed., *Historie van Mejuffrouw Sara Burgerhart*, 2 vols. (1782; 1980). Anthology: Vieu-Kuik, H.J., ed., *Keur uit het werk van Betje Wolff en Aagje Deken* (1969).

Henk Vynckier

Mary Wollstonecraft (Godwin)
1759–1797

Born April 27, 1759, London
Died September 10, 1797, London
Genre(s): tract, translation, review, history, novel
Language(s): English

Mary Wollstonecraft was the second child and first daughter of seven children born to Edward Wollstonecraft, an unsuccessful farmer and brutal, drunken father. In 1775 Wollstonecraft met Fanny Blood, a painter two years older, who became a powerful influence and friend and who later died in childbirth in Mary's arms. *Mary, A Fiction* (1788), Wollstonecraft's only complete novel, depicts Blood's situation and conveys Wollstonecraft's literary and life theme of distrust of marriage.

Wollstonecraft wrote *Thoughts on the Education of Daughters* in 1786 following the failure of a school at Islington that had been established by her, her sister Eliza, and Fanny Blood. In *Thoughts . . .* Wollstonecraft counseled women to seek tranquility through reason and self-discipline; she questioned the underlying purposes of education and concludes: "In a comfortable situation, a cultivated mind is necessary to render a woman contented; and in a miserable one, it is her only consolation."

Following her dismissal as governess to the daughters of Lord and Lady Kingsborough, she became involved in the radical publication *Analytical Review*, edited by Joseph Johnson. Johnson published her *The Cave of Fancy, or Sagesta* (1787) and *The Female Reader* (1789). At Johnson's home she met Thomas Holcroft, Henry Fuseli, William Blake, Anna Laetitia Barbauld, Thomas Paine, and William Godwin, and she wrote translations and reviews revealing her increasing awareness of women's secondary status.

In answer to Edmund Burke, Wollstonecraft wrote *A Vindication of the Rights of Men* (1790), first published anonymously and in her name in a second edition. In this she set herself up as the voice of reason (although she argues emotionally) and spoke out for the rights of the poor, the oppressed, and the degraded of either sex.

A Vindication of the Rights of Women, Wollstonecraft's best-known work, was published in 1792. Wollstonecraft has been called the first major feminist because of this work, in which she discussed all aspects of women's education, status, and position in society and dramatically argues that true freedom necessitates equality of men and women.

Following the uproar caused by this publication,

Wollstonecraft left for Paris, traveling first with the Fuselis, then alone. There she met Gilbert Imlay, observed the French Revolution, conceived her first child (fathered by Imlay), and wrote *An Historical and Moral View of the Origin and Progress of the French Revolution, and the Effect It Has Produced in Europe* (1794). Her daughter Fanny was born May 14, 1795. Imlay's subsequent indifference led to two suicide attempts, the first in May, the second in October. To rid himself of her, Imlay sent Wollstonecraft on a business trip to Scandinavia, resulting in *Letters Written During a Short Residence in Sweden, Norway, and Denmark* (1796).

Her parting from Imlay was softened by the renewal of her acquaintance with William Godwin, then at the height of his fame as a philosopher and writer; they proved to be a match politically, intellectually, and emotionally. Pregnant since December 1796, Wollstonecraft married Godwin March 29, 1797, despite both having been opposed to marriage. While pregnant, she wrote *The Wrongs of Woman* (1798) and led an unconventionally separate marriage.

Wollstonecraft's daughter, Mary Godwin (who married Percy Bysshe Shelley), was born August 30, 1797. On September 10, Wollstonecraft died of septicemia, the result of the placenta remaining in her for several days and becoming gangrenous. Her death, then, reflected her life: the constraints that held her sex won her final struggle.

Works

Female Reader (1787). *The Cave of Fancy: Sagesta* (1787). *Thoughts on the Education of Daughters; with Reflections on Female Conduct, in the More Important Duties of Life* (1787). *Mary, a Fiction* (1788). *Original Stories from Real Life; with Conversations, Calculated to Regulate the Affections, and Form the Mind to Truth and Goodness* (1788). (trans.) *On the Importance of Religious Opinions*, by J. Necker (1789). *The Female Reader; or Miscellaneous-Pieces, in Prose and Verse; Selected from the Best Writers, and Disposed Under Proper Heads; for the Improvement of Young Women* (1789). *A Vindication of the Rights of Men, in a Letter to the Right Honourable Edmund Burke* (1790). (trans.) *Young Grandison*, by Mme. de Cambon (1790). (trans.) *Elements of Morality for the Use of Children*, by C.G. Salzmann (1790). *A Vindication of the Rights of Women with Strictures on Political and Moral Subjects* (1792). *An Historical and Moral View of the Origin and Progress of the French Revolution, and the Effect It Has Produced in Europe* (1794). *Letters Written During a Short Residence in Sweden, Norway, and Denmark*

(1796). *The Wrongs of Woman* (1798). *Posthumous Works of The Author of "A Vindication of the Rights of Women"* (1798). *Mary Wollstonecraft's Original Stories with Five Illustrations by William Blake*, ed. E.V. Lucas (1906). *The Love Letters of Mary Wollstonecraft to Gilbert Imlay, with a Prefatory Memoir*, ed. R. Ingpen (1908). *Memoirs of Mary Wollstonecraft*, ed. W.C. Durant (1927). *Four New Letters of Mary Wollstonecraft and Helen Maria Williams*, ed. B.P. Kurtz and C.C. Autrey (1937). *Letters*, ed. F.L. Jones (1944). *Journal*, ed. F.L. Jones (1947). *Godwin and Mary: Letters of William Godwin and Mary Wollstonecraft*, ed. R.M. Wardle. *Maria, or The Wrongs of Woman* (1975; as *The Wrongs of Woman; or Maria* (part of *Posthumous* Works, 1978). *Collected Letters of Mary Wollstonecraft*, ed. R.M. Wardle (1979).

Anne-Marie Ray

Virginia Woolf
1882–1941

Born January 25, 1882, London
Died March 28, 1941, Monk's House, Rodmell
Genre(s): novel, criticism, essay
Language(s): English

Woolf survives as several distinct and familiar voices. Her most public voice during her lifetime, the voice in her book reviews and essays on literature, is calm, witty, rational, candid. The voice in her letters to friends and family is sometimes defensive, sometimes caustic, but nearly always clever, charming, and warm. In her diaries, though, the voice seems stricken cold with terror—dread of potential public and critical rejection of her work and fear of the physical and emotional collapses that recurred throughout her life, finally driving her to suicide. Widely read as all these voices have been, however, Woolf earned her fame with her artist's voice, the voice that speaks in her stories and novels.

From childhood Woolf knew that she would become a novelist. Her heritage certainly suggested a literary career: her father, Sir Leslie Stephen, literary critic, frustrated philosopher, and original editor of the *Dictionary of National Biography*, was married to one of Thackeray's daughters before he married Woolf's mother, and the Stephens' friends included Henry James, George Meredith, Robert Lowell, and Edward Burne-Jones. Woolf has preserved an evocative though

fictionalized version of her family's life in *To the Lighthouse* (1927). Woolf modelled the characters of Mr. and Mrs. Ramsay in this novel so closely on her own late parents' personalities that her sister Vanessa, in reading the novel, felt her mother had been "raised from the dead" and said she was shattered to find herself "face to face with those two again."

As a child in London and in Cornwall, Woolf read voraciously, studied languages, and wrote articles for a weekly family newspaper. When her mother died of influenza in 1895, it was, as Woolf later remarked, "the greatest disaster that could happen," and a few months later Woolf had her first breakdown, hearing voices, avoiding food, and suffering from the physical symptoms of extreme anxiety. Her grief over her mother's loss may have been exacerbated by the sexual fondlings of her half-brother, George Duckworth, which certainly upset her during her adolescence and may have contributed to her lifelong inability to respond sexually to men.

Her father's death marked a change in the children's lives; emerging from under his depressed and inhibiting influence, Woolf and her siblings began "a voyage out" from their eminently Victorian background. Resisting George Duckworth's attempts to introduce them into polite society, they began associating with her brother Thoby's Cambridge friends, the Apostles, a group greatly influenced by the rationalist philosopher G.E. Moore. Clive Bell (later Vanessa's husband), Saxon Sidney-Turner, Lytton Strachey, Desmond MacCarthy, and Leonard Woolf became frequent visitors, first at the Stephens' Gordon Square home and then at the house in Bloomsbury which Woolf and her brother Adrian rented in 1907. Though the group was diminished by Thoby's death in 1906, it later expanded to include John Maynard Keynes, Duncan Grant, Roger Fry, and—more peripherally—Bertrand Russell, E.M. Forster, and T.S. Eliot. The Bloomsbury Group, bound by no particular philosophy or discipline, came to represent a high level of intellectual discourse; an intense interest in current literary, philosophical, historical, and artistic issues; and a commitment to destroying "all barriers of reticence and reserve."

Associated with new ideas, artistic experimentation, homosexuality, and a certain degree of class snobbery, Bloomsbury was a controversial but nevertheless fertile atmosphere for Woolf's writing. In 1907, during that autumn when Bloomsbury began meeting in Fitzroy Square, Woolf started *Melymbrosia*, which was to become her first novel, *The Voyage Out*, accepted for publication in 1913 after extensive revisions. The six years of labor indicate the difficulties that novel writing always presented to Woolf. Her habitual reaction to stress persisted in her professional life: upon completing each of her major novels, she would collapse in more or less serious breakdowns and, after recovering, would pursue less demanding writing projects to build her strength toward the next important novel.

Woolf's most serious breakdown—and her first attempt at suicide—came after her marriage to Leonard Woolf in 1912. Six months after their marriage Woolf's condition deteriorated from severe headaches into the violent ravings that her friends and biographers have called "madness" and she tried to overdose on sleeping pills. One of Leonard Woolf's inspirations was to found and operate the Hogarth Press at their London home. Woolf worked as a reader and typesetter for the press from 1917 until 1937, when she sold her half of the concern to John Lehmann. Woolf's first Hogarth publication, "The Mark on the Wall" (1917), is a miniaturized model of her experiments in fiction. Having no action, it can hardly be called a "story," but at the same time, it is too fanciful to be called an "essay."

It is a highly controlled, brief "stream of consciousness," tracing a narrator's thoughts as she observes a spot on the wall across the room from her chair. When in the end her companion makes a complaint about the world war, remarking in passing that there is a snail on the wall, the narrator reacts only to the dissolution of her reverie and the mention of the snail. The relative unimportance of the war typifies Woolf's characteristic treatment of the world of politics and events. She criticized the "materialist" novelists of the previous generation—Wells, Galsworthy, and Bennett—for focusing too exclusively on externalities of setting, costume, and behavior; her fiction depicts instead her characters' inner realities or that "life" which Woolf calls, in her essay "Modern Fiction" (1925), "a luminous halo, a semi-transparent envelope surrounding us from the beginning of consciousness to the end."

Each of Woolf's novels takes a different approach in depicting that reality through those "moments of being" when her characters become fleetingly conscious of their memories, their emotions, their perceptions, their constantly shifting selves. Her experiments in narrative technique seldom involve a literal "stream of consciousness" but venture instead into forms of free indirect discourse, following the thoughts of various characters from an external point of view and shifting frequently from observing one character's mind to another's. In *Mrs. Dalloway* (1925), the narrator depicts the inner lives of two very different Lon-

doners: Clarissa Dalloway, a lovely, unhappy, successful socialite whom Woolf had originally created in *The Voyage Out,* and Septimus Warren Smith, a mad, miserable, "seedy" man who—the novel's structure suggests—has much more in common with Clarissa than is immediately obvious. Touching upon shared public experiences (for instance, watching a sky-writer over London), Woolf makes transitions among the overtly separate external worlds in the novel.

To the Lighthouse (1927) takes the experiment a step further, ranging among the consciousnesses of many characters but focusing especially on Mr. and Mrs. Ramsay, Woolf's portraits of her parents. The novel explores their modes of thinking: Mr. Ramsay's egocentric, intellectual, self-pitying and ambitious grapplings with philosophy; Mrs. Ramsay's maternal, emotional, manipulative, and affectionate attempts to achieve connections among the members of her extended family circle. We observe them from their own points of view as well as through the eyes of their children and friends, especially Lily Briscoe, an unmarried painter who tries simultaneously to come to terms with the Ramsays' relationship and with the frustrations of being a woman artist.

The novel is rich with symbolic significances, though Woolf herself claimed she couldn't "manage Symbolism except in this vague, generalised way. . . . directly I'm told what a thing means, it becomes hateful to me." Though some early critics, particularly those of the *Scrutiny* school under the influence of F.R. Leavis, condemned Woolf's novels as too ethereal, rarified, and amoral, sympathetic readers have found that her symbolism and narrative structure are not at all vague but rather poetically suggestive.

Woolf's most ambitious and unconventional novel, *The Waves* (1931), is still more poetic than *To the Lighthouse.* Following the internal lives of a group of friends from schooldays to adulthood as they come to terms individually and collectively with one friend's death, the novel alternates articulations of each character's thoughts with passages describing a seascape in meticulous, almost impersonally observed, densely symbolic detail. Inspired by a recurring mental image of a shark's fin emerging from beneath a wave, this novel most graphically explores the darker corners of consciousness that were such a perpetual source of terror, as well as inspiration, for Woolf.

Self-consciously experimental, Woolf is also very emphatically a *woman* writer. In essays and lectures like *A Room of One's Own* (1929) or "Professions for Women" (published posthumously, 1942), Woolf enunciates the difficulties of any woman who wishes to overcome cultural expectations; to throttle the specter of "the Angel in the House" who insists that she maintain charming, unassertive domesticity; and to write. Highly amusing and influential, *A Room* explores the traditional barriers to women artists— from family expectations to educational segregation to self-doubt—and concludes that women can write if they can achieve certain conditions: privacy (represented by their own rooms), independence (represented by a minimum annual income), and an ability to use "the androgynous mind." A crux in Woolf's feminism, the androgynous mind would—like Shakespeare's—draw on both its "masculine" and "feminine" creative powers while writing without any self-consciousness of gender or any sense of grievance against the opposite sex. If a woman writer were to achieve this, she would be free to write her vision of life whole and undistorted, finding "a woman's sentence" and new fictional forms in which to express herself. Whether or not the argument is theoretically consistent, it certainly provides insight into Woolf's view of the uncharted literary ground that she was to explore so courageously and at so high a cost to her emotional equilibrium.

In March 1941, discouraged by the ominous progress of World War II and its implications for her pacifist Jewish husband, dreading the critical reception of her last novel, *Between the Acts,* and faced with yet another emotional collapse, Woolf gave in to her despair and drowned herself in the River Ouse near her home. As an artist, critic, diarist, and literary theoretician, it is unlikely that she could possibly have made a greater contribution than in fact she made to English literature and to women's literature at large.

Works

The Voyage Out (1915). *The Mark on the Wall* (1917). *Kew Gardens* (1919). *Night and Day* (1919). *Monday or Tuesday* (1921). *Jacob's Room* (1922). *Mr. Bennett and Mrs. Brown* (1924). *The Common Reader* (1925). *Mrs. Dalloway* (1925). *To the Lighthouse* (1927). *Orlando: A Biography* (1928). *A Room of One's Own* (1929). *The Waves* (1931). *Letter to a Young Poet* (1932). *The Common Reader: Second Series* (1932). *Flush: A Biography* (1933). *Walter Sickert: A Conversation* (1934). *The Years* (1937). *Three Guineas* (1938). *Roger Fry: A Biography* (1940). *Between the Acts* (1941).

Posthumously published works and collections: *The Death of the Moth and Other Essays* (1942). *A Haunted House and Other Short Stories* (1943). *The Moment and Other Essays* (1947). *The Captain's Death Bed and Other Essays* (1950). *Granite and Rainbow* (1958). *Contemporary Writers* (1965). *Collected Essays* (4 vols., 1966–1967). *Mrs. Dalloway's Party: A Short Story Sequence by Virginia Woolf* (edited by S. McNichol, 1973). *The Waves: The Two Holograph Drafts* (edited by J.W. Graham, 1976). *Freshwater: A Comedy* (edited by L.P. Ruotolo, 1976). *Books and Portraits: Some Further Selections from the Literary and Biographical Writings of Virginia Woolf* (edited by M. Lyon, 1978). "Virginia Woolf's *The Journal of Mistress Joan Martyn*" (edited by S.M. Squier and L. DeSalvo, *TCL,* 1979). *The Complete Shorter Fiction of Virginia Woolf,* ed. S. Dick (1985). *Essays,* ed. A. McNeillie, vol. 1 (1986), vol. 2 (1987).

Letters and diaries: *A Writer's Diary* (edited by L. Woolf, 1953). *Virginia Woolf and Lytton Strachey: Letters* (edited by L. Woolf and J. Strachey, 1956). *The Letters of Virginia Woolf* (edited by N. Nicolson and J. Trautmann, 6 vols., 1975). *The Diary of Virginia Woolf* (edited by A.O. Bell, 1977).

Note: For a complete bibliography of Virginia Woolf's writings, including reviews, see B.J. Kirkpatrick, *A Bibliography of Virginia Woolf* (1980).

Robyn R. Warhol

Dorothy Wordsworth
1771–1855

Born December 25, 1771, Cockermouth
Cumberland, England
Died January 25, 1855, Rydal Mount, England
Genre(s): poem, journalism
Language(s): English

The early loss of both parents bound Wordsworth closely to her brothers John and especially to William. In 1795 Dorothy and William took up residence together at Racedown in Dorset, and two years later they moved to Alfoxden to be near Coleridge at Nether Stowey. After the publication of *William's Lyrical Ballads,* Dorothy and William spent a winter in Germany, after which they settled at Dove Cottage in Grasmere. When William married Mary Hutchinson, Dorothy's longtime and intimate friend, in 1802 Dorothy lived with her brother and his wife, taking an active interest in their domestic life and their children. The last twenty years of Dorothy's life were spent as an invalid, afflicted in both body and mind. She survived William by five years.

Despite her literary gifts, Dorothy never became an author in her own right during her lifetime. Yet family and friends, including some of the finest literary minds of the period, recognized her abilities. In one journal entry, Dorothy speaks of a scene making her "more than half a poet," but elsewhere she insists, "I should detest the idea of setting myself up as an Author." She wrote fewer than twenty poems, only five of which were published during her lifetime, and these were incorporated into her brother William's work, as were short extracts from her journals and letters. And although her *Narrative Concerning George and Sarah Green* was meant to be part of the public record of Grasmere Vale, she refused to have it published. Only her *Recollections of a Tour in Scotland,* although actually published posthumously in 1874, was ever intended for publication.

It is for her journal writing that Dorothy is now praised, especially for the journals kept at Alfoxden (January-May 1798) and Grasmere (May 1800–January 1803); she also kept a journal during her stay in Germany (1798) before her residence at Grasmere. After Grasmere, the intimate record of daily life stops, but Dorothy continues to keep a number of journals about various expeditions: a Scotland tour in 1803; excursions on the banks of Ullswater and up Scawfell Pike in 1805 and 1818, respectively; an 1820 tour of the continent; a second tour of Scotland in 1822; and an 1828 tour of the Isle of Man.

The Alfoxden and Grasmere journals are characterized by a naturalness and spontaneity that seem to bridge the prosaic and poetic details of everyday life with effortlessness and ease. Throughout her writing there is evident what Coleridge described as "her eye watchful in minutest observation of nature" and what De Quincey called her quick and ready "sympathy with either joy or sorrow, with laughter or with tears, with the realities of life or the larger realities of the poets." In her journals, Dorothy tells of making shoes, weeding the garden, copying her brother's poems, packing mattresses, reading Shakespeare, gathering firewood, walking with Coleridge, ironing linen. The poetic and the prosaic, the ready sympathy for the unfortunate, and the keen observation of nature are all brought together in her May 18, 1800, entry. In this representative entry, Dorothy begins by a passing mention of church-going and the weather, moves on to an appreciation of the surrounding valley and mountains with their bare ashes and emerging corn and follows with a tale of a beggar girl turned out of doors overnight by her stepmother.

Dorothy clearly influenced and inspired some of her brother's poetry. She continued her journal at Grasmere "because I shall give Wm Pleasure by it," and he sometimes had her read aloud journal pas-

sages to revive his memory. His poems "I Wandered Lonely as a Cloud," "Beggars," and "Resolution and Independence," among others, all owe a profound debt to Dorothy's prose descriptions. Not only did her journals give William poetic inspiration but her daily attention to the responsibilities of domestic life (as her journal readily attests) freed him to pursue his poetry. Her ready concern in her brother's labors, illnesses, and achievements provided an important source of emotional support, for which he remembers her in *The Prelude:* "She, in the midst of all, preserved me still / A Poet" (Book XI). For Dorothy, in her modesty, it seems to have been enough to have inspired her brother as a poet rather than to have emerged as one herself.

Works

George and Sarah Green: A Narrative (1808, under title *A Narrative Concerning George and Sarah Green of the Parish of Grasmere Addressed to a Friend,* ed. E. de Selincourt, 1936). *Recollections of a Tour in Scotland* (1874). *The Journals of Dorothy Wordsworth* (ed. E. de Selincourt, 1941). *The Early Letters of William and Dorothy Wordsworth* (ed. E. de Selincourt, 1935). *The Letters of William and Dorothy Wordsworth: The Middle Years* (1806–1820) (ed. E. de Selincourt, 1937). *The Letters of William and Dorothy Wordsworth: The Later Years* (1821–1850) (ed. E. de Selincourt, 1939). *The Grasmere Journal* (rev. text ed. J. Wordsworth, 1987).

Eileen Finan

Pauline Frederikke Worm
1825–1883
Born November 29, 1825, Hyllested, Denmark
Died December 13, 1883, Copenhagen
Genre(s): novel, poetry, essay, lecture
Language(s): Danish

As an engaged, concerned teacher and school administrator, Pauline Frederikke Worm played an active role in the educational, cultural, and social debates of her day. Along with Louise Bjørnsen, Mathilde Fibiger, and Athalie Schwartz, Worm was an outspoken critic of the education afforded young women; she also spoke out on feminist and equal rights issues, on the untenable position of Danish governesses and private tutors, on the rising tide of Danish nationalism, and on the Danish resistance to

German and Prussian political and military pressures, particularly evident after the War of 1864 and Denmark's loss of the Holstein-Schleswig Provinces. Pauline Worm has aptly and accurately described herself as a bit of a poet, perhaps a little more of a thinker, and even still more of a Valkyrie.

Pauline Frederikke Worm was born in Hyllested, Denmark, on November 29, 1825. She was the daughter of the parish priest of Kristrup (Randers area) Church, Peter Worm (1788–1865) and his wife, Louise Theodora Petrine Hjort (1800–1881). Pauline Worm received her first schooling from her father, then entered a girls' school in Randers in 1838. In 1841, when she was only just confirmed and barely sixteen years old, Worm became a teacher at the Randers school; she continued teaching in Randers until she accepted a post as private tutor in Præstø in 1847. In Præstø, Worm's significant talents for poetry and creative writing came to the fore, first in a poem in honor of the coronation of Frederik VII (in the nationalist journal, *Fædrelandet*), and in a collection of poems, *En Krands af ni Blade* (1850; A Wreath of Nine Leaves), and, then, in her expansive, engaging *De fornuftige I–II* (1850; The Wise Ones I–II, published 1857). Worm wrote a response to Mathilde Fibiger's stimulating, thought-provoking letters on women's liberation, equal rights, and education: *Tolv Breve af Clara Raphael* (Twelve Letters of Clara Raphael); Worm's response of 1851, *Fire Breve om Clara Raphael til en ung Pige fra hendes Søster* (Four Letters on Clara Raphael to a Young Girl from her Sister) generally supported Fibiger's thoughts on the status of women and the need to prepare for educational reform, but Worm's letters also recognized the importance of marriage and family. Worm's articles in *Fædrelandet*, "Om Kvindens Kald og Kvindens Opdragelse" (On the Calling and Education of Women), provided a more detailed explanation of her views and her concern for improved schooling as the very first goal of the feminist cause. In 1852, Worm received a degree in school administration and began her own school in Randers; from 1857 to 1863, she ran a similar school in Århus, where she was recognized for her fine, just mind, her impracticality, and her overwhelming, sometimes excessive, industry and endeavor. In 1859, Pauline Worm proposed a professional degree program enabling women to work as teachers in public schools; her recommendation was approved by the government, and women were allowed to pursue teaching as a viable, meaningful, rewarding career. In 1863, Worm sold her school and returned home to Randers, where she continued teaching and writing poetry;

she contributed a poem in memory of Frederik VII (1863), several poems for Christian Winter's collection, *Nye Digte af danske Digtere* (1864; New Poems by Danish Poets), and her own collection of poems, *Vaar og Høst* (1864, 2 ed. 1874; Spring and Autumn). Although shy, Worm became a very successful lecturer on feminist, historical, educational, and particularly, Danish nationalist causes. She wrote several articles on women in society and in the work force, and, as a proponent for equal rights for women, Worm joined *Dansk Kvindesamfund* (Society of Danish Women), "discussed . . . the possibility of organizing a university for women" (1875), and, through a written referendum campaign, sought to win support for the improvement of Danish naval defenses (1875–1876). From 1865 to 1868, Worm also engaged in volatile written exchanges with Vilhelm Beck, the leader of the *Indre Mission* (Home Mission); Worm's ideas concerning the Home Mission, inspired by N.F.S. Grundtvig, became the basis for her polemic, *Den indre Mission under Vilhelm Beck. Et Nutids-og Fremtidsbillede* (1868; The Home Mission under Vilhelm Beck. A Current and Future Depiction). Worm also rose to defend Danish independence and integrity and Nordic unity in her poem, "Forandrer Signalerne!" (1872; Change the Signals, *Fædrelandet*); she wrote against the conciliatory words of the Norwegian poet, Bjørnstjerne Bjørnson, who urged peace and reconciliation with Germany. Worm's spirited national defense invoked poetic response from Andreas Munch ("Gjensvar," Response) and from no less a literary giant than Henrik Ibsen ("Nordens Signaler," Nordic Signals). Worm's last work, *En Brevvexling* (1878; A Correspondence), recorded only too clearly the difficulties women encountered in pursuing a literary career. Pauline Worm's efforts and literary accomplishments won her official recognition and honor: together with nine other women writers, Worm received a government bursary in 1883, the year she died, and a Worm endowment fund for young women teachers was established by friends and colleagues. Never married, Worm died in Copenhagen on December 13, 1883.

From a literary and social viewpoint, Pauline Worm's most important work is her lengthy, involved novel, *De fornuftige*. The protagonist of the work, Alvilda, is the intelligent, promising, orphaned daughter of a cabinet official and his wife. As a dependent minor, Alvilda lives first with her aunt, then with a government-appointed official in the War Office, Minister Bigum, and his wife. What mainly concerned Worm in writing *De fornuftige* was the education of young women, and Alvilda became an illustration of the flaws in the Danish educational system: Alvilda enters school with a solid background from her parents, with a large measure of self-respect and concern for duty, hard work, and truth, but the system excludes Alvilda *a priori* from a meaningful and fair role in school and in the larger society, and society hardly values truth, mutual respect, and a meaningful role for each individual. Alvilda looks to art, to a career on the stage, as a means of expressing her inner life. In *De fornuftige*, Worm also describes marriage and family relations in changing social settings: Alvilda's own parents were linked "in a common land-based family structure where work [was the] integral element, where men's and women's work had equal value and equal respect . . . [where] marriage was based on mutual sensitive understanding." In the city, Alvilda meets a more negative marriage and family structure and a dissimilar work pattern, all based on the dependent woman in a marriage of security. In describing the young couple, Alvilda and Viggo of *De fornuftige*, Worm presents still another pattern of filial dedication, mutual respect, shared opinions and values, and innocent regard for personal qualities and attributes. The lively use of satire, the piquant sketches of secondary and central characters, the direct dialogue, and the intriguing dramatic sequences of *De fornuftige* all bring to mind the works of Charles Dickens: Pauline Worm has mastered satire as an artistic medium unlike her women contemporaries. With *De fornuftige*, her essays, lectures, educational and social agenda, and her poetry, Pauline Worm was an admirable, persistent, and active Valkyrie, eagerly promoting a new meaningful, substantive education for young women and a new social respect for their talents, efforts, and work within Danish society.

Works

"Hyldestdigt, Frederik VIIs Tronbestigelse," *Fædrelandet* (1847). *En Krands af ni Blade: Digtsamling* (1850). *De fornuftige I–II* (1850, published 1857). *Fire Breve om Clara Raphael til en ung Pige af hendes Søster* (1851). "Om Kvindens Kald og Kvindens Opdragelse," *Fædrelandet* (1851). *Digte i Christian Winters Nye Digte af danske Digtere* (1864). *Vaar og Høst* (1864; 2 ed., 1874). *Den indre Mission under Vilhelm Beck. Et Nutids-og Fremtidsbillede* (1868). "Forandrer Signalerne!" *Fædrelandet* (1872). *En Brevvexling* (1878).

Lanae Hjortsvang Isaacson

Lady Mary Wroth
ca. 1586–ca. 1653
Born 1586 or 1587, England
Died 1651 or 1653, England
Genre(s): poetry, drama, novel
Language(s): English

Wroth was the eldest daughter of Barbara Gamage, a Welsh heiress, and of Robert Sidney, Earl of Leicester, the younger brother of Sir Philip Sidney and Mary Sidney, Countess of Pembroke. Robert Sidney's letters frequently mention "my daughter Wroth" with particular affection, and he often visited her after her marriage in 1604. In that year Wroth became part of the court and acted in masques, including Ben Jonson's *The Masque of Blackness*. Her poetry was circulated in manuscript and was praised by such contemporary writers as Nathaniel Baxter, Joshua Sylvester, George Chapman, and Ben Jonson, who said that he had become "a better lover and much better Poet" after reading her sonnets. Jonson dedicated *The Alchemist* to her and praised her as "a Sydney" who incorporated the virtues of all the goddesses; in "To Sir Robert Wroth" Jonson praised Wroth's husband and estate much as he had praised her parents in "To Penshurst."

Her extravagant husband died in 1614, leaving the young widow with an infant son and a staggering debt of some £23,000. She undertook to pay off the debt herself and was in financial difficulties throughout the rest of her life. She never remarried, but she bore two illegitimate children to her cousin, William Herbert, third Earl of Pembroke.

Although she wrote a pastoral tragicomedy, *Love's Victorie*, only one of her works was published, *Urania* (1621), an intricate romance patterned on her uncle's *Arcadia*. The first full-length work of fiction by an Englishwoman, its central tale concerns the love of Queen Pamphilia, the image of Constancy, for Amphilanthus ("Lover-of-two"). The female protagonist is condemned to passive suffering more often than active redress, reflecting contemporary gender roles. Love is usually false and the romance has a disillusioned, even cynical, tone; inconstancy appears an almost inevitable male attribute, which is sometimes presented comically: "being a man, it was necessary for him to exceed a woman in all things, so much as inconstancie was found fit for him to excell her in, hee left her for a new." Eventually Pamphilia, like Queen Elizabeth, chose to marry only her kingdom; however, in the unpublished second part, she and Amphilanthus each marry someone else. *Urania* caused a scandal since it supposedly satirized various court intrigues. Wroth apologized and withdrew the book from sale; it has never been reprinted.

In addition to poems scattered through the text in the manner of Sidney's *Arcadia*, a series of 19 songs and 83 sonnets entitled *Pamphilia to Amphilanthus* is appended to the text, presenting the Petrarchan courtly love traditions from a female perspective. Significantly, Wroth wrote in an Elizabethan mode like her father's *Rosis and Lysa* and her uncle's *Astrophil and Stella*. The poems have a melancholy tone; Pamphilia is constant in her love to the faithless Amphilanthus. Much of the imagery is Petrarchan, but the tone of suffering seems from the heart. Pamphilia finally turns from love of Amphilanthus to the love of God. The concluding poem speaks of Venus's praise as proper to "young beeginers"; Pamphilia vows to progress now to "truth, which shall eternall goodnes prove; / enjoying of true joye, the most . . . The endles gaine which never will remove."

Wroth was the first Englishwoman to write a full-length work of prose fiction and the first to write a significant body of secular poetry, but she was castigated for that achievement. Lord Denny admonished her to imitate her "vertuous & learned Aunt, who translated so many godly bookes, & especially the holy Psalms of David" rather than creating "lascivious tales & amarous toyes"; translation, not creation, was the province of a learned woman. Wroth gave a spirited reply to Denny, but she apparently was forced to learn the womanly virtue of silence; if she did write more after she withdrew her *Urania*, it has not survived.

Works

Love's Victorie (MS, n.d. *Lady Mary Wroth's Love's Victory*, ed. M.G. Brennan, 1988). *Urania* (1621, including *Pamphilia to Amphilanthus*, a series of 19 songs and 83 sonnets. *Pamphilia to Amphilanthus* is available in two modern editions: *Pamphilia to Amphilanthus*, ed. G. Waller [1977] and *The Poems of Lady Mary Wroth*, ed. J.A. Roberts [1983]). *Urania*, ed. J.A. Roberts (1995).

Margaret P. Hannay

Hella Maria Wuolijoki
1886–1954

a.k.a. Juhani Tervapää, Felix Tuli
Born July 22, 1886, Valja-district of Estonia
Died February 2, 1954, Helsinki, Finland
Genre(s): drama, autobiography
Language(s): Estonian, Finnish

Hella Wuolijoki was born in the southern part of Estonia, in a district that was known as the birthplace of Estonian nationalism. The family moved to the city of Valga, where Hella started school in 1897. Four years later we find her in the Puśkin grammar school at Dorpat. She passed her matriculation exam and went to a university for women in St. Petersburg, a place she was admitted to only through influential contacts, and from there she asked for a transfer to the University of Helsinki to study folklore.

She spent her first summer in Finland in 1903 and returned to study at the university in 1904. The general Strike of 1905 in Finland changed her life entirely: she committed herself to socialism, to Finland, and to marriage, and the three were so intertwined that it would be hard to separate them. Her husband, Sulo Wuolijoki, was then a leading figure in the socialist student movement; they became engaged in 1906 and married two years later. After the parliamentary election of 1907, life became hard for young couples of the Wuolijoki-type. Following a fashion among young intellectuals of the day, they bought a house outside town and settled there when her husband had become a member of parliament. She had a daughter, and planned her first play. As soon as she had got hold of a nurse to take care of her daughter, she began to write the play. *Talu lapsed* (The Children of the House) was printed in Estonia in 1912 and performed there at the Estonia Theatre in Reval (Tallinn) in the autumn of that year. Its first performance in Finland took place in February 1914. In both places it was immediately forbidden as being too revolutionary. At about this time she also decided to give up her plans for a doctorate. In 1913, she was asked to run in the election but refused. Her energetic studies of Marxist theories at this time did not in the least change her bourgeois attitudes and habits: she hated the office where she had to work and was not interested in a housewife's duties. For 17 years, 1915–1932, she worked in business, first for other people, then as a representative for the Finnish Government, trying to procure wheat from the United States, and finally operating on her own account. In the aftermath of the Civil War, she stated: "The year

1918 made me a Finn." At that time her drawing room was the meeting place of literary people and politicians alike. Her international business and political contacts and the flow of people who passed through her drawing room kept her and a good many Finnish politicians up to date on European points of view. Her husband was imprisoned for his political views, and she herself was considered a suspicious person.

In 1920 she bought a mansion, Marlebäck, and in the process of restoring it, she acquired the experience and insight that makes her Niskavuori series of plays a description of genuine Finnish country life, mirroring the full specter of class and language differences and difficulties. She divorced her husband in 1923 and founded two businesses of her own in the same year. Both firms flourished until the Depression put an end to them in 1931. But she retained Marlebäck, and became in her own words "a capitalist employer with a Marxist view of the world and a belief in the bankruptcy of capitalism."

Her first play in the Niskavuori series, *Niskavuoren naiset* (The Women of Niskavuori), was refused, and when finally accepted, people thought it might run for only two or three performances. It ran for a hundred performances and eventually brought in more cash than all the other plays at that theatre that season. The playwright used the pseudonym "Juhani Tervapää" and continued using it for the plays that followed during the next few years.

The Finnish Winter War began in 1939, and Hella Wuolijoki knew influential people both in the east and in the west. As things became critical, she offered to contact Madame Alexandra Kollontay in Stockholm and try to get her cooperation to bring about peace negotiations. She carried out this mission successfully and eventually helped secure peace. In April, immediately after the end of the war, she housed Bertolt Brecht and the people that accompanied him while they waited for visas to the United States. They produced a play together, which each of them, however, revised and re-named later. Hella Wuolijoki's version was called *Iso-Heikkilän isäntä* (The Farmer of Iso-Heikkilä).

Before World War II started, her plays were performed in many European countries, including England and Germany. But in 1941 Finland again had to defend herself, and this time Hella Wuolijoki was endangered. In 1943 she was imprisoned, accused of espionage and high treason, and given a life sentence, a sentence that the High Martial Court upheld in 1944. When the war ended, she was freed and immediately resumed her political activities. The first of the series of autobiographical works, written or at least drafted

in prison, was published the same year: *Enkä ollut vanki* (And Prisoner I Was Not). In 1945 her memoirs *Koulutyttönä Tartossa* (Schoolgirl in Dorpat), *Yliopistovuodet Helsinginssä* (The Student Years in Helsinki), and a few short plays appeared. In 1945 she was also appointed President of the Finnish Broadcasting Corporation, a post she held until 1949, when she was dismissed.

Before the parliamentary elections she published a lean volume called *Luottamukselliset neuvottelut Suomen ja Neuvostoliiton välillä vuosina 1938, –39, –40, –41* (Confidential Negotiations Between Finland and the U.S.S.R. in the Years 1938–1941). In the election she only gained deputy status, but due to a substitution later on, she actually became a member of parliament in 1946. In 1946, the play she wrote in cooperation with Brecht was published, *Iso-Heikkilän isäntä ja hänen renkinsä Kalle* (The Farmer of Iso-Heikkilä and His Farmhand Kalle). She was not re-elected in 1948.

The fourth volume of her memoirs, *Kummituksia ja kajavia* (Ghosts and Gulls), was published in 1947. Then a few quiet years followed. Fortunately she was able to finish her Niskavuori series of plays in 1953 (Niskavuori is the name of the farm on which the events recounted take place). Within these plays she managed to cover almost every aspect of controversy and social debate going on in Finland at the time. The women of Niskavuori show a peculiar strength, which may be an unconscious transfer of the vital womanly strength she herself radiated. These plays seemed to be written out of the heart of the Finnish people, and they are still able to convey this impression of something most genuinely Finnish. The Estonian writer of these plays died on February 2, 1954. She was a colorful woman, always active, she loved social occasions and having lots of people around her. As a playwright she is a keen observer of character and capable of conveying the atmosphere and the feelings of the place and the people she describes. Her plays may seem purely realistic, but they also contain an almost mythic vigor. Her political activities may remain controversial for a long time; as a playwright she was and will remain one of the most popular ones in this century in Finland.

Works

In Estonian: *Talu lapsed* [The Children of the House] (1912). *Udutagused* (1914). *Koidula* [Lydia Koidula, Estonian writer, 1843–1886] (1932).

In Finnish: *Ministeri ja kommunisti* [The Minister and the Communist] (1936). *Laki ja Järjestys* [Law and Order] (1933). The Niskavuori series of plays: *Niskavuoren naiset* [The Women of Niska-vuori] (1936). *Niskavuoren leipä* [The Bread of Niskavuori] (1938). *Niskavuroen nuori emäntä* [The Young Mistress of Niskavuori] (1940). *Niskavuoren Heta* [Heta of Niskavuori] (1953). *Entäs nyt, Niskavuori* [What Next, Niskavuori?] (1953). *Palava maa* [The Burning Land] (1936). *Juurakon Hulda* [Hulda of Juurakko], filmed in the United States and given the film title *The Daughter of Parliament* (1937). *Justiina* (1937). *Naiset ja naamarit* [The Women and the Masks] (1937). *Vihreä kulta* [Green Gold] (1938). *Vastamyrkky* [Antidote] (1939).

Kuningas hovinarrina [The King as the Court's Jester], about the writer Eino Leino (1946). *Iso-Heikkilän isäntä ja hänen renkinsä Kalle* [The Farmer of Iso-Heikkilä and His Farmhand Kalle], originally written in cooperation with Bertolt Brecht (1947).

Memoirs: *Enkä ollut vanki* [And Prisoner I Was Not] (1944). *Koulutyttönä Tartossa* [Schoolgirl in Dorpat] (1945). *Yliopistovuodet Helsingissä* [The Student Years in Helsinki] (1945). *Kummituksia ja kajavia* [Ghosts and Gulls] (1947). *Minusta tuli liikenainen* [I Became a Business Woman] (1953).

Gunnel Cleve

Charlotte Mary Yonge
1823–1901

Born August 11, 1823, Otterbourne, Hampshire, England
Died March 20, 1901, Otterbourne, Hampshire
Genre(s): novel, history, biography, tract, translation
Language(s): English

Born the oldest of two children to High Church, upper-middle-class parents, Yonge passed her entire life in Otterbourne, the village where she taught Sunday school for seventy of her seventy-eight years. Beloved by school girls and the Victorian reading public alike, she published over two hundred works, including nearly one hundred novels and over thirty histories, as well as stories of village life, biographies, books of religious instruction, natural histories, editions, and translations. *The Heir of Redclyff* (1853), an enormous success in its day, has proved to be the most enduring of her novels. Yonge created several fictional families, and the sagas of the Mays, in *The Daisy Chain* (1856) and *The Trial* (1864), and the Underwoods, in *The Pillars of the House* (1873), were among her most popular. In her last novel, *Modern Broods* (1900), various Mays, Underwoods, Mohuns, and Merrifields make their final appearances. Over the course of fifty years, Yonge also edited and contributed to three journals: the *Monthly Packet* (1851–1894), the *Monthly Paper of Sunday Teaching* (1860–1875), and the *Mothers in Council* (1890–1900). Yonge perceived of herself as an "instrument for popularizing Church views," views that were molded by her parents and, more significantly, by John Keble, one of the founders of the Oxford Movement and vicar of the neighboring parish of Hursley. Hers is certainly edifying fiction; nonetheless, her best novels offer lively portraits of Victorian family life, well-delineated characters, and skillful dialogue.

While her upbringing strikes the modern reader as unduly harsh, Yonge spoke of her childhood as a happy one and remained devoted to her parents, particularly to her father. Fearful lest they spoil their spirited, pretty, intelligent daughter, the Yonges imposed strict controls on the child. She was given a diet of dry bread and milk for both breakfast and supper, and her mother discouraged vanity and selfishness by minimizing Charlotte's attractiveness and by chastising her for selfish, though typically childish, desires. Her home education, supervised entirely by her father, was a rigorous affair. From the time she was seven, she rose for an hour of math before breakfast, followed by lessons in Greek, science, and history. Evenings were devoted to an hour of Bible reading, followed by an hour of history. Yonge's many "romantic" histories were written as by a teacher attempting to provide adequate texts for young people.

The absolute necessity of submission and self-sacrifice is both the theme that informs her novels as well as the precept by which she lives her life. In Yonge's world, moral obligation is clear: children must submit to the wisdom of their parents; women must submit to the superior judgment of men; mankind must submit to the will of God. Yonge drew support for her belief in the inferiority of women from the biblical account of the fall of man. When her maternal grandmother objected to writing as a suspicious and unfeminine occupation and nearly prevented the publication of *Abbey Church* (1844), Yonge agreed to donate the profits from her works to the missions. She submitted her writing for criticism to her father and to Keble; Keble read to assure that "delicacy and reverence" were observed. Not unexpectedly then, characters in her novels are judged and dealt with according to the degree to which they submit to and obey those wiser than themselves, and female characters who act independently are often made to suffer quite severely.

The life of the shy, socially awkward, spinster "Aunt Charlotte," who is said to have remained fixed in adolescence, was possibly uneventful; nonetheless, the sheer volume and variety of her writing bespeak a rich and active imaginative life. Her first novel, *Abbey Church* (1844), was a frankly Tractarian work. Over the following decade, she published several works; however, it was *The Heir of Redclyff* (1853) that earned her a wide and devoted audience. The tale of Sir Guy Morville, heir to Redclyff and to an ancestral curse that blights the happiness of all the Morvilles, was admired by Dante Gabriel Rossetti, William Morris, and Henry James, who praised the novel and called Yonge a writer with "a force of genius." By 1868, *Heir* was in its seventeenth edition. Even Jo, in *Little Women*, wept over Sir Guy's death. The novel centers on Guy's struggle to subdue his self-destructive temper and to suffer patiently the false attacks of his cousin, Philip. Though Guy is vindicated by the truth and wed to his beloved Amy, his is the ultimate self-sacrifice, for on their honeymoon, he nurses the intolerable Philip through a terrible fever which he then catches and dies. Amy later gives birth to a daughter, whereupon Redclyff is passed on to Philip, now a grief-stricken, guilt-ridden man.

As is often noted, Yonge's characters are punished for their transgressions of the moral code as Yonge herself perceived it. In *The Clever Woman of the Family* (1865), Rachel Curtis tries to ameliorate the working conditions of girls in the lacemaking trade, but, by ignoring the advice of others, she ends up placing the girls in homes where they are mistreated and loses the money she has collected for them to an embezzler. In *Magnum Bonum* (1879), Janet Brownlow studies medicine in order to continue her father's discoveries, but her carelessness and poor judgment bring about the deaths of several people, including her child. Her own death, a result of her work to control an epidemic, serves as a penitential act of self-sacrifice, a pattern reflecting Yonge's deeply held religious convictions, convictions apparently shared by many of her readers. Yet her novels offered those readers more than a series of didactic plots, for much of her appeal lay in her characters and depictions of life in the Victorian hearth and home.

After 1875, Yonge wrote fewer novels and a greater number of children's books and school texts. In her lifetime she was much admired, and devoted readers would make pilgrimages to her home, to her dismay. In the 1940s, her novels enjoyed a revival in England, but today her novels are discussed chiefly in terms of their religious sentiments and their conservative response to the Victorian crisis of faith, of the patterns and concerns characteristic of the fiction of nineteenth-century women novelists, and of their domestic realism.

Works

Le Château de Melville (1838). *Abbey Church* (1844). *Scenes and Characters* (1847). *Kings of England* (1848). *Henrietta's Wish* (1850). *Kenneth* (1850). *Langley School* (1850). *Landmarks of History* (1852–1857). *The Two Guardians* (1852). *The Heir of Redclyff* (1853). *The Herb of the Field* (1853). *The Castle Builders* (1854). *Heartsease* (1854). *The Little Duke* (1854). *The History of the Life and Death of the Good Knight Sir Thomas Thumb* (1855). *The Lancer of Lynwood* (1855). *The Railroad Children* (1855). *Ben Sylvester's Word* (1856). *The Daisy Chain* (1856). *Harriet and her Sister* (1856?). *Leonard the Lionheart* (1856). *Dynevor Terrace* (1857). *The Instructive Picture Book* (1857). *The Christmas Mummers* (1858). *Friarswood Post Office* (1860). *Hopes and Fears* (1860). *The Mice at Play* (1860). *The Strayed Falcon* (1860). *Pigeon Pie* (1860). *The Stokesley Secret* (1861). *The Young Stepmother* (1861). *Biographies of Good Women*, 2 series (1862–5). *The Chosen People* (1862). *Countess Kate* (1862). *Sea Spleenwort and Other Stories* (1862). *A History of Christian Names* (1863). *The Apple of Discord* (1864). *A Book of Golden Deeds of All Times and All Lands* (1864). *Historical Dramas* (1864). *Readings from Standard Authors* (1864). *The Trial* (1864). *The Wars of Wapsburgh* (1864). *The Clever Woman of the Family* (1865). *The Dove in the Eagle's Nest* (1866). *The Prince and the Page* (1866). *The Danvers Papers* (1867). *A Shilling's Book of Golden Deeds* (1867). *The Six Cushions* (1867). *Cameos from English History*, 9 vols. (1868–1899). *The Chaplet of Pearls* (1868). *Historical Selection* (1868–1870). *New Ground* (1868). *The Pupils of St. John the Divine* (1868). *A Book of Worthies* (1869). *Keynotes of the First Lessons for Every Day in the Year* (1869). *The Seal* (1869). *The Caged Lion* (1870). *A Storehouse of Stories*, 2 series (1870–1872). *Little Lucy's Wonderful Glove* (1871). *Musings over the Christian Year and Lyra Innocentium* (1871). *A Parallel History of France and England* (1871). *Pioneers and Founders* (1871). *Scripture Readings for Schools* (1871–1879). *A History of France* (1872). *In Memoriam Bishop Patterson* (1872). *P's and Q's* (1872). *Questions on the Prayerbook* (1872). *Aunt Charlotte's Stories of English History for the Little Ones* (1873). *Life of John Coleridge Paterson* (1873). *The Pillars of the House* (1873). *Aunt Charlotte's Stories of French History for the Little Ones* (1874). *Lady Hester* (1874). *Questions on the Col-*

lects (1874). *Questions on the Epistles* (1874). *Questions on the Gospels* (1874). *Aunt Charlotte's Stories of Bible History for the Little Ones* (1875). *My Young Alcides* (1875). *Aunt Charlotte's Stories of Greek History for the Little Ones* (1875). *Eighteen Centuries of Beginnings of Church History* (1876). *The Three Brides* (1876). *Aunt Charlotte's Stories of German History for the Little Ones* (1877). *Aunt Charlotte's Stories of Roman History for the Little Ones* (1877). *The Disturbing Element* (1878). *A History of France* (1878). *The Story of the Christians and Moors of Spain* (1878). *Burnt Out* (1879). *Magnum Bonum* (1879). *Short English Grammar for Use in Schools* (1879). *Byewords* (1880). *Love and Life* (1880). *Nelly and Margaret* (1880?). *Verses on the Gospel for Sundays and Holy Days* (1880). *Aunt Charlotte's Evenings at Home with the Poets* (1881). *Cheap Jack* (1881). *Frank's Debt* (1881). *How to Teach the New Testament* (1881). *Lads and Lasses of Langley* (1881). *Practical Work in Sunday Schools* (1881). *Question on the Psalms* (1881). *Wolf* (1881). *Given to Hospitality* (1882). *Historical Ballads* (1882). *Langley Little Ones* (1882). *Pickle and His Page Boy* (1882). *Sowing and Sewing* (1882). *Talks about the Laws We Live Under* (1882). *Unknown to History* (1882). *Aunt Charlotte's Stories of American History* (1883). *English Church History* (1883). *Landmarks of Recent History 1770–1883* (1883). *Langley Adventures* (1883). *The Miz Maze*, with F. Awdry, M. Bramston, C.R. Coleridge, F.M. Peard, et al. (1883). *Shakespeare's Plays for School* (1883). *Stray Pearls* (1883). *The Armourer's 'Prentices* (1884). *The Daisy Chain Birthday Book* (1885). *Higher Reading-book for Schools, Colleges and General Use* (1885). *Nuttie's Father* (1885). *Pixie Lawn* (1885). *The Two Sides of the Shield* (1885). *Astray*, with M. Bramston, C. Coleridge, and E. Stuart (1886). *Chantry House* (1886). *Just One Tale More*, with Others (1886). *The Little Rick-burners* (1886). *A Modern Telemachus* (1886). *Teachings on the Catechism* (1886). *Victorian Half-Century* (1886). *Under the Storm* (1887). *What Books to Lend and What to Give* (1887). *Womankind* (1887). *Beechcroft at Rochstone* (1887). *Conversations on the Prayer Book* (1888). *Deacon's Book of Dates* (1888). *Hannah More* (1888). *Nurse's Memories* (1888). *Our New Mistress* (1888). *Preparation of Prayerbook Lessons* (1888). *The Cunning Woman's Grandson* (1889). *Neighbor's Fare* (1889). *The Parent's Power* (1889). *A Reputed Changeling* (1889). *Life of HRH the Prince Consort* (1890). *More Bywords* (1890). *The Slaves of Sabinns* (1890). *The Constable's Tower* (1891). *Old Timer at Otterbourne* (1891). *Seven Heroines of Christendom* (1891). *Simple Stories Relating to English History* (1891). *Twelve Stories from Early English History* (1891). *Twenty Stories and Biographies from 1066 to 1485* (1891). *Two Penniless Princesses* (1891). *Westminster Historical Reading Books* (1891–1892). *The Cross Roads* (1892). *The Hanoverian Period* (1892). *The Stuart Period* (1892). *That Stick* (1892). *The Tudor Period* (1892). *Chimes for the Mothers* (1893). *The Girl's Little Book* (1893). *Grisly Grisell* (1893). *The Strolling Players*, with C. Coleridge (1893). *The Treasure in the Marches* (1893). *The Cook and the Captive* (1894). *The Rubies of St. Lo* (1894). *The Story of Easter* (1894). *The Carbonels* (1895). *The Long Vacation* (1895). *The Release* (1896). *The Wardship of Steepcombe* (1896). *The Pilgrimage of the Ben Beriah* (1897). *Founded on Paper* (1898). *John Keble's Parishes* (1898). *The Patriots of Palestine* (1898). *Scenes with Kenneth* (1899). *The Herd Boy and His Hermit* (1900). *The Making of a Missionary* (1900). *Modern Broods* (1900). *Reasons Why I Am a Catholic, and Not a Roman Catholic* (1901).

Patricia A. O'Hara

Marguerite Yourcenar
1903–1987

Born June 8, 1903, Brussels, Belgium
Died December 18, 1987
Genre(s): novel, short fiction, autobiographical texts, poetry, prose poem, essay, translation from Greek, English, and Japanese
Language(s): French

Born in Brussels of a French father and a Belgian mother who died ten days after her birth, Marguerite de Crayencour spent much of her childhood and subsequent life traveling: the North of France, England, Paris, Switzerland, Italy, Greece, etc. In 1939 she came to the United States upon the invitation of Grace Frick, a doctoral student at Yale, who became a lifelong companion and who translated many of her works into English. As a return to Europe was made impossible by the coming of World War II, she remained in the U.S. throughout the war years and became a part-time instructor at Sarah Lawrence—a position which she held intermittently until 1949. When in 1947 she became a U.S. citizen, she adopted her *nom de plume* Yourcenar, an incomplete anagram of Crayencour, as her legal name. In 1950 she and Grace Frick purchased "Petite Plaisance," a house on Mount Desert

Island off the coast of Maine where Yourcenar spent the rest of her life.

Marguerite Yourcenar's career as a writer started at the age of eighteen, when, with the enthusiastic support of her father, she privately published a volume of poems entitled *Le Jardin des Chimères* (1921; The Garden of the Chimerae). A second privately published collection of poems, *Les Dieux ne sont pas morts* (The Gods Are Not Dead), followed one year later. Yet, the earliest work of Yourcenar's that the author approved of is the novel *Alexis ou le Traité du vain combat* (1929; Alexis or the Story of a Vain Struggle). Also noticeable among her early works are the novel *Denier du rêve* of 1934 (translated into English as *A Coin in Nine Hands*), the volume of prose poems *Feux* (1936; Fires), and her retellings of classical Arabic, Persian, Indian, and Chinese tales entitled *Nouvelles orientales* (1938; Oriental Tales). Fame came, however, in 1951, with *Mémoires d'Hadrien* (Memoirs of Hadrian), a novel about the Roman emperor Hadrian which was awarded the Prix Fémina-Vacaresco at the time of its publication and translated into English in 1954. She repeated her critical success in 1968 with *L'Oeuvre au noir* (The Work in Black), the story of an alchemist's physical and intellectual journeys in the Europe of the early Renaissance. Marguerite Yourcenar is also an accomplished playwright (her dramatic *oeuvre* has been published in two volumes, *Théâtre I* and *Théâtre II*), essayist (*The Dark Brain of Piranesi and Other Essays*, 1984, and *Mishima. A Vision of the Void*, 1986) and translator from Greek, English, and Japanese. Especially her translation of Virginia Woolf's *The Waves* (*Les Vagues*, 1937), of the Greek poet Cavafy (*Présentation critique de Constantin Cavafy [1863–1933]*, 1958), of negro spirituals (*Fleuve Profond, Sombre Rivière*, 1962) and her anthology of translations from classical Greek literature, *La Couronne et la Lyre* (1979; The Crown and the Lyre), deserve mention.

This prolific intellectual creativity could not but rouse interest in and admiration for Marguerite Yourcenar's *oeuvre* and, indeed, few honors have escaped her over the years. In 1970, she was elected to the Belgian Royal Academy of Language and Literature, in 1971 she received the Légion d'honneur, and in 1980 she became the first woman to be elected into the Académie Française. In 1981 followed an Honorary Doctorate from Harvard, and in 1982 membership in the American Academy of Arts and Letters. She also received numerous literary awards and prizes. Not all of these honors, however, came without controversy and especially her election into the French Academy was accompanied by a heated polemic between excited admirers and angry critics. Her critics

referred to the fact that she relinquished her French citizenship in 1939 and that she had been living in the U.S. for several decades. Some members of the Academy were also disturbed that Yourcenar did not follow the traditional procedure for being elected into the Academy—a procedure that demands that candidates call on the members of the Academy and petition them for their vote. A few "Immortals" even maintained that, as in the past, no woman should be admitted to the exclusively male French Academy. Finally, there was the vexed question of which dress Yourcenar would wear during the induction ceremony as she objected to the traditional green and gold livery with sword and cocked hat.

The publication in 1982 of Marguerite Yourcenar's work in the prestigious *Bibliothèque de la Pléiade* with a first volume containing her novels and other prose fiction (*Oeuvres romanesques de Marguerite Yourcenar*), and the publication of her essayistic and biographical works in a second volume, signals her public and critical success. A certain amount of literary image building, however, has seemed inescapable. American biographical sketches mention that Yourcenar became a U.S. citizen in 1947 (Farell and Farell; Horn), whereas the chronology of the *Pléiade* passes over this fact. Similarly, whereas American biographers review some of the controversial events surrounding her election into the French Academy, the French chronology neglects to mention these. In addition, Yourcenar submitted her texts to continuous rewriting and did not hesitate to radically revamp or outright reject some of her earlier writings. In the preface to the *Pléiade* edition she states that "The duration of the literary labor coincides with that of the existence of the author himself." Thus the novel *La Nouvelle Eurydice* (1931; The New Euridice) has been excluded from the *Pléiade* edition, and she also announced in that preface her intention to exclude her study *Pindare* (1932) from the forthcoming second *Pléiade* volume.

The quality, however, of Yourcenar's work and its erudition, eclecticism, and cross-cultural richness have generally not been doubted. Her works succeed in merging asceticism and excess, refined skepticism and an avid search for absolute truths, classical myth and modern political discourse, and the East and the West. The author herself often used the notion of "sympathetic magic" to describe the process which enables her to penetrate so thoroughly the mind of her characters—whether they be Roman emperors, Flemish alchemists, Chinese painters, Italian anti-fascist revolutionaries or classical heroes—and the complex historical and cultural frameworks within which they exist. Commenting on the *magnum opus* of Zeno, the protagonist of her *The Work in Black*, and the alchemists of the late Middle Ages and Renaissance during an interview, she stated, "in postulating a world in flux, a world which is perpetually coming into being, irrational *at least in appearance*, the philosophers of alchemy prefigured Hegel and contemporary physicists; this becoming world, they have also situated even more audaciously in the internal being of man." It is this fluctuating world which is ever coming into being and dissolving again in the realm of history and in the inner being of man which she has tried to delineate and interpret in her complex *oeuvre*.

Works

Marguerite Yourcenar's novels, short fiction, and prose poems were published in 1982 in the *Bibliothèque de la Pléiade*, Yvon Bernier, ed., *Oeuvres romanesques de Marguerite Yourcenar*. This volume contains: *Alexis ou le Traité du vain combat* (1929); *Denier du rêve* (1934); the collection of prose poems *Feux* (1936); *Nouvelles orientales* (1938); *Le Coup de Grâce* (1939); *Mémoires d'Hadrien* (1951); *L'Oeuvre au noir* (1968); *Comme l'eau qui coule* (1982), and a collection of 3 novellas: *Anna, soror . . . , Un homme obscur*, and *Une belle matinée*. The early works *La Nouvelle Eurydice* (1931) and *La Mort conduit l'attelage* (1934) were excluded on the request of the author.

Poetry: *Les Charités d'Alcippe et autres poèmes* (1956).

Plays: *Le Dialogue dans le Marécage. Pièce en un acte* (1930). *Rendre à César. Pièce en trois actes* (1961). *La Petite Sirène. Divertissement dramatique d'après le conte de Hans-Christian Andersen* (1942; rpt. in *Théâtre I*; *Electre ou la Chute des masques* [1954]). *Le Mystère d'Alceste. Pièce en un acte* (1963). *Qui n'a pas son Minotaure? Divertissement sacré en dix scènes* (1963; rpt. in *Théâtre II*).

Biography: *Le Labyrinthe du monde, I: Souvenirs Pieux* (1974). *Le Labyrinthe du Monde, II: Archives du Nord* (1977).

Essays: *Les Songes et les sorts* (1938). *Sous Bénéfice d'inventaire* (1962). *Mishima ou la vision du vide* (1981). *Le Temps, ce grand sculpteur* (1983).

Translations: *Memoirs of Hadrian*, tr. Gabrielle Frick (1954). *Coup de Grâce*, tr. Gabrielle Frick (1957). *The Abyss*, tr. Gabrielle Frick (1976). *Fires*, tr. Dori Katz (1981). *The Alms of Alcippe*, tr. Edith R. Farrell (1982). *A Coin in Nine Hands*, tr. Dori Katz (1982). *Alexis*, tr. Walter Kaiser (1984). *Plays*, tr. Dori Katz (1984) (contains translations of all of the above six plays except *Le Dialogue dans le Marécage* and *Le Mystère d'Alceste*). *The Dark Brain of Piranesi and Other Essays*, tr. Richard Howard (1984). *Oriental Tales*, tr. Alberto Manguel (1985). *Mishima. A Vision of the Void*, tr. Alberto Manguel (1986).

Translations into French: Virginia Woolf, *Les Vagues* (1937). Henry James, *Ce Que Savait Maisie* (1947). *Présentation critique de Constantin Cavafy (1863–1933)* (1958). *Fleuve Profond, Sombre Rivière* (1962). *Présentation critique d'Hortense Flexner* (1970). *La Couronne et la Lyre* (1979). James Baldwin, *Le Coin des "Amen"* (1983). *Blues et Gospels* (1984). M. Yourcenar and Jun Shiragi, tr., Yukio Mishima, *Cinq Nô modernes* (1983).

Miscellaneous: *Discours de réception de Marguerite Yourcenar à l'Académie royale belge de langue et de littérature française* (1971). *Discours de réception à l'Académie française de Marguerite Yourcenar. Et réponse de Jean D'Ormesson* (1981). Marie Métailler and Marie-Magdeleine Brumagne, *Le Poudre de sourire, précédé de lettres de Marguerite Yourcenar de l'académie française* (1982) (contains two letters by M. Yourcenar). *Notre Dame des hirondelles. Contes de Noël*, collection of tales for children (1982).

Henk Vynckier

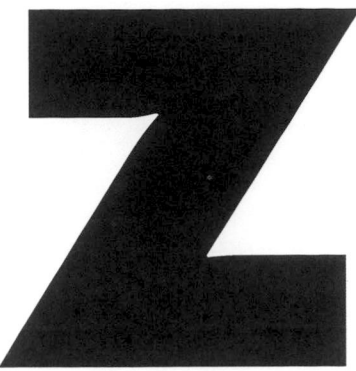

María de Zayas y Sotomayor
1590–1661/1669
Born September 12, 1590, Madrid, Spain
Died 1661/1669 (?), Spain
Genre(s): short story
Language(s): Spanish

The life of María de Zayas is wrapped in mystery. Her father was a captain in the infantry and a member of the military order of Santiago; thus she evidently belonged to a distinguished Spanish family. Certainly the fictional world of her stories reflects aristocratic values and a cultivated mind. Zayas may have traveled with the Court to Valladolid (1601–1606) and, possibly, to Italy with the entourage of Count Lemos in 1610. But we cannot be sure of these facts. We do know she played an active part in the cultural life of Madrid, participating in literary academies and gatherings, writing encomiastic poems for her friends, and receiving high praise from such luminaries as Lope de Vega and Pérez de Montalbán. Did she marry? Bear children? Or was her life a solitary one? We do not know. But her stories disclose a strong personality, exceptionally sensitive to the effects of passion and the cruel, unjust treatment of women.

Zayas was already known for her verses and a play, *Traición en la amistad* (Treachery in Friendship; published in Serrano y Sanz), by the time her first collection of *novellas* appeared in 1637. The ten stories included in *Novelas amorosas y ejemplares* (Exemplary Tales of Love) are: "Aventurarse perdiendo" (Nothing Ventured, Nothing Gained), "La burlada Aminta y Venganza del honor" (Aminta Deceived, or Honor Avenged), "El castigo de la miseria" (A Miser's Punishment), "El prevenido engañado" (The Foolish Wise Man), "La fuerza del amor" (The Power of Love), "El desengaño amando y Premio de la virtud" (The Deceits of Love, or Virtue's Reward), "Al fin se paga todo" (In the End We Always Pay), "El imposible vencido" (The Impossible Conquered), "El juez de su causa" (Judge and Jury), and "El jardín engañoso" (The Garden of Deceit). Ten years later, her second and last collection of stories appeared: *Parte segunda del Sarao y entretenimiento honesto, Desengaños amorosos* (The Second Part of an Evening's Honest Entertainments, or the Deceits of Love). The ten stories comprising her *Desengaños amorosos* are: "La esclava de su amante" (Her Lover's Slave), "La más infame venganza" (The Most Infamous Revenge), "El verdugo de su esposa" (His Wife's Executioner), "Tarde llega el desengaño" (A Tardy Lesson), "La inocencia castigada" (Innocence Castigated), "Amar sólo por vencer" (Love Conquers All), "Mal presagio casar lejos" (Beware of a Foreign Wedding), "El traidor contra su sangre" (Blood Betrayed), "La perseguida triunfante" (Virtue Triumphant), and "Estragos que causa el vicio" (The Wreckage of Sin).

Zayas's fictions were popular well into the eighteenth century. Subsequent Victorian hostility to her supposed libertine excesses persisted until fairly recently. While utilizing the conventional frame tale and topoi of love and honor lost, she turned escapist literature into a serious critique of counter-reformation values. Her feminist voice of dissent contrasts sharply with the more conformist, less daring narrations of Mariana de Carvajal. Readers loved her stories for their narrative deftness and for the extraordinary passion and vehemence brought to bear upon the frequently violent and cruel depiction of the darker side of Spanish culture. Zayas shunned a cultivated, rhetorical style, she said, because she wanted to be understood by everyone. Yet there is nothing simple either in the style or vision of María de Zayas's work. In her stories, women are guilty even when innocent, and punishment is extreme. Women are murdered, beaten, drained of their blood, even walled up to die an agonizingly protracted living death. When, for example, the married protagonist Inés of "La inocencia castigada" becomes the victim of a would-be seducer's hypnotic enchantment, both the character and the narrator claim her innocence, while her husband and family, believing she has dishonored them, plan an exemplary and horrific punishment: to be walled up and barely kept alive for years. Zayas brilliantly plays out her narrative between the poles of fictional verisimilitude, or convention (the victim's hard-to-believe enchantment), and a dominant cultural code that demands "guilt." The reader, tempted at first to doubt Inés's innocence, is later appalled at her imprisoned, emaciated condition. Thus Zayas circumvents the cultural code, subverting it even as she imaginatively and dramatically exploits belief in that same code. Her fictions, which she fittingly called *maravillas*, or marvels, have drawn a new readership, intrigued by her capacity to create passion within artifice, violence, and other irrational acts within a conflicting framework of grace and repression.

Works

Novelas amorosas y ejemplares (1637). *Parte segunda del Sarao y entretenimiento honesto, Desengaños amorosos* (1647; modern eds. 1948, 1973, 1983, 1989).

Translations: *A Shameful Revenge and Other Stories* (1963; title story: "La más infame venganza") in *Women Writers of the Seventeenth Century*, ed. K. Wilson and F. Warnke (1989).

Noël M. Valis

Žemaitė
1845–1921

Born June 4, 1845 on the estate of Bukantė, near Plungė, Lithuania
Died December 7, 1921, Marijampolė, Lithuania
Genre(s): novella, short story, drama, essay, journalism, children's literature
Language(s): Lithuanian

One of the classic writers of Lithuanian realism, Žemaitė (Julija Beniuševičiūtė), in her novellas, short stories, and sketches, gave a detailed and critical portrayal of rural Lithuanian life at the end of the nineteenth and the beginning of the twentieth centuries. She focused particularly on family relationships and on the status of women in the family. Other themes are the social and economic conflicts between the

peasants and the landed gentry, the repressions of the Czarist regime, and the rising nationalist movement. In addition to their literary value, her works are of ethnographic interest for their accurate depictions of folk customs and traditions in the Lithuanian province of Samogitia.

The daughter of impoverished gentry, Beniuševičiūtė was raised in a family that emphasized class traditions and status. As was typical for the gentry of the time, her family spoke Polish, espoused Polish culture, and maintained a distance from the Lithuanian-speaking peasantry. At an early age she rejected these family attitudes, empathizing with the exploited peasants. Marriage to a commoner, Laurynas Žymantas, completed her estrangement from the gentry class. For the next 35 years she lived the difficult life of a farm-wife, struggling with poverty, engulfed by endless chores, and by the cares of child-raising. These experiences later provided her with raw material for her portrayals of peasant life. She began to write at the age of forty-nine, encouraged and aided by a patriotic student, Povilas Višinskis. Her lack of formal education was partly compensated for by extensive reading and by her keen observation of life. Her first prose work, "Rudens vakaras" (1894; Autumn Evening), was published in a farmers' almanac. After her husband's death, in about 1900, Žemaitė became active in the Lithuanian cultural resistance movement directed against the Russian Czarist regime. She also took part in early efforts for women's emancipation, participating in the first Lithuanian women's conference in 1907 and the first Russian women's conference in St. Petersburg in 1908. In 1912 she settled in Vilnius, working as administrator and editor for several journals. Her involvement in relief work during World War I led her to undertake a fund-raising journey to the United States in 1916. She remained there for five years, touring the Lithuanian communities in an effort to raise funds for war victims and refugees. Always sensitive to social injustice, she espoused the socialist movement while remaining skeptical of the Soviet revolution in Russia. Returning to Lithuania in 1921, she died that same year.

Žemaitė's best works are short sketches from everyday life, with particular attention to dialogue and description. Most of her subjects are derived from her own experience and keen observation of the country people surrounding her, whose defects she depicts in great variety: their predominantly materialistic orientation, illiteracy, passivity, and alcoholism. She denounces forced marriages based on economic calculations and shows great concern for lack of intimate family ties. On the other hand, she strongly criticizes the Polonized landlords and clergymen who exploit the naive peasant. Noteworthy, although not always organically incorporated, are her descriptions of nature. In them, she often transmits the peasants' point of view, which is not founded on aesthetic contemplation but on their relation to daily-life chores and farm inventory, thus showing nature to be the core of their lives. She excels even more in creating dynamic scenes consisting of almost pure dialogue. Her sharp pen equally chides the Russian occupant and the imposed administrative system. In all her writing, readers discern her acute class-consciousness. She tried her hand at drama, developing the same topics, but lack of technical knowledge was not easy to surmount, although the works had some success as did those she later produced in collaboration with Gabrielė Petkevičaitė-Bitė.

Among her best stories are those included in her first cycle of narratives entitled *Laimė nutekėjimo* (1896–1898; Marital Fortunes). A representative short story is "Marti" (Daughter-in-law), which depicts the fate of a young woman forced to marry into a backward, slovenly, and hard-hearted family. Efforts to reform the family prove futile and lead to her own demise. The daughter-in-law is caught between the traditional woman's stance of acceptance and resignation and her desire to fight, which she, however, dismisses. In her, Zemaitė creates a very positive character (many of her women are morally and culturally superior to men), with a sensitivity that those surrounding her are lacking. Her personality is enhanced by almost lyrical descriptions of nature and, on the other hand, by extraordinarily dynamic scenes from daily life.

The denial of basic human rights to women, their mistreatment and exploitation by the patriarchal order, is explored further in the story "Topylis." In "Petras Kurmelis" she portrays the destructive forces of greed and narrow materialism that lead to loveless marriages and to moral decadence. While most of these works analyze negative family relationships, the stories "Sučiuptas velnias" (The Captured Devil) and "Sutkai" describe mutually supportive families in their struggles against a hostile environment. Narratives written in the years just prior to the 1905–1906 revolution present sharper social conflicts and stronger anti-Czarist sentiments. For instance, in the story "Prie dvaro" (1902; At the Estate) the peasants, embroiled in a dispute with local gentry, naively believe that the institutions of justice will uphold their rights. Concerned with the deprivations suffered by peasant children, Zemaitė wrote a number of stories about these children, such as "Kaip Jonelis raides pa'ino" (1914; How

Johnny Learned His Letters). Her keen-eyed, unflinchingly honest perceptions of the world around her are especially evident in her prose sketches, such as those reflecting her impressions of the United States, in her unfinished autobiography, and in her extensive correspondence. Although not equal to her prose in quality, a number of her comedies and farces were popular with amateur theatrical groups during the early decades of the twentieth century.

Zemaitė's best prose is characterized by a laconic, energetic, often ironic style, the use of concrete vocabulary, and dramatically intense dialogues, finely tuned to the patterns of oral speech. Her language is colored by folk proverbs and by metaphors rooted in colloquial speech. Her less successful works are marred by tendentiousness, overt didacticism, and sentimentality. Her unique contribution to Lithuanian literature was her ability to depict broad social conditions and relationships through the portrayal of seemingly insignificant individual fates.

Works

Raštai [Collected Works], 4 vols. (1924–1931). *Rinktiniai raštai* [Selected Works], 4 vols. *Raštai* [Collected Works], 6 vols. (1956–1957). *Autobiografija* (1946). *Apie Ameriką* (1953).

Translations: "The Devil Captured," tr. Althea von Boskirk and Clark Mills, in *Selected Lithuanian Short Stories*, ed. Stepas Zobarskas (1963), pp. 15–30.

Audronė B. Willeke
Birutė Ciplijauskaitė

Iulia Zhadovskaia
1824–1883
Born June 29, 1824
Died July 23, 1883, Kostroma province, Russia
Genre(s): lyric poetry, fiction
Language(s): Russian

Iulia Zhadovskaia carried the tradition of Russian lyric poetry into the civic-minded mid-nineteenth century. She was born with no left arm and only a few rudimentary fingers on her right, but she overcame this handicap with a determination, charm, and intelligence that seem to have impressed all who knew her. Her mother died before she was two, and she was brought up by her maternal grandmother and her aunt, the minor poet Anna Gotovtseva. When she was sixteen, her autocratic father hired the future historian of Russian literature, Petr Perevlessky, to tutor Iulia. He was horrified when they fell in love, however, and refused to permit his noble daughter to marry the young plebeian. To console Iulia, he took her to Petersburg and introduced her into the literary circles of the mid-1840s.

There, under her own name or initials, Zhadovskaia began publishing poems that are still remarkable for the naked intensity with which she mourns her thwarted love ("Vse ty unosish', neshchadnoe vremia" (1846; You take away everything, merciless time); "Da, ia vizhu—bezumstvo to bylo" (1856; Yes, I see—it was madness). A softer elegiac mood is reflected in nature verse ["Priblizhaiushchaiasia tucha" (1845; The Approaching Storm-Cloud)], in which: . . . "Before the grandeur of the storm / My soul's perturbation is stilled") and philosophical poems like "Na puti" (1856–1859; On My Way). Her diction is harsh, often deliberately unpoetic, and many of her poems have only proximate rhyme or none at all. These features, seen as defects by some mid-nineteenth-century critics, stem from a mastery of technique as versatile as her emotional range is limited. Although Zhadovskaia found the conservatism of Moscow and the quiet of Iaroslavl' more compatible than the ferment of Petersburg, she was not unsympathetic to social concerns. She wrote a few poems suggesting that poetry has a civic function such as "N.F. Shcherbine" (1857; addressed to a fellow poet). In "Grustnaia kartina" (1847; A Sad Picture) and "Niva" (1857; Grainfield), she depicted the hard life of the peasantry. Many of her poems were turned into popular or art songs. Mikhail Glinka wrote music for "Ty skoro menia pozabudesh'" (You'll soon forget me), and Aleksandr Dargomyzhsky set to music "Ia vse eshche ego, bezumnaia, liubliu" (Mad woman that I am, I can't stop loving him).

Zhadovskaia also produced prose tales of lovers thwarted by circumstance or social inequality. Titles like "Prostoi sluchai" (1847; A Simple Case), "Nepriniataia zhertva" (1848; A Sacrifice Refused), and "Sila proshedshego" (1851; The Force of the Past) indicate their general tone and themes. She was slow to master fiction. Her early tales alternate the telegraphic terseness of verse with passionate narratorial interpolation to produce an uneven, occasionally ludicrous, effect. Two later, more polished tales, published in Dostoyevsky's journal *Vremia* in 1861, "Zhenskaia istoriia" (A Woman's Story) and "Otstalaia" (Behind the Times), have strong female protagonists who manage to win happiness for themselves or others in the spirit of the "rational egotism" then being preached in radical circles. Zhadovskaia's most successful prose work was her largely autobiographical novel, *V storone*

ot bol'shogo sveta (1857; Apart from the Great World); it was still in print over twenty-five years later.

In 1863 Zhadovskaia married a family friend, Dr. Karl Seven, and retired to Iaroslavl'. At about the same time she stopped writing, due both to failing health and to the fact that, as she told her cousin and ward Nastas'ia Fedorova, "love has vanished from my heart, and poetry has deserted me." After Zhadovskaia's death, her brother oversaw the publication of her complete works just in time to bring her lyric legacy to the attention of the nascent Symbolist movement. In 1887 Fedorova wrote the brief memoir that is the most reliable account of Zhadovskaia's life.

Works

Polnoe sobranie sochinenii, 4 vols. (1885–1886). *Izbrannye stikhi* (1958). *Poety 1840–1850kh gg.* (1972), pp. 271–293.

Mary F. Zirin

Maria Zhukova
1804–1851

Born 1804, Nizhegorod province, Russia
Died April 13, 1851, Saratov
Genre(s): fiction, travel sketch
Language(s): Russian

Zhukova began writing in the late 1830s and, with Elena Gan and Nadezhda Durova, was among the first women in Russia to publish a substantial body of prose fiction. Little is known about her life. Her talent as a watercolorist and the prominent role artists and works of art play in her stories suggest that she may have studied with teachers from the Academy of Art in Arzamas where she grew up. Judging from her fiction, her marriage to a local landowner was unhappy. Sometime after 1830 Zhukova separated from her husband and moved to St. Petersburg. For health reasons, between 1838 and 1842 she spent long periods in the milder climates of Europe.

Zhukova's first published work, *Vechera na Karpovke* (1837–1838; Evenings at Karpovka), was an untendentious, often humorous set of stories rich in details of the life of the provincial Russian nobility. It brought her instant fame. Her heroines are refreshingly unstereotyped. In "Samopozhertvoznie," (1839; Self-Sacrifice), Liza, the poor young ward of a countess, became possibly the first independent woman in Russian fiction when, instead of fading under calumny, she returns home to found a girls' boarding school. Zhukova also used more conventionally Romantic themes and rhetoric: the son of a noble family, deprived of his birthright and true identity, has a near escape from incest in "Padaiushchaia zvezda" (1839; Falling Star); a married woman makes the hard choice between love and fidelity to her marital vows in "Sud serdtsa" (1840; The Judgment of the Heart). "Chernyi demon" (1840; The Black Demon) depicts a woman tainted by the Romantic affliction, more common in Russian male protagonists, of a cold intelligence that leads her to suspect and distrust all around her. Zhukova's feeling for the natural world is as genuine as her sympathy with her characters and her love of art, and she often uses extended landscape descriptions to retard a convoluted narrative and build suspense.

The critic Vissarion Belinsky found Zhukova's *Evenings* the epitome of popular light fiction—artless and prolix but enjoyable. The reader, he felt, could not help but respond to the conviction of her warm, engaging voice. Her closely observed, modest travel sketches of southern France and Nice were universally praised and widely read.

Works

Vechera na Karpovke, 2 vols. (1837–1838). *Povesti*, 2 vols. (1840). *Ocherki iuzhnoi Frantsii i Nitstsy*, 2 vols. (1844).

Mary F. Zirin

Pseudonyms, or lesser-known names

List of Entries by Country

Australia
Stead, Christina (Ellen)

Austria
Aichinger, Ilse
Grazie, Marie Eugenie delle
Kerschbaumer, Marie-Thérèse
Mayröcker, Friederike
Nöstlinger, Christine
Pataki, Heidi
Popp, Adelheid
Suttner, Berta von
Tielsch, Ilse
Ujvary, Liesl

Belgium
Belpaire, Maria Elisa
Bijns, Anna
Boudewijns, Katharina
Dentière, Marie
Hadewijch
Loveling, Virginie
Margaret of Austria
Méricourt, Théroigne de
Paemel, Monika van
Yourcenar, Marguerite

Bulgaria
Gabe, Dora Petrova
Mutafčieva, Vera

Byzantium
Kassia
Moero

Croatia
Brlić-Ma'uranić, Ivana
Budmani, Lukrecija Bogašinović

Czechoslovakia
(see also Slovakia)
Němcová, Božena

Denmark
Baden, Sophie Louise Charlotte
   (von Klenow)

Biehl, Charlotte Dorothea
Bjørnsen, Louise Cathrine Elisabeth
Brøgger, Suzanne
Brun, Friederike (Frederikke)
Christensen, Inger
Dinesen, Isak
Gyllembourg, Thomasine
Hansen, Aase
Hauch, Frederikke (Rinna/Renna)
   Elisabeth Brun Juul
Lasson, Anna Margrethe
Rode, Edith
Ryum, Ulla
Ulfeldt, Leonora Christina
Worm, Pauline Frederikke

Dutch Indies
Haasse, Hella
Vreede, Henny de

England
Austen, Jane
Behn, Aphra
Bowen, Elizabeth (Dorothea Cole)
Brittain, Vera
Brontë, Anne
Brontë, Charlotte
Brontë, Emily
Brookner, Anita
Browning, Elizabeth Barrett
Burney, Frances (Fanny)
Carlyle, Jane Welsh
Cartland, Barbara
Cavendish, Margaret, Duchess of
   Newcastle
Christie, Agatha
Churchill, Caryl
Clifford, Lady Anne
Compton-Burnett, Ivy
Delaney, Shelagh
Drabble, Margaret
Eden, Emily
Edgeworth, Maria
Eliot, George

Elizabeth I, Queen
Gaskell, Elizabeth
Gore, Catherine Grace Frances Moody
Greenaway, Kate
Hall, Radclyffe
Heyer, Georgette
Hill, Octavia
Hutchinson, Lucy Apsley
Inchbald, Elizabeth Simpson
Julian of Norwich
Kemble, Frances Anne
Kempe, Margery
Lamb, Lady Caroline
Lamb, Mary Ann
Lee, Sophia
Lehmann, Rosamond
Lessing, Doris
Linton, Elizabeth Lynn
Macaulay, (Emilie) Rose
Manley, (Mary) Delariviere
Manning, Olivia
Marryat, Florence
Marsh-Caldwell, Anne
Martineau, Harriet
Mew, Charlotte
Meynell, Alice
Mitford, Mary Russell
Mitford, Nancy
Montagu, Elizabeth
Montagu, Mary Wortley
More, Hannah
Nightingale, Florence
Oliphant, Margaret
Paston, Margaret
Philips, Katherine
Porter, Jane
Potter, Beatrix
Pym, Barbara
Radcliffe, Ann Ward
Ramée, Marie Louise de la
Renault, Mary
Rhys, Jean
Richardson, Dorothy
Ritchie, Lady Anne Thackeray

Robinson, Mary Darby
Rossetti, Christina
Sackville-West, Vita (Victoria Mary)
Sayers, Dorothy L.
Sewell, Anna
Shelley, Mary Wollstonecraft
Sidney, Mary, Countess of Pembroke
Sitwell, Dame Edith
Smith, Florence Margaret
Southcott, Joanna
Stanhope, Lucy Hester
Stevenson, Anne
Taylor, Elizabeth
Tennant, Emma
Trollope, Frances Milton
Warner, Sylvia Townsend
Webb, Beatrice Potter
Webb, (Gladys) Mary
Weldon, Fay
West, Rebecca
Woolf, Virginia
Wollstonecraft (Godwin), Mary
Wordsworth, Dorothy
Wroth, Lady Mary
Yonge, Charlotte Mary

Finland
Canth, Wilhelmina "Minna" Ulrika
 (Johnson)
Kallas, Aino
Manner, Eeva-Liisa
Meriluoto, Aila
Paraske, Larin
Tikkanen, Märta Eleonora
Vartio, Marja-Liisa
Wuolijoki, Hella Maria

France
Aulnoy, Marie-Catherine le Jumel de
 Barneville, Baronne d'
Barney, Natalie Clifford
Beaumont, Madame Jeanne-Marie Le
 Prince de
Beauvoir, Simone de
Bernard, Catherine
Bocage, Anne-Marie Fiquet du
Briet, Marguerite
Châtelet-Lomont, Gabrielle-Emilie le
 Tonnilier de Breteuil
Christine de Pizan
Cixous, Hélène
Colette, Sidonie-Gabrielle
Deffand, Madame du
Dia, the Countess of
Ducrest, Stéphanie, Countess of Genlis
Dupin, Amandine-Aurore-Lucie,
 Baronne Dudevant
Duras, Marguerite
Gacon-Dufour, Madame
Gouges, Marie Olympe de
Gournay, Marie le Jars de

Guyon, Jeanne-Marie Bouvier de la
 Motte, Mme
Heloise
Irigaray, Luce
Labé, Louise
Lacombe, Claire (Rose)
Lafayette, Marie-Madeleine, Pioche
 de la Vergne, Comtesse de
Lambert, Anne-Therese de Marguenat
 de Courcelles, Marquise de
Leduc, Violette
Le Prince de Beaumont, Madame
 Jeanne-Marie
Maintenon, Françoise d'Aubigné,
 Marquise de
Marguerite de Navarre
Marguerite de Valois
Michel, Louise
Montpensier, Anne-Marie Louise
 d'Orléans, Duchesse de
Motteville, François Bertaut, Dame
 Langlois de
Noialles (de Brancovan), Anna-
 Elizabeth de
Pascal, Françoise
Quoirez, Françoise
Rachilde
Radegunde
Roches, Dames des
Sablière, Marguerite Hessein de la
Sarrazin, Albertine
Scudery, Madeleine de
Séverine
Sévigné, Marie de Rabutin-Chantal,
 Marquise de
Staal, Marguerite-Jeanne Cordier de
 Launay, Baronne de
Staël-Holstein, Germaine Necker,
 Baronne de
Suze, Henriette de Coligny, Comtesse
 de la
Tastu, Sabine-Casimir-Amable
 Voïart
Teyssiéras, Anne
Tristan, Flora Célestine Thérèse
 Henriette
Villedieu, Madame de
Villeneuve, Gabrielle-Suzanne Barbot
 Gallon, dame de
Vivien, Renée
Voilquin, Suzanne
Weil, Simone

Germany
Arendt, Hannah
Arnim, Bettine von
Blumenthal-Weiss, Ilse
Borchers, Elisabeth
Elisabeth Charlotte Pfalzgräfin,
 Herzogin von Orléans

Elisabeth of Nassau-Saarbrücken
Elisabeth von Schönau
Françoise, Marie Louise von
Frank, Anneliese ("Anne")
Gertrud of Helfta
Goll, Claire
Gottsched, Luise Adelgunde Victoria
Heymair, Magdalena
Hildegard von Bingen
Hrotsvit of Gandersheim
Jhabvala, Ruth Prawer
Kempff, Diana
Kollwitz, Käthe
Krechel, Ursula
Magdeburg, Mechthild von
Mendelssohn-Veit-Schlegel, Dorothea
Mereau, Sophie
Modersohn-Becker, Paula
Morgner, Irmtraud
Naubert, Christiane Benedikte Eugenie
Reinshagen, Gerlind
Reventlow, Franziska von
Rinser, Luise
Sachs, Nelly
Schwartzer, Alice
Schwarz, Sibylle
Seghers, Anna
Susman, Margarete
Unzer, Johanna Charlotte
Wander, Maxie
Winsloe, Christa
Wolf, Christa

Greece
Anagnostaki, Loula
Anyte
Corinna
Erinna
Ikonomidou, Fotini
Karapanou, Margarita
Karelli, Zoe
Nossis
Parren, Callirhoe
Sappho
Sarantë, Galateia
Vakalo, Helenē

Holland/Netherlands
Bertken, Sister
Bosboom-Toussaint, Anna Louisa
 Geertruida
Dessaur, Catharina Irma
Groot, Maria de
Haasse, Hella
Hadewijch
Hillesum, Esther ("Etty")
Petijt, Maria
Savornin Lohman, Catherina Anna
 Maria de
Schurman, Anna-Maria van
Tesselschade, Maria

Vreede, Henny de
Wolff-Bekker, Elizabeth

Hungary
Bethlen, Kata
Ráskai, Lea
Szabó, Magda

Iceland
Miðjumdal, Jóreiðr Hermundardóttir í

Ireland
Bowen, Elizabeth (Dorothea Cole)
Gregory, Lady Augusta
Hemans, Felicia Dorothea Browne
Murdoch, (Jean) Iris
O'Brien, Edna
Sheridan, Frances
Somerville and Ross
Starkie, Enid (Mary)
Vesey, Elizabeth

Italy
Aleramo, Sibilla
Aragona, Tullia d'
Bandettini, Teresa Landucci
Bembo, Illuminata
Caterina da Siena
Cereta, Laura
Clare of Assisi
Deledda, Grazia
Faa' Gonzaga, Camilla
Fallaci, Oriana
Fedele, Cassandra
Gambara, Veronica
Ginzburg, Natalia
Manzini, Gianna
Matraini, Chiara
Morandini, Giuliana
Morante, Elsa
Negri, Ada
Nogarola, Isotta
Odaldi, Annalena
Percoto, Caterina
Pozzo, Modesta
Sanvitale, Francesca
Spaziani, Maria Luisa
Stampa, Gaspara
Strozzi, Lorenza
Tarabotti, Arcangela
Terracina, Laura
Umiltà of Faenza
Wertmuller, Lina

Latvia
Aspāzija
Brigadere, Anna
Niedra, Aīda
Strēlerte, Veronica

Lithuania
Bčinskaitė-Bučienė, Salomėja

Goldberg, Leah
Jasukaitytė, Vidmantė
Simonaitytė, Ieva
Žemaitė

New Zealand
Mansfield, Katherine

Norway
Collett, Camilla
Engelbretsdatter, Dorothe
Jølsen, Ragnhild
Moe, Karin
Sandel, Cora
Skram, Amalie
Sveen, Karin
Undset, Sigrid
Vik, Björg

Poland
Brzostowska, Janina
Dąbrowska, Maria
Luxemburg, Rosa
Przybyszewska, Stanisława
Sadowska, Barbara
Stanislawska, Anna
Stein, Edith
Szymborska, Wislawa

Portugal
Almeida de Portugal,
   Leonor de
Correia, Natalia de Oliveira
Espanca, Florbela de Alma
   da Conceição
Horta, Maria Teresa

Provence
Castelloza

Roman Empire
Egeria
Perpetua, Vibia
Sulpicia

Romania
Blandiana, Ana
Buzea, Constanţa
Lovinescu, Monica
Papadat-Bengescu, Hortensia
Smara

Russia
Akhmadúlina, Bélla Akhátovna
Akhmatova, Anna
Catherine II (the Great), Empress
   of Russia
Gippius, Zinaida
Khvoshchinskaia, Nadezhda
Kovalevskaia, Sofia
Mandelshtam, Nadezhda
Panova, Vera

Pavlova, Karolina
Ratushinskaia, Irina
Rostopchina, Evdokiia
Sarraute, Nathalie
Ségur, Sophie de
Shaginian, Marietta
Sokhanskaia, Nadezhda
Tolstaia, Tat'iana
Tsvetaeva, Marina
Zhadovskaia, Iulia
Zhukova, Maria

Scotland
Carlyle, Jane Welsh
Ferrier, Susan Edmonstone
Mackintosh, Elizabeth
Somerville, Mary
Spark, Muriel
Stuart, Mary, Queen of Scots

Slovakia
(now Czechoslovakia)
Figuli, Margita
Hal'amová, Maša
Maróthy-Šoltésová, Elena
Slančiková, Božena

South Africa
Schreiner, Olive Emilie Albertina

Spain
Alós, Concha
Bazán, Emilia Pardo
Böhl de Faber y Larrea, Cecilia
Caro Mallen de Soto, Ana
Champourcin, Ernestina de
   (y Móran de Loredo)
Espina, Concha
Martín-Gaite, Carmen
Martínez Sierra, María
Monserdà de Macía, Dolors
Nelken, Margarita
Pardo Bazán, Emilia
Quiroga, Elena
Sinués de Marco, Pilar de
Teresa de Cartagena
Teresa of Jesus, Saint
Tusquets, Esther
Uceda, Julia
Valenti, Helena
Wallādah bint al-Mustakfī
Zayas y Sotomayor, Maria de

Sweden
Boye, Karin
Brenner, Sophia Elisabet (Weber)
Bridget of Sweden
Flygare-Carlén, Emilie
Horn, Agneta
Lenngren, Anna Maria
   (Malmstedt)

Lindgren, Astrid
Nordenflycht, Hedvig Charlotta
Schoultz, Solveig Margareta von
Södergran, Edith Irene
Trotzig, Birgitta
Under, Marie

Switzerland

Dentière, Marie
Ehrmann, Marianne
Maillart, Ella
Schwarzenbach, Annemarie
Speyr, Adrienne von
Stagel, Elsbeth C.
Ullmann, Regina

Ukraine

Kosac, Ljarissa

Wales

Piozzi, Hester Lynch
  Salsubury Thrale

List of Entries by Century

Ulfeldt, Leonora Christina
Villedieu, Madame de
Wroth, Lady Mary
Zayas y Sotomayor, Maria de

18th Century

Almeida de Portugal, Leonor de
Baden, Sophie Louise Charlotte
  (von Klenow)
Beaumont, Madame Jeanne-Marie
  Le Prince de
Bethlen, Kata
Biehl, Charlotte Dorothea
Bocage, Anne-Marie Fiquet du
Brun, Friederike (Frederikke)
Budmani, Lukrecija Bogašinović
Burney, Frances (Fanny)
Catherine II (the Great), Empress
  of Russia
Châtelet-Lomont, Gabrielle-Emilie
  le Tonnilier de Breteuil
Deffand, Madame du
Ducrest, Stéphanie, Countess of Genlis
Ehrmann, Marianne
Gacon-Dufour, Madame
Gottsched, Luise Adelgunde Victoria
Gouges, Marie-Olympe de
Inchbald, Elizabeth Simpson
Lacombe, Claire (Rose)
Lambert, Anne-Therese de Marguenat
  de Courcelles, Marquise de
Lasson, Anna Margrethe
Lee, Sophia
Lenngren, Anna Maria (Malmstedt)
Le Prince de Beaumont, Madame
  Jeanne-Marie
Mendelssohn-Veit-Schlegel, Dorothea
Mereau, Sophie
Méricourt, Théroigne de
Montagu, Elizabeth
Montagu, Mary Wortley
More, Hannah
Naubert, Christiane Benedikte
  Eugenie
Nordenflycht, Hedvig Charlotta
Piozzi, Hester Lynch Salsubury Thrale
Radcliffe, Ann Ward
Robinson, Mary Darby
Sheridan, Frances
Staal, Marguerite-Jeanne Cordier de
  Launay, Baronne de
Staël-Holstein, Germaine Necker,
  Baronne de
Stanhope, Lucy Hester
Unzer, Johanna Charlotte
Vesey, Elizabeth
Villeneuve, Gabrielle-Suzanne Barbot
  Gallon, dame de
Wolff-Bekker, Elizabeth
Wollstonecraft (Godwin), Mary

19th Century

Arnim, Bettine von
Austen, Jane
Bandettini, Teresa Landucci
Bazán, Emilia Pardo
Bjørnsen, Louise Cathrine Elisabeth
Böhl de Faber y Larrea, Cecilia
Bosboom-Toussaint, Anna Louisa
  Geertruida
Brigadere, Anna
Brontë, Anne
Brontë, Charlotte
Brontë, Emily
Browning, Elizabeth Barrett
Canth, Wilhelmina "Minna" Ulrika
  (Johnson)
Carlyle, Jane Welsh
Collett, Camilla
Dupin, Amandine-Aurore-Lucie,
  Baronne Dudevant
Eden, Emily
Edgeworth, Maria
Eliot, George
Ferrier, Susan Edmonstone
Flygare-Carlén, Emilie
Françoise, Marie Louise von
Gaskell, Elizabeth
Gore, Catherine Grace Frances Moody
Grazie, Marie Eugenie delle
Greenaway, Kate
Gregory, Lady Augusta
Gyllembourg, Thomasine
Hauch, Frederikke (Rinna/Renna)
  Elisabeth Brun Juul
Hemans, Felicia Dorothea Browne
Hill, Octavia
Ikonomidou, Fotini
Kemble, Frances Anne
Khvoshchinskaia, Nadezhda
Kosac, Ljarissa
Kovalevskaia, Sofia
Lamb, Lady Caroline
Lamb, Mary Ann
Linton, Elizabeth Lynn
Loveling, Virginie
Luxemburg, Rosa
Marryat, Florence
Marsh-Caldwell, Anne
Martineau, Harriet
Mew, Charlotte
Meynell, Alice
Michel, Louise
Mitford, Mary Russell
Modersohn-Becker, Paula
Monserdà de Macía, Dolors
More, Hannah
Němcová, Božena
Nightingale, Florence
Oliphant, Margaret
Paraske, Larin

Pardo Bazan, Emilia
Parren, Callirhoe
Pavlova, Karolina
Percoto, Caterina
Popp, Adelheid
Porter, Jane
Ramée, Marie Louise de la
Reventlow, Franziska von
Ritchie, Lady Anne Thackeray
Rossetti, Christina
Rostopchina, Evdokiia
Savornin Lohman, Catherina Anna
  Maria de
Schreiner, Olive Emilie Albertina
Ségur, Sophie de
Séverine
Sewell, Anna
Shelley, Mary Wollstonecraft
Sinués de Marco, Pilar de
Skram, Amalie
Smara
Sokhanskaia, Nadezhda
Somerville and Ross
Somerville, Mary
Southcott, Joanna
Staël-Holstein, Germaine Necker,
  Baronne de
Stanhope, Lucy Hester
Suttner, Berta von
Tastu, Sabine-Casimir-Amable Voïart
Tristan, Flora Célestine Thérèse
  Henriette
Trollope, Frances Milton
Vivien, Renée
Voilquin, Suzanne
Wordsworth, Dorothy
Worm, Pauline Frederikke
Yonge, Charlotte Mary
Zhadovskaia, Iulia
Zhukova, Maria

20th Century

Aichinger, Ilse
Akhmadúlina, Bélla Akhátovna
Akhmatova, Anna
Aleramo, Sibilla
Alós, Concha
Anagnostaki, Loula
Arendt, Hannah
Aspāzija
Barney, Natalie Clifford
Bčinskaitė-Bučiené, Saloméja
Beauvoir, Simone de
Belpaire, Maria Elisa
Blandiana, Ana
Bluménthal-Weiss, Ilse
Borchers, Elisabeth
Bowen, Elizabeth (Dorothea Cole)
Boye, Karin
Brittain, Vera

Brlić-Ma'uranić, Ivana
Brøgger, Suzanne
Brookner, Anita
Brzostowska, Janina
Buzea, Constanţa
Cartland, Barbara
Champourcin, Ernestina de
 (y Morán de Loredo)
Christensen, Inger
Christie, Agatha
Churchill, Caryl
Cixous, Hélène
Colette, Sidonie-Gabrielle
Compton-Burnett, Ivy
Correia, Natalia de Oliveira
Dąbrowska, Maria
Delaney, Shelagh
Deledda, Grazia
Dessaur, Catharina Irma
Dinesen, Isak
Drabble, Margaret
Duras, Marguerite
Espanca, Florbela de Alma da
 Conceição
Espina, Concha
Fallaci, Oriana
Figuli, Margita
Frank, Anneliese ("Anne")
Gabe, Dora Petrova
Ginzburg, Natalia
Gippius, Zinaïda
Goldberg, Leah
Goll, Claire
Gregory, Lady Augusta
Groot, Maria de
Haasse, Hella
Hal'amová, Maša
Hall, Radclyffe
Hansen, Aase
Heyer, Georgette
Hillesum, Esther ("Etty")
Horta, Maria Teresa
Irigaray, Luce
Jasukaityté, Vidmanté
Jhabvala, Ruth Prawer
Jølsen, Ragnhild
Kallas, Aino
Karapanou, Margarita
Karelli, Zoe
Kempff, Diana
Kerschbaumer, Marie-Thérèse
Kollwitz, Käthe
Krechel, Ursula
Leduc, Violette
Lehmann, Rosamond
Lessing, Doris
Lindgren, Astrid
Lovinescu, Monica
Macaulay, (Emilie) Rose
Mackintosh, Elizabeth

Maillart, Ella
Mandelshtam, Nadezhda
Manner, Eeva-Liisa
Manning, Olivia
Mansfield, Katherine
Manzini, Gianna
Maróthy-Šoltésová, Elena
Martín-Gaite, Carmen
Martínez Sierra, María
Mayröcker, Friederike
Meriluoto, Aila
Mitford, Nancy
Moe, Karin
Morandini, Giuliana
Morante, Elsa
Morgner, Irmtraud
Murdoch, (Jean) Iris
Mutafčieva, Vera
Negri, Ada
Nelken, Margarita
Niedra, Aïda
Noailles (de Brancovan), Anna-
 Elizabeth de
Nöstlinger, Christine
O'Brien, Edna
Paemel, Monika van
Panova, Vera
Papadat-Bengescu, Hortensia
Parren, Callirhoe
Pataki, Heidi
Popp, Adelheid
Potter, Beatrix
Przybyszewska, Stanisława
Pym, Barbara
Quiroga, Elena
Quoirez, Françoise
Rachilde
Ratushinskaia, Irina
Reinshagen, Gerlind
Renault, Mary
Rhys, Jean
Richardson, Dorothy
Rinser, Luise
Rode, Edith
Ryuum, Ulla
Sachs, Nelly
Sackville-West, Vita (Victoria Mary)
Sadowska, Barbara
Sandel, Cora
Sanvitale, Francesca
Sarantë, Galateia
Sarraute, Nathalie
Sarrazin, Albertine
Savornin Lohman, Catherina Anna
 Maria de
Sayers, Dorothy L.
Schoultz, Solveig Margareta
Schreiner, Olive Emilie Albertina
Schwartzer, Alice
Schwarzenbach, Annemarie

Seghers, Anna
Séverine
Shaginian, Marietta
Simonaitytė, Ieva
Sitwell, Dame Edith
Slančiková, Božena
Smara
Smith, Florence Margaret
Södergran, Edith Irene
Somerville and Ross
Spark, Muriel
Spaziani, Maria Luisa
Speyr, Adrienne von
Starkie, Enid (Mary)
Stead, Christina (Ellen)
Stein, Edith
Stevenson, Anne
Strēlerte, Veronica
Susman, Margarete
Sveen, Karin
Szabó, Magda
Szymborska, Wislawa
Taylor, Elizabeth
Tennant, Emma
Teyssiéras, Anne
Tielsch, Ilse
Tikkanen, Märta Eleonora
Tolstaia, Tat'iana
Trotzig, Birgitta
Tsvetaeva, Marina
Tusquets, Esther
Uceda, Julia
Ujvary, Liesl
Ullmann, Regina
Under, Marie
Undset, Sigrid
Vakalo, Helenē
Valenti, Helena
Varţio, Marja-Liisa
Vik, Björg
Vreede, Henny de
Wander, Maxie
Warner, Sylvia Townsend
Webb, Beatrice Potter
Webb, (Gladys) Mary
Weil, Simone
Weldon, Fay
Wertmuller, Lina
West, Rebecca
Winsloe, Christa
Wolf, Christa
Woolf, Virginia
Wuolijoki, Hella Maria
Yourcenar, Marguerite
Zemaitė

▪ For Students

MyAccountingLab provides students with a personalized interactive learning environment, where they can learn at their own pace and measure their progress.

Interactive Tutorial Exercises ▼

MyAccountingLab's homework and practice questions are correlated to the textbook, and they regenerate algorithmically to give students unlimited opportunity for practice and mastery. Questions include guided solutions, DemoDoc examples, and learning aids for extra help at point-of-use, and they offer helpful feedback when students enter incorrect answers.

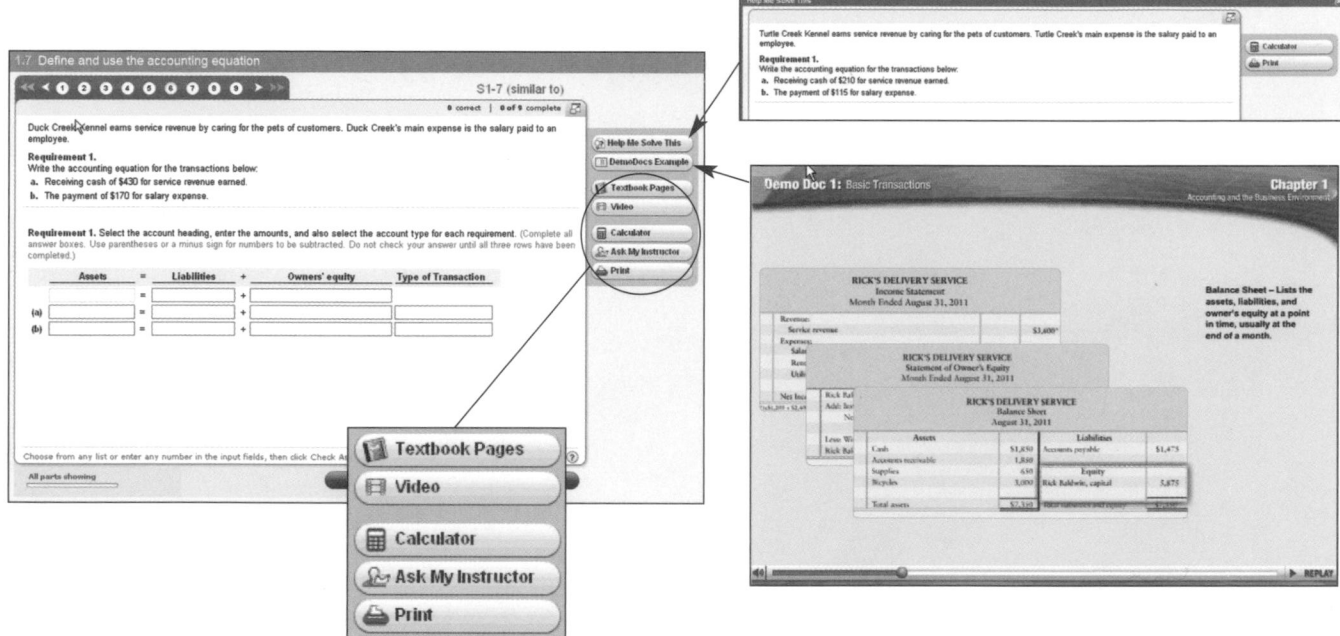

Study Plan for Self-Paced Learning ▶

MyAccountingLab's study plan helps students monitor their own progress, letting them see at a glance exactly which topics they need to practice. MyAccountingLab generates a personalized study plan for each student based on his or her test results, and the study plan links directly to interactive, tutorial exercises for topics the student hasn't yet mastered. Students can regenerate these exercises with new values for unlimited practice, and the exercises include guided solutions and multimedia learning aids to give students the extra help they need.

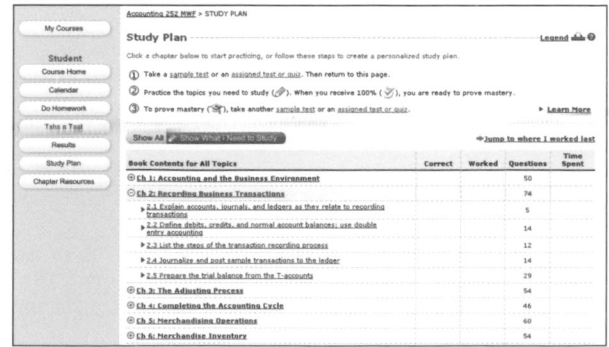

View a guided tour of MyAccountingLab at http://www.myaccountinglab.com/support/tours.

FINANCIAL ACCOUNTING

Eighth Edition

Walter T. Harrison Jr.
Baylor University

Charles T. Horngren
Stanford University

C. William (Bill) Thomas
Baylor University

Pearson Education

Boston   Columbus   Indianapolis   New York   San Francisco   Upper Saddle River
Amsterdam   Cape Town   Dubai   London   Madrid   Milan   Munich   Paris   Montreal   Toronto
Delhi   Mexico City   Sao Paulo   Sydney   Hong Kong   Seoul   Singapore   Taipei   Tokyo

AVP/Executive Editor: Jodi McPherson
VP/Publisher: Natalie E. Anderson
Acquisitions Editor: Jodi Bolognese
Director of Marketing, Intro Markets: Kate Valentine
AVP/Executive Editor, Media: Richard Keaveny
AVP/Executive Producer, Media: Lisa Strite
Director, Product Development: Pamela Hersperger
Editorial Project Manager: Rebecca Knauer
Editorial Media Project Manager: Allison Longley
Editorial Assistant: Terenia McHenry
Development Editor: Karen Misler
Supplements Development Editor: Claire Hunter
Marketing Manager: Maggie Moylan
Marketing Assistant: Justin Jacob
Senior Managing Editor, Production: Cynthia Zonneveld
Production Project Manager: Carol O'Rourke

Production Media Project Manager: John Cassar
Permissions Coordinator: Charles Morris
Senior Operations Specialist: Diane Peirano
Senior Art Director: Jonathan Boylan
Cover Design: Jonathan Boylan
Director, Image Resource Center: Melinda Patelli
Manager, Rights and Permissions: Zina Arabia
Manager, Visual Research: Beth Brenzel
Manager, Cover Visual Research & Permissions:
    Karen Sanatar
Image Permission Coordinator: Jan Marc Quisumbing
Photo Researcher: Kathy Ringrose
Composition: GEX Publishing Services
Full-Service Project Management: GEX Publishing Services
Printer/Binder: Courier
Typeface: Berkley Book 11/13.5

Credits and acknowledgments borrowed from other sources and reproduced, with permission, in this textbook appear on appropriate page within text.

Chapter 1: Alamy Images, p. 1; Chapter 2: Jupiter Images/Comstock Images, p. 63; Chapter 3: James Leynse/CORBIS, p. 137; Chapter 4: iStockPhoto, pp. 231, 256; David R. Frazier/Photolibrary, Inc./Photo Researchers, Inc., p. 242; Chapter 5: Jean Claude Moschetti/REA Agency, p. 289; Chapter 6: Getty Images, p. 341; Chapter 7: Alamy Images, p. 409; Chapter 8: Southwest Airlines Co., p. 467; Chapter 9: Alamy Images, p. 533; Chapter 10: Robert Clare/Photographer's Choice/Getty Images, Inc., p. 603; Chapter 11: Alamy Images, p. 653; Chapter 12: David Grossman/Photo Researchers, Inc., p. 701; Chapter 13: Ken James/Landov Media, p. 775.

All real company financial data presented in chapters 1–13 has been based on the most recent information reported by each company.

Many of the designations by manufacturers and seller to distinguish their products are claimed as trademarks. Where those designations appear in this book, and the publisher was aware of a trademark claim, the designations have been printed in initial caps or all caps.

Library of Congress Cataloging-in-Publication Data
Harrison, Walter T.
    Financial accounting / Walter T. Harrison Jr., Charles T.
Horngren, C. William (Bill) Thomas. — 8th ed.
        p. cm.
    Includes index.
    ISBN-13: 978-0-13-610886-3
    ISBN-10: 0-13-610886-5
    1. Accounting. I. Horngren, Charles T., – II. Thomas, C. William. III. Title.
HF5636.H37 2010
657--dc22   2009020390

10 9 8 7 6 5 4 3 2

Prentice Hall
is an imprint of

www.pearsonhighered.com

ISBN-13: 978-0-13-610886-3
ISBN-10: 0-13-610886-5

For our wives,

Nancy, Joan, and Mary Ann

About the Authors

Walter T. Harrison, Jr. is professor emeritus of accounting at the Hankamer School of Business, Baylor University. He received his BBA from Baylor University, his MS from Oklahoma State University, and his PhD from Michigan State University.

Professor Harrison, recipient of numerous teaching awards from student groups as well as from university administrators, has also taught at Cleveland State Community College, Michigan State University, the University of Texas, and Stanford University.

A member of the American Accounting Association and the American Institute of Certified Public Accountants, Professor Harrison has served as chairman of the Financial Accounting Standards Committee of the American Accounting Association, on the Teaching/Curriculum Development Award Committee, on the Program Advisory Committee for Accounting Education and Teaching, and on the Notable Contributions to Accounting Literature Committee.

Professor Harrison has lectured in several foreign countries and published articles in numerous journals, including *Journal of Accounting Research*, *Journal of Accountancy*, *Journal of Accounting and Public Policy*, *Economic Consequences of Financial Accounting Standards*, *Accounting Horizons*, *Issues in Accounting Education*, and *Journal of Law and Commerce*.

He is co-author of *Financial & Managerial Accounting*, second edition, 2009 and *Accounting*, eighth edition, 2009 (with Charles T. Horngren and M. Suzanne Oliver), published by Pearson Prentice Hall. Professor Harrison has received scholarships, fellowships, and research grants or awards from PricewaterhouseCoopers, Deloitte & Touche, the Ernst & Young Foundation, and the KPMG Foundation.

Charles T. Horngren is the Edmund W. Littlefield professor of accounting, emeritus, at Stanford University. A graduate of Marquette University, he received his MBA from Harvard University and his PhD from the University of Chicago. He is also the recipient of honorary doctorates from Marquette University and DePaul University.

A certified public accountant, Horngren served on the Accounting Principles Board for six years, the Financial Accounting Standards Board Advisory Council for five years, and the Council of the American Institute of Certified Public Accountants for three years. For six years he served as a trustee of the Financial Accounting Foundation, which oversees the Financial Accounting Standards Board and the Government Accounting Standards Board.

Horngren is a member of the Accounting Hall of Fame.

A member of the American Accounting Association, Horngren has been its president and its director of research. He received its first annual Outstanding Accounting Educator Award.

The California Certified Public Accountants Foundation gave Horngren its Faculty Excellence Award and its Distinguished Professor Award. He is the first person to have received both awards.

The American Institute of Certified Public Accountants presented its first Outstanding Educator Award to Horngren.

Horngren was named Accountant of the Year, in Education, by the national professional accounting fraternity, Beta Alpha Psi.

Professor Horngren is also a member of the Institute of Management Accountants, from whom he has received its Distinguished Service Award. He was a member of the institute's Board of Regents, which administers the Certified Management Accountant examinations.

Horngren is the author of these other accounting books published by Pearson Prentice Hall: *Cost Accounting: A Managerial Emphasis*, thirteenth edition, 2008 (with Srikant Datar and George Foster); *Introduction to Financial Accounting*, ninth edition, 2006 (with Gary L. Sundem and John A. Elliott); *Introduction to Management Accounting*, fourteenth edition, 2008 (with Gary L. Sundem and William Stratton); *Financial & Managerial Accounting*, second edition, 2009 and *Accounting*, eighth edition, 2009 (with Walter T. Harrison, Jr. and M. Suzanne Oliver).

Horngren is the consulting editor for Pearson Prentice Hall's Charles T. Horngren Series in Accounting.

Charles William (Bill) Thomas is the KPMG/Thomas L. Holton Chair, the J. E. Bush Professor of Accounting, and a Master Teacher at Baylor University. A Baylor University alumnus, he received both his BBA and MBA there and went on to earn his PhD from The University of Texas at Austin.

With primary interests in the areas of financial accounting and auditing, Bill Thomas has served as the J.E. Bush Professor of Accounting since 1995 and the KPMG/Thomas L. Holton Chair since 2006. He has been a member of the faculty of the Accounting and Business Law Department of the Hankamer School of Business since 1971, and served as chair of the department from 1983 until 1995. He was recognized as an Outstanding Faculty Member of Baylor University in 1984 and Distinguished Professor for the Hankamer School of Business in 2002. Dr. Thomas has received several awards for outstanding teaching, including the Outstanding Professor in the Executive MBA Programs in 2001, 2002, and 2006. In 2004, he received the designation as Master Teacher, an honor that has only been bestowed on 21 persons since the University's inception in 1845.

Thomas is the author of textbooks in auditing and financial accounting, as well as many articles in auditing, financial accounting and reporting, taxation, ethics and accounting education. His scholarly work focuses on the subject of fraud prevention and detection, as well as ethical issues among accountants in public practice. His most recent publication of national prominence is "The Rise and Fall of the Enron Empire" which appeared in the April 2002 *Journal of Accountancy*, and which was selected by Encyclopedia Britannica for inclusion in its *Annals of American History*. He presently serves as both technical and accounting and auditing editor of *Today's CPA*, the journal of the Texas Society of Certified Public Accountants, with a circulation of approximately 28,000.

Thomas is a certified public accountant in Texas. Prior to becoming a professor, Thomas was a practicing accountant with the firms of KPMG, LLP, and BDO Seidman, LLP. He is a member of the American Accounting Association, the American Institute of Certified Public Accountants, and the Texas Society of Certified Public Accountants.

Brief Contents

Brief Contents

Contents

Chapter 7

Plant Assets & Intangibles   409

Chapter 8

Liabilities   467

Chapter 9

Stockholders' Equity   533

Chapter 10

Long-Term Investments & International Operations   603

Chapter 11

The Income Statement & the Statement of Stockholders' Equity   653

With
Financial Accounting
Student Text, Study Resources,
and MyAccountingLab
students will have more
"I get it!"
moments!

Students will "get it" anytime, anywhere

Students understand (or "get it") right after you do a problem in class. Once they leave the classroom, however, students often struggle to complete the homework on their own. This frustration can cause students to quit on the material altogether and fall behind in the course, resulting in an entire class falling behind as the instructor attempts to keep everyone on the same page.

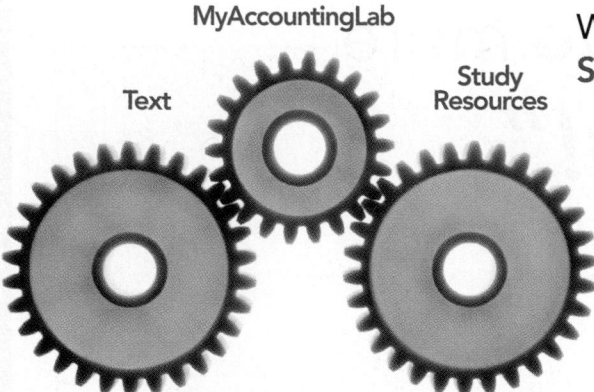

MyAccountingLab

Text

Study Resources

With the *Financial Accounting*, Eighth Edition, **Student Learning System**, all the features of the student textbook, study resources, and online homework system are designed to work together to provide students with the consistency, repetition, and high level of detail that will keep both instructors and students on track, providing more "I get it!" moments inside and outside the classroom.

Replicating the Classroom Experience with Demo Doc Examples

The Demo Doc examples consist of entire problems, worked through step-by-step, from start to finish, narrated with the kind of comments that instructors would say in class. The Demo Docs are available in the accounting cycle chapters of the text and in the study guide. In addition to the printed Demo Docs, Flash-animated versions are available so that students can watch the problems as they are worked through while listening to the explanations and details. Demo Docs will aid students when they are trying to solve exercises and problems on their own, duplicating the classroom experience outside of class.

Demo Doc

Debit/Credit Transaction Analysis

Demo Doc: To make sure you understand this material, work through the following demonstration "demo doc" with detailed comments to help you see the concept within the framework of a worked-through problem.

Learning Objectives 1, 2, 3, 4

On September 1, 2008, Michael Moe incorporated Moe's Mowing, Inc., a company that provides mowing and landscaping services. During the month of September, the business incurred the following transactions:

a. To begin operations, Michael deposited $10,000 cash in the business's bank account. The business received the cash and issued common stock to Michael.

b. The business purchased equipment for $3,500 on account.

c. The business purchased office supplies for $800 cash.

d. The business provided $2,600 of services to a customer on account.

e. The business paid $500 cash toward the equipment previously purchased on account in transaction b.

f. The business received $2,000 in cash for services provided to a new customer.

g. The business paid $200 cash to repair equipment.

h. The business paid $900 cash in salary expense.

i. The business received $2,100 cash from a customer on account.

j. The business paid cash dividends of $1,500.

with the Student Learning System!

Consistency, Repetition, and a High Level of Detail Throughout the Learning Process

The concepts, materials, and practice problems are presented with clarity and consistency across all mediums—textbook, study resources, and online homework system. No matter which platform students use they will continually experience the same look, feel, and language, minimizing confusion and ensuring clarity.

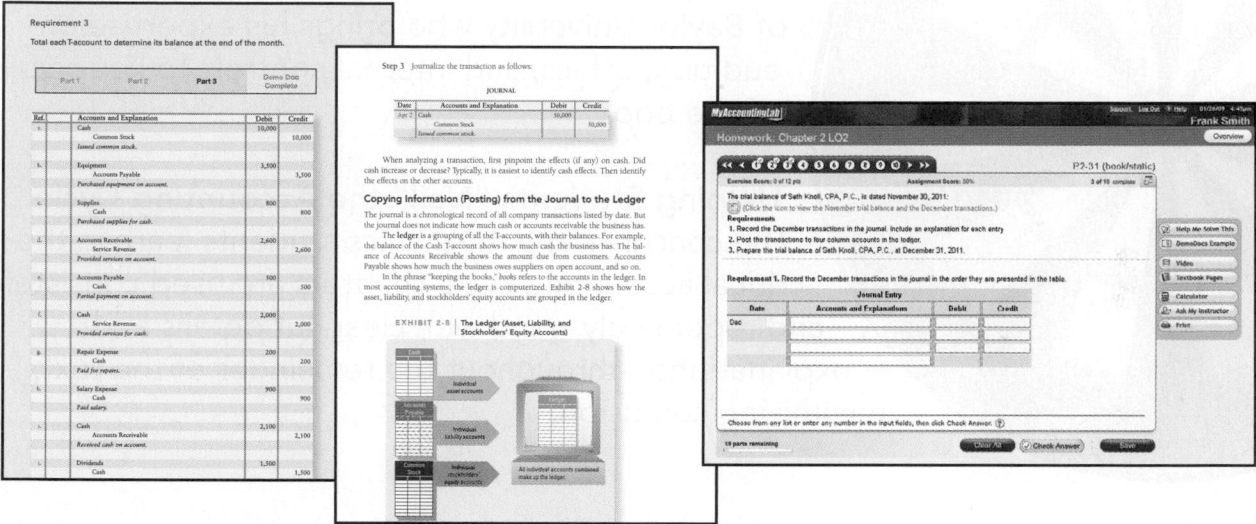

Experiencing the Power of Practice with MyAccountingLab: www.myaccountinglab.com

MyAccountingLab is an online homework system that gives students more "I get it!" moments through the power of practice. With MyAccountingLab, students can

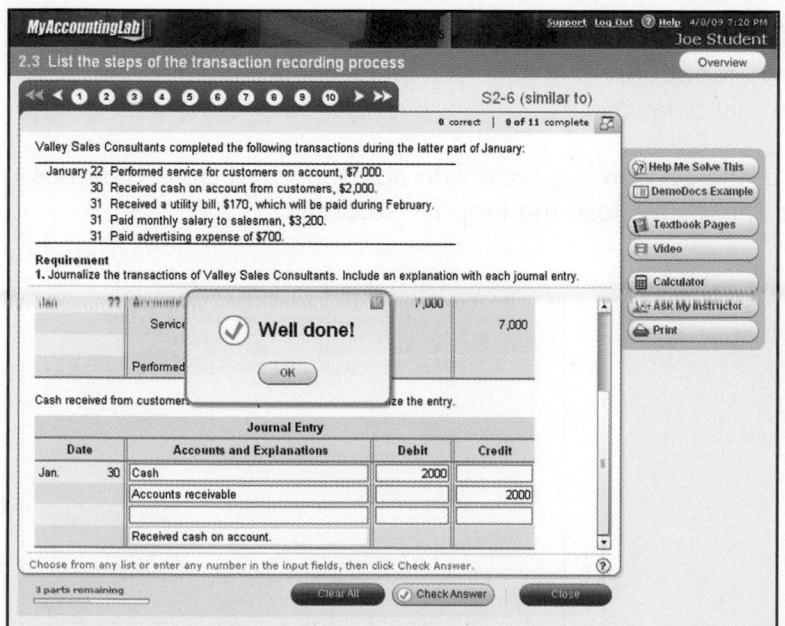

- Work on problems assigned by the instructor that are either exact matches or algorithmic versions of the end-of-chapter material.
- Use the Study Plan for self-assessment and customized study outlines.
- Use the Help Me Solve This for a step-by-step tutorial.
- View the Demo Docs example to see an animated demonstration of where the numbers came from.
- Watch a video to see additional information pertaining to the lecture.
- Open textbook pages to find the material they need to get help on specific problems.

Financial Accounting helps students

Financial Accounting helps students "nail" the accounting cycle up front in order to increase success and retention later on.

The Eighth Edition features new coauthor Bill Thomas of Baylor University who brings his expertise on auditing, ethics, and internal controls to key sections of the book.

Helping Students "Nail" the Accounting Cycle

The concepts and mechanics students learn in the critical accounting cycle chapters are used consistently and repetitively—and with clear-cut details and explanations—throughout the remainder of the text, minimizing confusion.

Better Coverage of the Accounting Cycle from Start to Finish

Chapter 1 introduces the accounting cycle with a brief financial statement overview, using the financial statements of J.Crew Group, Inc. This first exposure to accounting explores financial statements in depth, familiarizes students with using real business data, and points out basic relationships between the different types of statements.

Chapter 2 continues the discussion of the accounting cycle by explaining how to analyze and record basic transactions, and builds in repetition to ensure that students understand the fundamentals when they prepare the trial balance.

Chapter 3 concludes the discussion of the accounting cycle with adjusting and closing entries, and preparation of the related trial balances to close the loop for students.

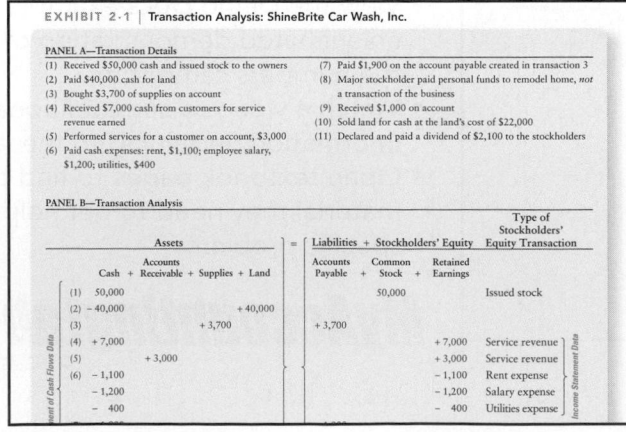

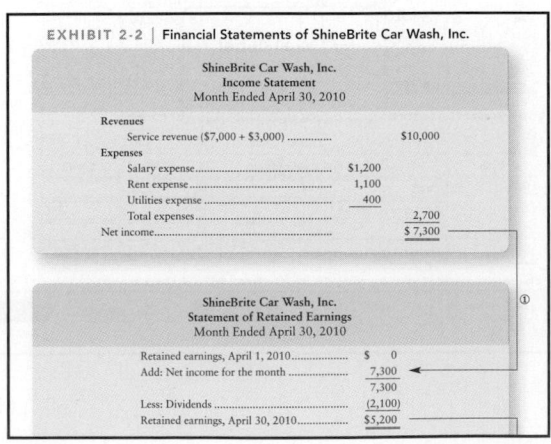

"nail" the accounting cycle!

Consistency, Repetition, and a High Level of Detail

Throughout the text, the core concepts and mechanics are brought together using consistent language, format, and formulas. Students also receive thorough explanations and details that show the meaning behind each concept and how to do the computation following it, providing an in-depth understanding of the fundamentals.

Whether it's the first transaction or the last, students perform the analysis in the same way, thus reinforcing their understanding, reducing the level of confusion and frustration, and helping them capture those "I get it!" moments.

For example, in Chapter 2 students see the impact of transactions and how the transactions are eventually summarized into the income statement, statement of retained earnings, and balance sheet.

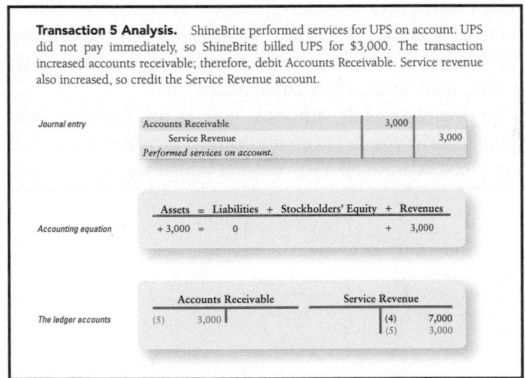

A **Mid-Chapter Summary Problem** provides a stopping point for students—it gives them an opportunity to repeat the entire process again, using data from a different company, to make sure they've "got it." The **End-of-Chapter Summary Problem** closes out the chapter and allows students to practice the process again and really "nail" these fundamental skills.

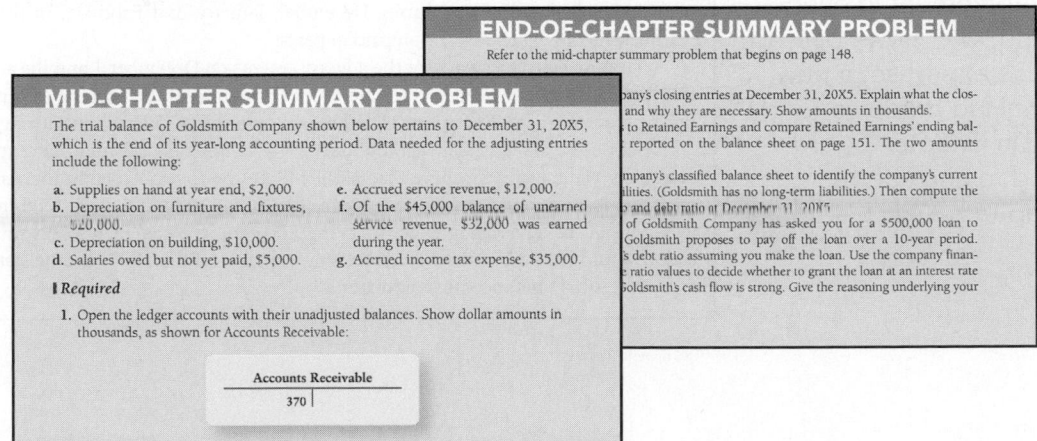

www.pearsonhighered.com/harrison

New to the Eighth Edition

New International Financial Reporting Standards (IFRS)

In order to increase student awareness of the most important potential shift in the future of financial accounting, information on IFRS is introduced in Chapter 1, where appropriate throughout chapters in the new Global View feature, and in a new appendix.

 **GLOBAL VIEW** One of the most significant differences between U.S. GAAP and International Financial Reporting Standards (IFRS) is the permitted reported carrying values of property, plant, and equipment. Recall from Chapter 1 that U.S. GAAP has long advocated the historical cost principle as most appropriate for plant assets because it results in a more objective (non-biased) and therefore a more reliable (auditable) figure. It also supports the continuity assumption, which states that we expect the entity to remain in business long enough to recover the cost of its plant assets through depreciation.

In contrast, while historical cost is the primary basis of accounting under IFRS, it permits the periodic revaluation of plant assets to fair market value. The primary justification for this position is that the historical cost of plant assets pur-

When students practice or complete their homework in **MyAccountingLab**, they will also be exposed to IFRS. The content is designed to raise student awareness of IFRS and to be a companion for the IFRS text coverage.

New and Updated Content on Ethics

Sound ethical judgment is important for every major financial decision—which is why this text provides consistent ethical reinforcement in every chapter. And, with new coauthor Bill Thomas's expertise, a new decision-making model is introduced in Chapter 1 and applied to each of the end-of-chapter cases.

Ethical Issues in Accrual Accounting

Accrual accounting provides some ethical challenges that cash accounting avoids. For example, suppose that in 2008, Starbucks Corporation prepays a $3 million advertising campaign to be conducted by a large advertising agency. The advertisements are scheduled to run during December, January, and February. In this case, Starbucks is buying an asset, a prepaid expense.

Suppose Starbucks pays for the advertisements on December 1 and the ads start running immediately. Starbucks should record one-third of the expense ($1 million) during the year ended December 31, 2008, and two-thirds ($2 million) during 2009.

Suppose 2008 is a great year for Starbucks—net income is better than expected. Starbucks' top managers believe that 2009 will not be as profitable. In this case, the company has a strong incentive to expense the full $3 million during 2008 in order to report all the advertising expense in the 2008 income statement. This unethical action would keep $2 million of advertising expense off the 2009 income statement and make 2009's net income look better.

Enhanced Coverage of Cash Flows

The current economy has created a shift in how we view money—specifically, cash. Cash flow is the lifeblood of any business, so in the Eighth Edition of *Financial Accounting*, coverage of Cash Flows has been increased and highlighted in Chapters 4–10 so that students can easily see the connections and understand the significance.

IMPACT OF REPORTING STOCKHOLDER FINANCING ACTIVITIES ON CASH FLOWS

At the end of the period, the business reports its financial statements. This process begins with the trial balance introduced in Chapter 2. We refer to this trial balance as unadjusted because the accounts are not yet ready for the financial statements. In most cases the simple label "Trial Balance" means "unadjusted."

Which Accounts Need to Be Updated (Adjusted)?

The stockholders need to know how well Genie Car Wash is performing. The financial statements report this information, and all accounts must be up-to-date. That

New Fraud Coverage

In an age of public scandals, understanding fraud is a key component of *Financial Accounting*. Chapter 4 now includes the concept of fraud, and introduces students to the "fraud triangle" (motivation, opportunity, and rationalization) and a discussion of internal controls as the primary way companies prevent fraud.

For example, **Cooking the Books** sections highlight real fraud cases in relevant sections throughout the text, giving students real-life business context. Examples include the following:

- Crazy Eddie (Chapters 6 and 8)
- WorldCom and Waste Management (Chapter 7)
- Enron (Chapters 8, 9, and 10)

COOKING THE BOOKS
by Improper Capitalization

WorldCom

It is one thing to accidentally capitalize a plant asset but quite another to do it intentionally, thus deliberately understating expenses and overstating net income. One well-known company committed one of the biggest financial statement frauds in history.

In 2002, WorldCom, Inc., was one of the largest telecommunications service providers in the world. The company had grown rapidly from a small, regional telephone company in 1983 to a giant corporation in 2002 by acquiring an ever-increasing number of other such companies. But 2002 was a bad year for WorldCom, as well as for many others in the "telecom" industry. The United States was reeling from the effects of a deep economic recession spawned by the "bursting dot-com bubble" in 2000 and intensified by the terrorist attacks on the World Trade Center and the U.S. Pentagon in 2001. Wall Street was looking high and low for positive signs, pressuring public companies to keep profits trending upward in order to support share prices, without much success, at least for the honest companies.

Hallmark Features

Summary Problems and Solutions appear in both the middle and end-of-chapter sections, providing students with additional guided learning. By presenting these problems and solutions twice in one chapter, this text breaks up the information, enabling students to absorb and master the material in more manageable pieces.

END-OF-CHAPTER SUMMARY PROBLEM

Refer to the mid-chapter summary problem that begins on page 148.

I Required

1. Make Goldsmith Company's closing entries at December 31, 20X5. Explain what the closing entries accomplish and why they are necessary. Show amounts in thousands.
2. Post the closing entries to Retained Earnings and compare Retained Earnings' ending balance with the amount reported on the balance sheet on page 151. The two amounts should be the same.

MID-CHAPTER SUMMARY PROBLEM

The trial balance of Goldsmith Company shown below pertains to December 31, 20X5, which is the end of its year-long accounting period. Data needed for the adjusting entries include the following:

a. Supplies on hand at year end, $2,000.
b. Depreciation on furniture and fixtures, $20,000.
c. Depreciation on building, $10,000.
d. Salaries owed but not yet paid, $5,000.

e. Accrued service revenue, $12,000.
f. Of the $45,000 balance of unearned service revenue, $32,000 was earned during the year.
g. Accrued income tax expense, $35,000.

I Required

1. Open the ledger accounts with their unadjusted balances. Show dollar amounts in thousands, as shown for Accounts Receivable:

Accounts Receivable
370

STOP & THINK . . .

1. A customer pays Starbucks $100 on March 15 for coffee to be served at a party in April. Has Starbucks earned revenue on March 15? When will Starbucks earn the revenue?
2. Starbucks pays $4,500 on July 1 for store rent for the next 3 months. Has Starbucks incurred an expense on July 1?

Answers:

1. No. Starbucks has received the cash but will not deliver the coffee until later. Starbucks earns the revenue when it gives the goods to the customer.

Stop & Think sections relate concepts to everyday life so that students can see the immediate relevance.

Demo Docs in the accounting cycle chapters offer fully worked-through problems that weave computation and concepts together in a step-by-step format, helping students understand the "how" and "why." Additional Demo Docs, including animated versions, are available in the study guide and in **MyAccountingLab**.

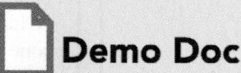 **Demo Doc**

Debit/Credit Transaction Analysis

Demo Doc: To make sure you understand this material, work through the following demonstration "demo doc" with detailed comments to help you see the concept within the framework of a worked through problem.

Learning Objectives 1, 2, 3, 4

On September 1, 2008, Michael Moe incorporated Moe's Mowing, Inc., a company that provides mowing and landscaping services. During the month of September, the business incurred the following transactions.

a. To begin operations, Michael deposited $10,000 cash in the business's bank account. The business received the cash and issued common stock to Michael.
b. The business purchased equipment for $3,500 on account.
c. The business purchased office supplies for $800 cash.
d. The business provided $2,600 of services to a customer on account.
e. The business paid $500 cash toward the equipment previously purchased on account in transaction b.
f. The business received $2,000 in cash for services provided to a new customer.
g. The business paid $200 cash to repair equipment.
h. The business paid $900 cash in salary expense.
i. The business received $2,100 cash from a customer on account.
j. The business paid cash dividends of $1,500.

Decision Guidelines in the end-of-chapter material summarize the chapter's key terms, concepts, and formulas in the context of business decisions. Not only does this help students read more actively in the question and answer format, but it also reinforces how the accounting information they are learning is used to make decisions in business.

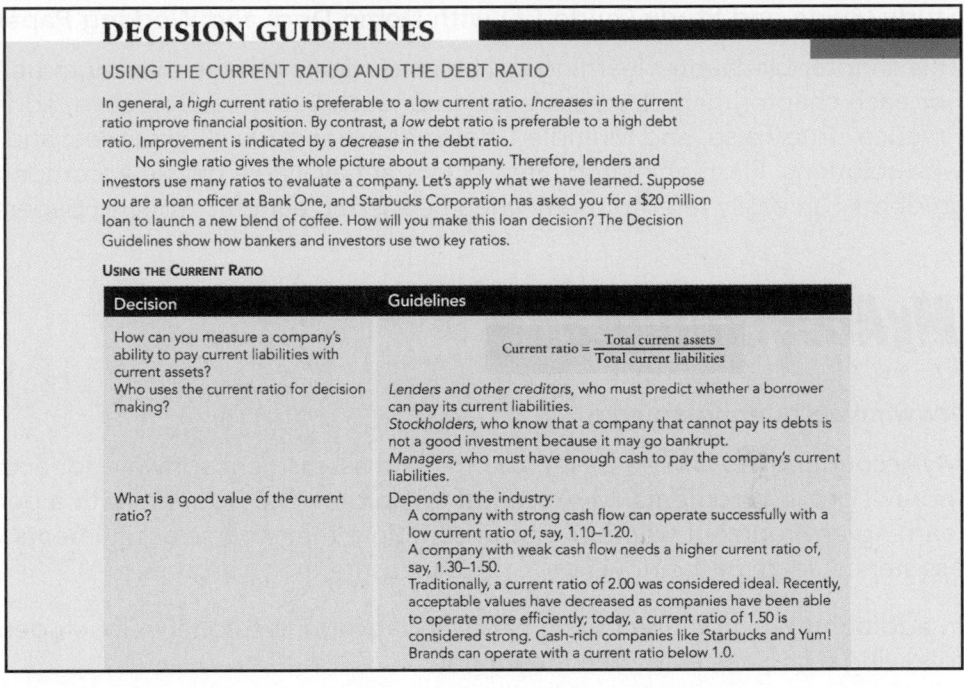

DECISION GUIDELINES

USING THE CURRENT RATIO AND THE DEBT RATIO

In general, a *high* current ratio is preferable to a low current ratio. *Increases* in the current ratio improve financial position. By contrast, a *low* debt ratio is preferable to a high debt ratio. Improvement is indicated by a *decrease* in the debt ratio.

No single ratio gives the whole picture about a company. Therefore, lenders and investors use many ratios to evaluate a company. Let's apply what we have learned. Suppose you are a loan officer at Bank One, and Starbucks Corporation has asked you for a $20 million loan to launch a new blend of coffee. How will you make this loan decision? The Decision Guidelines show how bankers and investors use two key ratios.

USING THE CURRENT RATIO

Decision	Guidelines
How can you measure a company's ability to pay current liabilities with current assets?	$\text{Current ratio} = \dfrac{\text{Total current assets}}{\text{Total current liabilities}}$
Who uses the current ratio for decision making?	*Lenders and other creditors*, who must predict whether a borrower can pay its current liabilities. *Stockholders*, who know that a company that cannot pay its debts is not a good investment because it may go bankrupt. *Managers*, who must have enough cash to pay the company's current liabilities.
What is a good value of the current ratio?	Depends on the industry: A company with strong cash flow can operate successfully with a low current ratio of, say, 1.10–1.20. A company with weak cash flow needs a higher current ratio of, say, 1.30–1.50. Traditionally, a current ratio of 2.00 was considered ideal. Recently, acceptable values have decreased as companies have been able to operate more efficiently; today, a current ratio of 1.50 is considered strong. Cash-rich companies like Starbucks and Yum! Brands can operate with a current ratio below 1.0.

MyAccountingLab ®

NEW! End-of-Chapter Material Integrated with MyAccountingLab at www.myaccountinglab.com

Students need practice and repetition in order to successfully learn the fundamentals of financial accounting. *Financial Accounting*, Eighth Edition, now contains an additional set of exercises in the text for professors to choose from. Also available in MyAccountingLab are three static alternatives for all exercises and problems, as well as algorithmic versions, providing students with unlimited practice. In addition, IFRS coverage has been added so students can see how IFRS will impact decisions in accounting. (For more information, visit www.myaccountinglab.com.)

End-of-Chapter Materials include Quick Check multiple-choice review questions, short exercises, A and B exercises and problems, serial and challenge exercises, multiple-choice quiz questions, decision cases, ethical cases, Focus on Financials (with real financial statement analysis), Focus on Analysis (with real financial statement analysis), and group projects.

www.pearsonhighered.com/harrison

Student Resources

Study Guide and Study Guide CD with Demo Docs and Working Papers

This chapter-by-chapter learning aid helps students get the maximum benefit from their study time. For each chapter there is an explanation of each Learning Objective; additional Demo Docs; Quick Practice, True/False, and Multiple Choice questions; Quick Exercises; and a Do It Yourself question, all with solutions. Flash-animated Demo Docs are available on the accompanying study guide CD so students can easily refer to them when needed. Electronic working papers are also included.

www.myaccountinglab.com

MyAccountingLab is Web-based tutorial and assessment software for accounting that gives students more "I get it!" moments. **MyAccountingLab** provides students with a personalized interactive learning environment where they can complete their course assignments with immediate tutorial assistance, learn at their own pace, and measure their progress.

In addition to completing assignments and reviewing tutorial help, students have access to the following resources in **MyAccountingLab**:

- The Flash-based eBook
- Study Guide
- Animated Demo Docs
- General Ledger Student Data Files
- Excel in Practice
- Videos and MP3 files
- Audio and Student PowerPoints
- Working Papers
- Flashcards

Student Resource Web site: www.pearsonhighered.com/harrison

- General Ledger Student Data Files
- Working Papers
- Excel in Practice

Student Reference Cards

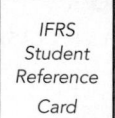

International Financial Reporting Standards Student Reference Card

This four-page laminated reference card includes an overview of IFRS, why they matter and how they compare to U.S. standards, and highlights key differences between IFRS and U.S. GAAP.

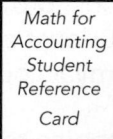

Math for Accounting Student Reference Card

This six-page laminated reference card provides students with a study tool for the basic math they will need to be successful in accounting, such as rounding, fractions, converting decimals, calculating interest, break-even analysis, and more!

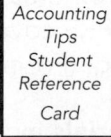

Accounting Tips Student Reference Card

This four-page laminated reference card illustrates the key steps in the accounting cycle.

Instructor Resources

The primary goal of the Instructor Resources is to help instructors deliver their course with ease, using any delivery method—traditional, self-paced, or online.

www.myaccountinglab.com

MyAccountingLab is Web-based tutorial and assessment software for accounting that not only gives students more "I get it!" moments, but also provides instructors the flexibility to make technology an integral part of their course. And, because practice makes perfect, **MyAccountingLab** offers exactly the same end-of-chapter material found in the text with algorithmic options that instructors can assign for homework. **MyAccountingLab** also replicates the text's exercises and problems with journal entries and financial statements so that students are familiar and comfortable working with the material.

Instructor's Manual

The Instructor's Manual, available electronically or in print, offers course-specific content including a guide to available resources, a road map for using **MyAccountingLab**, a first-day handout for students, sample syllabi, and guidelines for teaching an online course, as well as content-specific material including chapter overviews, teaching outlines, student summary handouts, lecture outline tips, assignment grids, ten-minute quizzes, and more!

Instructor Resource Center: www.pearsonhighered.com/harrison

For your convenience, many of our instructor supplements are available for download from the textbook's catalog page or your **MyAccountingLab** account. Available resources include the following:

- Solutions Manual containing the fully worked-through and accuracy-checked solutions for every question, exercise, and problem in the text
- Test Item File with TestGen Software providing over 1,600 multiple choice, true/false, and problem-solving questions correlated by Learning Objective and difficulty level as well as AACSB and AICPA standards
- Four sets of PowerPoint presentations give instructors flexibility and choices for their courses. There are 508 Compliant Instructor PowerPoints with extensive notes for on-campus or online classes, Student PowerPoints, Clicker Response System (CRS) PowerPoints, and Audio Narrated PowerPoints.
- Data and Solution Files—General Ledger
- Working Papers and Solutions
- Instructor's Manual
- Excel in Practice
- Image Library

Course Cartridges

Course Cartridges for BlackBoard, WebCT, CourseCompass, and other learning management systems are available upon request.

www.pearsonhighered.com/harrison

Changes to the Eighth Edition

Students and instructors will benefit from a variety of new content and features in the Eighth Edition of *Financial Accounting*. To reflect the most recent developments in the economy and in the accounting industry, the following content additions or changes have been made:

The first chapter has been rewritten to introduce the new **Joint Conceptual Framework for Accounting** from the Financial Accounting Standards Board (FASB) and the International Accounting Standards Board (IASB).

In order to increase student awareness of the most important potential shift in the future of financial accounting, **International Financial Reporting Standards (IFRS)** have been integrated into the Eighth Edition. Chapter 1 introduces the topic and summarizes the current plan for U.S. adoption of IFRS by 2014. This discussion lays the foundation for integration of IFRS in appropriate chapters throughout the book, including highlighting key differences between U.S. GAAP and IFRS. A new appendix (F) was added with a table highlighting the IFRS coverage topic by topic. A Global View feature was added in relevant chapters to specifically explain how IFRS integration will impact financial accounting. IFRS Student Study Guide by Marlene Plumlee at the University of Utah is a chapter long supplement that discusses the general context of U.S. GAAP and IFRS, providing background information about the use of U.S. GAAP and IFRS and "players" that will ultimately affect how and when IFRS will be adopted internationally. Included also is an overview of the conceptual frameworks that underlie the formation of U.S. GAAP and IFRS. A comparison of two companies is offered, one that employs U.S. GAAP to prepare its financial report and one that employs IFRS to prepare its financial report.

With the recent changes and events in the economy, educating students on the importance of **ethics and ethical decision making** is critical. The discussion of ethics in accounting has been updated and moved to Chapter 1, placing greater emphasis on the importance of ethics at the very beginning of the text. The Eighth Edition also introduces an expanded decision-making model in Chapter 1 and integrates the model throughout the entire text with economic, legal, and ethical dimensions. The Ethical Cases in the end-of-chapter material have been rewritten to unify and better integrate coverage on this important topic so that the material is reinforced consistently in every chapter.

In an age of public scandals, understanding **fraud** is a key component of financial accounting. Chapter 4 now includes the concept of fraud, and introduces students to the "fraud triangle" (motivation, opportunity, and rationalization) that leads to the discussion of internal controls as the primary way that companies prevent fraud—which has also been updated. The discussion of fraud in Chapter 4 also lays the foundation for the new Cooking the Books sections (found in appropriate chapters later on in the book), which add real-life relevance and interest to otherwise dry accounting concepts by presenting real-world fraud cases such as Crazy Eddie (Chapters 6 and 8), WorldCom and Waste Management (Chapter 7), and Enron (Chapters 8, 9, and 10).

To help students understand accounting topics that are currently impacting **the global economy**, Chapter 11 includes a new discussion on quality of earnings, revenue recognition, and fraud. The quality of earnings section focuses on evaluating a company's financial position to help in decision making, which students will need when they enter the workforce. There is also an expanded discussion on the elements of the income statement and revenue recognition. The revenue recognition and extraordinary items sections are key points that highlight the difference between IFRS and U.S. GAAP, and are critical to understanding the convergence of global accounting standards. The new Cooking the Books feature uses Bristol-Myers Squibb to highlight improper revenue recognition.

To keep examples and data current and accurate, all **financial statements** for the companies covered have been updated. All real company financial data now refers to 2007 or 2008.

Both of the **focus companies are new** (Amazon.com, Inc., and Foot Locker, Inc.) so that students see examples of statements and accounting practices that are as current as possible. As a result, the annual reports in the book's appendices are new, and all the Focus on Financials and Focus on Analysis questions in the end-of-chapter material have been updated throughout the text.

Understanding cash flows is a critical concept for students in today's economy, which is why there is a new and increased emphasis on the use of **cash flow information** in selected chapters. By highlighting this coverage from chapter to chapter, this edition helps students make the connection between cash and other accounting concepts so they understand the significance of cash flow as the lifeblood of a business.

To provide students with more opportunities to practice important concepts, and to provide instructors with additional choices of material to assign, all of the **end-of-chapter content** has been revised, including the following:

- 100% of values and dates in the end-of-chapter questions are new.
- A new set of "B" exercises has been added in every chapter, giving students more opportunities to practice important concepts.
- Every end-of-chapter question in the Assess Your Progress sections is now available in **MyAccountingLab** for students to complete and receive immediate tutorial feedback and help when they need it. Alternative, static exercises and problems were also added in **MyAccountingLab** (www.myaccountinglab.com) to give students and instructors more options for assignments and practice.

ACKNOWLEDGMENTS

In revising previous editions of *Financial Accounting*, we had the help of instructors from across the country who have participated in online surveys, chapter reviews, and focus groups. Their comments and suggestions for both the text and the supplements have been a great help in planning and carrying out revisions, and we thank them for their contributions.

Financial Accounting, Eighth Edition

Revision Plan Reviewers

Elizabeth Ammann, Lindenwood University
Brenda Anderson, Brandeis University
Patrick Bauer, DeVry University, Kansas City
Amy Bourne, Oregon State University
Elizabeth Brown, Keene State College
Scott Bryant, Baylor University
Marci Butterfield, University of Utah
Dr. Paul Clikeman, University of Richmond
Sue Counte, Saint Louis Community College-Meramec
Julia Creighton, American University
Sue Cullers, Buena Vista University
Betty David, Francis Marion University
Peter DiCarlo, Boston College
Allan Drebin, Northwestern University
Carolyn Dreher, Southern Methodist University
Emily Drogt, Grand Valley State University
Dr. Andrew Felo, Penn State Great Valley
Dr. Caroline Ford, Baylor University
Clayton Forester, University of Minnesota
Timothy Gagnon, Northeastern University
Marvin Gordon, University of Illinois at Chicago
Anthony Greig, Purdue University
Dr. Heidi Hansel, Kirkwood Community College
Michael Haselkorn, Bentley University
Mary Hollars, Vincennes University
Grace Johnson, Marietta College
Celina Jozsi, University of South Florida
John Karayan, Woodbury University
Robert Kollar, Duquesne University
Elliott Levy, Bentley University
Joseph Lupino, Saint Mary's College of California
Anthony Masino, Queens University / NC Central
Lizbeth Matz, University of Pittsburgh, Bradford
Mary Miller, University of New Haven
Scott Miller, Gannon University
Dr. Birendra (Barry) K. Mishra, University of California, Riverside
Lisa Nash, Vincennes University

Rosemary Nurre, College of San Mateo
Stephen Owen, Hamilton College
Rama Ramamurthy, College of William and Mary
Barb Reeves, Cleary University
Anwar Salimi, California State Polytechnic University, Pomona
Philippe Sammour, Eastern Michigan University
Albert A Schepanski, University of Iowa
Lily Sieux, California State University, East Bay
Vic Stanton, Stanford University
Martin Taylor, University of Texas at Arlington
Vincent Turner, California State Polytechnic University, Pomona
Craig Weaver, University of California, Riverside
Betsy Willis, Baylor University
Dr. Jia Wu, University of Massachusetts, Dartmouth
Barbara Yahvah, University of Montana-Helena

Chapter Reviewers

Florence Atiase, University of Texas at Austin
Amy Bourne, Oregon State University
Rada Brooks, University of California, Berkeley
Marci Butterfield, University of Utah
Carolyn Dreher, Southern Methodist University
Lisa Gillespie, Loyola University, Chicago
Mary Hollars, Vincennes University
Constance Malone Hylton, George Mason University
Barry Mishra, University of California, Riverside
Virginia Smith, Saint Mary's College of California
Betsy Willis, Baylor University

Supplements Authors

Excel in Practice Templates: Jennie Mitchell, Saint Mary-of-the-Woods College
Excel Data Files: Jennie Mitchell, Saint Mary-of-the-Woods College
General Ledger Templates: Jamie McCracken, Saint Mary-of-the-Woods College

Instructor's Manual: Denise Wooten, Erie Community
  College–North
PowerPoints: Courtney Baillie, Nebraska
  Wesleyan University
Study Guide: Helen Brubeck, San Jose State University
Solutions Manual: Richard J. Pettit, Mountain
  View College
Test Item File: Sandra Augustine, Hilbert College

Supplements Reviewers

Linda Abernathy, Kirkwood Community College
Brenda Bindschatel, Green River Community College
Allan Sheets, International Business College
Richard J. Pettit, Mountain View College

Previous Edition

Online Reviewers

Lucille Berry, Webster University, MO
Patrick Bouker, North Seattle Community College
Michael Broihahn, Barry University, FL
Kam Chan, Pace University
Hong Chen, Northeastern Illinois University
Charles Coate, St. Bonaventure University, NY
Bryan Church, Georgia Tech at Atlanta
Terrie Gehman, Elizabethtown College, PA
Brian Green, University of Michigan at Dearborn
Chao-Shin Liu, Notre Dame
Herb Martin, Hope College, MI
Bruce Maule, College of San Mateo
Michelle McEacharn, University of Louisiana at Monroe
Bettye Rogers-Desselle, Prairie View A&M University, TX
Norlin Rueschhoff, Notre Dame
William Schmul, Notre Dame
Arnie Schnieder, Georgia Tech at Atlanta
J. B. Stroud, Nicholls State Univesity, LA
Bruce Wampler, Louisiana State University, Shreveport
Myung Yoon, Northeastern Illinois University
Lin Zeng, Northeastern Illinois University

Focus Group Participants

Ellen D. Cook, University of Louisiana at Lafayette
Theodore D. Morrison III, Wingate University, NC
Alvin Gerald Smith, University of Northern Iowa

Carolyn R. Stokes, Frances Marion University, SC
Suzanne Ward, University of Louisiana at Lafayette

Chapter Reviewers

Kim Anderson, Indiana University of Pennsylvania
Peg Beresewski, Robert Morris College, IL
Helen Brubeck, San Jose State University, CA
Mark Camma, Atlantic Cape Community College, NJ
Freddy Choo, San Francisco State University, CA
Laurie Dahlin, Worcester State College, MA
Ronald Guidry, University of Louisiana at Monroe
Ellen Landgraf, Loyola University, Chicago
Nick McGaughey, San Jose State University, CA
Mark Miller, University of San Francisco, CA
Craig Reeder, Florida A&M University
Brian Stanko, Loyola University, Chicago
Marcia Veit, University of Central Florida
Ronald Woan, Indiana University of Pennsylvania

Online Supplement Reviewers

Shawn Abbott, College of the Siskiyous, CA
Sol Ahiarah, SUNY College at Buffalo (Buffalo State)
M. J. Albin, University of Southern Mississippi
Gary Ames, Brigham Young University, Idaho
Walter Austin, Mercer University, Macon GA
Brad Badertscher, University of Iowa
Sandra Bailey, Oregon Institute of Technology
Barbara A. Beltrand, Metropolitan State University, MN
Jerry Bennett, University of South
  Carolina–Spartanburg
John Bildersee, New York University, Stern School
Candace Blankenship, Belmont University, TN
Charlie Bokemeier, Michigan State University
Scott Boylan, Washington and Lee University, VA
Robert Braun, Southeastern Louisiana University
Linda Bressler, University of Houston Downtown
Carol Brown, Oregon State University
Marcus Butler, University of Rochester, NY
Kay Carnes, Gonzaga University, WA
Brian Carpenter, University of Scranton, PA
Sandra Cereola, James Madison University, VA
Hong Chen, Northeastern Illinois University
Shifei Chung, Rowan University, NJ
Bryan Church, Georgia Tech

Charles Christy, Delaware Tech and Community College, Stanton Campus
Carolyn Clark, Saint Joseph's University, PA
Dianne Conry, University of California State College Extension–Cupertino
John Coulter, Western New England College
Donald Curfman, McHenry County College, IL
Alan Czyzewski, Indiana State University
Bonita Daly, University of Southern Maine
Patricia Derrick, George Washington University
Charles Dick, Miami University
Barbara Doughty, New Hampshire Community Technical College
Carol Dutton, South Florida Community College
James Emig, Villanova University, PA
Ellen Engel, University of Chicago
Alan Falcon, Loyola Marymount University, CA
Janet Farler, Pima Community College, AZ
Andrew Felo, Penn State Great Valley
Ken Ferris, Thunderbird College, AZ
Lou Fowler, Missouri Western State College
Lucille Genduso, Nova Southeastern University, FL
Frank Gersich, Monmouth College, IL
Bradley Gillespie, Saddleback College, CA
Brian Green, University of Michigan–Dearborn
Konrad Gunderson, Missouri Western State College
William Hahn, Southeastern College, FL
Jack Hall, Western Kentucky University
Gloria Halpern, Montgomery College, MD
Kenneth Hart, Brigham Young University, Idaho
Al Hartgraves, Emory University
Thomas Hayes, University of North Texas
Larry Hegstad, Pacific Lutheran University, WA
Candy Heino, Anoka-Ramsey Community College, MN
Anit Hope, Tarrant County College, TX
Thomas Huse, Boston College
Fred R. Jex, Macomb Community College, MI
Beth Kern, Indiana University, South Bend
Hans E. Klein, Babson College, MA
Willem Koole, North Carolina State University
Emil Koren, Hillsborough Community College, FL
Dennis Kovach, Community College of Allegheny County–North Campus

Ellen Landgraf, Loyola University Chicago
Howard Lawrence, Christian Brothers University, TN
Barry Leffkov, Regis College, MA
Chao Liu, Notre Dame University
Barbara Lougee, University of California, Irvine
Heidemarie Lundblad, California State University, Northridge
Anna Lusher, West Liberty State College, WV
Harriet Maccracken, Arizona State University
Carol Mannino, Milwaukee School of Engineering
Aziz Martinez, Harvard University, Harvard Business School
Cathleen Miller, University of Michigan–Flint
Frank Mioni, Madonna University, MI
Bruce L. Oliver, Rochester Institute of Technology
Charles Pedersen, Quinsigamond Community College, MA
George Plesko, Massachusetts Institute of Technology
David Plumlee, University of Utah
Gregory Prescott, University of South Alabama
Craig Reeder, Florida A&M University
Darren Roulstone, University of Chicago
Angela Sandberg, Jacksonville State University, AL
George Sanders, Western Washington University, WA
Betty Saunders, University of North Florida
Arnie Schneider, Georgia Tech
Gim Seow, University of Connecticut
Itzhak Sharav, CUNY–Lehman Graduate School of Business
Gerald Smith, University of Northern Iowa
James Smith, Community College of Philadelphia
Beverly Soriano, Framingham State College, MA
J. B. Stroud, Nicholls State University, LA
Al Taccone, Cuyamaca College, CA
Diane Tanner, University of North Florida
Howard Toole, San Diego State University
Bruce Wampler, Louisiana State University, Shreveport
Frederick Weis, Claremont McKenna College, CA
Frederick Weiss, Virginia Wesleyan College
Allen Wright, Hillsborough Community College, FL
Tony Zordan, University of St. Francis, IL

Supplement Authors and Preparers

Excel templates: Al Fisher, Community College of Southern Nevada
General Ledger templates: Lanny Nelms, the Landor Group
Instructor's Edition: Helen Brubeck, San Jose State University
Interactive Powerpoints: Courtney Baillie
Solutions Manual preparer: Diane Colwyn
Study Guide: Helen Brubeck, San Jose State University
Test Item File: Calvin Fink
Working Papers, Essentials of Excel: Dr. L. Murphy Smith, Texas A&M University; Dr. Katherine T. Smith
Videos: Beverly Amer, Northern Arizona University; Lanny Nelms, The Landor Group

The author would like to thank the following faculty members at Baylor University who provided valuable input for improvements in various sections of the eighth edition of this text: Suzanne Abbe, Jane Baldwin, Scott Bryant, Gia Chevis, Carie Ford, David Hurtt, Becky Jones, and Betsy Willis. The author would like to extend special thanks to Dr. Marty Stuebs, who helped develop the model for ethical decision-making introduced in Chapter 1 and used in problems throughout the remainder of the eighth edition.

Prologue

Accounting Careers: Much More Than Counting Things

What kind of career can you have in accounting? Almost any kind you want. A career in accounting lets you use your analytical skills in a variety of ways, and it brings both monetary and personal rewards. According to the Jobs Rated Almanac, "accountant" was the fifth best job in terms of low stress, high compensation, lots of autonomy, and tremendous hiring demand.[1]

Accounting as an art is widely believed to have been invented by Fra Luca Bartolomeo de Pacioli, an Italian mathematician and Franciscan friar in the 16th Century. Pacioli was a close friend of Leonardo da Vinci, and collaborated with him on many projects.

Accounting as the profession we know today has its roots in the Industrial Revolution during the 18th and 19th centuries, mostly in England. However, accounting did not attain the stature of other professions such as law, medicine, or engineering until early in the 20th Century. Professions are distinguished from trades by the following characteristics: (1) a unifying body of technical literature; (2) standards of competence; (3) codes of professional conduct; and (4) dedication to service to the public.

Today's accountants obtain years of formal education at the college level which, for most, culminates in taking a very rigorous professional exam that qualifies them to hold the designation *certified public accountant* (CPA). There are other professional designations that accountants may obtain as well, each with its own professional exam and set of professional standards. Examples are certified management accountant (CMA), certified internal auditor (CIA), and certified fraud examiner (CFE).

WHERE ACCOUNTANTS WORK

Where can you work as an accountant? There are four kinds of employers.

Public Practice

You can work for a public accounting firm, which could be a large international firm or a variety of medium to small-sized firms. Within the CPA firm, you can specialize in areas such as audit, tax, or consulting. In this capacity, you'll be serving as an external accountant to many different clients. At present, the largest six international firms are Deloitte, Ernst &Young, KPMG, PricewaterhouseCoopers, Grant Thornton, and RSM McGladrey. However, there are many other firms with international and national scope of practice. Most CPAs start their career at a large CPA firm. From there, they move on to obtain positions of leadership in the corporate finance world, industry, or just about anywhere there is a demand for persons who like solving complex problems.

Managerial Accounting

Instead of working for a wide variety of clients, you can work within one corporation or nonprofit enterprise. Your role may be to analyze financial information and communicate that information to managers, who use it to plot strategy and make decisions. You may be called upon to help allocate corporate resources or improve financial performance. For example, you might do a cost-benefit analysis to help decide whether to acquire a company or build a factory. Or you might describe the financial implications of choosing one strategy over another. You might work in areas such as internal auditing, financial management, financial reporting, treasury management, and tax planning. The highest position in management accounting is the chief financial officer (CFO) position, with some CFOs rising to become chief executive officers (CEOs).

Government and Not-for-Profit Entities

As an accountant, you might work for the government—federal, state, or local. Like your counterparts in public accounting and business, your role as a government accountant includes responsibilities in the areas of auditing, financial reporting, and management accounting. You'll evaluate how government agencies are being managed. You may advise decision makers on how to allocate resources to promote efficiency. The FBI hires CPAs to investigate the financial aspects of white-collar crime. You might find yourself working for the IRS, the Securities and Exchange Commission, the Department of Treasury, or even the White House.

The Government Accountability Office (GAO)—formerly called the General Accounting Office—is an agency that works for Congress and the American people. Congress asks GAO to study federal government programs and expenditures. GAO studies how the federal government spends taxpayer dollars and advises Congress and the heads of executive agencies (such as the Environmental Protection Agency, Department of Defense, and Health and Human Services) about ways to make government more effective and responsive.

As an accountant, you might also decide to work in the not-for-profit sector. Colleges, universities, public and private primary and secondary schools, hospitals, and charitable organizations such as churches and the United Way all have accounting functions. Accountants for these types of entities prepare financial statements as well as budgets and projections. Most have special training in accounting standards specially designed for work in the not-for-profit sector.

Education

Finally, you can work at a college or university, advancing the thought and theory of accounting and teaching future generations of new accountants. On the research side of education, you might study how companies use accounting information. You might develop new ways of categorizing financial data, or study accounting practices in different countries. You then publish your ideas in journals and books and present them to colleagues at meetings around the world. On the education side, you can help others learn about accounting and give them the tools they need to be their best.

CPA: THREE LETTERS THAT SPEAK VOLUMES

When employers see the CPA designation, they know what to expect about your education, knowledge, abilities, and personal attributes. They value your analytic skills and extensive training. Your CPA credential gives you a distinct advantage in the job market and instant credibility and respect in the workplace. It's a plus when dealing with other professionals such as bankers, attorneys, auditors, and federal regulators. In addition, your colleagues in private industry tend to defer to you when dealing with complex business matters, particularly those involving financial management.[2]

THE HOTTEST GROWTH AREAS IN ACCOUNTING

Recent legislation, such as the Sarbanes-Oxley Act of 2002, has brought rising demand for accountants of all kinds. In addition to strong overall demand, certain areas of accounting are especially hot.[3]

Sustainability Reporting

Sustainability reporting involves reporting on an organization's performance with respect to health, safety, and environmental (HSE) issues. As businesses take a greater interest in environmental issues, CPAs are getting involved in reporting on such matters as employee health, on-the-job accident rates, emissions of certain pollutants, spills, volumes of waste generated, and initiatives to reduce and minimize such incidents and releases. Utilities, manufacturers, and chemical companies are particularly affected by environmental issues. As a result, they turn to CPAs to set up a preventive system to ensure compliance and avoid future claims or disputes or to provide assistance once legal implications have arisen.

Corporate social responsibility reporting (CSR) is similar to HSE reporting but with a broadened emphasis on social matters such as ethical labor practices, training, education, and diversity of workforce and corporate philanthropic initiatives. Most of the world's largest corporations have extensive CSR initiatives.

Assurance Services

Assurance services are services provided by a CPA that improve the quality of information, or its context, for decision makers. Such information can be financial or nonfinancial, and it can be about past events or about ongoing processes or systems. This broad concept includes audit and attestation services and is distinct from consulting because it focuses primarily on improving information rather than on providing advice or installing systems. You can use your analytical and information-processing expertise by providing assurance services in areas ranging from electronic commerce to elder care, comprehensive risk assessment, business valuations, entity performance measurement, and information systems quality assessment.

Information Technology Services

Companies can't compete effectively if their information technology systems don't have the power or flexibility to perform essential functions. Companies need accountants with strong computer skills who can design and implement advanced systems to fit a company's specific needs and to find ways to protect and insulate data. CPAs skilled in software research and development (including multimedia technology) are also highly valued.

International Accounting

Globalization means that cross-border transactions are becoming commonplace. Countries in Eastern Europe and Latin America, which previously had closed economies, are opening up and doing business with new trading partners. The passage of the North American Free Trade Agreement (NAFTA) and the General Agreement on Tariffs and Trade (GATT) facilitates trade, and the economic growth in areas such as the Pacific Rim further brings greater volumes of trade and financial flows. Organizations need accountants who understand international trade rules, accords, and laws; cross-border merger and acquisition issues; and foreign business customs, languages, cultures, and procedures.

Forensic Accounting

Forensic accounting is in growing demand after scandals such as the collapse of Enron and WorldCom, which are featured in this text. Forensic accountants look at a company's financial records for evidence of criminal activity. This could be anything from securities fraud to overvaluation of inventory to money laundering and improper capitalization of expenses.

Whether you seek a career in business, government, the not-for-profit sector, or a charity, **accounting** has a career for you. Every organization, from the smallest mom-and-pop music retailer to the biggest government in the world, needs accountants to help manage its resources. Global trade demands accountability, and ever-more complex tax laws mean an ever-increasing need for the skills and services of accountants.

ENDNOTES

[1]Alba, Jason, and Manisha Bathija. *Vault Career Guide to Accounting.* (New York: Vault, 2002).
[2]http://www.startheregoplaces.com/news/news_half5.asp.
[3]AICPA, the American Institute of Certified Public Accountants, http://www.aicpa.org.

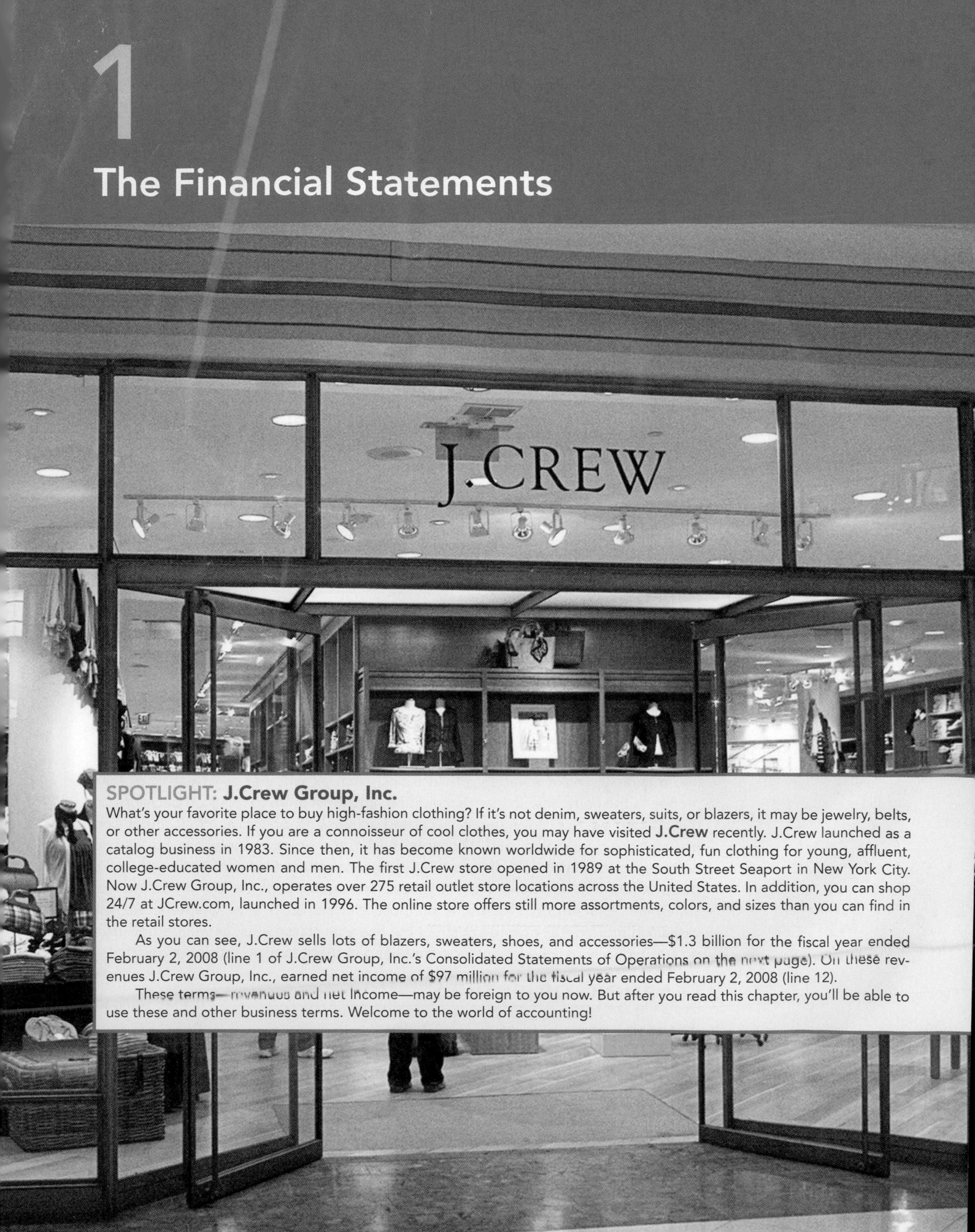

1

The Financial Statements

SPOTLIGHT: J.Crew Group, Inc.

What's your favorite place to buy high-fashion clothing? If it's not denim, sweaters, suits, or blazers, it may be jewelry, belts, or other accessories. If you are a connoisseur of cool clothes, you may have visited **J.Crew** recently. J.Crew launched as a catalog business in 1983. Since then, it has become known worldwide for sophisticated, fun clothing for young, affluent, college-educated women and men. The first J.Crew store opened in 1989 at the South Street Seaport in New York City. Now J.Crew Group, Inc., operates over 275 retail outlet store locations across the United States. In addition, you can shop 24/7 at JCrew.com, launched in 1996. The online store offers still more assortments, colors, and sizes than you can find in the retail stores.

As you can see, J.Crew sells lots of blazers, sweaters, shoes, and accessories—$1.3 billion for the fiscal year ended February 2, 2008 (line 1 of J.Crew Group, Inc.'s Consolidated Statements of Operations on the next page). On these revenues J.Crew Group, Inc., earned net income of $97 million for the fiscal year ended February 2, 2008 (line 12).

These terms—revenues and net income—may be foreign to you now. But after you read this chapter, you'll be able to use these and other business terms. Welcome to the world of accounting!

J.Crew Group, Inc.
Consolidated Statements of Operations (adapted)

(In millions)	Year Ended February 3, 2007	Year Ended February 2, 2008
Revenues		
1 Net sales	$1,117	$1,292
2 Other revenue	35	43
3 Total revenues	1,152	1,335
4 Cost of goods sold	652	746
5 Gross profit	500	589
6 Selling, general and administrative expense	375	416
7 Income from operations	125	173
8 Interest expense, net	44	11
9 Loss on debt refinancing	10	
10 Income before income taxes	71	162
11 Income tax expense	(7)	65
12 Net income	$ 78	$ 97

Each chapter of this book begins with an actual financial statement.
In this chapter, it's the income statements (or Consolidated Statements of
Operations) of J.Crew Group, Inc. The core of financial accounting revolves around
the basic financial statements:

- Income statement (the statement of operations)
- Statement of retained earnings
- Balance sheet (the statement of financial position)
- Statement of cash flows

   Financial statements are the business documents that companies use to report
the results of their activities to various user groups, which can include managers,
investors, creditors, and regulatory agencies. In turn, these parties use the reported
information to make a variety of decisions, such as whether to invest in or loan
money to the company. To learn accounting, you must learn to focus on decisions. In
this chapter we explain generally accepted accounting principles, their underlying
assumptions, principles, and concepts, and the bodies responsible for issuing
accounting standards. We discuss the judgment process that is necessary to make
good accounting decisions. We also discuss the contents of the four basic financial
statements that report the results of those decisions. In later chapters, we will
explain in more detail how to construct the financial statements, as well as how user
groups typically use the information contained in them to make business decisions.

LEARNING OBJECTIVES

1 **Use** accounting vocabulary

2 **Learn** underlying concepts, assumptions, and principles of accounting

3 **Apply** the accounting equation to business organizations

4 **Evaluate** business operations

5 **Use** information in financial statements to make business decisions, which are informed
by economic, legal, and ethical guidelines

> For more practice and review of accounting cycle concepts, use ACT, the Accounting Cycle Tutorial, online at www.myaccountinglab.com. Margin logos like this one, directing you to the appropriate ACT section and material, appear throughout Chapters 1, 2, and 3. When you enter the tutorial, you'll find three buttons on the opening page of each chapter module. Here's what the buttons mean: **Tutorial** gives you a review of the major concepts, **Application** gives you practice exercises, and **Glossary** reviews important terms.

BUSINESS DECISIONS

J.Crew Group, Inc., managers make lots of decisions. Which is selling faster—pants, suits, blazers, or shoes? Are jeans bringing in more profits than blazers? Should J.Crew expand into Europe or Asia? Accounting information helps companies make these decisions.

Take a look at J.Crew Group, Inc.'s Consolidated Statement of Operations on page 2. Focus on net income (line 12). Net income (profit) is the excess of revenues over expenses. You can see that J.Crew Group, Inc., earned a $97 million profit in the year ended February 2, 2008. That's good news because it means that J.Crew had $97 million more revenues than expenses for the year.

J.Crew's Consolidated Statement of Operations conveys more good news. Net income for fiscal 2007 (year ended February 2, 2008) increased by 24% over net income for the previous year (about $78 million). J.Crew is growing, and investors buy stocks of growing companies.

Suppose you have $5,000 to invest. What information would you need before deciding to invest that money in J.Crew Group, Inc.? Let's see how accounting works.

ACCOUNTING IS THE LANGUAGE OF BUSINESS

Accounting is an information system. It measures business activities, processes data into reports, and communicates results to decision makers. Accounting is "the language of business." The better you understand the language, the better you can manage your finances as well as those of your business.

Accounting produces financial statements, which report information about a business entity. The financial statements measure performance and communicate where a business stands in financial terms. In this chapter we focus on J.Crew Group, Inc. After completing this chapter, you'll begin to understand financial statements.

Don't confuse bookkeeping and accounting. Bookkeeping is a mechanical part of accounting, just as arithmetic is a part of mathematics. Exhibit 1-1 on the following page illustrates the flow of accounting information and helps illustrate accounting's role in business. The accounting process begins and ends with people making decisions.

OBJECTIVE

1 Use accounting vocabulary

EXHIBIT 1-1 | The Flow of Accounting Information

1. People make decisions.   2. Business transactions occur.   3. Companies report their results.

Who Uses Accounting Information?

Decision makers use many types of information. A banker decides who gets a loan. J.Crew Group, Inc., decides where to locate a new store. Let's see how decision makers use accounting information.

- *Individuals.* People like you manage their personal bank accounts, decide whether to rent an apartment or buy a house, and budget the monthly income and expenditures of their businesses. Accounting provides the necessary information to allow individuals to make these decisions.
- *Investors and Creditors.* Investors and creditors provide the money to finance J.Crew Group, Inc. Investors want to know how much income they can expect to earn on an investment. Creditors want to know when and how J.Crew Group, Inc., is going to pay them back. These decisions also require accounting information.
- *Regulatory Bodies.* All kinds of regulatory bodies use accounting information. For example, the Internal Revenue Service (IRS) and various state and local governments require businesses, individuals, and other types of organizations to pay income, property, excise, and other taxes. The U.S. Securities and Exchange Commission (SEC) requires companies whose stock is traded publicly to provide it with many kinds of periodic financial reports. All of these reports contain accounting information.
- *Nonprofit Organizations.* Nonprofit organizations—churches, hospitals, and charities such as Habitat for Humanity and the Red Cross—base many of their operating decisions on accounting data. In addition, these organizations have to file periodic reports of their activities with the IRS and state governments, even though they may owe no taxes.

Two Kinds of Accounting: Financial Accounting and Management Accounting

Both *external* and *internal users* of accounting information exist. We can therefore classify accounting into two branches.

Financial accounting provides information for decision makers outside the entity, such as investors, creditors, government agencies, and the public. This information must be relevant for the needs of decision makers and must faithfully give an accurate picture of the entity's economic activities. This textbook focuses on financial accounting.

Management accounting provides information for managers of J.Crew Group, Inc. Examples of management accounting information include budgets, forecasts, and projections that are used in making strategic decisions of the entity. Internal information must still be accurate and relevant for the decision needs of managers. Management accounting is covered in a separate course that usually follows this one.

[handwritten: get mgmt accounting textbook]

Organizing a Business

Accounting is used in every type of business. A business generally takes one of the following forms:

- proprietorship
- partnership
- limited-liability company (LLC)
- corporation

Exhibit 1-2 compares ways to organize a business.

EXHIBIT 1-2 | The Various Forms of Business Organization

	Proprietorship	Partnership	LLC	Corporation
1. *Owner(s)*	Proprietor—one owner	Partners—two or more owners	Members	Stockholders—generally many owners
2. *Personal liability of owner(s) for business debts*	Proprietor is personally liable	General partners are personally liable; limited partners are not	Members are *not* personally liable	Stockholders are *not* personally liable

Proprietorship.   A **proprietorship** has a single owner, called the proprietor. Dell Computer started out in the college dorm room of Michael Dell, the owner. Proprietorships tend to be small retail stores or solo providers of professional services—physicians, attorneys, or accountants. Legally, the business *is* the proprietor, and the proprietor is personally liable for all the business's debts. But for accounting purposes, a proprietorship is a distinct entity, separate from its proprietor. Thus, the business records should not include the proprietor's personal finances.

Partnership.   A **partnership** has two or more parties as co-owners, and each owner is a partner. Individuals, corporations, partnerships, or other types of entities can be partners. Income and loss of the partnership "flows through" to the partners and they recognize it based on their agreed-upon percentage interest in the business. The partnership is not a taxpaying entity. Instead, each partner takes a proportionate share of the entity's taxable income and pays tax according to that partner's individual or corporate rate. Many retail establishments, professional service firms (law, accounting, etc.), real estate, and oil and gas exploration companies operate as partnerships. Many partnerships are small or medium-sized, but some are gigantic, with thousands of partners. Partnerships are governed by agreement, usually spelled out in writing in the form of a contract between the partners. General partnerships have mutual agency and unlimited liability, meaning that each partner may conduct business in the name of the entity and can make agreements that legally bind all partners without limit for the partnership's debts. Partnerships are therefore quite risky, because an irresponsible partner can create large debts for the other general partners without their knowledge or permission. This feature of general partnerships has spawned the creation of limited-liability partnerships (LLPs).

A *limited-liability partnership* is one in which a wayward partner cannot create a large liability for the other partners. In LLPs, each partner is liable for partnership debts only up to the extent of his or her investment in the partnership, plus his or her proportionate share of the liabilities. Each LLP, however, must have one general partner with unlimited liability for all partnership debts.

Limited-Liability Company (LLC).   A *limited-liability company* is one in which the business (and not the owner) is liable for the company's debts. An LLC may have one owner or many owners, called *members*. Unlike a proprietorship or a general partnership, the members of an LLC do *not* have unlimited liability for the LLC's debts. An LLC pays no business income tax. Instead, the LLC's income "flows through" to the members, and they pay income tax at their own tax rates, just as they would if they were partners. Today, many multiple-owner businesses are organized as LLCs, because members of an LLC effectively enjoy limited liability while still being taxed like members of a partnership.

Corporation.   A **corporation** is a business owned by the **stockholders**, or **shareholders**, who own **stock** representing shares of ownership in the corporation. One of the major advantages of doing business in the corporate form is the ability to raise large sums of capital from issuance of stock to the public. All types of entities (individuals, partnerships, corporations, or other types) may be shareholders in a corporation. Even though proprietorships and partnerships are more numerous, corporations transact much more business and are larger in terms of assets, income, and number of employees. Most well-known companies, such as J.Crew Group, Inc., Google, Toyota, and Apple, Inc., are corporations. Their full names include *Corporation* or *Incorporated* (abbreviated *Corp.* and *Inc.*) to indicate that they are corporations—for example, J.Crew Group, Inc., and Starbucks Corporation. Some bear the name *Company*, such as Ford Motor Company.

A corporation is formed under state law. Unlike proprietorships and partnerships, a corporation is legally distinct from its owners. The corporation is like an artificial person and possesses many of the same rights that a person has. The stockholders have no personal obligation for the corporation's debts. So, stockholders of a corporation have limited liability, as do limited partners and members of an LLC. However, unlike partnerships or LLCs, a corporation pays a business income tax as well as many other types of taxes. Furthermore, the shareholders of a corporation are effectively taxed twice on distributions received from the corporation (called dividends). Thus, one of the major disadvantages of the corporate form of business is *double taxation of distributed profits*.

Ultimate control of a corporation rests with the stockholders, who generally get one vote for each share of stock they own. Stockholders elect the **board of directors**, which sets policy and appoints officers. The board elects a chairperson, who holds the most power in the corporation and often carries the title chief executive officer (CEO). The board also appoints the president as chief operating officer (COO). Corporations also have vice presidents in charge of sales, accounting, and finance (called the chief financial officer or CFO), and other key areas.

ACCOUNTING PRINCIPLES, ASSUMPTIONS, AND CONCEPTS

Accountants follow professional guidelines for measurement and disclosure of financial information. These are called **generally accepted accounting principles (GAAP.)**. In the United States, the **Financial Accounting Standards Board (FASB)** formulates GAAP. The **International Accounting Standards Board (IASB)** sets global—or International—Financial Reporting Standards (IFRS), as discussed in a later section.

Exhibit 1-3 gives an overview of the joint conceptual framework of accounting developed by the FASB and the IASB. Financial reporting standards (whether U.S. or international), at the bottom, follow the conceptual framework. The overall *objective* of accounting is to provide financial information that is useful to present and potential capital providers in making investment and lending decisions. In this sense, *capital* means resources (usually cash). The two basic types of external providers of capital include investors (who exchange cash for stock) and creditors (who loan cash) to the entity.

OBJECTIVE

2 **Learn** underlying concepts, assumptions, and principles of accounting

EXHIBIT 1-3 | Conceptual Foundations of Accounting

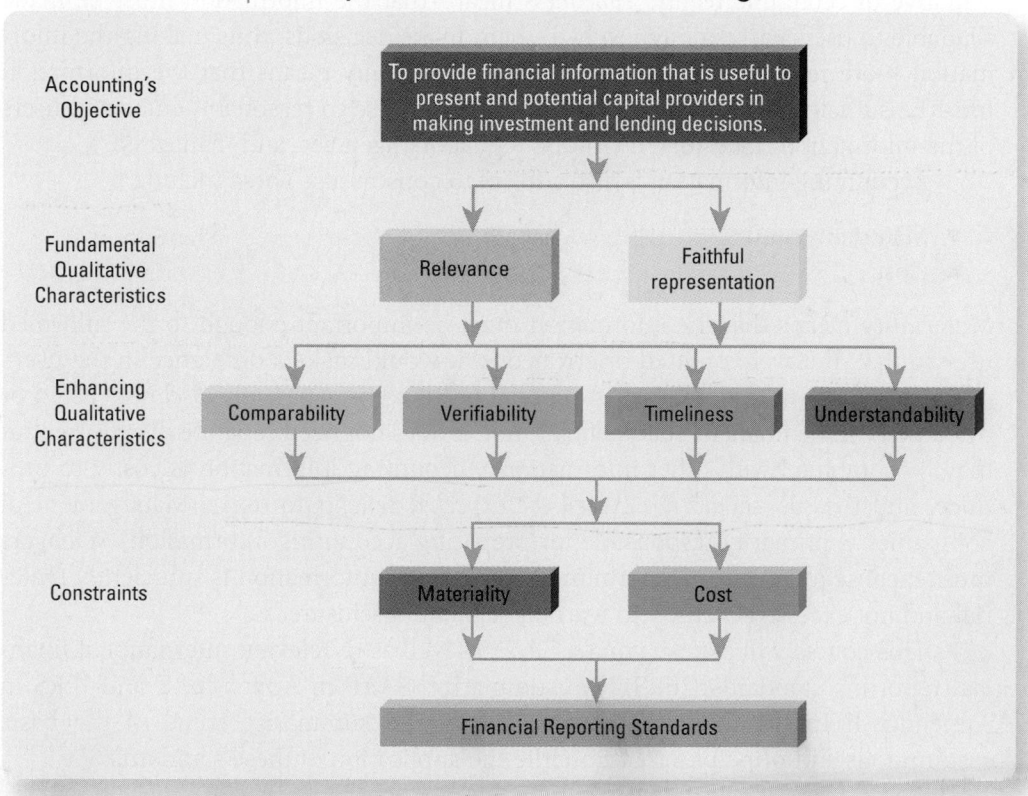

Source: FASB, IASB, Joint Conceptual Framework for Reporting (Exposure Draft), 2008.

To be useful, information must have the fundamental qualitative characteristics. Those include:

- Relevance; and
- Faithful representation

To be relevant, information must be capable of making a difference to the decision maker, having predictive or confirming value. To faithfully represent, the information must be complete, neutral (free from bias), and without material error (accurate). Accounting information must focus on the *economic substance* of a transaction, event, or circumstance, which may or may not always be the same as its legal form. Faithful representation makes the information *reliable* to users.

Accounting information must also have a number of *enhancing qualitative characteristics*. These include

- Comparability;
- Verifiability;
- Timeliness; and
- Understandability.

Comparability means that the accounting information for a company must be prepared in such a way as to be capable of being both compared with information from other companies in the same period, and *consistent* with similar information for that company in previous periods. *Verifiability* means that the information must be capable of being checked for accuracy, completeness, and reliability. The process of verifying information is often done by *internal* as well as *external auditors*. Verifiability enhances the reliability of information, and thus makes the information more representative of economic reality. *Timeliness* means that the information must be made available to users early enough to help them make decisions, thus making the information more relevant to their needs. *Understandability* means that the information must be sufficiently transparent so that it makes sense to reasonably informed users of the information (investors, creditors, regulatory agencies, and managers).

Accounting information is also subject to constraints. These include

- Materiality; and
- Cost

Materiality means that the information must be important enough to the informed user so that, if it were omitted or erroneous, it would make a difference in the user's decision. Only information that is material needs to be separately *disclosed* (listed or discussed) in the financial statements. If not, it does not need separate disclosure, but may be combined with other information. Accounting information is costly to produce, and the *cost should not exceed the expected benefits* to users. Management of companies is primarily responsible for preparing accounting information. Managers must exercise judgment in determining whether the information is sufficiently material and not excessively costly to warrant separate disclosure.

This course will expose you to GAAP as well as to relevant international financial reporting standards (IFRS). We summarize GAAP in Appendix E and IFRS in Appendix F. In the following section, we briefly summarize some of the basic assumptions and principles that underlie the application of these standards.

The Entity Assumption

The most basic accounting assumption (underlying idea) is the **entity**, which is any organization that stands apart as a separate economic unit. Sharp boundaries are drawn around each entity so as not to confuse its affairs with those of others.

Consider Millard S. Drexler, chairman of the board and CEO of J.Crew Group, Inc. Mr. Drexler owns a home and several automobiles. In addition, he may owe money on some personal loans. All these assets and liabilities belong to Mr. Drexler and have nothing to do with J.Crew Group, Inc. Likewise, J.Crew Group, Inc.'s cash, computers, and inventories belong to the company and not to Drexler. Why? Because the entity assumption draws a sharp boundary around each entity; in this case J.Crew Group, Inc., is one entity, and Millard S. Drexler is a second, separate entity.

Let's consider the various types of stores that make up J.Crew Group, Inc. Top managers evaluate the retail stores separately from the outlet stores. If retail-store sales were dropping, J.Crew should identify the reason. But if sales figures from all the retail and outlet stores were combined in a single total, managers couldn't tell how differently each unit was performing. To correct the problem, managers need accounting information for each division (entity) in the company. Thus, each store, both retail and outlet, keeps its own records in order to be evaluated separately.

The Continuity (Going-Concern) Assumption

In measuring and reporting accounting information, we assume that the entity will continue to operate long enough to use existing assets—land, buildings, equipment, and supplies—for its intended purposes. This is called the **continuity (going-concern) assumption**.

Consider the alternative to the **going-concern assumption**: the quitting concern, or going out of business. An entity that is not continuing would have to sell all of its assets in the process. In that case, the most *relevant* measure of the value of the assets would be their current fair market values (the amount the company would receive for the assets when sold). But going out of business is the exception rather than the rule. Therefore, the continuity assumption says that a business should stay in business long enough to recover the cost of those assets by allocating that cost through a process called *depreciation* to business operations over the assets' economic lives.

The Historical Cost Principle

The **historical cost principle** states that assets should be recorded at their *actual cost,* measured on the date of purchase as the amount of cash paid plus the dollar value of all non-cash consideration (other assets, privileges, or rights) also given in exchange. For example, suppose J.Crew Group, Inc., purchases a building for a new store. The building's current owner is asking for $600,000 for the building. The management of J.Crew believes the building is worth $585,000, and offers the present owner that amount. Two real estate professionals appraise the building at $610,000. The two parties compromise and agree on a price of $590,000 for the building. The historical cost principle requires J.Crew to initially record the building at its actual cost of $590,000, not at $585,000, $600,000 or $610,000, even though those amounts were what some people believed the building was worth. At the point of purchase, $590,000 is both the *relevant* amount for the building's worth and the amount that *faithfully represents* a reliable figure for the price the company paid for it.

The *historical cost principle*, and the *continuity assumption* (discussed above), also maintain that J.Crew's accounting records should continue to use historical cost to value the asset for as long as the business holds it. Why? Because cost is a *verifiable* measure that is relatively *free from bias*. Suppose that J.Crew Group, Inc., owns the building for six years. Real estate prices increase during this period. As a result, at the end of the period, the building can be sold for $650,000. Should J.Crew increase the carrying value of the building on the company's books to $650,000? No. According to the historical cost principle, the building remains on J.Crew Group, Inc.'s books at its historical cost of $590,000. According to the continuity assumption, J.Crew intends to stay in business and keep the building, not to sell it, so its historical cost is the most relevant and the most faithful representation of its carrying value. It is also the most easily verifiable (auditable) amount. Should the company decide to sell the building later at a price above or below its carrying value, it will record the cash received, remove the carrying value of the building from the books, and record a gain or a loss for the difference at that time.

The historical cost principle is not used as pervasively in the United States as it once was. Accounting is moving in the direction of reporting more and more assets and liabilities at their fair values. **Fair value** is the amount that the business could sell the asset for, or the amount that the business could pay to settle the liability. The FASB has issued guidance for companies to report many assets and liabilities at fair values. Moreover, in recent years, the FASB has agreed to align GAAP with International Financial Reporting Standards (IFRS). These standards generally allow for more liberal measurement of different types of assets with fair values than GAAP, which may cause more assets to be re-valued periodically to fair market values. We will discuss the trend toward globalization of accounting standards in a later part of this chapter, and illustrate it in later chapters throughout the book.

The Stable-Monetary-Unit Assumption

In the United States, we record transactions in dollars because that is our medium of exchange. British accountants record transactions in pounds sterling, Japanese in yen, and Europeans in euros.

Unlike a liter or a mile, the value of a dollar changes over time. A rise in the general price level is called *inflation*. During inflation, a dollar will purchase less food, less toothpaste, and less of other goods and services. When prices are stable—there is little inflation—a dollar's purchasing power is also stable.

Under the **stable-monetary-unit assumption**, accountants assume that the dollar's purchasing power is stable over time. We ignore inflation, and this allows us to add and subtract dollar amounts as though dollars over successive years have a consistent amount of purchasing power. This is important because businesses that report their financial information publicly usually report comparative financial information (that is, the current year along with one or more prior years). If we could not assume a stable monetary unit, assets and liabilities denominated in prior years' dollars would have to be adjusted to current year price levels. Since inflation is considered to be relatively minor over time, those adjustments do not have to be made.

GLOBAL VIEW — INTERNATIONAL FINANCIAL REPORTING STANDARDS (IFRS)

We live in a global economy! The global credit crisis of 2008 originated in the United States but rapidly spread throughout the world. U.S. investors can easily trade stocks on the Hong Kong, London, and Brussels stock exchanges over the Internet. Each year, American companies such as Starbucks, The Gap, McDonald's, Microsoft, and Disney conduct billions of dollars of business around the globe. Conversely, foreign companies such as Nokia, Samsung, Toyota, and Nestlé conduct billions of dollars of business in the United States. American companies have merged with foreign companies to create international conglomerates such as Pearson (publisher of this textbook) and Anheuser-Busch InBev. No matter where your career starts, it is very likely that it will eventually take you into global markets.

Until recently, one of the major challenges of conducting global business has been the fact that different countries have adopted different accounting standards for business transactions. Historically, the major developed countries in the world (United States, U.K., Japan, Germany, etc.) have all had their own versions of GAAP. As investors seek to compare financial results across entities from different countries, they have had to re-state and convert accounting data from one country to the next in order to make them comparable. This takes time and can be expensive.

The solution to this problem lies with the IASB, which has developed International Financial Reporting Standards (IFRS). These standards are now being used by most countries around the world. For years, accountants in the United States did not pay much attention to IFRS because our GAAP was considered to be the strongest single set of accounting standards in the world. In addition, the application of GAAP for public companies in the United States is overseen carefully by the U.S. Securities and Exchange Commission (SEC), a body which at present has no global counterpart.

Nevertheless, in order to promote consistency in global financial reporting, the SEC announced in November 2008 that it intends to require all U.S. public companies to adopt IFRS within the next few years. Some companies can choose to begin implementing IFRS by the end of 2009. Mandatory U.S. adoption of IFRS is currently slated to begin in stages from 2014 through 2016, beginning with the largest companies.

The advantage to adopting IFRS is that financial statements from a U.S. company (say, Hershey Corporation in Pennsylvania) will be comparable to those of a foreign company (say, Nestlé in Switzerland). It will be far easier for investors and businesspeople to evaluate information of various companies in the same industries from across the globe, and companies will only have to prepare one set of financial statements, instead of multiple versions. Thus, in the long run, global use of IFRS should significantly reduce costs of doing global business.

These are impressive goals, but what do these changes mean for U.S. GAAP? It could mean that U.S. GAAP will no longer exist, being replaced by international standards within the next decade. Alternatively, it could mean that U.S. GAAP will remain, and will become a domestic interpretation of IFRS for businesses operating solely within the United States.

Does this mean that the accounting information you are studying in this textbook will soon become outdated? Fortunately, no. For one thing, the vast majority of the material you learn from this textbook, including the underlying conceptual framework outlined in the previous section, is *already* part of IFRS. The most commonly used accounting practices are essentially the same under both U.S. GAAP and IFRS. Additionally, the FASB is working hand-in-hand with the IASB toward *convergence* of standards: that is, gradually adjusting both sets of standards to more closely align them over time so that, when transition to IFRS in the United States occurs, it will occur smoothly. Over the past few years, all newly-issued U.S. accounting standards have conformed U.S. practices to IFRS.

As of the publication of this text, there are still some areas of disagreement between GAAP and IFRS. For example, certain widely accepted U.S. practices, such as the use of the last-in, first-out (LIFO) inventory costing method (discussed in Chapter 6), are disallowed under IFRS. Other differences exist as well. These differences must be resolved before IFRS can be fully adopted in the United States.

In general, the main difference between U.S. GAAP and IFRS is that U.S. GAAP has become rather "rules-based" over its long history, while IFRS (not in existence as long) allows more professional judgment on the part of companies. In many areas, the international regulations allow accountants and managers to apply the rules in ways they think is best. For example, revenue recognition is one area where IFRS provides significantly less guidance and allows more judgment than U.S. GAAP. We will discuss this concept further in Chapters 3 and 11.

The other major difference between IFRS and U.S. GAAP lies in the valuation of long-term assets (plant assets and intangibles) and liabilities. In U.S. GAAP, the historical cost principle tells us to value assets at historical cost. In contrast, IFRS prefers more of a fair-value approach, which reports assets and liabilities on the balance sheet at their up-to-date values, rather than at historical cost. This may seem like a big difference, but U.S. GAAP already allows for a partial fair-value approach with rules such as lower-of-cost-or-market, accounting for the impairment of long-term assets, and adjusting certain investments to fair values. We cover these concepts in more depth in later chapters.

In past years, there have been many more lawsuits over accounting disputes in the United States than in other countries. This has led to more detailed U.S. accounting rules, so that American accountants and managers have clear guidelines to follow. Once IFRS is adopted, U.S. GAAP may be used as "secondary" guidance, in instances where IFRS is vague. As of the date of this text, it's unclear exactly how the eventual interaction between IFRS and U.S. GAAP will play out.

There are also terminology differences between IFRS and GAAP. Americans may have to get used to some new words that replace old familiar ones. The underlying concepts probably won't change, but there will probably be new terms and phrasings. Portions of the income statement and balance sheet may also be rearranged, as IFRS presentation is slightly different than the financial statements of U.S. GAAP. The information would still be on the same financial statement, but might appear in a new location.

Of course, everyone focuses on what is different, not on what stays the same. What will we have to adjust as the United States adopts international standards? Throughout the remainder of this textbook, in chapters that cover concepts where major differences between GAAP and IFRS exist, we will discuss those differences. Because this is an introductory textbook in financial accounting, our discussion will be brief, in order to focus on the changes that are relevant for this course. Appendix F includes a table, cross-referenced by chapter, that summarizes all of these differences, as well as their impacts on financial statements once IFRS is fully adopted.

You can expect to hear more about the adoption of IFRS, as well as global harmonization of accounting standards, in the future. When you do, the most important things to remember will be that these changes will be beneficial for financial statement users in the long run, and that most of what you learned in this accounting course will still apply. Remember that there are far more areas of common ground than of disagreement. Whatever may come, your knowledge of international accounting principles will benefit you in the future. The globalization of the world economy provides a wonderful opportunity for you to succeed in the business world.

THE ACCOUNTING EQUATION

J.Crew Group, Inc.'s financial statements tell us how the business is performing and where it stands. But how do we arrive at the financial statements? Let's examine the *elements of financial statements*, which are the building blocks on which these statements rest.

OBJECTIVE

3 **Apply** the accounting equation to business organizations

Assets and Liabilities

The financial statements are based on the **accounting equation**. This equation presents the resources of a company and the claims to those resources.

- **Assets** are economic resources that are expected to produce a benefit in the future. J.Crew Group, Inc.'s cash, merchandise inventory, and equipment are examples of assets.

  Claims on assets come from two sources:

- **Liabilities** are "outsider claims." They are debts that are payable to outsiders, called *creditors*. For example, a creditor who has loaned money to J.Crew Group, Inc., has a claim—a legal right—to a part of J.Crew's assets until J.Crew repays the debt.
- **Owners' equity** (also called **capital**, or **stockholders' equity for a corporation**) represents the "insider claims" of a business. Equity means ownership, so J.Crew Group, Inc.'s stockholders' equity is the stockholders' interest in the assets of the corporation.

The accounting equation shows the relationship among assets, liabilities, and owners' equity. Assets appear on the left side and liabilities and owners' equity on the right. As Exhibit 1-4 shows, the two sides must be equal:

EXHIBIT 1-4 | The Accounting Equation

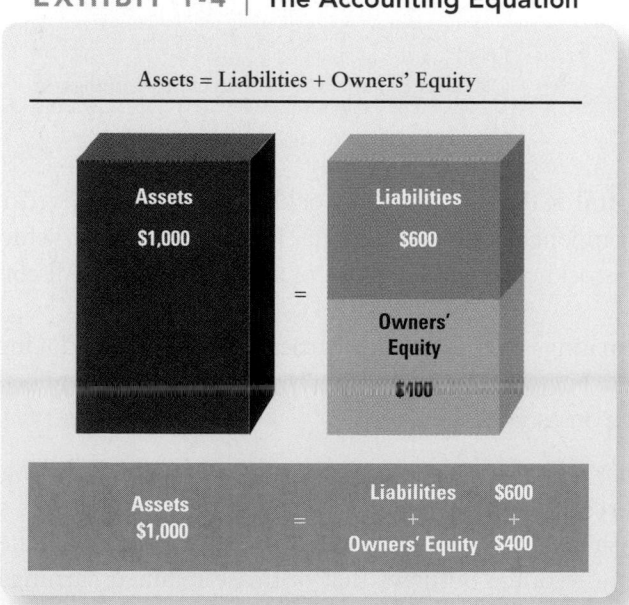

What are some of J.Crew Group, Inc.'s assets? The first asset is **cash** and cash equivalents, the liquid assets that are the medium of exchange. Another important asset is **merchandise inventory** (often called inventories)—the clothing and accessory items—that J.Crew's stores sell. J.Crew also has assets in the form of **property, plant, and equipment**, or **fixed assets**. These are the long-lived assets the company uses to do business—store equipment, buildings, computers, and so on.

J.Crew Group, Inc.'s liabilities include a number of payables, such as accounts payable and federal and state income taxes payable. The word *payable* always signifies a liability. An **account payable** is a liability for goods or services purchased on credit and supported by the credit standing of the purchaser. A **note payable** is a written promise to pay on a certain date. **Long-term debt** is a liability that's payable beyond one year from the date of the financial statements.

Owners' Equity

The owners' equity of any business is its assets minus its liabilities. We can write the accounting equation to show that owners' equity is what's left over when we subtract liabilities from assets.

Assets − Liabilities = Owners' Equity

A corporation's equity—called **stockholders' equity**—has two main subparts:

- paid-in capital and
- retained earnings

The accounting equation can be written as

Assets = Liabilities + Stockholders' Equity
Assets = Liabilities + Paid-in Capital + Retained Earnings

Paid-in capital is the amount the stockholders have invested in the corporation. The basic component of paid-in capital is **common stock**, which the corporation issues to the stockholders as evidence of their ownership. All corporations have common stock.

Retained earnings is the amount earned by income-producing activities and kept for use in the business. Three major types of transactions affect retained earnings: revenues, expenses, and dividends.

- **Revenues** are inflows of resources that increase retained earnings by delivering goods or services to customers. For example, a J.Crew store's sale of a blazer brings in cash revenue and increases J.Crew Group, Inc.'s retained earnings.
- **Expenses** are resource outflows that decrease retained earnings due to operations. For example, the wages that J.Crew pays employees are an expense and

decrease retained earnings. Expenses represent the costs of doing business; they are the opposite of revenues. Expenses include cost of goods sold, building rent, salaries, and utility payments. Expenses also include the depreciation of display cases, racks, shelving, and other equipment.

- **Dividends** decrease retained earnings, because they are distributions to stockholders of assets (usually cash) generated by net income, A successful business may pay dividends to shareholders as a return on their investments. Remember: **Dividends are not expenses. Dividends never affect net income. Instead of being subtracted from revenues to compute net income, dividends are recorded as direct reductions of retained earnings.**

Businesses strive for **profits**, the excess of revenues over expenses.

- When total revenues exceed total expenses, the result is called **net income**, **net earnings**, or **net profit**.
- When expenses exceed revenues, the result is a **net loss**.
- Net income or net loss is the "bottom line" on an income statement. J.Crew Group, Inc.'s bottom line reports net income for the year ended February 2, 2008, of $97 million (line 12 on the Consolidated Statement of Operations on page 2).

Exhibit 1-5 shows the relationships among

- Retained earnings
- Revenues – Expenses = Net income (or net loss)
- Dividends

EXHIBIT 1-5 | The Components of Retained Earnings

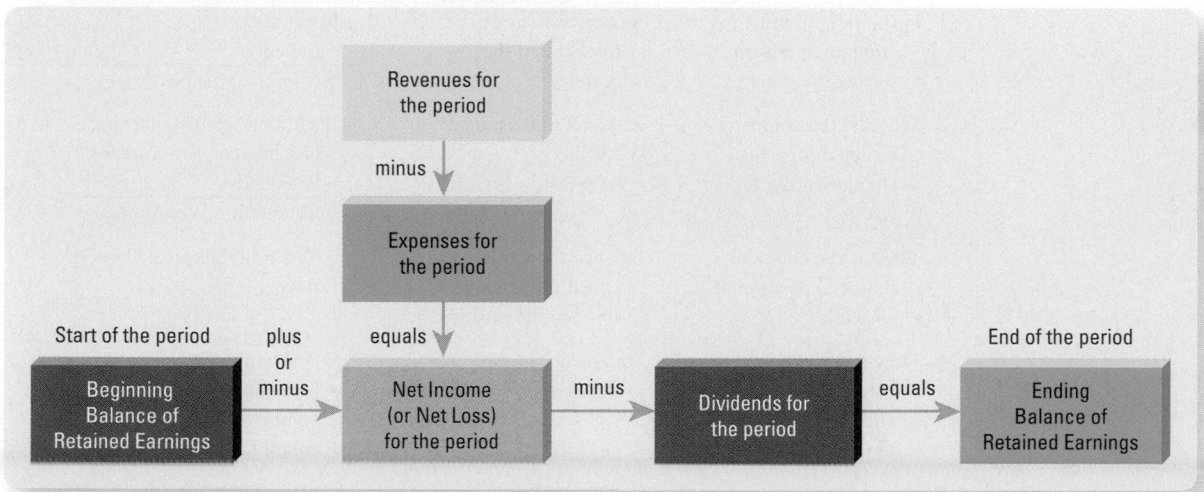

The owners' equity of proprietorships and partnerships is different from that of corporations. Proprietorships and partnerships don't identify paid-in capital and retained earnings separately. Instead, they use a single heading—Capital. Examples include: Randall Waller, Capital, for a proprietorship; and Powers, Capital, and Salazar, Capital, for a partnership.

STOP & THINK...

1. If the assets of a business are $240,000 and the liabilities are $80,000, how much is the owners' equity?
2. If the owners' equity in a business is $160,000 and the liabilities are $130,000, how much are the assets?
3. A company reported monthly revenues of $129,000 and expenses of $85,000. What is the result of operations for the month?
4. If the beginning balance of retained earnings is $100,000, revenue is $75,000, expenses total $50,000, and the company pays a $10,000 dividend, what is the ending balance of retained earnings?

Answers:

1. $160,000 ($240,000 − $80,000)
2. $290,000 ($160,000 + $130,000)
3. Net income of $44,000 ($129,000 − $85,000); revenues minus expenses
4. $115,000 [$100,000 beginning balance + net income $25,000 ($75,000 − $50,000) − dividends $10,000]

THE FINANCIAL STATEMENTS

OBJECTIVE

4 **Evaluate** business operations

The financial statements present a company to the public in financial terms. Each financial statement relates to a specific date or time period. What would investors want to know about J.Crew Group, Inc., at the end of its fiscal year? Exhibit 1-6 lists four questions decision makers may ask. Each answer comes from one of the financial statements.

EXHIBIT 1-6 | Information Reported in the Financial Statements

Question	Financial Statement	Answer
1. How well did the company perform during the year?	Income statement (also called the Statement of operations)	Revenues − Expenses Net income (or Net loss)
2. Why did the company's retained earnings change during the year?	Statement of retained earnings	Beginning retained earnings + Net income (or − Net loss) − Dividends Ending retained earnings
3. What is the company's financial position at December 31?	Balance sheet (also called the Statement of financial position)	Assets = Liabilities + Owners' Equity
4. How much cash did the company generate and spend during the year?	Statement of cash flows	Operating cash flows ± Investing cash flows ± Financing cash flows Increase (decrease) in cash

To learn how to use financial statements, let's work through J.Crew Group, Inc.'s statements for 2007 fiscal year (year ended February 2, 2008). The following diagram shows how the data flow from one financial statement to the next. The order is important.

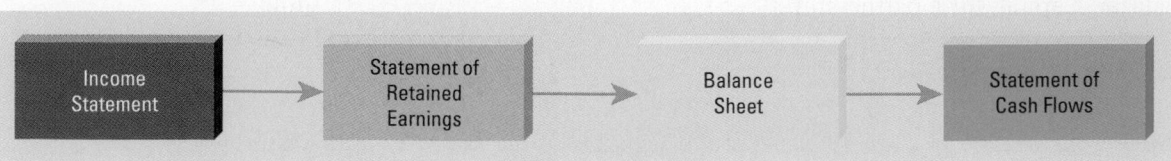

We begin with the income statement in Exhibit 1-7.

EXHIBIT 1-7 | J.Crew Group, Inc., Consolidated Statements of Operations

J.Crew Group, Inc.
Consolidated Statements of Operations (adapted)

(In millions)	Year Ended February 3, 2007	Year Ended February 2, 2008
Revenues		
1 Net sales	$1,117	$1,292
2 Other revenue	35	43
3 Total revenues	1,152	1,335
4 Cost of goods sold	652	746
5 Gross profit	500	589
6 Selling, general and administrative expense	375	416
7 Income from operations	125	173
8 Interest expense, net	44	11
9 Loss on debt refinancing	10	
10 Income before income taxes	71	162
11 Income tax expense	(7)	65
12 Net income	$ 78	$ 97

The Income Statement Measures Operating Performance

The **income statement**, or **statement of operations**, reports revenues and expenses for the period. The bottom line is net income or net loss *for the period*. At the top of Exhibit 1-7 is the company's name, J.Crew Group, Inc. On the second line is the term "Consolidated Statements of Operations." J.Crew Group, Inc., is actually made up of several corporations that are owned by a common group of shareholders. Commonly controlled corporations like this are required to combine, or consolidate, all of their revenues, expenses, assets, liabilities, and stockholders' equity, and to report them all as one.

The dates of J.Crew Group, Inc.'s Consolidated Statements of Operations are "Years Ended February 3, 2007 (fiscal year 2006) and February 2, 2008 (fiscal year 2007)." J.Crew uses a *fiscal year* consisting of 52 (or 53) weeks ending on the closest day to January 31 as its accounting year. This is because the holiday season is the busiest time of the year and includes Christmas, when the company typically earns the largest amount of revenue. In contrast, January is typically the slowest month of the year for retailers, allowing the company time to get its books in order. Companies often adopt a fiscal year that ends at the low point of their operations. Wal-Mart uses the same fiscal year as J.Crew. Whole Foods Markets, Inc., uses a fiscal year consisting of the 52 weeks ending closest to September 30. FedEx's year-end falls on May 31. About 60% of the largest companies use a fiscal year ending on December 31.

J.Crew Group, Inc.'s Consolidated Statements of Operations in Exhibit 1-7 report operating results for two fiscal years: 2006 (53 weeks ended February 3, 2007); and 2007 (52 weeks ended February 2, 2008), to show trends for revenues, expenses, and net income. To avoid clutter, J.Crew reports in millions of dollars. During fiscal 2007, J.Crew increased total revenues (line 3) from $1,152 million to

$1,335 million. Net income rose from $78 million to $97 million (line 12). J.Crew Group, Inc., stores sold more pants, coats, and accessories in 2007, and that boosted profits. Focus on fiscal 2007. (We show 2006 for comparative purposes.) An income statement reports two main categories:

- Revenues and gains
- Expenses and losses

We measure net income as follows:

> **Net Income = Total Revenues and Gains – Total Expenses and Losses**

In accounting, the word *net* refers to an amount after a subtraction. *Net* income is the profit left over after subtracting expenses and losses from revenues and gains. **Net income is the single most important item in the financial statements.**

Revenues.   J.Crew Group, Inc., has two kinds of revenue: Net sales and Other revenue. Revenues (lines 1, 2, and 3) do not always carry the term *revenue* in their titles. For example, net sales revenue is often abbreviated as *net sales*. *Net* sales means sales revenue after subtracting all the goods customers have returned to the company. J.Crew, Wal-Mart, Best Buy, and The Gap get some goods back from customers due to product defects, or items that customers do not want for other reasons. Other revenue consists principally of shipping and handling fees from catalog and Internet sales.

Expenses.   Not all expenses have the word *expense* in their title. For example, J.Crew Group, Inc.'s largest expense is for Cost of goods sold (line 4). Another title of this expense is *cost of sales*. This expense represents the direct cost of making sales. This includes J.Crew's cost of the merchandise it sold to customers, as well as occupancy costs (rent and maintenance) for leased stores. For example, suppose a sweater costs J.Crew $30. Assume J.Crew sells the sweater for $75. Sales revenue is $75, and cost of goods sold is $30. Cost of goods sold is the major expense of merchandising entities such as J.Crew, Best Buy, Wal-Mart, and Whole Foods Markets.
J.Crew has some other expenses:

- Selling, general and administrative expenses (line 6) are the costs of everyday operations that are not directly related to merchandise purchases and occupancy. Many expenses may be included in this category, including sales commissions paid to employees, catalog production, mailing costs, warehousing expenses, depreciation, credit card fees, executive salaries, and other home-office expenses. These expenses amounted to $416 million in fiscal 2007.
- Interest expense (line 8) was $11 million for 2007. This is J.Crew's cost of borrowing money. For J.Crew Group, Inc., interest revenue has been *netted* against interest expense. Companies are allowed to offset items like interest income and interest expense against each other and show only the difference (in this case the larger item is interest expense, and so the net amount appears as an expense).
- Income tax expense (line 11) is the expense levied on J.Crew Group, Inc.'s income by the government. This is often one of a corporation's largest expenses.

J.Crew's income tax expense for fiscal 2007 is a whopping $65 million (40% of its net income before taxes)! Compare this to fiscal 2006 when J. Crew had a tax benefit (income) of $7 million. The tax benefit occurred because, before 2006, J.Crew had reported net operating *losses* rather than net operating *income*, for tax purposes. Corporations are allowed a 20-year carry-forward for net operating losses, and are allowed to offset those losses against taxable income in profitable years. In fiscal 2006, the second year of profitable operations, the company used up the last of its net operating loss carry-forward, and showed net income, rather than expense, from income taxes.

J.Crew Group, Inc., reports Income from operations (line 7) of $173 million and Net income (line 12) of $97 million in fiscal 2007. Some investors use operating income to measure operating performance. Others use the "bottom-line" net income. A company whose net income from operations is consistently growing is regarded by the financial markets as a healthy and growing company. In the long run, that company's stock price should increase. We will explain this trend in greater detail in Chapter 11.

Now let's examine the statement of retained earnings (accumulated deficit) in Exhibit 1-8.

The Statement of Retained Earnings Shows What a Company Did with Its Net Income

Retained earnings means exactly what the term implies, that portion of net income the company has kept over a period of years. If, historically, revenue exceeds expenses, the result will be a positive balance in retained earnings. On the other hand, if, historically, expenses have exceeded sales revenues, the accumulation of these losses will result in an accumulated **deficit** in retained earnings (usually shown in parentheses). Net income or net loss flows from the income statement to the **statement of retained earnings** (lines 3 and 5 in Exhibit 1-8).

Net income increases retained earnings, and net losses and dividends decrease retained earnings.

Accounting Cycle Tutorial Income Statement Accounts

EXHIBIT 1-8 | **J.Crew Group, Inc., Consolidated Statement of Retained Earnings**

J.Crew Group, Inc.
Consolidated Statement of Retained Earnings (adapted)

(In millions)	Accumulated deficit
1 Balance 28-Jan-06...............	$(583)
2 Reclassifications..................	(3)
3 Net income 2006	78
4 Balance 3-Feb-07	$(508)
5 Net income 2007	97
6 Balance 2-Feb-08	$(411)

J.Crew Group, Inc.'s Consolidated Statements of Retained Earnings need explanation. Start with fiscal 2006. At the beginning of 2006 (January 28, 2006), J.Crew Group, Inc., had an accumulated deficit of $583 million (line 1) caused by the company's accumulated losses during its early years of operation (not uncommon for a young company). However, as the company turned profitable in more recent years, those deficits have been shrinking. During fiscal 2006, J.Crew earned net income of $78 million (line 3) and made another adjustment of $3 million (line 2). J.Crew ended fiscal 2006 with an accumulated deficit of $508 million (-$583 + $78 - $3, line 4). That deficit carried over and became the beginning balance of retained earnings in fiscal 2007.

In fiscal 2007, the company earned net income of $97 million (line 5) to end fiscal 2007 (February 2, 2008) with an accumulated deficit of about $411 million (line 6). If the company remains profitable for a few more years, it will erase the accumulated deficit, and retained earnings will start to show a positive balance (one of the signs of a maturing healthy company).

Which item on the statement of retained earnings comes directly from the income statement? It's net income. Lines 3 and 5 of the retained earnings statement come directly from line 12 of the income statement for fiscal years 2006 and 2007, respectively. Take a moment to trace this amount from one statement to the other.

Give yourself a pat on the back. You're already learning how to analyze financial statements!

After a company earns net income, the board of directors decides whether to pay a dividend to the stockholders. Corporations are not obligated to pay dividends unless their boards decide to pay (i.e., declare) them. Usually, companies who are in development stages or growth mode (like J.Crew Group, Inc.) elect not to pay dividends, opting instead to plow the money back into the company to expand operations or purchase property, plant, and equipment. Established companies usually have enough accumulated retained earnings (and cash) to pay dividends. Dividends decrease retained earnings because they represent a distribution of a company's assets (usually cash) to its stockholders.

The Balance Sheet Measures Financial Position

A company's **balance sheet**, also called the **statement of financial position**, reports three items: assets (line 9), liabilities (line 16), and stockholders' equity, (line 21). J.Crew Group, Inc.'s Consolidated Balance Sheets, shown in Exhibit 1-9, are dated at the *moment in time* when the accounting periods end (February 3, 2007, for fiscal 2006, and February 2, 2008, for fiscal 2007).

EXHIBIT 1-9 | J.Crew, Group, Inc., Consolidated Balance Sheets (Adapted)

J.Crew Group, Inc.
Consolidated Balance Sheets (adapted)

(In millions)	February 3, 2007	February 2, 2008
Assets		
1 Cash and cash equivalents	$ 89	$ 131
2 Merchandise inventories	141	159
3 Prepaid expenses..	47	43
4 Total current assets...	277	333
5 Property and equipment at cost	252	305
6 Less accumulated depreciation and amoritzation........	(130)	(137)
7 Net property and equipment.....................................	122	168
8 Other assets	29	34
9 Total assets	$ 428	$ 535
Liabilities and Stockholders' Equity		
10 Accounts payable..	$ 78	$ 101
11 Other current liabilities...	77	92
12 Federal and state income taxes payable......................	5	2
13 Total current liabilities..	160	195
14 Long-term debt..	200	125
15 Other liabilities...	62	75
16 Total liabilities..	422	395
Stockholders' equity:		
17 Common stock	1	1
18 Additional paid-in capital	516	553
19 Accumulated deficit..	(508)	(411)
20 Treasury stock, at cost	(3)	(3)
21 Total stockholders' equity.......................................	6	140
22 Total liabilities and stockholders' equity....................	$ 428	$ 535

Assets. There are two main categories of assets: current and long-term. **Current assets** are assets that are expected to be converted to cash, sold, or consumed during the next 12 months or within the business's operating cycle if longer than a year. Current assets include Cash, Short-term investments, Accounts and Notes receivable, Merchandise inventory, and Prepaid expenses. J.Crew's current assets at

February 2, 2008, total $333 million (line 4). Let's examine each current asset that J.Crew Group, Inc., holds.

- All companies have cash. Cash is the liquid asset that's the medium of exchange, and *cash equivalents* include money-market accounts or other financial instruments that are easily convertible to cash. J.Crew owns $131 million in cash and cash equivalents at February 2, 2008 (line 1).
- *Short-term investments* include stocks and bonds of other companies that J.Crew intends to sell within the next year. J.Crew's only short-term investments as of February 2, 2008, are counted as cash equivalents.
- *Accounts receivable* are amounts the company expects to collect from customers. J.Crew doesn't have any accounts receivable. That's because, as a retailer, all of J.Crew's sales are made either in cash or with credit cards, which are treated like cash sales. We'll discuss accounts receivable further in Chapter 5.
- *Notes receivable* are amounts a company expects to collect from a party who has signed a promissory note to that company and therefore owes it money. J.Crew doesn't own any notes receivable.
- Cash, short-term investments, and current receivables are the most liquid assets, in that order.
- *Merchandise inventory* (line 2) is the company's most important, and probably the largest, current asset. For J.Crew, merchandise inventory at February 2, 2008, totals $159 million (about 48% of total current assets and 30% of total assets). *Inventory* is a common abbreviation for *merchandise inventory*, and the two terms are used interchangeably.
- *Prepaid expenses* (line 3) represent amounts paid in advance for advertisements, rent, insurance, and supplies. Prepaid expenses are current assets because J.Crew Group, Inc., will benefit from these expenditures in the next fiscal year. J.Crew owns $43 million in prepaid expenses and other current assets as of February 2, 2008.
- An asset always represents a future benefit.

The main categories of *long-term assets* are Property, Plant, and Equipment (also called **plant assets**, lines 5–7), and other assets (line 8). Long-term assets may also include intangibles and other investments that are expected to benefit the company for long periods of time.

- *Property, plant, and equipment (PP&E)* includes J.Crew Group, Inc.'s land, buildings, computers, store fixtures, and equipment. J.Crew reports PP&E on three lines. Line 5 shows the company's cost of PP&E, which is $305 million through February 2, 2008. Cost means the historical acquisition price of these assets to J.Crew. It does not mean that J.Crew could sell its PP&E for $305 million. After all, the company may have acquired the assets several years ago.
- Line 6 shows how much *accumulated depreciation* J.Crew has recorded on its PP&E. *Depreciation* reallocates an asset's cost from the balance sheet to expense in the income statement over time as the asset is used in producing revenue. Accumulated depreciation ($137 million) is the total amount of depreciation recorded on PP&E from acquisition (perhaps years ago) through the end of the most recent year. Thus, accumulated depreciation represents the used-up portion of the asset. We subtract accumulated depreciation from the cost of PP&E to determine its book value ($168 million on line 7).

- *Intangibles* are assets with no physical form, such as patents, trademarks, and goodwill. J.Crew doesn't own any of these assets.
- *Long-term investments* are those investments the company does not intend to sell within the next year. J.Crew doesn't own any long-term investments.
- *Other assets* (line 8) is a catchall category for assets that are difficult to classify. J.Crew owns about $34 million of these assets. For J.Crew Group, Inc., these primarily represent long-term tax benefits, due to differences between the way the company keeps its books for financial reporting purposes and the way it keeps its books for tax purposes.
- Overall, J.Crew Group, Inc., reports total assets of $535 million at February 2, 2008 (line 9).

Liabilities.   Liabilities are also divided into current and long-term categories. **Current liabilities** (lines 10–13) are debts payable within one year or within J.Crew's operating cycle if longer than a year. Chief among the current liabilities are Accounts payable, Federal and state income taxes payable, and other liabilities like short-term notes payable, and accrued salaries and wages payable. *Long-term liabilities* are payable after one year.

- *Accounts payable* (line 10) of $101 million represents amounts owed to J.Crew's vendors and suppliers for purchases of inventory.
- *Income taxes payable* are tax debts owed to the government. J.Crew owes $2 million of federal and state income taxes as of February 2, 2008 (line 12).
- *Short-term notes payable* are amounts that a company has promised to pay back within one year or less. J.Crew doesn't owe any of these as of February 2, 2008.
- *Other current liabilities* (line 11). Included in this $92 million are interest payable on borrowed money, accrued liabilities for salaries, utilities, and other expenses that J.Crew has not yet paid.
- At February 2, 2008, J.Crew's current liabilities total $195 million (line 13). J.Crew also owes $125 million in long-term liabilities (line 14). These liabilities include long-term debt and other payables due after one year.
- At the end of fiscal 2007, total liabilities are $395 million (line 16). This is high relative to total assets of $535 million (about 74% of line 9) and indicates a not-so-strong financial position.

Stockholders' Equity.   The accounting equation states that

$$\text{Assets} - \text{Liabilities} = \text{Owners' Equity}$$

The assets (resources) and the liabilities (debts) of J.Crew Group, Inc., are fairly easy to understand. Owners' equity is harder to pin down. Owners' equity is simple to calculate, but what does it *mean*?

J.Crew Group, Inc., calls its owners' equity *Stockholders' equity* (line 21), and this title is descriptive. Remember that a company's owners' equity represents the stockholders' ownership of the business's assets. J.Crew's equity consists of

- *Common Stock* (line 17), represented by shares issued to stockholders for about $1 million through February 2, 2008. This amount represents the face amount (par value) of the stock. Par value is an artificial amount set by the company for the stock. Par value is explained in Chapter 9.

- *Additional paid-in capital* (line 18) represents amounts of cash received on initial sale of the company's stock in excess of the par value. This amounts to about $553 million at February 2, 2008.

- *Retained earnings* at February 2, 2008, is negative, or a *deficit* of $411 million (line 19). A year earlier J.Crew Group, Inc., had a deficit of $508 million. We saw these figures on the statement of retained earnings in Exhibit 1-8 (line 6). Retained earnings' final resting place is the balance sheet.

- J.Crew Group, Inc.'s stockholders' equity holds another item, Treasury Stock (line 20), which represents amounts paid by the company to repurchase its own stock. We will discuss the reasons for this in Chapter 9. For now, focus on the two main components of stockholders' equity: common stock and retained earnings.

- At February 2, 2008, J.Crew Group, Inc., has Total stockholders' equity of $140 million (line 21). We can now prove that J.Crew's total assets equal total liabilities and equity (amounts in millions):

Accounting Cycle Tutorial Balance Sheet Accounts

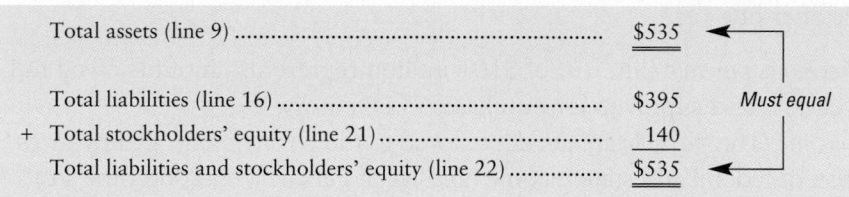

Total assets (line 9)	$535	
Total liabilities (line 16)	$395	*Must equal*
+ Total stockholders' equity (line 21)	140	
Total liabilities and stockholders' equity (line 22)	$535	

The statement of cash flows is the fourth required financial statement.

THE STATEMENT OF CASH FLOWS MEASURES CASH RECEIPTS AND PAYMENTS

Companies engage in three basic types of activities:

1. **Operating activities**

2. **Investing activities**

3. **Financing activities**

The **statement of cash flows** reports cash flows under each of these activities. Think about the cash flows (receipts and payments) in each category:

- *Companies operate by selling goods and services to customers.* **Operating activities** result in net income or net loss, and they either increase or decrease cash. The income statement tells whether the company is profitable. The statement of cash flows reports whether operations increased cash. Operating activities are most important, and they should be the company's main source of cash. Continuing negative cash flow from operations can lead to bankruptcy.

- *Companies invest in long-term assets.* J.Crew Group, Inc., buys store fixtures and equipment, and when these assets wear out, the company sells them. Both purchases and sales of long-term assets are investing cash flows. Investing cash flows are the next most important after operations.

- *Companies need money for financing.* Financing includes both issuing stock and borrowing. J.Crew Group, Inc., issues stock to its shareholders and borrows from banks. These are cash receipts. The company may also pay loans and repurchase its own stock. These payments are financing cash flows.

Overview.   Each category of cash flows—operating, investing, and financing—either increases or decreases cash. In Exhibit 1-10, which shows J.Crew Group, Inc.'s Consolidated Statements of Cash Flows, operating activities provided cash of $168 million in fiscal 2007 (line 4). This signals strong cash flow from operations. 2007's investing activities (purchase of property, plant, and equipment) used cash of about $81 million (line 6). That signals expansion. Financing activities used another $45 million (line 14). J.Crew paid off some debt and also issued some stock during the year. On a statement of cash flows, cash receipts appear as positive amounts. Cash payments are negative and enclosed by parentheses.

EXHIBIT 1-10 | J.Crew Group, Inc., Consolidated Statements of Cash Flows

J.Crew Group, Inc.
Consolidated Statements of Cash Flows (adapted)

	Years Ended	
(In millions)	February 3, 2007	February 2, 2008
1 Cash flows from operating activities:		
2 Net income	$ 78	$ 97
3 Adjustments to reconcile to cash provided by operations...............	43	71
4 Net cash provided by operating activities.....................................	121	168
5 Cash flows from investing activities:		
6 Purchases of property, plant and equipment	(46)	(81)
7 Cash flows from financing activities:		
8 Costs incurred in connection with amended credit agreement...............		(1)
9 Repayments and redemption of long-term debt	(386)	(75)
10 Redemption of preferred stock..	(358)	
11 Proceeds from issuance of long-term debt...................................	276	
12 Proceeds from issuance of common stock	421	32
13 Repurchase of common stock		(1)
14 Net cash provided by (used in) financing activities......................	(47)	(45)
15 Increase in cash and cash equivalents...	28	42
16 Cash and cash equivalents, beginning of year	61	89
17 Cash and cash equivalents, end of year	$ 89	$131

Overall, J.Crew's cash increased by about $42 million during 2007 (line 15) and ended the year at $131 million (line 17). Trace ending cash back to the balance sheet in Exhibit 1-9 (line 1). Cash links the statement of cash flows to the balance sheet. You've just performed more financial-statement analysis!

Let's now summarize the relationships that link the financial statements.

RELATIONSHIPS AMONG THE FINANCIAL STATEMENTS

Exhibit 1-11 summarizes the relationships among the financial statements of ABC Company for 2010. These statements are summarized with all amounts assumed for the illustration. Study the exhibit carefully because these relationships apply to all organizations. Specifically, note the following:

1. The income statement for the year ended December 31, 2010
   a. Reports revenues and expenses of the year. Revenues and expenses are reported *only* on the income statement.
   b. Reports net income if total revenues exceed total expenses. If expenses exceed revenues, there is a net loss.

2. The statement of retained earnings for the year ended December 31, 2010
   a. Opens with the beginning retained earnings balance.
   b. Adds net income (or subtracts net loss). Net income comes directly from the income statement (arrow ① in Exhibit 1-11).
   c. Subtracts dividends.
   d. Reports the retained earnings balance at the end of the year.

3. The balance sheet at December 31, 2010, end of the accounting year
   a. Reports assets, liabilities, and stockholders' equity at the end of the year. Only the balance sheet reports assets and liabilities.
   b. Reports that assets equal the sum of liabilities plus stockholders' equity. This balancing feature follows the accounting equation and gives the balance sheet its name.
   c. Reports retained earnings, which comes from the statement of retained earnings (arrow ② in Exhibit 1-11).

4. The statement of cash flows for the year ended December 31, 2010
   a. Reports cash flows from operating, investing, and financing activities. Each category results in net cash provided (an increase) or used (a decrease).
   b. Reports whether cash increased (or decreased) during the year. The statement shows the ending cash balance, as reported on the balance sheet (arrow ③ in Exhibit 1-11).

EXHIBIT 1-11 | **Relationships Among the Financial Statements**

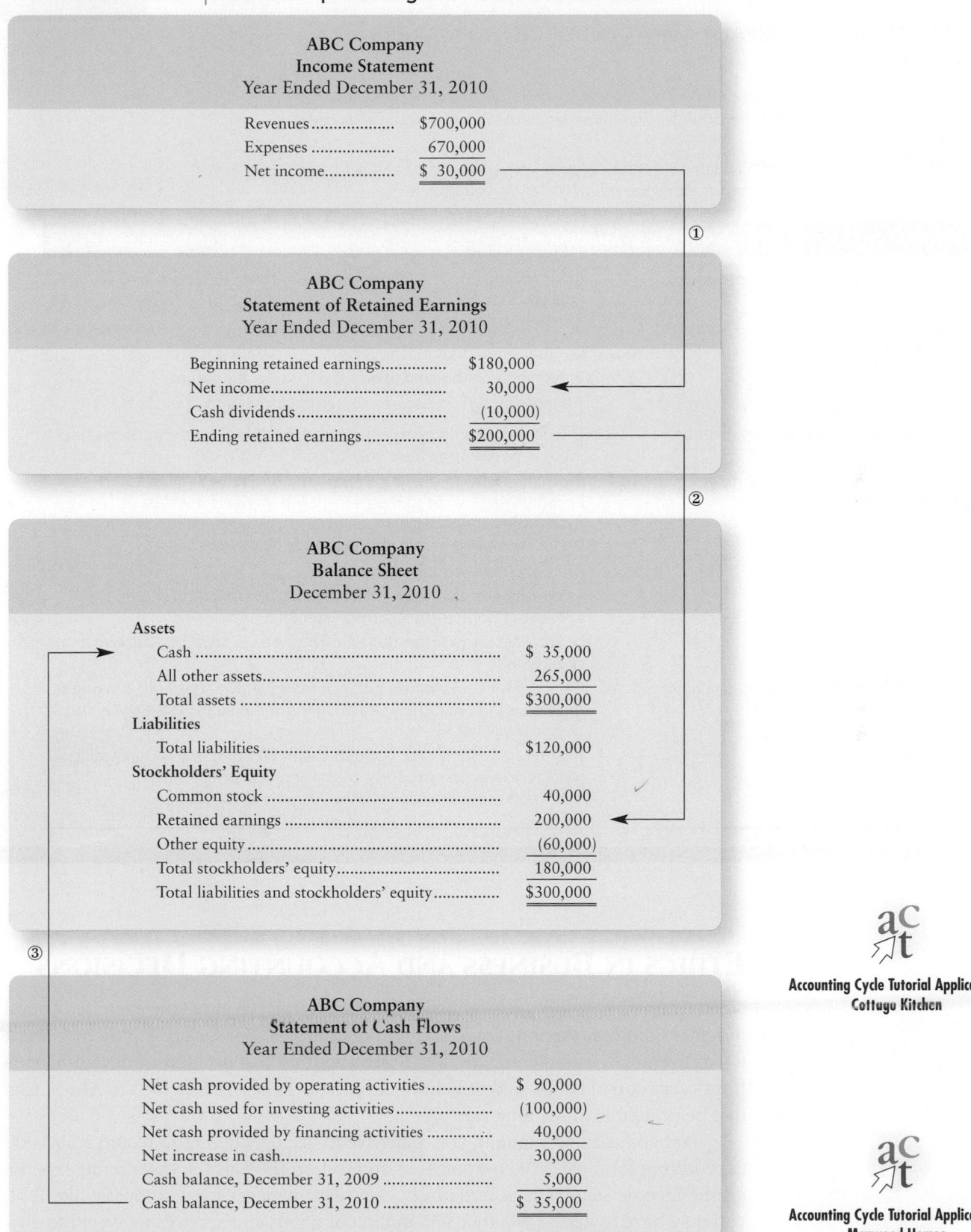

ABC Company
Income Statement
Year Ended December 31, 2010

Revenues....................	$700,000
Expenses	670,000
Net income................	$ 30,000

①

ABC Company
Statement of Retained Earnings
Year Ended December 31, 2010

Beginning retained earnings................	$180,000
Net income...	30,000
Cash dividends....................................	(10,000)
Ending retained earnings....................	$200,000

②

ABC Company
Balance Sheet
December 31, 2010

Assets

Cash	$ 35,000
All other assets...................................	265,000
Total assets	$300,000

Liabilities

Total liabilities...................................	$120,000

Stockholders' Equity

Common stock	40,000
Retained earnings	200,000
Other equity..	(60,000)
Total stockholders' equity....................	180,000
Total liabilities and stockholders' equity..............	$300,000

③

ABC Company
Statement of Cash Flows
Year Ended December 31, 2010

Net cash provided by operating activities................	$ 90,000
Net cash used for investing activities........................	(100,000)
Net cash provided by financing activities	40,000
Net increase in cash...	30,000
Cash balance, December 31, 2009	5,000
Cash balance, December 31, 2010	$ 35,000

ac
t
Accounting Cycle Tutorial Applications
Cottage Kitchen

ac
t
Accounting Cycle Tutorial Applications
Marwood Homes

DECISION GUIDELINES

IN EVALUATING A COMPANY, WHAT DO DECISION MAKERS LOOK FOR?

These Decision Guidelines illustrate how people use financial statements. Decision Guidelines appear throughout the book to show how accounting information aids decision making.

Suppose you are considering an investment in J.Crew Group, Inc., stock. How do you proceed? Where do you get the information you need? What do you look for?

Decision	Guidelines
1. Can the company sell its products?	1. Sales revenue on the income statement. Are sales growing or falling?
2. What are the main income measures to watch for trends?	2. a. Gross profit (Sales – Cost of goods sold) b. Operating income (Gross profit – Operating expenses) c. Net income (bottom line of the income statement) All three income measures should be increasing over time.
3. What percentage of sales revenue ends up as profit?	3. Divide net income by sales revenue. Examine the trend of the net income percentage from year to year.
4. Can the company collect its receivables?	4. From the balance sheet, compare the percentage increase in accounts receivable to the percentage increase in sales. If receivables are growing much faster than sales, collections may be too slow, and a cash shortage may result.
5. Can the company pay its a. Current liabilities? b. Current and long-term liabilities?	5. From the balance sheet, compare a. Current assets to current liabilities. Current assets should be somewhat greater than current liabilities. b. Total assets to total liabilities. Total assets must be somewhat greater than total liabilities.
6. Where is the company's cash coming from? How is cash being used?	6. On the cash-flows statement, operating activities should provide the bulk of the company's cash during most years. Otherwise, the business will fail. Examine investing cash flows to see if the company is purchasing long-term assets—property, plant, and equipment and intangibles (this signals growth).

ETHICS IN BUSINESS AND ACCOUNTING DECISIONS

Good business requires decision making, which in turn requires the exercise of good judgment, both at the individual and corporate levels. For example, you may work for or eventually run a company like **Starbucks** that has decided to devote 5 cents from every cup of coffee sold to helping save the lives of AIDS victims in Africa. Can that be profitable in the long run?

Perhaps as an accountant, you may have to decide whether to record a $50,000 expenditure for a piece of equipment as an asset on the balance sheet or an expense on the income statement. Alternatively, as a sales manager for a company like IBM, you may have to decide whether $25 million of goods and services delivered to customers in 2010 would be more appropriately recorded as revenue in 2010 or 2011.

As mentioned earlier, the transition from U.S. GAAP to IFRS *will require increased emphasis on judgment*, because IFRS contains fewer rules than U.S. GAAP. Depending on the type of business, the facts and circumstances surrounding accounting decisions may not always make them clear cut, and yet the decision may determine whether the company shows a profit or a loss in a particular period! What are the factors that influence business and accounting decisions, and how should these factors be weighed? Generally, three factors influence business and accounting decisions: **economic, legal, and ethical**.

The *economic* factor states that the decision being made should *maximize the economic benefits* to the decision maker. Based on most economic theory, every rational person faced with a decision will choose the course of action that maximizes his or her own welfare, without regard to how that decision impacts others. In summary, the combined outcome of each person acting in his or her own self-interest will maximize the benefits to society as a whole.

The *legal* factor is based on the proposition that free societies are governed by laws. Laws are written to provide clarity and to prevent abuse of the rights of individuals or society. Democratically enacted laws both contain and express society's collective moral standards. Legal analysis involves applying the relevant laws to each decision, and then choosing the action that complies with those laws. A complicating factor for a global business may be that what is legal in one country might not be legal in another. In that case, it is usually best to abide by the laws of the most restrictive country.

The *ethical* factor recognizes that while certain actions might be both economically profitable and legal, they may still not be right. Therefore, most companies, and many individuals, have established standards for themselves to enforce a higher level of conduct than that imposed by law. These standards govern how we treat others and the way we restrain our selfish desires. This behavior and its underlying beliefs are the essence of ethics. **Ethics** are shaped by our cultural, socioeconomic, and religious backgrounds. An *ethical analysis* is needed to guide judgment for making decisions.

The decision rule in an ethical analysis is to choose the action that fulfills ethical duties—responsibilities of the members of society to each other. The challenge in an ethical analysis is to identify specific ethical duties and stakeholders to whom you owe these duties. As with legal issues, a complicating factor in making global ethical decisions may be that what is considered ethical in one country is not considered ethical in another.

Among the questions you may ask in making an ethical analysis are:

- *Which options are most honest, open, and truthful?*

- *Which options are most kind, compassionate, and build a sense of community?*

- *Which options create the greatest good for the greatest number of stakeholders?*

- *Which options result in treating others as I would want to be treated?*

Ethical training starts at home and continues throughout our lives. It is reinforced by the teaching that we receive in our church, synagogue, or mosque; the schools we attend; and by the persons and companies we associate with.

A thorough understanding of ethics requires more study than we can accomplish in this book. However, remember that, when making accounting decisions, do not check your ethics at the door!

DECISION GUIDELINES

DECISION FRAMEWORK FOR MAKING ETHICAL JUDGMENTS

Weighing tough ethical judgments in business and accounting requires a decision framework. Answering the following four questions will guide you through tough decisions:

Decision	Guidelines
1. What is the issue?	1. The issue will usually deal with making a judgment about an accounting measurement or disclosure that results in economic consequences, often to numerous parties.
2. Who are the stakeholders, and what are the consequences of the decision to each?	2. Stakeholders are anyone who might be impacted by the decision—you, your company, and potential users of the information (investors, creditors, regulatory agencies). Consequences can be economic, legal, or ethical in nature.
3. Weigh the alternatives.	3. Analyze the impact of the decision on all stakeholders, using economic, legal, and ethical criteria. Ask "Who will be helped or hurt, whose rights will be exercised or denied, and in what way?"
4. Make the decision and be prepared to deal with the consequences.	4. Exercise the courage to either defend the decision or to change it, depending on its positive or negative impact. How does your decision make you feel afterward?

To simplify, we might ask three questions:

1. Is the action legal? If not, steer clear, unless you want to go to jail or pay monetary damages to injured parties. If the action is legal, go on to questions (2) and (3).
2. Who will be affected by the decision and how? Be as thorough about this analysis as possible, and analyze it from all three standpoints (economic, legal, and ethical).
3. How will this decision make me feel afterward? How would it make me feel if my family reads about it in the newspaper?

In later chapters throughout the book, we will apply this model to different accounting decisions.

In the business setting, ethics work best when modeled "from the top." Ethisphere Institute (www.ethisphere.com) has recently established the Business Ethics Leadership Alliance (BELA), aimed at "reestablishing ethics as the foundation of everyday business practices." BELA members agree to embrace and uphold four core values that incorporate ethics and integrity into all their practices: (1) Legal compliance; (2) Transparency; (3) Conflict identification; and (4) Accountability. Each year, Ethisphere Institute publishes a list of the World's Most Ethical Companies. The 2008 list includes corporations like UPS, Starbucks, McDonald's, The Gap, Target, and Pearson (the publisher of this textbook). Excerpts from many of these companies' financial statements will be featured in later chapters of this text. As you begin to make your decisions about future employers, put these companies on your list! It's easier to act ethically when those you work for recognize the importance of ethics in business practices. These companies have learned from experience that, in the long run, ethical conduct pays big rewards, not only socially, morally, and spiritually, but economically as well!

END-OF-CHAPTER SUMMARY PROBLEM

ShineBrite Car Wash, Inc., began operations on April 1, 2010. During April, the business provided services for customers. It is now April 30, and investors wonder how well ShineBrite performed during its first month. The investors also want to know the company's financial position at the end of April and its cash flows during the month.

The following data are listed in alphabetical order. Prepare the ShineBrite financial statements at the end of April 2010.

Accounts payable	$ 1,800	Land	$18,000
Accounts receivable	2,000	Payments of cash:	
Adjustments to reconcile net		Acquisition of land	40,000
income to net cash provided		Dividends	2,100
by operating activities	(3,900)	Rent expense	1,100
Cash balance at beginning of April	0	Retained earnings at beginning	
Cash balance at end of April	?	of April	0
Cash receipts:		Retained earnings at end of April	?
Issuance (sale) of stock to owners	50,000	Salary expense	1,200
Sale of land	22,000	Service revenue	10,000
Common stock	50,000	Supplies	3,700
		Utilities expense	400

Requirements

1. Prepare the income statement, the statement of retained earnings, and the statement of cash flows for the month ended April 30, 2010, and the balance sheet at April 30, 2010. Draw arrows linking the statements.
2. Answer the following questions:
   a. How well did ShineBrite perform during its first month of operations?
   b. Where does ShineBrite stand financially at the end of April?

Answers

Requirement 1
Financial Statements of ShineBrite Car Wash, Inc.

ShineBrite Car Wash, Inc.
Income Statement
Month Ended April 30, 2010

Revenue:		
Service revenue		$10,000
Expenses:		
Salary expense	$1,200	
Rent expense	1,100	
Utilities expense	400	
Total expenses		2,700
Net income		$ 7,300

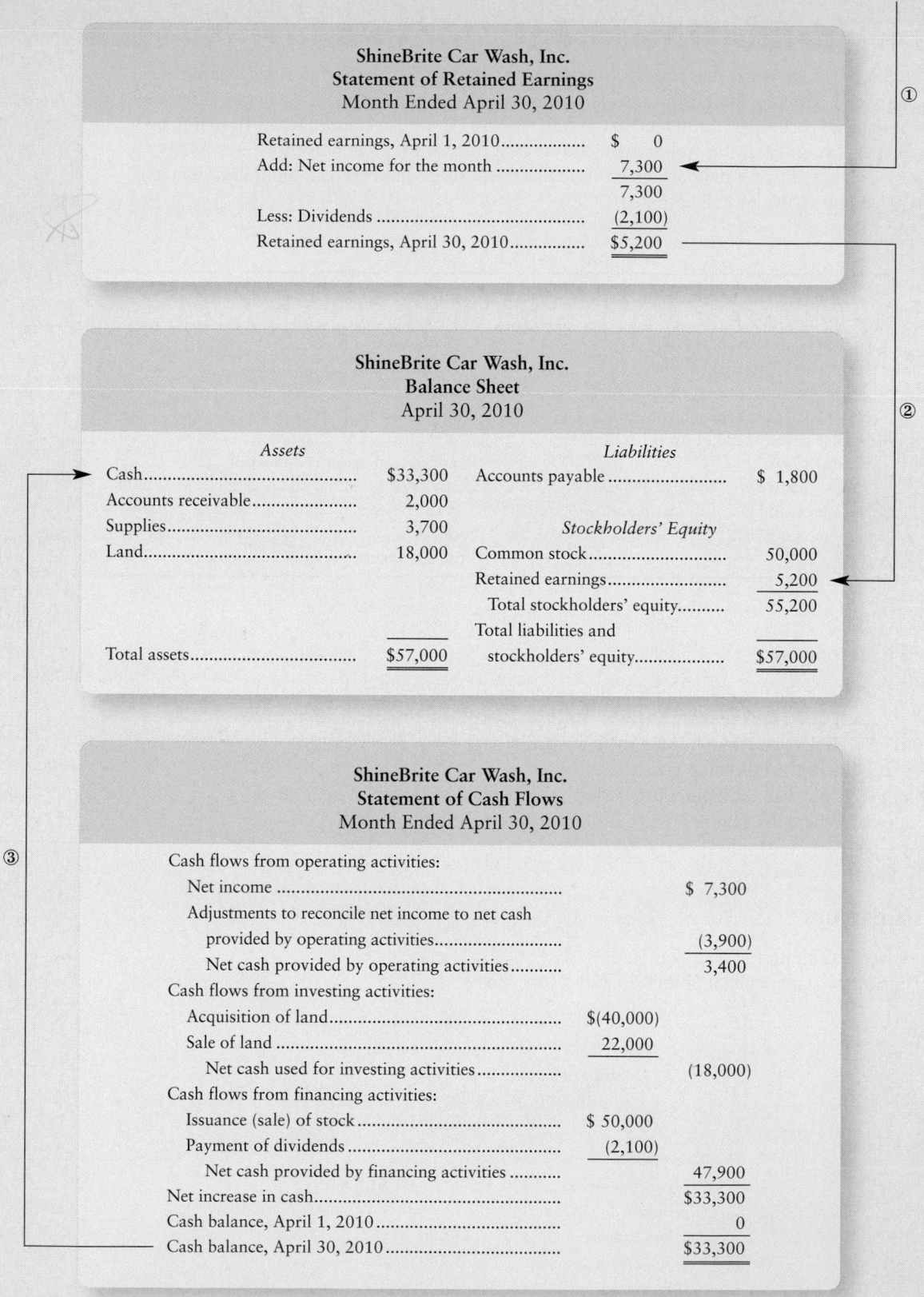

ShineBrite Car Wash, Inc.
Statement of Retained Earnings
Month Ended April 30, 2010

Retained earnings, April 1, 2010	$	0
Add: Net income for the month		7,300
		7,300
Less: Dividends		(2,100)
Retained earnings, April 30, 2010		$5,200

①

ShineBrite Car Wash, Inc.
Balance Sheet
April 30, 2010

Assets		*Liabilities*	
Cash	$33,300	Accounts payable	$ 1,800
Accounts receivable	2,000		
Supplies	3,700	*Stockholders' Equity*	
Land	18,000	Common stock	50,000
		Retained earnings	5,200
		Total stockholders' equity	55,200
		Total liabilities and	
Total assets	$57,000	stockholders' equity	$57,000

②

ShineBrite Car Wash, Inc.
Statement of Cash Flows
Month Ended April 30, 2010

③

Cash flows from operating activities:		
Net income		$ 7,300
Adjustments to reconcile net income to net cash		
provided by operating activities		(3,900)
Net cash provided by operating activities		3,400
Cash flows from investing activities:		
Acquisition of land	$(40,000)	
Sale of land	22,000	
Net cash used for investing activities		(18,000)
Cash flows from financing activities:		
Issuance (sale) of stock	$ 50,000	
Payment of dividends	(2,100)	
Net cash provided by financing activities		47,900
Net increase in cash		$33,300
Cash balance, April 1, 2010		0
Cash balance, April 30, 2010		$33,300

Requirement 2

 a. ShineBrite performed rather well in April. Net income was $7,300—very good in relation to service revenue of $10,000. The company was able to pay cash dividends of $2,100.

 b. ShineBrite ended April with cash of $33,300. Total assets of $57,000 far exceed total liabilities of $1,800. Stockholders' equity of $55,200 provides a good cushion for borrowing. The business's financial position at April 30, 2010, is strong.

REVIEW THE FINANCIAL STATEMENTS

Quick Check (Answers are given on page 58.)

1. All of the following statements are true except one. Which statement is false?
   a. The organization that formulates generally accepted accounting principles is the Financial Accounting Standards Board.
   b. A proprietorship is a business with several owners.
   c. Professional accountants are held to a high standard of ethical conduct.
   d. Bookkeeping is only a part of accounting.

2. The valuation of assets on the balance sheet is generally based on:
   a. current fair market value as established by independent appraisers.
   b. historical cost.
   c. selling price.
   d. what it would cost to replace the asset.

3. The accounting equation can be expressed as:
   a. Assets = Liabilities – Owners' Equity
   b. Assets + Liabilities = Owners' Equity
   c. Assets – Liabilities = Owners' Equity
   d. Owners' Equity - Assets = Liabilities

4. The nature of an asset is best described as:
   a. an economic resource that's expected to benefit future operations.
   b. something with physical form that's valued at cost in the accounting records.
   c. something owned by a business that has a ready market value.
   d. an economic resource representing cash or the right to receive cash in the future.

5. Which financial statement covers a period of time?
   a. Balance sheet   c. Statement of cash flows
   b. Income statement   d. Both b and c

6. How would net income be most likely to affect the accounting equation?
   a. Increase assets and increase liabilities
   b. Decrease assets and decrease liabilities
   c. Increase liabilities and decrease stockholders' equity
   d. Increase assets and increase stockholders' equity

7. During the year, EcoWash, Inc., has $120,000 in revenues, $50,000 in expenses, and $4,000 in dividend payments. Stockholders' equity changed by:
   a. +$66,000   c. –$66,000
   b. +$70,000   d. +$74,000

8. EcoWash in question 7 had net income (or net loss) of
   a. net loss of $50,000.
   b. net income of $70,000.
   c. net income of $66,000.
   d. net income of $120,000.
9. Rochester Corporation holds cash of $11,000 and owes $27,000 on accounts payable. Rochester has accounts receivable of $40,000, inventory of $34,000, and land that cost $55,000. How much are Rochester's total assets and liabilities?

	Total assets	Liabilities
a.	$129,000	$27,000
b.	$27,000	$140,000
c.	$140,000	$27,000
d.	$140,000	$93,000

10. Which item(s) is (are) reported on the balance sheet?
    a. Inventory
    b. Accounts payable
    c. Retained earnings
    d. All of the above
11. During the year, McKenna Company's stockholders' equity increased from $38,000 to $50,000. McKenna earned net income of $18,000. How much in dividends did McKenna declare during the year?
    a. $-0-
    b. $6,000
    c. $12,000
    d. $7,000
12. Javis Company had total assets of $340,000 and total stockholders' equity of $130,000 at the beginning of the year. During the year assets increased by $70,000 and liabilities increased by $25,000. Stockholders' equity at the end of the year is:
    a. $95,000.
    b. $175,000.
    c. $200,000.
    d. $155,000.
13. Which of the following is a true statement about International Financial Reporting Standards?
    a. They are more exact (contain more rules) than U.S. generally accepted accounting principles.
    b. They are not being applied anywhere in the world yet, but soon will be.
    c. They are converging gradually with U.S. standards.
    d. They are not needed for U.S. businesses since the United States already has the strongest accounting standards in the world.
14. Which of the following is the most accurate statement regarding ethics as applied to decision making in accounting?
    a. Ethics involves making difficult choices under pressure, and should be kept in mind in making every decision, including those involving accounting.
    b. Ethics has no place in accounting, since accounting deals purely with numbers.
    c. It is impossible to learn ethical decision making, since it is just something you decide to do or not to do.
    d. Ethics is becoming less and less important as a field of study in business.

Accounting Vocabulary

account payable (p. 14) A liability backed by the general reputation and credit standing of the debtor.

accounting (p. 3) The information system that measures business activities, processes that information into reports and financial statements, and communicates the results to decision makers.

accounting equation (p. 13) The most basic tool of accounting: Assets = Liabilities + Owners' Equity.

asset (p. 13) An economic resource that is expected to be of benefit in the future.

balance sheet (p. 20) List of an entity's assets, liabilities, and owners' equity as of a specific date. Also called the *statement of financial position*.

board of directors (p. 6) Group elected by the stockholders to set policy for a corporation and to appoint its officers.

capital (p. 13) Another name for the *owners' equity* of a business.

cash (p. 14) Money and any medium of exchange that a bank accepts at face value.

common stock (p. 14) The most basic form of capital stock.

continuity assumption (p. 9) See going-concern assumption.

corporation (p. 6) A business owned by stockholders. A corporation is a legal entity, an "artificial person" in the eyes of the law.

current asset (p. 21) An asset that is expected to be converted to cash, sold, or consumed during the next 12 months, or within the business's normal operating cycle if longer than a year.

current liability (p. 23) A debt due to be paid within one year or within the entity's operating cycle if the cycle is longer than a year.

deficit (p. 19) Negative balance in retained earnings caused by net losses over a period of years.

dividends (p. 15) Distributions (usually cash) by a corporation to its stockholders.

entity (p. 8) An organization or a section of an organization that, for accounting purposes, stands apart from other organizations and individuals as a separate economic unit.

ethics (p. 29) Standards of right and wrong that transcend economic and legal boundaries. Ethical standards deal with the way we treat others and restrain our own actions because of the desires, expectations, or rights of others, or with our obligations to them.

expenses (p. 14) Decrease in retained earnings that results from operations; the cost of doing business; opposite of revenues.

fair value (p. 10) The amount that a business could sell an asset for, or the amount that a business could pay to settle a liability.

financial accounting (p. 4) The branch of accounting that provides information to people outside the firm.

financial statements (p. 2) Business documents that report financial information about a business entity to decision makers.

financing activities (p. 24) Activities that obtain from investors and creditors the cash needed to launch and sustain the business; a section of the statement of cash flows.

fixed assets (p. 14) Another name for *property, plant, and equipment*.

generally accepted accounting principles (GAAP) (p. 7) Accounting guidelines, formulated by the Financial Accounting Standards Board, that govern how accounting is practiced.

going-concern assumption (p. 9) Holds that the entity will remain in operation for the foreseeable future.

historical cost principle (p. 9) Principle that states that assets and services should be recorded at their actual cost.

income statement (p. 17) A financial statement listing an entity's revenues, expenses, and net income or net loss for a specific period. Also called the *statement of operations*.

International Financial Reporting Standards (IFRS) (p. 7) Accounting guidelines, formulated by the International Accounting Standards Board (IASB). By 2014, U.S. GAAP is expected to be harmonized with IFRS. At that time, U.S. companies are expected to adopt these principles for their financial statements, so that they can be compared with those of companies from other countries.

investing activities (p. 24) Activities that increase or decrease the long-term assets available to the business; a section of the statement of cash flows.

liability (p. 13) An economic obligation (a debt) payable to an individual or an organization outside the business.

limited liability company (p. 6) A business organization in which the business (not the owner) is liable for the company's debts.

long-term debt (p. 14) A liability that falls due beyond one year from the date of the financial statements.

management accounting (p. 5) The branch of accounting that generates information for the internal decision makers of a business, such as top executives.

merchandise inventory (p. 14) The merchandise that a company sells to customers, also called *inventory*.

net earnings (p. 15) Another name for *net income*.

net income (p. 15) Excess of total revenues over total expenses. Also called *net earnings* or *net profit*.

net loss (p. 15) Excess of total expenses over total revenues.

net profit (p. 15) Another name for *net income*.

note payable (p. 14) A liability evidenced by a written promise to make a future payment.

operating activities (p. 24) Activities that create revenue or expense in the entity's major line of business; a section of the statement of cash flows. Operating activities affect the income statement.

owners' equity (p. 13) The claim of the owners of a business to the assets of the business. Also called *capital*, *stockholders' equity*, or *net assets*.

paid-in capital (p. 14) The amount of stockholders' equity that stockholders have contributed to the corporation. Also called *contributed capital*.

partnership (p. 5) An association of two or more persons who co-own a business for profit.

plant assets (p. 22) Another name for *property, plant, and equipment.*

property, plant, and equipment (p. 14) Long-lived assets, such as land, buildings, and equipment, used in the operation of the business. Also called *plant assets* or *fixed assets.*

proprietorship (p. 5) A business with a single owner.

retained earnings (p. 14) The amount of stockholders' equity that the corporation has earned through profitable operation and has not given back to stockholders.

revenues (p. 14) Increase in retained earnings from delivering goods or services to customers or clients.

shareholder (p. 6) Another name for *stockholder.*

stable-monetary-unit assumption (p. 10) The reason for ignoring the effect of inflation in the accounting records, based on the assumption that the dollar's purchasing power is relatively stable.

statement of cash flows (p. 24) Reports cash receipts and cash payments classified according to the entity's major activities: operating, investing, and financing.

statement of financial position (p. 20) Another name for the *balance sheet.*

statement of operations (p. 17) Another name for the *income statement.*

statement of retained earnings (p. 19) Summary of the changes in the retained earnings of a corporation during a specific period.

stock (p. 6) Shares into which the owners' equity of a corporation is divided.

stockholder (p. 6) A person who owns stock in a corporation. Also called a *shareholder.*

stockholders' equity (p. 13) The stockholders' ownership interest in the assets of a corporation.

ASSESS YOUR PROGRESS

Short Exercises

S1-1 (*Learning Objective 3: Using the accounting equation*) Suppose you manage a Pizza Sauce restaurant. Identify the missing amount for each situation:

	Total Assets	=	Total Liabilities	+	Stockholders' Equity
a.	$?		$130,000		$210,000
b.	250,000		70,000		?
c.	190,000		?		80,000

S1-2 (*Learning Objective 5: Making ethical judgments*) Good business and accounting practices require the exercise of good judgment. How should ethics be incorporated into making accounting judgments? Why is ethics important?

S1-3 (*Learning Objective 1: Organizing a business*) A Healthy Planet, Inc., needs funds, and Mary Barry, the president, has asked you to consider investing in the business. Answer the following questions about the different ways that Barry might organize the business. Explain each answer.

    a. What forms of organization will enable the owners of A Healthy Planet to limit their risk of loss to the amounts they have invested in the business?

    b. What form of business organization will give Barry the most freedom to manage the business as she wishes?

    c. What form of organization will give creditors the maximum protection in the event that A Healthy Planet fails and cannot pay its debts?

S1-4 (*Learning Objective 2: Applying accounting assumptions*) Daniel Newman is chairman of the board of Quality Food Brands, Inc. Suppose Mr. Newman has just founded Quality Food Brands, and assume that he treats his home and other personal assets as part of Quality Food Brands. Answer these questions about the evaluation of Quality Food Brands, Inc.

    1. Which accounting assumption governs this situation?

    2. How can the proper application of this accounting concept give Newman and others a realistic view of Quality Food Brands, Inc.? Explain in detail.

S1-5 (*Learning Objective 2: Applying accounting concepts, assumptions, and principles*) Identify the accounting concept, assumption or principle that best applies to each of the following situations:

    a. Arby's, the restaurant chain, sold a store location to McDonald's. How can Arby's determine the sale price of the store—by a professional appraisal, Arby's cost, or the amount actually received from the sale?

    b. Inflation has been around 6.25% for some time. Ridgeview Realtors is considering measuring its land values in inflation-adjusted amounts.

    c. Honda wants to determine which division of the company—Honda or Acura—is more profitable.

    d. You get an especially good buy on a television, paying only $1,100 for a television that normally costs $1,900. What is your accounting value for this television?

S1-6 (*Learning Objective 3: Using the accounting equation*)

    1. Use the accounting equation to show how to determine the amount of a company's owners' equity. How would your answer change if you were analyzing your own household or a single Denny's restaurant?

    2. If you know the assets and the owners' equity of a business, how can you measure its liabilities? Give the equation.

S1-7 (*Learning Objective 1: Defining key accounting terms*) Accounting definitions are precise, and you must understand the vocabulary to properly use accounting. Sharpen your understanding of key terms by answering the following questions:

    1. How do the assets and owners' equity of Microsoft Corporation differ from each other? Which one (assets or owners' equity) must be at least as large as the other? Which one can be smaller than the other?

    2. How are Microsoft's liabilities and owners' equity similar? Different?

S1-8 (*Learning Objective 1: Classifying assets, liabilities, and owners' equity*) Consider Target, a large retailer. Classify the following items as an Asset (A), a Liability (L), or Stockholders' Equity (S) for Target:

a. ___ Accounts payable		**g.** ___ Accounts receivable
b. ___ Common stock		**h.** ___ Long-term debt
c. ___ Supplies		**i.** ___ Merchandise inventory
d. ___ Retained earnings		**j.** ___ Notes payable
e. ___ Land		**k.** ___ Expenses payable
f. ___ Prepaid expenses		**l.** ___ Equipment

S1-9 (*Learning Objectives 1, 4: Using accounting vocabulary; using the income statement*)

    1. Identify the two basic categories of items on an income statement.

    2. What do we call the bottom line of the income statement?

S1-10 (*Learning Objective 4: Preparing an income statement*) Call Anywhere Wireless, Inc., began 2010 with total assets of $130 million and ended 2010 with assets of $165 million. During 2010 Call Anywhere earned revenues of $94 million and had expenses of $23 million. Call Anywhere paid dividends of $13 million in 2010. Prepare the company's income statement for the year ended December 31, 2010, complete with an appropriate heading.

S1-11 (*Learning Objective 4: Preparing a statement of retained earnings*) Roam Corp. began 2010 with retained earnings of $210 million. Revenues during the year were $380 million and expenses totaled $250 million. Roam declared dividends of $43 million. What was the company's ending balance of retained earnings? To answer this question, prepare Roam's statement of retained earnings for the year ended December 31, 2010, complete with its proper heading.

S1-12 (*Learning Objective 4: Preparing a balance sheet*) At December 31, 2010, Tommer Products has cash of $12,000, receivables of $5,000, and inventory of $42,000. The company's equipment totals $82,000. Tommer owes accounts payable of $17,000, and long-term notes payable of $78,000. Common stock is $14,800.

Prepare Tommer's balance sheet at December 31, 2010, complete with its proper heading. Use the accounting equation to compute retained earnings.

S1-13 *(Learning Objective 4: Preparing a statement of cash flows)* Lanos Medical, Inc., ended 2009 with cash of $25,000. During 2010, Lanos earned net income of $95,000 and had adjustments to reconcile net income to net cash provided by operations totaling $20,000 (this is a negative amount).

Lanos paid $35,000 to purchase equipment during 2010. During 2010, the company paid dividends of $15,000.

Prepare Lanos' statement of cash flows for the year ended December 31, 2010, complete with its proper heading.

S1-14 *(Learning Objectives 1, 4: Using accounting vocabulary; identifying items with the appropriate financial statement)* Suppose you are analyzing the financial statements of Murphy Radiology, Inc. Identify each item with its appropriate financial statement, using the following abbreviations: Income statement (IS), Statement of retained earnings (SRE), Balance sheet (BS), and Statement of cash flows (SCF). Three items appear on two financial statements, and one item shows up on three statements.

a. ____ Dividends
b. ____ Salary expense
c. ____ Inventory
d. ____ Sales revenue
e. ____ Retained earnings
f. ____ Net cash provided by operating activities
g. ____ Net income

h. ____ Cash
i. ____ Net cash used for financing activities
j. ____ Accounts payable
k. ____ Common stock
l. ____ Interest revenue
m. ____ Long-term debt
n. ____ Increase or decrease in cash

S1-15 *(Learning Objectives 2, 4: Applying accounting concepts, assumptions and principles to explain business activity)* Apply your understanding of the relationships among the financial statements to answer these questions.

a. How can a business earn large profits but have a small balance of retained earnings?
b. Give two reasons why a business can have a steady stream of net income over a six-year period and still experience a cash shortage.
c. If you could pick a single source of cash for your business, what would it be? Why?
d. How can a business lose money several years in a row and still have plenty of cash?

Exercises

All of the A and B exercises can be found within MyAccountingLab, an online homework and practice environment. Your instructor may ask you to complete these exercises using MyAccountingLab.

(Group A)

E1-16A *(Learning Objective 3, 4: Using the accounting equation; evaluating business operations)* Compute the missing amount in the accounting equation for each company (amounts in billions):

	Assets	Liabilities	Owners' Equity
Fresh Produce	$?	$ 9	$17
Hudson Bank	29	?	15
Pet Lovers	21	10	?

Which company appears to have the strongest financial position? Explain your reasoning.

E1-17A *(Learning Objectives 3, 4: Using the accounting equation; evaluating business operations)*   Hombran Doughnuts has current assets of $290 million; property, plant, and equipment of $490 million; and other assets totaling $150 million. Current liabilities are $150 million and long-term liabilities total $310 million.

I Requirements

1. Use these data to write Hombran Doughnuts' accounting equation.
2. How much in resources does Hombran have to work with?
3. How much does Hombran owe creditors?
4. How much of the company's assets do the Hombran stockholders actually own?

E1-18A *(Learning Objectives 3, 4: Using the accounting equation; evaluating business operations)*   Nelson, Inc.'s comparative balance sheet at January 31, 2011, and 2010, reports (in millions):

	2011	2010
Total assets	$39	$31
Total liabilities	10	9

I Requirements

Three situations about Nelson's issuance of stock and payment of dividends during the year ended January 31, 2011, follow. For each situation, use the accounting equation and the statement of retained earnings to compute the amount of Nelson's net income or net loss during the year ended January 31, 2011.

1. Nelson issued $11 million of stock and paid no dividends.
2. Nelson issued no stock but paid dividends of $11 million.
3. Nelson issued $55 million of stock and paid dividends of $32 million.

E1-19A *(Learning Objective 3: Using the accounting equation)* Answer these questions about two companies.

1. Clay, Inc., began the year with total liabilities of $50,000 and total stockholders' equity of $80,000. During the year, total assets increased by 35%. How much are total assets at the end of the year?
2. EastWest Airlines Ltd. began the year with total assets of $100,000 and total liabilities of $7,000. Net income for the year was $25,000, and dividends were zero. How much is stockholders' equity at the end of the year?

E1-20A *(Learning Objectives 4, 5: Evaluating business operations; making business decisions)* Assume Facebook is expanding into Ireland. The company must decide where to locate and how to finance the expansion. Identify the financial statement where these decision makers can find the following information about Facebook, Inc. In some cases, more than one statement will report the needed data.

a. Common stock
b. Income tax payable
c. Dividends
d. Income tax expense
e. Ending balance of retained earnings
f. Total assets
g. Long-term debt
h. Revenue

i. Cash spent to acquire the building
j. Selling, general, and administrative expenses
k. Adjustments to reconcile net income to net cash provided by operations
l. Ending cash balance
m. Current liabilities
n. Net income

E1-21A (*Learning Objectives 3, 4: Using the accounting equation; preparing a balance sheet*) Amounts of the assets and liabilities of Ellen Samuel Banking Company, as of January 31, 2010, are given as follows. Also included are revenue and expense figures for the year ended on that date (amounts in millions):

Total revenue	$ 37.8	Investment assets	$169.6
Receivables	0.9	Property and equipment, net	1.9
Current liabilities	151.1	Other expenses	6.9
Common stock	14	Retained earnings, beginning	8.6
Interest expense	0.8	Retained earnings, ending	?
Salary and other employee expenses	17.7	Cash	2.1
Long-term liabilities	2.8	Other assets	14.4

❘ *Requirement*

1. Prepare the balance sheet of Ellen Samuel Banking Company at January 31, 2010. Use the accounting equation to compute ending retained earnings.

E1-22A (*Learning Objective 4: Preparing an income statement and a statement of retained earnings*) This exercise should be used with Exercise 1-21A. Refer to the data of Ellen Samuel Banking Company in Exercise 1-21A.

❘ *Requirements*

1. Prepare the income statement of Ellen Samuel Banking Company, for the year ended January 31, 2010.
2. What amount of dividends did Ellen Samuel declare during the year ended January 31, 2010? Hint: Prepare a statement of retained earnings.

E1-23A (*Learning Objective 4: Preparing a statement of cash flows*) Lucky, Inc., began 2010 with $87,000 in cash. During 2010, Lucky earned net income of $410,000, and adjustments to reconcile net income to net cash provided by operations totaled $70,000, a positive amount. Investing activities used cash of $420,000, and financing activities provided cash of $72,000. Lucky ended 2010 with total assets of $260,000 and total liabilities of $115,000.

❘ *Requirement*

1. Prepare Lucky, Inc.'s statement of cash flows for the year ended December 31, 2010. Identify the data items given that do not appear on the statement of cash flows. Also identify the financial statement that reports the unused items.

E1-24A (*Learning Objective 4: Preparing an income statement and a statement of retained earnings*) Assume an Earl Copy Center ended the month of July 2010 with these data:

Payments of cash:			
Acquisition of equipment	$420,000	Cash balance, June 30, 2010	$ 0
Dividends	4,800	Cash balance, July 31, 2010	10,900
Retained earnings		Cash receipts:	
June 30, 2010	0	Issuance (sale) of stock	
Retained earnings		to owners	69,500
July 31, 2010	?	Rent expense	2,200
Utilities expense	10,000	Common stock	69,500
Adjustments to reconcile		Equipment	420,000
net income to net cash		Office supplies	14,800
provided by operations	2,200	Accounts payable	17,000
Salary expense	167,000	Service revenue	543,200

I *Requirement*

1. Prepare the income statement and the statement of retained earnings of Earl Copy Center, Inc., for the month ended July 31, 2010.

E1-25A (*Learning Objective 4: Preparing a balance sheet*) Refer to the data in Exercise 1-24A.

I *Requirement*

1. Prepare the balance sheet of Earl Copy Center, Inc., for July 31, 2010.

E1-26A (*Learning Objective 4: Preparing a statement of cash flows*) Refer to the data in Exercises 1-24A and 1-25A.

I *Requirement*

1. Prepare the statement of cash flows of Earl Copy Center, Inc., for the month ended July 31, 2010. Also explain the relationship among income statement, statement of retained earnings, balance sheet, and statement of cash flows.

E1-27A (*Learning Objectives 4, 5: Evaluating a business; advising a business*) This exercise should be used in conjunction with Exercises 1-24A through 1-26A.

writing assignment ■

The owner of Earl Copy Center seeks your advice as to whether he should cease operations or continue the business. Complete the report giving him your opinion of net income, dividends, financial position, and cash flows during his first month of operations. Cite specifics from the financial statements to support your opinion. Conclude your memo with advice on whether to stay in business or cease operations.

(Group B)

E1-28B (*Learning Objectives 3, 4: Using the accounting equation; evaluating business operations*)   Compute the missing amount in the accounting equation for each company (amounts in billions):

	Assets	Liabilities	Owners' Equity
DJ Video Rentals	$?	$ 8	$18
Ernie's Bank	34	?	14
Hudson Gift and Cards	20	12	?

Which company appears to have the strongest financial position? Explain your reasoning.

E1-29B (*Learning Objectives 3, 4: Using the accounting equation; evaluating business operations*)   Tinman Doughnuts has current assets of $270 million; property, plant, and equipment of $470 million; and other assets totaling $110 million. Current liabilities are $110 million and long-term liabilities total $370 million.

I *Requirements*

1. Use these data to write Tinman's accounting equation.
2. How much in resources does Tinman have to work with?
3. How much does Tinman owe creditors?
4. How much of the company's assets do the Tinman stockholders actually own?

E1-30B (*Learning Objectives 3, 4: Using the accounting equation; evaluating business operations*)   Winkler, Inc.'s comparative balance sheet at January 31, 2011, and 2010, reports (in millions):

	2011	2010
Total assets	$38	$24
Total liabilities	11	1

❙ Requirements

Three situations about Winkler's issuance of stock and payment of dividends during the year ended January 31, 2011, follow. For each situation, use the accounting equation and the statement of retained earnings to compute the amount of Winkler's net income or net loss during the year ended January 31, 2011.

1. Winkler issued $15 million of stock and paid no dividends.
2. Winkler issued no stock but paid dividends of $11 million.
3. Winkler issued $90 million of stock and paid dividends of $35 million.

E1-31B (*Learning Objective 3: Applying the accounting equation*) Answer these questions about two companies.

1. Sapphire, Inc., began the year with total liabilities of $90,000 and total stockholders' equity of $35,000. During the year, total assets increased by 30%. How much are total assets at the end of the year?
2. Southbound Airlines Ltd. began the year with total assets of $95,000 and total liabilities of $47,000. Net income for the year was $26,000, and dividends were zero. How much is stockholders' equity at the end of the year?

E1-32B (*Learning Objectives 4, 5: Evaluating business operations; making business decisions*) Assume Lesley, Inc., is expanding into Sweden. The company must decide where to locate and how to finance the expansion. Identify the financial statement where these decision makers can find the following information about Lesley, Inc. In some cases, more than one statement will report the needed data.

a. Income tax expense	i. Dividends
b. Net income	j. Total Assets
c. Current liabilities	k. Long-term debt
d. Common stock	l. Selling, general, and administrative expenses
e. Income tax payable	
f. Ending balance of retained earnings	m. Cash spent to acquire the building
g. Revenue	n. Adjustments to reconcile net income to net cash provided by operations
h. Ending cash balance	

■ spreadsheet

E1-33B (*Learning Objectives 3, 4: Using the accounting equation; preparing a balance sheet*) Amounts of the assets and liabilities of Eliza Bennet Banking Company, as of May 31, 2010, are given as follows. Also included are revenue and expense figures for the year ended on that date (amounts in millions):

Total revenue	$ 33.5	Investment assets	$169.8
Receivables	0.2	Property and equipment, net	1.6
Current liabilities	155.1	Other expenses	6.6
Common stock	14.9	Retained earnings, beginning	8.6
Interest expense	0.4	Retained earnings, ending	?
Salary and other employee expenses	17.5	Cash	2.7
Long-term liabilities	2.3	Other assets	14.9

❙ Requirement

1. Prepare the balance sheet of Eliza Bennet Banking Company at May 31, 2010. Use the accounting equation to compute ending retained earnings

■ spreadsheet

E1-34B (*Learning Objective 4: Preparing an income statement and a statement of retained earnings*) This exercise should be used with Exercise 1-33B.

❙ Requirements

1. Prepare the income statement of Eliza Bennet Banking Company, for the year ended May 31, 2010.

2. What amount of dividends did Eliza Bennet declare during the year ended May 31, 2010? Hint: Prepare a statement of retained earnings.

E1-35B (*Learning Objective 4: Preparing a statement of cash flows*) Fortune, Inc., began 2010 with $83,000 in cash. During 2010, Fortune earned net income of $440,000, and adjustments to reconcile net income to net cash provided by operations totaled $60,000, a positive amount. Investing activities used cash of $390,000, and financing activities provided cash of $65,000. Fortune ended 2010 with total assets of $300,000 and total liabilities of $120,000.

❚ *Requirement*

1. Prepare Fortune, Inc.'s statement of cash flows for the year ended December 31, 2010. Identify the data items given that do not appear on the statement of cash flows. Also identify the financial statement that reports each unused items.

E1-36B (*Learning Objective 4: Preparing an income statement and a statement of retained earnings*) Assume a Carson Copy Center ended the month of July 2011 with these data:

Payments of cash:			Cash balance, June 30, 2011	$ 0
Acquisition of equipment	$410,000		Cash balance, July 31, 2011	9,500
Dividends	4,100		Cash receipts:	
Retained earnings			Issuance (sale) of stock	
June 30, 2011	0		to owners	54,200
Retained earnings			Rent expense	2,900
July 31, 2011	?		Common stock	54,200
Utilities expense	10,800		Equipment	410,000
Adjustments to reconcile			Office supplies	15,000
net income to net cash			Accounts payable	17,900
provided by operations	2,900		Service revenue	542,200
Salary expense	162,000			

❚ *Requirement*

1. Prepare the income statement and the statement of retained earnings of Carson Copy Center, Inc., for the month ended July 31, 2011.

E1-37B (*Learning Objective 4: Preparing a balance sheet*) Refer to the data in Exercise 1-36B.

❚ *Requirement*

1. Prepare the balance sheet of Carson Copy Center, Inc., at July 31, 2011.

E1-38B (*Learning Objective 4: Preparing a statement of cash flows*) Refer to the data in Exercises 1-36B and 1-37B.

❚ *Requirement*

1. Prepare the statement of cash flows of Carson Copy Center, Inc., for the month ended July 31, 2011. Also explain the relationship among income statement, statement of retained earnings, balance sheet, and statement of cash flows.

E1-39B (*Learning Objectives 4, 5: Evaluating a business; advising a business*) This exercise should be used in conjunction with Exercises 1-36B through 1-38B.

writing assignment ■

The owner of Carson Copy Center now seeks your advice as to whether he should cease operations or continue the business. Complete the report giving him your opinion of net income, dividends, financial position, and cash flows during his first month of operations. Cite specifics from the financial statements to support your opinion. Conclude your memo with advice on whether to stay in business or cease operations.

Quiz

Test your understanding of the financial statements by answering the following questions. Select the best choice from among the possible answers given.

Q1-40 The *primary* objective of financial reporting is to provide information
a. useful for making investment and credit decisions.
b. about the profitability of the enterprise.
c. to the federal government.
d. on the cash flows of the company.

Q1-41 Which type of business organization provides the least amount of protection for bankers and other creditors of the company?
a. Partnership
b. Proprietorship
c. Corporation
d. Both a and b

Q1-42 Assets are usually reported at their
a. historical cost.
b. current market value.
c. appraised value.
d. none of the above (fill in the blank).

Q1-43 During March, assets increased by $19,000 and liabilities increased by $6,000. Stockholders' equity must have
a. increased by $13,000.
b. decreased by $13,000.
c. increased by $25,000.
d. decreased by $25,000.

Q1-44 The amount a company expects to collect from customers appears on the
a. statement of cash flows.
b. balance sheet in the current assets section.
c. income statement in the expenses section.
d. balance sheet in the stockholders' equity section.

Q1-45 All of the following are current assets except
a. Inventory.
b. Sales Revenue.
c. Cash.
d. Accounts Receivable.

Q1-46 Revenues are
a. decreases in liabilities resulting from paying off loans.
b. increases in paid-in capital resulting from the owners investing in the business.
c. increases in retained earnings resulting from selling products or performing services.
d. all of the above.

Q1-47 The financial statement that reports revenues and expenses is called the
a. statement of cash flows.
b. income statement.
c. statement of retained earnings.
d. balance sheet.

Q1-48 Another name for the balance sheet is the
a. statement of financial position
b. statement of operations.
c. statement of profit and loss.
d. statement of earnings.

Q1-49 Pinker Corporation began the year with cash of $30,000 and a computer that cost $25,000. During the year Pinker earned sales revenue of $135,000 and had the following expenses: salaries, $57,000; rent, $11,000; and utilities, $4,000. At year-end Pinker's cash balance was down to $18,000. How much net income (or net loss) did Pinker experience for the year?
a. ($12,000)
b. $135,000
c. $63,000
d. $123,000

Q1-50 Advanced Instruments had retained earnings of $155,000 at December 31, 2009. Net income for 2010 totaled $100,000, and dividends for 2010 were $25,000. How much retained earnings should Advanced report at December 31, 2010?

a. $255,000
b. $180,000

c. $230,000
d. $155,000

Q1-51 Net income appears on which financial statement(s)?

a. Income statement
b. Statement of retained earnings

c. Balance sheet
d. Both a and b

Q1-52 Cash paid to purchase a building appears on the statement of cash flows among the

a. Stockholders' equity.
b. Investing activities.

c. Financing activities.
d. Operating activities.

Q1-53 The stockholders' equity of Diakovsky Company at the beginning and end of 2010 totaled $15,000 and $20,000, respectively. Assets at the beginning of 2010 were $27,000. If the liabilities of Diakovsky Company increased by $9,000 in 2010, how much were total assets at the end of 2010? Use the accounting equation.

a. $45,000
b. $34,000

c. $50,000
d. $41,000

Q1-54 Robbin Company had the following on the dates indicated:

	12/31/10	12/31/09
Total assets	$740,000	$510,000
Total liabilities	290,000	190,000

Robbin had no stock transactions in 2010 and, thus, the change in stockholders' equity for 2010 was due to net income and dividends. If dividends were $55,000, how much was Robbin's net income for 2010? Use the accounting equation and the statement of retained earnings.

a. $185,000
b. $245,000

c. $155,000
d. $215,000

Problems

All of the following A and B problems can be found within MyAccountingLab, an online homework and practice environment. Your instructor may ask you to complete these problems using MyAccountingLab.

MyAccountingLab

(Group A)

P1-55A (*Learning Objectives 1, 2, 4: Applying accounting vocabulary, concepts, and principles; evaluating business operations*) Assume that the A division of Smith Corporation experienced the following transactions during the year ended December 31, 2011:

a. Suppose division A supplied copy products for a customer for the discounted price of $252,000. Under normal conditions they would have provided these services for $300,000. Other revenues totaled $52,000.

b. Salaries cost the division $21,000 to provide these services. The division had to pay employees overtime occasionally. Ordinarily the salary cost for these services would have been $18,000.

c. All other expenses totaled $247,000 for the year. Income tax expense was 35% of income before tax.

d. The A division has two operating subdivisions: basic retail and special contracts. Each subdivision is accounted for separately to indicate how well each is performing. However the A division combines the statements of all subdivisions to show results for the A division as a whole.

e. Inflation affects the amounts that the A division must pay for copy machines. To show the effects of inflation, net income would drop by $4,000.

f. If the A division were to go out of business, the sale of its assets would bring in $147,000 in cash.

❙ Requirements

1. Prepare the A division's income statement for the year ended December 31, 2011.
2. For items a through f, identify the accounting concept, assumption, or principle that provides guidance in accounting for the item. State how you have applied the concept or principle in preparing the income statement.

P1-56A (*Learning Objectives 3, 4: Using the accounting equation; evaluating business operations*) Compute the missing amount (?) for each company—amounts in millions.

	Sapphire Corp.	Lance Co.	Branch Inc.
Beginning			
Assets	$83	$35	$?
Liabilities	47	23	2
Common stock	2	2	1
Retained earnings	?	10	4
Ending			
Assets	$?	$54	$8
Liabilities	49	34	?
Common stock	2	?	1
Retained earnings	33	?	?
Income statement			
Revenues	$221	$?	$18
Expenses	213	152	?
Net income	?	?	?
Statement of retained earnings			
Beginning RE	$34	$10	$ 4
+ Net income	?	10	3
– Dividends	(9)	(2)	(3)
= Ending RE	$33	$18	$ 4

At the end of the year, which company has the

- Highest net income?
- Highest percent of net income to revenues?

P1-57A (*Learning Objectives 3, 4, 5: Using the accounting equation; preparing a balance sheet; making decisions*) The manager of Headlines, Inc., prepared the company's balance sheet while the accountant was ill. The balance sheet contains numerous errors. In particular, the manager knew that the balance sheet should balance, so he plugged in the stockholders' equity amount needed to achieve this balance. The stockholders' equity amount is *not* correct. All other amounts are accurate.

Headlines, Inc.
Balance Sheet
For the Month Ended June 30, 2010

Assets		Liabilities	
Cash..	$ 8,000	Notes receivable......................	$ 13,000
Equipment.................................	39,500	Interest expense........................	1,800
Accounts payable	5,000	Office supplies..........................	1,000
Utilities expense	1,700	Accounts receivable................	2,600
Advertising expense................	500	Note payable............................	55,500
Land...	77,000	Total	73,900
Salary expense..........................	4,000	**Stockholders' Equity**	
		Stockholders' equity	61,800
Total assets..............................	$135,700	Total liabilities	$135,700

Requirements

1. Prepare the correct balance sheet and date it properly. Compute total assets, total liabilities, and stockholders' equity.
2. Is Headlines actually in better (or worse) financial position than the erroneous balance sheet reports? Give the reason for your answer.
3. Identify the accounts listed on the incorrect balance sheet that should not be reported on the balance sheet. State why you excluded them from the correct balance sheet you prepared for Requirement 1. On which financial statement should these accounts appear?

P1-58A (*Learning Objectives 2, 4, 5: Preparing a balance sheet; applying the entity assumption; making business decisions*) Sandy Healey is a realtor. She organized the business as a corporation on April 16, 2011. The business received $95,000 cash from Healey and issued common stock. Consider the following facts as of April 30, 2011.

    a. Healey has $16,000 in her personal bank account and $71,000 in the business bank account.
    b. Healey owes $1,000 on a personal charge account with The Loft.
    c. Healey acquired business furniture for $41,000 on April 25. Of this amount, the business owes $33,000 on accounts payable at April 30.
    d. Office supplies on hand at the real estate office total $11,000.
    e. Healey's business owes $36,000 on a note payable for some land acquired for a total price of $110,000.
    f. Healey's business spent $24,000 for a Realty Universe franchise, which entitles her to represent herself as an agent. Realty Universe is a national affiliation of independent real estate agents. This franchise is a business asset.
    g. Healey owes $140,000 on a personal mortgage on her personal residence, which she acquired in 2003 for a total price of $340,000.

Requirements

1. Prepare the balance sheet of the real estate business of Sandy Healey Realtor, Inc., at April 30, 2011.
2. Does it appear that the realty business can pay its debts? How can you tell?
3. Identify the personal items given in the preceding facts that should not be reported on the balance sheet of the business.

P1-59A (*Learning Objectives 4, 5: Preparing an income statement, a statement of retained earnings and a balance sheet; using accounting information to make decisions*) The assets and liabilities of Post Maple, Inc., as of December 31, 2010, and revenues and expenses for the year ended on that date follow.

Land..................................	$ 8,200		Equipment..........................	$ 33,000
Note payable......................	28,000		Interest expense.................	4,200
Property tax expense...........	1,900		Interest payable.................	1,200
Rent expense......................	14,000		Accounts payable..............	11,000
Accounts receivable............	24,000		Salary expense...................	34,000
Service revenue...................	145,000		Building............................	126,000
Supplies.............................	2,200		Cash.................................	15,000
Utilities expense	3,000		Common stock..................	1,300

Beginning retained earnings was $117,000, and dividends totaled $38,000 for the year.

❚ Requirements

1. Prepare the income statement of Post Maple, Inc., for the year ended December 31, 2010.
2. Prepare the company's statement of retained earnings for the year.
3. Prepare the company's balance sheet at December 31, 2010.
4. Analyze Post Maple, Inc., by answering these questions:
   a. Was Post Maple profitable during 2010? By how much?
   b. Did retained earnings increase or decrease? By how much?
   c. Which is greater, total liabilities or total equity? Who owns more of Post Maple's assets, creditors of the company or the Post Maple's stockholders?

P1-60A (*Learning Objective 4: Preparing a statement of cash flows*) The following data come from the financial statements of The Water Sport Company for the year ended May 31, 2011 (in millions):

Purchases of property,			Other investing cash	
plant, and equipment	$ 3,515		payments...........................	$ 180
Net income..........................	3,030		Accounts receivable..............	500
Adjustments to reconcile net			Payment of dividends	290
income to net cash provided			Common stock......................	4,850
by operating activities	2,370		Issuance of common stock......	170
Revenues.............................	59,200		Sales of property, plant,	
Cash, beginning of year........	275		and equipment	30
end of year	1,890		Retained earnings.................	12,990
Cost of goods sold...............	37,450			

❚ Requirements

1. Prepare a cash flows statement for the year ended May 31, 2011. Not all items given appear on the cash flows statement.
2. What activities provided the largest source amount of cash? Is this a sign of financial strength or weakness?

P1-61A (*Learning Objective 4: Analyzing a company's financial statements*) Summarized versions of Cora Corporation's financial statements are given for two recent years.

	2010	2009
Income Statement	(In Thousands)	
Revenues	$ k	$15,750
Cost of goods sold	11,030	a
Other expenses	1,220	1,170
Income before income taxes	1,580	1,830
Income taxes (35% tax rate)	l	641
Net income	$ m	$ b
Statement of Retained Earnings		
Beginning balance	$ n	$ 2,660
Net income	o	c
Dividends	(98)	(120)
Ending balance	$ p	$ d
Balance Sheet		
Assets:		
Cash	$ q	$ e
Property, plant, and equipment	1,600	1,725
Other assets	r	10,184
Total assets	$ s	$13,239
Liabilities:		
Current liabilities	$ t	$ 5,650
Notes payable and long-term debt	4,350	3,380
Other liabilities	50	70
Total liabilities	$ 9,350	$ f
Stockholders' Equity:		
Common stock	$ 250	$ 250
Retained earnings	u	g
Other stockholders' equity	140	160
Total stockholders' equity	v	4,139
Total liabilities and stockholders' equity	$ w	$ h
Cash Flow Statement		
Net cash provided by operating activities	$ x	$ 950
Net cash used in investing activities	(230)	(300)
Net cash used in financing activities	(560)	(540)
Increase (decrease) in cash	(90)	i
Cash at beginning of year	y	1,220
Cash at end of year	$ z	$ j

I *Requirement*

1. Determine the missing amounts denoted by the letters.

(Group B)

P1-62B (*Learning Objectives 1, 2, 4: Applying accounting vocabulary, concepts, and principles to the income statement; evaluating business operations*) Assume that the A division of Perez Corporation experienced the following transactions during the year ended December 31, 2011:

a. Suppose division A supplied copy products for a customer for the discounted price of $263,000. Under normal conditions they would have provided these services for $296,000. Other revenues totaled $55,000.

b. Salaries cost the division $24,000 to provide these services. The division had to pay employees overtime occasionally. Ordinarily the salary cost for these services would have been $18,100.

c. All other expenses, excluding income taxes, totaled $235,000 for the year. Income tax expense was 33% of income before tax.

d. The A division has two operating subdivisions: basic retail and special contracts. Each division is accounted for separately to indicate how well each is performing. However, the A division combines the statements of all subdivisions to show results for the A division as a whole.

e. Inflation affects the amounts that the A division must pay for copy machines. To show the effects of inflation, net income would drop by $1,000.

f. If A division were to go out of business, the sale of its assets would bring in $145,000 in cash.

▌Requirements

1. Prepare the A division's income statement for the year ended December 31, 2011.

2. For items a through f, identify the accounting concept or principle that provides guidance in accounting for the item described. State how you have applied the concept or principle in preparing the income statement.

P1-63B (*Learning Objective 3, 4: Using the accounting equation; evaluating business operations*) Compute the missing amount (?) for each company—amounts in millions.

	Diamond Corp.	Lally Co.	Bryant Inc.
Beginning			
Assets	$82	$25	$?
Liabilities	48	21	5
Common stock	3	2	1
Retained earnings	?	2	2
Ending			
Assets	$?	$43	$10
Liabilities	50	34	?
Common stock	3	?	1
Retained earnings	30	?	?
Income statement			
Revenues	$223	$?	$26
Expenses	215	159	?
Net income	?	?	?
Statement of retained earnings			
Beginning RE	$31	$ 2	$ 2
+ Net income	?	7	4
– Dividends	(9)	(2)	(3)
= Ending RE	$30	$ 7	$ 3

Which company has the

- Highest net income?
- Highest percent of net income to revenues?

P1-64B (*Learning Objectives 3, 4, 5: Using the accounting equation; preparing a balance sheet; making decisions*) The manager of News Maker, Inc., prepared the company's balance sheet while the accountant was ill. The balance sheet contains numerous errors. In particular, the manager knew that the balance sheet should balance, so he plugged in the stockholders' equity amount needed to achieve this balance. The stockholders' equity amount is *not* correct. All other amounts are accurate.

News Maker, Inc.
Balance Sheet
For the Month Ended November 30, 2010

Assets		Liabilities	
Cash..............................	$ 7,500	Notes receivable......................	$ 14,500
Equipment..............................	39,000	Interest expense......................	1,600
Accounts payable..................	4,000	Office supplies.........................	900
Utilities expense......................	1,700	Accounts receivable................	3,400
Advertising expense................	400	Note payable..........................	55,000
Land..............................	82,000	Total	75,400
Salary expense.........................	4,500	**Stockholders' Equity**	
		Stockholders' equity	63,700
Total assets.............................	$139,100	Total liabilities	$139,100

❙ Requirements

1. Prepare the correct balance sheet and date it properly. Compute total assets, total liabilities, and stockholders' equity.
2. Is News Maker in better (or worse) financial position than the erroneous balance sheet reports? Give the reason for your answer.
3. Identify the accounts that should *not* be reported on the balance sheet. State why you excluded them from the correct balance sheet you prepared for Requirement 1. On which financial statement should these accounts appear?

P1-65B (*Learning Objectives 2, 4, 5: Preparing a balance sheet; applying the entity assumption; making business decisions*) Jeana Hart is a realtor. She organized her business as a corporation on September 16, 2011. The business received $95,000 from Hart and issued common stock. Consider these facts as of September 30, 2011.

   a. Hart has $15,000 in her personal bank account and $70,000 in the business bank account.
   b. Hart owes $2,000 on a personal charge account with The Gap.
   c. Hart acquired business furniture for $45,000 on September 25. Of this amount, the business owes $31,000 on accounts payable at September 30.
   d. Office supplies on hand at the real estate office total $7,000.
   e. Hart's business owes $36,000 on a note payable for some land acquired for a total price of $116,000.
   f. Hart's business spent $29,000 for a Realty Region franchise, which entitles her to represent herself as an agent. Realty Region is a national affiliation of independent real estate agents. This franchise is a business asset.
   g. Hart owes $140,000 on a personal mortgage on her personal residence, which she acquired in 2003 for a total price of $360,000.

❙ Requirements

1. Prepare the balance sheet of the real estate business of Jeana Hart Realtor, Inc., at September 30, 2011.
2. Does it appear that the realty business can pay its debts? How can you tell?
3. Identify the personal items given in the preceding facts that should not be reported on the balance sheet of the business.

■ spreadsheet

P1-66B (*Learning Objectives 4, 5: Preparing an income statement, a statement of retained earnings, and a balance sheet; using accounting information to make decisions*) The assets and liabilities of Post Shrub as of December 31, 2010, and revenues and expenses for the year ended on that date follow.

Land.................................	$ 9,000	Equipment..........................	$ 36,000
Note payable......................	33,000	Interest expense.................	4,950
Property tax expense...........	1,900	Interest payable.................	1,100
Rent expense......................	13,500	Accounts payable	14,000
Accounts receivable............	26,000	Salary expense...................	38,000
Service revenue..................	144,000	Building............................	129,000
Supplies.............................	2,000	Cash.................................	15,000
Utilities expense	3,200	Common stock..................	16,450

Beginning retained earnings was $112,000, and dividends totaled $42,000 for the year.

❙ Requirements

1. Prepare the income statement of Post Shrub, Inc., for the year ended December 31, 2010.
2. Prepare the company's statement of retained earnings for the year.
3. Prepare the company's balance sheet at December 31, 2010.
4. Analyze Post Shrub, Inc., by answering these questions:
   a. Was Post Shrub profitable during 2010? By how much?
   b. Did retained earnings increase or decrease? By how much?
   c. Which is greater, total liabilities or total equity? Who owns more of Post Shrub's assets, creditors of the company or Post Shrub's stockholders?

P1-67B (*Learning Objective 4: Preparing a statement of cash flows*) The following data come from the financial statements of The High Tide Company at the year ended May 31, 2011 (in millions).

Purchases of property,		Other investing cash	
plant, and equipment	$ 3,480	payments..........................	$ 170
Net income..........................	3,030	Accounts receivable...............	500
Adjustments to reconcile net		Payment of dividends............	285
income to net cash provided		Common stock......................	4,830
by operating activities	2,390	Issuance of common stock......	190
Revenues.............................	59,400	Sales of property, plant,	
Cash, beginning of year........	200	and equipment	25
end of year	1,900	Retained earnings..................	13,000
Cost of goods sold...............	37,550		

❙ Requirements

1. Prepare a cash flows statement for the year ended May 31, 2011. Not all the items given appear on the cash flows statement.
2. Which activities provided the largest amount of cash? Is this a sign of financial strength or weakness?

P1-68B (*Learning Objective 4: Analyzing a company's financial statements*) Summarized versions of Espinola Corporation's financial statements follow for two recent years.

	2011	2010
Income Statement	(In Thousands)	
Revenues	$ k	$15,250
Cost of goods sold	11,070	a
Other expenses	1,280	1,230
Income before income taxes	1,500	1,830
Income taxes (35% tax rate)	l	641
Net income	$ m	$ b
Statement of Retained Earnings		
Beginning balance	$ n	$ 2,720
Net income	o	c
Dividends	(84)	(140)
Ending balance	$ p	$ d
Balance Sheet		
Assets:		
Cash	$ q	$ e
Property, plant, and equipment	2,100	1,750
Other assets	r	10,404
Total assets	$ s	$13,419
Liabilities:		
Current liabilities	$ t	$ 5,690
Notes payable and long-term debt	4,300	3,340
Other liabilities	60	80
Total liabilities	$ 9,250	$ f
Stockholders' Equity:		
Common stock	$ 350	$ 350
Retained earnings	u	g
Other stockholders' equity	110	190
Total stockholders' equity	v	4,309
Total liabilities and stockholders' equity	$ w	$ h
Cash Flows Statement		
Net cash provided by operating activities	$ x	$ 850
Net cash used in investing activities	(240)	(325)
Net cash used in financing activities	(560)	(490)
Increase (decrease) in cash	(90)	i
Cash at beginning of year	y	1,230
Cash at end of year	$ z	$ j

I Requirement

1. Complete Espinola Corporation's financial statements by determining the missing amounts denoted by the letters.

APPLY YOUR KNOWLEDGE

Decision Cases

Case 1. *(Learning Objectives 1, 2, 5: Using financial statements to evaluate a loan request)* Two businesses, Blue Skies Corp., and Open Road, Inc., have sought business loans from you. To decide whether to make the loans, you have requested their balance sheets.

Blue Skies Corp.
Balance Sheet
August 31, 2011

Assets		Liabilities	
Cash	$ 5,000	Accounts payable	$ 50,000
Accounts receivable	10,000	Notes payable	80,000
Furniture	15,000	Total liabilities	130,000
Land	75,000	**Owners' Equity**	
Equipment	45,000	Owners' equity	20,000
		Total liabilities and	
Total assets	$150,000	owners' equity	$150,000

Open Road, Inc.
Balance Sheet
August 31, 2011

Assets		Liabilities	
Cash	$ 5,000	Accounts payable	$ 6,000
Accounts receivable	10,000	Note payable	9,000
Merchandise inventory	15,000	Total liabilities	15,000
Building	35,000	**Stockholders' Equity**	
		Stockholders' equity	50,000
		Total liabilities and	
Total assets	$65,000	stockholders' equity	$65,000

❙ Requirement

1. Using only these balance sheets, to which entity would you be more comfortable lending money? Explain fully, citing specific items and amounts from the respective balance sheets. (Challenge)

Case 2. (*Learning Objectives 2, 5: Analyzing a company as an investment*) A year out of college, you have $10,000 to invest. A friend has started GrandPrize Unlimited, Inc., and she asks you to invest in her company. You obtain the company's financial statements, which are summarized at the end of the first year as follows:

Grand Prize Unlimited, Inc. Income Statement Year Ended Dec. 31, 2010		
Revenues		$100,000
Expenses		80,000
Net income		$ 20,000

Grand Prize Unlimited, Inc. Balance Sheet Dec. 31, 2010			
Cash	$ 6,000	Liabilities	$ 60,000
Other assets	100,000	Equity	46,000
		Total liabilities	
Total assets	$106,000	and equity	$106,000

Visits with your friend turn up the following facts:

   a. Revenues and receivables of $40,000 were overlooked and omitted.
   b. Software costs of $50,000 were recorded as assets. These costs should have been expenses. GrandPrize Unlimited paid cash for these expenses and recorded the cash payment correctly.
   c. The company owes an additional $10,000 for accounts payable.

❙ Requirements

   1. Prepare corrected financial statements.
   2. Use your corrected statements to evaluate GrandPrize Unlimited's results of operations and financial position. (Challenge)
   3. Will you invest in Grand Prize Unlimited? Give your reason. (Challenge)

Ethical Issue

You are studying frantically for an accounting exam tomorrow. You are having difficulty in this course, and the grade you make on this exam can make the difference between receiving a final grade of B or C. If you receive a C, it will lower your grade point average to the point that you could lose your academic scholarship. An hour ago, a friend, also enrolled in the course but in a different section under the same professor, called you with some unexpected news. In her sorority test files, she has just found a copy of an old exam from the previous year. In looking at the exam, it appears to contain questions that come right from the class notes you have taken, even the very same numbers. She offers to make a copy for you and bring it over.

You glance at your course syllabus and find the following: "You are expected to do your own work in this class. Although you may study with others, giving, receiving, or obtaining information pertaining to an examination is considered an act of academic dishonesty, unless such action is authorized by the instructor giving the examination. Also, divulging the contents of an essay or objective examination designated by the instructor as an examination is considered an act of academic dishonesty. Academic dishonesty is considered a violation of the student honor code, and will subject the student to disciplinary procedures, which can include suspension from the University." Although you have heard a rumor that fraternities and sororities have cleared their exam files with professors, you are not sure.

❙ *Requirements*

1. What is the ethical issue in this situation?
2. Who are the stakeholders? What are the possible consequences to each?
3. Analyze the alternatives from the following standpoints: (a) economic, (b) legal, and (c) ethical.
4. What would you do? How would you justify your decision? How would your decision make you feel afterward?
5. How is this similar to a business situation?

Focus on Financials: ■ Amazon.com, Inc.

(Learning Objective 4: Identifying items from a company's financial statements) This and similar cases in succeeding chapters are based on the consolidated financial statements of **Amazon.com, Inc.** As you work with Amazon.com, Inc., throughout this course, you will develop the ability to use the financial statements of actual companies.

❙ *Requirements*

Refer to the Amazon.com, Inc., consolidated financial statements in Appendix A at the end of the book.

1. Suppose you own stock in Amazon.com, Inc. If you could pick one item on the company's Consolidated Statements of Operations to increase year after year, what would it be? Why is this item so important? Did this item increase or decrease during fiscal 2008? Is this good news or bad news for the company?
2. What was Amazon.com, Inc.'s largest expense each year? In your own words, explain the meaning of this item. Give specific examples of items that make up this expense. The chapter gives another title for this expense. What is it?
3. Use the Consolidated Balance Sheets of Amazon.com, Inc., in Appendix A to answer these questions: At the end of fiscal 2008, how much in total resources did Amazon.com, Inc., have to work with? How much did the company owe? How much of its assets did the company's stockholders actually own? Use these amounts to write Amazon.com, Inc.'s accounting equation at December 31, 2008.
4. How much cash did Amazon.com, Inc., have at the beginning of the most recent year? How much cash did Amazon.com have at the end of the year?

Focus on Analysis: ■ Foot Locker, Inc.

(Learning Objectives 3, 4: Evaluating a leading company) This and similar cases in each chapter are based on the consolidated financial statements of **Foot Locker, Inc.**, given in Appendix B at the end of this book. As you work with Foot Locker, Inc., you will develop the ability to analyze the financial statements of actual companies.

❙ *Requirements*

1. Write Foot Locker, Inc.'s accounting equation at February 2, 2008, the end of fiscal 2007 (express all items in millions and round to the nearest $1 million). Does Foot Locker, Inc.'s financial condition look strong or weak? How can you tell?
2. What was the result of Foot Locker, Inc.'s operations during fiscal 2007? Identify both the name and the dollar amount of the result of operations for fiscal 2007. Does an increase (decrease) signal good news or bad news for the company and its stockholders?
3. Examine retained earnings in the Consolidated Statements of Shareholders' Equity. What caused retained earnings to increase during fiscal 2007?
4. Which statement reports cash as part of Foot Locker, Inc.'s financial position? Which statement tells *why* cash increased (or decreased) during the year? What two individual items caused Foot Locker, Inc.'s cash to change the most during fiscal 2007?

Group Projects

Project 1. As instructed by your professor, obtain the annual report of a well-known company.

I *Requirements*

1. Take the role of a loan committee of Bank of America, a large banking company head-quartered in Charlotte, North Carolina. Assume the company has requested a loan from Bank of America. Analyze the company's financial statements and any other information you need to reach a decision regarding the largest amount of money you would be willing to lend. Go as deeply into the analysis and the related decision as you can. Specify the following:
   a. The length of the loan period—that is, over what period will you allow the company to pay you back?
   b. The interest rate you will charge on the loan. Will you charge the prevailing interest rate, a lower rate, or a higher rate? Why?
   c. Any restrictions you will impose on the borrower as a condition for making the loan.

Note: The long-term debt note to the financial statements gives details of the company's existing liabilities.

2. Write your group decision in a report addressed to the bank's board of directors. Limit your report to two double-spaced word-processed pages.
3. If your professor directs, present your decision and your analysis to the class. Limit your presentation to 10 to 15 minutes.

Project 2. You are the owner of a company that is about to "go public"—that is, issue its stock to outside investors. You wish to make your company look as attractive as possible to raise $1 million of cash to expand the business. At the same time, you want to give potential investors a realistic picture of your company.

I *Requirements*

1. Design a booklet to portray your company in a way that will enable outsiders to reach an informed decision as to whether to buy some of your stock. The booklet should include the following:
   a. Name and location of your company.
   b. Nature of the company's business (be as detailed as possible).
   c. How you plan to spend the money you raise.
   d. The company's comparative income statement, statement of retained earnings, balance sheet, and statement of cash flows for two years: the current year and the preceding year. Make the data as realistic as possible with the intent of receiving $1 million.
2. Word-process your booklet, not to exceed five pages.
3. If directed by your professor, make a copy for each member of your class. Distribute copies to the class and present your case with the intent of interesting your classmates in investing in the company. Limit your presentation to 10 to 15 minutes.

Quick Check Answers

1. *b*

2. *b*

3. *c* [This is not the typical way the accounting equation is expressed (Assets = Liabilities + Owners' Equity), but it may be rearranged this way].

4. *a*

5. *d*

6. *d*

7. *a* ($120,000 − $50,000 − $4,000 = $66,000)

8. *b* ($120,000 − $50,000 = $70,000)

9. *c* Total assets = $140,000 ($11,000 + $40,000 + $34,000 + $55,000). Liabilities = $27,000.

10. *d*

11. *b* $38,000 + Net income ($18,000) − Dividends = $50,000; Dividends = $6,000

12. *b*

	Assets =	Liabilities +	Equity
Beginning	$340,000 =	$210,000* +	$130,000
Increase	70,000 =	25,000 +	45,000*
Ending	$410,000* =	$235,000* +	$175,000*

*Must solve for these amounts.

13. *c*

14. *a*

Demo Doc

The Accounting Equation and Financial Statement Preparation

To make sure you understand this material, work through the following demonstration "Demo Doc" with detailed comments to help you see the concept within the framework of a worked-through problem.

Learning Objectives 3, 4, 5

David Richardson is the only shareholder of DR Painting, Inc., a painting business near a historical housing district. At March 31, 2010, DR Painting had the following information:

Cash	$27,300
Accounts receivable	1,400
Supplies	1,800
Truck	20,000
Accounts payable	1,000
Common stock	40,000
Retained earnings (March 1)	5,000
Retained earnings (March 31)	?
Dividends	1,500
Service revenue	7,000
Salary expense	1,000

Requirements

1. Prepare the income statement and statement of retained earnings for the month of March 2010 and the balance sheet of the business at March 31, 2010. Use Exhibits 1-7, 1-8, and 1-9 (pp. 17, 19, and 21) in the text as a guide.

2. Write the accounting equation of the business.

Demo Doc Solutions

Requirement 1

Prepare the income statement, statement of retained earnings, and balance sheet of the business. Use Exhibits 1-7, 1-8, and 1-9 (pp. 17, 19, and 21) in the text as a guide.

Part 1	Part 2	Demo Doc Complete

Income Statement

The income statement is the first statement to prepare because the other financial statements rely upon the net income number calculated on the income statement.

The income statement reports the profitability of the business. To prepare an income statement, begin with the proper heading. A proper heading includes the name of the company (DR Painting, Inc.), the name of the statement (Income Statement), and the time period covered (Month Ended March 31, 2010). Notice that we are reporting income for a period of time, rather than at a single date.

The income statement lists all revenues and expenses. It uses the following formula to calculate net income:

$$\text{Revenues} - \text{Expenses} = \text{Net income}$$

First, you should list revenues. Second, list the expenses. After you have listed and totaled the revenues and expenses, subtract the total expenses from total revenues to determine net income or net loss. A positive number means you earned net income (revenues exceeded expenses). A negative number indicates that expenses exceeded revenues, and this is a net loss.

DR Painting's total Service Revenue for the month was $7,000. The only expense is Salary Expense of $1,000. On the income statement, these would be reported as follows:

DR Painting, Inc.
Income Statement
Month Ended March 31, 2010

Revenue:		
Service revenue		$7,000
Expenses:		
Salary expense	$1,000	
Total expenses		1,000
Net income		$6,000

Note that the result is a net income of $6,000 ($7,000 − $1,000 = $6,000). You will also report net income on the statement of retained earnings, which comes next.

Statement of Retained Earnings

The statement of retained earnings shows the changes in Retained Earnings for a period of time. To prepare a statement of retained earnings, begin with the proper heading. A proper heading includes the name of the company (DR Painting, Inc.), the name of the statement (Statement of Retained Earnings), and the time period covered (Month Ended March 31, 2010). As with the income statement, we are reporting the changes in Retained Earnings for a period of time, rather than at a single date.

Net income is used on the statement of retained earnings to calculate the new balance in Retained Earnings. This calculation uses the following formula:

$$
\begin{array}{l}
\text{Beginning Retained Earnings} \\
+ \text{ Net Income (or } - \text{ Net Loss)} \\
\underline{- \text{ Dividends}} \\
= \text{Ending Retained Earnings}
\end{array}
$$

Start the body of the statement of retained earnings with the Retained Earnings at the beginning of the period (March 1). Then list net income. Observe that the amount of net income comes directly from the income statement. Following net income you will list the dividends declared and paid, which reduce Retained Earnings. Finally, total all amounts and compute the Retained Earnings at the end of the period.

The beginning Retained Earnings of $5,000 was given in the problem. Net income of $6,000 comes from the income statement and is added. Dividends of $1,500 are deducted. On the statement of retained earnings, these amounts are reported as follows:

DR Painting, Inc.
Statement of Retained Earnings
Month Ended March 31, 2010

Beginning retained earnings	$ 5,000
Add: Net income	6,000
	11,000
Less: Dividends	(1,500)
Retained earnings, March 31, 2010	$ 9,500

Note that Retained Earnings has a balance of $9,500 at March 31, 2010. You will also report Retained Earning's ending balance on the balance sheet, which you prepare last.

Balance Sheet

The balance sheet reports the financial position of the business at a moment in time. To prepare a balance sheet, begin with the proper heading. A proper heading includes the name of the company (DR Painting, Inc.), the name of the statement (Balance Sheet), and the time of the ending balances (March 31, 2010). Unlike the income statement and statement of retained earnings, we are reporting the financial position of the company at a specific date rather than for a period of time.

The balance sheet lists all assets, liabilities, and equity of the business, with the accounting equation verified at the bottom.

To prepare the body of the balance sheet, begin by listing assets. Then list all the liabilities and stockholders' equity. Notice that the balance sheet is organized in the same order as the accounting equation. The amount of Retained Earnings comes directly from the ending balance on your statement of retained earnings. You should then total both sides of the balance sheet to make sure that they are equal. If they are not equal, then you must correct an error.

In this case, assets accounts include cash of $27,300, accounts receivable of $1,400, $1,800 worth of supplies, and the truck, valued at $20,000. The only liability is accounts payable of $1,000. Stockholders' equity consists of common stock of $40,000, and the updated retained earnings of $9,500, from the statement of retained earnings.

DR Painting, Inc.
Balance Sheet
March 31, 2010

Assets		Liabilities	
Cash	$27,300	Accounts payable	$ 1,000
Accounts receivable	1,400		
Supplies	1,800	**Stockholders' Equity**	
Truck	20,000	Common stock	40,000
		Retained earnings	9,500
		Total stockholders' equity	49,500
		Total liabilities and	
Total assets	$50,500	stockholders' equity	$50,500

Assets   = Liabilities + Stockholders' Equity

Requirement 2

Write the accounting equation of the business

Part 1	Part 2	Demo Doc Complete

In this case, asset accounts total $50,500. Liabilities total $1,000—the balance of Accounts Payable, and stockholder's equity is $49,500. This gives us a total for liabilities and equity of $50,500 ($1,000 + $49,500).

The accounting equation is:

Assets of $50,500 = Liabilities of $1,000 + Stockholders' Equity of $49,500

Part 1	Part 2	**Demo Doc Complete**

2

Transaction Analysis

SPOTLIGHT: Apple, Inc.

How do you manage your messages? You may use Apple's iPhone for text messaging or surfing the Internet when you're on the go. The iPhone and iPod, in addition to the company's popular notebook computers, have generated billions of dollars in profits for the company.

Apple, Inc., is an American multinational corporation that designs and manufactures consumer electronics. The company started out 30 years ago with the name Apple Computer, Inc., but because the company has expanded its product line so much in the last few years, it dropped the "computer" from its name in 2007. The company's best-known hardware products include Macintosh computers, the iPod, and the iPhone. Apple software includes the Mac OS X operating system, the iTunes media browser, the iLife suite of multimedia and creativity software, the iWork suite of productivity software, and Final Cut Studio, a suite of professional audio and film-industry software products. The company operates more than 250 retail stores in nine countries and an online store where hardware and software products are sold.

How does Apple determine the amount of its revenues, expenses, and net income? Like all other companies, Apple has a comprehensive accounting system. Apple's income statement (statement of operations) is given at the start of this chapter. The income statement shows that during fiscal year 2008, Apple made over $32 billion of sales and earned net income of $4.8 billion. Where did those figures come from? In this chapter, we'll show you.

Apple, Inc.
Statement of Operations (Adapted)
Fiscal Year Ended September 30, 2008

(In billions)	2008
Net sales...	$32.4
Cost of goods sold...	21.3
Gross profit..	11.1
Operating expenses:	
Research and development expense	1.1
Selling, general, and administrative expense	3.7
Total operating expenses...	4.8
Operating income (loss)	6.3
Other income	.6
Income before income taxes	6.9
Income tax expense...	2.1
Net income..	$ 4.8

Chapter 1 introduced the financial statements. Chapter 2 will show you how companies actually record the transactions that eventually become part of the financial statements.

LEARNING OBJECTIVES

1 **Analyze** transactions

2 **Understand** how accounting works

3 **Record** transactions in the journal

4 **Use** a trial balance

5 **Analyze** transactions using only T-accounts

> ac/t For more practice and review of accounting cycle concepts, use ACT, the Accounting Cycle Tutorial, online at **www.myaccountinglab.com**. Margin logos like this one, directing you to the appropriate ACT section and material, appear throughout Chapters 1, 2, and 3. When you enter the tutorial, you'll find three buttons on the opening page of each chapter module. Here's what the buttons mean: **Tutorial** gives you a review of the major concepts, **Application** gives you practice exercises, and **Glossary** reviews important terms.

TRANSACTIONS

Business activity is all about transactions. A **transaction** is any event that has a financial impact on the business and can be measured reliably. For example, Apple, Inc., pays programmers to create iTunes® software. Apple sells computers, borrows money, and repays the loan—three separate transactions.

But not all events qualify as transactions. iTunes® may be featured in *Showtime Magazine* and motivate you to buy an Apple iPod. The magazine article may create lots of new business for Apple. But no transaction occurs until someone actually buys an Apple product. A transaction must occur before Apple records anything.

Transactions provide objective information about the financial impact on a company. Every transaction has two sides:

- You give something.
- You receive something.

In accounting we always record both sides of a transaction. And we must be able to measure the financial impact of the event on the business before recording it as a transaction.

THE ACCOUNT

As we saw in Chapter 1, the accounting equation expresses the basic relationships of accounting:

$$\text{Assets} = \text{Liabilities} + \text{Stockholders' (Owners') Equity}$$

For each asset, each liability, and each element of stockholders' equity, we use a record called the account. An **account** is the record of all the changes in a particular asset, liability, or stockholders' equity during a period. The account is the basic summary device of accounting. Before launching into transaction analysis, let's review the accounts that a company such as Apple, Inc., uses.

Assets

Assets are economic resources that provide a future benefit for a business. Most firms use the following asset accounts:

Cash.   Cash means money and any medium of exchange including bank account balances, paper currency, coins, certificates of deposit, and checks.

Accounts Receivable.   Apple, Inc., like most other companies, sells its goods and services and receives a promise for future collection of cash. The Accounts Receivable account holds these amounts.

Notes Receivable.   Apple may receive a note receivable from a customer, who signed the note promising to pay Apple. A note receivable is similar to an account receivable, but a note receivable is more binding because the customer signed the note. Notes receivable usually specify an interest rate.

Inventory.   Apple's most important asset is its inventory—the hardware and software Apple sells to customers. Other titles for this account include *Merchandise* and *Merchandise Inventory*.

Prepaid Expenses.   Apple pays certain expenses in advance, such as insurance and rent. A prepaid expense is an asset because the payment provides a *future* benefit for the business. Prepaid Rent, Prepaid Insurance, and Supplies are prepaid expenses.

Land.   The Land account shows the cost of the land Apple uses in its operations.

Buildings.   The costs of Apple's office building, manufacturing plant, and the like appear in the Buildings account.

Equipment, Furniture, and Fixtures.   Apple has a separate asset account for each type of equipment, for example, Manufacturing Equipment and Office Equipment. The Furniture and Fixtures account shows the cost of these assets, which are similar to equipment.

Liabilities

Recall that a *liability* is a debt. A payable is always a liability. The most common types of liabilities include:

Accounts Payable.   The Accounts Payable account is the direct opposite of Accounts Receivable. Apple's promise to pay a debt arising from a credit purchase of inventory or from a utility bill appears in the Accounts Payable account.

Notes Payable.   A note payable is the opposite of a note receivable. The Notes Payable account includes the amounts Apple must *pay* because Apple signed notes promising to pay a future amount. Notes payable, like notes receivable, also carry interest.

Accrued Liabilities.   An **accrued liability** is a liability for an expense you have not yet paid. Interest Payable and Salary Payable are accrued liability accounts for most companies. Income Tax Payable is another accrued liability.

Stockholders' (Owners') Equity

The owners' claims to the assets of a corporation are called *stockholders' equity, shareholders' equity*, or simply *owners' equity*. A corporation such as Apple, Inc., uses Common Stock, Retained Earnings, and Dividends accounts to record in the company's stockholders' equity. In a proprietorship, there is a single capital account. For a partnership, each partner has a separate owner equity account.

Common Stock.   The Common Stock account shows the owners' investment in the corporation. Apple, Inc., receives cash and issues common stock to its stockholders. A company's common stock is its most basic element of equity. All corporations have common stock.

STOP & THINK...

Name two things that (1) increase Apple, Inc.'s stockholders' equity and (2) decrease Apple's stockholders' equity.

Answer:
(1) Increases in equity: Sale of stock and net income (revenue greater than expenses).
(2) Decreases in equity: Dividends and net loss (expenses greater than revenue).

Retained Earnings.   The Retained Earnings account shows the cumulative net income earned by Apple, Inc., over the company's lifetime, minus its cumulative net losses and dividends.

Dividends.   Dividends are optional; they are decided (declared) by the board of directors. After profitable operations, the board of directors of Apple, Inc., may (or may not) declare and pay a cash dividend. The corporation may keep a separate account titled *Dividends*, which indicates a decrease in Retained Earnings.

Revenues.   The increase in stockholders' equity from delivering goods or services to customers is called *revenue*. The company uses as many revenue accounts as needed. Apple, Inc., uses a Sales Revenue account for revenue earned by selling its products. Apple has a Service Revenue account for the revenue it earns by providing services to customers. A lawyer provides legal services for clients and also uses a Service Revenue account. A business that loans money to an outsider needs an Interest Revenue account. If the business rents a building to a tenant, the business needs a Rent Revenue account.

Expenses.   The cost of operating a business is called *expense*. Expenses *decrease* stockholders' equity, the opposite effect of revenues. A business needs a separate account for each type of expense, such as Cost of Goods Sold, Salary Expense, Rent Expense, Advertising Expense, Insurance Expense, Utilities Expense, and Income Tax Expense. Businesses strive to minimize expenses and thereby maximize net income.

ACCOUNTING FOR BUSINESS TRANSACTIONS
Example: ShineBrite Car Wash, Inc.

To illustrate the accounting for transactions, let's return to ShineBrite Car Wash, Inc. In Chapter 1's End-of-Chapter Problem, Van Gray opened ShineBrite Car Wash, Inc., in April 2010.

OBJECTIVE

1 **Analyze** transactions

    We consider 11 events and analyze each in terms of its effect on ShineBrite Car Wash. We begin by using the accounting equation. In the second half of the chapter, we record transactions using the journal and ledger of the business.

Transaction 1.   Gray and a few friends invest $50,000 to open ShineBrite Car Wash, and the business issues common stock to the stockholders. The effect of this transaction on the accounting equation of ShineBrite Car Wash, Inc., is a receipt of cash and issuance of common stock, as follows:

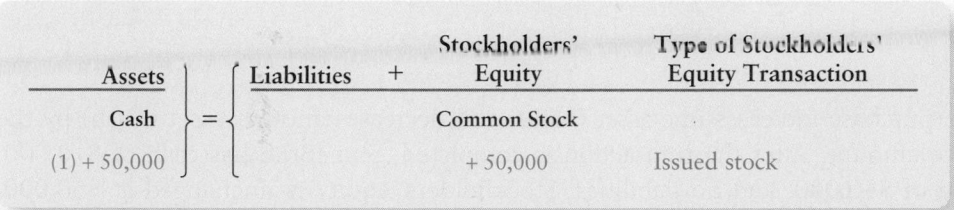

Assets		Liabilities	+	Stockholders' Equity	Type of Stockholders' Equity Transaction
Cash	} = {			Common Stock	
(1) + 50,000				+ 50,000	Issued stock

Every transaction's net amount on the left side of the equation must equal the net amount on the right side. The first transaction increases both the cash and the common stock of the business. To the right of the transaction we write "Issued stock" to show the reason for the increase in stockholders' equity.

Every transaction affects the financial statements of the business, and we can prepare financial statements after one, two, or any number of transactions. For example, ShineBrite Car Wash could report the company's balance sheet after its first transaction, shown here.

ShineBrite Car Wash, Inc.				
Balance Sheet				
April 1, 2010				
Assets		**Liabilities**		
Cash...............	$50,000	None		
		Stockholders' Equity		
		Common stock...............		$50,000
		Total stockholders' equity............		50,000
		Total liabilities and		
Total assets...............	$50,000	stockholders' equity............		$50,000

This balance sheet shows that the business holds cash of $50,000 and owes no liabilities. The company's equity (ownership) is denoted as *Common Stock* on the balance sheet. A bank would look favorably on this balance sheet because the business has $50,000 cash and no debt—a strong financial position.

As a practical matter, most entities report their financial statements at the end of the accounting period—not after each transaction. But an accounting system can produce statements whenever managers need to know where the business stands.

Transaction 2.   ShineBrite purchases land for a new location and pays cash of $40,000. The effect of this transaction on the accounting equation is:

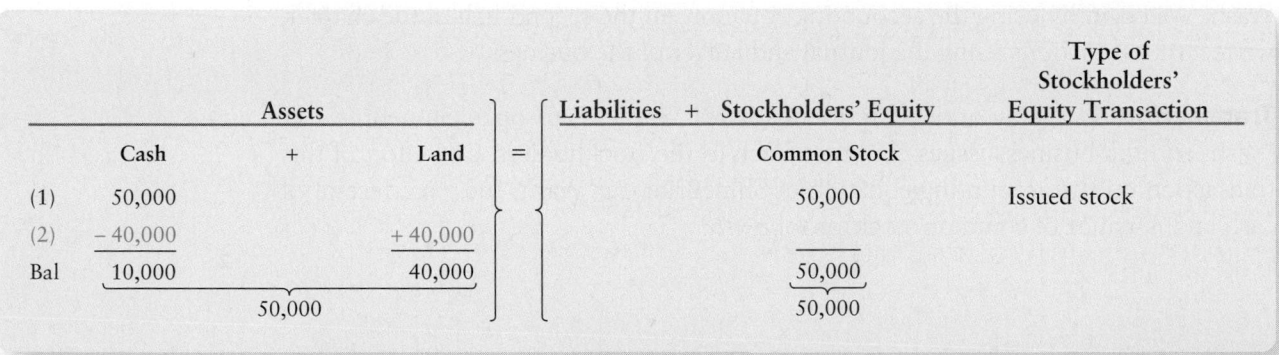

	Assets				Liabilities	+	Stockholders' Equity	Type of Stockholders' Equity Transaction
	Cash	+	Land	=			Common Stock	
(1)	50,000						50,000	Issued stock
(2)	− 40,000		+ 40,000					
Bal	10,000		40,000				50,000	
		50,000					50,000	

The purchase increases one asset (Land) and decreases another asset (Cash) by the same amount. After the transaction is completed, ShineBrite has cash of $10,000, land of $40,000, and no liabilities. Stockholders' equity is unchanged at $50,000. Note that total assets must always equal total liabilities plus equity.

Transaction 3.   The business buys supplies on account, agreeing to pay $3,700 within 30 days. This transaction increases both the assets and the liabilities of the business. Its effect on the accounting equation follows.

		Assets						Liabilities	+	Stockholders' Equity	
	Cash	+	Supplies	+	Land			Accounts Payable	+	Common Stock	
Bal	10,000				40,000	} = {				50,000	
(3)			+ 3,700					+ 3,700			
Bal	10,000		3,700		40,000			3,700		50,000	
			53,700							53,700	

The new asset is Supplies, and the liability is an Account Payable. ShineBrite signs no formal promissory note, so the liability is an account payable, not a note payable.

Transaction 4.   ShineBrite earns $7,000 of service revenue by providing services for customers. The business collects the cash. The effect on the accounting equation is an increase in the asset Cash and an increase in Retained Earnings, as follows:

		Assets						Liabilities	+	Stockholders' Equity			Type of Stockholders' Equity Transaction
	Cash	+	Supplies	+	Land			Accounts Payable	+	Common Stock	+	Retained Earnings	
Bal	10,000		3,700		40,000	} = {		3,700		50,000			
(4)	+ 7,000											+ 7,000	Service revenue
Bal	17,000		3,700		40,000			3,700		50,000		7,000	
			60,700							60,700			

To the right we record "Service revenue" to show where the $7,000 of increase in Retained Earnings came from.

Transaction 5.   ShineBrite performs service on account, which means that ShineBrite lets some customers pay later. ShineBrite earns revenue but doesn't receive the cash immediately. In transaction 5, ShineBrite cleans a fleet of UPS delivery trucks, and UPS promises to pay ShineBrite $3,000 within one month. This promise is an account receivable—an asset—of ShineBrite Car Wash. The transaction record follows.

			Assets					Liabilities	+	Stockholders' Equity			Type of Stockholders' Equity Transaction
	Cash	+	Accounts Receivable	+ Supplies + Land				Accounts Payable	+	Common Stock	+	Retained Earnings	
Bal	17,000			3,700	40,000	} = {		3,700		50,000		7,000	
(5)			+ 3,000									+ 3,000	Service revenue
Bal	17,000		3,000	3,700	40,000			3,700		50,000		10,000	
				63,700						63,700			

It's performing the service that earns the revenue—not collecting the cash. Therefore, ShineBrite records revenue when it performs the service—regardless of whether ShineBrite receives cash now or later.

Transaction 6.   During the month, ShineBrite Car Wash pays $2,700 for the following expenses: equipment rent, $1,100; employee salaries, $1,200; and utilities, $400. The effect on the accounting equation is as follows:

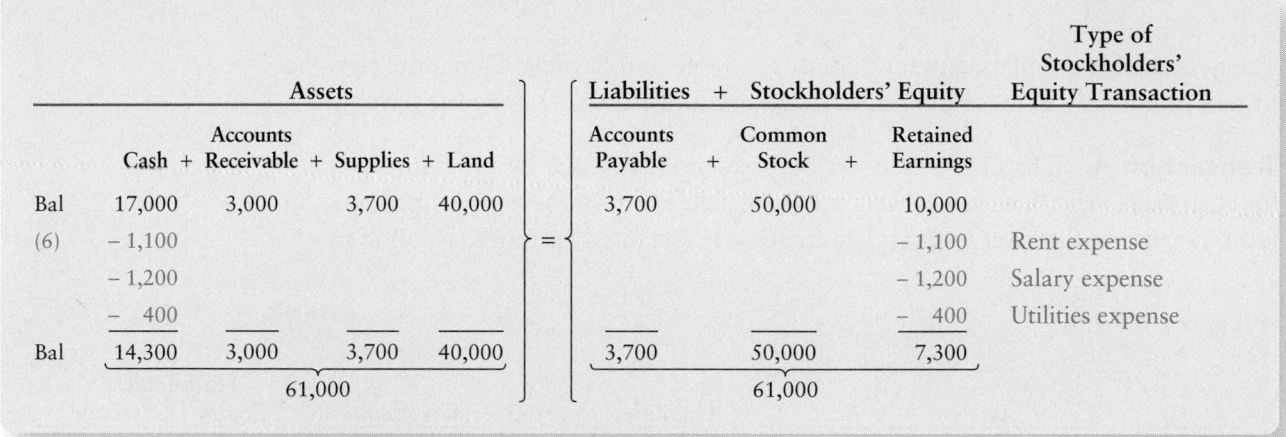

	Assets					Liabilities	+	Stockholders' Equity			Type of Stockholders' Equity Transaction
	Cash	+	Accounts Receivable	+ Supplies	+ Land	Accounts Payable	+	Common Stock	+	Retained Earnings	
Bal	17,000		3,000	3,700	40,000	3,700		50,000		10,000	
(6)	− 1,100									− 1,100	Rent expense
	− 1,200									− 1,200	Salary expense
	− 400									− 400	Utilities expense
Bal	14,300		3,000	3,700	40,000	3,700		50,000		7,300	
				61,000					61,000		

The expenses decrease ShineBrite's Cash and Retained Earnings. List each expense separately to keep track of its amount.

Transaction 7.   ShineBrite pays $1,900 on account, which means to pay off an account payable. In this transaction ShineBrite pays the store from which it purchased supplies in transaction 3. The transaction decreases Cash and also decreases Accounts Payable as follows:

	Assets								Liabilities	+	Stockholders' Equity		
	Cash	+	Accounts Receivable	+	Supplies	+	Land		Accounts Payable	+	Common Stock	+	Retained Earnings
Bal	14,300		3,000		3,700		40,000	=	3,700		50,000		7,300
(7)	− 1,900								− 1,900				
Bal	12,400		3,000		3,700		40,000		1,800		50,000		7,300
				59,100							59,100		

Transaction 8.   Van Gray, the major stockholder of ShineBrite Car Wash, paid $30,000 to remodel his home. This event is a personal transaction of the Gray family. It is not recorded by the ShineBrite Car Wash business. We focus solely on the business entity, not on its owners. This transaction illustrates the entity assumption from Chapter 1.

Transaction 9.   In transaction 5, ShineBrite performed services for UPS on account. The business now collects $1,000 from UPS. We say that ShineBrite *collects the cash on account*, which means that ShineBrite will record an increase in Cash and a decrease in

Accounts Receivable. This is not service revenue because ShineBrite already recorded the revenue in transaction 5. The effect of collecting cash on account is:

	Cash	+	Accounts Receivable	+	Supplies	+	Land		Accounts Payable	+	Common Stock	+	Retained Earnings
					Assets				**Liabilities**	+	**Stockholders' Equity**		
Bal	12,400		3,000		3,700		40,000	=	1,800		50,000		7,300
(9)	+ 1,000		− 1,000										
Bal	13,400		2,000		3,700		40,000		1,800		50,000		7,300
			59,100								59,100		

Transaction 10. ShineBrite sells some land for $22,000, which is the same amount that ShineBrite paid for the land. ShineBrite receives $22,000 cash, and the effect on the accounting equation is as follows:

	Cash	+	Accounts Receivable	+	Supplies	+	Land		Accounts Payable	+	Common Stock	+	Retained Earnings
					Assets				**Liabilities**	+	**Stockholders' Equity**		
Bal	13,400		2,000		3,700		40,000	=	1,800		50,000		7,300
(10)	+ 22,000						− 22,000						
Bal	35,400		2,000		3,700		18,000		1,800		50,000		7,300
			59,100								59,100		

Note that the company did not sell all its land; ShineBrite still owns $18,000 worth of land.

Transaction 11. ShineBrite Car Wash declares a dividend and pays the stockholders $2,100 cash. The effect on the accounting equation is as follows:

	Cash	+	Accounts Receivable	+	Supplies	+	Land		Accounts Payable	+	Common Stock	+	Retained Earnings	Type of Stockholders' Equity Transaction
				Assets					**Liabilities**	+	**Stockholders' Equity**			
Bal	35,400		2,000		3,700		18,000	=	1,800		50,000		7,300	
(11)	− 2,100												− 2,100	Dividends
Bal	33,300		2,000		3,700		18,000		1,800		50,000		5,200	
			57,000								57,000			

The dividend decreases both the Cash and the Retained Earnings of the business. *But dividends are not an expense.*

Transactions and Financial Statements

Exhibit 2-1 summarizes the 11 preceding transactions. Panel A gives the details of the transactions, and Panel B shows the transaction analysis. As you study the exhibit, note that every transaction maintains the equality:

Assets = Liabilities + Stockholders' Equity

Exhibit 2-1 provides the data for ShineBrite Car Wash's financial statements:

EXHIBIT 2-1 | Transaction Analysis: ShineBrite Car Wash, Inc.

PANEL A—Transaction Details

(1) Received $50,000 cash and issued stock to the owners
(2) Paid $40,000 cash for land
(3) Bought $3,700 of supplies on account
(4) Received $7,000 cash from customers for service revenue earned
(5) Performed services for a customer on account, $3,000
(6) Paid cash expenses: rent, $1,100; employee salary, $1,200; utilities, $400

(7) Paid $1,900 on the account payable created in transaction 3
(8) Major stockholder paid personal funds to remodel home, *not* a transaction of the business
(9) Received $1,000 on account
(10) Sold land for cash at the land's cost of $22,000
(11) Declared and paid a dividend of $2,100 to the stockholders

PANEL B—Transaction Analysis

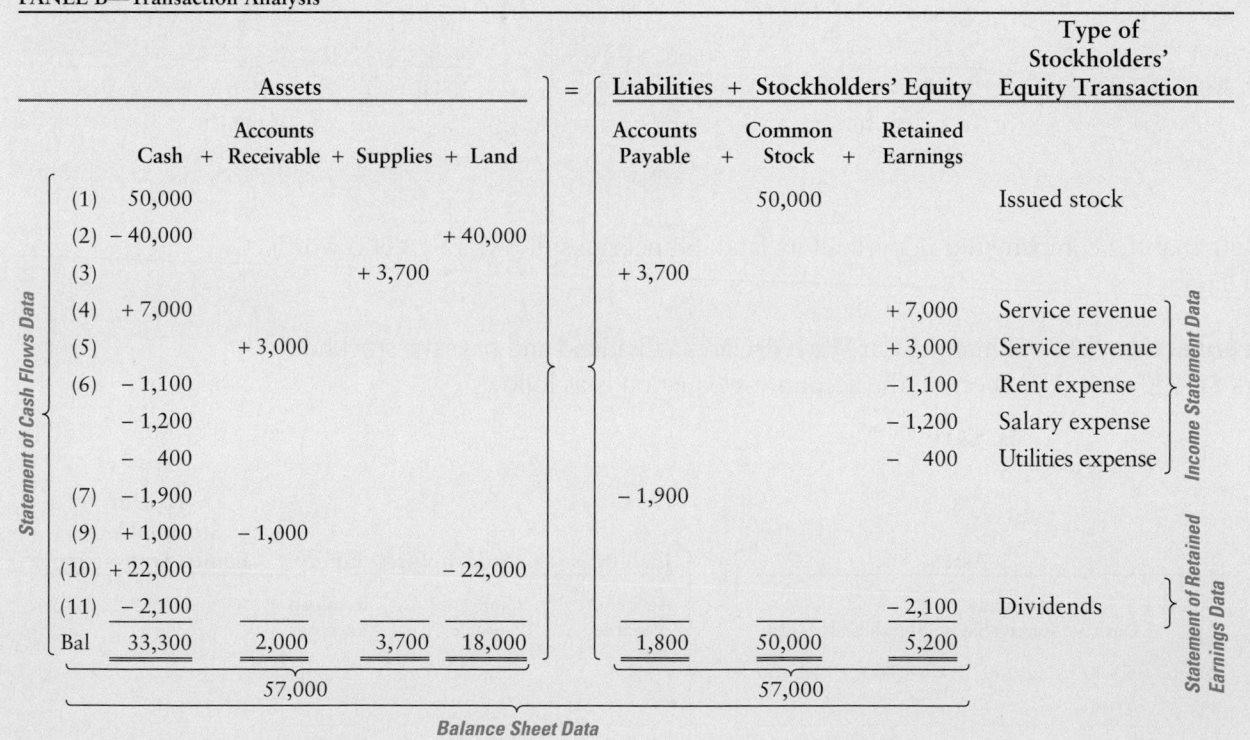

	Cash	+	Accounts Receivable	+	Supplies	+	Land	=	Accounts Payable	+	Common Stock	+	Retained Earnings	Type of Stockholders' Equity Transaction
(1)	50,000										50,000			Issued stock
(2)	– 40,000						+ 40,000							
(3)					+ 3,700				+ 3,700					
(4)	+ 7,000												+ 7,000	Service revenue
(5)			+ 3,000										+ 3,000	Service revenue
(6)	– 1,100												– 1,100	Rent expense
	– 1,200												– 1,200	Salary expense
	– 400												– 400	Utilities expense
(7)	– 1,900								– 1,900					
(9)	+ 1,000		– 1,000											
(10)	+ 22,000						– 22,000							
(11)	– 2,100												– 2,100	Dividends
Bal	33,300		2,000		3,700		18,000		1,800		50,000		5,200	

57,000 = 57,000

Balance Sheet Data

(Left margin: *Statement of Cash Flows Data*)
(Right margin: *Income Statement Data*, *Statement of Retained Earnings Data*)

- *Income statement* data appear as revenues and expenses under Retained Earnings. The revenues increase retained earnings; the expenses decrease retained earnings.
- The *balance sheet* data are composed of the ending balances of the assets, liabilities, and stockholders' equities shown at the bottom of the exhibit. The accounting equation shows that total assets ($57,000) equal total liabilities plus stockholders' equity ($57,000).
- The *statement of retained earnings* repeats net income (or net loss) from the income statement. Dividends are subtracted. Ending retained earnings is the final result.
- Data for the *statement of cash flows* are aligned under the Cash account. Cash receipts increase cash, and cash payments decrease cash.

Exhibit 2-2 on the following page shows the ShineBrite Car Wash financial statements at the end of April, the company's first month of operations. Follow the flow of data to observe the following:

1. The income statement reports revenues, expenses, and either a net income or a net loss for the period. During April, ShineBrite earned net income of $7,300. Compare ShineBrite's income statement with that of Apple, Inc., at the beginning of the chapter. The income statement includes only two types of accounts: revenues and expenses.

2. The statement of retained earnings starts with the beginning balance of retained earnings, (zero for a new business). Add net income for the period (arrow ①), subtract dividends, and compute the ending balance of retained earnings ($5,200).

3. The balance sheet lists the assets, liabilities, and stockholders' equity of the business at the end of the period. Included in stockholders' equity is retained earnings, which comes from the statement of retained earnings (arrow ②).

EXHIBIT 2-2 | **Financial Statements of ShineBrite Car Wash, Inc.**

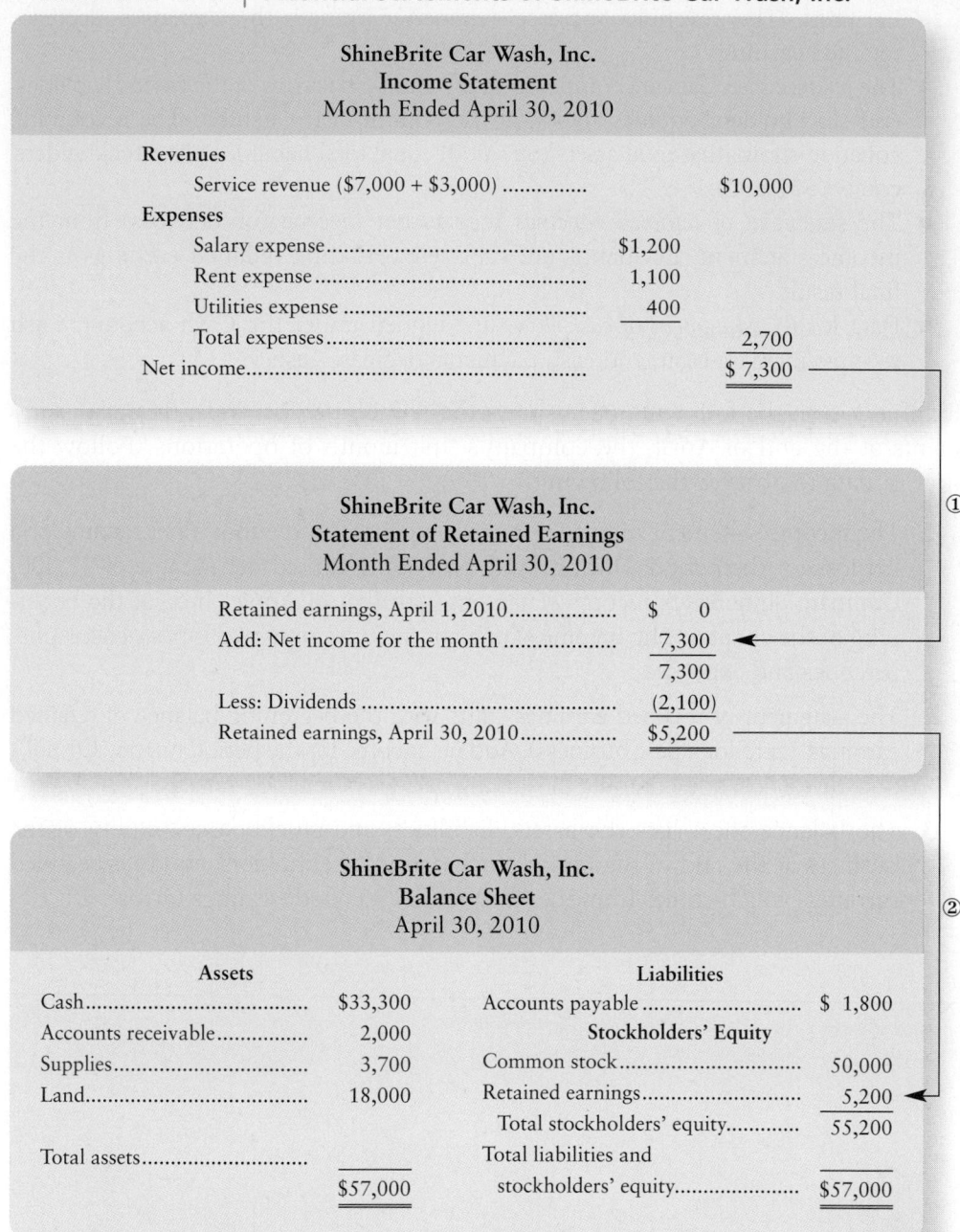

ShineBrite Car Wash, Inc.
Income Statement
Month Ended April 30, 2010

Revenues		
Service revenue ($7,000 + $3,000)		$10,000
Expenses		
Salary expense...	$1,200	
Rent expense...	1,100	
Utilities expense	400	
Total expenses...		2,700
Net income..		$ 7,300

①

ShineBrite Car Wash, Inc.
Statement of Retained Earnings
Month Ended April 30, 2010

Retained earnings, April 1, 2010...................	$ 0
Add: Net income for the month	7,300
	7,300
Less: Dividends	(2,100)
Retained earnings, April 30, 2010.................	$5,200

②

ShineBrite Car Wash, Inc.
Balance Sheet
April 30, 2010

Assets		Liabilities	
Cash..	$33,300	Accounts payable	$ 1,800
Accounts receivable...............	2,000	**Stockholders' Equity**	
Supplies.................................	3,700	Common stock................................	50,000
Land.......................................	18,000	Retained earnings...........................	5,200
		Total stockholders' equity............	55,200
Total assets............................		Total liabilities and	
	$57,000	stockholders' equity.....................	$57,000

Let's put into practice what you have learned thus far.

MID-CHAPTER SUMMARY PROBLEM

Shelly Herzog opens a research service near a college campus. She names the corporation Herzog Researchers, Inc. During the first month of operations, July 2010, the business engages in the following transactions:

a. Herzog Researchers, Inc., issues its common stock to Shelly Herzog, who invests $25,000 to open the business.

b. The company purchases on account office supplies costing $350.

c. Herzog Researchers pays cash of $20,000 to acquire a lot next to the campus. The company intends to use the land as a building site for a business office.

d. Herzog Researchers performs research for clients and receives cash of $1,900.

e. Herzog Researchers pays $100 on the account payable it created in transaction b.

f. Herzog pays $2,000 of personal funds for a vacation.

g. Herzog Researchers pays cash expenses for office rent ($400) and utilities ($100).

h. The business sells a small parcel of the land for its cost of $5,000.

i. The business declares and pays a cash dividend of $1,200.

▌Requirements

1. Analyze the preceding transactions in terms of their effects on the accounting equation of Herzog Researchers, Inc. Use Exhibit 2-1, Panel B as a guide.
2. Prepare the income statement, statement of retained earnings, and balance sheet of Herzog Researchers, Inc., after recording the transactions. Draw arrows linking the statements.

Answers

▌Requirement 1

PANEL B—Analysis of Transactions

	Assets			=	Liabilities +	Stockholders' Equity		Type of Stockholders' Equity Transaction
	Cash +	Office Supplies +	Land		Accounts Payable +	Common Stock +	Retained Earnings	
(a)	+ 25,000					+ 25,000		Issued stock
(b)		+ 350			+ 350			
(c)	− 20,000		+ 20,000					
(d)	+ 1,900						+ 1,900	Service revenue
(e)	− 100				− 100			
(f)	Not a transaction of the business							
(g)	− 400						− 400	Rent expense
	− 100						− 100	Utilities expense
(h)	+ 5,000		− 5,000					
(i)	− 1,200						− 1,200	Dividends
Bal	10,100	350	15,000		250	25,000	200	
		25,450				25,450		

Herzog Researchers, Inc.
Income Statement
Month Ended July 31, 2010

Revenues		
Service revenue.................		$1,900
Expenses		
Rent expense....................	$400	
Utilities expense	100	
Total expenses.................		500
Net income...............................		$1,400

Herzog Researchers, Inc.
Statement of Retained Earnings
Month Ended July 31, 2010

Retained earnings, July 1, 2010.................	$ 0
Add: Net income for the month	1,400
	1,400
Less: Dividends	(1,200)
Retained earnings, July 31, 2010...............	$ 200

Herzog Researchers, Inc.
Balance Sheet
July 31, 2010

Assets		Liabilities	
Cash...............................	$10,100	Accounts payable	$ 250
Office supplies................	350	**Stockholders' Equity**	
Land..............................	15,000	Common stock.................................	25,000
		Retained earnings............................	200
		Total stockholders' equity.............	25,200
		Total liabilities and	
Total assets.....................	$25,450	stockholders' equity.....................	$25,450

The analysis in the first half of this chapter can be used, but it is cumbersome. Apple, Inc., has hundreds of accounts and millions of transactions. The spreadsheet to account for Apple's transactions would be huge! In the second half of this chapter we discuss double-entry accounting as it is actually used in business.

DOUBLE-ENTRY ACCOUNTING

All business transactions include two parts:

OBJECTIVE

2 **Understand** how accounting works

- You give something.
- You receive something.

Accounting is, therefore, based on a double-entry system, which records the *dual effects* on the entity. *Each transaction affects at least two accounts.* For example, ShineBrite Car Wash's receipt of $50,000 cash and issuance of stock increased both Cash and Common Stock. It would be incomplete to record only the increase in Cash or only the increase in Common Stock.

The T-Account

An account can be represented by the letter T. We call them *T-accounts*. The vertical line in the letter divides the account into its two sides: left and right. The account title appears at the top of the T. For example, the Cash account can appear as follows:

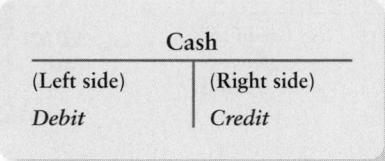

The left side of each account is called the **debit** side, and the right side is called the **credit** side. Often, students are confused by the words *debit* and *credit*. To become comfortable using these terms, remember that for every account

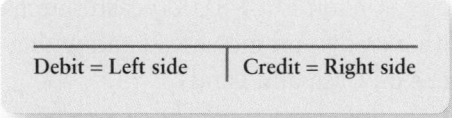

Every business transaction involves both a debit and a credit. *The debit side of an account shows what you received. The credit side shows what you gave.*

Increases and Decreases in the Accounts: The Rules of Debit and Credit

The type of account determines how we record increases and decreases. *The rules of debit and credit follow in Exhibit 2-3 on the next page.*

- Increases in *assets* are recorded on the left (debit) side of the account. Decreases in *assets* are recorded on the right (credit) side. You receive cash and debit the Cash account. You pay cash and credit the Cash account.
- Conversely, increases in *liabilities* and *stockholders' equity* are recorded by credits. Decreases in *liabilities* and *stockholders' equity* are recorded by debits.

EXHIBIT 2-3 | **Accounting Equation and the Rules of Debit and Credit**

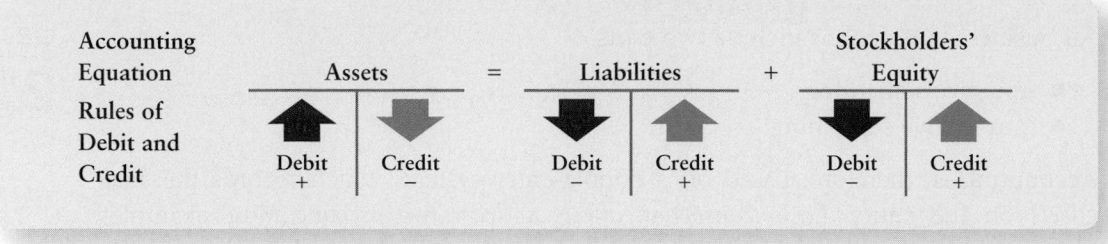

To illustrate the ideas diagrammed in Exhibit 2-3, let's review the first transaction. ShineBrite Car Wash received $50,000 and issued (gave) stock. Which accounts are affected? The Cash account and the Common Stock account will hold these amounts:

EXHIBIT 2-4 | **The Accounting Equation after ShineBrite Car Wash's First Transaction**

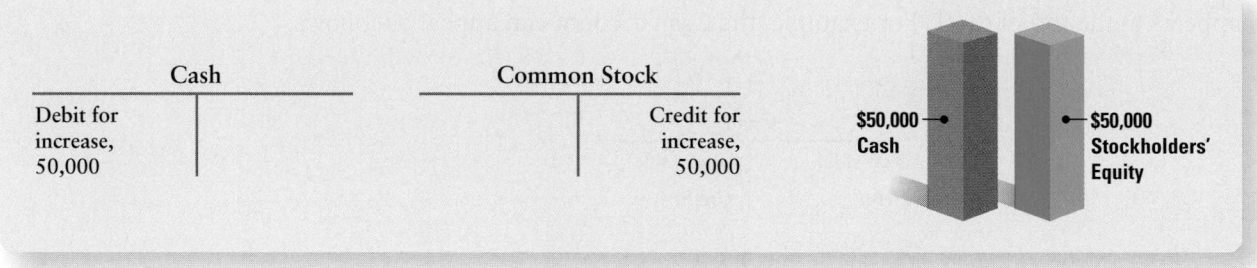

The amount remaining in an account is called its *balance*. This first transaction gives Cash a $50,000 debit balance and Common Stock a $50,000 credit balance. Exhibit 2-4 shows this relationship.

ShineBrite's second transaction is a $40,000 cash purchase of land. This transaction decreases Cash with a credit and increases Land with a debit, as shown in the following T-accounts (focus on Cash and Land):

	Cash				Common Stock	
Bal	50,000	Credit for decrease, 40,000			Bal	50,000
Bal	10,000					

	Land	
Debit for increase, 40,000		
Bal	40,000	

After this transaction, Cash has a $10,000 debit balance, Land has a debit balance of $40,000, and Common Stock has a $50,000 credit balance, as shown in Exhibit 2-5.

EXHIBIT 2-5 | The Accounting Equation after ShineBrite Car Wash's First Two Transactions

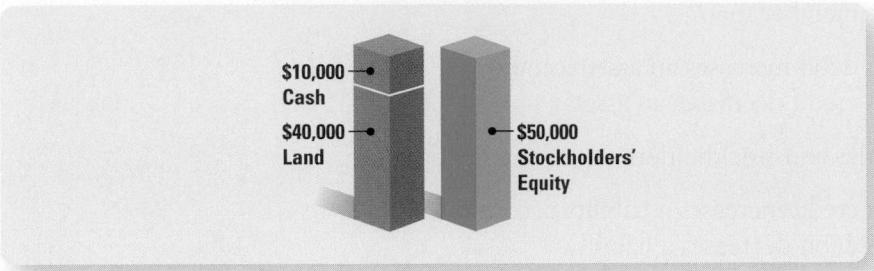

Additional Stockholders' Equity Accounts: Revenues and Expenses

Stockholders' equity also includes the two categories of income statement accounts, Revenues and Expenses:

- *Revenues* are increases in stockholders' equity that result from delivering goods or services to customers.
- *Expenses* are decreases in stockholders' equity due to the cost of operating the business.

Therefore, the accounting equation may be expanded as shown in Exhibit 2-6. Revenues and expenses appear in parentheses because their net effect—revenues minus expenses—equals net income, which increases stockholders' equity. If expenses exceed revenues, there is a net loss, which decreases stockholders' equity.

EXHIBIT 2-6 | Expansion of the Accounting Equation

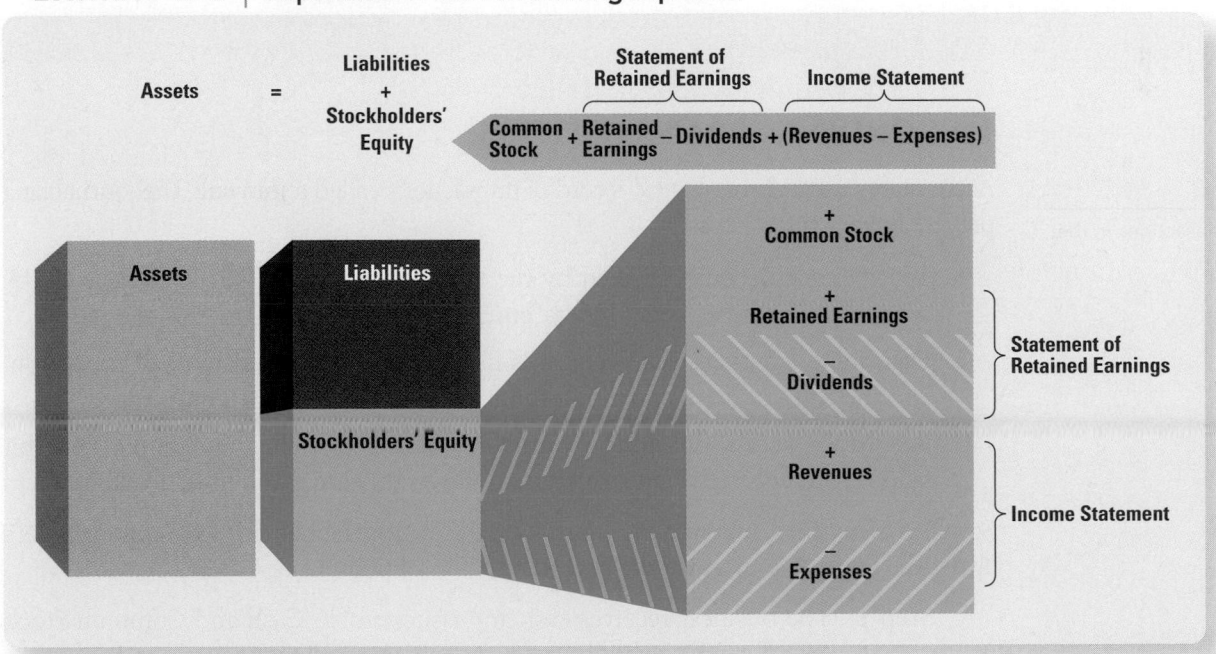

We can now express the final form of the rules of debit and credit, as shown in Exhibit 2-7. *You should not proceed until you have learned these rules.* For example, you must remember that

- A debit increases an asset account.
- A credit decreases an asset.

Liabilities and stockholders' equity are the opposite.

- A credit increases a liability account.
- A debit decreases a liability.

Dividends and Expense accounts are exceptions to the rule. <u>Dividends and Expenses are equity accounts that are increased by a deb</u>it. Dividends and Expense accounts are negative (or *contra*) equity accounts.

Revenues and Expenses are often treated as separate account categories because they appear on the income statement. Exhibit 2-7 shows Revenues and Expenses below the other equity accounts.

EXHIBIT 2-7 | **Final Form of the Rules of Debit and Credit**

ASSETS	=	LIABILITIES	+		STOCKHOLDERS' EQUITY		

Assets		Liabilities		Common Stock		Retained Earnings		Dividends	
Debit	Credit	Debit	Credit	Debit	Credit	Debit	Credit	Debit	Credit
+	−	−	+	−	+	−	+	+	−

						Revenues		Expenses	
						Debit	Credit	Debit	Credit
						−	+	+	−

RECORDING TRANSACTIONS

OBJECTIVE

3 **Record** transactions in the journal

Accountants use a chronological record of transactions called a **journal**. The journalizing process follows three steps:

1. Specify each account affected by the transaction and classify each account by type (asset, liability, stockholders' equity, revenue, or expense).

2. Determine whether each account is increased or decreased by the transaction. Use the rules of debit and credit to increase or decrease each account.

3. Record the transaction in the journal, including a brief explanation. The debit side is entered on the left margin, and the credit side is indented to the right.

Step 3 is also called "making the journal entry" or "journalizing the transaction." Let's apply the steps to journalize the first transaction of ShineBrite Car Wash.

Step 1 The business receives cash and issues stock. Cash and Common Stock are affected. Cash is an asset, and Common Stock is equity.

Step 2 Both Cash and Common Stock increase. Debit Cash to record an increase in this asset. Credit Common Stock to record an increase in this equity account.

Step 3 Journalize the transaction as follows:

JOURNAL

Date	Accounts and Explanation	Debit	Credit
Apr 2	Cash	50,000	
	Common Stock		50,000
	Issued common stock.		

When analyzing a transaction, first pinpoint the effects (if any) on cash. Did cash increase or decrease? Typically, it is easiest to identify cash effects. Then identify the effects on the other accounts.

Copying Information (Posting) from the Journal to the Ledger

The journal is a chronological record of all company transactions listed by date. But the journal does not indicate how much cash or accounts receivable the business has.

The **ledger** is a grouping of all the T-accounts, with their balances. For example, the balance of the Cash T-account shows how much cash the business has. The balance of Accounts Receivable shows the amount due from customers. Accounts Payable shows how much the business owes suppliers on open account, and so on.

In the phrase "keeping the books," *books* refers to the accounts in the ledger. In most accounting systems, the ledger is computerized. Exhibit 2-8 shows how the asset, liability, and stockholders' equity accounts are grouped in the ledger.

EXHIBIT 2-8 | The Ledger (Asset, Liability, and Stockholders' Equity Accounts)

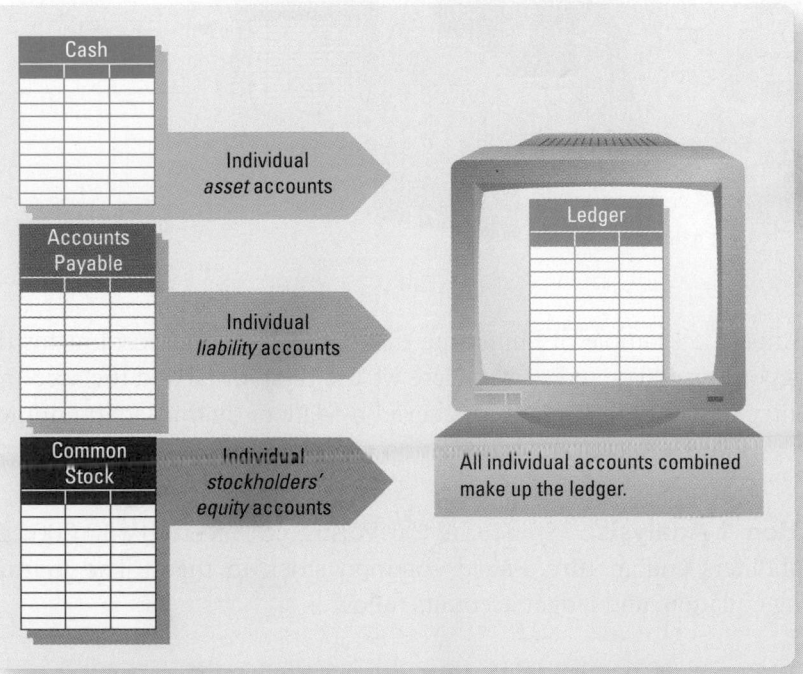

Entering a transaction in the journal does not get the data into the ledger. Data must be copied to the ledger—a process called **posting**. Debits in the journal are always posted as debits in the accounts, and likewise for credits. Exhibit 2-9 shows how ShineBrite Car Wash's stock issuance transaction is posted to the accounts.

EXHIBIT 2-9 | Journal Entry and Posting to the Accounts

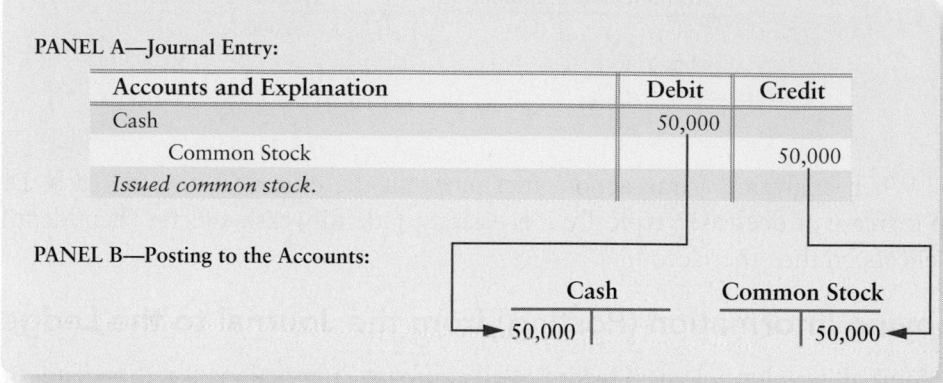

PANEL A—Journal Entry:

Accounts and Explanation	Debit	Credit
Cash	50,000	
Common Stock		50,000
Issued common stock.		

PANEL B—Posting to the Accounts:

Cash	Common Stock
50,000	50,000

The Flow of Accounting Data

Exhibit 2-10 summarizes the flow of accounting data from the business transaction to the ledger.

EXHIBIT 2-10 | Flow of Accounting Data

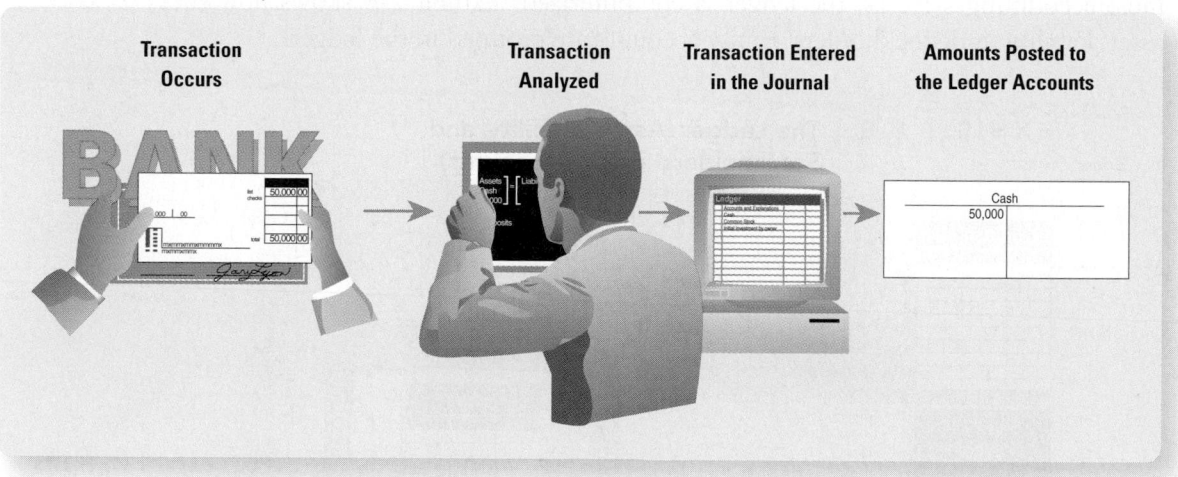

Transaction Occurs	Transaction Analyzed	Transaction Entered in the Journal	Amounts Posted to the Ledger Accounts

Let's continue the example of ShineBrite Car Wash, Inc., and account for the same 11 transactions we illustrated earlier. Here we use the journal and the accounts. Each journal entry posted to the accounts is keyed by date or by transaction number. This linking allows you to locate any information you may need.

Transaction 1 Analysis.   ShineBrite Car Wash, Inc., received $50,000 cash from the stockholders and in turn issued common stock to them. The journal entry, accounting equation, and ledger accounts follow.

Journal entry	Cash	50,000	
	Common Stock		50,000
	Issued common stock.		

Accounting equation	Assets	=	Liabilities	+	Stockholders' Equity
	50,000	=	0	+	50,000

	Cash		Common Stock	
The ledger accounts	(1) 50,000			(1) 50,000

Transaction 2 Analysis.

The business paid $40,000 cash for land. The purchase decreased cash; therefore, credit Cash. The purchase increased the asset land; to record this increase, debit Land.

Journal entry			
Land		40,000	
Cash			40,000
Paid cash for land.			

Accounting equation	Assets	=	Liabilities	+	Stockholders' Equity
	+ 40,000	=	0	+	0
	− 40,000				

	Cash		Land	
The ledger accounts	(1) 50,000	(2) 40,000	(2) 40,000	

Transaction 3 Analysis.

The business purchased supplies for $3,700 on account payable. The purchase increased Supplies, an asset, and Accounts Payable, a liability.

Journal entry			
Supplies		3,700	
Accounts Payable			3,700
Purchased office supplies on account.			

Accounting equation	Assets	=	Liabilities	+	Stockholders' Equity
	+ 3,700	=	+ 3,700	+	0

	Supplies		Accounts Payable	
The ledger accounts	(3) 3,700			(3) 3,700

Transaction 4 Analysis.

The business performed services for clients and received cash of $7,000. The transaction increased cash and service revenue. To record the revenue, credit Service Revenue.

Journal entry	Cash		7,000	
	Service Revenue			7,000
	Performed services for cash.			

Accounting equation	Assets	=	Liabilities	+	Stockholders' Equity	+	Revenues
	+ 7,000	=	0			+	7,000

The ledger accounts		Cash				Service Revenue	
	(1)	50,000	(2)	40,000		(4)	7,000
	(4)	7,000					

Transaction 5 Analysis. ShineBrite performed services for UPS on account. UPS did not pay immediately, so ShineBrite billed UPS for $3,000. The transaction increased accounts receivable; therefore, debit Accounts Receivable. Service revenue also increased, so credit the Service Revenue account.

Journal entry	Accounts Receivable		3,000	
	Service Revenue			3,000
	Performed services on account.			

Accounting equation	Assets	=	Liabilities	+	Stockholders' Equity	+	Revenues
	+ 3,000	=	0			+	3,000

The ledger accounts		Accounts Receivable			Service Revenue	
	(5)	3,000			(4)	7,000
					(5)	3,000

Transaction 6 Analysis. The business paid $2,700 for the following expenses: equipment rent, $1,100; employee salary, $1,200; and utilities, $400. Credit Cash for the sum of the expense amounts. The expenses increased, so debit each expense account separately.

Journal entry	Rent Expense		1,100	
	Salary Expense		1,200	
	Utilities Expense		400	
	Cash			2,700
	Paid expenses.			

Accounting equation	Assets	=	Liabilities	+	Stockholders' Equity	–	Expenses
	– 2,700	=	0			–	2,700

The ledger accounts

	Cash				Rent Expense	
(1)	50,000	(2)	40,000	(6)	1,100	
(4)	7,000	(6)	2,700			

	Salary Expense			Utilities Expense	
(6)	1,200		(6)	400	

Transaction 7 Analysis.
The business paid $1,900 on the account payable created in transaction 3. Credit Cash for the payment. The payment decreased a liability, so debit Accounts Payable.

Journal entry

Accounts Payable	1,900	
Cash		1,900
Paid cash on account.		

Accounting equation	Assets	=	Liabilities	+	Stockholders' Equity
	– 1,900	=	– 1,900	+	0

The ledger accounts

	Cash				Accounts Payable		
(1)	50,000	(2)	40,000	(7)	1,900	(3)	3,700
(4)	7,000	(6)	2,700				
		(7)	1,900				

Transaction 8 Analysis.
Van Gray, the major stockholder of ShineBrite Car Wash, remodeled his personal residence. This is not a transaction of the car-wash business, so the business does not record the transaction.

Transaction 9 Analysis.
The business collected $1,000 cash on account from the clients in transaction 5. Cash increased so debit Cash. The asset accounts receivable decreased; therefore, credit Accounts Receivable.

Journal entry

Cash	1,000	
Accounts Receivable		1,000
Collected cash on account.		

Accounting equation

	Assets	=	Liabilities	+	Stockholders' Equity
	+ 1,000	=	0	+	0
	− 1,000				

The ledger accounts

	Cash				Accounts Receivable		
(1)	50,000	(2)	40,000	(5)	3,000	(9)	1,000
(4)	7,000	(6)	2,700				
(9)	1,000	(7)	1,900				

Transaction 10 Analysis.   The business sold land for its cost of $22,000, receiving cash. The asset cash increased; debit Cash. The asset land decreased; credit Land.

Journal entry

Cash	22,000	
Land		22,000
Sold land.		

Accounting equation

	Assets	=	Liabilities	+	Stockholders' Equity
	+ 22,000	=	0	+	0
	− 22,000				

The ledger accounts

	Cash				Land		
(1)	50,000	(2)	40,000	(2)	40,000	(10)	22,000
(4)	7,000	(6)	2,700				
(9)	1,000	(7)	1,900				
(10)	22,000						

Transaction 11 Analysis.   ShineBrite Car Wash paid its stockholders cash dividends of $2,100. Credit Cash for the payment. The transaction also decreased stockholders' equity and requires a debit to an equity account. Therefore, debit Dividends.

Journal entry

Dividends	2,100	
Cash		2,100
Declared and paid dividends.		

Accounting equation

Assets	=	Liabilities	+	Stockholders' Equity	−	Dividends
− 2,100	=	0			−	2,100

	Cash				Dividends	
(1)	50,000	(2)	40,000	(11)	2,100	
(4)	7,000	(6)	2,700			
(9)	1,000	(7)	1,900			
(10)	22,000	(11)	2,100			

The ledger accounts

Accounts After Posting to the Ledger

Exhibit 2-11 shows the accounts after all transactions have been posted to the ledger. Group the accounts under assets, liabilities, and equity.

Each account has a balance, denoted as Bal, which is the difference between the account's total debits and its total credits. For example, the Accounts Payable's balance of $1,800 is the difference between the credit ($3,700) and the debit ($1,900). Cash has a debit balance of $33,300.

A horizontal line separates the transaction amounts from the account balance. If an account's debits exceed its total credits, that account has a debit balance, as for Cash. If the sum of the credits is greater, the account has a credit balance, as for Accounts Payable.

Accounting Cycle Tutorial Application 1—
Xpert Driving School

Accounting Cycle Tutorial Application 2—
Small Business Services

EXHIBIT 2-11 | ShineBrite Car Wash's Ledger Accounts After Posting

Assets	=	Liabilities	+	Stockholders' Equity

Cash

(1)	50,000	(2)	40,000
(4)	7,000	(6)	2,700
(9)	1,000	(7)	1,900
(10)	22,000	(11)	2,100
Bal	33,300		

Accounts Payable

(7)	1,900	(3)	3,700
		Bal	1,800

Common Stock

		(1)	50,000
		Bal	50,000

Dividends

(11)	2,100	
Bal	2,100	

Accounts Receivable

(5)	3,000	(9)	1,000
Bal	2,000		

Revenue

Service Revenue

		(4)	7,000
		(5)	3,000
		Bal	10,000

Expenses

Rent Expense

(6)	1,100	
Bal	1,100	

Supplies

(3)	3,700	
Bal	3,700	

Salary Expense

(6)	1,200	
Bal	1,200	

Land

(2)	40,000	(10)	22,000
Bal	18,000		

Utilities Expense

(6)	400	
Bal	400	

THE TRIAL BALANCE

A **trial balance** lists all accounts with their balances—assets first, then liabilities and stockholders' equity. The trial balance summarizes all the account balances for the financial statements and shows whether total debits equal total credits. A trial balance

OBJECTIVE

4 **Use** a trial balance

may be taken at any time, but the most common time is at the end of the period. Exhibit 2-12 is the trial balance of ShineBrite Car Wash, Inc., after all transactions have been journalized and posted at the end of April.

Accounting Cycle Tutorial Glossary

Accounting Cycle Tutorial Glossary Quiz

EXHIBIT 2-12 | Trial Balance

ShineBrite Car Wash, Inc.
Trial Balance
April 30, 2010

	Balance	
Account Title	Debit	Credit
Cash	$33,300	
Accounts receivable	2,000	
Supplies	3,700	
Land	18,000	
Accounts payable		$ 1,800
Common stock		50,000
Dividends	2,100	
Service revenue		10,000
Rent expense	1,100	
Salary expense	1,200	
Utilities expense	400	
Total	$61,800	$61,800

Analyzing Accounts

You can often tell what a company did by analyzing its accounts. This is a powerful tool for a manager who knows accounting. For example, if you know the beginning and ending balance of Cash, and if you know total cash receipts, you can compute your total cash payments during the period.

In our chapter example, suppose ShineBrite Car Wash began May with cash of $1,000. During May ShineBrite received cash of $8,000 and ended the month with a cash balance of $3,000. You can compute total cash payments by analyzing ShineBrite's Cash account as follows:

Cash			
Beginning balance	1,000		
Cash receipts	8,000	Cash payments	$x = 6,000$
Ending balance	3,000		

Or, if you know Cash's beginning and ending balances and total payments, you can compute cash receipts during the period—for any company!

You can compute either sales on account or cash collections on account by analyzing the Accounts Receivable account as follows (using assumed amounts):

Accounts Receivable			
Beginning balance	6,000		
Sales on account	10,000	Collections on account	11,000
Ending balance	5,000		

Also, you can determine how much you paid on account by analyzing Accounts Payable as follows (using assumed amounts):

Accounts Payable			
		Beginning balance	9,000
Payments on account	4,000	Purchases on account	6,000
		Ending balance	11,000

Please master this powerful technique. It works for any company and for your own personal finances! You will find this tool very helpful when you become a manager.

Correcting Accounting Errors

Accounting errors can occur even in computerized systems. Input data may be wrong, or they may be entered twice or not at all. A debit may be entered as a credit, and vice versa. You can detect the reason or reasons behind many out-of-balance conditions by computing the difference between total debits and total credits. Then perform one or more of the following actions:

1. Search the records for a missing account. Trace each account back and forth from the journal to the ledger. A $200 transaction may have been recorded incorrectly in the journal or posted incorrectly to the ledger. Search the journal for a $200 transaction.

2. Divide the out-of-balance amount by 2. A debit treated as a credit, or vice versa, doubles the amount of error. Suppose ShineBrite Car Wash added $300 to Cash instead of subtracting $300. The out-of-balance amount is $600, and dividing by 2 identifies $300 as the amount of the transaction. Search the journal for the $300 transaction and trace to the account affected.

3. Divide the out-of-balance amount by 9. If the result is an integer (no decimals), the error may be a

   - *slide* (writing $400 as $40). The accounts would be out of balance by $360 ($400 − $40 = $360). Dividing $360 by 9 yields $40. Scan the trial balance in Exhibit 2-12 for an amount similar to $40. Utilities Expense (balance of $400) is the misstated account.

■ *transposition* (writing $2,100 as $1,200). The accounts would be out of balance by $900 ($2,100 − $1,200 = $900). Dividing $900 by 9 yields $100. Trace all amounts on the trial balance back to the T-accounts. Dividends (balance of $2,100) is the misstated account.

Chart of Accounts

As you know, the ledger contains the accounts grouped under these headings:

1. **Balance sheet accounts: Assets, Liabilities, and Stockholders' Equity**
2. **Income statement accounts: Revenues and Expenses**

Organizations use a **chart of accounts** to list all their accounts and account numbers. Account numbers usually have two or more digits. Asset account numbers may begin with 1, liabilities with 2, stockholders' equity with 3, revenues with 4, and expenses with 5. The second, third, and higher digits in an account number indicate the position of the individual account within the category. For example, Cash may be account number 101, which is the first asset account. Accounts Payable may be number 201, the first liability. All accounts are numbered by using this system.

Organizations with many accounts use lengthy account numbers. For example, the chart of accounts of Apple, Inc., may use five-digit account numbers. The chart of accounts for ShineBrite Car Wash appears in Exhibit 2-13. The gap between account numbers 111 and 141 leaves room to add another category of receivables, for example, Notes Receivable, which may be numbered 121.

EXHIBIT 2-13 | **Chart of Accounts—ShineBrite Car Wash, Inc.**

Balance Sheet Accounts					
Assets		**Liabilities**		**Stockholders' Equity**	
101	Cash	201	Accounts Payable	301	Common Stock
111	Accounts Receivable	231	Notes Payable	311	Dividends
141	Office Supplies			312	Retained Earnings
151	Office Furniture				
191	Land				

Income Statement Accounts (Part of Stockholders' Equity)			
Revenues		**Expenses**	
401	Service Revenue	501	Rent Expense
		502	Salary Expense
		503	Utilities Expense

Appendix D to this book gives two expanded charts of accounts that you will find helpful as you work through this course. The first chart lists the typical accounts that a *service* corporation, such as ShineBrite Car Wash, would have after a period of growth. The second chart is for a *merchandising* corporation, one that sells a product instead of a service.

The Normal Balance of an Account

An account's *normal balance* falls on the side of the account—debit or credit—where increases are recorded. The normal balance of assets is on the debit side, so assets are *debit-balance accounts*. Conversely, liabilities and stockholders' equity usually have a credit balance, so these are *credit-balance accounts*. Exhibit 2-14 illustrates the normal balances of all the assets, liabilities, and stockholders' equities, including revenues and expenses.

EXHIBIT 2-14 | **Normal Balances of the Accounts**

Assets	Debit	
Liabilities		Credit
Stockholders' Equity—overall		Credit
Common stock		Credit
Retained earnings		Credit
Dividends	Debit	
Revenues		Credit
Expenses	Debit	

As explained earlier, stockholders' equity usually contains several accounts. Dividends and expenses carry debit balances because they represent decreases in stockholders' equity. In total, the equity accounts show a normal credit balance.

Account Formats

So far we have illustrated accounts in a two-column T-account format, with the debit column on the left and the credit column on the right. Another format has four *amount* columns, as illustrated for the Cash account in Exhibit 2-15. The first pair of amount columns are for the debit and credit amounts of individual transactions. The last two columns are for the account balance. This four-column format keeps a running balance in the two right columns.

ac t

Accounting Cycle Tutorial
The Journal, the Ledger, and the Trial Balance

EXHIBIT 2-15 | **Account in Four-Column Format**

Account: Cash				Account No. 101	
				Balance	
Date	Item	Debit	Credit	Debit	Credit
2010 Apr 2		50,000		50,000	
3			40,000	10,000	

Analyzing Transactions Using Only T-Accounts

5 Analyze transactions using only T-accounts

Businesspeople must often make decisions without the benefit of a complete accounting system. For example, the managers of Apple, Inc., may consider borrowing $100,000 to buy equipment. To see how the two transactions [(a) borrowing cash and (b) buying equipment] affect Apple, the manager can go directly to T-accounts, as follows:

T-accounts:	Cash			Note Payable	
(a)	100,000			(a)	100,000

T-accounts:	Cash			Equipment			Note Payable	
(a)	100,000	(b) 100,000	(b)	100,000			(a)	100,000

This informal analysis shows immediately that Apple will add $100,000 of equipment and a $100,000 note payable. Assuming that Apple began with zero balances, the equipment and note payable transactions would result in the following balance sheet (date assumed for illustration only):

Apple, Inc.
Balance Sheet
September 12, 2010

Assets		Liabilities	
Cash................................	$ 0	Note payable............................	$100,000
Equipment......................	100,000		
		Stockholders' Equity	0
		Total liabilities and	
Total assets....................	$100,000	stockholders' equity...............	$100,000

Companies don't actually keep records in this shortcut fashion. But a decision maker who needs information quickly may not have time to journalize, post to the accounts, take a trial balance, and prepare the financial statements. A manager who knows accounting can analyze the transaction and make the decision quickly.

Now apply what you've learned. Study the Decision Guidelines, which summarize the chapter.

ac
↗t

Accounting Cycle Tutorial Application
Constanza Architect

DECISION GUIDELINES

HOW TO MEASURE RESULTS OF OPERATIONS AND FINANCIAL POSITION

Any entrepreneur must determine whether the venture is profitable. To do this, he or she needs to know its results of operations and financial position. If Steve Jobs, who founded Apple, Inc., wants to know whether the business is making money, the Guidelines that follow will help him.

Decision	Guidelines
Has a transaction occurred?	If the event affects the entity's financial position and can be reliably recorded—Yes. If either condition is absent—No.
Where to record the transaction?	In the *journal*, the chronological record of transactions
How to record an increase or decrease in the following accounts?	Rules of *debit* and *credit*:

	Increase	Decrease
Assets	Debit	Credit
Liabilities	Credit	Debit
Stockholders' equity	Credit	Debit
Revenues	Credit	Debit
Expenses	Debit	Credit

Decision	Guidelines
Where to store all the information for each account?	In the *ledger*, the book of accounts
Where to list all the accounts and their balances?	In the *trial* balance
Where to report the:	
Results of operations?	In the *income* statement (Revenues – Expenses = Net income or net loss)
Financial position?	In the balance sheet (Assets = Liabilities + Stockholders' equity)

END-OF-CHAPTER SUMMARY PROBLEM

The trial balance of Calderon Service Center, Inc., on March 1, 2010, lists the entity's assets, liabilities, and stockholders' equity on that date.

		Balance	
Account Title		Debit	Credit
Cash..		$26,000	
Accounts receivable...............		4,500	
Accounts payable			$ 2,000
Common stock.......................			10,000
Retained earnings..................			18,500
Total		$30,500	$30,500

During March, the business completed the following transactions:

a. Borrowed $45,000 from the bank, with Calderon signing a note payable in the name of the business.

b. Paid cash of $40,000 to a real estate company to acquire land.

c. Performed service for a customer and received cash of $5,000.

d. Purchased supplies on credit, $300.

e. Performed customer service and earned revenue on account, $2,600.

f. Paid $1,200 on account.

g. Paid the following cash expenses: salaries, $3,000; rent, $1,500; and interest, $400.

h. Received $3,100 on account.

i. Received a $200 utility bill that will be paid next week.

j. Declared and paid dividend of $1,800.

I Requirements

1. Open the following accounts, with the balances indicated, in the ledger of Calderon Service Center, Inc. Use the T-account format.
   - Assets—Cash, $26,000; Accounts Receivable, $4,500; Supplies, no balance; Land, no balance
   - Liabilities—Accounts Payable, $2,000; Note Payable, no balance
   - Stockholders' Equity—Common Stock, $10,000; Retained Earnings, $18,500; Dividends, no balance
   - Revenues—Service Revenue, no balance
   - Expenses—(none have balances) Salary Expense, Rent Expense, Interest Expense, Utilities Expense
2. Journalize the preceding transactions. Key journal entries by transaction letter.
3. Post to the ledger and show the balance in each account after all the transactions have been posted.
4. Prepare the trial balance of Calderon Service Center, Inc., at March 31, 2010.
5. To determine the net income or net loss of the entity during the month of March, prepare the income statement for the month ended March 31, 2010. List expenses in order from the largest to the smallest.

Answers

▌Requirement 1

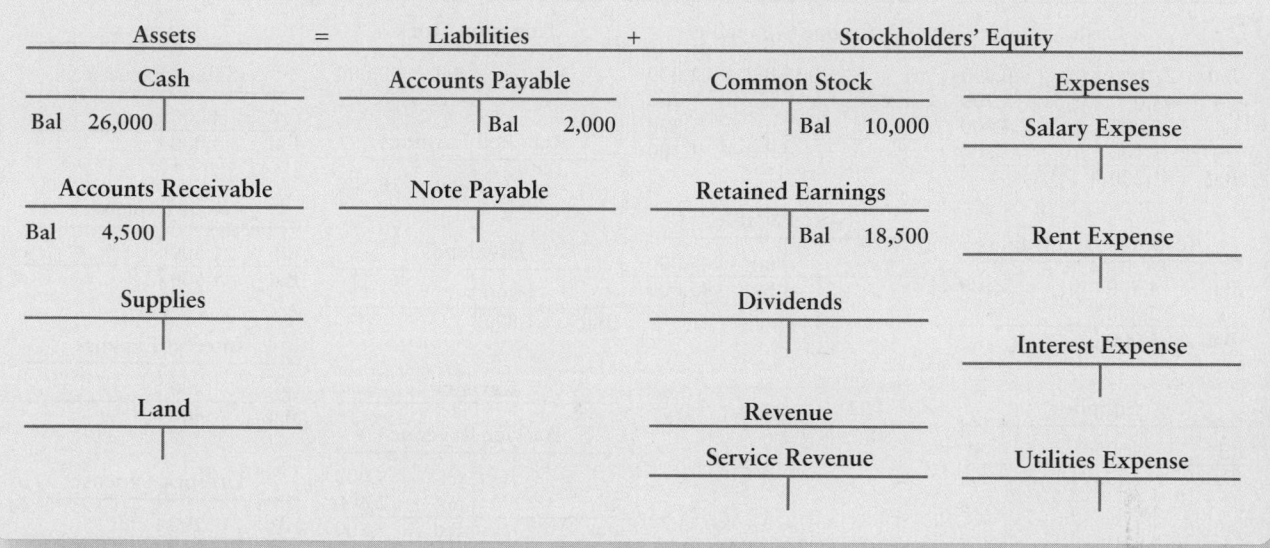

Assets	=	Liabilities	+	Stockholders' Equity	
Cash		**Accounts Payable**		**Common Stock**	**Expenses**
Bal 26,000		Bal 2,000		Bal 10,000	Salary Expense
Accounts Receivable		**Note Payable**		**Retained Earnings**	
Bal 4,500				Bal 18,500	Rent Expense
Supplies				**Dividends**	
					Interest Expense
Land				**Revenue**	
				Service Revenue	**Utilities Expense**

▌Requirement 2

Accounts and Explanation	Debit	Credit		Accounts and Explanation	Debit	Credit
a. Cash..	45,000		g.	Salary Expense	3,000	
Note Payable		45,000		Rent Expense	1,500	
Borrowed cash on note payable.				Interest Expense	400	
b. Land..	40,000			Cash		4,900
Cash		40,000		Paid cash expenses.		
Purchased land for cash.			h.	Cash..	3,100	
c. Cash..	5,000			Accounts Receivable		3,100
Service Revenue		5,000		Received on account.		
Performed service and received cash.			i.	Utilities Expense...........................	200	
d. Supplies....................................	300			Accounts Payable...................		200
Accounts Payable...............		300		Received utility bill.		
Purchased supplies on account.			j.	Dividends	1,800	
e. Accounts Receivable................	2,600			Cash		1,800
Service Revenue		2,600		Declared and paid dividends.		
Performed service on account.						
f. Accounts Payable	1,200					
Cash		1,200				
Paid on account.						

❚ Requirement 3

Assets		=	Liabilities		+		Stockholders' Equity	

Cash

Bal	26,000	(b)	40,000
(a)	45,000	(f)	1,200
(c)	5,000	(g)	4,900
(h)	3,100	(j)	1,800
Bal	31,200		

Accounts Payable

(f)	1,200	Bal	2,000
		(d)	300
		(i)	200
		Bal	1,300

Common Stock

		Bal	10,000

Retained Earnings

		Bal	18,500

Expenses

Salary Expense

(g)	3,000	
Bal	3,000	

Accounts Receivable

Bal	4,500	(h)	3,100
(e)	2,600		
Bal	4,000		

Note Payable

		(a)	45,000
		Bal	45,000

Dividends

(j)	1,800	
Bal	1,800	

Rent Expense

(g)	1,500	
Bal	1,500	

Interest Expense

(g)	400	
Bal	400	

Supplies

(d)	300	
Bal	300	

Revenue

Service Revenue

		(c)	5,000
		(e)	2,600
		Bal	7,600

Utilities Expense

(i)	200	
Bal	200	

Land

(b)	40,000	
Bal	40,000	

❚ Requirement 4

Calderon Service Center, Inc.
Trial Balance
March 31, 2010

	Balance	
Account Title	Debit	Credit
Cash..	$31,200	
Accounts receivable...............	4,000	
Supplies..................................	300	
Land..	40,000	
Accounts payable		$ 1,300
Note payable..........................		45,000
Common stock.......................		10,000
Retained earnings...................		18,500
Dividends...............................	1,800	
Service revenue......................		7,600
Salary expense........................	3,000	
Rent expense	1,500	
Interest expense.....................	400	
Utilities expense	200	
Total	$82,400	$82,400

I *Requirement 5*

Calderon Service Center, Inc.
Income Statement
Month Ended March 31, 2010

Revenue		
Service revenue.................		$7,600
Expenses		
Salary expense.................	$3,000	
Rent expense...................	1,500	
Interest expense..............	400	
Utilities expense	200	
Total expenses....................		5,100
Net income..........................		$2,500

REVIEW TRANSACTION ANALYSIS

Quick Check (Answers are given on page 122.)

1. A debit entry to an account
   a. increases liabilities.
   b. increases assets.
   c. increases stockholders' equity.
   d. both a and c.

2. Which account types normally have a credit balance?
   a. Revenues
   b. Liabilities
   c. Expenses
   d. Both a and b

3. An attorney performs services of $900 for a client and receives $100 cash with the remainder on account. The journal entry for this transaction would
   a. debit Cash, debit Service Revenue, credit Accounts Receivable.
   b. debit Cash, debit Accounts Receivable, credit Service Revenue.
   c. debit Cash, credit Service Revenue.
   d. debit Cash, credit Accounts Receivable, credit Service Revenue.

4. Accounts Payable had a normal beginning balance of $1,600. During the period, there were debit postings of $300 and credit postings of $900. What was the ending balance?
   a. $1,000 credit
   b. $2,200 debit
   c. $2,200 credit
   d. $1,000 debit

5. The list of all accounts with their balances is the
   a. balance sheet.
   b. journal.
   c. trial balance.
   d. chart of accounts.

6. The basic summary device of accounting is the
   a. account.
   b. ledger.
   c. trial balance.
   d. journal.

7. The beginning Cash balance was $9,000. At the end of the period, the balance was $11,000. If total cash paid out during the period was $25,000, the amount of cash receipts was
   a. $27,000.
   c. $23,000.
   b. $45,000.
   d. $5,000.

8. In a double-entry accounting system
   a. half of all the accounts have a normal credit balance.
   b. liabilities, owners' equity, and revenue accounts all have normal debit balances.
   c. a debit entry is recorded on the left side of a T-account.
   d. both a and c are correct.

9. Which accounts appear on which financial statement?
	Balance sheet	*Income statement*
a.	Receivables, land, payables	Revenues, supplies
b.	Cash, revenues, land	Expenses, payables
c.	Cash, receivables, payables	Revenues, expenses
d.	Expenses, payables, cash	Revenues, receivables, land

10. A doctor purchases medical supplies of $760 and pays $380 cash with the remainder on account. The journal entry for this transaction would be which of the following?
    a. Supplies
       Cash
          Accounts Payable
    c. Supplies
          Accounts Payable
          Cash
    b. Supplies
       Accounts Payable
       Cash
    d. Supplies
          Accounts Receivable
          Cash

11. Which is the correct sequence for recording transactions and preparing financial statements?
    a. Ledger, trial balance, journal, financial statements
    b. Financial statements, trial balance, ledger, journal
    c. Ledger, journal, trial balance, financial statements
    d. Journal, ledger, trial balance, financial statements

12. The error of posting $300 as $30 can be detected by
    a. totaling each account's balance in the ledger.
    b. dividing the out-of-balance amount by 2.
    c. examining the chart of accounts.
    d. dividing the out-of-balance amount by 9.

Accounting Vocabulary

account (p. 65) The record of the changes that have occurred in a particular asset, liability, or stockholders' equity during a period. The basic summary device of accounting.

accrued liability (p. 66) A liability for an expense that has not yet been paid by the company.

cash (p. 65) Money and any medium of exchange that a bank accepts at face value.

chart of accounts (p. 90) List of a company's accounts and their account numbers.

credit (p. 77) The right side of an account.

debit (p. 77) The left side of an account.

journal (p. 80) The chronological accounting record of an entity's transactions.

ledger (p. 81) The book of accounts and their balances.

posting (p. 81) Copying amounts from the journal to the ledger.

transaction (p. 64) Any event that has a financial impact on the business and can be measured reliably.

trial balance (p. 87) A list of all the ledger accounts with their balances.

ASSESS YOUR PROGRESS

Short Exercises

S2-1 (*Learning Objective 1: Explaining an asset versus an expense*) Brian Horton opened a software consulting firm that immediately paid $8,000 for a computer. Was Horton's computer an expense of the business? If not, explain.

S2-2 (*Learning Objective 1: Analyzing the effects of transactions*) Young Software began with cash of $13,000. Young then bought supplies for $1,800 on account. Separately, Young paid $4,000 for a computer. Answer these questions.

  a. How much in total assets does Young have?
  b. How much in liabilities does Young owe?

S2-3 (*Learning Objectives 1, 2: Analyzing transactions; understanding how accounting works*)
Hannah Lyle, MD, opened a medical practice. The business completed the following transactions:

> Aug 1   Lyle invested $31,000 cash to start her medical practice. The business issued common stock to Lyle.
> 1   Purchased medical supplies on account totaling $9,200.
> 2   Paid monthly office rent of $3,000.
> 3   Recorded $10,000 revenue for service rendered to patients, received cash of $2,000, and sent bills to patients for the remainder.

After these transactions, how much cash does the business have to work with? Use a T-account to show your answer.

S2-4 (*Learning Objective 1: Analyzing transactions*) Refer to Short Exercise 2-3. Which of the transactions of Hannah Lyle, MD, increased the total assets of the business? For each transaction, identify the asset that was increased.

S2-5 (*Learning Objective 1: Analyzing transactions*) Capri Design specializes in imported clothing. During May, Capri completed a series of transactions. For each of the following items, give an example of a transaction that has the described effect on the accounting equation of Capri Design.

  a. Increase one asset and decrease another asset.
  b. Decrease an asset and decrease owners' equity.
  c. Decrease an asset and decrease a liability.
  d. Increase an asset and increase owners' equity.
  e. Increase an asset and increase a liability.

S2-6 (*Learning Objectives 2, 3: Understanding how accounting works; journalizing transactions*) After operating for several months, architect Gwen Markum completed the following transactions during the latter part of July.

> Jul 15   Borrowed $34,000 from the bank, signing a note payable.
> 22   Performed service for clients on account totaling $8,500.
> 28   Received $6,500 cash on account from clients.
> 29   Received a utility bill of $700, an account payable that will be paid during August.
> 31   Paid monthly salary of $3,100 to employee.

Journalize the transactions of Gwen Markum, Architect. Include an explanation with each journal entry.

S2-7 (*Learning Objectives 2, 3: Understanding how accounting works; journalizing transactions; posting*) Architect David Delorme purchased supplies on account for $2,000. Later Delorme paid $500 on account.

1. Journalize the two transactions on the books of David Delorme, architect. Include an explanation for each transaction.
2. Open a T-account for Accounts Payable and post to Accounts Payable. Compute the balance and denote it as Bal.
3. How much does the Delorme business owe after both transactions? In which account does this amount appear?

S2-8 (*Learning Objectives 2, 3: Understanding how accounting works; journalizing transactions; posting*) Orman Unlimited performed service for a client who could not pay immediately. Orman expected to collect the $5,200 the following month. A month later, Orman received $2,400 cash from the client.

1. Record the two transactions on the books of Orman Unlimited. Include an explanation for each transaction.
2. Post to these T-accounts: Cash, Accounts Receivable, and Service Revenue. Compute each account balance and denote as Bal.

S2-9 (*Learning Objective 4: Preparing and using a trial balance*) Assume that Old Boardwalk reported the following summarized data at December 31, 2010. Accounts appear in no particular order; dollar amounts are in millions.

Other liabilities	$ 5	Revenues	$37
Cash	6	Other assets	13
Expenses	27	Accounts payable	1
Stockholders' equity	3		

Prepare the trial balance of Old Boardwalk at December 31, 2010. List the accounts in their proper order. How much was Old Boardwalk's net income or net loss?

S2-10 (*Learning Objective 4: Using a trial balance*) Redberry's trial balance follows.

Redberry, Inc.
Trial Balance
December 31, 2010

Account Title	Debit	Credit
	Balance	
Cash	$ 7,500	
Accounts receivable	12,000	
Supplies	5,000	
Equipment	24,000	
Land	52,000	
Accounts payable		$ 21,000
Note payable		32,000
Common stock		7,000
Retained earnings		9,000
Service revenue		63,000
Salary expense	23,000	
Rent expense	7,500	
Utilities expense	1,000	
Total	$132,000	$132,000

Compute these amounts for the business:

1. Total assets
2. Total liabilities
3. Net income or net loss during December

S2-11 (*Learning Objective 4: Using a trial balance*) Refer to Redberry's trial balance in Short Exercise 2-10. The purpose of this exercise is to help you learn how to correct three common accounting errors.

Error 1. Slide. Suppose the trial balance lists Land as $5,200 instead of $52,000. Recompute column totals, take the difference, and divide by 9. The result is an integer (no decimals), which suggests that the error is either a transposition or a slide.

Error 2. Transposition. Assume the trial balance lists Accounts Receivable as $21,000 instead of $12,000. Recompute column totals, take the difference, and divide by 9. The result is an integer (no decimals), which suggests that the error is either a transposition or a slide.

Error 3. Mislabeling an item. Assume that Redberry accidentally listed Accounts Receivable as a credit balance instead of a debit. Recompute the trial balance totals for debits and credits. Then take the difference between total debits and total credits, and divide the difference by 2. You get back to the original amount of Accounts Receivable.

S2-12 (*Learning Objective 2: Using key accounting terms*) Accounting has its own vocabulary and basic relationships. Match the accounting terms at left with the corresponding definition or meaning at right.

____	1. Debit	A.	The cost of operating a business; a decrease in stockholders' equity
____	2. Expense		
____	3. Net income	B.	Always a liability
____	4. Ledger	C.	Revenues − Expenses
____	5. Posting	D.	Grouping of accounts
____	6. Normal balance	E.	Assets − Liabilities
____	7. Payable	F.	Record of transactions
____	8. Journal	G.	Always an asset
____	9. Receivable	H.	Left side of an account
____	10. Owners' equity	I.	Side of an account where increases are recorded
		J.	Copying data from the journal to the ledger

S2-13 (*Learning Objective 5: Analyzing transactions without a journal*) Seventh Investments, Inc., began by issuing common stock for cash of $140,000. The company immediately purchased computer equipment on account for $100,000.

1. Set up the following T-accounts of Seventh Investments, Inc.: Cash, Computer Equipment, Accounts Payable, Common Stock.
2. Record the first two transactions of the business directly in the T-accounts without using a journal.
3. Show that total debits equal total credits.

Exercises

All of the A and B exercises can be found within MyAccountingLab, an online homework and practice environment. Your instructor may ask you to complete these exercises using MyAccountingLab.

MyAccountingLab

(Group A)

E2-14A (*Learning Objectives 1, 2: Analyzing transactions*) Assume M. Crew opened a store in Dallas, starting with cash and common stock of $94,000. Melissa Farino, the store manager, then signed a note payable to purchase land for $88,000 and a building for $123,000. Farino also paid $60,000 for equipment and $8,000 for supplies to use in the business.

writing assignment ■

Suppose the home office of M. Crew requires a weekly report from store managers. Write Farino's memo to the home office to report on her purchases. Include the store's balance sheet as the final part of your memo. Prepare a T-account to compute the balance for Cash.

E2-15A (*Learning Objective 1: Analyzing transactions*) The following selected events were experienced by either Solution Seekers, Inc., a corporation, or Paul Flynn, the major stockholder. State whether each event (1) increased, (2) decreased, or (3) had no effect on the total assets of the business. Identify any specific asset affected.

    a. Received $9,200 cash from customers on account.
    b. Flynn used personal funds to purchase a swimming pool for his home.
    c. Sold land and received cash of $65,000 (the land was carried on the company's books at $65,000).
    d. Borrowed $60,000 from the bank.
    e. Made cash purchase of land for a building site, $90,000.
    f. Received $25,000 cash and issued stock to a stockholder.
    g. Paid $70,000 cash on accounts payable.
    h. Purchased equipment and signed a $101,000 promissory note in payment.
    i. Purchased merchandise inventory on account for $17,000.
    j. The business paid Flynn a cash dividend of $5,000.

E2-16A (*Learning Objective 1: Analyzing transactions; using the accounting equation*) Harry Samson opened a medical practice specializing in surgery. During the first month of operation (March), the business, titled Harry Samson, Professional Corporation (P.C.), experienced the following events:

Mar	6	Samson invested $42,000 in the business, which in turn issued its common stock to him.
	9	The business paid cash for land costing $25,000. Samson plans to build an office building on the land.
	12	The business purchased medical supplies for $16,000 on account.
	15	Harry Samson, P.C., officially opened for business.
	15–31	During the rest of the month, Samson treated patients and earned service revenue of $7,700, receiving cash for half the revenue earned.
	15–31	The business paid cash expenses: employee salaries, $900; office rent, $900; utilities, $200.
	31	The business sold supplies to another physician for cost of $200.
	31	The business borrowed $18,000, signing a note payable to the bank.
	31	The business paid $1,100 on account.

❙ *Requirements*

  1. Analyze the effects of these events on the accounting equation of the medical practice of Harry Samson, P.C.
  2. After completing the analysis, answer these questions about the business.
    a. How much are total assets?
    b. How much does the business expect to collect from patients?
    c. How much does the business owe in total?
    d. How much of the business's assets does Samson really own?
    e. How much net income or net loss did the business experience during its first month of operations?

E2-17A (*Learning Objectives 2, 3: Understanding how accounting works; journalizing transactions*) Refer to Exercise 2-16A.

❙ *Requirement*

  1. Record the transactions in the journal of Harry Samson, P.C. List the transactions by date and give an explanation for each transaction.

E2-18A (*Learning Objectives 2, 3: Understanding how accounting works; journalizing transactions*) Harris Tree Cellular, Inc., completed the following transactions during April 2010, its first month of operations:

■ general ledger

Apr	1	Received $19,100 and issued common stock.
	2	Purchased $300 of office supplies on account.
	4	Paid $14,700 cash for land to use as a building site.
	6	Performed service for customers and received cash of $2,700.
	9	Paid $200 on accounts payable.
	17	Performed service for ShipEx on account totaling $1,000.
	23	Collected $200 from ShipEx on account.
	30	Paid the following expenses: salary, $1,300; rent, $500.

I Requirement

1. Record the transactions in the journal of Harris Tree Cellular, Inc. Key transactions by date and include an explanation for each entry.

E2-19A (*Learning Objectives 3, 4: Posting to the ledger; preparing and using a trial balance*) Refer to Exercise 2-18A.

■ general ledger

I Requirements

1. After journalizing the transactions of Exercise 2-18A, post the entries to the ledger, using T-accounts. Key transactions by date. Date the ending balance of each account April 30.
2. Prepare the trial balance of Harris Tree Cellular, Inc., at April 30, 2010.
3. How much are total assets, total liabilities, and total stockholders' equity on April 30?

E2-20A (*Learning Objectives 2, 3: Understanding how accounting works; journalizing transactions*) The first seven transactions of Fournier Advertising, Inc., have been posted to the company's accounts as follows:

Cash					Supplies				Equipment				Land	
(1)	10,200	(3)	6,000	(4)	500	(5)	150	(6)	5,100			(3)	30,000	
(2)	6,900	(6)	5,100											
(5)	150	(7)	100											

Accounts Payable				Note Payable			Common Stock		
(7)	100	(4)	500	(2)	6,900		(1)	10,200	
				(3)	24,000				

I Requirement

1. Prepare the journal entries that served as the sources for the seven transactions. Include an explanation for each entry. As Fournier moves into the next period, how much cash does the business have? How much does Fournier owe in total liabilities?

E2-21A (*Learning Objective 4: Preparing and using a trial balance*) The accounts of Deluxe Deck Service, Inc., follow with their normal balances at June 30, 2010. The accounts are listed in no particular order.

Account	Balance	Account	Balance
Common stock..................	$ 8,400	Dividends..........................	$ 6,100
Accounts payable..............	4,400	Utilities expense	2,100
Service revenue.................	22,400	Accounts receivable...........	15,900
Land.................................	29,800	Delivery expense	700
Note payable....................	10,500	Retained earnings..............	25,600
Cash.................................	8,500	Salary expense..................	8,200

❚ Requirements

1. Prepare the company's trial balance at June 30, 2010, listing accounts in proper sequence, as illustrated in the chapter. For example, Accounts Receivable comes before Land. List the expense with the largest balance first, the expense with the next largest balance second, and so on.

2. Prepare the financial statement for the month ended June 30, 2010, that will tell the company the results of operations for the month.

E2-22A *(Learning Objective 4: Correcting errors in a trial balance)* The trial balance of Carver, Inc., at September 30, 2010, does not balance:

Cash....................................	$ 4,500	
Accounts receivable...............	13,100	
Inventory..............................	16,600	
Supplies................................	200	
Land.....................................	52,000	
Accounts payable..................		$11,900
Common stock.......................		47,500
Service revenue.....................		30,500
Salary expense.......................	1,700	
Rent expense.........................	1,100	
Utilities expense	900	
Total....................................	$90,100	$89,900

The accounting records hold the following errors:

a. Recorded a $400 cash revenue transaction by debiting Accounts Receivable. The credit entry was correct.

b. Posted a $3,000 credit to Accounts Payable as $300.

c. Did not record utilities expense or the related account payable in the amount of $500.

d. Understated Common Stock by $500.

e. Omitted Insurance Expense of $3,000, from the trial balance.

❚ Requirement

1. Prepare the correct trial balance at September 30, 2010, complete with a heading. Journal entries are not required.

E2-23A *(Learning Objective 5: Recording transactions without a journal)* Set up the following T-accounts: Cash, Accounts Receivable, Office Supplies, Office Furniture, Accounts Payable, Common Stock, Dividends, Service Revenue, Salary Expense, and Rent Expense. Record the following transactions directly in the T-accounts without using a journal. Use the letters to identify the transactions.

a. Linda Oxford opened a law firm by investing $12,000 cash and office furniture valued at $8,600. Organized as a professional corporation, the business issued common stock to Oxford.

b. Paid monthly rent of $1,000.

c. Purchased office supplies on account, $700.

d. Paid employees' salaries of $2,000.

e. Paid $300 of the account payable created in Transaction c.

f. Performed legal service on account, $8,100.

g. Declared and paid dividends of $2,900.

writing assignment ■ **E2-24A** *(Learning Objective 4: Preparing and using a trial balance)* Refer to Exercise 2-23A.

1. After recording the transactions in Exercise 2-23A, prepare the trial balance of Linda Oxford, Attorney, at May 31, 2010. Use the T-accounts that have been prepared for the business.

2. How well did the business perform during its first month? Compute net income (or net loss) for the month.

(Group B)

E2-25B *(Learning Objectives 1, 2: Analyzing transactions)* Assume T. Crew opened a store in San Diego, starting with cash and common stock of $90,000. Barbara Breen, the store manager, then signed a note payable to purchase land for $91,000 and a building for $120,000. Breen also paid $62,000 for equipment and $13,000 for supplies to use in the business.

writing assignment ■

Suppose the home office of T. Crew requires a weekly report from store managers. Write Breen's memo to the head office to report on her purchases. Include the store's balance sheet as the final part of your memo. Prepare a T-account to compute the balance for Cash.

E2-26B *(Learning Objective 1: Analyzing transactions)* The following selected events were experienced by either Simple Solutions, Inc., a corporation, or Bob Gallagher, the major stockholder. State whether each event (1) increased, (2) decreased, or (3) had no effect on the total assets of the business. Identify any specific asset affected.

    a. Received $30,000 cash and issued stock to a stockholder.
    b. Purchased equipment for $75,000 cash.
    c. Paid $10,000 cash on accounts payable.
    d. Gallagher used personal funds to purchase a flat screen TV for his home.
    e. Purchased land for a building site and signed an $80,000 promissory note to the bank.
    f. Received $17,000 cash from customers for services performed.
    g. Sold land and received a note receivable of $55,000 (the land was carried on the company's books at $55,000).
    h. Earned $25,000 in revenue for services performed. The customer promises to pay Simple Solutions in one month.
    i. Purchased supplies on account for $5,000.
    j. The business paid Gallagher a cash dividend of $4,000.

E2-27B *(Learning Objective 1: Analyzing transactions; using the accounting equation)* Kyle Cohen opened a medical practice specializing in surgery. During the first month of operation (July), the business, titled Kyle Cohen, Professional Corporation (P.C.), experienced the following events:

Jul	6	Cohen invested $44,000 in the business, which in turn issued its common stock to him.
	9	The business paid cash for land costing $31,000. Cohen plans to build an office building on the land.
	12	The business purchased medical supplies for $1,700 on account.
	15	Kyle Cohen, P.C., officially opened for business.
	15–31	During the rest of the month, Cohen treated patients and earned service revenue of $7,600, receiving cash for half the revenue earned.
	15–31	The business paid cash expenses: employee salaries, $800; office rent, $800; utilities, $300.
	31	The business sold supplies to another physician for cost of $400.
	31	The business borrowed $16,000, signing a note payable to the bank.
	31	The business paid $700 on account.

I Requirements

  1. Analyze the effects of these events on the accounting equation of the medical practice of Kyle Cohen, P.C.
  2. After completing the analysis, answer these questions about the business.
    a. How much are total assets?
    b. How much does the business expect to collect from patients?
    c. How much does the business owe in total?
    d. How much of the business's assets does Cohen really own?
    e. How much net income or net loss did the business experience during its first month of operations?

E2-28B *(Learning Objectives 2, 3: Understanding how accounting works; journalizing transactions)* Refer to Exercise 2-27B.

I Requirement

1. Record the transactions in the journal of Kyle Cohen, P.C. List the transactions by date and give an explanation for each transaction.

E2-29B *(Learning Objectives 2, 3: Understanding how accounting works; journalizing transactions)* Green Tree Cellular, Inc., completed the following transactions during April 2010, its first month of operations:

Apr	1	Received $19,600 and issued common stock.
	2	Purchased $900 of office supplies on account.
	4	Paid $14,600 cash for land to use as a building site.
	6	Performed service for customers and received cash of $2,500.
	9	Paid $200 on accounts payable.
	17	Performed service for **UPS** on account totaling $1,200.
	23	Collected $900 from **UPS** on account.
	30	Paid the following expenses: salary, $1,900; rent, $1,400.

I Requirement

1. Record the transactions in the journal of Green Tree Cellular, Inc. Key transactions by date and include an explanation for each entry.

E2-30B *(Learning Objectives 3, 4: Posting to the ledger; preparing and using a trial balance)* Refer to Exercise 2-29B.

I Requirements

1. Post the entries to the ledger, using T-accounts. Key transactions by date. Date the ending balance of each account April 30.
2. Prepare the trial balance of Green Tree Cellular, Inc., at April 30, 2010.
3. How much are total assets, total liabilities, and total shareholders' equity on April 30?

E2-31B *(Learning Objectives 2, 3: Understanding how accounting works; journalizing transactions)* The first seven transactions of Portman Advertising, Inc., have been posted to the company's accounts as follows:

Cash				Supplies				Equipment			Land	
(1)	9,700	(3)	5,000	(4)	500	(5)	80	(6)	6,000		(3)	30,000
(2)	6,700	(6)	6,000									
(5)	80	(7)	90									

Accounts Payable				Note Payable			Common Stock	
(7)	90	(4)	500		(2)	6,700	(1)	9,700
					(3)	25,000		

I Requirement

1. Prepare the journal entries that served as the sources for the seven transactions. Include an explanation for each entry. As Portman moves into the next period, how much cash does the business have? How much does Portman owe in total liabilities?

E2-32B (*Learning Objective 4: Preparing and using a trial balance*) The accounts of Grand Pool Service, Inc., follow with their normal balances at June 30, 2010. The accounts are listed in no particular order.

Account	Balance	Account	Balance
Common stock...................	$ 8,000	Dividends...........................	$ 6,300
Accounts payable	4,500	Utilities expense	1,600
Service revenue..................	22,800	Accounts receivable...........	15,300
Land................................	29,400	Delivery expense	200
Note payable.....................	10,500	Retained earnings..............	24,600
Cash.................................	9,400	Salary expense...................	8,200

I Requirements

1. Prepare the company's trial balance at June 30, 2010, listing accounts in proper sequence, as illustrated in the chapter. For example, Accounts Receivable comes before Land. List the expense with the largest balance first, the expense with the next largest balance second, and so on.
2. Prepare the financial statement for the month ended June 30, 2010, that will tell the company the results of operations for the month.

E2-33B (*Learning Objective 4: Correcting errors in a trial balance*) The trial balance of Farris, Inc., at June 30, 2010, does not balance.

Cash..	$ 4,100	
Accounts receivable...............	13,300	
Inventory...............................	16,500	
Supplies.................................	700	
Land.......................................	53,000	
Accounts payable		$12,400
Common stock.......................		47,800
Service revenue......................		31,900
Salary expense.......................	2,200	
Rent expense.........................	600	
Utilities expense	300	
Total......................................	$90,700	$92,100

The accounting records hold the following errors:

    a. Recorded a $200 cash revenue transaction by debiting Accounts Receivable. The credit entry was correct.
    b. Posted a $2,000 credit to Accounts Payable as $200.
    c. Did not record utilities expense or the related account payable in the amount of $300.
    d. Understated Common Stock by $100.
    e. Omitted Insurance Expense of $3,300, from the trial balance.

I Requirement

1. Prepare the correct trial balance at June 30, 2010, complete with a heading. Journal entries are not required.

E2-34B (*Learning Objective 5: Recording transactions without a journal*) Set up the following T-accounts: Cash, Accounts Receivable, Office Supplies, Office Furniture, Accounts Payable, Common Stock, Dividends, Service Revenue, Salary Expense, and Rent Expense. Record the following transactions directly in the T-accounts without using a journal. Use the letters to identify the transactions.

    a. Linda Conway opened a law firm by investing $11,000 cash and office furniture valued at $9,100. Organized as a professional corporation, the business issued common stock to Conway.

    b. Paid monthly rent of $1,200.

    c. Purchased office supplies on account, $700.

    d. Paid employee salaries of $2,200.

    e. Paid $300 of the accounts payable created in Transaction c.

    f. Performed legal service on account, $8,300.

    g. Declared and paid dividends of $2,100.

E2-35B (*Learning Objective 4: Preparing and using a trial balance*) Refer to Exercise 2-34B.

❙ Requirements

    1. Prepare the trial balance of Linda Conway, Attorney, at January 31, 2010. Use the T-accounts that have been prepared for the business.

    2. How well did the business perform during its first month? Compute net income (or net loss) for the month.

Serial Exercise

Exercise 2-36 begins an accounting cycle that is completed in Chapter 3.

❙ general ledger

E2-36 (*Learning Objectives 2, 3, 4: Recording transactions; preparing a trial balance*) Jerome Smith, Certified Public Accountant, operates as a professional corporation (P.C.). The business completed these transactions during the first part of March, 2010:

Mar	2	Received $7,000 cash from Smith, and issued common stock to him.
	2	Paid monthly office rent, $600.
	3	Paid cash for a Dell computer, $2,400, with the computer expected to remain in service for five years.
	4	Purchased office furniture on account, $7,500, with the furniture projected to last for five years.
	5	Purchased supplies on account, $500.
	9	Performed tax service for a client and received cash for the full amount of $1,200.
	12	Paid utility expenses, $300.
	18	Performed consulting service for a client on account, $2,100.

❙ Requirements

    1. Journalize the transactions. Explanations are not required.

    2. Post to the T-accounts. Key all items by date and denote an account balance on March 18, 2010, as Bal.

    3. Prepare a trial balance at March 18, 2010. In the Serial Exercise of Chapter 3, we add transactions for the remainder of March and will require a trial balance at March 31.

Challenge Exercises

E2-37 (*Learning Objective 5: Computing financial statement amounts*) The manager of Pierce Furniture needs to compute the following amounts.

    a. Total cash paid during October.

    b. Cash collections from customers during October. Analyze Accounts Receivable.

    c. Cash paid on a note payable during October. Analyze Notes Payable.

Here's the additional data you need to analyze the accounts:

| | Balance | | Additional Information |
Account	Sep 30	Oct 31	for the Month of October
1. Cash..............................	$11,000	$ 6,000	Cash receipts, $83,000
2. Accounts Receivable.......	28,000	26,000	Sales on account, $47,000
3. Notes Payable	15,000	23,000	New borrowing, $24,000

I Requirement

1. Prepare a T-account to compute each amount, *a* through *c*.

E2-38 (*Learning Objectives 1, 4: Analyzing transactions; using a trial balance*) The trial balance of Circle 360, Inc., at October 31, 2010, does not balance.

Cash...................................	$ 4,400	Common stock....................	$20,700	
Accounts receivable.............	6,800	Retained earnings................	7,800	
Land...................................	34,000	Service revenue...................	9,000	
Accounts payable	6,300	Salary expense....................	3,200	
Note payable......................	5,400	Advertising expense............	1,000	

I Requirements

1. How much out of balance is the trial balance? Determine the out-of-balance amount. The error lies in the Accounts Receivable account. Add the out-of-balance amount to, or subtract it from, Accounts Receivable to determine the correct balance of Accounts Receivable.
2. After correcting Accounts receivable, advise the top management of Circle 360, Inc., on the company's
   a. total assets.
   b. total liabilities.
   c. net income or net loss for October.

E2-39 (*Learning Objective 1: Analyzing transactions*) This question concerns the items and the amounts that two entities, Nashua Co., and Ditka Hospital, should report in their financial statements.

During September, Ditka provided Nashua with medical exams for Nashua employees and sent a bill for $46,000. On October 7, Nashua sent a check to Ditka for $34,000. Nashua began September with a cash balance of $57,000; Ditka began with cash of $0.

I Requirements

1. For this situation, show everything that both Nashua and Ditka will report on their September and October income statements and on their balance sheets at September 30 and October 31.
2. After showing what each company should report, briefly explain how the Nashua and Ditka data relate to each other.

Quiz

Test your understanding of transaction analysis by answering the following questions. Select the best choice from among the possible answers.

Q2-40 An investment of cash into the business will
a. decrease total liabilities.
b. decrease total assets.
c. have no effect on total assets.
d. increase stockholders' equity.

Q2-41 Purchasing a laptop computer on account will
a. increase total liabilities.
b. have no effect on stockholders' equity.
c. increase total assets.
d. all of the above.

Q2-42 Performing a service on account will
a. increase stockholders' equity.
b. increase total assets.
c. increase total liabilities.
d. both a and b.

Q2-43 Receiving cash from a customer on account will
a. increase total assets.
b. decrease liabilities.
c. increase stockholders equity.
d. have no effect on total assets.

Q2-44 Purchasing computer equipment for cash will
a. decrease both total assets and stockholders' equity.
b. increase both total assets and total liabilities.
c. have no effect on total assets, total liabilities, or stockholders' equity.
d. decrease both total liabilities and stockholders' equity.

Q2-45 Purchasing a building for $110,000 by paying cash of $15,000 and signing a note payable for $95,000 will
a. increase both total assets and total liabilities by $95,000.
b. increase both total assets and total liabilities by $110,000.
c. decrease both total assets and total liabilities by $15,000.
d. decrease total assets and increase total liabilities by $15,000.

Q2-46 What is the effect on total assets and stockholders' equity of paying the telephone bill as soon as it is received each month?

Total assets	Stockholders' equity
a. No effect	No effect
b. Decrease	No effect
c. No effect	Decrease
d. Decrease	Decrease

Q2-47 Which of the following transactions will increase an asset and increase a liability?
a. Purchasing office equipment for cash
b. Issuing stock
c. Payment of an account payable
d. Buying equipment on account

Q2-48 Which of the following transactions will increase an asset and increase stockholders' equity?
a. Borrowing money from a bank
b. Purchasing supplies on account
c. Performing a service on account for a customer
d. Collecting cash from a customer on an account receivable

Q2-49 Where do we first record a transaction?
a. Journal
b. Trial balance
c. Account
d. Ledger

Q2-50 Which of the following is not an asset account?
a. Salary Expense
b. Service Revenue
c. Common Stock
d. None of the above accounts is an asset.

Q2-51 Which statement is false?
a. Assets are increased by debits.
b. Revenues are increased by credits.
c. Liabilities are decreased by debits.
d. Dividends are increased by credits.

Q2-52 The journal entry to record the receipt of land and a building and issuance of common stock
a. debits Land and credits Common Stock.
b. debits Land and Building and credits Common Stock.
c. debits Land, Building, and Common Stock.
d. debits Common Stock and credits Land and Building.

Q2-53 The journal entry to record the purchase of supplies on account
a. debits Supplies and credits Accounts Payable.
b. credits Supplies and debits Cash.
c. credits Supplies and debits Accounts Payable.
d. debits Supplies Expense and credits Supplies.

Q2-54 If the credit to record the purchase of supplies on account is not posted,
a. expenses will be overstated.
b. liabilities will be understated.
c. stockholders' equity will be understated.
d. assets will be understated.

Q2-55 The journal entry to record a payment on account will
a. debit Cash and credit Expenses.
b. debit Accounts Payable and credit Retained Earnings.
c. debit Accounts Payable and credit Cash.
d. debit Expenses and credit Cash.

Q2-56 If the credit to record the payment of an account payable is not posted,
a. expenses will be understated.
b. liabilities will be understated.
c. cash will be understated.
d. cash will be overstated.

Q2-57 Which statement is false?
a. A trial balance is the same as a balance sheet.
b. A trial balance can verify the equality of debits and credits.
c. A trial balance can be taken at any time.
d. A trial balance lists all the accounts with their current balances.

Q2-58 A business's receipt of a $120,000 building, with a $60,000 mortgage payable, and issuance of $60,000 of common stock will
a. increase stockholders' equity by $60,000.
b. increase assets by $60,000.
c. decrease assets by $60,000.
d. increase stockholders' equity by $120,000.

Q2-59 Gartex, a new company, completed these transactions. What will Gartex's total assets equal?
(1) Stockholders invested $54,000 cash and inventory worth $27,000.
(2) Sales on account, $15,000.
a. $66,000
b. $69,000
c. $96,000
d. $81,000

Problems

> All of the A and B problems can be found within MyAccountingLab, an online homework and practice environment. Your instructor may ask you to complete these problems using MyAccountingLab.

(Group A)

writing assignment ■

P2-60A (*Learning Objective 4: Analyzing a trial balance*) The trial balance of Luxury Specialties, Inc., follows.

Luxury Specialties Trial Balance December 31, 2010		
Cash..	$ 11,000	
Accounts receivable...............	48,000	
Prepaid expenses....................	5,000	
Equipment.............................	239,000	
Building..................................	105,000	
Accounts payable...................		$108,000
Note payable..........................		90,000
Common stock........................		35,000
Retained earnings...................		38,000
Dividends...............................	19,000	
Service revenue.......................		257,000
Rent expense..........................	28,000	
Advertising expense...............	4,000	
Wage expense.........................	61,000	
Supplies expense....................	8,000	
Total	$528,000	$528,000

Ashley Richards, your best friend, is considering investing in Luxury Specialties, Inc. Ashley seeks your advice in interpreting this information. Specifically, she asks how to use this trial balance to compute the company's total assets, total liabilities, and net income or net loss for the year.

❙ Requirement

1. Write a short note to answer Ashley's questions. In your note, state the amounts of Luxury Specialties' total assets, total liabilities, and net income or net loss for the year. Also show how you computed each amount.

P2-61A (*Learning Objective 1: Analyzing transactions with the accounting equation; preparing the financial statements*) The following amounts summarize the financial position of Mason Resources, Inc., on May 31, 2010:

		Assets					=	Liabilities	+	Stockholders' Equity		
	Cash	+	Accounts Receivable	+	Supplies	+	Land	=	Accounts Payable	+	Common Stock	+	Retained Earnings
Bal	1,150		1,350				11,900		7,600		4,400		2,400

During June 2010, Mason Resources completed these transactions:

a. The business received cash of $9,200 and issued common stock.
b. Performed services for a customer and received cash of $6,700.
c. Paid $4,500 on accounts payable.
d. Purchased supplies on account, $600.
e. Collected cash from a customer on account, $700.
f. Consulted on the design of a computer system and billed the customer for services rendered, $2,900.
g. Recorded the following business expenses for the month: (1) paid office rent—$1,100; (2) paid advertising—$1,000.
h. Declared and paid a cash dividend of $1,500.

❙ Requirements

1. Analyze the effects of the preceding transactions on the accounting equation of Mason Resources, Inc.
2. Prepare the income statement of Mason Resources, Inc., for the month ended June 30, 2010. List expenses in decreasing order by amount.
3. Prepare the entity's statement of retained earnings for the month ended June 30, 2010.
4. Prepare the balance sheet of Mason Resources, Inc., at June 30, 2010.

P2-62A (*Learning Objectives 2, 3: Recording transactions; posting*) This problem can be used in conjunction with Problem 2-61A. Refer to Problem 2-61A.

■ **general ledger**

❙ Requirements

1. Journalize the June transactions of Mason Resources, Inc. Explanations are not required.
2. Prepare T-Accounts for each account. Insert in each T-account its May 31 balance as given (example: Cash $1,150). Then, post the June transactions to the T-Accounts.
3. Compute the balance in each account.

P2-63A (*Learning Objectives 1, 2, 3: Analyzing transactions; understanding how accounting works; journalizing transactions*) Demers Real Estate Co. experienced the following events during the organizing phase and its first month of operations. Some of the events were personal for the stockholders and did not affect the business. Others were transactions of the business.

Nov	4	David Demers, the major stockholder of real estate company, received $100,000 cash from an inheritance.
	5	Demers deposited $57,000 cash in a new business bank account titled Demers Real Estate Co. The business issued common stock to Demers.
	6	The business paid $600 cash for letterhead stationery for the new office.
	7	The business purchased office equipment. The company paid cash of $12,000 and agreed to pay the account payable for the remainder, $8,000, within three months.
	10	Demers sold EVN stock, which he had owned for several years, receiving $76,500 cash from his stockbroker.
	11	Demers deposited the $76,500 cash from sale of the EVN stock in his personal bank account.
	12	A representative of a large company telephoned Demers and told him of the company's intention to transfer $15,500 of business to Demers.
	18	Demers finished a real estate deal for a client and submitted his bill for services, $3,500. Demers expects to collect from the client within two weeks.
	21	The business paid half its account payable on the equipment purchased on November 7.
	25	The business paid office rent of $1,300.
	30	The business declared and paid a cash dividend of $1,900.

❚ Requirements

1. Classify each of the preceding events as one of the following:

    a. A business-related event but not a transaction to be recorded by Demers Real Estate Co.

    b. A business transaction for a stockholder, not to be recorded by Demers Real Estate Co.

    c. A business transaction to be recorded by Demers Real Estate Co.

2. Analyze the effects of the preceding events on the accounting equation of Demers Real Estate Co.

3. Record the transactions of the business in its journal. Include an explanation for each entry.

■ general ledger

P2-64A (*Learning Objectives 2, 3: Understanding how accounting works; analyzing and recording transactions*) During December, Smith Auction Co. completed the following transactions:

Dec 1	Smith received $26,000 cash and issued common stock to the stockholders.
5	Paid monthly rent, $1,100.
9	Paid $8,500 cash and signed a $30,000 note payable to purchase land for an office site.
10	Purchased supplies on account, $1,700.
19	Paid $600 on account.
22	Borrowed $20,000 from the bank for business use. Smith signed a note payable to the bank in the name of the business.
31	Service revenue earned during the month included $12,000 cash and $8,000 on account.
31	Paid employees' salaries ($2,400), advertising expense ($1,500), and utilities expense ($1,400).
31	Declared and paid a cash dividend of $6,500.

Smith's business uses the following accounts: Cash, Accounts Receivable, Supplies, Land, Accounts Payable, Notes Payable, Common Stock, Dividends, Service Revenue, Salary Expense, Advertising Expense, and Utilities Expense.

❚ Requirements

1. Journalize each transaction of Smith Auction Co. Explanations are not required.

2. Post to these T-accounts: Cash, Accounts Payable, and Notes Payable.

3. After these transactions, how much cash does the business have? How much in total liabilities does it owe?

■ general ledger

P2-65A (*Learning Objectives 2, 3, 4: Understanding how accounting works; journalizing transactions; posting; preparing and using a trial balance*) During the first month of operations, Simmons Heating and Air Conditioning, Inc., completed the following transactions:

Jan 2	Simmons received $39,000 cash and issued common stock to the stockholders.
3	Purchased supplies, $200, and equipment, $3,100, on account.
4	Performed service for a customer and received cash, $1,600.
7	Paid cash to acquire land, $27,000.
11	Performed service for a customer and billed the customer, $900. We expect to collect within one month.
16	Paid for the equipment purchased January 3 on account.
17	Paid the telephone bill, $170.
18	Received partial payment from customer on account, $450.
22	Paid the water and electricity bills, $190.
29	Received $1,400 cash for servicing the heating unit of a customer.
31	Paid employee salary, $2,400.
31	Declared and paid dividends of $3,000.

❙ Requirements

1. Record each transaction in the journal. Key each transaction by date. Explanations are not required.
2. Post the transactions to the T-accounts, using transaction dates as posting references. Label the ending balance of each account Bal, as shown in the chapter.
3. Prepare the trial balance of Simmons Heating and Air Conditioning, Inc., at January 31 of the current year.
4. The manager asks you how much in total resources the business has to work with, how much it owes, and whether January was profitable (and by how much).

P2-66A (*Learning Objectives 4, 5: Recording transactions directly in T-accounts; preparing and using a trial balance*) During the first month of operations (November 2010), Stein Services Corporation completed the following selected transactions:

■ **general ledger**

    a. The business received cash of $28,000 and a building valued at $52,000. The corporation issued common stock to the stockholders.
    b. Borrowed $37,300 from the bank; signed a note payable.
    c. Paid $33,000 for music equipment.
    d. Purchased supplies on account, $500.
    e. Paid employees' salaries, $2,500.
    f. Received $1,600 for music service performed for customers.
    g. performed service for customers on account, $3,200.
    h. Paid $100 of the account payable created in Transaction d.
    i. Received an $800 bill for utility expense that will be paid in the near future.
    j. Received cash on account, $1,200.
    k. Paid the following cash expenses: (1) rent, $1,200; (2) advertising, $700.

❙ Requirements

1. Record each transaction directly in the T-accounts without using a journal. Use the letters to identify the transactions.
2. Prepare the trial balance of Stein Services Corporation at November 30, 2010.

(Group B)

P2-67B (*Learning Objective 4: Analyzing a trial balance*) The trial balance of Advantage Specialties, Inc., follows:

writing assignment ■

Advantage Specialties, Inc. **Trial Balance** **December 31, 2010**		
Cash..	$ 11,000	
Accounts receivable................	49,000	
Prepaid expenses	5,000	
Equipment..............................	234,000	
Building...................................	96,000	
Accounts payable		$102,000
Note payable...........................		95,000
Common stock........................		34,000
Retained earnings....................		36,000
Dividends...............................	23,000	
Service revenue.......................		252,000
Rent expense..........................	25,000	
Advertising expense................	4,000	
Wage expense.........................	65,000	
Supplies expense.....................	7,000	
Total	$519,000	$519,000

Rebecca Smith, your best friend, is considering making an investment in Advantage Specialties, Inc. Rebecca seeks your advice in interpreting the company's information. Specifically, she asks how to use this trial balance to compute the company's total assets, total liabilities, and net income or net loss for the year.

I Requirement

1. Write a short note to answer Rebecca's questions. In your note, state the amounts of Advantage Specialties' total assets, total liabilities, and net income or net loss for the year. Also show how you computed each amount.

P2-68B (*Learning Objective 1: Analyzing transactions with the accounting equation; preparing the financial statements*) The following amounts summarize the financial position of Rodriguez Resources on May 31, 2010:

	Cash	+	Accounts Receivable	+	Supplies	+	Land	=	Accounts Payable	+	Common Stock	+	Retained Earnings
					Assets			=	**Liabilities**	+	**Stockholders' Equity**		
Bal	1,450		1,650				11,500		7,800		4,000		2,800

During June, 2010, the business completed these transactions:

- **a.** Rodriguez Resources received cash of $8,600 and issued common stock.
- **b.** Performed services for a customer and received cash of $6,500.
- **c.** Paid $4,700 on accounts payable.
- **d.** Purchased supplies on account, $600.
- **e.** Collected cash from a customer on account, $200.
- **f.** Consulted on the design of a computer system and billed the customer for services rendered, $2,700.
- **g.** Recorded the following expenses for the month: (1) paid office rent—$900; (2) paid advertising—$800.
- **h.** Declared and paid a cash dividend of $2,300.

I Requirements

1. Analyze the effects of the preceding transactions on the accounting equation of Rodriguez Resources, Inc.
2. Prepare the income statement of Rodriguez Resources, Inc., for the month ended June 30, 2010. List expenses in decreasing order by amount.
3. Prepare the statement of retained earnings of Rodriguez Resources, Inc., for the month ended June 30, 2010.
4. Prepare the balance sheet of Rodriguez Resources, Inc., at June 30, 2010.

■ general ledger

P2-69B (*Learning Objectives 2, 3: Understanding how accounting works; journalizing transactions; posting*) This problem can be used in conjunction with Problem 2-68B. Refer to Problem 2-68B.

I Requirements

1. Journalize the transactions of Rodriguez Resources, Inc. Explanations are not required.
2. Prepare T-accounts for each account. Insert in each T-account its May 31 balance as given (example: Cash $1,450). Then, post the June transactions to the T-accounts.
3. Compute the balance in each account.

P2-70B (*Learning Objectives 1, 2, 3: Analyzing transactions; understanding how accounting works; journalizing transactions*) Smith Real Estate Co. experienced the following events during the organizing phase and its first month of operations. Some of the events were personal for the stockholders and did not affect the business. Others were transactions of the business.

Nov	4	John Smith, the major stockholder of real estate company, received $108,000 cash from an inheritance.
	5	Smith deposited $59,000 cash in a new business bank account titled Smith Real Estate Co. The business issued common stock to Smith.
	6	The business paid $500 cash for letterhead stationery for the new office.
	7	The business purchased office equipment. The company paid cash of $12,000 and agreed to pay the account payable for the remainder, $8,500, within three months.
	10	Smith sold DLD stock, which he owned for several years, receiving $74,000 cash from his stockbroker.
	11	Smith deposited the $74,000 cash from sale of the DLD stock in his personal bank account.
	12	A representative of a large company telephoned Smith and told him of the company's intention to transfer $12,500 of business to Smith.
	18	Smith finished a real estate deal for a client and submitted his bill for services, $3,000. Smith expects to collect from the client within two weeks.
	21	The business paid half its account payable for the equipment purchased on November 7.
	25	The business paid office rent of $500.
	30	The business declared and paid a cash dividend of $1,700.

I Requirements

1. Classify each of the preceding events as one of the following:
   a. A business-related event but not a transaction to be recorded by Smith Real Estate Co.
   b. A business transaction for a stockholder, not to be recorded by Smith Real Estate Co.
   c. A business transaction to be recorded by the Smith Real Estate Co.
2. Analyze the effects of the preceding events on the accounting equation of Smith Real Estate Co.
3. Record the transactions of the business in its journal. Include an explanation for each entry.

P2-71B (*Learning Objectives 2, 3: Analyzing and recording transactions*) During December, Swanson Auction Co. completed the following transactions:

■ **general ledger**

Dec	1	Swanson received $28,000 cash and issued common stock to the stockholders.
	5	Paid monthly rent, $2,000
	9	Paid $11,500 cash and signed a $33,000 note payable to purchase land for an office site.
	10	Purchased supplies on account, $1,700.
	19	Paid $800 on account.
	22	Borrowed $18,500 from the bank for business use. Swanson signed a note payable to the bank in the name of the business.
	31	Service revenue earned during the month included $14,500 cash and $4,500 on account.
	31	Paid employees' salaries ($2,100), advertising expense ($1,000), and utilities expense ($1,100).
	31	Declared and paid a cash dividend of $2,000.

Swanson's business uses the following accounts: Cash, Accounts Receivable, Supplies, Land, Accounts Payable, Notes Payable, Common Stock, Dividends, Service Revenue, Salary Expense, Rent Expense, Advertising Expense, and Utilities Expense.

I Requirements

1. Journalize each transaction of Swanson Auction Co. Explanations are not required.
2. Post to these T-accounts: Cash, Accounts Payable, and Notes Payable.
3. After these transactions, how much cash does the business have? How much does it owe in total liabilities?

■ **general ledger**

P2-72B (*Learning Objectives 2, 3, 4: Understanding how accounting works; journalizing transactions; posting; preparing and using a trial balance*) During the first month of operations, O'Shea Plumbing, Inc., completed the following transactions:

Jan	2	O'Shea received $33,000 cash and issued common stock to the stockholders.
	3	Purchased supplies, $400, and equipment, $2,900, on account.
	4	Performed service for a client and received cash, $1,700.
	7	Paid cash to acquire land, $22,000.
	11	Performed service for a customer and billed the customer, $1,100. We expect to collect within one month.
	16	Paid for the equipment purchased January 3 on account.
	17	Paid the telephone bill, $130.
	18	Received partial payment from customer on account, $550.
	22	Paid the water and electricity bills, $150.
	29	Received $1,100 cash for servicing the heating unit of a customer.
	31	Paid employee salary, $2,300.
	31	Declared and paid dividends of $2,900.

I Requirements

1. Record each transaction in the journal. Key each transaction by date. Explanations are not required.
2. Post the transactions to the T-accounts, using transaction dates as posting references.
3. Prepare the trial balance of O'Shea Plumbing, Inc., at January 31 of the current year.
4. The manager asks you how much in total resources the business has to work with, how much it owes, and whether January was profitable (and by how much).

P2-73B (*Learning Objectives, 4, 5: Recording transactions directly in T-accounts; preparing and using a trial balance*) During the first month of operations (March 2010), Silver Entertainment Corporation completed the following selected transactions:

a. The business received cash of $32,000 and a building valued at $52,000. The corporation issued common stock to the stockholders.
b. Borrowed $35,800 from the bank; signed a note payable.
c. Paid $32,000 for music equipment.
d. Purchased supplies on account, $200.
e. Paid employees' salaries, $2,300.
f. Received $1,700 for music service performed for customers.
g. Performed service for customers on account, $2,800.
h. Paid $100 of the account payable created in Transaction d.
i. Received a $900 bill for advertising expense that will be paid in the near future.
j. Received cash on account, $1,600.
k. Paid the following cash expenses: (1) rent, $1,200; (2) advertising, $800.

I Requirements

1. Record each transaction directly in the T-accounts without using a journal. Use the letters to identify the transactions.
2. Prepare the trial balance of Silver Entertainment Corporation, at March 31, 2010.

APPLY YOUR KNOWLEDGE

Decision Cases

Case 1. (*Learning Objectives 4, 5: Recording transactions directly in T-accounts; preparing a trial balance; measuring net income or loss*) A friend named Jay Barlow has asked what effect certain transactions will have on his company. Time is short, so you cannot apply the detailed procedures of journalizing and posting. Instead, you must analyze the transactions without the use of a journal. Barlow will continue the business only if he can expect to earn monthly net income of at least $5,000. The following transactions occurred this month:

   a. Barlow deposited $5,000 cash in a business bank account, and the corporation issued common stock to him.

   b. Borrowed $5,000 cash from the bank and signed a note payable due within 1 year.

   c. Paid $1,300 cash for supplies.

   d. Purchased advertising in the local newspaper for cash, $1,800.

   e. Purchased office furniture on account, $4,400.

   f. Paid the following cash expenses for 1 month: employee salary, $2,000; office rent, $1,200.

   g. Earned revenue on account, $7,000.

   h. Earned revenue and received $2,500 cash.

   i. Collected cash from customers on account, $1,200.

   j. Paid on account, $1,000.

❙ Requirements

1. Set up the following T-accounts: Cash, Accounts Receivable, Supplies, Furniture, Accounts Payable, Notes Payable, Common Stock, Service Revenue, Salary Expense, Advertising Expense, and Rent Expense.

2. Record the transactions directly in the accounts without using a journal. Key each transaction by letter.

3. Prepare a trial balance for Barlow Networks, Inc., at the current date. List expenses with the largest amount first, the next largest amount second, and so on.

4. Compute the amount of net income or net loss for this first month of operations. Why or why not would you recommend that Barlow continue in business?

Case 2. (*Learning Objective 2: Correcting financial statements; deciding whether to expand a business*) Sophia Loren opened an Italian restaurant. Business has been good, and Loren is considering expanding the restaurant. Loren, who knows little accounting, produced the following financial statements for Little Italy, Inc., at December 31, 2011, end of the first month of operations:

Little Italy, Inc. Income Statement Month Ended December 31, 2011	
Sales revenue	$42,000
Common stock	10,000
Total revenue	52,000
Accounts payable	$ 8,000
Advertising expense	5,000
Rent expense	6,000
Total expenses	19,000
Net income	$33,000

Little Italy, Inc. Balance Sheet December 31, 2011	
Assets	
Cash	$12,000
Cost of goods sold (expense)	22,000
Food inventory	5,000
Furniture	10,000
Total Assets	$49,000
Liabilities	
None	
Owners' Equity	$49,000

In these financial statements all *amounts* are correct, except for Owners' Equity. Loren heard that total assets should equal total liabilities plus owners' equity, so she plugged in the amount of owners' equity at $49,000 to make the balance sheet come out even.

❙ Requirement

1. Sophia Loren has asked whether she should expand the restaurant. Her banker says Loren may be wise to expand if (a) net income for the first month reached $10,000 and (b) total assets are at least $35,000. It appears that the business has reached these milestones, but Loren doubts whether her financial statements tell the true story. She needs your help in making this decision. Prepare a corrected income statement and balance sheet. (Remember that Retained Earnings, which was omitted from the balance sheet, should equal net income for the first month; there were no dividends.) After preparing the statements, give Sophia Loren your recommendation as to whether she should expand the restaurant.

Ethical Issues

Issue 1. Scruffy Murphy is the president and principal stockholder of Scruffy's Bar & Grill, Inc. To expand, the business is applying for a $250,000 bank loan. To get the loan, Murphy is considering two options for beefing up the owners' equity of the business:

Option 1. Issue $100,000 of common stock for cash. A friend has been wanting to invest in the company. This may be the right time to extend the offer.

Option 2. Transfer $100,000 of Murphy's personal land to the business, and issue common stock to Murphy. Then, after obtaining the loan, Murphy can transfer the land back to himself and zero out the common stock.

❙ Requirements

Use the ethical decision model in Chapter 1 to answer the following questions:

1. What is the ethical issue?
2. Who are the stakeholders? What are the possible consequences to each?
3. Analyze the alternatives from the following standpoints (a) economic, (b) legal, and (c) ethical
4. What would you do? How would you justify your decision? How would your decision make you feel afterward?

Issue 2. Part a. You have received your grade in your first accounting course, and to your amazement, it is an A. You feel the instructor must have made a big mistake. Your grade was a B going into the final, but you are sure that you really "bombed" the exam, which is worth 30% of the final grade. In fact, you walked out after finishing only 50% of the exam, and the grade report says you made 99% on the exam!

❙ Requirements

1. What is the ethical issue?
2. Who are the stakeholders? What are the possible consequences to each?
3. Analyze the alternatives from the following standpoints: (a) economic, (b) legal, and (c) ethical.
4. What would you do? How would you justify your decision? How would it make you feel afterward?

Part b. Now assume the same facts as above, except that you have received your final grade for the course and the grade is a B. You are confident that you "aced" the final. In fact, you stayed to the very end of the period, and checked every figure twice! You are confident that the instructor must have made a mistake grading the final.

❙ Requirements

1. What is the ethical issue?
2. Who are the stakeholders and what are the consequences to each?

3. Analyze the alternatives from the following standpoints: (a) economic, (b) legal, and (c) ethical.
4. What would you do? How would you justify your decision? How would it make you feel?

Part c. How is this situation like a financial accounting misstatement? How is it different?

Focus on Financials: ■ Amazon.com, Inc.

(*Learning Objectives 3, 4: Recording transactions; computing net income*) Refer to **Amazon.com, Inc.'s** financial statements in Appendix A at the end of the book. Assume that Amazon.com completed the following selected transactions during 2008.

   a. Made company sales (revenue) of $19,166 million, all on account (debit accounts receivable).
   b. Collected cash on accounts receivable $19,044.
   c. Purchased inventories, paying cash of $15,095 million.
   d. Incurred cost of sales in the amount of $14,896 million. Debit the Cost of sales (expense) account. Credit the Inventories account.
   e. Paid operating expenses of $3,428 million.
   f. Collected non-operating income (net) in cash, $59 million.
   g. Paid income taxes $247 million (debit provision for income taxes).
   h. Accounted for other investment activity net of taxes in the amount of $9 million. Debit equity method investment activity, net of taxes. Credit other assets.
   i. Paid cash for other assets, $103 million.

❙ *Requirements*

1. Set up T-accounts for: Cash (beginning debit balance of $2,539 million); Accounts Receivable, net and other (debit balance of $705 million); Inventories (debit balance $1,200 million); Other Assets ($0 balance); Net Sales ($0 balance); Cost of Sales ($0 balance); Operating expenses ($0 balance); Non-operating income (expense), net ($0 balance); Provision for income taxes ($0 balance); Equity method investment activity, net of tax ($0 balance).
2. Journalize Amazon.com's transactions a–i. Explanations are not required.
3. Post to the T-accounts, and compute the balance for each account. Key postings by transaction letters a–i.
4. For each of the following accounts, compare your computed balance to Amazon.com, Inc.'s actual balance as shown on its 2008 Consolidated Statement of Operations or Consolidated Balance Sheet in Appendix A. Your amounts should agree to the actual figures.

   a. Cash
   b. Accounts Receivable, net and other
   c. Inventories
   d. Net Sales
   e. Cost of sales
   f. Operating expenses
   g. Non-operating income (expenses), net
   h. Provision for income taxes
   i. Equity method investment activity, net of tax
5. Use the relevant accounts from requirement 4 to prepare a summary income statement for Amazon.com, Inc., for 2008. Compare the net income you computed to Amazon.com, Inc.'s actual net income. The two amounts should be equal.

Focus on Analysis: ■ Foot Locker, Inc.

(*Learning Objectives 1, 2: Analyzing a leading company's financial statements*) Refer to the **Foot Locker, Inc.**, financial statements in Appendix B at the end of the book. Suppose you are an investor considering buying Foot Locker, Inc., common stock. The following questions are important: **Show amounts in millions and round to the nearest $1 million**.

1. Explain whether Foot Locker, Inc., had more sales revenue, or collected more cash from customers, during 2007. Why is accounts receivable missing from its balance sheet? (Challenge)

2. Investors are vitally interested in a company's sales and profits, and its trends of sales and profits over time. Consider Foot Locker's sales and net income (net loss) during the period from 2005 through 2007. Compute the percentage increase or decrease in net sales and also in net income (net loss) from 2005 to 2007. Which item grew faster during this two-year period, net sales or net income (net loss)? Can you offer a possible explanation for these changes? (Challenge)

Group Projects

Project 1. You are promoting a rock concert in your area. Your purpose is to earn a profit, so you need to establish the formal structure of a business entity. Assume you organize as a corporation.

▌ *Requirements*

1. Make a detailed list of 10 factors you must consider as you establish the business.
2. Describe 10 of the items your business must arrange to promote and stage the rock concert.
3. Identify the transactions that your business can undertake to organize, promote, and stage the concert. Journalize the transactions, and post to the relevant T-accounts. Set up the accounts you need for your business ledger. Refer to Appendix D at the end of the book if needed.
4. Prepare the income statement, statement of retained earnings, and balance sheet immediately after the rock concert, that is, before you have had time to pay all the business bills and to collect all receivables.
5. Assume that you will continue to promote rock concerts if the venture is successful. If it is unsuccessful, you will terminate the business within three months after the concert. Discuss how to evaluate the success of your venture and how to decide whether to continue in business.

Project 2. Contact a local business and arrange with the owner to learn what accounts the business uses.

▌ *Requirements*

1. Obtain a copy of the business's chart of accounts.
2. Prepare the company's financial statements for the most recent month, quarter, or year. You may use either made-up account balances or balances supplied by the owner.

If the business has a large number of accounts within a category, combine related accounts and report a single amount on the financial statements. For example, the company may have several cash accounts. Combine all cash amounts and report a single Cash amount on the balance sheet.

You will probably encounter numerous accounts that you have not yet learned. Deal with these as best you can. The charts of accounts given in Appendix D at the end of the book can be helpful.

For online homework, exercises, and problems that provide you with immediate feedback, please visit www.myaccountinglab.com.

Quick Check Answers

1. *b*	5. *c*	8. *c*	11. *d*
2. *d*	6. *a*	9. *c*	12. *d*
3. *b*	7. *a* ($9,000 + x −$	10. *c*	
4. *c* ($1,600 +	$25,000 = 11,000;$		
900 − 300)	$x = 27,000$)		

Demo Doc

Debit/Credit Transaction Analysis

To make sure you understand this material, work through the following demonstration "Demo Doc" with detailed comments to help you see the concept within the framework of a worked-through problem.

Learning Objectives 1, 2, 3, 4

On September 1, 2010, Michael Moe incorporated Moe's Mowing, Inc., a company that provides mowing and landscaping services. During the month of September, the business incurred the following transactions:

a. To begin operations, Michael deposited $10,000 cash in the business's bank account. The business received the cash and issued common stock to Michael.

b. The business purchased equipment for $3,500 on account.

c. The business purchased office supplies for $800 cash.

d. The business provided $2,600 of services to a customer on account.

e. The business paid $500 cash toward the equipment previously purchased on account in transaction b.

f. The business received $2,000 in cash for services provided to a new customer.

g. The business paid $200 cash to repair equipment.

h. The business paid $900 cash in salary expense.

i. The business received $2,100 cash from a customer on account.

j. The business paid cash dividends of $1,500.

Requirements

1. Create blank T-accounts for the following accounts: Cash, Accounts Receivable, Supplies, Equipment, Accounts Payable, Common Stock, Dividends, Service Revenue, Salary Expense, Repair Expense.

2. Journalize the transactions and then post to the T-accounts. Use the table in Exhibit 2-16 to help with the journal entries.

EXHIBIT 2-16 | The Rules of Debit and Credit

	Increase	Decrease
Assets	debit	credit
Liabilities	credit	debit
Stockholders' Equity	credit	debit
Revenues	credit	debit
Expenses	debit	credit
Dividends	debit	credit

3. Total each T-account to determine its balance at the end of the month.

4. Prepare the trial balance of Moe's Mowing, Inc., at September 30, 2010.

Demo Doc Solutions

Requirement 1

Create blank T-accounts for the following accounts: Cash, Accounts Receivable, Supplies, Equipment, Accounts Payable, Common Stock, Dividends, Service Revenue, Salary Expense, Repair Expense.

Part 1	Part 2	Part 3	Part 4	Demo Doc Complete

Opening a T-account means drawing a blank account that looks like a capital "T" and putting the account title across the top. T-accounts show the additions and subtractions made to each account. For easy reference, the accounts are grouped into assets, liabilities, stockholders' equity, revenue, and expenses (in that order).

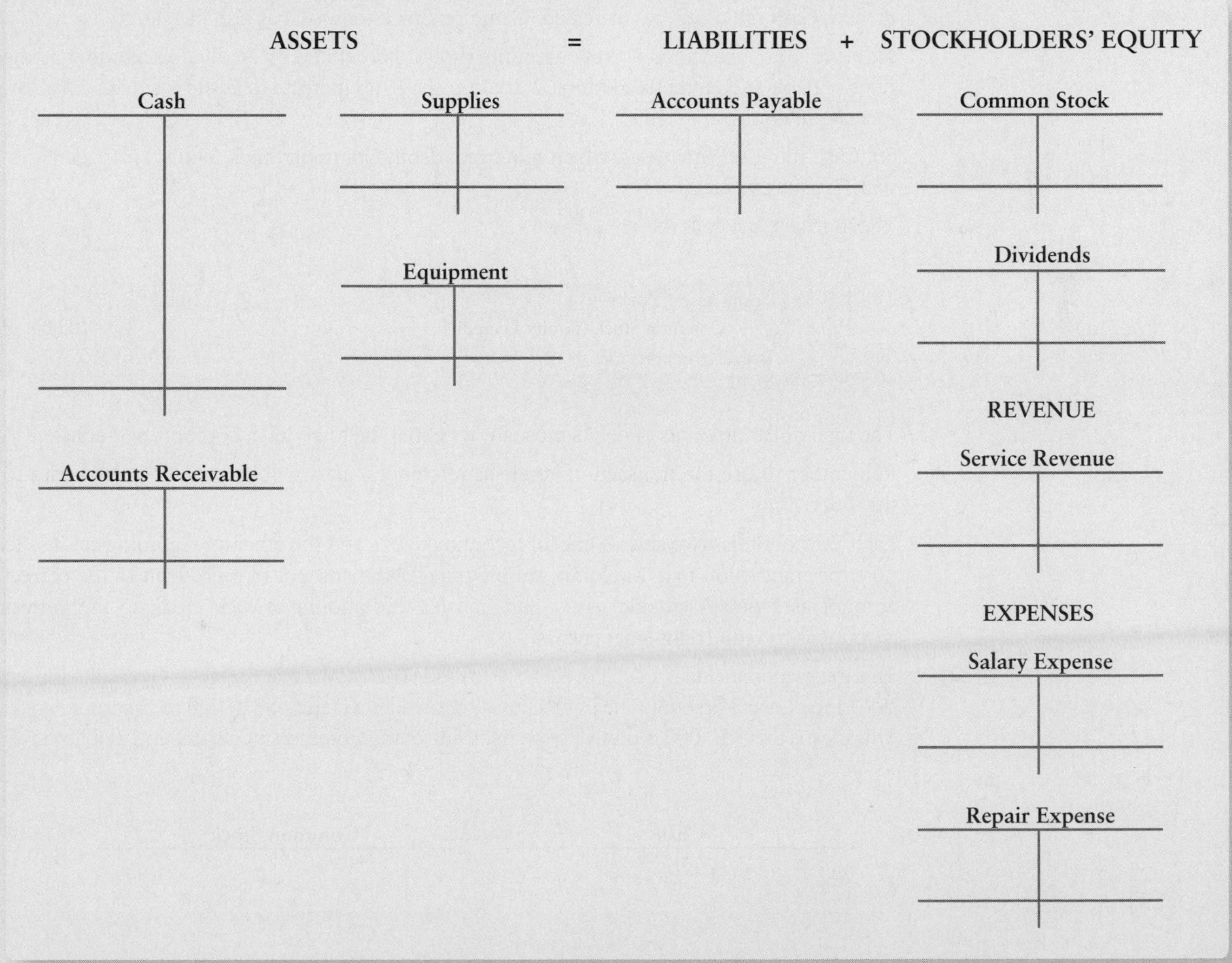

ASSETS   =   LIABILITIES   +   STOCKHOLDERS' EQUITY

Cash

Supplies

Accounts Payable

Common Stock

Equipment

Dividends

REVENUE

Accounts Receivable

Service Revenue

EXPENSES

Salary Expense

Repair Expense

Requirement 2

Journalize the transactions and show how they are recorded in T-accounts.

Part 1	**Part 2**	Part 3	Part 4	Demo Doc Complete

a. To begin operations, Michael deposited $10,000 cash in the business's bank account. The business received the cash and issued common stock to Michael.

First, we must determine which accounts are affected by the transaction.

The business received $10,000 cash from its principal stockholder (Michael Moe). In exchange, the business issued common stock to Michael. So, the accounts involved are Cash and Common Stock.

Remember that we are recording the transactions of Moe's Mowing, Inc., not the transactions of Michael Moe, the person. Michael and his business are two entirely separate accounting entities.

The next step is to determine what type of accounts these are. Cash is an asset, Common Stock is part of equity.

Next, we must determine if these accounts increased or decreased. From the business's point of view, Cash (an asset) has increased. Common Stock (equity) has also increased.

Now we must determine if these accounts should be debited or credited. According to the rules of debit and credit (see Exhibit 2-16 on p. 124), an increase in assets is a debit, while an increase in equity is a credit.

So, Cash (an asset) increases, which requires a debit. Common Stock (equity) also increases, which requires a credit.

The journal entry follows.

a.	Cash (Asset ↑; debit)	10,000	
	Common Stock (Equity ↑; credit)		10,000
	Issued common stock.		

The total dollar amounts of debits must always equal the total dollar amounts of credits.

Remember to use the transaction letters as references. This will help as we post entries to the T-accounts.

Each T-account has two sides—one for recording debits and the other for recording credits. To post the transaction to a T-account, simply transfer the amount of each debit to the correct account as a debit (left-side) entry, and transfer the amount of each credit to the correct account as a credit (right-side) entry.

This transaction includes a debit of $10,000 to cash. This means that $10,000 is posted to the left side of the Cash T-account. The transaction also includes a credit of $10,000 to Common Stock. This means that $10,000 is posted to the right side of the Common Stock account, as follows:

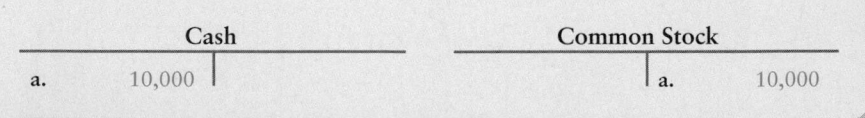

	Cash			Common Stock	
a.	10,000			a.	10,000

Now the first transaction has been journalized and posted. We repeat this process for every journal entry. Let's proceed to the next transaction.

126   Chapter 2   Transaction Analysis

b. The business purchased equipment for $3,500 on account.

The business received equipment in exchange for a promise to pay for the $3,500 cost at a future date. So the accounts involved in the transaction are Equipment and Accounts Payable.

Equipment is an asset and Accounts Payable is a liability.

The asset Equipment has increased. The liability Accounts Payable has also increased.

Looking at Exhibit 2-16, an increase in assets (in this case, the increase in Equipment) is a debit, while an increase in liabilities (in this case, Accounts Payable) is a credit.

The journal entry follows.

b.	Equipment (Asset ↑; debit)	3,500	
	Accounts Payable (Liability ↑; credit)		3,500
	Purchased equipment on account.		

$3,500 is then posted to the debit (left) side of the Equipment T-account. $3,500 is posted to the credit (right) side of Accounts Payable, as follows:

	Equipment			Accounts Payable	
b.	3,500			b.	3,500

c. The business purchased office supplies for $800 cash.

The business purchased supplies, paying cash of $800. So the accounts involved in the transaction are Supplies and Cash.

Supplies and Cash are both assets.

Supplies (an asset) has increased. Cash (an asset) has decreased.

Looking at Exhibit 2-16, an increase in assets is a debit, while a decrease in assets is a credit.

So the increase to Supplies (an asset) is a debit, while the decrease to Cash (an asset) is a credit.

The journal entry follows:

c.	Supplies (Asset ↑; debit)	800	
	Cash (Asset ↓; credit)		800
	Purchased supplies for cash.		

$800 is then posted to the debit (left) side of the Supplies T-account. $800 is posted to the credit (right) side of the Cash account, as follows:

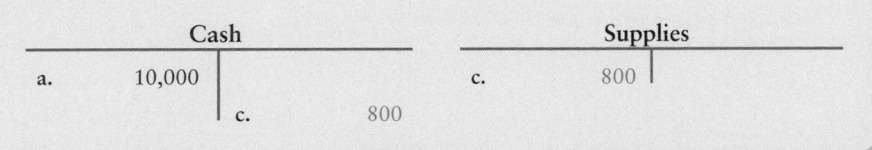

	Cash			Supplies	
a.	10,000		c.	800	
		c. 800			

Notice the $10,000 already on the debit side of the Cash account. This came from transaction a.

d. The business provided $2,600 of services to a customer on account.

The business rendered service for a customer and received a promise from the customer to pay us $2,600 cash next month. So the accounts involved in the transaction are Accounts Receivable and Service Revenue.

Accounts Receivable is an asset and Service Revenue is revenue.

Accounts Receivable (an asset) has increased. Service Revenue (revenue) has also increased.

Looking at Exhibit 2-16, an increase in assets is a debit, while an increase in revenue is a credit.

So the increase to Accounts Receivable (an asset) is a debit, while the increase to Service Revenue (revenue) is a credit.

The journal entry follows.

d.	Accounts Receivable (Asset ↑; debit)	2,600	
	Service Revenue (Revenue ↑; credit)		2,600
	Provided services on account.		

$2,600 is posted to the debit (left) side of the Accounts Receivable T-account. $2,600 is posted to the credit (right) side of the Service Revenue account, as follows:

Accounts Receivable		Service Revenue	
d. 2,600			**d.** 2,600

e. The business paid $500 cash toward the equipment previously purchased on account in transaction b.

The business paid some of the money that it owed on the purchase of equipment in transaction b. The accounts involved in the transaction are Accounts Payable and Cash.

Accounts Payable is a liability that has decreased. Cash is an asset that has also decreased.

Remember that Accounts Payable shows the amount the business must pay in the future (a liability). When the business pays these creditors, Accounts Payable will decrease because the business will then owe less (in this case, Accounts Payable drops from $3,500—in transaction b—to $3,000).

Looking at Exhibit 2-16, a decrease in liabilities is a debit, while a decrease in assets is a credit.

So Accounts Payable (a liability) decreases, which is a debit. Cash (an asset) decreases, which is a credit.

e.	Accounts Payable (Liability ↓; debit)	500	
	Cash (Asset ↓; credit)		500
	Partial payment on account.		

$500 is posted to the debit (left) side of the Accounts Payable T-account. $500 is posted to the credit (right) side of the Cash account, as follows:

Cash				Accounts Payable			
a.	10,000					b.	3,500
		c.	800	e.	500		
		e.	500				

Again notice the amounts already in the T-accounts from previous transactions. The reference letters show which transaction caused each amount to appear in the T-account.

f. The business received $2,000 in cash for services provided to a new customer.

The business received $2,000 cash in exchange for mowing and landscaping services rendered to a customer. The accounts involved in the transaction are Cash and Service Revenue.

Cash is an asset that has increased and Service Revenue is revenue, which has also increased.

Looking at Exhibit 2-16, an increase in assets is a debit, while an increase in revenue is a credit.

So the increase to Cash (an asset) is a debit. The increase to Service Revenue (revenue) is a credit.

f.	Cash (Asset ↑; debit)	2,000	
	Service Revenue (Revenue ↑; credit)		2,000
	Provided services for cash.		

$2,000 is then posted to the debit (left) side of the Cash T-account. $2,000 is posted to the credit (right) side of the Service Revenue account, as follows:

Cash				Service Revenue			
a.	10,000					d.	2,600
		c.	800			f.	2,000
		e.	500				
f.	2,000						

Notice how we keep adding onto the T-accounts. The values from previous transactions remain in their places.

g. The business paid $200 cash to repair equipment.

The business paid $200 cash to have equipment repaired. Because the benefit of the repairs has already been used, the repairs are recorded as Repair Expense. Because the repairs were paid in cash, the Cash account is also involved.

Repair Expense is an expense that has increased and Cash is an asset that has decreased.

Looking at Exhibit 2-16, an increase in expenses calls for a debit, while a decrease in an asset requires a credit.

So Repair Expense (an expense) increases, which is a debit. Cash (an asset) decreases, which is a credit.

g.	Repair Expense (Expense ↑ ; debit)	200	
	Cash (Asset ↓; credit)		200
	Paid for repairs.		

$200 is then posted to the debit (left) side of the Repair Expense T-account. $200 is posted to the credit (right) side of the Cash account, as follows:

	Cash					Repair Expense	
a.	10,000				g.	200	
		c.	800				
		e.	500				
f.	2,000						
		g.	200				

h. The business paid $900 cash for salary expense.

The business paid employees $900 in cash. Because the benefit of the employees' work has already been used, their salaries are recorded as Salary Expense. Because the salaries were paid in cash, the Cash account is also involved.

Salary Expense is an expense that has increased and Cash is an asset that has decreased.

Looking at Exhibit 2-16, an increase in expenses is a debit, while a decrease in an asset is a credit.

In this case, Salary Expense (an expense) increases, which is a debit. Cash (an asset) decreases, which is a credit.

h.	Salary Expense (Expense ↑; debit)	900	
	Cash (Asset ↓; credit)		900
	Paid salary.		

$900 is posted to the debit (left) side of the Salary Expense T-account. $900 is posted to the credit (right) side of the Cash account, as follows:

	Cash				Salary Expense	
a.	10,000			h.	900	
		c.	800			
		e.	500			
f.	2,000					
		g.	200			
		h.	900			

i. The business received $2,100 cash from a customer on account.

The business received cash of $2,100 from a customer for services previously provided in transaction d. The accounts affected by this transaction are Cash and Accounts Receivable.

Cash and Accounts Receivable are both assets.

The asset Cash has increased, and the asset Accounts Receivable has decreased.

Remember, Accounts Receivable shows the amount of cash the business has coming from customers. When the business receives cash from these customers, Accounts Receivable will decrease, because the business will have less to receive in the future (in this case, it reduces from $2,600—in transaction d—to $500).

Looking at Exhibit 2-16, an increase in assets is a debit, while a decrease in assets is a credit.

So Cash (an asset) increases, which is a debit. Accounts Receivable (an asset) decreases, which is a credit.

i.	Cash (Asset ↑; debit)	2,100	
	Accounts Receivable (Asset ↓; credit)		2,100
	Received cash on account.		

$2,100 is posted to the debit (left) side of the Cash T-account. $2,100 is posted to the credit (right) side of the Accounts Receivable account, as follows:

	Cash				Accounts Receivable	
a.	10,000			d.	2,600	
		c.	800			i.	2,100
		e.	500			
f.	2,000					
		g.	200			
		h.	900			
i.	2,100					

j. The business declared and paid cash dividends of $1,500.

The business paid Michael dividends from the earnings it had retained on his behalf. This caused Michael's ownership interest (equity) to decrease. The accounts involved in this transaction are Dividends and Cash.

Dividends have increased and Cash is an asset that has decreased.

Looking at Exhibit 2-16, an increase in dividends is a debit, while a decrease in an asset is a credit.

Remember that Dividends are a negative element of stockholders' equity. Therefore, when Dividends increase, stockholders' equity decreases. So in this case, Dividends decrease equity with a debit. Cash (an asset) decreases with a credit.

j.	Dividends (Dividends ↑; debit) ↓SE	1,500	
	Cash (Asset ↓; credit)		1,500
	Paid dividends.		

$1,500 is posted to the debit (left) side of the Dividends T-account. $1,500 is posted to the credit (right) side of the Cash account, as follows:

	Cash					Dividends	
a.	10,000				j.	1,500	
		c.	800				
		e.	500				
f.	2,000						
		g.	200				
		h.	900				
i.	2,100						
		j.	1,500				

Now we can summarize all of the journal entries during the month.

Ref.		Accounts and Explanation	Debit	Credit
a.		Cash	10,000	
		Common Stock		10,000
		Issued common stock.		
b.		Equipment	3,500	
		Accounts Payable		3,500
		Purchased equipment on account.		
c.		Supplies	800	
		Cash		800
		Purchased supplies for cash.		
d.		Accounts Receivable	2,600	
		Service Revenue		2,600
		Provided services on account.		
e.		Accounts Payable	500	
		Cash		500
		Partial payment on account.		
f.		Cash	2,000	
		Service Revenue		2,000
		Provided services for cash.		
g.		Repair Expense	200	
		Cash		200
		Paid for repairs.		
h.		Salary Expense	900	
		Cash		900
		Paid salary.		
i.		Cash	2,100	
		Accounts Receivable		2,100
		Received cash on account.		
j.		Dividends	1,500	
		Cash		1,500
		Paid dividends.		

Requirement 3

Total each T-account to determine its balance at the end of the month.

Part 1	Part 2	**Part 3**	Part 4	Demo Doc Complete

To compute the balance in a T-account (total the T-account), add up the numbers on the debit/left side of the account and (separately) add the credit/right side of the account. The difference between the total debits and the total credits is the account's balance, which is placed on the side that holds the larger total. This gives the balance in the T-account.

For example, for the Cash account, the numbers on the debit/left side total $10,000 + $2,000 + $2,100 = $14,100. The credit/right side = $800 + $500 + $200 + $900 + $1,500 = $3,900. The difference is $14,100 – $3,900 = $10,200. At the end of the period Cash has a debit balance of $10,200. We put the $10,200 at the bottom of the debit side because that was the side that showed the bigger total ($14,100). This is called a debit balance.

An easy way to think of totaling T-accounts is:

> Beginning balance in a T-account
>
> + Increases to the T-account
>
> – Decreases to the T-account
>
> T-account balance (net total)

T-accounts after posting all transactions and totaling each account are as follows:

	ASSETS		=	LIABILITIES	+	STOCKHOLDERS' EQUITY

Cash

a.	10,000		
		c.	800
		e.	500
f.	2,000		
		g.	200
		h.	900
i.	2,100		
		j.	1,500
Bal	10,200		

Accounts Receivable

d.	2,600		
		i.	2,100
Bal	500		

Supplies

c.	800	
Bal	800	

Equipment

b.	3,500	
Bal	3,500	

Accounts Payable

		b.	3,500
e.	500		
		Bal	3,000

Common Stock

		a.	10,000
		Bal	10,000

Dividends

j.	1,500	
Bal	1,500	

REVENUE

Service Revenue

		d.	2,600
		f.	2,000
		Bal	4,600

EXPENSES

Salary Expense

h.	900	
Bal	900	

Repair Expense

g.	200	
Bal	200	

Requirement 4

| Part 1 | Part 2 | Part 3 | **Part 4** | Demo Doc Complete |

The trial balance lists all the accounts along with their balances. This listing is helpful because it summarizes all the accounts in one place. Otherwise one must plow through all the T-accounts to find the balance of Accounts Payable, Salary Expense, or any other account.

The trial balance is an *internal* accounting document that accountants and managers use to prepare the financial statements. It's not like the income statement and balance sheet, which are presented to the public.

Data for the trial balance come directly from the T-accounts that we prepared in Requirement 3. A debit balance in a T-account remains a debit in the trial balance, and likewise for credits. For example, the T-account for Cash shows a debit balance of $10,200, and the trial balance lists Cash the same way. The Accounts Payable T-account shows a $3,000 credit balance, and the trial balance lists Accounts Payable correctly.

The trial balance for Moe's Mowing at September 30, 2010, appears as follows. Notice that we list the accounts in their proper order—assets, liabilities, stockholder's equity, revenues, and expenses.

Moe's Mowing, Inc.
Trial Balance
September 30, 2010

		Balance	
		Debit	Credit
Assets	Cash	$10,200	
	Accounts receivable	500	
	Supplies	800	
	Equipment	3,500	
Liabilities	Accounts payable...................		$ 3,000
Equity	Common stock		10,000
	Dividends..............................	1,500	
Revenues	Service revenue		4,600
Expenses	Salary expense	900	
	Repair expense......................	200	
	Total	$17,600	$17,600

You should trace each account from the T-accounts to the trial balance.

| Part 1 | Part 2 | Part 3 | Part 4 | Demo Doc Complete |

3

Accrual Accounting & Income

SPOTLIGHT: Starbucks Corporation

Starbucks has changed coffee from a breakfast drink to an experience. The corporation began in Seattle, Washington, in 1985 and now has over 10,000 locations in the United States alone, with almost 2,000 more abroad.

As you can see from Starbucks' Consolidated Statement of Earnings on the next page, the company sold over $10 billion of coffee and related products during the 2008 fiscal year. The company translated that revenue into about $316 million in profits. That's a lot of coffee!

But at Starbucks, the motto is "it's bigger than coffee." *Ethisphere* magazine has named Starbucks one of the 100 most ethical companies in the world. During the holiday season each year, the company donates five cents from every cup of certain specialty drinks to help feed starving HIV patients in Africa, where some of its coffee is grown. Through its Web site, the company also provides ways for customers to partner with Starbucks in donating to this and other worthy causes. The company sponsors community improvement projects for its coffee farmers in Central America and Africa. It has also developed standards for environmentally, socially, and economically responsible coffee-buying guidelines to help assure better prices for farmers who do business with it. Starbucks works with Conservation International to encourage coffee growers to use sustainable farming practices that help protect the environment. The company is developing reusable and recyclable cups. It also sponsors employee programs that contribute hundreds of thousands of service hours to the communities where Starbucks stores operate. All of these ethical practices cost money, which can be hard to justify during difficult economic times. But Starbucks is committed to using its resources for good as well as for gain. Think about that when you buy that next latte.

Starbucks Corporation
Consolidated Statement of Earnings (Adapted)
Year Ended September 28, 2008

	(In millions)
Revenues:	
Net operating revenues	$10,383
Other income	70
Total net revenues	10,453
Expenses:	
Cost of sales (cost of goods sold)	4,646
Store operating expenses	3,745
Other operating expenses	597
Depreciation and amortization expenses	549
General and administrative expenses	456
Total operating expenses	9,993
Income before income tax	460
Income tax expense	144
Net income	$ 316

This chapter completes our coverage of the accounting cycle. It gives the basics of what you need before tackling individual topics such as receivables, inventory, and cash flows.

LEARNING OBJECTIVES

1 **Relate** accrual accounting and cash flows

2 **Apply** the revenue and matching principles

3 **Adjust** the accounts

4 **Prepare** the financial statements

5 **Close** the books

6 **Use** two new ratios to evaluate a business

For more practice and review of accounting cycle concepts, use ACT, the accounting Cycle Tutorial, online at www.myaccountinglab.com. Margin logos like this one, directing you to the appropriate ACT section and material, appear throughout Chapters 1, 2, and 3. When you enter the tutorial, you'll find three buttons on the opening page of each chapter module. Here's what the buttons mean: **Tutorial** gives you a review of the major concepts, **Application** gives you practice exercises, and **Glossary** reviews important terms.

ACCRUAL ACCOUNTING VERSUS CASH-BASIS ACCOUNTING

Managers want to earn a profit. Investors search for companies whose stock prices will increase. Banks seek borrowers who'll pay their debts. Accounting provides the information these people use for decision making. Accounting can be based on either the

- accrual basis, or the
- cash basis.

Accrual accounting records the impact of a business transaction as it occurs. When the business performs a service, makes a sale, or incurs an expense, the accountant records the transaction even if it receives or pays no cash.

Cash-basis accounting records only cash transactions—cash receipts and cash payments. Cash receipts are treated as revenues, and cash payments are handled as expenses.

Generally accepted accounting principles (GAAP) require accrual accounting. The business records revenues as the revenues are earned and expenses as the expenses are incurred—not necessarily when cash changes hands. Consider a sale on account. Which transaction increases your wealth—making an $800 sale on account, or collecting the $800 cash? Making the sale increases your wealth by $300 because you gave up inventory that cost you $500 and you got a receivable worth $800. Collecting cash later merely swaps your $800 receivable for $800 cash—no gain on this transaction. Making the sale—not collecting the cash—increases your wealth.

The basic defect of cash-basis accounting is that the cash basis ignores important information. That makes the financial statements incomplete. The result? People using the statements make decisions based on incomplete information, which can lead to mistakes.

Suppose your business makes a sale *on account*. The cash basis does not record the sale because you received no cash. You may be thinking, "Let's wait until we collect cash and then record the sale. After all, we pay the bills with cash, so ignore transactions that don't affect cash."

What's wrong with this argument? There are two defects—one on the balance sheet and the other on the income statement.

Balance-Sheet Defect.   If we fail to record a sale on account, the balance sheet reports no account receivable. Why is this so bad? The receivable represents a claim to receive cash in the future, which is a real asset, and it should appear on the balance sheet. Without this information, assets are understated on the balance sheet.

Income-Statement Defect.   A sale on account provides revenue that increases the company's wealth. Ignoring the sale understates revenue and net income on the income statement.

The take-away lessons from this discussion are as follows:

- Companies that use the cash basis of accounting do not follow GAAP. Their financial statements omit important information.
- All but the smallest businesses use the accrual basis of accounting.

OBJECTIVE

1 **Relate** accrual accounting and cash flows

Accrual Accounting and Cash Flows

Accrual accounting is more complex—and, in terms of the Conceptual Foundations of Accounting (Exhibit 1-3), is a more faithful representation of economic reality—than cash-basis accounting. To be sure, accrual accounting records cash transactions, such as

- Collecting cash from customers
- Receiving cash from interest earned
- Paying salaries, rent, and other expenses
- Borrowing money
- Paying off loans
- Issuing stock

But accrual accounting also records *noncash* transactions, such as

- Sales on account
- Purchases of inventory on account
- Accrual of expenses incurred but not yet paid
- Depreciation expense
- Usage of prepaid rent, insurance, and supplies
- Earning of revenue when cash was collected in advance

Accrual accounting is based on a framework of additional concepts and principles to those we discussed in Chapter 1. We turn now to the time-period concept, the revenue principle, and the matching principle.

The Time-Period Concept

The only way for a business to know for certain how well it performed is to shut down, sell the assets, pay the liabilities, and return any leftover cash to the owners. This process, called liquidation, means going out of business. Ongoing companies can't wait until they go out of business to measure income! Instead, they need regular progress reports. Accountants, therefore, prepare financial statements for specific periods. The **time-period concept** ensures that accounting information is reported at regular intervals.

The basic accounting period is one year, and virtually all businesses prepare annual financial statements. Around 60% of large companies—including Amazon.com, eBay, and YUM! Brands—use the calendar year from January 1 through December 31.

A *fiscal* year ends on a date other than December 31. Most retailers, including Wal-Mart, J.Crew, and JCPenney, use a fiscal year that ends on or near January 31 because the low point in their business activity falls in January, after Christmas. Starbucks Corporation uses a fiscal year that ends on September 30.

Companies also prepare financial statements for interim periods of less than a year, such as a month, a quarter (three months), or a semiannual period (six months). Most of the discussions in this text are based on an annual accounting period.

The Revenue Principle

OBJECTIVE

2 **Apply** the revenue and matching principles

The **revenue principle** deals with two issues:

1. When to record revenue (make a journal entry); and
2. The amount of revenue to record.

When should you record revenue? After it has been earned—and not before. In most cases, revenue is earned when the business has delivered a good or service to a customer. It has done everything required to earn the revenue by transferring the good or service to the customer.

Revenue recognition is one of the areas in which a number of differences exist between U.S. GAAP and IFRS. Those differences deal with the two issues listed previously. U.S. GAAP is highly detailed and varies by industry. For example, the rules for timing and amount of revenue in the computer software industry differ from those in the construction industry. By contrast, IFRS is less detailed, leaving more room for interpretation on the part of the company. We will touch on these differences again in Chapter 11, where we discuss revenue in more detail. This book deals with retail businesses selling goods and services. Fortunately, in this industry, U.S. GAAP and IFRS are consistent with respect to general principles of revenue recognition.

Exhibit 3-1 shows two situations that provide guidance on when to record revenue for Starbucks Corporation. Situation 1 illustrates when not to record revenue. No transaction has occurred, so Starbucks Corporation records nothing. Situation 2 illustrates when revenue should be recorded—after a transaction has occurred.

EXHIBIT 3-1 | **When to Record Revenue**

The *amount* of revenue to record is the cash value of the goods or services transferred to the customer. Suppose that in order to promote business, Starbucks runs a promotion and sells lattes for the discount price of $2 per cup. Ordinarily Starbucks would charge $4 for this drink. How much revenue should Starbucks record? The answer is $2—the cash value of the transaction. The amount of the sale, $2, is the amount of revenue earned—not the regular price of $4.

The Matching Principle

The **matching principle** is the basis for recording expenses. Expenses are the costs of assets used up, and of liabilities created, in the earning of revenue. Expenses have no future benefit to the company. The matching principle includes two steps:

1. Identify all the expenses incurred during the accounting period.
2. Measure the expenses, and match expenses against the revenues earned.

To *match* expenses against revenues means to subtract expenses from revenues to compute net income or net loss. Exhibit 3-2 illustrates the matching principle.

EXHIBIT 3-2 | The Matching Principle

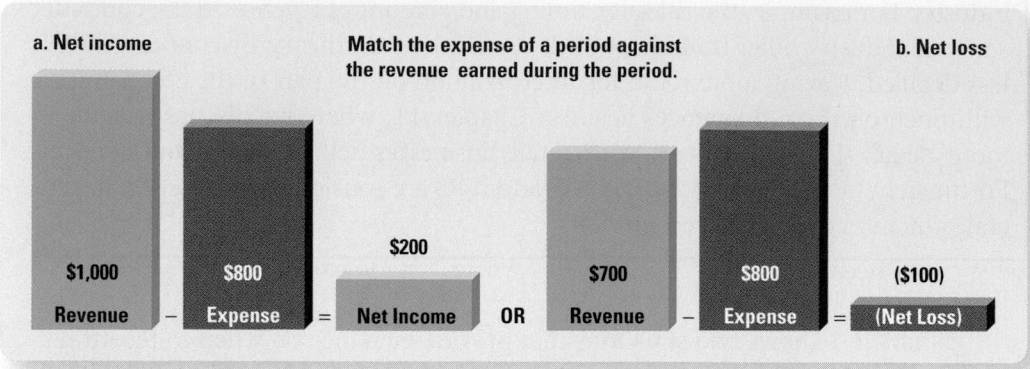

Some expenses are paid in cash. Other expenses arise from using up an asset such as supplies. Still other expenses occur when a company creates a liability. For example, Starbucks' salary expense occurs when employees work for the company. Starbucks may pay the salary expense immediately, or Starbucks may record a liability for the salary to be paid later. In either case, Starbucks has salary expense. The critical event for recording an expense is the employees' working for the company, not the payment of cash.

STOP & THINK. . .

1. A customer pays Starbucks $100 on March 15 for coffee to be served at a party in April. Has Starbucks earned revenue on March 15? When will Starbucks earn the revenue?
2. Starbucks pays $4,500 on July 1 for store rent for the next three months. Has Starbucks incurred an expense on July 1?

Answers:

1. No. Starbucks has received the cash but will not deliver the coffee until later. Starbucks earns the revenue when it gives the goods to the customer.
2. No. Starbucks has paid cash for rent in advance. There is no expense. This prepaid rent is an asset because Starbucks has the use of a store location in the future.

Ethical Issues in Accrual Accounting

Accrual accounting provides some ethical challenges that cash accounting avoids. For example, suppose that in 2010, Starbucks Corporation prepays a $3 million advertising campaign to be conducted by a large advertising agency. The advertisements are scheduled to run during September, October, and November. In this case, Starbucks is buying an asset, a prepaid expense.

Suppose Starbucks pays for the advertisements on September 1 and the ads start running immediately. Under accrual accounting, Starbucks should record one-third of the expense ($1 million) during the year ended September 30, 2010, and two-thirds ($2 million) during 2011.

Suppose fiscal 2010 is a great year for Starbucks—net income is better than expected. Starbucks' top managers believe that fiscal 2011 will not be as profitable.

In this case, the company has a strong incentive to expense the full $3 million during fiscal 2010 in order to report all the advertising expense in the fiscal 2010 income statement. This unethical action would keep $2 million of advertising expense off the fiscal 2011 income statement and make 2011's net income look $2 million better.

UPDATING THE ACCOUNTS: THE ADJUSTING PROCESS

At the end of the period, the business reports its financial statements. This process begins with the trial balance introduced in Chapter 2. We refer to this trial balance as unadjusted because the accounts are not yet ready for the financial statements. In most cases the simple label "Trial Balance" means "unadjusted."

OBJECTIVE

3 **Adjust** the accounts

Which Accounts Need to Be Updated (Adjusted)?

The stockholders need to know how well ShineBrite Car Wash is performing. The financial statements report this information, and all accounts must be up-to-date. That means some accounts must be adjusted. Exhibit 3-3 gives the trial balance of ShineBrite Car Wash, Inc., at June 30, 2010.

EXHIBIT 3-3 | Unadjusted Trial Balance

ShineBrite Car Wash, Inc.
Unadjusted Trial Balance
June 30, 2010

Cash...	$24,800	
Accounts receivable.........................	2,200	
Supplies...	700	
Prepaid rent....................................	3,000	
Equipment.......................................	24,000	
Accounts payable		$13,100
Unearned service revenue		400
Common stock................................		20,000
Retained earnings...........................		18,800
Dividends..	3,200	
Service revenue...............................		7,000
Salary expense................................	900	
Utilities expense	500	
Total	$59,300	$59,300

This trial balance is unadjusted. That means it's not completely up-to-date. It's not quite ready for preparing the financial statements for presentation to the public.

Cash, Equipment, Accounts Payable, Common Stock, and Dividends are up-to-date and need no adjustment at the end of the period. Why? Because the day-to-day transactions provide all the data for these accounts.

Accounts Receivable, Supplies, Prepaid Rent, and the other accounts are another story. These accounts are not yet up-to-date on June 30. Why? Because certain transactions have not yet been recorded. Consider Supplies. During June, ShineBrite Car Wash used cleaning supplies to wash cars. But ShineBrite didn't make a journal entry for supplies used every time it washed a car. That would waste time and money. Instead, ShineBrite waits until the end of the period and then records the supplies used up during the entire month.

The cost of supplies used up is an expense. An adjusting entry at the end of June updates both Supplies (an asset) and Supplies Expense. We must adjust all accounts whose balances are not yet up-to-date.

Categories of Adjusting Entries

Accounting adjustments fall into three basic categories: deferrals, depreciation, and accruals.

Deferrals. A **deferral** is an adjustment for an item that the business paid or received cash in advance. Starbucks purchases supplies for use in its operations. During the period, some supplies (assets) are used up and become expenses. At the end of the period, an adjustment is needed to decrease the Supplies account for the supplies used up. This is Supplies Expense. Prepaid rent, prepaid insurance, and all other prepaid expenses require deferral adjustments.

There are also deferral adjustments for liabilities. Companies such as Starbucks may collect cash from a grocery-store chain in advance of earning the revenue. When Starbucks receives cash up front, Starbucks has a liability to provide coffee for the customer. This liability is called Unearned Sales Revenue. Then, when Starbucks delivers the goods to the customer, it earns Sales Revenue. This earning process requires an adjustment at the end of the period. The adjustment decreases the liability and increases the revenue for the revenue earned. Publishers such as Time, Inc., and your cell-phone company collect cash in advance. They too must make adjusting entries for revenues earned later.

Depreciation. **Depreciation** allocates the cost of a plant asset to expense over the asset's useful life. Depreciation is the most common long-term deferral. Starbucks buys buildings and equipment. As Starbucks uses the assets, it records depreciation for wear-and-tear and obsolescence. The accounting adjustment records Depreciation Expense and decreases the asset's book value over its life. The process is identical to a deferral-type adjustment; the only difference is the type of asset involved.

Accruals. An **accrual** is the opposite of a deferral. For an accrued *expense*, Starbucks records the expense before paying cash. For an accrued *revenue*, Starbucks records the revenue before collecting cash.

Salary Expense can create an accrual adjustment. As employees work for Starbucks Corporation, the company's salary expense accrues with the passage of time. At September 30, 2008, Starbucks owed employees some salaries to be paid after year end. At September 30, Starbucks recorded Salary Expense and Salary Payable for the amount owed. Other examples of expense accruals include interest expense and income tax expense.

An accrued revenue is a revenue that the business has earned and will collect next year. At year end Starbucks must accrue the revenue. The adjustment debits a receivable and credits a revenue. For example, accrual of interest revenue debits Interest Receivable and credits Interest Revenue.

Let's see how the adjusting process actually works for ShineBrite Car Wash at June 30. We start with prepaid expenses.

Prepaid Expenses

A **prepaid expense** is an expense paid in advance. Therefore, prepaid expenses are assets because they provide a future benefit for the owner. Let's do the adjustments for prepaid rent and supplies.

Prepaid Rent.   Companies pay rent in advance. This prepayment creates an asset for the renter, who can then use the rented item in the future. Suppose ShineBrite Car Wash prepays three months' store rent ($3,000) on June 1. The entry for the prepayment of three months' rent debits Prepaid Rent as follows:

Jun 1	Prepaid Rent ($1,000 × 3)	3,000	
	Cash		3,000
	Paid three months' rent in advance.		

The accounting equation shows that one asset increases and another decreases. Total assets are unchanged.

Assets	=	Liabilities	+	Stockholders' Equity
3,000	=	0	+	0
− 3,000				

After posting, the Prepaid Rent account appears as follows:

Prepaid Rent

Jun 1	3,000	

Throughout June, the Prepaid Rent account carries this beginning balance, as shown in Exhibit 3-3 (p. 143). The adjustment transfers $1,000 from Prepaid Rent to Rent Expense as follows:*

Adjusting entry a

Jun 30	Rent Expense ($3,000 × 1/3)	1,000	
	Prepaid Rent		1,000
	To record rent expense.		

Both assets and stockholders' equity decrease.

Assets	=	Liabilities	+	Stockholders' Equity	−	Expenses
− 1,000	=	0				− 1,000

---

*See Exhibit 3-8, page 155, for a summary of adjustments a–g.

After posting, Prepaid Rent and Rent Expense appear as follows:

Prepaid Rent				Rent Expense	
Jun 1	3,000	Jun 30	1,000 →	Jun 30	1,000
Bal	2,000			Bal	1,000

This expense illustrates the matching principle. We record an expense in order to measure net income.

Supplies. Supplies are another type of prepaid expense. On June 2, ShineBrite Car Wash paid cash of $700 for cleaning supplies:

Jun 2	Supplies	700	
	Cash		700
	Paid cash for supplies.		

Assets	=	Liabilities	+	Stockholders' Equity
700	=	0	+	0
− 700				

The cost of the supplies ShineBrite used is supplies expense. To measure June's supplies expense, the business counts the supplies on hand at the end of the month. The count shows that $400 of supplies remain. Subtracting the $400 of supplies on hand from the supplies available ($700) measures supplies expense for the month ($300), as follows:

Asset Available During the Period	−	Asset on Hand at the End of the Period	=	Asset Used (Expense) During the Period
$700	−	$400	=	$300

The June 30 adjusting entry debits the expense and credits the asset, as follows:

Adjusting entry b

Jun 30	Supplies Expense ($700 − $400)	300	
	Supplies		300
	To record supplies expense.		

Assets	=	Liabilities	+	Stockholders' Equity	−	Expenses
− 300	=	0				− 300

After posting, the Supplies and Supplies Expense accounts appear as follows. The adjustment is highlighted for emphasis.

Supplies				Supplies Expense		
Jun 2	700	Jun 30	300 →	Jun 30	300	
Bal	400			Bal	300	

At the start of July, Supplies has this $400 balance, and the adjustment process is repeated each month.

STOP & THINK...

At the beginning of the month, supplies were $5,000. During the month, $7,000 of supplies were purchased. At month's end, $3,000 of supplies are still on hand. What is the

- adjusting entry?
- ending balance in the Supplies account?

Answer:

Supplies Expense ($5,000 + $7,000 − $3,000)	9,000	
Supplies		9,000
Ending balance of supplies = $3,000 (the supplies still on hand)		

Depreciation of Plant Assets

Plant assets are long-lived tangible assets, such as land, buildings, furniture, and equipment. All plant assets but land decline in usefulness, and this decline is an expense. Accountants spread the cost of each plant asset, except land, over its useful life. Depreciation is the process of allocating cost to expense for a long-term plant asset.

To illustrate depreciation, consider ShineBrite Car Wash. Suppose that on June 2 ShineBrite purchased car-washing equipment on account for $24,000:

Jun 3	Equipment	24,000	
	Accounts Payable		24,000
	Purchased equipment on account.		

Assets	=	Liabilities	+	Stockholders' Equity
24,000	=	24,000	+	0

After posting, the Equipment account appears as follows:

	Equipment
Jun 3 24,000	

ShineBrite records an asset when it purchases equipment. Then, as the asset is used, a portion of the asset's cost is transferred to Depreciation Expense. Accounting matches the expense against revenue—this is the matching principle. Computerized systems program the depreciation for automatic entry each period.

ShineBrite's equipment will remain useful for five years and then be worthless. One way to compute the amount of depreciation for each year is to divide the cost of the asset ($24,000 in our example) by its expected useful life (five years). This procedure—called the straight-line depreciation method—gives annual depreciation of $4,800. The depreciation amount is an estimate. (Chapter 7 covers plant assets and depreciation in more detail.)

$$\text{Annual Depreciation} = \$24,000/5 \text{ years} = \$4,800 \text{ per year}$$

Depreciation for June is $400.

$$\text{Monthly Depreciation} = \$4,800/12 \text{ months} = \$400 \text{ per month}$$

The Accumulated Depreciation Account. Depreciation expense for June is recorded as follows:

				Adjusting entry c
Jun 30	Depreciation Expense—Equipment	400	
	Accumulated Depreciation—Equipment		400
	To record depreciation.		

Total assets decrease by the amount of the expense:

Assets	=	Liabilities	+	Stockholders' Equity	−	Expenses
− 400	=	0				− 400

The Accumulated Depreciation account, (not Equipment) is credited to preserve the original cost of the asset in the Equipment account. Managers can then refer to the Equipment account if they ever need to know how much the asset cost.

The **Accumulated Depreciation** account shows the sum of all depreciation expense from using the asset. Therefore, the balance in the Accumulated Depreciation account increases over the asset's life.

Accumulated Depreciation is a contra asset account—an asset account with a normal credit balance. A **contra account** has two distinguishing characteristics:

1. It always has a companion account.
2. Its normal balance is opposite that of the companion account.

In this case, Accumulated Depreciation is the contra account to Equipment, so Accumulated Depreciation appears directly after Equipment on the balance sheet. A business carries an accumulated depreciation account for each depreciable asset, for example, Accumulated Depreciation—Building and Accumulated Depreciation—Equipment.

After posting, the plant asset accounts of ShineBrite Car Wash are as follows— with the adjustment highlighted:

Equipment		Accumulated Depreciation—Equipment		Depreciation Expense—Equipment	
Jun 3 24,000			Jun 30 400	Jun 30 400	
Bal 24,000			Bal 400	Bal 400	

Book Value.   The net amount of a plant asset (cost minus accumulated depreciation) is called that asset's **book value (of a plant asset)**, or carrying amount. Exhibit 3-4 shows how ShineBrite would report the book value of its equipment and building at June 30 (the building data are assumed for this illustration).

EXHIBIT 3-4 | Plant Assets on the Balance Sheet of ShineBrite Car Wash

ShineBrite Car Wash Plant Assets at June 30		
Equipment...	$24,000	
Less: Accumulated Depreciation	(400)	$23,600
Building...	$50,000	
Less: Accumulated Depreciation	(200)	49,800
Book value of plant assets		$73,400

At June 30, the book value of equipment is $23,600; the book value of the building is $49,800.

STOP & THINK...

What will be the book value of ShineBrite's equipment at the end of July?

Answer:
$24,000 − $400 − $400 = $23,200.

Exhibit 3-5 shows how Starbucks Corporation reports property, plant, and equipment in its annual report. Lines 1 to 6 list specific assets and their cost. Line 7 shows the cost of all Starbucks plant assets. Line 8 gives the amount of accumulated depreciation, and line 9 shows the assets' book value of $2,956 million.

EXHIBIT 3-5 | **Starbucks Corporation's Reporting of Property, Plant, and Equipment (Adapted, in millions)**

1	Land...	$ 59
2	Buildings	218
3	Leasehold improvements......................................	3,363
4	Store equipment	1,045
5	Roasting equipment	220
6	Furniture, fixtures, and other	812
7	Property, plant, and equipment, at cost..............	5,717
8	Less: Accumulated depreciation	(2,761)
9	Property, plant, and equipment, net	$ 2,956

Accrued Expenses

Businesses incur expenses before they pay cash. Consider an employee's salary. Starbucks' expense and payable grow as the employee works, so the liability is said to accrue. Another example is interest expense on a note payable. Interest accrues as the clock ticks. The term **accrued expense** refers to a liability that arises from an expense that has not yet been paid.

Companies don't record accrued expenses daily or weekly. Instead, they wait until the end of the period and use an adjusting entry to update each expense (and related liability) for the financial statements. Let's look at salary expense.

Most companies pay their employees at set times. Suppose ShineBrite Car Wash pays its employee a monthly salary of $1,800, half on the 15th and half on the last day of the month. The following calendar for June has the paydays circled:

June						
Sun.	Mon.	Tue.	Wed.	Thur.	Fri.	Sat.
						1
2	3	4	5	6	7	8
9	10	11	12	13	14	(15)
16	17	18	19	20	21	22
23	24	25	26	27	28	29
(30)						

Assume that if a payday falls on a Sunday, ShineBrite pays the employee on the following Monday. During June, ShineBrite paid its employees the first half-month salary of $900 and made the following entry:

Jun 15	Salary Expense	900	
	Cash		900
	To pay salary.		

Assets	=	Liabilities	+	Stockholders' Equity	–	Expenses
– 900	=	0				– 900

After posting, the Salary Expense account is

Salary Expense	
Jun 15	900

The trial balance at June 30 (Exhibit 3-3, p. 143) includes Salary Expense with its debit balance of $900. Because June 30, the second payday of the month, falls on a Sunday, the second half-month amount of $900 will be paid on Monday, July 1. At June 30, therefore, ShineBrite adjusts for additional salary expense and salary payable of $900 as follows:

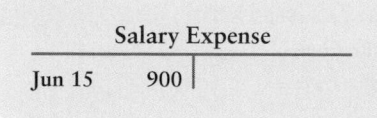

			Adjusting entry d
Jun 30	Salary Expense	900	
	Salary Payable		900
	To accrue salary expense.		

An accrued expense increases liabilities and decreases stockholders' equity:

Assets	=	Liabilities	+	Stockholders' Equity	–	Expenses
0	=	900				– 900

After posting, the Salary Payable and Salary Expense accounts appear as follows (adjustment highlighted):

Salary Payable				Salary Expense		
	Jun 30	900		Jun 15	900	
	Bal	900		Jun 30	900	
				Bal	1,800	

The accounts now hold all of June's salary information. Salary Expense has a full month's salary, and Salary Payable shows the amount owed at June 30. All accrued expenses are recorded this way—debit the expense and credit the liability.

Computerized systems contain a payroll module. Accrued salaries can be automatically journalized and posted at the end of each period.

Accrued Revenues

Businesses often earn revenue before they receive the cash. A revenue that has been earned but not yet collected is called an **accrued revenue**.

Assume that FedEx hires ShineBrite on June 15 to wash FedEx delivery trucks each month. Suppose FedEx will pay ShineBrite $600 monthly, with the first payment on July 15. During June, ShineBrite will earn half a month's fee, $300, for work done June 15 through June 30. On June 30, ShineBrite makes the following adjusting entry:

		Adjusting entry e	
Jun 30	Accounts Receivable ($600 × 1/2)	300	
	Service Revenue		300
	To accrue service revenue.		

Revenue increases both total assets and stockholders' equity:

Assets	=	Liabilities	+	Stockholders' Equity	+	Revenues
300	=	0				+ 300

Recall that Accounts Receivable has an unadjusted balance of $2,200, and Service Revenue's unadjusted balance is $7,000 (Exhibit 3-3, p. 143). This June 30 adjusting entry has the following effects (adjustment highlighted):

Accounts Receivable			Service Revenue	
	2,200			7,000
Jun 30	300		Jun 30	300
Bal	2,500		Bal	7,300

All accrued revenues are accounted for similarly—debit a receivable and credit a revenue.

STOP & THINK. . .

Suppose ShineBrite Car Wash holds a note receivable as an investment. At the end of June, $100 of interest revenue has been earned. Journalize the accrued revenue adjustment at June 30.

Answer:

Jun 30	Interest Receivable	100	
	Interest Revenue		100
	To accrue interest revenue.		

Unearned Revenues

Some businesses collect cash from customers before earning the revenue. This creates a liability called **unearned revenue**. Only when the job is completed does the business earn the revenue. Suppose **Home Depot** engages ShineBrite Car Wash to wash

Home Depot trucks, agreeing to pay ShineBrite $400 monthly, beginning immediately. If ShineBrite collects the first amount on June 15, then ShineBrite records this transaction as follows:

Jun 15	Cash	400	
	Unearned Service Revenue		400
	Received cash for revenue in advance.		

Assets	=	Liabilities	+	Stockholders' Equity
400	=	400	+	0

After posting, the liability account appears as follows:

Unearned Service Revenue	
Jun 15	400

Unearned Service Revenue is a liability because ShineBrite is obligated to perform services for Home Depot. The June 30 unadjusted trial balance (Exhibit 3-3, p. 143) lists Unearned Service Revenue with a $400 credit balance. During the last 15 days of the month, ShineBrite will earn one-half of the $400, or $200. On June 30, ShineBrite makes the following adjustment:

Adjusting entry f

Jun 30	Unearned Service Revenue ($400 × 1/2)	200	
	Service Revenue		200
	To record unearned service revenue that has been earned.		

Assets	=	Liabilities	+	Stockholders' Equity	+	Revenues
0	=	− 200	+			+ 200

This adjusting entry shifts $200 of the total amount received ($400) from liability to revenue. After posting, Unearned Service Revenue is reduced to $200, and Service Revenue is increased by $200, as follows (adjustment highlighted):

Unearned Service Revenue				Service Revenue	
Jun 30	200	Jun 15	400		7,000
		Bal	200	Jun 30	300
				Jun 30	200
				Bal	7,500

All revenues collected in advance are accounted for this way. An unearned revenue is a liability, not a revenue.

One company's prepaid expense is the other company's unearned revenue. For example, Home Depot's prepaid expense is ShineBrite Car Wash's liability for unearned revenue.

Exhibit 3-6 diagrams the distinctive timing of prepaids and accruals. Study prepaid expenses all the way across. Then study unearned revenues across, and so on.

EXHIBIT 3-6 | Prepaid and Accrual Adjustments

PREPAIDS—Cash First

	First			Later		
Prepaid expenses	*Pay cash and record an asset:* Prepaid Expense	XXX		*Record an expense and decrease the asset:* Expense	XXX	
	Cash		XXX	Prepaid Expense		XXX
Unearned revenues	*Receive cash and record unearned revenue:* Cash	XXX		*Record revenue and decrease unearned revenue:* Unearned Revenue	XXX	
	Unearned Revenue		XXX	Revenue		XXX

ACCRUALS—Cash Later

	First			Later		
Accrued expenses	*Accrue expense and a payable:* Expense	XXX		*Pay cash and decrease the payable:* Payable	XXX	
	Payable		XXX	Cash		XXX
Accrued revenues	*Accrue revenue and a receivable:* Receivable	XXX		*Receive cash and decrease the receivable:* Cash	XXX	
	Revenue		XXX	Receivable		XXX

The authors thank Professors Darrel Davis and Alfonso Oddo for suggesting this exhibit.

Summary of the Adjusting Process

Two purposes of the adjusting process are to

- measure income, and
- update the balance sheet.

Therefore, every adjusting entry affects at least one of the following:

- Revenue or expense—to measure income
- Asset or liability—to update the balance sheet

Exhibit 3-7 summarizes the standard adjustments.

EXHIBIT 3-7 | Summary of Adjusting Entries

	Type of Account	
Category of Adjusting Entry	Debit	Credit
Prepaid expense..................	Expense	Asset
Depreciation.......................	Expense	Contra asset
Accrued expense.................	Expense	Liability
Accrued revenue.................	Asset	Revenue
Unearned revenue...............	Liability	Revenue

Adapted from material provided by Beverly Terry.

Exhibit 3-8 summarizes the adjustments of ShineBrite Car Wash, Inc., at June 30—the adjusting entries we've examined over the past few pages.

- Panel A repeats the data for each adjustment.
- Panel B gives the adjusting entries.
- Panel C on the following page shows the accounts after posting the adjusting entries. The adjustments are keyed by letter.

EXHIBIT 3-8 | The Adjusting Process of ShineBrite Car Wash, Inc.

PANEL A—Information for Adjustments at June 30, 2010

PANEL B—Adjusting Entries

(a) Prepaid rent expired, $1,000.

(a) Rent Expense 1,000
    Prepaid Rent 1,000
    To record rent expense.

(b) Supplies used, $300.

(b) Supplies Expense 300
    Supplies.. 300
    To record supplies used.

(c) Depreciation on equipment, $400.

(c) Depreciation Expense—Equipment 400
    Accumulated Depreciation—Equipment 400
    To record depreciation.

(d) Accrued salary expense, $900.

(d) Salary Expense 900
    Salary Payable....................................... 900
    To accrue salary expense.

(e) Accrued service revenue, $300.

(e) Accounts Receivable................................. 300
    Service Revenue.................................... 300
    To accrue service revenue.

(f) Amount of unearned service revenue that has been earned, $200.

(f) Unearned Service Revenue......................... 200
    Service Revenue.................................... 200
    To record unearned revenue that has been earned.

(g) Accrued income tax expense, $600.

(g) Income Tax Expense 600
    Income Tax Payable.............................. 600
    To accrue income tax expense.

PANEL C—Ledger Accounts

| Assets | Liabilities | Stockholders' Equity | |

Cash

| Bal 24,800 | |

Accounts Receivable

2,200	
(e) 300	
Bal 2,500	

Supplies

| 700 | (b) 300 |
| Bal 400 | |

Prepaid Rent

| 3,000 | (a) 1,000 |
| Bal 2,000 | |

Equipment

| Bal 24,000 | |

Accumulated Depreciation— Equipment

| | (c) 400 |
| | Bal 400 |

Accounts Payable

| | Bal 13,100 |

Salary Payable

| | (d) 900 |
| | Bal 900 |

Unearned Service Revenue

| (f) 200 | 400 |
| | Bal 200 |

Income Tax Payable

| | (g) 600 |
| | Bal 600 |

Common Stock

| | Bal 20,000 |

Retained Earnings

| | Bal 18,800 |

Dividends

| Bal 3,200 | |

Revenue

Service Revenue

	7,000
(e)	300
(f)	200
	Bal 7,500

Expenses

Rent Expense

| (a) 1,000 | |
| Bal 1,000 | |

Salary Expense

900	
(d) 900	
Bal 1,800	

Supplies Expense

| (b) 300 | |
| Bal 300 | |

Depreciation Expense—Equipment

| (c) 400 | |
| Bal 400 | |

Utilities Expense

| Bal 500 | |

Income Tax Expense

| (g) 600 | |
| Bal 600 | |

Exhibit 3-8 includes an additional adjusting entry that we have not yet discussed—the accrual of income tax expense. Like individual taxpayers, corporations are subject to income tax. They typically accrue income tax expense and the related income tax payable as the final adjusting entry of the period. ShineBrite Car Wash accrues income tax expense with adjusting entry g, as follows:

			Adjusting entry g
Jun 30	Income Tax Expense	600	
	Income Tax Payable		600
	To accrue income tax expense.		

The income tax accrual follows the pattern for accrued expenses.

The Adjusted Trial Balance

This chapter began with the unadjusted trial balance (see Exhibit 3-3, p. 143). After the adjustments are journalized and posted, the accounts appear as shown in Exhibit 3-8, Panel C. A useful step in preparing the financial statements is to list the accounts, along with their adjusted balances, on an **adjusted trial balance**. This document lists all the accounts and their final balances in a single place. Exhibit 3-9 shows the adjusted trial balance of ShineBrite Car Wash.

EXHIBIT 3-9 | Adjusted Trial Balance

ShineBrite Car Wash, Inc.
Preparation of Adjusted Trial Balance
June 30, 2010

Account Title	Trial Balance Debit	Trial Balance Credit	Adjustments Debit		Adjustments Credit		Adjusted Trial Balance Debit	Adjusted Trial Balance Credit	
Cash	24,800						24,800		
Accounts receivable	2,200		(e)	300			2,500		
Supplies	700				(b)	300	400		
Prepaid rent	3,000				(a)	1,000	2,000		
Equipment	24,000						24,000		
Accumulated depreciation—equipment					(c)	400		400	**Balance Sheet** (*Exhibit 3-12*)
Accounts payable		13,100						13,100	
Salary payable					(d)	900		900	
Unearned service revenue		400	(f)	200				200	
Income tax payable					(g)	600		600	
Common stock		20,000						20,000	
Retained earnings		18,800						18,800	**Statement of Retained Earnings** (*Exhibit 3-11*)
Dividends	3,200						3,200		
Service revenue		7,000			(e)	300		7,500	
					(f)	200			
Rent expense			(a)	1,000			1,000		
Salary expense	900		(d)	900			1,800		**Income Statement** (*Exhibit 3-10*)
Supplies expense			(b)	300			300		
Depreciation expense			(c)	400			400		
Utilities expense	500						500		
Income tax expense			(g)	600			600		
	59,300	59,300	3,700		3,700		61,500	61,500	

Note how clearly the adjusted trial balance presents the data. The Account Title and the Trial Balance data come from the trial balance. The two Adjustments columns summarize the adjusting entries. The Adjusted Trial Balance columns then give the final account balances. Each adjusted amount in Exhibit 3-9 is the unadjusted balance plus or minus the adjustments. For example, Accounts Receivable starts with a balance of $2,200. Add the $300 debit adjustment to get Accounts Receivable's ending balance of $2,500. Spreadsheets are designed for this type of analysis.

Accounting Cycle Tutorial Glossary

PREPARING THE FINANCIAL STATEMENTS

The June financial statements of ShineBrite Car Wash can be prepared from the adjusted trial balance. At the far right, Exhibit 3-9 shows how the accounts are distributed to the financial statements.

- The income statement (Exhibit 3-10) lists the revenue and expense accounts.
- The statement of retained earnings (Exhibit 3-11) shows the changes in retained earnings.
- The balance sheet (Exhibit 3-12) reports assets, liabilities, and stockholders' equity.

The arrows in Exhibits 3-10, 3-11, and 3-12 (all on the following page) show the flow of data from one statement to the next.

OBJECTIVE

4 **Prepare** the financial statements

EXHIBIT 3-10 | **Income Statement**

ShineBrite Car Wash, Inc.
Income Statement
Month Ended June 30, 2010

Revenues:		
Service revenue		$7,500
Expenses:		
Salary expense	$1,800	
Rent expense............................	1,000	
Utilities expense	500	
Depreciation expense	400	
Supplies expense	300	4,000
Income before tax		3,500
Income tax expense		600
Net income..................................		$2,900

EXHIBIT 3-11 | **Statement of Retained Earnings**

ShineBrite Car Wash, Inc.
Statement of Retained Earnings
Month Ended June 30, 2010

Retained earnings, May 31, 2010................	$18,800
Add: Net income	2,900
	21,700
Less: Dividends	(3,200)
Retained earnings, June 30, 2010................	$18,500

①

EXHIBIT 3-12 | **Balance Sheet**

ShineBrite Car Wash, Inc.
Balance Sheet
June 30, 2010

Assets			Liabilities		
Cash..............................		$24,800	Accounts payable		$13,100
Accounts receivable........		2,500	Salary payable		900
Supplies.........................		400	Unearned service revenue		200
Prepaid rent...................		2,000	Income tax payable		600
Equipment.....................	$24,000		Total liabilities		14,800
Less: Accumulated					
depreciation	(400)	23,600	**Stockholders' Equity**		
			Common stock..........................		20,000
			Retained earnings.....................		18,500
			Total stockholders' equity		38,500
			Total liabilities and		
Total assets....................		$53,300	stockholders' equity...............		$53,300

②

Why is the income statement prepared first and the balance sheet last?

1. The income statement reports net income or net loss, the result of revenues minus expenses. Revenues and expenses affect stockholders' equity, so net income is then transferred to retained earnings. The first arrow tracks net income.

2. Retained Earnings is the final balancing element of the balance sheet. To solidify your understanding, trace the $18,500 retained earnings figure from Exhibit 3-11 to Exhibit 3-12. Arrow ❷ tracks retained earnings.

MID-CHAPTER SUMMARY PROBLEM

The trial balance of Goldsmith Company shown below pertains to December 31, 2010, which is the end of its year-long accounting period. Data needed for the adjusting entries include the following:

a. Supplies on hand at year end, $2,000.

b. Depreciation on furniture and fixtures, $20,000.

c. Depreciation on building, $10,000.

d. Salaries owed but not yet paid, $5,000.

e. Accrued service revenue, $12,000.

f. Of the $45,000 balance of unearned service revenue, $32,000 was earned during the year.

g. Accrued income tax expense, $35,000.

I *Requirements*

1. Open the ledger accounts with their unadjusted balances. Show dollar amounts in thousands, as shown for Accounts Receivable:

Accounts Receivable	
370	

2. Journalize the Goldsmith Company adjusting entries at December 31, 2010. Key entries by letter, as in Exhibit 3-8, page 155.
3. Post the adjusting entries.
4. Prepare an adjusted trial balance, as shown in Exhibit 3-9, page 157.
5. Prepare the income statement, the statement of retained earnings, and the balance sheet. (At this stage, it is not necessary to classify assets or liabilities as current or long term.) Draw arrows linking these three financial statements.

Goldsmith Company
Trial Balance
December 31, 2010

Cash	$ 198,000	
Accounts receivable	370,000	
Supplies	6,000	
Furniture and fixtures	100,000	
Accumulated depreciation—furniture and fixtures		$ 40,000
Building	250,000	
Accumulated depreciation—building		130,000
Accounts payable		380,000
Salary payable		
Unearned service revenue		45,000
Income tax payable		
Common stock		100,000
Retained earnings		193,000
Dividends	65,000	
Service revenue		286,000
Salary expense	172,000	
Supplies expense		
Depreciation expense—furniture and fixtures		
Depreciation expense—building		
Income tax expense		
Miscellaneous expense	13,000	
Total	$1,174,000	$1,174,000

Answers

Requirements 1 and 3

(Amounts in thousands)

Assets	Stockholders' Equity

Assets

Cash

Bal	198	

Accounts Receivable

	370	
(e)	12	
Bal	382	

Supplies

	6	(a)	4
Bal	2		

Furniture and Fixtures

Bal	100	

Accumulated Depreciation— Furniture and Fixtures

			40
		(b)	20
		Bal	60

Building

Bal	250	

Accumulated Depreciation—Building

			130
		(c)	10
		Bal	140

Liabilities

Accounts Payable

		Bal	380

Salary Payable

		(d)	5
		Bal	5

Unearned Service Revenue

(f)	32		45
		Bal	13

Income Tax Payable

		(g)	35
		Bal	35

Stockholders' Equity

Common Stock

		Bal	100

Retained Earnings

		Bal	193

Dividends

Bal	65	

Revenues

Service Revenue

			286
		(e)	12
		(f)	32
		Bal	330

Expenses

Salary Expense

	172	
(d)	5	
Bal	177	

Supplies Expense

(a)	4	
Bal	4	

Depreciation Expense— Furniture and Fixtures

(b)	20	
Bal	20	

Depreciation Expense— Building

(c)	10	
Bal	10	

Income Tax Expense

(g)	35	
Bal	35	

Miscellaneous Expense

Bal	13	

▌ *Requirement 2*

(a)	Dec 31	Supplies Expense ($6,000 – $2,000)	4,000	
		Supplies		4,000
		To record supplies used.		
(b)	31	Depreciation Expense—Furniture and Fixtures	20,000	
		Accumulated Depreciation—Furniture and Fixtures		20,000
		To record depreciation expense on furniture and fixtures.		
(c)	31	Depreciation Expense—Building	10,000	
		Accumulated Depreciation—Building		10,000
		To record depreciation expense on building.		
(d)	31	Salary Expense	5,000	
		Salary Payable		5,000
		To accrue salary expense.		
(e)	31	Accounts Receivable	12,000	
		Service Revenue		12,000
		To accrue service revenue.		
(f)	31	Unearned Service Revenue	32,000	
		Service Revenue		32,000
		To record unearned service revenue that has been earned.		
(g)	31	Income Tax Expense	35,000	
		Income Tax Payable		35,000
		To accrue income tax expense.		

Requirement 4

Goldsmith Company
Preparation of Adjusted Trial Balance
December 31, 2010

(Amounts in thousands)	Trial Balance		Adjustments				Adjusted Trial Balance	
Account Title	Debit	Credit	Debit		Credit		Debit	Credit
Cash	198						198	
Accounts receivable	370		(e)	12			382	
Supplies	6				(a)	4	2	
Furniture and fixtures	100						100	
Accumulated depreciation— furniture and fixtures		40			(b)	20		60
Building	250						250	
Accumulated depreciation—building		130			(c)	10		140
Accounts payable		380						380
Salary payable					(d)	5		5
Unearned service revenue		45	(f)	32				13
Income tax payable					(g)	35		35
Common stock		100						100
Retained earnings		193						193
Dividends	65						65	
Service revenue		286			(e)	12		330
					(f)	32		
Salary expense	172		(d)	5			177	
Supplies expense			(a)	4			4	
Depreciation expense— furniture and fixtures			(b)	20			20	
Depreciation expense—building			(c)	10			10	
Income tax expense			(g)	35			35	
Miscellaneous expense	13						13	
	1,174	1,174	118		118		1,256	1,256

❚ Requirement 5

Goldsmith Company
Income Statement
Year Ended December 31, 2010

(Amounts in thousands)

Revenue:

Service revenue		$330

Expenses:

Salary expense	$177	
Depreciation expense—furniture and fixtures	20	
Depreciation expense—building................................	10	
Supplies expense	4	
Miscellaneous expense..	13	224
Income before tax		106
Income tax expense..		35
Net income..		$ 71

Goldsmith Company
Statement of Retained Earnings
Year Ended December 31, 2010

(Amounts in thousands)

Retained earnings, December 31, 2009	$193
Add: Net income...	71
	264
Less: Dividends	(65)
Retained earnings, December 31, 2010	$199

① ②

Goldsmith Company
Balance Sheet
December 31, 2010

(Amounts in thousands)

Assets			Liabilities		
Cash..		$198	Accounts payable		$380
Accounts receivable..................		382	Salary payable		5
Supplies....................................		2	Unearned service revenue		13
Furniture and fixtures	$100		Income tax payable		35
Less: Accumulated			Total liabilities		433
depreciation.................	(60)	40			
			Stockholders' Equity		
Building....................................	$250		Common stock.............................		100
Less: Accumulated			Retained earnings..........................		199
depreciation.................	(140)	110	Total stockholders' equity............		299
			Total liabilities and		
Total assets..............................		$732	stockholders' equity...................		$732

Which Accounts Need to Be Closed?

It is now June 30, the end of the month. Van Gray, the manager, will continue ShineBrite Car Wash into July, August, and beyond. But wait—the revenue and the expense accounts still hold amounts for June. At the end of each accounting period, it is necessary to close the books.

Closing the books means to prepare the accounts for the next period's transactions. The **closing entries** set the revenue, expense, and dividends balances back to zero at the end of the period. The idea is the same as setting the scoreboard back to zero after a game.

Closing is easily handled by computers. Recall that the income statement for a particular year reports only one year's income. For example, net income for Starbucks 2008 relates exclusively to the year ended September 28, 2008. At each year end, Starbucks accountants close the company's revenues and expenses for that year.

Temporary Accounts.   Because revenues and expenses relate to a limited period, they are called **temporary accounts**. The Dividends account is also temporary. The closing process applies only to temporary accounts (revenues, expenses, and dividends).

Permanent Accounts.   Let's contrast the temporary accounts with the **permanent accounts**: assets, liabilities, and stockholders' equity. The permanent accounts are not closed at the end of the period because they carry over to the next period. Consider Cash, Receivables, Equipment, Accounts Payable, Common Stock, and Retained Earnings. Their ending balances at the end of one period become the beginning balances of the next period.

Closing entries transfer the revenue, expense, and dividends balances to Retained Earnings. Here are the steps to close the books of a company such as Starbucks Corporation or ShineBrite Car Wash:

① Debit each revenue account for the amount of its credit balance. Credit Retained Earnings for the sum of the revenues. Now the sum of the revenues is in Retained Earnings.

② Credit each expense account for the amount of its debit balance. Debit Retained Earnings for the sum of the expenses. The sum of the expenses is now in Retained Earnings.

③ Credit the Dividends account for the amount of its debit balance. Debit Retained Earnings. This entry places the dividends amount in the debit side of Retained Earnings. Remember that dividends are not expenses. Dividends never affect net income.

After closing the books, the Retained Earnings account of ShineBrite Car Wash appears as follows (data from page 158):

Retained Earnings			
		Beginning balance	18,800
Expenses	4,600	Revenues	7,500
Dividends	3,200		
		Ending balance	18,500

OBJECTIVE

5 **Close** the books

Assume that ShineBrite Car Wash closes the books at the end of June. Exhibit 3-13 presents the complete closing process for the business. Panel A gives the closing journal entries, and Panel B shows the accounts after closing.

EXHIBIT 3-13 | Journalizing and Posting the Closing Entries

PANEL A—Journalizing the Closing Entries   Page 5

			Closing Entries		
①	Jun 30	Service Revenue.................................	7,500	
		Retained Earnings		7,500
②	30	Retained Earnings	4,600	
		Rent Expense		1,000
		Salary Expense		1,800
		Supplies Expense		300
		Depreciation Expense...............		400
		Utilities Expense......................		500
		Income Tax Expense		600
③	30	Retained Earnings	3,200	
		Dividends...............................		3,200

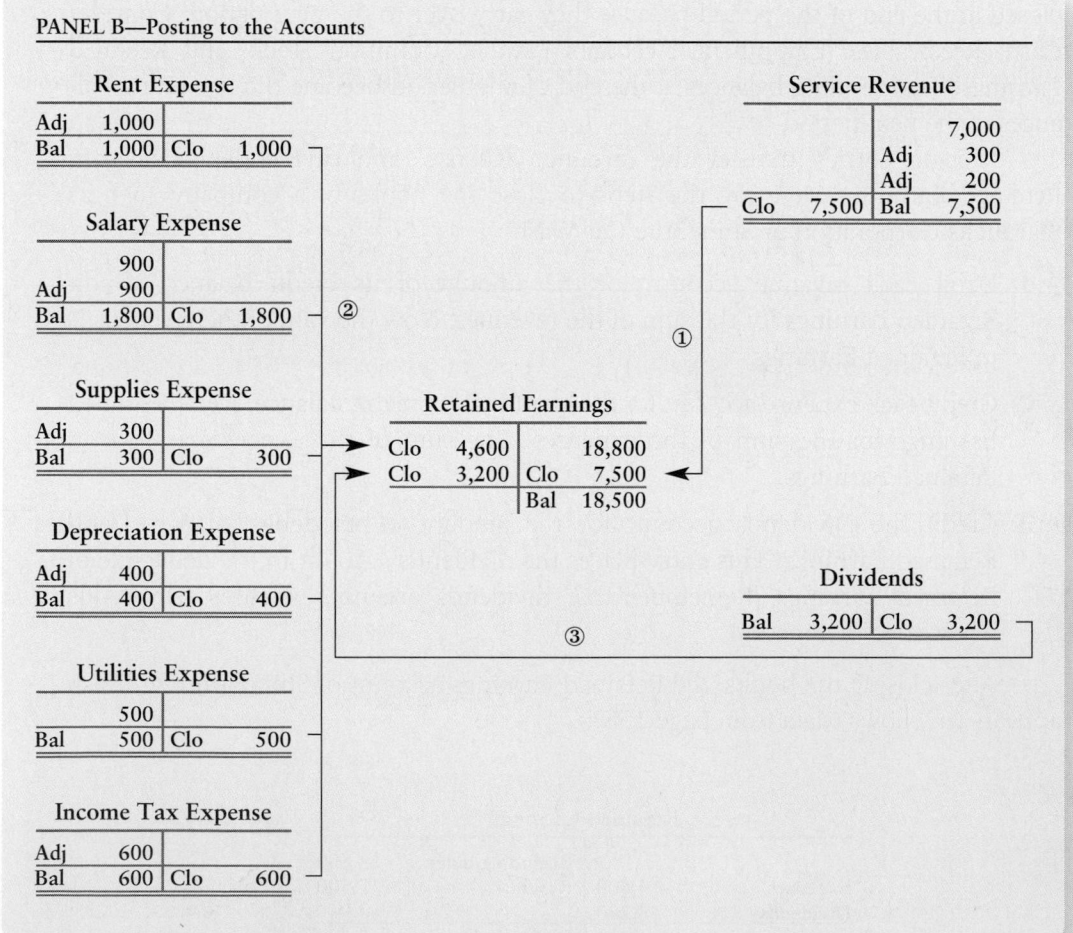

PANEL B—Posting to the Accounts

Rent Expense			
Adj	1,000		
Bal	1,000	Clo	1,000

Salary Expense			
	900		
Adj	900		
Bal	1,800	Clo	1,800

Supplies Expense			
Adj	300		
Bal	300	Clo	300

Depreciation Expense			
Adj	400		
Bal	400	Clo	400

Utilities Expense			
	500		
Bal	500	Clo	500

Income Tax Expense			
Adj	600		
Bal	600	Clo	600

Service Revenue			
			7,000
		Adj	300
		Adj	200
Clo	7,500	Bal	7,500

Retained Earnings			
Clo	4,600		18,800
Clo	3,200	Clo	7,500
		Bal	18,500

Dividends			
Bal	3,200	Clo	3,200

Adj = Amount posted from an adjusting entry
Clo = Amount posted from a closing entry
Bal = Balance
As arrow ② in Panel B shows, we can make a compound closing entry for all the expenses.

Classifying Assets and Liabilities Based on Their Liquidity

On the balance sheet, assets and liabilities are classified as current or long term to indicate their relative liquidity. **Liquidity** measures how quickly an item can be converted to cash. Cash is the most liquid asset. Accounts receivable are relatively liquid because cash collections usually follow quickly. Inventory is less liquid than accounts receivable because the company must first sell the goods. Equipment and buildings are even less liquid because these assets are held for use and not for sale. A balance sheet lists assets and liabilities in the order of relative liquidity.

Current Assets.   As we saw in Chapter 1, **current assets** are the most liquid assets. They will be converted to cash, sold, or consumed during the next 12 months or within the business's normal operating cycle if longer than a year. The **operating cycle** is the time span during which cash is paid for goods and services and these goods and services are sold to bring in cash.

For most businesses, the operating cycle is a few months. Cash, Short-Term Investments, Accounts Receivable, Merchandise Inventory, and Prepaid Expenses are the current assets.

Long-Term Assets.   **Long-term assets** are all assets not classified as current assets. One category of long-term assets is plant assets, often labeled Property, Plant, and Equipment. Land, Buildings, Furniture and Fixtures, and Equipment are plant assets. Of these, ShineBrite Car Wash has only Equipment. Long-Term Investments, Intangible Assets, and Other Assets (a catchall category for assets that are not classified more precisely) are also long-term.

Current Liabilities.   As we saw in Chapter 1, **current liabilities** are debts that must be paid within one year or within the entity's operating cycle if longer than a year. Accounts Payable, Notes Payable due within one year, Salary Payable, Unearned Revenue, Interest Payable, and Income Tax Payable are current liabilities.

Bankers and other lenders are interested in the due dates of an entity's liabilities. The sooner a liability must be paid, the more pressure it creates. Therefore, the balance sheet lists liabilities in the order in which they must be paid. Balance sheets usually report two liability classifications, current liabilities and long-term liabilities.

Long-Term Liabilities.   All liabilities that are not current are classified as **long-term liabilities**. Many notes payable are long term. Some notes payable are paid in installments, with the first installment due within one year, the second installment due the second year, and so on. The first installment is a current liability and the remainder is long term.

Let's see how Starbucks Corporation reports these asset and liability categories on its balance sheet.

Reporting Assets and Liabilities: Starbucks Corporation

Exhibit 3-14 on the following page shows a classified balance sheet: The Consolidated Balance Sheet of Starbucks Corporation. A **classified balance sheet** separates current assets from long-term assets and current liabilities from long-term liabilities. You should be familiar with most of Starbucks' accounts. Study the Starbucks balance sheet all the way through—line by line.

EXHIBIT 3-14 | **Classified Balance Sheet of Starbucks Corporation (Adapted, in millions)**

Starbucks Corporation
Consolidated Balance Sheet (Adapted)
September 28, 2008

(In millions)

Assets

Current assets:

Cash and cash equivalents	$ 270
Short-term investments	53
Accounts receivable	329
Inventories	693
Prepaid expenses and other current assets	403
Total current assets	1,748
Long-term investments	374
Property, plant, and equipment, net	2,956
Intangible assets	333
Other assets	262
Total assets	$5,673

Liabilities and Shareholders' Equity

Current liabilities:

Accounts payable	$ 325
Accrued expenses payable	783
Short-term notes payable	713
Current portion of long-term	1
Unearned revenue	368
Total current liabilities	2,190
Long-term debt	550
Other long-term liabilities	442
Total liabilities	3,182

Shareholders' equity:

Common stock	40
Retained earnings	2,402
Other equity	49
Total shareholders' equity	2,491
Total liabilities and shareholders' equity	$5,673

FORMATS FOR THE FINANCIAL STATEMENTS

Companies can format their financial statements in different ways. Both the balance sheet and the income statement can be formatted in two basic ways.

Balance Sheet Formats

The **report format** lists the assets at the top, followed by the liabilities and stock-holders' equity below. The Consolidated Balance Sheet of Starbucks Corporation in Exhibit 3-14 illustrates the report format. The report format is more popular, with approximately 60% of large companies using it.

The **account format** lists the assets on the left and the liabilities and stockholders' equity on the right in the same way that a T-account appears, with assets (debits) on the left and liabilities and equity (credits) on the right. Exhibit 3-12 (p. 158) shows an account-format balance sheet for ShineBrite Car Wash. Either format is acceptable.

Income Statement Formats

A **single-step income statement** lists all the revenues together under a heading such as Revenues, or Revenues and Gains. The expenses are listed together in a single category titled Expenses, or Expenses and Losses. There is only one step, the subtraction of Expenses and Losses from the sum of Revenues and Gains, in arriving at net income. Starbucks' income statement (p. 138) appears in single-step format.

A **multi-step income statement** reports a number of subtotals to highlight important relationships between revenues and expenses. Exhibit 3-15 shows Starbucks' income statement in multi-step format. Gross profit, income from operations, income before tax, and net income are highlighted for emphasis.

EXHIBIT 3-15 | Starbucks Corporation Income Statement in Multi-Step Format

Starbucks Corporation
Consolidated Statement of Earnings (Adapted)
Year Ended September 28, 2008

		Millions
Net operating revenues		$10,383
Cost of sales (Cost of goods sold)		4,646
Gross profit		5,737
Store operating expenses	$3,745	
Other operating expenses	597	
Depreciation and amortization expenses	549	
General and administrative expenses	456	
Total operating expenses		5,347
Income from operations		390
Other income		70
Income before income taxes		460
Income tax expense		144
Net income		$ 316

In particular, income from operations ($390 million) is separated from "Other income," which Starbucks did not earn by selling coffee. The other income was mainly interest revenue and other investment income. Most companies consider it important to report their operating income separately from nonoperating income such as interest and dividends.

Most companies' income statements do not conform to either a pure single-step format or a pure multi-step format. Business operations are too complex for all companies to conform to rigid reporting formats. We will discuss the components of the income statement in more detail in Chapter 11.

USING ACCOUNTING RATIOS

As we've seen, accounting provides information for decision making. A bank considering lending money must predict whether the borrower can repay the loan. If the borrower already has a lot of debt, the probability of repayment may be low. If the borrower owes little, the loan may go through. To analyze a company's financial position, decision makers use ratios computed from various items in the financial statements. Let's see how this process works.

OBJECTIVE

6 **Use** two new ratios to evaluate a business

Current Ratio

One of the most widely used financial ratios is the **current ratio**, which divides total current assets by total current liabilities, taken from the balance sheet.

$$\text{Current ratio} = \frac{\text{Total current assets}}{\text{Total current liabilities}}$$

For Starbucks Corporation (amounts in millions on page 168) is as follows:

$$\text{Current ratio} = \frac{\text{Total current assets}}{\text{Total current liabilities}} = \frac{\$1,748}{\$2,190} = 0.80$$

The current ratio measures the company's ability to pay current liabilities with current assets. A company prefers a high current ratio, which means that the business has plenty of current assets to pay liabilities. An increasing current ratio from period to period indicates improvement in financial position.

As a rule of thumb, a strong current ratio is 1.50, which indicates that the company has $1.50 in current assets for every $1.00 in current liabilities. A company with a current ratio of 1.50 would probably have little trouble paying its current liabilities. Most successful businesses operate with current ratios between 1.20 and 1.50. A current ratio of 1.00 is considered quite low.

Starbucks' current ratio of 0.80 is very low and indicates a relatively weak current position. How does Starbucks survive with so low a current ratio? The company makes most sales for cash, enough to pay off its accounts payable, accrued expenses, and the current portion of its long-term debt, which are the liabilities that must be met with cash immediately. In recent years, the company has borrowed increasing amounts on both a short-term and long-term basis to finance operations and expansion, which has somewhat weakened its debt position. However, in comparison to other companies in the retail business, Starbucks' level of total debt is still relatively low. That leads us to the next ratio.

Debt Ratio

A second aid to decision making is the **debt ratio**, which is the ratio of total liabilities to total assets.

$$\text{Debt ratio} = \frac{\text{Total liabilities}}{\text{Total assets}}$$

For Starbucks (amounts in millions on page 168),

$$\text{Debt ratio} = \frac{\text{Total liabilities}}{\text{Total assets}} = \frac{\$3,182}{\$5,673} = 0.56$$

The debt ratio indicates the proportion of a company's assets that is financed with debt. This ratio measures a business's ability to pay both current and long-term debts (total liabilities).

A low debt ratio is safer than a high debt ratio. Why? Because a company with few liabilities has low required debt payments. This company is unlikely to get into financial difficulty. By contrast, a business with a high debt ratio may have trouble paying its liabilities, especially when sales are low and cash is scarce.

Starbucks' debt ratio of 56% (0.56) is low compared to most companies in the United States. The norm for the debt ratio ranges from 60% to 70%. Starbucks' debt ratio indicates low risk for the company, and that partly offsets Starbucks' risky current ratio.

When a company fails to pay its debts, some of its creditors might be in a position to take the company away from its owners. Most bankruptcies result from high debt ratios. Companies that continue in this pattern are often forced out of business.

How Do Transactions Affect the Ratios?

Companies such as Starbucks are keenly aware of how transactions affect their ratios. Lending agreements often require that a company's current ratio not fall below a certain level. Another loan requirement is that the company's debt ratio may not rise above a threshold, such as 0.70. When a company fails to meet one of these conditions, it is said to default on its lending agreements. The penalty can be severe: The lender can require immediate payment of the loan. Starbucks has little enough debt that the company is not in much danger. But many companies are.

Let's use Starbucks Corporation to examine the effects of some transactions on the company's current ratio and debt ratio. As shown in the preceding section, Starbucks' ratios are as follows (dollar amounts in millions):[1]

$$\text{Current ratio} = \frac{\$1,748}{\$2,190} = 0.80 \qquad \text{Debt ratio} = \frac{\$3,182}{\$5,673} = 0.561$$

The managers of any company would be concerned about how inventory purchases, payments on account, expense accruals, and depreciation would affect its ratios. Let's see how Starbucks would be affected by some typical transactions. For each transaction, the journal entry helps identify the effects on the company.

a. Issued stock and received cash of $50 million.

Journal entry:	Cash	50	
	Common Stock		50

Cash, a current asset, affects both the current ratio and the debt ratio as follows:

$$\text{Current ratio} = \frac{\$1,748 + \$50}{\$2,190} = 0.82 \qquad \text{Debt ratio} = \frac{\$3,182}{\$5,673 + \$50} = 0.556$$

---

[1]Because of the relatively small amounts of these particular illustrative transactions compared to the original components, we have chosen to carry debt ratio computations to three decimals in order to illustrate the impact of individual transactions on the debt ratio. The larger the individual transaction in comparison with the original components (for example, see the End-of-Chapter Summary Problem) the less necessary this will be.

The issuance of stock improves both ratios.

b. Paid cash to purchase buildings for $20 million.

Journal entry:	Buildings	20	
	Cash		20

Cash, a current asset, decreases, but total assets stay the same. Liabilities are unchanged.

$$\text{Current ratio} = \frac{\$1,748 - \$20}{\$2,190} = 0.79 \qquad \text{Debt ratio} = \frac{\$3,182}{\$5,673 + \$20 - \$20} = 0.561; \text{ no change}$$

A cash purchase of a building hurts the current ratio, but doesn't affect the debt ratio.

c. Made a $30 million sale on account to a grocery chain.

Journal entry:	Accounts Receivable	30	
	Sales Revenue		30

The increase in Accounts Receivable increases current assets and total assets, as follows:

$$\text{Current ratio} = \frac{\$1,748 + \$30}{\$2,190} = 0.81 \qquad \text{Debt ratio} = \frac{\$3,182}{\$5,673 + \$30} = 0.558$$

A sale on account improves both ratios.

d. Collected the account receivable, $30 million.

Journal entry:	Cash	30	
	Accounts Receivable		30

This transaction has no effect on total current assets, total assets, or total liabilities. Both ratios are unaffected.

e. Accrued expenses at year end, $40 million.

Journal entry:	Expenses	40	
	Expenses Payable		40

$$\text{Current ratio} = \frac{\$1,748}{\$2,190 + \$40} = 0.78 \qquad \text{Debt ratio} = \frac{\$3,182 + \$40}{\$5,673} = 0.568$$

Most expenses hurt both ratios.

f. Recorded depreciation, $80 million.

Journal entry:	Depreciation Expense	80	
	Accumulated Depreciation		80

No current accounts are affected, so only the debt ratio is affected.

$$\text{Current ratio} = \frac{\$1,748}{\$2,190} = 0.80 \qquad \text{Debt ratio} = \frac{\$3,182}{\$5,673 - \$80} = 0.569$$

Depreciation decreases total assets and therefore hurts the debt ratio.

g. Earned interest revenue and collected cash, $40 million.

Journal entry:	Cash	40	
	Interest Revenue		40

Cash, a current asset, affects both the current ratio and the debt ratio as follows:

$$\text{Current ratio} = \frac{\$1,748 + \$40}{\$2,190} = 0.82 \qquad \text{Debt ratio} = \frac{\$3,182}{\$5,673 + \$40} = 0.557$$

A revenue improves both ratios.

Now, let's wrap up the chapter by seeing how to use the current ratio and the debt ratio for decision making. The Decision Guidelines feature offers some clues.

DECISION GUIDELINES

USING THE CURRENT RATIO AND THE DEBT RATIO

In general, a *high* current ratio is preferable to a low current ratio. *Increases* in the current ratio improve financial position. By contrast, a *low* debt ratio is preferable to a high debt ratio. Improvement is indicated by a *decrease* in the debt ratio.

No single ratio gives the whole picture about a company. Therefore, lenders and investors use many ratios to evaluate a company. Let's apply what we have learned. Suppose you are a loan officer at Bank of America, and Starbucks Corporation has asked you for a $20 million loan to launch a new blend of coffee. How will you make this loan decision? The Decision Guidelines show how bankers and investors use two key ratios.

USING THE CURRENT RATIO

Decision	Guidelines
How can you measure a company's ability to pay current liabilities with current assets?	$$\text{Current ratio} = \frac{\text{Total current assets}}{\text{Total current liabilities}}$$
Who uses the current ratio for decision making?	*Lenders and other creditors*, who must predict whether a borrower can pay its current liabilities. *Stockholders*, who know that a company that cannot pay its debts is not a good investment because it may go bankrupt. *Managers*, who must have enough cash to pay the company's current liabilities.
What is a good value of the current ratio?	Depends on the industry: A company with strong cash flow can operate successfully with a low current ratio of, say, 1.10–1.20. A company with weak cash flow needs a higher current ratio of, say, 1.30–1.50. Traditionally, a current ratio of 2.00 was considered ideal. Recently, acceptable values have decreased as companies have been able to operate more efficiently; today, a current ratio of 1.50 is considered strong. Cash-rich companies like Starbucks can operate with a current ratio below 1.0.

USING THE DEBT RATIO

Decision	Guidelines
How can you measure a company's ability to pay total liabilities?	$$\text{Debt ratio} = \frac{\text{Total liabilities}}{\text{Total assets}}$$
Who uses the debt ratio for decision making?	*Lenders and other creditors*, who must predict whether a borrower can pay its debts. *Stockholders*, who know that a company that cannot pay its debts is not a good investment because it may go bankrupt. *Managers*, who must have enough assets to pay the company's debts.
What is a good value of the debt ratio?	Depends on the industry: A company with strong cash flow can operate successfully with a high debt ratio of, say, 0.70–0.80 A company with weak cash flow needs a lower debt ratio of, say, 0.50–0.60. Traditionally, a debt ratio of 0.50 was considered ideal. Recently, values have increased as companies have been able to operate more efficiently; today, a normal value of the debt ratio is around 0.60–0.65.

END-OF-CHAPTER SUMMARY PROBLEM

Refer to the Mid-Chapter Summary Problem that begins on page 160. The adjusted trial balance appears on page 163.

Requirements

1. Make Goldsmith Company's closing entries at December 31, 2010. Explain what the closing entries accomplish and why they are necessary. Show amounts in thousands.
2. Post the closing entries to Retained Earnings and compare Retained Earnings' ending balance with the amount reported on the balance sheet on page 164. The two amounts should be the same.
3. Prepare Goldsmith Company's classified balance sheet to identify the company's current assets and current liabilities. (Goldsmith has no long-term liabilities.) Then compute the company's current ratio and debt ratio at December 31, 2010.
4. The top management of Goldsmith Company has asked you for a $500,000 loan to expand the business. Goldsmith proposes to pay off the loan over a 10-year period. Recompute Goldsmith's debt ratio assuming you make the loan. Use the company financial statements plus the ratio values to decide whether to grant the loan at an interest rate of 8%, 10%, or 12%. Goldsmith's cash flow is strong. Give the reasoning underlying your decision.

Answers

Requirement 1

2010			(In thousands)
Dec 31	Service Revenue..	330	
	Retained Earnings		330
31	Retained Earnings	259	
	Salary Expense		177
	Depreciation Expense—		
	Furniture and Fixtures............................		20
	Depreciation Expense—Building		10
	Supplies Expense		4
	Income Tax Expense		35
	Miscellaneous Expense...............................		13
31	Retained Earnings	65	
	Dividends...		65

Explanation of Closing Entries

The closing entries set the balance of each revenue, expense, and Dividends account back to zero for the start of the next accounting period. We must close these accounts because their balances relate only to one accounting period.

Requirement 2

Retained Earnings			
			193
Clo	259	Clo	330
Clo	65		
		Bal	199

The balance in the Retained Earnings account agrees with the amount reported on the balance sheet, as it should.

❙ Requirement 3

Goldsmith Company
Balance Sheet
December 31, 2010

(Amounts in thousands)

Assets			Liabilities		
Current assets:			Current liabilities:		
Cash		$198	Accounts payable		$380
Accounts receivable		382	Salary payable		5
Supplies		2	Unearned service revenue		13
Total current assets...............		582	Income tax payable		35
Furniture and			Total current liabilities..............		433
fixtures	$100				
Less: Accumulated			*Stockholders' Equity*		
depreciation.................	(60)	40	Common stock............................		100
Building...................................	$250		Retained earnings........................		199
Less: Accumulated			Total stockholders' equity............		299
depreciation.................	(140)	110	Total liabilities and		
Total assets..............................		$732	stockholders' equity..................		$732

$$\text{Current ratio} = \frac{\$582}{\$433} = 1.34 \qquad \text{Debt ratio} = \frac{\$433}{\$732} = 0.59$$

❙ Requirement 4

$$\frac{\text{Debt ratio assuming}}{\text{the loan is made}} = \frac{\$433 + \$500}{\$732 + \$500} = \frac{\$933}{\$1,232} = .76$$

Decision: Make the loan at 10%.

Reasoning: Prior to the loan, the company's financial position and cash flow are strong. The current ratio is in a middle range, and the debt ratio is not too high. Net income (from the income statement) is high in relation to total revenue. Therefore, the company should be able to repay the loan.

The loan will increase the company's debt ratio from 59% to 76%, which is more risky than the company's financial position at present. On this basis, a midrange interest rate appears reasonable—at least as the starting point for the negotiation between Goldsmith Company and the bank.

REVIEW ACCRUAL ACCOUNTING & INCOME

Quick Check (Answers are given on page 216.)

1. On October 1, River Place Apartments received $5,200 from a tenant for four months' rent. The receipt was credited to Unearned Rent Revenue. What adjusting entry is needed on December 31?

   a. Unearned Rent Revenue   1,300
        Rent Revenue   1,300

   b. Cash   1,300
        Rent Revenue   1,300

   c. Rent Revenue   1,300
        Unearned Rent Revenue   1,300

   d. Unearned Rent Revenue   3,900
        Rent Revenue   3,900

2. The following normal balances appear on the *adjusted* trial balance of Greenville National Company:

Equipment..	$110,000
Accumulated depreciation, equipment................	22,000
Depreciation expense, equipment........................	5,500

   The book value of the equipment is

   a. $82,500.   c. $88,000.
   b. $66,000.   d. $104,500.

3. Details, Inc., purchased supplies for $1,300 during 2010. At year end Details had $800 of supplies left. The adjusting entry should

   a. debit Supplies $800.   c. debit Supplies $500.
   b. credit Supplies $800.   d. debit Supplies Expense $500.

4. The accountant for Exeter Corp. failed to make the adjusting entry to record depreciation for the current year. The effect of this error is which of the following?

   a. Assets, net income, and stockholders' equity are all overstated.
   b. Assets and expenses are understated; net income is understated.
   c. Net income is overstated and liabilities are understated.
   d. Assets are overstated, stockholders' equity and net income are understated.

5. Interest earned on a note receivable at December 31 equals $375. What adjusting entry is required to accrue this interest?

   a. Interest Expense   375
        Interest Payable   375

   b. Interest Receivable   375
        Interest Revenue   375

   c. Interest Payable   375
        Interest Expense   375

   d. Interest Expense   375
        Cash   375

6. If a real estate company fails to accrue commission revenue,
   a. revenues are understated and net income is overstated.
   b. assets are understated and net income is understated.
   c. net income is understated and stockholders' equity is overstated.
   d. liabilities are overstated and owners' equity is understated.

7. All of the following statements are true except one. Which statement is false?
   a. A fiscal year ends on some date other than December 31.
   b. The matching principle directs accountants to identify and measure all expenses incurred and deduct them from revenues earned during the same period.
   c. Adjusting entries are required for a business that uses the cash basis.
   d. Accrual accounting produces better information than cash-basis accounting.

8. The account Unearned Revenue is a(n)
   a. asset.   c. revenue.
   b. expense.   d. liability.

9. Adjusting entries
   a. update the accounts.
   b. are needed to measure the period's net income or net loss.
   c. do not debit or credit cash.
   d. all of the above.

10. An adjusting entry that debits an expense and credits a liability is which type?
    a. Depreciation expense   c. Accrued expense
    b. Cash expense   d. Prepaid expense

Use the following data for questions 11 and 12.
Here are key figures from the balance sheet of Geneva, Inc., at the end of 2010 (amounts in thousands):

	December 31, 2010
Total assets (of which 50% are current)	$5,000
Current liabilities	500
Bonds payable (long-term)	1,400
Common stock	1,000
Retained earnings	2,100
Total liabilities and stockholders' equity	5,000

11. Geneva's current ratio at the end of 2010 is
    a. 10.00.   c. 1.32.
    b. 1.19.   d. 5.00.

12. Geneva's debt ratio at the end of 2010 is (all amounts are rounded)
    a. 1.32%.   c. 10.00%.
    b. 16%.   d. 38%.

13. On a trial balance, which of the following would indicate that an error has been made?
    a. Accumulated Depreciation has a credit balance.
    b. Salary Expense has a debit balance.
    c. Service Revenue has a debit balance.
    d. All of the above indicate errors.

14. The entry to close Management Fee Revenue would be which of the following?
    a. Management Fee Revenue
            Retained Earnings
    b. Management Fee Revenue does not need to be closed.
    c. Retained Earnings
            Management Fee Revenue
    d. Management Fee Revenue
            Service Revenue

15. Which of the following accounts is not closed?
   a. Dividends
   b. Depreciation Expense
   c. Interest Revenue
   d. Accumulated Depreciation
16. UPS earns service revenue of $800,000. How does this transaction affect UPS's ratios?
   a. Improves the current ratio and doesn't affect the debt ratio
   b. Hurts the current ratio and improves the debt ratio
   c. Hurts both ratios
   d. Improves both ratios
17. Suppose Green Mountain Corporation borrows $20 million on a 20-year note payable. How does this transaction affect Green Mountain's current ratio and debt ratio?
   a. Hurts both ratios
   b. Improves both ratios
   c. Improves the current ratio and hurts the debt ratio
   d. Hurts the current ratio and improves the debt ratio

Accounting Vocabulary

account format (p. 168) A balance-sheet format that lists assets on the left and liabilities and stockholders' equity on the right.

accrual (p. 144) An expense or a revenue that occurs before the business pays or receives cash. An accrual is the opposite of a deferral.

accrual accounting (p. 139) Accounting that records the impact of a business event as it occurs, regardless of whether the transaction affected cash.

accrued expense (p. 150) An expense incurred but not yet paid in cash.

accrued revenue (p. 151) A revenue that has been earned but not yet received in cash.

accumulated depreciation (p. 148) The cumulative sum of all depreciation expense from the date of acquiring a plant asset.

adjusted trial balance (p. 156) A list of all the ledger accounts with their adjusted balances.

book value (of a plant asset) (p. 149) The asset's cost minus accumulated depreciation.

cash-basis accounting (p. 139) Accounting that records only transactions in which cash is received or paid.

classified balance sheet (p. 167) A balance sheet that shows current assets separate from long-term assets, and current liabilities separate from long-term liabilities.

closing the books (p. 165) The process of preparing the accounts to begin recording the next period's transactions. Closing the accounts consists of journalizing and posting the closing entries to set the balances of the revenue, expense, and dividends accounts to zero. Also called closing the accounts.

closing entries (p. 165) Entries that transfer the revenue, expense, and dividends balances from these respective accounts to the Retained Earnings account.

contra account (p. 149) An account that always has a companion account and whose normal balance is opposite that of the companion account.

current asset (p. 167) An asset that is expected to be converted to cash, sold, or consumed during the next 12 months, or within the business's normal operating cycle if longer than a year.

current liability (p. 167) A debt due to be paid within one year or within the entity's operating cycle if the cycle is longer than a year.

current ratio (p. 170) Current assets divided by current liabilities. Measures a company's ability to pay current liabilities with current assets.

debt ratio (p. 170) Ratio of total liabilities to total assets. States the proportion of a company's assets that is financed with debt.

deferral (p. 144) An adjustment for which the business paid or received cash in advance. Examples include prepaid rent, prepaid insurance, and supplies.

depreciation (p. 144) Allocation of the cost of a plant asset to expense over its useful life.

liquidity (p. 167) Measure of how quickly an item can be converted to cash.

long-term asset (p. 167) An asset that is not a current asset.

long-term liability (p. 167) A liability that is not a current liability.

matching principle (p. 141) The basis for recording expenses. Directs accountants to identify all expenses incurred during the period, to measure the expenses, and to match them against the revenues earned during that same period.

multi-step income statement (p. 169) An income statement that contains subtotals to highlight important relationships between revenues and expenses.

operating cycle (p. 167) Time span during which cash is paid for goods and services that are sold to customers who pay the business in cash.

permanent accounts (p. 165) Asset, liability, and stockholders' equity accounts that are not closed at the end of the period.

plant assets (p. 147) Long-lived assets, such as land, buildings, and equipment, used in the operation of the business. Also called fixed assets.

prepaid expense (p. 145) A category of miscellaneous assets that typically expire or get used up in the near future. Examples include prepaid rent, prepaid insurance, and supplies.

report format (p. 168) A balance-sheet format that lists assets at the top, followed by liabilities and stockholders' equity below.

revenue principle (p. 140) The basis for recording revenues; tells accountants when to record revenue and the amount of revenue to record.

single-step income statement (p. 169) An income statement that lists all the revenues together under a heading such as Revenues or Revenues and Gains. Expenses appear in a separate category called Expenses or perhaps Expenses and Losses.

temporary accounts (p. 165) The revenue and expense accounts that relate to a limited period and are closed at the end of the period are temporary accounts. For a corporation, the Dividends account is also temporary.

time-period concept (p. 140) Ensures that accounting information is reported at regular intervals.

unearned revenue (p. 152) A liability created when a business collects cash from customers in advance of earning the revenue. The obligation is to provide a product or a service in the future.

ASSESS YOUR PROGRESS

Short Exercises

S3-1 (*Learning Objective 1: Linking accrual accounting and cash flows*) St. Pierre Corporation made sales of $960 million during 2010. Of this amount, St. Pierre collected cash for all but $25 million. The company's cost of goods sold was $270 million, and all other expenses for the year totaled $300 million. Also during 2010, St. Pierre paid $370 million for its inventory and $285 million for everything else. Beginning cash was $105 million. St. Pierre's top management is interviewing you for a job and they ask two questions:

    a. How much was St. Pierre's net income for 2010?
    b. How much was St. Pierre's cash balance at the end of 2010?

You will get the job only if you answer both questions correctly.

S3-2 (*Learning Objective 1: Linking accrual accounting and cash flows*) Capeside Corporation began 2010 owing notes payable of $3.9 million. During 2010 Capeside borrowed $2.3 million on notes payable and paid off $2.0 million of notes payable from prior years. Interest expense for the year was $1.8 million, including $0.1 million of interest payable accrued at December 31, 2010.

Show what Capeside should report for these facts on the following financial statements:

    1. Income statement
        a. Interest expense
    2. Balance sheet
        a. Notes payable
        b. Interest payable

writing assignment ■

S3-3 (*Learning Objectives 1, 2: Linking accrual accounting and cash flows; applying accounting principles*) As the controller of Eden Consulting, you have hired a new employee, whom you must train. She objects to making an adjusting entry for accrued salaries at the end of the period. She reasons, "We will pay the salaries soon. Why not wait until payment to record the expense? In the end, the result will be the same." Write a reply to explain to the employee why the adjusting entry is needed for accrued salary expense.

S3-4 (*Learning Objective 2: Applying the revenue and the matching principles*) A large auto manufacturer sells large fleets of vehicles to auto rental companies, such as Acme and Harris. Suppose Acme is negotiating with the auto manufacturer to purchase 950 vehicles. Write a short paragraph to explain to the auto manufacturer when the company should, and should not, record this sales revenue and the related expense for cost of goods sold. Mention the accounting principles that provide the basis for your explanation.

writing assignment ■

S3-5 (*Learning Objective 2: Applying accounting concepts and principles*) Write a short paragraph to explain in your own words the concept of depreciation as used in accounting.

writing assignment ■

S3-6 (*Learning Objective 2: Applying accounting concepts and principles*) Identify the accounting concept or principle that gives the most direction on how to account for each of the following situations:

    a. Salary expense of $35,000 is accrued at the end of the period to measure income properly.

    b. May has been a particularly slow month, and the business will have a net loss for the second quarter of the year. Management is considering not following its customary practice of reporting quarterly earnings to the public.

    c. A physician performs a surgical operation and bills the patient's insurance company. It may take four months to collect from the insurance company. Should the physician record revenue now or wait until cash is collected?

    d. A construction company is building a highway system, and construction will take five years. When should the company record the revenue it earns?

    e. A utility bill is received on December 28 and will be paid next year. When should the company record utility expense?

S3-7 (*Learning Objective 3: Adjusting prepaid expenses*) Answer the following questions about prepaid expenses:

    a. On March 1, Blue & Green Travel prepaid $4,800 for six months' rent. Give the adjusting entry to record rent expense at March 31. Include the date of the entry and an explanation. Then post all amounts to the two accounts involved, and show their balances at March 31. Blue & Green Travel adjusts the accounts only at March 31, the end of its fiscal year.

    b. On December 1, Blue & Green Travel paid $900 for supplies. At March 31, Blue & Green Travel has $700 of supplies on hand. Make the required journal entry at March 31. Then post all amounts to the accounts and show their balances at March 31.

S3-8 (*Learning Objectives 1, 3: Recording depreciation; linking accrual accounting and cash flows*) Suppose that on January 1 Georgetown Golf Company paid cash of $80,000 for computers that are expected to remain useful for four years. At the end of four years, the computers' values are expected to be zero.

    1. Make journal entries to record (a) purchase of the computers on January 1 and (b) annual depreciation on December 31. Include dates and explanations, and use the following accounts: Computer Equipment; Accumulated Depreciation—Computer Equipment; and Depreciation Expense—Computer Equipment.

    2. Post to the accounts and show their balances at December 31.

    3. What is the computer equipment's book value at December 31?

S3-9 (*Learning Objective 2: Applying the matching principle and the time-period concept*) During 2010, Northwest Airlines paid salary expense of $38.3 million. At December 31, 2010, Northwest accrued salary expense of $2.8 million. Northwest then paid $1.8 million to its employees on January 3, 2011, the company's next payday after the end of the 2010 year. For this sequence of transactions, show what Northwest would report on its 2010 income statement and on its balance sheet at the end of 2010.

S3-10 *(Learning Objective 3: Accruing and paying interest expense)* Resort Travel borrowed $80,000 on October 1 by signing a note payable to Texas First Bank. The interest expense for each month is $500. The loan agreement requires Resort to pay interest on December 31.

1. Make Resort's adjusting entry to accrue monthly interest expense at October 31, at November 30, and at December 31. Date each entry and include its explanation.
2. Post all three entries to the Interest Payable account. You need not take the balance of the account at the end of each month.
3. Record the payment of three months' interest at December 31.

S3-11 *(Learning Objective 3: Accruing and receiving cash from interest revenue)* Return to the situation in Short Exercise 3-10. Here you are accounting for the same transactions on the books of Texas First Bank, which lent the money to Resort Travel.

1. Make Texas First Bank's adjusting entry to accrue monthly interest revenue at October 31, at November 30, and at December 31. Date each entry and include its explanation.
2. Post all three entries to the Interest Receivable account. You need not take the balance of the account at the end of each month.
3. Record the receipt of three months' interest at December 31.

writing assignment ■

S3-12 *(Learning Objectives 1, 3: Relating accrual accounting to cash flows; adjusting the accounts)* Write a paragraph to explain why unearned revenues are liabilities instead of revenues. In your explanation, use the following actual example: *The Globe and Trail*, a national newspaper, collects cash from subscribers in advance and later delivers newspapers to subscribers over a one-year period. Explain what happens to the unearned revenue over the course of a year as *The Globe and Trail* delivers papers to subscribers. Into what account does the earned subscription revenue go as *The Globe and Trail* delivers papers? Give the journal entries that The Globe and Trail would make to (a) collect $50,000 of subscription revenue in advance and (b) record earning $50,000 of subscription revenue. Include an explanation for each entry, as illustrated in the chapter.

S3-13 *(Learning Objective 3, 4: Adjusting the accounts; reporting prepaid expenses)* Crow Golf Co. prepaid three years' rent ($24,000) on January 1, 2010. At December 31, 2010, Crow prepared a trial balance and then made the necessary adjusting entry at the end of the year. Crow adjusts its accounts once each year—on December 31.

What amount appears for Prepaid Rent on

a. Crow's *unadjusted* trial balance at December 31, 2010?
b. Crow's *adjusted* trial balance at December 31, 2010?

What amount appears for Rent Expense on

a. Crow's *unadjusted* trial balance at December 31?
b. Crow's *adjusted* trial balance at December 31?

S3-14 *(Learning Objective 3: Adjusting the accounts)* Bryson, Inc., collects cash from customers two ways:

a. **Accrued revenue.** Some customers pay Bryson after Bryson has performed service for the customer. During 2010, Bryson made sales of $60,000 on account and later received cash of $45,000 on account from these customers.
b. **Unearned revenue.** A few customers pay Bryson in advance, and Bryson later performs the service for the customer. During 2010 Bryson collected $7,500 cash in advance and later earned $3,500 of this amount.

Journalize for Bryson

a. Earning service revenue of $60,000 on account and then collecting $45,000 on account.
b. Receiving $7,500 in advance and then earning $3,500 as service revenue.

S3-15 (*Learning Objective 4: Preparing the financial statements*) Suppose Vulture Sporting Goods Company reported the following data at March 31, 2010, with amounts in thousands:

Retained earnings, March 31, 2009	$ 2,000	Cost of goods sold	$136,800
Accounts receivable	28,200	Cash	1,300
Net revenues	174,000	Property and equipment, net	6,000
Total current liabilities	53,000	Common stock	27,000
All other expenses	26,000	Inventories	37,000
Other current assets	5,200	Long-term liabilities	12,500
Other assets	28,000	Dividends	0

Use these data to prepare Vulture Sporting Goods Company's income statement for the year ended March 31, 2010; statement of retained earnings for the year ended March 31, 2010; and classified balance sheet at March 31, 2010. Use the report format for the balance sheet. Draw arrows linking the three statements.

S3-16 (*Learning Objective 5: Making closing entries*) Use the Vulture Sporting Goods Company data in Short Exercise 3-15 to make the company's closing entries at March 31, 2010.

Then set up a T-account for Retained Earnings and post to that account. Compare Retained Earnings' ending balance to the amount reported on Vulture's statement of retained earnings and balance sheet. What do you find?

S3-17 (*Learning Objective 6: Computing the current ratio and the debt ratio*) Vulture Sporting Goods reported the following data at March 31, 2010, with amounts adapted in thousands:

Vulture Sporting Goods Company
Income Statement
For the Year Ended March 31, 2010

(Amounts in thousands)

Net revenues	$174,000
Cost of goods sold	136,800
All other expenses	26,000
Net income	$ 11,200

Vulture Sporting Goods Company
Statement of Retained Earnings
For the Year Ended March 31, 2010

(Amounts in thousands)

Retained earnings, March 31, 2009	$ 2,000
Add: Net income	11,200
Retained earnings, March 31, 2010	$13,200

Vulture Sporting Goods Company
Balance Sheet
March 31, 2010

(Amounts in thousands)

ASSETS

Current:

Cash	$ 1,300
Accounts receivable	28,200
Inventories	37,000
Other current assets	5,200
Total current assets	71,700
Property and equipment, net	6,000
Other assets	28,000
Total assets	$105,700

LIABILITIES

Total current liabilites	$ 53,000
Long-term liabilities	12,500
Total liabilities	65,500

STOCKHOLDERS' EQUITY

Common stock	27,000
Retained earnings	13,200
Total stockholders' equity	40,200
Total liabilities and stockholders' equity	$105,700

1. Compute Vulture's current ratio. Round to two decimal places.
2. Compute Vulture's debt ratio. Round to two decimal places.

Do these ratio values look strong, weak, or middle-of-the-road?

S3-18 (*Learning Objective 6: Using the current ratio and the debt ratio*) Refer to the Vulture Sporting Goods Company data in Short Exercise 3-17.

At March 31, 2010, Vulture Sporting Goods Company's current ratio was 1.35 and their debt ratio was 0.62. Compute Vulture's (a) current ratio and (b) debt ratio after each of the following transactions (all amounts in thousands, as in the Vulture financial statements):

1. Vulture earned revenue of $8,000 on account.
2. Vulture paid off accounts payable of $8,000.

When calculating the revised ratios, treat each of the above scenarios independently. Round ratios to two decimal places.

Exercises

> All of the A and B exercises can be found within MyAccountingLab, an online homework and practice environment. Your instructor may ask you to complete these exercises using MyAccountingLab.

(Group A)

E3-19A *(Learning Objective 1: Linking accrual accounting and cash flows)* During 2010 Galaxy Corporation made sales of $4,100 (assume all on account) and collected cash of $4,900 from customers. Operating expenses totaled $1,400, all paid in cash. At year end, 2010, Galaxy customers owed the company $700. Galaxy owed creditors $1,300 on account. All amounts are in millions.

1. For these facts, show what Galaxy reported on the following financial statements:

   • Income statement   • Balance sheet

2. Suppose Galaxy had used the cash basis of accounting. What would Galaxy have reported for these facts?

E3-20A *(Learning Objective 1: Linking accrual accounting and cash flows)* During 2010 Prairie Sales, Inc., earned revenues of $580,000 on account. Prairie collected $590,000 from customers during the year. Expenses totaled $480,000, and the related cash payments were $460,000. Show what Prairie would report on its 2010 income statement under the

   a. cash basis.
   b. accrual basis.

Compute net income under both bases of accounting. Which basis measures net income better? Explain your answer.

E3-21A *(Learning Objectives 1, 2: Using the accrual basis of accounting; applying accounting principles)* During 2010, Carson Network, Inc., which designs network servers, earned revenues of $800 million. Expenses totaled $590 million. Carson collected all but $28 million of the revenues and paid $610 million on its expenses. Carson's top managers are evaluating 2010, and they ask you the following questions:

   a. Under accrual accounting, what amount of revenue should Carson Network report for 2010? Is the revenue the $800 million earned or is it the amount of cash actually collected? How does the revenue principle help to answer these questions?
   b. Under accrual accounting, what amount of total expense should Carson Network report for 2010—$590 million or $610 million? Which accounting principle helps to answer this question?
   c. Which financial statement reports revenues and expenses? Which statement reports cash receipts and cash payments?

■ general ledger

E3-22A (*Learning Objectives 1, 3: Journalizing adjusting entries and analyzing their effects on net income; comparing accrual and cash basis*) An accountant made the following adjustments at December 31, the end of the accounting period:

 a. Prepaid insurance, beginning, $500. Payments for insurance during the period, $1,500. Prepaid insurance, ending, $1,000.
 b. Interest revenue accrued, $1,100.
 c. Unearned service revenue, beginning, $1,200. Unearned service revenue, ending, $400.
 d. Depreciation, $4,900.
 e. Employees' salaries owed for three days of a five-day work week; weekly payroll, $14,000.
 f. Income before income tax, $22,000. Income tax rate is 25%.

I Requirements

 1. Journalize the adjusting entries.
 2. Suppose the adjustments were not made. Compute the overall overstatement or understatement of net income as a result of the omission of these adjustments.

■ spreadsheet

E3-23A (*Learning Objectives 2, 3: Applying the revenue and matching principles; allocating supplies cost between the asset and the expense*) Bird-Bath, Inc., experienced four situations for its supplies. Compute the amounts that have been left blank for each situation. For situations 1 and 2, journalize the needed transaction. Consider each situation separately.

	Situation			
	1	2	3	4
Beginning supplies	$ 100	$ 600	$ 1,400	$ 900
Payments for supplies during the year	?	600	?	700
Total amount to account for	1,400	?	?	1,600
Ending supplies	(200)	(200)	(1,000)	?
Supplies Expense	$1,200	$?	$ 1,200	$1,300

■ general ledger

E3-24A (*Learning Objective 3: Journalizing adjusting entries*) Jenkins Motor Company faced the following situations. Journalize the adjusting entry needed at December 31, 2010, for each situation. Consider each fact separately.

 a. The business has interest expense of $9,500 that it must pay early in January 2011.
 b. Interest revenue of $4,500 has been earned but not yet received.
 c. On July 1, when we collected $13,600 rent in advance, we debited Cash and credited Unearned Rent Revenue. The tenant was paying us for two years' rent.
 d. Salary expense is $1,800 per day—Monday through Friday—and the business pays employees each Friday. This year, December 31 falls on a Wednesday.
 e. The unadjusted balance of the Supplies account is $3,300. The total cost of supplies on hand is $1,200.
 f. Equipment was purchased at the beginning of this year at a cost of $100,000. The equipment's useful life is five years. There is no residual value. Record depreciation for this year and then determine the equipment's book value.

E3-25A (*Learning Objective 3: Making adjustments in T-accounts*) The accounting records of Fletcher Publishing Company include the following unadjusted balances at May 31: Accounts Receivable, $1,600; Supplies, $600; Salary Payable, $0; Unearned Service Revenue, $900; Service Revenue, $4,800; Salary Expense, $2,500; Supplies Expense, $0.

Fletcher's accountant develops the following data for the May 31 adjusting entries:

 a. Supplies on hand, $100
 b. Salary owed to employees, $300
 c. Service revenue accrued, $800
 d. Unearned service revenue that has been earned, $200

Open the foregoing T-accounts with their beginning balances. Then record the adjustments directly in the accounts, keying each adjustment amount by letter. Show each account's adjusted balance. Journal entries are not required.

E3-26A (*Learning Objective 4: Preparing the financial statements*) The adjusted trial balance of Delicious Hams, Inc., follows.

Delicious Hams, Inc.
Adjusted Trial Balance
December 31, 2010

(Amounts in thousands)	Adjusted Trial Balance	
Account	Debit	Credit
Cash	$ 3,800	
Accounts receivable	1,500	
Inventories	1,100	
Prepaid expenses	1,700	
Property, plant and equipment	6,500	
Accumulated depreciation		$ 2,300
Other assets	9,300	
Accounts payable		7,600
Income tax payable		600
Other liabilities		2,200
Common stock		4,700
Retained earnings (beginning, December 31, 2009)		4,700
Dividends	1,500	
Sales revenue		41,400
Cost of goods sold	25,100	
Selling, administrative, and general expenses	10,700	
Income tax expense	2,300	
Total	$63,500	$63,500

❙ Requirement

1. Prepare Delicious Hams, Inc.'s income statement and statement of retained earnings for the year ended December 31, 2010, and its balance sheet on that date.

E3-27A (*Learning Objectives 3, 4: Measuring financial statement amounts; preparing financial statement amounts*) The adjusted trial balances of Dickens Corporation at March 31, 2010, and March 31, 2009, include these amounts (in millions):

	2010	2009
Receivables	$390	$270
Prepaid insurance	190	160
Accrued liabilities payable (for other operating expenses)	730	610

Dickens completed these transactions during the year ended March 31, 2010.

Collections from customers	$20,200
Payment of prepaid insurance	420
Cash payments for other operating expenses	4,100

Compute the amount of sales revenue, insurance expense, and other operating expenses to report on the income statement for the year ended March 31, 2010.

E3-28A *(Learning Objective 4: Reporting on the financial statements)* This question deals with the items and the amounts that two entities, Mother Meghan Hospital (Mother Meghan) and City of Boston (Boston) should report in their financial statements. Fill in the blanks.

I *Requirements*

1. On July 1, 2010, Mother Meghan collected $6,000 in advance from Boston, a client. Under the contract, Mother Meghan is obligated to perform medical exams for City of Boston employees evenly during the 12 months ending June 30, 2011. Assume you are Mother Meghan.
   Mother Meghan's income statement for the year ended December 31, 2010, will report _____ of $ _____.
   Mother Meghan's balance sheet at December 31, 2010, will report _____ of $ _____.
2. Assume now that you are Boston.
   Boston's income statement for the year ended December 31, 2010, will report _____ of $ _____.
   Boston's balance sheet at December 31, 2010, will report _____ of $ _____.

E3-29A *(Learning Objectives 1, 3: Linking deferrals and cash flows)* Nanofone, the British wireless phone service provider, collects cash in advance from customers. All amounts are in millions of pounds sterling (£), the British monetary unit. Assume Nanofone collected £460 in advance during 2010 and at year end still owed customers phone service worth £110.

I *Requirements*

1. Show what Nanofone will report for 2010 on its income statement and balance sheet.
2. Use the same facts for Nanofone as in Requirement 1. Further, assume Nanofone reported unearned service revenue of £55 back at the end of 2009. Show what Nanofone will report for 2010 on the same financial statements. Explain why your answer here differs from your answer to Requirement 1.

E3-30A *(Learning Objective 5: Closing the accounts)* Prepare the closing entries from the following selected accounts from the records of Sunnydale Corporation at December 31, 2010:

Cost of services sold	$11,300	Service revenue	$24,000
Accumulated depreciation	40,900	Depreciation expense	4,800
Selling, general, and		Other revenue	300
administrative expenses	6,700	Dividends	600
Retained earnings,		Income tax expense	800
December 31, 2009	2,100	Income tax payable	300

How much net income did Sunnydale earn during 2010? Prepare a T-account for Retained Earnings to show the December 31, 2010, balance of Retained Earnings.

E3-31A (*Learning Objectives 3, 5: Identifying and recording adjusting and closing entries*)
The unadjusted trial balance and income statement amounts from the December 31 adjusted
trial balance of Draper Production Company follow.

Draper Production Company

Account	Unadjusted Trial Balance		From the Adjusted Trial Balance	
Cash..	14,800			
Prepaid rent......................................	1,000			
Equipment...	44,000			
Accumulated depreciation................		3,100		
Accounts payable		5,100		
Salary payable...................................				
Unearned service revenue.................		9,300		
Income tax payable				
Notes payable, long-term		13,000		
Common stock..................................		8,500		
Retained earnings.............................		14,100		
Dividends..	1,300			
Service revenue.................................		13,600		20,100
Salary expense..................................	4,600		5,100	
Rent expense.....................................	1,000		1,300	
Depreciation expense			400	
Income tax expense..........................			1,000	
Total	66,700	66,700	7,800	20,100

Requirement

1. Journalize the adjusting and closing entries of Draper Production Company at
December 31. There was only one adjustment to Service Revenue.

E3-32A (*Learning Objectives 4, 6: Preparing a classified balance sheet; using the ratios*)
Refer to Exercise 3-31A.

Requirements

1. Use the data in the partial worksheet to prepare Draper Production Company's classified
balance sheet at December 31 of the current year. Use the report format. First you must
compute the adjusted balance for several of the balance sheet accounts.
2. Compute Draper Production Company's current ratio and debt ratio at December 31. A
year ago, the current ratio was 1.70 and the debt ratio was 0.30. Indicate whether the
company's ability to pay its debts—both current and total—improved or deteriorated
during the current year.

E3-33A (*Learning Objective 6: Measuring the effects of transactions on the ratios*) Ben Williams Company reported these ratios at December 31, 2010 (dollar amounts in millions):

$$\text{Current ratio} = \frac{\$30}{\$20} = 1.50$$

$$\text{Debt ratio} = \frac{\$30}{\$60} = 0.50$$

Ben Williams Company completed these transactions during 2011:

    a. Purchased equipment on account, $8
    b. Paid long-term debt, $11
    c. Collected cash from customers in advance, $6
    d. Accrued interest expense, $3
    e. Made cash sales, $11

Determine whether each transaction improved or hurt Williams' current ratio and debt ratio.

(Group B)

E3-34B (*Learning Objective 1: Linking accrual accounting and cash flows*) During 2010 Nebula Corporation made sales of $4,800 (assume all on account) and collected cash of $4,900 from customers. Operating expenses totaled $1,100, all paid in cash. At year end, 2010, Nebula customers owed the company $300. Nebula owed creditors $500 on account. All amounts are in millions.

    1. For these facts, show what Nebula reported on the following financial statements:

       • Income statement   • Balance sheet

    2. Suppose Nebula had used the cash basis of accounting. What would Nebula have reported for these facts?

E3-35B (*Learning Objective 1: Linking accrual accounting and cash flows*) During 2010 Mountain Sales, Inc., earned revenues of $510,000 on account. Mountain collected $580,000 from customers during the year. Expenses totaled $470,000, and the related cash payments were $440,000. Show what Mountain would report on its 2010 income statement under the

    a. cash basis.
    b. accrual basis.

Compute net income under both bases of accounting. Which basis measures net income better? Explain your answer.

E3-36B (*Learning Objectives 1, 2: Using the accrual basis of accounting; applying accounting principles*) During 2010 Carlton Network, Inc., which designs network servers, earned revenues of $740 million. Expenses totaled $560 million. Carlton collected all but $24 million of the revenues and paid $580 million on its expenses. Carlton's top managers are evaluating 2010, and they ask you the following questions:

    a. Under accrual accounting, what amount of revenue should Carlton Network report for 2010? Is it the revenue of $740 million earned or is it the amount of cash actually collected? How does the revenue principle help to answer these questions?
    b. Under accrual accounting, what amount of total expense should Carlton report for 2010—$560 million or $580 million? Which accounting principle helps to answer this question?
    c. Which financial statement reports revenues and expenses? Which statement reports cash receipts and cash payments?

E3-37B (*Learning Objectives 1, 3: Journalizing adjusting entries and analyzing their effects on net income; comparing accrual and cash basis*) An accountant made the following adjustments at December 31, the end of the accounting period:

   a. Prepaid insurance, beginning, $800. Payments for insurance during the period, $2,400. Prepaid insurance, ending, $1,600.
   b. Interest revenue accrued, $1,000.
   c. Unearned service revenue, beginning, $1,500. Unearned service revenue, ending, $400.
   d. Depreciation, $4,600.
   e. Employees' salaries owed for three days of a five-day work week; weekly payroll, $16,000.
   f. Income before income tax, $21,000. Income tax rate is 25%.

■ **general ledger**

❙ Requirements

   1. Journalize the adjusting entries.
   2. Suppose the adjustments were not made. Compute the overall overstatement or understatement of net income as a result of the omission of these adjustments.

E3-38B (*Learning Objectives 2, 3: Applying the revenue and matching principles; allocating supplies cost between the asset and the expense*) Bird-Brain, Inc., experienced four situations for its supplies. Compute the amounts that have been left blank for each situation. For situations 1 and 2, journalize the needed transaction. Consider each situation separately.

■ **spreadsheet**

	Situation			
	1	2	3	4
Beginning supplies.....................................	$ 100	$ 400	$ 1,200	$ 800
Payments for supplies during the year.......	?	1,000	?	800
Total amount to account for	1,500	?	?	1,600
Ending supplies	(400)	(500)	(700)	?
Supplies Expense.......................................	$1,100	$?	$ 1,300	$1,100

E3-39B (*Learning Objective 3: Journalizing adjusting entries*) Folton Motor Company faced the following situations. Journalize the adjusting entry needed at December 31, 2010, for each situation. Consider each fact separately.

■ **general ledger**

   a. The business has interest expense of $9,200 that it must pay early in January 2011.
   b. Interest revenue of $4,200 has been earned but not yet received.
   c. On July 1, when we collected $12,600 rent in advance, we debited Cash and credited Unearned Rent Revenue. The tenant was paying us for two years' rent.
   d. Salary expense is $1,900 per day—Monday through Friday—and the business pays employees each Friday. This year, December 31 falls on a Wednesday.
   e. The unadjusted balance of the Supplies account is $2,600. The total cost of supplies on hand is $1,200.
   f. Equipment was purchased at the beginning of this year at a cost of $160,000. The equipment's useful life is five years. There is no residual value. Record depreciation for this year and then determine the equipment's book value.

E3-40B (*Learning Objective 3: Making adjustments in T-accounts*) The accounting records of Harris Publishing Company include the following unadjusted balances at May 31: Accounts Receivable, $1,200; Supplies, $300; Salary Payable, $0; Unearned Service Revenue, $800; Service Revenue, $4,400; Salary Expense, $1,900; Supplies Expense, $0.

Harris' accountant develops the following data for the May 31 adjusting entries:

   a. Supplies on hand, $200
   b. Salary owed to employees, $600
   c. Service revenue accrued, $800
   d. Unearned service revenue that has been earned, $100

Open the foregoing T-accounts with their beginning balances. Then record the adjustments directly in the accounts, keying each adjustment amount by letter. Show each account's adjusted balance. Journal entries are not required.

E3-41B (*Learning Objective 4: Preparing the financial statements*) The adjusted trial balance of Holiday Hams, Inc., follows.

Holiday Hams, Inc. Adjusted Trial Balance December 31, 2010		
(Amounts in thousands)	**Adjusted Trial Balance**	
Account	**Debit**	**Credit**
Cash...	$ 3,500	
Accounts receivable...	1,700	
Inventories	1,200	
Prepaid expenses	1,600	
Property, plant and equipment	6,700	
Accumulated depreciation..		$ 2,700
Other assets...	9,500	
Accounts payable		7,900
Income tax payable		900
Other liabilities		2,700
Common stock...		4,800
Retained earnings (beginning, December 31, 2009)...............		4,700
Dividends..	1,200	
Sales revenue..		39,900
Cost of goods sold...	25,400	
Selling, administrative, and general expenses........................	10,400	
Income tax expense	2,400	
Total	$63,600	$63,600

Requirement

1. Prepare Holiday Hams, Inc.'s income statement and statement of retained earnings for the year ended December 31, 2010, and its balance sheet on that date. Draw the arrows linking the three statements.

E3-42B (*Learning Objectives 3, 4: Measuring financial statement amounts; preparing financial statement amounts*) The adjusted trial balances of Victory Corporation at March 31, 2010, and March 31, 2009, include these amounts (in millions):

	2010	2009
Receivables..	$330	$250
Prepaid insurance...	140	130
Accrued liabilities payable (for other operating expenses)	760	600

Victory completed these transactions during the year ended March 31, 2010.

Collections from customers...	$20,600
Payment of prepaid insurance	450
Cash payments for other operating expenses...............	4,100

Compute the amount of sales revenue, insurance expense, and other operating expenses to report on the income statement for the year ended March 31, 2010.

E3-43B (*Learning Objective 4: Reporting on the financial statements*) This question deals with the items and the amounts that two entities, Mother Elizabeth Hospital (Mother Elizabeth) and City of Portland (Portland) should report in their financial statements. Fill in the blanks.

I *Requirements*

1. On July 1, 2010, Mother Elizabeth collected $9,600 in advance from Portland, a client. Under the contract, Mother Elizabeth is obligated to perform medical exams for City of Portland employees evenly during the 12 months ending June 30, 2011. Assume you are Mother Elizabeth.
   Mother Elizabeth's income statement for the year ended December 31, 2010, will report ___ of $ ___.
   Mother Elizabeth's balance sheet at December 31, 2010, will report ___ of $ ___
2. Assume now that you are Portland.
   Portland's income statement for the year ended December 31, 2010, will report ___ of $ ___.
   Portland's balance sheet at December 31, 2010, will report ___ of $ ___.

E3-44B (*Learning Objectives 1, 3: Linking deferrals and cash flows*) Direct, the British wireless phone service provider, collects cash in advance from customers. All amounts are in millions of pounds sterling (£), the British monetary unit. Assume Direct collected £400 in advance during 2010 and at year end still owed customers phone service worth £105.

I *Requirements*

1. Show what Direct will report for 2010 on its income statement balance sheet.
2. Use the same facts for Direct as in Requirement 1. Further, assume Direct reported unearned service revenue of £95 back at the end of 2009. Show what Direct will report for 2010 on the same financial statements. Explain why your answer here differs from your answer to Requirement 1.

E3-45B (*Learning Objective 5: Closing the accounts*) Prepare the closing entries from the following selected accounts from the records of East Shore Corporation at December 31, 2010:

Cost of services sold............	$11,200	Service revenue........................	$24,100
Accumulated depreciation...	41,800	Depreciation expense	4,800
Selling, general, and		Other revenue	500
administrative expenses....	6,100	Dividends...............................	900
Retained earnings,		Income tax expense................	400
December 31, 2009.........	2,400	Income tax payable	900

How much net income did East Shore earn during 2010? Prepare a T-account for Retained Earnings to show the December 31, 2010, balance of Retained Earnings.

E3-46B (*Learning Objectives 3, 5: Identifying and recording adjusting and closing entries*)
The unadjusted trial balance and income statement amounts from the December 31 adjusted trial balance of Wallace Production Company follow.

Wallace Production Company

Account	Unadjusted Trial Balance		From the Adjusted Trial Balance	
Cash	$13,600			
Prepaid rent	1,100			
Equipment	48,000			
Accumulated depreciation		$ 3,600		
Accounts payable		4,400		
Salary payable				
Unearned service revenue		8,500		
Income tax payable				
Notes payable, long-term		10,000		
Common stock		8,400		
Retained earnings		20,800		
Dividends	1,000			
Service revenue		13,400		$19,900
Salary expense	4,500		$4,900	
Rent expense	900		1,400	
Depreciation expense			600	
Income tax expense			1,700	
Total	$69,100	$69,100	$8,600	$19,900

❙ Requirement

1. Journalize the adjusting and closing entries of Wallace Production Company at December 31. There was only one adjustment to Service Revenue.

E3-47B (*Learning Objectives 4, 6: Preparing a classified balance sheet; using the ratios*)
Refer to Exercise 3-46B.

❙ Requirements

1. Use the data in the partial worksheet to prepare Wallace Production Company's classified balance sheet at December 31 of the current year. Use the report format. First you must compute the adjusted balance for several of the balance-sheet accounts.
2. Compute Wallace Production Company's current ratio and debt ratio at December 31. A year ago, the current ratio was 1.45 and the debt ratio was 0.35. Indicate whether the company's ability to pay its debts—both current and total—improved or deteriorated during the current year.

E3-48B (*Learning Objective 6: Measuring the effects of transactions on the ratios*) Brent Landry Company reported these ratios at December 31, 2010 (dollar amounts in millions):

$$\text{Current ratio} = \frac{\$40}{\$30} = 1.33$$

$$\text{Debt ratio} = \frac{\$30}{\$60} = 0.50$$

Brent Landry Company completed these transactions during 2011:

    a. Purchased equipment on account, $6
    b. Paid long-term debt, $11
    c. Collected cash from customers in advance, $8
    d. Accrued interest expense, $7
    e. Made cash sales, $11

Determine whether each transaction improved or hurt Landry's current ratio and debt ratio.

Serial Exercise

Exercise 3-49 continues the Jerome Smith, Certified Public Accountant, P.C., situation begun in Exercise 2-36 of Chapter 2.

E3-49 (*Learning Objectives 3, 4, 5, 6: Adjusting the accounts; preparing the financial statements; closing the accounts; evaluating the business*) Refer to Exercise 2-36 of Chapter 2. Start from the trial balance and the posted T-accounts that Jerome Smith, Certified Public Accountant, Professional Corporation (P.C.), prepared for his accounting practice at March 18. A professional corporation is not subject to income tax. Later in March, the business completed these transactions:

■ **general ledger**

Mar 21	Received $1,800 in advance for tax work to be performed over the next 30 days.
21	Hired a secretary to be paid on the 15th day of each month.
26	Paid $500 for the supplies purchased on March 5.
28	Collected $2,100 from the client on March 18.
31	Declared and paid dividends of $1,400.

❚ Requirements

1. Journalize the transactions of March 21 through 31.
2. Post the March 21 to 31 transactions to the T-accounts, keying all items by date.
3. Prepare a trial balance at March 31.
4. At March 31, gathers the following information for the adjusting entries:
    a. Accrued service revenue, $1,600
    b. Earned $600 of the service revenue collected in advance on March 21
    c. Supplies on hand, $100
    d. Depreciation expense equipment, $40; furniture, $125
    e. Accrued expense for secretary's salary, $600

    Make these adjustments in the adjustments columns and complete the adjusted trial balance at January 31.

5. Journalize and post the adjusting entries. Denote each adjusting amount as Adj and an account balance as Bal.
6. Prepare the income statement and statement of retained earnings of Jerome Smith Certified Public Accountant, P.C., for the month ended March 31 and the classified balance sheet at that date.
7. Journalize and post the closing entries at March 31. Denote each closing amount as Clo and an account balance as Bal.
8. Compute the current ratio and the debt ratio of Jerome Smith Certified Public Accountant, P.C., and evaluate these ratio values as indicative of a strong or weak financial position.

Challenge Exercises

E3-50 (*Learning Objective 6: Evaluating the current ratio*) Worthy Hills Corporation reported the following current accounts at December 31, 2010 (amounts in thousands):

Cash	$1,800
Receivables	5,300
Inventory	2,300
Prepaid expenses	1,100
Accounts payable	2,800
Unearned revenue	1,100
Accrued expenses payable	2,000

During 2011, Worthy Hills completed these selected transactions:

- Sold services on account, $8,700
- Depreciation expense, $700
- Paid for expenses, $7,400
- Collected from customers on account, $7,500
- Accrued expenses, $300
- Paid on account, $1,500
- Used up prepaid expenses, $400

Compute Worthy Hills's current ratio at December 31, 2010, and again at December 31, 2011. Did the current ratio improve or deteriorate during 2011? Comment on the level of the company's current ratio.

E3-51 (*Learning Objectives 3, 4: Computing financial statement amounts*) The accounts of Greatbrook Company prior to the year-end adjustments follow.

Cash	$ 16,600	Common stock	$ 14,000
Accounts receivable	7,000	Retained earnings	45,000
Supplies	4,200	Dividends	12,000
Prepaid insurance	3,400	Service revenue	160,000
Building	107,000	Salary expense	34,000
Accumulated depreciation—		Depreciation expense—	
building	15,000	building	
Land	52,000	Supplies expense	
Accounts payable	6,500	Insurance expense	
Salary payable		Advertising expense	7,600
Unearned service revenue	5,400	Utilities expense	2,100

Adjusting data at the end of the year include which of the following?

- **a.** Unearned service revenue that has been earned, $1,620
- **b.** Accrued service revenue, $32,000
- **c.** Supplies used in operations, $3,600
- **d.** Accrued salary expense, $3,200
- **e.** Prepaid insurance expired, $1,200
- **f.** Depreciation expense—building, $2,500

Rorie Lacourse, the principal stockholder, has received an offer to sell Greatbrook Company. He needs to know the following information within one hour:

    a. Net income for the year covered by these data

    b. Total assets

    c. Total liabilities

    d. Total stockholders' equity

    e. Prove that Total assets = Total liabilities + Total stockholders' equity after all items are updated.

❙ *Requirement*

    1. Without opening any accounts, making any journal entries, or using a work sheet, provide Mr. Lacourse with the requested information. The business is not subject to income tax.

Practice Quiz

Test your understanding of accrual accounting by answering the following questions. Select the best choice from among the possible answers given.

Questions 52–54 are based on the following facts:

Frank Dunn began a music business in January 2010. Dunn prepares monthly financial statements and uses the accrual basis of accounting. The following transactions are Dunn Company's only activities during January through April:

Jan 14	Bought music on account for $23, with payment to the supplier due in 90 days.
Feb 3	Performed a job on account for Jimmy Jones for $38, collectible from Jones in 30 days. Used up all the music purchased on Jan 14.
Mar 16	Collected the $38 receivable from Jones.
Apr 22	Paid the $23 owed to the supplier from the January 14 transaction.

Q3-52 In which month should Dunn record the cost of the music as an expense?

a. January   c. March

b. February   d. April

Q3-53 In which month should Dunn report the $38 revenue on its income statement?

a. January   c. March

b. February   d. April

Q3-54 If Dunn Company uses the *cash* basis of accounting instead of the accrual basis, in what month will Dunn report revenue and in what month will it report expense?

Revenue	Expense
a. March	February
b. February	April
c. February	February
d. March	April

Q3-55 In which month should revenue be recorded?

a. In the month that cash is collected from the customer

b. In the month that goods are shipped to the customer

c. In the month that goods are ordered by the customer

d. In the month that the invoice is mailed to the customer

Q3-56 On January 1 of the current year, Bambi Company paid $1,200 rent to cover six months (January–June). Bambi recorded this transaction as follows:

Journal Entry			
Date	Accounts	Debit	Credit
Jan 1	Prepaid Rent	1,200	
	Cash		1,200

Bambi adjusts the accounts at the end of each month. Based on these facts, the adjusting entry at the end of January should include
a. a credit to Prepaid Rent for $1,000.
b. a credit to Prepaid Rent for $200.
c. a debit to Prepaid Rent for $1,000.
d. a debit to Prepaid Rent for $200.

Q3-57 Assume the same facts as in question 3-56. Bambi's adjusting entry at the end of February should include a debit to Rent Expense in the amount of
a. $200.   **c.** $400.
b. $1,000.   **d.** $0.

Q3-58 What effect does the adjusting entry in question 3-57 have on Bambi's net income for February?
a. Increase by $200   **c.** Increase by $400
b. Decrease by $200   **d.** Decrease by $400

Q3-59 An adjusting entry recorded April salary expense that will be paid in May. Which statement best describes the effect of this adjusting entry on the company's accounting equation?
a. Assets are decreased, liabilities are increased, and stockholders' equity is decreased.
b. Assets are not affected, liabilities are increased, and stockholders' equity is decreased.
c. Assets are decreased, liabilities are not affected, and stockholders' equity is decreased.
d. Assets are not affected, liabilities are increased, and stockholders' equity is increased.

Q3-60 On April 1, 2010, Rural Insurance Company sold a one-year insurance policy covering the year ended April 1, 2011. Rural collected the full $2,700 on April 1, 2010. Rural made the following journal entry to record the receipt of cash in advance:

Journal Entry			
Date	Accounts	Debit	Credit
Apr 1	Cash	2,700	
	Unearned Revenue		2,700

Nine months have passed, and Rural has made no adjusting entries. Based on these facts, the adjusting entry needed by Rural at December 31, 2010, is

	Accounts	Debit	Credit
a.	Insurance Revenue	675	
	Unearned Revenue		675
b.	Unearned Revenue	2,025	
	Insurance Revenue		2,025
c.	Insurance Revenue	2,025	
	Unearned Revenue		2,025
d.	Unearned Revenue	675	
	Insurance Revenue		675

Q3-61 The Unearned Revenue account of Super Incorporated began 2010 with a normal balance of $2,000 and ended 2010 with a normal balance of $17,000. During 2010, the Unearned Revenue account was credited for $26,000 that Super will earn later. Based on these facts, how much revenue did Super earn in 2010?

a. $11,000

b. $28,000

c. $2,000

d. $26,000

Q3-62 What is the effect on the financial statements of *recording* depreciation on equipment?

a. Net income is not affected, but assets and stockholders' equity are decreased.

b. Net income and assets are decreased, but stockholders' equity is not affected.

c. Net income, assets, and stockholders' equity are all decreased.

d. Assets are decreased, but net income and stockholders' equity are not affected.

Q3-63 For 2010, Matthews Company had revenues in excess of expenses. Which statement describes Matthews' closing entries at the end of 2010?

a. Revenues will be credited, expenses will be debited, and retained earnings will be credited.

b. Revenues will be debited, expenses will be credited, and retained earnings will be debited.

c. Revenues will be credited, expenses will be debited, and retained earnings will be debited.

d. Revenues will be debited, expenses will be credited, and retained earnings will be credited.

Q3-64 Which of the following accounts would *not* be included in the closing entries?

a. Depreciation Expense

b. Accumulated Depreciation

c. Retained Earnings

d. Service Revenue

Q3-65 A major purpose of preparing closing entries is to

a. zero out the liability accounts.

b. close out the Supplies account.

c. adjust the asset accounts to their correct current balances.

d. update the Retained Earnings account.

Q3-66 Selected data for the Blossom Company follow:

Current assets..............	$ 29,333	Current liabilities	$ 24,800
Long-term assets	187,430	Long-term liabilities	112,738
Total revenues..............	196,651	Total expenses.................	169,015

Based on these facts, what are Blossom's current ratio and debt ratio?

Current ratio	Debt ratio
a. 1.633 to 1	0.742 to 1
b. 0.694 to 1	6.815 to 1
c. 1.183 to 1	0.635 to 1
d. 1.633 to 1	0.601 to 1

Q3-67 Unadjusted net income equals $7,500. Calculate what net income will be after the following adjustments:

1. Salaries payable to employees, $660

2. Interest due on note payable at the bank, $100

3. Unearned revenue that has been earned, $950

4. Supplies used, $300

Q3-68 Salary Payable at the beginning of the month totals $28,000. During the month salaries of $126,000 were accrued as expense. If ending Salary Payable is $15,000, what amount of cash did the company pay for salaries during the month?

a. $124,000

b. $139,000

c. $126,000

d. $154,000

Problems

All of the A and B problems can be found within MyAccountingLab, an online home-work and practice environment. Your instructor may ask you to complete these prob-lems using MyAccountingLab.

(Group A)

P3-69A (*Learning Objective 1: Linking accrual accounting and cash flows*) Labear Corporation earned revenues of $41 million during 2011 and ended the year with net income of $5 million. During 2011, Labear collected $23 million from customers and paid cash for all of its expenses plus an additional $5 million for amounts payable at December 31, 2010. Answer these questions about Labear's operating results, financial position, and cash flows during 2011:

I *Requirements*

1. How much were Labear's total expenses? Show your work.
2. Identify all the items that Labear will report on its 2011 income statement. Show each amount.
3. Labear began 2011 with receivables of $4 million. All sales are on account. What was the company's receivables balance at the end of 2011? Identify the appropriate finan-cial statement, and show how Labear will report ending receivables in the 2011 annual report.
4. Labear began 2011 owing accounts payable of $8 million. All expenses are incurred on account. During 2011 Labear paid $41 million on account. How much in accounts payable did the company owe at the end of 2011? Identify the appropriate financial state-ment and show how Labear will report accounts payable in its 2011 annual report.

P3-70A (*Learning Objective 1: Comparing cash basis and accrual basis*) Elders Consulting had the following selected transactions in August:

Aug	1	Prepaid insurance for August through December, $500.
	4	Purchased software for cash, $800.
	5	Performed services and received cash, $700.
	8	Paid advertising expense, $500.
	11	Performed service on account, $3,500.
	19	Purchased computer on account, $1,700.
	24	Collected for August 11 service.
	26	Paid account payable from August 19.
	29	Paid salary expense, $800.
	31	Adjusted for August insurance expense (see Aug 1).
	31	Earned revenue of $600 that was collected in advance back in July.

I *Requirements*

1. Show how each transaction would be handled using the cash basis and the accrual basis.
2. Compute August income (loss) before tax under each accounting method.
3. Indicate which measure of net income or net loss is preferable. Use the transactions on August 11 and August 24 to explain.

writing assignment ■ **P3-71A** (*Learning Objective 3: Making accounting adjustments*) Journalize the adjusting entry needed on December 31, end of the current accounting period, for each of the follow-ing independent cases affecting Rowling Corp. Include an explanation for each entry.

a. Details of Prepaid Insurance are shown in the account:

Prepaid Insurance		
Jan 1 Bal	900	
Mar 31	3,600	

Rowling prepays insurance on March 31 each year. At December 31, $1,300 is still prepaid.

b. Rowling pays employees each Friday. The amount of the weekly payroll is $6,100 for a five-day work week. The current accounting period ends on Tuesday.

c. Rowling has a note receivable. During the current year, Rowling has earned accrued interest revenue of $400 that it will collect next year.

d. The beginning balance of supplies was $2,700. During the year, Rowling purchased supplies costing $6,400, and at December 31 supplies on hand total $2,200.

e. Rowling is providing services for Orca Investments, and the owner of Orca paid Rowling $12,000 as the annual service fee. Rowling recorded this amount as Unearned Service Revenue. Rowling estimates that it has earned 70% of the total fee during the current year.

f. Depreciation for the current year includes Office Furniture, $3,000, and Equipment, $5,400. Make a compound entry.

P3-72A (*Learning Objectives 3, 4: Preparing an adjusted trial balance and the financial statements*)   Consider the unadjusted trial balance of London, Inc., at December 31, 2010, and the related month-end adjustment data.

London, Inc.
Trial Balance Work Sheet
December 31, 2010

Account	Trial Balance		Adjustments		Adjusted Trial Balance	
	Debit	Credit	Debit	Credit	Debit	Credit
Cash	8,900					
Accounts receivable	1,200					
Prepaid rent	2,400					
Supplies	2,500					
Furniture	72,000					
Accumulated depreciation		3,900				
Accounts payable		3,300				
Salary payable						
Common stock		12,000				
Retained earnings		63,110				
Dividends	3,500					
Service revenue		11,000				
Salary expense	2,300					
Rent expense						
Utilities expense	510					
Depreciation expense						
Supplies expense						
Total	93,310	93,310				

Adjustment data December 31, 2010:

a. Accrued service revenue at December 31, $2,100.

b. Prepaid rent expired during the month. The unadjusted prepaid balance of $2,400 relates to the period December 1, 2010 through February, 2011.

c. Supplies used during December, $2,170.

d. Depreciation on furniture for the month. The estimated useful life of the furniture is three years.

e. Accrued salary expense at December 31 for Monday, Tuesday, and Wednesday. The five-day weekly payroll of $4,800 will be paid on Friday.

I Requirements

1. Using Exhibit 3-9 as an example, prepare the adjusted trial balance of London, Inc., at December 31, 2010. Key each adjusting entry by letter.

2. Prepare the monthly income statement, the statement of retained earnings, and the classified balance sheet. Draw arrows linking the three statements.

■ general ledger

P3-73A (*Learning Objective 3: Analyzing and recording adjustments*) Peachtree Apartments, Inc.'s unadjusted and adjusted trial balances at April 30, 2010, follow.

Peachtree Apartments, Inc.
Adjusted Trial Balance
April 30, 2010

Account	Trial Balance Debit	Trial Balance Credit	Adjusted Trial Balance Debit	Adjusted Trial Balance Credit
Cash	$ 8,900		$ 8,900	
Accounts receivable	5,900		6,810	
Interest receivable			200	
Note receivable	4,400		4,400	
Supplies	1,800		600	
Prepaid insurance	2,300		600	
Building	70,000		70,000	
Accumulated depreciation		$ 7,400		$ 8,800
Accounts payable		6,700		6,700
Wages payable				1,000
Unearned rental revenue		2,100		1,600
Common stock		17,000		17,000
Retained earnings		40,000		40,000
Dividends	3,300		3,300	
Rental revenue		25,100		26,510
Interest revenue		400		600
Depreciation expense			1,400	
Supplies expense			1,200	
Utilities expense	400		400	
Wage expense	1,300		2,300	
Property tax expense	400		400	
Insurance expense			1,700	
Total	$98,700	$98,700	$102,210	$102,210

Requirements

1. Make the adjusting entries that account for the differences between the two trial balances.
2. Compute Peachtree's total assets, total liabilities, total equity, and net income.

P3-74A (*Learning Objectives 4, 6: Preparing the financial statements; using the debt ratio*)   The adjusted trial balance of Schneider Corporation at July 31, 2010, follows.

■ **spreadsheet**

Schneider Corporation
Adjusted Trial Balance
July 31, 2010

Account	Debit	Credit
Cash...	$ 2,000	
Accounts receivable........................	9,400	
Supplies..	2,400	
Prepaid rent....................................	1,200	
Equipment.......................................	36,600	
Accumulated depreciation...............		$ 4,200
Accounts payable............................		3,400
Interest payable..............................		200
Unearned service revenue		700
Income tax payable		2,000
Note payable...................................		18,900
Common stock................................		4,000
Retained earnings...........................		5,000
Dividends.......................................	21,000	
Service revenue..............................		102,100
Depreciation expense	1,700	
Salary expense................................	39,800	
Rent expense...................................	10,300	
Interest expense..............................	3,300	
Insurance expense	3,500	
Supplies expense.............................	2,800	
Income tax expense........................	6,500	
Total	$140,500	$140,500

Requirements

1. Prepare Schneider Corporation's 2010 income statement, statement of retained earnings, and balance sheet. List expenses (except for income tax) in decreasing order on the income statement and show total liabilities on the balance sheet. Draw arrows linking the three financial statements.
2. Schneider's lenders require that the company maintain a debt ratio no higher than 0.60. Compute Schneider's debt ratio at July 31, 2010, to determine whether the company is in compliance with this debt restriction. If not, suggest a way that Schneider could have avoided this difficult situation.

P3-75A (*Learning Objective 5: Closing the books; evaluating retained earnings*) The accounts of Spa View Service, Inc., at March 31, 2010, are listed in alphabetical order.

Accounts payable	$14,400	Interest expense	$ 900
Accounts receivable	16,100	Note payable, long term	6,100
Accumulated depreciation—		Other assets	14,400
equipment	6,900	Prepaid expenses	6,000
Advertising expense	10,900	Retained earnings,	
Cash	7,900	March 31, 2009	22,000
Common stock	5,600	Salary expense	17,800
Current portion of note		Salary payable	2,900
payable	1,000	Service revenue	95,000
Depreciation expense	1,700	Supplies	3,600
Dividends	31,200	Supplies expense	4,400
Equipment	41,700	Unearned service revenue	2,700

Requirements

1. All adjustments have been journalized and posted, but the closing entries have not yet been made. Journalize Spa View's closing entries at March 31, 2010.
2. Set up a T-account for Retained Earnings and post to that account. Then compute Spa View's net income for the year ended March 31, 2010. What is the ending balance of Retained Earnings?
3. Did Retained Earnings increase or decrease during the year? What caused the increase or the decrease?

P3-76A (*Learning Objectives 4, 6: Preparing a classified balance sheet; using the ratios to evaluate the business*) Refer back to Problem 3-75A.

Requirements

1. Use the Spa View data in Problem 3-75A to prepare the company's classified balance sheet at March 31, 2010. Show captions for total assets, total liabilities, and total liabilities and stockholders' equity.
2. Compute Spa View's current ratio and debt ratio at March 31, 2010, rounding to two decimal places. At March 31, 2009, the current ratio was 1.25 and the debt ratio was 0.20. Did Spa View's ability to pay both current and total debts improve or deteriorate during 2010? Evaluate Spa View's debt position as strong or weak and give your reason.

P3-77A (*Learning Objective 6: Analyzing financial ratios*) This problem demonstrates the effects of transactions on the current ratio and the debt ratio of Hartford Company. Hartford's condensed and adapted balance sheet at December 31, 2010, follows.

	(In millions)
Total current assets	$15.6
Properties, plant, equipment, and other assets	16.1
	$31.7
Total current liabilities	$ 9.6
Total long-term liabilities	5.8
Total stockholders' equity	16.3
	$31.7

Assume that during the first quarter of the following year, 2011, Hartford completed the following transactions:

 a. Paid half the current liabilities.

 b. Borrowed $6.0 million on long-term debt.

 c. Earned revenue, $2.5 million, on account.

 d. Paid selling expense of $0.6 million.

 e. Accrued general expense of $0.7 million. Credit General Expense Payable, a current liability.

 f. Purchased equipment for $4.2 million, paying cash of $1.5 million and signing a long-term note payable for $2.7 million.

 g. Recorded depreciation expense of $0.8 million.

❙ Requirements

1. Compute Hartford's current ratio and debt ratio at December 31, 2010. Round to two decimal places.
2. Consider each transaction separately. Compute Hartford's current ratio and debt ratio after each transaction during 2011, that is, seven times. Round ratios to two decimal places.
3. Based on your analysis, you should be able to readily identify the effects of certain transactions on the current ratio and the debt ratio. Test your understanding by completing these statements with either "increase" or "decrease":

 a. Revenues usually _____ the current ratio.

 b. Revenues usually _____ the debt ratio.

 c. Expenses usually _____ the current ratio. (*Note:* Depreciation is an exception to this rule.)

 d. Expenses usually _____ the debt ratio.

 e. If a company's current ratio is greater than 1.0, as it is for Hartford, paying off a current liability will always _____ the current ratio.

 f. Borrowing money on long-term debt will always the current ratio and _____ the debt ratio.

(Group B)

P3-78B (*Learning Objective 1: Linking accrual accounting and cash flows*) Gauge Corporation earned revenues of $33 million during 2010 and ended the year with net income of $6 million. During 2010 Gauge collected cash of $24 million from customers and paid cash for all of its expenses plus an additional $1 million on account for amounts payable at December 31, 2009. Answer these questions about Gauge's operating results, financial position, and cash flows during 2010:

❙ Requirements

1. How much were Gauge's total expenses? Show your work.
2. Identify all the items that Gauge will report on its 2010 income statement. Show each amount.
3. Gauge began 2010 with receivables of $9 million. All sales are on account. What was Gauge's receivables balance at the end of 2010? Identify the appropriate financial statement and show how Gauge will report its ending receivables balance in the company's 2010 annual report.
4. Gauge began 2010 owing accounts payable of $11 million. All expenses are incurred on account. During 2010, Gauge paid $28 million on account. How much in accounts payable did Gauge owe at the end of 2010? Identify the appropriate financial statement and show how Gauge will report accounts payable in its 2010 annual report.

P3-79B (*Learning Objective 1: Comparing cash basis and accrual basis*) Kings Consulting had the following selected transactions in May:

May	1	Prepaid insurance for May through September, $500.
	4	Purchased software for cash, $600.
	5	Performed services and received cash, $1,000.
	8	Paid advertising expense, $400.
	11	Performed service on account, $3,100.
	19	Purchased computer on account, $2,000.
	24	Collected for May 11 service.
	26	Paid account payable from May 19.
	29	Paid salary expense, $1,500.
	31	Adjusted for May insurance expense (see May 1).
	31	Earned revenue of $500 that was collected in advance back in April.

▌*Requirements*

1. Show how each transaction would be handled using the cash basis and the accrual basis.
2. Compute May income (loss) before tax under each accounting method.
3. Indicate which measure of net income or net loss is preferable. Use the transactions on May 11 and May 24 to explain.

writing assignment ■

P3-80B (*Learning Objective 3: Making accounting adjustments*) Journalize the adjusting entry needed on December 31, the end of the current accounting period, for each of the following independent cases affecting Irons Corp. Include an explanation for each entry.

a. Details of Prepaid Insurance are shown in the account:

Prepaid Insurance	
Jan 1 Bal 500	
Mar 31 3,800	

Irons prepays insurance on March 31 each year. At December 31, $900 is still prepaid.

b. Irons pays employees each Friday. The amount of the weekly payroll is $5,800 for a five-day work week. The current accounting period ends on Wednesday.

c. Irons has a note receivable. During the current year, has earned accrued interest revenue of $700 that it will collect next year.

d. The beginning balance of supplies was $2,700. During the year, Irons purchased supplies costing $6,100, and at December 31 supplies on hand total $2,200.

e. Irons is providing services for Orca Investments, and the owner of Orca paid Irons $12,100 as the annual service fee. Irons recorded this amount as Unearned Service Revenue. Irons estimates that it has earned 60% of the total fee during the current year.

f. Depreciation for the current year includes Office Furniture, $3,500, and Equipment, $5,400. Make a compound entry.

P3-81B *(Learning Objectives 3, 4: Preparing an adjusted trial balance and the financial statements)* Consider the unadjusted trial balance of Kings, Inc., at August 31, 2010, and the related month-end adjustment data.

Kings, Inc.
Trial Balance Work Sheet
August 31, 2010

Account	Trial Balance Debit	Trial Balance Credit	Adjustments Debit	Adjustments Credit	Adjusted Trial Balance Debit	Adjusted Trial Balance Credit
Cash	9,200					
Accounts receivable	1,500					
Prepaid rent	2,400					
Supplies	2,200					
Furniture	81,000					
Accumulated depreciation		3,900				
Accounts payable		3,500				
Salary payable						
Common stock		15,000				
Retained earnings		71,020				
Dividends	3,600					
Service revenue		10,000				
Salary expense	3,000					
Rent expense						
Utilities expense	520					
Depreciation expense						
Supplies expense						
Total	103,420	103,420				

Adjustment data at August 31, 2010 include the following:

a. Accrued advertising revenue at August 31, $2,000
b. Prepaid rent expired during the month. The unadjusted prepaid balance of $2,400 relates to the period August 2010 through October 2010.
c. Supplies used during August, $1,820
d. Depreciation on furniture for the month. The furniture's expected useful life is five years.
e. Accrued salary expense at August 31 for Monday, Tuesday, and Wednesday. The five-day weekly payroll is $5,200 and will be paid on Friday.

I Requirements

1. Using Exhibit 3-9 as an example, prepare the adjusted trial balance of Kings, Inc., at August 31, 2010. Key each adjusting entry by letter.
2. Prepare the monthly income statement, the statement of retained earnings, and the classified balance sheet. Draw arrows linking the three statements.

■ general ledger   **P3-82B** (*Learning Objective 3: Analyzing and recording adjustments*) Fairview Apartments, Inc.'s unadjusted and adjusted trial balances at April 30, 2010, follow:

Fairview Apartments, Inc.
Adjusted Trial Balance
April 30, 2010

Account	Trial Balance Debit	Trial Balance Credit	Adjusted Trial Balance Debit	Adjusted Trial Balance Credit
Cash	$ 7,900		$ 7,900	
Accounts receivable	6,000		6,880	
Interest receivable			500	
Note receivable	5,000		5,000	
Supplies	1,500		600	
Prepaid insurance	2,500		800	
Building	67,000		67,000	
Accumulated depreciation		$ 8,800		$10,300
Accounts payable		6,500		6,500
Wages payable				800
Unearned rental revenue		1,500		1,200
Common stock		17,000		17,000
Retained earnings		43,300		43,300
Dividends	3,200		3,200	
Rental revenue		18,300		19,480
Interest revenue		200		700
Depreciation expense			1,500	
Supplies expense			900	
Utilities expense	300		300	
Wage expense	1,900		2,700	
Property tax expense	300		300	
Insurance expense			1,700	
Total	$95,600	$95,600	$99,280	$99,280

I Requirements

1. Make the adjusting entries that account for the differences between the two trial balances.
2. Compute Fairview's total assets, total liabilities, total equity, and net income.

P3-83B *(Learning Objectives 4, 6: Preparing the financial statements; using the debt ratio)*   The adjusted trial balance of Sneed Corporation at October 31, 2010, follows: ■ spreadsheet

Sneed Corporation
Adjusted Trial Balance
October 31, 2010

Account	Debit	Credit
Cash...	$ 1,600	
Accounts receivable.........................	8,800	
Supplies...	2,100	
Prepaid rent.....................................	1,000	
Equipment.......................................	36,700	
Accumulated depreciation...............		$ 4,400
Accounts payable............................		3,800
Interest payable..............................		400
Unearned service revenue		900
Income tax payable		2,500
Note payable....................................		18,600
Common stock.................................		8,000
Retained earnings............................		4,000
Dividends..	25,000	
Service revenue................................		101,700
Depreciation expense	1,200	
Salary expense.................................	40,500	
Rent expense...................................	10,200	
Interest expense..............................	3,200	
Insurance expense	3,600	
Supplies expense.............................	2,900	
Income tax expense.........................	7,500	
Total	$144,300	$144,300

I Requirements

1. Prepare Sneed's 2010 income statement, statement of retained earnings, and balance sheet. List expenses (except for income tax) in decreasing order on the income statement and show total liabilities on the balance sheet.
2. Sneed's lenders require that the company maintain a debt ratio no higher than 0.60. Compute Sneed's debt ratio at October 31, 2010, to determine whether the company is in compliance with this debt restriction. If not, suggest a way Sneed could have avoided this difficult situation.

P3-84B (*Learning Objective 5: Making closing entries; evaluating retained earnings*) The accounts of Sunny Stream Service, Inc., at March 31, 2010, are listed in alphabetical order.

Accounts payable	$14,300	Interest expense	$ 800
Accounts receivable	16,400	Note payable, long term	5,900
Accumulated depreciation—		Other assets	14,500
equipment	7,300	Prepaid expenses	5,700
Advertising expense	11,100	Retained earnings,	
Cash	7,300	March 31, 2009	22,000
Common stock	6,700	Salary expense	18,100
Current portion of note		Salary payable	2,600
payable	500	Service revenue	94,100
Depreciation expense	2,000	Supplies	3,300
Dividends	30,000	Supplies expense	4,300
Equipment	42,500	Unearned service revenue	2,600

❙ Requirements

1. All adjustments have been journalized and posted, but the closing entries have not yet been made. Journalize Sunny Stream's closing entries at March 31, 2010.
2. Set up a T-account for Retained Earnings and post to that account. Then compute Sunny Stream's net income for 2010. What is the ending balance of Retained Earnings?
3. Did Retained Earnings increase or decrease during the year? What caused the increase or decrease?

P3-85B (*Learning Objectives 4, 6: Preparing a classified balance sheet; using the ratios*) Refer back to Problem 3-84B.

❙ Requirements

1. Prepare the company's classified balance sheet in report form at March 31, 2010. Show captions for total assets, total liabilities, and total liabilities and stockholders' equity.
2. Compute Sunny Stream's current ratio and debt ratio at March 31, 2010, rounding to two decimal places. At March 31, 2009, the current ratio was 1.40 and the debt ratio was 0.25. Did Sunny Stream's ability to pay both current and total liabilities improve or deteriorate during 2010? Evaluate Sunny Stream's debt position as strong or weak and give your reason.

P3-86B (*Learning Objective 6: Analyzing financial ratios*) This problem demonstrates the effects of transactions on the current ratio and the debt ratio of Hillsboro Company. Hillsboro's condensed and adapted balance sheet at December 31, 2009, follows.

	(In millions)
Total current assets	$15.3
Properties, plant, equipment, and other assets	16.4
	$31.7
Total current liabilities	$ 8.6
Total long-term liabilities	5.4
Total shareholders' equity	17.7
	$31.7

Assume that during the first quarter of the following year 2010, Hillsboro completed the following transactions:

    a. Paid half of the current liabilities.
    b. Borrowed $7.0 million on long-term debt.
    c. Earned revenue of $2.5 million, on account.
    d. Paid selling expense of $3.0 million.
    e. Accrued general expense of $0.7 million. Credit General Expense Payable, a current liability.
    f. Purchased equipment for $4.7 million, paying cash of $1.9 million and signing a long-term note payable for $2.8 million.
    g. Recorded depreciation expense of $0.6 million.

Requirements

1. Compute Hillsboro's current ratio and debt ratio at December 31, 2009. Round to two decimal places.
2. Consider each transaction separately. Compute Hillsboro's current ratio and debt ratio after each transaction during 2010, that is, seven times. Round ratios to two decimal places.
3. Based on your analysis, you should be able to readily identify the effects of certain transactions on the current ratio and the debt ratio. Test your understanding by completing these statements with either "increase" or "decrease."
   a. Revenues usually _____ the current ratio.
   b. Revenues usually _____ the debt ratio.
   c. Expenses usually _____ the current ratio. (*Note*: Depreciation is an exception to this rule.)
   d. Expenses usually _____ the debt ratio.
   e. If a company's current ratio is greater than 1.0, as for Hillsboro, paying off a current liability will always _____ the current ratio.
   f. Borrowing money on long-term debt will always _____ the current ratio and _____ the debt ratio.

APPLY YOUR KNOWLEDGE

Decision Cases

Case 1. (*Learning Objectives 3, 6: Adjusting and correcting the accounts; computing and evaluating the current ratio*) The unadjusted trial balance of Good Times, Inc., at January 31, 2010, does not balance. In addition, the trial balance needs to be adjusted before the financial statements at January 31, 2010 can be prepared. The manager of Good Times needs to know the business's current ratio.

Cash	$ 8,000
Accounts receivable	4,200
Supplies	800
Prepaid rent	1,200
Land	43,000
Accounts payable	12,000
Salary payable	0
Unearned service revenue	700
Note payable, due in three years	23,400
Common stock	5,000
Retained earnings	9,300
Service revenue	9,100
Salary expense	3,400
Rent expense	0
Advertising expense	900
Supplies expense	0

Requirements

1. How much *out of balance* is the trial balance? Notes Payable (the only error) is understated.
2. Good Times needs to make the following adjustments at January 31:
   a. Supplies of $400 were used during January.
   b. The balance of Prepaid Rent was paid on January 1 and covers the whole year 2010. No adjustment was made on January 31.
   c. At January 31, Good Times owes employees $1,000.
   d. Unearned service revenue of $500 was earned during January.
   Prepare a corrected, adjusted trial balance. Give Notes Payable its correct balance.

3. After the error is corrected and after these adjustments are made, compute the current ratio of Good Times, Inc. If your business had this current ratio, could you sleep at night?

Case 2. (*Learning Objectives 4: Preparing financial statements; deciding to continue or shut down the business*) On October 1, Lou Marks opened Eagle Restaurant, Inc. Marks is now at a crossroads. The October financial statements paint a glowing picture of the business, and Marks has asked you whether he should expand the business. To expand the business, Marks wants to be earning net income of $10,000 per month and have total assets of $50,000. Marks believes he is meeting both goals.

To start the business, Marks invested $25,000, not the $15,000 amount reported as "Common stock" on the balance sheet. The business issued $25,000 of common stock to Marks. The bookkeeper plugged the $15,000 "Common stock" amount into the balance sheet to make it balance. The bookkeeper made some other errors too. Marks shows you the following financial statements that the bookkeeper prepared:

Eagle Restaurant, Inc.
Income Statement
Month Ended October 31, 2011

Revenues:		
Investments by owner	$25,000	
Unearned banquet sales revenue	3,000	
		$28,000
Expenses:		
Wages expense	$ 5,000	
Rent expense	4,000	
Dividends	3,000	
Depreciation expense—fixtures	1,000	
		13,000
Net income		$15,000

Eagle Restaurant, Inc.
Balance Sheet
October 31, 2011

Assets:		Liabilities:	
Cash	$ 8,000	Accounts payable	$ 7,000
Prepaid insurance	1,000	Sales revenue	32,000
Insurance expense	1,000	Acuumulated depreciation—	
Food inventory	5,000	fixtures	1,000
Cost of goods sold (expense)	12,000		40,000
Fixtures (tables, chairs, etc.)	24,000	**Owners' equity:**	
Dishes and silverware	4,000	Common stock	15,000
	$55,000		$55,000

❙ Requirement

1. Prepare corrected financial statements for Eagle Restaurant, Inc.: Income Statement, Statement of Retained Earnings, and Balance Sheet. Then, based on Marks' goals and your corrected statements, recommend to Marks whether he should expand the restaurant.

Case 3. *(Learning Objectives 3, 4: Valuing a business on the basis of its net income)* Stanley Williams has owned and operated SW Advertising, Inc., since its beginning 10 years ago. Recently, Williams mentioned that he would consider selling the company for the right price.

Assume that you are interested in buying this business. You obtain its most recent monthly trial balance, which follows. Revenues and expenses vary little from month to month, and June is a typical month. Your investigation reveals that the trial balance does not include the effects of monthly revenues of $4,000 and expenses totaling $1,100. If you were to buy SW Advertising, you would hire a manager so you could devote your time to other duties. Assume that your manager would require a monthly salary of $5,000.

SW Advertising, Inc.
Trial Balance
June 30, 2010

Cash	$ 12,000	
Accounts receivable	6,900	
Prepaid expenses	3,200	
Plant assets	125,000	
Accumulated depreciation		$ 81,500
Land	158,000	
Accounts payable		13,800
Salary payable		
Unearned advertising revenue		58,700
Common stock		50,000
Retained earnings		93,000
Dividends	9,000	
Advertising revenue		22,000
Rent expense		
Salary expense	4,000	
Utilities expense	900	
Depreciation expense		
Supplies expense		
Total	$319,000	$319,000

❙ Requirements

1. Assume that the most you would pay for the business is 16 times the amount of monthly net income *you could expect to earn* from it. Compute this possible price.
2. Williams states that the least he will take for the business is two times its stockholders' equity on June 30. Compute this amount.
3. Under these conditions, how much should you offer Williams? Give your reason. (Challenge)

Ethical Issues

Issue 1. Cross Timbers Energy Co. is in its third year of operations, and the company has grown. To expand the business, Cross Timbers borrowed $15 million from Bank of Fort Worth. As a condition for making this loan, the bank required that Cross Timbers maintain a current ratio of at least 1.50 and a debt ratio of no more than 0.50.

Business recently has been worse than expected. Expenses have brought the current ratio down to 1.47 and the debt ratio up to 0.51 at December 15. Lane Collins, the general manager, is considering the result of reporting this current ratio to the bank. Collins is considering recording this year some revenue on account that Cross Timbers will earn next year. The contract for this job has been signed, and Cross Timbers will deliver the natural gas during January of next year.

I *Requirements*

1. Journalize the revenue transaction (without dollar amounts), and indicate how recording this revenue in December would affect the current ratio and the debt ratio.
2. Analyze this transaction according to the decision framework for making ethical judgments in Chapter 1:
   a. What is the issue?
   b. Who are the stakeholders and what are the alternatives? Weigh them from the standpoint of economic, legal, and ethical implications.
   c. What decision would you make?
3. Propose for Cross Timbers a course of action that is ethical.

Issue 2.   The net income of Solas Photography Company decreased sharply during 2010. Lisa Almond, owner of the company, anticipates the need for a bank loan in 2011. Late in 2010, Almond instructed Brad Lail, the accountant and a personal friend of yours, to record a $10,000 sale of portraits to the Almond family, even though the photos will not be shot until January 2011. Almond also told Lail *not* to make the following December 31, 2010, adjusting entries:

> Salaries owed to employees $10,000
> Prepaid insurance that has expired 1,000

I *Requirements*

1. Compute the overall effect of these transactions on the company's reported income for 2010. Is reported net income overstated or understated?
2. Why did Almond take these actions? Are they ethical? Give your reason, identifying the parties helped and the parties harmed by Almond's action. Consult the Decision Framework for Making Ethical Judgments in Chapter 1. Which factor (economic, legal, or ethical) seems to be taking precedence? Identify the stakeholders and the potential consequences to each.
3. As a personal friend of Brad's, what advice would you give him?

Focus on Financials: ■ Amazon.com, Inc.

(Learning Objectives 3, 6: Tracing account balances to the financial statements) **Amazon.com, Inc.**—like all other businesses—adjusts accounts prior to year end to get correct amounts for the financial statements. Examine Amazon.com, Inc.'s Consolidated Balance Sheets in Appendix A, and pay particular attention to "accrued expenses and other."

I *Requirements*

1. Why does a company have accrued expenses payable at year end?
2. Open a T-account for "accrued expenses and other." Insert Amazon.com, Inc.'s balance (in millions) at December 31, 2007.
3. Journalize the following transactions for the year ended December 31, 2008. Key entries by letter, and show amounts in millions. Explanations are not required.
   a. Paid off the beginning balance of "accrued expenses and other"
   b. Recorded operating expenses of $3,428 million, paying $2,335 million in cash and accruing the remainder
4. Post these entries to "accrued expenses and other" and show that the ending balance of the account agrees with the corresponding amount reported in Amazon.com, Inc.'s December 31, 2008, Consolidated Balance Sheets.
5. Compute the current ratios and debt ratios for Amazon.com, Inc., at December 31, 2007, and December 31, 2008. Did the ratio values improve, deteriorate, or hold steady during 2008? Do Amazon.com, Inc.'s ratio values indicate relative financial strength or weakness?

Focus on Analysis: ■ Foot Locker, Inc.

(Learning Objective 3: Explaining accruals and deferrals) During 2007, **Foot Locker, Inc.**, had numerous accruals and deferrals. As a new member of Foot Locker, Inc.'s accounting staff, it is your job to explain the effects of accruals and deferrals on net income for 2007. The accrual and deferral data follow, along with questions that Foot Locker, Inc.'s stockholders have raised (all amounts in millions):

1. Examine Footnote 8 to Foot Locker's consolidated financial statements (Other Current Assets) in Appendix B. Notice that included in this total are "net receivables." Ending net receivables for 2006 (beginning balance of 2007) were $59 million. Ending net receivables for 2007 were $50 million. Which of these amounts did Foot Locker, Inc., earn in 2006? Which amount is included in Foot Locker, Inc.'s 2007 net income?

2. In Footnote 8, examine the line entitled "prepaid rent." The beginning balance is $62 million and the ending balance is $65 million. Which of these amounts impacted Foot Locker, Inc.'s 2007 net income? Which amount impacted Foot Locker, Inc.'s 2008 net income?

3. Examine Footnote 9 (Property and Equipment, Net). Notice that accumulated depreciation stood at $870 million at the end of 2006 and at $903 million at year end 2007. Assume that depreciation expense for 2007 was $100. Explain what must have happened to account for the remainder of the change in the accumulated depreciation account during 2007. (Challenge)

4. Examine Footnote 13 (Accrued and Other Liabilities). Foot Locker, Inc., reports an account titled Customer deposits. The attached footnote states that customer deposits include unredeemed gift cards and certificates, merchandise credits. and deferred revenue related to undelivered merchandise, including layaway sales. This account carried credit balances of $33 million at the end of 2006 and $34 million at the end of 2007. What type of account is Customer deposits? Make a single journal entry to show how this account could have increased its balance during 2007. Then explain the event in your own words.

Group Project

Mark Davis formed a lawn service company as a summer job. To start the business on May 1, he deposited $2,000 in a new bank account in the name of the corporation. The $2,000 consisted of a $1,600 loan from his father and $400 of his own money. The corporation issued 200 shares of common stock to Davis.

Davis rented lawn equipment, purchased supplies, and hired high school students to mow and trim his customers' lawns. At the end of each month, Davis mailed bills to his customers. On August 31, Davis was ready to dissolve the business and return to Rutgers University for the fall semester. Because he had been so busy, he had kept few records other than his checkbook and a list of amounts owed by customers.

At August 31, Davis' checkbook shows a balance of $2,040, and his customers still owe him $600. During the summer, he collected $5,600 from customers. His checkbook lists payments for supplies totaling $400, and he still has gasoline, weedeater cord, and other supplies that cost a total of $50. He paid his employees wages of $1,900, and he still owes them $200 for the final week of the summer.

Davis rented some equipment from Ludwig Tool Company. On May 1, he signed a six-month lease on mowers and paid $600 for the full lease period. Ludwig will refund the unused portion of the prepayment if the equipment is in good shape. To get the refund, Davis has kept the mowers in excellent condition. In fact, he had to pay $300 to repair a mower that ran over a hidden tree stump.

To transport employees and equipment to jobs, Davis used a trailer that he bought for $300. He figures that the summer's work used up one-third of the trailer's service potential. The business checkbook lists an expenditure of $460 for dividends paid to Davis during the summer. Also, Davis paid his father back during the summer.

❙ Requirements

1. Prepare the income statement of Davis Lawn Service, Inc., for the four months May through August. The business is not subject to income tax.
2. Prepare the classified balance sheet of Davis Lawn Service, Inc., at August 31.

For online homework, exercises, and problems that provide you with immediate feedback, please visit www.myaccountinglab.com.

Quick Check Answers

1. *d*	6. *b*	10. *c*	14. *a*
2. *c*	7. *c*	11. *d*	15. *d*
3. *d*	8. *d*	12. *d*	16. *d*
4. *a*	9. *d*	13. *c*	17. *c*
5. *b*			

Demo Doc

Preparation of Adjusting Entries, Closing Entries, and Financial Statements

To make sure you understand this material, work through the following demonstration "Demo Doc" with detailed comments to help you see the concept within the framework of a worked-through problem.

Learning Objectives 2–5

Cloud Break Consulting, Inc., has the following information at June 30, 2010:

		Balance	
	Account Title	Debit	Credit
	Cash	$131,000	
	Accounts receivable	104,000	
	Supplies	4,000	
	Prepaid rent	27,000	
	Land	45,000	
	Building	300,000	
	Accumulated depreciation—building		$155,000
	Accounts payable		159,000
	Unearned service revenue		40,000
	Common stock		50,000
	Retained earnings		52,000
	Dividends	7,000	
	Service revenue		450,000
	Salary expense	255,000	
	Rent expense	25,000	
	Miscellaneous expense	8,000	
	Total	$906,000	$906,000

Cloud Break Consulting, Inc.
Unadjusted Trial Balance
June 30, 2010

June 30 is Cloud Break's fiscal year end; accordingly, it must make adjusting entries for the following items:

a. Supplies on hand at year-end, $1,000.

b. Nine months of rent totaling $27,000 were paid in advance on April 1, 2010. Cloud Break has recorded no rent expense yet.

c. Depreciation expense has not been recorded on the building for the 2010 fiscal year. The building has a useful life of 25 years.

d. Employees work Monday through Friday. The weekly payroll is $5,000 and is paid every Friday. June 30, 2010, falls on a Thursday.

e. Service revenue of $15,000 must be accrued.

f. Cloud Break received $40,000 in advance for consulting services to be provided evenly from January 1, 2010 through August 31, 2010. Cloud Break has recorded none of this revenue.

Requirements

1. Open the T-accounts with their unadjusted balances.

2. Journalize Cloud Break's adjusting entries at June 30, 2010, and post the entries to the T-accounts.

3. Total each T-account in the ledger.

4. Journalize and post Cloud Break's closing entries.

5. Prepare Cloud Break's income statement and statement of retained earnings for the year ended June 30, 2010, and the balance sheet at June 30, 2010. Draw arrows linking the three financial statements.

Demo Doc Solutions

Requirement 1

Open the T-accounts with their unadjusted balances.

Part 1	Part 2	Part 3	Part 4	Part 5	Demo Doc Complete

Remember from Chapter 2 that opening a T-account means drawing a blank account that looks like a capital "T" and putting the account title across the top. To help find the accounts later, they are grouped into assets, liabilities, stockholders' equity, revenues, and expenses (in that order). If the account has a starting balance, it *must* appear on the correct side.

Remember that debits are always on the left side of the T-account and credits are always on the right side. This is true for *every* account.

The correct side to enter each account's starting balance is the side of *increase* in the account. This is because we expect all accounts to have a *positive* balance (that is, more increases than decreases).

For assets, an increase is a debit, so we would expect all assets (except contra assets such as Accumulated Depreciation) to have a debit balance. For liabilities and stockholders' equity, an increase is a credit, so we would expect all liabilities and equities (except Dividends) to have a credit balance. By the same reasoning, we expect revenues to have credit balances and expenses and dividends to have debit balances.

The unadjusted balances appearing in the T-accounts are simply the amounts from the starting trial balance.

ASSETS	STOCKHOLDERS' EQUITY	EXPENSES

ASSETS

Cash
Bal 131,000 |

Building
Bal 300,000 |

Accounts Receivable
Bal 104,000 |

Accumulated Depreciation—Building
| Bal 155,000

Supplies
Bal 4,000 |

Prepaid Rent
Bal 27,000 |

Land
Bal 45,000 |

LIABILITIES

Accounts Payable
| Bal 159,000

Unearned Service Revenue
| Bal 40,000

STOCKHOLDERS' EQUITY

Common Stock
| Bal 50,000

Retained Earnings
| Bal 52,000

Dividends
Bal 7,000 |

REVENUE

Service Revenue
| Bal 450,000

EXPENSES

Salary Expense
Bal 255,000 |

Rent Expense
Bal 25,000 |

Miscellaneous Expense
Bal 8,000 |

Requirement 2

Journalize Cloud Break's adjusting entries at June 30, 2010, and post the entries to the T-accounts.

Part 1	**Part 2**	Part 3	Part 4	Part 5	Demo Doc Complete

a. Supplies on hand at year-end, $1,000.

On June 30, 2010, the unadjusted balance in the Supplies account was $4,000. However, a count shows that only $1,000 of supplies actually remains on hand. The supplies that are no longer there have been used. When assets/benefits are used, an expense is created.

Cloud Break will need to make an adjusting journal entry in order to report the correct amount of supplies on the balance sheet.

Looking at the Supplies T-account:

	Supplies		
	4,000		
		Used up	X
Bal	1,000		

The supplies have decreased because they have been used up. The amount of the decrease is **X**. **X** = $4,000 − $1,000 = $3,000.

$3,000 of supplies expense must be recorded to show the value of supplies that have been used.

a.	Jun 30	Supplies Expense ($4,000 − $1,000) (Expense ↑; debit)	3,000	
		Supplies (Asset ↓; credit)		3,000
		To record supplies expense.		

After posting, Supplies and Supplies Expense hold their correct ending balances:

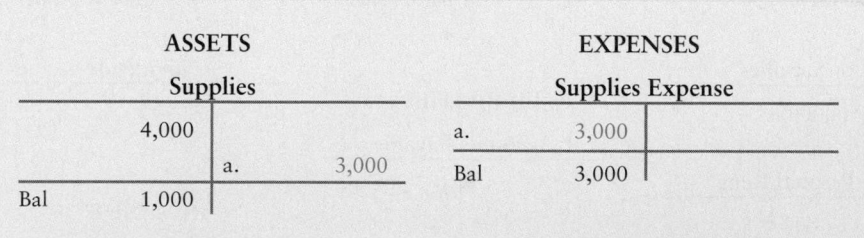

ASSETS			EXPENSES		
Supplies			**Supplies Expense**		
4,000			a.	3,000	
	a.	3,000	Bal	3,000	
Bal	1,000				

b. Nine months of rent (totalling $27,000) were paid in advance on April 1, 2010. Cloud Break has recorded no rent expense yet.

A prepayment for something, such as for rent or insurance, creates a *future* benefit (an asset) because the business is now entitled to receive the prepaid goods or services. Once those goods or services are received (in this case, once Cloud Break has occupied the building being rented), the benefit expires, and the prepaid cost becomes an expense.

Cloud Break prepaid $27,000 for nine months of rent on April 1. This means that Cloud Break pays $27,000/9 = $3,000 a month for rent. At June 30, Prepaid Rent is adjusted for the amount of the asset that has been used up. Because Cloud Break has occupied the building being rented for three months (April, May, and June), three months of the prepayment have been used. The amount of rent used is 3 × $3,000 = $9,000. Because that portion of the past benefit (asset) has expired, it becomes an expense (in this case, the adjustment transfers $9,000 from Prepaid Rent to Rent Expense).

This means that Rent Expense must be increased (a debit) and Prepaid Rent (an asset) must be decreased (a credit), with the following journal entry:

b.	Jun 30	Rent Expense (Expense ↑; debit)	9,000	
		Prepaid Rent (Asset ↓; credit)		9,000
		To record rent expense.		

Posting places $9,000 in each account, as follows:

	ASSETS				EXPENSES		
	Prepaid Rent				**Rent Expense**		
	27,000				25,000		
		b.	9,000	b.	9,000		
Bal	18,000			Bal	34,000		

c. **Depreciation expense has not been recorded on the building for the 2010 fiscal year. The building has a useful life of 25 years.**

Depreciation expense per year is calculated as:

$$\text{Depreciation expense per year} = \frac{\text{Original cost of asset}}{\text{Useful life of asset (in years)}}$$

The cost principle compels us to keep the original cost of a plant asset in that asset account. Because there is $300,000 in the Building account, we know that this is the original cost of the building. We are told in the question that the building's useful life is 25 years.

$$\text{Depreciation expense per year} = \$300,000/25 \text{ years} = \$12,000 \text{ per year}$$

We will record depreciation of $12,000 in an adjusting journal entry. The journal entry for depreciation expense is *always* the same. Only the dollar amount changes. There is always an increase to Depreciation Expense (a debit) and an increase to the contra asset account of Accumulated Depreciation (a credit).

c.	Jun 30	Depreciation Expense—Building (Expense ↑; debit)	12,000	
		Accumulated Depreciation—Building		
		(Contra Asset ↑; credit)		12,000
		To record depreciation on building.		

	ASSETS					EXPENSES	

	ASSET	CONTRA ASSET				
	Building	**Accumulated Depreciation— Building**			**Depreciation Expense— Building**	
	300,000		155,000	c.	12,000	
		c.	12,000			
Bal	300,000	Bal	167,000	Bal	12,000	

The book value of the building is its original cost (the amount in the Building T-account) minus the accumulated depreciation on the building.

Book value of plant assets:	
Building...	$300,000
Less: Accumulated depreciation	(167,000)
Book value of the building	$133,000

d. Employees work Monday through Friday. The weekly payroll is $5,000 and is paid every Friday. June 30, 2010, falls on a Thursday.

Salary is an accrued expense. That is, it's a liability that comes from an *expense* that hasn't been paid yet. Most employers pay their employees *after* the work has been done, so the work is a past benefit to the employer. This expense (Salary Expense, in this case) grows until payday.

Cloud Break's employees are paid $5,000 for five days of work. That means they earn $5,000/5 = $1,000 per day. By the end of the day on Thursday, June 30, they have earned $1,000/day × 4 days = $4,000 of salary.

If the salaries have not been paid, then they are pay*able* (or in other words, they are *owed*) and must be recorded as some kind of payable account. You might be tempted to use Accounts Payable, but this account is usually reserved for *bills* received. But employees don't bill employers for their paychecks. The appropriate payable account for salaries is Salary Payable.

The accrual of salary expense creates an increase to Salary Expense (a debit) and an increase to the liability Salary Payable (a credit) of $4,000.

d.	Jun 30	Salary Expense (Expense ↑; debit)	4,000	
		Salary Payable (Liability ↑; credit)		4,000
		To accrue salary expense.		

	EXPENSES			LIABILITIES	
	Salary Expense			**Salary Payable**	
	255,000		d.	4,000	
d.	4,000				
Bal	259,000		Bal	4,000	

e. Service revenue of $15,000 must be accrued.

Accrued revenue is another way of saying "accounts receivable" (or receipt in the future). When *accrued* revenue is recorded, it means that accounts receivable are also recorded (that is, the business gave goods or services to customers, but the business has not yet received the cash). The business is entitled to these receivables because the revenue has been earned.

Service Revenue must be increased by $15,000 (a credit) and the Accounts Receivable asset must be increased by $15,000 (a debit).

e.	Jun 30	Accounts Receivable (Asset ↑; debit)	15,000	
		Service Revenue (Revenue ↑; credit)		15,000
		To accrue service revenue.		

ASSETS		REVENUES	
Accounts Receivable		**Service Revenue**	
	104,000		450,000
e.	15,000	e.	15,000
Bal	119,000	Bal	465,000

f. Cloud Break received $40,000 in advance for consulting services to be provided evenly from January 1, 2010, through August 31, 2010. Cloud Break has recorded none of this revenue.

Cloud Break received cash in advance for work to be performed in the future. By accepting the cash, Cloud Break also accepted the obligation to perform that work (or provide a refund). In accounting, an obligation is a liability. We call this liability "unearned revenue" because it *will* be revenue (after the work is performed) but it is not revenue *yet*.

The $40,000 collected in advance is still in the Unearned Service Revenue account. However, some of the revenue has been earned as of June 30. Six months of the earnings period have passed (January through June), so Cloud Break has earned six months of the revenue.

The entire revenue-earning period is eight months (January through August), so the revenue earned per month is $40,000/8 = $5,000. The six months of revenue that Cloud Break has earned through the end of June totals $30,000 (6 × $5,000).

So Unearned Service Revenue, a liability, must be decreased by $30,000 (a debit). Because that portion of the revenue is now earned, Service Revenue is increased by $30,000 (a credit).

f.	Jun 30	Unearned Service Revenue (Liability ↓; debit)	30,000	
		Service Revenue (Revenue ↑; credit)		30,000
		To record the earning of service revenue that was		
		collected in advance.		

Essentially, the $30,000 has been shifted from "unearned revenue" to "earned" revenue.

	LIABILITIES		REVENUES	
	Unearned Service Revenue		**Service Revenue**	
		40,000		450,000
f.	30,000		e.	15,000
			f.	30,000
		Bal 10,000		Bal 495,000

Now we can summarize all of the adjusting journal entries:

Ref.	Date	Accounts and Explanation	Debit	Credit
	2010			
a.	Jun 30	Supplies Expense ($4,000 – $1,000)	3,000	
		Supplies		3,000
		To record supplies expense.		
b.	30	Rent Expense	9,000	
		Prepaid Rent		9,000
		To record rent expense.		
c.	30	Depreciation Expense—Building	12,000	
		Accumulated Depreciation—Building		12,000
		To record depreciation on building.		
d.	30	Salary Expense	4,000	
		Salary Payable		4,000
		To accrue salary expense.		
e.	30	Accounts Receivable	15,000	
		Service Revenue		15,000
		To accrue service revenue.		
f.	30	Unearned Service Revenue	30,000	
		Service Revenue		30,000
		To record the earning of service revenue that was collected in advance.		

Requirement 3

Total each T-account in the ledger.

Part 1	Part 2	**Part 3**	Part 4	Part 5	Demo Doc Complete

After posting all of these entries and totaling all of the T-accounts, we have:

ASSETS		STOCKHOLDERS' EQUITY	EXPENSES

ASSETS

Cash

Bal	131,000	

Accounts Receivable

	104,000	
e.	15,000	
Bal	119,000	

Supplies

	4,000	
		a. 3,000
Bal	1,000	

Prepaid Rent

	27,000	
		b. 9,000
Bal	18,000	

Land

Bal	45,000	

Building

Bal	300,000	

Accumulated Depreciation—Building

		155,000
		c. 12,000
		Bal 167,000

LIABILITIES

Accounts Payable

		Bal 159,000

Salary Payable

		d. 4,000
		Bal 4,000

Unearned Service Revenue

		40,000
f.	30,000	
		Bal 10,000

STOCKHOLDERS' EQUITY

Common Stock

		Bal 50,000

Retained Earnings

		Bal 52,000

Dividends

Bal	7,000	

REVENUE

Service Revenue

		450,000
		e. 15,000
		f. 30,000
		Bal 495,000

EXPENSES

Salary Expense

	255,000	
d.	4,000	
Bal	259,000	

Supplies Expense

a.	3,000	
Bal	3,000	

Rent Expense

	25,000	
b.	9,000	
Bal	34,000	

Depreciation Expense—Building

c.	12,000	
Bal	12,000	

Miscellaneous Expense

Bal	8,000	

Requirement 4

Journalize and post Cloud Break's closing entries.

Part 1	Part 2	Part 3	**Part 4**	Part 5	Demo Doc Complete

We prepare closing entries to (1) clear out the revenue, expense, and dividends accounts to a zero balance in order to get them ready for the next period. They must begin the next period empty so that we can evaluate each period's income separately from all other periods. We also need to (2) update the Retained Earnings account by transferring all revenues, expenses, and dividends into it.

The Retained Earnings balance is calculated each year using the following formula:

Beginning retained earnings
+ Net income (or – Net loss)
– Dividends declared
= Ending retained earnings

You can see this in the Retained Earnings T-account as well:

Retained Earnings	
	Beginning retained earnings
	Net income
Dividends	
	Ending retained earnings

This formula is the key to preparing the closing entries. We will use this formula, but we will do it *inside* the Retained Earnings T-account.

From the trial balance given in the problem, we know that beginning Retained Earnings is $52,000. The first component of the formula is already in the T-account.

The next component is net income, which is *not* yet in the Retained Earnings account. There is no T-account with net income in it, but we can place all the components of net income into the Retained Earnings account and come out with the net income number at the bottom. Remember:

Revenues – Expenses = Net income

This means that we need to get all of the revenues and expenses into the Retained Earnings account.

a. We start with our revenue T-account (service revenue as shown)

Service Revenue		
	Bal	495,000

In order to clear out all the income statement accounts so that they are empty to begin the next year, the first step is to *debit* each revenue account for the amount of its *credit* balance. Service Revenue has a *credit* balance of $495,000, so to bring that to zero, we need to *debit* Service Revenue for $495,000.

This means that we have part of our first closing entry:

1.		Service Revenue	495,000	
		???		495,000

What is the credit side of this entry? The reason we started with Service Revenue was to help calculate net income in the Retained Earnings account. So the other side of the entry must go to Retained Earnings:

1.	Service Revenue	495,000	
	Retained Earnings		495,000

b. The second step is to *credit* each expense account for the amount of its *debit* balance to bring each expense account to zero. In this case, we have five different expenses:

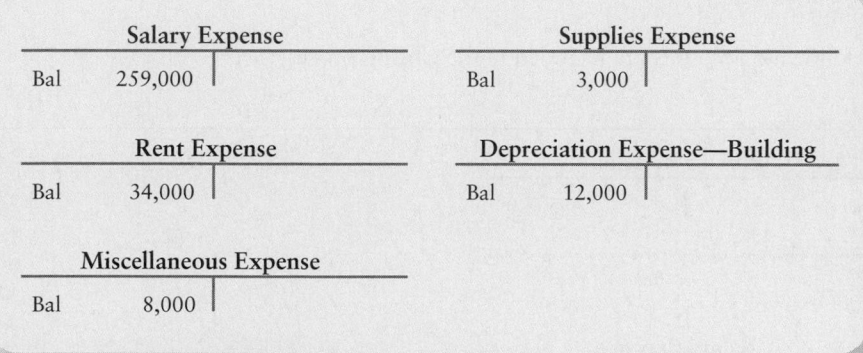

	Salary Expense			Supplies Expense	
Bal	259,000		Bal	3,000	

	Rent Expense			Depreciation Expense—Building	
Bal	34,000		Bal	12,000	

	Miscellaneous Expense	
Bal	8,000	

The sum of all the expenses will go to the debit side of the Retained Earnings account:

2.	Retained Earnings	316,000	
	Salary Expense		259,000
	Supplies Expense		3,000
	Rent Expense		34,000
	Depreciation Expense—Building		12,000
	Miscellaneous Expense		8,000

The last component of the Retained Earnings formula is dividends. There is a Dividends account:

	Dividends	
Bal	7,000	

c. The final step in the closing process is to transfer Dividends to the debit site of the Retained Earnings account. The Dividends account has a *debit* balance of $7,000, so to bring that to zero, we need to *credit* Dividends by $7,000. The balancing debit will go to Retained Earnings:

3.	Retained Earnings	7,000	
	Dividends		7,000

This entry subtracts Dividends from Retained Earnings. Retained Earnings now holds the following data:

					Retained Earnings
				52,000	**Beginning retained earnings**
Expenses	2.	316,000	1.	495,000	Revenue } Net income
Dividends	3.	7,000			
			Bal	224,000	**Ending retained earnings**

The formula to update Retained Earnings has now been re-created inside the Retained Earnings T-account.

The following accounts are included in the closing process:

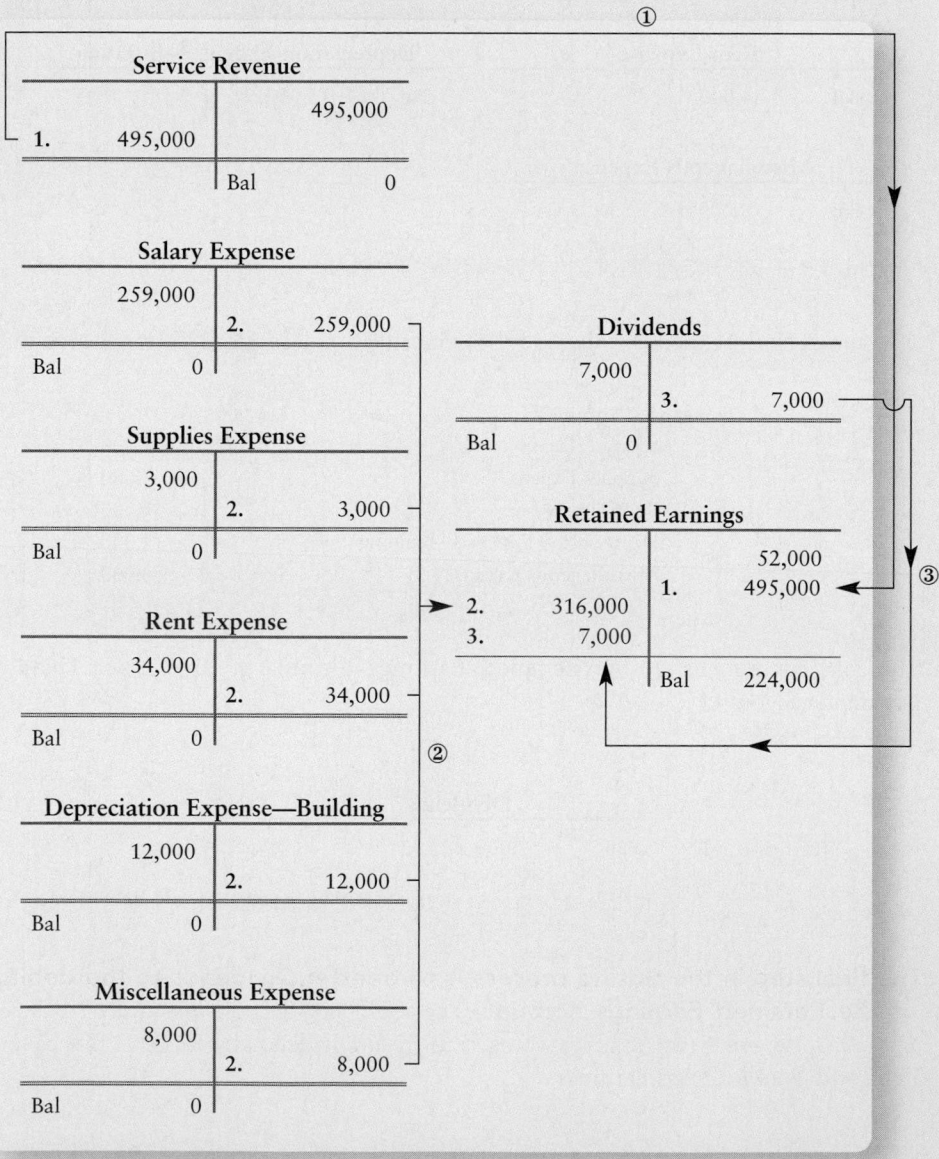

Notice that each temporary account (the Revenues, the Expenses, and Dividends), now has a zero balance.

Requirement 5

Prepare Cloud Break's income statement and the statement of retained earnings for the year ended June 30, 2010, and the balance sheet at June 30, 2010. Draw arrows linking the three financial statements.

Part 1	Part 2	Part 3	Part 4	**Part 5**	Demo Doc Complete

Cloud Break Consulting, Inc.
Income Statement
Year Ended June 30, 2010

Revenue:		
Service revenue		$495,000
Expenses:		
Salary expense	$259,000	
Rent expense	34,000	
Depreciation expense—building	12,000	
Supplies expense	3,000	
Miscellaneous expense	8,000	
Total expenses		316,000
Net income		$179,000

Cloud Break Consulting, Inc.
Statement of Retained Earnings
Year Ended June 30, 2010

Retained earnings, June 30, 2007	$ 52,000
Add: Net income	179,000
	231,000
Less: Dividends	(7,000)
Retained earnings, June 30, 2008	$224,000

Cloud Break Consulting, Inc.
Balance Sheet
June 30, 2010

Assets			Liabilities	
Cash		$131,000	Accounts payable	$159,000
Accounts receivable		119,000	Salary payable	4,000
Supplies		1,000	Unearned service revenue	10,000
Prepaid rent		18,000	Total liabilities	173,000
Land		45,000		
Building	$300,000		**Stockholders' Equity**	
Less: Accumulated			Common stock	50,000
depreciation	(167,000)	133,000	Retained earnings	224,000
			Total stockholders' equity	274,000
			Total liabilities and	
Total assets		$447,000	stockholders' equity	$447,000

RELATIONSHIPS AMONG THE FINANCIAL STATEMENTS

The arrows in these statements show how the financial statements relate to each other. Follow the arrow that takes the ending balance of Retained Earnings to the balance sheet.

1. Net income from the income statements is reported as an increase to Retained Earnings on the statement of retained earnings. A net loss would be reported as a decrease to Retained Earnings.

2. Ending Retained Earnings from the statement of retained earnings is transferred to the balance sheet. The ending Retained Earnings is the final balancing amount for the balance sheet.

Part 1	Part 2	Part 3	Part 4	Part 5	**Demo Doc Complete**

4

Internal Control & Cash

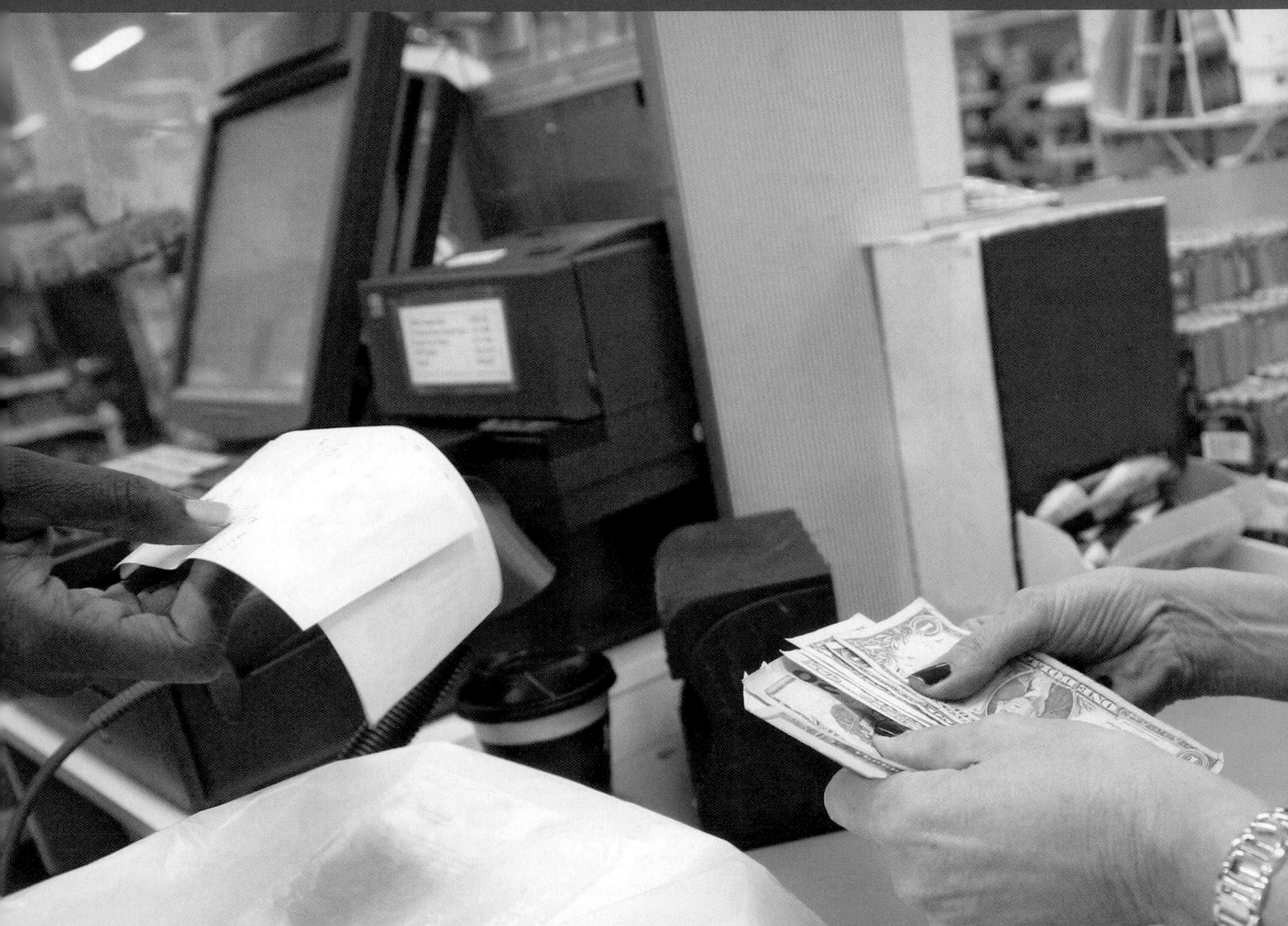

SPOTLIGHT: Cooking the Books: AMEX Products Takes a Hit

The following is adapted from a true story:

"I've never been so shocked in my life!" exclaimed Lee Riffe, manager of the **AMEX Products** office in Palo Alto, California. "I never thought this could happen to us. We are such a close-knit organization where everyone trusts everyone else. Why, people at AMEX feel like family! I feel betrayed, violated."

Riffe had just returned from the trial of Melissa Price, who had been convicted of embezzling over $600,000 from AMEX over a six-year period. Price had been one of AMEX's most trusted employees for 10 years. A single mom with two teenage daughters, Price had pulled herself up by her own bootstraps, putting herself through community college where she had obtained an associate's degree in accounting. Riffe had hired her as a part-time bookkeeper at AMEX while Price was in college to help her out. She had done such a good job that, when she completed her degree, Riffe asked her to stay on and assigned her the additional role of cashier, in charge of accumulating the daily cash receipts from customers and taking them to the night depository at the bank each day after work. Through the years, he also awarded her what he considered good raises, compensating her at a rate that was generally higher than other employees with her education and experience levels.

(continued on next page)

Price rapidly became the company's "go-to" financial employee. She was eager to learn, dependable, responsible. In 10 years she never took a day of vacation, choosing instead to take advantage of the company's policy that allowed employees to draw additional compensation for vacation accrued but not taken at the end of each year. Riffe grew to depend on Price more and more each month, as the business grew to serve over 1,000 customers. Price's increased involvement on the financial side of the business freed Riffe to spend his time working on new business, spending less and less time on financial matters. Riffe had noticed that, in the past few years, Price had begun to wear better clothes and drive a shiny late-model convertible around town. Both of her teenagers also drove late-model automobiles, and the family had recently moved into a new home in an upscale subdivision of the city. Riffe had been pleased that he had contributed to Price's success. But in recent months, Riffe was becoming worried because, in spite of increasing revenues, the cash balances and cash flows from operations at AMEX had been steadily deteriorating, sometimes causing the company difficulty in paying its bills on time.

Price, on the other hand, had felt underappreciated and underpaid for all of her hard work. Having learned the system well, and observing that no one was monitoring her, Price fell into a simple but deadly trap. As cashier, she was in charge of receiving customer payments that came in by mail. Unknown to Riffe, Price had been **lapping** accounts receivable, an embezzlement scheme nicknamed "robbing Peter to pay Paul." Price began by misappropriating (stealing) some of the customers' checks, endorsing them, and depositing them to her own bank account. To cover up the shortage in a particular customer's account, Price would apply the collections received later from another customer's account. She would do this just before the monthly statements were mailed to the first customer, so that the customer wouldn't notice when he or she received the statement that someone else's payment was being applied to the amount owed AMEX. Of course, this left the second customer's account short, so Price had to misapply the collection from a third customer to straighten out the discrepancy in the second customer's account. She did this for many customers, over a period of many months, boldly stealing more and more each month. With unlimited access to both cash and customer accounts, and with careful planning and constant diligence, Price became very proficient at juggling entries in the books to keep anyone from discovering her scheme. This embezzlement went on for six years, allowing Price to misappropriate $622,000 from the company. The customer accounts that were misstated due to the fraud eventually had to be written off.

What tipped off Riffe to the embezzlement? Price was involved in an automobile accident and couldn't work for two weeks. The employee covering for Price was swamped with telephone calls from customers wanting to discuss unexplained differences in their billing statements for amounts they could prove had been paid. The ensuing investigation pointed straight to Price, and Riffe turned the case over to the authorities.

The excerpt from the AMEX Products balance sheet on the following page reports the company's assets. Focus on the top line, Cash and cash equivalents. At December 31, 2010, AMEX reported cash of $6,260. Due to Price's scheme, the company had been cheated of $622,000 over several years that it could have used to buy new equipment, expand operations, or pay off debts.

AMEX Products has now revamped its internal controls. The company has hired a separate person, with no access to cash, to keep customer accounts receivable records. The company now uses a **lock-box system** for all checks received by mail. They are sent to AMEX's bank lock box, where they are gathered by a bank employee and immediately deposited. The remittance advices accompanying the checks are electronically scanned and forwarded to AMEX's accounts receivable bookkeeper where they are used as the source documents for posting amounts collected from customers. A summary of cash received goes to Riffe, who reviews it for reasonableness and compares it with the daily bank deposit total. Another employee, who has neither cash handling nor customer bookkeeping responsibilities, reconciles AMEX's monthly bank statement, and reconciles the total cash deposited per the daily listings with the total credits to customer accounts receivable. Now Riffe requires every employee to take time off for earned vacation, and rotates other employees through those positions while those employees are away.

AMEX Products, Inc.
Balance Sheet (Partial, Adapted)

Assets	December 31, 2010
Cash and cash equivalents	$ 6,260
Cash pledged as collateral	2,000
Accounts receivable	8,290
Inventories	36,200
Prepaid expenses	1,400
Investments	10,000
Equipment and facilities (net of accumulated depreciation of ($2,400)	13,170
Other assets	3,930
Total assets	$81,250

Lapping is a type of fraud known as misappropriation of assets. Although it doesn't take a genius to accomplish, lapping requires some *motivation*, and is usually *rationalized* by distorted and unethical thinking. The *opportunity* to commit this type and other types of frauds arises through a weak internal control system. In this case, the fact that Price had access to cash and the customer accounts receivable, along with the fact that Riffe failed to monitor Price's activities, proved to be the deadly combination that provided the opportunity for this fraud.

This chapter begins with a discussion of fraud, its types, and common characteristics. We then discuss internal controls, which are the primary means by which fraud as well as unintentional financial statement errors are prevented. We also discuss how to account for cash. These three topics—fraud, internal control, and cash—go together. Internal controls help prevent fraud. Cash is probably the asset that is most often misappropriated through fraud.

LEARNING OBJECTIVES

1 **Learn** about fraud and how much it costs

2 **Set up** an internal control system

3 **Prepare** and **use** a bank reconciliation

4 **Apply** internal controls to cash receipts and cash payments

5 **Use** a budget to manage cash

FRAUD AND ITS IMPACT

Fraud is an intentional misrepresentation of facts, made for the purpose of persuading another party to act in a way that causes injury or damage to that party. For example, in the chapter opening story, Melissa Price intentionally misappropriated money from AMEX and covered it up by making customer accounts look different than they actually were. In the end, her actions caused $622,000 in damages to AMEX.

OBJECTIVE

1 **Learn** about fraud and how much it costs

Fraud is a huge problem and is getting bigger, not only in the United States, but across the globe. Recent surveys of large and medium-sized companies in the United States and Canada revealed the following:

- Over 75% of businesses surveyed had experienced fraud;
- Over 50% of companies had experienced six or more instances of fraud in only one year;
- In 2007, companies lost an average of $2.4 million each to fraud (up from $1.7 million each in 2005);
- One out of every five American workers indicated personal awareness of fraud in the workplace.

Since small businesses and those in countries outside the United States and Canada were omitted from these surveys, we can be sure that the actual incidence of fraud is even higher! Another recent survey taken by the Association for Certified Fraud Examiners (ACFE) reveals that occupational fraud and abuse in America alone results in losses equal to about 6% of total business revenue. When applied to the U.S. gross domestic product, this means that about $600 billion per year is lost due to fraud, an astonishing $4,500 per employee! If you think that fraud occurs only in the for-profit sector, think again. About 13.4% of the ACFE survey cases are not-for-profit organizations, amounting to about $50 billion in fraud through not-for-profit organizations each year.

Fraud has literally exploded with the expansion of e-commerce via the Internet. In addition, studies have shown that the percentage of losses related to fraud from transactions originating in "third world" or developing countries via the Internet is even higher than in economically-developed countries.

What are the most common types of fraud? What causes fraud? What can be done to prevent it?

There are many types of fraud. Some of the most common types are insurance fraud, check forgery, Medicare fraud, credit card fraud, and identity theft. The two most common types of fraud that impact financial statements are:

- **Misappropriation of assets.** *This type of fraud is committed by employees of an entity who steal money from the company and cover it up* through erroneous entries in the books. The AMEX case is an example. Other examples of asset misappropriation include employee theft of inventory, bribery or kickback schemes in the purchasing function, or employee overstatement of expense reimbursement requests.
- **Fraudulent financial reporting.** *This type of fraud is committed by company managers who make false and misleading entries in the books*, making financial results of the company appear to be better than they actually are. The purpose of this type of fraud is to deceive investors and creditors into investing or loaning money to the company that they might not otherwise have invested or loaned.

Both of these types of fraud involve making false or misleading entries in the books of the company. We call this *cooking the books*. Of these two types, asset misappropriation is the most common, but fraudulent financial reporting is by far the most expensive. Perhaps the two most notorious recent cases involving fraudulent financial reporting in the United States involved **Enron Corporation** in 2001 and **WorldCom Corporation** in 2002. These two scandals alone rocked the U.S. economy and impacted financial markets across the world. Enron (discussed in Chapter 10) committed fraudulent financial reporting by overstating profits through bogus sales of nonexistent assets with inflated values.

When Enron's banks found out, they stopped loaning the company money to operate, causing it to go out of business almost overnight. WorldCom (discussed in Chapter 7) reported expenses as plant assets and overstated both profits and assets. The company's internal auditor blew the whistle on WorldCom, resulting in the company's eventual collapse. Sadly, the same international accounting firm, Arthur Andersen, LLP, had audited both companies' financial statements. Because of these and other failed audits, the once mighty firm of Arthur Andersen was forced to close its doors in 2002.

Each of these frauds, and many others revealed about the same time, involved losses in the billions of dollars and thousands of jobs when the companies went out of business. Widespread media coverage sparked adverse market reaction, loss of confidence in the financial reporting system, and losses through declines in stock values that ran in the trillions of dollars! We will discuss some of these cases throughout the remaining chapters of the text as examples of how accounting principles were deliberately misapplied, through cooking the books, in environments characterized by *weak internal controls*.

Exhibit 4-1 explains in graphic form the elements that make up virtually every fraud. We call it the **fraud triangle**.

EXHIBIT 4-1 | The Fraud Triangle

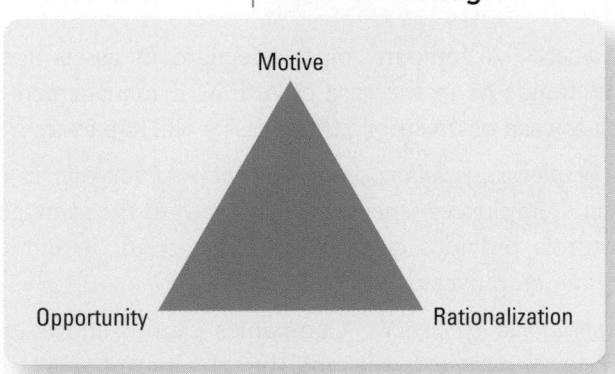

The first element in the fraud triangle is *motive*. This usually results from either critical need or greed on the part of the person who commits the fraud (the perpetrator). Sometimes it is a matter of just never having enough (because some persons who commit fraud are already rich by most people's standards). Other times the perpetrator of the fraud might have a legitimate financial need, such as a medical emergency, but he or she uses illegitimate means to meet that need. A recent article in the *Wall Street Journal* indicated that employee theft was on the rise due to economic hard times. In any case, the prevailing attitude on the part of the perpetrator is, "I want it, and someone else has it, so I'm going to do whatever I have to do to get it."

The second element in the fraud triangle is *opportunity*. As in the case of AMEX, the opportunity to commit fraud usually arises through weak internal controls. It might be a breakdown in a key element of controls, such as improper *segregation of duties* and/or *improper access to assets*. Or it might result from a weak *control environment*, such as a domineering CEO, a weak or conflicted board of directors, or lax ethical practices, allowing top management to override whatever controls the company has placed in operation for other transactions.

The third element in the triangle is *rationalization*. The perpetrator engages in distorted thinking, such as: "I deserve this;" "Nobody treats me fairly;" "No one will ever know;" "Just this once, I won't let it happen again;" or "Everyone else is doing it."

Fraud and Ethics

As we pointed out in our decision model for making ethical accounting and business judgments introduced in Chapter 1, the decision to engage in fraud is an act with economic, legal, and ethical implications. The perpetrators of fraud usually do so for their own short-term *economic gain*, while others incur *economic losses* that may far outstrip the gains of the fraudsters. Moreover, fraud is defined by state, federal, and international law as *illegal*. Those who are caught and found guilty of fraud ultimately face penalties which include imprisonment, fines, and monetary damages. Finally, from an *ethical* standpoint, fraud violates the rights of many for the temporary betterment of a few, and for the ultimate betterment of no one. At the end of the day, everyone loses! **Fraud is the ultimate unethical act in business!**

INTERNAL CONTROL

The primary way that fraud, as well as unintentional errors, is prevented, detected, or corrected in an organization is through a proper system of internal control. **Internal control** is a plan of organization and a system of procedures implemented by company management and the board of directors, and designed to accomplish the following five objectives:

1. *Safeguard assets.* A company must safeguard its assets against waste, inefficiency, and fraud. As in the case of AMEX, if management fails to safeguard assets such as cash or inventory, those assets will slip away.

2. *Encourage employees to follow company policy.* Everyone in an organization—managers and employees—needs to work toward the same goals. A proper system of controls provides clear policies that result in fair treatment of both customers and employees.

3. *Promote operational efficiency.* Companies cannot afford to waste resources. They work hard to make a sale, and they don't want to waste any of the benefits. If the company can buy something for $30, why pay $35? Effective controls minimize waste, which lowers costs and increases profits.

4. *Ensure accurate, reliable accounting records.* Accurate records are essential. Without proper controls, records may be unreliable, making it impossible to tell which part of the business is profitable and which part needs improvement. A business could be losing money on every product it sells—unless it keeps accurate records for the cost of its products.

5. *Comply with legal requirements.* Companies, like people, are subject to laws, such as those of regulatory agencies like the SEC, the IRS, and state, local, and international governing bodies. When companies disobey the law, they are subject to fines, or in extreme cases, their top executives may even go to prison. Effective internal controls help ensure compliance with the law and avoidance of legal difficulties.

How critical are internal controls? They're so important that the U.S. Congress has passed a law to require public companies—those that sell their stock to the public—to maintain a system of internal controls and to require that their auditors examine those controls and issue audit reports as to their reliability. Exhibit 4-2 is AMEX Products' Management Discussion of Financial Responsibility.

EXHIBIT 4-2 | **AMEX Products, Inc., Management's Discussion of Financial Responsibility**

Management's Discussion of Financial Responsibility

AMEX Products regularly reviews its framework of internal controls, which includes the company's policies, procedures and organizational structure. Corrective actions are taken to address any control deficiencies, and improvements are implemented as appropriate.

The Sarbanes-Oxley Act (SOX)

As the Enron and WorldCom scandals unfolded, many people asked, "How can these things happen? If such large companies that we have trusted commit such acts, how can we trust any company to be telling the truth in its financial statements? Where were the auditors?" To address public concerns, Congress passed the Sarbanes-Oxley Act of 2002 (SOX). SOX revamped corporate governance in the United States and profoundly affected the way that accounting and auditing is done in public companies. Here are some of the SOX provisions:

1. Public companies must issue an internal control report, and the outside auditor must evaluate and report on the soundness of the company's internal controls.

2. A new body, the Public Company Accounting Oversight Board, has been created to oversee the audits of public companies.

3. An accounting firm may not both audit a public client and also provide certain consulting services for the same client.

4. Stiff penalties await violators—25 years in prison for securities fraud; 20 years for an executive making false sworn statements.

The former CEO of WorldCom was convicted of securities fraud and sentenced to 25 years in prison. The top executives of Enron were also sent to prison. You can see that internal controls and related matters can have serious consequences.

Exhibit 4-3 diagrams the shield that internal controls provide for an organization. Protected by this shield, which provides protection from fraud, waste, and inefficiency, companies can do business in a trustworthy manner that ensures public confidence, an extremely important element in maintaining the stability of financial markets around the world.

EXHIBIT 4-3 | **The Shield of Internal Control**

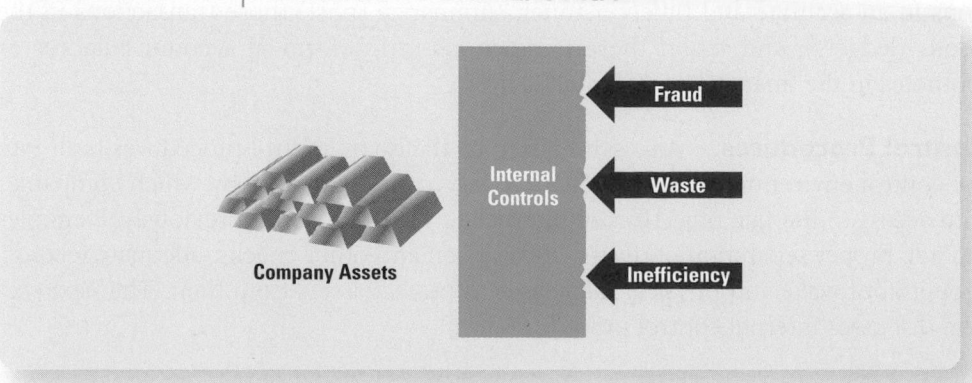

How does a business achieve good internal controls? The next section identifies the components of internal control.

The Components of Internal Control

OBJECTIVE

2 Set up an internal
control system

Internal control can be broken down into five components:

- Control environment
- Risk assessment
- Information system
- Control procedures
- Monitoring of controls

Exhibit 4-4 (p. 239) diagrams the components of internal control.

Control Environment.   The control environment, symbolized by the roof over the building in Exhibit 4-4, is the "tone at the top" of the business. It starts with the owner and the top managers. They must behave honorably to set a good example for company employees. The owner must demonstrate the importance of internal controls if he or she expects employees to take the controls seriously. A key ingredient in the control environment of many companies is a corporate code of ethics, modeled by top management, which includes such provisions as prohibition against giving or taking bribes or kickbacks from customers or suppliers, prohibition of transactions that involve conflicts of interest, and provisions that encourage good citizenship and corporate social responsibility.

Risk Assessment.   Symbolized by the smoke rising from the chimney, assessment of risks that a company faces offers hints of where mistakes or fraud might arise. A company must be able to identify its business risks, as well as to establish procedures for dealing with those risks to minimize their impacts on the company. For example, Kraft Foods faces the risk that its food products may harm people. American Airlines planes may crash. And all companies face the risk of bankruptcy. The managements of companies, supported by their boards, have to identify these risks and do what they can to prevent those risks from causing financial or other harm to the company, its employees, its owners, and its creditors.

Information System.   Symbolized by the door of the building, the information system is the means by which accounting information enters and exits. The owner of a business needs accurate information to keep track of assets and measure profits and losses. Every system within the business that processes accounting data should have the ability to capture transactions as they occur, record (journalize) those transactions in an accurate and timely manner, summarize (post) those transactions in the books (ledgers), and report those transactions in the form of account balances or footnotes in the financial statements.

Control Procedures.   Also symbolized by the door, control procedures built into the control environment and information system are the means by which companies gain access to the five objectives of internal controls discussed previously. Examples include proper separation of duties, comparison and other checks, adequate records, proper approvals, and physical safeguards to protect assets from theft. The next section discusses internal control procedures.

Monitoring of Controls.   Symbolized by the windows of the building, monitoring provides "eyes and ears," so that no one person or group of persons can process a transaction completely without being seen and checked by another person or group. With modern computerized systems, much of the monitoring of day-to-day activity is done through controls programmed into a company's information technology. Computer programs dealing with such systems as cash receipts and cash disbursements can be automatically programmed to generate *exception reports* for transactions that exceed certain pre-defined guidelines (such as disbursements in excess of $15,000 in a payroll) for special management scrutiny. In addition, companies hire auditors to monitor their controls. Internal auditors monitor company controls from the inside to safeguard the company's assets, and external auditors test the controls from the outside to ensure that the accounting records are accurate and reliable. Audits are discussed more thoroughly in the next section.

EXHIBIT 4-4 | The Components of Internal Control

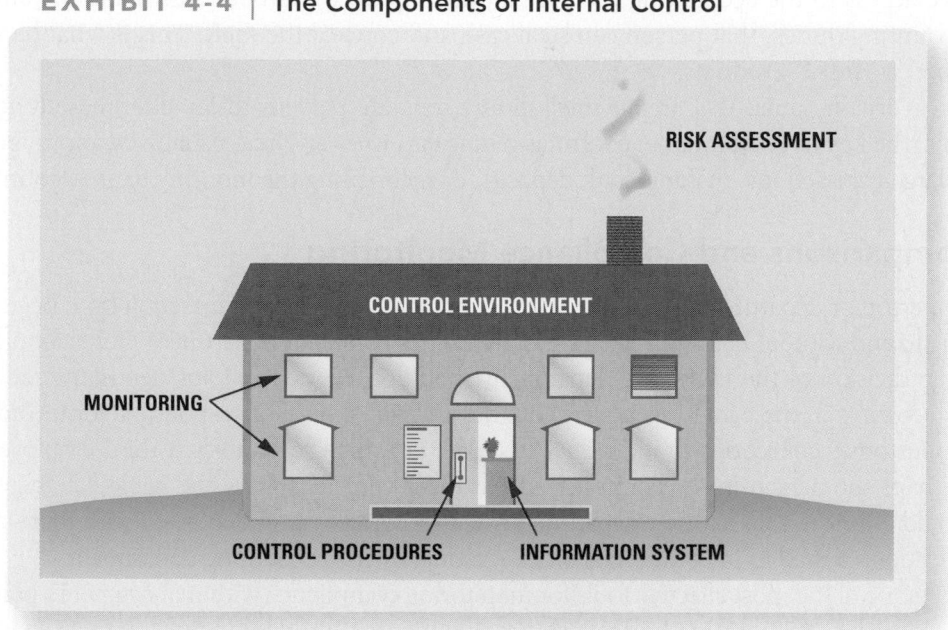

INTERNAL CONTROL PROCEDURES

Whether the business is AMEX Products, Microsoft, or a Starbucks store, every major class of transactions needs to have the following *internal control procedures*.

Smart Hiring Practices and Separation of Duties

In a business with good internal controls, no important duty is overlooked. Each person in the information chain is important. The chain should start with hiring. Background checks should be conducted on job applicants. Proper training and supervision, as well as paying competitive salaries, helps ensure that all employees are sufficiently competent for their jobs. Employee responsibilities should be clearly laid out in position descriptions. For example, the **treasurer**'s department should be in charge of cash handling, as well as signing and approving checks. Warehouse personnel should be in charge of storing and keeping track of inventory. With clearly assigned responsibilities, all important jobs get done.

In processing transactions, smart management *separates three key duties: asset handling, record keeping, and transaction approval.* For example, in the case of AMEX Products, separation of the duties of cash handling from record keeping for customer accounts receivable would have removed Melissa Price's incentive to engage in fraud, because it would have made it impossible for her to have lapped accounts receivable if another employee had been keeping the books. Ideally, someone else should also review customer accounts for collectability and be in charge of writing them off if they become completely uncollectible.

The accounting department should be completely separate from the operating departments, such as production and sales. What would happen if sales personnel, who were compensated based on a percentage of the amount of sales they made, approved the company's sales transactions to customers? Sales figures could be inflated and might not reflect the eventual amount collected from customers.

At all costs, accountants must not handle cash, and cash handlers must not have access to the accounting records. If one employee has both cash-handling and accounting duties, that person can steal cash and conceal the theft. This is what happened at AMEX Products.

For companies that are *too small* to hire separate persons to do all of these functions, the key to good internal control is *getting the owner involved*, usually by approving all large transactions, making bank deposits, or reconciling the monthly bank account.

Comparisons and Compliance Monitoring

No person or department should be able to completely process a transaction from beginning to end without being cross-checked by another person or department. For example, some division of the treasurer's department should be responsible for depositing daily cash receipts in the bank. The **controller**'s department should be responsible for recording customer collections to individual customer accounts receivable. A third employee (perhaps the person in the controller's department who reconciles the bank statement) should compare the treasurer department's daily records of cash deposited with totals of collections posted to individual customer accounts by the accounting department.

One of the most effective tools for monitoring compliance with management's policies is the use of **operating budgets** and **cash budgets**. A **budget** is a quantitative financial plan that helps control day-to-day management activities. Management may prepare these budgets on a yearly, quarterly, monthly, or more frequent basis. Operating budgets are budgets of future periods' net income. They are prepared by line item of the income statement. Cash budgets, discussed in depth later in this chapter, are budgets of future periods' cash receipts and cash disbursements. Often these budgets are "rolling," being constantly updated by adding a time period a year away while dropping the time period that has just passed. Computer systems are programmed to prepare exception reports for data that are out of line with expectations. This data can include variances for each account from budgeted amounts. Department managers are required to explain the variances, and to take corrective actions in their operating plans to keep the budgets in line with expectations. This is an example of the use of **exception reporting**.

To validate the accounting records and monitor compliance with company policies, most companies have an audit. An **audit** is an examination of the company's financial statements and its accounting system, including its controls.

Audits can be internal or external. *Internal auditors* are employees of the business. They ensure that employees are following company policies and operations are running efficiently. Internal auditors also determine whether the company is following legal requirements.

External auditors are completely independent of the business. They are hired to determine whether or not the company's financial statements agree with generally accepted accounting principles. Auditors examine the client's financial statements and the underlying transactions in order to form a professional opinion on the accuracy and reliability of the company's financial statements.

Adequate Records

Accounting records provide the details of business transactions. The general rule is that all major groups of transactions should be supported by either hard copy documents or electronic records. Examples of documents include sales invoices, shipping records, customer remittance advices, purchase orders, vendor invoices, receiving reports, and canceled (paid) checks. Documents should be pre-numbered to assure completeness of processing and proper transaction cutoff, and to prevent theft and inefficiency. A gap in the numbered document sequence draws attention to the possibility that transactions might have been omitted from processing.

Limited Access

To complement segregation of duties, company policy should limit access to assets only to those persons or departments that have custodial responsibilities. For example, access to cash should be limited to persons in the treasurer's department. Cash receipts might be processed through a lock-box system. Access to inventory should be limited to persons in the company warehouse where inventories are stored, or to persons in the shipping and receiving functions. Likewise, the company should limit access to records to those persons who have record keeping responsibilities. All manual records of the business should be protected by lock and key and electronic records should be protected by passwords. Only authorized persons should have access to certain records. Individual computers in the business should be protected by user identification and password. Electronic data files should be encrypted (processed through a special code) to prevent their recognition if accessed by a "hacker" or other unauthorized person.

Proper Approvals

No transaction should be processed without management's general or specific approval. The bigger the transaction, the more specific approval it should have. For individual small transactions, management might delegate approval to a specific department. For example:

- Sales to customers on account should all be approved by a separate *credit department* that reviews all customers for creditworthiness before goods are shipped to customers on credit. This helps assure that the company doesn't make sales to customers who cannot afford to pay their bills.
- Purchases of all items on credit should be approved by a separate *purchasing department* that specializes in that function. Among other things, a purchasing department should only buy from approved vendors, on the basis of competitive bids, to assure that the company gets the highest quality products for the most competitive prices.
- All personnel decisions, including hiring, firing, and pay adjustments, should be handled by a separate *human resources (HR) department* that specializes in personnel-related matters.

Very large (material) transactions should generally be approved by top management, and may even go to the board of directors.

What's an easy way to remember the basic control procedures for any class of transactions? Look at the first letters of each of the headings in this section:

Smart hiring practices and **S**egregation of duties

Comparisons and compliance monitoring

Adequate records

Limited access to both assets and records

Proper approvals (either general or specific) for each class of transaction

So, if you can remember SCALP and how to apply each of these attributes, you can have great controls in your business!

Information Technology

Accounting systems are relying less on manual procedures and more on information technology (IT) than ever before for record keeping, asset handling, approval, and monitoring, as well as physically safeguarding the assets. For example, retailers such as Target Stores and Macy's control inventory by attaching an *electronic sensor* to merchandise. The cashier must remove the sensor before the customer can walk out of the store. If a customer tries to leave the store with the sensor attached, an alarm sounds. According to Checkpoint Systems, these devices reduce theft by as much as 50%. *Bar codes* speed checkout at retail stores, performing multiple operations in a single step. When the sales associate scans the merchandise at the register, the computer records the sale, removes the item from inventory, and computes the amount of cash tendered.

When a company employs sophisticated IT, the basic attributes of internal control (SCALP) do not change, but the procedures by which these attributes are implemented change substantially. For example, segregation of duties is often accomplished by separating mainframe computer departments from other user departments (i.e., controller, sales, purchasing, receiving, credit, HR, treasurer) and restricting access to the IT department only to authorized personnel. Within the computer department, programmers should be separated from computer operators and data librarians. Access to sensitive data files is protected by **password** and data encryption. Electronic records must be saved routinely, or they might be written over or erased. Comparisons of data (such as cash receipts with total credits to customer accounts) that might otherwise be done by hand are performed by the computer. Computers can monitor inventory levels by item, generating a purchase order for inventory when it reaches a certain level.

The use of computers has the advantage of speed and accuracy (when programmed correctly). However, a computer that is *not* programmed correctly can corrupt *all* the data, making it unusable. It is therefore important to hire experienced and competent people to run the IT department, to restrict access to sensitive data and the IT department only to authorized personnel, to check data entered into and retrieved from the computer for accuracy and completeness, and to test and retest programs on a regular basis to assure data integrity and accuracy.

Safeguard Controls

Businesses keep important documents in *fireproof vaults. Burglar alarms* safeguard buildings, and *security cameras* safeguard other property. *Loss-prevention specialists* train employees to spot suspicious activity.

Employees who handle cash are in a tempting position. Many businesses purchase **fidelity bonds** on cashiers. The bond is an insurance policy that reimburses the company for any losses due to employee theft. Before issuing a fidelity bond, the insurance company investigates the employee's background.

Mandatory vacations and *job rotation* improve internal control. Companies move employees from job to job. This improves morale by giving employees a broad view of the business. Also, knowing someone else will do your job next month keeps you honest. AMEX Products didn't rotate employees to different jobs, and it cost the company $622,000.

INTERNAL CONTROLS FOR E-COMMERCE

E-commerce creates its own risks. Hackers may gain access to confidential information such as account numbers and passwords.

Pitfalls

E-commerce pitfalls include the following:

- Stolen credit card numbers
- Computer viruses and Trojan Horses
- Phishing expeditions

Stolen Credit Card Numbers.   Suppose you buy CDs from EMusic.com. To make the purchase, your credit card number must travel through cyberspace. Wireless networks (Wi-Fi) are creating new security hazards.

Amateur hacker Carlos Salgado, Jr., used his home computer to steal 100,000 credit card numbers with a combined limit exceeding $1 billion. Salgado was caught when he tried to sell the numbers to an undercover FBI agent.

Computer Viruses and Trojan Horses.   A **computer virus** is a malicious program that (a) enters program code without consent and (b) performs destructive actions in the victim's computer files or programs. A **Trojan Horse** is a malicious computer program that hides inside a legitimate program and works like a virus. Viruses can destroy or alter data, make bogus calculations, and infect files. Most firms have found a virus in their system at some point.

Suppose the U.S. Department of Defense takes bids for a missile system. Raytheon and Lockheed-Martin are competing for the contract. A hacker infects Raytheon's system and alters Raytheon's design. Then the government labels the Raytheon design as flawed and awards the contract to Lockheed.

Phishing Expeditions. Thieves **phish** by creating bogus Web sites, such as AOL4Free.com and BankAmerica.com. The neat-sounding Web site attracts lots of visitors, and the thieves obtain account numbers and passwords from unsuspecting people. The thieves then use the data for illicit purposes.

Security Measures

To address the risks posed by e-commerce, companies have devised a number of security measures, including

- encryption
- firewalls

Encryption. The server holding confidential information may not be secure. One technique for protecting customer data is encryption. **Encryption** rearranges messages by a mathematical process. The encrypted message can't be read by those who don't know the code. An accounting example uses check-sum digits for account numbers. Each account number has its last digit equal to the sum of the previous digits. For example, consider Customer Number 2237, where $2 + 2 + 3 = 7$. Any account number that fails this test triggers an error message.

Firewalls. **Firewalls** limit access into a local network. Members can access the network but nonmembers can't. Usually several firewalls are built into the system. Think of a fortress with multiple walls protecting the company's computerized records in the center. At the point of entry, passwords, PINs (personal identification numbers), and signatures are used. More sophisticated firewalls are used deeper in the network. Start with Firewall 1, and work toward the center.

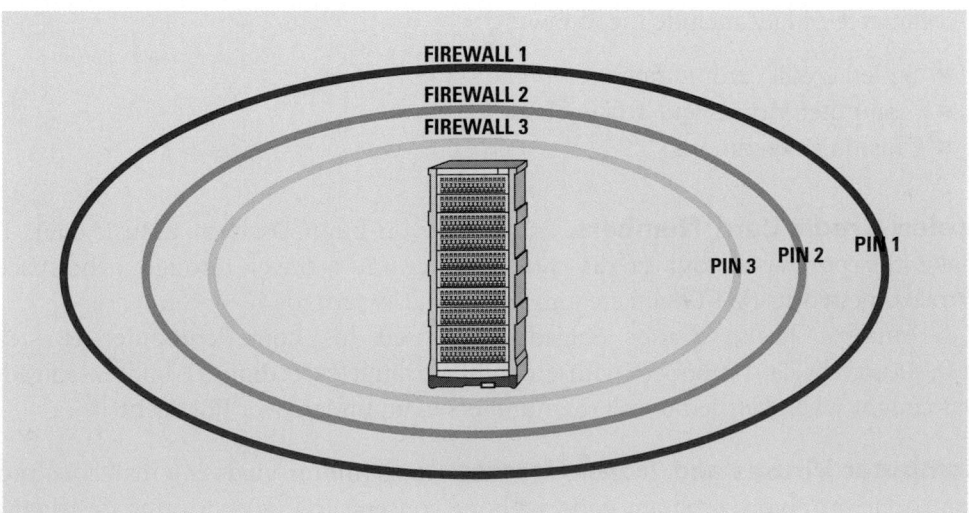

The Limitations of Internal Control—Costs and Benefits

Unfortunately, most internal controls can be overcome. Collusion—two or more people working together—can beat internal controls. Consider AMEX Products, discussed in the chapter opening. Even if Riffe were to hire a new person to keep the books, if that person had a relationship with Price and if they conspired with each other, they could design a scheme to lap accounts receivable, the same as Price did, and split the take. Other ways to circumvent a good system of internal controls include management override, human limitations such as fatigue and negligence, and gradual deterioration over time due to neglect. Because of the cost/benefit principle, discussed in the next paragraph, internal controls are not generally designed to detect these types of breakdowns. The best a company can do in this regard is to exercise care in hiring honest persons who have no conflicts of interest with existing employees, and to exercise constant diligence in monitoring the system to assure it continues to work properly.

The stricter the internal control system, the more it costs. An overly complex system of internal control can strangle the business with red tape. How tight should the controls be? Internal controls must be judged in light of their costs and benefits. An example of a good cost/benefit relationship: A part-time security guard at a **Wal-Mart** store costs about $28,000 a year. On average, each part-time guard prevents about $50,000 of theft. The net savings to Wal-Mart is $22,000. Most people would say the extra guard is well worth the cost!

THE BANK ACCOUNT AS A CONTROL DEVICE

Cash is the most liquid asset because it's the medium of exchange. Cash is easy to conceal and relatively easy to steal. As a result, most businesses create specific controls for cash.

Keeping cash in a bank account helps control cash because banks have established practices for safeguarding customers' money. The documents used to control a bank account include the following:

- Signature card
- Bank statement
- Deposit ticket
- Bank reconciliation
- Check

Signature Card

Banks require each person authorized to sign on an account to provide a *signature card*. This protects against forgery.

Deposit Ticket

Banks supply standard forms such as *deposit tickets*. The customer fills in the amount of each deposit. As proof of the transaction, the customer keeps a deposit receipt.

Check

To pay cash, the depositor can write a **check**, which tells the bank to pay the designated party a specified amount. There are three parties to a check:

- The maker, who signs the check
- The payee, to whom the check is paid
- The bank on which the check is drawn

Exhibit 4-5 shows a check drawn by AMEX Products, the maker. The check has two parts, the check itself and the **remittance advice** below. This optional attachment, which may often be scanned electronically, tells the payee the reason for the payment and is used as the source document for posting to proper accounts.

EXHIBIT 4-5 | **Check with Remittance Advice**

Date	Description	Amount
12/28/10	Office Supplies	$320.00

Bank Statement

Banks send monthly statements to customers. A **bank statement** reports what the bank did with the customer's cash. The statement shows the account's beginning and ending balances, cash receipts, and payments. Included with the statement are copies of the maker's *canceled checks* (or the actual paid checks). Exhibit 4-6 is the December bank statement of the Palo Alto office of AMEX Products.

EXHIBIT 4-6 | **Bank Statement**

	BANK STATEMENT

BAY AREA NATIONAL BANK

SOUTH PALO ALTO #136 P.O. BOX 22985 PALO ALTO, CA 94306

AMEX Products
3814 Glenwood Parkway
Palo Alto, CA 94306

CHECKING ACCOUNT 136–213733

DECEMBER 31, 2010

BEGINNING BALANCE	TOTAL DEPOSITS	TOTAL WITHDRAWALS	SERVICE CHARGES	ENDING BALANCE
6,550	4,370	5,000	20	5,900

— TRANSACTIONS —

DEPOSITS	DATE	AMOUNT
Deposit	12/04	1,150
Deposit	12/08	190
EFT—Receipt of cash dividend	12/17	900
Bank Collection	12/26	2,100
Interest	12/31	30

CHARGES	DATE	AMOUNT
Service Charge	12/31	20

CHECKS

Number	Amount	Number	Amount	Number	Amount
307	100	333	150	335	100
332	3,000	334	100	336	1,100

OTHER DEDUCTIONS	DATE	AMOUNT
NSF	12/04	50
EFT—Insurance	12/20	400

Electronic funds transfer (EFT) moves cash by electronic communication. It is cheaper to pay without having to mail a check, so many people pay their mortgage, rent, utilities, and insurance by EFT.

Bank Reconciliation

There are two records of a business's cash:

1. The Cash account in the company's general ledger. Exhibit 4-7 on the following page shows that AMEX Products' ending cash balance is $3,340.

EXHIBIT 4-7 | Cash Records of AMEX Products

General Ledger:

ACCOUNT Cash

Date	Item	Debit	Credit	Balance
2010				
Dec 1	Balance			6,550
2	Cash receipt	1,150		7,700
7	Cash receipt	190		7,890
31	Cash payments		6,150	1,740
31	Cash receipt	1,600		3,340

Cash Payments:

Check No.	Amount	Check No.	Amount
332	$3,000	337	$ 280
333	510	338	320
334	100	339	250
335	100	340	490
336	1,100	Total	$6,150

2. The bank statement, which shows the cash receipts and payments transacted through the bank. In Exhibit 4-6 the bank shows an ending balance of $5,900 for AMEX.

The books and the bank statement usually show different cash balances. Differences arise because of a time lag in recording transactions—two examples follow:

- When you write a check, you immediately deduct it in your checkbook. But the bank does not subtract the check from your account until the bank pays the check a few days later. And you immediately add the cash receipt for all your deposits. But it may take a day or two for the bank to add deposits to your balance.
- Your EFT payments and cash receipts are recorded by the bank before you learn of them.

To ensure accurate cash records, you need to update your cash record—either online or after you receive your bank statement. The result of this updating process creates a **bank reconciliation**, which you must prepare. The bank reconciliation explains all differences between your cash records and your bank balance. The person who prepares the bank reconciliation should have no other cash duties. Otherwise, he or she can steal cash and manipulate the reconciliation to conceal the theft.

Preparing the Bank Reconciliation

Here are the items that appear on a bank reconciliation. They all cause differences between the bank balance and the book balance. We call your cash record (also known as a "checkbook") the "Books."

Bank Side of the Reconciliation

1. Items to show on the *Bank* side of the bank reconciliation include the following:

   a. **Deposits in transit** (outstanding deposits). You have recorded these deposits, but the bank has not. Add deposits in transit on the bank reconciliation.

   b. **Outstanding checks**. You have recorded these checks, but the bank has not yet paid them. Subtract outstanding checks.

   c. **Bank errors.** Correct all bank errors on the Bank side of the reconciliation. For example, the bank may erroneously subtract from your account a check written by someone else.

Book Side of the Reconciliation

2. Items to show on the *Book* side of the bank reconciliation include the following:

   a. **Bank collections.** Bank collections are cash receipts that the bank has recorded for your account. But you haven't recorded the cash receipt yet. Many businesses have their customers pay directly to their bank. This is called a *lock-box system* and reduces theft. An example is a bank collecting an account receivable for you. Add bank collections on the bank reconciliation.

   b. **Electronic funds transfers.** The bank may receive or pay cash on your behalf. An EFT may be a cash receipt or a cash payment. Add EFT receipts and subtract EFT payments.

   c. **Service charge.** This cash payment is the bank's fee for processing your transactions. Subtract service charges.

   d. **Interest revenue on your checking account.** On certain types of bank accounts, you earn interest if you keep enough cash in your account. The bank statement tells you of this cash receipt. Add interest revenue.

   e. **Nonsufficient funds (NSF) checks.** These are cash receipts from customers for which there are not sufficient funds in the bank to cover the amount. NSF checks (sometimes called hot checks) are treated as cash payments on your bank reconciliation. Subtract NSF checks.

   f. **The cost of printed checks.** This cash payment is handled like a service charge. Subtract this cost.

   g. **Book errors.** Correct all book errors on the Book side of the reconciliation. For example, you may have recorded a $150 check that you wrote as $510.

Bank Reconciliation Illustrated. The bank statement in Exhibit 4-6 shows that the December 31 bank balance of AMEX Products is $5,900 (upper right corner). However, the company's Cash account has a balance of $3,340, as shown in Exhibit 4-7. This situation calls for a bank reconciliation. Exhibit 4-8, panel A, on the following page, lists the reconciling items for easy reference, and panel B shows the completed reconciliation.

EXHIBIT 4-8 | Bank Reconciliation

PANEL A—Reconciling Items

Bank side:

1. Deposit in transit, $1,600.
2. Bank error: The bank deducted $100 for a check written by another company. Add $100 to the bank balance.
3. Outstanding checks—total of $1,340.

Check No.	Amount
337	$280
338	320
339	250
340	490

Book side:

4. EFT receipt of your dividend revenue earned on an investment, $900.
5. Bank collection of your account receivable, $2,100.
6. Interest revenue earned on your bank balance, $30.
7. Book error: You recorded check no. 333 for $510. The amount you actually paid on account was $150. Add $360 to your book balance.
8. Bank service charge, $20.
9. NSF check from a customer, $50. Subtract $50 from your book balance.
10. EFT payment of insurance expense, $400.

PANEL B—Bank Reconciliation

AMEX Products
Bank Reconciliation
December 31, 2010

Bank			Books		
Balance, December 31		$5,900	Balance, December 31		$3,340
Add:			Add:		
1. Deposit in transit		1,600	4. EFT receipt of dividend revenue		900
2. Correction of bank error		100	5. Bank collection of account		
		7,600	receivable		2,100
			6. Interest revenue earned on		
			bank balance		30
			7. Correction of book error—		
			overstated our check no. 333		360
Less:					6,730
3. Outstanding checks					
No. 337	$280		Less:		
No. 338	320		8. Service charge	$ 20	
No. 339	250		9. NSF check	50	
No. 340	490	(1,340)	10. EFT payment of insurance expense	400	(470)
Adjusted bank balance		**$6,260**	**Adjusted bank balance**		**$6,260**

These amounts should agree.

SUMMARY OF THE VARIOUS RECONCILING ITEMS:

BANK BALANCE—ALWAYS

- *Add* deposits in transit.
- *Subtract* outstanding checks.
- *Add* or *subtract* corrections of bank errors.

BOOK BALANCE—ALWAYS

- *Add* bank collections, interest revenue, and EFT receipts.
- *Subtract* service charges, NSF checks, and EFT payments.
- *Add* or *subtract* corrections of book errors.

Journalizing Transactions from the Bank Reconciliation.   The bank reconciliation is an accountant's tool separate from the journals and ledgers. It does *not* account for transactions in the journal. To get the transactions into the accounts, we must make journal entries and post to the ledger. All items on the *Book* side of the bank reconciliation require journal entries.

The bank reconciliation in Exhibit 4-8 requires AMEX Products to make journal entries to bring the Cash account up-to-date. The numbers in red correspond to the reconciling items listed in Exhibit 4-8, Panel A.

4.	Dec 31	Cash	900	
		Dividend Revenue		900
		Receipt of dividend revenue earned on investment.		
5.	31	Cash	2,100	
		Accounts Receivable		2,100
		Account receivable collected by bank.		
6.	31	Cash	30	
		Interest Revenue		30
		Interest earned on bank balance.		
7.	31	Cash	360	
		Accounts Payable		360
		Correction of check no. 333.		
8.	31	Miscellaneous Expense[1]	20	
		Cash		20
		Bank service charge.		
9.	31	Accounts Receivable	50	
		Cash		50
		NSF check returned by bank.		
10.	31	Insurance Expense	400	
		Cash		400
		Payment of monthly insurance.		

[1]Miscellaneous Expense is debited for the bank service charge because the service charge pertains to no particular expense category.

The entry for the NSF check (entry 9) needs explanation. Upon learning that a customer's $50 check to us was not good, we must credit Cash to update the Cash account. Unfortunately, we still have a receivable from the customer, so we must debit Accounts Receivable to reinstate our receivable.

Online Banking

Online banking allows you to pay bills and view your account electronically. You don't have to wait until the end of the month to get a bank statement. With online banking you can reconcile transactions at any time and keep your account current whenever you wish. Exhibit 4-9 shows a page from the account history of Toni Anderson's bank account.

EXHIBIT 4-9 | **Online Banking—Account History (like a Bank Statement)**

Account History for Toni Anderson Checking # 5401-632-9 as of Close of Business 07/27/2010

Account Details

Current Balance $4,136.08

Date ↓	Description	Withdrawals	Deposits	Balance
	Current Balance			**$4,136.08**
07/27/10	DEPOSIT		1,170.35	
07/26/10	28 DAYS INTEREST		2.26	
07/25/10	Check #6131 View Image	443.83		
07/24/10	Check #6130 View Image	401.52		
07/23/10	EFT PYMT CINGULAR	61.15		
07/22/10	EFT PYMT CITICARD PAYMENT	3,172.85		
07/20/10	Check #6127 View Image	550.00		
07/19/10	Check #6122 View Image	50.00		
07/16/10	Check #6116 View Image	2,056.75		
07/15/10	Check #6123 View Image	830.00		
07/13/10	Check #6124 View Image	150.00		
07/11/10	ATM 4900 SANGER AVE	200.00		
07/09/10	Check #6119 View Image	30.00		
07/05/10	Check #6125 View Image	2,500.00		
07/04/10	ATM 4900 SANGER AVE	100.00		
07/01/10	DEPOSIT		9,026.37	

FDIC   EQUAL HOUSING LENDER   E-Mail

The account history—like a bank statement—lists deposits, checks, EFT payments, ATM withdrawals, and interest earned on your bank balance.

But the account history doesn't show your beginning balance, so you can't work from your beginning balance to your ending balance.

STOP & THINK...

The bank statement balance is $4,500 and shows a service charge of $15, interest earned of $5, and an NSF check for $300. Deposits in transit total $1,200; outstanding checks are $575. The bookkeeper recorded as $152 a check of $125 in payment of an account payable. This created a book error of $27 (positive amount to correct the error).

1. What is the adjusted bank balance?
2. What was the book balance of cash before the reconciliation?

Answers:

1. $5,125 ($4,500 + $1,200 − $575).
2. $5,408 ($5,125 + $15 − $5 + $300 − $27). The adjusted book and bank balances are the same. The answer can be determined by working backward from the adjusted balance.

Using the Bank Reconciliation to Control Cash. The bank reconciliation can be a powerful control device. Randy Vaughn is a CPA in Houston, Texas. He owns several apartment complexes that are managed by his aunt. His aunt signs up tenants, collects the monthly rents, arranges maintenance work, hires and fires employees, writes the checks, and performs the bank reconciliation. In short, she does it all. This concentration of duties in one person is evidence of weak internal control. Vaughn's aunt could be stealing from him, and as a CPA he is aware of this possibility.

Vaughn trusts his aunt because she is a member of the family. Nevertheless, Vaughn exercises some controls over his aunt's management of his apartments. Vaughn periodically drops by the apartments to see whether the maintenance staff is keeping the property in good condition. To control cash, Vaughn occasionally examines the bank reconciliation that his aunt has performed. Vaughn would know immediately if his aunt were writing checks to herself. By examining the copy of each check, Vaughn establishes control over cash payments.

Vaughn has a simple method for controlling cash receipts. He knows the occupancy level of his apartments. He also knows the monthly rent he charges. Vaughn multiplies the number of apartments—say 20—by the monthly rent (which averages $500 per unit) to arrive at expected monthly rent revenue of $10,000. By tracing the $10,000 revenue to the bank statement, Vaughn can tell if all his rent money went into his bank account. To keep his aunt on her toes, Vaughn lets her know that he periodically audits her work.

Control activities such as these are critical. If there are only a few employees, separation of duties may not be feasible. The manager must control operations, or the assets will slip away.

MID-CHAPTER SUMMARY PROBLEM

The cash account of Baylor Associates at February 28, 2011, follows.

Cash				
Feb 1	Bal 3,995	Feb 3		400
6	800	12		3,100
15	1,800	19		1,100
23	1,100	25		500
28	2,400	27		900
Feb 28	Bal 4,095			

Baylor Associates received the bank statement on February 28, 2011 (negative amounts are in parentheses):

Bank Statement for February 2011		
Beginning balance		$3,995
Deposits:		
Feb 7	$ 800	
15	1,800	
24	1,100	3,700
Checks (total per day):		
Feb 8	$ 400	
16	3,100	
23	1,100	(4,600)
Other items:		
Service charge		(10)
NSF check from M. E. Crown		(700)
Bank collection of note receivable for the company		1,000
EFT—monthly rent expense		(330)
Interest revenue earned on account balance		15
Ending balance		$3,070

Additional data:
Baylor deposits all cash receipts in the bank and makes all payments by check.

❚ Requirements

1. Prepare the bank reconciliation of Baylor Associates at February 28, 2011.
2. Journalize the entries based on the bank reconciliation.

Answers

❙ *Requirement 1*

Baylor Associates
Bank Reconciliation
February 28, 2011

Bank:				
Balance, February 28, 2011				$3,070
Add: Deposit of February 28 in transit				2,400
				5,470
Less: Outstanding checks issued on Feb 25 ($500)				
and Feb 27 ($900)				(1,400)
Adjusted bank balance, February 28, 2011				$4,070
Books:				
Balance, February 28, 2011				$4,095
Add: Bank collection of note receivable				1,000
Interest revenue earned on bank balance				15
				5,110
Less: Service charge		$ 10		
NSF check		700		
EFT—Rent expense		330		(1,040)
Adjusted book balance, February 28, 2011				$4,070

❙ *Requirement 2*

Feb 28	Cash		1,000	
	Note Receivable			1,000
	Note receivable collected by bank.			
28	Cash		15	
	Interest Revenue			15
	Interest earned on bank balance.			
28	Miscellaneous Expense		10	
	Cash			10
	Bank service charge.			
28	Accounts Receivable		700	
	Cash			700
	NSF check returned by bank.			
28	Rent Expense		330	
	Cash			330
	Monthly rent expense.			

OBJECTIVE

4 **Apply** internal controls to cash receipts and cash payments

INTERNAL CONTROL OVER CASH RECEIPTS

Cash requires some specific internal controls because cash is relatively easy to steal and it's easy to convert to other forms of wealth. Moreover, all transactions ultimately affect cash. That's why cash is called the "eye of the needle." Let's see how to control cash receipts.

All cash receipts should be deposited for safekeeping in the bank—quickly. Companies receive cash over the counter and through the mail. Each source of cash has its own security measures.

Cash Receipts over the Counter

Exhibit 4-10 illustrates the purchase of products in a grocery store. The point-of-sale terminal provides control over the cash receipts, while also recording the sale and relieving inventory for the appropriate cost of the goods sold. Consider a **Whole Foods Market** store. For each transaction, the Whole Foods sales associate issues a receipt to the customer as proof of purchase. The cash drawer opens when the sales associate enters a transaction, and the machine electronically transmits a record of the sale to the store's main computer. At the end of each shift, the sales associate delivers his or her cash drawer to the office, where it is combined with cash from all other terminals and delivered by armored car to the bank for deposit, as explained in the next section. Later, a separate employee in the accounting department reconciles the electronic record of the sales per terminal to the record of the cash turned in. These measures, coupled with oversight by a manager, discourage theft.

EXHIBIT 4-10 | **Cash Receipts over the Counter**

Point-of-sale terminals also provide effective control over inventory. For example, in a restaurant, these devices track sales by menu item and total sales by cash, type of credit card, gift card redeemed, etc. They create the daily sales journal for that store, which, in turn, interfaces with the general ledger. Managers can use records produced by point-of-sale terminals to check inventory levels and compare them against sales records for accuracy. For example, in a restaurant, an effective way to monitor sales of expensive wine is for a manager to perform a quick count of the bottles on hand at the end of the day and compare it with the count at the end of the previous day, plus the record of any purchased. The count at the end of the previous day, plus the record of bottles purchased, minus the count at the end of the current day should equal the amount sold as recorded by the point-of-sale terminals in the restaurant.

An effective control for many chain retail businesses, such as restaurants, grocery stores, or clothing stores, to prevent unauthorized access to cash as well as to allow for more efficient management of cash, is the use of "depository bank accounts." Cash receipts for an individual store are deposited into a local bank account (preferably delivered by armored car for security reasons) on a daily basis. The corporate headquarters arranges for its centralized bank to draft the local depository accounts on a frequent (perhaps daily) basis to get the money concentrated into the company's centralized account, where it can be used to pay the corporation's bills. Depository accounts are "one-way" accounts where the local management may only make deposits. They have no authority to write checks on the account or take money out of the store's account.

Cash Receipts by Mail

Many companies receive cash by mail. Exhibit 4-11 shows how companies control cash received by mail. All incoming mail is opened by a mailroom employee. The mailroom then sends all customer checks to the treasurer, who has the cashier deposit the money in the bank. The remittance advices go to the accounting department for journal entries to Cash and customer accounts receivable. As a final step, the controller compares the following records for the day:

- Bank deposit amount from the treasurer
- Debit to Cash from the accounting department

The debit to Cash should equal the amount deposited in the bank. All cash receipts are safe in the bank, and the company books are up-to-date.

EXHIBIT 4-11 | Cash Receipts by Mail

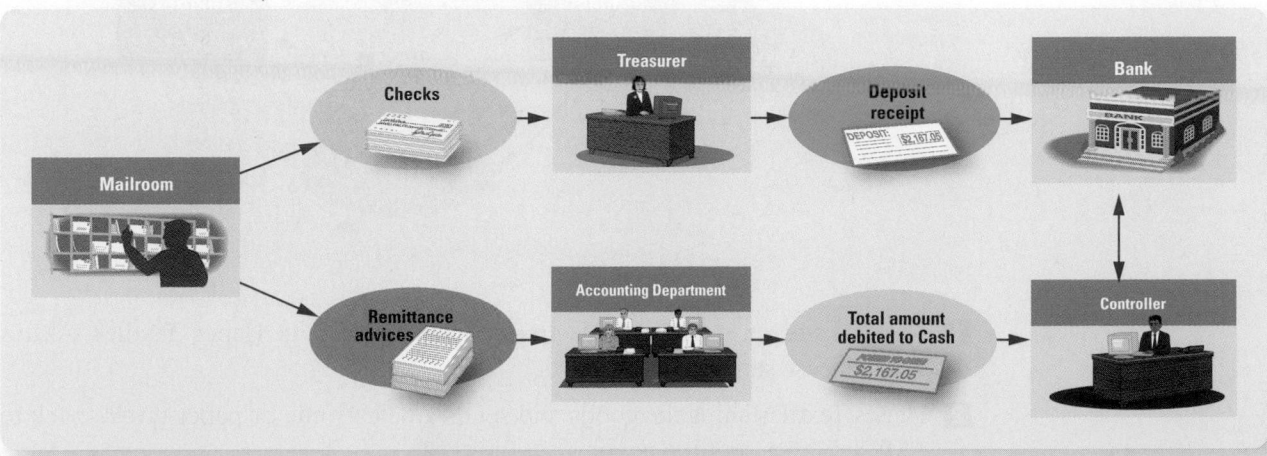

To prevent unauthorized access to cash, many companies use a bank lock-box system, rather than risk processing checks through the mailroom. Customers send their checks by return mail directly to a post office box controlled by the company's bank. The bank sends a detailed record of cash received, by customer, to the company for use in posting collections to accounts receivable. Internal control is tight because company personnel never touch incoming cash. The lock-box system also gets the cash to the bank in a more timely manner, allowing the company to put the cash to work faster than would be possible if it were processed by the company's mailroom.

INTERNAL CONTROL OVER CASH PAYMENTS

Companies make most payments by check. Let's see how to control cash payments by check.

Controls over Payment by Check

As we have seen, you need a good separation of duties between (a) operations and (b) writing checks for cash payments. Payment by check is an important internal control, as follows:

- The check provides a record of the payment.
- The check must be signed by an authorized official.
- Before signing the check, the official should study the evidence supporting the payment.

Controls over Purchase and Payment.   To illustrate the internal control over cash payments by check, suppose AMEX Products buys some of its inventory from Hanes Textiles. The purchasing and payment process follows these steps, as shown in Exhibit 4-12. Start with the box for AMEX Products on the left side.

EXHIBIT 4-12 | **Cash Payments by Check**

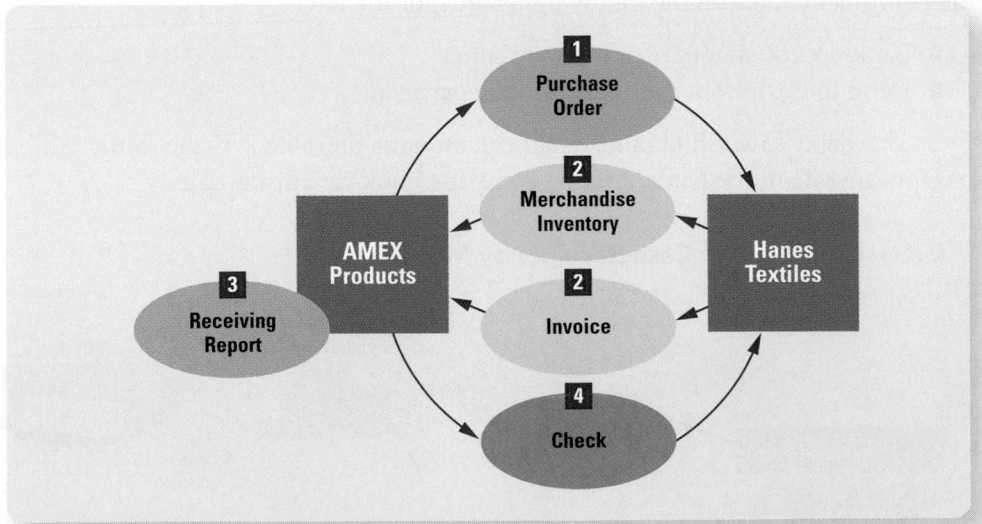

1 AMEX faxes or e-mails an electronic *purchase order* to Hanes Textiles. AMEX says, "Please send us 100 T-shirts."

2 Hanes Textiles ships the goods and sends an electronic or paper *invoice* back to AMEX. Hanes sent the goods.

3 AMEX receives the *inventory* and prepares a *receiving report* to list the goods received. AMEX got its T-shirts.

4 After approving all documents, AMEX sends a *check* to Hanes, or authorizes an electronic funds transfer (EFT) directly from its bank to Hanes' bank. By this action, AMEX says, "Okay, we'll pay you."

For good internal control, the purchasing agent should neither receive the goods nor approve the payment. If these duties aren't separated, a purchasing agent can buy goods and have them shipped to his or her home. Or a purchasing agent can spend too much on purchases, approve the payment, and split the excess with the supplier. To avoid these problems, companies split the following duties among different employees:

- Purchasing goods
- Receiving goods
- Approving and paying for goods

Exhibit 4-13 shows AMEX's payment packet of documents. Before signing the check or approving the EFT, the treasurer's department should examine the packet to prove that all the documents agree. Only then does the company know that

1. it received the goods ordered.

2. it is paying only for the goods received.

EXHIBIT 4-13 | Payment Packet

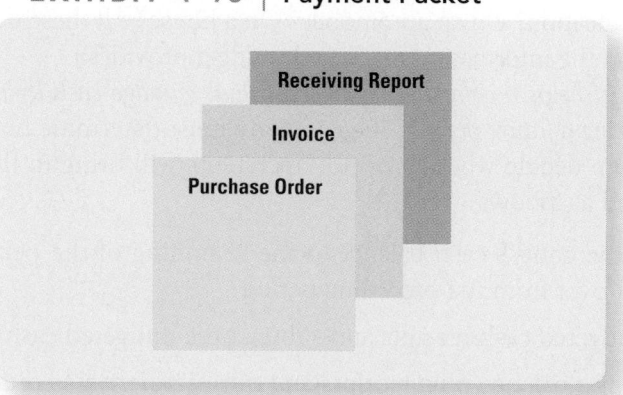

After payment, the person in the treasurer's department who has authorized the disbursement stamps the payment packet "paid" or punches a hole through it to prevent it from being submitted a second time. Dishonest people have tried to run a bill through twice for payment. The stamp or hole shows that the bill has been paid. If checks are used, they should then be mailed directly to the payee without being allowed to return to the department that prepared them. To do so would violate separation of the duties of cash handling and record keeping, as well as unauthorized access to cash.

Petty Cash. It would be wasteful to write separate checks for an executive's taxi fare, name tags needed right away, or delivery of a package across town. Therefore, companies keep a **petty cash** fund on hand to pay such minor amounts. The word "petty" means small. That's what petty cash is—a small cash fund kept by a single employee for the purpose of making such on-the-spot minor purchases.

The petty cash fund is opened with a particular amount of cash. A check for that amount is then issued to the custodian of the petty cash fund, who is solely responsible for accounting for it. Assume that on February 28 **Cisco Systems**, the worldwide leader in networks for the Internet, establishes a petty cash fund of $500 in a sales department by writing a check to the designated custodian. The custodian of the petty cash fund cashes the check and places $500 in the fund, which may be a cash box or other device.

For each petty cash payment, the custodian prepares a petty cash voucher to list the item purchased. The sum of the cash in the petty cash fund plus the total of the paid vouchers in the cash box should equal the opening balance at all times—in this case, $500. The Petty Cash account keeps its $500 balance at all times. Maintaining the Petty Cash account at this balance, supported by the fund (cash plus vouchers), is how an **imprest system** works. The control feature is that it clearly identifies the amount for which the custodian is responsible.

Using a Budget to Manage Cash

OBJECTIVE

5 **Use** a budget to manage cash

As mentioned earlier in the chapter, a budget is a financial plan that helps coordinate business activities. Managers control operations with an operating budget. They also control cash receipts and cash payments, as well as ending cash balances, through use of a cash budget.

How, for example, does AMEX Products decide when to invest in new inventory-tracking technology? How will AMEX decide how much to spend? Will borrowing be needed, or can AMEX finance the purchase with internally generated cash? What do ending cash balances need to be in order to provide a "safety margin" so the company won't unexpectedly run out of cash? A cash budget for a business works on roughly the same concept as a personal budget. By what process do you decide how much to spend on your education? On an automobile? On a house? All these decisions depend to some degree on the information that a cash budget provides.

A *cash budget helps a company or an individual manage cash by planning receipts and payments during a future period.* The company must determine how much cash it will need and then decide whether or not operations will bring in the needed cash. Managers proceed as follows:

1. Start with the entity's cash balance at the beginning of the period. This is the amount left over from the preceding period.

2. Add the budgeted cash receipts and subtract the budgeted cash payments.

3. The beginning balance plus receipts and minus payments equals the expected cash balance at the end of the period.

4. Compare the cash available before new financing to the budgeted cash balance at the end of the period. Managers know the minimum amount of cash they need (the budgeted balance). If the budget shows excess cash, managers can invest the excess. But if the cash available falls below the budgeted balance, the company will need additional financing. The company may need to borrow the shortfall amount. The budget is a valuable tool for helping the company plan for the future.

The budget period can span any length of time—a day, a week, a month, or a year. Exhibit 4-14 shows a cash budget for AMEX Products, Inc., for the year ended December 31, 2011. Study it carefully, because at some point you will use a cash budget.

AMEX Products' cash budget in Exhibit 4-14 begins with $6,260 of cash at the end of the previous year (line 1). Then add budgeted cash receipts and subtract budgeted payments for the current year. In this case, AMEX expects to have $3,900 of cash available at year-end (line 10). AMEX managers need to maintain a cash balance of at least $5,000 (line 11). Line 12 shows that AMEX must arrange $1,100 of financing in order to achieve its goals for 2011.

Internal Control Over Cash Payments **261**

EXHIBIT 4-14 | **Cash Budget**

AMEX Products, Inc.
Cash Budget
For the Year Ended December 31, 2011

(1)	Cash balance, December 31, 2010.................................		$ 6,260
	Budgeted cash receipts:		
(2)	Collections from customers		55,990
(3)	Dividends on investments		1,200
(4)	Sale of store fixtures		5,700
			69,150
	Budgeted cash payments:		
(5)	Purchases of inventory..	$33,720	
(6)	Operating expenses..	11,530	
(7)	Expansion of store...	12,000	
(8)	Payment of long-term debt	5,000	
(9)	Payment of dividends...	3,000	65,250
(10)	Cash available (needed) before new financing...............		$ 3,900
(11)	Budgeted cash balance, December 31, 2011..................		(5,000)
(12)	Cash available for additional investments, or		
	(New financing needed)		$ (1,100)

Reporting Cash on the Balance Sheet

Most companies have numerous bank accounts, but they usually combine all cash amounts into a single total called "Cash and Cash Equivalents." **Cash equivalents** include liquid assets such as time deposits, certificates of deposit, and high-grade government securities. These are interest-bearing accounts that can be withdrawn with no penalty, or interest-bearing securities. Slightly less liquid than cash, cash equivalents are sufficiently similar to be reported along with cash. The balance sheet of AMEX Products reported the following:

AMEX Products, Inc.
Balance Sheet (Excerpts, adapted)
For the Year Ended December 31, 2010

Assets

Cash and cash equivalents................	$ 6,260
Cash pledged as collateral................	2,000

Compensating Balance Agreements

The Cash account on the balance sheet reports the liquid assets available for day-to-day use. None of the Cash balance is restricted in any way.

Any restricted amount of cash should *not* be reported as Cash on the balance sheet. For example, on the AMEX Products balance sheet, *cash pledged as collateral* is reported separately because that cash is not available for day-to-day use. Instead, AMEX has pledged the cash as security (collateral) for a loan. If AMEX fails to pay the loan, the lender can take the pledged cash. For this reason, the pledged cash is less liquid.

Also, banks often lend money under a compensating balance agreement. The borrower agrees to maintain a minimum balance in a checking account at all times. This minimum balance becomes a long-term asset and is therefore not cash in the normal sense.

Suppose AMEX Products borrowed $10,000 at 8% from First Interstate Bank and agreed to keep 20% ($2,000) on deposit at all times. The net result of the compensating balance agreement is that AMEX actually borrowed only $8,000. And by paying 8% interest on the full $10,000, AMEX's actual interest rate is really 10%, as shown here:

$$\$10,000 \times .08 = \$800 \text{ interest}$$
$$\$800/\$8,000 = .10 \text{ interest rate}$$

END-OF-CHAPTER SUMMARY PROBLEM

Assume the following situation for PepsiCo, Inc.: PepsiCo ended 2010 with cash of $200 million. At December 31, 2010, Bob Detmer, the CFO of PepsiCo, is preparing the budget for 2011.

During 2011, Detmer expects PepsiCo to collect $26,400 million from customers and $80 million from interest earned on investments. PepsiCo expects to pay $12,500 million for its inventories and $5,400 million for operating expenses. To remain competitive, PepsiCo plans to spend $2,200 million to upgrade production facilities and an additional $350 million to acquire other companies. PepsiCo also plans to sell older assets for approximately $300 million and to collect $220 million of this amount in cash. PepsiCo is budgeting dividend payments of $550 million during the year. Finally, the company is scheduled to pay off $1,200 million of long-term debt plus the $6,600 million of current liabilities left over from 2010.

Because of the growth planned for 2011, Detmer budgets the need for a minimum cash balance of $300 million.

❙ *Requirement*

1. How much must PepsiCo borrow during 2011 to keep its cash balance from falling below $300 million? Prepare the 2011 cash budget to answer this important question.

Answer

PepsiCo, Inc.
Cash Budget
For the Year Ended December 31, 2011

(In millions)

Cash balance, December 31, 2010		$ 200
Estimated cash receipts:		
Collections from customers		26,400
Receipt of interest		80
Sales of assets		220
		26,900
Estimated cash payments:		
Purchases of inventory	$12,500	
Payment of operating expenses	5,400	
Upgrading of production facilities	2,200	
Acquisition of other companies	350	
Payment of dividends	550	
Payment of long-term debt and other		
liabilities ($1,200 + $6,600)	7,800	(28,800)
Cash available (needed) before new financing		$ (1,900)
Budgeted cash balance, December 31, 2011		(300)
Cash available for additional investments, or		
(New financing needed)		$ (2,200)

PepsiCo. must borrow $2,200 million.

REVIEW INTERNAL CONTROL AND CASH

Quick Check (Answers are given on page 287.)

1. Internal control has its own terminology. On the left are some key internal control concepts. On the right are some key terms. Match each internal control concept with its term by writing the appropriate letter in the space provided. Not all letters are used.

___ This procedure limits access to sensitive data.	**a.** Competent personnel
___ This type of insurance policy covers losses due to employee theft.	**b.** Encryption
	c. Separation of duties
___ Trusting your employees can lead you to overlook this procedure.	**d.** Safeguarding assets
	e. Fidelity bond
___ The most basic purpose of internal control.	**f.** Collusion
___ Internal control cannot always safeguard against this problem.	**g.** Firewalls
	h. Supervision
	i. External audits
___ Often mentioned as the cornerstone of a good system of internal control.	
___ Pay employees enough to require them to do a good job.	

2. Each of the following is an example of a control procedure, *except*
   a. sound personnel procedures.
   b. a sound marketing plan.
   c. separation of duties.
   d. limited access to assets.

3. Which of the following is an example of poor internal control?
   a. Employees must take vacations.
   b. Rotate employees through various jobs.
   c. The accounting department compares goods received with the related purchase order.
   d. The mailroom clerk records daily cash receipts in the journal.

Lowell Corporation has asked you to prepare its bank reconciliation at the end of the current month. Answer questions 4–8 using the following code letters to indicate how the item described would be reported on the bank reconciliation.
   a. Deduct from the book balance
   b. Does not belong on the bank reconciliation
   c. Add to the bank balance
   d. Deduct from the bank balance
   e. Add to the book balance

4. A check for $835 written by Lowell during the current month was erroneously recorded as a $358 payment.

5. A $400 deposit made on the last day of the current month did not appear on this month's bank statement.

6. The bank statement showed interest earned of $65.

7. The bank statement included a check from a customer that was marked NSF.

8. The bank statement showed the bank had credited Lowell's account for an $800 deposit made by Lawrence Company.

9. Which of the following reconciling items does not require a journal entry?
   a. Bank service charge   c. NSF check
   b. Bank collection of note receivable   d. Deposit in transit

10. A check was written for $754 to purchase supplies. The check was recorded in the journal as $745. The entry to correct this error would
   a. increase Supplies, $9.   c. decrease Cash, $9.
   b. decrease Supplies, $9.   d. both a. and c.

11. A cash budget helps control cash by
   a. helping to determine whether additional cash is available for investments or new financing is needed.
   b. developing a plan for increasing sales.
   c. ensuring accurate cash records.
   d. all of the above.

Accounting Vocabulary

audit (p. 240) A periodic examination of a company's financial statements and the accounting systems, controls, and records that produce them. Audits may be either external or internal. External audits are usually performed by certified public accountants (CPAs).

bank collections (p. 249) Collection of money by the bank on behalf of a depositor.

bank reconciliation (p. 248) A document explaining the reasons for the difference between a depositor's records and the bank's records about the depositor's cash.

bank statement (p. 246) Document showing the beginning and ending balances of a particular bank account listing the month's transactions that affected the account.

budget (p. 240) A quantitative expression of a plan that helps managers coordinate the entity's activities.

cash budget (p. 240) A budget that projects the entity's future cash receipts and cash disbursements.

cash equivalent (p. 261) Investments such as time deposits, certificates of deposit, or high-grade government securities that are considered so similar to cash that they are combined with cash for financial disclosure purposes on the balance sheet.

check (p. 246) Document instructing a bank to pay the designated person or business the specified amount of money.

computer virus (p. 243) A malicious program that enters a company's computer system by e-mail or other means and destroys program and data files.

controller (p. 240) The chief accounting officer of a business.

deposits in transit (p. 249) A deposit recorded by the company but not yet by its bank.

electronic fund transfer (EFT) (p. 247) System that transfers cash by electronic communication rather than by paper documents.

encryption (p. 244) Mathematical rearranging of data within an electronic file to prevent unauthorized access to information.

exception reporting (p. 240) Identifying data that is not within "normal limits" so that managers can follow up and take corrective action. Exception reporting is used in operating and cash budgets to keep company profits and cash flow in line with management's plans.

fidelity bond (p. 243) An insurance policy taken out on employees who handle cash.

firewall (p. 244) An electronic barrier, usually provided by passwords, around computerized data files to protect local area networks of computers from unauthorized access.

fraud (p. 233) An intentional misrepresentation of facts, made for the purpose of persuading another party to act in a way that causes injury or damage to that party.

fraud triangle (p. 235) The three elements that are present in almost all cases of fraud. These elements are motive, opportunity, and rationalization on the part of the perpetrator.

fraudulent financial reporting (p. 234) Fraud perpetrated by management by preparing misleading financial statements.

imprest system (p. 260) A way to account for petty cash by maintaining a constant balance in the petty cash account, supported by the fund (cash plus payment tickets) totaling the same amount.

internal control (p. 236) Organizational plan and related measures adopted by an entity to safeguard assets, encourage adherence to company policies, promote operational efficiency, and ensure accurate and reliable accounting records.

lapping (p. 232) A fraudulent scheme to steal cash through misappropriating certain customer payments and posting payments from other customers to the affected accounts to cover it up. Lapping is caused by weak internal controls (i.e., not segregating the duties of cash handling and accounts receivable bookkeeping, allowing the bookkeeper improper access to cash, and not appropriately monitoring the activities of those who handle cash).

lock-box system (p. 232) A system of handling cash receipts by mail whereby customers remit payment directly to the bank, rather than through the entity's mail system.

misappropriation of assets (p. 234) Fraud committed by employees by stealing assets from the company.

nonsufficient funds (NSF) check (p. 249) A "hot" check, one for which the payer's bank account has insufficient money to pay the check. NSF checks are cash receipts that turn out to be worthless.

operating budget (p. 240) A budget of future net income. The operating budget projects a company's future revenue and expenses. It is usually prepared by line item of the company's income statement.

outstanding checks (p. 249) A check issued by the company and recorded on its books but not yet paid by its bank.

password (p. 242) A special set of characters that must be provided by the user of computerized program or data files to prevent unauthorized access to those files.

petty cash (p. 259) Fund containing a small amount of cash that is used to pay minor amounts.

phishing (p. 244) Creating bogus Web sites for the purpose of stealing unauthorized data, such as names, addresses, social security numbers, bank account, and credit card numbers.

remittance advice (p. 246) An optional attachment to a check (sometimes a perforated tear-off document and sometimes capable of being electronically scanned) that indicates the payer, date, and purpose of the cash payment. The remittance advice is often used as the source documents for posting cash receipts or payments.

treasurer (p. 239) In a large company, the department that has total responsibility for cash handling and cash management. This includes cash budgeting, cash collections, writing checks, investing excess funds, and making proposals for raising additional cash when needed.

Trojan Horse (p. 243) A malicious program that hides within legitimate programs and acts like a computer virus.

ASSESS YOUR PROGRESS

Short Exercises

S4-1 (*Learning Objective 1: Defining fraud*) Define "fraud." List and briefly discuss the three major components of the "fraud triangle."

S4-2 (*Learning Objective 2: Listing components of internal control*) List the components of internal control. Briefly describe each component.

writing assignment ■

S4-3 (*Learning Objective 2: Explaining and describing characteristics of an effective system of internal control*) Explain why separation of duties is often described as the cornerstone of internal control for safeguarding assets. Describe what can happen if the same person has custody of an asset and also accounts for the asset.

S4-4 (*Learning Objective 2: Identifying internal control characteristics*) Identify the other control procedures usually found in a company's system of internal control besides separation of duties, and tell why each is important.

S4-5 (*Learning Objective 2: Explaining e-commerce internal control pitfalls*) How do computer viruses, Trojan Horses, and phishing expeditions work? How can these e-commerce pitfalls hurt you? Be specific.

S4-6 (*Learning Objective 2: Explaining the role of internal control*) Cash may be a small item on the financial statements. Nevertheless, internal control over cash is very important. Why is this true?

S4-7 (*Learning Objectives 2, 4: Explaining the role of internal control; identifying controls over cash payments*) Crow Company requires that all documents supporting a check be cancelled by punching a hole through the packet. Why is this practice required? What might happen if it were not?

S4-8 (*Learning Objective 3: Preparing a bank reconciliation*) The Cash account of Randell Corp. reported a balance of $2,400 at October 31. Included were outstanding checks totaling $500 and an October 31 deposit of $200 that did not appear on the bank statement. The bank statement, which came from Park Bank, listed an October 31 balance of $3,180. Included in the bank balance was an October 30 collection of $530 on account from a customer who pays the bank directly. The bank statement also shows a $20 service charge, $10 of interest revenue that Randell earned on its bank balance, and an NSF check for $40.

Prepare a bank reconciliation to determine how much cash Randell actually has at October 31.

S4-9 (*Learning Objective 3: Recording transactions from a bank reconciliation*) After preparing Randell Corp.'s bank reconciliation in Short Exercise 4-8, make the company's journal entries for transactions that arise from the bank reconciliation. Date each transaction October 31, and include an explanation with each entry.

S4-10 (*Learning Objective 3: Using a bank reconciliation as a control device*) Barbara Smith manages Jones Advertising. Smith fears that a trusted employee has been stealing from the company. This employee receives cash from clients and also prepares the monthly bank reconciliation. To check up on the employee, Smith prepares her own bank reconciliation, as follows:

writing assignment ■

Jones Advertising
Bank Reconciliation
October 31, 2010

Bank		Books	
Balance, October 31...................	$4,400	Balance, October 31...................	$3,920
Add:		Add:	
Deposits in transit	500	Bank collections	900
		Interest revenue	20
Less:		Less:	
Outstanding checks	(900)	Service charge..........................	(40)
Adjusted bank balance	$4,000	Adjusted book balance...............	$4,800

Does it appear that the employee has stolen from the company? If so, how much? Explain your answer. Which side of the bank reconciliation shows the company's true cash balance?

S4-11 (*Learning Objective 4: Applying internal controls over cash receipts*) Greta Cassidy sells memberships to the Phoenix Symphony Association in Phoenix, Arizona. The Symphony's procedure requires Cassidy to write a patron receipt for all memberships sold. The receipt forms are prenumbered. Cassidy is having personal financial problems and she stole $400 received from a customer. To hide her theft, Cassidy destroyed the company copy of the receipt that she gave the patron. What will alert manager Stephanie Stevens that something is wrong?

S4-12 (*Learning Objective 4: Applying internal control over cash payments by check*) Answer the following questions about internal control over cash payments:

1. Payment by check carries three controls over cash. What are they?
2. Suppose a purchasing agent receives the goods that he purchases and also approves payment for the goods. How could a dishonest purchasing agent cheat his company? How do companies avoid this internal control weakness?

S4-13 (*Learning Objective 5: Using a cash budget*) Briefly explain how a cash budget works and what it accomplishes with its last few lines of data.

writing assignment ■

S4-14 (*Learning Objective 5: Preparing a cash budget*) Crescent Artichoke Growers (CAG) is a major food cooperative. Suppose CAG begins 2010 with cash of $11 million. CAG estimates cash receipts during 2010 will total $104 million. Planned payments will total $93 million. To meet daily cash needs next year, CAG must maintain a cash balance of at least $17 million. Prepare the organization's cash budget for 2010.

writing assignment ■

S4-15 (*Learning Objectives 1, 5: Learning about fraud; making an ethical judgment related to internal controls*) Gretchen Rourke, an accountant for Dublin Limited, discovers that her supervisor, Billy Dunn, made several errors last year. In total, the errors overstated the company's net income by 25%. It is not clear whether the errors were deliberate or accidental. What should Rourke do?

Exercises

MyAccountingLab

All of the Group A and Group B exercises can be found within MyAccountingLab, an online homework and practice environment. Your instructor may ask you to complete these exercises using MyAccountingLab.

(Group A)

writing assignment ■

E4-16A (*Learning Objectives 1, 2: Learning about fraud; identifying internal control weaknesses*) Identify the internal control weakness in the following situations. State how the person can hurt the company.

a. James Mason works as a security guard at SAFETY parking in Detroit. Mason has a master key to the cash box where customers pay for parking. Each night Mason prepares the cash report that shows (a) the number of cars that parked on the lot and (b) the day's cash receipts. Louise Carrington, the SAFETY treasurer, checks Mason's figures by multiplying the number of cars by the parking fee per car. Carrington then deposits the cash in the bank.

b. Elizabeth Fleming is the purchasing agent for Marshfield Golf Equipment. Fleming prepares purchase orders based on requests from division managers of the company. Fleming faxes the purchase order to suppliers who then ship the goods to Marshfield. Fleming receives each incoming shipment and checks it for agreement with the purchase order and the related invoice. She then routes the goods to the respective division managers and sends the receiving report and the invoice to the accounting department for payment.

E4-17A (*Learning Objective 2: Identifying internal control strengths and weaknesses*) The following situations describe two cash payment situations and two cash receipt situations. In each pair, one set of internal controls is better than the other. Evaluate the internal controls in each situation as strong or weak, and give the reason for your answer.

Cash payments:

a. Tim McDermott Construction policy calls for construction supervisors to request the equipment needed for their jobs. The home office then purchases the equipment and has it shipped to the construction site.

b. Gravel & Sand, Inc., policy calls for project supervisors to purchase the equipment needed for jobs. The supervisors then submit the paid receipts to the home office for reimbursement. This policy enables supervisors to get the equipment quickly and keep construction jobs moving.

Cash receipts:

a. At Carlisle Auto Parts, cash received by mail goes straight to the accountant, who debits Cash and credits Accounts Receivable to record the collections from customers. The Carlisle accountant then deposits the cash in the bank.

b. Cash received by mail at Sole Orthopedic Clinic goes to the mail room, where a mail clerk opens envelopes and totals the cash receipts for the day. The mail clerk forwards customer checks to the cashier for deposit in the bank and forwards the remittance advices to the accounting department for posting credits to customer accounts.

writing assignment ■

E4-18A (*Learning Objectives 1, 2: Learning about fraud; correcting an internal control weakness*) Bobby Flynn served as executive director of Downtown Kalamazoo, an organization created to revitalize Kalamazoo, Michigan. Over the course of 13 years Flynn embezzled

$333,000. How did Flynn do it? By depositing subscriber cash receipts in his own bank account, writing Downtown Kalamazoo checks to himself, and creating phony entities that Downtown Kalamazoo wrote checks to.

Downtown Kalamazoo was led by a board of directors comprised of civic leaders. Flynn's embezzlement went undetected until Downtown Kalamazoo couldn't pay its bills.

Give four ways Flynn's embezzlement could have been prevented.

E4-19A (*Learning Objective 3: Classifying bank reconciliation items*) The following items appear on a bank reconciliation:

1. ___ Outstanding checks
2. ___ Bank error: The bank credited our account for a deposit made by another bank customer.
3. ___ Service charge
4. ___ Deposits in transit
5. ___ NSF check
6. ___ Bank collection of a note receivable on our behalf
7. ___ Book error: We debited Cash for $200. The correct debit was $2,000.

Classify each item as (a) an addition to the bank balance, (b) a subtraction from the bank balance, (c) an addition to the book balance, or (d) a subtraction from the book balance.

E4-20A (*Learning Objective 3: Preparing a bank reconciliation*) D. J. Hunter's checkbook lists the following:

Date	Check No.	Item	Check	Deposit	Balance
6/1					$ 525
4	622	Art Cafe	$ 30		495
9		Dividends received		$ 110	605
13	623	General Tire Co.	35		570
14	624	QuickMobil	68		502
18	625	Cash	55		447
26	626	Woodway Baptist Church	85		362
28	627	Bent Tree Apartments	285		77
30		Paycheck		1,210	1,287

The June bank statement shows

Balance				$525
Add: Deposits				110
Debit checks:	No.	Amount		
	622	$30		
	623	35		
	624	86*		
	625	55		(206)
Other charges:				
NSF check			$20	
Service charge			10	(30)
Balance				$399

*This is the correct amount for check number 624.

▌ Requirement

1. Prepare Hunter's bank reconciliation at June 30.

E4-21A (*Learning Objective 3: Preparing a bank reconciliation*) Evan Root operates a bowling alley. He has just received the monthly bank statement at April 30 from City National Bank, and the statement shows an ending balance of $565. Listed on the statement are an EFT rent collection of $320, a service charge of $7, two NSF checks totaling $115, and an $11 charge for printed checks. In reviewing his cash records, Root identifies outstanding checks totaling $602 and an April 30 deposit in transit of $1,790. During April, he recorded a $290 check for the salary of a part-time employee as $29. Root's Cash account shows an April 30 cash balance of $1,827. How much cash does Root actually have at April 30?

E4-22A (*Learning Objective 3: Making journal entries from a bank reconciliation*) Use the data from Exercise 4-21 to make the journal entries that Root should record on April 30 to update his Cash account. Include an explanation for each entry.

writing assignment ■

E4-23A (*Learning Objective 4: Evaluating internal control over cash receipts*) McCall stores use point-of-sale terminals as cash registers. The register shows the amount of each sale, the cash received from the customer, and any change returned to the customer. The machine also produces a customer receipt but keeps no record of transactions. At the end of the day, the clerk counts the cash in the register and gives it to the cashier for deposit in the company bank account.

Write a memo to convince the store manager that there is an internal control weakness over cash receipts. Identify the weakness that gives an employee the best opportunity to steal cash and state how to prevent such a theft.

E4-24A (*Learning Objective 4: Evaluating internal control over cash payments*) Green Grass Golf Company manufactures a popular line of golf clubs. Green Grass Golf employs 188 workers and keeps their employment records on time sheets that show how many hours the employee works each week. On Friday the shop foreman collects the time sheets, checks them for accuracy, and delivers them to the payroll department for preparation of paychecks. The treasurer signs the paychecks and returns the checks to the payroll department for distribution to the employees.

Identify the main internal control weakness in this situation, state how the weakness can hurt Green Grass Golf, and propose a way to correct the weakness.

■ spreadsheet

E4-25A (*Learning Objective 5: Preparing a cash budget*) Cole Communications, Inc., is preparing its cash budget for 2011. Cole ended 2010 with cash of $86 million, and managers need to keep a cash balance of at least $82 million for operations.

Collections from customers are expected to total $11,305 million during 2011, and payments for the cost of services and products should reach $6,167 million. Operating expense payments are budgeted at $2,544 million.

During 2011, Cole expects to invest $1,826 million in new equipment and sell older assets for $118 million. Debt payments scheduled for 2011 will total $603 million. The company forecasts net income of $885 million for 2011 and plans to pay dividends of $347 million.

Prepare Cole Communications' cash budget for 2011. Will the budgeted level of cash receipts leave Cole with the desired ending cash balance of $82 million, or will the company need additional financing? If so, how much?

E4-26A (*Learning Objective 5: Compensating balance agreement*) Assume Lenny's Lanes borrowed $14 million from Greenback Bank and agreed to (a) pay an interest rate of 7.7% and (b) maintain a compensating balance amount equal to 5.7% of the loan. Determine Lenny's Lanes' actual effective interest rate on this loan.

(Group B)

E4-27B (*Learning Objectives 1, 2: Learning about fraud; identifying internal control weaknesses*) Identify the internal control weakness in the following situations. State how the person can hurt the company.

    a. Jason Monroe works as a security guard at CITY parking in Dayton. Monroe has a master key to the cash box where customers pay for parking. Each night Monroe prepares the cash report that shows (a) the number of cars that parked on the lot and (b) the day's cash receipts. Linda Cooper, the CITY treasurer, checks Monroe's figures by multiplying the number of cars by the parking fee per car. Cooper then deposits the cash in the bank.

    b. Ashley Adams is the purchasing agent for Superior Golf Equipment. Adams prepares purchase orders based on requests from division managers of the company. Adams faxes the purchase order to suppliers who then ship the goods to Superior. Adams receives each incoming shipment and checks it for agreement with the purchase order and the related invoice. She then routes the goods to the respective division managers and sends the receiving report and the invoice to the accounting department for payment.

E4-28B (*Learning Objective 2: Identifying internal control strengths and weaknesses*) The following situations describe two cash payment situations and two cash receipt situations. In each pair, one set of internal controls is better than the other. Evaluate the internal controls in each situation as strong or weak, and give the reason for your answer.

Cash payments:

    a. Mike Milford Construction policy calls for construction supervisors to request the equipment needed for their jobs. The home office then purchases the equipment and has it shipped to the construction site.

    b. Superior Structures, Inc., policy calls for project supervisors to purchase the equipment needed for jobs. The supervisors then submit the paid receipts to the home office for reimbursement. This policy enables supervisors to get the equipment quickly and keep construction jobs moving.

Cash receipts:

    a. At Cramer Auto Parts, cash received by mail goes straight to the accountant, who debits Cash and credits Accounts Receivable to record the collections from customers. The Cramer accountant then deposits the cash in the bank.

    b. Cash received by mail at Better Vision Eye Clinic goes to the mail room, where a mail clerk opens envelopes and totals the cash receipts for the day. The mail clerk forwards customer checks to the cashier for deposit in the bank and forwards the remittance slips to the accounting department for posting credits to customer accounts.

E4-29B (*Learning Objectives 1, 2: Learning about fraud; correcting an internal control weakness*) Sam Smith served as executive director of Downtown Scanlon, an organization created to revitalize Scanlon, Minnesota. Over the course of 11 years Smith embezzled $297,000. How did Smith do it? He did it by depositing subscriber cash receipts in his own bank account, writing Downtown Scanlon checks to himself, and creating phony entities that Downtown Scanlon wrote checks to.

    Downtown Scanlon was led by a board of directors comprised of civic leaders. Smith's embezzlement went undetected until Downtown Scanlon couldn't pay its bills.

    Give four ways Smith's embezzlement could have been prevented.

E4-30B (*Learning Objective 3: Classifying bank reconciliation items*) The following items appear on a bank reconciliation.

Classify each item as (a) an addition to the bank balance, (b) a subtraction from the bank balance, (c) an addition to the book balance, or (d) a subtraction from the book balance.

1. ___ Outstanding checks
2. ___ Bank error: The bank credited our account for a deposit made by another bank customer.
3. ___ Service charge
4. ___ Deposits in transit
5. ___ NSF check
6. ___ Bank collection of a note receivable on our behalf
7. ___ Book error: We debited Cash for $300. The correct debit was $3,000.

E4-31B (*Learning Objective 3: Preparing a bank reconciliation*) D. J. Hill's checkbook and February bank statement show the following:

Date	Check No.	Item	Check	Deposit	Balance
2/1					$ 515
4	622	Art Cafe	$ 15		500
9		Dividends received		$ 115	615
13	623	General Tire Co.	40		575
14	624	QuickMobil	78		497
18	625	Cash	70		427
26	626	Woodway Baptist Church	85		342
28	627	Bent Tree Apartments	275		67
28		Paycheck		1,215	1,282

Balance				$515
Add: Deposits				115
Debit checks:	No.	Amount		
	622	$15		
	623	40		
	624	87*		
	625	70		(212)
Other charges:				
NSF check			$20	
Service charge			15	(35)
Balance				$383

*This is the correct amount for check number 624.

❚ Requirement

1. Prepare Hill's bank reconciliation at February 28.

E4-32B (*Learning Objective 3: Preparing a bank reconciliation*) Harry Smith operates a bowling alley. He has just received the monthly bank statement at September 30 from City National Bank, and the statement shows an ending balance of $545. Listed on the statement are an EFT rent collection of $325, a service charge of $8, two NSF checks totaling $125, and a $10 charge for printed checks. In reviewing his cash records, Smith identifies outstanding checks totaling $609 and a September 30 deposit in transit of $1,790. During September, he recorded a $310 check for the salary of a part-time employee as $31. Smith's Cash account shows a September 30 cash balance of $1,823. How much cash does Smith actually have at September 30?

E4-33B (*Learning Objective 3: Making journal entries from a bank reconciliation*) Use the data from Exercise 4-32B to make the journal entries that Smith should record on September 30 to update his Cash account. Include an explanation for each entry.

E4-34B (*Learning Objective 4: Evaluating internal control over cash receipts*) Radley stores use point-of-sale terminals as cash registers. The register shows the amount of each sale, the cash received from the customer, and any change returned to the customer. The machine also produces a customer receipt but keeps no record of transactions. At the end of the day, the clerk counts the cash in the register and gives it to the cashier for deposit in the company bank account.

writing assignment ■

Write a memo to convince the store manager that there is an internal control weakness over cash receipts. Identify the weakness that gives an employee the best opportunity to steal cash and state how to prevent such a theft.

E4-35B (*Learning Objective 4: Evaluating internal control over cash payments*) Beautiful Meadows Golf Company manufactures a popular line of golf clubs. Beautiful Meadows Golf employs 173 workers and keeps their employment records on time sheets that show how many hours the employee works each week. On Friday the shop foreman collects the time sheets, checks them for accuracy, and delivers them to the payroll department for preparation of paychecks. The treasurer signs the paychecks and returns the checks to the payroll department for distribution to the employees.

Identify the main internal control weakness in this situation, state how the weakness can hurt Beautiful Meadows Golf, and propose a way to correct the weakness.

E4-36B (*Learning Objective 5: Preparing a cash budget*) Fallon Communications, Inc., is preparing its cash budget for 2011. Fallon ended 2010 with cash of $82 million, and managers need to keep a cash balance of at least $81 million for operations.

■ **spreadsheet**

Collections from customers are expected to total $11,307 million during 2011, and payments for the cost of services and products should reach $6,174 million. Operating expense payments are budgeted at $2,545 million.

During 2011, Fallon expects to invest $1,831 million in new equipment and sell older assets for $121 million. Debt payments scheduled for 2011 will total $604 million. The company forecasts net income of $883 million for 2011 and plans to pay dividends of $341 million.

Prepare Fallon Communications' cash budget for 2011. Will the budgeted level of cash receipts leave Fallon with the desired ending cash balance of $81 million, or will the company need additional financing? If so, how much?

E4-37B (*Learning Objective 5: Compensating balance agreement*) Assume Dan's Drums borrowed $19 million from Need It Now Bank and agreed to (a) pay an interest rate of 7.1% and (b) maintain a compensating balance amount equal to 5.8% of the loan. Determine Dan's Drums' actual effective interest rate on this loan.

Challenge Exercises

E4-38 (*Learning Objectives 1, 2, 4: Learning about fraud; evaluating internal controls over cash payments; focusing on ethical considerations*) Susan Healey, the owner of Susan's Perfect Presents, has delegated management of the business to Louise Owens, a friend. Healey drops by to meet customers and check up on cash receipts, but Owens buys the merchandise and handles cash payments. Business has been very good lately, and cash receipts have kept pace with the apparent level of sales. However, for a year or so, the amount of cash on hand has been too low. When asked about this, Owens explains that suppliers are charging more for goods than in the past. During the past year, Owens has taken two expensive vacations, and Healey wonders how Owens can afford these trips on her $59,000 annual salary and commissions.

List at least three ways Owens could be defrauding Healey of cash. In each instance also identify how Healey can determine whether Owens' actions are ethical. Limit your answers to the store's cash payments. The business pays all suppliers by check (no EFTs).

E4-39 (*Learning Objective 5: Preparing and using a cash budget*) Dan Davis, the chief financial officer, is responsible for The Furniture Mart's cash budget for 2010. The budget will help Davis determine the amount of long-term borrowing needed to end the year with a cash balance of $130,000. Davis's assistants have assembled budget data for 2010, which the computer printed in alphabetical order. Not all the data items reproduced below are used in preparing the cash budget.

(Assumed Data)	(In thousands)
Actual cash balance, December 31, 2009	$ 130
Budgeted total assets	22,377
Budgeted total current assets	7,976
Budgeted total current liabilities	4,260
Budgeted total liabilities	11,088
Budgeted total stockholders' equity	7,197
Collections from customers	21,800
Dividend payments	317
Issuance of stock	647
Net income	1,183
Payment of long-term and short-term debt	980
Payment of operating expenses	2,349
Purchases of inventory items	14,545
Purchase of property and equipment	1,528

❙ Requirements

1. Prepare the cash budget of The Furniture Mart, Inc.
2. Compute The Furniture Mart's budgeted current ratio and debt ratio at December 31, 2010. Based on these ratio values, and on the cash budget, would you lend $100,000 to The Furniture Mart? Give the reason for your decision.

Quiz

Test your understanding of internal control and cash by answering the following questions. Answer each question by selecting the best choice from among the answers given.

Q4-40 All of the following are objectives of internal control except
a. to comply with legal requirements.
b. to maximize net income.
c. to ensure accurate and reliable accounting records.
d. to safeguard assets.

Q4-41 All of the following are internal control procedures except
a. Sarbanes-Oxley reforms.
b. electronic devices.
c. assignment of responsibilities.
d. internal and external audits.

Q4-42 Requiring that an employee with no access to cash do the accounting is an example of which characteristic of internal control?

a. Assignment of responsibility
b. Competent and reliable personnel
c. Monitoring of controls
d. Separation of duties

Q4-43 All of the following are controls for cash received over the counter except
a. the cash drawer should open only when the salesclerk enters an amount on the keys.
b. a printed receipt must be given to the customer.
c. the customer should be able to see the amounts entered into the cash register.
d. the sales clerk must have access to the cash register tape.

Q4-44 In a bank reconciliation, an outstanding check is

a. deducted from the book balance.
b. added to the bank balance.
c. added to the book balance.
d. deducted from the bank balance.

Q4-45 In a bank reconciliation, a bank collection of a note receivable is

a. deducted from the bank balance.
b. added to the book balance.
c. added to the bank balance.
d. deducted from the book balance.

Q4-46 In a bank reconciliation, an EFT cash payment is

a. deducted from the bank balance.
b. deducted from the book balance.
c. added to the book balance.
d. added to the bank balance.

Q4-47 If a bookkeeper mistakenly recorded a $35 deposit as $53, the error would be shown on the bank reconciliation as a

a. $53 deduction from the book balance.
b. $53 addition to the book balance.
c. $18 deduction from the book balance.
d. $18 addition to the book balance.

Q4-48 If a bank reconciliation included a deposit in transit of $880, the entry to record this reconciling item would include a

a. credit to cash for $880.
b. debit to cash for $880.
c. credit to prepaid insurance for $880.
d. no entry is required.

Q4-49 In a bank reconciliation, interest revenue earned on your bank balance is

a. deducted from the book balance.
b. deducted from the bank balance.
c. added to the bank balance.
d. added to the book balance.

Q4-50 Before paying an invoice for goods received on account, the controller or treasurer should ensure that
a. the company has not already paid this invoice.
b. the company is paying for the goods it ordered.
c. the company is paying for the goods it actually received.
d. all of the above.

Q4-51 The Little French Bakery is budgeting cash for 2011. The cash balance at December 31, 2010, was $6,000. The Little French Bakery budgets 2011 cash receipts at $83,000. Estimated cash payments include $36,000 for inventory, $26,000 for operating expenses, and $19,000 to expand the store. The Little French Bakery needs a minimum cash balance of $15,000 at all times. The Little French Bakery expects to earn net income of $78,000 during 2011. What is the final result of the company's cash budget for 2011?
a. Pay off $14,000 of debt.
b. $7,000 available for additional investments.
c. Must arrange new financing for $7,000.
d. $14,000 available for additional investments.

Problems

All of the Group A and Group B problems can be found within MyAccountingLab, an online homework and practice environment. Your instructor may ask you to complete these problems using MyAccountingLab.

(Group A)

writing assignment ■

P4-52A *(Learning Objectives 1, 2: Learning about fraud; identifying internal control weaknesses)* Celtic Imports is an importer of silver, brass, and furniture items from Ireland. Eileen Sullivan is the general manager of Celtic Imports. Sullivan employs two other people in the business. Mary McNicholas serves as the buyer for Celtic Imports. In her work McNicholas travels throughout Ireland to find interesting new products. When McNicholas finds a new product, she arranges for Celtic Imports to purchase and pay for the item. She helps the Irish artisans prepare their invoices and then faxes the invoices to Sullivan in the company office.

Sullivan operates out of an office in Boston, Massachusetts. The office is managed by Margaret Sweeney, who handles the mail, keeps the accounting records, makes bank deposits, and prepares the monthly bank reconciliation. Virtually all of Celtic Imports' cash receipts arrive by mail—from sales made to Target, Pier 1 Imports, and Macy's.

Sweeney also prepares checks for payment based on invoices that come in from the suppliers who have been contacted by McNicholas. To maintain control over cash payments, Sullivan examines the paperwork and signs all checks.

❙ Requirement

1. Identify all the major internal control weaknesses in Celtic Imports' system and how the resulting action could hurt Celtic Imports. Also state how to correct each weakness.

writing assignment ■

P4-53A *(Learning Objectives 1, 4: Learning about fraud; identifying internal control weakness)* Each of the following situations reveals an internal control weakness:

a. In evaluating the internal control over cash payments of Framingham Manufacturing, an auditor learns that the purchasing agent is responsible for purchasing diamonds for use in the company's manufacturing process, approving the invoices for payment, and signing the checks. No supervisor reviews the purchasing agent's work.

b. Leslie Joyce owns an architectural firm. Joyce's staff consists of 18 professional architects, and Joyce manages the office. Often, Joyce's work requires her to travel to meet with clients. During the past six months, Joyce has observed that when she returns from a business trip, the architecture jobs in the office have not progressed satisfactorily. Joyce learns that when she is away, two of her senior architects take over office management and neglect their normal duties. One employee could manage the office.

c. J. T. Durfee has been an employee of the City of Maron for many years. Because the city is small, Durfee performs all accounting duties, plus opening the mail, preparing the bank deposit, and preparing the bank reconciliation.

❙ Requirements

1. Identify the missing internal control characteristic in each situation.
2. Identify each firm's possible problem.
3. Propose a solution to the problem.

P4-54A *(Learning Objective 3: Using the bank reconciliation as a control device)* The cash data of Dunlap Automotive for July 2010 follow:

Cash					Account No. 101
Date	Item	Jrnl. Ref.	Debit	Credit	Balance
Jul 1	Balance				7,900
31		CR6	9,124		17,024
31		CP11		9,087	7,937

Cash Receipts (CR)		Cash Payments (CP)	
Date	Cash Debit	Check No.	Cash Credit
Jul 2	$2,771	3113	$1,503
8	516	3114	1,149
10	1,682	3115	1,630
16	871	3116	19
22	352	3117	825
29	924	3118	91
30	2,008	3119	440
Total	$9,124	3120	965
		3121	205
		3122	2,260
		Total	$9,087

Dunlap received the following bank statement on July 31, 2010:

Bank Statement for July 2010

Beginning balance		$ 7,900
Deposits and other additions:		
Jul 1............................	$ 750 EFT	
4............................	2,771	
9............................	516	
12............................	1,682	
17............................	871	
22............................	352	
23............................	1,250 BC	8,192
Checks and other deductions:		
Jul 7............................	$1,503	
13............................	1,360	
14............................	407 US	
15............................	1,149	
18............................	19	
21............................	334 EFT	
26............................	825	
30............................	91	
30............................	25 SC	(5,713)
Ending balance.....................		$10,379

Explanation: BC—bank collection, EFT—electronic funds transfer, US—unauthorized signature, SC—service charge

Additional data for the bank reconciliation include the following:

    a. The EFT deposit was a receipt of monthly rent. The EFT debit was a monthly insurance payment.

    b. The unauthorized signature check was received from a customer.

    c. The correct amount of check number 3115, a payment on account, is $1,360. (Dunlap's accountant mistakenly recorded the check for $1,630.)

❚ Requirements

    1. Prepare the Dunlap Automotive bank reconciliation at July 31, 2010.

    2. Describe how a bank account and the bank reconciliation help the general manager control Dunlap's cash.

■ spreadsheet

P4-55A (*Learning Objective 3: Preparing a bank reconciliation and the related journal entries*) The August 31 bank statement of Dickson Engineering Associates has just arrived from Carolina First Bank. To prepare the Dickson bank reconciliation, you gather the following data:

    a. Dickson's Cash account shows a balance of $8,152.71 on August 31.

    b. The August 31 bank balance is $8,879.24.

    c. The bank statement shows that Dickson earned $15.85 of interest on its bank balance during August. This amount was added to Dickson's bank balance.

    d. Dickson pays utilities ($730) and insurance ($280) by EFT.

    e. The following Dickson checks did not clear the bank by August 31:

Check No.	Amount
237	$401.00
288	74.82
291	33.25
293	165.55
294	236.00
295	47.75
296	107.85

    f. The bank statement includes a deposit of $899.15, collected on account by the bank on behalf of Dickson.

    g. The bank statement lists a $5.50 bank service charge.

    h. On August 31, the Dickson treasurer deposited $383.54, which will appear on the September bank statement.

    i. The bank statement includes a $398.00 deposit that Dickson did not make. The bank added $398.00 to Dickson's account for another company's deposit.

    j. The bank statement includes two charges for returned checks from customers. One is a $185.50 check received from a customer with the imprint "Unauthorized Signature." The other is a nonsufficient funds check in the amount of $68.15 received from another customer.

❚ Requirements

    1. Prepare the bank reconciliation for Dickson Engineering Associates.

    2. Journalize the August 31 transactions needed to update Dickson's Cash account. Include an explanation for each entry.

writing assignment ■

P4-56A (*Learning Objectives 2, 4: Identifying internal control weakness in sales and cash receipts*) Fresh Skin Care makes all sales on credit. Cash receipts arrive by mail, usually within 30 days of the sale. Kate Martin opens envelopes and separates the checks from the accompanying remittance advices. Martin forwards the checks to another employee, who makes the daily bank deposit but has no access to the accounting records. Martin sends the remittance advices, which show the amount of cash received, to the accounting department for entry in the accounts receivable. Martin's only other duty is to grant allowances to customers. (An *allowance* decreases the amount that the customer must pay.) When Martin receives a customer check for less than the full amount of the invoice, she records the allowance in the accounting records and forwards the document to the accounting department.

I Requirement

1. You are a new employee of Fresh Skin Care. Write a memo to the company president identifying the internal control weakness in this situation. State how to correct the weakness.

P4-57A (*Learning Objective 5: Preparing a cash budget and using cash-flow information*) John Watson, chief financial officer of Jasper Wireless, is responsible for the company's budgeting process. Watson's staff is preparing the Jasper cash budget for 2011. A key input to the budgeting process is last year's statement of cash flows, which follows (amounts in thousands):

Jasper Wireless
Statement of Cash Flows
2010

(In thousands)

Cash Flows from Operating Activities

Collections from customers	$ 64,000
Interest received	300
Purchases of inventory	(49,000)
Operating expenses	(13,500)
Net cash provided by operating activities	1,800

Cash Flows from Investing Activities

Purchases of equipment	(4,800)
Purchases of investments	(400)
Sales of investments	500
Net cash used for investing activities	(4,700)

Cash Flows from Financing Activities

Payment of long-term debt	(400)
Issuance of stock	1,700
Payment of cash dividends	(300)
Net cash provided by financing activities	1,000

Cash

Increase (decrease) in Cash	(1,900)
Cash, beginning of year	3,400
Cash, end of year	$ 1,500

I Requirements

1. Prepare the Jasper Wireless cash budget for 2011. Date the budget simply "2011" and denote the beginning and ending cash balances as "beginning" and "ending." Assume the company expects 2011 to be the same as 2010, but with the following changes:
   a. In 2011, the company expects a 10% increase in collections from customers and a 20% increase in purchases of inventory.
   b. There will be no sales of investments in 2011.
   c. Jasper plans to issue no stock in 2011.
   d. Jasper plans to end the year with a cash balance of $3,800.
2. Does the company's cash budget for 2011 suggest that Jasper is growing, holding steady, or decreasing in size? (Challenge)

(Group B)

writing assignment ■

P4-58B (*Learning Objectives 1, 2: Learning about fraud; identifying internal control weaknesses*) International Imports is an importer of silver, brass, and furniture items from France. Elaine Spencer is the general manager of International Imports. Spencer employs two other people in the business. Marie Walsh serves as the buyer for International Imports. In her work Walsh travels throughout France to find interesting new products. When Walsh finds a new product, she arranges for International Imports to purchase and pay for the item. She helps the French artisans prepare their invoices and then faxes the invoices to Spencer in the company office.

Spencer operates out of an office in Brooklyn, New York. The office is managed by Donna Durkin, who handles the mail, keeps the accounting records, makes bank deposits, and prepares the monthly bank reconciliation. Virtually all of International Imports' cash receipts arrive by mail—from sales made to Target, Crate and Barrel, and Williams-Sonoma.

Durkin also prepares checks for payment based on invoices that come in from the suppliers who have been contacted by Walsh. To maintain control over cash payments, Spencer examines the paperwork and signs all checks.

❙ *Requirement*

1. Identify all the major internal control weaknesses in International Imports' system and how the resulting action could hurt International Imports. Also state how to correct each weakness.

writing assignment ■

P4-59B (*Learning Objectives 1, 4: Learning about fraud; identifying internal control weakness*) Each of the following situations reveals an internal control weakness:

Situation a. In evaluating the internal control over cash payments of York Manufacturing, an auditor learns that the purchasing agent is responsible for purchasing diamonds for use in the company's manufacturing process, approving the invoices for payment, and signing the checks. No supervisor reviews the purchasing agent's work.

Situation b. Rita White owns an architectural firm. White's staff consists of 16 professional architects, and White manages the office. Often, White's work requires her to travel to meet with clients. During the past six months, White has observed that when she returns from a business trip, the architecture jobs in the office have not progressed satisfactorily. White learns that when she is away, two of her senior architects take over office management and neglect their normal duties. One employee could manage the office.

Situation c. M. J. Dowd has been an employee of the City of Northport for many years. Because the city is small, Dowd performs all accounting duties, plus opening the mail, preparing the bank deposit, and preparing the bank reconciliation.

❙ *Requirements*

1. Identify the missing internal control characteristic in each situation.
2. Identify each firm's possible problem.
3. Propose a solution to the problem.

P4-60B (*Learning Objective 3: Using the bank reconciliation as a control device*) The cash data of Donald Automotive for January 2010 follow:

writing assignment ■

■ **spreadsheet**

Cash					Account No. 101
Date	Item	Jrnl. Ref.	Debit	Credit	Balance
Jan 1	Balance				7,200
31		CR 6	9,127		16,327
31		CP 11		9,983	6,344

Cash Receipts (CR)		Cash Payments (CP)	
Date	Cash Debit	Check No.	Cash Credit
Jan 2	$2,726	3113	$1,475
8	572	3114	1,925
10	1,647	3115	1,530
16	837	3116	32
22	436	3117	870
29	856	3118	132
30	2,053	3119	493
Total	$9,127	3120	985
		3121	219
		3122	2,322
		Total	$9,983

Donald received the following bank statement on January 31, 2010:

Bank Statement for January 2010

Beginning balance		$ 7,200
Deposits and other additions:		
Jan 1	$ 650 EFT	
4	2,726	
9	572	
12	1,647	
17	837	
22	436	
23	1,350 BC	8,218
Checks and other deductions:		
Jan 7	$1,475	
13	1,350	
14	466 US	
15	1,925	
18	32	
21	331 EFT	
26	870	
30	132	
30	20 SC	(6,601)
Ending balance....................		$ 8,817

Explanation: BC—bank collection, EFT—electronic funds transfer, US—unauthorized signature, SC—service charge

Additional data for the bank reconciliation include the following:

a. The EFT deposit was a receipt of monthly rent. The EFT debit was a monthly insurance expense.

b. The unauthorized signature check was received from a customer.

c. The correct amount of check number 3115, a payment on account, is $1,350. (Donald's accountant mistakenly recorded the check for $1,530.)

❙ Requirements

1. Prepare the Donald Automotive bank reconciliation at January 31, 2010.
2. Describe how a bank account and the bank reconciliation help the general manager control Donald's cash.

■ spreadsheet

P4-61B *(Learning Objective 3: Preparing a bank reconciliation and the related journal entries)* The October 31 bank statement of Dunlap Engineering Associates has just arrived from Carolina First Bank. To prepare the Dunlap bank reconciliation, you gather the following data:

a. Dunlap's Cash account shows a balance of $7,605.86 on October 31.

b. The October 31 bank balance is $8,343.87.

c. The bank statement shows that Dunlap earned $15.45 of interest on its bank balance during October. This amount was added to Dunlap's bank balance.

d. Dunlap pays utilities ($770) and insurance ($250) by EFT.

e. The following Dunlap checks did not clear the bank by October 31:

Check No.	Amount
237	$403.15
288	78.98
291	36.39
293	155.45
294	234.00
295	47.50
296	106.79

f. The bank statement includes a deposit of $915.20, collected on account by the bank on behalf of Dunlap.

g. The bank statement lists a $6.25 bank service charge.

h. On October 31, the Dunlap treasurer deposited $380.50, which will appear on the November bank statement.

i. The bank statement includes a $405.00 deposit that Dunlap did not make. The bank added $405.00 to Dunlap's account for another company's deposit.

j. The bank statement includes two charges for returned checks from customers. One is a $185.50 check received from a customer with the imprint "Unauthorized Signature." The other is a nonsufficient funds check in the amount of $67.65 received from another customer.

❙ Requirements

1. Prepare the bank reconciliation for Dunlap Engineering Associates.
2. Journalize the October 31 transactions needed to update Dunlap's Cash account. Include an explanation for each entry.

■ writing assignment

P4-62B *(Learning Objective 4: Identifying internal control weakness in sales and cash receipts)* Flawless Skin Care makes all sales on credit. Cash receipts arrive by mail, usually within 30 days of the sale. Elizabeth Nelson opens envelopes and separates the checks from the accompanying remittance advices. Nelson forwards the checks to another employee, who makes the daily bank deposit but has no access to the accounting records. Nelson sends the remittance advices, which show the amount of cash received, to the accounting department for entry in the accounts receivable. Nelson's only other duty is to grant allowances to customers. (An *allowance* decreases the amount that the customer must pay.) When Nelson receives a customer check for less than the full amount of the invoice, she records the allowance in the accounting records and forwards the document to the accounting department.

❙ Requirement

1. You are a new employee of Flawless Skin Care. Write a memo to the company president identifying the internal control weakness in this situation. State how to correct the weakness.

P4-63B (*Learning Objective 5: Preparing a cash budget and using cash-flow information*) Don Beecher, chief financial officer of Carvel Wireless, is responsible for the company's budgeting process. Beecher's staff is preparing the Carvel cash budget for 2011. A key input to the budgeting process is last year's statement of cash flows, which follows (amount in thousands):

Carvel Wireless
Statement of Cash Flows
2010

(In thousands)

Cash Flows from Operating Activities	
Collections from customers	$ 62,000
Interest received	700
Purchases of inventory	(47,000)
Operating expenses	(13,700)
Net cash provided by operating activities	2,000
Cash Flows from Investing Activities	
Purchases of equipment	(4,100)
Purchases of investments	(300)
Sales of investments	900
Net cash used for investing activities	(3,500)
Cash Flows from Financing Activities	
Payment of long-term debt	(500)
Issuance of stock	1,500
Payment of cash dividends	(400)
Net cash provided by financing activities	600
Cash	
Increase (decrease) in Cash	(900)
Cash, beginning of year	2,800
Cash, end of year	$ 1,900

❙ Requirements

1. Prepare the Carvel Wireless cash budget for 2011. Date the budget simply "2011" and denote the beginning and ending cash balances as "beginning" and "ending." Assume the company expects 2011 to be the same as 2010, but with the following changes:
   a. In 2011, the company expects a 14% increase in collections from customers and a 25% increase in purchases of inventory.
   b. There will be no sales of investments in 2011.
   c. Carvel plans to issue no stock in 2011.
   d. Carvel plans to end the year with a cash balance of $3,550.
2. Does the company's cash budget for 2011 suggest that Carvel is growing, holding steady, or decreasing in size?

APPLY YOUR KNOWLEDGE

Decision Cases

Case 1. (*Learning Objectives 1, 2, 3: Learning about fraud; using a bank reconciliation to detect a theft*) Environmental Concerns, Inc., has poor internal control. Recently, Oscar Benz, the manager, has suspected the bookkeeper of stealing. Details of the business's cash position at September 30 follow.

    a. The Cash account shows a balance of $10,402. This amount includes a September 30 deposit of $3,794 that does not appear on the September 30 bank statement.

    b. The September 30 bank statement shows a balance of $8,224. The bank statement lists a $200 bank collection, an $8 service charge, and a $36 NSF check. The accountant has not recorded any of these items.

    c. At September 30, the following checks are outstanding:

Check No.	Amount
154	$116
256	150
278	853
291	990
292	206
293	145

    d. The bookkeeper receives all incoming cash and makes the bank deposits. He also reconciles the monthly bank statement. Here is his September 30 reconciliation:

Balance per books, September 30...............		$10,402
Add: Outstanding checks		1,460
Bank collection..................................		200
Subtotal..		12,062
Less: Deposits in transit.............................	$3,794	
Service charge	8	
NSF check...	36	(3,838)
Balance per bank, September 30.................		$ 8,224

❙ Requirement

    1. Benz has requested that you determine whether the bookkeeper has stolen cash from the business and, if so, how much. He also asks you to explain how the bookkeeper attempted to conceal the theft. To make this determination, you perform a proper bank reconciliation. There are no bank or book errors. Benz also asks you to evaluate the internal controls and to recommend any changes needed to improve them.

Case 2. (*Learning Objectives 1, 2: Learning about fraud; correcting an internal control weakness*) This case is based on an actual situation experienced by one of the authors. Gilead Construction, headquartered in Topeka, Kansas, built a motel in Kansas City. The construction foreman, Slim Pickins, hired the workers for the project. Pickins had his workers fill out the necessary tax forms and sent the employment documents to the home office.

Work on the motel began on May 1 and ended in December. Each Thursday evening, Pickins filled out a time card that listed the hours worked by each employee during the five-day work-week ended at 5 p.m. on Thursday. Pickins faxed the time sheets to the home office, which prepared the payroll checks on Friday morning. Pickins drove to the home office after lunch on Friday, picked up the payroll checks, and returned to the construction site. At 5 p.m. on Friday, Pickins distributed the paychecks to the workers.

a. Describe in detail the internal control weakness in this situation. Specify what negative result could occur because of the internal control weakness.
b. Describe what you would do to correct the internal control weakness.

Ethical Issues

For each of the following situations, answer the following questions:

1. What is the ethical issue in this situation?
2. What are the alternatives?
3. Who are the stakeholders? What are the possible consequences to each? Analyze from the following standpoints: (a) economic, (b) legal, and (c) ethical.
4. Place yourself in the role of the decision maker. What would you do? How would you justify your decision?

Issue 1. Sunrise Bank recently appointed the accounting firm of Smith, Godfroy, and Hannaford as the bank's auditor. Sunrise quickly became one of Smith, Godfroy, and Hannaford's largest clients. Subject to banking regulations, Sunrise must provide for any expected losses on notes receivable that Sunrise may not collect in full.

During the course of the audit, Smith, Godfroy, and Hannaford determined that three large notes receivable of Sunrise seem questionable. Smith, Godfroy, and Hannaford discussed these loans with Susan Carter, controller of Sunrise. Carter assured the auditors that these notes were good and that the makers of the notes will be able to pay their notes after the economy improves.

Smith, Godfroy, and Hannaford stated that Sunrise must record a loss for a portion of these notes receivable to account for the likelihood that Sunrise may never collect their full amount. Carter objected and threatened to dismiss Smith, Godfroy, and Hannaford if the auditor demands that the bank record the loss. Smith, Godfroy, and Hannaford want to keep Sunrise as a client. In fact, Smith, Godfroy, and Hannaford were counting on the revenue from the Sunrise audit to finance an expansion of the firm.

Issue 2. Barry Galvin is executive vice president of Community Bank. Active in community affairs, Galvin serves on the board of directors of The Salvation Army. The Salvation Army is expanding rapidly and is considering relocating. At a recent meeting, The Salvation Army decided to buy 250 acres of land on the edge of town. The owner of the property is Olga Nadar, a major depositor in Community Bank. Nadar is completing a bitter divorce, and Galvin knows that Nadar is eager to sell her property. In view of Nadar's difficult situation, Galvin believes Nadar would accept a low offer for the land. Realtors have appraised the property at $3.6 million.

Issue 3. Community Bank has a loan receivable from IMS Chocolates. IMS is six months late in making payments to the bank, and Jan French, a Community Bank vice president, is assisting IMS to restructure its debt.

French learns that IMS is depending on landing a contract with Snicker Foods, another Community Bank client. French also serves as Snicker Foods' loan officer at the bank. In this capacity, French is aware that Snicker is considering bankruptcy. No one else outside Snicker Foods knows this. French has been a great help to IMS and IMS's owner is counting on French's expertise in loan workouts to advise the company through this difficult process. To help the bank collect on this large loan, French has a strong motivation to alert IMS of Snicker's financial difficulties.

Focus on Financials: ■ Amazon.com, Inc.

(*Learning Objectives 2, 3: Cash and internal control*) Refer to the **Amazon.com, Inc.**, consolidated financial statements in Appendix A at the end of this book. The cash and cash equivalents section of the Consolidated Balance Sheet shows a balance of $2,769 as of December 31, 2008, and is made up of many different bank accounts, as well as time deposits, certificates of deposit, and perhaps government securities that are equivalent to cash. Suppose Amazon.com's year-end bank statement for the operating bank account, dated December 31, 2008, has just arrived at company headquarters. Further assume the bank statement shows Amazon.com's cash balance at $324 million and that Amazon.com, Inc.'s operating bank account has a balance of $316 million on the books (since this is only one of many bank accounts, it will not be possible to match it to the $2,769 that is shown.)

1. You must determine the correct balance for cash in the operating bank account on December 31, 2008. Suppose you uncover the following reconciling items (all amounts are assumed and are stated in millions):
   a. Interest earned on bank balance, $1
   b. Outstanding checks, $8
   c. Bank collections of various items, $2
   d. Deposits in transit, $3

   Prepare a bank reconciliation to show how Amazon.com, Inc., arrived at the correct amount of cash in the operating bank account at December 31, 2008. Journal entries are not required.

2. Study Amazon.com, Inc.'s Management's Report on Internal Control over Financial Reporting in Item 9A of its annual report, paragraph two. Indicate how that report links to specific items of internal control discussed in this chapter. (Challenge)

Focus on Analysis: ■ Foot Locker, Inc.

(*Learning Objectives 2, 5: Analyzing internal control and cash flows*) Refer to the **Foot Locker, Inc.**, Consolidated Financial Statements in Appendix B at the end of this book.

1. Focus on cash and cash equivalents. Why did cash change during 2007? The statement of cash flows holds the answer to this question. Analyze the seven largest *individual* items on the statement of cash flows (not the summary subtotals such as "net cash provided by operating activities"). For each of the seven individual items, state how Foot Locker, Inc.'s action affected cash. Show amounts in millions and round to the nearest $1 million. (Challenge)

2. Foot Locker, Inc.'s Report of Management describes the company's internal controls. Show how the management report corresponds to three of the five objectives of internal control included in this chapter. (Challenge)

Group Project

You are promoting a rock concert in your area. Assume you organize as a corporation, with each member of your group purchasing $10,000 of the corporation's stock. Therefore, each of you is risking some hard-earned money on this venture. Assume it is April 1 and that the concert will be performed on June 30. Your promotional activities begin immediately, and ticket sales start on May 1. You expect to sell all of the firm's assets, pay all the liabilities, and distribute all remaining cash to the group members by July 31.

❚ *Requirements*

Write an internal control manual that will help to safeguard the assets of the business. The manual should address the following aspects of internal control:

1. Assign responsibilities among the group members.
2. Authorize individuals, including group members and any outsiders that you need to hire to perform specific jobs.

3. Separate duties among the group and any employees.
4. Describe all documents needed to account for and safeguard the business's assets.

For online homework, exercises, and problems that provide you with immediate feedback, please visit www.myaccountinglab.com

---

Quick Check Answers

1. g, e, h, d, f, c, a   3. d   6. e   9. d
   Unused: b, i   4. a   7. a   10. d
2. b   5. c   8. d   11. a

5
Short-Term Investments & Receivables

SPOTLIGHT: Receivables and Investments Account for Over Half of PepsiCo's Current Assets!

What comes to mind when you think of **PepsiCo**? Do you think of a soft drink or a snack chip? PepsiCo's two main products are soft drinks and snack foods. PepsiCo also owns Frito Lay, the snack-food company. That might lead you to believe that inventories are the company's largest current asset. However, as of December 31, 2007, short-term investments and receivables account for about 59% of PepsiCo's current assets.

Take a look at PepsiCo's comparative balance sheets for 2007 and 2006 on the following page. Does it surprise you that receivables are PepsiCo's largest current asset? It turns out that receivables are the largest current asset for lots of companies, including **FedEx** and **The Boeing Company**.

Another important current asset is short-term investments. As you can see from PepsiCo's 2007 balance sheet, PepsiCo had about $1.5 billion of short-term investments at the end of 2007. You'll notice that short-term investments are listed on the balance sheet immediately after cash and before receivables. Let's see why.

PepsiCo, Inc.
Balance Sheets (Excerpt, Adapted)
December 31, 2007 and 2006

(In millions)	2007	2006
ASSETS		
Current Assets		
Cash and cash equivalents..	$ 910	$1,651
Short-term investments...	1,571	1,171
Accounts receivable, net of allowance for doubtful		
accounts of $75 in 2007 and $64 in 2006...............	4,389	3,725
Inventories	2,290	1,926
Prepaid expenses and other current assets	991	657
Total Current Assets	$10,151	$9,130

This chapter shows how to account for short-term investments and receivables. We cover short-term investments along with receivables to emphasize their relative liquidity. Short-term investments are the next-most-liquid current assets after cash. (Recall that liquid means close to cash.) We begin our discussion with short-term investments.

LEARNING OBJECTIVES

1 **Account** for short-term investments

2 **Account** for, and control, accounts receivable

3 **Use** the allowance method for uncollectible receivables

4 **Account** for notes receivable

5 **Use** two new ratios to evaluate a business

SHORT-TERM INVESTMENTS

OBJECTIVE

1 **Account** for short-term investments

Short-term investments are also called **marketable securities**. These are investments in marketable securities easily convertible to cash that a company plans to hold for one year or less. They allow the company to invest cash for a short period of time and earn a return until the cash is needed.

Short-term investments are the next-most-liquid asset after cash. This is why we report short-term investments in marketable securities immediately after cash and before receivables on the balance sheet. Short-term investments in marketable securities falls into one of three categories:

Three Categories of Short-Term Investments		
Trading Securities	**Available-for-Sale Securities**	**Held-to-Maturity Securities**
Covered in this section of the chapter	Covered in Chapter 10	Same as accounting for a note receivable, starting on page 307

The investor, such as PepsiCo, expects to sell a trading security within a very short time—a few months at most. Therefore, all trading securities are included in current assets. The other two categories of securities can be either current or long-term, depending on how long management intends to hold them. Let's begin with trading securities.

Trading Securities

The purpose of owning a **trading security** is to hold it for a short time and then sell it for more than its cost. Trading securities can be in the form of stock or debt securities of another company. Suppose PepsiCo purchases **IBM** stock, intending to sell the stock within a few months. If the market value of the IBM stock increases, PepsiCo will have a gain; if IBM's stock price drops, PepsiCo will have a loss. Along the way, PepsiCo will receive dividend revenue from IBM.

Suppose PepsiCo buys the IBM stock on November 18, paying $100,000 cash. PepsiCo records the purchase of the investment at cost:

2010			
Nov 18	Investment in IBM stock	100,000	
	Cash		100,000
	Purchased investment.		

Investment in IBM Stock	
100,000	

Assume that PepsiCo receives a cash dividend of $4,000 from IBM. PepsiCo records the dividend revenue as follows:

2010			
Nov 27	Cash	4,000	
	Dividend Revenue		4,000
	Received cash dividend.		

Assets	=	Liabilities	+	Stockholders' Equity	+	Revenues
+ 4,000	=				+	4,000

Unrealized Gains and Losses. PepsiCo's fiscal year ends on December 31, and PepsiCo prepares financial statements. The IBM stock has risen in value, and on December 31 PepsiCo's investment has a current market value of $102,000. Market value is the amount the owner can sell the securities for. PepsiCo has an *unrealized gain* on the investment:

- *Gain* because the market value ($102,000) of the securities is greater than PepsiCo's cost of the securities ($100,000). A gain has the same effect as a revenue.
- *Unrealized gain* because PepsiCo has not yet sold the securities.

Trading securities are reported on the balance sheet at their current market value, because market value is the amount the investor can receive by selling the securities. Prior to preparing financial statements on December 31, PepsiCo adjusts the investment in IBM securities to its current market value with this year-end journal entry:

2010			
Dec 31	Investment in IBM stock	2,000	
	Unrealized Gain on Investments		2,000
	Adjusted investment to market value.		

Investment in IBM Stock		Unrealized Gain on Investments	
100,000			
2,000			2,000
102,000			

After the adjustment, PepsiCo's Short-Term Investments account is ready to be reported on the balance sheet—at current market value of $102,000.

If PepsiCo's investment in IBM stock had decreased in value, say to $95,000, then PepsiCo would have reported an unrealized loss. A *loss* has the same effect as an expense. In that case, PepsiCo would have made a different entry at December 31. For an *unrealized* loss of $5,000, the entry would have been as follows:

Unrealized Loss on Investments	5,000	
Investment in IBM Stock		5,000
Adjusted investment to market value.		

Investment in IBM Stock		Unrealized Loss on Investments	
100,000	5,000	5,000	
95,000			

Reporting on the Balance Sheet and the Income Statement

The Balance Sheet.   Short-term investments are current assets. They appear on the balance sheet immediately after cash because short-term investments are almost as liquid as cash. Report **trading investments** at their *current market value*.

Income Statement.   Investments in debt and equity securities earn interest revenue and dividend revenue. Investments also create gains and losses. For trading investments these items are reported on the income statement as Other revenue, gains, and (losses), as shown in Exhibit 5-1.

EXHIBIT 5-1 | Reporting Short-Term Investments and the Related Revenues, Gains, and Losses

Balance sheet		Income statement	
Current assets:.....................		Revenues...........................	$ XXX
Cash....................................	$ XXX	Expenses	XXX
Short-term investments, at		Other revenue, gains	
market value	102,000	and (losses):	
Accounts receivable...............	XXX	Interest revenue............	XXX
		Dividend revenue	4,000
		Unrealized gain on	
		investment...............	2,000
		Net income...................	$ XXX

Realized Gains and Losses. A *realized* gain or loss occurs only when the investor sells an investment. This gain or loss is different from the unrealized gain that we reported for PepsiCo above. The result may be a

- Realized gain = Sale price is *greater than* the Investment carrying amount
- Realized loss = Sale price is *less than* the Investment carrying amount

Suppose PepsiCo sells its IBM stock during 2011. The sale price is $98,000, and PepsiCo makes this journal entry:

2011			
Jan 19	Cash	98,000	
	Loss on Sale of Investments	4,000	
	Investment in IBM Stock		102,000
	Sold investments at a loss.		

Investment in IBM Stock		Loss on Sale of Investments	
100,000		4,000	
2,000	102,000		

Accountants rarely use the word "Realized" in the account title. A gain (or a loss) is understood to be a realized gain (or loss) arising from a sale transaction. Unrealized gains and losses are clearly labeled as *unrealized*. PepsiCo would report Gain (or Loss) on Sale of Investments among the "Other" items of the income statement, as shown in Exhibit 5-1.

Lending Agreements and the Current Ratio

Lending agreements often require the borrower to maintain a current ratio at some specified level, say 1.50 or greater. What happens when the borrower's current ratio falls below 1.50? The consequences can be severe:

- The lender can call the loan for immediate payment.
- If the borrower cannot pay, then the lender may take over the company.

Suppose it's December 10 and it looks like Health Corporation of America's (HCA's) current ratio will end the year at a value of 1.48. That would put HCA in default on the lending agreement and create a bad situation. With three weeks remaining in the year, how can HCA improve its current ratio?

Recall that the current ratio is computed as

$$\text{Current ratio} = \frac{\text{Total current assets}}{\text{Total current liabilities}}$$

There are several strategies for increasing the current ratio, such as:

1. Launch a major sales effort. The increase in cash and receivables will more than offset the decrease in Inventory, total current assets will increase, and the current ratio will improve.

2. Pay off some current liabilities before year end. Both current assets in the numerator and current liabilities in the denominator will decrease by the same amount. The proportionate impact on current liabilities in the denominator will be greater than the impact on current assets in the numerator, and the current ratio will increase. This strategy increases the current ratio when the current ratio is already above 1.0, as for HCA and PepsiCo.

3. A third strategy is questionable, and we wish to alert you to one of the accounting games that companies sometimes play. Suppose HCA has some long-term investments (investments that HCA plans to hold for longer than a year—these are long-term assets). Before year end HCA might choose to reclassify these long-term investments as current assets. The reclassification of these investments increases HCA's current assets, and that increases the current ratio. This strategy would be okay if HCA does in fact plan to sell the investments within the next year. But the strategy would be unethical and dishonest if HCA in fact plans to keep the investments for longer than a year.

From this example you can see that accounting is not cut-and-dried or all black-and-white. It takes good judgment—which includes ethics—to become a successful accountant.

MID-CHAPTER SUMMARY PROBLEM

The largest current asset on Waverly Corporation's balance sheet is Short-Term Investments. The investments consist of stock in other corporations and cost Waverly $8,660. At the balance sheet date, the fair market value of these securities is $9,000 (amounts in millions).

Suppose Waverly holds the stock investments in the hope of selling at a profit within a few months. How will Waverly classify the investments? What will Waverly report on the balance sheet at December 31, 2010? What will Waverly report on its 2010 income statement? Show a T-account for Short-Term Investments.

Answer

These investments in trading securities are *current assets* as reported on the 2010 balance sheet, and Waverly's 2010 income statement will report as follows (amounts in millions):

Balance sheet		Income statement	
Current assets:		Other revenue and expense:	
Cash.................................	$ XX	Unrealized gain on investments	
Short-term investments,		($9,000 – $8,660)	$ 340
at market value	9,000		

Short-Term Investments	
8,660	
340	

Suppose Waverly sells the investment in securities for $8,700 in 2011. Journalize the sale and then show the Short-Term Investments T-account as it appears after the sale.

Answer

	(In millions)
Cash..	8,700
Loss on Sale of Investments.........	300
Short-Term Investments	9,000
Sold investments at a loss.	

Short-Term Investments	
8,660	
340	9,000

ACCOUNTS AND NOTES RECEIVABLE

Receivables are the third most liquid asset—after cash and short-term investments. Most of the remainder of this chapter shows how to account for receivables.

Types of Receivables

Receivables are monetary claims against others. Receivables are acquired mainly by selling goods and services (accounts receivable) and by lending money (notes receivable). The journal entries to record the receivables can be shown as follows:

Performing a Service on Account		Lending Money on a Note Receivable	
Accounts Receivable.................... XXX		Note Receivable XXX	
Service Revenue......................	XXX	Cash...	XXX
Performed a service on account.		*Loaned money to another company.*	

The two major types of receivables are accounts receivable and notes receivable. A business' *accounts receivable* are the amounts collectible from customers from the sale of goods and services. Accounts receivable, which are *current assets*, are sometimes called *trade receivables* or merely *receivables*.

The Accounts Receivable account in the general ledger serves as a *control account* that summarizes the total amount receivable from all customers. Companies also keep a *subsidiary record* of accounts receivable with a separate account for each customer, illustrated as follows:

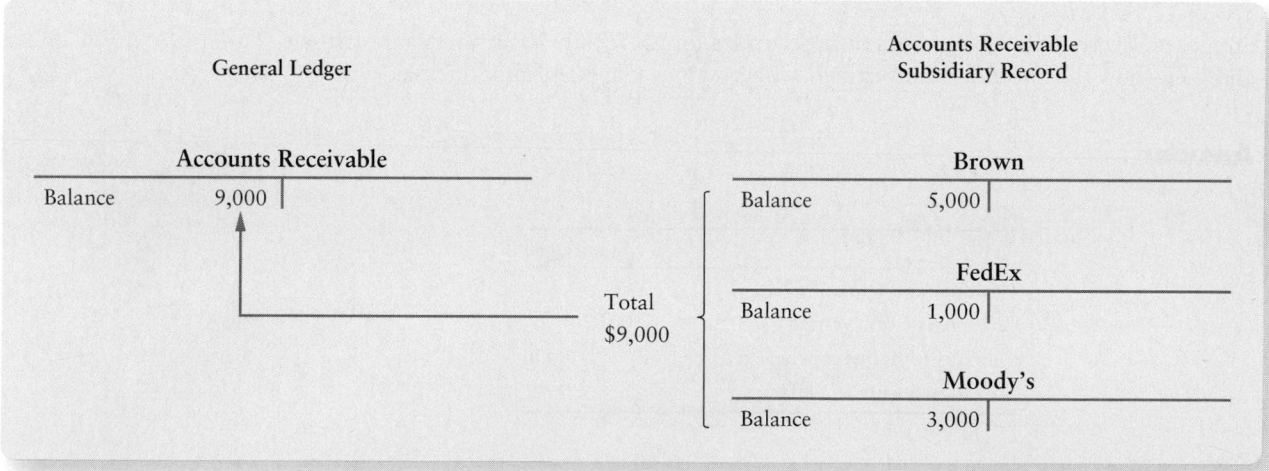

Notes receivable are more formal contracts than accounts receivable. For a note, the borrower signs a written promise to pay the lender a definite sum at the **maturity** date, plus interest. This is why notes are also called promissory notes. The note may require the borrower to pledge *security* for the loan. This means that the borrower gives the lender permission to claim certain assets, called *collateral*, if the borrower fails to pay the amount due. We cover the details of notes receivable starting on page 306.

Other receivables is a miscellaneous category for all receivables other than accounts receivable and notes receivable. Examples include loans to employees and to related companies.

Internal Controls over Cash Collections on Account

Businesses that sell on credit receive most of their cash receipts from collections of accounts receivable. Internal control over collections on account is important. Chapter 4 discusses control procedures for cash receipts, but another element of internal control deserves emphasis here—the separation of cash-handling and cash-accounting duties. Consider the following case:

> **Central Paint Company is a small, family-owned business that takes pride in the loyalty of its workers. Most employees have been with Central for 10 or more years. The company makes 90% of its sales on account and receives most of its cash by mail.**
>
> **The office staff consists of a bookkeeper and an office supervisor. The bookkeeper maintains the general ledger and a subsidiary record of individual customer accounts receivable. The bookkeeper also makes the daily bank deposit.**
>
> **The supervisor prepares monthly financial statements and any special reports the company needs. The supervisor also takes sales orders from customers and serves as office manager.**

Can you identify the internal control weakness here? The problem is that the bookkeeper makes the bank deposit. Remember the AMEX case in Chapter 4? With this cash-handling duty, the bookkeeper could lap accounts receivable. Alternatively, he or she could steal an incoming customer check and write off the customer's account as uncollectible. The customer doesn't complain because the bookkeeper wrote off the customer's account, and Central therefore stops pursuing collection.

How can this weakness be corrected? The supervisor—not the bookkeeper—could open incoming mail and make the daily bank deposit. The bookkeeper should *not* be allowed to handle cash. Only the remittance advices should be forwarded to the bookkeeper to credit customer accounts receivable. Removing cash handling from the bookkeeper and keeping the accounts away from the supervisor separates duties and strengthens internal control.

Using a bank lockbox achieves the same separation of duties. Customers send their payments directly to Central Paint Company's bank, which records cash as the cash goes into Central's bank account. The bank then forwards the remittance advice to Central's bookkeeper, who credits the customer account. No Central Paint employee even touches incoming cash.

How Do We Manage the Risk of Not Collecting?

In Chapters 1 to 4, we use many different companies to illustrate how to account for a business. Chapter 1 began with J.Crew Group, Inc., a high fashion clothing retailer. J.Crew, like other exclusively retail businesses, doesn't own any receivables, because it makes all of its sales in cash, which includes credit card sales. However, for most types of businesses, strictly cash sales are the exception rather than the rule. Chapter 2 featured Apple, Inc., Chapter 3 Starbucks Corporation, and Chapter 4 AMEX Products. This chapter features PepsiCo. All of these companies hold substantial amounts of receivables.

By selling on credit, companies run the risk of not collecting some receivables. Unfortunately, some customers don't pay their debts. The prospect of failing to collect from a customer provides the biggest challenge in accounting for receivables. The Decision Guidelines address this challenge.

DECISION GUIDELINES

MANAGING AND ACCOUNTING FOR RECEIVABLES

Here are the management and accounting issues a business faces when the company extends credit to customers. For each issue, the Decision Guidelines propose a plan of action. Let's look at a business situation: Suppose you open a health club near your college. Assume you will let customers use the club and bill them for their monthly dues. What challenges will you encounter by extending credit to customers?

The main issues in *managing* receivables, along with plans of action, are

Issues	Plan of Action
1. What are the benefits and the costs of extending credit to customers?	1. Benefit—Increase in sales. Cost—Risk of not collecting.
2. Extend credit only to creditworthy customers.	2. Run a credit check on prospective customers.
3. Separate cash-handling and accounting duties to keep employees from stealing the cash collected from customers.	3. Design the internal control system to separate duties.
4. Pursue collection from customers to maximize cash flow.	4. Keep a close eye on customer pay habits. Send second and third statements to slow-paying customers, if necessary.

The main issues in accounting for receivables, and the related plans of action, are (amounts are assumed)

Issues	Plan of Action
1. Measure and report receivables on the balance sheet at their net realizable value, the amount we expect to collect. This is the appropriate amount to report for receivables.	Report receivables at their net realizable value: **Balance sheet** Receivables... $1,000 Less: Allowance for uncollectibles.............. (80) Receivables, net... $ 920
2. Measure and report the expense associated with failure to collect receivables. This expense is called *uncollectible-account expense* and is reported on the income statement.	Measure the expense of not collecting from customers: **Income statement** Sales (or service) revenue............................. $8,000 Expenses: Uncollectible-account expense................. 190

These guidelines lead to our next topic, Accounting for Uncollectible Receivables.

ACCOUNTING FOR UNCOLLECTIBLE RECEIVABLES

A company gets an account receivable only when it sells its product or service on credit (on account). You'll recall that the entry to record the earning of revenue on account is (amount assumed)

Accounts Receivable	1,000	
Sales Revenue (or Service Revenue)		1,000
Earned revenue on account.		

Ideally, the company would collect cash for all of its receivables. But unfortunately the entry to record cash collections on account is for only $950.

Cash	950	
Accounts Receivable		950
Collections on account.		

You can see that companies rarely collect all of their accounts receivables. So companies must account for their uncollectible accounts—$50 in this example. Selling on credit creates both a benefit and a cost:

- *Benefit*: Customers who cannot pay cash immediately can buy on credit, so sales and profits increase.
- *Cost*: The company cannot collect from some customers. Accountants label this cost **uncollectible-account expense**, **doubtful-account expense**, or **bad-debt expense**.

PepsiCo reports receivables as follows on its 2007 balance sheet (in millions):

Accounts and notes receivable, net of allowance for doubtful accounts of $75 .... $4,389

The allowance ($75) represents the amount that PepsiCo does *not* expect to collect. The net amount of the receivables ($4,389) is the amount that PepsiCo *does* expect to collect. This is called the *net realizable value* because it's the amount of cash PepsiCo expects to realize in cash receipts.

Uncollectible-account expense is an operating expense along with salaries, depreciation, rent, and utilities. To measure uncollectible-account expense, accountants use the allowance method or, in certain limited cases, the direct write-off method (p. 305).

Allowance Method

The best way to measure bad debts is by the **allowance method**. This method records collection losses based on estimates developed from the company's collection experience. PepsiCo doesn't wait to see which customers will not pay. Instead, PepsiCo records the estimated amount as Uncollectible-Account Expense and also sets up **Allowance for Uncollectible Accounts**. Other titles for this account are **Allowance for Doubtful Accounts** and *Allowance for Bad Debts*. This is a contra

OBJECTIVE

3 **Use** the allowance method for uncollectible receivables account to Accounts Receivable. The allowance shows the amount of the receivables the business expects *not* to collect.

In Chapter 3 we used the Accumulated Depreciation account to show the amount of a plant asset's cost that has been expensed—the portion of the asset that's no longer a benefit to the company. Allowance for Uncollectible Accounts serves a similar purpose for Accounts Receivable. The allowance shows how much of the receivable has been expensed. You'll find this diagram helpful (amounts are assumed):

Equipment............................	$100,000	Accounts receivable....................	$10,000
Less: Accumulated		Less: Allowance for	
depreciation	(40,000)	uncollectible accounts	(900)
Equipment, net....................	60,000	Accounts receivable, net.............	9,100

Focus on Accounts Receivable. Customers owe this company $10,000, but it expects to collect only $9,100. The *net realizable value* of the receivables is therefore $9,100. Another way to report these receivables is

Accounts receivable, less allowance of $900.................	$9,100

You can work backward to determine the full amount of the receivable, $10,000 (net realizable value of $9,100 plus the allowance of $900).

The income statement reports Uncollectible-Account Expense among the operating expenses, as follows (using assumed figures):

Income statement (partial):

Expenses:
      Uncollectible-account expense:................ $2,000

STOP & THINK...

Refer to the PepsiCo balance sheet on page 290. At December 31, 2007, how much in total did customers owe PepsiCo? How much did PepsiCo expect *not* to collect? How much did PepsiCo expect to collect? What was the net realizable value of PepsiCo's receivables?

Answer:

	Millions
Customers owed PepsiCo..	$4,464 ($4,389 + 75)
PepsiCo expected not to collect the allowance of	(75)
PepsiCo expected to collect—net realizable value........	$4,389

Notice that, to determine the *total* (*gross*) amount customers owed, you have to add the amount of the allowance back to the "net realizable value" ($4,389 + $75 = $4,464). Although this amount is not shown in the financial statements, it is useful for analysis purposes, as shown in the following section.

The best way to estimate uncollectibles uses the company's history of collections from customers. There are two basic ways to estimate uncollectibles:

- Percent-of-sales method
- Aging-of-receivables method

Percent-of-Sales. The **percent-of-sales method** computes uncollectible-account expense as a percent of revenue. This method takes an *income-statement approach* because it focuses on the amount of expense to be reported on the income statement. Assume it is December 31, 2007, and PepsiCo's accounts have these balances *before the year-end adjustments* (amounts in millions):

Accounts Receivable		Allowance for Uncollectible Accounts	
4,464			15

Customers owe PepsiCo $4,464, and the Allowance amount on the books is $15. But PepsiCo's top managers know that the company will fail to collect more than $15. Suppose PepsiCo's credit department estimates that uncollectible-account expense is 1/10 of 1% (0.001) of total revenues, which were $46,000. The entry that records uncollectible-account expense for the year also updates the allowance as follows (using PepsiCo figures):

2007			
Dec 31	Uncollectible-Account Expense		
	($46,000 × .001)	46	
	Allowance for Uncollectible Accounts		46
	Recorded expense for the year.		

The expense decreases PepsiCo's assets, as shown by the accounting equation.

Assets	=	Liabilities	+	Stockholders' Equity	–	Expenses
– 46	=	0			–	46

The percentage-of-sales method employs the matching concept to estimate, probably on a monthly or quarterly basis, the amount of cost that has been incurred in order to earn a certain amount of revenue, and to recognize both in the same time period.

Accounts Receivable		Allowance for Uncollectible Accounts		Uncollectible-Account Expense	
4,464			15	46	
		Adj	46		
		End Bal	61		

Net accounts receivable, $4,403

Using the percentage-of-sales method, the net realizable value of accounts receivable, or the amount ultimately expected to be collected from customers, would be $4,403 ($4,464 − $61). This method will usually result in a different amount of estimated uncollectible accounts expense and net realizable value than the aging method, discussed next.

Aging-of-Receivables.   The other popular method for estimating uncollectibles is called **aging-of-receivables**. The aging method is a *balance-sheet approach* because it focuses on what should be the most relevant and faithful representation of accounts receivable as of the balance sheet date. In the aging method, individual receivables from specific customers are analyzed based on how long they have been outstanding.

Suppose it is December 31, 2007, and PepsiCo's receivables accounts show the following before the year-end adjustment (amounts in millions):

Accounts Receivable	Allowance for Uncollectible Accounts
$4,464	15

These accounts are not yet ready for the financial statements because the allowance balance is not realistic.

PepsiCo's computerized accounting package ages the company's accounts receivable. Exhibit 5-2 shows a representative aging schedule at December 31, 2007. PepsiCo's receivables total $4,464. Of this amount, the aging schedule shows that the company will *not* collect $75 (lower right corner).

EXHIBIT 5-2 | Aging the Accounts Receivable of PepsiCo.

	Age of Account (Dollar amounts rounded to the nearest million)				
Customer	1–30 Days	31–60 Days	61–90 Days	Over 90 Days	Total Balance
Taco Bell					
Pizza Hut					
⋮	⋮	⋮	⋮	⋮	⋮
Totals.................................	$3,600	$ 600	$ 200	$ 64	$4,464
Estimated percent uncollectible.............................	× 1%	× 2%	× 7%	× 20%	
Allowance for Uncollectible Accounts balance should be	$ 36 +	$ 12 +	$ 14 +	$ 13* =	$ 75

*Rounded to the nearest million

The aging method will bring the balance of the allowance account ($15) to the needed amount as determined by the aging schedule ($75). The lower right corner of the aging schedule gives the needed balance in the allowance account. To update the allowance, PepsiCo would make this adjusting entry at year end:

2007			
Dec 31	Uncollectible-Account Expense	60	
	Allowance for Uncollectible Accounts		
	($75 – $15)		60
	Recorded expense for the year.		

The expense decreases PepsiCo's assets and net income, as shown by the accounting equation.

Assets	=	Liabilities	+	Stockholders' Equity	–	Expenses
– 60	=	0			–	60

Now the balance sheet can report the amount that PepsiCo actually expects to collect from customers: $4,389 ($4,464 – $75). This is the net realizable value of PepsiCo's accounts receivable.

Accounts Receivable		Allowance for Uncollectible Accounts		Uncollectible-Account Expense
4,464		Beg Bal	15	60
		Adj	60	
		End Bal	75	

Net accounts receivable, $4,389

Writing Off Uncollectible Accounts.   Assume that at the beginning of 2010 a division of PepsiCo had these accounts receivable (amounts in thousands):

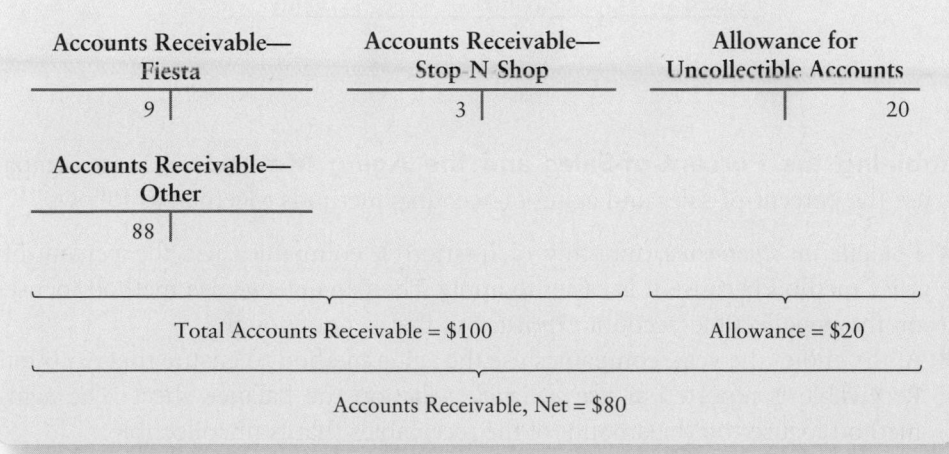

Accounts Receivable— Fiesta	Accounts Receivable— Stop N Shop	Allowance for Uncollectible Accounts
9	3	20

Accounts Receivable— Other		
88		

Total Accounts Receivable = $100   Allowance = $20

Accounts Receivable, Net = $80

Suppose that early in 2010, PepsiCo's credit department determines that PepsiCo cannot collect from customers Fiesta and Stop–N–Shop. PepsiCo then writes off the receivables from these customers with the following entry:

2010			
Jan 31	Allowance for Uncollectible Accounts	12	
	Accounts Receivable—Fiesta		9
	Accounts Receivable—Stop-N-Shop		3
	Wrote off uncollectible receivables.		

After the write-off, PepsiCo's accounts show these amounts:

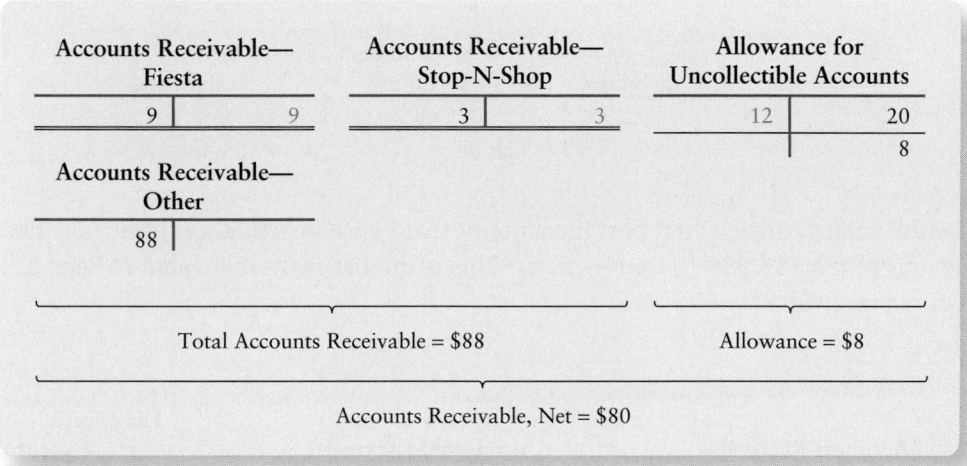

The accounting equation shows that the write-off of uncollectibles has no effect on PepsiCo's total assets, no effect on current assets, and no effect on net accounts receivable. Notice that Accounts Receivable, Net is still $80. There is no effect on net income either. Why is there no effect on net income? Net income is unaffected because the write-off of uncollectibles affects no expense account. If the company uses the allowance method as discussed in the previous section, expenses would have been properly recognized in the period they were incurred, which is the same period in which the related sales took place.

Assets	=	Liabilities	+	Stockholders' Equity
+ 12				
− 12	=	0	+	0

Combining the Percent-of-Sales and the Aging Methods. Most companies use the percent-of-sales and aging-of-accounts methods together, as follows:

- For *interim statements* (monthly or quarterly), companies use the percent-of-sales method because it is easier to apply. The percent-of-sales method focuses on the uncollectible-account *expense*, but that is not enough.
- At the end of the year, companies use the aging method to ensure that Accounts Receivable is reported at *net realizable value* on the balance sheet. The aging method focuses on the amount of the receivables that is uncollectible.
- Using the two methods together provides good measures of both the *expense* and the *asset*. Exhibit 5-3 compares the two methods.

EXHIBIT 5-3 | **Comparing the Percent-of-Sales and Aging Methods for Estimating Uncollectibles**

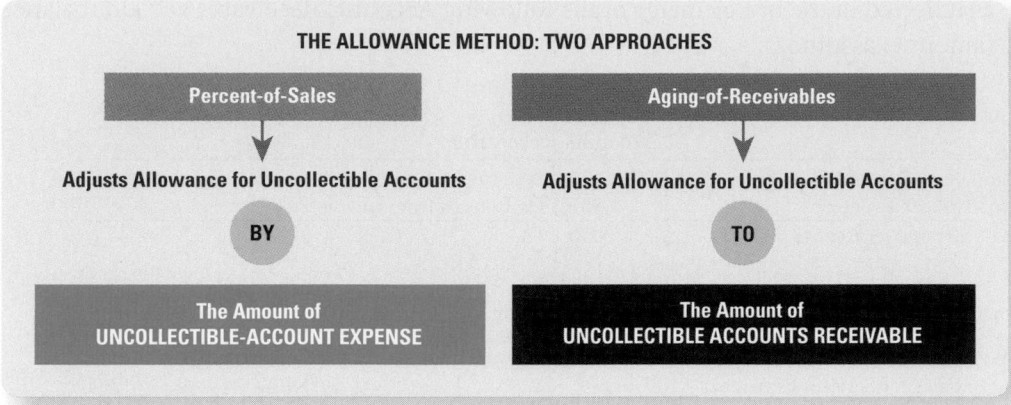

Direct Write-Off Method

There is another, less preferable, way to account for uncollectible receivables. Under the **direct write-off method**, the company waits until a specific customer's receivable proves uncollectible. Then the accountant writes off the customer's account and records Uncollectible-Account Expense, as follows (using assumed data):

2010			
Jan 2	Uncollectible-Account Expense	12	
	Accounts Receivable—Fiesta		9
	Accounts Receivable—Stop-N-Shop		3
	Wrote off bad accounts by direct write-off method.		

The direct write-off method is not considered generally accepted accounting for financial statement purposes. It is considered defective for two reasons:

1. It uses no allowance for uncollectibles. As a result, receivables are always reported at their full amount, which is more than the business expects to collect. *Assets on the balance sheet may be overstated.*

2. It causes a poor matching of uncollectible-account expense against revenue. In this example, PepsiCo made the sales to Fiesta and Stop–N–Shop in 2009 and should have recorded the uncollectible-account expense during 2009, not in 2010 when it wrote off the accounts.

Because of these deficiencies, PepsiCo and virtually all other large companies use the allowance method for preparing their financial statements.

The direct write-off method is the *required* method of accounting for uncollectible accounts for federal income tax purposes. It is one of several sources of timing differences that may arise between net income for financial reporting purposes and net income for federal income tax purposes. We will discuss other differences between book and taxable income in later chapters.

Computing Cash Collections from Customers

A company earns revenue and then collects the cash from customers. For PepsiCo and most other companies, there is a time lag between earning the revenue and collecting the cash. Collections from customers are the single most important source of cash for any business. You can compute a company's collections from customers by analyzing its Accounts Receivable account. Receivables typically hold only five items, as reflected in the five elements of the following Accounts Receivable account balance (amounts assumed):

Accounts Receivable			
Beg Bal (left over from last period)	200	Write-offs of uncollectibles	100**
Sales (or service) revenue	1,800*	Collections from customers	X = 1,500†
End Bal (carries over to next period)	400		

*The journal entry that places revenue into the receivable account is

Accounts Receivable	1,800	
Sales (or Service) Revenue		1,800

**The journal entry for write-offs is

Allowance for Uncollectibles	100	
Accounts Receivable		100

†The journal entry that places collections into the receivable account is

Cash	1,500	
Accounts Receivable		1,500

Suppose you know all these amounts *except* collections from customers. You can compute collections by solving for X in the T-account.[1] Often write-offs are unknown and must be omitted. Then the computation of collections becomes an approximation.

NOTES RECEIVABLE

As stated earlier, notes receivable are more formal than accounts receivable. Notes receivable due within one year or less are current assets. Notes due beyond one year are *long-term receivables* and are reported as long-term assets. Some notes receivable are collected in installments. The portion due within one year is a current asset and the remainder is long term. PepsiCo may hold a $20,000 note receivable from a customer, but only the $6,000 the customer must pay within one year is a current asset of PepsiCo.

Before launching into the accounting for notes receivable, let's define some key terms:

Creditor. The party to whom money is owed. The creditor is also called the *lender*.

Debtor. The party that borrowed and owes money on the note. The debtor is also called the *maker* of the note or the *borrower*.

Interest. Interest is the cost of borrowing money. The interest is stated in an annual percentage rate.

Maturity date. The date on which the debtor must pay the note.

Maturity value. The sum of principal and interest on the note.

---

[1]An equation may help you solve for X. The equation is $200 + $1,800 − X − $100 = $400. X = $1,500.

Principal. The amount of money borrowed by the debtor.

Term. The length of time from when the note was signed by the debtor to when the debtor must pay the note.

There are two parties to a note:

- The *creditor* has a note receivable.
- The *debtor* has a note payable.

Exhibit 5-4 is a typical promissory note.

EXHIBIT 5-4 | A Promissory Note

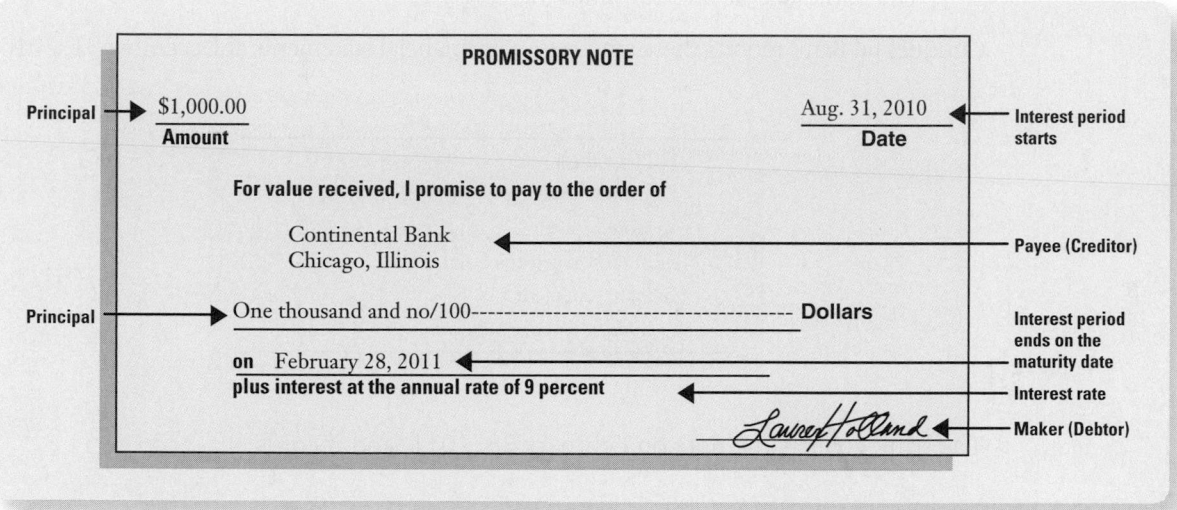

The **principal** amount of the note ($1,000) is the amount borrowed by the debtor, lent by the creditor. This six-month note receivable runs from August 31, 2010, to February 28, 2011, when Lauren Holland (the maker) promises to pay Continental Bank (the creditor) the principal of $1,000 plus 9% interest. Interest is revenue to the creditor (Continental Bank, in this case).

Accounting for Notes Receivable

Consider the promissory note in Exhibit 5-4. After Lauren Holland signs the note, Continental Bank gives her $1,000 cash. The bank's entries follow, assuming a December 31 year end for Continental Bank:

2010			
Aug 31	Note Receivable—L. Holland	1,000	
	Cash		1,000
	Made a loan.		

Note Receivable— L. Holland	
1,000	

The bank gave one asset, cash, in return for another asset, a note receivable, so total assets did not change.

Continental Bank earns interest revenue during September, October, November, and December. At December 31, the bank accrues 9% interest revenue for four months as follows:

2010			
Dec 31	Interest Receivable ($1,000 × .09 × 4/12)	30	
	Interest Revenue		30
	Accrued interest revenue.		

The bank's assets and revenues increase.

Continental Bank reports these amounts in its financial statements at December 31, 2010:

Balance sheet
Current assets:
    Note receivable $1,000
    Interest receivable............... 30
Income statement
    Interest revenue.................. $ 30

The bank collects the note on February 28, 2011, and records

2011			
Feb 28	Cash	1,045	
	Note Receivable—L. Holland		1,000
	Interest Receivable		30
	Interest Revenue ($1,000 × .09 × 2/12)		15
	Collected note at maturity.		

This entry zeroes out Note Receivable and Interest Receivable and also records the interest revenue earned in 2011.

Note Receivable—
L. Holland

1,000	1,000

In its 2011 financial statements the only item that Continental Bank will report is the interest revenue of $15 that was earned in 2011. There's no note receivable or interest receivable on the balance sheet because those items were zeroed out when the bank collected the note at maturity.

Three aspects of the interest computation deserve mention:

1. Interest rates are always for an annual period, unless stated otherwise. In this example, the annual interest rate is 9%. At December 31, 2010, Continental Bank accrues interest revenue for four months. The interest computation is

Principal	×	Interest Rate	×	Time	=	Amount of Interest
$1,000	×	.09	×	4/12	=	$30

2. The time element (4/12) is the fraction of the year that the note has been in force during 2010.

3. Interest is often completed for a number of days. For example, suppose you loaned out $10,000 on April 10. The note receivable runs for 90 days and specifies interest at 8%.

   a. Interest starts accruing on April 11 and runs for 90 days, ending on the due date, July 9, as follows:

Month	Number of Days That Interest Accrues
April	20
May	31
June	30
July	9
Total	90

   b. The interest computation is

   $10,000 × .08 × 90/365 = $197

Some companies sell goods and services on notes receivable (versus selling on accounts receivable). This often occurs when the payment term extends beyond the customary accounts receivable period of 30 to 60 days.

Suppose that on March 20, 2011, PepsiCo sells a large amount of food to Wal-Mart. PepsiCo gets Wal-Mart's three-month promissory note plus 10% annual interest. At the outset, PepsiCo would debit Notes Receivable and credit Sales Revenue.

A company may also accept a note receivable from a trade customer whose account receivable is past due. The company then debits Notes Receivable and credits Accounts Receivable. We would say the company "received a note receivable on account." Now let's examine some strategies to speed up cash flow.

How to Speed Up Cash Flow

All companies want speedy cash receipts. Rapid cash flow finances new products, research, and development. Thus, companies such as PepsiCo find ways to collect cash quickly. Two common strategies generate cash quickly.

Credit Card or Bankcard Sales

The merchant sells merchandise and lets the customer pay with a credit card, such as Discover or American Express, or with a bankcard, such as VISA or MasterCard. This strategy may dramatically increase sales, but the added revenue comes at a cost, which is typically about 2% to 3% of the total amount of the sale. Let's see how credit cards and bankcards work from the seller's perspective.

Suppose Dell, Inc., sells computers for $5,000, and the customer pays with a VISA card. Dell records the sale as follows:

Cash	4,900	
Credit Card Discount Expense	100	
Sales Revenue		5,000
Recorded bankcard sales.		

Assets	=	Liabilities	+	Stockholders' Equity	+	Revenues	–	Expenses
+ 4,900	=	0	+			+ 5,000		– 100

Dell enters the transaction in the credit card machine. The machine, linked to a VISA server, automatically credits Dell's account for a discounted portion, say $4,900, of the $5,000 sale amount. Two percent ($100) goes to VISA. To Dell, the credit card discount expense is an operating expense similar to interest expense.

Selling (Factoring) Receivables

PepsiCo makes some large sales to grocery chains on account, debiting Accounts Receivable and crediting Sales Revenue. PepsiCo might then sell these accounts receivable to another business, called a *factor*. The factor earns revenue by paying a discounted price for the receivable and then hopefully collecting the full amount from the customer. The benefit to PepsiCo is the immediate receipt of cash. The biggest disadvantage of factoring is that it is often quite expensive, when compared to the costs of retaining the receivable on the books and ultimately collecting the full amount. In addition, the company that factors its receivables loses control over the collection process. For these reasons, factoring is often not used by companies who have other less costly means to raise cash, such as short-term borrowing from banks. Factoring may be used by start-up companies with insufficient credit history to obtain loans at a reasonable cost, by companies with weak credit history, or by companies that are already saddled with a significant amount of debt.

To illustrate selling, or *factoring*, accounts receivable, suppose a company wishes to speed up cash flow and therefore sells $100,000 of accounts receivables, receiving cash of $95,000. The company would record the sale of the receivables as follows:

Cash	95,000	
Financing Expense	5,000	
Accounting Receivable		100,000
Sold accounts receivable.		

Again, Financing Expense is an operating expense, with the same effect as a loss. Some companies may debit a Loss account. Discounting a note receivable is similar to selling an account receivable. However, the credit is to Notes Receivable (instead of Accounts Receivable).

Notice the high price (5% of the face amount, or $5,000) the company has had to pay in order to collect the cash immediately, as opposed to waiting 30 to 60 days to collect the full amount. Therefore, if the company can afford to wait, it will probably not engage in factoring in order to collect the full amount of the receivables.

Reporting on the Statement of Cash Flows

Receivables and short-term investments appear on the balance sheet as assets. We saw these in PepsiCo's balance sheet at the beginning of the chapter. We've also seen how to report the related revenues, expenses, gains, and losses on the income statement. Because receivable and investment transactions affect cash, their effects must also be reported on the statement of cash flows.

Receivables bring in cash when the business collects from customers. These transactions are reported as *operating activities* on the statement of cash flows because they result from sales. Investment transactions show up as *investing activities* on the statement of cash flows. Chapter 12 shows how companies report their cash flows on the statement of cash flows. In that chapter we will see exactly how to report cash flows related to receivables and investment transactions.

USING TWO KEY RATIOS TO MAKE DECISIONS

Investors and creditors use ratios to evaluate the financial health of a company. We introduced the current ratio in Chapter 3. Other ratios, including the **quick** (or *acid-test*) **ratio** and the number of days' sales in receivables, help investors measure liquidity.

OBJECTIVE

5 **Use** two new ratios to evaluate a business

Acid-Test (or Quick) Ratio

The balance sheet lists assets in the order of relative liquidity:

1. Cash and cash equivalents
2. Short-term investments
3. Accounts (or notes) receivable

PepsiCo's balance sheet in the chapter-opening story lists these accounts in order. Managers, stockholders, and creditors care about the liquidity of a company's assets. The current ratio measures ability to pay current liabilities with current assets. A more stringent measure of ability to pay current liabilities is the **acid-test** (or *quick*) **ratio**:

PepsiCo 2007
(Dollars in millions, taken from PepsiCo balance sheet)

$$\text{Acid-test ratio} = \frac{\text{Cash} + \text{Short-term investments} + \text{Net current receivables}}{\text{Total current liabilities}} = \frac{\$910 + \$1,571 + \$4,389}{\$7,753} = 0.89$$

The higher the acid-test ratio, the easier it is to pay current liabilities. PepsiCo's acid-test ratio of 0.89 means that it has 89 cents of quick assets to pay each $1 of current liabilities. This ratio value is considered reasonably good, but not excellent. Traditionally, companies have wanted an acid-test ratio of at least 1.0 to be safe. The ratio needs to be high enough for safety, but not too high. After all, cash and the other liquid assets don't earn very high rates of return, as inventory and plant assets do.

What is an acceptable acid-test ratio? The answer depends on the industry. Auto dealers can operate smoothly with an acid-test ratio of 0.20, roughly one-fourth of PepsiCo's ratio value. How can auto dealers survive with so low an acid-test ratio? The auto manufacturers help finance their dealers' inventory. Most dealers, therefore, have a financial safety net provided through the manufacturers. During the recent business recession, General Motors' sales slumped and the company ran dangerously low of cash. One of the many consequences of GM's cash shortage was that it deprived dealerships of these safety nets and put them in jeopardy of bankruptcy and insolvency as well as the company. You can see the "domino effect" of arrangements like this, and why a number of GM dealerships were forced to close, even after GM received about $25 billion in "bailout money" from the United States government.

Days' Sales in Receivables

After a business makes a credit sale, the *next* step is collecting the receivable. **Days' sales in receivables**, also called the *collection period*, tells a company how long it takes to collect its average level of receivables. Shorter is better because cash is coming in quickly. The longer the collection period, the less cash is available to pay bills and expand.

Days' sales in receivables can be computed in two logical steps. First, compute one day's sales (or total revenues). Then divide one day's sales into average receivables for the period. We show days' sales in receivables for PepsiCo.

(Dollars in millions, taken from PepsiCo's financial statements)
Days' Sales in Receivables — PepsiCo

1. One day's sales = $\frac{\text{Net sales}}{365 \text{ days}}$ = $\frac{\$39{,}474}{365 \text{ days}}$ = $108 per day

2. Days' sales in average receivables = $\frac{\text{Average receivables *}}{\text{One day's sales}}$ = $\frac{\$4{,}057*}{\$108 \text{ per day}}$ = 38 days

*Average net receivables = $\frac{\text{Beginning net receivables + Ending net receivables}}{2}$ = $\frac{\$3{,}725 + \$4{,}389}{2}$ = $4,057

Net sales come from the income statement, and the receivables amounts are taken from the balance sheet. Average receivables is the simple average of the beginning and ending balance.

It takes PepsiCo 38 days to collect its average level of receivables. To evaluate PepsiCo's collection period of 38 days, we need to compare 38 days to the credit terms that PepsiCo offers customers when the company makes a sale, as well as the number of days on average that creditors typically allow PepsiCo to pay them without penalty.

Suppose PepsiCo makes sales on "net 30" terms, which means that customers should pay PepsiCo within 30 days of the sale. PepsiCo's collection period of 38 days is pretty good in comparison to the ideal measure of 30 days. After all, some customers drag out their payments. And, as we've seen, some customers don't pay at all. On the other hand, if PepsiCo's short-term creditors expect payment of their accounts payable within 30 days, PepsiCo might be forced to borrow cash at banks in order to pay its creditors on time, which could prove to be expensive.

Companies watch their collection periods closely. Whenever collections slow down, the business must find other sources of financing, such as borrowing or selling receivables. During recessions, customers pay more slowly, and a longer collection period may be unavoidable.[2]

---

[2]Another ratio, **accounts receivable turnover**, captures the same information as days' sales in receivables. Receivable turnover is computed as follows: Net sales/Average net accounts receivable. During 2007, PepsiCo had a receivable turnover rate of 9.7 times ($39,474/$4,057 = 9.7). Days sales in average receivables can then be computed by dividing 365 by the receivable turnover (365/9.7 = 37.63). You can see that this method merely rearranges the equations in the body of the text, "going through the back door" to achieve the same result. The authors prefer days' sales in receivables to receivables turnover because days' sales in receivable can be compared directly to the company's credit sale terms.

END-OF-CHAPTER SUMMARY PROBLEM

Superior Technical Resources' (STR's) balance sheet at December 31, 2010, reported

	(In millions)
Accounts receivable...............................	$382
Allowance for doubtful accounts...............	(52)

STR uses both the percent-of-sales and the aging approaches to account for uncollectible receivables.

Requirements

1. How much of the December 31, 2010, balance of accounts receivables did STR expect to collect? Stated differently, what was the net realizable value of STR's receivables?
2. Journalize, without explanations, 2011 entries for STR:
   a. Estimated doubtful-account expense of $40 million, based on the percent-of-sales method, all during the year.
   b. Write-offs of uncollectible accounts receivable totaling $58 million. Prepare a T-account for Allowance for Doubtful Accounts and post to this account. Show its unadjusted balance at December 31, 2011.
   c. December 31, 2011, aging of receivables, which indicates that $47 million of the total receivables of $409 million is uncollectible at year end. Post to Allowance for Doubtful Accounts, and show its adjusted balance at December 31, 2011.
3. Show how STR's receivables and the related allowance will appear on the December 31, 2011, balance sheet.
4. Show what STR's income statement will report for the foregoing transactions.

Answers

Requirement 1

	(In millions)
Net realizable value of receivables ($382 – $52)	$330

Requirement 2

		(In millions)	
a.	Doubtful-Account Expense	40	
	Allowance for Doubtful Accounts		40
b.	Allowance for Doubtful Accounts	58	
	Accounts Receivable		58

Allowance for Doubtful Accounts

		Dec 31, 2010	52
2011 Write-offs	58	2011 Expense	40
		Unadjusted balance at Dec 31, 2011	34

c.	Doubtful-Account Expense ($47 – $34)	13	
	Allowance for Doubtful Accounts		13

Allowance for Doubtful Accounts

	Dec 31, 2011 Unadj bal	34
	2011 Expense	13
	Dec 31, 2011 Adj bal	47

I Requirement 3

	(In millions)
Accounts receivable	$409
Allowance for doubtful accounts	(47)

I Requirement 4

	(In millions)
Expenses: Doubtful-account expense for 2011 ($40 + $13)	$53

REVIEW RECEIVABLES AND INVESTMENTS

Quick Check (Answers are given on page 340.)

1. Henry Funaro Golf Academy held investments in trading securities valued at $40,000 at December 31, 2010. These investments cost Henry Funaro $33,000. What is the appropriate amount for Henry Funaro to report for these investments on the December 31, 2010, balance sheet?
   a. $40,000
   b. $7,000 gain
   c. 33,000
   d. Cannot be determined from the data given

2. Return to Henry Funaro Golf Academy in question 1. What should appear on the Henry Funaro income statement for the year ended December 31, 2010, for the trading securities?
   a. $7,000 unrealized gain
   b. $33,000
   c. $40,000
   d. Cannot be determined from the data given

Use the following information to answer questions 3–7.

Anderson Company had the following information relating to credit sales in 2010.

Accounts receivable 12/31/10..	$10,000
Allowance for uncollectible accounts 12/31/10 (before adjustment).........	600
Credit sales during 2010	40,000
Cash sales during 2010	15,000
Collections from customers on account during 2010..............................	44,000

3. Uncollectible accounts are determined by the percent-of-sales method to be 4% of credit sales. How much is uncollectible-account expense for 2010?
   a. $2,200   c. $1,600
   b. $400   d. $1,760

4. Uncollectible-account expense for 2010 is $1,600. What is the adjusted balance in the Allowance account at year-end 2010?
   a. $3,800   c. $1,600
   b. $2,200   d. $600

5. If uncollectible accounts are determined by the aging-of-receivables method to be $1,030, the uncollectible account expense for 2010 would be
   a. $1,630.   c. $430.
   b. $600.   d. $1,030.

6. Using the aging-of-receivables method, the balance of the Allowance account after the adjusting entry would be
   a. $600.   c. $1,630.
   b. $1,030.   d. $430.

7. Using the aging-of-receivables method, the net realizable value of accounts receivable on the 12/31/10 balance sheet would be
   a. $8,370.   c. $8,400.
   b. $10,000.   d. $8,970.

8. Accounts Receivable has a debit balance of $2,800, and the Allowance for Uncollectible Accounts has a credit balance of $400. A $90 account receivable is written off. What is the amount of net receivables (net realizable value) after the write-off?
   a. $2,490   c. $2,310
   b. $2,710   d. $2,400

9. Magnolia Corporation began 2010 with Accounts Receivable of $575,000. Sales for the year totaled $2,200,000. Magnolia ended the year with accounts receivable of $725,000. Magnolia's bad-debt losses are minimal. How much cash did Magnolia collect from customers in 2010?
   a. $2,925,000   c. $2,200,000
   b. $2,050,000   d. $2,350,000

10. Neptune Company received a four-month, 9%, $2,800 note receivable on December 1. The adjusting entry on December 31 will
    a. debit Interest Receivable $21.   c. both a and b.
    b. credit Interest Revenue $21.   d. credit Interest Revenue $252.

11. What is the maturity value of a $70,000, 12%, six-month note?
    a. $70,000   c. $65,800
    b. $78,400   d. $74,200

12. If the adjusting entry to accrue interest on a note receivable is omitted, then
    a. assets, net income, and stockholders' equity are understated.
    b. assets are overstated, net income is understated, and stockholders' equity is understated.
    c. liabilities are understated, net income is overstated, and stockholders' equity is overstated.
    d. assets, net income, and stockholders' equity are overstated.
13. Net sales total $803,000. Beginning and ending accounts receivable are $80,000 and $74,000, respectively. Calculate days' sales in receivables.
    a. 35 days   c. 30 days
    b. 36 days   d. 34 days
14. From the following list of accounts, calculate the quick ratio.

Cash	$ 6,000	Accounts payable	$10,000
Accounts receivable	9,000	Salary payable	4,000
Inventory	11,000	Notes payable (due in two years)	13,000
Prepaid insurance	1,000	Short-term note investments	3,000

    a. 1.3   c. 1.1
    b. 2.1   d. 1.8

Accounting Vocabulary

acid-test ratio (p. 311) Ratio of the sum of cash plus short-term investments plus net current receivables to total current liabilities. Tells whether the entity can pay all its current liabilities if they come due immediately. Also called the *quick ratio*.

accounts receivable turnover (p. 313) Net sales divided by average net accounts receivable.

aging-of-receivables (p. 302) A way to estimate bad debts by analyzing individual accounts receivable according to the length of time they have been receivable from the customer.

Allowance for Doubtful Accounts (p. 299) Another name for *Allowance for Uncollectible Accounts*.

Allowance for Uncollectible Accounts (p. 299) The estimated amount of collection losses. Another name for *Allowance for Doubtful Accounts*.

allowance method (p. 299) A method of recording collection losses based on estimates of how much money the business will not collect from its customers.

bad-debt expense (p. 299) Another name for *uncollectible-account expense*.

creditor (p. 306) The party to whom money is owed.

days' sales in receivables (p. 312) Ratio of average net accounts receivable to one day's sales. Indicates how many days' sales remain in Accounts Receivable awaiting collection. Also called the *collection period*.

debtor (p. 306) The party who owes money.

direct write-off method (p. 305) A method of accounting for bad debts in which the company waits until a customer's account receivable proves uncollectible and then debits

Uncollectible-Account Expense and credits the customer's Account Receivable.

doubtful-account expense (p. 299) Another name for *uncollectible-account expense*.

interest (p. 306) The borrower's cost of renting money from a lender. Interest is revenue for the lender and expense for the borrower.

marketable securities (p. 290) Another name for *short-term investments*.

maturity (p. 296) The date on which a debt instrument must be paid.

maturity date (p. 306) The date on which the debtor must pay the note.

maturity value (p. 306) The sum of principal and interest on the note.

percent-of-sales method (p. 301) Computes uncollectible-account expense as a percentage of net sales. Also called the income statement approach because it focuses on the amount of expense to be reported on the income statement.

principal (p. 307) The amount borrowed by a debtor and lent by a creditor.

quick ratio (p. 311) Another name for *acid-test ratio*.

receivables (p. 296) Monetary claims against a business or an individual, acquired mainly by selling goods or services and by lending money.

short-term investments (p. 290) Investments that a company plans to hold for one year or less. Also called *marketable securities*.

term (p. 307) The length of time from inception to maturity.

trading securities (p. 291) Stock investments that are to be sold in the near future with the intent of generating profits on the sale.

uncollectible-account expense (p. 299) Cost to the seller of extending credit. Arises from the failure to collect from credit customers. Also called doubtful-account expense or bad-debt expense.

ASSESS YOUR PROGRESS

Short Exercises

S5-1 (*Learning Objective 1: Reporting trading investments*)   Answer these questions about investments.

1. What is the amount to report on the balance sheet for a trading security?
2. Why is a trading security always a current asset? Explain.

S5-2 (*Learning Objective 1: Accounting for a trading investment*)   Newsome Corp. holds a portfolio of trading securities. Suppose that on November 1, Newsome paid $87,000 for an investment in Quark shares to add to its portfolio. At December 31, the market value of Quark shares is $98,000. For this situation, show everything that Newsome would report on its December 31 balance sheet and on its income statement for the year ended December 31.

S5-3 (*Learning Objective 1: Accounting for a trading investment*)   McCarver Investments purchased Hoffman shares as a trading security on December 18 for $103,000.

1. Suppose the Hoffman shares decreased in value to $96,000 at December 31. Make the McCarver journal entry to adjust the Short-Term Investment account to market value.
2. Show how McCarver would report the short-term investment on its balance sheet and the unrealized gain or loss on its income statement.

S5-4 (*Learning Objective 2: Applying internal controls over the collection of receivables*) Susan Perry keeps the Accounts Receivable T-account of Abraham & Paige, a partnership. What duty will a good internal control system withhold from Perry? Why?

writing assignment ■

S5-5 (*Learning Objective 2: Controlling cash receipts from customers*)   As a recent college graduate, you land your first job in the customer collections department of Countryroads Publishing. Zach Peters, the manager, asked you to propose a system to ensure that cash received from customers by mail is handled properly. Draft a short memorandum to explain the essential element in your proposed plan. State why this element is important.

writing assignment ■

S5-6 (*Learning Objective 3: Applying the allowance method [percent-of-sales] to account for uncollectibles*)   During its first year of operations, Turning Leaves Furniture Restoration, Inc., had sales of $312,000, all on account. Industry experience suggests that Turning Leaves Furniture Restoration's uncollectibles will amount to 4% of credit sales. At December 31, 2010, accounts receivable total $38,000. The company uses the allowance method to account for uncollectibles.

1. Make Turning Leaves Furniture Restoration's journal entry for uncollectible-account expense using the percent-of-sales method.
2. Show how Turning Leaves Furniture Restoration should report accounts receivable on its balance sheet at December 31, 2010.

S5-7 (*Learning Objective 3: Applying the allowance method [percent-of-sales] to account for uncollectibles*)   During 2011, Turning Leaves Furniture Restoration completed these transactions:

1. Sales revenue on account, $1,000,000
2. Collections on account, $870,000
3. Write-offs of uncollectibles, $12,000
4. Uncollectible-account expense, 4% of sales revenue

Journalize Turning's 2011 transactions. Explanations are not required

S5-8 (*Learning Objective 3: Applying the allowance method to account for uncollectibles*) Use the information from the following journal entries of Turning Leaves Furniture Restoration to answer the questions below:

	Journal Entry		
	Accounts	Debit	Credit
1.	Accounts Receivable	1,000,000	
	Sales Revenue		1,000,000
2.	Cash	870,000	
	Accounts Receivable		870,000
3.	Allowance for Uncollectible Accounts	12,000	
	Accounts Receivable		12,000
4.	Uncollectible-Account Expense	40,000	
	Allowance for Uncollectible Accounts		40,000

I Requirements

1. Start with Accounts Receivable's beginning balance ($38,000) and then post to the Accounts Receivable T-account. How much do Turning Leaves Furniture Restoration's customers owe the company at December 31, 2011?
2. Start with the Allowance account's beginning credit balance ($12,480) and then post to the Allowance for Uncollectible Accounts T-account. How much of the receivables at December 31, 2011, does Turning Leaves Furniture Restoration expect *not* to collect?
3. At December 31, 2011, how much cash does Turning Leaves Furniture Restoration expect to collect on its accounts receivable?

S5-9 (*Learning Objective 3: Applying the allowance method [aging-of-accounts-receivable] to account for uncollectibles*)   Gray and Dumham, a law firm, started 2010 with accounts receivable of $31,000 and an allowance for uncollectible accounts of $4,000. The 2010 service revenues on account totaled $175,000, and cash collections on account totaled $128,000. During 2010, Gray and Dumham wrote off uncollectible accounts receivable of $2,800. At December 31, 2010, the aging of accounts receivable indicated that Gray and Dumham will not collect $1,850 of its accounts receivable.

Journalize Gray and Dumham's (a) service revenue, (b) cash collections on account, (c) write-offs of uncollectible receivables, and (d) uncollectible-account expense for the year. Explanations are not required. Prepare a T-account for Allowance for Uncollectible Accounts to show your computation of uncollectible-account expense for the year.

S5-10 (*Learning Objective 3: Applying the allowance method to account for uncollectibles*) Perform the following accounting for the receivables of Evans and Tanner, a law firm, at December 31, 2010.

I Requirements

1. Start with the beginning balances for these T-accounts:
   - Accounts Receivable, $97,000   • Allowance for Uncollectible Accounts, $5,000

   Post the following 2010 transactions to the T-accounts:
   a. Service revenue of $698,000, all on account
   b. Collections on account, $722,000
   c. Write-offs of uncollectible accounts, $8,000
   d. Uncollectible-account expense (allowance method), $14,000
2. What are the ending balances of Accounts Receivable and Allowance for Uncollectible Accounts?
3. Show how Evans and Tanner will report accounts receivable on its balance sheet at December 31, 2010.

S5-11 *(Learning Objectives 3, 4: Answering practical questions about receivables)* Answer these questions about receivables and uncollectibles. For the true-false questions, explain any answers that turn out to be false.

1. True or false? Credit sales increase receivables. Collections and write-offs decrease receivables.
2. Which receivables figure, the *total* amount that customers *owe* the company, or the *net* amount the company expects to collect, is more interesting to investors as they consider buying the company's stock? Give your reason.
3. Show how to determine net accounts receivable.
4. True or false? The direct write-off method of accounting for uncollectibles understates assets.
5. California Bank lent $200,000 to Sacramento Company on a six-month, 8% note. Which party has interest receivable? Which party has interest payable? Interest expense? Interest revenue? How much interest will these organizations record one month after Sacramento Company signs the note?
6. When California Bank accrues interest on the Sacramento Company note, show the directional effects on the bank's assets, liabilities, and equity (increase, decrease, or no effect).

S5-12 *(Learning Objective 4: Accounting for a note receivable)* Northend Bank & Trust Company lent $130,000 to Sylvia Peters on a six-month, 9% note. Record the following for bank (explanations are not required):

a. Lending the money on May 6.
b. Collecting the principal and interest at maturity. Specify the date.

S5-13 *(Learning Objective 4: Computing note receivable amounts)*

1. Compute the amount of interest during 2010, 2011, and 2012 for the following note receivable: On April 30, 2010, BCDE Bank lent $170,000 to Carl Abbott on a two-year, 7% note.
2. Which party has a (an)
   a. note receivable?
   b. note payable?
   c. interest revenue?
   d. interest expense?
3. How much in total would BCDE Bank collect if Carl Abbott paid off the note early—say, on November 30, 2010?

S5-14 *(Learning Objective 4: Accruing interest receivable and collecting a note receivable)* On August 31, 2010, Nancy Thompson borrowed $2,000 from Green Interstate Bank. Thompson signed a note payable, promising to pay the bank principal plus interest on August 31, 2011. The interest rate on the note is 10%. The accounting year of Green Interstate Bank ends on June 30, 2011. Journalize Green Interstate Bank's (a) lending money on the note receivable at August 31, 2010, (b) accrual of interest at June 30, 2011, and (c) collection of principal and interest August 31, 2011, the maturity date of the note.

S5-15 *(Learning Objective 4: Reporting receivables amounts)* Using your answers to Short Exercise 5-14, show how the Green Interstate Bank will report the following:

a. Whatever needs to be reported on its classified balance sheet at June 30, 2011.
b. Whatever needs to be reported on its income statement for the year ended June 30, 2011.
c. Whatever needs to be reported on its classified balance sheet at June 30, 2012. Ignore Cash.
d. Whatever needs to be reported on its income statement for the year ended June 30, 2012.

S5-16 *(Learning Objective 5: Evaluating the acid-test ratio and days' sales in receivables)* West Highland Clothiers reported the following amounts in its 2011 financial statements. The 2010 amounts are given for comparison.

	2011		2010	
Current assets:				
Cash..		$ 9,700		$ 9,700
Short-term investments................		17,000		14,000
Accounts receivable.....................	$84,000		$77,000	
Less: Allowance for				
uncollectibles......................	(7,100)	76,900	(6,100)	70,900
Inventory......................................		189,000		190,500
Prepaid insurance.........................		2,300		2,300
Total current assets		294,900		287,400
Total current liabilities...................		99,000		111,000
Net sales.....................................		802,000		736,000

I Requirements

1. Compute West Highland's acid-test ratio at the end of 2011. Round to two decimal places.
   How does the acid-test ratio compare with the industry average of 0.97?
2. Compare days' sales in receivables measure for 2011 with the company's credit terms of net 30 days.

S5-17 *(Learning Objectives 2, 3, 5: Reporting receivables and other accounts in the financial statements; using ratios to evaluate a business)*   Norbert Medical Service reported the following items, (amounts in thousands):

Unearned revenues (current)................	$ 607	Service revenue.....................................	$23,653
Allowance for		Other assets..	1,707
doubtful accounts............................	309	Property, plant, and equipment...........	25,376
Other expenses....................................	12,559	Operating expense...............................	11,610
Accounts receivable.............................	4,467	Cash..	289
Accounts payable	2,255	Notes payable (long term)..................	18,729

I Requirements

1. Classify each item as (a) income statement or balance sheet and as (b) debit balance or credit balance.
2. How much net income (or net loss) did Norbert report for the year?
3. Compute Norbert's quick (acid-test) ratio. Round to two decimal places. Evaluate Norbert Medical Service's liquidity position.

Exercises

All of A and B exercises can be found within MyAccountingLab, an online homework and practice environment. Your instructor may ask you to complete these exercises using MyAccountingLab.

(Group A)

E5-18A *(Learning Objective 1: Accounting for a trading investment)* Northern Corporation, the investment banking company, often has extra cash to invest. Suppose Northern buys 800 shares of Andy, Inc., stock at $54 per share. Assume Northern expects to hold the Andy stock for one month and then sell it. The purchase occurs on December 15, 2010. At December 31, the market price of a share of Andy stock is $66 per share.

▎Requirements

1. What type of investment is this to Northern? Give the reason for your answer.
2. Record Northern's purchase of the Andy stock on December 15 and the adjustment to market value on December 31.
3. Show how Northern would report this investment on its balance sheet at December 31 and any gain or loss on its income statement for the year ended December 31, 2010.

E5-19A *(Learning Objective 1: Reporting a trading investment)* On November 16, ACA, Inc., paid $95,000 for an investment in the stock of American Pacific Railway (APR). ACA plans to account for these shares as trading securities. On December 12, ACA received a $400 cash dividend from APR. It is now December 31, and the market value of the APR stock is $92,000. For this investment, show what ACA should report in its income statement and balance sheet.

E5-20A *(Learning Objective 1: Accounting for a trading investment)* Sponsor Corporation reports short-term investments on its balance sheet. Suppose a division of Sponsor completed the following short-term investment transactions during 2010:

2010	
Dec 12	Purchased 600 shares of Disc, Inc., stock for $21,600. Sponsor plans to sell the stock at a profit in the near future.
21	Received a cash dividend of $0.81 per share on the Disc, Inc., stock.
31	Adjusted the investment in Disc, Inc., stock. Current market value is $27,000. Sponsor still plans to sell the stock in early 2011.
2011	
Jan 16	Sold the Disc, Inc., stock for $35,670.

▎Requirement

1. Prepare T-accounts for Cash, Short-Term Investment, Dividend Revenue, Unrealized Gain (Loss) on Investment, and Gain on Sale of Investment. Show the effects of Sponsor's investment transactions. Start with a cash balance of $97,000; all the other accounts start at zero.

E5-21A *(Learning Objective 3: Reporting bad debts by the allowance method)* At December 31, 2010, Darci's Travel has an accounts receivable balance of $88,000. Allowance for Doubtful Accounts has a credit balance of $900 before the year-end adjustment. Service revenue for 2010 was $900,000. Darci's Travel estimates that doubtful-account expense for the year is 3% of sales. Make the year-end entry to record doubtful-account expense. Show how the accounts receivable and the allowance for doubtful accounts are reported on the balance sheet.

E5-22A *(Learning Objective 3: Using the allowance method for bad debts)* On September 30, Hilly Mountain Party Planners had a $30,000 balance in Accounts Receivable and a $2,000 credit balance in Allowance for Uncollectible Accounts. During October, the store made credit sales of $161,000. October collections on account were $137,000, and write-offs of uncollectible receivables totaled $2,300. Uncollectible-account expense is estimated as 4% of revenue.

▎Requirements

1. Journalize sales, collections, write-offs of uncollectibles, and uncollectible-account expense by the allowance method during October. Explanations are not required.
2. Show the ending balances in Accounts Receivable, Allowance for Uncollectible Accounts, and *Net* Accounts Receivable at October 31. How much does the store expect to collect?
3. Show how the store will report Accounts Receivable on its October 31 balance sheet.

E5-23A (*Learning Objective 3: Using the direct write-off method for bad debts*)   Refer to Exercise 5-22A.

I Requirements

1. Record uncollectible-account expense for October by the direct write-off method.
2. What amount of accounts receivable would Hilly Mountain report on its October 31 balance sheet under the direct write-off method? Does it expect to collect the full amount?

E5-24A (*Learning Objective 3: Using the aging approach to estimate bad debts*)   At December 31, 2010, before any year-end adjustments, the Accounts Receivable balance of Alpha Company is $210,000. The Allowance for Doubtful Accounts has a $13,500 credit balance. Alpha Company prepares the following aging schedule for Accounts Receivable:

■ **spreadsheet**

		Age of Accounts			
Total Balance		1–30 Days	31–60 Days	61–90 Days	Over 90 Days
$210,000		$80,000	$60,000	$40,000	$30,000
Estimated uncollectible		0.6%	4.0%	5.0%	40.0%

I Requirements

1. Based on the aging of accounts receivable, is the unadjusted balance of the allowance account adequate? Too high? Too low?
2. Make the entry required by the aging schedule. Prepare a T-account for the allowance.
3. Show how Alpha Company will report Accounts Receivable on its December 31 balance sheet.

E5-25A (*Learning Objective 3: Measuring and accounting for uncollectibles*)   Assume Dogwood Leaf Foods, Inc., experienced the following revenue and accounts receivable write-offs:

	Service	Accounts Receivable Write-Offs in Month			
Month	Revenue	January	February	March	Totals
January	$ 6,700	$54	$ 89		$143
February	6,900		101	$ 34	135
March	7,000			112	112
	$20,600	$54	$190	$146	$390

Suppose Dogwood Leaf estimates that 1% of revenues will become uncollectible.

I Requirement

1. Journalize service revenue (all on account), bad-debt expense, and write-offs during March. Include explanations.

E5-26A (*Learning Objective 4: Recording notes receivable and accruing interest revenue*)   Record the following note receivable transactions in the journal of Aegean Realty. How much interest revenue did Aegean earn this year? Use a 365-day year for interest computations, and round interest amounts to the nearest dollar.

Sep	1	Loaned $15,000 cash to Carroll Fadal on a one-year, 10% note.
Nov	6	Performed service for Turf Masters, receiving a 90-day, 8% note for $12,000.
	16	Received a $4,000, six-month, 11% note on account from Voleron, Inc.
	30	Accrued interest revenue for the year.

E5-27A (*Learning Objective 4: Reporting the effects of note receivable transactions on the balance sheet and income statement*) Assume Port City Credit Union completed these transactions:

2010		
Apr	1	Loaned $125,000 to Lee Franz on a one-year, 12% note.
Dec	31	Accrued interest revenue on the Franz note.
2011		
Apr	1	Collected the maturity value of the note from Franz (principal plus interest).

Show what the company would report for these transactions on its 2010 and 2011 balance sheets and income statements.

E5-28A (*Learning Objective 5: Using the acid-test ratio and days' sales in receivables to evaluate a company*) Cherokee, Inc., reported the following items at December 31, 2010 and 2009:

Balance Sheets (Summarized)

	Year End			Year End	
	2010	2009		2010	2009
Current assets:			**Current liabilities:**		
Cash...	$ 3,000	$ 9,000	Accounts payable	$ 19,000	$ 20,500
Marketable securities	20,000	9,000	Other current liabilities	103,000	105,000
Accounts receivable, net	55,000	69,000	Long-term liabilities	15,000	16,000
Inventory	192,000	188,000			
Other current assets	2,000	2,000	Stockholders' equity......................	135,000	135,500
Long-term assets					
Total assets....................................	$272,000	$277,000	Total liabilities and equity..............	$272,000	$277,000

Income Statement (partial):	2010
Sales revenue..............................	$730,000

▌Requirement

1. Compute Cherokee's (a) acid-test ratio and (b) days' sales in average receivables for 2010. Evaluate each ratio value as strong or weak. Cherokee sells on terms of net 30 days.

E5-29A (*Learning Objective 5: Analyzing a company's financial statements*) Modern Co., Inc., the electronics and appliance chain, reported these figures in millions of dollars:

	2011	2010
Net sales...	$573,000	$604,000
Receivables at end of year	3,910	4,710

Requirements

1. Compute Modern's average collection period during 2011.
2. Is Modern's collection period long or short? Viflex Networks takes 40 days to collect its average level of receivables. Domarko, the overnight shipper, takes 34 days. What causes Modern's collection period to be so different?

(Group B)

E5-30B (*Learning Objective 1: Accounting for a trading investment*)   River Corporation, the investment banking company, often has extra cash to invest. Suppose River buys 600 shares of Eathen, Inc., stock at $40 per share. Assume River expects to hold the Eathen stock for one month and then sell it. The purchase occurs on December 15, 2010. At December 31, the market price of a share of Eathen stock is $48 per share.

Requirements

1. What type of investment is this to River? Give the reason for your answer.
2. Record River's purchase of the Eathen stock on December 15 and the adjustment to market value on December 31.
3. Show how River would report this investment on its balance sheet at December 31 and any gain or loss on its income statement for the year ended December 31, 2010.

E5-31B (*Learning Objective 1: Reporting a trading investment*)   On November 16, SRO, Inc., paid $98,000 for an investment in the stock of Northwest Pacific Railway (NPR). SRO intends to account for these shares as trading securities. On December 12, SRO received a $700 cash dividend from NPR. It is now December 31, and the market value of the NPR stock is $94,000. For this investment, show what SRO should report in its income statement and balance sheet.

E5-32B (*Learning Objective 1: Accounting for a trading investment*)   Eastern Corporation reports short-term investments on its balance sheet. Suppose a division of Eastern completed the following short-term investment transactions during 2010:

2010	
Dec 12	Purchased 600 shares of Music, Inc., stock for $46,800. Eastern plans to sell the stock at a profit in the near future.
21	Received a cash dividend of $0.52 per share on the Music, Inc., stock.
31	Adjusted the investment in Music, Inc., stock. Current market value is $48,600. Eastern still plans to sell the stock in early 2011.
2011	
Jan 16	Sold the Music, Inc., stock for $66,465.

Requirement

1. Prepare T-accounts for Cash, Short-Term Investment, Dividend Revenue, Unrealized Gain (Loss) on Investment, and Gain on Sale of Investment. Show the effects of Eastern's investment transactions. Start with a cash balance of $94,000; all the other accounts start at zero.

E5-33B (*Learning Objective 3: Reporting bad debts by the allowance method*)   At December 31, 2010, White's Travel has an accounts receivable balance of $92,000. Allowance for Doubtful Accounts has a credit balance of $820 before the year-end adjustment. Service revenue for 2010 was $500,000. White's Travel estimates that doubtful-account expense for the year is 4% of sales. Make the December 31 entry to record doubtful-account expense. Show how the Accounts Receivable and the Allowance for Doubtful Accounts are reported on the balance sheet.

E5-34B (*Learning Objective 3: Using the allowance method for bad debts*) On April 30, Hilltop Party Planners had a $33,000 balance in Accounts Receivable and a $4,000 credit balance in Allowance for Uncollectible Accounts. During May, the store made credit sales of $156,000. May collections on account were $132,000, and write-offs of uncollectible receivables totaled $2,300. Uncollectible-account expense is estimated as 2% of revenue.

▌Requirements

1. Journalize sales, collections, write-offs of uncollectibles, and uncollectible-account expense by the allowance method during May. Explanations are not required.
2. Show the ending balances in Accounts Receivable, Allowance for Uncollectible Accounts, and *Net* Accounts Receivable at May 31. How much does the store expect to collect?
3. Show how the store will report Accounts Receivable on its May 31 balance sheet.

E5-35B (*Learning Objective 3: Using the direct write-off method for bad debts*) Refer to Exercise 5-34B.

▌Requirements

1. Record uncollectible-account expense for May by the direct write-off method.
2. What amount of accounts receivable would Hilltop report on its May 31 balance sheet under the direct write-off method? Does it expect to collect the full amount?

■ spreadsheet

E5-36B (*Learning Objective 3: Using the aging approach to estimate bad debts*) At December 31, 2010, before any year-end adjustments, the accounts receivable balance of Digital Electronics Company is $150,000. The allowance for doubtful accounts has a $6,800 credit balance. Digital Electronics Company prepares the following aging schedule for accounts receivable:

	Age of Accounts			
Total Balance	1–30 Days	31–60 Days	61–90 Days	Over 90 Days
$150,000	$60,000	$50,000	$30,000	$10,000
Estimated uncollectible	0.6%	4.0%	7.0%	40.0%

▌Requirements

1. Based on the aging of accounts receivable, is the unadjusted balance of the allowance account adequate? Too high? Too low?
2. Make the entry required by the aging schedule. Prepare a T-account for the allowance.
3. Show how Digital Electronics Company will report Accounts Receivable on its December 31 balance sheet.

E5-37B (*Learning Objective 3: Measuring and accounting for uncollectibles*) Assume Birch Leaf Foods, Inc., experienced the following revenue and accounts receivable write-offs:

Month	Service Revenue	Accounts Receivable Write-Offs in Month			
		January	February	March	Totals
January	$ 6,550	$53	$ 85		$138
February	6,750		100	$ 35	135
March	6,850			110	110
	$20,150	$53	$185	$145	$383

Suppose Birch Leaf estimates that 1% of revenues will become uncollectible.

Ⅰ Requirement

1. Journalize service revenue (all on account), bad-debt expense, and write-offs during March. Include explanations.

E5-38B (*Learning Objective 4: Recording notes receivable and accruing interest revenue*) Record the following note receivable transactions in the journal of Celtic Realty. How much interest revenue did Celtic earn this year? Use a 365-day year for interest computations, and round interest amounts to the nearest dollar.

Apr	1	Loaned $11,000 cash to Britt Durant on a one-year, 6% note.
Jun	6	Performed service for Putt Masters, receiving a 90-day, 7% note for $14,000.
	16	Received a $3,000, six-month, 12% note on account from Voleron, Inc.
	30	Accrued interest revenue for the year.

E5-39B (*Learning Objective 4: Reporting the effects of note receivable transactions on the balance sheet and income statement*)   Assume Tradesmen Credit Union completed these transactions:

2010		
Apr	1	Loaned $50,000 to Leanne Harold on a one-year, 7% note.
Dec	31	Accrued interest revenue on the Harold note.
2011		
Apr	1	Collected the maturity value of the note from Harold (principal plus interest).

Show what the company would report for these transactions on its 2010 and 2011 balance sheets and income statements.

E5-40B (*Learning Objective 5: Using the acid-test ratio and days' sales in receivables to evaluate a company*)   Navajo, Inc., reported the following items at December 31, 2010 and 2009:

Balance Sheets (Summarized)

	Year End 2010	Year End 2009		Year End 2010	Year End 2009
Current assets:			**Current liabilities:**		
Cash...	$ 4,000	$ 10,000	Accounts payable........................	$ 15,000	$ 16,500
Marketable securities	23,000	12,000	Other current liabilities..............	105,000	107,000
Accounts receivable, net..............	56,000	70,000	Long-term liabilities	15,000	16,000
Inventory	192,000	188,000			
Other current assets	6,000	6,000	Stockholders' equity......................	146,000	146,500
Long-term assets					
Total assets.....................................	$281,000	$286,000	Total liabilities and equity..............	$281,000	$286,000

Income Statement (partial):	2010
Sales revenue.............................	$727,000

❙ *Requirement*

1. Compute Navajo's (a) acid-test ratio and (b) days' sales in average receivables for 2010. Evaluate each ratio value as strong or weak. Navajo sells on terms of net 30 days.

E5-41B (*Learning Objective 5: Analyzing a company's financial statements*) Contemporary Co., Inc., the electronics and appliance chain, reported these figures in millions of dollars:

	2011	2010
Net sales..	$572,000	$601,000
Receivables at end of year	3,880	4,810

❙ *Requirements*

1. Compute Contemporary's average collection period during 2011.
2. Is Contemporary's collection period long or short? Kurzwel Networks takes 36 days to collect its average level of receivables. Damascus, the overnight shipper, takes 35 days. What causes Contemporary's collection period to be so different?

Challenge Exercises

E5-42 (*Learning Objective 2: Determining whether to sell on bankcards*)   Radical Shirt Company sells on credit and manages its own receivables. Average experience for the past three years has been as follows:

	Cash	Credit	Total
Sales..	$350,000	$350,000	$700,000
Cost of goods sold.............................	192,500	192,500	385,000
Uncollectible-account expense...........	—	18,000	18,000
Other expenses..................................	87,500	87,500	175,000

Jack Ryan, the owner, is considering whether to accept bankcards (VISA, MasterCard). Ryan expects total sales to increase by 12% but cash sales to remain unchanged. If Ryan switches to bankcards, the business can save $9,000 on other expenses, but VISA and MasterCard charge 2% on bankcard sales. Ryan figures that the increase in sales will be due to the increased volume of bankcard sales.

❙ *Requirement*

1. Should Radical Shirt Company start selling on bankcards? Show the computations of net income under the present plan and under the bankcard plan.

E5-43 (*Learning Objective 3: Reconstructing receivables and bad-debt amounts*) Suppose Diamond, Inc., reported net receivables of $2,586 million and $2,268 million at January 31, 2011, and 2010, after subtracting allowances of $70 million and $64 million at these respective dates. Diamond earned total revenue of $53,333 million (all on account) and recorded doubtful-account expense of $16 million for the year ended January 31, 2011.

❙ *Requirement*

1. Use this information to measure the following amounts for the year ended January 31, 2011:
   a. Write-offs of uncollectible receivables
   b. Collections from customers

Quiz

Test your understanding of receivables by answering the following questions. Select the best choice from among the possible answers given.

Q5-44 United First Bank, the nationwide banking company, owns many types of investments. Assume that United First Bank paid $700,000 for trading securities on December 3. Two weeks later United First Bank received a $37,000 cash dividend. At December 31, these trading securities were quoted at a market price of $705,000. United First Bank's December income statement should report:

a. unrealized loss of $5,000.   c. both a and b.
b. unrealized loss of $3,000.   d. none of the above.

Q5-45 Refer to the United First Bank data in Quiz question 5-44. At December 31, United First Bank's balance sheet should report:

a. dividend revenue of $37,000.   c. short-term investment of $705,000.
b. short-term investment of $700,000.   d. unrealized gain of $5,000.

Q5-46 Under the allowance method for uncollectible receivables, the entry to record uncollectible-account expense has what effect on the financial statements?

a. Decreases owners' equity and increases liabilities
b. Increases expenses and increases owners' equity
c. Decreases assets and has no effect on net income
d. Decreases net income and decreases assets

Q5-47 Vincent Company uses the aging method to adjust the allowance for uncollectible accounts at the end of the period. At December 31, 2010, the balance of accounts receivable is $200,000 and the allowance for uncollectible accounts has a credit balance of $4,000 (before adjustment). An analysis of accounts receivable produced the following age groups:

Current	$160,000
60 days past due........................	32,000
Over 60 days past due...............	8,000
	$200,000

Based on past experience, Vincent estimates that the percentage of accounts that will prove to be uncollectible within the three age groups is 4%, 10%, and 21%, respectively. Based on these facts, the adjusting entry for uncollectible accounts should be made in the amount of

a. $7,280.   c. $16,280.
b. $11,280.   d. $2,000.

Q5-48 Refer to Question 5-47. The net receivables on the balance sheet is _____.

Q5-49 Graham Company uses the percent-of-sales method to estimate uncollectibles. Net credit sales for the current year amount to $130,000 and management estimates 3% will be uncollectible. Allowance for doubtful accounts prior to adjustment has a credit balance of $2,000. The amount of expense to report on the income statement will be

a. $3,900.   c. $1,000.
b. $5,200.   d. $5,900.

Q5-50 Refer to question 5-49. The balance of Allowance for Doubtful Accounts, after adjustment, will be

a. $7,900.
b. $1,000.
c. $5,900.
d. $5,200.
e. Cannot be determined from the information given.

Q5-51 Refer to Quiz questions 5-49 and 5-50. The following year, Graham Company wrote off $3,900 of old receivables as uncollectible. What is the balance in the Allowance account now?

Questions 5-52 through 5-56 use the following data:

On August 1, 2010, Botores, Inc., sold equipment and accepted a six-month, 12%, $50,000 note receivable. Botores' year-end is December 31.

Q5-52 How much interest revenue should Botores accrue on December 31, 2010?

a. $6,000

b. $3,000

c. $2,500

d. Some other amount

Q5-53 If Botores, Inc., fails to make an adjusting entry for the accrued interest,

a. net income will be overstated and liabilities will be understated.

b. net income will be overstated and assets will be overstated.

c. net income will be understated and liabilities will be overstated.

d. net income will be understated and assets will be understated.

Q5-54 How much interest does Botores, Inc., expect to collect on the maturity date (February 1, 2011)?

a. $3,000

b. $6,000

c. $2,500

d. Some other amount

Q5-55 Which of the following accounts will Botores credit in the journal entry at maturity on February 1, 2011, assuming collection in full?

a. Cash

b. Interest Payable

c. Note Payable

d. Interest Receivable

Q5-56 Write the journal entry on the maturity date (February 1, 2011).

Q5-57 Which of the following is included in the calculation of the acid-test ratio?

a. Prepaid expenses and cash

b. Cash and accounts receivable

c. Inventory and prepaid expenses

d. Inventory and short-term investment

Q5-58 A company with net sales of $1,017,000, beginning net receivables of $110,000, and ending net receivables of $120,000, has days' sales in accounts receivable of

a. 38 days.

b. 47 days.

c. 41 days.

d. 44 days.

Q5-59 A company sells on credit terms of "net 30 days" and has days' sales in account receivable of 30 days. Its days' sales in receivables is

a. too high.

b. too low.

c. about right.

d. cannot be evaluated from the data given.

Problems

MyAccountingLab | All of the A and B problems can be found within MyAccountingLab, an online homework and practice environment. Your instructor may ask you to complete these problems using MyAccountingLab.

(Group A)

P5-60A (*Learning Objective 1: Accounting for a trading investment*) During the fourth quarter of 2010, Cable, Inc., generated excess cash, which the company invested in trading securities as follows:

2010	
Nov 18	Purchased 900 common shares as an investment in trading securities, paying $12 per share.
Dec 15	Received cash dividend of $0.48 per share on the trading securities.
Dec 31	Adjusted the trading securities to their market value of $8 per share.

❙ Requirements

1. Open T-accounts for Cash (including its beginning balance of $15,000), Short-Term Investments, Dividend Revenue, and Unrealized Gain (Loss) on Investment.
2. Journalize the foregoing transactions and post to the T-accounts.
3. Show how to report the short-term investment on Cable's balance sheet at December 31.
4. Show how to report whatever should appear on Cable's income statement for the year ended December 31, 2010.
5. Cable sold the trading securities for $8,388 on January 12, 2011. Journalize the sale.

P5-61A (*Learning Objective 2: Controlling cash receipts from customers*) Laptop Delivery, Inc., makes all sales on account. Sarah Carter, accountant for the company, receives and opens incoming mail. Company procedure requires Carter to separate customer checks from the remittance slips, which list the amounts that Carter posts as credits to customer accounts receivable. Carter deposits the checks in the bank. At the end of each day she computes the day's total amount posted to customer accounts and matches this total to the bank deposit slip. This procedure ensures that all receipts are deposited in the bank.

writing assignment ■

❙ Requirement

1. As a consultant hired by Laptop Delivery, Inc., write a memo to management evaluating the company's internal controls over cash receipts from customers. If the system is effective, identify its strong features. If the system has flaws, propose a way to strengthen the controls.

P5-62A (*Learning Objective 3: Accounting for revenue, collections, and uncollectibles; percent-of-sales method*)   This problem takes you through the accounting for sales, receivables, and uncollectibles for Mail Time Corp., the overnight shipper. By selling on credit, the company cannot expect to collect 100% of its accounts receivable. At May 31, 2010, and 2011, respectively, Mail Time Corp. reported the following on its balance sheet (in millions of dollars):

writing assignment ■

	May 31,	
	2011	2010
Accounts receivable	$3,697	$3,434
Less: Allowance for uncollectible accounts	(126)	(155)
Accounts receivable, net	$3,571	$3,279

During the year ended May 31, 2011, Mail Time Corp. earned service revenue and collected cash from customers. Assume uncollectible-account expense for the year was 1% of service revenue and that Mail Time wrote off uncollectible receivables. At year-end Mail Time ended with the foregoing May 31, 2011, balances.

❙ Requirements

1. Prepare T-accounts for Accounts Receivable and Allowance for Uncollectibles and insert the May 31, 2010, balances as given.
2. Journalize the following assumed transactions of Mail Time Corp. for the year ended May 31, 2011 (explanations are not required): Reference pg 306
   a. Service revenue on account, $32,481 million
   b. Collections from customers on account, $31,864 million
   c. Uncollectible-account expense, 2% of service revenue
   d. Write-offs of uncollectible accounts receivable, $354 million
3. Post your entries to the Accounts Receivable and the Allowance for Uncollectibles T-accounts.
4. Compute the ending balances for the two T-accounts and compare your balances to the actual May 31, 2011, amounts. They should be the same.
5. Show what Mail Time would report on its income statement for the year ended May 31, 2011.

P5-63A (*Learning Objective 3: Using the aging approach for uncollectibles*) The September 30, 2011, records of Perfecto Communications include these accounts:

Accounts Receivable.....................................	$250,000
Allowance for Doubtful Accounts..............	(8,200)

During the year, Perfecto Communications estimates doubtful-account expense at 1% of credit sales. At year-end (December 31), the company ages its receivables and adjusts the balance in Allowance for Doubtful Accounts to correspond to the aging schedule. During the last quarter of 2011, the company completed the following selected transactions:

Nov 30	Wrote off as uncollectible the $1,400 account receivable from Black Carpets and the $600 account receivable from Old Timer Antiques.
Dec 31	Adjusted the Allowance for Doubtful Accounts and recorded doubtful-account expense at year-end, based on the aging of receivables, which follows.

	Age of Accounts			
Accounts Receivable	1–30 Days	31–60 Days	61–90 Days	Over 90 Days
$232,000	$140,000	$45,000	$18,000	$29,000
Estimated percent uncollectible	0.1%	1%	10%	30%

❚ *Requirements*

1. Record the transactions in the journal. Explanations are not required.
2. Prepare a T-account for Allowance for Doubtful Accounts and post to that account.
3. Show how Perfecto Communications will report its accounts receivable in a comparative balance sheet for 2010 and 2011. Use the three-line reporting format. At December 31, 2010, the company's Accounts Receivable balance was $214,000 and the Allowance for Doubtful Accounts stood at $4,600.

P5-64A (*Learning Objectives 1, 3, 5: Correcting current asset accounts and recomputing ratios*)   Assume Smith & Jones, the accounting firm, advises Ocean Mist Seafood that its financial statements must be changed to conform to GAAP. At December 31, 2010, Ocean Mist's accounts include the following:

Cash...	$ 53,000
Short-term investment in trading securities, at cost..............	24,000
Accounts receivable...	36,000
Inventory...	63,000
Prepaid expenses	10,000
Total current assets	$186,000
Accounts payable...	$ 67,000
Other current liabilities..	39,000
Total current liabilities...	$106,000

The accounting firm advised Ocean Mist that

- Cash includes $17,000 that is deposited in a compensating balance account that is tied up until 2012.

- The market value of the trading securities is $10,000. Ocean Mist purchased the investments a couple of weeks ago.
- Ocean Mist has been using the direct write-off method to account for uncollectible receivables. During 2010, Ocean Mist wrote off bad receivables of $7,500. Smith & Jones determines that uncollectible-account expense should be 3% of sales revenue, which totaled $600,000 in 2010. The aging of Ocean Mist's receivables at year-end indicated uncollectibles of $10,500.
- Ocean Mist reported net income of $92,000 in 2010.

I Requirements

1. Restate Ocean Mist's current accounts to conform to GAAP. (Challenge)
2. Compute Ocean Mist's current ratio and acid-test ratio both before and after your corrections.
3. Determine Ocean Mist's correct net income for 2010. (Challenge)

P5-65A (*Learning Objective 4: Accounting for notes receivable and accrued interest revenue*)   Healthy Meal completed the following selected transactions.

■ **general ledger**

2010	
Oct 31	Sold goods to Buy Low Foods, receiving a $34,000, three-month, 5.25% note.
Dec 31	Made an adjusting entry to accrue interest on the Buy Low Foods note.
2011	
Jan 31	Collected the Buy Low Foods note.
Feb 18	Received a 90-day, 7.75%, $7,600 note from Dutton Market on account.
19	Sold the Dutton Market note to Amherst Bank, receiving cash of $7,400. (Debit the difference to financing expense.)
Nov 11	Lent $14,600 cash to Street Provisions, receiving a 90-day, 10.00% note.
Dec 31	Accrued the interest on the Street Provisions note.

I Requirements

1. Record the transactions in Healthy Meal's journal. Round interest amounts to the nearest dollar. Explanations are not required.
2. Show what Healthy Meal will report on its comparative classified balance sheet at December 31, 2011, and December 31, 2010.

P5-66A (*Learning Objective 5: Using ratio data to evaluate a company's financial position*) The comparative financial statements of Highland Pools, Inc., for 2011, 2010, and 2009 included the following select data:

■ **spreadsheet**

	(In millions)		
	2011	**2010**	**2009**
Balance sheet			
Current assets:			
Cash...	$ 80	$ 70	$ 60
Short-term investments	145	170	120
Receivables, net of allowance for doubtful accounts of $7, $6, and $4, respectively	270	250	240
Inventories	355	345	300
Prepaid expenses	60	30	55
Total current assets	$ 910	$ 865	$ 775
Total current liabilities....................	$ 580	$ 620	$ 690
Income statement			
Net sales	$5,880	$5,130	$4,220

Requirements

1. Compute these ratios for 2011 and 2010:
   a. Current ratio
   b. Acid-test ratio
   c. Days' sales in receivables
2. Which ratios improved from 2010 to 2011 and which ratios deteriorated? Is this trend favorable or unfavorable?

(Group B)

P5-67B (*Learning Objective 1: Accounting for a trading investment*)   During the fourth quarter of 2010, Main St., Inc., generated excess cash, which the company invested in trading securities, as follows:

2010	
Nov 13	Purchased 1,200 common shares as an investment in trading securities, paying $10 per share.
Dec 14	Received cash dividend of $0.48 per share on the trading securities.
Dec 31	Adjusted the securities to their market value of $7 per share.

Requirements

1. Open T-accounts for Cash (including its beginning balance of $22,000), Short-Term Investment, Dividend Revenue, and Unrealized Gain (Loss) on Investment.
2. Journalize the foregoing transactions and post to the T-accounts.
3. Show how to report the short-term investment on Main St.'s balance sheet at December 31.
4. Show how to report whatever should appear on Main St.'s income statement for the year ended December 31, 2010.
5. Main St. sold the trading securities for $10,512 on January 21, 2011. Journalize the sale.

writing assignment ■

P5-68B (*Learning Objective 2: Controlling cash receipts from customers*)   Lakeview Software Solutions makes all sales on account, so virtually all cash receipts arrive in the mail. Larry Higgins, the company president, has just returned from a trade association meeting with new ideas for the business. Among other things, Higgins plans to institute stronger internal controls over cash receipts from customers.

Requirement

1. Take the role of Larry Higgins, the company president. Write a memo to employees outlining procedures to ensure that all cash receipts are deposited in the bank and that the total amounts of each day's cash receipts are posted to customer accounts receivable.

writing assignment ■

P5-69B (*Learning Objective 3: Accounting for revenue, collections, and uncollectibles; percent-of-sales method*)   This problem takes you through the accounting for sales, receivables, and uncollectibles for Dependable Delivery Corp, the overnight shipper. By selling on credit, the company cannot expect to collect 100% of its accounts receivable. At May 31, 2010, and 2011, respectively, Dependable Delivery Corp. reported the following on its balance sheet (in millions of dollars):

	May 31, 2011	May 31, 2010
Accounts receivable	$3,693	$3,435
Less: Allowance for uncollectible accounts	(129)	(156)
Accounts receivable, net	$3,564	$3,279

During the year ended May 31, 2011, Dependable Delivery Corp. earned sales revenue and collected cash from customers. Assume uncollectible-account expense for the year was 1% of service revenue and Dependable Delivery wrote off uncollectible receivables. At year end, Dependable Delivery ended with the foregoing May 31, 2011 balances.

I Requirements

1. Prepare T-accounts for Accounts Receivable and Allowance for Uncollectibles, and insert the May 31, 2010, balances as given.
2. Journalize the following transactions of Dependable Delivery for the year ended May 31, 2011. (Explanations are not required.)
   a. Service revenue on account, $32,487 million.
   b. Collections from customers on account, $31,877 million.
   c. Uncollectible-account expense, 1% of service revenue.
   d. Write-offs of uncollectible accounts receivable, $352 million.
3. Post to the Accounts Receivable and Allowance for Uncollectibles T-accounts.
4. Compute the ending balances for the two T-accounts and compare your balances to the actual May 31, 2011, amounts. They should be the same.
5. Show what Dependable Delivery should report on its income statement for the year ended May 31, 2011.

P5-70B (*Learning Objective 3: Using the aging approach for uncollectibles*) The September 30, 2011, records of Image Communications include these accounts:

■ **general ledger**

Accounts Receivable......................................	$260,000
Allowance for Doubtful Accounts..............	(8,100)

During the year, Image Communications estimates doubtful-account expense at 1% of credit sales. At year-end, the company ages its receivables and adjusts the balance in Allowance for Doubtful Accounts to correspond to the aging schedule. During the last quarter of 2011, the company completed the following selected transactions:

Dec 28	Wrote off as uncollectible the $1,500 account receivable from Blue Carpets and the $400 account receivable from Show-N-Tell Antiques.
Dec 31	Adjusted the Allowance for Doubtful Accounts and recorded doubtful-account expense at year-end, based on the aging of receivables, which follows.

	Age of Accounts			
Accounts Receivable	1–30 Days	31–60 Days	61–90 Days	Over 90 Days
$230,000	$160,000	$35,000	$14,000	$21,000
Estimated percent uncollectible	0.2%	1%	5%	30%

I Requirements

1. Record the transactions in the journal. Explanations are not required.
2. Prepare a T-account for Allowance for Doubtful Accounts and post to that account.
3. Show how Image Communications will report its accounts receivable in a comparative balance sheet for 2011 and 2010. Use the three line reporting format. At December 31, 2010, the company's Accounts Receivable balance was $213,000 and the Allowance for Doubtful Accounts stood at $4,200.

P5-71B (*Learning Objectives 1, 3, 5: Correcting current asset accounts and recomputing ratios*)   Assume Smith & Jones, the accounting firm, advises Catch of the Day Seafood that its financial statement must be changed to conform to GAAP. At December 31, 2010, Catch of the Day's accounts include the following:

Cash...	$ 56,000
Short-term trading securities, at cost	18,000
Accounts receivable.......................................	44,000
Inventory...	55,000
Prepaid expenses	16,000
Total current assets	$189,000
Accounts payable	$ 58,000
Other current liabilities.................................	38,000
Total current liabilities..............................	$ 96,000

The accounting firm advised Catch of the Day that

- Cash includes $24,000 that is deposited in a compensating balance account that will be tied up until 2012.
- The market value of the trading securities is $11,000. Catch of the Day purchased the trading securities a couple of weeks ago.
- Catch of the Day has been using the direct write-off method to account for uncollectible receivables. During 2010, Catch of the Day wrote off bad receivables of $5,500. Smith & Jones determines that uncollectible-account expense should be 3% of service revenue, which totaled $670,000 in 2010. The aging of Catch of the Day's receivables at year-end indicated uncollectibles of $14,600.
- Catch of the Day reported net income of $99,000 for 2010.

❙ Requirements

1. Restate Catch of the Day's current accounts to conform to GAAP. (Challenge)
2. Compute Catch of the Day's current ratio and acid-test ratio both before and after your corrections.
3. Determine Catch of the Day's correct net income for 2010. (Challenge)

❚ general ledger

P5-72B (*Learning Objective 4: Accounting for notes receivable and accrued interest revenue*)   Quick Meals completed the following selected transactions:

2010	
Nov 30	Sold goods to Bragg Market, receiving a $32,000, three-month, 4.00% note.
Dec 31	Made an adjusting entry to accrue interest on the Bragg Market note.
2011	
Feb 28	Collected the Bragg Market note.
Mar 1	Received a 90-day, 8.00%, $7,200 note from Don's Market on account.
1	Sold the Don's Market note to Chelmsford Bank, receiving cash of $7,000. (Debit the difference to financing expense.)
Dec 16	Lent $15,400 cash to Stratford Provisions, receiving a 90-day, 9.50% note.
Dec 31	Accrued the interest on the Stratford Provisions note.

❙ Requirements

1. Record the transactions in Quick Meals' journal. Round all amounts to the nearest dollar. Explanations are not required.
2. Show what Quick Meals will report on its comparative classified balance sheet at December 31, 2011, and December 31, 2010.

P5-73B (*Learning Objective 5: Using ratio data to evaluate a company's financial position*)   The comparative financial statements of Gold Pools, Inc., for 2011, 2010, and 2009 included the following select data:

	(In millions)		
	2011	2010	2009
Balance sheet			
Current assets:			
Cash...	$ 70	$ 80	$ 50
Short-term investments	145	160	110
Receivables, net of allowance for doubtful accounts of $7, $6, and $4, respectively	290	260	230
Inventories	360	345	310
Prepaid expenses.........................	70	10	40
Total current assets	$ 935	$ 855	$ 740
Total current liabilities...................	$ 560	$ 610	$ 680
Income statement			
Net sales	$5,890	$5,150	$4,200

I **Requirements**

1. Compute these ratios for 2011 and 2010:
   a. Current ratio
   b. Acid-test ratio
   c. Days' sales in receivables
2. Which ratios improved from 2010 to 2011 and which ratios deteriorated? Is this trend favorable or unfavorable?

APPLY YOUR KNOWLEDGE

Decision Cases

Case 1. (*Learning Objective 3: Using accounts receivable data to reconstruct revenues, collections, and bad debts on receivables*)   A fire during 2010 destroyed most of the accounting records of Clearview Cablevision, Inc. The only accounting data for 2010 that Clearview can come up with are the following balances at December 31, 2010. The general manager also knows that bad-debt expense should be 5% of service revenue.

Accounts receivable	$180,000
Less: Allowance for bad debts.................................	(22,000)
Total expenses, excluding bad-debt expense.............	670,000
Collections from customers.....................................	840,000
Write-offs of bad receivables...................................	30,000
Accounts receivable, December 31, 2009	110,000

Prepare a summary income statement for Clearview Cablevision, Inc., for the year ended December 31, 2010. The stockholders want to know whether the company was profitable in 2010. Use a T-account for Accounts Receivable to compute service revenue.

Case 2. (*Learning Objective 3: Estimating the collectibility of accounts receivable*) Suppose you work in the loan department of Superior Bank. Dean Young, owner of Dean Young Beauty Aids, has come to you seeking a loan for $500,000 to expand operations. Young proposes to use accounts receivable as collateral for the loan and has provided you with the following information from the company's most recent financial statements:

	2011	2010	2009
	(In thousands)		
Sales	$1,475	$1,001	$902
Cost of goods sold	876	647	605
Gross profit	599	354	297
Other expenses	518	287	253
Net profit or (loss) before taxes	$ 81	$ 67	$ 44
Accounts receivable	$ 128	$ 107	$ 94
Allowance for doubtful accounts	13	11	9

❚ Requirement

1. Analyze the trends of sales, days' sales in receivables, and cash collections from customers for 2011 and 2010. Would you make the loan to Young? Support your decision with facts and figures.

Ethical Issue

Sunnyvale Loan Company is in the consumer loan business. Sunnyvale borrows from banks and loans out the money at higher interest rates. Sunnyvale's bank requires Sunnyvale to submit quarterly financial statements to keep its line of credit. Sunnyvale's main asset is Notes Receivable. Therefore, Uncollectible-Account Expense and Allowance for Uncollectible Accounts are important accounts for the company.

Kimberly Burnham, the company's owner, prefers that net income reflect a steady increase in a smooth pattern, rather than increase in some periods and decrease in other periods. To report smoothly increasing net income, Burnham underestimates Uncollectible-Account Expense in some periods. In other periods, Burnham overestimates the expense. She reasons that the income overstatements roughly offset the income understatements over time.

❚ Requirements

1. What is the ethical issue in this situation?
2. Who are the stakeholders? What are the possible consequences to each?
3. Analyze the alternatives from the following standpoints: (a) economic, (b) legal, (c) ethical.
4. What would you do? How would you justify your decision?

Focus on Financials: ■ Amazon.com, Inc.

(*Learning Objectives 2, 3: Accounting for receivables*) Refer to **Amazon.com, Inc.'s** Consolidated Balance Sheets as well as Note 1—Description of Business and Accounting Policies, in Appendix A at the end of this book.

1. The fourth account listed on Amazon.com's Consolidated Balance Sheet is called "accounts receivable, net and other." What does the "net" mean? The "other"?
2. Refer to Note 1. What kinds of accounts receivable are included in Amazon.com, Inc.'s receivables?
3. How much is the allowance for doubtful accounts in 2008 and 2007?

Focus on Analysis: ■ Foot Locker, Inc.

(*Learning Objective 1: Analyzing short-term investments*) This case is based on the **Foot Locker, Inc.'s** consolidated balance sheets, consolidated statements of cash flows, and Footnote 6 of its financial statements in Appendix B at the end of this book.

1. What securities are included in Foot Locker's Short-term investments? What type of securities are they?

2. Make a T-account for Short-term investments. Record $249 as the balance in the account as of the end of 2006. Using the information in the investments section of the Consolidated Statement of Cash Flows, record the cash purchases and sales of short-term investments during 2007. Why doesn't the ending balance equal the amount shown on the balance sheet as of the end of 2007?

Group Project

Jillian Michaels and Dee Childress worked for several years as sales representatives for Xerox Corporation. During this time, they became close friends as they acquired expertise with the company's full range of copier equipment. Now they see an opportunity to put their expertise to work and fulfill lifelong desires to establish their own business. Navarro Community College, located in their city, is expanding, and there is no copy center within five miles of the campus. Business in the area is booming, office buildings and apartments are springing up, and the population of the Navarro section of the city is growing.

Michaels and Childress want to open a copy center, similar to FedEx Kinko's, near the Navarro campus. A small shopping center across the street from the college has a vacancy that would fit their needs. Michaels and Childress each have $35,000 to invest in the business, but they forecast the need for $200,000 to renovate the store and purchase some of the equipment they will need. Xerox Corporation will lease two large copiers to them at a total monthly rental of $6,000. With enough cash to see them through the first six months of operation, they are confident they can make the business succeed. The two women work very well together, and both have excellent credit ratings. Michaels and Childress must borrow $130,000 to start the business, advertise its opening, and keep it running for its first six months.

▌ Requirements

Assume two roles: (1) Michaels and Childress, the partners who will own Navarro Copy Center; and (2) loan officers at Synergy Bank.

1. As a group, visit a copy center to familiarize yourselves with its operations. If possible, interview the manager or another employee. Then write a loan request that Michaels and Childress will submit to Synergy Bank with the intent of borrowing $130,000 to be paid back over three years. The loan will be a personal loan to the partnership of Michaels and Childress, not to Navarro Copy Center. The request should specify all the details of Michaels' and Childress' plan that will motivate the bank to grant the loan. Include a budget for each of the first six months of operation of the proposed copy center.

2. As a group, interview a loan officer in a bank. Write Synergy Bank's reply to the loan request. Specify all the details that the bank should require as conditions for making the loan.

3. If necessary, modify the loan request or the bank's reply in order to reach agreement between the two parties.

For online homework, exercises, and problems that provide you with immediate feedback, please visit www.myaccountinglab.com.

Quick Check Answers

1. *a*
2. *a*
3. *c* ($40,000 × .04)
4. *b* ($600 + $1,600)
5. *c* ($1,030 − $600)
6. *b*
7. *d* ($10,000 − $1,030)
8. *d* ($2,800 − $90) − ($400 − $90)
9. *b* ($575,000 + $2,200,000 − $725,000)
10. *c* ($2,800 × .09 × 4/12 × 1/4)
11. *d* $70,000 + ($70,000 × .12 × 6/12)
12. *a*
13. *a* [($80,000 + $74,000)/2] ÷ ($803,000/365)
14. *a* ($6,000 + $3,000 + $9,000) ÷ ($10,000 + $4,000)

SPOTLIGHT: Williams-Sonoma, Inc.

You've just graduated from college, taken a job, and you're moving into an apartment. The place is unfurnished, so you'll need everything: furniture, rugs, dishes, pots, pans, and everything that goes with them. Where will you find these things? Williams-Sonoma, Inc., stores, its subsidiaries (Pottery Barn, Pottery Barn Bed and Bath, West Elm, Williams-Sonoma Home), and its e-commerce Web sites may get some of your business.

Williams-Sonoma, Inc., is a specialty retailer of high-style products for the home. As of February 3, 2008, the company operated 600 stores in 44 states, Washington, D.C., and Canada.

Williams-Sonoma, Inc.'s Consolidated Balance Sheets are summarized on the following page. You can see that the merchandise inventory is Williams-Sonoma's largest current asset. That's not surprising since Williams-Sonoma, like other retailers, attracts customers with the latest styles in home furnishings that they can purchase and take home immediately.

We also present Williams-Sonoma's Consolidated Statements of Earnings for the comparative fiscal years 2008 and 2007. As of the fiscal year ended 2008, a difficult economic recession was beginning to hit the company, as it did virtually all retail businesses. A few quick computations will show that, while net revenues increased by $217 million, total costs (cost of goods sold and selling, general, and administrative expenses) went up by a total of $231 million, causing the company's pre-tax earnings to decline by $21 million year-over-year.

Williams-Sonoma, Inc.
Consolidated Balance Sheets (Adapted)
Fiscal years 2008 and 2007

(in thousands)	2008	2007
ASSETS		
Current assets		
Cash and cash equivalents.................................	$ 118,950	$ 275,429
Accounts receivable..	48,052	48,821
Merchandise inventories	693,661	610,599
Prepaid expenses..	87,183	88,180
Other current assets	101,929	77,934
Total current assets	1,049,775	1,100,963
Property and equipment, net	981,075	912,582
Other non-current assets	63,004	34,786
Total assets..	$2,093,854	$2,048,331
LIABILITIES AND STOCKHOLDERS' EQUITY		
Current liabilities	$ 611,534	$ 627,734
Long-term liabilities	316,597	269,166
Total liabilities	928,131	896,900
Stockholders' equity..	1,165,723	1,151,431
Total liabilities and stockholders' equity	$2,093,854	$2,048,331

Williams-Sonoma, Inc.
Consolidated Statements of Earnings (Adapted)
Fiscal years 2008 and 2007

(in thousands)	2008	2007
Net revenues	$3,944,934	$3,727,513
Cost of goods sold...	2,408,963	2,240,226
Gross margin (gross profit)	1,535,971	1,487,287
Selling, general, and administrative expenses..............	1,222,573	1,159,786
Interest (income), net..	(2,942)	(9,685)
Earnings before income taxes.............................	316,340	337,186
Income taxes	120,583	128,318
Net earnings..	$ 195,757	$ 208,868

You can see that cost of goods sold is by far Williams-Sonoma's largest expense. The title *Cost of Goods Sold* perfectly describes that expense. In short,

- Williams-Sonoma buys inventory, an asset carried on the books at cost.
- The goods that Williams-Sonoma sells are no longer Williams-Sonoma's assets. The cost of inventory that's sold gets shifted into the expense account, Cost of Goods Sold.

Merchandise inventory is the heart of a merchandising business, and cost of goods sold is the most important expense for a company that sells goods rather than services. Gross profit (or gross margin) is the difference between net sales and cost of goods sold. This chapter covers the accounting for inventory and cost of goods sold. It also shows you how to analyze financial statements. Here we focus on inventory, cost of goods sold, and gross profit.

LEARNING OBJECTIVES

1 **Account** for inventory

2 **Understand** the various inventory methods

3 **Use** gross profit percentage and inventory turnover to evaluate operations

4 **Estimate** inventory by the gross profit method

5 **Show** how inventory errors affect the financial statements

ACCOUNTING FOR INVENTORY

We begin by showing how the financial statements of a merchandiser such as Williams-Sonoma, Inc., or The Gap, Inc., differ from those of service entities such as FedEx and Century 21 Real Estate. The financial statements in Exhibit 6-1 (p. 344) highlight how service entities differ from merchandisers (dollar amounts are assumed).

> OBJECTIVE
>
> **1** **Account** for inventory

The basic concept of accounting for merchandise inventory can be illustrated with an example. Suppose Pottery Barn (a subsidiary company of Williams-Sonoma, Inc.) has in stock three chairs that cost $300 each. Pottery Barn marks the chairs up by $200 and sells two of the chairs for $500 each.

- Pottery Barn's balance sheet reports the one chair that the company still holds in inventory.
- The income statement reports the cost of the two chairs sold, as shown in Exhibit 6-2 (p. 344).

Here is the basic concept of how we identify **inventory**, the asset, from **cost of goods sold**, the expense.

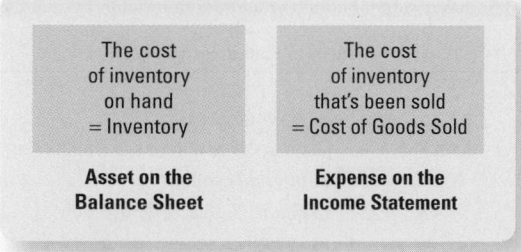

The cost of inventory on hand = Inventory

Asset on the Balance Sheet

The cost of inventory that's been sold = Cost of Goods Sold

Expense on the Income Statement

EXHIBIT 6-1 | **Contrasting a Service Company with a Merchandiser**

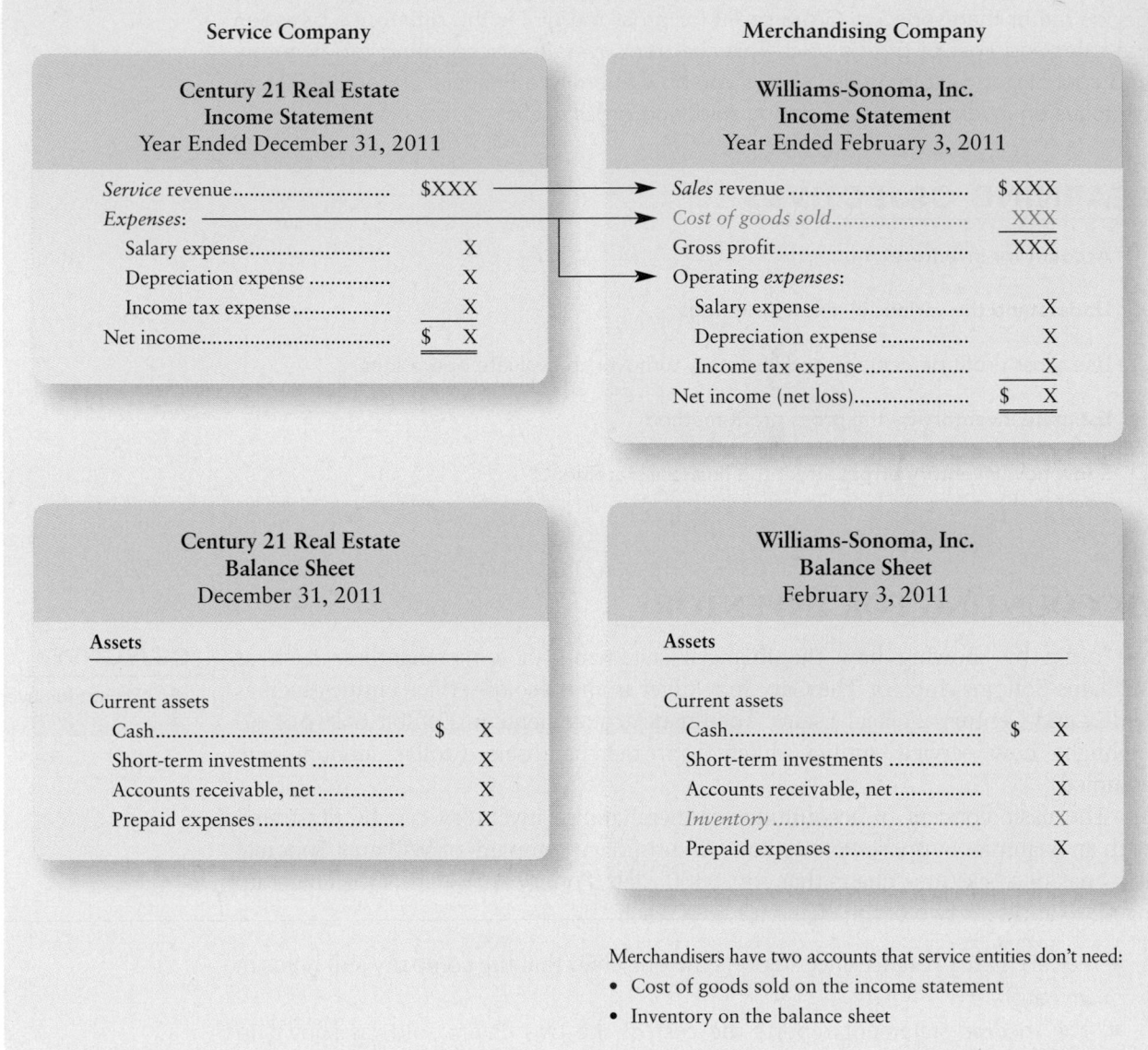

Service Company	Merchandising Company

Century 21 Real Estate
Income Statement
Year Ended December 31, 2011

Service revenue.............................	$XXX
Expenses:	
Salary expense..........................	X
Depreciation expense	X
Income tax expense.................	X
Net income...............................	$ X

Williams-Sonoma, Inc.
Income Statement
Year Ended February 3, 2011

Sales revenue	$ XXX
Cost of goods sold..........................	XXX
Gross profit....................................	XXX
Operating *expenses:*	
Salary expense............................	X
Depreciation expense	X
Income tax expense.....................	X
Net income (net loss)......................	$ X

Century 21 Real Estate
Balance Sheet
December 31, 2011

Assets

Current assets		
Cash..	$	X
Short-term investments		X
Accounts receivable, net...............		X
Prepaid expenses		X

Williams-Sonoma, Inc.
Balance Sheet
February 3, 2011

Assets

Current assets		
Cash..	$	X
Short-term investments		X
Accounts receivable, net...............		X
Inventory		X
Prepaid expenses		X

Merchandisers have two accounts that service entities don't need:
- Cost of goods sold on the income statement
- Inventory on the balance sheet

EXHIBIT 6-2 | **Inventory and Cost of Goods Sold When Inventory Cost Is Constant**

Balance Sheet (partial)		Income Statement (partial)	
Current assets		Sales revenue	
Cash...	$XXX	(2 chairs @ sale price of $500 each)	$1,000
Short-term investments	XXX	Cost of goods sold	
Accounts receivable................................	XXX	(2 chairs @ cost of $300 each)...............	600
Inventory (1 chair @ cost of $300)	300	Gross profit...	$ 400
Prepaid expenses	XXX		

The cost of the inventory sold shifts from asset to expense when the seller delivers the goods to the buyer.

Sale Price vs. Cost of Inventory

Note the difference between the sale price of inventory and the cost of inventory. In our example,

- Sales revenue is based on the *sale price* of the inventory sold ($500 per chair).
- Cost of goods sold is based on the *cost* of the inventory sold ($300 per chair).
- Inventory on the balance sheet is based on the *cost* of the inventory still on hand ($300 per chair).

Exhibit 6-2 shows these items.

Gross profit, also called **gross margin**, is the excess of sales revenue over cost of goods sold. It is called *gross* profit because operating expenses have not yet been subtracted. Exhibit 6-3 shows actual inventory and cost of goods sold data adapted from the financial statements of Williams-Sonoma.

EXHIBIT 6-3 | **Williams-Sonoma, Inc., Inventory and Cost of Goods Sold (Cost of Sales)**

Williams-Sonoma, Inc.
Consolidated Balance Sheet (Adapted)
February 3, 2008

Assets (In millions)

Current assets
Cash and cash equivalents................	$119
Receivables, net...............................	48
Inventories	694

Williams-Sonoma, Inc.
Consolidated Statement of Income (Adapted)
Year Ended February 3, 2008

(In millions)

Net sales	$3,945
Cost of sales (same as Cost of goods sold)...............	2,409
Gross profit..	$1,536

Williams-Sonoma, Inc.'s inventory of $694 million represents

$$\frac{\text{Inventory}}{\text{(balance sheet)}} = \frac{\text{Number of units of}}{\text{inventory } on \ hand} \times \frac{\text{Cost per unit}}{\text{of inventory}}$$

Williams-Sonoma's cost of goods sold ($2,409 million) represents

$$\text{Cost of goods sold} \atop \text{(income statement)} = {\text{Number of units of} \atop \text{inventory } \textit{sold}} \times {\text{Cost per unit} \atop \text{of inventory}}$$

Let's see what "units of inventory" and "cost per unit" mean.

Number of Units of Inventory.   The number of inventory units on hand is determined from the accounting records, backed up by a physical count of the goods at year end. Companies do not include in their inventory any goods they hold on consignment because those goods belong to another company. But they do include their own inventory that is out on consignment and held by another company. Companies include inventory in transit from suppliers or in transit to customers that, according to shipping terms, legally belong to them as of the year end. Shipping terms, otherwise known as *FOB terms*, indicate who owns the goods at a particular time and, therefore, who must pay for the shipping costs. The term **FOB** stands for *free on board*. When the vendor invoice specifies *FOB shipping point* (the most common business practice), legal title to the goods passes from the seller to the purchaser when the inventory leaves the seller's place of business. The purchaser therefore owns the goods while they are in transit and must pay the transportation costs. In the case of goods purchased FOB shipping point, the company purchasing the goods must include goods in transit from suppliers as units in inventory as of the year end. In the case of goods purchased *FOB destination*, title to the goods does not pass from the seller to the purchaser until the goods arrive at the purchaser's receiving dock. Therefore, these goods are not counted in year-end inventory of the purchasing company. Rather, the cost of these goods is included in inventory of the seller until the goods reach their destination.

Cost Per Unit of Inventory.   The cost per unit of inventory poses a challenge because companies purchase goods at different prices throughout the year. Which unit costs go into ending inventory? Which unit costs go to cost of goods sold?

The next section shows how different accounting methods determine amounts on the balance sheet and the income statement. First, however, you need to understand how inventory accounting systems work.

Accounting for Inventory in the Perpetual System

There are two main types of inventory accounting systems: the periodic system and the perpetual system. The **periodic inventory system**, discussed in more detail in Appendix 6A, is used for inexpensive goods. A fabric store or a lumber yard won't keep a running record of every bolt of fabric or every two-by-four. Instead, these stores count their inventory periodically—at least once a year—to determine the quantities on hand. Businesses such as restaurants and hometown nurseries also use the periodic system because the accounting cost of a periodic system is low.

A **perpetual inventory system** uses computer software to keep a running record of inventory on hand. This system achieves control over goods such as Pottery Barn furniture, automobiles, jewelry, apparel, and most other types of inventory. Most businesses use the perpetual inventory system.

Even with a perpetual system, the business still counts the inventory on hand annually. The physical count establishes the correct amount of ending inventory for the financial statements and also serves as a check on the perpetual records. Here is a quick summary of the two main inventory accounting systems.

Perpetual Inventory System	Periodic Inventory System
• Used for all types of goods • Keeps a running record of all goods bought, sold, and on hand • Inventory counted at least once a year	• Used for inexpensive goods • Does *not* keep a running record of all goods bought, sold, and on hand • Inventory counted at least once a year

How the Perpetual System Works.   Let's use an everyday situation to show how a perpetual inventory system works. When you check out of a Foot Locker, a Best Buy, or a Pottery Barn store, the clerk scans the bar codes on the labels of the items you buy. Exhibit 6-4 illustrates a typical bar code. Suppose you are buying a desk lamp from Pottery Barn. The bar code on the product label holds lots of information. The optical scanner reads the bar code, and the computer records the sale and updates the inventory records.

EXHIBIT 6-4 | Bar Code for Electronic Scanner

0 72512 06581 5

Recording Transactions in the Perpetual System.   All accounting systems record each purchase of inventory. When Pottery Barn makes a sale, two entries are needed in the perpetual system:

- The company records the sale—debits Cash or Accounts Receivable and credits Sales Revenue for the sale price of the goods.
- Pottery Barn also debits Cost of Goods Sold and credits Inventory for the cost of the inventory sold.

Exhibit 6-5, on the following page, shows the accounting for inventory in a perpetual system. Panel A gives the journal entries and the T-accounts, and Panel B shows the income statement and the balance sheet. All amounts are assumed. (Appendix 6A illustrates the accounting for these same transactions for a periodic inventory system.)

In Exhibit 6-5, the first entry to Inventory summarizes a lot of detail. The cost of the inventory, $560,000, is the *net* amount of the purchases, determined as follows (using assumed amounts):

Purchase price of the inventory	$600,000
+ **Freight-in** (the cost to transport the goods from the seller to the buyer)	4,000
− **Purchase returns** for unsuitable goods returned to the seller............................	(25,000)
− **Purchase allowances** granted by the seller	(5,000)
− **Purchase discounts** for early payment by the buyer.......................................	(14,000)
= Net purchases of inventory—Cost to the buyer...	$560,000

EXHIBIT 6-5 | **Recording and Reporting Inventory—Perpetual System (Amounts Assumed)**

PANEL A—Recording Transactions and the T-accounts (All amounts are assumed)

Journal Entry

1.	Inventory	560,000	
	Accounts Payable BS		560,000
	Purchased inventory on account. BS		
2.	Accounts Receivable BS	900,000	
	Sales Revenue IS		900,000
	Sold inventory on account.		
	Cost of Goods Sold IS	540,000	
	Inventory BS		540,000
	Recorded cost of goods sold.		

Inventory

Beginning balance	100,000*		
Purchases	560,000	Cost of goods sold	540,000
Ending balance	120,000		

*Beginning inventory was $100,000

Cost of Goods Sold

Cost of goods sold	540,000

PANEL B—Reporting in the Financial Statements

Income Statement (partial)		Ending Balance Sheet (partial)	
Sales revenue	$900,000	Current assets:	
Cost of goods sold	540,000	Cash	$ XXX
Gross profit	$360,000	Short-term investments	XXX
		Accounts receivable	XXX
		Inventory	120,000
		Prepaid expenses	XXX

Freight-in is the transportation cost, paid by the buyer, under terms FOB shipping point, to move goods from the seller to the buyer. Freight-in is accounted for as part of the cost of inventory. A **purchase return** is a decrease in the cost of inventory because the buyer returned the goods to the seller (vendor). A **purchase allowance** also decreases the cost of inventory because the buyer got an allowance (a deduction) from the amount owed. To document approval of purchase returns, management issues a **debit memorandum**, meaning that accounts payable are reduced (debited) for the amount of the return. The offsetting credit is to inventory as the goods are shipped back to the seller (vendor). Purchase discounts and allowances are usually documented on the final invoice received from the vendor. Throughout this book, we often refer to net purchases simply as Purchases.

A **purchase discount** is a decrease in the buyer's cost of inventory earned by paying quickly. Many companies offer payment terms of "2/10 n/30." This means the buyer can take a 2% discount for payment within 10 days, with the final amount due within 30 days. Another common credit term is "net 30," which tells the customer to pay the full amount within 30 days. In summary,

> Net purchases = Purchases
>   − Purchase returns and allowances
>   − Purchase discounts
>   + Freight-in

Net sales are computed exactly the same as net purchases, but with no freight-in, as follows:

> Net sales = Sales revenue
> – Sales returns and allowances
> – Sales discounts

Freight-out paid by the *seller*, under shipping terms FOB destination, is not part of the cost of inventory. Instead, freight-out is delivery expense. It's the seller's expense of delivering merchandise to customers.

INVENTORY COSTING

Inventory is the first asset for which a manager can decide which accounting method to use. The accounting method selected affects the profits to be reported, the amount of income tax to be paid, and the values of the ratios derived from the balance sheet.

What Goes into Inventory Cost?

The cost of inventory on Williams-Sonoma, Inc.'s balance sheet represents all the costs that the company incurred to bring its inventory to the point of sale. The following cost principle applies to all assets:

> **The cost of any asset, such as inventory, is the sum of all the costs incurred to bring the asset to its intended use, less any discounts.**

As we have seen, inventory's cost includes its basic purchase price, plus freight-in, insurance while in transit, and any fees or taxes paid to get the inventory ready to sell, less returns, allowances, and discounts.

After a Pottery Barn chair is sitting in the showroom, other costs, such as advertising and sales commissions, are *not* included as the cost of inventory. Advertising, sales commissions, and delivery costs are selling expenses that go in the income statement, rather than in the balance sheet.

The Various Inventory Costing Methods

Determining the cost of inventory is easy when the unit cost remains constant, as in Exhibit 6-2. But the unit cost usually changes. For example, prices often rise. The desk lamp that cost Pottery Barn $10 in January may cost $14 in June and $18 in October. Suppose Pottery Barn sells 1,000 lamps in November. How many of those lamps cost $10, how many cost $14, and how many cost $18?

OBJECTIVE

2 **Understand** the various inventory methods

To compute cost of goods sold and the cost of ending inventory still on hand, we must assign unit cost to the items. Accounting uses four generally accepted inventory methods:

1. **Specific unit cost**   2. **Average cost**
3. **First-in, first-out (FIFO) cost**   4. **Last-in, first-out (LIFO) cost**

A company can use any of these methods. The methods can have very different effects on reported profits, income taxes, and cash flow. Therefore, companies select their inventory method with great care.

Specific Unit Cost.   Some businesses deal in unique inventory items, such as automobiles, antique furniture, jewels, and real estate. These businesses cost their inventories at the specific cost of the particular unit. For instance, a Toyota dealer may have two vehicles in the showroom—a "stripped-down" model that cost the dealer $19,000 and a "loaded" model that cost the dealer $24,000. If the dealer sells the loaded model, the cost of goods sold is $24,000. The stripped-down auto will be the only unit left in inventory, and so ending inventory is $19,000.

The **specific-unit-cost method** is also called the *specific identification method*. This method is too expensive to use for inventory items that have common characteristics, such as bushels of wheat, gallons of paint, or auto tires.

The other inventory accounting methods—average, FIFO, and LIFO—are fundamentally different. These other methods do not use the specific cost of a particular unit. Instead, they assume different flows of inventory costs. To illustrate average, FIFO, and LIFO costing, we use a common set of data, given in Exhibit 6-6.

EXHIBIT 6-6 | **Inventory Data Used to Illustrate the Various Inventory Costing Methods**

Inventory					
Beg bal	(10 units @ $10)	100			
Purchases:			Cost of goods sold		
No. 1	(25 units @ $14)	350	(40 units @ ?)		?
No. 2	(25 units @ $18)	450			
End bal	(20 units @ ?)	?			

In Exhibit 6-6, Pottery Barn began the period with 10 lamps that cost $10 each; the beginning inventory was therefore $100. During the period Pottery Barn bought 50 more lamps, sold 40 lamps, and ended the period with 20 lamps, summarized in the T-account as follows:

Goods Available		Number of Units	Total Cost
Goods available	=	10 + 25 + 25 = 60 units	$100 + $350 + $450 = $900
Cost of goods sold	=	40 units	?
Ending inventory	=	20 units	?

The big accounting questions are

1. What is the cost of goods sold for the income statement?
2. What is the cost of the ending inventory for the balance sheet?

It all depends on which inventory method Pottery Barn uses. Pottery Barn, like other Williams-Sonoma, Inc., companies, actually uses the average-cost method, so let's look at average costing first.

Average Cost. The **average-cost method**, sometimes called the **weighted-average method**, is based on the average cost of inventory during the period. Average cost per unit is determined as follows (data from Exhibit 6-6):

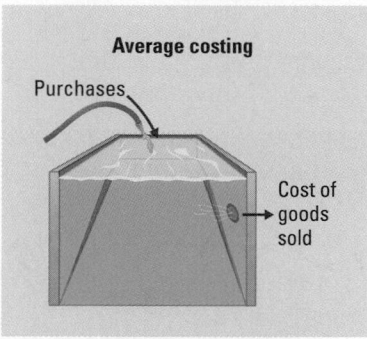

$$\text{Average cost per unit} = \frac{\text{Cost of goods available*}}{\text{Number of units available*}} = \frac{\$900}{60} = \$15$$

*Goods available = Beginning inventory + Purchases

Cost of goods sold =	Number of units sold	× Average cost per unit	
=	40 units	× $15	= $600

Ending inventory =	Number of units on hand	× Average cost per unit	
=	20 units	× $15	= $300

The following T-account shows the effects of average costing:

Inventory (at Average Cost)				
Beg bal	(10 units @ $10)	100		
Purchases:				
No. 1	(25 units @ $14)	350		
No. 2	(25 units @ $18)	450	Cost of goods sold (40 units	
			@ average cost of $15 per unit)	600
End bal	(20 units @ average			
	cost of $15 per unit)	300		

FIFO Cost. Under the FIFO method, the first costs into inventory are the first costs assigned to cost of goods sold—hence, the name *first-in, first-out*. The diagram near the bottom of the page shows the effect of FIFO costing. The following T-account shows how to compute FIFO cost of goods sold and ending inventory for the Pottery Barn lamps (data from Exhibit 6-6):

Inventory (at FIFO cost)					
Beg bal	(10 units @ $10)	100			
Purchases:			Cost of goods sold (40 units):		
No. 1	(25 units @ $14)	350	(10 units @ $10)	100	
No. 2	(25 units @ $18)	450	(25 units @ $14)	350	540
			(5 units @ $18)	90	
End bal	(20 units @ $18)	360			

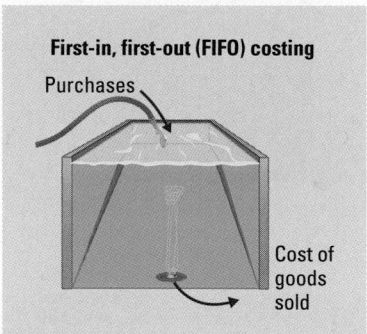

First-in, first-out (FIFO) costing
Purchases
Cost of goods sold

Under FIFO, the cost of ending inventory is always based on the latest costs incurred—in this case $18 per unit.

LIFO Cost. LIFO costing is the opposite of FIFO. Under LIFO, the last costs into inventory go immediately to cost of goods sold, as shown in the diagram on the following page. Compare LIFO and FIFO, and you will see a vast difference.

The following T-account shows how to compute the LIFO inventory amounts for the Pottery Barn lamps (data from Exhibit 6-6):

Inventory (at LIFO cost)					
Beg bal	(10 units @ $10)	100			
Purchases:			Cost of goods sold (40 units):		
No. 1	(25 units @ $14)	350	(25 units @ $18)	450	660
No. 2	(25 units @ $18)	450	(15 units @ $14)	210	
End bal	(10 units @ $10)				
	(10 units @ $14)	240			

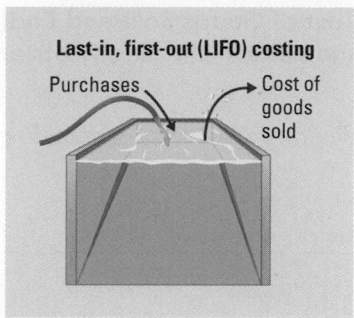

Under LIFO, the cost of ending inventory is always based on the oldest costs—from beginning inventory plus the early purchases of the period—$10 and $14 per unit.

The Effects of FIFO, LIFO and Average Cost on Cost of Goods Sold, Gross Profit, and Ending Inventory

In our Pottery Barn example, the cost of inventory rose from $10 to $14 to $18. When inventory unit costs change this way, the various inventory methods produce different cost-of-goods sold figures. Exhibit 6-7 summarizes the income effects (sales – cost of goods sold = gross profit) of the three inventory methods (remember that prices are rising). Study Exhibit 6-7 carefully, focusing on cost of goods sold and gross profit.

EXHIBIT 6-7 | **Income Effects of the FIFO, LIFO, and Average Inventory Methods**

	FIFO	LIFO	Average
Sales revenue (assumed)	$1,000	$1,000	$1,000
Cost of goods sold........................	540 (lowest)	660 (highest)	600
Gross profit.................................	$ 460 (highest)	$ 340 (lowest)	$ 400

Exhibit 6-8 on the following page shows the impact of both FIFO and LIFO costing methods on cost of goods sold and inventories during both increasing costs (Panel A) and decreasing costs (Panel B). Study this exhibit carefully; it will help you *really* understand FIFO and LIFO.

EXHIBIT 6-8 | **Cost of Goods Sold and Ending Inventory—FIFO and LIFO; Increasing Costs and Decreasing Costs**

Panel A—When Inventory Costs Are Increasing

	Cost of Goods Sold (COGS)	Ending Inventory (EI)
FIFO	FIFO COGS is lowest because it's based on the oldest costs, which are low. Gross profit is, therefore, the highest.	FIFO EI is highest because it's based on the most recent costs, which are high.
LIFO	LIFO COGS is highest because it's based on the most recent costs, which are high. Gross profit is, therefore, the lowest.	LIFO EI is lowest because it's based on the oldest costs, which are low.

Panel B—When Inventory Costs Are Decreasing

	Cost of Goods Sold (COGS)	Ending Inventory (EI)
FIFO	FIFO COGS is highest because it's based on the oldest costs, which are high. Gross profit is, therefore, the lowest.	FIFO EI is lowest because it's based on the most recent costs, which are low.
LIFO	LIFO COGS is lowest because it's based on the most recent costs, which are low. Gross profit is, therefore, the highest.	LIFO EI is highest because it's based on the oldest costs, which are high.

Financial analysts search the stock markets for companies with good prospects for income growth. Analysts sometimes need to compare the net income of a company that uses LIFO with the net income of a company that uses FIFO. Appendix 6B, pages 407-408, shows how to convert a LIFO company's net income to the FIFO basis in order to compare the companies.

The Tax Advantage of LIFO

The Internal Revenue Service requires all U.S. companies to use the same method of pricing inventories for tax purposes that they use for financial reporting purposes. Thus, the choice of inventory methods directly affects income taxes, which must be paid in cash. When prices are rising, LIFO results in the *lowest taxable income* and thus the *lowest income taxes*. Let's use the gross profit data of Exhibit 6-7 to illustrate.

	FIFO	LIFO
Gross profit (from Exhibit 6-7)	$460	$340
Operating expenses (assumed)	260	260
Income before income tax	$200	$ 80
Income tax expense (40%)	$ 80	$ 32

Income tax expense is lowest under LIFO ($32). **This is the most attractive feature of LIFO—low income tax payments**, which is why about one-third of all U.S. companies use LIFO. During periods of inflation, many companies switch to LIFO for its tax and cash-flow advantage. Exhibit 6-9, based on an American Institute of Certified Public Accountants (AICPA) survey of 600 companies, indicates that FIFO remains the most popular inventory method.

EXHIBIT 6-9 | **Use of the Various Inventory Methods**

Comparison of the Inventory Methods

Let's compare the average, FIFO, and LIFO inventory methods.

1. Measuring Cost of Goods Sold. How well does each method match inventory expense—cost of goods sold—against revenue? LIFO results in the most realistic net income figure because LIFO assigns the most recent inventory costs to expense. In contrast, FIFO matches old inventory costs against revenue—a poor measure of expense. FIFO income is therefore less realistic than LIFO income.

2. Measuring Ending Inventory. Which method reports the most up-to-date inventory cost on the balance sheet? FIFO. LIFO can value inventory at very old costs because LIFO leaves the oldest prices in ending inventory.

LIFO and Managing Reported Income.   LIFO allows managers to manipulate net income by timing their purchases of inventory. When inventory prices are rising rapidly and a company wants to show less income (in order to pay less taxes), managers can buy a large amount of inventory near the end of the year. Under LIFO, these high inventory costs go straight to cost of goods sold. As a result, net income is decreased.

If the business is having a bad year, management may wish to report higher income. The company can delay the purchase of high-cost inventory until next year. This avoids decreasing current-year income. In the process, the company draws down inventory quantities, a practice known as *LIFO inventory liquidation*.

LIFO Liquidation.   When LIFO is used and inventory quantities fall below the level of the previous period, the situation is called a *LIFO liquidation*. To compute cost of goods sold, the company must dip into older layers of inventory cost. Under LIFO, and when prices are rising, that action shifts older, lower costs into cost of goods sold. The result is higher net income. Managers try to avoid a LIFO liquidation because it increases income taxes.

INTERNATIONAL PERSPECTIVE

Many U.S. companies that currently use LIFO must use another method in foreign countries. Why? LIFO is not allowed in Australia, the United Kingdom, and some other British commonwealth countries. Virtually all countries permit FIFO and the average cost method.

These differences can create comparability problems for financial analysts when comparing a U.S. company against a foreign competitor. As discussed earlier, Appendix 6B illustrates how analysts convert reported income for a company that uses LIFO to reported income under FIFO.

International Financial Reporting Standards (IFRS) also do not permit the use of LIFO, although they do permit FIFO and other methods. When U.S. GAAP and IFRS are fully integrated in a few years, U.S. companies that use LIFO will be forced to convert their inventory pricing to another method. As we discussed earlier in the chapter, in periods of rising prices, the use of LIFO inventories results in the lowest amount of reported income and, thus, the lowest amount of income taxes. If the statistics in Figure 6-9 continue to hold through the next few years, conversion of inventories to methods other than LIFO may substantially increase reported income for up to 30 percent of U.S. companies. This change has potentially far-reaching implications. For example, if the Internal Revenue Service continues to require companies to use the same inventory pricing methods for income tax purposes and financial statement purposes, conversion of LIFO inventories to another method will greatly increase the tax burden on many U.S. companies, including small and medium-sized businesses that can least afford it.

The disallowance of LIFO inventories under IFRS is only one of several rather thorny issues that must be resolved before the United States can adopt IFRS. Resolution of these differences will likely have political as well as financial implications. We will cover other key differences between GAAP and IFRS in later chapters. Appendix F to the book summarizes all of these differences.

MID-CHAPTER SUMMARY PROBLEM

Suppose a division of **Texas Instruments** that sells computer microchips has these inventory records for January 2011:

Date		Item	Quantity	Unit Cost	Total cost
Jan	1	Beginning inventory	100 units	$ 8	$ 800
	6	Purchase	60 units	9	540
	21	Purchase	150 units	9	1,350
	27	Purchase	90 units	10	900

Company accounting records show sales of 310 units for revenue of $6,770. Operating expense for January was $1,900.

I Requirements

1. Prepare the January income statement, showing amounts for LIFO, average, and FIFO cost. Label the bottom line "Operating income." Round average cost per unit to three decimal places and all other figures to whole-dollar amounts. Show your computations.

2. Suppose you are the financial vice president of Texas Instruments. Which inventory method will you use if your motive is to
   a. Minimize income taxes?
   b. Report the highest operating income?
   c. Report operating income between the extremes of FIFO and LIFO?
   d. Report inventory on the balance sheet at the most current cost?
   e. Attain the best measure of net income for the income statement?
   State the reason for each of your answers.

Answers

I Requirement 1

Texas Instruments Incorporated
Income Statement for Microchip
Month Ended January 31, 2011

	LIFO	Average	FIFO
Sales revenue........................	$6,770	$6,770	$6,770
Cost of goods sold................	2,870	2,782	2,690
Gross profit..........................	3,900	3,988	4,080
Operating expenses	1,900	1,900	1,900
Operating income.................	$2,000	$2,088	$2,180

Cost of goods sold computations:
   LIFO: (90 @ $10) + (150 @ $9) + (60 @ $9) + (10 @ $8) = $2,870
   Average: 310 × $8.975* = $2,782
   FIFO: (100 @ $8) + (60 @ $9) + (150 @ $9) = $2,690

$$*\frac{(\$800 + \$540 + \$1,350 + \$900)}{(100 + 60 + 150 + 90)} = \$8.975$$

I *Requirement 2*

a. Use LIFO to minimize income taxes. Operating income under LIFO is lowest when inventory unit costs are increasing, as they are in this case (from $8 to $10). (If inventory costs were decreasing, income under FIFO would be lowest.)

b. Use FIFO to report the highest operating income. Income under FIFO is highest when inventory unit costs are increasing, as in this situation.

c. Use the average cost method to report an operating income amount between the FIFO and LIFO extremes. This is true in this situation and in others when inventory unit costs are increasing or decreasing.

d. Use FIFO to report inventory on the balance sheet at the most current cost. The oldest inventory costs are expensed as cost of goods sold, leaving in ending inventory the most recent (most current) costs of the period.

e. Use LIFO to attain the best measure of net income. LIFO produces the best matching of current expense with current revenue. The most recent (most current) inventory costs are expensed as cost of goods sold.

ACCOUNTING PRINCIPLES RELATED TO INVENTORY

Several accounting principles have special relevance to inventories:

- Consistency   ■ Disclosure   ■ Conservatism

Consistency Principle

The **consistency principle** states that businesses should use the same accounting methods and procedures from period to period. Consistency enables investors to compare a company's financial statements from one period to the next.

Suppose you are analyzing Interfax Corporation's net income pattern over a two-year period. Interfax switched from LIFO to FIFO during that time. Its net income increased dramatically but only because of the change in inventory method. If you did not know of the accounting change, you might believe that Interfax's income increased due to improved operations, but that's not the case.

The consistency principle does not mean that a company is not permitted to change its accounting methods. However, a company making an accounting change must disclose the effect of the change on net income. American-Saudi Oil Company, Inc., disclosed the following in a note to its annual report:

> **EXCERPT FROM NOTE 6 OF THE FINANCIAL STATEMENTS**
> . . . American-Saudi changed its method of accounting for the cost of crude oil . . . from the FIFO method to the LIFO method. The company believes that the LIFO method better matches current costs with current revenues. . . . The change decreased the Company's 2007 net income . . . by $3 million. . . .

Disclosure Principle

The **disclosure principle** holds that a company's financial statements should report enough information for outsiders to make informed decisions about the company. The company should report *relevant* and *representationally faithful* information about itself. That means properly disclosing inventory accounting methods, as well as the substance of all material transactions impacting the existence and proper valuation of inventory, using *comparable* methods from period to period. The financial statements typically contain a footnote describing the inventory pricing method used, as well as the fact that inventory was valued at the lower of that method or market. The lower-of-cost-or-market rule is described later. Without knowledge of the accounting method and without clear, complete disclosures in the financial statements, a banker could make an unwise lending decision. Suppose the banker is comparing two companies—one using LIFO and the other, FIFO. The FIFO company reports higher net income but only because it uses FIFO. Without knowing this, the banker could loan money to the wrong business.

Accounting Conservatism

Conservatism in accounting means reporting financial statement amounts that paint the most cautious or moderate immediate picture of the company. If faced with a choice of overstatement or understatement, accounting chooses to err on the side of caution in order to protect investors from inflated or overly positive results. However, this should not be interpreted to mean that companies must deliberately understate assets or profits, or overstate liabilities. These are still misstatements! What advantage does conservatism give a business? Many accountants regard conservatism as a brake on management's optimistic tendencies. The goal of accounting conservatism is representational faithfulness.

Conservatism appears in accounting guidelines such as "anticipate no gains, but provide for all probable losses" and "if in doubt, record an asset at the lowest reasonable amount and report a liability at the highest reasonable amount." Conservatism directs accountants to decrease the accounting value of an asset if it appears unrealistically high. Assume that **Texas Instruments** paid $35,000 for inventory that has become outdated and whose current value is only $12,000. Conservatism dictates that Texas Instruments must record a $23,000 loss immediately and write the inventory down to $12,000.

Lower-of-Cost-or-Market Rule

The **lower-of-cost-or-market rule** (abbreviated as **LCM**) is based on accounting conservatism. LCM requires that inventory be reported in the financial statements at whichever is lower—the inventory's historical cost or its market value. Applied to inventories, *market value* generally means *current replacement cost* (that is, how much the business would have to pay now to replace its inventory). If the replacement cost of inventory falls below its historical cost, the business must write down the value of its goods to market value. **The business reports ending inventory at its LCM value on the balance sheet**. All this can be done automatically by a computerized accounting system. How is the write-down accomplished?

Suppose Williams-Sonoma, Inc., paid $3,000 for inventory on September 26. By February 3, its fiscal year-end, the inventory can be replaced for $2,000. Williams-Sonoma's year-end balance sheet must report this inventory at LCM value of $2,000. Exhibit 6-10 on the following page presents the effects of LCM on the balance sheet and the income statement. Before any LCM effect, cost of goods sold is $9,000. An LCM write-down decreases Inventory and increases Cost of Goods Sold, as follows:

	Debit	Credit
Cost of Goods Sold	1,000	
Inventory		1,000
Wrote inventory down to market value.		

EXHIBIT 6-10 | Lower-of-Cost-or-Market (LCM) Effects on Inventory and Cost of Goods Sold

Balance Sheet

Current assets:	
Cash	$ XXX
Short-term investments	XXX
Accounts receivable	XXX
Inventories, at market	
(which is lower than $3,000 cost)	2,000
Prepaid expenses	XXX
Total current assets	$X,XXX

Income Statement

Sales revenue	$21,000
Cost of goods sold ($9,000 + $1,000)	10,000
Gross profit	$11,000

If the market value of Williams-Sonoma's inventory had been above cost, it would have made no adjustment for LCM. In that case, simply report the inventory at cost, which is the lower of cost or market.

Companies disclose LCM in notes to their financial statements, as shown below for Williams-Sonoma, Inc.:

NOTE 1: ACCOUNTING POLICIES
- *Inventories.* Inventories are . . . stated at the *lower of average cost or market.* [Emphasis added.]

LCM is not optional. It is required by GAAP.

ANOTHER IFRS DIFFERENCE

IFRS defines "market" differently than U.S. GAAP. Under IFRS, "market" is always defined as "net realizable value," which, for inventories, is current market value. Once IFRS is adopted in the United States, inventory write-downs may become less common than they are now, due to the fact that selling prices are usually greater than replacement cost.

Under U.S. GAAP, once the LCM rule is applied to write inventories down to replacement cost, the write-downs may never be reversed. In contrast, under IFRS, some LCM write-downs may be reversed, and inventory may be subsequently written up again, not to exceed original cost. This may cause more fluctuation in the reported incomes of companies that sell inventories than we currently see.

INVENTORY AND THE FINANCIAL STATEMENTS

Detailed Income Statement

Exhibit 6-11 provides an example of a detailed income statement, complete with all the discounts and expenses in their proper places. Study it carefully.

EXHIBIT 6-11 | Detailed Income Statement

New Jersey Technology, Inc.
Income Statement
Year Ended December 31, 2011

Sales revenue	$100,000	
Less: Sales discounts	(2,000)	
Sales returns and allowances	(3,000)	
Net sales		$95,000*
Cost of goods sold		45,000
Gross profit		50,000
Operating expenses:		
Selling:		
Sales commission expense	$ 5,000	
Freight-out (delivery expense)	1,000	
Other expenses (detailed)	6,000	12,000
Administrative:		
Salary expense	$ 2,000	
Depreciation expense	2,000	
Other expenses (detailed)	4,000	8,000
Income before income tax		30,000
Income tax expense (40%)		12,000
Net income		$18,000

*Most companies report only the net sales figure, $95,000.

Analyzing Financial Statements

Owners, managers, and investors use ratios to evaluate a business. Two ratios relate directly to inventory: gross profit percentage and the rate of inventory turnover.

Gross Profit Percentage. Gross profit—sales minus cost of goods sold—is a key indicator of a company's ability to sell inventory at a profit. Merchandisers strive to increase **gross profit percentage**, also called the **gross margin percentage**. Gross profit percentage is markup stated as a percentage of sales. Gross profit percentage is computed as follows for Williams-Sonoma, Inc. Data (in millions) for 2008 are taken from Exhibit 6-3, page 345.

OBJECTIVE

3 Use gross profit percentage and inventory turnover to evaluate operations

$$\text{Gross profit percentage} = \frac{\text{Gross profit}}{\text{Net sales revenue}} = \frac{\$1,536}{\$3,945} = 0.389 = 38.9\%$$

The gross profit percentage is watched carefully by managers and investors. A 38.9% gross margin means that each dollar of sales generates about $0.39 of gross profit. On average, cost of goods sold consumes $0.61 of each sales dollar for Williams-Sonoma, Inc. For most firms, the gross profit percentage changes little from year to year, so a small downturn may signal trouble. Williams-Sonoma's gross profit in 2007 was 39.8%, so the company experienced almost a 1% decline in gross margin year over year. In 2008 and 2009, a severe economic recession hit retail sales hard. In order to sell inventories, many retailers have had to cut selling prices, thus reducing gross margins.

Williams-Sonoma's gross profit percentage of 39% is greater than that of Wal-Mart Stores, Inc. (23%), but similar to the gross profit percentage of Nordstrom, Inc. (37.4%). Both Williams-Sonoma and Nordstrom handle higher-priced merchandise than Wal-Mart, thus resulting in higher gross profit. Exhibit 6-12 graphs the gross profit percentages for these three companies.

EXHIBIT 6-12 | **Gross Profit Percentages of Three Leading Retailers**

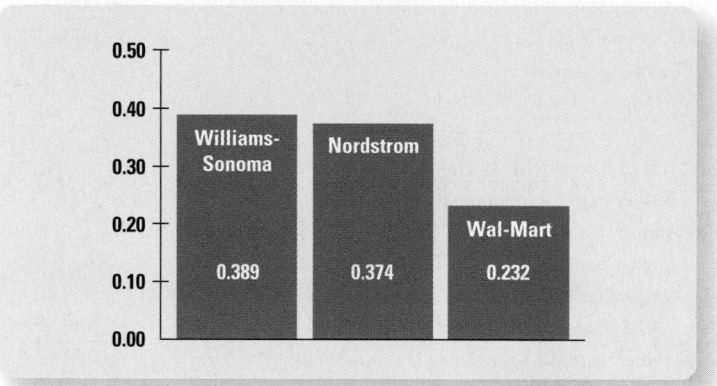

Inventory Turnover. Williams-Sonoma, Inc., strives to sell its inventory as quickly as possible because the goods generate no profit until they're sold. The faster the sales, the higher the income, and vice versa, for slow-moving goods. Ideally, a business could operate with zero inventory, but most businesses, especially retailers, must keep some goods on hand. **Inventory turnover**, the ratio of cost of goods sold to average inventory, indicates how rapidly inventory is sold. The 2008 computation for Williams-Sonoma, Inc., follows (data in millions from the Consolidated Balance Sheets and Statements of Income, page 342):

$$\text{Inventory turnover} = \frac{\text{Cost of goods sold}}{\text{Average inventory}} = \frac{\text{Cost of goods sold}}{\left(\dfrac{\text{Beginning}}{\text{inventory}} + \dfrac{\text{Ending}}{\text{inventory}}\right) \div 2}$$

$$= \frac{\$2,409}{(\$611 + \$694)/2} = \frac{3.7 \text{ times per year}}{\text{(every 99 days)}}$$

The inventory turnover statistic shows how many times the company sold (or turned over) its average level of inventory during the year. Inventory turnover varies from industry to industry.

Exhibit 6-13 graphs the rates of inventory turnover for the same three companies. Let's compare Williams-Sonoma's turnover with that of Nordstrom and Wal-Mart department stores. You can see that both Nordstrom and Wal-Mart turn inventory over faster than Williams-Sonoma. Both Nordstrom and Wal-Mart are department stores. They sell a variety of products (Nordstrom sells clothing and Wal-Mart sells virtually every kind of consumer item) that sell faster than the specialty home furnishings of Williams-Sonoma, Inc. Thus, both Nordstrom and Wal-Mart, Inc., report higher gross profit and net income than Williams-Sonoma.

EXHIBIT 6-13 | Inventory Turnover of Three Leading Retailers

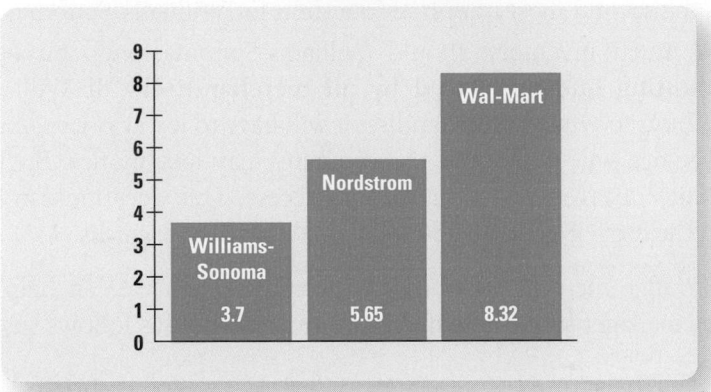

STOP & THINK...

Examine Exhibits 6-12 and 6-13. What do those ratio values say about the merchandising (pricing) strategies of Nordstrom, Inc., and Wal-Mart Stores, Inc.?

Answer:
It's obvious that Nordstrom sells high-end merchandise. Nordstrom's profit percentage is higher than Wal-Mart's. Wal-Mart has a much faster rate of inventory turnover. The lower the price, the faster the turnover, and vice versa.

ADDITIONAL INVENTORY ISSUES
Using the Cost-of-Goods-Sold Model

Exhibit 6-14 presents the **cost-of-goods-sold model.** Some may view this model as related to the periodic inventory system. But the cost-of-goods-sold model is used by all companies, regardless of their accounting system. The model is extremely powerful because it captures all the inventory information for an entire accounting period. Study this model carefully (all amounts are assumed).

EXHIBIT 6-14 | The Cost-of-Goods-Sold Model

Cost of goods sold:	
Beginning inventory	$1,200
+ Purchases	6,300
= Goods available	7,500
− Ending inventory	(1,500)
= Cost of goods sold	$6,000

Williams-Sonoma, Inc., uses a perpetual inventory accounting system. Let's see how the company can use the cost-of-goods-sold model to manage the business effectively.

1. What's the single most important question for Williams-Sonoma, Inc., to address?

   ■ What merchandise should Williams-Sonoma, Inc., offer to its customers? This is a *marketing* question that requires market research. If Williams-Sonoma and its affiliated stores continually stock up on the wrong merchandise, sales will suffer and profits will drop.

2. What's the second most important question for Williams-Sonoma, Inc.?

   ■ How much inventory should Williams-Sonoma, Inc., buy? **This is an accounting question faced by all merchandisers**. If Williams-Sonoma, Inc., buys too much merchandise, it will have to lower prices, the gross profit percentage will suffer, and the company may lose money. Buying the right quantity of inventory is critical for success. This question can be answered with the cost-of-goods-sold model. Let's see how it works.

We must rearrange the cost-of-goods-sold formula. Then we can help a Williams-Sonoma store manager know how much inventory to buy, as follows (using amounts from Exhibit 6-14):

1	Cost of goods sold (based on the plan for the next period)...................	$6,000
2 +	Ending inventory (based on the plan for the next period).......................	1,500
3 =	Goods available as planned...	7,500
4 −	Beginning inventory (actual amount left over from the prior period)......	(1,200)
5 =	Purchases (how much inventory the manager needs to buy)...................	$6,300

In this case the manager should buy $6,300 of merchandise to work his plan for the upcoming period.

Estimating Inventory by the Gross Profit Method

Often a business must *estimate* the value of its goods. A fire may destroy inventory, and the insurance company requires an estimate of the loss. In this case, the business must estimate the cost of ending inventory because it was destroyed.

The **gross profit method**, also known as the **gross margin method**, is widely used to estimate ending inventory. This method uses the familiar cost-of-goods-sold model (amounts are assumed):

	Beginning inventory	$ 4,000
+	Purchases	16,000
=	Goods available.......................................	20,000
−	Ending inventory......................................	(5,000)
=	Cost of goods sold...................................	$15,000

Know this formula (handwritten note)

For the gross-profit method, we rearrange *ending inventory* and *cost of goods sold* as follows:

Beginning inventory	$ 4,000
+ Purchases	16,000
= Goods available.....................................	20,000
– Cost of goods sold...............................	(15,000)
= Ending inventory....................................	$ 5,000

Suppose a fire destroys some of Williams-Sonoma's inventory. To collect insurance, the company must estimate the cost of the ending inventory lost. Using its *actual gross profit rate* of 39%, you can estimate the cost of goods sold. Then subtract cost of goods sold from goods available to estimate the amount of ending inventory. Exhibit 6-15 shows the calculations for the gross profit method, with new amounts assumed for the illustration.

EXHIBIT 6-15 | **Gross Profit Method of Estimating Inventory**

Beginning inventory		$ 38,000
Purchases		72,000
Goods available..		110,000
Estimated cost of goods sold:		
Net sales revenue	$100,000	
Less estimated gross profit of 39%	(39,000)	
Estimated cost of goods sold		61,000
Estimated cost of *ending inventory* lost.............		$ 49,000

You can also use the gross profit method to test the overall reasonableness of an ending inventory amount. This method also helps to detect large errors.

STOP & THINK...

Beginning inventory is $70,000, net purchases total $365,000, and net sales are $500,000. With a normal gross profit rate of 40% of sales (cost of goods sold = 60%), how much is ending inventory?

Answer:

$135,000 = [$70,000 + $365,000 – (0.60 × $500,000)]

Effects of Inventory Errors

Inventory errors sometimes occur. An error in ending inventory creates errors for two accounting periods. In Exhibit 6-16 on the following page, start with period 1 in which ending inventory is *overstated* by $5,000 and cost of goods sold is therefore *understated* by $5,000. Then compare period 1 with period 3, which is correct. *Period 1 should look exactly like period 3.*

Inventory errors counterbalance in two consecutive periods. Why? Recall that period 1's ending inventory becomes period 2's beginning amount. Thus, the period 1 error carries over into period 2. Trace the ending inventory of $15,000 from period 1 to period 2. Then compare periods 2 and 3. *All three periods should look exactly like period 3.* The Exhibit 6-16 amounts in color are incorrect.

EXHIBIT 6-16 | **Inventory Errors: An Example**

	Period 1		Period 2		Period 3	
	Ending Inventory Overstated by $5,000		Beginning Inventory Overstated by $5,000		Correct	
Sales revenue.............................		$100,000		$100,000		$100,000
Cost of goods sold:						
Beginning inventory	$10,000		$15,000		$10,000	
Purchases	50,000		50,000		50,000	
Cost of goods available	60,000		65,000		60,000	
Ending inventory..........................	(15,000)		(10,000)		(10,000)	
Cost of goods sold		45,000		55,000		50,000
Gross profit.................................		$ 55,000		$ 45,000		$ 50,000
			100,000			

The authors thank Professor Carl High for this example.

Beginning inventory and ending inventory have opposite effects on cost of goods sold (beginning inventory is added; ending inventory is subtracted). Therefore, after two periods, an inventory error washes out (counterbalances). Notice that total gross profit is correct for periods 1 and 2 combined ($100,000) even though each year's gross profit is off by $5,000. The correct gross profit is $50,000 for each period, as shown in Period 3.

We must have accurate information for all periods. Exhibit 6-17 summarizes the effects of inventory accounting errors.

EXHIBIT 6-17 | **Effects of Inventory Errors**

	Period 1		Period 2	
Inventory Error	Cost of Goods Sold	Gross Profit and Net Income	Cost of Goods Sold	Gross Profit and Net Income
Period 1				
Ending inventory **overstated**	Understated	Overstated	Overstated	Understated
Period 1				
Ending inventory **understated**	Overstated	Understated	Understated	Overstated

COOKING THE BOOKS
with Inventory
Crazy Eddie

It is one thing to make honest mistakes in accounting for inventory, but quite another to use inventory to commit fraud. The two most common ways to "cook the books" with inventory are:

1. inserting fictitious inventory, thus overstating quantities; and

2. deliberately overstating unit prices used in the computation of ending inventory amounts.

Either one of these tricks has exactly the same effect on income as inventory errors, discussed in the previous section. The difference is that honest inventory errors are often corrected as soon as they are detected, thus minimizing their impact on income. In contrast, deliberate overstatement of inventories tends to be repeated over and over again throughout the course of months, or even years, thus causing the misstatement to grow ever higher until it is discovered. By that time, it can be too late for the company.

Crazy Eddie, Inc.[1] was a retail consumer electronics store in 1987, operating 43 retail outlets in the New York City area, with $350 million in reported sales and reported profits of $10.5 million. Its stock was a Wall Street "darling," with a collective market value of $600 million. The only problem was that the company's reported profits had been grossly overstated since 1984, the year that the company went public.

Eddie Antar, the company's founder and major stockholder, became preoccupied with the price of his company's stock in 1984. Antar realized that the company, in an extremely competitive retail market in the largest city in the United States, had to keep posting impressive operating profits in order to maintain the upward trend in the company's stock price.

Within the first six months, Antar ordered a subordinate to double count about $2 million of inventory in the company's stores and warehouses. Using Exhibits 6-16 and 6-17, you can see that the impact of this inventory overstatement went straight to the "bottom line," overstating profits by the same amount. Unfortunately, the company's auditors failed to detect the inventory overstatement. The following year, emboldened by the audit error, Antar ordered subordinates (now accomplices) to bump the overstatement to $9 million. In addition, he ordered employees to destroy incriminating documents to conceal the inventory shortage. When auditors asked for these documents, employees told them they had been lost. Antar also ordered that the company scrap its sophisticated computerized perpetual inventory system and return to an outdated manual system that was easier to manipulate. The auditors made the mistake of telling Antar which company stores and warehouses they were going to visit in order to observe the year-end physical count of inventory. Antar shifted sufficient inventory to those locations just before the counts to conceal the shortages. By 1988, when the fraud was discovered, the inventory shortage (overstatement) was larger than the total profits the company had reported since it went public in 1984.

In June 1989, Crazy Eddie, Inc., filed for Chapter 11 bankruptcy protection. Later that year, the company closed its stores and sold off its assets. Eddie Antar became a fugitive from justice, moved to Israel, and took an assumed name. He was arrested in 1992, extradited to the United States, and convicted on 17 counts of fraudulent financial reporting in 1993. He was ordered to pay $121 million in restitution to former stockholders and creditors.

A series of missteps by the courts led to a plea bargain agreement in 1996, a condition of which Antar admitted, for the first time, that he had defrauded investors by manipulating the company's accounting records. One of the prosecuting attorneys was quoted as saying, "Crazy Eddie wasn't crazy, just crooked." ▲

The following Decision Guidelines summarize the situations that call for (a) a particular inventory system and (b) the motivation for using each costing method.

---

[1]Michael C. Knapp, *Contemporary Auditing: Real Issues and Cases*, 6th edition, Mason, Ohio: Thomson Southwestern, 2009.

DECISION GUIDELINES

ACCOUNTING FOR INVENTORY

Suppose a Williams-Sonoma store stocks two basic categories of merchandise:

- Furniture pieces, such as tables and chairs
- Small items of low value, near the checkout stations, such as cupholders and bottle openers

Jacob Stiles, the store manager, is considering how accounting will affect the business. Let's examine several decisions Stiles must make to properly account for the store's inventory.

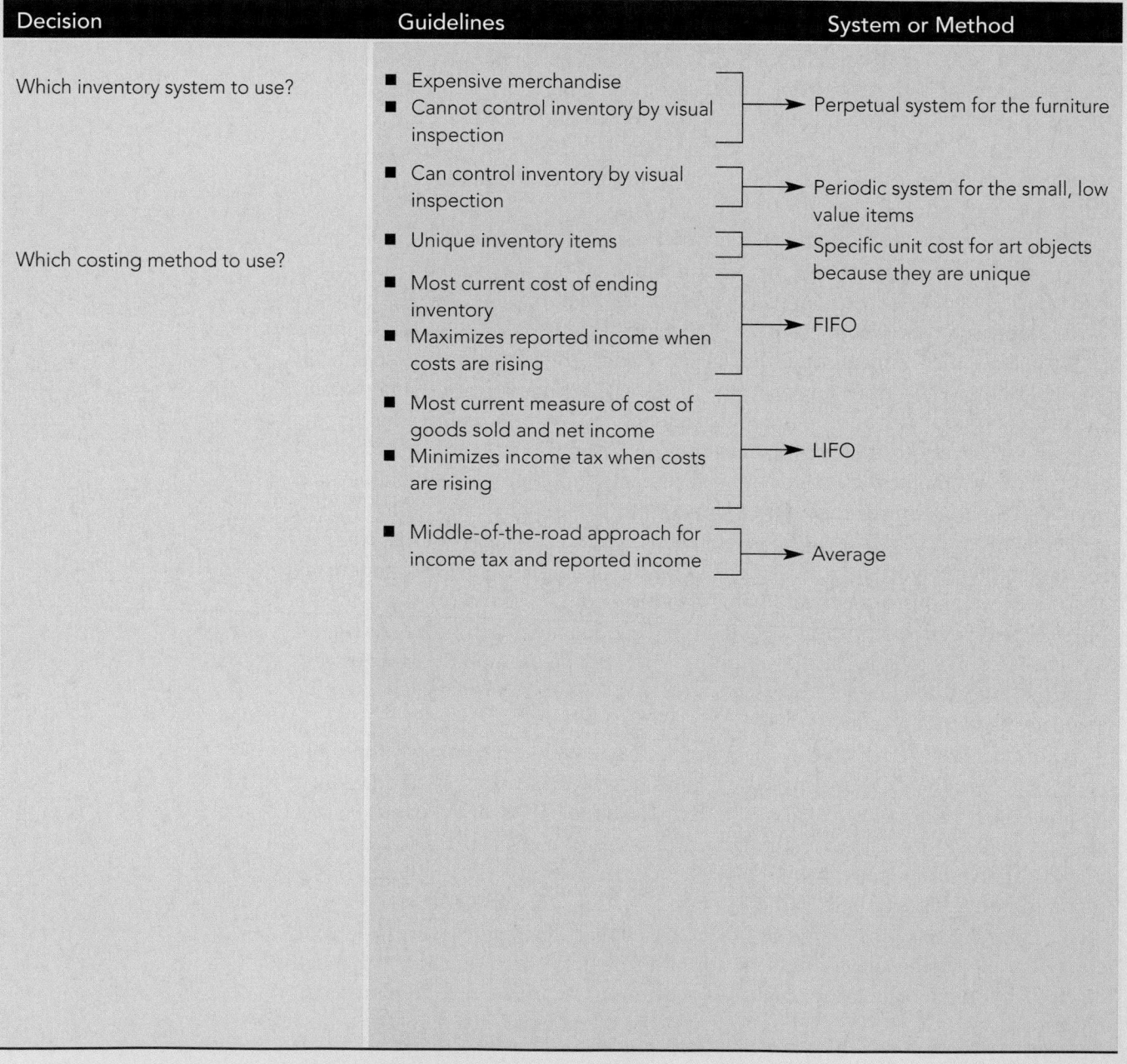

Decision	Guidelines	System or Method
Which inventory system to use?	■ Expensive merchandise ■ Cannot control inventory by visual inspection	Perpetual system for the furniture
	■ Can control inventory by visual inspection	Periodic system for the small, low value items
Which costing method to use?	■ Unique inventory items	Specific unit cost for art objects because they are unique
	■ Most current cost of ending inventory ■ Maximizes reported income when costs are rising	FIFO
	■ Most current measure of cost of goods sold and net income ■ Minimizes income tax when costs are rising	LIFO
	■ Middle-of-the-road approach for income tax and reported income	Average

END-OF-CHAPTER SUMMARY PROBLEM

Town & Country Gift Ideas began 2010 with 60,000 units of inventory that cost $36,000. During 2010, Town & Country purchased merchandise on account for $352,500 as follows:

Purchase 1	(100,000 units costing)	$ 65,000
Purchase 2	(270,000 units costing)	175,500
Purchase 3	(160,000 units costing)	112,000

Cash payments on account totaled $326,000 during the year.

Town & Country's sales during 2010 consisted of 520,000 units of inventory for $660,000, all on account. The company uses the FIFO inventory method.

Cash collections from customers were $630,000. Operating expenses totaled $240,500, of which Town & Country paid $211,000 in cash. Town & Country credited Accrued Liabilities for the remainder. At December 31, Town & Country accrued income tax expense at the rate of 35% of income before tax.

I Requirements

1. Make summary journal entries to record Town & Country's transactions for the year, assuming the company uses a perpetual inventory system.
2. Determine the FIFO cost of Town & Country's ending inventory at December 31, 2010 two ways:
   a. Use a T-account.
   b. Multiply the number of units on hand by the unit cost.
3. Show how Town & Country would compute cost of goods sold for 2010. Follow the FIFO example on page 352.
4. Prepare Town & Country's income statement for 2010. Show totals for the gross profit and income before tax.
5. Determine Town & Country's gross profit percentage, rate of inventory turnover, and net income as a percentage of sales for the year. In Town & Country's industry, a gross profit percentage of 40%, an inventory turnover of six times per year, and a net income percentage of 7% are considered excellent. How well does Town & Country compare to these industry averages?

Answers

▌*Requirement 1*

Inventory ($65,000 + $175,500 + $112,000)	$352,500	
Accounts Payable		352,500
Accounts Payable	326,000	
Cash		326,000
Accounts Receivable	660,000	
Sales Revenue		660,000
Cost of Goods Sold (see Requirement 3)	339,500	
Inventory		339,500
Cash	630,000	
Accounts Receivable		630,000
Operating Expenses	240,500	
Cash		211,000
Accrued Liabilities		29,500
Income Tax Expense (see Requirement 4)	28,000	
Income Tax Payable		28,000

▌*Requirement 2*

Inventory

Beg bal	36,000		
Purchases	352,500	Cost of goods sold	339,500
End bal	49,000		

Number of units in ending inventory (60,000 + 100,000 + 270,000 + 160,000 − 520,000)	70,000
Unit cost of ending inventory at FIFO ($112,000 ÷ 160,000 from Purchase 3).....	× $ 0.70
FIFO cost of ending inventory.......................	$49,000

❙ Requirement 3

Cost of goods sold (520,000 units):	
60,000 units costing...	$ 36,000
100,000 units costing..	65,000
270,000 units costing..	175,500
90,000 units costing $0.70 each*.................................	63,000
Cost of goods sold...	$339,500

*From Purchase 3: $112,000/160,000 units = $0.70 per unit.

❙ Requirement 4

Town & Country Gift Ideas
Income Statement
Year Ended December 31, 2010

Sales revenue	$660,000
Cost of goods sold..	339,500
Gross profit..	320,500
Operating expenses	240,500
Income before tax	80,000
Income tax expense (35%)...	28,000
Net income..	$ 52,000

❙ Requirement 5

		Industry Average
Gross profit percentage:	$320,500 ÷ $660,000 = 48.6%	40%
Inventory turnover:	$\dfrac{\$339,500}{(\$36,000 + \$49,000)/2} = 8$ times	6 times
Net income as a percent of sales:	$52,000 ÷ $660,000 = 7.9%	7%

Town & Country's statistics are better than the industry averages.

REVIEW INVENTORY & COST OF GOODS SOLD

Quick Check (Answers are given on page 400.)

1. Which statement is true?
    a. The invoice is the purchaser's request for collection from the customer.
    b. Gross profit is the excess of sales revenue over cost of goods sold.
    c. The Sales account is used to record only sales on account.
    d. A service company purchases products from suppliers and then sells them.
2. Sales discounts should appear in the financial statements:
    a. as a deduction from sales.
    b. among the current liabilities.
    c. as an addition to inventory.
    d. as an addition to sales.
    e. as an operating expense.
3. How is inventory classified in the financial statements?
    a. As a contra account to Cost of Goods Sold
    b. As an expense
    c. As a liability
    d. As a revenue
    e. As an asset

Questions 4–6 use the following data of Tortoise, Inc.:

	Units	Unit Cost	Total Cost	Units Sold
Beginning inventory	15	$5	$ 75	
Purchase on Apr 25	40	8	320	
Purchase on Nov 13	10	9	90	
Sales	40	?	?	

4. Tortoise uses a FIFO inventory system. Cost of goods sold for the period is:
    a. $360.   c. $275.
    b. $298.   d. $330.
5. Tortoise's LIFO cost of ending inventory would be:
    a. $187.   c. $210.
    b. $155.   d. $200.
6. Tortoise's average cost of ending inventory is:
    a. $210.   c. $187.
    b. $155.   d. $200.
7. When applying lower-of-cost-or-market to inventory, "market" generally means
    a. original cost, less physical deterioration.
    b. original cost.
    c. replacement cost.
    d. resale value.
8. During a period of rising prices, the inventory method that will yield the highest net income and asset value is:
    a. FIFO.   c. average cost.
    b. LIFO.   d. specific identification.

9. Which statement is true?
   a. When prices are rising, the inventory method that results in the lowest ending inventory value is FIFO.
   b. The inventory method that best matches current expense with current revenue is FIFO.
   c. Application of the lower-of-cost-or-market rule often results in a lower inventory value.
   d. An error overstating ending inventory in 2010 will understate 2010 net income.

10. The ending inventory of Misty Harbor Co. is $57,000. If beginning inventory was $68,000 and goods available totaled $117,000, the cost of goods sold is:
    a. $60,000.   d. $49,000.
    b. $128,000.   e. none of the above.
    c. $68,000.

11. Lantern Company had cost of goods sold of $145,000. The beginning and ending inventories were $15,000 and $25,000, respectively. Purchases for the period must have been:
    a. $136,000.   d. $170,000.
    b. $160,000.   e. $185,000.
    c. $155,000.

Use the following information for questions 12–14.

   Fairway Company had a $28,000 beginning inventory and a $35,000 ending inventory. Net sales were $184,000; purchases, $93,000; purchase returns and allowances, $7,000; and freight-in, $3,000.

12. Cost of goods sold for the period is
    a. $98,000.   d. $81,000.
    b. $82,000.   e. none of the above.
    c. $96,000.

13. What is Fairway's gross profit percentage (rounded to the nearest percentage)?
    a. 55%   c. 45%
    b. 15%   d. None of the above

14. What is Fairway's rate of inventory turnover?
    a. 5.3 times   c. 2.3 times
    b. 2.6 times   d. 3.0 times

15. Beginning inventory is $110,000, purchases are $260,000 and sales total $470,000. The normal gross profit is 40%. Using the gross profit method, how much is ending inventory?
    a. $210,000   d. $88,000
    b. $132,000   e. None of the above
    c. $188,000

16. An overstatement of ending inventory in one period results in:
    a. an understatement of net income of the next period.
    b. no effect on net income of the next period.
    c. an understatement of the beginning inventory of the next period.
    d. an overstatement of net income of the next period.

Accounting Vocabulary

average-cost method (p. 351) Inventory costing method based on the average cost of inventory during the period. Average cost is determined by dividing the cost of goods available by the number of units available. Also called the *weighted-average method.*

consignment (p. 346) An inventory arrangement where the seller sells inventory that belongs to another party. The seller does not include consigned merchandise on hand in its balance sheet, because the seller does not own this inventory.

conservatism (p. 359) The accounting concept by which the least favorable figures are presented in the financial statements.

consistency principle (p. 358) A business must use the same accounting methods and procedures from period to period.

cost of goods sold (p. 343) Cost of the inventory the business has sold to customers.

cost-of-goods-sold model (p. 363) Formula that brings together all the inventory data for the entire accounting period: Beginning inventory + Purchases = Goods available. Then, Goods available − Ending inventory = Cost of goods sold.

debit memorandum (p. 348) A document issued to the seller (vendor) when an item of inventory that is unwanted or damaged is returned. This document authorizes a reduction (debit) to accounts payable for the amount of the goods returned.

disclosure principle (p. 358) A business's financial statements must report enough information for outsiders to make knowledgeable decisions about the business. The company should report relevant, reliable, and comparable information about its economic affairs.

first-in, first-out (FIFO) cost (method) (p. 352) Inventory costing method by which the first costs into inventory are the first costs out to cost of goods sold. Ending inventory is based on the costs of the most recent purchases.

FOB (p. 346) Stands for *free on board*, a legal term that designates the point at which title passes for goods sold. FOB shipping point means that the buyer owns, and therefore is legally obligated to pay for goods at the point of shipment, including transportation costs. In this case, the buyer owns the goods while they are in transit from the seller and must include their costs, including freight, in inventory at that point. FOB destination means that the seller pays the transportation costs, so the goods do not belong to the buyer until they reach the buyer's place of business.

gross margin (p. 345) Another name for *gross profit*.

gross margin method (p. 364) Another name for the *gross profit method*.

gross margin percentage (p. 361) Another name for the *gross profit percentage*.

gross profit (p. 345) Sales revenue minus cost of goods sold. Also called *gross margin*.

gross profit method (p. 364) A way to estimate inventory based on a rearrangement of the cost-of-goods-sold model: Beginning inventory + Net purchases = Goods available − Cost of goods sold = Ending inventory. Also called the *gross margin method*.

gross profit percentage (p. 361) Gross profit divided by net sales revenue. Also called the *gross margin percentage*.

inventory (p. 343) The merchandise that a company sells to customers.

inventory turnover (p. 362) Ratio of cost of goods sold to average inventory. Indicates how rapidly inventory is sold.

last-in, first-out (LIFO) cost (method) (p. 352) Inventory costing method by which the last costs into inventory are the first costs out to cost of goods sold. This method leaves the oldest costs—those of beginning inventory and the earliest purchases of the period—in ending inventory.

lower-of-cost-or-market (LCM) rule (p. 359) Requires that an asset be reported in the financial statements at whichever is lower—its historical cost or its market value (current replacement cost for inventory).

periodic inventory system (p. 346) An inventory system in which the business does not keep a continuous record of the inventory on hand. Instead, at the end of the period, the business makes a physical count of the inventory on hand and applies the appropriate unit costs to determine the cost of the ending inventory.

perpetual inventory system (p. 346) An inventory system in which the business keeps a continuous record for each inventory item to show the inventory on hand at all times.

purchase allowance (p. 348) A decrease in the cost of purchases because the seller has granted the buyer a subtraction (an allowance) from the amount owed.

purchase discount (p. 348) A decrease in the cost of purchases earned by making an early payment to the vendor.

purchase return (p. 348) A decrease in the cost of purchases because the buyer returned the goods to the seller.

specific-unit-cost method (p. 350) Inventory cost method based on the specific cost of particular units of inventory.

weighted-average method (p. 351) Another name for the *average-cost method*.

ASSESS YOUR PROGRESS

Short Exercises

S6-1 (*Learning Objective 1: Accounting for inventory transactions*)   Journalize the following assumed transactions for The Pepson Company. Show amounts in billions.

  a. Cash purchases of inventory, $3.8 billion
  b. Sales on account, $19.7 billion
  c. Cost of goods sold (perpetual inventory system), $4.5 billion
  d. Collections on account, $18.8 billion

S6-2 (*Learning Objective 1: Accounting for inventory transactions*)   Summer Kluxon, Inc., purchased inventory costing $120,000 and sold 75% of the goods for $150,000. All purchases and sales were on account. Kluxon later collected 30% of the accounts receivable.

1. Journalize these transactions for Kluxon, which uses the perpetual inventory system.
2. For these transactions, show what Kluxon will report for inventory, revenues, and expenses on its financial statements. Report gross profit on the appropriate statement.

S6-3 (*Learning Objective 2: Applying the average, FIFO, and LIFO methods*)   Continental Sporting Goods started April with an inventory of nine sets of golf clubs that cost a total of $1,260. During April Continental purchased 25 sets of clubs for $4,000. At the end of the month, Continental had 8 sets of golf clubs on hand. The store manager must select an inventory costing method, and he asks you to tell him both cost of goods sold and ending inventory under these three accounting methods:

    a. Average cost (round average unit cost to the nearest cent)
    b. FIFO
    c. LIFO

S6-4 (*Learning Objective 2: Applying the average, FIFO, and LIFO methods*)   Jefferson's Copy Center uses laser printers. Assume Jefferson started the year with 92 containers of ink (average cost of $9.00 each, FIFO cost of $8.90 each, LIFO cost of $8.05 each). During the year, Jefferson purchased 680 containers of ink at $9.80 and sold 580 units for $20.25 each. Jefferson paid operating expenses throughout the year, a total of $3,750. Jefferson is not subject to income tax.

    Prepare Jefferson's income statement for the current year ended December 31 under the average, FIFO, and LIFO inventory costing methods. Include a complete statement heading.

S6-5 (*Learning Objective 2: Computing income tax effects of the inventory costing methods*)   This exercise should be used in conjunction with Short Exercise 6-4. Jefferson is a corporation subject to a 30% income tax. Compute Jefferson's income tax expense under the average, FIFO, and LIFO inventory costing methods. Which method would you select to (a) maximize income before tax and (b) minimize income tax expense?

S6-6 (*Learning Objective 2: Computing income and income tax effects of LIFO*)   Microdata.com uses the LIFO method to account for inventory. Microdata is having an unusually good year, with net income well above expectations. The company's inventory costs are rising rapidly. What can Microdata do immediately before the end of the year to decrease net income? Explain how this action decreases reported income, and tell why Microdata might want to decrease its net income.   **writing assignment ■**

S6-7 (*Learning Objective 2: Applying the lower-of-cost-or-market rule to inventory*)   It is December 31, end of the year, and the controller of Reed Corporation is applying the lower-of-cost-or-market (LCM) rule to inventories. Before any year-end adjustments Reed reports the following data:

Cost of goods sold...	$440,000
Historical cost of ending inventory, as determined by a physical count..............	57,000

Reed determines that the replacement cost of ending inventory is $42,000. Show what Reed should report for ending inventory and for cost of goods sold. Identify the financial statement where each item appears.

S6-8 (*Learning Objective 2: Managing income taxes under the LIFO method*)   Smith Saxophone Company is nearing the end of its worst year ever. With two weeks until year-end, it appears that net income for the year will have decreased by 25% from last year. Joe Smith, the president and principal stockholder, is distressed with the year's results. Smith asks you, the financial vice president, to come up with a way to increase the business's net income. Inventory quantities are a little higher than normal because sales have been slow during the last few months. Smith uses the LIFO inventory method, and inventory costs have risen dramatically during the latter part of the year.   **writing assignment ■**

Complete the memorandum to Joe Smith to explain how the company can increase its net income for the year. Explain your reasoning in detail. Smith is a man of integrity, so your plan must be completely ethical.

S6-9 (*Learning Objective 2: Identifying income, tax, and other effects of the inventory methods*)   This exercise tests your understanding of the four inventory methods. List the name of the inventory method that best fits the description. Assume that the cost of inventory is rising.

1. _____ Generally associated with saving income taxes.
2. _____ Results in a cost of ending inventory that is close to the current cost of replacing the inventory.
3. _____ Used to account for automobiles, jewelry, and art objects.
4. _____ Provides a middle-ground measure of ending inventory and cost of goods sold.
5. _____ Maximizes reported income.
6. _____ Matches the most current cost of goods sold against sales revenue.
7. _____ Results in an old measure of the cost of ending inventory.
8. _____ Writes inventory down when replacement cost drops below historical cost.
9. _____ Enables a company to buy high-cost inventory at year end and thereby decrease reported income and income tax.
10. _____ Enables a company to keep reported income from dropping lower by liquidating older layers of inventory.

S6-10 (*Learning Objective 3: Using ratio data to evaluate operations*)   Mountain Company made sales of $35,482 million during 2010. Cost of goods sold for the year totaled $15,333 million. At the end of 2009, Mountain's inventory stood at $1,641 million, and Mountain ended 2010 with inventory of $1,945 million.

Compute Mountain's gross profit percentage and rate of inventory turnover for 2010.

S6-11 (*Learning Objective 4: Estimating ending inventory by the gross profit method*)   City Technology began the year with inventory of $244,000 and purchased $1,540,000 of goods during the year. Sales for the year are $4,000,000, and City's gross profit percentage is 60% of sales. Compute City's estimated cost of ending inventory by using the gross profit method.

S6-12 (*Learning Objective 5: Assessing the effect of an inventory error—one year only*)   ABC, Inc., reported these figures for its fiscal year (amounts in millions):

Net sales.............................	$ 1,900
Cost of goods sold...............	1,130
Ending inventory..................	450

Suppose ABC later learns that ending inventory was overstated by $14 million. What are the correct amounts for (a) net sales, (b) ending inventory, (c) cost of goods sold, and (d) gross profit?

S6-13 (*Learning Objective 5: Assessing the effect of an inventory error on 2 years*)   Binder's $5.8 million cost of inventory at the end of last year was understated by $1.7 million.

1. Was last year's reported gross profit of $3.8 million overstated, understated, or correct? What was the correct amount of gross profit last year?
2. Is this year's gross profit of $5.5 million overstated, understated, or correct? What is the correct amount of gross profit for the current year?

S6-14 (*Learning Objectives 2, 4: Considering ethical implications of inventory actions*)   Determine whether each of the following actions in buying, selling, and accounting for inventories is ethical or unethical. Give your reason for each answer.

1. In applying the lower-of-cost-or-market rule to inventories, Tewksbury Financial Industries recorded an excessively low market value for ending inventory. This allowed the company to pay less income tax for the year.

2. Livingston Pharmaceuticals purchased lots of inventory shortly before year-end to increase the LIFO cost of goods sold and decrease reported income for the year.

3. Mulberry, Inc., delayed the purchase of inventory until after December 31, 2010, to keep 2010's cost of goods sold from growing too large. The delay in purchasing inventory helped net income of 2010 to reach the level of profit demanded by the company's investors.

4. Dunn Sales Company deliberately overstated ending inventory in order to report higher profits (net income).

5. Burke Corporation deliberately overstated purchases to produce a high figure for cost of goods sold (low amount of net income). The real reason was to decrease the company's income tax payments to the government.

Exercises

All of the A and B exercises can be found within MyAccountingLab, an online homework and practice environment. Your instructor may ask you to complete these exercises using MyAccountingLab.

(Group A)

E6-15A (*Learning Objectives 1, 2: Accounting for inventory transactions under FIFO costing*) Accounting records for Richmond Corporation yield the following data for the year ended December 31, 2010:

■ **general ledger**

Inventory, December 31, 2009	$ 8,000
Purchases of inventory (on account)	47,000
Sales of inventory—79% on account; 21% for cash (cost $41,000)	79,000
Inventory at FIFO, December 31, 2010	14,000

❚ Requirements

1. Journalize Richmond's inventory transactions for the year under the perpetual system.

2. Report ending inventory, sales, cost of goods sold, and gross profit on the appropriate financial statement.

E6-16A (*Learning Objectives 1, 2: Analyzing inventory transactions under FIFO costing*) Ken's, Inc.'s inventory records for a particular development program show the following at December 31:

■ **spreadsheet**

Dec	1	Beginning inventory	5 units @ $150	=	$ 750
	15	Purchase	4 units @ 150	=	$ 600
	26	Purchase	12 units @ 160	=	$1,920

At December 31, nine of these programs are on hand. Journalize for Ken's:

1. Total December purchases in one summary entry. All purchases were on credit.

2. Total December sales and cost of goods sold in two summary entries. The selling price was $550 per unit, and all sales were on credit. Assume that Ken's uses the FIFO inventory method.

3. Under FIFO, how much gross profit would Ken's earn on these transactions? What is the FIFO cost of Ken's ending inventory?

E6-17A (*Learning Objective 2: Determining ending inventory and cost of goods sold by four methods*)   Use the data for Ken's in Exercise 6-16A to answer the following:

I Requirements

1. Compute cost of goods sold and ending inventory, using each of the following methods:
   a. Specific unit cost, with three $150 units and six $160 units still on hand at the end.
   b. Average cost.
   c. First-in, first-out.
   d. Last-in, first-out.
2. Which method produces the highest cost of goods sold? Which method produces the lowest cost of goods sold? What causes the difference in cost of goods sold?

E6-18A (*Learning Objective 2: Computing the tax advantage of LIFO over FIFO*)   Use the data for Ken's in Exercise 6-16A to illustrate Ken's income tax advantage from using LIFO over FIFO. Sales revenue is $6,600, operating expenses are $1,500, and the income tax rate is 35%. How much in taxes would Ken's save by using the LIFO method versus FIFO?

E6-19A (*Learning Objective 2: Determining ending inventory and cost of goods sold— FIFO vs. LIFO*)   MusicPlace.net specializes in sound equipment. Because each inventory item is expensive, MusicPlace uses a perpetual inventory system. Company records indicate the following data for a line of speakers:

Date		Item	Quantity	Unit Cost	Sale Price
Apr	1	Balance..................	16	$32	
Apr	2	Purchase...............	5	63	
Apr	7	Sale	7		$112
Apr	13	Sale	5		112

I Requirements

1. Determine the amounts that MusicPlace should report for cost of goods sold and ending inventory two ways:
   a. FIFO
   b. LIFO
2. MusicPlace uses the FIFO method. Prepare MusicPlace's income statement for the month ended April 30, 2010, reporting gross profit. Operating expenses totaled $260, and the income tax rate was 35%.

E6-20A (*Learning Objective 2: Measuring gross profit—FIFO vs. LIFO; Falling prices*)   Suppose a Waldorf store in Atlanta, Georgia, ended November 2010 with 900,000 units of merchandise that cost an average of $5 each. Suppose the store then sold 800,000 units for $4.8 million during December. Further, assume the store made two large purchases during December as follows:

Dec 11	200,000 units @ $4.00	= $ 800,000
24	500,000 units @ $3.00	= $1,500,000

I Requirements

1. At December 31, the store manager needs to know the store's gross profit under both FIFO and LIFO. Supply this information.
2. What caused the FIFO and LIFO gross profit figures to differ?
3. Assume that the store uses FIFO to value inventories, and that the store manager, whose bonus is based on profits, decides to change the unit cost on inventory to $5 for all units. What impact will this have on gross profit and net income? Does GAAP allow this?

E6-21A (*Learning Objective 2: Applying the lower-of-cost-or-market rule to inventories*)   Thames Garden Supplies uses a perpetual inventory system. Thames Garden Supplies has these account balances at July 31, 2010, prior to making the year-end adjustments:

Inventory		Cost of Goods Sold		Sales Revenue	
Beg bal 11,500					
End bal 15,000		Bal 67,000		Bal	116,000

A year ago, the replacement cost of ending inventory was $12,000, which exceeded cost of $11,500. Thames Garden Supplies has determined that the replacement cost of the July 31, 2010, ending inventory is $10,800.

▌ *Requirement*

1. Prepare Thames Garden Supplies' 2010 income statement through gross profit to show how the company would apply the lower-of-cost-or-market rule to its inventories.

E6-22A (*Learning Objective 2: Using the cost-of-goods-sold model*)   Supply the missing income statement amounts for each of the following companies (amounts adapted, in millions or billions):

Company	Net Sales	Beginning Inventory	Net Purchases	Ending Inventory	Cost of Goods Sold	Gross Profit
Crane	$105,000	$19,000	$65,000	$18,000	(a)	(b)
Foster	138,000	27,000	(c)	28,000	(d)	45,000
Allen	(e)	(f)	56,000	21,000	60,000	32,000
Matthews	84,000	11,000	30,000	(g)	36,000	(h)

▌ *Requirement*

1. Prepare the income statement for Crane Company, for the year ended December 31, 2010. Use the cost-of-goods-sold model to compute cost of goods sold. Crane's operating and other expenses, as adapted, for the year were $41,000. Ignore income tax.

Note: Exercise E6-23A builds on Exercise 6-22A with a profitability analysis of these actual companies.

E6-23A (*Learning Objective 3: Measuring profitability*)   Refer to the data in Exercise 6-22A. Compute all ratio values to answer the following questions:

■ general ledger

- Which company has the highest, and which company has the lowest, gross profit percentage?
- Which company has the highest, and the lowest rate of inventory turnover?

Based on your figures, which company appears to be the most profitable?

E6-24A (*Learning Objective 3: Computing gross profit percentage and inventory turnover*)   Thurston & Talty, a partnership, had the following inventory data:

	2009	2010
Ending inventory at:		
FIFO Cost	$21,000	$ 23,000
LIFO Cost	8,000	17,000
Cost of goods sold at:		
FIFO Cost		$ 85,200
LIFO Cost		92,800
Sales revenue		144,000

Thurston & Talty need to know the company's gross profit percentage and rate of inventory turnover for 2010 under

1. FIFO   **2.** LIFO

Which method makes the business look better on

3. Gross profit percentage?   **4.** Inventory turnover?

E6-25A (*Learning Objective 2: Budgeting inventory purchases*)   Toys Plus prepares budgets to help manage the company. Toys Plus is budgeting for the fiscal year ended January 31, 2010. During the preceding year ended January 31, 2009, sales totaled $9,300 million and cost of goods sold was $6,500 million. At January 31, 2009, inventory stood at $2,100 million. During the upcoming 2010 year, suppose Toys Plus expects cost of goods sold to increase by 10%. The company budgets next year's ending inventory at $2,400 million.

I Requirement

1. One of the most important decisions a manager makes is how much inventory to buy. How much inventory should Toys Plus purchase during the upcoming year to reach its budgeted figures?

■ spreadsheet

E6-26A (*Learning Objective 4: Estimating inventory by the gross profit method*)   J R Company began May with inventory of $47,500. The business made net purchases of $30,900 and had net sales of $62,100 before a fire destroyed the company's inventory. For the past several years, J R's gross profit percentage has been 35%. Estimate the cost of the inventory destroyed by the fire. Identify another reason owners and managers use the gross profit method to estimate inventory.

E6-27A (*Learning Objective 5: Correcting an inventory error*)   Big Blue Sea Marine Supply reported the following comparative income statement for the years ended September 30, 2010, and 2009:

Big Blue Sea Marine Supply
Income Statements
For the Years Ended September 30, 2010, and 2009

	2010		2009	
Sales revenue		$143,000		$120,000
Cost of goods sold:				
Beginning inventory	$ 14,500		$ 9,000	
Net purchases	74,000		67,000	
Cost of goods available	88,500		76,000	
Ending inventory	(19,000)		(14,500)	
Cost of goods sold		69,500		61,500
Gross profit		73,500		58,500
Operating expenses		28,000		24,000
Net income		$ 45,500		$ 34,500

Big Blue Sea's president and shareholders are thrilled by the company's boost in sales and net income during 2010. Then the accountants for the company discover that ending 2009 inventory was understated by $6,500. Prepare the corrected comparative income statement for the 2-year period, complete with a heading for the statement. How well did Big Blue Sea really perform in 2010, as compared with 2009?

(Group B)

E6-28B *(Learning Objectives 1, 2: Accounting for inventory transactions under FIFO costing)* Accounting records for Rockford Corporation yield the following data for the year ended December 31, 2010:

Inventory, December 31, 2009..	$ 8,000
Purchases of inventory (on account)...	49,000
Sales of inventory—76% on account; 24% for cash (cost $40,000).........	74,000
Inventory at FIFO, December 31, 2010..	17,000

I Requirements

1. Journalize Rockford's inventory transactions for the year under the perpetual system.
2. Report ending inventory, sales, cost of goods sold, and gross profit on the appropriate financial statement.

E6-29B *(Learning Objectives 1, 2: Analyzing inventory transactions under FIFO costing)* Ron's, Inc.'s inventory records for a particular development program show the following at May 31:

May	1	Beginning inventory	7 units @ $160	=	$1,120
	15	Purchase.................................	6 units @ 160	=	960
	26	Purchase.................................	11 units @ 170	=	1,870

At May 31, 10 of these programs are on hand. Journalize for Ron's:

1. Total May purchases in one summary entry. All purchases were on credit.
2. Total May sales and cost of goods sold in two summary entries. The selling price was $625 per unit and all sales were on credit. Assume that Ron's uses the FIFO inventory method.
3. Under FIFO, how much gross profit would Ron's earn on these transactions? What is the FIFO cost of Ron's, Inc.'s ending inventory?

E6-30B *(Learning Objective 2: Determining ending inventory and cost of goods sold by four methods)* Use the data for Ron's, Inc., in Exercise 6-29B to answer the following.

I Requirements

1. Compute cost of goods sold and ending inventory using each of the following methods:
   a. Specific unit cost, with five $160 units and five $170 units still on hand at the end.
   b. Average cost.
   c. FIFO.
   d. LIFO.
2. Which method produces the highest cost of goods sold? Which method produces the lowest cost of goods sold? What causes the difference in cost of goods sold?

E6-31B *(Learning Objective 2: Computing the tax advantage of LIFO over FIFO)* Use the data for Ron's, Inc., in Exercise 6-29B to illustrate Ron's income tax advantage from using LIFO over FIFO. Sales revenue is $8,750, operating expenses are $2,000, and the income tax rate is 32%. How much in taxes would Ron's save by using the LIFO method versus FIFO?

E6-32B (*Learning Objective 2: Determining ending inventory and cost of goods sold—FIFO vs. LIFO*) MusicLife.net specializes in sound equipment. Because each inventory item is expensive, MusicLife uses a perpetual inventory system. Company records indicate the following data for a line of speakers:

Date		Item	Quantity	Unit Cost	Sale Price
Apr	1	Balance..................	16	$39	
Apr	2	Purchase...............	6	66	
Apr	7	Sale	7		$105
Apr	13	Sale	6		96

I **Requirements**

1. Determine the amounts that MusicLife should report for cost of goods sold and ending inventory two ways:
   a. FIFO
   b. LIFO
2. MusicLife uses the FIFO method. Prepare MusicLife's income statement for the month ended April 30, 2010, reporting gross profit. Operating expenses totaled $340, and the income tax rate was 30%.

E6-33B (*Learning Objective 2: Measuring gross profit—FIFO vs. LIFO; falling prices*) Suppose a Williams store in Cleveland, Ohio, ended September 2010 with 1,100,000 units of merchandise that cost an average of $9.00 each. Suppose the store then sold 1,000,000 units for $9.7 million during October. Further, assume the store made two large purchases during October as follows:

Oct 12	100,000 units @ $8.00 = $ 800,000
24	600,000 units @ $7.00 = $4,200,000

I **Requirements**

1. At October 31, the store manager needs to know the store's gross profit under both FIFO and LIFO. Supply this information.
2. What caused the FIFO and LIFO gross profit figures to differ?
3. Assume that the store uses FIFO, and that the store manager, whose bonus is based on profits, decides to value all units in ending inventory at $9 per unit. What impact will this action have on gross profit and net income? Does GAAP allow this?

E6-34B (*Learning Objective 2: Applying the lower-of-cost-or-market rule to inventories*) Ontario Garden Supplies uses a perpetual inventory system. Ontario Garden Supplies has these account balances at May 31, 2010, prior to making the year-end adjustments:

Inventory		Cost of Goods Sold		Sales Revenue	
Beg bal 12,500					
End bal 13,500		Bal 73,000			Bal 115,000

A year ago, the replacement cost of ending inventory was $13,400, which exceeded the cost of $12,500. Ontario Garden Supplies has determined that the replacement cost of the May 31, 2010, ending inventory is $13,000.

I Requirement

1. Prepare Ontario Garden Supplies' 2010 income statement through gross profit to show how the company would apply the lower-of-cost-or-market rule to its inventories.

E6-35B (*Learning Objective 2: Using the cost-of-goods-sold model*)   Supply the missing amounts for each of the following companies:

Company	Net Sales	Beginning Inventory	Net Purchases	Ending Inventory	Cost of Goods Sold	Gross Profit
Fisher	$101,000	$22,000	$61,000	$17,000	(a)	(b)
Hults	132,000	26,000	(c)	27,000	(d)	40,000
Franklin	(e)	(f)	56,000	20,000	65,000	30,000
Ogden	86,000	8,000	37,000	(g)	39,000	(h)

I Requirement

1. Prepare the income statement for Fisher Company, for the year ended December 31, 2010. Use the cost-of-goods-sold model to compute cost of goods sold. Fisher's operating and other expenses for the year were $46,000. Ignore income tax.

Note: Exercise E6-36B builds on Exercise E6-35B with a profitability analysis of these actual companies.

E6-36B (*Learning Objective 3: Measuring profitability*)   Refer to the data in Exercise 6-35B. Compute all ratio values to answer the following questions:

general ledger ■

■ Which company has the highest, and which company has the lowest, gross profit percentage?
■ Which company has the highest, and the lowest rate of inventory turnover?

Based on your figures, which company appears to be the most profitable?

E6-37B (*Learning Objective 3: Computing gross profit percentage and inventory turnover*)   Durkin & Davis, a partnership, had these inventory data:

	2009	2010
Ending inventory at:		
FIFO Cost...............	$17,000	$ 21,000
LIFO Cost...............	15,000	23,000
Cost of goods sold at:		
FIFO Cost...............		$ 85,700
LIFO Cost...............		92,500
Sales revenue...............		141,000

Durkin & Davis need to know the company's gross profit percentage and rate of inventory turnover for 2010 under
1. FIFO   2. LIFO

Which method makes the business look better on
3. Gross profit percentage?   4. Inventory turnover?

E6-38B (*Learning Objective 2: Budgeting inventory purchases*)   Toyland prepares budgets to help manage the company. Toyland is budgeting for the fiscal year ended January 31, 2010. During preceding year ended January 31, 2009, sales totaled $9,700 million and cost of goods sold was $6,200 million. At January 31, 2009, inventory stood at $1,800 million. During the upcoming 2010 year, suppose Toyland expects cost of goods sold to increase by 10%. The company budgets next year's inventory at $2,100 million.

I Requirement

1. One of the most important decisions a manager makes is how much inventory to buy. How much inventory should Toyland purchase during the upcoming year to reach its budgeted figures?

■ spreadsheet

E6-39B (*Learning Objective 4: Estimating inventory by the gross profit method*) R B Company began June with inventory of $45,800. The business made net purchases of $31,900 and had net sales of $64,500 before a fire destroyed the company's inventory. For the past several years, R B's gross profit percentage has been 45%. Estimate the cost of the inventory destroyed by the fire. Identify another reason owners and managers use the gross profit method to estimate inventory.

E6-40B (*Learning Objective 5: Correcting an inventory error*) Harbour Master Marine Supply reported the following comparative income statement for the years ended September 30, 2010, and 2009:

Harbour Master Marine Supply
Income Statements
For the Years Ended September 30, 2010, and 2009

	2010		2009	
Sales revenue		$139,000		$121,000
Cost of goods sold:				
Beginning inventory	$ 13,000		$ 12,000	
Net purchases	74,000		69,000	
Cost of goods available	87,000		81,000	
Ending inventory	(18,500)		(13,000)	
Cost of goods sold		68,500		68,000
Gross profit		70,500		53,000
Operating expenses		26,000		19,000
Net income		$ 44,500		$ 34,000

Harbour Master's president and shareholders are thrilled by the company's boost in sales and net income during 2010. Then the accountants for the company discover that ending 2009 inventory was understated by $7,000. Prepare the corrected comparative income statement for the two-year period, complete with a heading for the statement. How well did Harbour Master really perform in 2010, as compared with 2009?

Challenge Exercises

E6-41 (*Learning Objective 2: Making inventory policy decisions*) For each of the following situations, identify the inventory method that you would use or, given the use of a particular method, state the strategy that you would follow to accomplish your goal:

   a. Inventory costs are increasing. Your company uses LIFO and is having an unexpectedly good year. It is near year-end, and you need to keep net income from increasing too much in order to save on income tax.
   b. Suppliers of your inventory are threatening a labor strike, and it may be difficult for your company to obtain inventory. This situation could increase your income taxes.

   c. Company management, like that of IBM and Pier 1 Imports, prefers a middle-of-the-road inventory policy that avoids extremes.

   d. Inventory costs are *decreasing*, and your company's board of directors wants to minimize income taxes.

   e. Inventory costs are *increasing*, and the company prefers to report high income.

   f. Inventory costs have been stable for several years, and you expect costs to remain stable for the indefinite future. (Give the reason for your choice of method.)

E6-42 (*Learning Objective 2: Measuring the effect of a LIFO liquidation*)   Suppose Trendy Now Fashions, a specialty retailer, had these records for ladies' evening gowns during 2010.

Beginning inventory (40 @ $1,075)....................	$ 43,000
Purchase in February (22 @ $1,200)	26,400
Purchase in June (53 @ $1,275)	67,575
Purchase in December (26 @ $1,325)................	34,450
Goods available for sale	$171,425

Assume sales of evening gowns totaled 130 units during 2010 and that Trendy Now uses the LIFO method to account for inventory. The income tax rate is 40%.

❙ Requirements

   1. Compute Trendy Now's cost of goods sold for evening gowns in 2010.

   2. Compute what cost of goods sold would have been if Trendy Now had purchased enough inventory in December—at $1,325 per evening gown—to keep year-end inventory at the same level it was at the beginning of the year.

E6-43 (*Learning Objective 3: Evaluating a company's profitability*)   T Mart, Inc., declared bankruptcy. Let's see why. T Mart reported these figures:

T Mart, Inc. **Statement of Income** **Years Ended December 31**				
Millions	**2010**	**2009**	**2008**	**2007**
Sales...	$36.1	$36.0	$34.6	
Cost of sales............................	28.7	27.9	26.9	
Selling expenses.......................	7.6	6.7	6.1	
Other expenses........................	0.1	0.9	0.7	
Net income (net loss)..............	$ (0.3)	$ 0.5	$ 0.9	
Additional data:				
Ending inventory..................	$ 8.8	$ 7.4	$ 7.6	$ 6.6

❙ Requirement

   1. Evaluate the trend of T Mart's results of operations during 2008 through 2010. Consider the trends of sales, gross profit, and net income. Track the gross profit percentage (to three decimal places) and the rate of inventory turnover (to one decimal place) in each year. Also discuss the role that selling expenses must have played in T Mart's difficulties.

Quiz

Test your understanding of accounting for inventory by answering the following questions. Select the best choice from among the possible answers given.

Q6-44 Oceanview Software began January with $3,200 of merchandise inventory. During January, Oceanview made the following entries for its inventory transactions:

Inventory		6,400	
	Accounts Payable		6,400
Accounts Receivable		7,400	
	Sales Revenue		7,400
Cost of Goods Sold		5,400	
	Inventory		5,400

How much was Oceanview's inventory at the end of January?

a. $5,200   c. $4,200
b. Zero   d. $4,700

Q6-45 What is Oceanview's gross profit for January?

a. Zero   c. $5,400
b. $7,400   d. $2,000

Q6-46 When does the cost of inventory become an expense?

a. When inventory is purchased from the supplier.
b. When cash is collected from the customer.
c. When payment is made to the supplier.
d. When inventory is delivered to a customer.

The next two questions use the following facts. Perfect Corner Frame Shop wants to know the effect of different inventory costing methods on its financial statements. Inventory and purchases data for April follow:

		Units	Unit Cost	Total Cost
Apr 1	Beginning inventory	2,700	$14.00	$37,800
4	Purchase	1,500	$14.40	21,600
9	Sale	(1,600)		

Q6-47 If Perfect Corner uses the FIFO method, the *cost of the ending inventory* will be

a. $37,000.   c. $22,400.
b. $22,700.   d. $21,600.

Q6-48 If Perfect Corner uses the LIFO method, *cost of goods sold* will be

a. $22,700.   c. $22,400.
b. $23,000.   d. $21,600.

Q6-49 In a period of rising prices,

a. Net income under LIFO will be higher than under FIFO.
b. Gross profit under FIFO will be higher than under LIFO.
c. LIFO inventory will be greater than FIFO inventory.
d. Cost of goods sold under LIFO will be less than under FIFO.

Q6-50 The income statement for Feel Good Health Foods shows gross profit of $151,000, operating expenses of $126,000, and cost of goods sold of $215,000. What is the amount of net sales revenue?

a. $277,000
b. $366,000

c. $492,000
d. $341,000

Q6-51 The word "market" as used in "the lower of cost or market" generally means

a. retail market price.
b. Replacement cost.

c. Retail market price.
d. Liquidation price.

Q6-52 The sum of (a) ending inventory and (b) cost of goods sold is

a. beginning inventory.
b. goods available.

c. net purchases.
d. gross profit.

Q6-53 The following data come from the inventory records of Draper Company:

Net sales revenue..	$623,000
Beginning inventory	64,000
Ending inventory..	45,000
Net purchases...	460,000

Based on these facts, the gross profit for Draper Company is

a. $130,000.
b. $163,000.

c. $134,000.
d. Some other amount.

Q6-54 Eleanor Barker Cosmetics ended the month of May with inventory of $25,000. Eleanor Barker expects to end June with inventory of $12,000 after cost of goods sold of $102,000. How much inventory must Eleanor Barker purchase during June in order to accomplish these results?

a. $89,000
b. $114,000

c. $115,000
d. Cannot be determined from the data given

Q6-55 Two financial ratios that clearly distinguish a discount chain such as Kmart from a high-end retailer such as Saks Fifth Avenue are the gross profit percentage and the rate of inventory turnover. Which set of relationships is most likely for Saks Fifth Avenue?

Gross profit percentage	**Inventory turnover**
a. High	Low
b. High	High
c. Low	Low
d. Low	High

Q6-56 Sales are $540,000 and cost of goods sold is $330,000. Beginning and ending inventories are $29,000 and $34,000, respectively. How many times did the company turn its inventory over during this period?

a. 17.1 times
b. 6.7 times

c. 7.2 times
d. 10.5 times

Q6-57 Trigger, Inc., reported the following data:

Freight in.....................	$ 25,000	Sales returns..............	$ 7,000
Purchases	208,000	Purchase returns........	6,200
Beginning inventory	57,000	Sales revenue.............	450,000
Purchase discounts	4,300	Ending inventory........	46,000

Trigger's gross profit percentage is

a. 46.3.   c. 47.3.
b. 52.7.   d. 57.4.

Q6-58 Shipley Tank Company had the following beginning inventory, net purchases, net sales, and gross profit percentage for the first quarter of 2010:

Beginning inventory, $52,000	Net purchases, $73,000
Net sales revenue, $94,000	Gross profit rate, 50%

By the gross profit method, the ending inventory should be

a. $80,000.   c. $81,000.
b. $78,000.   d. $79,000.

Q6-59 An error understated Regan Corporation's December 31, 2010, ending inventory by $42,000. What effect will this error have on total assets and net income for 2010?

	Assets	Net income
a.	Understate	No effect
b.	No effect	No effect
c.	Understate	Understate
d.	No effect	Overstate

Q6-60 An error understated Regan Corporation's December 31, 2010, ending inventory by $42,000. What effect will this error have on net income for 2011?
a. Overstate
b. Understate
c. No effect

Problems

All of the A and B problems can be found within MyAccountingLab, an online homework and practice environment. Your instructor may ask you to complete these problems using MyAccountingLab.

(Group A)

■ **general ledger**

P6-61A (*Learning Objectives 1, 2: Accounting for inventory in a perpetual system using average costing method*)   Nice Buy purchases inventory in crates of merchandise; each crate of inventory is a unit. The fiscal year of Nice Buy ends each February 28. Assume you are dealing with a single Nice Buy store in Dallas, Texas. The Dallas store began 2010 with an inventory of 21,000 units that cost a total of $1,050,000. During the year, the store purchased merchandise on account as follows:

April (31,000 units at $51)...............................	$1,581,000
August (51,000 units at $55).............................	2,805,000
November (61,000 units at $61)	3,721,000
Total purchases..	$8,107,000

Cash payments on account totaled $7,707,000. During fiscal year 2010, the store sold 148,000 units of merchandise for $14,208,000, of which $4,900,000 was for cash and the balance was on account. Nice Buy uses the average cost method for inventories. Operating expenses for the year were $3,750,000. Nice Buy paid 70% in cash and accrued the rest as accrued liabilities. The store accrued income tax at the rate of 30%.

I Requirements

1. Make summary journal entries to record the store's transactions for the year ended February 28, 2010. Nice Buy uses a perpetual inventory system.
2. Prepare a T-account to show the activity in the Inventory account.
3. Prepare the store's income statement for the year ended February 28, 2010. Show totals for gross profit, income before tax, and net income.

P6-62A (*Learning Objective 2: Measuring cost of goods sold and ending inventory—perpetual system*)   Assume a Tiger Sports outlet store began October 2010 with 48 pairs of running shoes that cost the store $34 each. The sale price of these shoes was $69. During October, the store completed these inventory transactions:

		Units	Unit Cost	Units Sales Price
Oct 3	Sale	11	$34	$69
8	Purchase	83	35	
11	Sale	37	34	69
19	Sale	6	35	71
24	Sale	38	35	71
30	Purchase	25	36	

I Requirements

1. The preceding data are taken from the store's perpetual inventory records. Which cost method does the store use? Explain how you arrived at your answer.
2. Determine the store's cost of goods sold for October. Also compute gross profit for October.
3. What is the cost of the store's October 31 inventory of running shoes?

P6-63A (*Learning Objective 2: Computing inventory by three methods—perpetual system*)   Fatigues Surplus began October with 72 tents that cost $17 each. During the month, Fatigues Surplus made the following purchases at cost:

Oct 4	103 tents @ $19 = $1,957
19	158 tents @ $21 = 3,318
25	43 tents @ $22 = 946

Fatigues Surplus sold 324 tents and at October 31 the ending inventory consists of 52 tents. The sale price of each tent was $51.

I Requirements

1. Determine the cost of goods sold and ending inventory amounts for October under the average cost, FIFO cost, and LIFO cost. Round average cost per unit four decimal places, and round all other amounts to the nearest dollar.
2. Explain why cost of goods sold is highest under LIFO. Be specific.
3. Prepare Fatigues Surplus' income statement for October. Report gross profit. Operating expenses totaled $5,000. Fatigues Surplus uses average costing for inventory. The income tax rate is 40%.

P6-64A (*Learning Objective 2: Applying the different inventory costing methods—perpetual system*)   The records of Bell Aviation include the following accounts for inventory of aviation fuel at December 31 of the current year:

Inventory			
Jan 1	Balance	790 units @ $7.70	$ 6,083
Mar 6	Purchase	320 units @ $7.80	2,496
Jun 22	Purchase	8,350 units @ $8.20	68,470
Oct 4	Purchase	530 units @ $9.20	4,876

Sales Revenue		
Dec 31	9,010 units	$132,447

❙ Requirements

1. Prepare a partial income statement through gross profit under the average, FIFO, and LIFO methods. Round average cost per unit to four decimal places and all other amounts to the nearest dollar.
2. Which inventory method would you use to minimize income tax? Explain why this method causes income tax to be the lowest.

P6-65A (*Learning Objective 2: Applying the lower-of-cost-or-market rule to inventories—perpetual system*)   ELV Trade Mart has recently had lackluster sales. The rate of inventory turnover has dropped, and the merchandise is gathering dust. At the same time, competition has forced ELV's suppliers to lower the prices that ELV will pay when it replaces its inventory. It is now December 31, 2010, and the current replacement cost of ELV's ending inventory is $75,000 below what ELV actually paid for the goods, which was $220,000. Before any adjustments at the end of the period, the Cost of Goods Sold account has a balance of $770,000.

a. What accounting action should ELV take in this situation?
b. Give any journal entry required.
c. At what amount should ELV report Inventory on the balance sheet?
d. At what amount should the company report Cost of Goods Sold on the income statement?
e. Discuss the accounting principle or concept that is most relevant to this situation.

P6-66A (*Learning Objective 3: Using gross profit percentage and inventory turnover to evaluate two companies*)   Sprinkle Top and Coffee Shop are both specialty food chains. The two companies reported these figures, in millions:

Sprinkle Top, Inc. Income Statement (Adapted) Years Ended December 31		
(Amounts in millions)	2010	2009
Revenues:		
Net sales	$544	$707
Costs and Expenses:		
Cost of goods sold	478	594
Selling, general, and administrative expenses	60	55

Sprinkle Top, Inc.
Balance Sheet (Adapted)
December 31

(Amounts in millions)	2010	2009
Assets		
Current assets:		
Cash and cash equivalents................	$12	$27
Receivables.....................................	28	40
Inventories	26	36

Coffee Shop Corporation
Income Statement (Adapted)
Years Ended December 31

(Amounts in millions)	2010	2009
Net sales	$7,700	$6,300
Cost of goods sold..............................	3,160	2,604
Selling, general, and administrative expenses.......	2,950	2,390

Coffee Shop Corporation
Balance Sheet (Adapted)
December 31

(Amounts in millions)	2010	2009
Assets		
Current assets:		
Cash and temporary investments................	$313	$172
Receivables, net..	230	188
Inventories	627	544

▌ Requirements

1. Compute the gross profit percentage and the rate of inventory turnover for Sprinkle Top and Coffee Shop for 2010.
2. Based on these statistics, which company looks more profitable? Why? What other expense category should we consider in evaluating these two companies?

P6-67A *(Learning Objectives 1, 4: Estimating inventory by the gross profit method; preparing the income statement)*   Assume Thompson Company, a copy center, lost some inventory in a fire. To file an insurance claim, Thompson Company must estimate its inventory by the gross profit method. Assume that for the past two years that Thompson

■ **spreadsheet**

Company's gross profit has averaged 41% of net sales. Suppose the Thompson Company's inventory records reveal the following data:

Inventory, October 1................	$ 57,100
Transactions during October:	
Purchases	490,200
Purchase discounts	11,000
Purchase returns.......................	70,900
Sales..	667,000
Sales returns............................	11,000

I Requirements

1. Estimate the cost of the lost inventory, using the gross profit method.
2. Prepare the October income statement for this product through gross profit. Show the detailed computations of cost of goods sold in a separate schedule.

P6-68A (*Learning Objective 3: Determining the amount of inventory to purchase*) Maroney's Convenience Store's income statement and balance sheet reported the following.

Maroney's Convenience Stores
Income Statement
Year Ended December 31, 2009

Sales	$957,000
Cost of sales	720,000
Gross profit	237,000
Operating expenses	114,000
Net income	$123,000

Maroney's Convenience Stores
Balance Sheet
December 31, 2009

Assets		Liabilities	
Cash	$ 44,000	Accounts payable	$ 31,000
Inventories	68,000	Note payable.................	187,000
Land and		Total liabilities	218,000
buildings, net	273,000	Owner, capital...............	167,000
		Total liabilities	
Total assets...................	$385,000	and capital	$385,000

The business is organized as a proprietorship, so it pays no corporate income tax. The owner is budgeting for 2010. He expects sales and cost of goods sold to increase by 6%. To meet customer demand, ending inventory will need to be $76,000 at December 31, 2010. The owner hopes to earn a net income of $154,000 next year.

I Requirements

1. One of the most important decisions a manager makes is the amount of inventory to purchase. Show how to determine the amount of inventory to purchase in 2010.
2. Prepare the store's budgeted income statement for 2010 to reach the target net income of $154,000. To reach this goal, operating expenses must decrease by $16,780.

P6-69A (*Learning Objective 5: Correcting inventory errors over a three-year period*) The accounting records of R.B. Video Sales show the data on the following page (in millions). The shareholders are very happy with R.B.'s steady increase in net income.

Auditors discovered that the ending inventory for 2008 was understated by $3 million and that the ending inventory for 2009 was also understated by $3 million. The ending inventory at December 31, 2010, was correct.

	2010		2009		2008	
Net sales revenue.............................		$39		$36		$33
Cost of goods sold:						
Beginning inventory..................	$ 5		$ 4		$ 3	
Net purchases	27		25		23	
Cost of goods available..............	32		29		26	
Less ending inventory................	(6)		(5)		(4)	
Cost of goods sold		26		24		22
Gross profit....................................		13		12		11
Operating expenses........................		6		6		6
Net income.....................................		$ 7		$ 6		$ 5

I *Requirements*

1. Show corrected income statements for each of the three years.
2. How much did these assumed corrections add to or take away from R.B.'s total net income over the three-year period? How did the corrections affect the trend of net income?
3. Will R.B.'s shareholders still be happy with the company's trend of net income? Give the reason for your answer.

(Group B)

P6-70B (*Learning Objectives 1, 2: Accounting for inventory in a perpetual system using average costing method*)   Best Guy purchases inventory in crates of merchandise; each crate of inventory is a unit. The fiscal year of Best Guy ends each February 28. Assume you are dealing with a single Best Guy store in Denver, Colorado. The Denver store began 2010 with an inventory of 17,000 units that cost a total of $850,000. During the year, the store purchased merchandise on account as follows:

■ **general ledger**

April (33,000 units at $60).....................................	$1,980,000
August (53,000 units at $64)................................	3,392,000
November (63,000 units at $70)	4,410,000
Total purchases..	$9,782,000

Cash payments on account totaled $9,382,000. During fiscal 2010, the store sold 152,000 units of merchandise for $14,592,000, of which $4,500,000 was for cash and the balance was on account. Best Guy uses the average cost method for inventories. Operating expenses for the year were $2,750,000. Best Guy paid 60% in cash and accrued the rest as accrued liabilities. The store accrued income tax at the rate of 35%.

I *Requirements*

1. Make summary journal entries to record the store's transactions for the year ended February 28, 2010. Best Guy uses a perpetual inventory system.
2. Prepare a T-account to show the activity in the Inventory account.
3. Prepare the store's income statement for the year ended February 28, 2010. Show totals for gross profit, income before tax, and net income.

P6-71B *(Learning Objective 2: Measuring cost of goods sold and ending inventory—perpetual system)* Assume a Championship Sports outlet store began March 2010 with 46 pairs of running shoes that cost the store $39 each. The sale price of these shoes was $65. During March the store completed these inventory transactions:

		Units	Unit Cost	Units Sale Price
Mar 3	Sale	17	$39	$65
8	Purchase......	78	40	
11	Sale	29	39	65
19	Sale	11	40	67
24	Sale	36	40	67
30	Purchase......	19	41	

❚ Requirements

1. The preceding data are taken from the store's perpetual inventory records. Which cost method does the store use? Explain how you arrived at your answer.
2. Determine the store's cost of goods sold for March. Also compute gross profit for March.
3. What is the cost of the store's March 31 inventory of running shoes?

P6-72B *(Learning Objective 2: Computing inventory by three methods—perpetual system)* SWAT Team Surplus began July with 66 tents that cost $23 each. During the month, SWAT Team Surplus made the following purchases at cost:

Jul 4	105 tents @ $25 =	$2,625
19	157 tents @ $27 =	4,239
25	37 tents @ $28 =	1,036

SWAT Team Surplus sold 310 tents, and at July 31 the ending inventory consists of 55 tents. The sale price of each tent was $53.

❚ Requirements

1. Determine the cost of goods sold and ending inventory amounts for July under the average cost, FIFO cost, and LIFO cost. Round average cost per unit four decimal places, and round all other amounts to the nearest dollar.
2. Explain why cost of goods sold is highest under LIFO. Be specific.
3. Prepare SWAT Team Surplus income statement for July. Report gross profit. Operating expenses totaled $3,000. SWAT Team Surplus uses average costing for inventory. The income tax rate is 32%.

writing assignment ■

P6-73B *(Learning Objective 2: Applying the different inventory costing methods—perpetual system)* The records of Buzz Aviation include the following accounts for inventory of aviation fuel at December 31 of the current year:

			Inventory		
Jan 1	Balance	730 units @ $7.60	$ 5,548		
Mar 6	Purchase	310 units @ $7.70	2,387		
Jun 22	Purchase	8,370 units @ $8.10	67,797		
Oct 4	Purchase	520 units @ $9.10	4,732		

		Sales Revenue		
	Dec 31	9,030 units		$128,226

▌ Requirements

1. Prepare a partial income statement through gross profit under the average, FIFO, and LIFO methods. Round average cost per unit to four decimal places and all other amounts to the nearest whole dollar.
2. Which inventory method would you use to minimize income tax? Explain why this method causes income tax to be the lowest.

P6-74B (*Learning Objective 2: Applying the lower-of-cost-or-market rule to inventories— perpetual system*)   Aquarium Trade Mart has recently had lackluster sales. The rate of inventory turnover has dropped, and the merchandise is gathering dust. At the same time, competition has forced Aquarium's suppliers to lower the prices that Aquarium will pay when it replaces its inventory. It is now December 31, 2010, and the current replacement cost of Aquarium's ending inventory is $70,000 below what Aquarium actually paid for the goods, which was $280,000. Before any adjustments at the end of the period, the Cost of Goods Sold account has a balance of $800,000.

writing assignment ■

    a. What accounting action should Aquarium take in this situation?
    b. Give any journal entry required.
    c. At what amount should Aquarium report Inventory on the balance sheet?
    d. At what amount should the company report Cost of Goods Sold on the income statement?
    e. Discuss the accounting principle or concept that is most relevant to this situation.

P6-75B (*Learning Objective 3: Using gross profit percentage and inventory turnover to evaluate two companies*)   Pastry People and Coffee Grind are both specialty food chains. The two companies reported these figures, in millions:

Pastry People, Inc.
Income Statement (Adapted)
Years Ended December 31

(Amounts in millions)	2010	2009
Revenues:		
Net sales	$548	$701
Costs and Expenses:		
Cost of goods sold.......................................	477	593
Selling, general, and administrative expenses...............	61	51

Pastry People, Inc.
Balance Sheet (Adapted)
December 31

(Amounts in millions)	2010	2009
Assets		
Current assets:		
Cash and cash equivalents................	$17	$22
Receivables.......................................	21	34
Inventories	17	33

Coffee Grind Corporation
Income Statement (Adapted)
Years Ended December 31

(Amounts in millions)	2010	2009
Net sales	$7,171	$6,369
Cost of goods sold...	3,190	2,603
Selling, general, and administrative expenses.......	2,955	2,360

Coffee Grind Corporation
Balance Sheet (Adapted)
December 31

(Amounts in millions)	2010	2009
Assets		
Current assets:		
Cash and temporary investments................	$310	$171
Receivables, net..	227	193
Inventories	631	546

▌Requirements

1. Compute the gross profit percentage and the rate of inventory turnover for Pastry People and Coffee Grind for 2010.
2. Based on these statistics, which company looks more profitable? Why? What other expense category should we consider in evaluating these two companies?

P6-76B (*Learning Objectives 1, 4: Estimating inventory by the gross profit method; preparing the income statement*) Assume Ross Company, a sporting goods store, lost some inventory in a fire. To file an insurance claim, Ross Company must estimate its ending inventory by the gross profit method. Assume that for the past two years, Ross Company's gross profit has averaged 43% of net sales. Suppose Ross Company's inventory records reveal the following data:

Inventory, January 1	$ 57,500
Transactions during January:	
Purchases	490,500
Purchase discounts	12,000
Purchase returns........................	70,300
Sales...	664,000
Sales returns..............................	16,000

▌Requirements

1. Estimate the cost of the lost inventory, using the gross profit method.
2. Prepare the January income statement for this product through gross profit. Show the detailed computation of cost of goods sold in a separate schedule.

P6-77B (*Learning Objective 3: Determining the amount of inventory to purchase*) Dave's Convenience Store's income statement and balance sheet reported the following. The business is organized as a proprietorship, so it pays no corporate income tax. The owner is budgeting for 2010. He expects sales and cost of goods sold to increase by 9%. To meet customer demand, ending inventory will need to be $78,000 at December 31, 2010. The owner hopes to earn a net income of $156,000 next year.

Dave's Convenience Stores
Income Statement
Year Ended December 31, 2009

Sales	$964,000
Cost of sales	722,000
Gross profit	242,000
Operating expenses	110,000
Net income	$132,000

Dave's Convenience Stores
Balance Sheet
December 31, 2009

Assets		Liabilities	
Cash	$ 35,000	Accounts payable	$ 28,000
Inventories	65,000	Note payable	193,000
Land and		Total liabilities	221,000
buildings, net	268,000	Owner, capital	147,000
		Total liabilities	
Total assets	$368,000	and capital	$368,000

I Requirements

1. One of the most important decisions a manager makes is the amount of inventory to purchase. Show how to determine the amount of inventory to purchase in 2010.
2. Prepare the store's budgeted income statement for 2010 to reach the target net income of $156,000. To reach this goal, operating expenses must decrease by $2,220.

P6-78B (*Learning Objective 5: Correcting inventory errors over a three-year period*)   The accounting records of Waterville Video Sales show these data (in millions). The shareholders are very happy with Waterville's steady increase in net income.

	2010		2009		2008	
Net sales revenue		$42		$39		$36
Cost of goods sold:						
Beginning inventory	$ 10		$ 9		$ 8	
Net purchases	33		31		29	
Cost of goods available	43		40		37	
Less ending inventory	(11)		(10)		(9)	
Cost of goods sold		32		30		28
Gross profit		10		9		8
Operating expenses		5		5		5
Net income		$ 5		$ 4		$ 3

Auditors discovered that the ending inventory for 2008 was understated by $2 million and that the ending inventory for 2009 was also understated by $2 million. The ending inventory at December 31, 2010 was correct.

I Requirements

1. Show corrected income statements for each of the three years.
2. How much did these assumed corrections add to or take away from Waterville's total net income over the three-year period? How did the corrections affect the trend of net income?
3. Will Waterville's shareholders still be happy with the company's trend of net income? Give the reason for your answer.

APPLY YOUR KNOWLEDGE

Decision Cases

writing assignment ■

Case 1. *(Learning Objectives 1, 2: Assessing the impact of a year-end purchase of inventory)* Duracraft Corporation is nearing the end of its first year of operations. Duracraft made inventory purchases of $745,000 during the year, as follows:

January	1,000 units @	$100.00 =	$100,000
July	4,000	121.25	485,000
November	1,000	160.00	160,000
Totals	6,000		$745,000

Sales for the year are 5,000 units for $1,200,000 of revenue. Expenses other than cost of goods sold and income taxes total $200,000. The president of the company is undecided about whether to adopt the FIFO method or the LIFO method for inventories. The income tax rate is 40%.

▮ Requirements

1. To aid company decision making, prepare income statements under FIFO and under LIFO.
2. Compare the net income under FIFO with net income under LIFO. Which method produces the higher net income? What causes this difference? Be specific.

writing assignment ■

Case 2. *(Learning Objective 2: Assessing the impact of the inventory costing method on the financial statements)* The inventory costing method a company chooses can affect the financial statements and thus the decisions of the people who use those statements.

▮ Requirements

1. Company A uses the LIFO inventory method and discloses its use of the LIFO method in notes to the financial statements. Company B uses the FIFO method to account for its inventory. Company B does *not* disclose which inventory method it uses. Company B reports a higher net income than Company A. In which company would you prefer to invest? Give your reason.
2. Conservatism is an accepted accounting concept. Would you want management to be conservative in accounting for inventory if you were a shareholder or a creditor of a company? Give your reason.

Ethical Issue

During 2010, Vanguard, Inc., changed to the LIFO method of accounting for inventory. Suppose that during 2011, Vanguard changes back to the FIFO method and the following year Vanguard switches back to LIFO again.

▮ Requirements

1. What would you think of a company's ethics if it changed accounting methods every year?
2. What accounting principle would changing methods every year violate?
3. Who can be harmed when a company changes its accounting methods too often? How?

Focus on Financials: ■ Amazon.com, Inc.

(Learning Objectives 2, 3: Analyzing inventories) The notes are part of the financial statements. They give details that would clutter the statements. This case will help you learn to use a

company's inventory notes. Refer to **Amazon.com, Inc.'s** consolidated financial statements and related notes in Appendix A at the end of the book and answer the following questions:

1. How much was Amazon.com, Inc.'s merchandise inventory at December 31, 2008? At December 31, 2007? Does Amazon.com, Inc., include all inventory that it handles in the inventory account on its balance sheet?

2. How does Amazon.com, Inc., *value* its inventories? Which *cost* method does the company use?

3. How much were Amazon.com, Inc.'s purchases of inventory during the year ended December 31, 2008?

4. Did Amazon.com, Inc.'s gross profit percentage on company sales improve or deteriorate in the year ended February 2, 2008, compared to the previous year?

5. Would you rate Amazon.com, Inc.'s rate of inventory turnover for the years ended February 2, 2008, and February 3, 2007, as fast or slow in comparison to most other companies in its industry? Explain your answer.

6. Go to the SEC's Web site (www.sec.gov). Find Amazon.com, Inc.'s most recent consolidated balance sheet and consolidated statement of operations. What has happened to the company's inventory turnover and gross profit percentages since December 31, 2008? Can you explain the reasons? Where would you find the company's explanations for these changes? (Challenge)

Focus on Analysis: ■ Foot Locker, Inc.

(*Learning Objectives 1, 2, 3: Measuring critical inventory amounts*) Refer to the **Foot Locker, Inc.**, consolidated financial statements in Appendix B at the end of this book. Show amounts in millions and round to the nearest $1 million.

1. Three important pieces of inventory information are (a) the cost of inventory on hand, (b) the cost of sales, and (c) the cost of inventory purchases. Identify or compute each of these items for Foot Locker, Inc., at the end of its fiscal 2007 year.

2. Which item in requirement 1 is most directly related to cash flow? Why? (Challenge)

3. Assume that all inventory purchases were made on account, and that only inventory purchases increased Accounts Payable. Compute Foot Locker, Inc.'s cash payments for inventory during fiscal 2007.

4. How does Foot Locker, Inc., *value* its inventories? Which *costing* method does Foot Locker, Inc., use?

5. Did Foot Locker, Inc.'s gross profit percentage and rate of inventory turnover improve or deteriorate in fiscal 2007 (versus fiscal 2006)? Consider the overall effect of these two ratios. Did Foot Locker, Inc., improve during fiscal 2007? How did these factors affect the net income for fiscal 2007? Foot Locker, Inc.'s inventories totaled $1,254 million at the end of fiscal 2005. Round decimals to three places.

Group Project

(*Learning Objective 3: Comparing companies' inventory turnover ratios*) Obtain the annual reports of 10 companies, two from each of five different industries. Most companies' financial statements can be downloaded from their Web sites.

writing assignment ■

1. Compute each company's gross profit percentage and rate of inventory turnover for the most recent two years. If annual reports are unavailable or do not provide enough data for multiple-year computations, you can gather financial statement data from *Moody's Industrial Manual*.

2. For the industries of the companies you are analyzing, obtain the industry averages for gross profit percentage and inventory turnover from Robert Morris Associates, *Annual Statement Studies*; Dun and Bradstreet, *Industry Norms and Key Business Ratios*; or Leo Troy, *Almanac of Business and Industrial Financial Ratios*.

3. How well does each of your companies compare to the other company in its industry? How well do your companies compare to the average for their industry? What insight about your companies can you glean from these ratios?
4. Write a memo to summarize your findings, stating whether your group would invest in each of the companies it has analyzed.

For online homework, exercises, and problems that provide you with immediate feedback, please visit www.myaccountinglab.com.

Quick Check Answers

1. *b*
2. *a*
3. *e*
4. *c* [(15 × $5) + (25 × $8)]
5. *b* (15 × $5) + ($10 × $8)
6. *c* 25 × [($75 + $320 + $90) ÷ 65]
7. *c*
8. *a*
9. *c*
10. *a* ($117,000 − $57,000)
11. *c* ($145,000 + $25,000 − $15,000)
12. *b* ($28,000 + $93,000 + $3,000 − $7,000 − $35,000)
13. *a* ($184,000 − $82,000)/$184,000
14. *b* [$82,000 ÷ ($28,000 + $35,000)/2]
15. *d* $110,000 + $260,000 − [$470,000 × (1 − .40)]
16. *a*

APPENDIX 6A

Accounting for Inventory in the Periodic System

In the periodic inventory system, the business keeps no running record of the merchandise. Instead, at the end of the period, the business counts inventory on hand and applies the unit costs to determine the cost of ending inventory. This inventory figure appears on the balance sheet and is used to compute cost of goods sold.

Recording Transactions in the Periodic System

In the periodic system, throughout the period the Inventory account carries the beginning balance left over from the preceding period. The business records purchases of inventory in the Purchases account (an expense). Then, at the end of the period, the Inventory account must be updated for the financial statements. A journal entry removes the beginning balance by crediting Inventory and debiting Cost of Goods Sold. A second journal entry sets up the ending inventory balance, based on the physical count. The final entry in this sequence transfers the amount of Purchases to Cost of Goods Sold. These end-of-period entries can be made during the closing process.

Exhibit 6A-1 illustrates the accounting in the periodic system. After the process is complete, Inventory has its correct ending balance of $120,000, and Cost of Goods Sold shows $540,000.

EXHIBIT 6-A1 | Recording and Reporting Inventories—Periodic System (Amounts Assumed)

PANEL A—Recording Transactions and the T-accounts (All amounts are assumed)

1.	Purchases	560,000	
	Accounts Payable		560,000
	Purchased inventory on account.		
2.	Accounts Receivable	900,000	
	Sales Revenue		900,000
	Sold inventory on account.		
3.	End-of-period entries to update Inventory and record Cost of Goods Sold:		
a.	Cost of Goods Sold	100,000	
	Inventory (beginning balance)		100,000
	Transferred beginning inventory to COGS.		
b.	Inventory (ending balance)	120,000	
	Cost of Goods Sold		120,000
	Set up ending inventory based on physical count.		
c.	Cost of Goods Sold	560,000	
	Purchases		560,000
	Transferred purchases to COGS.		

The T-accounts show the following:

Inventory		Cost of Goods Sold	
100,000*	100,000	100,000	120,000
120,000		560,000	
		540,000	

*Beginning inventory was $100,000

PANEL B—Reporting in the Financial Statements

Income Statement (Partial)			Ending Balance Sheet (Partial)		
Sales revenue		$900,000	Current assets:		
Cost of goods sold:			Cash	$	XXX
Beginning inventory	$ 100,000		Short-term investments		XXX
Purchases	560,000		Accounts receivable		XXX
Goods available	660,000		Inventory		120,000
Ending inventory	(120,000)		Prepaid expenses		XXX
Cost of goods sold		540,000			
Gross profit		$360,000			

Appendix Assignments

Short Exercises

S6A-1 (*Recording inventory transactions in the periodic system*)   Saxton Technologies began the year with inventory of $480. During the year, Saxton purchased inventory costing $1,180 and sold goods for $3,200, with all transactions on account. Saxton ended the year with inventory of $610. Journalize all the necessary transactions under the periodic inventory system.

S6A-2 (*Computing cost of goods sold and preparing the income statement—periodic system*)   Use the data in Short Exercise 6A-1 to do the following for Saxton Technologies:

❚ Requirements

1. Post to the Inventory and Cost of Goods Sold accounts.
2. Compute cost of goods sold by the cost-of-goods-sold model.
3. Prepare the income statement of Saxton Technologies through gross profit.

Exercises

> All of these exercises can be found within MyAccountingLab, an online homework and practice environment. Your instructor may ask you to complete these exercises using MyAccountingLab.

(Group A)

E6A-3A (*Computing amounts for the GAAP inventory methods—periodic system*)   Suppose Halton Corporation's inventory records for a particular computer chip indicate the following at July 31:

Jul	1	Beginning inventory	5 units @ $59 = $295
	8	Purchase.................................	3 units @ $59 = 177
	15	Purchase.................................	13 units @ $69 = 897
	26	Purchase.................................	1 units @ $79 = 79

The physical count of inventory at July 31 indicates that seven units of inventory are on hand.

❚ Requirements

Compute ending inventory and cost of goods sold, using each of the following methods:

1. Specific unit cost, assuming two $59 units and five $69 units are on hand
2. Average cost (round average unit cost to the nearest cent)
3. First-in, first-out
4. Last-in, first-out

E6A-4A (*Journalizing inventory transactions in the periodic system; computing cost of goods sold*)   Use the data in Exercise 6A-3A.

❚ Requirements

Journalize the following for the periodic system:

1. Total July purchases in one summary entry. All purchases were on credit.
2. Total July sales in a summary entry. Assume that the selling price was $295 per unit and that all sales were on credit.
3. July 31 entries for inventory. Halton uses LIFO. Post to the Cost of Goods Sold T-account to show how this amount is determined. Label each item in the account.
4. Show the computation of cost of goods sold by the cost-of-goods-sold model.

(Group B)

E6A-5B (*Computing amounts for the GAAP inventory methods—periodic system*)   Suppose Saxton Corporation's inventory records for a particular computer chip indicate the following at December 31:

Dec	1	Beginning inventory	6 units @ $60 = $360
	8	Purchase................................	4 units @ $60 = 240
	15	Purchase................................	13 units @ $70 = 910
	26	Purchase................................	2 units @ $80 = 160

The physical count of inventory at December 31 indicates that nine units of inventory are on hand.

❙ Requirements

Compute ending inventory and cost of goods sold, using each of the following methods:

1. Specific unit cost, assuming four $60 units and five $70 units are on hand
2. Average cost (round average unit cost to the nearest cent)
3. First-in, first-out
4. Last-in, first-out

E6A-6B (*Journalizing inventory transactions in the periodic system; computing cost of goods sold*)   Use the data in Exercise 6A-5B.

❙ Requirements

Journalize the following for the periodic system:

1. Total December purchases in one summary entry. All purchases were on credit.
2. Total December sales in a summary entry. Assume that the selling price was $315 per unit and that all sales were on credit.
3. December 31 entries for inventory. Saxton uses LIFO. Post to the Cost of Goods Sold T-account to show how this amount is determined. Label each item in the account.
4. Show the computation of cost of goods sold by the cost-of-goods-sold model.

Problems

All of these problems can be found within MyAccountingLab, an online homework and practice environment. Your instructor may ask you to complete these problems using MyAccountingLab.

MyAccountingLab

(Group A)

P6A-7A *(Computing cost of goods sold and gross profit on sales—periodic system)*   Assume a Watercrest outlet store began July 2010 with 48 units of inventory that cost $16 each. The sale price of these units was $69. During July, the store completed these inventory transactions:

		Units	Unit Cost	Units Sale Price
Jul 3	Sale	19	$16	$69
8	Purchase	80	17	71
11	Sale	29	16	69
19	Sale	3	17	71
24	Sale	35	17	71
30	Purchase	22	18	72
31	Sale	4	17	71

I *Requirements*

1. Determine the store's cost of goods sold for July under the periodic inventory system. Assume the FIFO method.
2. Compute gross profit for July.

P6A-8A *(Recording transactions in the periodic system; reporting inventory items in the financial statements)*   Accounting records for Halton Desserts, Inc., yield the following data for the year ended December 31, 2010 (amounts in thousands):

Inventory, December 31, 2009	$ 560
Purchases of inventory (on account)	2,040
Sales of inventory—70% on account; 30% for cash	3,400
Inventory at the lower of FIFO cost or market, December 31, 2010	680

I *Requirements*

1. Journalize Halton Desserts' inventory transactions for the year under the periodic system. Show all amounts in thousands.
2. Report ending inventory, sales, cost of goods sold, and gross profit on the appropriate financial statement (amounts in thousands). Show the computation of cost of goods sold.

(Group B)

P6A-9B *(Computing cost of goods sold and gross profit on sales—periodic system)* Assume a Championship outlet store began January 2010 with 50 units of inventory that cost $19 each. The sale price of these units was $71. During January the store completed these inventory transactions:

		Units	Unit Cost	Units Sale Price
Jan 3	Sale	17	$19	$71
8	Purchase	77	20	73
11	Sale	33	19	71
19	Sale	2	20	73
24	Sale	39	20	73
30	Purchase	19	21	74
31	Sale	5	20	73

I Requirements

1. Determine the store's cost of goods sold for January under the periodic inventory system. Assume the FIFO method.
2. Compute gross profit for January.

P6A-10B *(Recording transactions in the periodic system; reporting inventory items in the financial statements)* Accounting records for Just Desserts, Inc., yield the following data for the year ended December 31, 2010 (amounts in thousands):

Inventory, December 31, 2009	$ 530
Purchases of inventory (on account)	2,000
Sales of inventory—75% on account, 25% for cash	3,800
Inventory at the lower of FIFO cost or market, December 31, 2010	650

I Requirements

1. Journalize Just Desserts' inventory transactions for the year under the periodic system. Show all amounts in thousands.
2. Report ending inventory, sales, cost of goods sold, and gross profit on the appropriate financial statement (amounts in thousands). Show the computation of cost of goods sold.

APPENDIX 6B

The LIFO Reserve—Converting a LIFO Company's Net Income to the FIFO Basis

Suppose you are a financial analyst, and it is your job to recommend stocks for your clients to purchase as investments. You have narrowed your choice to **Wal-Mart Stores, Inc.**, and **Gap, Inc.** Wal-Mart uses the LIFO method for inventories and the GAP uses FIFO. The two companies' net incomes are not comparable because they use different inventory methods. To compare the two companies, you need to place them on the same footing.

The Internal Revenue Service allows companies to use LIFO for income tax purposes only if they use LIFO for financial reporting, but companies may also report an alternative inventory amount in the financial statements. Doing so presents a rare opportunity to convert a company's net income from the LIFO basis to what the income would have been if the business had used FIFO. Fortunately, you can convert Wal-Mart's income from the LIFO basis, as reported in the company's financial statements, to the FIFO basis. Then you can compare Wal-Mart and Gap.

Like many other companies that use LIFO, Wal-Mart reports the FIFO cost, a LIFO Reserve, and the LIFO cost of ending inventory. The LIFO Reserve[1] is the difference between the LIFO cost of an inventory and what the cost of that inventory would be under FIFO. Assume that Wal-Mart reported the following amounts:

Wal-Mart Uses LIFO		
	(In millions)	
	2011	2010
From the Wal-Mart balance sheet:		
Inventories (approximate FIFO cost)...............	$ 25,056	$22,749
Less LIFO reserve...	(165)	(135)
LIFO cost...	24,891	22,614
From the Wal-Mart income statement:		
Cost of goods sold...	$191,838	
Net income...	8,039	
Income tax rate	35%	

Converting Wal-Mart's 2011 net income to the FIFO basis focuses on the LIFO Reserve because the reserve captures the difference between Wal-Mart's ending inventory costed at LIFO and at FIFO. Observe that during each year, the FIFO cost of ending inventory exceeded the LIFO cost. During 2011, the LIFO Reserve increased by $30 million ($165 million − $135 million). *The LIFO Reserve can increase only when inventory costs are rising.* Recall that during a period of rising costs, LIFO produces the highest cost of goods sold and the lowest net income. Therefore, for 2011, Wal-Mart's cost of goods sold would have been lower if the company had used the FIFO method for inventories. Wal-Mart's net income would have been higher, as the following computations show:

---

[1]The LIFO Reserve account is widely used in practice even though the term "reserve" is poor terminology.

If Wal-Mart Had Used FIFO in 2011	
	(In millions)
Cost of goods sold, as reported under LIFO...	$191,838
− Increase in LIFO Reserve ($165 − $135)	(30)
= Cost of goods sold, if Wal-Mart had used FIFO.......................................	$191,808
Lower cost of goods sold → Higher pretax income by...............................	$ 30
Minus income taxes (35%)	11
Higher net income under FIFO........................	19
Net income as reported under LIFO...............	8,039
Net income Wal-Mart would have reported for 2011 if using FIFO.....................................	$ 8,058

Now you can compare Wal-Mart's net income with that of The Gap, Inc. All the ratios used for the analysis—current ratio, inventory turnover, and so on—can be compared between the two companies as though they both used the FIFO inventory method.

The LIFO Reserve provides another opportunity for managers and investors to answer a key question about a company.

How much income tax has the company saved over its lifetime by using the LIFO method to account for inventory?

Using Wal-Mart as an example, the computation at the end of 2011 is (amounts in millions):

Income tax saved by using LIFO = LIFO Reserve × Income tax rate
$$\$58 \quad = \quad \$165 \quad \times \quad .35$$

With these price changes, by the end of 2011 Wal-Mart has saved a total of $58 million by using the LIFO method to account for its merchandise inventory. Had Wal-Mart used the FIFO method, Wal-Mart would have almost $58 million less cash to invest in the opening of new stores.

In recent years many companies have experienced decreases in the cost of their inventories. When prices decline, cost of goods sold under FIFO is greater (LIFO cost of goods sold is less). This makes gross profit and net income less under FIFO.

7

Plant Assets & Intangibles

SPOTLIGHT: FedEx Corporation

If you need a document delivered across the country overnight, FedEx can handle it. FedEx Corporation sets the standard for quick delivery. As you can see from the company's Consolidated Balance Sheets on the following page, FedEx moves packages using aircraft, package-handling equipment, computers, and vehicles. These are FedEx's most important assets (lines 8–16).

This chapter covers long-term plant assets to complete our coverage of assets, except for long-term investments in Chapter 10. Let's begin by examining the various types of long-term assets.

FedEx Corporation
Consolidated Balance Sheets (Partial, Adapted)

(In millions)	May 31, 2008	2007
1 ASSETS		
2 CURRENT ASSETS		
3 Cash and cash equivalents....................................	$ 1,539	$ 1,569
4 Receivables, less allowances of $158 and $136	4,359	3,942
5 Spare parts, supplies and fuel	435	338
6 Prepaid expenses and other	911	780
7 Total current assets...	7,244	6,629
8 PROPERTY AND EQUIPMENT, AT COST		
9 Aircraft and related equipment...........................	10,165	9,593
10 Package handling and ground support equipment....	4,817	3,889
11 Computer and electronic equipment..................	5,040	4,685
12 Vehicles	2,754	2,561
13 Facilities and other...	6,529	6,362
14 Total cost...	29,305	27,090
15 Less: Accumulated depreciation	(15,827)	(14,454)
16 Net property and equipment...........................	13,478	12,636
17 OTHER LONG-TERM ASSETS		
18 Goodwill...	3,165	3,497
19 Prepaid pension cost..	827	—
20 Intangible and other assets	919	1,238
21 Total other long-term assets...........................	4,911	4,735
22 TOTAL ASSETS	$ 25,633	$ 24,000

LEARNING OBJECTIVES

1 **Determine** the cost of a plant asset

2 **Account** for depreciation

3 **Select** the best depreciation method

4 **Analyze** the effect of a plant asset disposal

5 **Account** for natural resources and depletion

6 **Account** for intangible assets and amortization

7 **Report** plant asset transactions on the statement of cash flows

TYPES OF ASSETS

Businesses use several types of long-lived assets, as shown in Exhibit 7-1. We also show the expense that applies to each asset. For example, buildings, airplanes, and equipment depreciate. Natural resources deplete, and intangible assets are amortized.

- **Plant assets**, or *fixed assets*, are long-lived assets that are tangible—for instance, land, buildings, and equipment. The expense associated with plant assets is called *depreciation*. Of the plant assets, land is unique. Land is not expensed over time because its usefulness does not decrease. Most companies report plant assets as property, plant, and equipment on the balance sheet. **FedEx** uses the heading Property and Equipment (lines 8–16).

■ **Intangible assets** are useful because of the special rights they carry. They have no physical form. Patents, copyrights, and trademarks are intangible assets; so is goodwill. Accounting for intangibles is similar to accounting for plant assets. FedEx reports Goodwill and Intangible Assets on its balance sheet (lines 18 and 20). Prepaid pension cost (line 19) is a type of long-term prepaid expense that's covered in later courses.

Accounting for plant assets and intangibles has its own terminology. Different names apply to the individual plant assets and their corresponding expenses, as shown in Exhibit 7-1.

EXHIBIT 7-1 | **Plant Assets Terminology**

Asset Account (Balance Sheet)	Related Expense Account (Income Statement)
Plant Assets	
Land	None
Buildings, Machinery and Equipment	Depreciation
Furniture and Fixtures	Depreciation
Land Improvements	Depreciation
Natural Resources	Depletion
Intangibles	Amortization

Unless stated otherwise, we describe accounting that follows generally accepted accounting principles (GAAP) for the financial statements. Later, we cover depreciation for income-tax purposes. Before examining the various types of plant assets, let's see how to value them.

Measuring the Cost of a Plant Asset

Here is a basic working rule for determining the cost of an asset:

The cost of any asset is the sum of all the costs incurred to bring the asset to its intended use. The cost of a plant asset includes purchase price, plus any taxes, commissions, and other amounts paid to make the asset ready for use. Because the specific costs differ for the various types of plant assets, we discuss the major groups individually.

OBJECTIVE

1 **Determine** the cost of a plant asset

Land

The cost of land includes its purchase price (cash plus any note payable given), brokerage commission, survey fees, legal fees, and any back property taxes that the purchaser pays. Land cost also includes expenditures for grading and clearing the land and for removing unwanted buildings.

The cost of land does *not* include the cost of fencing, paving, security systems, and lighting. These are separate plant assets—called *land improvements*—and they are subject to depreciation.

Suppose FedEx signs a $300,000 note payable to purchase 20 acres of land for a new shipping site. FedEx also pays $10,000 for real estate commission,

$8,000 of back property tax, $5,000 for removal of an old building, a $1,000 survey fee, and $260,000 to pave the parking lot—all in cash. What is FedEx's cost of this land?

Purchase price of land		$300,000
Add related costs:		
Real estate commission	$10,000	
Back property tax........................	8,000	
Removal of building....................	5,000	
Survey fee..................................	1,000	
Total related costs......................		24,000
Total cost of land..........................		$324,000

Note that the cost to pave the parking lot, $260,000, is *not* included in the land's cost, because the pavement is a land improvement. FedEx would record the purchase of this land as follows:

Land	324,000	
Note Payable		300,000
Cash		24,000

Assets	=	Liabilities	+	Stockholders' Equity
+ 324,000 – 24,000	=	+ 300,000	+	0

This purchase of land increases both assets and liabilities. There is no effect on equity.[1]

Buildings, Machinery, and Equipment

The cost of constructing a building includes architectural fees, building permits, contractors' charges, and payments for material, labor, and overhead. If the company constructs its own building, the cost will also include the cost of interest on money borrowed to finance the construction.

When an existing building (new or old) is purchased, its cost includes the purchase price, brokerage commission, sales and other taxes paid, and all expenditures to repair and renovate the building for its intended purpose.

The cost of FedEx's package-handling equipment includes its purchase price (less any discounts), plus transportation from the seller to FedEx, insurance while in transit, sales and other taxes, purchase commission, installation costs, and any expenditures to test the asset before it's placed in service. The equipment cost will also include the cost of any special platforms. Then after the asset is up and running, insurance, taxes, and maintenance costs are recorded as expenses, not as part of the asset's cost.

---

[1]We show the accounting equation along with each journal entry—where the accounting equation aids your understanding of the transaction.

Land Improvements and Leasehold Improvements

For a FedEx shipping terminal, the cost to pave a parking lot ($260,000) would be recorded in a separate account entitled Land Improvements. This account includes costs for such other items as driveways, signs, fences, and sprinkler systems. Although these assets are located on the land, they are subject to decay, and their cost should therefore be depreciated.

FedEx may lease some of its airplanes and other assets. The company customizes these assets for its special needs. For example, FedEx paints its logo on delivery trucks. These improvements are assets of FedEx even though the company may not own the truck. The cost of leasehold improvements should be depreciated over the term of the lease. Most companies call the depreciation on leasehold improvements *amortization*, which is the same concept as *depreciation*.

Lump-Sum (or Basket) Purchases of Assets

Businesses often purchase several assets as a group, or a "basket," for a single lump-sum amount. For example, FedEx may pay one price for land and a building. The company must identify the cost of each asset. The total cost is divided among the assets according to their relative sales (or market) values. This technique is called the *relative-sales-value method*.

Suppose FedEx purchases land and a building in Denver. The building sits on two acres of land, and the combined purchase price of land and building is $2,800,000. An appraisal indicates that the land's market value is $300,000 and that the building's market value is $2,700,000.

FedEx first figures the ratio of each asset's market value to the total market value. Total appraised value is $2,700,000 + $300,000 = $3,000,000. Thus, the land, valued at $300,000, is 10% of the total market value. The building's appraised value is 90% of the total. These percentages are then used to determine the cost of each asset, as follows:

Asset	Market (Sales) Value		Total Market Value		Percentage of Total Market Value		Total Cost	Cost of Each Asset
Land	$ 300,000	÷	$3,000,000	=	10%	×	$2,800,000	$ 280,000
Building	2,700,000	÷	3,000,000	=	90%	×	$2,800,000	2,520,000
Total	$3,000,000				100%			$2,800,000

If FedEx pays cash, the entry to record the purchase of the land and building is

Land	280,000	
Building	2,520,000	
Cash		2,800,000

Assets	=	Liabilities	+	Stockholders' Equity
+ 280,000	=			
+ 2,520,000	=	0	+	0
− 2,800,000	=			

Total assets don't change—merely the makeup of FedEx's assets.

STOP & THINK...

How would FedEx divide a $120,000 lump-sum purchase price for land, building, and equipment with estimated market values of $40,000, $95,000, and $15,000, respectively?

Answer:

	Estimated Market Value	Percentage of Total Market Value	×	Total Cost	=	Cost of Each Asset
Land..................	$ 40,000	26.7%*	×	$120,000	=	$ 32,040
Building.............	95,000	63.3%	×	$120,000	=	75,960
Equipment.........	15,000	10.0%	×	$120,000	=	12,000
Total	$150,000	100.0%				$120,000

*$40,000/$150,000 = 0.267, and so on

Capital Expenditure vs. Immediate Expense

When a company spends money on a plant asset, it must decide whether to record an asset or an expense. Examples of these expenditures range from FedEx's purchase of an airplane to replacing the tires on a FedEx truck.

Expenditures that increase the asset's capacity or extend its useful life are called **capital expenditures**. For example, the cost of a major overhaul that extends the useful life of a FedEx truck is a capital expenditure. Capital expenditures are said to be *capitalized, which means the cost is added to an asset account* and not expensed immediately. A major decision in accounting for plant assets is whether to capitalize or to expense a certain cost.

Costs that do not extend the asset's capacity or its useful life, but merely maintain the asset or restore it to working order, are recorded as expenses. For example, Repair Expense is reported on the income statement and matched against revenue. The costs of repainting a FedEx delivery truck, repairing a dented fender, and replacing tires are also expensed immediately. Exhibit 7-2 shows the distinction between capital expenditures and immediate expenses for delivery truck expenditures.

EXHIBIT 7-2 | **Capital Expenditure or Immediate Expense for Costs Associated with a Delivery Truck**

Record an Asset for Capital Expenditures	Record Repair and Maintenance Expense (Not an Asset) for an Expense
Extraordinary repairs:	**Ordinary repairs:**
Major engine overhaul	Repair of transmission or other mechanism
Modification of body for new use of truck	Oil change, lubrication, and so on
	Replacement of tires and windshield,
Addition to storage capacity of truck	or a paint job

The distinction between a capital expenditure and an expense requires judgment: Does the cost extend the asset's usefulness or its useful life? If so, record an asset. If the cost merely repairs the asset or returns it to its prior condition, then record an expense.

Most companies expense all small costs, say, below $1,000. For higher costs, they follow the rule we gave above: capitalize costs that extend the asset's usefulness or its useful life, and expense all other costs. A conservative policy is one that avoids overstating assets and profits. A company that overstates its assets may get into trouble and have to defend itself in court. Whenever investors lose money because a company overstated its profits or its assets, the investors file a lawsuit. The courts tend to be sympathetic to investor losses caused by shoddy accounting.

Accounting errors sometimes occur for plant asset costs. For example, a company may

- expense a cost that should have been capitalized. This error overstates expenses and understates net income in the year of the error.
- capitalize a cost that should have been expensed. This error understates expenses and overstates net income in the year of the error.

COOKING THE BOOKS
by Improper Capitalization

WorldCom

It is one thing to accidentally capitalize a plant asset but quite another to do it intentionally, thus deliberately overstating assets, understating expenses, and overstating net income. One well-known company committed one of the biggest financial statement frauds in U.S. history in this way.

In 2002, WorldCom, Inc., was one of the largest telecommunications service providers in the world. The company had grown rapidly from a small, regional telephone company in 1983 to a giant corporation in 2002 by acquiring an ever-increasing number of other such companies. But 2002 was a bad year for WorldCom, as well as for many others in the "telecom" industry. The United States was reeling from the effects of a deep economic recession spawned by the "bursting dot-com bubble" in 2000 and intensified by the terrorist attacks on U.S. soil in 2001. Wall Street was looking high and low for positive signs, pressuring public companies to keep profits trending upward in order to support share prices, without much success, at least for the honest companies.

Bernard J. ("Bernie") Ebbers, WorldCom's chief executive officer, was worried. He began to press his chief financial officer, Scott Sullivan, to find a way to make the company's income statement look healthier. After all legitimate attempts to improve earnings failed, Sullivan concocted a scheme to cook the books.

Like all telecommunications companies, WorldCom had signed contracts with other telephone companies, paying them fees so that WorldCom customers could use their lines for telephone calls and Internet usage. GAAP require such fees to be expensed as incurred, rather than capitalized. Overestimating the growth of its business, WorldCom had incurred billions of dollars in such costs, about 15% more than its customers would ever use.

In direct violation of GAAP, Sullivan rationalized that the excessive amounts WorldCom had spent on line costs would eventually lead to the company's recognizing revenue in future years (thus extending their usefulness and justifying, in his mind, their classification as assets). Sullivan directed the accountants working under him to reclassify line costs as property, plant, and equipment assets, rather than as expenses, and to amortize (spread) the costs over several years rather than to expense them in the periods in which they were incurred. Over several quarters, Mr. Sullivan and his assistants transferred a total of $3.1 billion in such charges from operating expense accounts to property, plant, and equipment, resulting in the transformation of what would have been a net loss for all of 2001 and the first quarter of 2002 into a sizeable profit. It was the largest single fraud in U.S. history to that point.

Sullivan's fraudulent scheme was discovered by the company's internal audit staff during a routine spot-check of the company's records for capital expenditures. The staff members reported Sullivan's (and his staff's) fraudulent activities to the head of the company's audit committee and its external auditor, setting in motion a chain of events that resulted in Ebbers' and Sullivan's firing, and the company's eventual bankruptcy. Ebbers, Sullivan, and several of their assistants went to prison for their participation in this fraudulent scheme.

Shareholders of WorldCom lost billions of dollars in share value when the company went down, and more than 500,000 people lost their jobs.

The WorldCom scandal rocked the financial world, causing global stock markets to plummet from lack of confidence. This prompted action on the part of the U.S. Congress and President George W. Bush that eventually led to the passage of the Sarbanes-Oxley Act, the most significant piece of shareholder protection legislation since the Great Depression in the 1930s.

MEASURING DEPRECIATION ON PLANT ASSETS

As we've seen in previous chapters, plant assets are reported on the balance sheet at book value, which is

> Book Value of a Plant Asset = Cost − Accumulated Depreciation

Plant assets wear out, grow obsolete, and lose value over time. To account for this process we allocate a plant asset's cost to expense over its life—a process called *depreciation*. The depreciation process matches the asset's expense against revenue to measure income, as the matching principle directs. Exhibit 7-3 illustrates the accounting for a Boeing 737 jet by FedEx.

EXHIBIT 7-3 | **Depreciation and the Matching of Expense with Revenue**

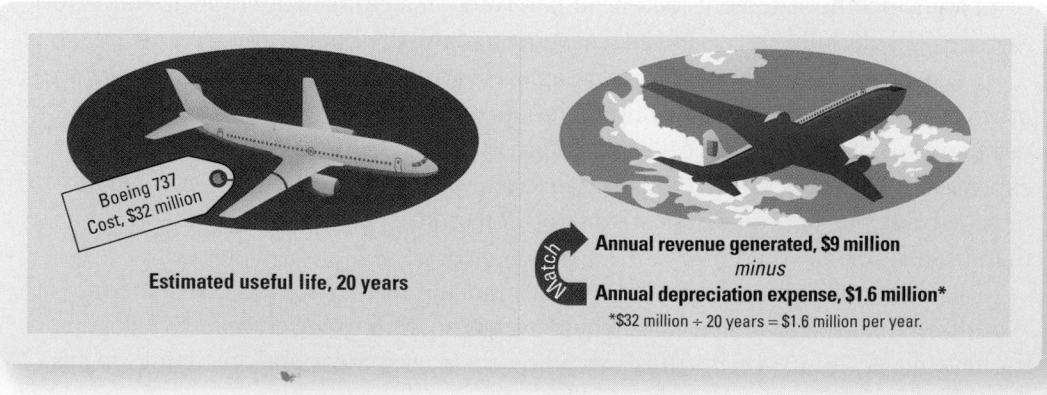

Boeing 737
Cost, $32 million

Estimated useful life, 20 years

Match

Annual revenue generated, $9 million
minus
Annual depreciation expense, $1.6 million*

*$32 million ÷ 20 years = $1.6 million per year.

Recall that depreciation expense (not accumulated depreciation) is reported on the income statement.

Only land has an unlimited life and is not depreciated for accounting purposes. For most plant assets, depreciation is caused by:

- *Physical wear and tear.* For example, physical deterioration takes its toll on the usefulness of FedEx airplanes, equipment, delivery trucks, and buildings.
- *Obsolescence.* Computers and other electronic equipment may become *obsolete* before they deteriorate. An asset is obsolete when another asset can do the job more efficiently. An asset's useful life may be shorter than its physical life. FedEx and other companies depreciate their computers over a short period of time—perhaps four years—even though the computers will remain in working condition much longer.

Suppose FedEx buys a computer for use in tracking packages. FedEx believes it will get four years of service from the computer, which will then be worthless. Under straight-line depreciation, FedEx expenses one-quarter of the asset's cost in each of its four years of use.

You've just seen what depreciation is. Let's see what depreciation is *not.*

1. **Depreciation is not a process of valuation.** Businesses do *not* record depreciation based on changes in the market value of their plant assets. Instead, businesses allocate the asset's *cost* to the period of its useful life.

2. **Depreciation does not mean setting aside cash to replace assets as they wear out.** Any cash fund is entirely separate from depreciation.

How to Measure Depreciation

To measure depreciation for a plant asset, we must know three things about the asset:

1. Cost   2. Estimated useful life   3. Estimated residual value

We have discussed cost, which is a known amount. The other two factors must be estimated.

Estimated useful life is the length of service expected from using the asset. Useful life may be expressed in years, units of output, miles, or some other measure. For example, the useful life of a building is stated in years. The useful life of a FedEx airplane or delivery truck may be expressed as the number of miles the vehicle is expected to travel. Companies base estimates on their experience and trade publications.

Estimated residual value—also called *scrap value* or *salvage value*—is the expected cash value of an asset at the end of its useful life. For example, FedEx may believe that a package-handling machine will be useful for seven years. After that time, FedEx may expect to sell the machine as scrap metal. The amount FedEx believes it can get for the machine is the estimated residual value. In computing depreciation, the estimated residual value is *not* depreciated because FedEx expects to receive this amount from selling the asset. If there's no expected residual value, the full cost of the asset is depreciated. A plant asset's **depreciable cost** is measured as follows:

Depreciable Cost = Asset's cost − Estimated residual value

Depreciation Methods

There are three main depreciation methods:

- Straight-line
- Units-of-production
- Double-declining-balance—an accelerated depreciation method

These methods allocate different amounts of depreciation to each period. However, they all result in the same total amount of depreciation, which is the asset's depreciable cost. Exhibit 7-4 presents the data we use to illustrate depreciation computations for a FedEx truck.

EXHIBIT 7-4 | **Data for Depreciation Computations—A FedEx Truck**

Data Item	Amount
Cost of truck...	$41,000
Less: Estimated residual value	(1,000)
Depreciable cost....................................	$40,000
Estimated useful life:	
Years	5 years
Units of production	100,000 units [miles]

Straight-Line Method. In the **straight-line (SL) method**, an equal amount of depreciation is assigned to each year (or period) of asset use. Depreciable cost is divided by useful life in years to determine the annual depreciation expense. Applied to the FedEx truck data from Exhibit 7-4, SL depreciation is

$$\text{Straight-line depreciation per year} = \frac{\text{Cost} - \text{Residual value}}{\text{Useful life, in years}}$$

$$= \frac{\$41,000 - \$1,000}{5}$$

$$= \$8,000$$

The entry to record depreciation is

Depreciation Expense		8,000	
Accumulated Depreciation			8,000

Assets	=	Liabilities	+	Stockholders' Equity	−	Expenses
− 8,000	=	0				− 8,000

Observe that depreciation decreases the asset (through Accumulated Depreciation) and also decreases equity (through Depreciation Expense). Let's assume that FedEx purchased this truck on January 1, 2009. Assume that FedEx's accounting year ends on December 31. Exhibit 7-5 gives a *straight-line depreciation schedule* for the truck. The final column of the exhibit shows the *asset's book value*, which is cost less accumulated depreciation.

EXHIBIT 7-5 | **Straight-Line Depreciation for a FedEx Truck**

Date	Asset Cost	Depreciation for the Year			Accumulated Depreciation	Asset Book Value
		Depreciation Rate	Depreciable Cost	Depreciation Expense		
1- 1-2009	$41,000					$41,000
12-31-2009		0.20* ×	$40,000 =	$8,000	$ 8,000	33,000
12-31-2010		0.20 ×	40,000 =	8,000	16,000	25,000
12-31-2011		0.20 ×	40,000 =	8,000	24,000	17,000
12-31-2012		0.20 ×	40,000 =	8,000	32,000	9,000
12-31-2013		0.20 ×	40,000 =	8,000	40,000	1,000

*⅕ year = .20 per year

As an asset is used in operations,

- accumulated depreciation increases.
- the book value of the asset decreases.

An asset's final book value is its *residual value* ($1,000 in Exhibit 7-5). At the end of its useful life, the asset is said to be *fully depreciated*.

STOP & THINK...

A FedEx sorting machine that cost $10,000, has a useful life of five years, and residual value of $2,000, was purchased on January 1. What is SL depreciation for each year?

Answer:

$1,600 = ($10,000 – $2,000)/5 $1600 a year

Units-of-Production Method. In the **units-of-production (UOP) method**, a fixed amount of depreciation is assigned to each *unit of output*, or service, produced by the asset. Depreciable cost is divided by useful life—in units of production—to determine this amount. This per-unit depreciation expense is then multiplied by the number of units produced each period to compute depreciation. The UOP depreciation for the FedEx truck data in Exhibit 7-4 (p. 418) is

$$\text{Units-of-production depreciation per unit of output} = \frac{\text{Cost} - \text{Residual value}}{\text{Useful life, in units of production}}$$

$$= \frac{\$41,000 - \$1,000}{100,000 \text{ miles}} = \$0.40 \text{ per mile}$$

Assume that FedEx expects to drive the truck 20,000 miles during the first year, 30,000 during the second, 25,000 during the third, 15,000 during the fourth, and 10,000 during the fifth. Exhibit 7-6 on the following page shows the UOP depreciation schedule.

EXHIBIT 7-6 | Units-of-Production Depreciation for a FedEx Truck

Date	Asset Cost	Depreciation for the Year			Accumulated Depreciation	Asset Book Value
		Depreciation Per Unit	Number of Units	Depreciation Expense		
1- 1-2009	$41,000					$41,000
12-31-2009		$0.40* ×	20,000 =	$ 8,000	$ 8,000	33,000
12-31-2010		0.40 ×	30,000 =	12,000	20,000	21,000
12-31-2011		0.40 ×	25,000 =	10,000	30,000	11,000
12-31-2012		0.40 ×	15,000 =	6,000	36,000	5,000
12-31-2013		0.40 ×	10,000 =	4,000	40,000	1,000

*($41,000 – $1,000)/100,000 miles = $0.40 per mile.

The amount of UOP depreciation varies with the number of units the asset produces. In our example, the total number of units produced is 100,000. UOP depreciation does not depend directly on time, as do the other methods.

Double-Declining-Balance Method. An **accelerated depreciation method** writes off a larger amount of the asset's cost near the start of its useful life than the straight-line method does. Double-declining-balance is the main accelerated depreciation method. **Double-declining-balance (DDB) depreciation** computes annual depreciation by multiplying the asset's declining book value by a constant percentage, which is two times the straight-line depreciation rate. DDB amounts are computed as follows:

- *First*, compute the straight-line depreciation rate per year. A 5-year truck has a straight-line depreciation rate of 1/5, or 20% each year. A 10-year asset has a straight-line rate of 1/10, or 10%, and so on.
- *Second*, multiply the straight-line rate by 2 to compute the DDB rate. For a 5-year asset, the DDB rate is 40% (20% × 2). A 10-year asset has a DDB rate of 20% (10% × 2).
- *Third*, multiply the DDB rate by the period's beginning asset book value (cost less accumulated depreciation). Under the DDB method, ignore the residual value of the asset in computing depreciation, except during the last year. The DDB rate for the FedEx truck in Exhibit 7-4 (p. 418) is

$$\text{DDB depreciation rate per year} = \frac{1}{\text{Useful life, in years}} \times 2$$

$$= \frac{1}{5 \text{ years}} \times 2$$

$$= 20\% \times 2 = 40\%$$

- *Fourth*, determine the final year's depreciation amount—that is, the amount needed to reduce asset book value to its residual value. In Exhibit 7-7, the fifth and final year's DDB depreciation is $4,314—book value of $5,314 less the $1,000 residual value. *The residual value should not be depreciated* but should remain on the books until the asset is disposed of.

EXHIBIT 7-7 | Double-Declining-Balance Depreciation for a FedEx Truck

Date	Asset Cost	DDB Rate	Asset Book Value	Depreciation Expense	Accumulated Depreciation	Asset Book Value
			Depreciation for the Year			
1- 1-2009	$41,000					$41,000
12-31-2009		0.40 ×	$41,000 =	$16,400	$16,400	24,600
12-31-2010		0.40 ×	24,600 =	9,840	26,240	14,760
12-31-2011		0.40 ×	14,760 =	5,904	32,144	8,856
12-31-2012		0.40 ×	8,856 =	3,542	35,686	5,314
12-31-2013				4,314*	40,000	1,000

*Last-year depreciation is the "plug" amount needed to reduce asset book value (far right column) to the residual amount ($5,314 – $1,000 = $4,314).

The DDB method differs from the other methods in two ways:

1. Residual value is ignored initially; first-year depreciation is computed on the asset's full cost.

2. Depreciation expense in the final year is the "plug" amount needed to reduce the asset's book value to the residual amount.

STOP & THINK. . .

What is the DDB depreciation each year for the asset in the Stop & Think on page 419?

Answers:

Yr. 1: $4,000 ($10,000 × 40%)
Yr. 2: $2,400 ($6,000 × 40%)
Yr. 3: $1,440 ($3,600 × 40%)
Yr. 4: $160 ($10,000 – $4,000 – $2,400 – $1,440 – $2,000 = $160)*
Yr. 5: $0

*The asset is not depreciated below residual value of $2,000.

Comparing Depreciation Methods

Let's compare the three methods in terms of the yearly amount of depreciation. The yearly amount varies by method, but the total $40,000 depreciable cost is the same under all methods.

Year	Straight-Line	Units-of-Production	Accelerated Method Double-Declining Balance
		Amount of Depreciation per Year	
1	$ 8,000	$ 8,000	$16,400
2	8,000	12,000	9,840
3	8,000	10,000	5,904
4	8,000	6,000	3,542
5	8,000	4,000	4,314
Total	$40,000	$40,000	$40,000

GAAP say to match an asset's depreciation against the revenue the asset produces. For a plant asset that generates revenue evenly over time, the straight-line method best meets the matching principle. The units-of-production method best fits those assets that wear out because of physical use rather than obsolescence. The accelerated method (DDB) applies best to assets that generate more revenue earlier in their useful lives and less in later years.

Exhibit 7-8 graphs annual depreciation amounts for the straight-line, units-of-production, and accelerated depreciation (DDB) methods. The graph of straight-line depreciation is flat through time because annual depreciation is the same in all periods. Units-of-production depreciation follows no particular pattern because annual depreciation depends on the use of the asset. Accelerated depreciation is greatest in the first year and less in the later years.

EXHIBIT 7-8 | **Depreciation Patterns Through Time**

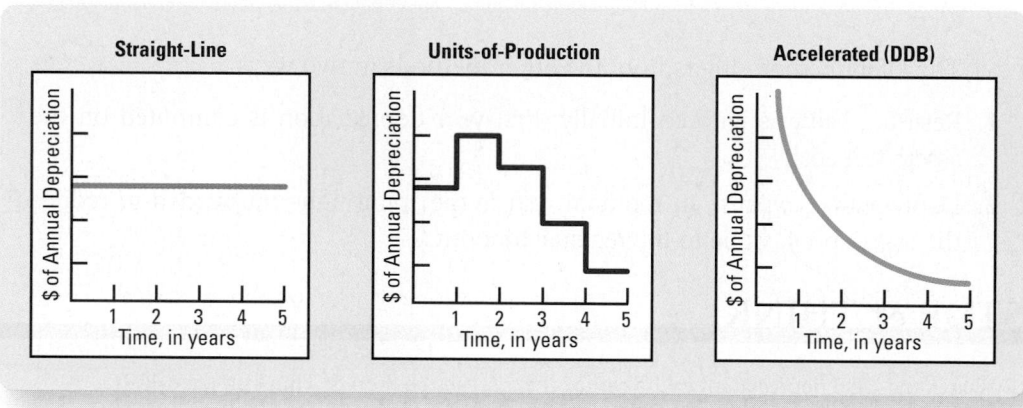

Exhibit 7-9 shows the percentage of companies that use each depreciation method from a survey of 600 companies by the American Institute of Certified Public Accountants (AICPA).

EXHIBIT 7-9 | **Depreciation Methods Used by 600 Companies**

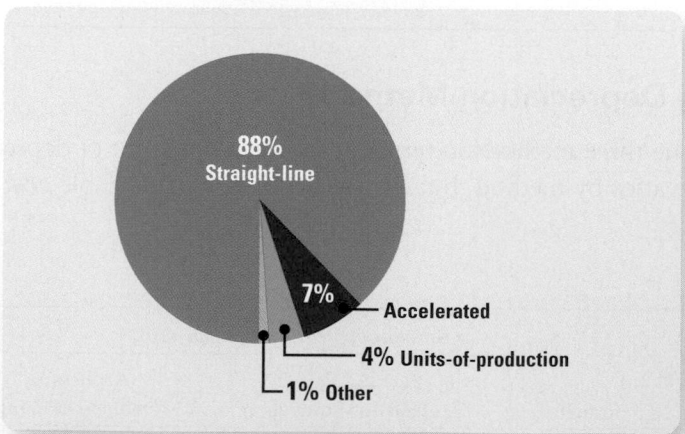

For reporting in the financial statements, straight-line depreciation is most popular. As we shall see, however, accelerated depreciation is most popular for income-tax purposes.

MID-CHAPTER SUMMARY PROBLEM

Suppose FedEx purchased equipment on January 1, 2010, for $44,000. The expected useful life of the equipment is 10 years or 100,000 units of production, and its residual value is $4,000. Under three depreciation methods, the annual depreciation expense and the balance of accumulated depreciation at the end of 2010 and 2011 are as follows:

| | Method A | | Method B | | Method C | |
Year	Annual Depreciation Expense	Accumulated Depreciation	Annual Depreciation Expense	Accumulated Depreciation	Annual Depreciation Expense	Accumulated Depreciation
2010	$4,000	$4,000	$8,800	$ 8,800	$1,200	$1,200
2011	4,000	8,000	7,040	15,840	5,600	6,800

▌Requirements

1. Identify the depreciation method used in each instance, and show the equation and computation for each. (Round to the nearest dollar.)
2. Assume continued use of the same method through year 2012. Determine the annual depreciation expense, accumulated depreciation, and book value of the equipment for 2010 through 2012 under each method, assuming 12,000 units of production in 2012.

Answers

▌Requirement 1

Method A: Straight-Line

$$\text{Depreciable cost} = \$40,000(\$44,000 - \$4,000)$$
$$\text{Each year: } \$40,000/10 \text{ years} = \$4,000$$

Method B: Double-Declining-Balance

$$\text{Rate} = \frac{1}{10 \text{ years}} \times 2 = 10\% \times 2 = 20\%$$
$$2010: 0.20 \times \$44,000 = \$8,800$$
$$2011: 0.20 \times (\$44,000 - \$8,800) = \$7,040$$

Method C: Units-of-Production

$$\text{Depreciation per unit} = \frac{\$44,000 - \$4,000}{100,000 \text{ units}} = \$0.40$$
$$2010: \$0.40 \times 3,000 \text{ units} = \$1,200$$
$$2011: \$0.40 \times 14,000 \text{ units} = \$5,600$$

❙ Requirement 2

Method A: Straight-Line

Year	Annual Depreciation Expense	Accumulated Depreciation	Book Value
Start			$44,000
2010	$4,000	$ 4,000	40,000
2011	4,000	8,000	36,000
2012	4,000	12,000	32,000

Method B: Double-Declining-Balance

Year	Annual Depreciation Expense	Accumulated Depreciation	Book Value
Start			$44,000
2010	$8,800	$ 8,800	35,200
2011	7,040	15,840	28,160
2012	5,632	21,472	22,528

Method C: Units-of-Production

Year	Annual Depreciation Expense	Accumulated Depreciation	Book Value
Start			$44,000
2010	$1,200	$ 1,200	42,800
2011	5,600	6,800	37,200
2012	4,800	11,600	32,400

Computations for 2012

Straight-line	$40,000/10 years = $4,000
Double-declining-balance	$28,160 × 0.20 = $5,632
Units-of-production	12,000 units × $0.40 = $4,800

OTHER ISSUES IN ACCOUNTING FOR PLANT ASSETS

OBJECTIVE

3 **Select** the best depreciation method

Plant assets are complex because

- they have long lives.
- depreciation affects income taxes.
- companies may have gains or losses when they sell plant assets.
- international accounting changes in the future may affect the recognition as well as the carrying values of assets.

Depreciation for Tax Purposes

FedEx and most other companies use straight-line depreciation for reporting to stockholders and creditors on their financial statements. But for their income taxes they also keep a separate set of depreciation records. For tax purposes, FedEx and most other companies use an accelerated depreciation method. This is legal, ethical, and honest. U.S. law permits it.

Suppose you are a business manager, and the IRS allows an accelerated depreciation method. Why do FedEx managers prefer accelerated over straight-line depreciation for income-tax purposes? Accelerated depreciation provides the fastest tax deductions, thus decreasing immediate tax payments. FedEx can reinvest the tax savings back into the business. FedEx has a choice—pay taxes or buy equipment. This choice is easy.

To understand the relationships between cash flow, depreciation, and income tax, recall our depreciation example of a FedEx truck:

- First-year depreciation is $8,000 under straight-line and $16,400 under double-declining-balance (DDB).
- DDB is permitted for income tax purposes.

Assume that this FedEx office has $400,000 in revenue and $300,000 in cash operating expenses during the truck's first year and an income tax rate of 30%. The cash-flow analysis appears in Exhibit 7-10.

EXHIBIT 7-10 | **The Cash-Flow Advantage of Accelerated Depreciation over Straight-Line Depreciation for Income Tax Purposes**

		SL	Accelerated
1	Cash revenue...	$400,000	$400,000
2	Cash operating expenses	300,000	300,000
3	Cash provided by operations before income tax................	100,000	100,000
4	Depreciation expense (a noncash expense).............................	8,000	16,400
5	Income before income tax	$ 92,000	$ 83,600
6	Income tax expense (30%)...	$ 27,600	$ 25,080
	Cash-flow analysis:		
7	Cash provided by operations before tax	$100,000	$100,000
8	Income tax expense	27,600	25,080
9	Cash provided by operations	$ 72,400	$ 74,920
10	Extra cash available for investment if DDB is used ($74,920 – $72,400)............................		$ 2,520

You can see that, for income-tax purposes, accelerated depreciation helps conserve cash for the business. That's why virtually all companies use accelerated depreciation to compute their income tax.

There is a special depreciation method—used only for income tax purposes—called the **Modified Accelerated Cost Recovery System (MACRS)**. Under MACRS each fixed asset is classified into one of eight classes identified by asset life (Exhibit 7-11 on the following page). Depreciation for the first four classes is computed by the double-declining-balance method. Depreciation for 15-year assets and 20-year assets is computed by the 150%-declining-balance method. Under 150% DB, annual depreciation is computed by multiplying the straight-line rate by 1.50 (instead of 2.00, as for DDB). For a 20-year asset, the straight-line rate is 0.05 per year ($1/20 = 0.05$), so the annual MACRS depreciation rate is 0.075 ($0.05 \times 1.50 = 0.075$). The taxpayer computes annual depreciation by multiplying asset book value by 0.075, in a manner similar to how DDB works.

Most real estate is depreciated by the straight-line method (see the last two categories in Exhibit 7-11).

EXHIBIT 7-11 | MACRS Depreciation Method

Class Identified by Asset Life (years)	Representative Assets	Depreciation Method
3	Race horses	DDB
5	Automobiles, light trucks	DDB
7	Equipment	DDB
10	Equipment	DDB
15	Sewage-treatment plants	150% DDB
20	Certain real estate	150% DDB
27½	Residential rental property	SL
39	Nonresidential rental property	SL

Depreciation for Partial Years

Companies purchase plant assets whenever they need them, not just at the beginning of the year. Therefore, companies must compute *depreciation for partial years*. Suppose UPS purchases a warehouse building on April 1 for $500,000. The building's estimated life is 20 years, and its estimated residual value is $80,000. UPS's accounting year ends on December 31. Let's consider how UPS computes depreciation for April through December:

- First, compute depreciation for a full year.
- Second, multiply full-year depreciation by the fraction of the year that you held the asset—in this case, 9/12. Assuming the straight-line method, the year's depreciation for this UPS building is $15,750, as follows:

$$\text{Full-year depreciation} \qquad \frac{\$500,000 - \$80,000}{20} = \$21,000$$

$$\text{Partial year depreciation} \qquad \$21,000 \times 9/12 = \$15,750$$

What if UPS bought the asset on April 18? Many businesses record no monthly depreciation on assets purchased after the 15th of the month, and they record a full month's depreciation on an asset bought on or before the 15th.

Most companies use computerized systems to account for fixed assets. Each asset has a unique identification number, and the system will automatically calculate the asset's depreciation expense. Accumulated Depreciation is automatically updated.

Changing the Useful Life of a Depreciable Asset

After an asset is in use, managers may change its useful life on the basis of experience and new information. **Disney Enterprises, Inc.**, made such a change, called a *change in accounting estimate*. Disney recalculated depreciation on the basis of revised useful lives of several of its theme park assets. The following note in Disney Enterprises, Inc.'s financial statements reports this change in accounting estimate:

> **Note 5**
> ...[T]he Company extended the estimated useful lives of certain theme park ride and attraction assets based upon historical data and engineering studies. The effect of this change was to decrease depreciation by approximately $8 million (an increase in net income of approximately $4.2 million...).

Assume that a Disney hot dog stand cost $50,000 and that the company originally believed the asset had a 10-year useful life with no residual value. Using the straight-line method, the company would record $5,000 depreciation each year ($50,000/10 years = $5,000). Suppose Disney used the asset for four years. Accumulated depreciation reached $20,000, leaving a remaining depreciable book value (cost less accumulated depreciation less residual value) of $30,000 ($50,000 – $20,000). From its experience, management believes the asset will remain useful for an *additional* 10 years. The company would spread the remaining depreciable book value over the asset's remaining life as follows:

Asset's remaining depreciable book value	÷	(New) Estimated useful life remaining	=	(New) Annual depreciation
$30,000	÷	10 years	=	$3,000

The yearly depreciation entry based on the new estimated useful life is

Depreciation Expense—Hot Dog Stand			3,000	
Accumulated Depreciation—Hot Dog Stand				3,000

Depreciation decreases both assets and equity.

Assets	=	Liabilities	+	Stockholders' Equity	–	Expenses
– 3,000	=	0				– 3,000

COOKING THE BOOKS
Through Depreciation

Waste Management

Since plant assets usually involve relatively large amounts and relatively large numbers of assets, sometimes a seemingly subtle change in the way they are accounted for can have a tremendous impact on the financial statements. When these changes are made in order to cook the books, the results can be devastating.

Waste Management, Inc., is North America's largest integrated waste service company, providing collection, transfer, recycling, disposal, and waste-to-energy services for commercial, industrial, municipal, and residential customers from coast to coast.

Starting in 1992, six top executives of the company, including its founder and chairman of the board, its chief financial officer, its corporate controller, its top lawyer, and its vice president of finance, decided that the company's profits were not growing fast enough to meet "earnings targets," which were tied to their executive bonuses. Among several fraudulent financial tactics these top executives employed to cook the books were: (1) assigning unsupported and inflated salvage values to garbage trucks; (2) unjustifiably extending the estimated useful lives of their garbage trucks; and (3) assigning arbitrary salvage values to other fixed assets that previously had no salvage values. All of these tactics had the effect of decreasing the amount of depreciation expense in the income statements and increasing net income by a corresponding amount. While practices like this might seem relatively subtle and even insignificant when performed on an individual asset, remember that there were thousands of trash trucks and dumpsters involved, so the dollar amount grew huge in a short time. In addition, the company continued these practices for five years, overstating earnings by $1.7 billion.

The Waste Management fraud was the largest of its kind in history until the WorldCom scandal, discussed earlier in this chapter. In 1997, the company fired the officers involved and hired a new CEO who ordered a review of these practices, which uncovered the fraud. In the meantime, these dishonest executives had profited handsomely, receiving performance-based bonuses based on the company's inflated earnings, retaining their high-paying jobs, and receiving enhanced retirement benefits. One of the executives took the fraud to another level. Just 10 days before the fraud was disclosed, he enriched himself with a tax benefit by donating inflated company stock to his alma mater to fund a building in his name! Although the men involved were sued for monetary damages, none of them ever went to jail.

When the fraud was disclosed, Waste Management shareholders lost over $6 billion in the market value of their investments when the stock price plummeted by more than 33%. The company and these officers eventually settled civil lawsuits for approximately $700 million because of the fraud.

You might ask, "Where were the auditors while this was occurring?" The company's auditor was Arthur Andersen, LLP, whose partners involved on the audit engagement were eventually found to be complicit in the scheme. In fact, a few of the Waste Management officers who perpetrated the scheme had been ex-partners of the audit firm. As it turns out, the auditors actually identified many of the improper accounting practices of Waste Management. However, rather than insisting that the company fix the errors, or risk exposure, they merely "persuaded" management to agree not to repeat these practices in the future, and entered into an agreement with them to write off the accumulated balance sheet overstatement over a period of 10 years. In June 2001, the SEC fined Arthur Andersen $7 million for "knowingly and recklessly issuing false and misleading audit reports" for Waste Management from 1993 through 1996.

In October 2001, immediately on the heels of these disclosures, the notorious Enron scandal broke. Enron, as well as WorldCom, were Arthur Andersen clients at the time. The Enron scandal finally put the firm out of business. Many people feel that, had it not been for Andersen's involvement in the Waste Management affair, the SEC might have been more lenient toward the company in the Enron scandal.

The Enron scandal is discussed in Chapter 10.

Fully Depreciated Assets

A *fully depreciated asset* is one that has reached the end of its estimated useful life. Suppose FedEx has fully depreciated equipment with zero residual value (cost was $60,000). FedEx accounts will appear as follows:

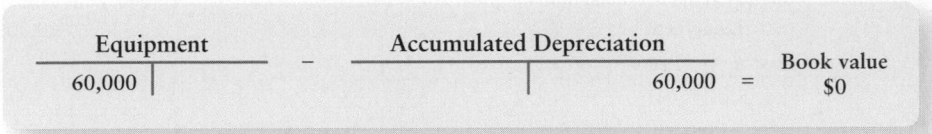

Equipment	−	Accumulated Depreciation		Book value
60,000			60,000 =	$0

The equipment's book value is zero, but that doesn't mean the equipment is worthless. FedEx may use the equipment for a few more years, but FedEx will not record any more depreciation on a fully depreciated asset.

When FedEx disposes of the equipment, FedEx will remove both the asset's cost ($60,000) and its accumulated depreciation ($60,000) from the books. The next section shows how to account for plant asset disposals.

Accounting for Disposal of Plant Assets

Eventually, a plant asset ceases to serve a company's needs. The asset may wear out or become obsolete. Before accounting for the disposal of the asset, the business should bring depreciation up to date to

- measure the asset's final book value and
- record the expense up to the date of sale.

OBJECTIVE

4 Analyze the effect of a plant asset disposal

To account for disposal, remove the asset and its related accumulated depreciation from the books. Suppose the final year's depreciation expense has just been recorded for a machine that cost $60,000 and is estimated to have zero residual value. The machine's accumulated depreciation thus totals $60,000. Assuming that this asset is junked, the entry to record its disposal is:

Accumulated Depreciation—Machinery		60,000	
Machinery			60,000
To dispose of a fully depreciated machine.			

Assets	=	Liabilities	+	Stockholders' Equity
+ 60,000 − 60,000	=	0	+	0

There is no gain or loss on this disposal, and there's no effect on total assets, liabilities, or equity.

If assets are junked before being fully depreciated, the company incurs a loss on the disposal. Suppose FedEx disposes of equipment that cost $60,000. This asset's accumulated depreciation is $50,000, and book value is, therefore, $10,000. Junking this equipment results in a loss equal to the book value of the asset, as follows:

Accumulated Depreciation—Equipment	50,000	
Loss on Disposal of Equipment	10,000	
Equipment		60,000
To dispose of equipment.		

Assets	=	Liabilities	+	Stockholders' Equity	−	Losses
+ 50,000 − 60,000	=	0				− 10,000

FedEx got rid of an asset with $10,000 book value and received nothing. The result is a $10,000 loss, which decreases both total assets and equity.

The Loss on Disposal of Equipment is reported as Other income (expense) on the income statement. Losses decrease net income exactly as expenses do. Gains increase net income the same as revenues.

Selling a Plant Asset. Suppose FedEx sells equipment on September 30, 2012, for $7,300 cash. The equipment cost $10,000 when purchased on January 1, 2009, and has been depreciated straight-line. FedEx estimated a 10-year useful life and no residual value. Prior to recording the sale, FedEx accountants must update the asset's depreciation. Assume that FedEx uses the calendar year as its accounting period. Partial-year depreciation must be recorded for the asset's depreciation from January 1, 2012, to the sale date. The straight-line depreciation entry at September 30, 2012, is

Sep 30	Depreciation Expense ($10,000/10 years × 9/12)	750	
	Accumulated Depreciation—Equipment		750
	To update depreciation.		

The Equipment account and the Accumulated Depreciation account appear as follows. Observe that the equipment's book value is $6,250 ($10,000 − $3,750).

Equipment			Accumulated Depreciation		
Jan 1, 2009	10,000		Dec 31, 2009	1,000	
		−	Dec 31, 2010	1,000	= Book value
			Dec 31, 2011	1,000	$6,250
			Sep 30, 2012	750	
			Balance	3,750	

The gain on the sale of the equipment for $7,300 is $1,050, computed as follows:

Cash received from sale of the asset		$7,300
Book value of asset sold:		
Cost	$10,000	
Less: Accumulated depreciation	(3,750)	6,250
Gain on sale of the asset................................		$1,050

The entry to record sale of the equipment is

Sep 30	Cash	7,300	
	Accumulated Depreciation—Equipment	3,750	
	Equipment		10,000
	Gain on Sale of Equipment		1,050
	To sell equipment.		

Total assets increase, and so does equity—by the amount of the gain.

Assets	=	Liabilities	–	Stockholders' Equity	+	Gains
+ 7,300						
+ 3,750	=	0			+	1,050
–10,000						

Gains are recorded as credits, as revenues are. Gains and losses on asset disposals appear on the income statement as Other income (expense), or Other gains (losses).

Exchanging Plant Assets. Managers often trade in old assets for new ones. This is called a *nonmonetary exchange*. The accounting for nonmonetary exchanges is based on the *fair values of the assets involved.* Thus, the cost of an asset like plant and equipment received in a nonmonetary exchange is equal to the fair values of the assets given up (including the old asset and any cash paid). Any difference between the fair value of the old asset from its book value is recognized as gain (fair value of old asset exceeds book value) or loss (book value of old asset exceeds fair value) on the exchange. For example, assume Papa John's Pizza's

- old delivery car cost $9,000 and has accumulated depreciation of $8,000. Thus, the old car's book value is $1,000.

Assume Papa John's trades in the old automobile for a new one with a fair market value of $15,000 and pays cash of $10,000. Thus, the implied fair value of the old car is $5,000 ($15,000 − $10,000). This amount is treated as cash paid by the seller for the old vehicle.

- The cost of the new delivery car is $15,000 (fair value of the old asset, $5,000, plus cash paid, $10,000).

The pizzeria records the exchange transaction as follows:

Delivery Auto (new)	15,000	
Accumulated Depreciation (old)	8,000	
Delivery Auto (old)		9,000
Cash		10,000
Gain on Exchange of Delivery Auto		4,000
Traded in old delivery car for new auto.		

Assets	=	Liabilities	+	Stockholders' Equity
+15,000				
+ 8,000	=	0	+	4,000
− 9,000				
−10,000				

There was a net increase in total assets of $4,000 and a corresponding increase in stockholders' equity, to reflect the gain on the exchange. Notice that this amount represents the excess of the fair value of the old asset over its book value. Some special rules may apply here, but they are reserved for more advanced courses.

T-Accounts for Analyzing Plant Asset Transactions

You can perform quite a bit of analysis if you know how transactions affect the plant asset accounts. Here are the accounts with descriptions of the activity in each account.

Building (or Equipment)		Accumulated Depreciation	
Beg bal		Accum deprec	Beg bal
Cost of assets purchased	Cost of assets disposed of	of assets disposed of	Depreciation expense for the current period
End bal			End bal

Depreciation Expense		Gain on Sale of Building (or Equipment)	
Depreciation expense for the current period			Gain on sale
		Loss on Sale of Building (or Equipment)	
		Loss on sale	

Example: Suppose you started the year with buildings that cost $100,000. During the year you bought another building for $150,000 and ended the year with buildings that cost $180,000. What was the cost of the building you sold?

Building			
Beg bal	100,000		
Cost of assets purchased	150,000	Cost of assets sold	? = $70,000*
End bal	180,000		

*100,000 + 150,000 − $180,000

You can perform similar analyses to answer other interesting questions about what the business did during the period.

 **GLOBAL VIEW**

One of the most significant differences between U.S. GAAP and International Financial Reporting Standards (IFRS) is the permitted reported carrying values of property, plant, and equipment. Recall from Chapter 1 that U.S. GAAP has long advocated the historical cost principle as most appropriate for plant assets because it results in a more objective (nonbiased) and therefore a more reliable (auditable) figure. It also supports the continuity assumption, which states that we expect the entity to remain in business long enough to recover the cost of its plant assets through depreciation.

In contrast, while historical cost is the primary basis of accounting under IFRS, it permits the periodic revaluation of plant assets to fair market value. The primary justification for this position is that the historical cost of plant assets purchased years ago does not properly reflect their current values. Thus, the amounts shown on the balance sheet for these assets do not reflect a relevant measure of what these assets are worth. For example, suppose a business bought a building in downtown Orlando, Florida, in 1960 for $1 million. Assume that this year that building has been appraised for $20 million. IFRS would permit the company to revalue the building on its balance sheet.

The primary objection to use of fair values on the balance sheet for plant assets is that these values are subjective, and subject to change, sometimes quite rapidly. Consider, for example, residential and commercial real estate in California during the credit crisis of 2008 and 2009. The fair market values of these assets dropped by double-digit percentages in a period of less than one year. If these assets had been valued at fair market values on the books of the companies that held them, assets would have to have been adjusted accordingly, causing the balance sheet amounts to fluctuate wildly. Furthermore, if the assets had been depreciated, it is likely that both the depreciation expense and the allowance for depreciation would also have had to be adjusted more frequently.

ACCOUNTING FOR NATURAL RESOURCES

OBJECTIVE

5 **Account** for natural resources and depletion

Natural resources are plant assets of a special type, such as iron ore, petroleum (oil), and timber. As plant assets are expensed through depreciation, so natural resource assets are expensed through *depletion*. **Depletion expense** is that portion of the cost of a natural resource that is used up in a particular period. Depletion expense is computed in the same way as units-of-production depreciation.

An oil lease may cost **ExxonMobil** $100,000 and contain an estimated 10,000 barrels of oil. The depletion rate would be $10 per barrel ($100,000/10,000 barrels). If 3,000 barrels are extracted, depletion expense is $30,000 (3,000 barrels × $10 per barrel). The depletion entry is

Depletion Expense (3,000 barrels × $10)	30,000	
Accumulated Depletion—Oil		30,000

This entry is almost identical to a depreciation entry using the units-of-production method.

If 4,500 barrels are removed the next year, that period's depletion is $45,000 (4,500 barrels × $10 per barrel). Accumulated Depletion is a contra account similar to Accumulated Depreciation.

Natural resource assets can be reported on ExxonMobil's balance sheet as follows (amounts assumed):

Property, Plant, and Equipment:		
Equipment...	$960,000	
Less: Accumulated depreciation	(410,000)	$550,000
Oil...	$340,000	
Less: Accumulated depletion	(140,000)	200,000
Total property, plant, and equipment...............		$750,000

ACCOUNTING FOR INTANGIBLE ASSETS

OBJECTIVE

6 **Account** for intangible assets and amortization

As we've seen, *intangible assets* are long-lived assets with no physical form. Intangibles are valuable because they carry special rights from patents, copyrights, trademarks, franchises, leaseholds, and goodwill. Like buildings and equipment, an intangible asset is recorded at its acquisition cost. Intangibles are the most valuable assets of high-tech companies and those that depend on research and development. The residual value of most intangibles is zero.

Intangible assets fall into two categories:

- Intangibles with *finite lives* that can be measured. We record amortization for these intangibles. **Amortization** expense is the title of the expense associated with intangibles. Amortization works like depreciation and is usually computed on a straight-line basis. Amortization can be credited directly to the asset account, as we shall see.
- Intangibles with *indefinite lives*. Record no amortization for these intangibles. Instead, check them annually for any loss in value (impairment), and record a loss when it occurs. Goodwill is the most prominent example of an intangible asset with an indefinite life.

In the following discussions, we illustrate the accounting for both categories of intangibles.

Accounting for Specific Intangibles

Each type of intangible asset is unique, and the accounting can vary from one asset to another.

Patents.   Patents are federal government grants that give the holder the exclusive right for 20 years to produce and sell an invention. The invention may be a product or a process—for example, Sony compact disc players and the Dolby noise-reduction process. Like any other asset, a patent may be purchased. Suppose **Sony** pays $170,000 to acquire a patent on January 1, and the business believes the expected useful life of the patent is five years—not the entire 20-year period. Amortization expense is $34,000 per year ($170,000/5 years). Sony records the acquisition and amortization for this patent as follows:

Jan 1	Patents	170,000	
	Cash		170,000
	To acquire a patent.		

Dec 31	Amortization Expense—Patents ($170,000/5)	34,000	
	Patents		34,000
	To amortize the cost of a patent.		

You can see that we credited the Patents account directly (no Accumulated Amortization account).

Assets	=	Liabilities	+	Stockholders' Equity	−	Expenses
− 34,000	=	0				− 34,000

Amortization for an intangible decreases both assets and equity exactly as depreciation does for equipment or a building.

Copyrights.   Copyrights are exclusive rights to reproduce and sell a book, musical composition, film, or other work of art. Copyrights also protect computer software programs, such as **Microsoft**'s Windows® and Excel. Issued by the federal government, copyrights extend 70 years beyond the author's (composer's, artist's, or programmer's) life. The cost of obtaining a copyright from the government is low, but a company may pay a large sum to purchase an existing copyright from the owner. For example, a publisher may pay the author of a popular novel $1 million or more for the book copyright. Because the useful life of a copyright is usually no longer than two or three years, each period's amortization amount is a high proportion of the copyright cost.

Trademarks and Trade Names.   Trademarks and trade names (or *brand names*) are distinctive identification of a product or service. The "eye" symbol that flashes across our television screens is the trademark that identifies the **CBS** television network. You are probably also familiar with **NBC**'s peacock. Advertising slogans that are legally protected include **United Airlines'** "Fly the friendly skies®" and **Avis Rental Car's** "We try harder®." These are distinctive identifications of products or services, marked with the symbol ™ or ®.

Some trademarks may have a definite useful life set by contract. We should amortize the cost of this type of trademark over its useful life. But a trademark or a trade name may have an indefinite life and not be amortized.

Franchises and Licenses. **Franchises** and **licenses** are privileges granted by a private business or a government to sell a product or service in accordance with specified conditions. The Chicago Cubs baseball organization is a franchise granted to its owner by the National League. **McDonald's** restaurants and **Holiday Inns** are popular franchises. The useful lives of many franchises and licenses are indefinite and, therefore, are not amortized.

Goodwill. In accounting, **goodwill** has a very specific meaning.

> **Goodwill is defined as the excess of the cost of purchasing another company over the sum of the market values of the acquired company's net assets (assets minus liabilities).**

A purchaser is willing to pay for goodwill when the purchaser buys another company that has abnormal earning power.

FedEx operates in several foreign countries. Suppose FedEx acquires Europa Company at a cost of $10 million. Europa's assets have a market value of $9 million, and its liabilities total $2 million so Europa's net assets total $7 million at current market value. In this case, FedEx paid $3 million for goodwill, computed as follows:

Purchase price paid for Europa Company		$10 million
Sum of the market values of Europa Company's assets	$9 million	
Less: Europa Company's liabilities....................................	(2 million)	
Market value of Europa Company's net assets....................		7 million
Excess is called *goodwill*		$ 3 million

FedEx's entry to record the acquisition of Europa Company, including its goodwill, would be

Assets (Cash, Receivables, Inventories, Plant Assets, all at market value)	9,000,000	
Goodwill	3,000,000	
Liabilities		2,000,000
Cash		10,000,000

Goodwill in accounting has special features, as follows:

1. Goodwill is recorded *only* when it is purchased in the acquisition of another company. A purchase transaction provides objective evidence of the value of goodwill. Companies never record goodwill that they create for their own business.

2. According to GAAP, goodwill is not amortized because the goodwill of many entities increases in value.

Accounting for the Impairment of an Intangible Asset

Some intangibles—such as goodwill, licenses, and some trademarks—have indefinite lives and therefore are not subject to amortization. But all intangibles are subject to a write-down when their value decreases. The decline in value of an asset is called an **impairment**.

PepsiCo is a major company with vast amounts of purchased goodwill due to its acquisition of other companies. Each year, PepsiCo determines whether the goodwill it has purchased has increased or decreased in value. If PepsiCo's goodwill is worth more at the end of the year than at the beginning, no increase in the asset is permitted. But if PepsiCo's goodwill has decreased in value, say from $500 million to $470 million, then PepsiCo will record a $30 million impairment loss and write down the book value of the goodwill, as follows (in millions):

2011			
Dec 31	Impairment Loss on Goodwill ($500 – $470)	30	
	Goodwill		30

Both assets (Goodwill) and equity decrease (through the Loss account). Under U.S. GAAP, once a long-term asset like goodwill has been written down because of impairment, it may never again be written back up, should it increase in value.

Assets	=	Liabilities	+	Stockholders' Equity	–	Losses
– 30	=	0				– 30

PepsiCo's financial statements will report the following (in millions):

	2011	2010
Balance sheet		
Intangible assets:		
Goodwill.....................................	$470	$500
Income statement		
Impairment (Loss) on goodwill	(30)	—

Accounting for Research and Development Costs

Accounting for research and development (R&D) costs is one of the most difficult issues in accounting. R&D is the lifeblood of companies such as **Procter & Gamble**, **General Electric**, **Intel**, and **Boeing**. R&D is one of these companies' most valuable (intangible) assets. But, in general, U.S. companies do not report R&D assets on their balance sheets.

GAAP requires companies to expense R&D costs as they incur them. Only in limited circumstances may the company capitalize R&D cost as an asset and amortize it over future periods as sales revenue from the product is earned. For example, a computer software company may incur R&D cost under a contract whereby the company will recover R&D costs through future sales revenue. This R&D cost is an asset, and the company records an intangible R&D asset when it incurs the cost. But this is the exception to the general rule.

 **GLOBAL VIEW** Accounting for research and development costs represents another prominent difference between U.S. GAAP and IFRS. Whereas under GAAP, in general, both research and development costs are expensed as incurred, under IFRS, costs associated with the creation of intangible assets are classified into research phase costs and development phase costs. Costs in the research phase are always expensed. However, costs in the development phase are capitalized if the company can demonstrate meeting all of the following six criteria:

- the technical feasibility of completing the intangible asset;
- the intention to complete the intangible asset;
- the ability to use or sell the intangible asset;
- the future economic benefits (e.g., the existence of a market or, if for internal use, the usefulness of the intangible asset);
- the availability of adequate resources to complete development of the asset; and
- the ability to reliably measure the expenditure attributable to the intangible asset during its development.

Thus, IFRS are generally more permissive than U.S. GAAP toward capitalization of research and development costs. Adoption of IFRS should result in generally higher reported incomes for companies that incur research and development costs in periods in which these costs are incurred.

The Financial Accounting Standards Board (FASB) is currently working on a new accounting standard aimed at eliminating the differences between U.S. GAAP and IFRS in the area of research and development costs.

Still another difference between IFRS and U.S. GAAP lies in the capitalization of internally-generated intangible assets such as brand names and patents. U.S. GAAP only permits capitalization when they are purchased from a source outside the company. The cost of internally-generated brand names and patents must be expensed on the income statement. In contrast, IFRS allows the capitalization of internally-generated intangible assets like these as long as it is probable (i.e., more likely than not) that the company will receive future benefits from them. Adoption of IFRS by U.S. companies is therefore expected to result in the recognition of more intangible assets on their balance sheets than presently exist. These assets may be either amortized over the assets' estimated useful lives or tested for impairment as they are held, depending on the asset.

REPORTING PLANT ASSET TRANSACTIONS ON THE STATEMENT OF CASH FLOWS

OBJECTIVE

7 **Report** plant asset transactions on the statement of cash flows

Three main types of plant asset transactions appear on the statement of cash flows:

- acquisitions,
- sales, and
- depreciation (including amortization and depletion).

Acquisitions and sales are *investing* activities. A company invests in plant assets. The payments for equipment and buildings are investing activities that appear on the statement of cash flows. The sale of plant assets results in a cash receipt, as illustrated in Exhibit 7-12, which excerpts data from the cash-flow statement of FedEx Corporation. Depreciation, acquisitions, and sales of plant assets are denoted in color (lines 2, 5, and 6).

EXHIBIT 7-12 | **Reporting Plant Asset Transactions on FedEx's Statement of Cash Flows**

> **FedEx Corporation**
> **Statement of Cash Flows (partial, adapted)**
> **Year Ended May 31, 2008**
>
> | | | (In millions) |
> |---|---|---|
> | **Cash Flows from Operating Activities:** | | |
> | 1 | Net income.. | $1,125 |
> | | Adjustments to reconcile net income | |
> | | to net cash provided by operating activities: | |
> | 2 | Depreciation and amortization............................. | 1,946 |
> | 3 | Other items (summarized)..................................... | 413 |
> | 4 | Cash provided by operating activities.................... | 3,484 |
> | **Cash Flows from Investing Activities:** | | |
> | 5 | Capital expenditures .... | (2,947) |
> | 6 | Proceeds from asset dispositions........................... | 50 |
> | 7 | Cash (used in) investing activities.......................... | (2,897) |
> | **Cash Flows from Financing Activities:** | | |
> | 8 | Cash (used in) financing activities .... | (617) |
> | 9 | **Net (decrease) in cash and cash equivalents......................** | (30) |
> | 10 | **Cash and cash equivalents, beginning of period ....** | 1,569 |
> | 11 | **Cash and cash equivalents, end of period.........................** | $1,539 |

Let's examine FedEx's investing activities first. During 2008, FedEx paid $2,947 million for plant assets (line 5). FedEx also sold property and equipment, receiving cash of $50 million (line 6). FedEx labels the cash received as Proceeds from asset dispositions.

FedEx's statement of cash flows reports Depreciation and amortization (line 2). Observe that "Depreciation and amortization" is listed as a positive item under Adjustments to reconcile net income to Cash provided by operating activities. Since depreciation does not affect cash, you may be wondering why depreciation appears on the Statement of Cash Flows. In this format, the operating activities section of the Statement of Cash Flows starts with net income (line 1) and reconciles to cash provided by operating activities (line 4). Depreciation decreases net income but does not affect cash. Depreciation is therefore added back to net income to measure cash flow from operations. The add-back of depreciation to net income offsets the earlier subtraction of the expense. The sum of net income plus depreciation, therefore, helps to reconcile net income (on the accrual basis) to cash flow from operations (a cash-basis amount). We revisit this topic in the full context of the statement of cash flows in Chapter 12.

FedEx's cash flows are strong, but you can tell from reading the Statement of Cash Flows that the recession of 2008 and 2009 has taken its toll on FedEx. Cash flows from operations has declined over the past two fiscal years (not shown). Capital expenditures have grown, signaling that the company has invested much of its cash in the plant and equipment needed to run its business. However, the company has also had to borrow money to help finance these purchases. The company's debt payments ($617) have grown substantially over the past two years as well. This has resulted in a decline in cash and cash equivalents of $30 million in 2008. However, the company's cash position at the end of the year, in the amount of $1,539, is still very strong.

DECISION GUIDELINES

PLANT ASSETS AND RELATED EXPENSES

FedEx Corporation, like all other companies, must make some decisions about how to account for its plant assets and intangibles. Let's review some of these decisions.

Decision	Guidelines
Capitalize or expense a cost?	General rule: Capitalize all costs that provide *future* benefit for the business such as a new package-handling system. Expense all costs that provide no *future* benefit, such as a repair to an airplane.
Capitalize or expense:	
• Cost associated with a new asset?	Capitalize all costs that bring the asset to its intended use, including asset purchase price, transportation charges, and taxes paid to acquire the asset.
• Cost associated with an existing asset?	Capitalize only those costs that add to the asset's usefulness or to its useful life. Expense all other costs as maintenance or repairs.
Which depreciation method to use:	
• For financial reporting?	Use the method that best matches depreciation expense against the revenues produced by the asset. Most companies use the straight-line method.
• For income tax?	Use the method that produces the fastest tax deductions (MACRS). A company can use different depreciation methods for financial reporting and for income-tax purposes. In the United States, this practice is both legal and ethical.
• How to account for natural resources?	Capitalize the asset's acquisition cost and all later costs that add to the natural resource's future benefit. Then record depletion expense, as computed by the units-of-production method.
• How to account for intangibles?	Capitalize acquisition cost and all later costs that add to the asset's future benefit. For intangibles with finite lives, record amortization expense. For intangibles with indefinite lives, do not record amortization. But if an intangible asset loses value, then record a loss in the amount of the decrease in asset value.

END-OF-CHAPTER SUMMARY PROBLEM

The figures that follow appear in the *Answers to the Mid-Chapter Summary Problem*, Requirement 2, on page 424.

Year	*Method A: Straight-Line*			*Method B: Double-Declining-Balance*		
	Annual Depreciation Expense	Accumulated Depreciation	Book Value	Annual Depreciation Expense	Accumulated Depreciation	Book Value
Start			$44,000			$44,000
2009	$4,000	$ 4,000	40,000	$8,800	$ 8,800	35,200
2010	4,000	8,000	36,000	7,040	15,840	28,160
2011	4,000	12,000	32,000	5,632	21,472	22,528

▌ Requirements

1. Suppose the income tax authorities permitted a choice between these two depreciation methods. Which method would FedEx select for income-tax purposes? Why?
2. Suppose FedEx purchased the equipment described in the table on January 1, 2009. Management has depreciated the equipment by using the double-declining-balance method. On July 1, 2011, FedEx sold the equipment for $27,000 cash.

Record depreciation for 2011 and the sale of the equipment on July 1, 2011.

Answers

▌ Requirement 1

For tax purposes, most companies select the accelerated method because it results in the most depreciation in the earliest years of the asset's life. Accelerated depreciation minimizes income tax payments in the early years of the asset's life. That maximizes the business's cash at the earliest possible time.

▌ Requirement 2

Entries to record depreciation to date of sale, and then the sale of the equipment, follow:

2011			
Jul 1	Depreciation Expense—Equipment ($5,632 × 1/2 year)	2,816	
	Accumulated Depreciation—Equipment		2,816
	To update depreciation.		
Jul 1	Cash	27,000	
	Accumulated Depreciation—Equipment		
	($15,840 + $2,816)	18,656	
	Equipment		44,000
	Gain on Sale of Equipment		1,656
	To record sale of equipment.		

REVIEW PLANT ASSETS AND INTANGIBLES

Quick Check (Answers are given on page 466.)

1. Bartman, Inc., purchased a tract of land, a small office building, and some equipment for $1,900,000. The appraised value of the land was $1,380,000, the building $575,000, and the equipment $345,000. What is the cost of the land?

   a. $633,333   **c.** $1,380,000

   b. $1,140,000   **d.** None of the above

2. Which statement is false?

   a. Depreciation is a process of allocating the cost of a plant asset over its useful life.

   b. Depreciation is based on the matching principle because it matches the cost of the asset with the revenue generated over the asset's useful life.

   c. The cost of a plant asset minus accumulated depreciation equals the asset's book value.

   d. Depreciation creates a fund to replace the asset at the end of its useful life.

Use the following data for questions 3–6.

On July 1, 2010, Horizon Communications purchased a new piece of equipment that cost $45,000. The estimated useful life is 10 years and estimated residual value is $5,000.

3. What is the depreciation expense for 2010 if Horizon uses the straight-line method?

   a. $4,000   **c.** $4,500

   b. $2,000   **d.** $2,250

4. Assume Horizon Communications purchased the equipment on January 1, 2010. If Horizon uses the straight-line method for depreciation, what is the asset's book value at the end of 2011?

   a. $42,000   **c.** $32,000

   b. $36,000   **d.** $37,000

5. Assume Horizon Communications purchased the equipment on January 1, 2010. If Horizon uses the double-declining-balance method, what is depreciation for 2011?

   a. $9,000   **c.** $16,200

   b. $6,400   **d.** $7,200

6. Return to Horizon's original purchase date of July 1, 2010. Assume that Horizon uses the straight-line method of depreciation and sells the equipment for $36,500 on July 1, 2014. The result of the sale of the equipment is a gain (loss) of

   a. ($3,500).   **c.** $2,500.

   b. $7,500.   **d.** $0.

7. A company bought a new machine for $24,000 on January 1. The machine is expected to last five years and have a residual value of $4,000. If the company uses the double-declining-balance method, accumulated depreciation at the end of year 2 will be:

   a. $12,800.   **c.** $19,200.

   b. $15,360.   **d.** $16,000.

8. Which of the following is *not* a capital expenditure?

   a. The addition of a building wing   **d.** Replacement of an old motor with a

   b. A tune-up of a company vehicle   new one in a piece of equipment

   c. A complete overhaul of an air-   **e.** The cost of installing a piece of

       conditioning system   equipment

9. Which of the following assets is *not* subject to a decreasing book value through depreciation, depletion, or amortization?

   a. Land improvements   **c.** Intangibles

   b. Goodwill   **d.** Natural resources

10. Why would a business select an accelerated method of depreciation for tax purposes?

   a. MACRS depreciation follows a specific pattern of depreciation.

   b. Accelerated depreciation generates higher depreciation expense immediately, and therefore lowers tax payments in the early years of the asset's life.

   c. Accelerated depreciation is easier to calculate because salvage value is ignored.

   d. Accelerated depreciation generates a greater amount of depreciation over the life of the asset than does straight-line depreciation.

11. A company purchased an oil well for $270,000. It estimates that the well contains 90,000 barrels, has an eight-year life, and no salvage value. If the company extracts and sells 10,000 barrels of oil in the first year, how much depletion expense should be recorded?
    a. $33,750
    b. $135,000
    c. $27,000
    d. $30,000
12. Which item among the following is not an intangible asset?
    a. A copyright
    b. A patent
    c. A trademark
    d. Goodwill
    e. All of the above are intangible assets.

Accounting Vocabulary

accelerated depreciation method (p. 420) A depreciation method that writes off a relatively larger amount of the asset's cost nearer the start of its useful life than the straight-line method does.

amortization (p. 434) The systematic reduction of a lump-sum amount. Expense that applies to intangible assets in the same way depreciation applies to plant assets and depletion applies to natural resources.

capital expenditure (p. 414) Expenditure that increases an asset's capacity or efficiency or extends its useful life. Capital expenditures are debited to an asset account.

copyright (p. 435) Exclusive right to reproduce and sell a book, musical composition, film, other work of art, or computer program. Issued by the federal government, copyrights extend 70 years beyond the author's life.

depletion expense (p. 434) That portion of a natural resource's cost that is used up in a particular period. Depletion expense is computed in the same way as units-of-production depreciation.

depreciable cost (p. 417) The cost of a plant asset minus its estimated residual value.

double-declining-balance (DDB) method (p. 420) An accelerated depreciation method that computes annual depreciation by multiplying the asset's decreasing book value by a constant percentage, which is two times the straight-line rate.

estimated residual value (p. 417) Expected cash value of an asset at the end of its useful life. Also called *residual value, scrap value,* or *salvage value.*

estimated useful life (p. 417) Length of service that a business expects to get from an asset. May be expressed in years, units of output, miles, or other measures.

franchises and licenses (p. 436) Privileges granted by a private business or a government to sell a product or service in accordance with specified conditions.

goodwill (p. 436) Excess of the cost of an acquired company over the sum of the market values of its net assets (assets minus liabilities).

impairment (p. 437) The condition that exists when the carrying amount of a long-lived asset exceeds its fair value. Whenever long-term assets have been impaired, they have to be written down to fair market values. Under U.S. GAAP, once impaired, the carrying value of a long-lived asset may never again be increased. Under IFRS, if the fair value of impaired assets recovers in the future, the values may be increased.

intangible assets (p. 411) An asset with no physical form, a special right to current and expected future benefits.

Modified Accelerated Cost Recovery System (MACRS) (p. 425) A special depreciation method used only for income-tax purposes. Assets are grouped into classes, and for a given class depreciation is computed by the double-declining-balance method, the 150%-declining balance method, or, for most real estate, the straight-line method.

patent (p. 435) A federal government grant giving the holder the exclusive right for 20 years to produce and sell an invention.

plant assets (p. 410) Long-lived assets, such as land, buildings, and equipment, used in the operation of the business. Also called *fixed assets.*

straight-line (SL) method (p. 418) Depreciation method in which an equal amount of depreciation expense is assigned to each year of asset use.

trademark, trade name (p. 435) A distinctive identification of a product or service. Also called a *brand name.*

units-of-production (UOP) method (p. 419) Depreciation method by which a fixed amount of depreciation is assigned to each unit of output produced by the plant asset.

ASSESS YOUR PROGRESS

Short Exercises

S7-1 (*Learning Objective 1: Determining cost and book value of a company's plant assets*)   Examine Round Rock's assets.

(In millions)	May 31, 2011	2010
Round Rock Corporation		
Consolidated Balance Sheets (Partial, Adapted)		
1 Assets		
2 Current assets		
3 Cash and cash equivalents...	$ 2,098	$ 246
4 Receivables, less allowances of $144 and $125	2,772	2,610
5 Spare parts, supplies, and fuel	4,670	4,510
6 Prepaid expenses and other...	468	411
7 Total current assets	10,008	7,777
8 Property and equipment, at cost		
9 Aircraft	2,394	2,394
10 Package handling and ground support equipment..............	12,225	12,139
11 Computer and electronic equipment...................................	28,165	26,115
12 Vehicles..	586	453
13 Facilities and other...	1,435	1,594
14 Total cost..	44,805	42,695
15 Less: Accumulated depreciation	(14,903)	(12,942)
16 Net property and equipment...	29,902	29,753
17 Other long-term assets		
18 Goodwill...	724	724
19 Prepaid pension cost..	1,341	1,275
20 Intangible and other assets	324	329
21 Total other long-term assets..	2,389	2,328
22 Total assets	$ 42,299	$ 39,858

1. What is Round Rock's largest category of assets? List all 2011 assets in the largest category and their amounts as reported by Round Rock.
2. What was Round Rock's cost of property and equipment at May 31, 2011? What was the book value of property and equipment on this date? Why is book value less than cost?

S7-2 (*Learning Objective 1: Measuring the cost of a plant asset*)   This chapter lists the costs included for the acquisition of land on pages 411–412. First is the purchase price of the land, which is obviously included in the cost of the land. The reasons for including the other costs are not so obvious. For example, property tax is ordinarily an expense, not part of the cost of an asset. State why the other costs listed are included as part of the cost of the land. After the land is ready for use, will these related costs be capitalized or expensed?

S7-3 (*Learning Objective 1: Determining the cost of individual assets in a lump-sum purchase of assets*)   Foley Distribution Service pays $140,000 for a group purchase of land, building, and equipment. At the time of acquisition, the land has a current market value of $75,000, the building's current market value is $45,000, and the equipment's current market value is $30,000. Journalize the lump-sum purchase of the three assets for a total cost of $140,000. You sign a note payable for this amount.

S7-4 (*Learning Objective 1: Capitalizing versus expensing plant asset costs*)   Assume Nation Airlines repaired a Boeing 777 aircraft at a cost of $1.5 million, which Nation paid in cash. Further, assume the Nation accountant erroneously capitalized this expense as part of the cost of the plane.

Show the effects of the accounting error on Nation Airlines' income statement. To answer this question, determine whether revenues, total expenses, and net income were overstated or understated by the accounting error.

S7-5 (*Learning Objective 2: Computing depreciation by three methods—first year only*)   Assume that at the beginning of 2010, Northeast USA, a FedEx competitor, purchased a used Boeing 737 aircraft at a cost of $53,000,000. Northeast USA expects the plane to remain useful for five years (six million miles) and to have a residual value of $5,000,000. Northeast USA expects to fly the plane 775,000 miles the first year, 1,275,000 miles each year during the second, third, and fourth years, and 1,400,000 miles the last year.

1. Compute Northeast USA's first-year depreciation on the plane using the following methods:
   a. Straight-line
   b. Units-of-production
   c. Double-declining-balance
2. Show the airplane's book value at the end of the first year under each depreciation method.

S7-6 (*Learning Objective 2: Computing depreciation by three methods—third year only*)   Use the Northeast USA data in Short Exercise 7-5 to compute Northeast USA's third-year depreciation on the plane using the following methods:

   a. Straight-line
   b. Units-of-production
   c. Double-declining balance

S7-7 (*Learning Objective 3: Selecting the best depreciation method for income tax purposes*)   This exercise uses the assumed Northeast USA data from Short Exercise 7-5. Assume Northeast USA is trying to decide which depreciation method to use for income tax purposes. The company can choose from among the following methods: (a) straight-line, (b) units of production, or (c) double-declining-balance.

1. Which depreciation method offers the tax advantage for the first year? Describe the nature of the tax advantage.
2. How much income tax will Northeast USA save for the first year of the airplane's use under the method you selected above as compared with using the straight-line depreciation method? The income tax rate is 32%. Ignore any earnings from investing the extra cash.

S7-8 (*Learning Objectives 2, 3: Computing partial year depreciation; selecting the best depreciation method*)   Assume that on September 30, 2010, LoganAir, the national airline of Switzerland, purchased an Airbus aircraft at a cost of €45,000,000 (€ is the symbol for the euro). LoganAir expects the plane to remain useful for six years (4,500,000 miles) and to have a residual value of €5,400,000. LoganAir will fly the plane 410,000 miles during the remainder of 2010.

Compute LoganAir's depreciation on the plane for the year ended December 31, 2010, using the following methods:

    a. Straight-line
    b. Units-of-production
    c. Double-declining-balance

Which method would produce the highest net income for 2010? Which method produces the lowest net income?

S7-9 *(Learning Objectives 2, 3: Computing and recording depreciation after a change in useful life of the asset)* Ten Flags over Georgia paid $100,000 for a concession stand. Ten Flags started out depreciating the building straight-line over 20 years with zero residual value. After using the concession stand for three years, Ten Flags determines that the building will remain useful for only six more years. Record Ten Flags' depreciation on the concession stand for year 4 by the straight-line method.

S7-10 *(Learning Objectives 2, 4: Computing depreciation; recording a gain or loss on disposal)* On January 1, 2010, ABC Airline Service purchased an airplane for $37,700,000. ABC Airline Service expects the plane to remain useful for six years and to have a residual value of $2,900,000. ABC Airline Service uses the straight-line method to depreciate its airplanes. ABC Airline Service flew the plane for three years and sold it on January 1, 2013, for $8,300,000.

    1. Compute accumulated depreciation on the airplane at January 1, 2013 (same as December 31, 2012).
    2. Record the sale of the plane on January 1, 2013.

S7-11 *(Learning Objective 5: Accounting for the depletion of a company's natural resources)* North Coast Petroleum, the giant oil company, holds reserves of oil and gas assets. At the end of 2010, assume the cost of North Coast Petroleum's mineral assets totaled $120 billion, representing 10 billion barrels of oil in the ground.

    1. Which depreciation method is similar to the depletion method that North Coast Petroleum and other oil companies use to compute their annual depletion expense for the minerals removed from the ground?
    2. Suppose North Coast Petroleum removed 0.4 billion barrels of oil during 2011. Record depletion expense for the year. Show amounts in billions.
    3. At December 31, 2010, North Coast Petroleum's Accumulated Depletion account stood at $38 billion. Report Mineral Assets and Accumulated Depletion at December 31, 2011. Do North Coast Petroleum's Mineral Assets appear to be plentiful or mostly used up? Give your reason.

S7-12 *(Learning Objective 6: Measuring and recording goodwill)* Vector, Inc., dominates the snack-food industry with its Tangy-Chip brand. Assume that Vector, Inc., purchased Concord Snacks, Inc., for $8.8 million cash. The market value of Concord Snacks' assets is $15 million, and Concord Snacks has liabilities of $8 million.

❚ Requirements

    1. Compute the cost of the goodwill purchased by Vector.
    2. Explain how Vector will account for goodwill in future years.

S7-13 *(Learning Objective 6: Accounting for patents and research and development cost)* This exercise summarizes the accounting for patents, which like copyrights, trademarks, and franchises, provide the owner with a special right or privilege. It also covers research and development costs.

Suppose Solar Automobiles Limited paid $600,000 to research and develop a new global positioning system. Solar also paid $350,000 to acquire a patent on a new motor. After readying the motor for production, Solar's sales revenue for the first year totaled

$5,200,000. Cost of goods sold was $3,800,000, and selling expenses totaled $480,000. All these transactions occurred during 2010. Solar expects the patent to have a useful life of seven years.

Prepare Solar Automobiles' income statement for the year ended December 31, 2010, complete with a heading. Ignore income tax.

S7-14 (*Learning Objective 7: Reporting investing activities on the statement of cash flows*)   During 2010, Northern Satellite Systems, Inc., purchased two other companies for $16 million. Also during 2010, Northern made capital expenditures of $7 million to expand its market share. During the year, Northern sold its North American operations, receiving cash of $14 million. Overall, Northern reported a net income of $2 million during 2010.

Show what Northern would report for cash flows from investing activities on its statement of cash flows for 2010. Report a total amount for net cash provided by (used in) investing activities.

Exercises

All of the A and B exercises can be found within MyAccountingLab, an online homework and practice environment. Your instructor may ask you to complete these exercises using MyAccountingLab.

(Group A)

E7-15A (*Learning Objective 1: Determining the cost of plant assets*)   Ayer Self Storage purchased land, paying $175,000 cash as a down payment and signing a $190,000 note payable for the balance. Ayer also had to pay delinquent property tax of $3,500, title insurance costing $3,000, and $9,000 to level the land and remove an unwanted building. The company paid $59,000 to add soil for the foundation and then constructed an office building at a cost of $650,000. It also paid $55,000 for a fence around the property, $14,000 for the company sign near the property entrance, and $8,000 for lighting of the grounds. Determine the cost of Ayer's land, land improvements, and building.

E7-16A (*Learning Objectives 1, 4: Allocating costs to assets acquired in a lump-sum purchase; disposing of a plant asset*)   Deadwood Manufacturing bought three used machines in a $167,000 lump-sum purchase. An independent appraiser valued the machines as shown in the table.

Machine No.	Appraised Value
1	$38,250
2	73,100
3	58,650

What is each machine's individual cost? Immediately after making this purchase, Deadwood sold machine 2 for its appraised value. What is the result of the sale? (Round decimals to three places when calculating proportions, and use your computed percentages throughout.)

E7-17A (*Learning Objective 1: Distinguishing capital expenditures from expenses*)   Assume Candy Corner, Inc., purchased conveyor-belt machinery. Classify each of the following expenditures as a capital expenditure or an immediate expense related to machinery:

  a. Sales tax paid on the purchase price
  b. Transportation and insurance while machinery is in transit from seller to buyer
  c. Purchase price
  d. Installation

e. Training of personnel for initial operation of the machinery
f. Special reinforcement to the machinery platform
g. Income tax paid on income earned from the sale of products manufactured by the machinery
h. Major overhaul to extend the machinery's useful life by three years
i. Ordinary repairs to keep the machinery in good working order
j. Lubrication of the machinery before it is placed in service
k. Periodic lubrication after the machinery is placed in service

E7-18A *(Learning Objectives 1, 2: Measuring, depreciating, and reporting plant assets)*   During 2010, Chun Book Store paid $487,000 for land and built a store in Akron. Prior to construction, the city of Akron charged Chun $1,400 for a building permit, which Chun paid. Chun also paid $15,320 for architect's fees. The construction cost of $690,000 was financed by a long-term note payable, with interest cost of $28,300 paid at completion of the project. The building was completed September 30, 2010. Chun depreciates the building by the straight-line method over 35 years, with estimated residual value of $337,000.

1. Journalize transactions for
   a. Purchase of the land
   b. All the costs chargeable to the building in a single entry
   c. Depreciation on the building

Explanations are not required.

2. Report Chun Book Store's plant assets on the company's balance sheet at December 31, 2010.
3. What will Chun's income statement for the year ended December 31, 2010, report for this situation?

writing assignment ■

■ spreadsheet

E7-19A *(Learning Objectives 2, 3: Determining depreciation amounts by three methods)*
West Side's Pizza bought a used Nissan delivery van on January 2, 2010, for $19,000. The van was expected to remain in service for four years (36,000 miles). At the end of its useful life, West Side's officials estimated that the van's residual value would be $2,800. The van traveled 11,000 miles the first year, 13,000 miles the second year, 5,000 miles the third year, and 7,000 miles in the fourth year. Prepare a schedule of *depreciation expense* per year for the van under the three depreciation methods. (For units-of-production and double-declining-balance, round to the nearest two decimals after each step of the calculation.)

Which method best tracks the wear and tear on the van? Which method would West Side's prefer to use for income tax purposes? Explain in detail why West Side's prefers this method.

E7-20A *(Learning Objectives 1, 2, 7: Reporting plant assets, depreciation, and investing cash flows)*   Assume that in January 2010, an Oatmeal House restaurant purchased a building, paying $56,000 cash and signing a $107,000 note payable. The restaurant paid another $61,000 to remodel the building. Furniture and fixtures cost $53,000, and dishes and supplies—a current asset—were obtained for $9,200.

Oatmeal House is depreciating the building over 20 years by the straight-line method, with estimated residual value of $55,000. The furniture and fixtures will be replaced at the end of five years and are being depreciated by the double-declining-balance method, with zero residual value. At the end of the first year, the restaurant still has dishes and supplies worth $1,700.

Show what the restaurant will report for supplies, plant assets, and cash flows at the end of the first year on its

■ Income statement
■ Balance sheet
■ Statement of cash flows (investing only)

Note: The purchase of dishes and supplies is an operating cash flow because supplies are a current asset.

E7-21A *(Learning Objective 3: Selecting the best depreciation method for income tax purposes)* On June 30, 2010, Rockwell Corp. paid $220,000 for equipment that is expected to have an eight-year life. In this industry, the residual value of equipment is approximately 10% of the asset's cost. Rockwell's cash revenues for the year are $115,000 and cash expenses total $75,000.

Select the appropriate MACRS depreciation method for income tax purposes. Then determine the extra amount of cash that Rockwell can invest by using MACRS depreciation, versus straight-line, for the year ended December 31, 2010. The income tax rate is 40%.

E7-22A *(Learning Objectives 2, 3: Changing a plant asset's useful life)* Assume G-1 Designing Consultants purchased a building for $400,000 and depreciated it on a straight-line basis over 40 years. The estimated residual value was $55,000. After using the building for 20 years, G-1 realized that the building will remain useful only 15 more years. Starting with the 21st year, G-1 began depreciating the building over a revised total life of 35 years and decreased the residual value to $10,000. Record depreciation expense on the building for years 20 and 21.

E7-23A *(Learning Objectives 2, 3, 4: Analyzing the effect of a sale of a plant asset; DDB depreciation)* Assume that on January 2, 2010, Maxwell of Michigan purchased fixtures for $8,800 cash, expecting the fixtures to remain in service for five years. Maxwell has depreciated the fixtures on a double-declining-balance basis, with $1,300 estimated residual value. On August 31, 2011, Maxwell sold the fixtures for $2,900 cash. Record both the depreciation expense on the fixtures for 2011 and the sale of the fixtures. Apart from your journal entry, also show how to compute the gain or loss on Maxwell' disposal of these fixtures.

E7-24A *(Learning Objectives 1, 2, 4: Measuring a plant asset's cost; using UOP depreciation; trading in a used asset)* Honest Truck Company is a large trucking company that operates throughout the United States. Honest Truck Company uses the units-of-production (UOP) method to depreciate its trucks.

Honest Truck Company trades in trucks often to keep driver morale high and to maximize fuel economy. Consider these facts about one Mack truck in the company's fleet: When acquired in 2010, the tractor-trailer rig cost $380,000 and was expected to remain in service for 10 years or 1,000,000 miles. Estimated residual value was $100,000. During 2010, the truck was driven 76,000 miles; during 2011, 116,000 miles; and during 2012, 156,000 miles. After 37,000 miles in 2013, the company traded in the Mack truck for a less-expensive Freightliner with a sticker price of $300,000. Honest Truck Company paid cash of $28,000. Determine Honest's gain or loss on the transaction. Prepare the journal entry to record the trade-in of the old truck on the new one.

E7-25A *(Learning Objective 5: Recording natural resource assets and depletion)* Rocky Mines paid $426,000 for the right to extract ore from a 275,000-ton mineral deposit. In addition to the purchase price, Rocky Mines also paid a $120 filing fee, a $2,100 license fee to the state of Colorado, and $64,030 for a geologic survey of the property. Because the company purchased the rights to the minerals only, it expects the asset to have zero residual value when fully depleted. During the first year of production, Rocky Mines removed 40,000 tons of ore. Make journal entries to record (a) purchase of the mineral rights, (b) payment of fees and other costs, and (c) depletion for first-year production. What is the mineral asset's book value at the end of the year?

E7-26A *(Learning Objectives 3, 6: Recording intangibles, amortization, and a change in the asset's useful life)*

1. Morris Printers purchased for $900,000 a patent for a new laser printer. Although the patent gives legal protection for 20 years, it is expected to provide Morris Printers with a competitive advantage for only 10 years. Assuming the straight-line method of amortization, make journal entries to record (a) the purchase of the patent and (b) amortization for year 1.

2. After using the patent for five years, Morris Printers learns at a industry trade show that Super Printers is designing a more-efficient printer. On the basis of this new information, Morris Printers determines that the patent's total useful life is only seven years. Record amortization for year 6.

E7-27A (*Learning Objective 6: Computing and accounting for goodwill*) Assume Haledan paid $16 million to purchase Northshore.com. Assume further that Northshore had the following summarized data at the time of the Haledan acquisition (amounts in millions):

Northshore.com			
Assets		**Liabilities and Equity**	
Current assets	$13	Total liabilities	$25
Long-term assets	23	Stockholders' equity	11
	$36		$36

Northshore's long-term assets had a current market value of only $18 million.

❚ Requirements

1. Compute the cost of goodwill purchased by Haledan.
2. Journalize Haledan's purchase of Northshore.
3. Explain how Haledan will account for goodwill in the future.

E7-28A (*Learning Objective 7: Reporting cash flows for property and equipment*) Assume Shoe Warehouse Corporation completed the following transactions:

   a. Sold a store building for $650,000. The building had cost Shoe Warehouse $1,700,000, and at the time of the sale its accumulated depreciation totaled $1,050,000.
   b. Lost a store building in a fire. The building cost $380,000 and had accumulated depreciation of $190,000. The insurance proceeds received by Shoe Warehouse totaled $130,000.
   c. Renovated a store at a cost of $160,000.
   d. Purchased store fixtures for $70,000. The fixtures are expected to remain in service for 10 years and then be sold for $20,000. Shoe Warehouse uses the straight-line depreciation method.

For each transaction, show what Shoe Warehouse would report for investing activities on its statement of cash flows. Show negative amounts in parentheses.

(Group B)

E7-29B (*Learning Objective 1: Determining the cost of plant assets*) Lavallee Self Storage purchased land, paying $155,000 cash as a down payment and signing a $195,000 note payable for the balance. Lavallee also had to pay delinquent property tax of $4,000, title insurance costing $3,500, and $5,000 to level the land and remove an unwanted building. The company paid $53,000 to add soil for the foundation and then constructed an office building at a cost of $600,000. It also paid $45,000 for a fence around the property, $20,000 for the company sign near the property entrance, and $3,000 for lighting of the grounds. Determine the cost of Lavallee's land, land improvements, and building.

E7-30B (*Learning Objectives 1, 4: Allocating costs to assets acquired in a lump-sum purchase; disposing of a plant asset*) Eastwood Manufacturing bought three used machines in a $216,000 lump-sum purchase. An independent appraiser valued the machines as shown in the table.

Machine No.	Appraised Value
1	$ 77,000
2	116,600
3	26,400

What is each machine's individual cost? Immediately after making this purchase, Eastwood sold machine 2 for its appraised value. What is the result of the sale? (Round decimals to three places when calculating proportions, and use your computed percentages throughout.)

E7-31B (*Learning Objective 1: Distinguishing capital expenditures from expenses*)   Assume Delicious Desserts, Inc., purchased conveyor-belt machinery. Classify each of the following expenditures as a capital expenditure or an immediate expense related to machinery:

    a. Sales tax paid on the purchase price
    b. Transportation and insurance while machinery is in transit from seller to buyer
    c. Purchase price
    d. Installation
    e. Training of personnel for initial operation of the machinery
    f. Special reinforcement to the machinery platform
    g. Income tax paid on income earned from the sale of products manufactured by the machinery
    h. Major overhaul to extend the machinery's useful life by three years
    i. Ordinary repairs to keep the machinery in good working order
    j. Lubrication of the machinery before it is placed in service
    k. Periodic lubrication after the machinery is placed in service

E7-32B (*Learning Objectives 1, 2: Measuring, depreciating, and reporting plant assets*)   During 2010, Tao Book Store paid $488,000 for land and built a store in Detroit. Prior to construction, the city of Detroit charged Tao $1,800 for a building permit, which Tao paid. Tao also paid $15,800 for architect's fees. The construction cost of $710,000 was financed by a long-term note payable, with interest cost of $30,180 paid at completion of the project. The building was completed September 30, 2010. Tao depreciates the building by the straight-line method over 35 years, with estimated residual value of $341,000.

    1. Journalize transactions for
        a. Purchase of the land
        b. All the costs chargeable to the building in a single entry
        c. Depreciation on the building

Explanations are not required.

    2. Report Tao Book Store's plant assets on the company's balance sheet at December 31, 2010.
    3. What will Tao's income statement for the year ended December 31, 2010, report for this situation?

E7-33B (*Learning Objectives 2, 3: Determining depreciation amounts by three methods*)   Southern's Pizza bought a used Nissan delivery van on January 2, 2010, for $19,200. The van was expected to remain in service four years (30,000 miles). At the end of its useful life, Southern's officials estimated that the van's residual value would be $2,400. The van traveled 8,000 miles the first year, 8,500 miles the second year, 5,500 miles the third year, and 8,000 miles in the fourth year. Prepare a schedule of *depreciation expense* per year for the van under the three depreciation methods. (For units-of-production and double-declining-balance, round to the nearest two decimals after each step of the calculation.)

writing assignment ■

■ spreadsheet

Which method best tracks the wear and tear on the van? Which method would Southern's prefer to use for income tax purposes? Explain in detail why Southern's prefers this method.

E7-34B (*Learning Objectives 1, 2, 7: Reporting plant assets, depreciation, and investing cash flows*)   Assume that in January 2010, an International Eatery restaurant purchased a building, paying $52,000 cash and signing a $106,000 note payable. The restaurant paid another $62,000 to remodel the building. Furniture and fixtures cost $57,000, and dishes and supplies—a current asset—were obtained for $8,800.

International Eatery is depreciating the building over 20 years by the straight-line method, with estimated residual value of $54,000. The furniture and fixtures will be replaced at the end of five years and are being depreciated by the double-declining-balance method, with zero residual value. At the end of the first year, the restaurant still has dishes and supplies worth $1,600.

Show what the restaurant will report for supplies, plant assets, and cash flows at the end of the first year on its

- Income statement
- Balance sheet
- Statement of cash flows (investing only)

Note: The purchase of dishes and supplies is an operating cash flow because supplies are a current asset.

E7-35B *(Learning Objective 3: Selecting the best depreciation method for income tax purposes)* On June 30, 2010, Roy Corp. paid $200,000 for equipment that is expected to have an eight-year life. In this industry, the residual value is approximately 10% of the asset's cost. Roy's cash revenues for the year are $140,000 and cash expenses total $100,000.

Select the appropriate MACRS depreciation method for income tax purposes. Then determine the extra amount of cash that Roy can invest by using MACRS depreciation, versus straight-line, for the year ended December 31, 2010. The income tax rate is 30%.

E7-36B *(Learning Objectives 2, 3: Changing a plant asset's useful life)* Assume B – 1 Accounting Consultants purchased a building for $435,000 and depreciated it on a straight-line basis over 40 years. The estimated residual value was $73,000. After using the building for 20 years, B – 1 realized that the building will remain useful only 15 more years. Starting with the 21st year, B – 1 began depreciating the building over the newly revised total life of 35 years and decreased the estimated residual value to $14,000. Record depreciation expense on the building for years 20 and 21.

E7-37B *(Learning Objectives 2, 3, 4: Analyzing the effect of a sale of a plant asset; DDB depreciation)* Assume that on January 2, 2010, McKnight of Wyoming purchased fixtures for $8,300 cash, expecting the fixtures to remain in service for five years. McKnight has depreciated the fixtures on a double-declining-balance basis, with $1,700 estimated residual value. On September 30, 2011, McKnight sold the fixtures for $2,300 cash. Record both the depreciation expense on the fixtures for 2011 and then the sale of the fixtures. Apart from your journal entry, also show how to compute the gain or loss on McKnight's disposal of these fixtures.

E7-38B *(Learning Objectives 1, 2, 4: Measuring a plant asset's cost; using UOP depreciation; trading in a used asset)* Trusty Truck Company is a large trucking company that operates throughout the United States. Trusty Truck Company uses the units-of-production (UOP) method to depreciate its trucks.

Trusty Truck Company trades in trucks often to keep driver morale high and to maximize fuel economy. Consider these facts about one Mack truck in the company's fleet: When acquired in 2010, the rig cost $370,000 and was expected to remain in service for 10 years or 1,000,000 miles. Estimated residual value was $100,000. During 2010, the truck was driven 77,000 miles; during 2011, 117,000 miles; and during 2012, 157,000 miles. After 42,000 miles in 2013, the company traded in the Mack truck for a less-expensive Freightliner with a sticker price of $300,000. Trusty Truck Company paid cash of $25,000. Determine Trusty's gain or loss on the transaction. Prepare the journal entry to record the trade-in of the old truck on the new one.

E7-39B *(Learning Objective 5: Recording natural resource assets and depletion)* Mighty Mines paid $432,000 for the right to extract ore from a 425,000-ton mineral deposit. In addition to the purchase price, Mighty Mines also paid a $150 filing fee, a $2,700 license fee to the state of Colorado, and $92,150 for a geologic survey of the property. Because the company purchased the rights to the minerals only, it expected the asset to have zero residual value when fully depleted. During the first year of production, Mighty Mines removed 70,000 tons of ore. Make journal entries to record (a) purchase of the mineral rights, (b) payment of fees and other costs, and (c) depletion for first-year production. What is the mineral asset's book value at the end of the year?

E7-40B (*Learning Objectives 3, 6: Recording intangibles, amortization, and a change in the asset's useful life*)

1. Miracle Printers purchased for $700,000 a patent for a new laser printer. Although the patent gives legal protection for 20 years, it is expected to provide Miracle Printers with a competitive advantage for only eight years. Assuming the straight-line method of amortization, make journal entries to record (a) the purchase of the patent and (b) amortization for year 1.

2. After using the patent for four years, Miracle Printers learns at an industry trade show that Speedy Printers is designing a more-efficient printer. On the basis of this new information, Miracle Printers determines that the patent's total useful life is only six years. Record amortization for year 5.

E7-41B (*Learning Objective 6: Computing and accounting for goodwill*)   Assume Kaledan paid $18 million to purchase Southwest.com. Assume further that Southwest had the following summarized data at the time of the Kaledan acquisition (amounts in millions):

Southwest.com			
Assets		**Liabilities and Equity**	
Current assets	$10	Total liabilities	$25
Long-term assets	22	Stockholders' equity	7
	$32		$32

Southwest's long-term assets had a current market value of only $17 million.

❙ Requirements

1. Compute the cost of goodwill purchased by Kaledan.
2. Journalize Kaledan's purchase of Southwest.
3. Explain how Kaledan will account for goodwill in the future.

E7-42B (*Learning Objective 7: Reporting cash flows for property and equipment*)   Assume Shoes-R-Us Corporation completed the following transactions:

   a. Sold a store building for $610,000. The building had cost Shoes-R-Us $1,300,000, and at the time of the sale its accumulated depreciation totaled $690,000.

   b. Lost a store building in a fire. The building cost $350,000 and had accumulated depreciation of $170,000. The insurance proceeds received by Shoes-R-Us totaled $110,000.

   c. Renovated a store at a cost of $120,000.

   d. Purchased store fixtures for $90,000. The fixtures are expected to remain in service for 10 years and then be sold for $10,000. Shoes-R-Us uses the straight-line depreciation method.

For each transaction, show what Shoes-R-Us would report for investing activities on its statement of cash flows. Show negative amounts in parentheses.

Challenge Exercises

E7-43 (*Learning Objective 2: Computing units-of-production depreciation*)   Buff Gym purchased exercise equipment at a cost of $107,000. In addition, Buff paid $3,000 for a special platform on which to stabilize the equipment for use. Freight costs of $1,600 to ship the equipment were borne by the seller. Buff will depreciate the equipment by the units-of-production method, based on an expected useful life of 55,000 hours of exercise. The estimated residual value of the equipment is $11,000. How many hours did Buff Gym use the machine if depreciation expense is $4,320?

E7-44 (*Learning Objective 4: Determining the sale price of property and equipment*)   Wilson Corporation reported the following for property and equipment (in millions, adapted):

	Year End	
	2011	**2010**
Property and equipment..................	$24,073	$22,011
Accumulated depreciation...............	(13,306)	(12,087)

During 2011, Wilson paid $2,510 million for new property and equipment. Depreciation for the year totaled $1,546 million. During 2011, Wilson sold property and equipment for cash of $48 million. How much was Wilson's gain or loss on the sale of property and equipment during 2011?

E7-45 (*Learning Objectives 2, 3: Determining net income after a change in depreciation method*)   Norzani, Inc., has a popular line of sunglasses. Norzani reported net income of $66 million for 2010. Depreciation expense for the year totaled $32 million. Norzani, Inc., depreciates plant assets over eight years using the straight-line method and no residual value.

Norzani, Inc., paid $256 million for plant assets at the beginning of 2010. Then at the start of 2011, Norzani switched over to double-declining-balance (DDB) depreciation. 2011 is expected to be the same as 2010 except for the change in depreciation method. If Norzani had been using DDB depreciation all along, how much net income can Norzani, Inc., expect to earn during 2011? Ignore income tax.

E7-46 (*Learning Objective 1: Capitalizing versus expensing; measuring the effect of an error*)   All French Press (AFP) is a major French telecommunication conglomerate. Assume that early in year 1, AFP purchased equipment at a cost of 8 million euros (€8 million). Management expects the equipment to remain in service for four years and estimated residual value to be negligible. AFP uses the straight-line depreciation method. *Through an accounting error, AFP expensed the entire cost of the equipment at the time of purchase.* Because AFP is operated as a partnership, it pays no income tax.

❙ Requirements

Prepare a schedule to show the overstatement or understatement in the following items at the end of each year over the four-year life of the equipment:

1. Total current assets
2. Equipment, net
3. Net income

Quiz

Test your understanding of accounting for plant assets, natural resources, and intangibles by answering the following questions. Select the best choice from among the possible answers given.

Q7-47 A capital expenditure
a. adds to an asset.
b. is expensed immediately.
c. is a credit like capital (owners' equity).
d. records additional capital.

Q7-48 Which of the following items should be accounted for as a capital expenditure?
a. The monthly rental cost of an office building
b. Taxes paid in conjunction with the purchase of office equipment
c. Maintenance fees paid with funds provided by the company's capital
d. Costs incurred to repair leaks in the building roof

Q7-49 Suppose you buy land for $2,900,000 and spend $1,200,000 to develop the property. You then divide the land into lots as follows:

Catergory	Sale Price per Lot
10 Hilltop lots................	$525,000
10 Valley lots	350,000

How much did each hilltop lot cost you?
a. $246,000
b. $175,715
c. $234,285
d. $410,000

Q7-50 Which statement about depreciation is false?
a. Depreciation should not be recorded in years that the market value of the asset has increased.
b. Depreciation is a process of allocating the cost of an asset to expense over its useful life.
c. A major objective of depreciation accounting is to match the cost of using an asset with the revenues it helps to generate.
d. Obsolescence as well as physical wear and tear should be considered when determining the period over which an asset should be depreciated.

Q7-51 Boston Corporation acquired a machine for $33,000 and has recorded depreciation for two years using the straight-line method over a five-year life and $6,000 residual value. At the start of the third year of use, Boston revised the estimated useful life to a total of 10 years. Estimated residual value declined to $0.

What is the book value of the machine at the end of two full years of use?
a. $13,200
b. $16,800
c. $10,800
d. $22,200

Q7-52 Boston Corporation acquired a machine for $33,000 and has recorded depreciation for two years using the straight-line method over a five-year life and $6,000 residual value. At the start of the third year of use, Boston revised the estimated useful life to a total of 10 years. Estimated residual value declined to $0.

How much depreciation should Boston record in each of the asset's last eight years (that is, year 3 through year 10), following the revision?
a. $13,200
b. $3,300
c. $2,775
d. Some other amount

Q7-53 King Company failed to record depreciation of equipment. How does this omission affect King's financial statements?

a. Net income is overstated and assets are understated.
b. Net income is overstated and assets are overstated.
c. Net income is understated and assets are overstated.
d. Net income is understated and assets are understated.

Q7-54 Jimmy's DVD, Inc., uses the double-declining-balance method for depreciation on its computers. Which item is not needed to compute depreciation for the first year?

a. Original cost
b. Expected useful life in years
c. Estimated residual value
d. All the above are needed.

Q7-55 Which of the following costs is reported on a company's income statement?
a. Land
b. Accumulated depreciation
c. Depreciation expense
d. Accounts payable

Q7-56 Which of the following items is reported on the balance sheet?
a. Gain on disposal of equipment
b. Accumulated depreciation
c. Cost of goods sold
d. Net sales revenue

Use the following information to answer questions 7-57 through 7-59.

Hill Company purchased a machine for $8,600 on January 1, 2010. The machine has been depreciated using the straight-line method over a 10-year life and $600 residual value. Hill sold the machine on January 1, 2012, for $7,700.

Q7-57 What gain or loss should Hill record on the sale?
a. Gain, $1,300   c. Gain, $300
b. Loss, $900   d. Gain, $700

Q7-58 Journalize Hill's sale of the machine.

Q7-59 What is straight-line depreciation for the year ended December 31, 2010, and what is the book value on December 31, 2011?

Q7-60 A company purchased mineral assets costing $840,000, with estimated residual value of $30,000, and holding approximately 300,000 tons of ore. During the first year, 48,000 tons are extracted and sold. What is the amount of depletion for the first year?
a. $114,500
b. $129,600
c. $109,400
d. Cannot be determined from the data given

Q7-61 Suppose Timely Delivery pays $64 million to buy Guaranteed Overnight. Guaranteed's assets are valued at $74 million, and its liabilities total $16 million. How much goodwill did Timely Delivery purchase in its acquisition of Guaranteed Overnight?
a. $48 million   c. $26 million
b. $16 million   d. $6 million

Problems

> All of the A and B problems can be found within MyAccountingLab, an online homework and practice environment. Your instructor may ask you to complete these problems using MyAccountingLab.

(Group A)

P7-62A (*Learning Objectives 1, 2, 3: Identifying the elements of a plant asset's cost*) Assume Online, Inc., opened an office in Clearwater, Florida. Further assume that Online incurred the following costs in acquiring land, making land improvements, and constructing and furnishing the new sales building:

a. Purchase price of land, including an old building that will be used for a garage (land market value is $315,000; building market value is $85,000)	$360,000
b. Landscaping (additional dirt and earth moving)	8,500 *Land*
c. Fence around the land	31,800 LA ①
d. Attorney fee for title search on the land	900 L
e. Delinquent real estate taxes on the land to be paid by Online	5,600 L
f. Company signs at entrance to the property	1,200 LA
g. Building permit for the sales building	400 SB
h. Architect fee for the design of the sales building	19,600 SB
i. Masonry, carpentry, and roofing of the sales building	515,000 SB
j. Renovation of the garage building	41,200 GB
k. Interest cost on construction loan for sales building	9,100 SB
l. Landscaping (trees and shrubs)	6,600 LA or L
m. Parking lot and concrete walks on the property	52,100 LA
n. Lights for the parking lot and walkways	7,500 LA
o. Salary of construction supervisor (86% to sales building; 11% to land improvements; and 3% to garage building renovations)	44,000 ←
p. Office furniture for the sales building	79,400 F
q. Transportation and installation of furniture	1,900 F

Handwritten notes: ⚹ Land / ⚹ Land Approvements / ⚹ Sales Building / ⚹ Garage Building / ⚹ Furniture / 11% LI = 4840 / 86% SA 37,840

Assume Online depreciates buildings over 40 years, land improvements over 20 years, and furniture over 10 years, all on a straight-line basis with zero residual value.

❙ Requirements

1. Show how to account for each of Online's costs by listing the cost under the correct account. Determine the total cost of each asset.
2. All construction was complete and the assets were placed in service on May 2. Record depreciation for the year ended December 31. Round to the nearest dollar.
3. How will what you learned in this problem help you manage a business?

P7-63A (*Learning Objectives 2, 3: Recording plant asset transactions; reporting on the balance sheet*) Romano Lakes Resort reported the following on its balance sheet at December 31, 2010:

■ **general ledger**

Property, plant, and equipment, at cost:	
Land	$ 146,000
Buildings	709,000
Less: Accumulated depreciation	(342,000)
Equipment	405,000
Less: Accumulated depreciation	(265,000)

In early July 2011, the resort expanded operations and purchased additional equipment at a cost of $102,000. The company depreciates buildings by the straight-line method over 20 years with residual value of $89,000. Due to obsolescence, the equipment has a useful life of only 10 years and is being depreciated by the double-declining-balance method with zero residual value.

❙ Requirements

1. Journalize Romano Lakes Resort's plant asset purchase and depreciation transactions for 2011.
2. Report plant assets on the December 31, 2011, balance sheet.

P7-64A *(Learning Objectives 1, 2, 3, 4: Recording plant asset transactions, exchanges, and changes in useful life)* Carr, Inc., has the following plant asset accounts: Land, Buildings, and Equipment, with a separate accumulated depreciation account for each of these except land. Carr completed the following transactions:

Jan 2	Traded in equipment with accumulated depreciation of $65,000 (cost of $136,000) for similar new equipment with a cash cost of $175,000. Received a trade-in allowance of $75,000 on the old equipment and paid $100,000 in cash.
Jun 30	Sold a building that had a cost of $655,000 and had accumulated depreciation of $130,000 through December 31 of the preceding year. Depreciation is computed on a straight-line basis. The building has a 40-year useful life and a residual value of $275,000. Carr received $115,000 cash and a $405,250 note receivable.
Oct 29	Purchased land and a building for a single price of $390,000. An independent appraisal valued the land at $221,100 and the building at $180,900.
Dec 31	Recorded depreciation as follows:
	Equipment has an expected useful life of 5 years and an estimated residual value of 6% of cost. Depreciation is computed on the double-declining-balance method.
	Depreciation on buildings is computed by the straight-line method. The new building carries a 40-year useful life and a residual value equal to 20% of its cost.

I **Requirement**

1. Record the transactions in Carr, Inc.'s journal

P7-65A *(Learning Objective 2: Explaining the concept of depreciation)* The board of directors of Gold Structures, Inc., is reviewing the 2010 annual report. A new board member—a wealthy woman with little business experience—questions the company accountant about the depreciation amounts. The new board member wonders why depreciation expense has decreased from $220,000 in 2008 to $204,000 in 2009 to $196,000 in 2010. She states that she could understand the decreasing annual amounts if the company had been disposing of properties each year, but that has not occurred. Further, she notes that growth in the city is increasing the values of company properties. Why is the company recording depreciation when the property values are increasing?

P7-66A *(Learning Objectives 1, 2, 3: Computing depreciation by three methods; identifying the cash-flow advantage of accelerated depreciation for tax purposes)* On January 9, 2010, J.T. Outtahe Co. paid $230,000 for a computer system. In addition to the basic purchase price, the company paid a setup fee of $1,000, $6,000 sales tax, and $28,000 for a special platform on which to place the computer. J.T. Outtahe management estimates that the computer will remain in service for five years and have a residual value of $15,000. The computer will process 30,000 documents the first year, with annual processing decreasing by 2,500 documents during each of the next four years (that is, 27,500 documents in year 2011; 25,000 documents in year 2012; and so on). In trying to decide which depreciation method to use, the company president has requested a depreciation schedule for each of the three depreciation methods (straight-line, units-of-production, and double-declining-balance).

I **Requirements**

1. For each of the generally accepted depreciation methods, prepare a depreciation schedule showing asset cost, depreciation expense, accumulated depreciation, and asset book value.
2. J.T. Outtahe reports to stockholders and creditors in the financial statements using the depreciation method that maximizes reported income in the early years of asset use. For income tax purposes, the company uses the depreciation method that minimizes income tax payments in those early years. Consider the first year J.T. Outtahe Co. uses the computer. Identify the depreciation methods that meet Outtahe's objectives, assuming the income tax authorities permit the use of any of the methods.

3. Cash provided by operations before income tax is $156,000 for the computer's first year. The income tax rate is 28%. For the two depreciation methods identified in Requirement 2, compare the net income and cash provided by operations (cash flow). Show which method gives the net-income advantage and which method gives the cash-flow advantage.

P7-67A (*Learning Objectives 2, 4, 7: Analyzing plant asset transactions from a company's financial statements*)   Floral, Inc., sells electronics and appliances. The excerpts that follow are adapted from Floral's financial statements for 2010 and 2009.

Balance Sheet (dollars in millions)	February 28, 2010	2009
Assets		
Total current assets	$7,980	$6,900
Property, plant, and equipment	4,830	4,199
Less: Accumulated depreciation	2,126	1,726
Goodwill..	558	519

Statement of Cash Flows (dollars in millions)	Year Ended February 28, 2010	2009
Operating activities:		
Net income	$1,146	$ 981
Noncash items affecting net income:		
Depreciation	460	457
Investing activities:		
Additions to property, plant, and equipment................	(707)	(615)

❙ Requirements

1. How much was Floral's cost of plant assets at February 28, 2010? How much was the book value of plant assets? Show computations.
2. The financial statements give three evidences that Floral purchased plant assets and goodwill during fiscal year 2010. What are they?
3. Prepare T-accounts for Property, Plant, and Equipment; Accumulated Depreciation; and Goodwill. Then show all the activity in these accounts during 2010. Label each increase or decrease and give its dollar amount. During 2010, Floral sold plant assets that had cost the company $76 million (accumulated depreciation on these assets was $60 million). Assume there were no losses on goodwill during 2010.

P7-68A (*Learning Objective 5: Accounting for natural resources, and the related expense*) Northeastern Energy Company's balance sheet includes the asset Iron Ore. Northeastern Energy paid $2.5 million cash for a lease giving the firm the right to work a mine that contained an estimated 197,000 tons of ore. The company paid $65,000 to remove unwanted buildings from the land and $75,000 to prepare the surface for mining. Northeastern Energy also signed a $37,230 note payable to a landscaping company to return the land surface to its original condition after the lease ends. During the first year, Northeastern Energy removed 33,500 tons of ore, which it sold on account for $35 per ton. Operating expenses for the first year totaled $250,000, all paid in cash. In addition, the company accrued income tax at the tax rate of 32%.

❙ Requirements

1. Record all of Northeastern Energy's transactions for the year.
2. Prepare the company's income statement for its iron ore operations for the first year. Evaluate the profitability of the company's operations.

P7-69A *(Learning Objectives 4, 7: Reporting plant asset transactions on the statement of cash flows)* At the end of 2009, Solving Engineering Associates (SEA) had total assets of $17.1 billion and total liabilities of $9.7 billion. Included among the assets were property, plant, and equipment with a cost of $4.4 billion and accumulated depreciation of $3.2 billion.

SEA completed the following selected transactions during 2010: The company earned total revenues of $26.4 billion and incurred total expenses of $21.2 billion, which included depreciation of $1.9 billion. During the year, SEA paid $1.8 billion for new property, plant, and equipment and sold old plant assets for $0.3 billion. The cost of the assets sold was $1.1 billion, and their accumulated depreciation was $0.6 billion.

❚ Requirements

1. Explain how to determine whether SEA had a gain or loss on the sale of old plant assets during the year. What was the amount of the gain or loss, if any?
2. Show how SEA would report property, plant, and equipment on the balance sheet at December 31, 2010, after all the year's activity. What was the book value of property, plant, and equipment?
3. Show how SEA would report its operating activities and investing activities on its statement of cash flows for 2010. Ignore gains and losses.

(Group B)

P7-70B *(Learning Objectives 1, 2, 3: Identifying the elements of a plant asset's cost)* Assume Lance Pharmacy, Inc., opened an office in Vero Beach, Florida. Further assume that Lance Pharmacy incurred the following costs in acquiring land, making land improvements, and constructing and furnishing the new sales building:

a.	Purchase price of land, including an old building that will be used for a garage (land market value is $310,000; building market value is $90,000)...	$340,000
b.	Landscaping (additional dirt and earth moving).....................................	8,900
c.	Fence around the land..	31,000
d.	Attorney fee for title search on the land	400
e.	Delinquent real estate taxes on the land to be paid by Lance Pharmacy	5,800
f.	Company signs at entrance to the property	1,400
g.	Building permit for the sales building..	700
h.	Architect fee for the design of the sales building..................................	19,900
i.	Masonry, carpentry, and roofing of the sales building...........................	510,000
j.	Renovation of the garage building...	41,900
k.	Interest cost on construction loan for sales building.............................	9,000
l.	Landscaping (trees and shrubs)	6,300
m.	Parking lot and concrete walks on the property	52,900
n.	Lights for the parking lot and walkways	7,000
o.	Salary of construction supervisor (86% to sales building; 10% to land improvements; and 4% to garage building renovations)..............	41,000
p.	Office furniture for the sales building..	79,200
q.	Transportation and installation of furniture...	1,100

Assume Lance Pharmacy depreciates buildings over 30 years, land improvements over 15 years, and furniture over eight years, all on a straight-line basis with zero residual value.

❚ Requirements

1. Show how to account for each of Lance Pharmacy's costs by listing the cost under the correct account. Determine the total cost of each asset.
2. All construction was complete and the assets were placed in service on May 2. Record depreciation for the year ended December 31. Round to the nearest dollar.
3. How will what you learned in this problem help you manage a business?

P7-71B (*Learning Objectives 2, 3: Recording plant asset transactions; reporting on the balance sheet*)   Rossi Lakes Resort reported the following on its balance sheet at December 31, 2010:

Property, plant, and equipment, at cost:	
Land...	$ 149,000
Buildings	704,000
Less: Accumulated depreciation	(342,000)
Equipment..	401,000
Less: Accumulated depreciation	(268,000)

In early July 2011, the resort expanded operations and purchased additional equipment at a cost of $105,000. The company depreciates buildings by the straight-line method over 20 years with residual value of $89,000. Due to obsolescence, the equipment has a useful life of only 10 years and is being depreciated by the double-declining-balance method with zero residual value.

I Requirements

1. Journalize Rossi Lakes Resort's plant asset purchase and depreciation transactions for 2011.
2. Report plant assets on the December 31, 2011, balance sheet.

P7-72B (*Learning Objectives 1, 2, 3, 4: Recording plant asset transactions, exchanges, and changes in useful life*)   Tarrier, Inc., has the following plant asset accounts: Land, Buildings, and Equipment, with a separate accumulated depreciation account for each of these except land. Tarrier completed the following transactions:

Jan 2	Traded in equipment with accumulated depreciation of $64,000 (cost of $138,000) for similar new equipment with a cash cost of $179,000. Received a trade-in allowance of $73,000 on the old equipment and paid $106,000 in cash.
Jun 30	Sold a building that had a cost of $645,000 and had accumulated depreciation of $155,000 through December 31 of the preceding year. Depreciation is computed on a straight-line basis. The building has a 40-year useful life and a residual value of $285,000. Tarrier received $135,000 cash and a $350,500 note receivable.
Oct 29	Purchased land and a building for a single price of $340,000. An independent appraisal valued the land at $108,900 and the building at $254,100.
Dec 31	Recorded depreciation as follows: Equipment has an expected useful life of 4 years and an estimated residual value of 4% of cost. Depreciation is computed on the double-declining-balance method. Depreciation on buildings is computed by the straight-line method. The new building carries a 40-year useful life and a residual value equal to 10% of its cost.

I Requirement

1. Record the transactions in Tarrier, Inc.'s journal.

P7-73B (*Learning Objective 2: Explaining the concept of depreciation*)   The board of directors of Cooper Structures, Inc., is reviewing the 2010 annual report. A new board member—a wealthy woman with little business experience—questions the company accountant about the depreciation amounts. The new board member wonders why depreciation expense has decreased from $190,000 in 2008 to $174,000 in 2009 to $166,000 in 2010. She states that she could understand the decreasing annual amounts if the company had been disposing of properties each year, but that has not occurred. Further, she notes that growth in the city is increasing the values of company properties. Why is the company recording depreciation when the property values are increasing?

P7-74B *(Learning Objectives 1, 2, 3: Computing depreciation by three methods; identifying the cash-flow advantage of accelerated depreciation for tax purposes)* On January 6, 2010, K.P. Scott Co. paid $245,000 for a computer system. In addition to the basic purchase price, the company paid a setup fee of $800, $6,400 sales tax, and $27,800 for a special platform on which to place the computer. K.P. Scott management estimates that the computer will remain in service for five years and have a residual value of $20,000. The computer will process 45,000 documents the first year, with annual processing decreasing by 2,500 documents during each of the next four years (that is, 42,500 documents in 2011; 40,000 documents in 2012; and so on). In trying to decide which dep-reciation method to use, the company president has requested a depreciation schedule for each of the three depreciation methods (straight-line, units-of-production, and double-declining-balance).

I *Requirements*

1. For each of the generally accepted depreciation methods, prepare a depreciation schedule showing asset cost, depreciation expense, accumulated depreciation, and asset book value.
2. K.P. Scott reports to stockholders and creditors in the financial statements using the depreciation method that maximizes reported income in the early years of asset use. For income tax purposes, the company uses the depreciation method that minimizes income tax payments in those early years. Consider the first year K.P. Scott Co. uses the computer. Identify the depreciation methods that meet Scott's objectives, assuming the income tax authorities permit the use of any of the methods.
3. Cash provided by operations before income tax is $155,000 for the computer's first year. The income tax rate is 35%. For the two depreciation methods identified in Requirement 2, compare the net income and cash provided by operations (cash flow). Show which method gives the net-income advantage and which method gives the cash-flow advantage.

P7-75B *(Learning Objectives 2, 4, 7: Analyzing plant asset transactions from a company's financial statements)* Parem, Inc., sells electronics and appliances. The excerpts that follow are adapted from Parem's financial statements for 2010 and 2009.

Balance Sheet (dollars in millions)	February 28, 2010	2009
Assets		
Total current assets	$7,986	$6,901
Property, plant, and equipment	4,836	4,198
Less: Accumulated depreciation	2,123	1,727
Goodwill	553	511

Statement of Cash Flows (dollars in millions)	Year Ended February 28, 2010	2009
Operating activities:		
Net income	$1,147	$ 989
Noncash items affecting net income:		
Depreciation	458	460
Investing activities:		
Additions to property, plant, and equipment	(716)	(617)

Requirements

1. How much was Parem's cost of plant assets at February 28, 2010? How much was the book value of plant assets? Show computations.
2. The financial statements give three evidences that Parem purchased plant assets and goodwill during fiscal year 2010. What are they?
3. Prepare T-accounts for Property, Plant, and Equipment; Accumulated Depreciation; and Goodwill. Then show all the activity in these accounts during 2010. Label each increase or decrease and give its dollar amount. During 2010, Parem sold plant assets that had cost the company $78 million (accumulated depreciation on these assets was $62 million). Assume there were no losses on goodwill during 2010.

P7-76B (*Learning Objective 5: Accounting for natural resources and the related expense*)   South Pacific Energy Company's balance sheet includes the asset Iron Ore. South Pacific Energy paid $2.2 million cash for a lease giving the firm the right to work a mine that contained an estimated 190,000 tons of ore. The company paid $61,000 to remove unwanted buildings from the land and $71,000 to prepare the surface for mining. South Pacific Energy also signed a $24,000 note payable to a landscaping company to return the land surface to its original condition after the lease ends. During the first year, South Pacific Energy removed 31,500 tons of ore, which it sold on account for $31 per ton. Operating expenses for the first year totaled $242,000, all paid in cash. In addition, the company accrued income tax at the tax rate of 25%.

Requirements

1. Record all of South Pacific Energy's transactions for the year.
2. Prepare the company's income statement for its iron ore operations for the first year. Evaluate the profitability of the company's operations.

P7-77B (*Learning Objectives 4, 7: Reporting plant asset transactions on the statement of cash flows*)   At the end of 2009, Great Financial Associates (GFA) had total assets of $17.4 billion and total liabilities of $9.9 billion. Included among the assets were property, plant, and equipment with a cost of $4.5 billion and accumulated depreciation of $3.3 billion.

GFA completed the following selected transactions during 2010: The company earned total revenues of $26.1 billion and incurred total expenses of $21.0 billion, which included depreciation of $1.9 billion. During the year, GFA paid $1.6 billion for new property, plant, and equipment and sold old plant assets for $0.4 billion. The cost of the assets sold was $1.2 billion, and their accumulated depreciation was $0.5 billion.

Requirements

1. Explain how to determine whether GFA had a gain or loss on the sale of old plant assets during the year. What was the amount of the gain or loss, if any?
2. Show how GFA would report property, plant, and equipment on the balance sheet at December 31, 2010, after all the year's activity. What was the book value of property, plant, and equipment?
3. Show how GFA would report its operating activities and investing activities on its statement of cash flows for 2010. Ignore gains and losses.

APPLY YOUR KNOWLEDGE

Decision Cases

writing assignment ■

Case 1. *(Learning Objectives 2, 3: Measuring profitability based on different inventory and depreciation methods)* Suppose you are considering investing in two businesses, La Petite France Bakery and Burgers Ahoy!. The two companies are virtually identical, and both began operations at the beginning of the current year. During the year, each company purchased inventory as follows:

Jan	4	10,000 units at $4 =	40,000
Apr	6	5,000 units at 5 =	25,000
Aug	9	7,000 units at 6 =	42,000
Nov	27	10,000 units at 7 =	70,000
	Totals	32,000	$177,000

During the first year, both companies sold 25,000 units of inventory.

In early January, both companies purchased equipment costing $150,000 that had a 10-year estimated useful life and a $20,000 residual value. La Petite France uses the inventory and depreciation methods that maximize reported income. By contrast, Burgers uses the inventory and depreciation methods that minimize income tax payments. Assume that both companies' trial balances at December 31 included the following:

Sales revenue.........................	$350,000
Operating expenses	50,000

The income tax rate is 40%.

❙ Requirements

1. Prepare both companies' income statements.
2. Write an investment newsletter to address the following questions: Which company appears to be more profitable? Which company has more cash to invest in promising projects? If prices continue rising over the long term, which company would you prefer to invest in? Why? (Challenge)

writing assignment ■

Case 2. *(Learning Objectives 1, 6: Accounting for plant assets and intangible assets)* The following questions are unrelated except that they all apply to plant assets and intangible assets:

1. The manager of Carpet World regularly debits the cost of repairs and maintenance of plant assets to Plant and Equipment. Why would she do that, since she knows she is violating GAAP?
2. The manager of Horizon Software regularly buys plant assets and debits the cost to Repairs and Maintenance Expense. Why would he do that, since he knows this action violates GAAP?
3. It has been suggested that because many intangible assets have no value except to the company that owns them, they should be valued at $1.00 or zero on the balance sheet. Many accountants disagree with this view. Which view do you support? Why?

Ethical Issue

United Jersey Bank of Princeton purchased land and a building for the lump sum of $6.0 million. To get the maximum tax deduction, the bank's managers allocated 80% of the purchase price to the building and only 20% to the land. A more realistic allocation would have been 60% to the building and 40% to the land.

❚ *Requirements*

1. What is the ethical issue in this situation?
2. Who are the stakeholders? What are the possible consequences to each?
3. Analyze the alternatives from the following standpoints: (a) economic, (b) legal, and (c) ethical.
4. What would you do? How would you justify your decision?

Focus on Financials: ■ Amazon.com, Inc.

(*Learning Objectives 2, 3, 6: Analyzing plant assets*) Refer to **Amazon.com, Inc.**'s Consolidated Financial Statements in Appendix A at the end of the book, and answer the following questions:

1. Refer to Note 1 and Note 3 of the Notes to Consolidated Financial Statements. What kinds of assets are included in fixed assets of Amazon.com, Inc?
2. Which depreciation method does Amazon.com, Inc., use for reporting to stockholders and creditors in the financial statements? What type of depreciation method does the company probably use for income tax purposes? Why is this method preferable for tax purposes?
3. Depreciation expense is embedded in the expense amounts listed on the income statement. It is reported on the Consolidated Statements of Cash Flows. How much was Amazon.com, Inc.'s depreciation and amortization expense during 2008? Now refer to Note 3 of the Notes to Consolidated Financial Statements. How much was Amazon.com, Inc.'s accumulated depreciation and amortization at the end of 2008? Explain why accumulated depreciation and amortization exceeds depreciation and amortization expense for the current year.
4. How much did Amazon.com, Inc., spend on fixed assets, including internal-use software and website development, during 2008? In 2007? Evaluate the trend in these capital expenditures as to whether it conveys good news or bad news for Amazon.com, Inc. Explain.
5. Refer to Notes 1 and 4 of the Notes to Consolidated Financial Statements. What are Amazon.com, Inc.'s intangible assets? How does the company account for each of these intangibles over its lifetime?

Focus on Analysis: ■ Foot Locker, Inc.

(*Learning Objectives 2, 4, 7: Explaining plant asset activity*) Refer to the **Foot Locker, Inc.**, Consolidated Financial Statements in Appendix B at the end of this book. This case leads you through a comprehensive analysis of Foot Locker, Inc.'s long-term assets. Its purpose is to show you how to account for plant asset (properties) transactions in summary form.

1. On the statement of cash flows, how much did Foot Locker, Inc., pay for capital expenditures during fiscal 2007? In what section of the cash flows statement do you find this amount? How much cash did Foot Locker, Inc., pay to repay capital leases in fiscal 2007? In what section of the cash flows statement was this recorded?
2. Explain Foot Locker, Inc.'s policy for capitalization of fixed assets. You can find this in Note 1 to the Consolidated Financial Statements (Summary of Significant Accounting Policies).
3. Which depreciation method does Foot Locker, Inc., use? Over what useful life does Foot Locker, Inc., depreciate various types of fixed assets?
4. Were Foot Locker, Inc.'s plant assets proportionately newer or older at the end of fiscal 2007 (versus 2006)? Explain your answer. (Challenge)

Group Project

Visit a local business.

❘ *Requirements*

1. List all its plant assets.
2. If possible, interview the manager. Gain as much information as you can about the business's plant assets. For example, try to determine the assets' costs, the depreciation method the company is using, and the estimated useful life of each asset category. If an interview is impossible, then develop your own estimates of the assets' costs, useful lives, and book values, assuming an appropriate depreciation method.
3. Determine whether the business has any intangible assets. If so, list them and gain as much information as possible about their nature, cost, and estimated useful lives.
4. Write a detailed report of your findings and be prepared to present your results to the class.

For online homework, exercises, and problems that provide you with immediate feedback, please visit www.myaccountinglab.com.

Quick Check Answers

1. *b* {[$1,380/($1,380 + $575 + $345)] × $1,900 = $1,140}
2. *d*
3. *b* ($45,000 − $5,000)/10 × 6/12 = $2,000)
4. *d* [($45,000 − $5,000)/10 × 2 = $8,000; $45,000 = $8,000 = $37,000]
5. *d* [$45,000 × .2 = $9,000; ($45,000 − $9,000) × .2 = $7,200]
6. *b* [($45,000 − $5,000)/5 × 4 = $16,000; $45,000 − $16,000 = $29,000; $36,500 − $29,000 = gain of $7,500]
7. *b* [$24,000 × 2/5 = $9,600; ($24,000 − $9,600) × 2/5 = $5,760; $9,600 + $5,760 = $15,360]
8. *b*
9. *b*
10. *b*
11. *d* [$270,000 × (3,000/90,000) = $30,000]
12. *e*

8
Liabilities

SPOTLIGHT: Southwest Airlines: A Success Story

Southwest Airlines has been a maverick in the airline industry from the start. In recent years, despite turmoil in the industry, Southwest has managed to stay profitable while other airlines have been in bankruptcy or close to it.

The airlines have some interesting liabilities. Southwest's Rapid Rewards program provides free flights to the company's frequent fliers. Southwest accrues frequent-flier liability for this program and reports "Accrued Liabilities" on the company's consolidated balance sheet.

Southwest collects cash in advance and then provides flights for customers later. This creates unearned revenue that Southwest reports as "Unearned Ticket Revenue." The company also has notes payable and bonds payable that it reports under "Long-Term Debt."

Southwest Airlines Co.
Consolidated Balance Sheet (Adapted)
December 31, 2008

(In millions)

Assets		Liabilities and Stockholders' Equity	
Current Assets		Current Liabilities	
Cash	$ 1,368	Accounts payable	$ 668
Other current assets	1,525	Accrued liabilities	1,012
Total current assets	2,893	Unearned ticket revenue	963
Equipment and		Current maturities of	
property, net	11,040	long-term debt	163
Other assets	375	Total current liabilities	2,806
		Long-term debt	3,498
		Other long-term liabilities	3,051
		Stockholders' Equity	4,953
Total assets	$14,308	Total liabilities and equity	$14,308

This chapter shows how to account for liabilities—both current and long-term. We begin with current liabilities.

LEARNING OBJECTIVES

1 Account for current liabilities and contingent liabilities

2 Account for bonds payable

3 Measure interest expense

4 Understand the advantages and disadvantages of borrowing

5 Report liabilities on the balance sheet

CURRENT LIABILITIES

OBJECTIVE

1 Account for current liabilities and contingent liabilities

Current liabilities are obligations due within one year or within the company's normal operating cycle if longer than a year. Obligations due beyond that period of time are classified as *long-term liabilities*.

Current liabilities are of two kinds:

- Known amounts
- Estimated amounts

We look first at current liabilities of a known amount.

Current Liabilities of Known Amount

Current liabilities of known amount include accounts payable, short-term notes payable, sales tax payable, accrued liabilities, payroll liabilities, unearned revenues, and current portion of long-term debt.

Accounts Payable. Amounts owed for products or services purchased on account are *accounts payable*. For example, Southwest Airlines purchases soft drinks and napkins on accounts payable. We have seen many other accounts payable examples in preceding chapters. One of a merchandiser's most common transactions is the credit purchase of inventory. **Best Buy** and **Wal-Mart** buy their inventory on account.

Short-Term Notes Payable. **Short-term notes payable**, a common form of financing, are notes payable due within one year. **Starbucks** lists its short-term notes payable as *short-term borrowings*. Starbucks may issue short-term notes payable to borrow cash or to purchase assets. On its notes payable, Starbucks must accrue interest expense and interest payable at the end of the period. The following sequence of entries covers the purchase of inventory, accrual of interest expense, and payment of a 10% short-term note payable that's due in one year.

2010			
Jan 1	Inventory	8,000	
	Note Payable, Short-Term		8,000
	Purchase of inventory by issuing a note payable.		

This transaction increases both an asset and a liability.

Assets	=	Liabilities	+	Stockholders' Equity
+ 8,000	=	+ 8,000	+	0

The Starbucks fiscal year ends each September 30. At year-end, Starbucks must accrue interest expense at 10% for January through September:

Sep 30	Interest Expense ($8,000 × .10 × 9/12)	600	
	Interest Payable		600
	Accrual of interest expense at year-end.		

Liabilities increase and equity decreases because of the expense.

Assets	=	Liabilities	+	Stockholders' Equity	–	Expenses
0	=	+ 600				– 600

The balance sheet at year-end will report the Note Payable of $8,000 and the related Interest Payable of $600 as current liabilities. The income statement will report interest expense of $600.

The following entry records the note's payment at maturity on January 1, 2011:

2011			
Jan 1	Note Payable, Short-Term	8,000	
	Interest Payable	600	
	Interest Expense ($8,000 × .10 × 3/12)	200	
	Cash [$8,000 + ($8,000 × .10)]		8,800
	Payment of a note payable and interest at maturity.		

The debits zero out the payables and also record Starbucks' interest expense for October, November, and December.

Sales Tax Payable. Most states levy a sales tax on retail sales. Retailers collect the tax from customers and thus owe the state for sales tax collected. Suppose one Saturday's sales at a Home Depot store totaled $200,000. Home Depot collected an additional 5% ($10,000) of sales tax. The store would record that day's sales as follows:

Cash ($200,000 × 1.05)	210,000	
Sales Revenue		200,000
Sales Tax Payable ($200,000 × .05)		10,000
To record cash sales and the related sales tax.		

Assets, liabilities, and equity all increase—equity because of the revenues.

Assets	=	Liabilities	+	Stockholders' Equity	+	Revenues
+ 210,000	=	+ 10,000				+ 200,000

Accrued Liabilities (Accrued Expenses). An **accrued liability** usually results from an expense the business has incurred but not yet paid. Therefore, an accrued expense creates a liability, which explains why it is also called an **accrued expense**.

For example, Southwest Airlines' salary expense and salary payable occur as employees work for the company. Interest expense accrues with the passage of time. There are several categories of accrued expenses:

- Salaries and Wages Payable
- Interest Payable
- Income Taxes Payable

Salaries and Wages Payable is the liability for payroll expenses not yet paid at the end of the period. This category includes salaries, wages, and payroll taxes withheld from employee paychecks. *Interest Payable* is the company's interest payable on notes payable. *Income Taxes Payable* is the amount of income tax the company still owes at year-end.

Payroll Liabilities. **Payroll**, also called *employee compensation*, is a major expense. For service organizations—such as law firms, real estate companies, and airlines—compensation is *the* major expense, just as cost of goods sold is the largest expense for a merchandising company.

Employee compensation takes many different forms. A *salary* is employee pay stated at a monthly or yearly rate. A *wage* is employee pay stated at an hourly rate. Sales employees earn a *commission*, which is a percentage of the sales the employee has made. A *bonus* is an amount over and above regular compensation. Accounting for all forms of compensation follows the pattern illustrated in Exhibit 8-1 (using assumed figures).

EXHIBIT 8-1 | Accounting for Payroll Expenses and Liabilities

Salary Expense	10,000	
Employee Income Tax Payable		1,200
FICA Tax Payable		800
Salary Payable to Employees [take-home pay]		8,000
To record salary expense.		

Every expense accrual has the same effect: Liabilities increase and equity decreases because of the expense. The accounting equation shows these effects.

Assets	=	Liabilities	+	Stockholders' Equity	−	Expenses
		+ 1,200				− 10,000
0	=	+ 800				
		+ 8,000				

Salary expense represents *gross pay* (that is, employee pay before subtractions for taxes and other deductions). Salary expense creates several payroll liabilities:

- *Employee Income Tax Payable* is the employees' income tax that has been withheld from paychecks.
- *FICA Tax Payable* includes the employees' Social Security tax and Medicare tax, which also are withheld from paychecks. (FICA stands for the Federal Insurance Contributions Act, which created the Social Security tax.)
- *Salary Payable* to employees is their net (take-home) pay.

Companies must also pay some *employer* payroll taxes and expenses for employee benefits. Accounting for these expenses is similar to the illustration in Exhibit 8-1.

Unearned Revenues.   *Unearned revenues* are also called *deferred revenues* and *revenues collected in advance.* For all unearned revenue the business has received cash from customers before earning the revenue. The company has a liability—an obligation to provide goods or services to the customer. Let's consider an example.

Southwest Airlines sells tickets and collects cash in advance. Southwest therefore reports Unearned Ticket Revenue for airline tickets sold in advance.[1] At December 31, 2008, Southwest owed customers $963 million of air travel (see page 468). Let's see how Southwest accounts for unearned ticket revenue.

---

[1]Some airlines call this liability "Air Traffic Liability."

Assume that Southwest collects $300 for a round-trip ticket from Dallas to Los Angeles and back. Southwest records the cash collection and related liability as follows:

2010			
Dec 15	Cash	300	
	Unearned Ticket Revenue		300
	Received cash in advance for ticket sales.		

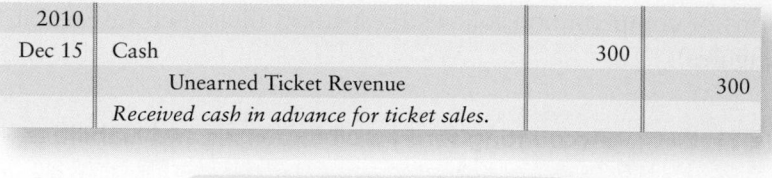

Suppose the customer flies to Los Angeles late in December. Southwest records the revenue earned as follows:

2010			
Dec 28	Unearned Ticket Revenue	150	
	Ticket Revenue ($300 × 1/2)		150
	Earned revenue that was collected in advance.		

The liability decreases and the revenue goes up.

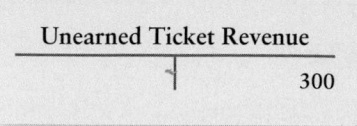

At year-end, Southwest reports

- $150 of unearned ticket revenue (a liability) on the balance sheet
- $150 of ticket revenue on the income statement

The customer returns to Dallas in January 2011, and Southwest records the revenue earned with this journal entry:

2011			
Jan 4	Unearned Ticket Revenue	150	
	Ticket Revenue ($300 × 1/2)		150
	Earned revenue that was collected in advance.		

Now the liability balance is zero because Southwest has earned all the revenue it collected in advance.

Unearned Ticket Revenue	
150	300
150	
	Bal 0

Current Portion of Long-Term Debt.   Some long-term debt must be paid in installments. The **current portion of long-term debt** (also called *current maturity* or *current installment*) is the amount of the principal that is payable within one year. At the end of each year, a company reclassifies (from long-term debt to a current liability) the amount of its long-term debt that must be paid next year.

Southwest Airlines reports Current Maturities of Long-Term Debt as a current liability. Southwest also reports a long-term liability for Long-Term Debt, which excludes the current maturities. *Long-term debt* refers to long-term notes payable and bonds payable, which we cover in the second half of this chapter.

Current Liabilities That Must Be Estimated

A business may know that a liability exists but not know its exact amount. The business must report the liability on the balance sheet. Estimated liabilities vary among companies. Let's look first at Estimated Warranty Payable, a liability account that most merchandisers have.

Estimated Warranty Payable.   Many companies guarantee their products under *warranty* agreements. The warranty period may extend for 90 days to a year for consumer products. Automobile companies—General Motors, BMW, and Toyota—accrue liabilities for vehicle warranties.

Whatever the warranty's life, the matching principle demands that the company record the *warranty expense* in the same period that the business records sales revenue. After all, the warranty motivates customers to buy products, so the company must record warranty expense. At the time of the sale, however, the company doesn't know which products are defective. The exact amount of warranty expense cannot be known with certainty, so the business must estimate warranty expense and the related liability.

Assume that **Black & Decker**, which manufactures power tools, made sales of $100,000 subject to product warranties. Assume that in past years between 2% and 4% of products proved defective. Black & Decker could estimate that 3% of sales will require repair or replacement. In this case Black & Decker would estimate warranty expense of $3,000 ($100,000 × 0.03) for the year and make the following entry:

Warranty Expense	3,000	
Estimated Warranty Payable		3,000
To accrue warranty expense.		

Estimated Warranty Payable	
	3,000

Assume that defects add up to $2,800, and Black & Decker will replace the defective products. Black & Decker then records the following:

Estimated Warranty Payable	2,800	
Inventory		2,800
To replace defective products sold under warranty.		

Estimated Warranty Payable

2,800		3,000
	Bal	200

At the end of the year Black & Decker will report Estimated Warranty Payable of $200 as a current liability. The income statement reports Warranty Expense of $3,000 for the year. Then, next year Black & Decker will repeat this process. The Estimated Warranty Payable account probably won't ever zero out.

If Black & Decker paid cash to satisfy the warranty, then the credit would be to Cash rather than to Inventory. Vacation pay is another expense that must be estimated. And income taxes must be estimated because the final amount isn't determined until early the next year.

Contingent Liabilities

A *contingent liability* is not an actual liability. Instead, it's a potential liability that depends on the future outcome of past events. Examples of contingent liabilities are future obligations that may arise because of lawsuits, tax disputes, or alleged violations of environmental protection laws. The principle of conservatism, discussed in Chapter 6, requires that companies avoid painting too "rosy" a picture of their financial positions. With liabilities, that principle says "When in doubt, disclose. When necessary, accrue." The Financial Accounting Standards Board (FASB) provides these guidelines to account for contingent liabilities:[2]

1. *Accrue* (i.e., make an adjusting journal entry for) a contingent liability if it's *probable* that the loss (or expense) will occur **and** the *amount can be reasonably estimated.* Warranty expense, illustrated on the previous page, is an example. Another example is a lawsuit that has been settled as of the balance sheet date but has not yet been paid.

2. *Disclose* a contingency in a financial statement note if it's *reasonably possible* that a loss (or expense) will occur. Lawsuits in progress are a prime example. Southwest Airlines includes a note in its financial statements to report contingent liabilities from examinations of its past income tax returns by the IRS.

---

[2]The FASB is currently reconsidering its disclosure requirements for contingent liabilities. If the new requirements are adopted, entities will be required to greatly expand disclosures of their loss contingencies. Specifically, *regardless of likelihood*, entities will be required to *disclose* loss contingencies (a) if they are expected to be resolved within the next year; and (b) if, in the opinion of management, they could have a *severe impact* on the entity's financial position, cash flows, or results of operation. An example of such a situation is a lawsuit that could put the company out of business within the next year. Both quantitative (dollar amounts) and qualitative (descriptive) information would be included. In addition, for all amounts *accrued*, the entity would have to include a table and explanations that show how these accruals have changed from the previous period.

> **Note 17, Contingencies**
> The Company is subject to various legal proceedings [...] including [...] examinations by the Internal Revenue Service (IRS). The IRS regularly examines the Company's federal income tax returns and, in the course thereof, proposes adjustments to the Company's federal income tax liability reported on such returns.
> The Company's management does not expect that [...] any of its currently ongoing legal proceedings or [...] any proposed adjustments [...] by the IRS [...] will have a material adverse effect on the Company's financial condition, results of operations or cash flow.

3. There is no need to report a contingent loss that is unlikely to occur. Instead, wait until an actual transaction clears up the situation. For example, suppose **Del Monte Foods** grows vegetables in Nicaragua, and the Nicaraguan government threatens to confiscate the assets of all foreign companies. Del Monte will report nothing about the contingency if the probability of a loss is considered remote.

A contingent liability may arise from lawsuits that claim wrongdoing by the company. The plantiff may seek damages through the courts. If the court or the IRS rules in favor of Southwest, there is no liability. But if the ruling favors the plaintiff, then Southwest will have an actual liability. It would be unethical to omit these disclosures from the financial statements because investors need this information to properly evaluate a company.

 The international accounting standard for loss contingencies requires accrual (i.e., journal entries) for **both** probable and possible contingent liabilities.

The IASB is studying its existing standard with a view toward harmonizing it with the changes that are being contemplated by the FASB (discussed in the footnote on p. 474). Regardless of the outcome of the changes that are being proposed by both the IASB and FASB, it is likely that future financial statements of all companies will include **more disclosures of both quantitative and qualitative information** for contingent liabilities than are presently required.

Appendix F summarizes differences between U.S. GAAP and IFRS, cross-referenced by chapter.

Are All Liabilities Reported on the Balance Sheet?

The big danger with liabilities is that you may fail to report a large debt on your balance sheet. What is the consequence of missing a large liability? You will definitely understate your liabilities and your debt ratio. By failing to accrue interest on the liability, you'll probably overstate your net income as well. In short, your financial statements will make you look better than you really are. Any such error, if significant, hurts a company's credibility.

Contingent liabilities are very easy to overlook because they aren't actual debts. How would you feel if you owned stock in a company that failed to report a contingency that put the company out of business? If you had known of the contingency, you could have sold the stock and avoided the loss. In this case, you would hire a lawyer to file suit against the company for negligent financial reporting.

COOKING THE BOOKS
with Liabilities
Crazy Eddie, Inc.

Accidentally understating liabilities is one thing, but doing it intentionally is quite another. When unethical management decides to cook the books in the area of liabilities, its strategy is to **deliberately understate recorded liabilities**. This can be done by intentionally under-recording the amount of existing liabilities, or by omitting certain liabilities altogether.

Crazy Eddie, Inc., first discussed in Chapter 6, used *multiple tactics* to overstate its financial position from 1984 through 1987. In addition to overstating inventory (thus understating cost of goods sold and overstating income), the management of the company deliberately *understated accounts payable* by issuing fictitious (false) debit memoranda from suppliers (vendors). A debit memo is issued for goods returned to a vendor, such as Sony. When a debit memorandum is issued, accounts payable are debited (reduced), thus reducing current liabilities and increasing the current ratio. Eventually, expenses are also decreased, and profits are correspondingly increased through reduction of expenses. Crazy Eddie, Inc., issued $3 million of fictitious debit memoranda in 1985, making the company's current ratio and debt ratio look better than they actually were, and eventually overstating profits.

Summary of Current Liabilities

Let's summarize what we've covered thus far. A company can report its current liabilities on the balance sheet as follows:

Accounting, Inc.
Balance Sheet
December 31, 2010

Assets		Liabilities	
Current Assets:		Current liabilities:	
Cash		Accounts payable	
Short-term investments		Salary payable*	
Etc.		Interest payable*	
		Income tax payable*	
Property, plant, and equipment:		Unearned revenue	
Land		Estimated warranty payable*	
Etc.		Notes payable, short-term	
		Current portion of long-term debt	
Other assets		Total current liabilities	
		Long-term liabilities	
		Stockholders' Equity	
		Common stock	
		Retained earnings	
Total assets	$XXX	Total liabilities and stockholders equity	$XXX

*These items are often combined and reported in a single total as "Accrued Liabilities" or "Accrued Expenses Payable."

On its income statement this company would report

- *Expenses* related to some of the current liabilities. Examples include Salary Expense, Interest Expense, Income Tax Expense, and Warranty Expense.
- *Revenue* related to the unearned revenue. Examples include Service Revenue and Sales Revenue that were collected in advance.

MID-CHAPTER SUMMARY PROBLEM

Assume that the Estée Lauder Companies, Inc., faced the following liability situations at June 30, 2010, the end of the company's fiscal year. Show how Estée Lauder would report these liabilities on its balance sheet at June 30, 2010.

a. Salary expense for the last payroll period of the year was $900,000. Of this amount, employees' withheld income tax totaled $88,000 and FICA taxes were $61,000. These payroll amounts will be paid in early July.

b. On fiscal-year 2010 sales of $400 million, management estimates warranty expense of 2%. One year ago, at June 30, 2009, Estimated Warranty Payable stood at $3 million. Warranty payments were $9 million during the year ended June 30, 2010.

c. The company pays royalties on its purchased trademarks. Royalties for the trademarks are equal to a percentage of Estée Lauder's sales. Assume that sales in 2010 were $400 million and were subject to a royalty rate of 3%. At June 30, 2010, Estée Lauder owes two-thirds of the year's royalty, to be paid in July.

d. Long-term debt totals $100 million and is payable in annual installments of $10 million each. The interest rate on the debt is 7%, and the interest is paid each December 31.

Answer

Liabilities at June 30, 2010:

a. Current liabilities:

Salary payable ($900,000 − $88,000 − $61,000)	$ 751,000
Employee income tax payable	88,000
FICA tax payable	61,000

b. Current liabilities:

Estimated warranty payable	2,000,000
[$3,000,000 + ($400,000,000 × 0.02) − $9,000,000]	

c. Current liabilities:

Royalties payable ($400,000,000 × 0.03 × 2/3)	8,000,000

d. Current liabilities:

Current installment of long-term debt	10,000,000
Interest payable ($100,000,000 × 0.07 × 6/12)	3,500,000
Long-term debt ($100,000,000 − $10,000,000)	90,000,000

LONG-TERM LIABILITIES: BONDS AND NOTES PAYABLE

Large companies such as Southwest Airlines, Home Depot, and **Toyota** cannot borrow billions from a single lender. So how do corporations borrow huge amounts? They issue (sell) bonds to the public. **Bonds payable** are groups of notes payable issued to multiple lenders, called *bondholders*. Southwest Airlines needs airplanes and can borrow large amounts by issuing bonds to thousands of individual investors, who each lend Southwest a modest amount. Southwest receives the cash it needs, and each investor limits risk by diversifying investments—not putting all the investor's "eggs in one basket." Here we treat bonds payable and notes payable together because their accounting is the same.

Bonds: An Introduction

Each bond payable is, in effect, a note payable. Bonds payable are debts of the issuing company.

Purchasers of bonds receive a bond's certificate, which carries the issuing company's name. The certificate also states the *principal*, which is typically stated in units of $1,000; principal is also called the bond's *face value*, *maturity value*, or *par value*. The bond obligates the issuing company to pay the debt at a specific future time called the *maturity date*.

Interest is the rental fee on borrowed money. The bond certificate states the interest rate that the issuer will pay the holder and the dates that the interest payments are due (generally twice a year). Exhibit 8-2 shows an actual bond certificate.

Issuing bonds usually requires the services of a securities firm, such as Merrill Lynch, to act as the underwriter of the bond issue. The **underwriter** purchases the bonds from the issuing company and resells them to its clients, or it may sell the bonds to its clients and earn a commission on the sale.

EXHIBIT 8-2 | **Bond (Note) Certificate (Adapted)**

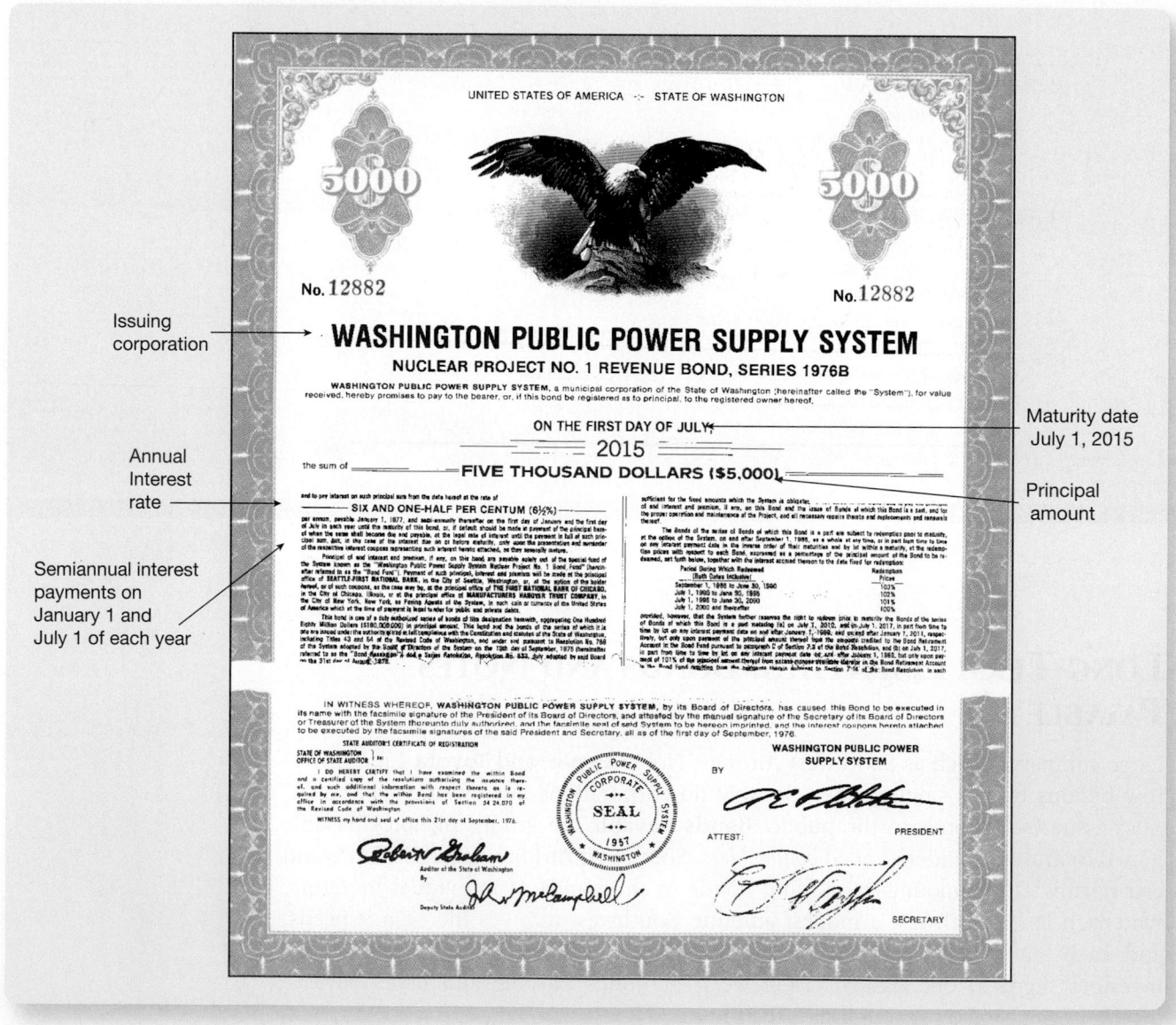

Types of Bonds. All the bonds in a particular issue may mature at the same time (**term bonds**) or in installments over a period of time (**serial bonds**). Serial bonds are like installment notes payable. Some of Southwest Airlines' long-term debts are serial in nature because they are payable in installments.

Secured, or *mortgage*, *bonds* give the bondholder the right to take specified assets of the issuer if the company *defaults*—that is, fails to pay interest or principal. *Unsecured bonds*, called **debentures**, are backed only by the good faith of the borrower. Debentures carry a higher rate of interest than secured bonds because debentures are riskier investments.

Bond Prices. Investors may buy and sell bonds through bond markets. Bond prices are quoted at a percentage of their maturity value. For example,

- A $1,000 bond quoted at 100 is bought or sold for $1,000, which is 100% of its face value.
- The same bond quoted at 101.5 has a market price of $1,015 (101.5% of face value = $1,000 × 1.015).
- A $1,000 bond quoted at 88.375 is priced at $883.75 ($1,000 × 0.88375).

Bond Premium and Bond Discount. A bond issued at a price above its face (par) value is said to be issued at a **premium**, and a bond issued at a price below face (par) value has a **discount**.

Premium on Bonds Payable has a *credit* balance and Discount on Bonds Payable carries a *debit* balance. Bond Discount is therefore a contra liability account.

As a bond nears maturity, its market price moves toward par value. Therefore, the price of a bond issued at a

- premium decreases toward maturity value.
- discount increases toward maturity value.

On the maturity date, a bond's market value exactly equals its face value because the company that issued the bond pays that amount to retire the bond.

The Time Value of Money. A dollar received today is worth more than a dollar to be received in the future. You can invest today's dollar immediately and earn income from it. But if you must wait to receive the dollar, you forgo the interest revenue. Money earns income over time, a fact called the *time value of money*. Let's examine how the *time value of money* affects the pricing of bonds.

Assume that a Southwest Airlines bond with a face value of $1,000 reaches maturity three years from today and carries no interest. Would you pay $1,000 today to purchase this bond? No, because the payment of $1,000 today to receive the same amount in the future provides you with no income on the investment. Just how much would you pay today to receive $1,000 at the end of three years? The answer is some amount *less* than $1,000. Let's suppose that you feel $750 is a good price. By investing $750 now to receive $1,000 later, you earn $250 interest revenue over the three years. The issuing company such as Southwest Airlines, sees the transaction this way: Southwest will pay you $250 interest to use your $750 for three years.

The amount to invest *now* to receive more later is called the **present value** of a future amount. In our example, $750 is the present value, and $1,000 is the future amount.

Our $750 bond price is a reasonable estimate. The exact present value of any future amount depends on

1. the amount of the future payment ($1,000 in our example).
2. the length of time from the investment date to the date when the future amount is to be collected (three years).
3. the interest rate during the period (say 10%).

In this case the present value is very close to $750. Present value is always less than the future amount. We discuss how present value is computed in Appendix C at the end of the book (pp. 885–894).

Bond Interest Rates Determine Bond Prices. Bonds are always sold at their *market price*, which is the amount investors will pay for the bond. **Market price is the bond's present value**, which equals the present value of the principal payment plus the present value of the cash interest payments. Interest is usually paid semiannually (twice a year). Some companies pay interest annually or quarterly.

Two interest rates work to set the price of a bond:

- The **stated interest rate**, also called the coupon rate, is the interest rate printed on the bond certificate. The stated interest rate determines the amount of cash interest the borrower pays—and the investor receives—each year. Suppose Southwest Airlines bonds have a stated interest rate of 9%. Southwest would pay $9,000 of interest annually on each $100,000 bond. Each semiannual payment would be $4,500 ($100,000 × 0.09 × 6/12).
- The **market interest rate**, or *effective interest rate*, is the rate that investors demand for loaning their money. The market interest rate varies by the minute.

A company may issue bonds with a stated interest rate that differs from the prevailing market interest rate. In fact, the two interest rates often differ.

Exhibit 8-3 shows how the stated interest rate and the market interest rate interact to determine the issue price of a bond payable for three separate cases.

EXHIBIT 8-3 | **How the Stated Interest Rate and the Market Interest Rate Interact to Determine the Price of a Bond**

Issue Price of Bonds Payable

Case A:

Stated interest rate on a bond payable	equals	Market interest rate	Therefore,	Price of face (par, or maturity) value
Example: 9%	=	9%	→	*Par: $1,000 bond issued for $1,000*

Case B:

Stated interest rate on a bond payable	less than	Market interest rate	Therefore,	Discount price (price below face value)
Example: 9%	<	10%	→	*Discount: $1,000 bond issued for a price below $1,000*

Case C:

Stated interest rate on a bond payable	greater than	Market interest rate	Therefore,	Premium price (price above face value)
Example: 9%	>	8%	→	*Premium: $1,000 bond issued for a price above $1,000*

Southwest Airlines may issue 9% bonds when the market rate has risen to 10%. Will the Southwest 9% bonds attract investors in this market? No, because investors can earn 10% on other bonds of similar risk. Therefore, investors will purchase Southwest bonds only at a price less than their face value. The difference between the lower price and face value is a *discount* (Exhibit 8-3). Conversely, if the market interest rate is 8%, Southwest's 9% bonds will be so attractive that investors will pay more than face value to purchase them. The difference between the higher price and face value is a *premium*.

Issuing Bonds Payable at Par (Face Value)

We start with the most straightforward situation—issuing bonds at their par value. There is no premium or discount on these bonds payable.

Suppose Southwest Airlines has $50,000 of 9% bonds payable that mature in five years. Assume that Southwest issued these bonds at par on January 1, 2010. The issuance entry is

OBJECTIVE

2 **Account** for bonds payable

2010			
Jan 1	Cash	50,000	
	Bonds Payable		50,000
	To issue bonds at par.		

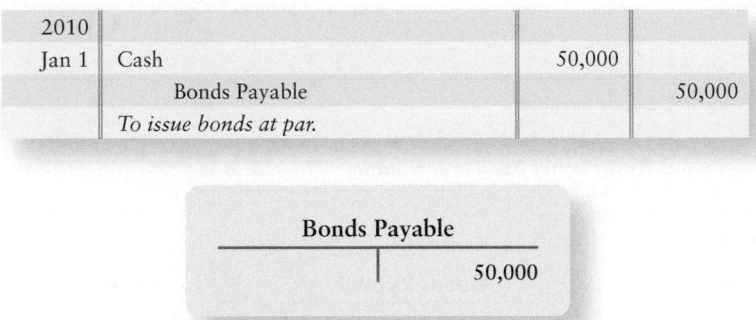

Bonds Payable

	50,000

Assets and liabilities increase when a company issues bonds payable.

Assets	=	Liabilities	+	Stockholders' Equity
+ 50,000	=	+ 50,000	+	0

Southwest, the borrower, makes a one-time entry to record the receipt of cash and the issuance of bonds. Afterward, investors buy and sell the bonds through the bond markets. These later buy-and-sell transactions between outside investors do *not* involve Southwest at all.

Interest payments occur each January 1 and July 1. Southwest's entry to record the first semiannual interest payment is

2010			
Jul 1	Interest Expense ($50,000 × 0.09 × 6/12)	2,250	
	Cash		2,250
	To pay semiannual interest.		

The payment of interest expense decreases assets and equity. Bonds payable are not affected.

Assets	=	Liabilities	+	Stockholders' Equity	−	Expenses
− 2,250	=	0	+			− 2,250

At year-end, Southwest accrues interest expense and interest payable for six months (July through December), as follows:

2010			
Dec 31	Interest Expense ($50,000 × 0.09 × 6/12)	2,250	
	Interest Payable		2,250
	To accrue interest.		

Liabilities increase, and equity decreases.

Assets	=	Liabilities	+	Stockholders' Equity	−	Expenses
0	=	+ 2,250	+			− 2,250

On January 1, Southwest will pay the interest, debiting Interest Payable and crediting Cash. Then, at maturity, Southwest pays off the bonds as follows:

2015			
Jan 1	Bonds Payable	50,000	
	Cash		50,000
	To pay bonds payable at maturity.		

Bonds Payable

50,000	50,000
	Bal 0

Assets	=	Liabilities	+	Stockholders' Equity
− 50,000	=	− 50,000		

Issuing Bonds Payable at a Discount

Market conditions may force a company to issue bonds at a discount. Suppose Southwest Airlines issued $100,000 of 9%, five-year bonds when the market interest rate is 10%. The market price of the bonds drops, and Southwest receives $96,149[3] at issuance. The transaction is recorded as follows:

2010			
Jan 1	Cash	96,149	
	Discount on Bonds Payable	3,851	
	Bonds Payable		100,000
	To issue bonds at a discount.		

[3]Appendix C at the end of this book shows how to determine the price of this bond.

The accounting equation shows that Southwest has a net liability of $96,149—not $100,000.

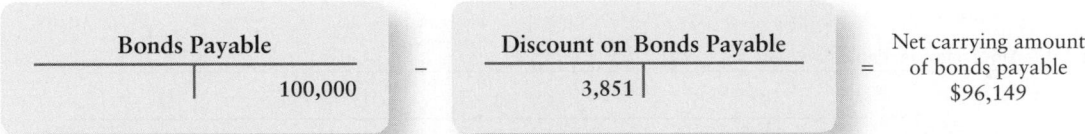

Assets	=	Liabilities	+	Stockholders' Equity
+ 96,149	=	− 3,851	+	0
		+ 100,000		

The bonds payable accounts have a net balance of $96,149 as follows:

Bonds Payable				Discount on Bonds Payable			Net carrying amount
	100,000	−		3,851		=	of bonds payable $96,149

Southwest's balance sheet immediately after issuance of the bonds would report the following:

Total current liabilities...................................		$ XXX
Long-term liabilities:		
Bonds payable, 9%, due 2015....................	$100,000	
Less: Discount on bonds payable...............	(3,851)	96,149

Discount on Bonds Payable is a contra account to Bonds Payable, a decrease in the company's liabilities. Subtracting the discount from Bonds Payable yields the *carrying amount* of the bonds. Thus, Southwest's liability is $96,149, which is the amount the company borrowed.

What Is the Interest Expense on These Bonds Payable?

Southwest pays interest on bonds semiannually, which is common practice. Each semiannual *interest payment* is set by the bond contract and therefore remains the same over the life of the bonds:

OBJECTIVE

3 **Measure** interest expense

$$\text{Semiannual interest payment} = \$100,000 \times 0.09 \times 6/12$$
$$= \$4,500$$

But Southwest's *interest expense* increases as the bonds march toward maturity. Remember: These bonds were issued at a discount.

Panel A of Exhibit 8-4 on the following page repeats the Southwest Airlines bond data we've been using. Panel B provides an amortization table that does two things:

- Determines the periodic interest expense (column B)
- Shows the bond carrying amount (column E)

Study the exhibit carefully because the amounts we'll be using come directly from the amortization table. This exhibit shows the *effective-interest method of amortization*, which is the correct way to measure interest expense.

EXHIBIT 8-4 | Debt Amortization for a Bond Discount

Panel A—Bond Data

Issue date—January 1, 2010	Maturity date—January 1, 2015
Face (par or *maturity*) value—$100,000	Market interest rate at time of issue—10% annually, 5% semiannually
Stated interest rate—9%	Issue price—$96,149
Interest paid—4½% semiannually, $4,500 = $100,000 × 0.09 × 6/12	

Panel B—Amortization Table

	A	B	C	D	E
Semiannual Interest Date	Interest Payment (4 1/2% of Maturity Value)	Interest Expense (5% of Preceding Bond Carrying Amount)	Discount Amortization (B – A)	Discount Account Balance (Preceding D – C)	Bond Carrying Amount ($100,000 – D)
Jan 1, 2010				$3,851	$ 96,149
Jul 1	$4,500	$4,807	$307	3,544	96,456
Jan 1, 2011	4,500	4,823	323	3,221	96,779
Jul 1	4,500	4,839	339	2,882	97,118
Jan 1, 2012	4,500	4,856	356	2,526	97,474
Jul 1	4,500	4,874	374	2,152	97,848
Jan 1, 2013	4,500	4,892	392	1,760	98,240
Jul 1	4,500	4,912	412	1,348	98,652
Jan 1, 2014	4,500	4,933	433	915	99,085
Jul 1	4,500	4,954	454	461	99,539
Jan 1, 2015	4,500	4,961*	461	-0-	100,000

*Adjusted for effect of rounding

Notes
- Column A   The semiannual interest payments are constant—fixed by the bond contract.
- Column B   The interest expense each period = the preceding bond carrying amount × the market interest rate.
  Interest expense increases as the bond carrying amount (E) increases.
- Column C   The discount amortization (C) is the excess of interest expense (B) over interest payment (A).
- Column D   The discount balance (D) decreases when amortized.
- Column E   The bond carrying amount (E) increases from $96,149 at issuance to $100,000 at maturity.

Interest Expense on Bonds Issued at a Discount

In Exhibit 8-4, Southwest Airlines borrowed $96,149 cash but must pay $100,000 when the bonds mature. What happens to the $3,851 balance of the discount account over the life of the bond issue?

The $3,851 is additional interest expense to Southwest over and above the stated interest that Southwest pays each six months. Exhibit 8-5 graphs the interest expense and the interest payment on the Southwest bonds over their lifetime. Observe that the semiannual interest payment is fixed—by contract—at $4,500. But the amount of interest expense increases as the discount bond marches upward toward maturity.

EXHIBIT 8-5 | **Interest Expense on Bonds Payable Issued at a Discount**

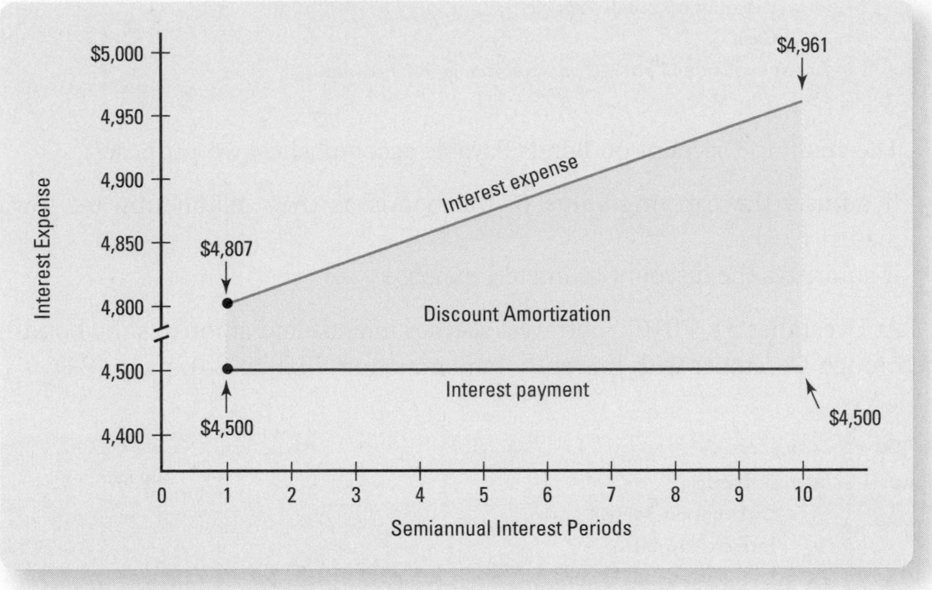

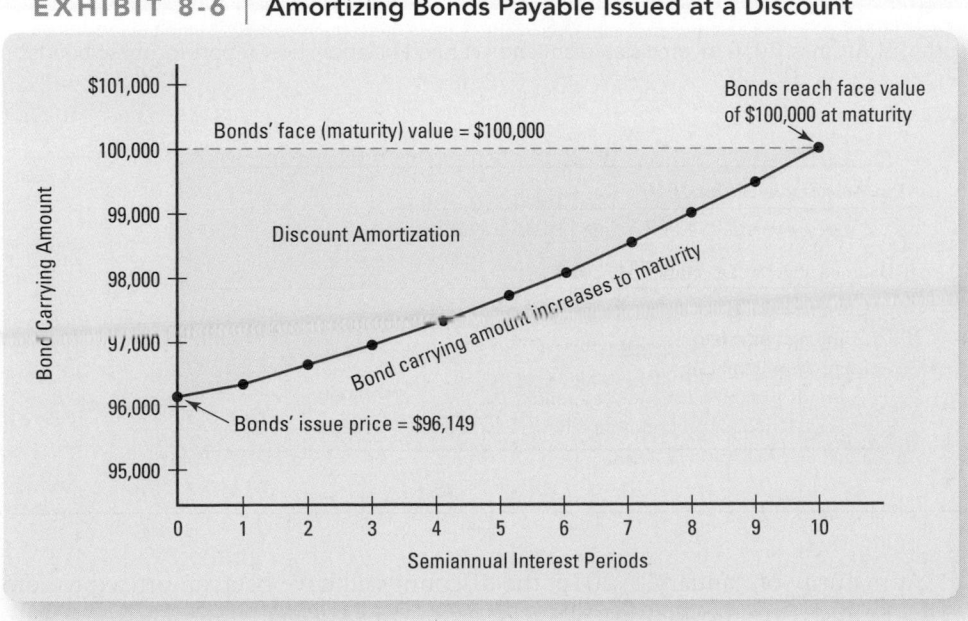

The discount is allocated to interest expense through amortization over the term of the bonds. Exhibit 8-6 illustrates the amortization of the bonds from $96,149 at the start to $100,000 at maturity. These amounts come from Exhibit 8-4, column E (p. 484).

Now let's see how Southwest would account for these bonds issued at a discount. In our example, Southwest issued its bonds on January 1, 2010. On July 1, Southwest made the first semiannual interest payment. But Southwest's interest expense is greater than its payment of $4,500. Southwest's journal entry to record interest expense and the interest payment for the first 6 months follows (with all amounts taken from Exhibit 8-4):

EXHIBIT 8-6 | **Amortizing Bonds Payable Issued at a Discount**

2010			
Jul 1	Interest Expense	4,807	
	Discount on Bonds Payable		307
	Cash		4,500
	To pay semiannual interest and amortize bond discount.		

The credit to Discount on Bonds Payable accomplishes two purposes:

- It adjusts the carrying value of the bonds as they march upward toward maturity value.
- It amortizes the discount to interest expense.

At December 31, 2010, Southwest accrues interest and amortizes the bonds for July through December with this entry (amounts from Exhibit 8-4, page 484):

2010			
Dec 31	Interest Expense	4,823	
	Discount on Bonds Payable		323
	Interest Payable		4,500
	To accrue semiannual interest and amortize bond discount.		

At December 31, 2010, Southwest's bond accounts appear as follows:

Bonds Payable		Discount on Bonds Payable	
	100,000	3,851	307
			323
		Bal 3,221	

Bond carrying amount, $96,779 = $100,000 − $3,221 from Exhibit 8-4, page 484.

STOP & THINK...

What would Southwest Airlines' 2010 income statement and year-end balance sheet report for these bonds?

Answer:

Income Statement for 2010		
Interest expense ($4,807 + $4,823)		$ 9,630
Balance Sheet at December 31, 2010		
Current liabilities:		
Interest payable...		$ 4,500
Long-term liabilities:		
Bonds payable...	$100,000	
Less: Discount on bonds payable..............	(3,221)	96,779

At maturity on January 1, 2015, the discount will have been amortized to zero, and the bonds' carrying amount will be face value of $100,000. Southwest will retire the bonds by paying $100,000 to the bondholders.

Partial-Period Interest Amounts

Companies don't always issue bonds at the beginning or the end of their accounting year. They issue bonds when market conditions are most favorable, and that may be on May 16, August 1, or any other date. To illustrate partial-period interest, assume **Google Inc.** issues $100,000 of 8% bonds payable at 96 on August 31, 2010. The market rate of interest was 9%, and these bonds pay semiannual interest on February 28 and August 31 each year. The first few lines of Google's amortization table are

Semiannual Interest Date	4% Interest Payment	4 ½% Interest Expense	Discount Amortization	Discount Account Balance	Bond Carrying Amount
Aug 31, 2010				$4,000	$96,000
Feb 28, 2011	$4,000	$4,320	$320	3,680	96,320
Aug 31, 2011	4,000	4,334	334	3,346	96,654

Google's accounting year ends on December 31, so at year-end Google must accrue interest and amortize bond discount for four months (September through December). At December 31, 2010, Google will make this entry:

2010			
Dec 31	Interest Expense ($4,320 × 4/6)	2,880	
	Discount on Bonds Payable ($320 × 4/6)		213
	Interest Payable ($4,000 × 4/6)		2,667
	To accrue interest and amortize discount at year-end.		

The year-end entry at December 31, 2010, uses 4/6 of the upcoming semiannual amounts at February 28, 2011. This example clearly illustrates the benefit of an amortization schedule.

Issuing Bonds Payable at a Premium

Let's modify the Southwest Airlines bond example to illustrate issuance of the bonds at a premium. Assume that Southwest issues $100,000 of five-year, 9% bonds that pay interest semiannually. If the 9% bonds are issued when the market interest rate is 8%, their issue price is $104,100.[4] The premium on these bonds is $4,100, and Exhibit 8-7 on the following page shows how to amortize the bonds by the effective-interest method. In practice, bond premiums are rare because few companies issue their bonds to pay cash interest above the market interest rate. We cover bond premiums for completeness.

Southwest's entries to record issuance of the bonds on January 1, 2010, and to make the first interest payment and amortize the bonds on July 1, are as follows:

2010			
Jan 1	Cash	104,100	
	Bonds Payable		100,000
	Premium on Bonds Payable		4,100
	To issue bonds at a premium.		

---

[4]Appendix C at the end of this book shows how to determine the price of this bond.

At the beginning, Southwest's liability is $104,100—not $100,000. The accounting equation makes this clear.

Assets	=	Liabilities	+	Stockholders' Equity
+ 104,100	=	+ 100,000	+	0
		+ 4,100		

2010			
Jul 1	Interest Expense (from Exhibit 8-7)	4,164	
	Premium on Bonds Payable	336	
	Cash		4,500
	To pay semiannual interest and amortize bond premium.		

EXHIBIT 8-7 | Debt Amortization for a Bond Premium

Panel A—Bond Data

Issue date—January 1, 2010	Maturity date—January 1, 2015
Face (par or *maturity*) value—$100,000	Market interest rate at time of issue—8% annually, 4% semiannually
Stated interest rate—9%	Issue price—$104,100
Interest paid—4½% semiannually, $4,500 = $100,000 × 0.09 × 6/12	

Panel B—Amortization Table

	A	B	C	D	E
Semiannual Interest Date	Interest Payment (4 1/2% of Maturity Value)	Interest Expense (4% of Preceding Bond Carrying Amount)	Premium Amortization (A − B)	Premium Account Balance (Preceding D − C)	Bond Carrying Amount ($100,000 + D)
Jan 1, 2010				$4,100	$ 104,100
Jul 1	$4,500	$4,164	$336	3,764	103,764
Jan 1, 2011	4,500	4,151	349	3,415	103,415
Jul 1	4,500	4,137	363	3,052	103,052
Jan 1, 2012	4,500	4,122	378	2,674	102,674
Jul 1	4,500	4,107	393	2,281	102,281
Jan 1, 2013	4,500	4,091	409	1,872	101,872
Jul 1	4,500	4,075	425	1,447	101,447
Jan 1, 2014	4,500	4,058	442	1,005	101,005
Jul 1	4,500	4,040	460	545	100,545
Jan 1, 2015	4,500	3,955*	545	-0-	100,000

*Adjusted for effect of rounding

Notes
- Column A   The semiannual interest payments are constant—fixed by the bond contract.
- Column B   The interest expense each period = the preceding bond carrying amount × the market interest rate. Interest expense decreases as the bond carrying amount (E) decreases.
- Column C   The premium amortization (C) is the excess of interest payment (A) over interest expense (B).
- Column D   The premium balance (D) decreases when amortized.
- Column E   The bond carrying amount (E) decreases from $104,100 at issuance to $100,000 at maturity.

Immediately after issuing the bonds at a premium on January 1, 2010, Southwest would report the bonds payable on the balance sheet as follows:

Total current liabilities............................		$ XXX
Long-term liabilities:		
Bonds payable..	$100,000	
Premium on bonds payable....................	4,100	104,100

A premium is *added* to the balance of bonds payable to determine the carrying amount.

In Exhibit 8-7 Southwest borrowed $104,100 cash but must pay back only $100,000 at maturity. The $4,100 premium is a reduction in Southwest's interest expense over the term of the bonds. Exhibit 8-8 graphs Southwest's interest payments (column A from Exhibit 8-7) and interest expense (column B).

EXHIBIT 8-8 | **Interest Expense on Bonds Payable Issued at a Premium**

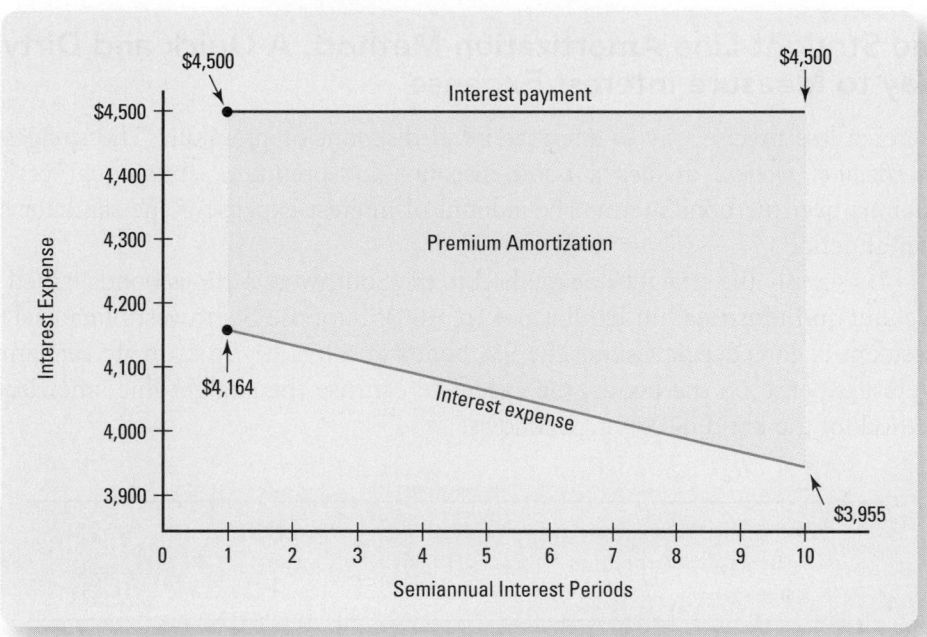

Through amortization the premium decreases interest expense each period over the term of the bonds. Exhibit 8-9 on the following page diagrams the amortization of the bonds from the issue price of $104,100 to maturity value of $100,000. All amounts are taken from Exhibit 8-7.

EXHIBIT 8-9 | Amortizing Bonds Payable Issued at a Premium

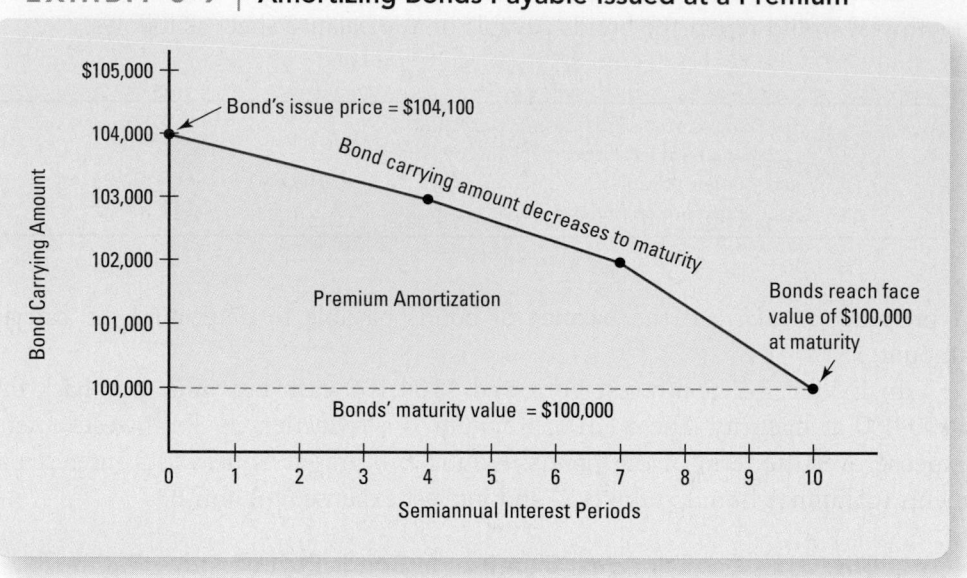

The Straight-Line Amortization Method: A Quick and Dirty Way to Measure Interest Expense

There's a less precise way to amortize bond discount or premium. The *straight-line amortization method* divides a bond discount (or premium) into equal periodic amounts over the bond's term. The amount of interest expense is the same for each interest period.

Let's apply the straight-line method to the Southwest Airlines bonds issued at a discount and illustrated in Exhibit 8-4 (p. 484). Suppose Southwest's financial vice president is considering issuing the 9% bonds at $96,149. To estimate semiannual interest expense on the bonds, the executive can use the straight-line amortization method for the bond discount, as follows:

Semiannual cash interest payment ($100,000 × 0.09 × 6/12)...............	$4,500
+ Semiannual amortization of discount ($3,851 ÷ 10)...........................	385
= Estimated semiannual interest expense...	$4,885

The straight-line amortization method uses these same amounts every period over the term of the bonds.

Southwest's entry to record interest and amortization of the bond discount under the straight-line amortization method would be

2010				
Jul 1	Interest Expense	4,885	
	Discount on Bonds Payable		385
	Cash		4,500
	To pay semiannual interest and amortize bond discount.		

Generally accepted accounting principles (GAAP) permit the straight-line amortization method only when its amounts differ insignificantly from the amounts determined by the effective-interest method.

Should We Retire Bonds Payable Before Their Maturity?

Normally, companies wait until maturity to pay off, or *retire*, their bonds payable. But companies sometimes retire bonds early. The main reason for retiring bonds early is to relieve the pressure of making high interest payments. Also, the company may be able to borrow at a lower interest rate.

Some bonds are **callable**, which means that the issuer may *call*, or pay off, those bonds at a prearranged price (this is the *call price*) whenever the issuer chooses. The call price is often a percentage point or two above the par value, perhaps 101 or 102. Callable bonds give the issuer the benefit of being able to pay off the bonds whenever it is most favorable to do so. The alternative to calling the bonds is to purchase them in the open market at their current market price.

Southwest Airlines has $300 million of debenture bonds outstanding. Assume the unamortized discount is $30 million. Lower interest rates may convince management to pay off these bonds now. Assume that the bonds are callable at 101. If the market price of the bonds is 99, will Southwest call the bonds at 101 or purchase them for 99 in the open market? Market price is the better choice because the market price is lower than the call price. Let's see how to account for an early retirement of bonds payable. Retiring the bonds at 99 results in a loss of $27 million, computed as follows:

	Millions
Par value of bonds being retired	$300
Less: Unamortized discount	(30)
Carrying amount of the bonds being retired	270
Market price ($300 × .99)	297
Loss on retirement of bonds payable	$ 27

Gains and losses on early retirement of bonds payable are reported as Other income (loss) on the income statement.

Convertible Bonds and Notes

Some corporate bonds may be converted into the **issuing** company's common stock. These bonds are called **convertible bonds** (or **convertible notes**). For investors these bonds combine the safety of (a) assured receipt of interest and principal on the bonds with (b) the opportunity for gains on the stock. The conversion feature is so attractive that investors usually accept a lower interest rate than they would on nonconvertible bonds. The lower cash interest payments benefit the issuer. If the market price of the issuing company's stock gets high enough, the bondholders will convert the bonds into stock.

Suppose Southwest Airlines has convertible notes payable of $100 million. If Southwest's stock price rises high enough, the noteholders will convert the notes into the company's common stock. Conversion of the notes payable into stock will decrease Southwest's liabilities and increase its equity.

Assume the noteholders convert the notes into 4 million shares of Southwest Airlines common stock ($1 par) on May 14. Southwest makes the following entry in its accounting records:

May 14	Notes Payable	100,000,000	
	Common Stock (4,000,000 × $1 par)		4,000,000
	Paid-in Capital in Excess of		
	Par—Common		96,000,000
	To record conversion of notes payable.		

The accounting equation shows that liabilities decrease and equity goes up.

Assets	=	Liabilities	+	Stockholders' Equity
0	=	− 100,000,000		+ 4,000,000 + 96,000,000

The carrying amount of the notes ($100 million) ceases to be debt and becomes stockholders' equity. Common Stock is recorded at its *par value*, which is a dollar amount assigned to each share of stock. In this case, the credit to Common Stock is $4,000,000 (4,000,000 shares × $1 par value per share). The extra carrying amount of the notes payable ($96,000,000) is credited to another stockholders' equity account, Paid-in Capital in Excess of Par—Common. We'll be using this account in various ways in the next chapter.

Financing Operations with Bonds or Stock?

OBJECTIVE

4 **Understand** the advantages and disadvantages of borrowing

Managers must decide how to get the money they need to pay for assets. There are three main ways to finance operations:

- By retained earnings
- By issuing stock
- By issuing bonds (or notes) payable

Each strategy has its advantages and disadvantages.

1. *Financed by retained earnings* means that the company already has enough cash to purchase the needed assets. There's no need to issue more stock or to borrow money. This strategy is low-risk to the company.

2. *Issuing stock* creates no liabilities or interest expense and is less risky to the issuing corporation. But issuing stock is more costly, as we shall see.

Long-Term Liabilities: Bonds and Notes Payable **493**

3. *Issuing bonds or notes payable* does not dilute control of the corporation. It often results in higher earnings per share because the earnings on borrowed money usually exceed interest expense. But creating more debt increases the risk of the company.

Earnings per share (EPS) is the amount of a company's net income for each share of its stock. EPS is the single most important statistic for evaluating companies because EPS is a standard measure of operating performance that applies to companies of different sizes and from different industries.

Suppose Southwest Airlines needs $500,000 for expansion. Assume Southwest has net income of $300,000 and 100,000 shares of common stock outstanding. Management is considering two financing plans. Plan 1 is to issue $500,000 of 6% bonds payable, and plan 2 is to issue 50,000 shares of common stock for $500,000. Management believes the new cash can be invested in operations to earn income of $200,000 before interest and taxes.

Exhibit 8-10 shows the earnings-per-share advantage of borrowing. As you can see, Southwest's EPS amount is higher if the company borrows by issuing bonds (compare lines 9 and 10). Southwest earns more on the investment ($102,000) than the interest it pays on the bonds ($30,000). This is called **trading on the equity**, or using **leverage**. It is widely used to increase earnings per share of common stock.

EXHIBIT 8-10 | **Earnings-Per-Share Advantage of Borrowing**

	Plan 1		Plan 2	
	Borrow $500,000 at 6%		Issue 50,000 Shares of Common Stock for $500,000	
1 Net income before expansion		$300,000		$300,000
2 Expected project income before interest and income tax	$200,000		$200,000	
3 Less interest expense ($500,000 × .06)	(30,000)		0	
4 Expected project income before income tax	170,000		200,000	
5 Less income tax expense (40%)	(68,000)		(80,000)	
6 Expected project net income		102,000		120,000
7 Total company net income		$402,000		$420,000
8 Earnings per share after expansion:				
9 Plan 1 Borrow ($402,000/100,000 shares)		$4.02		
10 Plan 2 Issue Stock ($420,000/150,000 shares)				$2.80

In this case borrowing results in higher earnings per share than issuing stock. Borrowing has its disadvantages, however. Interest expense may be high enough to eliminate net income and lead to losses. Also, borrowing creates liabilities that must be paid during bad years as well as good years. In contrast, a company that issues stock can omit its dividends during a bad year. The Decision Guidelines provide some help in deciding how to finance operations.

DECISION GUIDELINES

FINANCING WITH DEBT OR WITH STOCK

El Chico is the leading chain of Tex-Mex restaurants in the United States, begun by the Cuellar family in the Dallas area. Suppose El Chico is expanding into neighboring states. Take the role of Miguel Cuellar and assume you must make some key decisions about how to finance the expansion.

Decision	Guidelines
How will you finance El Chico's expansion?	Your financing plan depends on El Chico's ability to generate cash flow, your willingness to give up some control of the business, the amount of financing risk you are willing to take, and El Chico's credit rating.
Do El Chico's operations generate enough cash to meet all its financing needs?	If yes, the business needs little outside financing. There is no need to borrow. If no, the business will need to issue additional stock or borrow the money.
Are you willing to give up some of your control of the business?	If yes, then issue stock to other stockholders, who can vote their shares to elect the company's directors. If no, then borrow from bondholders, who have no vote in the management of the company.
How much financing risk are you willing to take?	If much, then borrow as much as you can, and you may increase El Chico's earnings per share. But this will increase the business's debt ratio and the risk of being unable to pay its debts. If little, then borrow sparingly. This will hold the debt ratio down and reduce the risk of default on borrowing agreements. But El Chico's earnings per share may be lower than if you were to borrow.
How good is the business's credit rating?	The better the credit rating, the easier it is to borrow on favorable terms. A good credit rating also makes it easier to issue stock. Neither stockholders nor creditors will entrust their money to a company with a bad credit rating.

The Times-Interest-Earned Ratio

We have just seen how borrowing can increase EPS. But too much debt can lead to bankruptcy if the business cannot pay liabilities as they come due. UAL, Inc., the parent company of United Airlines, fell into the debt trap.

The **debt ratio** measures the effect of debt on the company's *financial position* but says nothing about the ability to pay interest expense. Analysts use a second ratio—the **times-interest-earned ratio**—to relate income to interest expense. To compute this ratio, we divide *income from operations* (also called *operating income*) by interest expense. This ratio measures the number of times that operating income can *cover* interest expense. The times-interest-earned ratio is also called the **interest-coverage** *ratio*. A high times-interest-earned ratio indicates ease in paying interest expense; a low value suggests difficulty. Let's see how competing airlines, Southwest and United (UAL), compare on the times-interest-earned ratio (dollar amounts in millions taken from the companies' 2008 financial statements):

Times–interest earned ratio	=	$\dfrac{\text{Operating income}}{\text{Interest expense}}$
Southwest		$\dfrac{\$449}{\$130} = 3.5$ times
United		$\dfrac{\$(4{,}438)}{\$523} = (8.5)$ times

Southwest's income from operations covers its interest expense 3.5 times. In contrast, UAL incurred a $4.4 billion loss for 2008, which dwarfs its interest expense by 8.5 times. It is obvious that UAL is experiencing difficulty staying in business. Paying interest on its outstanding debt is just the beginning of its worries.

STOP & THINK...

Which company, Southwest or UAL, would you expect to have the higher debt ratio? Compute the two companies' debt ratios to confirm your opinion. Summarized balance sheets follow at December 31, 2008.

	(In millions)	
	Southwest	UAL
Total assets	$14,308	$19,461
Total liabilities	$ 9,355	$21,926
Stockholders' equity	4,953	(2,465)
Total liabilities and equity	$14,308	$19,461

Answer:
As expected, UAL has a much higher debt ratio than Southwest, as follows (dollar amounts in millions). UAL actually has 13% more liabilities than assets! The company is literally awash in debt, resulting in a negative balance in stockholders' equity as of December 31, 2008. In comparison, although Southwest's leverage, as expressed by the debt ratio, is getting higher (its was 0.521 in 2006) Southwest is still far less leveraged than UAL, or any other major airline, as of December 31, 2008:

	Southwest	UAL
Debt ratio $= \dfrac{\text{Total liabilities}}{\text{Total assets}} =$	$\dfrac{\$9{,}355}{\$14{,}308}$	$\dfrac{\$21{,}926}{\$19{,}461}$
	= 0.654	= 1.13

LONG-TERM LIABILITIES: LEASES AND PENSIONS

A **lease** is a rental agreement in which the tenant (**lessee**) agrees to make rent payments to the property owner (**lessor**) in exchange for the use of the asset. Leasing allows the lessee to acquire the use of a needed asset without having to make the large up-front payment that purchase agreements require. Accountants distinguish between two types of leases: operating leases and capital leases.

Types of Leases

Operating leases are sometimes short-term or cancelable. However, often operating lease agreements are noncancelable and require the lessee to commit funds to pay the lessor for use of property for years. They give the lessee the right to use the asset but provide no continuing rights to the asset. Instead, the lessor retains the usual risks and rewards of owning the leased asset. To account for an operating lease, the lessee debits Rent Expense (or Lease Expense) and credits Cash for the amount of the lease payment. Operating leases require the lessee to make rent payments, so an operating lease creates a liability even though that liability does not appear on the lessee's balance sheet. In recent years, Southwest Airlines has begun to lease many of its facilities (hangars, buildings, and equipment, including airplanes) under operating lease agreements. Following is an excerpt from Note 8 of Southwest's 2008 financial statements:

Note 8 Leases (partial)

The majority of the Company's terminal operations space, as well as 82 aircraft, were under operating leases at December 31, 2008. Future minimum lease payments under noncancelable operating leases with initial or remaining terms in excess of one year at December 31, 2008, were (in millions):

2009	$ 376
2010	324
2011	249
2012	203
2013	152
After 2013	728
Total	$2,032

This essentially means that, although the company has merely signed rental agreements for these assets, it has an obligation over several years in an amount exceeding $2 billion to the companies from which it is leasing these assets. Neither the obligation nor the associated assets are included in Southwest's balance sheet.

    Capital leases. Sometimes businesses use capital leases to finance the acquisition of some assets. A **capital lease** is a long-term noncancelable debt. How do we distinguish a capital lease from an operating lease? *FASB Statement No. 13* provides the U.S. GAAP guidelines. To be classified as a capital lease, the lease must meet any *one* of the following criteria:

1. The lease transfers title of the leased asset to the lessee at the end of the lease term. Thus, the lessee becomes the legal owner of the leased asset.

2. The lease contains a *bargain purchase option*. The lessee can be expected to purchase the leased asset and become its legal owner.

3. The lease term is 75% or more of the estimated useful life of the leased asset. The lessee uses up most of the leased asset's service potential.

4. The present value of the lease payments is 90% or more of the market value of the leased asset. In effect, the lease payments are the same as installment payments for the leased asset.

If the lease does not meet one of these exact criteria, it is classified as an operating lease by default.

Accounting for a capital lease is much like accounting for the purchase of an asset. The lessee enters the asset into the lessee's long-term asset accounts and records a long-term lease liability at the beginning of the lease term. Thus, the lessee capitalizes the asset even though the lessee may never take legal title to the asset, because the lease agreement makes the lessee assume the risks and rewards of ownership of the assets and the associated obligations.

Most companies lease some of their plant assets. Southwest Airlines leases airplanes under capital leases. At December 31, 2008, Southwest Airlines reported its capital leases in Note 8 of its financial statements, excerpted as follows:

Note 8 Leases (partial)
Southwest's "future minimum lease payments under capital leases [...] as of December 31, 2008, were" (in millions):

Year Ending December 31	Capital Lease Payments	
2009	$ 16	
2010	15	
2011	12	
after 2011	–	
	43	*This is Southwest's*
Less amount representing interest	(4)	*liability under its*
Present value of...lease payments	$ 39 ←	*capital leases.*

The note shows that Southwest must pay a total of $43 million on its capital leases through 2011. The present value of this liability (gross amount less the amount attributable to interest on the liability) is $39 million. The present value is the net amount that's included in the liability figures reported on Southwest's balance sheet.

Do Lessees Prefer Operating Leases or Capital Leases?

Suppose you were the chief financial officer (CFO) of Southwest Airlines. Southwest leases some of its planes. Suppose the leases can be structured either as operating leases or as capital leases. Which type of lease would you prefer for Southwest? Why? Consider what would happen to Southwest's debt ratio if its operating leases in footnote 8 were capitalized, and the related liabilities recognized. Computing Southwest's debt ratio two ways (*operating* leases versus reclassifying them as *capital* leases) will make your decision clear (using Southwest's actual figures in millions):

		Operating Leases as Stated	Operating Leases Reclassified as Capital Leases	
Debt ratio =	$\frac{\text{Total liabilities}}{\text{Total assets}}$ =	$\frac{\$9,355}{\$14,308}$	$\frac{\$9,355 + \$2,032}{\$14,308 + \$2,032}$ =	$\frac{\$11,387}{\$16,340}$
	=	0.654	=	0.697

You can see that a capital lease increases the debt ratio—by about five percentage points for Southwest, but a lot more for UAL and AMR (parent company of American Airlines). By contrast, notice that operating leases don't affect the debt ratio that's reported on the balance sheet. For this reason, companies prefer operating leases. It is easy to see why Southwest's long-term commitment for operating leases, as disclosed in Note 8, far outweighs that of its capital lease agreements.

Ethical Challenge.   Because of the relatively mechanical nature of the accounting criteria for capitalization of leases, it is possible under existing U.S. GAAP to purposely structure a company's lease agreements so that they barely miss meeting the third criterion (75% test) or the fourth criterion (90% test) for capitalization. Many U.S. companies have taken advantage of these mechanical rules, quite legally, to their economic advantage, thus obtaining almost all the same economic benefits associated with ownership of long-term assets, but avoiding the detrimental impact that recording those assets and obligations can have on their debt ratios.

 In contrast to U.S. GAAP with its mechanical, or "bright line" tests for capitalization of leases, IFRS adopts a much broader approach. Rather than rules, IFRS employs "guidance" that focuses on the overall substance of the transaction, rather than on the mechanical form, and that leaves more to the judgment of the preparer of the financial statement. If, in the judgment of the company's accountants, the lease transfers "substantially all of the risks and rewards of ownership to the lessee," IFRS says the lease should be capitalized. Otherwise, the lease should be expensed as an operating lease.

As of the publication date of this textbook, the FASB and IASB are in discussions about adopting consistent criteria for disclosures of leases on the financial statements of both lessors and lessees. A revised statement is expected sometime in 2010 or 2011. The impact of eventual adoption of IFRS on U.S. financial statements in the area of leases is hard to predict. Switching to current IFRS could result in more or fewer lease agreements being capitalized, depending on the judgment of financial statement preparers. If given the choice, what would you do?

Pensions and Postretirement Liabilities

Most companies have retirement plans for their employees. A **pension** is employee compensation that will be received during retirement. Companies also provide postretirement benefits, such as medical insurance for retired former employees. Because employees earn these benefits by their service, the company records pension and retirement-benefit expense while employees work for the company.

Pensions are one of the most complex areas of accounting. As employees earn their pensions and the company pays into the pension plan, the plan's assets grow. The obligation for future pension payments to employees also accumulates. At the end of each period, the company compares

- the fair market value of the assets in the retirement plans—cash and investments—with
- the plans' *accumulated benefit obligation*, which is the present value of promised future payments to retirees.

If the plan assets exceed the accumulated benefit obligation, the plan is said to be *overfunded*. In this case, the asset and obligation amounts are to be reported only in the notes to the financial statements. However, if the accumulated benefit obligation (the liability) exceeds plan assets, the plan is *underfunded*, and the company must report the excess liability amount as a long-term liability on the balance sheet.

Southwest Airlines' retirement plans don't create large liabilities for Southwest. To illustrate pension liabilities let's see the pension plan of AMR Corp., the parent company of American Airlines.

At December 31, 2007, the retirement plans of AMR Corporation were underfunded. They had

- assets with a fair market value of $9,323 million.
- accumulated benefit obligations totaling $13,123 million.

AMR's balance sheet, therefore, included a Pension and Post-Retirement Liability of $3,800 million ($13,123 – $9,323). This liability was split between current and long-term liabilities, in accordance with the due dates for the obligations.

REPORTING LIABILITIES

Reporting on the Balance Sheet

This chapter began with the liabilities reported on the consolidated balance sheets of Southwest Airlines. Exhibit 8-11 shows a standard way for Southwest to report its long-term debt.

OBJECTIVE

5 **Report** liabilities on the balance sheet

EXHIBIT 8-11 | **Reporting the Liabilities of Southwest Airlines Co.**

Southwest Airlines Co. Consolidated Balance Sheet (Partial, adapted)		Note 10 Financial Instruments (adapted) Long-term debt consists of (in millions);	
Liabilities (in millions)		Revolving credit facility	$ 400
Current Liabilities:		10.5% notes due 2011	400
Accounts payable	$ 668	Term agreement due 2020	585
Accrued liabilities	1,012	French credit agreements due 2012	26
Unearned ticket revenue	963	6½% notes due 2012	410
Current maturities of long-term debt	163	5¼% notes due 2014	391
Total current liabilities	2,806	5¾% notes due 2016	300
Long-term debt	3,498	5⅛% notes due 2017	358
Other long-term liabilities	3,051	French credit agreements due 2017	87
		Other long-term debt	704
		Total long-term debt	3,661
		Less current maturities	(163)
		Long-term debt	$3,498

Exhibit 8-11 includes Note 10 from Southwest's consolidated financial statements. The note gives additional details about the company's liabilities. Note 10 shows the interest rates and the maturity dates of Southwest's long-term debt. Investors need these data to evaluate the company. The note also reports

- current maturities of long-term debt ($163 million) as a current liability.
- long-term debt (excluding current maturities) of $3,498 million.

Trace these amounts from the Note to the balance sheet. Working back and forth between the financial statements and the related notes is an important part of financial analysis. You now have the tools to understand the liabilities reported on an actual balance sheet.

Reporting the Fair Market Value of Long-Term Debt

Generally accepted accounting principles require companies to report the fair market value of their long-term debt. At December 31, 2008, Southwest Airlines' Note 11 included this excerpt:

> **The estimated fair value of the Company's long-term debt was $3,163 million.**

Overall, the fair market value of Southwest's long-term debt is about $335 million less than its carrying amount on books ($3,498). Fair market values of publicly-traded debt are based on quoted market prices, which fluctuate with interest rates and overall market conditions. Therefore, at any one time, fair market values for various obligations can either exceed or be less than their carrying amounts.

Reporting Financing Activities on the Statement of Cash Flows

The Southwest Airlines consolidated balance sheet (p. 468) shows that the company finances 65% of its operations with debt. Southwest's debt ratio is 65%. Let's examine Southwest's financing activities as reported on its statement of cash flows. Exhibit 8-12 is an excerpt from Southwest's consolidated statement of cash flows.

EXHIBIT 8-12 | **Consolidated Statement of Cash Flows (partial; adapted) for Southwest Airlines Co.**

Southwest Airlines Co.
Consolidated Statement of Cash Flows (Adapted)

(In millions)	Year Ended December 31, 2008
Cash Flow from Operating Activities:	
Net cash provided by operating activities	$(1,521)
Cash Flow from Investing Activities:	
Net cash used for investing activities	$ (978)
Cash Flow from Financing Activities:	
Issuance of long-term debt	$ 1,491
Payments of long-term debt	(55)
Other financing sources	218
Net cash from financing activities	$ 1,654
Net decrease in Cash	$ (845)

Southwest used more cash from operations than it provided in 2008 by over $1.5 billion. This was largely due to a global economic recession made worse by a four-month spike in fuel prices. During 2008, Southwest's major source of cash ($1,654 million) was from financing, mostly with long-term debt. Southwest borrowed $1.5 billion and paid off only $55 million. You can see that Southwest is greatly increasing its debt position. Borrowing on a long-term basis enabled Southwest to invest $978 million, mostly in equipment, in order to keep growing during turbulent times. The company ended 2008 with a net decrease of $845 (−$1,521 − $978 + $1,654) million in cash.

END-OF-CHAPTER SUMMARY PROBLEM

The **Cessna Aircraft Company** has outstanding an issue of 8% convertible bonds that mature in 2018. Suppose the bonds are dated October 1, 2010, and pay interest each April 1 and October 1.

I Requirements

1. Complete the following effective-interest amortization table through October 1, 2012.

   Bond Data

   Maturity (face) value—$100,000

   Stated interest rate—8%

   Interest paid—4% semiannually, $4,000 ($100,000 × 0.08 × 6/12)

   Market interest rate at the time of issue—9% annually, 4 1/2% semiannually

   Issue price—93.5

	Amortization Table				
	A	B	C	D	E
Semiannual Interest Date	Interest Payment (4% of Maturity Amount)	Interest Expense (4½% of Preceding Bond Carrying Amount)	Discount Amortization (B – A)	Discount Account Balance (Preceding D – C)	Bond Carrying Amount ($100,000 – D)
10-1-10					
4-1-11					
10-1-11					
4-1-12					
10-1-12					

2. Using the amortization table, record the following transactions:
   a. Issuance of the bonds on October 1, 2010.
   b. Accrual of interest and amortization of the bonds on December 31, 2010.
   c. Payment of interest and amortization of the bonds on April 1, 2011.
   d. Conversion of one-third of the bonds payable into no-par stock on October 2, 2012. For no-par stock, transfer the bond carrying amount into the Common Stock account. There is no Additional Paid-in Capital account.
   e. Retirement of two-thirds of the bonds payable on October 2, 2012. Purchase price of the bonds was based on their call price of 102.

Answers

I Requirement 1

	A	B	C	D	E
Semiannual Interest Date	Interest Payment (4% of Maturity Amount)	Interest Expense (4½% of Preceding Bond Carrying Amount)	Discount Amortization (B – A)	Discount Account Balance (Preceding D – C)	Bond Carrying Amount ($100,000 – D)
10-1-10				$6,500	$93,500
4-1-11	$4,000	$4,208	$208	6,292	93,708
10-1-11	4,000	4,217	217	6,075	93,925
4-1-12	4,000	4,227	227	5,848	94,152
10-1-12	4,000	4,237	237	5,611	94,389

❚ Requirement 2

a.	2010				
	Oct 1	Cash ($100,000 × 0.935)		93,500	
		Discount on Bonds Payable		6,500	
		Bonds Payable			100,000
		To issue bonds at a discount.			
b.	Dec 31	Interest Expense ($4,208 × 3/6)		2,104	
		Discount on Bonds Payable ($208 × 3/6)			104
		Interest Payable ($4,000 × 3/6)			2,000
		To accrue interest and amortize the bonds.			
c.	2011				
	Apr 1	Interest Expense ($4,208 × 3/6)		2,104	
		Interest Payable		2,000	
		Discount on Bonds Payable ($208 × 3/6)			104
		Cash			4,000
		To pay semiannual interest, part of which was			
		accrued, and amortize the bonds.			
d.	2012				
	Oct 2	Bonds Payable ($100,000 × 1/3)		33,333	
		Discount on Bonds Payable ($5,611 × 1/3)			1,870
		Common Stock ($94,389 × 1/3)			31,463
		To record conversion of bonds payable.			
e.	Oct 2	Bonds Payable ($100,000 × 2/3)		66,667	
		Loss on Retirement of Bonds		5,074	
		Discount on Bonds Payable ($5,611 × 2/3)			3,741
		Cash ($100,000 × 2/3 × 1.02)			68,000
		To retire bonds payable before maturity.			

REVIEW LIABILITIES

Quick Check (Answers are given on page 531.)

1. Which of the following is *not* an estimated liability?
   a. Product warranties
   b. Vacation pay
   c. Income taxes
   d. Allowance for bad debts

2. Recording estimated warranty expense in the current year *best* follows which accounting principle?

   a. Historical cost
   b. Consistency
   c. Full disclosure
   d. Materiality
   e. Matching

3. Crank the Volume grants a 120-day warranty on all stereos. Historically, approximately 1% of all sales prove to be defective. Sales in March are $450,000. In March, $3,800 of defective units are returned for replacement. What entry must Crank the Volume make at the end of March to record the warranty expense?
   a. Debit Warranty Expense and credit Estimated Warranty Payable, $3,800.
   b. Debit Warranty Expense and credit Estimated Warranty Payable, $4,500.
   c. Debit Warranty Expense and credit Cash, $4,500.
   d. No entry is needed at March 31.

4. Expedition Camera Co. was organized to sell a single product that carries a 45-day warranty against defects. Engineering estimates indicate that 4% of the units sold will prove defective and require an average repair cost of $25 per unit. During Expedition's first month of operations, total sales were 900 units; by the end of the month, 15 defective units had been repaired. The liability for product warranties at month-end should be
   a. $1,275.   **d.** $900.
   b. $375.   **e.** none of these.
   c. $525.

5. A contingent liability should be recorded in the accounts
   a. if the amount can be reasonably estimated.
   b. if the amount is due in cash within one year.
   c. if the related future event will probably occur.
   d. Both b and c
   e. Both a and c

6. An unsecured bond is a
   a. mortgage bond.   **d.** serial bond.
   b. debenture bond.   **e.** term bond.
   c. registered bond.

7. The Discount on Bonds Payable account
   a. is expensed at the bond's maturity.   **d.** is a contra account to Bonds Payable.
   b. is a miscellaneous revenue account.   **e.** is an expense account.
   c. has a normal credit balance.

8. The discount on a bond payable becomes
   a. a reduction in interest expense over the life of the bonds.
   b. a liability in the year the bonds are sold.
   c. additional interest expense over the life of the bonds.
   d. a reduction in interest expense the year the bonds mature.
   e. additional interest expense the year the bonds are sold.

9. A bond that matures in installments is called a
   a. term bond.   **d.** zero coupon.
   b. secured bond.   **e.** callable bond.
   c. serial bond.

10. The carrying value of Bonds Payable equals
    a. Bonds Payable + Accrued Interest.
    b. Bonds Payable + Discount on Bonds Payable.
    c. Bonds Payable – Premium on Bonds Payable.
    d. Bonds Payable – Discount on Bonds Payable.

11. A corporation issues bonds that pay interest each May 1 and November 1. The corporation's December 31 adjusting entry may include a
    a. credit to Discount on Bonds Payable.   **d.** debit to Interest Payable.
    b. credit to Cash.   **e.** debit to Cash.
    c. credit to Interest Expense.

Use this information to answer questions 12–16.

McCabe Corporation issued $550,000 of 7% 10-year bonds. The bonds are dated and sold on January 1, 2011. Interest payment dates are January 1 and July 1. The bonds are issued for $512,408 to yield the market interest rate of 8%. Use the effective-interest method for questions 12–15.

12. What is the amount of interest expense that McCabe Corporation will record on July 1, 2011, the first semiannual interest payment date? (All amounts rounded to the nearest dollar.)
    a. $20,496   c. $19,250
    b. $38,500   d. $22,000

13. What is the amount of discount amortization that McCabe Corporation will record on July 1, 2011, the first semiannual interest payment date?
    a. $0   c. $1,246
    b. $2,562   d. $1,504

14. What is the total cash payment for interest for each 12-month period? (All amounts rounded to the nearest dollar.)
    a. $22,000   c. $40,993
    b. $38,500   d. $44,000

15. What is the carrying amount of the bonds on the January 1, 2012 balance sheet?
    a. $514,950   c. $512,408
    b. $513,654   d. $516,167

16. Using straight-line amortization, the carrying amount of McCabe Corporation's bonds at December 31, 2011, is
    a. $513,654.   c. $514,950.
    b. $512,408.   d. $516,167.

Accounting Vocabulary

accrued expense (p. 470) An expense incurred but not yet paid in cash. Also called *accrued liability*.

accrued liability (p. 470) A liability for an expense that has not yet been paid. Also called *accrued expense*.

bonds payable (p. 477) Groups of notes payable issued to multiple lenders called *bondholders*.

callable bond (p. 491) Bonds that are paid off early at a specified price at the option of the issuer.

capital lease (p. 496) Lease agreement in which the lessee assumes, in substance, the risks and rewards of asset ownership. In the United States, a lease is assumed to be a capital lease if it meets any one of four criteria: (1) The lease transfers title of the leased asset to the lessee. (2) The lease contains a bargain purchase option. (3) The lease term is 75% or more of the estimated useful life of the leased asset. (4) The present value of the lease payments is 90% or more of the market value of the leased asset.

convertible bonds (or notes) (p. 491) Bonds or notes that may be converted into the issuing company's common stock at the investor's option.

current portion of long-term debt (p. 473) The amount of the principal that is payable within one year.

debentures (p. 479) Unsecured bonds—bonds backed only by the good faith of the borrower.

discount (on a bond) (p. 479) Excess of a bond's face (par) value over its issue price.

earnings per share (EPS) (p. 493) Amount of a company's net income per share of its outstanding common stock.

interest-coverage ratio (p. 494) Another name for the *times-interest-earned ratio*.

lease (p. 495) Rental agreement in which the tenant (lessee) agrees to make rent payments to the property owner (lessor) in exchange for the use of the asset.

lessee (p. 495) Tenant in a lease agreement.

lessor (p. 495) Property owner in a lease agreement.

leverage (p. 493) Using borrowed funds to increase the return on equity. Successful use of leverage means earning more income on borrowed money than the related interest expense, thereby increasing the earnings for the owners of the business. Also called *trading on the equity*.

market interest rate (p. 480) Interest rate that investors demand for loaning their money. Also called *effective interest rate*.

operating lease (p. 496) A lease in which the lessee does not assume the risks or rewards of asset ownership.

payroll (p. 470) Employee compensation, a major expense of many businesses.

pension (p. 498) Employee compensation that will be received during retirement.

premium (on a bond) (p. 479) Excess of a bond's issue price over its face (par) value.

present value (p. 479) Amount a person would invest now to receive a greater amount at a future date.

serial bonds (p. 479) Bonds that mature in installments over a period of time.

short-term notes payable (p. 469) Note payable due within one year.

stated interest rate (p. 480) Interest rate that determines the amount of cash interest the borrower pays and the investor receives each year.

term bonds (p. 479) Bonds that all mature at the same time for a particular issue.

times-interest-earned ratio (p. 494) Ratio of income from operations to interest expense. Measures the number of times that operating income can cover interest expense. Also called the *interest-coverage ratio*.

trading on the equity (p. 493) Earning more income on borrowed money than the related interest expense, thereby increasing the earnings for the owners of the business. Also called *leverage*.

underwriter (p. 478) Organization that purchases the bonds from an issuing company and resells them to its clients or sells the bonds for a commission, agreeing to buy all unsold bonds.

ASSESS YOUR PROGRESS

Short Exercises

S8-1 *(Learning Objective 1: Accounting for a note payable)* Franklin Sports Authority purchased inventory costing $5,000 by signing an 8% short-term note payable. The purchase occurred on September 30, 2010. Franklin pays annual interest each year on September 30. Journalize the company's (a) purchase of inventory, (b) accrual of interest expense on June 30, 2011, which is the year-end, and (c) payment of the note plus interest on September 30, 2011. (Round your answers to the nearest whole number.)

S8-2 *(Learning Objective 1: Reporting a short-term note payable and the related interest in the financial statements)* This short exercise works with Short Exercise 8-1.

1. Refer to the data in Short Exercise 8-1. Show what the company would report on its balance sheet at June 30, 2011, and on its income statement for the year ended on that date.
2. What single item will the financial statements for the year ended June 30, 2012, report? Identify the financial statement, the item, and its amount.

S8-3 *(Learning Objective 1: Accounting for warranty expense and estimated warranty payable)* Trekster USA guarantees automobiles against defects for five years or 55,000 miles, whichever comes first. Suppose Trekster USA can expect warranty costs during the five-year period to add up to 6% of sales. Assume that Trekster USA dealer in Atlanta, Georgia, made sales of $483,000 during 2010. Trekster USA received cash for 30% of the sales and took notes receivable for the remainder. Payments to satisfy customer warranty claims totaled $19,000 during 2010.

1. Record the sales, warranty expense, and warranty payments for Trekster USA.
2. Post to the Estimated Warranty Payable T-account. The beginning balance was $11,000. At the end of 2010, how much in estimated warranty payable does Trekster USA owe to its customers?

S8-4 *(Learning Objective 1: Applying GAAP; reporting warranties in the financial statements)* Refer to the data given in Short Exercise 8-3. What amount of warranty expense will Trekster USA report during 2010? Which accounting principle addresses this situation? Does the warranty expense for the year equal the year's cash payments for warranties? Explain the relevant accounting principle as it applies to measuring warranty expense.

S8-5 (*Learning Objective 1: Interpreting a company's contingent liabilities*)   Marley-David, Inc., the motorcycle manufacturer, included the following note in its annual report:

> **NOTES TO CONSOLIDATED FINANCIAL STATEMENTS**
> **7 (In Part): Commitments and Contingencies**
> The Company self-insures its product liability losses in the United States up to $3.2 million (catastrophic coverage is maintained for individual claims in excess of $3.2 million up to $25.2 million). Outside the United States, the Company is insured for product liability up to $25.2 million per individual claim and in the aggregate.

1. Why are these *contingent* (versus *real*) liabilities?
2. In the United States, how can the contingent liability become a real liability for Marley-David? What are the limits to the company's product liabilities in the United States?
3. How can a contingency outside the United States become a real liability for the company? How does Marley-David's potential liability differ for claims outside the United States?

S8-6 (*Learning Objective 2: Pricing bonds*)   Compute the price of the following bonds:

a. $300,000 issued at 75.75
b. $300,000 issued at 102.75
c. $300,000 issued at 94.50
d. $300,000 issued at 104.50

S8-7 (*Learning Objective 2: Determining bond prices at par, discount, or premium*) Determine whether the following bonds payable will be issued at maturity value, at a premium, or at a discount:

a. The market interest rate is 5%. Carlisle Corp. issues bonds payable with a stated rate of 4 1/2%.
b. Oiler, Inc., issued 7% bonds payable when the market rate was 6 3/4%.
c. Toronto Corporation issued 5% bonds when the market interest rate was 5%.
d. Ontario Company issued bonds payable that pay stated interest of 6%. At issuance, the market interest rate was 7 1/4%.

S8-8 (*Learning Objective 2: Journalizing basic bond payable transactions; bonds issued at par*)   Deer Corp. issued 15-year bonds payable with a face amount of $80,000, when the market interest rate was 5.5%. Assume that the accounting year of Deer ends on December 31. Journalize the following transactions for Deer. Include an explanation for each entry.

a. Issuance of the bonds payable at par on July 1, 2010.
b. Accrual of interest expense on December 31, 2010 (rounded to the nearest dollar).
c. Payment of cash interest on January 1, 2011.
d. Payment of the bonds payable at maturity. (Give the date.)

S8-9 (*Learning Objectives 2, 3: Issuing bonds payable; amortizing bonds by the effective-interest method*)   GIT, Inc., issued $600,000 of 5%, 12-year bonds payable at a price of 77 on March 31, 2010. The market interest rate at the date of issuance was 8%, and the GIT bonds pay interest semiannually.

1. Prepare an effective-interest amortization table for the bonds through the first three interest payments. Round amounts to the nearest dollar.
2. Record GIT, Inc.'s issuance of the bonds on March 31, 2010, and payment of the first semiannual interest amount and amortization of the bond discount on September 30, 2010. Explanations are not required.

S8-10 (*Learning Objectives 2, 3: Accounting for bonds payable; analyzing data on long-term debt*)   Use the amortization table that you prepared for GIT's bonds in Short Exercise 8-9 to answer the following questions:

1. How much cash did GIT borrow on March 31, 2010? How much cash will GIT pay back at maturity on March 31, 2022?

2. How much cash interest will GIT pay each six months?

3. How much interest expense will GIT report on September 30, 2010, and on March 31, 2011? Why does the amount of interest expense increase each period?

S8-11 (*Learning Objectives 2, 3: Determining bonds payable amounts; amortizing bonds by the straight-line method*)   Sunset Drive-Ins Ltd. borrowed money by issuing $5,000,000 of 3% bonds payable at 36.5 on July 1, 2010. The bonds are 10-year bonds and pay interest each January 1 and July 1.

1. How much cash did Sunset receive when it issued the bonds payable?
2. How much must Sunset pay back at maturity? When is the maturity date?
3. How much cash interest will Sunset pay each six months?
4. How much interest expense will Sunset report each six months? Assume the straight-line amortization method.

S8-12 (*Learning Objectives 2, 3: Issuing bonds payable; accruing interest; amortizing bonds by the straight-line method*)   Sunset Drive-Ins Ltd. issued a $500,000, 8%, 10-year bond payable on July 1, 2010, at a price of 94. Also assume that Sunset's accounting year ends on December 31. Journalize the following transactions for Sunset Drive-Ins Ltd., including an explanation for each entry:

a. Issuance of the bond payable on July 1, 2010.
b. Accrual of interest expense and amortization of bonds on December 31, 2010. (Use the straight-line amortization method, and round amounts to the nearest dollar.)
c. Payment of the first semiannual interest amount on January 1, 2011.

S8-13 (*Learning Objective 4: Computing earnings-per-share effects of financing with bonds versus stock*)   Speedtown Marina needs to raise $3 million to expand the company. Speedtown Marina is considering the issuance of either:

- $3,000,000 of 8% bonds payable to borrow the money, or
- 100,000 shares of common stock at $30 per share.

Before any new financing, Speedtown Marina expects to earn net income of $300,000, and the company already has 100,000 shares of common stock outstanding. Speedtown Marina believes the expansion will increase income before interest and income tax by $500,000. The income tax rate is 35%.

Prepare an analysis to determine which plan is likely to result in the higher earnings per share. Based solely on the earnings-per-share comparison, which financing plan would you recommend for Speedtown Marina?

S8-14 (*Learning Objective 4: Computing the times-interest-earned ratio*)   Houle Plumbing Products Ltd. reported the following data in 2010 (in billions):

writing assignment ■

	2010
Net operating revenues...............	$29.7
Operating expenses	24.7
Operating income.......................	5.0
Nonoperating items:	
Interest expense......................	(1.6)
Other	(0.1)
Net income.................................	$ 3.3

Compute Houle's times-interest-earned ratio, and write a sentence to explain what the ratio value means. Would you be willing to lend Houle $1 billion? State your reason.

S8-15 (*Learning Objective 5: Reporting liabilities, including capital lease obligations*) Like Home, Inc., includes the following selected accounts in its general ledger at December 31, 2010:

Bonds payable	$400,000
Equipment	112,000
Current portion of bonds payable	51,000
Notes payable, long-term	300,000
Interest payable (due March 1, 2011)	1,000
Accounts payable	36,000
Discount on bonds payable (all long-term)	12,000
Accounts receivable	27,000

Prepare the liabilities section of Like Home, Inc.'s balance sheet at December 31, 2010, to show how the company would report these items. Report total current liabilities and total liabilities.

Exercises

All of the A and B exercises can be found within MyAccountingLab, an online homework and practice environment. Your instructor may ask you to complete these exercises using MyAccountingLab.

(Group A)

E8-16A (*Learning Objective 1: Accounting for warranty expense and the related liability*) The accounting records of From the Earth Ceramics included the following balances at the end of the period:

Estimated Warranty Payable	Sales Revenue	Warranty Expense
Beg bal 3,000	161,000	

In the past, From the Earth's warranty expense has been 7% of sales. During 2010 the business paid $8,000 to satisfy the warranty claims.

❚ *Requirements*

1. Journalize From the Earth's warranty expense for the period and the company's cash payments to satisfy warranty claims. Explanations are not required.
2. Show what From the Earth will report on its income statement and balance sheet for this situation.
3. Which data item from Requirement 2 will affect From the Earth's current ratio? Will From the Earth's current ratio increase or decrease as a result of this item?

E8-17A *(Learning Objective 1: Recording and reporting current liabilities)*   TransWorld Publishing completed the following transactions for one subscriber during 2010:

Oct 1	Sold a one-year subscription, collecting cash of $1,400, plus sales tax of 8%.
Nov 15	Remitted (paid) the sales tax to the state of Massachusetts.
Dec 31	Made the necessary adjustment at year-end.

❙ Requirement

1. Journalize these transactions (explanations not required). Then report any liability on the company's balance sheet at December 31, 2010.

E8-18A *(Learning Objective 1: Reporting payroll expense and liabilities)*   Perform Talent Search has an annual payroll of $200,000. In addition, the company incurs payroll tax expense of 8%. At December 31, Perform owes salaries of $8,100 and FICA and other payroll tax of $800. The company will pay these amounts early next year. Show what Perform will report for the foregoing on its income statement and year-end balance sheet.

E8-19A *(Learning Objective 1: Recording note payable transactions)*   Assume that Crandell Company completed the following note-payable transactions.

2010	
May 1	Purchased delivery truck costing $83,000 by issuing a one-year, 6% note payable.
Dec 31	Accrued interest on the note payable.
2011	
May 1	Paid the note payable at maturity.

❙ Requirements

1. How much interest expense must be accrued at December 31, 2010? (Round your answer to the nearest whole dollar.)
2. Determine the amount of Crandell's final payment on May 1, 2011.
3. How much interest expense will Crandell report for 2010 and for 2011? (Round your answer to the nearest whole dollar.)

E8-20A *(Learning Objective 1: Accounting for income tax)*   At December 31, 2010, Souza Real Estate reported a current liability for income tax payable of $180,000. During 2011, Souza earned income of $1,200,000 before income tax. The company's income tax rate during 2011 was 36%. Also during 2011, Souza paid income taxes of $370,000.

How much income tax payable did Souza Real Estate report on its balance sheet at December 31, 2011? How much income tax expense did Souza report on its 2011 income statement?

E8-21A *(Learning Objectives 1, 5: Analyzing liabilities)* Mountainside Manors, Inc., builds environmentally sensitive structures. The company's 2010 revenues totaled $2,760 million, and at December 31, 2010, the company had $650 million in current assets. The December 31, 2010 and 2009, balance sheets reported the liabilities and stockholders' equity as follows:

At year-end (In millions)	2010	2009
Liabilities and Stockholders' Equity		
Current Liabilities		
Accounts payable	$ 138	$ 179
Accrued expenses	155	172
Employee compensation and benefits	38	20
Current portion of long-term debt.......................	9	24
Total Current Liabilities...................................	340	395
Long-Term Debt	1,494	1,323
Post-Retirement Benefits Payable	122	123
Other Liabilities	12	8
Stockholders' Equity	2,027	1,784
Total Liabilities and Stockholders' Equity..............	$3,995	$3,633

❚ Requirements

1. Describe each of Mountainside Manors, Inc.'s liabilities and state how the liability arose.
2. What were the company's total assets at December 31, 2010? Was the company's debt ratio at the end of 2010 high, low, or in a middle range?

E8-22A *(Learning Objective 1: Reporting a contingent liability)* Roden Security Systems' revenues for 2010 totaled $6.3 million. As with most companies, Roden is a defendant in lawsuits related to its products. Note 14 of the Roden Annual Report for 2010 reported:

> **14. Contingencies**
> The company is involved in various legal proceedings.... It is the Company's policy to accrue for amounts related to these legal matters if it is probable that a liability has been incurred and an amount is reasonably estimable.

❚ Requirements

1. Suppose Roden's lawyers believe that a significant legal judgment against the company is reasonably possible. How should Roden report this situation in its financial statements?
2. Suppose Roden's lawyers believe it is probable that a $1.5 million judgment will be rendered against the company. Report this situation in Roden's financial statements. Journalize any entry requirements by GAAP. Explanations are not required.

E8-23A *(Learning Objectives 1, 5: Reporting current and long-term liabilities)* Assume that McKinley Electronics completed these selected transactions during June 2010:

a. Sales of $2,200,000 are subject to estimated warranty cost of 7%. The estimated warranty payable at the beginning of the year was $34,000, and warranty payments for the year totaled $50,000.
b. On June 1, McKinley Electronics signed a $55,000 note payable that requires annual payments of $13,750 plus 6% interest on the unpaid balance each June 2.

c. Music For You, Inc., a chain of music stores, ordered $125,000 worth of CD players. With its order, Music For You, Inc., sent a check for $125,000 in advance, and McKinley shipped $70,000 of the goods. McKinley will ship the remainder of the goods on July 3, 2010.

d. The June payroll of $260,000 is subject to employee withheld income tax of $30,000 and FICA tax of 7.65%. On June 30, McKinley pays employees their take-home pay and accrues all tax amounts.

I Requirement

1. Report these items on McKinley Electronics' balance sheet at June 30, 2010.

E8-24A (*Learning Objectives 2, 3: Issuing bonds payable (discount); paying and accruing interest; amortizing the bonds by the straight-line method*) On January 31, Driftwood Logistics, Inc., issued 10-year, 6% bonds payable with a face value of $13,000,000. The bonds were issued at 94 and pay interest on January 31 and July 31. Driftwood Logistics, Inc., amortizes bonds by the straight-line method. Record (a) issuance of the bonds on January 31, (b) the semiannual interest payment and amortization of bond discount on July 31, and (c) the interest accrual and discount amortization on December 31.

E8-25A (*Learning Objectives 2, 3: Measuring cash amounts for a bond payable (premium); amortizing the bonds by the straight-line method*) Federal Bank has $500,000 of 7% debenture bonds outstanding. The bonds were issued at 103 in 2010 and mature in 2030.

I Requirements

1. How much cash did Federal Bank receive when it issued these bonds?
2. How much cash in *total* will Federal Bank pay the bondholders through the maturity date of the bonds?
3. Take the difference between your answers to Requirements 1 and 2. This difference represents Federal Bank's total interest expense over the life of the bonds.
4. Compute Federal Bank's annual interest expense by the straight-line amortization method. Multiply this amount by 20. Your 20-year total should be the same as your answer to Requirement 3.

E8-26A (*Learning Objectives 2, 3: Issuing bonds payable (discount); recording interest payments and the related bond amortization*) Goal Sports Ltd. is authorized to issue $3,000,000 of 10%, 10-year bonds payable. On December 31, 2010, when the market interest rate is 12%, the company issues $2,400,000 of the bonds and receives cash of $2,128,800. Goal Sports Ltd. amortizes bond discounts by the effective-interest method. The semiannual interest dates are June 30 and December 31.

■ spreadsheet

I Requirements

1. Prepare a bond amortization table for the first four semiannual interest periods.
2. Record issuance of the bonds payable on December 31, 2010, the first semiannual interest payment on June 30, 2011, and the second payment on December 31, 2011.

E8-27A (*Learning Objectives 2, 3: Issuing bonds payable (premium); recording interest accrual and payment and the related bond amortization*) On June 30, 2010, the market interest rate is 4%. Score Sports Ltd. issues $800,000 of 5%, 30-year bonds payable at 117.38. The bonds pay interest on June 30 and December 31. Score Sports Ltd. amortizes bonds by the effective-interest method.

■ spreadsheet

I Requirements

1. Prepare a bond amortization table for the first four semiannual interest periods.
2. Record the issuance of bonds payable on June 30, 2010, the payment of interest on December 31, 2010, and the payment of interest on June 30, 2011.

■ **spreadsheet**

E8-28A *(Learning Objective 3: Creating a bond amortization schedule (discount))* Dracut Co. issued $100,000 of 8% (0.08), 10-year bonds payable on January 1, 2010, when the market interest rate was 10% (0.10). The company pays interest annually at year-end. The issue price of the bonds was $87,711.

❙ Requirement

1. Create a spreadsheet model to prepare a schedule to amortize the bonds. Use the effective-interest method of amortization. (Round to the nearest dollar).

E8-29A *(Learning Objective 2: Recording conversion of notes payable)* Coastalview Imaging Ltd. issued $3,300,000 of 6% notes payable on December 31, 2010, at a price of 95. The notes' term to maturity is 20 years. After four years, the notes may be converted into Coastalview common stock. Each $1,000 face amount of notes is convertible into 50 shares of $1 par common stock. On December 31, 2015, note holders exercised their right to convert all the notes into common stock.

❙ Requirements

1. Without making journal entries, compute the carrying amount of the notes payable at December 31, 2015, immediately before the conversion. Coastalview Imaging Ltd. uses the straight-line method to amortize bonds.
2. All amortization has been recorded properly. Journalize the conversion transaction at December 31, 2015.

E8-30A *(Learning Objective 4: Measuring the times-interest-earned ratio)* Companies that operate in different industries may have very different financial ratio values. These differences may grow even wider when we compare companies located in different countries.

Compare three leading companies on their current ratio, debt ratio, and times-interest-earned ratio. Compute three ratios for Company A, Company N, and Company S.

(Amounts in millions or billions)	Company A	Company N	Company S
Income data			
Total revenues.............................	$9,723	¥7,311	€136,431
Operating income........................	291	222	5,581
Interest expense...........................	42	31	671
Net income..................................	27	15	441
Asset and liability data			
(Amounts in millions or billions)			
Total current assets	431	5,932	170,140
Long-term assets	139	39	45,315
Total current liabilities................	197	2,197	72,400
Long-term liabilities	137	2,341	110,737
Stockholders' equity....................	236	1,433	32,318

Based on your computed ratio values, which company looks the least risky?

writing assignment ■

E8-31A *(Learning Objective 4: Analyzing alternative plans for raising money)* First Bank Financial Services is considering two plans for raising $800,000 to expand operations. Plan A is to borrow at 10%, and plan B is to issue 200,000 shares of common stock at $4.00 per share. Before any new financing, First Bank Financial Services has net income of $600,000 and 200,000 shares of common stock outstanding. Assume you own most of First Bank Financial Services' existing stock. Management believes the company can use the new funds to earn additional income of $800,000 before interest and taxes. First Bank Financial Services' income tax rate is 25%.

❚ Requirements

1. Analyze First Bank Financial Services situation to determine which plan will result in higher earnings per share.
2. Which plan results in the higher earnings per share? Which plan allows you to retain control of the company? Which plan creates more financial risk for the company? Which plan do you prefer? Why? Present your conclusion in a memo to First Bank Financial Services board of directors.

(Group B)

E8-32B (*Learning Objective 1: Accounting for warranty expense and the related liability*)   The accounting records of Made from Clay Ceramics included the following balances at the end of the period:

Estimated Warranty Payable	Sales Revenue	Warranty Expense
Beg bal 4,000	160,000	

In the past, Made from Clay's warranty expense has been 4% of sales. During 2010 the business paid $5,000 to satisfy the warranty claims.

❚ Requirements

1. Journalize Made from Clay's warranty expense for the period and the company's cash payments to satisfy warranty claims. Explanations are not required.
2. Show what Made from Clay will report on its income statement and balance sheet for this situation.
3. Which data item from Requirement 2 will affect Made from Clay's current ratio? Will Made from Clay's current ratio increase or decrease as a result of this item?

E8-33B (*Learning Objective 1: Recording and reporting current liabilities*)   Trevor Publishing completed the following transactions for one subscriber during 2010:

Oct 1	Sold a one-year subscription, collecting cash of $1,300, plus sales tax of 9%.
Nov 15	Remitted (paid) the sales tax to the state of Massachusetts.
Dec 31	Made the necessary adjustment at year-end.

❚ Requirement

1. Journalize these transactions (explanations not required). Then report any liability on the company's balance sheet at December 31.

E8-34B (*Learning Objective 1: Reporting payroll expense and liabilities*)   Potvin Talent Search has an annual payroll of $160,000. In addition, the company incurs payroll tax expense of 9%. At December 31, Potvin owes salaries of $7,900 and FICA and other payroll tax of $850. The company will pay these amounts early next year.

Show what Potvin will report for the foregoing on its income statement and year-end balance sheet.

E8-35B (*Learning Objective 1: Recording note payable transactions*)   Assume that Concilio Company completed the following note-payable transactions:

2010	
Mar 1	Purchased delivery truck costing $82,000 by issuing a one-year, 5% note payable.
Dec 31	Accrued interest on the note payable.
2011	
Mar 1	Paid the note payable at maturity.

I *Requirements*

1. How much interest expense must be accrued at December 31, 2010? (Round your answer to the nearest whole dollar.)
2. Determine the amount of Concilio's final payment on March 1, 2011.
3. How much interest expense will Concilio report for 2010 and for 2011? (Round your answer to the nearest whole dollar.)

E8-36B (*Learning Objective 1: Accounting for income tax*)   At December 31, 2010, Saglio Real Estate reported a current liability for income tax payable of $190,000. During 2011, Saglio earned income of $1,500,000 before income tax. The company's income tax rate during 2011 was 25%. Also during 2011, Saglio paid income taxes of $300,000.

How much income tax payable did Saglio Real Estate report on its balance sheet at December 31, 2011? How much income tax expense did Saglio report on its 2011 income statement?

writing assignment ■

E8-37B (*Learning Objectives 1, 5: Analyzing liabilities*)   New Planet Structures, Inc., builds environmentally sensitive structures. The company's 2010 revenues totaled $2,815 million, and at December 31, 2010, the company had $654 million in current assets. The December 31, 2010 and 2009, balance sheets reported the liabilities and stockholders' equity as follows.

At Year-end (In millions)	2010	2009
Liabilities and Stockholders' Equity		
Current Liabilities..		
Accounts payable..	$ 145	$ 183
Accrued expenses..	161	182
Employee compensation and benefits..................	31	15
Current portion of long-term debt.......................	3	9
Total Current Liabilities...................................	340	389
Long-Term Debt	1,488	1,317
Post-Retirement Benefits Payable	129	135
Other Liabilities..	11	7
Stockholders' Equity	2,030	1,776
Total Liabilities and Stockholders' Equity..............	$3,998	$3,624

I *Requirements*

1. Describe each of New Planet Structures, Inc.'s liabilities and state how the liability arose.
2. What were the company's total assets at December 31, 2010? Was the company's debt ratio at the end of 2010 high, low, or in a middle range?

E8-38B (*Learning Objective 1: Reporting a contingent liability*) Peterson Security Systems' revenues for 2010 totaled $26.2 million. As with most companies, Peterson is a defendant in lawsuits related to its products. Note 14 of the Peterson Annual Report for 2010 reported the following:

> **14. Contingencies**
> The company is involved in various legal proceedings.... It is the Company's policy to accrue for amounts related to these legal matters if it is probable that a liability has been incurred and an amount is reasonably estimable.

I **Requirements**

1. Suppose Peterson's lawyers believe that a significant legal judgment against the company is reasonably possible. How should Peterson report this situation in its financial statements?
2. Suppose Peterson's lawyers believe it is probable that a $2.5 million judgment will be rendered against the company. Report this situation in Peterson's financial statements. Journalize any entry required by GAAP. Explanations are not required.

E8-39B (*Learning Objectives 1, 5: Reporting current and long-term liabilities*) Assume Five Mile Electronics completed these selected transactions during September 2010.

    a. Sales of $2,150,000 are subject to estimated warranty cost of 5%. The estimated warranty payable at the beginning of the year was $33,000, and warranty payments for the year totaled $57,000.
    b. On September 1, Five Mile Electronics signed a $40,000 note payable that requires annual payments of $10,000 plus 4% interest on the unpaid balance each September 2.
    c. Music For You, Inc., a chain of music stores, ordered $110,000 worth of CD players. With its order, Music For You, Inc., sent a check for $110,000, and Five Mile Electronics shipped $90,000 of the goods. Five Mile Electronics will ship the remainder of the goods on October 3, 2010.
    d. The September payroll of $240,000 is subject to employee withheld income tax of $30,000 and FICA tax of 7.65%. On September 30, Five Mile Electronics pays employees their take-home pay and accrues all tax amounts.

I **Requirement**

1. Report these items on Five Mile Electronics' balance sheet at September 30, 2010.

E8-40B (*Learning Objectives 2, 3: Issuing bonds payable (discount); paying and accruing interest; amortizing the bonds by the straight-line method*) On January 31, Daughtry Logistics, Inc., issued five-year, 5% bonds payable with a face value of $11,000,000. The bonds were issued at 95 and pay interest on January 31 and July 31. Daughtry Logistics, Inc., amortizes bond discounts by the straight-line method. Record (a) issuance of the bonds on January 31, (b) the semiannual interest payment and amortization of bond discount on July 31, and (c) the interest accrual and discount amortization on December 31.

E8-41B (*Learning Objectives 2, 3: Measuring cash amounts for a bond payable (premium); amortizing the bonds by the straight-line method*) Commonwealth Bank has $400,000 of 9% debenture bonds outstanding. The bonds were issued at 104 in 2010 and mature in 2030.

I **Requirements**

1. How much cash did Commonwealth Bank receive when it issued these bonds?
2. How much cash in *total* will Commonwealth Bank pay the bondholders through the maturity date of the bonds?
3. Take the difference between your answers to Requirements 1 and 2. This difference represents Commonwealth Bank's total interest expense over the life of the bonds.
4. Compute Commonwealth Bank's annual interest expense by the straight-line amortization method. Multiply this amount by 20. Your 20-year total should be the same as your answer to Requirement 3.

■ **spreadsheet**

E8-42B (*Learning Objectives 2, 3: Issuing bonds payable (discount); recording interest payments and the related bond amortization*)   First Place Sports Ltd. is authorized to issue $1,000,000 of 9%, 10-year bonds payable. On December 31, 2010, when the market interest rate is 10%, the company issues $800,000 of the bonds and receives cash of $750,232. First Place Sports amortizes bonds by the effective-interest method. The semiannual interest dates are June 30 and December 31.

I Requirements

1. Prepare a bond amortization table for the first four semiannual interest periods.
2. Record issuance of the bonds payable on December 31, 2010, the first semiannual interest payment on June 30, 2011, and the second payment on December 31, 2011.

■ **spreadsheet**

E8-43B (*Learning Objectives 2, 3: Issuing bonds payable (premium); recording interest accrual and payment and the related bond amortization*)   On June 30, 2010, the market interest rate is 9%. Team Sports Ltd. issues $3,200,000 of 10%, 10-year bonds payable at 106.5. The bonds pay interest on June 30 and December 31. Team Sports Ltd. amortizes bonds by the effective-interest method.

I Requirements

1. Prepare a bond amortization table for the first four semiannual interest periods.
2. Record the issuance of bonds payable on June 30, 2010, the payment of interest on December 31, 2010, and the payment of interest on June 30, 2011.

■ **spreadsheet**

E8-44B (*Learning Objective 3: Creating a bond amortization schedule (discount)*)   Tewksbury Co. issued $720,000 of 11% (0.11), 10-year bonds payable on January 1, 2010, when the market interest rate was 12% (0.12). The company pays interest annually at year-end. The issue price of the bonds was $679,318.

I Requirement

1. Create a spreadsheet model to prepare a schedule to amortize the bonds. Use the effective-interest method of amortization. (Round to the nearest dollar.)

E8-45B (*Learning Objective 2: Recording conversion of notes payable*)   Worldview Imaging Ltd. issued $3,600,000 of 9% notes payable on December 31, 2010, at a price of 94. The notes' term maturity is 10 years. After four years, the notes may be converted into Worldview common stock. Each $1,000 face amount of notes is convertible into 60 shares of $1 par common stock. On December 31, 2015, noteholders exercised their right to convert all the notes into common stock.

I Requirements

1. Without making journal entries, compute the carrying amount of the notes payable at December 31, 2015, immediately before conversion. Worldview uses the straight-line method to amortize bonds.
2. All amortization has been recorded properly. Journalize the conversion transaction at December 31, 2015.

E8-46B (*Learning Objective 4: Measuring the times-interest-earned ratio*)   Companies that operate in different industries may have very different financial ratio values. These differences may grow even wider when we compare companies located in different countries.

Compare three leading companies on their current ratio, debt ratio, and times-interest-earned ratio. Compute three ratios for Company F, Company L, and Company V.

(Amounts in millions or billions)	Company F	Company L	Company V
Income data			
Total revenues............................	$9,728	¥7,312	€136,377
Operating income.......................	294	229	5,627
Interest expense...........................	43	29	687
Net income.................................	25	12	443
Asset and liability data			
(Amounts in millions or billions)			
Total current assets	433	5,414	147,378
Long-term assets	137	731	61,153
Total current liabilities................	227	2,237	72,600
Long-term liabilities	107	2,310	110,907
Stockholders' equity	236	1,598	25,024

Based on your computed ratio values, which company looks the least risky?

E8-47B (*Learning Objective 4: Analyzing alternative plans for raising money*)   First Federal Financial Services is considering two plans for raising $600,000 to expand operations. Plan A is to borrow at 5%, and plan B is to issue 100,000 shares of common stock at $6.00 per share. Before any new financing, First Federal Financial Services has net income of $400,000 and 100,000 shares of common stock outstanding. Assume you own most of First Federal Financial Services existing stock. Management believes the company can use the new funds to earn additional income of $550,000 before interest and taxes. First Federal Financial Services' income tax rate is 40%.

writing assignment ■

I Requirements

1. Analyze First Federal Financial Services situation to determine which plan will result in the higher earnings per share.
2. Which plan results in the higher earnings per share? Which plan allows you to retain control of the company? Which plan creates more financial risk for the company? Which plan do you prefer? Why? Present your conclusion in a memo to First Federal Financial Services board of directors.

Challenge Exercises

E8-48 (*Learning Objectives 1, 5: Reporting current liabilities*)   The top management of Pratt Marketing Services examines the following company accounting records at August 29, immediately before the end of the year, August 31.

Total current assets	$ 324,700
Noncurrent assets........................	1,067,500
	$1,392,200
Total current liabilities...............	$ 193,400
Noncurrent liabilities	253,400
Owners' equity............................	945,400
	$1,392,200

Suppose Pratt's management wants to achieve a current ratio of 2.25. How much in current liabilities should Pratt's pay off within the next two days in order to achieve its goal?

E8-49 *(Learning Objectives 2, 3, 5: Refinancing old bonds payable with new bonds)* Great Brands completed one of the most famous debt refinancings in history. A debt refinancing occurs when a company issues new bonds payable to retire old bonds. The company debits the old bonds payable and credits the new bonds payable.

Great Brands had $140 million of 5 3/4% bonds payable outstanding, with 21 years to maturity. Great retired these old bonds by issuing $77 million of new 11% bonds payable to the holders of the old bonds and paying the bondholders $8 million in cash. Great issued both groups of bonds at face value. At the time of the debt refinancing, Great Brands had total assets of $497 million and total liabilities of $357 million. Net income for the most recent year was $6.2 million on sales of $1 billion.

Ι Requirements

1. Journalize the debt refinancing transaction.
2. Compute annual interest expense for both the old and the new bond issues.
3. Why did Great Brands refinance the old bonds 5 3/4% payable with the new 11% bonds? Consider interest expense, net income, and the debt ratio.

writing assignment ■

E8-50 *(Learning Objectives 2, 3: Analyzing bond transactions)* This (adapted) advertisement appeared in the *Wall Street Chronicle*.

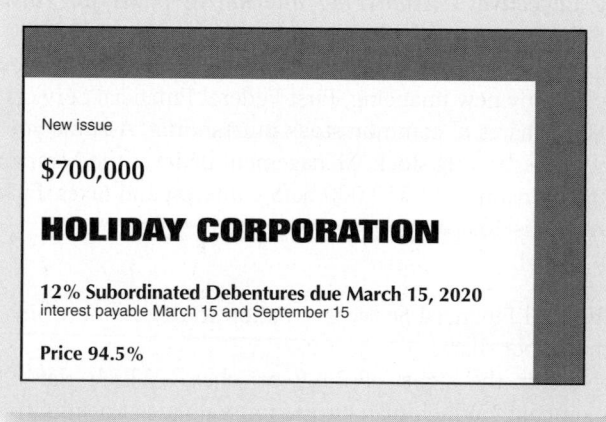

New issue

$700,000

HOLIDAY CORPORATION

12% Subordinated Debentures due March 15, 2020
interest payable March 15 and September 15

Price 94.5%

(Note: A *subordinated debenture* is an unsecured bond payable whose rights are less than the rights of other bondholders.)

Ι Requirements

1. Journalize Holiday's issuance of these bonds payable on March 15, 2010. No explanation is required, but describe the transaction in detail, indicating who received cash, who paid cash, and how much.
2. Why is the stated interest rate on these bonds so high?
3. Compute the semiannual cash interest payment on the bonds.
4. Compute the semiannual interest expense under the straight-line amortization method.
5. Compute both the first-year (from March 15, 2010, to March 15, 2011) and the second-year interest expense (March 15, 2011, to March 15, 2012) under the effective-interest amortization method. The market rate of interest at the date of issuance was 13%. Why is interest expense greater in the second year?

Quiz

Test your understanding of accounting for liabilities by answering the following questions. Select the best choice from among the possible answers given.

Q8-51 For the purpose of classifying liabilities as current or noncurrent, the term *operating cycle* refers to
a. the average time period between business recessions.
b. the time period between date of sale and the date the related revenue is collected.
c. the time period between purchase of merchandise and the conversion of this merchandise back to cash.
d. a period of one year.

Q8-52 Failure to accrue interest expense results in
a. an understatement of net income and an understatement of liabilities.
b. an understatement of net income and an overstatement of liabilities.
c. an overstatement of net income and an overstatement of liabilities.
d. an overstatement of net income and an understatement of liabilities.

Q8-53 FastscarsWarehouse operates in a state with a 5.5% sales tax. For convenience, Fastscars Warehouse credits Sales Revenue for the total amount (selling price plus sales tax) collected from each customer. If Fastscars Warehouse fails to make an adjustment for sales taxes,
a. net income will be overstated and liabilities will be understated.
b. net income will be understated and liabilities will be overstated.
c. net income will be understated and liabilities will be understated.
d. net income will be overstated and liabilities will be overstated.

Q8-54 What kind of account is Unearned Revenue?
a. Asset account
b. Liability account
c. Expense account
d. Revenue account

Q8-55 An end-of-period adjusting entry that debits Unearned Revenue most likely will credit
a. an asset.
b. a liability.
c. a revenue.
d. an expense.

Q8-56 Alexander, Inc., manufactures and sells computer monitors with a three-year warranty. Warranty costs are expected to average 7% of sales during the warranty period. The following table shows the sales and actual warranty payments during the first two years of operations:

Year	Sales	Warranty Payments
2010	$450,000	$ 3,150
2011	750,000	30,000

Based on these facts, what amount of warranty liability should Alexander, Inc., report on its balance sheet at December 31, 2011?
a. $33,150
b. $30,000
c. $84,000
d. $50,850

Q8-57 Yesterday's Fashions has a debt that has been properly reported as a long-term liability up to the present year (2010). Some of this debt comes due in 2010. If Yesterday's Fashions continues to report the current position as a long-term liability, the effect will be to
a. overstate net income.
b. understate total liabilities.
c. overstate the current ratio.
d. understate the debt ratio.

Q8-58 A bond with a face amount of $10,000 has a current price quote of 104.885. What is the bond's price?
a. $10,488.50
b. $1,048,850
c. $1,048.85
d. $10,104.89

Q8-59 Bond carrying value equals Bonds Payable
a. minus Premium on Bonds Payable.
b. plus Discount on Bonds Payable.
c. minus Discount on Bonds Payable.
d. plus Premium on Bonds Payable.
e. Both a and b
f. Both c and d

Q8-60 What type of account is *Discount on Bonds Payable* and what is its normal balance?
a. Adjusting amount;   Credit
b. Reversing account;   Debit
c. Contra liability;   Credit
d. Contra liability;   Debit

Questions 61–64 use the following data:

Spring Company sells $200,000 of 12%, 10-year bonds for 96 on April 1, 2010. The market rate of interest on that day is 12.5%. Interest is paid each year on April 1.

Q8-61 The entry to record the sale of the bonds on April 1 would be

a.	Cash	192,000	
	Discount on Bonds Payable	8,000	
	Bonds Payable		200,000
b.	Cash	200,000	
	Discount on Bonds Payable		8,000
	Bonds Payable		192,000
c.	Cash	200,000	
	Bonds Payable		200,000
d.	Cash	192,000	
	Bonds Payable		192,000

Q8-62 Spring Company uses the straight-line amortization method. The amount of interest expense on April 1 of each year will be
a. $24,000.   d. $32,000.
b. $25,000.   e. none of these.
c. $24,800.

Q8-63 Write the adjusting entry required at December 31, 2010.

Q8-64 Write the journal entry requirements at April 1, 2011.

Q8-65 McPartlin Corporation issued $300,000 of 10%, 10-year bonds payable on January 1, 2010, for $236,370. The market interest rate when the bonds were issued was 14%. Interest is paid semiannually on January 1 and July 1. The first interest payment is July 1, 2010. Using the effective-interest amortization method, how much interest expense will McPartlin record on July 1, 2010?

a. $15,500

b. $15,000

c. $14,500

d. $21,000

e. $16,546

Q8-66 Using the facts in the preceding question, McPartlin's journal entry to record the interest expense on July 1, 2010 will include a

a. debit to Bonds Payable.

b. credit to Discount on Bonds Payable.

c. credit to Interest Expense.

d. debit to Premium on Bonds Payable.

Q8-67 Amortizing the discount on bonds payable

a. reduces the semiannual cash payment for interest.

b. is necessary only if the bonds were issued at more than face value.

c. reduces the carrying value of the bond liability.

d. increases the recorded amount of interest expense.

Q8-68 The journal entry on the maturity date to record the payment of $500,000 of bonds payable that were issued at a $50,000 discount includes

a. a debit to Bonds Payable for $500,000.

b. a credit to Cash for $550,000.

c. a debit to Discount on Bonds Payable for $50,000.

d. all of the above.

Q8-69 Is the payment of the face amount of a bond on its maturity date regarded as an operating activity, an investing activity, or a financing activity?

a. Financing activity

b. Investing activity

c. Operating activity

Problems

All of the A and B problems can be found within MyAccountingLab, an online homework and practice environment. Your instructor may ask you to complete these problems using MyAccountingLab.

MyAccountingLab

(Group A)

P8-70A (*Learning Objective 1: Measuring current liabilities*)   Big Wave Marine experienced these events during the current year.

  a. December revenue totaled $120,000, and in addition, Big Wave collected sales tax of 5%. The tax amount will be sent to the state of Florida early in January.

  b. On August 31, Big Wave signed a six-month, 4% note payable to purchase a boat costing $85,000. The note requires payment of principal and interest at maturity.

  c. On August 31, Big Wave received cash of $2,400 in advance for service revenue. This revenue will be earned evenly over six months.

  d. Revenues of $850,000 were covered by Big Wave's service warranty. At January 1, estimated warranty payable was $11,600. During the year, Big Wave recorded warranty expense of $34,000 and paid warranty claims of $34,800.

  e. Big Wave owes $70,000 on a long-term note payable. At December 31, 12% interest for the year plus $35,000 of this principal are payable within one year.

I *Requirement*

1. For each item, indicate the account and the related amount to be reported as a current liability on the Big Wave Marine balance sheet at December 31.

P8-71A *(Learning Objective 1: Recording liability-related transactions)*   The following transactions of Harmony Music Company occurred during 2010 and 2011:

2010		
Mar	3	Purchased a piano (inventory) for $70,000, signing a six-month, 4% note payable.
May 31		Borrowed $75,000 on a 4% note payable that calls for annual installment payments of $15,000 principal plus interest. Record the short-term note payable in a separate account from the long-term note payable.
Sep	3	Paid the six-month, 4% note at maturity.
Dec 31		Accrued warranty expense, which is estimated at 3.0% of sales of $190,000.
	31	Accrued interest on the outstanding note payable.
2011		
May 31		Paid the first installment and interest for one year on the outstanding note payable.

I *Requirement*

1. Record the transactions in Harmony's journal. Explanations are not required.

P8-72A *(Learning Objectives 2, 3: Recording bond transactions (at par); reporting bonds payable on the balance sheet)*   The board of directors of Monitors Plus authorizes the issue of $9,000,000 of 10%, five-year bonds payable. The semiannual interest dates are May 31 and November 30. The bonds are issued on May 31, 2010, at par.

I *Requirements*

1. Journalize the following transactions:
   a. Issuance of half of the bonds on May 31, 2010.
   b. Payment of interest on November 30, 2010.
   c. Accrual of interest on December 31, 2010.
   d. Payment of interest on May 31, 2011.
2. Report interest payable and bonds payable as they would appear on the Monitors Plus balance sheet at December 31, 2010.

P8-73A *(Learning Objectives 2, 3, 5: Issuing bonds at a discount; amortizing by the straight-line method; reporting bonds payable on the balance sheet)*   On February 28, 2010, Marlin Corp. issues 8%, 10-year bonds payable with a face value of $900,000. The bonds pay interest on February 28 and August 31. Marlin Corp. amortizes bonds by the straight-line method.

I *Requirements*

1. If the market interest rate is 7% when Marlin Corp. issues its bonds, will the bonds be priced at par, at a premium, or at a discount? Explain.
2. If the market interest rate is 9% when Marlin Corp. issues its bonds, will the bonds be priced at par, at a premium, or at a discount? Explain.
3. Assume that the issue price of the bonds is 99. Journalize the following bonds payable transactions.
   a. Issuance of the bonds on February 28, 2010.
   b. Payment of interest and amortization of the bonds on August 31, 2010.
   c. Accrual of interest and amortization of the bonds on December 31, 2010.
   d. Payment of interest and amortization of the bonds on February 28, 2011.
4. Report interest payable and bonds payable as they would appear on the Marlin Corp. balance sheet at December 31, 2010.

P8-74A (*Learning Objectives 2, 3: Accounting for bonds payable at a discount; amortizing by the straight-line method*)

I Requirements

1. Journalize the following transactions of Laporte Communications, Inc.:

2010		
Jan	1	Issued $7,000,000 of 9%, 10-year bonds payable at 96.
Jul	1	Paid semiannual interest and amortized bonds by the straight-line method on the 9% bonds payable.
Dec 31		Accrued semiannual interest expense and amortized bonds by the straight-line method on the 9% bonds payable.
2011		
Jan	1	Paid semiannual interest.
2020		
Jan	1	Paid the 9% bonds at maturity.

2. At December 31, 2010, after all year-end adjustments, determine the carrying amount of Laporte Communications bonds payable, net.
3. For the six months ended July 1, 2010, determine for Laporte Communications, Inc.:
   a. Interest expense   **b.** Cash interest paid

What causes interest expense on the bonds to exceed cash interest paid?

P8-75A (*Learning Objectives 2, 3, 5: Analyzing a company's long-term debt; reporting long-term debt on the balance sheet (effective-interest method)*)   The notes to the Helping Charities financial statements reported the following data on December 31, Year 1 (end of the fiscal year):

■ **spreadsheet**

Note 6. Indebtedness		
Bonds payable, 7% due in Year 7	$3,000,000	
Less: Discount..	(138,686)	$2,861,314
Notes payable, 6%, payable in amounts of $55,000		
annual installments starting in Year 5...............		330,000

Helping Charities amortizes bonds by the effective-interest method and pays all interest amounts at December 31.

I Requirements

1. Answer the following questions about Helping Charities' long-term liabilities:
   a. What is the maturity value of the 7% bonds?
   b. What are Helping Charities' annual cash interest payments on the 7% bonds?
   c. What is the carrying amount of the 7% bonds at December 31, year 1?
2. Prepare an amortization table through December 31, Year 4, for the 7% bonds. The market interest rate on the bonds was 8%. (Round all amounts to the nearest dollar.) How much is Helping Charities' interest expense on the 7% bonds for the year ended December 31, Year 4?
3. Show how Helping Charities would report the 7% bonds payable and the 6% notes payable at December 31, Year 4.

P8-76A (*Learning Objectives 2, 3, 5: Issuing convertible bonds at a discount; amortizing by the effective-interest method; converting bonds; reporting the bonds payable on the balance sheet*)   On December 31, 2010, Mugaboo Corp. issues 7%, 10-year convertible bonds payable with a maturity value of $3,000,000. The semiannual interest dates are June 30 and December 31. The market interest rate is 8%, and the issue price of the bonds is 93.165. Mugaboo Corp. amortizes bonds by the effective-interest method.

I Requirements

1. Prepare an effective-interest method amortization table for the first four semiannual interest periods.
2. Journalize the following transactions:
    a. Issuance of the bonds on December 31, 2010. Credit Convertible Bonds Payable.
    b. Payment of interest and amortization of the bonds on June 30, 2011.
    c. Payment of interest and amortization of the bonds on December 31, 2011.
    d. Conversion by the bondholders on July 1, 2012, of bonds with face value of $1,200,000 into 40,000 shares of Mugaboo Corp.'s $1-par common stock.
3. Show how Mugaboo Corp. would report the remaining bonds payable on its balance sheet at December 31, 2012.

P8-77A (*Learning Objective 4: Financing operations with debt or with stock*)   Paulus Sporting Goods is embarking on a massive expansion. Assume plans call for opening 25 new stores during the next three years. Each store is scheduled to be 40% larger than the company's existing locations, offering more items of inventory, and with more elaborate displays. Management estimates that company operations will provide $1.5 million of the cash needed for expansion. Paulus must raise the remaining $6.5 million from outsiders. The board of directors is considering obtaining the $6.5 million either through borrowing or by issuing common stock.

I Requirement

1. Write a memo to Paulus' management discussing the advantages and disadvantages of borrowing and of issuing common stock to raise the needed cash. Which method of raising the funds would you recommend?

P8-78A (*Learning Objectives 4, 5: Reporting liabilities on the balance sheet; calculating the times-interest-earned ratio*)   The accounting records of Barnstable Foods, Inc., include the following items at December 31, 2010:

Mortgage note payable, current	$ 94,000		Accumulated depreciation, equipment	$164,000
Accumulated pension benefit obligation	465,000		Discount on bonds payable (all long-term)	27,000
Bonds payable, long-term	1,200,000		Operating income	400,000
Mortgage note payable, long-term	319,000		Equipment	745,000
Bonds payable, current portion	400,000		Pension plan assets (market value)	405,000
Interest expense	222,000		Interest payable	72,000

I Requirements

1. Show how each relevant item would be reported on the Barnstable Foods, Inc., classified balance sheet, including headings and totals for current liabilities and long-term liabilities.
2. Answer the following questions about Barnstable's financial position at December 31, 2010:
    a. What is the carrying amount of the bonds payable (combine the current and long-term amounts)?
    b. Why is the interest-payable amount so much less than the amount of interest expense?
3. How many times did Barnstable cover its interest expense during 2010?

(Group B)

P8-79B (*Learning Objective 1: Measuring current liabilities*)   Sea Breeze Marine experienced these events during the current year.

   a. December revenue totaled $110,000, and in addition, Sea Breeze collected sales tax of 8%. The tax amount will be sent to the state of Georgia early in January.
   b. On August 31, Sea Breeze signed a six-month, 4% note payable to purchase a boat costing $82,000. The note requires payment of principal and interest at maturity.
   c. On August 31, Sea Breeze received cash of $1,200 in advance for service revenue. This revenue will be earned evenly over six months.
   d. Revenues of $750,000 were covered by Sea Breeze's service warranty. At January 1, estimated warranty payable was $11,400. During the year, Sea Breeze recorded warranty expense of $30,000 and paid warranty claims of $34,600.
   e. Sea Breeze owes $85,000 on a long-term note payable. At December 31, 10% interest for the year plus $25,000 of this principal are payable within one year.

I Requirement

1. For each item, indicate the account and the related amount to be reported as a current liability on the Sea Breeze Marine balance sheet at December 31.

P8-80B (*Learning Objective 1: Recording liability-related transactions*)   The following transactions of Soft Sounds Music Company occurred during 2010 and 2011:

2010	
Mar 3	Purchased a piano (inventory) for $30,000, signing a six-month, 10% note payable.
May 31	Borrowed $75,000 on a 6% note payable that calls for annual installment payments of $15,000 principal plus interest. Record the short-term note payable in a separate account from the long-term note payable.
Sep 3	Paid the six-month, 10% note at maturity.
Dec 31	Accrued warranty expense, which is estimated at 1.5% of sales of $196,000.
31	Accrued interest on the outstanding note payable.
2011	
May 31	Paid the first installment and interest for one year on the outstanding note payable.

I Requirement

1. Record the transactions in Soft Sounds Music Company's journal. Explanations are not required.

P8-81B (*Learning Objectives 2, 3: Recording bond transactions (at par); reporting bonds payable on the balance sheet*)   The board of directors of Pictures Plus authorizes the issue of $6,000,000 of 8%, 15-year bonds payable. The semiannual interest dates are May 31 and November 30. The bonds are issued on May 31, 2010, at par.

I Requirements

1. Journalize the following transactions:
   a. Issuance of half of the bonds on May 31, 2010.
   b. Payment of interest on November 30, 2010.
   c. Accrual of interest on December 31, 2010.
   d. Payment of interest on May 31, 2011.
2. Report interest payable and bonds payable as they would appear on the Pictures Plus balance sheet at December 31, 2010.

P8-82B *(Learning Objectives 2, 3, 5: Issuing bonds at a discount; amortizing by the straight-line method; reporting notes payable on the balance sheet)* On February 28, 2010, Mackerel Corp. issues 6%, 20-year bonds payable with a face value of $1,800,000. The bonds pay interest on February 28 and August 31. Mackerel Corp. amortizes bonds by the straight-line method.

❙ Requirements

1. If the market interest rate is 5% when Mackerel Corp. issues its bonds, will the bonds be priced at par, at a premium, or at a discount? Explain.
2. If the market interest rate is 7% when Mackerel Corp. issues its bonds, will the bonds be priced at par, at a premium, or at a discount? Explain.
3. Assume that the issue price of the bonds is 96. Journalize the following bond transactions.
   a. Issuance of the bonds on February 28, 2010.
   b. Payment of interest and amortization of the bonds on August 31, 2010.
   c. Accrual of interest and amortization of the bonds on December 31, 2010, the year-end.
   d. Payment of interest and amortization of the bonds on February 28, 2011.
4. Report interest payable and bonds payable as they would appear on the Mackerel Corp. balance sheet at December 31, 2010.

P8-83B *(Learning Objectives 2, 3: Accounting for bonds payable at a discount; amortizing by the straight-line method)*

❙ Requirements

1. Journalize the following transactions of Lamore Communications, Inc.:

2010		
Jan	1	Issued $4,000,000 of 7%, 10-year bonds payable at 96.
Jul	1	Paid semiannual interest and amortized the bonds by the straight-line method on the 7% bonds payable.
Dec	31	Accrued semiannual interest expense and amortized the bonds by the straight-line method on the 7% bonds payable.
2011		
Jan	1	Paid semiannual interest.
2020		
Jan	1	Paid the 7% bonds at maturity.

2. At December 31, 2010, after all year-end adjustments, determine the carrying amount of Lamore Communications bonds payable, net.
3. For the six months ended July 1, 2010, determine the following for Lamore Communications Inc:
   a. Interest expense   b. Cash interest paid
   What causes interest expense on the bonds to exceed cash interest paid?

❚ spreadsheet

P8-84B *(Learning Objectives 2, 3, 5: Analyzing a company's long-term debt; reporting the long-term debt on the balance sheet (effective-interest method))* The notes to the Helpful Charities financial statements reported the following data on December 31, Year 1 (end of the fiscal year):

Note 6. Indebtedness		
Bonds payable, 4% due in Year 7	$6,000,000	
Less: Discount	(304,542)	$5,695,458
Notes payable, 7%, payable in $60,000		
annual installments starting in Year 5		360,000

Helpful Charities amortizes bonds by the effective-interest method and pays all interest amounts at December 31.

I Requirements

1. Answer the following questions about Helpful Charities long-term liabilities:
   a. What is the maturity value of the 4% bonds?
   b. What is Helpful Charities' annual cash interest payment on the 4% bonds?
   c. What is the carrying amount of the 4% bonds at December 31, Year 1?
2. Prepare an amortization table through December 31, Year 4, for the 4% bonds. The market interest rate on the bonds was 5%. Round all amounts to the nearest dollar. How much is Helpful Charities' interest expense on the 4% bonds for the year ended December 31, Year 4?
3. Show how Helpful Charities would report the 4% bonds and the 7% notes payable at December 31, Year 4.

P8-85B *(Learning Objectives 2, 3, 5: Issuing convertible bonds at a discount; amortizing by the effective-interest method; converting bonds; reporting the bonds payable on the balance sheet)*   On December 31, 2010, Rugaboo Corp. issues 9%, 10-year convertible bonds payable with a maturity value of $2,000,000. The semiannual interest dates are June 30 and December 31. The market interest rate is 10%, and the issue price of the bonds is 93.779. Rugaboo Corp. amortizes bonds by the effective-interest method.

■ **spreadsheet**

I Requirements

1. Prepare an effective-interest method amortization table for the first four semiannual interest periods.
2. Journalize the following transactions:
   a. Issuance of the bonds on December 31, 2010. Credit Convertible Bonds Payable.
   b. Payment of interest and amortization of the bonds on June 30, 2011.
   c. Payment of interest and amortization of the bonds on December 31, 2011.
   d. Conversion by the bondholders on July 1, 2012, of bonds with face value of $800,000 into 90,000 shares of Rugaboo Corp. $1-par common stock.
3. Show how Rugaboo Corp. would report the remaining bonds payable on its balance sheet at December 31, 2012.

P8-86B *(Learning Objective 4: Financing operations with debt or with stock)*   Fitzpatrick Sporting Goods is embarking on a massive expansion. Assume plans call for opening 30 new stores during the next four years. Each store is scheduled to be 45% larger than the company's existing locations, offering more items of inventory, and with more elaborate displays. Management estimates that company operations will provide $1.75 million of the cash needed for expansion. Fitzpatrick must raise the remaining $7 million from outsiders. The board of directors is considering obtaining the $7 million either through borrowing or by issuing common stock.

writing assignment ■

I Requirement

1. Write a memo to Fitzpatrick's management discussing the advantages and disadvantages of borrowing and of issuing common stock to raise the needed cash. Which method of raising the funds would you recommend?

P8-87B *(Learning Objectives 4, 5: Reporting liabilities on the balance sheet; calculating the times-interest-earned ratio)*   The accounting records of Brilliant Foods, Inc., include the following items at December 31, 2010:

Mortgage note payable, current	$ 95,000	Accumulated depreciation, equipment	$165,000
Accumulated pension benefit obligation	460,000	Discount on bonds payable (all long-term)	23,000
Bonds payable, long-term	200,000	Operating income	360,000
Mortgage note payable, long-term	313,000	Equipment	746,000
Bonds payable, current portion	500,000	Pension plan assets (market value)	410,000
Interest expense	224,000	Interest payable	72,000

❙ *Requirements*

1. Show how each relevant item would be reported on the Brilliant Foods, Inc., classified balance sheet, including headings and totals for current liabilities and long-term liabilities.
2. Answer the following questions about Brilliant's financial position at December 31, 2010:
   a. What is the carrying amount of the bonds payable (combine the current and long-term amounts)?
   b. Why is the interest-payable amount so much less than the amount of interest expense?
3. How many times did Brilliant cover its interest expense during 2010?

APPLY YOUR KNOWLEDGE

Decision Cases

Case 1. (*Learning Objective 2: Exploring an actual bankruptcy*) In 2002, **Enron Corporation** filed for Chapter 11 bankruptcy protection, shocking the business community: How could a company this large and this successful go bankrupt? This case explores the causes and the effects of Enron's bankruptcy.

At December 31, 2000, and for the four years ended on that date, Enron reported the following (amounts in millions):

Balance Sheet (summarized)			
Total assets			$65,503
Total liabilities			54,033
Total stockholders' equity			11,470

Income Statements (excerpts)			
	2000	1999	1998	1997
Net income	$979*	$893	$703	$105

*Operating income = $1,953
Interest expense = $838

Unknown to investors and lenders, Enron also controlled hundreds of partnerships that owed vast amounts of money. These special-purpose entities (SPEs) did not appear on the Enron financial statements. Assume that the SPEs' assets totaled $7,000 million and their liabilities stood at $6,900 million; assume a 10% interest rate on these liabilities.

During the four-year period up to December 31, 2000, Enron's stock price shot up from $17.50 to $90.56. Enron used its escalating stock price to finance the purchase of the SPEs by guaranteeing lenders that Enron would give them Enron stock if the SPEs could not pay their loans.

In 2001, the SEC launched an investigation into Enron's accounting practices. It was alleged that Enron should have been including the SPEs in its financial statements all along. Enron then restated net income for years up to 2000, wiping out nearly $600 million of total net income (and total assets) for this four-year period. Enron's stock price tumbled, and the guarantees to the SPEs' lenders added millions to Enron's liabilities (assume the full amount of the SPEs' debt). To make matters worse, the assets of the SPEs lost much of their value; assume that their market value is only $500 million.

❙ *Requirements*

1. Compute the debt ratio that Enron reported at the end of 2000. Recompute this ratio after including the SPEs in Enron's financial statements. Also compute Enron's times-interest-earned ratio both ways for 2000. Assume that the changes to Enron's financial position occurred during 2000.
2. Why does it appear that Enron failed to include the SPEs in its financial statements? How do you view Enron after including the SPEs in the company's financial statements? (Challenge)

Case 2. *(Learning Objective 4: Analyzing alternative ways of raising $5 million)* Business is going well for **Park 'N Fly**, the company that operates remote parking lots near major airports. The board of directors of this family-owned company believes that Park 'N Fly could earn an additional $1.5 million income before interest and taxes by expanding into new markets. However, the $5 million that the business needs for growth cannot be raised within the family. The directors, who strongly wish to retain family control of the company, must consider issuing securities to outsiders. The directors are considering three financing plans.

Plan A is to borrow at 6%. Plan B is to issue 100,000 shares of common stock. Plan C is to issue 100,000 shares of nonvoting, $3.75 preferred stock ($3.75 is the annual dividend paid on each share of preferred stock).[5] Park 'N Fly presently has net income of $3.5 million and 1 million shares of common stock outstanding. The company's income tax rate is 35%.

❙ Requirements

1. Prepare an analysis to determine which plan will result in the highest earnings per share of common stock.
2. Recommend a plan to the board of directors. Give your reasons.

Ethical Issues

Issue 1. Microsoft Corporation is the defendant in numerous lawsuits claiming unfair trade practices. Microsoft has strong incentives not to disclose these contingent liabilities. However, GAAP requires that companies report their contingent liabilities.

❙ Requirements

1. Why would a company prefer not to disclose its contingent liabilities?
2. Identify the parties involved in the decision and the potential consequences to each.
3. Analyze the issue of whether to report contingent liabilities from lawsuits from the following standpoints:
   a. economic
   b. legal
   c. ethical
4. What impact will future changes in accounting standards, both at the U.S. level and the international level, likely have on the issue of disclosure of loss contingencies?

Issue 2. WHEN IS A LEASE A CAPITAL IDEA? Laurie Gocker, Inc., entered into a lease arrangement with Nathan Morgan Leasing Corporation for an industrial machine. Morgan's primary business is leasing. The cash purchase price of the machine is $1,000,000. Its economic life is six years.

Gocker's balance sheet reflects total assets of $10 million and total liabilities of $7.5 million. Among the liabilities is a $2.5 million long-term note outstanding at Last National Bank. The note carries a restrictive covenant that requires the company's debt ratio to be no higher than 75%. The company's revenues have been falling of late and the shareholders are concerned about profitability.

Gocker and Morgan are engaging in negotiations for terms of the lease. Some relevant other facts:

1. Morgan wants to take possession of the machine at the end of the initial lease term.
2. The term may run from four to five years, at Gocker's discretion.
3. Morgan estimates the machine will have no residual value, and Gocker will not purchase it at the end of the lease term.
4. The present value of minimum lease payments on the machine is $890,000.

❙ Requirements

1. What is (are) the ethical issue(s) in this case?
2. Who are the stakeholders? Analyze the consequences for each stakeholder from the following standpoints: (a) economic, (b) legal, and (c) ethical.

---

[5]For a discussion of preferred stock, see Chapter 9.

3. How should Gocker structure the lease agreement?

4. How will the analysis of this case change when IFRS are adopted in the United States? Would your decision be different? Why or why not?

Focus on Financials: ■ Amazon.com, Inc.

(*Learning Objectives 1, 2, 5: Analyzing current and contingent liabilities*) Refer to **Amazon.com, Inc.**'s consolidated financial statements in Appendix A at the end of this book.

1. Did accounts payable for Amazon.com, Inc., increase or decrease in 2008? What was the amount? What might have caused this change?

2. Examine Note 12—Income Taxes—in the Notes to Consolidated Financial Statements. Income tax provision is another title for income tax expense. What was Amazon.com, Inc.'s income tax provision in 2008? How much did the company pay in federal income taxes? How much was income taxes payable as of December 31, 2008? In general, why were these amounts different? (Challenge)

3. Did Amazon.com, Inc., borrow more or pay off more long-term debt during 2008? How can you tell? (Challenge)

4. Examine Note 7—Commitments and Contingencies—in the Notes to Consolidated Financial Statements. Describe some of Amazon.com, Inc.'s contingent liabilities as of December 31, 2008.

5. How would you rate Amazon.com, Inc.'s overall debt position—risky, safe, or average? Compute the ratio at December 31, 2008, that answers this question.

Focus on Analysis: ■ Foot Locker, Inc.

(*Learning Objectives 1, 2, 3, 5: Analyzing current liabilities and long-term debt*) **Foot Locker, Inc.**'s consolidated financial statements in Appendix B at the end of this book report a number of liabilities. Show amounts in thousands.

1. The current liability section of Foot Locker, Inc.'s Consolidated Balance Sheet as of February 2, 2008 (the end of fiscal 2007) lists accrued and other liabilities totaling $268 million. Find the details of this total in the Notes to Consolidated Financial Statements. What are the four principal items comprising this total? (Challenge)

2. Refer to Note 15 of the Notes to Consolidated Financial Statements—Long-Term Debt and Obligations under Capital Leases. Why do you think the company has combined these two totals? Summarize the contents of this section of the balance sheet as of the end of the fiscal 2007 year, as well as the changes that have occurred during fiscal 2007. When do the company's long-term liabilities of $221 million mature? (Challenge)

3. How would you rate Foot Locker, Inc.'s overall debt position at the end of fiscal 2007—risky, safe, or average? Compute the ratios that enable you to answer this question. (Challenge)

4. Access Foot Locker, Inc.'s most recent financial statements from its Web site (www.footlocker.com). You will find a link called "about us" under the customer service section of the website, which will lead you to the latest financial statements filed with the SEC. What has happened to Foot Locker, Inc.'s debt position since the end of fiscal 2007? Why?

Group Projects

Project 1. Consider three different businesses:

1. A bank
2. A magazine publisher
3. A department store

For each business, list all of its liabilities—both current and long-term. Then compare the three lists to identify the liabilities that the three businesses have in common. Also identify the liabilities that are unique to each type of business.

Project 2.   Alcenon Corporation leases the majority of the assets that it uses in operations. Alcenon prefers operating leases (versus capital leases) in order to keep the lease liability off its balance sheet and maintain a low debt ratio.

Alcenon is negotiating a 10-year lease on an asset with an expected useful life of 15 years. The lease requires Alcenon to make 10 annual lease payments of $20,000 each, with the first payment due at the beginning of the lease term. The leased asset has a market value of $135,180. The lease agreement specifies no transfer of title to the lessee and includes no bargain purchase option.

Write a report for Alcenon's management to explain what conditions must be present for Alcenon to be able to account for this lease as an operating lease.

For online homework, exercises, and problems that provide you with immediate feedback, please visit www.myaccountinglab.com.

Quick Check Answers

1. *d*

2. *e*

3. *b* ($450,000 × 0.01 = $4,500)

4. *c* [900 × 0.04 × $25 = warranty expense of $900; repaired $25 × 15 = $375; year-end liability = $525 ($900 - $375)]

5. *e*

6. *b*

7. *d*

8. *c*

9. *c*

10. *d*

11. *a*

12. *a* ($512,408 × 0.08 × 6/12 = $20,496)

13. *c* [Int. exp. = $20,496 Int. payment = $19,250 ($550,000 × 0.07 × 6/12) $20,496 − $19,250 = $1,246]

14. *b* ($550,000 × 0.07 = $38,500)

15. *a* (See Amortization Schedule)

Date	Interest Payment	Interest Expense	Discount Amortiz.	Bond Carry Amt.
1/1/2011				$512,408
7/1/2011	$19,250	$20,496	$1,246	513,654
1/1/2012	19,250	20,546	1,296	514,950

16. *d* {$512,408 + [($550,000 − $512,408) × 1/10] = $516,167}

9

Stockholders' Equity

SPOTLIGHT: DineEquity: Where IHOP meets Applebee's

It's late and you have a history exam tomorrow morning at 8. Where do you go for a quick bite? Either **IHOP** or **Applebee's** may be your choice, because both of these popular restaurants locate near college campuses.

IHOP started in 1958 and first offered the company's stock to the public in 1991. Now IHOP operates 1,350 restaurants in 49 states. In November 2007, IHOP bought Applebee's International, the world's largest casual dining restaurant, with more than 1,900 restaurants. To help finance the transaction, IHOP issued some new preferred stock. In May 2008, IHOP changed its corporate name to **DineEquity**. These events bring together two leading restaurant chains under one umbrella, creating the largest full-service franchise restaurant corporation in the world. In 2007, the corporation racked up sales of $484 million. However, Applebee's operating losses, combined with a long and deep business recession, have forced DineEquity to incur big losses for the past fiscal year, and have distorted its rate of return on stockholders' equity (ROE), as will be discussed later.

In this chapter we'll show you how to account for the issuance of corporate capital stock to investors. We'll also cover the other elements of stockholders' equity—Additional Paid-in Capital, Retained Earnings, and Treasury Stock, plus dividends and stock splits. By the time you finish this chapter, you may be hungry for a stack of IHOP pancakes or a steak from Applebee's. Or you may go out and buy some DineEquity stock. The consolidated balance sheet on the next page is for December 31, 2007, the last year before IHOP changed its name to DineEquity.

IHOP Corp.
Consolidated Balance Sheet (Adapted)
December 31, 2007

(In thousands, except number of shares)

Assets

Current assets:

Total current assets	$ 433,678
Long-term receivables	288,452
Property and equipment, net	1,139,616
Goodwill	730,728
Other intangibles, net	1,011,457
Other assets	227,231
Total assets	$3,831,162

Liabilities and Stockholders' Equity

Current liabilities:

	Total current liabilities	$ 381,340
	Long-term debt	2,432,129
	Other long-term liabilities	621,270
1	Perpetual Preferred stock, series A, $1 par value, 220,000 shares authorized; 190,000 shares issued and outstanding	187,050
2	Stockholders' equity:	
3	Preferred stock, series B, $1 par value, 10,000,000 shares authorized; 35,000 shares issued and outstanding: 35,000 shares	35
4	Common stock, $.01 par value, 40,000,000 shares authorized; 23,359,664 shares issued and 17,105,469 shares outstanding	230
5	Additional paid-in capital	184,710
6	Retained earnings	338,790
7	Treasury stock, at cost (6,254,195 shares)	(277,654)
8	Other equity	(36,738)
9	Total stockholders' equity	209,373
	Total liabilities and stockholders' equity	$3,831,162

Chapters 4 to 8 discussed accounting for assets and liabilities. By this time, you should be familiar with all the assets and liabilities listed on IHOP's balance sheet. Let's focus now on IHOP's stockholders' equity. In this chapter we discuss some of the decisions a company faces when:

- paying dividends
- issuing stock
- buying back its stock

Let's begin with the organization of a corporation.

LEARNING OBJECTIVES

1 **Explain** the features of a corporation

2 **Account** for the issuance of stock

3 **Describe** how treasury stock affects a company

4 **Account** for dividends

5 **Use** stock values in decision making

6 **Compute** return on assets and return on equity

7 **Report** equity transactions on the statement of cash flows

WHAT'S THE BEST WAY TO ORGANIZE A BUSINESS?

Anyone starting a business must decide how to organize the company. Corporations differ from proprietorships and partnerships in several ways.

OBJECTIVE

1 **Explain** the features of a corporation

Separate Legal Entity.   A corporation is a business entity formed under state law. It is a distinct entity, an artificial person that exists apart from its owners, the **stockholders**, or **shareholders**. The corporation has many of the rights that a person has. For example, a corporation may buy, own, and sell property. Assets and liabilities in the business belong to the corporation and not to its owners. The corporation may enter into contracts, sue, and be sued.

Nearly all large companies, such as DineEquity, **Toyota**, and **Wal-Mart**, are corporations. Their full names may include *Corporation* or *Incorporated* (abbreviated *Corp.* and *Inc.*) to indicate that they are corporations, for example, DineEquity Corp. and Williams-Sonoma, Inc. Corporations can also use the word *Company*, such as Ford Motor Company.

Continuous Life and Transferability of Ownership.   Corporations have *continuous lives* regardless of changes in their ownership. The stockholders of a corporation may buy more of the stock, sell the stock to another person, give it away, or bequeath it in a will. The transfer of the stock from one person to another does not affect the continuity of the corporation. In contrast, proprietorships and partnerships terminate when their ownership changes.

Limited Liability.   Stockholders have **limited liability** for the corporation's debts. They have no personal obligation for corporate liabilities. The most that a stockholder can lose on an investment in a corporation's stock is the cost of the investment. Limited liability is one of the most attractive features of the corporate form of organization. It enables corporations to raise more capital from a wider group of investors than proprietorships and partnerships can. By contrast, proprietors and partners are personally liable for all the debts of their businesses.[1]

---

[1]Unless the business is organized as a limited-liability company (LLC) or a limited-liability partnership (LLP).

Separation of Ownership and Management. Stockholders own the corporation, but the *board of directors*—elected by the stockholders—appoints officers to manage the business. Thus, stockholders may invest $1,000 or $1 million in the corporation without having to manage it.

Management's goal is to maximize the firm's value for the stockholders. But the separation between owners and managers may create problems. Corporate officers may run the business for their own benefit and not for the stockholders. For example, the CEO of **Tyco Corporation** was accused of looting Tyco of $600 million. The CFO of **Enron Corporation** set up outside partnerships and paid himself millions to manage the partnerships—unknown to Enron stockholders. Both men went to prison.

Corporate Taxation. Corporations are separate taxable entities. They pay several taxes not borne by proprietorships or partnerships, including an annual franchise tax levied by the state. The franchise tax keeps the corporate charter in force. Corporations also pay federal and state income taxes.

Corporate earnings are subject to **double taxation** on their income to the extent they are distributed to shareholders in the form of dividends.

- First, corporations pay income taxes on their corporate income.
- Then stockholders pay income tax on the cash dividends received from corporations. Proprietorships and partnerships pay no business income tax. Instead, the business' tax falls solely on the owners.

Government Regulation. Because stockholders have only limited liability for corporation debts, outsiders doing business with the corporation can look no further than the corporation if it fails to pay. To protect a corporation's creditors and stockholders, both federal and state governments monitor corporations. The regulations mainly ensure that corporations disclose the information that investors and creditors need to make informed decisions. Accounting provides much of this information.

Exhibit 9-1 summarizes the advantages and disadvantages of the corporate form of business organization.

EXHIBIT 9-1 | **Advantages and Disadvantages of the Corporation**

Advantages	Disadvantages
1. Can raise more capital than a proprietorship or partnership can	1. Separation of ownership and management
2. Continuous life	2. Corporate taxation
3. Ease of transferring ownership	3. Government regulation
4. Limited liability of stockholders	

ORGANIZING A CORPORATION

The creation of a corporation begins when its organizers, called the *incorporators*, obtain a charter from the state. The charter includes the authorization for the corporation to issue a certain number of shares of stock. A share of stock is the basic unit of ownership for a corporation. The incorporators

- pay fees,
- sign the charter,

- file documents with the state, and
- agree to a set of **bylaws**, which act as the constitution for governing the company.

The corporation then comes into existence.

Ultimate control of the corporation rests with the stockholders who elect a **board of directors** that sets company policy and appoints officers. The board elects a **chairperson**, who usually is the most powerful person in the organization. The chairperson of the board of directors has the title chief executive officer (CEO). The board also designates the **president**, who is the chief operating officer (COO) in charge of day-to-day operations. Most corporations also have vice presidents in charge of sales, manufacturing, accounting and finance (the chief financial officer, or CFO), and other key areas. Exhibit 9-2 shows the authority structure in a corporation.

EXHIBIT 9-2 | **Authority Structure in a Corporation**

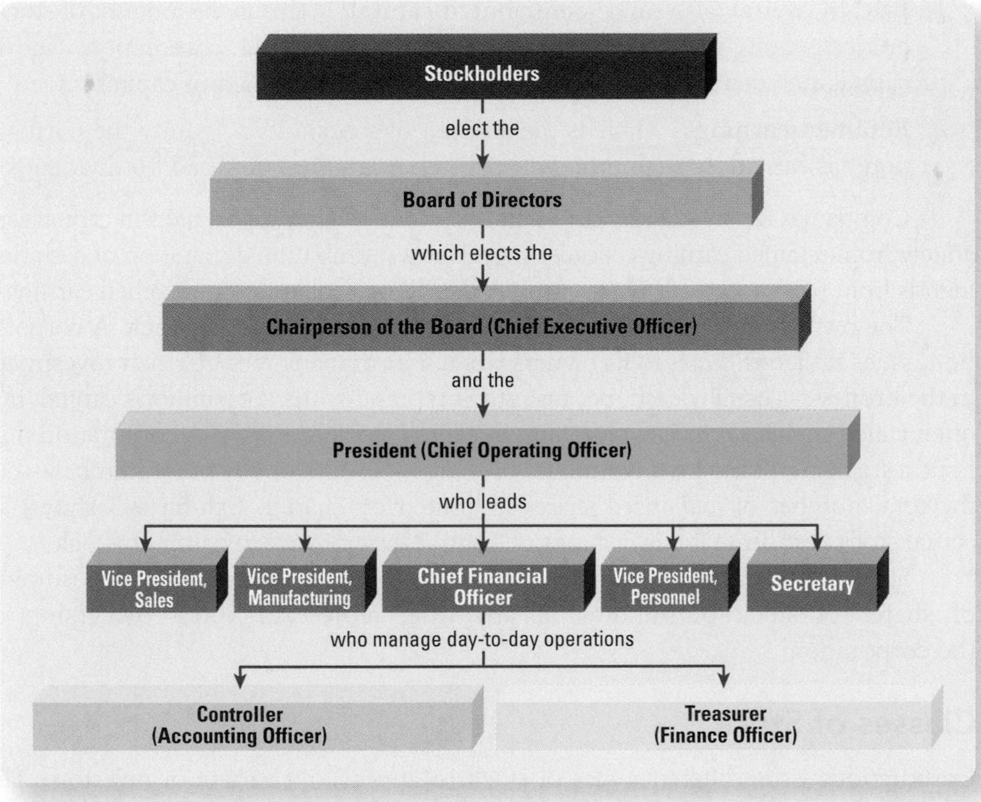

Stockholders' Rights

Ownership of stock entitles stockholders to four basic rights, unless a specific right is withheld by agreement with the stockholders:

1. *Vote.* The right to participate in management by voting on matters that come before the stockholders. This is the stockholder's sole voice in the management of the corporation. A stockholder gets one vote for each share of stock owned.

2. *Dividends.* The right to receive a proportionate part of any dividend. Each share of stock in a particular class receives an equal dividend.

3. *Liquidation.* The right to receive a proportionate share of any assets remaining after the corporation pays its liabilities in liquidation. Liquidation means to go

out of business, sell the assets, pay all liabilities, and distribute any remaining cash to the owners.

4. *Preemption.* The right to maintain one's proportionate ownership in the corporation. Suppose you own 5% of a corporation's stock. If the corporation issues 100,000 new shares, it must offer you the opportunity to buy 5% (5,000) of the new shares. This right, called the *preemptive right*, is usually withheld from the stockholders.

Stockholders' Equity

As we saw in Chapter 1, **stockholders' equity** represents the stockholders' ownership interest in the assets of a corporation. Stockholders' equity is divided into two main parts:

1. **Paid-in capital**, also called **contributed capital.**   This is the amount of stockholders' equity the stockholders have contributed to the corporation. Paid-in capital includes the stock accounts and any additional paid-in capital.

2. **Retained earnings.**   This is the amount of stockholders' equity the corporation has earned through profitable operations and has not used for dividends.

Companies report stockholders' equity by source. They report paid-in capital separately from retained earnings because most states prohibit the declaration of cash dividends from paid-in capital. Thus, cash dividends are declared from retained earnings.

The owners' equity of a corporation is divided into shares of **stock.** A corporation issues *stock certificates* to its owners when the company receives their investment in the business—usually cash. Because stock represents the corporation's capital, it is often called *capital stock.* The basic unit of capital stock is a *share.* A corporation may issue a stock certificate for any number of shares—1, 100, or any other number—but the total number of *authorized* shares is limited by charter. Exhibit 9-3 shows an actual stock certificate for 288 shares of Central Jersey Bancorp common stock.

Stock in the hands of a stockholder is said to be *outstanding*. The total number of shares of stock outstanding at any time represents 100% ownership of the corporation.

Classes of Stock

Corporations issue different types of stock to appeal to a variety of investors. The stock of a corporation may be either

- Common or preferred
- Par or no-par

Common and Preferred.   Every corporation issues **common stock**, the basic form of capital stock. Unless designated otherwise, the word *stock* is understood to mean "common stock." Common stockholders have the four basic rights of stock ownership, unless a right is specifically withheld. The common stockholders are the owners of the corporation. They stand to benefit the most if the corporation succeeds because they take the most risk by investing in common stock.

Preferred stock gives its owners certain advantages over common stockholders. Preferred stockholders receive dividends before the common stockholders and they also receive assets before the common stockholders if the corporation liquidates. Owners of preferred stock also have the four basic stockholder rights, unless a right

EXHIBIT 9-3 | Stock Certificate

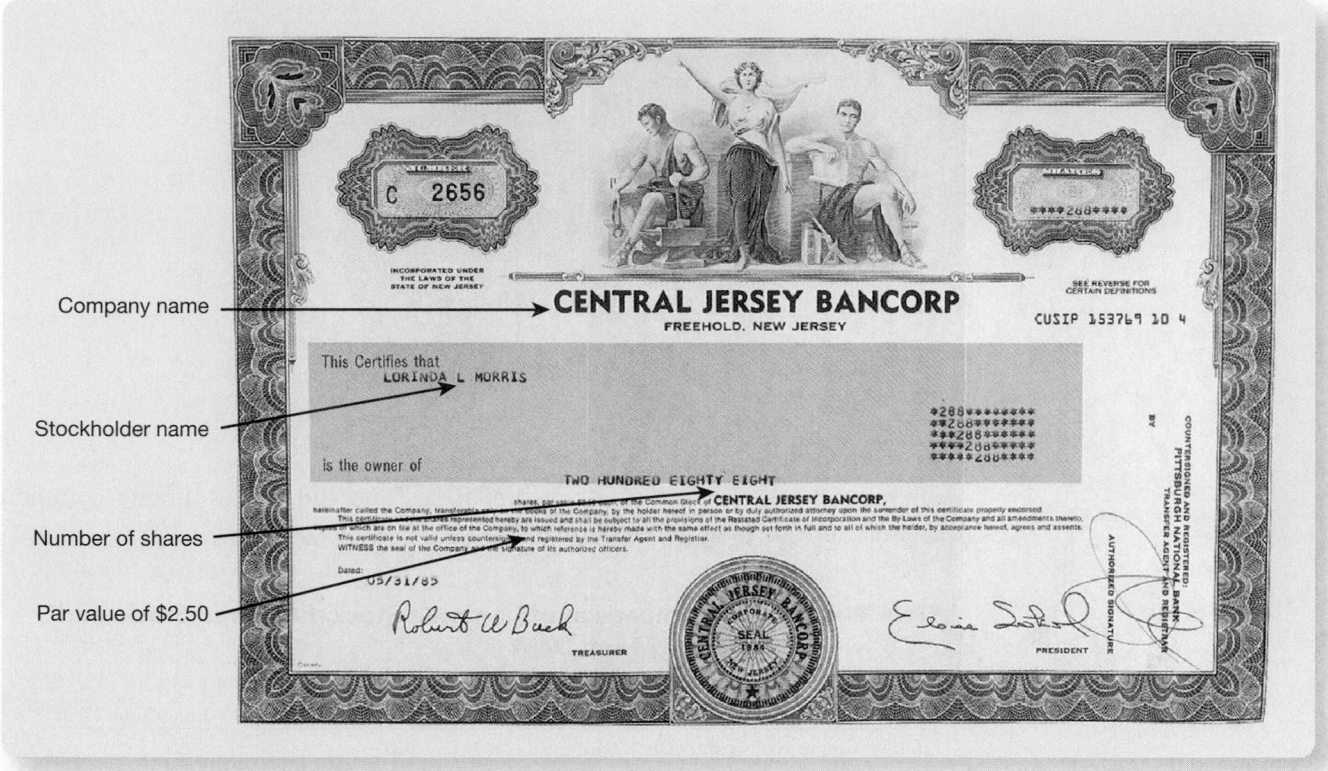

Company name

Stockholder name

Number of shares

Par value of $2.50

is specifically denied. Companies may issue different classes of preferred stock (Class A and Class B or Series A and Series B, for example). Each class of stock is recorded in a separate account. The most preferred stockholders can expect to earn on their investments is a fixed dividend.

Preferred stock is a hybrid between common stock and long-term debt. Like interest on debt, preferred stock pays a fixed dividend. But unlike interest on debt, the dividend is not required to be paid unless the board of directors declares the dividend. Also, companies have no obligation to pay back true preferred stock. Preferred stock that must be redeemed (paid back) by the corporation is a liability masquerading as a stock.

Preferred stock is rare. A recent survey of 600 corporations revealed that only 9% of them had preferred stock (Exhibit 9-4 on the following page). All corporations have common stock. The balance sheet of IHOP Corp. (p. 534) shows that IHOP actually has two classes of preferred stock: Series A and Series B. Both of these classes of stock were issued in November 2007, in connection with IHOP's acquisition of Applebee's International Corp. The Class A preferred stock, recorded at a net amount of $187,050,000 ($190,000,000 par value less $2,950,000 issuance costs) is called "perpetual preferred stock." It has so many features that are like long-term debt (i.e., fixed but potentially increasing dividend amounts, cumulative as to dividends) that the company actually classifies it between the long-term debt and stockholders' equity sections of the balance sheet, rather than in stockholders' equity per se. IHOP also has authorized 10 million shares of Series B $1 convertible preferred stock. As of December 31, 2007, 35,000 of these shares have been issued and are outstanding. The company received approximately $35 million for these shares. We will explain the meanings of the terms "cumulative" and "convertible" later.

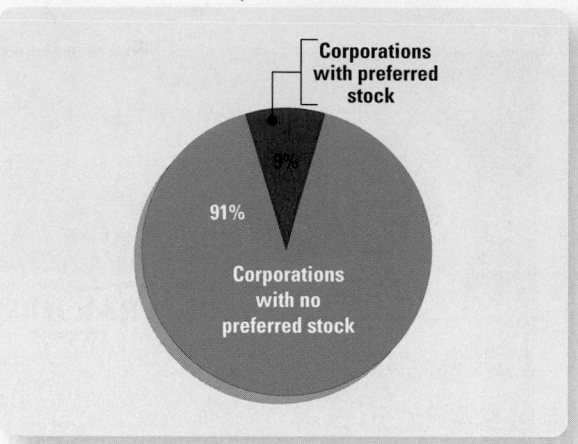

EXHIBIT 9-4 | Preferred Stock

Exhibit 9-5 shows some of the similarities and differences among common stock, preferred stock, and long-term debt.

EXHIBIT 9-5 | Comparison of Common Stock, Preferred Stock, and Long-Term Debt

	Common Stock	Preferred Stock	Long-Term Debt
1. Obligation to repay principal	No	No	Yes
2. Dividends/interest	Dividends are not tax-deductible	Dividends are not tax-deductible	Interest expense is tax-deductible
3. Obligation to pay dividends/interest	Only after declaration	Only after declaration	At fixed rates and dates

Par Value and No-Par. Stock may be par-value stock or no-par stock. **Par value** is an arbitrary amount assigned by a company to a share of its stock. Most companies set the par value of their common stock low to avoid legal difficulties from issuing their stock below par. Most states require companies to maintain a minimum amount of stockholders' equity for the protection of creditors, and this minimum is often called the corporation's legal capital. For corporations with par-value stock, **legal capital** is the par value of the shares issued.

The par value of **PepsiCo** common stock is $0.0166 (1 2/3 cents) per share. **Best Buy** common stock carries a par value of $1 per share, and **IHOP**'s common stock has par value of $0.01 per share. Par value of preferred stock is sometimes higher. IHOP's December 31, 1997, balance sheet lists Series B preferred stock with $1 par value.

No-par stock does not have par value. But some no-par stock has a **stated value**, which makes it similar to par-value stock. The stated value is an arbitrary amount similar to par value. In a recent survey, only 9% of the companies had no-par stock outstanding. Apple, Inc., Krispy Kreme Doughnuts, and Sony have no-par stock.

ISSUING STOCK

OBJECTIVE

2 **Account** for the issuance of stock

Large corporations such as **IHOP**, **PepsiCo**, and **Microsoft** need huge quantities of money to operate. Corporations may sell stock directly to the stockholders or use the service of an *underwriter*, such as the investment banking firms **UBS** and **Goldman**

Sachs. Companies often advertise the issuance of their stock to attract investors. *The Wall Street Journal* is the most popular medium for such advertisements, which are also called *tombstones*. Exhibit 9-6 is a reproduction of IHOP's tombstone, which appeared in *The Wall Street Journal*.

EXHIBIT 9-6 | Announcement of Public Offering of IHOP Stock (Adapted)

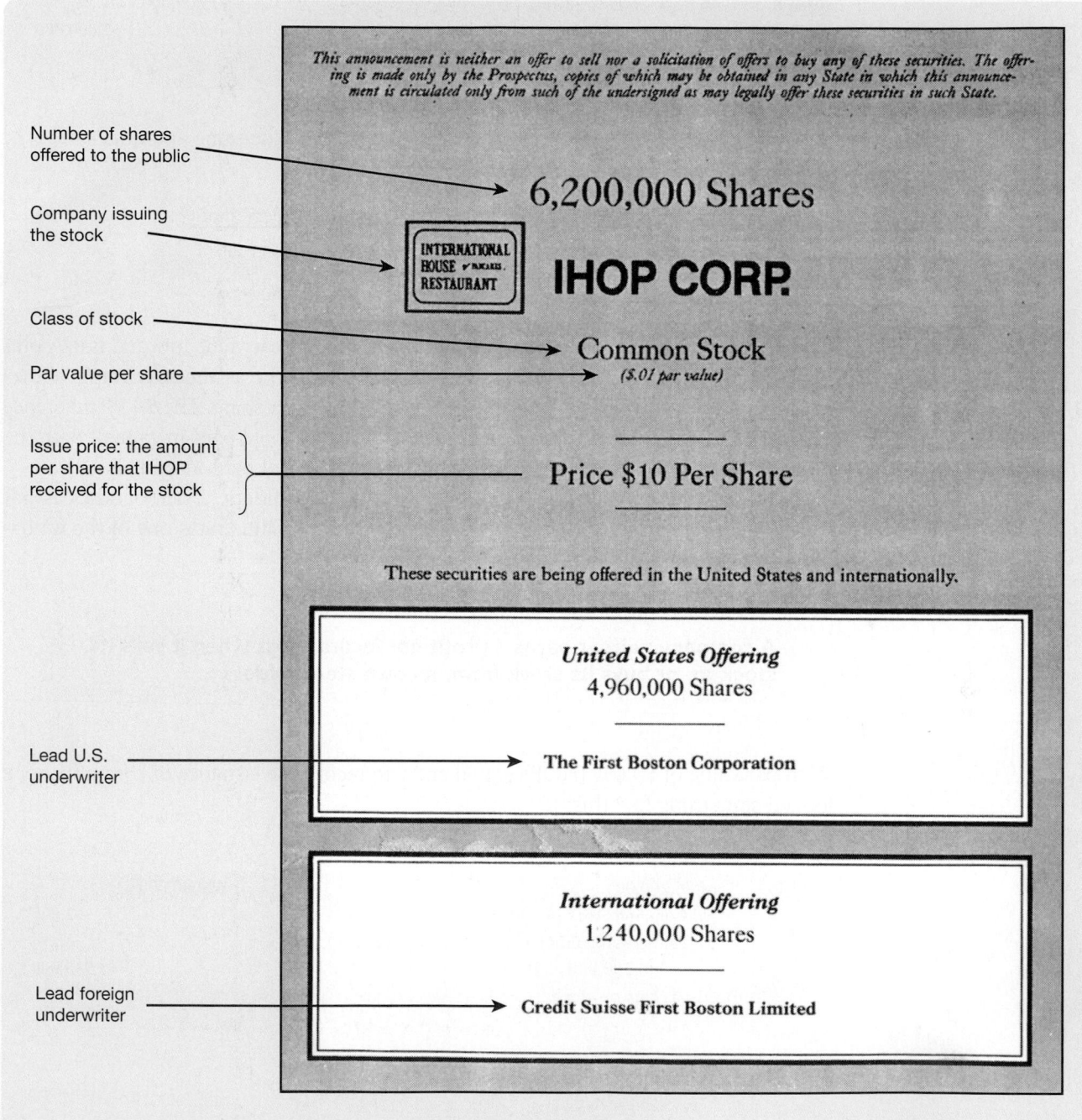

The lead underwriter of IHOP's public offering was First Boston Corporation. Outside the United States, Credit Suisse First Boston Limited led the way. Several other domestic brokerage firms and investment bankers sold IHOP stock to their clients. In its initial public offering (Exhibit 9-6), IHOP sought to raise $62 million of capital (6.2 million shares at the offering price of $10 per share). Let's see how a stock issuance works.

Common Stock

Common Stock at Par.   Suppose IHOP's common stock had carried a par value equal to its issuance price of $10 per share. The entry for issuance of 6.2 million shares of stock at par would be

Jan 8	Cash (6,200,000 × $10)	62,000,000	
	Common Stock		62,000,000
	To issue common stock.		

IHOP's assets and stockholders' equity increase by the same amount.

Assets	=	Liabilities	+	Stockholders' Equity
+ 62,000,000	=	0		+ 62,000,000

Common Stock Above Par.   Most corporations set par value low and issue common stock for a price above par. Rather than $10 as in the assumed example above, IHOP's common stock has a par value of $0.01 (1 cent) per share. The $9.99 difference between issue price ($10) and par value ($0.01) is additional paid-in capital. Both the par value of the stock and the additional amount are part of paid-in capital.

Because the entity is dealing with its own stockholders, a sale of stock is not gain, income, or profit to the corporation. This situation illustrates one of the fundamentals of accounting:

> **A company neither earns a profit nor incurs a loss when it sells its stock to, or buys its stock from, its own stockholders.**

With par value of $0.01, IHOP's actual entry to record the issuance of common stock looked something like this:

Jul 23	Cash (6,200,000 × $10)	62,000,000	
	Common Stock (6,200,000 × $0.01)		62,000
	Paid-in Capital in Excess of Par—Common		
	(6,200,000 × $9.99)		61,938,000
	To issue common stock.		

Both assets and equity increase by the same amount.

Assets	=	Liabilities	+	Stockholders' Equity
+ 62,000,000	=	0		+ 62,000
				+ 61,938,000

Another title for Paid-in Capital in Excess of Par—Common is Additional Paid-in Capital, as used by IHOP Corporation (p. 534, line 5). At the end of the year, IHOP could report stockholders' equity on its balance sheet as follows:

Stockholders' Equity	
Common stock, $0.01 par, 40 million shares authorized, 6.2 million shares issued	$ 62,000
Paid-in capital in excess of par	61,938,000
Total paid-in capital	62,000,000
Retained earnings	338,790
Total stockholders' equity	$62,338,790

All the transactions in this section include a receipt of cash by the corporation as it issues *new* stock. The transactions we illustrate are different from those reported in the daily news. In those transactions, one stockholder sold stock to another investor. The corporation doesn't record those transactions because they were between two outside parties.

STOP & THINK...

Examine IHOP's balance sheet at December 31, 2007 (p. 534). Answer these questions about IHOP's actual stock transactions (amounts in thousands, except per share):

1. What was IHOP's total paid-in capital at December 31, 2007?
2. How many shares of common stock had IHOP issued through the end of 2007 (in thousands)?
3. What was the average issue price of the IHOP common stock that the company had issued through the end of 2007?

Answers:

		December 31, 2007
1.	Total paid-in capital (in thousands)	$35 + $230 + $184,710 = $184,975
2.	Number of shares of common stock issued (in thousands)	23,360

3.
$$\frac{\text{Average issue price of common stock through the end of 2007}}{} = \frac{\text{Total received from issuance of common stock}}{\text{Common shares issued}} = \frac{\$230 + (\$184,710 - \$34,215^1)}{23,360} = \$150,725$$
$$= \$6.45 \text{ per share}$$

[1] A total of $34,215 in additional paid-in capital came from the issuance of the series B preferred stock. It must be subtracted to compute the total received from issuance of common stock.

IHOP has issued its common stock at an average price of $6.45 per share.

No-Par Common Stock. To record the issuance of no-par stock, the company debits the asset received and credits the stock account for the cash value of the asset received. Suppose Apple, Inc., issues 855 million shares of no-par common stock for $4,355 million. Apple's stock issuance entry is (in millions)

Aug 14	Cash	4,355	
	Common Stock		4,355
	To issue no-par common stock.		

Assets	=	Liabilities	+	Stockholders' Equity
+ 4,355	=	0		+ 4,355

Apple's charter authorizes the company to issue 1,800 million shares of no-par stock, and the company has approximately $5,629 in retained earnings. Apple, Inc., reports stockholders' equity on the balance sheet as follows (in millions):

Stockholders' Equity	
Common stock, no par, 1,800 shares	
authorized, 855 shares issued.................	$4,355
Retained earnings...	5,629
Total stockholders' equity	$9,984

You can see that a company with true no-par stock has no Additional Paid-in Capital account.

No-Par Common Stock with a Stated Value. Accounting for no-par stock with a stated value is identical to accounting for par-value stock. The excess over stated value is credited to Additional Paid-in Capital.

Common Stock Issued for Assets Other Than Cash. When a corporation issues stock and receives assets other than cash, the company records the assets received at their current market value and credits the stock and additional paid-in capital accounts accordingly. The assets' prior book value isn't relevant because the stockholder will demand stock equal to the market value of the asset given. On November 12, Kahn Corporation issued 15,000 shares of its $1 par common stock for equipment worth $4,000 and a building worth $120,000. Kahn's entry is

Nov 12	Equipment	4,000	
	Building	120,000	
	Common Stock (15,000 × $1)		15,000
	Paid-in Capital in Excess of Par—Common		
	($124,000 − $15,000)		109,000
	To issue no-par common stock in exchange for equipment		
	and a building.		

Assets and equity both increase by $124,000.

Assets	=	Liabilities	+	Stockholders' Equity
+ 4,000 + 120,000	=	0		+ 15,000 + 109,000

Common Stock Issued for Services. Sometimes a corporation will issue shares of common stock in exchange for services rendered, either by employees or outsiders. In this case, no cash is exchanged. However, the transaction is recognized at fair market value. The corporation usually recognizes an expense for the fair market value of the services rendered. Common stock is increased for its par value (if any) and additional paid-in capital is increased for any difference. For example, assume that Kahn Corporation engages an attorney to represent the company on a legal matter. The attorney bills the corporation $25,000 for services, and agrees to accept 2,500 shares of $1 par common stock, rather than cash, in settlement of the fee. The fair market value of the stock is $10 per share. The journal entry to record the transaction is

Legal Expense	25,000	
Common Stock		2,500
Paid-in Capital in Excess of Par—Common ($25,000 – $2,500)		22,500

In this case, retained earnings (stockholders' equity) is eventually decreased by $25,000, and paid-in capital (stockholders' equity) is increased for the same amount.

A Stock Issuance for Other Than Cash Can Create an Ethical Challenge

Generally accepted accounting principles require a company to record its stock at the fair market value of whatever the corporation receives in exchange for the stock. When the corporation receives cash, there is clear evidence of the value of the stock because cash is worth its face amount. But when the corporation receives an asset other than cash, the value of the asset can create an ethical challenge.

A computer whiz may start a new company by investing computer software. The software may be market-tested or it may be new. The software may be worth millions or worthless. The corporation must record the asset received and the stock given with a journal entry such as the following:

Software	500,000	
Common Stock		500,000
Issued stock in exchange for software.		

If the software is really worth $500,000, the accounting records are okay. But if the software is new and untested, the assets and equity may be overstated.

Suppose your computer-whiz friend invites you to invest in the new business and shows you this balance sheet:

Gee-Whiz Computer Solutions, Inc.
Balance Sheet
December 31, 2011

Assets		Liabilities	
Computer software	$500,000		$ -0-
		Stockholders' Equity	
		Common stock............................	500,000
Total assets............................	$500,000	Total liabilities and equity............	$500,000

Companies like to report large asset and equity amounts on their balance sheets. That makes them look prosperous and creditworthy. Gee-Whiz looks debt-free and appears to have a valuable asset. Will you invest in this new business? Here are two takeaway lessons:

- Some accounting values are more solid than others.
- Not all financial statements mean exactly what they say—unless they are audited by independent CPAs.

Preferred Stock

Accounting for preferred stock follows the same pattern we illustrated for common. When a company issues preferred stock, it credits Preferred Stock at its par value, with any excess credited to Paid-in Capital in Excess of Par—Preferred.

There may be separate accounts for paid-in capital in excess of par for preferred and common stock, but not necessarily. Some companies, such as DineEquity (formerly IHOP), combine paid-in capital in excess of par from both preferred and common stock transactions into one account. Accounting for no-par preferred follows the pattern for no-par common stock. When reporting stockholders' equity on the balance sheet, a corporation lists its accounts in this order:

- preferred stock
- common stock
- additional paid-in capital
- retained earnings

as illustrated for IHOP on page 534.

In Chapter 8 we saw how to account for convertible bonds payable (p. 491). Companies also issue convertible preferred stock. The preferred stock is usually convertible into the company's common stock at the discretion of the preferred stockholders. For example, in November 2007, IHOP issued 35,000 shares of Class B preferred stock. This stock is convertible into shares of DineEquity (formerly IHOP) stock according to a formula based on the relative values of preferred and common stock, during the first five years after issuance. On the 5th anniversary (November 2012), all the shares automatically convert into shares of the company's common stock, without any action on the part of the stockholder. The journal entry to record the transaction was

2007	Cash	34,250,000	
	Preferred Stock, Series B		35,000
	Additional Paid-in Capital		34,215,000
	Issued 35,000 shares of series B preferred stock.		

Whenever the common stock's market price gets high enough—or the preferred's market price gets low enough—holders of convertible preferred will convert their stock into common. Here are some representative journal entries for convertible preferred stock, using assumed amounts:

2008	Cash	50,000	
	Convertible Preferred Stock		50,000
	Issued convertible preferred stock.		

2010	Convertible Preferred Stock	50,000	
	Common Stock		8,000
	Paid-in Capital in Excess of Par—Common		42,000
	Investors converted preferred into common.		

As you can see, we merely remove Preferred Stock from the books and give the new Common Stock the prior book value of the preferred.

MID-CHAPTER SUMMARY PROBLEM

1. Test your understanding of the first half of this chapter by deciding whether each of the following statements is true or false.
   a. The policy-making body in a corporation is called the board of directors.
   b. The owner of 100 shares of preferred stock has greater voting rights than the owner of 100 shares of common stock.
   c. Par-value stock is worth more than no-par stock.
   d. Issuance of 1,000 shares of $5 par-value stock at $12 increases contributed capital by $12,000.
   e. The issuance of no-par stock with a stated value is fundamentally different from issuing par-value stock.
   f. A corporation issues its preferred stock in exchange for land and a building with a combined market value of $200,000. This transaction increases the corporation's owners' equity by $200,000 regardless of the assets' prior book values.
   g. Preferred stock is a riskier investment than common stock.
2. Adolfo Company has two classes of common stock. Only the Class A common stockholders are entitled to vote. The company's balance sheet included the following presentation:

Stockholders' Equity	
Capital stock:	
Class A common stock, voting, $1 par value,	
authorized and issued 1,260,000 shares..................	$ 1,260,000
Class B common stock, nonvoting, no par value,	
authorized and issued 46,200,000 shares...............	11,000,000
	12,260,000
Additional paid-in capital..	2,011,000
Retained earnings...	872,403,000
	$886,674,000

❙ Requirements
a. Record the issuance of the Class A common stock. Use the Adolfo account titles.
b. Record the issuance of the Class B common stock. Use the Adolfo account titles.
c. How much of Adolfo's stockholders' equity was contributed by the stockholders? How much was provided by profitable operations? Does this division of equity suggest that the company has been successful? Why or why not?
d. Write a sentence to describe what Adolfo's stockholders' equity means.

Answers

1. a. True   b. False   c. False   d. True   e. False   f. True   g. False
2. a.

Cash	3,271,000	
Class A Common Stock		1,260,000
Additional Paid-in Capital		2,011,000
To record issuance of Class A common stock.		

b.

Cash	11,000,000	
Class B Common Stock		11,000,000
To record issuance of Class B common stock.		

c. Contributed by the stockholders: $14,271,000 ($12,260,000 + $2,011,000). Provided by profitable operations: $872,403,000.
   This division suggests that the company has been successful because most of its stockholders' equity has come from profitable operations.

d. Adolfo's stockholders' equity of $886,674,000 means that the company's stockholders own $886,674,000 of the business's assets.

AUTHORIZED, ISSUED, AND OUTSTANDING STOCK

It's important to distinguish among three distinctly different numbers of a company's stock. The following examples use IHOP's actual data from page 534.

- **Authorized stock** is the maximum number of shares the company can issue under its charter. As of December 31, 2007, IHOP was authorized to issue 40 million shares of common stock.
- **Issued stock** is the number of shares the company has issued to its stockholders. This is a cumulative total from the company's beginning up through the current date. As of December 31, 2007, IHOP had issued 23,359,664 shares of its common stock.
- **Outstanding stock** is the number of shares that the stockholders own (that is, the number of shares outstanding in the hands of the stockholders). Outstanding stock is issued stock minus treasury stock. At December 31, 2007, IHOP had 17,105,469 shares of common stock outstanding, computed as follows:

Issued shares (line 4)	23,359,664
Less: Treasury shares (line 7)...............	(6,254,195)
Outstanding shares (line 4)..................	17,105,469

Now let's learn about treasury stock.

TREASURY STOCK

A company's own stock that it has issued and later reacquired is called **treasury stock**.[2] In effect, the corporation holds this stock in its treasury. Many public companies spend millions of dollars each year to buy back their own stock. Corporations purchase their own stock for several reasons:

OBJECTIVE

3 Describe how treasury stock affects a company

1. The company has issued all its authorized stock and needs some stock for distributions to employees under stock purchase plans.

2. The business wants to increase net assets by buying its stock low and hoping to resell it for a higher price.

3. Management wants to avoid a takeover by an outside party.

[2]In this text, we illustrate the *cost* method of accounting for treasury stock because it is used most widely. Other methods are presented in intermediate accounting courses.

4. Management wants to increase its reported earnings per share (EPS) of common stock (net income/number of common shares outstanding). Purchasing shares removes them from outstanding shares, thus decreasing the denominator of this fraction and increasing EPS. We cover the computation of EPS in more depth in Chapter 11.

How is Treasury Stock Recorded?

Treasury stock is recorded at cost (the market value of the stock on the date of the purchase) without regard to stock's par value. Treasury stock is a *contra stockholders' equity* account. Therefore, the treasury stock account carries a debit balance, the opposite of the other equity accounts. It is reported beneath the retained earnings account on the balance sheet as a negative amount.

To understand the way treasury stock transactions work, it is helpful to analyze the changes that occur in the treasury stock account during the year. Let's start with the company's stockholders' equity at the end of the previous year, December 31, 2006 (we use rounded amounts in thousands, except for shares):

IHOP, Inc.
Stockholders' Equity
December 31, 2006

Common stock...	$ 227
Additional paid-in capital............................	131,748
Retained earnings..	358,975
Treasury stock (4,944,459 shares)...............	(201,604)
Other equity..	(133)
Total stockholders' equity..........................	$289,213

Notice that, up to the end of 2006, IHOP had spent $201,604,000 to repurchase 4,944,459 shares of its own stock throughout the company's history. The average price it paid for the shares was therefore about $40.77 ($201,604,000/4,944,459). Assume that during 2007, IHOP paid $76,050,000 to purchase 1,309,736 additional shares of its common stock as treasury stock. Therefore, it paid $58.065 per share for the stock ($76,050,000/1,309,736 shares). IHOP would record the purchase of treasury stock as follows (in thousands):

2007			
Nov 12	Treasury Stock	76,050	
	Cash		76,050
	Purchased treasury stock.		

Assets	=	Liabilities	+	Stockholders' Equity
– 76,050	=	0		– 76,050

Notice that treasury stock is recorded at cost, which is the market price of the stock on the day IHOP purchased it ($58.065 per share). The financial statement impact of the transaction is to decrease cash as well as stockholders' equity by $76,050,000.

Now let's examine the stockholders' equity section of IHOP on December 31, 2007. In addition to purchasing treasury stock, the company issued both preferred stock and common stock during 2007. It also reported a net loss for 2007 and had some other reductions in retained earnings. The stockholders' equity account balances (rounded amounts in thousands, except for shares) at December 31, 2007, follow. For now, focus only on the treasury stock account:

IHOP, Inc. Stockholders' Equity December 31, 2007	
Preferred stock	$ 35
Common stock	230
Paid-in capital in excess of par	184,710
Retained earnings	338,790
Less Treasury stock (at cost) 6,254,195 shares	(277,654)
Other equity	(36,738)
Total stockholders' equity	$ 209,373

The treasury stock purchase increased the contra account treasury stock by $76,050,000. Therefore, it decreased IHOP's stockholders' equity by $76,050,000. The new number of treasury shares is now 6,254,195 (4,944,459 + 1,309,736). The new average purchase price of treasury shares is $44.39, reflecting the higher amount paid for the newly acquired shares.

In summary, the purchase of treasury stock has the opposite effect of issuing stock:

- Issuing stock *grows* assets and equity.
- Purchasing treasury stock *shrinks* assets and equity.

Treasury stock is so named because it is held in the company treasury awaiting resale. Now let's see how to account for the resale of treasury stock.

Resale of Treasury Stock

Reselling treasury stock grows assets and equity exactly as issuing new stock does. Suppose that, on July 22, 2008, IHOP resells all of the treasury stock it purchased in 2007 for $100,000,000. The sale increases assets and equity by the full amount of cash received. Notice that the company **never records gains or losses on transactions involving its own treasury stock**. Rather, amounts received in excess of amounts originally paid for treasury stock are recorded as paid-in capital from treasury stock transactions, thus bypassing the income statement. If amounts received from resale of treasury stock were less than amounts originally paid, the difference would be debited to paid-in capital to the extent of that balance, and after that, to retained earnings. IHOP would record this sale of treasury stock as follows (in thousands):

2008			
Jul 22	Cash	100,000	
	Treasury Stock		76,050
	Paid-in Capital from Treasury Stock Transactions		
	(or Additional Paid-in Capital—Common)		23,950
	Sold treasury stock.		

Assets	=	Liabilities	+	Stockholders' Equity
+ 100,000	=	0		+ 76,050
				+ 23,950

If IHOP had sold the treasury stock for a price below cost, then IHOP could have debited Retained Earnings for the difference.

Issuing Treasury Stock as Compensation

Sometimes companies supplement their employee salaries by granting them stock rather than cash. If, in the preceding example, IHOP had chosen to distribute $100,000,000 in stock as compensation, the account debited would have been salary expense, rather than cash. The credit side of the transaction would have been the same.

Summary of Treasury-Stock Transactions

There are only two types of treasury-stock transactions:

- Buying treasury stock. Assets and equity *decrease* by an amount equal to the cost of treasury stock purchased.
- Selling treasury stock. Assets and equity *increase* by an amount equal to the sale price of the treasury stock sold.

Retirement of Stock

A corporation may purchase its own stock and *retire* it by canceling the stock certificates. Companies retire their preferred stock to avoid paying dividends on the preferred stock. The retired stock cannot be reissued. When a company retires its stock, the journal entry credits Cash and debits the stock account and any additional paid-in capital on the stock. Retirements of common stock are rare.

Retained Earnings, Dividends, and Splits

The Retained Earnings account carries the balance of the business's net income, less its net losses and less any declared dividends that have been accumulated over the corporation's lifetime. *Retained* means "held onto." Successful companies grow by reinvesting back into the business the assets they generate through profitable operations. IHOP Corp. is an example. Take another look at its stockholders' equity as of December 31, 2007 (p. 534). Notice that the Retained Earnings account ($338,790,000) is the largest account balance in stockholders' equity as of the end of 2007. In fact, because historically the company has spent so much money on treasury stock, retained earnings actually *exceeds* total stockholders' equity ($209,373,000) as of the end of 2007.

The Retained Earnings account is not a reservoir of cash for paying dividends to the stockholders. In fact, the corporation may have a large balance in Retained Earnings but not have enough cash to pay a dividend. Cash and Retained Earnings are two entirely separate accounts with no particular relationship. Retained Earnings says nothing about the company's Cash balance.

A *credit* balance in Retained Earnings is normal, indicating that the corporation's lifetime earnings exceed lifetime losses and dividends. A *debit* balance in Retained Earnings arises when a corporation's lifetime losses and dividends exceed lifetime earnings. Called a **deficit**, this amount is subtracted to determine total stockholders' equity. In a recent survey, 15.5% of companies had a retained earnings deficit (Exhibit 9-7).

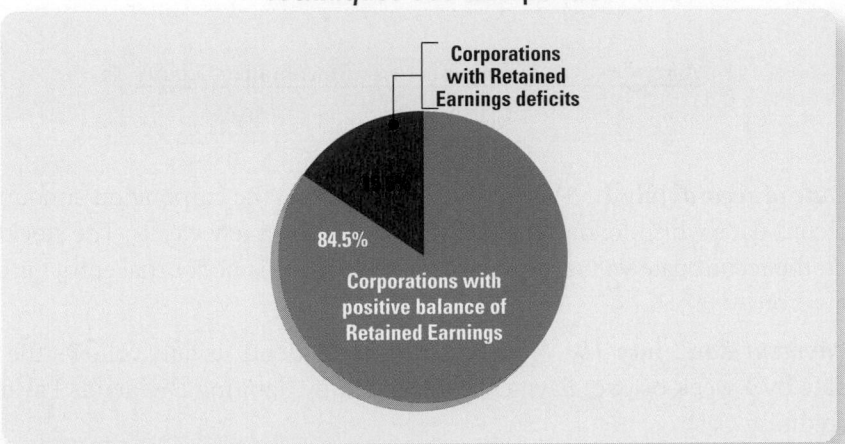

EXHIBIT 9-7 | **Retained Earnings of the** *Accounting Trends &* *Techniques 600* **Companies**

Should the Company Declare and Pay Cash Dividends?

A **dividend** is a distribution by a corporation to its stockholders, usually based on earnings. Dividends usually take one of three forms:

OBJECTIVE

4 **Account** for dividends

- Cash
- Stock
- Noncash assets

In this section we focus on cash dividends and stock dividends because noncash dividends are rare. For a noncash asset dividend, debit Retained Earnings and credit the asset (for example, Long-Term Investment) for the current market value of the asset given.

Cash Dividends   *I will give you cash*

Most dividends are cash dividends. Finance courses discuss how a company decides on its dividend policy. Accounting tells a company if it can pay a dividend. To do so, a company must have both

- Enough Retained Earnings   and   ▪ Enough Cash to *pay*
  to *declare* the dividend   the dividend

A corporation declares a dividend before paying it. Only the board of directors has the authority to declare a dividend. The corporation has no obligation to pay a dividend until the board declares one, but once declared, the dividend becomes a legal liability of the corporation. There are three relevant dates for dividends (using assumed amounts):

1. *Declaration date, June 19.*   On the declaration date, the board of directors announces the dividend. Declaration of the dividend creates a liability for the corporation. Declaration is recorded by debiting Retained Earnings and crediting Dividends Payable. Assume a $50,000 dividend.

Jun 19	Retained Earnings[3]	50,000	
	Dividends Payable		50,000
	Declared a cash dividend.		

Liabilities increase, and equity goes down.

Assets	=	Liabilities	+	Stockholders' Equity
0	=	+ 50,000		− 50,000

2. **Date of record, July 1.**   As part of the declaration, the corporation announces the record date, which follows the declaration date by a few weeks. The stockholders on the record date will receive the dividend. There is no journal entry for the date of record.

3. **Payment date, July 10.**   Payment of the dividend usually follows the record date by a week or two. Payment is recorded by debiting Dividends Payable and crediting Cash.

Jul 10	Dividends Payable	50,000	
	Cash		50,000
	Paid cash dividend.		

Both assets and liabilities decrease. The corporation shrinks.

Assets	=	Liabilities	+	Stockholders' Equity
− 50,000	=	− 50,000		

The net effect of a dividend declaration and its payment, as shown in steps 1, 2, and 3, is a decrease in assets and a corresponding decrease in stockholders' equity.

Analyzing the Stockholder's Equity Accounts

By knowing accounting you can look at a company's comparative year-to-year financial statements and tell a lot about what the company did during the current year. For example, IHOP reported the following for Retained Earnings (in thousands):

| | December 31, | |
	2007	2006
Retained earnings...............	$338,790	$358,975

What do these figures tell you about IHOP's results of operations during 2007—was it a net income or a net loss? How can you tell? Remember that

- Net income is the only item that increases retained earnings;
- Net losses decrease retained earnings;
- Dividends decrease retained earnings; and
- Other adjustments to retained earnings are usually relatively minor and relatively rare.

---

[3] In the early part of this book, we debited a Dividends account to clearly identify the purpose of the payment. From here on, we follow the more common practice of debiting the Retained Earnings account for dividend declarations.

In most cases, if you know the amount of either net income or dividends, but not both, and if you know both beginning and ending balances of retained earnings, you can figure out the amount you don't know by analyzing the Retained Earnings account.

For example, let's assume that IHOP's net income for 2007 had been $10,000,000, and that there were no other changes besides dividends. How much in dividends did the company pay?

If you know accounting—if you know IHOP's net income (assumed to be $10,000,000), you can compute IHOP's dividend declarations during 2007, as follows (in thousands):

Retained Earnings

		Beg bal	358,975
Dividends	?	Net income	10,000
		End bal	338,790

Dividends (x) would have been $30,185 ($358,975 + $10,000 − x = $338,790; x = $30,185). It really helps to be able to use accounting in this way!

Unfortunately, in IHOP's case, 2007 wasn't that simple. Every change to IHOP's retained earnings in 2007 was negative:

1. The company incurred a net loss of $480,000.

2. It paid dividends on common stock in the amount of $17,293,000, and dividends on preferred stock in the amount of $1,742,000 (total $19,035,000).

3. It had to make two other relatively minor negative adjustments to retained earnings that totaled $670,000.

Therefore, an analysis of IHOP's ending balance in retained earnings as of December 31, 2007 is as follows (in thousands):

Retained Earnings

Net loss	480	Beg bal	358,975
Dividends	19,035		
Other adj	670		
		End bal	338,790

Common stock Holders are the last to be paid. normally do not see any money.

Dividends on Preferred Stock

As shown in the previous section, IHOP paid dividends on its preferred stock in 2007 in the amount of $1,742,000. When a company has issued both preferred and common stock, the preferred stockholders receive their dividends first. The common stockholders receive dividends only if the total dividend is large enough to pay the preferred stockholders first.

Avant Garde, Inc., has 100,000 shares of $1.50 preferred stock outstanding in addition to its common stock. The $1.50 designation means that the preferred stockholders receive an annual cash dividend of $1.50 per share. In 2010, Avant Garde declares an annual dividend of $500,000. The allocation to preferred and common stockholders is:

Preferred dividend (100,000 shares × $1.50 per share)...........	$150,000
Common dividend (remainder: $500,000 − $150,000)	350,000
Total dividend...	$500,000

 *know this*

If Avant Garde declares only a $200,000 dividend, preferred stockholders receive $150,000, and the common stockholders get the remainder, $50,000 ($200,000 – $150,000).

Two Ways to Express the Dividend Rate on Preferred Stock.   Dividends on preferred stock are stated either as a

- Percent of par value   or   ▪ Dollar amount per share

For example, preferred stock may be "6% preferred," which means that owners of the preferred stock receive an annual dividend equal to 6% of the stock's par value. If par value is $100 per share, preferred stockholders receive an annual cash dividend of $6 per share (6% of $100). Alternatively, the preferred stock may be "$3 preferred," which means that the preferred stockholders receive an annual dividend of $3 per share regardless of the stock's par value. The dividend rate on no-par preferred stock is stated in a dollar amount per share.

Dividends on Cumulative and Noncumulative Preferred Stock.   The balance sheet classification of preferred stock, as well as the allocation of dividends, may be complex if the preferred stock is *cumulative*. IHOP's balance sheet (p. 534), for example, reflects that it has issued 190,000 shares of Series A, $1 par value cumulative preferred stock. The cumulative feature gives this series of preferred stock sufficient debt features that the company has opted to report the $187 million carrying value immediately after long-term liabilities, but has omitted it from stockholders' equity. Why? Corporations sometimes fail to pay a dividend to preferred stockholders. This is called *passing the dividend*, and the passed dividends are said to be *in arrears*. The owners of **cumulative preferred stock** must receive all dividends in arrears plus the current year's dividend before any dividends go to the common stockholders. In this sense, cumulative dividends almost take on the flavor of accrued interest on long-term debt, but not quite. Although cumulative dividends must be paid before other dividends, they must still be declared by the company's board of directors.

In contrast, interest on long-term debt doesn't have to go through a formal approval process by the board. Nevertheless, the similarity of cumulative dividends on preferred stock with interest on long-term debt are one feature that justify classifying such instruments as debt, rather than equity financing. Hence, IHOP has recorded the Series A preferred stock between its long-term debt and stockholders' equity. It doesn't quite fit in either section, so it is classified between them. *In most states preferred stock is cumulative unless it is specifically labeled as noncumulative.*

Here's an example of how cumulative dividends work. The preferred stock of Avant Garde, Inc., is cumulative. Suppose Avant Garde passed the preferred dividend of $150,000 in 2010. Before paying dividends to common in 2011, Avant Garde must first pay preferred dividends of $150,000 for both 2010 and 2011, a total of $300,000. On September 6, 2011, Avant Garde declares a $500,000 dividend. The entry to record the declaration is

Sep 6	Retained Earnings	500,000	
	Dividends Payable, Preferred ($150,000 × 2)		300,000
	Dividends Payable, Common ($500,000 – $300,000)		200,000
	To declare a cash dividend.		

If the preferred stock is *noncumulative*, the corporation is not obligated to pay dividends in arrears—until the board of directors declares the dividend.

Stock Dividends   I will give you stock

A **stock dividend** is a proportional distribution by a corporation of its own stock to its stockholders. Stock dividends increase the stock account and decrease Retained Earnings. Total equity is unchanged, and no asset or liability is affected.

The corporation distributes stock dividends to stockholders in proportion to the number of shares they already own. If you own 300 shares of IHOP common stock and IHOP distributes a 10% common stock dividend, you get 30 (300 × .10) additional shares. You would then own 330 shares of the stock. All other IHOP stockholders would also receive 10% more shares, leaving all stockholders' ownership unchanged.

In distributing a stock dividend, the corporation gives up no assets. Why, then, do companies issue stock dividends? A corporation may choose to distribute stock dividends for these reasons:

1. **To continue dividends but conserve cash.**   A company may need to conserve cash and yet wish to continue dividends in some form. So the corporation may distribute a stock dividend. Stockholders pay no income tax on stock dividends.

2. **To reduce the per-share market price of its stock.**   Distribution of a stock dividend usually causes the stock's market price to fall because of the increased number of outstanding shares that result from it. The objective is to make the stock less expensive and therefore attractive to more investors.

Generally accepted accounting principles (GAAP) label a stock dividend of 25% or less as *small* and suggest that the dividend be recorded at the market value of the shares distributed. Suppose DineEquity (formerly IHOP) declared a 10% common stock dividend in 2011. At the time, assume DineEquity had 20,000,000 shares of common stock outstanding, and DineEquity's stock is trading for $10 per share. DineEquity would record this stock dividend as follows:

2011			
May 19	Retained Earnings[4] (20,000,000 shares of common outstanding × 0.10 stock dividend × $10 market value per share of common)	20,000,000	
	Common Stock (20,000,000 × 0.10 × $0.01 per value per share)		20,000
	Paid-in Capital in Excess of Par—Common		19,980,000
	Distributed a 10% stock dividend.		

The accounting equation clearly shows that a stock dividend has no effect on total assets, liabilities, or equity. The increases in equity offset the decreases, and the net effect is zero.

Assets	=	Liabilities	+	Stockholders' Equity
0	=	0		− 20,000,000
				+ 20,000
				+ 19,980,000

[4]Many companies debit Additional Paid-in Capital for their stock dividends.

GAAP identifies stock dividends above 25% as *large* and permits large stock dividends to be recorded at par value. For a large stock dividend, therefore, IHOP would debit Retained Earnings and credit Common Stock for the par value of the shares distributed in the dividend.

Stock Splits

A **stock split** is an increase in the number of shares of stock authorized, issued, and outstanding, coupled with a proportionate reduction in the stock's par value. For example, if the company splits its stock 2 for 1, the number of outstanding shares is doubled and each share's par value is halved. A stock split, like a large stock dividend, decreases the market price of the stock—with the intention of making the stock more attractive in the market. Most leading companies in the United States—including **IBM**, **PepsiCo**, and **Best Buy**—have split their stock.

The market price of a share of Best Buy common stock has been approximately $50. Assume that Best Buy wishes to decrease the market price to approximately $25 per share. Best Buy can split its common stock 2 for 1, and the stock price will fall to around $25. A 2-for-1 stock split means that

- the company will have twice as many shares of stock authorized, issued, and outstanding after the split as it had before.
- each share's par value will be cut in half.

Before the split, Best Buy had approximately 500 million shares of $0.10 (10 cents) par common stock issued and outstanding. Compare Best Buy's stockholders' equity before and after a 2-for-1 stock split:

Best Buy Co., Inc., Stockholders' Equity (Adapted)

Before 2-for-1 Stock Split	(In millions)	After 2-for-1 Stock Split	(In millions)
Common stock, $0.10 par, 1,000 shares authorized, 500 shares issued.........	$ 50	Common stock, $0.05 par, 2,000 shares authorized, 1,000 shares issued......	$ 50
Additional paid-in capital....................	643	Additional paid-in capital....................	643
Retained earnings................................	4,304	Retained earnings................................	4,304
Other equity...	260	Other...	260
Total stockholders' equity..................	$5,257	Total stockholders' equity..................	$5,257

All account balances are the same after the stock split as before. Only three Best Buy items are affected:

- Par value per share drops from $0.10 to $0.05.
- Shares *authorized* double from 1,000 to 2,000 (both in millions).
- Shares *issued* double from 500 to 1,000 (both in millions).

Total equity doesn't change, nor do any assets or liabilities.

Summary of the Effects on Assets, Liabilities, and Stockholders' Equity

We've seen how to account for the basic stockholders' equity transactions:

- Issuance of stock—common and preferred (pp. 540–547)
- Purchase and sale of treasury stock (pp. 549–552)
- Cash dividends (pp. 553–554)
- Stock dividends and stock splits (pp. 557–558)

How do these transactions affect assets, liabilities, and equity? Exhibit 9-8 provides a helpful summary.

EXHIBIT 9-8 | Effects on Assets, Liabilities, and Equity

Transaction	Assets	=	Liabilities	+	Stockholders' Equity
Issuance of stock—common and preferred	Increase		No effect		Increase
Purchase of treasury stock	Decrease		No effect		Decrease
Sale of treasury stock	Increase		No effect		Increase
Declaration of cash dividend	No effect		Increase		Decrease
Payment of cash dividend	Decrease		Decrease		No effect
Stock dividend—large and small	No effect		No effect		No effect*
Stock split	No effect		No effect		No effect

*The stock accounts increase and retained earnings decrease by offsetting amounts that net to zero.

MEASURING THE VALUE OF STOCK

The business community measures *stock values* in various ways, depending on the purpose of the measurement. These values include market value, redemption value, liquidation value, and book value.

OBJECTIVE

5 Use stock values in decision making

Market, Redemption, Liquidation, and Book Value

A stock's **market value**, or *market price*, is the price a person can buy or sell 1 share of the stock for. Market value varies with the corporation's net income, financial position, and future prospects, and with general economic conditions. *In almost all cases, stockholders are more concerned about the market value of a stock than any other value.*

DineEquity's stock price has been quoted recently at $31.50 per share. Therefore, if DineEquity were issuing 100,000 shares of its common stock, it would receive cash of $3,150,000 (100,000 shares × $31.50 per share). This is the market value of the stock DineEquity issued.

Preferred stock that requires the company to redeem the stock at a set price is called **redeemable preferred stock**. The company is *obligated* to redeem (pay to retire) the preferred stock. Therefore, redeemable preferred stock is really not stockholders' equity. Instead it's a liability. The price the corporation agrees to pay for the stock, set when the stock is issued, is called the **redemption value**. **Liquidation value** is the amount that a company must pay a preferred stockholder in the event the company liquidates (sells out) and goes out of business.

The **book value** per share of common stock is the amount of owners' equity on the company's books for each share of its stock. If the company has only common stock outstanding, its book value is computed by dividing total equity by the number of shares of common *outstanding*. Recall that *outstanding* stock is *issued* stock minus *treasury* stock. For example, a company with stockholders' equity of $150,000 and 5,000 shares of common stock outstanding has a book value of $30 per share ($150,000 ÷ 5,000 shares).

If the company has both preferred and common outstanding, the preferred stockholders have the first claim to owners' equity. Preferred stock often has a specified redemption value. The preferred equity is its redemption value plus any cumulative preferred dividends in arrears. Book value per share of common is then computed as follows:

$$\text{Book value per share of common stock} = \frac{\text{Total stockholders' equity} - \text{Preferred equity}}{\text{Number of shares of common stock outstanding}}$$

Crusader Corporation's balance sheet reports the following amounts:

Stockholders' Equity	
Preferred stock, 5%, $100 par, 400 shares issued, redemption value $130 per share	$ 40,000
Common stock, $10 par, 5,500 shares issued	55,000
Additional paid-in capital—common	72,000
Retained earnings	88,000
Treasury stock—common, 500 shares at cost	(15,000)
Total stockholders' equity	$240,000

Cumulative preferred dividends are in arrears for four years (including the current year). Crusader's preferred stock has a redemption value of $130 per share. The book-value-per-share computations for Crusader Corporation are:

Preferred Equity	
Redemption value (400 shares × $130)	$52,000
Cumulative dividends ($40,000 × 0.05 × 4 years)	8,000
Preferred equity	$60,000*

Common Equity	
Total stockholders' equity	$240,000
Less preferred equity	(60,000)
Common equity	$180,000
Book value per share [$180,000 ÷ 5,000 shares outstanding (5,500 shares issued minus 500 treasury shares)]	$ 36.00

*If the preferred stock had no redemption value, then preferred equity would be $40,000 + preferred dividends in arrears.

Some investors search for stocks whose market price is below book value. They believe this indicates a good buy. Financial analysts often shy away from companies with a stock price at or below book value. To these investors, such a company is in trouble. As you can see, not all investors agree on a stock value. In fact, wise investors base their decisions on more than a single ratio. In Chapter 13 you'll see the full range of financial ratios, plus a few more analytical techniques.

Relating Profitability to a Company's Stock

Investors search for companies whose stocks are likely to increase in value. They're constantly comparing companies. But a comparison of IHOP with a new restaurant chain is not meaningful. IHOP's profits run into the millions, which far exceed a new company's net income. Does this automatically make IHOP a better investment? Not necessarily. To compare companies of different size, investors use some standard profitability measures, including

OBJECTIVE

6 **Compute** return on assets and return on equity

- return on assets
- return on equity

Return on Assets. The **rate of return on total assets**, or simply **return on assets (ROA)**, measures a company's use of its assets to earn income for the two groups who finance the business:

- Creditors to whom the corporation owes money. Creditors want interest.
- Stockholders who own the corporation's stock. Stockholders want net income.

The sum of interest expense and net income is the return to the two groups who finance a corporation. This sum is the numerator of the return-on-assets ratio. The denominator is average total assets. ROA is computed as follows, using actual data (in thousands) from the 2007 annual report of IHOP Corp.:

$$\text{Rate of return on total assets} = \frac{\text{Net income} + \text{Interest expense}}{\text{Average total assets}}$$

$$= \frac{\$(480) + \$28,654}{\$(3,831,162 + 766,250)/2} = .012$$

Net income and interest expense come from the income statement. Average total assets is computed from the beginning and ending balance sheets. Notice that total assets for 2007 increased by five times over total assets in 2006 (not shown), because of the purchase of Applebee's International. In addition, the tidy net income of $45 million that IHOP earned in 2006 (not shown) has turned into a loss ($480 thousand) when combined with Applebee's results in 2007.

What is a good rate of return on total assets? Ten percent is considered strong in most industries. However, rates of return vary by industry. Some high-technology companies earn much higher returns than do utility companies, groceries, and manufacturers of consumer goods such as toothpaste and paper towels. IHOP's return on assets (1.2%) is very low due to two factors. First, the company's total assets increased by five times when IHOP bought Applebee's in November 2007, thus greatly increasing the denominator of the ROA fraction. In addition, after operating at a profit for many years, the combined entity reflected an operating loss of $480,000 in 2007. This was mostly due to excessive operating costs associated with Applebee's that, by December 31, 2007, management hadn't yet had a chance to trim. Hopefully, within a few years operating as DineEquity, the company can cut these costs and return to profitability.

Return on Equity. **Rate of return on common stockholders' equity**, often called **return on equity (ROE)**, shows the relationship between net income available to common and average common stockholders' equity. Return on equity is computed only on common stock because the return to preferred stockholders is the specified dividend (for example, 5%).

The numerator of return on equity is net income minus preferred dividends. The denominator is *average common stockholders' equity*—total stockholders' equity minus preferred equity. IHOP Corp.'s ROE for 2007 is computed as follows (dollars in thousands):

$$\text{Rate of return on common stockholder's equity} = \frac{\text{Net income (loss)} - \text{Preferred dividends}}{\text{Average common stockholders' equity}}$$

$$= \frac{\$(480) - (1,742)}{\$(289,213 + 175,123^5)/2} = \frac{\$(2,222)}{\$232,168} = (0.957\%)$$

The common stockholders' equity for 2007 is total stockholders' equity of $209,373 less the portion attributable to preferred stock ($35 stock + $34,215 additional paid-in capital) or $175,123 (all amounts in thousands).

IHOP's return on equity (about −1%) is less than its return on assets, which is, in itself, very small (1.2%). This is not a good signal. In contrast, IHOP's ROE for the 2006 year was 15.4%. It appears that the acquisition of Applebee's International in 2007 has, at least in the short run, placed a great deal of pressure on the income of DineEquity, while greatly multiplying the amount of assets under management. ROE is always higher than ROA for a successful company in the long run. Stockholders take a lot more investment risk than bondholders, so the stockholders demand that ROE exceed ROA. They expect the return on their investment to exceed the amount they are having to pay their creditors for borrowed funds. Since ROA is higher in the case of IHOP, that means that the creditors' return on debt—interest—is higher than the return on equity—net income.

The common stockholders of DineEquity cannot permit this situation to persist for a long period of time, or they will sell their stock! It is no wonder that the market price of the company's common stock has fallen from the high $50s to $31.50 per share recently. Common stockholders are going to demand some changes in the way the company is run, cutting costs, finding new ways to increase profitability, and possibly closing a large number of marginally profitable restaurants.

Investors and creditors use ROE in much the same way they use ROA—to compare companies. The higher the rate of return, the more successful the company. In many industries, 15% is considered a good ROE.

The Decision Guidelines feature (p. 565) offers suggestions for what to consider when investing in stock.

---

[5] Ending equity comes from page 534. Beginning equity comes from the 2006 balance sheet, which is not shown.

REPORTING STOCKHOLDERS' EQUITY TRANSACTIONS

Statement of Cash Flows

Many of the transactions we've covered are reported on the statement of cash flows. Equity transactions are *financing activities* because the company is dealing with its owners. Financing transactions that affect both cash and equity fall into three main categories:

- issuance of stock
- treasury stock
- dividends

Issuances of Stock. During 2007, IHOP Corp. issued preferred stock as well as common stock. This is as a financing activity, as shown in Exhibit 9-9

EXHIBIT 9-9 | **IHOP Corp's Financing Activities (Adapted from the consolidated statement of cash flows)**

Cash Flows from Financing Activities	(In thousands)
Issuance of preferred stock	$222,800
Issuance of common stock..........................	8,928
Purchase of treasury stock..........................	(76,050)
Payment of dividends	(17,293)

Treasury Stock. During 2007, IHOP purchased treasury stock and reported the payment as a financing activity.

Dividends. Most companies, including IHOP, pay cash dividends to their stockholders. Dividend payments are a type of financing transaction because the company is paying its stockholders for the use of their money. Stock dividends are not reported on the statement of cash flows because the company pays no cash for them.

In Exhibit 9-9, cash receipts appear as positive amounts and cash payments as negative amounts, denoted by parentheses.

Reporting Stockholders' Equity on the Balance Sheet

Businesses may report stockholders' equity in a way that differs from our examples. We use a detailed format in this book to help you learn all the components of stockholders' equity.

One of the most important skills you will take from this course is the ability to understand the financial statements of real companies. Exhibit 9-10 presents a side-by-side comparison of our general teaching format and the format you are likely to encounter in real-world balance sheets, such as IHOP's. All amounts are assumed for this illustration.

EXHIBIT 9-10 | **Formats for Reporting Stockholders' Equity**

General Teaching Format		Real-World Format	
Stockholders' Equity		**Stockholders' Equity**	
Paid-in capital:		Preferred stock, 8%, $10 par, 30,000	
Preferred stock, 8%, $10 par, 30,000		shares authorized and issued	$ 330,000
shares authorized and issued	$ 300,000	Common stock, $1 par, 100,000 shares	
Paid-in capital in excess of		authorized, 60,000 shares issued	60,000
par—preferred	30,000	Additional paid-in capital	2,150,000
Common stock, $1 par, 100,000 shares		Retained earnings	1,500,000
authorized, 60,000 shares issued	60,000	Less treasury stock, common	
Paid-in capital in excess of		(1,400 shares at cost)	(40,000)
par—common	2,100,000	Total stockholders' equity	$4,000,000
Paid-in capital from treasury stock			
transactions, common	20,000		
Paid-in capital from retirement of			
preferred stock	30,000		
Total paid-in capital	2,540,000		
Retained earnings	1,500,000		
Subtotal	4,040,000		
Less treasury stock, common			
(1,400 shares at cost)	(40,000)		
Total stockholders' equity	$4,000,000		

In general:

- Preferred Stock comes first and is usually reported as a single amount
- Common Stock lists par value per share, the number of shares authorized and the number of shares issued. The balance of the Common Stock account is determined as follows:

  Common stock = Number of shares *issued* × Par value per share

- Additional paid-in capital combines Paid-in Capital in Excess of Par plus Paid-in Capital from Treasury Stock Transactions plus Paid-in Capital from Retirement of Preferred Stock. Additional paid-in capital belongs to the common stockholders.
- Outstanding stock equals issued stock minus treasury stock.
- Retained Earnings comes after the paid-in capital accounts.
- Treasury Stock can come last, as a subtraction in arriving at total stockholders' equity.

DECISION GUIDELINES

INVESTING IN STOCK

Suppose you've saved $5,000 to invest. You visit a nearby **Edward Jones** office, where the broker probes for your risk tolerance. Are you investing mainly for dividends or for growth in the stock price? You must make some key decisions.

Investor Decision	Guidelines
Which category of stock to buy for:	
■ A safe investment?	Preferred stock is safer than common, but for even more safety, invest in high-grade corporate bonds or government securities.
■ Steady dividends?	Cumulative preferred stock. However, the company is not obligated to declare preferred dividends, and the dividends are unlikely to increase.
■ Increasing dividends?	Common stock, as long as the company's net income is increasing and the company has adequate cash flow to pay a dividend after meeting all obligations and other cash demands.
■ Increasing stock price?	Common stock, but again only if the company's net income and cash flow are increasing.
How to identify a good stock to buy?	There are many ways to pick stock investments. One strategy that works reasonably well is to invest in companies that consistently earn higher rates of return on assets and on equity than competing firms in the same industry. Also, select industries that are expected to grow.

END-OF-CHAPTER SUMMARY PROBLEM

1. The balance sheet of Trendline Corp. reported the following at December 31, 2010.

Stockholders' Equity

Preferred stock, 4%, $10 par, 10,000 shares authorized and issued (redemption value, $110,000)................	$100,000
Common stock, no-par, $5 stated value, 100,000 shares authorized, 50,000 shares issued.............................	250,000
Paid-in capital in excess of par or stated value:	
Common stock	239,500
Retained earnings..	395,000
Less: Treasury stock, common (1,000 shares)...............	(8,000)
Total stockholders' equity	$976,500

Requirements

   a. Is the preferred stock cumulative or noncumulative? How can you tell?
   b. What is the total amount of the annual preferred dividend?
   c. How many shares of common stock are outstanding?
   d. Compute the book value per share of the common stock. No preferred dividends are in arrears, and Trendline has not yet declared the 2010 dividend.

2. Use the following accounts and related balances to prepare the classified balance sheet of Whitehall, Inc., at September 30, 2011. Use the account format of the balance sheet.

Common stock, $1 par, 50,000 shares authorized, 20,000 shares issued...................	20,000	Long-term note payable	80,000	
		Inventory......................................	85,000	
Dividends payable..........................	4,000	Property, plant, and		
Cash..	9,000	equipment, net	226,000	
Accounts payable	28,000	Accounts receivable, net..............	23,000	
Paid-in capital in excess		Preferred stock, $3.75, no-par,		
of par—common.......................	115,000	10,000 shares authorized,		
		2,000 shares issued..................	24,000	
Treasury stock, common,		Accrued liabilities........................	3,000	
1,000 shares at cost....................	6,000	Retained earnings........................	75,000	

Answers

1. **a.** The preferred stock is cumulative because it is not specifically labeled otherwise.
   b. Total annual preferred dividend: $4,000 ($100,000 × 0.04).

c. Common shares outstanding: 49,000 (50,000 issued − 1,000 treasury).
d. Book value per share of common stock:

Common:	
Total stockholders' equity	$976,500
Less stockholders' equity allocated to preferred	(114,000)*
Stockholders' equity allocated to common	$862,500
Book value per share ($862,500 ÷ 49,000 shares)..............	$17.60

*Redemption value	$110,000
Cumulative dividend ($100,000 × 0.04)...	4,000
Stockholders' equity allocated to preferred...	$114,000

2.

Whitehall, Inc.
Balance Sheet
September 30, 2011

Assets		Liabilities	
Current		Current	
Cash	$ 9,000	Account payable	$ 28,000
Accounts receivable, net..............	23,000	Dividends payable........................	4,000
Inventory.....................................	85,000	Accrued liabilities	3,000
Total current assets	117,000	Total current liabilities	35,000
Property, plant, and equipment, net.....	226,000	Long-term note payable	80,000
		Total liabilities	115,000
		Stockholders' Equity	
		Preferred stock, $3.75, no par,	
		10,000 shares authorized,	
		2,000 shares issued	$ 24,000
		Common stock, $1 par,	
		50,000 shares authorized,	
		20,000 shares issued	20,000
		Paid-in capital in excess of	
		par—common............................	115,000
		Retained earnings............................	75,000
		Treasury stock, common,	
		1,000 shares at cost	(6,000)
		Total stockholders' equity...........	228,000
		Total liabilities and	
Total assets......................................	$343,000	stockholders' equity....................	$343,000

REVIEW STOCKHOLDERS' EQUITY

Quick Check (Answers are given on page 601.)

1. Lurvey Company is authorized to issue 50,000 shares of $25 par common stock. On May 30, 2010, Lurvey issued 20,000 shares at $45 per share. Lurvey's journal entry to record these facts should include a
   a. credit to Common Stock for $500,000.
   b. debit to Common Stock for $900,000.
   c. credit to Paid-in Capital in Excess of Par for $900,000.
   d. both a and c.

Questions 2–5 use the following account balances of Machado Co. at August 31, 2010:

Dividends Payable	$ 12,500	Cash	$111,000
Preferred Stock, $150 par	375,000	Common Stock, $5 par	600,000
Paid-in Capital in Excess of Par—		Retained Earnings	325,000
Common	60,000		

2. How many shares of common stock has Machado issued?
   a. 111,000   c. 120,000
   b. 660,000   d. Some other amount

3. Machado's total paid-in capital at August 31, 2010, is
   a. $1,347,500.   c. 1,458,500.
   b. $1,022,500.   d. $1,035,000.

4. Machado's total stockholders' equity as of August 31, 2010, is
   a. $1,035,000.   c. $1,458,500.
   b. $1,347,500.   d. $1,360,000.

5. What would Machado's total stockholders' equity be if Machado had $10,000 of treasury stock?
   a. $1,448,500   c. $1,350,000
   b. $1,025,000   d. $1,337,500

6. Syracuse Corporation purchased treasury stock in 2010 at a price of $15 per share and resold the treasury stock in 2011 at a price of $35 per share. What amount should Syracuse report on its income statement for 2011?
   a. $20 gain per share   c. $35 gain per share
   b. $15 gain per share   d. $0

7. The stockholders' equity section of a corporation's balance sheet reports
   Discount on Bonds Payable   *Treasury Stock*
   a. No   Yes
   b. Yes   No
   c. No   No
   d. Yes   Yes

8. The purchase of treasury stock
   a. decreases total assets and increases total stockholders' equity.
   b. decreases total assets and decreases total stockholder's equity.
   c. has no effect on total assets, total liabilities, or total stockholders' equity.
   d. increases one asset and decreases another asset.

9. When does a cash dividend become a legal liability?
   a. It never becomes a liability because it is paid.
   b. On date of payment.
   c. On date of record.
   d. On date of declaration.

10. When do dividends increase stockholders' equity?
    a. On date of declaration.   c. Never.
    b. On date of payment.   d. On date of record.

11. Maple Tree Mall, Inc., has 2,500 shares of 2%, $25 par cumulative preferred stock and 125,000 shares of $2 par common stock outstanding. At the beginning of the current year, preferred dividends were four years in arrears. Maple Tree's board of directors wants to pay a $2.50 cash dividend on each share of outstanding common stock in the current year. To accomplish this, what total amount of dividends must Maple Tree declare?
    a. $250,000   c. $256,250
    b. $255,000   d. Some other amount

12. Stock dividends
    a. have no effect on total stockholders' equity.
    b. increase the corporation's total liabilities.
    c. reduce the total assets of the company.
    d. are distributions of cash to stockholders.

13. What is the effect of a stock dividend and a stock split on total assets?

Stock dividend	Stock split
a. No effect	Decrease
b. Decrease	Decrease
c. No effect	No effect
d. Decrease	No effect

14. A 2-for-1 stock split has the same effect on the number of shares being issued as a
    a. 50% stock dividend.   c. 100% stock dividend.
    b. 200% stock dividend.   d. 20% stock dividend.

15. The numerator for computing the rate of return on total assets is
    a. net income.
    b. net income minus preferred dividends.
    c. net income minus interest expense.
    d. net income plus interest expense.

16. The numerator for computing the rate of return on common equity is
    a. net income.
    b. net income minus interest expense.
    c. net income minus preferred dividends.
    d. net income plus preferred dividends.

Accounting Vocabulary

authorized stock (p. 549) Maximum number of shares a corporation can issue under its charter.

board of directors (p. 537) Group elected by the stockholders to set policy for a corporation and to appoint its officers.

book value (of a stock) (p. 560) Amount of owners' equity on the company's books for each share of its stock.

bylaws (p. 537) Constitution for governing a corporation.

chairperson (p. 537) Elected by a corporation's board of directors, usually the most powerful person in the corporation.

common stock (p. 538) The most basic form of capital stock. The common stockholders own a corporation.

contributed capital (p. 538) The amount of stockholders' equity that stockholders have contributed to the corporation. Also called *paid-in capital*.

cumulative preferred stock (p. 556) Preferred stock whose owners must receive all dividends in arrears before the corporation can pay dividends to the common stockholders.

deficit (p. 553) Debit balance in the Retained Earnings account.

dividend (p. 553) Distribution (usually cash) by a corporation to its stockholders.

double taxation (p. 536) Corporations pay income taxes on corporate income. Then, the stockholders pay personal income tax on the cash dividends that they receive from corporations.

issued stock (p. 549) Number of shares a corporation has issued to its stockholders.

legal capital (p. 540) Minimum amount of stockholders' equity that a corporation must maintain for the protection of creditors. For corporations with par-value stock, legal capital is the par value of the stock issued.

limited liability (p. 535) No personal obligation of a stockholder for corporation debts. A stockholder can lose no more on an investment in a corporation's stock than the cost of the investment.

liquidation value (p. 560) The amount a corporation must pay a preferred stockholder in the event the company liquidates and goes out of business.

market value (of a stock) (p. 559) Price for which a person could buy or sell a share of stock.

outstanding stock (p. 549) Stock in the hands of stockholders.

paid-in capital (p. 538) The amount of stockholders' equity that stockholders have contributed to the corporation. Also called *contributed capital*.

par value (p. 540) Arbitrary amount assigned by a company to a share of its stock.

preferred stock (p. 538) Stock that gives its owners certain advantages, such as the priority to receive dividends before the common stockholders and the priority to receive assets before the common stockholders if the corporation liquidates.

president (p. 537) Chief operating officer in charge of managing the day-to-day operations of a corporation.

rate of return on common stockholders' equity (p. 562) Net income minus preferred dividends, divided by average common stockholders' equity. A measure of profitability. Also called *return on equity*.

rate of return on total assets (p. 561) Net income plus interest expense divided by average total assets. This ratio measures a company's success in using its assets to earn income for the persons who finance the business. Also called *return on assets*.

redeemable preferred stock (p. 559) A corporation reserves the right to buy an issue of stock back from its shareholders, with the intent to retire the stock.

redemption value (p. 560) The price a corporation agrees to eventually pay for its redeemable preferred stock, set when the stock is issued.

retained earnings (p. 538) The amount of stockholders' equity that the corporation has earned through profitable operation of the business and has not given back to stockholders.

return on assets (ROA) (p. 561) Another name for *rate of return on total assets*.

return on equity (ROE) (p. 562) Another name for *rate of return on common stockholders' equity*.

shareholders (p. 535) Persons or other entities that own stock in a corporation. Also called *stockholders*.

stated value (p. 540) An arbitrary amount assigned to no-par stock; similar to par value.

stock (p. 538) Shares into which the owners' equity of a corporation is divided.

stock dividend (p. 557) A proportional distribution by a corporation of its own stock to its stockholders.

stockholder (p. 535) A person who owns stock in a corporation. Also called a *shareholder*.

stockholders' equity (p. 538) The stockholders' ownership interest in the assets of a corporation.

stock split (p. 558) An increase in the number of authorized, issued, and outstanding shares of stock coupled with a proportionate reduction in the stock's par value.

treasury stock (p. 549) A corporation's own stock that it has issued and later reacquired.

ASSESS YOUR PROGRESS

Short Exercises

S9-1 (*Learning Objective 1: Explaining advantages and disadvantages of a corporation*) What are two main advantages that a corporation has over a proprietorship and a partnership? What are two main disadvantages of a corporation?

S9-2 (*Learning Objective 1: Describing the authority structure in a corporation*) Consider the authority structure in a corporation, as diagrammed in Exhibit 9-2.

1. What group holds the ultimate power in a corporation?
2. Who is the most powerful person in the corporation? What's the abbreviation of this person's title?
3. Who's in charge of day-to-day operations? What's the abbreviation of this person's title?
4. Who's in charge of accounting and finance? What's the abbreviation of this person's title?

S9-3 (*Learning Objective 1: Describing characteristics of preferred and common stock*)
Answer the following questions about the characteristics of a corporation's stock:

1. Who are the real owners of a corporation?
2. What privileges do preferred stockholders have over common stockholders?
3. Which class of stockholders reap greater benefits from a highly profitable corporation? Explain.

S9-4 (*Learning Objective 1: Organizing a corporation*)   Karen Scanlon and Jennifer Shaw are opening a Submarine's deli. Scanlon and Shaw need outside capital, so they plan to organize the business as a corporation. They come to you for advice. Write a memorandum informing them of the steps in forming a corporation. Identify specific documents used in this process, and name the different parties involved in the ownership and management of a corporation.

S9-5 (*Learning Objective 2: Describing the effect of a stock issuance on paid-in capital*)
SHOE received $73,000,000 for the issuance of its stock on April 24. The par value of the SHOE stock was only $73,000. Was the excess amount of $72,927,000 a profit to SHOE? If not, what was it?

Suppose the par value of the SHOE stock had been $2 per share, $12 per share, or $15 per share. Would a change in the par value of the company's stock affect SHOE's total paid-in capital? Give the reason for your answer.

S9-6 (*Learning Objective 2: Issuing stock—par value stock and no-par stock*)   At fiscal year-end 2010, Horris Printer and Delectable Doughnuts reported these adapted amounts on their balance sheets (amounts in millions):

Horris Printer:		
Common stock, 1 cent par value, 2,300 shares issued		$ 23
Additional paid-in capital		17,100

Delectable Doughnuts:		
Common stock, no par value, 63 shares issued		$ 292

Assume each company issued its stock in a single transaction. Journalize each company's issuance of its stock, using its actual account titles. Explanations are not required.

S9-7 (*Learning Objective 2: Issuing stock to finance the purchase of assets*)   This short exercise demonstrates the similarity and the difference between two ways to acquire plant assets.

Case A—Issue stock and buy the assets in separate transactions:

Ashley, Inc., issued 12,000 shares of its $20 par common stock for cash of $800,000. In a separate transaction, Ashley used the cash to purchase a building for $550,000 and equipment for $250,000. Journalize the two transactions.

Case B—Issue stock to acquire the assets in a single transaction:

Ashley, Inc., issued 12,000 shares of its $20 par common stock to acquire a building valued at $550,000 and equipment worth $250,000. Journalize this transaction.

Compare the balances in all the accounts after making both sets of entries. Are the account balances similar or different?

S9-8 *(Learning Objective 2: Preparing the stockholders' equity section of a balance sheet)* The financial statements of Mountainpeak Employment Services, Inc., reported the following accounts (adapted, with dollar amounts in thousands except for par value):

Paid-in capital in excess of par.................	$196	Total revenues......................	$1,340
Other stockholders' equity (negative)........	(22)	Accounts payable	440
Common stock, $0.01 par		Retained earnings................	647
400 shares issued.................................	4	Other current liabilities........	2,569
Long-term debt	27	Total expenses......................	806

Prepare the stockholders' equity section of Mountainpeak's balance sheet. Net income has already been closed to Retained Earnings.

S9-9 *(Learning Objective 2: Using stockholders' equity data)* Use the Mountainpeak Employment Services data in Short Exercise 9-8 to compute Mountainpeak's

    a. Net income.
    b. Total liabilities.
    c. Total assets (use the accounting equation).

S9-10 *(Learning Objective 3: Accounting for the purchase and sale of treasury stock)* Genius Marketing Corporation reported the following stockholders' equity at December 31 (adapted and in millions):

Common stock...................................	$ 225
Additional paid-in capital..................	245
Retained earnings.............................	2,149
Treasury stock..................................	(621)
Total stockholders' equity.................	$1,998

During the next year, Genius Marketing purchased treasury stock at a cost of $29 million and resold treasury stock for $8 million (this treasury stock had cost Genius Marketing $2 million). Record the purchase and resale of Genius Marketing's treasury stock. Overall, how much did stockholders' equity increase or decrease as a result of the two treasury stock transactions?

S9-11 *(Learning Objective 3: Purchasing treasury stock to fight off a takeover of the corporation)* Susan Smith Exports, Inc., is located in Birmingham, Alabama. Smith is the only company with reliable sources for its imported gifts. The company does a brisk business with specialty stores such as Bloomingdale's. Smith's recent success has made the company a prime target for a takeover. An investment group in Mobile is attempting to buy 52% of Smith's outstanding stock against the wishes of Smith's board of directors. Board members are convinced that the Mobile investors would sell the most desirable pieces of the business and leave little of value.

At the most recent board meeting, several suggestions were advanced to fight off the hostile takeover bid. The suggestion with the most promise is to purchase a huge quantity of treasury stock. Smith has the cash to carry out this plan.

I *Requirements*

    1. Suppose you are a significant stockholder of Susan Smith Exports, Inc. Write a memorandum to explain to the board how the purchase of treasury stock would make it difficult for the Mobile group to take over Smith. Include in your memo a discussion of the effect that purchasing treasury stock would have on stock outstanding and on the size of the corporation.

2. Suppose Smith management is successful in fighting off the takeover bid and later sells the treasury stock at prices greater than the purchase price. Explain what effect these sales will have on assets, stockholders' equity, and net income.

S9-12 (*Learning Objective 4: Accounting for cash dividends*)   Greentea Corporation earned net income of $95,000 during the year ended December 31, 2010. On December 15, Greentea declared the annual cash dividend on its 6% preferred stock (11,000 shares with total par value of $110,000) and a $1.00 per share cash dividend on its common stock (45,000 shares with total par value of $450,000). Greentea then paid the dividends on January 4, 2011.

Journalize for Greentea Corporation:
   a. Declaring the cash dividends on December 15, 2010.
   b. Paying the cash dividends on January 4, 2011.

Did Retained Earnings increase or decrease during 2010? By how much?

S9-13 (*Learning Objective 4: Dividing cash dividends between preferred and common stock*)   Access Garde, Inc., has 200,000 shares of $1.80 preferred stock outstanding in addition to its common stock. The $1.80 designation means that the preferred stockholders receive an annual cash dividend of $1.80 per share. In 2010, Access Garde declares an annual dividend of $500,000. The allocation to preferred and common stockholders is:

Preferred dividend, (200,000 shares × $1.80 per share)............	$360,000
Common dividend (remainder: $500,000 – $360,000)	140,000
Total dividend...	$500,000

Answer these questions about Access Garde's cash dividends.

   1. How much in dividends must Access Garde declare each year before the common stockholders receive any cash dividends for the year?
   2. Suppose Access Garde, Inc., declares cash dividends of $400,000 for 2010. How much of the dividends goes to preferred? How much goes to common?
   3. Is Access Garde's preferred stock cumulative or noncumulative? How can you tell?
   4. Access Garde, Inc., passed the preferred dividend in 2009 and 2010. Then in 2011, Access Garde declares cash dividends of $1,500,000. How much of the dividends goes to preferred? How much goes to common?

S9-14 (*Learning Objective 4: Recording a small stock dividend*)   Centerville Bancshares has 13,000 shares of $3 par common stock outstanding. Suppose Centerville distributes a 15% stock dividend when the market value of its stock is $25 per share.

   1. Journalize Centerville's distribution of the stock dividend on May 11. An explanation is not required.
   2. What was the overall effect of the stock dividend on Centerville's total assets? On total liabilities? On total stockholders' equity?

S9-15 (*Learning Objective 5: Computing book value per share*)   Fools Gold, Inc., has the following stockholders' equity:

Preferred stock, 4%, $5 par,	
33,000 shares authorized and issued.....................................	$ 195,000
Common stock, $2 par, 100,000 shares authorized	
63,000 shares issued	126,000
Additional paid-in capital..	2,170,000
Retained earnings..	1,700,000
Less treasury stock, common (1,400 shares at cost)	(45,000)
Total stockholders' equity	$4,146,000

That company has passed its preferred dividends for three years including the current year. Compute the book value per share of the company's common stock.

S9-16 (*Learning Objective 6: Computing and explaining return on assets and return on equity*)   Give the formula for computing (a) rate of return on total assets (ROA) and (b) rate of return on common stockholders' equity (ROE). Then answer these questions about the rate-of-return computations.

1. Why is interest expense added to net income in the computation of ROA?
2. Why are preferred dividends subtracted from net income to compute ROE?

S9-17 (*Learning Objective 6: Computing return on assets and return on equity for a leading company*)   Godhi Corporation's 2010 financial statements reported the following items, with 2009 figures given for comparison (adapted and in millions).

	2010	2009
Balance Sheet		
Total assets	¥10,624	¥9,515
Total liabilities	¥ 7,412	¥6,637
Total stockholders' equity (all common)	3,212	2,878
Total liabilities and equity	¥10,624	¥9,515
Income Statement		
Revenues and other income	¥ 7,633	
Operating expense	7,286	
Interest expense	31	
Other expense	196	
Net income	¥ 120	

Compute Godhi's return on assets and return on common equity for 2011. Evaluate the rates of return as strong or weak. ¥ is the symbol for the Japanese yen.

S9-18 (*Learning Objectives 1, 2, 5: Explaining the features of a corporation's stock*)   McGahan Corporation is conducting a special meeting of its board of directors to address some concerns raised by the stockholders. Stockholders have submitted the following questions. Answer each question.

1. Why are common stock and retained earnings shown separately in the shareholders' equity section of the balance sheet?
2. Linda Leary, a McGahan shareholder, proposes to transfer some land she owns to the company in exchange for shares of the company stock. How should McGahan Corporation determine the number of shares of our stock to issue for the land?
3. Preferred shares generally are preferred with respect to dividends and in the event of our liquidation. Why would investors buy our common stock when preferred stock is available?
4. What does the redemption value of our preferred stock require us to do?
5. One of our stockholders owns 200 shares of McGahan stock and someone has offered to buy her shares for their book value. Our stockholder asks us the formula for computing the book value of her stock.

S9-19 (*Learning Objective 7: Measuring cash flows from financing activities*)   During 2010, Dwyer Corporation earned net income of $5.8 billion and paid off $2.4 billion of long-term notes payable. Dwyer raised $1.1 billion by issuing common stock, paid $3.5 billion to purchase treasury stock, and paid cash dividends of $1.6 billion. Report Dwyer's *cash flows from financing* activities on the statement of cash flows for 2010.

Exercises

All of the A and B exercises can be found within MyAccountingLab, an online homework and practice environment. Your instructor may ask you to complete these exercises using MyAccountingLab.

(Group A)

E9-20A (*Learning Objective 2: Issuing stock and reporting stockholders' equity*)   Bread & Butter, Inc., is authorized to issue 120,000 shares of common stock and 7,000 shares of preferred stock. During its first year, the business completed the following stock issuance transactions:

Jan 19	Issued 12,000 shares of $2.00 par common stock for cash of $6.00 per share.
Apr 3	Issued 400 shares of $1.00 no-par preferred stock for $54,000 cash.
11	Received inventory valued at $16,000 and equipment with market value of $9,500 for 3,700 shares of the $2.00 par common stock.

I Requirements

1. Journalize the transactions. Explanations are not required.
2. Prepare the stockholders' equity section of Bread & Butter's balance sheet. The ending balance of retained earnings is a deficit of $43,000.

E9-21A (*Learning Objective 2: Preparing stockholders' equity section of a balance sheet*) Army Navy Sporting Goods is authorized to issue 10,000 shares of preferred stock and 19,000 shares of common stock. During a two-month period, Army Navy completed these stock-issuance transactions:

Apr 23	Issued 1,700 shares of $1.50 par common stock for cash of $16.50 per share.
May 2	Issued 600 shares of $2.50, no-par preferred stock for $22,000 cash.
12	Received inventory valued at $19,000 and equipment with market value of $41,000 for 3,300 shares of the $1.50 par common stock.

I Requirement

1. Prepare the stockholders' equity section of the Army Navy Sporting Goods' balance sheet for the transactions given in this exercise. Retained Earnings has a balance of $45,000. Journal entries are not required.

E9-22A (*Learning Objective 2: Measuring the paid-in capital of a corporation*)   Travel Publishing was recently organized. The company issued common stock to an attorney who provided legal services worth $23,000 to help organize the corporation. Travel also issued common stock to an inventor in exchange for his patent with a market value of $82,000. In addition, Travel received cash both for the issuance of 2,000 shares of its preferred stock at

$120 per share and for the issuance of 22,000 of its common shares at $1 per share. During the first year of operations, Travel earned net income of $50,000 and declared a cash dividend of $29,000. Without making journal entries, determine the total paid-in capital created by these transactions.

E9-23A (*Learning Objectives 2, 3: Preparing stockholders' equity section of a balance sheet*) Patterson Software had the following selected account balances at December 31, 2010 (in thousands, except par value per share).

Inventory	$ 651	Common stock, $0.75 par per share, 800 shares authorized, 320 shares	
Property, plant, and equipment, net	900		
Paid-in capital in excess of par	899	issued	$ 240
Treasury stock,		Retained earnings	2,220
100 shares at cost	1,150	Accounts receivable, net	1,000
Other stockholders' equity	(730)*	Notes payable	1,100

*Debit balance

I Requirements

1. Prepare the stockholders' equity section of Patterson's balance sheet (in thousands).
2. How can Patterson have a larger balance of treasury stock than the sum of Common Stock and Paid-in Capital in Excess of Par?

E9-24A (*Learning Objectives 2, 3: Recording treasury stock transactions and measuring their effects on stockholders' equity*) Journalize the following transactions of Aliant Productions:

Jan 17	Issued 2,200 shares of $2.50 par common stock at $10 per share.
May 23	Purchased 300 shares of treasury stock at $12 per share.
Jul 11	Sold 200 shares of treasury stock at $20 per share.

What was the overall effect of these transactions on Aliant's stockholders' equity?

E9-25A (*Learning Objectives 2, 3, 4: Recording stock issuance, treasury stock, and dividend transactions*) At December 31, 2010, Northeast Corporation reported the stockholders' equity accounts shown here (with dollar amounts in millions, except per share amounts).

Common stock $2.00 par value per share, 2,100 million shares issued	$ 4,200
Capital in excess of par value	8,400
Retained earnings	250
Treasury stock, at cost	(70)
Total stockholders' equity	$12,780

Northeast's 2011 transactions included the following:

a. Net income, $446 million.
b. Issuance of 8 million shares of common stock for $13.50 per share.
c. Purchase of 2 million shares of treasury stock for $16 million.
d. Declaration and payment of cash dividends of $31 million.

I Requirement

1. Journalize Northeast's transactions in b, c, and d. Explanations are not required.

E9-26A *(Learning Objectives 2, 3, 4: Reporting stockholders' equity after a sequence of transactions)*   Use the Northeast Corporation data in Exercise 9-25A to prepare the stockholders' equity section of the company's balance sheet at December 31, 2011.

E9-27A *(Learning Objectives 2, 3, 4, 5: Inferring transactions from a company's stockholders' equity)*   Theta Products Company reported the following stockholders' equity on its balance sheet:

Stockholders' Equity	December 31,	
(Dollars and shares in millions)	2011	2010
Preferred stock—$0.50 par value; authorized 30 shares;		
Convertible Preferred Stock; issued and outstanding:		
2011 and 2010—6 and 12 shares, respectively	$ 3	$ 6
Common stock—$2 per share par value; authorized		
1,400 shares; issued: 2011 and 2010—300		
and 200 shares, respectively	600	400
Additional paid-in capital	1,950	1,200
Retained earnings	6,270	5,066
Treasury stock, common—at cost		
2011—52 shares; 2010—12 shares	(1,144)	(228)
Total stockholders' equity	7,679	6,444
Total liabilities and stockholders' equity	$48,299	$45,294

I Requirements

1. What caused Theta's preferred stock to decrease during 2011? Cite all possible causes.
2. What caused Theta's common stock to increase during 2011? Identify all possible causes.
3. How many shares of Theta's common stock were outstanding at December 31, 2011?
4. Theta's net income during 2011 was $1,380 million. How much were Theta's dividends during the year?
5. During 2011, Theta sold no treasury stock. What average price per share did Theta pay for the treasury stock the company purchased during the year?

E9-28A *(Learning Objective 4: Computing dividends on preferred and common stock)*   Huron Manufacturing, Inc., reported the following:

Stockholders' Equity	
Preferred stock, cumulative, $0.50 par, 9%, 40,000 shares issued	$ 20,000
Common stock, $0.10 par, 9,170,000 shares issued	917,000

Huron Manufacturing has paid all preferred dividends through 2007.

I Requirement

1. Compute the total amounts of dividends to both preferred and common for 2010 and 2011 if total dividends are $60,000 in 2010 and $120,000 in 2011.

E9-29A (*Learning Objective 4: Recording a stock dividend and reporting stockholders' equity*)   The stockholders' equity for Heavenly Desserts Drive-Ins (HD) on December 31, 2010, follows:

Stockholders' Equity	
Common stock, $0.80 par, 2,600,000 shares	
authorized, 300,000 shares issued......................	$ 240,000
Paid-in capital in excess of par—common	307,200
Retained earnings..	7,122,000
Other equity..	(200,000)
Total stockholders' equity.................................	$7,469,200

On May 11, 2011, the market price of HD common stock was $19 per share. Assume HD distributed a 15% stock dividend on this date.

❙ Requirements

1. Journalize the distribution of the stock dividend.
2. Prepare the stockholders' equity section of the balance sheet after the stock dividend.
3. Why is total stockholders' equity unchanged by the stock dividend?
4. Suppose HD had a cash balance of $560,000 on May 12, 2011. What is the maximum amount of cash dividends HD can declare?

E9-30A (*Learning Objectives 2, 3, 4: Measuring the effects of stock issuance, dividends, and treasury stock transactions*)   Identify the effects—both the direction and the dollar amount—of these assumed transactions on the total stockholders' equity of Athol Corporation. Each transaction is independent.

a. Declaration of cash dividends of $78 million.
b. Payment of the cash dividend in a.
c. A 25% stock dividend. Before the dividend, 70 million shares of $2.00 par common stock were outstanding; the market value was $8.250 at the time of the dividend.
d. A 50% stock dividend. Before the dividend, 70 million shares of $2.00 par common stock were outstanding; the market value was $15.50 at the time of the dividend.
e. Purchase of 1,900 shares of treasury stock (par value $2.00) at $5.25 per share.
f. Sale of 900 shares of the treasury stock for $7.00 per share. Cost of the treasury stock was $5.25 per share.
g. A 2-for-1 stock split. Prior to the split, 70 million shares of $2.00 par common stock were outstanding.

E9-31A (*Learning Objective 4: Reporting stockholders' equity after a stock split*)   Clublink Corp. had the following stockholders' equity at October 31 (dollars in millions, except par value per share):

Stockholders' Equity	
Common stock, $1.50 par, 750 million shares	
authorized, 420 million shares issued.................	$ 630
Additional paid-in capital...	318
Retained earnings..	2,399
Other equity..	(148)
Total stockholders' equity.................................	$3,199

On December 6, Clublink split its $1.50 par common stock 3-for-1.

I Requirement

1. Prepare the stockholders' equity section of the balance sheet immediately after the split.

E9-32A (*Learning Objective 5: Measuring the book value per share of common stock*)   The balance sheet of Luxury Rug Company reported the following:

Redeemable preferred stock, 4%, $60 par value,	
redemption value $45,000; outstanding 500 shares.................	$30,000
Common stockholders' equity:	
6,000 shares issued and outstanding	66,000
Total stockholders' equity..	$96,000

I Requirements

1. Compute the book value per share for the common stock, assuming all preferred dividends are fully paid up (none in arrears).
2. Compute the book value per share of the common stock, assuming that three years' cumulative preferred dividends including the current year, are in arrears.
3. Luxury Rug's common stock recently traded at a market price of $6.00 per share. Does this mean that Luxury Rug's stock is a good buy at $6.00?

E9-33A (*Learning Objective 6: Evaluating profitability*)   Luna Inns reported these figures for 2011 and 2010 (in millions):

	2011	2010
Balance sheet		
Total assets	$15,906	$13,700
Common stock and additional paid-in capital	44	390
Retained earnings	11,522	16,490
Other equity...	(3,010)	(9,044)
Income statement		
Operating income	$ 4,023	$ 3,818
Interest expense	222	269
Net income	1,525	1,549

I Requirement

1. Compute Luna's return on assets and return on common stockholders' equity for 2011. Do these rates of return suggest strength or weakness? Give your reason.

E9-34A (*Learning Objective 6: Evaluating profitability*)   Littleton Company included the following items in its financial statements for 2010, the current year (amounts in millions):

Payment of long-term debt..........	$17,060	Dividends paid	$ 230
Proceeds from issuance		Interest expense:	
of common stock.....................	8,500	Current year.....................	1,439
Total liabilities:		Preceding year.................	601
Current year-end....................	32,315	Net income:	
Preceding year-end	38,025	Current year.....................	1,878
Total stockholders' equity:		Preceding year.................	2,003
Current year-end.....................	23,475	Operating income:	
Preceding year-end	14,033	Current year.....................	4,884
Borrowings...............................	6,580	Preceding year.................	4,006

I *Requirement*

1. Compute Littleton's return on assets and return on common equity during 2010 (the current year). Littleton has no preferred stock outstanding. Do the company's rates of return look strong or weak? Give your reason.

E9-35A *(Learning Objective 7: Reporting cash flows from financing activities)* Use the Littleton Company data in Exercise E9-34A to show how the company reported cash flows from financing activities during 2010 (the current year). List items in descending order from largest to smallest dollar amount.

(Group B)

E9-36B *(Learning Objective 2: Issuing stock and reporting stockholders' equity)* Sweet & Sour, Inc., is authorized to issue 110,000 shares of common stock and 5,000 shares of preferred stock. During its first year, the business completed the following stock issuance transactions:

Aug	19	Issued 15,000 shares of $3.50 par common stock for cash of $7.50 per share.
Nov	3	Issued 400 shares of $2.00 no-par preferred stock for $55,000 cash.
	11	Received inventory valued at $18,000 and equipment with market value of $10,500 for 4,000 shares of the $3.50 par common stock.

I *Requirements*

1. Journalize the transactions. Explanations are not required.
2. Prepare the stockholders' equity section of Sweet & Sour's balance sheet. The ending balance of retained earnings is a deficit of $47,000.

E9-37B *(Learning Objective 2: Preparing stockholders' equity section of a balance sheet)* Honcho Sporting Goods is authorized to issue 7,000 shares of preferred stock and 16,000 shares of common stock. During a two-month period, Honcho completed these stock-issuance transactions:

Jun	23	Issued 1,500 shares of $2.00 par common stock for cash of $17.50 per share.
Jul	2	Issued 400 shares of $5.50, no-par preferred stock for $30,000 cash.
	12	Received inventory valued at $15,000 and equipment with market value of $44,000 for 3,700 shares of the $2.00 par common stock.

I *Requirement*

1. Prepare the stockholders' equity section of the Honcho Sporting Goods balance sheet for the transactions given in this exercise. Retained Earnings has a balance of $46,000. Journal entries are not required.

E9-38B *(Learning Objective 2: Measuring the paid-in capital of a corporation)* Journey Publishing was recently organized. The company issued common stock to an attorney who provided legal services worth $24,000 to help organize the corporation. Journey also issued common stock to an inventor in exchange for his patent with a market value of $85,000. In addition, Journey received cash both for the issuance of 3,000 shares of its preferred stock at $90 per share and for the issuance of 17,000 shares of its common shares at $18 per share. During the first year of operations, Journey earned net income of $65,000 and declared a cash dividend of $23,000. Without making journal entries, determine the total paid-in capital created by these transactions.

E9-39B *(Learning Objectives 2, 3: Stockholders' equity section of a balance sheet)*   Bukala Software had the following selected account balances at December 31, 2010 (in thousands, except par value per share):

Inventory...	$ 705	Common stock, $0.50 par	
Property, plant, and		per share, 900 shares	
equipment, net	903	authorized, 300 shares	
Paid-in capital in excess of par	897	issued	$ 150
Treasury stock,		Retained earnings................	2,270
140 shares at cost......................	1,610	Accounts receivable, net......	200
Other stockholders' equity	(726)*	Notes payable	1,166

*Debit balance

I Requirements

1. Prepare the stockholders' equity section of Bukala Software's balance sheet (in thousands).
2. How can Bukala have a larger balance of treasury stock than the sum of Common Stock and Paid-in Capital in Excess of Par?

E9-40B *(Learning Objectives 2, 3: Recording treasury stock transactions and measuring their effects on stockholders' equity)*   Journalize the following assumed transactions of Applebug Productions:

Mar 16	Issued 2,400 shares of $1.50 par common stock at $7 per share.
Apr 20	Purchased 800 shares of treasury stock at $16 per share.
Aug 8	Sold 600 shares of treasury stock at $17 per share.

What was the overall effect of these transactions on Applebug's stockholders' equity?

E9-41B *(Learning Objectives 2, 3, 4: Recording stock issuance, treasury stock, and dividend transactions)*   At December 31, 2010, Eastern Corporation reported the stockholders' equity accounts shown here (with dollar amounts in millions, except per share amounts).

Common stock $1.50 par value per share,	
1,700 million shares issued................	$ 2,550
Capital in excess of par value................	7,650
Retained earnings....................................	260
Treasury stock, at cost	(10)
Total stockholders' equity.................	$10,450

Eastern's 2011 transactions included the following:

    a. Net income, $447 million.
    b. Issuance of 9 million shares of common stock for $12.50 per share.
    c. Purchase of 3 million shares of treasury stock for $15 million.
    d. Declaration and payment of cash dividends of $34 million.

❙ Requirement

    1. Journalize Eastern's transactions in b, c, and d. Explanations are not required.

E9-42B *(Learning Objectives 2, 3, 4: Reporting stockholders' equity after a sequence of transactions)* Use the Eastern Corporation data in Exercise 9-41B to prepare the stockholders' equity section of the company's balance sheet at December 31, 2011.

E9-43B *(Learning Objectives 2, 3, 4, 5: Inferring transactions from a company's stockholders' equity)* Supreme Products Company reported the following stockholders' equity on its balance sheet:

Stockholders' Equity (Dollars and shares in millions)	December 31, 2011	2010
Preferred stock—$1.50 par value; authorized 40 shares; Convertible Preferred Stock; issued and outstanding: 2011 and 2010—8 and 16 shares, respectively	$ 12	$ 24
Common stock—$4 per share par value; authorized 1,200 shares; issued: 2011 and 2010—500 and 400 shares, respectively	2,000	1,600
Additional paid-in capital	2,750	2,000
Retained earnings	6,300	5,025
Treasury stock, common—at cost 2011—54 shares; 2010—14 shares	(1,242)	(280)
Total stockholders' equity	9,820	8,369
Total liabilities and stockholders' equity	$50,320	$47,215

❙ Requirements

    1. What caused Supreme's preferred stock to decrease during 2011? Cite all possible causes.
    2. What caused Supreme's common stock to increase during 2011? Identify all possible causes.
    3. How many shares of Supreme's common stock were outstanding at December 31, 2011?
    4. Supreme's net income during 2011 was $1,475 million. How much were Supreme's dividends during the year?
    5. During 2011, Supreme sold no treasury stock. What average price per share did Supreme pay for the treasury stock the company purchased during the year?

E9-44B *(Learning Objective 4: Computing dividends on preferred and common stock)* Eerie Manufacturing, Inc., reported the following:

Stockholders' Equity	
Preferred stock, cumulative, $1.50 par, 7%, 50,000 shares issued	$ 75,000
Common stock, $0.20 par, 9,110,000 shares issued	1,822,000

Eerie Manufacturing has paid all preferred dividends through 2007.

❙ Requirement

1. Compute the total amounts of dividends to both preferred and common for 2010 and 2011 if total dividends are $100,000 in 2010 and $200,000 in 2011.

E9-45B (*Learning Objective 4: Recording a stock dividend and reporting stockholders' equity*)   The stockholders' equity for Icy Pop Drive-Ins (IP) on December 31, 2010, follows:

Stockholders' Equity	
Common stock, $0.30 par, 2,200,000 shares authorized, 400,000 shares issued......................	$ 120,000
Paid-in capital in excess of par—common...............	409,600
Retained earnings...	7,133,000
Other equity...	(185,000)
Total stockholders' equity.................................	$7,477,600

On August 15, 2011, the market price of IP common stock was $15 per share. Assume IP distributed a 20% stock dividend on this date.

❙ Requirements

1. Journalize the distribution of the stock dividend.
2. Prepare the stockholders' equity section of the balance sheet after the stock dividend.
3. Why is total stockholders' equity unchanged by the stock dividend?
4. Suppose IP had a cash balance of $590,000 on August 16, 2011. What is the maximum amount of cash dividends IP can declare?

E9-46B (*Learning Objectives 2, 3, 4: Measuring the effects of stock issuance, dividends, and treasury stock transactions*)   Identify the effects—both the direction and the dollar amount—of these assumed transactions on the total stockholders' equity of Dracut Corporation. Each transaction is independent.

　　a. Declaration of cash dividends of $85 million.
　　b. Payment of the cash dividend in a.
　　c. A 5% stock dividend. Before the dividend, 72 million shares of $3.00 par common stock were outstanding; the market value was $9.185 at the time of the dividend.
　　d. A 30% stock dividend. Before the dividend, 72 million shares of $3.00 par common stock were outstanding; the market value was $13.75 at the time of the dividend.
　　e. Purchase of 1,800 shares of treasury stock (par value $3.00) at $6.25 per share.
　　f. Sale of 900 shares of the treasury stock for $9.00 per share. Cost of the treasury stock was $6.25 per share.
　　g. A 3-for-1 stock split. Prior to the split, 72 million shares of $3.00 par common stock were outstanding.

E9-47B (*Learning Objective 4: Reporting stockholders' equity after a stock split*) Griffin Corp. had the following stockholders' equity at March 31 (dollars in millions, except par value per share):

Stockholders' Equity	
Common stock, $0.30 par, 500 million shares authorized, 450 million shares issued................	$ 135
Additional paid-in capital..	315
Retained earnings..	2,393
Other equity..	(146)
Total stockholders' equity.................................	$2,697

On May 3, Griffin split its $0.30 par common stock 3-for-1.

I Requirement

1. Prepare the stockholders' equity section of the balance sheet immediately after the split.

E9-48B (*Learning Objective 5: Measuring the book value per share of common stock*) The balance sheet of Eclectic Rug Company reported the following:

Redeemable preferred stock, 10%, $30 par value, redemption value $25,000; outstanding 700 shares................	$ 21,000
Common stockholders' equity:	
10,000 shares issued and outstanding	100,000
Total stockholders' equity	$121,000

I Requirements

1. Compute the book value per share for the common stock, assuming all preferred dividends are fully paid up (none in arrears).
2. Compute the book value per share of the common stock, assuming that three years' cumulative preferred dividends, including the current year, are in arrears.
3. Eclectic Rug's common stock recently traded at a market price of $7.10 per share. Does this mean that Eclectic Rug's stock is a good buy at $7.10?

E9-49B (*Learning Objective 6: Evaluating profitability*) LaSalle Inns reported these figures for 2011 and 2010 (in millions):

	2011	2010
Balance sheet		
Total assets	$16,000	$13,790
Common stock and additional paid-in capital	38	384
Retained earnings	11,528	16,530
Other equity..	(2,962)	(9,112)
Income statement		
Operating income	$ 4,022	$ 3,815
Interest expense	219	273
Net income..	1,530	1,544

I *Requirement*

1. Compute LaSalle's return on assets and return on common stockholders' equity for 2011. Do these rates of return suggest strength or weakness? Give your reason.

E9-50B (*Learning Objective 6: Evaluating profitability*)   Lawrence Company included the following items in its financial statements for 2010, the current year (amounts in millions):

Payment of long-term debt..........	$17,100	Dividends paid......................	$ 215
Proceeds from issuance		Interest expense:	
of common stock.....................	8,495	Current year.....................	1,443
Total liabilities:		Preceding year.................	603
Current year-end.....................	32,315	Net income:	
Preceding year-end.................	38,031	Current year.....................	1,872
Total stockholders' equity:		Preceding year.................	1,993
Current year-end.....................	23,477	Operating income:	
Preceding year-end.................	14,043	Current year.....................	4,876
Borrowings................................	6,590	Preceding year.................	3,996

I *Requirement*

1. Compute Lawrence's return on assets and return on common equity during 2010 (the current year). Lawrence has no preferred stock outstanding. Do the company's rates of return look strong or weak? Give your reason.

E9-51B (*Learning Objective 7: Reporting cash flows from financing activities*)   Use the Lawrence data in Exercise E9-50B to show how the company reported cash flows from financing activities during 2010 (the current year). List items in descending order from largest to smallest dollar amount.

Challenge Exercises

E9-52 (*Learning Objectives 2, 3, 4: Reconstructing transactions from the financial statements*)   D-4 Networking Solutions began operations on January 1, 2010, and immediately issued its stock, receiving cash. D-4's balance sheet at December 31, 2010, reported the following stockholders' equity:

Common stock, $1 par.....................	$ 51,000
Additional paid-in capital.................	102,000
Retained earnings.............................	35,000
Treasury stock, 850 shares...............	(7,650)
Total stockholders' equity...........	$180,350

During 2010, D-4

a. Issued stock for $3 per share.
b. Purchased 950 shares of treasury stock, paying $9 per share.
c. Resold some of the treasury stock.
d. Earned net income of $58,000 and declared and paid cash dividends. Revenues were $172,000 and expenses totaled $114,000.

I *Requirement*

1. Journalize all of D-4's stockholders' equity transactions during the year. D-4's entry to close net income to Retained Earnings was:

Revenues	172,000	
Expenses		114,000
Retained Earnings		58,000

E9-53 (*Learning Objective 7: Reporting financing activities on the statement of cash flows*)
Use the D-4 Networking Solutions data in Exercise 9-52 to show how the company reported
cash flows from financing activities during 2010.

E9-54 (*Learning Objectives 2, 3, 4: Explaining the changes in stockholders' equity*)   Space
Walk Corporation reported the following stockholders' equity data (all dollars in millions except
par value per share):

	December 31,	
	2010	2009
Preferred stock	$ 609	$ 740
Common stock, $1 par value	905	889
Additional paid-in capital.....................	1,514	1,482
Retained earnings.................................	20,625	19,100
Treasury stock, common	(2,777)	(2,600)

Space Walk earned net income of $2,980 during 2010. For each account except Retained
Earnings, one transaction explains the change from the December 31, 2009, balance to the
December 31, 2010, balance. Two transactions affected Retained Earnings. Give a full explanation,
including the dollar amount, for the change in each account.

E9-55 (*Learning Objectives 2, 3, 4: Accounting for changes in stockholders' equity*)   Clubhouse,
Inc., ended 2010 with 7 million shares of $1 par common stock issued and outstanding.
Beginning additional paid-in capital was $10 million, and retained earnings totaled $35 million.

- In April 2011, Clubhouse issued 5 million shares of common stock at a price of
  $3 per share.
- In June, the company distributed a 10% stock dividend at a time when Clubhouse's
  common stock had a market value of $6 per share.
- Then in September, Clubhouse's stock price dropped to $2 per share and the company
  purchased 5 million shares of treasury stock.
- For the year, Clubhouse earned net income of $22 million and declared cash divi-
  dends of $12 million.

❚ Requirement

1. Complete the following tabulation to show what Clubhouse should report for stockholders'
   equity at December 31, 2011. Journal entries are not required.

(Amounts in millions)	Common Stock	+	Additional Paid-In Capital	+	Retained Earnings	−	Treasury Stock	=	Total Equity
Balance, Dec 31, 2010......................	$7		$10		$35		0		$52
Issuance of stock									
Stock dividend....................................									
Purchase of treasury stock................									
Net income...									
Cash dividends...................................									
Balance, Dec 31, 2011......................									

Quiz

Test your understanding of stockholders' equity by answering the following questions. Select the best choice from among the possible answers given.

Q9-56 Which of the following is a characteristic of a corporation?

a. No income tax
b. Mutual agency
c. Limited liability of stockholders
d. Both a and b

Q9-57 Spirit World, Inc., issues 280,000 shares of no-par common stock for $9 per share. The journal entry is:

a.	Cash	2,520,000	
	Common Stock		560,000
	Paid-In Capital in Excess of Par		1,960,000
b.	Cash	2,520,000	
	Common Stock		2,520,000
c.	Cash	2,520,000	
	Common Stock		280,000
	Gain on the Sale of Stock		2,240,000
d.	Cash	280,000	
	Common Stock		280,000

Q9-58 Par value

a. represents the original selling price for a share of stock.
b. is established for a share of stock after it is issued.
c. may exist for common stock but not for preferred stock.
d. represents what a share of stock is worth.
e. is an arbitrary amount that establishes the legal capital for each share.

Q9-59 The paid-in capital portion of stockholders' equity does not include

a. Common Stock.
b. Preferred Stock.
c. Retained Earnings.
d. Paid-in Capital in Excess of Par Value.

Q9-60 Preferred stock is least likely to have which of the following characteristics?

a. Extra liability for the preferred stockholders
b. The right of the holder to convert to common stock
c. Preference as to dividends
d. Preference as to assets on liquidation of the corporation

Q9-61 Which of the following classifications represents the most shares of common stock?

a. Authorized shares
b. Outstanding shares
c. Unissued shares
d. Treasury shares
e. Issued shares

Use the following information for Questions Q9-62 to Q9-64:

These account balances at December 31 relate to Sportworld, Inc.:

Accounts Payable	$ 51,500	Paid-in Capital in Excess	
Accounts Receivable	81,550	of Par—Common	$220,000
Common Stock	317,000	Preferred Stock, 10%, $100 Par	85,000
Treasury Stock	5,200	Retained Earnings	71,300
Bonds Payable	3,800	Notes Receivable	12,100

Q9-62 What is total paid-in capital for Sportworld, Inc.?

a. $634,445   d. $693,300
b. $622,000   e. None of the above
c. $641,345

Q9-63 What is total stockholders' equity for Sportworld, Inc.?

a. $688,100   d. $698,500
b. $641,345   e. None of the above
c. $693,300

Q9-64 Sportworld's net income for the period is $119,100 and beginning common stockholders' equity is $681,500. Calculate Sportworld's return on common stockholders' equity.

a. 17.2%   c. 18.2%
b. 16.4%   d. 19.3%

Q9-65 A company paid $24 per share to purchase 600 shares of its common stock as treasury stock. The stock was originally issued at $16 per share. The journal entry to record the purchase of the treasury stock is:

a.	Treasury Stock	14,400	
	Cash		14,400
b.	Treasury Stock	9,600	
	Retained Earnings	4,800	
	Cash		14,400
c.	Treasury Stock	7,200	
	Paid-in Capital in Excess of Par	7,200	
	Cash		14,400
d.	Common Stock	14,000	
	Cash		14,000

Q9-66 When treasury stock is sold for less than its cost, the entry should include a debit to:

a. Paid-in Capital in Excess of Par.   c. Gain on Sale of Treasury Stock.
b. Retained Earnings.   d. Loss on Sale of Treasury Stock.

Q9-67 A company purchased 100 shares of its common stock at $50 per share. It then sells 35 of the treasury shares at $56 per share. The entry to sell the treasury stock includes a

a. credit to Paid-in Capital, Treasury Stock for $210.
b. debit to Retained Earnings for $210.
c. credit to Retained Earnings for $600.
d. credit to Treasury Stock for $1,960.
e. credit to Cash for $1,960.

Q9-68 Stockholders are eligible for a dividend if they own the stock on the date of:

a. record.

b. issuance.

c. declaration.

d. payment.

Q9-69 Luca's Foods has outstanding 600 shares of 7% preferred stock, $100 par value, and 1,600 shares of common stock, $30 par value. Luca's declares dividends of $15,800. The correct entry is:

a.	Dividends Payable, Preferred	4,200	
	Dividends Payable, Common	11,600	
	Cash		15,800
b.	Dividends Expense	15,800	
	Cash		15,800
c.	Retained Earnings	15,800	
	Dividends Payable, Preferred		4,200
	Dividends Payable, Common		11,600
d.	Retained Earnings	15,800	
	Dividends Payable, Preferred		7,900
	Dividends Payable, Common		7,900

Q9-70 A corporation has 40,000 shares of 10% preferred stock outstanding. Also, there are 40,000 shares of common stock outstanding. Par value for each is $100. If a $500,000 dividend is paid, how much goes to the preferred stockholders?

a. None

b. $400,000

c. $50,000

d. $380,000

e. $500,000

Q9-71 Assume the same facts as in question 70. What is the amount of dividends per share on common stock?

a. $1.00

b. $5.50

c. $2.50

d. $12.50

e. None of these

Q9-72 Which of the following is *not* true about a 10% stock dividend?

a. The market value of the stock is needed to record the stock dividend.

b. Total stockholders' equity remains the same.

c. Paid-in Capital increases.

d. Retained Earnings decreases.

e. Par value decreases.

Q9-73 A company declares a 5% stock dividend. The debit to Retained Earnings is an amount equal to

a. the excess of the market price over the original issue price of the shares to be issued.

b. the market value of the shares to be issued.

c. the par value of the shares to be issued.

d. the book value of the shares to be issued.

Q9-74 Which of the following statements is *not* true about a 3-for-1 stock split?

a. The market price of each share of stock will decrease.

b. Total stockholders' equity increases.

c. A stockholder with 10 shares before the split owns 30 shares after the split.

d. Par value is reduced to one-third of what it was before the split.

e. Retained Earnings remains the same.

Q9-75 Antonio Company's net income and interest expense are $27,000 and $3,000, respectively, and average total assets are $600,000. How much is Antonio's return on assets?

a. 5.0%

b. 4.5%

c. 6.2%

d. 4.0%

Problems

MyAccountingLab

All of these A and B problems can be found within MyAccountingLab (MAL), an online homework and practice environment. Your instructor may ask you to complete these problems using MyAccountingLab.

(Group A)

P9-76A (*Learning Objective 2: Recording corporate transactions and preparing the stockholders' equity section of the balance sheet*) The partners who own Cohen Canoes Co. wished to avoid the unlimited personal liability of the partnership form of business, so they incorporated as Cohen Canoes Inc. The charter from the state of Utah authorizes the corporation to issue 9,000 shares of $2 no-par preferred stock and 100,000 shares of $5 par common stock. In its first month, Cohen Canoes completed the following transactions:

May	6	Issued 900 shares of common stock to the promoter for assistance with issuance of the common stock. The promotional fee was $22,500. Debit Organization Expense.
	9	Issued 10,000 shares of common stock to Ben Cohen and 12,000 shares to Bill Cohen in return for cash equal to the stock's market value of $25 per share. The Cohens were partners in Cohen Canoes Co.
	10	Issued 800 shares of preferred stock to acquire a patent with a market value of $20,000.
	26	Issued 1,000 shares of common stock for $25 cash per share.

I Requirements

1. Record the transactions in the journal.
2. Prepare the stockholders' equity section of the Cohen Canoes, Inc., balance sheet at May 31. The ending balance of Retained Earnings is $55,000.

P9-77A (*Learning Objectives 2, 4: Preparing the stockholders' equity section of the balance sheet*) Garman Corp. has the following stockholders' equity information:

Garman's charter authorizes the company to issue 8,000 shares of 5% preferred stock with par value of $130 and 600,000 shares of no-par common stock. The company issued 1,600 shares of the preferred stock at $130 per share. It issued 120,000 shares of the common stock for a total of $513,000. The company's retained earnings balance at the beginning of 2010 was $74,000, and net income for the year was $94,000. During 2010, Garman declared the specified dividend on preferred and a $0.20 per-share dividend on common. Preferred dividends for 2009 were in arrears.

▌Requirement

1. Prepare the stockholders' equity section of Garman Corp.'s balance sheet at December 31, 2010. Show the computation of all amounts. Journal entries are not required.

P9-78A (*Learning Objectives 2, 3, 4: Measuring the effects of stock issuance, treasury stock, and dividend transactions on stockholders' equity*)   Good Foods, Inc., is authorized to issue 5,500,000 shares of $5.00 par common stock.

In its initial public offering during 2010, Good issued 475,000 shares of its $5.00 par common stock for $7.00 per share. Over the next year, Good's stock price increased, and the company issued 380,000 more shares at an average price of $10.00.

During 2012, the price of Good's common stock dropped to $7.25, and Good purchased 58,000 shares of its common stock for the treasury. After the market price of the common stock rose in 2013, Good sold 41,000 shares of the treasury stock for $10.00 per share.

During the five years 2010 to 2015, Good earned net income of $1,010,000 and declared and paid cash dividends of $610,000. Stock dividends of $645,570 were distributed to the stockholders in 2011, with $358,650 credited to common stock and $286,920 credited to additional paid-in capital. At December 31, 2015, total assets of the company are $14,600,000, and liabilities add up to $7,085,500.

▌Requirement

1. Show the computation of Good's total stockholders' equity at December 31, 2015. Present a detailed computation of each element of stockholders' equity. Use the end-of-chapter summary problem on pages 566–567 to format your answer.

P9-79A (*Learning Objectives 2, 4: Analyzing the stockholders' equity and dividends of a corporation*)   Elegant Outdoor Furniture Company included the following stockholders' equity on its year-end balance sheet at February 28, 2011:

Stockholders' Equity	
Preferred stock, 6.5% cumulative—par value $35 per share; authorized 110,000 shares in each class	
Class A—issued 78,000 shares	$ 2,730,000
Class B—issued 89,000 shares..............................	3,115,000
Common stock—$3 par value:..	
authorized 1,200,000 shares,	
issued 290,000 shares..	870,000
Additional paid-in capital—common	5,530,000
Retained earnings...	8,390,000
	$20,635,000

▌Requirements

1. Identify the different issues of stock Elegant Outdoor Furniture Company has outstanding.
2. Give the summary entries to record issuance of all the Elegant stock. Assume that all the stock was issued for cash. Explanations are not required.
3. Suppose Elegant passed its preferred dividends for three years. Would the company have to pay those dividends in arrears before paying dividends to the common stockholders? Give your reason.
4. What amount of preferred dividends must Elegant declare and pay each year to avoid having preferred dividends in arrears?
5. Assume that preferred dividends are in arrears for 2010. Record the declaration of an $860,000 dividend on February 28, 2011. An explanation is not required.

P9-80A *(Learning Objectives 2, 3, 4: Accounting for stock issuance, dividends, and treasury stock)* Moscow Jewelry Company reported the following summarized balance sheet at December 31, 2010:

Assets	
Current assets..	$ 33,600
Property and equipment, net	74,000
Total assets..	$107,600
Liabilities and Equity	
Liabilities	$ 37,300
Stockholders' equity:	
$0.70 cumulative preferred stock, $5 par, 300 shares issued	1,500
Common stock, $4 par, 6,500 shares issued........................	26,000
Paid-in capital in excess of par	17,800
Retained earnings..	25,000
Total liabilities and equity....................................	$107,600

During 2011, Moscow completed these transactions that affected stockholders' equity:

Feb	13	Issued 5,400 shares of common stock for $5 per share.
Jun	7	Declared the regular cash dividend on the preferred stock.
	24	Paid the cash dividend.
Aug	9	Distributed a 10% stock dividend on the common stock. Market price of the common stock was $6 per share.
Oct	26	Reacquired 500 shares of common stock as treasury stock, paying $7 per share.
Nov	20	Sold 200 shares of the treasury stock for $11 per share.

I Requirements

1. Journalize Moscow's transactions. Explanations are not required.
2. Report Moscow's stockholders' equity at December 31, 2011. Net income for 2011 was $28,000.

P9-81A *(Learning Objectives 3, 4: Measuring the effects of dividend and treasury stock transactions on a company)* Assume Dessert Destination of Montana, Inc., completed the following transactions during 2010, the company's 10th year of operations:

Feb	3	Issued 15,000 shares of company stock ($1.00 par) for cash of $435,000.
Mar	19	Purchased 2,600 shares of the company's own common stock at $24 per share.
Apr	24	Sold 1,300 shares of treasury common stock for $32 per share.
Aug	15	Declared a cash dividend on the 18,000 shares of $0.40 no-par preferred stock.
Sep	1	Paid the cash dividends.
Nov	22	Distributed a 8% stock dividend on the 92,000 shares of $1.00 par common stock outstanding. The market value of the common stock was $26 per share.

I *Requirement*

1. Analyze each transaction in terms of its effect on the accounting equation of Dessert Destination of Montana, Inc.

P9-82A *(Learning Objectives 3, 6: Preparing a corporation's balance sheet; measuring profitability)* The following accounts and related balances of Seagull Designers, Inc., as of December 31, 2010, are arranged in no particular order.

Cash	$55,000	Interest expense	$ 15,600
Accounts receivable, net	34,000	Property, plant, and	
Paid-in capital in excess		equipment, net	364,000
of par—common	20,000	Common stock, $2 par,	
Accrued liabilities	24,000	600,000 shares authorized,	
Long-term note payable	99,000	116,000 shares issued	232,000
Inventory	93,000	Prepaid expenses	13,000
Dividends payable	6,000	Common stockholders'	
Retained earnings	?	equity, December 31, 2009	222,000
Accounts payable	136,000	Net income	32,000
Trademarks, net	4,000	Total assets,	
Preferred stock, $.50,		December 31, 2009	493,000
no-par, 11,000 shares		Treasury stock,	
authorized and issued	29,700	21,000 shares at cost	24,000
Goodwill	13,000		

I *Requirements*

1. Prepare Seagull's classified balance sheet in the account format at December 31, 2010.
2. Compute rate of return on total assets and rate of return on common stockholders' equity for the year ended December 31, 2010.
3. Do these rates of return suggest strength or weakness? Give your reason.

P9-83A *(Learning Objective 7: Analyzing the statement of cash flows)* The statement of cash flows of Frappe, Inc., reported the following (adapted) for the year ended December 31, 2010:

Cash flows from financing activities (amounts in millions)	
Cash dividends paid	$(1,918)
Issuance of common stock at par value	1,000
Proceeds from issuance of long-term notes payable	54
Purchases of treasury stock	(3,030)
Payments of long-term notes payable	(163)

I *Requirement*

1. Make the journal entry that Frappe would use to record each of these transactions.

(Group B)

P9-84B *(Learning Objective 2: Recording corporate transactions and preparing the stockholders' equity section of the balance sheet)* The partners who own Liard Canoes Co. wished to avoid the unlimited personal liability of the partnership form of business, so they incorporated as Liard Canoes, Inc. The charter from the state of Texas authorizes the corporation to issue 5,000 shares of $1 no-par preferred stock and 140,000 shares of $5 par common stock. In its first month, Liard Canoes completed the following transactions:

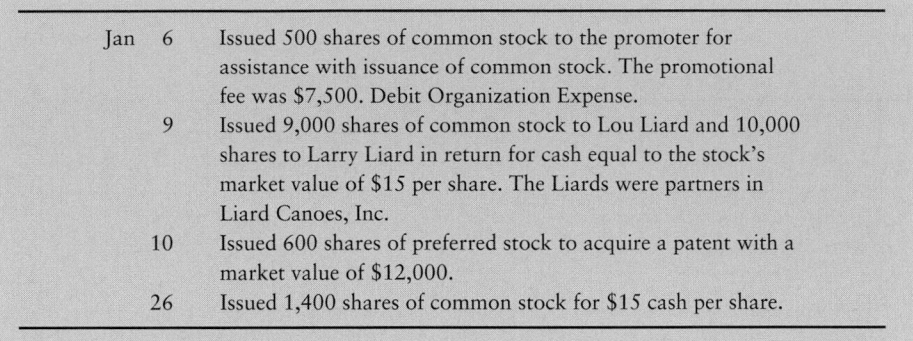

Jan	6	Issued 500 shares of common stock to the promoter for assistance with issuance of common stock. The promotional fee was $7,500. Debit Organization Expense.
	9	Issued 9,000 shares of common stock to Lou Liard and 10,000 shares to Larry Liard in return for cash equal to the stock's market value of $15 per share. The Liards were partners in Liard Canoes, Inc.
	10	Issued 600 shares of preferred stock to acquire a patent with a market value of $12,000.
	26	Issued 1,400 shares of common stock for $15 cash per share.

▌ Requirements

1. Record the transactions in the journal.
2. Prepare the stockholders' equity section of the Liard Canoes, Inc., balance sheet at January 31. The ending balance of Retained Earnings is $56,000.

P9-85B (*Learning Objectives 2, 4: Preparing the stockholders' equity section of the balance sheet*) Holman Corp. has the following stockholders' equity information:

Holman's charter authorizes the company to issue 5,000 shares of 8% preferred stock with par value of $110 and 400,000 shares of no-par common stock. The company issued 1,000 shares of the preferred stock at $110 per share. It issued 80,000 shares of the common stock for a total of $512,000. The company's retained earnings balance at the beginning of 2010 was $71,000, and net income for the year was $92,000. During 2010, Holman declared the specified dividend on preferred and a $0.60 per-share dividend on common. Preferred dividends for 2009 were in arrears.

▌ Requirement

1. Prepare the stockholders' equity section of Holman Corp.'s balance sheet at December 31, 2010. Show the computation of all amounts. Journal entries are not required.

P9-86B (*Learning Objectives 2, 3, 4: Measuring the effects of stock issuance, treasury stock, and dividend transactions on stockholders' equity*) Hearty Foods, Inc., is authorized to issue 5,000,000 shares of $2.00 par common stock.

In its initial public offering during 2010, Hearty issued 500,000 shares of its $2.00 par common stock for $5.00 per share. Over the next year, Hearty's stock price increased, and the company issued 395,000 more shares at an average price of $9.00.

During 2012, the price of Hearty's common stock dropped to $7.25, and Hearty purchased 61,000 shares of its common stock for the treasury. After the market price of the common stock rose in 2013, Hearty sold 38,000 shares of the treasury stock for $8.00 per share.

During the 5 years 2010 to 2015, Hearty earned net income of $1,150,000 and declared and paid cash dividends of $700,000. Stock dividends of $600,480 were distributed to the stockholders in 2011, with $150,120 credited to common stock and $450,360 credited to additional paid-in capital. At December 31, 2015, total assets of the company are $14,200,000, and liabilities add up to $7,833,250.

▌ Requirement

1. Show the computation of Hearty's total stockholders' equity at December 31, 2015. Present a detailed computation of each element of stockholders' equity. Use the end-of-chapter summary problem on pages 566 and 567 to format your answer.

P9-87B (*Learning Objectives 2, 4: Analyzing the stockholders' equity and dividends of a corporation*) Seasonal Outdoor Furniture Company included the following stockholders' equity on its year-end balance sheet at February 28, 2011:

Stockholders' Equity	
Preferred stock, 4.0% cumulative—par value $20 per share authorized 100,000 shares in each class	
Class A—issued 76,000 shares	$ 1,520,000
Class B—issued 97,000 shares......................................	1,940,000
Common stock—$4 par value:......................................	
authorized 1,500,000 shares,	
issued 250,000 shares..	1,000,000
Additional paid-in capital—common	5,520,000
Retained earnings...	8,320,000
	$18,300,000

▌ Requirements

1. Identify the different issues of stock Seasonal Outdoor Furniture Company has outstanding.
2. Give the summary entries to record issuance of all the Seasonal stock. Assume that all the stock was issued for cash. Explanations are not required.
3. Suppose Seasonal passed its preferred dividends for three years. Would the company have to pay these dividends in arrears before paying dividends to the common stockholders? Give your reasons.
4. What amount of preferred dividends must Seasonal declare and pay each year to avoid having preferred dividends in arrears?
5. Assume that preferred dividends are in arrears for 2010. Record the declaration of an $840,000 dividend on February 28, 2011. An explanation is not required.

P9-88B (*Learning Objectives 2, 3, 4: Accounting for stock issuance, dividends, and treasury stock*) London Jewelry Company reported the following summarized balance sheet at December 31, 2010:

Assets	
Current assets...	$33,500
Property and equipment, net	63,100
Total assets...	$96,600
Liabilities and Equity	
Liabilities	$37,600
Stockholders' equity:	
$0.80 cumulative preferred stock, $15 par,	
400 shares issued...................................	6,000
Common stock, $2 par, 6,300 shares issued...............	12,600
Paid-in capital in excess of par	17,400
Retained earnings...	23,000
Total liabilities and equity...	$96,600

During 2011, London completed these transactions that affected stockholders' equity:

Feb	13	Issued 5,200 shares of common stock for $6 per share.
Jun	7	Declared the regular cash dividend on the preferred stock.
	24	Paid the cash dividend.
Aug	9	Distributed a 20% stock dividend on the common stock. Market price of the common stock was $7 per share.
Oct	26	Reacquired 900 shares of common stock as treasury stock, paying $8 per share.
Nov	20	Sold 600 shares of the treasury stock for $12 per share.

❙ Requirements

1. Journalize London's transactions. Explanations are not required.
2. Report London's stockholders' equity at December 31, 2011. Net income for 2011 was $25,000.

P9-89B (*Learning Objectives 3, 4: Measuring the effects of dividend and treasury stock transactions on a company*)   Assume Cookie Corner of Wisconsin, Inc., completed the following transactions during 2010, the company's 10th year of operations:

Feb	4	Issued 14,000 shares of company stock ($1.00 par) for cash of $350,000.
Mar	20	Purchased 2,200 shares of the company's own common stock at $21 per share.
Apr	25	Sold 900 shares of treasury stock for $30 per share.
Aug	17	Declared a cash dividend on the 14,000 shares of $0.80 no-par preferred stock.
Sep	4	Paid the cash dividends.
Nov	28	Distributed a 5% stock dividend on the 99,000 shares of $1.00 par common stock outstanding. The market value of the common stock was $22 per share.

❙ Requirement

1. Analyze each transaction in terms of its effect on the accounting equation of Cookie Corner of Wisconsin, Inc.

P9-90B (*Learning Objectives 3, 6: Preparing a corporation's balance sheet; measuring profitability*)   The following accounts and related balances of Hawk Designers, Inc., as of December 31, 2010, are arranged in no particular order.

Cash..	$43,000	Interest expense..........................	$ 16,000
Accounts receivable, net................	22,000	Property, plant, and	
Paid-in capital in excess		equipment, net	359,000
of par—common........................	17,000	Common stock, $2 par,	
Accrued liabilities..........................	27,000	300,000 shares authorized,	
Long-term note payable	96,000	117,000 shares issued.............	234,000
Inventory.......................................	94,000	Prepaid expenses	16,000
Dividends payable.........................	12,000	Common stockholders'	
Retained earnings..........................	?	equity, December 31, 2009	225,000
Accounts payable	133,000	Net income................................	30,000
Trademarks, net............................	10,000	Total assets,	
Preferred stock, $.50,		December 31, 2009................	496,000
no-par, 12,000 shares		Treasury stock, common,	
authorized and issued...............	32,400	19,000 shares at cost.............	22,000
Goodwill......................................	11,000		

Requirements

1. Prepare Hawk's classified balance sheet in the account format at December 31, 2010.
2. Compute rate of return on total assets and rate of return on common stockholders' equity for the year ended December 31, 2010.
3. Do these rates of return suggest strength or weakness? Give your reason.

P9-91B *(Learning Objective 7: Analyzing the statement of cash flows)*   The statement of cash flows of Smoothie, Inc., reported the following (adapted) for the year ended December 31, 2010:

Cash flows from financing activities (amounts in millions)	
Cash dividends paid	$(1,890)
Issuance of common stock at par value	1,234
Proceeds from issuance of long-term notes payable	58
Purchases of treasury stock	(3,080)
Payments of long-term notes payable	(162)

Requirement

1. Make the journal entry that Smoothie would use to record each of these transactions.

APPLY YOUR KNOWLEDGE

Decision Cases

Case 1. *(Learning Objective 2: Evaluating alternative ways of raising capital)* Nate Smith and Darla Jones have written a computer program for a video game that may rival Playstation and Xbox. They need additional capital to market the product, and they plan to incorporate their business. Smith and Jones are considering alternative capital structures for the corporation. Their primary goal is to raise as much capital as possible without giving up control of the business. Smith and Jones plan to receive 50,000 shares of the corporation's common stock in return for the net assets of their old business. After the old company's books are closed and the assets adjusted to current market value, Smith's and Jones' capital balances will each be $25,000.

writing assignment ■

The corporation's plans for a charter include an authorization to issue 10,000 shares of preferred stock and 500,000 shares of $1 par common stock. Smith and Jones are uncertain about the most desirable features for the preferred stock. Prior to incorporating, Smith and Jones are discussing their plans with two investment groups. The corporation can obtain capital from outside investors under either of the following plans:

- *Plan 1.*   Group 1 will invest $80,000 to acquire 800 shares of 6%, $100 par nonvoting, preferred stock.
- *Plan 2.*   Group 2 will invest $55,000 to acquire 500 shares of $5, no-par preferred stock and $35,000 to acquire 35,000 shares of common stock. Each preferred share receives 50 votes on matters that come before the stockholders.

Requirements

Assume that the corporation is chartered.

1. Journalize the issuance of common stock to Smith and Jones. Debit each person's capital account for its balance.
2. Journalize the issuance of stock to the outsiders under both plans.
3. Assume that net income for the first year is $120,000 and total dividends are $30,000. Prepare the stockholders' equity section of the corporation's balance sheet under both plans.
4. Recommend one of the plans to Smith and Jones. Give your reasons. (Challenge)

Case 2. *(Learning Objective 4: Analyzing cash dividends and stock dividends)* **United Parcel Service (UPS), Inc.**, had the following stockholders' equity amounts on December 31, 2010 (adapted, in millions):

Common stock and additional paid-in capital; 1,135 shares issued...............	$ 278
Retained earnings...	9,457
Total stockholders' equity	$9,735

During 2010, UPS paid a cash dividend of $0.715 per share. Assume that, after paying the cash dividends, UPS distributed a 10% stock dividend. Assume further that the following year UPS declared and paid a cash dividend of $0.65 per share.

Suppose you own 10,000 shares of UPS common stock, acquired three years ago, prior to the 10% stock dividend. The market price of UPS stock was $61.02 per share before the stock dividend.

I *Requirements*

1. How does the stock dividend affect your proportionate ownership in UPS? Explain.
2. What amount of cash dividends did you receive last year? What amount of cash dividends will you receive after the above dividend action?
3. Assume that immediately after the stock dividend was distributed, the market value of UPS's stock decreased from $61.02 per share to $55.473 per share. Does this decrease represent a loss to you? Explain.
4. Suppose UPS announces at the time of the stock dividend that the company will continue to pay the annual $0.715 *cash* dividend per share, even after distributing the *stock* dividend. Would you expect the market price of the stock to decrease to $55.473 per share as in Requirement 3? Explain.

Case 3. *(Learning Objectives 2, 3, 4, 5: Evaluating financial position and profitability)* At December 31, 2000, **Enron Corporation** reported the following data (condensed in millions):

Total assets	$65,503
Total liabilities	54,033
Stockholders' equity	11,470
Net income, as reported, for 2000................	979

During 2001, Enron restated company financial statements for 1997 to 2000, after reporting that some data had been omitted from those prior-year statements. Assume that the startling events of 2001 included the following:

■ Several related companies should have been, but were not, included in the Enron statements for 2000. These companies had total assets of $5,700 million, liabilities totaling $5,600 million, and net losses of $130 million.
■ In January 2001, Enron's stockholders got the company to give them $2,000 million of 12% long-term notes payable in return for their giving up their common stock. Interest is accrued at year-end.

Take the role of a financial analyst. It is your job to analyze Enron Corporation and rate the company's long-term debt.

I *Requirements*

1. Measure Enron's expected net income for 2001 two ways:
   a. Assume 2001's net income should be the same as the amount of net income that Enron actually reported for 2000. (Given)
   b. Recompute expected net income for 2001 taking into account the new developments of 2001. (Challenge)
   c. Evaluate Enron's likely trend of net income for the future. Discuss *why* this trend is developing. Ignore income tax. (Challenge)

2. Write Enron's accounting equation two ways:
   a. As actually reported at December 31, 2000.
   b. As adjusted for the events of 2001. (Challenge)
3. Measure Enron's debt ratio as reported at December 31, 2000, and again after making the adjustments for the events of 2001.
4. Based on your analysis, make a recommendation to the Debt-Rating Committee of Moody's Investor Services. Would you recommend upgrading, downgrading, or leaving Enron's debt rating undisturbed (currently, it is "high-grade"). (Challenge)

Ethical Issues

Ethical Issue 1.   *Note:* This case is based on a real situation.

writing assignment ■

   George Campbell paid $50,000 for a franchise that entitled him to market Success Associates software programs in the countries of the European Union. Campbell intended to sell individual franchises for the major language groups of western Europe—German, French, English, Spanish, and Italian. Naturally, investors considering buying a franchise from Campbell asked to see the financial statements of his business.

   Believing the value of the franchise to be greater than $50,000, Campbell sought to capitalize his own franchise at $500,000. The law firm of McDonald & LaDue helped Campbell form a corporation chartered to issue 500,000 shares of common stock with par value of $1 per share. Attorneys suggested the following chain of transactions:

   a. A third party borrows $500,000 and purchases the franchise from Campbell.
   b. Campbell pays the corporation $500,000 to acquire all its stock.
   c. The corporation buys the franchise from the third party, who repays the loan.

In the final analysis, the third party is debt-free and out of the picture. Campbell owns all the corporation's stock, and the corporation owns the franchise. The corporation balance sheet lists a franchise acquired at a cost of $500,000. This balance sheet is Campbell's most valuable marketing tool.

❙ Requirements

1. What is the ethical issue in this situation?
2. Who are the stakeholders to the suggested transaction?
3. Analyze this case from the following standpoints: (a) economic, (b) legal, (c) ethical. What are the consequences to each stakeholder?
4. How should the transaction be reported?

Ethical Issue 2.   St. Genevieve Petroleum Company is an independent oil producer in Baton Parish, Louisiana. In February, company geologists discovered a pool of oil that tripled the company's proven reserves. Prior to disclosing the new oil to the public, St. Genevieve quietly bought most of its stock as treasury stock. After the discovery was announced, the company's stock price increased from $6 to $27.

writing assignment ■

❙ Requirements

1. What is the ethical issue in this situation? What accounting principle is involved?
2. Who are the stakeholders?
3. Analyze the facts from the following standpoints: (a) economic, (b) legal, and (c) ethical. What is the impact to each stakeholder?
4. What decision would you have made?

Focus on Financials: ■ Amazon.com, Inc.

*(**Learning Objectives 2, 3, 6:** Analyzing common stock, retained earnings, return on equity, and return on assets)* **Amazon.com's** consolidated financial statements appear in Appendix A at the end of this book.

1. Refer to the Consolidated Balance Sheets and Note 8 (Stockholders' Equity). Describe the classes of stock that Amazon.com, Inc., has authorized. How many shares of each class have been issued? How many are outstanding as of December 31, 2008?

2. Refer to the Consolidated Balance Sheets and the Consolidated Statements of Stockholders' Equity. (Note: The Statement of Stockholders' Equity is discussed in detail in Chapter 11, pages 667 through 675.) How many shares of treasury stock did the company purchase during the year ended December 31, 2008? How much did it pay for it in total? How much per share?

3. Examine Amazon.com's consolidated statement of shareholders' equity. Analyze the change that occurred in the company's Retained Earnings account during the year ended December 31, 2008. Can you trace the change to any of its other financial statements? Is this a good thing or a bad thing? (Note: The Statement of Stockholders' Equity is discussed in detail in Chapter 11, pages 667 through 675.)

4. Compute Amazon.com's return on equity and return on assets for 2008. Which is larger? Is this a sign of financial strength or weakness? Explain.

Focus on Analysis: ■ Foot Locker, Inc.

(*Learning Objectives 2, 3, 4: Analyzing treasury stock and retained earnings*) This case is based on the consolidated financial statements of **Foot Locker, Inc.**, given in Appendix B at the end of this book. In particular, this case uses Foot Locker, Inc.'s consolidated statement of shareholders' equity for the year 2007. (Note: The Statement of Stockholders' Equity is discussed in detail in Chapter 11, pages 667 through 675.)

1. As of the end of fiscal 2007, how many classes of stock does Foot Locker, Inc., have authorized? Issued? Outstanding?

2. During 2007, Foot Locker, Inc., repurchased its treasury stock. How many shares did it purchase? How much did it pay for the stock? How much per share? Compare the price it paid for these shares with the market price of the company's stock at the end of each quarter (see footnote 26). Does it look like the company was getting a "good deal" on the purchase of its stock? Why do you think it did it? (Challenge)

3. Did Foot Locker, Inc., issue any new shares of common stock during fiscal 2007? Briefly explain the reasons. (Challenge)

4. Prepare a T-account to show the beginning and ending balances, plus all the activity in Retained Earnings for fiscal 2007.

Group Project in Ethics

writing assignment ■

The global economic recession that started in 2007 has impacted every business, but it was especially hard on banks, automobile manufacturing, and retail companies. Banks were largely responsible for the recession. Some of the biggest banks made excessively risky investments collateralized by real estate mortgages, and many of these investments soured when the real estate markets collapsed. When banks had to write these investments down to market values, the regulatory authorities notified them that they had inadequate capital ratios on their balance sheets to operate. Banks stopped loaning money. Because stock prices were depressed, companies could not raise capital by selling stock. With both debt and stock financing frozen, many businesses had to close their doors.

Fearing collapse of the whole economy, the central governments of the United States and several European nations loaned money to banks to prop up their capital ratios and keep them open. The government also loaned massive amounts to the largest insurance company in the United States (AIG), as well as to General Motors and Chrysler, to help them stay in business. When asked why, many in government replied "these businesses were too important to fail." In several cases, the U.S. government has taken an "equity stake" in some banks and businesses by taking preferred stock in exchange for the cash infusion.

Because of the recession, corporate downsizing has occurred on a massive scale throughout the world. While companies in the retail sector provide more jobs than the banking and automobile industry combined, the government has not chosen to "bail out" any retail businesses. Each company or industry mentioned in this book has pared down plant and equipment, laid off employees, or restructured operations. Some companies have been forced out of business altogether.

❙ *Requirements*

1. Identify all the stakeholders of a corporation. A *stakeholder* is a person or a group who has an interest (that is, a stake) in the success of the organization.
2. Do you believe that some entities are "too important to fail?" Should the federal government help certain businesses to stay afloat during economic recessions, and allow others to fail?
3. Identify several measures by which a company may be considered deficient and in need of downsizing. How can downsizing help to solve this problem?
4. Debate the bailout issue. One group of students takes the perspective of the company and its stockholders, and another group of students takes the perspective of the other stakeholders of the company (the community in which the company operates and society at large).
5. What is the problem with the government taking an equity position such as preferred stock in a private enterprise?

For online homework, exercises, and problems that provide you with immediate feedback, please visit www.myaccountinglab.com.

Quick Check Answers

1. *a* (20,000 shares × $25 = $500,000)
2. *c* ($600,000/$5 par = 120,000 shares)
3. *d* ($375,000 + $60,000 + $600,000)
4. *d* ($375,000 + $60,000 + $600,000 + $325,000)
5. *c* ($1,360,000 − $10,000)
6. *d* [No gain or loss (for the income statement) on treasury stock transactions]
7. *a*
8. *b*
9. *d*
10. *c*
11. *d* [First, annual preferred dividend = $1,250 (2,500 × $25 × .02)]. Five years of preferred dividends must be paid (four in arrears plus the current year).
    [($1,250 × 5) + ($125,000 × $2.50 per share common dividend) = $318,750]
12. *a*
13. *c*
14. *c*
15. *d*
16. *c*

10

Long-Term Investments & International Operations

SPOTLIGHT: **Intel Holds Several Different Types of Investments**

After college you'll start investing through a retirement or savings plan at work, and you may make some investments on your own. The reasons people invest are for current income (interest and dividends) and appreciation of the investment's value (stocks, bonds, and real estate, for example). Some very wealthy individuals invest in order to obtain significant influence over, or even to control, corporate entities.

Businesses like **Intel**, **General Electric**, and **Coca-Cola** invest for the same reasons. In this chapter you'll learn how to account for investments of all types. We use Intel Corporation as our example company because Intel has so many interesting investments. You'll also learn how companies like this do business across international borders, and the impact that business has on their financial statements.

Intel Corporation Consolidated Balance Sheet (partial; adapted) December 31, 2007	
(In millions)	2007
1 Assets	
2 Current assets:	
3 Cash and cash equivalents......................................	$ 7,307
4 Short-term investments...	5,490
5 Trading assets..	2,566
6 Accounts receivable, net of allowance for doubtful accounts of $27	2,576
7 Inventories..	3,370
8 Other current assets...	2,576
9 Total current assets..	23,885
10 Property, plant and equipment, net..........................	16,918
11 Marketable strategic equity securities	987
12 Other long-term investments...................................	4,398
13 Goodwill..	3,916
14 Other long-term assets	5,547
15 Total assets	$55,651

What comes to mind when you think of Intel? Computer processors and microchips? Yes, Intel produces processors and computer chips. But, interestingly, 24.2% ($5,490 + $2,566 + $987 + $4,398/$55,651) of Intel's assets are tied up in investments in other companies. The assets section of Intel's 2007 balance sheet reports these investments on lines 4, 5, 11, and 12. Some of Intel's other asset categories also include investments.

Throughout this course, you've become increasingly familiar with the financial statements of companies such as **Intel**, **Southwest Airlines**, and **Starbucks**. You've seen most of the items that appear in a set of financial statements. One of your learning goals should be to develop the ability to analyze whatever you encounter in real-company statements. This chapter will help you advance toward that goal.

The first half of this chapter shows how to account for long-term investments, including a brief overview of consolidated financial statements. The second half of the chapter covers accounting for international operations.

LEARNING OBJECTIVES

1 **Account** for available-for-sale investments

2 **Use** the equity method for investments

3 **Understand** consolidated financial statements

4 **Account** for long-term investments in bonds

5 **Account** for international operations

6 **Report** investing transactions on the statement of cash flows

STOCK INVESTMENTS: AN OVERVIEW

Investments come in all sizes and shapes—from a few shares of stock to a controlling interest in multiple companies. In earlier chapters, we discussed stocks and bonds from the perspective of the company that issued the securities. In this chapter, we examine *long-term* investments.

To consider investments, we need to define two key terms. The entity that owns the stock of a corporation is the *investor*. The corporation that issued the stock is the *investee*. If you own some shares of Intel common stock, you are an investor and Intel is the investee.

Stock Prices

You can log onto the Internet to learn Intel's current stock price. Exhibit 10-1 presents information on Intel. During the previous 52 weeks, Intel common stock had a high price of $25.29 and a low of $12.06 per share. The annual cash dividend is $0.56 per share. During the previous day, 51.3 million shares of Intel common stock were traded. At day's end the price of the stock closed at $13.36, up $0.15 from the closing price of the preceding day.

EXHIBIT 10-1 | Stock Price Information for Intel Corporation

52-Week Hi	Lo	Stock (sym)	Div	Volume	Close	Net Change
$25.29	$12.06	INTC	$0.56	51,305,000	$13.36	+ $0.15

Reporting Investments on the Balance Sheet

An investment is an asset to the investor. The investment may be short-term or long-term. **Short-term investments** in marketable securities are current assets. They can be classified as either *trading*, *held-to-maturity*, or *available for sale*, depending on management's intent and ability to hold them until they mature. To be listed as short-term on the balance sheet,

- the investment must be *liquid* (readily convertible to cash).
- the investor must intend either to convert the investment to cash within one year or to use it to pay a current liability.

We saw how to account for short-term investments in Chapter 5.

Investments that aren't short-term are listed as **long-term investments**, a category of noncurrent assets. Long-term investments include stocks and bonds that the investor expects to hold for longer than one year. Exhibit 10-2 on the following page shows where short-term and long-term investments appear on the balance sheet.

EXHIBIT 10-2 | **Reporting Investments on the Balance Sheet**

Current Assets:		
Cash	$X	
Short-term investments	X	
Accounts receivable	X	
Inventories	X	
Prepaid expenses	X	
Total current assets		X
Long-term investments [or simply Investments]		X
Property, plant, and equipment		X
Intangible assets		X
Other assets		X

Assets are listed in order of liquidity. Long-term investments are less liquid than current assets but more liquid than property, plant, and equipment. Intel also reports short-term investments immediately after cash (p. 604, lines 4 and 5).

The accounting rules for long-term investments in stock depend on the percentage of ownership by the investor. The accounting methods typically used are shown in Exhibit 10-3.

EXHIBIT 10-3 | **Accounting Methods for Long-Term Investments Based on Level of Ownership**

Percentage Ownership by the Investor	GAAP Accounting Method
Up to 20% (Available-for-Sale)	→ Fair Market Value
20–50%	→ Equity
Greater than 50%	→ Consolidation

An investment up to 20% is considered available-for-sale because the investor usually has little or no influence on the investee, in which case the strategy would be to hold the investment, making it available for sale in periods beyond the end of the fiscal year. Ownership between 20% and 50% provides the investor with the opportunity to significantly influence the investee's operating decisions and policies over the long run. An investment above 50% allows the investor a great deal of long-term influence—perhaps control—over the investee company. Let's see how these methods apply to long-term investments in stock.

AVAILABLE-FOR-SALE INVESTMENTS

Available-for-sale investments are stock investments other than trading securities. They are classified as current assets if the business expects to sell them within the next year. All other available-for-sale investments are classified as long term (Exhibit 10-2).

Accounting for Available-for-Sale Investments

Available-for-sale investments are accounted for at fair market value because the company expects to sell the investment at its market price. *Cost* is used only as the initial amount for recording the investments. These investments are reported on the balance sheet at current **fair market values**.

Suppose Intel purchases 1,000 shares of **Hewlett-Packard** common stock at the market price of $44.00. Intel intends to hold this investment for longer than a year and therefore treats it as an available-for-sale investment. Intel's entry to record the investment is:

2010			
Oct 23	Long-Term Investment (1,000 × $44)	44,000	
	Cash		44,000
	Purchased investment.		

Assets	=	Liabilities	+	Stockholders' Equity
+ 44,000 − 44,000	=	0	+	0

Assume that Intel receives a $0.20 cash dividend on the Hewlett-Packard stock. Intel's entry to record receipt of the dividend is

2010			
Nov 14	Cash (1,000 × $0.20)	200	
	Dividend Revenue		200
	Received cash dividend.		

Assets	=	Liabilities	+	Stockholders' Equity	+	Revenues
+200	=	0	+			+200

Receipt of a *stock* dividend is different from receipt of a cash dividend. For a stock dividend, the investor records no dividend revenue. Instead, the investor makes a memorandum entry in the accounting records to denote the new number of shares of stock held as an investment. Because the number of shares of stock held has increased, the investor's cost per share decreases. To illustrate, suppose Intel receives a 10% stock dividend from Hewlett-Packard Company. Intel would receive 100 shares (10% of 1,000 shares previously held) and make this memorandum entry in its accounting records:

> **MEMORANDUM—Receipt of stock dividend: Received 100 shares of Hewlett-Packard common stock in 10% stock dividend. New cost per share is $40.00 (cost of $44,000 ÷ 1,100 shares).**

In all future transactions affecting this investment, Intel's cost per share is now $40.00.

What Value of an Investment Is Most Relevant?

Fair market value is the amount that a seller would receive on the sale of an investment to a willing purchaser on a given date. Because of the relevance of fair market values for decision making, available-for-sale investments in stock are reported on the balance sheet at their fair market values. On the balance-sheet date we therefore adjust available-for-sale investments from their last carrying amount to current fair market value. Assume that the fair market value of the Hewlett-Packard common stock is $46,500 on December 31, 2010. In this case, Intel makes the following entry to bring the investment to fair market value.

2010			
Dec 31	Allowance to Adjust Investment to Market		
	($46,500 − $44,000)	2,500	
	Unrealized Gain on Investment		2,500
	Adjusted investment to fair market value.		

The increase in the investment's fair market value creates additional equity for the investor.

Assets	=	Liabilities	+	Stockholders' Equity
+ 2,500	=	0		+ 2,500

Allowance to Adjust Investment to Market is a companion account to Long-Term Investment. In this case, the investment's cost ($44,000) plus the Allowance ($2,500) equals the investment fair market value carrying amount ($46,500), as follows:

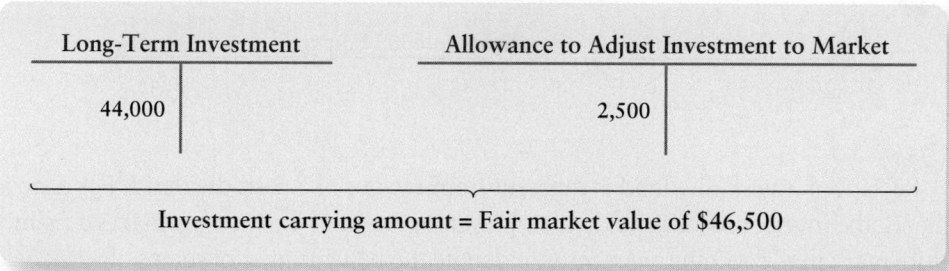

Here the Allowance has a debit balance because the fair market value of the investment increased. If the investment's fair market value declines, the Allowance is credited. In that case the carrying amount is its cost minus the Allowance.

The other side of this adjustment entry is a credit to Unrealized Gain on Investment. If the fair market value of the investment declines, the company debits Unrealized Loss on Investment. *Unrealized* gains and losses result from changes in fair market value, not from sales of investments. For available-for-sale investments, the Unrealized Gain account or the Unrealized Loss account is reported in either of two places in the financial statements:

- *Other comprehensive income*, which can be reported on the *income statement* in a separate section below net income
- *Accumulated other comprehensive income*, which is a separate section of stockholders' equity, below retained earnings, on the *balance sheet*

The following display shows how Intel could report its investment and the related unrealized gain in its financial statements at the end of 2010 (all other figures are assumed for this illustration):

Balance sheet		Income statement		
Assets:				
Total current assets	$ XXX	Revenues		$50,000
Long-term investments—		Expenses, including		
at market value		income tax		36,000
($44,000 + $2,500	46,500	Net income		$14,000
Property, plant, and equipment,		Other comprehensive income:		
net	XXX	Unrealized gain on		
Stockholders' equity:		investments	$ 2,500	
Common stock	1,000	Less Income tax		
Retained earnings	2,000	40%	(1,000)	1,500
Accumulated other		Comprehensive income		$15,500
comprehensive income:				
Unrealized gain on investments	2,500			
Total stockholders' equity	$ 5,500			

The preceding example assumes that the investor holds an investment in only one security of another company. Usually companies invest in a portfolio of securities (more than one). In this case, the periodic adjustment to fair market value must be made for the portfolio as a whole. See the "Stop & Think" exercise at the end of this section (p. 610) for an example.

Selling an Available-for-Sale Investment

The sale of an available-for-sale investment usually results in a *realized* gain or loss. Realized gains and losses measure the difference between the amount received from the sale and the cost of the investment.

Suppose Intel sells its investment in Hewlett-Packard stock for $43,000 during 2011. Intel would record the sale as follows:

2011	Cash	43,000	
May 19	Loss on Sale of Investment	1,000	
	Long-Term Investment (cost)		44,000
	Sold investment.		

Assets	=	Liabilities	+	Stockholders' Equity	−	Losses
+ 43,000	=	0			−	1,000
− 44,000						

Intel would report Loss on Sale of Investments as an "Other" item on the income statement. Then at December 31, 2011, Intel must make adjusting entries to update the Allowance to Adjust Investment to Market and the Unrealized Gain on Investment accounts to their current balances (in this case, these accounts have been reduced to zero since the entire investment was sold). These adjustments are covered in intermediate accounting courses.

STOP & THINK...

Suppose Intel Corporation holds the following available-for-sale securities as long-term investments at December 31, 2011:

Stock	Cost	Current Fair Market Value
The Coca-Cola Company.........	$ 85,000	$71,000
Eastman Kodak Company........	16,000	12,000
	$101,000	$83,000

Show how Intel will report long-term investments on its December 31, 2011, balance sheet.

Answer:

Assets	
Long-term investments, at fair market value	$83,000

When Should We Sell an Investment?

Companies control when they sell investments, and that helps them control when they record gains and losses. Suppose a bad year hits and Intel holds an investment that has appreciated in value. Intel can sell the investment, raise cash, record the gain, and boost reported income.

The cost principle of accounting provides this opportunity to "manage" earnings. If companies had to account for all investments at pure market value, there would be no gain or loss on the sale. Instead, all gains and losses would be recorded when the market value of the asset changes. That would eliminate part of management's ability to "manage" earnings. But the business community may not be ready to fully embrace fair-market-value accounting.

EQUITY-METHOD INVESTMENTS

OBJECTIVE

2 Use the equity method for investments

We use the **equity method** to account for investments in which the investor owns 20% to 50% of the investee's stock.

Buying a Large Stake in Another Company

An investor with a stock holding between 20% and 50% of the investee's voting stock may significantly influence the investee. Such an investor can probably affect dividend policy, product lines, and other important matters.

Intel holds equity-method investments in IM Flash Technologies and Clearwire Corporation. These investee companies are often referred to as *affiliates*; thus Clearwire is an affiliate of Intel. And because Intel has a voice in shaping the policy and operations of Clearwire, some measure of Clearwire's profits and losses should be included in Intel's income.

Accounting for Equity-Method Investments

Investments accounted for by the equity method are recorded initially at cost. Suppose Intel pays $400 million for 30% of the common stock of Clearwire Corporation. Intel's entry to record the purchase of this investment follows (in millions):

2010			
Jan 6	Long-Term Investment	400	
	Cash		400
	To purchase equity–method investment.		

Assets	=	Liabilities	+	Stockholders' Equity
+ 400	=	0	+	0
− 400				

The Investor's Percentage of Investee Income.   Under the equity method, Intel, as the investor, applies its percentage of ownership—30%, in our example—in recording its share of the investee's net income and dividends. If Clearwire reports net income of $250 million for the year, Intel records 30% of this amount as follows (in millions):

2010			
Dec 31	Long-Term Investment ($250 × 0.30)	75	
	Equity-Method Investment Revenue		75
	To record investment revenue.		

Assets	=	Liabilities	+	Stockholders' Equity
+ 75	=	0		+ 75

Because of the close relationship between Intel and Clearwire, Intel the investor, increases the Investment account and records Investment Revenue when Clearwire the investee, reports income. As Clearwire's owners' equity increases, so does the Investment account on Intel's books.

Receiving Dividends Under the Equity Method.   Intel records its proportionate part of cash dividends received from Clearwire. When Clearwire declares and pays a cash dividend of $100 million, Intel receives 30% of this dividend and records this entry (in millions):

2010			
Dec 31	Cash ($100 × 0.30)	30	
	Long-Term Investment		30
	To receive cash dividend on equity-method investment.		

Assets	=	Liabilities	+	Stockholders' Equity
+ 30	=	0	+	0
− 30				

The Investment account is *decreased* for the receipt of a dividend on an equity-method investment. Why? Because the dividend decreases the investee's owners' equity and thus the investor's investment.

After the preceding entries are posted, Intel's Investment account at December 31, 2010, shows Intel's equity in the net assets of Clearwire (in millions):

Long-Term Investment					
Jan 6	Purchase	400	Dec 31	Dividends	30
Dec 31	Net income	75			
Dec 31	Balance	445			

Intel would report the long-term investment on the balance sheet and the equity-method investment revenue on the income statement as follows:

	Millions
Balance sheet (partial):	
Assets	
Total current assets..	$XXX
Long-term investments, at equity.......................	445
Property, plant, and equipment, net....................	XXX
Income statement (partial):	
Income from operations......................................	$XXX
Other revenue:	
Equity-method investment revenue.................	75
Net income...	$XXX

Gain or loss on the sale of an equity-method investment is measured as the difference between the sale proceeds and the carrying amount of the investment. For example, Intel's sale of 20% of the Clearwire common stock for $81 million would be recorded as follows:

2011			
Feb 13	Cash	81	
	Loss on Sale of Investment	8	
	Long-Term Investment ($445,000 × 0.20)		89
	Sold 20% of investment.		

Assets	=	Liabilities	+	Stockholders' Equity	−	Losses
+ 81	=	0			−	8
− 89						

Summary of the Equity Method. The following T-account illustrates the accounting for equity-method investments:

Equity-Method Investment	
Original cost	Share of losses
Share of income	Share of dividends
Balance	

CONSOLIDATED SUBSIDIARIES

Companies buy a significant stake in another company in order to *influence* the other company's operations. In this section we cover the situation in which a corporation buys enough of another company to actually *control* that company. Intel's ownership of Intel Capital is an example.

OBJECTIVE

3 **Understand** consolidated financial statements

Why Buy Another Company?

Most large corporations own controlling interests in other companies. A **controlling** (or **majority**) **interest** is the ownership of more than 50% of the investee's voting stock. Such an investment enables the investor to elect a majority of the members of the investee's board of directors and thus control the investee. The investor is called the **parent company**, and the investee company is called the **subsidiary**. For example, **Intel Capital** is a subsidiary of Intel Corporation, the parent. Therefore, the stockholders of Intel control Intel Capital, as diagrammed in Exhibit 10-4.

EXHIBIT 10-4 | **Ownership Structure of Intel Corporation and Intel Capital**

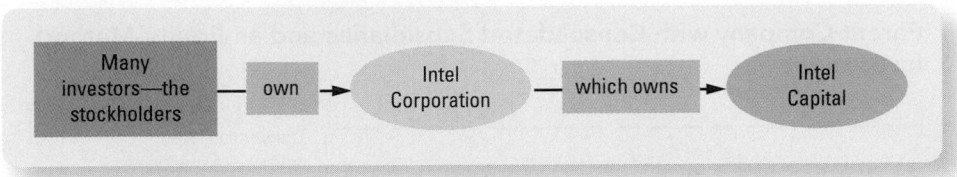

Exhibit 10-5 shows some of the subsidiaries of Intel Corporation.

EXHIBIT 10-5 | **Selected Subsidiaries of Intel**

Intel Capital	Intel Americas, Inc.
Componentes Intel de Costa Rica, S.A.	Intel Europe, Inc.
Intel Asia Holding Limited	Intel Kabushiki Kaisha

Consolidation Accounting

Consolidation accounting is a method of combining the financial statements of all the companies controlled by the same stockholders. This method reports a single set of financial statements for the consolidated entity, which carries the name of the parent company. Exhibit 10-6 summarizes the accounting methods used for stock investments.

EXHIBIT 10-6 | **Accounting Methods for Stock Investment by Percentage of Ownership**

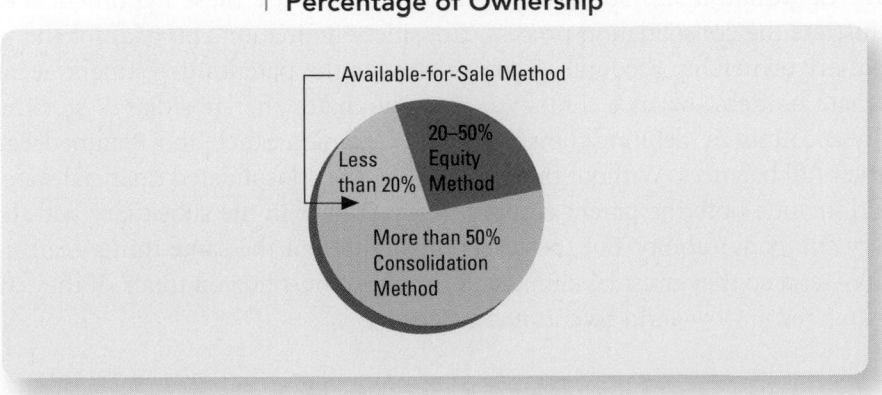

Consolidated statements combine the balance sheets, income statements, and cash-flow statements of the parent company with those of its subsidiaries. The result is a single set of statements as if the parent and its subsidiaries were one company. Investors can gain a better perspective on total operations than they could by examining the reports of the parent and each individual subsidiary.

In consolidated statements the assets, liabilities, revenues, and expenses of each subsidiary are added to the parent's accounts. For example, the balance in Intel Capital's Cash account is added to the balance in the Intel Corporation Cash account and to the cash of all other subsidiaries. The sum of all of the cash amounts is presented as a single amount in the Intel consolidated balance sheet. Each account balance of a subsidiary, such as Intel Capital or Intel Europe, Inc., loses its identity in the consolidated statements, which bear the name of the parent, Intel Corporation. When a subsidiary's financial statements get consolidated into the parent company's statements, the subsidiary's statements are no longer available to the public.

Exhibit 10-7 diagrams a corporate structure for a parent corporation that owns controlling interests in five subsidiaries and an equity-method investment in another investee company.

EXHIBIT 10-7 | **Parent Company with Consolidated Subsidiaries and an Equity-Method Investment**

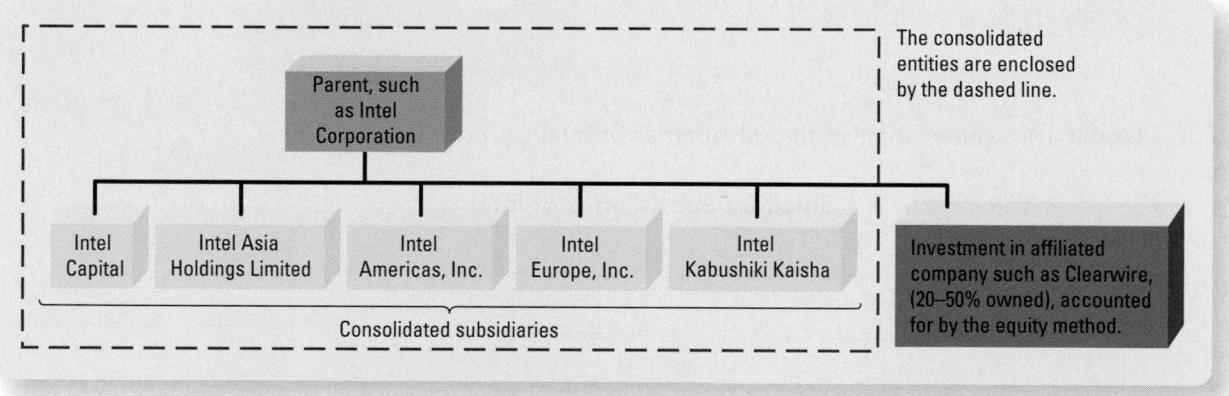

The Consolidated Balance Sheet and the Related Work Sheet

Intel owns all (100%) the outstanding common stock of Intel Capital. Both Intel and Intel Capital keep separate sets of books. Intel, the parent company, uses a work sheet to prepare the consolidated statements of Intel and its consolidated subsidiaries. Then Intel's consolidated balance sheet shows the combined assets and liabilities of both Intel and all its subsidiaries.

Exhibit 10-8 shows the work sheet for consolidating the balance sheets of Parent Corporation and Subsidiary Corporation. We use these hypothetical entities to illustrate the consolidation process. Consider elimination entry (a) for the parent-subsidiary ownership accounts. Entry (a) credits the parent's Investment account to eliminate its debit balance. Entry (a) also eliminates the subsidiary's stockholders' equity accounts by debiting the subsidiary's Common Stock and Retained Earnings for their full balances. Without this elimination, the consolidated financial statements would include both the parent company's investment in the subsidiary and the subsidiary company's equity. But these accounts represent the same thing—Subsidiary's equity—and so they must be eliminated from the consolidated totals. If they weren't, the same resources would be counted twice.

EXHIBIT 10-8 | Work Sheet for a Consolidated Balance Sheet

	Parent Corporation	Subsidiary Corporation	Eliminations Debit	Eliminations Credit	Parent and Subsidiary Consolidated Amounts
Assets					
Cash	12,000	18,000			30,000
Note receivable from Subsidiary	80,000	—		(b) 80,000	—
Inventory	104,000	91,000			195,000
Investment in Subsidiary	150,000	—		(a) 150,000	—
Other assets	218,000	138,000			356,000
Total	564,000	247,000			581,000
Liabilities and Stockholders' Equity					
Accounts payable	43,000	17,000			60,000
Notes payable	190,000	80,000	(b) 80,000		190,000
Common stock	176,000	100,000	(a) 100,000		176,000
Retained earnings	155,000	50,000	(a) 50,000		155,000
Total	564,000	247,000	230,000	230,000	581,000

The resulting Parent and Subsidiary consolidated balance sheet (far-right column) reports no Investment in Subsidiary account. Moreover, the consolidated totals for Common Stock and Retained Earnings are those of Parent Corporation only. Study the final column of the consolidation work sheet.

In this example, Parent Corporation has an $80,000 note receivable from Subsidiary, and Subsidiary has a note payable to Parent. The parent's receivable and the subsidiary's payable represent the same resources—all entirely within the consolidated entity. Both, therefore, must be eliminated and entry (b) accomplishes this.

- The $80,000 credit in the Elimination column of the work sheet zeros out Parent's Note Receivable from Subsidiary.
- The $80,000 debit in the Elimination column zeros out the Subsidiary's Note Payable to Parent.
- The resulting consolidated amount for notes payable is the amount owed to creditors outside the consolidated entity, which is appropriate.

After the work sheet is complete, the consolidated amount for each account represents the total asset, liability, and equity amounts controlled by Parent Corporation.

STOP & THINK...

Examine Exhibit 10-8. Why does the consolidated stockholders' equity ($176,000 + $155,000) *exclude* the equity of Subsidiary Corporation?

Answer:

The stockholders' equity of the consolidated entity is that of the parent only. To include the stockholders' equity of the subsidiary as well as the investment in the subsidiary on the parent's books would be double counting.

Goodwill and Noncontrolling Interest

Goodwill and Noncontrolling (minority) Interest are two accounts that only a consolidated entity can have. *Goodwill*, which we studied in Chapter 7, arises when a parent company pays more to acquire a subsidiary company than the market value of the subsidiary's net assets. As we saw in Chapter 7, goodwill is the intangible asset that represents the parent company's excess payment over and above the fair market value of assets to acquire the subsidiary. GE reports goodwill as an intangible asset on its balance sheet.

Noncontrolling (minority) interest arises when a parent company owns less than 100% of the stock of a subsidiary. For example, General Electric (GE) owns less than 100% of some of the companies it controls. The remainder of the subsidiaries' stock is noncontrolling (minority) interest to GE. Noncontrolling Interest is reported as a separate account in the stockholders' equity section of the consolidated balance sheet of the parent company. The amount of noncontrolling interest in subsidiaries' stock must be clearly identified and labeled as such. GE reports noncontrolling interest in the stockholders' equity section on its balance sheet. By contrast, Intel reports no noncontrolling interest, so that suggests that Intel owns 100% of all its subsidiaries.

Income of a Consolidated Entity

The income of a consolidated entity is the net income of the parent plus the parent's proportion of the subsidiaries' net income. Suppose Parent Company owns all the stock of Subsidiary S-1 and 60% of the stock of Subsidiary S-2. During the year just ended, Parent earned net income of $330,000, S-1 earned $150,000, and S-2 had a net loss of $100,000. Parent Company would report net income of $420,000, computed as follows:

	Net Income (Net Loss) of Each Company		Parent's Ownership of Each Company		Parent's Consolidated Net Income (Net Loss)
Parent Company	$330,000	×	100%	=	$330,000
Subsidiary S-1	150,000	×	100%	=	150,000
Subsidiary S-2	(100,000)	×	60%	=	(60,000)
Consolidated net income					$420,000

COOKING THE BOOKS with Investments and Debt

Enron Corporation

In 2000, Enron Corporation in Houston, Texas, employed approximately 22,000 people and was one of the world's leading electricity, natural gas, pulp and paper, and communications companies, with reported revenues of nearly $101 billion. *Fortune* had named Enron "America's Most Innovative Company" for six consecutive years. To many outside observers, Enron was the model corporation.

Enron's financial statements showed that the company was making a lot of money, but in reality, most of its profits were merely on paper. Rather than from operations, the great majority of the cash Enron needed to operate on a day-to-day basis came from bank loans. It was very important, therefore, that Enron keep its debt ratio (discussed in Chapter 8) as well as its return on assets (ROA, discussed in Chapter 9) at acceptable levels, so the banks would continue to view the company as creditworthy. Enron's balance sheets contained large misstatements in the liabilities and stockholders' equity sections over a period of years. Many of the offsetting misstatements were in long-term assets. Specifically, Enron owned numerous long-term investments, including power plants, water, broadband cable, and sophisticated, complex, and somewhat dubious derivative financial instruments in such unusual things as the weather! Many of these investments actually had questionable value, but Enron had abused fair market value accounting to estimate them at grossly inflated values.

To create paper profits, Andrew Fastow, Enron's chief financial officer, created a veritable maze of "special purpose entities" (SPEs), financed with bank debt. He then "sold" the dubious investments to the SPEs to get them off Enron's books. Enron recorded millions of dollars in "profits" from these transactions. Fastow then used Enron stock to collateralize the bank debt of the SPEs, making the transactions entirely circular. Unknown to Enron's board of directors, Fastow or members of his own family owned most of these entities, making them related parties to Enron. Enron was, in fact, the owner of the assets, and was, in fact, obligated for the debts of the SPEs since those debts were collateralized with Enron stock. When Enron's fraud was discovered in late 2001, the company was forced to consolidate the assets of the SPEs, as well as all of their bank debt, into its own financial statements. The end result of the restatement so depressed Enron's debt ratio and ROA that the banks refused to loan the company any more money to operate. Enron's energy trading business virtually dried up overnight, and it was bankrupt within 60 days. An estimated $60 billion in shareholder value, and 22,000 jobs, were lost. Enron's CEO, Jeffrey Skilling, its CFO, Andrew Fastow, and Board Chairman Kenneth Lay were all convicted of fraud. Skilling and Fastow both went to prison. Lay died suddenly of a heart attack before being sentenced.

Enron's audit firm, Arthur Andersen, was accused of trying to cover up its knowledge of Enron's practices by shredding documents. The firm was indicted by the U.S. Justice Department in March 2002. Because of the indictment, Andersen lost all of its public clients and was forced out of business. As a result, over 58,000 persons lost their jobs worldwide. A U.S. Supreme Court decision in 2005 eventually led to withdrawal of the indictment, but it came much too late for the once "gold plated" CPA firm. Allegations about the quality of its work on Enron, as well as other well-publicized cases such as Waste Management (p. 427) and WorldCom (p. 415), who were also clients, doomed Arthur Andersen.

Decision Case 1 in Chapter 8 (p. 528) and Decision Case 3 in Chapter 9 (p. 598) illustrate the financial statement impact of Enron's fraudulent transactions.

Long-Term Investments in Bonds

The major investors in bonds are financial institutions—pension plans, mutual funds, and insurance companies such as Intel Capital. The relationship between the issuing corporation and the investor (bondholder) may be diagrammed as follows:

OBJECTIVE

4 **Account** for long-term investments in bonds

An investment in bonds is classified either as short-term (a current asset) or as long-term. Short-term investments in bonds are relatively rare. Here, we focus on long-term investments called **held-to-maturity investments**.

Bond investments are recorded at cost. Years later, at maturity, the investor will receive the bonds' face value. Often bond investments are purchased at a premium or a discount. When there is a premium or discount, held-to-maturity investments are amortized to account for interest revenue and the bonds' carrying amount. Held-to-maturity investments are reported by the *amortized cost method*, which determines the carrying amount.

Suppose Intel Capital purchases $10,000 of 6% CBS bonds at a price of 95.2 on April 1, 2010. The investor intends to hold the bonds as a long-term investment until their maturity. Interest dates are April 1 and October 1. Because these bonds mature on April 1, 2014, they will be outstanding for four years (48 months). In this case the investor paid a discount price for the bonds (95.2% of face value). Intel Capital must amortize the bonds' carrying amount from cost of $9,520 up to $10,000 over their term to maturity. Assume amortization of the bonds by the straight-line method. The following are the entries for this long-term investment:

2010			
Apr 1	Long-Term Investment in Bonds ($10,000 × 0.952)	9,520	
	Cash		9,520
	To *purchase bond investment.*		
Oct 1	Cash ($10,000 × 0.06 × 6/12)	300	
	Interest Revenue		300
	To *receive semiannual interest.*		
Oct 1	Long-Term Investment in Bonds [($10,000 − $9,520)/48] × 6	60	
	Interest Revenue		60
	To *amortize bond investment.*		

At December 31, Intel Capital's year-end adjustments are

2010			
Dec 31	Interest Receivable ($10,000 × 0.06 × 3/12)	150	
	Interest Revenue		150
	To *accrue interest revenue.*		
Dec 31	Long-Term Investment in Bonds [($10,000 − $9,520)/48] × 3	30	
	Interest Revenue		30
	To *amortize bond investment.*		

This amortization entry has two effects:

- It increases the Long-Term Investment account on its march toward maturity value.
- It records the interest revenue earned from the increase in the carrying amount of the investment.

The financial statements of Intel Capital at December 31, 2010, would report the following for this investment in bonds:

Balance sheet at December 31, 2010:		
Current assets:		
Interest receivable...	$	150
Long-term investments in bonds ($9,520 + $60 + $30)		9,610
Property, plant, and equipment..		X,XXX
Income statement for the year ended December 31, 2010:		
Other revenues:		
Interest revenue ($300 + $60 + $150 + $30)............................	$	540

DECISION GUIDELINES

ACCOUNTING METHODS FOR LONG-TERM INVESTMENTS

These guidelines show which accounting method to use for each type of long-term investment.
Intel has all types of investments—stocks, bonds, 25% interests, and controlling interests. How should Intel account for its various investments?

Type of Long-Term Investment	Accounting Method
Intel owns less than 20% of investee stock	Available-for-sale
Intel owns between 20% and 50% of investee/affiliate stock	Equity
Intel owns more than 50% of investee stock	Consolidation
Intel owns long-term investment in bonds (held-to-maturity investment)	Amortized cost

MID-CHAPTER SUMMARY PROBLEMS

1. Identify the appropriate accounting method for each of the following situations:
   a. Investment in 25% of investee's stock
   b. 10% investment in stock
   c. Investment in more than 50% of investee's stock
2. At what amount should the following available-for-sale investment portfolio be reported on the December 31 balance sheet? All the investments are less than 5% of the investee's stock.

Stock	Investment Cost	Current Market Value
DuPont	$ 5,000	$ 5,500
ExxonMobil	61,200	53,000
Procter & Gamble	3,680	6,230

   Journalize any adjusting entry required by these data.
3. Investor paid $67,900 to acquire a 40% equity-method investment in the common stock of Investee. At the end of the first year, Investee's net income was $80,000, and Investee declared and paid cash dividends of $55,000. What is Investor's ending balance in its Equity-Method Investment account? Use a T-account to answer.
4. Parent company paid $85,000 for all the common stock of Subsidiary Company, and Parent owes Subsidiary $20,000 on a note payable. Complete the consolidation work sheet below.

	Parent Company	Subsidiary Company	Eliminations Debit	Credit	Consolidated Amounts
Assets					
Cash	7,000	4,000			
Note receivable					
from Parent	—	20,000			
Investment in					
Subsidiary	85,000	—			
Other assets	108,000	99,000			
Total	200,000	123,000			
Liabilities and Stockholders' Equity					
Accounts payable	15,000	8,000			
Notes payable	20,000	30,000			
Common stock	120,000	60,000			
Retained earnings	45,000	25,000			
Total	200,000	123,000			

Answers

1. a. Equity   b. Available-for-sale   c. Consolidation
2. Report the investments at market value: $64,730, as follows:

Stock	Investment Cost	Current Market Value
DuPont	$ 5,000	$ 5,500
ExxonMobil	61,200	53,000
Procter & Gamble	3,680	6,230
Totals	$69,880	$64,730

Adjusting entry:

Unrealized Loss on Investments ($69,880 − $64,730)	5,150	
Allowance to Adjust Investment to Market		5,150
To adjust investments to current market value.		

3.

Equity-Method Investment			
Cost	67,900	Dividends	22,000**
Income	32,000*		
Balance	77,900		

* $80,000 × .40 = $32,000
** $55,000 × .40 = $22,000

4. Consolidation work sheet:

	Parent Company	Subsidiary Company	Eliminations Debit	Eliminations Credit	Consolidated Amounts
Assets					
Cash	7,000	4,000			11,000
Note receivable from Parent	—	20,000		(a) 20,000	—
Investment in Subsidiary	85,000	—		(b) 85,000	—
Other assets	108,000	99,000			207,000
Total	200,000	123,000			218,000
Liabilities and Stockholders' Equity					
Accounts payable	15,000	8,000			23,000
Notes payable	20,000	30,000	(a) 20,000		30,000
Common stock	120,000	60,000	(b) 60,000		120,000
Retained earnings	45,000	25,000	(b) 25,000		45,000
Total	200,000	123,000	105,000	105,000	218,000

GLOBAL VIEW | ACCOUNTING FOR INTERNATIONAL OPERATIONS

Many U.S. companies do a large part of their business abroad. Intel, General Electric, and PepsiCo, among others, are very active in other countries. In fact, Intel earns 84% of its revenue outside the United States. Exhibit 10-9 shows the percentages of international revenues for these companies.

EXHIBIT 10-9 | Extent of International Business

Company	Percentage of International Revenues
Intel...	84%
General Electric......................	87%
PepsiCo..................................	41%

Accounting for business activities across national boundaries is called *international accounting*. Electronic communication makes international accounting important because investors around the world need the same data to make decisions. Therefore, the accounting in Australia needs to be the same as in Brazil and the United Kingdom. The International Accounting Standards Board (IASB) is working on a uniform set of accounting standards for the whole world. At present, over 130 countries either permit or require the use of international financial reporting standards (IFRS).

U.S. accounting standards are being gradually harmonized with IFRS. As new U.S. standards are being written, they are being made to conform in substance with corresponding IFRS, and vice versa.

In 2008, the U.S. Securities and Exchange Commission (SEC) removed a significant barrier for use of IFRS in the United States when it removed the requirement for foreign-registered companies that prepare their financial statements in accordance with IFRS to provide reconciling schedules with U.S. GAAP. A short time later, the SEC provided a "road map" for U.S. companies to transition from U.S. GAAP to IFRS by 2014. As of the publication date of this textbook, IFRS are expected to supersede U.S. GAAP by 2014.

Recent turmoil in the global credit markets and a global recession, followed by political changes in the United States, may slow the process of abandoning U.S. GAAP in favor of IFRS. Therefore, the exact date for U.S. companies to transition to IFRS is not known. However, because of the advantages of efficiency and consistency provided by a single global set of accounting standards, it is likely that this transition will occur.

As emphasized throughout this text, many U.S. GAAP requirements are already consistent with IFRS. In relevant chapters, we have discussed key differences that remain as of this text's publication date. Appendix F summarizes these differences and cross-references them to discussion in relevant chapters.

Foreign Currencies and Exchange Rates

Most countries use their own national currency. An exception is the European Union nations—France, Germany, Italy, Belgium, and others use a common currency, the *euro*, whose symbol is €. If Intel, a U.S. company, sells computer processors to software developers in France, will Intel receive U.S. dollars or euros? If the transaction is in dollars, the company in France must buy dollars to pay Intel in U.S. currency. If the transaction is in euros, then Intel will collect euros and must sell euros for dollars.

The price of one nation's currency can be stated in terms of another country's monetary unit. This measure of one currency against another is called the **foreign-currency exchange rate**. In Exhibit 10-10, the dollar value of a euro is $1.27. This means that one euro can be bought for $1.27. Other currencies are also listed in Exhibit 10-10.

EXHIBIT 10-10 | Foreign-Currency Exchange Rates

Country	Monetary Unit	U.S. Dollar Value	Country	Monetary Unit	U.S. Dollar Value
Brazil	Real (R)	$0.43	United Kingdom	Pound (£)	$1.44
Canada	Dollar ($)	0.80	China	Yuan (元)	0.146
France	Euro (€)	1.27	Japan	Yen (¥)	0.012
Germany	Euro (€)	1.27	Mexico	Peso (P)	0.069

Source: *The Wall Street Journal* (February 19, 2009).

We can convert the cost of an item stated in one currency to its cost in a second currency. We call this conversion a *translation*. Suppose an item costs 200 euros. To compute its cost in dollars, we multiply the euro amount by the conversion rate: 200 euros × $1.27 = $254.

Two main factors affect the price (the exchange rate) of a particular currency:

1. the ratio of a country's imports to its exports, and
2. the rate of return available in the country's capital markets.

The Import/Export Ratio. Japanese exports often exceed Japan's imports. Customers of Japanese companies must buy yen (the Japanese unit of currency) to pay for their purchases. This strong demand drives up the price of the yen. In contrast, the United States imports more goods than it exports. Americans must sell dollars to buy the foreign currencies needed to pay for the foreign goods. As the supply of dollars increases, the price of the dollar falls.

The Rate of Return. The rate of return available in a country's capital markets affects the amount of investment funds flowing into the country. When rates of return are high in a politically stable country such as the United States, international investors buy stocks, bonds, and real estate in that country. This activity increases the demand for the nation's currency and drives up its exchange rate.

Currencies are often described as "strong" or "weak." The exchange rate of a **strong currency** is rising relative to other nations' currencies. The exchange rate of a **weak currency** is falling relative to other currencies.

The *Wall Street Journal* listed the exchange rate for the British pound as $1.44 on February 19, 2009. On February 20, that rate may rise to $1.45. We would say that the dollar has weakened against the pound. The pound has become more expensive, and that makes travel in England more expensive for Americans.

Managing Cash in International Transactions. International transactions are common. **D.E. Shipp Belting**, a family-owned company in Waco, Texas, provides an example. Shipp Belting makes conveyor belts used in a variety of industries. Farmers along the Texas–Mexico border use Shipp conveyor belts to process vegetables. Some of these customers are in Mexico, so Shipp makes sales in pesos, the Mexican monetary unit. Shipp Belting purchases inventory from Swiss companies, and some of these transactions are in Swiss francs.

Do We Collect Cash in Dollars or in Foreign Currency? Do We Pay in Dollars or in Foreign Currency?

Consider Shipp Belting's sale of conveyor belts to Artes de Mexico, a vegetable grower in Matamoros, Mexico. The sale can be conducted in dollars or in pesos. If Artes de Mexico agrees to pay in dollars, Shipp avoids the complication of dealing in a foreign currency, and the transaction is the same as selling to M&M Mars across town. But suppose Artes de Mexico orders 1 million pesos (approximately $90,000) worth of conveyor belts from Shipp. Further suppose Artes demands to pay in pesos and Shipp agrees to receive pesos instead of dollars.

Shipp will need to convert the pesos to dollars, so the transaction poses a challenge. What if the peso weakens before Shipp collects from Artes? In that case, Shipp will not collect as many dollars as expected. The following example shows how to account for international sales stated in a foreign currency.

Shipp Belting sells goods to Artes de Mexico for a price of 1 million pesos on July 28. On that date, a peso is worth $0.086. One month later, on August 28, the peso has weakened against the dollar so that a peso is worth only $0.083. Shipp receives 1 million pesos from Artes on August 28, but the dollar value of Shipp's cash receipt is $3,000 less than expected. Shipp ends up earning less than hoped for on the transaction. The following journal entries show how Shipp would account for these transactions:

Jul 28	Accounts Receivable—Artes (1,000,000 pesos × $0.086)	86,000	
	Sales Revenue		86,000
	Sale on account.		

Aug 28	Cash (1,000,000 pesos × $0.083)	83,000	
	Foreign-Currency Transaction Loss	3,000	
	Accounts Receivable—Artes		86,000
	Collection on account.		

If Shipp had required Artes to pay at the time of the sale, Shipp would have received pesos worth $86,000. But by selling on account, Shipp exposed itself to *foreign-currency exchange risk*. Shipp therefore had a $3,000 foreign-currency transaction loss when it received $3,000 less cash than expected. If the peso had increased in value, Shipp would have had a foreign-currency transaction gain.

When a company holds a receivable denominated in a foreign currency, it wants the foreign currency to strengthen so that it can be converted into more dollars. Unfortunately, that did not occur for Shipp Belting.

Purchasing in a foreign currency also exposes a company to foreign-currency exchange risk. To illustrate, assume Shipp Belting buys inventory from Gesellschaft Ltd., a Swiss company. The price is 20,000 Swiss francs. On September 15 Shipp receives the goods, and the Swiss franc is quoted at $0.80. When Shipp pays two weeks later, the Swiss franc has weakened against the dollar—to $0.78. Shipp would record the purchase and payment as follows:

Sep 15	Inventory (20,000 Swiss francs × $0.80)	16,000	
	Accounts Payable—Gesellschaft Ltd.		16,000
	Purchase on account.		

Sep 29	Accounts Payable—Gesellschaft Ltd.	16,000	
	Cash (20,000 Swiss francs × $0.78)		15,600
	Foreign-Currency Transaction Gain		400
	Payment on account.		

The Swiss franc could have strengthened against the dollar, and Shipp would have had a foreign-currency transaction loss. A company with a payable denominated in a foreign currency wants the dollar to get stronger: The payment then costs fewer dollars.

Reporting Gains and Losses on the Income Statement

The Foreign-Currency Transaction Gain account holds gains on transactions settled in a foreign currency. Likewise, the Foreign-Currency Transaction Loss account holds losses on transactions conducted in foreign currencies. Report the *net amount* of these two accounts on the income statement as Other Revenues and Gains, or Other Expenses and Losses, as the case may be. For example, Shipp Belting would combine its $3,000 foreign-currency loss and the $400 gain and report the net loss of $2,600 on the income statement as follows:

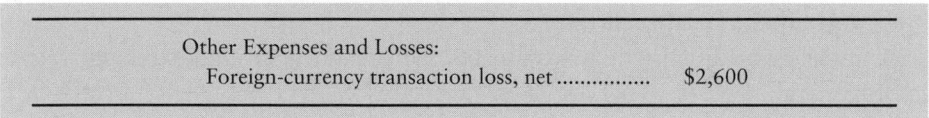

Other Expenses and Losses:
Foreign-currency transaction loss, net $2,600

These gains and losses fall into the "Other" category because they arise from buying and selling foreign currencies, not from the company's main business (in the case of D.E. Shipp Belting, selling conveyor belts).

Should We Hedge Our Foreign-Currency-Transaction Risk?

One way for U.S. companies to avoid foreign-currency transaction losses is to insist that international transactions be settled in dollars. This requirement puts the burden of currency translation on the foreign party. But this approach may alienate customers and decrease sales. Another way for a company to protect itself is by hedging. **Hedging** means to protect oneself from losing money in one transaction by engaging in a counterbalancing transaction.

A U.S. company selling goods to be collected in Mexican pesos expects to receive a fixed number of pesos. If the peso is losing value, the U.S. company would expect the pesos to be worth fewer dollars than the amount of the receivable—an expected loss situation, as we saw for Shipp Belting.

The U.S. company may have accumulated payables in a foreign currency, such as Shipp's payable to the Swiss company. Losses on pesos may be offset by gains on Swiss francs. Most companies do not have equal amounts of receivables and payables in foreign currency. To obtain a more precise hedge, companies can buy *futures contracts*. These are contracts for foreign currencies to be received in the future. Futures contracts can create a payable to exactly offset a receivable, and vice versa. Many companies that do business internationally use hedging techniques.

Consolidation of Foreign Subsidiaries

A U.S. company with a foreign subsidiary must consolidate the subsidiary's financial statements into its own statements for reporting to the public. The consolidation of a foreign subsidiary poses two special challenges:

1. Some foreign countries require accounting treatments that differ from American accounting principles. For example, the foreign subsidiary's financial statements might be prepared in accordance with international financial reporting standards (IFRS). For reporting to the American public, if those differences are material, the subsidiary's statements must be adjusted to conform to U.S. generally accepted accounting principles (GAAP).

2. The subsidiary's statements may be expressed in a foreign currency. First, we must translate the subsidiary's statements into dollars. Then the two companies' financial statements can be consolidated as illustrated in Exhibit 10-8.

The process of translating a foreign subsidiary's financial statements into dollars usually creates a *foreign-currency translation adjustment*. This item appears in the financial statements of most multinational companies and is reported as part of other comprehensive income on the income statement and as part of stockholders' equity on the consolidated balance sheet.

A translation adjustment arises due to changes in the foreign exchange rate over time. In general,

- *assets* and *liabilities* are translated into dollars at the current exchange rate on the date of the statements.
- *stockholders' equity* is translated into dollars at older, historical exchange rates. Paid-in capital accounts are translated at the historical exchange rate when the subsidiary was acquired. Retained earnings is translated at the average exchange rates applicable over the period that interest in the subsidiary has been held.

This difference in exchange rates creates an out-of-balance condition on the balance sheet. The translation adjustment brings the balance sheet back into balance. Let's see how the translation adjustment works.

Suppose Intel has an Italian subsidiary whose financial statements are expressed in euros (the European currency). Intel must consolidate the Italian subsidiary's financials into its own statements. When Intel acquired the Italian company in 2009, a euro was worth $1.35. When the Italian firm earned its retained income during 2009–2012, the average exchange rate was $1.30. On the balance sheet date in 2012, a euro is worth only $1.20. Exhibit 10-11 shows how to translate the Italian company's balance sheet into dollars.

EXHIBIT 10-11 | **Translation of a Foreign-Currency Balance Sheet into Dollars**

Italian Imports, Inc., Accounts	Euros	Exchange Rate	Dollars
Assets	800,000	$1.20	$960,000
Liabilities	500,000	1.20	$600,000
Stockholders' equity			
Common stock	100,000	1.35	135,000
Retained earnings	200,000	1.30	260,000
Accumulated other comprehensive income:			
Foreign-currency translation adjustment			(35,000)
	800,000		$960,000

The **foreign-currency translation adjustment** is the balancing amount that brings the dollar amount of liabilities and equity of a foreign subsidiary into agreement with the dollar amount of total assets (in Exhibit 10-11, total assets equal $960,000). Only after the translation adjustment of $35,000 do total liabilities and equity equal total assets stated in dollars.

What caused the negative translation adjustment? The euro weakened after the acquisition of the Italian company.

- When Intel acquired the foreign subsidiary in 2009, a euro was worth $1.35.
- When the Italian company earned its income during 2009 through 2012, the average exchange rate was $1.30.
- On the balance sheet date in 2012, a euro is worth only $1.20.
- Thus, the Italian company's equity (assets minus liabilities) are translated into only $360,000 ($960,000 – $600,000).
- To bring stockholders' equity to $360,000 requires a $35,000 negative adjustment.

In a sense, a negative translation adjustment is like a loss, reported as a contra item in the stockholders' equity section of the balance sheet, as in Exhibit 10-11. The Italian firm's dollar figures in Exhibit 10-11 are what Intel would include in its consolidated balance sheet. The consolidation procedures would follow those illustrated beginning on page 613.

6 **Report** investing transactions on the statement of cash flows

IMPACT OF INVESTING ACTIVITIES ON THE STATEMENT OF CASH FLOWS

Investing activities include many types of transactions. In Chapter 7, we covered the purchase and sale of long-term assets such as plant and equipment. In this chapter, we examine investments in stocks and bonds.

Exhibit 10-12 provides excerpts from Intel's 2007 consolidated statement of cash flows. During 2007, Intel sold available-for-sale investments and received $8 billion in cash. Intel bought available-for-sale investments for $11.8 billion and equity-method investments for $1.4 billion. These actual investing activities relate directly to the topics you studied in this chapter.

EXHIBIT 10-12 | **Intel Corporation Statement of Cash Flows (Partial, Adapted)**

Intel Corporation
Consolidated Statement of Cash Flows (Partial, Adapted)

(In billions)	2007
Cash flows provided by (used for) investing activities:	
Sales of available-for-sale investments	$ 8.0
Purchases of available-for-sale investments...................	(11.8)
Additions to property, plant, and equipment...............	(5.0)
Purchases of equity-method investments	(1.4)
Proceeds from selling subsidiary companies	0.3
Net cash (used for) investing activities.............................	**$ (9.9)**

END-OF-CHAPTER SUMMARY PROBLEM

Translate the balance sheet of the Brazilian subsidiary of **Wrangler Corporation**, a U.S. company, into dollars. When Wrangler acquired this subsidiary, the exchange rate of the Brazilian currency, the real, was $0.40. The average exchange rate applicable to retained earnings is $0.41. The real's current exchange rate is $0.43.

Before performing the translation, predict whether the translation adjustment will be positive or negative. Does this situation generate a foreign-currency translation gain or loss? Give your reasons.

	Reals
Assets	900,000
Liabilities	600,000
Stockholders' equity:	
Common stock	30,000
Retained earnings	270,000
	900,000

Answer

Translation of foreign-currency balance sheet:

This situation will generate a *positive* translation adjustment, which is like a gain. The gain occurs because the real's current exchange rate, which is used to translate net assets (assets minus liabilities), exceeds the historical exchange rates used for stockholders' equity. The calculation follows.

	Reals	Exchange Rate	Dollars
Assets	900,000	0.43	$387,000
Liabilities	600,000	0.43	$258,000
Stockholders' equity:			
Common stock	30,000	0.40	12,000
Retained earnings	270,000	0.41	110,700
Accumulated other comprehensive income:			
Foreign-currency translation adjustment	—		6,300
	900,000		$387,000

REVIEW LONG-TERM INVESTMENTS AND INTERNATIONAL OPERATIONS

Quick Check (Answers are given on page 651.)

1. Apple's investment in less than 2% of Ford's stock, which Apple expects to hold for three years and then sell, is what type of investment?
   - **a.** Available-for-sale
   - **b.** Equity
   - **c.** Consolidation
   - **d.** Trading

2. Jacques Corporation purchased an available-for-sale investment in 1,500 shares of Home Central stock for $24 per share. On the next balance-sheet date, Home Central stock is quoted at $27 per share. Jacques' *balance sheet* should report
   - **a.** unrealized gain of $36,000.
   - **b.** investments of $40,500.
   - **c.** unrealized loss of $4,500.
   - **d.** investments of $36,000.

3. Use the Jacques Corporation data in question 2. Jacques' *income statement* should report
   - **a.** unrealized loss of $4,500.
   - **b.** investments of $36,000.
   - **c.** unrealized gain of $4,500.
   - **d.** nothing because Jacques hasn't sold the investment.

4. Use the Jacques Corporation data in question 2. Jacques sold the Home Central stock for $45,000 two years later. Jacques' *income statement* should report
   - **a.** investments of $45,000.
   - **b.** unrealized gain of $4,500.
   - **c.** gain on sale of $9,000.
   - **d.** gain on sale of $4,500.

5. Patrick Moving & Storage Co. paid $180,000 for 30% of the common stock of McDonough Co. McDonough earned net income of $50,000 and paid dividends of $20,000. The carrying value of Patrick's investment in McDonough is
   - **a.** $180,000.
   - **b.** $230,000.
   - **c.** $210,000.
   - **d.** $189,000.

6. Tidal, Inc., owns 70% of Granite Corporation, and Granite owns 70% of Shaw Company. During 2010, these companies' net incomes are as follows before any consolidations:
   - ▪ Tidal $200,000
   - ▪ Granite $64,000
   - ▪ Shaw $55,000

   How much net income should Tidal report for 2010?
   - **a.** $283,300
   - **b.** $200,000
   - **c.** $271,750
   - **d.** $319,000

7. Royalston, Inc., holds an investment in Daley bonds that pay interest each October 31. Royalston's *balance sheet* at December 31 should report
   - **a.** Interest expense.
   - **b.** Interest revenue.
   - **c.** Interest payable.
   - **d.** Interest receivable.

8. You are taking a vacation to Italy, and you buy euros for $1.50. On your return you cash in your unused euros for $1.20. During your vacation
   - **a.** the euro rose against the dollar.
   - **b.** the euro gained value.
   - **c.** the dollar rose against the euro.
   - **d.** the dollar lost value.

9. Coleman County, Texas, purchased earth-moving equipment from a Canadian company. The cost was $1,600,000 Canadian, and the Canadian dollar was quoted at $0.90. A month later, Coleman County paid its debt, and the Canadian dollar was quoted at $0.92. What was Coleman County's cost of the equipment?
   - **a.** $1,472,000
   - **b.** $32,000
   - **c.** $1,632,000
   - **d.** $1,440,000

10. Insight owns numerous foreign subsidiary companies. When Insight consolidates its British subsidiary, Insight should translate the subsidiary's assets into dollars at the
    - **a.** current exchange rate.
    - **b.** average exchange rate during the period Insight owned the British subsidiary.
    - **c.** historical exchange rate when Insight purchased the British company.
    - **d.** none of the above. There's no need to translate the subsidiary's assets into dollars.

Accounting Vocabulary

available-for-sale investments (p. 606) All investments not classified as held-to-maturity or trading securities.

consolidated statements (p. 614) Financial statements of the parent company plus those of majority-owned subsidiaries as if the combination were a single legal entity

controlling (majority) interest (p. 613) Ownership of more than 50% of an investee company's voting stock.

equity method (p. 610) The method used to account for investments in which the investor has 20–50% of the investee's voting stock and can significantly influence the decisions of the investee.

fair market value (p. 607) The amount that a seller would receive on the sale of an investment to a willing purchaser on a given date. Securities and available-for-sale securities are valued at fair market values on the balance sheet date. Other assets may be recorded at fair market value on occasion.

foreign-currency exchange rate (p. 623) The measure of one country's currency against another country's currency.

foreign-currency translation adjustment (p. 627) The balancing figure that brings the dollar amount of the total liabilities and stockholders' equity of the foreign subsidiary into agreement with the dollar amount of its total assets.

hedging (p. 625) To protect oneself from losing money in one transaction by engaging in a counterbalancing transaction.

held-to-maturity investments (p. 617) Bonds and notes that an investor intends to hold until maturity.

long-term investments (p. 605) Any investment that does not meet the criteria of a short-term investment; any investment that the investor expects to hold longer than a year or that is not readily marketable.

noncontrolling (minority) interest (p. 616) A subsidiary company's equity that is held by stockholders other than the parent company (i.e., less than 50%).

parent company (p. 613) An investor company that owns more than 50% of the voting stock of a subsidiary company.

short-term investments (p. 605) Investment that a company plans to hold for 1 year or less. Also called *marketable securities*.

strong currency (p. 623) A currency whose exchange rate is rising relative to other nations' currencies.

subsidiary (p. 613) An investee company in which a parent company owns more than 50% of the voting stock.

weak currency (p. 623) A currency whose exchange rate is falling relative to that of other nations.

ASSESS YOUR PROGRESS

Short Exercises

S10-1 (*Learning Objective 1: Accounting for an available-for-sale investment; recording unrealized gain or loss*)   Ship Your Way completed these long-term available-for-sale investment transactions during 2010:

2010	
Apr 10	Purchased 400 shares of Naradon stock, paying $22 per share. Ship Your Way intends to hold the investment for the indefinite future.
Jul 22	Received a cash dividend of $1.26 per share on the Naradon stock.
Dec 31	Adjusted the Naradon investment to its current market value of $5,200.

1. Journalize Ship Your Way's investment transactions. Explanations are not required.
2. Show how to report the investment and any unrealized gain or loss on Ship Your Way's balance sheet at December 31, 2010. Ignore income tax.

S10-2 (*Learning Objective 1: Accounting for the sale of an available-for-sale investment*)
Use the data given in Short Exercise 10-1. On May 21, 2011, Ship Your Way sold its investment in Naradon stock for $27 per share.

1. Journalize the sale. No explanation is required.
2. How does the gain or loss that you recorded here differ from the gain or loss that was recorded at December 31, 2010?

S10-3 (*Learning Objective 2: Accounting for a 40% investment in another company*)
Suppose on February 1, 2010, Fall Motors paid $420 million for a 40% investment in Yuza Motors. Assume Yuza earned net income of $50 million and paid cash dividends of $25 million during 2010.

1. What method should Fall Motors use to account for the investment in Yuza? Give your reason.
2. Journalize these three transactions on the books of Fall Motors. Show all amounts in millions of dollars and include an explanation for each entry.
3. Post to the Long-Term Investment T-account. What is its balance after all the transactions are posted?

S10-4 (*Learning Objective 2: Accounting for the sale of an equity-method investment*)
Use the data given in Short Exercise 10-3. Assume that in November 2011, Fall Motors sold half its investment in Yuza Motors. The sale price was $155 million. Compute Fall Motors' gain or loss on the sale.

S10-5 (*Learning Objective 3: Understanding consolidated financial statements*)   Answer these questions about consolidation accounting:

1. Define "parent company." Define "subsidiary company."
2. How do consolidated financial statements differ from the financial statements of a single company?
3. Which company's name appears on the consolidated financial statements? How much of the subsidiary's shares must the parent own before reporting consolidated statements?

writing assignment ■

S10-6 (*Learning Objective 3: Understanding goodwill and minority interest*)   Two accounts that arise from consolidation accounting are goodwill and noncontrolling interest.

1. What is goodwill, and how does it arise? Which company reports goodwill, the parent or the subsidiary? Where is goodwill reported?
2. What is noncontrolling interest, and which company reports it, the parent or the subsidiary? Where is noncontrolling interest reported?

S10-7 (*Learning Objective 4: Working with a bond investment*)   Hopter Khan (HK) owns vast amounts of corporate bonds. Suppose HK buys $1,100,000 of Tyconix bonds at a price of 104. The Tyconix bonds pay cash interest at the annual rate of 6% and mature at the end of five years.

1. How much did HK pay to purchase the bond investment? How much will HK collect when the bond investment matures?
2. How much cash interest will HK receive each year from Tyconix?
3. Will HK's annual interest revenue on the bond investment be more or less than the amount of cash interest received each year? Give your reason.
4. Compute HK's annual interest revenue on this bond investment. Use the straight-line method to amortize the investment.

S10-8 (*Learning Objective 4: Recording bond investment transactions*)   Return to Short Exercise 10-7, the Hopter Khan (HK) investment in Tyconix bonds. Journalize on HK's books:

a. Purchase of the bond investment on June 30, 2010. HK expects to hold the investment to maturity.
b. Receipt of semiannual cash interest on December 31, 2010.
c. Amortization of the bonds on December 31, 2010. Use the straight-line method.

   d. Collection of the investment's face value at the maturity date on June 30, 2015. (Assume the receipt of 2015 interest and the amortization of bonds for 2015 have already been recorded, so ignore these entries.)

S10-9 (*Learning Objective 5: Accounting for transactions stated in a foreign currency*) Suppose Pepson sells soft drink syrup to a Russian company on September 12. Pepson agrees to accept 500,000 Russian rubles. On the date of sale, the ruble is quoted at $0.36. Pepson collects half the receivable on October 18, when the ruble is worth $0.33. Then on November 15, when the foreign-exchange rate of the ruble is $0.39, Pepson collects the final amount.

   Journalize these three transactions for Pepson.

S10-10 (*Learning Objective 5: Accounting for transactions stated in a foreign currency*) Ocean Belting sells goods for 1,100,000 Mexican pesos. The foreign-exchange rate for a peso is $0.086 on the date of sale. Ocean Belting then collects cash on April 24, when the exchange rate for a peso is $0.089. Record Ocean's cash collection.

   Ocean Belting buys inventory for 28,000 Swiss francs. A Swiss franc costs $0.82 on the purchase date. Record Ocean Belting's payment of cash on October 25, when the exchange rate for a Swiss Franc is $0.87.

   In these two scenarios, which currencies strengthened? Which currencies weakened?

S10-11 (*Learning Objective 6: Reporting cash flows*)   Companies divide their cash flows into three categories for reporting on the cash flows statement.

1. List the three categories of cash flows in the order they appear on the cash flows statement. Which category of cash flows is most closely related to this chapter?
2. Identify two types of transactions that companies report as cash flows from investing activities.

S10-12 (*Learning Objective 6: Using a statement of cash flows*)   Excerpts from The ABC Company statement of cash flows, as adapted, appear as follows:

writing assignment ■

The ABC Company and Subsidiaries Consolidated Statement of Cash Flows (Adapted)		
	Years Ended December 31,	
(In millions)	2011	2009
Operating Activities		
Net cash provided by operating activities.....................................	$ 4,222	$ 1,170
Investing Activities		
Purchases of property, plant, and equipment......................................	(782)	(743)
Acquisitions and investments, principally trademarks and		
bottling companies..	(665)	(407)
Purchases of investments...	(461)	(522)
Proceeds from disposals of investments...	475	300
Proceeds from disposals of property, plant, and equipment...............	100	56
Other investing activities..	143	139
Net cash used in investing activities	(1,190)	(1,177)
Financing Activities		
Issuances of debt (borrowing)	3,021	3,675
Payments of debt..	(4,017)	(4,279)
Issuances of stock...	172	342
Purchases of stock for treasury..	(280)	(145)
Dividends...	(1,795)	(1,697)
Net cash used in financing activities..	(2,899)	(2,104)

As the chief executive officer of The ABC Company, your duty is to write the management letter to your stockholders explaining ABC's major investing activities during 2011. Compare the company's level of investment with previous years and indicate how the company financed its investments during 2011. Net income for 2011 was $3,971 million.

Exercises

> All of the A and B exercises can be found within MyAccountingLab, an online homework and practice environment. Your instructor may ask you to complete these exercises using MyAccountingLab.

(Group A)

■ general ledger

E10-13A (*Learning Objective 1: Journalizing transactions for an available-for-sale investment*)   Journalize the following long-term available-for-sale investment transactions of Cullen Brothers Department Stores:

    a. Purchased 470 shares of Potter Foods common stock at $31 per share, with the intent of holding the stock for the indefinite future.
    b. Received cash dividend of $1.70 per share on the Potter investment.
    c. At year-end, adjusted the investment account to fair market value of $36 per share.
    d. Sold the Potter stock for the market price of $22 per share.

E10-14A (*Learning Objective 1: Accounting for long-term investments*)   Osborn Co. bought 3,400 shares of Stockholm common stock at $35; 660 shares of London stock at $46.50; and 1,200 shares of Glasgow stock at $74—all as available-for-sale investments. At December 31, Hoover's Online reports Stockholm stock at $28.375, London at $48.25, and Glasgow at $68.75.

❚ Requirements

    1. Determine the cost and the fair market value of the long-term investment portfolio at December 31.
    2. Record Osborn's adjusting entry at December 31.
    3. What would Osborn report on its income statement and balance sheet for the information given? Make the necessary disclosures. Ignore income tax.

E10-15A (*Learning Objective 2: Accounting for transactions under the equity method*)   Nelson Corporation owns equity-method investments in several companies. Suppose Nelson paid $1,500,000 to acquire a 25% investment in Payton Software Company. Payton Software reported net income of $670,000 for the first year and declared and paid cash dividends of $400,000.

❚ Requirements

    1. Record the following in Nelson's journal: (a) purchase of the investment, (b) Nelson's proportion of Payton Software's net income, and (c) receipt of the cash dividends.
    2. What is the ending balance in Nelson's investment account?

E10-16A (*Learning Objective 2: Measuring gain or loss on the sale of an equity-method investment*)   Without making journal entries, record the transactions of Exercise 10-15A directly in the Nelson account, Long-Term Investment in Payton Software. Assume that after all the noted transactions took place, Nelson sold its entire investment in Payton Software for cash of $1,100,000. How much is Nelson's gain or loss on the sale of the investment?

E10-17A (*Learning Objective 2: Applying the appropriate accounting method for a 30% investment*)   Ashcroft Financial paid $590,000 for a 30% investment in the common stock of Sonic, Inc. For the first year, Sonic reported net income of $200,000 and at year-end declared and paid cash dividends of $125,000. On the balance-sheet date, the market value of Ashcroft's investment in Sonic stock was $390,000.

❙ Requirements

1. Which method is appropriate for Ashcroft Financial to use in accounting for its investment in Sonic? Why?
2. Show everything that Ashcroft would report for the investment and any investment revenue in its year-end financial statements.

E10-18A (*Learning Objective 3: Preparing a consolidated balance sheet*)   XYZ, Inc., owns Cressida Corp. The two companies' individual balance sheets follow:

■ **spreadsheet**

XYZ, Inc.
Consolidation Work Sheet

	XYZ, Inc.	Cressida Corp.	Elimination Debit	Elimination Credit
Assets				
Cash	$ 51,000	$ 18,000		
Accounts receivable, net	85,000	58,000		
Note receivable from XYZ	—	40,000		
Inventory	57,000	81,000		
Investment in Cressida	103,000	—		
Plant assets, net	291,000	96,000		
Other assets	22,000	9,000		
Total	$609,000	$302,000		
Liabilities and Stockholders' Equity				
Accounts payable	$ 46,000	$ 29,000		
Notes payable	147,000	35,000		
Other liabilities	79,000	135,000		
Common stock	113,000	81,000		
Retained earnings	224,000	22,000		
Total	$609,000	$302,000		

❙ Requirements

1. Prepare a consolidated balance sheet of XYZ, Inc. It is sufficient to complete the consolidation work sheet.
2. What is the amount of stockholders' equity for the consolidated entity?

E10-19A (*Learning Objective 4: Recording bond investment transactions*)   Assume that on September 30, 2010, Newtex, Inc., paid 98 for 8% bonds of Teague Corporation as a long-term held-to-maturity investment. The maturity value of the bonds will be $30,000 on September 30, 2015. The bonds pay interest on March 31 and September 30.

Requirements

1. What method should Newtex use to account for its investment in the Teague bonds?
2. Using the straight-line method of amortizing the bonds, journalize all of Newtex's transactions on the bonds for 2010.
3. Show how Newtex would report everything related to the bond investment on its balance sheet at December 31, 2010.

writing assignment ■

E10-20A (*Learning Objective 5: Managing and accounting for foreign-currency transactions*) Assume that Computer City Stores completed the following foreign-currency transactions:

Sep 9	Purchased DVD players as inventory on account from Sona, a Japanese company. The price was 800,000 yen, and the exchange rate of the yen was $0.0085.
Oct 18	Paid Sona when the exchange rate was $0.0084.
22	Sold merchandise on account to CoCo, a French company, at a price of 50,000 euros. The exchange rate was $1.25.
28	Collected from CoCo when the exchange rate was $1.21.

Requirements

1. Journalize these transactions for Computer City. Focus on the gains and losses caused by changes in foreign-currency rates. (Round your answers to the nearest whole dollar.)
2. On September 10, immediately after the purchase, and on October 23, immediately after the sale, which currencies did Computer City want to strengthen? Which currencies did in fact strengthen? Explain your reasoning.

■ spreadsheet

E10-21A (*Learning Objective 5: Translating a foreign-currency balance sheet into dollars*) Translate into dollars the balance sheet of Utah Leather Goods' Spanish subsidiary. When Utah Leather Goods acquired the foreign subsidiary, a euro was worth $1.01. The current exchange rate is $1.38. During the period when retained earnings were earned, the average exchange rate was $1.18 per euro.

	Euros
Assets	800,000
Liabilities	550,000
Stockholders' equity:	
Common stock	70,000
Retained earnings	180,000
	800,000

During the period covered by this situation, which currency was stronger, the dollar or the euro?

E10-22A (*Learning Objective 6: Preparing and using the statement of cash flows*) During fiscal year 2010, Sugar Land Doughnuts reported net loss of $129.6 million. Sugar Land received $1.7 million from the sale of other businesses. Sugar Land made capital expenditures of $10.0 million and sold property, plant, and equipment for $6.9 million. The company purchased long-term investments at a cost of $11.5 million and sold other long-term investments for $2.6 million.

I Requirement

1. Prepare the investing activities section of Sugar Land Doughnuts' statement of cash flows. Based solely on Sugar Land Doughnuts' investing activities, does it appear that the company is growing or shrinking? How can you tell?

E10-23A (*Learning Objective 6: Using the statement of cash flows*) At the end of the year, Crown King Properties' statement of cash flows reported the following for investment activities:

Crown King Properties Consolidated Statement of Cash Flows (Partial)	
Cash flows from Investing Activities:	
Notes receivable collected	$ 3,117,000
Purchases of short-term investments	(3,465,000)
Proceeds from sales of equipment	1,599,000*
Proceeds from sales of investments (cost of $470,000)	487,000
Expenditures for property and equipment	(1,741,000)
Net used by investing activities	$ (3,000)

*Cost $5,300,000; Accumulated depreciation, $3,701,000.

I Requirement

1. For each item listed, make the journal entry that placed the item on Crown King's statement of cash flows.

(Group B)

E10-24B (*Learning Objective 1: Journalizing transactions for an available-for-sale investment*) Journalize the following long-term available-for-sale investment transactions of Johnson Brothers Department Stores:

■ **general ledger**

   a. Purchased 460 shares of Jefferson Foods common stock at $30 per share, with the intent of holding the stock for the indefinite future.
   b. Received cash dividend of $1.20 per share on the Jefferson investment.
   c. At year-end, adjusted the investment account to fair market value of $39 per share.
   d. Sold the Jefferson stock for the market price of $21 per share.

E10-25B (*Learning Objective 1: Accounting for long-term investments*) Leary Co. bought 3,800 shares of Canada common stock at $38; 640 shares of Chile stock at $47.25; and 1,500 shares of Milan stock at $77—all as available-for-sale investments. At December 31, Hoover's Online reports Canada stock at $29.125, Chile at $49.25, and Milan at $69.50.

I Requirements

1. Determine the cost and the market value of the long-term investment portfolio at December 31.
2. Record Leary's adjusting entry at December 31.
3. What would Leary report on its income statement and balance sheet for the information given? Make the necessary disclosures. Ignore income tax.

E10-26B (*Learning Objective 2: Accounting for transactions under the equity method*) Watson Corporation owns equity-method investments in several companies. Suppose Watson paid $1,200,000 to acquire a 35% investment in Smith Software Company. Smith Software reported net income of $650,000 for the first year and declared and paid cash dividends of $440,000.

Requirements

1. Record the following in Watson's journal: (a) purchase of the investment, (b) Watson's proportion of Smith Software's net income, and (c) receipt of the cash dividends.
2. What is the ending balance in Watson's investment account?

E10-27B (*Learning Objective 2: Measuring gain or loss on the sale of an equity-method investment*) Without making journal entries, record the transactions of Exercise 10-26B directly in the Watson account, Long-Term Investment in Smith Software. Assume that after all the noted transactions took place, Watson sold its entire investment in Smith Software for cash of $3,000,000. How much is Watson's gain or loss on the sale of the investment?

E10-28B (*Learning Objective 2: Applying the appropriate accounting method for a 20% investment*) Ever Financial paid $560,000 for a 20% investment in the common stock of Laker, Inc. For the first year, Laker reported net income of $220,000 and at year-end declared and paid cash dividends of $105,000. On the balance-sheet date, the market value of Ever's investment in Laker stock was $410,000.

Requirements

1. Which method is appropriate for Ever Financial to use in its accounting for its investment in Laker? Why?
2. Show everything that Ever would report for the investment and any investment revenue in its year-end financial statements.

■ **spreadsheet**

E10-29B (*Learning Objective 3: Preparing a consolidated balance sheet*) Gamma, Inc., owns Hamlet Corp. These two companies' individual balance sheets follow:

Gamma, Inc.
Consolidation Work Sheet

	Gamma, Inc.	Hamlet Corp.	Elimination Debit	Elimination Credit
Assets				
Cash	$ 50,000	$ 19,000		
Accounts receivable, net	79,000	54,000		
Note receivable from Gamma	—	43,000		
Inventory	55,000	78,000		
Investment in Hamlet	93,000	—		
Plant assets, net	284,000	90,000		
Other assets	24,000	5,000		
Total	$585,000	$289,000		
Liabilities and Stockholders' Equity				
Accounts payable	$ 48,000	$ 27,000		
Notes payable	154,000	31,000		
Other liabilities	80,000	138,000		
Common stock	111,000	78,000		
Retained earnings	192,000	15,000		
Total	$585,000	$289,000		

Requirements

1. Prepare a consolidated balance sheet of Gamma, Inc. It is sufficient to complete the consolidation work sheet.
2. What is the amount of stockholders' equity for the consolidated entity?

E10-30B *(Learning Objective 4: Recording bond investment transactions)* Assume that on September 30, 2010, Baytex, Inc., paid 96 for 7.5% bonds of Collins Corporation as a long-term held-to-maturity investment. The maturity value of the bonds will be $40,000 on September 30, 2015. The bonds pay interest on March 31 and September 30.

Ⅰ Requirements

1. What method should Baytex use to account for its investment in the Collins bonds?
2. Using the straight-line method of amortizing the bonds, journalize all of Baytex's transactions on the bonds for 2010.
3. Show how Baytex would report everything related to the bond investment on its balance sheet at December 31, 2010.

E10-31B *(Learning Objective 5: Managing and accounting for foreign-currency transactions)* Assume that Tech Know Stores completed the following foreign-currency transactions:

writing assignment ■

Jul 17	Purchased DVD players as inventory on account from Toshikar, a Japanese company. The price was 700,000 yen, and the exchange rate of the yen was $0.0088.	
Aug 16	Paid Toshikar when the exchange rate was $0.0079.	
19	Sold merchandise on account to Magnificent, a French company, at a price of 20,000 euros. The exchange rate was $1.19.	
30	Collected from Magnificent when the exchange rate was $1.12.	

Ⅰ Requirements

1. Journalize these transactions for Tech Know. Focus on the gains and losses caused by changes in foreign-currency rates. (Round your answers to the nearest whole dollar.)
2. On July 18, immediately after the purchase, and on August 20, immediately after the sale, which currencies did Tech Know want to strengthen? Which currencies did in fact strengthen? Explain your reasoning.

E10-32B *(Learning Objective 5: Translating a foreign-currency balance sheet into dollars)* Translate into dollars the balance sheet of Wyoming Leather Goods' Spanish subsidiary. When Wyoming Leather Goods acquired the foreign subsidiary, a euro was worth $1.07. The current exchange rate is $1.31. During the period when retained earnings were earned, the average exchange rate was $1.19 per euro.

■ spreadsheet

	Euros
Assets.....................................	700,000
Liabilities	500,000
Stockholders' equity:	
Common stock...................	65,000
Retained earnings...............	135,000
	700,000

During the period covered by this situation, which currency was stronger, the dollar or the euro?

E10-33B *(Learning Objective 6: Preparing and using the statement of cash flows)* During fiscal year 2010, Frosted Doughnuts reported net loss of $131.1 million. Frosted received $1.8 million from the sale of other businesses. Frosted made capital expenditures of $10.9 million and sold property, plant, and equipment for $7.2 million. The company purchased long-term investments at a cost of $11.4 million and sold other long-term investments for $2.2 million.

❙ Requirement

1. Prepare the investing activities section of Frosted Doughnuts' statement of cash flows. Based solely on Frosted Doughnuts investing activities, does it appear that the company is growing or shrinking? How can you tell?

E10-34B *(Learning Objective 6: Using the statement of cash flows)* At the end of the year, Elite Properties' statement of cash flows reported the following for investment activities:

Elite Properties Consolidated Statement of Cash Flows (Partial)	
Cash flows from Investing Activities:	
Notes receivable collected	$ 3,113,000
Purchases of short-term investments......................................	(3,453,000)
Proceeds from sales of equipment	1,529,000*
Proceeds from sales of investments (cost of $490,000)..........	498,000
Expenditures for property and equipment.............................	(1,720,000)
Net used for investing activities...	$ (33,000)

*Cost $5,200,000; Accumulated depreciation, $3,671,000.

❙ Requirement

1. For each item listed, make the journal entry that placed the item on Elite's statement of cash flows.

Challenge Exercises

E10-35 *(Learning Objectives 1, 2, 3, 5: Accounting for various types of investments)* Suppose ChatNow owns the following investments at December 31, 2010:

a. 100% of the common stock of ChatNow United Kingdom, which holds assets of £1,400,000 and owes a total of £1,200,000. At December 31, 2010, the current exchange rate of the pound (£) is £1 = $2.01. The translation rate of the pound applicable to stockholders' equity is £1 = $1.64. During 2010, ChatNow United Kingdom earned net income of £120,000 and the average exchange rate for the year was £1 = $1.92. ChatNow United Kingdom paid cash dividends of £20,000 during 2010.

b. Investments that ChatNow is holding to sell. These investments cost $1,500,000 and declined in value by $350,000 during 2010, but they paid cash dividends of $23,000 to ChatNow. One year ago, at December 31, 2009, the market value of these investments was $1,500,000.

c. 45% of the common stock of ChatNow Financing Associates. During 2010, ChatNow Financing earned net income of $500,000 and declared and paid cash dividends of $25,000. The carrying amount of this investment was $500,000 at December 31, 2009.

❙ Requirements

1. Which method is used to account for each investment?
2. By how much did each of these investments increase or decrease ChatNow's net income during 2010?
3. For investments b and c, show how ChatNow would report these investments on its balance sheet at December 31, 2010.

E10-36 (*Learning Objectives 1, 6: Explaining and analyzing accumulated other comprehensive income*) In-the-Box Retail Corporation reported stockholders' equity on its balance sheet at December 31, as follows:

In-the-Box Retail Balance Sheet (Partial)	
Shareholder's Equity:	
Common stock, $1.00 par value—	
600 million shares authorized,	
200 shares issued	$ 200
Additional paid-in capital	1,080
Retained earnings	6,350
Accumulated other comprehensive (loss)	(?)
Less: Treasury stock, at cost	(60)

I Requirements

1. Identify the two components that typically make up accumulated other comprehensive income.
2. For each component of accumulated other comprehensive income, describe the event that can cause a *positive* balance. Also describe the events that can cause a *negative* balance for each component.
3. At December 31, 2010, In-the-Box Retail's accumulated other comprehensive loss was $54 million. Then during 2011, In-the-Box Retail had a positive foreign-currency translation adjustment of $24 million and an unrealized loss of $11 million on available-for-sale investments. What was In-the-Box Retail's balance of accumulated other comprehensive income (loss) at December 31, 2011?

Quiz

Test your understanding of long-term investments and international operations by answering the following questions. Select the best choice from among the possible answers given.

Questions 37–39 use the following data:

Assume that Clear Networks owns the following long-term available-for-sale investments:

Company	Number of Shares	Cost per Share	Current Market Value per Share	Dividend per Share
ABC Corp.	1,200	$60	$74	$2.10
Good Food, Inc.	150	11	13	1.40
Lesley Ltd.	700	22	26	0.80

Q10-37 Clear's balance sheet should report
a. investments of $108,950.
b. unrealized loss of $19,900.
c. investments of $89,050.
d. dividend revenue of $3,290.

Q10-38 Clear's income statement should report
a. gain on sale of investment of $19,900.
b. unrealized gain of $19,900.
c. dividend revenue of $3,290.
d. investments of $89,050.

Q10-39 Suppose Clear sells the ABC stock for $73 per share. Journalize the sale.

Q10-40 Dividends received on an equity-method investment
a. decrease the investment account.
b. increase dividend revenue.
c. increase the investment account.
d. increase owners' equity.

Q10-41 The starting point in accounting for all investments is
a. cost.
b. equity value.
c. cost minus dividends.
d. market value on the balance-sheet date.

Q10-42 Consolidation accounting
a. reports the receivables and payables of the parent company only.
b. eliminates all liabilities.
c. combines the accounts of the parent company and those of the subsidiary companies.
d. all of the above.

Q10-43 On January 1, 2010, Microspace, Inc., purchased $80,000 face value of the 5% bonds of Mail Frontier, Inc., at 107. The bonds mature on January 1, 2015. For the year ended December 31, 2015, Microspace received cash interest of
a. $2,000.
b. $3,000.
c. $4,000.
d. $5,000.

Q10-44 Return to Microspace, Inc.'s bond investment in the preceding question. For the year ended December 31, 2013, Microspace received cash interest of $4,000. What was the interest revenue that Microspace earned in this period?
a. $3,000
b. $5,000
c. $2,880
d. $2,000

Q10-45 Providence Systems purchased inventory on account from Megasonic. The price was ¥100,000, and a yen was quoted at $0.0088. Providence paid the debt in yen a month later, when the price of a yen was $0.0093. Providence
a. debited Inventory for $930.
b. recorded a Foreign-Currency Transaction Gain of $50.
c. debited Inventory for $880.
d. none of the above.

Q10-46 One way to hedge a foreign-currency transaction loss is to
a. offset foreign-currency inventory and plant assets.
b. collect in your own currency.
c. pay debts as late as possible.
d. pay in the foreign currency.

Q10-47 Foreign-currency transaction gains and losses are reported on the
a. income statement.
b. consolidation work sheet.
c. balance sheet.
d. statement of cash flows.

Q10-48 Consolidation of a foreign subsidiary usually results in a
a. foreign-currency translation adjustment.
b. gain or loss on consolidation.
c. LIFO/FIFO difference.
d. foreign-currency transaction gain or loss.

Problems

All of the A and B problems can be found within MyAccountingLab, an online home-work and practice environment. Your instructor may ask you to complete these problems using MyAccountingLab.

(Group A)

P10-49A (*Learning Objectives 1, 2: Reporting investments on the balance sheet and the related revenue on the income statement*)   Oregon Exchange Company completed the following long-term investment transactions during 2010:

2010	
May 12	Purchased 17,500 shares, which make up 30% of the common stock of Woburn Corporation at total cost of $380,000.
Jul 9	Received annual cash dividend of $1.26 per share on the Woburn investment.
Sep 16	Purchased 900 share of Columbus, Inc., common stock as an available-for-sale investment, paying $41.00 per share.
Oct 30	Received cash dividend of $0.38 per share on the Columbus investment.
Dec 31	Received annual report from Woburn Corporation. Net income for the year was $580,000.

At year-end the fair market value of the Columbus stock is $30,000. The fair market value of the Woburn stock is $658,000.

I Requirements

1. For which investment is fair market value used in the accounting? Why is fair market value used for one investment and not the other?
2. Show what Oregon would report on its year-end balance sheet and income statement for these investment transactions. It is helpful to use a T-account for the Long-Term Investment in Woburn Stock account. Ignore income tax.

P10-50A (*Learning Objectives 1, 2: Accounting for available-for-sale and equity-method investments*)   The beginning balance sheet of Noram Corporation included the following:

Long-Term Investment in Rockaway Software (equity-method investment)..............	$612,000

■ **general ledger**

Noram completed the following investment transactions during the year:

Mar 16	Purchase 1,400 shares of Canton, Inc., common stock as a long-term available-for-sale investment, paying $13.00 per share.
May 21	Received cash dividend of $1.75 per share on the Canton investment.
Aug 17	Received cash dividend of $86,000 from Rockaway Software.
Dec 31	Received annual reports from Rockaway Software, net income for the year was $520,000. Of this amount Noram's proportion is 21%.

At year-end, the fair market values of Noram's investments are: Canton, $26,600; Rockaway, $698,000.

Requirements

1. Record the transactions in the journal of Noram Corporation.
2. Post entries to the T-account for Long-Term Investment in Rockaway and determine its balance at December 31.
3. Show how to report the Long-Term Available-for-Sale Investments and the Long-Term Investment in Rockaway accounts on Noram's balance sheet at December 31.

P10-51A *(Learning Objective 3: Analyzing consolidated financial statements)* This problem demonstrates the dramatic effect that consolidation accounting can have on a company's ratios. Fixed Motor Company (Fixed) owns 100% of Fixed Motor Credit Corporation (FMCC), its financing subsidiary. Fixed's main operations consist of manufacturing automotive products. FMCC mainly helps people finance the purchase of automobiles from Fixed and its dealers. The two companies' individual balance sheets are adapted and summarized as follows (amounts in billions):

	Fixed (Parent)	FMCC (Subsidiary)
Total assets	$89.7	$170.7
Total liabilities	$65.1	$156.6
Total stockholders' equity	24.6	14.1
Total liabilities and equity...............	$89.7	$170.7

Assume that FMCC's liabilities include $1.2 billion owed to Fixed, the parent company.

Requirements

1. Compute the debt ratio of Fixed Motor Company considered alone.
2. Determine the consolidated total assets, total liabilities, and stockholders' equity of Fixed Motor Company after consolidating the financial statements of FMCC into the totals of Fixed, the parent company.
3. Recompute the debt ratio of the consolidated entity. Why do companies prefer not to consolidate their financing subsidiaries into their own financial statements?

■ spreadsheet

P10-52A *(Learning Objective 3: Consolidating a wholly owned subsidiary)* Assume Rose, Inc., paid $453,000 to acquire all the common stock of Mountain Corporation, and Mountain owes Rose $175,000 on a note payable. Immediately after the purchase on September 30, 2010, the two companies' balance sheets follow.

	Rose	Mountain
Assets		
Cash..	$ 60,000	$ 59,000
Accounts receivable, net........................	194,000	86,000
Note receivable from Mountain	175,000	—
Inventory...	305,000	458,000
Investment in Mountain........................	453,000	—
Plant assets, net	403,000	524,000
Total..	$1,590,000	$1,127,000
Liabilities and Stockholders' Equity		
Accounts payable	$ 122,000	$ 67,000
Notes payable	410,000	312,000
Other liabilities	216,000	295,000
Common stock.......................................	556,000	268,000
Retained earnings.................................	286,000	185,000
Total...	$1,590,000	$1,127,000

Requirement

1. Prepare the worksheet for the consolidated balance sheet of Rose, Inc.

P10-53A *(Learning Objective 4: Accounting for a bond investment purchased at a premium)*
Insurance companies and pension plans hold large quantities of bond investments. Sea Insurance
Corp. purchased $2,400,000 of 4.0% bonds of Sheehan, Inc., for 110 on January 1, 2010. These
bonds pay interest on January 1 and July 1 each year. They mature on January 1, 2014. At
October 31, 2010, the market price of the bonds is 108.

Requirements

1. Journalize Sea's purchase of the bonds as a long-term investment on January 1, 2010 (to
be held to maturity), receipt of cash interest, and amortization of the bond investment at
July 1, 2010. The straight-line method is appropriate for amortizing the bond investment.
2. Show all financial statement effects of this long-term bond investment on Sea Insurance
Corp.'s balance sheet and income statement at October 31, 2010.

P10-54A *(Learning Objective 5: Recording foreign-currency transactions and reporting the
transaction gain or loss)*   Suppose Turquoise Corporation completed the following international transactions:

■ **general ledger**

May	1	Sold inventory on account to Fiat, the Italian automaker, for €65,000. The exchange rate of the euro was $1.32, and Fiat demands to pay in euros.
	10	Purchased supplies on account from a Canadian company at a price of Canadian $59,000. The exchange rate of the Canadian dollar was $0.77, and the payment will be in Canadian dollars.
	17	Sold inventory on account to an English firm for 134,000 British pounds. Payment will be in pounds, and the exchange rate of the pound was $1.97.
	22	Collected from Fiat. The exchange rate is €1 = $1.35.
Jun	18	Paid the Canadian company. The exchange rate of the Canadian dollar is $0.76.
	24	Collected from the English firm. The exchange rate of the British pound was $1.94.

Requirements

1. Record these transactions in Turquoise's journal and show how to report the transaction
gain or loss on the income statement.
2. How will what you learned in this problem help you structure international transactions?

P10-55A *(Learning Objective 5: Measuring and explaining the foreign-currency translation
adjustment)*   Assume that Folgate has a subsidiary company based in Japan.

Requirements

1. Translate into dollars the foreign-currency balance sheet of the Japanese subsidiary of Folgate.

	Yen
Assets......................................	480,000,000
Liabilities	115,000,000
Stockholders' equity:	
Common stock....................	40,000,000
Retained earnings...............	325,000,000
	480,000,000

When Folgate acquired this subsidiary, the Japanese yen was worth $0.0095. The current exchange rate is $0.0110. During the period when the subsidiary earned its income, the average exchange rate was $0.0100 per yen. Before you perform the foreign-currency translation calculations, indicate whether Folgate has experienced a positive or a negative translation adjustment. State whether the adjustment is a gain or a loss, and show where it is reported in the financial statements.

2. To which company does the foreign-currency translation adjustment "belong"? In which company's financial statements will the translation adjustment be reported?

(Group B)

P10-56B (*Learning Objectives 1, 2: Reporting investments on the balance sheet and the related revenue on the income statement*)   Colorado Exchange Company completed the following long-term investment transactions during 2010:

2010	
May 12	Purchased 18,200 shares, which make up 40% of the common stock of Brentwood Corporation at total cost of $330,000.
Jul 9	Received annual cash dividend of $1.24 per share on the Brentwood investment.
Sep 16	Purchased 900 shares of Bangkok, Inc., common stock as an available-for-sale investment, paying $42.00 per share.
Oct 30	Received cash dividend of $0.33 per share on the Bangkok investment.
Dec 31	Received annual report from Brentwood Corporation. Net income for the year was $530,000.

At year-end the fair market value of the Bangkok stock is $30,300. The fair market value of the Brentwood stock is $655,000.

I Requirements

1. For which investment is fair market value used in the accounting? Why is fair market value used for one investment and not the other?
2. Show what Colorado would report on its year-end balance sheet and income statement for these investment transactions. It is helpful to use a T-account for the Long-Term Investment in Brentwood Stock account. Ignore income tax.

P10-57B (*Learning Objectives 1, 2: Accounting for available-for-sale and equity-method investments*)   The beginning balance sheet of Segui Corporation included the following:

Long-Term Investment in NEW Software (equity-method investment)...................... $616,000

Segui completed the following investment transactions during the year:

Mar 16	Purchase 1,600 shares of Hubbardston, Inc., common stock as a long-term available-for-sale investment, paying $12.75 per share.
May 21	Received cash dividend of $1.50 per share on the Hubbardston investment.
Aug 17	Received cash dividend of $85,000 from NEW Software.
Dec 31	Received annual reports from NEW Software, net income for the year was $500,000. Of this amount Segui's proportion is 23%.

At year-end, the fair market values of Segui's investments are: Hubbardston, $26,100; NEW, $701,000.

I *Requirements*

1. Record the transactions in the journal of Segui Corporation.
2. Post entries to the T-account for Long-Term Investment in NEW and determine its balance at December 31.
3. Show how to report the Long-Term Available-for-Sale Investments and the Long-Term Investment in NEW accounts on Segui's balance sheet at December 31.

P10-58B (*Learning Objective 3: Analyzing consolidated financial statements*) This problem demonstrates the dramatic effect that consolidation accounting can have on a company's ratios. Space Motor Company (Space) owns 100% of Space Motor Credit Corporation (SMCC), its financing subsidiary. Space's main operations consist of manufacturing automotive products. SMCC mainly helps people finance the purchase of automobiles from Space and its dealers. The two companies' individual balance sheets are adapted and summarized as follows (amounts in billions):

	Space (Parent)	SMCC (Subsidiary)
Total assets	$89.5	$170.8
Total liabilities	$65.7	$156.1
Total stockholders' equity	23.8	14.7
Total liabilities and equity................	$89.5	$170.8

Assume that SMCC's liabilities include $1.7 billion owed to Space, the parent company.

I *Requirements*

1. Compute the debt ratio of Space Motor Company considered alone.
2. Determine the consolidated total assets, total liabilities, and stockholders' equity of Space Motor Company after consolidating the financial statements of SMCC into the totals of Space, the parent company.
3. Recompute the debt ratio of the consolidated entity. Why do companies prefer not to consolidate their financing subsidiaries into their own financial statements?

P10-59B (*Learning Objective 3: Consolidating a wholly owned subsidiary*) Assume Ronny, Inc., paid $346,000 to acquire all the common stock of Dinette Corporation, and Dinette owes Ronny $192,000 on a note payable. Immediately after the purchase on September 30, 2010, the two companies' balance sheets follow.

■ spreadsheet

	Ronny	Dinette
Assets		
Cash..	$ 54,000	$ 52,000
Accounts receivable, net.........................	195,000	89,000
Note receivable from Dinette	192,000	—
Inventory...	278,000	452,000
Investment in Dinette	346,000	—
Plant assets, net.....................................	397,000	457,000
Total	$1,462,000	$1,050,000
Liabilities and Stockholders' Equity		
Accounts payable	$ 127,000	$ 79,000
Notes payable	399,000	329,000
Other liabilities	249,000	296,000
Common stock..	577,000	259,000
Retained earnings..................................	110,000	87,000
Total	$1,462,000	$1,050,000

I *Requirement*

1. Prepare the worksheet for the consolidated balance sheet of Ronny, Inc.

P10-60B (*Learning Objective 4: Accounting for a bond investment purchased at a premium*) Insurance companies and pension plans hold large quantities of bond investments. Safe Insurance Corp. purchased $2,700,000 of 8.0% bonds of Sherman, Inc., for 118 on January 1, 2010. These bonds pay interest on January 1 and July 1 each year. They mature on January 1, 2014. At October 31, 2010, the market price of the bonds is 104.

I *Requirements*

1. Journalize Safe's purchase of the bonds as a long-term investment on January 1, 2010 (to be held to maturity), receipt of cash interest, and amortization of the bond investment at July 1, 2010. The straight-line method is appropriate for amortizing the bond investment.
2. Show all financial statement effects of this long-term bond investment on Safe Insurance Corp.'s balance sheet and income statement at October 31, 2010.

■ **general ledger**

P10-61B (*Learning Objective 5: Recording foreign-currency transactions and reporting the transaction gain or loss*) Suppose Lavender Corporation completed the following international transactions:

May	1	Sold inventory on account to Palermo, the Italian automaker, for €60,000. The exchange rate of the euro was $1.38, and Palermo demands to pay in euros.
	10	Purchased supplies on account from a Canadian company at a price of Canadian $57,000. The exchange rate of the Canadian dollar was $0.78, and the payment will be in Canadian dollars.
	17	Sold inventory on account to an English firm for 148,000 British pounds. Payment will be in pounds, and the exchange rate of the pound was $1.94.
	22	Collected from Palermo. The exchange rate is €1 = $1.41.
Jun	18	Paid the Canadian company. The exchange rate of the Canadian dollar is $0.77.
	24	Collected from the English firm. The exchange rate of the British pound was $1.91.

I *Requirements*

1. Record these transactions in Lavender's journal and show how to report the transaction gain or loss on the income statement.
2. How will what you learned in this problem help you structure international transactions?

P10-62B (*Learning Objective 5: Measuring and explaining the foreign-currency translation adjustment*) Assume that Mason has a subsidiary company based in Japan.

I *Requirements*

1. Translate into dollars the foreign-currency balance sheet of the Japanese subsidiary of Mason.

	Yen
Assets.......................................	410,000,000
Liabilities	100,000,000
Stockholders' equity:	
Common stock....................	18,000,000
Retained earnings...............	292,000,000
	410,000,000

When Mason acquired this subsidiary, the Japanese yen was worth $0.0075. The current exchange rate is $0.0090. During the period when the subsidiary earned its income, the average exchange rate was $0.0088 per yen. Before you perform the foreign-currency translation calculations, indicate whether Mason has experienced a positive or a negative translation adjustment. State whether the adjustment is a gain or a loss, and show where it is reported in the financial statements.

2. To which company does the foreign-currency translation adjustment "belong?" In which company's financial statements will the translation adjustment be reported?

APPLY YOUR KNOWLEDGE

Decision Cases

Case 1. (*Learning Objectives 1, 5: Making an investment decision*) Infografix Corporation's consolidated sales for 2010 were $26.6 billion, and expenses totaled $24.8 billion. Infografix operates worldwide and conducts 37% of its business outside the United States. During 2010, Infografix reported the following items in its financial statements (amounts in billions):

Foreign-currency translation adjustments...	$(202)
Unrealized holding _____ on available-for-sale investments.............	(328)

As you consider an investment in Infografix stock, some concerns arise. Answer each of the following questions:

1. What do the parentheses around the two dollar amounts signify?
2. Are these items reported as assets, liabilities, stockholders' equity, revenues, or expenses? Are they normal-balance accounts, or are they contra accounts?
3. Did Infografix include these items in net income? in retained earnings? In the final analysis, how much net income did Infografix report for 2010?
4. Should these items scare you away from investing in Infografix stock? Why or why not? (Challenge)

Case 2. (*Learning Objectives 1, 2, 4: Making an investment sale decision*) Cathy Talbert is the general manager of Barham Company, which provides data-management services for physicians in the Columbus, Ohio, area. Barham Company is having a rough year. Net income trails projections for the year by almost $75,000. This shortfall is especially important. Barham plans to issue stock early next year and needs to show investors that the company can meet its earnings targets.

Barham holds several investments purchased a few years ago. Even though investing in stocks is outside Barham's core business of data-management services, Talbert thinks these investments may hold the key to helping the company meet its net income goal for the year. She is considering what to do with the following investments:

1. Barham owns 50% of the common stock of Ohio Office Systems, which provides the business forms that Barham uses. Ohio Office Systems has lost money for the past two years but still has a retained earnings balance of $550,000. Talbert thinks she can get Ohio's treasurer to declare a $160,000 cash dividend, half of which would go to Barham.
2. Barham owns a bond investment purchased eight years ago for $250,000. The purchase price represents a discount from the bonds' maturity value of $400,000. These bonds mature two years from now, and their current market value is $380,000. Ms. Talbert has checked with a **Charles Schwab** investment representative, and Talbert is considering selling the bonds. Schwab would charge a 1% commission on the sale transaction.

3. Barham owns 5,000 shares of **Microsoft** stock valued at $53 per share. One year ago, Microsoft stock was worth only $28 per share. Barham purchased the Microsoft stock for $37 per share. Talbert wonders whether Barham should sell the Microsoft stock.

▌Requirement

1. Evaluate all three actions as a way for Barham Company to generate the needed amount of income. Recommend the best way for Barham to achieve its net income goal.

Ethical Issue

writing assignment ■

Media One owns 18% of the voting stock of Web Talk, Inc. The remainder of the Web Talk stock is held by numerous investors with small holdings. Austin Cohen, president of Media One and a member of Web Talk's board of directors, heavily influences Web Talk's policies.

Under the market value method of accounting for investments, Media One's net income increases as it receives dividend revenue from Web Talk. Media One pays President Cohen a bonus computed as a percentage of Media One's net income. Therefore, Cohen can control his personal bonus to a certain extent by influencing Web Talk's dividends.

A recession occurs in 2010, and Media One's income is low. Cohen uses his power to have Web Talk pay a large cash dividend. The action requires Web Talk to borrow in order to pay the dividend.

▌Requirements

1. What are the ethical issues in the Media One case?
2. Who are the stakeholders? What are the possible consequences to each?
3. What are the alternatives for Austin Cohen to consider? Analyze each alternative from the following standpoints: (a) economic, (b) legal, (c) ethical.
4. If you were Cohen, what would you do?
5. Discuss how using the equity method of accounting for investment would decrease Cohen's potential for manipulating his bonus.

Focus on Financials: ■ Amazon.com, Inc.

(Learning Objectives 2, 3, 5: Analyzing investments, consolidated subsidiaries, and international operations) The consolidated financial statements of **Amazon.com, Inc.**, are given in Appendix A at the end of this book.

1. Refer to Note 1—Description of Business and Accounting Policies, under *Investments*. Describe the method of accounting used for investments over which the company can exercise significant influence, but not control. How does the company classify these investments on its balance sheet? How does the company account for these investments on its income statement?
2. Does Amazon.com have any other types of investments other than the ones described in (1)? How does the company account for them? Does it adjust for periodic changes in fair market value of these investments? If so, where do these adjustments appear?
3. Continue looking in Note 1, under the caption *Foreign Currency*. Describe the nature of Amazon.com's business dealings with foreign currencies. What has been the impact of this activity on its financial statements? On which financial statement is the impact of this activity reflected?
4. Which monetary currency was stronger, the U.S. dollar or Amazon.com, Inc.'s foreign currencies, during 2008, 2007, and 2006? Give the basis for your answers.

Focus on Analysis: ■ Foot Locker, Inc.

(Learning Objectives 3, 5: Analyzing consolidated statements and international operations)
This case is based on the consolidated financial statements of **Foot Locker, Inc.,** given in Appendix B at the end of this book. Refer specifically to Note 1, Summary of Significant Accounting Policies.

1. What indicates that Foot Locker, Inc., owns foreign subsidiaries? Identify the item that proves your point and the financial statement on which the item appears.
2. Which currency, the U.S. dollar, or the currency of foreign countries in which Foot Locker did business, was stronger in each fiscal year 2007, 2006, and 2005? Give the evidence to support each answer.
3. At February 2, 2008, did Foot Locker, Inc., have a cumulative net gain or a cumulative net loss from translating its foreign subsidiaries' financial statements into dollars? How can you tell?

Group Project

Pick a stock from The *Wall Street Journal* or other database or publication. Assume that your group purchases 1,000 shares of the stock as a long-term investment and that your 1,000 shares are less than 20% of the company's outstanding stock. Research the stock in *Value Line, Moody's Investor Record*, or other source to determine whether the company pays cash dividends and, if so, how much and at what intervals.

❚ *Requirements*

1. Track the stock for a period assigned by your professor. Over the specified period, keep a daily record of the price of the stock to see how well your investment has performed. Each day, search the Corporate Dividend News in The *Wall Street Journal* to keep a record of any dividends you've received. End the period of your analysis with a month end, such as September 30 or December 31.
2. Journalize all transactions that you have experienced, including the stock purchase, dividends received (both cash dividends and stock dividends), and any year-end adjustment required by the accounting method that is appropriate for your situation. Assume you will prepare financial statements on the ending date of your study.
3. Show what you will report on your company's balance sheet, income statement, and statement of cash flows as a result of your investment transactions.

For online homework, exercises, and problems that provide you with immediate feedback, please visit www.myaccountinglab.com.

Quick Check Answers

11

The Income Statement & the Statement of Stockholders' Equity

SPOTLIGHT: The Gap Encounters Headwinds

The Gap, Inc., is a leading international specialty retailer with a strong portfolio of casual apparel, accessories, and personal care products for men, women, and children under The Gap, Old Navy, Banana Republic, and Piperlime brands. The company is encountering "top line" headwinds. Its revenues have been declining slowly but steadily over the past few years. In spite of successes in controlling costs, revenue declines are eroding profits. In fiscal 2007, the company earned revenues of $15.8 billion and net earnings of $833 million. By the end of 2008 (not reflected in the chapter because the financial statements had not yet been released) a global recession caused revenues (and profit from operations) to plummet still further. In its 2007 annual report, the company stated a commitment to serve the needs of customers while delivering "quality earnings and long-term value to shareholders." When you finish this chapter, you will have a better understanding of both of these terms and how you can use a company's income statement to estimate them.

This chapter rounds out your coverage of the corporate income statement. After studying this chapter, you will have seen all the types of items that typically appear on an income statement. You'll study the components of *net income from continuing operations,* which is the basis for many analysts' predictions about companies' future operations, as well as their current values. You'll also learn about earnings per share, the most often-mentioned statistic in business. Finally, you'll learn about the statement of stockholders' equity, of which a component is the analysis of changes in retained earnings. The knowledge you get from this chapter will help you analyze financial statements and use the information in decision making.

We begin with a basic question: How do we evaluate the quality of a company's earnings? The term *quality of earnings* refers to the characteristics of an earnings number that make it most useful for decision making.

LEARNING OBJECTIVES

1 **Analyze** a corporate income statement

2 **Account** for a corporation's income tax

3 **Analyze** a statement of stockholders' equity

4 **Understand** managers' and auditors' responsibilities for the financial statements

EVALUATING THE QUALITY OF EARNINGS

A corporation's net income (including earnings per share) receives more attention than any other item in the financial statements. To stockholders, the larger the net income, the greater the likelihood of dividends. In addition, an upward trend in net income generally translates sooner or later to a higher stock price.

Suppose you are considering investing in either the stock of **The Gap, Inc.**, or Brand X Superstore. How do you make the decision? A knowledgeable investor will want to assess each company's **earnings quality**. The higher the quality of earnings in the current period as compared to its recent past, the more likely it is that the company is executing a successful business strategy to generate healthy earnings in the future, which is a key component in its stock price.

There are many components of earnings quality. Among the most prominent are (1) proper revenue and expense recognition, (2) high and improving gross margin/sales ratio, (3) low operating expenses compared to sales, and (4) high and improving operating earnings/sales. To explore the makeup and the quality of earnings, let's examine its various sources. Exhibit 11-1 shows the Consolidated Statements of Earnings of The Gap, Inc., for fiscal years 2007, 2006, and 2005. We'll use this statement as a basis for our discussion of earnings quality.

EXHIBIT 11-1 | Consolidated Statements of Earnings

The Gap, Inc.
Consolidated Statements of Earnings

($ and shares in millions except per share amounts)	52 Weeks Ended February 2, 2008	52 Weeks Ended February 3, 2007	52 Weeks Ended January 28, 2006
1 Net sales	$15,763	$15,923	$16,019
2 Cost of goods sold and occupancy expenses	10,071	10,266	10,145
3 Gross profit	5,692	5,657	5,874
4 Operating expenses	4,377	4,432	4,099
5 Interest expense	26	41	45
6 Interest income	(117)	(131)	(93)
7 Earnings from continuing operations before income taxes	1,406	1,315	1,823
8 Income taxes	539	506	692
9 Earnings from continuing operations, net of income taxes	867	809	1,131
10 Loss from discontinued operation, net of income tax benefit	(34)	(31)	(18)
11 Net earnings	$ 833	$ 778	$ 1,113
12 Weighted-average number of shares—basic	791	831	881
13 Weighted-average number of shares—diluted	794	836	902
Basic earnings per share:			
14 Earnings from continuing operations, net of income taxes	$ 1.10	$ 0.97	$ 1.28
15 Loss from discontinued operation, net of income tax benefit	(0.05)	(0.03)	(0.02)
16 Net earnings per share	$ 1.05	$ 0.94	$ 1.26
Diluted earnings per share:			
17 Earnings from continuing operations, net of income taxes	$ 1.09	$ 0.97	$ 1.26
18 Loss from discontinued operation, net of income tax benefit	(0.04)	(0.04)	(0.02)
19 Net earnings per share	$ 1.05	$ 0.93	$ 1.24

Revenue Recognition

The first component of earnings quality, and the top line of the income statement, is proper recognition of net revenue, or *net sales*. You learned a little about revenue in Chapters 3 through 6. The *revenue principle*, discussed in Chapter 3 (p. 140) states that, under accrual accounting, revenue should be recognized when it is *earned*—that is, when the selling business has done everything it has to do to either deliver the product or the service to the customer. In recognizing revenue, several important events have to occur: (1) the seller delivers the product or service to the customer, (2) the customer takes both possession and ownership of the product or service, and (3) the seller either collects cash or is reasonably assured of collecting the cash in the near future. In Chapter 4 (p. 256), you learned the process by which cash collected over the counter is entered into the accounting system. In Chapter 5 (pp. 297 through 305), you learned that credit sales, or sales on account, have to go through the process of collection, that some would ultimately not be collectible, and that a company must make allowances for doubtful accounts. In Chapter 6 (p. 346), you studied the concept of *free on board* (F.O.B.) terms, which governs the issue of who owns the goods during the shipment process, and therefore the timing of revenue. You must understand all of these concepts in order to grasp the meaning of revenue recognition.

Proper revenue recognition in a retail business, like The Gap, Inc., is relatively straightforward. As explained in its Notes to Consolidated Financial Statements, The Gap, Inc., properly recognizes revenue, as well as related cost of goods sold, at the time customers receive the products. In the stores, revenue is recognized at the registers when the customers receive and pay for merchandise. For online sales (which comprise about 5.7% of the total) the company has to estimate how long it takes the merchandise to reach customers by mail or courier. For both over-the-counter and Internet sales, the company estimates an allowance for returns and deducts it from gross sales, to report *net sales*.

Let's examine Exhibit 11-1 and analyze the trend in The Gap's net sales revenue (line 1). Notice that, over the past three years, net sales for the company have been declining by about 1% per year ($16,019, $15,923, and $15,763, respectively). Same-store sales, a key factor in growth for retail stores, have declined each year. Competition from other specialty retailers has contributed to the "top line" decline. This has reflected negatively on the company's earnings and, as a result, on its stock price.

 Although the general definition and principles are the same under U.S. GAAP and IFRS, revenue recognition remains one of the principal areas of difference between U.S. GAAP and IFRS. Over its 70-year existence, U.S. GAAP has built up very specific rules for revenue recognition by industry and type of contract. For example, U.S. GAAP contains detailed guidance on revenue recognition for the computer software and real estate industries. When a sales contract contains multiple elements, revenue may be recognized differently for each element. In the construction industry, revenue may be recognized under either the completed-contract method or the percentage-of-completion method. In contrast, IFRS recognizes revenue based mainly on a single standard that contains general principles applied to all industries and all types of contracts. Whereas IFRS literature on revenue recognition contains about 250 pages, U.S. GAAP in this area contains over 2,500 pages! Fortunately for us, this textbook focuses mostly on the retail sector, in which U.S. GAAP and IFRS for revenue recognition are similar. Later courses will address more complex U.S. GAAP and IFRS revenue recognition differences.

COOKING THE BOOKS
with Revenue

Research has shown that roughly half of all financial statement fraud over the past two decades has involved improper revenue recognition.[1] Following are several of the more significant revenue recognition issues involving fraud from the SEC's files:

- **Recognizing revenue prematurely (before it is earned).** One of the common fraud techniques is **channel stuffing**, where a company may ship inventory to regular customers in excess of amounts ordered. **Bristol-Myers Squibb**, a global pharmaceuticals company, was sued by the SEC in 2004 for channel stuffing during 2000 and 2001. The company allegedly stuffed its distribution channels with excess inventory near the end of every quarter in amounts sufficient to meet company sales targets (tied to executive bonuses), overstating revenue by about $1.5 billion. The company paid a civil fine of $100 million and established a $50 million fund to compensate shareholders for their losses.[2]
- **Providing incentives for customers to purchase more inventory than is needed**, in exchange for future discounts and other benefits.
- **Reporting revenue when significant services are still to be performed or goods delivered.**
- **Reporting sales to fictitious or nonexistent customers.** This may include falsified shipping and inventory records.

Cost of Goods Sold and Gross Profit (Gross Margin)

After revenue, the next two important components in earnings quality are cost of goods sold and resulting gross profit. Before we get to these components, however, it is important to emphasize that, just as it is important to avoid premature or improper revenue recognition, it is equally important to make sure that *all expenses are accurately, completely, and transparently included* in the computation of net income. We saw with the example of the WorldCom fraud in Chapter 7 what can happen when a company manipulates reported earnings by deliberately understating expenses. Without the integrity that comes through full and complete disclosures of all existing expenses, and without matching those expenses against the revenues they are incurred to earn, trends in earnings are at best meaningless, and at worst, downright misleading.

Cost of Goods Sold.   Covered in Chapter 6, cost of goods sold represents the direct cost of the goods sold to customers. In the case of The Gap, Inc., cost of goods sold also includes the cost of occupying the space used to sell the product, or store

---

[1]*CPA Letter* (February 2003). American Institute of Certified Public Accountants. See www.aicpa.org/pubs/cpaltr/feb2003/financial.htm.

[2]Accounting and Auditing Enforcement Release No. 2075, August 4, 2004. *Securities and Exchange Commission v. Bristol-Myers Squibb Company,* 04-3680 DNJ (2004). See www.sec.gov.

rent. As shown on line 2 of Exhibit 11-1, cost of goods sold and occupancy costs represents the largest single operating expense for The Gap, Inc., ranging from 63% to 65% of each revenue dollar. In general, assuming cost of goods sold are accurately measured each period, steadily decreasing cost of goods sold as a percentage of net sales revenue is regarded as a sign of increasing earnings quality. Unfortunately for The Gap, Inc., rather than a steady trend downward, we observe a rather erratic trend, first upward and then downward, from fiscal 2005 through fiscal 2007.

Gross Profit (Gross Margin).   Gross profit (gross margin) represents the difference between net sales and cost of goods sold. Conversely with steadily decreasing cost of goods sold, steadily increasing gross profit as a percentage of net sales revenue is considered a sign of increasing earnings quality. For The Gap, Inc., gross profit was 36.7% in fiscal 2005 (52 weeks ended January 28, 2006). Fiscal 2006 (the 53 weeks ended February 3, 2007) was a particularly tough year for The Gap, Inc. Sales declined by 0.6%, and cost of goods sold and occupancy expenses went up by 1.2%, causing gross profit to fall to 35.5%. By the end of fiscal 2007, the company improved its control over gross margin by cutting costs of goods sold and rental expense. Although the company's net sales fell by another 1% in fiscal 2007, cost of goods sold and occupancy expenses fell by 1.9%, causing gross profit to rise to 36.1%.

Operating and Other Expenses

As implied in the title, operating expenses are the ongoing expenses incurred by the entity, other than direct expenses for merchandise and other costs directly related to sales. The largest operating expenses generally include salaries, wages, utilities, and supplies. Again, given that the entity takes care to accurately measure operating expenses, the lower these costs are relative to sales, the more efficiently and, therefore, the more profitably, we can assume management is operating the business. As shown in line 4 of Exhibit 11-1, operating expenses of The Gap, Inc., have followed a rather erratic pattern in relation to sales over the three-year period. From fiscal 2005 to fiscal 2006, operating expenses increased from $4,099 to $4,432, while revenue slipped from $16,019 to $15,923. In fiscal 2007, company management apparently began to exercise tighter control, and operating expenses thus began to follow the same downward trend as sales, representing an improvement relative to fiscal 2006.

The next two ingredients in operating earnings are interest expense and interest income. Covered in Chapters 8, 5, and 10, respectively, interest expense and interest income represent the charges for borrowed money, and the return earned on invested money. As shown in lines 5 and 6 of Exhibit 11-1, interest expense declined over the three-year period and interest income increased, representing a positive trend.

The next important ingredient of operating earnings is corporate income tax expense, which must be subtracted in arriving at income from continuing operations. The current maximum federal income tax rate for corporations is 35%. State income taxes run about 5% in many states. The Gap, Inc.'s fiscal 2007 income tax expense of $539 amounts to about 38.3% of earnings from continuing operations before income taxes. Thus, we use a rate of 40% to approximate income taxes in our illustrations later in the chapter. Effective tax planning, both by in-house tax staff, and externally, through the counsel of the company's independent outside accountants and attorneys, can help lower the company's tax burden, and can contribute substantially to improved operating profits.

Operating Earnings

Given the integrity that comes with accuracy and transparency of reported revenues and expenses, a trend of high and improving operating earnings in relation to net sales reflects increasing earnings quality. Operating earnings are a function of all of its individual ingredients: revenue, cost of goods sold, gross margin, operating and other expenses, interest income and expense, and income tax expense. Unfortunately for The Gap, Inc., for the reasons outlined previously, the trend in earnings from continuing operations (line 9 of Exhibit 11-1) has fallen short of the goal of high and improving operating earnings. Rather than follow a steady path upward over time, earnings from continuing operations for The Gap, Inc., has followed a rather erratic path downward over the fiscal 2005–fiscal 2007 period.

Which Income Number Predicts Future Profits?

How is income from continuing operations used in investment analysis? Suppose Kimberly Kuhl, an analyst with **Morgan Stanley**, is estimating the value of The Gap, Inc.'s common stock. Kuhl believes that The Gap, Inc., can earn annual income each year equal to its income from continuing operations—$1,406 million for The Gap, Inc.

To estimate the value of The Gap, Inc.'s common stock, financial analysts determine the present value (present value means the value *today*) of The Gap, Inc.'s stream of future income. Blume must use some interest rate to compute the present value. Assume that an appropriate interest rate (*i*) for the valuation of The Gap, Inc., is 12%. This rate is based on the risk that The Gap, Inc., might not be able to earn annual income of $1,406 million for the indefinite future. The rate is also called the **investment capitalization rate** because it is used to estimate the value of an investment. The higher the risk, the higher the rate, and vice versa. The computation of the estimated value of the stock of The Gap, Inc., is

$$\text{Estimated value of The Gap, Inc., common stock} = \frac{\text{Estimated annual income in the future}}{\text{Investment capitalization rate}} = \frac{\$1,406 \text{ million}}{0.12} = \$11.717 \text{ billion}$$

Kuhl thus estimates that The Gap, Inc., as a company is worth $11.72 billion. She then computes the company's market capitalization. The Gap, Inc.'s balance sheet at February 2, 2008, reports that the company has 734 million shares of common stock outstanding. The market price of The Gap, Inc., common stock at the beginning of February 2008 is about $19 per share. The current market value of The Gap, Inc., as a company (market capitalization) is thus

$$\text{Current market value of the company} = \text{Number of shares of common stock outstanding} \times \text{Current market price per share}$$
$$\$13.946 \text{ billion} = 734 \text{ million} \times \$19$$

The investment decision rule may be

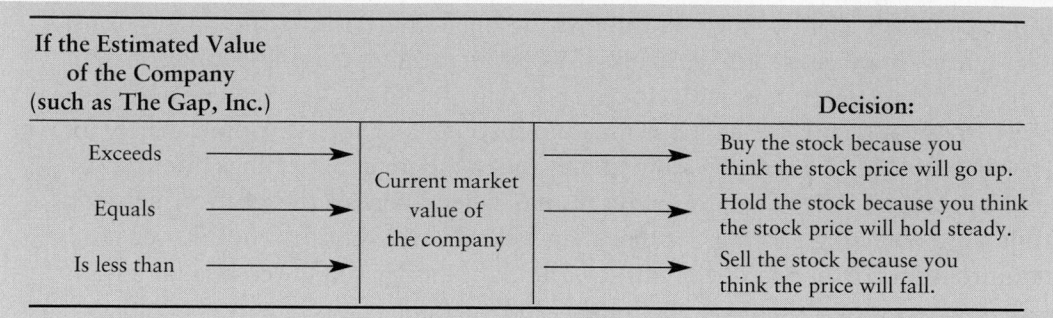

If the Estimated Value of the Company (such as The Gap, Inc.)		Decision:
Exceeds	→ Current market value of the company →	Buy the stock because you think the stock price will go up.
Equals		Hold the stock because you think the stock price will hold steady.
Is less than		Sell the stock because you think the price will fall.

In this case,

			Decision:
Estimated Value of The Gap, Inc. $11.717 billion	Is less than	Current market value of The Gap, Inc. $13.946 billion	→ Sell the stock
$15.96 per share*	Is less than	$19 per share	

*$11.717 billion/734 million = $15.96

Kuhl believes The Gap, Inc.'s stock price should fall below its current market value of $19 to somewhere in a range near $15.96. Based on this analysis, Morgan Stanley would recommend that investors holding The Gap, Inc., stock should sell it.

Discontinued Operations

Most large companies engage in several lines of business. For example, The Gap, Inc., owns The Gap stores, its mid-line store; as well as **Old Navy**, its less expensive lines; **Banana Republic**, its upscale lines; and **Piperlime**, a specialty line of women's shoes and handbags. **General Electric** makes household appliances and jet engines and owns **NBC**, the media network. We call each identifiable part of a company a segment of the business.

A company may sell a segment of its business. During fiscal 2007 The Gap, Inc., closed its Forth and Towne stores, which were designed to appeal to women 35 and older. The discontinuance of a business segment, either through sale or closure, is viewed as a one-time transaction. The Gap, Inc.'s income statement reports the loss from the closure of Forth and Towne stores under the heading Discontinued Operations (line 10 in Exhibit 11-1). The loss is reported net of the income tax benefit that the company receives from being allowed to deduct it on its corporate income tax return.

Financial analysts typically do *not* include discontinued operations in predictions of future corporate income because the discontinued segments will not continue to generate income for the company.

GLOBAL VIEW — EXTRAORDINARY ITEMS: ANOTHER IFRS DIFFERENCE

Extraordinary gains and losses, also called **extraordinary items**, are both *unusual* for the company and *infrequent*. Losses from natural disasters (such as earthquakes, floods, and tornadoes) and the expropriation of company assets by a foreign government are extraordinary. The Gap, Inc., had no extraordinary items on its income statement for fiscal year 2007.

Gains and losses due to lawsuits, restructuring, and the sale of plant assets are *not* extraordinary items. These gains and losses are considered normal business occurrences and are reported as Other Gains and Losses. The Gap, Inc., had none of these items on its income statement for fiscal 2007.

International Financial Reporting Standards (IFRS) do not give special treatment to extraordinary items. Instead, items that are "unusual" in nature or "infrequent" in occurrence are combined with operating income and expenses on the income statement. The result of U.S. companies' adoption of IFRS will be that extraordinary items will eventually disappear from the income statement. In fact, due to the narrow definition, extraordinary items are very rare even under current U.S. GAAP.

Accounting Changes

Companies sometimes change from one accounting method to another, such as from double-declining-balance (DDB) to straight-line depreciation, or from first-in, first-out (FIFO) to average cost for inventory. An accounting change makes it difficult to compare one period with preceding periods. Without detailed information, investors can be misled into thinking that the current year is better or worse than the preceding year, when in fact the only difference is a change in accounting method.

Two types of accounting changes are most relevant to introductory accounting:[3]

a. *Changes in accounting estimates* include changing the estimated life of a building or equipment and the collectibility of receivables. For these changes, companies report amounts for the *current and future* periods on the new basis. There is no looking back to the past. A change in depreciation method is treated as a change in estimate.

b. *Changes in accounting principles* include most changes in accounting methods, such as from FIFO to average cost for inventory and from one method to another for a revenue or an expense. For these changes the company reports figures for all periods presented in the income statement—*past as well as current*—on the new basis. The company *retrospectively restates* (looks back and restates) all prior-period amounts that are presented for comparative purposes with the current year, as though the new accounting method had been in effect all along. This lets investors compare all periods that are presented on the same accounting basis. If an accounting change impacts periods prior to the earliest one presented in the current income statement, an adjustment to retained earnings must be made. The Gap, Inc., reports one of these in its Consolidated Statement of Stockholders' Equity, which is covered later in this chapter.

[3]FASB Statement No. 154, "Accounting Changes and Error Corrections," May 2005.

Watch Out for Voluntary Accounting Changes That Increase Reported Income

Investment analysts follow companies to see if they meet their forecasted earnings targets. And managers sometimes take drastic action to increase reported earnings. Assume it's late in November and our earnings may fall *below* the target for the year. A reasonable thing to do is to try to increase sales and net income. Managers can also cut expenses. These actions are ethical and honest. Profits earned by these actions are real. Managers can take another action that is honest and legal, but its ethics are questionable. Suppose the company has been using the double-declining-balance method for depreciation. Changing to straight-line depreciation can increase reported income.

Accounting changes are a quick-and-dirty way to create profits when the company can't earn enough from continuing operations. This is why GAAP requires companies to report all accounting changes, along with their effects on earnings—to let investors know where the income came from.

Earnings per Share of Common Stock

The final segment of the income statement reports earnings per share. **Earnings per share (EPS)** is the amount of a company's net income per share of its *outstanding common stock*. EPS is a key measure of a business's success because it shows how much income the company earned for each share of stock. Stock prices are quoted at an amount per share, and investors buy a certain number of shares. EPS is used to help determine the value of a share of stock. EPS is computed as follows:

$$\text{Earnings per share} = \frac{\text{Net income} - \text{Preferred dividends}}{\text{Average number of shares of common stock outstanding}}$$

The corporation lists its various sources of income separately: continuing operations, discontinued operations, and so on. It also lists the EPS figure for each element of net income. Consider the EPS of The Gap, Inc. The final section of Exhibit 11-1 (lines 14 through 19) shows how companies report EPS. Notice that two EPS computations are made: one for "basic" (the currently outstanding shares) and one for "diluted" (which takes into account potential increases in outstanding shares). Companies must first compute a weighted average number of shares outstanding. This computation, which is beyond the scope of this textbook, takes into account the changes that might occur in the number of shares outstanding during the year from such things as treasury stock purchases or reissuances. According to Exhibit 11-1, The Gap, Inc., has a "basic" weighted average of 791 million shares of common stock outstanding.

Basic earnings per share of common stock (791 weighted average shares outstanding) (in millions):

14	Income from continuing operations ($867/791)	$1.10
15	Loss from discontinued operations, net of tax ($(34)/791)	(0.05)
16	Net income ($833/791)	$1.05

Effect of Preferred Dividends on Earnings per Share. Recall that EPS is earnings per share of *common* stock. But the holders of preferred stock have first claim on dividends. Therefore, preferred dividends must be subtracted from net income to compute EPS. Preferred dividends are not subtracted from discontinued operations or extraordinary items.

Suppose that The Gap, Inc., had 10,000,000 shares of preferred stock outstanding, each with a $1.00 dividend. The Gap, Inc.'s annual preferred dividends would be $10,000,000 (10,000,000 × $1.00). The $10,000,000 is subtracted from each income subtotal, resulting in the following EPS amounts (recall that The Gap, Inc., has a weighted average of 791 million shares of common stock outstanding):

Basic earnings per share of common stock (791 weighted average shares outstanding) (in millions):	
Income from continuing operations ($867 − $10)/791	$1.08
Loss from discontinued operations ($(34)/791)	(0.05)*
Net income ($833 − $10)/791	$1.03

*rounded up to agree with company's actual financial statements

Earnings per Share Dilution.

Some corporations have convertible preferred stock, which may be exchanged for common stock. For example, The Gap, Inc., is authorized to issue 30 million shares of one or more series of common stock, as well as Class B common stock, which is convertible into shares of its current common stock. The company has not yet issued any of these shares, but could, at some date in the future. When preferred is converted to common, the EPS is *diluted*—reduced—because more common shares are divided into net income. Corporations with complex capital structures present two sets of EPS figures:

- EPS based on actual outstanding common shares (*basic* EPS)
- EPS based on outstanding common shares plus the additional shares that can arise from conversion of the preferred stock into common (*diluted* EPS)

The Gap, Inc.'s weighted average diluted number of shares as of February 2, 2008, (the end of fiscal 2007) is 794 million. The computations for diluted EPS are similar to those illustrated previously for basic EPS.

What Should You Analyze to Gain an Overall Picture of a Company?

Two key figures used in financial analysis are

- net income (or income from continuing operations), and
- cash flow from operations.

For a given period, The Gap, Inc.'s net income and net cash flow from operating activities may chart different paths. Accounting income arises from the accrual process as follows:

Total revenues and gains − Total expenses and losses = Net income (or Net loss)

As we have seen, revenues and gains are recorded when they occur, regardless of when the company receives or pays cash.

Net cash flow, on the other hand, is based solely on cash receipts and cash payments. During 2011, a company may have lots of revenues and expenses and a hefty net income. But the company may have weak cash flow because it cannot collect from customers. The reverse may also be true: The company may have abundant cash but little income.

The income statement and the cash flows statement often paint different pictures of the company. Which statement provides better information? Neither: Both statements are needed, along with the balance sheet and statement of stockholders' equity, for an overall view of the business. In Chapter 12 we'll cover the statement of cash flows in detail.

ACCOUNTING FOR CORPORATE INCOME TAXES

Corporations pay income tax as individuals do, but corporate and personal tax rates differ. The current federal tax rate on most corporate income is 35%. Most states also levy income taxes on corporations, so most corporations have a combined federal and state income tax rate of approximately 40%.

To account for income tax, the corporation measures

- *Income tax expense*, an expense on the income statement. Income tax expense helps measure net income.
- *Income tax payable*, a current liability on the balance sheet. Income tax payable is the amount of tax to pay the government in the next period.

Accounting for income tax follows the principles of accrual accounting. Suppose at the end of fiscal 2010 The Gap, Inc., reports net income before tax (also called **pretax accounting income**) of $1 billion. The Gap, Inc.'s combined income tax rate is close to 40%. To start this discussion, assume income tax expense and income tax payable are the same. Then The Gap, Inc., would record income tax for the year as follows (amounts in millions):

2011			
Jan 28	Income Tax Expense ($1,000 × 0.40)	400	
	Income Tax Payable		400
	Recorded income tax for the year.		

The Gap, Inc.'s financial statements for fiscal 2010 would report these figures (partial, in millions):

Income statement		Balance sheet	
Income before income tax	$1,000	Current liabilities:	
Income tax expense	(400)	Income tax payable	$400
Net income................................	$ 600		

In general, income tax expense and income tax payable can be computed as follows:*

Income tax expense	=	Income before income tax (from the income statement)	×	Income tax rate		Income tax payable	=	Taxable income (from the *income tax return* filed with the IRS)	×	Income tax rate

*The authors thank Jean Marie Hudson for suggesting this presentation.

The income statement and the income tax return are entirely separate documents:

- The *income statement* reports the results of operations.
- The *income tax return* is filed with the Internal Revenue Service (IRS) to measure how much tax to pay the government in the current period.

For most companies, tax expense and tax payable differ. Some revenues and expenses affect income differently for accounting and for tax purposes. The most common difference between accounting income and **taxable income** occurs when a corporation uses straight-line depreciation in its financial statements and accelerated depreciation for the tax return.

Continuing with the The Gap, Inc., illustration, suppose for fiscal 2010 that it had

- pretax accounting income of $1 billion on its income statement, and
- taxable income of $800 million on its income tax return.

Taxable income is less than accounting income because The Gap, Inc., uses

- straight-line depreciation for accounting purposes (say $100 million), and
- accelerated depreciation for tax purposes (say $300 million).

The Gap, Inc., would record income tax for fiscal 2010 as follows (dollar amounts in millions and an income tax rate of 40%):

2011			
Jan 28	Income Tax Expense ($1,000 × 0.40)	400	
	Income Tax Payable ($800 × 0.40)		320
	Deferred Tax Liability		80
	Recorded income tax for the year.		

Deferred Tax Liability is usually long-term.

The Gap, Inc.'s financial statements for fiscal 2010 will report the following:

Income statement		Balance sheet	
Income before income tax	$1,000	Current liabilities:	
Income tax expense	(400)	Income tax payable	$320
Net income..................................	$ 600	Long-term liabilities:	
		Deferred tax liability	80*

*The beginning balance of Deferred tax liability was zero.

In March 2011, The Gap, Inc., would pay income tax payable of $320 million because this is a current liability. The deferred tax liability can be paid later.

For a given year, Income Tax Payable can exceed Income Tax Expense. This occurs when, because of differences in revenue and expenses for book and tax purposes, taxable income exceeds book income. When that occurs, the company debits a Deferred Tax Asset. The remainder of this topic is reserved for a more advanced course.

CORRECTING RETAINED EARNINGS

Occasionally a company records a revenue or an expense incorrectly. If the error is corrected in a later period, the balance of Retained Earnings is wrong until corrected. Corrections to Retained Earnings for errors of an earlier period are called

prior-period adjustments. The prior-period adjustment appears on the statement of retained earnings.

Assume that NPR Corporation recorded 2010 income tax expense as $30,000, but the correct amount was $40,000. This error understated expenses by $10,000 and overstated net income by $10,000. The government sent a bill in 2011 for the additional $10,000, and this alerted NPR to the mistake.

This accounting error requires a prior-period adjustment. Prior-period adjustments are not reported on the income statement because they relate to an earlier accounting period. This prior-period adjustment would appear on the statement of retained earnings, as shown in Exhibit 11-2, with all amounts assumed:

EXHIBIT 11-2 | **Reporting a Prior-Period Adjustment**

NPR Corporation
Statement of Retained Earnings
Year Ended December 31, 2011

Retained earnings balance, December 31, 2010, as originally reported	$390,000
Prior-period adjustment—debit to correct error in recording income tax expense of 2010	(10,000)
Retained earnings balance, December 31, 2010, as adjusted	380,000
Net income for 2011	110,000
	490,000
Dividends for 2011	(40,000)
Retained earnings balance, December 31, 2011	$450,000

Reporting Comprehensive Income

All companies report net income or net loss on their income statements. As we saw in Chapter 10, companies with unrealized gains and losses on certain investments and foreign-currency translation adjustments also report another income figure. **Comprehensive income** is the company's change in total stockholders' equity from all sources other than from the owners of the business. Comprehensive income includes net income plus

- unrealized gains (losses) on available-for-sale investments, and
- foreign-currency translation adjustments.

These items do not enter into the determination of net income or of earnings per share. Exhibit 11-3 shows the statement of comprehensive earnings presented as a part of the Consolidated Statements of Stockholders' Equity of The Gap, Inc., as of February 2, 2008 (end of fiscal 2007). Comprehensive earnings are listed in the far right column. Notice that they include net earnings of $833 million from the income statement in Exhibit 11-1, plus a foreign currency translation adjustment of $84 million, and two negative adjustments for changes in the fair value of derivative financial instruments (available-for-sale securities) of $18 million each.

EXHIBIT 11-3 | Consolidated Statements of Stockholders' Equity

The Gap, Inc.
Consolidated Statements of Stockholders' Equity

($ and shares in millions except per share amounts)	Common Stock		Additional Paid-in Capital	Retained Earnings	Accumulated Other Comprehensive Earnings	Deferred Compensation	Treasury Stock		Total	Comprehensive Earnings
	Shares	Amount					Shares	Amount		
1 Balance at February 3, 2007	1,093	$55	$2,631	$8,646	$ 77	—	(279)	$(6,235)	$ 5,174	$804
2 Net earnings				833					833	$833
3 Foreign currency translation					84				84	84
4 Change in fair value of derivative financial instruments, net of tax of $17					(18)				(18)	(18)
5 Reclassification adjustment for realized gains on derivative financial instruments, net of tax of $11					(18)				(18)	(18)
6 Cumulative effect of adoption of FIN 48				(4)					(4)	
7 Issuance of common stock pursuant to stock option and other stock award plans and related tax benefit of $8	7	—	101						101	
8 Amortization of unrecognized share-based compensation, net of estimated forfeiture..........			49						49	
9 Repurchase of common stock							(89)	(1,700)	(1,700)	
10 Reissuance of treasury stock			2				2	23	25	
11 Cash dividends ($0.32 per share)........				(252)					(252)	
12 Balance at February 2, 2008	1,100	$55	$2,783	$9,223	$125	$—	(366)	$(7,912)	$ 4,274	$881

ANALYZING THE STATEMENT OF STOCKHOLDERS' EQUITY

The **statement of stockholders' equity** reports the reasons for all the changes in the stockholders' equity section of the balance sheet during the period.

Take another look at Exhibit 11-3, the Consolidated Statements of Stockholders' Equity for The Gap, Inc. Study its format. There is a column for each element of equity, starting with Common Stock on the left. The second column from the far right reports the total. The top row (line 1) reports beginning balances as of February 3, 2007, taken from last period's statement of stockholders' equity. The rows then report the various transactions that affected equity, starting with net earnings (line 2). The statement ends with the February 2, 2008, balances (line 12). All the amounts on the bottom line appear on the ending balance sheet, given in Exhibit 11-4 on page 669.

OBJECTIVE

3 **Analyze** a statement of stockholders' equity

Let's examine the changes in The Gap, Inc.'s stockholders' equity during fiscal 2007.

Net Income (Line 2). During 2007, The Gap, Inc., earned net income (net earnings) of $833 million, which increased Retained Earnings. Trace net income from the Consolidated Statements of Earnings (Exhibit 11-1, p. 655) to the Consolidated Statements of Stockholders' Equity (Exhibit 11-3).

Accumulated Other Comprehensive Income (Lines 3 Through 5). Two categories of other comprehensive income are unrealized gains and losses on available-for-sale investments and the foreign-currency translation adjustment.

At February 2, 2007, The Gap, Inc. had an accumulated other comprehensive earnings from previous years of $77 million (line 1). This was made up of $63 million from foreign currency translation sources, and $14 million from fluctuations in the fair market value of derivative (available-for-sale) securities. During fiscal 2007, it made a foreign-currency translation adjustment that increased accumulated other comprehensive earnings by $84 million (line 3). Also, during fiscal 2007, the company recognized an unrealized loss from the change in fair value of derivative financial instruments (available-for-sale) and made another adjustment to reclassified realized gains from these investments. Two negative adjustments for $18 million each resulted, for a total of $36 million. The company ended fiscal 2007 with accumulated other comprehensive earnings of $125 ($147 million accumulated from foreign currency translation adjustments, netted against a $22 million accumulated unrealized loss from the fluctuations in fair market value of derivative—available-for-sale—investments).

Cumulative Effect of Adoption of New Accounting Principle (Line 6). Earlier in the chapter we discussed the impact of accounting changes on current year financial statements. The normal way to account for changes in accounting principles (or methods) is to report them "retrospectively," meaning that, for each prior period presented in the comparative financial statements of the current year, income is restated to incorporate the new method's impact as if the new principle had been in effect in those years as well. When changes in accounting principle impact income of periods that were prior to the earliest presented, the cumulative impact on those periods is reported as an adjustment to retained earnings in the current period. In Exhibit 11-3, The Gap, Inc., adopted Financial Interpretation (FIN) 48 of the FASB during fiscal 2007. The net impact on net income of prior periods is negative $4 million.

Issuance of Stock (Lines 7 and 8). During fiscal 2007, The Gap, Inc., in conjunction with its stock option plan to compensate employees, issued 7 million shares of common stock. The impact of the issuance of the stock was to increase additional paid-in capital, and total stockholders' equity, in the amount of $101 million. The company amortized an additional $49 million of previously unrecognized share-based compensation in the amount of $49 million. This topic is beyond the scope of this textbook, and a discussion of it is reserved for future accounting courses.

Treasury Stock Transactions (Lines 9 and 10). The company repurchased 89 million shares of its own stock for $1.7 billion in fiscal 2007, resulting in a reduction to total stockholders' equity. It then reissued 2 million shares for $25 million, resulting in a reduction in treasury stock in the amount of $23 million and an increase in additional paid-in-capital of $2 million.

Declaration of Cash Dividends (Line 11).   The Gap, Inc., declared cash dividends of $0.32 per share in fiscal 2007. This resulted in a reduction in retained earnings of $252 million.

EXHIBIT 11-4 | Stockholders' Equity Section of the Balance Sheet

The Gap, Inc.
Consolidated Balance Sheet (Partial)
February 2, 2008

(In millions)

Total assets	$7,838
Total liabilities	$3,564
Stockholders' equity:	
Common stock, $0.05 par, shares issued—1,100	55
Additional paid-in capital	2,783
Retained earnings	9,223
Accumulated other comprehensive income	125
Treasury stock	(7,912)
Total stockholders' equity	4,274
Total liabilities and stockholders' equity	$7,838

RESPONSIBILITY FOR THE FINANCIAL STATEMENTS

Management's Responsibility

Management issues a report on internal control over financial reporting, along with the company's financial statements. Exhibit 11-5 is an excerpt from the report of management for The Gap, Inc.

OBJECTIVE

4 **Understand** managers' and auditors' responsibilities for the financial statements

EXHIBIT 11-5 | Excerpt from Management's Responsibility for Financial Reporting

Management is responsible for establishing and maintaining an adequate system of internal control over financial reporting. Management conducted an assessment of internal control over financial reporting based on the framework established by the Committee of Sponsoring Organizations of the Treadway Commission in *Internal Control—Integrated Framework*. Based on the assessment, management concluded that, as of February 2, 2008, our internal control over financial reporting is effective. The Company's internal control over financial reporting as of February 2, 2008, has been audited by Deloitte & Touche, LLP, an independent registered public accounting firm, as stated in their report which is included herein.

Management declares its responsibility for the internal controls over financial reporting in accordance with the Securities Exchange Act of 1934. Management also states that it has conducted an assessment of internal controls over financial reporting based on the framework established by the Committee of Sponsoring Organizations (COSO) of the Treadway Commission, and has concluded that, as of February 2, 2008, internal controls over financial reporting are effective. In addition, management states that the internal controls of the company have been audited by the company's outside auditors, and refers to their report, an excerpt of which is contained in Exhibit 11-6 in the next section.

Auditor Report

The Securities Exchange Act of 1934 requires companies that issue their stock publicly to file audited financial statements with the SEC. Companies engage outside auditors who are certified public accountants to examine their financial statements as well as their internal controls over financial reporting. The independent auditors decide whether the company's financial statements comply with GAAP. They must also decide whether the internal controls of the company meet certain standards. They then issue a combined audit report on both the financial statements and the company's system of internal controls over financial reporting. Exhibit 11-6 contains this report for The Gap, Inc., and its subsidiaries as of February 2, 2008.

EXHIBIT 11-6 | **Excerpt of Report of Independent Registered Public Accounting Firm**

To the Board of Directors and Stockholders of The Gap, Inc.

We have audited the accompanying consolidated balance sheets of The Gap, Inc. and subsidiaries (the "Company") as of February 2, 2008 and February 3, 2007, and the related consolidated statements of earnings, stockholders' equity, and cash flows for each of the three fiscal years in the period ended February 2, 2008. We also have audited the Company's internal control over financial reporting as of February 2, 2008, based on criteria established by *Internal Control—Integrated Framework* issued by the Committee of Sponsoring Organizations of the Treadway Commission. The Company's management is responsible for these financial statements, for maintaining effective internal control over financial reporting, and for its assessment of the effectiveness of internal control over financial reporting, included in the accompanying Management's Report on Internal Control over Financial Reporting. Our responsibility is to express an opinion on these financial statements and opinion on the Company's internal control over financial reporting based on our audits.

We conducted our audits in accordance with the standards of the Public Company Accounting Oversight Board (United States). Those standards require that we plan and perform the audit to obtain reasonable assurance about whether the financial statements are free from material misstatements and whether effective internal control over financial reporting was maintained in all material respects.....We believe that our audits provide a reasonable basis for our opinions.

A company's internal control over financial reporting is a process designed by, or under the supervision of, the company's...financial officers...and effected by the Company's board of directors...to provide reasonable assurance regarding the reliability of financial reporting and the preparation of financial statements....in accordance with generally accepted accounting principles.

Because of the inherent limitations of internal control over financial reporting, including the possibility of collusion or improper management override of controls, material misstatements due to error or fraud may not be prevented or detected on a timely basis. Also, projections of any evaluation of the effectiveness of internal control over financial reporting to future periods are subject to the risk that the controls may become inadequate because of changes in conditions, or that the degree of compliance with the policies or procedures may deteriorate.

In our opinion, the consolidated financial statement referred to above present fairly, in all material respects, the financial position of The Gap, Inc. and subsidiaries as of February 2, 2008 and February 3, 2007, and the results of their operations and their cash flows for each of the three years in the period ended February 2, 2008, in conformity with accounting principles generally accepted in the United States of America. Also, in our opinion, the Company maintained, in all material respects, effective internal control over financial reporting as of February 2, 2008, based on the criteria established in *Internal Control—Integrated Framework* issued by the Committee of Sponsoring Organizations of the Treadway Commission.

/s/ Deloitte & Touche, LLP

San Francisco, California

March 28, 2008

The audit report is addressed to the board of directors and stockholders of the company. A partner of the auditing firm signs the firm's name to the report. In this case, the auditing firm is the San Francisco office of **Deloitte & Touche, LLP** (limited liability partnership).

The combined audit report on financial statements and internal control over financial reporting typically contains five paragraphs:

- The first paragraph identifies the audited financial statements as well as the company being audited. It also states the responsibility of the company's management as well as the auditor's responsibilities.
- The second paragraph describes how the audit was performed in accordance with generally accepted auditing standards of the Public Company Accounting Oversight Board (an independent regulatory body with SEC oversight). These are the standards used by auditors as the benchmark for evaluating audit quality.
- The third paragraph describes in detail what a system of internal controls is, that it should be designed to provide reasonable assurance that transactions are recorded to permit preparation of financial statements that are fairly presented in conformity with GAAP.
- The fourth paragraph describes inherent limitations in the system of internal controls and, that at best, the system of internal controls can only provide reasonable assurance that financial statements are fairly presented.
- The fifth paragraph expresses the auditor's combined opinion on both the fairness of financial statements, in all material respects, in conformity with GAAP, and the effectiveness of the company's internal controls over financial reporting. Deloitte & Touche, LLP, is expressing an **unqualified (clean) opinion** on both the fairness of the financial statements and the effectiveness of The Gap, Inc.'s internal controls. The unqualified opinion is the highest statement of assurance that an independent certified public accountant can express.

The independent audit adds credibility to the financial statements of a company as well as to its system of internal controls. It is no accident that financial reporting and auditing are more advanced in the United States than anywhere else in the world and that U.S. capital markets are the envy of the world.

DECISION GUIDELINES

USING THE INCOME STATEMENT AND RELATED NOTES IN INVESTMENT ANALYSIS

Suppose you've completed your studies, taken a job, and been fortunate to save $10,000. Now you are ready to start investing. These guidelines provide a framework for using accounting information for investment analysis.

Decision	Factors to Consider		Decision Variable or Model
Which measure of profitability should be used for investment analysis?	Are you interested in accounting income?⟶	Income, including all revenues, expenses, gains, and losses?	Net income (bottom line)
		Income that can be expected to repeat from year to year?	Income from continuing operations
	Are you interested in cash flows? ⟶		Cash flows from operating activities (Chapter 12)

Note: A conservative strategy may use both income and cash flows and compare the two sets of results.

What is the estimated value of the stock?	If you believe the company can earn the income (or ⟶ cash flow) indefinitely	$\text{Estimated value} = \dfrac{\text{Annual income}}{\text{Investment capitalization rate}}$
	If you believe the company can earn the income (or ⟶ cash flow) for a finite number of years	$\text{Estimated value} = \text{Annual income} \times \begin{matrix}\text{Present value of annuity}\\ \text{(See Appendix C)}\end{matrix}$

How does risk affect the value of the stock?	If the investment is high risk⟶	Increase the investment capitalization rate
	If the investment is low risk⟶	Decrease the investment capitalization rate

END-OF-CHAPTER SUMMARY PROBLEM

The following information was taken from the ledger of Maxim, Inc.:

Prior-period adjustment—		Treasury stock, common	
credit to Retained Earnings	$ 5,000	(5,000 shares at cost)	$ 25,000
Gain on sale of plant assets	21,000	Selling expenses................................	78,000
Cost of goods sold...........................	380,000	Common stock, no par,	
Income tax expense (saving):		45,000 shares issued....................	180,000
Continuing operations.................	32,000	Sales revenue	620,000
Discontinued operations..............	8,000	Interest expense................................	30,000
Extraordinary gain	10,000	Extraordinary gain	26,000
Preferred stock, 8%, $100 par,		Income from discontinued	
500 shares issued.........................	50,000	operations	20,000
Dividends..	16,000	Loss due to lawsuit...........................	11,000
Retained earnings, beginning,		General expenses..............................	62,000
as originally reported	103,000		

❚ *Requirement*

1. Prepare a single-step income statement (with all revenues and gains grouped together) and a statement of retained earnings for Maxim, Inc., for the current year ended December 31, 2010. Include the earnings-per-share presentation and show computations. Assume no changes in the stock accounts during the year.

Answers

Maxim, Inc.
Income Statement
Year Ended December 31, 2010

Revenue and gains:		
Sales revenue..		$620,000
Gain on sale of plant assets...		21,000
Total revenues and gains		641,000
Expenses and losses:		
Cost of goods sold	$380,000	
Selling expenses	78,000	
General expenses	62,000	
Interest expense	30,000	
Loss due to lawsuit	11,000	
Income tax expense...	32,000	
Total expenses and losses		593,000
Income from continuing operations...................................		48,000
Discontinued operations, $20,000, less income tax, $8,000		12,000
Income before extraordinary item		60,000
Extraordinary gain, $26,000, less income tax, $10,000		16,000
Net income...		$ 76,000
Earnings per share:*		
Income from continuing operations		
[($48,000 − $4,000)/40,000 shares]		$ 1.10
Income from discontinued operations		
($12,000/40,000 shares)...		0.30
Income before extraordinary item		
[($60,000 − $4,000)/40,000 shares]		1.40
Extraordinary gain ($16,000/40,000 shares)..............................		0.40
Net income [($76,000 − $4,000)/40,000 shares].........................		$ 1.80

*Computations:

$$\text{EPS} = \frac{\text{Income} - \text{Preferred dividends}}{\text{Common shares outstanding}}$$

Preferred dividends: $50,000 × 0.08 = $4,000
Common shares outstanding:
   45,000 shares issued − 5,000 treasury shares = 40,000 shares outstanding

Maxim, Inc.
Statement of Retained Earnings
Year Ended December 31, 2010

Retained earnings balance, beginning, as originally reported................	$103,000
Prior-period adjustment—credit	5,000
Retained earnings balance, beginning, as adjusted...............................	108,000
Net income for current year..	76,000
	184,000
Dividends for current year..	(16,000)
Retained earnings balance, ending..	$168,000

REVIEW THE INCOME STATEMENT

Quick Check (Answers are given on page 700.)

1. The quality of earnings suggests that
   a. net income is the best measure of the results of operations.
   b. continuing operations and one-time transactions are of equal importance.
   c. stockholders want the corporation to earn enough income to be able to pay its debts.
   d. income from continuing operations is better than income from one-time transactions.

2. Which statement is true?
   a. Extraordinary items are part of discontinued operations.
   b. Discontinued operations are a separate category on the income statement.
   c. Extraordinary items are combined with continuing operations on the income statement.
   d. All of the above are true.

3. Stafford Corporation earned $5.12 per share of its common stock. Suppose you capitalize Stafford's income at 4%. How much are you willing to pay for a share of Stafford stock?
   a. $125.00   c. $5.12
   b. $20.48   d. $128.00

4. The following is a selected portion of Trendy Trinkets' income statement.

	Year Ended		
	2011	2010	2009
Income (loss) from continuing operations	$(50,000)	$55,000	$145,000
Income (loss) from discontinued operations	(10,000)	(5,000)	1,000
Net income (loss)	$(60,000)	$50,000	$146,000
Earnings (loss) per share from continuing operations:			
Basic..	$ (0.33)	$ 0.37	$ 0.92
Earnings (loss) per share from discontinued operations:			
Basic..	$ (0.07)	$ (0.03)	$ 0.01
Earnings (loss) per share:			
Basic..	$ (0.40)	$ 0.34	$ 0.93

Trendy Trinkets has no preferred stock outstanding. How many shares of common stock did Trendy Trinkets have outstanding during fiscal year 2011?
   a. 175,000 shares   c. 181,818 shares
   b. 125,000 shares   d. 150,000 shares

5. Why is it important for companies to report their accounting changes to the public?
   a. It is important for the results of operations to be compared between periods.
   b. Most accounting changes increase net income, and investors need to know why the increase in net income occurred.
   c. Some accounting changes are more extraordinary than others.
   d. Accounting changes affect dividends, and investors want dividends.

6. Other comprehensive income
   a. includes unrealized gains and losses on investments.
   b. has no effect on income tax.
   c. affects earnings per share.
   d. includes extraordinary gains and losses.

7. Never Lost Systems earned income before tax of $190,000. Taxable income was $165,000, and the income tax rate was 35%. Never Lost recorded income tax with this journal entry:

a.	Income Tax Expense	66,500	
	Income Tax Payable		57,750
	Deferred Tax Liability		8,750
b.	Income Tax Expense	66,500	
	Income Tax Payable		66,500
c.	Income Tax Payable	66,500	
	Income Tax Expense		57,750
	Deferred Tax Liability		8,750
d.	Income Tax Expense	57,750	
	Income Tax Payable		57,750

8. Deferred Tax Liability is usually

Type of Account	Reported on the
a. Long-term	Income statement
b. Long-term	Balance sheet
c. Short-term	Statement of stockholders' equity
d. Short-term	Income statement

9. The main purpose of the statement of stockholders' equity is to report
   a. reasons for changes in the equity accounts.
   b. results of operations.
   c. financial position.
   d. comprehensive income.

10. An auditor report by independent accountants
    a. gives investors assurance that the company's financial statements conform to GAAP.
    b. is ultimately the responsibility of the management of the client company.
    c. ensures that the financial statements are error-free.
    d. gives investors assurance that the company's stock is a safe investment.

Accounting Vocabulary

channel stuffing (p. 657) A type of financial statement fraud that is accomplished by shipping more to customers (usually around the end of the year) than they ordered, with the expectation that they may return some or all of it. The objective is to record more revenue than the company has actually earned with legitimate sales and shipments.

clean opinion (p. 672) An *unqualified opinion*.

comprehensive income (p. 666) A company's change in total stockholders' equity from all sources other than from the owners of the business.

earnings per share (EPS) (p. 662) Amount of a company's net income per share of its outstanding common stock.

earnings quality (p. 654) The characteristics of an earnings number that make it most useful for decision making. The degree to which earnings are an accurate reflection of underlying economic events for both revenues and expenses, and the extent to which earnings from a company's core operations are improving over time. Assuming that revenues and expenses are measured accurately, high-quality earnings are reflected in steadily improving sales and steadily declining costs over time, so that income from continuing operations follows a high and improving pattern over time.

extraordinary gains and losses (p. 661) Also called *extraordinary items*, these gains and losses are both unusual for the company and infrequent.

extraordinary items (p. 661) An *extraordinary gain or loss*.

investment capitalization rate (p. 659) An earnings rate used to estimate the value of an investment in stock.

pretax accounting income (p. 664) Income before tax on the income statement.

prior-period adjustment (p. 666) A correction to beginning balance of retained earnings for an error of an earlier period.

statement of stockholders' equity (p. 667) Reports the changes in all categories of stockholders' equity during the period.

taxable income (p. 665) The basis for computing the amount of tax to pay the government.

unqualified (clean) opinion (p. 672) An audit opinion stating that the financial statements are reliable.

ASSESS YOUR PROGRESS

Short Exercises

S11-1 (*Learning Objective 1: Analyzing a corporate income statement*) Research has shown that over 50% of financial statement frauds are committed by companies that improperly recognize revenue. What does this mean? Describe the most common ways companies improperly recognize revenue.

writing assignment ■

S11-2 (*Learning Objective 1: Analyzing items on an income statement*) Study the 2010 (not 2011) income statement of Household Imports, Inc., and answer these questions about the company:

Household Imports, Inc.
Consolidated Statement of Operations (Adapted)

	Year Ended	
(In thousands except per share amounts)	2010	2009
1 Net sales	$1,825,775	$1,806,293
Operating costs and expenses:		
2 Cost of sales (including buying and store occupancy costs)	1,121,697	1,045,380
3 Selling, general, and administrative expenses	549,250	526,550
4 Depreciation and amortization	55,275	48,750
	1,726,222	1,620,680
5 Operating income (loss)	99,553	185,613
Nonoperating (income) and expenses:		
6 Interest and investment income	(2,665)	(2,760)
7 Interest expense	1,785	1,610
	(880)	(1,150)
8 Income (loss) from continuing operations before income taxes	100,433	186,763
9 Provision (benefit) for income taxes	36,384	69,515
10 Income (loss) from continuing operations	64,049	117,248
11 Discontinued operations:		
12 Income (loss) from discontinued operations (including write down of assets held for sale of $7,993 in 2011)	(2,500)	270
13 Income tax savings	—	—
14 Income (loss) from discontinued operations	(2,500)	270
15 Net income (loss)	$ 61,549	$ 117,518
Earnings (loss) per share from continuing operations:		
16 Basic	$ 0.69	$ 1.52
Earnings (loss) per share from discontinued operations:		
17 Basic	$ (0.06)	$ 0.00
Earnings (loss) per share:		
18 Basic	$ 0.63	$ 1.52

1. How much gross profit did Household earn on the sale of its products? How much was income from continuing operations? Net income?

2. At the end of 2010, what dollar amount of net income would most sophisticated investors use to predict Household's net income for 2011 and beyond? Name this item, give its amount, and state your reason.

S11-3 *(Learning Objective 1: Preparing a complex income statement)* Knowledge King, Inc., reported the following items, listed in no particular order at December 31, 2010 (in thousands):

Other gains (losses)	$ (21,000)	Extraordinary gain................	$ 4,000
Net sales revenue...................	184,000	Cost of goods sold.................	72,000
Loss on discontinued		Operating expenses	60,000
operations	17,000	Accounts receivable..............	16,000

Income tax of 30% applies to all items.

Prepare Knowledge King's income statement for the year ended December 31, 2010. Omit earnings per share.

S11-4 *(Learning Objective 1: Reporting earnings per share)* Return to the Knowledge King data in Short Exercise 11-3. Knowledge King had 10,000 shares of common stock outstanding during 2010. Knowledge King declared and paid preferred dividends of $1,000 during 2010.

Report Knowledge King's earnings per share on the income statement. (Round all calculations to two decimal places.)

S11-5 *(Learning Objective 1: Reporting comprehensive income)* Use the Knowledge King data in Short Exercise S11-3. In addition, Knowledge King had unrealized gains of $1,100 on investments and a $2,400 foreign-currency translation adjustment (a gain) during 2010. Both amounts are net of tax. Start with Knowledge King's net income from S11-3 and show how the company could report other comprehensive income on its 2010 income statement.

Should Knowledge King report earnings per share for other comprehensive income? State why or why not.

S11-6 *(Learning Objective 1: Valuing a company's stock)* For fiscal year 2010, Kiwi Computer, Inc., reported net sales of $19,322 million, net income of $1,993 million, and no significant discontinued operations, extraordinary items, or accounting changes. Earnings per share was $2.10. At a capitalization rate of 10%, how much should one share of Kiwi stock be worth? Compare your estimated stock price with the market price of $71.04 as quoted in the newspaper. Based on your estimated market value, should you buy, hold, or sell Kiwi stock?

S11-7 *(Learning Objective 1: Interpreting earnings-per-share data)* Scorzelli Motor Company has preferred stock outstanding and issued additional common stock during the year.   **writing assignment ■**

1. Give the basic equation to compute earnings per share of common stock for net income.
2. List the income items for which Scorzelli must report earnings-per-share data.
3. What makes earnings per share so useful as a business statistic?

S11-8 *(Learning Objective 1: Using an income statement)* Christianson Cruise Lines, Inc., reported the following income statement for the year ended December 31, 2010:   **writing assignment ■**

	Millions
Operating revenues	$80,998
Operating expenses	71,300
Operating income...	9,698
Other revenue (expense), net...	887
Income from continuing operations.....................................	10,585
Discontinued operations, net of tax......................................	908
Net income...	$11,493

❙ Requirements

1. Were Christianson's discontinued operations more like an expense or revenue? How can you tell?
2. Should the discontinued operations of Christianson be included in or excluded from net income? State your reason.
3. Suppose you are working as a financial analyst and your job is to predict Christianson's net income for 2011 and beyond. Which item from the income statement will you use for your prediction? Identify its amount. Why will you use this item?

S11-9 *(Learning Objective 2: Accounting for a corporation's income tax)* Freeman Marine, Inc., had income before income tax of $122,000 and taxable income of $94,000 for 2010, the company's first year of operations. The income tax rate is 30%.

1. Make the entry to record Freeman Marine's income taxes for 2010.
2. Show what Freeman Marine will report on its 2010 income statement starting with income before income tax. Also show what Freeman Marine will report for current and long-term liabilities on its December 31, 2010, balance sheet.

S11-10 *(Learning Objective 3: Reporting a prior-period adjustment)* iPlace, Inc., was set to report the following statement of retained earnings for the year ended December 31, 2010:

iPlace, Inc. Statement of Retained Earnings Year Ended December 31, 2010	
Retained earnings, December 31, 2009	$ 71,000
Net income for 2010	97,000
Dividends for 2010	(26,000)
Retained earnings, December 31, 2010	$142,000

Before issuing its 2010 financial statements, iPlace learned that net income of 2009 was overstated by $19,000. Prepare iPlace's 2010 statement of retained earnings to show the correction of the error—that is, the prior-period adjustment.

S11-11 *(Learning Objective 3: Using the statement of stockholders' equity)*   Use the statement of stockholders' equity to answer the following questions about Mason Electronics Corporation:

					Accumulated Other Comprehensive Income		
	Common Stock $2 Par	Additional Paid-in Capital	Retained Earnings	Treasury Stock	Unrealized Gain (Loss) on Investments	Foreign-Currency Translation Adjustment	Total Stockholders' Equity
1 Balance, December 31, 2009	$20,000	$ 140,000	$185,000	$(24,000)	$21,000	$(11,000)	$ 331,000
2 Issuance of stock........................	40,000	1,100,000					1,140,000
3 Net income			93,000				93,000
4 Cash dividends..........................			(23,000)				(23,000)
5 Stock dividends—10%..............	6,000	78,000	(84,000)				0
6 Purchase of treasury stock				(8,000)			(8,000)
7 Sale of treasury stock		7,000		5,000			12,000
8 Unrealized gain on investments					6,000		6,000
9 Foreign-currency translation adjustment...........						3,000	3,000
10 Balance, December 31, 2010	$66,000	$1,325,000	$171,000	$(27,000)	$27,000	$ (8,000)	$1,554,000

Mason Electronics Corporation
Statement of Stockholders' Equity
For the Year Ended December 31, 2010

1. How much cash did the issuance of common stock bring in during 2010?
2. What was the effect of the stock dividends on Mason's retained earnings? On total paid-in capital? On total stockholders' equity? On total assets?
3. What was the cost of the treasury stock that Mason purchased during 2010? What was the cost of the treasury stock that Mason sold during the year? For how much did Mason sell the treasury stock during 2010?

S11-12 *(Learning Objective 4: Identifying responsibility and standards for the financial statements)* The annual report of Ashburnham Computer, Inc., included the following:

Management's Annual Report on Internal Control over Financial Reporting

The Company's management is responsible for establishing and maintaining adequate control over financial reporting [....] Management conducted an evaluation of the effectiveness of the Company's internal control over financial reporting [....] Based on this evaluation, management has concluded that the Company's internal control over financial reporting was effective as of September 30, 2010....

Report of Independent Registered Public Accounting Firm
The Board of Directors and Shareholders
Ashburnham Computer, Inc.:

We have audited the accompanying consolidated balance sheets of Ashburnham Computer, Inc., and subsidiaries (the Company) as of September 30, 2010, and September 30, 2009, and the related consolidated statements of operations, shareholders' equity, and cash flows for each of the years in the three-year period ended September 30, 2010. These consolidated financial statements are the responsibility of the Company's management. Our responsibility is to express an opinion on these consolidated financial statements based on our audits.
We conducted our audits in accordance with the standards of the Public Company Accounting Oversight Board (United States)....
In our opinion, the consolidated financial statements referred to above present fairly, in all material respects, the financial position of the Company as of September 30, 2010, and September 30, 2009, and the results of their operations and their cash flows for each of the years in the three-year period ended September 30, 2010, in conformity with accounting principles generally accepted in the United States of America.

/S/ SLMA LLP

Portage, Michigan
December 28, 2010

---

1. Who is responsible for Ashburnham's financial statements?
2. By what accounting standard are the financial statements prepared?
3. Identify one concrete action that Ashburnham management takes to fulfill its responsibility for the reliability of the company's financial information.
4. Which entity gave an outside, independent opinion on the Ashburnham financial statements? Where was this entity located, and when did it release its opinion to the public?
5. Exactly what did the audit cover? Give names and dates.
6. By what standard did the auditor conduct the audit?
7. What was the auditor's opinion of Ashburnham's financial statements?

Exercises

All of the A and B exercises can be found within MyAccountingLab, an online homework and practice environment. Your instructor may ask you to complete these exercises using MyAccountingLab.

(Group A)

E11-13A (*Learning Objective 1: Preparing and using a complex income statement*)   Suppose Dighton Cycles, Inc., reported a number of special items on its income statement. The following data, listed in no particular order, came from Dighton's financial statements (amounts in thousands):

Income tax expense (saving):		Net sales...	$14,000
Continuing operations..................	$295	Foreign-currency translation	
Discontinued operations...............	56	adjustment	320
Extraordinary loss........................	(2)	Extraordinary loss.................................	10
Unrealized gain on		Income from discontinued operations	280
available-for-sale investments.......	35	Dividends declared and paid	600
Short-term investments....................	25	Total operating expenses.......................	12,800

❙ Requirement

1. Show how the Dighton Cycles, Inc., income statement for the year ended September 30, 2010, should appear. Omit earnings per share.

E11-14A (*Learning Objective 1: Preparing and using a complex income statement*)   The Regan Books Company accounting records include the following for 2010 (in thousands):

■ spreadsheet

Other revenues...	$ 2,400
Income tax expense—extraordinary gain	1,600
Income tax expense—income from continuing operations............	2,880
Extraordinary gain..	4,000
Sales revenue...	102,000
Total operating expenses..	97,200

❙ Requirements

1. Prepare Regan Books' single-step income statement for the year ended December 31, 2010, including EPS. Regan Books had 1,800 thousand shares of common stock and no preferred stock outstanding during the year.
2. Assume investors capitalize Regan Books' earnings at 5%. Estimate the price of one share of the company's stock.

E11-15A (*Learning Objective 1: Using income data for investment analysis*) During 2010, Prime, Inc., had sales of $7.26 billion, operating profit of $2.20 billion, and net income of $3.30 billion. EPS was $4.80. On March 13, 2011, one share of Prime's common stock was priced at $53.80 on the New York Stock Exchange.

What investment capitalization rate did investors appear to be using to determine the value of one share of Prime stock? The formula for the value of one share of stock uses EPS in the calculation.

E11-16A (*Learning Objective 1: Computing earnings per common share*) Jetty Loan Company's balance sheet reports the following:

Preferred stock, $60 par value, 3%, 12,000 shares issued	$720,000
Common stock, $0.75 par, 1,100,000 shares issued....................	825,000
Treasury stock, common, 90,000 shares at cost	540,000

During 2010 Jetty earned net income of $6,100,000. Compute Jetty's earnings per common share for 2010. (Round EPS to two decimal places.)

E11-17A (*Learning Objective 1: Computing and using earnings per share*) Athens Holding Company operates numerous businesses, including motel, auto rental, and real estate companies. Year 2010 was interesting for Athens, which reported the following on its income statement (in millions):

Net revenues	$3,932
Total expenses and other...	3,358
Income from continuing operations.............................	574
Discontinued operations, net of tax savings	(89)
Income before extraordinary item and cumulative	
effect of accounting change, net of tax................	485
Extraordinary loss, net of tax savings..........................	(7)
Net income...	$ 478

During 2010, Athens had the following (in millions, except for par value per share):

Common stock, $0.05 par value, 900 shares issued	$ 45
Treasury stock, 300 shares at cost..	(3,649)

I Requirement

1. Show how Athens should report earnings per share for 2010. (Round EPS to the nearest cent.)

E11-18A (*Learning Objective 2: Accounting for income tax by a corporation*) For 2010, its first year of operations, Quinn Advertising, Inc., earned pretax accounting income (on the income statement) of $375,000. Taxable income (on the tax return filed with the Internal Revenue Service) is $300,000. The income tax rate is 30%. Record Quinn's income tax for the year. Show what Quinn will report on its 2010 income statement and balance sheet for this situation. Start the income statement with income before tax.

E11-19A (*Learning Objective 2: Accounting for income tax by a corporation*) During 2010, the Alvin Heights Corp. income statement reported income of $330,000 before tax. The company's income tax return filed with the IRS showed taxable income of $280,000. During 2010, Alvin Heights was subject to an income tax rate of 30%.

I Requirements

1. Journalize Alvin Heights' income taxes for 2010.
2. How much income tax did Alvin Heights have to pay currently for the year 2010?
3. At the beginning of 2010, Alvin Heights' balance of Deferred Tax Liability was $36,000. How much Deferred Tax Liability did Alvin Heights report on its balance sheet at December 31, 2010?

E11-20A (*Learning Objective 3: Reporting a prior-period adjustment on the statement of retained earnings*) Domicile, Inc., a household products chain, reported a prior-period adjustment in 2010. An accounting error caused net income of 2009 to be overstated by $16 million. Retained earnings at December 31, 2009, as previously reported, stood at $342 million. Net income for 2010 was $96 million, and 2010 dividends were $68 million.

■ spreadsheet

I Requirement

1. Prepare the company's statement of retained earnings for the year ended December 31, 2010. How does the prior-period adjustment affect Domicile's net income for 2010?

E11-21A (*Learning Objective 3: Preparing a statement of stockholders' equity*) At December 31, 2010, Pacheco Mall, Inc., reported stockholders' equity as follows:

Common stock, $1.75 par, 400,000 shares authorized, 310,000 shares issued	$ 542,500
Additional paid-in capital.......................................	700,000
Retained earnings...	630,000
	$1,872,500

During 2011, Pacheco Mall completed these transactions (listed in chronological order):

a. Declared and issued a 2% stock dividend on the outstanding stock. At the time, Pacheco Mall stock was quoted at a market price of $20 per share.
b. Issued 2,000 shares of common stock at the price of $18 per share.
c. Net income for the year, $342,000.
d. Declared cash dividends of $187,000.

I Requirement

1. Prepare Pacheco Mall, Inc.'s statement of stockholders' equity for 2011.

E11-22A (*Learning Objective 3: Using a company's statement of stockholders' equity*) Clean Water Company reported the following items on its statement of shareholders' equity for the year ended December 31, 2010:

	$3 Par Common Stock	Additional Paid-in Capital	Retained Earnings	Accumulated Other Comprehensive Income	Total Shareholders' Equity
Balance, December 31, 2009.............	$405	$1,695	$3,600	$12	$5,712
Net earnings......................................			950		
Unrealized gain on investments.........					
Issuance of stock	60	240		5	
Cash dividends..................................			(50)		
Balance, December 31, 2010.............					

❙ Requirements

1. Determine the December 31, 2010, balances in Clean Water's shareholders' equity accounts and total shareholders' equity on this date.
2. Clean Water's total liabilities on December 31, 2010, are $8,000. What is Clean Water's debt ratio on this date?
3. Was there a profit or a loss for the year ended December 31, 2010? How can you tell?
4. At what price per share did Clean Water issue common stock during 2010?

(Group B)

E11-23B (*Learning Objective 1: Preparing and using a complex income statement*) Suppose Searstown Cycles, Inc., reported a number of special items on its income statement. The following data, listed in no particular order, came from Searstown's financial statements (amounts in thousands):

Income tax expense (saving):		Net sales...	$13,300
Continuing operations..................	$300	Foreign-currency translation	
Discontinued operations..............	(62)	adjustment	330
Extraordinary loss.......................	(8)	Extraordinary loss.................................	14
Unrealized gain on		Income from discontinued operations	310
available-for-sale investments.......	38	Dividends declared and paid	610
Short-term investments....................	50	Total operating expenses.......................	12,400

❙ Requirement

1. Show how the Searstown Cycles, Inc., income statement for the year ended September 30, 2010, should appear. Omit earnings per share.

E11-24B (*Learning Objective 1: Preparing and using a complex income statement*) The Beemer Books Company accounting records include the following for 2010 (in thousands):

Other revenues...	$ 2,100
Income tax expense—extraordinary gain	1,440
Income tax expense—income from continuing operations............	4,840
Extraordinary gain...	3,600
Sales revenue..	107,000
Total operating expenses..	97,000

❙ Requirements

1. Prepare Beemer Books' single-step income statement for the year ended December 31, 2010, including EPS. Beemer Books had 1,500 thousand shares of common stock and no preferred stock outstanding during the year.
2. Assume investors capitalize Beemer Books earnings at 6%. Estimate the price of one share of the company's stock.

E11-25B (*Learning Objective 1: Using income data for investment analysis*) During 2010, Doppler, Inc., had sales of $7.36 billion, operating profit of $2.10 billion, and net income of $3.10 billion. EPS was $4.20. On April 12, 2011, one share of Doppler's common stock was priced at $54.40 on the New York Stock Exchange.

What investment capitalization rate did investors appear to be using to determine the value of one share of Doppler stock? The formula for the value of one share of stock uses EPS in the calculation.

E11-26B (*Learning Objective 1: Computing earnings per share*) Tidepool Loan Company's balance sheet reports the following:

Preferred stock, $40 par value, 4%, 9,000 shares issued	$ 360,000
Common stock, $2.00 par, 1,000,000 shares issued....................	2,000,000
Treasury stock, common, 200,000 shares at cost	1,200,000

During 2010 Tidepool earned net income of $6,000,000. Compute Tidepool's earnings per common share for 2010. (Round EPS to two decimal places.)

E11-27B (*Learning Objective 1: Computing and using earnings per share*) Helenic Holding Company operates numerous businesses, including motel, auto rental, and real estate companies. Year 2010 was interesting for Helenic, which reported the following on its income statement (in millions):

Net revenues	$3,934
Total expenses and other..	3,357
Income from continuing operations.............................	577
Discontinued operations, net of tax.............................	88
Income before extraordinary item and cumulative	
effect of accounting change, net of tax................	665
Extraordinary gain, net of tax.....................................	10
Net income..	$ 675

During 2010, Helenic had the following (in millions, except for par value per share):

Common stock, $0.30 par value, 600 shares issued	$ 180
Treasury stock, 200 shares at cost..	(3,542)

❙ Requirement

1. Show how Helenic should report earnings per share for 2010. (Round EPS to the nearest cent.)

E11-28B (*Learning Objective 2: Accounting for income tax by a corporation*) For 2010, its first year of operations, Johnson Advertising earned pretax accounting income (on the income statement) of $750,000. Taxable income (on the tax return filed with the Internal Revenue Service) is $650,000. The income tax rate is 35%. Record Johnson's income tax for the year. Show what Johnson will report on its 2010 income statement and balance sheet for this situation. Start the income statement with income before tax.

E11-29B (*Learning Objective 2: Accounting for income tax by a corporation*) During 2010, Florimax Heights Corp. income statement reported income of $410,000 before tax. The company's income tax return filed with the IRS showed taxable income of $360,000. During 2010, Florimax Heights was subject to an income tax rate of 32%.

❙ Requirements

1. Journalize Florimax Heights' income taxes for 2010.
2. How much income tax did Florimax Heights have to pay for the year 2010?
3. At the beginning of 2010, Florimax Heights' balance of Deferred Tax Liability was $34,000. How much Deferred Tax Liability did Florimax Heights report on its balance sheet at December 31, 2010?

E11-30B (*Learning Objective 3: Reporting a prior-period adjustment on the statement of retained earnings*) Tidy, Inc., a household products chain, reported a prior-period adjustment in 2010. An accounting error caused net income of 2009 to be understated by $8 million. Retained earnings at December 31, 2009, as previously reported, stood at $343 million. Net income for 2010 was $98 million, and 2010 dividends were $65 million.

I Requirement

1. Prepare the company's statement of retained earnings for the year ended December 31, 2010. How does the prior-period adjustment affect Tidy's net income for 2010?

E11-31B (*Learning Objective 3: Preparing a statement of stockholders' equity*) At December 31, 2010, Cox Mall, Inc., reported stockholders' equity as follows:

Common stock, $2.00 par, 600,000 shares authorized, 280,000 shares issued	$ 560,000
Additional paid-in capital......................................	700,000
Retained earnings...	645,000
	$1,905,000

During 2011, Cox Mall completed these transactions (listed in chronological order):

a. Declared and issued a 1% stock dividend on the outstanding stock. At the time, Cox Mall stock was quoted at a market price of $28 per share.
b. Issued 2,100 shares of common stock at the price of $14 per share.
c. Net income for the year, $343,000.
d. Declared cash dividends of $180,000.

I Requirement

1. Prepare Cox Mall, Inc.'s statement of stockholders' equity for 2011.

E11-32B (*Learning Objective 3: Using a company's statement of stockholders' equity*) Rockaway Water Company reported the following items on its statement of shareholders' equity for the year ended December 31, 2010:

	$2 Par Common Stock	Additional Paid-in Capital	Retained Earnings	Accumulated Other Comprehensive Income	Total Shareholders' Equity
Balance, December 31, 2009.............	$390	$1,710	$5,000	$9	$7,109
Net earnings......................................			1,170		
Unrealized gain on investments.........				2	
Issuance of stock..............................	90	270			
Cash dividends..................................			(50)		
Balance, December 31, 2010.............					

I Requirements

1. Determine the December 31, 2010, balances in Rockaway Water's shareholders' equity accounts and total stockholders' equity on this date.
2. Rockaway Water's total liabilities on December 31, 2010, are $6,700. What is Rockaway Water's debt ratio on this date?
3. Was there a profit or a loss for the year ended December 31, 2010? How can you tell?
4. At what price per share did Rockaway Water issue common stock during 2010?

Quiz

Test your understanding of the corporate income statement and the statement of stockholders' equity by answering the following questions. Select the best choice from among the possible answers given.

Q11-33 What is the best source of income for a corporation?
a. Discontinued operations
b. Continuing operations
c. Extraordinary items
d. Prior-period adjustments

Michael's Lotion Company reports several earnings numbers on its current-year income statement (parentheses indicate a loss):

Gross profit	$150,000	Income from continuing operations	$33,000
Net income	43,000	Extraordinary gains	16,000
Income before income tax	62,000	Discontinued operations	(6,000)

Q11-34 How much net income would most investment analysts predict for Michael's to earn next year?
a. $43,000
b. $16,000
c. $33,000
d. $49,000

Q11-35 Return to the preceding question. Suppose you are evaluating Michael's Lotion Company stock as an investment. You require an 8% rate of return on investments, so you capitalize Michael's earnings at 8%. How much are you willing to pay for all of Michael's stock?
a. $1,875,000
b. $412,500
c. $537,500
d. $775,000

Q11-36 Superior Value Corporation had the following items that were labeled "extraordinary" on its income statement:

Extraordinary flood loss	$100,000
Extraordinary gain on lawsuit	150,000

Net income from operations, before income tax and before these "extraordinary" items, totals $240,000, and the income tax rate is 30%. Superior Value's "bottom line" net income after tax is
a. $273,000.
b. $203,000.
c. $290,000.
d. $168,000.

Q11-37 Superior Value Corporation in question 36 has 9,000 shares of 7%, $100 par preferred stock, and 200,000 shares of common stock outstanding. Earnings per share for net income is
a. $0.58.
b. $1.20.
c. $1.51.
d. $0.70.

Q11-38 Earnings per share is *not* reported for
a. extraordinary items.
b. discontinued operations.
c. continuing operations.
d. comprehensive income.

Q11-39 Copyhouse Corporation has income before income tax of $160,000 and taxable income of $120,000. The income tax rate is 30%. Copyhouse's income statement will report net income of
a. $142,000.
b. $48,000.
c. $112,000.
d. $36,000.

Q11-40 Copyhouse Corporation in the preceding question must immediately pay income tax of
a. $112,000.
b. $36,000.
c. $48,000.
d. $84,000.

Q11-41 Use the Copyhouse Corporation data in question 39. At the end of its first year of operations, Copyhouse's deferred tax liability is

a. $12,000.

b. $20,000.

c. $36,000.

d. $28,000.

Q11-42 Which of the following items is most closely related to prior-period adjustments?

a. Preferred stock dividends

b. Retained earnings

c. Accounting changes

d. Earnings per share

Q11-43 Examine the statement of stockholders' equity of Mason Electronics Corporation.

Mason Electronics Corporation
Statement of Stockholders' Equity
Year Ended December 31, 2010

	Common Stock $2 Par	Additional Paid-in Capital	Retained Earnings	Treasury Stock	Accumulated Other Comprehensive Income		Total Stockholders' Equity
					Unrealized Gain (Loss) on Investments	Foreign-Currency Translation Adjustment	
1 Balance, December 31, 2009.....	$20,000	$ 140,000	$185,000	$(24,000)	$21,000	$(11,000)	$ 331,000
2 Issuance of stock........................	40,000	1,100,000					1,140,000
3 Net income			93,000				93,000
4 Cash dividends..........................			(23,000)				(23,000)
5 Stock dividend—10%	6,000	78,000	(84,000)				0
6 Purchase of treasury stock				(8,000)			(8,000)
7 Sale of treasury stock................		7,000		5,000			12,000
8 Unrealized gain on investments					6,000		6,000
9 Foreign-currency translation adj........................						3,000	3,000
10 Balance, December 31, 2010	$66,000	$1,325,000	$171,000	$ 27,000	$27,000	$ (8,000)	$1,554,000

What was the market value of each share of the stock that Mason gave its stockholders in the stock dividend?

a. $3,000

b. $28

c. $42,000

d. $56

Q11-44 Which statement is true?

a. Independent auditors prepare the financial statements.

b. Management audits the financial statements.

c. GAAP governs the form and content of the financial statements.

d. The Public Company Oversight Board evaluates internal controls.

Problems

All of the A and B problems can be found within MyAccountingLab, an online homework and practice environment. Your instructor may ask you to complete these problems using MyAccountingLab.

(Group A)

P11-45A *(Learning Objective 1: Preparing a complex income statement)*   The following information was taken from the records of Daughtry Cosmetics, Inc., at December 31, 2010:

Prior-period adjustment—		Dividends on common stock	$24,000
debit to Retained Earnings.............	$ 1,000	Interest expense..................................	30,000
Income tax expense (saving):		Gain on lawsuit settlement................	14,000
Continuing operations	33,980	Dividend revenue	20,000
Income from discontinued		Treasury stock, common	
operations......................................	8,680	(3,000 shares at cost)...............	17,000
Extraordinary loss	(12,280)	General expenses...............................	85,000
Loss on sale of plant assets.....................	15,000	Sales revenue	610,000
Income from discontinued		Retained earnings, beginning,	
operations......................................	21,000	as originally reported...............	195,000
Preferred stock, 4%, $20 par,		Selling expenses..................................	105,000
3,000 shares issued	60,000	Common stock, no par,	
Extraordinary loss..................................	29,400	25,000 shares authorized	
Cost of goods sold..................................	324,000	and issued.................................	400,000

I Requirements

1. Prepare Daughtry Cosmetics' single-step income statement, which lists all revenues together and all expenses together, for the fiscal year ended December 31, 2010. Include earnings-per-share data.
2. Evaluate income for the year ended December 31, 2010. Daughtry's top managers hoped to earn income from continuing operations equal to 12% of sales.

P11-46A *(Learning Objective 3: Preparing a statement of retained earnings)*   Use the data in Problem P11-45A to prepare the Daughtry Cosmetics statement of retained earnings for the year ended December 31, 2010. Use the Statement of Retained Earnings for Maxim, Inc., in the End-of-Chapter Summary Problem as a model.

P11-47A *(Learning Objective 1: Using income data to make an investment decision)*   Daughtry Cosmetics in Problem P11-45A holds significant promise for carving a niche in its industry. A group of Irish investors is considering purchasing the company's outstanding common stock. Daughtry's stock is currently selling for $43 per share.

A *BetterLife Magazine* story predicted the company's income is bound to grow. It appears that Daughtry can earn at least its current level of income for the indefinite future. Based on this information, the investors think that an appropriate investment capitalization rate for estimating the value of Daughtry's common stock is 5%. How much will this belief lead the investors to offer for Daughtry Cosmetics? Will Daughtry's existing stockholders be likely to accept this offer? Explain your answers.

P11-48A *(Learning Objective 1: Computing earnings per share and estimating the price of a stock)* Overhaul Experts, Ltd., (OEL) specializes in taking underperforming companies to a higher level of performance. OEL's capital structure at December 31, 2009, included 11,000 shares of $2.30 preferred stock and 125,000 shares of common stock. During 2010, OEL issued common stock and ended the year with 131,000 shares of common stock outstanding. Average common shares outstanding during 2010 were 128,000. Income from continuing operations during 2010 was $220,000. The company discontinued a segment of the business at a loss of $67,000, and an extraordinary item generated a gain of $50,000. All amounts are after income tax.

▌*Requirements*

1. Compute OEL's earnings per share. Start with income from continuing operations.
2. Analysts believe OEL can earn its current level of income for the indefinite future. Estimate the market price of a share of OEL common stock at investment capitalization rates of 10%, 12%, and 14%. Which estimate presumes an investment in OEL is the most risky? How can you tell?

P11-49A *(Learning Objective 1: Preparing a corrected income statement, including comprehensive income)* Jim Heller, accountant for Perfect Pie Foods, was injured in an auto accident. Another employee prepared the following income statement for the fiscal year ended June 30, 2010:

Perfect Pie Foods, Inc.
Income Statement
June 30, 2010

Revenue and gains:		
Sales		$896,000
Paid-in capital in excess of par—common		15,000
Total revenues and gains		911,000
Expenses and losses:		
Cost of goods sold	$387,000	
Selling expenses	101,000	
General expenses	93,000	
Sales returns	23,000	
Unrealized loss on available-for-sale investments	13,000	
Dividends paid	16,000	
Sales discounts	12,000	
Income tax expense	35,000	
Total expenses and losses		680,000
Income from operations		231,000
Other gains and losses:		
Extraordinary loss	(42,000)	
Income from discontinued operations	27,000	
Total other gains (losses)		(15,000)
Net income		$216,000
Earnings per share		$ 10.80

The individual *amounts* listed on the income statement are correct. However, some *accounts* are reported incorrectly, and some accounts do not belong on the income statement at all. Also, income tax (40%) has not been applied to all appropriate figures. Perfect Pie Foods issued 24,000 shares of common stock back in 2004 and held 4,000 shares as treasury stock all during the fiscal year 2010.

▌Requirement

1. Prepare a corrected statement of income (single-step, which lists all revenues together and all expenses together), including comprehensive income, for fiscal year 2010. Include earnings per share.

P11-50A *(Learning Objective 2: Accounting for a corporation's income tax)* The accounting (not the income tax) records of Crowley Publications, Inc., provide the comparative income statement for 2010 and 2011, respectively:

	2010	2011
Total revenue	$930,000	$1,020,000
Expenses:		
Cost of goods sold..............................	$410,000	$ 440,000
Operating expenses	290,000	300,000
Total expenses before tax....................	700,000	740,000
Pretax accounting income	$230,000	$ 280,000

Taxable income for 2010 includes these modifications from pretax accounting income:

a. Additional taxable income of $18,000 for accounting income earned in 2011 but taxed in 2010.

b. Additional depreciation expense of $30,000 for MACRS tax depreciation.

The income tax rate is 30%.

▌Requirements

1. Compute Crowley's taxable income for 2010.
2. Journalize the corporation's income taxes for 2010.
3. Prepare the corporation's income statement for 2010.

P11-51A *(Learning Objective 3: Using a statement of stockholders' equity)* Falmouth Food Specialties, Inc., reported the following statement of stockholders' equity for the year ended October 31, 2010:

Falmouth Food Specialties, Inc.
Statement of Stockholders' Equity
For the Year Ended October 31, 2010

(In millions)	Common Stock	Additional Paid-in Capital	Retained Earnings	Treasury Stock	Total
Balance, October 31, 2009...........	$450	$1,670	$ 911	$(114)	$2,917
Net income..................................			280		280
Cash dividends............................			(197)		(197)
Issuance of stock (25 shares)........	50	200			250
Stock dividend.............................	100	400	(500)		—
Sale of treasury stock		12		13	25
Balance, October 31, 2010...........	$600	$2,282	$ 494	$(101)	$3,275

| Requirements

Answer these questions about Falmouth Food Specialties' stockholders' equity transactions.

1. The income tax rate is 30%. How much income before income tax did Falmouth Food Specialties report on the income statement?
2. What is the par value of the company's common stock?
3. At what price per share did Falmouth Food Specialties issue its common stock during the year?
4. What was the cost of treasury stock sold during the year? What was the selling price of the treasury stock sold? What was the increase in total stockholders' equity?
5. Falmouth Food Specialties' statement of stockholders' equity lists the stock transactions in the order in which they occurred. What was the percentage of the stock dividend? (Round to the nearest percentage.)

(Group B)

P11-52B *(Learning Objective 1: Preparing a complex income statement)* The following information was taken from the records of Ahern Cosmetics, Inc., at December 31, 2010:

Prior-period adjustment—			Dividends on common stock	$23,000
debit to Retained Earnings	$ 3,000		Interest expense	25,000
Income tax expense (saving):			Gain on lawsuit settlement	9,000
Continuing operations	24,450		Dividend revenue	15,000
Income from discontinued			Treasury stock, common	
operations	7,190		(4,000 shares at cost)	12,000
Extraordinary loss	(12,910)		General expenses	80,000
Loss on sale of plant assets	13,000		Sales revenue	560,000
Income from discontinued			Retained earnings, beginning,	
operations	18,000		as originally reported	193,000
Preferred stock, 10%, $15 par,			Selling expenses	90,000
500 shares issued	7,500		Common stock, no par,	
Extraordinary loss	32,000		27,000 shares authorized	
Cost of goods sold	314,000		and issued	380,000

| Requirements

1. Prepare Ahern Cosmetics' single-step income statement, which lists all revenues together and all expenses together, for the fiscal year ended December 31, 2010. Include earnings-per-share data.
2. Evaluate income for the year ended December 31, 2010. Ahern's top managers hoped to earn income from continuing operations equal to 14% of sales.

P11-53B *(Learning Objective 3: Preparing a statement of retained earnings)* Use the data in Problem P11-52B to prepare the Ahern Cosmetics statement of retained earnings for the year ended December 31, 2010. Use the Statement of Retained Earnings for Maxim, Inc., in the End-of-Chapter Summary Problem as a model.

P11-54B *(Learning Objective 1: Using income data to make an investment decision)* Ahern Cosmetics in Problem P11-52B holds significant promise for carving a niche in its industry. A group of Swedish investors is considering purchasing the company's outstanding common stock. Ahern's stock is currently selling for $19 per share.

A *Dollars and Sense* story predicted the company's income is bound to grow. It appears that Ahern can earn at least its current level of income for the indefinite future. Based on this information, the investors think that an appropriate investment capitalization rate for estimating the value of Ahern's common stock is 10%. How much will this belief lead the investors to offer for Ahern Cosmetics? Will Ahern's existing stockholders be likely to accept this offer? Explain your answers.

P11-55B (*Learning Objective 1: Computing earnings per share and estimating the price of a stock*)   New Ventures Ltd. (NVL) specializes in taking underperforming companies to a higher level of performance. NVL's capital structure at December 31, 2009, included 12,000 shares of $2.20 preferred stock and 130,000 shares of common stock. During 2010, NVL issued common stock and ended the year with 138,000 shares of common stock outstanding. Average common shares outstanding during 2010 were 134,000. Income from continuing operations during 2010 was $225,000. The company discontinued a segment of the business at a loss of $66,000, and an extraordinary item generated a gain of $48,000. All amounts are after income tax.

I Requirements

1. Compute NVL's earnings per share. Start with income from continuing operations.
2. Analysts believe NVL can earn its current level of income for the indefinite future. Estimate the market price of a share of NVL common stock at investment capitalization rates of 9%, 11%, and 13%. Which estimate presumes an investment in NVL is the most risky? How can you tell?

P11-56B (*Learning Objective 1: Preparing a corrected income statement, including comprehensive income*)   Jack Hodges, accountant for Edible Pie Foods, was injured in an auto accident. Another employee prepared the following income statement for the fiscal year ended June 30, 2010:

Edible Pie Foods, Inc. Income Statement June 30, 2010		
Revenue and gains:		
Sales		$894,000
Paid-in capital in excess of par—common		14,000
Total revenues and gains		908,000
Expenses and losses:		
Cost of goods sold	$382,000	
Selling expenses	106,000	
General expenses	95,000	
Sales returns	26,000	
Unrealized loss on available-for-sale investments	12,000	
Dividends paid	17,000	
Sales discounts	14,000	
Income tax expense	33,000	
Total expenses and losses		685,000
Income from operations		223,000
Other gains and losses:		
Extraordinary gain	40,000	
Loss on discontinued operations	(26,000)	
Total other gains (losses)		14,000
Net income		$237,000
Earnings per share		$ 23.70

The individual *amounts* listed on the income statement are correct. However, some *accounts* are reported incorrectly, and some accounts do not belong on the income statement at all. Also, income tax (30%) has not been applied to all appropriate figures. Edible Pie Foods issued 13,000 shares of common stock back in 2004 and held 3,000 shares as treasury stock all during the fiscal year 2010.

I *Requirement*

1. Prepare a corrected statement of income (single-step, which lists all revenues together and all expenses together), including comprehensive income for 2010. Include earnings per share.

P11-57B (*Learning Objective 2: Accounting for a corporation's income tax*)   The accounting (not the income tax) records of Consolidated Publications, Inc., provide the comparative income statement for 2010 and 2011, respectively:

	2010	2011
Total revenue	$920,000	$1,010,000
Expenses:		
Cost of goods sold..............................	$470,000	$ 500,000
Operating expenses	270,000	280,000
Total expenses before tax...................	740,000	780,000
Pretax accounting income	$180,000	$ 230,000

Taxable income for 2010 includes these modifications from pretax accounting income:

 a. Additional taxable income of $13,000 for accounting income earned in 2011 but taxed in 2010.
 b. Additional depreciation expense of $40,000 for MACRS tax depreciation.

The income tax rate is 35%.

I *Requirements*

1. Compute Consolidated's taxable income for 2010.
2. Journalize the corporation's income taxes for 2010.
3. Prepare the corporation's income statement for 2010.

P11-58B (*Learning Objective 3: Using a statement of stockholders' equity*)   Franklin Food Specialties Inc. reported the following statement of stockholders' equity for the year ended October 31, 2010:

Franklin Food Specialties, Inc.
Statement of Stockholders' Equity
For the Year Ended October 31, 2010

(In millions)	Common Stock	Additional Paid-in Capital	Retained Earnings	Treasury Stock	Total
Balance, October 31, 2009...........	$440	$1,680	$ 907	$(114)	$2,913
Net income..................................			420		420
Cash dividends.............................			(190)		(190)
Issuance of stock (10 shares)	10	220			230
Stock dividend.............................	45	990	(1,035)		—
Sale of treasury stock		16		11	27
Balance, October 31, 2010...........	$495	$2,906	$ 102	$(103)	$3,400

I *Requirements*

Answer these questions about Franklin Food Specialties' stockholders' equity transactions.

1. The income tax rate is 40%. How much income before income tax did Franklin Food Specialties report on the income statement?

2. What is the par value of the company's common stock?
3. At what price per share did Franklin Food Specialties issue its common stock during the year?
4. What was the cost of treasury stock sold during the year? What was the selling price of the treasury stock sold? What was the increase in total stockholders' equity?
5. Franklin Food Specialties' statement of stockholders' equity lists the stock transactions in the order in which they occurred. What was the percentage of the stock dividend? (Round to the nearest percentage).

APPLY YOUR KNOWLEDGE

Decision Cases

Case 1. (*Learning Objective 1: Evaluating the components of income*) Prudhoe Bay Oil Co. is having its initial public offering (IPO) of company stock. To create public interest in its stock, Prudhoe Bay's chief financial officer has blitzed the media with press releases. One, in particular, caught your eye. On November 19, Prudhoe Bay announced unaudited earnings per share (EPS) of $1.19, up 89% from last year's EPS of $0.63. An 89% increase in EPS is outstanding!

Before deciding to buy Prudhoe Bay stock, you investigated further and found that the company omitted several items from the determination of unaudited EPS, as follows:

- Unrealized loss on available-for-sale investments, $0.06 per share
- Gain on sale of building, $0.05 per share
- Prior-period adjustment, increase in retained earnings $1.10 per share
- Restructuring expenses, $0.29 per share
- Loss on settlement of lawsuit begun five years ago, $0.12 per share
- Lost income due to employee labor strike, $0.24 per share
- Income from discontinued operations, $0.09 per share

Wondering how to treat these "special items," you called your stockbroker at **Merrill Lynch**. She thinks that these items are nonrecurring and outside Prudhoe Bay's core operations. Furthermore, she suggests that you ignore the items and consider Prudhoe Bay's earnings of $1.19 per share to be a good estimate of long-term profitability.

❚ *Requirement*

1. What EPS number will you use to predict Prudhoe Bay's future profits? Show your work, and explain your reasoning for each item.

Case 2. (*Learning Objective 1: Using the financial statements in investment analysis*) Mike Magid Toyota is an automobile dealership. Magid's annual report includes Note 1—Summary of Significant Accounting Policies as follows:

> **Income Recognition**
>
> **Sales are recognized when cash payment is received or, in the case of credit sales, which represent the majority of . . . sales, when a down payment is received and the customer enters into an installment sales contract. These installment sales contracts . . . are normally collectible over 36 to 60 months. . . .**
>
> **Revenue from auto insurance policies sold to customers are recognized as income over the life of the contracts.**

Bay Area Nissan, a competitor of Mike Magid Toyota, includes the following note in its Summary of Significant Accounting Policies:

> **Accounting Policies for Revenues**
>
> Sales are recognized when cash payment is received or, in the case of credit sales, which represent the majority of . . . sales, when the customer enters into an installment sales contract. Customer down payments are rare. Most of these installment sales contracts are normally collectible over 36 to 60 months. . . . Revenue from auto insurance policies sold to customers are recognized when the customer signs an insurance contract. Expenses are recognized over the life of the insurance contracts.

Suppose you have decided to invest in an auto dealership and you've narrowed your choices to Magid and Bay Area. Which company's earnings are of higher quality? Why? Will their accounting policies affect your investment decision? If so, how? Mention specific accounts in the financial statements that will differ between the two companies. (Challenge)

Ethical Issue

The income statement of Royal Bank of Singapore reported the following results of operations:

Earnings before income taxes and extraordinary gain	$187,046
Income tax expense	72,947
Earnings before extraordinary gain	114,099
Extraordinary gain, net of income tax	419,557
Net earnings	$533,656

Suppose Royal Bank's management, in violation of International Financial Reporting Standards (IFRS), had reported the company's results of operations in this manner:

Earnings before income taxes	$847,111
Income tax expense	352,651
Net earnings	$494,460

❙ Requirements

1. Identify the ethical issue in this situation.
2. Who are the stakeholders?
3. Evaluate the issue from the standpoint of (a) economic, (b) legal or regulatory, and (c) ethical dimensions. What are the possible effects on all stakeholders you identified?
4. Put yourself in the position of the controller of the bank. Your boss, the CEO, tries to pressure you to make the disclosure that violates IFRS. What would you do? What are the potential consequences?

Focus on Financials: ■ Amazon.com, Inc.

(*Learning Objective 1: Analyzing income and investments*) Refer to the **Amazon.com, Inc.**, consolidated financial statements in Appendix A at the end of this book.

1. Amazon.com, Inc.'s consolidated statements of operations do not mention income from continuing operations. Why not?
2. Take the role of an investor, and suppose you are determining the price to pay for a share of Amazon.com, Inc., stock. Assume you are considering three investment capitalization rates that depend on the risk of an investment in Amazon.com: 5%, 6%, and 7%. Compute your estimated value of a share of Amazon.com, Inc., stock using each of the three capitalization rates. Which estimated value would you base your investment strategy on if you rate Amazon.com, Inc., risky? If you consider Amazon.com, Inc., a safe investment? Use basic earnings per share for 2008.
3. Go to Amazon.com's Web site and compare your computed estimates to its actual stock price. Which of your prices is most realistic? (Challenge)

Focus on Analysis: ■ Foot Locker, Inc.

(*Learning Objectives 1, 3: Evaluating the quality of earnings, valuing investments, and analyzing stock outstanding*) This case is based on the **Foot Locker, Inc.**, consolidated financial statements in Appendix B at the end of this book.

1. Foot Locker, Inc.'s consolidated statements of operations report only one special item. What is it, and what is its amount for 2007?
2. What is your evaluation of the quality of Foot Locker, Inc.'s earnings? State how you formed your opinion.
3. At the end of 2006, how much would you have been willing to pay for one share of Foot Locker, Inc.'s stock if you had rated the investment as high risk? As low risk? Use even-numbered investment capitalization rates in the range of 4%–10% for your analysis, and use basic earnings per share for continuing operations.
4. Go to Foot Locker, Inc.'s Web site and get the current price of a share of its common stock. Which value that you estimated in Requirement 2 is closest to the company's actual stock price? (Challenge)

Group Project

Select a company and research its business. Search the Internet for articles about this company. Obtain its latest available annual report from the company's Web site or from www.sec.gov. Use the link entitled "Search for Company Filings."

I *Requirements*

1. Based on your group's analysis, come to class prepared to instruct the class on six interesting facts about the company that can be found in its financial statements and the related notes. Your group can mention only the obvious, such as net sales or total revenue, net income, total assets, total liabilities, total stockholders' equity, and dividends, in conjunction with other terms. Once you use an obvious item, you may not use that item again.
2. The group should write a paper discussing the facts that it has uncovered. Limit the paper to two double-spaced word-processed pages.

For online homework, exercises, and problems that provide you with immediate
feedback, please visit www.myaccountinglab.com.

Quick Check Answers

1. *d*
2. *b*
3. *d* ($5.12/.04)
4. *d* (($60,000)/(.40)) (rounding causes slight differences for computations of other lines)
5. *a*
6. *a*
7. *a*
8. *b*
9. *a*
10. *a*

12

The Statement of Cash Flows

SPOTLIGHT: Google: The Ultimate Answer Machine

What Internet search engine do you use? It's probably Google, the world's largest search engine. Google was created by Larry Page and Sergey Brin when they were students at Stanford University. From small beginnings, Google has grown to become a global technology leader that has helped transform the way people connect with information. The company generates revenue primarily by delivering cost-effective online advertising. Google maintains an index of billions of Web pages, which it makes freely available via its search engine to anyone with an Internet connection. Recently the market value of Google stock surpassed that of Wal-Mart, the world's largest retailer.

The beauty of Google is that it's so easy to use. Access the Internet at www.google.com, and you can simply enter what you want to find in the search box. You get a whole list of helpful Web sites. The world is literally at your fingertips. Google may be the ultimate answer machine, and lately, it has become a cash machine as well! In 2008, its cash flow from operations exceeded its net income by more than $3.6 billion!

Google Inc.
Consolidated Statement of Cash Flows (Adapted; in millions)
Year Ended December 31, 2008

Cash Flows from Operating Activities		
Net income	$ 4,227	
Adjustments to reconcile net income to net cash		
provided by operating activities:		
Depreciation and amortization...	1,500	
Stock-based compensation, net of taxes	961	
Impairment of equity investments	1,095	
Change in assets and liabilities, net of acquired businesses:		
Accounts receivable	(334)	
Other current assets...	(147)	
Accounts payable..	(212)	
Accrued expenses and other liabilities.......................	339	
Unearned revenue	41	
Income taxes payable..	401	
Other, net...	(18)	
Net cash provided by operating activities..........................		$ 7,853
Cash Flows from Investing Activities		
Purchases of property and equipment	$ (2,358)	
Purchases of investments..	(15,403)	
Sales of investments	15,762	
Acquisitions of other companies	(3,320)	
Net cash used in investing activities		(5,319)
Cash Flows from Financing Activities (net)		87
Other, net...		(46)
Net increase (decrease) in cash and cash equivalents		2,575
Cash and cash equivalents at beginning of year....................		6,082
Cash and cash equivalents at end of year..............................		$ 8,657

In preceding chapters, we covered cash flows as they related to various topics: receivables, plant assets, and so on. In this chapter, we show you how to prepare and use the statement of cash flows. We begin with the statement format used by the vast majority (98.7%) of companies, called the *indirect method*. We end with the alternate format of the statement of cash flows, the *direct method*, used by 1.3% of companies in a recent survey. After working through this chapter, you can analyze the cash flows of actual companies.

This chapter has three distinct sections:

- Introduction, beginning on this page
- Preparing the Statement of Cash Flows: Indirect Method, page 706
- Preparing the Statement of Cash Flows: Direct Method, page 720

The introduction applies to all the cash-flow topics. Professors who wish to cover only the indirect method can assign the first two parts of the chapter. Those interested only in the direct method can proceed from the introduction, which ends on page 706, to the direct method, on page 720.

LEARNING OBJECTIVES

1 **Identify** the purposes of the statement of cash flows

2 **Distinguish** among operating, investing, and financing cash flows

3 **Prepare** a statement of cash flows by the indirect method

4 **Prepare** a statement of cash flows by the direct method

BASIC CONCEPTS: THE STATEMENT OF CASH FLOWS

The balance sheet reports financial position, and balance sheets from two periods show whether cash increased or decreased. But that doesn't tell *why* the cash balance changed. The income statement reports net income and offers clues about cash, but the income statement doesn't tell *why* cash increased or decreased. We need a third financial statement.

The **statement of cash flows** reports **cash flows**—cash receipts and cash payments—in other words, where cash came from (receipts) and how it was spent (payments). The statement covers a span of time and therefore is dated "Year Ended December 31, 2010" or "Month Ended June 30, 2011." Exhibit 12-1 illustrates the relative timing of the four basic statements.

OBJECTIVE

1 **Identify** the purposes of the statement of cash flows

EXHIBIT 12-1 | Timing of the Financial Statements

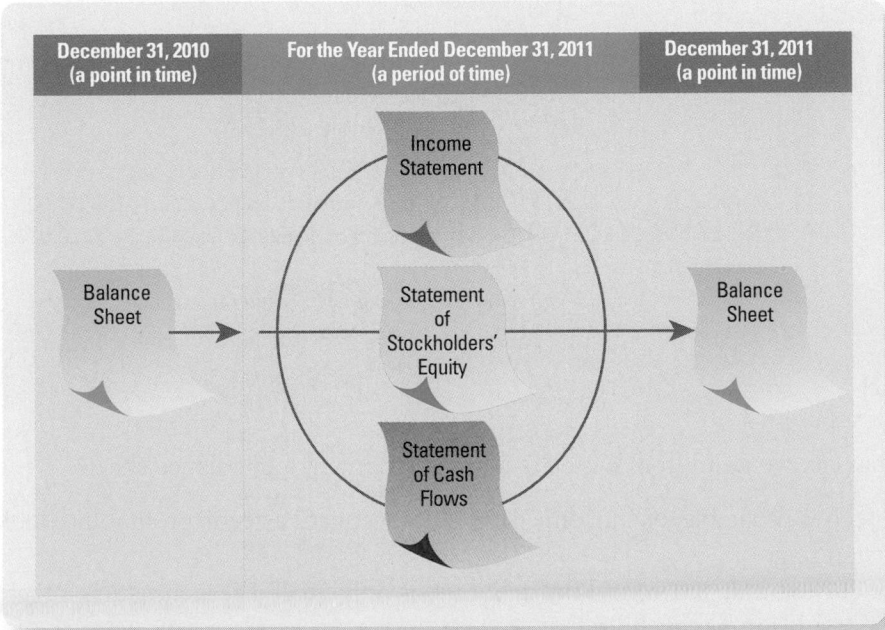

The statement of cash flows serves these purposes:

1. *Predicts future cash flows.*   Past cash receipts and payments are reasonably good predictors of future cash flows.
2. *Evaluates management decisions.*   Businesses that make wise decisions prosper, and those that make unwise decisions suffer losses. The statement of cash flows reports how managers got cash and how they used cash to run the business.

3. ***Determines ability to pay dividends and interest.*** Stockholders want dividends on their investments. Creditors demand interest and principal on their loans. The statement of cash flows reports on the ability to make these payments.

4. ***Shows the relationship of net income to cash flows.*** Usually, high net income leads to an increase in cash, and vice versa. But cash flow can suffer even when net income is high.

On a statement of cash flows, *cash* means more than just cash in the bank. It includes **cash equivalents**, which are highly liquid short-term investments that can be converted into cash immediately. Examples include money-market accounts and investments in U.S. Government securities. Throughout this chapter, the term cash refers to cash and cash equivalents.

How's Your Cash Flow? Telltale Signs of Financial Difficulty

Companies want to earn net income because profit measures success. Without net income, a business sinks. There will be no dividends, and the stock price suffers. High net income attracts investors, but you can't pay bills with net income. That requires cash.

A company needs both net income and strong cash flow. Income and cash flow usually move together because net income generates cash. Sometimes, however, net income and cash flow take different paths. To illustrate, consider Fastech Company:

Fastech Company
Income Statement
Year Ended December 31, 2010

Sales revenue	$100,000
Cost of goods sold	30,000
Operating expenses	10,000
Net income	$ 60,000

Fastech Company
Balance Sheet
December 31, 2010

Cash	$ 3,000	Total current liabilities	$ 50,000
Receivables	37,000	Long-term liabilities	20,000
Inventory	40,000		
Plant assets, net	60,000	Stockholders' equity	70,000
Total assets	$140,000	Total liabilities and equity	$140,000

What can we glean from Fastech's income statement and balance sheet?

- Fastech is profitable. Net income is 60% of revenue. Fastech's profitability looks outstanding.
- The current ratio is 1.6, and the debt ratio is only 50%. These measures suggest little trouble in paying bills.
- But Fastech is on the verge of bankruptcy. Can you spot the problem? Can you see what is causing the problem? Three trouble spots leap out to a financial analyst.

1. The cash balance is very low. Three thousand dollars isn't enough cash to pay the bills of a company with sales of $100,000.

2. Fastech isn't selling inventory fast enough. Fastech turned over its inventory only 0.75 times during the year. As we saw in Chapter 6, inventory turnover rates of

3–8 times a year are common. A turnover ratio of 0.75 times means it takes Fastech far too long to sell its inventory, and that delays cash collections.

3. Fastech's days' sales in receivables ratio is 135 days. Very few companies can wait that long to collect from customers.

The takeaway lesson from this discussion is this:

- You need both net income and strong cash flow to succeed in business.

Let's turn now to the different categories of cash flows.

Operating, Investing, and Financing Activities

A business engages in three types of business activities:

- Operating activities
- Investing activities
- Financing activities

OBJECTIVE

2 **Distinguish** among operating, investing, and financing cash flows

Google's statement of cash flows reports cash flows under these three headings, as shown for Google on page 702.

Operating activities create revenues, expenses, gains, and losses—*net income*, which is a product of accrual-basis accounting. The statement of cash flows reports on operating activities. Operating activities are the most important of the three categories because they reflect the core of the organization. *A successful business must generate most of its cash from operating activities.*

Investing activities increase and decrease *long-term assets*, such as computers, land, buildings, equipment, and investments in other companies. Purchases and sales of these assets are investing activities. Investing activities are important, but they are less critical than operating activities.

Financing activities obtain cash from investors and creditors. Issuing stock, borrowing money, buying and selling treasury stock, and paying cash dividends are financing activities. Paying off a loan is another example. Financing cash flows relate to *long-term liabilities* and *owners' equity*. They are the least important of the three categories of cash flows, and that's why they come last. Exhibit 12-2 shows how operating, investing, and financing activities relate to the various parts of the balance sheet.

EXHIBIT 12-2 | **How Operating, Investing, and Financing Cash Flows Affect the Balance Sheet**

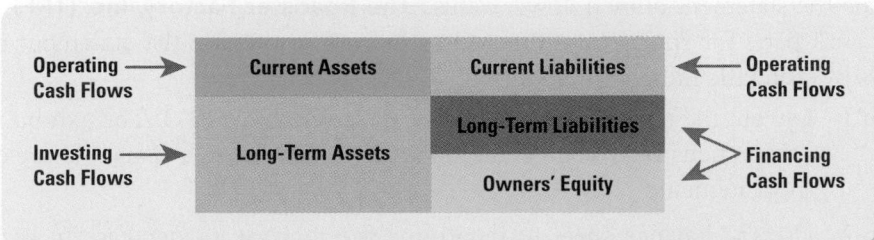

Examine Google's statement of cash flows on page 702. Focus on the final line of each section: Operating, Investing, and Financing. Google has very strong cash flows. During 2008, Google's operating activities provided $7.8 billion of cash. Google invested $5.3 billion and received $87 million in financing. These figures show that

- *Operations* are Google's largest source of cash.
- The company is *investing* in the future.
- People are willing to *finance* Google.

Two Formats for Operating Activities

There are two ways to format operating activities on the statement of cash flows:

- **Indirect method**, which reconciles from net income to net cash provided by operating activities. (pp. 706–717)
- **Direct method**, which reports all cash receipts and cash payments from operating activities. (pp. 720–732)

The two methods use different computations, but they produce the same figure for cash from *operating activities*. The two methods do not affect *investing* or *financing activities*. The following table summarizes the differences between the indirect and direct methods:

Indirect Method		Direct Method	
Net income.................................	$600	Collections from customers..........	$2,000
Adjustments:		*Deductions:*	
Depreciation, etc.	300	Payments to suppliers, etc.	(1,100)
Net cash provided by		Net cash provided by	
operating activities	$900	operating activities	$ 900

——— same ———

We begin with the indirect method because 98 out of 100 companies use it.

PREPARING THE STATEMENT OF CASH FLOWS: INDIRECT METHOD

OBJECTIVE

3 Prepare a statement of cash flows by the indirect method

To illustrate the statement of cash flows, we use **The Roadster Factory, Inc. (TRF)**, a dealer in auto parts for sports cars. Proceed as follows to prepare the statement of cash flows by using the indirect method:

Step 1 Lay out the template as shown in Part 1 of Exhibit 12-3. The exhibit is comprehensive. The diagram in Part 2 (p. 708) gives a visual picture of the statement.

Step 2 Use the balance sheet to determine the increase or decrease in cash during the period. The change in cash is the "check figure" for the statement of cash flows. Exhibit 12-4 (p. 709) gives The Roadster

Factory's (TRF's) comparative balance sheet, with cash highlighted. TRF's cash decreased by $8,000 during 2011. *Why* did cash decrease? The statement of cash flows will provide the answer.

Step 3 From the income statement, take net income, depreciation, depletion, and amortization expense, and any gains or losses on the sale of long-term assets. Print these items on the statement of cash flows. Exhibit 12-5 (p. 709) gives TRF's income statement, with relevant items highlighted.

Step 4 Use the income statement and balance sheet data to prepare the statement of cash flows. The statement of cash flows is complete only after you have explained the year-to-year changes in all the balance sheet accounts.

EXHIBIT 12-3 | **Part 1: Template of the Statement of Cash Flows: Indirect Method**

The Roadster Factory, Inc. (TRF)
Statement of Cash Flows
Year Ended December 31, 2011

Cash flows from operating activities
  Net income
    Adjustments to reconcile net income to net cash provided by operating activities:
    + Depreciation/depletion/amortization expense
    + Loss on sale of long-term assets
    − Gain on sale of long-term assets
    − Increases in current assets other than cash
    + Decreases in current assets other than cash
    + Increases in current liabilities
    − Decreases in current liabilities
        Net cash provided by (used for) operating activities
Cash flows from investing activities:
  + Sales of long-term assets (investments, land, building, equipment, and so on)
  − Purchases of long-term assets
  + Collections of notes receivable
  − Loans to others
        Net cash provided by (used for) investing activities
Cash flows from financing activities:
  + Issuance of stock
  + Sale of treasury stock
  − Purchase of treasury stock
  + Borrowing (issuance of notes or bonds payable)
  − Payment of notes or bonds payable
  − Payment of dividends
        Net cash provided by (used for) financing activities
Net increase (decrease) in cash during the year
  + Cash at December 31, 2010
  = Cash at December 31, 2011

Go to "Cash Flows from Operating Activities" on page 710.

EXHIBIT 12-3 | **Part 2: Positive and Negative Items on the Statement of Cash Flows: Indirect Method**

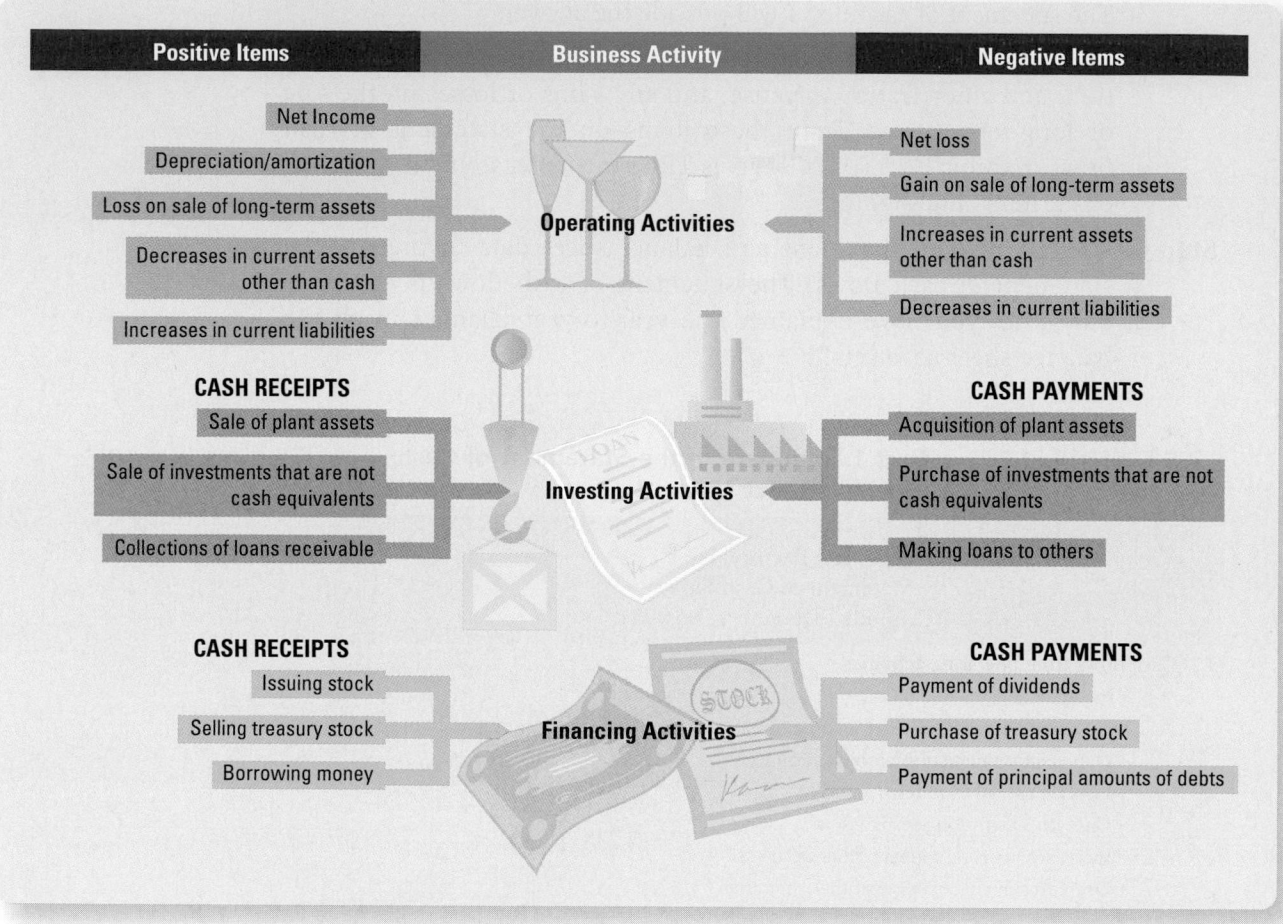

EXHIBIT 12-4 | **Comparative Balance Sheet**

The Roadster Factory, Inc. (TRF)
Comparative Balance Sheets
December 31, 2011 and 2010

(In thousands)	2011	2010	Increase (Decrease)	
Assets				
Current:				
Cash..	$ 34	$ 42	$ (8)	⎫
Accounts receivable.................	96	81	15	⎬ Changes in current assets—*Operating*
Inventory	35	38	(3)	
Prepaid expenses	8	7	1	⎭
Notes receivable	21	—	21	⎫ Changes in noncurrent assets—*Investing*
Plant assets, net of depreciation...	343	219	124	⎭
Total	$537	$387	$150	
Liabilities				
Current:				
Accounts payable	$ 91	$ 57	$ 34	⎫
Salary and wage payable	4	6	(2)	⎬ Changes in current liabilities—*Operating*
Accrued liabilities....................	1	3	(2)	⎭
Long-term debt	160	77	83	⎫ Changes in long-term liabilities and paid-in capital accounts—*Financing*
Stockholders' Equity				
Common stock...........................	162	158	4	⎭
Retained earnings.......................	119	86	33	⎬ Changes due to net income—*Operating* Change due to dividends—*Financing*
Total	$537	$387	$150	

EXHIBIT 12-5 | **Income Statement**

The Roadster Factory, Inc. (TRF)
Income Statement
Year Ended December 31, 2011

	(In thousands)	
Revenues and gains:		
Sales revenue	$303	
Interest revenue	2	
Gain on sale of plant assets	8	
Total revenues and gains		$313
Expenses:		
Cost of goods sold	$150	
Salary and wage expense................	56	
Depreciation expense	18	
Other operating expense	17	
Income tax expense.........................	15	
Interest expense...............................	7	
Total expenses.............................		263
Net income..		$ 50

EXHIBIT 12-6 | Statement of Cash Flows—Operating Activities by the Indirect Method

The Roadster Factory, Inc. (TRF)
Statement of Cash Flows (Indirect Method)
For the Year Ended December 31, 2011

		(In thousands)
Cash flows from operating activities:		
Net income		$50
Adjustments to reconcile net income to net cash provided by operating activities:		
ⒶⒶ* Depreciation	$ 18	
Ⓑ Gain on sale of plant assets	(8)	
Increase in accounts receivable..................................	(15)	
Decrease in inventory..	3	
Ⓒ Increase in prepaid expenses	(1)	
Increase in accounts payable	34	
Decrease in salary and wage payable.........................	(2)	
Decrease in accrued liabilities.....................................	(2)	27
Net cash provided by operating activities.............		$77

*Adjustments A, B, and C are explained in the following section.

Cash Flows from Operating Activities

Operating activities are related to the transactions that make up net income.[1]

The operating section begins with the net income, taken from the income statement, (Exhibit 12-5) and is followed by "Adjustments to reconcile net income to net cash provided by operating activities." Let's discuss these adjustments.

Ⓐ **Depreciation, Depletion, and Amortization Expenses.** These expenses are added back to net income to convert net income to cash flow. Let's see why. Depreciation is recorded as follows:

Depreciation Expense	18,000	
Accumulated Depreciation		18,000

Depreciation has no effect on cash. But depreciation, like all other expenses, decreases net income. Therefore, to convert net income to cash flows, we add depreciation back to net income. The add-back cancels the earlier deduction.

---

[1] The authors thank Professor Alfonso Oddo for suggesting this summary.

Example: Suppose you had only two transactions, a $1,000 cash sale and depreciation expense of $300. Cash flow from operations is $1,000, and net income is $700 ($1,000 – $300). To go from net income ($700) to cash flow ($1,000), we add back the depreciation ($300). Depletion and amortization are treated like depreciation.

Ⓑ Gains and Losses on the Sale of Assets.   Sales of long-term assets are *investing* activities and there's often a gain or loss on the sale. On the statement of cash flows, the gain or loss is an adjustment to net income. Exhibit 12-6 includes an adjustment for a gain. During 2011, The Roadster Factory sold equipment for $62,000. The book value was $54,000, so there was a gain of $8,000.

The $62,000 cash received from the sale is an investing activity (Exhibit 12-7), and the $62,000 includes the $8,000 gain. Net income also includes the gain, so we must subtract the gain from net cash provided by operations, so that it may be added to the net book value of equipment removed in the investing section ($54,000 + $8,000 = $62,000). (We explain investing activities in the next section.)

A loss on the sale of plant assets also creates an adjustment in the operating section. Since the cash received from the sale of a long-term asset at a loss is less than the asset's book value, the amount of cash received reflects the loss. Losses are deducted from net income. Therefore, in order to show the amount of cash received from the sale of the asset in the investments section, losses are *added back* to net income to compute cash flow from operations.

Ⓒ Changes in the Current Asset and Current Liability Accounts.   Most current assets and current liabilities result from operating activities. For example, accounts receivable result from sales, inventory relates to cost of goods sold, and so on. Changes in the current accounts are adjustments to net income on the cash-flow statement. The reasoning follows:

1. *An increase in another current asset decreases cash.*   It takes cash to acquire assets. Suppose you make a sale on account. Accounts receivable are increased, but cash isn't affected yet. Exhibit 12-4 (p. 709) reports that during 2011, The Roadster Factory's Accounts Receivable increased by $15,000. To compute cash flow from operations, we must subtract the $15,000 increase in Accounts Receivable, as shown in Exhibit 12-6. The reason is this: We have *not* collected this $15,000 in cash. Similar logic applies to all the other current assets. If they increase, cash decreases.

2. *A decrease in another current asset increases cash.*   Suppose TRF's Accounts Receivable balance decreased by $4,000. Cash receipts caused Accounts Receivable to decrease, so we add decreases in Accounts Receivable and the other current assets to net income.

3. *A decrease in a current liability decreases cash.*   Payment of a current liability decreases both cash and the liability, so we subtract decreases in current liabilities from net income. In Exhibit 12-6, the $2,000 decrease in Accrued Liabilities is *subtracted* to compute net cash provided by operations.

4. *An increase in a current liability increases cash.*   The Roadster Factory's Accounts Payable increased. That can occur only if cash was not spent to pay this debt. Cash payments are therefore less than expenses and TRF has more cash on hand. Thus, increases in current liabilities increase cash.

EXHIBIT 12-7 | Statement of Cash Flows—Indirect Method

The Roadster Factory, Inc. (TRF)
Statement of Cash Flows (Indirect Method)
For the Year Ended December 31, 2011

			(In thousands)
Cash flows from operating activities:			
Net income			$ 50
Adjustments to reconcile net income to net cash provided by operating activities:			
Ⓐ Depreciation		$ 18	
Ⓑ Gain on sale of plant assets		(8)	
Increase in accounts receivable		(15)	
Decrease in inventory		3	
Ⓒ Increase in prepaid expenses		(1)	
Increase in accounts payable		34	
Decrease in salary and wage payable		(2)	
Decrease in accrued liabilities		(2)	27
Net cash provided by operating activities			77
Cash flows from investing activities:			
Acquisition of plant assets		$(196)	
Loan to another company		(21)	
Proceeds from sale of plant assets		62	
Net cash used for investing activities			(155)
Cash flows from financing activities:			
Proceeds from issuance of long-term debt		$ 94	
Proceeds from issuance of common stock		4	
Payment of long-term debt		(11)	
Payment of dividends		(17)	
Net cash provided by financing activities			70
Net (decrease) in cash			$ (8)
Cash balance, December 31, 2010			42
Cash balance, December 31, 2011			$ 34

Evaluating Cash Flows from Operating Activities.   Let's step back and evaluate The Roadster Factory's operating cash flows during 2011. TRF's operations provided net cash flow of $77,000. This amount exceeds net income, which is one sign of a healthy company. Now let's examine TRF's investing and financing activities, as reported in Exhibit 12-7.

Cash Flows from Investing Activities

> Investing activities affect long-term assets, such as Plant Assets, Investments, and Notes Receivable.

Most of the data come from the balance sheet.

Computing Purchases and Sales of Plant Assets.   Companies keep a separate account for each plant asset. But for computing cash flows, it is helpful to combine all the plant assets into a single summary account. Also, we subtract accumulated depreciation and use the net figure. It's easier to work with a single plant asset account.

To illustrate, observe that The Roadster Factory's

- balance sheet reports beginning plant assets, net of accumulated depreciation, of $219,000. The ending balance is $343,000 (Exhibit 12-4).
- income statement shows depreciation expense of $18,000 and an $8,000 gain on sale of plant assets (Exhibit 12-5).

TRF's purchases of plant assets total $196,000 (take this amount as given; see Exhibit 12-7). How much, then, are the proceeds from the sale of plant assets? First, we must determine the book value of the plant assets sold, as follows:

Plant Assets, Net								
Beginning balance	+	Acquisitions	−	Depreciation	−	Book value of assets sold	=	Ending balance
$219,000	+	$196,000	−	$18,000		−X	=	$343,000
						−X	=	$343,000 − $219,000 − $196,000 + $18,000
						X	=	$54,000

The sale proceeds are $62,000, determined as follows:

Sale proceeds	=	Book value of assets sold	+	Gain	−	Loss
X	=	$54,000	+	$8,000	−	$0
X	=	$62,000				

Trace the sale proceeds of $62,000 to the statement of cash flows in Exhibit 12-7. The Plant Assets T-account provides another look at the computation of the book value of the assets sold.

Plant Assets, Net			
Beginning balance	219,000	Depreciation	18,000
Acquisitions	196,000	Book value of assets sold	54,000
Ending balance	343,000		

If the sale resulted in a loss of $3,000, the sale proceeds would be $51,000 ($54,000 − $3,000), and the statement of cash flows would report $51,000 as a cash receipt from this investing activity.

Computing Purchases and Sales of Investments, and Loans and Collections.

The cash amounts of investment transactions can be computed in the manner illustrated for plant assets. Investments are easier because there is no depreciation, as shown in the following equation:

Investments (amounts assumed for illustration only)						
Beginning balance	+	Purchases	−	Book value of investments sold	=	Ending balance
$100,000	+	$50,000		−X	=	$140,000
				−X	=	$140,000 − $100,000 − $50,000
				X	=	$10,000

The Investments T-account provides another look (amounts assumed).

Investments			
Beginning balance	100		
Purchases	50	Book value of investments sold	10
Ending balance	140		

The Roadster Factory has a long-term receivable, and the cash flows from loan transactions on notes receivable can be determined as follows (data from Exhibit 12-4):

Notes Receivable							
Beginning balance	+	New loans made	−	Collections	=	Ending balance
$0	+	X		−0	=	$21,000
		X			=	$21,000

Notes Receivable			
Beginning balance	0		
New loans made	21	Collections	0
Ending balance	21		

Exhibit 12-8 summarizes the cash flows from investing activities, highlighted in color.

EXHIBIT 12-8 | Computing Cash Flows from Investing Activities

Receipts

From sale of plant assets	Beginning plant assets, net	+	Acquisition cost	−	Depreciation	−	Book value of assets sold	=	Ending plant assets, net
	Cash received	=	Book value of assets sold	+ or −	Gain on sale Loss on sale				
From sale of investments	Beginning investments	+	Purchase cost of investments	−	Cost of investments sold			=	Ending investments
	Cash received	=	Cost of investments sold	+ or −	Gain on sale Loss on sale				
From collection of notes receivable	Beginning notes receivable	+	New loans made	−	Collections			=	Ending notes receivable

Payments

For acquisition of plant assets	Beginning plant assets, net	+	Acquisition cost	−	Depreciation	−	Book value of assets sold	=	Ending plant assets, net
For purchase of investments	Beginning investments	+	Purchase cost of investments	−	Cost of investments sold			=	Ending investments
For new loans made	Beginning notes receivable	+	New loans made	−	Collections			=	Ending notes receivable

Cash Flows from Financing Activities

> Financing activities affect liabilities and stockholders' equity, such as Notes Payable, Bonds Payable, Long-Term Debt, Common Stock, Paid-in Capital in Excess of Par, and Retained Earnings. Most of the data come from the balance sheet.

Computing Issuances and Payments of Long-Term Debt.   The beginning and ending balances of Long-Term Debt, Notes Payable, or Bonds Payable come from the balance sheet. If either new issuances or payments are known, the other amount can be computed. The Roadster Factory's new debt issuances total $94,000 (take this amount as given; Exhibit 12-7). Debt payments are computed from the Long-Term Debt account (see Exhibit 12-4).

Long-Term Debt (Notes Payable, Bonds Payable)

Beginning balance	+	Issuance of new debt	−	Payments of debt	=	Ending balance
$77,000	+	$94,000		−X	=	$160,000
				−X	=	$160,000 − $77,000 − $94,000
				X	=	$11,000

Long-Term Debt

		Beginning balance	77,000
Payments	11,000	Issuance of new debt	94,000
		Ending balance	160,000

Computing Issuances of Stock and Purchases of Treasury Stock.   These cash flows can be determined from the stock accounts. For example, cash received from issuing common stock is computed from Common Stock and Capital in Excess of Par. We use a single summary Common Stock account as we do for plant assets. The Roadster Factory data are

Common Stock

Beginning balance	+	Issuance of new stock	=	Ending balance
$158,000	+	$4,000	=	$162,000

Common Stock

	Beginning balance	158,000
	Issuance of new stock	4,000
	Ending balance	162,000

The Roadster Factory has no treasury stock, but cash flows from purchasing treasury stock can be computed as follows (using assumed amounts):

Treasury Stock (amounts assumed for illustration only)				
Beginning balance	+	Purchase of treasury stock	=	Ending balance
$16,000	+	$3,000	=	$19,000

Treasury Stock		
Beginning balance	16,000	
Purchase of treasury stock	3,000	
Ending balance	19,000	

Computing Dividend Declarations and Payments.   If dividend declarations and payments are not given elsewhere, they can be computed. For The Roadster Factory, this computation is

Retained Earnings						
Beginning balance	+	Net income	−	Dividend declarations and payments	=	Ending balance
$86,000	+	$50,000		−X	=	$119,000
				−X	=	$119,000 − $86,000 − $50,000
				X	=	$17,000

The T-account also shows the dividend computation.

Retained Earnings			
Dividend declarations and payments	17,000	Beginning balance	86,000
		Net income	50,000
		Ending balance	119,000

Exhibit 12-9 summarizes the cash flows from financing activities, highlighted in color.

EXHIBIT 12-9 | **Computing Cash Flows from Financing Activities**

Receipts

From borrowing—issuance of long-term debt (notes payable)	Beginning long-term debt (notes payable)	+	Cash received from issuance of long-term debt	−	Payment of debt	=	Ending long-term debt (notes payable)
From issuance of stock	Beginning stock	+	Cash received from issuance of new stock			=	Ending stock

Payments

Of long-term debt	Beginning long-term debt (notes payable)	+	Cash received from issuance of long-term debt	−	Payment of debt	=	Ending long-term debt (notes payable)
To purchase treasury stock	Beginning treasury stock + Purchase cost of treasury stock = Ending treasury stock						
Of dividends	Beginning retained earnings + Net income − Dividend declarations and payments = Ending retained earnings						

STOP & THINK. . .

Classify each of the following as an operating activity, an investing activity, or a financing activity as reported on the statement of cash flows prepared by the *indirect* method.

a. Issuance of stock	g. Paying bonds payable
b. Borrowing	h. Interest expense
c. Sales revenue	i. Sale of equipment
d. Payment of dividends	j. Cost of goods sold
e. Purchase of land	k. Purchase of another company
f. Purchase of treasury stock	l. Making a loan

Answers:

a. Financing	e. Investing	i. Investing
b. Financing	f. Financing	j. Operating
c. Operating	g. Financing	k. Investing
d. Financing	h. Operating	l. Investing

Noncash Investing and Financing Activities

Companies make investments that do not require cash. They also obtain financing other than cash. Our examples have included none of these transactions. Now suppose The Roadster Factory issued common stock valued at $300,000 to acquire a warehouse. TRF would journalize this transaction as follows:

Warehouse Building	300,000	
Common Stock		300,000

This transaction would not be reported as a cash payment because TRF paid no cash. But the investment in the warehouse and the issuance of stock are important. These noncash investing and financing activities can be reported in a separate schedule under the statement of cash flows. Exhibit 12-10 illustrates noncash investing and financing activities (all amounts are assumed).

EXHIBIT 12-10 | **Noncash Investing and Financing Activities (All Amounts Assumed)**

	Thousands
Noncash Investing and Financing Activities:	
Acquisition of building by issuing common stock	$300
Acquisition of land by issuing note payable	70
Payment of long-term debt by issuing common stock	100
Total noncash investing and financing activities	$470

Now let's apply what you've learned about the statement of cash flows prepared by the indirect method.

MID-CHAPTER SUMMARY PROBLEM

Lucas Corporation reported the following income statement and comparative balance sheets, along with transaction data for 2011:

Lucas Corporation
Income Statement
Year Ended December 31, 2011

Sales revenue		$662,000
Cost of goods sold		560,000
Gross profit		102,000
Operating expenses		
Salary expenses	$46,000	
Depreciation expense— equipment	7,000	
Amortization expense— patent	3,000	
Rent expense	2,000	
Total operating expenses		58,000
Income from operations		44,000
Other items:		
Loss on sale of equipment		(2,000)
Income before income tax		42,000
Income tax expense		16,000
Net income		$ 26,000

Lucas Corporation
Comparative Balance Sheets
December 31, 2011 and 2010

Assets	2011	2010	Liabilities	2011	2010
Current:			Current:		
Cash and equivalents	$ 19,000	$ 3,000	Accounts payable	$ 35,000	$ 26,000
Accounts receivable	22,000	23,000	Accrued liabilities	7,000	9,000
Inventories	34,000	31,000	Income tax payable	10,000	10,000
Prepaid expenses	1,000	3,000	Total current liabilities	52,000	45,000
Total current assets	76,000	60,000	Long-term note payable	44,000	—
Long-term investments	18,000	10,000	Bonds payable	40,000	53,000
Equipment, net	67,000	52,000	Owners' Equity		
Patent, net	44,000	10,000	Common stock	52,000	20,000
			Retained earnings	27,000	19,000
			Less: Treasury stock	(10,000)	(5,000)
Total assets	$205,000	$132,000	Total liabilities and equity	$205,000	$132,000

Transaction Data for 2011:

Purchase of equipment	$ 98,000	Issuance of long-term note payable to purchase patent	$ 37,000
Payment of cash dividends	18,000		
Issuance of common stock to retire bonds payable	13,000	Issuance of long-term note payable to borrow cash	7,000
Purchase of long-term investment	8,000	Issuance of common stock for cash	19,000
Purchase of treasury stock	5,000	Sale of equipment (book value, 76,000)	74,000

❚ Requirement

1. Prepare Lucas Corporation's statement of cash flows (indirect method) for the year ended December 31, 2011. Follow the four steps outlined below. For Step 4, prepare a T-account to show the transaction activity in each long-term balance sheet account. For each plant asset, use a single account, net of accumulated depreciation (for example: Equipment, Net).

Step 1 Lay out the template of the statement of cash flows.

Step 2 From the comparative balance sheet, determine the increase in cash during the year, $16,000.

Step 3 From the income statement, take net income, depreciation, amortization, and the loss on sale of equipment to the statement of cash flows.

Step 4 Complete the statement of cash flows. Account for the year-to-year change in each balance sheet account.

Answer

Lucas Corporation
Statement of Cash Flows
Year Ended December 31, 2011

Cash flows from operating activities:		
Net income		$ 26,000
Adjustments to reconcile net income to		
net cash provided by operating activities:		
Depreciation	$ 7,000	
Amortization	3,000	
Loss on sale of equipment	2,000	
Decrease in accounts receivable	1,000	
Increase in inventories	(3,000)	
Decrease in prepaid expenses	2,000	
Increase in accounts payable	9,000	
Decrease in accrued liabilities	(2,000)	19,000
Net cash provided by operating activities		45,000
Cash flows from investing activities:		
Purchase of equipment	$(98,000)	
Sale of equipment	74,000	
Purchase of long-term investment	(8,000)	
Net cash used for investing activities		(32,000)
Cash flows from financing activities:		
Issuance of common stock	$ 19,000	
Payment of cash dividends	(18,000)	
Issuance of long-term note payable	7,000	
Purchase of treasury stock	(5,000)	
Net cash provided by financing activities		3,000
Net increase in cash		**16,000**
Cash balance, December 31, 2010		3,000
Cash balance, December 31, 2011		$ 19,000
Noncash investing and financing activities:		
Issuance of long-term note payable to purchase patent...		$ 37,000
Issuance of common stock to retire bonds payable		13,000
Total noncash investing and financing activities		$ 50,000

Long-Term Investments

Bal	10,000		
	8,000		
Bal	18,000		

Equipment, Net

Bal	52,000		
	98,000	76,000	
		7,000	
Bal	67,000		

Patent, Net

Bal	10,000		
	37,000	3,000	
Bal	44,000		

Long-Term Note Payable

		Bal	0
			37,000
			7,000
		Bal	44,000

Bonds Payable

		Bal	53,000
	13,000		
		Bal	40,000

Common Stock

		Bal	20,000
			13,000
			19,000
		Bal	52,000

Retained Earnings

		Bal	19,000
	18,000		26,000
		Bal	27,000

Treasury Stock

Bal	5,000	
	5,000	
Bal	10,000	

PREPARING THE STATEMENT OF CASH FLOWS: DIRECT METHOD

OBJECTIVE

4 **Prepare** a statement of cash flows by the direct method

The Financial Accounting Standards Board (FASB) prefers the direct method of reporting operating cash flows because it provides clearer information about the sources and uses of cash. But only about 1% of companies use this method because it requires more computations than the indirect method. Investing and financing cash flows are unaffected by the operating cash flows.

To illustrate the statement of cash flows, we use The Roadster Factory, Inc. (TRF), a dealer in auto parts for sports cars. To prepare the statement of cash flows by the direct method, proceed as follows:

Step 1 Lay out the template of the statement of cash flows by the direct method, as shown in Part 1 of Exhibit 12-11. Part 2 (p. 722) gives a visual presentation of the statement.

Step 2   Use the balance sheet to determine the increase or decrease in cash during the period. The change in cash is the "check figure" for the statement of cash flows. The Roadster Factory's comparative balance sheet shows that cash decreased by $8,000 during 2011 (Exhibit 12-4, p. 709). *Why* did cash fall during 2011? The statement of cash flows explains.

EXHIBIT 12-11 | **Part 1: Template of the Statement of Cash Flows—Direct Method**

The Roadster Factory, Inc. (TRF)
Statement of Cash Flows
Year Ended December 31, 2011

Cash flows from operating activities:
  Receipts:
    Collections from customers
    Interest received on notes receivable
    Dividends received on investments in stock
      Total cash receipts
  Payments:
    To suppliers
    To employees
    For interest
    For income tax
      Total cash payments
  Net cash provided by (used for) operating activities
Cash flows from investing activities:
    Sales of long-term assets (investments, land, building, equipment, and so on)
  − Purchases of long-term assets
  + Collections of notes receivable
  − Loans to others
  Net cash provided by (used for) investing activities
Cash flows from financing activities:
    Issuance of stock
  + Sale of treasury stock
  − Purchase of treasury stock
  + Borrowing (issuance of notes or bonds payable)
  − Payment of notes or bonds payable
  − Payment of dividends
  Net cash provided by (used for) financing activities
Net increase (decrease) in cash during the year
  + Cash at December 31, 2010
  = Cash at December 31, 2011

EXHIBIT 12-11 | Part 2: Cash Receipts and Cash Payments on the Statement of Cash Flows—Direct Method

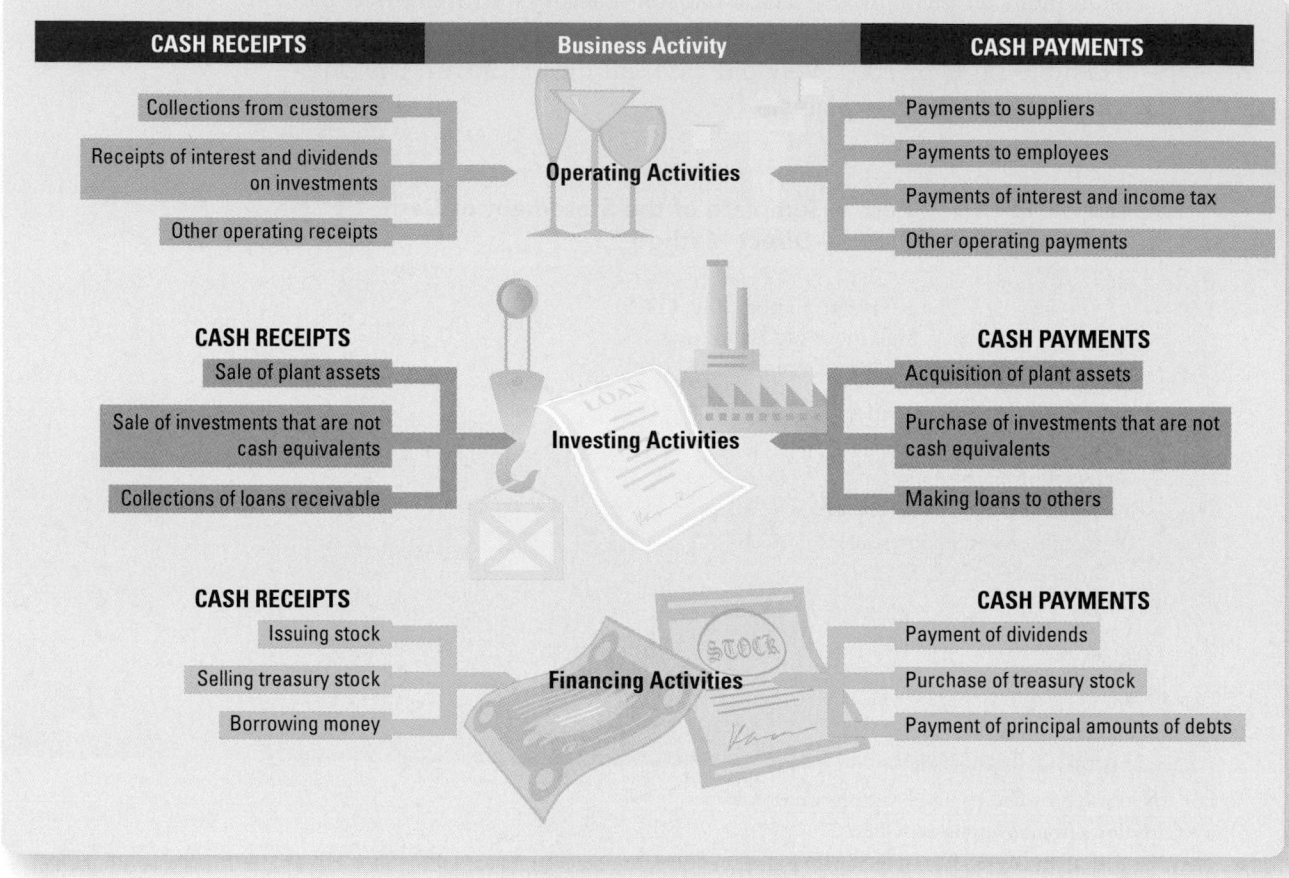

Step 3 Use the available data to prepare the statement of cash flows. The Roadster Factory's transaction data appear in Exhibit 12-12. These transactions affected both the income statement (Exhibit 12-5, p. 709) and the statement of cash flows. Some transactions affect one statement and some affect the other. For example, sales (item 1) are reported on the income statement. Cash collections (item 2) go on the statement of cash flows. Other transactions, such as interest expense and payments (item 11) affect both statements. *The statement of cash flows reports only those transactions with cash effects* (those with an asterisk in Exhibit 12-12). Exhibit 12-13 (on p. 724) gives The Roadster Factory's statement of cash flows for 2011.

Cash Flows from Operating Activities

Operating cash flows are listed first because they are the most important. Exhibit 12-13 shows that The Roadster Factory is sound; operating activities were the largest source of cash.

Cash Collections from Customers Both cash sales and collections of accounts receivable are reported on the statement of cash flows as "Collections from customers . . . $288,000" in Exhibit 12-13.

Cash Receipts of Interest and Dividends   The income statement reports interest revenue and dividend revenue. Only the cash receipts of interest and dividends appear on the statement of cash flows—$2,000 of interest received in Exhibit 12-13.

EXHIBIT 12-12 | **Summary of The Roadster Factory's 2011 Transactions**

Operating Activities
1. Sales on credit, $303,000
*2. Collections from customers, $288,000
*3. Interest revenue and receipts, $2,000
4. Cost of goods sold, $150,000
5. Purchases of inventory on credit, $147,000
*6. Payments to suppliers, $133,000
7. Salary and wage expense, $56,000
*8. Payments of salary and wages, $58,000
9. Depreciation expense, $18,000
10. Other operating expense, $17,000
*11. Income tax expense and payments, $15,000
*12. Interest expense and payments, $7,000

Investing Activities
*13. Cash payments to acquire plant assets, $196,000
*14. Loan to another company, $21,000
*15. Proceeds from sale of plant assets, $62,000, including $8,000 gain

Financing Activities
*16. Proceeds from issuance of long-term debt, $94,000
*17. Proceeds from issuance of common stock, $4,000
*18. Payment of long-term debt, $11,000
*19. Declaration and payment of cash dividends, $17,000

*Indicates a cash flow to be reported on the statement of cash flows.
Note: Income statement data are taken from Exhibit 12-16, page 727.

Payments to Suppliers   Payments to suppliers include all expenditures for inventory and operating expenses except employee pay, interest, and income taxes. *Suppliers* are those entities that provide inventory and essential services. For example, a clothing store's suppliers may include **Tommy Hilfiger, Adidas,** and **Ralph Lauren**. Other suppliers provide advertising, utilities, and office supplies. Exhibit 12-13 shows that The Roadster Factory paid suppliers $133,000.

Payments to Employees   This category includes salaries, wages, and other forms of employee pay. Accrued amounts are excluded because they have not yet been paid. The statement of cash flows reports only the cash payments of $58,000.

Payments for Interest Expense and Income Tax Expense Interest and income tax payments are reported separately. The Roadster Factory paid cash for all its interest and income taxes. Therefore, the same amount goes on the income statement and the statement of cash flows. These payments are operating cash flows because the interest and income tax are expenses.

EXHIBIT 12-13 | **Statement of Cash Flows— Direct Method**

The Roadster Factory, Inc. (TRF)
Statement of Cash Flows (Direct Method)
For Year Ended December 31, 2011

	(In thousands)	
Cash flows from operating activities:		
Receipts:		
Collections from customers......................................	$ 288	
Interest received	2	
Total cash receipts		$ 290
Payments:		
To suppliers..	$(133)	
To employees	(58)	
For income tax...	(15)	
For interest...	(7)	
Total cash payments		(213)
Net cash provided by operating activities................		77
Cash flows from investing activities:		
Acquisition of plant assets..	$(196)	
Loans to another company..	(21)	
Proceeds from sale of plant assets	62	
Net cash used for investing activities........................		(155)
Cash flows from financing activities:		
Proceeds from issuance of long-term debt	$ 94	
Proceeds from issuance of common stock....................	4	
Payment of long-term debt..	(11)	
Payment of dividends..	(17)	
Net cash provided by financing activities		70
Net (decrease) in cash..		(8)
Cash balance, December 31, 2010		42
Cash balance, December 31, 2011		$ 34

Depreciation, Depletion, and Amortization Expense

These expenses are *not* listed on the direct-method statement of cash flows because they do not affect cash.

Cash Flows from Investing Activities

Investing is critical because a company's investments affect the future. Large purchases of plant assets signal expansion. Meager investing activity means the business is not growing.

Purchasing Plant Assets and Investments and Making Loans to Other Companies. These cash payments acquire long-term assets. The Roadster Factory's first investing activity in Exhibit 12-13 is the purchase of plant assets ($196,000). TRF also made a $21,000 loan and thus got a note receivable.

Proceeds from Selling Plant Assets and Investments and from Collecting Notes Receivable. These cash receipts are also investing activities. The sale of the plant assets needs explanation. The Roadster Factory received $62,000 cash from the sale of plant assets, and there was an $8,000 gain on this transaction. What is the appropriate amount to show on the cash-flow statement? It is $62,000, the cash received from the sale, not the $8,000 gain.

Investors are often critical of a company that sells large amounts of its plant assets. That may signal an emergency. For example, problems in the airline industry have caused some companies to sell airplanes to generate cash.

Cash Flows from Financing Activities

Cash flows from financing activities include the following:

Proceeds from Issuance of Stock and Debt (Notes and Bonds Payable). Issuing stock and borrowing money are two ways to finance a company. In Exhibit 12-13, The Roadster Factory received $4,000 when it issued common stock. TRF also received $94,000 cash when it issued long-term debt (such as a note payable) to borrow money.

Payment of Debt and Purchasing the Company's Own Stock. Paying debt (notes payable) is the opposite of borrowing. TRF reports long-term debt payments of $11,000. The purchase of treasury stock is another example of a use of cash.

Payment of Cash Dividends. Paying cash dividends is a financing activity, as shown by The Roadster Factory's $17,000 payment in Exhibit 12-13. A *stock* dividend has no effect on Cash and is *not* reported on the cash-flow statement.

Noncash Investing and Financing Activities

Companies make investments that do not require cash. They also obtain financing other than cash. Our examples thus far have included none of these transactions. Now suppose that The Roadster Factory issued common stock valued at $300,000 to acquire a warehouse. TRF would journalize this transaction as follows:

Warehouse Building	300,000	
Common Stock		300,000

This transaction would not be reported as a cash payment because TRF paid no cash. But the investment in the warehouse and the issuance of stock are important.

These noncash investing and financing activities can be reported in a separate schedule under the statement of cash flows. Exhibit 12-14 illustrates noncash investing and financing activities (all amounts are assumed).

EXHIBIT 12-14 | **Noncash Investing and Financing Activities (All Amounts Assumed)**

	Thousands
Noncash Investing and Financing Activities:	
Acquisition of building by issuing common stock	$300
Acquisition of land by issuing note payable	70
Payment of long-term debt by issuing common stock	100
Total noncash investing and financing activities	$470

STOP & THINK...

Classify each of the following as an operating activity, an investing activity, or a financing activity. Also identify those items that are not reported on the statement of cash flows prepared by the *direct* method.

a. Net income
b. Payment of dividends
c. Borrowing
d. Payment of cash to suppliers
e. Making a loan
f. Sale of treasury stock
g. Depreciation expense
h. Purchase of equipment

i. Issuance of stock
j. Purchase of another company
k. Payment of a note payable
l. Payment of income taxes
m. Collections from customers
n. Accrual of interest revenue
o. Expiration of prepaid expense
p. Receipt of cash dividends

Answers:

a. Not reported
b. Financing
c. Financing
d. Operating

e. Investing
f. Financing
g. Not reported
h. Investing

i. Financing
j. Investing
k. Financing
l. Operating

m. Operating
n. Not reported
o. Not reported
p. Operating

Now let's see how to compute the operating cash flows by the direct method.

Computing Operating Cash Flows by the Direct Method

To compute operating cash flows by the direct method, we use the income statement and the *changes* in the balance sheet accounts. Exhibit 12-15 diagrams the process. Exhibit 12-16 is The Roadster Factory's income statement, and Exhibit 12-17 is the comparative balance sheet.

EXHIBIT 12-15 | **Direct Method of Computing Cash Flows from Operating Activities**

RECEIPTS / PAYMENTS	Income Statement Account	Change in Related Balance Sheet Account	
RECEIPTS:			
From customers	Sales Revenue	+ Decrease in Accounts Receivable − Increase in Accounts Receivable	
Of interest	Interest Revenue	+ Decrease in Interest Receivable − Increase in Interest Receivable	
PAYMENTS:			
To suppliers	Cost of Goods Sold	+ Increase in Inventory − Decrease in Inventory	+ Decrease in Accounts Payable − Increase in Accounts Payable
	Operating Expense	+ Increase in Prepaids − Decrease in Prepaids	+ Decrease in Accrued Liabilities − Increase in Accrued Liabilities
To employees	Salary (Wage) Expense	+ Decrease in Salary (Wage) Payable − Increase in Salary (Wage) Payable	
For interest	Interest Expense	+ Decrease in Interest Payable − Increase in Interest Payable	
For income tax	Income Tax Expense	+ Decrease in Income Tax Payable − Increase in Income Tax Payable	

*We thank Professor Barbara Gerrity for suggesting this exhibit.

EXHIBIT 12-16 | **Income Statement**

The Roadster Factory, Inc. (TRF)
Income Statement
Year Ended December 31, 2011

	(In thousands)	
Revenues and gains:		
Sales revenue	$303	
Interest revenue	?	
Gain on sale of plant assets	8	
Total revenues and gains		$313
Expenses:		
Cost of goods sold	$150	
Salary and wage expense	56	
Depreciation expense	18	
Other operating expense	17	
Income tax expense	15	
Interest expense	7	
Total expenses		263
Net income		$ 50

EXHIBIT 12-17 | Comparative Balance Sheets

The Roadster Factory, Inc. (TRF)
Comparative Balance Sheets
December 31, 2011 and 2010

(In thousands)	2011	2010	Increase (Decrease)	
Assets				
Current:				
Cash..	$ 34	$ 42	$ (8)	⎫
Accounts receivable................	96	81	15	⎪
Inventory	35	38	(3)	⎬ Changes in current assets—*Operating*
Prepaid expenses	8	7	1	⎭
Notes receivable.........................	21	—	21	⎫
Plant assets, net of depreciation...	343	219	124	⎬ Changes in noncurrent assets—*Investing*
Total	$537	$387	$150	
Liabilities				
Current:				
Accounts payable	$ 91	$ 57	$ 34	⎫
Salary and wage payable	4	6	(2)	⎬ Changes in current liabilities—*Operating*
Accrued liabilities....................	1	3	(2)	⎭
Long-term debt	160	77	83	⎫ Changes in long-term liabilities and
Stockholders' Equity				⎬ paid-in capital accounts—*Financing*
Common stock..........................	162	158	4	⎭
Retained earnings......................	119	86	33	⎫ Change due to net income—*Operating*
Total	$537	$387	$150	⎭ Change due to dividends—*Financing*

Computing Cash Collections from Customers. Collections start with sales revenue (an accrual-basis amount). The Roadster Factory's income statement (Exhibit 12-16) reports sales of $303,000. Accounts receivable increased from $81,000 at the beginning of the year to $96,000 at year-end, a $15,000 increase (Exhibit 12-17). Based on those amounts, Cash Collections equal $288,000, as follows. We must solve for cash collections (X):

Accounts Receivable

Beginning balance	+	Sales	−	Collections	=	Ending balance
$81,000	+	$303,000		−X	=	$96,000
				−X	=	$96,000 − $81,000 − $303,000
				X	=	$288,000

The T-account for Accounts Receivable provides another view of the same computation.

Accounts Receivable			
Beginning balance	81,000		
Sales	303,000	Collections	288,000
Ending balance	96,000		

Accounts Receivable increased, so collections must be less than sales.

All collections of receivables are computed this way. Let's turn now to cash receipts of interest revenue. In our example, The Roadster Factory earned interest revenue and collected cash of $2,000. The amounts of interest revenue and cash receipts of interest often differ and Exhibit 12-15 shows how to make this computation.

Computing Payments to Suppliers.   This computation includes two parts:

- Payments for inventory
- Payments for operating expenses (other than interest and income tax)

Payments for inventory are computed by converting cost of goods sold to the cash basis. We use Cost of Goods Sold, Inventory, and Accounts Payable. First, we must solve for purchases. All the amounts come from Exhibits 12-16 and 12-17.

Cost of Goods Sold					
Beginning inventory	+	Purchases	−	Ending inventory	=	Cost of goods sold
$38,000	+	X	−	$35,000	=	$150,000
		X			=	$150,000 − $38,000 + $35,000
		X			=	$147,000

Now we can compute cash payments for inventory (Y), as follows:

Accounts Payable					
Beginning balance	+	Purchases	−	Payments for inventory	=	Ending balance
$57,000	+	$147,000		−Y	=	$91,000
				−Y	=	$91,000 − $57,000 − $147,000
				Y	=	$113,000

The T-accounts show where the data come from. Start with Cost of Goods Sold.

Cost of Goods Sold					Accounts Payable			
Beg inventory	38,000	End inventory	35,000		Payments for		Beg bal	57,000
Purchases	147,000				inventory	113,000	Purchases	147,000
Cost of goods sold	150,000						End bal	91,000

Accounts Payable increased, so payments for inventory are less than purchases.

Computing Payments for Operating Expenses. Payments for operating expenses other than interest and income tax are computed from three accounts: Prepaid Expenses, Accrued Liabilities, and Other Operating Expenses. All The Roadster Factory data come from Exhibits 12-16 and 12-17.

Prepaid Expenses

Beginning balance	+	Payments	−	Expiration of prepaid expense (assumed)	=	Ending balance
$7,000	+	X	−	$7,000	=	$8,000
		X			=	$8,000 − $7,000 + $7,000
		X			=	$8,000

Accrued Liabilities

Beginning balance	+	Accrual of expense at year-end (assumed)	−	Payments	=	Ending balance
$3,000	+	$1,000		−X	=	$1,000
				−X	=	$1,000 − $3,000 − $1,000
				X	=	$3,000

Other Operating Expenses

Accrual of expense at year-end	+	Expiration of prepaid expense	−	Payments	=	Ending balance
$1,000	+	$7,000		X	=	$17,000
				X	=	$17,000 − $1,000 − $7,000
				X	=	$9,000
		Total payments for operating expenses			=	$8,000 + $3,000 + $9,000
					=	$20,000

The T-accounts give another picture of the same data.

Prepaid Expenses				Accrued Liabilities				Other Operating Expenses		
Beg bal	7,000	Expiration of				Beg bal	3,000	Accrual of	1,000	
Payments	8,000	prepaid		Payment	3,000	Accrual of		expense at		
		expense	7,000			expense at		year-end		
End bal	8,000					year-end	1,000	Expiration of		
						End bal	1,000	prepaid		
								expense	7,000	
								Payments	9,000	
								End bal	17,000	

Total payments for operating expenses = $20,000($8,000 + $3,000 + $9,000)

Now we can compute Payments to Suppliers as follows:

Payments to Suppliers	=	Payments for Inventory	+	Payments for Operating Expenses
$133,000	=	$113,000	+	$20,000

Computing Payments to Employees.   It is convenient to combine all payments to employees into one account, Salary and Wage Expense. We then adjust the expense for the change in Salary and Wage Payable, as shown here:

Salary and Wage Payable						
Beginning balance	+	Salary and wage expense	–	Payments	=	Ending balance
$6,000	+	$56,000		–X	=	$4,000
				–X	=	$4,000 – $6,000 – $56,000
				X	=	$58,000

Salary and Wage Payable		
	Beginning balance	6,000
Payments to employees 58,000	Salary and wage expense	56,000
	Ending balance	4,000

Computing Payments of Interest and Income Taxes.   The Roadster Factory's expense and payment amounts are the same for interest and income tax, so no analysis is required. If the expense and the payment differ, the payment can be computed as shown in Exhibit 12-15.

Computing Investing and Financing Cash Flows

Investing and financing activities are explained on pages 712–716. These computations are the same for both the direct and the indirect methods.

STOP & THINK. . .

Fidelity Company reported the following for 2011 and 2010 (in millions):

At December 31,	2011	2010
Receivables, net	$3,500	$3,900
Inventory	5,200	5,000
Accounts payable	900	1,200
Income taxes payable	600	700

Year Ended December 31,	2011
Revenues...	$23,000
Cost of goods sold........................	14,100
Income tax expense......................	900

Based on these figures, how much cash did
- Fidelity collect from customers during 2011?
- Fidelity pay for inventory during 2011?
- Fidelity pay for income taxes during 2011?

Answers

	Beginning Receivables	+	Revenues	−	Collections	=	Ending Receivables
Collections from customers = $23,400:	$3,900	+	$23,000	−	$23,400	=	$3,500

	Cost of Goods Sold	+	Increase in Inventory	+	Decrease in Accounts Payable	=	Payments
Payments for inventory = $14,600:	$14,100	+ ($5,200 − $5,000) +			($1,200 − $900)	=	$14,600

	Beginning Income Taxes Payable	+	Income Tax Expense	−	Payment	=	Ending Income Taxes Payable
Payment of income taxes = $1,000:	$700	+	$900	−	$1,000	=	$600

MEASURING CASH ADEQUACY: FREE CASH FLOW

Throughout this chapter, we have focused on cash flows from operating, investing, and financing activities. Some investors want to know how much cash a company can "free up" for new opportunities. **Free cash flow** is the amount of cash available from operations after paying for planned investments in plant assets. Free cash flow can be computed as follows:

$$\text{Free cash flow} = \frac{\text{Net cash provided}}{\text{by operating activities}} - \frac{\text{Cash payments earmarked for}}{\text{investments in plant assets}}$$

PepsiCo, Inc., uses free cash flow to manage its operations. Suppose PepsiCo expects net cash inflow of $2.3 billion from operations. Assume PepsiCo plans to spend $1.9 billion to modernize its bottling plants. In this case, PepsiCo's free cash flow would be $0.4 billion ($2.3 billion − $1.9 billion). If a good investment opportunity comes along, PepsiCo should have $0.4 billion to invest in the other company. **Shell Oil Company** also uses free-cash-flow analysis. A large amount of free cash flow is preferable because it means that a lot of cash is available for new investments. The Decision Guidelines that follow show some ways to use cash-flow and income data for investment and credit analysis.

DECISION GUIDELINES

INVESTORS' AND CREDITORS' USE OF CASH-FLOW AND RELATED INFORMATION

Jan Childres is a private investor. Through years of experience she has devised some guidelines for evaluating both stock investments and bond investments. Childres uses a combination of accrual-accounting data and cash-flow information. Here are her decision guidelines for both investors and creditors.

INVESTORS

Questions	Factors to Consider	Financial Statement Predictor/Decision Model*
1. How much in dividends can I expect to receive from an investment in stock?	Expected future net income	Income from continuing operations**
	Expected future cash balance	Net cash flows from (in order): ■ Operating activities ■ Investing activities ■ Financing activities
	Future dividend policy	Current and past dividend policy
2. Is the stock price likely to increase or decrease?	Expected future net income	Income from continuing operations**
	Expected future cash flows from operating activities	Income from continuing operations** Net cash flow from operating activities
3. What is the future stock price likely to be?	Expected future income from ■ continuing operations, and ■ net cash flow from operating activities	$\frac{\text{Expected future price}}{\text{of a share of stock}} = \frac{\text{Net cash flow from operations per share}}{\text{Investment capitalization rate**}}$ $\frac{\text{Expected future price}}{\text{of a share of stock}} = \frac{\text{Expected future earnings per share**}}{\text{Investment capitalization rate**}}$

CREDITORS

Questions	Factors to Consider	Financial Statement Predictor
Can the company pay the interest and principal at the maturity of a loan?	Expected future net cash flow from operating activities	Income from continuing operations** Net cash flow from operating activities

*There are many other factors to consider in making these decisions. These are some of the more common.
**See Chapter 11.

END-OF-CHAPTER SUMMARY PROBLEM

Adeva Health Foods, Inc., reported the following comparative balance sheet and income statement for 2011.

Adeva Health Foods, Inc.
Comparative Balance Sheets
December 31, 2011 and 2010

	2011	2010
Cash..	$ 19,000	$ 3,000
Accounts receivable...............	22,000	23,000
Inventories	34,000	31,000
Prepaid expenses	1,000	3,000
Equipment, net.......................	90,000	79,000
Intangible assets	9,000	9,000
	$175,000	$148,000
Accounts payable	$ 14,000	$ 9,000
Accrued liabilities..................	16,000	19,000
Income tax payable	14,000	12,000
Notes payable	45,000	50,000
Common stock.......................	31,000	20,000
Retained earnings..................	64,000	40,000
Treasury stock.......................	(9,000)	(2,000)
	$175,000	$148,000

Adeva Health Foods, Inc.
Income Statement
Year Ended December 31, 2011

Sales revenue	$190,000
Gain on sale of equipment..................	6,000
Total revenue and gains	196,000
Cost of goods sold.............................	85,000
Depreciation expense	19,000
Other operating expenses...................	36,000
Total expenses	140,000
Income before income tax	56,000
Income tax expense............................	18,000
Net income..	$ 38,000

Assume that **Berkshire Hathaway** is considering buying Adeva. Berkshire Hathaway requests the following cash-flow data for 2011. There were no noncash investing and financing activities.

a. Collections from customers
b. Cash payments for inventory
c. Cash payments for operating expenses
d. Cash payment for income tax
e. Cash received from the sale of equipment. Adeva paid $40,000 for new equipment during the year.

f. Issuance of common stock
g. Issuance of notes payable. Adeva paid off $20,000 during the year.
h. Cash dividends. There were no stock dividends.

Provide the requested data. Show your work.

Answers

a. Analyze Accounts Receivable (let X = Collections from customers):

Beginning	+	Sales	−	Collections	=	Ending
$23,000	+	$190,000	−	X	=	$22,000
				X	=	$191,000

b. Analyze Inventory and Accounts Payable (let X = Purchases, and let Y = Payments for inventory):

Beginning Inventory	+	Purchases	−	Ending Inventory	=	Cost of Goods Sold
$31,000	+	X	−	$34,000	=	$85,000
		X			=	$88,000

Beginning Accounts Payable	+	Purchases	−	Payments	=	Ending Accounts Payable
$9,000	+	$88,000	−	Y	=	$14,000
				Y	=	$83,000

c. Start with Other Operating Expenses, and adjust for the changes in Prepaid Expenses and Accrued Liabilities:

Other Operating Expenses	− Decrease in Prepaid Expenses	+ Decrease in Accrued Liabilities	=	Payments for Operating Expenses
$36,000	− $2,000	+ $3,000	=	$37,000

d. Analyze Income Tax Payable (let X = Payment of income tax):

Beginning	+	Income Tax Expense	−	Payments	=	Ending
$12,000	+	$18,000	−	X	=	$14,000
				X	=	$16,000

e. Analyze Equipment, Net (let X = Book value of equipment sold. Then combine with the gain or loss to compute cash received from the sale.)

Beginning	+	Acquisitions	–	Depreciation	–	Book Value Sold	=	Ending
$79,000	+	$40,000	–	$19,000	–	X	=	$90,000
						X	=	$10,000

Cash Received from Sale	=	Book Value Sold	+	Gain on Sale
$16,000	=	$10,000	+	$6,000

f. Analyze Common Stock (let X = Issuance)

Beginning	+	Issuance	=	Ending
$20,000	+	X	=	$31,000
		X	=	$11,000

g. Analyze Notes Payable (let X = Issuance):

Beginning	+	Issuance	–	Payment	=	Ending
$50,000	+	X	–	$20,000	=	$45,000
		X			=	$15,000

h. Analyze Retained Earnings (let X = Dividends)

Beginning	+	Net Income	–	Dividends	=	Ending
$40,000	+	$38,000	–	X	=	$64,000
				X	=	$14,000

REVIEW STATEMENT OF CASH FLOWS

Quick Check (Answers are given on page 774.)

1. All of the following activities are reported on the statement of cash flows except:
   a. marketing activities.   c. operating activities.
   b. investing activities.   d. financing activities.

2. Activities that create long-term liabilities are usually
   a. financing activities.
   b. operating activities.
   c. noncash investing and financing activities.
   d. investing activities.

3. Activities affecting long-term assets are
   a. financing activities.   c. operating activities.
   b. marketing activities.   d. investing activities.

4. In 2010, PMW Corporation borrowed $110,000, paid dividends of $34,000, issued 10,000 shares of stock for $45 per share, purchased land for $240,000, and received dividends of $10,000. Net income was $150,000, and depreciation for the year totaled $8,000. How much should be reported as net cash provided by operating activities by the indirect method?

   a. $194,000   c. $234,000
   b. $158,000   d. $134,000

5. Activities that obtain the cash needed to launch and sustain a company are
   a. marketing activities.   c. investing activities.
   b. income activities.   d. financing activities.

6. The exchange of stock for land would be reported as
   a. Exchanges are not reported on the statement of cash flows.
   b. financing activities.
   c. noncash investing and financing activities.
   d. investing activities.

Use the following Montana Company information for questions 7–10.

Net income..	$50,000	Increase in accounts payable	$ 9,000
Depreciation expense	10,000	Acquisition of equipment	35,000
Payment of dividends	1,000	Sale of treasury stock	4,000
Increase in accounts receivable	8,000	Payment of long-term debt	16,000
Collection of long-term notes receivable..........	5,000	Proceeds from sale of land..........	40,000
Loss on sale of land..	15,000	Decrease in inventories..............	3,000

7. Under the indirect method, net cash provided by operating activities would be
   a. $84,000.   c. $79,000.
   b. $76,000.   d. $89,000.

8. Net cash provided by (used for) investing activities would be
   a. $20,000.   c. $(15,000).
   b. $10,000.   d. $(10,000).

9. Net cash provided by (used for) financing activities would be
   a. $3,000.   c. $(21,000).
   b. $(13,000).   d. $1,000.

10. The cost of land must have been
   a. $40,000.
   b. $55,000.
   c. $25,000.
   d. cannot be determined from the data given.

11. Sweet Treat Ice Cream began the year with $60,000 in accounts receivable and ended the year with $50,000 in accounts receivable. If sales for the year were $700,000, the cash collected from customers during the year amounted to
   a. $690,000.   c. $750,000.
   b. $760,000.   d. $710,000.

12. Nassau Farms, Ltd., made sales of $750,000 and had cost of goods sold of $410,000. Inventory decreased by $10,000 and accounts payable decreased by $12,000. Operating expenses were $180,000. How much was Nassau Farms' net income for the year?
   a. $150,000.   c. $148,000.
   b. $160,000.   d. $340,000.

13. Use the Nassau Farms data from question 12. How much cash did Nassau Farms pay for inventory during the year?
   a. $410,000.   c. $422,000.
   b. $400,000.   d. $412,000.

Accounting Vocabulary

cash equivalents (p. 704) Highly liquid short-term investments that can be converted into cash immediately.

cash flows (p. 703) Cash receipts and cash payments (disbursements).

direct method (p. 706) Format of the operating activities section of the statement of cash flows; lists the major categories of operating cash receipts (collections from customers and receipts of interest and dividends) and cash disbursements (payments to suppliers, to employees, for interest and income taxes).

financing activities (p. 705) Activities that obtain from investors and creditors the cash needed to launch and sustain the business; a section of the statement of cash flows.

free cash flow (p. 732) The amount of cash available from operations after paying for planned investments in plant assets.

indirect method (p. 706) Format of the operating activities section of the statement of cash flows; starts with net income and reconciles to cash flows from operating activities.

investing activities (p. 705) Activities that increase or decrease the long-term assets available to the business; a section of the statement of cash flows.

operating activities (p. 705) Activities that create revenue or expense in the entity's major line of business; a section of the statement of cash flows. Operating activities affect the income statement.

statement of cash flows (p. 703) Reports cash receipts and cash payments classified according to the entity's major activities: operating, investing, and financing.

ASSESS YOUR PROGRESS

Short Exercises

S12-1 (*Learning Objectives 1, 2, 3: Explaining the purposes of the statement of cash flows*) State how the statement of cash flows helps investors and creditors perform each of the following functions:

    a. Predict future cash flows.

    b. Evaluate management decisions.

writing assignment ■

S12-2 (*Learning Objectives 1, 2, 3: Explaining the purposes of the statement of cash flows*) U.S. Rondeau, Inc., has experienced an unbroken string of nine years of growth in net income. Nevertheless, the company is facing bankruptcy. Creditors are calling all of U.S. Rondeau's loans for immediate payment, and the cash is simply not available. It is clear that the company's top managers overemphasized profits and gave too little attention to cash flows.

❙ Requirement

    1. Write a brief memo, in your own words, to explain to the managers of U.S. Rondeau, Inc., the purposes of the statement of cash flows.

S12-3 (*Learning Objective 2: Evaluating operating cash flows—indirect method*)   Examine the statement of cash flows of Clock, Inc.

Clock, Inc.		
Consolidated Statement of Cash Flows (Adapted; in millions)		
Year Ended December 31, 2010		
Cash Flows from Operating Activities		
Net income...	$ 983	
Adjustment to reconcile net income to net cash provided by operating activities:		
Depreciation and amortization	278	
Change in assets and liabilities, net of acquired businesses:		
Accounts receivable...	(587)	
Other current assets...	(200)	
Accounts payable	(98)	
Accrued expenses and other liabilities	(298)	
Unearned revenue..	31	
Income taxes payable	(333)	
Other, net	33	
Net cash used in operating activities............................		(191)
Cash Flows from Investing Activities		
Purchase of property and equipment................................	$ (1,991)	
Purchase of investments	(26,603)	
Sale of investments...	24,108	
Acquisitions of other companies	(454)	
Net cash used in investing activities............................		(4,940)
Cash Flows from Financing Activities		
Proceeds from the issuance of common stock, net.............	$ 1,043	
Other, net..	473	
Net cash provided by financing activities.......................		1,516
Other, net..		22
Net increase (decrease) in cash and cash equivalents		(3,593)
Cash and cash equivalents at beginning of year..................		5,194
Cash and cash equivalents at end of year...........................		$ 1,601

Suppose Clock's operating activities *provided*, rather than *used*, cash. Identify three things under the indirect method that could cause operating cash flows to be positive.

S12-4 (*Learning Objectives 1, 2: Using cash-flow data to evaluate performance*)   Top managers of Tranquility Inns are reviewing company performance for 2010. The income statement reports a 25% increase in net income over 2009. However, most of the increase resulted from an extraordinary gain on insurance proceeds from fire damage to a building. The balance sheet shows a large increase in receivables. The cash flows statement, in summarized form, reports the following:

writing assignment ■

Net cash used for operating activities......................	$(50,000)
Net cash provided by investing activities................	30,000
Net cash provided by financing activities................	25,000
Increase in cash during 2010.................................	$ 5,000

❚ Requirement

1. Write a memo giving Tranquility Inns' managers your assessment of 2010 operations and your outlook for the future. Focus on the information content of the cash flows data.

S12-5 (*Learning Objective 3: Reporting cash flows from operating activities—indirect method*) Beautiful America Transportation (BAT) began 2010 with accounts receivable, inventory, and prepaid expenses totaling $58,000. At the end of the year, BAT had a total of $55,000 for these current assets. At the beginning of 2010, BAT owed current liabilities of $20,000, and at year-end current liabilities totaled $32,000.

Net income for the year was $12,000. Included in net income were a $2,000 loss on the sale of land and depreciation expense of $8,000.

Show how BAT should report cash flows from operating activities for 2010. BAT uses the *indirect* method.

S12-6 (*Learning Objectives 2, 3: Identifying items for reporting cash flows from operations—indirect method*) Campbell Clinic, Inc., is preparing its statement of cash flows (*indirect* method) for the year ended March 31, 2010. Consider the following items in preparing the company's statement of cash flows. Identify each item as an operating activity—addition to net income (O+) or subtraction from net income (O-), an investing activity (I), a financing activity (F), or an activity that is not used to prepare the cash flows statement by the indirect method (N). Place the appropriate symbol in the blank space.

	a. Increase in accounts payable
	b. Purchase of equipment
	c. Decrease in prepaid expense
	d. Collection of cash from customers
	e. Net income
	f. Retained earnings
	g. Payment of dividends
	h. Decrease in accrued liabilities
	i. Issuance of common stock
	j. Gain on sale of building
	k. Loss on sale of land
	l. Depreciation expense
	m. Increase in inventory
	n. Decrease in accounts receivable

S12-7 (*Learning Objective 3: Computing operating cash flows—indirect method*) Ethan Corporation accountants have assembled the following data for the year ended June 30, 2010.

Net income................................	$?	Cost of goods sold....................	$116,000
Payment of dividends	5,600	Other operating expenses.........	33,000
Proceeds from the issuance		Purchase of equipment.............	43,000
of common stock	26,000	Increase in current liabilities.....	7,000
Sales revenue............................	228,000	Payment of note payable	32,000
Decrease in current assets		Proceeds from sale of land........	29,000
other than cash	35,000	Depreciation expense	11,000
Purchase of treasury stock........	6,000		

Prepare the *operating activities section* of Ethan's statement of cash flows for the year ended June 30, 2010. Ethan uses the *indirect* method for operating cash flows.

S12-8 (*Learning Objective 3: Preparing a statement of cash flows—indirect method*) Use the data in Short Exercise 12-7 to prepare Ethan Corporation's statement of cash flows for the year ended June 30, 2010. Ethan uses the *indirect* method for operating activities.

S12-9 (*Learning Objective 3: Computing investing cash flows*) Motorsports of Miami, Inc., reported the following financial statements for 2010:

Motorsports of Miami, Inc.
Income Statement
Year Ended December 31, 2010

(In thousands)

Service revenue	$770
Cost of goods sold	330
Salary expense	40
Depreciation expense	30
Other expenses	170
Total expenses	570
Net income	$200

Motorsports of Miami, Inc.
Comparative Balance Sheets
December 31, 2010 and 2009

(In thousands)

Assets	2010	2009	Liabilities	2010	2009
Current:			Current:		
Cash	$ 28	$ 11	Accounts payable	$ 48	$ 43
Accounts receivable	54	43	Salary payable	26	24
Inventory	77	89	Accrued liabilities	16	19
Prepaid expenses	6	5	Long-term notes payable	69	54
Long-term investments	54	79			
Plant assets, net	229	188	**Stockholders' Equity**		
			Common stock	48	38
			Retained earnings	241	237
Total	$448	$415	Total	$448	$415

Compute the following investing cash flows: (Enter all amounts in thousands.)

a. Acquisitions of plant assets (all were for cash). Motorsports of Miami sold no plant assets.

b. Proceeds from the sale of investments. Motorsports of Miami purchased no investments.

S12-10 (*Learning Objective 3: Computing financing cash flows*) Use the Motorsports of Miami data in Short Exercise 12-9 to compute the following: (Enter all amounts in thousands.)

a. New borrowing or payment of long-term notes payable. Motorsports of Miami had only one long-term note payable transaction during the year.

b. Issuance of common stock or retirement of common stock. Motorsports of Miami had only one common stock transaction during the year.

c. Payment of cash dividends (same as dividends declared).

S12-11 *(Learning Objective 4: Computing operating cash flows—direct method)* Use the Motorsports of Miami data in Short Exercise 12-9 to compute the following: (Enter all amounts in thousands.)

    a. Collections from customers
    b. Payments for inventory

S12-12 *(Learning Objective 4: Computing operating cash flows—direct method)* Use the Motorcars of Miami data in Short Exercise 12-9 to compute the following: (Enter all amounts in thousands).

    a. Payments to employees
    b. Payments of other expenses

S12-13 *(Learning Objective 4: Preparing a statement of cash flows—direct method)* Horse Heaven Horse Farm, Inc., began 2010 with cash of $170,000. During the year, Horse Heaven earned service revenue of $590,000 and collected $480,000 from customers. Expenses for the year totaled $320,000, with $310,000 paid in cash to suppliers and employees. Horse Heaven also paid $136,000 to purchase equipment and a cash dividend of $49,000 to stockholders. During 2010, Horse Heaven borrowed $26,000 by issuing a note payable. Prepare the company's statement of cash flows for the year. Format operating activities by the *direct* method.

S12-14 *(Learning Objective 4: Computing operating cash flows—direct method)* Middleton Golf Club, Inc., has assembled the following data for the year ended September 30, 2010:

Cost of goods sold............................	$104,000	Payment of dividends..........................	$ 8,000
Payments to suppliers........................	90,000	Proceeds from issuance	
Purchase of equipment	42,000	of common stock	16,000
Payments to employees.....................	75,000	Sales revenue......................................	211,000
Payment of note payable	15,000	Collections from customers................	203,000
Proceeds from sale of land................	61,000	Payment of income tax.......................	14,000
Depreciation expense	6,000	Purchase of treasury stock.................	5,700

Prepare the *operating activities section* of Middleton Golf Club, Inc.'s statement of cash flows for the year ended September 30, 2010. Middleton uses the *direct* method for operating cash flows.

S12-15 *(Learning Objective 4: Preparing a statement of cash flows—direct method)* Use the data in Short Exercise 12-14 to prepare Middleton Golf Club, Inc.'s statement of cash flows for the year ended September 30, 2010. Middleton uses the *direct* method for operating activities.

Exercises

All of the A and B exercises can be found within MyAccountingLab, an online homework and practice environment. Your instructor may ask you to complete these exercises using MyAccountingLab.

(Group A)

E12-16A *(Learning Objectives 2, 3: Identifying activities for the statement of cash flows—indirect method)* Tucker-Breen Investments specializes in low-risk government bonds. Identify each of Tucker-Breen's transactions as operating (O), investing (I), financing (F), noncash investing and financing (NIF), or a transaction that is not reported on the statement of cash flows (N). Indicate whether each item increases (+) or decreases (–) cash. The *indirect* method is used for operating activities.

☐	a. Sale of long-term investment
☐	b. Issuance of long-term note payable to borrow cash
☐	c. Increase in prepaid expenses
☐	d. Payment of cash dividend
☐	e. Loss of sale of equipment
☐	f. Decrease in merchandise inventory
☐	g. Acquisition of equipment by issuance of note payable
☐	h. Increase in accounts payable
☐	i. Amortization of intangible assets
☐	j. Net income
☐	k. Payment of long-term debt
☐	l. Accrual of salary expense
☐	m. Cash sale of land
☐	n. Purchase of long-term investment
☐	o. Acquisition of building by cash payment
☐	p. Purchase of treasury stock
☐	q. Issuance of common stock for cash
☐	r. Decrease in accrued liabilities
☐	s. Depreciation of equipment

E12-17A (*Learning Objectives 2, 3: Classifying transactions for the statement of cash flows—indirect method*)   Indicate whether each of the following transactions records an operating activity, an investing activity, a financing activity, or a noncash investing and financing activity.

a.	Depreciation Expense	11,000		h.	Cash	50,000	
	Accumulated Depreciation		11,000		Accounts Receivable	9,000	
b.	Treasury Stock	7,800			Service Revenue		59,000
	Cash		7,800	i.	Bonds Payable	47,000	
c.	Land	83,000			Cash		47,000
	Cash		83,000	j.	Cash	74,000	
d.	Equipment	19,000			Common Stock		11,000
	Cash		19,000		Capital in Excess of Par		63,000
e.	Salary Expense	24,000		k.	Dividends Payable	17,100	
	Cash		24,000		Cash		17,100
f.	Furniture and Fixtures	24,200		l.	Loss on Disposal of Equipment	1,200	
	Cash		24,200		Equipment, Net		1,200
g.	Building	159,000		m.	Cash	6,900	
	Note Payable, Long-Term		159,000		Long-Term Investment		6,900

E12-18A (*Learning Objective 3: Computing cash flows from operating activities—indirect method*)   The accounting records of North East Distributors, Inc., reveal the following: **writing assignment ■**

Net income..	$38,000	Depreciation..................................	$17,000
Collection of dividend revenue..........	7,800	Decrease in current liabilities..........	19,000
Payment of interest............................	11,000	Increase in current assets	
Sales revenue......................................	13,000	other than cash	24,000
Loss on sale of land...........................	22,000	Payment of dividends	7,800
Acquisition of land	42,000	Payment of income tax...................	15,000

❙ Requirement

1. Compute cash flows from operating activities by the *indirect* method. Use the format of the operating activities section of Exhibit 12-6. Also evaluate the operating cash flow of North East Distributors. Give the reason for your evaluation.

E12-19A (*Learning Objective 3: Computing cash flows from operating activities—indirect method*) The accounting records of Wilderness Fur Traders include these accounts:

Cash		
May 1	90,000	
Receipts	440,000	Payments 445,000
May 31	85,000	

Accounts Receivable		
May 1	1,000	
Receipts	540,000	Collections 440,000
May 31	101,000	

Inventory		
May 1	3,000	
Purchases	438,000	Cost of sales 336,000
May 31	105,000	

Equipment	
May 1	185,000
Acquisition	5,000
May 31	190,000

Accumulated Deprec.—Equipment		
	May 1	55,000
	Depreciation	5,000
	May 31	60,000

Accounts Payable		
	May 1	14,500
Payments 327,000	Purchases	438,000
	May 31	125,500

Accrued Liabilities		
	May 1	19,000
Payments 32,000	Receipts	26,000
	May 31	13,000

Retained Earnings		
Quarterly	May 1	63,000
Dividend 16,000	Net Income	20,000
	May 31	67,000

❚ Requirement

1. Compute Wilderness net cash provided by (used for) operating activities during May. Use the *indirect* method. Does Wilderness have trouble collecting receivables or selling inventory? How can you tell?

writing assignment ■

E12-20A (*Learning Objective 3: Preparing the statement of cash flows—indirect method*) The income statement and additional data of Newbury Travel Products, Inc., follow:

Newbury Travel Products, Inc.
Income Statement
Year Ended December 31, 2010

Revenues:		
Service revenue	$283,000	
Dividend revenue	8,000	$291,000
Expenses:		
Cost of goods sold	103,000	
Salary expense	78,000	
Depreciation expense	26,000	
Advertising expense	4,500	
Interest expense	2,600	
Income tax expense	8,000	222,100
Net income		$ 68,900

Additional data:

a. Acquisition of plant assets was $212,000. Of this amount, $160,000 was paid in cash and $52,000 by signing a note payable.
b. Proceeds from sale of land totaled $27,000.
c. Proceeds from issuance of common stock totaled $80,000.
d. Payment of long-term note payable was $17,000.
e. Payment of dividends was $13,000.
f. From the balance sheets:

	December 31,	
	2010	2009
Current Assets:		
Cash	$30,000	$10,800
Accounts receivable	42,000	59,000
Inventory...............................	30,000	91,000
Prepaid expenses....................	9,400	8,700
Current Liabilities:		
Accounts payable...................	$38,000	$27,000
Accrued liabilities	18,000	99,000

Requirements

1. Prepare Newbury's statement of cash flows for the year ended December 31, 2010, using the *indirect* method.
2. Evaluate Newbury's cash flows for the year. In your evaluation, mention all three categories of cash flows and give the reason for your evaluation.

E12-21A (*Learning Objective 3: Interpreting a statement of cash flows—indirect method*)   Consider three independent cases for the cash flows of 579 Pavilion Shoes. For each case, identify from the statement of cash flows how 579 Pavilion Shoes generated the cash to acquire new plant assets. Rank the three cases from the most healthy financially to the least healthy.

	Case A	Case B	Case C
Cash flows from operating activities			
Net income	$ 20,000	$ 20,000	$ 20,000
Depreciation and amortization	9,000	9,000	9,000
Increase in current assets	(22,000)	(2,000)	(11,000)
Decrease in current liabilities	(10,000)	(4,000)	(1,000)
	(3,000)	23,000	17,000
Cash flows from investing activities:			
Acquisition of plant assets	(83,000)	(83,000)	(83,000)
Sales of plant assets	9,000	37,000	90,000
	(74,000)	(46,000)	7,000
Cash flows from financing activities:			
Issuance of stock............................	97,000	62,000	15,000
Payment of debt............................	(22,000)	(38,000)	(23,000)
	75,000	24,000	(8,000)
Net increase (decrease) in cash	$ (2,000)	$ 1,000	$ 16,000

E12-22A (*Learning Objectives 3, 4: Computing investing and financing amounts for the statement of cash flows*)   Compute the following items for the statement of cash flows:

a. Beginning and ending Plant Assets, Net, are $110,000 and $106,000, respectively. Depreciation for the period was $9,000, and purchases of new plant assets were $33,000. Plant assets were sold at a $4,000 loss. What were the cash proceeds of the sale?

b. Beginning and ending Retained Earnings are $49,000 and $74,000, respectively. Net income for the period was $58,000, and stock dividends were $7,000. How much were cash dividends?

writing assignment ■

E12-23A (*Learning Objective 4: Computing cash flows from operating activities—direct method*)   The accounting records of Princeton Pharmaceuticals, Inc., reveal the following:

Payment of salaries and wages	$35,000	Net income	$60,000
Depreciation	20,000	Payment of income tax	24,000
Decrease in current liabilities	22,000	Collection of dividend revenue	10,000
Increase in current assets other than cash	23,000	Payment of interest	17,000
Payment of dividends	7,000	Cash sales	33,000
Collection of accounts receivable	50,000	Loss on sale of land	6,000
		Acquisition of land	38,000
		Payment of accounts payable	58,000

❚ Requirement

1. Compute cash flows from operating activities by the *direct* method. Also evaluate Princeton's operating cash flow. Give the reason for your evaluation.

E12-24A (*Learning Objective 4: Identifying items for the statement of cash flows—direct method*)   Selected accounts of Ashley Antiques show the following:

Salary Payable

		Beginning balance	10,000
Payments	30,000	Salary expense	28,000
		Ending balance	8,000

Buildings

Beginning balance	80,000	Depreciation	20,000
Acquisitions	120,000	Book value of building sold	119,000*
Ending balance	61,000		

*Sale price was 150,000.

Notes Payable

		Beginning balance	234,000
Payments	67,000	Issuance of note payable for cash	74,000
		Ending balance	241,000

❚ Requirement

1. For each account, identify the item or items that should appear on a statement of cash flows prepared by the *direct* method. State where to report the item.

E12-25A (*Learning Objective 4: Preparing the statement of cash flows—direct method*)   The
income statement and additional data of Cobbs Hill, Inc., follow:

Cobbs Hill, Inc.
Income Statement
Year Ended April 30, 2010

Revenues:
Sales revenue......................	$232,000	
Dividend revenue...............	11,000	$243,000
Expenses:		
Cost of goods sold..............	108,000	
Salary expense	46,000	
Depreciation expense..........	31,000	
Advertising expense............	11,500	
Interest expense	2,100	
Income tax expense.............	9,000	207,600
Net income		$ 35,400

Additional data:

  a. Collections from customers are $13,000 more than sales.
  b. Payments to suppliers are $1,300 less than the sum of cost of goods sold plus advertising expense.
  c. Payments to employees are $2,000 more than salary expense.
  d. Dividend revenue, interest expense, and income tax expense equal their cash amounts.
  e. Acquisition of plant assets is $143,000. Of this amount, $100,000 is paid in cash and $43,000 by signing a note payable.
  f. Proceeds from sale of land total $28,000.
  g. Proceeds from issuance of common stock total $93,000.
  h. Payment of long-term note payable is $17,000.
  i. Payment of dividends is $8,500.
  j. Cash balance, April 30, 2009, was $21,000.

❚ Requirements

  1. Prepare Cobbs Hill, Inc.'s statement of cash flows and accompanying schedule of noncash investing and financing activities. Report operating activities by the *direct* method.
  2. Evaluate Cobbs Hill's cash flows for the year. In your evaluation, mention all three categories of cash flows and give the reason for your evaluation.

E12-26A (*Learning Objective 4: Computing amounts for the statement of cash flows—direct method*)   Compute the following items for the statement of cash flows:

  a. Beginning and ending Accounts Receivable are $25,000 and $20,000, respectively. Credit sales for the period total $62,000. How much are cash collections from customers?
  b. Cost of goods sold is $79,000. Beginning Inventory was $26,000, and ending Inventory balance is $29,000. Beginning and ending Accounts Payable are $11,000 and $9,000, respectively. How much are cash payments for inventory?

(Group B)

E12-27B (*Learning Objectives 2, 3: Identifying activities for the statement of cash flows—indirect method*) Burke-Cassidy Investments specializes in low-risk government bonds. Identify each of Burke-Cassidy's transactions as operating (O), investing (I), financing (F), noncash investing and financing (NIF), or a transaction that is not reported on the statement of cash flows (N). Indicate whether each item increases (+) or decreases (−) cash. The *indirect* method is used for operating activities.

a. Acquisition of building by cash payment
b. Decrease in merchandise inventory
c. Depreciation of equipment
d. Decrease in accrued liabilities
e. Payment of cash dividend
f. Purchase of long-term investment
g. Issuance of long-term note payable to borrow cash
h. Increase in prepaid expenses
i. Accrual of salary expense
j. Acquisition of equipment by issuance of note payable
k. Sale of long-term investment
l. Issuance of common stock for cash
m. Increase in accounts payable
n. Amortization of intangible assets
o. Loss of sale of equipment
p. Payment of long-term debt
q. Cash sale of land
r. Purchase of treasury stock
s. Net income

E12-28B (*Learning Objectives 2, 3: Classifying transactions for the statement of cash flows—indirect method*) Indicate whether each of the following transactions records an operating activity, an investing activity, a financing activity, or a noncash investing and financing activity.

a.	Cash	85,000		g.	Equipment	15,600	
	Common Stock		14,000		Cash		15,600
	Capital in Excess of Par		71,000	h.	Dividends Payable	18,200	
b.	Furniture and Fixtures	25,600			Cash		18,200
	Cash		25,600	i.	Salary Expense	19,400	
c.	Cash	72,000			Cash		19,400
	Accounts Receivable	15,000		j.	Building	146,000	
	Service Revenue		87,000		Note Payable—Long-Term		146,000
d.	Cash	9,100		k.	Dividends Payable	17,100	
	Long-Term Investment		9,100		Cash		17,100
e.	Loss on Disposal of Equipment	1,500		l.	Depreciation Expense	7,000	
	Equipment, Net		1,500		Accumulated Depreciation		7,000
f.	Land	20,300		m.	Bonds Payable	49,000	
	Cash		20,300		Cash		49,000

E12-29B (*Learning Objective 3: Computing cash flows from operating activities—indirect*   <u>**writing assignment ■**</u>
method)   The accounting records of Central Distributors, Inc., reveal the following:

Net income...	$40,000	Depreciation....................................	$15,000
Collection of dividend revenue..........	6,900	Increase in current liabilities...........	23,000
Payment of interest..........................	14,000	Decrease in current assets	
Sales revenue....................................	12,000	other than cash....................	28,000
Loss on sale of land..........................	19,000	Payment of dividends....................	7,200
Acquisition of land	43,000	Payment of income tax..................	12,000

▌Requirement

1. Compute cash flows from operating activities by the *indirect* method. Use the format of the operating activities section of Exhibit 12-6. Also evaluate the operating cash flow of Central Distributors. Give the reason for your evaluation.

E12-30B (*Learning Objective 3: Computing cash flows from operating activities—indirect method*)   The accounting records of Lawrence Fur Traders include these accounts:

Cash				Accounts Receivable				Inventory			
Oct 1	11,000			Oct 1	8,000			Oct 1	4,000		
Receipts	537,000	Payments	446,000	Receipts	538,000	Collections	537,000	Purchases	437,000	Cost of sales	434,000
Oct 31	102,000			Oct 31	9,000			Oct 31	7,000		

Equipment				Accumulated Deprec.—Equipment				Accounts Payable			
Oct 1	188,000					Oct 1	52,000			Oct 1	14,000
Acquisition	7,000					Depreciation	9,000	Payments	328,000	Purchases	437,000
Oct 31	195,000					Oct 31	61,000			Oct 31	123,000

Accrued Liabilities				Retained Earnings			
		Oct 1	12,000	Quarterly		Oct 1	66,000
Payments	28,000	Receipts	22,000	Dividend	18,000	Net Income	35,000
		Oct 31	6,000			Oct 31	83,000

▌Requirement

1. Compute Lawrence's net cash provided by (used for) operating activities during October. Use the *indirect* method. Does Lawrence have trouble collecting receivables or selling inventory? How can you tell?

writing assignment ■ **E12-31B** (*Learning Objective 3: Preparing the statement of cash flows—indirect method*) The income statement and additional data of Norton Travel Products, Inc., follow:

Norton Travel Products, Inc.
Income Statement
Year Ended December 31, 2010

Revenues:		
Service revenue	$235,000	
Dividend revenue	8,300	$243,300
Expenses:		
Cost of goods sold	102,000	
Salary expense	62,000	
Depreciation expense	33,000	
Advertising expense	4,300	
Interest expense	2,400	
Income tax expense	7,000	210,700
Net income		$ 32,600

Additional data:

  a. Acquisition of plant assets was $170,000. Of this amount, $140,000 was paid in cash and $30,000 by signing a note payable.
  b. Proceeds from sale of land totaled $48,000.
  c. Proceeds from issuance of common stock totaled $31,000.
  d. Payment of long-term note payable was $16,000.
  e. Payment of dividends was $10,000.
  f. From the balance sheets:

	December 31,	
	2010	**2009**
Current Assets:		
Cash	$32,000	$13,300
Accounts receivable	41,000	57,000
Inventory	48,000	87,000
Prepaid expenses	9,100	8,200
Current Liabilities:		
Accounts payable	$32,000	$17,000
Accrued liabilities	14,000	43,000

❙ Requirements

  1. Prepare Norton's statement of cash flows for the year ended December 31, 2010, using the *indirect* method.
  2. Evaluate Norton's cash flows for the year. In your evaluation, mention all three categories of cash flows and give the reason for your evaluation.

E12-32B (*Learning Objective 3: Interpreting a statement of cash flows—indirect method*) Con-sider three independent cases for the cash flows of 424 Promenade Shoes. For each case, identify from the statement of cash flows how 424 Promenade Shoes generated the cash to acquire new plant assets. Rank the three cases from the most healthy financially to the least healthy.

	Case A	Case B	Case C
Cash flows from operating activities			
Net income	$ 10,000	$ 10,000	$ 10,000
Depreciation and amortization	12,000	12,000	12,000
Increase in current assets	1,000	(5,000)	2,000
Decrease in current liabilities	2,000	(19,000)	3,000
	25,000	(2,000)	27,000
Cash flows from investing activities:			
Acquisition of plant assets	(99,000)	(99,000)	(99,000)
Sales of plant assets	104,000	20,000	33,000
	5,000	(79,000)	(66,000)
Cash flows from financing activities:			
Issuance of stock	18,000	105,000	73,000
Payment of debt	(27,000)	(20,000)	(32,000)
	(9,000)	85,000	41,000
Net increase (decrease) in cash	$ 21,000	$ 4,000	$ 2,000

E12-33B (*Learning Objectives 3, 4: Computing investing and financing amounts for the statement of cash flows*) Compute the following items for the statement of cash flows:

a. Beginning and ending Plant Assets, Net, are $102,000 and $97,000, respectively. Depreciation for the period was $12,000, and purchases of new plant assets were $30,000. Plant assets were sold at a $5,000 gain. What were the cash proceeds of the sale?

b. Beginning and ending Retained Earnings are $46,000 and $70,000, respectively. Net income for the period was $48,000, and stock dividends were $11,000. How much were cash dividends?

E12-34B (*Learning Objective 4: Computing cash flows from operating activities—direct method*) The accounting records of One Stop Pharmaceuticals, Inc., reveal the following:

writing assignment ■

Payment of salaries and wages	$40,000	Net income	$20,000
Depreciation	25,000	Payment of income tax	8,000
Increase in current liabilities	27,000	Collection of dividend revenue	7,000
Increase in current assets other than cash	28,000	Payment of interest	13,000
Payment of dividends	6,000	Cash sales	36,000
Collection of accounts receivable	80,000	Gain on sale of land	2,000
		Acquisition of land	35,000
		Payment of accounts payable	51,000

I Requirement

1. Compute cash flows from operating activities by the *direct* method. Also evaluate One Stop's operating cash flow. Give the reason for your evaluation.

E12-35B *(Learning Objective 4: Identifying items for the statement of cash flows—direct method)*   Selected accounts of Elizabeth Antiques show the following:

Salary Payable

		Beginning balance	14,000
Payments	20,000	Salary expense	42,000
		Ending balance	36,000

Buildings

Beginning balance	100,000	Depreciation	22,000
Acquisitions	155,000	Book value of building sold	117,000*
Ending balance	116,000		

*Sale price was 160,000.

Notes Payable

		Beginning balance	244,000
Payments	72,000	Issuance of note payable for cash	90,000
		Ending balance	262,000

I *Requirement*

1. For each account, identify the item or items that should appear on a statement of cash flows prepared by the *direct* method. State where to report the item.

E12-36B *(Learning Objective 4: Preparing the statement of cash flows—direct method)*   The income statement and additional data of Happy Life, Inc., follow:

Happy Life, Inc.
Income Statement
Year Ended November 30, 2010

Revenues:		
Sales revenue......................	$223,000	
Dividend revenue................	10,500	$233,500
Expenses:		
Cost of goods sold..............	102,000	
Salary expense	42,000	
Depreciation expense..........	19,000	
Advertising expense	14,000	
Interest expense	4,500	
Income tax expense.............	8,000	189,500
Net income		$ 44,000

Additional data:

a. Collections from customers are $16,500 more than sales.
b. Payments to suppliers are $1,200 more than the sum of cost of goods sold plus advertising expense.

c. Payments to employees are $1,700 less than salary expense.
d. Dividend revenue, interest expense, and income tax expense equal their cash amounts.
e. Acquisition of plant assets is $154,000. Of this amount, $108,000 is paid in cash and $46,000 by signing a note payable.
f. Proceeds from sale of land total $21,000.
g. Proceeds from issuance of common stock total $86,000.
h. Payment of long-term note payable is $13,000.
i. Payment of dividends is $9,000.
j. Cash balance, November 30, 2009, was $23,000.

❚ Requirements

1. Prepare Happy Life, Inc.'s statement of cash flows and accompanying schedule of non-cash investing and financing activities. Report operating activities by the *direct* method.
2. Evaluate Happy Life's cash flows for the year. In your evaluation, mention all three categories of cash flows and give the reason for your evaluation.

E12-37B (*Learning Objective 4: Computing amounts for the statement of cash flows—direct method*)   Compute the following items for the statement of cash flows:

a. Beginning and ending Accounts Receivable are $20,000 and $17,000, respectively. Credit sales for the period total $61,000. How much are cash collections from customers?
b. Cost of goods sold is $79,000. Beginning Inventory balance is $28,000, and ending Inventory balance is $24,000. Beginning and ending Accounts Payable are $12,000 and $13,000, respectively. How much are cash payments for inventory?

Challenge Exercises

E12-38 (*Learning Objectives 3, 4: Computing cash-flow amounts*)   Tip Top, Inc., reported the following in its financial statements for the year ended May 30, 2010 (in thousands):

	2010	2009
Income Statement		
Net sales	$23,984	$21,674
Cost of sales	18,026	15,432
Depreciation	266	227
Other operating expenses	3,875	4,254
Income tax expense	536	488
Net income	$ 1,281	$ 1,273
Balance Sheet		
Cash and equivalents	$ 16	$ 15
Accounts receivable	603	614
Inventory	3,140	2,872
Property and equipment, net	4,346	3,436
Accounts payable	1,551	1,371
Accrued liabilities	935	632
Income tax payable	197	193
Long-term liabilities	480	468
Common stock	515	445
Retained earnings	4,427	3,828

❙ Requirement

1. Determine the following cash receipts and payments for Tip Top, Inc., during 2010: (Enter all amounts in thousands.)
   a. Collections from customers
   b. Payments for inventory
   c. Payments for other operating expenses
   d. Payment of income tax
   e. Proceeds from issuance of common stock
   f. Payment of cash dividends

E12-39 (*Learning Objective 3: Using the balance sheet and the statement of cash flows together*)   Delorme Specialties reported the following at December 31, 2010 (in thousands):

	2010	2009
From the comparative balance sheet:		
Property and equipment, net...	$10,950	$9,630
Long-term notes payable...	4,500	3,040
From the statement of cash flows:		
Depreciation	$ 1,950	
Capital expenditures..	(4,090)	
Proceeds from sale of property and equipment	740	
Proceeds from issuance of long-term note payable.......	1,250	
Payment of long-term note payable.............................	(80)	
Issuance of common stock	389	

❙ Requirement

1. Determine the following items for Delorme Specialties during 2010:
   a. Gain or loss on the sale of property and equipment
   b. Amount of long-term debt issued for something other than cash

Quiz

Test your understanding of the statement of cash flows by answering the following questions. Select the best choice from among the possible answers given.

Q12-40 Paying off bonds payable is reported on the statement of cash flows under
a. noncash investing and financing activities.
b. investing activities.
c. operating activities.
d. financing activities.

Q12-41 The sale of inventory for cash is reported on the statement of cash flows under
a. financing activities.
b. noncash investing and financing activities.
c. investing activities.
d. operating activities.

Q12-42 Selling equipment is reported on the statement of cash flows under
a. financing activities.
b. investing activities.
c. noncash investing and financing activities.
d. operating activities.

Q12-43 Which of the following terms appears on a statement of cash flows—indirect method?
a. Cash receipt of interest revenue
b. Collections from customers
c. Depreciation expense
d. Payments to suppliers

Q12-44 On an indirect method statement of cash flows, an increase in a prepaid insurance would be
a. added to increases in current assets.
b. included in payments to suppliers.
c. deducted from net income.
d. added to net income.

Q12-45 On an indirect method statement of cash flows, an increase in accounts payable would be
a. reported in the financing activities section.
b. reported in the investing activities section.
c. added to net income in the operating activities section.
d. deducted from net income in the operating activities section.

Q12-46 On an indirect method statement of cash flows, a gain on the sale of plant assets would be
a. reported in the investing activities section.
b. added to net income in the operating activities section.
c. deducted from net income in the operating activities section.
d. ignored, since the gain did not generate any cash.

Q12-47 Select an activity for each of the following transactions:
1. Paying cash dividends is a/an _____ activity.
2. Receiving cash dividends is a/an _____ activity.

Q12-48 Click Camera Co. sold equipment with a cost of $21,000 and accumulated depreciation of $9,000 for an amount that resulted in a gain of $1,000. What amount should Click report on the statement of cash flows as "proceeds from sale of plant assets"?
a. $10,000   c. $13,000
b. $20,000   d. Some other amount

Questions 49–57 use the following data. Sheehan Corporation formats operating cash flows by the *indirect* method.

Sheehan's Income Statement for 2010

Sales revenue	$177,000	
Gain on sale of equipment	9,000*	$186,000
Cost of goods sold	114,000	
Depreciation	6,500	
Other operating expenses	24,000	144,500
Net income		$ 41,500

*The book value of equipment sold during 2010 was $21,000.

Sheehan's Comparative Balance Sheet at the end of 2010

	2010	2009		2010	2009
Cash	$ 5,500	$ 3,000	Accounts payable	$ 8,000	$ 9,000
Accounts receivable	5,000	13,000	Accrued liabilities	6,000	4,000
Inventory	11,000	10,000	Common stock	18,000	9,000
Plant and equipment, net	97,000	71,000	Retained earnings	86,500	75,000
	$118,500	$97,000		$118,500	$97,000

Q12-49 How many items enter the computation of Sheehan's net cash provided by operating activities?
a. 3   c. 7
b. 2   d. 5

Q12-50 How do Sheehan's accrued liabilities affect the company's statement of cash flows for 2010?
a. Increase in cash used by investing activities.
b. Increase in cash provided by operating activities.
c. Increase in cash used by financing activities.
d. They don't because the accrued liabilities are not yet paid.

Q12-51 How do accounts receivable affect Sheehan's cash flows from operating activities for 2010?
a. Decrease in cash provided by operating activities.
b. Decrease in cash used by investing activities.
c. Increase in cash provided by operating activities.
d. They don't because accounts receivable result from investing activities.

Q12-52 Sheehan's net cash provided by operating activities during 2010 was
a. $53,000.   c. $47,000.
b. $50,000.   d. $44,000.

Q12-53 How many items enter the computation of Sheehan's net cash flow from investing activities for 2010?

a. 5   c. 7
b. 3   d. 2

Q12-54 The book value of equipment sold during 2010 was $21,000. Sheehan's net cash flow from investing activities for 2010 was
a. net cash used of $23,500.
b. net cash used of $53,000.
c. net cash used of $50,000.
d. net cash used of $44,000.

Q12-55 How many items enter the computation of Sheehan's net cash flow from financing activities for 2010?
a. 7   c. 5
b. 3   d. 2

Q12-56 Sheehan's largest financing cash flow for 2010 resulted from
a. payment of dividends.   c. purchase of equipment.
b. sale of equipment.   d. issuance of common stock.

Q12-57 Sheehan's net cash flow from financing activities for 2010 was
a. net cash used of $21,000.   c. net cash provided of $9,000.
b. net cash used of $50,000.   d. net cash used of $44,000.

Q12-58 Sales totaled $820,000, accounts receivable increased by $50,000, and accounts payable decreased by $30,000. How much cash did the company collect from customers?
a. $800,000   c. $770,000
b. $820,000   d. $870,000

Q12-59 Income Tax Payable was $4,500 at the end of the year and $3,000 at the beginning. Income tax expense for the year totaled $59,500. What amount of cash did the company pay for income tax during the year?
a. $62,500   c. $61,000
b. $58,000   d. $59,500

Problems

All of the A and B problems can be found within MyAccountingLab, an online homework and practice environment. Your instructor may ask you to complete these problems using MyAccountingLab.

(Group A)

P12-60A (*Learning Objectives 2, 3: Preparing an income statement, balance sheet, and statement of cash flows—indirect method*) Antique Automobiles of Dallas, Inc., was formed on January 1, 2010. The following transactions occurred during 2010:

On January 1, 2010, Antique issued its common stock for $440,000. Early in January, Antique made the following cash payments:

- **a.** $180,000 for equipment
- **b.** $203,000 for inventory (seven cars at $29,000 each)
- **c.** $17,000 for 2010 rent on a store building

In February, Antique purchased two cars for inventory on account. Cost of this inventory was $80,000 ($40,000.00 each). Before year-end, Antique paid $56,000 of this debt. Antique uses the FIFO method to account for inventory.

During 2010, Antique sold eight vintage autos for a total of $488,000. Before year-end, Antique collected 80% of this amount.

The business employs five people. The combined annual payroll is $125,000, of which Antique owes $7,000 at year-end. At the end of the year, Antique paid income tax of $12,600.

Late in 2010, Antique declared and paid cash dividends of $12,000.

For equipment, Antique uses the straight-line depreciation method, over five years, with zero residual value.

❚ Requirements

1. Prepare Antique Automobiles of Dallas, Inc.'s income statement for the year ended December 31, 2010. Use the single-step format, with all revenues listed together and all expenses together.
2. Prepare Antique's balance sheet at December 31, 2010.
3. Prepare Antique's statement of cash flows for the year ended December 31, 2010. Format cash flows from operating activities by using the *indirect* method.

P12-61A (*Learning Objectives 2, 4: Preparing an income statement, balance sheet, and statement of cash flows—direct method*)   Use the Antique Automobiles of Dallas, Inc., data from Problem 12-60A.

❚ Requirements

1. Prepare Antique's income statement for the year ended December 31, 2010. Use the single-step format, with all revenues listed together and all expenses together.
2. Prepare Antique's balance sheet at December 31, 2010.
3. Prepare Antique's statement of cash flows for the year ended December 31, 2010. Format cash flows from operating activities by using the *direct* method.

P12-62A (*Learning Objectives 2, 3: Preparing the statement of cash flows—indirect method*) Morgensen Software Corp. has assembled the following data for the years ending December 31, 2010 and 2009.

	December 31,	
	2010	2009
Current Accounts:		
Current assets:		
Cash and cash equivalents	$120,400	$30,000
Accounts receivable	69,900	64,400
Inventories..	8,600	80,000
Prepaid expenses..............................	3,100	1,500
Current liabilities:		
Accounts payable.............................	$ 57,200	$55,800
Income tax payable...........................	18,600	16,700
Accrued liabilities	15,500	27,200

Transaction Data for 2010:			
Acquisition of land by issuing		Purchase of treasury stock	$10,700
long-term note payable	$201,000	Loss on sale of equipment	5,000
Stock dividends	31,400	Payment of cash dividends	9,300
Collection of loan..................	10,600	Issuance of long-term note	
Depreciation expense	17,000	payable to borrow cash.....	34,500
Purchase of building..............	97,000	Net income...........................	6,500
Retirement of bonds payable		Issuance of common stock	
by issuing common stock	64,000	for cash	36,500
Purchase of long-term		Proceeds from sale of	
investment........................	44,600	equipment	81,000
		Amortization expense..........	5,000

❙ *Requirement*

1. Prepare Morgensen Software Corp.'s statement of cash flows using the *indirect* method to report operating activities. Include an accompanying schedule of noncash investing and financing activities.

writing assignment ■

■ **spreadsheet**

P12-63A (*Learning Objectives 2, 3: Preparing the statement of cash flows—indirect method*) The comparative balance sheets of Maynard Movie Theater Company at June 30, 2010 and 2009, reported the following:

	June 30,	
	2010	2009
Current assets:		
Cash and cash equivalents	$52,600	$17,000
Accounts receivable	14,500	21,600
Inventories..	63,500	61,100
Prepaid expenses..............................	3,100	8,000
Current liabilities:		
Accounts payable.............................	$57,800	$56,200
Accrued liabilities	37,300	17,300
Income tax payable...........................	9,100	10,100

Maynard Movie Theater's transactions during the year ended June 30, 2010, included the following:

Acquisition of land		Sale of long-term investment....	$12,700
by issuing note payable	$100,000	Depreciation expense	15,700
Amortization expense............	9,000	Cash purchase of building.....	44,000
Payment of cash dividend......	29,000	Net income...........................	54,000
Cash purchase of		Issuance of common	
equipment	79,000	stock for cash....................	24,000
Issuance of long-term note		Stock dividend......................	11,000
payable to borrow cash.....	42,000		

Requirements

1. Prepare Maynard Movie Theater Company's statement of cash flows for the year ended June 30, 2010, using the *indirect* method to report cash flows from operating activities. Report noncash investing and financing activities in an accompanying schedule.
2. Evaluate Maynard Movie Theater's cash flows for the year. Mention all three categories of cash flows and give the reason for your evaluation.

P12-64A (*Learning Objectives 2, 3: Preparing the statement of cash flows—indirect method*)   The 2010 and 2009 comparative balance sheets and 2010 income statement of Affordable Supply Corp. follow:

■ spreadsheet

writing assignment ■

Affordable Supply Corp.
Comparative Balance Sheets

	December 31, 2010	2009	Increase (Decrease)
Current assets:			
Cash and cash equivalents	$ 17,300	$ 4,000	$ 13,300
Accounts receivable	45,700	44,500	1,200
Inventories....................................	61,400	47,000	14,400
Prepaid expenses...........................	1,800	3,900	(2,100)
Plant assets:			
Land	69,100	22,600	46,500
Equipment, net	53,100	49,500	3,600
Total assets...................................	$248,400	$171,500	$ 76,900
Current liabilities:			
Accounts payable..........................	$ 35,200	$ 26,900	$ 8,300
Salary payable	24,000	13,100	10,900
Other accrued liabilities................	22,100	23,700	(1,600)
Long-term liabilities:			
Notes payable...............................	51,000	34,000	17,000
Stockholders' equity:			
Common stock, no-par..................	88,600	65,900	22,700
Retained earnings	27,500	7,900	19,600
Total liabilities and stockholders' equity.....	$248,400	$171,500	$ 76,900

Affordable Supply Corp.
Income Statement
Year Ended December 31, 2010

Revenues:		
Sales revenue		$446,000
Expenses:		
Cost of goods sold	$186,600	
Salary expense	76,000	
Depreciation expense....................	17,700	
Other operating expense...............	49,700	
Interest expense	24,100	
Income tax expense	29,000	
Total expenses..........................		383,100
Net income..		$ 62,900

Affordable Supply had no noncash investing and financing transactions during 2010. During the year, there were no sales of land or equipment, no payment of notes payable, no retirements of stock, and no treasury stock transactions.

▌Requirements

1. Prepare the 2010 statement of cash flows, formatting operating activities by using the *indirect* method.
2. How will what you learned in this problem help you evaluate an investment?

writing assignment ▮

▮ spreadsheet

P12-65A (*Learning Objectives 2, 4: Preparing the statement of cash flows—direct method*)   Use the Affordable Supply Corp. data from Problem 12-64A.

▌Requirements

1. Prepare the 2010 statement of cash flows by using the *direct* method.
2. How will what you learned in this problem help you evaluate an investment?

writing assignment ▮

P12-66A (*Learning Objectives 2, 4: Preparing the statement of cash flows—direct method*)   Ramirez Furniture Gallery, Inc., provided the following data from the company's records for the year ended May 31, 2010:

a. Credit sales, $584,500
b. Loan to another company, $12,300
c. Cash payments to purchase plant assets, $72,100
d. Cost of goods sold, $312,400
e. Proceeds from issuance of common stock, $7,000
f. Payment of cash dividends, $48,300
g. Collection of interest, $4,600
h. Acquisition of equipment by issuing short-term note payable, $16,000
i. Payments of salaries, $78,000
j. Proceeds from sale of plant assets, $22,600, including $6,900 loss
k. Collections on accounts receivable, $428,500
l. Interest revenue, $3,500
m. Cash receipt of dividend revenue, $8,900
n. Payments to suppliers, $368,000

o. Cash sales, $191,300
p. Depreciation expense, $40,100
q. Proceeds from issuance of note payable, $24,500
r. Payments of long-term notes payable, $83,000
s. Interest expense and payments, $13,400
t. Salary expense, $75,800
u. Loan collections, $11,900
v. Proceeds from sale of investments, $9,500, including $4,400 gain
w. Payment of short-term note payable by issuing long-term note payable, $94,000
x. Amortization expenses, $3,100
y. Income tax expense and payments, $38,300
z. Cash balance: May 31, 2009, $19,100; May 31, 2010, $14,500

❙ Requirements

1. Prepare Ramirez Furniture Gallery, Inc.'s statement of cash flows for the year ended May 31, 2010. Use the *direct* method for cash flows from operating activities. Include an accompanying schedule of noncash investing and financing activities.

2. Evaluate 2010 from a cash-flows standpoint. Give your reasons.

P12-67A (*Learning Objectives 2, 3, 4: Preparing the statement of cash flows—direct and indirect methods*)   To prepare the statement of cash flows, accountants for Daisy Electric Company have summarized 2010 activity in two accounts as follows:

■ spreadsheet

Cash

Beginning balance	49,600	Payments on accounts payable	402,000
Sale of long-term investment	14,600	Payments of dividends	47,900
Collections from customers	661,800	Payments of salaries and wages	143,600
Issuance of common stock	61,000	Payments of interest	26,600
Receipts of dividends	16,900	Purchase of equipment	31,000
		Payments of operating expenses	34,500
		Payment of long-term note payable	41,500
		Purchase of treasury stock	22,400
		Payment of income tax	17,000
Ending Balance	37,400		

Common Stock

Beginning balance	74,200
Issuance for cash	61,000
Issuance to acquire land	80,800
Issuance to retire note payable	20,000
Ending balance	236,000

Daisy's 2010 income statement and balance sheet data follow:

Daisy Electric Company
Income Statement
Year Ended December 31, 2010

Revenues:		
Sales revenue		$689,200
Dividend revenue		16,900
Total revenue		706,100
Expenses and losses:		
Cost of goods sold	$334,000	
Salary and wage expense	135,800	
Depreciation expense	19,000	
Other operating expense	23,700	
Interest expense	29,100	
Income tax expense	14,500	
Loss on sale of investments	22,100	
Total expenses and losses		578,200
Net income		$127,900

Daisy Electric Company
Selected Balance Sheet Data
December 31, 2010

	Increase (Decrease)
Current assets:	
Cash and cash equivalents	$(12,200)
Accounts receivable	27,400
Inventories..	59,700
Prepaid expenses...............................	600
Long-term investments..............................	(36,700)
Equipment, net...	12,000
Land	80,800
Current liabilities:	
Accounts payable.............................	(8,300)
Interest payable	2,500
Salary payable	(7,800)
Other accrued liabilities...................	(10,200)
Income tax payable..........................	(2,500)
Long-term note payable	(61,500)
Common stock..	161,800
Retained earnings.....................................	80,000
Treasury stock..	(22,400)

▌*Requirements*

1. Prepare the statement of cash flows of Daisy Electric Company for the year ended December 31, 2010, using the *direct* method to report operating activities. Also prepare the accompanying schedule of noncash investing and financing activities.
2. Use Daisy's 2010 income statement and balance sheet to prepare a supplementary schedule of cash flows from operating activities by using the *indirect* method.

P12-68A (*Learning Objectives 2, 3, 4: Preparing the statement of cash flows—indirect and direct methods*) The comparative balance sheets of Stephen Summers Design Studio, Inc., at June 30, 2010 and 2009, and transaction data for fiscal 2010 are as follows:

Stephen Summers Design Studio
Comparative Balance Sheets

	June 30, 2010	June 30, 2009	Increase (Decrease)
Current assets:			
Cash	$ 28,900	$ 21,000	$ 7,900
Accounts receivable	48,800	31,700	17,100
Inventories	78,400	80,700	(2,300)
Prepaid expenses	3,100	2,200	900
Long-term investment	10,300	5,600	4,700
Equipment, net	74,000	73,300	700
Land	33,100	94,500	(61,400)
	$276,600	$309,000	$(32,400)
Current liabilities:			
Notes payable, short-term	$ 14,000	$19,000	$(5,000)
Accounts payable	29,400	40,400	(11,000)
Income tax payable	13,200	14,400	(1,200)
Accrued liabilities	3,700	9,400	(5,700)
Interest payable	3,400	2,400	1,000
Salary payable	1,000	4,400	(3,400)
Long-term note payable	47,200	94,000	(46,800)
Common stock	59,400	52,000	7,400
Retained earnings	105,300	73,000	32,300
	$276,600	$309,000	$(32,400)

Transaction data for the year ended June 30, 2010:

   a. Net income, $80,700
   b. Depreciation expense on equipment, $13,900
   c. Purchased long-term investment, $4,700
   d. Sold land for $54,900, including $6,500 loss
   e. Acquired equipment by issuing long-term note payable, $14,600
   f. Paid long-term note payable, $61,400
   g. Received cash for issuance of common stock, $2,400
   h. Paid cash dividends, $48,400
   i. Paid short-term note payable by issuing common stock, $5,000

❙ Requirements

1. Prepare the statement of cash flows of Stephen Summers Design Studio, Inc., for the year ended June 30, 2010, using the *indirect* method to report operating activities. Also prepare the accompanying schedule of noncash investing and financing activities. All current accounts except short-term notes payable result from operating transactions.
2. Prepare a supplementary schedule showing cash flows from operations by the *direct* method. The accounting records provide the following: collections from customers, $241,700; interest received, $1,700; payments to suppliers, $118,600; payments to employees, $41,900; payments for income tax, $12,900; and payment of interest, $4,900.

(Group B)

P12-69B (*Learning Objectives 2, 3: Preparing an income statement, balance sheet, and statement of cash flows—indirect method*)   Sweet Automobiles of Pepperell, Inc., was formed on January 1, 2010. The following transactions occurred during 2010:

On January 1, 2010, Sweet issued its common stock for $350,000. Early in January, Sweet made the following cash payments:

   a. $140,000 for equipment
   b. $175,000 for inventory (five cars at $35,000 each)
   c. $19,000 for 2010 rent on a store building

In February, Sweet purchased six cars for inventory on account. Cost of this inventory was $282,000 ($47,000 each). Before year end, Sweet paid $197,400 of this debt. Sweet uses the FIFO method to account for inventory.

During 2010, Sweet sold six vintage autos for a total of $426,000. Before year-end, Sweet collected 90% of this amount.

The business employs three people. The combined annual payroll is $90,000, of which Sweet owes $5,000 at year-end. At the end of the year, Sweet paid income tax of $14,000.

Late in 2010, Sweet declared and paid cash dividends of $16,000.

For equipment, Sweet uses the straight-line depreciation method, over five years, with zero residual value.

❙ Requirements

1. Prepare Sweet Automobiles of Pepperell, Inc.'s income statement for the year ended December 31, 2010. Use the single-step format, with all revenues listed together and all expenses together.
2. Prepare Sweet's balance sheet at December 31, 2010.
3. Prepare Sweet's statement of cash flows for the year ended December 31, 2010. Format cash flows from operating activities by using the *indirect* method.

P12-70B (*Learning Objectives 2, 4: Preparing an income statement, balance sheet, and statement of cash flows—direct method*)   Use the Sweet Automobiles of Pepperell, Inc., data from Problem 12-69B.

❙ Requirements

1. Prepare Sweet's income statement for the year ended December 31, 2010. Use the single-step format, with all revenues listed together and all expenses together.
2. Prepare Sweet's balance sheet at December 31, 2010.
3. Prepare Sweet's statement of cash flows for the year ended December 31, 2010. Format cash flows from operating activities by using the *direct* method.

P12-71B (*Learning Objectives 2, 3: Preparing the statement of cash flows—indirect method*)   Neighbor Software Corp. has assembled the following data for the year ended December 31, 2010:

	December 31,	
	2010	2009
Current Accounts:		
Current assets:		
Cash and cash equivalents	$60,000	$26,000
Accounts receivable	22,000	64,100
Inventories...	88,500	85,000
Prepaid expenses................................	3,200	2,400
Current liabilities:		
Accounts payable..............................	57,700	55,500
Income tax payable...........................	29,000	16,900
Accrued liabilities	15,500	7,600

Transaction Data for 2010:

Acquisition of land by issuing		Purchase of treasury stock	$14,400
long-term note payable	$198,000	Loss on sale of equipment	3,000
Stock dividends	31,600	Payment of cash dividends	18,800
Collection of loan..................	11,000	Issuance of long-term note	
Depreciation expense	17,000	payable to borrow cash.....	34,000
Purchase of building..............	159,000	Net income...........................	58,000
Retirement of bonds payable		Issuance of common stock	
by issuing common stock	71,000	for cash	74,200
Purchase of long-term		Proceeds from sale of	
investment.........................	49,900	equipment	12,900
		Amortization expense..........	6,000

Requirement

1. Prepare Neighbor Software Corp.'s statement of cash flows using the *indirect* method to report operating activities. Include an accompanying schedule of noncash investing and financing activities.

P12-72B (*Learning Objectives 2, 3: Preparing the statement of cash flows—indirect method*)   The comparative balance sheets of Medford Movie Theater Company at June 30, 2010 and 2009, reported the following:

writing assignment ■

■ **spreadsheet**

	June 30,	
	2010	2009
Current assets:		
Cash and cash equivalents	$ 5,800	$16,000
Accounts receivable	14,000	21,700
Inventories...	63,000	60,800
Prepaid expenses................................	17,200	8,000
Current liabilities:		
Accounts payable..............................	$58,000	$55,900
Accrued liabilities	57,400	47,400
Income tax payable...........................	6,500	10,500

Medford's transactions during the year ended June 30, 2010, included the following:

Acquisition of land by issuing note payable	$115,000	Sale of long-term investment....	$13,400
Amortization expense............	6,000	Depreciation expense	15,600
Payment of cash dividend......	34,000	Cash purchase of building.....	59,000
		Net income...........................	50,000
Cash purchase of equipment	45,600	Issuance of common stock for cash	13,000
Issuance of long-term note payable to borrow cash.....	26,000	Stock dividend......................	9,000

Requirements

1. Prepare Medford Movie Theater Company's statement of cash flows for the year ended June 30, 2010, using the *indirect* method to report cash flows from operating activities. Report noncash investing and financing activities in an accompanying schedule.
2. Evaluate Medford's cash flows for the year. Mention all three categories of cash flows and give the reason for your evaluation.

writing assignment ■

■ **spreadsheet**

P12-73B (*Learning Objectives 2, 3: Preparing the statement of cash flows—indirect method*)   The 2010 and 2009 comparative balance sheets and 2010 income statement of King Supply Corp. follow:

King Supply Corp.
Comparative Balance Sheets

	December 31, 2010	December 31, 2009	Increase (Decrease)
Current assets:			
Cash and cash equivalents	$ 17,600	$ 5,000	$ 12,600
Accounts receivable	45,500	44,500	1,000
Inventories.....................................	79,100	67,500	11,600
Prepaid expenses............................	2,100	6,000	(3,900)
Plant assets:			
Land	69,100	21,900	47,200
Equipment, net	53,100	49,200	3,900
Total assets......................................	$266,500	$194,100	$ 72,400
Current liabilities:			
Accounts payable...........................	$ 35,800	$ 25,600	$ 10,200
Salary payable	22,000	15,600	6,400
Other accrued liabilities................	22,900	24,200	(1,300)
Long-term liabilities:			
Notes payable	50,000	37,000	13,000
Stockholders' equity:			
Common stock, no-par..................	88,600	64,300	24,300
Retained earnings	47,200	27,400	19,800
Total liabilities and stockholders' equity.....	$266,500	$194,100	$ 72,400

King Supply Corp.
Income Statement
Year Ended December 31, 2010

Revenues:		
Sales revenue		$445,000
Expenses:		
Cost of goods sold	$185,100	
Salary expense	76,400	
Depreciation expense.....................	17,400	
Other operating expense...............	49,800	
Interest expense	24,800	
Income tax expense	29,500	
Total expenses...........................		383,000
Net income..		$ 62,000

King Supply had no noncash investing and financing transactions during 2010. During the year, there were no sales of land or equipment, no payment of notes payable, no retirements of stock, and no treasury stock transactions.

❙ Requirements

1. Prepare the 2010 statement of cash flows, formatting operating activities by using the *indirect* method.
2. How will what you learned in this problem help you evaluate an investment?

P12-74B (*Learning Objectives 2, 4: Preparing the statement of cash flows—direct method*) Use the King Supply Corp. data from Problem P12-73B.

writing assignment ■

■ spreadsheet

❙ Requirements

1. Prepare the 2010 statement of cash flows by using the *direct* method.
2. How will what you learned in this problem help you evaluate an investment?

P12-75B (*Learning Objectives 2, 4: Preparing the statement of cash flows—direct method*) Dunleavy Furniture Gallery, Inc., provided the following data from the company's records for the year ended December 31, 2010:

writing assignment ■

a. Credit sales, $567,000
b. Loan to another company, $12,800
c. Cash payments to purchase plant assets, $59,900
d. Cost of goods sold, $382,700
e. Proceeds from issuance of common stock, $7,000
f. Payment of cash dividends, $48,000
g. Collection of interest, $4,200
h. Acquisition of equipment by issuing short-term note payable, $16,500
i. Payments of salaries, $93,700
j. Proceeds from sale of plant assets, $22,300, including $7,000 loss
k. Collections on accounts receivable, $406,000
l. Interest revenue, $3,300
m. Cash receipt of dividend revenue, $4,000
n. Payments to suppliers, $387,200

o. Cash sales, $201,000
p. Depreciation expense, $40,100
q. Proceeds from issuance of note payable, $19,300
r. Payments of long-term notes payable, $69,000
s. Interest expense and payments, $13,700
t. Salary expense, $91,600
u. Loan collections, $12,100
v. Proceeds from sale of investments, $11,200, including $3,800 gain
w. Payment of short-term note payable by issuing long-term note payable, $68,000
x. Amortization expenses, $3,200
y. Income tax expense and payments, $36,800
z. Cash balance: December 31, 2009, $40,000; December 31, 2010, $6,000

I *Requirements*

1. Prepare Dunleavy Furniture Gallery, Inc.'s statement of cash flows for the year ended December 31, 2010. Use the *direct* method for cash flows from operating activities. Include an accompanying schedule of noncash investing and financing activities.
2. Evaluate 2010 from a cash-flows standpoint. Give your reasons.

■ spreadsheet

P12-76B (*Learning Objectives 2, 3, 4: Preparing the statement of cash flows—direct and indirect methods*)   To prepare the statement of cash flows, accountants for Spencer Electric Company have summarized 2010 activity in two accounts as follows:

Cash

Beginning balance	71,500	Payments on accounts payable	399,500
Sale of long-term investment	20,000	Payments of dividends	27,600
Collections from customers	661,600	Payments of salaries and wages	143,300
Issuance of common stock	22,200	Payments of interest	27,100
Receipts of dividends	16,800	Purchase of equipment	31,700
		Payments of operating expenses	34,900
		Payment of long-term note payable	41,300
		Purchase of treasury stock	26,300
		Payment of income tax	18,600
Ending Balance	41,800		

Common Stock

		Beginning balance	73,200
		Issuance for cash	22,200
		Issuance to acquire land	61,700
		Issuance to retire note payable	17,000
		Ending balance	174,100

Spencer's 2010 income statement and balance sheet data follow:

Spencer Electric Company
Income Statement
Year Ended December 31, 2010

Revenues:		
Sales revenue		$647,200
Dividend revenue		16,800
Total revenue		664,000
Expenses and losses:		
Cost of goods sold	$404,600	
Salary and wage expense	150,500	
Depreciation expense	16,400	
Other operating expense	30,500	
Interest expense	24,900	
Income tax expense	16,100	
Loss on sale of investments	16,700	
Total expenses and losses		659,700
Net income		$ 4,300

Spencer Electric Company Selected Balance Sheet Data December 31, 2010	
	Increase (Decrease)
Current assets:	
Cash and cash equivalents	$(29,700)
Accounts receivable	(14,400)
Inventories.......................................	(12,900)
Prepaid expenses..............................	(6,000)
Long-term investments..............................	(36,700)
Equipment, net..	15,300
Land	61,700
Current liabilities:	
Accounts payable..............................	(7,800)
Interest payable	(2,200)
Salary payable	7,200
Other accrued liabilities...................	(10,400)
Income tax payable...........................	(2,500)
Long-term note payable	(58,300)
Common stock...	100,900
Retained earnings......................................	(23,300)
Treasury stock...	(26,300)

▎*Requirements*

1. Prepare the statement of cash flows of Spencer Electric Company for the year ended December 31, 2010, using the *direct* method to report operating activities. Also prepare the accompanying schedule of noncash investing and financing activities.

2. Use Spencer's 2010 income statement and balance sheet to prepare a supplementary schedule of cash flows from operating activities by using the *indirect* method.

P12-77B (*Learning Objectives 2, 3, 4: Preparing the statement of cash flows—indirect and direct methods*) The comparative balance sheets of Franny Franklin Design Studio, Inc., at June 30, 2010 and 2009, and transaction data for fiscal 2010 are as follows:

Franny Franklin Design Studio
Comparative Balance Sheets

	June 30, 2010	June 30, 2009	Increase (Decrease)
Current assets:			
Cash	$ 28,900	$ 2,400	$ 26,500
Accounts receivable	59,000	22,300	36,700
Inventories	98,200	40,400	57,800
Prepaid expenses	3,500	2,500	1,000
Long-term investment	10,000	5,000	5,000
Equipment, net	74,900	73,600	1,300
Land	58,100	98,900	(40,800)
	$332,600	$245,100	$ 87,500)
Current liabilities:			
Notes payable, short-term	$ 13,200	$20,200	$ (7,000)
Accounts payable	42,300	41,300	1,000
Income tax payable	13,300	14,400	(1,100)
Accrued liabilities	97,400	9,300	88,100
Interest payable	3,500	2,500	1,000
Salary payable	400	3,100	(2,700)
Long-term note payable	48,700	94,200	(45,500)
Common stock	79,700	51,600	28,100
Retained earnings	34,100	8,500	25,600
	$332,600	$245,100	$ 87,500

Transaction data for the year ended June 30, 2010:

a. Net income, $73,400
b. Depreciation expense on equipment, $13,900
c. Purchased long-term investment, $5,000
d. Sold land for $33,800, including $7,000 loss
e. Acquired equipment by issuing long-term note payable, $15,200
f. Paid long-term note payable, $60,700
g. Received cash for issuance of common stock, $21,100
h. Paid cash dividends, $47,800
i. Paid short-term note payable by issuing common stock, $7,000

▌Requirements

1. Prepare the statement of cash flows of Franny Franklin Design Studio, Inc., for the year ended June 30, 2010, using the *indirect* method to report operating activities. Also prepare the accompanying schedule of noncash investing and financing activities. All current accounts except short-term notes payable result from operating transactions.
2. Prepare a supplementary schedule showing cash flows from operations by the *direct* method. The accounting records provide the following: collections from customers, $272,300; interest received, $1,400; payments to suppliers, $130,900; payments to employees, $40,000; payments for income tax, $12,500; and payment of interest, $5,200.

APPLY YOUR KNOWLEDGE

Decision Cases

Case 1. (*Learning Objective 3: Preparing and using the statement of cash flows to evaluate operations*) The 2011 income statement and the 2011 comparative balance sheet of T-Bar-M Camp, Inc., have just been distributed at a meeting of the camp's board of directors. The directors raise a fundamental question: Why is the cash balance so low? This question is especially troublesome since 2011 showed record profits. As the controller of the company, you must answer the question.

T–Bar–M Camp, Inc.
Income Statement
Year Ended December 31, 2011

(In thousands)

Revenues:

Sales revenue	$436

Expenses:

Cost of goods sold	$221
Salary expense	48
Depreciation expense	46
Interest expense	13
Amortization expense	11
Total expenses	339
Net income	$ 97

T–Bar–M Camp, Inc.
Comparative Balance Sheets
December 31, 2011 and 2010

(In thousands)	2011	2010
Assets		
Cash	$ 17	$ 63
Accounts receivable, net	72	61
Inventories	194	181
Long-term investments	31	0
Property, plant, and equipment	369	259
Accumulated depreciation	(244)	(198)
Patents	177	188
Totals	$ 616	$ 554
Liabilities and Owners' Equity		
Accounts payable	$ 63	$ 56
Accrued liabilities	12	17
Notes payable, long-term	179	264
Common stock, no par	149	61
Retained earnings	213	156
Totals	$ 616	$ 554

I Requirements

1. Prepare a statement of cash flows for 2011 in the format that best shows the relationship between net income and operating cash flow. The company sold no plant assets or long-term investments and issued no notes payable during 2011. There were *no* noncash investing and financing transactions during the year. Show all amounts in thousands.
2. Answer the board members' question: Why is the cash balance so low? Point out the two largest cash payments during 2011. (Challenge)
3. Considering net income and the company's cash flows during 2011, was it a good year or a bad year? Give your reasons.

writing assignment ■

Case 2. *(Learning Objectives 1, 2: Using cash-flow data to evaluate an investment)* Applied Technology, Inc., and Four-Star Catering are asking you to recommend their stock to your clients. Because Applied and Four-Star earn about the same net income and have similar financial positions, your decision depends on their statements of cash flows, summarized as follows:

	Applied		Four–Star	
Net cash provided by operating activities:......................		$ 30,000		$ 70,000
Cash provided by (used for) investing activities:				
Purchase of plant assets	$(20,000)		$(100,000)	
Sale of plant assets...	40,000	20,000	10,000	(90,000)
Cash provided by (used for) financing activities:				
Issuance of common stock		—		30,000
Paying off long-term debt		(40,000)		—
Net increase in cash...		$ 10,000		$10,000

Based on their cash flows, which company looks better? Give your reasons. (Challenge)

Ethical Issue

writing assignment ■

Columbia Motors is having a bad year. Net income is only $37,000. Also, two important overseas customers are falling behind in their payments to Columbia, and Columbia's accounts receivable are ballooning. The company desperately needs a loan. The Columbia board of directors is considering ways to put the best face on the company's financial statements. Columbia's bank closely examines cash flow from operations. Daniel Peavey, Columbia's controller, suggests reclassifying as long-term the receivables from the slow-paying clients. He explains to the board that removing the $80,000 rise in accounts receivable from current assets will increase net cash provided by operations. This approach may help Columbia get the loan.

I Requirements

1. Using only the amounts given, compute net cash provided by operations, both without and with the reclassification of the receivables. Which reporting makes Columbia look better?
2. Identify the ethical issue(s).
3. Who are the stakeholders?
4. Analyze the issue from the (a) economic, (b) legal, and (c) ethical standpoints. What is the potential impact on all stakeholders?
5. What should the board do?
6. Under what conditions would the reclassification of the receivables be considered ethical?

Focus on Financials: ■ Amazon.com, Inc.

(Learning Objectives 1, 2, 3, 4: Using the statement of cash flows) Use **Amazon.com, Inc.'s** consolidated statement of cash flows along with the company's other consolidated financial statements, all in Appendix A at the end of the book, to answer the following questions.

I *Requirements*

1. By which method does Amazon.com, Inc., report cash flows from *operating* activities? How can you tell?
2. Suppose Amazon.com, Inc., reported net cash flows from operating activities by using the direct method. Compute these amounts for the year ended December 31, 2008 (ignore the statement of cash flows, and use only Amazon.com, Inc.'s income statement and balance sheet).

    a. Collections from vendors, customers, and others. Use the information in Note 1—Description of Business and Accounting Policies. Prepare a T-Account for Gross Accounts Receivable. Prepare another T-Account for Allowance for Doubtful Accounts. Calculate the beginning and ending gross amounts of gross accounts receivable by adding the beginning and ending balances of allowance for doubtful accounts ($81 and $64, respectively) to the net accounts receivable at both the beginning and end of the year. Assume that all sales are on account. Also assume that the company uses the percentage of net sales method for estimating doubtful accounts expense, and that the company estimates this amount at 0.5%.

    b. Payments to suppliers. Amazon.com, Inc., calls its Cost of Goods Sold "Cost of Sales." For this computation, use the format provided in Exhibit 12-15. Assume all inventory is purchased on account, and that all cash payments to suppliers are made from accounts payable.

3. Prepare a T-account for Net Fixed Assets (Fixed Assets minus Accumulated Depreciation). In this account, analyze all activity in the fixed assets and accumulated depreciation accounts for 2008. Use the information in Note 3—Fixed Assets to analyze this activity. Assume that Amazon.com, Inc., did not sell any fixed assets during the year. Compare your computation of fixed asset additions with the amount reflected in the investments section of the balance sheet. What is the difference? Where might that difference be reflected in Amazon's Consolidated Statement of Cash Flows? (Challenge)

4. Evaluate 2008 for Amazon.com, Inc., in terms of net income, total assets, stockholders' equity, cash flows from operating activities, and overall results. Be specific. (Challenge)

Focus on Analysis: ■ Foot Locker, Inc.

(*Learning Objectives 1, 2, 3, 4: Analyzing cash flows*) Refer to the **Foot Locker, Inc.**, consolidated financial statements in Appendix B at the end of this book. Focus on fiscal 2007 (year ended February 2, 2008).

1. What is Foot Locker, Inc.'s main source of cash? Is this good news or bad news to Foot Locker managers, stockholders, and creditors? What is Foot Locker's main use of cash? Good news or bad news? Explain all answers in detail.
2. Explain briefly the three main reasons why net cash provided by operations differs from net income.
3. Did Foot Locker, Inc., buy or sell more fixed assets during fiscal 2007? How can you tell?
4. Identify the largest two items in the financing activities section of the Consolidated Statement of Cash Flows. Explain the company's probable reasoning behind these two expenditures.

Group Projects

Project 1.   Each member of the group should obtain the annual report of a different company. Select companies in different industries. Evaluate each company's trend of cash flows for the most recent two years. In your evaluation of the companies' cash flows, you may use any other information that is publicly available—for example, the other financial statements (income statement, balance sheet, statement of stockholders' equity, and the related notes) and news stories from magazines and newspapers. Rank the companies' cash flows from best to worst and write a two-page report on your findings.

Project 2.   Select a company and obtain its annual report, including all the financial statements. Focus on the statement of cash flows and, in particular, the cash flows from operating activities. Specify whether the company uses the direct method or the indirect method to report operating cash flows. As necessary, use the other financial statements (income statement, balance sheet, and statement of stockholders' equity) and the notes to prepare the company's cash flows from operating activities by using the *other* method.

For online homework, exercises, and problems that provide you with immediate feedback, please visit www.myaccountinglab.com.

Quick Check Answers

1. *a*
2. *a*
3. *d*
4. *b* ($150,000 + $8,000)
5. *d*
6. *c*
7. *c* ($50,000 + $10,000 − $8,000 + $15,000 + $9,000 + $3,000)
8. *b* ($5,000 − $35,000 + $40,000)
9. *b* (− $1,000 + $4,000 − $16,000)
10. *b* ($40,000 + $15,000)
11. *d* ($60,000 + $700,000 − $50,000)
12. *b* ($750,000 − $410,000 − $180,000)
13. *d* ($410,000 − $10,000 + $12,000)

13

Financial Statement Analysis

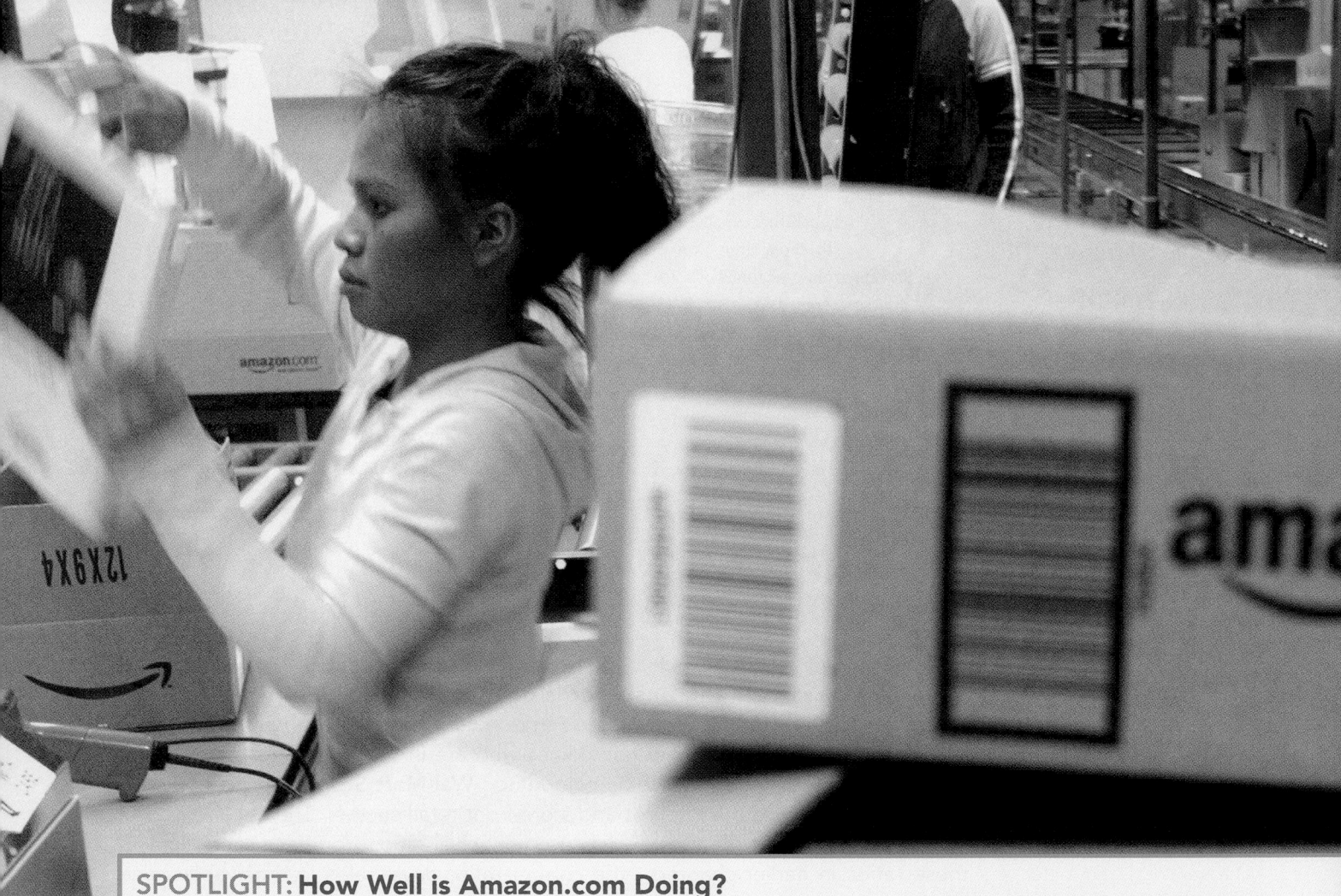

SPOTLIGHT: How Well is Amazon.com Doing?

Throughout this book we have shown how to account for companies such as **Apple, Inc.**, **Starbucks**, **PepsiCo**, **Southwest Airlines**, and **Google**. Only one aspect of the course remains: the overall analysis of financial statements. In this chapter, we cover this process, using the financial statements of Amazon.com, one of the book's focus companies, whose annual report is in Appendix A.

Amazon.com is the largest virtual supermarket on the globe. Since its inception as mostly a bookseller in 1995, the company has become synonymous with Internet retailing, expanding its lines of merchandise to cover almost every conceivable consumer item. Its Web site (www.amazon.com) offers the Earth's biggest selection of merchandise: books; movies, music, and games; computer hardware and software; electronics; home and garden supplies; grocery, health, and beauty products; children's toys and apparel; adult apparel; sports and recreational gear; and auto and industrial tools. In fact, it is hard to think of any consumer item Amazon.com does not sell at competitive prices! How well has Amazon.com been performing during the most severe economic recession in 70 years? We can answer that question by financial statement analysis. We begin with the analysis of Amazon.com, Inc.'s comparative Consolidated Statements of Operations for years ended December 31, 2008, 2007, and 2006. In 2008, Amazon.com earned revenues of about $19.2 billion. Is that positive or negative news? One of several things we can do to answer that question is to compare 2008 results to 2007. We also need to compare Amazon.com's results with those of some of its competitors.

Amazon.com, Inc.
Consolidated Statements of Operations

(In millions, except per share data)	Year ended December 31		
	2008	2007	2006
Net sales	$19,166	$14,835	$10,711
Cost of sales	14,896	11,482	8,255
Gross profit	4,270	3,353	2,456
Operating expenses:			
Fulfillment	1,658	1,292	937
Marketing	482	344	263
Technology and content	1,033	818	662
General and administrative	279	235	195
Other operating expense (income), net	(24)	9	10
Total operating expenses	3,428	2,698	2,067
Income from operations	842	655	389
Interest income	83	90	59
Interest expense	(71)	(77)	(78)
Other income (expense), net	47	(8)	7
Total non-operating income (expense)	59	5	(12)
Income before income taxes	901	660	377
Provision for income taxes	(247)	(184)	(187)
Equity-method investment activity, net of tax	(9)	—	—
Net income	$ 645	$ 476	$ 190
Basic earnings per share	$ 1.52	$ 1.15	$ 0.46

This chapter covers the basic tools of financial analysis. The first part of the chapter shows how to evaluate Amazon.com from year to year and how to compare Amazon.com to other companies who are in the same lines of business. For this comparison we use a retail competitor, **Wal-Mart Stores, Inc.,** a company that operates in both the Internet and store-front retail sectors. The second part of the chapter discusses the most widely used financial ratios. You have seen many of these ratios in earlier chapters—the current ratio, days' sales in receivables, and inventory turnover, return on assets, and return on equity.

By studying all these ratios together,

- You will learn the basic tools of financial analysis.
- You will enhance your business education.

Regardless of your chosen field—marketing, management, finance, entrepreneurship, or accounting—you will find these analytical tools useful as you move through your career.

LEARNING OBJECTIVES

1 Perform a horizontal analysis of financial statements

2 Perform a vertical analysis of financial statements

3 Prepare common-size financial statements

4 Use the statement of cash flows for decisions

5 Compute the standard financial ratios

6 Use ratios in decision making

7 Measure the economic value added by operations

HOW DOES AN INVESTOR EVALUATE A COMPANY?

Investors and creditors cannot evaluate a company by examining only one year's data. This is why most financial statements are comparative, that is, they cover at least two periods, like Amazon.com's Consolidated Statements of Operations that begins this chapter. In fact, most financial analysis covers trends of three to ten years. Since one of the goals of financial analysis is to predict the future, it makes sense to start by mapping the trends of the past. This is particularly true of income statement data such as net sales and net income.

The graphs in Exhibit 13-1 show Amazon.com's three-year trend of net sales and income from operations.

EXHIBIT 13-1 | Representative Financial Data of Amazon.com, Inc.

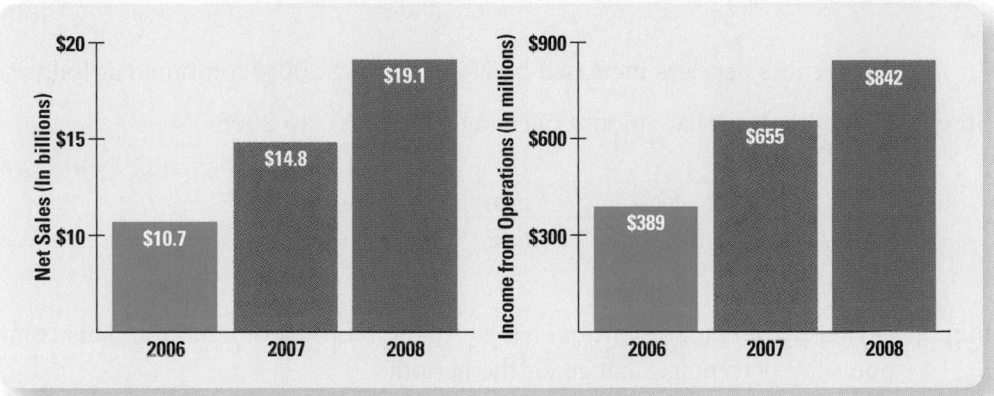

Amazon.com's net sales and income from operations (see Chapter 11 for discussion) both increased at a healthy pace during 2007 and 2008. These are good signs, because they may point the way to growth in company value in future years. How would you predict Amazon.com's net sales and income from operations for 2009 and beyond? Based on the recent past, you would probably extend the net sales line and the income from operations line upward. Let's examine some financial analysis tools. We begin with horizontal analysis.

HORIZONTAL ANALYSIS

Many decisions hinge on the trend of revenues, expenses, income from operations, and so on. Have revenues increased from last year? By how much? Suppose net sales have increased by $50,000. Considered alone this fact is not very helpful, but knowing the long-term *percentage change* in net sales helps a lot. It's better to know that net sales have increased by 20% than to know that the increase is $50,000. It's even better to know that percentage increases in net sales for the past several years have been rising year over year.

The study of percentage changes from year to year is called **horizontal analysis**. Computing a percentage change takes two steps:

1. Compute the dollar amount of the change from one period (the base period) to the next.

2. Divide the dollar amount of change by the base-period amount.

Illustration: Amazon.com, Inc.

Horizontal analysis is illustrated for Amazon.com, Inc., as follows (using the 2007 and 2008 figures, dollars in millions):

	2008	2007	Increase (Decrease) Amount	Increase (Decrease) Percentage
Net sales...............	$19,166	$14,835	$4,331	29.2%

Amazon.com's net sales increased by 29.2% during 2008, computed as follows:

Step 1 Compute the dollar amount of change from 2007 to 2008:

2008		2007		Increase
$19,166	−	$14,835	=	$4,331

Step 2 Divide the dollar amount of change by the base-period amount. This computes the percentage change for the period:

$$\text{Percentage change} = \frac{\text{Dollar amount of change}}{\text{Base-year amount}}$$
$$= \frac{\$4,331}{\$14,835} = 29.2\%$$

Exhibits 13-2 and 13-3 (on the following page) are detailed horizontal analysis for Amazon.com, Inc. The comparative Consolidated Statements of Operations show that net sales increased by 29.2% during 2008. In addition, Amazon.com's net income on the bottom line grew by 35.5%. Why the difference? Amazon.com was successful in increasing net sales while at the same time controlling, or even reducing, rates of increases in some expenses in 2008. In the operating expense category, only marketing expenses grew at a faster pace than net sales. Other operating items actually generated $24 million in income in 2008. Non-operating income items turned in a ten-fold positive change as well. The result was a 35.5% increase in net income after taxes, which is good news for shareholders!

EXHIBIT 13-2 | **Comparative Consolidated Statements of Operations—Horizontal Analysis**

Amazon.com, Inc.
Consolidated Statements of Operations

(In millions, except per share data)	Year ended December 31 2008	2007	Increase (decrease) Amount	Percentage
Net sales	$19,166	$14,835	$4,331	29.2%
Cost of sales	14,896	11,482	3,414	29.7
Gross profit	4,270	3,353	917	27.3
Operating expenses:				
Fulfillment	1,658	1,292	366	28.3
Marketing	482	344	138	40.1
Technology and content	1,033	818	215	26.3
General and administrative	279	235	44	18.7
Other operating expense (income), net	(24)	9	(33)	−366.7
Total operating expenses	3,428	2,698	730	27.1
Income from operations	842	655	187	28.5
Interest income	83	90	(7)	−7.8
Interest expense	(71)	(77)	6	−7.8
Other income (expense), net	47	(8)	55	687.5
Total non-operating income (expense)	59	5	54	1080.0
Income before income taxes	901	660	241	36.5
Provision for income taxes	(247)	(184)	(63)	34.2
Equity-method investment activity, net of tax	(9)	—		
Net income	$ 645	$ 476	$ 169	35.5%
Basic earnings per share	$ 1.52	$ 1.15	$ 0.37	32.2%

EXHIBIT 13-3 | Comparative Balance Sheets—Horizontal Analysis

Amazon.com, Inc.
Consolidated Balance Sheets

(in millions, except per share data)	December 31, 2008	December 31, 2007	Increase (decrease) Amount	Increase (decrease) Percentage
ASSETS				
Current assets:				
Cash and cash equivalents	$2,769	$2,539	$ 230	9.1%
Marketable securities	958	573	385	67.2
Inventories	1,399	1,200	199	16.6
Accounts receivable, net and other	827	705	122	17.3
Deferred tax assets	204	147	57	38.8
Total current assets	6,157	5,164	993	19.2
Fixed assets, net	854	543	311	57.3
Deferred tax assets	145	260	(115)	–44.2
Goodwill	438	222	216	97.3
Other assets	720	296	424	143.2
Total assets	$8,314	$6,485	$1,829	28.2%
LIABILITIES AND STOCKHOLDERS' EQUITY				
Current liabilities:				
Accounts payable	$3,594	$2,795	$ 799	28.6%
Accrued expenses and other	1,093	902	191	21.2
Current portion of long-term debt	59	17	42	247.1
Total current liabilities	4,746	3,714	1,032	27.8
Long-term debt	409	1,282	(873)	–68.1
Other long-term liabilities	487	292	195	66.8
Commitments and contingencies				
Stockholders' equity:				
Preferred stock, $0.01 par value:				
Authorized shares—500				
Issued and outstanding shares—none	—	—		
Common stock, $0.01 par value:				
Authorized shares—5,000				
Issued shares—445 and 431				
Outstanding shares—428 and 416	4	4	—	0.0
Treasury stock, at cost	(600)	(500)	(100)	20.0
Additional paid-in capital	4,121	3,063	1,058	34.5
Accumulated other comprehensive income (loss)	(123)	5	(128)	–2560.0
Accumulated deficit	(730)	(1,375)	645	–46.9
Total stockholders' equity	2,672	1,197	1,475	123.2
Total liabilities and stockholders' equity	$8,314	$6,485	$1,829	28.2%

Studying changes in balance sheet accounts can enhance our total understanding of the current and long-term financial position of the entity. Let's look at a few balance sheet changes. First, cash increased by a healthy 9.1% in 2008, and marketable securities increased by 67.2%. These changes indicate that the company's liquidity has significantly improved. Inventories and accounts receivable increased (16.6% and 17.3%, respectively), but not as fast as net sales (29.2%). Accounts payable increased by about the same rate as net sales (28.6%) indicating that the company's payments of short-term debt has about kept pace with its overall rate of growth in net sales. The aggregate impact of these changes in the current section of the balance sheet indicates that the company is improving in its ability to operate in the short run, which is a healthy sign, especially when one considers that 2008 was a period of deep global economic recession. Long-term assets increased by rates in excess of 50%, indicating that the company is growing. It also appears that the company refinanced some of its long-term debt (likely at lower interest rates), and incurred additional current maturities, which it can well afford to pay off in the near future. The company used some of its excess cash to purchase additional treasury stock from its shareholders. In summary, the net impact of all of these changes reduced its accumulated deficit (from the company's early years) by 46.9%. Overall, it appears that 2008 was a very good year for Amazon.com, Inc., while other companies (especially retailers) were struggling to survive.

STOP & THINK...

Examine Exhibits 13-2 and 13-3. Which items had the largest percentage fluctuations during 2008? Should these fluctuations cause alarm? Explain your reasoning.

Answer:

On the Consolidated Statements of Operations, both for operating and non-operating income and expenses, the category Other Income and Expense had the largest percentage increases (in both categories, net expenses turned to net income, causing huge percentage swings). On the balance sheet, the categories Other Assets, Current Portion of Long-Term Debt, and Accumulated Other Comprehensive Income or Loss experienced huge percentage fluctuations. These fluctuations would *not* cause alarm because the dollar amount of the category is relatively small to begin with, causing year over year percentage changes to look very large. This illustrates the materiality concept, which says to give major consideration to big items and less attention to small (immaterial) items. In this case, these items are immaterial to the analysis of Amazon.com, Inc.

Trend Percentages

Trend percentages are a form of horizontal analysis. Trends indicate the direction a business is taking. How have revenues changed over a five-year period? What trend does net income show? These questions can be answered by trend percentages over a representative period, such as the most recent five years.

Trend percentages are computed by selecting a base year whose amounts are set equal to 100%. The amount for each following year is stated as a percentage of the base amount. To compute a trend percentage, divide an item for a later year by the base year amount.

$$\text{Trend } \% = \frac{\text{Any year \$}}{\text{Base year \$}}$$

Recall that, in Chapter 11, we established that income from operations is often viewed as the primary measure of a company's earnings quality. This is because operating income represents a company's best predictor of the future net inflows from its core business units. Net income from operations is often used in estimating the current value of the business.

Amazon.com, Inc., showed income from operations for 2003–2008 years as follows:

(In millions)	2008	2007	2006	2005	2004	Base 2003
Income from operations	$842	$655	$389	$432	$440	$270

We want to calculate a trend for the five-year period 2003 through 2008. The first year in the series (2003) is set as the base year. Trend percentages are computed by dividing each year's amount by the 2003 amount. The resulting trend percentages follow (2003 = 100%):

	2008	2007	2006	2005	2004	Base 2003
Income from operations	312	243	144	160	163	100

Income from operations followed a downward trend from 2004 through 2006. In 2007, however, operating income took almost a 100% jump, relative to the base year, and it took another 69% jump in 2008. The most likely cause for these results is that Internet sales were just getting started in 2003. In the early years, people were generally reluctant to use the computer for their purchases because of concerns over Internet security. However, in recent years, improvements in security, as well as the relative convenience and lower cost of shopping from home as opposed to traveling to the store, have made Internet sales boom.

You can perform a trend analysis on any item you consider important. Trend analysis using income statement data is widely used for predicting the future.

Horizontal analysis highlights changes over time. However, no single technique gives a complete picture of a business.

VERTICAL ANALYSIS

OBJECTIVE

2 **Perform** a vertical analysis of financial statements

Vertical analysis shows the relationship of a financial-statement item to its base, which is the 100% figure. All items on the particular financial statement are reported as a percentage of the base. For the income statement, total revenue (sales) is usually the base. Suppose under normal conditions a company's net income is 8% of revenue. A drop to 6% may cause the company's stock price to fall.

Illustration: Amazon.com, Inc.

Exhibit 13-4 shows the vertical analysis of Amazon.com, Inc.'s income statement as a percentage of revenue (net sales). In this case,

$$\text{Vertical analysis \%} = \frac{\text{Each income statement item}}{\text{Total revenue}}$$

EXHIBIT 13-4 | Comparative Income Statements—Vertical Analysis

Amazon.com, Inc.
Consolidated Statements of Operations

		Year ended December 31		
(In millions, except per share data)	2008	% of total	2007	% of total
Net sales	$19,166	100.0%	$14,835	100.0%
Cost of sales	14,896	77.7	11,482	77.4
Gross profit	4,270	22.3	3,353	22.6
Operating expenses:				
Fulfillment	1,658	8.7	1,292	8.7
Marketing	482	2.5	344	2.3
Technology and content	1,033	5.4	818	5.5
General and administrative	279	1.5	235	1.6
Other operating expense (income), net	(24)	–0.1	9	0.1
Total operating expenses	3,428	17.9	2,698	18.2
Income from operations	842	4.4	655	4.4
Interest income	83	0.4	90	0.6
Interest expense	(71)	–0.4	(77)	–0.5
Other income (expense), net	47	0.2	(8)	–0.1
Total non-operating income (expense)	59	0.3	5	0.0
Income before income taxes	901	4.7	660	4.4
Provision for income taxes	(247)	–1.3	(184)	–1.2
Equity-method investment activity, net of tax	(9)	0.0	—	
Net income	$ 645	3.4%	$ 476	3.2%

For Amazon.com, Inc., in 2008, the vertical-analysis percentage for cost of sales is 77.7% ($14,896/$19,166), up slightly from 77.4% in 2007. Therefore, the company's gross margin percentage declined slightly from 2007 to 2008, from 22.6% to 22.3%. However, the company was successful in controlling operating costs in 2008 at approximately the same as or slightly lower percentages of net sales than in 2007. Operating expenses declined from 18.2% to 17.9% of net sales, causing income from operations as a percentage of net sales to remain stable at 4.4% over the two years.

Exhibit 13-5 on the following page shows the vertical analysis of Amazon.com's Consolidated Balance Sheets. The base amount (100%) is total assets for each year. The vertical analysis of Amazon.com's balance sheet reveals several things about Amazon.com's financial position at December 31, 2008, relative to 2007:

- Cash increased nicely in 2008, but declined as a percentage of total assets, while marketable (likely trading) securities increased as a percentage of total assets. Amazon.com, Inc., invested its excess cash in short-term investments expected to earn a higher return than interest-bearing cash accounts.
- Inventories as a percentage of total assets fell from 18.5% to 16.8%, indicating that inventory turnover is increasing, because sales (and related cost of sales) are increasing. Accounts receivable increased from 10.9% to 23% of total assets, reflecting an increase in net sales activity. Overall, current assets make up a large percentage of total assets (74.1%, down from 79.6% in 2007).
- The company's debt to total assets (57.1% + 4.9% + 5.9% = 67.9%) improved significantly in 2008 from 81.6% in 2007. Although current liabilities stayed about the same (57%) over the two years, the percentage of total assets financed with long-term

debt declined significantly, reflecting the company's substantially improved cash position and repayment of a good portion of its long-term debt. Amazon.com, Inc., grew substantially healthier from the standpoint of leverage in 2008.

How Do We Compare One Company to Another?

OBJECTIVE

3 **Prepare** common-size financial statements

Exhibits 13-4 and 13-5 can be modified to report only percentages (no dollar amounts). Such financial statements are called **common-size statements**. In order to perform vertical analysis, you must first convert the financial statements to common-size format.

EXHIBIT 13-5 | **Comparative Balance Sheets—Vertical Analysis**

Amazon.com, Inc.
Consolidated Balance Sheets

	Year ended December 31			
(In millions, except per share data)	2008	% of total	2007	% of total
ASSETS				
Current assets:				
Cash and cash equivalents	$2,769	33.3%	$2,539	39.2%
Marketable securities	958	11.5	573	8.8
Inventories	1,399	16.8	1,200	18.5
Accounts receivable, net and other	827	10.0	705	10.9
Deferred tax assets	204	2.5	147	2.3
Total current assets	6,157	74.1	5,164	79.6
Fixed assets, net	854	10.3	543	8.4
Deferred tax assets	145	1.7	260	4.0
Goodwill	438	5.3	222	3.4
Other assets	720	8.7	296	4.6
Total assets	$8,314	100.0%	$6,485	100.0%
LIABILITIES AND STOCKHOLDERS' EQUITY				
Current liabilities:				
Accounts payable	$3,594	43.2%	$2,795	43.1%
Accrued expenses and other	1,093	13.1	902	13.9
Current portion of long-term debt	59	0.7	17	0.3
Total current liabilities	4,746	57.1	3,714	57.3
Long-term debt	409	4.9	1,282	19.8
Other long-term liabilities	487	5.9	292	4.5
Commitments and contingencies				
Stockholders' equity:				
Preferred stock, $0.01 par value:				
Authorized shares—500				
Issued and outstanding shares—none	—		—	
Common stock, $0.01 par value:				
Authorized shares—5,000				
Issued shares—445 and 431				
Outstanding shares—428 and 416	4	0.05	4	0.1
Treasury stock, at cost	(600)	–7.2	(500)	–7.7
Additional paid-in capital	4,121	49.6	3,063	47.2
Accumulated other comprehensive income (loss)	(123)	–1.5	5	0.1
Accumulated deficit	(730)	–8.8	(1,375)	–21.2
Total stockholders' equity	2,672	32.1	1,197	18.5
Total liabilities and stockholders' equity	$8,314	100.0%	$6,485	100.0%

On a common-size income statement, each item is expressed as a percentage of the revenue (net sales) amount. Total revenue is therefore the *common size*. In the balance sheet, the common size is total assets. A common-size financial statement aids the comparison of different companies because all amounts are stated in percentages, thus expressing the financial results of each comparative company in terms of a common denominator.

STOP & THINK...

Calculate the common-size percentages for the following income statement:

Net sales..................................	$150,000
Cost of goods sold.................	60,000
Gross profit............................	90,000
Operating expense..................	40,000
Operating income...................	50,000
Income tax expense................	15,000
Net income.............................	$ 35,000

Answer:

Net sales.................................	100%	(= $150,000 ÷ $150,000)
Cost of goods sold.................	40	(= $ 60,000 ÷ $150,000)
Gross profit............................	60	(= $ 90,000 ÷ $150,000)
Operating expense..................	27	(= $ 40,000 ÷ $150,000)
Operating income...................	33	(= $ 50,000 ÷ $150,000)
Income tax expense................	10	(= $ 15,000 ÷ $150,000)
Net income.............................	23%	(= $ 35,000 ÷ $150,000)

BENCHMARKING

Benchmarking compares a company to some standard set by others. The goal of benchmarking is improvement. Suppose you are a financial analyst for **Goldman Sachs**, a large investment bank. You are considering investing in one of two different retailers, say Amazon.com, Inc., or Wal-Mart Stores, Inc. A direct comparison of these companies' financial statements is not meaningful, in part because Wal-Mart, Inc., is so much larger than Amazon.com. However, you can convert the companies' income statements to common size and compare the percentages. This comparison is meaningful, as we shall see.

Benchmarking Against a Key Competitor

Exhibit 13-6 on the following page presents the common-size income statements of Amazon.com, Inc., benchmarked against Wal-Mart Stores, Inc. The companies are not exactly comparable because of differences in their business models. For example, Wal-Mart has physical stores as well as online retail services. However, if you look at their Web sites, the two companies are very similar, organized in much the same way. They are close enough to illustrate the value of common-size vertical analysis. In this comparison, the results of the two companies are strikingly similar. Amazon.com's cost of sales is 1.2% higher than Wal-Mart's, but its operating expenses are about a percentage point lower. Their net incomes as a percentage of net sales are identical. Of course, Wal-Mart comes out far ahead in terms of total earnings because of its sheer size ($12.7 billion vs. $645 million for Amazon.com).

EXHIBIT 13-6 | **Common-Size Income Statement Compared with a Key Competitor**

Amazon.com, Inc.
Common-Size Income Statement for Comparison with Key Competitor (Adapted)
Year Ended During 2008

	Amazon.com	Wal-Mart
Net sales	100.0%	100.0%
Cost of sales	77.7	76.5
Operating expenses	17.9	18.8
Other expenses (income), net	1.0	1.3
Net income	3.4%	3.4%

OBJECTIVE

4 Use the statement of cash flows for decisions

Using the Statement of Cash Flows

This chapter has focused on the income statement and balance sheet. We may also perform horizontal and vertical analyses on the statement of cash flows. To continue our discussion of its role in decision making, let's use Exhibit 13-7, the statement of cash flows of Unix Corporation.

EXHIBIT 13-7 | **Statement of Cash Flows**

Unix Corporation
Statement of Cash Flows
Year Ended June 30, 2010

(In millions)

Operating activities:		
Net income		$ 35,000
Adjustments for noncash items:		
Depreciation	$ 14,000	
Net increase in current assets other than cash	(24,000)	
Net increase in current liabilities	8,000	(2,000)
Net cash provided by operating activities		33,000
Investing activities:		
Sale of property, plant, and equipment	$ 91,000	
Net cash provided by investing activities		91,000
Financing activities:		
Borrowing	$ 22,000	
Payment of long-term debt	(90,000)	
Purchase of treasury stock	(9,000)	
Payment of dividends	(23,000)	
Net cash used for financing activities		(100,000)
Increase (decrease) in cash		$ 24,000

Analysts find the statement of cash flows more helpful for spotting weakness than for gauging success. Why? Because a *shortage* of cash can throw a company into bankruptcy, but lots of cash doesn't ensure success. The statement of cash flows in Exhibit 13-7 reveals the following:

- Unix's operations provide less cash than net income. That's strange. Ordinarily, cash provided by operations exceeds net income because of the add-back of depreciation and amortization. The increases in current assets and current liabilities should cancel out over time. For Unix Corporation, current assets increased far more than current liabilities during the year. This may be harmless. But it may signal difficulty in collecting receivables or selling inventory. Either event will cause trouble.
- The sale of plant assets is Unix's major source of cash. This is okay if this is a one-time situation. Unix may be shifting from one line of business to another, and it may be selling off old assets. But if the sale of plant assets is the major source of cash for several periods, Unix will face a cash shortage. A company can't sell off its plant assets forever. Soon it will go out of business.
- The only strength shown by the statement of cash flows is that Unix paid off more long-term debt than it did new borrowing. This will improve the debt ratio and Unix's credit standing.

Here are some cash-flow signs of a healthy company:

- Operations are the major *source* of cash (not a *use* of cash).
- Investing activities include more purchases than sales of long-term assets.
- Financing activities are not dominated by borrowing.

MID-CHAPTER SUMMARY PROBLEM

Perform a horizontal analysis and a vertical analysis of the comparative income statement of Hard Rock Products, Inc., which makes metal detectors. State whether 2011 was a good year or a bad year, and give your reasons.

Hard Rock Products, Inc.
Comparative Income Statements
Years Ended December 31, 2011 and 2010

	2011	2010
Total revenues	$275,000	$225,000
Expenses:		
Cost of goods sold	194,000	165,000
Engineering, selling, and administrative expenses	54,000	48,000
Interest expense	5,000	5,000
Income tax expense	9,000	3,000
Other expense (income)	1,000	(1,000)
Total expenses	263,000	220,000
Net income	$ 12,000	$ 5,000

Answer

The horizontal analysis shows that total revenues increased 22.2%. This was greater than the 19.5% increase in total expenses, resulting in a 140% increase in net income.

Hard Rock Products, Inc.
Horizontal Analysis of Comparative Income Statements
Years Ended December 31, 2011 and 2010

			Increase (Decrease)	
	2011	2010	Amount	Percent
Total revenues	$275,000	$225,000	$50,000	22.2%
Expenses:				
Cost of goods sold	194,000	165,000	29,000	17.6
Engineering, selling, and administrative expenses	54,000	48,000	6,000	12.5
Interest expense	5,000	5,000	—	—
Income tax expense	9,000	3,000	6,000	200.0
Other expense (income)	1,000	(1,000)	2,000	—*
Total expenses	263,000	220,000	43,000	19.5
Net income	$ 12,000	$ 5,000	$ 7,000	140.0%

*Percentage changes are typically not computed for shifts from a negative to a positive amount and vice versa.

The vertical analysis on the next page shows decreases in the percentages of net sales consumed by the cost of goods sold (from 73.3% to 70.5%) and by the engineering, selling, and administrative expenses (from 21.3% to 19.6%). Because these two items are Hard Rock's largest dollar expenses, their percentage decreases are quite important. The relative reduction in expenses raised 2011 net income to 4.4% of sales, compared with 2.2% the preceding year. The overall analysis indicates that 2011 was significantly better than 2010.

Hard Rock Products, Inc.
Vertical Analysis of Comparative Income Statements
Years Ended December 31, 2011 and 2010

	2011		2010	
	Amount	Percent	Amount	Percent
Total revenues	$275,000	100.0 %	$225,000	100.0 %
Expenses:				
Cost of goods sold	194,000	70.5	165,000	73.3
Engineering, selling, and				
administrative expenses........	54,000	19.6	48,000	21.3
Interest expense	5,000	1.8	5,000	2.2
Income tax expense..................	9,000	3.3	3,000	1.4**
Other expense (income)	1,000	0.4	(1,000)	(0.4)
Total expenses.....................	263,000	95.6	220,000	97.8
Net income..................................	$ 12,000	4.4 %	$ 5,000	2.2 %

**Number rounded up.

USING RATIOS TO MAKE BUSINESS DECISIONS

Ratios are a major tool of financial analysis. We have discussed the use of many ratios in financial analysis in various chapters throughout the book. A ratio expresses the relationship of one number to another. Suppose your balance sheet shows current assets of $100,000 and current liabilities of $50,000. The ratio of current assets to current liabilities is $100,000 to $50,000. We can express this ratio as 2 to 1, or 2:1. The current ratio is 2.0.

Many companies include ratios in a special section of their annual reports. RubberMate Corporation displays ratio data in the Summary section. Exhibit 13-8 shows data from that summary section. Investment services—**Moody's, Standard & Poor's, Risk Management Association**, and others—report these ratios.

OBJECTIVE

5 Compute the standard financial ratios

EXHIBIT 13-8 | **Financial Summary of RubberMate Corporation (Dollar Amounts in Millions Except per-share Amounts)**

Year Ended December 31	2011	2010	2009
Operating Results			
Net income..	$ 218	$ 164	$ 163
Per common share.................................	$1.32	$1.02	$1.02
Percent of sales....................................	10.8%	9.1%	9.8%
Return on average shareholders' equity...............	20.0%	17.5%	19.7%
Financial Position			
Current assets.....................................	$ 570	$ 477	$ 419
Current liabilities	$ 359	$ 323	$ 345
Working capital....................................	$ 211	$ 154	$ 74
Current ratio	1.59	1.48	1.21

The ratios we discuss in this chapter are classified as follows:

1. Ability to pay current liabilities
2. Ability to sell inventory and collect receivables
3. Ability to pay long-term debt
4. Profitability
5. Analyze stock as an investment

How much can a computer help in analyzing financial statements for investment purposes? Time yourself as you complete the problems in this chapter. Multiply your efforts by 10 as though you were comparing 10 companies. Now rank these 10 companies on the basis of four or five ratios.

Measuring Ability to Pay Current Liabilities

Working capital is defined as follows:

$$\text{Working capital} = \text{Current assets} - \text{Current liabilities}$$

Working capital measures the ability to pay current liabilities with current assets. In general, the larger the working capital, the better the ability to pay debts. Recall that capital is total assets minus total liabilities. Working capital is like a "current" version of total capital. Consider two companies with equal working capital:

	Company	
	Jones	Smith
Current assets......................	$100,000	$200,000
Current liabilities	50,000	150,000
Working capital	$ 50,000	$ 50,000

Both companies have working capital of $50,000, but Jones' working capital is as large as its current liabilities. Smith's working capital is only one-third as large as current liabilities. Jones is in a better position because its working capital is a higher percentage of current liabilities. Two decision-making tools based on working-capital data are the *current ratio* and the *acid-test ratio*.

Current Ratio.   The most common ratio evaluating current assets and current liabilities is the **current ratio**, which is current assets divided by current liabilities. As discussed in Chapter 3, the current ratio measures the ability to pay current liabilities with current assets. Exhibit 13-9 gives the income statement and balance sheet data of Palisades Furniture.

The current ratios of Palisades Furniture, Inc., at December 31, 2011 and 2010, follow, along with the average for the retail furniture industry:

Formula	*Palisades' Current Ratio*		Industry Average
	2011	2010	
Current ratio = $\dfrac{\text{Current assets}}{\text{Current liabilities}}$	$\dfrac{\$262,000}{\$142,000} = 1.85$	$\dfrac{\$236,000}{\$126,000} = 1.87$	1.50

EXHIBIT 13-9 | Comparative Financial Statements

Palisades Furniture, Inc.
Comparative Income Statements
Years Ended December 31, 2011 and 2010

	2011	2010
Net sales	$858,000	$803,000
Cost of goods sold	513,000	509,000
Gross profit	345,000	294,000
Operating expenses:		
Selling expenses	126,000	114,000
General expenses	118,000	123,000
Total operating expenses	244,000	237,000
Income from operations	101,000	57,000
Interest revenue	4,000	—
Interest (expense)	(24,000)	(14,000)
Income before income taxes	81,000	43,000
Income tax expense	33,000	17,000
Net income	$ 48,000	$ 26,000

Palisades Furniture, Inc.
Comparative Balance Sheets
December 31, 2011 and 2010

	2011	2010
Assets		
Current Assets:		
Cash	$ 29,000	$ 32,000
Accounts receivable, net	114,000	85,000
Inventories	113,000	111,000
Prepaid expenses	6,000	8,000
Total current assets	262,000	236,000
Long-term investments	18,000	9,000
Property, plant, and equipment, net	507,000	399,000
Total assets	$787,000	$644,000
Liabilities		
Current Liabilities:		
Notes payable	$ 42,000	$ 27,000
Accounts payable	73,000	68,000
Accrued liabilities	27,000	31,000
Total current liabilities	142,000	126,000
Long-term debt	289,000	198,000
Total liabilities	431,000	324,000
Stockholders' Equity		
Common stock, no par	186,000	186,000
Retained earnings	170,000	134,000
Total stockholders' equity	356,000	320,000
Total liabilities and stockholders' equity	$787,000	$644,000

The current ratio decreased slightly but not significantly during 2011. In general, a higher current ratio indicates a stronger financial position. The business has sufficient current assets to maintain its operations. Palisades Furniture's current ratio of 1.85 compares favorably with the current ratios of some well-known companies:

Company	Current Ratio
Wal-Mart Stores, Inc.	0.8
Hewlett-Packard Company................	0.98
eBay	1.70

Note: These figures show that ratio values vary widely from one industry to another.

What is an acceptable current ratio? The answer depends on the industry. The norm for companies in most industries is around 1.50, as reported by the Risk Management Association. Palisades Furniture's current ratio of 1.85 is better than average.

The Limitations of Ratio Analysis

Business decisions are made in a world of uncertainty. As useful as ratios are, they aren't a cure-all. Consider a physician's use of a thermometer. A reading of 102.0° Fahrenheit tells a doctor something is wrong with the patient, but that doesn't indicate what the problem is or how to cure it.

In financial analysis, a sudden drop in the current ratio signals that *something* is wrong, but that doesn't identify the problem. A manager must analyze the figures to learn what caused the ratio to fall. A drop in current assets may mean a cash shortage or that sales are slow. The manager must evaluate all the ratios in the light of factors such as increased competition or a slowdown in the economy.

Legislation, international affairs, scandals, and other factors can turn profits into losses. To be useful, ratios should be analyzed over a period of years to consider all relevant factors. Any one year, or even any two years, may not represent the company's performance over the long term.

Acid-Test Ratio.   As discussed in Chapter 5, the **acid-test** (or **quick**) **ratio** tells us whether the entity could pass the acid test of paying all its current liabilities if they came due immediately. The acid-test ratio uses a narrower base to measure liquidity than the current ratio does.

To compute the acid-test ratio, we add cash, short-term investments, and net current receivables (accounts and notes receivable, net of allowances) and divide by current liabilities. Inventory and prepaid expenses are excluded because they are less liquid. A business may be unable to convert inventory to cash immediately.

Palisades Furniture's acid-test ratios for 2011 and 2010 follow:

Formula	Palisades' Acid-Test Ratio		Industry Average
	2011	**2010**	
Acid-test ratio = $\dfrac{\text{Cash + Short-term investments + Net current receivables}}{\text{Current liabilities}}$	$\dfrac{\$29,000 + \$0 + \$114,000}{\$142,000} = 1.01$	$\dfrac{\$32,000 + \$0 + \$85,000}{\$126,000} = 0.93$	0.40

The company's acid-test ratio improved during 2011 and is significantly better than the industry average. Compare Palisades' acid test ratio with the values of some leading companies.

Company	Acid-Test Ratio
Best Buy	0.30
DineEquity (IHOP).........	1.41
Foot Locker, Inc.	0.98

An acid-test ratio of 0.90 to 1.00 is acceptable in most industries. How can a company such as Best Buy function with such a low acid-test ratio? Best Buy prices its inventory to turn it over quickly. And most of Best Buy's sales are for cash or credit cards, so the company collects cash quickly. This points us to the next two ratios.

Measuring Ability to Sell Inventory and Collect Receivables

The ability to sell inventory and collect receivables is critical. In this section, we discuss three ratios that measure this ability.

Inventory Turnover. Companies generally strive to sell their inventory as quickly as possible. The faster inventory sells, the sooner cash comes in.

Inventory turnover, discussed in Chapter 6, measures the number of times a company sells its average level of inventory during a year. A fast turnover indicates ease in selling inventory; a low turnover indicates difficulty. A value of 6 means that the company's average level of inventory has been sold six times during the year, and that's usually better than a turnover of three times. But too high a value can mean that the business is not keeping enough inventory on hand, which can lead to lost sales if the company can't fill orders. Therefore, a business strives for the most *profitable* rate of turnover, not necessarily the *highest* rate.

To compute inventory turnover, divide cost of goods sold by the average inventory for the period. We use the cost of goods sold—*not sales*—in the computation because both cost of goods sold and inventory are stated *at cost*. Palisades Furniture's inventory turnover for 2011 is

Formula	Palisades' Inventory Turnover	Industry Average
Inventory turnover = $\dfrac{\text{Cost of goods sold}}{\text{Average inventory}}$	$\dfrac{\$513,000}{\$112,000} = 4.6$	1.50

Cost of goods sold comes from the income statement (Exhibit 13-9). Average inventory is the average of beginning ($111,000) and ending inventory ($113,000). (See the balance sheet, Exhibit 13-9.) If inventory levels vary greatly from month to month, you should compute the average by adding the 12 monthly balances and dividing the sum by 12.

Inventory turnover varies widely with the nature of the business. For example, YUM! Brands, owner of fast food restaurants Pizza Hut, Taco Bell, KFC, and Long John Silver's, has an inventory turnover ratio of 29 times per year because food spoils so quickly. Williams-Sonoma, Inc., on the other hand, turns its inventory over only about 3.7 times per year. Williams-Sonoma keeps enough inventory on hand for customers to make their selections.

To evaluate inventory turnover, compare the ratio over time. A sharp decline suggests the need for corrective action.

Accounts Receivable Turnover. **Accounts receivable turnover** measures the ability to collect cash from customers. In general, the higher the ratio, the better. However, a receivable turnover that is too high may indicate that credit is too tight, and that may cause you to lose sales to good customers.

To compute accounts receivable turnover, divide net sales by average net accounts receivable. The ratio tells how many times during the year average receivables were turned into cash. Palisades Furniture's accounts receivable turnover ratio for 2011 is

Formula	Palisades' Accounts Receivable Turnover	Industry Average
$\dfrac{\text{Accounts}}{\text{receivable turnover}} = \dfrac{\text{Net sales}}{\substack{\text{Average net} \\ \text{accounts receivable}}}$	$\dfrac{\$858,000}{\$99,500} = 8.6$	51.0

Average net accounts receivable is figured by adding beginning ($85,000) and ending receivables ($114,000), then dividing by 2. If accounts receivable vary widely during the year, compute the average by using the 12 monthly balances.

Palisades' receivable turnover of 8.6 times per year is much slower than the industry average. Why the slow collection? Palisades is a hometown store that sells to local people who pay bills over a period of time. Many larger furniture stores sell their receivables to other companies called *factors*. This practice, discussed in Chapter 6, keeps receivables low and receivable turnover high. But companies that factor (sell) their receivables receive less than face value of the receivables. Palisades Furniture follows a different strategy.

Days' Sales in Receivables. Businesses must convert accounts receivable to cash. All else being equal, the lower the receivable balance, the better the cash flow.

The **days'-sales-in-receivables** ratio, also discussed in Chapter 6, shows how many days' sales remain in Accounts Receivable. Compute the ratio by a two-step process:

1. Divide net sales by 365 days to figure average sales per day.

2. Divide average net receivables by average sales per day.

The data to compute this ratio for Palisades Furniture, Inc., are taken from the 2011 income statement and the balance sheet (Exhibit 13-9):

Formula	Palisades' Days' Sales in Accounts Receivable	Industry Average
Days' sales in average accounts receivable:		
1. One day's sales = $\dfrac{\text{Net sales}}{365 \text{ days}}$	$\dfrac{\$858,000}{365 \text{ days}} = \$2,351$	
$\substack{\text{Days' sales in} \\ \text{2. average accounts} \\ \text{receivable}} = \dfrac{\substack{\text{Average net} \\ \text{accounts receivable}}}{\text{One day's sales}}$	$\dfrac{\$99,500}{\$2,351} = 42 \text{ days}$	7 days

Days' sales in average receivables can also be computed in a single step: $99,500/($858,000/365 days) = 42 days.

Measuring Ability to Pay Debts

The ratios discussed so far relate to current assets and current liabilities. They measure the ability to sell inventory, collect receivables, and pay current bills. Two indicators of the ability to pay total liabilities are the *debt ratio* and the *times-interest-earned ratio*.

Debt Ratio.   Suppose you are a bank loan officer and you have received $500,000 loan applications from two similar companies. The first company already owes $600,000, and the second owes only $250,000. Which company gets the loan? Company 2, because it owes less.

This relationship between total liabilities and total assets is called the **debt ratio**. Discussed in Chapters 3 and 8, the debt ratio tells us the proportion of assets financed with debt. A debt ratio of 1 reveals that debt has financed all the assets. A debt ratio of 0.50 means that debt finances half the assets. The higher the debt ratio, the greater the pressure to pay interest and principal. The lower the ratio, the lower the risk.

The debt ratios for Palisades Furniture in 2011 and 2010 follow:

| Formula | Palisades' Debt Ratio | | Industry Average |
	2011	2010	
Debt ratio = $\frac{\text{Total liabilities}}{\text{Total assets}}$	$\frac{\$431,000}{\$787,000} = 0.55$	$\frac{\$324,000}{\$644,000} = 0.50$	0.64

Risk Management Association reports that the average debt ratio for most companies ranges around 0.62, with relatively little variation from company to company. Palisades' 0.55 debt ratio indicates a fairly low-risk debt position compared with the retail furniture industry average of 0.64.

Times-Interest-Earned Ratio.   Analysts use a second ratio—the **times-interest-earned ratio** (introduced in Chapter 8)—to relate income to interest expense. To compute the times-interest-earned ratio, divide income from operations (operating income) by interest expense. This ratio measures the number of times operating income can *cover* interest expense and is also called the *interest-coverage ratio*. A high ratio indicates ease in paying interest; a low value suggests difficulty.

Palisades' times-interest-earned ratios are

| Formula | Palisades' Times-Interest-Earned Ratio | | Industry Average |
	2011	2010	
Times-interest-earned ratio = $\frac{\text{Income from operations}}{\text{Interest expense}}$	$\frac{\$101,000}{\$24,000} = 4.21$	$\frac{\$57,000}{\$14,000} = 4.07$	2.80

The company's times-interest-earned ratio increased in 2011. This is a favorable sign.

Measuring Profitability

The fundamental goal of business is to earn a profit, and so the ratios that measure profitability are reported widely.

Rate of Return on Sales.   In business, *return* refers to profitability. Consider the **rate of return on net sales**, or simply *return on sales* (ROS). (The word *net* is usually omitted for convenience.) This ratio shows the percentage of each sales dollar earned as net income. The return-on-sales ratios for Palisades Furniture are

		Palisades' Rate of Return on Sales		Industry
	Formula	2011	2010	Average
Rate of return on sales	$= \dfrac{\text{Net income}}{\text{Net sales}}$	$\dfrac{\$48,000}{\$858,000} = 0.056$	$\dfrac{\$26,000}{\$803,000} = 0.032$	0.008

Companies strive for a high rate of return on sales. The higher the percentage, the more profit is being generated by sales dollars. Palisades Furniture's return on sales is higher than the average furniture store. Compare Palisades' rate of return on sales to the rates of some leading companies:

Company	Rate of Return on Sales
FedEx	0.056
PepsiCo	0.119
Intel	0.141

Rate of Return on Total Assets.   Also introduced in Chapter 9, the **rate of return on total assets**, or simply *return on assets* (ROA), measures a company's success in using assets to earn a profit. Creditors have loaned money, and the interest they receive is their return on investment. Shareholders have bought the company's stock, and net income is their return. The sum of interest expense and net income is the return to the two groups that have financed the company. This sum is the numerator of the ratio. Average total assets is the denominator. The return-on-assets ratio for Palisades Furniture is

	Formula	Palisades' 2011 Rate of Return on Total Assets	Industry Average
Rate of return on assets	$= \dfrac{\text{Net income} + \text{Interest expense}}{\text{Average total assets}}$	$\dfrac{\$48,000 + \$24,000}{\$715,500} = 0.101$	0.078

To compute average total assets, add the beginning and ending balances and divide by 2. Compare Palisades Furniture's rate of return on assets to the rates of these leading companies:

Company	Rate of Return on Assets
General Electric	0.055
Starbucks	0.066
Google	0.108

Rate of Return on Common Stockholders' Equity. A popular measure of profitability is **rate of return on common stockholders' equity**, often shortened to *return on equity* (ROE). Also discussed in Chapter 9, this ratio shows the relationship between net income and common stockholders' investment in the company—how much income is earned for every $1 invested.

To compute this ratio, first subtract preferred dividends from net income to measure income available to the common stockholders. Then divide income available to common by average common equity during the year. Common equity is total equity minus preferred equity. The 2011 return on common equity for Palisades Furniture is

Formula		Palisades' 2011 Rate of Return on Common Stockholders' Equity	Industry Average
Rate of return on common stockholders' equity	$= \dfrac{\text{Net income} - \text{Preferred dividends}}{\text{Average common stockholders' equity}}$	$\dfrac{\$48,000 - \$0}{\$338,000} = 0.142$	0.121

Average equity uses the beginning and ending balances [($320,000 + $356,000)/2 = $338,000].

Observe that Palisades' return on equity (0.142) is higher than its return on assets (0.101). This is a good sign. The difference results from borrowing at one rate—say, 8%—and investing the funds to earn a higher rate, such as the firm's 14.2% return on equity. This practice is called using **leverage**, or **trading on the equity**. The higher the debt ratio, the higher the leverage. Companies that finance operations with debt are said to *leverage* their positions.

For Palisades Furniture, leverage increases profitability. This is not always the case, because leverage can hurt profits. If revenues drop, debts still must be paid. Therefore, leverage is a double-edged sword. It increases profits during good times but compounds losses during bad times.

Palisades Furniture's rate of return on equity lags behind that of GE, but exceeds those of Google and Starbucks.

Company	Rate of Return on Common Equity
General Electric.................	0.158
Google	0.121
Starbucks	0.132

Earnings per Share of Common Stock. Discussed in Chapters 8 and 11, *earnings per share of common stock*, or simply **earnings per share (EPS)**, is the amount of net income earned for each share of outstanding *common* stock. EPS is the most widely quoted of all financial statistics. It's the only ratio that appears on the income statement.

Earnings per share is computed by dividing net income available to common stockholders by the average number of common shares outstanding during the year. Preferred dividends are subtracted from net income because the preferred stockholders have a prior claim to their dividends. Palisades Furniture has no preferred stock and thus has no preferred dividends. The firm's EPS for 2011 and 2010 follows (Palisades has 10,000 shares of common stock outstanding).

	Formula	Palisades' Earnings per Share	
		2011	2010
Earnings per share of common stock	$= \dfrac{\text{Net income} - \text{Preferred dividends}}{\text{Average number of shares of common stock outstanding}}$	$\dfrac{\$48,000 - \$0}{10,000} = \$4.80$	$\dfrac{\$26,000 - \$0}{10,000} = \$2.60$

Palisades Furniture's EPS increased 85% during 2011, and that's good news. The Palisades stockholders should not expect such a significant boost every year. Most companies strive to increase EPS by 10% to 15% annually.

Analyzing Stock Investments

OBJECTIVE

6 **Use** ratios in decision making

Investors buy stock to earn a return on their investment. This return consists of two parts: (1) gains (or losses) from selling the stock and (2) dividends.

Price/Earnings Ratio. The **price/earnings ratio** is the ratio of common stock price to earnings per share. This ratio, abbreviated P/E, appears in *The Wall Street Journal* stock listings and online. It shows the market price of $1 of earnings.

Calculations for the P/E ratios of Palisades Furniture, Inc., follow. The market price of Palisades' common stock was $60 at the end of 2011 and $35 at the end of 2010. Stock prices can be obtained from a company's Web site, a financial publication, or a stockbroker.

	Formula	Palisades' Price/Earnings Ratio	
		2011	2010
P/E ratio $=$	$\dfrac{\text{Market price per share of common stock}}{\text{Earnings per share}}$	$\dfrac{\$60.00}{\$4.80} = 12.5$	$\dfrac{\$35.00}{\$2.60} = 13.5$

Given Palisades Furniture's 2011 P/E ratio of 12.5, we would say that the company's stock is selling at 12.5 times earnings. Each $1 of Palisades' earnings is worth $12.50 to the stock market.

Dividend Yield. **Dividend yield** is the ratio of dividends per share of stock to the stock's market price. This ratio measures the percentage of a stock's market value returned annually to the stockholders as dividends. *Preferred* stockholders pay special attention to this ratio because they invest primarily to receive dividends.

Palisades Furniture paid annual cash dividends of $1.20 per share in 2011 and $1.00 in 2010. The market prices of the company's common stock were $60 in 2011 and $35 in 2010. The firm's dividend yields on common stock are

	Formula	Dividend Yield on Palisades' Common Stock	
		2011	2010
Dividend yield on common stock* $=$	$\dfrac{\text{Dividend per share of common stock}}{\text{Market price per share of common stock}}$	$\dfrac{\$1.20}{\$60.00} = 0.020$	$\dfrac{\$1.00}{\$35.00} = 0.029$

*Dividend yields may also be calculated for preferred stock.

An investor who buys Palisades Furniture common stock for $60 can expect to receive around 2% of the investment annually in the form of cash dividends. Dividend yields vary widely, from 5% to 8% for older, established firms (such as **Procter & Gamble** and **General Electric**) down to the range of 0% to 3% for young, growth-oriented companies. **Google**, **Starbucks**, and **eBay** pay no cash dividends.

Book Value per Share of Common Stock.   Book value per share of common stock is simply common stockholders' equity divided by the number of shares of common stock outstanding. Common equity equals total equity less preferred equity. Palisades Furniture has no preferred stock outstanding. Calculations of its book value per share of common follow. Recall that 10,000 shares of common stock were outstanding.

		Book Value per Share of Palisades' Common Stock	
	Formula	2011	2010
Book value per share of common stock	$= \dfrac{\text{Total stockholders' equity} - \text{Preferred equity}}{\text{Number of shares of common stock outstanding}}$	$\dfrac{\$356,000 - \$0}{10,000} = \$35.60$	$\dfrac{\$320,000 - \$0}{10,000} = \$32.00$

Book value indicates the recorded accounting amount for each share of common stock outstanding. Many experts believe book value is not useful for investment analysis because it bears no relationship to market value and provides little information beyond what's reported on the balance sheet. But some investors base their investment decisions on book value. For example, some investors rank stocks by the ratio of market price to book value. The lower the ratio, the more attractive the stock. These investors are called "value" investors, as contrasted with "growth" investors, who focus more on trends in net income.

What does the outlook for the future look like for Palisades Furniture? If the company can stay on the same path it has followed for the past two years, it looks bright. It appears that its earnings per share are solid, and its ROS, ROA, and ROE ratios are all above average for its industry. From the standpoint of liquidity and leverage, it also appears to be in good shape, with higher liquidity, excellent debt and interest coverage, and lower debt ratios than its industry. The company's P/E ratio of 12:1 is relatively low, and it pays a 2% dividend. All of these factors make Palisades Furniture stock look like a good investment.

OTHER MEASURES
Economic Value Added (EVA®)

The top managers of **Coca-Cola**, **Quaker Oats**, and other leading companies use **economic value added (EVA®)** to evaluate operating performance. EVA® combines accounting and finance to measure whether operations have increased stockholder wealth. EVA® can be computed as follows:

OBJECTIVE

7 **Measure** the economic value added by operations

$$\text{EVA}^® = \text{Net income} + \text{Interest expense} - \text{Capital charge}$$

$$\text{Capital charge} = \begin{pmatrix} & & \text{(Beginning balances)} & & \\ & & \text{Current} & & \\ \text{Notes} & + & \text{maturities} & + & \text{Long-term} & + & \text{Stockholders'} \\ \text{payable} & & \text{of long-} & & \text{debt} & & \text{equity} \\ & & \text{term debt} & & & & \end{pmatrix} \times \begin{array}{c} \text{Cost of} \\ \text{capital} \end{array}$$

All amounts for the EVA® computation, except the cost of capital, come from the financial statements. The **cost of capital** is a weighted average of the returns demanded by the company's stockholders and lenders. Cost of capital varies with the company's level of risk. For example, stockholders would demand a higher return from a start-up company than from Amazon.com, Inc., because the new company is untested and therefore more risky. Lenders would also charge the new company a higher interest rate because of its greater risk. Thus, the new company has a higher cost of capital than Amazon.com, Inc.

The cost of capital is a major topic in finance classes. In the following discussions we assume a value for the cost of capital (such as 10%, 12%, or 15%) to illustrate the computation of EVA®.

The idea behind EVA® is that the returns to the company's stockholders (net income) and to its creditors (interest expense) should exceed the company's capital charge. The **capital charge** is the amount that stockholders and lenders *charge* a company for the use of their money. A positive EVA® amount suggests an increase in stockholder wealth, and so the company's stock should remain attractive to investors. If EVA® is negative, stockholders will probably be unhappy with the company and sell its stock, resulting in a decrease in the stock's price. Different companies tailor the EVA® computation to meet their own needs.

Let's apply EVA® to Amazon.com, Inc. The company's EVA® for 2008 can be computed as follows, assuming a 10% cost of capital (dollars in millions):

		Net income	+	Interest expense	−	(Beginning balances)					×	Cost of capital
						Short-term borrowings	+	Long-term debt	+	Stockholders' equity		
Amazon.com, Inc.'s EVA®	=	$645	+	$71	−	[($3,714	+	$1,574	+	$1,197)	×	0.10]
	=	$716			−			$6,485			×	0.10
	=	$716			−					$648		
	=					$68						

By this measure, Amazon.com, Inc.'s operations added $68 million of value to its stockholders' wealth after meeting the company's capital charge. This performance is considered strong.

Red Flags in Financial Statement Analysis

Recent accounting scandals have highlighted the importance of *red flags* in financial analysis. The following conditions may mean a company is very risky.

- *Earnings Problems.*   Have income from continuing operations and net income decreased for several years in a row? Has income turned into a loss? This may be okay for a company in a cyclical industry, such as an airline or a home builder, but a company such as Amazon.com, Inc., may be unable to survive consecutive loss years.

■ *Decreased Cash Flow.*   Cash flow validates earnings. Is cash flow from operations consistently lower than net income? Are the sales of plant assets a major source of cash? If so, the company may be facing a cash shortage.

■ *Too Much Debt.*   How does the company's debt ratio compare to that of major competitors and to the industry average? If the debt ratio is much higher than average, the company may be unable to pay debts during tough times. As we saw earlier, Amazon.com, Inc.'s debt ratio of 67.9% in 2008 (while still high) is much improved over its 81.6% debt ratio in 2007.

■ *Inability to Collect Receivables.*   Are days' sales in receivables growing faster than for other companies in the industry? A cash shortage may be looming. Amazon.com, Inc.'s cash collections are very strong.

■ *Buildup of Inventories.*   Is inventory turnover slowing down? If so, the company may be unable to move products, or it may be overstating inventory as reported on the balance sheet. Recall from the cost-of-goods-sold model that one of the easiest ways to overstate net income is to overstate ending inventory. Amazon.com, Inc., has no problem here.

■ *Trends of Sales, Inventory, and Receivables.*   Sales, receivables, and inventory generally move together. Increased sales lead to higher receivables and require more inventory in order to meet demand. Strange movements among these items may spell trouble. Amazon.com, Inc.'s relationships look normal.

Efficient Markets

An **efficient capital market** is one in which market prices fully reflect all information available to the public. Because stock prices reflect all publicly accessible data, it can be argued that the stock market is efficient. Market efficiency has implications for management action and for investor decisions. It means that managers cannot fool the market with accounting gimmicks. If the information is available, the market as a whole can set a "fair" price for the company's stock.

Suppose you are the president of Anacomp Corporation. Reported earnings per share are $4, and the stock price is $40—so the P/E ratio is 10. You believe Anacomp's stock is underpriced. To correct this situation, you are considering changing your depreciation method from accelerated to straight-line. The accounting change will increase earnings per share to $5. Will the stock price then rise to $50? Probably not; the company's stock price will probably remain at $40 because the market can understand the accounting change. After all, the company merely changed its method of computing depreciation. There is no effect on Anacomp's cash flows, and the company's economic position is unchanged: An efficient market interprets data in light of their true underlying meaning.

In an efficient market, the search for "underpriced" stock is fruitless unless the investor has relevant *private* information. But it is unlawful as well as unethical to invest on the basis of *inside* information. An appropriate strategy seeks to manage risk, diversify investments, and minimize transaction costs. Financial analysis helps mainly to identify the risks of various stocks and then to manage the risk.

The Decision Guidelines feature summarizes the most widely used ratios.

DECISION GUIDELINES

USING RATIOS IN FINANCIAL STATEMENT ANALYSIS

Lane and Kay Collins operate a financial services firm. They manage other people's money and do most of their own financial-statement analysis. How do they measure companies' ability to pay bills, sell inventory, collect receivables, and so on? They use the standard ratios we have covered throughout this book.

Ratio	Computation	Information Provided
Measuring ability to pay current liabilities:		
1. Current ratio	$$\dfrac{\text{Current assets}}{\text{Current liabilities}}$$	Measures ability to pay current liabilities with current assets
2. Acid-test (quick) ratio	$$\dfrac{\text{Cash} + \dfrac{\text{Short-term}}{\text{investments}} + \dfrac{\text{Net current}}{\text{receivables}}}{\text{Current liabilities}}$$	Shows ability to pay all current liabilities if they come due immediately
Measuring ability to sell inventory and collect receivables:		
3. Inventory turnover	$$\dfrac{\text{Cost of goods sold}}{\text{Average inventory}}$$	Indicates saleability of inventory—the number of times a company sells its average level of inventory during a year
4. Accounts receivable turnover	$$\dfrac{\text{Net credit sales}}{\text{Average net accounts receivable}}$$	Measures ability to collect cash from credit customers
5. Days' sales in receivables	$$\dfrac{\text{Average net accounts receivable}}{\text{One day's sales}}$$	Shows how many days' sales remain in Accounts Receivable—how many days it takes to collect the average level of receivables
Measuring ability to pay long-term debt:		
6. Debt ratio	$$\dfrac{\text{Total liabilities}}{\text{Total assets}}$$	Indicates percentage of assets financed with debt
7. Times-interest-earned ratio	$$\dfrac{\text{Income from operations}}{\text{Interest expense}}$$	Measures the number of times operating income can cover interest expense
Measuring profitability:		
8. Rate of return on net sales	$$\dfrac{\text{Net income}}{\text{Net sales}}$$	Shows the percentage of each sales dollar earned as net income
9. Rate of return on total assets	$$\dfrac{\text{Net income} + \text{Interest expense}}{\text{Average total assets}}$$	Measures how profitably a company uses its assets
10. Rate of return on common stockholders' equity	$$\dfrac{\text{Net income} - \text{Preferred dividends}}{\text{Average common stockholders' equity}}$$	Gauges how much income is earned with the money invested by the common shareholders
11. Earnings per share of common stock	$$\dfrac{\text{Net income} - \text{Preferred dividends}}{\text{Average number of shares of common stock outstanding}}$$	Gives the amount of net income earned for each share of the company's common stock outstanding

Ratio	Computation	Information Provided
Analyzing stock as an investment:		
12. Price/earnings ratio	$\dfrac{\text{Market price per share of common stock}}{\text{Earnings per share}}$	Indicates the market price of $1 of earnings
13. Dividend yield	$\dfrac{\begin{array}{c}\text{Dividend per share of}\\ \text{common (or preferred) stock}\end{array}}{\begin{array}{c}\text{Market price per share of}\\ \text{common (or preferred) stock}\end{array}}$	Shows the percentage of a stock's market value returned as dividends to stockholders each period
14. Book value per share of common stock	$\dfrac{\text{Total stockholders' equity} - \text{Preferred equity}}{\text{Number of shares of common stock outstanding}}$	Indicates the recorded accounting amount for each share of common stock outstanding

END-OF-CHAPTER SUMMARY PROBLEM

The following financial data are adapted from the annual reports of Lampeer Corporation:

Lampeer Corporation
Four-Year Selected Financial Data
Years Ended January 31, 2010, 2009, 2008, and 2007

Operating Results*	2010	2009	2008	2007
Net Sales	$13,848	$13,673	$11,635	$9,054
Cost of goods sold and occupancy expenses excluding depreciation and amortization......................	9,704	8,599	6,775	5,318
Interest expense	109	75	45	46
Income from operations...............	338	1,445	1,817	1,333
Net earnings (net loss)	(8)	877	1,127	824
Cash dividends............................	76	75	76	77
Financial Position				
Merchandise inventory	1,677	1,904	1,462	1,056
Total assets	7,591	7,012	5,189	3,963
Current ratio................................	1.48:1	0.95:1	1.25:1	1.20:1
Stockholders' equity....................	3,010	2,928	2,630	1,574
Average number of shares of common stock outstanding (in thousands)	860	879	895	576

*Dollar amounts are in thousands.

I Requirement

1. Compute the following ratios for 2008 through 2010, and evaluate Lampeer's operating results. Are operating results strong or weak? Did they improve or deteriorate during the three-year period? Your analysis will reveal a clear trend.

a. Gross profit percentage*	**d.** Inventory turnover
b. Net income as a percentage of sales	**e.** Times-interest-earned ratio
c. Earnings per share	**f.** Rate of return on stockholders' equity

*Refer to Chapter 6 if necessary.

Answer

	2010	2009	2008
1. Gross profit percentage	$\dfrac{\$13,848 - \$9,704}{\$13,848} = 29.9\%$	$\dfrac{\$13,673 - \$8,599}{\$13,673} = 37.1\%$	$\dfrac{\$11,635 - \$6,775}{\$11,635} = 41.8\%$
2. Net income as a percentage of sales	$\dfrac{\$(8)}{\$13,848} = (0.06)\%$	$\dfrac{\$877}{\$13,673} = 6.4\%$	$\dfrac{\$1,127}{\$11,635} = 9.7\%$
3. Earnings per share	$\dfrac{\$(8)}{860} = \$(0.01)$	$\dfrac{\$877}{879} = \$1.00$	$\dfrac{\$1,127}{895} = \$1.26$
4. Inventory turnover	$\dfrac{\$9,704}{(\$1,677 + \$1,904)/2} = 5.4$ times	$\dfrac{\$8,599}{(\$1,904 + \$1,462)/2} = 5.1$ times	$\dfrac{\$6,775}{(\$1,462 + \$1,056)/2} = 5.4$ times
5. Times-interest-earned ratio	$\dfrac{\$338}{\$109} = 3.1$ times	$\dfrac{\$1,445}{\$75} = 19.3$ times	$\dfrac{\$1,817}{\$45} = 40.4$ times
6. Rate of return on stockholders' equity	$\dfrac{\$(8)}{(\$3,010 + \$2,928)/2} = (0.3\%)$	$\dfrac{\$877}{(\$2,928 + \$2,630)/2} = 31.6\%$	$\dfrac{\$1,127}{(\$2,630 + \$1,574)/2} = 53.6\%$

Evaluation: During this period, Lampeer's operating results deteriorated on all these measures except inventory turnover. The gross profit percentage is down sharply, as are the times-interest-earned ratio and all the return measures. From these data it is clear that Lampeer could sell its merchandise, but not at the markups the company enjoyed in the past. The final result, in 2010, was a net loss for the year.

REVIEW FINANCIAL STATEMENT ANALYSIS

Quick Check (Answers are given on page 841.)

Analyze the Oullette Company financial statements by answering the questions that follow. Oullette owns a chain of restaurants.

Oullette Company
Consolidated Statements of Income (Adapted)
Years Ended December 31, 2011 and 2010

(In millions, except per share data)	2011	2010
Revenues		
Sales by Company-operated restaurants	$13,200	11,100
Revenues from franchised and affiliated restaurants	4,500	3,700
Total revenues	17,700	14,800
Food and paper (Cost of goods sold)	3,300	3,108
Payroll and employee benefits	3,200	3,000
Occupancy and other operating expenses	2,900	2,800
Franchised restaurants—occupancy expenses	949	850
Selling, general, and administrative expenses	1,820	1,730
Other operating expense, net	510	855
Total operating expenses	12,679	12,343
Operating income	5,021	2,457
Interest expense	370	345
Other nonoperating expense, net	140	168
Income before income taxes	4,511	1,944
Income tax expense	1,820	820
Net income	$ 2,691	$ 1,124
Per common-share basic:		
Net income	$ 2.69	$ 1.15
Dividends per common share	$ 0.50	$ 0.24

Oulette Company
Consolidated Balance Sheets
December 31, 2011 and 2010

(In millions, except per share data)	2011	2010
Assets		
Current Assets		
Cash and equivalents	$ 690	$ 455
Accounts and notes receivable	780	840
Inventories, at cost, not in excess of market	140	120
Prepaid expense and other current assets	580	440
Total current assets	2,190	1,855
Other Assets		
Investments in affiliates	1,150	1,055
Goodwill, net	1,780	1,590
Miscellaneous	990	1,100
Total other assets	3,920	3,745
Property and Equipment		
Property and equipment, at cost	28,800	26,500
Accumulated depreciation and amortization	(8,850)	(7,900)
Net property and equipment	19,950	18,600
Total assets	$26,060	$24,200
Liabilities and Stockholders' Equity		
Current liabilities		
Accounts payable	$ 520	$ 675
Income taxes	70	14
Other taxes	230	180
Accrued interest	189	196
Accrued restructuring and restaurant closing costs	110	385
Accrued payroll and other liabilities	890	795
Current maturities of long-term debt	365	305
Total current liabilities	2,374	2,550
Long-term debt	8,700	9,500
Other long-term liabilities and minority interests	690	520
Deferred income taxes	1,005	1,015
Stockholders' Equity		
Preferred stock, no par value; authorized—140.0 million shares; issued—none	—	—
Common stock, $0.01 par value; authorized—2.0 billion shares; issued—1,400 million shares	14	14
Additional paid-in capital	1,786	1,662
Unearned ESOP compensation	(85)	(101)
Retained earnings	21,741	19,550
Accumulated other comprehensive income (loss)	(815)	(1,570)
Common stock in treasury, at cost; 400 and 420 million shares	(9,350)	(8,940)
Total stockholders' equity	13,291	10,615
Total liabilities and stockholders' equity	$26,060	$24,200

1. Horizontal analysis of Oullette's income statement for 2011 would show which of the following for Selling, General, and Administrative expenses?
   a. 0.95
   b. 1.05
   c. 0.68
   d. None of the above

2. Vertical analysis of Oullette's income statement for 2011 would show which of the following for Selling, General, and Administrative expenses?
   a. 0.103
   b. 0.144
   c. 0.138
   d. None of the above

3. Which item on Oullette's income statement has the most favorable trend during 2010–2011?
   a. Food and paper costs
   b. Total revenues
   c. Payroll and employee benefits
   d. Net income

4. On Oullette's common-size balance sheet, Goodwill would appear as
   a. $1,780 million.
   b. up by 11.9%.
   c. 0.068.
   d. 10.06% of total revenues.

5. A good benchmark for Oullette Company would be
   a. Volvo.
   b. Microsoft.
   c. Whataburger.
   d. All of the above.

6. Oullette's inventory turnover for 2011 was
   a. 17 times.
   b. 61 times.
   c. 25 times.
   d. 72 times.

7. Oullette's acid-test ratio at the end of 2011 was
   a. 0.62.
   b. 2.83.
   c. 0.92.
   d. 0.06.

8. Oullette's average collection period for accounts and notes receivables is
   a. 32 days.
   b. 2 days.
   c. 17 days.
   d. 1 day.

9. The average debt ratio for most companies is 0.64. Oullette's total debt position looks
   a. risky.
   b. middle-ground.
   c. safe.
   d. cannot tell from the financials.

10. Oullette's return on total revenues for 2011 was
    a. $2.69.
    b. $1.16.
    c. 10.33%.
    d. 15.2%.

11. Oullette's return on stockholders' equity for 2011 was
    a. 15.2%.
    b. 22.5%.
    c. 10.33%.
    d. $2,691 million.

12. On May 31, 2011, Oullette's common stock sold for $30 per share. At that price, how much did investors say $1 of the company's net income was worth?
    a. $1.00
    b. $30.00
    c. $11.15
    d. $10.99

13. On May 31, 2011, Oullette's common stock sold for $30 per share and dividends per share were $0.50. Compute Oullette's dividend yield during 2011.
    a. 2.9%
    b. 4.1%
    c. 1.7%
    d. 5.0%

14. How much EVA® did Oullette generate for investors during 2011? Assume the cost of capital was 5%.
    a. $2,040 million
    b. $1,943 million
    c. $3,061 million
    d. $2,691 million

Accounting Vocabulary

accounts receivable turnover (p. 794) Measures a company's ability to collect cash from credit customers. To compute accounts receivable turnover, divide net credit sales by average net accounts receivable.

acid-test ratio (p. 792) Ratio of the sum of cash plus short-term investments plus net current receivables to total current liabilities. Tells whether the entity can pay all its current liabilities if they come due immediately. Also called the *quick ratio*.

benchmarking (p. 785) The comparison of a company to a standard set by other companies, with a view toward improvement.

book value per share of common stock (p. 799) Common stockholders' equity divided by the number of shares of common stock outstanding. The recorded amount for each share of common stock outstanding.

capital charge (p. 800) The amount that stockholders and lenders charge a company for the use of their money. Calculated as (Notes payable + Loans payable + Long-term debt + Stockholders' equity) × Cost of capital.

common-size statement (p. 784) A financial statement that reports only percentages (no dollar amounts).

cost of capital (p. 800) A weighted average of the returns demanded by the company's stockholders and lenders.

current ratio (p. 790) Current assets divided by current liabilities. Measures a company's ability to pay current liabilities with current assets.

days' sales in receivables (p. 794) Ratio of average net accounts receivable to one day's sales. Indicates how many days' sales remain in Accounts Receivable awaiting collection. Also called the *collection period*.

debt ratio (p. 795) Ratio of total liabilities to total assets. States the proportion of a company's assets that is financed with debt.

dividend yield (p. 798) Ratio of dividends per share of stock to the stock's market price per share. Tells the percentage of a stock's market value that the company returns to stockholders as dividends.

earnings per share (EPS) (p. 797) Amount of a company's net income earned for each share of its outstanding common stock.

economic value added (EVA®) (p. 799) Used to evaluate a company's operating performance. EVA combines the concepts of accounting income and corporate finance to measure whether the company's operations have increased stockholder wealth. EVA = Net income + Interest expense − Capital charge.

efficient capital market (p. 801) A capital market in which market prices fully reflect all information available to the public.

horizontal analysis (p. 778) Study of percentage changes in comparative financial statements.

inventory turnover (p. 793) Ratio of cost of goods sold to average inventory. Indicates how rapidly inventory is sold.

leverage (p. 797) Earning more income on borrowed money than the related interest expense, thereby increasing the earnings for the owners of the business. Also called *trading on the equity*.

price/earnings ratio (p. 798) Ratio of the market price of a share of common stock to the company's earnings per share. Measures the value that the stock market places on $1 of a company's earnings.

quick ratio (p. 792) Another name for the *acid-test ratio*.

rate of return on common stockholders' equity (p. 797) Net income minus preferred dividends, divided by average common stockholders' equity. A measure of profitability. Also called *return on equity*.

rate of return on net sales (p. 796) Ratio of net income to net sales. A measure of profitability. Also called *return on sales*.

rate of return on total assets (p. 796) Net income plus interest expense, divided by average total assets. This ratio measures a company's success in using its assets to earn income for the persons who finance the business. Also called *return on assets*.

return on equity (p. 797) Another name for *rate of return on common stockholders' equity*.

times-interest-earned ratio (p. 795) Ratio of income from operations to interest expense. Measures the number of times that operating income can cover interest expense. Also called the *interest-coverage ratio*.

trading on the equity (p. 797) Another name for *leverage*.

trend percentages (p. 781) A form of horizontal analysis that indicates the direction a business is taking.

vertical analysis (p. 782) Analysis of a financial statement that reveals the relationship of each statement item to a specified base, which is the 100% figure.

working capital (p. 790) Current assets minus current liabilities; measures a business's ability to meet its short-term obligations with its current assets.

ASSESS YOUR PROGRESS

Short Exercises

S13-1 (*Learning Objective 1: Performing horizontal analysis of revenues and net income*) Fitzgerald Corporation reported the following amounts on its 2010 comparative income statement:

(In thousands)	2010	2009	2008
Revenues	$10,473	$9,998	$9,111
Total expenses	5,822	5,422	5,110

Perform a horizontal analysis of revenues and net income—both in dollar amounts and in percentages—for 2010 and 2009.

S13-2 (*Learning Objective 1: Performing trend analysis of sales and net income*) Fenton, Inc., reported the following sales and net income amounts:

(In thousands)	2010	2009	2008	2007
Sales	$10,020	$8,960	$8,740	$8,490
Net income	620	530	420	330

Show Fenton's trend percentages for sales and net income. Use 2007 as the base year.

S13-3 (*Learning Objective 2: Performing vertical analysis to correct a cash shortage*) Craft Software reported the following amounts on its balance sheets at December 31, 2010, 2009, and 2008:

	2010	2009	2008
Cash	$ 7,500	$ 2,195	$ 1,990
Receivables, net	35,000	21,950	23,880
Inventory	260,000	193,160	147,260
Prepaid expenses	10,000	17,560	11,940
Property, plant, and equipment, net	187,500	204,135	212,930
Total assets	$500,000	$439,000	$398,000

Sales and profits are high. Nevertheless, Craft is experiencing a cash shortage. Perform a vertical analysis of Craft Software's assets at the end of years 2010, 2009, and 2008. Use the analysis to explain the reason for the cash shortage.

S13-4 (*Learning Objective 3: Comparing common-size income statements of two companies*) Hartigan, Inc., and Pintal Corporation are competitors. Compare the two companies by converting their condensed income statements to common size.

(In millions)	Hartigan	Pintal
Net sales..	$10,800	$8,752
Cost of goods sold..	6,469	6,065
Selling and administrative expenses................	3,110	1,698
Interest expense..	54	35
Other expenses..	32	44
Income tax expense...	432	210
Net income..	$ 703	$ 700

Which company earned more net income? Which company's net income was a higher percentage of its net sales? Explain your answer.

S13-5 (*Learning Objectives 5, 6: Evaluating the trend in a company's current ratio*)   Examine the financial data of Jacob Corporation.

Year Ended December 31	2010	2009	2008
Operating Results			
Net income...	$ 220	$ 120	$ 119
Per common share.....................................	$1.23	$0.93	$0.63
Percent of sales..	15.6%	17.6%	19.6%
Return on average stockholders' equity...............	14.0	17.0	20.0
Financial Position			
Current assets...	$ 550	$ 445	$ 435
Current liabilities	$ 360	$ 333	$ 356
Working capital	$ 190	$ 112	$ 79
Current ratio...	1.53	1.34	1.22

Show how to compute Jacob's current ratio for each year 2008 through 2010. Is the company's ability to pay its current liabilities improving or deteriorating?

S13-6 (*Learning Objectives 5, 6: Evaluating a company's acid-test ratio*)   Use the Gagnon, Inc., balance sheet data on the following page.

❙ Requirements

1. Compute Gagnon, Inc.'s acid-test ratio at December 31, 2010 and 2009.
2. Use the comparative information from the table on the bottom of page 811 for Horner, Inc., Isaacson Company, and Jona Companies Limited. Is Gagnon, Inc.'s acid-test ratio for 2010 and 2009 strong, average, or weak in comparison?

Gagnon, Inc.
Balance Sheets (Adapted)
December 31, 2010 and 2009

(Dollar amounts in millions)	2010	2009	Increase (Decrease) Amount	Percentage
Assets				
Current Assets				
Cash and cash equivalents	$1,203	$ 903	$ 300	33.2 %
Short-term investments	7	84	(77)	(91.7)
Receivables, net	246	256	(10)	(3.9)
Inventories..	91	81	10	12.3
Prepaid expenses and other assets...........................	203	343	(140)	(40.8)
Total current assets..	1,750	1,667	83	5.0
Property, plant, and equipment, net	3,619	3,396	223	6.6
Intangible assets..	1,089	841	248	29.5
Other assets	824	718	106	14.8
Total assets...	$7,282	$6,622	$ 660	10.0 %
Liabilities and Stockholders' Equity				
Current Liabilities				
Accounts payable..	$ 977	$ 884	$ 93	10.5 %
Income tax payable..	39	69	(30)	(43.5)
Short-term debt..	121	115	6	5.2
Other...	70	73	(3)	(4.1)
Total current liabilities	1,207	1,141	66	5.8
Long-term debt...	3,544	2,982	562	18.8
Other liabilities..	1,177	1,046	131	12.5
Total liabilities..	5,928	5,169	759	14.7
Stockholders' Equity				
Common stock	—	—	—	—
Retained earnings	1,513	1,629	(116)	(7.1)
Accumulated other comprehensive (loss)	(159)	(176)	17	9.7
Total stockholders' equity	1,354	1,453	(99)	(6.8)
Total liabilities and stockholders' equity.............	$7,282	$6,622	$ 660	10.0 %

Company	Acid-Test Ratio
Horner, Inc. (Utility)	0.73
Isaacson Company (Department store)..................	0.68
Jona Companies Limited (Grocery store)	0.72

S13-7 *(Learning Objectives 5, 6: Computing and evaluating inventory turnover and days' sales in receivables)*   Use the Gagnon 2010 income statement below and balance sheet from Short Exercise 13-6 to compute the following:

Gagnon, Inc. Statements of Income (Adapted) Year Ended December 31, 2010 and 2009		
(Dollar amounts in millions)	2010	2009
Revenues	$9,500	$9,068
Expenses:		
Food and paper (Cost of goods sold)	2,200	2,236
Payroll and employee benefits	2,138	2,001
Occupancy and other operating expenses	2,778	2,745
General and administrative expenses	1,171	1,135
Interest expense	150	133
Other expense (income), net	11	(29)
Income before income taxes	1,052	847
Income tax expense	273	251
Net income	$ 779	$ 596

  a. Gagnon's rate of inventory turnover for 2010.
  b. Days' sales in average receivables during 2010. (Round dollar amounts to one decimal place.)

Do these measures look strong or weak? Give the reason for your answer.

S13-8 *(Learning Objectives 5, 6: Measuring ability to pay long-term debt)*   Use the financial statements of Gagnon, Inc., in Short Exercises 13-6 and 13-7.

▌ Requirements

  1. Compute the company's debt ratio at December 31, 2010.
  2. Compute the company's times-interest-earned ratio for 2010. For operating income, use income before both interest expense and income taxes. You can simply add interest expense back to income before taxes.
  3. Is Gagnon's ability to pay liabilities and interest expense strong or weak? Comment on the value of each ratio computed for questions 1 and 2.

S13-9 *(Learning Objectives 5, 6: Measuring profitability)*   Use the financial statements of Gagnon, Inc., in Short Exercises 13-6 and 13-7 to compute these profitability measures for 2010. Show each computation.

  a. Rate of return on sales.
  b. Rate of return on total assets.
  c. Rate of return on common stockholders' equity.

S13-10 *(Learning Objective 5: Computing EPS and the price/earnings ratio)*   The annual report of Tri-State Cars, Inc., for the year ended December 31, 2010, included the following items (in millions):

Preferred stock outstanding, 6%	$400
Net income	$500
Number of shares of common stock outstanding	100

I *Requirements*

1. Compute earnings per share (EPS) and the price/earnings ratio for Tri-State Cars' stock. Round to the nearest cent. The price of a share of Tri-State Car stock is $57.12.
2. How much does the stock market say $1 of Tri-State Cars' net income is worth?

S13-11 (*Learning Objective 5: Using ratio data to reconstruct an income statement*)   A skeleton of Athol Country Florist's income statement appears as follows (amounts in thousands):

Income Statement

Net sales	$7,500
Cost of goods sold........................	(a)
Selling expenses............................	1,511
Administrative expenses...............	328
Interest expense...........................	(b)
Other expenses.............................	154
Income before taxes	1,046
Income tax expense......................	(c)
Net income..................................	$ (d)

Use the following ratio data to complete Athol Country Florist's income statement:

a. Inventory turnover was 4 (beginning inventory was $784; ending inventory was $762).
b. Rate of return on sales is 0.10.

S13-12 (*Learning Objective 5: Using ratio data to reconstruct a balance sheet*)   A skeleton of Athol Country Florist's balance sheet appears as follows (amounts in thousands):

Balance Sheet

Cash......................................	$ 85		Total current liabilities	$1,900
Receivables.............................	(a)		Long-term debt	(e)
Inventories	762		Other long-term liabilities	720
Prepaid expenses	(b)			
Total current assets	(c)			
Plant assets, net....................	(d)		Common stock...........................	185
Other assets...........................	2,100		Retained earnings......................	3,165
Total assets...........................	$7,300		Total liabilities and equity..........	$ (f)

Use the following ratio data to complete Athol Country Florist's balance sheet:

a. Debt ratio is 0.50.
b. Current ratio is 1.30.
c. Acid-test ratio is 0.40.

writing assignment ■   **S13-13** *(Learning Objective 6: Analyzing a company based on its ratios)*   Take the role of an investment analyst at Merrimack Lowell. It is your job to recommend investments for your client. The only information you have is the following ratio values for two companies in the graphics software industry.

Ratio	Graphit.net	Data Doctors
Days' sales in receivables	44	50
Inventory turnover	6	10
Gross profit percentage	69%	60%
Net income as a percent of sales	13%	14%
Times interest earned	17	11
Return on equity	36%	28%
Return on assets	15%	20%

Write a report to the Merrimack Lowell investment committee. Recommend one company's stock over the other. State the reasons for your recommendation.

S13-14 *(Learning Objective 7: Measuring economic value added)*   Compute economic value added (EVA®) for Beverly Software. The company's cost of capital is 5%. Net income was $770 thousand, interest expense $409 thousand, beginning long-term debt $700 thousand, and beginning stockholders' equity was $3,060 thousand. Round all amounts to the nearest thousand dollars.

Should the company's stockholders be happy with the EVA®?

Exercises

> All of the A and B exercises can be found within MyAccountingLab, an online homework and practice environment. Your instructor may ask you to complete these exercises using MyAccountingLab.

MyAccountingLab

(Group A)

E13-15A *(Learning Objective 1: Computing year-to-year changes in working capital)*   What were the dollar amount of change and the percentage of each change in Wilderness Lodge's working capital during 2010 and 2009? Is this trend favorable or unfavorable?

	2010	2009	2008
Total current assets	$270,000	$320,000	$340,000
Total current liabilities	125,000	160,000	170,000

■ **spreadsheet**   **E13-16A** *(Learning Objective 1: Performing horizontal analysis of an income statement)* Prepare a horizontal analysis of the comparative income statements of Sensible Music Co. Round percentage changes to the nearest one-tenth percent (three decimal places).

Sensible Music Co.
Comparative Income Statements
Years Ended December 31, 2010 and 2009

	2010	2009
Total revenue	$852,000	$912,000
Expenses:		
Cost of goods sold	$402,000	$408,000
Selling and general expenses	232,000	261,000
Interest expense	9,200	10,500
Income tax expense	83,000	84,000
Total expenses	726,200	763,500
Net income	$125,800	$148,500

E13-17A (*Learning Objective 1: Computing trend percentages*)   Compute trend percentages for Palm Valley Sales & Service's total revenue, and net income for the following five-year period, using year 0 as the base year. Round to the nearest full percent.

(In thousands)	Year 4	Year 3	Year 2	Year 1	Year 0
Total revenue	$1,414	$1,203	$1,101	$999	$1,020
Net income	104	99	86	74	88

Which grew faster during the period, total revenue or net income?

E13-18A (*Learning Objective 2: Performing vertical analysis of a balance sheet*)   Fore Golf Company has requested that you perform a vertical analysis of its balance sheet to determine the component percentages of its assets, liabilities, and stockholders' equity.

Fore Golf Company
Balance Sheet
December 31, 2010

Assets
Total current assets	$ 43,000
Property, plant, and equipment, net	117,000
Other assets	38,000
Total assets	$198,000

Liabilities
Total current liabilities	$ 49,000
Long-term debt	109,000
Total liabilities	158,000

Stockholders' Equity
Total stockholders' equity	40,000
Total liabilities and stockholders' equity	$198,000

■ **spreadsheet**

E13-19A *(Learning Objective 3: Preparing a common-size income statement)* Prepare a comparative common-size income statement for Sensible Music Co., using the 2010 and 2009 data of Exercise 13-16A and rounding to four decimal places.

writing assignment ■

E13-20A *(Learning Objective 4: Analyzing the statement of cash flows)* Identify any weaknesses revealed by the statement of cash flows of California Fruit Growers, Inc.

California Fruit Growers, Inc.
Statement of Cash Flows
For the Current Year

Operating activities:			
Income from operations..			$ 61,000
Add (subtract) noncash items:			
Depreciation		$ 11,000	
Net increase in current assets other than cash		(52,000)	
Net decrease in current liabilities			
exclusive of short-term debt.........................		(19,000)	(60,000)
Net cash provided by operating activities.........			1,000
Investing activities:			
Sale of property, plant, and equipment			115,000
Financing activities:			
Issuance of bonds payable		$ 113,000	
Payment of short-term debt		(174,000)	
Payment of long-term debt		(86,000)	
Payment of dividends..		(38,000)	
Net cash used for financing activities...............			(185,000)
Increase (decrease) in cash			$ (69,000)

■ **spreadsheet**

E13-21A *(Learning Objective 5: Computing five ratios)* The financial statements of Smith News, Inc., include the following items:

	Current Year	Preceding Year
Balance sheet:		
Cash	$ 26,000	$ 32,000
Short-term investments	14,000	20,000
Net receivables	50,000	73,000
Inventory......................................	94,000	76,000
Prepaid expenses.........................	9,000	8,000
Total current assets	193,000	209,000
Total current liabilities................	129,000	96,000
Income statement:		
Net credit sales	$490,000	
Cost of goods sold	274,000	

❙ *Requirement*

1. Compute the following ratios for the current year:

    a. Current ratio   **d.** Accounts receivable turnover
    b. Acid-test ratio   **e.** Days' sales in average receivables
    c. Inventory turnover

(Round your answers to a through d to two decimal points. Round your answer to e to the nearest whole number.)

E13-22A (*Learning Objectives 5, 6: Analyzing the ability to pay current liabilities*)   Dorman Furniture Company has requested that you determine whether the company's ability to pay its current liabilities and long-term debts improved or deteriorated during 2010. To answer this question, compute the following ratios for 2010 and 2009:

a. Current ratio
b. Acid-test ratio

c. Debt ratio
d. Times-interest-earned ratio

Summarize the results of your analysis in a written report.

	2010	2009
Cash	$ 21,000	$ 53,000
Short-term investments	32,000	15,000
Net receivables	117,000	127,000
Inventory	243,000	272,000
Prepaid expenses	18,000	4,000
Total assets	500,000	531,000
Total current liabilities	247,000	312,000
Long-term debt	27,000	134,000
Income from operations	191,000	160,000
Interest expense	39,000	45,000

E13-23A (*Learning Objectives 5, 6: Analyzing profitability*)   Compute four ratios that measure the ability to earn profits for Harmon Decor, Inc., whose comparative income statements follow:

Harmon Decor, Inc.
Comparative Income Statements
Years Ended December 31, 2010 and 2009

	2010	2009
Net sales	$100,000	$90,000
Cost of goods sold	53,000	46,000
Gross profit	47,000	44,000
Selling and general expenses	20,000	18,000
Income from operations	27,000	26,000
Interest expense	3,000	2,000
Income before income tax	24,000	24,000
Income tax expense	8,000	7,000
Net income	$ 16,000	$17,000

Additional data:

	2010	2009	2008
Total assets	$104,000	$100,000	$83,000
Common stockholders' equity	$ 72,000	$ 70,000	$69,000
Preferred dividends	$ 3,000	$ 2,000	$ 1,000
Common shares outstanding during the year	10,000	9,000	4,000

Did the company's operating performance improve or deteriorate during 2010?

writing assignment ■

E13-24A *(Learning Objectives 5, 6: Evaluating a stock as an investment)* Evaluate the common stock of Regal Distributing Company as an investment. Specifically, use the three common stock ratios to determine whether the common stock increased or decreased in attractiveness during the past year.

	2010	2009
Net income	$ 83,000	$ 60,000
Dividends to common	22,000	23,000
Total stockholders' equity at year-end	300,000	510,000
(includes 90,000 shares of common stock)		
Preferred stock, 5%	80,000	80,000
Market price per share of common		
stock at year-end	$ 24.50	$ 17.50

E13-25A *(Learning Objective 7: Using economic value added to measure corporate performance)* Two companies with different economic-value-added (EVA®) profiles are Barton Oil Pipeline Incorporated and Crompton Bank Limited. Adapted versions of the two companies' financial statements are presented here (in millions):

	Barton Oil Pipeline Inc.	Crompton Bank Limited
Balance sheet data:		
Total assets	$ 4,338	$14,000
Interest-bearing debt	$ 1,257	$ 13
All other liabilities	2,675	2,605
Stockholders' equity	406	11,382
Total liabilities and equity	$ 4,338	$14,000
Income statement data:		
Total revenue	$11,007	$ 3,819
Interest expense	76	7
Net income	$ 180	$ 1,219

❙ Requirements

1. Before performing any calculations, which company do you think represents the better investment? Give your reason.
2. Compute the EVA® for each company and then decide which company's stock you would rather hold as an investment. Assume both companies' cost of capital is 8.5%.

(Group B)

E13-26B *(Learning Objective 1: Computing year-to-year changes in working capital)* What were the dollar amount of change and the percentage of each change in Ricardo Lodge's working capital during 2010 and 2009? Is this trend favorable or unfavorable?

	2010	2009	2008
Total current assets	$400,000	$300,000	$240,000
Total current liabilities	190,000	150,000	120,000

■ spreadsheet

E13-27B *(Learning Objective 1: Performing horizontal analysis of an income statement)* Prepare a horizontal analysis of the comparative income statements of Fashion Music Co. Round percentage changes to the nearest one-tenth percent (three decimal places).

Fashion Music Co.
Comparative Income Statements
Years Ended December 31, 2010 and 2009

	2010	2009
Total revenue	$1,080,000	$919,000
Expenses:		
Cost of goods sold	$ 479,000	$400,450
Selling and general expenses	289,000	269,000
Interest expense	24,500	14,500
Income tax expense	106,500	86,850
Total expenses	899,000	770,800
Net income	$181,000	$148,200

E13-28B (*Learning Objective 1: Computing trend percentages*)   Compute trend percentages for Andover Valley Sales & Service's total revenue, and net income for the following five-year period, using year 0 as the base year. Round to the nearest full percent.

(in thousands)	Year 4	Year 3	Year 2	Year 1	Year 0
Total revenue	$1,433	$1,251	$1,067	$1,008	$1,022
Net income	120	112	81	69	83

Which grew faster during the period, total revenue or net income?

E13-29B (*Learning Objective 2: Performing vertical analysis of a balance sheet*)   Epsilon Golf Company has requested that you perform a vertical analysis of its balance sheet to determine the component percentages of its assets, liabilities, and stockholders' equity.

Epsilon Golf Company
Balance Sheet
December 31, 2010

Assets	
Total current assets	$ 45,000
Property, plant, and equipment, net	210,000
Other assets	42,000
Total assets	$297,000
Liabilities	
Total current liabilities	$ 53,000
Long-term debt	111,000
Total liabilities	164,000
Stockholders' Equity	
Total stockholders' equity	133,000
Total liabilities and stockholders' equity	$297,000

E13-30B (*Learning Objective 3: Preparing a common-size income statement*)   Prepare a comparative common-size income statement for Fashion Music Co. using the 2010 and 2009 data of Exercise 13-27B and rounding to four decimal places.

■ **spreadsheet**

writing assignment ■

E13-31B (*Learning Objective 4: Analyzing the statement of cash flows*)   Identify any weaknesses revealed by the statement of cash flows of Massachusetts Chowder Distributors, Inc.

Massachusetts Chowder Distributors, Inc. Statement of Cash Flows For the Current Year			
Operating activities:			
Income from operations...			$ 77,000
Add (subtract) noncash items:			
Depreciation		$ 30,000	
Net increase in current assets other than cash		(61,000)	
Net decrease in current liabilities			
exclusive of short-term debt.........................		(22,000)	(53,000)
Net cash provided by operating activities.........			24,000
Investing activities:			
Sale of property, plant, and equipment			126,000
Financing activities:			
Issuance of bonds payable		$ 99,000	
Payment of short-term debt		(166,000)	
Payment of long-term debt		(90,000)	
Payment of dividends..		(50,000)	
Net cash used for financing activities...............			(207,000)
Increase (decrease) in cash			$ (57,000)

■ spreadsheet

E13-32B (*Learning Objective 5: Computing five ratios*)   The financial statements of Advent News, Inc., include the following items:

	Current Year	Preceding Year
Balance sheet:		
Cash	$ 65,000	$ 91,000
Short-term investments	13,000	25,000
Net receivables	79,000	82,000
Inventory......................................	93,000	75,000
Prepaid expenses..........................	6,000	12,000
Total current assets	256,000	285,000
Total current liabilities.................	133,000	97,000
Income statement:		
Net credit sales	$494,000	
Cost of goods sold	277,000	

❙ Requirement

1. Compute the following ratios for the current year:

   a. Current ratio
   b. Acid-test ratio
   c. Inventory turnover

   d. Accounts receivable turnover
   e. Days' sales in average receivables

(Round your answers to a through d to two decimal points. Round your answer to e to the nearest whole number.)

E13-33B (*Learning Objectives 5, 6: Analyzing the ability to pay current liabilities*)   Jalbert
Furniture Company has requested that you determine whether the company's ability to pay its current liabilities and long-term debts improved or deteriorated during 2010. To answer this question,
compute the following ratios for 2010 and 2009. (Round your answers to two decimal places.)

writing assignment ■

■ **spreadsheet**

a. Current ratio
b. Acid-test ratio

c. Debt ratio
d. Times-interest-earned ratio

Summarize the results of your analysis in a written report.

	2010	2009
Cash	$ 27,000	$ 47,000
Short-term investments	33,000	4,000
Net receivables	120,000	135,000
Inventory	238,000	271,000
Prepaid expenses	22,000	8,000
Total assets	590,000	510,000
Total current liabilities	187,000	332,000
Long-term debt	147,000	84,000
Income from operations	191,000	169,000
Interest expense	41,000	43,000

E13-34B (*Learning Objectives 5, 6: Analyzing profitability*)   Compute four ratios that measure the ability to earn profits for Jarvis Decor, Inc., whose comparative income statements follow:

Jarvis Decor, Inc.
Comparative Income Statements
Years Ended December 31, 2010 and 2009

	2010	2009
Net sales	$254,000	$217,000
Cost of goods sold	125,000	111,000
Gross profit	129,000	106,000
Selling and general expenses	50,000	46,000
Income from operations	79,000	60,000
Interest expense	7,000	6,000
Income before income tax	72,000	54,000
Income tax expense	25,000	19,000
Net income	$ 47,000	$ 35,000

Additional data:

	2010	2009	2008
Total assets	$249,000	$239,000	$227,000
Common stockholders' equity	$106,000	$104,000	$102,000
Preferred dividends	$ 17,000	$ 15,000	$ 13,000
Common shares outstanding during the year	19,000	17,000	11,000

Did the company's operating performance improve or deteriorate during 2010?

E13-35B *(Learning Objectives 5, 6: Evaluating a stock as an investment)*   Evaluate the common stock of Basic Distributing Company as an investment. Specifically, use the three common stock ratios to determine whether the common stock increased or decreased in attractiveness during the past year.

	2010	2009
Net income...	$ 91,000	$ 99,000
Dividends to common	28,000	13,000
Total stockholders' equity at year-end................	565,000	515,000
(includes 80,000 shares of common stock)		
Preferred stock, 6%..	90,000	90,000
Market price per share of common		
stock at year-end	$ 24.00	$ 25.16

E13-36B *(Learning Objective 7: Using economic value added to measure corporate performance)*   Two companies with different economic-value-added (EVA®) profiles are Houle Oil Pipeline, Inc., and Johnson Bank Limited. Adapted versions of the two companies' financial statements are presented here (in millions):

	Houle Oil Pipeline, Inc.	Johnson Bank Limited
Balance sheet data:		
Total assets	$ 4,338	$14,451
Interest-bearing debt	$ 1,250	$ 5
All other liabilities............................	2,900	2,585
Stockholders' equity.........................	188	11,861
Total liabilities and equity...............	$ 4,338	$14,451
Income statement data:		
Total revenue	$10,991	$ 3,697
Interest expense................................	80	7
Net income..	$ 200	$ 1,197

I *Requirements*

1. Before performing any calculations, which company do you think represents the better investment? Give your reason.
2. Compute the EVA® for each company and then decide which company's stock you would rather hold as an investment. Assume both companies' cost of capital is 11.0%. (Round your EVA® calculation to the nearest whole number.)

Challenge Exercises

E13-37 *(Learning Objectives 2, 3, 5: Using ratio data to reconstruct a company's balance sheet)*   The following data (dollar amounts in millions) are taken from the financial statements of Floor 1 Industries, Inc.:

Total liabilities	$12,600
Preferred stock	$ 0
Total current assets	$11,900
Accumulated depreciation	$ 1,700
Debt ratio	60%
Current ratio	1.70

I Requirement

1. Complete the following condensed balance sheet. Report amounts to the nearest million dollars.

		(In millions)
Current assets		☐
Property, plant, and equipment	☐	
Less: Accumulated depreciation	☐	☐
Total assets		☐
Current liabilities		☐
Long-term liabilities		☐
Stockholders' equity		☐
Total liabilities and stockholders' equity		☐

E13-38 *(Learning Objectives 2, 3, 5: Using ratio data to reconstruct a company's income statement)*   The following data (dollar amounts in millions) are from the financial statements of County Corporation:

Average stockholders' equity	$3,400
Interest expense	$ 800
Preferred stock	$ 0
Operating income as a percent of sales	20%
Rate of return on stockholders' equity	10%
Income tax rate	30%

▌Requirement

1. Complete the following condensed income statement. Report amounts to the nearest million dollars.

Sales...	☐
Operating expense.................	☐
Operating income...................	☐
Interest expense......................	☐
Pretax income	☐
Income tax expense................	☐
Net income..............................	☐

Quiz

Use the Hialeah Bell Corporation financial statements that follow to answer questions 13–39 through 13–50.

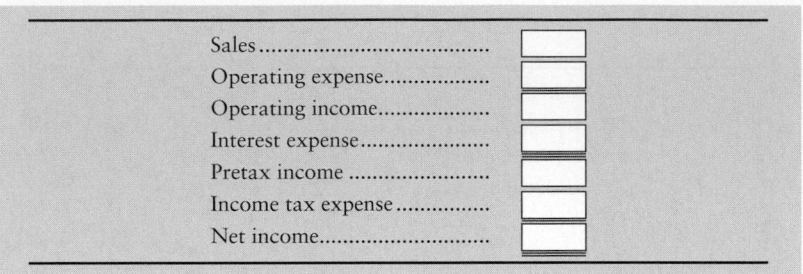

Hialeah Bell Corporation
Consolidated Statements of Income
(In millions, except per share amounts)

	Year ended December 31,		
	2010	2009	2008
Net revenue...	$42,788	$35,299	$30,968
Cost of goods sold......................................	34,000	29,111	26,061
Gross profit	8,788	6,188	4,907
Operating expenses:			
Selling, general, and administrative......	3,341	3,000	2,581
Research, development, and			
engineering.....................................	574	556	542
Special charges....................................	—	—	502
Total operating expenses	3,915	3,556	3,625
Operating income...........................	4,873	2,632	1,282
Investment and other income (loss), net	170	212	(78)
Income before income taxes................	5,043	2,844	1,204
Income tax expense.....................................	1,100	912	472
Net income..	$ 3,943	$ 1,932	$ 732
Earnings per common share:			
Basic...	$ 1.33	$ 0.94	$ 0.42

Hialeah Bell Corporation
Consolidated Statements of Financial Position
(In millions)

	December 31, 2010	2009
Assets		
Current assets:		
Cash and cash equivalents..................................	$ 4,301	$ 4,138
Short-term investments......................................	830	512
Accounts receivable, net....................................	3,402	2,401
Inventories	427	410
Other	1,638	1,213
Total current assets	10,598	8,674
Property, plant, and equipment, net	1,517	932
Investments..	6,613	5,323
Other noncurrent assets......................................	301	144
Total assets..	$19,029	$15,073
Liabilities and Stockholders' Equity		
Current liabilities:		
Accounts payable	$ 7,702	$ 6,002
Accrued and other	3,676	3,044
Total current liabilities.....................................	11,378	9,046
Long-term debt...	301	302
Other noncurrent liabilities.................................	1,701	1,167
Commitments and contingent liabilities (Note 7)......	—	—
Total liabilities	13,380	10,515
Stockholders' equity:		
Preferred stock and capital in excess of $0.02 par value; shares issued and outstanding: none	—	—
Common stock and capital in excess of $0.05 par value; shares authorized: 6,000; shares issued: 3,240 and 2,989, respectively...........	7,801	7,004
Treasury stock, at cost; 175 and 124 shares, respectively...	(6,333)	(4,404)
Retained earnings...	4,321	2,054
Other comprehensive loss..................................	(104)	(50)
Other..	(36)	(46)
Total stockholders' equity	5,649	4,558
Total liabilities and stockholders' equity	$19,029	$15,073

Q13-39 During 2010, Hialeah Bell's total assets
a. increased by $9,390 million.　　c. both a and b.
b. increased by 26.2%.　　d. increased by 20.8%.

Q13-40 Hialeah Bell's current ratio at year end 2010 is closest to
a. 1.2.　　c. 20.8.
b. 9,390.　　d. 0.9.

Q13-41 Hialeah Bell's acid-test ratio at year-end 2010 is closest to
a. $0.68.　　c. $8,533 million.
b. $0.75.　　d. 0.45.

Q13-42 What is the largest single item included in Hialeah Bell's debt ratio at December 31, 2010?
a. Cash and cash equivalents　　c. Accounts payable
b. Investments　　d. Common stock

Q13-43 Using the earliest year available as the base year, the trend percentage for Hialeah Bell's net revenue during 2010 was
a. 121%.
b. up by 21.2%.
c. up by $11,820 million.
d. 138%.

Q13-44 Hialeah Bell's common-size income statement for 2010 would report cost of goods sold as
a. 79.5%.
b. Up by 16.8%.
c. 130.5%.
d. $34,000 million.

Q13-45 Hialeah Bell's days' sales in average receivables during 2010 was
a. 29 days.
b. 117 days.
c. 21 days.
d. 25 days.

Q13-46 Hialeah Bell's inventory turnover during fiscal year 2010 was
a. 130 times.
b. 81 times.
c. 41 times.
d. very slow.

Q13-47 Hialeah Bell's long-term debt bears interest at 11%. During the year ended December 31, 2010, Bell's times-interest-earned ratio was
a. 137 times.
b. 144 times.
c. 147 times.
d. 150 times.

Q13-48 Hialeah Bell's trend of return on sales is
a. worrisome.
b. declining.
c. improving.
d. stuck at 20.8%.

Q13-49 How many shares of common stock did Hialeah Bell have outstanding, on average, during 2010? Hint: Compute earnings per share.
a. 2,947 million
b. 5,258 million
c. 5,244 million
d. 2,965 million

Q13-50 Book value per share of Hialeah Bell's common stock outstanding at December 31, 2010, was
a. $5,649.
b. $1.84.
c. $1.96.
d. $2.08.

Problems

MyAccountingLab

All of the A and B problems can be found within MyAccountingLab, an online homework and practice environment. Your instructor may ask you to complete these problems using MyAccountingLab.

(Group A)

■ spreadsheet

P13-51A (*Learning Objectives 1, 5, 6: Computing trend percentages, return on sales, and comparison with the industry*)   Net sales, net income, and total assets for Amble Shipping, Inc., for a five-year period follow:

(In thousands)	2010	2009	2008	2007	2006
Net sales.....................	$902	$800	$492	$313	$303
Net income.................	42	39	15	39	33
Total assets	305	268	256	221	203

Requirements

1. Compute trend percentages for each item for 2007 through 2010. Use 2006 as the base year and round to the nearest percent.

2. Compute the rate of return on net sales for 2008 through 2010, rounding to three decimal places.

3. How does Amble Shipping's return on net sales compare with that of the industry? In the shipping industry, rates above 5% are considered good, and rates above 7% are outstanding.

P13-52A (*Learning Objectives 3, 5, 6: Preparing common-size statements; analyzing profitability; making comparisons with the industry*) Top managers of McDonough Products, Inc., have asked for your help in comparing the company's profit performance and financial position with the average for the industry. The accountant has given you the company's income statement and balance sheet and also the following data for the industry:

writing assignment ■

■ **spreadsheet**

McDonough Products, Inc.
Income Statement Compared with Industry Average
Year Ended December 31, 2010

	McDonough	Industry Average
Net sales..................................	$700,000	100.0%
Cost of goods sold.................	490,000	57.3
Gross profit...........................	210,000	42.7
Operating expenses	175,000	29.4
Operating income..................	35,000	13.3
Other expenses......................	7,000	2.5
Net income	$ 28,000	10.8%

McDonough Products, Inc.
Balance Sheet Compared with Industry Average
December 31, 2010

	McDonough	Industry Average
Current assets..........................	$471,200	72.1%
Fixed assets, net	114,700	19.0
Intangible assets, net	21,080	4.8
Other assets...........................	13,020	4.1
Total	$620,000	100.0%
Current liabilities	$240,560	47.2%
Long-term liabilities	135,160	21.0
Stockholders' equity................	244,280	31.8
Total	$620,000	100.0%

Requirements

1. Prepare a common-size income statement and balance sheet for McDonough Products. The first column of each statement should present McDonough Products' common-size statement, and the second column should show the industry averages.

2. For the profitability analysis, compute McDonough Products' (a) ratio of gross profit to net sales (b) ratio of operating income to net sales, and (c) ratio of net income to net sales. Compare these figures with the industry averages. Is McDonough Products' profit performance better or worse than the average for the industry?

3. For the analysis of financial position, compute McDonough Products' (a) ratios of current assets and current liabilities to total assets and (b) ratio of stockholders' equity to total assets. Compare these ratios with the industry averages. Is McDonough Products' financial position better or worse than the average for the industry?

writing assignment ■   **P13-53A** (*Learning Objective 4: Using the statement of cash flows for decision making*) You are evaluating two companies as possible investments. The two companies, similar in size, are commuter airlines that fly passengers up and down the West Coast. All other available information has been analyzed and your investment decision depends on the statements of cash flows.

Friendly Airlines
Statements of Cash Flows
Years Ended November 30, 2011 and 2010

	2011	2010
Operating activities:		
Net income (net loss)	$ (48,000)	$121,000
Adjustments for noncash items:		
Total	60,000	(10,000)
Net cash provided by operating activities	12,000	111,000
Investing activities:		
Purchase of property, plant, and equipment	$ (51,000)	$(106,000)
Sale of long-term investments	44,000	7,000
Net cash provided by (used for) investing activities	(7,000)	(99,000)
Financing activities:		
Issuance of short-term notes payable	$ 150,000	$ 165,000
Payment of short-term notes payable	(186,000)	(139,000)
Payment of cash dividends	(39,000)	(70,000)
Net cash used for financing activities	(75,000)	(44,000)
Increase (decrease) in cash	$ (70,000)	$ (32,000)
Cash balance at beginning of year	80,000	112,000
Cash balance at the end of year	$ 10,000	$ 80,000

Cloudview, Inc.
Statements of Cash Flows
Years Ended September 30, 2011 and 2010

	2011	2010
Operating activities:		
Net income	$ 200,000	$ 146,000
Adjustments for noncash items:		
Total	51,000	60,000
Net cash provided by operating activities	251,000	206,000
Investing activities:		
Purchase of property, plant,		
and equipment	$(299,000)	$(462,000)
Sale of property, plant, and equipment	52,000	90,000
Net cash used for investing activities	(247,000)	(372,000)
Financing activities:		
Issuance of long-term notes payable	$ 150,000	$ 99,000
Payment of short-term notes payable	(72,000)	(20,000)
Net cash provided by financing activities	78,000	79,000
Increase (decrease) in cash	$ 82,000	$ (87,000)
Cash balance at beginning of year	133,000	220,000
Cash balance at end of year	$ 215,000	$ 133,000

❙ Requirement

1. Discuss the relative strengths and weaknesses of Friendly and Cloudview. Conclude your discussion by recommending one of the companies' stocks as an investment.

P13-54A (*Learning Objectives 5, 6: Computing effects of business transactions on selected ratios*)   Financial statement data of Greatland Engineering include the following items:

Cash	$ 25,000	Accounts payable	$101,000
Short-term investments	38,000	Accrued liabilities	37,000
Accounts receivable, net	82,000	Long-term notes payable	160,000
Inventories	149,000	Other long-term liabilities	37,000
Prepaid expenses	6,000	Net income	96,000
Total assets	674,000	Number of common	
Short-term notes payable	41,000	shares outstanding	52,000

I Requirements

1. Compute Greatland's current ratio, debt ratio, and earnings per share. (Round all ratios to two decimal places.)
2. Compute the three ratios after evaluating the effect of each transaction that follows. Consider each transaction *separately*.
   a. Borrowed $135,000 on a long-term note payable.
   b. Issued 40,000 shares of common stock, receiving cash of $360,000.
   c. Paid short-term notes payable, $28,000.
   d. Purchased merchandise of $44,000 on account, debiting Inventory.
   e. Received cash on account, $16,000.

P13-55A (*Learning Objectives 5, 6: Using ratios to evaluate a stock investment*)   Comparative financial statement data of Bloomfield Optical Mart follow:

Bloomfield Optical Mart
Comparative Income Statements
Years Ended December 31, 2010 and 2009

	2010	2009
Net sales...	$690,000	$590,000
Cost of goods sold.............................	375,000	283,000
Gross profit..	315,000	307,000
Operating expenses	126,000	141,000
Income from operations	189,000	166,000
Interest expense.................................	36,000	50,000
Income before income tax	153,000	116,000
Income tax expense............................	40,000	53,000
Net income	$113,000	$ 63,000

Bloomfield Optical Mart
Comparative Balance Sheets
December 31, 2010 and 2009

	2010	2009	2008*
Current assets:			
Cash	$ 38,000	$ 40,000	
Current receivables, net	217,000	149,000	$140,000
Inventories..	298,000	285,000	181,000
Prepaid expenses..	9,000	25,000	
Total current assets	562,000	499,000	
Property, plant, and equipment, net	284,000	276,000	
Total assets...	$846,000	$775,000	710,000
Total current liabilities	$281,000	$267,000	
Long-term liabilities..	241,000	236,000	
Total liabilities	522,000	503,000	
Preferred stockholders' equity, 5%, $10 par................	70,000	70,000	
Common stockholders' equity, no par.........................	254,000	202,000	195,000
Total liabilities and stockholders' equity	$846,000	$775,000	

*Selected 2008 amounts.

Other information:

1. Market price of Bloomfield common stock: $82.20 at December 31, 2010, and $52.96 at December 31, 2009.
2. Common shares outstanding: 20,000 during 2010 and 18,000 during 2009.
3. All sales on credit.

I Requirements

1. Compute the following ratios for 2010 and 2009:
   a. Current ratio
   b. Inventory turnover
   c. Times-interest-earned ratio
   d. Return on assets
   e. Return on common stockholders' equity
   f. Earnings per share of common stock
   g. Price/earnings ratio
2. Decide whether (a) Bloomfield's financial position improved or deteriorated during 2010 and (b) the investment attractiveness of Bloomfield's common stock appears to have increased or decreased.
3. How will what you learned in this problem help you evaluate an investment?

P13-56A (*Learning Objectives 5, 6, 7: Using ratios to decide between two stock investments; measuring economic value added*) Assume that you are considering purchasing stock as an investment. You have narrowed the choice to DVR.com and Express Shops and have assembled the following data.

writing assignment ■

Selected income statement data for the current year:

	DVR	Express
Net sales (all on credit).................	$602,000	$517,000
Cost of goods sold.........................	449,000	382,000
Income from operations	88,000	73,000
Interest expense.............................	—	16,000
Net income....................................	61,000	39,000

Selected balance sheet and market price data at *end* of current year:

	DVR	Express
Current assets:		
Cash	$ 22,000	$ 38,000
Short-term investments	10,000	14,000
Current receivables, net	182,000	167,000
Inventories..	210,000	181,000
Prepaid expenses..	21,000	8,000
Total current assets	445,000	408,000
Total assets...	981,000	935,000
Total current liabilities	362,000	333,000
Total liabilities	673,000	700,000
Preferred stock, 5%, $150 par		30,000
Common stock, $1 par (100,000 shares).................	100,000	
$5 par (15,000 shares)...................		75,000
Total stockholders' equity	308,000	235,000
Market price per share of common stock	$ 6.10	$ 55.00

Selected balance sheet data at *beginning* of current year:

	DVR	Express
Balance sheet:		
Current receivables, net...	$144,000	$195,000
Inventories	205,000	199,000
Total assets...	853,000	908,000
Long-term debt	—	299,000
Preferred stock, 5%, $150 par		30,000
Common stock, $1 par (100,000 shares)................	100,000	
$5 par (15,000 shares).................		75,000
Total stockholders' equity	260,000	221,000

Your strategy is to invest in companies that have low price/earnings ratios but appear to be in good shape financially. Assume that you have analyzed all other factors and that your decision depends on the results of ratio analysis.

I Requirements

1. Compute the following ratios for both companies for the current year and decide which company's stock better fits your investment strategy.
   a. Acid-test ratio
   b. Inventory turnover
   c. Days' sales in average receivables
   d. Debt ratio
   e. Times-interest-earned ratio
   f. Return on common stockholders' equity
   g. Earnings per share of common stock
   h. Price/earnings ratio
2. Compute each company's economic-value-added (EVA®) measure and determine whether the companies' EVA®s confirm or alter your investment decision. Each company's cost of capital is 10%.

(Group B)

■ spreadsheet

P13-57B (*Learning Objectives 1, 5, 6: Computing trend percentages, return on common equity, and comparison with the industry*)   Net sales, net income, and total assets for Amaze Shipping, Inc., for a five-year period follow:

(In thousands)	2010	2009	2008	2007	2006
Net sales...	$616	$503	$358	$309	$300
Net income...	33	30	45	34	27
Total assets.......................................	300	268	255	231	204

I Requirements

1. Compute trend percentages for each item for 2007 through 2010. Use 2006 as the base year and round to the nearest percent.
2. Compute the rate of return on net sales for 2008 through 2010, rounding to three decimal places.
3. How does Amaze Shipping's return on net sales compare with that of the industry? In the shipping industry, rates above 5% are considered good, and rates above 7% are outstanding.

writing assignment ■
■ spreadsheet

P13-58B (*Learning Objectives 3, 5, 6: Preparing common-size statements; analyzing profitability; making comparisons with the industry*)   Top managers of Walsh Products, Inc., have asked for your help in comparing the company's profit performance and financial position with the average for the industry. The accountant has given you the company's income statement and balance sheet and also the following data for the industry:

Walsh Products, Inc.
Income Statement Compared with Industry Average
Year Ended December 31, 2010

	Walsh	Industry Average
Net sales................................	$900,000	100.0%
Cost of goods sold.................	648,000	57.3
Gross profit...........................	252,000	42.7
Operating expenses...............	216,000	29.4
Operating income..................	36,000	13.3
Other expenses......................	13,500	2.5
Net income	$ 22,500	10.8%

Walsh Products, Inc.
Balance Sheet Compared with Industry Average
December 31, 2010

	Walsh	Industry Average
Current assets..........................	$408,100	72.1%
Fixed assets, net	99,640	19.0
Intangible assets, net	20,140	4.8
Other assets............................	2,120	4.1
Total	$530,000	100.0%
Current liabilities	$205,640	47.2%
Long-term liabilities	112,360	21.0
Stockholders' equity................	212,000	31.8
Total	$530,000	100.0%

I Requirements

1. Prepare a common-size income statement and balance sheet for Walsh Products. The first column of each statement should present Walsh Products' common-size statement, and the second column should show the industry averages.

2. For the profitability analysis, compute Walsh Products' (a) ratio of gross profit to net sales (b) ratio of operating income to net sales, and (c) ratio of net income to net sales. Compare these figures with the industry averages. Is Walsh Products' profit performance better or worse than the average for the industry?

3. For the analysis of financial position, compute Walsh Products' (a) ratios of current assets and current liabilities to total assets and (b) ratio of stockholders' equity to total assets. Compare these ratios with the industry averages. Is Walsh Products' financial position better or worse than the average for the industry?

P13-59B (*Learning Objective 4: Using the statement of cash flows for decision making*)   You are evaluating two companies as possible investments. The two companies, similar in size, are commuter airlines that fly passengers across the United States of America. All other available information has been analyzed and your investment decision depends on the statements of cash flows.

writing assignment ■

Zoom Airlines
Statements of Cash Flows
Years Ended May 31, 2011 and 2010

	2011	2010
Operating activities:		
Net income (net loss)	$(78,000)	$160,000
Adjustments for noncash items:		
Total	88,000	(33,000)
Net cash provided by operating activities	10,000	127,000
Investing activities:		
Purchase of property, plant, and equipment	$ (70,000)	$(110,000)
Sale of long-term investments	73,000	22,000
Net cash provided by (used for) investing activities	3,000	(88,000)
Financing activities:		
Issuance of short-term notes payable	$ 111,000	$ 138,000
Payment of short-term notes payable	(191,000)	(100,000)
Payment of cash dividends	(50,000)	(79,000)
Net cash used for financing activities	(130,000)	(41,000)
Increase (decrease) in cash	$(117,000)	$ (2,000)
Cash balance at beginning of year	125,000	127,000
Cash balance at end of year	$ 8,000	$125,000

Skyview, Inc.
Statements of Cash Flows
Years Ended May 31, 2011 and 2010

	2011	2010
Operating activities:		
Net income	$ 150,000	$ 110,000
Adjustments for noncash items:		
Total	69,000	49,000
Net cash provided by operating activities	219,000	159,000
Investing activities:		
Purchase of property, plant, and equipment	$(334,000)	$(470,000)
Sales of property, plant, and equipment	65,000	84,000
Net cash used for investing activities	(269,000)	(386,000)
Financing activities:		
Issuance of long-term notes payable	$ 182,000	$ 125,000
Payment of short-term notes payable	(80,000)	(12,000)
Net cash provided by financing activities	102,000	113,000
Increase (decrease) in cash	$ 52,000	$(114,000)
Cash balance at beginning of year	101,000	215,000
Cash balance at end of year	$ 153,000	$ 101,000

I *Requirement*

1. Discuss the relative strengths and weaknesses of Zoom and Skyview. Conclude your discussion by recommending one of the companies' stocks as an investment.

P13-60B *(Learning Objectives 5, 6: Computing effects of business transactions on selected ratios)*   Financial statement data of Trinton Engineering include the following items:

Cash	$ 26,000	Accounts payable	$106,000
Short-term investments	34,000	Accrued liabilities	34,000
Accounts receivable, net	87,000	Long-term notes payable	165,000
Inventories	145,000	Other long-term liabilities	32,000
Prepaid expenses	8,000	Net income	98,000
Total assets	677,000	Number of common	
Short-term notes payable	48,000	shares outstanding	47,000

I *Requirements*

1. Compute Trinton's current ratio, debt ratio, and earnings per share. (Round all ratios to two decimal places.)
2. Compute the three ratios after evaluating the effect of each transaction that follows. Consider each transaction *separately*.
   a. Borrowed $115,000 on a long-term note payable.
   b. Issued 20,000 shares of common stock, receiving cash of $365,000.
   c. Paid short-term notes payable, $26,000.
   d. Purchased merchandise of $45,000 on account, debiting Inventory.
   e. Received cash on account, $19,000.

P13-61B *(Learning Objectives 5, 6: Using ratios to evaluate a stock investment)*   Comparative financial statement data of Rourke Optical Mart follow:

<u>**writing assignment ■**</u>

Rourke Optical Mart **Comparative Income Statements** **Years Ended December 31, 2010 and 2009**		
	2010	2009
Net sales	$688,000	$593,000
Cost of goods sold	376,000	283,000
Gross profit	312,000	310,000
Operating expenses	131,000	144,000
Income from operations	181,000	166,000
Interest expense	31,000	50,000
Income before income tax	150,000	116,000
Income tax expense	42,000	47,000
Net income	$108,000	$ 69,000

Rourke Optical Mart
Comparative Balance Sheets
December 31, 2010 and 2009

	2010	2009	2008*
Current assets:			
Cash	$ 32,000	$ 36,000	
Current receivables, net	211,000	154,000	$134,000
Inventories	291,000	288,000	188,000
Prepaid expenses	6,000	30,000	
Total current assets	540,000	508,000	
Property, plant, and equipment, net	288,000	278,000	
Total assets	$828,000	$786,000	704,000
Total current liabilities	$280,000	$293,000	
Long-term liabilities	240,000	231,000	
Total liabilities	520,000	524,000	
Preferred stockholders' equity, 3%, $5 par	65,000	65,000	
Common stockholders' equity, no par	243,000	197,000	198,000
Total liabilities and stockholders' equity	$828,000	$786,000	

*Selected 2008 amounts.

Other information:

1. Market price of Rourke common stock: $78.12 at December 31, 2010, and $59.10 at December 31, 2009.
2. Common shares outstanding: 19,000 during 2010 and 17,000 during 2009.
3. All sales on credit.

❙ Requirements

1. Compute the following ratios for 2010 and 2009:
   a. Current ratio
   b. Inventory turnover
   c. Times-interest-earned ratio
   d. Return on common stockholders' equity
   e. Earnings per share of common stock
   f. Price/earnings ratio
2. Decide whether (a) Rourke's financial position improved or deteriorated during 2010 and (b) the investment attractiveness of Rourke's common stock appears to have increased or decreased.
3. How will what you learned in this problem help you evaluate an investment?

writing assignment ■

P13-62B (*Learning Objectives 5, 6, 7: Using ratios to decide between two stock investments; measuring economic value added*) Assume that you are considering purchasing stock as an investment. You have narrowed the choice to CDROM.com and E-shop Stores and have assembled the following data.

Selected income statement data for current year:

	CDROM	E-Shop
Net sales (all on credit)	$597,000	$516,000
Cost of goods sold	455,000	388,000
Income from operations	89,000	70,000
Interest expense	—	13,000
Net income	68,000	39,000

Selected balance sheet and market price data at the *end* of the current year:

	CDROM	E-Shop
Current assets:		
Cash	$ 24,000	$ 41,000
Short-term investments	5,000	15,000
Current receivables, net	185,000	165,000
Inventories...	219,000	187,000
Prepaid expenses...	21,000	11,000
Total current assets	454,000	419,000
Total assets..	978,000	928,000
Total current liabilities	363,000	332,000
Total liabilities	663,000	693,000
Preferred stock: 6%, $150 par		30,000
Common stock, $1 par (100,000 shares)...............	100,000	
$5 par (10,000 shares)..................		50,000
Total stockholders' equity	315,000	235,000
Market price per share of common stock	$ 8.84	$ 70.68

Selected balance sheet data at the *beginning* of the current year:

	CDROM	E-Shop
Balance sheet:		
Current receivables, net...	$143,000	$190,000
Inventories	202,000	195,000
Total assets...	843,000	914,000
Long-term debt	—	300,000
Preferred stock, 6%, $150 par		30,000
Common stock, $1 par (100,000 shares)...............	100,000	
$5 par (10,000 shares).................		50,000
Total stockholders' equity.......................................	259,000	220,000

Your strategy is to invest in companies that have low price/earnings ratios but appear to be in good shape financially. Assume that you have analyzed all other factors and that your decision depends on the results of ratio analysis.

❙ *Requirements*

1. Compute the following ratios for both companies for the current year and decide which company's stock better fits your investment strategy.
   a. Acid-test ratio
   b. Inventory turnover
   c. Days' sales in average receivables
   d. Debt ratio
   e. Times-interest-earned ratio
   f. Return on common stockholders' equity
   g. Earnings per share of common stock
   h. Price/earnings ratio
2. Compute each company's economic-value-added (EVA®) measure and determine whether the companies' EVA®s confirm or alter your investment decision. Each company's cost of capital is 12%.

APPLY YOUR KNOWLEDGE

Decision Cases

Case 1. (*Learning Objectives 5, 6: Assessing the effects of transactions on a company*) Suppose **AOL Time Warner, Inc.**, is having a bad year in 2011, as the company has incurred a $4.9 billion net loss. The loss has pushed most of the return measures into the negative column and the current ratio dropped below 1.0. The company's debt ratio is still only 0.27. Assume top management of AOL Time Warner is pondering ways to improve the company's ratios. In particular, management is considering the following transactions:

1. Sell off the cable television segment of the business for $30 million (receiving half in cash and half in the form of a long-term note receivable). Book value of the cable television business is $27 million.
2. Borrow $100 million on long-term debt.
3. Purchase treasury stock for $500 million cash.
4. Write off one-fourth of goodwill carried on the books at $128 million.
5. Sell advertising at the normal gross profit of 60%. The advertisements run immediately.
6. Purchase trademarks from **NBC**, paying $20 million cash and signing a one-year note payable for $80 million.

❙ Requirements

1. Top management wants to know the effects of these transactions (increase, decrease, or no effect) on the following ratios of AOL Time Warner:
   a. Current ratio
   b. Debt ratio
   c. Times-interest-earned ratio (measured as [net income + interest expense]/interest expense)
   d. Return on equity
   e. Book value per share of common stock
2. Some of these transactions have an immediately positive effect on the company's financial condition. Some are definitely negative. Others have an effect that cannot be judged as clearly positive or negative. Evaluate each transaction's effect as positive, negative, or unclear. (Challenge)

writing assignment ■

Case 2. (*Learning Objectives 5, 6: Analyzing the effects of an accounting difference on the ratios*) Assume that you are a financial analyst. You are trying to compare the financial statements of **Caterpillar, Inc.**, with those of **CNH Global**, an international company that uses international financial reporting standards (IFRS). Caterpillar, Inc., uses the last-in, first-out (LIFO) method to account for its inventories. IFRS does not permit CNH Global to use LIFO. Analyze the effect of this difference in accounting method on the two companies' ratio values. For each ratio discussed in this chapter, indicate which company will have the higher (and the lower) ratio value. Also identify those ratios that are unaffected by the FIFO/LIFO difference. Ignore the effects of income taxes, and assume inventory costs are increasing. Then, based on your analysis of the ratios, summarize your conclusions as to which company looks better overall.

writing assignment ■

Case 3. (*Learning Objectives 2, 5, 6: Identifying action to cut losses and establish profitability*) Suppose you manage Outward Bound, Inc., a Vermont sporting goods store that lost money during the past year. To turn the business around, you must analyze the company and industry data for the current year to learn what is wrong. The company's data follow:

Outward Bound, Inc.
Common-Size Balance Sheet Data

	Outward Bound	Industry Average
Cash and short-term investments	3.0%	6.8%
Trade receivables, net	15.2	11.0
Inventory	64.2	60.5
Prepaid expenses	1.0	0.0
Total current assets	83.4%	78.3%
Fixed assets, net	12.6	15.2
Other assets	4.0	6.5
Total assets	100.0%	100.0%
Notes payable, short-term, 12%	17.1%	14.0%
Accounts payable	21.1	25.1
Accrued liabilities	7.8	7.9
Total current liabilities	46.0	47.0
Long-term debt, 11%	19.7	16.4
Total liabilities	65.7	63.4
Common stockholders' equity	34.3	36.6
Total liabilities and stockholders' equity	100.0%	100.0%

Outward Bound, Inc.
Common-Size Income Statement Data

	Outward Bound	Industry Average
Net sales	100.0%	100.0%
Cost of sales	(68.2)	(64.8)
Gross profit	31.8	35.2
Operating expense	(37.1)	(32.3)
Operating income (loss)	(5.3)	2.9
Interest expense	(5.8)	(1.3)
Other revenue	1.1	0.3
Income (loss) before income tax	(10.0)	1.9
Income tax (expense) saving	4.4	(0.8)
Net income (loss)	(5.6)%	1.1%

I *Requirement*

1. On the basis of your analysis of these figures, suggest four courses of action Outward Bound might take to reduce its losses and establish profitable operations. Give your reason for each suggestion. (Challenge)

Ethical Issue

Turnberry Golf Corporation's long-term debt agreements make certain demands on the business. For example, Turnberry may not purchase treasury stock in excess of the balance of retained earnings. Also, long-term debt may not exceed stockholders' equity, and the current ratio may not fall below 1.50. If Turnberry fails to meet any of these requirements, the company's lenders have the authority to take over management of the company.

Changes in consumer demand have made it hard for Turnberry to attract customers. Current liabilities have mounted faster than current assets, causing the current ratio to fall to 1.47. Before releasing financial statements, Turnberry management is scrambling to improve the current ratio. The controller points out that the company owns an investment that is currently classified as long-term. The investment can be classified as either long-term or short-term, depending on management's intention. By deciding to convert an investment to cash within one year, Turnberry can classify the investment as short-term—a current asset. On the controller's recommendation, Turnberry's board of directors votes to reclassify long-term investments as short-term.

I *Requirements*

writing assignment ■

1. What is the accounting issue in this case? What ethical decision needs to be made?
2. Who are the stakeholders?
3. Analyze the potential impact on the stakeholders from the following standpoints: (a) economic, (b) legal, and (c) ethical.
4. Shortly after the financial statements are released, sales improve; so, too, does the current ratio. As a result, Turnberry management decides not to sell the investments it had reclassified as short term. Accordingly, the company reclassifies the investments as long term. Has management acted unethically? Give the reasoning underlying your answer.

Focus on Financials: ■ Amazon.com, Inc.

writing assignment ■

(*Learning Objectives 4, 5, 6: Computing standard financial ratios; using the statement of cash flows; measuring liquidity and profitability; analyzing stock as an investment*) Use the consolidated financial statements and the data in **Amazon.com, Inc.'s** annual report (Appendix A at the end of the book) to evaluate the company's comparative performance for 2008 versus 2007. Does the company appear to be improving or declining in the following dimensions?

I *Requirements*

1. The ability to pay its current liabilities
2. The ability to sell inventory and collect receivables
3. The ability to pay long-term debts
4. Profitability
5. Cash flows from operations
6. The potential of the company's stock as a long-term investment (Challenge)

Focus on Analysis: ■ Foot Locker, Inc.

writing assignment ■

(*Learning Objectives 1, 5, 6: Analyzing trend data; computing the standard financial ratios and using them to make decisions*) Use the **Foot Locker, Inc.**, consolidated financial statements in Appendix B at the end of this book to address the following questions.

1. Perform a trend analysis of Foot Locker's net sales, gross profit, operating income, and net income. Use 2005 as the base year, and compute trend figures for 2006 and 2007.
2. Find Foot Locker, Inc.'s annual report for 2008 at www.sec.gov. Also perform research at a popular investment Web site such as www.msnmoney.com or www.yahoofinance.com to update the information from part 1. (Challenge)
3. What in your opinion is the company's outlook for the future? Would you buy the company's stock as an investment? Why or why not? (Challenge)

Group Projects

Project 1.   Select an industry you are interested in, and use the leading company in that industry as the benchmark. Then select two other companies in the same industry. For each category of ratios in the Decision Guidelines feature on pages 802 and 803, compute at least two ratios for all three companies. Write a two-page report that compares the two companies with the benchmark company.

writing assignment ■

Project 2.   Select a company and obtain its financial statements. Convert the income statement and the balance sheet to common size and compare the company you selected to the industry average. **Risk Management Association's** *Annual Statement Studies*, **Dun & Bradstreet's** *Industry Norms & Key Business Ratios*, and **Prentice Hall's** *Almanac of Business and Industrial Financial Ratios* by Leo Troy, publish common-size statements for most industries.

For online homework, exercises, and problems that provide you with immediate feedback, please visit www.myaccountinglab.com.

Quick Check Answers

1. *b* ($1,820/$1,730)
2. *a* ($1,820/$17,700)
3. *d* ($2,691 − $1,124)/$1,124 = 139.4%
4. *c* ($1,780/$26,060)
5. *c*
6. *c* $\left[\dfrac{\$3,300}{(\$140 + \$120)/2}\right] = 25.4 \approx 25$ times
7. *a* [($690 + $780)/ $2,374 = 0.62]
8. *c* $\left[\dfrac{\$780 + \$840/2}{\$17,700/365}\right] = 16.9 \approx 17$ days
9. *c* (Debt ratio is ($26,060 − $13,291)/$26,060 = 0.49. This debt ratio is lower than the average for most companies, given in the chapter as 0.64.)
10. *d* ($2,691/$17,700 = 0.152)
11. *b* $\left[\dfrac{\$2,691}{(\$13,291 + 10,615)/2}\right] = 0.225$
12. *c* ($30/$2.69)
13. *c* ($0.50/$30)
14. *a* [$2,691 + $370 − ($305 + $9,500 + $10,615) × 0.05] = $2,040

2 0 0 8

ANNUAL REPORT

Report of Ernst & Young LLP, Independent Registered Public Accounting Firm

The Board of Directors and Stockholders
Amazon.com, Inc.

We have audited the accompanying consolidated balance sheets of Amazon.com, Inc. as of December 31, 2008 and 2007, and the related consolidated statements of operations, stockholders' equity, and cash flows for each of the three years in the period ended December 31, 2008. Our audits also included the financial statement schedule listed in the Index at Item 15(a)(2). These financial statements and schedule are the responsibility of the Company's management. Our responsibility is to express an opinion on these financial statements and schedule based on our audits.

We conducted our audits in accordance with the standards of the Public Company Accounting Oversight Board (United States). Those standards require that we plan and perform the audit to obtain reasonable assurance about whether the financial statements are free of material misstatement. An audit includes examining, on a test basis, evidence supporting the amounts and disclosures in the financial statements. An audit also includes assessing the accounting principles used and significant estimates made by management, as well as evaluating the overall financial statement presentation. We believe that our audits provide a reasonable basis for our opinion.

In our opinion, the financial statements referred to above present fairly, in all material respects, the consolidated financial position of Amazon.com, Inc. at December 31, 2008 and 2007, and the consolidated results of its operations and its cash flows for each of the three years in the period ended December 31, 2008, in conformity with U.S. generally accepted accounting principles. Also, in our opinion, the related financial statement schedule, when considered in relation to the basic financial statements taken as a whole, presents fairly in all material respects the information set forth therein.

As discussed in Note 1 to the consolidated financial statements, the Company adopted FASB Interpretation No. 48 *Accounting for Uncertainty in Income Taxes*, effective January 1, 2007, and FASB No. 157 *Fair Value Measurements*, effective January 1, 2008.

We also have audited, in accordance with the standards of the Public Company Accounting Oversight Board (United States), the effectiveness of Amazon.com, Inc.'s internal control over financial reporting as of December 31, 2008, based on criteria established in Internal Control—Integrated Framework issued by the Committee of Sponsoring Organizations of the Treadway Commission and our report dated January 29, 2009 expressed an unqualified opinion thereon.

/s/ Ernst & Young LLP

Seattle, Washington
January 29, 2009

AMAZON.COM, INC.

CONSOLIDATED STATEMENTS OF CASH FLOWS
(in millions)

	Year Ended December 31,		
	2008	2007	2006
CASH AND CASH EQUIVALENTS, BEGINNING OF PERIOD	$ 2,539	$1,022	$ 1,013
OPERATING ACTIVITIES:			
Net income	645	476	190
Adjustments to reconcile net income to net cash from operating activities:			
Depreciation of fixed assets, including internal-use software and website development, and other amortization	287	246	205
Stock-based compensation	275	185	101
Other operating expense (income), net	(24)	9	10
Losses (gains) on sales of marketable securities, net	(2)	1	(2)
Other expense (income), net	(34)	12	(6)
Deferred income taxes	(5)	(99)	22
Excess tax benefits from stock-based compensation	(159)	(257)	(102)
Changes in operating assets and liabilities:			
Inventories	(232)	(303)	(282)
Accounts receivable, net and other	(218)	(255)	(103)
Accounts payable	812	928	402
Accrued expenses and other	247	429	241
Additions to unearned revenue	449	244	206
Amortization of previously unearned revenue	(344)	(211)	(180)
Net cash provided by operating activities	1,697	1,405	702
INVESTING ACTIVITIES:			
Purchases of fixed assets, including internal-use software and website development	(333)	(224)	(216)
Acquisitions, net of cash acquired, and other	(494)	(75)	(32)
Sales and maturities of marketable securities and other investments	1,305	1,271	1,845
Purchases of marketable securities and other investments	(1,677)	(930)	(1,930)
Net cash provided by (used in) investing activities	(1,199)	42	(333)
FINANCING ACTIVITIES:			
Proceeds from exercises of stock options	11	91	35
Excess tax benefits from stock-based compensation	159	257	102
Common stock repurchased	(100)	(248)	(252)
Proceeds from long-term debt and other	87	24	98
Repayments of long-term debt and capital lease obligations	(355)	(74)	(383)
Net cash provided by (used in) financing activities	(198)	50	(400)
Foreign-currency effect on cash and cash equivalents	(70)	20	40
Net increase in cash and cash equivalents	230	1,517	9
CASH AND CASH EQUIVALENTS, END OF PERIOD	$ 2,769	$2,539	$ 1,022
SUPPLEMENTAL CASH FLOW INFORMATION:			
Cash paid for interest	$ 64	$ 67	$ 86
Cash paid for income taxes	53	24	15
Fixed assets acquired under capital leases and other financing arrangements	148	74	69
Fixed assets acquired under build-to-suit leases	72	15	—
Conversion of debt	605	1	—

See accompanying notes to consolidated financial statements.

AMAZON.COM, INC.

CONSOLIDATED STATEMENTS OF OPERATIONS
(in millions, except per share data)

	Year Ended December 31,		
	2008	2007	2006
Net sales	$19,166	$14,835	$10,711
Cost of sales	14,896	11,482	8,255
Gross profit	4,270	3,353	2,456
Operating expenses (1):			
Fulfillment	1,658	1,292	937
Marketing	482	344	263
Technology and content	1,033	818	662
General and administrative	279	235	195
Other operating expense (income), net	(24)	9	10
Total operating expenses	3,428	2,698	2,067
Income from operations	842	655	389
Interest income	83	90	59
Interest expense	(71)	(77)	(78)
Other income (expense), net	47	(8)	7
Total non-operating income (expense)	59	5	(12)
Income before income taxes	901	660	377
Provision for income taxes	(247)	(184)	(187)
Equity-method investment activity, net of tax	(9)	—	—
Net income	$ 645	$ 476	$ 190
Basic earnings per share	$ 1.52	$ 1.15	$ 0.46
Diluted earnings per share	$ 1.49	$ 1.12	$ 0.45
Weighted average shares used in computation of earnings per share:			
Basic	423	413	416
Diluted	432	424	424

(1)   Includes stock-based compensation as follows:

Fulfillment	$ 61	$ 39	$ 24
Marketing	13	8	4
Technology and content	151	103	54
General and administrative	50	35	19

See accompanying notes to consolidated financial statements.

AMAZON.COM, INC.

CONSOLIDATED BALANCE SHEETS
(in millions, except per share data)

	December 31, 2008	2007
ASSETS		
Current assets:		
Cash and cash equivalents	$2,769	$ 2,539
Marketable securities	958	573
Inventories	1,399	1,200
Accounts receivable, net and other	827	705
Deferred tax assets	204	147
Total current assets	6,157	5,164
Fixed assets, net	854	543
Deferred tax assets	145	260
Goodwill	438	222
Other assets	720	296
Total assets	$8,314	$ 6,485
LIABILITIES AND STOCKHOLDERS' EQUITY		
Current liabilities:		
Accounts payable	$3,594	$ 2,795
Accrued expenses and other	1,093	902
Current portion of long-term debt	59	17
Total current liabilities	4,746	3,714
Long-term debt	409	1,282
Other long-term liabilities	487	292
Commitments and contingencies		
Stockholders' equity:		
Preferred stock, $0.01 par value:		
Authorized shares—500		
Issued and outstanding shares—none	—	—
Common stock, $0.01 par value:		
Authorized shares—5,000		
Issued shares—445 and 431		
Outstanding shares—428 and 416	4	4
Treasury stock, at cost	(600)	(500)
Additional paid-in capital	4,121	3,063
Accumulated other comprehensive income (loss)	(123)	5
Accumulated deficit	(730)	(1,375)
Total stockholders' equity	2,672	1,197
Total liabilities and stockholders' equity	$8,314	$ 6,485

See accompanying notes to consolidated financial statements.

AMAZON.COM, INC.
CONSOLIDATED STATEMENTS OF STOCKHOLDERS' EQUITY
(in millions)

	Common Stock Shares	Common Stock Amount	Treasury Stock	Additional Paid-In Capital	Accumulated Other Comprehensive Income (Loss)	Accumulated Deficit	Total Stockholders' Equity
Balance at January 1, 2006	416	4	$—	$2,263	$ 6	$(2,027)	$ 246
Net income						190	190
Foreign currency translation losses, net of tax					(13)		(13)
Change in unrealized losses on available-for-sale securities, net of tax					4		4
Amortization of unrealized loss on terminated Euro Currency Swap, net of tax					2		2
Comprehensive income							183
Exercise of common stock options	6			35			35
Repurchase of common stock	(8)		(252)				(252)
Excess tax benefits from stock-based compensation				102			102
Stock-based compensation and issuance of employee benefit plan stock				117			117
Balance at December 31, 2006	414	4	(252)	2,517	(1)	(1,837)	431
Net income						476	476
Foreign currency translation losses, net of tax					(3)		(3)
Change in unrealized losses on available-for-sale securities, net of tax					8		8
Amortization of unrealized loss on terminated Euro Currency Swap, net of tax					1		1
Comprehensive income							482
Change in accounting principle				2		(14)	(12)
Unrecognized excess tax benefits from stock-based compensation				4			4
Exercise of common stock options and conversion of debt	8			92			92
Repurchase of common stock	(6)		(248)				(248)
Excess tax benefits from stock-based compensation				257			257
Stock-based compensation and issuance of employee benefit plan stock				191			191
Balance at December 31, 2007	416	4	(500)	3,063	5	(1,375)	1,197
Net income						645	645
Foreign currency translation losses, net of tax					(127)		(127)
Change in unrealized losses on available-for-sale securities, net of tax					(1)		(1)
Comprehensive income							517
Unrecognized excess tax benefits from stock-based compensation				(8)			(8)
Exercise of common stock options and conversion of debt	14			624			624
Repurchase of common stock	(2)		(100)				(100)
Excess tax benefits from stock-based compensation				154			154
Stock-based compensation and issuance of employee benefit plan stock				288			288
Balance at December 31, 2008	428	4	$(600)	$4,121	$(123)	$ (730)	$2,672

See accompanying notes to consolidated financial statements.

AMAZON.COM, INC.

NOTES TO CONSOLIDATED FINANCIAL STATEMENTS

Note 1—DESCRIPTION OF BUSINESS AND ACCOUNTING POLICIES

Description of Business

Amazon.com opened its virtual doors on the World Wide Web in July 1995 and we offer Earth's Biggest Selection. We seek to be Earth's most customer-centric company for three primary customer sets: consumer customers, seller customers and developer customers. We serve our consumer customers through our retail websites and focus on selection, price, and convenience. We offer programs that enable seller customers to sell their products on our websites and their own branded websites and to fulfill orders through us. We serve developer customers through Amazon Web Services, which provides access to technology infrastructure that developers can use to enable virtually any type of business. In addition, we generate revenue through co-branded credit card agreements and other marketing and promotional services, such as online advertising.

We have organized our operations into two principal segments: North America and International. See "Note 13—Segment Information."

Principles of Consolidation

The consolidated financial statements include the accounts of the Company, its wholly-owned subsidiaries, and those entities (relating primarily to *www.amazon.cn*) in which we have a variable interest. Intercompany balances and transactions have been eliminated.

Use of Estimates

The preparation of financial statements in conformity with U.S. GAAP requires estimates and assumptions that affect the reported amounts of assets and liabilities, revenues and expenses, and related disclosures of contingent liabilities in the consolidated financial statements and accompanying notes. Estimates are used for, but not limited to, valuation of investments, receivables valuation, sales returns, incentive discount offers, inventory valuation, depreciable lives of fixed assets, internally-developed software, valuation of acquired intangibles and goodwill, income taxes, stock-based compensation, and contingencies. Actual results could differ materially from those estimates.

Earnings per Share

Basic earnings per share is calculated using our weighted-average outstanding common shares. Diluted earnings per share is calculated using our weighted-average outstanding common shares including the dilutive effect of stock awards as determined under the treasury stock method.

Our convertible debt instrument is excluded from the calculation of diluted earnings per share as its effect under the if-converted method is anti-dilutive. See "Note 5—Long-Term Debt."

The following table shows the calculation of diluted shares (in millions):

	Year Ended December 31,		
	2008	**2007**	**2006**
Shares used in computation of basic earnings per share	423	413	416
Total dilutive effect of outstanding stock awards (1)	9	11	8
Shares used in computation of diluted earnings per share	432	424	424

AMAZON.COM, INC.

NOTES TO CONSOLIDATED FINANCIAL STATEMENTS—(Continued)

(1) Calculated using the treasury stock method that assumes proceeds available to reduce the dilutive effect of outstanding stock awards, which include the exercise price of stock options, the unrecognized deferred compensation of stock awards, and assumed tax proceeds from excess stock-based compensation deductions.

Treasury Stock

We account for treasury stock under the cost method and include treasury stock as a component of stockholders' equity.

Cash and Cash Equivalents

We classify all highly liquid instruments, including money market funds that comply with Rule 2a-7 of the Investment Company Act of 1940, with an original maturity of three months or less at the time of purchase as cash equivalents.

Inventories

Inventories, consisting of products available for sale, are accounted for using the FIFO method, and are valued at the lower of cost or market value. This valuation requires us to make judgments, based on currently-available information, about the likely method of disposition, such as through sales to individual customers, returns to product vendors, or liquidations, and expected recoverable values of each disposition category. Based on this evaluation, we adjust the carrying amount of our inventories to lower of cost or market value.

We provide fulfillment-related services in connection with certain of our sellers' programs. In those arrangements, as well as all other product sales by other sellers, the seller maintains ownership of the related products. As such, these amounts are not included in our consolidated balance sheets.

Accounts Receivable, Net, and Other

Included in "Accounts receivable, net, and other" on our consolidated balance sheets are amounts primarily related to vendor receivables and customer receivables. At December 31, 2008 and 2007, vendor receivables, net, were $400 million and $280 million, and customer receivables, net, were $311 million and $296 million.

Allowance for Doubtful Accounts

We estimate losses on receivables based on known troubled accounts, if any, and historical experience of losses incurred. The allowance for doubtful customer and vendor receivables was $81 million and $64 million at December 31, 2008 and 2007.

Internal-use Software and Website Development

Costs incurred to develop software for internal use are required to be capitalized and amortized over the estimated useful life of the software in accordance with Statement of Position (SOP) 98-1, *Accounting for the Costs of Computer Software Developed or Obtained for Internal Use*. Costs related to design or maintenance of internal-use software are expensed as incurred. For the years ended 2008, 2007, and 2006, we capitalized $187 million (including $27 million of stock-based compensation), $129 million (including $21 million of stock-based compensation), and $123 million (including $16 million of stock-based compensation) of costs associated with internal-use software and website development. Amortization of previously capitalized amounts was $143 million, $116 million, and $86 million for 2008, 2007, and 2006.

AMAZON.COM, INC.

NOTES TO CONSOLIDATED FINANCIAL STATEMENTS—(Continued)

Depreciation of Fixed Assets

Fixed assets include assets such as furniture and fixtures, heavy equipment, technology infrastructure, internal-use software and website development. Depreciation is recorded on a straight-line basis over the estimated useful lives of the assets (generally two years or less for assets such as internal-use software, two or three years for our technology infrastructure, five years for furniture and fixtures, and ten years for heavy equipment). Depreciation expense is generally classified within the corresponding operating expense categories on our consolidated statements of operations, and certain assets are amortized as "Cost of sales."

Leases and Asset Retirement Obligations

We account for our lease agreements pursuant to Statement of Financial Accounting Standards (SFAS) No. 13, *Accounting for Leases*, which categorizes leases at their inception as either operating or capital leases depending on certain defined criteria. On certain of our lease agreements, we may receive rent holidays and other incentives. We recognize lease costs on a straight-line basis without regard to deferred payment terms, such as rent holidays that defer the commencement date of required payments. Additionally, incentives we receive are treated as a reduction of our costs over the term of the agreement. Leasehold improvements are capitalized at cost and amortized over the lesser of their expected useful life or the life of the lease, without assuming renewal features, if any, are exercised. We account for build-to-suit lease arrangements in accordance with EITF 97-10, *The Effect of Lessee Involvement in Asset Construction,* to the extent we are involved in the construction of structural improvements prior to commencement of a lease.

In accordance with SFAS No. 143, *Accounting for Asset Retirement Obligations,* we establish assets and liabilities for the present value of estimated future costs to return certain of our leased facilities to their original condition. Such assets are depreciated over the lease period into operating expense, and the recorded liabilities are accreted to the future value of the estimated restoration costs.

Goodwill

We evaluate goodwill for impairment annually and when an event occurs or circumstances change to suggest that the carrying amount may not be recoverable. Impairment of goodwill is tested at the reporting unit level by comparing the reporting unit's carrying amount, including goodwill, to the fair value of the reporting unit. The fair values of the reporting units are estimated using discounted projected cash flows. If the carrying amount of the reporting unit exceeds its fair value, goodwill is considered impaired and a second step is performed to measure the amount of impairment loss, if any. We conduct our annual impairment test as of October 1 of each year, and have determined there to be no impairment in 2008 or 2007. There were no events or circumstances from the date of our assessment through December 31, 2008 that would impact this conclusion.

See "Note 4—Acquisitions, Goodwill, and Acquired Intangible Assets."

Other Assets

Included in "Other assets" on our consolidated balance sheets are amounts primarily related to marketable securities restricted for longer than one year, the majority of which are attributable to collateralization of bank guarantees and debt related to our international operations; acquired intangible assets, net of amortization; deferred costs; certain equity investments; and intellectual property rights.

AMAZON.COM, INC.

NOTES TO CONSOLIDATED FINANCIAL STATEMENTS—(Continued)

Investments

The initial carrying cost of our investments is the price we paid. Investments are accounted for using the equity method of accounting if the investment gives us the ability to exercise significant influence, but not control, over an investee. The total of these investments in equity-method investees, including identifiable intangible assets, deferred tax liabilities and goodwill, are classified on our consolidated balance sheets as "Other assets" and our share of the investees' earnings or losses along with amortization of the related intangible assets, if any, as "Equity-method investment activity, net of tax" on our consolidated statements of operations.

All other equity investments consist of investments for which we do not have the ability to exercise significant influence. Under the cost method of accounting, investments in private companies are carried at cost and are adjusted only for other-than-temporary declines in fair value, distributions of earnings, and additional investments. For public companies that have readily determinable fair values, we classify our equity investments as available-for-sale and, accordingly, record these investments at their fair values with unrealized gains and losses, net of tax, included in "Accumulated other comprehensive income (loss)," a separate component of stockholders' equity.

We generally invest our excess cash in investment grade short to intermediate term fixed income securities and AAA-rated money market funds. Such investments are included in "Cash and cash equivalents," or "Marketable securities" on the accompanying consolidated balance sheets, are classified as available-for-sale, and reported at fair value with unrealized gains and losses included in "Accumulated other comprehensive income (loss)." The weighted average method is used to determine the cost of Euro-denominated securities sold, and the specific identification method is used to determine the cost of all other securities.

We periodically evaluate whether declines in fair values of our investments below their cost are other-than-temporary. This evaluation consists of several qualitative and quantitative factors regarding the severity and duration of the unrealized loss as well as our ability and intent to hold the investment until a forecasted recovery occurs. Factors considered include quoted market prices; recent financial results and operating trends; other publicly available information; implied values from any recent transactions or offers of investee securities; or other conditions that may affect the value of our investments.

Long-Lived Assets

Long-lived assets, other than goodwill, are reviewed for impairment whenever events or changes in circumstances indicate that the carrying amount of the assets might not be recoverable. Conditions that would necessitate an impairment assessment include a significant decline in the observable market value of an asset, a significant change in the extent or manner in which an asset is used, or any other significant adverse change that would indicate that the carrying amount of an asset or group of assets may not be recoverable.

For long-lived assets used in operations, impairment losses are only recorded if the asset's carrying amount is not recoverable through its undiscounted, probability-weighted future cash flows. We measure the impairment loss based on the difference between the carrying amount and estimated fair value.

Long-lived assets are considered held for sale when certain criteria are met, including when management has committed to a plan to sell the asset, the asset is available for sale in its immediate condition, and the sale is probable within one year of the reporting date. Assets held for sale are reported at the lower of cost or fair value less costs to sell. Assets held for sale were not significant at December 31, 2008 or 2007.

AMAZON.COM, INC.

NOTES TO CONSOLIDATED FINANCIAL STATEMENTS—(Continued)

Accrued Expenses and Other

Included in "Accrued expenses and other" at December 31, 2008 and 2007 were liabilities of $270 million and $230 million for unredeemed gift certificates. We recognize revenue from a gift certificate when a customer redeems it. If a gift certificate is not redeemed, we recognize revenue when it expires or, for a certificate without an expiration date, when the likelihood of its redemption becomes remote, generally two years from date of issuance.

Unearned Revenue

Unearned revenue is recorded when payments are received in advance of performing our service obligations and is recognized over the service period. Current unearned revenue is included in "Accrued expenses and other" and non-current unearned revenue is included in "Other long-term liabilities" on our consolidated balance sheets. Current unearned revenue was $191 million and $91 million at December 31, 2008 and 2007. Non-current unearned revenue was $46 million and $19 million at December 31, 2008 and 2007.

Income Taxes

Income tax expense includes U.S. and international income taxes. We do not provide for U.S. taxes on our undistributed earnings of foreign subsidiaries, totaling $328 million at December 31, 2008, since we intend to invest such undistributed earnings indefinitely outside of the U.S. If such amounts were repatriated, determination of the amount of U.S. income taxes that would be incurred is not practicable due to the complexities associated with this calculation.

Deferred income tax balances reflect the effects of temporary differences between the carrying amounts of assets and liabilities and their tax bases and are stated at enacted tax rates expected to be in effect when taxes are actually paid or recovered. At December 31, 2008, our deferred tax assets, net of deferred tax liabilities and valuation allowance, were $349 million, which includes $165 million relating to net operating loss carryforwards that were primarily attributed to stock-based compensation. The majority of our net operating loss carryforwards begin to expire in 2021 and thereafter.

SFAS No. 109, *Accounting for Income Taxes,* requires that deferred tax assets be evaluated for future realization and reduced by a valuation allowance to the extent we believe a portion will not be realized. We consider many factors when assessing the likelihood of future realization of our deferred tax assets, including our recent cumulative earnings experience and expectations of future taxable income by taxing jurisdiction, the carry-forward periods available to us for tax reporting purposes, and other relevant factors. In accordance with SFAS No. 109, we allocate our valuation allowance to current and long-term deferred tax assets on a pro-rata basis.

Effective January 1, 2007, we adopted the provisions of FIN No. 48, *Accounting for Uncertainty in Income Taxes—an Interpretation of FASB Statement No. 109.* FIN 48 contains a two-step approach to recognizing and measuring uncertain tax positions (tax contingencies) accounted for in accordance with SFAS No. 109. The first step is to evaluate the tax position for recognition by determining if the weight of available evidence indicates it is more likely than not that the position will be sustained on audit, including resolution of related appeals or litigation processes, if any. The second step is to measure the tax benefit as the largest amount which is more than 50% likely of being realized upon ultimate settlement. We consider many factors when evaluating and estimating our tax positions and tax benefits, which may require periodic adjustments and which may not accurately forecast actual outcomes. Our policy is to include interest and penalties related to our tax contingencies in income tax expense. Implementation of FIN 48 was not material.

AMAZON.COM, INC.

NOTES TO CONSOLIDATED FINANCIAL STATEMENTS—(Continued)

Fair Value of Financial Instruments

Effective January 1, 2008, we adopted SFAS No. 157, except as it applies to the nonfinancial assets and nonfinancial liabilities subject to FSP No. 157-2. SFAS No. 157 clarifies the definition of fair value, prescribes methods for measuring fair value, establishes a fair value hierarchy based on the inputs used to measure fair value, and expands disclosures about fair value measurements. The three-tier fair value hierarchy, which prioritizes the inputs used in the valuation methodologies, is:

Level 1—Valuations based on quoted prices for identical assets and liabilities in active markets.

Level 2—Valuations based on observable inputs other than quoted prices included in Level 1, such as quoted prices for similar assets and liabilities in active markets, quoted prices for identical or similar assets and liabilities in markets that are not active, or other inputs that are observable or can be corroborated by observable market data.

Level 3—Valuations based on unobservable inputs reflecting our own assumptions, consistent with reasonably available assumptions made by other market participants. These valuations require significant judgment.

Revenue

We recognize revenue from product sales or services rendered when the following four revenue recognition criteria are met: persuasive evidence of an arrangement exists, delivery has occurred or services have been rendered, the selling price is fixed or determinable, and collectability is reasonably assured. Additionally, revenue arrangements with multiple deliverables are divided into separate units of accounting if the deliverables in the arrangement meet the following criteria: the delivered item has value to the customer on a standalone basis; there is objective and reliable evidence of the fair value of undelivered items; and delivery of any undelivered item is probable.

We evaluate the criteria outlined in EITF Issue No. 99-19, *Reporting Revenue Gross as a Principal Versus Net as an Agent,* in determining whether it is appropriate to record the gross amount of product sales and related costs or the net amount earned as commissions. Generally, when we are primarily obligated in a transaction, are subject to inventory risk, have latitude in establishing prices and selecting suppliers, or have several but not all of these indicators, revenue is recorded gross. If we are not primarily obligated and amounts earned are determined using a fixed percentage, a fixed-payment schedule, or a combination of the two, we generally record the net amounts as commissions earned.

Product sales and shipping revenues, net of promotional discounts, rebates, and return allowances, are recorded when the products are shipped and title passes to customers. Retail sales to customers are made pursuant to a sales contract that provides for transfer of both title and risk of loss upon our delivery to the carrier. Return allowances, which reduce product revenue, are estimated using historical experience. Revenue from product sales and services rendered is recorded net of sales taxes. Amounts received in advance for subscription services, including amounts received for Amazon Prime and other membership programs, are deferred and recognized as revenue over the subscription term. For our products with multiple elements, where a standalone value for each element cannot be established, we recognize the revenue and related cost over the estimated economic life of the product.

We periodically provide incentive offers to our customers to encourage purchases. Such offers include current discount offers, such as percentage discounts off current purchases, inducement offers, such as offers for future discounts subject to a minimum current purchase, and other similar offers. Current discount offers, when

AMAZON.COM, INC.
NOTES TO CONSOLIDATED FINANCIAL STATEMENTS—(Continued)

accepted by our customers, are treated as a reduction to the purchase price of the related transaction, while inducement offers, when accepted by our customers, are treated as a reduction to purchase price based on estimated future redemption rates. Redemption rates are estimated using our historical experience for similar inducement offers. Current discount offers and inducement offers are presented as a net amount in "Net sales."

Commissions and per-unit fees received from sellers and similar amounts earned through other seller sites are recognized when the item is sold by seller and our collectability is reasonably assured. We record an allowance for estimated refunds on such commissions using historical experience.

Shipping Activities

Outbound shipping charges to customers are included in "Net sales" and were $835 million, $740 million, and $567 million for 2008, 2007, and 2006. Outbound shipping-related costs are included in "Cost of sales" and totaled $1.5 billion, $1.2 billion, and $884 million for 2008, 2007, and 2006. The net cost to us of shipping activities was $630 million, $434 million, and $317 million for 2008, 2007 and 2006.

Cost of Sales

Cost of sales consists of the purchase price of consumer products and content sold by us, inbound and outbound shipping charges, packaging supplies, and costs incurred in operating and staffing our fulfillment and customer service centers on behalf of other businesses. Shipping charges to receive products from our suppliers are included in our inventory, and recognized as "Cost of sales" upon sale of products to our customers. Payment processing and related transaction costs, including those associated with seller transactions, are classified in "Fulfillment" on our consolidated statements of operations.

Vendor Agreements

We have agreements to receive cash consideration from certain of our vendors, including rebates and cooperative marketing reimbursements. We generally presume amounts received from our vendors are a reduction of the prices we pay for their products and, therefore, we reflect such amounts as either a reduction of "Cost of sales" on our consolidated statements of operations, or, if the product inventory is still on hand, as a reduction of the carrying value of inventory. Vendor rebates are typically dependent upon reaching minimum purchase thresholds. We evaluate the likelihood of reaching purchase thresholds using past experience and current year forecasts. When volume rebates can be reasonably estimated, we record a portion of the rebate as we make progress towards the purchase threshold.

When we receive direct reimbursements for costs incurred by us in advertising the vendor's product or service, the amount we receive is recorded as an offset to "Marketing" on our consolidated statements of operations.

Fulfillment

Fulfillment costs represent those costs incurred in operating and staffing our fulfillment and customer service centers, including costs attributable to buying, receiving, inspecting, and warehousing inventories; picking, packaging, and preparing customer orders for shipment; payment processing and related transaction costs, including costs associated with our guarantee for certain seller transactions; and responding to inquiries from customers. Fulfillment costs also include amounts paid to third parties that assist us in fulfillment and customer service operations. Certain of our fulfillment-related costs that are incurred on behalf of other businesses are classified as cost of sales rather than fulfillment.

AMAZON.COM, INC.

NOTES TO CONSOLIDATED FINANCIAL STATEMENTS—(Continued)

Foreign Currency

We have the following internationally-focused websites: *www.amazon.co.uk, www.amazon.de, www.amazon.fr, www.amazon.co.jp, www.amazon.ca*, and *www.amazon.cn*. Net sales generated from internationally-focused websites, as well as most of the related expenses directly incurred from those operations, are denominated in the functional currencies of the resident countries. Additionally, the functional currency of our subsidiaries that either operate or support these international websites is the same as the local currency of the United Kingdom, Germany, France, Japan, Canada, and China. Assets and liabilities of these subsidiaries are translated into U.S. Dollars at period-end exchange rates, and revenues and expenses are translated at average rates prevailing throughout the period. Translation adjustments are included in "Accumulated other comprehensive income (loss)," a separate component of stockholders' equity, and in the "Foreign currency effect on cash and cash equivalents," on our consolidated statements of cash flows. Transaction gains and losses arising from transactions denominated in a currency other than the functional currency of the entity involved are included in "Other income (expense), net" on our consolidated statements of operations. See "Note 11—Other Income (Expense), Net."

Gains and losses arising from intercompany foreign currency transactions are included in net income. In connection with the remeasurement of intercompany balances, we recorded gains of $23 million, $32 million and $50 million in 2008, 2007 and 2006.

Note 2—CASH, CASH EQUIVALENTS, AND MARKETABLE SECURITIES

As of December 31, 2008 and 2007 our cash, cash equivalents, and marketable securities primarily consisted of cash, government and government agency securities, AAA-rated money market funds and other investment grade securities. Such amounts are recorded at fair value. The following table summarizes, by major security type, our cash, cash equivalents and marketable securities (in millions):

	December 31, 2008			
	Cost or Amortized Cost	Gross Unrealized Gains	Gross Unrealized Losses (1)	Total Estimated Fair Value
Cash	$ 355	$—	$—	$ 355
Money market funds	1,682	—	—	1,682
Foreign government and agency securities	1,120	8	—	1,128
Corporate debt securities (2)	194	2	(2)	194
U.S. government and agency securities	589	5	—	594
Asset-backed securities	62	—	(4)	58
Other fixed income securities	23	—	—	23
Equity securities	2	—	(1)	1
	$4,027	$ 15	$ (7)	$4,035
Less: Long-term marketable securities (3)				(308)
Total cash, cash equivalents, and marketable securities				$3,727

AMAZON.COM, INC.

NOTES TO CONSOLIDATED FINANCIAL STATEMENTS—(Continued)

	December 31, 2007			
	Cost or Amortized Cost	Gross Unrealized Gains	Gross Unrealized Losses (1)	Total Estimated Fair Value
Cash	$ 813	$—	$—	$ 813
Money market funds	1,558	—	—	1,558
Foreign government and agency securities	358	—	(1)	357
Corporate debt securities (2)	128	1	(1)	128
U.S. government and agency securities	326	5	—	331
Asset-backed securities	106	1	(1)	106
Other fixed income securities	4	—	—	4
Equity securities	5	7	—	12
	$3,298	$ 14	$ (3)	$3,309
Less: Long-term marketable securities (3)				(197)
Total cash, cash equivalents, and marketable securities				$3,112

(1) As of December 31, 2008, the cost and fair value of investments with loss positions was $761 million and $753 million. As of December 31, 2007, the cost and fair value of investments with loss positions was $550 million and $547 million. We evaluated the nature of these investments, credit worthiness of the issuer, and the duration of these impairments to determine if an other-than-temporary decline in fair value has occurred and concluded that these losses were temporary. Investments that have continuously been in loss positions for more than twelve months have gross unrealized losses of $2 million and $2 million as of December 31, 2008 and 2007.

(2) Corporate debt securities include investments in financial, insurance, and corporate institutions. No single issuer represents a significant portion of the total corporate debt securities portfolio.

(3) We are required to pledge or otherwise restrict a portion of our marketable securities as collateral for standby letters of credit, guarantees, debt, and real estate lease agreements. We classify cash and marketable securities with use restrictions of twelve months or longer as non-current "Other assets" on our consolidated balance sheets. See "Note 7—Commitments and Contingencies."

The following table summarizes contractual maturities of our cash equivalent and marketable fixed-income securities as of December 31, 2008 (in millions):

	Amortized Cost	Estimated Fair Value
Due within one year	$3,089	$3,090
Due after one year through five years	578	589
	$3,667	$3,679

Gross gains of $9 million, $2 million, and $18 million and gross losses of $7 million, $3 million and $16 million were realized on sales of available-for-sale marketable securities, including Euro-denominated securities, for 2008, 2007, and 2006. Realized gains and losses are included in "Other income (expense), net" on our consolidated statements of operations.

AMAZON.COM, INC.

NOTES TO CONSOLIDATED FINANCIAL STATEMENTS—(Continued)

Note 3—FIXED ASSETS

Fixed assets, at cost, consisted of the following (in millions):

	December 31,	
	2008	2007
Gross Fixed Assets:		
Fulfillment and customer service	$ 564	$ 464
Technology infrastructure	348	196
Internal-use software, content, and website development	331	285
Construction in progress (1)	87	15
Other corporate assets	79	63
Gross fixed assets	1,409	1,023
Accumulated Depreciation :		
Fulfillment and customer service	254	216
Technology infrastructure	82	74
Internal-use software, content, and website development	159	146
Other corporate assets	60	44
Total accumulated depreciation	555	480
Total fixed assets, net	$ 854	$ 543

---

(1) We capitalize construction in progress and record a corresponding long-term liability for certain lease agreements, including our Seattle, Washington corporate office space subject to leases scheduled to begin in 2010 and 2011. See "Note 6—Other Long-Term Liabilities" and "Note 7—Commitments and Contingencies" for further discussion.

Depreciation expense on fixed assets was $311 million, $258 million, and $200 million, which includes amortization of fixed assets acquired under capital lease obligations of $50 million, $40 million, and $26 million for 2008, 2007, and 2006. Gross assets remaining under capital leases were $304 million and $150 million at December 31, 2008 and 2007. Accumulated depreciation associated with capital leases was $116 million and $64 million at December 31, 2008 and 2007.

AMAZON.COM, INC.

NOTES TO CONSOLIDATED FINANCIAL STATEMENTS—(Continued)

Note 4—ACQUISITIONS, GOODWILL, AND ACQUIRED INTANGIBLE ASSETS

In 2008, we acquired certain companies for an aggregate purchase price of $432 million. For each acquisition, the purchase price has been allocated to the tangible assets, liabilities assumed, and identifiable intangible assets acquired based on estimated fair values on the acquisition date. The excess of purchase price over the fair value of the net assets acquired is classified as "Goodwill" on our consolidated balance sheets.

The following summarizes the allocation of the purchase price for companies acquired in 2008 (in millions):

Goodwill	$210
Internal-use software	31
Other assets, net	104
Deferred tax liabilities net	(75)
Intangible assets (1):	
Marketing-related	12
Contract-based	60
Technology and content	2
Customer-related	88
	$432

---

(1) Acquired intangible assets have estimated useful lives of between 2 and 13 years.

We acquired certain companies during 2007 for an aggregate purchase price of $33 million, resulting in goodwill of $21 million and acquired intangible assets of $18 million. We also made principal payments of $13 million on acquired debt in connection with one of these acquisitions.

We acquired certain companies during 2006 for an aggregate purchase price of $50 million, resulting in goodwill of $33 million and acquired intangible assets of $17 million.

The results of operations of each of the businesses acquired in 2008, 2007, and 2006 have been included in our consolidated results from each transaction closing date forward. The effect of these acquisitions on consolidated net sales and operating income during 2008, 2007, and 2006 was not significant.

At December 31, 2008 and December 31, 2007, approximately 22% and 36% of our acquired goodwill related to our International segment.

Note 5—LONG-TERM DEBT

Our long-term debt is summarized as follows:

	December 31,	
	2008	**2007**
	(in millions)	
6.875% PEACS due February 2010	$335	$ 350
4.75% Convertible Subordinated Notes		899
Other long-term debt	133	50
	468	1,299
Less current portion of long-term debt	(59)	(17)
	$409	$1,282

In 2008, we called for redemption of the remaining principal amount of $899 million of our outstanding 4.75% Convertible Subordinated Notes. Holders elected to convert $605 million in principal amount of the 4.75% Convertible Subordinated Notes, and we issued 7.8 million shares of our common stock as a result; we redeemed the remaining $294 million of the called principal amount for cash.

AMAZON.COM, INC.

NOTES TO CONSOLIDATED FINANCIAL STATEMENTS—(Continued)

Note 6—OTHER LONG-TERM LIABILITIES

Our other long-term liabilities are summarized as follows:

	December 31,	
	2008	2007
	(in millions)	
Tax contingencies	$144	$ 98
Long-term capital lease obligations	124	62
Construction liabilities	87	15
Other	132	117
	$487	$292

Tax Contingencies

As of December 31, 2008 and 2007, we have provided tax reserves for tax contingencies of approximately $144 million and $98 million for U.S. and foreign income taxes, which primarily relate to restructuring of certain foreign operations and intercompany pricing between our subsidiaries. See "Note 12—Income Taxes" for discussion of tax contingencies.

Capital Leases

Certain of our equipment fixed assets, primarily related to technology, have been acquired under capital leases. Long-term capital lease obligations were as follows:

	December 31, 2008
	(in millions)
Gross capital lease obligations	$219
Less imputed interest	(23)
Present value of net minimum lease payments	196
Less current portion	(72)
Total long-term capital lease obligations	$124

Construction Liabilities

We capitalize construction in progress and record a corresponding long-term liability for certain lease agreements, including our Seattle, Washington corporate office space subject to leases scheduled to begin in 2010 and 2011.

In accordance with EITF No. 97-10, for build-to-suit lease arrangements where we are involved in the construction of structural improvements prior to the commencement of the lease or take some level of construction risk, we are considered the owner of the assets during the construction period under U.S. GAAP.

Accordingly, as the landlord incurs the construction project costs, the assets and corresponding financial obligation are recorded in "Fixed assets, net" and "Other long-term liabilities" on our consolidated balance sheet. Once the construction is completed, if the lease meets certain "sale-leaseback" criteria in accordance with SFAS No. 98, *Accounting for Leases*, we will remove the asset and related financial obligation from the balance sheet and treat the building lease as an operating lease. If upon completion of construction, the project does not meet the "sale-leaseback" criteria, the leased property will be treated as a capital lease for financial reporting purposes.

The remainder of our other long-term liabilities primarily include deferred tax liabilities, unearned revenue, asset retirement obligations, and deferred rental liabilities.

AMAZON.COM, INC.

NOTES TO CONSOLIDATED FINANCIAL STATEMENTS—(Continued)

Note 7—COMMITMENTS AND CONTINGENCIES

Commitments

We lease office and fulfillment center facilities and fixed assets under non-cancelable operating and capital leases. Rental expense under operating lease agreements was $158 million, $141 million, and $132 million for 2008, 2007, and 2006.

In December 2007, we entered into a series of leases and other agreements for the lease of corporate office space to be developed in Seattle, Washington with initial terms of up to 16 years commencing on completion of development in 2010 and 2011 and options to extend for two five year periods. At December 31, 2008, under the agreements we committed to occupy approximately 1,360,000 square feet of office space. In addition, we have the right to occupy up to an additional approximately 330,000 square feet subject to a termination fee, estimated to be up to approximately $10 million, if we elect not to occupy the additional space. We also have an option to lease up to an additional approximately 500,000 square feet at rates based on fair market values at the time the option is exercised, subject to certain conditions. In addition, if interest rates exceed a certain threshold, we have the option to provide financing for some of the buildings.

The following summarizes our principal contractual commitments, excluding open orders for inventory purchases that support normal operations, as of December 31, 2008:

	Year Ended December 31,					Thereafter	Total
	2009	2010	2011	2012	2013		
	(in millions)						
Operating and capital commitments:							
Debt principal (1)	$ 59	$335	$ 41	$ 33	$—	$ —	$ 468
Debt interest (1)	30	28	5	1	—	—	64
Capital leases, including interest	86	77	44	7	4	1	219
Operating leases	146	127	105	93	84	261	816
Other commitments (2)(3)	96	143	88	84	76	1,005	1,492
Total commitments	$417	$710	$283	$218	$164	$1,267	$3,059

(1) Under our 6.875% PEACS, the principal payment due in 2010 and the annual interest payments fluctuate based on the Euro/U.S. Dollar exchange ratio. At December 31, 2008, the Euro to U.S. Dollar exchange rate was 1.3974. Due to changes in the Euro/U.S. Dollar exchange ratio, our remaining principal debt obligation under this instrument since issuance in February 2000 has increased by $99 million as of December 31, 2008. The principal and interest commitments at December 31, 2008 reflect the partial redemption of the 6.875% PEACS and full redemption of the 4.75% Convertible Subordinated Notes.

AMAZON.COM, INC.

NOTES TO CONSOLIDATED FINANCIAL STATEMENTS—(Continued)

(2) Includes the estimated timing and amounts of payments for rent, operating expenses, and tenant improvements associated with approximately 1,360,000 square feet of corporate office space being developed in Seattle, Washington and also includes the $10 million termination fee related to our right to occupy up to an additional approximately 330,000 square feet. The amount of space available and our financial and other obligations under the lease agreements are affected by various factors, including government approvals and permits, interest rates, development costs and other expenses and our exercise of certain rights under the lease agreements.

(3) Excludes $166 million of such tax contingencies for which we cannot make a reasonably reliable estimate of the amount and period of payment, if at all. See Item 8 of Part II, "Financial Statements and Supplementary Data—Note 12—Income Taxes."

Pledged Securities

We are required to pledge or otherwise restrict a portion of our cash and marketable securities as collateral for standby letters of credit, guarantees, debt, and real estate leases. We classify cash and marketable securities with use restrictions of twelve months or longer as non-current "Other assets" on our consolidated balance sheets. The balance of pledged securities at December 31, 2008 consisted of $308 million included in "Other assets." The amount required to be pledged for certain real estate lease agreements changes over the life of our leases based on our credit rating and changes in our market capitalization (common shares outstanding multiplied by the closing price of our common stock). Information about collateral required to be pledged under these agreements is as follows:

	Standby and Trade Letters of Credit and Guarantees	Debt (1)	Real Estate Leases (2)	Total
		(in millions)		
Balance at December 31, 2007	$138	$ 60	$13	$211
Net change in collateral pledged	—	100	(3)	97
Balance at December 31, 2008	$138	$160	$10	$308

(1) Represents collateral for certain debt related to our international operations.

(2) At December 31, 2007, our market capitalization was $22.0 billion. The required amount of collateral to be pledged will increase by $5 million if our market capitalization is equal to or below $18.0 billion and by an additional $6 million if our market capitalization is equal to or below $13.0 billion.

Legal Proceedings

The Company is involved from time to time in claims, proceedings and litigation, including the following:

In June 2001, Audible, Inc., our subsidiary acquired in March 2008, was named as a defendant in a securities class-action filed in United States District Court for the Southern District of New York related to its initial public offering in July 1999. The lawsuit also named certain of the offering's underwriters, as well as Audible's officers and directors as defendants. Approximately 300 other issuers and their underwriters have had similar suits filed against them, all of which are included in a single coordinated proceeding in the Southern District of New York. The complaints allege that the prospectus and the registration statement for Audible's offering failed to disclose that the underwriters allegedly solicited and received "excessive" commissions from investors and that some investors allegedly agreed with the underwriters to buy additional shares in the aftermarket in order to inflate the price of the Company's stock. Audible and its officers and directors were named in the suits pursuant to Section 11 of the Securities Act of 1933, Section 10(b) of the Securities Exchange Act of 1934, and other related provisions. The complaints seek unspecified damages, attorney and expert fees,

AMAZON.COM, INC.

NOTES TO CONSOLIDATED FINANCIAL STATEMENTS—(Continued)

and other unspecified litigation costs. The Court has directed that the litigation proceed with a number of "focus cases" rather than all of the consolidated cases at once. Audible's case is not one of these focus cases. We dispute the allegations of wrongdoing in the complaint against Audible and its officers and directors and intend to vigorously defend ourselves in this matter.

Beginning in March 2003, we were served with complaints filed in several different states, including Illinois, by a private litigant, Beeler, Schad & Diamond, P.C., purportedly on behalf of the state governments under various state False Claims Acts. The complaints allege that we (along with other companies with which we have commercial agreements) wrongfully failed to collect and remit sales and use taxes for sales of personal property to customers in those states and knowingly created records and statements falsely stating we were not required to collect or remit such taxes. In December 2006, we learned that one additional complaint was filed in the state of Illinois by a different private litigant, Matthew T. Hurst, alleging similar violations of the Illinois state law. All of the complaints seek injunctive relief, unpaid taxes, interest, attorneys' fees, civil penalties of up to $10,000 per violation, and treble or punitive damages under the various state False Claims Acts. It is possible that we have been or will be named in similar cases in other states as well. We dispute the allegations of wrongdoing in these complaints and intend to vigorously defend ourselves in these matters.

In May 2004, Toysrus.com LLC filed a complaint against us for breach of contract in the Superior Court of New Jersey. The complaint alleged that we breached our commercial agreement with Toysrus.com LLC by selling, and by permitting other third parties to sell, products that Toysrus.com LLC alleged it has an exclusive right to sell on our website. We disputed the allegations in the complaint and brought counterclaims alleging breach of contract and seeking damages and declaratory relief. The trial of both parties' claims concluded in November 2005. In March 2006, the Court entered a judgment in favor of Toysrus.com LLC, terminating the contract but declining to award damages to either party. We are pursuing an appeal of the lower court's rulings terminating the contract, declining to award us damages, and denying our motion to compel Toysrus.com to pay certain fees incurred during the wind-down period.

In December 2005, Registrar Systems LLC filed a complaint against us and Target Corporation for patent infringement in the United States District Court for the District of Colorado. The complaint alleges that our website technology, including the method by which Amazon.com enables customers to use Amazon.com account information on websites that Amazon.com operates for third parties, such as Target.com, infringes two patents obtained by Registrar Systems purporting to cover methods and apparatuses for a "World Wide Web Registration Information Processing System" (U.S. Patent Nos. 5,790,785 and 6,823,327) and seeks injunctive relief, monetary damages in an amount no less than a reasonable royalty, prejudgment interest, costs, and attorneys' fees. We dispute the allegations of wrongdoing in this complaint and intend to vigorously defend ourselves in this matter. In September 2006, the Court entered an order staying the lawsuit pending the outcome of the Patent and Trademark Office's re-examination of the patents in suit.

In August 2006, Cordance Corporation filed a complaint against us for patent infringement in the United States District Court for the District of Delaware. The complaint alleges that our website technology, including our 1-Click ordering system, infringes a patent obtained by Cordance purporting to cover an "Object-Based Online Transaction Infrastructure" (U.S. Patent No. 6,757,710) and seeks injunctive relief, monetary damages in an amount no less than a reasonable royalty, treble damages for alleged willful infringement, prejudgment interest, costs, and attorneys' fees. In response, we asserted a declaratory judgment counterclaim in the same action alleging that a service that Cordance has advertised its intent to launch infringes a patent owned by us entitled "Networked Personal Contact Manager" (U.S. Patent No. 6,269,369). We dispute Cordance's allegations of wrongdoing and intend to vigorously defend ourselves in this matter.

AMAZON.COM, INC.

NOTES TO CONSOLIDATED FINANCIAL STATEMENTS—(Continued)

In October 2007, Digital Reg of Texas, LLC filed a complaint against our subsidiary, Audible, Inc., and several other defendants in the United States District Court for the Eastern District of Texas. The complaint alleges that Audible's digital rights management technology infringes a patent obtained by Digital Reg purporting to cover a system for "Regulating Access to Digital Content" (U.S. Patent No. 6,389,541) and seeks injunctive relief, monetary damages, enhanced damages for alleged willful infringement, prejudgment and post-judgment interest, costs and attorneys' fees. We dispute the allegations of wrongdoing and intend to vigorously defend ourselves in the matter.

In December 2008, Quito Enterprises, LLC filed a complaint against us for patent infringement in the United States District Court for the Southern District of Florida. The complaint alleges that our website technology infringes a patent obtained by Quito purporting to cover a "Personal Feedback Browser for Obtaining Media Files" (U.S. Patent No. 5,890,152) and seeks injunctive relief and monetary damages. We dispute the allegations of wrongdoing and intend to vigorously defend ourselves in this matter.

In January 2009, we learned that the United States Postal Service, including the Postal Service Office of Inspector General, is investigating our compliance with Postal Service rules, and we are cooperating.

Depending on the amount and the timing, an unfavorable resolution of some or all of these matters could materially affect our business, results of operations, financial position, or cash flows.

See also "Note 12—Income Taxes."

Inventory Suppliers

During 2008, no vendor accounted for 10% or more of our inventory purchases. We do not have long-term contracts or arrangements with most of our vendors to guarantee the availability of merchandise, particular payment terms, or the extension of credit limits.

Note 8—STOCKHOLDERS' EQUITY

Preferred Stock

We have authorized 500 million shares of $0.01 par value Preferred Stock. No preferred stock was outstanding for any period presented.

Stock Conversion Activity

Holders of our 4.75% Convertible Subordinated Notes elected to convert a total of $605 million in outstanding principal amount under called redemptions during 2008, and we issued 7.8 million shares of common stock as a result of such elections.

Stock Repurchase Activity

We repurchased 2.2 million shares of common stock for $100 million in 2008 under the $1 billion repurchase program authorized by our Board of Directors in February 2008. We repurchased 6.3 million shares of common stock for $248 million in 2007, and 8.2 million shares of common stock for $252 million in 2006, under the $500 million repurchase program authorized by our Board of Directors in August 2006.

AMAZON.COM, INC.

NOTES TO CONSOLIDATED FINANCIAL STATEMENTS—(Continued)

Note 9—OTHER COMPREHENSIVE INCOME (LOSS)

The changes in the components of other comprehensive income (loss) were as follows:

	Year Ended December 31,		
	2008	2007	2006
	(in millions)		
Net income	$ 645	$476	$190
Net change in unrealized gains/losses on available-for-sale securities	(1)	8	4
Foreign currency translation adjustment, net of tax	(127)	(3)	(13)
Amortization of net unrealized losses on terminated Euro Currency Swap, net of tax	—	1	2
Other comprehensive income (loss)	(128)	6	(7)
Comprehensive income	$ 517	$482	$183

Accumulated balances within other comprehensive income (loss) were as follows:

	December 31,	
	2008	2007
	(in millions)	
Net unrealized losses on foreign currency translation, net of tax	$(128)	$(1)
Net unrealized gains on available-for-sale securities, net of tax	6	7
Net unrealized losses on terminated Euro Currency Swap, net of tax	(1)	(1)
Total accumulated other comprehensive income (loss)	$(123)	$ 5

AMAZON.COM, INC.

NOTES TO CONSOLIDATED FINANCIAL STATEMENTS—(Continued)

Note 10—OTHER OPERATING EXPENSE (INCOME), NET

Other operating expense (income), net, was $(24) million, $9 million and $10 million in 2008, 2007 and 2006. The increase in other operating income in 2008 compared to the comparable prior years is primarily attributable to the $53 million non-cash gain recognized on the sale in 2008 of our European DVD rental assets, partially offset by increased amortization of intangible assets. Other operating expense in 2007 and 2006 was primarily attributable to amortization of intangible assets.

Note 11—OTHER INCOME (EXPENSE), NET

Other income (expense), net, was $47 million, $(8) million, and $7 million in 2008, 2007 and 2006, and consisted primarily of gains and losses on sales of marketable securities, foreign currency transaction gains and losses, and other miscellaneous losses.

Foreign currency transaction gains and losses primarily relate to remeasurement of our 6.875% PEACS and remeasurement of intercompany balances.

Note 12—INCOME TAXES

In 2008, 2007 and 2006 we recorded net tax provisions of $247 million, $184 million, and $187 million. A majority of this provision is non-cash. We have current tax benefits and net operating losses relating to excess stock-based compensation that are being utilized to reduce our U.S. taxable income. As such, cash taxes paid were $53 million, $24 million, and $15 million for 2008, 2007, and 2006.

The components of the provision for income taxes, net were as follows:

	Year Ended December 31,		
	2008	2007	2006
	(in millions)		
Current taxes:			
U.S. and state	$227	$275	$162
International	25	8	3
Current taxes	252	283	165
Deferred taxes	(5)	(99)	22
Provision for income taxes, net	$247	$184	$187

AMAZON.COM, INC.

NOTES TO CONSOLIDATED FINANCIAL STATEMENTS—(Continued)

Item 9.   *Changes in and Disagreements with Accountants On Accounting and Financial Disclosure*

None.

Item 9A.   *Controls and Procedures*

Evaluation of Disclosure Controls and Procedures

We carried out an evaluation required by the 1934 Act, under the supervision and with the participation of our principal executive officer and principal financial officer, of the effectiveness of the design and operation of our disclosure controls and procedures, as defined in Rule 13a-15(e) of the 1934 Act, as of December 31, 2008. Based on this evaluation, our principal executive officer and principal financial officer concluded that, as of December 31, 2008, our disclosure controls and procedures were effective to provide reasonable assurance that information required to be disclosed by us in the reports that we file or submit under the 1934 Act is recorded, processed, summarized, and reported within the time periods specified in the SEC's rules and forms and to provide reasonable assurance that such information is accumulated and communicated to our management, including our principal executive officer and principal financial officer, as appropriate to allow timely decisions regarding required disclosures.

Management's Report on Internal Control over Financial Reporting

Management is responsible for establishing and maintaining adequate internal control over financial reporting, as defined in Rule 13a-15(f) of the 1934 Act. Management has assessed the effectiveness of our internal control over financial reporting as of December 31, 2008 based on criteria established in Internal Control—Integrated Framework issued by the Committee of Sponsoring Organizations of the Treadway Commission. As a result of this assessment, management concluded that, as of December 31, 2008, our internal control over financial reporting was effective in providing reasonable assurance regarding the reliability of financial reporting and the preparation of financial statements for external purposes in accordance with generally accepted accounting principles. Ernst & Young has independently assessed the effectiveness of our internal control over financial reporting and its report is included below.

Changes in Internal Control Over Financial Reporting

There were no changes in our internal control over financial reporting during the quarter ended December 31, 2008 that materially affected, or are reasonably likely to materially affect, our internal control over financial reporting.

Limitations on Controls

Our disclosure controls and procedures and internal control over financial reporting are designed to provide reasonable assurance of achieving their objectives as specified above. Management does not expect, however, that our disclosure controls and procedures or our internal control over financial reporting will prevent or detect all error and fraud. Any control system, no matter how well designed and operated, is based upon certain assumptions and can provide only reasonable, not absolute, assurance that its objectives will be met. Further, no evaluation of controls can provide absolute assurance that misstatements due to error or fraud will not occur or that all control issues and instances of fraud, if any, within the Company have been detected.

FOOT LOCKER, INC.

2007 ANNUAL REPORT   OUR BRAND IDENTITY

Foot Locker

Lady Foot Locker

kids foot locker

CHAMPS

Eastbay

FOOTACTION

Item 8. Consolidated Financial Statements and Supplementary Data

MANAGEMENT'S REPORT

The integrity and objectivity of the financial statements and other financial information presented in this annual report are the responsibility of the management of the Company. The financial statements have been prepared in conformity with U.S. generally accepted accounting principles and include, when necessary, amounts based on the best estimates and judgments of management.

The Company maintains a system of internal controls designed to provide reasonable assurance, at appropriate cost, that assets are safeguarded, transactions are executed in accordance with management's authorization and the accounting records provide a reliable basis for the preparation of the financial statements. The system of internal accounting controls is continually reviewed by management and improved and modified as necessary in response to changing business conditions. The Company also maintains an internal audit function to assist management in evaluating and formally reporting on the adequacy and effectiveness of internal accounting controls, policies and procedures.

The Company's financial statements have been audited by KPMG LLP, the Company's independent registered public accounting firm, whose report expresses their opinion with respect to the fairness of the presentation of these financial statements.

The Audit Committee of the Board of Directors, which comprises solely independent non-management directors who are not officers or employees of the Company, meets regularly with the Company's management, internal auditors, legal counsel and KPMG LLP to review the activities of each group and to satisfy itself that each is properly discharging its responsibility. In addition, the Audit Committee meets on a periodic basis with KPMG LLP, without management's presence, to discuss the audit of the financial statements as well as other auditing and financial reporting matters. The Company's internal auditors and independent registered public accounting firm have direct access to the Audit Committee.

MATTHEW D. SERRA,
Chairman of the Board,
President and Chief Executive Officer

ROBERT W. MCHUGH,
Senior Vice President and
Chief Financial Officer

March 31, 2008

REPORT OF INDEPENDENT REGISTERED PUBLIC ACCOUNTING FIRM

The Board of Directors and Shareholders of
Foot Locker, Inc.:

We have audited the accompanying consolidated balance sheets of Foot Locker, Inc. and subsidiaries as of February 2, 2008 and February 3, 2007, and the related consolidated statements of operations, comprehensive income, shareholders' equity, and cash flows for each of the years in the three-year period ended February 2, 2008. These consolidated financial statements are the responsibility of the Company's management. Our responsibility is to express an opinion on these consolidated financial statements based on our audits.

We conducted our audits in accordance with the standards of the Public Company Accounting Oversight Board (United States). Those standards require that we plan and perform the audit to obtain reasonable assurance about whether the financial statements are free of material misstatement. An audit also includes examining, on a test basis, evidence supporting the amounts and disclosures in the financial statements, assessing the accounting principles used and significant estimates made by management, as well as evaluating the overall financial statement presentation. We believe that our audits provide a reasonable basis for our opinion.

In our opinion, the consolidated financial statements referred to above present fairly, in all material respects, the financial position of Foot Locker, Inc. and subsidiaries as of February 2, 2008 and February 3, 2007, and the results of their operations and their cash flows for each of the years in the three-year period ended February 2, 2008 in conformity with U.S. generally accepted accounting principles.

As discussed in the Notes to Consolidated Financial Statements, effective February 4, 2007, the Company adopted Statement of Financial Accounting Standards Interpretation ("FIN") No. 48, "Accounting for Uncertainty in Income Taxes." Effective February 3, 2007, the Company adopted Statement of Financial Accounting Standards ("SFAS") No 158, "Employers' Accounting for Defined Benefit Pension and Other Post Retirement Plans – An Amendment of FASB Statements No. 87, 88, 106, and 132(R)." In addition, effective January 29, 2006, the Company adopted SFAS No. 123(R), "Share-Based Payment," and SFAS No. 151, "Inventory Costs – An Amendment of ARB No. 43, Chapter 4," as well as changed their method for quantifying errors based on SEC Staff Accounting Bulletin No. 108, "Considering the Effects of Prior Year Misstatements when Quantifying Misstatements in Current Year Financial Statements."

We also have audited, in accordance with the standards of the Public Company Accounting Oversight Board (United States), the effectiveness of Foot Locker, Inc.'s internal control over financial reporting as of February 2, 2008, based on criteria established in Internal Control – Integrated Framework issued by the Committee of Sponsoring Organizations of the Treadway Commission (COSO), and our report dated March 31, 2008 expressed an unqualified opinion on the effectiveness of internal control over financial reporting.

KPMG LLP

New York, New York
March 31, 2008

CONSOLIDATED STATEMENTS OF OPERATIONS

	2007	2006	2005
	(in millions, except per share amounts)		
Sales	$ 5,437	$ 5,750	$ 5,653
Costs and expenses			
Cost of sales	4,017	4,014	3,944
Selling, general and administrative expenses	1,176	1,163	1,129
Depreciation and amortization	166	175	171
Impairment charges and store closing program costs	128	17	—
Interest expense, net	1	3	10
	5,488	5,372	5,254
Other income	(1)	(14)	(6)
	5,487	5,358	5,248
(Loss) Income from continuing operations before income taxes	(50)	392	405
Income tax (benefit) expense	(99)	145	142
Income from continuing operations	49	247	263
Income on disposal of discontinued operations, net of income tax expense (benefit) of $1, $1, and $(3), respectively	2	3	1
Cumulative effect of accounting change, net of income tax benefit of $ —	—	1	—
Net income	$ 51	$ 251	$ 264
Basic earnings per share:			
Income from continuing operations	$ 0.32	$ 1.59	$ 1.70
Income from discontinued operations	0.01	0.02	0.01
Cumulative effect of accounting change	—	0.01	—
Net income	$ 0.33	$ 1.62	$ 1.71
Diluted earnings per share:			
Income from continuing operations	$ 0.32	$ 1.58	$ 1.67
Income from discontinued operations	0.01	0.02	0.01
Cumulative effect of accounting change	—	—	—
Net income	$ 0.33	$ 1.60	$ 1.68

See Accompanying Notes to Consolidated Financial Statements.

CONSOLIDATED STATEMENTS OF COMPREHENSIVE INCOME

	2007	2006	2005
		(in millions)	
Net income...	$ 51	$ 251	$ 264
Other comprehensive income, net of tax			
Foreign currency translation adjustment:			
Translation adjustment arising during the period, net of tax...............	60	27	(25)
Cash flow hedges:			
Change in fair value of derivatives, net of income tax.....................	1	—	2
Reclassification adjustments, net of income tax.........................	—	—	(1)
Net change in cash flow hedges:	1	—	1
Minimum pension liability adjustment:			
Minimum pension liability adjustment, net of deferred tax expense of $-, $120 and $10 million, respectively	—	181	15
Pension and postretirement plan adjustments, net of income tax benefit of $11 million	(20)	—	—
Unrealized loss on available-for-sale securities........................	(2)	—	—
Comprehensive income.......................................	$ 90	$459	$ 255

CONSOLIDATED BALANCE SHEETS

	2007	2006
	(in millions)	
ASSETS		
Current assets		
Cash and cash equivalents	$ 488	$ 221
Short-term investments	5	249
Merchandise inventories	1,281	1,303
Other current assets	290	261
	2,064	2,034
Property and equipment, net	521	654
Deferred taxes	243	109
Goodwill	266	264
Intangible assets, net	96	105
Other assets	58	83
	$ 3,248	$ 3,249
LIABILITIES AND SHAREHOLDERS' EQUITY		
Current liabilities		
Accounts payable	$ 233	$ 256
Accrued and other liabilities	268	246
Current portion of long-term debt and obligations under capital leases	—	14
	501	516
Long-term debt and obligations under capital leases	221	220
Other liabilities	255	218
Total liabilities	977	954
Shareholders' equity	2,271	2,295
	$ 3,248	$ 3,249

See Accompanying Notes to Consolidated Financial Statements.

CONSOLIDATED STATEMENTS OF SHAREHOLDERS' EQUITY

	2007 Shares	2007 Amount	2006 Shares	2006 Amount	2005 Shares	2005 Amount
		(shares in thousands, amounts in millions)				
Common Stock and Paid-In Capital						
Par value $0.01 per share, 500 million shares authorized						
Issued at beginning of year	157,810	$ 653	157,280	$ 635	156,155	$ 608
Restricted stock issued under stock option and award plans	513	—	—	(3)	225	—
Forfeitures of restricted stock	—	—	—	—	—	2
Share-based compensation expense..........................	—	10	—	10	—	6
Issued under director and employee stock plans, net of tax	674	13	530	11	900	19
Issued at end of year	158,997	676	157,810	653	157,280	635
Common stock in treasury at beginning of year	(2,107)	(47)	(1,776)	(38)	(64)	(2)
Reissued under employee stock plans.........................	—	—	122	3	90	2
Restricted stock issued under stock option and award plans	—	—	157	3	—	—
Forfeitures/cancellations of restricted stock...................	(25)	—	(30)	(1)	(135)	(2)
Shares of common stock used to satisfy tax withholding obligations	(95)	(2)	(241)	(6)	(49)	(1)
Stock repurchases	(2,283)	(50)	(334)	(8)	(1,590)	(35)
Exchange of options.......................................	(13)	—	(5)	—	(28)	—
Common stock in treasury at end of year	(4,523)	(99)	(2,107)	(47)	(1,776)	(38)
	154,474	577	155,703	606	155,504	597
Retained Earnings						
Balance at beginning of year		1,785		1,601		1,386
Cumulative effect of adjustments resulting from the adoption of SAB 108, net of tax (see note 3)		—		(6)		—
Cumulative effect of adjustments resulting from the adoption of FIN 48, net of tax (see note 1)		1		—		—
Adjusted balance at beginning of year		1,786		1,595		1,386
Net income...		51		251		264
Cash dividends declared on common stock $0.50, $0.40 and $0.32 per share, respectively..............		(77)		(61)		(49)
Balance at end of year		1,760		1,785		1,601
Accumulated Other Comprehensive Loss						
Foreign Currency Translation Adjustment						
Balance at beginning of year		37		10		35
Translation adjustment arising during the period, net of tax		60		27		(25)
Balance at end of year		97		37		10
Cash Flow Hedges						
Balance at beginning of year		—		—		(1)
Change during year, net of tax		1		—		1
Balance at end of year		1		—		—
Minimum Pension Liability Adjustment						
Balance at beginning of year		—		(181)		(196)
Change during year, net of tax		—		181		15
Balance at end of year		—		—		(181)
Pension Adjustments						
Balance at beginning of year		(133)		—		—
Adoption of SFAS No. 158.................................		—		(133)		—
Change during year, net of tax		(29)		—		—
Balance at end of year		(162)		(133)		—
Unrealized loss on available-for-sale securities		(2)		—		—
Total Accumulated Other Comprehensive Loss		(66)		(96)		(171)
Total Shareholders' Equity.................................		$ 2,271		$ 2,295		$ 2,027

See Accompanying Notes to Consolidated Financial Statements.

CONSOLIDATED STATEMENTS OF CASH FLOWS

	2007	2006	2005
		(in millions)	
From Operating Activities			
Net income	$ 51	$ 251	$ 264
Adjustments to reconcile net income to net cash provided by operating activities of continuing operations:			
Income on disposal of discontinued operations, net of tax	(2)	(3)	(1)
Non-cash impairment charges and store closing program costs	124	17	—
Cumulative effect of accounting change, net of tax.	—	(1)	—
Depreciation and amortization	166	175	171
Share-based compensation expense	10	10	6
Deferred income taxes	(129)	21	24
Change in assets and liabilities:			
Merchandise inventories	55	(38)	(111)
Accounts payable and other accruals	(36)	(103)	14
Qualified pension plan contributions	—	(68)	(26)
Income taxes.	—	(3)	(8)
Other, net	44	(69)	16
Net cash provided by operating activities of continuing operations	283	189	349
From Investing Activities			
Acquisitions	—	—	1
Gain from lease termination.	1	4	—
Gain from insurance recoveries	1	4	3
Purchases of short-term investments.	(1,378)	(1,992)	(2,798)
Sales of short-term investments	1,620	2,041	2,767
Capital expenditures	(148)	(165)	(155)
Proceeds from investment and note.	21	—	—
Net cash provided by (used in) investing activities of continuing operations.	117	(108)	(182)
From Financing Activities			
Reduction in long-term debt	(7)	(86)	(35)
Repayment of capital lease	(14)	(1)	—
Dividends paid on common stock.	(77)	(61)	(49)
Issuance of common stock.	9	9	12
Treasury stock reissued under employee stock plans.	—	3	2
Purchase of treasury shares	(50)	(8)	(35)
Tax benefit on stock compensation	1	2	—
Net cash used in financing activities of continuing operations	(138)	(142)	(105)
Net Cash Used In operating activities of Discontinued Operations	—	(8)	—
Effect of Exchange Rate Fluctuations on Cash and Cash Equivalents	5	1	2
Net Change in Cash and Cash Equivalents	267	(68)	64
Cash and Cash Equivalents at Beginning of Year	221	289	225
Cash and Cash Equivalents at End of Year	$ 488	$ 221	$ 289
Cash Paid During the Year:			
Interest	$ 18	$ 20	$ 21
Income taxes	$ 52	$ 133	$ 93

See Accompanying Notes to Consolidated Financial Statements.

NOTES TO CONSOLIDATED FINANCIAL STATEMENTS

1. **Summary of Significant Accounting Policies**

Cash and Cash Equivalents

The Company considers all highly liquid investments with original maturities of three months or less, including commercial paper and money market funds, to be cash equivalents. Amounts due from third party credit card processors for the settlement of debit and credit cards transactions are included as cash equivalents as they are generally collected within three business days. Cash equivalents at February 2, 2008 and February 3, 2007 were $472 million and $208 million, respectively.

Short-Term Investments

The Company accounts for its short-term investments in accordance with SFAS No. 115, "Accounting for Certain Investments in Debt and Equity Securities." At February 2, 2008, the Company's auction rate security was classified as available-for-sale, and accordingly is reported at fair value. Auction rate securities are perpetual preferred or long-dated securities whose dividend/coupon resets periodically through a Dutch auction process. A Dutch auction is a competitive bidding process designed to determine a rate for the next term. As of February 2, 2008, the carrying value of the Company's short-term investment of $7 million was reduced by $2 million. The unrealized loss of $2 million was recorded to accumulated comprehensive loss without tax benefit. There were no unrealized gains or losses recognized in 2006 and 2005. Realized losses recognized in 2007 were not significant.

Merchandise Inventories and Cost of Sales

Merchandise inventories for the Company's Athletic Stores are valued at the lower of cost or market using the retail inventory method. Cost for retail stores is determined on the last-in, first-out (LIFO) basis for domestic inventories and on the first-in, first-out (FIFO) basis for international inventories. The retail inventory method is commonly used by retail companies to value inventories at cost and calculate gross margins due to its practicality. Under the retail method, cost is determined by applying a cost-to-retail percentage across groupings of similar items, known as departments. The cost-to-retail percentage is applied to ending inventory at its current owned retail valuation to determine the cost of ending inventory on a department basis. The Company provides reserves based on current selling prices when the inventory has not been marked down to market. Merchandise inventories of the Direct-to-Customers business are valued at the lower of cost or market using weighted-average cost, which approximates FIFO. Transportation, distribution center and sourcing costs are capitalized in merchandise inventories. In 2006, the Company adopted SFAS No. 151, "Inventory Costs- An Amendment of ARB 43, Chapter 4." This standard amends the guidance to clarify that abnormal amount of idle facility expense, freight, handling costs, and wasted materials (spoilage) should be recognized as current-period charges. With the adoption of this standard the Company no longer capitalized the freight associated with transfers between its store locations. The Company maintains an accrual for shrinkage based on historical rates.

Cost of sales is comprised of the cost of merchandise, occupancy, buyers' compensation and shipping and handling costs. The cost of merchandise is recorded net of amounts received from vendors for damaged product returns, markdown allowances and volume rebates, as well as cooperative advertising reimbursements received in excess of specific, incremental advertising expenses. Occupancy reflects the amortization of amounts received from landlords for tenant improvements.

Property and Equipment

Property and equipment are recorded at cost, less accumulated depreciation and amortization. Significant additions and improvements to property and equipment are capitalized. Maintenance and repairs are charged to current operations as incurred. Major renewals or replacements that substantially extend the useful life of an asset are capitalized and depreciated. Owned property and equipment is depreciated on a straight-line basis over the estimated useful lives of the assets: maximum of 50 years for buildings and 3 to 10 years for furniture, fixtures and equipment. Property and equipment under capital leases and improvements to leased premises are generally amortized on a straight-line basis over the shorter of the estimated useful life of the asset or the remaining lease term. Capitalized software reflects certain costs related to software developed for internal use that are capitalized and amortized. After substantial completion of the project, the costs are amortized on a straight-line basis over a 2 to 7 year period. Capitalized software, net of accumulated amortization, is included in property and equipment and was $22 million at February 2, 2008 and $29 million at February 3, 2007.

Recoverability of Long-Lived Assets

In accordance with SFAS No. 144, "Accounting for the Impairment or Disposal of Long-Lived Assets" ("SFAS No. 144"), an impairment loss is recognized whenever events or changes in circumstances indicate that the carrying amounts of long-lived tangible and intangible assets with finite lives may not be recoverable. Management's policy in determining whether an impairment indicator exists, a triggering event, comprises measurable operating performance criteria at the division level, as well as qualitative measures. The Company considers historical performance and future estimated results, which are predominately identified from the Company's three-year strategic plans, in its evaluation of potential store-level impairment and then compares the carrying amount of the asset with the estimated future cash flows expected to result from the use of the asset. If the carrying amount of the asset exceeds the estimated expected undiscounted future cash flows, the Company measures the amount of the impairment by comparing the carrying amount of the asset with its estimated fair value. The estimation of fair value is measured by discounting expected future cash flows at the Company's weighted-average cost of capital. The Company estimates fair value based on the best information available using estimates, judgments and projections as considered necessary.

Goodwill and Intangible Assets

The Company accounts for goodwill and other intangibles in accordance with SFAS No. 142, "Goodwill and Other Intangible Assets," which requires that goodwill and intangible assets with indefinite lives be reviewed for impairment if impairment indicators arise and, at a minimum, annually.

The Company performs its annual impairment review as of the beginning of each fiscal year. The fair value of each reporting unit is determined using a combination of market and discounted cash flow approaches. During the third and fourth quarters of 2007, the Company performed reviews of its U.S. Athletic stores' goodwill, as a result of the SFAS No. 144 recoverability analysis. These analyses did not result in an impairment charge. Separable intangible assets that are deemed to have finite lives will continue to be amortized over their estimated useful lives. Intangible assets with finite lives primarily reflect lease acquisition costs and are amortized over the lease term.

Derivative Financial Instruments

All derivative financial instruments are recorded in the Consolidated Balance Sheets at their fair values. Changes in fair values of derivatives are recorded each period in earnings, other comprehensive gain or loss, or as a basis adjustment to the underlying hedged item, depending on whether a derivative is designated and effective as part of a hedge transaction. The effective portion of the gain or loss on the hedging derivative instrument is reported as a component of other comprehensive income/loss or as a basis adjustment to the underlying hedged item and reclassified to earnings in the period in which the hedged item affects earnings.

The effective portion of the gain or loss on hedges of foreign net investments is generally not reclassified to earnings unless the net investment is disposed of. To the extent derivatives do not qualify as hedges, or are ineffective, their changes in fair value are recorded in earnings immediately, which may subject the Company to increased earnings volatility. The changes in the fair value of the Company's hedges of net investments in various foreign subsidiaries is computed using the spot method.

Fair Value of Financial Instruments

The fair value of financial instruments is determined by reference to various market data and other valuation techniques as appropriate. The carrying value of cash and cash equivalents, and other current receivables and payables approximates fair value due to the short-term nature of these assets and liabilities. Quoted market prices of the same or similar instruments are used to determine fair value of long-term debt and forward foreign exchange contracts. Discounted cash flows are used to determine the fair value of long-term investments and notes receivable if quoted market prices on these instruments are unavailable.

Income Taxes

On February 4, 2007, the Company adopted FASB Interpretation No. 48, "Accounting for Uncertainty in Income Taxes" ("FIN 48"). Interpretation No. 48 clarifies the accounting for uncertainty in income taxes recognized in an enterprise's financial statements in accordance with Statement of Financial Accounting Standards No. 109, "Accounting for Income Taxes." FIN 48 prescribes a recognition threshold and measurement standard for the financial statement recognition and measurement of a tax position taken or expected to be taken in a tax return. Upon the adoption of FIN 48, the Company recognized a $1 million increase to retained earnings to reflect the change of its liability for the unrecognized income tax benefits as required. At February 4, 2007, the total amount of gross unrecognized tax benefits was $33 million. The Company recognizes interest and penalties related to unrecognized tax benefits in income tax expense.

The Company determines its deferred tax provision under the liability method, whereby deferred tax assets and liabilities are recognized for the expected tax consequences of temporary differences between the tax bases of assets and liabilities and their reported amounts using presently enacted tax rates. Deferred tax assets are recognized for tax credits and net operating loss carryforwards, reduced by a valuation allowance, which is established when it is more likely than not that some portion or all of the deferred tax assets will not be realized. The effect on deferred tax assets and liabilities of a change in tax rates is recognized in income in the period that includes the enactment date.

A taxing authority may challenge positions that the Company adopted in its income tax filings. Accordingly, the Company may apply different tax treatments for transactions in filing its income tax returns than for income tax financial reporting. The Company regularly assesses its tax position for such transactions and records reserves for those differences when considered necessary.

Provision for U.S. income taxes on undistributed earnings of foreign subsidiaries is made only on those amounts in excess of the funds considered to be permanently reinvested.

Pension and Postretirement Obligations

The discount rate selected to measure the present value of the Company's U.S. benefit obligations as of February 2, 2008 was derived using a cash flow matching method whereby the Company compares the plans' projected payment obligations by year with the corresponding yield on the Citibank Pension Discount Curve. The cash flows are then discounted to their present value and an overall discount rate is determined. The discount rate selected to measure the present value of the Company's Canadian benefit obligations as of February 2, 2008 was developed by using the plan's bond portfolio indices which match the benefit obligations.

Insurance Liabilities

The Company is primarily self-insured for health care, workers' compensation and general liability costs. Accordingly, provisions are made for the Company's actuarially determined estimates of discounted future claim costs for such risks for the aggregate of claims reported and claims incurred but not yet reported. Self-insured liabilities totaled $17 million and $16 million at February 2, 2008 and February 3, 2007. The Company discounts its workers' compensation and general liability using a risk-free interest rate. Imputed interest expense related to these liabilities was $1 million in each of 2007, 2006 and 2005.

Accounting for Leases

The Company recognizes rent expense for operating leases as of the possession date for store leases or the commencement of the agreement for a non-store lease. Rental expense, inclusive of rent holidays, concessions and tenant allowances are recognized over the lease term on a straight-line basis. Contingent payments based upon sales and future increases determined by inflation related indices cannot be estimated at the inception of the lease and accordingly, are charged to operations as incurred.

Foreign Currency Translation

The functional currency of the Company's international operations is the applicable local currency. The translation of the applicable foreign currency into U.S. dollars is performed for balance sheet accounts using current exchange rates in effect at the balance sheet date and for revenue and expense accounts using the weighted-average rates of exchange prevailing during the year. The unearned gains and losses resulting from such translation are included as a separate component of accumulated other comprehensive loss within shareholders' equity.

Recent Accounting Pronouncements Not Previously Discussed Herein

In September 2006, the FASB issued SFAS No. 157, "Fair Value Measurements" ("SFAS No. 157") which is effective for fiscal years beginning after November 15, 2007 and for interim periods within those years. This statement defines fair value, establishes a framework for measuring fair value and expands the related disclosure requirements. However, the FASB issued FASB Staff Positions ("FSP") 157-1 and 157-2. FSP 157-1 amends SFAS No. 157 to exclude FASB No. 13, "Accounting for Leases," and its related interpretive accounting pronouncements that address leasing transactions, while FSP-2 delays the effective date of SFAS No. 157 for all nonfinancial assets and nonfinancial liabilities, except those that are recognized or disclosed at fair value in the financial statements on a recurring basis, until fiscal years beginning after November 15, 2008. The Company does not believe that this standard will significantly affect the Company's financial position or results of operations.

In February 2007, the FASB issued SFAS No. 159, "The Fair Value Option for Financial Assets and Financial Liabilities—Including an Amendment of FASB Statement No. 115." This statement permits, but does not require, entities to measure many financial instruments at fair value. The objective is to provide entities with an opportunity to mitigate volatility in reported earnings caused by measuring related assets and liabilities differently without having to apply complex hedge accounting provisions. The Company does not believe that this standard will significantly affect the Company's financial position or results of operations.

In December 2007, the FASB issued SFAS No. 141 (Revised 2007), "Business Combinations," ("SFAS No. 141(R)"). This standard will significantly change the accounting for business combinations. Under SFAS No. 141(R), an acquiring entity will be required to recognize all the assets acquired and liabilities assumed in a transaction at the acquisition-date fair value with limited exceptions. SFAS No. 141(R) also includes a substantial number of new disclosure requirements. SFAS No. 141(R) applies prospectively to business combinations for which the acquisition date is on or after the beginning of the first annual reporting period beginning on or after December 15, 2008.

In December 2007, the FASB issued SFAS No. 160, "Noncontrolling Interests in Consolidated Financial Statements - An Amendment of ARB No. 51" ("SFAS No. 160"), which establishes new accounting and reporting standards for the noncontrolling interest in a subsidiary and for the deconsolidation of a subsidiary. Specifically, this statement requires the recognition of a noncontrolling interest (minority interest) as equity in the consolidated financial statements and separate from the parent's equity. SFAS No. 160 is effective for fiscal years, and interim periods within those fiscal years, beginning on or after December 15, 2008. This standard does not currently affect the Company.

2. Impairment of Long-Lived Assets and Store Closing Program

During 2007, the Company concluded that triggering events had occurred at its U.S. retail store divisions, comprising Foot Locker, Lady Foot Locker, Kids Foot Locker, Footaction, and Champs Sports. Accordingly, the Company evaluated the long-lived assets of those operations for impairment and recorded non-cash impairment charges of $117 million primarily to write-down long-lived assets such as store fixtures and leasehold improvements for 1,395 stores at the Company's U.S. store operations pursuant to SFAS No. 144.

Additionally, in the third quarter of 2007, the Company identified 66 unproductive stores for closure. Accordingly, the Company evaluated the recoverability of long-lived assets considering the revised estimated future cash flows. The Company recorded an additional non-cash impairment charge of $7 million as a result of this analysis. Of the total stores identified for closure in the third quarter of 2007, 13 will remain in operation as the Company was able to negotiate more favorable lease terms. Exit costs related to 33 stores which closed during 2007, comprising primarily lease termination costs of $4 million, were recognized in accordance with SFAS No. 146, "Accounting for Costs Associated with Exit or Disposal Activities." During 2008, the Company currently expects to close the remaining 20 unproductive stores prior to normal lease expiration, depending on the Company's success in negotiating agreements with its landlords. The lease exit costs associated with these remaining closures is expected to total $5 million to $10 million. These charges will be recorded during 2008 in accordance with SFAS No. 146. The cash impact of the 2008 store closings is expected to be minimal, as the related cash lease costs are expected to be offset by associated inventory reductions. Under SFAS No. 144, store closings may constitute discontinued operations if migration of customers and cash flows are not expected. The Company has concluded that no store closings have met the criteria for discontinued operations treatment.

Included in the Athletic Stores division profit for 2006 is an impairment charge of $17 million related to the Company's European operations to write-down long-lived assets in 69 stores to their estimated fair value. During 2006, division profit declined primarily due to the fashion shift from higher priced marquee footwear to lower priced low-profile footwear styles and a highly competitive retail environment, particularly for the sale of low-profile footwear styles. The charge was comprised primarily of stores located in the U.K. and France.

6. Short-Term Investments

The Company's auction rate security investments are accounted for as available-for-sale securities. The following represents the composition of the Company's auction rate securities by underlying investment.

	2007	2006
	(in millions)	
Tax exempt municipal bonds	$ —	$ 44
Equity securities	5	205
	$ 5	$ 249

With the liquidity issues experienced in the global credit and capital markets, the Company's preferred stock auction rate security, having a face value of $7 million, has experienced failed auctions. The Company determined that a temporary impairment has occurred and therefore has recorded a charge of $2 million, with no tax benefit, to accumulated other comprehensive loss as of February 2, 2008. This security will continue to accrue interest at the contractual rate and will be auctioned every 90 days until the auction succeeds. Based on the relatively small size of this investment and the Company's ability to access cash and other short-term investments, and expected operating cash flows, we do not anticipate the lack of liquidity on this investment will affect our ability to operate our business as usual.

7. Merchandise Inventories

	2007	2006
	(in millions)	
LIFO inventories	$ 907	$ 967
FIFO inventories	374	336
Total merchandise inventories	$1,281	$1,303

The value of the Company's LIFO inventories, as calculated on a LIFO basis, approximates their value as calculated on a FIFO basis.

8. Other Current Assets

	2007	2006
	(in millions)	
Net receivables	$ 50	$ 59
Prepaid expenses and other current assets	34	36
Prepaid rent	65	62
Prepaid income taxes	70	67
Deferred taxes	53	21
Investments	—	14
Northern Group note receivable	14	1
Current tax asset	1	—
Fair value of derivative contracts	3	1
	$290	$ 261

9. **Property and Equipment, Net**

	2007	2006
	(in millions)	
Land..	$ 3	$ 3
Buildings:		
Owned	30	30
Furniture, fixtures and equipment:		
Owned	1,117	1,139
Leased	—	14
	1,150	1,186
Less: accumulated depreciation	(903)	(870)
	247	316
Alterations to leased and owned buildings,		
net of accumulated amortization	274	338
	$ 521	$ 654

13. **Accrued and Other Liabilities**

	2007	2006
	(in millions)	
Pension and postretirement benefits	$ 4	$ 4
Incentive bonuses	5	12
Other payroll and payroll related costs, excluding taxes	52	46
Taxes other than income taxes	44	46
Property and equipment..	23	24
Customer deposits[1]	34	33
Income taxes payable..	7	2
Fair value of derivative contracts	—	2
Current deferred tax liabilities	13	4
Sales return reserve	4	4
Current portion of repositioning and restructuring reserves	—	1
Current portion of reserve for discontinued operations......................	14	3
Other operating costs...	68	65
	$268	$246

(1) Customer deposits include unredeemed gift cards and certificates, merchandise credits and, deferred revenue related to undelivered merchandise, including layaway sales.

15. Long-Term Debt and Obligations under Capital Leases

In May 2004, the Company obtained a 5-year, $175 million amortizing term loan from the bank group participating in its existing revolving credit facility to finance a portion of the purchase price of the Footaction stores. The interest rate on the LIBOR-based, floating-rate loan was 5.4 percent on February 2, 2008 and 6.5 percent on February 3, 2007. The loan requires minimum principal payments each May, equal to a percentage of the original principal amount of 10 percent in 2006, 15 percent in years 2007 and 2008 and 50 percent in year 2009. Closing and upfront fees totaling approximately $1 million were paid for the term loan and these fees are being amortized using the interest rate method as determined by the principal repayment schedule. During 2007, 2006 and 2005 the Company repaid $2 million, $50 million, and $35 million, respectively, with the outstanding amount of $88 million due in 2009.

The Company purchased and retired $38 million of the $200 million 8.50 percent debentures payable in 2022 at a $2 million discount from face value during 2006. During 2007, the Company purchased and retired an additional $5 million bringing the outstanding amount to $129 million as of February 2, 2008. The Company has various interest rate swap agreements, which convert $100 million of the 8.50 percent debentures from a fixed interest rate to a variable interest rate, which are collectively classified as a fair value hedge. The net fair value of the interest rate swaps at February 2, 2008 was an asset of $4 million, which was included in other assets, the carrying value of the 8.50 percent debentures was increased by the corresponding amount. The net fair value of the interest rate swaps at February 3, 2007 was a liability of $4 million, which was included in other liabilities, the carrying value of the 8.50 percent debentures was decreased by the corresponding amount.

During 2007, the Company's $14 million Industrial Revenue Bond, which was accounted for as a capital lease matured. Accordingly, the Company repaid this amount.

Following is a summary of long-term debt and obligations under capital leases:

	2007	2006
	(in millions)	
8.50% debentures payable 2022	$133	$ 130
$175 million term loan	88	90
Total long-term debt	221	220
Obligations under capital leases	—	14
	221	234
Less: Current portion	—	14
	$221	$ 220

Maturities of long-term debt in future periods are:

	Long-Term Debt
	(in millions)
2008	$ —
2009	88
2010 -2012	—
Thereafter	133
Less: Current portion	—
	$ 221

Appendix C

TIME VALUE OF MONEY: FUTURE VALUE AND PRESENT VALUE

The following discussion of future value lays the foundation for our explanation of present value in Chapter 8 but is not essential. For the valuation of long-term liabilities, some instructors may wish to begin on page 889 of this appendix.

The term *time value of money* refers to the fact that money earns interest over time. *Interest* is the cost of using money. To borrowers, interest is the expense of renting money. To lenders, interest is the revenue earned from lending. We must always recognize the interest we receive or pay. Otherwise, we overlook an important part of the transaction. Suppose you invest $4,545 in corporate bonds that pay 10% interest each year. After one year, the value of your investment has grown to $5,000. The difference between your original investment ($4,545) and the future value of the investment ($5,000) is the amount of interest revenue you will earn during the year ($455). If you ignored the interest, you would fail to account for the interest revenue you have earned. Interest becomes more important as the time period lengthens because the amount of interest depends on the span of time the money is invested.

Let's consider a second example, this time from the borrower's perspective. Suppose you purchase a machine for your business. The cash price of the machine is $8,000, but you cannot pay cash now. To finance the purchase, you sign an $8,000 note payable. The note requires you to pay the $8,000 plus 10% interest one year from the date of purchase. Is your cost of the machine $8,000, or is it $8,800 [$8,000 plus interest of $800 ($8,000 × .10)]? The cost is $8,000. The additional $800 is interest expense and not part of the cost of the machine.

Future Value

The main application of future value is the accumulated balance of an investment at a future date. In our first example, the investment earned 10% per year. After one year, $4,545 grew to $5,000, as shown in Exhibit C-1.

EXHIBIT C-1 | Future Value: An Example

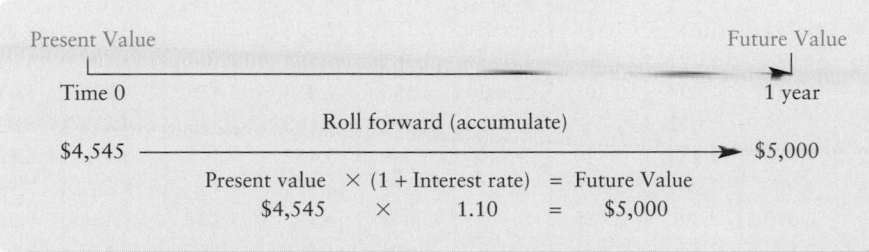

If the money were invested for five years, you would have to perform five such calculations. You would also have to consider the compound interest that your investment is earning. *Compound interest* is not only the interest you earn on your principal amount, but also the interest you receive on the interest you have already earned. Most business applications include compound interest. The following table shows the interest revenue earned on the original $4,545 investment each year for five years at 10%:

End of Year	Interest	Future Value
0	—	$4,545
1	$4,545 × 0.10 = $455	5,000
2	5,000 × 0.10 = 500	5,500
3	5,500 × 0.10 = 550	6,050
4	6,050 × 0.10 = 605	6,655
5	6,655 × 0.10 = 666	7,321

Earning 10%, a $4,545 investment grows to $5,000 at the end of one year, to $5,500 at the end of two years, and $7,321 at the end of five years. Throughout this appendix we round off to the nearest dollar.

Future-Value Tables

The process of computing a future value is called *accumulating* because the future value is *more* than the present value. Mathematical tables ease the computational burden. Exhibit C-2, Future Value of $1, gives the future value for a single sum (a present value), $1, invested to earn a particular interest rate for a specific number of periods. Future value depends on three factors: (1) the amount of the investment,

EXHIBIT C-2 | Future Value of $1

Periods	4%	5%	6%	7%	8%	9%	10%	12%	14%	16%
1	1.040	1.050	1.060	1.070	1.080	1.090	1.100	1.120	1.140	1.160
2	1.082	1.103	1.124	1.145	1.166	1.188	1.210	1.254	1.300	1.346
3	1.125	1.158	1.191	1.225	1.260	1.295	1.331	1.405	1.482	1.561
4	1.170	1.216	1.262	1.311	1.360	1.412	1.464	1.574	1.689	1.811
5	1.217	1.276	1.338	1.403	1.469	1.539	1.611	1.762	1.925	2.100
6	1.265	1.340	1.419	1.501	1.587	1.677	1.772	1.974	2.195	2.436
7	1.316	1.407	1.504	1.606	1.714	1.828	1.949	2.211	2.502	2.826
8	1.369	1.477	1.594	1.718	1.851	1.993	2.144	2.476	2.853	3.278
9	1.423	1.551	1.689	1.838	1.999	2.172	2.358	2.773	3.252	3.803
10	1.480	1.629	1.791	1.967	2.159	2.367	2.594	3.106	3.707	4.411
11	1.539	1.710	1.898	2.105	2.332	2.580	2.853	3.479	4.226	5.117
12	1.601	1.796	2.012	2.252	2.518	2.813	3.138	3.896	4.818	5.936
13	1.665	1.886	2.133	2.410	2.720	3.066	3.452	4.363	5.492	6.886
14	1.732	1.980	2.261	2.579	2.937	3.342	3.798	4.887	6.261	7.988
15	1.801	2.079	2.397	2.759	3.172	3.642	4.177	5.474	7.138	9.266
16	1.873	2.183	2.540	2.952	3.426	3.970	4.595	6.130	8.137	10.748
17	1.948	2.292	2.693	3.159	3.700	4.328	5.054	6.866	9.276	12.468
18	2.026	2.407	2.854	3.380	3.996	4.717	5.560	7.690	10.575	14.463
19	2.107	2.527	3.026	3.617	4.316	5.142	6.116	8.613	12.056	16.777
20	2.191	2.653	3.207	3.870	4.661	5.604	6.728	9.646	13.743	19.461

(2) the length of time between investment and future accumulation, and (3) the interest rate. Future-value and present-value tables are based on $1 because unity (the value 1) is so easy to work with.

In business applications, interest rates are always stated for the annual period of one year unless specified otherwise. In fact, an interest rate can be stated for any period, such as 3% per quarter or 5% for a six-month period. The length of the period is arbitrary. For example, an investment may promise a return (income) of 3% per quarter for six months (two quarters). In that case, you would be working with 3% interest for two periods. It would be incorrect to use 6% for one period because the interest is 3% compounded quarterly, and that amount differs from 6% compounded semiannually. *Take care in studying future-value and present-value problems to align the interest rate with the appropriate number of periods.*

Let's see how a future-value table like the one in Exhibit C-2 is used. The future value of $1.00 invested at 8% for one year is $1.08 ($1.00 × 1.080, which appears at the junction of the 8% column and row 1 in the Periods column). The figure 1.080 includes both the principal (1.000) and the compound interest for one period (0.080).

Suppose you deposit $5,000 in a savings account that pays annual interest of 8%. The account balance at the end of one year will be $5,400. To compute the future value of $5,000 at 8% for one year, multiply $5,000 by 1.080 to get $5,400. Now suppose you invest in a 10-year, 8% certificate of deposit (CD). What will be the future value of the CD at maturity? To compute the future value of $5,000 at 8% for 10 periods, multiply $5,000 by 2.159 (from Exhibit C-2) to get $10,795. This future value of $10,795 indicates that $5,000, earning 8% interest compounded annually, grows to $10,795 at the end of 10 years. Using Exhibit C-2, you can find any present amount's future value at a particular future date. Future value is especially helpful for computing the amount of cash you will have on hand for some purpose in the future.

Future Value of an Annuity

In the preceding example, we made an investment of a single amount. Other investments, called *annuities*, include multiple investments of an equal periodic amount at fixed intervals over the duration of the investment. Consider a family investing for a child's education. The Dietrichs can invest $4,000 annually to accumulate a college fund for 15-year-old Helen. The investment can earn 7% annually until Helen turns 18—a three-year investment. How much will be available for Helen on the date of the last investment? Exhibit C-3 shows the accumulation—a total future value of $12,860.

EXHIBIT C-3 | **Future Value of an Annuity**

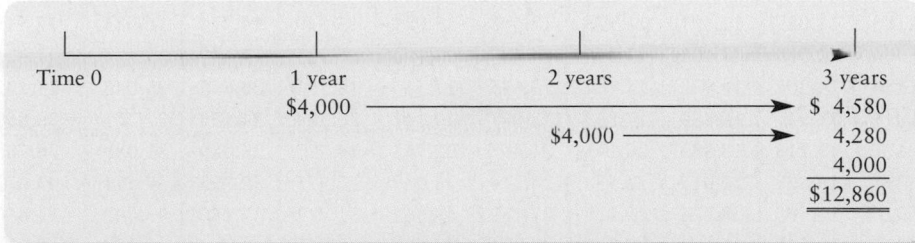

The first $4,000 invested by the Dietrichs grows to $4,580 over the investment period. The second amount grows to $4,280, and the third amount stays at $4,000 because it has no time to earn interest. The sum of the three future values

($4,580 + $4,280 + $4,000) is the future value of the annuity ($12,860), which can also be computed as follows:

End of Year	Annual Investment	Interest	Increase for the Year	Future Value of Annuity
0	—	—	—	0
1	$4,000	—	$4,000	$ 4,000
2	4,000	+ ($4,000 × 0.07 = $280) =	4,280	8,280
3	4,000	+ ($8,280 × 0.07 = $580) =	4,580	12,860

These computations are laborious. As with the Future Value of $1 (a lump sum), mathematical tables ease the strain of calculating annuities. Exhibit C-4, Future Value of Annuity of $1, gives the future value of a series of investments, each of equal amount, at regular intervals.

What is the future value of an annuity of three investments of $1 each that earn 7%? The answer, 3.215, can be found at the junction of the 7% column and row 3 in Exhibit C-4. This amount can be used to compute the future value of the investment for Helen's education, as follows:

Amount of each periodic investment	×	Future value of annuity of $1 (Exhibit C-4)	×	Future value of investment
$4,000	×	3.215	×	$12,860

EXHIBIT C-4 | Future Value of Annuity of $1

Future Value of Annuity of $1

Periods	4%	5%	6%	7%	8%	9%	10%	12%	14%	16%
1	1.000	1.000	1.000	1.000	1.000	1.000	1.000	1.000	1.000	1.000
2	2.040	2.050	2.060	2.070	2.080	2.090	2.100	2.120	2.140	2.160
3	3.122	3.153	3.184	3.215	3.246	3.278	3.310	3.374	3.440	3.506
4	4.246	4.310	4.375	4.440	4.506	4.573	4.641	4.779	4.921	5.066
5	5.416	5.526	5.637	5.751	5.867	5.985	6.105	6.353	6.610	6.877
6	6.633	6.802	6.975	7.153	7.336	7.523	7.716	8.115	8.536	8.977
7	7.898	8.142	8.394	8.654	8.923	9.200	9.487	10.089	10.730	11.414
8	9.214	9.549	9.897	10.260	10.637	11.028	11.436	12.300	13.233	14.240
9	10.583	11.027	11.491	11.978	12.488	13.021	13.579	14.776	16.085	17.519
10	12.006	12.578	13.181	13.816	14.487	15.193	15.937	17.549	19.337	21.321
11	13.486	14.207	14.972	15.784	16.645	17.560	18.531	20.655	23.045	25.733
12	15.026	15.917	16.870	17.888	18.977	20.141	21.384	24.133	27.271	30.850
13	16.627	17.713	18.882	20.141	21.495	22.953	24.523	28.029	32.089	36.786
14	18.292	19.599	21.015	22.550	24.215	26.019	27.975	32.393	37.581	43.672
15	20.024	21.579	23.276	25.129	27.152	29.361	31.772	37.280	43.842	51.660
16	21.825	23.657	25.673	27.888	30.324	33.003	35.950	42.753	50.980	60.925
17	23.698	25.840	28.213	30.840	33.750	36.974	40.545	48.884	59.118	71.673
18	25.645	28.132	30.906	33.999	37.450	41.301	45.599	55.750	68.394	84.141
19	27.671	30.539	33.760	37.379	41.446	46.018	51.159	63.440	78.969	98.603
20	29.778	33.066	36.786	40.995	45.762	51.160	57.275	72.052	91.025	115.380

This one-step calculation is much easier than computing the future value of each annual investment and then summing the individual future values. In this way, you can compute the future value of any investment consisting of equal periodic amounts at regular intervals. Businesses make periodic investments to accumulate funds for equipment replacement and other uses—an application of the future value of an annuity.

Present Value

Often a person knows a future amount and needs to know the related present value. Recall Exhibit C-1, in which present value and future value are on opposite ends of the same time line. Suppose an investment promises to pay you $5,000 at the *end* of one year. How much would you pay *now* to acquire this investment? You would be willing to pay the present value of the $5,000 future amount.

Like future value, present value depends on three factors: (1) the *amount of payment (or receipt)*, (2) the length of *time* between investment and future receipt (or payment), and (3) the *interest rate*. The process of computing a present value is called *discounting* because the present value is *less* than the future value.

In our investment example, the future receipt is $5,000. The investment period is one year. Assume that you demand an annual interest rate of 10% on your investment. With all three factors specified, you can compute the present value of $5,000 at 10% for one year:

$$\text{Present value} = \frac{\text{Future value}}{1 + \text{Interest rate}} = \frac{\$5,000}{1.10} = \$4,545$$

By turning the data around into a future-value problem, we can verify the present-value computation:

Amount invested (present value)	$4,545
Expected earnings ($4,545 × 0.10)...	455
Amount to be received one year from now (future value)..............	$5,000

This example illustrates that present value and future value are based on the same equation:

$$\text{Future value} = \text{Present value} \times (1 + \text{Interest rate})$$

$$\text{Present value} = \frac{\text{Future value}}{1 + \text{Interest rate}}$$

If the $5,000 is to be received two years from now, you will pay only $4,132 for the investment, as shown in Exhibit C-5 on the following page. By turning the data around, we verify that $4,132 accumulates to $5,000 at 10% for two years:

Amount invested (present value)	$4,132
Expected earnings for first year ($4,132 × 0.10)..........................	413
Value of investment after one year	4,545
Expected earnings for second year ($4,545 × 0.10)	455
Amount to be received two years from now (future value)..........	$5,000

EXHIBIT C-5 | Present Value: An Example

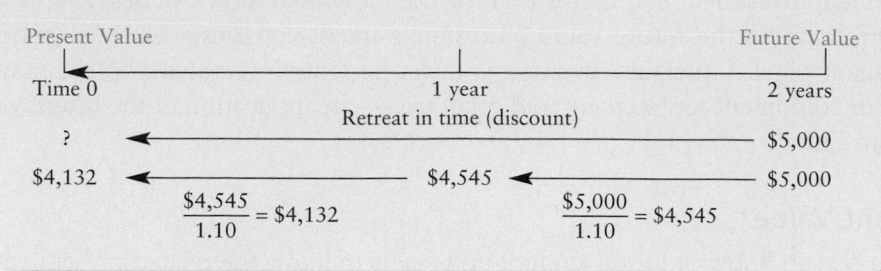

You would pay $4,132—the present value of $5,000—to receive the $5,000 future amount at the end of two years at 10% per year. The $868 difference between the amount invested ($4,132) and the amount to be received ($5,000) is the return on the investment, the sum of the two interest receipts: $413 + $455 = $868.

Present-Value Tables

We have shown the simple formula for computing present value. However, figuring present value "by hand" for investments spanning many years is time-consuming and presents too many opportunities for arithmetic errors. Present-value tables ease our work. Let's reexamine our examples of present value by using Exhibit C-6, Present Value of $1, given below.

EXHIBIT C-6 | Present Value of $1

Present Value of $1

Periods	4%	5%	6%	7%	8%	10%	12%	14%	16%
1	0.962	0.952	0.943	0.935	0.926	0.909	0.893	0.877	0.862
2	0.925	0.907	0.890	0.873	0.857	0.826	0.797	0.769	0.743
3	0.889	0.864	0.840	0.816	0.794	0.751	0.712	0.675	0.641
4	0.855	0.823	0.792	0.763	0.735	0.683	0.636	0.592	0.552
5	0.822	0.784	0.747	0.713	0.681	0.621	0.567	0.519	0.476
6	0.790	0.746	0.705	0.666	0.630	0.564	0.507	0.456	0.410
7	0.760	0.711	0.665	0.623	0.583	0.513	0.452	0.400	0.354
8	0.731	0.677	0.627	0.582	0.540	0.467	0.404	0.351	0.305
9	0.703	0.645	0.592	0.544	0.500	0.424	0.361	0.308	0.263
10	0.676	0.614	0.558	0.508	0.463	0.386	0.322	0.270	0.227
11	0.650	0.585	0.527	0.475	0.429	0.350	0.287	0.237	0.195
12	0.625	0.557	0.497	0.444	0.397	0.319	0.257	0.208	0.168
13	0.601	0.530	0.469	0.415	0.368	0.290	0.229	0.182	0.145
14	0.577	0.505	0.442	0.388	0.340	0.263	0.205	0.160	0.125
15	0.555	0.481	0.417	0.362	0.315	0.239	0.183	0.140	0.108
16	0.534	0.458	0.394	0.339	0.292	0.218	0.163	0.123	0.093
17	0.513	0.436	0.371	0.317	0.270	0.198	0.146	0.108	0.080
18	0.494	0.416	0.350	0.296	0.250	0.180	0.130	0.095	0.069
19	0.475	0.396	0.331	0.277	0.232	0.164	0.116	0.083	0.060
20	0.456	0.377	0.312	0.258	0.215	0.149	0.104	0.073	0.051

For the 10% investment for one year, we find the junction of the 10% column and row 1 in Exhibit C-6. The figure 0.909 is computed as follows: 1/1.10 = 0.909. This work has been done for us, and only the present values are given in the table. To figure the present value for $5,000, we multiply 0.909 by $5,000. The result is $4,545, which matches the result we obtained by hand.

For the two-year investment, we read down the 10% column and across row 2. We multiply 0.826 (computed as 0.909/1.10 = 0.826) by $5,000 and get $4,130, which confirms our earlier computation of $4,132 (the difference is due to rounding in the present-value table). Using the table, we can compute the present value of any single future amount.

Present Value of an Annuity

Return to the investment example near the bottom of page 889 of this appendix. That investment provided the investor with only a single future receipt ($5,000 at the end of two years). *Annuity investments* provide multiple receipts of an equal amount at fixed intervals over the investment's duration.

Consider an investment that promises *annual* cash receipts of $10,000 to be received at the end of three years. Assume that you demand a 12% return on your investment. What is the investment's present value? That is, what would you pay today to acquire the investment? The investment spans three periods, and you would pay the sum of three present values. The computation follows.

Year	Annual Cash Receipt	Present Value of $1 at 12% (Exhibit C-6)	Present Value of Annual Cash Receipt
1	$10,000	0.893	$ 8,930
2	10,000	0.797	7,970
3	10,000	0.712	7,120
Total present value of investment...............			$24,020

The present value of this annuity is $24,020. By paying this amount today, you will receive $10,000 at the end of each of the three years while earning 12% on your investment.

This example illustrates repetitive computations of the three future amounts, a time-consuming process. One way to ease the computational burden is to add the three present values of $1 (0.893 + 0.797 + 0.712) and multiply their sum (2.402) by the annual cash receipt ($10,000) to obtain the present value of the annuity ($10,000 × 2.402 = $24,020).

An easier approach is to use a present-value-of-an-annuity table. Exhibit C-7 on the following page shows the present value of $1 to be received periodically for a given number of periods. The present value of a three-period annuity at 12% is 2.402 (the junction of row 3 and the 12% column). Thus, $10,000 received annually at the end of each of three years, discounted at 12%, is $24,020 ($10,000 × 2.402), which is the present value.

EXHIBIT C-7 | **Present Value Annuity of $1**

Present Value of Annuity of $1

Periods	4%	5%	6%	7%	8%	10%	12%	14%	16%
1	0.962	0.952	0.943	0.935	0.926	0.909	0.893	0.877	0.862
2	1.886	1.859	1.833	1.808	1.783	1.736	1.690	1.647	1.605
3	2.775	2.723	2.673	2.624	2.577	2.487	2.402	2.322	2.246
4	3.630	3.546	3.465	3.387	3.312	3.170	3.037	2.914	2.798
5	4.452	4.329	4.212	4.100	3.993	3.791	3.605	3.433	3.274
6	5.242	5.076	4.917	4.767	4.623	4.355	4.111	3.889	3.685
7	6.002	5.786	5.582	5.389	5.206	4.868	4.564	4.288	4.039
8	6.733	6.463	6.210	5.971	5.747	5.335	4.968	4.639	4.344
9	7.435	7.108	6.802	6.515	6.247	5.759	5.328	4.946	4.608
10	8.111	7.722	7.360	7.024	6.710	6.145	5.650	5.216	4.833
11	8.760	8.306	7.887	7.499	7.139	6.495	5.938	5.453	5.029
12	9.385	8.863	8.384	7.943	7.536	6.814	6.194	5.660	5.197
13	9.986	9.394	8.853	8.358	7.904	7.103	6.424	5.842	5.342
14	10.563	9.899	9.295	8.745	8.244	7.367	6.628	6.002	5.468
15	11.118	10.380	9.712	9.108	8.559	7.606	6.811	6.142	5.575
16	11.652	10.838	10.106	9.447	8.851	7.824	6.974	6.265	5.669
17	12.166	11.274	10.477	9.763	9.122	8.022	7.120	6.373	5.749
18	12.659	11.690	10.828	10.059	9.372	8.201	7.250	6.467	5.818
19	13.134	12.085	11.158	10.336	9.604	8.365	7.366	6.550	5.877
20	13.590	12.462	11.470	10.594	9.818	8.514	7.469	6.623	5.929

Present Value of Bonds Payable

The present value of a bond—its market price—is the present value of the future principal amount at maturity plus the present value of the future stated interest payments. The principal is a *single amount* to be paid at maturity. The interest is an *annuity* because it occurs periodically.

Let's compute the present value of the assumed 9% five-year bonds of **Southwest Airlines** (discussed on pages 482–483). The face value of the bonds is $100,000, and they pay 4½%—stated (cash) interest semiannually (that is, twice a year).[1] At issuance, the market interest rate is expressed as 10% annually, but it is computed at 5% semiannually. Therefore, the effective interest rate for each of the 10 semiannual periods is 5%. We thus use 5% in computing the present value (PV) of the maturity and of the interest. The market price of these bonds is $96,149, as follows:

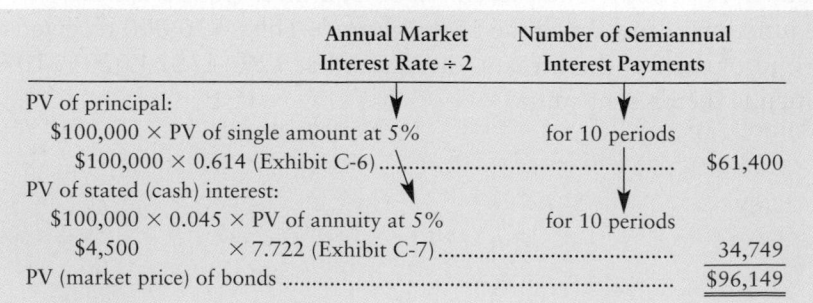

	Annual Market Interest Rate ÷ 2	Number of Semiannual Interest Payments	
PV of principal:			
$100,000 × PV of single amount at 5%		for 10 periods	
$100,000 × 0.614 (Exhibit C-6)			$61,400
PV of stated (cash) interest:			
$100,000 × 0.045 × PV of annuity at 5%		for 10 periods	
$4,500 × 7.722 (Exhibit C-7)			34,749
PV (market price) of bonds			$96,149

---

[1]For a definition of stated interest rate, see page 480.

The market price of the Southwest bonds shows a discount because the contract (stated) interest rate on the bonds (9%) is less than the market interest rate (10%).

Let's consider a premium price for the 9% Southwest bonds. Assume that the market interest rate is 8% (rather than 10%) at issuance. The effective interest rate is thus 4% for each of the 10 semiannual periods:

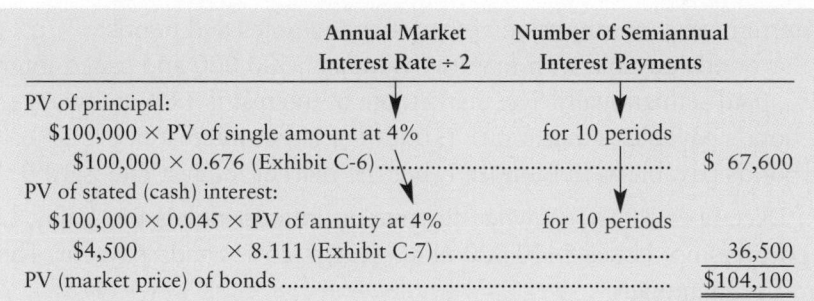

	Annual Market Interest Rate ÷ 2	Number of Semiannual Interest Payments	
PV of principal:			
$100,000 × PV of single amount at 4%		for 10 periods	
$100,000 × 0.676 (Exhibit C-6)			$ 67,600
PV of stated (cash) interest:			
$100,000 × 0.045 × PV of annuity at 4%		for 10 periods	
$4,500 × 8.111 (Exhibit C-7)			36,500
PV (market price) of bonds			$104,100

We discuss accounting for these bonds on pages 483–486. It may be helpful for you to reread this section ("Present Value of Bonds Payable") after you've studied those pages.

Capital Leases

How does a lessee compute the cost of an asset acquired through a capital lease? (See page 496 for the definition of *capital leases*.) Consider that the lessee gets the use of the asset but does *not* pay for the leased asset in full at the beginning of the lease. A capital lease is therefore similar to an installment purchase of the leased asset. The lessee must record the leased asset at the present value of the lease liability. The time value of money must be weighed.

The cost of the asset to the lessee is the sum of any payment made at the beginning of the lease period plus the present value of the future lease payments. The lease payments are equal amounts occurring at regular intervals—that is, they are annuity payments.

Consider a 20-year building lease that requires 20 annual payments of $10,000 each, with the first payment due immediately. The interest rate in the lease is 10%, and the present value of the 19 future payments is $83,650 ($10,000 × PV of annuity at 10% for 19 periods, or 8.365 from Exhibit C-7). The lessee's cost of the building is $93,650 (the sum of the initial payment, $10,000, plus the present value of the future payments, $83,650). The lessee would base its accounting for the leased asset (and the related depreciation) and for the lease liability (and the related interest expense) on the cost of the building that we have just computed.

Appendix Problems

PC-1. For each situation, compute the required amount.
a. **Kellogg Corporation** is budgeting for the acquisition of land over the next several years. Kellogg can invest $100,000 today at 9%. How much cash will Kellogg have for land acquisitions at the end of five years? At the end of six years?
b. Davidson, Inc., is planning to invest $50,000 each year for five years. The company's investment adviser believes that Davidson can earn 6% interest without taking on too much risk. What will be the value of Davidson's investment on the date of the last deposit if Davidson can earn 6%? If Davidson can earn 8%?

PC-2. For each situation, compute the required amount.
a. **Intel Corporation** operations are generating excess cash that will be invested in a special fund. During 2009, Intel invests $5,643,341 in the fund for a planned

advertising campaign on a new product to be released six years later, in 2015. If Intel's investments can earn 10% each year, how much cash will the company have for the advertising campaign in 2015?

b. Intel will need $10 million to advertise a new type of chip in 2015. How much must Intel invest in 2009 to have the cash available for the advertising campaign? Intel's investments can earn 10% annually.

c. Explain the relationship between your answers to a and b.

PC-3. Determine the present value of the following notes and bonds:

1. Ten-year bonds payable with maturity value of $500,000 and stated interest rate of 12%, paid semiannually. The market rate of interest is 12% at issuance.
2. Same bonds payable as in number 1, but the market interest rate is 14%.
3. Same bonds payable as in number 1, but the market interest rate is 10%.

PC-4. On December 31, 2010, when the market interest rate is 8% Libby, Libby, & Short, a partnership, issues $400,000 of 10-year, 7.25% bonds payable. The bonds pay interest semiannually.

I Requirements

1. Determine the present value of the bonds at issuance.
2. Assume that the bonds are issued at the price computed in Requirement 1. Prepare an effective-interest-method amortization table for the first two semiannual interest periods.
3. Using the amortization table prepared in Requirement 2, journalize issuance of the bonds and the first two interest payments and amortization of the bonds.

PC-5. St. Mere Eglise Children's Home needs a fleet of vans to transport the children to singing engagements throughout Normandy. **Renault** offers the vehicles for a single payment of €630,000 due at the end of four years. **Peugeot** prices a similar fleet of vans for four annual payments of €150,000 at the end of each year. The children's home could borrow the funds at 6%, so this is the appropriate interest rate. Which company should get the business, Renault or Peugeot? Base your decision on present value, and give your reason.

PC-6. American Family Association acquired equipment under a capital lease that requires six annual lease payments of $40,000. The first payment is due when the lease begins, on January 1, 2010. Future payments are due on January 1 of each year of the lease term. The interest rate in the lease is 16%.

I Requirement

1. Compute the association's cost of the equipment.

Answers

PC-1   a. 5 yrs. $153,900
            6 yrs. $167,700
        b. 6% $281,850
            8% $293,350
PC-2   a. $10,000,000
        b. $5,640,000
PC-3   1. $500,100   2. $446,820   3. $562,360
PC-4   1. $379,455   2. Bond
            carry. amt. at 12-31-11 $380,838
PC-5   Renault PV €498,960
        Peugeot PV €519,750
PC-6   Cost $170,960

Appendix D

TYPICAL CHARTS OF ACCOUNTS FOR DIFFERENT TYPES OF BUSINESSES

A Simple Service Corporation

Assets	Liabilities	Stockholders' Equity
Cash	Accounts Payable	Common Stock
Accounts Receivable	Notes Payable, Short-Term	Retained Earnings
Allowance for Uncollectible Accounts	Salary Payable	Dividends
Notes Receivable, Short-Term	Wages Payable	**Revenues and Gains**
Interest Receivable	Payroll Taxes Payable	
Supplies	Employee Benefits Payable	Service Revenue
Prepaid Rent	Interest Payable	Interest Revenue
Prepaid Insurance	Unearned Service Revenue	Gain on Sale of Land (Furniture,
Notes Receivable, Long-Term	Notes Payable, Long-Term	Equipment, or Building)
Land		**Expenses and Losses**
Furniture		
Accumulated Depreciation—Furniture		Salary Expense
Equipment		Payroll Tax Expense
Accumulated Depreciation—Equipment		Employee Benefits Expense
Building		Rent Expense
Accumulated Depreciation—Building		Insurance Expense
		Supplies Expense
		Uncollectible Account Expense
		Depreciation Expense—Furniture
		Depreciation Expense—Equipment
		Depreciation Expense—Building
		Property Tax Expense
		Interest Expense
		Miscellaneous Expense
		Loss on Sale (or Exchange) of Land
		(Furniture, Equipment, or Building)

Service Partnership

Same as service corporation, except for owners' equity

Owners' Equity

Partner 1, Capital
Partner 2, Capital
.
.
.
Partner N, Capital

Partner 1, Drawing
Partner 2, Drawing
.
.
.
Partner N, Drawing

A Complex Merchandising Corporation

Assets	Liabilities	Stockholders' Equity

Assets	Liabilities	Stockholders' Equity	Expenses and Losses
Cash	Accounts Payable	Preferred Stock	Cost of Goods Sold
Short-Term Investments	Notes Payable, Short-Term	Paid-in Capital in Excess of Par—Preferred	Salary Expense
Accounts Receivable	Current Portion of Bonds Payable	Common Stock	Wage Expense
Allowance for Uncollectible Accounts	Salary Payable	Paid-in Capital in Excess of Par—Common	Commission Expense
Notes Receivable, Short-Term	Wages Payable	Paid-in Capital from Treasury Stock Transactions	Payroll Tax Expense
Interest Receivable	Payroll Taxes Payable	Paid-in Capital from Retirement of Stock	Employee Benefits Expense
Inventory	Employee Benefits Payable	Retained Earnings	Rent Expense
Supplies	Interest Payable	Unrealized Gain (or Loss) on Investments	Insurance Expense
Prepaid Rent	Income Tax Payable	Foreign Currency Translation Adjustment	Supplies Expense
Prepaid Insurance	Unearned Sales Revenue	Treasury Stock	Uncollectible Account Expense
Notes Receivable, Long-Term	Notes Payable, Long-Term		Depreciation Expense—Land Improvements
Investments in Subsidiaries	Bonds Payable		Depreciation Expense—Furniture and Fixtures
Investments in Stock (Available-for-Sale Securities)	Lease Liability		Depreciation Expense—Equipment
Investments in Bonds (Held-to-Maturity Securities)	Minority Interest		Depreciation Expense—Buildings
Other Receivables, Long-Term			Organization Expense
Land			Amortization Expense—Franchises
Land Improvements			Amortization Expense—Leasholds
Furniture and Fixtures			Amortization Expense—Goodwill
Accumulated Depreciation—Furniture and Fixtures			Income Tax Expense
Equipment			Unrealized Holding Loss on Trading Investments
Accumulated Depreciation—Equipment			Loss on Sale of Investments
Buildings			Loss on Sale (or Exchange) of Land (Furniture and Fixtures, Equipment, or Buildings)
Accumulated Depreciation—Buildings			Discontinued Operations—Loss
Franchises			Extraordinary Losses
Patents			
Leaseholds			
Goodwill			

Revenues and Gains

Sales Revenue
Interest Revenue
Dividend Revenue
Equity-Method Investment Revenue
Unrealized Holding Gain on Trading Investments
Gain on Sale of Investments
Gain on Sale of Land (Furniture and Fixtures, Equipment, or Buildings)
Discontinued Operations—Gain
Extraordinary Gains

A Manufacturing Corporation

Same as merchandising corporation, except for Assets

Assets

Inventories:
  Materials Inventory
  Work-in-Process Inventory
  Finished Goods Inventory
Factory Wages
Factory Overhead

Appendix E

SUMMARY OF GENERALLY ACCEPTED ACCOUNTING PRINCIPLES (GAAP)

Every technical area has professional associations and regulatory bodies that govern the practice of the profession. Accounting is no exception. In the United States, generally accepted accounting principles (GAAP) are influenced most by the Financial Accounting Standards Board (FASB). The FASB has five full-time members and a large staff. Its financial support comes from professional associations such as the American Institute of Certified Public Accountants (AICPA).

The FASB is an independent organization with no government or professional affiliation. The FASB's pronouncements, called *Statements of Financial Accounting Standards*, specify how to account for certain business transactions. Each new *Standard* becomes part of GAAP, the "accounting law of the land." In the same way that our laws draw authority from their acceptance by the people, GAAP depends on general acceptance by the business community. Throughout this book, we refer to GAAP as the proper way to do financial accounting.

The U.S. Congress has given the Securities and Exchange Commission (SEC), a government organization that regulates the trading of investments, ultimate responsibility for establishing accounting rules for companies that are owned by the general investing public. However, the SEC has delegated much of its rule-making power to the FASB. Exhibit E-1 outlines the flow of authority for developing GAAP.

EXHIBIT E-1 | Flow of Authority for Developing GAAP

United States Congress → Securities and Exchange Commission → Financial Accounting Standards Board → Pronouncements that make up generally accepted accounting principles (GAAP)

The Objective of Financial Reporting

The basic objective of financial reporting is to provide information that is useful in making investment and lending decisions. The FASB believes that accounting information can be useful in decision making only if it is *relevant* and if it *faithfully represents* economic reality.

Relevant information is useful in making predictions and for evaluating past performance—that is, the information has feedback value. For example, PepsiCo's disclosure of the profitability of each of its lines of business is relevant for investor evaluations of the company. To be relevant, information must be timely. To faithfully represent, the information must be complete, neutral (free from bias), and without material error (accurate). Accounting information must focus on the *economic substance* of a transaction, event, or circumstance, which may or may not always be the same as its legal form. Faithful represenation makes the information *reliable* to users.

Exhibit 1-3 on page 7 of Chapter 1 presents the objectives of accounting, its fundamental and enhancing qualitative characteristics, as well as its contraints. These characteristics and contraints combine to shape the concepts and principles that make up GAAP. Exhibit E-2 summarizes the assumptions, concepts, and principles that accounting has developed to provide useful information for decision making.

EXHIBIT E-2 | Summary of Important Accounting Concepts, Principles, and Financial Statements

Assumptions, Concepts, Principles, and Financial Statements	Quick Summary	Text Reference
Assumptions and Concepts		
Entity assumption	Accounting draws a boundary around each organization to be accounted for.	Chapter 1, page 8
Continuity (going concern) assumption	Accountants assume the business will continue operating for the foreseeable future.	Chapter 1, page 9
Stable-monetary-unit assumption	Accounting information is expressed primarily in monetary terms that ignore the effects of inflation.	Chapter 1, page 10
Time-period concept	Ensures that accounting information is reported at regular intervals.	Chapter 3, page 140
Conservatism concept	Accountants report items in the financial statements in a way that avoids overstating assets, owners' equity, and revenues and avoids understating liabilities and expenses.	Chapter 6, page 359
Materiality	A constraint of accounting. Accountants perform strictly proper accounting only for items that are significant to the company's financial statements.	Chapter 1, page 8
Cost	A constraint of accounting, meaning that the cost of producing information should not exceed the expected benefits to users.	Chapter 1, page 8
Principles		
Historical cost principle	Assets, services, revenues, and expenses are recorded at their actual historical cost.	Chapter 1, page 9
Revenue principle	Tells accountants when to record revenue (only after it has been earned) and the amount of revenue to record (the cash value of what has been received).	Chapter 3, page 140, and Chapter 11
Matching principle	Directs accountants to (1) identify and measure all expenses incurred during the period and (2) match the expenses against the revenues earned during the period. The goal is to measure net income.	Chapter 3, page 141
Consistency principle	Businesses should use the same accounting methods from period to period.	Chapter 6, page 358
Disclosure principle	A company's financial statements should report enough information for outsiders to make informed decisions about the company.	Chapter 6, page 358
Financial Statements		
Balance sheet	Assets = Liabilities + Owners' Equity at a point in time.	Chapter 1
Income statement	Revenues and gains – Expenses and losses = Net income or net loss for the period	Chapters 1 and 11
Statement of cash flows	Cash receipts – Cash payments = Increase or decrease in cash during the period, grouped under operating, investing, and financing activities	Chapters 1 and 12
Statement of retained earnings	Beginning retained earnings + Net income (or – Net loss) – Dividends = Ending retained earnings	Chapters 1 and 11
Statement of stockholders' equity	Shows the reason for the change in each stockholders' equity account, including retained earnings.	Chapter 11
Financial statement notes	Provide information that cannot be reported conveniently on the face of the financial statements. The notes are an integral part of the statements.	Chapter 11

Appendix F

SUMMARY OF DIFFERENCES BETWEEN U.S. GAAP AND IFRS CROSS REFERENCED TO CHAPTER

The following table describes some of the current differences between U.S. GAAP and International Financial Reporting Standards (IFRS) that relate to topics (by chapter) covered in this textbook. The U.S. Securities and Exchange Commission (SEC) has adopted a timetable whereby U.S. public companies may adopt IFRS by 2014. Because of a global economic recession and a crisis in the financial markets, a significant number of informed persons believe that this time table may be delayed. Nevertheless, most people believe that the integration of GAAP and IFRS will eventually become a reality. The last column of the table explains what *could* happen if the U.S. GAAP of today were to switch to IFRS as they currently exist. This will help you assess the impact of these changes on U.S. financial statements.

Accounts	Topic	U.S. GAAP Position	IFRS Position	Implications of Switch to IFRS
Inventory and Cost of Goods Sold Chapter 6	Inventory costing	Companies can choose to use LIFO inventory costing, if desired. Approximately 30% of U.S. companies currently use LIFO for its tax benefits.	LIFO is not allowed under any circumstances.	LIFO could be eliminated. Companies could still choose to use FIFO, average, or specific identification methods.
	Lower-of-cost-or market (LCM)	Market is usually determined to be replacement cost. LCM write-downs cannot be reversed.	Market is always net realizable value (fair market value). LCM write-downs can be reversed under certain conditions.	LCM write-downs may become less common, as selling prices are usually greater than replacement costs. Some write-downs might be reversed over time.
Property, Plant, and Equipment Chapter 7	Asset impairment and revaluation	If long-term assets are impaired, they are written down. Write-downs may not be reversed.	Long-term assets may be written up or down, based on fair market value (appraisals). Adjustments may be potentially reversed.	The cost principle might not apply to long-term assets as strongly. Assets could be evaluated by independent appraisers and adjusted either up or down.
Research and Development Chapter 7	Development costs	All research and development costs are expensed. Only exception is for computer software development costs, which can be capitalized and amortized over future sales revenues.	All research is expensed, but all development costs are capitalized and amortized over future sales revenues.	Standards already developed by U.S. GAAP might be extended to apply to all development costs, not just computer software development.
Intangible Assets Chapter 7	Capitalization and recognition of intangible assets on balance sheet	Only recognized when purchased. Internally developed not recognized.	Recognized if future benefit is probable and reliably measurable (same criteria as recognition of contingencies). May be purchased or internally developed.	More intangible assets could be recognized on balance sheet. Adjusted for amortization or impairment over time.
Contingent Liabilities Chapter 8	Recording of contingent liabilities	Accrued (recorded in journal entry) if probable and reliably measurable. Contingent liabilities that are possible are disclosed in notes to financial statements.	Both probable and possible contingent liabilities are recorded in journal entries.	More liabilities will likely be recorded, regardless of the outcome of proposals being studied by FASB and IASB.

Accounts	Topic	U.S. GAAP Position	IFRS Position	Implications of Switch to IFRS
Contingent Liabilities Chapter 8	Disclosure of contingencies	The FASB has proposed that the standard for disclosure of loss contingencies be increased to include all such matters that are expected to be resolved in the near term (i.e., within the next year) and that could have a severe impact (higher than material, disruptive to the business). In addition, the proposal requires a quantitative tabular reconciliation of accrued loss contingencies that includes increases or decreases in such amounts during the most recent year.	IASB is studying its present requirements with a view to increase required disclosures in the next few years.	More liabilities will likely be recorded, regardless of the outcome of proposals being studied by the FASB and IASB.
Lease Liabilities Chapter 8	Classification of leases	To be classified as a capital lease, one of four quantitative "bright line" tests must be met. If not, lease is classified as an operating lease by default.	Guidance focuses on the overall substance of the transaction. Classification as capital lease depends on whether lease transfers substantially all risks and rewards of ownership to lessee. More judgment required on the part of preparer. No quantitative guidelines exist.	More leases could be classified as capital leases, resulting in more frequent recognition of long-term assets as well as long-term liabilities.
Revenue Chapter 11	Revenue recognition	Many different ways to recognize revenues, depending on the industry and the type of contract.	Revenue recognition based mainly on a single standard that contains general principles applied to different types of transactions.	It will standardize the way in which revenues are recognized, resulting in changes in the timing of revenue recognition.
Extraordinary Items Chapter 11	Recording of extraordinary items	Allows separate disclosure of extraordinary items (unusual in nature and infrequent in occurrence) after income from continuing operations.	Extraordinary items do not have special treatment. Even "unusual and infrequent" items are reported in income from continuing operations.	Extraordinary items may disappear from the income statement, to be reclassified as "ordinary" revenues and expenses.
Interest Revenue and Interest Expense Chapter 12	Indirect method cash flows statement presentation Direct method cash flows statement presentation	Interest revenue and interest expense are part of net income, and as such are included in operating activities (as part of net income) on an indirect method cash flows statement. Interest is not reported under investing activities.	Interest revenue and interest expense are removed from net income (as an adjustment, similar to the adjustment for depreciation expense) in the operating activities section of the indirect method cash flows statement. Interest income is reported under financing activities, and interest expense is reported under investing activities for both direct and indirect methods.	Interest revenue and interest expense reclassified to different sections of the cash flows statement.

Company Index

Glindex
A Combined Glossary and Subject Index

Double-entry accounting, T-accounts
   analyzing transactions, 92
      credit side, 77
      debit and credit, exercise, 123–135
      debit and credit, rules for, 77–80
      debit side, 77
      defined, 77
      grouping. *See* Ledger.
Doubtful-account expense. Another name
   for *uncollectible-account expense*, 299. *See
   also* Uncollectible-account expense.
Drexler, Millard S., 8

E

Earnings per share (EPS). Amount of a
   company's net income earned for each
   share of its outstanding common stock.
      defined, 493, 662
      dilution, 663
      effect of preferred dividends, 662–663
      ratio analysis, 797–798
Earnings quality. The characteristics of an
   earnings number that make it most useful
   for decision making. The degree to which
   earnings are an accurate reflection of
   underlying economic events for both revenues and expenses, and the extent to
   which earnings from a company's core
   operations are improving over time.
   Assuming that revenues and expenses are
   measured accurately, high-quality earnings
   are reflected in steadily improving sales and
   steadily declining costs over time, so that
   income from continuing operations follows
   a high and improving pattern over time,
   654–655
Ebbers, Bernard, 415–416
E-commerce
      pitfalls, 243–244
      security measures, 244
Economic value added (EVA®). Used to
   evaluate a company's operating performance.
   EVA combines the concepts of accounting
   income and corporate finance to measure
   whether the company's operations have
   increased stockholder wealth. EVA = Net
   income + Interest expense – Capital charge.
      ratio analysis, 799–800
Effective interest rates, bonds payable,
      480–481
Effective-interest amortization, 483–484
Efficient capital market. A capital market
   in which market prices fully reflect all
   information available to the public, 801
EFT (electronic funds transfer), 247
Electronic funds transfer (EFT). System
   that transfers cash by electronic communication rather than by paper documents, 247
Employee benefit expenses, current
      liabilities, 471

Employee compensation, current liabilities,
      470–471
Employee income tax payable, current
      liabilities, 471
Employee payments, statement of cash flows,
      723, 731
Employer income tax payable, current liabili-
      ties, 471
Encryption. Mathematical rearranging of
   data within an electronic file to prevent
   unauthorized access to information,
      242–244
Ending inventory
      effects of inventory costing, 353–354
      FIFO method, effects of, 353–354
      LIFO method, effects of, 353–354
Entity. An organization or a section of an
   organization that, for accounting purposes,
   stands apart from other organizations and
   individuals as a separate economic unit, 8
Entity assumption, 8–9
EPS (earnings per share). *See* Earnings per
   share (EPS).
Equipment, plant assets, 412
Equipment accounts, 66
Equity method. The method used to
   account for investments in which the
   investor has 20—50% of the investee's voting stock and can significantly influence the
   decisions of the investee, 610
Error correction, 89–90
Errors, inventory
      deliberate, 366–367
      effects of, 365–366
Estimated current liabilities, 473–474
Estimated residual value. Expected cash
   value of an asset at the end of its useful life.
   Also called *residual value*, *scrap value*, or
   salvage value, 417
Estimated useful life. Length of service that
   a business expects to get from an asset. May
   be expressed in years, units of output,
   miles, or other measures, 417, 426–427
Ethics. Standards of right and wrong that
   transcend economic and legal boundaries.
   Ethical standards deal with the way we treat
   others and restrain our own actions because
   of the desires, expectations, or rights of others, or with our obligations to them.
      in accrual accounting, 142–143
      BELA (Business Ethics Leadership
         Alliance), 30
      bonus manipulation, 650
      decision guidelines, 30
      in decision making, 29
      defined, 29
      disclosure of contingent liabilities, 529
      economic factors, 29
      ethical analyses, 29
      Ethisphere Institute, 30

   franchise capitalization, 599
   and fraud, 236
   income statements, 673
   inventory, 398
   issuing common stock, 545–546
   leases, 498
   legal factors, 29
   plant assets, 465
   ratio analysis, 840
   World's Most Ethical Companies, 30
Euro, 622
EVA® (economic value added), 799–800
Exception reporting. Identifying data that is
   not within "normal limits" so that managers
   can follow up and take corrective action.
   Exception reporting is used in operating
   and cash budgets to keep company profits
   and cash flow in line with management's
   plans, 240
Exchanging plant assets, 431–432
Expense accounts, 67, 80
Expenses. Decrease in retained earnings that
   results from operations; the cost of doing
   business; opposite of revenues.
      accrual accounting, 141–142
      administrative, 18
      cost of sales, 18
      debits and credits, 80
      decreases, recording, 80
      defined, 14
      in financial statements, 14–15
      general, 18
      in income statements, 18
      income tax, 18
      increases, recording, 80
      interest paid, 18
      of plant assets, decision guidelines, 440
      selling, 18
      vs. dividends, 15
External users of accounting information, 4–5
Extraordinary gains and losses. Also called
   extraordinary items, these gains and losses
   are both unusual for the company and infrequent, 661
Extraordinary items. An *extraordinary gain
   or loss*, 661

F

Face value, bonds (notes) payable, 478
Factoring receivables, 310–311
Fair market value. The amount that a seller
   would receive on the sale of an investment
   to a willing purchaser on a given date.
   Securities and available-for-sale securities
   are valued at fair market values on the balance sheet date. Other assets may be
   recorded at fair market value on occasion.
      defined, 607
      of long-term debt, 500